ARIZONA PRACTICE SERIES™

ARIZONA CIVIL RULES HANDBOOK

Volume 2B

2014 Edition

Issued in March 2014

by

DANIEL J. McAULIFFE

SHIRLEY J. McAULIFFE

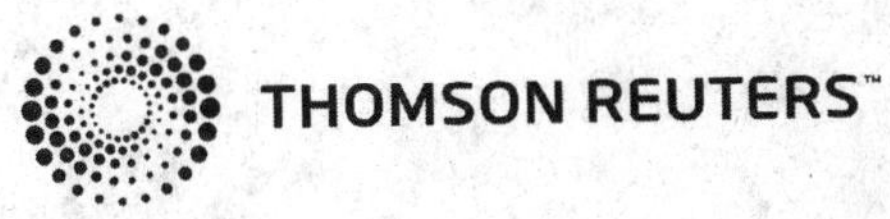

For Customer Assistance Call 1-800-328-4880

Mat #41416068

ISBN: 978–0–314–62157–3

Remembering Daniel J. McAuliffe 1945 - 2010

Dan McAuliffe, my wonderful husband, best friend and sole author of the **Arizona Civil Rules Handbook** from its inception in 1993 to 2009, passed away in March 2010. He was a brilliant lawyer, innovative problem solver and gifted writer, who left a legacy of six books on civil procedure, evidence, civil trial practice and ethics. These legal reference books reside on the bookshelves of practitioners and members of the judiciary alike—at least when the books aren't being used!

Dan was born in New York City in 1945. He graduated at the top of his class from Regis High School, one of New York's most prestigious high schools. He then attended Fordham University, graduating Phi Beta Kappa, with a major in Russian. Following his graduation from Fordham, Dan attended Harvard Law School, graduated in 1969 with honors and promptly went to work with the U.S. Department of Justice in Washington, D.C.

In 1973, Dan left his position with the Justice Department to join Snell & Wilmer in Phoenix, Arizona. Over Dan's 37 years with Snell & Wilmer, Dan focused his practice in the areas of commercial litigation and civil appeals.

While Dan was an accomplished lawyer and author, he also was committed to giving of his time and talent to his community and the legal profession. Dan served on countless community and professional committees concerned with legal reform and public access to justice. He chaired the Arizona State Bar's Professionalism Course Committee. He served several terms on the Arizona State Bar's Board of Governors and then led the State Bar of Arizona as its President from July 2007 to June 2008. In 2009, the Arizona State Bar recognized Dan's substantial contributions and accomplishments by renaming its continuing legal education conference center in Dan's honor. The center is now the *Daniel J. McAuliffe CLE Center*.

Dan was a true legal giant and a good honest man with an unforgettable laugh. Dan was the best of the best; first among equals. He is truly missed by all of us who knew, respected and loved him.

Shirley J. McAuliffe

For Danny-

Forever in my heart

PREFACE

The 2014 Edition of the **Arizona Civil Rules Handbook** adheres to the time-tested goal and standards established in 1993 by Dan McAuliffe: to provide Arizona practitioners, and judges alike, with a basic tool in the conduct of a civil litigation practice—a readily available source of answers and/or explanations for the questions that most frequently arise in the conduct of a civil case, in a one-volume work that can be used as readily in the courtroom as in the office.

As in the past, the 2014 Edition contains updated discussions of recent decisions by the Arizona Supreme Court and Arizona Court of Appeals, and discussions of the relevant changes to the Arizona Rules of Civil Procedure and Arizona Rules of Evidence, adopted after the publication of the 2013 Edition and effective in 2014, including the 2014 amendments to the case management/ trial setting rules.

The decisional updates, of course, are subject to the limitations imposed by the fact that published material appears at a discrete point in time, while the development of the law, particularly in the procedural arena, is ongoing and dynamic. For that reason, those who use this work in their practice are reminded to cite check and update all information before relying on that information. In short, this Handbook is a starting point for further research, not the end point.

In closing, I extend the long-standing invitation to readers to provide comments and suggestions for items to be included, excluded and/or discussed in this work. Please direct comments or suggestions to: shirley.mcauliffe@azbar.org.

Shirley J. McAuliffe

Related Products

ARIZONA PRACTICE SERIES™

Arizona Family Law Rules Handbook

Mark W. Armstrong, Annette T. Burns,
Daniel J. McAuliffe and Shirley J. McAuliffe

Arizona Law of Evidence

Daniel J. McAuliffe and Shirley J. Wahl

Arizona Civil Trial Practice

Daniel J. McAuliffe and Shirley J. Wahl

Arizona Civil Rules Handbook

Daniel J. McAuliffe and Shirley J. McAuliffe

Arizona Real Estate Law

Ronald W. Messerly

Arizona Construction Law Annotated

Ronald W. Messerly

Arizona Marriage Dissolution Practice

Charles M. Smith and Irwin Cantor

Arizona Community Property Law

Thomas A. Jacobs

Arizona Estate Planning and Probate Handbook

Darren T. Case, Brent W. Nelson, T.J. Ryan

Arizona Juvenile Law and Practice

Thomas A. Jacobs

Arizona Corporate Practice

Terence W. Thompson, John L. Hay, James P. O'Sullivan,
Robert A. Royal and Thomas J. McDonald

Arizona Trial Handbook

Bennett Evan Cooper, Kevin M. Judiscak, and Leslie Kyman Cooper

Arizona Business Law Deskbook

Lisa C. Thompson and Brent A. Olson

Arizona Business Regulations—State and Federal

Lisa C. Thompson and Brent A. Olson

ARIZONA LEGAL FORMS™

Arizona Civil Procedure Forms

Daniel J. McAuliffe and Shirley J. McAuliffe

Arizona Debtor–Creditor Forms

Lisa C. Thompson

Arizona Domestic Relations Forms

Catherine A. Creighton

Arizona Commercial Transactions Forms

Douglas S. John

Arizona Criminal Procedure Forms

Crane McClennen

Arizona Business Organizations—Corporations Forms

Thomas H. Curzon

Arizona Business Organizations—Limited Liability Companies and Partnerships Forms

Lisa C. Thompson

Other West Products

West's Arizona Revised Statutes—Annotated

West's Arizona Revised Statutes—Compact Edition

West's Arizona Legislative Service

West's Arizona Civil Practice Law Pamphlet

West's Arizona Criminal and Motor Vehicle Law Pamphlet

West's Arizona Criminal Law and Rules Pamphlet

RELATED PRODUCTS

West's Arizona Education Code Pamphlet

West's Arizona Probate Law and Rules Pamphlet

West's Arizona Rules of Court—State

West's Arizona Rules of Court—Federal

West's Arizona Reports

West's Arizona Digest

West's Arizona Law Finder

Westlaw®
WestCheck.com®

Thomson Reuters® thanks you for subscribing to this product. Should you have any questions regarding this product please contact Customer Service at 1-800-328-4880 or by fax at 1-800-340-9378. If you would like to inquire about related publications or place an order, please contact us at 1–800–344–5009.

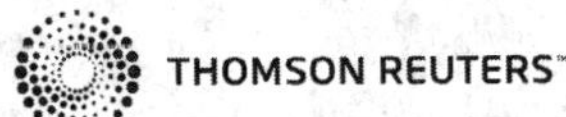

Thomson Reuters
610 Opperman Drive
Eagan, MN 55123

legalsolutions.thomsonreuters.com

Summary of Contents

ARIZONA RULES OF CIVIL PROCEDURE WITH COMMENTS

Effective January 1, 1956

Including Amendments Effective in 2014.

Research Note

See Arizona Revised Statutes Annotated, *Volume 16, Part 1 and 2 for historical notes and judicial constructions.*

See McAuliffe & Wahl, Arizona Practice—Civil Trial Practice (Second Edition) *for discussion of the Rules of Civil Procedure.*

See McAuliffe & Wahl, Arizona Practice—Law of Evidence (Revised and Edited, Fourth Edition).

See Arizona Rules of Court—State and Federal for the complete text of court rules governing State and Federal practice in Arizona.

Use Westlaw® *to find recent cases citing provisions of the Rules of Civil Procedure. In addition, use* Westlaw *to find a specific term or to update a rule; see the AZ-RULES and AZ-ORDERS SCOPE screens for further information.*

I. SCOPE OF RULES—ONE FORM OF ACTION

II. COMMENCEMENT OF ACTION; SERVICE OF PROCESS, PLEADINGS, MOTIONS AND ORDERS; DUTIES OF COUNSEL

III. PLEADINGS AND MOTIONS; PRETRIAL PROCEDURES

IV. PARTIES

V. DEPOSITIONS AND DISCOVERY

VI. TRIALS

VII. JUDGMENT

VIII. PROVISIONAL AND FINAL REMEDIES AND SPECIAL PROCEEDINGS

IX. COMPULSORY ARBITRATION

X. GENERAL PROVISIONS

I. SCOPE OF RULES—ONE FORM OF ACTION

Rule 1. Scope of rules

These rules govern the procedure in the superior courts of Arizona in all suits of a civil nature whether cognizable as cases at law or in equity. They shall be construed to secure the just, speedy, and inexpensive determination of every action.

AUTHORS' COMMENTS

Analysis

1. Scope and Purpose of Rule.
2. Similarity to Federal Rules of Civil Procedure.
3. Comparison With Federal Rule.
4. Other Procedural Rules.
5. Rulemaking Authority; Effect of Statutory Provisions.
6. Jurisdiction of the Superior Court; Justice Courts.
7. Visiting Judges.
8. Time Limits for Decisions.

1. *Scope and Purpose of Rule.* Rule 1 establishes that the Arizona Rules of Civil Procedure are to govern procedure in the Superior Court in all civil actions, whether legal or equitable in nature. The applicability of the Arizona Rules of Civil Procedure to "domestic relations" cases, however, is limited by the provisions of the Arizona Rules of Family Law Procedure, which "govern the procedure in the Superior Court of Arizona in all family law cases, including paternity, and all other matters arising out of Title 25, Arizona Revised Statutes." *See,* Rule 1, Arizona Rules of Family Law Procedure. Rule 2 of those Rules specifies that, in such cases, the Arizona Rules of Civil Procedure apply only where they are incorporated by reference into the Rules of Family Law Procedure.

The Arizona Rules of Civil Procedure also may be inapplicable in certain ways in special statutory proceedings, such as forcible detainer actions, which have procedural provisions that are an integral part of the substantive rights conferred by the statute. *Byrd v. Peterson*, 66 Ariz. 253, 186 P.2d 955 (1947); *Hinton v. Hotchkiss*, 65 Ariz. 110, 174 P.2d 749 (1946); *Jenkins v. First Baptist Church of Scottsdale*, 166 Ariz. 243, 801 P.2d 478 (Ct. App. Div. 1 1990). These rules do not apply to proceedings before the Industrial Commission. *Martens v. Industrial Com'n of*

Arizona, 211 Ariz. 319, 121 P.3d 186 (Ct. App. Div. 1 2005).

The stated purpose of the Rules of Civil Procedure is to "secure the just, speedy and inexpensive determination of every action," and they are to be construed with that goal in mind. *Union Interchange, Inc. v. Van Aalsburg*, 102 Ariz. 461, 432 P.2d 589 (1967); *Union Interchange, Inc. v. Benton*, 100 Ariz. 33, 410 P.2d 477 (1966).

2. *Similarity to Federal Rules of Civil Procedure.* As promulgated effective January 1, 1956 by the Arizona Supreme Court, the Arizona Rules of Civil Procedure incorporated most of the provisions of the Federal Rules of Civil Procedure, and since that time there has been a conscious and continuous effort to maintain, where possible, uniformity between the Arizona and Federal Rules. For a variety of reasons, however, the two bodies of Rules remain only substantially similar, and not identical.

Initially, at the time the Arizona Rules were adopted, they carried forward and incorporated a number of procedural provisions from the 1939 Arizona Code which had no counterparts in the Federal Rules. In addition, since 1956 the maintenance of uniformity between the Arizona Rules of Civil Procedure and Federal Rules of Civil Procedure has been a persuasive guideline rather than a fixed requirement, and some intervening amendments to the Federal Rules have either been modified to facilitate their incorporation into pre-existing Arizona practice, or at times rejected as inappropriate or unnecessary. Finally, Arizona has in several instances adopted amendments to its Rules of Civil Procedure which had not been prompted by corresponding amendments to the Federal Rules. The discovery reform amendments to the Arizona Rules of Civil Procedure, which became effective July 1, 1992, and the "jury reform" amendments, which became effective December 1, 1995, are perhaps the most dramatic, example of the latter phenomenon.

The *Authors' Comments* to each of the Rules will devote a section to a comparison of the Rule under discussion with the corresponding federal rule. Federal interpretations of a procedural rule that corresponds to one adopted by Arizona are persuasive, but not binding on Arizona's courts. *U S West Communications, Inc. v. Arizona Dept. of Revenue*, 199 Ariz. 101, 14 P.3d 292 (2000); *Anserv Ins. Services, Inc. v. Albrecht In and For County of Maricopa*, 192 Ariz. 48, 960 P.2d 1159 (1998), as corrected, (July 7, 1998) and as corrected, (July 31, 1998); *Orme School v. Reeves*, 166 Ariz. 301, 802 P.2d 1000, 64 Ed. Law Rep. 1221 (1990); *Ritchie v. Grand Canyon Scenic Rides*, 165 Ariz. 460, 799 P.2d 801 (1990); *Edwards v. Young*, 107 Ariz. 283, 486 P.2d 181 (1971); *Byers-Watts v. Parker*, 199 Ariz. 466, 18 P.3d 1265 (Ct. App. Div. 1 2001), as amended, (Mar. 29, 2001); *Estate of Page v. Litzenburg*,

177 Ariz. 84, 865 P.2d 128 (Ct. App. Div. 1 1993); *Bayham v. Funk*, 3 Ariz. App. 220, 413 P.2d 279 (1966).

3. *Comparison With Federal Rule.* ARCP 1 is virtually identical to FRCP 1. The only substantive difference is the phrase "and administered" added to FRCP 1 by the 1993 amendments to the Federal Rules of Civil Procedure.

4. *Other Procedural Rules.* Recent years have witnessed a proliferation of procedural rules and rule amendments that may apply to particular aspects, or particular types, of civil proceedings. This phenomenon was, at least in part, the catalyst for the Supreme Court entering an Order, in October 2000, which abrogated the Uniform Rules of Practice of the Superior Court, the Uniform Rules of Procedure for Arbitration and the Uniform Rules of Practice for Medical Malpractice Cases as separate sets of procedural rules, and transferring most of their former provisions to either the Arizona Rules of Civil Procedure or the Rules of the Arizona Supreme Court. Provisions from the sets of rules thus abrogated that dealt with the processing of civil cases were transferred to the Arizona Rules of Civil Procedure; rule provisions that primarily concerned the internal administration of the Superior Court were placed in the Rules of the Arizona Supreme Court.

The *2000 Rules Consolidation Correlation Table,* which follows the Arizona Rules of Civil Procedure in this Volume, shows what disposition was made of the abrogated rules. This Handbook contains the procedural rules which have the most frequent and broad-based impact on civil cases—the Arizona Rules of Civil Procedure and the Arizona Rules of Evidence.

Despite the effort to consolidate the procedural rules governing civil cases, there remain, and indeed have been affirmatively adopted, other, more specialized sets of procedural rules which may have a bearing on a particular case or issue. These specialized sets of rules include at least the following: the Arizona Rules of Civil Appellate Procedure, the Rules of Procedure for Special Actions, the Rules of Procedure for Judicial Review of Administrative Decisions, the Rules of Practice for the Arizona Tax Court, the Superior Court Rules of Appellate Procedure—Civil, the Rules of Procedure for the Juvenile Court, the Rules of Procedure for Direct Appeals from Decisions of the Corporation Commission to the Arizona Court of Appeals, the Rules of Procedure for Recognition of Tribal Court Civil Judgments, the Arizona Rules of Protective Order Procedure and the Rules of Procedure for Eviction Cases. In addition, the Superior Courts in each of the fifteen counties have adopted their own sets of Local Rules that govern certain aspects of civil proceedings.

The most significant separate set of Rules, in terms of the volume of cases to which they will apply and which they will govern, is the Arizona Rules of Family Law Procedure, which became effective January 1, 2006. The Arizona Rules of Family Law Procedure "govern the procedure in the Superior Court of Arizona in all family law cases, including paternity, and all other matters arising out of Title 25, Arizona Revised Statutes . . . " Rule 1, Arizona Rules of Family Law Procedure. Effective January 2009, the Arizona Supreme Court adopted the Arizona Rules of Probate Procedure, which also will have significant impact in terms of the number of cases to which they will apply.

5. *Rulemaking Authority; Effect of Statutory Provisions.* The doctrine of the primacy of the Supreme Court of Arizona in procedural matters has evolved from somewhat tentative beginnings. Shortly after the promulgation of what were the predecessors to the Arizona Rules of Civil Procedure and the Arizona Rules of Criminal Procedure, the Court held that the judiciary has "the inherent power to prescribe rules of practice and rules to regulate their own proceedings," confirmed by the fact that Article VI, § 1 of the Arizona Constitution gives the judicial branch of government exclusive power "to make rules of practice and procedure governing the courts." *Burney v. Lee*, 59 Ariz. 360, 363, 129 P.2d 308, 309 (1942). *See also State v. Pierce*, 59 Ariz. 411, 129 P.2d 916 (1942). The Court buttressed this assertion of its exclusive procedural prerogatives, however, with the observation that the Arizona Legislature, by adopting what is now A.R.S. § 12-109(A), had "withdrawn from the field of court procedure." *Burney v. Lee*, 59 Ariz. 360, 367, 129 P.2d 308, 311 (1942); *State v. Pierce*, 59 Ariz. 411, 414, 129 P.2d 916, 917 (1942).

The adoption in 1960 of Section 5 of Article VI of the Constitution, which conferred on the Supreme Court the power "to make rules relative to all procedural matters in any court," confirmed that the Court has the exclusive power, free of legislative restraints, to adopt and promulgate procedural rules. *Cullen v. Auto-Owners Ins. Co.*, 218 Ariz. 417, 189 P.3d 344 (2008); *State, ex rel. Romley v. Ballinger*, 209 Ariz. 1, 97 P.3d 101 (2004); *Daou v. Harris*, 139 Ariz. 353, 678 P.2d 934 (1984); *Arizona Podiatry Ass'n v. Director of Ins.*, 101 Ariz. 544, 422 P.2d 108 (1966); *Heat Pump Equipment Co. v. Glen Alden Corp.*, 93 Ariz. 361, 380 P.2d 1016 (1963); *Bertleson v. Sacks Tierney, P.A.*, 204 Ariz. 124, 60 P.3d 703 (Ct. App. Div. 1 2002); *In re Jonah T.*, 196 Ariz. 204, 994 P.2d 1019 (Ct. App. Div. 1 1999); *Graf v. Whitaker*, 192 Ariz. 403, 966 P.2d 1007 (Ct. App. Div. 1 1998); *Pompa v. Superior Court In and For the County of Maricopa*, 187 Ariz. 531, 931 P.2d 431 (Ct. App. Div. 1 1997).

The Arizona Supreme Court's power to make procedural rules may not be reduced or repealed by legislation, and the absence of action by the Supreme Court does not *ipso facto* authorize the legislature to act in the Court's place. *Phoenix Newspapers, Inc. v. Superior Court In and For County of Maricopa*, 180 Ariz. 159, 882 P.2d 1285, 22 Media L. Rep. (BNA) 1531 (Ct. App. Div. 1 1993). Rules promulgated by the Arizona Supreme Court are subject to general rules of statutory interpretation. *Haywood Securities, Inc. v. Ehrlich*, 214 Ariz. 114, 149 P.3d 738 (2007).

While the legislature retains the prerogative to declare, modify or abrogate (subject to separate constitutional constraints) substantive rights, the judicial branch may prescribe the method or manner in which those rights are enforced or made effective. *State v. Fletcher*, 149 Ariz. 187, 717 P.2d 866 (1986); *State v. Birmingham*, 96 Ariz. 109, 392 P.2d 775 (1964); *Rackmaster Systems, Inc. v. Maderia*, 219 Ariz. 60, 193 P.3d 314 (Ct. App. Div. 1 2008); *Encinas v. Pompa*, 189 Ariz. 157, 939 P.2d 435, R.I.C.O. Bus. Disp. Guide (CCH) P 9287 (Ct. App. Div. 1 1997); *Del Castillo v. Wells*, 22 Ariz. App. 41, 523 P.2d 92 (Div. 1 1974). The Court's exclusive authority to regulate matters of court procedure is subject only to the limitation that a procedural rule may not diminish, abridge or modify a substantive right. *In re Marriage of Waldren*, 217 Ariz. 173, 171 P.3d 1214 (2007); *State v. Pierce*, 59 Ariz. 411, 129 P.2d 916 (1942); *Jenkins v. First Baptist Church of Scottsdale*, 166 Ariz. 243, 801 P.2d 478 (Ct. App. Div. 1 1990); A.R.S. § 12-109(A).

Traditionally, rules of court have not been viewed as impermissibly diminishing a litigant's right of action or appeal merely because the rules include, among the permissible sanctions for failure to comply, the possibility of the dismissal of a party's claim or defense. *Graf v. Whitaker*, 192 Ariz. 403, 966 P.2d 1007 (Ct. App. Div. 1 1998). If a rule and a substantive statute appear to conflict, the rule is to be construed, if possible, to be consistent with the statute. *Brush Wellman, Inc. v. Lee*, 196 Ariz. 344, 996 P.2d 1248 (Ct. App. Div. 2 2000); *Rosner v. Denim & Diamonds, Inc.*, 188 Ariz. 431, 937 P.2d 353 (Ct. App. Div. 2 1996). While the legislature may regulate the practice of law, it may not adopt regulations which are inconsistent with the mandates of the Supreme Court. *Scheehle v. Justices of the Supreme Court of the State of Arizona*, 211 Ariz. 282, 120 P.3d 1092 (2005).

The determination of whether a statute unduly infringes upon the rulemaking power of the court requires an analysis of both the challenged statute and the rule then at issue. *Seisinger v. Siebel*, 220 Ariz. 85, 203 P.3d 483 (2009). The first step in the analysis is to determine whether the rule and the statute can be harmonized; if it is possible to harmonize the statute with the rule, then there is no conflict and the analysis ends. *See Seisinger v. Siebel*, 220 Ariz. 85, 203 P.3d 483 (2009). If the statute and the rule cannot be harmonized, then the analysis turns to whether the statute at issue is substantive or procedural in nature.

Seisinger v. Siebel, 220 Ariz. 85, 203 P.3d 483 (2009). Substantive law, which is the province of the Legislative branch, "creates, defines and regulates rights." *Seisinger v. Siebel*, 220 Ariz. 85, 203 P.3d 483 (2009).

The Arizona Revised Statutes, and particularly Title 12, contain a number of provisions that purport to regulate pleading, practice and procedure in the court system. Such procedural statutes are considered to be rules of court which remain in effect until modified by rules promulgated by the Supreme Court, at which point the procedural rule takes precedence over any inconsistent procedure previously prescribed by statute. *State ex rel. Purcell v. Superior Court In and For Maricopa County*, 107 Ariz. 224, 485 P.2d 549 (1971); *State v. Blazak*, 105 Ariz. 216, 462 P.2d 84 (1969); *Gonzales v. Whitney*, 90 Ariz. 324, 367 P.2d 668 (1961); *Bertleson v. Sacks Tierney, P.A.*, 204 Ariz. 124, 60 P.3d 703 (Ct. App. Div. 1 2002); *Encinas v. Pompa*, 189 Ariz. 157, 939 P.2d 435, R.I.C.O. Bus. Disp. Guide (CCH) P 9287 (Ct. App. Div. 1 1997); *Pompa v. Superior Court In and For the County of Maricopa*, 187 Ariz. 531, 931 P.2d 431 (Ct. App. Div. 1 1997); *State v. Jackson*, 184 Ariz. 296, 908 P.2d 1081 (Ct. App. Div. 1 1995); *Matter of Maricopa County, Juvenile Action No. JS-834*, 26 Ariz. App. 485, 549 P.2d 580 (Div. 1 1976); *Del Castillo v. Wells*, 22 Ariz. App. 41, 523 P.2d 92 (Div. 1 1974); A.R.S. § 12-111.

Rules of evidence have been held to be a species of "procedural rule" that fall within the Supreme Court's plenary authority to regulate matters of procedure. *Seisinger v. Siebel*, 220 Ariz. 85, 203 P.3d 483 (2009); *Matter of One (1) Rolex Brand Man's Watch*, 176 Ariz. 294, 860 P.2d 1347 (Ct. App. Div. 1 1993). The relationship between statutes that deal with evidentiary matters and the Arizona Rules of Evidence is discussed further in Section 4 of the *Authors' Comments* to Ariz. R. Evid. 101.

The occasions on which the Court has declared a "procedural" statute unconstitutional as an invasion of its rule-making authority have been relatively infrequent. *State v. Bejarano*, 158 Ariz. 253, 762 P.2d 540 (1988); *In re Property at 6757 S. Burcham Ave.*, 204 Ariz. 401, 64 P.3d 843 (Ct. App. Div. 2 2003); *State v. Fowler*, 156 Ariz. 408, 752 P.2d 497 (Ct. App. Div. 1 1987). This "rule" is inoperative where the nominally procedural provisions of a statute are found to be an integral part of the substantive rights created, and necessary to make them effective, as in the forcible entry and detainer statutes. *Byrd v. Peterson*, 66 Ariz. 253, 186 P.2d 955 (1947); *Hinton v. Hotchkiss*, 65 Ariz. 110, 174 P.2d 749 (1946); *Jenkins v. First Baptist Church of Scottsdale*, 166 Ariz. 243, 801 P.2d 478 (Ct. App. Div. 1 1990). Finally, the legislature has been granted the constitutional authority, by Article II, § 2.1(D) of the Constitution, to enact "procedural laws" to effectuate the victims' rights created by that Section.

Procedures for the adoption of procedural rules and amendments to existing ones are governed by Rule 28 of the Rules of the Supreme Court, which generally requires the filing of a formal petition and the circulation, for public comment, of the proposed rule or amendment sought by that petition. Although A.R.S. § 12-109(C) purports to require that procedural rules or amendments not become effective until at least sixty (60) days after their adoption and promulgation, Rule 28(g), Rules of the Supreme Court authorizes the Court to adopt rules on an emergency basis.

A procedural rule of court is one that prescribes a course of conduct that litigants are required to follow such that the failure to comply with it may deprive the parties of substantial rights. *State, ex rel. Romley v. Ballinger*, 209 Ariz. 1, 97 P.3d 101 (2004). An "administrative order," on the other hand, generally embodies an internal statement of policy not directly applicable to litigants or their counsel, which is adopted to provide more efficient management and disposition of cases. *State, ex rel. Romley v. Ballinger*, 209 Ariz. 1, 97 P.3d 101 (2004).

The Arizona Supreme Court amended Rule 28 to prescribe a schedule for consideration of proposed rules and amendments under which the Court, absent an emergency, will only consider such proposals once a year. Under the "annual rule-making cycle" set forth in the amended Rule, petitions for the adoption of new rules or rule amendments must be filed by January 10 in any year.

If the Court determines to open the matter for public comment, the petition is circulated in the manner provided in Rule 28(C). Supreme Court Rule 28(D) governs comments to rule petitions, and provides among other matters, for the submission of comments on or before May 20 of each year, unless the Court specifies a different date in its request for comments. The Court will then consider them at its "Rules Agenda" in September, and any new Rules or Rule amendments adopted will be given an effective date of the following January 1.

It should be noted, however, that over the last several years, the Court has considered certain Rule 28 petitions at a rules agenda meeting held in early December and has adopted rule amendments at that December meeting effective January 1 of the then upcoming year. Adhering to the "you never know" philosophy, practitioners would be well-served to check the Court's website at frequent intervals.

Under Rule 83, the Superior Courts in individual counties may promulgate Local Rules applicable to cases pending in that Superior Court. Such Local Rules may not be inconsistent with the Arizona Rules of Civil Procedure, and do not become effective until approved by the Supreme Court. *State, ex rel. Romley v.*

Ballinger, 209 Ariz. 1, 97 P.3d 101 (2004).

On appeal, the court reviews *de novo* questions involving the interpretation of court rules and "evaluates procedural rules using principles of statutory construction." *Haroutunian v. Valueoptions, Inc.*, 218 Ariz. 541, 189 P.3d 1114 (Ct. App. Div. 2 2008). Thus, when interpreting the language of an ambiguous court rule, an appellate court considers "a variety of elements, including the rule's context, the language used, the subject matter, the historical background, the effects and consequences, and its spirit and purpose," to determine the framers' intent. *State ex rel. Romley v. Superior Court In and For County of Maricopa*, 168 Ariz. 167, 812 P.2d 985 (1991); *Haroutunian v. Valueoptions, Inc.*, 218 Ariz. 541, 189 P.3d 1114 (Ct. App. Div. 2 2008); *Vega v. Sullivan*, 199 Ariz. 504, 19 P.3d 645 (Ct. App. Div. 2 2001).

6. *Jurisdiction of the Superior Court; Justice Courts.* The Superior Court is Arizona's court of general jurisdiction. *Marvin Johnson, P.C. v. Myers*, 184 Ariz. 98, 907 P.2d 67 (1995); *State ex rel. Neely v. Brown*, 177 Ariz. 6, 864 P.2d 1038 (1993). By Constitution, the Superior Court is a court of record and has original jurisdiction of, *inter alia:*

(1) all cases and proceedings for which exclusive jurisdiction has not been vested in another court,

(2) other cases in which the demand or amount in controversy is $1,000 or more, and

(3) special cases and proceedings not otherwise provided for.

Ariz. Const. Art. VI, §§ 14(1), (3), (11) and § 30(A); A.R.S. § 12-123.

Although the Superior Court has nominally separate "Divisions" or "Sections" sitting in each of Arizona's fifteen counties, it remains a single, unitary Court. *Lerette v. Adams*, 186 Ariz. 628, 925 P.2d 1079 (Ct. App. Div. 1 1996). Although Judges of the Superior Court sit primarily in their "home county," they are qualified and eligible to serve in any Division of the Court. *Lerette v. Adams*, 186 Ariz. 628, 925 P.2d 1079 (Ct. App. Div. 1 1996); *State v. Patterson*, 222 Ariz. 574, 218 P.3d 1031 (Ct. App. Div. 1 2009). The superior court is bound by appellate decisions, regardless of the division out of which they arise. *State v. Patterson*, 222 Ariz. 574, 218 P.3d 1031 (Ct. App. Div. 1 2009).

This constitutional grant of jurisdiction includes original jurisdiction over all probate matters. *Matter of Wilcox Revocable Trust*, 192 Ariz. 337, 965 P.2d 71 (Ct. App. Div. 1 1998). In Arizona, there is no such thing as a distinct Probate Court. *Marvin Johnson, P.C. v. Myers*, 184 Ariz. 98, 907 P.2d 67 (1995); *In re Estate of Newman*, 219 Ariz. 260, 196 P.3d 863 (Ct. App. Div. 1 2008), as amended on other grounds, (July 17, 2008). The single trial court of general jurisdiction is the Superior Court, and a judge of the Superior Court presiding over a probate proceeding has the power to order the consolidation of that probate proceeding with a civil matter connected with it. *Marvin Johnson, P.C. v. Myers*, 184 Ariz. 98, 907 P.2d 67 (1995); *Huerta v. Nelson*, 222 Ariz. 44, 213 P.3d 193 (Ct. App. Div. 1 2009); *In re Estate of Newman*, 219 Ariz. 260, 196 P.3d 863 (Ct. App. Div. 1 2008), as amended on other grounds, (July 17, 2008); *Roden v. Roden*, 190 Ariz. 407, 949 P.2d 67 (Ct. App. Div. 1 1997) (Domestic relations court had jurisdiction in dissolution action to consider wife's contract claim).

In dissolution proceedings, the jurisdiction of the Superior Court includes jurisdiction to adjudicate contract claims that involve separate property interests. *Roden v. Roden*, 190 Ariz. 407, 949 P.2d 67 (Ct. App. Div. 1 1997). An action for dissolution abates, however, and the Superior Court loses jurisdiction over it when one of the spouses involved dies before any order is entered, other than one for a preliminary injunction. *Van Emmerik v. Colosi*, 193 Ariz. 398, 972 P.2d 1034 (Ct. App. Div. 1 1998).

The failure of a party to resort to and exhaust available administrative remedies deprives the Superior Court of jurisdiction to hear that party's claim. *McNutt v. Department of Revenue of State of Ariz.*, 196 Ariz. 255, 995 P.2d 691 (Ct. App. Div. 1 1998). It has also been held that the enactment and amendment of zoning ordinances are exclusively legislative functions, and a Superior Court has neither jurisdiction nor authority to order a rezoning of property. *Mehlhorn v. Pima County*, 194 Ariz. 140, 978 P.2d 117 (Ct. App. Div. 2 1998).

(Justice Court Jurisdiction)

Justice courts are not courts of record and their civil jurisdiction is constitutionally limited to matters where the amount in controversy, exclusive of interest and costs, does not exceed $10,000. Ariz.Const. Art. VI, §§ 32(B), (c). Effective January 1, 2013, the Arizona Supreme Court adopted the Justice Court Rules of Civil Procedure, which are based on the Arizona Rules of Civil Procedure. The Justice Court Rules of Civil Procedure do not apply to evictions, civil traffic or civil boating proceedings, or to protective orders or injunctions against harassment in justice court. Further, Rule 113(i) [dismissal due to lack of service] and Rule 140 [entry of default judgment] apply only in small claims cases.

The 'Introduction to the Justice Court Rules of Civil Procedure' explains that the wording of a justice court rule may differ from a corresponding superior court rule, but that such differences "are intended only to make the justice court rule simpler and easier to understand." The Introduction also notes that case law interpreting a rule of civil procedure is authoritative unless a justice court rule "expressly adds a requirement or provides a right" not found in a rule of civil procedure.

By statute, the justice courts have exclusive original jurisdiction in civil actions where the amount in controversy is $10,000 or less. A.R.S. § 22-201(B). In determining whether the amount in controversy exceeds $10,000, A.R.S. § 22-201(B) specifies that "interest, costs and awarded attorney's fees when authorized by law" should not be considered. Prior case law, however, suggests that attorney's fees that are claimed pursuant to a contractual provision that specifically provides for the award of such fees may be included. *Metro Collections v. Meggers*, 180 Ariz. 570, 886 P.2d 649 (Ct. App. Div. 1 1994).

If, in an action properly commenced in justice court, a verified counterclaim seeking a recovery greater than $10,000 is filed, the matter is to be transferred to the Superior Court. A.R.S. § 22-201(G).

Justice courts also have jurisdiction to try the right to possession of real property, but not if title to or ownership of the property becomes in issue. A.R.S. § 22-201(D). The justice courts have concurrent jurisdiction with the Superior Court in forcible entry and detained cases where the damages sought are $10,000 or less. A.R.S. § 22-201(C), except that in counties where the population is more than two million persons (presently only Maricopa County), that jurisdiction is "original." A.R.S. § 22-201(E)(4).

Under A.R.S. §§ 22-501 *et seq.*, each justice court is to have a small claims division, which has concurrent original jurisdiction with the justice court over civil matters, with certain statutory exceptions, in which the amount in controversy does not exceed $3,500. *See,* A.R.S. § 22-503(A), as amended effective December 31, 2013. The Superior Court retains at least concurrent original jurisdiction in forfeiture cases in which the property in question has a value of between $1,000 and $5,000. *State ex rel. Neely v. Brown*, 177 Ariz. 6, 864 P.2d 1038 (1993).

In criminal cases, when a Justice Court elects to utilize the method for summoning jurors set forth in A.R.S. § 21-331(C), the jurors must be residents of the precinct in which the Justice Court sits. *State ex rel. Romley v. Johnson*, 196 Ariz. 52, 993 P.2d 453 (Ct. App. Div. 1 1998). When the Justice Court elects to use the county-wide system for juror selection authorized by A.R.S. § 21-331(A), however, no such limitation exists and the jurors need only be residents of the County, but not necessarily the precinct, where the Justice Court sits. *State ex rel. Romley v. Johnson*, 196 Ariz. 52, 993 P.2d 453 (Ct. App. Div. 1 1998).

The Superior Court has appellate jurisdiction over all cases arising in the justice and other inferior courts. Ariz. Const. Art.

VI, § 16; A.R.S. § 12-124(A). Such appeals are governed by the Superior Court Rules of Appellate Procedure—Civil and the Superior Court Rules of Appellate Procedure—Criminal.

7. *Visiting Judges.* It is not uncommon for a matter pending in the Superior Court for one county to be heard by a Judge of the Superior Court for a different county. A Judge of the Superior Court must serve in another county if directed to do so by the Chief Justice of the Supreme Court, and may do so if requested by the Presiding Judge of the other county. Ariz. Const. Art. VI, Sec. 19. The transfer of a case filed in one Superior Court to a Judge from another county does not represent an improper change of venue. *Lerette v. Adams*, 186 Ariz. 628, 925 P.2d 1079 (Ct. App. Div. 1 1996). The Superior Court is a single, unified trial court that is separated into divisions by county. *Lerette v. Adams*, 186 Ariz. 628, 925 P.2d 1079 (Ct. App. Div. 1 1996); A.R.S. § 12-121(A). Although Judges of the Superior Court serve primarily in their "home county," they are qualified and eligible to serve in any division of the Court. *State v. Patterson*, 222 Ariz. 574, 218 P.3d 1031 (Ct. App. Div. 1 2009); *Lerette v. Adams*, 186 Ariz. 628, 925 P.2d 1079 (Ct. App. Div. 1 1996).

Under Rule 95(d) of the Rules of the Supreme Court, if a visiting judge hears a proceeding in another county and takes the matter under advisement, the judge must transmit the decision or order to the Clerk of the Superior Court in the county in which the action is pending *only* if the judge is in that county at the time the order or decision is signed. Otherwise, the judge is to transmit the decision or order to the Clerk of the Superior Court in the county of the judge's residence. The Clerk is to file the decision, which becomes effective upon filing, and notify the parties and, if necessary, the Clerk of the Superior Court in which the action is pending. If the decision is upon a matter tried to the Court, judgment thereon may be entered ten (10) days following the Clerk's notice and the judgment may be signed by a Judge of the Superior Court in the county in which the action is pending.

A visiting judge may extend the dates for hearing and determining, but not the date for filing, a motion for new trial or a motion to set aside a judgment. A visiting judge, however, may extend the date for filing a certified transcript or statement of the evidence or proceedings.

All requests for a visiting judge to be assigned to a Superior Court in a county are to be initiated by the Presiding Judge in that county. All requests for a judge of a Superior Court to sit as a visiting judge in another county are to be supervised by the Presiding Judge in the county where the requested judge is regularly assigned. The Presiding Judge or Court Administrator, if any, are to keep records of judges visiting from and to other counties.

A Superior Court judge also may substitute for a member of the Arizona Supreme Court or the Arizona Court of Appeals in a particular case. Ariz. Const. Art. 6, § 3. Retired judges are subject to call to serve as trial or appellate judges. Ariz. Const. Art. 6, § 20. The state pays the expenses of a visiting judge for appellate service; the county in which the visiting judge serves as a trial judge pays his or her expenses. A.R.S. § 12-129. A justice of the peace may act in any precinct in the county or in any adjoining precinct in another county. A.R.S. § 22-114(A). When the justice acts in another county, that county pays the expense. A.R.S. § 22-114(B). Upon disqualification, a justice may request another justice of the peace in the county to conduct the trial where the action is pending. A.R.S. § 22-204(A).

8. *Time Limits for Decision*. Article VI, Sec. 21 of the Arizona Constitution provides that every matter submitted to a Judge of the Superior Court for decision shall be decided within sixty (60) days of the date it is submitted. This constitutional provision further requires the Arizona Supreme Court provide by rule for the speedy disposition of all matters not decided within the specified 60-day period of time. Rule 91(e) of the Rules of the Arizona Supreme Court, which in effect replaces former Rules 39(*l*) and 77(i), Ariz. R. Civ. P., and former Rule XIII of the now abrogated Uniform Rules of Practice of the Superior Court, reiterates this constitutional directive. It has been held that the requirement is directory rather than mandatory, but should be observed as a matter of course in all but the most extraordinary circumstances. *Wustrack v. Clark*, 18 Ariz. App. 407, 502 P.2d 1084 (Div. 1 1972). The failure to issue a decision on a submitted matter within the requisite 60 days, however, does not deprive the Superior Court of jurisdiction. *In re Appleton's Estate*, 15 Ariz. App. 490, 489 P.2d 864 (Div. 1 1971); *Western Sav. and Loan Ass'n v. Diamond Lazy K Guest Ranch, Inc.*, 18 Ariz. App. 256, 501 P.2d 432 (Div. 1 1972).

Although the constitutional provision also specifies that the Supreme Court is to provide by rule for the speedy disposition of all matters not decided within the specified sixty (60) day period, no rules specifically addressing that situation have been adopted. Rule 91(e), Rules of the Supreme Court requires the Clerk of the Superior Court in each county to provide the Administrative Director of the Courts with detailed quarterly reports of matters in that Court that remain undecided for sixty (60) days or more on the date of report, but does not elaborate on what steps are to be taken with respect to such undecided matters. There is also no effective enforcement mechanism available to the parties in a case where a matter has gone undecided for over sixty (60) days.

Rule 2.10(c) of the Maricopa County Superior Court Local Rules requires counsel in a case to notify the Presiding Judge when a matter submitted for decision in the case has gone undecided for in excess of sixty (60) days. Alternatively, counsel may confer with the Deputy Clerk regularly assigned to the Division in question to ascertain whether the matter is still under advisement or has been inadvertently overlooked.

The Court of Appeals has suggested that parties should make a record in the trial court, before a decision is issued, urging compliance with the 60-day rule. *Western Sav. and Loan Ass'n v. Diamond Lazy K Guest Ranch, Inc.*, 18 Ariz. App. 256, 501 P.2d 432 (Div. 1 1972). In extraordinary cases, relief by special action in the nature of mandamus may also be available. *Western Sav. and Loan Ass'n v. Diamond Lazy K Guest Ranch, Inc.*, 18 Ariz. App. 256, 501 P.2d 432 (Div. 1 1972); *Wustrack v. Clark*, 18 Ariz. App. 407, 502 P.2d 1084 (Div. 1 1972).

Rule 2. One form of action

There shall be one form of action to be known as "civil action."

AUTHORS' COMMENTS

Analysis

1. *Scope and Purpose of Rule.* In prescribing that there is to be one form of action known as a "civil action," Ariz. R. Civ. P. 2 intends to abolish distinctions between courts of law and courts of equity for procedural purposes and abandon the common law notion of distinct forms of action with distinct procedural requirements. *Manor v. Stevens*, 61 Ariz. 511, 152 P.2d 133 (1944); *Day v. Wiswall*, 11 Ariz. App. 306, 464 P.2d 626 (Div. 2 1970) (rejected on other grounds by, Grynberg v. Shaffer, 216 Ariz. 256, 165 P.3d 234 (Ct. App. Div. 1 2007)). The common law forms of action may, however, be the reference point used in determining whether all the requisite elements of a claim have been alleged or established. *First Nat. Bank of Arizona v. Superior Court of Maricopa County*, 112 Ariz. 292, 541 P.2d 392 (1975).

The Rule does not abolish, however, all procedural distinctions between legal and equitable claims. For example, in the case of claims traditionally heard in equity, the parties retain the right to trial by jury, but the jury's verdict is merely advisory and not binding. *Graham v. Shooke*, 107 Ariz. 79, 482 P.2d 446 (1971); *Kostolansky v. Lesher*, 95 Ariz. 103, 387 P.2d 804 (1963); *Stukey v. Stephens*, 37 Ariz. 514, 295 P. 973 (1931); *Timmons v. City of Tucson*, 171 Ariz. 350, 830 P.2d 871, 63 Fair Empl. Prac. Cas. (BNA) 11 (Ct. App. Div. 2 1991); *Slonsky v. Hunter*, 17 Ariz. App. 231, 496 P.2d 874 (Div. 1 1972); *Zimmer v. Salcido*, 9 Ariz. App. 416, 453 P.2d 245 (1969).

2. *Comparison With Federal Rule.* ARCP 2 is, for all practical purposes, identical to FRCP 2.

3. *Legal and Equitable Remedies.* Ariz. R. Civ. P. 2 merely merges the separate law and equity court divisions for procedural purposes and leaves unchanged the substantive distinctions between legal and equitable claims and remedies. *Evans v. Mason*, 82 Ariz. 40, 308 P.2d 245, 65 A.L.R.2d 936 (1957). Thus, "laches,"

a defense only to claims in equity, is specifically listed in Rule 8(c) as an affirmative defense that must be pled. The Rules of Civil Procedure merely provide a uniform method for the presentation of claims, whether characterized as legal or equitable in nature.

4. *Special Statutory Actions.* While there is nominally only one form of action, Arizona has a number of statutory provisions that specify procedural requirements for particular types of civil actions. These include actions for declaratory judgments, A.R.S. §§ 12-1831 *et seq.;* consumer fraud actions, A.R.S. §§ 44-1521 *et seq.;* actions for dissolution of marriage, A.R.S. §§ 25-311 *et seq.;* paternity and maternity proceedings, A.R.S. §§ 25-801 *et seq.;* replevin actions, A.R.S. §§ 12-1801 *et seq.;* forcible detainer actions, A.R.S. §§ 12-1171 *et seq.;* and actions to quiet title, A.R.S. §§ 12-1101 *et seq.*

II. COMMENCEMENT OF ACTION; SERVICE OF PROCESS, PLEADINGS, MOTIONS AND ORDERS; DUTIES OF COUNSEL

Rule 3. Commencement of action

A civil action is commenced by filing a complaint with the court.

AUTHORS' COMMENTS

Analysis

1. Scope and Purpose of Rule.
2. Comparison With Federal Rule.
3. Civil Cover Sheets.
4. Arbitration Certificates.
5. Pre-complaint Activities; Claims Against Governmental Entities.
6. Lis Pendens.

1. *Scope and Purpose of Rule.* Ariz. R. Civ. P. 3 provides the test for determining when an action is effectively commenced. An action is commenced by the filing of a complaint and service need not be completed to cease the running of any applicable statute of limitations. *City of Tucson v. Clear Channel Outdoor, Inc.*, 209 Ariz. 544, 105 P.3d 1163 (2005); *Murphey v. Valenzuela*, 95 Ariz. 30, 386 P.2d 78 (1963). Merely obtaining an order to show cause will not suffice; only the filing of a complaint invokes the Court's jurisdiction. *Bryant v. Bloch Companies*, 166 Ariz. 46, 800 P.2d 33 (Ct. App. Div. 1 1990).

The date of filing determines when the court initially acquires jurisdiction. *Allen v. Superior Court of Maricopa County*, 86 Ariz. 205, 344 P.2d 163 (1959). An action which, due to some defect, is not validly commenced, *i.e.*, where the complaint is not signed by a party or an attorney, does not halt the running of the statute of limitations. *Peters v. M & O Const., Inc.*, 119 Ariz. 34, 579 P.2d 72 (Ct. App. Div. 1 1978); *Safeway Stores, Inc. v. Maricopa County Superior Court*, 19 Ariz. App. 210, 505 P.2d 1383 (Div. 1 1973).

The complaint is merely a statement of the plaintiff's claim; the summons issued under the seal of the Court announces the presence of the Court in the dispute and gives notice to the defendant that the Court is assuming jurisdiction for purposes of resolving the controversy. *Spiegel v. Board of Sup'rs of Maricopa County*, 175 Ariz. 479, 857 P.2d 1333 (Tax Ct. 1993). While the action is technically "commenced" upon filing, service of a summons and of the complaint by one of the means authorized in Rule 4.1 or 4.2 is necessary to maintain the viability of the action.

The time limit for securing service of process domestically is within one hundred and twenty (120) days after the filing of the complaint. If service is not made upon a defendant within that period, the action is to be dismissed as to that defendant without prejudice, unless the party on whose behalf service was to be made demonstrates good cause why service was not made. This time limit does not apply to service in a foreign country. Rule 4(i).

Arizona follows the "notice pleading" regime of the Federal Rules of Civil Procedure and it is not necessary to allege the evidentiary details of plaintiff's claim for relief. *Hogan v. Washington Mut. Bank, N.A.*, 230 Ariz. 584, 277 P.3d 781 (2012) (Although Rule 8 requires only a short and plain statement of the claim showing the party is entitled to relief, in analyzing a pleading under Rule 12(b) (6), the court will assume the truth of such statements.); *Coleman v. City of Mesa*, 230 Ariz. 352, 284 P.3d 863 (2012) ("Arizona follows a notice pleading standard."); *Cullen v. Auto-Owners Ins. Co.*, 218 Ariz. 417, 189 P.3d 344 (2008); *Maldonado v. Southern Pac. Transp. Co.*, 129 Ariz. 165, 629 P.2d 1001 (Ct. App. Div. 2 1981); *Schmidt v. Mel Clayton Ford*, 124 Ariz. 65, 601 P.2d 1349 (Ct. App. Div. 1 1979); *Folk v. City of Phoenix*, 27 Ariz. App. 146, 551 P.2d 595 (Div. 1 1976).

A complaint which is overly conclusory, however, will be subject to a motion for more definite statement and, possibly a motion to dismiss for failure to state a claim. *Belen Loan Investors, LLC v. Bradley*, 231 Ariz. 448, 296 P.3d 984 (Ct. App. Div. 2 2012) (A complaint that sets forth only factually unsupported legal conclusions does not satisfy Rule 8(a)'s notice pleading standard.). The complaint should set forth sufficient facts to satisfy the Court that a claim for relief has been stated and to permit the framing of discovery into the particulars of that claim.

2. *Comparison With Federal Rule.* ARCP 3 is textually identical to FRCP 3.

3. *Civil Cover Sheets.* Ariz. R. Civ. P. 8(h)(1) was amended in 2009 to eliminate the requirement that a complaint specify one of four classifications into which the civil action could be categorized, and to substitute in its place a requirement that the plaintiff complete and submit a Civil Cover Sheet in a form approved by the Supreme Court. The amended Rule specifies that the Civil Cover Sheet is to contain at least the following information: the plaintiff's correct name and mailing address, the name and State Bar number of plaintiff's attorney, the names(s) of the defendant(s), the nature of the action, the applicable main case cate-

gory and subcategory designated by the Director of the Administrative Office of the Courts, and whether the action qualifies as complex under the criteria specified in Rule 8(i). Individual Superior Courts may, by Local Rule, require that an Addendum contain additional information. The basic form of Civil Cover Sheet is to be maintained on the Administrative Office of the Court's Internet Web site. The Rule 8(i) certification of complex case is Form 10, Ariz. R. Civ. P. 84.

4. *Arbitration Certificates.* Ariz. R. Civ. P. 5(i) requires that both the complaint and the answer be accompanied by the certificate required by Rule 72(e). That Rule requires the filing of a separate certificate, or controverting certificate, on compulsory arbitration certifying whether or not the action is subject to court-annexed mandatory arbitration. The requirement for such certificates is discussed further in Section 4 of the *Authors' Comments* to Rule 72.

5. *Pre-complaint Activities; Claims Against Governmental Entities.* Although an action is formally commenced by the filing of a complaint, there are instances where statutes prescribe certain steps to be taken before that point which may affect a claimant's right to recover and/or the scope of relief available. That may be the case in pursuing claims against public entities or officials. Under the Arizona Constitution, the Legislature may restrict the right to sue governmental entities and employees, and prescribe the manner in which such a suit may be maintained. *Flood Control Dist. of Maricopa County v. Gaines*, 202 Ariz. 248, 43 P.3d 196 (Ct. App. Div. 1 2002); *Landry v. Superior Court In and For Pima County*, 125 Ariz. 337, 609 P.2d 607 (Ct. App. Div. 2 1980).

A.R.S. § 12-821 formerly provided that persons with claims against public entities or employees were to submit them within twelve months after the cause of action accrued. No action on such a claim could be maintained, even though brought within the time prescribed by the applicable statute of limitations, unless there was a showing of excusable neglect in failing to submit a timely claim or a showing that the absence of excusable neglect was due to the conduct of the claimant's attorney. In the latter case, the action could proceed but the public entity or employee defendant had a right of indemnity against the attorney involved. *Cf., Hauskins v. McGillicuddy*, 175 Ariz. 42, 852 P.2d 1226 (Ct. App. Div. 1 1992).

As part of comprehensive "tort reform" legislation, the Arizona Legislature in April 1993 repealed existing A.R.S. § 12-821, and replaced it with a new A.R.S. § 12-821 which simply prescribes a one-year statute of limitations for personal injury actions against public entities or public employees alleged to be acting within the scope of their public employment. This statute has been found to be constitutional. *Stulce v. Salt River Project Agr. Imp. and Power Dist.*, 197 Ariz. 87, 3 P.3d 1007 (Ct. App. Div. 1 1999).

Although this statute was amended in 1994 to remove the language referring to acts performed within the scope of employment, the one-year statute of limitations for claims against public employees (and, by implication, the notice of claim statute, A.R.S. § 12-821.01 as well) applies only to claims arising out of acts performed within the scope of the public employee's employment. *Dube v. Desai*, 218 Ariz. 362, 186 P.3d 587, 233 Ed. Law Rep. 954 (Ct. App. Div. 2 2008); *McCloud v. State, Ariz. Dept. of Public Safety*, 217 Ariz. 82, 170 P.3d 691 (Ct. App. Div. 2 2007).

In 1994, the Legislature also adopted a new A.R.S. § 12-821.01, which generally requires that persons with claims against a public entity or employee must file such claims with an authorized public official within 180 days after the cause of action accrues, except minors may file such notices within 180 days after turning 18. *See* A.R.S. § 12-821.01(D). *Estate of DeSela v. Prescott Unified School Dist. No. 1*, 226 Ariz. 387, 249 P.3d 767, 265 Ed. Law Rep. 1241 (2011); *Haab v. County of Maricopa*, 219 Ariz. 9, 191 P.3d 1025 (Ct. App. Div. 1 2008). *Cf. Clark Equipment Co. v. Arizona Property and Cas. Ins. Guar. Fund*, 189 Ariz. 433, 943 P.2d 793 (Ct. App. Div. 1 1997). Another statute, A.R.S. § 12-821, states the deadline for commencing a lawsuit, *i.e.*, within one year after the "cause of action accrues and not afterward." A minor may bring such action within one year after turning eighteen as prescribed by A.R.S. § 12-502.

The limitations periods set forth in A.R.S. § 12-821.01 is not extended by the fact that a case, if filed, will be subject to mandatory arbitration. *Andress v. City of Chandler*, 198 Ariz. 112, 7 P.3d 121 (Ct. App. Div. 1 2000).

The limitations period may be tolled, however, by the doctrine of equitable tolling, which requires a showing of excusable neglect and/or that the defendant improperly caused the claimant to delay in submitting the notice of claim. *Kosman v. State*, 199 Ariz. 184, 16 P.3d 211 (Ct. App. Div. 1 2000). Such claims remain subject to the one-year statute of limitations in A.R.S. § 12-821. If a notice of claim is not properly filed within the statutory time limit, the claim is barred by statute. *Mayer Unified School Dist. v. Winkleman*, 219 Ariz. 562, 201 P.3d 523, 241 Ed. Law Rep. 436 (2009); *Deer Valley Unified School Dist. No. 97 v. Houser*, 214 Ariz. 293, 152 P.3d 490, 25 I.E.R. Cas. (BNA) 1491 (2007); *Falcon ex rel. Sandoval v. Maricopa County*, 213 Ariz. 525, 144 P.3d 1254 (2006).

The "mail delivery rule" applies to such notices, and there is a presumption that a notice that has been mailed has been properly filed. *Lee v. State*, 218 Ariz. 235, 182 P.3d 1169 (2008); *Lee v. State*, 225 Ariz. 576, 242 P.3d 175 (Ct. App. Div. 1 2010), review denied, (May 24, 2011), on appeal from remand, (holding, "a filing under A.R.S. § 12-821.01(A) may be accomplished through regular mail, and proof of mailing is evidence the governmental entity actually received the notice"). If, however, the governmental agency in question denies receipt of the notice, that presumption may cease to operate. The fact of mailing, however, will still have evidentiary value and will preclude dismissal of a suit for failure to submit a prior claim. *Lee v. State*, 218 Ariz. 235, 182 P.3d 1169 (2008). See also, *Lee v. State*, 225 Ariz. 576, 242 P.3d 175 (Ct. App. Div. 1 2010), review denied, (May 24, 2011), on appeal from remand, (holding the jury, and not the trial court, must decide factual dispute as to whether state had received plaintiff's notice of claim required by A.R.S. § 12-821.01).

The State Compensation Fund has been held to be a "public entity" within the meaning of A.R.S. § 12-821.01. *State Compensation Fund v. Superior Court In and For County of Maricopa (EnerGCorp, Inc.)*, 190 Ariz. 371, 948 P.2d 499 (Ct. App. Div. 1 1997). Similarly, because the statute defines the term "public entity" to include "any political subdivision of this state," it applies to claims against the Salt River Project Agricultural Improvement and Power District, which is, by statute, a political subdivision of the state. *Stulce v. Salt River Project Agr. Imp. and Power Dist.*, 197 Ariz. 87, 3 P.3d 1007 (Ct. App. Div. 1 1999).

Deputy clerks of the Superior Court are officers, agents or employees of the Judicial Department of the State of Arizona, and a party wishing to pursue claims against them arising out of the performance of their official duties must first submit a notice of claim to the State under the statute. *Salerno v. Espinoza*, 210 Ariz. 586, 115 P.3d 626 (Ct. App. Div. 1 2005). The notice of claim statute and the one-year statute of limitations cannot be applied to claims based upon 42 U.S.C. § 1983. *Mulleneaux v. State*, 190 Ariz. 535, 950 P.2d 1156 (Ct. App. Div. 1 1997).

A claimant who asserts that a public employee's conduct giving rise to a claim for damages was committed within the course of the public employment must give notice of the claim to *both* the employer and the employee individually. *Harris v. Cochise Health Systems*, 215 Ariz. 344, 160 P.3d 223 (Ct. App. Div. 2 2007); *Crum v. Superior Court In and For County of Maricopa*, 186 Ariz. 351, 922 P.2d 316 (Ct. App. Div. 1 1996). The purpose of notice of claim statutes is to allow the public entity to investigate and assess liability, to permit the possibility of settlement before litigation, and to assist the public entity in financial planning and budgeting. *Backus v. State*, 220 Ariz. 101, 203 P.3d 499 (2009); *Deer Valley Unified School Dist. No. 97 v. Houser*, 214 Ariz. 293, 152 P.3d 490, 25 I.E.R. Cas. (BNA) 1491 (2007); *Falcon ex rel.*

Sandoval v. Maricopa County, 213 Ariz. 525, 144 P.3d 1254 (2006); *Vasquez v. State*, 220 Ariz. 304, 206 P.3d 753 (Ct. App. Div. 2 2008); *Havasupai Tribe of Havasupai Reservation v. Arizona Bd. of Regents*, 220 Ariz. 214, 204 P.3d 1063, 243 Ed. Law Rep. 889 (Ct. App. Div. 1 2008); *Yollin v. City of Glendale*, 219 Ariz. 24, 191 P.3d 1040 (Ct. App. Div. 1 2008); *Haab v. County of Maricopa*, 219 Ariz. 9, 191 P.3d 1025 (Ct. App. Div. 1 2008); *Martineau v. Maricopa County*, 207 Ariz. 332, 86 P.3d 912 (Ct. App. Div. 1 2004); *Crum v. Superior Court In and For County of Maricopa*, 186 Ariz. 351, 922 P.2d 316 (Ct. App. Div. 1 1996).

A party who has filed such a notice of claim must amend the notice or file a new notice to preserve claims which arose after, or which were otherwise omitted from, the original notice. *Haab v. County of Maricopa*, 219 Ariz. 9, 191 P.3d 1025 (Ct. App. Div. 1 2008). Although a notice of claim filed pursuant to A.R.S. § 12-821.01 (or A.R.S. § 12-1134) may be amended to cure a defect, such amendment must be made within 180 days "after the cause of action accrues," at least when the defect concerns a matter known to the claimant. *Turner v. City of Flagstaff*, 226 Ariz. 341, 247 P.3d 1011 (Ct. App. Div. 1 2011), as corrected, (Mar. 3, 2011).

The current claims statute permits an action against a public entity to proceed only if a claimant files a timely notice of claim that includes: (1) facts sufficient to permit the public entity to understand the basis upon which liability is claimed, (2) a specific amount for which the claim can be settled, and (3) the facts supporting the amount claimed. *Backus v. State*, 220 Ariz. 101, 203 P.3d 499 (2009). These requirements in the claims statute allow the public entity to investigate and assess liability, permit the possibility of settlement before litigation and assist the public entity in financial planning and budgeting. *Backus v. State*, 220 Ariz. 101, 203 P.3d 499 (2009). Such a notice is not required, however, where the claim arises from purely private acts of persons who happen to be public employees and which are not within the course and scope of their employment. *Crum v. Superior Court In and For County of Maricopa*, 186 Ariz. 351, 922 P.2d 316 (Ct. App. Div. 1 1996).

Where the sole relief sought on a claim is a declaratory, rather than a monetary, judgment, compliance with the notice of claim statute is not required. *Arpaio v. Maricopa County Bd. of Supervisors*, 225 Ariz. 358, 238 P.3d 626 (Ct. App. Div. 1 2010), review denied, (Jan. 4, 2011); *Home Builders Ass'n of Cent. Arizona v. Kard*, 219 Ariz. 374, 381, 199 P.3d 629, 636 (Ct. App. Div. 1 2008), as amended on other grounds, (July 10, 2008); *Martineau v. Maricopa County*, 207 Ariz. 332, 86 P.3d 912 (Ct. App. Div. 1 2004) (notice of claim statute did not apply in declaratory judgment action because (1) relief did not seek damages, (2) would not result in any monetary award even if successful (absent possible costs and attorneys' fees), (3) would have no direct effect upon financial planning or budgeting and (4) evaluation of the claim did not depend upon the availability of witnesses or evidence).

As noted, the current claims statute, A.R.S. § 12-821.01, also requires that the claim "contain a specific amount for which the claim can be settled and the facts supporting that amount." That requirement is not satisfied by a notice which uses qualifying language, such as "approximately," "no less than," or "in excess of," and an action based on such a claim will be barred by statute. *Deer Valley Unified School Dist. No. 97 v. Houser*, 214 Ariz. 293, 152 P.3d 490, 25 I.E.R. Cas. (BNA) 1491 (2007). Claimants are required to include in the notice a particular and certain amount of money that, if agreed to by the governmental entity involved, will settle the claim. *Backus v. State*, 220 Ariz. 101, 203 P.3d 499 (2009); *Deer Valley Unified School Dist. No. 97 v. Houser*, 214 Ariz. 293, 152 P.3d 490, 25 I.E.R. Cas. (BNA) 1491 (2007); *Yollin v. City of Glendale*, 219 Ariz. 24, 191 P.3d 1040 (Ct. App. Div. 1 2008).

To satisfy this requirement of the statute where a claim is presented on behalf of a purported class, the putative class representative must include in the notice of claim a specific amount for which that individual's claim can be settled, and also a statement that, if litigation ensues, that individual intends to seek certification of a plaintiff class; then if a class is later certified, the notice of claim will serve as a representative notice for the other class members. *City Of Phoenix v. Fields*, 219 Ariz. 568, 201 P.3d 529 (2009). A notice of claim that provides no facts whatsoever to explain or justify a particular damage claim may be legally deficient, and any claim based on that notice statutorily barred. *See*, discussion in *Vasquez v. State*, 220 Ariz. 304, 206 P.3d 753 (Ct. App. Div. 2 2008).

The intent of A.R.S. § 12-821.01, enacted in 1994, was to reinsert the "discovery rule" into the concept of accrual of a cause of action against a public employee or agency. *Stulce v. Salt River Project Agr. Imp. and Power Dist.*, 197 Ariz. 87, 3 P.3d 1007 (Ct. App. Div. 1 1999). Thus, a cause of action accrues for purposes of this statute when the claimant knows or should have known of the claim, and not on the date when the claim is denied by the public agency or employee to which it is submitted. *Stulce v. Salt River Project Agr. Imp. and Power Dist.*, 197 Ariz. 87, 3 P.3d 1007 (Ct. App. Div. 1 1999). Far more importantly, the one-year statute of limitations now applicable to such claims, is not tolled by the filing of the notice of a claim or during the period that the public agency or employee involved is considering it. *Stulce v. Salt River Project Agr. Imp. and Power Dist.*, 197 Ariz. 87, 3 P.3d 1007 (Ct. App. Div. 1 1999).

The provisions of A.R.S. § 12-820.02 provide a qualified immunity, which should probably be plead as a affirmative defense, in that those provisions specify that, in performing certain specified functions, a public employee cannot be held liable absent a showing that the public employee was grossly negligent or intended to cause injury. *Clouse ex rel. Clouse v. State*, 199 Ariz. 196, 16 P.3d 757 (2001). This statute has also been held to be constitutional. *Clouse ex rel. Clouse v. State*, 199 Ariz. 196, 16 P.3d 757 (2001). The statute is not limited in its application to claims by third parties for injuries caused by someone a law enforcement officer failed to keep in custody, but applies as well to claims of injury sustained by persons while held in custody by a law enforcement officer. *Luchanski v. Congrove*, 193 Ariz. 176, 971 P.2d 636 (Ct. App. Div. 1 1998).

Failure to comply with the former "claims statute," A.R.S. § 12-821, was not jurisdictional, and it was not appropriate to raise the issue whether there had been compliance with the statute by a motion to dismiss for lack of subject matter jurisdiction. *Pritchard v. State*, 163 Ariz. 427, 788 P.2d 1178 (1990); *Howland v. State*, 169 Ariz. 293, 818 P.2d 1169 (Ct. App. Div. 1 1991). The requirement that a claim be submitted before instituting suit was held to be more analogous to a statute of limitations, and to be raised by a motion to dismiss for failure to state a claim. *Pritchard v. State*, 163 Ariz. 427, 788 P.2d 1178 (1990); *Howland v. State*, 169 Ariz. 293, 818 P.2d 1169 (Ct. App. Div. 1 1991).

It has now been established that the assertion that a claimant has failed to comply with the notice of claim statute is an affirmative defense, which is waived unless asserted in the answer or a motion to dismiss. *City Of Phoenix v. Fields*, 219 Ariz. 568, 201 P.3d 529 (2009). Even if a party preserves this defense in its answer, that party may waive this defense by its subsequent conduct during the litigation. *City Of Phoenix v. Fields*, 219 Ariz. 568, 201 P.3d 529 (2009).

In addition to A.R.S. § 12-821.01, which applies to state agencies and officers, there is a separate statute, A.R.S. § 11-622, which applies only to county agencies and officers. This statute serves essentially the same purpose as A.R.S. § 12-821.01—to allow the public entity opportunity to investigate and assess liability, to permit the possibility of settlement before litigation, and to assist the public entity in financial planing and budgeting. *Martineau v. Maricopa County*, 207 Ariz. 332, 86 P.3d 912 (Ct. App. Div. 1 2004); *Crum v. Superior Court In and For County of Maricopa*, 186 Ariz. 351, 922 P.2d 316 (Ct. App. Div. 1 1996). Specifically, A.R.S. § 11-622 provides that a claim must be presented to the board of supervisors "within six months after the last item of the account accrues." While this statute refers to claims based on contract, it has not been consistently applied in that fashion. *See, American Credit Bureau v. Pima County*, 122 Ariz. 545, 596 P.2d 380 (Ct. App. Div. 2 1979). And, so, prudence would dictate in favor of complying with the statute even in the case of tort claims to insure the claim is not forfeited. An action upon a rejected or partially disallowed claim is to be commenced within six months after final action on the claim by the board of supervisors. *See,* A.R.S. § 11-630(A).

A procedure somewhat analogous to the "notice of claim" procedure is now imposed by statute with respect to actions brought by purchasers against sellers of dwellings which arise out of or are related to the design, construction, condition or sale of the dwelling. *See* A.R.S. §§ 12-1361 *et seq.* Whether the action concerns a single dwelling, or a multiunit dwelling, the purchaser must provide the seller, before instituting the action, with a written notice (by certified mail, return receipt requested) specifying in reasonable detail the basis of the action. A.R.S. §§ 12-1363(A), (B). If the purchaser institutes such a "dwelling action" without providing the requisite notice, the action may be stayed. A.R.S. § 12-1362.

Following receipt of the "dwelling action" notice, the seller has the right to inspect the dwelling, and must make a good faith written response to the purchaser's notice. A.R.S. §§ 12-1363(C), (D). If the seller fails to provide such a response, then the purchaser may proceed immediately to suit. A.R.S. § 12-1363(E). In any contested dwelling action, the court is to award the prevailing party reasonable attorney's fees, reasonable expert witness fees and taxable costs. A.R.S. § 12-1364. If the seller, during the "inspection period" makes the purchaser an offer, and the judgment eventually obtained by the purchaser is not more favorable than that offer, then the seller is deemed the prevailing party from the date of that offer. A.R.S. § 12-1364.

6. *Lis Pendens.* The purpose of a *lis pendens* is to provide notice to interested parties that a judicial action is pending with respect to certain real property and that title to the property may thereby be affected. *Pueblo Santa Fe Townhomes Owners' Ass'n v. Transcontinental Ins. Co.*, 218 Ariz. 13, 178 P.3d 485 (Ct. App. Div. 1 2008); *West Pinal Family Health Center, Inc. v. McBryde*, 162 Ariz. 546, 785 P.2d 66 (Ct. App. Div. 2 1989). A *lis pendens* also prevents third parties from acquiring interests in the affected property, during the pendency of the litigation, that might hinder the court's ability to grant suitable and effective relief. *HCZ Const., Inc. v. First Franklin Financial Corp.*, 199 Ariz. 361, 18 P.3d 155 (Ct. App. Div. 1 2001); *Hatch Companies Contracting, Inc. v. Arizona Bank*, 170 Ariz. 553, 826 P.2d 1179 (Ct. App. Div. 1 1991). A litigant may properly file a notice of *lis pendens* with respect to real property in Arizona in connection with litigation pending in another jurisdiction that potentially affects title to

that property. *TWE Retirement Fund Trust v. Ream*, 198 Ariz. 268, 8 P.3d 1182 (Ct. App. Div. 1 2000).

Although it is typically prepared in the format of a pleading, a *lis pendens* need not be filed with the Court, but must be recorded, to be effective, with the Recorder for the county in which the property is located. A.R.S. § 12-1191(A). The recording of a *lis pendens* is proper, however, *only* where the relief sought will affect the title to the property. *Wyatt v. Wehmueller*, 163 Ariz. 12, 785 P.2d 581 (Ct. App. Div. 1 1989), opinion vacated in part on other grounds, 167 Ariz. 281, 806 P.2d 870 (1991); *Coventry Homes, Inc. v. Scottscom Partnership*, 155 Ariz. 215, 745 P.2d 962 (Ct. App. Div. 1 1987) (holding that because an equitable lien is an encumbrance on real property, an action to impose such a lien is one affecting title to property); *Santa Fe Ridge Homeowners' Ass'n v. Bartschi*, 219 Ariz. 391, 199 P.3d 646 (Ct. App. Div. 1 2008); *Hatch Companies Contracting, Inc. v. Arizona Bank*, 170 Ariz. 553, 826 P.2d 1179 (Ct. App. Div. 1 1991) (a *lis pendens* filed in an action that does not affect title to real property is a groundless document and improper under A.R.S. § 33-420).

The fact that the plaintiff seeks and may eventually secure a monetary judgment which, if recorded, will constitute a lien on the defendant's property and/or can cause an execution sale of the property is not sufficient grounds for recording a *lis pendens,* even where the plaintiff has applied for a prejudgment attachment of the property. *Wyatt v. Wehmueller*, 163 Ariz. 12, 785 P.2d 581 (Ct. App. Div. 1 1989), opinion vacated in part on other grounds, 167 Ariz. 281, 806 P.2d 870 (1991). Similarly, because Arizona law does not recognize an action to set aside a Trustee's Sale of property under a Deed of Trust on the grounds of the inadequacy of the price paid, a *lis pendens* recorded in connection with such a claim is unauthorized. *Security Sav. and Loan Ass'n v. Fenton*, 167 Ariz. 268, 806 P.2d 362 (Ct. App. Div. 2 1990).

A suit by a homeowners' association to enforce compliance with deed restrictions regarding property maintenance does not affect title to real property within the meaning of the statute. *Pueblo Santa Fe Townhomes Owners' Ass'n v. Transcontinental Ins. Co.*, 218 Ariz. 13, 178 P.3d 485 (Ct. App. Div. 1 2008). An action by a creditor under Arizona's version of the Uniform Fraudulent Transfer Act, A.R.S. §§ 44-1001 to 44-1010, to void a debtor's allegedly fraudulent transfer of real property, on the other hand, is an action "affecting title to real property." *Farris v. Advantage Capital Corp.*, 217 Ariz. 1, 170 P.3d 250 (2007). A party who elects not to pursue a specific performance remedy is not required to file a notice of *lis pendens* in order to mitigate damages. *West Pinal Family Health Center, Inc. v. McBryde*, 162 Ariz. 546, 785 P.2d 66 (Ct. App. Div. 2 1989).

There are a variety of ways to secure the removal of an

improperly recorded *lis pendens,* certain of which are governed by separate and somewhat confusing statutory provisions. Initially, removal of an improper *lis pendens* can be secured through motion or application in the action in connection with which it was filed. In addition, A.R.S. § 12-1191(C) provides that, where a *lis pendens* has been recorded and the underlying action is dismissed without prejudice for lack of prosecution, the plaintiff must furnish the defendant with a release of the *lis pendens,* in recordable form, or is subject to liability in the amount of one thousand dollars and for actual damages.

In addition, A.R.S. § 33-420(A) provides that a person who causes the recordation of a document purporting to claim an interest in real property which is false or groundless is liable to the owner or beneficial title holder of the property for treble the actual damages caused or five thousand dollars, whichever is greater, together with costs and attorney's fees. A.R.S. § 33-420(C) subjects any person named in such a recorded document to liability for treble the actual damages caused or one thousand dollars, whichever is greater, and for costs and attorneys' fees if that person willfully refuses to release or correct the document within twenty days of a formal request to do so. Finally, A.R.S. § 33-420(B) authorizes the owner or beneficial title holder of the real property affected to bring an independent action to clear title to the property and for damages. The purpose of the statute is to protect property owners from actions clouding title to their property. *Lebaron Properties, LLC v. Jeffrey S. Kaufman, Ltd.*, 223 Ariz. 227, 221 P.3d 1041 (Ct. App. Div. 1 2009).

A *lis pendens* which is filed without justification has been held to be a groundless document purporting to claim an interest in real property within the scope of A.R.S. § 33-420. *Wyatt v. Wehmueller*, 163 Ariz. 12, 785 P.2d 581 (Ct. App. Div. 1 1989), opinion vacated in part on other grounds, 167 Ariz. 281, 806 P.2d 870 (1991); *Richey v. Western Pacific Development Corp.*, 140 Ariz. 597, 684 P.2d 169 (Ct. App. Div. 2 1984). In order to prevail in a statutory special action to remove a *lis pendens,* however, the plaintiff must establish that the defendant: (1) caused a document to be recorded, (2) in which an interest in, or a lien or encumbrance against, real property was claimed, (3) which was forged, groundless or contained a material misstatement or a false or otherwise invalid claim. *Evergreen West, Inc. v. Boyd*, 167 Ariz. 614, 810 P.2d 612 (Ct. App. Div. 2 1991). A *lis pendens* should only be found to be "groundless" where the claim that the underlying action is one affecting title to real property has no arguable basis or is not supported by any credible evidence. *Mining Investment Group, LLC v. Roberts*, 217 Ariz. 635, 177 P.3d 1207 (Ct. App. Div. 1 2008); *Evergreen West, Inc. v. Boyd*, 167 Ariz. 614, 810 P.2d 612 (Ct. App. Div. 2 1991).

The denial of a motion to quash a *lis pendens* is not an appealable order. *Muchesko v. Muchesko*, 191 Ariz. 265, 955 P.2d 21 (Ct. App. Div. 1 1997). Relief may be available, however, through a petition for special action where the denial of the motion to quash was an abuse of discretion. *Muchesko v. Muchesko*, 191 Ariz. 265, 955 P.2d 21 (Ct. App. Div. 1 1997).

Rule 4. Process

(a) Summons; Issuance. When the complaint or any other pleading which requires service of a summons is filed, the clerk shall endorse thereon the day and hour on which it was filed and the number of the action, and shall forthwith issue a summons. The party filing the pleading may present a summons to the clerk for signature and seal. If in proper form, the clerk shall sign and seal the summons and issue it to the party for service or for delivery to a person authorized by Rule 4(d) to serve it. A summons, or a copy of the summons if addressed to multiple persons, shall be issued for each person to be served.

Former Rule 4 abrogated and new Rule 4 promulgated April 16, 1991, effective July 1, 1991. Amended Oct. 9, 1996, effective Dec. 1, 1996.

(b) Summons; Form; Replacement Summons. The summons shall be signed by the clerk, be under the seal of the court, contain the name of the court and the names of the parties, be directed to the person to be served, state the name and address of the attorney, if any, for the party on whose behalf service is being made, and otherwise that party's address. The summons shall state the time within which these Rules require the person being served to appear and defend, and shall notify that person that in case of a failure to do so judgment by default will be rendered against that person for the relief demanded in the pleading served. A summons, or a copy of the summons in the case of multiple persons to be served, shall be served together with a copy of the pleading to be served. If a summons is returned without being served, or if it has been lost, the clerk may upon request issue a replacement summons in the same form as the original. A replacement summons shall be issued and served within the time prescribed by Rule 4(i) of these Rules for service of the original summons. The summons shall state that "requests for reasonable accommodation for persons with disabilities must be made to the court by parties at least 3 working days in advance of a scheduled court proceeding."

Former Rule 4 abrogated and new Rule 4 promulgated April 16, 1991, effective July 1, 1991. Amended June 1, 1995, effective Dec. 1, 1995; Oct. 9, 1996, effective Dec. 1, 1996.

(c) Summons; Parties Named Fictitiously; Return. When a pleading which requires service of a summons designates a party whose true name is unknown by a fictitious name pursuant to Rule 10(f) of these Rules, the summons may issue directed to the fictitious name employed for that purpose. The return of service of process upon a person designated therein by a fictitious name shall state the true name of the person or party upon whom it was served.

Former Rule 4 abrogated and new Rule 4 promulgated April 16, 1991, effective July 1, 1991.

(d) Process; By Whom Served. Service of process shall be by a sheriff, a sheriff's deputy, a constable, a constable's deputy, a private process server certified pursuant to the Arizona Code of Judicial Administration § 7-204: Private Process Server and subpart (e) of this Rule, or any other person specially appointed by the court, except that a subpoena may be served as provided in Rule 45. Service of process may also be made by a party or that party's attorney where expressly authorized by these Rules. A specially appointed person shall be not less than twenty-one (21) years of age and shall not be a party, an attorney, or the employee of an attorney in the action whose process is being served. Special appointments to serve process shall be requested by motion to the presiding Superior Court judge and the motion shall be accompanied by a proposed form of order. The party submitting the proposed form of order shall comply with Rule 5(j)(2) under which the filing party includes the appropriate number of copies to be addressed to each party who has entered an appearance in the case and stamped, addressed envelopes for distribution of the resulting order, unless otherwise provided by the Presiding Judge. If the proposed form of order is signed, no minute entry shall issue. Special appointments shall be granted freely, are valid only for the cause specified in the motion, and do not constitute an appointment as a certified private process server.

Former Rule 4 abrogated and new Rule 4 promulgated April 16, 1991, effective July 1, 1991. Amended Sept. 20, 2006, effective Jan. 1, 2007; August 30, 2012, effective January 1, 2013; amended August 28, 2013, effective January 1, 2014.

(e) State-Wide Certification of Private Process Servers. A person who files with the clerk of the court an application for certification as a private process server, pursuant to the Arizona Code of Judicial Administration § 7-204, as adopted by the Supreme Court, shall, upon approval of the court or presiding judge thereof, in the County where the application is filed, be registered with the clerk as a certified private process server until such certification is withdrawn by the court. The clerk shall maintain a register for this purpose. Such certified private process server shall be entitled to serve in such capacity for any court of the state anywhere within the State.

Former Rule 4 abrogated and new Rule 4 promulgated April 16, 1991, effective July 1, 1991. Amended Feb. 2, 1993, effective June 1, 1993; August 30, 2012, effective January 1, 2013.

(f) Service; Acceptance or Waiver; Voluntary

Appearance. The person to whom a summons or other process is directed may accept service, or waive issuance or service thereof, in writing, signed by that person or by that person's authorized agent or attorney, and the acceptance or waiver shall be filed in the action. A person upon whom service is required may, in person or by attorney or by an authorized agent, enter an appearance in open court, and the appearance shall be noted by the clerk upon the docket and entered in the minutes. Such waiver, acceptance or appearance shall have the same force and effect as if a summons had been issued and served. The filing of a pleading responsive to a pleading allowed under Rule 7(a) of these Rules shall constitute an appearance.

Former Rule 4 abrogated and new Rule 4 promulgated April 16, 1991, effective July 1, 1991.

(g) Return of Service. If service is not accepted or waived, then the person effecting service shall make proof thereof to the court. When the process is served by a sheriff or a sheriff's deputy, the return shall be officially endorsed on or attached thereto and returned to the court promptly. If served by a person other than the sheriff or a deputy sheriff, return and proof of service shall be made promptly by affidavit thereof. Each such affidavit of a registered private process server shall include clear reference to the county where that private process server is registered. When the summons is served by publication, the return of the person making such service shall be made in the manner specified in Rules 4.1(n) and 4.2(e) [*sic*, Rules 4.1(*l*) and 4.2(f)], of these Rules. Proof of service in a place not within any judicial district of the United States shall, if effected under paragraph (1) of Rule 4.2(h) [*sic*, 4.2(i)], be made pursuant to the applicable treaty or convention; and shall, if effected under paragraph (2) or (3) thereof, include a receipt signed by the addressee or other evidence of delivery to the addressee satisfactory to the court. In any event the return shall be made within the time during which the person served must respond to process. Failure to make proof of service does not affect the validity thereof.

Former Rule 4 abrogated and new Rule 4 promulgated April 16, 1991, effective July 1, 1991. Amended Oct. 9, 1996, effective Dec. 1, 1996.

(h) Amendment of Process or Amendment of Proof of Service. At any time in its discretion and upon such terms as it deems just, the court may allow any process or proof of service thereof to be amended, unless it clearly appears that material prejudice would result to the substantial rights of the party against whom the process issued.

Former Rule 4 abrogated and new Rule 4 promulgated April 16, 1991, effective July 1, 1991. Amended Oct. 9, 1996, effective Dec. 1, 1996.

(i) Summons; Time Limit for Service. If service of the summons and complaint is not made upon a defendant within 120 days after the filing of the complaint, the court, upon motion or on its own initiative after notice to the plaintiff, shall dismiss the action without prejudice as to that defendant or direct that service be effected within a specified time; provided that if the plaintiff shows good cause for the failure, the court shall extend the time for service for an appropriate period. This subdivision does not apply to service in a foreign country pursuant to Rule 4.2(h), (i), (j) and (k) [*sic*, Rule 4.2(i), (j), (k) and [*(l)*]] of these rules.

Former Rule 4 abrogated and new Rule 4 promulgated December 20, 1991 (corrected nunc pro tunc July 7, 1992), effective July 1, 1991. Amended Oct. 9, 1996, effective Dec. 1, 1996.

Applicability

[Rule 4(i)] *Applicable to cases filed on or after July 1, 1992.*

STATE BAR COMMITTEE NOTES

April 1991 Promulgation Amendments

Former Rule 4 and portions of former Rule 5 were revised and restated in new Rules 4, 4.1 and 4.2, which were promulgated and adopted in 1991. Piecemeal amendments to these former Rules had rendered them ambiguous, confusing and difficult to apply, and had blurred the intended distinction between them. The purpose of the revisions and restatement was to clarify the appropriate procedural manner for accomplishing service of process at the inception of the action, but some substantive changes were made in the process, as noted herein and in the Committee Notes to the new Rules. In addition, throughout the new and restated Rules, an effort was made to eliminate specific references such as "plaintiff", "defendant" or "complaint" in favor of generic terms such as "pleading" or "person to be served," etc., in recognition of the fact that there are a number of instances where a pleading allowed under Rule 7(a) other than the complaint requires service by a summons.

Rule 4

As revised and restated, Rules 4(a) and (b) are essentially the same as the corresponding subparts of the former Rule. Provisions have been added to Rule 4(a) to recognize and authorize the current practice under which the summons is actually prepared by the party, presented to the clerk for issuance, and returned to the party who then arranges for service. In addition, Rule 4(b) was slightly revised in the restatement process to eliminate reference to an alias summons, the proper use of which was generally misunderstood. Where an original summons is lost or is returned without being served, the clerk may issue, upon request, what is termed a replacement summons, which will be considered, for purposes of determining whether service has been timely made under Rule 6(f), as having been issued on the same date as the original.

A new Rule 4(c) has been added to address specifically the form of a summons directed to a party designated in the pleading being served by a fictitious name, as permitted by Rule 10(f). The summons should be addressed to the fictitious name or designation employed for that purpose, e.g., "John Doe," "White Corporation," but the return of service of such a summons must specify the true name of the party served. Under prior practice, an alias summons was generally, but improperly, used for this purpose.

New Rule 4(d) is a portion of former Rule 4(c), with some editorial revisions for the sake of clarity. New Rule 4(d) specifies that service may be made by a party or that party's attorney where specifically authorized by other provisions of the Rules. Such authority is provided where service is made by mail, under new Rules 4.1(c) and 4.2(c), and where service is made by publication, under new Rules 4.1(e) and 4.2(e). The provisions of former Rule 4(c) dealing with the registration of private process servers have been incorporated into a separate new Rule 4(e).

New Rule 4(f) is former Rule 5(e) which has been placed here because it deals with service of process upon initiation of the action rather than service of pleadings and other papers generated during the course of the action. The placement of this provision in Rule 4 makes clear that a person may voluntarily accept service of a summons regardless of where that person is located. Rules 4(g) and (h) are essentially the same as former Rules 4(g) and (i). The provisions of former Rule 4(h) have been incorporated into new Rule 4(g) and into the provisions of new Rules 4.1(e) and 4.2(e) dealing with service by publication.

Rule 4(i) Dec 1991, State Bar Committee Notes.

STATE BAR COMMITTEE NOTES

December 1991 Amendments

[Rule 4(i)] This rule addition is intended to bring the state rules into conformity with the federal rules. It is also consistent with the philosophy of Rule 11. It eliminates the necessity for Rule 6(f).

Rule 4(i), Dec 1991 Court Comment.

COURT COMMENT

December 1991 Amendment

[Rule 4(i)] The above rule change was part of a comprehensive set of rule revisions proposed by the Special Bar Committee to Study Civil Litigation Abuse, Cost and Delay, which was specifically charged in March, 1990 with the task of proposing rules to reduce discovery abuse and to make the judicial system in Arizona more efficient, expeditious, and accessible to the people.

For more complete background information on the rule changes proposed by the Committee, see Court Comment to Rule 26.1.

1993 Amendment

[Rule 4(e)] State guidelines for the registration of private process servers will be adopted separately by administrative action.

AUTHORS' COMMENTS

Analysis

1. Scope and Purpose of Rule.
2. History of Amendments to the Service of Process Rules.
3. Comparison With Federal Rule.
4. General Requirement of Service; Time for Service.
5. Preparation and Issuance of Summons.
6. Fictitious Defendants.
7. Replacement Summons.
8. Use of Process Servers.
9. Service by Party or Attorney.
10. Return of Service.
11. Voluntary Appearance; Acceptance of Service.

12. Amendment of Process.

1. *Scope and Purpose of Rule.* Ariz. R. Civ. P. 4, 4.1 and 4.2 contain the provisions specifying the procedural requirements for accomplishing effective service of process. Rule 4 contains provisions dealing with service of process generally. Rule 4.1 contains those provisions dealing with service of process that is accomplished on defendants within the State of Arizona; Rule 4.2 deals with service upon parties located outside the State of Arizona.

2. *History of Amendments to the Service of Process Rules.* The governing provisions for accomplishing effective service were formerly contained, in large part, in Rule 4. Piecemeal amendments to that Rule, and to Rule 5 had rendered them ambiguous, confusing and difficult to apply, and had blurred the intended distinction between them.

Accordingly, former Rule 4 and portions of Rule 5 were revised and restated in 1991 as new Rules 4, 4.1 and 4.2. The purpose of the revisions and restatement was to clarify the appropriate procedural manner for accomplishing service at the inception of the action, and only a very few substantive changes were made in the process. The following table shows the correlation between the restated Rules and the provisions of former Rules 4 and 5:

'New' 1991 Rule	**Former Rule**	**'New' 1991 Rule**	**Former Rule**
4(a)	4(a)	4.1(a)	4(f)
4(b)	4(b)	4.1(b)(1)	4(d)(1)
4(c)	None	4.1(b)(2)	4(d)(2)
4(d)	4(c)	4.1(b)(3)	4(d)(3)
4(e)	4(c)	4.1(b)(4)	4(d)(4)
4(f)	4(h), 5(e)	4.1(b)(5)	4(d)(7)
4(g)	4(g)	4.1(f)	5(f)
4(h)	4(i)	4.2(a)	4(e)(2)
4.1(b)(6)	4(d)(8)	4.2(b)	4(e)(2)
4.1(b)(7)	None	4.2(c)	4(e)(2)(a)
4.1(b)(8)	4(d)(6)	4.2(d)	4(d)(5), 4(e)(5)
4.1(b)(9)	4(d)(10)	4.2(e)	4(e)(3)
4.1(c)	4(e)(7)	4.2(f)	5(f)
4.1(d)	4(d)(11)	4.2(g)	4(e)(6)
4.1(e)	4(e)(1), (3)	4.2(h)	4(e)(4)

An effort was made, as part of the process, to eliminate specific references such as "plaintiff", "defendant" or "complaint" in favor of generic terms such as "pleading" or "person to be served" to recognize the fact that there are a number of instances where a pleading allowed under Rule 7(a) other than the complaint may require service by a summons.

New Rule 4(i) was added as part of the general discovery and court reform amendments that became effective July 1, 1992.

The Rules were once again extensively amended, effective December 1, 1996, as part of an omnibus effort to bring various provisions in the Arizona Rules of Civil Procedure into greater conformity with their counterparts in the Federal Rules of Civil Procedure, as the latter had been amended in 1993. New provisions (Rules 4.1(c) and 4.2(c)) dealing with waivers of service were added and the provisions allowing direct service by mail were eliminated. Certain provisions in Rules 4.1 and 4.2 were also renumbered or relettered. Rules 4.1 and 4.2 were then again amended in 1997 to delete certain provisions which imposed a duty to seek waivers of service that had not been contained in the corresponding Federal Rule, and to restore the provisions authorizing service by mail on out-of-state defendants which the 1996 amendments had deleted. The following table shows the correlation between the provisions of the Rules impacted by the 1996 and 1997 amendments and the provisions as they were contained in the 1991 restatement of the service of process rules:

'New' 1997 Rule	1991 Rule	'New' 1997 Rule	1991 Rule
4.1(c)	None	4.1(*o*)	4.1(f)
4.1(d)	4.1(b)(1)	4.2(c)	4.2(c)
4.1(e)	4.1(b)(2)	4.2(d)	None
4.1(f)	4.1(b)(3)	4.2(e)	4.2(d)
4.1(g)	4.1(b)(4)	4.2(f)	4.2(e)
4.1(h)	4.1(b)(5)	4.2(g)	4.2(f)
4.1(i)	4.1(b)(6)	4.2(h)	None
4.1(j)	4.1(b)(7)	4.2(i)	4.2(g)
4.1(k)	4.1(b)(8)	4.2(j)	None
4.1(*l*)	4.1(b)(9)	4.2(k)	None
4.1(m)	4.1(d)	4.2(*l*)	None
4.1(n)	4.1(e)	4.2(m)	4.2(h)

3. *Comparison With Federal Rule.* While the Arizona service of process rules contain certain provisions adopted from FRCP 4, there are marked substantive and stylist differences between that Rule and ARCP 4, 4.1 and 4.2.

The differences between the two sets of Rules created by the 1993 amendments to the Federal Rules of Civil Procedure were largely, but not entirely, eliminated by the 1996 amendments to Rules 4, 4.1 and 4.2 of the Arizona Rules. These amendments retained the title "Process" for Rule 4 of the Arizona Rules, whereas the Federal Rule's title was changed to "Summons."

Arizona has not adopted a Rule comparable to FRCP 4.1, which federal rule deals with the service of process other than a summons.

In 2007, the language of FRCP 4 was amended as part of the general restyling of the Federal Rules of Civil Procedure to make those rules more easily understood and to make style and terminology consistent throughout the Federal Rules of Civil Procedure. Those stylist modifications have not been incorporated into ARCP 4.

4. *General Requirement of Service; Time for Service.* While the filing of the complaint constitutes the formal commencement of the action, and ceases the running of the statute of limitations, service must be accomplished by one of the means authorized by Rules 4.1 or 4.2. The complaint is merely the statement of the plaintiff's claim. The summons, which is issued under the seal of the Court, announces the presence of the Court and gives the defendant notice that the Court is assuming jurisdiction for purposes of resolving the controversy. *Spiegel v. Board of Sup'rs of Maricopa County*, 175 Ariz. 479, 857 P.2d 1333 (Tax Ct. 1993).

The time limit for securing service of process domestically is within one hundred and twenty (120) days after the filing of the complaint. The provisions of Rule 6(a) apply to the computation of this one hundred and twenty (120) day period, so that the day on which the complaint was filed is not counted, and weekends and holidays are included. *AA Mechanical v. Superior Court In and For County of Maricopa (Vree)*, 190 Ariz. 364, 948 P.2d 492 (Ct. App. Div. 1 1997). If service is not made upon a defendant within that period, the court may, either on motion or on its own initiative, dismiss the action without prejudice as to the unserved defendant or direct that service be accomplished within a specified time.

The plaintiff is not entitled to notice that a defendant has not been properly served before the defendant files a motion to dismiss. *Corbett v. ManorCare of America, Inc.*, 213 Ariz. 618, 146 P.3d 1027 (Ct. App. Div. 2 2006). As an alternative to dismissing the action, Rule 4(i), as amended in 1996, provides that the trial court may direct that service be accomplished within a specified time, even without a finding of good cause for failure to secure service within one hundred and twenty (120) days. *Maher v. Urman*, 211 Ariz. 543, 124 P.3d 770 (Ct. App. Div. 2 2005).

If the plaintiff demonstrates good cause for the failure to accomplish service within the one hundred and twenty day period, the court must extend the time for service for an appropriate period. Rule 4(i). To show good cause for such an extension, a plaintiff must demonstrate the exercise of due diligence in trying to secure service on the defendant. *Maher v. Urman*, 211 Ariz. 543, 124 P.3d 770 (Ct. App. Div. 2 2005). Whether a party has shown such good cause is a matter left to the trial court's discretion. *Maher v. Urman*, 211 Ariz. 543, 124 P.3d 770 (Ct. App. Div. 2 2005).

This time limit does not apply to service in a foreign country. When the plaintiff has secured, before the time for securing service has expired, an Order from the Court extending the time in which to effect service, the Court may deny a subsequent motion to dismiss for untimely service, even if the Court concludes that the Order granting the extension was improvident. *Toy v. Katz*, 192 Ariz. 73, 961 P.2d 1021 (Ct. App. Div. 1 1997).

The repeal of former Rule 6(f) and its replacement with current Rule 4(i) did not eliminate the defense of abatement entirely; this rule change simply shortened the time limit for service of the summons from one (1) year to one hundred and twenty (120) days. *Schwartz v. Arizona Primary Care Physicians*, 192 Ariz. 290, 964 P.2d 491 (Ct. App. Div. 1 1998). Abatement occurs when defendants receive no summons or complaint within the requisite time period to put them on notice of the pending case. *Schwartz v. Arizona Primary Care Physicians*, 192 Ariz. 290, 964 P.2d 491 (Ct. App. Div. 1 1998). The abatement rule gives effect to the statute of limitations and prevents a plaintiff who files an action within the statute of limitations, but fails to timely serve the defendants, from gaining a tactical advantage over defendants who are not on notice that they should begin preparing to respond to a lawsuit. *Schwartz v. Arizona Primary Care Physicians*, 192 Ariz. 290, 964 P.2d 491 (Ct. App. Div. 1 1998). Abatement should not be applied where the claimed defect is not a failure to serve, but rather the insufficiency of service. *Schwartz v. Arizona Primary Care Physicians*, 192 Ariz. 290, 964 P.2d 491 (Ct. App. Div. 1 1998).

Where there has been a dismissal or abatement for failure to secure timely service, relief may be available under the "savings statute," A.R.S. § 12–504. To obtain relief under that statute where the action has abated, the plaintiff must show an inability to effect service despite diligent efforts to do so. *Maher v. Urman*, 211 Ariz. 543, 124 P.3d 770 (Ct. App. Div. 2 2005). A grant or denial of relief under the statute is reviewed only for an abuse of discretion. *Maher v. Urman*, 211 Ariz. 543, 124 P.3d 770 (Ct. App. Div. 2 2005).

Rule 4, rather than Rule 5, governs service of the complaint and service is not effective until process is either served upon, or accepted by an authorized representative of, the person or entity to be served. *Morgan v. Foreman ex rel. County of Maricopa*, 193 Ariz. 405, 973 P.2d 616 (Ct. App. Div. 1 1999). Service of a claim instituted against a person or entity that is already a party to the action (*e.g.*, a counterclaim or cross-claim), on the other hand, may be accomplished by one of the methods authorized by Rule 5. Service of process upon an attorney who has entered a special appearance in an action to contest personal jurisdiction, however, is not sufficient service upon the client. *Rouzaud v. Marek*, 166 Ariz. 375, 802 P.2d 1074 (Ct. App. Div. 1 1990).

The purpose of process is to provide effective notice that the defendant is being called to Court by the plaintiff to account for the matters set forth in the complaint. Such notice is required by the Due Process Clauses of both the United States and Arizona Constitutions. Where service of process on a defendant does not comply with prescribed procedural requirements, the Court does not obtain jurisdiction, and any judgment rendered against that defendant is void for lack of jurisdiction. *Postal Instant Press, Inc. v. Corral Restaurants, Inc.*, 186 Ariz. 535, 925 P.2d 260 (1996), opinion supplemented on reconsideration, 187 Ariz. 487, 930 P.2d 1001 (1997); *Wells v. Valley Nat. Bank of Arizona*, 109 Ariz. 345, 509 P.2d 615 (1973); *Barlage v. Valentine*, 210 Ariz. 270, 110 P.3d 371 (Ct. App. Div. 2 2005); *Hilgeman v. American Mortg. Securities, Inc.*, 196 Ariz. 215, 994 P.2d 1030 (Ct. App. Div. 2 2000); *Ellman Land Corp. v. Maricopa County*, 180 Ariz. 331, 884 P.2d 217 (Ct. App. Div. 1 1994); *Sprang v. Petersen Lumber, Inc.*, 165 Ariz. 257, 798 P.2d 395 (Ct. App. Div. 1 1990); *Kadota v. Hosogai*, 125 Ariz. 131, 608 P.2d 68 (Ct. App. Div. 1 1980); *Spiegel v. Board of Sup'rs of Maricopa County*, 175 Ariz. 479, 857 P.2d 1333 (Tax Ct. 1993).

Any defect in service is waived if the defendant voluntarily appears in, and defends, the action. *Hill Bros. Chemical Co. v. Grandinetti*, 123 Ariz. 84, 597 P.2d 987 (Ct. App. Div. 1 1979). The filing of a responsive pleading that does not contest the exercise of personal jurisdiction over the defendant will operate as a waiver of the defense and a submission to the jurisdiction of the Court. *Martin v. Martin*, 156 Ariz. 452, 752 P.2d 1038 (1988). On the other hand, a party's participation in proceedings after the unsuccessful pursuit of a motion to dismiss for insufficient service, under circumstances where the party does not evidence an intention to submit to the Court's jurisdiction, does not constitute a voluntary appearance. *Ellman Land Corp. v. Maricopa County*, 180 Ariz. 331, 884 P.2d 217 (Ct. App. Div. 1 1994).

An Arizona court has statutory jurisdiction to enter a decree of dissolution of a marriage when one of the parties was domiciled in the state for ninety (90) days before the filing of the petition for dissolution. The Court may exercise this limited jurisdiction to dissolve the marriage without violating due process, even though it lacks personal jurisdiction over the nonresident party, so long as the Court does not determine the monetary obligations of the parties. *Taylor v. Jarrett*, 191 Ariz. 550, 959 P.2d 807 (Ct. App. Div. 1 1998). Similarly, under the Uniform Child Custody Jurisdiction Act, an Arizona court need not secure personal jurisdiction over a nonresident party in order to adjudicate child custody and visitation issues. *Taylor v. Jarrett*, 191 Ariz. 550, 959 P.2d 807 (Ct. App. Div. 1 1998). Technical personal jurisdiction must be acquired, however, before the Court can decide issues of child support, spousal maintenance or the division of marital property. Of course, a nonresident party may waive objection to the absence of personal jurisdiction by appearing and seeking affirmative relief, but does not do so in this context simply by participating in the proceedings concerning the proper custodial determination. *Taylor v. Jarrett*, 191 Ariz. 550, 959 P.2d 807 (Ct. App. Div. 1 1998).

On the other hand, an Arizona court does have jurisdiction in a child support action over a father who does not reside in Arizona but was personally served while in the state on vacation and visiting his child. *Rutherford v. Rutherford*, 193 Ariz. 173, 971 P.2d 220 (Ct. App. Div. 1 1998). Physical presence in the forum, where not procured by coercion or trickery, satisfies personal jurisdiction requirements. A minimum contacts analysis is not necessary when a defendant is served with process within Arizona because physical presence is one of the continuing traditions of our legal system that define the due process standard of traditional notions of fair play and substantial justice. *Rutherford v. Rutherford*, 193 Ariz. 173, 971 P.2d 220 (Ct. App. Div. 1 1998).

5. *Preparation and Issuance of Summons.* As part of the 1991 restatement and revision of the service of process rules, provisions were added to Rule 4(a) to recognize and authorize the prevailing practice under which the summons is physically prepared by the party or the party's attorney, presented to the clerk for issuance (if it is in proper form), and returned to the party, who then makes arrangements for service. Effective December 1, 1995, every summons must contain a specific notice, the contents of which are prescribed in amended Rule 4(b), concerning requests to accommodate persons with disabilities.

Under the 1996 amendments, it is no longer necessary, in cases involving multiple defendants, to have an original summons issued and served on each separate defendant. Rather, the clerk can issue a single original summons addressed to the multiple parties defendant, and copies of that summons may be served on the multiple parties named therein.

6. *Fictitious Defendants.* Ariz. R. Civ. P. 10(f) authorizes the

designation of a defendant whose name is unknown by any name. Ariz. R. Civ. P. 4(c) authorizes the issuance of a summons directed to the fictitious name employed, as authorized by Rule 10(f). The return of service, however, must state the true name of the person or entity upon whom such a "fictitious defendant" summons was served and, if it is the party named fictitiously, the pleadings are to be amended accordingly. Rule 10(f).

7. *Replacement Summons.* Amended Rule 4(b) eliminated the prior Rule's reference to an "alias summons," the proper use of which was generally misunderstood. The Rule now authorizes the issuance of what is termed a "replacement summons," where the original summons is lost or is, for some reason, returned without being served. For purposes of determining whether service has been accomplished within the time specified by Rule 4(i), however, a replacement summons is deemed to have been issued on the same date as the original summons.

8. *Use of Process Servers.* The common practice is to use the sheriff or a certified (formerly, "registered") private process server to serve a summons and complaint. Before June 1993, private process server could only serve process in the county or counties in which that individual had been registered and approved.

Under an amendment to Ariz. R. Civ. P. 4(e) which became effective June 1, 1993, private process servers were able to register to serve process throughout the state, by complying with procedures set forth in an Administrative Order of the Supreme Court.

Effective January 1, 2013, Ariz. R. Civ. P. 4(d) and (e) were further amended to change any reference to "registered" private process server to "certified" private process server to conform with the Arizona Code of Judicial Administration § 704, as adopted by the Arizona Supreme Court. This amendment also deleted language from Rule 4(e) regarding the stated qualifications for certification and limitations on certified private process servers as such provisions are specified in Arizona Code of Judicial Administration § 704.

Ariz. R. Civ. P. 4(d) was amended again, effective January 1, 2014, to add "constables" and "constable's deputy" to the list of persons authorized to serve process.

A person specially appointed to serve process, may not be a party or attorney in the action and must be at least twenty-one years of age. A subpoena, however, may be served by "any person who is not a party and is not less than eighteen years of age." Ariz. R. Civ. P. 45(d)(1) (2011). The State Bar Committee Note to the 1961 Amendment to former Rule 4(c) [now Rule 4(d)] indicates that a higher minimum age requirement for service of process was purposely adopted.

Requests for the appointment of a special process server must be made by/ motion to the Presiding Judge, and must be accompanied by a proposed form of order. The party submitting the motion and proposed order must also comply with the requirements of Rule 5(j)(2).

Service of process by the sheriff on a non-Native American, if made within that part of a Native American reservation that lies within the boundaries of Arizona, is valid. *State v. Zaman*, 194 Ariz. 442, 984 P.2d 528 (1999). A State officer not authorized by the sovereign Native American tribe in question cannot, however, effect valid service of process on a Native American within the appropriate reservation. *Dixon v. Picopa Const. Co.*, 160 Ariz. 251, 772 P.2d 1104 (1989); *Francisco v. State*, 113 Ariz. 427, 556 P.2d 1 (1976). Such service may be secured, however, through registered mail under Rule 4.2(c). *State v. Zaman*, 194 Ariz. 442, 984 P.2d 528 (1999).

9. *Service by Party or Attorney.* Rule 4(d) added a provision permitting service to be made by a party or a party's attorney where specifically authorized by other provisions of Rule 4.1 or Rule 4.2. The only situations where such authority is currently granted is where service is made by mail on an out-of-state defendant pursuant to Rule 4.2(c), or where service is made by publication under Rules 4.1(*l*), 4.1(m), and 4.2(f) or 4.2(g).

10. *Return of Service.* A return of service must be made within the time during which the person served must respond. The return of service made by a person other than the sheriff or deputy sheriff must be made by affidavit. The affidavit of a private process server must clearly specify the county in which that process server is registered. Where service is made by publication, Rules 4.1(*l*) and 4.2(f) require that the return or affidavit specify the manner and dates of publication and mailing (or a statement that no mailing was made because the residence address of the party being served was unknown), and the circumstances warranting the use of service by publication. A printed copy of the publication must accompany the return.

The return of service by the sheriff or duly appointed or certified (formerly, "registered") private process server may be impeached only by clear and convincing evidence. *Hilgeman v. American Mortg. Securities, Inc.*, 196 Ariz. 215, 994 P.2d 1030 (Ct. App. Div. 2 2000); *General Elec. Capital Corp. v. Osterkamp*, 172 Ariz. 191, 836 P.2d 404 (Ct. App. Div. 2 1992); *Mayhew v. McDougall*, 16 Ariz. App. 125, 491 P.2d 848 (Div. 2 1971); *Phoenix Airport Travelodge v. Dolgin*, 12 Ariz. App. 358, 470 P.2d 506 (Div. 2 1970).

11. *Voluntary Appearance; Acceptance of Service.* Rule 4(f) [former Rule 5(e)] provides that a person may voluntarily accept ser-

vice either by formally executing an acceptance or waiver of service, which must be in writing, or by entering a general appearance in the action. Rule 4(f) is not limited in its application to situations where the defendant does not have an attorney and is asked directly to waive or accept service. *Morgan v. Foreman ex rel. County of Maricopa*, 193 Ariz. 405, 973 P.2d 616 (Ct. App. Div. 1 1999). This provision was left untouched by the 1996 and 1997 amendments, which added specific provisions concerning the waiver of service (Rules 4.1(c) and 4.2(d)), and the relationship between them is yet to be explored. Specifically, it is unclear whether, where a party merely agrees to accept service, and the procedures of Rule 4.1(c) or 4.2(d) are not employed, that party receives the additional time to answer or otherwise respond for which those Rules provide.

A general appearance by a party or counsel has the same effect as timely and valid service of a summons. *Montano v. Scottsdale Baptist Hospital, Inc.*, 119 Ariz. 448, 581 P.2d 682 (1978). Mere physical presence in court, however, without participation in the proceedings, does not constitute an appearance. *Austin v. State ex rel. Herman*, 10 Ariz. App. 474, 459 P.2d 753 (Div. 2 1969).

Similarly, an appearance to defend against a garnishment does not constitute an appearance in the main action in which the writ issued. *Knox v. Knox*, 137 Ariz. 494, 671 P.2d 935 (Ct. App. Div. 2 1983). Service of process upon an attorney who has entered a special appearance in the action to contest personal jurisdiction is not sufficient to secure service upon the client. *Rouzaud v. Marek*, 166 Ariz. 375, 802 P.2d 1074 (Ct. App. Div. 1 1990).

A party's participation in proceedings after the unsuccessful pursuit of a motion to dismiss for insufficient service, under circumstances where the party does not evidence an intention to submit to the Court's jurisdiction, does not constitute a voluntary appearance. *Ellman Land Corp. v. Maricopa County*, 180 Ariz. 331, 884 P.2d 217 (Ct. App. Div. 1 1994). However, a party's conduct may constitute consent to jurisdiction. Thus, the Arizona Supreme Court found that a party consented to personal jurisdiction in post-decree proceedings "by appearing, requesting affirmative relief and failing to challenge personal jurisdiction in a timely fashion." *Davis v. Davis*, 230 Ariz. 333, 284 P.3d 23 (Ct. App. Div. 1 2012).

12. *Amendment of Process.* The court may permit an amendment to process or to the proof of service thereof, unless the amendment would result in material prejudice to the substantial rights of the party against whom the process issued.

Rule 4.1. Service of process within Arizona

(a) Territorial Limits of Effective Service. All process may be served anywhere within the territorial limits of the state.

(b) Summons; Service With Complaint. The summons and pleading being served shall be served together. The party procuring service is responsible for service of a summons and the pleading being served within the time allowed under Rule 4(i) of these Rules and shall furnish the person effecting service with the necessary copies of the pleading to be served.

(c) Waiver of Service; Duty to Save Costs of Service; Request to Waive.

(1) A defendant who waives service of a summons does not thereby waive any objection to the venue or to the jurisdiction of the court over the person of such defendant.

(2) An individual, governmental entity, corporation, partnership or unincorporated association that is subject to service under paragraph (d), (h)(1)–(4)(A), or (i) of this Rule 4.1 and that receives notice of an action in the manner provided in this paragraph has a duty to avoid unnecessary costs of serving the summons. To avoid costs, the plaintiff may notify such a defendant of the commencement of the action and request that the defendant waive service of a summons. The notice and request:

(A) shall be in writing and shall be addressed directly to the defendant in accordance with paragraph (d), (h)(1)–(4)(A), or (i) of this Rule 4.1, as applicable;

(B) shall be dispatched through first-class mail or other reliable means;

(C) shall be accompanied by a copy of the complaint and shall identify the court in which it has been filed;

(D) shall inform the defendant, by means of a text prescribed in an official form promulgated pursuant to Rule 84, of the consequences of compliance and of a failure to comply with the request;

(E) shall set forth the date on which the request is sent;

(F) shall allow the defendant a reasonable time to return the waiver, which shall be at least 30 days from the date on which the request is sent; and

(G) shall provide the defendant with an extra copy of the notice and request, as well as a prepaid means of compliance in writing.

If a defendant fails to comply with a request for waiver made by a plaintiff located within the United States, the court shall impose the costs subsequently incurred in effecting service on the defendant unless good cause for the failure be shown.

(3) A defendant that, before being served with process, timely returns a waiver so requested is not required to serve an answer to the complaint until 60 days after the date on which the request for waiver of service was sent.

(4) When the plaintiff files a waiver of service with the court, the action shall proceed, except as provided in paragraph (3), as if a summons and the complaint had been served at the time of filing the waiver, and no proof of service shall be required.

(5) The costs to be imposed on a defendant under paragraph (2) for failure to comply with a request to waive service of a summons shall include the costs subsequently incurred in effecting service under paragraph (d), (h) or (i) of this Rule 4.1, together with the costs, including a reasonable attorney's fee, of any motion required to collect the costs of service.

Amended Dec. 10, 2012, effective Jan. 1, 2013.

(d) Service of Summons Upon Individuals. Service upon an individual from whom a waiver has not been obtained and filed, other than those specified in paragraphs (e), (f) and (g) of this Rule 4.1, shall be effected by delivering a copy of the summons and of the pleading to that individual personally or by leaving copies thereof at that individual's dwelling house or usual place of abode with some person of suitable age and discretion then residing therein or by delivering a copy of the summons and of the pleading to an agent authorized by appointment or by law to receive service of process.

(e) Service of Summons Upon Minors. Service upon a minor under the age of sixteen years shall be effected by service in the manner set forth in paragraph (d) of this Rule 4.1 upon the minor and upon the minor's father, mother or guardian, within this state, or if none is found therein, then upon any person having the care and control of such minor, or with whom the minor resides.

(f) Service of Summons Upon a Minor With Guardian or Conservator. Service upon a minor for whom a guardian or conservator has been appointed in this state shall be effected by service in the manner set forth in paragraph (d) of this Rule 4.1 upon such guardian or conservator and minor.

(g) Service of Summons Upon Incompetent Persons. Service upon a person who has been judicially declared to be insane, gravely disabled, incapacitated or mentally incompetent to manage that person's property and for whom a guardian or conservator has been appointed in this state shall be effected by service in the manner set forth in paragraph (d) of this Rule 4.1 upon such person and also upon that person's guardian or conservator, or if no guardian or conservator has been appointed, upon such person as the court designates.

(h) Service of Summons Upon a Governmental Entity. Service upon a governmental entity subject to suit, and from which a waiver has not been obtained and filed, shall be effected by delivering a copy of the summons and of the pleading to the following individuals:

(1) For service upon the State, the Attorney General;

(2) For service upon a County, the Clerk of the Board of Supervisors thereof;

(3) For service upon a Municipal Corporation, the Clerk thereof; and

(4) For service upon any other governmental entity:

(A) The individual designated by the entity pursuant to statute to receive service of process; or

(B) If the entity has not pursuant to statute designated a person to receive service of process, then the chief executive officer(s), or, alternatively, the official secretary, clerk, or recording officer of the entity as established by law.

Formerly Rules 4.1(h), (i), (j); combined, amended and renumbered as Rule 4.1(h) Dec. 10, 2012, effective Jan. 1, 2013.

(i) Service of Summons Upon Corporations, Partnerships or Other Unincorporated Associations. Service upon a domestic or foreign corporation or upon a partnership or other unincorporated association which is subject to suit in a common name, and from which a waiver has not been obtained and filed, shall be effected by delivering a copy of the summons and of the pleading to a partner, an officer, a managing or general agent, or to any other agent authorized by appointment or by law to receive service of process and, if the agent is one authorized by statute to receive service and the statute so requires, by also mailing a copy to the party on whose behalf the agent accepted or received service.

Formerly Rule 4.1(k); renumbered as Rule 4.1(i) Dec. 10, 2012, effective Jan. 1, 2013.

(j) Service of Summons Upon a Domestic Corporation if Authorized Officer or Agent Not Found Within the State. When a domestic corporation does not have an officer or agent in this state upon whom legal service of process can be made, service upon such domestic corporation shall be effected by depositing two copies of the summons and of the pleading being served in the office of the Corporation Commission, which shall be deemed personal service on such corporation. The return of the sheriff of the county in which the action or proceeding is brought that after diligent search or inquiry the sheriff has been unable to find any officer or agent of such corporation upon whom process may be served, shall be prima facie evidence that the corporation does not have such an officer or agent in this state. The Corporation Commission shall file one of the copies in its office and immediately mail the other copy, postage prepaid, to the office of the corporation, or to the president, secretary or any director or officer of such corporation as appears or is ascertained by the Corporation Commission from the articles of incorporation or other papers on file in its office, or otherwise.

Formerly Rule 4.1(*l*); renumbered as Rule 4.1(j) Dec. 10, 2012, effective Jan. 1, 2013.

(k) Alternative or Substituted Service. If service by one of the means set forth in the preceding paragraphs of this Rule 4.1 proves impracticable, then service may be accomplished in such manner, other than by publication, as the court, upon motion and without notice, may direct. Whenever the court allows an alternate or substitute form of service pursuant to this subpart, reasonable efforts shall be undertaken by the party making service to assure that actual notice of the commencement of the action is provided to the person to be served and, in any event, the summons and the pleading to be served, as well as any order of the court authorizing an alternative method of service, shall be mailed to the last known business or residence address of the person to be served. Service by publication may be employed only under the circumstances, and in accordance with the procedures, specified in Rules 4.1(*l*), 4.1(m), 4.2(f) and 4.2(g) of these Rules.

Formerly Rule 4.1(m); amended and renumbered as Rule 4.1(k) Dec. 10, 2012, effective Jan. 1, 2013.

***(l)* Service by Publication; Return.** Where the person to be served is one whose residence is unknown to the party seeking service but whose last known residence address was within the state, or has avoided service of process, and service by publication is the best means practicable under the circumstances for providing notice of the institution of the action, then service may be made by publication in accordance with the requirements of this subpart. Such service shall be made by publication of the summons, and of a statement as to the manner in which a copy of the pleading being served may be obtained, at least once a week for four successive weeks (1) in a newspaper published in the county where the action is pending, and (2) in a newspaper published in the county of the last known residence of the person to be served if different from the county where the action is pending. If no newspaper is published in any such county, then the required publications shall be made in a newspaper published in an adjoining county. The service shall be complete thirty days after the first publication. When the residence of the person to be served is known, the party or officer making service shall also, on or before the date of the first publication, mail the summons and a copy of the pleading being served, postage prepaid, to that person at that person's place of residence. Service by publication and the return thereof may be made by the party procuring service or that party's attorney in the same manner as though made by an officer. The party or officer making service shall file an affidavit showing the manner and dates of the publication and mailing, and the circumstances warranting the utilization of the procedure authorized by this subpart, which shall be prima facie evidence of compliance herewith. A printed copy of the publication shall accompany the affidavit. If the residence of the party being served is unknown, and for that reason no mailing was made, the affidavit shall so state.

Formerly Rule 4.1(n); renumbered as Rule 4.1(*l*) Dec. 10, 2012, effective Jan. 1, 2013.

(m) Service by Publication; Unknown Heirs in Real Property Actions. When in an action for the foreclosure of a mortgage on real property or in any action involving title to real property, it is necessary for a complete determination of the action that the unknown heirs of a deceased person be made parties, they may be sued as the unknown heirs of the decedent, and service of a summons may be made on them by publication in the county where the action is pending, as provided in subpart (*l*) of this Rule 4.1.

Formerly Rule 4.1(o); renumbered as Rule 4.1(m) Dec. 10, 2012, effective Jan. 1, 2013.

Rule 4.1 added April 16, 1991, effective July 1, 1991. Amended Oct. 9, 1996, effective Dec. 1, 1996; Oct. 14, 1997, effective Oct. 15, 1997.

STATE BAR COMMITTEE NOTES

1991 Promulgation

New Rule 4.1 contains, with some revisions, those provisions of former Rules 4 and 5 that dealt with service of process on defendants within the State of Arizona. Rule 4.1(a) is former Rule 4(f) which specifies that process may be served anywhere within the territorial limits of the state. This provision does not limit the scope of the intended exercise of extraterritorial jurisdiction by an Arizona court which, under Rule 4.2(a), may be to the maximum extent permitted by the Arizona and United States Constitutions.

Rule 4.1(b) is former Rule 4(d) with the exception of those subparts previously abrogated, of former Rule 4(d)(5), which has been incorporated in new Rule 4.2(d), and of former Rule 4(d)(11), which has been incorporated as new Rule 4.1(d). The subparts have been reordered for purposes of clarity, and a new subpart (7) has been added, which derives largely from Rule 4.2(14) of the Ohio Rules of Civil Procedure and specifies the person to be served where service is made upon a governmental entity, foreign or domestic, not specifically mentioned in subparts (5) and (6). The subparts of this new Rule, like those in its precursor, do not purport to set forth an exhaustive list of the categories of persons and entities that are amenable to suit in the Arizona courts.

Rule 4.1(c) authorizes service by mail within the state in lieu of personal service, but only upon certain classes of persons and only in accordance with the procedures set forth therein. It is identical to former Rule 4(e)(7) which was adopted in 1985 as an adaptation of the provisions of Rule 4(c)(2)(C), (D), and (E) of the Federal Rules of Civil Procedure. An acceptable form for the acknowledgment of service is Form 18-A in the Appendix of Forms to the Federal Rules of Civil Procedure.

Rule 4.1(e) incorporates certain provisions of former Rules 4(e)(1) and 4(e)(3) dealing with the circumstances where service by publication is permissible. The provisions of this new Rule may be invoked only where the person to be served is a person whose residence is unknown but whose last known address was within Arizona or is attempting to avoid service. The additional requirement that personal service not be required by law, which found its theoretical origins in the distinction between actions in personam and actions in rem, has been eliminated.

Even where the conditions specified in the Rule are present, service by publication must also satisfy due process standards of being the best means of notice practicable under the circumstances and reasonably calculated to apprise interested parties of the institution and/or pendency of the proceedings. *Mullane v. Central Hanover Bank & Trust Co.*, 339 U.S. 306, 70 S. Ct. 652, 94 L. Ed. 865 (1950). The party who elects to make service by publication is at risk that the service will be subject to a subsequent successful constitutional challenge. Where the last known address of the person to be served by publication is outside Arizona, the procedures set forth in new Rule 4.2(e) are to be followed. The provision requiring a supplementary mailing of a copy of the summons and of the pleading being served where the person's address is known has been retained, but it is stressed that service by publication on a person whose current address is known is only to be employed where it can be shown that that person is attempting to evade service. While the new Rule retains the provision that only the summons need be published, it adds the requirement that the publication contain a statement as to the manner in which a copy of the pleading being served may be obtained.

Rule 4.1(f) is former Rule 5(f), the specific provision authorizing service of process by publication upon the unknown heirs of a decedent in certain actions involving real property. The Rule is included here because it deals with service of process at the initiation of the action rather than the service of pleadings and other papers generated during the course of the action. Because, by definition, both the identities and the residences of these heirs, if any, will be unknown, publication under this Rule need only be made in the county where the action is pending.

AUTHORS' COMMENTS

Analysis

8. Service Upon Governmental Entities.
9. Alternative or Substitute Service.
10. Service by Publication Generally.
11. Service Upon Unknown Heirs by Publication.

1. *Scope and Purpose of Rule.* Ariz. R. Civ. P. 4.1 contains, with some revisions, those provisions of former Rules 4 and 5 that dealt with service of process on defendants within the State of Arizona. The origin and history of the Rule is discussed in Section 2 of the *Authors' Comments* to Rule 4.

2. *Comparison With Federal Rule.* ARCP 4.1 contains many provisions adopted from FRCP 4, but there remain some differences between the two rules. The 1993 amendments to the Federal Rules of Civil Procedure added a new FRCP 4.1, which governs the service of process other than a summons or a subpoena and is not at all similar to ARCP 4.1.

3. *Territorial Limits of Service.* Process may be served anywhere within the territorial limits of the state.

4. *Waivers of Service.* The 1996 amendments added a new Rule 4.1(c), modeled on Rule 4(d) of the Federal Rules of Civil Procedure, dealing with waivers of service. As a predicate for the new Rule, a provision was also initially added to Rule 4.1(b) specifying that the party responsible for procuring service had a duty to avoid incurring unnecessary service costs and should, where the request for waiver of service procedure is available, attempt to secure a waiver of service. That particular provision had not been contained in the corresponding Federal Rule and was, as a consequence, deleted from Rule 4.1(b) by the 1997 amendment.

The request for waiver of service of procedure may only be used where the defendant to be served is an individual (but not a minor or incompetent), a governmental entity, corporation, partnership or unincorporated association. To comply with new Rule 4.1(c), the plaintiff is to send to the defendant, by first class mail, a copy of the complaint or other pleading to be served, together with a notice of initiation of the action and a written request that the defendant waive the requirement of service of a summons. The Rule, as adopted, requires that the notice inform the defendant, "by means of a text prescribed in an official form promulgated pursuant to Rule 84," of the consequences of compliance and of a failure to comply with the request. By subsequent Order, the Arizona Supreme Court promulgated what are in actuality two official Forms—"Form 1. Notice of Lawsuit and Request for Waiver of Service of Summons" and "Form 2. Waiver of Service of Summons" which will be sufficient to comply with the requirements of Rule 4.1(c). (As promulgated, Form 2 was separated into two separate Forms, but they comprise only a single "Waiver of Service of Summons.").

The request for waiver of service must specify the date on which it was sent and allow the defendant a reasonable time, which must be at least thirty (30) days, to return the waiver of service. *Morgan v. Foreman ex rel. County of Maricopa*, 193 Ariz. 405, 973 P.2d 616 (Ct. App. Div. 1 1999). The plaintiff must provide the defendant with an extra copy of the notice and request and a prepaid means for complying with the request. New Rule 4.1(c)(2) provides that defendants from whom such waivers of service may be requested have a duty to avoid unnecessary service costs. Defendants are also given incentives to agree to waive the requirement of service as well.

If the defendant does not return the requested waiver, the plaintiff can then proceed to secure service in one of the traditional ways and the defendant is to be responsible for the costs thereby incurred. If the waiver of service of summons is returned, the plaintiff is to file it and the action then proceeds as if a summons had been served, *but* the defendant has up to sixty (60) days from the date on which the request for waiver was mailed in which to respond to the complaint. By executing and returning the waiver of service, the defendant does not thereby waive any objections to jurisdiction or venue.

The 1996 amendments deleted former Rule 4.1(c), which authorized alternative service by mail in Arizona. *Cf. Postal Instant Press, Inc. v. Corral Restaurants, Inc.*, 186 Ariz. 535, 925 P.2d 260 (1996), opinion supplemented on reconsideration, 187 Ariz. 487, 930 P.2d 1001 (1997). In addition, conforming amendments were also adopted to Rule 12(a) to reflect the fact that a defendant who has agreed to waive service of the summons has additional time to respond to a complaint, and to the provisions of Rules 33, 34 and 36 which specify when a response must be made to interrogatories, requests for production and requests for admissions that are served together with the complaint.

5. *Service Upon Individuals; Marital Communities.* In-state service on a party who has not made a general appearance in the action is governed by Rule 4.1. *Kline v. Kline*, 221 Ariz. 564, 212 P.3d 902 (Ct. App. Div. 1 2009). Service upon an individual, other than a minor or an incompetent, may be accomplished (1) by delivering a copy of the summons to the individual personally, (2) by leaving a copy at the individual's residence or usual place of abode with a person of suitable age and discretion then residing there, or (3) by delivering a copy to an agent authorized to accept it on behalf of the individual.

An attorney retained by an individual does not automatically qualify as an agent authorized to receive service on the individual's behalf. *Kline v. Kline*, 221 Ariz. 564, 212 P.3d 902 (Ct. App. Div. 1 2009). Such agency, however, can be implied from the circumstances accompanying the attorney's appearance and conduct of the action. *Kline v. Kline*, 221 Ariz. 564, 212 P.3d 902 (Ct. App. Div. 1 2009).

When a summons is left with a person, either at a residence or office, the person must be aware that the papers are being left for the purpose of accomplishing service of process. *Tonelson v. Haines*, 2 Ariz. App. 127, 406 P.2d 845 (1965). In an action against a husband and wife, service must be accomplished upon both to bind the marital community and community assets. *Spudnuts, Inc. v. Lane*, 139 Ariz. 35, 676 P.2d 669 (Ct. App. Div. 2 1984).

6. *Service Upon Minors.* A guardian of a minor is not ipso facto authorized to accept service of process on that minor's behalf. *Bowen v. Graham*, 140 Ariz. 593, 684 P.2d 165 (Ct. App. Div. 1 1984). And, the appointment of a guardian is not a predicate to the commencement of an action against a minor. *Montano v. Browning*, 202 Ariz. 544, 48 P.3d 494 (Ct. App. Div. 2 2002).

Montano v. Browning, 202 Ariz. 544, 48 P.3d 494 (Ct. App. Div. 2 2002).

For minors who are under 16 years of age, Ariz.R.Civ.P. 4.1(e) requires that service be made not only on the minor but also on the minor's parent, guardian, or person having care or control of the minor. *See also*, *Montano v. Browning*, 202 Ariz. 544, 48 P.3d 494 (Ct. App. Div. 2 2002).

For minors of any age for whom a guardian or conservator has already been appointed in this state, Ariz.R.Civ.P. 4.1(f) requires service on both the minor and the guardian or conservator. *See also, Montano v. Browning*, 202 Ariz. 544, 48 P.3d 494 (Ct. App. Div. 2 2002).

Rule 4.1(d), the general rule governing service of process by delivery on persons of unspecified age, implicitly applies to minors between 16 and 18 years of age and for whom a conservator or guardian has not been appointed. In such instance, Rule 4.1(d) permits service of process on the minor—and, only the minor. *See also, Montano v. Browning*, 202 Ariz. 544, 48 P.3d 494 (Ct. App. Div. 2 2002).

7. *Service Upon Corporations.* Corporations which are organized under the laws of Arizona, and foreign corporations which qualify to conduct business in Arizona, are required by statute to appoint a resident of Arizona as an agent to accept service of process. *See* A.R.S. §§ 10-202, 10-501, 10-504, 10-1503 and 10-1510.

The usual manner of accomplishing service upon such a corporation is to serve that "statutory agent." Under Ariz. R. Civ. P. 4.1(i) (amended 2013), however, service also may be effected upon an officer or managing or general agent. The officer or agent served, on the other hand, must be of a character and rank that assures that the corporate defendant will receive actual notice of the service. *American Motors Sales Corp. v. Superior Court In and For Pima County*, 16 Ariz. App. 494, 494 P.2d 394 (Div. 2 1972); *Safeway Stores, Inc. v. Ramirez*, 1 Ariz. App. 117, 400 P.2d 125 (1965), aff'd in part, 99 Ariz. 372, 409 P.2d 292 (1965). Service upon the sole stockholder who shares an address with the corporate party has been held to satisfy the requirements of due process and of former Rule 4(d)(6). *Dixon v. Picopa Const. Co.*, 160 Ariz. 251, 772 P.2d 1104 (1989).

8. *Service Upon Governmental Entities.* Effective January 1, 2013, Ariz. R. Civ. P. 4.1(h) governs the service of process upon a governmental entity. The topics governed by former Rules 4.1(h), (i) and (j) were amended and then consolidated into Ariz. R. Civ. P. 4.1(h). The remaining subparagraphs of Rule 4.1 were renumbered as appropriate. As a result of the 2013 amendment, Rule 4.1(h) now governs service of process upon *all* governmental entities.

Ariz. R. Civ, P. 4.1(h) provides that, in the absence of a waiver, service is effected by delivering a copy of the summons and pleading upon governmental entities as follows:

(1) For service upon the State: the Attorney General;

(2) For service upon a County: the Clerk of the Board of Supervisors thereof;

(3) For service upon a Municipal Corporation: the Clerk thereof; and

(4) For service upon any other governmental entity:

(a) The individual designated by the entity pursuant to statute to receive service of process; or

(b) If the entity has designated a person to receive service of process, pursuant to statute, then the chief executive officer(s), or, alternatively, the official secretary, clerk, or recording officer of the entity as established by law.

As noted above, Ariz. R. Civ. P. 4.1(h)(2) (2013) governs service of process upon a county and provides that service shall be upon the Clerk of the Board of Supervisors of such county. As a result of the 2013 amendment, it is no longer necessary to serve the entire board of supervisors. *Contra*, *Falcon ex rel. Sandoval v. Maricopa County*, 213 Ariz. 525, 144 P.3d 1254 (2006); *Maricopa County v. Arizona Tax Court*, 162 Ariz. 64, 781 P.2d 41 (Ct. App. Div. 1 1989).

Service upon any other governmental entity is governed by Ariz. R. Civ. P. 4.1(h)(4) (2013). Under this new provision service must be made upon the individual designated by the entity pursuant to statute to receive such service. *See,* Ariz. R. Civ. P. 4.1(h)(4)(A). If the entity has not designated a person to receive service, then service must be made on either the chief executive officer(s) or, alternatively, the official secretary, clerk or recording officer of the entity as established by law. *See,* Ariz. R. Civ. P. 4.1 (h)(4)(B). *But see, Batty v. Glendale Union High School Dist. No. 205*, 221 Ariz. 592, 212 P.3d 930, 247 Ed. Law Rep. 456 (Ct. App. Div. 1 2009) (In the case of a defendant school district, the party to be served is the entire governing board of the school district; service upon the superintendent is not sufficient under A.R.S. 12-821.01.).

9. *Alternative or Substitute Service.* Ariz. R. Civ. P. 4.1(k) [former Rule 4(d)(11) the predecessor to now former Rule 4.1(m)] was added to the Arizona Rules of Civil Procedure in 1989 to provide authority for the Court to direct an alternative method of service of process where all other methods of service authorized by the rules of procedure had proven impracticable. *Blair v. Burgener*, 226 Ariz. 213, 245 P.3d 898 (Ct. App. Div. 2 2010). While Rule 4.1(k) is primarily addressed to the situation where a third party, such as a residential security guard or office receptionist, denies access to the person on whom service is sought, it is not limited in its application to such situations.

Rule 4.1(k) permits alternative service when traditional service is "impracticable." *Blair v. Burgener*, 226 Ariz. 213, 245 P.3d 898 (Ct. App. Div. 2 2010) (interpreting former Rule 4.1(m)). The "impracticable" standard requires something less than the "due diligence" showing required before service by publication under Ariz. R. Civ. P. 4.1(*l*) [formerly, Rule 4.1(n)] is authorized; something less than a complete inability to serve the defendant. *Blair v. Burgener*, 226 Ariz. 213, 245 P.3d 898 (Ct. App. Div. 2 2010).

An application must be made to the Court for authority to employ alternative service under this subpart of the Rule and, regardless of the alternative method of service the Court authorizes, a copy of the summons, the complaint and the Order authorizing alternative service must be mailed to the last known business or residence address of the person on whom effective service is sought.

The Rule should not be invoked when service can be effectively accomplished under Rules 4.1(d) to (j). Further, Ariz. R. Civ. P. 4.1(k) [formerly, Rule 4.1(m)] does not provide a separate basis for a court to authorize service by publication. Thus, a court may not authorize service by publication under Ariz. R. Civ. P. 4.1(k) in circumstances where such service would not be permitted by Rule 4.1(*l*). *Blair v. Burgener*, 226 Ariz. 213, 245 P.3d 898 (Ct. App. Div. 2 2010) (interpreting former Rule 4.1(m)).

10. *Service by Publication Generally.* Although authorized by the rules of civil procedure, it is well settled that actual notice via publication is not a preferred means of service because it is less certain than direct personal service. *Ritchie v. Salvatore Gatto Partners, L.P.*, 223 Ariz. 304, 222 P.3d 920 (Ct. App. Div. 1 2010). For that reason, personal service is generally preferred because it insures the named party receives actual and timely notice of the action. *Ritchie v. Salvatore Gatto Partners, L.P.*, 223 Ariz. 304, 222 P.3d 920 (Ct. App. Div. 1 2010).

As renumbered effective January 1, 2013, Ariz. R. Civ. P. 4.1(*l*) [formerly, Rule 4.1(n)] governs the procedure for securing service of process by publication upon defendants whose present or last-known residence was within Arizona. Under Rule 4.1(*l*), a person seeking to utilize service by publication must demonstrate that personal service was not practicable, because either the person's whereabouts in the state is unknown or that person is actively avoiding attempts to achieve personal service.

Under Rule 4.1(*l*), service by publication where the defendant's residence is *unknown* is only proper where the defendant's address cannot be ascertained after diligent efforts to do so. In the *Matter of Rights to Use of Gila River*, 171 Ariz. 230, 830 P.2d 442 (1992); *Walker v. Dallas*, 146 Ariz. 440, 706 P.2d 1207 (1985); *Pioneer Federal Sav. Bank v. Driver*, 166 Ariz. 585, 804 P.2d 118 (Ct. App. Div. 1 1990); *Omega II Inv. Co. v. McLeod*, 153 Ariz. 341, 736 P.2d 824 (Ct. App. Div. 2 1987); *Saucedo v. Engelbrecht*, 149 Ariz. 18, 716 P.2d 79 (Ct. App. Div. 2 1986); *Brennan v. Western Sav. and Loan Ass'n*, 22 Ariz. App. 293, 526 P.2d 1248 (Div. 1 1974). The exercise of "due diligence" requires such measures as the examination of telephone company records, utility company records, and records maintained by the county treasurer, county recorder or similar agency, to locate the defendant's whereabouts. *Sprang v. Petersen Lumber, Inc.*, 165 Ariz. 257, 798 P.2d 395 (Ct. App. Div. 1 1990). The efforts made to ascertain the defendant's address or location must be set forth in an affidavit filed before service by publication is accomplished. *Sprang v. Petersen Lumber, Inc.*, 165 Ariz. 257, 798 P.2d 395 (Ct. App. Div. 1 1990). An affidavit which merely asserts, in conclusory fashion, that a duly diligent effort to locate the defendant had been made is insufficient. *Barlage v. Valentine*, 210 Ariz. 270, 110 P.3d 371 (Ct. App. Div. 2 2005).

The publication must be of the summons and of a statement as to the manner in which a copy of the pleading being served may be obtained. The publication is to be for four (4) successive weeks in a newspaper of general circulation in the county where the action is pending and, if the last-known residence address of the defendant was in another county, in a newspaper of general circulation in that county. If either of these counties does not have a newspaper of general circulation, then the required publication is to be made in a newspaper in an adjoining county. Where the defendant's residence is known, in addition to the publication, the summons and a copy of the complaint must be mailed to the defendant at that address.

The requirements of the Rule are to be satisfied for each person to be served. The seeming burden of multiple publications where there is more than one person to be served in this fashion is alleviated by the fact that the entire pleading being served need not be published. Under the Rule, what is published may consist only of the summons and of a statement as to the manner in which a copy of the pleading being served can be obtained.

Incomplete service by publication is neither adequate nor perfected for purposes of triggering deadlines established under the rules of civil procedure or as contained in statutes that require service of process. *Ritchie v. Salvatore Gatto Partners, L.P.*, 223 Ariz. 304, 222 P.3d 920 (Ct. App. Div. 1 2010) (holding entitlement to award of attorneys' fees and costs under A.R.S. § 42-18206 (2006) requires completion of service).

A plaintiff pursuing a monetary judgment against a defendant whose residence is unknown, but whose last known residence was within the state, or who has avoided service, can serve that defendant by publication in accordance with the requirements of Rule 4.1(*l*). *Master Financial, Inc. v. Woodburn*, 208 Ariz. 70, 90 P.3d 1236 (Ct. App. Div. 1 2004), as amended, (June 7, 2004). The deletion from that Rule of the phrase "where by law personal service is not required," which appeared in former Rule 4(e)(3), was intended to eliminate the distinction between *in personam* and *in rem* actions. *Master Financial, Inc. v. Woodburn*, 208 Ariz. 70, 90 P.3d 1236 (Ct. App. Div. 1 2004), as amended on other grounds, (June 7, 2004).

In addition to satisfying the requirements of Rule 4.1(*l*), a plaintiff seeking service by publication must also satisfy due process minimums. *Master Financial, Inc. v. Woodburn*, 208 Ariz. 70, 90 P.3d 1236 (Ct. App. Div. 1 2004), as amended on other grounds, (June 7, 2004). Publication satisfies due process minimum notice requirements if it is the best means of notice under the circumstances and is reasonably calculated to apprise the interested parties of the pendency of the action. *Master Financial, Inc. v. Woodburn*, 208 Ariz. 70, 90 P.3d 1236 (Ct. App. Div. 1 2004), as amended on other grounds, (June 7, 2004). Service by publication is constitutionally sufficient for a defendant who willfully leaves the state to evade service of process. *Master Financial, Inc. v. Woodburn*, 208 Ariz. 70, 90 P.3d 1236 (Ct. App. Div. 1 2004), as amended on other grounds, (June 7, 2004).

Service by publication is likewise sufficient when a plaintiff has exercised due diligence to personally serve a resident defendant at a last known address and has complied with the publication procedures of Rule 4.1(*l*). *Master Financial, Inc. v. Woodburn*, 208 Ariz. 70, 90 P.3d 1236 (Ct. App. Div. 1 2004), as amended on other grounds, (June 7, 2004). When service of process is by publication, a party against whom a default judgment has been entered may seek relief, under Rule 59(j), within one (1) year after the entry of judgment. *Master Financial, Inc. v. Woodburn*, 208 Ariz. 70, 90 P.3d 1236 (Ct. App. Div. 1 2004), as amended on other grounds, (June 7, 2004). Even after one year has elapsed, the party may still seek relief under Rule 60(c)(4). *Master Financial, Inc. v. Woodburn*, 208 Ariz. 70, 90 P.3d 1236 (Ct. App. Div. 1 2004), as amended on other grounds, (June 7, 2004).

11. *Service Upon Unknown Heirs by Publication.* As renumbered effective January 1, 2013, Ariz. R. Civ. P. 4.1(m) codifies one specific instance where service may be accomplished by publication, in actions involving real property where the joinder as parties of unknown heirs of a decedent is necessary to the complete determination of the action. The requirements of Ariz. R. Civ. P. 4.1(*l*) must be satisfied, but publication need only be made in the county where the action is pending because, by definition, there will be no last known residences of the heirs in question. The party utilizing such service must explain, if challenged, the circumstances warranting service by publication and the efforts made to identify and locate the unknown heirs. *Roberts v. Robert*, 215 Ariz. 176, 158 P.3d 899 (Ct. App. Div. 1 2007).

Rule 4.2. Service of process outside the state

(a) Extraterritorial Jurisdiction; Personal Service Out of State. A court of this state may exercise personal jurisdiction over parties, whether found within or outside the state, to the maximum extent permitted by the Constitution of this state and the Constitution of the United States. Service upon any such party located outside the state may be made as provided in this Rule 4.2, and when so made shall be of the same effect as personal service within the state.

Added April 16, 1991, effective July 1, 1991. Amended Oct. 9, 1996, effective Dec. 1, 1996; Oct. 14, 1997, effective Oct. 15, 1997.

(b) Direct Service. Service of process may be made outside the state but within the United States in the same manner provided in Rule 4.1(d)–(j) of these Rules by a person authorized to serve process under the law of the state where such service is made. Such service shall be complete when made and time for purposes of Rule 4.2(m) shall begin to run at that time, provided that before any default may be had on such service, there shall be filed an affidavit of service showing the circumstances warranting the utilization of this procedure and attaching an affidavit of the process server showing the fact and circumstances of the service.

Added April 16, 1991, effective July 1, 1991. Amended Oct. 9, 1996, effective Dec. 1, 1996; Oct. 14, 1997, effective Oct. 15, 1997. Technical amendment correcting cross-reference to Rule 4.1 subparagraphs, effective Jan. 1, 2014.

(c) Service by Mail; Return. When the whereabouts of a party outside the state is known, service may be made by depositing the summons and a copy of the pleading being served in the post office, postage prepaid, to be sent to the person to be served by any form of mail requiring a signed and returned receipt. Service by mail pursuant to this subpart and the return thereof may be made by the party procuring service or by that party's attorney. Upon return through the post office of the signed receipt, the serving party shall file an affidavit with the court stating (1) that the party being served is known to be located outside the state; (2) that the summons and a copy of the pleading were dispatched to the party being served; (3) that such papers were in fact received by the party as evidenced by the receipt, a copy of which shall be attached to the affidavit; and (4) the date of receipt by the party being served and the date of the return of the receipt to the sender. This affidavit shall be prima facie evidence of personal service of the summons and the pleading and service shall be deemed complete and time shall begin to run for the purposes of Rule 4.2(m) of these Rules from the date of receipt by the party being served, provided that no default may be had on such service until such an affidavit has been filed.

Added Oct. 14, 1997, effective Oct. 15, 1997.

(d) Waiver of Service; Duty to Save Costs of Service; Request to Waive.

(1) A defendant who waives service of a summons does not thereby waive any objection to the venue or to the jurisdiction of the court over the person of such defendant.

(2) An individual, corporation or association that is subject to service under paragraph (b), (c), (h), (i) or (k) of this Rule 4.2 and that receives notice of an action in the manner provided in this paragraph has a duty to avoid unnecessary costs of serving the summons. To avoid costs, the plaintiff may notify such a defendant of the commencement of the action and request that the defendant waive service of the summons. The notice and request:

(A) shall be in writing and shall be addressed directly to the defendant in accordance with paragraph (b), (c), (h), (i) or (k) of this Rule 4.2, as applicable;

(B) shall be dispatched through first-class mail or other reliable means;

(C) shall be accompanied by a copy of the complaint and shall identify the court in which it has been filed;

(D) shall inform the defendant, by means of a text prescribed in an official form promulgated pursuant to Rule 84, of the consequences of compliance and of a failure to comply with the request;

(E) shall set forth the date on which request is sent;

(F) shall allow the defendant a reasonable time to return the waiver, which shall be at least 30 days from the date the notice is sent, or 60 days from that date if the defendant is addressed outside any judicial district of the United States; and

(G) shall provide the defendant with an extra copy of the notice and request, as well as prepaid means of compliance in writing.

If a defendant located within the United States fails to comply with a request for waiver made by a plaintiff located within the United States, the court shall impose the costs subsequently incurred in effecting service on the defendant unless good cause for the failure be shown.

(3) A defendant that, before being served with process, timely returns a waiver so requested is not required to serve an

answer to the complaint until 60 days after the date on which the request for waiver of service was sent, or 90 days after that date if the defendant was addressed outside any judicial district of the United States.

(4) When the plaintiff files a waiver of service with the court, the action shall proceed, except as provided in paragraph (3), as if a summons and complaint had been served at the time of filing the waiver, and no proofs of service shall be required.

(5) The costs to be imposed on a defendant under paragraph (2) for failure to comply with a request to waive service of a summons shall include the costs subsequently incurred in effecting service under paragraph (b), (c), (h), (i) or (k) of this Rule 4.2, together with the costs, including reasonable attorney's fees, of any motion required to collect the costs of service.

Added as Rule 4.2(c) Oct. 9, 1996, effective Dec. 1, 1996. Renumbered as Rule 4.2(d) Oct. 14, 1997, effective Oct. 15, 1997.

(e) Service Under Nonresident Motorist Act. In an action involving operation of a motor vehicle in this state, a nonresident minor, insane or incompetent person may be served in the manner provided by A.R.S. §§ 28-2321 through 28-2327 for service upon a nonresident in such cases as if that person were sui juris. When service of a copy of the summons and complaint is made pursuant to A.R.S. § 28-2327, the service shall be deemed complete thirty days after filing defendant's return receipt and plaintiff's affidavit of compliance, as required by A.R.S. § 28-2327, subsection A, paragraph 1, or, in case of personal service out of the state under A.R.S. § 28-2327, subsection A, paragraph 2, thirty days after filing the officer's return of such personal service. The defendant shall appear and answer within thirty days after completion of such service in the same manner and under the same penalties as if the defendant had been personally served with a summons within the county in which the action is pending.

Added as Rule 4.2(d) April 16, 1991, effective July 1, 1991. Renumbered as Rule 4.2(e) Oct. 14, 1997, effective Oct. 15, 1997. Amended Oct. 2, 1998, effective Dec. 2 1998.

(f) Service by Publication; Return. Where the person to be served is one whose present residence is unknown but whose last known residence was outside the state, or has avoided service of process, and service by publication is the best means practicable under the circumstances for providing notice of institution of the action, then service may be made by publication in accordance with the requirements of this subpart. Such service shall be made by publication of the summons, and of a statement as to the manner in which a copy of the pleading being served may be obtained, at least once a week for four successive weeks in a newspaper published in the county where the action is pending. If no newspaper is published in any such county, then the required publications shall be made in a newspaper published in an adjoining county. The service shall be complete thirty days after the first publication. When the residence of the person to be served is known, the party or officer making service shall also, on or before the date of the first publication, mail the summons and a copy of the pleading being served, postage prepaid, directed to that person at that person's place of residence.

Service by publication and the return thereof may be made by the party procuring service or that party's attorney in the same manner as though made by an officer. The party or officer making service shall file an affidavit showing the manner and dates of publication and mailing, and the circumstances warranting utilization of the procedure authorized by this subpart which shall be prima facie evidence of compliance herewith. A printed copy of the publication shall accompany the affidavit. If the residence of the person to be served is unknown, and for that reason no mailing was made, the affidavit shall so state.

Added as Rule 4.2(e) April 16, 1991, effective July 1, 1991. Amended May 25, 1994, effective Dec. 1, 1994. Renumbered as Rule 4.2(f) Oct. 14, 1997, effective Oct. 15, 1997.

(g) Service by Publication; Unknown Heirs in Real Property Actions. When in an action for the foreclosure of a mortgage on real property or in any action involving title to real property, it is necessary for a complete determination of the action that the unknown heirs of a deceased person be made parties, they may be sued as the unknown heirs of the decedent, and service of a summons may be made on them by publication in the county where the action is pending, as provided in subpart (e) of this Rule.

Added as Rule 4.2(f) April 16, 1991, effective July 1, 1991. Renumbered as Rule 4.2(g) Oct. 14, 1997, effective Oct. 15, 1997.

(h) Service of Summons Upon Corporations, Partnerships or Unincorporated Associations Located Outside Arizona but Within the United States. In case of a corporation or partnership or unincorporated association located outside the state but within the United States, service under this Rule shall be made on one of the persons specified in Rule 4.1(i).

Add as Rule 4.2(g) Oct. 9, 1996, effective Dec. 1, 1996. Renumbered as Rule 4.2(h) Oct. 14, 1997, effective Oct. 15, 1997.

(i) Service Upon Individuals in a Foreign Country. Unless otherwise provided by federal law, service upon an individual from whom a waiver has not been obtained and filed, other than an infant or an incompetent person, may be effected in a place not within any judicial district of the United States:

(1) by any internationally agreed means reasonably calculated to give notice, such as those means authorized by the Hague Convention on the Service Abroad of Judicial and Extrajudicial Documents; or

(2) if there is no internationally agreed means of service or the applicable international agreement allows other means of service, provided that service is reasonably calculated to give notice:

(A) in the manner prescribed by the law of the foreign country for service in that country in an action in any of its courts of general jurisdiction; or

(B) as directed by the foreign authority in response to a letter rogatory or letter of request; or

(C) unless prohibited by the law of the foreign country, by

(i) delivery to the party to be served personally of a copy of the summons and of the pleading; or

(ii) any form of mail requiring a signed receipt, to be addressed and dispatched by the clerk of the court to the party to be served; or

(3) by other means not prohibited by international agreement as may be directed by the court.

Added as Rule 4.2(g) April 16, 1991, effective July 1, 1991. Renumbered as Rule 4.2(h) and amended Oct. 9, 1996, effective Dec. 1, 1996. Renumbered as Rule 4.2(i) Oct. 14, 1997, effective Oct. 15, 1997.

(j) Service of Summons Upon Minors and Incompetent Persons in a Foreign Country. Service upon a minor, a minor with a guardian or an incompetent person in a place not within any judicial district of the United States shall be effected in the manner prescribed by paragraph (2)(A) or (2)(B) of subdivision (i) of this Rule 4.2 or by such means as the court may direct.

Added as Rule 4.2(i) Oct. 9, 1996, effective Dec. 1, 1996. Renumbered as Rule 4.2(j) Oct. 14, 1997, effective Oct. 15, 1997.

(k) Service of Summons Upon Corporation and Associations in a Foreign Country. Unless otherwise provided by federal law, service upon a corporation or upon a partnership or other unincorporated association that is subject to suit under a common name, and from which a waiver of service has not been obtained and filed, shall be effected in a place not within any judicial district of the United States in any manner prescribed for individuals by subdivision (i) of this Rule 4.2, except personal delivery as provided in paragraph (2)(C)(i) thereof.

Added as Rule 4.2(j) Oct. 9, 1996, effective Dec. 1, 1996. Renumbered as Rule 4.2(k) Oct. 14, 1997, effective Oct. 15, 1997.

(*l*) Service of Summons Upon a Foreign State or Political Subdivision Thereof. Service of a summons upon a foreign state or a political subdivision, agency, or instrumentality thereof shall be effected pursuant to 28 U.S.C. § 1608.

Added as Rule 4.2(k) Oct. 9, 1996, effective Dec. 1, 1996. Renumbered as Rule 4.2(*l*) Oct. 14, 1997, effective Oct. 15, 1997.

(m) Time for Appearance After Service Outside State. Where service of the summons and of a copy of a pleading requiring service by summons is made outside the state by any means authorized by this Rule 4.2, other than subsection (d), the person served shall appear and answer within thirty days after completion thereof in the same manner and under the same penalties as if that person had been personally served with a summons within the county in which the action is pending.

Added as Rule 4.2(h) April 16, 1991, effective July 1, 1991. Renumbered as Rule 4.2(*l*) and amended Oct. 9, 1996, effective Dec. 1, 1996. Renumbered as Rule 4.2(m) Oct. 14, 1997, effective Oct. 15, 1997.

STATE BAR COMMITTEE NOTES

1991 Promulgation

New Rule 4.2 contains, with minor revisions, those provisions of former Rule 4(e) that dealt with service of process outside the State of Arizona. New Rule 4.2(a), which incorporates certain of the provisions of former Rule 4(e)(2), codifies the rule that Arizona courts may exercise extraterritorial jurisdiction to the maximum extent permitted by the Arizona and United States Constitutions. *Batton v. Tennessee Farmers Mut. Ins. Co.*, 153 Ariz. 268, 736 P.2d 2 (1987).

New Rule 4.2(b) incorporates the pertinent provisions of former Rule 4(e)(2), and particularly those of former Rule 4(e)(2)(b), authorizing direct personal service of process outside the state in accordance with the applicable laws of the state where such service is made.

New Rule 4.2(c) [d] is based upon former Rule 4(e)(2)(a), which authorized service by registered mail where the out-of-state party's residence address is known. Specific reference to a particular classification of mail service has been eliminated in favor of a generic reference to any form of mail which requires a signed and returned receipt. See A.R.S. § 1-205. The provision of the former Rule that service by this means was not complete until the affidavit of service was filed operated to unnecessarily elongate the time for responding and has been deleted. It has been replaced with a provision, consistent with a similar provision in new Rule 4.2(b), that such service is complete, and the time for responding begins to run, upon receipt by the party served but that a default may not be entered upon such service unless and until an affidavit complying with the terms of the Rule is filed. Service under this new Rule, and the return thereof, may be made by a party or by that party's attorney.

New Rule 4.2(d) [e] is former Rule 4(e)(5), with the addition by incorporation of the provisions of former Rule 4(d)(5) which deals with the same statutory procedure for serving nonresident motorists.

New Rule 4.2(e) [f] is based on former Rule 4(e)(3) and is similar to new Rule 4.1(e), but applies where the present location of the person to be served cannot be ascertained but the last known residence address of that person was outside the state, or a person outside the state is attempting to avoid service. In that instance, publication must occur not only in the county where the action is pending but also in the county of the person's last known residence address. A copy of the summons and pleading being served must also be mailed to the last known address. Once again, service by publication must still satisfy the constitutional standard as being the best means practicable under the circumstances for providing notice. See Comment to new Rule 4.1(f). In addition, the publication must contain a statement as to the manner in which a copy of the pleading being served may be obtained.

New Rule 4.2(f) [g] is identical to new Rule 4.1(f), which itself derives from former Rule 5(f), and has now been repeated here only to make clear that this manner of service is effective even if it develops that the unknown heirs are located outside Arizona, rather than to impose any additional service requirement. It is contemplated that service accomplished in accordance with either Rule 4.1(f) or 4.2(g) will satisfy both. Again, publication under these particular Rules need only be made in the county where the action is pending.

New Rule 4.2(g) [h] dealing with service of process in a foreign country, is adapted from a preliminary draft of proposed amendments to provisions of the Federal Rules of Civil Procedure on the same subject. The principal purpose of these amendments is to call attention to the Hague Convention on the Service Abroad of Judicial and Extrajudicial Documents, which entered into force for the United States on February 10, 1969. The procedures for foreign service specified in the Convention must be employed where they are available and where service requires the transmittal of documents for service abroad. See *Volkswagenwerk Aktiengesellschaft v. Schlunk*, 486 U.S. 694, 108 S. Ct. 2104, 100 L. Ed. 2d 722, 11 Fed. R. Serv. 3d 417 (1988).

New Rule 4.2(h) [i] is essentially identical to former Rule 4(e)(4) and provides a slightly longer time for a party to appear and defend when service is made outside the state than when service is accomplished within Arizona.

COURT COMMENT

1994 Amendment

[Rule 4.2(f)] In adopting the amendment deleting the out-of-state publication requirement, the Court is aware that in a small category of cases out-of-state publication might yield the best practicable notice under the circumstances. However, the Court acted out of concern for the unnecessary expense in the vast majority of cases in which out-of-state publication is ineffective as a means of providing notice. Counsel should always consider whether, in a given case, out-of-state publication may nevertheless be indicated.

1998 Amendment

[Rule 4.2(e)] In 1997 the Transportation Code was amended, resulting in renumbering of its provisions. Rule 4.2(e), which refers to certain provisions of the Transportation Code, was amended correspondingly to refer to the renumbered statutory provisions.

AUTHORS' COMMENTS

Analysis

7. Forum Selection Clauses.
8. Nonresident Motorists.
9. Service by Publication.
10. Service Upon Unknown Heirs by Publication.
11. Service in Foreign Countries.
12. Time for Appearance.

1. *Scope and Purpose of Rule.* Ariz. R. Civ. P. 4.2 contains the provisions governing service of process outside the State of Arizona that were, for the most part, contained in former Rule 4(e). A discussion of the origins and history of the Rule can be found in Section 2 of the *Authors' Comments* to Rule 4.

2. *Comparison With Federal Rule.* FRCP 4(e) and 4(k) merely authorize extraterritorial service under the circumstances and in the manner authorized by federal statute or by a statute or court rule of the forum state. In Arizona, that rule is ARCP 4.2.

3. *Waivers of Service.* The 1996 amendments added what was then a new Rule 4.2(c), subsequently redesignated Rule 4.2(d) in 1997, modeled on Rule 4(d) of the Federal Rules of Civil Procedure, dealing with waivers of service by parties who are to be served outside the State of Arizona. (These amendments also added a virtually identical new Rule 4.1(c), but that Rule only applies to defendants to be served within Arizona.) As a predicate for the new Rule, a provision was also initially added to Rule 4.2(a) specifying that the party responsible for procuring service has a duty to avoid incurring unnecessary service costs and should, where the request for waiver of service procedure is available, attempt to secure a waiver of service. That particular provision had not been contained in the corresponding Federal Rule and was, as a consequence, deleted from Rule 4.2(a) by the 1997 amendment.

The request for waiver of service of procedure may only be used where the out-of-state defendant is an individual, corporation, partnership or unincorporated association. To comply with new Rule 4.2(d), the plaintiff is to send to the defendant, by first class mail, a copy of the complaint or other pleading to be served, together with a notice of initiation of the action and a written request that the defendant waive the requirement of service of a summons. The Rule, as adopted, requires that the notice inform the defendant, "by means of a text prescribed in an official form promulgated pursuant to Rule 84," of the consequences of compliance and of a failure to comply with the request. By subsequent Order, the Arizona Supreme Court promulgated two official Forms—"Form 1. Notice of Lawsuit and Request for Waiver of Service of Summons" and "Form 2. Waiver of Service of

Summons." which will be sufficient to comply with the requirements of Rule 4.2(d). (As promulgated, Form 2 was separated into two separate Forms, but they comprise only a single "Waiver of Service of Summons.").

The request for waiver of service must specify the date on which it was sent and allow the defendant a reasonable time, which must be at least thirty (30) days for defendants located within the United States and at least sixty (60) days for defendants located in foreign countries, to return the waiver of service. The plaintiff must provide the defendant with an extra copy of the notice and request and a prepaid means for complying with the request. New Rule 4.2(d)(2) provides that defendants from whom such waivers of service may be requested have a duty to avoid unnecessary service costs. Defendants are also given incentives to agree to waive the service requirement as well.

If a defendant located outside Arizona but within the United States does not return the requested waiver, the plaintiff can then proceed to secure service in one of the traditional ways and the defendant is to be responsible for the costs thereby incurred. (This cost assessment provision does not apply to defendants located in foreign countries who are requested to waive service.) If the waiver of service of summons is returned, the plaintiff is to file it and the action then proceeds as if a summons had been served, *but* a defendant located outside Arizona but within the United States has up to sixty (60) days from the date on which the request for waiver was mailed in which to respond to the complaint. Defendants located in foreign countries who execute and return a requested waiver of service are given ninety (90) days from the date of mailing to respond to the complaint. By executing and returning the waiver of service, the defendant does not thereby waive any objections to jurisdiction or venue.

Conforming amendments were also adopted to Rule 12(a) to reflect the fact that a defendant who has agreed to waive service of the summons has additional time to respond to a complaint, and to the provisions of Rules 33, 34 and 36 which specify when a response must be made to interrogatories, requests for production and requests for admissions that are served together with the complaint.

4. *Authorized Methods of Service.* Service upon persons located outside Arizona may be made by direct service, by a form of mail requiring a signed and returned receipt, or by publication under specified circumstances. Direct service of process may be made by a person authorized to serve process under the law of the state where service is made, but must be made upon the persons and in the manner specified in Ariz. R. Civ. P. 4.1(d) through (j). Thus, service on a corporation located outside Arizona must be

made upon one of the persons specified in Ariz. R. Civ. P. 4.1(i). *Hilgeman v. American Mortg. Securities, Inc.*, 196 Ariz. 215, 994 P.2d 1030 (Ct. App. Div. 2 2000). Such direct service is completed when made.

Rule 4.2(b) specifies that, where direct service is made on a defendant outside the State of Arizona, an affidavit of service must be filed "before any default may be had on such service." The affidavit is to show the circumstances that warranted use of direct out-of-state service and must attach a separate affidavit from the process server who secured direct service on the defendant. The provision requiring submission of such an affidavit before a default may be taken was not intended, however, to confer any substantive rights on a defendant who is properly served in that fashion. The fact that the specified affidavits are not filed until after a default is taken is not grounds for setting that default aside. *Creach v. Angulo*, 186 Ariz. 548, 925 P.2d 689 (Ct. App. Div. 1 1996), decision approved, 189 Ariz. 212, 941 P.2d 224 (1997).

5. *Service by Mail*. The 1996 amendments deleted the provisions of former Rule 4.2(c), which authorized service outside the state by certain forms of mail. After a brief absence, this provision was restored, in virtually the same form, by an amendment to Rule 4.2 which was made effective October 15, 1997. To accomplish service under Rule 4.2(c), the party or attorney must send a summons and a copy of the pleading being served to the party being served by a form of mail that requires a signed and returned receipt. Execution of that receipt by a commercial mail-receiving agency, such as the UPS Store, which the defendant has authorized to receive restricted delivery mail, will be sufficient. *Barlage v. Valentine*, 210 Ariz. 270, 110 P.3d 371 (Ct. App. Div. 2 2005).

Upon return of the signed receipt, the party procuring service must file an affidavit stating (1) that the party served was known to be located outside the state, (2) that the summons and a copy of the pleading being served were dispatched to that party, (3) that the papers served were in fact received, as evidenced by the signed receipt, and (4) the date the receipt was signed and the date it was returned to the sender. Such service is deemed complete on the date of receipt by the party being served, but no default on such service can be taken until the specified affidavit is filed. *But cf. Creach v. Angulo*, 186 Ariz. 548, 925 P.2d 689 (Ct. App. Div. 1 1996), decision approved, 189 Ariz. 212, 941 P.2d 224 (1997). While the affidavit establishes only a rebuttable presumption of personal service upon the defendant, that presumption can only be overcome by clear and convincing evidence. *Barlage v. Valentine*, 210 Ariz. 270, 110 P.3d 371 (Ct. App. Div. 2 2005). Such service by mail can be employed to secure service on an

Indian reservation located within the physical boundaries of Arizona, or any other state. *State v. Zaman*, 190 Ariz. 208, 946 P.2d 459 (1997).

6. *Scope of Extraterritorial Jurisdiction.* Rule 4.2(a) [former Rule 4(e)(2)] codifies the rule established in prior case law and authorizes Arizona courts to exercise extraterritorial jurisdiction over nonresident defendants to the maximum extent possible consistent with the Arizona Constitution and the Due Process Clause of the Fourteenth Amendment to the United States Constitution. *Planning Group of Scottsdale, L.L.C. v. Lake Mathews Mineral Properties, Ltd.*, 226 Ariz. 262, 246 P.3d 343 (2011); *Williams v. Lakeview Co.*, 199 Ariz. 1, 13 P.3d 280 (2000); *A. Uberti and C. v. Leonardo*, 181 Ariz. 565, 892 P.2d 1354, Prod. Liab. Rep. (CCH) P 14198 (1995); *Northern Propane Gas Co. v. Kipps*, 127 Ariz. 522, 622 P.2d 469 (1980); *Van Heeswyk v. Jabiru Aircraft Pty., Ltd.*, 229 Ariz. 412, 276 P.3d 46 (Ct. App. Div. 2 2012), review denied, (Sept. 25, 2012); *Cohen v. Barnard, Vogler & Co.*, 199 Ariz. 16, 13 P.3d 758 (Ct. App. Div. 1 2000); *G.T. Helicopters, Inc. v. Helicopters, Ltd.*, 135 Ariz. 380, 661 P.2d 230 (Ct. App. Div. 1 1983); *Bach v. McDonnell Douglas, Inc.*, 468 F. Supp. 521 (D. Ariz. 1979).

Accordingly, the resolution of any personal jurisdiction issue "hinges on federal law." *Planning Group of Scottsdale, L.L.C. v. Lake Mathews Mineral Properties, Ltd.*, 226 Ariz. 262, 246 P.3d 343 (2011) (citing, *A. Uberti and C. v. Leonardo*, 181 Ariz. 565, 892 P.2d 1354, Prod. Liab. Rep. (CCH) P 14198 (1995); *Van Heeswyk v. Jabiru Aircraft Pty., Ltd.*, 229 Ariz. 412, 276 P.3d 46 (Ct. App. Div. 2 2012), review denied, (Sept. 25, 2012).

While the "long-arm" provisions of Rule 4.2 are fully applicable to Native American reservations, a state officer not authorized by the sovereign Indian tribe in question cannot effect valid service of process on a non-Native American within a Native American reservation. *Dixon v. Picopa Const. Co.*, 160 Ariz. 251, 772 P.2d 1104 (1989); *Francisco v. State*, 113 Ariz. 427, 556 P.2d 1 (1976). Such service may be secured, however, through registered mail under Rule 4.2(c). Service of process by a Sheriff on a non-Indian, however, if made within that part of an Indian reservation that lies within the boundaries of Arizona, is valid. *State v. Zaman*, 194 Ariz. 442, 984 P.2d 528 (1999).

Service on an out-of-state corporation under Rule 4.2 must be made in a manner that also complies with Ariz. R. Civ. P. 4.1(i) (2013), *i.e.*, on an officer, managing agent or agent authorized by law to accept service. *Hilgeman v. American Mortg. Securities, Inc.*, 196 Ariz. 215, 994 P.2d 1030 (Ct. App. Div. 2 2000). The "law" referred to is the law of the jurisdiction where service is to be made. *Hilgeman v. American Mortg. Securities, Inc.*, 196 Ariz.

215, 994 P.2d 1030 (Ct. App. Div. 2 2000). Generally, however, a foreign corporation consents to jurisdiction by appointing a statutory agent as a condition of doing business in the forum state. If service upon a defendant is not proper, then any resulting judgment is void and must be vacated upon request. *Hilgeman v. American Mortg. Securities, Inc.*, 196 Ariz. 215, 994 P.2d 1030 (Ct. App. Div. 2 2000).

Formerly, the Arizona courts, in assessing challenges to the exercise of extraterritorial jurisdiction, pursued a two-step inquiry which entailed determining, first, whether the provisions of former Rule 4(e)(2) were satisfied, and then whether the exercise of jurisdiction was constitutionally permissible. *Meyers v. Hamilton Corp.*, 143 Ariz. 249, 693 P.2d 904 (1984); *Manufacturers' Lease Plans, Inc. v. Alverson Draughon College*, 115 Ariz. 358, 565 P.2d 864 (1977). This approach has now been both explicitly and implicitly abandoned in favor of analysis of the single issue of whether the defendant had sufficient contacts with Arizona to sustain its exercise of extraterritorial jurisdiction. *Batton v. Tennessee Farmers Mut. Ins. Co.*, 153 Ariz. 268, 736 P.2d 2 (1987); *Northern Propane Gas Co. v. Kipps*, 127 Ariz. 522, 622 P.2d 469 (1980); *Maake v. L & J Press Corp.*, 147 Ariz. 362, 710 P.2d 472 (Ct. App. Div. 2 1985).

There are now two recognized categories of extraterritorial jurisdiction—general and specific. The first category, general jurisdiction, is available for any claim whether or not related to the defendant's activities in Arizona, but may be exercised only when the defendant's contacts with, or activities in, Arizona are substantial, continuous and systematic. *Planning Group of Scottsdale, L.L.C. v. Lake Mathews Mineral Properties, Ltd.*, 226 Ariz. 262, 246 P.3d 343 (2011); *Williams v. Lakeview Co.*, 199 Ariz. 1, 13 P.3d 280 (2000); *Batton v. Tennessee Farmers Mut. Ins. Co.*, 153 Ariz. 268, 736 P.2d 2 (1987); *Helicopteros Nacionales de Colombia, S.A. v. Hall*, 466 U.S. 408, 104 S. Ct. 1868, 80 L. Ed. 2d 404 (1984); *Van Heeswyk v. Jabiru Aircraft Pty., Ltd.*, 229 Ariz. 412, 276 P.3d 46 (Ct. App. Div. 2 2012), review denied, (Sept. 25, 2012); *Arizona Tile, L.L.C. v. Berger*, 223 Ariz. 491, 224 P.3d 988 (Ct. App. Div. 1 2010), as amended on other grounds, (Feb. 8, 2010); *In re Consolidated Zicam Product Liability Cases*, 212 Ariz. 85, 127 P.3d 903 (Ct. App. Div. 1 2006); *Rollin v. William V. Frankel & Co., Inc.*, 196 Ariz. 350, 996 P.2d 1254 (Ct. App. Div. 2 2000); *Taylor v. Fireman's Fund Ins. Co. of Canada*, 161 Ariz. 432, 778 P.2d 1328 (Ct. App. Div. 2 1989).

The second category, specific jurisdiction, exists only for the particular claim asserted and only where the activities in Arizona giving rise to the claim establish the necessary minimum contacts with Arizona to make the exercise of jurisdiction reasonable and just with respect to that claim. *Planning Group of Scottsdale,*

L.L.C. v. Lake Mathews Mineral Properties, Ltd., 226 Ariz. 262, 246 P.3d 343 (2011) (discussing at length the analysis to be employed when several claims arise from a single set of facts); *Williams v. Lakeview Co.*, 199 Ariz. 1, 13 P.3d 280 (2000); *Batton v. Tennessee Farmers Mut. Ins. Co.*, 153 Ariz. 268, 736 P.2d 2 (1987); *Burger King Corp. v. Rudzewicz*, 471 U.S. 462, 105 S. Ct. 2174, 85 L. Ed. 2d 528 (1985); *Keeton v. Hustler Magazine, Inc.*, 465 U.S. 770, 104 S. Ct. 1473, 79 L. Ed. 2d 790, 10 Media L. Rep. (BNA) 1405 (1984); *Van Heeswyk v. Jabiru Aircraft Pty., Ltd.*, 229 Ariz. 412, 276 P.3d 46 (Ct. App. Div. 2 2012), review denied, (Sept. 25, 2012); *In re Consolidated Zicam Product Liability Cases*, 212 Ariz. 85, 127 P.3d 903 (Ct. App. Div. 1 2006); *Rollin v. William V. Frankel & Co., Inc.*, 196 Ariz. 350, 996 P.2d 1254 (Ct. App. Div. 2 2000).

Thus, Arizona's courts have jurisdiction over an out-of-state law firm and lawyer retained by Arizona residents to provide an opinion letter. *Beverage v. Pullman & Comley, LLC*, 232 Ariz. 414, 306 P.3d 71 (Ct. App. Div. 1 2013), affirmed, as clarified, in *Beverage v. Pullman & Comley, LLC*, 234 Ariz. 1, 316 P.3d 590 (2014) (nature of jurisdictional contact under facts presented more precisely termed "Arizona-client-specific contacts" because such contacts do not relate to Arizona, but rather such contacts relate to the client). In that case, the defendants' contacts with the Arizona clients, as opposed to Arizona, were sufficient to confer specific jurisdiction over the defendants.

An individual must have fair warning that particular activity may subject that individual to the jurisdiction of a foreign court. *Bils v. Nixon, Hargrave, Devans & Doyle*, 179 Ariz. 523, 880 P.2d 743 (Ct. App. Div. 2 1994), redesignated as opinion, (Aug. 30, 1994). That fair warning requirement is met where the defendant has purposely directed activities at residents of Arizona and litigation results from alleged injuries that arise out of or relate to those activities. *Beverage v. Pullman & Comley, LLC*, 232 Ariz. 414, 306 P.3d 71 (Ct. App. Div. 1 2013), affirmed, as clarified, in *Beverage v. Pullman & Comley, LLC*, 234 Ariz. 1, 316 P.3d 590 (2014); *Macpherson v. Taglione*, 158 Ariz. 309, 762 P.2d 596 (Ct. App. Div. 2 1988). The exercise of such jurisdiction must also be reasonable. *Beverage v. Pullman & Comley, LLC*, 232 Ariz. 414, 306 P.3d 71 (Ct. App. Div. 1 2013), affirmed, as clarified, in *Beverage v. Pullman & Comley, LLC*, 234 Ariz. 1, 316 P.3d 590 (2014);; *Austin v. CrystalTech Web Hosting*, 211 Ariz. 569, 125 P.3d 389 (Ct. App. Div. 1 2005).

The retention of an Arizona law firm to defend litigation pending in Arizona has been held sufficient contact to justify the exercise of extraterritorial jurisdiction in subsequent action brought by that law firm to enforce its fee agreement against non-resident client. *O'Connor, Cavanagh, Anderson, Westover,*

Killingsworth & Beshears, P.A. v. Bonus Utah, Inc., 156 Ariz. 171, 750 P.2d 1374 (Ct. App. Div. 2 1988).

The domestication of a foreign judgment in Arizona, however, for purposes of according it full faith and credit does not transfer the *in personam* jurisdiction of the foreign court to the Arizona courts. *Polacke v. Superior Court In and For County of Maricopa*, 170 Ariz. 217, 823 P.2d 84 (Ct. App. Div. 1 1991).

When the only nexus with Arizona is the effect of a damage-causing event, the requisite minimum contacts for the exercise of extraterritorial jurisdiction do not exist. *Cohen v. Barnard, Vogler & Co.*, 199 Ariz. 16, 13 P.3d 758 (Ct. App. Div. 1 2000). Thus, an audit performed in Nevada of a Nevada company by a Nevada auditor does not give Arizona jurisdiction over that auditor, even though the audit report caused harm to an Arizona resident. *Cohen v. Barnard, Vogler & Co.*, 199 Ariz. 16, 13 P.3d 758 (Ct. App. Div. 1 2000). Similarly, the commission of an intentional tort that causes harm to an Arizona resident will not be sufficient, in and of itself, to confer personal jurisdiction over the tortfeasor. *Bils v. Bils*, 200 Ariz. 45, 22 P.3d 38 (2001).

A nonresident who contracted with an Arizona Internet Web hosting service to maintain an allegedly defamatory article on its Web server, and sent the offending article to the service in Arizona, has purposefully availed himself of the benefits of Arizona law. *Austin v. CrystalTech Web Hosting*, 211 Ariz. 569, 125 P.3d 389 (Ct. App. Div. 1 2005). The exercise of personal jurisdiction over such a defendant, however, would not be reasonable. *Austin v. CrystalTech Web Hosting*, 211 Ariz. 569, 125 P.3d 389 (Ct. App. Div. 1 2005).

The mere fact that the exercise of extraterritorial jurisdiction may be foreseeable is not sufficient, however, to satisfy due process if the defendant has not had sufficient contacts to justify the exercise of specific personal jurisdiction. *Williams v. Lakeview Co.*, 199 Ariz. 1, 13 P.3d 280 (2000); *Hoskinson Through Fleming v. State of Cal.*, 168 Ariz. 250, 812 P.2d 1068 (Ct. App. Div. 2 1990).

A foreign defendant cannot, however, insulate itself from the exercise of such jurisdiction simply by the use of an intermediary. *A. Uberti and C. v. Leonardo*, 181 Ariz. 565, 892 P.2d 1354, Prod. Liab. Rep. (CCH) P 14198 (1995).

A trial court's dismissal for lack of personal jurisdiction is reviewed on appeal *de novo*, and the facts are viewed in the light most favorable to the plaintiff. *Rollin v. William V. Frankel & Co., Inc.*, 196 Ariz. 350, 996 P.2d 1254 (Ct. App. Div. 2 2000).

7. *Forum Selection Clauses.* A defendant may consent to the exercise of jurisdiction over that defendant, by implication through the entry of a general appearance, or expressly through

advance agreement. Enforcement of forum selection contractual provisions does not offend due process where they have been fully negotiated and are not unreasonable and unjust. *Bennett v. Appaloosa Horse Club*, 201 Ariz. 372, 35 P.3d 426 (Ct. App. Div. 1 2001); *Morgan Bank (Delaware) v. Wilson*, 164 Ariz. 535, 794 P.2d 959 (Ct. App. Div. 2 1990). Where such a forum selection provision is found to be enforceable, the necessity for a due process analysis of the type and extent of the defendant's contacts with the forum is eliminated. *Morgan Bank (Delaware) v. Wilson*, 164 Ariz. 535, 794 P.2d 959 (Ct. App. Div. 2 1990). The party claiming oppression or unfairness as a basis for refusing to enforce a forum selection clause must meet a heavy burden of proof, even when the forum designated in the clause is in a geographically remote location. *Bennett v. Appaloosa Horse Club*, 201 Ariz. 372, 35 P.3d 426 (Ct. App. Div. 1 2001).

8. *Nonresident Motorists.* A nonresident motorist defendant may also be served by publication, and such service will be constitutionally sufficient to confer personal jurisdiction, where diligent efforts have been made to locate and serve the defendant, but have proved unsuccessful. *Walker v. Dallas*, 146 Ariz. 440, 706 P.2d 1207 (1985); *Saucedo v. Engelbrecht*, 149 Ariz. 18, 716 P.2d 79 (Ct. App. Div. 2 1986). Rule 4.2(e) also provides that a nonresident minor or insane or incompetent person may be served, in an action involving the operation of a motor vehicle within Arizona, in the manner specified in pertinent provisions of the Transportation Code. A 1997 amendment to the Transportation Code produced, *inter alia*, a renumbering of certain of its provisions, and Rule 4.2(e) was correspondingly amended in 1998 to refer to the proper renumbered statutory provisions, A.R.S. §§ 28-2321 through 28-2327. Those statutory provisions authorize substituted service on *any* non resident who operates an automobile on a public highway in Arizona, or permits an automobile owned by that nonresident to be so operated.

9. *Service by Publication.* Service by publication upon persons whose present or last-known residence was outside Arizona is governed by Rule 4.2(f). The 1994 amendment to its predecessor, then Rule 4.2(e), deleted the prior requirement that the summons, and a statement as to the manner in which a copy of the pleading being served can be obtained, be published in a newspaper published in the county of the defendant's last known residence. For such out-of-state service by publication attempted after December 1, 1994, publication need only be made in the county where the action is pending.

Service by publication must still meet constitutional standards as the best means practicable for providing notice to the defendant under the circumstances. See Section 10 of the *Authors' Comments* to Rule 4.1. The Court Comment which accompanied the 1994 amendment to this Rule cautioned counsel to consider whether, under the circumstances of a particular case, out-of-state publication should nevertheless be done, in order to satisfy due process requirements.

Rule 4.2(f) permits service by publication when an out-of-state defendant has avoided service, and requires the party securing service in that manner to file an affidavit showing the manner and dates of publication and facts indicating that party made a duly diligent effort to effect personal service. An affidavit which merely asserts, in conclusory fashion, that a duly diligent effort to locate the defendant had been made is insufficient. *Barlage v. Valentine*, 210 Ariz. 270, 110 P.3d 371 (Ct. App. Div. 2 2005).

10. *Service Upon Unknown Heirs by Publication.* Ariz. R. Civ. P. 4.2(g) is identical to Ariz. R. Civ. P. 4.1(m), as renumbered effective January 1, 2013, and was repeated only to make clear that the manner of service authorized is effective even if it develops that the unknown heirs are located outside Arizona. It does not seek to impose any additional service requirement in the types of actions where it is applicable. Service accomplished under either Rule 4.1(m) or 4.2(g) will satisfy both. See Section 11 of the *Authors' Comments* to Rule 4.1.

11. *Service in Foreign Countries.* Ariz. R. Civ. P. 4.2(i) [added as 4.2(g) in 1991; renumbered as 4.2(h) in 1996; and renumbered again in 1997 as 4.2(i)] deals with service in foreign countries. The rule was amended in 1996 to more closely conform to the provisions of Fed. R. Civ. P. 4(f).

In addition, recently renumbered Rules 4.2(j), (k) and (*l*) were added to deal specifically with service abroad on minors, incompetent persons, corporations, partnerships, unincorporated associations and foreign states. The provisions conform closely to the provisions of Fed. R. Civ. P. 4(g), (h)(2) and (j). Ariz. R. Civ. P. 4.2(h)(1) essentially invokes the provisions of the Hague Convention on the Service Abroad of Judicial and Extrajudicial Documents.

The procedures for foreign service specified in the Convention must be employed where they are available and where service requires the transmittal abroad of documents for service. *Volkswagenwerk Aktiengesellschaft v. Schlunk*, 486 U.S. 694, 108 S. Ct. 2104, 100 L. Ed. 2d 722, 11 Fed. R. Serv. 3d 417 (1988); *Cardona v. Kreamer*, 225 Ariz. 143, 235 P.3d 1026 (2010).

12. *Time for Appearance.* Rule 4.2(m) provides a slightly longer time (thirty (30) days) for a party to appear and defend when service is made outside the state than when service is accomplished within Arizona. The time begins to run once service is complete, not from the date when the affidavit or return of service is filed. This provision only applies where service must be made, and not

where the defendant has executed and returned a waiver of service. *But see,* discussion at Section 3: Waivers of Service, *infra.*

Rule 5. Service and filing of pleadings and other papers

(a) Service: When Required. Except as otherwise provided in these rules, every order required by its terms to be served, every pleading subsequent to the original complaint unless the court otherwise orders because of numerous defendants, every paper relating to discovery required to be served upon a party unless the court otherwise orders, every written motion other than one which may be heard ex parte, and every written notice, appearance, demand, offer of judgment, designation of record on appeal, and similar paper shall be served upon each of the parties. No service need be made on parties in default for failure to appear except that pleadings asserting new or additional claims for relief against them shall be served upon them in the manner provided for service of summons in Rule 4, Rule 4.1, or Rule 4.2 as applicable.

Amended March 26, 1963, effective June 1, 1963; July 17, 1970, effective Nov. 1, 1970; Oct. 9, 1996, effective Dec. 1, 1996.

(b) Service; Parties Served; Continuance. When there are several defendants, and some are served with summons and others are not, the plaintiff may proceed against those served or continue the action. The court may order the plaintiff to proceed against those served.

(c) Service After Appearance; Service After Judgment; How Made.

(1) *Serving an Attorney*. If a party is represented by an attorney, service under this rule must be made on the attorney unless the court orders service on the party.

(2) *Service in General*. A paper is served under this rule by:

(A) handing it to the person;

(B) leaving it:

(i) at the person's office with a clerk or other person in charge or, if no one is in charge, in a conspicuous place in the office; or

(ii) if the person has no office or the office is closed, at the person's dwelling or usual place of abode with someone of suitable age and discretion who resides there;

(C) Mailing it via U.S. mail to the person's last known address—in which event service is complete upon mailing; or

(D) delivering the paper by any other means, including electronic means, if the recipient consents in writing to that method of service or if the court orders service in that manner—in which event service is complete upon transmission.

(3) *Certificate of Service*. The date and manner of service shall be noted on the original of the paper served or in a separate certificate. If the precise manner in which service has actually been made is not so noted, it will be conclusively presumed that the paper was served by mail. This conclusive presumption shall only apply if service in some form has actually been made.

(4) *Service After Judgment*. After the time for appeal from a judgment has expired or a judgment has become final after appeal, the service of a motion, petition, complaint or other pleading required to be served and requesting modification, vacation or enforcement of that judgement, shall be served pursuant to Rules 4, 4.1 or 4.2, as applicable, of these rules as if serving a summons and complaint.

Amended Oct. 28, 1980, effective Jan. 1, 1981; Sept. 15, 1987, effective Nov. 15, 1987; Dec. 21, 1990, effective Feb. 1, 1991; Oct. 2, 1991, effective Dec. 1, 1991; Jan. 26, 1994, effective June 1, 1994; Jan. 20, 2006, effective June 1, 2006; Sept. 5, 2007, effective Jan. 1, 2008; Sept. 3, 2009, effective Jan. 1, 2010.

(d) Service; Numerous Defendants. In any action in which there are unusually large numbers of defendants, the court, upon motion or of its own initiative, may order that service of the pleadings of the defendants and replies thereto need not be made as between the defendants and that any cross-claim, counterclaim, or matter constituting an avoidance or affirmative defense contained therein shall be deemed denied or avoided by all other parties and that the filing of any such pleading and service thereof upon the plaintiff constitutes due notice of it to the parties. A copy of every such order shall be served upon the parties in such manner and form as the court directs.

(e) [Abrogated April 16, 1991, effective July 1, 1991].

(f) Sensitive Data.

(1) A person making a filing with the court shall refrain from including the following sensitive data in all pleadings or other documents filed with the court, including exhibits thereto, whether filed electronically or in paper, unless otherwise ordered by the court or as otherwise provided by law:

(A) Social Security Numbers. If an individual's social security number must be included in a pleading or other document, only the last four digits of that number shall be used.

(B) Financial Account Numbers. If financial account records are relevant or set forth in a pleading or other document, only the last four digits of these numbers shall be used.

(2) The responsibility for redacting sensitive data shall rest solely with a person making a filing with the court. The clerk

of the court or the court is not required to review documents for compliance with this rule, seal documents that contain sensitive data on the clerk's own initiative, or redact pleadings or other documents. However, if a document is subject to availability by remote electronic access pursuant to Rule 123, Rules of the Supreme Court of Arizona, any party or their attorney may request that the court order, or the court on its own initiative may order, that the document be sealed and/or replaced with an identical document with the sensitive data redacted or removed.

(3) For violation of this rule, the court may impose sanctions against counsel or the parties to ensure future compliance with this rule.

Former Rule 5(f) abrogated April 16, 1991, effective July 1, 1991. New Rule 5(f) added Sept. 3, 2009, effective Jan. 1, 2010.

(g) Filing; Attachments.

(1) *Filing.* All papers after the complaint required to be served upon a party or to be filed with the Court within a specified time shall be both filed with the Court and served within that specified time;

(2) *Papers Not to Be Filed.* The following papers shall not be filed separately and may be filed as attachments or exhibits to other documents only when relevant to the determination of an issue before the Court:

(A) Subpoena Papers. Any praecipe used solely for issuance of a subpoena or subpoena duces tecum, any subpoena or subpoena duces tecum, and any affidavit of service of a subpoena, except for post-judgment proceedings;

(B) Discovery Papers. Notices of deposition; depositions, interrogatories and answers; requests for production, inspection or admission, and responses; requests for physical and mental examination; and notices of service of any discovery or discovery response;

(C) Proposed Pleadings. Any proposed pleading, except such pleadings may be filed after ruling by the Court if necessary to preserve the record on appeal;

(D) Prior Filings. Any paper which previously has been filed in the case. If a party desires to call the Court's attention to anything contained in a previously filed paper, the party shall do so by incorporation by reference;

(E) Authorities Cited in Memoranda. Copies of authorities cited in memoranda, unless necessary to preserve the record on appeal; and

(F) Offers of Judgment Under Rule 68.

(3) *Attachments to Judge.* Except for proposed orders and

proposed judgments, a party may attach copies of papers not otherwise to be filed under this rule to a copy of a motion or memorandum of points and authorities delivered to the judge to whom the case has been assigned. Any such papers provided to the judge must also be provided to all other parties.

(4) *Sanctions.* For violation of this Rule, the Court may order the removal of the offending document and charge the offending party or counsel such costs or fees as may be necessary to cover the Clerk's costs of filing, preservation, or storage, and the Court may impose any additional sanctions provided in Rule 16(f).

Amended July 23, 1976, effective Oct. 1, 1976; July 6, 1983, effective Sept. 7, 1983; March 2, 1993, effective June 1, 1993; Jan. 29, 1999, effective June 1, 1999.

(h) Filing With the Court Defined. The filing of pleadings and other papers with the court as required by these Rules shall be made by filing them with the clerk of the court, except that the judge may permit the papers to be filed with the judge and in that event the judge shall note thereon the filing date and forthwith transmit them to the office of the clerk.

Amended Sept. 15, 1987, effective Nov. 15, 1987.

(i) Compulsory Arbitration. A complaint and an answer shall be accompanied by such certificate as may be required by Rule 72(e) of these Rules and such other certificates as may be required by local rule.

Added July 16, 1992, effective Dec. 1, 1992. Amended Oct. 10, 2000, effective Dec. 1, 2000.

(j) Proposed Orders and Proposed Judgments.

(1) *Required Format.* A proposed order or proposed judgment shall be prepared as a separate document and shall not be included as an integral part of a motion, stipulation or other document. The proposed order or proposed judgment shall be prepared in accordance with this subsection and Rule 10(d), and shall contain the following information as single-spaced text on the first page of the document:

(A) To the left of the center of the page starting at line one, the filing party's typed or printed name, address, telephone number, State Bar of Arizona attorney identification number, and any State Bar of Arizona law firm identification number, along with an identification of the party being represented by the attorney, e.g., plaintiff, defendant, third party plaintiff, etc. (Note: If the document is being presented by a litigant representing himself or herself, all of this information shall be included except the State Bar of Arizona identification numbers);

(B) Centered on or below line six (6) of the page, the typed or printed title of the court;

(C) Below the title of the court and to the left of the center of the paper, the typed or printed title of the action or proceeding;

(D) Opposite the title, in the space to the right of the center of the page, the typed or printed case number of the action or proceeding; and

(E) Immediately below the case number, a brief typed or printed description of the nature of the document. There shall be at least two lines of text on the signature page. Any proposed form of order or proposed form of judgment shall be served upon all parties and counsel simultaneous with its submission to the Court for consideration. Proposed orders and proposed judgments shall not be filed or docketed by the Clerk of the Court until after judicial review and decision to sign, modify or reject. A party may file an unsigned order or judgment to preserve the record on appeal.

(2) *Stipulations and Motions; Proposed Forms of Order.*

(A) All written stipulations shall be accompanied by a proposed form of order. The party submitting the stipulation shall include with it copies to be conformed, together with envelopes stamped and addressed to each party who has entered an appearance in the case, unless otherwise provided for by the presiding judge. If the proposed form of order is signed, no minute entry shall issue.

(B) Any motion that is accompanied by a proposed form of order shall also include with it copies to be conformed, together with envelopes stamped and addressed to each party who has entered an appearance in the case. If the proposed form of order is signed, no minute entry shall issue.

Amended Jan. 1, 1999, effective, June 1, 1999; June 8, 2004, effective Dec. 1, 2004.

STATE BAR COMMITTEE NOTES

1963 Amendment

[Rule 5(a)] The words "affected thereby," stricken out by the amendment, introduced a problem of interpretation. See 1 Barron & Holtzoff, Federal Practice & Procedure 760–61 (Wright ed. 1960) [Now, 4 Wright & Miller, Federal Practice & Procedure § 1142]. The amendment eliminates this difficulty and promotes full exchange of information among the parties by requiring service of papers on all parties to the action, except as otherwise provided in the rules. So, for example, a third-party defendant is required to serve his answer to the third-party complaint not only upon the defendant but also upon the plaintiff.

As to the method of serving papers upon a party whose address is unknown, see Rule 5(c).

1970 Amendment

[Rule 5(a)] The 1970 revision, requiring that papers relating to discovery shall be served upon all of the parties unless the court otherwise orders, accords with common Arizona practice.

1991 Amendments

[Rule 5(e) and (f)] As part of the 1991 restructuring of former Rule 4, which included the adoption of new Rules 4.1 and 4.2, former Rules 5(e) and 5(f) were abrogated. The intent of the abrogation was to limit Rule 5 to its originally intended scope, i.e., to define the procedures for serving pleadings and other papers generated during the course of the action subsequent to the original complaint. The substance of former Rule 5(e) has been incorporated into new Rule 4(f), and that of former Rule 5(f) into new Rule 4.1(f) and 4.2(f).

AUTHORS' NOTE: Effective January 1, 2010, the Court adopted, and thereby replaced the previously abrogated Rule 5(f) with a new Rule 5(f), which now governs sensitive data contained in pleadings and other court documents.

2000 Amendment

[Rule 5(i)] In the 2000 effort to consolidate formerly separate sets of procedural rules into either the Arizona Rules of Civil Procedure or the Rules of the Arizona Supreme Court, the former Uniform Rules of Procedure for Arbitration were in effect transferred to a renamed Section IX of these Rules. Rule 5(i) 's reference to former Rule 1(e) of the Uniform Rules of Procedure for Arbitration was amended to reflect the new location of that former Rule.

2006 Amendment

[Previous State Bar Committee Note is deleted.]

[Rule 5(c)] Rule 5(c) was amended: (i) to make the rule easier to understand; (ii) to transfer and slightly modify the electronic service provisions in Rule 124(e) and (g) of the Rules of the Supreme Court of Arizona to Rule 5(c); and (iii) to authorize service by other means if the recipient consents in writing or the court so orders.

Like the former Rule 124(e), the amended rule authorizes service by electronic means if the recipient consents to such service in writing. As with other methods of service, an electronically served paper must be in final form, which may be signified by the serving party's signature or by a notation or action that is deemed by agreement, local rule or court order as being the equivalent of the serving party's signature. The consent to electronic service must be express, and may not be implied from conduct. For example, an attorney's listing of his or her e-mail address on court filings, correspondence or on a website does not constitute "consent" within the meaning of this rule. Consent may be communicated by electronic means. The amended rule eliminates the provision in former Rule 124(e) requiring the consent to be filed with the court. The amended rule also authorizes service by "other means" if the recipient consents to such service in writing. "Other means" includes facsimile transmission and transmission by an overnight delivery service. Again, consent must be express, and may not be implied from conduct.

Parties are encouraged to specify the scope and duration of the consent to electronic service and service by "other means." The specification should include at least the names of the persons to whom service should be made, the appropriate address or location for such service (such as the e-mail address or facsimile machine number), and the format to be used for attachments.

The amended rule also authorizes courts to order service by "any other means, including electronic means." The prior rule already authorized courts to permit service by facsimile, and this authority has been extended to authorize a court to permit other methods of service. In some instances, it may be appropriate to authorize alternative service methods over a party's objection because of the exigencies of the case, difficulties of hand-delivery or other factors. In deciding whether to authorize such methods, a court should consider whether: (i) an additional copy of the paper must be served by another method specifically authorized by Rule 5(c) (such as mailing or hand-delivery); (ii) whether page limitations should be imposed (such as in the case of facsimile service); and (iii) whether the recipient's costs associated with an alternative service method (such as in the case of facsimile delivery) should be included as a taxable cost.

Service by electronic means or by "other means" is complete upon transmission, which occurs when the sender does the last act that must be performed by the sender. For example, electronic service is complete when the sender executes the "send" command on a computer to transmit the paper to the recipient. Similarly, facsimile service is complete when transmission of the paper on a facsimile machine is completed. Likewise, service by an overnight delivery service is complete when the sender makes delivery to the service designated to make the overnight delivery to the recipient. As with other modes of service, evidence that the intended recipient did not receive a paper served by these methods may defeat the presumption that service has been effected.

The amended rule also eliminates the requirement that certificates of service must be filed with the court whenever service is effected under this rule. The amended rule, however, is not intended to modify the requirement that a certificate of service accompany any paper that is served on a party or is filed with a court.

COURT COMMENT

1993 Amendment

[Rule 5(g)] The 1993 amendment to Rule 5(g), proscribing the filing of certain documents, and a related amendment to Rule XVII, Uniform Rules of Practice, were intended to have a positive impact on the Superior Court clerks' offices, making their operations both more efficient and less costly. Since parties are no longer required to file Notices of Service of Interrogatories, and since all parties receive copies of Nonuniform Interrogatories [see Uniform Rule XVII(c)(1)], there is no longer a need for the preparation of Notices of Service of Nonuniform Interrogatories. In the interests of conservation and cost-savings, it is hoped that parties will discontinue the practice of preparing and exchanging these notices.

AUTHORS' COMMENTS

Analysis

1. *Scope and Purpose of Rule.* While Ariz. R. Civ. P. 4, 4.1 and 4.2 are concerned primarily with the methods for securing service of original process as the next step after commencement of the action, Rule 5 deals primarily with the service of pleadings and other papers in subsequent stages of the action, where, in most instances, service is made upon counsel as the representative of the party served. In fact, former Rules 5(e) and (f) were abrogated in 1991, and incorporated into new Rule 4, because they dealt with initial service of process. Rule 5 defines the post-complaint papers that must be served and the methods by which such service is to be accomplished. *See Mara M. v. Arizona Dept. of Economic Sec.*, 201 Ariz. 503, 38 P.3d 41 (Ct. App. Div. 1 2002); *Morgan v. Foreman ex rel. County of Maricopa*, 193 Ariz. 405, 973 P.2d 616 (Ct. App. Div. 1 1999).

2. *Comparison With Federal Rule.* ARCP 5 is generally comparable to FRCP 5, but there are substantive and stylistic differences. ARCP 5 does not have a provision for service of papers in *in rem* actions such as is found in FRCP 5(a). Similarly, the Arizona Rule does not have provisions similar to the final three sentences of FRCP 5(e) which authorize individual District Courts to provide for the filing, signing or verification of papers by electronic means and which preclude the clerk from refusing to accept papers for filing simply because they are not presented in proper form.

In addition, FRCP 5, does not have a presumption that service was accomplished by mail unless otherwise specified and no provision similar to ARCP 5(c)(4), dealing with service after a judgment has become final. FRCP 5 also does not contain provisions which correspond to ARCP 5(b), 5(i) and 5(j).

Finally, ARCP 5(g) specifically exempts offers of judgment under ARCP 68 from the filing requirement while the corresponding Federal Rule, FRCP 5(d)(1), does not.

In 2007, the language of FRCP 5 was amended as part of the general restyling of the Federal Rules of Civil Procedure to make the Federal Rules more easily understood and to make style and terminology consistent throughout the Federal Rules of Civil Procedure. ARCP 5 has not been amended to conform to the stylistic amendments made to FRCP 5.

3. *Papers Required to Be Served.* Rule 5(a) is comprehensive in defining the papers that are to be served upon other parties to the action, unless the court otherwise directs, and includes all orders, pleadings, discovery papers, motions and similar papers. *Kline v. Kline*, 221 Ariz. 564, 212 P.3d 902 (Ct. App. Div. 1 2009). If a party has made a general appearance, then service is made on that party pursuant to Rule 5. *Kline v. Kline*, 221 Ariz. 564,

212 P.3d 902 (Ct. App. Div. 1 2009).

Service upon parties in default for failure to appear is not required, except for pleadings asserting new or additional claims for relief, which must be served as prescribed in Rules 4, 4.1 or 4.2. This service exception obviously does not apply to the application for entry of default which must be served by mail on a party claimed to be in default whose whereabouts or attorney are known under Rule 55(a)(1). In addition, Rule 55(a)(1)(iv), added effective January 1, 2012, requires a party requesting entry of default provide notice to all other parties consistent with Rule 5(a).

4. *Manner of Service After Appearance.* In most instances, service is made upon counsel as the representative of the party served. In fact, Rule 5(c)(1) expressly requires that service be made upon an attorney of record rather than the party represented, unless the court orders that service be made directly on the party. It has been held that counsel making service of a pleading or other paper has an obligation to ascertain whether a party to be served has an attorney of record upon whom service must be made. *Biaett v. Phoenix Title & Trust Co.*, 70 Ariz. 164, 217 P.2d 923, 22 A.L.R.2d 615 (1950).

Service upon a party under Rule 5 may only be made upon an attorney who was an attorney of record for that party at the time the pleading was mailed, or who agreed to accept service on that party's behalf. *Kline v. Kline*, 221 Ariz. 564, 212 P.3d 902 (Ct. App. Div. 1 2009). The fact that the attorney subsequently appeared for the party does not signify that the prior service was effective when made. *Morrison v. Shanwick Intern. Corp.*, 167 Ariz. 39, 804 P.2d 768 (Ct. App. Div. 1 1990). Even an informal indication that counsel of record no longer represents the party being served is sufficient to render service ineffective. *Schatt v. O. S. Stapley Co.*, 84 Ariz. 58, 323 P.2d 953 (1958). Moreover, before a party or an attorney for that party has entered an appearance in an action, service on that party of any pleadings or other papers filed in the action must be made as prescribed by Rule 4 rather than under Rule 5. *Maricopa County v. Arizona Tax Court*, 162 Ariz. 64, 781 P.2d 41 (Ct. App. Div. 1 1989).

Service upon an attorney of record may be made by delivery to the attorney personally, by delivery to the attorney's office, or by mail. Where service is made by mail, any prescribed period for responding to the papers served is extended by five *calendar* days, under Rule 6(e). Service by mail is complete upon mailing and receipt is not a condition of its effectiveness. *Phoenix Metals Corp. v. Roth*, 79 Ariz. 106, 284 P.2d 645 (1955) (overruled in part on other grounds by, Coulas v. Smith, 96 Ariz. 325, 395 P.2d 527 (1964)); *McEvoy v. Aerotek, Inc.*, 201 Ariz. 300, 34 P.3d 979

(Ct. App. Div. 1 2001); *Columbia Group, Inc. v. Jackson*, 151 Ariz. 86, 725 P.2d 1120 (Ct. App. Div. 2 1985), opinion aff'd, 151 Ariz. 76, 725 P.2d 1110 (1986).

A strong presumption of receipt arises upon proof of proper mailing as a means of service. *Ulibarri v. Gerstenberger*, 178 Ariz. 151, 871 P.2d 698 (Ct. App. Div. 1 1993) (rejected by, Logerquist v. Danforth, 188 Ariz. 16, 932 P.2d 281 (Ct. App. Div. 2 1996)). The trial court retains discretion, however, to relieve a party of the consequences of failing to respond to a paper, including an offer of judgment, that was served by mail, if that party provides proof that the paper was not in fact received. *McEvoy v. Aerotek, Inc.*, 201 Ariz. 300, 34 P.3d 979 (Ct. App. Div. 1 2001).

While a natural person can always appear *in propria persona*, a corporation is an entity unto itself quite separate from its officers and directors. *Boydston v. Strole Development Co.*, 193 Ariz. 47, 969 P.2d 653 (1998). Thus, there is a long-standing rule that a corporation cannot appear in court except through a lawyer. *Ramada Inns, Inc. v. Lane & Bird Advertising, Inc.*, 102 Ariz. 127, 426 P.2d 395 (1967); *Boydston v. Strole Development Co.*, 193 Ariz. 47, 969 P.2d 653 (1998); *State v. Eazy Bail Bonds*, 224 Ariz. 227, 229 P.3d 239 (Ct. App. Div. 1 2010). (*But see*, exceptions set forth in Rule 31, Rules of the Supreme Court, which permit corporate officers to represent corporations in specified instances). When it does so, however, its actions are not automatically a nullity. A reasonable opportunity should be given to cure the problem. *Boydston v. Strole Development Co.*, 193 Ariz. 47, 969 P.2d 653 (1998).

5. *Service by Other Means*. The 2006 amendment to Rule 5(c)(2) restructured the Rule, but also added what is now subpart (D). Subpart (D) authorizes service "by any other means, including electronic means," but only if the recipient has consented in writing to that method of service or if the court has ordered that service be accomplished in that fashion. An amendment also was made to Rule 6(e) to provide that, where service is accomplished by electronic means or some other means authorized by this Rule, the party served has five (5) additional days to respond.

The State Bar Committee Note that accompanies the 2006 amendment states that the phrase "other means" in Rule 5(c)(2)(D) authorizes the court to permit service by electronic means and other methods, including overnight delivery. The State Bar Committee Note to the 1994 amendments, which provided that service by facsimile transmission was not authorized, was expressly deleted.

The Rule itself specifies that service by one of these "other means" is "complete upon transmission." The accompanying State Bar Committee Note explains that this means service is complete when the "sender does the last act that must be performed" to effect transmission, such as executing the "send" command on a computer or making delivery of the paper to the overnight delivery service that will accomplish actual delivery.

By Administrative Order 2014-23, the Arizona Supreme Court has modified the procedures set forth in Ariz. R. Civ. P. 5(c)(2)(D). Thus, effective March 8, 2014, for those attorneys using e-service through AZTurboCourt, the consent requirement has been waived. Consent or a court order is still required to deliver papers by any other means, as contemplated by Rule 5(c)(2)(D).

The Administrative Order states that "filers" are permitted to choose whether or not to effect service through AZTurboCourt and cautions that any attorney who receives service through AZTurboCourt must accept service in that way. Service is complete upon transmission.

The Administrative Order also clarifies the application of Ariz. R. Civ. P. 6(e) (mailing rule). Thus, Rule 6(e) applies to papers served electronically as well as those served by U.S. Mail.

A rule petition has been filed with the Court seeking the amendment of Rule 5(c)(2) and Rule 6(e) to conform with the Administrative Order. The rule petition is out for comments, which are due May 20, 2014.

6. *Certificate of Service.* Before its amendment in 1991, Rule 5(c)(1) did not expressly require the filing of any proof or certificate of service. As amended in 1991, that Rule now requires that the date and manner of service be noted on the original of the paper served or in a separately filed certificate. While such proof of service can be made by separate certificate or an acknowledgment of receipt, the most common technique is by an endorsement at the conclusion of the paper being served as to the fact and manner of service upon counsel.

It can be important to know the precise manner in which service was accomplished because, if service was by mail, the time for response is extended by Rule 6(e). The practice of using so-called "all purpose certificates," which simply listed alternatives, was discouraged by the 1991 amendment. That amendment also added the provision that, if the certificate of service fails to specify the precise manner in which service was accomplished, then it is conclusively presumed that service was accomplished by mail.

7. *Manner of Service After Judgment.* Rule 5(c)(2) expressly provides that service of any pleading or paper filed after a judgment has become final must be made pursuant to Rule 4, rather than simply upon counsel. *Mara M. v. Arizona Dept. of Economic Sec.*, 201 Ariz. 503, 38 P.3d 41 (Ct. App. Div. 1 2002).

8. *Actions Involving Numerous Defendants.* Rule 5(d) recog-

nizes that, in cases where there are multiple defendants, the requirement that all pleadings and other papers be served upon all parties can become quite burdensome, and lead to the service upon some parties of papers in which they have little or no interest. The Rule authorizes the Court to limit the extent to which defendants in such cases are required to serve pleadings on other defendants.

9. *Filing Procedure.* Papers required to be filed by the rules are ordinarily to be submitted to the clerk of the court. Under Rule 5(h), the judge to whom a case assigned may accept papers for filing in that action, but must note the filing date and transmit them to the clerk. The duty to file a paper is discharged when a party places it in the hands of the proper custodian of such papers at the proper time and in the proper place. *Crye v. Edwards*, 178 Ariz. 327, 873 P.2d 665 (Ct. App. Div. 1 1993).

10. *Filing Exceptions; Notices of Service of Discovery Papers.* Essentially on its own motion, the Arizona Supreme Court adopted an amendment to Rule 5(g), effective June 1, 1993, which drastically curtailed the requirement for filing papers following the Complaint in a civil action. Under the amended Rule, the following categories of papers are not to be filed with the Clerk of the Court as a matter of course:

(1) papers associated with the issuance of subpoenas, including praecipes, subpoenas, and affidavits of service, except for those secured in connection with post-judgment proceedings;

(2) discovery papers generally, including notices of depositions, depositions themselves, discovery requests and responses, and notices of service of any discovery requests and responses;

(3) proposed pleadings, except such pleadings may be filed if necessary to preserve an appellate record;

(4) papers previously filed in the action;

(5) copies of authorities cited in legal memoranda, unless necessary to preserve the appellate record; and,

(6) offers of judgment under Ariz. R. Civ. P. 68.

Under Rule 5(g), copies of papers that may not be filed as a matter of course, may be attached to copies of motions or memoranda of points and authorities that are delivered to the judge to whom the case is assigned.

11. *Arbitration Certificates.* Ariz. R. Civ. P. 5(i) provides that any complaint and answer must be accompanied by any certificate required by Rule 72(e) or any other certificate required by Local Rule. Rule 72(e) requires the parties to file a certificate, or controverting certificate, as to whether the case is subject to mandatory court-annexed arbitration. This requirement is

discussed further in Section 3 of the *Authors' Comments* to Rule 72.

12. *Proposed Forms of Orders; Proposed Forms of Judgments.* An amendment to Rule 5 which became effective June 1, 1999 added a new Rule 5(j), which imposes some very specific and detailed requirements for the form of proposed orders and judgments. A 2004 amendment to the Rule added a new subparagraph (2)(B), which makes clear that the requirements of the Rule apply to any proposed form of order that accompanies a motion. They are to be prepared as a separate document, and cannot be included as part of any motion, stipulation or other document that is filed. To the left of the center of the page starting at line one, the submitting attorney must place, single-spaced, that attorney's name, address, telephone number, State Bar of Arizona attorney identification number, State Bar of Arizona law firm identification number (if applicable), and an identification of the party being represented by the submitting attorney.

The title of the Court is to be centered on line six (6), again single-spaced. The title of the action or proceeding is to be below the title of the Court and to the left of the center of the page. Opposite the title, in the space to the right of the center of the page, the submitting party is to place the case number of the action or proceeding. Immediately below the case number, there is to be a brief description of the nature of the document. Finally, the new Rule requires that there must be at least two lines of text on the signature page.

Proposed forms of orders and judgments are to be served upon all parties and counsel simultaneously with their submission for consideration. (Rule 58(a) imposes an identical requirement, but is limited in its application to proposed judgments.) They are not to be filed or docketed until after the Judge has decided to sign, modify or reject them. At that point, an unsigned order or form of judgment may be filed, if necessary, to preserve the record on an issue for appeal.

13. *Written Stipulations.* Rule 5(j) was amended in 2004 and, as part of that amendment, a new Rule 5(j)(2)(A) was added. This Rule requires that *all* written stipulations be accompanied by a proposed form of order, and the party submitting it must furnish sufficient copies to be conformed, together with envelopes stamped and addressed to each party who has entered an appearance in the case.

14. *Filing Sensitive Data.* Effective January 1, 2010, the Supreme Court amended extensively its Rule 123, to deal with the issue of public access, including electronic access, to judicial records. As a companion, the Court also adopted new Rule 5(f) to protect sensitive personal and financial data which might be rele-

vant and included within those records.

The Rule provides that filings made with the courts are not to contain, unless otherwise ordered by the court or required by other law, social security numbers and financial account numbers. If either of these types of data is required to be included in a filing—a pleading, paper or attachment or exhibit thereto—then only the last four digits of the numbers may be used. Although the court is given authority, where the rule is not followed, to order that the document be sealed and/or replaced with a document that redacts or removes the sensitive data, the Rule is clear that the responsibility for removing or redacting such sensitive data rests solely with the person making the filing. For violations of the Rule, the court may impose sanctions against counsel or the parties to ensure future compliance.

Rule 5.1. Duties of counsel

(a) Attorney of Record: Withdrawal and Substitution of Counsel.

(1) *Attorney of Record: Duties of Counsel.* No attorney shall appear in any action or file anything in any action without first appearing as counsel of record. In any matter, even if it has proceeded to judgment, there must be a formal substitution or association of counsel before any attorney, who is not an attorney of record, may appear. An attorney of record shall be deemed responsible as attorney of record in all matters before and after judgment until the time for appeal from a judgment has expired or a judgment has become final after appeal or until there has been a formal withdrawal from or substitution in the case.

(2) *Withdrawal and Substitution.* Except where provided otherwise in any local rules pertaining to domestic relations cases, no attorney shall be permitted to withdraw, or be substituted, as attorney of record in any pending action except by formal written order of the court, supported by written application setting forth the reasons therefor together with the name, residence and telephone number of the client, as follows:

(A) Where such application bears the written approval of the client, it shall be accompanied by a proposed written order and may be presented to the court ex parte. The withdrawing attorney shall give prompt notice of the entry of such order, together with the name and residence of the client, to all other parties or their attorneys.

(B) Where such application does not bear the written approval of the client, it shall be made by motion and shall be served upon the client and all other parties or their attorneys. The motion shall be accompanied by a certificate of the attorney making the motion that (i) the client has been notified in writing of the status of the case including the dates and times of any court hearings or trial settings, pending compliance with any existing court orders, and the possibility of sanctions, or (ii) the client cannot be located or for whatever other reason cannot be notified of the pendency of the motion and the status of the case.

(C) No attorney shall be permitted to withdraw as attorney of record after an action has been set for trial, (i) unless there shall be endorsed upon the application therefor either the signature of a substituting attorney stating that such attorney is advised of the trial date and will be prepared for trial, or the signature of the client stating that the client is advised of the trial date and has made suitable arrangements to be prepared for trial, or (ii) unless the court is satisfied for good cause shown that the attorney should be permitted to withdraw.

Added Oct. 10, 2000, effective Dec. 1, 2000.

(b) Responsibility to Court. Each attorney shall be responsible for keeping advised of the status of cases in which that attorney has appeared, or their positions on the calendars of the court and of any assignments for hearing or argument. Upon relocation, each attorney shall advise the clerk of court and court administrator, in each of the counties in which that attorney has cases that are pending, of the attorney's current office address and telephone number.

Added Oct. 10, 2000, effective Dec. 1, 2000.

(c) Limited Appearance. In accordance with ER 1.2, Arizona Rules of Professional Conduct, an attorney may undertake limited representation of a person involved in a court proceeding.

(1) An attorney may make a limited appearance by filing and serving a Notice of Limited Scope Representation. The notice shall:

(A) state that the attorney and the party have a written agreement that the attorney will provide limited scope representation to the party for the purpose of representing the party in such an action; and

(B) specify the matters, hearings, or issues with regard to which the attorney will represent the party.

(2) Service on an attorney making a limited appearance on behalf of a party shall constitute effective service on that party under Rule 5(c) with respect to all matters in the action, but shall not extend the attorney's responsibility for representing the party beyond the specific matters, hearings, or issues for which the attorney has appeared.

(3) Upon an attorney's completion of the representation specified in the Notice of Limited Scope Representation, the attorney may withdraw from the action as follows:

(A) *With Consent.* If the client consents to withdrawal, the attorney may withdraw from the action by filing a Notice of Withdrawal with Consent, signed by both the attorney and the client, stating:

(i) the attorney has completed the representation specified in the Notice of Limited Scope Representation and will no longer be representing the party; and

(ii) the last known address and telephone number of the

party who will no longer be represented.

The attorney shall serve a copy of the notice on the party who will no longer be represented and on all other parties. The attorney's withdrawal from the action shall be effective upon the filing and service of the Notice of Withdrawal with Consent.

(B) *Without Consent*. If the client does not consent to withdrawal or to sign a Notice of Withdrawal with Consent, the attorney may file a motion to withdraw, which shall be served upon the client and all other parties, along with a proposed form of order.

(i) If no objection is filed within ten (10) days from the date the motion is served on the client, the court shall sign the order unless it determines that good cause exists to hold a hearing on whether the attorney has completed the limited scope representation for which the attorney has appeared. If the court signs the order, the withdrawing attorney shall serve a copy of the order on the client. The withdrawing attorney also shall promptly serve a written notice of the entry of such order, together with the name, last known address and telephone number of the client, on all other parties.

(ii) If an objection is filed within ten (10) days of the service of the motion, the court shall conduct a hearing to determine whether the attorney has completed the limited scope representation for which the attorney appeared.

Rule 5.1(c) added on an emergency basis Dec. 5, 2012, effective Jan. 1, 2013. Adopted on a permanent basis August 27, 2013.

(d) Notice of Settlement. It shall be the duty of counsel, or any party if unrepresented by counsel, to give the judge or the commissioner assigned the case or matter, the clerk of court and court administrator prompt notice of the settlement of any case or matter set for trial, hearing or argument before the trial, hearing, argument or matter awaiting court ruling. In the event of any unreasonable delay in the giving of such notice, the court may impose sanctions against counsel or the parties to insure future compliance with this rule. Jury fees may be taxed as costs pursuant to statute and local rule.

Added as Rule 5.1(c) Oct. 10, 2000, effective Dec. 1, 2000. Renumbered as Rule 5.1(d) on an emergency basis Dec. 5, 2012, effective Jan. 1, 2013. Renumbered as Rule 5.1(d) on a permanent basis August 27, 2013.

STATE BAR COMMITTEE NOTES

2000 Promulgation

Rule 5.1 was promulgated in 2000 as part of the effort to consolidate formerly separate sets of procedural rules into either the Arizona Rules of Civil Procedure or the Rules of the Arizona Supreme Court, and essentially incorporates, in a different order but without substantive change, the provisions of former Rule XII of the Uniform Rules of Practice of the Superior Court. New Rule 5.1(a) is former Rule XII(c) of the Uniform Rules of Practice; new Rules 5.1(b) and (c) are former Rules XII(a) and (b) of the Uniform Rules of Practice, respectively.

AUTHORS' COMMENTS

Analysis

1. Scope and Purpose of Rule.
2. Comparison With Federal Rule.
3. History and Origin of Rule.
4. Requirement of Appearance by Counsel; Duties of Counsel of Record.
5. *Pro Hac Vice* Admission of Counsel.
6. Withdrawal and/or Substitution of Counsel of Record.
7. Limited (Scope) Appearance.
8. Notices of Settlement.

1. *Scope and Purpose of Rule.* Ariz. R. Civ. P. 5.1 defines the responsibilities of counsel who has entered an appearance as counsel of record for a party in a civil action, and establishes the procedures for securing the approval of the Court for the withdrawal of counsel of record and/or for the substitution of new counsel of record.

2. *Comparison With Federal Rule.* The Federal Rules of Civil Procedure do not have a provision that corresponds to ARCP 5.1.

3. *History and Origin of Rule.* Rule 5.1 was added to the Arizona Rules of Civil Procedure, effective December 1, 2000, as a consequence of the Arizona Supreme Court's approval of the recommendations of what was known as the Civil Rules Consolidation Project. By an Order entered in October 2000, the Supreme Court abrogated the Uniform Rules of Practice of the Superior Court, the Uniform Rules of Procedure for Medical Malpractice Cases, and the Uniform Rules of Procedure for Arbitration, as separate sets of procedural rules, and transferred their provisions to either the Arizona Rules of Civil Procedure or the Rules of the Arizona Supreme Court. The rationale used for determining the placement of rules was that rules affecting the processing of civil cases should be placed in the Arizona Rules of Civil Procedure, while rules that concerned only internal court administration should be placed in the Rules of the Arizona Supreme Court. Application of this rationale resulted, in some instances, in the transfer of certain provisions of the Arizona Rules of Civil Procedure to the Rules of the Arizona Supreme Court.

Rule 5.1 essentially incorporates, in a different order but

without substantive change, the provisions of former Rule XII of the Uniform Rules of Practice of the Superior Court. Rule 5.1(a) is former Rule XII(c) of the Uniform Rules of Practice; Rules 5.1(b) and (c) are former Rules XII(a) and (b) of the Uniform Rules of Practice, respectively.

4. *Requirement of Appearance by Counsel; Duties of Counsel of Record.* Rule 5.1(a)(1) provides that an attorney representing a party in a civil action may not make an appearance or file any papers without first appearing as counsel of record for that party. It is generally assumed that the filing of papers on behalf of a party or participating in any proceedings constitutes a representation that the attorney involved is appearing as counsel of record.

Rule 5(c)(1) generally requires that service of papers following the complaint be made upon an attorney of record rather than directly upon the party represented unless the court orders that service be made directly upon the party. It has been held that counsel making service of a pleading or other paper has an obligation to ascertain whether a party to be served has an attorney of record upon whom service can be made. *Biaett v. Phoenix Title & Trust Co.*, 70 Ariz. 164, 217 P.2d 923, 22 A.L.R.2d 615 (1950).

Attorneys are responsible for keeping themselves advised of the status of all cases in which they have appeared as counsel of record and of any court appearances required. *Troxler v. Holohan*, 9 Ariz. App. 304, 451 P.2d 662 (1969). An attorney must also keep the Clerk of the Court or Court Administrator, if there is one, in each county in which that attorney has cases pending, apprised of the attorney's current office address and telephone number.

5. *Pro Hac Vice Admission of Counsel.* An attorney who is a member in good standing of the bar of another state or territory or insular possession of the United States or the District of Columbia, but who is not admitted to practice in Arizona, may appear as counsel *pro hac vice* by following the procedures specified in what is now Rule 38(a), Rules of the Arizona Supreme Court.

Under the revised amended Rule, before applying for *pro hac vice* admission, the out-of-state lawyer must *first* obtain from the State Bar of Arizona a form of Notice specified in the amended Rule. To obtain that Notice, the lawyer must submit the following documentation to the State Bar:

1. the original and one copy of a verified application,
2. a certificate from the state bar or clerk of the highest admitting court of each state in which the nonresident attorney has been admitted to practice, certifying the lawyer's date of admission and the lawyer's current membership status or eligibility to practice in that jurisdiction, and

3. a non-refundable application fee equal to the current annual dues paid by active members of the State Bar of Arizona for the calendar year in which the application is made.

Where *pro hac vice* admission is sought in many cases which constitute "consolidated or related matters," only one application and application fee is required per nonresident attorney. In the discretion of the State Bar, the application fee requirement may also be waived to permit *pro bono* representation of an indigent client by a nonresident attorney.

The verified application must be on a form approved by the State Bar Board of Governors, and must provide the following information:

(1) the title of the case or cause, court, board or agency or docket number in which the nonresident attorney will be seeking to appear *pro hac vice* and whether that case is related to or consolidated with a matter in which the attorney has previously applied to appear *pro hac vice*;

(2) the nonresident attorney's residence and office address;

(3) the courts to which the nonresident attorney has been admitted and the dates of such admission;

(4) that the nonresident attorney is a member in good standing in such courts;

(5) that the nonresident attorney is not currently suspended or disbarred in any court;

(6) whether the nonresident attorney is currently subject to any pending disciplinary proceeding by any court, agency or similar organization and, if so, the jurisdiction where such proceeding is pending, the nature of the matter under investigation and the name and address of the disciplinary authority investigating the matter;

(7) whether the nonresident attorney has ever been disciplined by any court, agency or organization authorized to discipline lawyers;

(8) the title of the court and cause and docket number of any case in Arizona in which the nonresident attorney, has filed an application to appear as counsel in the preceding three (3) years, the date of such application, and whether it was granted;

(9) the name, address and telephone number of local counsel;

(10) the name of each party in the case (in which the nonresident attorney will seek to appear), and the name and address of counsel of record for each such party;

(11) a certification by the nonresident attorney that he or she will be subject to the jurisdiction of the courts and agen-

cies of the State of Arizona and of the State Bar of Arizona with respect to the law governing the conduct of attorneys to the same extent as an active member of the State Bar of Arizona;

(12) a statement that the nonresident attorney will review and comply with appropriate rules of procedure as required in the case in question, and

(13) a statement that the nonresident attorney understands and will comply with the standards of professional conduct required of members of the State Bar of Arizona.

Upon receipt of the verified application and application fee from the nonresident attorney, the State Bar will issue, *to local counsel*, a Notice of Receipt of Complete Application ("Notice") which states:

(1) whether the nonresident attorney has previously submitted an application for *pro hac vice* admission in Arizona within the preceding three (3) years,

(2) the date of such application or motion, and

(3) whether the application or motion was granted or denied.

The Notice is to include as exhibits the nonresident attorney's original verified application and the original certificates of good standing that accompanied it.

Local counsel must then file a motion to associate the nonresident attorney *pro hac vice* and serve the motion on all parties. The motion must be accompanied by

(1) the original verified application submitted to the State Bar by the nonresident attorney,

(2) the original certificates of good standing for the nonresident attorney,

(3) the Notice issued to local counsel by the State Bar, and

(4) a proposed order granting or denying the motion.

The order granting or denying the motion to associate must be entered by the court or administrative agency in which it is filed within twenty (20) days after the motion is filed, and local counsel is required to send a copy of the order entered to the State Bar of Arizona.

The revised amended Rule does contain a provision which permits a court, board or administrative agency to allow a nonresident attorney to appear *pro hac vice* on a temporary basis pending completion of the application procedures specified in the Rule. Where such a temporary *pro hac vice* admission is granted, however, the court, board or administrative agency must specify a time period for the nonresident attorney to complete the application procedures, and any temporary *pro hac vice* admission is revoked if the nonresident attorney fails to do so.

The revised amended Rule specifically states that whether to grant a motion to associate a nonresident attorney *pro hac vice* is discretionary with the court or administrative agency to which it is submitted, and a nonresident attorney must associate local counsel who is a member in good standing of the State Bar of Arizona. The name of such local counsel must appear on all notices, orders, pleadings and other documents filed in the matter involved, and local counsel must accept joint responsibility with the nonresident attorney for the matter to the client, to opposing parties and counsel, and to the court or administrative agency in which the matter is pending. Local counsel may also be required to appear and participate in pretrial conferences, hearings, trials and other proceedings where the tribunal in question deems such appearance and participation appropriate.

Interestingly, the amended Rule specifies that a motion to associate nonresident counsel may be denied, or the authority of nonresident counsel to appear *pro hac vice* may be revoked, for "repeated appearances by any person or firm of attorneys pursuant to this rule," absent special circumstances such as a showing that the matter involves a complex area of the law in which the nonresident attorney possesses a special expertise or a lack of local counsel with expertise in the area of law involved in the case.

The order granting the associated nonresident attorney permission to appear *pro hac vice* is valid and effective *only for a period of one (1) year*, and must be renewed. In order to secure a renewal of the authority to appear, local counsel must certify to the State Bar of Arizona, on the anniversary date of the nonresident attorney's submission of the original verified application, whether

(1) the nonresident attorney continues to act as counsel in the case, or

(2) that the case has been fully adjudicated or otherwise concluded.

If the nonresident attorney continues to act as counsel in the case, then that attorney must remit to the State Bar of Arizona a renewal fee equal to current annual dues paid by active members of the State Bar of Arizona for the calendar year in which renewal is sought. Such renewals are also only valid and effective for a period of one (1) year, so that the renewal requirements must be followed and satisfied for each year that the nonresident attorney continues to act as counsel in the case.

Failure to comply with the renewal procedures and requirements will result in the suspension of the nonresident attorney's authority to appear in any case in Arizona. The Executive Director of the State Bar is to notify the nonresident attorney, local counsel and any court or administrative agency involved of any such suspension. The nonresident attorney's authority to appear may then be reinstated by complying with the renewal procedures and requirements, and by paying the prescribed renewal fee *plus* a $50 late penalty. The revised amended Rule does not address the question whether its annual renewal provisions, which did not appear in the former Rule 33(d), apply to *pro hac vice* admissions granted before its September 1, 2002 effective date.

Former Rule 33(d) provided that counsel admitted *pro hac vice* "consents to the jurisdiction of the court for any alleged misconduct which occurs during the course of the matter," but did not define what constituted "misconduct." *Speer v. Donfeld*, 193 Ariz. 28, 969 P.2d 193 (Ct. App. Div. 2 1998). A *pro hac vice* admission should only be revoked for instances of behavior that, collectively or individually, amount to conduct that was intentionally wrong or that deliberately violated any law, court rule or order. *Speer v. Donfeld*, 193 Ariz. 28, 969 P.2d 193 (Ct. App. Div. 2 1998).

6. *Withdrawal and/or Substitution of Counsel of Record.* Rule 5.1(a)(2) does not draw a substantive distinction between withdrawals and substitutions of counsel of record. Any withdrawal of an attorney who has entered an appearance as counsel of record must be approved by a formal written order of the Court, whether there is to be a substitution of new counsel or not. Correspondingly, a stipulation for the substitution of counsel must be approved by the court and comply with the requirements of the Rule concerning withdrawal of counsel.

If the application for withdrawal or substitution contains the written approval of the client, it may be submitted to the Court *ex parte* with a proposed written order approving the withdrawal and/or substitution. If the application does not bear the written approval of the client, counsel seeking to withdraw must proceed by motion which must be served upon the client and all other parties. Notwithstanding that the foregoing are the only two methods specifically sanctioned by the Rule for accomplishing the withdrawal and/or substitution of counsel, there is a relatively prevalent practice, to which the Superior Courts generally do not object, of submitting stipulations for the substitution of counsel without the client's written endorsement.

After an action has been set for trial, a withdrawal or substitution of counsel will not be permitted unless the client or the new attorney acknowledges in writing, as part of the application, an awareness of the trial date and that new counsel will be prepared for trial. The requirement of such a written acknowledgment by the client or substitute counsel may be waived by the Court if the attorney seeking permission to withdraw certifies that the client cannot be located or notified and the Court finds good cause for permitting the attorney to withdraw.

Under the Rule as it existed before the 1989 and 1990 amendments to former Rule XII, it was held that it was within the trial court's discretion whether to grant a continuance of trial where counsel had been permitted to withdraw. *Hackin v. First Nat. Bank of Ariz., Phoenix*, 5 Ariz. App. 379, 427 P.2d 360 (1967); *Evans v. Scottsdale Plumbing Co.*, 10 Ariz. App. 184, 457 P.2d 724 (Div. 1 1969). The purpose of adding the requirement of a written acknowledgment from the client or the substitute attorney of an ability to be prepared for trial on the date set was to reduce to a minimum the cases where a continuance would be required.

7. *Limited (Scope) Appearance.* On August 28, 2013, the Arizona Supreme Court adopted on a permanent basis Ariz. R. Civ. P. 5.1(c), which is entitled "Limited Appearance." In addition to adopting Rule 5.1(c), the Court amended various other rules necessary to facilitate the ability of counsel to engage in limited scope representation.

Despite its title, this Rule 5.1(c) does not govern those circumstances where a limited appearance is made for the purpose of taking some action in a judicial matter without subjecting the client to the jurisdiction of the court. Rather, Rule 5.1(c) sets forth a general rule by which an attorney may provide limited scope *representation* in any civil matter.

Rule 5.1(c) is substantially identical to Ariz. R. Civ. P. 5.2, which addresses the limited scope representation of clients who desire to pursue claims under the Arizona Vulnerable Adult statute, A.R.S. §§ 46-451, et seq., but who are either unwilling or unable to bear the expense of retaining counsel to handle every aspect of such an action.

For that reason, the procedure under Ariz. R. Civ. P. 5.1(c) also is virtually identical to that set forth in Ariz. R. Civ. 5.2, albeit without a corresponding form of notice. *See,* Ariz. R. Civ. P. 84, Form 8. Thus, under Rule 5.1(c), a lawyer wishing to make a limited scope appearance on behalf of a client must file and serve a Notice of Limited Scope Representation. This Notice must:

1. state that the lawyer and the client have a written agreement that the attorney will provide limited scope representation to the party in the action; and

2. specify the matters, hearings or issues with respect to which the attorney will represent the party.

While the adoption of Rule 5.1(c) was not accompanied by a corresponding adoption of a form of Notice of Limited Scope Representation, Rule 84, Form 8, which did accompany the adoption of Rule 5.2, provides a useful template for the Notice of Limited

Representation under Rule 5.1(c).

A lawyer who has appeared in the action pursuant to such a Notice may be served with papers on behalf of the client, but acceptance of such service does not extend the attorney's responsibility for representing the party beyond the scope of the previously agreed to representation. Rule 5.1(c) does not expressly require the lawyer forward to the client papers served on the lawyer outside the scope of representation. Such requirement, however, is implicit and governed by the Arizona Rules of Professional Conduct.

Once the lawyer has completed the limited scope representation for which the lawyer was engaged, the lawyer may withdraw, either upon notice, or on motion if the client does not consent. While the Rule contemplates that there may be situations where the client objects to the lawyer's withdrawal, its language suggests that withdrawal should be permitted if the Court determines that the lawyer has completed the matters for which engaged.

8. *Notices of Settlement.* The coverage of Ariz. R. Civ. P. 5.1(d), formerly Rule 5.1(c), which deals with the obligation to furnish the Court with notice of the settlement of any civil case, was expanded significantly by an amendment to former Rule XII(b) of the Uniform Rules of Practice which became effective December 1, 1997. The obligation to provide "prompt notice" of such a settlement is now imposed upon unrepresented parties as well as counsel, and applies, not just to settlements reached shortly before trial, but to the settlement of any case or matter that is set for trial, hearing or argument. The notice must be provided before the trial, hearing, argument or matter awaiting court ruling, and must be furnished to the Judge or Commissioner to whom the case or matter is assigned, in addition to the Clerk and Court Administrator, if any. The Court is authorized, but no longer required, to impose sanctions for violations of the Rule, which may include the taxation of jury fees.

The Superior Courts in several counties have adopted, by Local Rule, more specific requirements concerning the timing of a notice of settlement before trial and, for that reason, must be consulted.

Rule 5.2. Limited scope representation in vulnerable adult exploitation actions brought under A.R.S. § 46-451, et seq.

(a) Limited Appearance. An attorney may make a limited appearance on behalf of a claimant in a vulnerable adult exploitation action brought under A.R.S. § 46-451, et seq., by filing and serving a Notice of Limited Scope Representation in the form prescribed in Rule 84, Form 8. The notice shall:

(1) state that the attorney and the party have a written agreement that the attorney will provide limited scope representation to the party for the purpose of representing the party in such an action; and

(2) specify the matters, hearings or issues with regard to which the attorney will represent the party.

(b) Service; Limits on Scope of Appearance. Service on an attorney making a limited appearance on behalf of a party shall constitute effective service on that party under Rule 5(c) with respect to all matters in the action, but shall not extend the attorney's responsibility for representing the party beyond the specific matters, hearings or issues for which the attorney has appeared. Nothing in this Rule shall limit an attorney's ability to provide limited services to a client without appearing of record in any judicial proceedings.

(c) Withdrawal. Upon an attorney's completion of the representation specified in the Notice of Limited Scope Representation, the attorney may withdraw from the action as follows:

(1) *With Consent.* If the client consents to withdrawal, the attorney may withdraw from the action by filing a Notice of Withdrawal with Consent, signed by both the attorney and the client, stating: (i) the attorney has completed the representation specified in the Notice of Limited Scope Representation and will no longer be representing the party: and (ii) the last known address and telephone number of the party who will no longer be represented. The attorney shall serve a copy of the notice on the party who will no longer be represented and on all other parties. The attorney's withdrawal from the action shall be effective upon the filing and service of the Notice of Withdrawal with Consent.

(2) *Without Consent.* If the client does not consent to withdrawal or sign a Notice of Withdrawal with Consent, the attorney may file a motion to withdraw, which shall be served upon the client and all other parties, along with a proposed form of order.

(i) If no objection is filed within ten (10) days from the date the motion is served on the client, the court shall sign the order unless it determines that good cause exists to hold a hearing on whether the attorney has completed the limited scope representation for which the attorney has appeared. If the court signs the order, the withdrawing attorney shall serve a copy of the order on the client. The withdrawing attorney also shall promptly serve a written notice of the entry of such order, together with the name, last known address and telephone number of the client, on all other parties.

(ii) If an objection is filed within ten (10) days of the service of the motion, the court shall conduct a hearing to determine whether the attorney has completed the limited scope representation for which the attorney appeared.

(d) Experimental Rule. This rule shall be deemed experimental in nature and shall be reviewed in approximately four years by a committee to be appointed by the Supreme Court.

Rule 5.2 added September 2008, effective January 1, 2009.

AUTHORS' COMMENTS

Analysis

1. Scope and Purpose of Rule.
2. Comparison With Federal Rule.

1. *Scope and Purpose of Rule.* Ariz. R. Civ. P. 5.2 was added to the Arizona Rules of Civil Procedure in 2009 to facilitate so-called "limited scope" appearances by counsel representing clients who desired to pursue claims under the Arizona Vulnerable Adult statute, A.R.S. §§ 46-451, et seq., but who were either unwilling or unable to bear the expense of retaining counsel to handle every aspect of such an action. In that regard, Rule ER 1.2(c) of the Arizona Rules of Professional Conduct, as amended in 2003, specifically permits a lawyer to limit the scope of representation of a client "if the limitation is reasonable under the circumstances and the client gives informed consent."

Under the Rule, a lawyer wishing to make a limited scope appearance on behalf of a client pursuing a covered claim must file and serve a Notice of Limited Scope Representation, using the form specified in Form 8 under Rule 84. The Notice must state that the lawyer and the client have a written agreement that the attorney will provide limited scope representation to the party in the action, and specify the matters, hearings or issues with respect to which the attorney will represent the party. This mirrors the requirement in Rule ER 1.5(b) of the Arizona Rules of Professional Conduct that a lawyer communicates the "scope of the representation" to a client in writing. A lawyer who has appeared in the action pursuant to such a Notice may be served with papers on behalf of the client, but acceptance of such service does not extend the attorney's responsibility for representing the party beyond the scope previously agreed to.

Once the lawyer has completed the limited scope representation for which the lawyer was engaged, the lawyer may withdraw, either upon notice or on motion, if the client does not consent. While the Rule contemplates that there may be situations where the client objects to the lawyer's withdrawal, its language suggests that withdrawal should be permitted if the Court determines that the lawyer has completed the matters for which engaged.

The Rule specifically states that it is being adopted on an experimental basis, and is to be reviewed by a Supreme Court Committee appointed for that purpose in approximately four (4) years (in or around 2013).

2. *Comparison With Federal Rule.* The Federal Rules of Civil Procedure do not have a provision that corresponds to ARCP 5.2.

Rule 6. Time

(a) Computation. In computing any period of time specified or allowed by these rules, by any local rules, by order of court, or by any applicable statute, the day of the act, event or default from which the designated period of time begins to run shall not be included. When the period of time specified or allowed, exclusive of any additional time allowed under subdivision (e) of this rule, is less than 11 days, intermediate Saturdays, Sundays and legal holidays shall not be included in the computation. When the period of time is 11 days or more, intermediate Saturdays, Sundays and legal holidays shall be included in the computation. The last day of the period so computed shall be included, unless it is a Saturday, a Sunday or a legal holiday, in which event the period runs until the end of the next day which is not a Saturday, a Sunday or a legal holiday.is less than 11 days, intermediate Saturdays, Sundays and legal holidays shall not be included in the computation. When that period of time is 11 days or more, intermediate Saturdays, Sundays and legal holidays shall be included in the computation. The last day of the period so computed shall be included, unless it is a Saturday, a Sunday or a legal holiday, in which event the period runs until the end of the next day which is not a Saturday, a Sunday or a legal holiday.

Amended July 14, 1961, effective Oct. 31, 1961; March 26, 1963, effective June 1, 1963; July 2, 1985, effective Oct. 1, 1985; Sept. 15, 1987, effective Nov. 15, 1987; May 1, 1989, effective July 1, 1989; Sept. 1, 2010, effective Jan. 1, 2011.

(b) Enlargement. When by these rules or by a notice given thereunder or by order of court an act is required or allowed to be done at or within a specified time, the court for cause shown may at any time in its discretion (1) with or without motion or notice order the period enlarged if request therefor is made before the expiration of the period originally prescribed or as extended by a previous order or (2) upon motion made after the expiration of the specified period permit the act to be done where the failure to act was the result of excusable neglect; but it may not extend the time for taking any action under Rules 50(b), 52(b), 59(d), (g) and (*l*), and 60(c), except to the extent and under the conditions stated in them, unless the court finds (a) that a party entitled to notice of the entry of judgment or order did not receive such notice from the clerk or any party within 21 days of its entry, and (b) that no party would be prejudiced, in which case the court may, upon motion filed within thirty days after the expiration of the period originally prescribed or within 7 days of receipt of such notice, whichever is earlier, extend the time for taking such action for a period of 10 days from the date of entry of the order extending the time for taking such action.

Amended March 26, 1963, effective June 1, 1963; Sept. 23, 1994, effective Dec. 1, 1994.

(c) [Abrogated Oct. 1, 2000, effective Dec. 1, 2000].

(d) Orders to Show Cause. A judge of the superior court, upon application supported by affidavit showing cause therefor, may issue an order requiring a party to show cause why the party applying for the order should not have the relief therein requested, and may make the order returnable at such time as the judge designates. Any such order to show cause shall be served in accordance with the requirements of Rules 4, 4.1 or 4.2, as applicable, of these rules or, if the party to whom the order is directed has entered an appearance in the action, in accordance with the requirements of Rule 5 of these Rules, within such time as the judge shall direct.

Amended Feb. 25, 1991, effective May 1, 1991; Oct. 2, 1991, effective Dec. 1, 1991.

(e) Additional Time After Service under Rule 5(c)(2)(C) or (D). Whenever a party has the right or is required to do some act or take some proceedings within a prescribed period after the service of a notice or other paper upon the party and the notice or paper is served by a method authorized by Rule 5(c)(2)(C) or (D), five calendar days are added after the prescribed period would otherwise expire under Rule 6(a). This rule has no application to the distribution of notice of entry of judgment required by Rule 58(e).

Amended July 23, 1976, effective Oct. 1, 1976; Sept. 15, 1987, effective Nov. 15, 1987; Oct. 1, 1991, effective Dec. 1, 1991. Amended and effective May 7, 2001. Amended Jan. 20, 2006, effective June 1, 2006; Sept. 3, 2009, effective Jan. 1, 2010; Sept. 2, 2010, effective Jan. 1, 2011.

(f) [Abrogated Dec. 20, 1991, effective July 1, 1992].

STATE BAR COMMITTEE NOTES

1961 Amendment

[Rule 6(a)] The exclusion of Saturday in computing any period of time has been added because of the permissive five (5) day week authorized by A.R.S. § 11-413.01.

1963 Amendments

[Rule 6(a)] This change is for conformity purposes only. It alters nothing which had not been the previous rule in Arizona and simply makes the words the same as in the federal rule. However, the Arizona draft deletes the list of particular holidays contained in the federal rule on the ground that this is unnecessary under our statutes.

[Rule 6(b)] This is a conforming change because the change proposed in connection with Rule 25 (Substitution of Parties) permits the courts to extend time on that subject.

2000 Amendment

[Rule 6(c), abrogated in 2000] As part of the 2000 effort to consolidate formerly separate sets of procedural rules into either the Arizona Rules of Civil Procedure or the Rules of the Supreme Court, Rule 6(c), Ariz. R. Civ. P. was abrogated, because its provisions, which were obviously carried forward from Rule 6(d), Fed. R. Civ. P. were, with one exception, plainly inconsistent with Rule IV of the Uniform Rules of Practice of the Superior Court, and with actual civil motion practice. A modified version of the provision of former Rule 6(c) dealing with the time for filing affidavits in support of, or in opposition to, civil motions was incorporated into new Rule 7.1(a).

2006 Amendment

[Rule 6(e)] Rule 6(e) was amended (i) to transfer and slightly modify the computation of time provision for electronic service and delivery in Rule 124(g) of the Rules of the Supreme Court of Arizona to Rule 6(e); (ii) to adopt a similar rule for service made under the other methods authorized under amended Rule 5(c)(2)(D) and (E); and (iii) to clarify an ambiguity in the rule arising from a 2004 amendment to Rule 58(e).

As amended, the five-day "mailing rule" applies to service authorized by Rule 5(c)(2)(C), (D), or (E). Rule 6(e)'s reference to the mailing of a notice of entry of judgment under Rule 58(e)) was changed to "distribution" to reflect that Rule 58(e) now allows a notice of entry of judgment to be "distributed" by the clerk by mail, electronic mail or delivery to an attorney drop-box.

Previously, Rule 124(g) provided that a document which was served electronically after 5:00 p.m. was to be treated as if served or delivered the following day. Rather than have a time computation rule that applies only to electronic service, this provision was not incorporated into the amendments to Rule 6(e).

COURT COMMENT

1994 Amendment

[Rule 6(b)] The 1994 amendment to this rule and Rule 9(a), ARCAP, and Rules 58(a) and 77(g), Rules of Civil Procedure, were designed to address a problem experienced by practitioners, whereby they were not receiving notice of entry of judgment in some cases and their clients' rights to appeal were jeopardized.

2011 Amendment

[Rule 6(e)] Rule 6(e) is amended to remove any doubt as to the method for extending the time to respond after service by mail or other means, including electronic means, if consented to in writing by the recipient or ordered by the court. Five days are added after the prescribed period otherwise expires under Rule 6(a). Intermediate Saturdays, Sundays, and legal holidays are included in counting these added five days. If the fifth day is a Saturday, Sunday, or legal holiday, the last day to act is the next day that is not a Saturday, Sunday, or legal holiday. The effect of invoking the day when the prescribed period would otherwise expire under Rule 6(a) can be illustrated by assuming that the thirtieth day of a thirty-day period is a Saturday. Under Rule 6(a) the period expires on the next day that is not a Sunday or legal holiday. If the following Monday is a legal holiday, under Rule 6(a) the period expires on Tuesday. Five calendar days are then added-Wednesday, Thursday, Friday, Saturday and Sunday. As the fifth and final day falls on a Sunday, by operation of Rule 6(a), the fifth and final day to act is the following Monday. If Monday is a legal holiday, the next day that is not a legal holiday is the fifth and final day to act. If the period prescribed expires on a Wednesday, the five added calendar days are Thursday, Friday, Saturday, Sunday, and Monday, which is the fifth and final day to act unless it is a legal holiday. If Monday is a legal holiday, the next day that is not a legal holiday is the fifth and final day to act.

Application of Rule 6(e) to a period that is less than eleven days can be illustrated by a paper that is served by mailing on a Wednesday. If ten days are allowed to respond, intermediate Saturdays, Sundays, and legal holidays are excluded in determining when the period expires under Rule 6(a). If there is no legal holiday, the period expires on the Wednesday two weeks after the paper was mailed. The five added Rule 6(e) days are Thursday, Friday, Saturday, Sunday, and Monday, which is the fifth and final day to act unless it is a legal holiday. If Monday is a legal holiday, the next day that is not a legal holiday is the final day to act.

AUTHORS' COMMENTS

Analysis

1. *Scope and Purpose of Rule.* Ariz. R. Civ. P. 6 deals generally with the methods for computing, or for seeking changes to, the time periods prescribed for taking action by the Rules of Civil Procedure or applicable statutes.

2. *Comparison With Federal Rule.* Effective January 1, 2011, ARCP 6(e) was amended such that the method for calculating extra time after service by mail set forth in ARCP 6(e) corresponds to the method set forth in FRCP 6(d). Thus, ARCP 6(e) now provides that five (5) calendar days "are added *after* the prescribed time would otherwise expire under Rule 6(a)." Intermediate Saturdays, Sundays and legal holidays are included in counting these additional five (5) days. The Comment to the 2011 Amendment succinctly explains the amended method for calculating extra time and includes illustrations applying ARCP 6(e) under different circumstances.

Finally, FRCP 6(d) continues to provide three (3) extra days when a paper is served by mail, while ARCP 6(e) continues to provide 5 extra calendar days when a paper is served by mail. Effective March 8, 2014, ARCP 6(e) also applies to e-service through AZTurboCourt. See, Administrative Order 2014-23.

3. *Method for Computing Time.* In computing time periods, the first day is generally excluded and the last day is included, unless it is a Saturday, Sunday or legal holiday. The provisions of Rule 6(a), however, specify the method for counting days whether

one is required to count forward or backward from a precipitating event to a date by which action is required. *Maciborski v. Chase Service Corp. of Arizona*, 161 Ariz. 557, 779 P.2d 1296 (Ct. App. Div. 1 1989). If the applicable statute or rule, accordingly, requires that an action be taken within a time period *before* a certain date or event, then it is that date or event that is excluded from the computation. *Maciborski v. Chase Service Corp. of Arizona*, 161 Ariz. 557, 779 P.2d 1296 (Ct. App. Div. 1 1989). Rule 6(a) does not apply in computing time periods prescribed by election statutes. *Barry v. Alberty*, 173 Ariz. 387, 843 P.2d 1279 (Ct. App. Div. 1 1992).

If the prescribed period for acting is eleven (11) days or more, then intermediate Saturdays, Sundays and legal holidays are counted; if the period prescribed is less than eleven (11) days, weekends and holidays are excluded from the calculation.

4. *Enlargement of Time by Court Generally.* Rule 6(b) confers upon the court the authority to extend or enlarge the period of time within which an act must be performed. Whether to grant such an extension or enlargement is a matter committed to the trial court's discretion. *Strategic Development and Const., Inc. v. 7th & Roosevelt Partners, LLC*, 224 Ariz. 60, 226 P.3d 1046 (Ct. App. Div. 1 2010); *Perry v. County of Maricopa*, 167 Ariz. 458, 808 P.2d 343 (Ct. App. Div. 2 1991). If the request is made before expiration of the time period in question, the court may act with or without motion or notice. If the request is made after expiration of the time period, a motion is required and there must be a showing that the failure to act during the specified time period was the result of excusable neglect.

Rule 6(b) provides the trial court with limited authority to enlarge the time for filing motions under Rules 50(b), 52(b), 59(d), 59(g), 59(l), and 60(c), except to the extent and under the circumstances stated in such rules. *See also*, *Andrew R. v. Arizona Dept. of Economic Sec.*, 223 Ariz. 453, 224 P.3d 950 (Ct. App. Div. 1 2010) (addressing the limitation on extending time for filing motions under Rule 60(c)). Rule 6(b), nonetheless, permits the trial court to order such an extension if the court makes two separate findings: (1) that a party entitled to notice of the entry of judgment did not receive it within twenty-one (21) days of its entry, and (2) that no party would be prejudiced by granting such an extension. There is no requirement that good cause or excusable neglect be shown, and it is an abuse of discretion for the trial court to require one. *Haroutunian v. Valueoptions, Inc.*, 218 Ariz. 541, 189 P.3d 1114 (Ct. App. Div. 2 2008).

The Court may, under Rule 6, enlarge the time prescribed for responding to an offer of judgment under Rule 68. *Digirolamo v. Superior Court In and For County of Mohave*, 173 Ariz. 7, 839

P.2d 427 (Ct. App. Div. 1 1991). Rule 68(e) was amended in 1993, however, to provide that, where the Court does enlarge the time period during which an offer of judgment is effective and may be accepted, the party who made the offer may withdraw it after the initial unextended effective period and before it is accepted.

5. *Enlargement of Time to File Post-trial Motions and/or Notices of Appeal.* With a fair degree of uniformity, the Rules governing the renewal of motions for judgment as a matter of law, motions to amend findings, motions for new trial, and motions to alter or amend a judgment require that any such motion be filed no later than fifteen (15) days after the formal entry of judgment. Similarly, under Rule 9(a), Ariz. R. Civ. App. P., a notice of appeal in civil cases must be filed within thirty (30) days after the formal entry of judgment, or after disposition of a timely filed post-trial motion.

While former Rule 77(f), Ariz. R. Civ. P. (which was renumbered in 2000 as Rule 58(e)) long required that the Clerk mail to the parties a notice that judgment has been entered, it has also long been the rule in Arizona that the failure to receive such a notice does not relieve a party of the obligation to file post-trial motions and/or notices of appeal within the specified time period following the entry of judgment. *Park v. Strick*, 137 Ariz. 100, 669 P.2d 78 (1983); *Old Pueblo Transit Co. v. Corp. Com'n of Ariz.*, 73 Ariz. 32, 236 P.2d 1018 (1951); *Lone Mountain Ranch, Inc. v. Dillingham Inv., Inc.*, 131 Ariz. 583, 643 P.2d 28 (Ct. App. Div. 2 1982). Moreover, Rule 6(b) formerly precluded a Court from extending the time for filing post-trial motions and/or notices of appeal.

A 1994 amendment to Rule 6(b) provides the trial court with limited authority to enlarge the time for filing motions under Rules 50(b), 52(b), 59(d), 59(g) and 59(l), Ariz. R. Civ. P. Under that amendment, the trial court may order such an extension if it makes two separate findings: (1) that a party entitled to notice of the entry of judgment did not receive it within twenty-one (21) days of its entry, and (2) that no party would be prejudiced by granting such an extension. There is no requirement that good cause or excusable neglect be shown, and it is an abuse of discretion for the trial court to require one. *Haroutunian v. Valueoptions, Inc.*, 218 Ariz. 541, 189 P.3d 1114 (Ct. App. Div. 2 2008).

A motion seeking such an enlargement of time must be filed within thirty (30) days after expiration of the period when such a post-trial motion would have been due under the normal operation of the Rules, or within seven (7) days of the receipt of notice of entry of judgment, whichever is earlier. The trial court may only extend the period for filing post-trial motions for a period of ten (10) days from the date of its order granting the extension.

Any motion filed within the extended period thus permitted by the trial court will operate to extend the time period for filing a notice of appeal until thirty (30) days from its disposition. Rule 9(b)(2), Ariz. R. Civ. App. P.

Under both of these Rules, the condition for granting relief is when notice of the entry of judgment has not been "received," not whether it was sent. *United Metro Materials, Inc. v. Pena Blanca Properties, L.L.C.*, 197 Ariz. 479, 4 P.3d 1022 (Ct. App. Div. 1 2000). An avowal of counsel that notice of the entry of judgment was not received may be sufficient evidence to allow an extension when all the other circumstances called for by the Rules are demonstrated. *United Metro Materials, Inc. v. Pena Blanca Properties, L.L.C.*, 197 Ariz. 479, 4 P.3d 1022 (Ct. App. Div. 1 2000).

With respect to notices of appeal, similar authority to extend the time for filing them was granted to the Court of Appeals by a simultaneous amendment to Rule 9(a), Ariz. R. Civ. App. P. The Court of Appeals must make the same two findings as are prescribed in Rule 6(b), and the relief must be requested no later than thirty (30) days after the expiration of the normal time for taking an appeal, or within seven (7) days of receipt of notice of the entry of judgment, whichever is earlier. Under the amendment, the Court of Appeals can grant an extension of the time for filing a notice of appeal of up to fourteen (14) days from the date of the order granting the extension. An extension of the time for taking an appeal may also be secured by asking the trial court, under Rule 60(c), to vacate the entry of judgment and re-enter it, but a showing of due diligence is required. *Haroutunian v. Valueoptions, Inc.*, 218 Ariz. 541, 189 P.3d 1114 (Ct. App. Div. 2 2008).

As a practical matter, these amendments place formally entered judgments in an uncertain status for a longer period of time than was formerly the case. A motion seeking a re-opening of the time for filing post-trial motions can now potentially be filed up to forty-five (45) days, and a motion seeking to re-open the time for taking an appeal can now be filed up to sixty (60) days, after judgment is formally entered. In an effort to minimize the number of instances where such extensions can be sought and secured, a provision was simultaneously added to Rule 58(a), requiring that proposed forms of judgment be served upon all parties and counsel. In addition, a sentence was added to Rule 58(e), which authorizes any party to serve a notice of entry of judgment. Under this latter provision, a party can avoid the situation where the Clerk of the Court does not provide an effective notice of entry of judgment by providing one of its own. If that notice is received within twenty-one (21) days after entry of judgment, the conditions for securing an extension cannot be met. In addition, any motion seeking such an extension would have to be filed within seven (7) days of receipt of such a notice.

6. *Extra Time Where Service Accomplished by Mail or Other Authorized Means*. There had been a lingering question concerning the relationship between the method of computing time under the last sentence of Rule 6(a) and the provision granting additional time to act, prescribed in Rule 6(e), where service is accomplished by mail. Rule 6(a) was amended in 1987, to include an express provision that the additional five (5) days prescribed by Rule 6(e) should be included in "any period of time prescribed or allowed by these rules . . ." under Rule 6(a). Subsequent decisions interpreting the corresponding provisions of the Federal Rules of Civil Procedure, however, including one rendered by the United States Court of Appeals for the Ninth Circuit (which includes Arizona), *Tushner v. U.S. Dist. Court for the Cent. Dist. of California*, 829 F.2d 853, 9 Fed. R. Serv. 3d 554 (9th Cir. 1987), reached precisely the opposite result.

To avoid conflict with those decisions, Rule 6(a) was again amended, effective July 1, 1989, to specify that the additional time provided where service is made by mail is to be excluded from "any period of time prescribed or allowed by these rules . . ." in computing response times under Rule 6(a), and then added after the Rule 6(a) computation is made. Rule 6(e) was amended in 1991 to specify that the additional time allowed where service is accomplished by mail is five (5) *calendar* days rather than business days.

Rule 6(e) sets forth a five-day "mailing rule" applicable to papers served by a method authorized by Rule 5(c)(2)(C) [U.S. mail delivery] or (D) [electronic delivery]. Former Rule 5(c)(2)(D), which provided for service upon the court clerk, if a party's address was unknown, was deleted in 2006, and former Rule 5(c)(2)(E) [service by other means, including electronic] was renumbered as "Rule 5(c)(2)(D)."

By Administrative Order 2014-23, the Arizona Supreme Court has modified the procedures set forth in Ariz. R. Civ. P. 5(c)(2)(D). Thus, effective March 8, 2014, for those attorneys using e-service through AZTurboCourt, the consent requirement has been waived. Consent or a court order is still required to deliver papers by any other means, as contemplated by Rule 5(c)(2)(D).

The Administrative Order states that "filers" are permitted to choose whether or not to effect service through AZTurboCourt and cautions that any attorney who receives service through AZTurboCourt must accept service in that way. Service is complete upon transmission.

The Administrative Order also clarifies the application of Ariz. R. Civ. P. 6(e) (mailing rule). Thus, Rule 6(e) applies to papers served electronically as well as those served by U.S. Mail.

A rule petition has been filed with the Court seeking the amendment of Rule 5(c)(2) and Rule 6(e) to conform with the Administrative Order. The rule petition is out for comment. Comments are due May 20, 2014.

In 2011, Rule 6(e) was further amended to remove "any doubt as to the method for extending the time to respond after service by mail or other means, including electronic means, ..." *See* Comment to 2011 Amendment. Rule 6(e) now makes clear that the extra time is to be added *after* the prescribed time period otherwise expires under Rule 6(a). The Comment to the 2011 Amendment is helpful in that it provides detailed explanation as to the application of the rule, as amended.

Rule 6(e), however, applies only when a party has the right or is required to take some action after the *service* of a notice or other paper, and does not purport to apply where the prescribed period runs from the *filing* of such a notice or paper. *Baker Intern. Associates, Inc. v. Shanwick Intern. Corp.*, 174 Ariz. 580, 851 P.2d 1379 (Ct. App. Div. 1 1993). Rule 6(e), accordingly, does not apply to extend the ten-day grace period provided for filing an answer by Rules 55(a)(2) and 55(a)(3), as that period runs from the filing, not the service, of the application for entry of default. *Baker Intern. Associates, Inc. v. Shanwick Intern. Corp.*, 174 Ariz. 580, 851 P.2d 1379 (Ct. App. Div. 1 1993). The Rule, however, does extend the time for filing a complaint in Superior Court seeking judicial review of an administrative decision when that decision has been served by mail. *Thielking v. Kirschner*, 176 Ariz. 154, 859 P.2d 777 (Ct. App. Div. 1 1993).

7. *Orders to Show Cause.* Unlike the Federal Rules of Civil Procedure, the Arizona Rules of Civil Procedure contain a specific provision authorizing judges of the Superior Court to issue orders requiring a party to show cause why certain requested relief should not be granted against the party to whom it is addressed. This provision has, for some reason, been codified as Rule 6(d), Rule 6(d) was amended in 1991 to provide that orders to show cause must be served in accordance with the requirements of Rules 4, 4.1, 4.2 or 5, as applicable, within such time as the Court directs.

III. PLEADINGS AND MOTIONS; PRETRIAL PROCEDURES

Rule 7. Pleadings allowed

(a) Pleadings Allowed. There shall be a complaint and an answer; a reply to a counterclaim denominated as such; an answer to a cross-claim, if the answer contains a cross-claim; a third-party complaint, if a person who was not an original party is summoned under the provisions of Rule 14; and a third-party answer, if a third-party complaint is served. No other pleading shall be allowed, except that the court may order a reply to an answer or a third-party answer.

Amended March 26, 1963, effective June 1, 1963.

(b) Demurrers, Pleas, and Exceptions for Insufficiency Abolished. Demurrers, pleas, and exceptions for insufficiency of a pleading shall not be used.

Formerly 7(c). Redesignated 7(b) Oct. 10, 2000, effective Dec. 1, 2000.

STATE BAR COMMITTEE NOTES

1963 Amendment

[Rule 7(a)] Certain redundant words are eliminated and the subdivision is modified to reflect the amendment of Rule 14(a) which in certain cases eliminates the requirement of obtaining leave to bring in a third-party defendant.

2000 Amendment

[Rule 7(b)] Rule 7 was amended in 2000 as part of the effort to consolidate formerly separate sets of procedural rules into either the Arizona Rules of Civil Procedure or the Rules of the Arizona Supreme Court. The title of the Rule was changed, and the provisions of Rule 7(b) were abrogated, incorporated into a new Rule 7.1 and combined with certain provisions of former Rule IV of the Uniform Rules of Practice of the Superior Court. Former Rule 7(c) was redesignated as Rule 7(b).

AUTHORS' COMMENTS

Analysis

1. Scope and Purpose of Rule.
2. Comparison With Federal Rule.
3. Pleadings Allowed; Replies to Answers.
4. Motion as Pleading.
5. Affidavits and Declarations.

1. *Scope and Purpose of Rule.* Ariz. R. Civ. P. 7 is the first of

several rules that define the structure of Arizona's simplified system of pleading. The purpose of Rule 7 is to simplify and shorten the pleading process and to permit the issues in an action to be presented and developed free from technicalities.

Rule 7(a) delineates the pleadings permitted without court order and the pleadings permitted only upon court order. Rule 7(b) abolishes the technical forms of demurrers, pleas and exceptions for insufficiency of a pleading. Most of the functions of these common law technical forms have been replaced by motion practice. *See also, Associated Aviation Underwriters v. Wood*, 209 Ariz. 137, 98 P.3d 572 (Ct. App. Div. 2 2004) (citing, Daniel J. McAuliffe, Arizona Civil Rules Handbook, at 94 (2004)).

2. *Comparison With Federal Rule.* Although both the language and the structure differ, ARCP 7(a) is substantively identical to FRCP 7(a).

Nonetheless, ARCP 7 no longer contains a provision corresponding to FRCP 7(b); and, FRCP 7 no longer contains a provision corresponding to ARCP 7(b).

3. *Pleadings Allowed; Replies to Answers.* Rule 7(a) permits the following pleadings, and no others, without court order:

1. a complaint;
2. an answer;
3. a counterclaim;
4. a cross-claim (stated within the answer);
5. a third-party complaint;
6. a reply to a counterclaim designated as such;
7. an answer to a cross-claim; and
8. an answer to a third-party complaint.

A reply to an answer is not required, even if that answer contains allegations seeking relief against the plaintiff in the nature of a counterclaim where the answer is not designated as a counterclaim. *Bohmfalk v. Vaughan*, 89 Ariz. 33, 357 P.2d 617 (1960); *Eggerth v. Forselius*, 82 Ariz. 256, 311 P.2d 964 (1957). In its discretion, however, the Court may direct that there be a reply, either to an answer or to an answer to a third-party complaint.

4. *Motion as Pleading.* A motion is *not* a pleading within the meaning of Rule 7(a). *Mallamo v. Hartman*, 70 Ariz. 294, 219 P.2d 1039 (1950), opinion modified on reh'g, 70 Ariz. 420, 222 P.2d 797 (1950); *Coulas v. Smith*, 96 Ariz. 325, 329, 395 P.2d 527, 529 (1964); *Prutch v. Town of Quartzsite*, 231 Ariz. 431, 296 P.3d 94 (Ct. App. Div. 1 2013), as amended, (Feb. 26, 2013) (a motion to dismiss is not a pleading, but it does satisfy the "otherwise defends" requirement for avoiding entry of default);

King v. Titsworth, 221 Ariz. 597, 212 P.3d 935 (Ct. App. Div. 1 2009).

Similarly, a motion seeking attorney fees filed after a decision on the merits does not constitute a "pleading" as required by Rule 54(g). *Balestrieri v. Balestrieri*, 232 Ariz. 25, 300 P.3d 560 (Ct. App. Div. 1 2013); *King v. Titsworth*, 221 Ariz. 597, 212 P.3d 935 (Ct. App. Div. 1 2009).

An attorney's fees request will be deemed timely, however, if asserted at the time a Rule 12(b) motion to dismiss is filed in lieu of an answer. *Balestrieri v. Balestrieri*, 232 Ariz. 25, 300 P.3d 560 (Ct. App. Div. 1 2013) (motion to dismiss is not a pleading, but court may grant a request for attorney fees made in a motion to dismiss filed in lieu of a responsive pleading).

A defendant does not submit itself to the jurisdiction of the court by filing a request for fees with the motion to dismiss. *Balestrieri v. Balestrieri*, 232 Ariz. 25, 300 P.3d 560 (Ct. App. Div. 1 2013).

5. *Affidavits and Declarations.* An affidavit is a statement reduced to writing and sworn to or affirmed before an authorized officer. An affidavit should be made by one with knowledge of the facts and may be made by a party for whose benefit it is to be used.

Counsel of record, instead of the party represented, may make an affidavit, where the facts set forth in such affidavit are within the attorney's knowledge. *See Huff v. Flynn*, 48 Ariz. 175, 60 P.2d 931 (1936). Generally, however, an attorney is not in a position to have personal knowledge concerning the material facts underlying a civil action and, therefore, is not often in a position to make such an affidavit. An attorney who submits an affidavit based upon personal knowledge concerning the facts underlying the action runs the risk of being called as a witness, either at trial or deposition.

Rule 80(i) permits the use of "unsworn declarations" under penalty of perjury in the place of formal sworn affidavits.

Rule 7.1. Civil motion practice

(a) Formal Requirements. An application to the court for an order shall be by motion which, unless made during a hearing or trial, shall be in writing, shall state with particularity the grounds therefor, and shall set forth the relief or order sought. The requirement of a writing is fulfilled if the motion is stated in a written notice of the hearing of the motion.

All motions made before or after trial shall be accompanied by a memorandum indicating, as a minimum, the precise legal points, statutes and authorities relied on, citing the specific portions or pages thereof, and shall be served on the opposing parties. Unless otherwise ordered by the court, affidavits supporting the motion shall be filed and served together with the motion. Each opposing party shall within ten days thereafter serve and file any answering memorandum. Within five days thereafter the moving party may serve and file a memorandum in reply, which shall be directed only to matters raised in the answering memorandum. Affidavits submitted in support of any answering memorandum or memorandum in reply shall be filed and served together with that memorandum, unless the court permits them to be filed and served at some other time. The trial court may in its discretion waive these requirements as to motions made in open court.

The time and manner of service shall be noted on all such filings, and shall be governed by Rule 6 of these Rules. If the precise manner in which service has actually been made is not noted on any such filing, it will be conclusively presumed that the filing was served by mail, and the provisions of Rule 6(e) of these Rules shall apply. This conclusive presumption shall only apply if service in some form has actually been made. The time periods specified in this paragraph shall not apply where specific times for motions, affidavits or memoranda are otherwise provided by statute, the Rules of Civil Procedure, or order of court.

The rules applicable to captions and other matters of form of pleadings apply to all motions and other papers provided for by this Rule, and all such motions and other papers shall be signed in accordance with Rule 11.

Rule 7.1(a) added Oct. 10, 2000, effective Dec. 1, 2000.

(b) Effect of Non-compliance. If a motion does not conform in all substantial respects with the requirements of this rule, or if the opposing party does not serve and file the required answering memorandum, or if counsel for any moving or opposing party fails to appear at the time and place assigned for oral argument, such non-compliance may be deemed a consent to the denial or granting of the motion, and the court may dispose of the motion summarily.

Rule 7.1(b) added Oct. 10, 2000, effective Dec. 1, 2000.

(c) Law and Motion Day.

(1) Unless local conditions make it impracticable, each superior court shall establish regular times and places, at intervals sufficiently frequent for the prompt dispatch of business, at which motions requiring notice and hearing may be heard and disposed of. The judge at any time or place and on such notice, if any, as the judge considers reasonable may make orders for the advancement, conduct, and hearing of actions.

(2) To expedite its business, the court may make provision by rule or order for the submission and determination of motions without oral hearing upon brief written statements of reasons in support and opposition.

Rule 7.1(c) added Oct. 10, 2000, effective Dec. 1, 2000.

(d) Oral Argument. Oral argument shall be limited, in accordance with local rules, to a prescribed number of minutes, which shall not be exceeded without special permission in advance.

Rule 7.1(d) added Oct. 10, 2000, effective Dec. 1, 2000.

(e) Motions for Reconsideration. A party seeking reconsideration of a ruling of the court may file a motion for reconsideration. All motions for reconsideration, however denominated, shall be submitted without oral argument and without response or reply, unless the court otherwise directs. No motion for reconsideration shall be granted, however, without the court providing an opportunity for response. A motion authorized by this Rule may not be employed as a substitute for a motion pursuant to Rule 50(b), 52(b), 59 or 60 of these Rules, and shall not operate to extend the time within which a notice of appeal must be filed.

Rule 7.1(e) added Oct. 10, 2000, effective Dec. 1, 2000.

(f) Limitations on Motions to Strike.

(1) *Generally*. Unless made at trial or an evidentiary hearing, a motion to strike may be filed only if it is expressly authorized by statute or other rule, or if it seeks to strike any part of a filing or submission on the ground that it is prohibited, or not authorized, by a specific statute, rule, or court order. Unless the motion to strike is expressly authorized by statute or rule: (a) it may not exceed two (2) pages in length, including any supporting memorandum; (b) any responsive memorandum

must be filed within five (5) days of service of the motion and may not exceed two (2) pages in length; and (c) no reply memorandum may be filed unless authorized by the court.

(2) *Objections to Admission of Evidence on Written Motions.* Subject to Rule 56(c)(4), governing motions for summary judgment, any objections to, and any arguments regarding the admissibility of, evidence offered in support of or in opposition to a motion must be presented in the objecting party's responsive or reply memorandum and may not be presented in a separate motion to strike or other separate filing. Any response to an objection must be included in the responding party's reply memorandum for the underlying motion and may not be presented in a separate responsive memorandum. If the evidence is offered for the first time in connection with a reply memorandum, the objecting party may file a separate objection limited to addressing the new evidence and not exceeding three (3) pages in length, within five (5) days after service of the reply memorandum. No responsive memorandum may be filed unless authorized by the court.

Rule 7.1(f) added Aug. 28, 2013, effective Jan. 1, 2014.

(g) Agreed Extensions of Time for Filing Memorandum. Subject to the court's power to reject any such agreement, parties may agree to any extension of the dates upon which response and reply memoranda are due when the extension does not otherwise conflict with other scheduling dates set by the court of these Rules. To make an extension effective under this subsection, a notice of the extension to which the parties have agreed must be filed, setting out the dates on which the response or reply briefs shall then be due. The notice shall set forth in its title the number of extensions agreed to to with respect to that filing (e.g., First Extension of Time to File Response on Motion To Dismiss). No extension shall be effective without court approval if it purports to make a reply or other final memorandum due less than five days before a hearing or oral argument date previously set by the court, or if the notice of that extension is filed after the memorandum is due. No order is necessary to obtain an extension under this subsection, and the extension shall be effective upon filing, unless and until the court disapproves the change. The provisions of the subsection do not apply to motion practice under Rule 56.

Rule 7.1(g) added Aug. 28, 2013, effective Jan. 1, 2014.

STATE BAR COMMITTEE NOTES

2000 Promulgation

Rule 7.1 was promulgated in 2000 as part of the process of consolidating formerly separate sets of procedural rules into either the Arizona Civil Rules of

Civil Procedure or the Rules of the Arizona Supreme Court, and represents an effort to incorporate into a single Rule the provisions of several prior rules that applied generally to civil motion practice and procedure. Rule 7.1(a) combines the provisions of former Rule 7(b) of the Arizona Rules of Civil Procedure and the provisions of former Rule IV(a) of the Uniform Rules of Practice of the Superior Court. It also incorporates a modified version of the provision in former Rule 6(c), which was abrogated, dealing with the time for service and filing of any affidavits submitted in support of, or in opposition to, a civil motion. Rules 7.1(b), (d), and (e) contain the provisions formerly set forth in Rules IV(b), (d), and (h) of the Uniform Rules of Practice of the Superior Court. Rule 7.1(c) is what was formerly Rule 78 of the Arizona Rules of Civil Procedure. The retention of former Rule IV(e) of the Uniform Rules of Practice of the Superior Court, which authorized the scheduling of a special pretrial conference for the hearing of repeated or multiple motions, was deemed unnecessary, and potentially confusing, in light of the expanded permissible scope of pretrial conferences scheduled pursuant to Rule 16 of the Arizona Rules of Civil Procedure.

AUTHORS' COMMENTS

Analysis

1. *Scope and Purpose of Rule.* Ariz. R. Civ. P. 7.1 establishes the general procedures applicable to motions made other than during the course of trial.

2. *Comparison With Federal Rule.* Effective December 1, 2002, FRCP 7.1 was added to the Federal Rules of Civil Procedure. FRCP 7.1, however, deals with an entirely different subject matter than ARCP 7.1. FRCP 7.1 requires nongovernmental corporate parties to submit certain disclosures to the Court concerning corporate ownership. The Arizona Rules of Civil Procedure do not contain a rule similar to FRCP 7.1.

3. *History and Origin of Rule.* Rule 7.1 was added to the Arizona Rules of Civil Procedure, effective December 1, 2000, as

a consequence of the Arizona Supreme Court's approval of the recommendations of what was known as the Civil Rules Consolidation Project. By an Order entered in October 2000, the Supreme Court abrogated the Uniform Rules of Practice of the Superior Court, the Uniform Rules of Procedure for Medical Malpractice Cases, and the Uniform Rules of Procedure for Arbitration, as separate sets of procedural rules, and transferred their provisions to either the Arizona Rules of Civil Procedure or the Rules of the Arizona Supreme Court.

The rationale used for determining the placement of rules was that rules affecting the processing of civil cases should be placed in the Arizona Rules of Civil Procedure, while rules that concerned only internal court administration should be placed in the Rules of the Arizona Supreme Court. Application of this rationale resulted, in some instances, in the transfer of certain provisions of the Arizona Rules of Civil Procedure to the Rules of the Arizona Supreme Court.

Rule 7.1 represents an effort to incorporate into a single Rule the provisions of several prior rules that applied generally to civil motion practice and procedure. Briefly summarized:

1. Rule 7.1(a) combines the provisions of former Rule 7(b) of the Arizona Rules of Civil Procedure and the provisions of former Rule IV(a) of the Uniform Rules of Practice of the Superior Court. It also incorporates a modified version of the provision in former Rule 6(c), which was abrogated, dealing with the time for service and filing of any affidavits submitted in support of, or in opposition to, a civil motion.

2. Rules 7.1(b), (d), and (e) contain the provisions formerly set forth in now former Rules IV(b), (d), and (h) of the Uniform Rules of Practice of the Superior Court. Rule 7.1(c) is what was formerly Rule 78 of the Arizona Rules of Civil Procedure.

4. *Formal Requirements for Motions and Responses; Consequences of Failure to Comply.* All motions made before and after trial must be in writing, and must be accompanied by a memorandum of points and authorities setting forth the grounds for the motion and the authorities relied upon in support of the relief requested. Any party who desires to oppose the motion must file an answering memorandum, which sets forth the grounds for resisting the motion and the authorities relied upon. The prevailing practice is for such an answering memorandum to be captioned as a "Memorandum of Points and Authorities in Opposition to" the motion being opposed. The moving party then has the right and the option to file a memorandum in reply, which is only to address matters raised in the answering memorandum. The trial court may waive any of these requirements for motions made in open court.

The Superior Courts in Maricopa, Gila and Pima Counties have adopted an identical Local Rule which limits the length of memoranda submitted in support of and in opposition to civil motions. Rule 3.2(f), Maricopa County Superior Court Local Rules; Rule 18, Gila County Superior Court Local Rules; and Rule 3.7. These Rules prescribe that a motion and its supporting memorandum and the answering memorandum may not exceed fifteen (15) pages, exclusive of attachments and any required statement of facts. A memorandum in reply may not exceed ten (10) pages, exclusive of attachments. These page limitations may only be exceeded with permission of the Court. The Santa Cruz County Superior Court has adopted an identical requirement by Local Rule, but it exempts from its provisions motions for summary judgment. Rule 8.3, Santa Cruz County Superior Court Local Rules.

Generally, a party must file a written response whenever a motion is filed. *Schwab v. Ames Const.*, 207 Ariz. 56, 83 P.3d 56 (Ct. App. Div. 1 2004). Under Rule 7.1(b), the failure of the moving or opposing party to comply with the procedural requirements applicable to civil motions may be deemed a consent to the granting or denial of the motion, as the case may be, and the Court may dispose of the motion summarily. *Arnold v. Van Ornum*, 4 Ariz. App. 89, 417 P.2d 723 (1966); *BCAZ Corp. v. Helgoe*, 194 Ariz. 11, 976 P.2d 260 (Ct. App. Div. 1 1998), opinion supplemented on reh'g, (Mar. 25, 1999); *but cf.*, *Choisser v. State ex rel. Herman*, 12 Ariz. App. 259, 469 P.2d 493 (Div. 1 1970). Rule 7.1(b), however, is not mandatory, and the failure to respond does not in and of itself require a judgment against the nonmoving party if the motion fails to demonstrate the moving party's entitlement to the requested relief. *Zimmerman v. Shakman*, 204 Ariz. 231, 62 P.3d 976 (Ct. App. Div. 1 2003). No such consequences attach to the failure of the moving party to file a memorandum in reply as such a memorandum is not, strictly speaking, required by the Rule.

While, as noted in the foregoing paragraph, Rule 7.1(b) gives the trial court discretion to dispose of a motion summarily where there has been a failure to comply with Rule 7.1's requirements, there are limitations on the exercise of that discretion, especially if the motion is one for summary judgment. *Schwab v. Ames Const.*, 207 Ariz. 56, 83 P.3d 56 (Ct. App. Div. 1 2004). Rule 56(e) says that a party opposing a motion for summary judgment may not rest on the allegations and denials in its pleadings. This language simply means that a nonmoving party who fails to respond does so at its peril. *Schwab v. Ames Const.*, 207 Ariz. 56, 83 P.3d 56 (Ct. App. Div. 1 2004). Nonetheless, if a moving party's summary judgment motion fails to show an entitlement to judgment, the nonmoving party need not respond to controvert the motion, and the trial court is still required to determine the moving party's entitlement to the relief requested. *Schwab v. Ames Const.*, 207 Ariz. 56, 83 P.3d 56 (Ct. App. Div. 1 2004).

5. *Service of Motions and Responses; Certificates of Service.* All motions and memoranda filed in support of or in opposition to a motion are to be served on all parties to the action so that they may determine whether to resist the relief sought. *Edgar v. Garrett*, 10 Ariz. App. 98, 456 P.2d 944 (1969). For parties that have appeared, service may be accomplished by one of the means authorized under Rule 5. If a party has not yet appeared in the action, service must be accomplished by one of the means authorized under Rules 4, 4.1 or 4.2.

Rule 7.1(a) requires that the time and manner of service be noted on all papers filed in connection with motions. While the language of the Rule requires that the manner of service be noted on the paper itself, a separate certificate of service would probably be deemed sufficient. The prevalent practice is to include a service certificate on the paper itself after the signatures of counsel. If the precise manner of service is not noted, it is conclusively presumed that service was accomplished by mail and the adverse party will have the additional five (5) calendar days to respond prescribed by Rule 6(e). Rule 93(b), Rules of the Arizona Supreme Court contemplates that the Court Administrator, in those counties where one has been appointed, will review and determine the timeliness and propriety of service of motion papers.

6. *Briefing Schedule for Civil Motions; Agreed Upon Extensions.* Rule 7.1(a) provides that a party opposing a motion has ten (10) days in which to file and serve an answering memorandum, and the moving party has five (5) days thereafter in which to file and serve a memorandum in reply. These periods are extended by an additional five (5) calendar days where service of the motion or answering memorandum is accomplished by mail, or where the precise manner of service is not noted in the service certificate. The Court may, of course, extend or shorten these periods.

Ariz. R. Civ. P. 7.1(a) specifies that these time periods will not apply where a different time for filing a motion, affidavit or response is prescribed by statute or the Arizona Rules of Civil Procedure. One instance where the Arizona Rules of Civil Procedure do prescribe a different schedule is for motions for summary judgment. *See,* Ariz. R. Civ. P. 56(c).

Rule 56(c) provides that a party opposing a motion for summary judgment has thirty (30) days after service of the motion to serve opposing memoranda and/or supporting material and the moving party has fifteen (15) days to serve a reply memorandum and any supporting material.

Ariz. R. Civ. P. 7.1(g), adopted effective January 1, 2014, sets forth procedures by which litigants may secure stipulated extensions of time on briefing schedules for motions, other than motions for summary judgment. Parties must now file a "notice of extension" setting forth the dates of the agreed upon briefing schedule and stating the number of previous agreed upon extensions.

An agreed upon extension does not require court approval and is effective upon the filing of the notice, except that the court may vacate and disapprove such extension at any time. Accordingly, practitioners may want to consider submitting a proposed form of order requesting the court approve the stipulated briefing schedule.

Additionally, court approval is needed for an agreed upon extension that would "make a reply or other final memorandum due less that 5 days before" a scheduled hearing on the matter.

7. *Procedure for Requesting Oral Argument; Scheduling of Hearings; Length of Oral Argument.* The procedures for requesting oral argument of motions, for scheduling of hearings on motions, and the length of permissible oral argument are governed by the Local Rules of the particular Superior Court in which the action is pending. Where there are factual issues that must be addressed, the Court may, under Ariz. R. Civ. P. 43(i), either hear the matter on affidavits submitted by the parties or direct that the matter be heard wholly or partially on oral testimony or depositions.

The procedure for *securing* a hearing and oral argument on civil motions varies widely between the counties. The Superior Courts in several counties require that the notation "(Oral Argument Requested)" be included as part of the caption of one of the motion papers or in a separate document filed with the Clerk. Rule 10(c), Apache County Superior Court Local Rules; Rule 2(d), Cochise County Superior Court Local Rules; Rule 4(D), Coconino County Superior Court Local Rules; Rule 16(B), Gila County Superior Court Local Rules; Rule 1.13(B), Graham County Superior Court Local Rules; Rule 2(b), La Paz County Superior Court Local Rules; Rule 3.2(d), Maricopa County Superior Court Local Rules; Rule CV-1(B), Mohave County Superior Court Local Rules; Rule 2.5(b), Pinal County Superior Court Local Rules; Rule 8.2(a), Santa Cruz County Superior Court Local Rules; Rule 2(C), Yavapai County Superior Court Local Rules. (In Santa Cruz County, if oral argument is requested through use of this notation, the motion must also be accompanied by a Notice of Hearing which contains an estimate of the time that will be required to hear it. Rule 8.1, Santa Cruz County Superior Court Local Rules.

The procedures for *scheduling* oral argument on motions also vary widely between counties. The Superior Courts in fourteen counties have, by Local Rule, set a regular day as "Law and Motion Day." In Apache, Cochise, Gila, Pinal, Santa Cruz, and Yavapai Counties, Law and Motion Day is set as Monday of each week, or the following Tuesday, if Monday is a holiday. Rule 2, Apache County Superior Court Local Rules; Rule 2(a), Cochise County Superior Court Local Rules; Rule 2, Gila County Superior Court Local Rules, Rule 1.3(a), Pinal County Superior Court Local Rules; Rule 1.2(a), Santa Cruz County Superior Court Local Rules; and Rule 2(B), Yavapai County Superior Court Local Rules. Rule 2(a), La Paz County Superior Court Local Rules, Rule CV-1(A), Mohave County Superior Court Local Rules, and Rule 2.1, Pima County Superior Court Local Rules provide that oral argument of motions is heard on Monday, or the following day if Monday is a Holiday, but do not specifically refer to Monday as "Law and Motion Day." Rule 2(a) of the Yuma County Superior Court Local Rules designates "the first working day of each week" as Law and Motion Day. In Navajo County, Law and Motion Day is the second Monday in each month. Rule 2(a), Navajo County Superior Court Local Rules.

The published Local Rules for the Greenlee County Superior Court sets the first Monday of each month as Law and Motion Day, *cf.* Rule 2(a), Greenlee County Superior Court Local Rules, but the actual practice is different, presumably due to Administrative Order. In the Greenlee County Superior Court, Law and Motion Day is every Monday, or the following Tuesday, if Monday is a holiday. The Superior Court in Maricopa County has not established a formal Law and Motion Day, by Local Rule or otherwise. The Coconino County Superior Court and the Graham County Superior Court have established, by local rule, a Criminal Law and Motion Day, but not a Civil Law and Motion Day.

The actual *scheduling* of a motion for oral argument is done by the Clerk, in Cochise, Pinal and Yavapai Counties. Rule 2(c), Cochise County Superior Court Local Rules; Rule 1.3(b), Pinal County Superior Court Local Rules; and Rule 2(E), Yavapai County Superior Court Local Rules. In Pima, Santa Cruz and Yuma Counties, a hearing is to be scheduled by stipulation or by a notice of hearing provided by one of the parties. Rule 3.8(a), Pima County Superior Court Local Rules; Rule 8.1, Santa Cruz County Superior Court Local Rules; and, Rule 2(a), Yuma County Superior Court Local Rules. Rule 2(b), La Paz County Superior Court Local Rules specifies that the Court will schedule and give notice of the time for oral argument on motions. Rule CV-1(B), Mohave County Superior Court Local Rules suggests, but does not explicitly state, that the Court schedules hearing and argument on motions, when requested.

Rule 3.2(d) of the Maricopa County Superior Court Local Rules provides that the party desiring oral argument is to secure a time for hearing and provide a notice of the hearing to other parties. The operation of that Rule, however, has been suspended indefinitely, and the practice is for each Division to schedule hearings on motions in cases assigned to that Division, and notify the parties by minute entry. The Local Rules of the Apache, and Coconino County Superior Courts do not specify how hearings on civil motions are to be scheduled.

Under Rule 7.1(b), the failure to appear for oral argument may be deemed consent to the Court's granting or denial of the motion summarily. The actual practice for requesting and scheduling oral argument of motions may not always conform to the literal provisions of the published Local Rules, and the prudent course is to contact the Clerk of the Court or the Division of the Superior Court to which the case is assigned to ascertain the proper procedure to follow.

In the Superior Courts of those counties which require the notation "(Oral Argument Requested)" on the motion papers in order to secure oral argument, it is generally provided that the failure to do so results in the motion being submitted for determination without oral argument. There are other instances where the presumption is against allowing oral argument. Under Ariz. R. Civ. P. 58(d)(2), objections to a proposed form of judgment are to be submitted for determination without oral argument unless the Court otherwise directs.

Rule 7.1(e) provides that motions for reconsideration of a prior ruling are submitted without oral argument and without response or reply unless the Court directs. Such a motion may not be granted, however, without affording the opponent an opportunity to respond.

8. *Motions for Reconsideration.* Motions for reconsideration of a prior ruling are recognized by Ariz. R. Civ. P. 7.1(e), but they are to be submitted for decision without response or reply, unless the Court otherwise directs. No such motion may be granted without the Court affording the adverse party an opportunity to respond. The general, though not inflexible, rule is that a trial court should not reconsider a motion already decided by another judge of the Superior Court unless the moving party can demonstrate new circumstances warranting such reconsideration. *Powell-Cerkoney v. TCR-Montana Ranch Joint Venture, II*, 176 Ariz. 275, 860 P.2d 1328 (Ct. App. Div. 1 1993); *Dunlap v. City of Phoenix*, 169 Ariz. 63, 817 P.2d 8 (Ct. App. Div. 1 1990); *Hibbs v. Calcot, Ltd.*, 166 Ariz. 210, 801 P.2d 445 (Ct. App. Div. 1 1990); *Shade v. U.S. Fidelity and Guar. Co. (USF & G)*, 166 Ariz. 206, 801 P.2d 441 (Ct. App. Div. 2 1990); *Smoole v. Maricopa County*, 177 Ariz. 185, 866 P.2d 167 (Tax Ct.1993).

The denial of a motion for reconsideration is reviewed on appeal only for an abuse of discretion. *Tilley v. Delci*, 220 Ariz. 233, 204 P.3d 1082 (Ct. App. Div. 1 2009). "Abuse of discretion" is "discretion manifestly unreasonable, or exercised on untenable grounds, or for untenable reasons." *Tilley v. Delci*, 220 Ariz. 233, 204 P.3d 1082 (Ct. App. Div. 1 2009) (citing, *Torres for and on Behalf of Torres v. North American Van Lines, Inc.*, 135 Ariz. 35, 658 P.2d 835 (Ct. App. Div. 2 1982)).

This general rule finds its origins in the doctrine of the "law of the case," which is merely a practice that protects the ability of the court to build to its final judgment by cumulative rulings, with reconsideration or review postponed until after final judgment is rendered. *Zimmerman v. Shakman*, 204 Ariz. 231, 62 P.3d 976 (Ct. App. Div. 1 2003), quoting the Arizona Supreme Court in *State v. King*, 180 Ariz. 268, 883 P.2d 1024 (1994). The doctrine does not prevent, however, a judge from reconsidering nonfinal rulings; nor does it prevent a different judge, sitting on the same case, from reconsidering a preceding judge's prior, nonfinal rulings. *Bogard v. Cannon & Wendt Elec. Co., Inc.*, 221 Ariz. 325, 212 P.3d 17 (Ct. App. Div. 1 2009); *Zimmerman v. Shakman*, 204 Ariz. 231, 62 P.3d 976 (Ct. App. Div. 1 2003).

9. *Limitations on Motions to Strike; Objections to Admission of Evidence On Written Motions.* Ariz. R. Civ. P. 7.1(f) was adopted, effective January 1, 2014, to impose limitations on motions to strike and provide procedures for stating objections to admission of evidence on written motions.

Rule 7.1(f)(1) prohibits the filing of a motion to strike that is not authorized by statute, rule, or "seeks to strike any part of a filing or submission on the grounds that it is prohibited, or not authorized, by a specific statute, rule or court order." *See, Sitton v. Deutsche Bank Nat. Trust Co.*, 233 Ariz. 215, 311 P.3d 237 (Ct. App. Div. 1 2013) (discussing the impact of the 2014 adoption of Rule 7.1(f)).

As to those motions to strike part of a filing/submission on the grounds that such part is not authorized, Rule 7.1(f)(1) limits the motion to two pages, including the supporting memorandum, and limits the responsive memorandum to two pages.

Subject to Ariz. R. Civ. P. 56(c)(4) (added 2014), Ariz. R. Civ. P. 7.1(f)(2) states the requirements and procedures for objecting to evidence on written motion as follows:

1. objections to the admissibility of evidence offered in support of, or opposition to, a motion must be made in the objecting party's response or reply and *not* in a separate filing;
2. any response to such objection must be in a party's reply memorandum and *not* in a separate filing;
3. where evidence is offered for the first time in the reply,

the objecting party, within five days after service of the reply, may file a separate objection limited in scope to the newly offered evidence and limited in length to three pages; and

4. no other briefing is permitted unless authorized by the court.

With respect to evidentiary objections on motions for summary judgment, Ariz. R. Civ. P. 56(c)(4), adopted effective January 1, 2014, states that Ariz. R. Civ. 7.1(f)(2) (added 2014), applies. Rule 56(c)(4) also allows a party, however, to include "concisely" stated objections in that party's response to the opposing party's separate statement of facts.

10. *Affidavits in Support of Motions*. Rule 7.1(a) specifies that affidavits submitted in supported of a motion must be filed and served together with the motion. Similarly, any affidavits submitted in support of an answering memorandum or a memorandum in reply also must filed and served at the same time as the memorandum.

In contrast, former Rule 6(c), Ariz. R. Civ. P. provided that written motions and notices of hearing were to be served not later than five (5) days before the hearing date. It also required affidavits supporting a motion to be filed and served together with the motion, but permitted affidavits submitted in opposition to the motion to be served not later than one (1) day before the hearing. These provisions were obviously carried forward from FRCP Rule 6(d), but they were plainly inconsistent with former Rule IV of the Uniform Rules of the Superior Court, and with actual motion practice.

At the time the provisions of former Rule IV of the Uniform Rules of Practice were transferred to Rule 7.1, and other rule provisions dealing with motion practice were incorporated into that rule, Rule 6(c) was abrogated.

Rule 7.2. Motions *in limine*

(a) Within sufficient time to comply with subsection (b) of this rule, the parties shall confer to identify disputed evidentiary issues that are anticipated to be the subject of motions *in limine.*

(b) Unless a different schedule is ordered by the court, no later than 30 days before either a final pretrial conference or, if no final pretrial conference is set, then the date of the trial, the parties shall file all motions *in limine* for which pretrial rulings are desired.

(c) The moving party shall not file a reply in support of its motion *in limine.*

(d) All motions *in limine* submitted in accordance with subsection (b) of this rule shall be ruled upon before trial unless the court determines the particular issue is better considered at trial.

(e) Motions *in limine* not filed in accordance with subsection (b) of this rule shall be deemed untimely and shall not be ruled upon prior to trial except for good cause shown.

(f) The failure to file a motion *in limine* in compliance with this rule shall not operate as a waiver of the right to object to evidence at trial.

Rule 7.2 added October 4, 2004, effective December 1, 2004.

STATE BAR COMMITTEE COMMENT

"*In limine*" means "on or at the threshold; at the very beginning; preliminary." The purpose of a motion *in limine* is to obtain a pretrial ruling on evidentiary disputes and to avoid the admission of unduly prejudicial evidence to a jury. *State ex rel. Berger v. Superior Court In and For Maricopa County*, 108 Ariz. 396, 499 P.2d 152 (1972). Where a sufficiently specific motion *in limine* is made and ruled upon on the merits, the objection raised in that motion is preserved for appeal, without the need for specific objection at trial. *State v. Burton*, 144 Ariz. 248, 697 P.2d 331 (1985).

Subsection (a) of the rule imposes a requirement that parties meet and confer about evidentiary issues likely to arise at trial. One of the purposes of this requirement is to eliminate motions *in limine* that are directed to evidence the opponent does not intend to offer or are otherwise unnecessary. It is anticipated that the parties will provide the court with a written report of agreements reached at the conference so that the court can enforce such agreements at trial.

A response to a motion *in limine* should be filed in accordance with Rule 7.1. No leave of court is necessary to file a motion *in limine* more than 30 days before either the date of trial or a final pretrial conference, whichever is earlier. Parties are encouraged to do so, particularly if an early ruling on admissibility would advance settlement.

AUTHORS' COMMENTS

Analysis

1. Scope and Purpose of Rule.
2. Comparison With Federal Rule.
3. Function of, and Standards for, Motions *In Limine*.

1. *Scope and Purpose of Rule*. Ariz. R. Civ. P. 7.2 was promulgated in 2004, at least in part, to impose a structure on what was perceived as a proliferation of motions *in limine* seeking pretrial rulings on the admissibility of categories of evidence, many of which were at times unnecessary. Thus, subpart (a) of the Rule requires that the parties confer, within sufficient time to meet the deadlines established by the Rule, to identify any disputed evidentiary issues that are anticipated to be the subject of motions *in limine*. While not specified in the Rule, the accompanying State Bar Committee Comment anticipates "that the parties will provide the court with a written report of agreements reached at the conference so that the court can enforce such agreements at trial."

Motions *in limine* must be filed no later than thirty (30) days before a final pretrial conference or, if none is set, no later than thirty (30) days before trial, unless the Court sets a different schedule. Such motions can be filed earlier than those deadlines, without leave of court. A response to the motion is to be filed within the time frames set forth in Ariz. R. Civ. P. 7.1, but there is to be no reply memorandum. All timely filed motions are to be decided before trial, unless the Court determines that the issue the motion raises is better considered at trial. A motion that is not filed within the time frames set forth in the Rule will not be ruled upon before trial except for good cause shown. The failure to file a motion *in limine* that complies with the Rule does not operate as a waiver of the right to object to evidence at trial.

2. *Comparison With Federal Rule*. The Federal Rules of Civil Procedure do not have a rule or provision that corresponds with ARCP 7.2.

3. *Function of, and Standards for, Motions In limine*. Rule 7.2 both recognizes and authorizes what has been a common and time-honored practice where a party anticipates an evidentiary problem in advance of trial. While it has been held that the primary purpose of motions *in limine* is to avoid having disclosed to the jury prejudicial matters that might result in a mistrial, and that they are not to be used except where evidence is clearly shown to be inadmissible, *State ex rel. Berger v. Superior Court In and For Maricopa County*, 108 Ariz. 396, 499 P.2d 152 (1972),

they are nevertheless frequently employed and entertained in situations which do not rise to that standard. *Cf. Shuck v. Texaco Refining & Marketing, Inc.*, 178 Ariz. 295, 872 P.2d 1247 (Ct. App. Div. 1 1994). A motion *in limine* directed to specific categories or types of evidence, which is denied, obviates the necessity for making repeated objections to the evidence during the course of the trial, and preserves the issue for appeal. *State v. Burton*, 144 Ariz. 248, 697 P.2d 331 (1985); *Gibson v. Gunsch*, 148 Ariz. 416, 714 P.2d 1311 (Ct. App. Div. 1 1985).

Motions *in limine* have been employed in civil cases as a means to exclude evidence for violations of the disclosure rules. *Zimmerman v. Shakman*, 204 Ariz. 231, 62 P.3d 976 (Ct. App. Div. 1 2003). When a motion *in limine* is used to enforce the provisions of Rule 26.1, it is effectively a request for sanctions under Rule 37(c), and will be considered and reviewed using the standards developed under those Rules. *Zimmerman v. Shakman*, 204 Ariz. 231, 62 P.3d 976 (Ct. App. Div. 1 2003). The granting of a motion *in limine* for a violation of the disclosure rules, followed by a dismissal for lack of evidence, is the equivalent of a dismissal for nondisclosure and must be preceded by a hearing to determine whether the party or the party's attorney was at fault. *Zimmerman v. Shakman*, 204 Ariz. 231, 62 P.3d 976 (Ct. App. Div. 1 2003). While a trial court's order of dismissal for discovery or disclosure violations will be upheld absent a clear abuse of discretion, the trial court's discretion to dismiss a case for such violations is more limited than when it employs lesser sanctions. *Zimmerman v. Shakman*, 204 Ariz. 231, 62 P.3d 976 (Ct. App. Div. 1 2003). Sanctions for abuses of discovery or disclosure must be appropriate and must be preceded by due process. *Zimmerman v. Shakman*, 204 Ariz. 231, 62 P.3d 976 (Ct. App. Div. 1 2003). There is little reason to completely bar the use of evidence when no trial or case dispositive motion is pending. *Zimmerman v. Shakman*, 204 Ariz. 231, 62 P.3d 976 (Ct. App. Div. 1 2003). On the other hand, if a trial is set or imminent, the possibility of prejudice increases. *Zimmerman v. Shakman*, 204 Ariz. 231, 62 P.3d 976 (Ct. App. Div. 1 2003).

Rule 8. General rules of pleading

(a) Claims for Relief. A pleading which sets forth a claim for relief, whether an original claim, counterclaim, cross-claim, or third-party claim, shall contain:

1. A short and plain statement of the grounds upon which the court's jurisdiction depends, unless the court already has jurisdiction and the claim needs no new grounds of jurisdiction to support it.

2. A short and plain statement of the claim showing that the pleader is entitled to relief.

3. A demand for judgment for the relief the pleader seeks. Relief in the alternative or of several different types may be demanded.

Amended Sept. 15, 1987, effective Nov. 15, 1987.

(b) Defenses; Form of Denials. A party shall state in short and plain terms the party's defenses to each claim asserted and shall admit or deny the averments upon which the adverse party relies. If a party is without knowledge or information sufficient to form a belief as to the truth of an averment, the party shall so state and this has the effect of a denial. Denials shall fairly meet the substance of the averments denied. When a pleader intends in good faith to deny only a part or a qualification of an averment, the pleader shall specify so much of it as is true and material and shall deny only the remainder. Unless the pleader intends in good faith to controvert all the averments of the preceding pleading, the pleader may make denials as specific denials of designated averments or paragraphs, or may generally deny all the averments except such designated averments or paragraphs as the pleader expressly admits, but when the pleader does so intend to controvert all its averments, including averments of the grounds upon which the court's jurisdiction depends, the pleader may do so by general denial subject to the obligations set forth in Rule 11(a).

Amended Sept. 15, 1987, effective Nov. 15, 1987.

(c) Affirmative Defenses. In pleading to a preceding pleading, a party shall set forth affirmatively accord and satisfaction, arbitration and award, assumption of risk, contributory negligence, duress, estoppel, failure of consideration, fraud, illegality, laches, license, payment, release, res judicata, statute of frauds, statute of limitations, waiver, and any other matter constituting an avoidance or affirmative defense. When a party has mistakenly designated a defense as a counterclaim or a counterclaim as a defense, the court on terms, if justice so requires, shall treat the pleading as if there had been a proper designation.

Formerly 8(d). Redesignated 8(c) by amendment of Sept. 26, 1991, effective Dec. 1, 1991. Amended August 30, 2012, effective January 1, 2013.

(d) Effect of Failure to Deny. Averments in a pleading to which a responsive pleading is required, other than those as to the amount of damage, are admitted when not denied in the responsive pleading. Averments in a pleading to which no responsive pleading is required or permitted shall be taken as denied or avoided.

Formerly 8(e). Redesignated 8(d) by amendment of Sept. 26, 1991, effective Dec. 1, 1991.

(e) Pleading to Be Concise and Direct; Consistency.

1. Each averment of a pleading shall be simple, concise, and direct. No technical forms of pleading or motions are required.

2. A party may set forth two or more statements of a claim or defense alternatively or hypothetically, either in one count or defense or in separate counts or defenses. When two or more statements are made in the alternative and one of them if made independently would be sufficient, the pleading is not made insufficient by the insufficiency of one or more of the alternative statements. A party may also state as many separate claims or defenses as the party has regardless of consistency and whether based on legal or equitable grounds or both. All statements shall be made subject to the obligations set forth in Rule 11(a).

Formerly 8(f). Amended Sept. 15, 1987, effective Nov. 15, 1987. Redesignated 8(e) by amendment of Sept. 26, 1991, effective Dec. 1, 1991.

(f) Construction of Pleadings. All pleadings shall be so construed as to do substantial justice.

Formerly 8(g). Redesignated 8(f) by amendment of Sept. 26, 1991, effective Dec. 1, 1991.

(g) Claims for Damages. In all cases in which a party is pursuing a claim other than for a sum certain or for a sum which can by computation be made certain, no dollar amount or figure for damages sought shall be stated in any pleading allowed under Rule 7(a) of these Rules. The pleading setting forth the claim may include a statement reciting that the minimum jurisdictional amount established for filing the action has been satisfied.

Added as 8(h) May 9, 1990, effective Sept. 1, 1990. Redesignated 8(g) by amendment of Sept. 26, 1991, effective Dec. 1, 1991.

(h) Civil Cover Sheets; Classification of Civil Actions.

(1) When filing the initial complaint or petition in a civil action, the plaintiff shall complete and submit a Civil Cover Sheet in a form approved by the Supreme Court. The Civil Cover Sheet shall contain the following: plaintiff's correct name and mailing address; the name of plaintiff's attorney and bar number; the defendant's name(s), the nature of the civil action or proceeding; the main case categories and subcategories designated by the Administrative Director; whether the action meets the criteria for a complex action listed in Rule 8(i); and such other information as the Supreme Court may require. The superior court in each county may, with the approval of the Supreme Court, adopt a local rule requiring that additional information be provided in an Addendum to the Civil Cover Sheet. The Civil Cover Sheet shall be maintained on the website of the Administrative Office of the Courts.

(2) Writs of garnishment do not require a Civil Cover Sheet. Writs of garnishment shall include under the caption of the petition or complaint whichever one of the following notations is applicable:

(A) Federal exemption

(B) Enforce order of support

(C) Enforce order of bankruptcy

(D) Enforce collection of taxes

(E) Non-earnings.

(3) In those counties in which a complex civil litigation program has been established, in addition to the Civil Cover Sheet designation required by subsection (1), the caption shall also identify the action as complex if the action meets the criteria listed in Rule 8(i).

Added Oct. 10, 2000, effective Dec. 1, 2000. Amended Nov. 3, 2005, effective on an experimental basis nunc pro tunc from Nov. 22, 2002. Amended Sept. 16, 2009, effective Jan. 1, 2009. Amended Sept. 1, 2011, effective on a permanent basis Jan. 1, 2012.

(i) Complex Civil Litigation Program Designation

(1) **Definition**. In those counties in which a complex civil litigation program has been established, a "complex case" is a civil action that requires continuous judicial management to avoid placing unnecessary burdens on the court or the litigants and to expedite the case, keep costs reasonable, and promote an effective decision making process by the court, the parties, and counsel.

(2) **Factors**. In deciding whether a civil action is a complex case under subsection (1), the court shall consider the following factors:

(A) numerous pretrial motions raising difficult or novel

legal issues that will be time-consuming to resolve;

(B) management of a large number of witnesses or a substantial amount of documentary evidence;

(C) management of a large number of separately represented parties;

(D) coordination with related actions pending in one or more courts in other counties, states or countries, or in a federal court;

(E) substantial postjudgment judicial supervision;

(F) the case would benefit from permanent assignment to a judge who would have acquired a substantial body of knowledge in a specific area of the law;

(G) inherently complex legal issues;

(H) factors justifying the expeditious resolution of an otherwise complex dispute; and

(I) any other factor which in the interests of justice warrants a complex designation or as otherwise required to serve the interests of justice.

(3) **Procedure for designating a complex case**. At the time of filing the initial complaint, a plaintiff may designate an action as a complex case by filing a motion and separate certification of complex case identifying the case attributes outlined in paragraph (2) justifying the designation. The certification shall be in a form approved by the Supreme Court as set forth in paragraph (8) of this rule and must be served on the defendant along with the motion at the time of service of the complaint. Plaintiff's certification, and any controverting certificate of a party represented by an attorney, shall be signed by at least one attorney of record in the attorney's individual name. A party who is not represented by an attorney shall sign the party's certification of complexity or controverting certification.

The signature of an attorney or party constitutes a certification by the signer that the signer has considered the applicability of Rule 8(i) of the Arizona Rules of Civil Procedure; that the signer has read the certificate of complexity or controverting certificate; that to the best of the signer's knowledge, information and belief, formed after reasonable inquiry, it is warranted; and that the allegation as to complexity is not set forth for any improper purpose. The provisions of Rule 11(a) of these Rules apply to every certification of complexity filed under this Rule.

(4) **Procedure for opposing designation**. If a plaintiff has certified a case as complex and the court has not previously declared the action to be a complex case, and the defendant disagrees with the plaintiff's assertion as to complexity, the

defendant shall file and serve no later than that party's first responsive pleading a response to plaintiff's motion and a controverting certification that specifies the particular reason for the defendant's disagreement with plaintiff's certificate.

(5) **Designation by defendant or joint designation**. A defendant may designate an action as a complex case if the plaintiff has not done so and if the court has not already made a ruling in this matter by filing a motion and the certification of complex case described in subsection (3) at or before the time of filing defendant's first responsive pleading and serving them upon the plaintiff. The parties may join in designating an action as a complex case by filing a joint motion and certification of complex case with or before the filing of defendant's first responsive pleading.

(6) **Action by court**. The presiding judge of the court or designee shall decide, with or without a hearing, whether the action is a complex case within 30 days after the filing of the response to the designating party's motion. The court may decide on its own motion, or on a noticed motion by any party, that a civil action is a complex case or that an action previously declared to be a complex case is not a complex case. This ruling may be made at any time during the pendency of an action, for good cause shown. If the court finds that an attorney or party has made an allegation as to complexity which was not made in good faith, the court, upon motion or upon its own initiative, shall make such orders with regard to such conduct as are just, including, among others, any action authorized under Rule 11(a) of these Rules.

(7) **Not Appealable.** Parties shall not have the right to appeal the court's decision regarding the designation of an action as complex or noncomplex.

(8) **Program Designation Certification Form.** The certification of a complex case shall be substantially in the form set forth in Rule 84, Form 10.

Rule 8(i) added Nov. 3, 2005, effective on an experimental basis nunc pro tunc from Nov. 22, 2002. Amended Sept. 1, 2011, effective on a permanent basis Jan. 1, 2012.

STATE BAR COMMITTEE NOTES

2000 Amendment

[Rule 8(h)] New Rule 8(h) was adopted as part of the effort to consolidate formerly separate sets of procedural rules into either the Arizona Rules of Civil Procedure or the Rules of the Arizona Supreme Court, and contains the provisions of former Rule XII(d) of the Uniform Rules of Practice of the Superior Court.

COURT COMMENT TO RULE 8(I)

[Rule 8(i)] Rule 8(i) is intended to establish a process by which the parties can alert the court to the complex nature of their dispute. However, the determination that a case is, in fact, eligible for the complex litigation program is to be made by the presiding judge or designee. The parties are not to self-select in the absence of a determination by the court on good cause shown.

Justification for this rule. This rule sets the standard for determining whether a case is eligible for participation in the complex case program. It also sets out a process for designating a case as complex and for contesting the designation. A ruling on whether a case is eligible for the complex case program is not appealable to promote early final resolution of the issue of eligibility for participation in the program. This is in keeping with one of the overall goals of the program: to achieve finality for complex cases in an expedited manner.

AUTHORS' COMMENTS

Analysis

1. *Scope and Purpose of Rule.* Ariz. R. Civ. P. 8 generally governs the form, nature, scope and construction of pleadings that assert claims or defenses, and is the cornerstone of the simplified pleading system contemplated by the Arizona Rules of Civil Procedure. Arizona is a "notice pleading" jurisdiction and extensive pleading of facts is not required. *Hogan v. Washington Mut. Bank, N.A.*, 230 Ariz. 584, 277 P.3d 781 (2012), as amended, (July 11, 2012) (Rule 8 requires only a short and plain statement of the claim showing the party is entitled to relief); *Coleman v. City of Mesa*, 230 Ariz. 352, 284 P.3d 863 (2012) ("Arizona follows a notice pleading standard."); *Cullen v. Auto-Owners Ins. Co.*, 218 Ariz. 417, 189 P.3d 344 (2008); *Rosenberg v. Rosenberg*, 123 Ariz. 589, 601 P.2d 589 (1979); *Folk v. City of Phoenix*, 27 Ariz. App. 146, 551 P.2d 595 (Div. 1 1976); *Horne v. Timbanard*, 6 Ariz. App. 518, 434 P.2d 520 (1967). The function of pleadings is simply to provide notice of the claims asserted, and not their evidentiary details. *Cullen v. Auto-Owners Ins. Co.*, 218 Ariz. 417, 189 P.3d 344 (2008); *Schmidt v. Mel Clayton Ford*, 124 Ariz. 65, 601 P.2d 1349 (Ct. App. Div. 1 1979).

In Arizona, the statute of limitations is tolled when suit is commenced, and a suit is commenced by the filing of a complaint. *City of Tucson v. Clear Channel Outdoor, Inc.*, 209 Ariz. 544, 105 P.3d 1163 (2005). In order to accomplish that, a complaint need only have a statement of the ground upon which the court's jurisdiction depends, a statement of the claim showing that the pleader is entitled to relief, and a demand for judgment. *Rowland v. Kellogg Brown and Root, Inc.*, 210 Ariz. 530, 115 P.3d 124 (Ct. App. Div. 2 2005).

2. *Comparison With Federal Rule.* As a consequence of the 2007 and the 2010 amendments to the Federal Rules of Civil Procedure, there are now significant differences between ARCP 8 and FRCP 8 in content, structure and style. With minor differences in language, ARCP 8(a) continues to mirror its federal counterpart both in content and form. Nonetheless, and despite the virtually identical language, the Arizona Supreme Court and the United States Supreme Court have reached different conclusions as to the pleading requirement set forth in Rule 8(a)(2). *Compare discussion in*, *Cullen v. Auto-Owners Ins. Co.*, 218 Ariz. 417, 189 P.3d 344 (2008), with *Bell Atlantic Corp. v. Twombly*, 550 U.S. 544, 127 S. Ct. 1955, 167 L. Ed. 2d 929, 2007-1 Trade Cas. (CCH) ¶ 75709, 68 Fed. R. Serv. 3d 661 (2007).

FRCP 8(c) lists "injury by fellow servant" as an affirmative defense that must be pled, while ARCP 8(c) does not. Effective January 1, 2013, ARCP 8(c) was amended to delete "discharge in bankruptcy" as an affirmative defense, which brings Arizona's rule in line with its federal counterpart on this issue.

The federal counterpart to ARCP 8(d) [*Effect of Failure to Deny*] is found in FRCP 8(b)(6).

The Federal Rules of Civil Procedure do not have provisions that correspond to ARCP 8(g) [Claims for Damages], ARCP 8(h) [*Civil Cover Sheets; Classification of Civil Actions*], or ARCP 8(i) [*Complex Civil Litigation Program Designation*]. The form that accompanies ARCP 8(i) concerning the certification of a complex case is also unique to Arizona practice.

In 2007, the language of FRCP 8 was amended as part of the general restyling of the Federal Rules of Civil Procedure to make the Federal Rules more easily understood and to make style and terminology consistent throughout the Federal Rules of Civil Procedure. Those stylistic modifications have not been incorporated into ARCP 8.

3. *General Requirements for Complaints and Other Pleadings Making a Claim for Relief.* To set forth a proper claim for relief, Rule 8(a) requires:

(1) a short and plain statement of jurisdiction;
(2) a short and plain statement of the claim entitling the pleader to relief; and
(3) a demand for judgment for relief to which the pleader believes the pleader is entitled.

Steinberger v. McVey ex rel. County of Maricopa, — P.3d —, 2014 WL 333575 (Ct. App. Div. 1 2014); *Hogan v. Washington Mut. Bank, N.A.*, 230 Ariz. 584, 277 P.3d 781 (2012), as amended, (July 11, 2012) (Rule 8 requires only a short and plain statement of the claim showing the party is entitled to relief); *Tritschler v. Allstate Ins. Co.*, 213 Ariz. 505, 144 P.3d 519 (Ct. App. Div. 2 2006), as corrected, (Dec. 19, 2006).

This aspect of the Rule is straightforward—"short" can be defined as "having little length" or "not lengthy or drawn out," and its synonyms include "concise," "condensed," and "direct." *Anserv Ins. Services, Inc. v. Albrecht In and For County of Maricopa*, 192 Ariz. 48, 960 P.2d 1159 (1998), as corrected, (July 7, 1998) and as corrected, (July 31, 1998). A three-sentence letter from a *pro se* plaintiff was found sufficient in *Rowland v. Kellogg Brown and Root, Inc.*, 210 Ariz. 530, 115 P.3d 124 (Ct. App. Div. 2 2005).

A complaint that sets forth only factually unsupported legal conclusions does not satisfy Rule 8(a)'s notice pleading standard.

Belen Loan Investors, LLC v. Bradley, 231 Ariz. 448, 296 P.3d 984 (Ct. App. Div. 2 2012).

The purpose of a pleading is to give the opponent fair notice of the nature and basis of the claim and indicate generally the type of litigation involved—if a pleading does not comply with these requirements of Rule 8, it may be subject to dismissal for failure to state a claim upon which relief can be granted. *Cullen v. Auto-Owners Ins. Co.*, 218 Ariz. 417, 189 P.3d 344 (2008). Conclusory statements do not satisfy Arizona's notice pleading standard and "are insufficient to state a claim upon which relief can be granted." *Cullen v. Auto-Owners Ins. Co.*, 218 Ariz. 417, 189 P.3d 344 (2008); *Belen Loan Investors, LLC v. Bradley*, 231 Ariz. 448, 296 P.3d 984 (Ct. App. Div. 2 2012) (A complaint that sets forth only factually unsupported legal conclusions does not satisfy Rule 8(a)'s notice pleading standard.).

Rule 8(a)(3) permits demands for relief in the alternative, or for several different types of relief.

Under Rule 8(g), adopted in 1990 as then Rule 8(h), a pleading may not set forth a dollar amount or figure for damages sought in the action unless the claim is for a sum certain or a sum which can be made certain by computation. Additionally, Rule 5(i) requires that any complaint and answer must be accompanied by any certificate required by Rule 72(e), or any other certificate required by Local Rule.

Counterclaims, cross-claims and third-party complaints also must contain every allegation needed in a complaint founded on the same cause of action. The allegations in a pleading are to be simple, concise and direct, and all pleadings are to be construed to do substantial justice. Rules 8(e), (f); *Bishop v. Marks*, 117 Ariz. 50, 570 P.2d 821 (Ct. App. Div. 2 1977). A complaint or other pleading setting forth a claim for relief is not subject to dismissal if there is any viable theory susceptible of proof under the allegations that would entitle the plaintiff to relief. *Mackey v. Spangler*, 81 Ariz. 113, 301 P.2d 1026 (1956); *AMCOR Inv. Corp. v. Cox Ariz. Publications, Inc.*, 158 Ariz. 566, 764 P.2d 327, 16 Media L. Rep. (BNA) 1059 (Ct. App. Div. 2 1988); *McClanahan v. Cochise College*, 25 Ariz. App. 13, 540 P.2d 744 (Div. 2 1975); *Bates v. Bates*, 1 Ariz. App. 165, 400 P.2d 593 (1965).

Parties are, however, generally bound by their pleadings and may not introduce evidence which contradicts the allegations in those pleadings. *Armer v. Armer*, 105 Ariz. 284, 463 P.2d 818 (1970). Further, a litigant is entitled to no greater relief if the legal theories change after the factual issues have been explored in full. *Horne v. Timbanard*, 6 Ariz. App. 518, 434 P.2d 520 (1967).

Under A.R.S. § 12-341.01, the court may award reasonable attorneys' fees to the prevailing party in an action "arising out of a contract, express or implied . . . ." Rule 54(g)(1), requires that a claim for attorneys' fees, to be preserved, be stated in the pleadings. The procedures for seeking an award of attorneys' fees are discussed at length in Section 12 of the *Authors' Comments* under Rule 54.

4. *Technical Requirements for Complaints and Similar Pleadings.* With respect to technical requirements, every complaint must have a caption setting forth the name of the court, the title of the action, the file number (if known), the names of the parties, and an identification of the nature of the pleading. Rule 10. The plaintiff's claim must be set forth in numbered paragraphs, followed by the demand for relief. If the party is represented by counsel, the counsel must sign the pleading and provide a current office address. Rule 11.

The Maricopa County Superior Court requires that complaints for harassment be prepared and filed on a prescribed form available from the Clerk's office.

5. *Sufficiency of Complaints and Similar Pleadings.* On the question of the sufficiency of pleadings, the standards enunciated in Rule 8 must be read in conjunction with the standards developed under Rule 12. The purpose of Arizona's liberal pleading standards is to avoid technicalities and to give the opposing party notice of the basis for the claim and of its general nature. *Guerrero v. Copper Queen Hospital*, 112 Ariz. 104, 537 P.2d 1329 (1975). Accordingly, the Arizona courts do not look with favor upon motions to dismiss for failure to state a claim for relief. *Maldonado v. Southern Pac. Transp. Co.*, 129 Ariz. 165, 629 P.2d 1001 (Ct. App. Div. 2 1981).

In determining the sufficiency of a pleading on a motion to dismiss for failure to state a claim, the court will consider all well-pleaded facts to be true, but not conclusions of law or unwarranted deductions. *Cullen v. Auto-Owners Ins. Co.*, 218 Ariz. 417, 189 P.3d 344 (2008); *Folk v. City of Phoenix*, 27 Ariz. App. 146, 551 P.2d 595 (Div. 1 1976). The test is whether enough is stated to entitle the pleader to relief on some theory of law susceptible of proof under the allegations made. *Cullen v. Auto-Owners Ins. Co.*, 218 Ariz. 417, 189 P.3d 344 (2008). The demand for relief will not be considered in determining the pleading's sufficiency. *McClanahan v. Cochise College*, 25 Ariz. App. 13, 540 P.2d 744 (Div. 2 1975). A complaint need not anticipate, and attempt to negate or avoid, affirmative defenses. *Keck v. Kelley*, 16 Ariz. App. 163, 492 P.2d 412 (Div. 1 1972).

6. *Statutory Requirements.* There are a number of instances where Arizona has adopted statutory provisions which set forth detailed requirements for specific types of actions. A practitioner preparing a pleading asserting such a claim should consult the

statutory requirements to insure full compliance therewith. Examples of such actions covered by statutory enactments include: wrongful death actions, A.R.S. §§ 611 *et seq.;* actions to quiet title, A.R.S. §§ 12-1101 *et seq.;* actions for forcible entry and detainer, A.R.S. §§ 12-1171, *et seq.;* actions for partition, A.R.S. §§ 12-1211, *et seq.;* receivership actions, A.R.S. §§ 12-1241, *et seq.;* replevin actions, A.R.S. §§ 12-1301, *et seq.;* actions seeking injunctions, A.R.S. §§ 12-1801, *et seq.;* and, declaratory judgment actions, A.R.S. §§ 12-1831, *et seq.*

The Arizona Legislature enacted A.R.S. § 12-2602, which purported to require that the complaint in an action for negligence against a contractor, architect, engineer or other "registered professional" be accompanied by a supporting affidavit from an expert "who is competent to testify against" the defendant. That statute, was declared unconstitutional by the Arizona Court of Appeals and was subsequently repealed and replaced in 1999 by a statute which prescribes the procedures for asserting claims against licensed professionals and the circumstances under which expert testimony will be necessary to prove the standard of care. *AA Mechanical v. Superior Court In and For County of Maricopa (Vree)*, 190 Ariz. 364, 948 P.2d 492 (Ct. App. Div. 1 1997); *Hunter Contracting Co., Inc. v. Superior Court In and For County of Maricopa*, 190 Ariz. 318, 947 P.2d 892 (Ct. App. Div. 1 1997).

The amended version of A.R.S. § 12-2602 has been found to be constitutional. *Bertleson v. Sacks Tierney, P.A.*, 204 Ariz. 124, 60 P.3d 703 (Ct. App. Div. 1 2002). Nonetheless, a claim grounded on *respondeat superior* liability is not a "claim" as contemplated by the statute, and does not require expert testimony to prove the principal's liability. *Warner v. Southwest Desert Images, LLC*, 218 Ariz. 121, 180 P.3d 986 (Ct. App. Div. 2 2008).

Under A.R.S. § 12-2603(a), a plaintiff who asserts a claim against a health care professional in a civil action must certify whether or not expert opinion testimony is necessary to prove the health care professional's standard of care or liability for the claim, and serve a preliminary expert opinion affidavit at the time of the initial disclosures under Rule 26.1, if the claimant certifies such an opinion is needed. *See Jilly v. Rayes*, 221 Ariz. 40, 209 P.3d 176 (Ct. App. Div. 1 2009), upholding constitutionality of A.R.S. § 12-2603. An affidavit must contain, at a minimum, four elements:

(1) the expert's qualifications for providing an opinion on the standard of care;
(2) the factual basis for the claim;
(3) the acts that are claimed to have violated the standard of care, and
(4) the manner in which those acts harmed the claimant.

Sanchez v. Old Pueblo Anesthesia, P.C., 218 Ariz. 317, 183 P.3d 1285 (Ct. App. Div. 2 2008). There is no exception for cases which proceed on a theory of res ipsa loquitur. *Sanchez v. Old Pueblo Anesthesia, P.C.*, 218 Ariz. 317, 183 P.3d 1285 (Ct. App. Div. 2 2008).

7. *Requirements for Answers Generally.* The function of the answer is to define, on an initial basis, the factual and legal matters that will be in dispute. The party answering must admit or deny the allegations that have been made in support of the claims asserted and set forth, in short and plain terms, whatever defenses will be raised to each claim. Under Rule 8(b), an elaborate or explanatory reply to every allegation of the complaint is not required and a defendant is not bound for all time to the responses made. *State ex rel. La Prade v. Smith*, 43 Ariz. 343, 31 P.2d 102 (1934). Ordinarily, it is not necessary to file a responsive pleading to an answer. Allegations in an answer, which does not contain a counterclaim designated as such, are deemed to be denied. *Young v. Bishop*, 88 Ariz. 140, 353 P.2d 1017 (1960).

The failure to deny an allegation when a responsive pleading is required, however, results in the allegation being deemed admitted. Rule 8(d). To avoid such a result from inadvertence, it is common practice to include a paragraph in answers to the effect that all allegations not specifically admitted are denied. It is also good practice to include an allegation asserting any of the defenses listed in Rule 12(b), that will be waived if not asserted in the initial responsive pleading to the complaint and which appear to be available, consistently with the requirements of Rule 11(a).

8. *General Denials.* A general denial puts into issue every allegation of the complaint which plaintiff is required to prove to sustain a cause of action, including jurisdiction. *Wingfoot California Homes Co. v. Valley Nat. Bank of Phoenix*, 80 Ariz. 133, 294 P.2d 370 (1956). Rule 8(b) permits general denials, but only when the pleader intends, in good faith, to controvert all of the allegations in the opponent's pleading. Such a general denial, however, is subject to the "good faith" obligations of Rule 11(a), Rule 11(a) requires an attorney to undertake a reasonable investigation to determine whether an answer is well grounded in fact, and an answer denying liability complies with Rule 11 only if a prefiling investigation uncovers some evidence to support the assertions in the answer. *James, Cooke & Hobson, Inc. v. Lake Havasu Plumbing & Fire Protection*, 177 Ariz. 316, 868 P.2d 329 (Ct. App. Div. 1 1993).

9. *Partial or Qualified Denials.* Rule 8(b) provides that, when a pleader intends to deny only a part of, or to qualify the response to, an allegation, the pleader shall specify so much of it as is true

and deny only the remainder. The pleader may make denials as specific denials of designated allegations or paragraphs, or may generally deny all the allegations except such designated allegations or paragraphs as are expressly admitted. The particular language or form of the specific denial is not important as long as it is clear which allegations are being negated and which are not. A denial where defendants admit certain stated allegations and allege that they are without knowledge or information sufficient to form a belief as to the truth of certain allegations, and deny generally other allegations, constitutes a "qualified general denial." *Wingfoot California Homes Co. v. Valley Nat. Bank of Phoenix*, 80 Ariz. 133, 294 P.2d 370 (1956).

Care, however, should be exercised in using qualified general denials as well as specific denials to make certain that the pleader's response to each allegation is clear; the responsive pleading should not impose an inordinate burden upon the Court and the opposing party in analyzing exactly what has been admitted and what has been denied.

10. *Denials on Information and Belief.* Rule 8(b) permits a party, who is without knowledge or information sufficient to form a belief as to the truth of an allegation, to so state and this statement has the nominal effect of a denial. *Equal Employment Opportunity Commission v. Wah Chang Albany Corp.*, 499 F.2d 187, 8 Fair Empl. Prac. Cas. (BNA) 203, 8 Empl. Prac. Dec. (CCH) P 9477, 18 Fed. R. Serv. 2d 1099 (9th Cir. 1974). A denial upon information and belief of a factual allegation whose accuracy can be ascertained from public records is not favored, however, and will be deemed an admission of that fact for purposes of a motion for summary judgment. *Washington Nat. Trust Co. v. W. M. Dary Co.*, 116 Ariz. 171, 568 P.2d 1069 (1977); *Sligh v. Watson*, 69 Ariz. 373, 214 P.2d 123 (1950) (overruled in part on other grounds by, Diamond v. Chiate, 81 Ariz. 86, 300 P.2d 583 (1956)).

11. *Negative Pregnants.* An overly specific denial may involve an affirmative implication favorable to the adversary. Classically, this technical defect in pleading is called a "negative pregnant," *i.e.,* the purported "negative" is "pregnant" with an admission. *Frank v. Solomon*, 94 Ariz. 55, 381 P.2d 591 (1963). For instance, a denial of the balance of a certain amount may admit one of any smaller amounts. *Eads v. Commercial Nat. Bank of Phoenix*, 33 Ariz. 499, 266 P. 14, 62 A.L.R. 183 (1928). Although such a denial should be carefully avoided, the Arizona courts will not penalize the pleader who, in good faith, is seeking to controvert certain allegations. *Frank v. Solomon*, 94 Ariz. 55, 381 P.2d 591 (1963). A clear admission in an answer, however, is binding on the party making it and conclusive as to the fact admitted. *Schwartz v. Schwerin*, 85 Ariz. 242, 336 P.2d 144 (1959); *Czarnecki v. Czarnecki*, 123 Ariz. 478, 600 P.2d 1110 (Ct. App. Div. 2 1978),

decision approved, 123 Ariz. 466, 600 P.2d 1098 (1979) and (disapproved of on other grounds by, Porter v. Estate of Pigg, 175 Ariz. 303, 856 P.2d 796 (1993)).

12. *Verification of Pleadings.* A pleading need not be verified unless an applicable statute or Rule of Civil Procedure requires that. *Colboch v. Aviation Credit Corp.*, 64 Ariz. 88, 166 P.2d 584 (1946). Rule 11(a) was intended to have an attorney's signature serve in lieu of a formal verification, but many provisions of the Rules of Civil Procedure and statutes requiring verification were retained.

A complaint must be verified in derivative actions, Rule 23.1; in actions seeking appointment of a receiver, Rule 66(a); in quiet title actions, A.R.S. § 12-1102; in forcible entry and detainer actions, A.R.S. § 12-1175; in replevin actions, A.R.S. § 12-1301; and, in actions for dissolution of marriage, A.R.S. § 25-314. An injunction, or temporary restraining order, may be granted either upon a verified complaint or on affidavit. A.R.S. § 12-1803; Rule 65(d). Claims in forfeiture proceedings must be verified by the claimant personally. *State ex rel. McDougall v. Superior Court In and For County of Maricopa*, 173 Ariz. 385, 843 P.2d 1277 (Ct. App. Div. 1 1992).

Ariz. R. Civ. P. 9(i) requires the verification of an answer which raises certain specified defenses. A.R.S. § 22-216 imposes the identical requirement for answers filed in justice courts. On the other hand, Ariz. R. Civ. P. 11(c), does not require that a complaint seeking injunctive relief be verified. Where the complaint in an action seeking equitable relief is verified, however, Rule 11(c) requires that the responsive pleading of the opposing party be verified as well. *Barnet v. Board of Medical Examiners*, 121 Ariz. 338, 590 P.2d 454 (1979).

Under Ariz. R. Civ. P. 80(i), what is termed an "unsworn declaration under penalty of perjury" may be used in place of a formal, sworn verification where a verification is required by the Rules.

13. *Affirmative Defenses Generally.* Ariz. R. Civ. P. 8(c), formerly Rule 8(d), requires that a responsive pleading set forth certain enumerated affirmative defenses and "any other matter constituting an avoidance or affirmative defense." This subdivision should be read in conjunction with, and distinguished from, Rule 8(b), which deals with denials or negative defenses. The specific affirmative defenses listed in Rule 8(c) are not, by any means, exclusive or exhaustive. Other matters which have been held to be affirmative defenses that must be pleaded or waived include the defense of *ultra vires*, *City of Phoenix v. Linsenmeyer*, 86 Ariz. 328, 346 P.2d 140 (1959); and, an agent's lack of authority, *State ex rel. Dandoy v. City of Phoenix*, 133 Ariz. 334, 651 P.2d 862 (Ct. App. Div. 1 1982). The defense of "undue influence" has

been held to be a separate species of fraud that must be separately alleged. *Brazee v. Morris*, 68 Ariz. 224, 204 P.2d 475 (1949). Similarly, the defense of usury has also been held to be an affirmative defense that must be pled. *Wieman v. Roysden*, 166 Ariz. 281, 802 P.2d 432 (Ct. App. Div. 1 1990).

The "tort reform" legislation passed in 1993 by the Arizona Legislature adopted a new A.R.S. § 12-711, which creates an "affirmative defense" which permits the trier of fact to find a defendant not liable if it finds that the claimant was under the influence of an intoxicating drug or liquor and, as a result, was at least 50% responsible for the accident or event that produced the claimant's injuries.

The provisions of A.R.S. § 12-820.02 provide a qualified immunity in that they specify that, in performing certain specified functions, a public employee cannot be held liable absent a showing that the public employee was grossly negligent or intended to cause injury. The statute, which has been held to be constitutional, is not limited in its application to third parties for injuries caused by someone a law enforcement officer failed to keep in custody, but also applies to claims for injuries sustained by persons while in the custody of a law enforcement officer. *Clouse ex rel. Clouse v. State*, 199 Ariz. 196, 16 P.3d 757 (2001); *Luchanski v. Congrove*, 193 Ariz. 176, 971 P.2d 636 (Ct. App. Div. 1 1998). The "qualified immunity" conferred by this statute is probably an affirmative defense that must be pled.

In determining what defenses other than those listed in Rule 8(c) must be pleaded affirmatively, the interpretations given to the corresponding Federal Rule are applicable. *Foremost-McKesson Corp. v. Allied Chemical Co.*, 140 Ariz. 108, 680 P.2d 818 (Ct. App. Div. 2 1983). Another highly relevant consideration is whether the plaintiff will be taken by surprise by the assertion at trial of a defense not pleaded affirmatively by the defendant.

14. *Failure to Plead Affirmative Defense.* Failure to plead an affirmative defense results in waiver of the defense, unless the trial court, in its discretion, allows an amendment of the answer to raise it. *O'Keefe v. Grenke*, 170 Ariz. 460, 825 P.2d 985, 16 U.C.C. Rep. Serv. 2d 746 (Ct. App. Div. 1 1992); *Sirek v. Fairfield Snowbowl, Inc.*, 166 Ariz. 183, 800 P.2d 1291 (Ct. App. Div. 1 1990); *Hughes Aircraft Co v. Industrial Commission*, 125 Ariz. 1, 606 P.2d 819 (Ct. App. Div. 1 1979). *But see, Gary Outdoor Advertising Co. v. Sun Lodge, Inc.*, 133 Ariz. 240, 650 P.2d 1222 (1982). A pretrial stipulation or statement which raises affirmative defenses not included in the answer effectively amends the pleadings to raise them. *Ries v. McComb*, 25 Ariz. App. 554, 545 P.2d 65 (Div. 1 1976).

The general rules of pleading that are applicable to the statement of a claim also govern the pleading of affirmative defenses. Thus, the pleading standards set out in Rule 8(e) must be consulted in connection with drafting affirmative defenses under Rule 8(c). It is not essential to allege evidentiary detail in support of affirmative defenses and, indeed, it is common, and acceptable, practice to simply plead the defense by its generic designation (*e.g.*, "accord and satisfaction," "failure of consideration," etc.). The party pleading an affirmative defense has the burden of proof with respect to it. *Millers Nat. Ins. Co. v. Taylor Freeman Ins. Agency*, 161 Ariz. 490, 779 P.2d 365 (Ct. App. Div. 2 1989).

The final sentence in Rule 8(c) provides that when a party has mistakenly designated a defense as a counterclaim or a counterclaim as a defense, the Court, in the interest of justice, may relabel the defense or counterclaim as appropriate.

15. *Contributory Negligence*. Rule 8(c) continues to list "contributory negligence" as one of the available affirmative defenses that must be plead or are waived. The Supreme Court has observed, however, that one of the reasons for the adoption of a modified version of the Uniform Contribution Among Tortfeasors Act in 1984, and the subsequent 1987 amendments, was to eliminate the harshness of the all-or-nothing contributory negligence defense. *Hutcherson v. City of Phoenix*, 192 Ariz. 51, 961 P.2d 449 (1998).

Other decisions of the Court dealing with related issues and analogous defenses also have strongly suggested that the defense of contributory negligence, if it has in fact survived and is successfully maintained, will no longer operate as a complete bar to a plaintiff's recovery. See *Gunnell v. Arizona Public Service Co.*, 202 Ariz. 388, 46 P.3d 399 (2002); *Williams v. Thude*, 188 Ariz. 257, 934 P.2d 1349 (1997) and *Jimenez v. Sears, Roebuck and Co.*, 183 Ariz. 399, 904 P.2d 861, Prod. Liab. Rep. (CCH) P 14382 (1995).

By reason of provisions in the Arizona Constitution (Art. 18, Sect. 5), the presence or absence of contributory negligence, and its related doctrine, assumption of the risk, and their effect, if any, on a plaintiff's recovery, are always matters for the jury exclusively to decide. *Estate of Reinen v. Northern Arizona Orthopedics, Ltd.*, 198 Ariz. 283, 9 P.3d 314 (2000). The giving of a peremptory instruction on either of these issues will constitute reversible error. *Estate of Reinen v. Northern Arizona Orthopedics, Ltd.*, 198 Ariz. 283, 9 P.3d 314 (2000).

The Arizona Supreme Court has also held that this constitutional provision, Article 18, § 5 of the Arizona Constitution, applies to the defense of comparative negligence as well. *Gunnell v. Arizona Public Service Co.*, 202 Ariz. 388, 46 P.3d 399 (2002). It also applies to express contractual assumptions of risk and/or prospective releases of liability, effectively precluding the award of summary judgment in cases presenting such issues. *Phelps v. Firebird Raceway, Inc.*, 210 Ariz. 403, 111 P.3d 1003 (2005).

A statute that purported to absolve a defendant from civil liability to a plaintiff injured while involved in a criminal act, A.R.S. § 12–712(B), was held to violate this constitutional mandate, because it triggered a statutory defense of nonliability based on the plaintiff's antecedent conduct. *Sonoran Desert Investigations, Inc. v. Miller*, 213 Ariz. 274, 141 P.3d 754 (Ct. App. Div. 2 2006). The background of Article 18, Section 5 suggests, however, that it was intended to address "assumption of risk" as a defense that effectively relieved a defendant of any duty of care by completely barring recovery by the injured party. *1800 Ocotillo, LLC v. WLB Group, Inc.*, 219 Ariz. 200, 196 P.3d 222, 62 A.L.R.6th 727 (2008). Accordingly, Article 18, Section 5 is not applicable to a provision in a professional services contract that merely limits the monetary amount of the professional's liability. *1800 Ocotillo, LLC v. WLB Group, Inc.*, 219 Ariz. 200, 196 P.3d 222, 62 A.L.R.6th 727 (2008).

Article 18, Section 5 of the Arizona Constitution does not give a defendant an unqualified right to right to raise assumption of the risk as a defense. Instead, to receive an instruction on the issue, a defendant must present evidence showing (1) a risk of harm to the plaintiff caused by the defendant's conduct; (2) plaintiff's actual knowledge of the risk and appreciation of its magnitude; and, (3) plaintiff's voluntary choice to accept the risk given the circumstances. *A Tumbling-T Ranches v. Flood Control Dist. of Maricopa County*, 222 Ariz. 515, 217 P.3d 1220 (Ct. App. Div. 1 2009).

16. *Duress.* An act or threat constitutes duress if it is wrongful and places the party entering into the transaction in such fear as to preclude the exercise of free will and independent judgment. *Dunbar v. Dunbar*, 102 Ariz. 352, 429 P.2d 949 (1967). Arizona uses the definition of "duress" articulated in Section 492 of the Restatement of Contracts. *Inter-Tel, Inc. v. Bank of America, Arizona*, 195 Ariz. 111, 985 P.2d 596 (Ct. App. Div. 1 1999). Under that definition, duress is present if one party is induced to assent to a contract by a wrongful threat or act of the other party. *Inter-Tel, Inc. v. Bank of America, Arizona*, 195 Ariz. 111, 985 P.2d 596 (Ct. App. Div. 1 1999). Normally, duress is not established merely because one party takes advantage of the financial difficulty of the other, unless the wrongful act of one party is what created the other party's financial difficulty. *Inter-Tel, Inc. v. Bank of America, Arizona*, 195 Ariz. 111, 985 P.2d 596 (Ct. App. Div. 1 1999).

17. *Estoppel.* The essential elements of an estoppel are conduct

by which one induces another to believe in certain material facts, which inducement results in acts in reliance thereon, justifiably taken, which cause injury. *Darner Motor Sales, Inc. v. Universal Underwriters Ins. Co.*, 140 Ariz. 383, 682 P.2d 388 (1984).

In Arizona, equitable estoppel has three elements:

(1) the party to be estopped has committed affirmative acts inconsistent with a position it later adopts;

(2) the other party has acted in reliance on such conduct; and

(3) the other party is injured as a result of the former's repudiation its prior conduct. *Valencia Energy Co. v. Arizona Dept. of Revenue*, 191 Ariz. 565, 959 P.2d 1256 (1998); *Gorman v. Pima County*, 230 Ariz. 506, 287 P.3d 800 (Ct. App. Div. 2 2012); *McBride v. Kieckhefer Associates, Inc.*, 228 Ariz. 262, 265 P.3d 1061 (Ct. App. Div. 1 2011), review denied, (Apr. 24, 2012); *Pueblo Santa Fe Townhomes Owners' Ass'n v. Transcontinental Ins. Co.*, 218 Ariz. 13, 178 P.3d 485 (Ct. App. Div. 1 2008); *Lowe v. Pima County*, 217 Ariz. 642, 177 P.3d 1214 (Ct. App. Div. 2 2008); *City of Tucson v. Whiteco Metrocom, Inc.*, 194 Ariz. 390, 983 P.2d 759 (Ct. App. Div. 2 1999), redesignated as opinion and publication ordered, (Apr. 14, 1999).

The doctrine of equitable estoppel is not applicable unless a party is injured by justifiably relying upon the conduct of another which was intended to induce such reliance. *Sherman v. First American Title Ins. Co.*, 201 Ariz. 564, 38 P.3d 1229 (Ct. App. Div. 2 2002); *LaBombard v. Samaritan Health System*, 195 Ariz. 543, 991 P.2d 246 (Ct. App. Div. 1 1998); *Villas at Hidden Lakes Condominiums Ass'n v. Geupel Const. Co., Inc.*, 174 Ariz. 72, 847 P.2d 117 (Ct. App. Div. 1 1992).

Estoppel may now be applied against the state and its political subdivisions, even when they are performing governmental functions, but with great caution and only when its application would promote rather than frustrate the basic intent of the statute involved and when the government's conduct threatens to work a serious injustice and the public interest would not be unduly damaged. *Lowe v. Pima County*, 217 Ariz. 642, 177 P.3d 1214 (Ct. App. Div. 2 2008); *City of Tucson v. Whiteco Metrocom, Inc.*, 194 Ariz. 390, 983 P.2d 759 (Ct. App. Div. 2 1999), redesignated as opinion and publication ordered, (Apr. 14, 1999); *Pingitore v. Town of Cave Creek*, 194 Ariz. 261, 981 P.2d 129 (Ct. App. Div. 1 1998); *Hansson v. Arizona State Bd. of Dental Examiners*, 195 Ariz. 66, 985 P.2d 551 (Ct. App. Div. 1 1998).

The rigid rule forbidding the application of estoppel against the government was the logical corollary to the previous notions of sovereign immunity, which have been significantly eroded. Accordingly, the doctrine of equitable estoppel may now be invoked against the government in tax matters, so that the Department of Revenue can be estopped from collecting back taxes owed because a Department agent previously advised a taxpayer in writing that the activity now being levied was not subject to tax. *Valencia Energy Co. v. Arizona Dept. of Revenue*, 191 Ariz. 565, 959 P.2d 1256 (1998).

The defense of estoppel may be established by proving that the Department's conduct was inconsistent with a position later assumed, the taxpayer relied and had a right to rely on the Department's conduct, and the taxpayer sustained damage that would make it unjust to allow the Department to maintain the later-taken position. *Valencia Energy Co. v. Arizona Dept. of Revenue*, 191 Ariz. 565, 959 P.2d 1256 (1998). Such an estoppel may not be based, however, on the casual acts, advice or instructions issued by nonsupervisory Department employees. *Valencia Energy Co. v. Arizona Dept. of Revenue*, 191 Ariz. 565, 959 P.2d 1256 (1998). Moreover, the detriment suffered by the taxpayer must involve some collateral loss other than payment of the tax due under the law as properly interpreted. *Valencia Energy Co. v. Arizona Dept. of Revenue*, 191 Ariz. 565, 959 P.2d 1256 (1998).

Judicial estoppel is a doctrine that protects the integrity of the judicial system by preventing a party from taking an inconsistent position in successive or separate actions. *Standage Ventures, Inc. v. State*, 114 Ariz. 480, 562 P.2d 360 (1977); *Bank of America Nat. Trust and Sav. Ass'n v. Maricopa County*, 196 Ariz. 173, 993 P.2d 1137 (Ct. App. Div. 1 1999); *State Farm Auto. Ins. Co. v. Civil Service Emp. Ins. Co.*, 19 Ariz. App. 594, 509 P.2d 725 (Div. 1 1973) ("the law will not allow a party 'to have his cake and eat it too' "). For judicial estoppel to apply, three requirements must be met:

(1) the parties must be the same;
(2) the question involved must be the same; and
(3) the party asserting the inconsistent position must have been successful in the prior proceeding. *Bank of America Nat. Trust and Sav. Ass'n v. Maricopa County*, 196 Ariz. 173, 993 P.2d 1137 (Ct. App. Div. 1 1999).

The doctrine of judicial estoppel is to be applied cautiously, and a party is not considered to have been successful in the prior proceeding unless (a) the court in that proceeding granted the party relief or accepted the party's earlier inconsistent position either as a preliminary matter or as part of a final disposition, and (b) the party's inconsistent position was a significant factor in the relief granted. *Standage Ventures, Inc. v. State*, 114 Ariz.

480, 562 P.2d 360 (1977) (defendant did not obtain judicial relief by taking one position, and, as a result, is not judicially estoppel from taking a different position in subsequent litigation); *Bank of America Nat. Trust and Sav. Ass'n v. Maricopa County*, 196 Ariz. 173, 993 P.2d 1137 (Ct. App. Div. 1 1999); *State Farm Auto. Ins. Co. v. Civil Service Emp. Ins. Co.*, 19 Ariz. App. 594, 509 P.2d 725 (Div. 1 1973) (defendants did not obtain any relief in the prior action as a result of their counsel's statement in the motion for summary judgment).

Estoppel and waiver are not synonymous. Waiver is the voluntary and intentional relinquishment, express or inferred, of a known right and must be shown by clear and convincing evidence. *Ray v. Mangum*, 163 Ariz. 329, 788 P.2d 62 (1989); *Angus Medical Co. v. Digital Equipment Corp.*, 173 Ariz. 159, 840 P.2d 1024, 17 U.C.C. Rep. Serv. 2d 724 (Ct. App. Div. 1 1992). Estoppel occurs where a party is prevented by that party's own conduct from claiming a right to the detriment of another party who is entitled to rely on such conduct and has acted accordingly; it does not necessarily require proof by clear and convincing evidence. *Fotinos v. Baker*, 164 Ariz. 447, 793 P.2d 1114 (Ct. App. Div. 2 1990); *Certainteed Corp. v. United Pacific Ins. Co.*, 158 Ariz. 273, 762 P.2d 560 (Ct. App. Div. 2 1988).

18. *Lack or Failure of Consideration.* A written contract presumes proper consideration; therefore, the burden of showing a lack or failure of consideration is on the party attacking the contract. *Dunlap v. Fort Mohave Farms, Inc.*, 89 Ariz. 387, 363 P.2d 194 (1961). An answer that raises the defense of a lack or failure of consideration, in whole or in part, must be verified. Rule 9(i)(8).

19. *Fraud or Undue Influence.* When fraud is raised as a defense to an action, the circumstances constituting fraud must be stated with particularity. *Fruth v. Divito*, 26 Ariz. App. 154, 546 P.2d 1163 (Div. 1 1976). The purpose of such pleading is to eliminate surprise at trial and to allow the issues to be properly developed before trial. *Fruth v. Divito*, 26 Ariz. App. 154, 546 P.2d 1163 (Div. 1 1976). The defense of "undue influence" is a separate species of fraud that must be separately alleged. *Brazee v. Morris*, 68 Ariz. 224, 204 P.2d 475 (1949).

20. *Illegality.* There is a division of authority in other jurisdictions as to whether the defenses of illegality and *ultra vires* are waived if not pled in the trial court. In Arizona, an appellate court has the discretion to permit the issue of the illegality of a contract to be raised initially on appeal, where that issue will dispose of the case without requiring a remand and will avoid having the courts enforce a contract that is contrary to law. *Bank One, Arizona v. Rouse*, 181 Ariz. 36, 887 P.2d 566 (Ct. App. Div. 1

1994).

21. *Laches.* Laches is a defense when lack of diligence on the part of the plaintiff results in injury or prejudice to the defendant. The mere passage of time without more, however, does not amount to the required prejudice. *Mobile Discount Corp. v. Schumacher*, 139 Ariz. 15, 676 P.2d 649 (Ct. App. Div. 2 1983). Laches thus differs in its application from a statute of limitations where the passage of a specified period of time will bar the action. For the doctrine of laches to apply, there must be an unreasonable delay after knowledge of the facts which works a hardship. *Jerger v. Rubin*, 106 Ariz. 114, 471 P.2d 726 (1970); *Prutch v. Town of Quartzsite*, 231 Ariz. 431, 296 P.3d 94 (Ct. App. Div. 1 2013), as amended, (Feb. 26, 2013) (noting defendant must show unreasonable delay and prejudice for laches to apply); *Summit Properties, Inc. v. Wilson*, 26 Ariz. App. 550, 550 P.2d 104 (Div. 1 1976); *Maricopa County v. Cities and Towns of Avondale, et al., Wickenburg*, 12 Ariz. App. 109, 467 P.2d 949 (Div. 1 1970); *but cf. Flynn v. Rogers*, 172 Ariz. 62, 834 P.2d 148 (1992).

Laches is, in a sense, a form of estoppel that applies when the party asserting the defense shows that, because of delay or lapse of time, he/she has been injured or has changed his/her position in justifiable reliance on the other party's inaction. *In re Paternity of Gloria*, 194 Ariz. 201, 979 P.2d 529 (Ct. App. Div. 1 1998), redesignated as opinion, (Feb. 4, 1999). A finding of laches is one committed to the sound discretion of the trial court. *Cyprus Bagdad Copper Corp. v. Arizona Dept. of Revenue*, 196 Ariz. 5, 992 P.2d 5 (Ct. App. Div. 1 1999).

22. *Payment.* Once payment is affirmatively alleged as a defense, the burden is upon the defendant to prove payment with some affirmative evidence. *Hegel v. O'Malley Ins. Co., Inc.*, 122 Ariz. 52, 593 P.2d 275 (1979); *B & R Materials, Inc. v. U. S. Fidelity and Guaranty Co.*, 132 Ariz. 122, 644 P.2d 276 (Ct. App. Div. 2 1982).

23. *Release.* Release is one of the affirmative defenses specifically listed in Rule 8(c), and must ordinarily be pled or it is waived. *Sirek v. Fairfield Snowbowl, Inc.*, 166 Ariz. 183, 800 P.2d 1291 (Ct. App. Div. 1 1990). A general release can be avoided on the grounds of mutual mistake. Arizona also recognizes that a unilateral mistake induced by misrepresentations may constitute grounds for avoiding a release if, at the time it was entered into, the party seeking to enforce the release knew or should have known of the mistake. *Parrish v. United Bank of Arizona*, 164 Ariz. 18, 790 P.2d 304 (Ct. App. Div. 2 1990).

When a party executes a release agreement, he or she abandons a claim or right to the person against whom the claim exists or the right may be enforced or exercised. *Cunningham v. Goettl Air*

Conditioning, Inc., 194 Ariz. 236, 980 P.2d 489 (1999); *A Tumbling-T Ranches v. Flood Control Dist. of Maricopa County*, 220 Ariz. 202, 204 P.3d 1051 (Ct. App. Div. 1 2008). The claim, once abandoned or released, is extinguished. A covenant not to execute, on the other hand, does not extinguish the plaintiff's cause of action and does not operate to release other joint tortfeasors. *Cunningham v. Goettl Air Conditioning, Inc.*, 194 Ariz. 236, 980 P.2d 489 (1999); *A Tumbling-T Ranches v. Flood Control Dist. of Maricopa County*, 220 Ariz. 202, 204 P.3d 1051 (Ct. App. Div. 1 2008).

The release of one joint tortfeasor does not automatically release all others. A release is a contract and other tortfeasors will be deemed released only if that was the intended result of the release or the release expressly so provided. For a release to be "express," the entity or person to be released must be named or otherwise specifically identified. *Spain v. General Motors Corp., Chevrolet Motor Div.*, 171 Ariz. 226, 829 P.2d 1272 (Ct. App. Div. 2 1992).

Arizona allows parties to agree in advance, through the vehicle of a release, that one party shall not be liable to the other for negligence. *Valley Nat. Bank v. National Ass'n for Stock Car Auto Racing, Inc.*, 153 Ariz. 374, 736 P.2d 1186 (Ct. App. Div. 2 1987). Arizona courts traditionally look upon such releases with disfavor out of concern they may encourage carelessness, and the limiting language of such a release is construed strictly against the party relying upon it. *Bothell v. Two Point Acres, Inc.*, 192 Ariz. 313, 965 P.2d 47 (Ct. App. Div. 2 1998). To be effective, such a release must *expressly* release liability caused by the negligence of the party securing it, and a general release of liability will not absolve the party obtaining it of a duty to disclose unexpected and extraordinary risks known to it, but not known to the party giving the release. *Bothell v. Two Point Acres, Inc.*, 192 Ariz. 313, 965 P.2d 47 (Ct. App. Div. 2 1998); *Morganteen v. Cowboy Adventures, Inc.*, 190 Ariz. 463, 949 P.2d 552 (Ct. App. Div. 1 1997); *Sirek v. Fairfield Snowbowl, Inc.*, 166 Ariz. 183, 800 P.2d 1291 (Ct. App. Div. 1 1990).

24. *Res Judicata; Collateral Estoppel; Law of the Case.* The term '*res judicata*' is now understood to encompass both the concept of *claim* preclusion and the related concept of *issue* preclusion. *Pettit v. Pettit*, 218 Ariz. 529, 189 P.3d 1102 (Ct. App. Div. 1 2008). Most of the cases cited in this Handbook use the term '*res judicata*' in its traditional sense as synonymous with claim preclusion and use the term 'collateral estoppel' in its traditional sense as issue preclusion. *In re General Adjudication of All Rights to Use Water In Gila River System and Source*, 212 Ariz. 64, 127 P.3d 882 (2006) ("We deal today with the issue of claim preclusion, formerly referred to as res judicata."); *Peterson*

v. Newton, 232 Ariz. 593, 307 P.3d 1020 (Ct. App. Div. 1 2013).

Res judicata is a judicially created doctrine grounded in public policy considerations to insure there will be an end to litigation, at some point. *Lee v. Johnson*, 70 Ariz. 122, 216 P.2d 722 (1950).

The failure to plead res judicata as an affrmative defense constitutes a waiver. *Salt River Project/Bechtel Corp. v. Industrial Com'n of Arizona*, 179 Ariz. 280, 877 P.2d 1336 (Ct. App. Div. 1 1994); *Nienstedt v. Wetzel*, 133 Ariz. 348, 651 P.2d 876, 33 A.L.R. 4th 635 (Ct. App. Div. 1 1982).

To prevail on the affirmative defense, a party must establish:

(1) identity or privity between the parties;

(2) identity of claims in the previous litigaton in which a judgment was entered and the current litigation; and

(3) a final judgment on the merits in the previous litigation.

In re General Adjudication of All Rights to Use Water In Gila River System and Source, 212 Ariz. 64, 127 P.3d 882 (2006); *Peterson v. Newton*, 232 Ariz. 593, 307 P.3d 1020 (Ct. App. Div. 1 2013); *Howell v. Hodap*, 221 Ariz. 543, 212 P.3d 881 (Ct. App. Div. 1 2009); *Hall v. Lalli*, 191 Ariz. 104, 952 P.2d 748 (Ct. App. Div. 2 1997), aff'd, 194 Ariz. 54, 977 P.2d 776 (1999); *Matusik v. Arizona Public Service Co.*, 141 Ariz. 1, 684 P.2d 882 (Ct. App. Div. 1 1984).

Under the doctrine of *res judicata,* a judgment on the merits in a prior suit involving the same parties or their privies bars a second suit based on the same cause of action, even when the judgment is entered after the second suit is filed. *Murphy v. Board of Medical Examiners of State of Ariz.*, 190 Ariz. 441, 949 P.2d 530 (Ct. App. Div. 1 1997).

The doctrine also applies to judgments entered in the small claims division of the justice court. *Peterson v. Newton*, 232 Ariz. 593, 307 P.3d 1020 (Ct. App. Div. 1 2013) (". . . we hold that a plaintiff who chooses to litigate a claim under the simplified procedures of small claims court may be barred by the doctrine of claim preclusion from bring a second lawsuit bases on the same claim alleged in the first lawsuit.").

A valid and final judgment rendered without fraud or collusion by a court of competent jurisdiction is generally conclusive as to every claim or issue actually litigated and every claim or issue that could have been litigated. *Pettit v. Pettit*, 218 Ariz. 529, 189 P.3d 1102 (Ct. App. Div. 1 2008); *Better Homes Const., Inc. v. Goldwater*, 203 Ariz. 295, 53 P.3d 1139 (Ct. App. Div. 1 2002), redesignated as opinion and publication ordered, (Sept. 19, 2002); *Hall v. Lalli*, 191 Ariz. 104, 952 P.2d 748 (Ct. App. Div. 2 1997), aff'd, 194 Ariz. 54, 977 P.2d 776 (1999); *Norriega v. Machado*, 179 Ariz. 348, 878 P.2d 1386 (Ct. App. Div. 1 1994).

A determination by a court that it lacks subject matter jurisdiction over a controversy thus does not have *res judicata* or collateral estoppel effect. *Washburn v. Pima County*, 206 Ariz. 571, 81 P.3d 1030 (Ct. App. Div. 2 2003). On the other hand, it has been held that two causes of action which arise out of the same transaction or occurrence are not the same for purposes of *res judicata* if proof of different or additional facts will be required to establish them. *E.C. Garcia and Co., Inc. v. Arizona State Dept. of Revenue*, 178 Ariz. 510, 875 P.2d 169 (Ct. App. Div. 1 1993).

Claims that were not ripe at the time of the prior adjudication cannot be barred by application of the *res judicata* doctrine. *Owens v. City of Phoenix*, 180 Ariz. 402, 884 P.2d 1100 (Ct. App. Div. 1 1994). Similarly, a confirmed arbitration award will not have preclusive effect on any subsequent litigation of claims that the arbitrator expressly reserved and/or claims that were outside the scope of the arbitrator's jurisdiction. *Heinig v. Hudman*, 177 Ariz. 66, 865 P.2d 110 (Ct. App. Div. 1 1993). A judgment dismissing an action against a parent corporation on the grounds that the action should have been brought against its subsidiaries does not bar a subsequent action against those subsidiaries. *Corbett v. ManorCare of America, Inc.*, 213 Ariz. 618, 146 P.3d 1027 (Ct. App. Div. 2 2006).

For an action to be barred by the affirmative defense of *res judicata* such action must be based on the same cause of action as was asserted in the prior proceeding. The Restatement (Second) of Judgments and the clear majority of courts in other jurisdictions employ a "transactional" test for determining whether the causes of action are the same. *Phoenix Newspapers, Inc. v. Department of Corrections, State of Ariz.*, 188 Ariz. 237, 934 P.2d 801 (Ct. App. Div. 1 1997) (comparing and contrasting the Restatement's *transactional* test with Arizona's *same evidence* test). *See also, Pettit v. Pettit*, 218 Ariz. 529, 189 P.3d 1102 (Ct. App. Div. 1 2008); *E.C. Garcia and Co., Inc. v. Arizona State Dept. of Revenue*, 178 Ariz. 510, 520, 875 P.2d 169, 179 (Ct. App. Div. 1 1993).

The *transactional* test focuses on whether the new claim arises out of the same transaction or occurrence as the claim that was the subject of the original action. *Phoenix Newspapers, Inc. v. Department of Corrections, State of Ariz.*, 188 Ariz. 237, 934 P.2d 801 (Ct. App. Div. 1 1997). This modern "transactional" rule prevents the relitigation of claims closely related to previously litigated claims which arise out of the same events and the revival of essentially the same cause of action under a new legal theory. *Phoenix Newspapers, Inc. v. Department of Corrections, State of Ariz.*, 188 Ariz. 237, 934 P.2d 801 (Ct. App. Div. 1 1997).

Arizona, however, follows a more restrictive same evidence

test, *e.g.*, only if no additional evidence is needed to prevail in the second action than that needed to prevail in the first is the action barred. *Phoenix Newspapers, Inc. v. Department of Corrections, State of Ariz.*, 188 Ariz. 237, 934 P.2d 801 (Ct. App. Div. 1 1997); *Pettit v. Pettit*, 218 Ariz. 529, 189 P.3d 1102 (Ct. App. Div. 1 2008) (citing Restatement Second, Judgments § 61). Under this test—the Arizona test—an action is barred only if no additional evidence is needed to prevail in the second action than was needed to prevail in the first action.

When a final judgment in an earlier action is issued by a federal court, federal law dictates the earlier judgment's preclusive effect. *Howell v. Hodap*, 221 Ariz. 543, 212 P.3d 881 (Ct. App. Div. 1 2009).

(Collateral Estoppel)

A defense related to, but distinct from that of, *res judicata* is "collateral estoppel," or "issue preclusion," which may be asserted defensively by one who was not a party in the action in which the prior judgment was entered. *Hullett v. Cousin*, 204 Ariz. 292, 63 P.3d 1029 (2003); *Beltran v. Harrah's Arizona Corp.*, 220 Ariz. 29, 202 P.3d 494 (Ct. App. Div. 2 2008); *Corbett v. ManorCare of America, Inc.*, 213 Ariz. 618, 146 P.3d 1027 (Ct. App. Div. 2 2006); *Bridgestone/Firestone North America Tire, L.L.C. v. Naranjo*, 206 Ariz. 447, 79 P.3d 1206, Prod. Liab. Rep. (CCH) P 16845 (Ct. App. Div. 2 2003); *PFS v. Industrial Com'n of Arizona*, 191 Ariz. 274, 955 P.2d 30 (Ct. App. Div. 1 1997).

Collateral estoppel operates to preclude only those issues that were actually litigated and determined and only if that determination was essential. *Western Cable v. Industrial Com'n of Arizona*, 144 Ariz. 514, 698 P.2d 759 (Ct. App. Div. 1 1985). Issue preclusion may not be invoked when the issue was neither essential nor necessary to the prior judgment. *King v. Superior Court*, 138 Ariz. 147, 673 P.2d 787 (1983).

Generally *res judicata* but not collateral estoppel, applies to consent judgments. *Suttle v. Seely*, 94 Ariz. 161, 382 P.2d 570 (1963); Modern Views of State Courts as to Whether Consent Judgment is Entitled to Res Judicata or Collateral Estoppel Effect, 91 A.L.R.3d 1170.

A stipulated dismissal does not result in issue preclusion. *Chaney Bldg. Co. v. City of Tucson*, 148 Ariz. 571, 716 P.2d 28 (1986). Issue preclusion does not apply when there is some overriding consideration of fairness involved. *Ferris v. Hawkins*, 135 Ariz. 329, 660 P.2d 1256 (Ct. App. Div. 1 1983).

Application of the doctrine of collateral estoppel requires that the following conditions be present:

(1) that the issue in question was actually litigated in a previ-

ous proceeding;

(2) that there was a full and fair opportunity to litigate the issue;

(3) that there was a final decision on the merits;

(4) that resolution of the issue in question was essential to that decision; and,

(5) that there be a common identity of the parties.

Pettit v. Pettit, 218 Ariz. 529, 189 P.3d 1102 (Ct. App. Div. 1 2008); *Beltran v. Harrah's Arizona Corp.*, 220 Ariz. 29, 202 P.3d 494 (Ct. App. Div. 2 2008); *Corbett v. ManorCare of America, Inc.*, 213 Ariz. 618, 146 P.3d 1027 (Ct. App. Div. 2 2006); *Robert Schalkenbach Foundation v. Lincoln Foundation, Inc.*, 208 Ariz. 176, 91 P.3d 1019 (Ct. App. Div. 1 2004), as amended, (July 9, 2004); *Better Homes Const., Inc. v. Goldwater*, 203 Ariz. 295, 53 P.3d 1139 (Ct. App. Div. 1 2002), redesignated as opinion and publication ordered, (Sept. 19, 2002); *Brown v. Industrial Com'n of Arizona*, 199 Ariz. 521, 19 P.3d 1237 (Ct. App. Div. 2 2001); *Irby Const. Co. v. Arizona Dept. of Revenue*, 184 Ariz. 105, 907 P.2d 74 (Ct. App. Div. 1 1995).

When a prior court has ruled, on a motion *in limine*, that an issue cannot be presented, and the case subsequently settled, the third and fourth prerequisites for application of collateral estoppel are not satisfied. *Garcia v. General Motors Corp.*, 195 Ariz. 510, 990 P.2d 1069 (Ct. App. Div. 1 1999). Collateral estoppel does not bar a later action asserting claims alleged as affirmative defenses in a prior action because affirmative defenses are not claims. *Airfreight Exp. Ltd v. Evergreen Air Center, Inc.*, 215 Ariz. 103, 158 P.3d 232 (Ct. App. Div. 2 2007).

The final element for the application of the doctrine of collateral estoppel is the "common identity of parties," but such element may not be required depending on whether the doctrine is being invoked "offensively" or "defensively." *Campbell v. SZL Properties, Ltd.*, 204 Ariz. 221, 62 P.3d 966 (Ct. App. Div. 1 2003). "Offensive" use of the doctrine of collateral estoppel occurs when a plaintiff seeks to prevent the defendant from relitigating an issue the defendant previously litigated unsuccessfully against another party. *Campbell v. SZL Properties, Ltd.*, 204 Ariz. 221, 62 P.3d 966 (Ct. App. Div. 1 2003). "Defensive" use occurs when a defendant seeks to prevent a plaintiff from asserting a claim the plaintiff previously litigated against another party. *Campbell v. SZL Properties, Ltd.*, 204 Ariz. 221, 62 P.3d 966 (Ct. App. Div. 1 2003). If only the first four elements of collateral estoppel are present, Arizona permits defensive, but not offensive, use of the doctrine. *Campbell v. SZL Properties, Ltd.*, 204 Ariz. 221, 62 P.3d 966 (Ct. App. Div. 1 2003). *See also Bridgestone/Firestone North America Tire, L.L.C. v. Naranjo*, 206 Ariz. 447, 79 P.3d 1206,

Prod. Liab. Rep. (CCH) P 16845 (Ct. App. Div. 2 2003).

The doctrine of collateral estoppel is not applicable unless a final judgment was entered. *Elia v. Pifer*, 194 Ariz. 74, 977 P.2d 796 (Ct. App. Div. 1 1998). The requirement of a "final" judgment, however, does not necessarily require that the judgment be appealable, and a judgment entered in a contempt proceeding, which is not appealable, but is subject to review by special action, can have collateral estoppel effect. *Elia v. Pifer*, 194 Ariz. 74, 977 P.2d 796 (Ct. App. Div. 1 1998). Similarly, a dismissal without prejudice is not an adjudication on the merits and does not bar a second action asserting the same claims. *Airfreight Exp. Ltd v. Evergreen Air Center, Inc.*, 215 Ariz. 103, 158 P.3d 232 (Ct. App. Div. 2 2007). The defenses of claim preclusion and collateral estoppel may apply to decisions rendered by administrative agencies acting in a quasi-judicial capacity. *Smith v. CIGNA HealthPlan of Arizona*, 203 Ariz. 173, 52 P.3d 205, 19 I.E.R. Cas. (BNA) 41, 170 L.R.R.M. (BNA) 2884, 147 Lab. Cas. (CCH) P 59642, 120 A.L.R.5th 757 (Ct. App. Div. 2 2002); *Hawkins v. State, Dept. of Economic Sec.*, 183 Ariz. 100, 900 P.2d 1236, 68 Fair Empl. Prac. Cas. (BNA) 1178 (Ct. App. Div. 2 1995).

A judgment that is vacated pursuant to a settlement between the parties to it while it is on appeal can have no preclusive effect. *Campbell v. SZL Properties, Ltd.*, 204 Ariz. 221, 62 P.3d 966 (Ct. App. Div. 1 2003).

Moreover, even in cases where the technical requirements for application of collateral estoppel exist, courts will not preclude the litigation of issues when special circumstances exist where the party to be precluded was deprived of an adequate opportunity or incentive to obtain a full and fair adjudication in the initial action. *In re Marriage of Gibbs*, 227 Ariz. 403, 258 P.3d 221 (Ct. App. Div. 2 2011), review denied, (Nov. 29, 2011), citing *Smith v. CIGNA HealthPlan of Arizona*, 203 Ariz. 173, 52 P.3d 205, 19 I.E.R. Cas. (BNA) 41, 170 L.R.R.M. (BNA) 2884, 147 Lab. Cas. (CCH) P 59642, 120 A.L.R.5th 757 (Ct. App. Div. 2 2002); *Hullett v. Cousin*, 204 Ariz. 292, 63 P.3d 1029 (2003).

(Law of the Case)

Finally, a doctrine related to both claim preclusion and collateral estoppel is that of "law of the case." This doctrine generally provides that, if an appellate court has ruled upon a legal question and remanded the case for further proceedings, that ruling is binding in all subsequent proceedings in the trial court and in any subsequent appeal, absent an intervening change in the controlling case law. *Paul R. Peterson Const., Inc. v. Arizona State Carpenters Health and Welfare Trust Fund*, 179 Ariz. 474, 880 P.2d 694, 17 Employee Benefits Cas. (BNA) 2624 (Ct. App. Div. 1 1994).

The doctrine of "law of the case" is a rule of policy, however, not a rule of law. *Martinez v. Industrial Com'n of Arizona*, 192 Ariz. 176, 962 P.2d 903 (1998); *Dancing Sunshines Lounge v. Industrial Com'n of Arizona*, 149 Ariz. 480, 720 P.2d 81 (1986); *Associated Aviation Underwriters v. Wood*, 209 Ariz. 137, 98 P.3d 572 (Ct. App. Div. 2 2004); *Davis v. Davis*, 195 Ariz. 158, 985 P.2d 643 (Ct. App. Div. 1 1999). Many exceptions to the rule have arisen, and it will generally not be applied where there has been error in the first appellate decision which renders it manifestly erroneous or unjust, where the initial appellate decision is ambiguous, or where the issue was not actually decided in the first decision. *Martinez v. Industrial Com'n of Arizona*, 192 Ariz. 176, 962 P.2d 903 (1998); *Johnson v. Mofford*, 193 Ariz. 540, 975 P.2d 130 (Ct. App. Div. 1 1998).

At the trial court level, the doctrine of the law of the case is merely a practice that protects the ability of the court to build to its final judgment by cumulative rulings, with reconsideration or review postponed until after the judgment is rendered. *Zimmerman v. Shakman*, 204 Ariz. 231, 62 P.3d 976 (Ct. App. Div. 1 2003). The doctrine does not prevent a trial judge from reconsidering nonfinal rulings; nor does it prevent a different judge, sitting on the same case, from reconsidering a preceding judge's prior, nonfinal rulings. *Zimmerman v. Shakman*, 204 Ariz. 231, 62 P.3d 976 (Ct. App. Div. 1 2003).

25. *Statute of Frauds.* Arizona's version of the Statute of Frauds, A.R.S. § 44-101, requires that the following agreements be memorialized in writing to be enforceable:

(1) agreements in consideration of marriage;
(2) promises by executors or administrators;
(3) promises to answer for the debt, default or miscarriage of another (guaranty or surety);
(4) agreements not to be performed within one year or during a lifetime;
(5) sale of goods worth more than $500; and
(6) agreements concerning the sale of an interest in real property, or the lease of real property for more than one year.

26. *Statute of Limitations.* The statute of limitations is an affirmative defense that must be pled or it is waived. *Academy Life Ins. Co. v. Odiorne*, 165 Ariz. 188, 797 P.2d 727 (Ct. App. Div. 1 1990); *Lewis R. Pyle Memorial Hosp. v. Gila County*, 161 Ariz. 82, 775 P.2d 1146 (Ct. App. Div. 2 1989). It has been held, however, that waiver should not be found if the defense is raised before judgment and the defendant should be permitted to amend the answer to assert it. *Uyleman v. D.S. Rentco*, 194 Ariz. 300, 981 P.2d 1081 (Ct. App. Div. 1 1999); *Romo v. Reyes*, 26 Ariz. App.

374, 548 P.2d 1186 (Div. 2 1976). The statute of limitations may also be raised, and frequently is, by a motion to dismiss. *McCloud v. State, Ariz. Dept. of Public Safety*, 217 Ariz. 82, 170 P.3d 691 (Ct. App. Div. 2 2007); *Pritchard v. State*, 163 Ariz. 427, 788 P.2d 1178 (1990). A party does not waive the defense by filing a notice of appearance in the action. *O'Keefe v. Grenke*, 170 Ariz. 460, 825 P.2d 985, 16 U.C.C. Rep. Serv. 2d 746 (Ct. App. Div. 1 1992).

The various Arizona statutes of limitations, which can be found in Chapter 5 of Article 12 of the Arizona Revised Statutes, serve the important public policy of protecting defendants and the courts from stale claims and from the evidentiary problems such claims engender, and of protecting defendants from economic uncertainty. *Nolde v. Frankie*, 192 Ariz. 276, 964 P.2d 477, 129 Ed. Law Rep. 837 (1998); *Logerquist v. Danforth*, 188 Ariz. 16, 932 P.2d 281 (Ct. App. Div. 2 1996); *Floyd v. Donahue*, 186 Ariz. 409, 923 P.2d 875 (Ct. App. Div. 1 1996). In determining whether a claim is barred by the statute of limitations, four factors must be examined: (1) when the plaintiff's cause of action accrued; (2) what is the applicable statute of limitations; (3) when did the plaintiff file the claim; and (4) was the running of the statute of limitations tolled for any reason. *La Canada Hills Ltd. Partnership v. Kite*, 217 Ariz. 126, 171 P.3d 195 (Ct. App. Div. 2 2007); *Logerquist v. Danforth*, 188 Ariz. 16, 932 P.2d 281 (Ct. App. Div. 2 1996).

Whether a particular statute of limitations applies to any given cause of action is an issue of law. *Occhino v. Occhino*, 164 Ariz. 482, 793 P.2d 1149 (Ct. App. Div. 2 1990). For tort actions, Arizona generally follows the "discovery rule," under which a cause of action in tort only arises when the plaintiff knows, or by the exercise of reasonable diligence should have known, of the defendant's tortious conduct. *Ritchie v. Krasner*, 221 Ariz. 288, 211 P.3d 1272 (Ct. App. Div. 1 2009); *Logerquist v. Danforth*, 188 Ariz. 16, 932 P.2d 281 (Ct. App. Div. 2 1996), (rejected on other grounds by *Logerquist v. Danforth*, 188 Ariz. 16, 932 P.2d 281 (Ct. App. Div. 2 1996); *Floyd v. Donahue*, 186 Ariz. 409, 923 P.2d 875 (Ct. App. Div. 1 1996); *Angus Medical Co. v. Digital Equipment Corp.*, 173 Ariz. 159, 840 P.2d 1024, 17 U.C.C. Rep. Serv. 2d 724 (Ct. App. Div. 1 1992); *Cooney v. Phoenix Newspapers, Inc.*, 160 Ariz. 139, 770 P.2d 1185 (Ct. App. Div. 2 1989). The purpose of a statute of limitations is to protect defendants and courts from stale claims where plaintiffs have slept on their rights. *Doe v. Roe*, 191 Ariz. 313, 955 P.2d 951 (1998). One does not sleep on his or her rights with respect to an unknown cause of action, and the presumed invalidity of a claim allowed to become stale is not present in the case where the injured plaintiff has no knowledge that such a claim exists. *Doe v. Roe*, 191 Ariz. 313, 955 P.2d 951 (1998).

In a tort action, the applicable statute of limitations, absent an enforceable agreement between the parties tolling it, is two years, and it is the plaintiff's burden to sustain any claim that the running of the statute has been tolled. *Doe v. Roe*, 191 Ariz. 313, 955 P.2d 951 (1998). Negligent misrepresentation is a claim which sounds in tort, and such claims are subject to this statute. *Hullett v. Cousin*, 204 Ariz. 292, 63 P.3d 1029 (2003).

The "discovery rule" also has been applied to the provisions of former A.R.S. § 12-502(B), which then tolled the statute of limitations for one year for the "disability" of imprisonment. *Vega v. Morris*, 183 Ariz. 526, 905 P.2d 535 (Ct. App. Div. 1 1995), opinion approved of, 184 Ariz. 461, 910 P.2d 6 (1996). Because of the particular wording of that statute, however, the prisoner's period of "disability" ended when the prisoner discovered, or reasonably should have discovered, the *right* to bring a cause of action, rather than the *conduct* that gave rise to the cause of action. *Vega v. Morris*, 183 Ariz. 526, 905 P.2d 535 (Ct. App. Div. 1 1995), opinion approved of, 184 Ariz. 461, 910 P.2d 6 (1996). In 1996, presumably in response to *Vega* decision, the Arizona Legislature "deleted" A.R.S. § 12-502(B) in its entirety.

The "discovery rule" requires only the discovery of the facts which give rise to a cause of action rather than discovery of the legal significance of those facts. *Doe v. Roe*, 191 Ariz. 313, 955 P.2d 951 (1998). For the statute to commence to run, it is not necessary that the claimant know *all* the facts; all that is required is that the claimant know enough facts as would prompt a reasonable person to investigate and discover the full extent of the claim. *Doe v. Roe*, 191 Ariz. 313, 955 P.2d 951 (1998). A defendant's wrongful concealment of facts that prevents the plaintiff from detecting the defendant's wrongful act is a separate and distinct theory for tolling the running of the statute of limitations. *Logerquist v. Danforth*, 188 Ariz. 16, 932 P.2d 281 (Ct. App. Div. 2 1996). While evidence of such fraudulent concealment may impact upon the application and analysis of the discovery rule, it is not a prerequisite to its operation. *Logerquist v. Danforth*, 188 Ariz. 16, 932 P.2d 281 (Ct. App. Div. 2 1996).

Under the discovery rule, for the statute of limitations to commence to run, the plaintiff must have also sustained actual, appreciable and non-speculative damages, rather than the threat of future harm. *CDT, Inc. v. Addison, Roberts & Ludwig, C.P.A., P.C.*, 198 Ariz. 173, 7 P.3d 979 (Ct. App. Div. 2 2000). This principle frequently comes into play in negligence claims against professionals, such as lawyers and accountants. *CDT, Inc. v. Addison, Roberts & Ludwig, C.P.A., P.C.*, 198 Ariz. 173, 7 P.3d 979 (Ct. App. Div. 2 2000).

The one-year statute of limitations in A.R.S. § 12-541(5) for liabilities created by statute applies only where a cause of action and liability would not exist but for a statute. *Andrews ex rel. Woodard v. Eddie's Place, Inc.*, 199 Ariz. 240, 16 P.3d 801 (Ct. App. Div. 2 2000). If a tort cause of action and liability exists at common law, then the applicable statute of limitations is the two-year statute of A.R.S. § 12-541(1), even if the cause of action has also been codified in a statute. *Andrews ex rel. Woodard v. Eddie's Place, Inc.*, 199 Ariz. 240, 16 P.3d 801 (Ct. App. Div. 2 2000). Causes of action for the negligent performance of, or the negligent failure to perform, an act required by statute, however, are subject to the one-year statute specified in A.R.S. § 12-541(5) rather than the two-year statute generally applicable to negligence actions. *Owens v. City of Phoenix*, 180 Ariz. 402, 884 P.2d 1100 (Ct. App. Div. 1 1994).

In legal malpractice actions, the statute of limitations begins to run when a cause of action accrues, which requires not only negligence but damage as well. Such claims are also subject to the "discovery rule," which in this context applies not only to the discovery of the facts giving rise to the claim of negligence, but to the discovery of causation and damage as well. *Commercial Union Ins. Co. v. Lewis and Roca*, 183 Ariz. 250, 902 P.2d 1354 (Ct. App. Div. 1 1995). A cause of action for legal malpractice, accordingly, accrues when the client both:

(1) has sustained appreciable, non-speculative harm as the result of such malpractice; and

(2) knows, or in the exercise of reasonable diligence, should know, that the harm or damage was the result of the attorney's negligence. *Kiley v. Jennings, Strouss & Salmon*, 187 Ariz. 136, 927 P.2d 796 (Ct. App. Div. 1 1996); *Reed v. Mitchell & Timbanard, P.C.*, 183 Ariz. 313, 903 P.2d 621 (Ct. App. Div. 1 1995); *Commercial Union Ins. Co. v. Lewis and Roca*, 183 Ariz. 250, 902 P.2d 1354 (Ct. App. Div. 1 1995).

Minor damages which are not the loss anticipated to result from the malpractice, or which are incurred in attempting to avoid damage, however, may not be sufficient to commence the running of the statute. *Myers v. Wood*, 174 Ariz. 434, 850 P.2d 672 (Ct. App. Div. 2 1992). In the majority of malpractice cases outside the litigation context, the damage or injury occurs contemporaneously with the malpractice. *Keonjian v. Olcott*, 216 Ariz. 563, 169 P.3d 927 (Ct. App. Div. 2 2007).

Where the claimed malpractice occurred during the course of litigation, the cause of action accrues when the plaintiff knew or reasonably should have known of the malpractice *and* when the plaintiff's damages are certain and not contingent on the outcome of an appeal. *Lansford v. Harris*, 174 Ariz. 413, 850 P.2d 126 (Ct.

App. Div. 1 1992). The claim does not accrue until an adverse judgment becomes final, either upon the rendering of the final appellate decision, or the expiration of any available period for taking an appeal. *Lansford v. Harris*, 174 Ariz. 413, 850 P.2d 126 (Ct. App. Div. 1 1992).

Where there is an appeal that is resolved by the Court of Appeals, and no petition for review by the Arizona Supreme Court is filed, the appellate process is not completed, and the statute of limitations on any malpractice that may have occurred during the course of that litigation does not begin to run, until the Court of Appeals issues its formal mandate which brings the appeal to its formal, final end. *Joel Erik Thompson, Ltd. v. Holder*, 192 Ariz. 348, 965 P.2d 82 (Ct. App. Div. 1 1998), as amended, (July 22, 1998).

The final judgment rule applies where the claimed malpractice occurred during the course of a criminal case as well; the cause of action does not accrue, and the statute of limitations does not begin to run, until the criminal proceedings are finally resolved favorably to the criminal defendant, either through direct appeal or through post-conviction relief proceedings. *Glaze v. Larsen*, 207 Ariz. 26, 83 P.3d 26 (2004). The final judgment rule will not necessarily apply, however, in situations where the litigation in which the malpractice allegedly occurred was settled. *Althaus v. Cornelio*, 203 Ariz. 597, 58 P.3d 973 (Ct. App. Div. 2 2002).

Claimed malpractice which occurs during the course of a non-adversarial bankruptcy proceeding does not take place "during the course of litigation" for purposes of applying this rule. *Cannon v. Hirsch Law Office, P.C.*, 222 Ariz. 171, 213 P.3d 320 (Ct. App. Div. 1 2009).

The statute of limitations for medical malpractice cases is two (2) years from the date the cause of action accrues. Such claims are subject to the "discovery rule," and the cause of action accrues when the plaintiff knew, or by the exercise of reasonable diligence should have known, of the facts which give rise to the malpractice claim. *Walk v. Ring*, 202 Ariz. 310, 44 P.3d 990 (2002); *Little v. State*, 225 Ariz. 466, 240 P.3d 861, 261 Ed. Law Rep. 835 (Ct. App. Div. 2 2010), review denied, (Apr. 19, 2011) (resolution of a complaint to the Arizona Medical Board is not relevant to the statute of limitations inquiry).

In professional negligence cases, however, the running of the statute of limitations is not automatically triggered each time a professional's services have failed to produce the desired result or have brought about an adverse result. *Walk v. Ring*, 202 Ariz. 310, 44 P.3d 990 (2002). While it is ordinarily sufficient when the plaintiff is aware of an injury and its causative agent, summary judgment is warranted only if the plaintiff's failure to go forward and investigate is not reasonably justified. *Walk v. Ring*, 202 Ariz. 310, 44 P.3d 990 (2002). The prospective plaintiff must have knowledge that would put a reasonable patient or client on notice to investigate whether the injury might be attributable to negligence on the part of the professional. *Walk v. Ring*, 202 Ariz. 310, 44 P.3d 990 (2002).

The "discovery rule" also applies to claims against public entities and employees, and the 180-day period for filing notice of such claims prescribed by Arizona's current "claims statute," A.R.S. § 12-821.01, does not begin to run until the claimant discovers, or should have discovered by the exercise of reasonable diligence, that the claimant's injury was caused by a public entity's or employee's negligent conduct. *Stulce v. Salt River Project Agr. Imp. and Power Dist.*, 197 Ariz. 87, 3 P.3d 1007 (Ct. App. Div. 1 1999). Because that statute defines the term "public entity" to include "any political subdivision of this state," it applies to claims against the Salt River Project Agricultural Improvement and Power District, which is, by statute, a "political subdivision" of the State of Arizona. *Stulce v. Salt River Project Agr. Imp. and Power Dist.*, 197 Ariz. 87, 3 P.3d 1007 (Ct. App. Div. 1 1999). This 180-day period may be tolled, however, by the doctrine of equitable tolling, which requires a showing of excusable neglect and/or that the defendant improperly caused the claimant to delay in submitting the notice. *Kosman v. State*, 199 Ariz. 184, 16 P.3d 211 (Ct. App. Div. 1 2000). *See also* the discussion of this statutory provision in Section 5 of the *Authors' Comments* under Rule 3.

A cause of action on a written contract accrues at the time of breach. *Enyart v. Transamerica Ins. Co.*, 195 Ariz. 71, 985 P.2d 556 (Ct. App. Div. 1,1998); *Angus Medical Co. v. Digital Equipment Corp.*, 173 Ariz. 159, 840 P.2d 1024, 17 U.C.C. Rep. Serv. 2d 724 (Ct. App. Div. 1 1992). *But see*, *HSL Linda Gardens Properties, Ltd. v. Freeman*, 176 Ariz. 206, 859 P.2d 1339 (Ct. App. Div. 2 1993) (general rule not applied). The applicable statute of limitations for actions or contracts is six (6) years for contracts executed within Arizona and four (4) years for contracts executed outside the state. *See*, A.R.S. §§ 12-548 and 12-544(3), respectively. An action for negligent performance of a contract, which sounds exclusively in tort, is not one "based on a contract" for purposes of determining the appropriate statute of limitations to apply. *Fry's Food Stores of Arizona, Inc. v. Mather and Associates, Inc.*, 183 Ariz. 89, 900 P.2d 1225 (Ct. App. Div. 1 1995).

Similarly, a first-party "bad faith" claim against an insurer for failure or refusal to settle a liability claim against its insured is governed by the two-year "tort" statute of limitations set forth in A.R.S. § 12-542. *Taylor v. State Farm Mut. Auto. Ins. Co.*, 185 Ariz. 174, 913 P.2d 1092 (1996). Such a claim does not accrue, however, until a judgment against the insured on the liability claim becomes final or non-appealable. *Taylor v. State Farm Mut. Auto. Ins. Co.*, 185 Ariz. 174, 913 P.2d 1092 (1996).

While the statutory limitations period for actions arising out of a written contract is six years, under A.R.S. § 20-1115(A)(3), a fire insurance policy may require that the insured file an action within a shorter period, so long as the statutory limitations period is not shortened to less than one year. *Nangle v. Farmers Ins. Co. of Arizona*, 205 Ariz. 517, 73 P.3d 1252 (Ct. App. Div. 1 2003). This is consistent with the general rule that contractual provisions which specify the period during which an action under the contract must be brought are enforceable. *Decca Design Build, Inc. v. American Auto. Ins. Co.*, 206 Ariz. 301, 77 P.3d 1251 (Ct. App. Div. 1 2003), as amended, (Oct. 7, 2003).

The prevailing doctrine had been that the "discovery rule" did not apply to actions for breach of contract and that, in such actions, the statute of limitations ran from the date of the breach of contract rather than from the date damage resulting therefrom was incurred. *HSL Linda Gardens Properties, Ltd. v. Freeman*, 176 Ariz. 206, 859 P.2d 1339 (Ct. App. Div. 2 1993). Thus, a contract claim on a promise to pay an obligation "when convenient" or "when able" was found to accrue when the debtor was out of debt and able to pay the obligation as a matter of fact, whether or not the creditor was aware of that fact at the time. *Estate of Page v. Litzenburg*, 177 Ariz. 84, 865 P.2d 128 (Ct. App. Div. 1 1993).

In certain circumstances, however, the statute was deemed to run only from the date damage was suffered because to require that an action be brought before significant damage is incurred may only prompt unnecessary litigation and entail the resolution of the difficult question of the present value of the risk of future harm that may or may not occur. *HSL Linda Gardens Properties, Ltd. v. Freeman*, 176 Ariz. 206, 859 P.2d 1339 (Ct. App. Div. 2 1993) (in the context of a covenant not to sell land with encumbrances, cause of action accrues for purposes of the limitations period either from the date the plaintiff discovered or reasonably should have discovered the breach or from the time the plaintiff was damaged by the breach); *see also Myers v. Wood*, 174 Ariz. 434, 850 P.2d 672 (Ct. App. Div. 2 1992).

The Arizona Supreme Court held, however, that the problem of stale claims was no more acute in the case of contract claims than it was in the case of tort claims, where the "discovery rule" does apply, and that the "discovery rule" should be applied to contract actions governed by A.R.S. § 12-548 as well. *Gust, Rosenfeld & Henderson v. Prudential Ins. Co. of America*, 182 Ariz. 586, 898 P.2d 964 (1995). In contract actions, accordingly, as in tort actions, the statute of limitations will not commence to run until the plaintiff knows or in the exercise of reasonable diligence should have known that it has suffered injury as a consequence of a breach of contract. *Gust, Rosenfeld & Henderson v. Prudential Ins. Co. of America*, 182 Ariz. 586, 898 P.2d 964 (1995).

Under Arizona's " Little Miller Act," A.R.S. §§ 34-221 to 34-226, and particularly A.R.S. § 34-223(B), a suit against a payment and performance bond on a publicly funded construction project must be commenced within one (1) year from the date on which the claimant performed the last of the labor, or supplied the last of the materials, for the project. *R.E. Monks Const. Co. v. Aetna Cas. & Sur. Co.*, 189 Ariz. 575, 944 P.2d 517 (Ct. App. Div. 1 1997).

Under A.R.S. § 12–552(A), claims for defective design or construction of improvements on property are barred if filed more than eight (8) years after substantial completion of the improvements. *Evans Withycombe, Inc. v. Western Innovations, Inc.*, 215 Ariz. 237, 159 P.3d 547 (Ct. App. Div. 1 2006). That statute does not apply, however, to a third-party complaint filed by a contractor asserting common law indemnity claims against subcontractors on the construction. *Evans Withycombe, Inc. v. Western Innovations, Inc.*, 215 Ariz. 237, 159 P.3d 547 (Ct. App. Div. 1 2006).

The statute of limitations for securities fraud claims, A.R.S. § 44-2004(B), provides that such a claim is barred "unless brought within two years after discovery of the fraudulent action on which the liability is based, or after the discovery should have been made by the exercise of reasonable diligence." Because damage is not an element of a securities fraud claim, the only thing that needs to be discovered is the alleged "fraudulent practice," and the statute commences to run from the date when it is, or should have been, discovered. *Aaron v. Fromkin*, 196 Ariz. 224, 994 P.2d 1039 (Ct. App. Div. 1 2000).

The statute of limitations pertaining to domestic judgments, A.R.S. § 12-1551(B), provides that execution or other process may not be issued upon a judgment after the expiration of five years from the date of its entry unless the judgment is renewed. In applying this provision and its predecessors to judgments payable in installments, such as judgments for child support or for alimony, etc., the rule has consistently been that the five-year limitations period begins to run from the period fixed for each installment as it becomes due. *Johnson v. Johnson*, 195 Ariz. 389, 988 P.2d 621 (Ct. App. Div. 1 1999).

An action to enforce a foreign judgment is subject to the four-year statute of limitations prescribed in A.R.S. § 12-544(3), even if the judgment has been domesticated pursuant to the procedures set forth in the Uniform Enforcement of Foreign Judgments Act, A.R.S. §§ 12-1701 *et seq. Citibank (South Dakota), N.A. v. Phifer*, 181 Ariz. 5, 887 P.2d 5 (Ct. App. Div. 2 1994). Arizona may apply its own statute of limitations to the enforcement of foreign judgments, even if it operates to bar the enforcement of them, without transgressing the Full Faith and Credit Clause of the United States Constitution. *Citibank (South Dakota), N.A. v. Phifer*, 181 Ariz. 5, 887 P.2d 5 (Ct. App. Div. 2 1994).

In cases where a choice of law as to which state's statute of limitations should be applied must be made, Arizona will now follow the approach of Section 142 of the *Restatement (Second) of Conflict of Laws*, and apply the statute of the state with the most significant relationship to the parties and the occurrence which gave rise to the litigation. *DeLoach v. Alfred*, 192 Ariz. 28, 960 P.2d 628 (1998).

The statute of limitations applicable to adverse condemnation actions is the one-year statute in A.R.S. § 12-821, which applies to suits against public entities or employees, and not the ten-year statute in A.R.S. § 12-526(A), which applies to actions to recover lands in the possession of another. *Flood Control Dist. of Maricopa County v. Gaines*, 202 Ariz. 248, 43 P.3d 196 (Ct. App. Div. 1 2002).

The defense of the statute of limitations is not favored, and where two constructions are possible, the one which favors the longer limitations period is preferred. *O'Malley v. Sims*, 51 Ariz. 155, 75 P.2d 50, 115 A.L.R. 634 (1938); *Keonjian v. Olcott*, 216 Ariz. 563, 169 P.3d 927 (Ct. App. Div. 2 2007); *Glaze v. Larsen*, 203 Ariz. 399, 55 P.3d 93 (Ct. App. Div. 2 2002), opinion vacated, 207 Ariz. 26, 83 P.3d 26 (2004); *Third & Catalina Associates v. City of Phoenix*, 182 Ariz. 203, 895 P.2d 115, 63 A.L.R.5th 879 (Ct. App. Div. 1 1994); *Guertin v. Dixon*, 177 Ariz. 40, 864 P.2d 1072 (Ct. App. Div. 2 1993). In fact, the Supreme Court declared unconstitutional, as an abrogation of the right to bring an action to recover damages for injuries, the provisions of A.R.S. § 12-551, which stated that no product liability action could be brought more than twelve (12) years after the product in question was first sold for use or consumption. *Hazine v. Montgomery Elevator Co.*, 176 Ariz. 340, 861 P.2d 625, Prod. Liab. Rep. (CCH) P 13676, 30 A.L.R.5th 729 (1993).

A defendant who raises the bar of the statute of limitations has the burden of establishing that the claim is barred by the statute. *Kiley v. Jennings, Strouss & Salmon*, 187 Ariz. 136, 927 P.2d 796 (Ct. App. Div. 1 1996). Once the defendant has made a *prima facie* showing, however, that the plaintiff's claim is untimely, the burden shifts to the plaintiff to establish that the "discovery rule" operates to delay commencement of the running of the statute, or that the running of the statute was otherwise tolled. *Doe v. Roe*, 191 Ariz. 313, 955 P.2d 951 (1998).

A defendant may not, however, use the statute of limitations as a shield for inequity, and the Arizona courts have recognized equitable exceptions to the application of the statute when necessary to prevent injustice. *Nolde v. Frankie*, 192 Ariz. 276, 964 P.2d 477, 129 Ed. Law Rep. 837 (1998); *McCloud v. State, Ariz. Dept. of Public Safety*, 217 Ariz. 82, 170 P.3d 691 (Ct. App. Div. 2 2007). One such exception applies when a defendant induces a plaintiff to forbear from filing suit. *Nolde v. Frankie*, 192 Ariz. 276, 964 P.2d 477, 129 Ed. Law Rep. 837 (1998); *McCloud v. State, Ariz. Dept. of Public Safety*, 217 Ariz. 82, 170 P.3d 691 (Ct. App. Div. 2 2007); *Roer v. Buckeye Irr. Co.*, 167 Ariz. 545, 809 P.2d 970 (Ct. App. Div. 2 1990).

To successfully invoke such an estoppel from inducement, a plaintiff must establish four factors:

(1) the plaintiff must identify specific promises, threats or inducements by the defendant that prevented the plaintiff from filing suit,

(2) the defendant's promises, threats or inducements must have actually induced the plaintiff to forbear from filing suit,

(3) the defendant's conduct must have *reasonably* caused the plaintiff to forbear filing the action in a timely fashion, and

(4) the plaintiff must file suit within a reasonable time after the termination of the conduct warranting estoppel.

Nolde v. Frankie, 192 Ariz. 276, 964 P.2d 477, 129 Ed. Law Rep. 837 (1998).

The running of the statute of limitations may also be tolled where the plaintiff presents evidence that the defendant concealed the facts giving rise to the cause of action and thereby prevented the plaintiff from filing the claim in a timely manner. *Mohave Elec. Co-op., Inc. v. Byers*, 189 Ariz. 292, 942 P.2d 451 (Ct. App. Div. 1 1997). If fraudulent concealment is established, the plaintiff is relieved of the duty of diligent investigation required by the discovery rule, and the statute of limitations is tolled until the concealment is discovered or reasonably should have been discovered. *Walk v. Ring*, 202 Ariz. 310, 44 P.3d 990 (2002).

In addition, constructive fraud is sufficient to toll the running of the statute of limitations until the plaintiff either knows, or through the exercise of due diligence should have known, of the fraud. *Lasley v. Helms*, 179 Ariz. 589, 880 P.2d 1135 (Ct. App. Div. 1 1994). Constructive fraud is defined as a breach of a legal or equitable duty which, without regard to the guilt or intent of the person charged, the law declares fraudulent. *Lasley v. Helms*, 179 Ariz. 589, 880 P.2d 1135 (Ct. App. Div. 1 1994). Constructive fraud requires the existence of a confidential relationship, but does not require a showing of either intent to deceive or dishonesty of purpose. *Lasley v. Helms*, 179 Ariz. 589, 880 P.2d 1135 (Ct. App. Div. 1 1994).

Finally, equitable tolling applies when the plaintiff is excusably ignorant of the limitations period and the defendant would not be prejudiced by the late filing. *Kyles v. Contractors/Engineers Supply, Inc.*, 190 Ariz. 403, 949 P.2d 63 (Ct. App. Div. 2 1997). Unlike equitable estoppel, equitable tolling does not require the plaintiff to show any misconduct on the defendant's part. *Kyles v. Contractors/Engineers Supply, Inc.*, 190 Ariz. 403, 949 P.2d 63 (Ct. App. Div. 2 1997). Whether to apply the equitable tolling doctrine is an issue committed to the trial court's discretion. *McCloud v. State, Ariz. Dept. of Public Safety*, 217 Ariz. 82, 170 P.3d 691 (Ct. App. Div. 2 2007).

A.R.S. §§ 12-1363(A), (B), which concerns actions brought by purchasers of single or multiunit dwellings, requires the purchasers/plaintiffs provide the seller, before instituting suit, with a written notice specifying in reasonable detail the basis of the action. This statute provides that the provision of such a notice tolls any applicable statute of limitations until ninety (90) days after the seller receives it. A.R.S. § 12-1363(J). The requirements of this statute, A.R.S. §§ 12-1361 *et seq.*, are discussed in more detail in Section 5 of the *Authors' Comments* under Rule 3.

Arizona's wrongful death statutes endow minors with their own cause of action. Accordingly, the provisions of A.R.S. § 12-502, which toll the running of the statute of limitations during the period of minority, apply to such a claim. *Porter v. Triad of Arizona (L.P.)*, 203 Ariz. 230, 52 P.3d 799 (Ct. App. Div. 1 2002). That statute, however, has no application to claims *against* minors, and does not operate to toll the statute of limitations because the defendant was a minor at the time the cause of action accrued. *Montano v. Browning*, 202 Ariz. 544, 48 P.3d 494 (Ct. App. Div. 2 2002). It is possible to both commence and serve an action against a minor even though no guardian for that minor has been appointed. *Montano v. Browning*, 202 Ariz. 544, 48 P.3d 494 (Ct. App. Div. 2 2002).

The state is not subject to the running of the statute of limitations. A political subdivision of the state, such as a county or a municipality, is similarly exempt from the running of the statute of limitations if it acts in a governmental capacity as an agent of the state in a matter of state-wide concern, or performs a governmental function akin to that of the state. *Tucson Unified School Dist. v. Owens-Corning Fiberglas Corp.*, 174 Ariz. 336, 849

P.2d 790, 82 Ed. Law Rep. 245 (1993), as amended, (May 7, 1993); *Pima County v. State*, 174 Ariz. 402, 850 P.2d 115 (Ct. App. Div. 1 1992).

In determining which state's statute of limitations to apply, in cases where that is an issue, Arizona follows the approach of Section 142 of the *Restatement (Second) of Conflict of Laws*, which permits the forum state to apply its own statute to a claim that would be barred by the statute with a more significant relationship to the dispute if application of the forum state's statute would serve a substantial interest of the forum state. *Jackson v. Chandler*, 204 Ariz. 135, 61 P.3d 17 (2003). Applying this analysis, Arizona was held to have a sufficient interest to warrant application of its own statute of limitations, rather than California's, to a personal injury action arising out of a motor vehicle accident which occurred in Arizona, but in which both drivers were California residents and domiciliaries, because Arizona has an interest in deterring wrongful conduct in the state, and in providing a forum to adjudicate disputes when such wrongful conduct occurs. *Jackson v. Chandler*, 204 Ariz. 135, 61 P.3d 17 (2003).

27. *Waiver.* "Waiver" is an intentional and voluntary relinquishment, express or inferred, of a known right, and must be shown by clear and convincing evidence. *Ray v. Mangum*, 163 Ariz. 329, 788 P.2d 62 (1989); *Minjares v. State*, 223 Ariz. 54, 219 P.3d 264 (Ct. App. Div. 1 2009); *Havasupai Tribe of Havasupai Reservation v. Arizona Bd. of Regents*, 220 Ariz. 214, 204 P.3d 1063, 243 Ed. Law Rep. 889 (Ct. App. Div. 1 2008); *Meineke v. Twin City Fire Ins. Co.*, 181 Ariz. 576, 892 P.2d 1365 (Ct. App. Div. 1 1994). It is not synonymous with estoppel. *Certainteed Corp. v. United Pacific Ins. Co.*, 158 Ariz. 273, 762 P.2d 560 (Ct. App. Div. 2 1988). A waiver need not be in writing. *Angus Medical Co. v. Digital Equipment Corp.*, 173 Ariz. 159, 840 P.2d 1024, 17 U.C.C. Rep. Serv. 2d 724 (Ct. App. Div. 1 1992).

Waiver generally requires a finding of intentional relinquishment of a known right or of conduct which would warrant such an inference. *Minjares v. State*, 223 Ariz. 54, 219 P.3d 264 (Ct. App. Div. 1 2009). Waiver also is generally an issue of fact and will not be set aside unless clearly erroneous. *Minjares v. State*, 223 Ariz. 54, 219 P.3d 264 (Ct. App. Div. 1 2009). *But see*, *City Of Phoenix v. Fields*, 219 Ariz. 568, 201 P.3d 529 (2009) (in case dealing with notices of claim against governmental entity, the Arizona Supreme Court found waiver as a matter of law based on conduct of governmental entity as supported by extensive litigation record).

28. *Product Misuse.* A.R.S. § 12-683(3) recognizes an affirmative defense of "product misuse" in product liability actions. The

Arizona Supreme Court reconciled a divergence of views between two Divisions of the Arizona Court of Appeals, and held that the "product misuse" defense is encompassed within principles of comparative fault and no longer constitutes an "all or nothing" defense. *Jimenez v. Sears, Roebuck and Co.*, 183 Ariz. 399, 904 P.2d 861, Prod. Liab. Rep. (CCH) P 14382 (1995).

29. *Comparative Negligence.* In 1984, Arizona adopted a modified version of the Uniform Contribution Among Tortfeasors Act, A.R.S. §§ 12-2501 *et seq.* As originally adopted, the Act, *inter alia*, adopted a comparative negligence rule for personal injury actions involving joint tortfeasors and abolished, to a limited extent, the prior common law rule which prohibited claims of contribution among joint tortfeasors. Each joint tortfeasor was made responsible for that tortfeasor's *pro rata* share of the entire liability, which was to be allocated according to "relative degrees of fault." A.R.S. § 12-2501. A right of contribution against other joint tortfeasors was created in favor of any tortfeasor who "has paid," or become responsible for, more than that tortfeasor's "pro rata share of the common liability." A.R.S. § 12-2501(B).

A 1987 amendment to the statute abolished the doctrine of joint and several liability among joint tortfeasors, except in those cases where the parties were acting in concert, where one party was acting as an agent or servant of another party, and in other cases relating to hazardous wastes or substances, or solid waste disposal sites. A.R.S. § 12-2504; *Yslava v. Hughes Aircraft Co.*, 188 Ariz. 380, 936 P.2d 1274, 45 Env't. Rep. Cas. (BNA) 1315 (1997); *Bill Alexander Ford, Lincoln Mercury, Inc. v. Casa Ford, Inc.*, 187 Ariz. 616, 931 P.2d 1126, Prod. Liab. Rep. (CCH) P 14727 (Ct. App. Div. 1 1996). (The exception for cases relating to hazardous wastes or substances, or solid waste disposal sites, was repealed in 1997, purportedly retroactively, and liability in these types of cases is now several as well.) It correspondingly limited the potential availability of a claim for contribution against another joint tortfeasor pursuant to A.R.S. § 12-2501. By abolishing joint and several liability, and by limiting recovery against any defendant to that percentage of the plaintiff's total damages which represents that defendant's relative degree of fault, the statute virtually insures that the conditions for claiming contribution cannot occur. *PAM Transport v. Freightliner Corp.*, 182 Ariz. 132, 893 P.2d 1295 (1995); *City of Tucson v. Superior Court In and For County of Pima*, 161 Ariz. 441, 778 P.2d 1337 (Ct. App. Div. 2 1989), opinion approved of, 165 Ariz. 236, 798 P.2d 374 (1990); *Cella Barr Associates, Inc. v. Cohen*, 177 Ariz. 480, 868 P.2d 1063 (Ct. App. Div. 1 1994); *Neil v. Kavena*, 176 Ariz. 93, 859 P.2d 203 (Ct. App. Div. 1 1993); *Roland v. Bernstein*, 171 Ariz. 96, 828 P.2d 1237 (Ct. App. Div. 2 1991).

The statute did not, however, change the law with regard to

vicarious liability. *Law v. Verde Valley Medical Center*, 217 Ariz. 92, 170 P.3d 701 (Ct. App. Div. 1 2007). An alleged tortfeasor and a party potentially liable vicariously for that person's tortious conduct are not joint tortfeasors under Arizona law. *Law v. Verde Valley Medical Center*, 217 Ariz. 92, 170 P.3d 701 (Ct. App. Div. 1 2007). When a judgment on the merits is entered in favor of a person for whose conduct a party is vicariously liable, there is no fault to impute or allocate. *Law v. Verde Valley Medical Center*, 217 Ariz. 92, 170 P.3d 701 (Ct. App. Div. 1 2007).

Guiding this statutory revision was a desire to increase the fairness of the tort system for both plaintiffs and defendants, and to eliminate the harshness of an all-or-nothing contributory negligence defense. *Hutcherson v. City of Phoenix*, 192 Ariz. 51, 961 P.2d 449 (1998). The 1987 amendments also broadened the scope of torts subject to the rules of comparative fault beyond those grounded on theories of negligence, and are fully applicable in product liability actions. *Jimenez v. Sears, Roebuck and Co.*, 183 Ariz. 399, 904 P.2d 861, Prod. Liab. Rep. (CCH) P 14382 (1995); *Zuern By and Through Zuern v. Ford Motor Co.*, 188 Ariz. 486, 937 P.2d 676 (Ct. App. Div. 2 1996). In such actions, accordingly, there must be an allocation of fault to each person or entity in the chain of distribution of the allegedly defective product. *State Farm Ins. Companies v. Premier Manufactured Systems, Inc.*, 213 Ariz. 419, 142 P.3d 1232, Prod. Liab. Rep. (CCH) P 17517 (Ct. App. Div. 1 2006), opinion aff'd, 217 Ariz. 222, 172 P.3d 410 (2007).

The amendment applies to actions filed on or after December 31, 1987, and has been held to be constitutional. *Jimenez v. Sears, Roebuck and Co.*, 183 Ariz. 399, 904 P.2d 861, Prod. Liab. Rep. (CCH) P 14382 (1995); *Larsen v. Nissan Motor Corp. in U.S.A.*, 194 Ariz. 142, 978 P.2d 119 (Ct. App. Div. 2 1998); *Lerma v. Keck*, 186 Ariz. 228, 921 P.2d 28 (Ct. App. Div. 1 1996); *Church v. Rawson Drug & Sundry Co.*, 173 Ariz. 342, 842 P.2d 1355 (Ct. App. Div. 1 1992). Under the Act as amended, Arizona follows a "pure comparative fault" regime, under which the trier of fact considers and apportions the fault of all persons who contributed to the harm to the plaintiff, and each tortfeasor is responsible only for his or her percentage of fault, and no more. *Hutcherson v. City of Phoenix*, 192 Ariz. 51, 961 P.2d 449 (1998); *Sanchez v. City of Tucson*, 191 Ariz. 128, 953 P.2d 168 (1998); *McKillip v. Smitty's Super Valu, Inc.*, 190 Ariz. 61, 945 P.2d 372 (Ct. App. Div. 1 1997); *Zuern By and Through Zuern v. Ford Motor Co.*, 188 Ariz. 486, 937 P.2d 676 (Ct. App. Div. 2 1996); *Standard Chartered PLC v. Price Waterhouse*, 190 Ariz. 6, 945 P.2d 317 (Ct. App. Div. 1 1996), as corrected on denial of reconsideration, (Jan. 13, 1997); *Rosner v. Denim & Diamonds, Inc.*, 188 Ariz. 431, 937 P.2d 353 (Ct. App. Div. 2 1996); *Natseway v. City of*

Tempe, 184 Ariz. 374, 909 P.2d 441 (Ct. App. Div. 1 1995). The trier of fact may even consider the fault of persons who are not parties to the action, even if the plaintiff would be prohibited from suing them directly or recovering damages from them. *Dietz v. General Elec. Co.*, 169 Ariz. 505, 821 P.2d 166 (1991); *Larsen v. Nissan Motor Corp. in U.S.A.*, 194 Ariz. 142, 978 P.2d 119 (Ct. App. Div. 2 1998).

The statutory definition of "fault" is extremely broad, and there is no authority for the proposition that intentional conduct must be given more weight than negligent conduct in the apportionment of fault. *Hutcherson v. City of Phoenix*, 192 Ariz. 51, 961 P.2d 449 (1998); *State Farm Ins. Companies v. Premier Manufactured Systems, Inc.*, 213 Ariz. 419, 142 P.3d 1232, Prod. Liab. Rep. (CCH) P 17517 (Ct. App. Div. 1 2006), opinion aff'd, 217 Ariz. 222, 172 P.3d 410 (2007). Thus, these comparative fault principles apply regardless of the relationship of the parties and the nature of the duty owed, and even where it is alleged that a negligent tortfeasor had a duty to prevent an intentional wrong from occurring. *Natseway v. City of Tempe*, 184 Ariz. 374, 909 P.2d 441 (Ct. App. Div. 1 1995).

The Act also permits the apportionment of fault between a negligent plaintiff and a defendant whose conduct is wanton or wilful. *Rosner v. Denim & Diamonds, Inc.*, 188 Ariz. 431, 937 P.2d 353 (Ct. App. Div. 2 1996); *Wareing v. Falk*, 182 Ariz. 495, 897 P.2d 1381 (Ct. App. Div. 1 1995). It even permits the allocation of fault between an allegedly negligent defendant and a nonparty who commits a criminal act. *Hutcherson v. City of Phoenix*, 192 Ariz. 51, 961 P.2d 449 (1998); *Thomas v. First Interstate Bank of Arizona, N.A.*, 187 Ariz. 488, 930 P.2d 1002, 54 A.L.R. 5th 827 (Ct. App. Div. 2 1996). Correspondingly, a plaintiff guilty of gross or wanton negligence in causing an accident will not necessarily be barred from any recovery. *Williams v. Thude*, 188 Ariz. 257, 934 P.2d 1349 (1997).

The provision of the Arizona Constitution, article 18, § 5, which requires that the defense of contributory negligence always be left to the jury to decide, applies to claims of comparative negligence as well, so that the issue of the proper allocation of fault will always be a jury issue, where a jury is demanded. *Gunnell v. Arizona Public Service Co.*, 202 Ariz. 388, 46 P.3d 399 (2002).

Arizona's adoption of the Uniform Contribution Among Tortfeasors Act left intact the common law doctrine of "indivisible injury." *Piner v. Superior Court In and For County of Maricopa*, 192 Ariz. 182, 962 P.2d 909 (1998); *Salica v. Tucson Heart Hosp.-Carondelet, L.L.C.*, 224 Ariz. 414, 231 P.3d 946 (Ct. App. Div. 2 2010). When the tortious conduct of more than one defendant contributes to one indivisible injury, the entire amount of damages resulting from all contributing causes is the total amount "of damages recoverable by the plaintiff," as that term is used in A.R.S. § 12-2506(A). *Piner v. Superior Court In and For County of Maricopa*, 192 Ariz. 182, 962 P.2d 909 (1998). The fault of all actors is then determined by the trier of fact, and each defendant is *severally* liable for damages allocated in direct proportion to that defendant's percentage of fault. *Piner v. Superior Court In and For County of Maricopa*, 192 Ariz. 182, 962 P.2d 909 (1998). In an indivisible injury case, the fact finder is to compute the total amount of damages sustained by the plaintiff, and the percentage of fault of each tortfeasor, and the maximum amount recoverable against each tortfeasor is computed by multiplying the first figure by the second. *Piner v. Superior Court In and For County of Maricopa*, 192 Ariz. 182, 962 P.2d 909 (1998). Further, in an indivisible injury case, the burden is on the defendants to apportion fault. *Piner v. Superior Court In and For County of Maricopa*, 192 Ariz. 182, 962 P.2d 909 (1998); *Salica v. Tucson Heart Hosp.-Carondelet, L.L.C.*, 224 Ariz. 414, 231 P.3d 946 (Ct. App. Div. 2 2010).

The doctrine of "satisfaction of judgment" provides that, if one joint tortfeasor satisfies a judgment obtained by the plaintiff, all other tortfeasors are discharged from liability and the plaintiff has no further cause of action. *Bridgestone/Firestone North America Tire, L.L.C. v. Naranjo*, 206 Ariz. 447, 79 P.3d 1206, Prod. Liab. Rep. (CCH) P 16845 (Ct. App. Div. 2 2003). This doctrine also survives the abolition of joint and several liability, and the adoption of a comparative fault regime, in situations where the plaintiff has obtained a judgment for the total damages suffered from an indivisible injury against only one party at fault, and that judgment is satisfied. *Bridgestone/Firestone North America Tire, L.L.C. v. Naranjo*, 206 Ariz. 447, 79 P.3d 1206, Prod. Liab. Rep. (CCH) P 16845 (Ct. App. Div. 2 2003). The satisfaction of that judgment extinguishes any claim against other parties at fault. *Bridgestone/Firestone North America Tire, L.L.C. v. Naranjo*, 206 Ariz. 447, 79 P.3d 1206, Prod. Liab. Rep. (CCH) P 16845 (Ct. App. Div. 2 2003).

Under A.R.S. § 12-2506(D), joint tortfeasors who act in concert remain jointly and severally liable for the resulting injury. *Chappell v. Wenholz*, 226 Ariz. 309, 247 P.3d 192 (Ct. App. Div. 1 2011); *Mein ex rel. Mein v. Cook*, 219 Ariz. 96, 193 P.3d 790 (Ct. App. Div. 1 2008); *Bishop v. Pecanic*, 193 Ariz. 524, 975 P.2d 114 (Ct. App. Div. 1 1998). A.R.S. § 12-2506(F)(1), however, defines "acting in concert" as, *inter alia*, being inapplicable to "any person whose conduct was negligent in any of its degrees rather than intentional." Thus, Arizona's "acting in concert" exception to the general rule of several liability has been held to apply, as a practical matter, only to intentional torts. *Security Title Agency, Inc. v.*

Pope, 219 Ariz. 480, 200 P.3d 977, 27 I.E.R. Cas. (BNA) 1811 (Ct. App. Div. 1 2008); *Mein ex rel. Mein v. Cook*, 219 Ariz. 96, 193 P.3d 790 (Ct. App. Div. 1 2008). In *Mein*, the court of appeals held that a *prima facie* case under A.R.S. § 12-2506(D)(1) requires evidence the parties: (1) knowingly agreed to commit an intentional tort, (2) they were certain or substantially certain their actions would result in the consequences complained of, and (3) they actively participated in the commission of the tort. *Mein ex rel. Mein v. Cook*, 219 Ariz. 96, 193 P.3d 790 (Ct. App. Div. 1 2008); *see also*, *Chappell v. Wenholz*, 226 Ariz. 309, 247 P.3d 192 (Ct. App. Div. 1 2011) (holding, "[a] conscious agreement need not be verbally expressed and may be implied from the conduct itself").

Joint liability and vicarious liability "are related but separate doctrines." *Wiggs v. City of Phoenix*, 198 Ariz. 367, 10 P.3d 625, 111 A.L.R.5th 815 (2000) (citing, *Srithong v. Total Investment Co.*, 23 Cal. App. 4th 721, 28 Cal. Rptr. 2d 672 (2d Dist. 1994); *State Farm Ins. Companies v. Premier Manufactured Systems, Inc.*, 213 Ariz. 419, 142 P.3d 1232, Prod. Liab. Rep. (CCH) P 17517 (Ct. App. Div. 1 2006), opinion aff'd, 217 Ariz. 222, 172 P.3d 410 (2007). The joint liability that was abolished by A.R.S. § 12-2506(D) is limited to "that class of joint tortfeasors whose independent negligence coalesced to form a single injury." *Wiggs v. City of Phoenix*, 198 Ariz. 367, 10 P.3d 625, 111 A.L.R.5th 815 (2000). The statute preserves joint liability both for true joint tortfeasors (those "acting in concert") and for those who are vicariously liable for the fault of others. *Wiggs v. City of Phoenix*, 198 Ariz. 367, 10 P.3d 625, 111 A.L.R.5th 815 (2000); *State Farm Ins. Companies v. Premier Manufactured Systems, Inc.*, 213 Ariz. 419, 142 P.3d 1232, Prod. Liab. Rep. (CCH) P 17517 (Ct. App. Div. 1 2006), opinion aff'd, 217 Ariz. 222, 172 P.3d 410 (2007).

The comparative fault statute, thus, preserves vicarious liability for the negligence of an independent contractor, when the employer of that independent contractor had a non-delegable duty. *Wiggs v. City of Phoenix*, 198 Ariz. 367, 10 P.3d 625, 111 A.L.R.5th 815 (2000). This will not operate to immunize independent contractors from the consequences of their own negligence, any more than in the case of a true employee. *Wiggs v. City of Phoenix*, 198 Ariz. 367, 10 P.3d 625, 111 A.L.R.5th 815 (2000). In either setting, the employer may seek indemnity against the employee or independent contractor, in cases of pure vicarious liability, or contribution in cases in which the employer has some degree of independent liability. *Wiggs v. City of Phoenix*, 198 Ariz. 367, 10 P.3d 625, 111 A.L.R.5th 815 (2000).

30. *Claims of Nonparty Liability*. Before the 1987 amendments to Arizona's version of the Uniform Contribution Among Tortfeasors Act, discussed in the preceding Section, fault was to be al-

located only among parties to the action. The remedy available to a joint tortfeasor who, because another joint tortfeasor had not been joined as a party, became responsible for more than his or her *pro rata* share of the common liability was an action for contribution against the absent joint tortfeasor.

That situation was changed by the 1987 amendments. A.R.S. § 12-2506(B) (as amended) specifies that the negligence or fault of a nonparty may be considered by the trier of fact in assessing percentages of fault if the plaintiff has settled with such nonparty or if "the defending party gives notice before trial, in accordance with requirements established by court rule, that a nonparty was wholly or partially at fault."

To serve as the "court rule" contemplated by this legislation, the Arizona Supreme Court adopted, effective July 1, 1989, Rule 26(b)(5), which adopts a general rule regarding the disclosure of such a claim. The disclosure must be specific, not generic, and include not only the identity and location of the nonparty claimed to be wholly or partially liable but also the facts relied upon to support that claim.

On the other hand, where the party making such a claim and disclosure has made duly diligent efforts to locate and specifically identify such non-parties and has been unsuccessful, it is not an abuse of discretion for the trial court to allow the jury to allocate fault to non-parties whose names and addresses have not been provided. *Rosner v. Denim & Diamonds, Inc.*, 188 Ariz. 431, 937 P.2d 353 (Ct. App. Div. 2 1996). *See also*, *Bowen Productions, Inc. v. French*, 231 Ariz. 424, 296 P.3d 87 (Ct. App. Div. 1 2013). Furthermore, a Rule 26(b)(5) notice of a non-party at fault, and timely Rule 26.1 disclosures must be read together, to determine the sufficiency of such notice. *Bowen Productions, Inc. v. French*, 231 Ariz. 424, 296 P.3d 87 (Ct. App. Div. 1 2013). A facially vague notice of non-party at fault, however, cannot be revived by facially vague Rule 26.1 disclosures. *Scottsdale Ins. Co. v. Cendejas*, 220 Ariz. 281, 205 P.3d 1128 (Ct. App. Div. 1 2009).

Rule 26(b)(5) requires that any party who claims a person or entity not *currently or formerly named as a party* is wholly or partially at fault for causing damages claimed for personal injury, property damage or wrongful death must file a notice of a non-party at fault. *LyphoMed, Inc. v. Superior Court In and For County of Maricopa*, 172 Ariz. 423, 837 P.2d 1158 (Ct. App. Div. 1 1992) (Neither the Rule nor the statute it implements, however, require notice of a claim that another party is wholly or partially at fault). *See also*, *Bowen Productions, Inc. v. French*, 231 Ariz. 424, 296 P.3d 87 (Ct. App. Div. 1 2013) (observing that "[c]omparative fault principles do not apply in breach of contract cases.", citing *Fidelity and Deposit Co. of Maryland v. Bondwriter*

Southwest, Inc., 228 Ariz. 84, 263 P.3d 633 (Ct. App. Div. 1 2011), review denied, (Oct. 30, 2012). A defendant is not relieved of the need to file such a notice because another defendant has done so, even though the other defendant's notice identifies all of the non-parties that the defendant who failed to file a notice would name.

In cases of vicarious liability, it does not make legal or tactical sense for the party whose liability is derivative to name as a non-party at fault the person or entity whose conduct is imputed to it, because the vicariously liable party will be fully liable for that fault in any event. *Wiggs v. City of Phoenix*, 198 Ariz. 367, 10 P.3d 625, 111 A.L.R.5th 815 (2000).

31. *Alternative Pleading; Joinder of Claims.* Rule 8(e)(2) permits a pleader to set forth two or more statements of a claim or defense alternately or hypothetically, either in one count or defense or in separate counts or defenses. *Musgrove v. Leonard*, 97 Ariz. 44, 396 P.2d 614 (1964). Where there are alternative statements, the pleading is not rendered insufficient by the insufficiency of one of the alternative statements. A party may state as many separate claims or defenses as that party has, regardless of consistency and whether based on legal or on equitable grounds or both. *Smith v. Superior Equipment Co.*, 102 Ariz. 320, 428 P.2d 998 (1967).

Where the plaintiff has set forth alternative claims or theories that are inconsistent and mutually exclusive, *e.g.*, a claim for damages for breach of contract and a claim for rescission of the same contract, an election of remedies must be made, but is not required until before the action is submitted to the jury. *Edward Greenband Enterprises of Arizona v. Pepper*, 112 Ariz. 115, 538 P.2d 389 (1975); *Dixon v. Feffer*, 84 Ariz. 308, 327 P.2d 994 (1958); *Tempe Corporate Office Bldg. v. Arizona Funding Services, Inc.*, 167 Ariz. 394, 807 P.2d 1130 (Ct. App. Div. 1 1991); *Vinson v. Marton & Associates*, 159 Ariz. 1, 764 P.2d 736 (Ct. App. Div. 1 1988); *Earven v. Smith*, 127 Ariz. 354, 621 P.2d 41 (Ct. App. Div. 2 1980).

Whenever a cause of action may be initiated only after another claim has been prosecuted to a conclusion, the two claims may be joined in a single action. In particular, a plaintiff may state a claim for money and a claim to have a fraudulent conveyance set aside, without first having obtained a judgment establishing the claim for money. See Rule 18(b).

32. *Complex Civil Litigation Rules.* On November 22, 2002, in Administrative Order No. 2002-107, the Arizona Supreme Court in effect approved a report from a Committee to Study Complex Litigation. By that same administrative order, the Court established a pilot program to experiment with a Complex Civil Litigation Court in the Maricopa County Superior Court and

proposed several new or amended rules of civil procedure, and a new form for identifying cases eligible for the program, which the Court set forth in an Appendix to the Order.

The Complex Civil Litigation Rules—designated as Rules 8(h)(3), 8(i), 16.3, and 39.1—were originally promulgated to facilitate the conduct of an experimental Complex Litigation Program in the Superior Court of Maricopa County, which was scheduled to run from January 1, 2003 and December 31, 2004. At the request of the Complex Civil Litigation Court Evaluation Committee, this experimental program was extended through December 31, 2010. On September 1, 2011, the Arizona Supreme Court made permanent the Complex Litigation pilot program. The Complex Civil Litigation Rules— Rule 8(h)(3), 8(i), 16.3, and 39.1—are effective January 1, 2012.

Rule 9. Pleading special matters

(a) Capacity. It is not necessary to aver the capacity of a party to sue or be sued or the authority of a party to sue or be sued in a representative capacity or the legal existence of an organized association of persons that is made a party, except to the extent required to show the jurisdiction of the court. When a party desires to raise an issue as to the legal existence of any party or the capacity of any party to sue or be sued or the authority of a party to sue or be sued in a representative capacity, the party desiring to raise the issue shall do so by specific negative averment, which shall include such supporting particulars as are peculiarly within the pleader's knowledge.

Amended Sept. 15, 1987, effective Nov. 15, 1987.

(b) Fraud, Mistake, Condition of the Mind. In all averments of fraud or mistake, the circumstances constituting fraud or mistake shall be stated with particularity. Malice, intent, knowledge, and other condition of mind of a person may be averred generally.

(c) Conditions Precedent. In pleading the performance or occurrence of conditions precedent, it is sufficient to aver generally that all conditions precedent have been performed or have occurred. A denial of performance or occurrence shall be made specifically and with particularity.

(d) Official Document or Act. In pleading an official document or official act it is sufficient to aver that the document was issued or the act done in compliance with law.

(e) Judgment. In pleading a judgment or decision of a domestic or foreign court, judicial or quasi-judicial tribunal, or of a board or officer, it is sufficient to aver the judgment or decision without setting forth matter showing jurisdiction to render it.

(f) Time and Place. For the purpose of testing the sufficiency of a pleading, averments of time and place are material and shall be considered like all other averments of material matter.

(g) Special Damage. When items of special damage are claimed, they shall be specifically stated.

(h) Complaint in Action for Libel or Slander. In an action for libel or slander, the complaint need not state the extrinsic facts applying to the plaintiff the defamatory matter out of which the claim arose, but may allege generally that the libel or slander was published or spoken concerning the plaintiff, and if the allegation is controverted the plaintiff shall establish on the trial that it was so published or spoken.

(i) Verification of Answer. Any responsive pleading setting up any of the following matters, unless the truth of the pleading appears of record, shall be verified by affidavit:

1. That the plaintiff does not have legal capacity to sue.
2. That the plaintiff is not entitled to recover in the capacity in which the plaintiff sues.
3. That there is another action pending in this state between the same parties for the same claim.
4. That there is a defect of parties, plaintiff or defendant.
5. A denial of partnership, or of incorporation, of the plaintiff or defendant.
6. A denial of the execution by the defendant or by the defendant's authority of any instrument in writing upon which any pleading is based, in whole or in part, and alleged to have been executed by the defendant or by the defendant's authority, and not alleged to be lost or destroyed. When the instrument is alleged to have been executed by a person then deceased, the affidavit may state that the affiant has reason to believe, and does believe, that such instrument was not executed by the decedent or by the decedent's authority.
7. A denial of the genuineness of the endorsement or assignment of a written instrument.
8. That a written instrument upon which a pleading is based is without consideration, or that the consideration therefor has failed in whole or in part.
9. That an account which is the basis of plaintiff's action, and supported by an affidavit, is not just, and in such case the answer shall set forth the items and particulars which are unjust.

Amended Sept. 15, 1987, effective Nov. 15, 1987.

AUTHORS' COMMENTS

Analysis

10. Foreign Judgments.
11. Special Damages.
12. Libel or Slander Actions.
13. Verification of Answer.

1. *Scope and Purpose of Rule.* Rule 9 sets forth particular requirements for pleading certain special matters and refines, for the situations to which it applies, the general rules of pleading set forth in Rule 8. Many of its provisions carry forward the same notion of simplicity in pleading as is found in Rule 8, for such matters as capacity, conditions of mind, conditions precedent, and the pleading of official acts. There are instances, however, in which Rule 9 requires detailed specificity, such as those provisions relating to specific negative averments, those requiring particularity in alleging the circumstances of fraud or mistake and in alleging the nonperformance of conditions, and those regarding special damages.

Rule 9 must be read in light of the basic pleading philosophy set forth in Rule 8 and in conjunction with the instructions as to pleading forms that appear in Rule 10. Even those portions of Rule 9 that mandate detailed or specific allegations should not be construed too literally; simplicity still governs pleading practice in Arizona. Although fraud and certain other allegations must be pled with particularity, the allegations still must be short, plain, simple, direct, and as concise as is reasonable under the circumstances.

Failure to comply with the special pleading provisions in Rule 9 will not necessarily result in the dismissal of the action or striking the pleading; rather, the courts are more likely to remedy a defect by requiring an amendment or a more definite statement or by requiring reliance upon the use of discovery. Finally, Rule 9 specifies those instances, *i.e.,* where certain matters are to be placed in issue, in which verification of the answer is required.

2. *Comparison With Federal Rule.* ARCP 9(a) through (g) are substantively identical to FRCP 9(a) through (g). The Federal Rule has no counterpart to ARCP 9(h), dealing with complaints in actions for libel or slander, or to ARCP 9(i), requiring the verification of answers raising certain specified matters. The Arizona Rule does not have a counterpart to FRCP 9(h), which deals with admiralty and maritime claims.

In 2007, the language of FRCP 9 was amended as part of the general restyling of the Federal Rules of Civil Procedure to make the Federal Rules more easily understood and to make style and terminology consistent throughout the Federal Rules of Civil Procedure. Those stylistic modifications have not been incorporated into ARCP 9.

3. *Capacity to Sue Generally.* As a general rule, the capacity or authority of a party to sue or be sued need not be specifically alleged. A party in a licensed profession or occupation, however, may be required to allege licensed status in an action arising out of licensed activities. Cf. A.R.S. § 32-1153 (contractors); A.R.S. § 32-2152 (real estate brokers).

A party desiring to raise an issue regarding legal existence, capacity, or authority of a party must do so "by specific negative averment." The specific negative averment must include "such supporting particulars as are peculiarly within the pleader's knowledge." Thereafter, the party claiming capacity, authority, or legal existence would have the burden of proof on that issue. *See, In re Cassidy's Estate*, 77 Ariz. 288, 270 P.2d 1079 (1954); *Aranda v. Cardenas*, 215 Ariz. 210, 159 P.3d 76 (Ct. App. Div. 2 2007).

Thus, an issue as to capacity cannot be raised by a general denial. The issue of legal existence, capacity, or authority must be specifically raised in the answer or in motions before answering; if not timely raised, it is deemed waived. *Gonzales v. Arizona Public Service Co.*, 161 Ariz. 84, 775 P.2d 1148 (Ct. App. Div. 2 1989); *Anderson v. Wilson*, 140 Ariz. 64, 680 P.2d 200 (Ct. App. Div. 1 1984) (disapproved of on other grounds by, Tarr v. Superior Court In and For Pima County, 142 Ariz. 349, 690 P.2d 68 (1984)); *Reeves v. Arizona Aggregate Ass'n Health and Welfare Fund*, 102 Ariz. 595, 435 P.2d 829, 67 L.R.R.M. (BNA) 2624, 57 Lab. Cas. (CCH) P 12387 (1967); *Baxter v. Harrison*, 83 Ariz. 354, 321 P.2d 1019 (1958).

A party's *capacity* to bring a lawsuit does not depend on the nature of a claim. The capacity to sue merely requires the legal authority to act. *State ex rel. Montgomery v. Mathis*, 231 Ariz. 103, 290 P.3d 1226 (Ct. App. Div. 1 2012). Thus, when a party has the legal authority to act, it also has the capacity to bring a lawsuit independent of whether such party has a justiciable interest in the controversy. *State ex rel. Montgomery v. Mathis*, 231 Ariz. 103, 290 P.3d 1226 (Ct. App. Div. 1 2012).

4. *Corporate Capacity.* A foreign corporation must be authorized to transact business by complying with A.R.S. §§ 10-110 and 10-111. A foreign corporation which is required to qualify to conduct business in Arizona, but fails or refuses to do so, may not maintain any action, suit or proceeding in any Arizona court, until such corporation is authorized to transact business. A.R.S. § 10-1502(A). This statutory mandate applies equally to any successor or assignee of such corporation. A.R.S. § 10-1502(B). It has been held, however, that compliance with the predecessors to these statutes, A.R.S. §§ 10-110 and 10-111, *after* an action has been commenced by the foreign corporation is sufficient to enable

the corporation to maintain the action. *Capin v. S & H Packing Co., Inc.*, 130 Ariz. 441, 636 P.2d 1223 (Ct. App. Div. 2 1981).

5. *Fraud or Mistake.* Rule 9(b) requires that the circumstances constituting alleged fraud or mistake be stated with particularity. One purpose of Rule 9(b)'s particularity requirement is so that the responding party is in a position to adequately answer or otherwise respond to the allegations. *Steinberger v. McVey ex rel. County of Maricopa*, — P.3d —, 2014 WL 333575 (Ct. App. Div. 1 2014). This requirement also is intended to "avoid surprise at trial." *Steinberger v. McVey ex rel. County of Maricopa*, — P.3d —, 2014 WL 333575 (Ct. App. Div. 1 2014); *Pruitt v. Pavelin*, 141 Ariz. 195, 685 P.2d 1347 (Ct. App. Div. 1 1984); *Spudnuts, Inc. v. Lane*, 131 Ariz. 424, 641 P.2d 912 (Ct. App. Div. 2 1982).

Pleading the "circumstances constituting fraud" generally means the time, the place, the substance of the false representations, the facts misrepresented, and the identification of the person making the misrepresentation and what was obtained thereby. This requirement applies whether fraud is asserted as a claim or as a defense. *Spudnuts, Inc. v. Lane*, 131 Ariz. 424, 641 P.2d 912 (Ct. App. Div. 2 1982); *Bender v. Bender*, 123 Ariz. 90, 597 P.2d 993 (Ct. App. Div. 1 1979); *Fruth v. Divito*, 26 Ariz. App. 154, 546 P.2d 1163 (Div. 1 1976).

Arizona law requires that the plaintiff establish the following elements by clear and convincing evidence to prevail on a claim for fraud:

(1) a representation;
(2) its falsity;
(3) its materiality;
(4) the speaker's knowledge of its falsity or ignorance of its truth;
(5) the speaker's intent that the representation should be acted upon by the person and in a manner reasonably contemplated;
(6) the hearer's ignorance of its falsity;
(7) the hearer's reliance on its truth;
(8) a right to rely thereon; and
(9) consequent and proximate injury and damages.

Steinberger v. McVey ex rel. County of Maricopa, — P.3d —, 2014 WL 333575 (Ct. App. Div. 1 2014); *Green v. Lisa Frank, Inc.*, 221 Ariz. 138, 211 P.3d 16 (Ct. App. Div. 2 2009); *Wagner v. Casteel*, 136 Ariz. 29, 663 P.2d 1020 (Ct. App. Div. 2 1983).

In pleading a claim for fraud, no particular or "magic" language is required so long as all the nine elements of fraud can be found in the facts alleged in the pleading viewed as a whole. *Steinberger v. McVey ex rel. County of Maricopa*, — P.3d —, 2014 WL

333575 (Ct. App. Div. 1 2014) ("[a]lthough there is no 'magic language' required to state a claim for fraud," a claimant must "plead all the essential elements of . . . fraud" in the complaint.", citing *Linder v. Brown & Herrick*, 189 Ariz. 398, 404–05, 943 P.2d 758, 764–65 (Ct. App. Div. 1 1997); *Ness v. Western Sec. Life Ins. Co.*, 174 Ariz. 497, 851 P.2d 122, R.I.C.O. Bus. Disp. Guide (CCH) P 8086 (Ct. App. Div. 1 1992); *Hall v. Romero*, 141 Ariz. 120, 685 P.2d 757 (Ct. App. Div. 1 1984); *Denbo v. Badger*, 18 Ariz. App. 426, 503 P.2d 384 (Div. 2 1972). Bare allegations that the defendant's conduct was "fraudulent" or that plaintiff "reasonably relied" are, however, insufficient. *Orca Communications Unlimited, LLC v. Noder*, 233 Ariz. 411, 314 P.3d 89 (Ct. App. Div. 1 2013); *Ness v. Western Sec. Life Ins. Co.*, 174 Ariz. 497, 851 P.2d 122, R.I.C.O. Bus. Disp. Guide (CCH) P 8086 (Ct. App. Div. 1 1992); *Hall v. Romero*, 141 Ariz. 120, 685 P.2d 757 (Ct. App. Div. 1 1984).

Failure to set forth a fraud claim with the specificity necessary to comply with Rule 9(b) will not necessarily cause a pleading to be subject to dismissal. The Arizona courts have proven relatively liberal in allowing amendments to pleadings when this rule is violated. *Spudnuts, Inc. v. Lane*, 131 Ariz. 424, 641 P.2d 912 (Ct. App. Div. 2 1982).

To set forth a claim of mistake, as for fraud, the circumstances and facts must be stated with particularity. The pleading must demonstrate what was intended, what was done, and how the mistake came to be made; mere conclusions of law are insufficient. *Glendale Union High School Dist. v. Peoria School Dist. No. 11*, 51 Ariz. 478, 78 P.2d 141 (1938). If any condition of mind is pertinent, however, the condition may be pleaded generally.

6. *Conditions of Mind.* Rule 9(b) provides, by its terms, that malice, intent, knowledge, and other condition of mind of a person may be alleged generally. The Rule recognizes that any attempt to require specificity in pleading a condition of mind would be unworkable and undesirable, because of the difficulty inherent in describing a state of mind. Therefore, while fraud itself must be stated with particularity, fraudulent intent may be alleged in general terms. *Cf. Haynes v. Anderson & Strudwick, Inc.*, 508 F. Supp. 1303, Fed. Sec. L. Rep. (CCH) P 97905 (E.D. Va. 1981).

7. *Conditions Precedent.* Because Rule 9(c) permits the use of general allegations of performance or occurrence of all conditions precedent, the allegation used in a complaint should be as broad as possible. *Cf. Equal Employment Opportunity Commission v. Wah Chang Albany Corp.*, 499 F.2d 187, 8 Fair Empl. Prac. Cas. (BNA) 203, 8 Empl. Prac. Dec. (CCH) P 9477, 18 Fed. R. Serv. 2d 1099 (9th Cir. 1974). The application of Rule 9(c) is not limited to contract actions and includes both the occurrence *and* the perfor-

mance of conditions precedent. The rule, however, does not apply to conditions subsequent, *Cf. Crosney v. Edward Small Productions*, 52 F. Supp. 559, 59 U.S.P.Q. 193 (S.D. N.Y. 1942), or to "procedural" conditions precedent. *Cf. Kirkland v. Bianco*, 595 F. Supp. 797, 39 Fair Empl. Prac. Cas. (BNA) 1306 (S.D. N.Y. 1984). Lack of fulfillment of conditions *subsequent* is an affirmative defense within the scope of Rule 8(c). *Cf. Reynolds-Fitzgerald v. Journal Pub. Co.*, 15 F.R.D. 403 (S.D. N.Y. 1954).

The express terms of Rule 9(c) refer only to "performance" or "occurrence" of conditions precedent. Therefore, if a waiver or excuse of conditions precedent is relied upon, such allegation must be pled with somewhat more particularity. *Cf. Lumbermens Mut. Ins. Co. v. Bowman*, 313 F.2d 381 (10th Cir. 1963).

A general denial will not put in issue the question of the fulfillment of a condition precedent; rather, denial of performance or occurrence of such a condition must be made specifically and with particularity. *Slovenic Nat. Ben. Soc. v. Dabcevich*, 30 Ariz. 294, 246 P. 765 (1926). The burden of proof, however, does not shift. When the defendant denies specifically and with particularity that any condition precedent to suit has been fulfilled, plaintiff is required to prove that the conditions precedent were, in fact, satisfied. *Cf. Mason v. State of Conn.*, 583 F. Supp. 729, 17 Ed. Law Rep. 509, 38 Fair Empl. Prac. Cas. (BNA) 1259 (D. Conn. 1984).

8. *Official Documents or Acts.* Rule 9(d) eliminates the need to allege the evidentiary facts that demonstrate that an official document was issued or an official act was done in compliance with the law. It is sufficient simply to allege compliance with the law in the pleading.

Official documents are records kept in the usual course of business by a government agency. An official act is any act done by an officer in an official capacity under color of and by virtue of the office held. *Weidler v. Arizona Power Co.*, 39 Ariz. 390, 7 P.2d 241 (1932).

9. *Judgments Generally.* Rule 9(e) abolishes the common law rule which required, when a judgment of a court of limited or special jurisdiction was the basis of an action, that the pleader allege facts showing that the court rendering the judgment had jurisdiction. The present rule makes it sufficient to allege that a judgment or decision of a domestic or foreign court, judicial or quasi-judicial tribunal, or of a board or officer was rendered. *Clark v. Wesendorf*, 35 Ariz. 172, 275 P. 925 (1929). Rule 9(e) also includes the decisions of administrative officers and tribunals. A decision by quasi-judicial bodies, boards or officers is enforceable in the Arizona courts where such decision was rendered in the course of such body, board or officer "acting in a judicial capacity."

City of Phoenix v. Sanner, 54 Ariz. 363, 95 P.2d 987 (1939).

Although Rule 9(e) is intended to discourage unnecessary pleading, sound pleading practice still requires the following: (1) name of the court, body or person rendering the judgment or decision; (2) name of the country, state, or other jurisdiction in which the judgment or decision was rendered; (3) name of the parties; (4) date of the judgment or decision; and (5) character and effect of the judgment or decision as is pertinent to the issues. If a defendant wishes to question the validity of the judgment or decision being sued upon, the defendant must do so specifically in the answer. A general denial is not sufficient. *Cf. Gull v. Constam*, 105 F. Supp. 107 (D. Colo. 1952).

The legal operation and effect of a judgment must be ascertained by the construction of its terms, and, if possible, a construction will be adopted that supports the judgment, rather than one that destroys it. *Title Ins. Co. of Minnesota v. Acumen Trading Co., Inc.*, 121 Ariz. 525, 591 P.2d 1302 (1979). The validity of an assignment of a judgment is determined by the law of the state where the judgment is recovered. *Emblen v. Southern Adjustment Bureau, Inc.*, 1 Ariz. App. 359, 403 P.2d 294 (1965).

10. *Foreign Judgments.* A foreign judgment is entitled to "full faith and credit" in the Arizona courts if the following elements are satisfied: (1) a court of competent jurisdiction; (2) a final judgment on the merits; and (3) the absence of fraud or some other factor invalidating the judgment. *Cho v. American Bonding Co.*, 190 Ariz. 593, 951 P.2d 468 (Ct. App. Div. 1 1997); *Oyakawa v. Gillett*, 175 Ariz. 226, 854 P.2d 1212 (Ct. App. Div. 1 1993); *Rotary Club of Tucson v. Chaprales Ramos de Pena*, 160 Ariz. 362, 773 P.2d 467 (Ct. App. Div. 2 1989). Foreign judgments are subject to attack if the rendering court lacked jurisdiction over the person or the subject matter, if the judgment was obtained through lack of due process or was the result of extrinsic fraud, or if the judgment is otherwise invalid and unenforceable. *Cho v. American Bonding Co.*, 190 Ariz. 593, 951 P.2d 468 (Ct. App. Div. 1 1997). If an Arizona court finds that the notice given to the defendant in the foreign proceedings failed to satisfy constitutional standards, it may properly refuse to grant the foreign judgment full faith and credit. *Pioneer Federal Sav. Bank v. Driver*, 166 Ariz. 585, 804 P.2d 118 (Ct. App. Div. 1 1990). The enforceability, and the procedures for securing enforcement, of foreign judgments are discussed more extensively in Section 11 of the *Authors' Comments* to Rule 69.

11. *Special Damages.* Although Rule 9(g) requires that "special" damages be specifically stated, an allegation of special damages is sufficient when it notifies the defendant of the nature of the claimed damages even though it does not delineate them with as

great a precision as might be possible or desirable. *Southern Arizona School For Boys, Inc. v. Chery*, 119 Ariz. 277, 580 P.2d 738 (Ct. App. Div. 2 1978). General damages are such as the law implies and presumes to have occurred from the wrong complained of, while special damages are those which are the natural, but not the necessary, consequence of the act complained of and usually stem from the particular circumstances of the case. *Southern Arizona School For Boys, Inc. v. Chery*, 119 Ariz. 277, 580 P.2d 738 (Ct. App. Div. 2 1978).

The following items are generally treated as special damages in personal injury actions:

(1) loss of time and earnings;
(2) loss or impairment of future earning capacity;
(3) expenses of drugs, hospitalization and physicians' fees; and
(4) aggravation of a pre-existing condition.

If the character of the injury demonstrates that the natural and probable consequences would be pain and suffering, then a specific allegation of pain and suffering is unnecessary. *Olsen v. Mading*, 45 Ariz. 423, 45 P.2d 23 (1935). In a defamation action, special damages must be alleged unless a publication constitutes libel per se. *Berg v. Hohenstein*, 13 Ariz. App. 583, 479 P.2d 730 (Div. 1 1971). A claim for punitive damages, on the other hand, does not require special pleading requirements. *Ezell v. Quon*, 224 Ariz. 532, 233 P.3d 645 (Ct. App. Div. 1 2010)(" 'a general prayer for punitive damages is sufficient. . . to put the defendant on notice' that punitive damages may be awarded."), citing *Kline v. Kline*, 221 Ariz. 564, 212 P.3d 902 (Ct. App. Div. 1 2009).

The failure to set out special damages with the requisite specificity may usually be cured by amendment under Rule 15. Moreover, special damages can be awarded, even if not pled, if evidence of them is admitted at trial without objection. *Gilmore v. Cohen*, 95 Ariz. 34, 386 P.2d 81, 11 A.L.R.3d 714 (1963); *Home Indem. Co. v. Bush*, 20 Ariz. App. 355, 513 P.2d 145 (Div. 1 1973).

12. *Libel or Slander Actions.* Rule 9(h) permits the plaintiff in an action for libel or slander to allege only generally that the libel or slander was published or spoken concerning the plaintiff; extrinsic facts establishing that the defamatory matter applied to or concerned the plaintiff need not be pleaded. *Central Arizona Light & Power Co. v. Akers*, 45 Ariz. 526, 46 P.2d 126 (1935). The Rule provides that, if the defendant controverts such allegation in the answer, then the plaintiff must establish at trial that it was so published or spoken. As noted earlier, special damages generally must be alleged unless a publication constitutes libel *per se. Berg v. Hohenstein*, 13 Ariz. App. 583, 479 P.2d 730 (Div. 1 1971).

13. *Verification of Answer.* Rule 9(i) requires verification of a responsive pleading setting up any of the following matters:

(1) plaintiff has no legal capacity to sue;
(2) plaintiff is not entitled to recover in the capacity in which plaintiff has sued;
(3) another action is pending in Arizona between the same parties for the same claim;
(4) defect of parties;
(5) denial of partnership or incorporation of parties;
(6) denial of execution of a written instrument by defendant or decedent;
(7) denial of genuineness of endorsement or assignment of a written instrument;
(8) failure of or lack of consideration supporting written instrument; and
(9) unjust account.

The purpose of requiring verification of the answer in certain circumstances is to enable the parties to determine the issues on which it will be necessary to present evidence. *Mendez v. Moya*, 54 Ariz. 44, 91 P.2d 870 (1939). When an issue concerning the justness of an account is raised, the answer must set forth the items and particulars which are unjust. The failure to verify an answer which denies execution of an instrument is an admission of any allegation of due execution in the complaint. *Wenrich v. Household Finance Corp.*, 5 Ariz. App. 335, 426 P.2d 671 (1967).

Under Rule 80(i), what is termed an "unsworn declaration under penalty of perjury" may be used in place of a formal, sworn verification where a verification is required by the Rules.

Rule 10. Form of pleading

(a) Caption; Names of Parties. Every pleading shall contain a caption setting forth the name of the court, the title of the action, the file number, and a designation as in Rule 7(a). In the complaint the title of the action shall include the names of all the parties, but in other pleadings it is sufficient to state the name of the first party on each side with an appropriate indication of other parties.

(b) Paragraphs; Separate Statements. All averments of claim or defense shall be made in numbered paragraphs, the contents of each of which shall be limited as far as practicable to a statement of a single set of circumstances, and a paragraph may be referred to by number in all succeeding pleadings. Each claim founded upon a separate transaction or occurrence and each defense other than denials shall be stated in a separate count or defense whenever a separation facilitates the clear presentation of the matters set forth.

(c) Adoption by Reference; Exhibits. Statements in a pleading may be adopted by reference in a different part of the same pleading or in another pleading or in a motion. A copy of a written instrument which is an exhibit to a pleading is a part thereof for all purposes.

(d) Method of Preparation and Filing. All pleadings and other papers filed in any action or proceeding shall be on white, opaque, unglazed paper measuring 8½ inches × 11 inches, with a margin at the top of the first page of not less than 2 inches; a margin at the top of each subsequent page of not less than 1½ inches; a left-hand margin of not less than 1 inch; a right-hand margin of not less than ½ inch; and a margin at the bottom of the page of not less than ½ inch.

Notwithstanding the foregoing, exhibits, attachments to pleadings, or pleadings from jurisdictions other than the State of Arizona which are larger than the specified size shall be folded to the specified size or folded and fastened to pages of the specified size. Exhibits or attachments to pleadings which are smaller than the specified size shall be fastened to pages of the specified size. An exhibit, attachment to a pleading or a pleading from a jurisdiction other than the State of Arizona not in compliance with the foregoing provisions may be filed only if it appears that compliance is not reasonably practicable.

All pleadings and other papers filed shall have the pages numbered and shall state the number of the action, the title of the court and action, the nature of the paper filed and the name, address, Arizona Bar Number and telephone number of the attorney. Originals only shall be filed, except that where it is necessary to file more than one copy of a pleading or other paper the additional copies may be photocopies or computer generated duplicates.

All pleadings and other papers filed, other than printed forms, shall be clearly handwritten or typewritten on one side of the page only. The body of all documents shall be double spaced and shall not exceed 28 lines per page, except for headings, quotations and footnotes which may be single spaced.

Printed forms may be single spaced except that those requiring the signature of a judge or commissioner shall be double spaced. Printed forms must be single sided. All printed forms shall be on paper of sufficient quality and weight to assure legibility upon duplication, microfilming or imaging.

The court may, on its own motion or on request of any party, waive any of the foregoing requirements or provisions.

Rule 10(d) amended April 2, 1981, effective July 1, 1982; Jan. 19, 1983, effective Feb. 1, 1983; Aug. 7, 1984, effective Nov. 1, 1984; June 8, 2004, effective December 1, 2004.

(e) [Deleted Sept. 15, 1987, effective Oct. 1, 1987].

(f) Designation of Defendant. When the name of the defendant is unknown to the plaintiff, the defendant may be designated in the pleadings or proceeding by any name. When the defendant's true name is discovered the pleading or proceeding may be amended accordingly.

Rule 10(f) amended April 2, 1981, effective July 1, 1982; Sept. 15, 1987, effective Nov. 15, 1987.

AUTHORS' COMMENTS

Analysis

1. *Scope and Purpose of Rule.* Rules 7, 8 and 9 prescribe the types of pleadings allowed and their substance. Rule 10 prescribes the form of such pleadings—as well as the form of other papers

filed with the court.

2. *Comparison With Federal Rule.* ARCP 10(a), (b) and (c) are essentially to FRCP 10(a), (b) and (c). The Federal Rule does not have a counterpart to ARCP 10(d), which prescribes the size and form of pleadings, or to ARCP 10(f), which permits the use of fictitious names to designate a defendant whose true name is unknown.

In 2007, the language of FRCP 10 was amended as part of the general restyling of the Federal Rules of Civil Procedure to make the Federal Rules more easily understood and to make style and terminology consistent throughout the Federal Rules of Civil Procedure. Those stylistic modifications have not been incorporated into ARCP 10.

3. *Caption; Requirements.* Ariz. R. Civ. P. 10(a) requires every pleading contain a caption which sets forth the name of the court, the title of the action, the file number, and a designation of the type of the pleading. The complaint must include the names of all of the parties, but subsequent pleadings require only identification of the first party on each side and appropriate identification of the other parties, (*e.g.*, "*et al.*," "*et ux.*").

While Rule 10(a), by its terms, applies only to "pleadings," Rule 10(d) imposes similar requirements on other papers filed in an action. Specifically, Rule 10(d) requires that all pleadings and other papers filed have numbered pages, and state the number of the action, the title of the court and action, the nature of the paper filed, and the name, address and telephone number of the attorney responsible for its filing.

The caption is not part of the pleading for purposes of determining the parties to the action or the Court's jurisdiction. See *Hoffman v. Halden*, 268 F.2d 280, 2 Fed. R. Serv. 2d 241 (9th Cir. 1959) (overruled on other grounds by, Cohen v. Norris, 300 F.2d 24 (9th Cir. 1962)).

4. *Amendments to Captions.* Although Rule 10(a) frames the specification of parties in a caption as a mandatory requirement, a defective caption is usually viewed as merely a formal error and not a fatal defect. *See, Kellner v. Lewis*, 130 Ariz. 465, 636 P.2d 1247 (Ct. App. Div. 2 1981). In any event, Ariz. R. Civ. P. 15, permits the amendment of the caption, like any part of the complaint.

An amendment merely to correct a name for proper identification or to name parties already sufficiently identified in the complaint's body will not usually prejudice the opponent and likely will be permitted. However, amending the caption to name new or different parties may involve the application of the rules concerning parties; the effect of the statute of limitations must also be considered. These issues are discussed more extensively in the *Authors' Comments* to Rule 15.

5. *Paragraphs.* The initial portion of Ariz. R. Civ. P. 10(b) requires that a pleading be divided into numbered paragraphs. Each paragraph should contain, insofar as practicable, a statement of a single set of circumstances. What constitutes a "single set of circumstances" depends upon the nature of the action and should be determined in light of the Rule's basic objective, which is to insure that the contents of each paragraph are drafted so as to produce a clear and succinct pleading. The pleading should be comprehensible and not present interpretative difficulties to the parties or the Court. In the same vein, the purpose of requiring that each paragraph be numbered is to provide an easy means of identification for later reference in subsequent pleadings.

Short titles for groups of paragraphs, although not required, may be helpful in comparatively long and complicated complaints. In any event, care should be taken to draft the complaint in a clear and succinct fashion; if the complaint sufficiently states plaintiff's claims and defendant has sufficient notice of the matter in controversy, then the complaint should withstand a technical motion requiring separate counts.

6. *Separate Statement of Claims or Defenses.* Rule 10(b) also requires that, where there are multiple claims or defenses, each claim founded upon a separate transaction or occurrence and each defense other than denials must be stated in a separate count or defense whenever such separation facilitates clear presentation. The purpose of requiring separate statement of claims or defenses is quite similar to the underlying goal of separate paragraphing, *i.e.,* to clarify the issues for the parties and the Court. *Cf. Williamson v. Columbia Gas & Elec. Corp.*, 186 F.2d 464 (3d Cir. 1950).

By its terms, the Rule requires separate counts only when necessary to "facilitate clear presentation" of the issues therein. For instance, affirmative defenses should be stated separately, as should counterclaims or cross-claims in the answer.

The plaintiff who fails to set forth claims in separate counts or paragraphs may be ordered to do so by the Court. *Patterson v. City of Phoenix*, 103 Ariz. 64, 436 P.2d 613 (1968). Usually, unless prejudice can be shown, a defect in the statement of claims and defenses is subject to amendment under Rule 15. Dismissal with prejudice is warranted, however, when the opportunity to amend the complaint could not cure its defects. *Sun World Corp. v. Pennysaver, Inc.*, 130 Ariz. 585, 589, 637 P.2d 1088, 1092 (Ct. App. Div. 1 1981). *See also*, *Young v. Rose*, 230 Ariz. 433, 286 P.3d 518 (Ct. App. Div. 1 2012), review denied, (Apr. 23, 2013) (Before dismissing a complaint for failure to state a claim, if requested, the plaintiff should be given an opportunity to amend the complaint if such an amendment cures its defects.); *Chalpin v. Snyder*, 220 Ariz. 413, 207 P.3d 666 (Ct. App. Div. 1 2008).

7. *Incorporation by Reference.* Rule 10(c) permits pleading by reference. The purpose of pleading by reference is to produce pleadings that are short, concise and non-repetitious. The reference to the exhibit, however, should clearly identify such exhibit to avoid confusion or other problems of interpretation.

Rule 10(c) also authorizes the incorporation of exhibits or writings attached to a pleading and makes them part of the pleading for all purposes. In effect, an exhibit attached to a complaint and made a part thereof has the same effect as alleging in the complaint the facts set forth in the exhibit. *Young v. Bishop*, 88 Ariz. 140, 353 P.2d 1017 (1960); *MM & A Productions, LLC v. Yavapai-Apache Nation*, — Ariz. —, 316 P.3d 1248 (Ct. App. Div. 2 2014); *Strategic Development and Const., Inc. v. 7th & Roosevelt Partners, LLC*, 224 Ariz. 60, 226 P.3d 1046 (Ct. App. Div. 1 2010). There is older authority to the effect, however, that an attached and incorporated exhibit can only enlarge upon allegations that are legally sufficient in themselves and that a statement in such an exhibit cannot supply a necessary allegation omitted from the body of the Complaint. *Beltran v. Roll*, 39 Ariz. 417, 7 P.2d 248 (1932); *State v. Superior Court, Pima County*, 14 Ariz. 126, 125 P. 707 (1912).

It should be noted that the pertinent Local Superior Court Rules should be researched before attaching exhibits or other writings to subsequent pleadings, motions or memorandums of points and authorities.

8. *Format of Pleadings and Other Papers.* Ariz. R. Civ. P. 10(d) governs the format of pleadings and other papers, and requires that such documents have the pages numbered, and state the number of the action, the title of the court and action, the nature of the paper filed, and the name, address, Arizona State Bar number and telephone number of the attorney responsible for its filing.

The Rule was amended in 2004 to delete the provision which permitted the body of documents to be one and one-half spaced. The body of a pleading or other paper must now be double spaced, except for headings, quotations and footnotes, and cannot exceed 28 lines per page. Rule 10(d) provides further that if printed forms are employed, they must be single sided to facilitate duplication, "microfilming" or imaging. The reference to "microfilming" seems quite dated.

9. *Fictitious Parties.* Ariz. R. Civ. P. 10(f) allows a plaintiff to designate a defendant whose name is unknown in the pleadings by a fictitious name. *Arizona Land & Stock Co. v. Markus*, 37 Ariz. 530, 296 P. 251 (1931). Under Rule 4(c), a summons may

also issue directed to the fictitious name employed in the pleadings but any return of service of such a summons must state the true name of the person on whom it was served. For a plaintiff to properly name an actual but unknown party as a fictitious defendant, however, the plaintiff's lack of knowledge of the defendant's true name must be real and not feigned, and must not be willful ignorance, or such as may be removed by some inquiry or by resort to information that is easily accessible. *Gonzalez v. Tidelands Motor Hotel Co., Inc.*, 123 Ariz. 217, 598 P.2d 1036 (Ct. App. Div. 2 1979). The plaintiff must have some idea that a defendant exists but be without knowledge of the defendant's name. *Scottsdale Memorial Health Systems, Inc. v. Clark*, 157 Ariz. 461, 759 P.2d 607 (1988).

Before the court has personal jurisdiction over a defendant designated by a fictitious name, the party being served must clearly be given notice that that party is being served as a defendant designated by a fictitious name. *Brennan v. Western Sav. and Loan Ass'n*, 22 Ariz. App. 293, 526 P.2d 1248 (Div. 1 1974). The pleading or proceeding should be amended once the true name is revealed, but an amendment is not mandatory. *Brennan v. Western Sav. and Loan Ass'n*, 22 Ariz. App. 293, 526 P.2d 1248 (Div. 1 1974).

A plaintiff who has named a fictitious defendant pursuant to Rule 10(f) bears the burden of showing the propriety of doing so, but only after that defendant raises the issue in an appropriate motion. *Lane v. Elco Industries, Inc.*, 134 Ariz. 361, 656 P.2d 650 (Ct. App. Div. 1 1982).

For statute of limitations purposes, an amendment substituting specifically named defendants for fictitious defendants relates back to the time of filing the complaint only where the defendants actually had, or should have had, notice of the pending action within the applicable limitations period plus the period allowed for service of process. *Ritchie v. Grand Canyon Scenic Rides*, 165 Ariz. 460, 799 P.2d 801 (1990); *Cook v. Superior Court of Maricopa County*, 135 Ariz. 1, 658 P.2d 801 (1983); *Grobe v. McBryde*, 105 Ariz. 577, 468 P.2d 936 (1970); *Gould v. Tibshraeny*, 21 Ariz. App. 146, 517 P.2d 104 (Div. 1 1973). This issue is discussed further in Section 11 of the *Authors' Comments* under Rule 15.

Rule 11. Signing of pleadings

(a) Signing of Pleadings, Motions and Other Papers; Sanctions. Every pleading, motion, and other paper of a party represented by an attorney shall be signed by at least one attorney of record in the attorney's individual name, whose address shall be stated. A party who is not represented by an attorney shall sign the party's pleading, motion, or other paper and state the party's address. Except when otherwise specifically provided by rule or statute, pleadings need not be verified or accompanied by affidavit. The rule in equity that the averments of an answer under oath must be overcome by the testimony of two witnesses or of one witness sustained by corroborating circumstances is abolished. The signature of an attorney or party constitutes a certificate by the signer that the signer has read the pleading, motion, or other paper; that to the best of the signer's knowledge, information, and belief formed after reasonable inquiry it is well grounded in fact and is warranted by existing law or a good faith argument for the extension, modification, or reversal of existing law; and that it is not interposed for any improper purpose, such as to harass or to cause unnecessary delay or needless increase in the cost of litigation. If a pleading, motion or other paper is not signed, it shall be stricken unless it is signed promptly after the omission is called to the attention of the pleader or movant. If a pleading, motion or other paper is signed in violation of this rule, the court, upon motion or upon its own initiative, shall impose upon the person who signed it, a represented party, or both, an appropriate sanction, which may include an order to pay to the other party or parties the amount of the reasonable expenses incurred because of the filing of the pleading, including a reasonable attorney's fee. An attorney may help to draft a pleading, motion or document filed by an otherwise self-represented person, and the attorney need not sign that pleading, motion, or document. In providing such drafting assistance, the attorney may rely on the otherwise self-represented person's representation of facts, unless the attorney has reason to believe that such representations are false or materially insufficient, in which instance the attorney shall make an independent reasonable inquiry into the facts.

Amended Aug. 7, 1984, effective Nov. 1, 1984; Sept. 15, 1987, effective Nov. 15, 1987. Amended on an emergency basis Dec. 5, 2012, effective Jan. 1, 2013. Adopted on a permanent basis Aug. 28, 2013.

(b) Verification of Pleading Generally. When in a civil action a pleading is required to be verified by the affidavit of the party, or when in a civil action an affidavit is required or permitted to be filed, the pleading may be verified, or the affidavit made, by the party or by a person acquainted with the facts, for and on behalf of such party.

(c) Verification of Pleading When Equitable Relief Demanded. When equitable relief is demanded, and the party demanding such relief makes oath that the allegations of the complaint, counterclaim, cross-claim, or third-party claim are true in substance and in fact, the responsive pleading of the opposite party shall be under oath, unless the oath is waived in the pleading to which the responsive pleading is filed, and each material allegation not denied under oath shall be taken as confessed.

STATE BAR COMMITTEE NOTES

1984 Amendment

[Rule 11(a)] The 1984 amendments to Rule 11(a) are intended to establish a better defined and more stringent standard of conduct for the signing attorney or party, and to expand the range of sanctions which a court may impose for its violation. The signing of a pleading, motion or other paper (which includes discovery papers) now constitutes a certification of a bona fide belief formed after reasonable inquiry that it is well grounded in fact and warranted by law or a good faith argument for extension, modification or reversal of existing law, and that it is not interposed for any improper purpose, including delay.

It is not the amended rule's intention to encourage or create satellite litigation over the propriety of pleadings, motions or other papers. The court's inquiry into violations of the rule should ordinarily be restricted to the record then before the court, including any discovery addressed to the substance of the challenged pleading, and should focus on what was reasonable for the signer to believe at the time the pleading was submitted. Discovery directed to the signer's conduct should be allowed only by leave of court and should not be permitted in the absence of clear appearance of abuse. The rule does not require disclosure of privileged communications or work product to demonstrate that the signing of the pleading, motion or other paper is justified.

The amended rule gives the court greater latitude to tailor sanctions, including the award of expenses to the signer's opponent, to the particular situation before it, and authorizes the imposition of sanctions on the court's own motion. The provisions in the original rule for striking pleadings have been deleted as unnecessary. The striking of a pleading, motion or other paper is now mandatory where a failure to sign is not cured after notice, and within the court's discretion in other appropriate cases.

AUTHORS' COMMENTS

Analysis

6. Statutory Remedies.
7. Verification of Pleadings.

1. *Scope and Purpose of Rule.* Ariz. R. Civ. P. 11 imposes upon attorneys and unrepresented parties the responsibility to insure that assertions made, and positions taken, in pleadings are done so in good faith and not for some improper purpose. The Rule's requirements apply not just to pleadings as defined in Rule 7(a), but to motions and other papers that are filed as well. It is intended to discourage frivolous and/or legally unreasonable claims, or pleadings that are without factual foundation, even though not filed in subjective bad faith. The pendency of a civil action, however, is not a jurisdictional prerequisite to the imposition of sanctions under Rule 11. *Bryant v. Bloch Companies*, 166 Ariz. 46, 800 P.2d 33 (Ct. App. Div. 1 1990). While Rule 11 was partially intended to obviate the need for formal verification of pleadings, there are instances where a verification requirement has been retained in the Rules or is imposed by statute. The Rule applies only to civil proceedings, and has no counterpart in the criminal procedural rules. *State v. Shipman*, 208 Ariz. 474, 94 P.3d 1169 (Ct. App. Div. 2 2004). Accordingly, the Rule does not authorize the imposition of sanctions in a special action arising out of criminal proceedings. *State v. Shipman*, 208 Ariz. 474, 94 P.3d 1169 (Ct. App. Div. 2 2004).

2. *Comparison With Federal Rule.* There are significant differences, both substantively and stylistically, between ARCP 11(a) and FRCP 11, as a consequence of the 1993 and 2007 amendments to the latter Rule.

FRCP 11 has been restructured into subparts that do not correspond to the any of the subparts in the Arizona rule. The nature of the representations implicit in signing a pleading or other paper, or in presenting a position to the Federal Court, have been made more specific and objective.

Under FRCP 11(c), sanction awards are now discretionary rather than mandatory, are to be limited to what is necessary to deter repetition of the conduct or comparable conduct by others, and may include nonmonetary directives or orders to pay a penalty to the Court. Awards of expenses or fees to another party are to be ordered as a sanction only where they are incurred as a result of the violation and are warranted for effective deterrence, and may not be awarded by the Court on its own initiative.

Under FRCP 11(c), any motion seeking sanctions is served, but not filed until at least 21 days after being served (or a time period set by the court). If, during this "safe harbor" period, the challenged claim, defense or contention is withdrawn or corrected, the motion should not be filed with the court. Arizona's Rule 11 does not contain these provisions.

FRCP 11(d) states that it does not apply to disclosures or discovery requests, which are addressed separately in the Federal Rules of Civil Procedure. The Arizona Rules of Civil Procedure do not have a counterpart.

The FRCP 11 does not have a provision, however, that corresponds to ARCP 11(b), which delineates the manner for verifying pleadings when verification is required, or to ARCP 11(c), dealing with verification of pleadings when equitable relief is demanded.

In 2007, the language of FRCP 11 was amended as part of the general restyling of the Federal Rules of Civil Procedure to make the Federal Rules more easily understood and to make style and terminology consistent throughout the Federal Rules of Civil Procedure. Those stylistic modifications have not been incorporated into ARCP 11.

3. *Standards; Duties of Counsel.* Rule 11(a) requires that every pleading, motion and other paper (which includes discovery papers) be signed by at least one attorney of record for the party on whose behalf it is submitted, or by the unrepresented party. Under the Rule as amended in 1984, the signature constitutes a certification by the party or attorney that the pleading "is well grounded in fact and is warranted by existing law or a good faith argument for the extension, modification, or reversal of existing law; and that it is not interposed for any improper purpose. . . ." *See also, Villa De Jardines Ass'n v. Flagstar Bank, FSB*, 227 Ariz. 91, 253 P.3d 288 (Ct. App. Div. 2 2011), review denied, (Oct. 25, 2011) ("The good faith component of Rule 11 is not based on whether an attorney subjectively pursues claims in good faith, but instead is judged on an objective standard of what a professional competent attorney would do in similar circumstances . . . .", citing *Standage v. Jaburg & Wilk, P.C.*, 177 Ariz. 221, 866 P.2d 889 (Ct. App. Div. 1 1993).).

Before signing a pleading, counsel is required to make reasonable efforts to assure that the matters asserted are not illusory, frivolous, unnecessary or insubstantial. *James, Cooke & Hobson, Inc. v. Lake Havasu Plumbing & Fire Protection*, 177 Ariz. 316, 868 P.2d 329 (Ct. App. Div. 1 1993). In addition, as the facts of a case develop, counsel is under a continuing obligation to assess the validity of claims asserted. *Standage v. Jaburg & Wilk, P.C.*, 177 Ariz. 221, 866 P.2d 889 (Ct. App. Div. 1 1993); *Gilbert v. Board of Medical Examiners of State of Ariz.*, 155 Ariz. 169, 745 P.2d 617 (Ct. App. Div. 1 1987), superseded by statute as stated in, *Goodman v. Samaritan Health System*, 195 Ariz. 502, 990 P.2d 1061 (Ct. App. Div. 1 1999).

In sum, Rule 11 requires that, before signing a pleading, an attorney must possess a good faith belief, formed on the basis of a reasonable inquiry, that a colorable claim or defense exists. *Villa De Jardines Ass'n v. Flagstar Bank, FSB*, 227 Ariz. 91, 253 P.3d 288 (Ct. App. Div. 2 2011), review denied, (Oct. 25, 2011) ("The good faith component of Rule 11 is not based on whether an attorney subjectively pursues claims in good faith, but instead is judged on an objective standard of what a professional competent attorney would do in similar circumstances . . . .," citing *Standage v. Jaburg & Wilk, P.C.*, 177 Ariz. 221, 866 P.2d 889 (Ct. App. Div. 1 1993).); *Wolfinger v. Cheche*, 206 Ariz. 504, 80 P.3d 783 (Ct. App. Div. 1 2003). An attorney violates the objective standard of Rule 11 when (1) there was no reasonable inquiry into the basis for the pleading or motion, (2) there was no chance of success under existing precedent, and (3) there was no reasonable argument to extend, modify or reverse controlling law. *See also, Villa De Jardines Ass'n v. Flagstar Bank, FSB*, 227 Ariz. 91, 253 P.3d 288 (Ct. App. Div. 2 2011), review denied, (Oct. 25, 2011); *Wolfinger v. Cheche*, 206 Ariz. 504, 80 P.3d 783 (Ct. App. Div. 1 2003). The fact that summary judgment has been granted against a party, however, is not dispositive of the issue whether sanctions against that party's attorney are warranted under Rule 11. *Sallomi v. Phoenix Newspapers, Inc.*, 160 Ariz. 144, 771 P.2d 469, 16 Media L. Rep. (BNA) 1529 (Ct. App. Div. 2 1989).

The "reasonable efforts" required in any specific instance will depend upon a variety of factors, including the facts already known to or readily ascertainable by counsel, the amount of time available for investigation, the need to rely upon others, including the client, for information, and the plausibility of the claim itself. *See also, Villa De Jardines Ass'n v. Flagstar Bank, FSB*, 227 Ariz. 91, 253 P.3d 288 (Ct. App. Div. 2 2011), review denied, (Oct. 25, 2011); *Boone v. Superior Court In and For Maricopa County*, 145 Ariz. 235, 700 P.2d 1335 (1985). The filing of an action or pleading is not frivolous simply because counsel has not first substantiated the facts or expects to develop critical evidence through discovery. *Smith v. Lucia*, 173 Ariz. 290, 842 P.2d 1303 (Ct. App. Div. 1 1992); *Roberts v. Kino Community Hosp.*, 159 Ariz. 333, 767 P.2d 56 (Ct. App. Div. 2 1988).

The test is nominally an objective one of reasonableness, but is also analogous to the standard of Rule ER 3.1 of the Arizona Rules of Professional Conduct. A common theme in both Rules is the need for an examination of whether a claim is frivolous by considering both the objective legal reasonableness of the theory and the subjective motive of the proponent of the claim. *Matter of Levine*, 174 Ariz. 146, 847 P.2d 1093 (1993), reinstatement granted, 176 Ariz. 535, 863 P.2d 254 (1993); *Hill v. Chubb Life American Ins. Co.*, 178 Ariz. 37, 870 P.2d 1133 (Ct. App. Div. 1

1993), vacated on other grounds, 182 Ariz. 158, 894 P.2d 701 (1995).

An attorney is also under a continuing duty to review and examine positions taken as the facts of the case are developed. If an attorney becomes aware of information which would lead a reasonable attorney to believe that there is no factual or legal basis for a position taken, the attorney may be obligated to reevaluate an earlier certification under Rule 11. *Standage v. Jaburg & Wilk, P.C.*, 177 Ariz. 221, 866 P.2d 889 (Ct. App. Div. 1 1993); *Wright v. Hills*, 161 Ariz. 583, 780 P.2d 416 (Ct. App. Div. 2 1989), abrogated on other grounds by *James, Cooke & Hobson, Inc. v. Lake Havasu Plumbing & Fire Protection*, 177 Ariz. 316, 868 P.2d 329 (Ct. App. Div. 1 1993), and *MacLean v. State Dept. of Educ.*, 195 Ariz. 235, 986 P.2d 903, 9 A.D. Cas. (BNA) 1284 (Ct. App. Div. 2 1999), as corrected, (Aug. 27, 1999); *Gilbert v. Board of Medical Examiners of State of Ariz.*, 155 Ariz. 169, 745 P.2d 617 (Ct. App. Div. 1 1987), superseded by statute as stated in, *Goodman v. Samaritan Health System*, 195 Ariz. 502, 990 P.2d 1061 (Ct. App. Div. 1 1999).

The trial court has broad discretion in fashioning an appropriate sanction where a violation of Rule 11 is found, including an award of expenses and attorneys' fees. *Corbett v. ManorCare of America, Inc.*, 213 Ariz. 618, 146 P.3d 1027 (Ct. App. Div. 2 2006). The Rule's prior specific reference to the striking of pleadings was eliminated solely because it was deemed unnecessary, and does not signify that the sanction of striking pleadings may not be employed.

A request for an award of sanctions under Rule 11 involves many of the same issues and concerns as are raised where a party invokes the provisions of A.R.S. § 12-349 (amended 2013). Effective January 1, 2013, the definition of "without substantial justification" set forth in subparagraph (F) was amended to delete the phrase "constitutes harassment." *See also*, *Harris v. Reserve Life Ins. Co.*, 158 Ariz. 380, 762 P.2d 1334 (Ct. App. Div. 1 1988). The sanctions imposed, however, must bear some relationship to the violation and, where a monetary sanction is imposed, it should be related to the expenses directly caused by the sanctioned conduct. *Taliaferro v. Taliaferro*, 188 Ariz. 333, 935 P.2d 911 (Ct. App. Div. 1 1996). An award of sanctions will be reviewed on appeal only for an abuse of discretion. *Taliaferro v. Taliaferro*, 188 Ariz. 333, 935 P.2d 911 (Ct. App. Div. 1 1996).

The availability of Rule 11 does not operate to deprive the trial court of its inherent power to impose sanctions for attorney misconduct before the Court and/or violations of the rules of practice. *Precision Components, Inc. v. Harrison, Harper, Christian & Dichter, P.C.*, 179 Ariz. 552, 880 P.2d 1098 (Ct. App. Div.

2 1993). That power arises from, and is governed by, the control necessarily vested in courts to manage their own affairs so as to accomplish the orderly and expeditious disposition of disputes. *Hmielewski v. Maricopa County*, 192 Ariz. 1, 960 P.2d 47 (Ct. App. Div. 1 1997). The imposition of sanctions should ordinarily be preceded by some form of notice and opportunity to be heard on the issue, but that may consist of the trial court explaining to the attorneys the reason for the proposed sanctions and the form they will take, and providing an opportunity for them to argue against them. *Hmielewski v. Maricopa County*, 192 Ariz. 1, 960 P.2d 47 (Ct. App. Div. 1 1997). Whether an additional hearing on sanctions should be conducted depends on the nature of the case, and the factors to be considered include (1) the general circumstances of the violation, (2) the type and severity of the sanctions being considered, (3) the trial court's degree of participation in the proceedings and knowledge of the underlying facts, and (4) the need, if any, for further inquiry. *Hmielewski v. Maricopa County*, 192 Ariz. 1, 960 P.2d 47 (Ct. App. Div. 1 1997).

The trial court's discretion as to when motions for sanctions may be heard is governed by Rule 11, not Rule 54. *Britt v. Steffen*, 220 Ariz. 265, 205 P.3d 357 (Ct. App. Div. 1 2008). A trial court may sanction conduct that violates Rule 11 before the merits of an action have been determined, and even when it never obtains jurisdiction to consider the merits. *Britt v. Steffen*, 220 Ariz. 265, 205 P.3d 357 (Ct. App. Div. 1 2008). While Rule 11 motions should be filed within a reasonable time, the trial court's discretion to impose sanctions does not end at some arbitrary period of time following a decision on the merits or even the entry of judgment. *Britt v. Steffen*, 220 Ariz. 265, 205 P.3d 357 (Ct. App. Div. 1 2008).

4. *Appeal From Award of Sanctions.* An attorney subjected to an award of sanctions under Rule 11 has standing to challenge that award on appeal, even though the attorney is technically not a party to the action. *Wieman v. Roysden*, 166 Ariz. 281, 802 P.2d 432 (Ct. App. Div. 1 1990); *Barrow v. Arizona Bd. of Regents*, 158 Ariz. 71, 761 P.2d 145, 49 Ed. Law Rep. 761 (Ct. App. Div. 2 1988); *Abril v. Harris*, 157 Ariz. 78, 754 P.2d 1353 (Ct. App. Div. 2 1987). The evidence will be viewed in a manner most favorable to sustaining the award of sanctions. *Heuisler v. Phoenix Newspapers, Inc.*, 168 Ariz. 278, 812 P.2d 1096, 18 Media L. Rep. (BNA) 2305 (Ct. App. Div. 1 1991).

The Court of Appeals has indicated that, in light of intervening United States Supreme Court precedent, the "three-tiered" standard of review articulated in *Wright v. Hills*, 161 Ariz. 583, 780 P.2d 416 (Ct. App. Div. 2 1989), abrogated on other grounds by *James, Cooke & Hobson, Inc. v. Lake Havasu Plumbing & Fire Protection*, 177 Ariz. 316, 868 P.2d 329 (Ct. App. Div. 1 1993), and *MacLean v. State Dept. of Educ.*, 195 Ariz. 235, 986 P.2d 903,

9 A.D. Cas. (BNA) 1284 (Ct. App. Div. 2 1999), as corrected, (Aug. 27, 1999), will no longer be employed, and that all aspects of orders imposing sanctions under Rule 11 will now be reviewed solely for abuse of the trial court's discretion. *James, Cooke & Hobson, Inc. v. Lake Havasu Plumbing & Fire Protection*, 177 Ariz. 316, 868 P.2d 329 (Ct. App. Div. 1 1993). *See also, Villa De Jardines Ass'n v. Flagstar Bank, FSB*, 227 Ariz. 91, 253 P.3d 288 (Ct. App. Div. 2 2011), review denied, (Oct. 25, 2011) (reviewing for abuse of discretion attorney fees awards under Rule 11; reviewing de novo the legal basis for such award). The trial court's personal contact with the attorneys involved, however, will entitle its views to some deference. *Sallomi v. Phoenix Newspapers, Inc.*, 160 Ariz. 144, 771 P.2d 469, 16 Media L. Rep. (BNA) 1529 (Ct. App. Div. 2 1989).

5. *Failure to Sign.* If a pleading or other paper is filed unsigned by either an attorney or the party, it is to be stricken unless it is signed promptly after the omission is called to the attention of the attorney or party. The failure of an unrepresented plaintiff to sign a complaint is a jurisdictional defect and results in the action not being validly instituted. Such an unsigned complaint does not cease the running of the statute of limitations. *Safeway Stores, Inc. v. Maricopa County Superior Court*, 19 Ariz. App. 210, 505 P.2d 1383 (Div. 1 1973). The omission of a party's or counsel's signature on a pleading or other paper does not automatically render the pleading invalid under Rule 11(a), or require that it be stricken, provided the omission is cured promptly after the omission is called to the attention of the filing party. *BCAZ Corp. v. Helgoe*, 194 Ariz. 11, 976 P.2d 260 (Ct. App. Div. 1 1998), opinion supplemented on reh'g, (Mar. 25, 1999).

6. *Statutory Remedies.* Various statutes also provide a vehicle for recovering attorney fees. A nominally separate basis for awarding sanctions for the bringing of meritless claims is provided by A.R.S. § 12-349 (amended 2013).

"Without substantial justification" is defined in the statute to mean that the claim or defense is groundless and is not made in good faith. A.R.S. § 12-349(F) (amended 2013). Effective January 1, 2013, the definition of "without substantial justification"was amended to delete the phrase "constitutes harassment."

1. Brings or defends a claim without substantial justification.
2. Brings or defends a claim solely or primarily for delay or harassment.
3. Unreasonably expands or delays the proceeding.
4. Engages in abuse of discovery.

This statute provides that, in any civil action commenced in a court of record, the court shall assess reasonable attorneys' fees and, at the court's discretion, double damages of not to exceed five thousand dollars ($5,000) against any attorney or party, including the state or any of its political subdivisions, who is found to have done any of the following:

Each element must be proven by a preponderance of the evidence, and the absence of one element renders the statute inapplicable. *Johnson v. Mohave County*, 206 Ariz. 330, 78 P.3d 1051 (Ct. App. Div. 1 2003). Subpart (C) of the statute also provides that attorneys' fees may not be assessed if, after filing an action, a voluntary dismissal is filed for any claim or defense within a reasonable time after the attorney or party filing the dismissal knew or reasonably should have known that the claim or defense was without substantial justification.

A.R.S. § 12-350 provides that, in awarding attorneys' fees under A.R.S. § 12-349 (amended 2013). The Court must set forth the specific reasons for the award, and may take into account the following factors in determining whether such an award is warranted:

1. The extent of any effort made to determine the validity of a claim before the claim was asserted;
2. The extent of any effort made after commencement of an action to reduce the number of claims or defenses being asserted or to dismiss claims or defenses found not to be valid;
3. The availability of facts to assist a party in determining the validity of a claim or defense;
4. The relative financial positions of the parties involved;
5. Whether the action was prosecuted, in whole or in part, in bad faith;
6. Whether issues of fact determinative of the validity of a party's claim or defense were reasonably in conflict;
7. The extent to which the party prevailed with respect to the amount and number of claims in controversy; and
8. The amount and conditions of any offer of judgment or settlement as related to the amount and conditions of the ultimate relief granted by the court.

It has been held that the same issues and concerns are involved, where a party requests sanctions under A.R.S. § 12-349 (amended 2013), as where the request is based upon Ariz. R. Civ. P. 11. *Harris v. Reserve Life Ins. Co.*, 158 Ariz. 380, 762 P.2d 1334 (Ct. App. Div. 1 1988).

In addition, attorneys who engage in abusive litigation tactics are subject to claims for abuse of process and/or malicious prosecution brought by the adverse party subjected to such tactics. *Chalpin v. Snyder*, 220 Ariz. 413, 207 P.3d 666 (Ct. App. Div. 1 2008); *Giles v. Hill Lewis Marce*, 195 Ariz. 358, 988 P.2d 143 (Ct.

App. Div. 2 1999). *See also Boone v. Superior Court In and For Maricopa County*, 145 Ariz. 235, 242, 700 P.2d 1335, 1342 (1985); *McElhanon v. Hing*, 151 Ariz. 386, 394, 728 P.2d 256, 264 (Ct. App. Div. 1 1985), judgment aff'd in part, vacated in part on other grounds, 151 Ariz. 403, 728 P.2d 273 (1986). Liability for such a claim, however, must be predicated on conduct that is intentional, rather than merely negligent or inadvertent. *Bird v. Rothman*, 128 Ariz. 599, 627 P.2d 1097 (Ct. App. Div. 2 1981); *Lewis v. Swenson*, 126 Ariz. 561, 617 P.2d 69 (Ct. App. Div. 1 1980).

7. *Verification of Pleadings.* A pleading need not be verified unless an applicable statute or Rule of Civil Procedure requires that. *Colboch v. Aviation Credit Corp.*, 64 Ariz. 88, 166 P.2d 584 (1946). A complaint must be verified in derivative actions, Rule 23.1; in actions seeking appointment of a receiver, Rule 66(a); in quiet title actions, A.R.S. § 12-1102; in forcible entry and detainer actions, A.R.S. § 12-1175; in replevin actions, A.R.S. § 12-1301; and, in actions for dissolution of marriage, A.R.S. § 25-314. An injunction, or temporary restraining order, may be granted either upon a verified complaint or on affidavit. Rule 65(d); A.R.S. § 12-1803. Claims in forfeiture proceedings must be verified by the claimant personally. *State ex rel. McDougall v. Superior Court In and For County of Maricopa*, 173 Ariz. 385, 843 P.2d 1277 (Ct. App. Div. 1 1992).

Rule 9(i) requires the verification of an answer which raises certain specified defenses. A.R.S. § 22-216 imposes the identical requirement for answers filed in justice court actions. *See also*, Justice Court Rules of Civil Procedure 109(c) (effective, Jan. 1, 2013). Rule 11(c) does not require that a complaint seeking equitable relief be verified. Where the complaint in an action seeking equitable relief is verified, however, Rule 11(c) requires that the responsive pleading of the opposing party be verified as well. *Barnet v. Board of Medical Examiners*, 121 Ariz. 338, 590 P.2d 454 (1979). In that instance, each material allegation of the verified complaint not denied under oath will be deemed admitted. The verification is to be made by the party or on the party's behalf by a person acquainted with the facts.

Under Rule 80(i), what is termed an "unsworn declaration under penalty of perjury" may be used in place of a formal, sworn verification where a verification is required by the Rules.

Rule 12. Defenses and objections; when and how presented; by pleading or motion; motion for judgment on pleadings

(a) When Presented.

(1) A defendant shall serve and file an answer

(A) within twenty days after the service of the summons and complaint upon the defendant, except as otherwise provided in Rules 4.2(d) and 4.2(m) of these rules; or

(B) if service of the summons has been timely waived on request under Rule 4.1(c) or 4.2(c), within sixty (60) days after the date when the request was sent, or within ninety (90) days after that date if the defendant was addressed outside any judicial district of the United States.

(2) A party served with a pleading stating a cross-claim against that party shall serve and file an answer thereto within twenty days after being served. The plaintiff shall serve and file a reply to a counterclaim in the answer within twenty days after service of the answer or, if a reply is ordered by the court, within twenty days after service of the order, unless the order otherwise directs.

(3) Unless a different time is fixed by court order, the service of a motion permitted under this rule alters these periods of time as follows:

(A) if the court denies the motion or postpones its disposition until the trial on the merits, the responsive pleading shall be served within ten days after notice of the court's action; or

(B) if the court grants a motion for a more definite statement, the responsive pleading shall be served within ten days after service of the more definite statement.

Amended Sept. 15, 1987, effective Nov. 15, 1987; Oct. 2, 1991, effective Dec. 1, 1991; Oct. 9, 1996, effective Dec. 1, 1996. Amended effective May 31, 2002.

(b) How Presented; Motion to Dismiss. Every defense, in law or fact, to a claim for relief in any pleading, whether a claim, counterclaim, cross-claim, or third-party claim, shall be asserted in the responsive pleading thereto if one is required, except that the following defenses may at the option of the pleader be made by motion:

1. Lack of jurisdiction over the subject matter.
2. Lack of jurisdiction over the person.
3. Improper venue.
4. Insufficiency of process.

5. Insufficiency of service of process.
6. Failure to state a claim upon which relief can be granted.
7. Failure to join a party under Rule 19.

A motion making any of these defenses shall be made before pleading if a further pleading is permitted. No defense or objection is waived by being joined with one or more other defenses or objections in a responsive pleading or motion. If a pleading sets forth a claim for relief to which the adverse party is not required to serve a responsive pleading, the adverse party may assert at the trial any defense in law or fact to that claim for relief. The defense numbered 3 may be made only if the action cannot be or could not have been transferred to the proper county pursuant to A.R.S., § 12-404. If, on a motion asserting the defense numbered 6 to dismiss for failure of the pleading to state a claim upon which relief can be granted, matters outside the pleading are presented to and not excluded by the court, the motion shall be treated as one for summary judgment and disposed of as provided in Rule 56, and all parties shall be given reasonable opportunity to present all material made pertinent to such a motion by Rule 56.

Amended July 14, 1961; July 1, 1966, effective Nov. 1, 1966; Sept. 15, 1987, effective Nov. 15, 1987.

(c) Motion for Judgment on the Pleadings. After the pleadings are closed but within such time as not to delay the trial, any party may move for judgment on the pleadings. If, on a motion for judgment on the pleadings, matters outside the pleadings are presented to and not excluded by the court, the motion shall be treated as one for summary judgment and disposed of as provided in Rule 56, and all parties shall be given reasonable opportunity to present all material made pertinent to such a motion by Rule 56.

(d) Preliminary Hearings. The defenses specifically enumerated as 1 through 7 in subdivision (b) of this Rule, whether made in a pleading or by motion, and the motion for judgment mentioned in subdivision (c) of this Rule shall be heard and determined before trial on application of any party, unless the court orders that the hearing and determination thereof be deferred until the trial.

(e) Motion for More Definite Statement. If a pleading to which a responsive pleading is permitted is so vague or ambiguous that a party cannot reasonably be required to frame a responsive pleading, the party may move for a more definite statement before interposing a responsive pleading. The motion shall point out the defects complained of and the details desired. If the motion is granted and the order of the court is not obeyed within ten days after notice of the order or within such other time as the court may fix, the court may strike the pleading to which the motion was directed or make such order as it deems just.

Amended Sept. 15, 1987, effective Nov. 15, 1987.

(f) Motion to Strike. Upon motion made by a party before responding to a pleading or, if no responsive pleading is permitted by these Rules, upon motion made by a party within twenty days after service of the pleading upon the party or upon the court's own initiative at any time, the court may order stricken from a pleading any insufficient defense or any redundant, immaterial, impertinent, or scandalous matter.

Formerly Rule 12(g). Amended Sept. 15, 1987, effective Nov. 15, 1987. Redesignated Rule 12(f) Oct. 15, 2001, effective Dec. 1, 2001.

(g) Consolidation of Defenses in Motion. A party who makes a motion under this rule may join with it any other motions herein provided for and then available to the party. If a party makes a motion under this rule but omits therefrom any defense or objection then available to the party which this rule permits to be raised by motion, the party shall not thereafter make a motion based on the defense or objection so omitted, except a motion as provided in subdivision (g)(2) hereof on any of the grounds there stated.

Formerly Rule 12(h). Amended July 1, 1966, effective Nov. 1, 1966; Sept. 15, 1987, effective Nov. 15, 1987. Redesignated Rule 12(g) and amended Oct. 15, 2001, effective Dec. 1, 2001.

(h) Waiver or Preservation of Certain Defenses. A party waives all defenses and objections which that party does not present either by motion as hereinbefore provided, or, if that party has made no motion, in that party's answer or reply, except

(1) A defense of lack of jurisdiction over the person, improper venue, insufficiency of process, or insufficiency of service of process is waived (A) if omitted from a motion in the circumstances described in subdivision (h), or (B) if it is neither made by motion under this rule nor included in a responsive pleading or an amendment thereof permitted by Rule 15(a) to be made as a matter of course.

(2) A defense of failure to state a claim upon which relief can be granted, a defense of failure to join a party indispensable under Rule 19, and an objection of failure to state a legal defense to a claim may be made in any pleading permitted or ordered under Rule 7(a), or by motion for judgment on the pleadings, or at the trial on the merits.

(3) Whenever it appears by suggestion of the parties or otherwise that the court lacks jurisdiction of the subject matter, the court shall dismiss the action.

Formerly Rule 12(i). Amended July 1, 1966, effective Nov. 1, 1966; Sept. 15,

1987, effective Nov. 15, 1987. Renumbered as Rule 12(h) and amended Oct. 15, 2001, effective Dec. 1, 2001.

(i) Renumbered as Rule 12(h)

STATE BAR COMMITTEE NOTES

1961 Amendment

[Rule 12(b)] The Committee recommends the retention of defense numbered 3 of Rule 12(b) because of possible situations involving improper venue that could not be remedied by transferring an action to another county.

The amended rule is designed expressly to settle the present conflict between this Rule and A.R.S. Section 12-404.

1966 Amendments

[Rule 12(b)] The terminology of subdivision 7 is changed to accord with the language of Rule 19. The subdivision is intended to provide for dismissal where there has been a failure to join a party who is indispensable under Rule 19.

[Rule 12(h)] The subdivision as amended continues to preclude piecemeal consideration of the case. For exceptions to the requirements of consolidation, see Rule 12(i)(2).

[Rule 12(i)] The first paragraph of this subdivision is not in the amended federal rule. Under the previous rule, numerous federal court decisions had divided on whether, when the party sees fit to offer a defensive motion, he may thereafter allege the defenses mentioned in this rule in his answer when he has not included them in his motion. The revised rule adopts the holding of those cases concluding that the defense is waived in such circumstances. The rule states that lack of jurisdiction over the person, improper venue, insufficiency of process, and insufficiency of service of process are waived if (a) a party offers a motion and (b) does not include them. This re-emphasizes the policy of avoiding piecemeal decisions.

This does not mean that the party must make a motion. He may leave these defenses to his answer if he wishes; the requirement of the rule is merely that if he does make a motion, he must include them all at once. However, the rule further provides that the same defenses are waived unless included in either a motion or an answer, subject only to amendments as a matter of course.

This waiver rule applies only to the defenses specified, some defenses being regarded as too important to be subject to such waiver. These are the defenses of failure to state a claim upon which relief can be granted; failure to join party who is indispensable under Rule 19; failure to state a legal defense; and want of jurisdiction over the subject matter. Each can be subsequently raised.

The amendment does not alter the results of existing Arizona decisions and is in accord for example with *Baxter v. Harrison*, 83 Ariz. 354, 321 P.2d 1019 (1958).

AUTHORS' COMMENTS

Analysis

1. Scope and Purpose of Rule.
2. Comparison With Federal Rule.
3. Time for Answer.
4. Rule 12(b) Defenses; Waiver.
5. Consolidation of Defenses in Rule 12 Motion.
6. Motions to Dismiss Generally.

7. Treatment of Motion to Dismiss as Motion for Summary Judgment.
8. Subject Matter Jurisdiction.
9. Personal Jurisdiction.
10. Resolution of Factual Issues Raised by Jurisdictional Motions.
11. Improper Venue.
12. Forum Non Conveniens.
13. Change of Venue in Actions Against the State.
14. Insufficiency of Process; Insufficiency of Service.
15. Failure to State a Claim for Relief.
16. Failure to Join Indispensable Party.
17. Raising Affirmative Defenses by Rule 12 Motion.
18. Statute of Limitations.
19. Statute of Frauds.
20. Motion for Judgment on the Pleadings.
21. Motion for More Definite Statement.
22. Motions to Strike.
23. Prior Pending Actions; Abatement.

1. *Scope and Purpose of Rule.* Ariz. R. Civ. P. 12 generally governs the time within which the defendant must appear and defend an action and prescribes the procedures for presenting, or preserving, certain defenses which question the sufficiency of the pleadings and/or the jurisdiction of the Court.

2. *Comparison With Federal Rule.* Despite structural differences, ARCP 12 is generally the same as FRCP 12, but there are important differences between the two rules, some of which are summarized here.

As a consequence of the 2009 amendments to FRCP 12, the times set in former FRCP 12 at 10 and 20 days were revised to 14 and 21 days.

FRCP 12(a) also states that the United States and federal officers and agencies have sixty (60) days to respond to actions brought against them. ARCP 12 does not have a provision giving the State of Arizona, its officers and agencies a greater period to respond.

ARCP 12(b) provides that the defense of improper venue can be raised only if the action cannot be, or could not have been, transferred pursuant to A.R.S. § 12-404. FRCP 12 has no such provision. ARCP 12(c), (e), (f), (g) and (h) are generally similar to FRCP 12(c), (e), (f), (g) and (h). The first paragraph of ARCP 12(h), however, is not contained in the corresponding FRCP 12(h). ARCP 12(d) is substantively identical to FRCP 12(i).

ARCP 12 also does not have a provision that corresponds to FRCP 12(d) [Result of Presenting Matters Outside the Pleadings].

In 2007, the language of FRCP 12 was amended as part of the general restyling of the Federal Rules of Civil Procedure to make the Federal Rules more easily understood and to make style and terminology consistent throughout the Federal Rules of Civil Procedure. Those stylistic modifications have not been incorporated into ARCP 12.

3. *Time for Answer.* Generally, the defendant must file and serve an answer within twenty (20) days after service of the summons and complaint within the state. *See* Ariz. R. Civ. P. 12(a)(1).

The service of a motion permitted by Rule 12 tolls the time to file a responsive pleading pending the resolution of a motion. See, Rule 12(a)(3). Moreover, the time for filing an answer is tolled pending the resolution of a motion for summary judgment. *Waltner v. JPMorgan Chase Bank, N.A.*, 231 Ariz. 484, 297 P.3d 176 (Ct. App. Div. 1 2013) (addressing issues associated with Rule 12(b) motion presenting matters outside the pleadings converted to Rule 56 motion for summary judgment). Similarly, the time for filing an answer is tolled pending the resolution of a motion to dismiss for improper venue filed within the time to permitted to answer. *Prutch v. Town of Quartzsite*, 231 Ariz. 431, 296 P.3d 94 (Ct. App. Div. 1 2013), as amended, (Feb. 26, 2013).

Ariz. R. Civ. P. 4.2(m) governs the time for answering when service is made upon a defendant outside the state, and it provides that the defendant shall appear and answer within thirty (30) days after *completion* of service. The date of "completion" of such service, however, is no longer the date on which the affidavit of service is filed although no default may be taken until it is. *But see Creach v. Angulo*, 186 Ariz. 548, 925 P.2d 689 (Ct. App. Div. 1 1996), decision approved, 189 Ariz. 212, 941 P.2d 224 (1997). The time for answering in a forcible entry and detainer action is controlled by statute and is considerably shorter. A.R.S. § 12-1175; *Byrd v. Peterson*, 66 Ariz. 253, 186 P.2d 955 (1947). The time for answering in a forcible entry and detainer action is controlled by statute and is considerably shorter. A.R.S. § 12-1175; *Byrd v. Peterson*, 66 Ariz. 253, 186 P.2d 955 (1947); the time for answering in.

Under the 1996 amendments to the Rule, additional time to respond is granted to defendants who execute and return a waiver of service requested under the authority provided in Rule 4.1(c) or Rule 4.2(c). Defendants located within the United States who waive service have until sixty (60) days from the date the request for waiver was mailed to respond to the complaint; for defendants in foreign countries, that period is ninety (90) days.

An answer to a cross-claim must be filed within twenty (20)

days of service of the pleading stating the cross-claim. A reply to a counterclaim stated in the defendant's answer must be filed within twenty (20) days of service of the answer or service of an order directing a reply. Under Rule 14(a), a third-party complaint, for purposes of determining the time for, and authorized methods of, responding is treated in the same fashion as the original complaint.

If the party responding to a complaint, counterclaim, cross-claim or third-party complaint initially files one of the motions authorized by Rule 12(b), and it is denied, an answer is due within ten (10) days of notice of the court's action. These time periods may, of course, be adjusted through stipulation of the parties, or by the Court under Rule 6. While the filing of a motion under Rule 12 may extend the time for filing an answer, it does not affect the deadline for filing a claim in a civil forfeiture proceeding, which is governed by statute. *State v. Five Thousand Five Hundred & 00/100 Dollars ($5,500.00) in U.S. Currency*, 169 Ariz. 156, 817 P.2d 960 (Ct. App. Div. 1 1991).

4. *Rule 12(b) Defenses; Waiver.* Rule 12(b) lists seven separate "legal" defenses which, at the defendant's option, may be presented by initial motion or preserved by appropriate allegation in the answer: lack of subject matter jurisdiction, lack of personal jurisdiction, improper venue, insufficiency of process, insufficiency of service, failure to state a claim and failure to join a party under Rule 19. Under the "once and for all" regime of Rule 12(h), the defendant must include all available Rule 12(b) defenses in the initial motion or the answer, or they are waived. See State Bar Committee Note to 1966 Amendment to former Rule 12(i); *cf. also Sirek v. Fairfield Snowbowl, Inc.*, 166 Ariz. 183, 800 P.2d 1291 (Ct. App. Div. 1 1990). This does not apply to the defenses of lack of subject matter jurisdiction, failure to state a claim and failure to join an indispensable party which may be raised at any time. *Mallamo v. Hartman*, 70 Ariz. 420, 222 P.2d 797 (1950); *Swichtenberg v. Brimer*, 171 Ariz. 77, 828 P.2d 1218 (Ct. App. Div. 1 1991); *Hibbs ex rel. Arizona Dept. of Revenue v. Chandler Ginning Co.*, 164 Ariz. 11, 790 P.2d 297 (Ct. App. Div. 1 1990); *Lightning A Ranch Venture v. Tankersley*, 161 Ariz. 497, 779 P.2d 812 (Ct. App. Div. 2 1989); *Carlson v. Brown*, 118 Ariz. 387, 576 P.2d 1387 (Ct. App. Div. 1 1978).

5. *Consolidation of Defenses in Rule 12 Motion.* As noted, Arizona has a "once and for all" regime with respect to the defenses listed in Rule 12(b)(2), (3), (4) and (5). If a defendant raises any of these matters by initial Rule 12 motion, then all other Rule 12 motions then available must also be made at the same time. If there has been a Rule 12 motion raising any of these defenses, then a subsequent answer may not allege them. A defendant may elect not to file a Rule 12 motion and allege these

defenses, if applicable, in the answer, but must do so or they are waived. This rule does not apply to the defenses of lack of subject matter jurisdiction, failure to join a party under Rule 19, or failure to state a claim or defense.

6. *Motions to Dismiss Generally.* Dismissal under Rule 12(b)(6) is appropriate only if "as a matter of law plaintiffs would not be entitled to relief under any interpretation of the facts susceptible of proof. *Coleman v. City of Mesa*, 230 Ariz. 352, 284 P.3d 863 (2012) ("In adjudicating a Rule 12(b)(6) motion to dismiss, . . ., a court does not resolve factual disputes between the parties on an undeveloped record."); *Fidelity Sec. Life Ins. Co. v. State, Dept. of Ins.*, 191 Ariz. 222, 954 P.2d 580 (1998).

A motion raising one of the defenses listed in Rule 12 is an appearance and defense, which precludes the entry of default. *See,* Ariz. R. Civ. P. 12(a)(3)(A). Under Rule 15(a), as amended effective January 12, 2012, a party confronted with a motion brought pursuant to Rule 12(b), (e) or (f) may amend its pleading once as a matter of course within 21 days of service of such motion.

The denial of a motion to dismiss is not an appealable order. Special action jurisdiction is rarely accepted when the petitioner seeks relief from the denial of a motion to dismiss, but an exception will be made when the petition reveals an absence of jurisdiction in the trial court, as an appeal is not an adequate remedy for the trial court's requiring a defense in a matter over which it has no jurisdiction. *Taylor v. Jarrett*, 191 Ariz. 550, 959 P.2d 807 (Ct. App. Div. 1 1998). The exercise of special action jurisdiction over the denial of a motion to dismiss may also be appropriate where the issue presented is of statewide importance. *Qwest Corp. v. Kelly*, 204 Ariz. 25, 59 P.3d 789 (Ct. App. Div. 2 2002).

The dismissal of a complaint under Rule 12(b)(6) is reviewed *de novo*. *Coleman v. City of Mesa*, 230 Ariz. 352, 284 P.3d 863 (2012); *Wilmot v. Wilmot*, 203 Ariz. 565, 58 P.3d 507 (2002). On review of the granting of a motion to dismiss, all material facts alleged by the non-moving party are taken to be true. *McMurray v. Dream Catcher USA, Inc.*, 220 Ariz. 71, 202 P.3d 536 (Ct. App. Div. 2 2009).

7. *Treatment of Motion to Dismiss as Motion for Summary Judgment.* The final sentence of Rule 12(b) provides that where a motion under the Rule is accompanied and supported by matters outside the pleadings which are considered by the Court, it is to be treated as a motion for summary judgment under Rule 56. *Smith v. Payne*, 156 Ariz. 506, 753 P.2d 1162 (1988); *Vasquez v. State*, 220 Ariz. 304, 206 P.3d 753 (Ct. App. Div. 2 2008); *Blanchard v. Show Low Planning and Zoning Com'n*, 196 Ariz. 114, 993 P.2d 1078 (Ct. App. Div. 1 1999). That treatment is not appropriate if the extraneous matters submitted in support of the motion

do not add to or subtract from the pleadings on file. *Strategic Development and Const., Inc. v. 7th & Roosevelt Partners, LLC*, 224 Ariz. 60, 226 P.3d 1046 (Ct. App. Div. 1 2010); *Brosie v. Stockton*, 105 Ariz. 574, 468 P.2d 933 (1970).

Moreover, a Rule 12(b)(6) motion that refers to a contract or other document attached to the complaint does not trigger Rule 56 treatment insofar as the referenced matter is not 'outside the pleading' within the meaning of the rule. *Strategic Development and Const., Inc. v. 7th & Roosevelt Partners, LLC*, 224 Ariz. 60, 226 P.3d 1046 (Ct. App. Div. 1 2010). Even if a document is not attached to the complaint, if it is a matter of public record or central to the claim, the court may consider the document without converting a Rule 12 motion to dismiss to a Rule 56 motion for summary judgment. *ELM Retirement Center, LP v. Callaway*, 226 Ariz. 287, 246 P.3d 938 (Ct. App. Div. 1 2010); *Strategic Development and Const., Inc. v. 7th & Roosevelt Partners, LLC*, 224 Ariz. 60, 226 P.3d 1046 (Ct. App. Div. 1 2010) (conversion not required when Rule 12(b) motion attaches extraneous documents that are a matter of public record). *But see, Canyon del Rio Investors, L.L.C. v. City of Flagstaff*, 227 Ariz. 336, 258 P.3d 154 (Ct. App. Div. 1 2011) (motion to dismiss converted to motion for summary judgment where responding party attached extraneous documents, which the trial court did not strike).

If the motion to dismiss is to be treated as a motion for summary judgment, all parties must be so advised by the Court and given a reasonable opportunity to present the underlying facts to the Court. *Gatecliff v. Great Republic Life Ins. Co.*, 154 Ariz. 502, 744 P.2d 29 (Ct. App. Div. 1 1987); *Parks v. Macro-Dynamics, Inc.*, 121 Ariz. 517, 591 P.2d 1005 (Ct. App. Div. 2 1979); *Davidson v. All State Materials Co.*, 101 Ariz. 375, 419 P.2d 732 (1966); *Allison v. State*, 101 Ariz. 418, 420 P.2d 289 (1966). *But see, Canyon del Rio Investors, L.L.C. v. City of Flagstaff*, 227 Ariz. 336, 258 P.3d 154 (Ct. App. Div. 1 2011) (on appeal, Rule 12(b) dismissal deemed Rule 56 summary judgment, even absent notice and express opportunity to present additional facts to the court).

A party must timely respond, nonetheless, to a motion to dismiss which may be subject to conversion and a party served with such motion may not wait to respond until the court signals whether it will treat the motion as a motion for summary judgment. *Strategic Development and Const., Inc. v. 7th & Roosevelt Partners, LLC*, 224 Ariz. 60, 226 P.3d 1046 (Ct. App. Div. 1 2010).

A party uncertain about whether the court will treat the Rule 12 (b)(6) motion as a Rule 56 motion "may confer with the moving party about a briefing schedule to be presented to the court," or may respond to the motion to dismiss in accordance with Rule 7.1(a) "and ask the court in its response for more time to present additional materials if the court determines to treat the motion as a motion for summary judgment." *Strategic Development and Const., Inc. v. 7th & Roosevelt Partners, LLC*, 224 Ariz. 60, 226 P.3d 1046 (Ct. App. Div. 1 2010). If the motion is supported by factual affidavits and the party opposing the motion fails to object to the court's consideration of matters outside the pleadings, the Court may take the facts stated therein as true. *Payne v. Pennzoil Corp.*, 138 Ariz. 52, 672 P.2d 1322 (Ct. App. Div. 2 1983).

8. *Subject Matter Jurisdiction.* The defense that the court lacks jurisdiction over the subject matter of the action is one that may be raised at any time. *Swichtenberg v. Brimer*, 171 Ariz. 77, 828 P.2d 1218 (Ct. App. Div. 1 1991); *Hibbs ex rel. Arizona Dept. of Revenue v. Chandler Ginning Co.*, 164 Ariz. 11, 790 P.2d 297 (Ct. App. Div. 1 1990); *Lightning A Ranch Venture v. Tankersley*, 161 Ariz. 497, 779 P.2d 812 (Ct. App. Div. 2 1989); *Carlson v. Brown*, 118 Ariz. 387, 576 P.2d 1387 (Ct. App. Div. 1 1978). The parties to an action cannot by consent confer upon a court subject matter jurisdiction which it otherwise would not have. *Solomon v. Findley*, 165 Ariz. 45, 796 P.2d 477 (Ct. App. Div. 2 1990), decision approved, 167 Ariz. 409, 808 P.2d 294 (1991).

The Superior Court loses subject matter jurisdiction over an action for dissolution, and the action abates, when one of the spouses involved dies before any order is entered, other than one for a preliminary injunction. *Van Emmerik v. Colosi*, 193 Ariz. 398, 972 P.2d 1034 (Ct. App. Div. 1 1998). A party's failure to resort to and exhaust available administrative remedies will also deprive the Superior Court of jurisdiction to hear that party's claim. *McNutt v. Department of Revenue of State of Ariz.*, 196 Ariz. 255, 995 P.2d 691 (Ct. App. Div. 1 1998).

Subject matter jurisdiction is an issue of law to be resolved by the trial court, and appellate review of that determination is *de novo*. *Mitchell v. Gamble*, 207 Ariz. 364, 86 P.3d 944, 186 Ed. Law Rep. 564 (Ct. App. Div. 2 2004); *Satterly v. Life Care Centers of America, Inc.*, 204 Ariz. 174, 61 P.3d 468, 29 Employee Benefits Cas. (BNA) 2713 (Ct. App. Div. 1 2003); *Rashedi v. General Bd. of Church of Nazarene*, 203 Ariz. 320, 54 P.3d 349 (Ct. App. Div. 1 2002); *Guminski v. Arizona State Veterinary Medical Examining Bd.*, 201 Ariz. 180, 33 P.3d 514 (Ct. App. Div. 1 2001); *Harris v. Harris*, 195 Ariz. 559, 991 P.2d 262 (Ct. App. Div. 1 1999); *Fairway Constructors, Inc. v. Ahern*, 193 Ariz. 122, 970 P.2d 954, 48 U.S.P.Q.2d 1951 (Ct. App. Div. 1 1998); *In re Marriage of Crawford*, 180 Ariz. 324, 884 P.2d 210 (Ct. App. Div. 2 1994). Once a court determines that it lacks subject matter jurisdiction, it has no authority to address the merits of a case. *Washburn v. Pima County*, 206 Ariz. 571, 81 P.3d 1030 (Ct. App. Div. 2 2003).

An issue related to, but also quite distinct from, that of subject matter jurisdiction is that of "standing to sue." In Arizona, which does not have a "case or controversy" requirement such as is found in the federal constitution, the issue is not one of constitutional dimension. *Armory Park Neighborhood Ass'n v. Episcopal Community Services in Arizona*, 148 Ariz. 1, 712 P.2d 914 (1985); *Arizona Association of Providers for Persons with Disabilities v. State*, 223 Ariz. 6, 219 P.3d 216 (Ct. App. Div. 1 2009); *Strawberry Water Co. v. Paulsen*, 220 Ariz. 401, 207 P.3d 654 (Ct. App. Div. 1 2008); *Karbal v. Arizona Dept. of Revenue*, 215 Ariz. 114, 158 P.3d 243 (Ct. App. Div. 1 2007). Rather, the issue is approached as one raising questions of judicial restraint, and courts will exercise that restraint to insure that the case is not moot and that the issues will be fully developed by true adversaries. *Armory Park Neighborhood Ass'n v. Episcopal Community Services in Arizona*, 148 Ariz. 1, 712 P.2d 914 (1985); *Blanchard v. Show Low Planning and Zoning Com'n*, 196 Ariz. 114, 993 P.2d 1078 (Ct. App. Div. 1 1999).

Generally, to have standing, a plaintiff must have suffered injury in fact, economic or otherwise, from the conduct complained of, and that injury must be distinct and palpable so that the plaintiff has a personal stake in the outcome. *Bennett v. Brownlow*, 211 Ariz. 193, 119 P.3d 460 (2005); *Fernandez v. Takata Seat Belts, Inc.*, 210 Ariz. 138, 108 P.3d 917 (2005); *Arizona Association of Providers for Persons with Disabilities v. State*, 223 Ariz. 6, 219 P.3d 216 (Ct. App. Div. 1 2009); *Strawberry Water Co. v. Paulsen*, 220 Ariz. 401, 207 P.3d 654 (Ct. App. Div. 1 2008); *Aegis of Arizona, L.L.C. v. Town of Marana*, 206 Ariz. 557, 81 P.3d 1016 (Ct. App. Div. 2 2003), redesignated as opinion, (Dec. 17, 2003) and as corrected, (Dec. 22, 2003).

Lack of standing is not a jurisdictional defect and will not bar consideration of the merits on appeal if the issue is not raised. If the issue is raised, however, the standing requirement will be waived only in exceptional circumstances. *Bennett v. Brownlow*, 211 Ariz. 193, 119 P.3d 460 (2005); *Fernandez v. Takata Seat Belts, Inc.*, 210 Ariz. 138, 108 P.3d 917 (2005). Whether a party has standing to sue is a question of law which is reviewed on appeal *de novo*. *Robert Schalkenbach Foundation v. Lincoln Foundation, Inc.*, 208 Ariz. 176, 91 P.3d 1019 (Ct. App. Div. 1 2004), as amended, (July 9, 2004), as amended, (July 9, 2004).

A person aggrieved by a zoning decision of a legislative body or board may appeal that decision by special action to the Superior Court, but must have suffered an injury in fact, economic or otherwise, in order to have standing to do so. *Center Bay Gardens, L.L.C. v. City of Tempe City Council*, 214 Ariz. 353, 153 P.3d 374 (Ct. App. Div. 1 2007), as amended, (Feb. 6, 2007). General economic losses or concerns regarding aesthetics in the affected area are not sufficient to confer standing. *Center Bay Gardens, L.L.C. v. City of Tempe City Council*, 214 Ariz. 353, 153 P.3d 374 (Ct. App. Div. 1 2007), as amended, (Feb. 6, 2007). Whether a party has standing to sue is a question of law which is reviewed on appeal *de novo*. *Robert Schalkenbach Foundation v. Lincoln Foundation, Inc.*, 208 Ariz. 176, 91 P.3d 1019 (Ct. App. Div. 1 2004), as amended, (July 9, 2004). A plaintiff who lacks standing to pursue a claim may not pursue such claims on behalf of a class of persons who would have standing to do so. *Fernandez v. Takata Seat Belts, Inc.*, 210 Ariz. 138, 108 P.3d 917 (2005). Standing issues are reviewed on appeal *de novo*. *Strawberry Water Co. v. Paulsen*, 220 Ariz. 401, 207 P.3d 654 (Ct. App. Div. 1 2008).

Arizona has adopted the doctrine of primary jurisdiction which determines whether a court or an administrative agency should make the initial decision in a particular case. The doctrine, which is distinct from the doctrine requiring the exhaustion of administrative remedies, is a discretionary rule created by the courts to effectuate the efficient handling of cases in specialized areas where an administrative agency's expertise may be helpful.

The doctrine of exhaustion of administrative remedies determines *when* judicial review is available; the doctrine of primary jurisdiction determines *who* should make the initial determination of the issues presented. *Wonders v. Pima County*, 207 Ariz. 576, 89 P.3d 810 (Ct. App. Div. 2 2004); *Qwest Corp. v. Kelly*, 204 Ariz. 25, 59 P.3d 789 (Ct. App. Div. 2 2002); *Southwest Soil Remediation, Inc. v. City of Tucson*, 201 Ariz. 438, 36 P.3d 1208 (Ct. App. Div. 2 2001). Both doctrines are techniques of sound judicial administration, rather than questions bearing on the court's subject matter jurisdiction. *Original Apartment Movers, Inc. v. Waddell*, 179 Ariz. 419, 880 P.2d 639 (Ct. App. Div. 1 1993).

To determine whether exhaustion of remedies is required, the court must decide whether an administrative agency has original jurisdiction over the subject matter of the action. *Moulton v. Napolitano*, 205 Ariz. 506, 73 P.3d 637 (Ct. App. Div. 1 2003). A litigant should not be required to exhaust administrative remedies when such an effort would be futile. *Moulton v. Napolitano*, 205 Ariz. 506, 73 P.3d 637 (Ct. App. Div. 1 2003).

The doctrine of primary jurisdiction applies when an initial decision by the judiciary could interfere with the effective operation of an agency created by a co-equal branch of government. *Coconino County v. Antco, Inc.*, 214 Ariz. 82, 148 P.3d 1155 (Ct. App. Div. 1 2006). The purpose of the doctrine requiring the exhaustion of administrative remedies is to allow an administrative agency to perform functions within its special competence—to make a factual record, to apply its expertise and to correct its own errors and possibly moot judicial controversies. *Arizona Association of Providers for Persons with Disabilities v. State*, 223 Ariz. 6, 219 P.3d 216 (Ct. App. Div. 1 2009); *Bailey-Null v. ValueOptions*, 221 Ariz. 63, 209 P.3d 1059 (Ct. App. Div. 1 2009). To determine whether exhaustion of administrative remedies is required, a court must first determine whether an administrative agency has original jurisdiction over the subject matter of the claims. *Bailey-Null v. ValueOptions*, 221 Ariz. 63, 209 P.3d 1059 (Ct. App. Div. 1 2009).

A Native American plaintiff may not bring an action against a non-Native American in *federal* court, when a tribal court also would have jurisdiction, without first exhausting such recourse as is available in the tribal courts. *Astorga v. Wing*, 211 Ariz. 139, 118 P.3d 1103 (Ct. App. Div. 1 2005). That principle, however, does not apply to *state* court proceedings. *Astorga v. Wing*, 211 Ariz. 139, 118 P.3d 1103 (Ct. App. Div. 1 2005). In instances where courts of separate sovereigns have concurrent jurisdiction, the two courts may proceed simultaneously until one reaches a judgment which will have *res judicata* effect in the other. *Astorga v. Wing*, 211 Ariz. 139, 118 P.3d 1103 (Ct. App. Div. 1 2005). While such an action may not be dismissed for failure to exhaust available tribal court remedies, the Superior Court does have discretion to stay it and, in exercising that discretion, it is appropriate for the Superior Court to give some degree of deference to tribal courts that may have jurisdiction over a parallel proceeding. *Astorga v. Wing*, 211 Ariz. 139, 118 P.3d 1103 (Ct. App. Div. 1 2005).

Under the former "claims statute," A.R.S. § 12-821, it was held that its requirement that a claim against a governmental entity be submitted to it before the institution of suit was analogous to a statute of limitations, and failure to comply with the requirement was not jurisdictional. Accordingly, it was not appropriate to raise the issue of noncompliance with the statute by a motion to dismiss for lack of subject matter jurisdiction. *Pritchard v. State*, 163 Ariz. 427, 788 P.2d 1178 (1990); *Howland v. State*, 169 Ariz. 293, 818 P.2d 1169 (Ct. App. Div. 1 1991). In April 1993 the Arizona Legislature, as part of comprehensive "tort reform" legislation, repealed this "claims statute," and replaced it with a new A.R.S. § 12-821, which now simply prescribes a one-year statute of limitations for actions against any public entity or public employee.

In 1994, however, the legislature adopted a new A.R.S. § 12-821.01, which provides that persons with claims against a public entity or employee must file such claims with an authorized public official within one hundred and eighty (180) days after the cause of action accrues. Such claims remain subject to the one-year statute of limitations in A.R.S. § 12-821. The requirements imposed by these "claims statutes" are discussed in Section 5 of the *Authors' Comments* to Rule 3, Ariz. R. Civ. P.

The First Amendment and the ecclesiastical abstention doctrine preclude civil courts from inquiring into ecclesiastical matters. *Rashedi v. General Bd. of Church of Nazarene*, 203 Ariz. 320, 54 P.3d 349 (Ct. App. Div. 1 2002). Civil courts must accept the decisions of the highest adjudicatory bodies of religious organizations of hierarchical structure on matters of discipline, faith, internal organization, or ecclesiastical rule, custom or law. *Rashedi v. General Bd. of Church of Nazarene*, 203 Ariz. 320, 54 P.3d 349 (Ct. App. Div. 1 2002). The doctrine does not preclude a civil court from adjudicating, however, a church-related dispute which can be resolved by applying neutral principles of law without inquiry into religious doctrine and without resolving a religious controversy. *Rashedi v. General Bd. of Church of Nazarene*, 203 Ariz. 320, 54 P.3d 349 (Ct. App. Div. 1 2002).

Where a case has been removed to federal District Court because it is related to a pending bankruptcy, and is then transferred to, but remanded by, the Bankruptcy Court, the Superior Court reacquires jurisdiction upon the entry of the order of remand, and not when the order is mailed by the Bankruptcy Court clerk. *Health For Life Brands, Inc. v. Powley*, 203 Ariz. 536, 57 P.3d 726 (Ct. App. Div. 1 2002).

9. *Personal Jurisdiction.* The defense of lack of personal jurisdiction must be asserted by initial motion or pleaded in the answer or it is waived. *Martin v. Martin*, 156 Ariz. 452, 752 P.2d 1038 (1988). The intent of the Rule was to abolish the distinction between a "general appearance" and a "special appearance," and an appearance by the defendant in the action without preserving the jurisdictional issue in the manner specified in Rule 12(b) constitutes a waiver of it. There is considerable confusion, however, concerning what type of appearance triggers the obligation to raise the defense on pain of waiver.

One case has held that a request for a stay and for conciliation by a defendant did not constitute an appearance which waived an as yet unasserted jurisdictional defense. *Rodriguez v. Rodriguez*, 8 Ariz. App. 5, 442 P.2d 169 (1968). A subsequent case held, however, that a defendant's request for stay under the Soldiers' and Sailors' Civil Relief Act did subject that defendant to the jurisdiction of the Court. *Skates v. Stockton*, 140 Ariz. 505, 683 P.2d 304 (Ct. App. Div. 2 1984). It has also been held that a defendant who appears and seeks affirmative relief waives any lack of personal jurisdiction defense. *National Homes Corp. v. Totem Mobile Home Sales, Inc.*, 140 Ariz. 434, 682 P.2d 439 (Ct. App. Div. 1 1984).

On the other hand, a defendant does not submit to the jurisdiction of the court by merely filing a compulsory counterclaim. *Aries v. Palmer Johnson, Inc.*, 153 Ariz. 250, 735 P.2d 1373, 4 U.C.C. Rep. Serv. 2d 85 (Ct. App. Div. 2 1987); *cf. also Cargill, Inc. v. Sabine Trading & Shipping Co., Inc.*, 756 F.2d 224, 1985 A.M.C. 1634, 40 Fed. R. Serv. 2d 1476 (2d Cir. 1985). Likewise, a defendant does not waive the right to assert a Rule 12(b)(2) personal jurisdiction defense by seeking the appointment of a guardian *ad litem* to defend the lawsuit. *Balestrieri v. Balestrieri*, 232 Ariz. 25, 300 P.3d 560 (Ct. App. Div. 1 2013) citing, *Kadota v. Hosogai*, 125 Ariz. 131, 608 P.2d 68 (Ct. App. Div. 1 1980). Similarly, an insurance carrier's assertion of the policy's forum selection clause in support of a motion to dismiss is not a general appearance. *Taylor v. Fireman's Fund Ins. Co. of Canada*, 161 Ariz. 432, 778 P.2d 1328 (Ct. App. Div. 2 1989).

An Arizona court has statutory jurisdiction to enter a decree of dissolution of a marriage when one of the parties was domiciled in the state for ninety (90) days prior to the filing of the petition for dissolution. The Court may exercise this limited jurisdiction to dissolve the marriage without violating due process, even though it lacks personal jurisdiction over the nonresident party, so long as the Court does not determine the monetary obligations of the parties. *Taylor v. Jarrett*, 191 Ariz. 550, 959 P.2d 807 (Ct. App. Div. 1 1998).

Similarly, under the Uniform Child Custody Jurisdiction Act, an Arizona court need not secure personal jurisdiction over a nonresident party in order to adjudicate child custody and visitation issues. *Taylor v. Jarrett*, 191 Ariz. 550, 959 P.2d 807 (Ct. App. Div. 1 1998). Technical personal jurisdiction must be acquired, however, before the Court can decide issues of child support, spousal maintenance or the division of marital property. Of course, a nonresident party may waive objection to the absence of personal jurisdiction by appearing and seeking affirmative relief, but does not do so in this context simply by participating in the proceedings concerning the proper custodial determination. *Taylor v. Jarrett*, 191 Ariz. 550, 959 P.2d 807 (Ct. App. Div. 1 1998).

An Arizona court does have jurisdiction, however, in a child support action over a father who does not reside in Arizona but was personally served while in the state on vacation and visiting his child. *Rutherford v. Rutherford*, 193 Ariz. 173, 971 P.2d 220 (Ct. App. Div. 1 1998). Physical presence in the forum, where not procured by coercion or trickery, satisfies personal jurisdiction requirements. A minimum contacts analysis is not necessary when a defendant is served with process within Arizona because physical presence is one of the continuing traditions of our legal system that define the due process standard of traditional notions of fair play and substantial justice. *Rutherford v. Rutherford*,

193 Ariz. 173, 971 P.2d 220 (Ct. App. Div. 1 1998).

Although it is the defendant's obligation to raise the issue of whether the Court has or may exercise jurisdiction over the defendant, the burden of demonstrating the propriety of exercising personal jurisdiction is on the plaintiff. *Arizona Tile, L.L.C. v. Berger*, 223 Ariz. 491, 224 P.3d 988 (Ct. App. Div. 1 2010), as amended on other grounds, (Feb. 8, 2010) (where defendant challenges the existence of personal jurisdiction, plaintiff must establish a *prima facie* showing of jurisdiction, after which the burden shifts to the defendant to rebut that showing); *In re Consolidated Zicam Product Liability Cases*, 212 Ariz. 85, 127 P.3d 903 (Ct. App. Div. 1 2006); *Coast to Coast Marketing Co., Inc. v. G & S Metal Products Co., Inc.*, 130 Ariz. 506, 637 P.2d 308 (Ct. App. Div. 2 1981). When the issue of a lack of personal jurisdiction is raised by motion, the plaintiff may not simply rest on the allegations of the complaint, but must come forward with sufficient facts to establish a *prima facie* showing that the exercise of jurisdiction is proper. *Macpherson v. Taglione*, 158 Ariz. 309, 762 P.2d 596 (Ct. App. Div. 2 1988). The permissible scope of extraterritorial jurisdiction that can be exercised over nonresident defendants is discussed in the *Authors' Comments* under Rule 4.2, Ariz. R. Civ. P.

10. *Resolution of Factual Issues Raised by Jurisdictional Motions.* Where resolution of a jurisdictional issue involves disputed factual questions that are intertwined with the merits of the case, the trial court should leave such jurisdictional questions for trial rather than determining them on a Rule 12 motion. *Bonner v. Minico, Inc.*, 159 Ariz. 246, 766 P.2d 598 (1988). Where jurisdictional fact issues are present but are not intertwined with factual issues raised by the claim on the merits, the resolution of those issues is to be made by the trial court. *MM & A Productions, LLC v. Yavapai-Apache Nation*, ___ Ariz. ___, 316 P.3d 1248 (Ct. App. Div. 2 2014). *Swichtenberg v. Brimer*, 171 Ariz. 77, 828 P.2d 1218 (Ct. App. Div. 1 1991). Although a trial court may consider and resolve jurisdictional fact issues when such facts are not intertwined with the merits of the case, the appellate court reviews the trial court's ultimate legal conclusion *de novo*. *Mitchell v. Gamble*, 207 Ariz. 364, 86 P.3d 944, 186 Ed. Law Rep. 564 (Ct. App. Div. 2 2004).

In resolving jurisdictional fact issues, the court may consider affidavits, depositions and exhibits. *MM & A Productions, LLC v. Yavapai-Apache Nation*, ___ Ariz. ___, 316 P.3d 1248 (Ct. App. Div. 2 2014). The fact that the Court considers such materials in resolving issues that are separable from the merits of the controversy does not convert a motion to dismiss made on jurisdictional grounds into one for summary judgment. *Swichtenberg v. Brimer*, 171 Ariz. 77, 828 P.2d 1218 (Ct. App. Div. 1 1991).

Where the underlying facts are undisputed, a determination whether personal jurisdiction can properly be exercised is a question of law, which is reviewable *de novo. Morgan Bank (Delaware) v. Wilson*, 164 Ariz. 535, 794 P.2d 959 (Ct. App. Div. 2 1990).

11. *Improper Venue.* The venue requirements for civil actions are set forth in A.R.S. § 12-401, and the remedies for improper venue are also specified by statute. The plaintiff has the option of bringing suit in any county in which venue is proper. *Cacho v. Superior Court In and For County of Maricopa*, 170 Ariz. 30, 821 P.2d 721 (1991). When an action is filed in a Court where venue is improper, the Court in which it is filed nevertheless has jurisdiction over the controversy. *Mohave County v. James R. Brathovde Family Trust*, 187 Ariz. 318, 928 P.2d 1247 (Ct. App. Div. 1 1996). Under A.R.S. § 12-404, the defendant must contest venue by appropriate affidavit and request a transfer of the action to a proper county, or the defect is waived.

This statutory scheme was inconsistent with Rule 12(b)(3), as originally adopted, which contemplated seeking the dismissal (rather than the transfer) of actions for improper venue. The Rule was amended in 1961 to resolve this conflict. The text of the amendment, and the accompanying State Bar Committee Note, make clear that a motion to dismiss for improper venue is available only in those limited situations where the venue defect cannot be cured by transfers to another county.

The procedures for challenging venue and requesting transfer to another county are set forth in A.R.S. § 12-404. The defendant must, before the time for filing an answer, submit an affidavit stating that the county in which the action is brought is not the proper county, identifying the county of the defendant's residence, and requesting transfer to the proper county. If the affidavit is not controverted within five (5) days, the action is to be transferred. If the affidavit is controverted, the trial court hears the issues and decides on transfer. Unless it specifically states otherwise, a stipulation extending the time to answer also extends the time for requesting a change of venue. *Goff v. Superior Courts In and For Pima and Maricopa Counties*, 2 Ariz. App. 344, 409 P.2d 60 (1965).

In Arizona, venue generally lies in the county in which the defendant resides, unless a statutory exception exists. *Yarbrough v. Montoya–Paez*, 214 Ariz. 1, 147 P.3d 755 (Ct. App. Div. 2 2006); *Amparano v. ASARCO, Inc.*, 208 Ariz. 370, 93 P.3d 1086 (Ct. App. Div. 2 2004); *Lakritz v. Superior Court In and For County of Coconino*, 179 Ariz. 598, 880 P.2d 1144 (Ct. App. Div. 1 1994). The exception in A.R.S. § 12-401(12) for real property actions, which must be brought in the county where the property is located, is based on the notion that it is more convenient for witnesses and prevents more than one county from acting on title to real property. *Amparano v. ASARCO, Inc.*, 208 Ariz. 370, 93 P.3d 1086 (Ct. App. Div. 2 2004).

Venue statutes, however, rarely fix venue immutably; rather, they create either limited venue choices for plaintiffs or presumptive venues. *Maricopa County v. Barkley*, 168 Ariz. 234, 812 P.2d 1052 (Ct. App. Div. 1 1990). In determining a venue question, the trial court looks to the allegations of the complaint, construing them liberally in favor of the plaintiff's choice of venue. *Lakritz v. Superior Court In and For County of Coconino*, 179 Ariz. 598, 880 P.2d 1144 (Ct. App. Div. 1 1994). If venue is brought in the proper county, the trial court may not legally direct a change of venue. *Cacho v. Superior Court In and For County of Maricopa*, 170 Ariz. 30, 821 P.2d 721 (1991); *Lakritz v. Superior Court In and For County of Coconino*, 179 Ariz. 598, 880 P.2d 1144 (Ct. App. Div. 1 1994). *But see*, *Behrens v. O'Melia*, 206 Ariz. 309, 78 P.3d 278 (Ct. App. Div. 1 2003) (even if venue is proper, trial court has authority under A.R.S. § 12-406(B)(3) to change venue where trial court finds "good and sufficient cause" for such change). Conversely, when a proper request for change of venue has been made on one of the grounds specified by statute, a transfer must be ordered. *Lakritz v. Superior Court In and For County of Coconino*, 179 Ariz. 598, 880 P.2d 1144 (Ct. App. Div. 1 1994); *Maricopa County v. Barkley*, 168 Ariz. 234, 812 P.2d 1052 (Ct. App. Div. 1 1990).

When the adversary of the moving party fails to dispute under oath statements made in the motion to transfer, the trial court has no choice but to transfer the action. *Morgan v. Foreman ex rel. County of Maricopa*, 193 Ariz. 405, 973 P.2d 616 (Ct. App. Div. 1 1999). The Superior Court is a single, unified trial court separated into divisions by county, and the transfer of a case filed in one Superior Court to a Superior Court judge regularly assigned to another county, as a visiting judge, does not represent an improper change of venue. *Lerette v. Adams*, 186 Ariz. 628, 925 P.2d 1079 (Ct. App. Div. 1 1996).

Under A.R.S. § 12-406(B)(3), a trial court has discretion to order the transfer of a case from one county, where venue is proper, to another county for "good and sufficient cause." There is "good and sufficient cause" for directing such a transfer so that the case can be consolidated with another case arising out of the same underlying event, because such a consolidation will serve the interests of judicial economy, and will ensure that 100% of all damages are awarded, and no more, and properly allocated among all parties at fault, as required by A.R.S. § 12-2506. *Behrens v. O'Melia*, 206 Ariz. 309, 78 P.3d 278 (Ct. App. Div. 1 2003).

A.R.S. § 12–408(A) entitles a party opponent of a county in a civil action to have venue of the action changed as a matter of right from that county to some other county. Unlike changes of venue pursuant to A.R.S. § 12–406 for which a moving party must show cause and as to which the trial court has discretion, changes of venue under Section 12–408 require no showing other than that the county is an opposing party and there is no discretion vested in the trial court whether to order a transfer. *Yarbrough v. Montoya–Paez*, 214 Ariz. 1, 147 P.3d 755 (Ct. App. Div. 2 2006).

The transfer is not required to be to a county in which venue would have been proper under Section 12–401. *Yarbrough v. Montoya-Paez*, 214 Ariz. 1, 147 P.3d 755 (Ct. App. Div. 2 2006). Nor is the selection of the county to which to transfer the action governed by Section 12–407, which requires that transfer be to the most convenient adjoining county. *Yarbrough v. Montoya-Paez*, 214 Ariz. 1, 147 P.3d 755 (Ct. App. Div. 2 2006). Section 12–407 applies only to transfers for cause ordered under Section 12–406. *Yarbrough v. Montoya-Paez*, 214 Ariz. 1, 147 P.3d 755 (Ct. App. Div. 2 2006). Rather the selection of the transferee county is governed by Section 12–411, which directs that the transfer be to the most convenient county to which the objections of the parties do not apply or are least applicable. *Yarbrough v. Montoya-Paez*, 214 Ariz. 1, 147 P.3d 755 (Ct. App. Div. 2 2006).

As a practical matter, because resolution of the venue issue will result either in transfer of the action or denial of the request therefor, and not dismissal, appellate review other than on appeal from the final judgment is available only by special action. Thus, denial of a motion for change of venue is appropriately reviewed by special action. *Yarbrough v. Montoya-Paez*, 214 Ariz. 1, 147 P.3d 755 (Ct. App. Div. 2 2006); *Curtis v. Richardson*, 212 Ariz. 308, 131 P.3d 480 (Ct. App. Div. 1 2006); *Behrens v. O'Melia*, 206 Ariz. 309, 78 P.3d 278 (Ct. App. Div. 1 2003); *Lakritz v. Superior Court In and For County of Coconino*, 179 Ariz. 598, 880 P.2d 1144 (Ct. App. Div. 1 1994); *Morgan v. Foreman ex rel. County of Maricopa*, 193 Ariz. 405, 973 P.2d 616 (Ct. App. Div. 1 1999). Appellate courts will generally not interfere with a venue ruling, however, in the absence of a clear abuse of the trial court's discretion. *Maricopa County v. Barkley*, 168 Ariz. 234, 812 P.2d 1052 (Ct. App. Div. 1 1990).

12. *Forum Non Conveniens*. A motion to dismiss for *forum non conveniens* is distinguishable from a motion for change of venue in that it assumes that the venue selected for the action by plaintiff is proper, but inconvenient. To obtain a dismissal based upon *forum non conveniens,* the defendant must show that there is an alternative forum available to hear the case and that, on balance, the alternative forum is a more convenient place to litigate the matter. *Parra v. Continental Tire North America, Inc.*, 222 Ariz. 212, 213 P.3d 361 (Ct. App. Div. 1 2009).

Generalized allegations as to the inconvenience of defending a suit in Arizona will not be sufficient to satisfy the defendant's burden of establishing that the plaintiff's selection of Arizona as a forum is unreasonable. *Bils v. Nixon, Hargrave, Devans & Doyle*, 179 Ariz. 523, 880 P.2d 743 (Ct. App. Div. 2 1994), redesignated as opinion, (Aug. 30, 1994). The issue is one committed to the trial court's discretion based on a balancing of factors. The fact that one of the parties is a citizen of Arizona does not preclude dismissal. While some deference should be given to the plaintiff's choice of forum, a forum that has no significant factual connection to the cause of action should not try the case. *Coonley & Coonley v. Turck*, 173 Ariz. 527, 844 P.2d 1177 (Ct. App. Div. 1 1993).

13. *Change of Venue in Actions Against the State.* A.R.S. § 12-822(B) provides that, in an action against the State, upon written demand of the Attorney General, the venue of the action is to be changed to Maricopa County. To be effective, the demand must be in writing and filed and served on or before the time for answer. The power to make such a demand may be delegated to and exercised by a private attorney retained to represent the State. *State, Dept. of Corrections v. Fenton*, 163 Ariz. 174, 786 P.2d 1025 (Ct. App. Div. 2 1989). The statute does not apply, however, to actions seeking judicial review of administrative rulings or actions. *Cochise County v. Borowiec*, 162 Ariz. 192, 781 P.2d 1379 (Ct. App. Div. 2 1989). A change of venue to Maricopa County, pursuant to a demand made pursuant to A.R.S. § 12-822(B), does not preclude a subsequent change of venue under A.R.S. § 12-406 (change of venue for cause), but the party moving for such relief must produce convincing evidence that Maricopa County is not a convenient venue. *Dunn v. Carruth*, 162 Ariz. 478, 784 P.2d 684 (1989).

14. *Insufficiency of Process; Insufficiency of Service.* Insufficiency of process is based on the *form* of papers used to accomplish service. *Schwartz v. Arizona Primary Care Physicians*, 192 Ariz. 290, 964 P.2d 491 (Ct. App. Div. 1 1998). Insufficiency of service of process, on the other hand, deals with the *manner* in which service was accomplished, which may result in a defendant not receiving actual notice of a pending action. *Schwartz v. Arizona Primary Care Physicians*, 192 Ariz. 290, 964 P.2d 491 (Ct. App. Div. 1 1998).

A challenge to the sufficiency of service of process cannot be raised after answering the complaint on the merits without expressly preserving it. *Montano v. Scottsdale Baptist Hospital, Inc.*, 119 Ariz. 448, 581 P.2d 682 (1978); and is waived if the defendant seeks affirmative relief in the action. *National Homes Corp. v. Totem Mobile Home Sales, Inc.*, 140 Ariz. 434, 682 P.2d 439 (Ct. App. Div. 1 1984).

If the true thrust of the motion is to challenge the exercise of personal jurisdiction, it will be treated as a motion to dismiss asserting that defense. *Pegler v. Sullivan*, 6 Ariz. App. 338, 432 P.2d 593 (1967). The return of service by the sheriff or duly appointed or certified (formerly, "registered") private process server may be impeached only by clear and convincing evidence. *General Elec. Capital Corp. v. Osterkamp*, 172 Ariz. 191, 836 P.2d 404 (Ct. App. Div. 2 1992); *Mayhew v. McDougall*, 16 Ariz. App. 125, 491 P.2d 848 (Div. 2 1971); *Phoenix Airport Travelodge v. Dolgin*, 12 Ariz. App. 358, 470 P.2d 506 (Div. 2 1970).

15. *Failure to State a Claim for Relief.* The defense of failure to state a claim for relief is so basic that it cannot be waived. *Mallamo v. Hartman*, 70 Ariz. 420, 222 P.2d 797 (1950). The Court can raise the issue *sua sponte* at trial even though the issue has not been listed in the pretrial statement. *Zuniga v. City of Tucson*, 5 Ariz. App. 220, 425 P.2d 122 (1967).

A motion to dismiss for failure to state a claim filed at the initial pleading stage, however, is not favored and *sua sponte* dismissals for failure to state a claim are strongly disfavored. *Acker v. CSO Chevira*, 188 Ariz. 252, 934 P.2d 816 (Ct. App. Div. 1 1997). In deciding a Rule 12(b)(6) motion to dismiss, a court must:

(1) limit its consideration to the well-pled factual allegations, ignoring conclusory allegations;
(2) assume the truth of the well-pled factual allegations set forth in the challenged pleading, and consider all reasonable inferences therefrom and
(3) dismiss only if the claimant "is not entitled to relief, as a matter of law, on any interpretation of the facts" as alleged in the challenged pleading. *Cullen v. Auto-Owners Ins. Co.*, 218 Ariz. 417, 189 P.3d 344 (2008).

In considering such a motion, all material allegations of the complaint are taken as true and read in the light most favorable to the plaintiff. *Logan v. Forever Living Products Intern., Inc.*, 203 Ariz. 191, 52 P.3d 760, 18 I.E.R. Cas. (BNA) 1555, 147 Lab. Cas. (CCH) P 59617 (2002); *Doe ex rel. Doe v. State*, 200 Ariz. 174, 24 P.3d 1269, 155 Ed. Law Rep. 1424 (2001); *Fidelity Sec. Life Ins. Co. v. State, Dept. of Ins.*, 191 Ariz. 222, 954 P.2d 580 (1998); *Mohave Disposal, Inc. v. City of Kingman*, 186 Ariz. 343, 922 P.2d 308 (1996); *Sensing v. Harris*, 217 Ariz. 261, 172 P.3d 856 (Ct. App. Div. 1 2007); *Yes on Prop 200 v. Napolitano*, 215 Ariz. 458, 160 P.3d 1216 (Ct. App. Div. 1 2007); *Harris v. Cochise Health Systems*, 215 Ariz. 344, 160 P.3d 223 (Ct. App. Div. 2 2007); *Turley v. Ethington*, 213 Ariz. 640, 146 P.3d 1282 (Ct. App. Div. 2 2006). For that purpose, however, the prayer for relief is not considered to be part of the complaint. *Citizens' Committee for Recall of Jack Williams v. Marston*, 109 Ariz. 188, 507 P.2d 113 (1973); *Husky v. Lee*, 2 Ariz. App. 129, 406 P.2d 847 (1965).

Similarly, allegations that represent merely conclusions of law or unwarranted deductions are not credited. *Cullen v. Auto-Owners Ins. Co.*, 218 Ariz. 417, 189 P.3d 344 (2008); *Aldabbagh v. Arizona Dept. of Liquor Licenses and Control*, 162 Ariz. 415, 783 P.2d 1207 (Ct. App. Div. 2 1989).

A motion to dismiss, thus, tests the formal sufficiency of a claim for relief; if a complaint is facially sufficient, but unpled facts establish a legal bar to relief, then the appropriate motion is one under Rule 56. *Moretto v. Samaritan Health System*, 190 Ariz. 343, 947 P.2d 917 (Ct. App. Div. 1 1997).

A motion to dismiss for failure to state a claim should not be granted unless it appears that the plaintiff would not be entitled to relief under any state of facts susceptible of proof under the claim as stated in the challenged pleading. *Cullen v. Auto-Owners Ins. Co.*, 218 Ariz. 417, 189 P.3d 344 (2008) (rejecting the standard established by the United States Supreme Court in *Bell Atlantic Corp. v. Twombly*, 550 U.S. 544, 127 S. Ct. 1955, 167 L. Ed. 2d 929, 2007-1 Trade Cas. (CCH) ¶ 75709, 68 Fed. R. Serv. 3d 661 (2007)); *Dressler v. Morrison*, 212 Ariz. 279, 130 P.3d 978 (2006); *Mohave Disposal, Inc. v. City of Kingman*, 186 Ariz. 343, 922 P.2d 308 (1996); *Veach v. City of Phoenix*, 102 Ariz. 195, 427 P.2d 335 (1967); *T.P. Racing, L.L.L.P. v. Arizona Department of Racing*, 223 Ariz. 257, 222 P.3d 280 (Ct. App. Div. 1 2009); *Yes on Prop 200 v. Napolitano*, 215 Ariz. 458, 160 P.3d 1216 (Ct. App. Div. 1 2007); *Airfreight Exp. Ltd v. Evergreen Air Center, Inc.*, 215 Ariz. 103, 158 P.3d 232 (Ct. App. Div. 2 2007); *Turley v. Ethington*, 213 Ariz. 640, 146 P.3d 1282 (Ct. App. Div. 2 2006); *Douglas v. Governing Bd. of Window Rock Consol. School Dist. No. 8*, 206 Ariz. 344, 78 P.3d 1065, 182 Ed. Law Rep. 624 (Ct. App. Div. 1 2003); *Universal Marketing and Entertainment, Inc. v. Bank One of Arizona, N.A.*, 203 Ariz. 266, 53 P.3d 191 (Ct. App. Div. 1 2002); *Widoff v. Wiens*, 202 Ariz. 383, 45 P.3d 1232 (Ct. App. Div. 1 2002); *Kremser v. Quarles & Brady, L.L.P.*, 201 Ariz. 413, 36 P.3d 761 (Ct. App. Div. 1 2001), as corrected, (Feb. 14, 2002); *Albers v. Edelson Technology Partners L.P.*, 201 Ariz. 47, 31 P.3d 821, 111 A.L.R.5th 715 (Ct. App. Div. 1 2001); *Leal v. Allstate Ins. Co.*, 199 Ariz. 250, 17 P.3d 95 (Ct. App. Div. 1 2000); *Luchanski v. Congrove*, 193 Ariz. 176, 971 P.2d 636 (Ct. App. Div. 1 1998).

If the deficiency in the complaint is one that can be cured by further pleading, the motion should be denied or, if granted, the plaintiff should be given leave to amend. *Republic Nat. Bank of New York v. Pima County*, 200 Ariz. 199, 25 P.3d 1 (Ct. App. Div.

2 2001); *Sun World Corp. v. Pennysaver, Inc.*, 130 Ariz. 585, 637 P.2d 1088 (Ct. App. Div. 1 1981); *In re Cassidy's Estate*, 77 Ariz. 288, 270 P.2d 1079 (1954).

The complaint must give the opponent fair notice of the nature and basis of the claim and indicate generally the type of litigation involved, and its failure to do so will render it subject to dismissal for failure to state a claim upon which relief can be granted. *Cullen v. Auto-Owners Ins. Co.*, 218 Ariz. 417, 189 P.3d 344 (2008). In *Cullen*, the Court expressly declined to adopt the more particularized pleading standard under the Federal Rules of Civil Procedure articulated by the United States Supreme Court in *Bell Atlantic Corp. v. Twombly*, 550 U.S. 544, 127 S. Ct. 1955, 167 L. Ed. 2d 929, 2007-1 Trade Cas. (CCH) ¶ 75709, 68 Fed. R. Serv. 3d 661 (2007).

Even under liberal notice pleading rules, a plaintiff's obligation to provide the grounds for entitlement to relief requires more than labels and conclusions, and a formulaic recitation of the elements of a cause of action is not sufficient. *Dube v. Likins*, 216 Ariz. 406, 167 P.3d 93, 224 Ed. Law Rep. 408 (Ct. App. Div. 2 2007). A wholly conclusory statement of a claim cannot survive a motion to dismiss simply because the pleadings leave open the possibility that the plaintiff might later establish some set of undisclosed facts to support a recovery. *Belen Loan Investors, LLC v. Bradley*, 231 Ariz. 448, 296 P.3d 984 (Ct. App. Div. 2 2012) (A complaint that sets forth only factually unsupported legal conclusions does not satisfy Rule 8(a)'s notice pleading standard.); *Cullen v. Auto-Owners Ins. Co.*, 218 Ariz. 417, 189 P.3d 344 (2008) (mere conclusory statements insufficient to state a claim upon which relief may be granted); *Dube v. Likins*, 216 Ariz. 406, 167 P.3d 93, 224 Ed. Law Rep. 408 (Ct. App. Div. 2 2007).

16. *Failure to Join Indispensable Party.* The defense of failure to join a party under Rule 19 may be asserted by motion under Rule 12 or preserved in the responsive pleading. It is never waived and can be raised for the first time on appeal. *Riley v. Cochise County*, 10 Ariz. App. 55, 455 P.2d 1005 (1969); *City of Flagstaff v. Babbitt*, 8 Ariz. App. 123, 443 P.2d 938 (1968). The terms "party under Rule 19," employed in Rule 12(b)(7), and "indispensable party" are not synonymous. Where a "party under Rule 19" has not been joined in the action, and is subject to the Court's jurisdiction, then joinder of that party should be ordered rather than dismissal.

Dismissal should result only where the party not joined is truly indispensable, and the test for indispensability in Arizona is quite restrictive. An absent party is deemed indispensable only where the absent party's interest in the controversy is such that no final judgment or decree can be entered that will do justice between the parties before the Court without injuring the rights of the absent party. *Town of Gila Bend v. Walled Lake Door Co.*, 107 Ariz. 545, 490 P.2d 551 (1971); *King v. Uhlmann*, 103 Ariz. 136, 437 P.2d 928 (1968).

17. *Raising Affirmative Defenses by Rule 12 Motion.* Affirmative defenses may be raised as the basis for, and resolved upon, a motion to dismiss if the facts supporting them appear on the face of the complaint. *Sierra Madre Development, Inc. v. Via Entrada Townhouses Ass'n*, 20 Ariz. App. 550, 514 P.2d 503 (Div. 2 1973); *Industrial Commission v. Superior Court In and For Pima County*, 5 Ariz. App. 100, 423 P.2d 375 (1967).

18. *Statute of Limitations.* The defense of the statute of limitations may be resolved on a motion to dismiss where the allegations of the complaint show conclusively that the plaintiff's claim is barred. *Pritchard v. State*, 163 Ariz. 427, 788 P.2d 1178 (1990); *Ross v. Ross*, 96 Ariz. 249, 393 P.2d 933 (1964); *Manterola v. Farmers Ins. Exchange*, 200 Ariz. 572, 30 P.3d 639 (Ct. App. Div. 2 2001); *Gomez v. Leverton*, 19 Ariz. App. 604, 509 P.2d 735, 85 A.L.R.3d 158 (Div. 2 1973); *Brand v. Dolgin*, 17 Ariz. App. 154, 496 P.2d 144 (Div. 1 1972). When a complaint shows on its face that the cause of action is barred by the statute of limitations, the burden is on the plaintiff to show that the statute should be tolled. *Ulibarri v. Gerstenberger*, 178 Ariz. 151, 871 P.2d 698 (Ct. App. Div. 1 1993) (rejected by, Logerquist v. Danforth, 188 Ariz. 16, 932 P.2d 281 (Ct. App. Div. 2 1996))). A motion to dismiss based on the bar of the statute of limitations is not one that is required by Rule 12(h) to be consolidated with other Rule 12(b) defenses. *Engle Bros., Inc. v. Superior Court In and For Pima County*, 23 Ariz. App. 406, 533 P.2d 714 (Div. 2 1975).

Under the former "claims statute," A.R.S. § 12-821, its requirement that a claim against a governmental entity be submitted to it prior to the institution of suit was held to be analogous to a statute of limitations. *Pritchard v. State*, 163 Ariz. 427, 788 P.2d 1178 (1990). That statute was repealed in 1993, but in 1994 the Legislature enacted a new "claims statute," A.R.S. § 12-821.01, which generally requires the filing of a notice of such claims with an authorized public official within 180 days after they accrue. *See* A.R.S. § 12-821.01(D). *Estate of DeSela v. Prescott Unified School Dist. No. 1*, 226 Ariz. 387, 249 P.3d 767, 265 Ed. Law Rep. 1241 (2011).

19. *Statute of Frauds.* Although the Arizona Supreme Court has not had an opportunity to pass on the matter, certain federal courts, under parallel rules, have permitted the statute of frauds to be asserted by a Rule 12(b) motion. *E.g., Price v. Reynolds Metals Co.*, 69 F. Supp. 82 (E.D. N.Y. 1946); *Butcher v. United Elec. Coal Co.*, 174 F.2d 1003 (7th Cir. 1949).

20. *Motion for Judgment on the Pleadings.* A motion for judgment on the pleadings can test either the sufficiency of the complaint or of the answer. *Mobile Community Council for Progress, Inc. v. Brock*, 211 Ariz. 196, 119 P.3d 463 (Ct. App. Div. 1 2005); *Emmett McLoughlin Realty, Inc. v. Pima County*, 203 Ariz. 557, 58 P.3d 39 (Ct. App. Div. 2 2002). In considering such a motion, all material allegations of the opposing party's pleadings are to be taken as true. *Shannon v. Butler Homes, Inc.*, 102 Ariz. 312, 428 P.2d 990, 26 A.L.R.3d 309 (1967); *Giles v. Hill Lewis Marce*, 195 Ariz. 358, 988 P.2d 143 (Ct. App. Div. 2 1999); *Boatman v. Samaritan Health Services, Inc.*, 168 Ariz. 207, 812 P.2d 1025 (Ct. App. Div. 2 1990); *American Federation of State, County and Mun. Employees, AFL-CIO, Council 97 v. Lewis*, 165 Ariz. 149, 797 P.2d 6 (Ct. App. Div. 1 1990); *Wenrich v. Household Finance Corp.*, 5 Ariz. App. 335, 426 P.2d 671 (1967).

Unlike a motion raising a defense enumerated in Rule 12(b), which is generally filed in response to a complaint, a motion for judgment on the pleadings is made after the pleadings are closed and is premature if filed before that time. *Colboch v. Aviation Credit Corp.*, 64 Ariz. 88, 166 P.2d 584 (1946). The allegations of the answer, to which no response or reply is required, are deemed denied. *Neiderhiser v. Henry's Drive-In, Inc.*, 96 Ariz. 305, 394 P.2d 420 (1964); *Food for Health Co., Inc. v. 3839 Joint Venture*, 129 Ariz. 103, 628 P.2d 986 (Ct. App. Div. 1 1981). A motion for summary judgment which is not accompanied by the separate statement of facts required by Ariz. R. Civ. P. 56(c)(2) is appropriately treated as a motion for judgment on the pleadings. *Wieman v. Roysden*, 166 Ariz. 281, 802 P.2d 432 (Ct. App. Div. 1 1990). On appeal from the entry of judgment on the pleadings, the facts are viewed in the light most favorable to the party against whom such a judgment was entered. *Napier v. Bertram*, 191 Ariz. 238, 954 P.2d 1389 (1998).

21. *Motion for More Definite Statement.* A defendant may move for a more definite statement if there is any doubt as to what is meant by the allegations of the complaint. *Boone v. Superior Court In and For Maricopa County*, 145 Ariz. 235, 700 P.2d 1335 (1985); *Folk v. City of Phoenix*, 27 Ariz. App. 146, 551 P.2d 595 (Div. 1 1976).

22. *Motions to Strike.* Rule 12 (f) motions to strike portions of pleadings are not favored.

A Rule 12(f) motion should not be granted unless it clearly appears that the matter challenged can have no possible relation to the subject matter of the litigation and the moving party demonstrates prejudice resulting from its retention. *Stone v. Arizona Highway Commission*, 93 Ariz. 384, 381 P.2d 107 (1963); *Blankenbaker v. Jonovich*, 203 Ariz. 226, 52 P.3d 795 (Ct. App.

Div. 1 2002), opinion vacated on other grounds, 205 Ariz. 383, 71 P.3d 910 (2003). Denial of a motion to strike will be reviewed on appeal only for an abuse of discretion. *Birth Hope Adoption Agency, Inc. v. Doe*, 190 Ariz. 285, 947 P.2d 859 (Ct. App. Div. 1 1997).

A motion to strike may not be used as a substitute for a motion to dismiss for failure to state a claim. *Colboch v. Aviation Credit Corp.*, 64 Ariz. 88, 166 P.2d 584 (1946). Similarly, the proper way to test the sufficiency of a motion for summary judgment is by responding to it, not by moving to strike it, and a motion to strike a motion for summary judgment that essentially challenges the merits of that motion is properly denied on that basis. *Birth Hope Adoption Agency, Inc. v. Doe*, 190 Ariz. 285, 947 P.2d 859 (Ct. App. Div. 1 1997).

The issue of whether a will should be voided because one of the beneficiaries helped prepare it and was thereby engaged in the unauthorized practice of law is not properly raised by a motion to strike; such an issue goes to the merits and should be raised by a motion for summary judgment. *In re Estate of Shumway*, 197 Ariz. 57, 3 P.3d 977 (Ct. App. Div. 1 1999), opinion vacated in part on other grounds, 198 Ariz. 323, 9 P.3d 1062 (2000). A motion to strike should be employed, however, where truly irrelevant and prejudicial matter is included in the pleadings which, under Arizona practice, may be read to the jury.

Rule 12(f) motions to strike are excluded from the provisions of Ariz. R. Civ. P. 7.1(f) (added 2014).

23. *Prior Pending Actions; Abatement.* In the majority of situations where identical or related actions have been filed in different jurisdictions, the appropriate remedy is to order a stay, rather than a dismissal, of the later filed action. While the pendency of an earlier filed, related action can cause abatement of a later filed action, such instances of abatement are limited to: (1) *in personam* actions that are brought *in the same jurisdiction*, and (2) *in rem* and *quasi-in-rem* actions. *Tonnemacher v. Touche Ross & Co.*, 186 Ariz. 125, 920 P.2d 5, R.I.C.O. Bus. Disp. Guide (CCH) P 9136 (Ct. App. Div. 1 1996). That abatement rule does not apply to personal actions that are pending in different jurisdictions. When related or identical actions are filed in different states, neither sovereign is required to yield to the other. The same rule applies when the actions are filed in state and federal courts in the same state. Because state and federal courts operate under different sovereigns, an action pending in federal court does not abate an identical action subsequently commenced in state court. The Superior Court, accordingly, has no authority to dismiss such a subsequently filed action, but it does have the discretion to stay it. *Tonnemacher v. Touche Ross & Co.*, 186 Ariz. 125, 920

P.2d 5, R.I.C.O. Bus. Disp. Guide (CCH) P 9136 (Ct. App. Div. 1 1996).

Rule 13. Counterclaim and cross-claim

(a) Compulsory Counterclaims. A pleading shall state as a counterclaim any claim which at the time of serving the pleading the pleader has against any opposing party, if it arises out of the transaction or occurrence that is the subject matter of the opposing party's claim and does not require for its adjudication the presence of third parties of whom the court cannot acquire jurisdiction. But the pleader need not state the claim if (1) at the time the action was commenced the claim was the subject of another pending action, or (2) the opposing party brought suit upon the claim by attachment or other process by which the court did not acquire jurisdiction to render a personal judgment on that claim, and the pleader is not stating any counterclaim under this Rule 13.

Amended March 26, 1963, effective June 1, 1963; Sept. 21, 1979, effective Dec. 1, 1979; Sept. 15, 1987, effective Nov. 15, 1987.

(b) Permissive Counterclaims. A pleading may state as a counterclaim any claim against an opposing party not arising out of the transaction or occurrence that is the subject matter of the opposing party's claim.

(c) Counterclaim Exceeding Opposing Claim. A counterclaim may or may not diminish or defeat the recovery sought by the opposing party. It may claim relief exceeding in amount or different in kind from that sought in the pleading of the opposing party.

(d) Counterclaim Against the State. These Rules shall not be construed to enlarge beyond the limits now fixed by law the right to assert counterclaims or to claim credits against the state or an officer or agency thereof.

(e) Counterclaim Maturing or Acquired After Pleading. A claim which either matured or was acquired by the pleader after serving a pleading may, with the permission of the court, be presented as a counterclaim by supplemental pleading.

(f) Abrogated Sept. 1, 2011, effective Jan. 1, 2012.

(g) Cross-Claim Against Co-party. A pleading may state as a cross-claim any claim by one party against a co-party arising out of the transaction or occurrence that is the subject matter either of the original action or of a counterclaim therein or relating to any property that is the subject matter of the original action. The cross-claim may include a claim that the party against whom it is asserted is or may be liable to the cross-claimant for all or part of a claim asserted in the action against the cross-claimant.

(h) Joinder of Additional Parties. Persons other than those made parties to the original action may be made parties to a counterclaim or cross-claim in accordance with the provisions of Rules 19 and 20.

Amended July 1, 1966, effective Nov. 1,1966.

(i) Separate Trials; Separate Judgments. If the court orders separate trials as provided in Rule 42(b), judgment on a counterclaim or cross-claim may be rendered in accordance with the terms of Rule 54(b) when the court has jurisdiction so to do, even if the claims of the opposing party have been dismissed or otherwise disposed of.

STATE BAR COMMITTEE NOTES

1963 Amendment

[Rule 13(a)] When a defendant, if he desires to defend his interest in property, is obliged to come in and litigate in a court to whose jurisdiction he could not ordinarily be subjected, fairness suggests that he should not be required to assert counterclaims, but should rather be permitted to do so at his election. If, however, he does elect to assert a counterclaim, it seems fair to require him to assert any other which is compulsory within the meaning of Rule 13(a). Clause (2), added by amendment to Rule 13(a), carries out this scheme. It will apply to various cases described in Rule 4(e), as amended, where service is effected through attachment or other process by which the court does not acquire jurisdiction to render a personal judgment against the defendant.

1966 Amendment

[Rule 13(h)] This conforms the rule to changes made in Rules 19 and 20.

AUTHORS' COMMENTS

Analysis

1. Scope and Purpose of Rule.
2. Comparison With Federal Rule.
3. Compulsory Counterclaims.
4. Permissive Counterclaims.
5. Counterclaim Maturing or Acquired After Original Pleading.
6. Omitted Counterclaims.
7. Cross-Claims.
8. Joinder of Additional Parties.
9. Separate Trials; Separate Judgments.
10. Contribution Claims.

1. *Scope and Purpose of Rule.* Ariz. R. Civ. P. 13 authorizes a defendant to assert claims held against the plaintiff, termed "counterclaims," as well as claims against other parties defendant, termed "cross-claims." Additional parties who are subject to the Court's jurisdiction may be joined if necessary to the adjudication

of counterclaims or cross-claims.

Rule 13 distinguishes between "compulsory" counterclaims, which must be raised or are barred, and "permissive" counterclaims, which may be raised at the defendant's option. The policy of the Rule, however, is to encourage the assertion of counterclaims so that all disputes existing between the parties may be resolved in a single action rather than through a multiplicity of suits. *O'Brien v. Scottsdale Discount Corp.*, 14 Ariz. App. 224, 482 P.2d 473 (Div. 2 1971); *Pacific Guano Co. v. Pinal County Land Co.*, 1 Ariz. App. 34, 399 P.2d 122 (1965).

Under Rule 13(c), the relief sought in a counterclaim may exceed that sought in the plaintiff's claim. A counterclaim which is barred by the applicable statute of limitations, however, may not be asserted unless it is in the nature of a recoupment, which may not exceed the plaintiff's claim, even if the complaint in the action was timely filed. *W. J. Kroeger Co. v. Travelers Indem. Co.*, 112 Ariz. 285, 541 P.2d 385 (1975); *Egan-Ryan Mechanical Co. v. Cardon Meadows Development Corp.*, 169 Ariz. 161, 818 P.2d 146 (Ct. App. Div. 1 1990); *Ness v. Greater Arizona Realty, Inc.*, 117 Ariz. 357, 572 P.2d 1195 (Ct. App. Div. 2 1977).

A counterclaim needs to be distinguished from an affirmative defense, which if successful will only defeat or diminish the plaintiff's recovery. A counterclaim is a cause of action for which the defendant might have brought a separate action against the plaintiff and recovered a judgment, and permits the defendant to secure affirmative relief or a setoff in the action in which it is asserted. *Turf Paradise, Inc. v. Maricopa County*, 179 Ariz. 337, 878 P.2d 1375 (Ct. App. Div. 1 1994).

Where a counterclaim is asserted as part of the defendant's answer, it should be specifically designated as such. This necessitates a reply by the plaintiff-counterdefendant under Rule 7(a) which helps frame the issues to be resolved.

2. *Comparison With Federal Rule.* Despite structural differences, ARCP 13 is generally identical to FRCP 13, but there are other differences. In 2007, the language of FRCP 13 was amended as part of the general restyling of the Federal Rules of Civil Procedure to make the Federal Rules more easily understood and to make style and terminology consistent throughout the Federal Rules of Civil Procedure. Those stylistic modifications have not been incorporated, as yet, into ARCP 13.

In addition to the stylistic amendments, in 2007, the language of FRCP 13(b) was amended to delete the phrase "not arising out of the transaction or the occurrence that is the subject matter of the opposing party's claim." ARCP 13(b) has not been amended to incorporate this 2007 amendment to the federal rule.

As a technical comparative difference, ARCP 13(d) refers to

counterclaims against the state while FRCP 13(d) refers to counterclaims against the United States.

In 2009, FRCP 13 was amended to delete subparagraph (f) [Omitted Counterclaim] because its provisions were deemed "largely redundant and misleading" insofar as a request to add an omitted counterclaim is governed by FRCP 15. *See* Comment to 2009 Amendment of FRCP 13. Effective January 1, 2012, ARCP 13(f) was abrogated to conform with the 2009 abrogation of FRCP 13(f).

3. *Compulsory Counterclaims.* A counterclaim which arises out of the same "transaction or occurrence" as the complaint is "compulsory," in that it must be asserted or it is barred. *Lansford v. Harris*, 174 Ariz. 413, 850 P.2d 126 (Ct. App. Div. 1, 1992); *O'Brien v. Scottsdale Discount Corp.*, 14 Ariz. App. 224, 482 P.2d 473 (Div. 2 1971).

The assertion that a claim in a newly instituted action was a compulsory counterclaim that should have been raised in a prior action between the parties is merely a particularized application of the doctrine of *res judicata. Biaett v. Phoenix Title & Trust Co.*, 70 Ariz. 164, 217 P.2d 923, 22 A.L.R.2d 615 (1950); *Lansford v. Harris*, 174 Ariz. 413, 850 P.2d 126 (Ct. App. Div. 1 1992).

The test is whether there is a logical or legal relationship between the claim and the counterclaim. *Technical Air Products, Inc. v. Sheridan-Gray, Inc.*, 103 Ariz. 450, 445 P.2d 426 (1968); *Occidental Chemical Co. v. Connor*, 124 Ariz. 341, 604 P.2d 605 (1979).

A compulsory counterclaim asserted in response to the initial complaint need not be re-pleaded in response to any amendment of that complaint. *Mohave Concrete and Materials, Inc. v. Scaramuzzo*, 154 Ariz. 28, 739 P.2d 1345 (Ct. App. Div. 1 1987). An otherwise compulsory counterclaim need not be asserted if it is already the subject of another pending action or if the court's jurisdiction on the plaintiff's claim is purely *in rem.* The assertion of a compulsory counterclaim, however, does not necessarily constitute a waiver of the lack-of-personal-jurisdictional defenses. *Aries v. Palmer Johnson, Inc.*, 153 Ariz. 250, 735 P.2d 1373, 4 U.C.C. Rep. Serv. 2d 85 (Ct. App. Div. 2 1987).

A counterclaim may not be asserted if it has not as yet matured. *O'Brien v. Scottsdale Discount Corp.*, 14 Ariz. App. 224, 482 P.2d 473 (Div. 2 1971). A counterclaim must be mature to be considered a compulsory counterclaim. *Lansford v. Harris*, 174 Ariz. 413, 850 P.2d 126 (Ct. App. Div. 1 1992). Once a counterclaim matures, it may be asserted in a supplemental pleading under Rule 13(e). Thus, there can be no counterclaim for malicious prosecution arising out of the filing of plaintiff's claim because such a counterclaim will not mature until the validity of plaintiff's claim is determined. *Bradshaw v. State Farm Mut. Auto. Ins. Co.*, 157 Ariz. 411, 758 P.2d 1313 (1988); *Nataros v. Superior Court of Maricopa County*, 113 Ariz. 498, 557 P.2d 1055 (1976).

An abuse of process claim, on the other hand, is a compulsory counterclaim in the action claimed to be abusive. *Pochiro v. Prudential Ins. Co. of America*, 827 F.2d 1246, 9 Fed. R. Serv. 3d 266 (9th Cir. 1987) (applying Arizona law).

4. *Permissive Counterclaims.* A counterclaim held by the defendant which does not arise out of the same transaction or occurrence as the plaintiff's claim is a permissive one and the defendant has the option of asserting it as a counterclaim or pursuing it independently.

5. *Counterclaim Maturing or Acquired After Original Pleading.* A counterclaim may not be asserted unless it has matured at the time the answer is filed. *Cochise Hotels, Inc. v. Douglas Hotel Operating Co.*, 83 Ariz. 40, 316 P.2d 290 (1957); *Lansford v. Harris*, 174 Ariz. 413, 850 P.2d 126 (Ct. App. Div. 1 1992); *O'Brien v. Scottsdale Discount Corp.*, 14 Ariz. App. 224, 482 P.2d 473 (Div. 2 1971). If a counterclaim matures or is acquired by the defendant after that point, the Court may permit it to be asserted in a supplemental pleading under Rule 13(e).

6. *Omitted Counterclaims.* Effective January 1, 2012, the Arizona Supreme Court abrogated, without comment, Rule 13(f), which had addressed omitted counterclaims. Although the Court did not give any reasons for the abrogation, the Petition giving rise to the Court's order urged the abrogation of Rule 13(f) to bring Arizona's rule in line with the recent abrogation of Fed. R. Civ. P. 13(f).

The Advisory Committee Note accompanying the 2009 abrogation of Fed. R. Civ. P. 13(f), explained that Fed. R. Civ. P. 15(a) already governed amendments to pleadings rendering Fed. R. Civ. P. 13(f) "largely redundant and potentially misleading." The Advisory Committee Note also noted that Fed. R. Civ. P. 13(f) also seemed to set forth a standard for allowing an amendment different than the standard set by Fed. R. Civ. P. 15. Finally, the Advisory Committee Note observed that Fed. R. Civ. P. 13(f) injected uncertainty into whether relation back of an amendment was available under Fed. R. Civ. P. 13(f).

The Petition acknowledged that Ariz. R. Civ. P. 13(f) differed from its federal counterpart, but urged that the reasons underlying the abrogation of the federal rule also supported the abrogation of Ariz. R. Civ. P. 13(f). The Arizona Supreme Court appears to have agreed with the Rule 28 Petition insofar as it abrogated Ariz. R. Civ. P. 13(f).

As a result, and effective January 1, 2012, motions to assert an omitted counterclaim are now governed by Ariz. R. Civ. P. 15.

7. *Cross-Claims.* A cross-claim may only be asserted if it arises out of the same "transaction or occurrence" as the plaintiff's claims—essentially the same test as for a compulsory counterclaim. *Hollar v. Wright*, 115 Ariz. 606, 566 P.2d 1352 (Ct. App. Div. 1 1977). The assertion of a cross-claim, however, is always permissive and there is no waiver or bar for failure to do so. While cross-claims are generally between co-defendants, a plaintiff may under the Rule assert against a co-plaintiff a cross-claim precipitated by a defendant's counterclaim.

8. *Joinder of Additional Parties.* A counterclaim or cross-claim may add new parties to the action if their joinder is consistent with the standards of Rules 19 and 20. A counterclaim will not be considered compulsory under Rule 13(a) if its adjudication requires the presence of third parties over whom the Court cannot acquire jurisdiction.

9. *Separate Trials; Separate Judgments.* Rule 42(b) grants express authority for the Court to direct that a counterclaim or cross-claim be tried separately to avoid prejudice or where separate trials would be conducive to expedition and economy. If there are separate trials ordered, judgment on a counterclaim or cross-claim may be entered separately in accordance with the terms of Rule 54(b).

10. *Contribution Claims.* The law in Arizona with respect to claims for contribution among joint tortfeasors has taken several divergent turns in recent years. Before 1984, Arizona adhered to the strict common law rule which prohibited claims for contribution among joint tortfeasors. *City of Tucson v. Superior Court In and For County of Pima*, 165 Ariz. 236, 798 P.2d 374 (1990); *Holmes v. Hoemako Hospital*, 117 Ariz. 403, 573 P.2d 477, 7 A.L.R.4th 1231 (1977); *Young v. Environmental Air Products, Inc.*, 136 Ariz. 206, 665 P.2d 88 (Ct. App. Div. 2 1982), aff'd as modified, 136 Ariz. 158, 665 P.2d 40 (1983); *Employers Mut. Liability Ins. Co. of Wis. v. Advance Transformer Co.*, 15 Ariz. App. 1, 485 P.2d 591 (Div. 2 1971); *Pinal County v. Adams*, 13 Ariz. App. 571, 479 P.2d 718 (Div. 1 1971). Because joint tortfeasors were subject to joint and several liability, the prohibition on contribution claims at times had the harsh result of permitting one of several joint tortfeasors to bear the entire financial responsibility for a loss produced by the concurrent negligence of all of them. *Bill Alexander Ford, Lincoln Mercury, Inc. v. Casa Ford, Inc.*, 187 Ariz. 616, 931 P.2d 1126, Prod. Liab. Rep. (CCH) P 14727 (Ct. App. Div. 1 1996); *Transcon Lines v. Barnes*, 17 Ariz. App. 428, 498 P.2d 502 (Div. 1 1972).

In 1984, Arizona adopted a modified version of the Uniform Contribution Among Tortfeasors Act, A.R.S. §§ 12-2501, *et seq.* The Act, *inter alia,* abolished the prior common law rule prohibiting claims of contribution among joint tortfeasors. Each joint tortfeasor was made responsible for that tortfeasor's *pro rata* share of the entire liability, which was to be allocated according to "relative degrees of fault." A.R.S. § 12-2502.

A right of contribution against other joint tortfeasors was created in favor of any tortfeasor who "has paid" more than that tortfeasor's "pro rata share of the common liability." A.R.S. § 12-2501(B). This right to contribution may be enforced by counterclaim or cross-claim in an action in which the joint tortfeasors have been named as defendants, through a third-party claim, or in a separate action. A.R.S. § 12-2503; *Nikolous v. Superior Court In and For Maricopa County*, 157 Ariz. 256, 756 P.2d 925 (1988). The Act applied to actions filed on or after August 30, 1984. The number of cases in which the right to contribution thereby created would be a viable issue, however, was severely limited by subsequent amendments to the statute.

In 1987, the Arizona Legislature enacted amendments to the Uniform Contribution Among Tortfeasors Act which abolished the doctrine of joint and several liability, except in cases where parties were acting in concert, where one party was acting as an agent or servant of another party, and in cases relating to hazardous wastes or substances or solid waste disposal sites. A.R.S. § 12-2506 (as amended). *Yslava v. Hughes Aircraft Co.*, 188 Ariz. 380, 936 P.2d 1274, 45 Env't. Rep. Cas. (BNA) 1315 (1997); *Bishop v. Pecanic*, 193 Ariz. 524, 975 P.2d 114 (Ct. App. Div. 1 1998). (The exception for cases relating to hazardous wastes or substances, or solid waste disposal sites, was repealed in 1997, purportedly retroactively, and liability in those type of cases is now several only as well.) Guiding this statutory revision was a desire to increase the fairness of the tort system for both plaintiffs and defendants, and to eliminate the harshness of an all-or-nothing contributory negligence defense. *Hutcherson v. City of Phoenix*, 192 Ariz. 51, 961 P.2d 449 (1998).

The 1987 amendments also broadened the scope of torts subject to the rules of comparative fault beyond those grounded on theories of negligence, and are fully applicable in product liability actions. *Jimenez v. Sears, Roebuck and Co.*, 183 Ariz. 399, 904 P.2d 861, Prod. Liab. Rep. (CCH) P 14382 (1995); *Zuern By and Through Zuern v. Ford Motor Co.*, 188 Ariz. 486, 937 P.2d 676 (Ct. App. Div. 2 1996). In such actions, accordingly, there must be an allocation of fault to each person or entity in the chain of distribution of the allegedly defective product. *State Farm Ins. Companies v. Premier Manufactured Systems, Inc.*, 217 Ariz. 222, 172 P.3d 410 (2007). The amendment applies to actions filed on or after December 31, 1987, and has been held to be constitutional. *Jimenez v. Sears, Roebuck and Co.*, 183 Ariz. 399, 904 P.2d 861, Prod. Liab. Rep. (CCH) P 14382 (1995); *Larsen v.*

Nissan Motor Corp. in U.S.A., 194 Ariz. 142, 978 P.2d 119 (Ct. App. Div. 2 1998); *Lerma v. Keck*, 186 Ariz. 228, 921 P.2d 28 (Ct. App. Div. 1 1996); *Church v. Rawson Drug & Sundry Co.*, 173 Ariz. 342, 842 P.2d 1355 (Ct. App. Div. 1 1992).

The statute did not, however, change the law with regard to vicarious liability. *Law v. Verde Valley Medical Center*, 217 Ariz. 92, 170 P.3d 701 (Ct. App. Div. 1 2007). An alleged tortfeasor and a party potentially liable vicariously for that person's tortious conduct are not joint tortfeasors under Arizona law. *Law v. Verde Valley Medical Center*, 217 Ariz. 92, 170 P.3d 701 (Ct. App. Div. 1 2007). When a judgment on the merits is entered in favor of a person for whose conduct a party is vicariously liable, there is no fault to impute or allocate. *Law v. Verde Valley Medical Center*, 217 Ariz. 92, 170 P.3d 701 (Ct. App. Div. 1 2007).

Under the Act as amended, Arizona follows a "comparative fault" regime, under which the trier of fact considers and apportions the fault of all persons who contributed to the harm to the plaintiff, and each tortfeasor is responsible only for his or her percentage of fault and no more. *Hutcherson v. City of Phoenix*, 192 Ariz. 51, 961 P.2d 449 (1998); *Sanchez v. City of Tucson*, 191 Ariz. 128, 953 P.2d 168 (1998); *McKillip v. Smitty's Super Valu, Inc.*, 190 Ariz. 61, 945 P.2d 372 (Ct. App. Div. 1 1997); *Zuern By and Through Zuern v. Ford Motor Co.*, 188 Ariz. 486, 937 P.2d 676 (Ct. App. Div. 2 1996); *Standard Chartered PLC v. Price Waterhouse*, 190 Ariz. 6, 945 P.2d 317 (Ct. App. Div. 1 1996), as corrected on denial of reconsideration, (Jan. 13, 1997); *Rosner v. Denim & Diamonds, Inc.*, 188 Ariz. 431, 937 P.2d 353 (Ct. App. Div. 2 1996); *Natseway v. City of Tempe*, 184 Ariz. 374, 909 P.2d 441 (Ct. App. Div. 1 1995).

The trier of fact may consider the fault of persons who are not parties to the action, even if the plaintiff would be prohibited from suing them directly or recovering damages from them. *Dietz v. General Elec. Co.*, 169 Ariz. 505, 821 P.2d 166 (1991); *A Tumbling-T Ranches v. Flood Control Dist. of Maricopa County*, 222 Ariz. 515, 217 P.3d 1220 (Ct. App. Div. 1 2009); *Larsen v. Nissan Motor Corp. in U.S.A.*, 194 Ariz. 142, 978 P.2d 119 (Ct. App. Div. 2 1998). Thus, an expert's opinion apportioning percentages of fault to the parties and non-parties improperly invades the province of the jury and is inadmissible, notwithstanding Rule 704, Ariz. R. Evid. *Webb v. Omni Block, Inc.*, 216 Ariz. 349, 166 P.3d 140 (Ct. App. Div. 1 2007).

There is no authority for the proposition that intentional conduct must be given more weight than negligent conduct in the apportionment of fault. *Hutcherson v. City of Phoenix*, 192 Ariz. 51, 961 P.2d 449 (1998). These comparative fault principles apply regardless of the relationship of the parties and the nature of the duty owed, and even where it is alleged that a negligent tortfeasor had a duty to prevent an intentional wrong from occurring. *Natseway v. City of Tempe*, 184 Ariz. 374, 909 P.2d 441 (Ct. App. Div. 1 1995). The Act permits the apportionment of fault between a negligent plaintiff and a defendant whose conduct is wanton or wilful. *Rosner v. Denim & Diamonds, Inc.*, 188 Ariz. 431, 937 P.2d 353 (Ct. App. Div. 2 1996); *Wareing v. Falk*, 182 Ariz. 495, 897 P.2d 1381 (Ct. App. Div. 1 1995). It even permits the allocation of fault between an allegedly negligent defendant and a nonparty who commits a criminal act. *Hutcherson v. City of Phoenix*, 192 Ariz. 51, 961 P.2d 449 (1998); *Thomas v. First Interstate Bank of Arizona, N.A.*, 187 Ariz. 488, 930 P.2d 1002, 54 A.L.R. 5th 827 (Ct. App. Div. 2 1996). Correspondingly, a plaintiff guilty of gross or wanton negligence in causing an accident will not necessarily be barred from any recovery. *Williams v. Thude*, 188 Ariz. 257, 934 P.2d 1349 (1997).

The statutory goal of having percentages of fault allocated to all responsible parties and nonparties in a single action provides "good and sufficient cause," under A.R.S. § 12-406(B)(3), for the transfer of an action from a county where venue is proper to another county so that it can be consolidated with another case arising out of the same underlying event. *Behrens v. O'Melia*, 206 Ariz. 309, 78 P.3d 278 (Ct. App. Div. 1 2003).

A claim that a jury's allocation of fault was against the weight of the evidence is properly presented as a motion for new trial under Rule 59(a)(8). *Hutcherson v. City of Phoenix*, 192 Ariz. 51, 961 P.2d 449 (1998). Similarly, where the parties stipulate that a non-party was the proximate cause of the plaintiff's injuries, the jury must allocate some degree of fault to that non-party, and the jury's disregard of the stipulation and assignment of 100% of the fault to the named defendants warrants a new trial on all issues. *Ogden v. J.M. Steel Erecting, Inc.*, 201 Ariz. 32, 31 P.3d 806 (Ct. App. Div. 1 2001).

The provision of the Arizona Constitution, article 18, § 5, which requires that the defense of contributory negligence always be left to the jury to decide, applies to claims of comparative negligence as well, so that the issue of the proper allocation of fault will always be a jury issue, where a jury is demanded. *Gunnell v. Arizona Public Service Co.*, 202 Ariz. 388, 46 P.3d 399 (2002).

The 1987 amendments severely limit the right of contribution granted by A.R.S. § 12-2501. By abolishing joint and several liability and limiting recovery against any defendant to that percentage of the plaintiff's total injuries which represents that defendant's degree of fault, the statute insures that the conditions for claiming contribution will not occur. *PAM Transport v. Freightliner Corp.*, 182 Ariz. 132, 893 P.2d 1295 (1995); *Cella*

Barr Associates, Inc. v. Cohen, 177 Ariz. 480, 868 P.2d 1063 (Ct. App. Div. 1 1994); *Neil v. Kavena*, 176 Ariz. 93, 859 P.2d 203 (Ct. App. Div. 1 1993); *Roland v. Bernstein*, 171 Ariz. 96, 828 P.2d 1237 (Ct. App. Div. 2 1991).

As a practical matter, accordingly, contribution claims among joint tortfeasors are potentially viable only in cases filed between August 30, 1984 and December 31, 1987. The issue of how pretrial settlements between the plaintiff and one or more of the joint tortfeasors are to be accounted for is discussed in Sections 5 and 6 of the *Authors' Comments* to Rule 16.1.

Arizona's adoption of the Uniform Contribution Among Tortfeasors Act left intact the common law doctrine of "indivisible injury." *Piner v. Superior Court In and For County of Maricopa*, 192 Ariz. 182, 962 P.2d 909 (1998); *Salica v. Tucson Heart Hosp.-Carondelet, L.L.C.*, 224 Ariz. 414, 231 P.3d 946 (Ct. App. Div. 2 2010). When the tortious conduct of more than one defendant contributes to one indivisible injury, the entire amount of damages resulting from all contributing causes is the total amount "of damages recoverable by the plaintiff," as that term is used in A.R.S. § 12-2506(A). *Piner v. Superior Court In and For County of Maricopa*, 192 Ariz. 182, 962 P.2d 909 (1998). The fault of all actors is then determined by the trier of fact, and each defendant is *severally* liable for damages allocated in direct proportion to that defendant's percentage of fault. *Piner v. Superior Court In and For County of Maricopa*, 192 Ariz. 182, 962 P.2d 909 (1998). In an indivisible injury case, the fact finder is to compute the total amount of damages sustained by the plaintiff, and the percentage of fault of each tortfeasor, and the maximum amount recoverable against each tortfeasor is computed by multiplying the first figure by the second. *Piner v. Superior Court In and For County of Maricopa*, 192 Ariz. 182, 962 P.2d 909 (1998).

The doctrine of "satisfaction of judgment" provides that, if one joint tortfeasor satisfies a judgment obtained by the plaintiff, all other tortfeasors are discharged from liability and the plaintiff has no further cause of action. *Bridgestone/Firestone North America Tire, L.L.C. v. Naranjo*, 206 Ariz. 447, 79 P.3d 1206, Prod. Liab. Rep. (CCH) P 16845 (Ct. App. Div. 2 2003). This doctrine also survives the abolition of joint and several liability, and the adoption of a comparative fault regime, in situations where the plaintiff has obtained a judgment for the total damages suffered from an indivisible injury against only one party at fault, and that judgment is satisfied. *Bridgestone/Firestone North America Tire, L.L.C. v. Naranjo*, 206 Ariz. 447, 79 P.3d 1206, Prod. Liab. Rep. (CCH) P 16845 (Ct. App. Div. 2 2003). The satisfaction of that judgment extinguishes any claim against other parties at fault. *Bridgestone/Firestone North America Tire, L.L.C. v. Naranjo*, 206 Ariz. 447, 79 P.3d 1206, Prod. Liab. Rep. (CCH)

P 16845 (Ct. App. Div. 2 2003).

Under A.R.S. § 12-2506(D), joint tortfeasors who act in concert remain jointly and severally liable for the resulting injury or damage. *Chappell v. Wenholz*, 226 Ariz. 309, 247 P.3d 192 (Ct. App. Div. 1 2011); *Mein ex rel. Mein v. Cook*, 219 Ariz. 96, 193 P.3d 790 (Ct. App. Div. 1 2008); *Bishop v. Pecanic*, 193 Ariz. 524, 975 P.2d 114 (Ct. App. Div. 1 1998). In *Mein*, the court of appeals held that a *prima facie* case under A.R.S. § 12-2506(D)(1) requires evidence the parties: (1) knowingly agreed to commit an intentional tort, (2) they were certain or substantially certain their actions would result in the consequences complained of, and (3) they actively participated in the commission of the tort. *Mein ex rel. Mein v. Cook*, 219 Ariz. 96, 193 P.3d 790 (Ct. App. Div. 1 2008); *see also*, *Chappell v. Wenholz*, 226 Ariz. 309, 247 P.3d 192 (Ct. App. Div. 1 2011) (holding, "[a] conscious agreement need not be verbally expressed and may be implied from the conduct itself"). A joint tortfeasor in such a situation who pays more than his or her share of the common liability is entitled to seek contribution from fellow tortfeasors. *Herstam v. Deloitte & Touche, LLP*, 186 Ariz. 110, 919 P.2d 1381 (Ct. App. Div. 1 1996).

When a complaint alleges concerted action that normally would subject all parties to joint and several liability, however, the injured party can, as part of a settlement with one or more of the joint tortfeasors, agree to waive the right to hold nonsettling parties jointly and severally liable and thereby bar the nonsettling parties from seeking contribution and/or indemnity from the settling parties. *Herstam v. Deloitte & Touche, LLP*, 186 Ariz. 110, 919 P.2d 1381 (Ct. App. Div. 1 1996). *See also*, *Bishop v. Pecanic*, 193 Ariz. 524, 975 P.2d 114 (Ct. App. Div. 1 1998). A.R.S. § 12-2506(F)(1) defines "acting in concert" as, *inter alia*, being inapplicable to "any person whose conduct was negligent in any of its degrees rather than intentional." In enacting this exception where parties are acting in concert, the Legislature did not, however, displace or alter the longstanding common law liability for aiding and abetting. *Security Title Agency, Inc. v. Pope*, 219 Ariz. 480, 200 P.3d 977, 27 I.E.R. Cas. (BNA) 1811 (Ct. App. Div. 1 2008).

Joint liability and vicarious liability "are related but separate doctrines." *Wiggs v. City of Phoenix*, 198 Ariz. 367, 10 P.3d 625, 111 A.L.R.5th 815 (2000) (citing, *Srithong v. Total Investment Co.*, 23 Cal. App. 4th 721, 28 Cal. Rptr. 2d 672 (2d Dist. 1994); *State Farm Ins. Companies v. Premier Manufactured Systems, Inc.*, 213 Ariz. 419, 142 P.3d 1232, Prod. Liab. Rep. (CCH) P 17517 (Ct. App. Div. 1 2006), opinion aff'd, 217 Ariz. 222, 172 P.3d 410 (2007)). The joint liability that was abolished by A.R.S. § 12-2506(D) is limited to "that class of joint tortfeasors whose independent negligence coalesced to form a single injury." *Wiggs v. City of Phoenix*, 198 Ariz. 367, 10 P.3d 625, 111 A.L.R.5th 815

(2000). The statute preserves joint liability both for true joint tortfeasors (those "acting in concert") and for those who are vicariously liable for the fault of others. *Wiggs v. City of Phoenix*, 198 Ariz. 367, 10 P.3d 625, 111 A.L.R.5th 815 (2000); *State Farm Ins. Companies v. Premier Manufactured Systems, Inc.*, 213 Ariz. 419, 142 P.3d 1232, Prod. Liab. Rep. (CCH) P 17517 (Ct. App. Div. 1 2006), opinion aff'd, 217 Ariz. 222, 172 P.3d 410 (2007).

The comparative fault statute, thus, preserves vicarious liability for the negligence of an independent contractor, when the employer of that independent contractor had a non-delegable duty. *Wiggs v. City of Phoenix*, 198 Ariz. 367, 10 P.3d 625, 111 A.L.R.5th 815 (2000). This will not operate to immunize independent contractors from the consequences of their own negligence, any more than in the case of a true employee. *Wiggs v. City of Phoenix*, 198 Ariz. 367, 10 P.3d 625, 111 A.L.R.5th 815 (2000). In either setting, the employer may seek indemnity against the employee or independent contractor, in cases of pure vicarious liability, or contribution in cases in which the employer has some degree of independent liability. *Wiggs v. City of Phoenix*, 198 Ariz. 367, 10 P.3d 625, 111 A.L.R.5th 815 (2000).

Rule 14. Third-party practice

(a) When Defendant May Bring in Third Party. At any time after commencement of the action a defendant, as a third-party plaintiff, may cause a summons and complaint to be served upon a person not a party to the action who is or may be liable to the third-party plaintiff for all or part of the plaintiff's claim against the third-party plaintiff. A copy of all previous pleadings, as defined in Rule 7(a) of these Rules, that have been filed in the action shall be served together with the third-party complaint or be provided by the third-party plaintiff to the person served promptly after service. The third-party plaintiff need not obtain leave to make the service if the third-party plaintiff files the third-party complaint not later than 10 days after serving the original answer. Otherwise the third-party plaintiff must obtain leave on motion upon notice to all parties to the action. The person served with the summons and third-party complaint, hereinafter called the third-party defendant, shall make any defenses to the third-party plaintiff's claim as provided in Rule 12, and any counterclaims against the third-party plaintiff and cross-claims against other third-party defendants as provided in Rule 13. The third-party defendant may assert against the plaintiff any defenses which the third-party plaintiff has to the plaintiff's claim. The third-party defendant may also assert any claim against the plaintiff arising out of the transaction or occurrence that is the subject matter of the plaintiff's claim against the third-party plaintiff. The plaintiff may assert any claim against the third-party defendant arising out of the transaction or occurrence that is the subject matter of the plaintiff's claim against the third-party plaintiff, and the third-party defendant thereupon shall assert any defenses as provided in Rule 12 and any counterclaims and cross-claims as provided in Rule 13. Any party may move to strike the third-party claim, or for its severance or separate trial. A third-party defendant may proceed under this rule against any person not a party to the action who is or may be liable to the third-party defendant for all or part of the claim made in the action against the third-party defendant.

Amended March 26, 1963, effective June 1, 1963; Sept. 15, 1987, effective Nov. 15, 1987; Sept. 25, 1990, effective Jan. 1, 1991.

(b) When Plaintiff May Bring in Third Party. When a counterclaim is asserted against a plaintiff, he may cause a third party to be brought in under circumstances which under this Rule would entitle a defendant to do so.

STATE BAR COMMITTEE NOTES

1963 Amendment

[Rule 14] Under the amendment of the initial sentences of the rule, a defendant as third-party plaintiff may freely and without leave of court bring in a third-party defendant if he files the third-party complaint not later than 10 days after he serves his answer. When the impleader comes so early in the case, there is little value in requiring a preliminary ruling by the court on the propriety of the impleader.

After the third-party defendant is brought in, the court has discretion to allow the impleader to stand or dismiss it, or to sever it or accord it separate trial. This discretion, applicable not merely to the cases covered by the amendment where the third-party defendant is brought in without leave, but to all impleaders under the rule is emphasized in the next-to-last sentence of the rule, added by amendment. It includes the power to strike a third-party complaint filed without leave for any reason for which leave might have been denied in the first instance. Because the amendment deals solely with the time of filing, it has no bearing on substance and leaves wholly unaffected the decision in *Blakely Oil, Inc. v. Crowder*, 80 Ariz. 72, 292 P.2d 842 (1956) or *Busy Bee Buffet, Inc. v. Ferrell*, 82 Ariz. 192, 310 P.2d 817 (1957).

AUTHORS' COMMENTS

Analysis

1. *Scope and Purpose of Rule.* Ariz. R. Civ. P. 14 creates the procedural device—the third-party claim—which permits the defendant to become in effect a plaintiff as against any person who is or may be liable for all or any part of the original plaintiff's claim. *Ewing v. Goettl's Metal Products Co.*, 116 Ariz. 484, 569 P.2d 1382 (Ct. App. Div. 1 1977); *Thornton v. Marsico*, 5 Ariz. App. 299, 425 P.2d 869 (1967). Under Rule 14(b), a plaintiff may also bring in a third party claimed to be responsible for claims asserted in a counterclaim in circumstances which would permit a defendant to do so. The Rule provides a convenient vehicle for the assertion of claims for partial or total indemnity, *Ewing v. Goettl's Metal Products Co.*, 116 Ariz. 484, 569 P.2d 1382 (Ct. App. Div. 1 1977), and serves the purpose of resolving in one proceeding all issues arising out of a particular dispute.

2. *Comparison With Federal Rule.* ARCP 14 is similar to FRCP 14, but there are both structural and substantive differences.

ARCP 14(a) has a provision that requires service on a third-party defendant of copies of all prior pleadings in the action. FRCP 14(a) does not contain a similar provision. Also, ARCP 14 does not contain provisions similar to FRCP 14(a)(6) and FRCP 14(c), relating to third-party practice in admiralty and maritime cases.

As a consequence of the 2009 amendments to FRCP 14(a), the time set in the former federal rule at 10 days was revised to 14 days. ARCP 14 has not been amended to alter this time period, which remains set at 10 days.

FRCP 14(b) was amended in 2007 to delete reference to the word "counterclaim" in favor of the word "claim," in order to place a plaintiff "on equal footing with the defendant in making third-party claims." *See* 2007 Comment to FRCP 14. ARCP 14(b) has not been amended to conform to its federal counterpart.

In addition, in 2007, the language of FRCP 14 was amended as part of the general restyling of the Federal Rules of Civil Procedure to make the Federal Rules more easily understood and to make style and terminology consistent throughout the Federal Rules of Civil Procedure. Those stylistic modifications have not been incorporated into ARCP 14.

3. *Procedures for Filing and Defending Third-Party Claims.* A defendant may file a third-party complaint without leave of court at any time prior to ten (10) days after serving the original answer (or reply to a counterclaim). Thereafter, leave of court is required. Where leave is required, it should be granted liberally, but it may be denied where the Court believes it would unduly complicate the issues in the action. *Smith v. Rabb*, 95 Ariz. 49, 386 P.2d 649 (1963). The 1990 amendments to Rule 14(a) added the requirement that all previous pleadings in the action (as "pleadings" is defined in Rule 7(a)) must be served together with the third-party complaint or provided to the person served promptly thereafter.

Rule 14 does not specify the time period in which an answer or other pleading responsive to a third-party complaint is to be filed other than by its incorporation of the provisions of Rules 12 and 13, which signifies that the time periods are the same as for responding to an original complaint. The third-party defendant may raise the defenses contemplated by Rule 12, may assert counterclaims against the third-party plaintiff and cross-claims against other third-party defendants, and may institute a third-party action. The third-party defendant may also raise any available defenses to the plaintiff's original claim, and may assert against the plaintiff any claim arising out of the transaction or occurrence that is the subject of the plaintiff's claim. The original plaintiff may similarly assert against the third-party defendant any claim arising out of that transaction or occurrence.

The standards of Rule 12 govern a motion to dismiss directed to a third-party complaint. All facts alleged in a third-party complaint are assumed to be true and are read in the light most favorable to the third-party plaintiff. *Truck Equipment Co. of Ariz. v. Vanlandingham*, 103 Ariz. 402, 442 P.2d 849 (1968).

4. *Joinder of Additional Parties.* A third-party defendant may expand the parties even further by bringing in any person not already a party to the action who is or may be liable to the third-party defendant for all or part of the third-party claim. In addition, if a counterclaim is asserted against the plaintiff, the plaintiff may bring in a third-party under the same circumstances as a defendant would be permitted to do so, but only to pass on part or all of the liability for a counterclaim asserted by a defendant. *State Compensation Fund v. Superior Court In and For Pima County*, 11 Ariz. App. 583, 466 P.2d 802 (Div. 2 1970).

5. *Limitations on Use of Rule.* While the Rule is to be construed broadly in favor of permitting third-party claims, *Chirco Const. Co., Inc. v. Stewart Title and Trust of Tucson*, 129 Ariz. 187, 629 P.2d 1023 (Ct. App. Div. 2 1981), it is not open-ended. There must be a claim that the third-party defendant bears some responsibility for the claim asserted against the third-party plaintiff.

The availability of third-party practice is not limited to cases of strict indemnity, but Rule 14 is not a device for bringing into the action any controversy that happens to have some relationship to the parties or the subject matter of the original claim. *Jobe v. King*, 129 Ariz. 195, 629 P.2d 1031 (Ct. App. Div. 2 1981). Quite obviously, Rule 14 does not create a right to indemnity; it merely provides a convenient vehicle for enforcing it. *Ewing v. Goettl's Metal Products Co.*, 116 Ariz. 484, 569 P.2d 1382 (Ct. App. Div. 1 1977).

6. *Indemnity Actions; Common Law Indemnity.* Actions for indemnity are generally based on contractual indemnity provisions. When there is an express indemnity agreement between the parties, that agreement determines the extent of the duty to indemnify. *MT Builders, L.L.C. v. Fisher Roofing, Inc.*, 219 Ariz. 297, 197 P.3d 758 (Ct. App. Div. 1 2008). Indemnification against a loss encompasses a loss incurred through a settlement of a claim as long as the loss is covered by the indemnity agreement. *MT Builders, L.L.C. v. Fisher Roofing, Inc.*, 219 Ariz. 297, 197 P.3d 758 (Ct. App. Div. 1 2008).

In the tort context, one issue that frequently arises is whether an indemnity contract or clause covers situations where the loss resulted, either in whole or in part, from the indemnitee's own negligence. An indemnity agreement will not be construed to provide indemnity for losses resulting from the indemnitee's own actively negligent conduct unless it expressly provides for that. *Estes Co. v. Aztec Const., Inc.*, 139 Ariz. 166, 677 P.2d 939 (Ct. App. Div. 1 1983). (Essentially the same rule applies to general releases of liability. See discussion in Section 23 of the *Authors' Comments* under Rule 8.)

Under a "general indemnity" agreement, i.e., one which does not specifically address the effect, if any, that the indemnitee's negligence will have on the indemnitor's obligation, the indemnitee will be entitled to indemnity only where the loss results from the indemnitee's "passive" negligence, and not where the indemnitee's negligence is active. *Grubb & Ellis Management Services, Inc. v. 407417 B.C., L.L.C.*, 213 Ariz. 83, 138 P.3d 1210 (Ct. App. Div. 1 2006); *Estes Co. v. Aztec Const., Inc.*, 139 Ariz. 166, 677 P.2d 939 (Ct. App. Div. 1 1983).

If, on the other hand, the language of an indemnity agreement clearly and unequivocally indicates that one party is to be indemnified, regardless of whether or not injury was caused by that party, indemnification is required notwithstanding the indemnitee's active negligence. *Cunningham v. Goettl Air Conditioning, Inc.*, 194 Ariz. 236, 980 P.2d 489 (1999); *Grubb & Ellis Management Services, Inc. v. 407417 B.C., L.L.C.*, 213 Ariz. 83, 138 P.3d 1210 (Ct. App. Div. 1 2006). Public policy precludes the indemnification of persons for losses resulting from their own *willful* wrongdoing. *Transamerica Ins. Group v. Meere*, 143 Ariz. 351, 694 P.2d 181 (1984); *Wilshire Ins. Co. v. S.A.*, 224 Ariz. 97, 227 P.3d 504 (Ct. App. Div. 1 2010); *American Family Mut. Ins. Co. v. White*, 204 Ariz. 500, 65 P.3d 449 (Ct. App. Div. 1 2003).

Similar treatment is given to so-called prospective exculpatory contractual provisions by which one party seeks to secure immunity against the consequences of its own torts. Such a clause will not be construed as relieving the party securing it from the consequences of its own, or its employees', negligence unless it provides for that expressly. *Cunningham v. Goettl Air Conditioning, Inc.*, 194 Ariz. 236, 980 P.2d 489 (1999); *Morganteen v. Cowboy Adventures, Inc.*, 190 Ariz. 463, 949 P.2d 552 (Ct. App. Div. 1 1997). In addition, the clause will be unenforceable unless it appears that it reflects an actual bargain that was made for the intentional relinquishment of a known right. *Morganteen v. Cowboy Adventures, Inc.*, 190 Ariz. 463, 949 P.2d 552 (Ct. App. Div. 1 1997).

In *Cunningham v. Goettl Air Conditioning, Inc.*, 194 Ariz. 236, 980 P.2d 489 (1999), the Supreme Court considered the issue whether an indemnitor was bound by a stipulated judgment that its indemnitee agreed could be entered, in connection with a covenant not to execute, where the judgment was for more than the indemnitee had paid in settlement for a release. The Court found that the issue was controlled by Section 57 of the *Restatement (Second) of Judgments*, which applies when an indemnity obligation exists and judgment has been entered against the indemnitee. Thus, if the indemnitor received reasonable notice of the action and was given an opportunity to assume or participate in its defense, and the indemnitee defended the action with due diligence and reasonable prudence, then the indemnitor is estopped from disputing the existence and extent of the indemnitee's liability to the injured person.

When the indemnitee settles an action, its obligation to defend with reasonable diligence and prudence also extends to the amount of the settlement. On the facts before it, the Court concluded that it was not reasonable and prudent for the indemnitee to agree to the entry of judgment on a claim that had already been released, for an amount greater than that paid in settlement, and the indemnitor was only liable for the lesser amount.

The same rule applies to settlement of claims covered by indemnity agreements—the indemnitee may still obtain indemnity from its indemnitor if it gave the indemnitor notice of the action and an opportunity to defend, and demonstrates that the decision to settle was, under the circumstances, reasonable and prudent. *A Tumbling-T Ranches v. Flood Control Dist. of Maricopa County*, 220 Ariz. 202, 204 P.3d 1051 (Ct. App. Div. 1 2008); *MT Builders, L.L.C. v. Fisher Roofing, Inc.*, 219 Ariz. 297, 197 P.3d 758 (Ct. App. Div. 1 2008).

Arizona also has recognized a form of "common law indemnity" which can be claimed by a tortfeasor whose negligence in producing a loss was purely "passive," from a tortfeasor whose negligence in producing the loss was "active." *Busy Bee Buffet, Inc. v. Ferrell*, 82 Ariz. 192, 310 P.2d 817 (1957); *Transamerica Ins. Co. v. Trico Intern., Inc.*, 149 Ariz. 104, 716 P.2d 1041 (Ct. App. Div. 2 1985); *Estes Co. v. Aztec Const., Inc.*, 139 Ariz. 166, 677 P.2d 939 (Ct. App. Div. 1 1983); *Employers Mut. Liability Ins. Co. of Wis. v. Advance Transformer Co.*, 15 Ariz. App. 1, 485 P.2d 591 (Div. 2 1971). The fact that the negligence alleged is that of an omission to act, however, will not necessarily cause it to be characterized as "passive" negligence. *Shea v. Superior Court of Maricopa County*, 150 Ariz. 271, 723 P.2d 89 (1986); *Salt River Project Agr. Imp. and Power Dist. v. City of Scottsdale*, 24 Ariz. App. 254, 537 P.2d 982 (Div. 1 1975).

In fact, this form of "common law indemnity" as between joint tortfeasors will be available only where

(1) the party claiming the indemnity is not personally at fault at all, or

(2) that party's causative contribution to the loss ended so that that party is held liable only because of the continuing conduct of the party from whom the indemnity is claimed, or

(3) the party claiming the indemnity is liable only because the law imposes on that party derivative liability for the torts of the putative indemnitor.

Shea v. Superior Court of Maricopa County, 150 Ariz. 271, 723 P.2d 89 (1986); *INA Ins. Co. of North America v. Valley Forge Ins. Co.*, 150 Ariz. 248, 722 P.2d 975 (Ct. App. Div. 1 1986); *King & Johnson Rental Equipment Co. v. Superior Court, In and For Pima County*, 123 Ariz. 256, 599 P.2d 212 (1979); *City of Phoenix v. Kenly*, 21 Ariz. App. 394, 519 P.2d 1159 (Div. 1 1974); *Allison Steel Mfg. Co. v. Superior Court of Maricopa County, Division Three*, 20 Ariz. App. 185, 511 P.2d 198 (Div. 1 1973); *Transcon Lines v. Barnes*, 17 Ariz. App. 428, 498 P.2d 502 (Div. 1 1972); *Chrysler Corp. v. McCarthy*, 14 Ariz. App. 536, 484 P.2d 1065 (Div. 1 1971); *Thornton v. Marsico*, 5 Ariz. App. 299, 425 P.2d 869 (1967).

While both common law and contractual indemnity concern a claimed obligation on the part of one party to make good a loss or damage another party has incurred, they are governed by independent legal principles. *Evans Withycombe, Inc. v. Western Innovations, Inc.*, 215 Ariz. 237, 159 P.3d 547 (Ct. App. Div. 1 2006). Contractual indemnity is based on principles of contract; common law or implied indemnity is based more on principles of equity. *Evans Withycombe, Inc. v. Western Innovations, Inc.*, 215 Ariz. 237, 159 P.3d 547 (Ct. App. Div. 1 2006).

Finally, Arizona has recognized the doctrine of "implied indemnity," based on theories of implied contractual indemnity and/or Section 76 of the *Restatement of Restitution*. *INA Ins. Co. of North America v. Valley Forge Ins. Co.*, 150 Ariz. 248, 722 P.2d 975 (Ct. App. Div. 1 1986); *American and Foreign Ins. Co. v. Allstate Ins. Co.*, 139 Ariz. 223, 677 P.2d 1331 (Ct. App. Div. 1 1983); *Henderson Realty v. Mesa Paving Co., Inc.*, 27 Ariz. App. 299, 554 P.2d 895 (Div. 1 1976); *First Bank of Ariz. v. Otis Elevator Co.*, 2 Ariz. App. 596, 411 P.2d 34 (1966). The cornerstone of such implied indemnity is a relationship between the parties such that the asserted indemnitor should be responsible for a duty discharged by, or a liability assessed against, the party invoking the doctrine, and it is not limited in its application to tort cases involving defective or dangerous products. *Schweber Electronics v. National Semiconductor Corp.*, 174 Ariz. 406, 850 P.2d 119 (Ct. App. Div. 1 1992).

Once again, however, the party invoking the doctrine must be without independent fault, and the doctrine is not applicable where there is an express indemnity contract or contractual indemnity provision. *Schweber Electronics v. National Semiconductor Corp.*, 174 Ariz. 406, 850 P.2d 119 (Ct. App. Div. 1 1992).

7. *Third-Party Claims for Contribution.* The law in Arizona with respect to claims for contribution among joint tortfeasors has taken several divergent turns.

Before 1984, Arizona adhered to the strict common law rule which prohibited claims for contribution among joint tortfeasors. *City of Tucson v. Superior Court In and For County of Pima*, 165 Ariz. 236, 798 P.2d 374 (1990); *Holmes v. Hoemako Hospital*, 117 Ariz. 403, 573 P.2d 477, 7 A.L.R.4th 1231 (1977); *Young v. Environmental Air Products, Inc.*, 136 Ariz. 206, 665 P.2d 88 (Ct. App. Div. 2 1982), aff'd as modified, 136 Ariz. 158, 665 P.2d 40 (1983); *Employers Mut. Liability Ins. Co. of Wis. v. Advance Transformer Co.*, 15 Ariz. App. 1, 485 P.2d 591 (Div. 2 1971); *Pinal County v. Adams*, 13 Ariz. App. 571, 479 P.2d 718 (Div. 1 1971). Because joint tortfeasors were subject to joint and several liability, the prohibition on contribution claims at times had the harsh result of permitting one of several joint tortfeasors to bear the entire financial responsibility for a loss produced by the concurrent negligence of all of them. *Bill Alexander Ford, Lincoln Mercury, Inc. v. Casa Ford, Inc.*, 187 Ariz. 616, 931 P.2d 1126, Prod. Liab. Rep. (CCH) P 14727 (Ct. App. Div. 1 1996); *Transcon Lines v. Barnes*, 17 Ariz. App. 428, 498 P.2d 502 (Div. 1 1972).

In 1984, Arizona adopted a modified version of the Uniform Contribution Among Tortfeasors Act, A.R.S. §§ 12-2501, *et seq.*, which abolished the prior common law rule prohibiting claims of contribution among joint tortfeasors and adopted a comparative negligence rule for personal injury actions involving joint tortfeasors. The Act was applicable to actions filed on and after August 31, 1984. In cases subject to the Act's original provisions, the responsibility for the plaintiff's injuries was to be allocated on the basis of "relative degrees of fault," A.R.S. § 12-2502, and there was a right of contribution against other joint tortfeasors in favor of any joint tortfeasor who had become responsible for, or paid, more than that joint tortfeasor's *pro rata* share of the common liability. A.R.S. § 12-2501(B).

In such cases, where plaintiff had failed to join all joint tortfeasors in the action, a third-party claim against an absent joint tortfeasor was an appropriate vehicle for insuring that the *pro rata* shares of liability were determined in a single action by one trier of fact. A.R.S. § 12-2503; *Nikolous v. Superior Court In and For Maricopa County*, 157 Ariz. 256, 756 P.2d 925 (1988); *but cf. Kriz v. Buckeye Petroleum Co., Inc.*, 145 Ariz. 374, 701 P.2d 1182 (1985). The 1987 amendments to the statute, however, and the passage of time will eventually make such third-party contribution claims an anachronism.

In 1987, the Arizona Legislature enacted amendments to the Uniform Contribution Among Tortfeasors Act which abolished the doctrine of joint and several liability, except in cases where parties were acting in concert, where one party was acting as an agent or servant of another party, and in cases relating to hazardous wastes or substances or solid waste disposal sites. A.R.S. § 12-2506 (as amended). *Yslava v. Hughes Aircraft Co.*, 188 Ariz. 380, 936 P.2d 1274, 45 Env't. Rep. Cas. (BNA) 1315 (1997); *Bishop v. Pecanic*, 193 Ariz. 524, 975 P.2d 114 (Ct. App. Div. 1 1998). (The exception for cases relating to hazardous wastes or substances, or solid waste disposal sites, was repealed in 1997, purportedly retroactively, and liability in these types of cases is now several only as well.) Guiding this statutory revision was a desire to increase the fairness of the tort system for both plaintiffs and defendants, and to eliminate the harshness of an all-or-nothing contributory negligence defense. *Hutcherson v. City of Phoenix*, 192 Ariz. 51, 961 P.2d 449 (1998).

The 1987 amendments, which apply to actions filed on or after December 31, 1987, also broadened the scope of torts subject to the rules of comparative fault beyond those grounded on theories of negligence, and are fully applicable in product liability actions. *Jimenez v. Sears, Roebuck and Co.*, 183 Ariz. 399, 904 P.2d 861, Prod. Liab. Rep. (CCH) P 14382 (1995); *Zuern By and Through Zuern v. Ford Motor Co.*, 188 Ariz. 486, 937 P.2d 676 (Ct. App. Div. 2 1996). In such actions, accordingly, there must be an allocation of fault to each person or entity in the chain of distribution of the allegedly defective product. *State Farm Ins. Companies v. Premier Manufactured Systems, Inc.*, 217 Ariz. 222, 172 P.3d 410 (2007). The constitutionality of this legislation has been upheld. *Jimenez v. Sears, Roebuck and Co.*, 183 Ariz. 399, 904 P.2d 861, Prod. Liab. Rep. (CCH) P 14382 (1995); *Larsen v. Nissan Motor Corp. in U.S.A.*, 194 Ariz. 142, 978 P.2d 119 (Ct. App. Div. 2 1998); *Lerma v. Keck*, 186 Ariz. 228, 921 P.2d 28 (Ct. App. Div. 1 1996); *Church v. Rawson Drug & Sundry Co.*, 173 Ariz. 342, 842 P.2d 1355 (Ct. App. Div. 1 1992).

The statute did not, however, change the law with regard to vicarious liability. *Law v. Verde Valley Medical Center*, 217 Ariz. 92, 170 P.3d 701 (Ct. App. Div. 1 2007). An alleged tortfeasor and a party potentially liable vicariously for that person's tortious conduct are not joint tortfeasors under Arizona law. *Law v. Verde Valley Medical Center*, 217 Ariz. 92, 170 P.3d 701 (Ct. App. Div. 1 2007). When a judgment on the merits is entered in favor of a person for whose conduct a party is vicariously liable, there is no fault to impute or allocate. *Law v. Verde Valley Medical Center*, 217 Ariz. 92, 170 P.3d 701 (Ct. App. Div. 1 2007).

Under the Act as amended, Arizona follows a "comparative fault" regime, under which the trier of fact considers and apportions the fault of all persons who contributed to the harm to the plaintiff, and each tortfeasor is responsible only for his or her percentage of fault and no more. *Hutcherson v. City of Phoenix*, 192 Ariz. 51, 961 P.2d 449 (1998); *Sanchez v. City of Tucson*, 191 Ariz. 128, 953 P.2d 168 (1998); *McKillip v. Smitty's Super Valu, Inc.*, 190 Ariz. 61, 945 P.2d 372 (Ct. App. Div. 1 1997); *Zuern By and Through Zuern v. Ford Motor Co.*, 188 Ariz. 486, 937 P.2d 676 (Ct. App. Div. 2 1996); *Standard Chartered PLC v. Price Waterhouse*, 190 Ariz. 6, 945 P.2d 317 (Ct. App. Div. 1 1996), as corrected on denial of reconsideration, (Jan. 13, 1997); *Rosner v. Denim & Diamonds, Inc.*, 188 Ariz. 431, 937 P.2d 353 (Ct. App. Div. 2 1996); *Natseway v. City of Tempe*, 184 Ariz. 374, 909 P.2d 441 (Ct. App. Div. 1 1995).

The trier of fact may consider the fault of persons who are not parties to the action, even if the plaintiff would be prohibited from suing them directly or recovering damages from them. *Dietz v. General Elec. Co.*, 169 Ariz. 505, 821 P.2d 166 (1991); *A Tumbling-T Ranches v. Flood Control Dist. of Maricopa County*, 222 Ariz. 515, 217 P.3d 1220 (Ct. App. Div. 1 2009); *Larsen v. Nissan Motor Corp. in U.S.A.*, 194 Ariz. 142, 978 P.2d 119 (Ct. App. Div. 2 1998). Thus, an expert's opinion apportioning percentages of fault to parties and non-parties improperly invades the province of the jury and is inadmissible, notwithstanding Rule 704, Ariz. R. Evid. *Webb v. Omni Block, Inc.*, 216 Ariz. 349, 166 P.3d 140 (Ct. App. Div. 1 2007).

There is no authority for the proposition that intentional conduct must be given more weight than negligent conduct in the apportionment of fault. *Hutcherson v. City of Phoenix*, 192 Ariz. 51, 961 P.2d 449 (1998). These comparative fault principles apply regardless of the relationship of the parties and the nature of the duty owed, and even where it is alleged that a negligent tortfeasor had a duty to prevent an intentional wrong from occurring. *Natseway v. City of Tempe*, 184 Ariz. 374, 909 P.2d 441 (Ct. App. Div. 1 1995).

The Act permits the apportionment of fault between a negligent plaintiff and a defendant whose conduct is wanton or wilful. *Rosner v. Denim & Diamonds, Inc.*, 188 Ariz. 431, 937 P.2d 353 (Ct. App. Div. 2 1996); *Wareing v. Falk*, 182 Ariz. 495, 897 P.2d 1381 (Ct. App. Div. 1 1995). It even permits the allocation of fault between an allegedly negligent defendant and a non-party who commits a criminal act. *Hutcherson v. City of Phoenix*, 192 Ariz. 51, 961 P.2d 449 (1998); *Thomas v. First Interstate Bank of Arizona, N.A.*, 187 Ariz. 488, 930 P.2d 1002, 54 A.L.R.5th 827 (Ct. App. Div. 2 1996). Correspondingly, a plaintiff guilty of gross or wanton negligence in causing an accident will not necessarily be barred from any recovery. *Williams v. Thude*, 188 Ariz. 257, 934 P.2d 1349 (1997).

The statutory goal of having percentages of fault allocated to all responsible parties and nonparties in a single action provides "good and sufficient cause," under A.R.S. § 12-406(B)(3), for the transfer of an action from a county where venue is proper to another county so that it can be consolidated with another case arising out of the same underlying event. *Behrens v. O'Melia*, 206 Ariz. 309, 78 P.3d 278 (Ct. App. Div. 1 2003). A claim that a jury's allocation of fault was against the weight of the evidence is properly presented as a motion for new trial under Rule 59(a)(8). *Hutcherson v. City of Phoenix*, 192 Ariz. 51, 961 P.2d 449 (1998). Similarly, where the parties stipulate that a non-party was the proximate cause of the plaintiff's injuries, the jury must allocate some degree of fault to that non-party, and the jury's disregard of the stipulation and assignment of 100% of the fault to the named defendants warrants a new trial on all issues. *Ogden v. J.M. Steel Erecting, Inc.*, 201 Ariz. 32, 31 P.3d 806 (Ct. App. Div. 1 2001).

The provision of the Arizona Constitution, article 18, § 5, which requires that the defense of contributory negligence always be left to the jury to decide, applies to claims of comparative negligence as well, so that the issue of the proper allocation of fault will always be a jury issue, where a jury is demanded. *Gunnell v. Arizona Public Service Co.*, 202 Ariz. 388, 46 P.3d 399 (2002).

The 1987 amendments severely limit the right of contribution granted by A.R.S. § 12-2501. By abolishing joint and several liability and limiting recovery against any defendant to that percentage of the plaintiff's total injuries which represents that defendant's degree of fault, the statute insures that the conditions for claiming contribution will not occur. *PAM Transport v. Freightliner Corp.*, 182 Ariz. 132, 893 P.2d 1295 (1995); *City of Tucson v. Superior Court In and For County of Pima*, 161 Ariz. 441, 778 P.2d 1337 (Ct. App. Div. 2 1989), opinion approved of, 165 Ariz. 236, 798 P.2d 374 (1990); *Cella Barr Associates, Inc. v. Cohen*, 177 Ariz. 480, 868 P.2d 1063 (Ct. App. Div. 1 1994); *Neil v. Kavena*, 176 Ariz. 93, 859 P.2d 203 (Ct. App. Div. 1 1993); *Roland v. Bernstein*, 171 Ariz. 96, 828 P.2d 1237 (Ct. App. Div. 2 1991).

As a practical matter, accordingly, third-party claims for contribution among joint tortfeasors under this statute are appropriate and necessary only in cases filed between August 30, 1984 and December 31, 1987. The issue of how pretrial settlements between the plaintiff and one or more of the joint tortfeasors are to be accounted for is discussed in Sections 6 and 7 of the *Authors' Comments* to Rule 16.2.

Arizona's adoption of the Uniform Contribution Among Tortfeasors Act left intact the common law doctrine of "indivisible injury." *Piner v. Superior Court In and For County of Maricopa*, 192 Ariz. 182, 962 P.2d 909 (1998); *Salica v. Tucson Heart Hosp.-Carondelet, L.L.C.*, 224 Ariz. 414, 231 P.3d 946 (Ct. App. Div. 2 2010). When the tortious conduct of more than one defendant contributes to one indivisible injury, the entire amount of damages resulting from all contributing causes is the total amount "of damages recoverable by the plaintiff," as that term is used in A.R.S. § 12-2506(A). *Piner v. Superior Court In and For County of Maricopa*, 192 Ariz. 182, 962 P.2d 909 (1998).

The fault of all actors is then determined by the trier of fact, and each defendant is *severally* liable for damages allocated in direct proportion to that defendant's percentage of fault. *Piner v. Superior Court In and For County of Maricopa*, 192 Ariz. 182, 962 P.2d 909 (1998). In an indivisible injury case, the fact finder is to compute the total amount of damages sustained by the plaintiff, and the percentage of fault of each tortfeasor, and the maximum amount recoverable against each tortfeasor is computed by multiplying the first figure by the second. *Piner v. Superior Court In and For County of Maricopa*, 192 Ariz. 182, 962 P.2d 909 (1998).

The doctrine of "satisfaction of judgment" provides that, if one joint tortfeasor satisfies a judgment obtained by the plaintiff, all other tortfeasors are discharged from liability and the plaintiff has no further cause of action. *Bridgestone/Firestone North America Tire, L.L.C. v. Naranjo*, 206 Ariz. 447, 79 P.3d 1206, Prod. Liab. Rep. (CCH) P 16845 (Ct. App. Div. 2 2003). This doctrine also survives the abolition of joint and several liability, and the adoption of a comparative fault regime, in situations where the plaintiff has obtained a judgment for the total damages suffered from an indivisible injury against only one party at fault, and that judgment is satisfied. *Bridgestone/Firestone North America Tire, L.L.C. v. Naranjo*, 206 Ariz. 447, 79 P.3d 1206, Prod. Liab. Rep. (CCH) P 16845 (Ct. App. Div. 2 2003). The satisfaction of that judgment extinguishes any claim against other parties at fault. *Bridgestone/Firestone North America Tire, L.L.C. v. Naranjo*, 206 Ariz. 447, 79 P.3d 1206, Prod. Liab. Rep. (CCH) P 16845 (Ct. App. Div. 2 2003).

Under A.R.S. § 12-2506(D), joint tortfeasors who act in concert remain jointly and severally liable for the resulting injury or damage. *Chappell v. Wenholz*, 226 Ariz. 309, 247 P.3d 192 (Ct. App. Div. 1 2011); *Mein ex rel. Mein v. Cook*, 219 Ariz. 96, 193 P.3d 790 (Ct. App. Div. 1 2008); *Bishop v. Pecanic*, 193 Ariz. 524, 975 P.2d 114 (Ct. App. Div. 1 1998). In *Mein*, the court of appeals held that a *prima facie* case under A.R.S. § 12-2506(D)(1) requires evidence the parties:

(1) knowingly agreed to commit an intentional tort,
(2) they were certain or substantially certain their actions would result in the consequences complained of, and
(3) they actively participated in the commission of the tort.

Mein ex rel. Mein v. Cook, 219 Ariz. 96, 193 P.3d 790 (Ct. App. Div. 1 2008); *see also*, *Chappell v. Wenholz*, 226 Ariz. 309, 247 P.3d 192 (Ct. App. Div. 1 2011) (holding, "[a] 'conscience agreement' need not be verbally expressed and may be implied from the conduct itself"). A joint tortfeasor in such a situation who pays more than his or her share of the common liability is entitled to seek contribution from fellow tortfeasors. *Herstam v. Deloitte & Touche, LLP*, 186 Ariz. 110, 919 P.2d 1381 (Ct. App. Div. 1 1996).

When a complaint alleges concerted action that normally would subject all parties to joint and several liability, however, the injured party can, as part of a settlement with one or more of the joint tortfeasors, agree to waive the right to hold nonsettling parties jointly and severally liable and thereby bar the nonsettling parties from seeking contribution and/or indemnity from the settling parties. *Herstam v. Deloitte & Touche, LLP*, 186 Ariz. 110, 919 P.2d 1381 (Ct. App. Div. 1 1996). *See also*, *Bishop v. Pecanic*, 193 Ariz. 524, 975 P.2d 114 (Ct. App. Div. 1 1998). A.R.S. § 12-2506(F)(1) defines "acting in concert" as, *inter alia*, being inapplicable to "any person whose conduct was negligent in any of its degrees rather than intentional." In enacting this exception where parties are acting in concert, the Legislature did not, however, displace or alter the longstanding common law liability for aiding and abetting. *Security Title Agency, Inc. v. Pope*, 219 Ariz. 480, 200 P.3d 977, 27 I.E.R. Cas. (BNA) 1811 (Ct. App. Div. 1 2008).

Joint liability and vicarious liability "are related but separate doctrines." *Wiggs v. City of Phoenix*, 198 Ariz. 367, 10 P.3d 625, 111 A.L.R.5th 815 (2000) (citing, *Srithong v. Total Investment Co.*, 23 Cal. App. 4th 721, 28 Cal. Rptr. 2d 672 (2d Dist. 1994); *State Farm Ins. Companies v. Premier Manufactured Systems, Inc.*, 213 Ariz. 419, 142 P.3d 1232, Prod. Liab. Rep. (CCH) P 17517 (Ct. App. Div. 1 2006), opinion aff'd, 217 Ariz. 222, 172 P.3d 410 (2007)). The joint liability that was abolished by A.R.S. § 12-2506(D) is limited to that "class of joint tortfeasors whose independent negligence coalesced to form a single injury." *Wiggs v. City of Phoenix*, 198 Ariz. 367, 10 P.3d 625, 111 A.L.R.5th 815 (2000).

The statute preserves joint liability both for true joint tortfeasors (those "acting in concert") and for those who are vicariously liable for the fault of others. *Wiggs v. City of Phoenix*, 198 Ariz. 367, 10 P.3d 625, 111 A.L.R.5th 815 (2000); *State Farm Ins.*

Companies v. Premier Manufactured Systems, Inc., 213 Ariz. 419, 142 P.3d 1232, Prod. Liab. Rep. (CCH) P 17517 (Ct. App. Div. 1 2006), opinion aff'd, 217 Ariz. 222, 172 P.3d 410 (2007). The comparative fault statute, thus, preserves vicarious liability for the negligence of an independent contractor, when the employer of that independent contractor had a non-delegable duty. *Wiggs v. City of Phoenix*, 198 Ariz. 367, 10 P.3d 625, 111 A.L.R.5th 815 (2000). This will not operate to immunize independent contractors from the consequences of their own negligence, any more than in the case of a true employee. *Wiggs v. City of Phoenix*, 198 Ariz. 367, 10 P.3d 625, 111 A.L.R.5th 815 (2000). In either setting, the employer may seek indemnity against the employee or independent contractor, in cases of pure vicarious liability, or contribution in cases in which the employer has some degree of independent liability. *Wiggs v. City of Phoenix*, 198 Ariz. 367, 10 P.3d 625, 111 A.L.R.5th 815 (2000).

8. *Vouching In.* Third-party claims under Rule 14 are similar to, but do not entirely replace, the common law procedural device of "vouching in." *Litton Systems, Inc. v. Shaw's Sales and Service, Ltd.*, 119 Ariz. 10, 579 P.2d 48 (Ct. App. Div. 2 1978). Vouching in, which is more commonly known as "tendering the defense," permits a defendant to conclusively bind a potential indemnitor to a judgment if certain requirements are met: the indemnitor must be given a timely and sufficient notice which provides full and fair information of the pending action, an unequivocal and explicit demand to undertake defense of the action, and an offer to surrender control of the action. The offer to surrender control should occur soon after initiation of the action to allow the indemnitor to control pretrial proceedings. Whether the requirements for vouching in have been met is a mixed question of fact and law which will be subject to a *de novo* review on appeal. *Falcon v. Beverly Hills Mortg. Corp.*, 166 Ariz. 311, 802 P.2d 1010 (Ct. App. Div. 2 1990), opinion vacated on other grounds, 168 Ariz. 527, 815 P.2d 896 (1991).

Rule 15. Amended and supplemental pleadings

(a) Amendments.

1. A party may amend the party's pleading once as a matter of course:

A. no later than twenty-one days after serving it, if the pleading is one to which no responsive pleading is permitted; or

B. no later than twenty-one days after service of a responsive pleading if the pleading is one to which a responsive pleading is required or, if a motion under Rule 12(b), (e), or (f) is served, on or before the date on which a response to the motion is due, whichever is earlier.

Otherwise a party may amend the party's pleading only by leave of court or by written consent of the adverse party. Leave to amend shall be freely given when justice requires. Amendment as a matter of course after service of a motion under Rule 12(b), (e), or (f) does not, by itself, moot the motion as to the adequacy of the allegations of the pleading as revised in the amended pleading and does not relieve a party opposing the motion from filing a timely response to the motion.

2. A party who moves for leave to amend a pleading must attach a copy of the proposed amended pleading as an exhibit to the motion, which shall indicate in what respect it differs from the pleading that it amends, by bracketing or striking through the text to be deleted and underlining the text to be added. If a motion for leave to amend is granted, the moving party shall file and serve the amended pleading within ten days of the order granting the motion, unless the court otherwise orders.

3. A party shall plead in response to an amended pleading within the time remaining for response to the original pleading or within ten days after service of the amended pleading, whichever period may be the longer, unless the court otherwise orders.

Amended Sept. 15, 1987, effective Nov. 15, 1987; Sept. 5, 2007, effective Jan. 1, 2008; Sept. 1, 2011, effective Jan. 1, 2012; Aug. 28, 2013, effective Jan. 1, 2014.

(b) Amendments to Conform to the Evidence. When issues not raised by the pleadings are tried by express or implied consent of the parties, they shall be treated in all respects as if they had been raised in the pleadings. Such amendment of the pleadings as may be necessary to cause them to conform to the evidence and to raise these issues may be made upon motion of any party at any time, even after judgment, but failure so to

amend does not affect the result of the trial of these issues. If evidence is objected to at the trial on the ground that it is not within the issues made by the pleadings, the court may allow the pleadings to be amended and shall do so freely when the presentation of the merits of the action will be subserved thereby and the objecting party fails to satisfy the court that the admission of such evidence would prejudice the party in maintaining the party's action or defense upon the merits. The court may grant a continuance to enable the objecting party to meet such evidence.
Amended Sept. 15, 1987, effective Nov. 15, 1987.

(c) Relation Back of Amendments. Whenever the claim or defense asserted in the amended pleading arose out of the conduct, transaction, or occurrence set forth or attempted to be set forth in the original pleading, the amendment relates back to the date of the original pleading. An amendment changing the party against whom a claim is asserted relates back if the foregoing provision is satisfied and, within the period provided by law for commencing the action against the party to be brought in by amendment, plus the period provided by Rule 4(i) for service of the summons and complaint, the party to be brought in by amendment, (1) has received such notice of the institution of the action that the party will not be prejudiced in maintaining a defense on the merits, and (2) knew or should have known that, but for a mistake concerning the identity of the proper party, the action would have been brought against the party. Service of process in compliance with Rule 4.1(h), (i) or (j) of these rules satisfies the requirement of clauses (1) and (2) hereof with respect to the state, county, municipal corporation or any agency or officer thereof to be brought into the action as a defendant.
Amended July 1, 1966, effective Nov. 1, 1966; Sept. 15, 1987, effective Nov. 15, 1987; Oct. 2, 1991, effective Dec. 1, 1991; Oct. 9, 1996, effective Dec. 1, 1996.

(d) Supplemental Pleadings. Upon motion of a party the court may, upon reasonable notice and upon such terms as are just, permit the party to serve a supplemental pleading setting forth transactions or occurrences or events which have happened since the date of the pleading sought to be supplemented. Permission may be granted even though the original pleading is defective in its statement of a claim for relief or defense. If the court deems it advisable that the adverse party plead to the supplemental pleading, it shall so order, specifying the time therefor.
Amended March 26, 1966, effective June 1, 1963; Sept. 15, 1987, effective Nov. 15, 1987.

STATE BAR COMMITTEE NOTES

1963 Amendment

Rule 15(d) is intended to give the court broad discretion in allowing a supplemental pleading. However, some cases opposed by other cases and criticized by the commentators, have taken the rigid and formalistic view that where the original complaint fails to state a claim upon which relief can be granted, leave to serve a supplemental complaint must be denied. Thus plaintiffs have sometimes been needlessly remitted to the difficulties of commencing a new action even though events occurring after the commencement of the original action may have made clear the right to relief.

Under the amendment the court has discretion to permit a supplemental pleading despite the fact that the original pleading is defective. As in other situations where a supplemental pleading is offered, the court is to determine in the light of the particular circumstances whether filing should be permitted, and if so, upon what terms. The amendment does not attempt to deal with such questions as the relation of the statute of limitations to supplemental pleadings, the operation of the doctrine of laches, or the availability of other defenses. All these questions are for decision in accordance with the principles applicable to supplemental pleadings generally.

1966 Amendment

[Rule 15(c)] The amendment to this rule provides for relation back of pleading amendments in cases in which a complainant makes a mistake in designating against whom his claim asserted. The amendment applies primarily but not exclusively to public officials, as where a party may mistakenly suppose that a particular person occupies an office when in fact by change of circumstances it is occupied by someone else; and it also covers cases in which a suit names an agency when it should name an individual. For example, a plaintiff might sue the "State Treasury Department" instead of the "State Treasurer." While this problem has not been substantial in Arizona, it has been substantial in the federal system, and the amendment is therefore adopted in the interest of conformity.

1991 Supplemental State Bar Committee Note

[Rule 15(c)] In *Ritchie v. Grand Canyon Scenic Rides*, 165 Ariz. 460, 799 P.2d 801 (1990), the Arizona Supreme Court held that the "period provided by law for commencing the action" referred to in the second sentence of Rule 15(c) includes the time allowed for service of process. Accordingly, when a party files a claim prior to the expiration of the statute of limitations, an amendment to the pleadings that adds a party, or changes the party, against whom the claim is asserted will relate back under Rule 15(c), if the new party is served within the time prescribed by the applicable statute of limitations plus the time allowed for service of process under Rule 4(i), and if the claim asserted in the amended pleading arose out of the same occurrence set forth in the original pleading.

1991 Supplemental State Bar Committee Note amended Jan. 26, 1994, effective June 1, 1994.

AUTHORS' COMMENTS

Analysis

1. *Scope and Purpose of Rule.* Ariz. R. Civ. P. 15 defines the circumstances under which the pleadings filed by the parties may be amended or supplemented. The policy of the law is to encourage permitting pleadings to be amended so as to facilitate the efficient and effective resolution of an entire controversy.

2. *Comparison With Federal Rule.* Despite structural and organizational differences, ARCP 15 and FRCP 15 are generally similar, but there are important differences.

Effective January 1, 2014, the substance, but not the language, of ARCP 15(a)(1)(A), (B) and FRCP 15(a)(1) (A), (B) are now essentially identical. The last sentence of ARCP 15(a) is unique, however, to Arizona practice. That provision states that, by itself, an amendment as a matter of course after service of a specified Rule 12 motion does not moot such Rule 12 motion. Meaning, a party opposing the Rule 12 motion must still file a timely response notwithstanding the timely submission of an amended pleading. FRCP 15 does not have a similar corresponding provision.

FRCP 15(a) does not contain a provision corresponding to ARCP 15(a)(2), which provides that a party seeking leave to amend must attach to its motion a copy of the proposed pleading showing in what respect the amended pleading differs from the underlying pleading.

Further, ARCP 15(a)(3) and FRCP 15(a)(3), which govern the time to respond to an amended pleading, differ in their provisions. ARCP 15(a)(3) requires a response to an amended pleading; FRCP 15(a)(3) applies only if a responsive pleading is required.

ARCP 15(b) and (d) are substantively identical to FRCP 15(b) and (d). ARCP 15(c) and FRCP 15(c) differ significantly following the 1991 amendment to the Federal Rule, but the 1991 amendment makes the provisions of FRCP 15(c) more consistent with the construction placed on ARCP 15(c) by the Arizona Supreme Court in *Ritchie v. Grand Canyon Scenic Rides*, 165 Ariz. 460, 799 P.2d 801 (1990).

As a consequence of the 2009 amendments to FRCP 15, the

times set in former FRCP 15 at 10 days and 20 days have been revised to 14 days and 21 days. The 2012 amendments to ARCP 15 did not consistently adopt these 2009 amendments to FRCP 15. The time proscribed in ARCP 15(a)(1) is now 21 days, identical to FRCP 15(a)(1). However, ARCP 15(a)(3) and FRCP 15(a)(3) provide slightly different time periods for responding to an amended pleading. ARCP 15(a)(3) requires a response within the time remaining for response to the original pleading or 10 days after service of the amended pleading, whichever is longer. FRCP 15(a)(3) provides that any required response must be made within the time remaining for response to the original pleading or 14 days after service of the amended pleading, whichever is later.

In addition, in 2007, the language of FRCP 15 was amended as part of the general restyling of the Federal Rules of Civil Procedure to make the Federal Rules more easily understood and to make style and terminology consistent throughout the Federal Rules of Civil Procedure. Those stylistic modifications also have not been incorporated into ARCP 15.

3. *Amendments as a Matter of Course.* After a brief 2-year hiatus caused by certain unintended consequences created by the 2012 amendment to Ariz. R. Civ. P. 15(a)(1), the rules governing the procedure for amendments as a matter of course have returned to their long-standing roots. Thus, effective January 1, 2014, a party again may amend its pleading once as a matter of course until a responsive pleading is filed. See, Ariz. R. Civ. P. 15(a)(1) (amended 2014). And, compliments of a residual 2012 amendment, which is consistent with current federal practice, a party also will be able to amend its pleading for a period of 21 days after service of a motion filed under Ariz. R. Civ. P. 12(b), (e) or (f).

In this latter regard, the last sentence of Ariz. R. Civ. P. 15(a) (amended 2012), which survived the 2014 amendments, provides that, by itself, an amendment as a matter of course after service of a specified Rule 12 motion does not moot such Rule 12 motion. And, a party opposing the Rule 12 motion must still file a timely response notwithstanding the timely submission of an amended pleading. Of course, such party might seek relief by securing an appropriate stipulation or by filing an appropriate motion.

4. *Amendments by Leave of Court.* Once the right to amend a pleading as a matter of course has expired, a party may amend its pleading only with a written stipulation of the parties or leave of court. *See,* Ariz. R. Civ. P 15(a). A request for leave to amend is one addressed to the discretion of the trial court, the policy of the Rule favors the liberal allowance of requests to amend. *Cagle v. Carr*, 101 Ariz. 225, 418 P.2d 381 (1966); *Frank v. Solomon*, 94 Ariz. 55, 381 P.2d 591 (1963); *Valley Farms, Ltd. v. Transconti-*

nental Ins. Co., 206 Ariz. 349, 78 P.3d 1070 (Ct. App. Div. 2 2003); *Dewey v. Arnold*, 159 Ariz. 65, 764 P.2d 1124 (Ct. App. Div. 2 1988); *Schmidt v. Mel Clayton Ford*, 124 Ariz. 65, 601 P.2d 1349 (Ct. App. Div. 1 1979). This holds true even in the instance where the plaintiff seeks leave to amend to plead new legal theories and to add wholly new defendants. *Green Reservoir Flood Control Dist. v. Willmoth*, 15 Ariz. App. 406, 489 P.2d 69 (Div. 2 1971). *But see*, *Grand v. Nacchio*, 225 Ariz. 171, 236 P.3d 398, Blue Sky L. Rep. (CCH) P 74862 (2010) (upholding denial of leave to amend in light of years of litigation and "considered decision to abandon" claim during course of litigation).

A request for leave to amend, however, must be made by separate motion that complies with the requirements of Rule 7.1. *Blumenthal v. Teets*, 155 Ariz. 123, 745 P.2d 181 (Ct. App. Div. 1 1987).

5. *Time for Seeking Leave; Standards.* There is no fixed time limit for filing a motion for leave to amend a pleading. *But see*, *Grand v. Nacchio*, 225 Ariz. 171, 236 P.3d 398, Blue Sky L. Rep. (CCH) P 74862 (2010) (upholiding denial of leave to amend in light of years of litigation and the "considered decision to abandon" claim during course of litigation). Whether the proposed amendment will be permitted is within the discretion of the Court. *Valley Farms, Ltd. v. Transcontinental Ins. Co.*, 206 Ariz. 349, 78 P.3d 1070 (Ct. App. Div. 2 2003); *Bujanda v. Montgomery Ward & Co., Inc.*, 125 Ariz. 314, 609 P.2d 584 (Ct. App. Div. 2 1980); *Romo v. Reyes*, 26 Ariz. App. 374, 548 P.2d 1186 (Div. 2 1976). The policy underlying the Rule, however, is liberal in favor of permitting amendments, and a motion to amend is generally granted unless there has been undue delay, bad faith, dilatory motive, repeated failure to cure deficiencies by previous amendments or undue prejudice to the adverse party. *Owen v. Superior Court of State of Ariz., In and For Maricopa County*, 133 Ariz. 75, 649 P.2d 278 (1982).

Denial of a motion for leave to amend is generally an abuse of discretion where the amendment merely seeks to add a new legal theory. *Uyleman v. D.S. Rentco*, 194 Ariz. 300, 981 P.2d 1081 (Ct. App. Div. 1 1999); *MacCollum v. Perkinson*, 185 Ariz. 179, 913 P.2d 1097, Blue Sky L. Rep. (CCH) P 74090 (Ct. App. Div. 1 1996), corrected, (Mar. 13, 1996). The fact that the claims to be added by the amendment are arguably inconsistent with claims already being asserted is not grounds for denying leave to amend, as parties are permitted to plead alternatively and/or inconsistently. *MacCollum v. Perkinson*, 185 Ariz. 179, 913 P.2d 1097, Blue Sky L. Rep. (CCH) P 74090 (Ct. App. Div. 1 1996), corrected, (Mar. 13, 1996). Delay alone is not ordinarily sufficient grounds for denying a request for leave to amend. *Uyleman v. D.S. Rentco*, 194 Ariz. 300, 981 P.2d 1081 (Ct. App. Div. 1 1999).

Ordinarily it is not proper, in evaluating a request to amend, for the Court to consider the factual basis for the proposed amended pleading. *Hernandez v. Maricopa County Superior Court*, 108 Ariz. 422, 501 P.2d 6 (1972). The better course is to allow the amendment and to permit the factual basis for it to be explored through discovery and addressed in a motion for summary judgment, if appropriate. Generally, it is reversible error to dismiss a complaint without granting leave to amend when such leave is requested. *Van Denburgh v. Tungsten Reef Mines Co.*, 48 Ariz. 540, 63 P.2d 647 (1936).

Leave to amend may be denied, however, where the proposed amendment is legally insufficient and would not affect the outcome. *Foman v. Davis*, 371 U.S. 178, 182, 83 S. Ct. 227, 230, 9 L. Ed. 2d 222, 6 Fed. R. Serv. 2d 1234 (1962); *Walls v. Arizona Dept. of Public Safety*, 170 Ariz. 591, 826 P.2d 1217 (Ct. App. Div. 1 1991); *Moore v. Toshiba Intern. Corp.*, 160 Ariz. 205, 772 P.2d 28 (Ct. App. Div. 1 1989); *Matter of Torstenson's Estate*, 125 Ariz. 373, 609 P.2d 1073 (Ct. App. Div. 1 1980); *Home Ins. Co. v. Balfour-Guthrie Ins. Co.*, 13 Ariz. App. 327, 476 P.2d 533 (Div. 1 1970). A request for leave to amend may also be denied if there has been undue delay, bad faith, dilatory motive, repeated failures to cure deficiencies by previous amendments or if it would demonstrably and unduly prejudice the adverse party. *Preston v. Kindred Hospitals West, L.L.C.*, 226 Ariz. 391, 249 P.3d 771 (2011); *Owen v. Superior Court of State of Ariz., In and For Maricopa County*, 133 Ariz. 75, 649 P.2d 278 (1982); *Haynes v. Syntek Finance Corp.*, 184 Ariz. 332, 909 P.2d 399 (Ct. App. Div. 1 1995); *Carrillo v. State*, 169 Ariz. 126, 817 P.2d 493 (Ct. App. Div. 1 1991). Finally, it is not an abuse of discretion for the trial court to refuse leave to file an amendment which seeks to assert a claim that the trial court has previously found to be without evidentiary support or which is merely the refiling of a pleading previously found to be without evidentiary support. *Tovrea v. Nolan*, 178 Ariz. 485, 875 P.2d 144 (Ct. App. Div. 2 1993).

6. *Amendments by Stipulation.* Ordinarily, leave of court is not required under Rule 15(a), to file an amended pleading stipulated to by the adverse party. The stipulation should indicate, however, either (1) the agreed upon date the amendment is to be considered effective for purposes of filing a responsive pleading, or (2) the agreed upon date the responsive pleading is due. In such instances, an order setting forth the dates agreed upon may be desirable.

7. *Procedure for Amending.* Rule 15(a)(2) provides that a party seeking leave to amend must attach to the motion a copy of the proposed amended pleading as an exhibit, and that exhibit must "indicate in what respect it differs from the pleading it amends, by bracketing or striking through text to be deleted and underlin-

ing text to be added." This Rule also adds the requirement that, when a motion for leave to amend is granted, the amended pleading must be both filed and served within ten (10) days of the order granting leave, unless the Court establishes a different time.

A party must plead in response to an amended pleading which requires one within the time remaining for responding to the original pleading, or within ten (10) days after service of the amended pleading, whichever is longer. The Court may, of course, establish a different date for responding. See further discussion of this topic in Section 12, *infra*.

8. *Effect of Amendment.* A pleading which is replaced and superseded by an amendment becomes a nullity. *Campbell v. Deddens*, 21 Ariz. App. 295, 518 P.2d 1012 (Div. 2 1974). An amended complaint, however, does not supersede a counterclaim asserted in the original answer, and such a counterclaim need not be repleaded. *Mohave Concrete and Materials, Inc. v. Scaramuzzo*, 154 Ariz. 28, 739 P.2d 1345 (Ct. App. Div. 1 1987).

9. *Relation Back of Amendments Generally.* Under Rule 15(c), an amendment will relate back to the date of the original pleading if it arises out of the same "conduct, transaction or occurrence," and any party brought in by the amendment had actual or constructive notice of the institution of the action. *North Star Development Corp. v. Wolfswinkel*, 146 Ariz. 406, 706 P.2d 732 (Ct. App. Div. 2 1985); *Green Reservoir Flood Control Dist. v. Willmoth*, 15 Ariz. App. 406, 489 P.2d 69 (Div. 2 1971). The concept of "relating back" is particularly important where the new claim (or the assertion of the initial claim as against substituted parties) would be barred by the statute of limitations at the time of the amendment but would have been timely if asserted in the original pleading.

10. *Amendments Adding New Claims.* An amended pleading will "relate back" if it merely asserts, as against the parties already named in the action, a new legal theory arising out of the same operative facts as the original pleading. *Huskie v. Ames Bros. Motor and Supply Co., Inc.*, 139 Ariz. 396, 678 P.2d 977, 38 U.C.C. Rep. Serv. 618 (Ct. App. Div. 1 1984); *Green Reservoir Flood Control Dist. v. Willmoth*, 15 Ariz. App. 406, 489 P.2d 69 (Div. 2 1971); *Arizona Title Ins. & Trust Co. v. O'Malley Lumber Co.*, 14 Ariz. App. 486, 484 P.2d 639 (Div. 1 1971). An amended pleading will not relate back if the claim in the requested amendment arises from a new transaction or event, *Marshall v. Superior Court, Maricopa County*, 131 Ariz. 379, 641 P.2d 867 (1982); or sets forth a wholly different legal obligation or liability, *Barnes v. Vozack*, 113 Ariz. 269, 550 P.2d 1070 (1976).

11. *Amendments Adding or Changing Parties.* In order for a claim in an amended pleading against a newly named defendant

to "relate back" to the date of the filing of the original pleading, the claim must arise out of the same transaction or occurrence set forth in the original pleading, and the new or newly identified defendant must receive actual notice of the institution of the action within the time period prescribed by Rule 15(c). An amendment adding or changing a party will relate back if the defendant is served within the time period prescribed by the applicable statute of limitations plus the time allowed for service of process. *Ritchie v. Grand Canyon Scenic Rides*, 165 Ariz. 460, 799 P.2d 801 (1990); *Cook v. Superior Court of Maricopa County*, 135 Ariz. 1, 658 P.2d 801 (1983); *Grobe v. McBryde*, 105 Ariz. 577, 468 P.2d 936 (1970). Prior service of the complaint upon other defendants through a statutory agent also employed by the new defendants will not, without more, constitute the requisite notice. *Hughes Air Corp. v. Maricopa County Superior Court*, 114 Ariz. 412, 561 P.2d 736 (1977) (disapproved of by, Ritchie v. Grand Canyon Scenic Rides, 165 Ariz. 460, 799 P.2d 801 (1990)). The substitution of a named defendant for one previously identified as a fictitious party is considered to be adding or changing parties and is governed by this Rule. *Cook v. Superior Court of Maricopa County*, 135 Ariz. 1, 658 P.2d 801 (1983); *Grobe v. McBryde*, 105 Ariz. 577, 468 P.2d 936 (1970).

Where the amended complaint changes the party against whom a claim is asserted, it will not relate back unless the newly-added defendant must have known that the failure to be named in the original complaint was due to a mistake in identity. *Levinson v. Jarrett ex rel. County of Maricopa*, 207 Ariz. 472, 88 P.3d 186 (Ct. App. Div. 1 2004); *Ellman Land Corp. v. Maricopa County*, 180 Ariz. 331, 884 P.2d 217 (Ct. App. Div. 1 1994); *Bisaillon v. Casares*, 165 Ariz. 359, 798 P.2d 1368 (Ct. App. Div. 2 1990). A "mistake concerning the identities of the proper party" within the meaning of Rule 15(c) does not include a mistake of counsel regarding whom to name in a suit. Where a plaintiff knows of the existence and identity of a defendant before the statute of limitations runs, and makes a conscious decision about whom to sue, that deliberate, though ultimately erroneous or unwise, tactical choice cannot be considered a "mistake" in identity of a party that would allow relation back of an amended pleading to defeat a statute of limitations defense. *O'Keefe v. Grenke*, 170 Ariz. 460, 825 P.2d 985, 16 U.C.C. Rep. Serv. 2d 746 (Ct. App. Div. 1 1992). The "mistake" must involve an element of negligence, carelessness or fault, and does not encompass a conscious decision not to name a party for strategic reasons, even where that decision turns out to be erroneous. *Tyman v. Hintz Concrete, Inc.*, 214 Ariz. 73, 148 P.3d 1146 (2006). In addition, the mistake must be one as to the identity of the proper party, and not as to whether the defendant is the appropriately liable party. *Tyman v. Hintz Concrete, Inc.*,

214 Ariz. 73, 148 P.3d 1146 (2006).

The "relation back" doctrine balances a plaintiff's right to a hearing on the merits of a claim, despite procedural or technical difficulties, with a defendant's right to be protected from stale claims and the attendant uncertainty they cause. *Pargman v. Vickers*, 208 Ariz. 573, 96 P.3d 571 (Ct. App. Div. 1 2004), as amended on denial of reconsideration, (Nov. 1, 2004). First, the plaintiff must show that the party to be brought in received notice of the institution of the action so that it will not be prejudiced in maintaining a defense. *Pargman v. Vickers*, 208 Ariz. 573, 96 P.3d 571 (Ct. App. Div. 1 2004), as amended on denial of reconsideration on other grounds, (Nov. 1, 2004). Second, the plaintiff must show that the to-be-named defendant knew, or should have known, that the plaintiff would have sued it but for a mistake. *Pargman v. Vickers*, 208 Ariz. 573, 96 P.3d 571 (Ct. App. Div. 1 2004), as amended on denial of reconsideration on other grounds, (Nov. 1, 2004). This insures that the new defendant knew its joinder was a distinct possibility. *Pargman v. Vickers*, 208 Ariz. 573, 96 P.3d 571 (Ct. App. Div. 1 2004), as amended on denial of reconsideration on other grounds, (Nov. 1, 2004). Third, the plaintiff must show that the to-be-added defendant received the required notice and knowledge within the original limitations period plus the time allowed for service. *Pargman v. Vickers*, 208 Ariz. 573, 96 P.3d 571 (Ct. App. Div. 1 2004), as amended on denial of reconsideration on other grounds, (Nov. 1, 2004). When a plaintiff mistakenly sues a defendant who is deceased, rather than the decedent's estate, but seeks to recover only against insurance proceeds, if the decedent's insurer had notice of the action and knowledge of the plaintiff's mistake within the period specified in Rule 15(c), an amended complaint against the estate will relate back to the date of the original complaint. *Pargman v. Vickers*, 208 Ariz. 573, 96 P.3d 571 (Ct. App. Div. 1 2004), as amended on denial of reconsideration on other grounds, (Nov. 1, 2004).

12. *Responding to Amended Complaints*. Rule 15(a) by its terms does not limit the matters that can be alleged in response to an amended pleading. The Rule does state, however, that the pleading must be "in response to the amended pleading." Rule 13(e) and Rule 15(d) contain special rules concerning later arising counterclaims. Such claims may be presented, with the court's permission, as a counterclaim by supplemental pleading.

13. *Amendments to Answers; Omitted Counterclaims*. Rule 15(a) (2012) provides that once the right to amend a pleading as a matter of course has expired, one must seek leave of court to amend a pleading, such as an answer. It is within the discretion of the trial court to permit an amendment to an answer to plead a previously omitted affirmative defense, such as the statute of

limitations. *Uyleman v. D.S. Rentco*, 194 Ariz. 300, 981 P.2d 1081 (Ct. App. Div. 1 1999); *Sirek v. Fairfield Snowbowl, Inc.*, 166 Ariz. 183, 800 P.2d 1291 (Ct. App. Div. 1 1990); *Trujillo v. Brasfield*, 119 Ariz. 8, 579 P.2d 46 (Ct. App. Div. 2 1978); *Romo v. Reyes*, 26 Ariz. App. 374, 548 P.2d 1186 (Div. 2 1976).

An amendment to an answer may also be sought to conform to the evidence, under Rule 15(b). Because of the undue prejudice to the plaintiff, however, an amendment to the answer should not be allowed when the amendment will, as a practical matter, deny the plaintiff the opportunity to file suit against the proper party in the proper forum within the limitations period. *Haynes v. Syntek Finance Corp.*, 184 Ariz. 332, 909 P.2d 399 (Ct. App. Div. 1 1995).

Effective January 1, 2012, the Arizona Supreme Court abrogated, without comment, Rule 13(f), which had concerned omitted counterclaims. Although the Court did not give any reasons for the abrogation, the Rule 28 Petition giving rise to the Court's order urged the abrogation of Rule 13(f) to bring Arizona's rule in line with recent abrogation of Rule 13(f) of the Federal Rules of Civil Procedure.

As a result, and effective January 1, 2012, Rule 13(f) was abrogated and the standards and procedures embraced by Rule 15(a) now govern motions to amend a pleading, such as an answer, to assert an omitted counterclaim.

14. *Amendments to Conform to Proof.* Requests for amendments to conform to the evidence are also addressed to the discretion of the trial court, but the same policy of liberal allowance of such amendments pertains. *Puntel v. Kirtides*, 89 Ariz. 361, 362 P.2d 737 (1961); *In re McCauley's Estate*, 101 Ariz. 8, 415 P.2d 431 (1966); *Parker v. City of Tucson*, 233 Ariz. 422, 314 P.3d 100 (Ct. App. Div. 2 2013) (A Rule 15(b) motion to amend should be granted absent a showing of prejudice, i.e., surprise.); *SWC Baseline & Crismon Investors, L.L.C. v. Augusta Ranch Ltd. Partnership*, 228 Ariz. 271, 265 P.3d 1070 (Ct. App. Div. 1 2011), review denied, (Apr. 24, 2012); *Vinson v. Marton & Associates*, 159 Ariz. 1, 764 P.2d 736 (Ct. App. Div. 1 1988).

The issue to be introduced by the amendment must, however, have actually been tried. *Hitching Post Lodge, Inc. v. Kerwin*, 101 Ariz. 402, 420 P.2d 273 (1966); *SWC Baseline & Crismon Investors, L.L.C. v. Augusta Ranch Ltd. Partnership*, 228 Ariz. 271, 265 P.3d 1070 (Ct. App. Div. 1 2011), review denied, (Apr. 24, 2012).

Generally, the failure to object to evidence at trial implies consent to trial of an issue. *In re McCauley's Estate*, 101 Ariz. 8, 415 P.2d 431 (1966). In that circumstance, where evidence pertaining to an issue not pleaded is admitted without objection, the pleadings will be treated on appeal as having been amended to conform to the proof. *Gilmore v. Cohen*, 95 Ariz. 34, 386 P.2d 81, 11 A.L.R.3d 714 (1963); *Beckwith v. Clevenger Realty Co.*, 89 Ariz. 238, 360 P.2d 596 (1961); *Sholes v. Fernando*, 228 Ariz. 455, 268 P.3d 1112 (Ct. App. Div. 2 2011) (issues not raised by the pleadings but tried by the express or implied consent of the parties treated as if they had been raised in the pleadings). Consent will not be implied, however, where the evidence admitted is pertinent to an existing issue framed by the pleadings and there is no indication that a new issue is being introduced. *Magma Copper Co. v. Industrial Com'n of Arizona*, 139 Ariz. 38, 676 P.2d 1096 (1983); *SWC Baseline & Crismon Investors, L.L.C. v. Augusta Ranch Ltd. Partnership*, 228 Ariz. 271, 265 P.3d 1070 (Ct. App. Div. 1 2011), review denied, (Apr. 24, 2012) (consent may not be implied by opposing party's failure to object to admission of evidence relevant to an issue within the pleadings); *Arizona Farmworkers Union v. Agricultural Employment Relations Bd.*, 158 Ariz. 411, 762 P.2d 1365, 124 Lab. Cas. (CCH) P 57172 (Ct. App. Div. 2 1988); *Bujanda v. Montgomery Ward & Co., Inc.*, 125 Ariz. 314, 609 P.2d 584 (Ct. App. Div. 2 1980).

The trial court may not *sua sponte* direct an amendment after trial to conform to the proof—it only has the power to suggest the need to request an amendment. *Smith v. Continental Bank*, 130 Ariz. 320, 636 P.2d 98 (1981). If requested and proper, however, leave to amend to conform to the proof may be granted even after judgment. *In re McCauley's Estate*, 101 Ariz. 8, 415 P.2d 431 (1966); *Vinson v. Marton & Associates*, 159 Ariz. 1, 764 P.2d 736 (Ct. App. Div. 1 1988).

15. *Supplemental Pleadings.* Rule 15(d) permits supplemental pleadings upon motion and order. A supplemental pleading is a pleading which sets forth transactions, occurrences or events which have taken place since the date the original pleading was filed. Rule 13(e) specifies, for example, that a counterclaim acquired or maturing after the filing of the original pleading is to be presented, with leave of court, by supplemental pleading. The function of the supplemental pleading is to bring forward new facts or events arising after the filing of an original pleading so that the entire controversy can be before the Court. Matters existing at the time of filing the original pleading, but omitted therefrom because overlooked or unknown, should be brought in by amendment rather than a supplemental pleading.

A trial court has the same broad discretion to allow a supplemental pleading under Rule 15(d) as it has in permitting the amendment of pleadings. *Southwest Soil Remediation, Inc. v. City of Tucson*, 201 Ariz. 438, 36 P.3d 1208 (Ct. App. Div. 2 2001). A party's failure to object to the filing of a supplemental complaint does not operate as a waiver of any defenses that party has to the merits of the claim. *Southwest Soil Remediation, Inc. v. City of Tucson*, 201 Ariz. 438, 36 P.3d 1208 (Ct. App. Div. 2 2001).

No responsive pleading to a supplemental pleading is necessary. If the Court deems it advisable that the adverse party respond to a supplemental pleading, it must order a responsive pleading and specify the time by which such responsive pleading should be filed.

Rule 16. Pretrial conferences; scheduling; management (pre-2014 amendment)

Text of Rule 16 applicable to those cases filed before April 15, 2014 that are not subject to the conditions stated in the November 27, 2013 Amended Order Regarding Applicability Provision, in R-13-0017.

See also, text of Rule 16 applicable to cases filed on or after April 15, 2014 and to those cases filed before April 15, 2014 that are subject to the conditions stated in the November 27, 2013, Amended Order Regarding Applicability Provision, in R-13-0017.

(a) Pretrial Conferences; Objectives. In any action, the court may in its discretion direct the parties, the attorneys for the parties and, if appropriate, representatives of the parties having authority to settle, to participate, either in person or, with leave of court, by telephone, in a conference or conferences before trial for such purposes as:

1. expediting the disposition of the action;

2. establishing early and continuing control so that the case will not be protracted because of lack of management;

3. discouraging wasteful pretrial activities;

4. improving the quality of the trial through more thorough preparation.

Amended Aug. 7, 1984, effective Nov. 1, 1984; Sept. 15, 1987, effective Nov. 15, 1987; Oct. 10, 2000, effective Dec. 1, 2000. Cases filed before April 15, 2014, may be subject to November 27, 2013, Amended Order Regarding Applicability Provision, entered In the Matter of Petition to Amend Rules 16, 16.1, 26, 37, 38, 38.1, 72, 73, 74 and 77, Arizona Rules of Civil Procedure, R-13-0017.

(b) Scheduling and Subjects to Be Discussed at Comprehensive Pretrial Conference in Non-Medical Malpractice Cases. Except in medical malpractice cases, upon written request of any party the court shall, or upon its own motion the court may, schedule a comprehensive pretrial conference. At any comprehensive pretrial conference under this rule, except for conferences conducted in medical malpractice cases, the court may:

(1) Determine the additional disclosures, discovery and related activities to be undertaken and a schedule therefor.

(A) The schedule shall include depositions to be taken and the time for taking same; production of documents or electronically stored information; non-uniform interrogatories; admissions; inspections or physical or mental examinations; and any other discovery pursuant to these rules.

(B) Among other orders the court may enter under this rule, the court may enter orders addressing one or more of the following:

(i) setting forth any requirements or limitations for the disclosure or discovery of electronically stored information, including the form or forms in which the electronically stored information should be produced;

(ii) setting forth any measures the parties must take to preserve discoverable documents or electronically stored information; and

(iii) adopting any agreements the parties reach for asserting claims of privilege or of protection as to trial preparation materials after production.

(2) Determine a schedule for the disclosure of expert witnesses. Such disclosure shall be within 90 days after the conference except upon good cause shown.

(3) Determine the number of expert witnesses or designate expert witnesses as set forth in Rule 26(b)(4).

(4) Determine a date for the disclosure of non-expert witnesses and the order of their disclosure; provided, however, that the date for disclosure of all witnesses, expert and non-expert, shall be at least 45 days before the completion of discovery. Any witnesses not so disclosed shall not be allowed to testify at trial unless there is a showing of good cause.

(5) Resolve any discovery disputes which have been presented to the court by way of motion not less than 10 days before the conference. The moving party shall set forth the requested discovery to which objection is made and the basis for the objection. The responding party may file a response not less than 3 days before the conference. No replies shall be filed unless ordered by the court. The court shall assess an appropriate sanction, including those permitted under Rule 16(f), against any party or attorney who has engaged in unreasonable, groundless, abusive or obstructionist discovery.

(6) Eliminate non-meritorious claims or defenses.

(7) Permit the amendment of the pleadings.

(8) Assist in identifying those issues of fact which are still at issue.

(9) Obtain stipulations as to the foundation or admissibility of evidence.

(10) Determine the desirability of special procedures for management of the case.

(11) Consider alternative dispute resolution.

(12) Determine whether any time limits or procedures set forth in the discovery rules or set forth in these Rules or Local

Rules of Practice should be modified or suspended.

(13) Determine whether Rule 26.1 has been appropriately complied with by the parties.

(14) Determine a date for a settlement conference if such a conference is requested by a party or deemed advisable by the court.

(15) Determine a date for compliance with subpart (d) of this Rule.

(16) Determine a trial date.

(17) Discuss the imposition of time limits on trial proceedings or portions thereof, the use of juror notebooks, the giving of brief pre-voir dire opening statements and preliminary jury instructions, and the effective management of documents and exhibits.

(18) Make such other orders as the court deems appropriate.

(19) Determine how verbatim record of future proceedings in the case will be made.

Formerly 16(c). Amended Aug. 7, 1984, effective Nov. 1, 1984; Dec. 1991, effective July 1, 1992. Redesignated 16(b) by amendment of Oct. 10, 2000, effective Dec. 1, 2000. Amended Sept. 18, 2006, effective Jan. 1, 2007; Sept. 5, 2007, effective Jan. 1, 2008. Cases filed before April 15, 2014, may be subject to November 27, 2013, Amended Order Regarding Applicability Provision, entered In the Matter of Petition to Amend Rules 16, 16.1, 26, 37, 38, 38.1, 72, 73, 74 and 77, Arizona Rules of Civil Procedure, R-13-0017.

(c) Scheduling and Subject Matter at Comprehensive Pretrial Conferences in Medical Malpractice Cases. In medical malpractice cases, within five days of receiving answers or motions from all defendants who have been served, plaintiff shall notify the court to whom the case has been assigned so that a comprehensive pretrial conference can be set. Within 60 days of receiving that notice, the court shall conduct a comprehensive pretrial conference. At that conference, the court and the parties shall:

(1) Determine the discovery to be undertaken and a schedule therefor. The schedule shall include the depositions to be taken, any medical examination which defendant desires to be made of plaintiff and what additional documents, electronically stored information, and other materials are to be exchanged. Only those depositions specifically authorized in the comprehensive pretrial conference shall be allowed except upon stipulation of the parties or upon motion and a showing of good cause. The court, upon request of any defendant, shall require an authorization to allow the parties to obtain copies of records previously produced under Rule 26.2(A)(2) of these Rules or records ordered to be produced by the court. If records are obtained pursuant to such authorization, the party obtaining the records

shall furnish complete copies to all other parties at the sole expense of the party obtaining the records.

(2) Determine a schedule for the disclosure of standard of care and causation expert witnesses. Except upon good cause shown, such disclosure shall be simultaneous and within 30 to 90 days after the conference, depending upon the number and complexity of the issues. No motion for summary judgment based upon the lack of expert testimony will be filed prior to the expiration of the date set for the simultaneous disclosure of expert witnesses except upon a showing of good cause.

(3) Determine the order of and dates for the disclosure of all other expert and non-expert witnesses, provided that the date for disclosure of all witnesses, expert and non-expert, shall be at least 45 days before the close of discovery. Any witnesses not appropriately disclosed shall be precluded from testifying at trial unless there is a showing of extraordinary circumstances.

(4) Limit the number of experts as provided in Rule 26(b)(4)(D) of these Rules.

(5) Determine whether additional non-uniform interrogatories and/or requests for admission or production are necessary and, if so, limit the number.

(6) Resolve any discovery disputes which have been presented to the court by way of motion within 10 days before the conference. The moving party shall set forth the question or answer to which objection is made and the basis for the objection. The responding party may file a response within 3 days of the conference. No replies shall be filed unless ordered by the court. The court shall assess an appropriate sanction, including any order under Rule 37(b)(2) of these Rules, against any party or attorney who has engaged in unreasonable, groundless, abusive or obstructionist discovery.

(7) Discuss alternative dispute resolution, including mediation, and binding and non-binding arbitration.

(8) Assure compliance with A.R.S. § 12-570.

(9) Set a date for a mandatory settlement conference.

(10) Set a date for filing the joint pretrial statement required by subpart (d) of this Rule.

(11) Set a trial date.

(12) Make such other orders as the court deems appropriate.

(13) Determine how verbatim record of future proceedings in the case will be made.

Added Oct. 10, 2000, effective Dec. 1, 2000. Amended Sept. 18, 2006, effective Jan. 1, 2007; Sept. 5, 2007, effective Jan. 1, 2008. Cases filed before April 15, 2014, may be subject to November 27, 2013, Amended Order Regarding Applicability Provision, entered In the Matter of Petition to Amend Rules 16, 16.1, 26, 37, 38, 38.1, 72, 73, 74 and 77, Arizona Rules of Civil Procedure, R-13-0017.

(d) Joint Pretrial Statement; Preparation; Final Pretrial Conference.

(1) Counsel or the parties who will try the case and who are authorized to make binding stipulations shall confer and prepare a written joint pretrial statement, signed by each counsel or party, that shall be filed five days before the date of the final pretrial conference, or if no conference is scheduled, five days before trial. Plaintiffs shall submit their portion of the joint pretrial statement to all parties no later than twenty days before the statement is due. All other parties shall submit their portions of the joint pretrial statement to all parties no later than fifteen days before the statement is due.

(2) The joint pretrial statement shall contain the following:

(A) Stipulations of material fact and law;

(B) Such contested issues of fact and law as counsel can agree are material or applicable;

(C) A separate statement by each party of other issues of fact and law believed by that party to be material;

(D) A list of the witnesses intended to be used by each party during the trial. Each party shall list any objections to a witness and the basis for that objection. No witness shall be used at trial other than those listed, except for good cause shown. Witnesses whose testimony will be received by deposition testimony only will be so indicated.

(E) Each party's final list of exhibits to be used at trial for any purpose, including impeachment. Plaintiffs shall deliver copies of all their exhibits to all parties twenty days before the final pretrial conference. All other parties shall deliver copies of all their exhibits to all parties fifteen days before the final pretrial conference. Any exhibit that cannot be reproduced must be made available for inspection to all parties on or before the deadlines stated above. Each party shall list any objections to an exhibit and the basis for that objection. No exhibits shall be used at trial other than those listed, except for good cause shown. The parties shall indicate any exhibits which the parties stipulate can be admitted into evidence, such stipulations being subject to court approval;

(F) A statement by each party indicating any proposed deposition summaries or designating portions of any deposition testimony to be offered by that party at trial, other than for impeachment purposes. Deposition testimony shall be designated by transcript page and line numbers. A copy of any proposed deposition summary and written transcript of designated deposition testimony shall be filed with the Joint Pretrial Statement. Each party shall list any objections to the proposed deposition summaries and designated deposition testimony and the basis for any objections. Except for good cause shown, no deposition testimony shall be used at trial other than that designated or counter-designated or for impeachment purposes.

(G) A brief statement of the case to be read to the jury during voir dire. If the parties cannot agree on this statement, then each party shall submit a separate statement to the judge who will decide the contents of the statement to be read to the jury;

(H) Technical equipment needed or interpreters requested;

(I) The number of jurors and alternates agreed upon, whether the alternates may deliberate, and the number of jurors required to reach a verdict;

(J) Whether any party will be invoking Rule 615 of the Arizona Rules of Evidence regarding exclusion of witnesses from the courtroom; and

(K) A brief description of settlement efforts.

(3) At the time of the filing of the joint pretrial statement, the parties shall file (A) an agreed-upon set of jury instructions, verdict forms, and voir dire questions and (B) any additional jury instructions, verdict forms, and voir dire questions requested, but not agreed upon, (C) a statement by each party on how a verbatim record of the trial will be made.

(4) Each party intending to submit a jury notebook to the jurors shall submit a copy of the notebook to opposing counsel five days before the final pretrial conference, or if no conference is scheduled, five days before the trial.

(5) Each party who will be submitting a trial memorandum shall file such memorandum five days before the final pretrial conference, or if no conference is scheduled, five days before the trial,

(6) Any final pretrial conference scheduled by the court shall be held as close to the time of trial as reasonable under the circumstances. The conference shall be attended by at least one of the attorneys who will conduct the trial for each of the parties any by any unrepresented parties.

(7) The provisions of this rule may be modified by order of the court.

Amended Aug. 7, 1984, effective Nov. 1, 1984; Oct. 10, 2000, effective Dec. 1, 2000; Oct. 16, 2003, effective Dec. 1, 2003; Sept. 18, 2006, effective Jan. 1, 2007; Sept. 5, 2007, effective Jan. 1, 2008. Cases filed before April 15, 2014, may be subject to November 27, 2013, Amended Order Regarding Applicability Provision, entered In the Matter of Petition to Amend Rules 16, 16.1, 26, 37, 38, 38.1, 72, 73, 74 and 77, Arizona Rules of Civil Procedure, R-13-0017.

(e) Pretrial Orders. After any conference held pursuant to this rule, an order shall be entered reciting the action taken. This order shall control the subsequent course of the action unless modified by a subsequent order. The order following a final pretrial conference shall be modified only to prevent manifest injustice.

Amended Aug. 7, 1984, effective Nov. 1, 1984. Cases filed before April 15, 2014, may be subject to November 27, 2013, Amended Order Regarding Applicability Provision, entered In the Matter of Petition to Amend Rules 16, 16.1, 26, 37, 38, 38.1, 72, 73, 74 and 77, Arizona Rules of Civil Procedure, R-13-0017.

(f) Sanctions. If a party or attorney fails to obey a scheduling or pretrial order, or if no appearance is made on behalf of a party at a scheduling or pretrial conference, or if a party or party's attorney is substantially unprepared to participate in the conference, or if a party or party's attorney fails to participate in good faith in a scheduling or pretrial conference or in the preparation of the joint pretrial statement, the judge, upon motion or the judge's own initiative, shall, except upon a showing of good cause, make such orders with regard to such conduct as are just, including, among others, any of the orders provided in Rule 37(b)(2)(B), (C), or (D). In lieu of or in addition to any other sanction, the judge shall require the party, or the attorney representing the party, or both, to pay the reasonable expenses incurred because of any noncompliance with this rule, including attorneys' fees, or payment of an assessment to the clerk of the court, or both, unless the judge finds that the noncompliance was substantially justified, or that other circumstances make an award of expenses unjust.

Amended Aug. 7, 1984, effective Nov. 1, 1984; Sept. 15, 1987, effective Nov. 15, 1987; Dec. 20, 1991, effective July 1, 1992; Oct. 10, 2000, effective Dec. 1, 2000. Cases filed before April 15, 2014, may be subject to November 27, 2013, Amended Order Regarding Applicability Provision, entered In the Matter of Petition to Amend Rules 16, 16.1, 26, 37, 38, 38.1, 72, 73, 74 and 77, Arizona Rules of Civil Procedure, R-13-0017.

(g) Alternative Dispute Resolution.

(1) Upon motion of any party, or upon its own initiative after consultation with the parties, the court may direct the parties in any action to submit the dispute which is the subject matter of the action to an alternative dispute resolution program created or authorized by appropriate local rules.

Added July 16, 1991, effective Oct. 1, 1991. Amended Oct. 6, 1994, effective Dec. 1, 1994; Oct. 22, 2001, effective Dec. 1, 2001. Rule 16(g)(2) abrogated August 30, 2012, effective January 1, 2013. Cases filed before April 15, 2014, may be subject to November 27, 2013, Amended Order Regarding Applicability Provision, entered In the Matter of Petition to Amend Rules 16, 16.1, 26, 37, 38, 38.1, 72, 73, 74 and 77, Arizona Rules of Civil Procedure, R-13-0017.

(h) Time Limitations. The Court may impose reasonable time limits on the trial proceedings or portions thereof.

Added Oct. 24, 1995, effective Dec. 1, 1995. Amended Oct. 10, 2000, effective Dec. 1, 2000. Cases filed before April 15, 2014, may be subject to November 27,

2013, Amended Order Regarding Applicability Provision, entered In the Matter of Petition to Amend Rules 16, 16.1, 26, 37, 38, 38.1, 72, 73, 74 and 77, Arizona Rules of Civil Procedure, R-13-0017.

STATE BAR COMMITTEE NOTES

1984 Amendments

[Rule 16(a)] The 1984 amendment thoroughly reorganizes Rule 16. The subject matter of Rule 16(a) is now transferred to 16(c). New Rule 16(a) emphasizes judicial management of the pretrial as well as the trial phase.

[Rule 16(b)] This section is new. It is an adaptation of Federal Rule 16(b), intended to retain as much conformity with the federal rule as is consistent with the needs of the state court system. The principal difference is that under the federal rule a scheduling order is mandatory in all cases not exempted by district court rule, while under the Arizona rule as conference will be held on motion of the parties or order of the court to determine whether a scheduling order is appropriate. Because the order is an option to be exercised in the discretion of the court, it can be employed where useful without incurring the administrative burdens of a mandatory rule.

Former 16(b) is deleted. Originally enacted as Ariz. Rev. Stat. Ann. § 21-454 (1939), it provided that no civil action shall be heard on its merits until all motions are disposed of, and that the setting of an action for trial shall be deemed to overrule all motions pending. There were no cases on this provision, and it had no apparent utility.

[Rule 16(d)] If there is more than one pretrial conference, Rule 16(d) makes clear that the time between the final pretrial conference and trial should be as short as possible; the Advisory Committee to the Judicial Conference of the United States cites authority to the effect that ten days to two weeks is the optimal period. See, Discussion, 1981 Proposed Amendments to the Federal Rules of Civil Procedure, Report of the Judicial Conference of the United States (1982). However, the timing is left to the court's discretion.

Rule 16(f) incorporates the sanctions which the court may now impose for failure to provide or permit discovery under Rule 37(b)(2). See, e.g., *B & R Materials, Inc. v. U. S. Fidelity and Guaranty Co.*, 132 Ariz. 122, 644 P.2d 276 (Ct. App. Div. 2 1982). In the four situations enumerated, sanctions may be imposed, either upon the court's initiative or upon a party's motion. In addition, the court shall require the payment of expenses, including attorneys' fees, by the uncooperative party, the attorney, or both, unless circumstances warrant otherwise. Compare, *Golleher v. Horton*, 119 Ariz. 604, 583 P.2d 260 (Ct. App. Div. 1 1978) and *Zakroff v. May*, 8 Ariz. App. 101, 443 P.2d 916 (1968). These sanctions are reviewable under the abuse-of-discretion standard. See, *Sears Roebuck and Co. v. Walker*, 127 Ariz. 432, 621 P.2d 938 (Ct. App. Div. 1 1980).

1991 Amendments

[Comment to former Rule 16(c); now Rule 16(b)]

[Rule 16(b)] The trial court may require the parties to file pretrial memoranda and may, by minute entry, prescribe the form and content thereof.

[Former Rule 16(c); currently 16(b))] The subjects to be discussed at the Comprehensive Pretrial Conference are within the discretion of the court. All 17 of the items listed may be the subject of discussion or the court may add to or delete from those suggested items.

Rule 16(c)(3) should be read in conjunction with Rules 26(b)(4) and 43(g) and the comments appended to those rules. It was not the intent of the Committee to limit parties from designating or calling at trial expert witnesses who are reasonably necessary. The goal of the Committee was to reduce the expense of the litigation by eliminating unnecessary or duplicative expert witnesses.

Rule 16(c)(6) is not intended to permit "lightning summary judgments," but to require the court to discuss with the parties in cases involving multiple parties, multiple theories, multiple causes of action, etc., whether all such claims or defenses are, in fact, necessary and whether they will ultimately be relied on. The court does not have the power over objection of the parties to dismiss any such claim or defense except upon motion as otherwise provided in these rules.

Rule 16(c)(10) is intended to encourage the court and the parties to consider whether or not their particular case requires special procedures for the management of the case. By way of example, discovery masters have proven useful. Judicial time may be preserved if the issues are bifurcated.

Rule 16(c)(11) is intended by the Committee to be a strong suggestion that the court explore the possibility of alternative dispute resolution including binding and non-binding arbitration, mediation and summary jury trials.

[Rule 16(f)] This rule expands the sanctions available to the court for noncompliance with not only the letter but the spirit of the rule. It makes available to the court any and all of the sanctions available under the rules. The sanctions are mandatory upon the finding by the court that Rule 16 has been breached. The rule also allows the court to enter an order requiring that all or a portion of the sanction be paid to the clerk of the court. It is contemplated that where the parties have incurred expenses and the sanction is intended to reimburse for those expenses or attorneys' fees, that portion of the payment at least will be ordered paid directly to the party incurring the expense. Where all or a portion of the sanction, however, is not intended to reimburse for an expense, such amount can be ordered paid to the clerk of the court. One of the purposes in such an order would be to see that, in fact, the sanction is paid rather than being waived by opposing counsel.

It should be noted that the court may be required, depending upon the circumstances, to hold an evidentiary hearing to determine the appropriate nature of the sanctions and whether the sanctions should be entered against the party, counsel, or both. See *Robinson v. Higuera*, 157 Ariz. 622, 760 P.2d 622 (Ct. App. Div. 1 1988).

1993 Amendment

[Rule 16(g)] Prior to any comprehensive pre-trial conference under this rule, counsel for each of the parties should confer regarding the feasibility of resolving the parties' dispute through alternative dispute resolution methods.

2000 Amendment

Rule 16 was amended in 2000 as part of the effort to consolidate formerly separate sets of procedural rules into either the Arizona Rules of Civil Procedure or the Rules of the Arizona Supreme Court. Rule 16(a)(5), which authorized the court to engage in ex parte communications, with the consent of all participating, at any settlement conference was removed from this Rule and incorporated into new Rule 16.1, dealing with the subject of settlement conferences generally.

Former Rule 16(c), dealing with comprehensive pretrial conferences, was renumbered as Rule 16(b), the provisions of what was former Rule 16(b) were incorporated therein, and its coverage was limited to cases other than medical malpractice cases. The provisions of former Rule 1(A) and most of the provisions of former Rule 1(D) of the Uniform Rules of Practice for Medical Malpractice Cases were incorporated into a new Rule 16(c), which deals with the scheduling and conduct of comprehensive pretrial conferences in medical malpractice cases. The provisions of former Rules 1(D)(9) and (10) were simply abrogated as outmoded and/or unnecessary.

The former Uniform Rules of Practice for Medical Malpractice Cases, which were promulgated in 1989, effective as of January 1, 1990, and amended in 1992, were the product of a special Committee appointed by the Arizona Supreme Court to study malpractice procedure. The consolidation of those

Rules into the Arizona Rules of Civil Procedure was not intended to abrogate or dilute the continuing vitality of the observations of the Preamble which accompanied the Uniform Rules of Practice for Medical Malpractice Cases when they were promulgated, and which provided:

PREAMBLE

The Governor and the Thirty Ninth Legislature requested the Supreme Court to appoint a special committee on malpractice procedure. The Committee was appointed by the Supreme Court with a specific charge to review the court and discovery procedures to determine whether a more efficient and less expensive system could be devised without doing violence to the rights of the parties. The Committee proposed the following rules for that purpose and with the further hope that if they are successful they might serve as a model for rules applicable to all civil litigation.

The Committee proposed certain presumptive limitations. The Committee did not intend to remove judicial discretion in these presumptive limits. It is intended, however, that variation from the presumptive limits would occur only where there is an affirmative demonstration of good cause. The courts shall strictly enforce the good cause requirement. The Committee considered and rejected presumptive limitations on the number of depositions which would be available to the parties. It is the intent of these rules however that the judge at the comprehensive pretrial conference will inquire of the parties as to the number of depositions contemplated and the reasons therefor. So long as the ends of justice will be served the judge shall limit the number of depositions to be taken. A voluntary exchange of information is to be encouraged by the judge presiding at the comprehensive pretrial conference.

Certain sanctions are provided in these rules. The Committee contemplated that these sanctions would be applied in the spirit of the rules, i.e., if the cooperation and compliance of counsel and the parties is not demonstrated then the sanctions shall be awarded. The award should be in a reasonable amount to compensate the party in compliance and to deter the non-complying party from such conduct in the future.

The Committee recognized that these rules will achieve the purpose intended only through effective judicial administration of the rules. The Committee sincerely hopes that counsel and the parties will act in the spirit of the rules and that the court will demand compliance.

In a comment to Rule 1 of the original Uniform Rules of Practice for Medical Malpractice Cases, effective January 1, 1990, and amended effective July 1, 1992, the special Committee stated the following, inter alia:

" Rule D(3) [sic: Rule 1(D)(4); now Rule 16(c)(4)] relating to the number of experts on standard-of-care contemplates that each party may have an expert for each standard-of-care issue. For instance, if the case involves issues of nursing care, anesthesia, and general surgery, the plaintiff should be entitled to three standard-of-care experts. Similarly, if the hospital employed the nurse, anesthesiologist and surgeon, and was the sole defendant, it would be entitled to three standard-of-care experts.

* * *

Under Rule D(6) [now Rule 16(c)(6)] any pending discovery dispute can be called to the court's attention. For instance, insufficient answers to any interrogatory or inadequate discovery under Uniform Rule 1(B) [now Rule 26.2(A)] should be resolved at the comprehensive pretrial conference.

Paragraph E [sic: Rule 1(D)(2); now Rule 16(c)(2)] pertaining to the establishment of a date for the simultaneous disclosure of experts at the comprehensive pretrial conference does not excuse either side from its obligation under Rule 26 to seasonably supplement answers to interrogatories in order to reveal the names of all witnesses, including experts, and to respond to interrogatories regarding the subject matter and substance of all expert opinions."

In a Court Comment to the 1992 amendment to former Rule 1(D)(3), the Supreme Court observed that the standard of "extraordinary circumstances" set forth in that Rule, which has been carried forward to new Rule 16(c)(3), is to be interpreted more stringently than the good cause exception in Rule 26(e) of the Arizona Rules of Civil Procedure. Under the "extraordinary circumstances" standard, courts are to evaluate the diligence of the party seeking to list a witness beyond the time limit, together with the reasons for the late listing and the listing party's need for the witness' testimony. While the absence of prejudice resulting from the late listing is a factor to be considered, it will not alone constitute grounds for permitting an untimely listing. Cf., *Aguirre v. Robert Forrest, P.A.*, 186 Ariz. 393, 923 P.2d 859 (Ct. App. Div. 2 1996).

The provisions of former Rules VI(a) and (b) of the Uniform Rules of Practice of the Superior Court, and one provision from former Rule VIII(a) of those Rules, were incorporated into an expanded Rule 16(d), the title of which was modified to reflect the changes effected by the amendment. The provisions of former Rule VI(c) of the Uniform Rules of Practice of the Superior Court were not retained because they were essentially duplicative of the existing provisions of Rule 16(a) of the Arizona Rules of Civil Procedure. Finally, a provision was added to Rule 16(f) to authorize the imposition of sanctions for the failure to participate in good faith in the preparation of the joint pretrial statement required by amended Rule 16(d). Such authority had been contained in former Rule VI(d), and referenced in former Rule VIII(a), of the Uniform Rules of Practice of the Superior Court.

Comment to 2001 Amendment to Rule 16(g)

[Rule 16(g)] Parties are cautioned that the 2001 amendment to Rule 16(g) must be read in light of Martinez v. Binsfield, 196 Ariz. 466, 999 P.2d 810 (2000), which held that Uniform Rule V(e) [now Rule 38.1(d)] applies to cases assigned to mandatory arbitration, and repeated continuances granted by the arbitrator in connection with mandatory arbitration did not provide good cause for continuing the case on the Inactive Calendar.

2008 Amendment

[Rule 16(b)] Rule 16(b) was amended to clarify that a court has the power under Rule 16 to enter orders governing the disclosure and discovery of electronically stored information, the preservation of discoverable documents and electronically stored information, and the enforcement of party agreements regarding postproduction assertions of privilege or work product protection. Because these issues typically arise at the beginning of a case, a court need not wait until the parties are ready to address other issues under Rule 16(b) before holding a hearing under this Rule on these and related subjects.

Orders regarding the disclosure or discovery of electronically stored information may specify the forms and manner in which such information shall be produced. The court may also enter orders limiting (or imposing conditions upon) the disclosure of such information, and may take into account the relative accessibility of the electronically stored information at issue, the costs and burdens on parties in making such information available, the probative value of such information, and the amount of damages (or the type of relief) at issue in the case. See CONFERENCE OF CHIEF JUSTICES, GUIDELINES FOR STATE TRIAL COURTS REGARDING DISCOVERY OF ELECTRONICALLY STORED INFORMATION 5 (approved August 2006) (noting that in determining discovery issues relating to electronically stored information, a court should consider these factors, among others).

Document retention and preservation issues are especially likely to arise with electronically stored information because the "ordinary operation of computers involves both the automatic creation and the automatic deletion or overwriting of certain information." Fed. R. Civ. P. 26(f),, Advisory Committee Notes on 2006 Amendment. A court has the power under this Rule to incorporate into an order any agreement the parties might reach regarding preservation issues or, absent an agreement, to enter an order in appropriate circumstances imposing such requirements and limitations. In considering such an order, a court should take into account not only the need to preserve potentially relevant evidence, but also any adverse effects such an order may have on a party's on-going activities and computer operations. A preservation order entered over objections should be narrowly tailored to address specific evidentiary needs in a case, and ex parte preservation orders should issue only in exceptional circumstances. Cf. Fed. R. Civ. P. 26(f),, Advisory Committee Notes on 2006 Amendment. (stating that preservation orders should be narrowly tailored where objections are made and cautioning against "blanket" or ex parte preservation orders); CONFERENCE OF CHIEF JUSTICES, GUIDELINES FOR STATE TRIAL COURTS REGARDING DISCOVERY OF ELECTRONICALLY-STORED INFORMATION

10 (approved August 2006) ("When issuing an order to preserve electronically stored information, a judge should carefully tailor the order so that it is no broader than necessary to safeguard the information in question.").

If the amount of documents and electronic data to be disclosed is voluminous, an agreement among the parties minimizing the risks associated with the inadvertent production of privileged or otherwise protected material may be helpful in lessening discovery costs and expediting the litigation. As with its counterpart in the Federal Rules of Civil Procedure, this Rule does not provide the court with authority to enter such an order without party agreement, or limit the court's authority to act on motions to resolve privilege issues. Cf. Fed. R. Civ. P. 26(f),, Advisory Committee Notes on 2006 Amendment (clarifying the rule's scope).

COURT COMMENT

1991 Amendments

[Comment to former Rule 16(c); renumbered Rule 16(b)]

The above rule change was part of a comprehensive set of rule revisions proposed by the Special Bar Committee to Study Civil Litigation Abuse, Cost and Delay, which was specifically charged in March, 1990 with the task of proposing rules to reduce discovery abuse and to make the judicial system in Arizona more efficient, expeditious, and accessible to the people.

For more complete background information on the rule changes proposed by the Committee, see Court Comment to Rule 26.1.

AUTHORS' COMMENTS

Analysis

1. *Scope and Purpose of Rule.* Ariz. R. Civ. P. 16 (pre-2014 amendment) authorizes the application by the Court of various pretrial case management procedures with a view toward simplifying and shortening the trial, and perhaps avoiding it entirely. Rule 16 was thoroughly revised in 1984 to conform generally to the then recent amendments to the corresponding provisions of the Federal Rules of Civil Procedure. As revised, it provides the trial court with broad powers of case management at the pretrial stage. A pretrial conference, and resulting order, may serve to shorten trial time, and to limit the issues to be tried. *Walters v. First Federal Sav. and Loan Ass'n of Phoenix*,

131 Ariz. 321, 641 P.2d 235 (1982); *Calderon v. Calderon*, 9 Ariz. App. 538, 454 P.2d 586 (1969). While some of the purposes for a Rule 16 pretrial conference are served by the Pretrial Statement required by subpart (d) of the Rule, Rule 16 deals with a variety of other matters and functions that may be accomplished in a pretrial conference.

In December 1991, the Arizona Supreme Court adopted, to become effective July 1, 1992, a comprehensive package of discovery and court reform proposals proposed by a Special Bar Committee to Study Civil Litigation Abuse, Cost and Delay. These proposals, as adopted, contemplate mandatory disclosure of pertinent facts and documents, and the imposition of presumptive limits on the amount of discovery to be conducted in the ordinary civil case. Rules 16(b) and (c) were also amended to authorize the conduct of a Comprehensive Pretrial Conference to facilitate case management, to monitor compliance with the new discovery rules and limitations, and to impose and exercise judicial control in those cases not suited for disposition according to the new limited discovery regime.

The Rule was further amended as part of the Supreme Court's adoption, in October 2000, of a proposal to abrogate the Uniform Rules of Practice of the Superior Court, the Uniform Rules of Practice for Medical Malpractice Cases, and the Uniform Rules of Procedure for Arbitration, and to transfer their provisions to either the Arizona Rules of Civil Procedure or the Rules of the Arizona Supreme Court. Rule 16(c) was in effect renumbered as Rule 16(b), and its coverage limited to cases other than medical malpractice cases. A new Rule 16(c) was added, dealing with the subject of comprehensive pretrial conferences in medical malpractice cases, and most of the provisions of former Rule 1(D) of the Uniform Rules of Practice for Medical Malpractice Cases were incorporated therein. In addition, the provisions of former Rules VI(a) and (b) of the Uniform Rules of Practice of the Superior Court, and one provision from former Rule VIII(a) of those Rules, were incorporated into an expanded Rule 16(d), the title of which was modified to reflect the changes made by that amendment.

2. *Comparison With Federal Rule.* As a consequence of the 1992 Arizona court and discovery reform amendments and of the 1993, 2006 and 2007 amendments to the Federal Rules of Civil Procedure, there are now significant differences between ARCP 16 and FRCP 16. ARCP 16(a) and ARCP 16(e) are similar to FRCP 16(a) and (d).

ARCP 16(b) and ARCP 16(c) authorize the conduct of, and delineate the subjects that may be considered at, a Comprehensive Pretrial Conference. The scheduling of future proceedings in the case is among the subjects that may be considered. FRCP 16(b) now requires the conduct of a scheduling conference and/or issuance of a scheduling order, after receipt of the discovery plan generated by the parties under FRCP 26(f), but no later than ninety (90) days after a defendant's appearance in the action and one hundred and twenty (120) days after service of the summons and complaint upon a defendant, except in categories of cases exempted by local rule. The scheduling order is to set deadlines for joining parties, filing motions, amending pleadings and completing discovery, and may also modify the time periods for making mandatory disclosures or the limitations on the amount of discovery permitted.

Also, the range of sanctions available to the Court under ARCP 16(f) is slightly greater than under the corresponding Federal Rule. Finally, the Federal Rules of Civil Procedure do not have a counterpart to ARCP 16(h).

In addition to these differences, and as a consequence of the 2014 amendments to the various rules governing case management/trial setting procedure, this version of ARCP 16 (pre-2014 amendment) will go the way of the dinosaur as soon as the last case subject to its provisions works its way through the process. FRCP 16 is not slated for a similar fate.

3. *Comprehensive Pretrial Conferences in Cases Other Than Medical Malpractice Cases.* The discovery and court reform amendments which became effective July 1, 1992 authorized the conduct of what is termed a Comprehensive Pretrial Conference to facilitate case management and judicial control. At a Comprehensive Pretrial Conference requested or ordered pursuant to Rule 16(b), the Court may consider and resolve any or all of the items specified in that Rule, the coverage of which was limited to cases other than medical malpractice cases by the 2000 amendments. A Comprehensive Pretrial Conference may be held upon written request of any party or upon the Court's own motion. Rule 16(a) authorizes the conduct of pretrial conferences by telephone, with leave of court. Presumably, that authority extends to the conduct of Comprehensive Pretrial Conferences as well.

A Comment with regard to Rule 16(g) was added in 1993, pointing out that, before the conduct of any Comprehensive Pretrial Conference, counsel for the parties should confer as to whether it is feasible to resolve the parties' disputes through alternative dispute resolution methods. Effective January 1, 2013, Ariz. R. Civ. P. 16(g)(2) was abrogated.

The 2008 amendments to the Rule specifically authorized the trial court, at or following a comprehensive pretrial conference, to enter orders establishing requirements for or limitations upon the disclosure or discovery of electronically stored information, including the form in which such information is to be produced, setting forth what measures the parties must take to preserve discoverable information that is electronically stored, and adopting any agreements between the parties concerning asserting privilege claims as to such information after its production. The accompanying State Bar Committee Note stresses that, in entering preservation orders that might adversely impact the ongoing operation of a party's computer system, a court should consider the amount in controversy or type of relief requested, that preservation orders entered over objection should be narrowly tailored to the needs of the case, and that ex parte preservation orders should only be entered in exceptional circumstances.

4. *Comprehensive Pretrial Conferences in Medical Malpractice Cases.* In October 2000, the Arizona Supreme Court entered an Order abrogating the Uniform Rules of Practice of the Superior Court, the Uniform Rules of Procedure for Medical Malpractice Cases, and the Uniform Rules of Procedure for Arbitration as separate sets of procedural rules, and transferring their provisions to either the Arizona Rules of Civil Procedure or the Rules of the Arizona Supreme Court. Former Rule 16(c) was redesignated as Rule 16(b), and its coverage was limited to cases other than medical malpractice cases. Most of the provisions of former Rule 1(D) of the Uniform Rules of Procedure for Medical Malpractice Cases were incorporated into a new Rule 16(c), which deals with the subject of scheduling and conducting comprehensive pretrial conferences in medical malpractice cases.

The Comprehensive Pretrial Conference is the centerpiece of the procedural scheme adopted by the former Medical Malpractice Rules and is the proceeding at which the Court determines the future procedural course of the litigation. Under Rule 16(c), the triggering mechanism for the scheduling of the Comprehensive Pretrial Conference is a notice to the Court from the plaintiff that answers or motions (presumably motions under Rule 12) have been received from "all defendants who have been served." The Court, upon receipt of that notice, is to schedule the Comprehensive Pretrial Conference which must be conducted within sixty (60) days of receipt of the notice.

The language of the Rule which specifies the date for providing the requisite notice to the Court is somewhat vague and difficult to apply in cases where there are multiple defendants. It does not tie the date for providing notice to the receipt of answers and/or motions from *all* defendants, but rather from the receipt of such pleadings from "all defendants who have been served." Under new Rule 4(i), the plaintiff has a period of one hundred and twenty (120) days in which to secure service on the defendants. An answer or motion from a defendant served expeditiously could be received before service is even attempted on other defendants, and would trigger the requirement for providing notice to the Court under the literal language of the Rule. Indeed, in that circumstance, given the requirements of Rule 16(c), the Court could be required to conduct a Comprehensive Pretrial Conference before all defendants are served with process.

Within five (5) days of providing notice to the Court that answers or motions have been received from all defendants who have been served, the plaintiff is required, by Rule 26.2(A), to serve upon the defendants copies of all the medical records of plaintiff that are available and that are relevant to the condition that is in issue in the case. Within ten (10) days of service of the plaintiff's medical records, each defendant is to serve on the plaintiff copies of medical records of the plaintiff which are relevant to the condition in issue. In lieu of serving copies of all such medical records, counsel may confer and agree to produce only those records which are specifically requested.

Rule 26.2(B) specifies the limited discovery that the parties may undertake prior to the conduct of the Comprehensive Pretrial Conference. The Appendix of Forms following Rule 84 now contains the three sets of uniform interrogatories for use in medical malpractice cases that were previously part of the Uniform Rules of Procedure for Medical Malpractice Cases. To view these sets of uniform interrogatories, please see the current Edition of the publication *Arizona Rules of Court—State and Federal*. (The Court of Appeals has held that, as formulated, Interrogatory No. 17 of Set B of these uniform interrogatories seeks information protected from disclosure by the "peer review privilege," created by A.R.S. § 36-445.01. *Yuma Regional Medical Center v. Superior Court In and For County of Yuma*, 175 Ariz. 72, 852 P.2d 1256 (Ct. App. Div. 1 1993).) Before the Comprehensive Pretrial Conference, the parties may exchange those uniform interrogatories and ten (10) additional non-uniform interrogatories. Any subpart of a non-uniform interrogatory is considered a separate interrogatory. In addition, the parties may also submit a request for production under Rule 34, but it may only seek production of documents reflecting a party's wage information, if relevant; written or recorded statements of a party or witness, including statements and reports of experts; exhibits intended to be used at trial; and, incident reports. Finally, the parties may conduct, during this period, the depositions of the parties and the depositions of any identified experts on the issue of liability. The Committee Comment to the Rule explains that the term "parties" encompasses managing agents of parties and any persons involved in the incident giving rise to the litigation.

Rule 26.2(B) specifically provides that no other discovery is permitted prior to the Comprehensive Pretrial Conference except by stipulation of the parties. The 1992 amendment to the predecessor to this Rule added a provision that stipulations for additional discovery during this period are not to be unreasonably withheld. Presumably, however, absent such a stipulation, requests for admissions under Rule 36 may not be served before the Conference.

The purpose of the Comprehensive Pretrial Conference is to permit the Court to assess the progress of the case to date and for the Court to establish a schedule for the future course of the litigation. While Rule 16(c) specifies certain matters that are to be considered at the Comprehensive Pretrial Conference, the listing is not exclusive of other matters affecting the course of the litigation that may be considered and resolved.

At the Comprehensive Pretrial Conference, the Court is to determine what further discovery may be undertaken in the case and establish a schedule for the completion of it. Rule 16(c)(5) also directs the Court to determine whether additional non-uniform interrogatories and/or requests for admission or production are necessary and, if so, the number that can be served. The use of the term "additional" in this subpart is partially inappropriate, as there will have been no requests for admissions propounded before the Comprehensive Pretrial Conference, unless the parties have stipulated to their use. The Court is also to resolve any discovery disputes that have been presented by appropriate motion at least ten (10) days prior to the conduct of the Conference.

The Court is also to establish a schedule for the disclosure of expert and non-expert witnesses which differs depending on the issue to which the expert's testimony will relate. Expert witnesses on the issues of the standard of care and of causation must be simultaneously disclosed on a date set by the Court within thirty (30) to ninety (90) days after the Conference. No motion for summary judgment based upon the lack of expert testimony may be filed before the date set for simultaneous disclosure absent a showing of good cause.

The language of Rule 16(c)(3) suggests that the disclosure of all other expert witnesses and all non-expert witnesses need not be simultaneous. The Court is to determine the order of and dates for such disclosures, but the final date for all disclosures must be at least forty-five (45) days before the date set for the completion of discovery. Any witness not thus disclosed is precluded from testifying at trial absent a showing of "extraordinary circumstances." The Court's Comment to the 1992 amendments to the Medical Malpractice Rules suggests that "extraordinary circumstances" require more than the showing of good cause which is the standard under Rule 26(e). On the other hand, the

Court of Appeals held that this provision is to be given the same flexible, common sense approach as pertains under the sanction provisions applicable to disclosures mandated under Rule 26.1. *Aguirre v. Robert Forrest, P.A.*, 186 Ariz. 393, 923 P.2d 859 (Ct. App. Div. 2 1996).

At the Comprehensive Pretrial Conference, the parties are to discuss the possibility of using alternative dispute resolution mechanisms for resolving the controversy, and the Court is to set the date for the conduct of the settlement conference required by Rule 16.1. The Court is also to set a date for trial and a date for the submission of the pretrial statement required by Rule 16(d). The Court has the authority, under Rule 16(f), to impose sanctions for the failure to appear for the Comprehensive Pretrial Conference, the failure to participate in good faith, or the failure to be substantially prepared to participate.

Finally, Rule 16(c)(8) retains the requirement that the Court, at the Comprehensive Pretrial Conference, assure that there has been compliance with the requirements of A.R.S. § 12-570, which formerly required that the plaintiff report the medical malpractice claim to the appropriate health care regulatory authority. That statute has been amended since the adoption of the Rule, and now only requires that the attorney for the plaintiff in a medical malpractice case notify, and provide certain specified information concerning the claim to, the board which regulates the defendant's health profession, within thirty (30) days after a settlement of the claim is reached or a monetary judgment is entered. Whether there has been compliance with the requirements of the statute, as thus amended, is obviously not a matter that can be determined at the time the Comprehensive Pretrial Conference is conducted.

The 1992 amendments to the Medical Malpractice Rules added a specific provision to what is now Rule 16(c)(1), limiting the depositions that could be conducted following the Comprehensive Pretrial Conference to those specifically authorized by the Court at the Conference, except upon stipulation of the parties or with leave of Court based upon a showing of good cause. The Rules contain no specific provision similarly limiting the use of other forms of discovery following the Comprehensive Pretrial Conference. The sense of the Rules, however, would suggest that, absent an agreement of the parties or leave of Court, the only discovery that can be conducted between the Comprehensive Pretrial Conference and the trial is that discussed at the Conference and included in the discovery schedule that is established at the Conference.

The Rules do contain a provision, added by the 1992 amendments, that stipulations to conduct additional discovery are not to be withheld unreasonably. That provision, however, was inserted into what is now Rule 26.2(B), which generally governs discovery *prior to* the Comprehensive Pretrial Conference, and it is not certain whether it was intended to apply to the conduct of discovery in subsequent stages of the case as well.

Rule 16(c)(4) specifies that the Court, at the Comprehensive Pretrial Conference, is to limit the number of expert witnesses that the parties may call to testify at trial, in accordance with the requirements of Rule 26(b)(4)(D). Each *party* is presumptively entitled to only one expert on the issue of the standard of care; each *side* is presumptively entitled to only one expert on any other issue. The Committee Comment points out that, if the case involves more than one medical discipline, each party may call an expert on the standard of care in each separate discipline involved.

The Rule says nothing about the listing or disclosure of experts. *Perguson v. Tamis*, 188 Ariz. 425, 937 P.2d 347 (Ct. App. Div. 2 1996). If a party lists more than one such expert, or lists overlapping experts, that party is to be ordered to limit the number of experts to what the Rule contemplates. *Perguson v. Tamis*, 188 Ariz. 425, 937 P.2d 347 (Ct. App. Div. 2 1996). It is the party, however, and not the Court or the adverse party, who should select what expert will or will not be used at trial. *Perguson v. Tamis*, 188 Ariz. 425, 937 P.2d 347 (Ct. App. Div. 2 1996).

Before the 1992 amendments, there was an issue as to whether, if the defendant health care provider testified and offered an opinion as to compliance with the applicable standard of care, that constituted the single expert witness to which that party was entitled. The 1992 amendment to former Rule 1(D)(4) answered that question clearly and definitively. A health care provider defendant may testify on the issue of that defendant's compliance with the applicable standard of care, and still be entitled to an additional independent expert witness on that issue. If both the defendant and an independent expert witness called by that defendant testify as to the standard of care issue, the Court is not *required* to allow the plaintiff an additional expert on the standard of care. The phrasing of the amendment implies that the Court is free to permit the plaintiff to call an additional expert in that situation, if circumstances warrant that. Similarly, when a treating physician testified about his or her treatment and whether another health care provider's treatment caused the harm to the plaintiff, the treating physician does not constitute that party's expert witness on causation, precluding testimony by any other expert on that issue, because the treating physician is not an "independent" or retained witness, which are the only types of expert witnesses the Rule is intended to limit. *Kuhn v. St. Joseph's Hosp. and Medical Center*, 194 Ariz. 465,

984 P.2d 551 (Ct. App. Div. 1 1998), review denied and opinion ordered not published, 195 Ariz. 574, 991 P.2d 804 (2000).

5. *Alternative Dispute Resolution.* Former Rule I(a) of the now abrogated Uniform Rules of Practice of the Superior Court, was amended in 1991 to give the presiding judge in each county the authority to identify and develop alternative dispute resolution programs to be governed by Local Rules approved by a majority of judges in the county. This authority is now provided by Rule 92(a) of the Rules of the Arizona Supreme Court.

Under Ariz.R.Civ.P. 16(g)(1), the Court, on motion of any party or on its own initiative after consultation with the parties, may direct the parties in a civil action to submit their dispute to such an authorized alternative dispute resolution program. It is probably the case that the Court cannot make the result of any such program binding on the parties without their consent. A 1994 amendment clarified that the trial court's authority to direct submission of a case to such an authorized alternative dispute resolution program applies even in cases which are already subject to compulsory arbitration.

Former Rule 16(g)(2), which set forth meet, confer and report requirements pertaining to alternative dispute resolution, was abrogated effective January 1, 2013, together with Form 3 [Joint Alternative Dispute Resolution Statement to the Court] located in the Appendix to Rule 84.

6. *Pretrial Statements.* In October 2000, the Arizona Supreme Court issued an Order which abrogated the Uniform Rules of Practice of the Superior Court, the Uniform Rules of Practice for Medical Malpractice Cases, and the Uniform Rules of Procedure for Arbitration as separate sets of procedural rules, and transferred most of their provisions to either the Arizona Rules of Civil Procedure or the Rules of the Arizona Supreme Court. The provisions of former Rules VI(a) and (b) of the Uniform Rules of Practice of the Superior Court, and one provision from former Rule VIII(a) of those Rules, were incorporated into an expanded Rule 16(d), the title of which was modified to reflect those changes.

Rule 16(d) was extensively amended in 2008 to change the procedure for accomplishing preparation of the final pretrial statement, and to significantly change its prescribed contents. A joint written pretrial statement must be prepared by the parties or counsel who will actually try the case, and it is to be filed five (5) days before the final pretrial conference or, if no such conference has been scheduled, five (5) days before trial. The provision that the pretrial statement was to be prepared at the initiative of counsel for the plaintiff was deleted. Under the Rule, as amended, the plaintiff is to submit plaintiff's portion of the joint pretrial statement to all parties no later than twenty (20) days before it is due, and all other parties are to submit their portions to all parties no later than fifteen (15) days before it is due.

The prescribed contents of the joint pretrial statement are now the following:

1) stipulations of material fact and law;

2) such contested issues of fact and law as counsel can agree are material;

3) a separate statement from each party as to any other issues of fact or law deemed material;

4) a list of witnesses intended to be used by each party at trial together with any objections a party has to a witness and the basis for such objection;

5) each party's final list of exhibits to be used at trial including those to be used for impeachment. Plaintiff is to deliver copies of the plaintiff's exhibits to all parties twenty (20) days before the final pretrial conference. All other parties are to deliver copies of all their exhibits to all parties fifteen (15) days before the final pretrial conference. Any exhibit that cannot be reproduced must be made available for inspection. Each party is to list in the joint pretrial statement any objections to an exhibit and the basis for it. The parties must also indicate any exhibits which they stipulate can be admitted into evidence;

6) a statement from each party indicating any proposed deposition summaries, or designating portions of any deposition testimony, to be offered by that party at trial, other than for impeachment purposes. Deposition testimony is to be designated by transcript page and line numbers, and a copy of any proposed deposition summary and/or of a written transcript of any designated deposition testimony, is to be filed together with the joint pretrial statement. The parties must also list any objections to the proposed deposition summaries and designated deposition testimony and the bases for them;

7) a brief statement of the case to be read to the jury during voir dire. If the parties cannot agree on such a statement, each is to submit a separate statement and the judge is to determine the contents of the statement to be read;

8) any technical equipment needed or interpreters requested;

9) the number of jurors and alternates agreed upon, whether the alternates may deliberate, and the number of jurors required to return a verdict;

10) whether any party will invoke Rule 615 of the Arizona Rules of Evidence concerning the exclusion of evidence; and

11) a brief description of settlement efforts.

In addition, the parties must file, at the same time as the joint pretrial statement is filed, an agreed-upon set of jury instructions, verdict forms and voir dire questions, any additional jury instructions, verdict forms and voir dire questions requested but not agreed to, and a statement by each party as to how a verbatim record of the trial will be made. Any party who intends to submit a jury notebook must submit a copy of it to opposing counsel five (5) days before the final pretrial conference, or five (5) days before trial, if no final pretrial conference is held. A party submitting a trial memorandum must file it at the same time.

Previously, former Rule VI of the Uniform Rules of Practice contained provisions exempting from the requirement of being listed in the pretrial statement witnesses and exhibits to be used solely for purposes of impeachment. *Zimmerman v. Superior Court In and For Maricopa County*, 98 Ariz. 85, 402 P.2d 212, 18 A.L.R.3d 909 (1965); *Helena Chemical Co. v. Coury Bros. Ranches, Inc.*, 126 Ariz. 448, 616 P.2d 908 (Ct. App. Div. 1 1980). The names of such "impeachment" witnesses and copies of such "impeachment" exhibits were to be submitted to the Clerk in a sealed envelope before the commencement of trial and revealed only when actually used for impeachment purposes. The restrictive definition given to what constituted evidence to be used solely for impeachment purposes, however, caused this regime to become a trap for the unwary and the exemption was consequently removed. All witnesses and exhibits intended to be used at trial, even those to be used for impeachment purposes, must now be listed in the pretrial statement.

In certain counties, the Superior Court has adopted a Local Rule specifying a different time for filing the pretrial statement, unless the trial judge sets a different schedule. In Yavapai County, the date for filing the pretrial statement is thirty (30) days before the date set for trial. Rule 6(A), Yavapai County Superior Court Local Rules. In La Paz County, the deadline is twenty (20) days before trial. Rule 4, La Paz County Superior Court Local Rules. In Apache County, the deadline is no later than fifteen (15) days before the date of trial. Rule 20(a), Apache County Superior Court Local Rules. Cochise County requires that the pretrial statement be filed at least ten (10) "working days" before the trial date. Rule 22, Cochise County Superior Court Local Rules. Finally, Mohave County requires that the pretrial statement be filed at least five (5) days before trial. Rule 7(B), Mohave County Superior Court Local Rules.

The joint pretrial statement controls the subsequent course of the litigation through trial unless it is modified by the Court to prevent manifest injustice. *Murcott v. Best Western Intern., Inc.*, 198 Ariz. 349, 9 P.3d 1088, 16 I.E.R. Cas. (BNA) 1277 (Ct. App. Div. 1 2000), as amended, (Oct. 16, 2000); *Carlton v. Emhardt*, 138 Ariz. 353, 674 P.2d 907 (Ct. App. Div. 2 1983); *Gertz v. Selin*,

11 Ariz. App. 495, 466 P.2d 46 (Div. 1 1970); *Loya v. Fong*, 1 Ariz. App. 482, 404 P.2d 826 (1965). Thus, under former Rule VI(a)(4) of the Uniform Rules of Practice of the Superior Court, and presumably under amended Rule 16(d), the trial court has the discretion to permit the calling of a witness not listed in the pretrial statement "for good cause." *Sheppard v. Crow-Barker Paul No. 1 Ltd. Partnership*, 192 Ariz. 539, 968 P.2d 612 (Ct. App. Div. 1 1998). Any stipulations made during a pretrial conference or in the pretrial statement are binding unless the parties are relieved from them by the Court. *Harsh Bldg. Co. v. Bialac*, 22 Ariz. App. 591, 529 P.2d 1185 (Div. 1 1975). The pretrial statement in effect amends the pleadings and can add for trial affirmative defenses not raised in the original pleadings. *Murcott v. Best Western Intern., Inc.*, 198 Ariz. 349, 9 P.3d 1088, 16 I.E.R. Cas. (BNA) 1277 (Ct. App. Div. 1 2000), as amended on other grounds, (Oct. 16, 2000); *Ries v. McComb*, 25 Ariz. App. 554, 545 P.2d 65 (Div. 1 1976). That will not be the case, however, unless the adverse party has stipulated in the pretrial statement that the issue in question is material and applicable. *Lake Havasu Community Hosp., Inc. v. Arizona Title Ins. and Trust Co.*, 141 Ariz. 363, 687 P.2d 371 (Ct. App. Div. 1 1984) (disapproved of on other grounds by, Barmat v. John and Jane Doe Partners A-D, 155 Ariz. 519, 747 P.2d 1218 (1987)).

7. *Trial Time Limitations.* Rule 16(h), added by a 1995 amendment to the Rule, provides that the Court may impose "reasonable time limits on the trial proceedings or portions thereof." While trial courts have the discretion to place time limitations on trial proceedings to avoid undue delay, waste of time or needless presentation of cumulative evidence, any limits imposed must be reasonable under the circumstances and rigid limits are disfavored. *Gamboa v. Metzler*, 223 Ariz. 399, 224 P.3d 215 (Ct. App. Div. 1 2010); *Brown v. U.S. Fidelity and Guar. Co.*, 194 Ariz. 85, 977 P.2d 807 (Ct. App. Div. 1 1998), as amended, (Nov. 25, 1998) and as corrected, (Aug. 5, 1999). Any time limits imposed should be sufficiently flexible to allow for adjustment during trial. *Gamboa v. Metzler*, 223 Ariz. 399, 224 P.3d 215 (Ct. App. Div. 1 2010); *Brown v. U.S. Fidelity and Guar. Co.*, 194 Ariz. 85, 977 P.2d 807 (Ct. App. Div. 1 1998), as amended, (Nov. 25, 1998) and as corrected, (Aug. 5, 1999).

The time limitations imposed will be reviewed on appeal for abuse of discretion. To merit reversal, a party must show they incurred some harm as a consequence of the court's time limitation. *Gamboa v. Metzler*, 223 Ariz. 399, 224 P.3d 215 (Ct. App. Div. 1 2010); *Brown v. U.S. Fidelity and Guar. Co.*, 194 Ariz. 85, 977 P.2d 807 (Ct. App. Div. 1 1998), as amended, (Nov. 25, 1998) and as corrected, (Aug. 5, 1999).

8. *Sanctions.* As part of the court and discovery reform amend-

ments, Rule 16(f) was also amended to enhance the Court's ability to insure meaningful participation in, and compliance with, pretrial case management procedures. Amended Rule 16(f) authorizes sanctions for failure to appear at a pretrial conference, failure to be substantially prepared to participate in a pretrial conference, failure to participate in good faith at a pretrial conference, and/or failure to comply with a pretrial or scheduling order. *See, Estate of Lewis v. Lewis*, 229 Ariz. 316, 275 P.3d 615 (Ct. App. Div. 2 2012) (under the facts presented, reversing Rule 16(f) sanctions of default and dismissal entered without a hearing for failure to comply with a court order to personally appear at a scheduled pretrial conference; finding the "non-aggravated circumstances of this case and the ambiguous nature of the trial court's order to appear would not permit the drastic sanctions imposed . . . .").

Sanctions are virtually mandatory unless there is a showing of good cause and may include an order to pay to the Clerk of the Court an assessment determined by the trial judge. *But see, Estate of Lewis v. Lewis*, 229 Ariz. 316, 275 P.3d 615 (Ct. App. Div. 2 2012). Any monetary sanctions imposed must bear some relationship to the expenses caused by the offending conduct. *Taliaferro v. Taliaferro*, 188 Ariz. 333, 935 P.2d 911 (Ct. App. Div. 1 1996). It has previously been held, however, that dismissal of an action may be too severe a sanction to impose for counsel's failure to attend a pretrial conference. *Stoyer v. Doctors Hospital, Inc.*, 15 Ariz. App. 255, 488 P.2d 191, 55 A.L.R.3d 295 (Div. 1 1971).

In addition, Rule 16(d) provides that a witness or exhibit not listed in the joint pretrial statement may not be used at trial except for good cause shown. The failure to comply with the Rule's requirement that all trial exhibits be listed and exchanged is sufficient basis for refusing to admit into evidence at trial an exhibit not so listed and exchanged. *Norman v. Del Elia*, 111 Ariz. 480, 533 P.2d 537 (1975). Generally, however, that is a discretionary decision with the trial court, and the exclusion of evidence for failure to list a witness or exhibit in the pretrial statement will only be ordered where there is no good reason advanced for the failure to do so, and there will be demonstrable prejudice to the opposing party from admitting it. *Sheppard v. Crow-Barker Paul No. 1 Ltd. Partnership*, 192 Ariz. 539, 968 P.2d 612 (Ct. App. Div. 1 1998); *Acosta v. Superior Court, In and For Pima County*, 146 Ariz. 437, 706 P.2d 763 (Ct. App. Div. 2 1985); *Calderon v. Calderon*, 9 Ariz. App. 538, 454 P.2d 586 (1969); *Wright v. Demeter*, 8 Ariz. App. 65, 442 P.2d 888 (1968); *cf. also, Grant v. Arizona Public Service Co.*, 133 Ariz. 434, 652 P.2d 507 (1982).

Rule 16. Scheduling and management of cases (2014 amendment)

Text of Rule 16 applicable to cases filed on or after April 15, 2014 and to those cases filed before April 15, 2014 that are subject to the conditions stated in the November 27, 2013, Amended Order Regarding Applicability Provision, in R-13-0017.

See also, text of Rule 16 applicable to those cases filed before April 15, 2014 that are not subject to the conditions stated in the November 27, 2013 Amended Order Regarding Applicability Provision, in R-13-0017.

(a) Objectives of Case Management. In accordance with Rule 1, the court shall manage a civil action with the following objectives:

(1) expediting a just disposition of the action;

(2) establishing early and continuing control so that the case will not be protracted because of lack of management;

(3) discouraging wasteful, expensive and duplicative pretrial activities;

(4) improving the quality of case resolution through more thorough and timely preparation;

(5) facilitating the appropriate use of alternative dispute resolution;

(6) conserving parties' resources;

(7) managing the court's calendar to eliminate unnecessary trial settings and continuances; and

(8) adhering to applicable standards for timely resolution of civil actions.

Amended Aug. 7, 1984, effective Nov. 1, 1984; Sept. 15, 1987, effective Nov. 15, 1987; Oct. 10, 2000, effective Dec. 1, 2000. Amended Aug. 28, 2013, effective April 15, 2014, subject to the conditions of Order No. R-13-0017.

(b) Joint Report and Proposed Scheduling Order.

(1) This section (b) applies to all civil actions except:

A. Medical malpractice cases;

B. Cases subject to compulsory arbitration under Rule 72(b);

C. Cases designated complex under Rule 8(i)(6); and

D. Cases seeking the following relief:

i. Change of name;

ii. Forcible entry and detainer;

iii. Enforcement, domestication, transcript, or renewal of a judgment;

iv. An order pertaining to a subpoena sought pursuant to Rule 45.1(e);

v. Restoration of civil rights;

vi. Injunction against harassment or workplace harassment;

vii. Delayed birth certificate;

viii. Amendment of birth certificate or marriage license;

ix. Civil forfeiture;

x. Distribution of excess proceeds;

xi. Review of a decision of an agency or a court of limited jurisdiction; and

xii. Declarations of factual innocence under Rule 57.1 or factual improper party status under Rule 57.2.

(2) No later than 60 days after any defendant has filed an answer to the complaint or 180 days after commencement of the action, whichever occurs first, the parties shall confer regarding the subjects set forth in Rule 16(d). No later than 14 days after the parties confer, they shall file a Joint Report and a Proposed Scheduling Order with the court stating, to the extent practicable, their positions on the subjects set forth in Rule 16(d) and proposing a Scheduling Order that specifies by calendar date, month, and year deadlines for the following:

(A) service of initial disclosures under Rule 26.1 if they have not already been served;

(B) identification of areas of expert testimony;

(C) identification of and disclosure of expert witnesses and their opinions in accordance with Rule 26.1(a)(6);

(D) propounding of written discovery;

(E) disclosure of non-expert witnesses;

(F) completion of depositions;

(G) completion of all discovery other than depositions;

(H) final supplementation of Rule 26.1 disclosures;

(I) holding a Rule 16.1 settlement conference or private mediation;

(J) filing of dispositive motions;

(K) a proposed trial date; and

(L) the anticipated number of days for trial.

Unless otherwise ordered by the court for good cause shown, the parties' Proposed Scheduling Order shall state the deadlines for completing discovery and for holding a Rule 16.1 settlement conference or private mediation to occur no more than 15 months after the commencement of the action. The Joint Report shall certify that the parties conferred regarding the subjects set forth in Rule 16(d). The attorneys of record and all unrepresented parties that have appeared in the case are jointly responsible for arranging and participating in the conference, for attempting in good faith to agree on a Proposed Scheduling Order, and for filing the Joint Report and the Proposed Scheduling Order with the court.

(3) The Joint Report and the Proposed Scheduling Order shall be filed using the forms approved by the Supreme Court and set forth in Forms 11-13, Rule 84, Appendix of Forms.

(A) *Expedited*: The parties shall use Forms 11(a) and (b) (Expedited Case) when all of the following factors apply:

(i) Every party except defaulted parties has filed an answer;

(ii) There are no third party claims;

(iii) The parties intend to have no more than one expert per side; and

(iv) Each party intends to call no more than four lay witnesses at trial.

(B) *Standard*: The parties shall use Forms 12(a) and (b) (Standard Case) if the case is not eligible for management as an Expedited Case or Complex Case.

(C) *Complex*: The parties shall use Forms 13(a) and (b) (Complex Case) if the factors enumerated in Rule 8(i)(2) apply, regardless of whether the case has been designated as complex by the court.Upon request of any party, the court may designate any case as expedited, standard, or complex. The court shall endeavor to conduct trial in expedited cases within twelve months after the commencement of the action.

Added Aug. 28, 2013, revised Sept. 6, 2013, effective April 15, 2014, subject to the conditions of Order No. R-13-0017.

(c) Scheduling Orders. The court shall issue a Scheduling Order as soon as practicable after receiving the parties' Joint Report and their Proposed Scheduling Order under Rule 16(b) or after holding a Scheduling Conference. The Scheduling Order shall establish calendar deadlines specifying the month, date, and year for each of the items included in the Proposed Scheduling Order submitted pursuant to Rule 16(b). The Scheduling Order shall also set either (1) a trial date or (2) a date for a Trial-Setting Conference under Rule 16(f) at which a trial date may be set. Absent leave of court, no trial shall be set unless the parties certify that they engaged in a settlement conference or private mediation or that they will do so by a date certain established by the court. The Scheduling Order may address other appropriate matters. The dates established in a Scheduling Order that govern court filings or hearings may be modified only for good cause and with the court's consent. Once a trial date is set, it may be modified only pursuant to Rule 38.1.

Added Aug. 28, 2013, effective April 15, 2014, subject to the conditions of Order No. R-13-0017.

Comment to 2014 Amendment

A primary goal of civil case management is the creation of public confidence in a predictable court calendar. Courts should avoid overlapping trial settings that necessitate continuances when the court is unable to hold a trial on the date scheduled. Continuances of scheduled trial dates impose unnecessary costs and inconvenience when counsel, parties, witnesses, and courts are required to engage in redundant preparation. Although early trial settings may be appropriate, a court should employ a case management system that ensures it will be in a position to conduct each trial on the date it has been set.

(d) Scheduling Conferences in Non-Medical Malpractice Cases. Except in medical malpractice cases, upon written request of any party the court shall, or upon its own motion the court may, set a Scheduling Conference. At any Scheduling Conference under this Rule 16(d), the court may:

(1) Determine the additional disclosures, discovery and related activities to be undertaken and a schedule therefor.

(2) Discuss which form of Joint Report and Scheduling Order is appropriate under Rule 16(b)(3).

(3) Determine whether the court should enter orders addressing one or more of the following:

(A) setting forth any requirements or limitations for the disclosure or discovery of electronically stored information, including the form or forms in which the electronically stored information should be produced;

(B) setting forth any measures the parties must take to preserve discoverable documents or electronically stored information; and

(C) adopting any agreements the parties reach for asserting claims of privilege or of protection as to trial preparation materials after production.

(4) Determine a schedule for the disclosure of expert witnesses and the method of such disclosure, including whether signed reports from the experts should be required.

(5) Determine the number of expert witnesses or designate expert witnesses as set forth in Rule 26(b)(4)(D).

(6) Determine a date for the disclosure of non-expert witnesses and the order of their disclosure.

(7) Determine a deadline for the filing of dispositive motions.

(8) Resolve any discovery disputes.

(9) Eliminate non-meritorious claims or defenses.

(10) Permit the amendment of the pleadings.

(11) Assist in identifying those issues of fact which are still at issue.

(12) Obtain stipulations as to the foundation or admissibility of evidence.

(13) Determine the desirability of special procedures for management of the case.

(14) Consider alternative dispute resolution and determine a deadline for the parties to participate in a settlement conference or private mediation.

(15) Determine whether any time limits or procedures set forth in the discovery rules or set forth in these rules or Local Rules of Practice should be modified or suspended.

(16) Determine whether Rule 26.1 has been appropriately complied with by the parties.

(17) Determine a date for filing the Joint Pretrial Statement required by section (g) of these Rules.

(18) Discuss the imposition of time limits on trial proceedings or portions thereof, the use of juror notebooks, the giving of brief pre-voir dire opening statements and preliminary jury instructions, and the effective management of documents and exhibits.

(19) Determine how verbatim record of future proceedings in the case will be made.

(20) Discuss such other matters and make such other orders as the court deems appropriate.

Formerly 16(c). Amended Aug. 7, 1984, effective Nov. 1, 1984; Dec. 1991, effective July 1, 1992. Redesignated 16(b) by amendment of Oct. 10, 2000, effective Dec. 1, 2000. Amended Sept. 18, 2006, effective Jan. 1, 2007; Sept. 5, 2007, effective Jan. 1, 2008. Renumbered Rule 16(d) and amended Aug. 28, 2013, effective April 15, 2014, subject to the conditions of Order No. R-13-0017.

(e) Scheduling and Subject Matter at Comprehensive Pretrial Conferences in Medical Malpractice Cases. In medical malpractice cases, within five days of receiving answers or motions from all defendants who have been served, plaintiff shall notify the court to whom the case has been assigned so that a comprehensive pretrial conference can be set. Within 60 days of receiving the notice, the court shall conduct a comprehensive pretrial conference. At that conference, the court and the parties shall:

(1) Determine the discovery to be undertaken and a schedule therefor. The schedule shall include the depositions to be taken, any medical examination which defendant desires to be made of plaintiff and what additional documents, electronically stored information, and other materials are to be exchanged. Only

those depositions specifically authorized in the comprehensive pretrial conference shall be allowed except upon stipulation of the parties or upon motion and a showing of good cause. The court, upon request of any defendant, shall require an authorization to allow the parties to obtain copies of records previously produced under Rule 26.2(A)(2) of these Rules or records ordered to be produced by the court. If records are obtained pursuant to such authorization, the party obtaining the records shall furnish complete copies to all other parties at the sole expense of the party obtaining the records.

(2) Determine a schedule for the disclosure of standard of care and causation expert witnesses. Except upon good cause shown, such disclosure shall be simultaneous and within 30 to 90 days after the conference, depending upon the number and complexity of the issues. No motion for summary judgment based upon the lack of expert testimony will be filed prior to the expiration of the date set for the simultaneous disclosure of expert witnesses except upon a showing of good cause.

(3) Determine the order of and dates for the disclosure of all other expert and non-expert witnesses, provided that the date for disclosure of all witnesses, expert and non-expert, shall be at least 45 days before the close of discovery. Any witnesses not appropriately disclosed shall be precluded from testifying at trial unless there is a showing of extraordinary circumstances.

(4) Limit the number of experts as provided in Rule 26(b)(4)(D) of these Rules.

(5) Determine whether additional non-uniform interrogatories and/or requests for admission or production are necessary and, if so, limit the number.

(6) Resolve any discovery disputes.

(7) Discuss alternative dispute resolution, including mediation, and binding and non-binding arbitration.

(8) Assure compliance with A.R.S. § 12-570.

(9) Set a date for a mandatory settlement conference.

(10) Set a date for filing the Joint Pretrial Statement required by subpart (g) of this Rule.

(11) Set a trial date.

(12) Determine how verbatim record of future proceedings in the case will be made.

(13) Discuss such other matters and make such other orders as the court deems appropriate.

Formerly Rule 16(c), added Oct. 10, 2000, effective Dec. 1, 2000. Amended Sept. 18, 2006, effective Jan. 1, 2007; Sept. 5, 2007, effective Jan. 1, 2008. Renumbered Rule 16(e) and amended, Aug. 28, 2013, effective April 15, 2014, subject to the conditions of Order No. R-13-0017.

(f) Trial-Setting Conference.

(1) If the Court has not already set a trial date in a Scheduling Order or otherwise, the court shall hold a Trial-Setting Conference, as set by the Scheduling Order, for the purpose of setting a trial date. The conference shall be attended in person or telephonically (as permitted by the court) by at least one of the attorneys who will conduct the trial for each of the parties and by any unrepresented parties.

(2) In addition to setting a trial date, the court may discuss at the Trial-Setting Conference:

(A) The status of discovery and any dispositive motions that have been or will be filed.

(B) A date for holding a Trial Management Conference under Rule 16(g).

(C) The imposition of time limits on trial proceedings or portions thereof.

(D) The use of juror questionnaires.

(E) The use of juror notebooks.

(F) The giving of brief pre-voir dire opening statements and preliminary jury instructions.

(G) The effective management of documents and exhibits.

(H) Such other matters as the court deems appropriate.

(3) If for any reason a trial date is not set at the Trial-Setting Conference, the court shall schedule another Trial-Setting Conference as soon as practicable for the setting of a trial date.

Added Aug. 28, 2013, effective April 15, 2014, subject to the conditions of Order No. R-13-0017.

(g) Joint Pretrial Statement: Preparation; Trial Management Conference.

(1) Counsel or the unrepresented parties who will try the case and who are authorized to make binding stipulations shall confer and prepare a written joint pretrial statement, signed by each counsel or party, that shall be filed ten days before the date of the Trial Management Conference, or if no conference is scheduled, ten days before trial. Plaintiffs shall submit their portion of the Joint Pretrial Statement to all parties no later than twenty days before the statement is due. All other parties shall submit their portion of the Joint Pretrial Statement to all parties no later than fifteen days before the statement is due.

(2) The Joint Pretrial Statement shall be prepared by the parties as a single document and contain the following:

(A) Stipulations of material fact and law;

(B) Such contested issues of fact and law as counsel can agree are material or applicable;

(C) A separate statement by each party of other issues of fact and law believed by that party to be material;

(D) A list of witnesses intended to be used by each party during trial. Each party shall list any objections to a witness and the basis for that objection. No witness shall be used at the trial other than those listed, except for good cause shown. Witnesses whose testimony will be received by deposition testimony only will be so indicated;

(E) Each party's final list of exhibits to be used at trial for any purpose, including impeachment. Plaintiffs shall deliver copies of all of their exhibits to all parties twenty days before the Trial Management Conference. All other parties shall deliver copies of all their exhibits to all parties fifteen days before the Trial Management Conference. Any exhibit that cannot be reproduced must be made available for inspection to all parties on or before the deadlines stated above. Each party shall list any objections to an exhibit and the basis for that objection. No exhibit shall be used at the trial other than those listed, except for good cause shown. The parties shall indicate any exhibits which the parties stipulate can be admitted into evidence, such stipulations being subject to court approval;

(F) A statement by each party indicating any proposed deposition summaries or designating portions of any deposition testimony to be offered by that party at trial, other than for impeachment purposes. Deposition testimony shall be designated by transcript page and line numbers. A copy of any proposed deposition summary and written transcript of designated deposition testimony should be filed with the Joint Pretrial Statement. Each party shall list any objections to the proposed deposition summaries and designated deposition testimony and the basis for any objections. Except for good cause shown, no deposition testimony shall be used at trial other than that designated or counter-designated or for impeachment purposes;

(G) A brief statement of the case to be read to the jury during voir dire. If the parties cannot agree on this statement, then each party shall submit a separate statement to the judge who will decide the contents of the statement to be read to the jury;

(H) Technical equipment needed or interpreters requested;

(I) The number of jurors and alternates agreed upon, whether the alternates may deliberate, and the number of jurors required to reach a verdict;

(J) Whether any party will be invoking Rule 615 of the Arizona Rules of Evidence regarding exclusion of witnesses from the courtroom; and

(K) A brief description of settlement efforts.

(3) At the time of the filing of the Joint Pretrial Statement, the parties shall file (A) an agreed-upon set of jury instructions, verdict forms, and voir dire questions, (B) any additional jury instructions, verdict forms, and voir dire questions requested, but not agreed upon, and (C) a statement by each party on how a verbatim record of the trial will be made.

(4) A party intending to submit a jury notebook to the jurors shall serve a copy of the notebook on the other parties five days before the Trial Management Conference, or, if no conference is scheduled, five days before the trial.

(5) Any trial memoranda shall be filed five days before the Trial Management Conference, or, if no conference is scheduled, five days before the trial.

(6) Any Trial Management Conference scheduled by the court shall be held as close to the time of trial as reasonable under the circumstances. The conference shall be attended by at least one of the attorneys who will conduct the trial for each of the parties and by any unrepresented parties.

(7) The provisions of this rule may be modified by order of the court.

Formerly Rule 16(d), amended Aug. 7, 1984, effective Nov. 1, 1984; Oct. 10, 2000, effective Dec. 1, 2000; Oct. 16, 2003, effective Dec. 1, 2003; Sept. 18, 2006, effective Jan. 1, 2007; Sept. 5, 2007, effective Jan. 1, 2008. Renumbered Rule 16(g) and amended, Aug. 28, 2014, effective April 15, 2014, subject to the conditions of Order No. R-13-0017.

(h) Pretrial Orders. After any conference held pursuant to this Rule, an order shall be entered reciting the action taken. This order shall control the subsequent course of the action unless modified by a subsequent order. The order following a Trial Management Conference under Rule 16(g) shall be modified only to prevent manifest injustice.

Formerly Rule 16(e), amended Aug. 7, 1984, effective Nov. 1, 1984. Renumbered Rule 16(h) and amended Aug. 28, 2013, effective April 15, 2014, subject to the conditions of Order No. R-13-0017.

(i) Sanctions. If a party or attorney fails to obey a scheduling or pretrial order or fails to meet the discovery, disclosure and other deadlines set forth therein, or if no appearance is made on behalf of a party at a Scheduling or Trial Management Conference, or if a party or party's attorney is substantially unprepared to participate in the conference, or if a party or party's attorney fails to participate in good faith in a Scheduling or Trial Management Conference or in the preparation of the Joint Report and Proposed Scheduling Order or Joint Pretrial Statement, the judge, upon motion or the judge's own initiative, shall, except upon a showing of good cause, make such orders with regard to such conduct as are just, including, among others, any of the orders provided in Rule 37(b)(2)(B), (C), or (D). The fact that a trial date has not been set does not preclude sanctions under this Rule, including the exclusion from evidence of untimely disclosed information. In lieu of or in addition to any other sanction, the judge shall require the party, or the attorney representing the party, or both, to pay the reasonable expenses incurred as the result of any noncompliance with this Rule, including attorneys' fees, or payment of an assessment to the clerk of the court, or both, unless the judge finds that the noncompliance was substantially justified, or that other circumstances make an award of expenses unjust.

Formerly Rule 16(f), amended Aug. 7, 1984, effective Nov. 1, 1984; Sept. 15, 1987, effective Nov. 15, 1987; Dec. 20, 1991, effective July 1, 1992; Oct. 10, 2000, effective Dec. 1, 2000. Renumbered Rule 16(i) and amended Aug. 28, 2013, effective April 15, 2014, subject to the conditions of Order No. R-13-0017.

(j) Alternative Dispute Resolution. Upon motion of any party, or upon its own initiative after consultation with the parties, the court may direct the parties in any action to submit the dispute which is the subject matter of the action to an alternative dispute resolution program created or authorized by appropriate local court rules.

Formerly Rule 16(g), added July 16, 1991, effective Oct. 1, 1991. Amended Oct. 6, 1994, effective Dec. 1, 1994; Oct. 22, 2001, effective Dec. 1, 2001. Rule 16(g)(2) abrogated August 30, 2012, effective January 1, 2013. Renumbered Rule 16(i) and amended Aug. 28, 2013, effective April 15, 2014, subject to the conditions of Order No. R-13-0017.

(k) Time Limitations. The court may impose reasonable time limits on the trial proceedings or portions thereof.

Rule 16(k) (2014) added Aug. 28, 2013, applicable April 15, 2014, subject to the conditions of Order No. R-13-0017.

HISTORICAL NOTES

[2014 Amendments]

[Rule 16] Arizona Supreme Court Order No. R-13-0017, issued Aug. 28, 2013, provided that the amendments of the order would be "effective on April 15, 2014 as to all cases filed on or after that date." The applicability provision of Order No. R-13-0017 was amended on Nov. 14, 2013, and subsequently amended on Nov. 27, 2013 to provide:

(1) The Amendments shall apply to all actions filed on or after April 15, 2014.

(2) Beginning on April 15, 2014, the Amendments also shall apply to any action filed prior to April 15, 2014 (a "pending action"), unless one of the following events has occurred before that date:

  (a) A party has filed a Motion to Set and Certificate of Readiness,

  (b) The parties have filed a Proposed Scheduling Order, or

  (c) The court has entered a Scheduling Order.

(3) If, in a pending action, one of the preceding events has not occurred

before April 15, 2014, the parties shall file a Joint Report and a Proposed Scheduling Order in accordance with the Amendments by June 30, 2014, or within 270 days after the commencement of the action, whichever date is later. Otherwise, the court will place the action on the Dismissal Calendar in accordance with the Amendments.

(4) A trial court, in its discretion, may apply any of the Amendments to a case pending before April 15, 2014, even if the Amendments would not otherwise apply under paragraph (2) above. For example, if a party filed a Motion to Set and Certificate of Readiness before April 15, 2014, the trial judge may set the matter for a trial setting conference under amended Rule 16(f), rather than place the case on the active calendar under pre-amendment Rule 38.1(c).

(5) Civil actions pending on the Inactive Calendar on April 15, 2014 shall be dismissed without prejudice on June 14, 2014, unless one of the actions set forth in subparts (1) - (4) of amended Rule 38.1(f) occurs before June 14, 2014.

AUTHORS' COMMENTS

Analysis

1. *Scope and Purpose of Rule.* Ariz. R. Civ. P. 16 (added 2014) was adopted as part of a larger project to align case management and trial setting procedures with current practice and, thereby, "acknowledge, by rule, what has become the reality in the vast majority of civil cases litigated in the State." *See,* Amended Petition filed In the Matter of Petition to Amend Rules 16, 16.1, 26, 37, 38, 38.1, 72, 73, 74 and 77, Arizona Rules of Civil Procedure, R-13-0017, page 2.

The general purpose of case management and trial setting procedures is discussed in the Authors' Comments to pre-amendment Rules 16 and 38.1 applicable to cases filed before April 15, 2014, which are not otherwise subject to the R-13-0017 rule amendments.

2. *Comparison With Federal Rule.* ARCP 16 (amended 2014) and FRCP 16 both concern pretrial case management matters, but there are significant differences between the rules. *See,* discussion in Section 2 of the Authors' Comments under Rule 16 ("Pretrial conferences; scheduling; management").

3. *2014 Rule Amendments: Effective Date and Applicability.* On August 28, 2013, the Arizona Supreme Court adopted sweeping amendments to the case management and trial setting rules governing civil cases. The Promulgating Order specified such rules were adopted "effective on April 15, 2014 as to all cases filed on or after that date." *See,* August 28, 2013 Order entered in

In the Matter of Petition to Amend Rules 16, 16.1, 26, 37, 38, 38.1, 72, 73, 74 and 77, Arizona Rules of Civil Procedure, R-13-0017. The applicability provision set forth in the Promulgating Order set up two procedural tracks for case management with the "new" rules governing cases file on or after April 15, 2014 and the "old" rules governing pre-April 15, 2014 cases.

To avoid any confusion potentially created by the two different tracks, the Court entered an order on November 14, 2013, amending the applicability provision. On November 27, 2013, the court entered a second order further refining the amended applicability provision. As a result, the 2014 case management/trial setting amendments are effective and applicable as follows:

"(1) The Amendments shall apply to all actions filed on or after April 15, 2014.

"(2) Beginning on April 15, 2014, the Amendments also shall apply to any action filed prior to April 15, 2014 (a "pending action"), unless one of the following events has occurred before that date:

(a) A party has filed a Motion to Set and Certificate of Readiness,

(b) The parties have filed a Proposed Scheduling Order, or

(c) The court has entered a Scheduling Order.

"(3) If, in a pending action, one of the preceding events has not occurred before April 15, 2014, the parties shall file a Joint Report and a Proposed Scheduling Order in accordance with the Amendments by June 30, 2014, or within 270 days after the commencement of the action, whichever date is later. Otherwise, the court will place the action on the Dismissal Calendar in accordance with the Amendments.

"(4) A trial court, in its discretion, may apply any of the Amendments to a case pending before April 15, 2014, even if the Amendments would not otherwise apply under paragraph (2) above. For example, if a party filed a Motion to Set and Certificate of Readiness before April 15, 2014, the trial judge may set the matter for a trial setting conference under amended Rule 16(f), rather than place the case on the active calendar under pre-amendment Rule 38.1(c).

"(5) Civil actions pending on the Inactive Calendar on April 15, 2014 shall be dismissed without prejudice on June 14, 2014, unless one of the actions set forth in subparts (1) - (4) of amended Rule 38.1(f) occurs before June 14, 2014."

Rule 16.1. Settlement conferences; objectives

Text of Rule 16.1(a) applicable to those cases filed before April 15, 2014 that are not subject to the conditions stated in the November 27, 2013 Amended Order Regarding Applicability Provision, in R-13-0017.

See also, text of Rule 16.1(a) applicable to cases filed on or after April 15, 2014 and to those cases filed before April 15, 2014 that are subject to the conditions stated in the November 27, 2013, Amended Order Regarding Applicability Provision, in R-13-0017.

(a) Mandatory Settlement Conferences. Except as to lower court appeals, medical malpractice cases, and cases subject to compulsory arbitration under A.R.S. § 12-133, in any action in which a motion to set and certificate of readiness is filed, the court, at the request of any party, shall, except for good cause shown, direct the parties, the attorneys for the parties and, if appropriate, representatives of the parties having authority to settle, to participate either in person or, with leave of court, by telephone, in a conference or conferences before trial for the purpose of facilitating settlement. Unless otherwise ordered by the court, all requests for settlement conferences shall be made not later than 60 days prior to trial. The court may also schedule a settlement conference upon its own motion.

In medical malpractice cases, the court shall conduct a mandatory settlement conference no earlier than four (4) months after the conduct of the comprehensive pretrial conference and no later than thirty (30) days before trial.

Rule 16.1(a) added Oct. 10, 2000, effective Dec. 1, 2000.

Text of Rule 16.1(a) applicable to cases filed on or after April 15, 2014 and to those cases filed before April 15, 2014 that are subject to the conditions stated in the November 27, 2013, Amended Order Regarding Applicability Provision, in R-13-0017.

See also, text of Rule 16.1(a) applicable to those cases filed before April 15, 2014 that are not subject to the conditions stated in the November 27, 2013 Amended Order Regarding Applicability Provision, in R-13-0017.

(a) Mandatory Settlement Conferences. Except in appeals from a lower court, medical malpractice cases, and cases subject to compulsory arbitration under Rule 72(b), at the request of any party, the court may direct the parties, the attorneys for the parties and, if appropriate, representatives of the parties having authority to settle, to participate either in person or, with leave of court, by telephone, in a conference or conferences before trial for the purpose of facilitating settlement. Unless otherwise ordered by the court, all requests for settlement conferences shall be made not later than 60 days prior to trial. The court may also schedule a settlement conference upon its own motion.

In medical malpractice cases, the court shall conduct a mandatory settlement conference no earlier than four (4) months after the Rule 16(e) conference and no later than thirty (30) days before trial.

Rule 16.1(a) added Oct. 10, 2000, effective Dec. 1, 2000. Amended Aug. 28, 2013, effective April 15, 2014, subject to the conditions of Order No. R-13-0017.

(b) Scheduling and Planning. The court shall enter an order that sets the date for the settlement conference, a deadline for furnishing settlement conference memoranda, and other matters appropriate in the circumstances of the case. An order setting a settlement conference shall not be modified except by leave of court upon a showing of good cause.

Rule 16.1(b) added Oct. 10, 2000, effective Dec. 1, 2000.

(c) Settlement Conference Memoranda. At least five (5) days prior to the settlement conference, each party shall furnish the court with a separate memorandum. In non-medical malpractice cases, the memorandum shall not be filed with the clerk of the court, and the parties shall furnish the memoranda sealed to the division assigned to the case. In medical malpractice cases, the settlement conference memoranda shall be filed and exchanged. Each memorandum shall address the following:

(1) a general description of the issues in the lawsuit, and the positions of each party with respect to each issue;

(2) a general description of the evidence that will be presented by each side with respect to each issue;

(3) a summary of the settlement negotiations that have previously occurred;

(4) an assessment by each party of the anticipated result if the matter did proceed to trial; and

(5) any other information each party believes will be helpful to the settlement process.

No part of any settlement conference memorandum shall be admissible at trial.

Rule 16.1(c) added Oct. 10, 2000, effective Dec. 1, 2000.

(d) Attendance. Settlement conferences shall be attended by all of the parties to the litigation and their counsel unless specifically excused for good cause by the court. In addition, the defendants shall have a representative present with actual authority to enter into a binding settlement agreement. All participants shall appear in person except pursuant to stipulation of the parties or order of the court.

Rule 16.1(d) added Oct. 10, 2000, effective Dec. 1, 2000.

(e) Confidentiality. The court shall order that discussions in settlement conferences shall be confidential among the parties, their counsel and the court.

Rule 16.1(e) added Oct. 10, 2000, effective Dec. 1, 2000.

(f) Discretion to Transfer. The court, upon its own motion, or upon the motion of a party, may transfer the settlement conference to another division of the court, willing to conduct the settlement conference.

Rule 16.1(f) added Oct. 10, 2000, effective Dec. 1, 2000.

(g) *Ex Parte* Communications. At any settlement conference conducted pursuant to this Rule, the court, with the consent of all those participating in the conference, may engage in ex parte communications if the court determines that will facilitate the settlement of the case.

Rule 16.1(g) added Oct. 10, 2000, effective Dec. 1, 2000.

(h) Sanctions. The provisions of Rule 16(f) of these Rules concerning sanctions shall apply to a conference provided for by this rule.

Rule 16.1(h) added Oct. 10, 2000, effective Dec. 1, 2000.

HISTORICAL NOTES

[2014 Amendments]

[Rule 16.1] Arizona Supreme Court Order No. R-13-0017, issued Aug. 28, 2013, provided that the amendments of the order would be "effective on April 15, 2014 as to all cases filed on or after that date." The applicability provision of Order No. R-13-0017 was amended on Nov. 14, 2013, and subsequently amended on Nov. 27, 2013 to provide:

(1) The Amendments shall apply to all actions filed on or after April 15, 2014.

(2) Beginning on April 15, 2014, the Amendments also shall apply to any action filed prior to April 15, 2014 (a "pending action"), unless one of the following events has occurred before that date:

- (a) A party has filed a Motion to Set and Certificate of Readiness,
- (b) The parties have filed a Proposed Scheduling Order, or
- (c) The court has entered a Scheduling Order.

(3) If, in a pending action, one of the preceding events has not occurred before April 15, 2014, the parties shall file a Joint Report and a Proposed Scheduling Order in accordance with the Amendments by June 30, 2014, or within 270 days after the commencement of the action, whichever date is later. Otherwise, the court will place the action on the Dismissal Calendar in accordance with the Amendments.

(4) A trial court, in its discretion, may apply any of the Amendments to a case pending before April 15, 2014, even if the Amendments would not otherwise apply under paragraph (2) above. For example, if a party filed a Motion to Set and Certificate of Readiness before April 15, 2014, the trial judge may set the matter for a trial setting conference under amended Rule 16(f), rather than place the case on the active calendar under pre-amendment Rule 38.1(c).

(5) Civil actions pending on the Inactive Calendar on April 15, 2014 shall be dismissed without prejudice on June 14, 2014, unless one of the actions set forth in subparts (1) - (4) of amended Rule 38.1(f) occurs before June 14, 2014.

STATE BAR COMMITTEE NOTES

2000 Promulgation

As part of the effort to consolidate formerly separate sets of procedural rules into either the Arizona Rules of Civil Procedure or the Rules of the Arizona Supreme Court, certain provisions of the former Uniform Rules of Practice of the Superior Court and of the former Uniform Rules of Practice for Medical Malpractice Cases which dealt with the subject of settlement conferences were combined into a new Rule 16.1 dealing with that subject generally. The provisions of subparts (a), (b), (c), (f), and (h) of this new Rule are taken largely from former Rule VI(e) of the Uniform Rules of Practice of the Superior Court; the provisions of subparts (d), (e) and (g) are taken from former Rule 2 of the Uniform Rules of Practice for Medical Malpractice Cases.

The provision making the conduct of a settlement conference mandatory in all medical malpractice cases was retained; in all other cases, a settlement conference may be set either at the request of any party or by the court, on its own motion. The new Rule also preserves the differing practice concerning the exchange of settlement conference memoranda. In medical malpractice cases, such memoranda are to be filed and exchanged; in other cases, they are not filed but are furnished under seal to the division to which the case is assigned.

In a Comment to the original Uniform Rules of Practice for Medical Malpractice Cases, which was effective January 1, 1990 and was amended effective July 1, 1992, the special Committee stated the following concerning the provisions of Rule 2 [now part of Rule 16.1]:

> "The committee recognizes that certain professional liability insurance policies require the consent of the insured before an insurer can settle a claim. All parties are encouraged to set forth in detail, orally or in writing, the basis of their positions with respect to their willingness to compromise disputed claims. A party who refuses to settle because that party insists on the right to trial cannot be found to have failed to comply with the provisions of this rule."

AUTHORS' COMMENTS

Analysis

1. *History and Origin of Rule.* Ariz. R. Civ. P. 16.1 was added to the Arizona Rules of Civil Procedure, effective December 1,

2000, as a consequence of the Arizona Supreme Court's approval of the recommendations of what was known as the Civil Rules Consolidation Project. [Then existing Rule 16.1 was simply renumbered as Rule 16.2]. By an Order entered in September 2000, the Supreme Court abrogated the Uniform Rules of Practice of the Superior Court, the Uniform Rules of Procedure for Medical Malpractice Cases, and the Uniform Rules of Procedure for Arbitration, as separate sets of procedural rules, and transferred their provisions to either the Arizona Rules of Civil Procedure or the Rules of the Arizona Supreme Court.

The rationale used for determining the placement of rules was that rules affecting the processing of civil cases should be placed in the Arizona Rules of Civil Procedure, while rules that concerned primarily internal court administration should be placed in the Rules of the Arizona Supreme Court. Application of this rationale resulted, in some instances, in the transfer of certain provisions of the Arizona Rules of Civil Procedure to the Rules of the Arizona Supreme Court.

Rules 16.1(a), (b), (c), (f) and (h) were taken largely from former Rule VI(e) of the Uniform Rules of Practice of the Superior Court; Rules 16.1(d), (e) and (g) were taken from former Rule 2 of the Uniform Rules of Practice for Medical Malpractice Cases. The provision making the conduct of a settlement conference mandatory in all medical malpractice cases was retained; in all other cases, a settlement conference may be set either at the request of any party or by the Court on its own motion. Rule 16.1 also preserves the differing practice concerning the exchange of settlement conference memoranda. In medical malpractice cases, such memoranda are to be filed and exchanged; in other cases, they are not filed but are furnished under seal to the Division to which the case is assigned, or to the Judge (if different) who will preside over the settlement conference.

2. *Comparison With Federal Rule.* The Federal Rules of Civil Procedure do not have a provision that corresponds to ARCP 16.1.

3. *Settlement Conferences in Non-Medical Malpractice Cases.* Rule 16.1(a) governs the scheduling of what are called "mandatory settlement conferences." In all civil cases, *except* appeals from justice courts, cases subject to mandatory arbitration, and medical malpractice cases, a settlement conference is not, strictly speaking, "mandatory," but is to be set by the Court if requested by any party, or by the Court on its own motion and at its discretion.

For cases filed before April 15, 2014, and not otherwise subject to conditions stated in the November 27, 2013 Amended Order Regarding Applicability Provision, in R-13-0017, any request for the conduct of a settlement conference must be made after a motion to set and certificate of readiness has been filed, but no later than sixty (60) days before trial. The Court is to issue a scheduling order setting the date for the settlement conference and the dates for submitting settlement conference memoranda. The scheduling of a settlement conference is one of the matters that may be considered at a Comprehensive Pretrial Conference held pursuant to Rule 16(b). The order is also to specify that discussions had at the settlement conference are to be confidential among the parties, their counsel and the court.

Ariz. R. Civ. P. 16.1(c) provides that before the settlement conference, in accordance with whatever schedule is set by the Court, each party is to provide the Court with a separate memorandum, addressing the following subjects:

(1) a description of the issues in the case, and each party's position on each issue;

(2) a description of the evidence that will be presented at trial with respect to each issue;

(3) a summary of the prior settlement negotiations conducted, if any;

(4) that party's assessment of the anticipated result if the matter proceeds to trial; and,

(5) any other information deemed helpful to the prospect of settlement.

The memoranda are to be furnished to the Division of the Superior Court to which the case is assigned under seal and are not to be filed. While the Rule does not specify, the memoranda presumably need not be served on the other parties to the case.

The settlement conference must be attended by the parties and their counsel and, if the Court deems it appropriate, by representatives of the parties with settlement authority. Attendance in person is required, unless the Court grants an individual leave to appear by telephone. The settlement conference may be conducted by the Judge who will preside over the trial unless that Judge, on motion of a party or *sua sponte,* transfers the settlement conference to another Judge who is willing to conduct it. Rule 16.1(g) permits the Court at a settlement conference to engage in *ex parte* communications, but only with the consent of all those participating. The sanction provisions of Rule 16(f) are specifically made applicable to settlement conferences conducted by Rule 16.1(h).

4. *Settlement Conferences in Medical Malpractice Cases; 2014 Rule Amendments.* In medical malpractice cases, settlement conferences are truly mandatory.

For cases filed before April 15, 2014, and not otherwise subject to the conditions stated in the November 27, 2013 Amended Order Regarding Applicability Provision, in R-13-0017, Rule 16.1(a) provides that settlement conferences in such cases must be conducted no earlier than four (4) months after the conduct of the Comprehensive Pretrial Conference, and no later than thirty (30) days before trial. In fact, the scheduling of the settlement conference is one of the matters that is to be discussed and agreed upon at the Comprehensive Pretrial Conference conducted pursuant to Rule 16(c).

For cases filed on or after April 15, 2014, and those cases subject to the November 27, 2013 Amended Order Regarding Applicability Provision, in R-13-0017, Rule 16.1(a) (amended 2014) provides that settlement conferences in such cases must be conducted no earlier than four (4) months after the Rule 16(e) (amended 2014) conference, and no later than thirty (30) days before trial.

Ariz. R. Civ. P. 16(c) also preserves the differing practice concerning the exchange of settlement conference memoranda. In medical malpractice cases, such memoranda are to be filed and exchanged; in other cases, they are not filed but are furnished under seal to the Division to which the case is assigned, or to the Judge (if different) who will preside over the settlement conference.

5. *2014 Rule Amendments: Effective Date and Applicability.* On August 28, 2013, the Arizona Supreme Court adopted sweeping amendments to the case management and trial setting rules governing civil cases. The promulgating order specified such rules were adopted "effective on April 15, 2014 as to all cases filed on or after that date." See, August 28, 2013 Order entered in In the Matter of Petition to Amend Rules 16, 16.1, 26, 37, 38, 38.1, 72, 73, 74 and 77, Arizona Rules of Civil Procedure, R-13-0017. The applicability provision set forth in the Promulgating Order set up two procedural tracks for case management with the new rules governing cases file on or after April 15, 2014 and the "old" rules governing pre-April 15, 2014 cases.

To avoid any confusion potentially created by the two different tracks, the Court entered an order on November 14, 2013, amending the applicability provision. On November 27, 2013, the Court entered a second order further refining the amended applicability provision. As a result, the Amendments are effective and applicable as follows:

(1) The Amendments shall apply to all actions led on or after April 15, 2014.

(2) Beginning on April 15, 2014, the Amendments also shall apply to any action filed prior to April 15, 2014 (a "pending action"), unless one of the following events has occurred

before that date:

(a) A party has filed a Motion to Set and Certificate of Readiness,

(b) The parties have filed a Proposed Scheduling Order, or

(c) The court has entered a Scheduling Order.

(3) If, in a pending action, one of the preceding events has not occurred before April 15, 2014, the parties shall file a Joint Report and a Proposed Scheduling Order in accordance with the Amendments by June 30, 2014, or within 270 days after the commencement of the action, whichever date is later. Otherwise, the court will place the action on the Dismissal Calendar in accordance with the Amendments.

(4) A trial court, in its discretion, may apply any of the Amendments to a case pending before April 15, 2014, even if the Amendments would not otherwise apply under paragraph (2) above. For example, if a party filed a Motion to Set and Certificate of Readiness before April 15, 2014, the trial judge may set the matter for a trial setting conference under amended Rule 16(f), rather than place the case on the active calendar under pre-amendment Rule 38.1(c).

(5) Civil actions pending on the Inactive Calendar on April 15, 2014 shall be dismissed without prejudice on June 14, 2014, unless one of the actions set forth in subparts (1) - (4) of amended Rule 38.1(f) occurs before June 14, 2014.

Rule 16.2. Good faith settlement hearings

(a) Petition. In any action where it is alleged that two or more parties are joint tortfeasors, and a settlement is entered into by any of the parties to the action, the court, upon petition of any party, shall make a formal determination whether the settlement is made in good faith. Any petition shall be accompanied by affidavits. If the petition is filed by the parties to the settlement, such affidavits shall set forth the terms of the settlement and the circumstances establishing the good faith of the settlement.

Added as 16.1(a) April 2, 1986, effective June 1, 1986. Renumbered as 16.2(a) Oct. 10, 2000, effective Dec. 1, 2000.

(b) Objection to Petition. Within ten days after a petition has been filed, any other party may file an objection to the petition, supported by accompanying affidavits. Replies to the objection shall be filed within ten days of service of the objection. The foregoing time periods may be shortened or enlarged by the court or by agreement of the parties.

Added as 16.1(b) April 2, 1986, effective June 1, 1986. Renumbered as 16.2(b) Oct. 10, 2000, effective Dec. 1, 2000.

(c) Hearing. Upon timely request of any party, the court shall set a time for hearing of the objection. If no request is made, the court may, in its discretion, set a time for such hearing, or rule without a hearing. If a hearing is set, the court shall consider the circumstances and evidence set forth in the parties' affidavits, and shall receive other evidence as presented.

Added as 16.1(c) April 2, 1986, effective June 1, 1986. Renumbered as 16.2(c) Oct. 10, 2000, effective Dec. 1, 2000.

STATE BAR COMMITTEE NOTES

2000 Amendment

As part of the effort to consolidate formerly separate sets of procedural rules into either the Arizona Rules of Civil Procedure or the Rules of the Arizona Supreme Court, former Rule 16.1 was simply renumbered as Rule 16.2, with no substantive change.

AUTHORS' COMMENTS

Analysis

1. Scope and Purpose of Rule.
2. Comparison With Federal Rule.
3. Procedures for Securing Approval of Settlements.
4. Burden of Proof.

1. *Scope and Purpose of Rule.* What is now Ariz. R. Civ. P. 16.2 was adopted in 1986 in response to the initial adoption in Arizona of the Uniform Contribution Among Tortfeasors Act, A.R.S. §§ 12-2501, *et seq.*, and applies primarily to actions governed by the provisions of that Act.

The Act adopted a comparative negligence rule for claims involving joint tortfeasors filed on or after August 31, 1984, and abolished the prior common law rule prohibiting claims of contribution among joint tortfeasors. The responsibility of joint tortfeasors, and of the plaintiff(s) as well, was to be allocated on the basis of "relative degrees of fault." A.R.S. § 12-2502. A right of contribution against other joint tortfeasors was created in favor of any tortfeasor who "has paid" more than that tortfeasor's "pro rata share of the common liability." A.R.S. § 12-2501(B). This right to contribution could be enforced in the action in which the joint tortfeasors are named, or in a separate action. The term "common liability," however, meant the total dollar amount of damages sustained for which the joint tortfeasors were legally answerable, and not necessarily the amount accepted in settlement from one joint tortfeasor by the claimant. *Parker v. Vanell*, 170 Ariz. 350, 824 P.2d 746 (1992) (disapproved of by, PAM Transport v. Freightliner Corp., 182 Ariz. 132, 893 P.2d 1295 (1995)).

This right, and the concomitant exposure, to a contribution claim could be limited by achieving a settlement with the plaintiff. If a settlement was reached between one of the joint tortfeasors and the plaintiff "in good faith," then that settlement "discharges the tortfeasor . . . from all liability for contribution to any other tortfeasor." To accomplish that, however, the settlement must have been reached in "good faith." A.R.S. § 12-2504.

The Rule was drafted to provide a vehicle for the parties to such an action to secure a determination from the Court as to whether a settlement reached between the plaintiff and less than all joining tortfeasors is a "good faith settlement." The Rule only specifies the procedures to be followed to secure a determination whether a settlement with a joint tortfeasor was reached in good faith—it does not prescribe the standards to be applied in making that determination. *City of Tucson v. Superior Court In and*

For County of Pima, 161 Ariz. 441, 778 P.2d 1337 (Ct. App. Div. 2 1989), opinion approved of, 165 Ariz. 236, 798 P.2d 374 (1990).

The Rule was originally adopted as a new Rule 16.1. As part of the consolidation of formerly separate sets of procedural rules into either the Arizona Rules of Civil Procedure or the Rules of the Arizona Supreme Court which occurred in 2000, the Rule was renumbered as Rule 16.2.

2. *Comparison With Federal Rule.* The Federal Rules of Civil Procedure do not have a provision that corresponds to ARCP 16.2.

3. *Procedures for Securing Approval of Settlements.* A petition for a determination whether a settlement was reached in good faith may be brought by "any party" to the action, including a litigant who is not a party to the settlement. The petition must be accompanied by affidavits. If the petition is brought by one of the parties to the settlement, the affidavits must "set forth the terms of the settlement and the circumstances establishing the good faith of the settlement."

Any objection to the petition must be filed within ten days thereafter, and must also be supported by affidavits. A hearing must be conducted pursuant to Rule 16.2(c) if it is requested in a timely manner by one of the parties. Absent a timely request, it is discretionary with the Court whether to conduct a hearing.

4. *Burden of Proof.* As originally drafted and proposed by the State Bar of Arizona, Rule 16.2 contained provisions that the parties seeking approval of the settlement had the burden of going forward with evidence, but that the party or parties challenging the settlement had the burden of proving the absence of good faith. These provisions were deleted from the version eventually promulgated by the Arizona Supreme Court, and Rule 16.2 is silent on these issues. The courts have now held, however, that the burden of proof rests on the party challenging the settlement to demonstrate that it was not reached in good faith. *Barmat v. John and Jane Doe Partners A-D*, 165 Ariz. 205, 797 P.2d 1223 (Ct. App. Div. 2 1990). There is nothing which precludes the plaintiff from settling with a third-party defendant, even though the plaintiff has not asserted any claims against that third-party defendant. *Barmat v. John and Jane Doe Partners A-D*, 165 Ariz. 205, 797 P.2d 1223 (Ct. App. Div. 2 1990).

5. *Effect of Determination.* If the Court finds that the settlement between the plaintiff and one or more of the tortfeasors was made in good faith, there are two consequences which flow by statute from that determination: (1) the plaintiff's claims against non-settling tortfeasors are reduced by the amount paid or agreed to be paid, and (2) the settling tortfeasors are released from liability for contribution to other tortfeasors. *Barmat v. John and*

Jane Doe Partners A-D, 165 Ariz. 205, 797 P.2d 1223 (Ct. App. Div. 2 1990). While the language of the Rule suggests that the determination of good faith which produces those results is binding only on parties to the action, judicial interpretation suggests that a determination that a settlement was reached in good faith is applicable to all parties to the agreement. *Barmat v. John and Jane Doe Partners A–D*, 165 Ariz. 205, 797 P.2d 1223 (Ct. App. Div. 2 1990).

The fact that a settlement is determined to be a good faith settlement, however, does not bar a nonsettling party, in a subsequent action for contribution brought against that nonsettling party by a settling party, from litigating the issue of the amount of damages suffered by the claimant. *City of Tucson v. Superior Court In and For County of Pima*, 161 Ariz. 441, 778 P.2d 1337 (Ct. App. Div. 2 1989), opinion approved of, 165 Ariz. 236, 798 P.2d 374 (1990).

Similarly, the finding that a settlement has been reached in good faith is pertinent and necessary only to insulate a settling tortfeasor from contribution claims by nonsettling parties; it does not condition or define that settling party's right to seek contribution. *City of Tucson v. Superior Court In and For County of Pima*, 165 Ariz. 236, 798 P.2d 374 (1990). Even though a joint tortfeasor has entered into a "bad faith" settlement with the plaintiff, that settling tortfeasor may still seek contribution, but the recovery will be limited to that authorized by A.R.S. § 12-2501. *City of Tucson v. Superior Court In and For County of Pima*, 165 Ariz. 236, 798 P.2d 374 (1990).

6. *Accounting Treatment of Settlements in Joint and Several Liability Cases*. In cases to which it is still applicable, A.R.S. § 12-2504 dictates that the amounts paid by any settling joint tortfeasors be applied to reduce the claim against the other nonsettling joint tortfeasors. Amounts paid in settlement are to be deducted, however, from the total damages found by the trier of fact, and not from that portion found to be attributable to the nonsettling parties. *Shelby v. Action Scaffolding, Inc.*, 171 Ariz. 1, 827 P.2d 462 (1992).

Under this "Settlement First Formula," the total damages found by the trier of fact are first reduced by any amounts paid in settlement, and responsibility for the balance that remains, if any, is assigned according to the jury's allocations of fault. *Shelby v. Action Scaffolding, Inc.*, 171 Ariz. 1, 827 P.2d 462 (1992). This treatment of sums paid in settlement is inapplicable in most cases instituted after December 31, 1987. *See*, *Gemstar Ltd. v. Ernst & Young*, 185 Ariz. 493, 917 P.2d 222 (1996) (noting that *Shelby* was decided before A.R.S. § 12-2506 was enacted). *See also*, discussion in Sections 7 and 8, *infra*.

This "Settlement First Formula" rule still pertains in cases where a defendant who proceeds to trial is made jointly and severally liable for an *intentional tort* with a settling co-tortfeasor, because the jury found they were acting in concert. *Bishop v. Pecanic*, 193 Ariz. 524, 975 P.2d 114 (Ct. App. Div. 1 1998). That defendant is entitled to have an adverse judgment reduced by the amount of any settlement reached with the settling co-tortfeasor. *Bishop v. Pecanic*, 193 Ariz. 524, 975 P.2d 114 (Ct. App. Div. 1 1998).

While it is true that A.R.S. §§ 12-2504 and 12-2501(C) specify that there is no right to contribution in a joint and several liability case in favor of an intentional tortfeasor, there are clear policy distinctions between the right to contribution, and the right to have a prior settlement credited against the eventual adverse judgment. *Bishop v. Pecanic*, 193 Ariz. 524, 975 P.2d 114 (Ct. App. Div. 1 1998). A.R.S. § 12-2506(F)(1) defines "acting in concert" as, *inter alia*, being inapplicable to "any person whose conduct was negligent in any of its degrees rather than intentional." The "Settlement First Formula" appears to still be the rule in cases where a plaintiff, seeking to recover damages arising out of one incident or transaction, alleges an alternative theory of recovery as to each of several defendants. *Pasco Industries, Inc. v. Talco Recycling, Inc.*, 195 Ariz. 50, 985 P.2d 535, 1998-2 Trade Cas. (CCH) ¶ 72377 (Ct. App. Div. 1 1998).

7. *Effect of Abolition of Joint and Several Liability.* In 1987, the Arizona Legislature enacted amendments to the Uniform Contribution Among Tortfeasors Act which abolished the doctrine of joint and several liability, except in cases where parties were acting in concert, where one party was acting as an agent or servant of another party, and in other cases relating to hazardous wastes or substances or solid waste disposal sites. A.R.S. § 12-2506. *Yslava v. Hughes Aircraft Co.*, 188 Ariz. 380, 936 P.2d 1274, 45 Env't. Rep. Cas. (BNA) 1315 (1997); *Bishop v. Pecanic*, 193 Ariz. 524, 975 P.2d 114 (Ct. App. Div. 1 1998). (The exception for cases relating to hazardous wastes or substances, or solid waste disposal sites, was repealed in 1997, purportedly retroactively, and liability in those type of cases is now several only as well.) These amendments apply to actions filed on or after December 31, 1987, and the constitutionality of this legislation has been upheld. *Jimenez v. Sears, Roebuck and Co.*, 183 Ariz. 399, 904 P.2d 861, Prod. Liab. Rep. (CCH) P 14382 (1995); *Larsen v. Nissan Motor Corp. in U.S.A.*, 194 Ariz. 142, 978 P.2d 119 (Ct. App. Div. 2 1998); *Lerma v. Keck*, 186 Ariz. 228, 921 P.2d 28 (Ct. App. Div. 1 1996); *Church v. Rawson Drug & Sundry Co.*, 173 Ariz. 342, 842 P.2d 1355 (Ct. App. Div. 1 1992).

Guiding this statutory revision was a desire to increase the fairness of the tort system for both plaintiffs and defendants, and to eliminate the harshness of an all-or-nothing contributory negligence defense. *Hutcherson v. City of Phoenix*, 192 Ariz. 51, 961 P.2d 449 (1998). The 1987 amendments also broadened the scope of torts subject to the rules of comparative fault beyond those grounded on theories of negligence, and are fully applicable in product liability actions. *Jimenez v. Sears, Roebuck and Co.*, 183 Ariz. 399, 904 P.2d 861, Prod. Liab. Rep. (CCH) P 14382 (1995); *State Farm Ins. Companies v. Premier Manufactured Systems, Inc.*, 217 Ariz. 222, 172 P.3d 410 (2007); *Zuern By and Through Zuern v. Ford Motor Co.*, 188 Ariz. 486, 937 P.2d 676 (Ct. App. Div. 2 1996).

Under the Act as amended, Arizona follows a "comparative fault" regime, under which the trier of fact considers and apportions the fault of all persons who contributed to the harm to the plaintiff, and each tortfeasor is responsible only for his or her percentage of fault and no more. *Hutcherson v. City of Phoenix*, 192 Ariz. 51, 961 P.2d 449 (1998); *Sanchez v. City of Tucson*, 191 Ariz. 128, 953 P.2d 168 (1998); *McKillip v. Smitty's Super Valu, Inc.*, 190 Ariz. 61, 945 P.2d 372 (Ct. App. Div. 1 1997); *Zuern By and Through Zuern v. Ford Motor Co.*, 188 Ariz. 486, 937 P.2d 676 (Ct. App. Div. 2 1996); *Standard Chartered PLC v. Price Waterhouse*, 190 Ariz. 6, 945 P.2d 317 (Ct. App. Div. 1 1996), as corrected on denial of reconsideration, (Jan. 13, 1997); *Rosner v. Denim & Diamonds, Inc.*, 188 Ariz. 431, 937 P.2d 353 (Ct. App. Div. 2 1996); *Natseway v. City of Tempe*, 184 Ariz. 374, 909 P.2d 441 (Ct. App. Div. 1 1995).

The trier of fact may consider the fault of persons who are not parties to the action, even if the plaintiff would be prohibited from suing them directly or recovering damages from them. *A Tumbling-T Ranches v. Flood Control Dist. of Maricopa County*, 222 Ariz. 515, 217 P.3d 1220 (Ct. App. Div. 1 2009); *Dietz v. General Elec. Co.*, 169 Ariz. 505, 821 P.2d 166 (1991); *Larsen v. Nissan Motor Corp. in U.S.A.*, 194 Ariz. 142, 978 P.2d 119 (Ct. App. Div. 2 1998). Thus, an expert's opinion apportioning percentages of fault to the parties and non-parties improperly invades the province of the jury and is inadmissible, notwithstanding the provisions of Rule 704, Ariz. R. Evid. *Webb v. Omni Block, Inc.*, 216 Ariz. 349, 166 P.3d 140 (Ct. App. Div. 1 2007).

There is no authority for the proposition that intentional conduct must be given more weight than negligent conduct in the apportionment of fault. *Hutcherson v. City of Phoenix*, 192 Ariz. 51, 961 P.2d 449 (1998). These comparative fault principles apply regardless of the relationship of the parties and the nature of the duty owed, and even where it is alleged that a negligent tortfeasor had a duty to prevent an intentional wrong from occurring. *Natseway v. City of Tempe*, 184 Ariz. 374, 909 P.2d 441 (Ct. App. Div. 1 1995).

The Act permits the apportionment of fault between a negligent plaintiff and a defendant whose conduct is wanton or wilful. *Rosner v. Denim & Diamonds, Inc.*, 188 Ariz. 431, 937 P.2d 353 (Ct. App. Div. 2 1996); *Wareing v. Falk*, 182 Ariz. 495, 897 P.2d 1381 (Ct. App. Div. 1 1995). It even permits the allocation of fault between an allegedly negligent defendant and a non-party who commits a criminal act. *Hutcherson v. City of Phoenix*, 192 Ariz. 51, 961 P.2d 449 (1998); *Thomas v. First Interstate Bank of Arizona, N.A.*, 187 Ariz. 488, 930 P.2d 1002, 54 A.L.R.5th 827 (Ct. App. Div. 2 1996). Correspondingly, a plaintiff guilty of gross or wanton negligence in causing an accident will not necessarily be barred from any recovery. *Williams v. Thude*, 188 Ariz. 257, 934 P.2d 1349 (1997).

The statute did not, however, change the law with regard to vicarious liability. *Law v. Verde Valley Medical Center*, 217 Ariz. 92, 170 P.3d 701 (Ct. App. Div. 1 2007). An alleged tortfeasor and a party potentially liable vicariously for that person's tortious conduct are not joint tortfeasors under Arizona law. *Law v. Verde Valley Medical Center*, 217 Ariz. 92, 170 P.3d 701 (Ct. App. Div. 1 2007). When a judgment on the merits is entered in favor of a person for whose conduct a party is vicariously liable, there is no fault to impute or allocate. *Law v. Verde Valley Medical Center*, 217 Ariz. 92, 170 P.3d 701 (Ct. App. Div. 1 2007).

The statute expressly permits fault to be allocated to nonparties to the action, even to those immune from suit. Thus, where an employer's negligence contributes to an employee's injury, any joint tortfeasors may require the employer's negligence to be considered in assessing relative degrees of fault under A.R.S. § 12-2506, even though the employer may be immune from suit under the workmen's compensation statutes. *Dietz v. General Elec. Co.*, 169 Ariz. 505, 821 P.2d 166 (1991).

Where the parties stipulate that a nonparty was the proximate cause of the plaintiff's injuries, the jury must allocate some degree of fault to that nonparty, and the jury's disregard of the stipulation and assignment of 100% of the fault to the named defendants warrants a new trial on all issues. *Ogden v. J.M. Steel Erecting, Inc.*, 201 Ariz. 32, 31 P.3d 806 (Ct. App. Div. 1 2001).

Under A.R.S. § 12-406(B)(3), the statutory goal of having percentages of fault allocated to all responsible parties and nonparties in a single action provides "good and sufficient cause" for the transfer of an action from a county where venue is proper to another county in order that it can be consolidated with another case arising out of the same underlying event. Such a consolidation will serve the interests of judicial economy and will ensure that 100% of all damages are awarded, and no more. *Behrens v. O'Melia*, 206 Ariz. 309, 78 P.3d 278 (Ct. App. Div. 1

2003).

The provision of the Arizona Constitution, article 18, § 5, which requires that the defense of contributory negligence always be left to the jury to decide, applies to claims of comparative negligence as well, so that the issue of the proper allocation of fault will always be a jury issue, where a jury is demanded. *Gunnell v. Arizona Public Service Co.*, 202 Ariz. 388, 46 P.3d 399 (2002). A claim that a jury's allocation of fault was against the weight of the evidence is properly presented as a motion for new trial under Rule 59(a)(8). *Hutcherson v. City of Phoenix*, 192 Ariz. 51, 961 P.2d 449 (1998).

Arizona's adoption of the Uniform Contribution Among Tortfeasors Act left intact the common law doctrine of "indivisible injury." *Piner v. Superior Court In and For County of Maricopa*, 192 Ariz. 182, 962 P.2d 909 (1998); *Salica v. Tucson Heart Hosp.-Carondelet, L.L.C.*, 224 Ariz. 414, 231 P.3d 946 (Ct. App. Div. 2 2010). When the tortious conduct of more than one defendant contributes to one indivisible injury, the entire amount of damages resulting from all contributing causes is the total amount "of damages recoverable by the plaintiff," as that term is used in A.R.S. § 12-2506(A). *Piner v. Superior Court In and For County of Maricopa*, 192 Ariz. 182, 962 P.2d 909 (1998). The fault of all actors is then determined by the trier of fact, and each defendant is *severally* liable for damages allocated in direct proportion to that defendant's percentage of fault. *Piner v. Superior Court In and For County of Maricopa*, 192 Ariz. 182, 962 P.2d 909 (1998). In an indivisible injury case, the fact finder is to compute the total amount of damages sustained by the plaintiff, and the percentage of fault of each tortfeasor, and the maximum amount recoverable against each tortfeasor is computed by multiplying the first figure by the second. *Piner v. Superior Court In and For County of Maricopa*, 192 Ariz. 182, 962 P.2d 909 (1998).

The doctrine of "satisfaction of judgment" provides that, if one joint tortfeasor satisfies a judgment obtained by the plaintiff, all other tortfeasors are discharged from liability and the plaintiff has no further cause of action. *Bridgestone/Firestone North America Tire, L.L.C. v. Naranjo*, 206 Ariz. 447, 79 P.3d 1206, Prod. Liab. Rep. (CCH) P 16845 (Ct. App. Div. 2 2003). This doctrine also survives the abolition of joint and several liability, and the adoption of a comparative fault regime, in situations where the plaintiff has obtained a judgment for the total damages suffered from an indivisible injury against only one party at fault, and that judgment is satisfied. *Bridgestone/Firestone North America Tire, L.L.C. v. Naranjo*, 206 Ariz. 447, 79 P.3d 1206, Prod. Liab. Rep. (CCH) P 16845 (Ct. App. Div. 2 2003). The satisfaction of that judgment extinguishes any claim against other parties at fault. *Bridgestone/Firestone North America Tire, L.L.C.*

v. Naranjo, 206 Ariz. 447, 79 P.3d 1206, Prod. Liab. Rep. (CCH) P 16845 (Ct. App. Div. 2 2003).

Joint liability and vicarious liability "are related but separate doctrines." *Wiggs v. City of Phoenix*, 198 Ariz. 367, 10 P.3d 625, 111 A.L.R.5th 815 (2000) (citing, *Srithong v. Total Investment Co.*, 23 Cal. App. 4th 721, 28 Cal. Rptr. 2d 672 (2d Dist. 1994); *State Farm Ins. Companies v. Premier Manufactured Systems, Inc.*, 213 Ariz. 419, 142 P.3d 1232, Prod. Liab. Rep. (CCH) P 17517 (Ct. App. Div. 1 2006), opinion aff'd, 217 Ariz. 222, 172 P.3d 410 (2007)). The joint liability that was abolished by A.R.S. § 12-2506(D) is limited to "that class of joint tortfeasors whose independent negligence coalesced to form a single injury." *Wiggs v. City of Phoenix*, 198 Ariz. 367, 10 P.3d 625, 111 A.L.R.5th 815 (2000).

The statute preserves joint liability both for true joint tortfeasors (those "acting in concert") and for those who are vicariously liable for the fault of others. *Wiggs v. City of Phoenix*, 198 Ariz. 367, 10 P.3d 625, 111 A.L.R.5th 815 (2000); *State Farm Ins. Companies v. Premier Manufactured Systems, Inc.*, 213 Ariz. 419, 142 P.3d 1232, Prod. Liab. Rep. (CCH) P 17517 (Ct. App. Div. 1 2006), opinion aff'd, 217 Ariz. 222, 172 P.3d 410 (2007). The comparative fault statute, thus, preserves vicarious liability for the negligence of an independent contractor, when the employer of that independent contractor had a non-delegable duty. *Wiggs v. City of Phoenix*, 198 Ariz. 367, 10 P.3d 625, 111 A.L.R.5th 815 (2000). This will not operate to immunize independent contractors from the consequences of their own negligence, any more than in the case of a true employee. *Wiggs v. City of Phoenix*, 198 Ariz. 367, 10 P.3d 625, 111 A.L.R.5th 815 (2000).

In either setting, the employer may seek indemnity against the employee or independent contractor, in cases of pure vicarious liability, or contribution in cases in which the employer has some degree of independent liability. *Wiggs v. City of Phoenix*, 198 Ariz. 367, 10 P.3d 625, 111 A.L.R.5th 815 (2000).

The 1987 amendments severely limit the right of contribution granted by A.R.S. § 12-2501. By abolishing joint and several liability and limiting recovery against any defendant to that percentage of the plaintiff's total injuries which represents that defendant's degree of fault, the statute insures that the conditions for claiming contribution will not occur. *PAM Transport v. Freightliner Corp.*, 182 Ariz. 132, 893 P.2d 1295 (1995); *City of Tucson v. Superior Court In and For County of Pima*, 161 Ariz. 441, 778 P.2d 1337 (Ct. App. Div. 2 1989), opinion approved of, 165 Ariz. 236, 798 P.2d 374 (1990); *Cella Barr Associates, Inc. v. Cohen*, 177 Ariz. 480, 868 P.2d 1063 (Ct. App. Div. 1 1994); *Neil v. Kavena*, 176 Ariz. 93, 859 P.2d 203 (Ct. App. Div. 1 1993);

Roland v. Bernstein, 171 Ariz. 96, 828 P.2d 1237 (Ct. App. Div. 2 1991). A determination that a settlement was reached in good faith in an action filed after December 31, 1987 will, accordingly, not have any effect on the settling tortfeasor's liability for contribution because that liability has theoretically been extinguished.

8. *Treatment of Pretrial Settlements in Several Liability Cases.* The accounting for pretrial settlements between the plaintiff and less than all of the defendants in several liability cases is also quite different than in cases under the statute prior to the 1987 amendments. See discussion in Section 6 of this Chapter. Except in the limited classes of cases to which the 1987 amendments do not apply, the liability of joint tortfeasors for injuries caused by their concurrent negligence is several only, and the plaintiff's recovery against any nonsettling joint tortfeasor defendant is limited, under A.R.S. § 12-2506, to an amount which equates to that defendant's share of the liability for the total damages, as determined by the trier of fact.

Any defendant's share of liability is determined by what the trier of fact finds to be that defendant's percentage degree of fault in causing the plaintiff's damages. Any amounts paid in settlement by any joint tortfeasor are irrelevant to, and are excluded from, the calculation of a nonsettling tortfeasor's monetary liability. *Neil v. Kavena*, 176 Ariz. 93, 859 P.2d 203 (Ct. App. Div. 1 1993); *Roland v. Bernstein*, 171 Ariz. 96, 828 P.2d 1237 (Ct. App. Div. 2 1991). This is essentially the same rule that now applies to settlements in federal admiralty tort cases. *McDermott, Inc. v. AmClyde*, 511 U.S. 202, 114 S. Ct. 1461, 128 L. Ed. 2d 148, Prod. Liab. Rep. (CCH) P 13826, 1994 A.M.C. 1521 (1994) (liability of nonsettling defendants in admiralty case to be calculated with reference to jury's allocation of proportionate responsibility, rather than by giving nonsettling defendants credit for dollar amount of settlement).

If the plaintiff settles before trial with one of multiple tortfeasors for an amount which exceeds the proportion of the plaintiff's damages determined to be recoverable from that defendant, the plaintiff receives the full benefit of that settlement, even if that results in the plaintiff receiving more than the total amount of damages found by the trier of fact to have been sustained. Conversely, the plaintiff bears the risk and the burden of agreeing to a disadvantageous settlement which turns out to be less than the amount that would have been recoverable from the settling defendant, because the recovery against the nonsettling parties will still be limited to their determined percentages of fault. *Neil v. Kavena*, 176 Ariz. 93, 859 P.2d 203 (Ct. App. Div. 1 1993); *Roland v. Bernstein*, 171 Ariz. 96, 828 P.2d 1237 (Ct. App. Div. 2 1991). *But see Pasco Industries, Inc. v. Talco Recycling, Inc.*, 195 Ariz. 50, 985 P.2d 535, 1998-2 Trade Cas. (CCH) ¶

72377 (Ct. App. Div. 1 1998), and *Bishop v. Pecanic*, 193 Ariz. 524, 975 P.2d 114 (Ct. App. Div. 1,1998).

Under A.R.S. § 12-2506(D), joint tortfeasors who act in concert remain jointly and severally liable for the resulting injury or damage. *Chappell v. Wenholz*, 226 Ariz. 309, 247 P.3d 192 (Ct. App. Div. 1 2011); *Mein ex rel. Mein v. Cook*, 219 Ariz. 96, 193 P.3d 790 (Ct. App. Div. 1 2008); *Bishop v. Pecanic*, 193 Ariz. 524, 975 P.2d 114 (Ct. App. Div. 1 1998). In *Mein*, the court of appeals held that a prima facie case under A.R.S. § 12-2506(D)(1) requires evidence the parties: (1) knowingly agreed to commit an intentional tort, (2) they were certain or substantially certain their actions would result in the consequences complained of, and (3) they actively participated in the commission of the tort. *Mein ex rel. Mein v. Cook*, 219 Ariz. 96, 193 P.3d 790 (Ct. App. Div. 1 2008); *see also*, *Chappell v. Wenholz*, 226 Ariz. 309, 247 P.3d 192 (Ct. App. Div. 1 2011) (holding, "[a] conscious agreement need not be verbally expressed and may be implied from the conduct itself").

Such a joint tortfeasor who pays more than its share of the common liability is entitled to seek contribution from fellow tortfeasors. *Herstam v. Deloitte & Touche, LLP*, 186 Ariz. 110, 919 P.2d 1381 (Ct. App. Div. 1 1996). When a complaint alleges concerted action that normally would subject all parties to joint and several liability, however, the injured party can, as part of a settlement with one or more of the joint tortfeasors, agree to waive the right to hold nonsettling parties jointly and severally liable and thereby bar the nonsettling parties from seeking contribution and/or indemnity from the settling parties. *Herstam v. Deloitte & Touche, LLP*, 186 Ariz. 110, 919 P.2d 1381 (Ct. App. Div. 1 1996). *See also*, *Bishop v. Pecanic*, 193 Ariz. 524, 975 P.2d 114 (Ct. App. Div. 1 1998). A.R.S. § 12-2506 (F)(1) defines "acting in concert" as, *inter alia*, being inapplicable to "any person whose conduct was negligent in any of its degrees rather than intentional." In enacting this exception where parties are acting in concert, the Legislature did not, however, displace or alter the longstanding common law liability for aiding and abetting. *Security Title Agency, Inc. v. Pope*, 219 Ariz. 480, 200 P.3d 977, 27 I.E.R. Cas. (BNA) 1811 (Ct. App. Div. 1 2008).

Where an allegedly partially negligent defendant is subject to an agreement requiring it to indemnify a co-defendant for the entire liability if it is found to be even partially at fault, that defendant may settle with the plaintiff for both itself and the co-defendant and seek restitution from the negligent nonsettling co-defendant on a theory of equitable subrogation. *Rowley Plastering Co., Inc. v. Marvin Gardens Development Corp.*, 180 Ariz. 212, 883 P.2d 449 (Ct. App. Div. 1 1994). One who settles under a threat of civil proceedings or to protect its own interests is not a mere volunteer. *Rowley Plastering Co., Inc. v. Marvin Gardens Development Corp.*, 180 Ariz. 212, 883 P.2d 449 (Ct. App. Div. 1 1994).

Rule 16.3. Initial case management conference in cases assigned to the complex civil litigation program

(a) Subjects for Consideration. Once a case is determined to be a complex civil case, an initial case management conference with all parties represented shall be conducted at the earliest practical date, and a Case Management Order issued by the court promptly thereafter. Among the subjects that should be considered at such a conference are:

(1) the status of parties and pleadings;

(2) determining whether severance, consolidation, or coordination with other actions is desirable;

(3) scheduling motions to dismiss or other preliminary motions;

(4) scheduling class certification motions, if applicable;

(5) scheduling discovery proceedings, setting limits on discovery and determining whether to appoint a discovery master;

(6) issuing protective orders;

(7) any requirements or limitations for the disclosure or discovery of electronically stored information, including the form or forms in which the electronically stored information should be produced;

(8) any measures the parties must take to preserve discoverable documents or electronically stored information;

(9) any agreements reached by the parties for asserting claims of privilege or of protection as to trial-preparation materials after production;

(10) appointing liaison counsel and admission of non-resident counsel;

(11) scheduling settlement conferences;

(12) notwithstanding Rule 26.1, the establishment and timing of disclosure requirements;

(13) scheduling expert disclosures and whether sequencing of expert disclosures is warranted;

(14) scheduling dispositive motions;

(15) adopting a uniform numbering system for documents and establishing a document depository;

(16) determining whether electronic service of discovery materials and pleadings is warranted;

(17) organizing a master list of contact information for

counsel;

(18) determining whether expedited trial proceedings are desired or appropriate

(19) Scheduling further conferences as necessary;

(20) use of technology, videoconferencing and/or teleconferencing;

(21) determination of whether the issues can be resolved by summary judgment, summary trial, trial to the court, jury trial, or some combination thereof; and

(22) such other matters as the court or the parties deem appropriate to manage or expedite the case.

(b) Meeting of Parties Before Conference. Before the date set by the court for the initial case management conference, all parties who have appeared in the action, or their attorneys, shall meet and confer concerning the matters to be raised at the conference, shall attempt in good faith to reach agreement on as many case management issues as possible, and shall submit a joint report to the court no later than seven (7) days before the initial case management conference. A party who fails to participate in good faith shall be subject to sanctions.

(c) Purpose of Conference. The purpose of the initial case management conference is to identify the essential issues in the litigation and to avoid unnecessary, burdensome or duplicative discovery and other pretrial procedures in the course of preparing for trial of those issues.

(d) Establishing Time Limits. Time limits should be regularly used to expedite major phases of complex civil cases. Time limits should be established early, tailored to the circumstances of each case, firmly and fairly maintained, and accompanied by other methods of sound judicial management. The date of the final pre-trial conference shall be set by the court as early as possible with a trial date to follow within 60 days of the final pre-trial conference.

(e) Commencement of Discovery. Absent an order of the court, or by stipulation of the parties filed with the court, no party may initiate discovery or disclosure in a complex civil case until the court has issued a Case Management Order following the initial case management conference.

Added Nov. 3, 2005, effective on an experimental basis nunc pro tunc from Nov. 22, 2002. Amended Sept. 5, 2007, effective Jan. 1, 2008. Amended Sept. 1, 2011, effective on a permanent basis Jan. 1, 2012.

COMMENT

Justification for this rule: Rule 16.3 is intended to supplement the Arizona Rules of Civil Procedure in a manner that will provide judges and litigants with appropriate procedural mechanisms for the fair, efficient and expeditious management of discovery, disclosures, motions, service of documents and pleadings, communications between and among counsel and the court, trial, and other aspects of complex civil litigation. Other than as specifically set forth, cases assigned to the complex litigation program are not exempt from any normally applicable rule of procedure, except to the extent the trial judge may order otherwise. Rule 16.3 should be available to any trial judge who wishes to follow it, in whole or in part, in managing a civil dispute, even in cases that are not formally assigned to a complex litigation program.

Case Management Resources. In considering procedures for management of a complex civil case, the court, in its discretion, may look for guidance to the Manual for Complex Litigation published by the Federal Judicial Center and to similar complex litigation manuals used by courts in other jurisdictions.

AUTHORS' COMMENTS

Analysis

1. *Scope and Purpose of Rule.* By administrative order effective November 22, 2002, the Arizona Supreme Court adopted Ariz. R. Civ. P. 16.3 on an experimental basis following the Court's approval of a report from the Complex Civil Litigation Court Evaluation Committee. *See*, Administrative Order No. 2002-107. By that same administrative order, the Court established a pilot program to experiment with a Complex Civil Litigation Court in the Maricopa County Superior Court and adopted, on an experimental basis, several rules of civil procedure to apply to cases in the Complex Civil Litigation Court. Administrative Order No. 2002-107 also adopted, on an experimental basis, a form for identifying cases eligible for the program, which the Court set forth in an Appendix to the Order. *See*, Rule 8(i)(8).

The Complex Civil Litigation Rules—designated as Rules 8(h)(3), 8(i), 16.3 and 39.1—were promulgated to facilitate the conduct of an experimental Complex Litigation Program in the Superior Court of Maricopa County, which was scheduled to run from January 1, 2003 and December 31, 2004. At the request of the Complex Civil Litigation Court Evaluation Committee, this experimental program was extended through December 31, 2010.

On September 1, 2011, the Arizona Supreme Court made permanent the Complex Litigation pilot program. The Complex Civil Litigation Rules— Rule 8(h)(3), 8(i), 16.3, and 39.1—are effective January 1, 2012.

2. *Comparison with Federal Rule.* The Federal Rules of Civil Procedure do not have a provision that corresponds to ARCP 16.3.

IV. PARTIES

Rule 17. Parties plaintiff and defendant; capacity

(a) Real Party in Interest. Every action shall be prosecuted in the name of the real party in interest. An executor, administrator, guardian, bailee, trustee of an express trust, a party with whom or in whose name a contract has been made for the benefit of another, or a party authorized by statute may sue in that person's own name without joining the party for whose benefit the action is brought; and when a statute of the state so provides, an action for the use or benefit of another shall be brought in the name of the State of Arizona. No action shall be dismissed on the ground that it is not prosecuted in the name of the real party in interest until a reasonable time has been allowed after objection for ratification of commencement of the action by, or joinder or substitution of, the real party in interest; and such ratification, joinder or substitution shall have the same effect as if the action had been commenced in the name of the real party in interest.

Amended July 1, 1966, effective Nov. 1, 1966; Sept. 15, 1987, effective Nov. 15, 1987.

(b) Actions by Personal Representatives; Setting Aside Judgment. Actions for the recovery of personal property, debts or damages, and for the title to or possession of lands, or for any right attached thereto or arising therefrom, or for an injury or damage thereto may be commenced by an executor, administrator, or guardian appointed in this state in the same manner as if commenced by the testator or intestate, and judgment therein shall be as conclusive as if rendered in favor of or against the testator or intestate. The judgment may be set aside upon the application of any person interested for fraud or collusion on the part of the executor, administrator or guardian.

(c) Actions By or Against Personal Representatives. Actions for the recovery or possession of property, real or personal, or to quiet title thereto, or to determine an adverse claim thereto, and all actions founded upon contracts, may be maintained by or against an executor or administrator in all cases in which such actions might have been maintained by or against the testator or intestate.

Amended Sept. 15, 1987, effective Nov. 15, 1987.

(d) Actions By or Against County, City or Town. Actions brought by or against a county or incorporated city or town shall be in its corporate name.

(e) [Deleted, effective June 1, 1985].

(f) Actions Against Surety, Assignor or Endorser. The assignor, endorser, guarantor and surety upon a contract, and the drawer of a bill which has been accepted, may be sued without the maker, acceptor or other principal obligor when the latter resides beyond the limits of the state, or in such part of the state that the latter cannot be reached by ordinary process of law, or when the latter's residence is unknown and cannot be ascertained by the use of reasonable diligence, or when the latter is dead, or insolvent.

Amended Sept. 15, 1987, effective Nov. 15, 1987.

(g) Infants or Incompetent Persons. Whenever an infant or incompetent person has a representative, such as a general guardian, or similar fiduciary, the representative may sue or defend on behalf of the infant or incompetent person. If an infant or incompetent person does not have a duly appointed representative the infant or incompetent may sue by a next friend or by a guardian ad litem. The court shall appoint a guardian ad litem for an infant or incompetent person not otherwise represented in an action or shall make such other order as it deems proper for the protection of the infant or incompetent person.

Amended Sept. 15, 1987, effective Nov. 15, 1987.

(h) Bond of Guardian Ad Litem or Next Friend. If an action is brought for the minor by a next friend or guardian ad litem, the next friend or guardian ad litem shall not receive any money or property of the minor until such friend or guardian files a bond as security therefor in such form and with such surety as the court may prescribe and approve.

Amended Sept. 15, 1987, effective Nov. 15, 1987.

(i) Consent of Guardian Ad Litem or Next Friend; Liability; Compensation. No person shall be appointed guardian ad litem or next friend except upon written consent filed in the action. A guardian or next friend shall not be personally liable for costs, unless by special order of the court. The court may allow the guardian or next friend a reasonable compensation for services to be taxed as part of the costs of the action.

Amended Sept. 15, 1987, effective Nov. 15, 1987.

(j) Partnerships. Any partnership may sue and be sued in the name which it has assumed or by which it is known.

Amended July 28, 1978, effective Sept. 1, 1978.

STATE BAR COMMITTEE NOTES

1966 Amendment

[Rule 17(a)] The provision that no action shall be dismissed on the ground that it is not prosecuted in the name of the real party in interest until a reasonable time has been allowed, after the objection has been raised, for ratification, substitution, etc., is added simply in the interests of justice. In its origin the rule concerning the real party in interest was permissive in purpose: it was designed to allow an assignee to sue in his own name. That having been accomplished, the modern function of the rule in its negative aspect is simply to protect the defendant against a subsequent action by the party actually entitled to recover, and to insure generally that the judgment will have its proper effect as res judicata.

The provision is intended to prevent forfeiture when determination of the proper party to sue is difficult or when an understandable mistake has been made. It does not mean, for example, that, following an airplane crash in which all aboard were killed, an action may be filed in the name of John Doe (a fictitious person), as personal representative of Richard Roe (another fictitious person), in the hope that at a later time the attorney filing the action may substitute the real name of the real personal representative of a real victim, and have the benefit of suspension of the limitation period. It does not even mean, when an action if filed by the personal representative of John Smith, of Buffalo, in the good faith belief that he was aboard the flight, that upon discovery that Smith is alive and well, having missed the fatal flight, the representative of James Brown, of San Francisco, an actual victim, can be substituted to take advantage of the suspension of the limitation period. It is, in cases of this sort, intended to insure against forfeiture and injustice—in short, to codify in broad terms the salutary principle of *Levinson v. Deupree*, 345 U.S. 648, 73 S. Ct. 914, 97 L. Ed. 2d 1319, 1953 A.M.C. 972 (1953), and *Link Aviation, Inc. v. Downs*, 325 F.2d 613, 7 Fed. R. Serv. 2d 264 (D.C. Cir. 1963).

The amendment will not alter the results of existing Arizona decisions.

AUTHORS' COMMENTS

Analysis

1. *Scope and Purpose of Rule.* Ariz. R. Civ. P. 17 is essentially a collection of separate provisions that are related to each other to the extent that they bear on the qualification of a person to serve as a plaintiff or defendant in an action. The provisions include those relating to real parties in interest, infants and incompetent persons, assignees, public corporations, sureties and partnerships.

2. *Comparison With Federal Rule.* ARCP 17(a) and (g) are substantially the same as FRCP 17(a) and (c). The Arizona Rules

of Civil Procedure do not have a provision that corresponds to FRCP 17(b); and, the Federal Rules of Civil Procedure do not have provisions that correspond to ARCP 17(b), (c), (d), (f), (h), (i) and (j). FRCP 17(d) is the same as ARCP 25(e)(2).

In addition, in 2007, the language of FRCP 17 was amended as part of the general restyling of the Federal Rules of Civil Procedure to make the Federal Rules more easily understood and to make style and terminology consistent throughout the Federal Rules of Civil Procedure. Those stylistic modifications have not been incorporated into ARCP 17.

3. *Real Party in Interest Generally.* The purpose of the requirement of Rule 17(a) that every action be prosecuted by the real party in interest is to insure the defendant may avail itself of the evidence and defenses it has against the real party in interest and to achieve finality of results through the doctrine of *res judicata*. *Preston v. Kindred Hospitals West, L.L.C.*, 225 Ariz. 223, 236 P.3d 450 (Ct. App. Div. 1 2010), review granted, (Jan. 4, 2011) and opinion aff'd, 226 Ariz. 391, 249 P.3d 771 (2011); *Colorado Cas. Ins. Co. v. Safety Control Co., Inc.*, 230 Ariz. 560, 288 P.3d 764 (Ct. App. Div. 1 2012), review denied, (Mar. 19, 2013); *Cruz v. Lusk Collection Agency*, 119 Ariz. 356, 580 P.2d 1210 (Ct. App. Div. 2 1978). Under Rule 9(a), however, it is not necessary to plead the basis of the plaintiff's capacity to sue as a representative of the real party in interest, except to the extent it may be necessary to establish the jurisdiction of the Court.

By its express terms, Rule 17(a) provides that an action may not be dismissed for a defect in the party plaintiff until the real party in interest is given a reasonable time to join in the action or to ratify its commencement. *See also*, *Preston v. Kindred Hospitals West, L.L.C.*, 226 Ariz. 391, 249 P.3d 771 (2011) (in a case of first impression, the Court held that "Rule 17(a) does not require a plaintiff to show that an initial failure to name the real party in interest resulted from an understandable mistake or difficulty in identifying the proper party"); *Safeway Ins. Co. v. Collins*, 192 Ariz. 262, 963 P.2d 1085 (Ct. App. Div. 1 1998). The provision in Rule 17(a) permitting ratification or joinder by the real party in interest is intended to prevent the forfeiture of claims when the determination of the real party to bring suit is difficult to make or when an understandable mistake has been made. *Toy v. Katz*, 192 Ariz. 73, 961 P.2d 1021 (Ct. App. Div. 1 1997).

Rule 17(a) does not require, however, a showing that the determination of the real party in interest is difficult to determine or that the plaintiff made an understandable mistake as to the determination of the real party in interest. *Preston v. Kindred Hospitals West, L.L.C.*, 226 Ariz. 391, 249 P.3d 771 (2011); *Safeway Ins. Co. v. Collins*, 192 Ariz. 262, 963 P.2d 1085 (Ct. App. Div. 1

1998); *Toy v. Katz*, 192 Ariz. 73, 961 P.2d 1021 (Ct. App. Div. 1 1997). The lack of capacity to sue, moreover, is not jurisdictional and is waived if not raised in a timely manner. *Safeway Ins. Co. v. Collins*, 192 Ariz. 262, 963 P.2d 1085 (Ct. App. Div. 1 1998); *Gonzales v. Arizona Public Service Co.*, 161 Ariz. 84, 775 P.2d 1148 (Ct. App. Div. 2 1989); *Ballard v. Lawyers Title of Arizona*, 27 Ariz. App. 168, 552 P.2d 455 (Div. 1 1976).

4. *Personal Representatives.* Read together, Rules 17(b) and (c) authorize an executor, administrator or similar personal representative to commence, maintain and/or defend virtually any action that might have been commenced or maintained by or against the testator or intestate. Under ordinary circumstances, a claim for medical malpractice and/or for violation of the Adult Protective Services Act survives death and can be brought by the decedent's personal representative. Personal representatives may bring claims based on the Adult Protective Services Act regardless of when they are appointed, and limitations placed on personal representatives by the Probate Code do not apply to such claims. *In re Estate of Winn*, 214 Ariz. 149, 150 P.3d 236 (2007).

5. *Assignees.* The assignee of a claim, whether by contract or operation of law, is the real party in interest to prosecute that claim. *General Acc. Fire & Life Assur. Corp. v. Little*, 103 Ariz. 435, 443 P.2d 690 (1968); *Moore v. Toshiba Intern. Corp.*, 160 Ariz. 205, 772 P.2d 28 (Ct. App. Div. 1 1989); *Cruz v. Lusk Collection Agency*, 119 Ariz. 356, 580 P.2d 1210 (Ct. App. Div. 2 1978).

6. *Insurers.* An insurer that pays a claim of its insured becomes, by reason of subrogation, the real party in interest to pursue the insured's claims against third parties. *Tri-City Property Management Services, Inc. v. Research Products Corp.*, 149 Ariz. 596, 721 P.2d 144, 42 U.C.C. Rep. Serv. 1606 (Ct. App. Div. 2 1986); *Hamman-McFarland Lumber Co. v. Arizona Equipment Rental Co.*, 16 Ariz. App. 188, 492 P.2d 437 (Div. 1 1972). The insurer may thus intervene in an action brought by its insureds which does not exclude recovery for losses previously paid by the insurer. *United Pacific/Reliance Ins. Co. v. Kelley*, 127 Ariz. 87, 618 P.2d 257 (Ct. App. Div. 1 1980).

7. *Unincorporated Associations.* An unincorporated association lacks capacity to sue unless it is conferred by statute either expressly or by necessary implication. *Associated Students of University of Arizona v. Arizona Bd. of Regents*, 120 Ariz. 100, 584 P.2d 564 (Ct. App. Div. 2 1978).

8. *Guardians.* Rules 17(g) and (h) recognize two separate classifications of guardians—general guardians and guardians *ad litem.* A general guardian has fiduciary responsibilities that extend beyond the parameters of a particular case; a guardian *ad*

litem is appointed in an action, and serves only for the purposes of that action. Where a guardian *ad litem* for a minor defendant has been appointed, the parents of the minor are not parties even though served with process on behalf of the minor, as required by Rule 4.1(b)(2). *Ackel v. Ackel*, 83 Ariz. 207, 318 P.2d 676 (1957). The Rule thus anticipates the problem created when minors or incompetent persons are named as defendants in civil actions, and empowers the trial court to take the necessary steps to ensure that minors or incompetent persons are adequately defended in actions brought against them. *Montano v. Browning*, 202 Ariz. 544, 48 P.3d 494 (Ct. App. Div. 2 2002). Although an order appointing a person as a guardian *ad litem* is preferable, the lack of such an order is not fatal to a person acting in that capacity. *Widoff v. Wiens*, 202 Ariz. 383, 45 P.3d 1232 (Ct. App. Div. 1 2002). A guardian *ad litem*, in the performance of duties related to that role, is entitled to judicial immunity. *Widoff v. Wiens*, 202 Ariz. 383, 45 P.3d 1232 (Ct. App. Div. 1 2002).

The proper party to bring an action for damages to recover the medical expenses of an injured child, however, are the parents, not the child through a guardian *ad litem*. *Lopez v. Cole*, 214 Ariz. 536, 155 P.3d 1060 (Ct. App. Div. 1 2007). A child may bring such a claim only with parental consent, and the parents' waiver of the claim by failure to pursue it does not constitute such consent. *Lopez v. Cole*, 214 Ariz. 536, 155 P.3d 1060 (Ct. App. Div. 1 2007).

Rule 17(g) underscores the inherent powers of the Superior Court regarding the substitution of parties in matters involving children. *Arizona Dept. of Economic Sec. v. Superior Court In and For County of Maricopa*, 178 Ariz. 236, 871 P.2d 1172 (Ct. App. Div. 1 1994). A parent, acting solely in that capacity, lacks the authority to settle the claim of a minor child, unless formally appointed as guardian *ad litem*. *Gomez v. Maricopa County*, 175 Ariz. 469, 857 P.2d 1323 (Ct. App. Div. 1 1993). In the case of wrongful death claims, the surviving spouse must obtain the consent of the other beneficiaries to settle the claim or the action and, if any of the beneficiaries are minors, a guardian must be appointed and the Court must approve the settlement. *Gomez v. Maricopa County*, 175 Ariz. 469, 857 P.2d 1323 (Ct. App. Div. 1 1993).

Rule 17(g) allows a general guardian, fiduciary or other representative to sue or defend on behalf of an infant or incompetent person. In Arizona, a minor is never allowed to bring an action in his or her own name, but must always sue through a representative, whatever the cause of action. *Porter v. Triad of Arizona (L.P.)*, 203 Ariz. 230, 52 P.3d 799 (Ct. App. Div. 1 2002). A guardian may even maintain an action for dissolution of marriage on behalf of an incapacitated adult ward. *Ruvalcaba By and Through*

Stubblefield v. Ruvalcaba, 174 Ariz. 436, 850 P.2d 674 (Ct. App. Div. 1 1993). The Rule does not, however, authorize a representative or guardian to file an action *in propria persona* on behalf of the infant or incompetent without employing counsel. *Byers-Watts v. Parker*, 199 Ariz. 466, 18 P.3d 1265 (Ct. App. Div. 1 2001), as amended, (Mar. 29, 2001). There is no indication that Rule 17(g) was intended to override the limitations on persons who can properly practice law contained in Rule 31 of the Rules of the Arizona Supreme Court. *Byers-Watts v. Parker*, 199 Ariz. 466, 18 P.3d 1265 (Ct. App. Div. 1 2001), as amended on other grounds, (Mar. 29, 2001).

Rule 17(i), specifically requires that no person may be appointed a guardian *ad litem* or next friend unless that person files with the Court a written consent to the appointment. The requirement that an appointed guardian *ad litem* file a bond as security, imposed by Rule 17(h), applies only where an action is "brought for" a minor and only as a condition of the guardian receiving any money or property of the minor.

9. *Actions on Bonds.* Unless one of the exceptions delineated in Rule 17(f) applies, a supplier suing on a payment bond must join the principal (general contractor) as a party defendant. *SCA Const. Supply v. Aetna Cas. and Sur. Co.*, 157 Ariz. 64, 754 P.2d 1339 (1988).

10. *Partnerships.* Rule 17(j), which provides that a partnership may sue or be sued in the partnership name, is essentially a codification of the common law rule that a partnership is a legal entity capable of suing or being sued in its own right, without naming the individual partners as plaintiffs or defendants. *Clogher v. Winston and Strawn*, 181 Ariz. 372, 891 P.2d 240 (Ct. App. Div. 2 1995); *Hunt Inv. Co. v. Eliot*, 154 Ariz. 357, 742 P.2d 858 (Ct. App. Div. 1 1987). Should a judgment be entered against the partnership, the assets of the individual partners are jointly and severally liable for it, regardless of whether the individual partners were named in the suit. *Clogher v. Winston and Strawn*, 181 Ariz. 372, 891 P.2d 240 (Ct. App. Div. 2 1995). In fact, Arizona's partnership statutes and the common law permit punitive damages to be awarded vicariously against a partnership for acts of a partner performed in the ordinary course of the partnership's business. *Hyatt Regency Phoenix Hotel Co. v. Winston & Strawn*, 184 Ariz. 120, 907 P.2d 506 (Ct. App. Div. 1 1995).

11. *Husband and Wife.* Arizona follows a community property regime, but the spouses have equal rights to manage, control and dispose of community property, except in the case of real property. A.R.S. § 25-214(B). Either spouse may maintain an action relating to community personal property and the other spouse is a

proper, but not a necessary, party. *Bristol v. Moser*, 55 Ariz. 185, 99 P.2d 706 (1940); *Dombey v. Phoenix Newspapers, Inc.*, 147 Ariz. 61, 708 P.2d 742, 12 Media L. Rep. (BNA) 1201 (Ct. App. Div. 1 1985), approved in part, vacated in part, 150 Ariz. 476, 724 P.2d 562, 13 Media L. Rep. (BNA) 1282 (1986). In actions involving community real property, except for unpatented mining claims and leases of less than a year, both spouses must join or be joined in the suit. A.R.S. § 25-214(C).

In an action which seeks to bind the community, or to recover from community assets, both spouses must be sued, even where the suit is to enforce a premarital obligation of one of the spouses. *Flexmaster Aluminum Awning Co., Inc. v. Hirschberg*, 173 Ariz. 83, 839 P.2d 1128 (Ct. App. Div. 1 1992); *Spudnuts, Inc. v. Lane*, 139 Ariz. 35, 676 P.2d 669 (Ct. App. Div. 2 1984). A judgment rendered in a foreign action to which one spouse was not made a party may not be enforced against community property, even if it is made an Arizona judgment in accordance with the procedures of the Uniform Enforcement of Foreign Judgments Act, A.R.S. §§ 12-1701 through 12-1708. *C & J Travel, Inc. v. Shumway*, 161 Ariz. 33, 775 P.2d 1097 (Ct. App. Div. 2 1989). Moreover, the spouse not named in the foreign action cannot be added as a party to an action on the judgment in Arizona. *C & J Travel, Inc. v. Shumway*, 161 Ariz. 33, 775 P.2d 1097 (Ct. App. Div. 2 1989).

On the other hand, a creditor, who has obtained a judgment against one of the marital partners for a separate premarital debt *prior* to the marriage, may enforce that judgment against the community without bringing an independent suit naming the nondebtor spouse. *CBM of Arizona, Inc. v. Sevier*, 184 Ariz. 503, 910 P.2d 654 (Ct. App. Div. 2 1996). In that circumstance, however, both spouses have the right to litigate the extent of the debtor spouse's contribution to the community and the corresponding amount of community property which may be reached to satisfy the judgment. *CBM of Arizona, Inc. v. Sevier*, 184 Ariz. 503, 910 P.2d 654 (Ct. App. Div. 2 1996). Issues concerning the enforcement of domestic and foreign judgments against community property in Arizona are discussed more extensively in Section 9 of the *Authors' Comments* under Rule 58, and Section 11 of the *Authors' Comments* under Rule 69.

Rule 18. Joinder of claims and remedies

(a) Joinder of Claims. A party asserting a claim to relief as an original claim, counterclaim, cross-claim, or third-party claim, may join,.either as independent or as alternate claims, as many claims, legal or equitable, as the party has against an opposing party.

Amended July 1, 1966, effective Nov. 1, 1966; Sept. 15, 1987, effective Nov. 15, 1987.

(b) Joinder of Remedies; Fraudulent Conveyances. Whenever a claim is one heretofore cognizable only after another claim has been prosecuted to a conclusion, the two claims may be joined in a single action, but the court shall grant relief in that action only in accordance with the relative substantive rights of the parties. In particular, a plaintiff may state a claim for money and a claim to have set aside a conveyance fraudulent as to that plaintiff, without first having obtained a judgment establishing the claim for money.

Amended Sept. 15, 1987, effective Nov. 15, 1987.

STATE BAR COMMITTEE NOTES

1966 Amendment

[Rule 18(a)] The former rule proved unduly restrictive in preventing joinder; see e.g., *Federal Housing Adm'r v. Christianson*, 26 F. Supp. 419, 1 Fed. R. Serv. 304, 1 Fed. R. Serv. 305 (D. Conn. 1939) and discussion; 2 Barron & Holtzoff, Federal Practice & Procedure, 553.1 (Wright ed. 1961); 3 Moore, Federal Practice, Para. 18.04(3).

Rule 18(a) as amended not only overcomes the Christianson decision and similar authority but also states clearly, as a comprehensive proposition, that a party asserting a claim (an original claim, counterclaim, cross-claim, or third-party claim) may join as many claims as he has against an opposing party. This permitted joinder is not affected by the fact that there are multiple parties in the action. Excessive joinders can be controlled by separate trials as authorized by Rule 42(b).

AUTHORS' COMMENTS

Analysis

1. Scope and Purpose of Rule.
2. Comparison With Federal Rule.
3. Joinder of Claims Generally; Limitations.

1. *Scope and Purpose of Rule.* The thrust of the Rules of Civil Procedure generally, and of this Rule in particular, is that, whenever possible, all claims should be disposed of in one action. *Staffco,*

Inc. v. Maricopa Trading Co., 122 Ariz. 353, 595 P.2d 31 (1979). Thus, Ariz. R. Civ. P. 18, particularly, alleviates the procedural problems associated with the distinct remedies available under law and equity, as well as the concern for avoiding premature and piecemeal judgments, by permitting a party to bring any and all claims and to request any and all remedies in one action in a court of general jurisdiction. *Sertich v. Moorman*, 162 Ariz. 407, 783 P.2d 1199 (1989).

2. *Comparison With Federal Rule.* ARCP 18 and FRCP 18 are essentially identical.

In 2007, the language of FRCP 18 was amended as part of the general restyling of the Federal Rules of Civil Procedure to make the Federal Rules more easily understood and to make style and terminology consistent throughout the Federal Rules of Civil Procedure. Those stylistic modifications have not been incorporated into ARCP 18.

In addition to the 2007 stylistic amendments, the first sentence of FRCP 18(b) was modified to clarify and restate the phrase "*heretofore cognizable only after another claim has been prosecuted to conclusion.*" This modification has not been incorporated into ARCP 18(b).

3. *Joinder of Claims Generally; Limitations.* Joinder of claims is freely permitted. The Rule authorizes the joinder of claims, counterclaims, cross-claims or third-party claims irrespective of their relationship to the principal claim asserted or their relationship to each other. A party may thus assert in the same action as many independent claims as that party has against the other parties. *Parsons v. Maricopa County*, 176 Ariz. 307, 860 P.2d 1360 (Tax Ct.1993). Rather than mandatory, the joinder of claims is permissive, even when such claims arise out of identical operative facts. *Wilson v. Bramblett*, 91 Ariz. 284, 371 P.2d 1014 (1962).

Specific instances of the joinder of claims which have been approved include: a claim for an account stated and on open account, *Merrick v. U. S. Rubber Co.*, 7 Ariz. App. 433, 440 P.2d 314 (1968); claims for an account stated and *quantum meruit, Musgrove v. Leonard*, 97 Ariz. 44, 396 P.2d 614 (1964), and contract and tort claims arising out of the same transaction or series of transactions, *Reese v. Cradit*, 12 Ariz. App. 233, 469 P.2d 467 (Div. 2 1970). If inconsistent claims and remedies are asserted, a binding election is required before the action is submitted to the jury. *Edward Greenband Enterprises of Arizona v. Pepper*, 112 Ariz. 115, 538 P.2d 389 (1975); *Dixon v. Feffer*, 84 Ariz. 308, 327 P.2d 994 (1958); *Vinson v. Marton & Associates*, 159 Ariz. 1, 764 P.2d 736 (Ct. App. Div. 1 1988); *Earven v. Smith*, 127 Ariz. 354, 621 P.2d 41 (Ct. App. Div. 2 1980).

The operation of Rule 18's permissive joinder of claims regime can render a single action quite complex where there are multiple parties. Under Rule 20, multiple parties may be joined when there is one claim common to all. Each of those parties, however, is free to join any and all unrelated claims against any of the other parties under Rule 18. If too liberal exercise of the right to join claims renders the action unwieldy, the Court, in its discretion, may order separate trials under the authority of Rule 42(b). *Parsons v. Maricopa County*, 176 Ariz. 307, 860 P.2d 1360 (Tax Ct.1993). The Court can also, in drastic cases, refuse to permit joinder, as where a plaintiff joined in a single action 294 separate claims against eleven different defendants. *Apache County v. Superior Court In and For County of Maricopa*, 163 Ariz. 54, 785 P.2d 1242 (Ct. App. Div. 1 1989).

Rule 19. Joinder of persons needed for just adjudication

(a) Persons to Be Joined if Feasible. A person who is subject to service of process and whose joinder will not deprive the court of jurisdiction over the subject matter of the action shall be joined as a party in the action if (1) in that person's absence complete relief cannot be accorded among those already parties, or (2) the person claims an interest relating to the subject of the action and is so situated that the disposition of the action in his absence may (i) as a practical matter impair or impede the person's ability to protect that interest (ii) leave any of the persons already parties subject to a substantial risk of incurring double, multiple, or otherwise inconsistent obligations by reason of the claimed interest. If the person has not been so joined, the court shall order that the person be made a party. If the person should join as a plaintiff but refuses to do so, the person may be made a defendant, or, in a proper case, an involuntary plaintiff. If the joined party objects to venue and joinder of that party would render the venue of the action improper, that party shall be dismissed from the action.

Amended July 1, 1966, effective Nov. 1, 1966; Sept. 15, 1987, effective Nov. 15, 1987.

(b) Determination by Court Whenever Joinder Not Feasible. If a person as described in subdivision (a)(1)–(2) hereof cannot be made a party, the court shall determine whether in equity and good conscience the action should proceed among the parties before it, or should be dismissed, the absent person being thus regarded as indispensable. The factors to be considered by the court include: first, to what extent a judgment rendered in the person's absence might be prejudicial to the person or those already parties; second, the extent to which, by protective provisions in the judgment, by the shaping of relief, or other measure, the prejudice can be lessened or avoided; third, whether a judgment rendered in the person's absence will be adequate; fourth, whether the plaintiff will have an adequate remedy if the action is dismissed for nonjoinder.

Amended July 1, 1966, effective Nov. 1, 1966; Sept. 15, 1987, effective Nov. 15, 1987.

(c) Pleading Reasons for Nonjoinder. A pleading asserting a claim for relief shall state the names, if known to the pleader, of any persons as described in subdivision (a)(1)–(2) hereof who are not joined, and the reasons why they are not joined.

Amended July 1, 1966, effective Nov. 1, 1966.

(d) Exception of Class Actions. This rule is subject to the provisions of Rule 23.
Amended July 1, 1966, effective Nov. 1, 1966.

STATE BAR COMMITTEE NOTES

1966 Amendment

[Rule 19] The present rule, with its judicial gloss in terms of indispensable, necessary, and proper parties, has proved confusing and difficult to apply. The revision seeks to substitute practical procedures to deal with problems where otherwise desirable joinder is difficult. At the same time, it retains the basic principle that parties must be joined where this is required by "equity and good conscience." *Shields v. Barrow*, 58 U.S. 130, 17 How. 130, 15 L. Ed. 158, 1854 WL 7514 (1854); *Bolin v. Superior Court In and For Maricopa County*, 85 Ariz. 131, 333 P.2d 295 (1958); *Smith v. Rabb*, 95 Ariz. 49, 386 P.2d 649 (1963); *State of Washington v. U.S.*, 87 F.2d 421 (C.C.A. 9th Cir. 1936).

The description is not at variance with the settled authorities holding that a tortfeasor with the usual "joint-and-several" liability is merely a permissive party to an action against another with like liability. Joinder of these tortfeasors continues to be regulated by Rule 20; compare Rule 14 on third-party practice.

If a person as described in subdivision (a)(1)–(2) is amenable to service of process and his joinder would not deprive the court of jurisdiction in the sense of competence over the action, he should be joined as a party; and if he has not been joined, the court should order him to be brought into the action. If a party joined has a valid objection to the venue and chooses to assert it, he will be dismissed from the action.

Under subdivision (b), when a person as described in subdivision (a)(1)–(2) cannot be made a party, the court is to determine whether in equity and good conscience the action should proceed among the parties already before it, or should be dismissed because the absent party is indispensable.

Subdivision (c) continues the requirement that a pleading asserting a claim for relief state the names of persons described in subdivision (c) who are not joined as parties and the reasons for their non-joinder.

The official comment of the federal advisory committee on civil rules on the change in Federal Rule 19 is comprehensive and should be consulted.

AUTHORS' COMMENTS

Analysis

1. *Scope and Purpose of Rule.* The purpose of Ariz. R. Civ. P. 19 is to insure the joinder of all interested parties in a single action and avoid a multiplicity of litigation. *Arizona Title Ins. & Trust Co. v. Kelly*, 11 Ariz. App. 254, 463 P.2d 838 (Div. 1 1970). The Rule discards the old distinctions between "proper," "necessary"

or "indispensable" parties, *cf. Oglesby v. Chandler*, 37 Ariz. 1, 288 P. 1034 (1930), in favor of an emphasis upon the practical realities of joinder. *Riley v. Cochise County*, 10 Ariz. App. 55, 455 P.2d 1005 (1969). The defense of failure to join a party required under Rule 19 is never waived and can be raised for the first time on appeal. *Riley v. Cochise County*, 10 Ariz. App. 55, 455 P.2d 1005 (1969); *City of Flagstaff v. Babbitt*, 8 Ariz. App. 123, 443 P.2d 938 (1968).

2. *Comparison With Federal Rules.* Despite structural differences, ARCP 19 is substantially the same as FRCP 19.

In 2007, the language of FRCP 19 was amended as part of the general restyling of the Federal Rules of Civil Procedure to make the Federal Rules more easily understood and to make style and terminology consistent throughout the Federal Rules of Civil Procedure. Consistent with this approach, FRCP 19(b) was amended to delete as redundant the phrase "*the absent person being thus regarded as indispensable.*" The stylistic modifications to FRCP 19 and the amendment to FRCP 19(b) have not been incorporated into ARCP 19.

3. *Compulsory Joinder of Parties.* The compulsory joinder of absent parties under Rule 19 requires a three-step analysis. *Copper Hills Enterprises, Ltd. v. Arizona Dept. of Revenue*, 214 Ariz. 386, 153 P.3d 407 (Ct. App. Div. 1 2007). First, the Court must apply Rule 19(a) to determine whether the absent party is conditionally necessary to the action. A party is necessary, under Rule 19(a)(2)(ii), if there is a substantial risk that the existing parties may be subjected to inconsistent obligations. The next step in the analysis is to determine whether the absent parties can be joined in the action. If joinder is feasible, then the action may not be dismissed until the plaintiff has an opportunity to add the absent parties. The final stage of the analysis is whether the absent party, if joinder is not feasible, is indispensable. *Copper Hills Enterprises, Ltd. v. Arizona Dept. of Revenue*, 214 Ariz. 386, 153 P.3d 407 (Ct. App. Div. 1 2007).

A party who should be joined, but refuses to participate, may be brought in as a defendant or as an involuntary plaintiff. *Vance v. Vance*, 124 Ariz. 1, 601 P.2d 605, 27 U.C.C. Rep. Serv. 728 (1979). The issue of the failure to join an indispensable party is not waivable and may be raised for the first time on appeal. *Gerow v. Covill*, 192 Ariz. 9, 960 P.2d 55 (Ct. App. Div. 1 1998), as amended, (Aug. 26, 1998).

A partially subrogated insurer is not an indispensable party whose joinder can be compelled under Rule 19, where the insured is a party and is seeking full recovery for both. *Tri-City Property Management Services, Inc. v. Research Products Corp.*, 149 Ariz. 596, 721 P.2d 144, 42 U.C.C. Rep. Serv. 1606 (Ct. App. Div. 2

1986). A creditor must join both spouses as defendants before the creditor may obtain and execute upon a judgment against the marital community, even where the claim is for a separate premarital debt. *Spudnuts, Inc. v. Lane*, 139 Ariz. 35, 676 P.2d 669 (Ct. App. Div. 2 1984); *Flexmaster Aluminum Awning Co., Inc. v. Hirschberg*, 173 Ariz. 83, 839 P.2d 1128 (Ct. App. Div. 1 1992). A judgment on such a claim will not be valid unless both spouses are joined in the action. The nondebtor spouse's interest in the community property includes a due process right to litigate both the premarital debt and the value of the debtor's contribution to the assets of the marital community. *Heinig v. Hudman*, 177 Ariz. 66, 865 P.2d 110 (Ct. App. Div. 1 1993); *Flexmaster Aluminum Awning Co., Inc. v. Hirschberg*, 173 Ariz. 83, 839 P.2d 1128 (Ct. App. Div. 1 1992). On the other hand, a creditor, who has obtained a judgment against one of the marital partners for a separate premarital debt *prior* to the marriage, may enforce that judgment against the community without bringing an independent action naming the nondebtor spouse. *CBM of Arizona, Inc. v. Sevier*, 184 Ariz. 503, 910 P.2d 654 (Ct. App. Div. 2 1996). In that circumstance, however, both spouses have the right to litigate the extent of the debtor spouse's contribution to the community estate and the corresponding amount of community property which may be reached to satisfy the judgment. *CBM of Arizona, Inc. v. Sevier*, 184 Ariz. 503, 910 P.2d 654 (Ct. App. Div. 2 1996).

4. *Indispensable Parties.* Dismissal of an action for nonjoinder of a party should occur only where the absent party is truly indispensable. The test for indispensability in Arizona is quite restrictive. An indispensable party is one who has such an interest in the subject matter of the action that no final judgment or decree can be entered that does justice between the parties before the court without injuriously affecting the absent party's rights. *Ivancovich v. Meier*, 122 Ariz. 346, 595 P.2d 24 (1979); *Town of Gila Bend v. Walled Lake Door Co.*, 107 Ariz. 545, 490 P.2d 551 (1971); *King v. Uhlmann*, 103 Ariz. 136, 437 P.2d 928 (1968); *Arizona Bd. of Regents for and on Behalf of University of Arizona v. State ex rel. State of Ariz. Public Safety Retirement Fund Manager Adm'r*, 160 Ariz. 150, 771 P.2d 880, 53 Ed. Law Rep. 260 (Ct. App. Div. 1 1989); *Tippit v. Lahr*, 132 Ariz. 406, 646 P.2d 291 (Ct. App. Div. 2 1982). If complete relief in an action cannot be granted without joinder of an Indian Tribe, and that Tribe has not waived its sovereign immunity with respect to the claim, the action should be dismissed and the parties left to their remedies in Tribal Court. *Beltran v. Harrah's Arizona Corp.*, 220 Ariz. 29, 202 P.3d 494 (Ct. App. Div. 2 2008). A necessary party does not become indispensable, even if that party cannot be joined in the action, if the Court determines that the action should

proceed. Before determining indispensability, the Court must also consider resulting prejudice and adequacy of remedy if joinder is not feasible. *Gerow v. Covill*, 192 Ariz. 9, 960 P.2d 55 (Ct. App. Div. 1 1998), as amended, (Aug. 26, 1998). A judgment rendered in the absence of an indispensable party is, however, merely voidable and not wholly void. *City of Flagstaff v. Babbitt*, 8 Ariz. App. 123, 443 P.2d 938 (1968).

Rule 20. Permissive joinder of parties

(a) Permissive Joinder. All persons may join in one action as plaintiffs if they assert any right to relief jointly, severally, or in the alternative in respect of or arising out of the same transaction, occurrence, or series of transactions or occurrences and if any question of law or fact common to all these persons will arise in the action. All persons may be joined in one action as defendants if there is asserted relief in respect of or arising out of the same transaction, occurrence, or series of transactions or occurrences and if any question of law or fact common to all defendants will arise in the action. A plaintiff or defendant need not be interested in obtaining or defending against all the relief demanded. Judgment may be given for one or more of the plaintiffs according to their respective rights to relief, and against one or more defendants according to their respective liabilities.

Amended July 1, 1966, effective Nov. 1, 1966.

(b) Separate Trials. The court may make such orders as will prevent a party from being embarrassed, delayed, or put to expense by the inclusion of a party against whom the party asserts no claim and who asserts no claim against the party, and may order separate trials or make other orders to prevent delay or prejudice.

Amended Sept. 15, 1987, effective Nov. 15, 1987.

STATE BAR COMMITTEE NOTES

1966 Amendment

[Rule 20(a)] This amendment is for purpose of conformity with the Federal Rule.

AUTHORS' COMMENTS

Analysis

1. Scope and Purpose of Rule.
2. Comparison With Federal Rule.
3. Joinder of Parties Generally; Limitations.

1. *Scope and Purpose of Rule.* Ariz. R. Civ. P. 20 carries forward the goal of encouraging the joinder of all appropriate and interested parties in a single action and thereby avoiding a multiplicity of litigation. *Staffco, Inc. v. Maricopa Trading Co.*, 122 Ariz. 353, 595 P.2d 31 (1979); *Arizona Title Ins. & Trust Co. v. Kelly*, 11 Ariz. App. 254, 463 P.2d 838 (Div. 1 1970). The Rule is

designed to expedite the determination of claims by permitting the inclusion of all parties interested in the subject matter of the controversy.

2. *Comparison With Federal Rule.* Despite structural differences, ARCP 20 is substantially identical to FRCP 20, except that FRCP 20(a) contains a provision permitting the joinder of vessels or cargo in admiralty or maritime actions, which provision is not found in the Arizona Rule.

In addition, in 2007, the language of FRCP 20 was amended as part of the general restyling of the Federal Rules of Civil Procedure to make the Federal Rules more easily understood and to make style and terminology consistent throughout the Federal Rules of Civil Procedure. Those stylistic modifications have not been incorporated into ARCP 20.

3. *Joinder of Parties Generally; Limitations.* Even though the purpose of the Rule is to encourage liberal joinder of parties to avoid a multiplicity of actions, the claims of or against the parties joined should arise out of the same litigable event, and there must be some common thread running between or through each of the claims joined. *Apache County v. Superior Court In and For County of Maricopa*, 163 Ariz. 54, 785 P.2d 1242 (Ct. App. Div. 1 1989). In cases where there are multiple parties joined, the concomitant operation of Rule 18, which permits any or all of those multiple parties to assert against any other party any or all claims it possesses, whether related to the original common claim or not, can render the action quite cumbersome. The Court has the power to avoid inconvenience and prejudice by ordering separate trials of claims where appropriate.

Rule 21. Misjoinder and nonjoinder of parties

Misjoinder of parties is not ground for dismissal of an action. Parties may be dropped or added by order of the court on motion of any party or of its own initiative at any stage of the action and on such terms as are just. Any claim against a party may be severed and proceeded with separately.

AUTHORS' COMMENTS

Analysis

1. *Scope and Purpose of Rule.* Ariz. R. Civ. P. 21 is primarily intended to give the Court flexibility in resolving situations where parties have been improperly joined in a single action. The Rule also covers "nonjoinder of parties," however, and provides that parties may be "added" by the Court as an alternative to dismissal.

2. *Comparison With Federal Rule.* ARCP 21 is substantially identical to FRCP 21.

In 2007, the language of FRCP 21 was amended as part of the general restyling of the Federal Rules of Civil Procedure to make the Federal Rules more easily understood and to make style and terminology consistent throughout the Federal Rules of Civil Procedure. Those stylistic modifications have not been incorporated into ARCP 21.

3. *Remedies for Misjoinder and Nonjoinder.* Where there has been a misjoinder of parties, the action should not be dismissed, but rather restructured through the Court's authority, either upon motion or *sua sponte,* to drop improperly joined parties. Due regard should be given, however, to the policies of Rule 20 and the Court's authority to sever claims and/or to order separate trials under Rule 20(b).

The Rule also covers "non-joinder of parties" and alludes to the Court's authority to "add" parties where there has been a nonjoinder, as an alternative to dismissal. That aspect of the Rule implicates, and must be harmonized with, the policies of Rules 15 and 19. The Rule does not permit the addition of defendants after the rendition of judgment. *Spudnuts, Inc. v. Lane*, 139 Ariz. 35, 676 P.2d 669 (Ct. App. Div. 2 1984).

A defect in parties may be waived by proceeding to trial without raising the objection unless the defect is the absence of an indispensable party that precludes a conclusive determination of the controversy. *Pioneer Nat. Trust Co. of Arizona v. Pioneer Nat. Trust Co. of Arizona*, 115 Ariz. 511, 566 P.2d 312 (Ct. App. Div. 2 1977).

Rule 22. Interpleader

(a) Interpleader. Persons having claims against the plaintiff may be joined as defendants and required to interplead when their claims are such that the plaintiff is or may be exposed to double or multiple liability. It is not ground for objection to the joinder that the claims of the several claimants or the titles on which their claims depend do not have a common origin or are not identical but are adverse to and independent of one another, or that the plaintiff avers that the plaintiff is not liable in whole or in part to any or all of the claimants. A defendant exposed to similar liability may obtain such interpleader by way of cross-claim or counterclaim. The provisions of this Rule supplement and do not in any way limit the joinder of parties permitted in Rule 20.

Amended Sept. 15, 1987, effective Nov. 15, 1987

(b) Release From Liability; Deposit or Delivery. Any party invoking the interpleader, as provided by subdivision (a) of this Rule, may move the court for an order discharging that party from liability to either party, and upon depositing in court the amount claimed, or by delivering the property to the party entitled thereto, or into court as the court may direct, that party may be discharged.

Amended Sept. 15, 1987, effective Nov. 15, 1987.

AUTHORS' COMMENTS

Analysis

1. Scope and Purpose of Rule.
2. Comparison With Federal Rule.
3. Purpose of Interpleader; Limitations.
4. Effect of Interpleader; Deposit With Court.

1. *Scope and Purpose of Rule.* Ariz. R. Civ. P. 22 states the circumstances under which persons having claims against the plaintiff may be joined and required to interplead their claims, and the limitations on the objections thereto. The conflicting claims need not be meritorious; the mere assertion of the claims or threat of litigation suffices. While an interpleader action is generally instituted by the stakeholder as plaintiff, the rule provides that a defendant may invoke interpleader as a counterclaim and/or cross-claim.

The purpose of interpleader is to provide a debtor or stakeholder with a convenient and effective vehicle for escaping from conflicting claims to a fund or property held for the account of another. This procedural mechanism is intended to relieve the stakeholder of the burden of attempting to resolve competing claims to money or property in which the stakeholder claims no interest. The interpleader plaintiff (counterclaimant, cross-complainant, third-party plaintiff), however, must be a mere stakeholder. *Hill v. Favour*, 52 Ariz. 561, 84 P.2d 575 (1938).

2. *Comparison With Federal Rule.* ARCP 22(a) is substantially identical to FRCP 22(a). The Arizona Rule does not contain FRCP 22(b) [Relation to Other Rules and Statutes] and the Federal Rule has no counterpart to ARCP 22(b) [Release from Liability; Deposit or Delivery], which, in Arizona, allows the party instituting the interpleader to secure a discharge from liability, with Court approval, upon depositing with the Court the property or amounts as to which there are competing claims.

In 2007, the language of FRCP 22 was amended as part of the general restyling of the Federal Rules of Civil Procedure to make the Federal Rules more easily understood and to make style and terminology consistent throughout the Federal Rules of Civil Procedure. Those stylistic modifications have not been incorporated into ARCP 22.

3. *Limitations.* Interpleader is not a substitute for a declaratory judgment action, and may not be maintained if the interpleader plaintiff has, or claims, any right to or interest in the fund or property as against the other claimants. *State Compensation Fund v. Superior Court In and For Pima County*, 11 Ariz. App. 583, 466 P.2d 802 (Div. 2 1970).

4. *Effect of Interpleader; Deposit With Court.* A successful interpleader forces the competing claimants to pursue judicial resolution of their claims and discharges the stakeholder from liability. *Canal Ins. Co. v. Pizer*, 183 Ariz. 162, 901 P.2d 1192 (Ct. App. Div. 1 1995); *Hill Bros. Chemical Co. v. Grandinetti*, 123 Ariz. 84, 597 P.2d 987 (Ct. App. Div. 1 1979). Indeed, it has been intimated that a debtor faced with conflicting demands for payment of a single debt may not simply refuse to pay, but must tender performance by pursuit of interpleader. *Hutchens v. Linden*, 159 Ariz. 388, 767 P.2d 1178 (Ct. App. Div. 2 1988).

Under Rule 22(b), the party invoking the interpleader may move the Court for an order discharging that party from liability upon deposit with the Court, or upon delivery to the party entitled thereto, of the money or property in dispute. The procedures governing such deposits with the Court are set out in Rules 67(a), (b) and (c). Ordinarily, the stakeholder need not deposit the funds or property in issue with the court until the court enters an order discharging it from liability. *Canal Ins. Co. v. Pizer*, 183 Ariz. 162, 901 P.2d 1192 (Ct. App. Div. 1 1995). The stakeholder is not liable for interest for any funds at issue during the pendency of the interpleader action, if the stakeholder properly and promptly files an interpleader action and actually pays the funds into the court or makes an unconditional offer to do so. *Canal Ins. Co. v. Pizer*, 183 Ariz. 162, 901 P.2d 1192 (Ct. App. Div. 1 1995).

Rule 23. Class actions

(a) Prerequisites to a Class Action. One or more members of a class may sue or be sued as representative parties on behalf of all only if (1) the class is so numerous that joinder of all members is impracticable, (2) there are questions of law or fact common to the class, (3) the claims or defenses of the representative parties are typical of the claims or defenses of the class, and (4) the representative parties will fairly and adequately protect the interests of the class.

Amended July 1, 1966, effective Nov. 1, 1966.

(b) Class Actions Maintainable. An action may be maintained as a class action if the prerequisites of subdivision (a) are satisfied, and in addition:

(1) the prosecution of separate actions by or against individual members of the class would create a risk of (A) inconsistent or varying adjudications with respect to individual members of the class which would establish incompatible standards of conduct for the party opposing the class, or (B) adjudications with respect to individual members of the class which would as a practical matter be dispositive of the interests of the other members not parties to the adjudications or substantially impair or impede their ability to protect their interests; or

(2) the party opposing the class has acted or refused to act on grounds generally applicable to the class, thereby making appropriate final injunctive relief or corresponding declaratory relief with respect to the class as a whole; or

(3) the court finds that the questions of law or fact common to the members of the class predominate over any questions affecting only individual members, and that a class action is superior to other available methods for the fair and efficient adjudication of the controversy. The matters pertinent to the findings include: (A) the interest of members of the class in individually controlling the prosecution or defense of separate actions; (B) the extent and nature of any litigation concerning the controversy already commenced by or against members of the class; (C) the desirability or undesirability of concentrating the litigation of the claims in the particular forum; (D) the difficulties likely to be encountered in the management of a class action.

Amended July 1, 1966, effective Nov. 1, 1966.

(c) Determination by Order Whether Class Action to Be

Maintained; Notice; Judgment; Actions Conducted Partially as Class Actions.

(1) As soon as practicable after the commencement of an action brought as a class action, the court shall hold a hearing and determine by written order whether it is to so maintained. The court shall set forth its reasons and shall describe all evidence in support of its determination. An order under this subdivision may be conditional, and may be altered or amended before the decision on the merits.

Amended July 1, 1966, effective Nov. 1, 1966; Sept. 15, 1987, effective Nov. 15, 1987. Amended on an expedited basis Aug. 28, 2013, effective Sept. 13, 2013; opened for comment until October 25, 2013, amendment adopted on a permanent basis, effective Nov. 14, 2013.

(2) In any class action maintained under subdivision (b)(3), the court shall direct to the members of the class the best notice practicable under the circumstances, including individual notice to all members who can be identified through reasonable effort. The notice shall advise each member that (A) the court will exclude the member from the class if the member so requests by a specified date; (B) the judgment, whether favorable or not, will include all members who do not request exclusion; and (C) any member who does not request exclusion may, if the member desires, enter an appearance through counsel.

(3) The judgment in an action maintained as a class action under subdivision (b)(1) or (b)(2), whether or not favorable to the class, shall include and describe those whom the court finds to be members of the class. The judgment in an action maintained as a class action under subdivision (b)(3), whether or not favorable to the class, shall include and specify or describe those to whom the notice provided in subdivision (c)(2) was directed, and who have not requested exclusion, and whom the court finds to be members of the class.

(4) When appropriate (A) an action may be brought or maintained as a class action with respect to particular issues, or (B) a class may be divided into subclasses and each subclass treated as a class, and the provisions of this rule shall then be construed and applied accordingly.

Amended July 1, 1966, effective Nov. 1, 1966; Sept. 15, 1987, effective Nov. 15, 1987.

(d) Orders in Conduct of Actions. In the conduct of actions to which this rule applies, the court may make appropriate orders: (1) determining the course of proceedings or prescribing measures to prevent undue repetition or complication in the presentation of evidence or argument; (2) requiring, for the protection of the members of the class or otherwise for the fair conduct of the action, that notice be given in such manner as the court may direct to some or all of the members of any step in the action, or of the proposed extent of the judgment, or of the opportunity of members to signify whether they consider the representation fair and adequate, to intervene and present claims or defenses, or otherwise to come into the action; (3) imposing conditions on the representative parties or on intervenors; (4) requiring that the pleadings be amended to eliminate therefrom allegations as to representation of absent persons, and that the action proceed accordingly; (5) dealing with similar procedural matters. The orders may be combined with an order under Rule 16, and may be altered or amended as may be desirable from time to time.

Amended July 1, 1966, effective Nov. 1, 1966

(e) Dismissal or Compromise. A class action shall not be dismissed or compromised without the approval of the court, and notice of the proposed dismissal or compromise shall be given to all members of the class in such manner as the court directs.

Amended July 1, 1966, effective Nov. 1, 1966.

(f) Appeals. The court's order certifying or denying class action status is appealable in the same manner as a final order or judgment. During the pendency of an appeal under A.R.S. § 12-1873, all discovery and other proceedings shall be stayed except that, on motion of a party, the court may permit discovery proceedings to continue.

Adopted on an expedited basis Aug. 28, 2013, effective Sept. 13, 2013; adopted on a permanent basis, effective Nov. 14, 2013.

STATE BAR COMMITTEE NOTES

1966 Amendment

[Rule 23] The present rule, with its obscure classifications in the cases and literature of "true," "hybrid," and "spurious" class actions with their various consequences as to res judicata, has proved hopelessly confusing and is completely replaced. The blending of shareholders' derivative actions with class actions under the previous rule, when in fact derivative action need not be a class action, has also proved confusing, and this confusion is eliminated by clearly separating the two.

The official comment of the federal advisory committee on civil rules on the change of Federal Rule 23 is comprehensive and should be consulted.

AUTHORS' COMMENTS

Analysis

5. Class Action Determinations.
6. Appeal from Class Action Determinations.
7. Requirements for Notice to Class Members.
8. Exhaustion of Administrative Remedies; Claims Against Governmental Entities.
9. Doctrine of Virtual Representation.
10. Communication With Potential Class Members by Parties and Counsel.
11. Settlement and Dismissal of Class Actions.
12. Settlement Classes.
13. Claim Forms.
14. Securities Fraud Class Actions.

1. *Scope and Purpose of Rule.* Ariz. R. Civ. P. 23, was substantially amended in 1966 to maintain conformity with the corresponding provisions of the Federal Rules of Civil Procedure. While the Rule, as amended, contemplates three distinct types of class actions, they do not correspond to the pre-1966 categories of "true," "hybrid" and "spurious" class actions, which were abandoned as "hopelessly confusing."

Class actions under the amended Rule are intended to provide a convenient method of litigating claims involving large numbers of people. In appropriate cases, they provide benefits to both claiming and defending parties, and serve as a practical tool for resolving multiple claims on a consistent basis at the least cost and with the least disruption to the judicial system. *Andrew S. Arena, Inc. v. Superior Court In and For County of Maricopa*, 163 Ariz. 423, 788 P.2d 1174 (1990). The Rule, accordingly, should be construed liberally and doubts concerning whether to certify a class should be resolved in favor of certification. *ESI Ergonomic Solutions, LLC v. United Artists Theatre Circuit, Inc.*, 203 Ariz. 94, 50 P.3d 844 (Ct. App. Div. 1 2002).

The fact that claims may be brought on behalf of a class does not render arbitration agreements unenforceable. *Harrington v. Pulte Home Corp.*, 211 Ariz. 241, 119 P.3d 1044 (Ct. App. Div. 1 2005).

2. *Comparison With Federal Rule.* ARCP 23 deals with the same subject matter as FRCP 23, and contains many provisions found in the Federal Rule, but there are differences. ARCP 23 does not contain a number of the 1998, 2003 or 2007 substantive amendments made to FRCP 23, which concern, among other things, the appointment of class counsel, procedures for settling or compromising class actions, the contents of class notices and the award of attorney's fees. In addition the certification procedures differ between the rule.

In response to the enactment of A.R.S. § 12-1871, and effective November 14, 2013, ARCP 23(f) was added to address interlocutory appeals from an order certifying or denying class action status. ARCP 23(f) concerns the same topic as FRCP 23(f), which was adopted in 1998, but the two provisions differ in important ways. The federal rule is discretionary and states that an appeal "does not stay proceedings" unless ordered otherwise by the district judge or court of appeal. The Arizona rule is not discretionary and states that an appeal "shall be stayed" unless, on motion, the court permits discovery to continue.

In 2007, the language of FRCP 23 was amended as part of the general restyling of the Federal Rules of Civil Procedure to make the Federal Rules more easily understood and to make style and terminology consistent throughout the Federal Rules of Civil Procedure. Those stylistic modifications have not been incorporated into ARCP 23. ARCP 23 and FRCP 23 also are structurally dissimilar.

3. *Requirements for All Class Actions— Rule 23(a).* To be properly maintainable as such, every class action must satisfy all the requirements of Rule 23(a), and, in addition, the requirements of one of the three subdivisions of Rule 23(b). While class actions are most frequently instituted on behalf of plaintiff classes, the Rule clearly authorizes and contemplates actions brought against a defendant class. Rule 23 provides that one or more members of a class may "sue *or be sued* as representative parties on behalf of all. . . ." (emphasis added).

The four prerequisites for every class action established in Rule 23(a) are: (1) that the class be so numerous that joinder of all members would be impracticable, (2) that there be questions of fact and law common to the class, (3) that the claims or defenses of the putative class representative be typical of those of the class members, and (4) that the putative class representative fairly and adequately protect the interests of the class. Whether these prerequisites are satisfied in any given case is a matter committed to the sound discretion of the trial court. *London v. Green Acres Trust*, 159 Ariz. 136, 765 P.2d 538 (Ct. App. Div. 1 1988); *Continental Townhouses East Unit One Ass'n v. Brockbank*, 152 Ariz. 537, 733 P.2d 1120, 73 A.L.R.4th 921 (Ct. App. Div. 1 1986); *Godbey v. Roosevelt School Dist. No. 66 of Maricopa County*, 131 Ariz. 13, 638 P.2d 235, 1 Ed. Law Rep. 1326, 25 Wage & Hour Cas. (BNA) 1011 (Ct. App. Div. 1 1981); *Carpinteiro v. Tucson School Dist. No. 1 of Pima County*, 18 Ariz. App. 283, 501 P.2d 459 (Div. 2 1972).

In the unique vernacular which class action litigation, primarily in the federal courts, has generated, the four requirements set forth in Rule 23(a) are generally referred to as "numerosity," "commonality," "typicality," and "adequacy." With respect to the first requirement, there is no bright line test for determining whether the membership of the class is so numerous that joinder of all members would be impracticable. *London v. Green Acres Trust*, 159 Ariz. 136, 765 P.2d 538 (Ct. App. Div. 1 1988). Although the "commonality" requirement of Rule 23(a)(2) literally only requires that there be one or more issues of either or law or fact that are common to the members of the class, there has been a tendency in Arizona to merge this analysis with the analysis required by Rule 23(b)(3) of whether those common questions predominate over questions affecting only individual class members. *See Reader v. Magma-Superior Copper Co.*, 110 Ariz. 115, 515 P.2d 860 (1973); *Lennon v. First Nat. Bank of Arizona*, 21 Ariz. App. 306, 518 P.2d 1230 (Div. 1 1974).

In assessing whether the "typicality" requirement is satisfied, the Arizona courts, relying on federal case law, have examined whether: (1) common issues of law and/or fact are presented; (2) the interests of the proposed class representative are antagonistic to those of members of the putative class; and, (3) absent class members have suffered the same type of injury as the class representative. *Lennon v. First Nat. Bank of Arizona*, 21 Ariz. App. 306, 518 P.2d 1230 (Div. 1 1974). Finally, determining that the class representative will adequately protect the interests of the class includes consideration of the quality and experience of the attorneys representing the class representative and the class. *London v. Green Acres Trust*, 159 Ariz. 136, 765 P.2d 538 (Ct. App. Div. 1 1988). A putative class representative who does not have standing to pursue a claim cannot maintain a class action on behalf of others who would have such standing. *Karbal v. Arizona Dept. of Revenue*, 215 Ariz. 114, 158 P.3d 243 (Ct. App. Div. 1 2007).

Arizona law permits class action lawsuits seeking tax refunds in the Tax Court on behalf of a class of affected taxpayers. *Arizona Dept. of Revenue v. Dougherty*, 200 Ariz. 515, 29 P.3d 862 (2001). *See also*, *City Of Phoenix v. Fields*, 219 Ariz. 568, 201 P.3d 529 (2009). It is not necessary that each taxpayer member of the class file an individual administrative refund claim with the Department of Revenue. *Arizona Dept. of Revenue v. Dougherty*, 200 Ariz. 515, 29 P.3d 862 (2001). The requirement that administrative remedies be exhausted may be satisfied by the filing of an administrative claim on behalf of class members by the representative party. *Arizona Dept. of Revenue v. Dougherty*, 200 Ariz. 515, 29 P.3d 862 (2001). The provisions of the "notice of claim" statute, A.R.S. § 12-821.01, with respect to claims against public agencies and officers are generally applicable to claims brought on behalf of a class. *City Of Phoenix v. Fields*, 219 Ariz. 568, 201 P.3d 529 (2009).

4. *Types of Class Actions; Additional Requirements—Rule 23(b).* In addition to meeting the four prerequisites of Rule 23(a), a class action must satisfy the criteria of one of the three subdivisions of Rule 23(b). Rule 23(b)(1) authorizes a class action where the prosecution of separate actions creates the possibility that such individual adjudications would, as a practical matter, dispose of the interests of other class members not party to the adjudications, or impair or impede their ability to protect those interests. *Cf. Godbey v. Roosevelt School Dist. No. 66 of Maricopa County*, 131 Ariz. 13, 638 P.2d 235, 1 Ed. Law Rep. 1326, 25 Wage & Hour Cas. (BNA) 1011 (Ct. App. Div. 1 1981).

Rule 23(b)(2) authorizes a class action where the party opposing the class has acted or refused to act on grounds generally applicable to the class. The presence of such a uniform policy or course of conduct applied to a class would also satisfy the requirements of Rule 23(a) that there be questions of law or fact common to class members and that the class representative's claims be typical of those of the class. *Lennon v. First Nat. Bank of Arizona*, 21 Ariz. App. 306, 518 P.2d 1230 (Div. 1 1974). This type of class action, however, is limited to instances where injunctive or declaratory relief is sought.

Rule 23(b)(3) permits a class action where questions of law or fact common to the class predominate over questions that affect only individual members, and the class action is the superior vehicle for resolving the controversy. These are again determinations committed to the discretion of the trial court, which is directed by the Rule to consider four nonexclusive considerations: (1) the interests of members of the class in prosecuting or defending separate actions, (2) the extent and nature of existing litigation concerning the controversy, (3) the desirability of concentrating litigation of the controversy in a single forum, and (4) the management difficulties likely to be encountered. *See Reader v. Magma-Superior Copper Co.*, 110 Ariz. 115, 515 P.2d 860 (1973).

It is not necessary that all questions of law or fact be common to class members—only that those issues that are common be predominant in the litigation. *Home Federal Sav. and Loan Ass'n v. Pleasants*, 23 Ariz. App. 467, 534 P.2d 275 (Div. 2 1975) (overruled on other grounds by, Hanania v. City of Tucson, 123 Ariz. 37, 597 P.2d 190 (Ct. App. Div. 2 1979)). That requirement may not be satisfied where the primary focus of the action is the recovery of individualized damages, or where there will be difficult issues as to the liability of the defendant(s) to some members of the class as defined. *See Godbey v. Roosevelt School Dist. No. 66 of Maricopa County*, 131 Ariz. 13, 638 P.2d 235, 1 Ed. Law Rep. 1326, 25 Wage & Hour Cas. (BNA) 1011 (Ct. App. Div. 1 1981); *Markiewicz v. Salt River Valley Water Users' Ass'n*, 118 Ariz. 329, 576 P.2d 517 (Ct. App. Div. 1 1978).

The four factors listed under Rule 23(b)(3) are not exclusive, and the trial court may consider other relevant factors. *ESI Ergonomic Solutions, LLC v. United Artists Theatre Circuit, Inc.*, 203 Ariz. 94, 50 P.3d 844 (Ct. App. Div. 1 2002). While one of those factors is the extent and nature of any litigation concerning the dispute already commenced, the absence of such litigation is consistent with individual claims and suits not being economically feasible, and typically supports the superiority of the class action vehicle. *ESI Ergonomic Solutions, LLC v. United Artists Theatre Circuit, Inc.*, 203 Ariz. 94, 50 P.3d 844 (Ct. App. Div. 1 2002). The fact that the class claim is brought under a statute that prescribes minimum penalties such that a recovery by the class might be economically ruinous for, or even annihilate, the defendants is not a proper basis for determining that the class action would not be superior to other means for resolving the dispute. *ESI Ergonomic Solutions, LLC v. United Artists Theatre Circuit, Inc.*, 203 Ariz. 94, 50 P.3d 844 (Ct. App. Div. 1 2002).

5. *Class Action Determinations.* As amended effective November 14, 2013, Ariz. R. Civ. P. 23(c)(1), directs the trial court, as soon as practicable after the commencement of a purported class action to hold a hearing and determine by written order whether the action is properly maintained as a class action. This is a change from past practice, and is the result of amendment to Rule 23, which was adopted on an expedited basis and in response to the the enactment of A.R.S. § 12-1871 *et seq.* concerning certification of class actions.

While Rule 23(c)(1) speaks in terms of a determination whether an action is to be maintained as a class action, that determination is commonly referred to, in the unique legal vernacular which Rule 23 has inspired, as a "certification" of the class, and a request for such a determination as a "motion to certify."

The issue may be brought before the Court by the purported class representative or by the adverse party. Regardless of the manner in which the issue is raised, the burden is on the purported class representative to demonstrate the propriety of the class action. *Carpinteiro v. Tucson School Dist. No. 1 of Pima County*, 18 Ariz. App. 283, 501 P.2d 459 (Div. 2 1972). The issue before the trial court, however, is whether the requirements of Rule 23 are met, however, and not whether the class representative has stated a claim or will prevail on the merits. *Home Federal Sav. and Loan Ass'n v. Pleasants*, 23 Ariz. App. 467, 534 P.2d 275 (Div. 2 1975) (overruled on other grounds by, Hanania v. City of Tucson, 123 Ariz. 37, 597 P.2d 190 (Ct. App. Div. 2 1979)). Rule 23(c)(4) authorizes the Court to limit a class action to particular issues presented, and to divide the overall class into subclasses for particular purposes.

The issue of whether an action may be maintained as a class

action is committed to the trial court's discretion and will only be disturbed on appeal for abuse of that discretion. *Godbey v. Roosevelt School Dist. No. 66 of Maricopa County*, 131 Ariz. 13, 638 P.2d 235, 1 Ed. Law Rep. 1326, 25 Wage & Hour Cas. (BNA) 1011 (Ct. App. Div. 1 1981); *Carpinteiro v. Tucson School Dist. No. 1 of Pima County*, 18 Ariz. App. 283, 501 P.2d 459 (Div. 2 1972).

A judgment entered in a class action is binding upon all members of the class, except those who have, after receipt of notice, excluded themselves from the class. *A.J. Bayless Markets, Inc. v. Superior Court of Pima County*, 145 Ariz. 285, 700 P.2d 1385 (Ct. App. Div. 2 1985). A plaintiff who does not have standing to pursue a claim may not bring a class action on behalf of persons who would have such standing. *Fernandez v. Takata Seat Belts, Inc.*, 210 Ariz. 138, 108 P.3d 917 (2005).

6. *Appeal from Class Action Determinations.* Effective January 1, 2014, and in response to the enactment of A.R.S. § 12-1871 *et seq.* relating to class actions, the Arizona Supreme Court adopted on an expedited basis new Ariz. R. Civ. P. 23(f) is a departure from past practice and case law. Specifically, Rule 23(f) does the following:

1. confirms a party's right to an interlocutory appeal of an order granting or denying class certification, as provided by A.R.S. §§ 12-1871 *et seq.*; and
2. operates to stay the trial proceedings pending appeal, except that on motion the court may permit discovery to proceed.

Although adopted on an expedited basis, the Arizona Supreme Court ordered the matter opened up for comment until October 25, 2013. Ariz. R. Civ. P. 23(f) was adopted on a permanent basis, effective November 14, 2013.

7. *Requirements for Notice to Class Members.* Rule 23(c)(2) requires that notice be given to class members in any class action permitted to be maintained under Rule 23(b)(3). A similar notice is not mandated for class actions brought pursuant to Rule 23(b)(1) or Rule 23(b)(2), but the Court has discretion to direct such a notice if deemed advisable.

The notice must advise class members of the pendency of the action, that class members may request to be excluded from the class, that any judgment entered will be binding upon class members who do not request exclusion, and that class members desiring to participate may enter an appearance through counsel. The notice should also describe the litigation, the nature of the claims being asserted, and the definition of the class.

The notice must be the "best notice practicable under the circumstances," which includes individual notice to all those class members who can be identified and located through reasonable efforts. *A.J. Bayless Markets, Inc. v. Superior Court of Pima County*, 145 Ariz. 285, 700 P.2d 1385 (Ct. App. Div. 2 1985). This generally entails notice by mail to those class members for whom a current or recent address is ascertainable without undue burden, supplemented by a notice through publication. A defendant cannot complain of a failure to give notice to members of the class whose names have been wrongfully withheld from the class representative by the defendant. *London v. Green Acres Trust*, 159 Ariz. 136, 765 P.2d 538 (Ct. App. Div. 1 1988).

Rule 23(c)(2) provides that "the court shall direct" the requisite notice to members of the class, but it is the general practice to place upon the parties the task of actually disseminating the notice. There has been some question whether the notice should purport to be from counsel, rather than the Court, *cf.*, Wright & Miller, *Federal Practice & Procedure: Civil* § 1788. The better view is that the notice should have the Court's *imprimatur,* regardless of the mechanics of its actual dissemination. It is settled that the plaintiff or plaintiffs must bear the original costs of providing notice.

8. *Exhaustion of Administrative Remedies; Claims Against Governmental Entities.* The general rule is that at least one member of the putative class must have exhausted applicable administrative remedies. *Estate of Bohn v. Waddell*, 174 Ariz. 239, 848 P.2d 324, 16 Employee Benefits Cas. (BNA) 2877 (Ct. App. Div. 1 1992). There is generally no requirement that all members of the class have done so. There was nothing in the former Arizona "claims statute," A.R.S. § 12-821, which precluded class actions against public entities. A claim against a governmental entity may be presented as a class claim and, if it is denied, may thereafter be entertained as a class action, provided it is otherwise a proper class action under applicable principles of law. *Andrew S. Arena, Inc. v. Superior Court In and For County of Maricopa*, 163 Ariz. 423, 788 P.2d 1174 (1990).

To satisfy the requirements of the statute where a claim is presented on behalf of a purported class, the putative class representative must include in the notice of claim a specific amount for which that individual's claim can be settled, and also a statement that, if litigation ensues, that individual intends to seek certification of a plaintiff class. *City Of Phoenix v. Fields*, 219 Ariz. 568, 201 P.3d 529 (2009). The same rule prevails in Tax Court proceedings seeking tax refunds on behalf of a class of similarly situated taxpayers. *Arizona Dept. of Revenue v. Dougherty*, 200 Ariz. 515, 29 P.3d 862 (2001).

9. *Doctrine of Virtual Representation.* At least one Arizona court

has given recognition to the doctrine of "virtual representation," which provides that a judgment or decree may adjudicate the rights of a person not a party to the adjudication, if that absent party's interests are so well represented by a party before the Court that they receive actual and efficient representation. The doctrine, which rests on consideration of necessity, convenience and efficiency in the administration of justice, is a descendant of the rule of equity known as the doctrine of representation, which is the historical root of the Court's power to administer class actions. As evidenced by the following Arizona case recognizing this doctrine, application of the doctrine of virtual representation, however, demands the utmost caution. *Bohn v. Waddell*, 164 Ariz. 74, 790 P.2d 772 (Tax Ct. 1990), on reconsideration, 167 Ariz. 344, 807 P.2d 1 (Tax Ct. 1991), opinion vacated, 174 Ariz. 239, 848 P.2d 324, 16 Employee Benefits Cas. (BNA) 2877 (Ct. App. Div. 1 1992) and (abrogated by, Harper v. Virginia Dept. of Taxation, 509 U.S. 86, 113 S. Ct. 2510, 125 L. Ed. 2d 74, 16 Employee Benefits Cas. (BNA) 2313 (1993)) and aff'd in part, vacated in part, 174 Ariz. 239, 848 P.2d 324, 16 Employee Benefits Cas. (BNA) 2877 (Ct. App. Div. 1 1992).

10. *Communication With Potential Class Members by Parties and Counsel.* The question of whether the named parties or their counsel should be permitted to communicate directly with members of the class is a sensitive one requiring a delicate balance of competing considerations.

On the one hand, class members are perhaps the best source of factual information concerning the merits of the claims in issue and a prohibition on communications may unduly hamper the ability of counsel to prepare their case. Perhaps more importantly, class members who receive notice of the class action will frequently have questions concerning the actions which are best and most efficiently handled by counsel for the parties. An order barring such communications deprives class members of a convenient source of accurate information, and may place upon the Court and its personnel the burden of responding to inquiries from class members.

On the other hand, there is always the danger that counsel may seize the opportunity to influence the decision by a class member whether or not to participate in the action. One solution to this dilemma is to allow limited communication with class members subject to monitoring by the Court to detect and deal with abuses.

11. *Settlement and Dismissal of Class Actions.* Rule 23(e) provides that a class action may not be dismissed or compromised without the Court's approval and with notice of the proposed dismissal or compromise to class members. This provision is

designed to protect absent class members against collusive settlements and does not apply to a dismissal on the merits. The requirement of prior judicial approval applies, even if the settlement is made prior to a determination by the Court that the action may proceed as a class action. *Cf. Simer v. Rios*, 661 F.2d 655, 32 Fed. R. Serv. 2d 781, 68 A.L.R. Fed. 235 (7th Cir. 1981).

Rule 23(e) does not by its terms require a hearing on the proposed settlement, but the common and more prudent practice is to conduct one where interested class members can present their views. Similarly, there is no specified procedure for "tentative approval" of a class action settlement, but the wisest course is to secure at least a preliminary indication as to whether the court considers the settlement fair and reasonable before the parties incur the burden and expense of providing notice to the class. A class representative has two legally cognizable interests—a cause of action against the defendant(s) and a claim to proceed on behalf of a class. *Douglas v. Governing Bd. of Window Rock Consol. School Dist. No. 8*, 221 Ariz. 104, 210 P.3d 1275, 246 Ed. Law Rep. 435 (Ct. App. Div. 1 2009). When a purported class representative accepts an unapportioned offer of judgment, that party relinquishes both claims, and lacks standing to appeal from the judgment entered on the offer and acceptance. *Douglas v. Governing Bd. of Window Rock Consol. School Dist. No. 8*, 221 Ariz. 104, 210 P.3d 1275, 246 Ed. Law Rep. 435 (Ct. App. Div. 1 2009).

12. *Settlement Classes.* It is not uncommon for proposed settlements of class actions to be reached before the Court makes a determination whether the action may proceed as a class action, and for the settlement agreement to contemplate the certification of a class for settlement purposes only. If the settlement is not approved, the agreement concerning formation and certification of a class is withdrawn. *Cf. Plummer v. Chemical Bank*, 668 F.2d 654, 27 Fair Empl. Prac. Cas. (BNA) 1169, 27 Empl. Prac. Dec. (CCH) P 32321 (2d Cir. 1982). It remains to be seen whether the Arizona courts will follow the rule enunciated by the United States Supreme Court, in *Amchem Products, Inc. v. Windsor*, 521 U.S. 591, 117 S. Ct. 2231, 138 L. Ed. 2d 689, 37 Fed. R. Serv. 3d 1017, 28 Envtl. L. Rep. 20173 (1997), that trial courts, when presented with a request to "certify" a class for settlement purposes only, must nevertheless conduct an inquiry into whether, considerations of trial management problems aside, the proposed settlement class meets the other requirements of Rule 23 for class certification.

13. *Claim Forms.* It is a fairly common practice to require class members who desire to participate in the proceeds of a proposed settlement to submit a claim evidencing that desire and providing some indication of the nature of their claim. This procedure is

not, however, required by the Rule and the Court is free to construct a mechanism for approving and effectuating settlements that is both efficient and fair to class members.

14. *Securities Fraud Class Actions*. A.R.S. § 44-2081 purports to impose a variety of procedural requirements on class actions alleging violations of Arizona's securities statutes, A.R.S. §§ 44-2001 *et seq.*, which would not necessarily be imposed by Rule 23. Initially, any plaintiff seeking to serve as a class representative in such a class action must file, together with the complaint, a sworn certification that: (1) the plaintiff reviewed and authorized the filing of the complaint; (2) the plaintiff did not purchase the security that is the subject of the action at the direction of counsel or in order to participate in the action; (3) the plaintiff is willing to serve as a class representative; and, (4) the plaintiff will not accept any remuneration for serving as class representative, beyond the plaintiff's share of any recovery, except as may be ordered or approved by the Court. The certification must also detail all the plaintiff's pertinent transactions in the securities that are the subject of the action, and identify any other securities fraud actions filed within the preceding three (3) years in which the plaintiff has sought to serve as a class representative. As of this date, there are no Arizona cases addressing the constitutionality of this statute.

Within twenty (20) days after the complaint is filed, the plaintiff must arrange for the publication, in a "widely circulated national business-oriented publication or wire service," of a notice that advises members of the purported class of the pendency of the action and the claims that have been asserted. In addition, the notice must advise purported class members that they may move the Court, within sixty (60) days of the date of publication, to serve as "lead plaintiff" for the purported class. If any such motion is filed, the Court is to consider it within ninety (90) days after the notice is published, and appoint the "most adequate" plaintiff as the "lead plaintiff" for the class. The "most adequate" plaintiff may be, but need not be, the plaintiff who originally instituted the action, and is the plaintiff who, subject to the Court's approval, is to select and retain counsel to represent the class. The statute also contains extensive provisions concerning the processing of settlements of these types of class actions.

Rule 23.1. Derivative actions by shareholders

In a derivative action brought by one or more shareholders or members to enforce a right of a corporation or of an unincorporated association, the corporation or association having failed to enforce a right which may properly be asserted by it, the complaint shall be verified and shall allege that the plaintiff was a shareholder or member at the time of the transaction of which the plaintiff complains or that the share or membership thereafter devolved on the plaintiff by operation of law. The complaint shall also allege with particularity the efforts, if any, made by the plaintiff to obtain the action the plaintiff desires from the directors or comparable authority and, if necessary, from the shareholders or members, and the reasons for the plaintiff's failure to obtain the action or for not making the effort. The derivative action may not be maintained if it appears that the plaintiff does not fairly and adequately represent the interests of the shareholders or members similarly situated in enforcing the right of the corporation or association. The action shall not be dismissed or compromised without the approval of the court, and notice of the proposed dismissal or compromise shall be given to shareholders or members in such manner as the court directs.

Added July 1, 1966, effective Nov. 1, 1966; amended Sept. 15, 1987, effective Nov. 15, 1987.

STATE BAR COMMITTEE NOTES

1966 Amendment

[Rule 23.1] A derivative action by a shareholder of a corporation or by a member of an unincorporated association has distinctive aspects which require the special provisions set forth in the proposed rule. The next-to-last sentence recognizes that the question of adequacy of representation may arise when the plaintiff is one of a group of shareholders or members.

The court has inherent power to provide for the conduct of the proceedings in a derivative action, including the power to determine the course of the proceedings and require that any appropriate notice be given to shareholders or members.

The amendment is in accord with *Funk v. Spalding*, 74 Ariz. 219, 246 P.2d 184 (1952) and *Goodman v. Cushman*, 92 Ariz. 276, 376 P.2d 394 (1962).

AUTHORS' COMMENTS

Analysis

1. *Scope and Purpose of Rule.* Ariz. R. Civ. P. 23.1, adopted in 1966 to conform to a corresponding amendment to the Federal Rules of Civil Procedure, provides a vehicle for stockholders of a corporation (or members of an unincorporated association) to pursue a claim which belongs to the corporation but which the corporation refuses to pursue or is not pursuing competently. It is quite frequently employed where the claim is for damages to the corporation resulting from mismanagement or other wrongdoing by the corporation's own officers and/or directors.

The Rule specifically requires that the Complaint in a derivative action be verified and must allege either that the plaintiff was a shareholder at the time of the transaction which is the subject of the litigation, or that the plaintiff's shares devolved upon the plaintiff by operation of law. The Rule also specifies that a derivative action may not be dismissed or compromised without Court approval, following notice to shareholders or class members of the proposed dismissal or compromise in such manner as the Court directs.

2. *Comparison With Federal Rule.* Despite structural differences, ARCP 23.1 is essentially the same as FRCP 23.1, except that the Arizona Rule does not contain the requirement contained in the Federal Rule that the complaint in a shareholders derivative action must allege that the action is not one brought to confer jurisdiction on a Federal court which it would not otherwise have.

In 2007, the language of FRCP 23.1 was amended as part of the general restyling of the Federal Rules of Civil Procedure to make the Federal Rules more easily understood and to make style and terminology consistent throughout the Federal Rules of Civil Procedure. Those stylistic modifications have not been incorporated into ARCP 23.1.

3. *Standards and Requirements for Derivative Actions.* The general rule is that, where the effect of mismanagement, or of a wrong by a third party, is to the value of the corporate stock, only the corporation has a right of action for damages. *Funk v. Spalding*, 74 Ariz. 219, 246 P.2d 184 (1952). The stockholders of the corporation may only intervene where the officers and/or directors refuse to pursue the claim or are guilty of fraud in pursuing it. *Rugee v. Hadley Products*, 73 Ariz. 362, 241 P.2d 798, 33 A.L.R.2d 468 (1952); *Funk v. Spalding*, 74 Ariz. 219, 246 P.2d 184 (1952).

There must first be a demand made upon the corporation to pursue the claim. *Callanan v. Sun Lakes Homeowners' Ass'n No. 1, Inc.*, 134 Ariz. 332, 656 P.2d 621 (Ct. App. Div. 1 1982) (dismissing a stockholder's derivative action without prejudice because the stockholder failed to make a demand on the corporate defendant or explain the futility of such effort, as required by

Rule 23.1). The purpose of this requirement is to ensure that prospective defendants are not exposed to multiple actions. *Funk v. Spalding*, 74 Ariz. 219, 246 P.2d 184 (1952).

The claim for relief is actually that of the corporation, and any judgment obtained is in favor of the corporation. The complaint must set forth with particularity the efforts of the plaintiff to secure from the management and, if necessary, from the shareholders, the action desired, and the reasons for the failure to obtain such action or the reasons for not making such effort.

Under A.R.S. § 10-742, no shareholder may commence a derivative action until two requirements are met: (1) a written demand has been made on the corporation to take suitable action, and (2) ninety (90) days have expired from the date the demand was made, unless the shareholder is notified within that ninety-day period that the demand has been rejected, and unless the statute of limitations applicable to the claim will expire within the ninety days or the corporation will suffer irreparable injury during that period. *Albers v. Edelson Technology Partners L.P.*, 201 Ariz. 47, 31 P.3d 821, 111 A.L.R.5th 715 (Ct. App. Div. 1 2001). The statute is clear and admits of no exception on the basis that a demand would be futile. *Albers v. Edelson Technology Partners L.P.*, 201 Ariz. 47, 31 P.3d 821, 111 A.L.R.5th 715 (Ct. App. Div. 1 2001). The statute effectively overrules the result reached in *Blumenthal v. Teets*, 155 Ariz. 123, 745 P.2d 181 (Ct. App. Div. 1 1987).

Rule 23.2. Actions relating to unincorporated associations

An action brought by or against the members of an unincorporated association as a class by naming certain members as representative parties may be maintained only if it appears that the representative parties will fairly and adequately protect the interests of the association and its members. In the conduct of the action the court may make appropriate orders corresponding with those described in Rule 23(d), and the procedure for dismissal or compromise of the action shall correspond with that provided in Rule 23(e).

Added July 1, 1966, effective Nov. 1, 1966.

STATE BAR COMMITTEE NOTES

1966 Addition

[Rule 23.2] Although an action by or against representatives of the membership of an unincorporated association has often been viewed as a class action, the real or main purpose of this characterization has been to give "entity treatment" to the association when for formal reasons it cannot sue or be sued as a jural person under Rule 17(b).

AUTHORS' COMMENTS

Analysis

1. Scope and Purpose of Rule.
2. Comparison With Federal Rule.

1. *Scope and Purpose of Rule.* The action authorized by Ariz. R. Civ. P. 23.2 is in essence a form of class action for the members of unincorporated associations. An unincorporated association may sue or be sued in its own name only where that jural status is conferred by statute, either expressly or by necessary implication. *Associated Students of University of Arizona v. Arizona Bd. of Regents*, 120 Ariz. 100, 584 P.2d 564 (Ct. App. Div. 2 1978). Absent such statutory authority, the association can pursue grievances (or be pursued) either in an action which joins all the association's members as parties plaintiff or defendant, or through a "representative" action by or against one of its members under Rule 23.2. The Rule thus eliminates the need to join in the action all the members of an association which lacks the authority to sue or be sued in its own name. Where the Rule 23.2 action is brought against members of an unincorporated association as a class, it eliminates jurisdictional, service and venue obstacles that might render joining all members individually

impracticable.

The only requirement of Rule 23(a) expressly carried forward to Rule 23.2 is that the representative members fairly and adequately protect the interests of the association and its members, and there is some debate whether Rule 23(a)'s other requirements of "commonality," "typicality," and "numerosity" apply as well. The categorization of the class action, required under Rule 23(b) for determining how it is to be governed, is not required for an action brought pursuant to Rule 23.2. The Rule also specifically incorporates Rule 23(d)'s authority for the Court to make appropriate orders concerning the conduct of these types of actions, and Rule 23(e)'s requirement that Court approval be obtained for any compromise or dismissal of an action on behalf of an unincorporated association.

2. *Comparison With Federal Rule.* ARCP 23.2 is substantively identical to FRCP 23.2. In 2007, the language of FRCP 23.2 was amended as part of the general restyling of the Federal Rules of Civil Procedure to make the Federal Rules more easily understood and to make style and terminology consistent throughout the Federal Rules of Civil Procedure. Those stylistic modifications have not been incorporated into ARCP 23.2.

Rule 24. Intervention

(a) Intervention of Right. Upon timely application anyone shall be permitted to intervene in an action: (1) when a statute confers an unconditional right to intervene; or (2) when the applicant claims an interest relating to the property or transaction which is the subject of the action and the applicant is so situated that the disposition of the action may as a practical matter impair or impede the applicant's ability to protect that interest, unless the applicant's interest is adequately represented by existing parties.

Amended July 1, 1966, effective Nov. 1, 1966; Sept. 15, 1987, effective Nov. 15, 1987; Oct. 9, 1996, effective Dec. 1, 1996.

(b) Permissive Intervention. Upon timely application anyone may be permitted to intervene in an action:

1. When a statute confers a conditional right to intervene.
2. When an applicant's claim or defense and the main action have a question of law or fact in common.

In exercising its discretion the court shall consider whether the intervention will unduly delay or prejudice the adjudication of the rights of the original parties.

(c) Procedure. A person desiring to intervene shall serve a motion to intervene upon the parties as provided in Rule 5. The motion shall state the grounds therefor and shall be accompanied by a pleading setting forth the claim or defense for which intervention is sought.

Amended March 26, 1963, effective June 1, 1963.

(d) Time to Answer. If the motion to intervene is granted, the plaintiff and defendant shall be allowed a reasonable time, not exceeding twenty days, in which to answer the pleading of the intervener.

STATE BAR COMMITTEE NOTES

1963 Amendment

[Rule 24(c)] This change is made to include the change made in Rule 5.

1966 Amendment

[Rule 24(a)] Present Rule 24(a)(2) makes it a condition of intervention that "the applicant is or may be bound by a judgment in the action," and this has recently created difficulties with intervention in class actions. If the "bound" language is read literally in the sense of res judicata, it can defeat intervention in some meritorious cases.

The amendment provides that an applicant is entitled to intervene in an action when his position is comparable to that of a person under Rule 19(a)(2)(i), as amended. The Rule 19(a)(2)(i) criterion imports practical considerations, and the deletion of the "bound" language similarly frees the rule from undue preoccupation with strict considerations of res judicata.

Whether a party is in fact so situated that the disposition of the action may as a practical matter impair or impede his ability to protect his interests is a question to be determined by the court; it is not sufficient that such an impairment or impediment is pleaded.

The amendment will not alter the results of existing Arizona decisions. See, for example, *John F. Long Homes, Inc. v. Holohan*, 97 Ariz. 31, 396 P.2d 394 (1964); *Miller v. City of Phoenix*, 51 Ariz. 254, 75 P.2d 1033 (1938).

It is intended to have no bearing on specialized problems of taxpayers suits which do not exist in the federal system. See *Mitchell v. City of Nogales*, 83 Ariz. 328, 320 P.2d 955 (1958).

AUTHORS' COMMENTS

Analysis

1. Scope and Purpose of Rule.
2. Comparison With Federal Rule.
3. Intervention as of Right.
4. Permissive Intervention.
5. Procedure for Seeking Intervention; Standards.
6. Timeliness Requirement.
7. Procedure After Intervention.
8. Appellate Review.

1. *Scope and Purpose of Rule.* Ariz. R. Civ. P. 24 specifies the circumstances under which third parties whose interests may be affected by pending litigation may move to intervene to assert or defend those interests. The right to intervene is mandatory if the conditions of Rule 24(a) are satisfied; otherwise, it is permissive.

The proposed intervenor has the burden of showing the propriety of and/or entitlement to intervention. *Morris v. Southwest Sav. & Loan Ass'n*, 9 Ariz. App. 65, 449 P.2d 301 (1969). Intervention in special actions under Rule 2(b) of the Rules of Procedure for Special Actions is governed by the same standards as intervention under Rule 24. *Mountain States Tel. & Tel. Co. v. Arizona Corp. Com'n*, 160 Ariz. 350, 773 P.2d 455 (1989). Rule 24 is remedial and should be liberally construed to assist parties in securing justice and protecting their rights. *Allen v. Chon-Lopez*, 214 Ariz. 361, 153 P.3d 382 (Ct. App. Div. 2 2007).

2. *Comparison With Federal Rule.* Both ARCP 24 and FRCP 24 deal with the subject of intervention and are similar, but there are significant differences between the two rules. ARCP 24(a) and (b) are essentially the same as FRCP 24(a) and (b)(1), (3). ARCP 24(d) provides that, if intervention is permitted, the existing parties shall have a reasonable time, not to exceed twenty (20) days, to respond to the pleadings of the intervener. FRCP 24 does not

have a corresponding provision.

FRCP 24(b)(2) provides that, where a party relies upon a federal or state statute, executive order or regulation as the basis for a claim or defense, the federal or state officer or agency concerned may be permitted to intervene. ARCP 24 does not have a similar provision.

In addition, in 2007, the language of FRCP 24 was amended as part of the general restyling of the Federal Rules of Civil Procedure to make the Federal Rules more easily understood and to make style and terminology consistent throughout the Federal Rules of Civil Procedure. Those stylistic modifications have not been incorporated into ARCP 24.

3. *Intervention as of Right.* Ariz. R. Civ. P. 24(a) provides for intervention as of right when: (1) a statute confers an unconditional right to intervene or (2) the applicant claims an interest relating to the property or transaction which is the subject of the action and the disposition of the action may, as a practical matter, impair or impede the applicant's ability to protect that interest, unless the applicant's interest is adequately represented by existing parties. To establish intervention as of right, a prospective intervenor must have such an interest in the case that the judgment would have a direct legal effect upon his or her rights and not merely a possible or contingent effect. *Dowling v. Stapley*, 221 Ariz. 251, 211 P.3d 1235 (Ct. App. Div. 1 2009).

For example, a party who claims to be the owner of property which is the subject of a replevin action has a right to intervene. *General Ins. Co. of America v. Deen*, 3 Ariz. App. 187, 412 P.2d 869 (1966). To intervene as of right, the intervenor's asserted interest must be based on a right which belongs to the proposed intervenor rather than to an existing party, and a bare allegation that one's interest may become impaired is not, without more, sufficient to confer a right to intervene. *Weaver v. Synthes, Ltd. (U.S.A.)*, 162 Ariz. 442, 784 P.2d 268 (Ct. App. Div. 1 1989). The appellate courts review *de novo* the issue of whether an applicant has established a right to intervene under Rule 24(a). *Dowling v. Stapley*, 221 Ariz. 251, 211 P.3d 1235 (Ct. App. Div. 1 2009).

Under the Rule as it existed before it was amended in December 1996, when intervention was sought as a matter of right, the fact that the parties already present in the action could adequately protect the intervenor's interests was irrelevant. *Winner Enterprises, Ltd. v. Superior Court in and for County of Yavapai*, 159 Ariz. 106, 765 P.2d 116 (Ct. App. Div. 1 1988). The 1996 amendment to Rule 24(a) added a provision which indicates that an application for intervention as of right may be denied where the interests of the applicant are being adequately represented by existing parties to the action.

4. *Permissive Intervention.* Rule 24(b) permits intervention, in the discretion of the trial court, where:

(1) a statute confers a conditional right to intervene and

(2) the claim or defense the proposed intervenor seeks to assert has a question of law or fact in common with the underlying action.

Dowling v. Stapley, 221 Ariz. 251, 211 P.3d 1235 (Ct. App. Div. 1 2009) (permissive intervention denied).

Before granting permissive intervention, the trial court must first decide whether Rule 24(b)(1) or (2) have been satisfied. *Bechtel v. Rose In and For Maricopa County*, 150 Ariz. 68, 722 P.2d 236 (1986); *Roberto F. v. Arizona Dept. of Economic Sec.*, 232 Ariz. 45, 301 P.3d 211 (Ct. App. Div. 1 2013), as amended, (June 20, 2013) and review denied, (Oct. 29, 2013); *Dowling v. Stapley*, 221 Ariz. 251, 211 P.3d 1235 (Ct. App. Div. 1 2009). While an application for permissive intervention is addressed to the trial court's discretion, the Rule directs the Court to consider whether intervention "will unduly delay or prejudice the adjudication of the rights of the original parties." Ariz. R. Civ. P. 24(b).

On appeal, the court reviews an order denying permissive intervention under Rule 24(b) for abuse of discretion. *Bechtel v. Rose In and For Maricopa County*, 150 Ariz. 68, 722 P.2d 236 (1986); *Dowling v. Stapley*, 221 Ariz. 251, 211 P.3d 1235 (Ct. App. Div. 1 2009).

5. *Procedure for Seeking Intervention; Standards.* The procedures for seeking intervention are specified in Rule 24(c). The intervenor's proposed pleading must accompany the motion for leave to intervene, and the failure to submit one is grounds for denial of the motion. *Lebrecht v. O'Hagan*, 96 Ariz. 288, 394 P.2d 216 (1964). The intervenor must take the action as it stands and may not seek to expand or contract the issues framed by the original parties. *Pintek v. Superior Court In and For Cochise County*, 78 Ariz. 179, 277 P.2d 265 (1954); *Arizona Real Estate Dept. v. Arizona Land Title & Trust Co.*, 9 Ariz. App. 54, 449 P.2d 71 (1968), superseded by statute on unrelated grounds as stated in, *Chaffin v. Commissioner of Arizona Dept. of Real Estate*, 164 Ariz. 474, 793 P.2d 1141 (Ct. App. Div. 1 1990).

The proposed intervenor has the burden of showing the propriety of and/or entitlement to intervention. *Morris v. Southwest Sav. & Loan Ass'n*, 9 Ariz. App. 65, 449 P.2d 301 (1969). Under Rule 24(d), if the Court grants a motion to intervene, the intervenor's adversary (plaintiff or defendant) must be given a reasonable time, but not exceeding twenty (20) days, to respond to the intervenor's pleading.

Arizona courts have repeatedly recognized that, because collateral estoppel generally will apply, an insurance company has the requisite interest under Rule 24(a) to be entitled to intervene. *Mora v. Phoenix Indem. Ins. Co.*, 196 Ariz. 315, 996 P.2d 116 (Ct. App. Div. 1 1999); *McGough v. Insurance Co. of North America*, 143 Ariz. 26, 691 P.2d 738 (Ct. App. Div. 1 1984); *United Pacific/Reliance Ins. Co. v. Kelley*, 127 Ariz. 87, 618 P.2d 257 (Ct. App. Div. 1 1980); *Lawrence v. Burke*, 6 Ariz. App. 228, 431 P.2d 302 (1967). An insurer may even intervene in an action against its insured which is in the process of being settled, so long as the insurer has not refused to defend. *Anderson v. Martinez*, 158 Ariz. 358, 762 P.2d 645 (Ct. App. Div. 1 1988).

An insurer that acknowledges its duty to defend, even if it reserves the right to contest coverage, has at least implicitly acknowledged that it might be required to indemnify the insured and retains an interest in the outcome of the litigation that would support a right to intervene. *Himes v. Safeway Ins. Co.*, 205 Ariz. 31, 66 P.3d 74 (Ct. App. Div. 1 2003); *Mora v. Phoenix Indem. Ins. Co.*, 196 Ariz. 315, 996 P.2d 116 (Ct. App. Div. 1 1999). Thus, an insurer that has agreed to defend subject to a reservation of rights has a right to intervene in the hearing on damages to be awarded following the entry of the insured's default pursuant to an agreement between the insured and the claimant. *Monterey Homes Arizona, Inc. v. Federated Mut. Ins. Co.*, 221 Ariz. 351, 212 P.3d 43 (Ct. App. Div. 1 2009); *H.B.H. v. State Farm Fire and Cas. Co.*, 170 Ariz. 324, 823 P.2d 1332 (Ct. App. Div. 1 1991).

That hearing, and the insurer's participation in it, are appropriately limited to the issue of damages, however, unless the insurer's motion to intervene is accompanied by a pleading raising the issue of the reasonableness of the settlement, as Rule 24(c) requires. *Waddell v. Titan Ins. Co., Inc.*, 207 Ariz. 529, 88 P.3d 1141 (Ct. App. Div. 1 2004). The insurer can still litigate the issue of the reasonableness of the settlement in a subsequent garnishment proceeding or a declaratory judgment action. *Waddell v. Titan Ins. Co., Inc.*, 207 Ariz. 529, 88 P.3d 1141 (Ct. App. Div. 1 2004).

Where an insurer asserts that it owes no duty to defend its insured, however, that implies that it has no duty to indemnify and the insurer has in effect asserted that its insurance policy does not apply to the claim. In that circumstance, the insurer has no interest in the litigation against its insured that would justify granting it a right to intervene. *Mora v. Phoenix Indem. Ins. Co.*, 196 Ariz. 315, 996 P.2d 116 (Ct. App. Div. 1 1999). It has been held, accordingly, that an insurer loses its right to intervene if it has breached the contract of insurance by refusing to provide a defense for its insured. *Purvis v. Hartford Acc. and Indem. Co.*, 179 Ariz. 254, 877 P.2d 827 (Ct. App. Div. 1 1994). Before such a refusal to defend can be found, however, it must first be shown that the insurer received sufficient notice that the insured was tendering to it the defense of the claim. *Purvis v. Hartford Acc. and Indem. Co.*, 179 Ariz. 254, 877 P.2d 827 (Ct. App. Div. 1 1994).

6. *Timeliness Requirement.* An application for intervention must be timely, whether it is for intervention as of right or for permissive intervention. *See*, Rules 24(a) and (b); *Weaver v. Synthes, Ltd. (U.S.A.)*, 162 Ariz. 442, 784 P.2d 268 (Ct. App. Div. 1 1989) (interpreting the timeliness requirement under Rule 24(a), which governs intervention as of right); *Zenith Electronics Corp. v. Ballinger*, 220 Ariz. 257, 204 P.3d 1106 (Ct. App. Div. 1 2009) (discussing the timeliness requirement under Rule 24(b), which governs permissive intervention). The timeliness requirement, however, is a flexible one committed to the trial court's broad discretion, and its decision on timeliness will be disturbed only for an abuse of that discretion. *William Z. v. Arizona Dept. of Economic Sec.*, 192 Ariz. 385, 965 P.2d 1224 (Ct. App. Div. 1 1998); *Purvis v. Hartford Acc. and Indem. Co.*, 179 Ariz. 254, 877 P.2d 827 (Ct. App. Div. 1 1994); *Weaver v. Synthes, Ltd. (U.S.A.)*, 162 Ariz. 442, 784 P.2d 268 (Ct. App. Div. 1 1989); *Winner Enterprises, Ltd. v. Superior Court in and for County of Yavapai*, 159 Ariz. 106, 765 P.2d 116 (Ct. App. Div. 1 1988); *State Farm Mut. Auto. Ins. Co. v. Paynter*, 118 Ariz. 470, 577 P.2d 1089 (Ct. App. Div. 1 1978).

The trial court can take into account the stage to which the action has progressed and whether the applicant had prior notice of the action and an opportunity to seek intervention. *State Farm Mut. Auto. Ins. Co. v. Paynter*, 118 Ariz. 470, 577 P.2d 1089 (Ct. App. Div. 1 1978). The most important consideration is whether the delay in seeking intervention will prejudice the existing parties. *State ex rel. Napolitano v. Brown & Williamson Tobacco Corp.*, 196 Ariz. 382, 998 P.2d 1055 (2000); *Weaver v. Synthes, Ltd. (U.S.A.)*, 162 Ariz. 442, 784 P.2d 268 (Ct. App. Div. 1 1989). *Compare State ex rel. Napolitano v. Brown & Williamson Tobacco Corp.*, 196 Ariz. 382, 998 P.2d 1055 (2000) (prejudice where case ongoing for two and one-half years and parties already had settled), with *Winner Enterprises, Ltd. v. Superior Court in and for County of Yavapai*, 159 Ariz. 106, 765 P.2d 116 (Ct. App. Div. 1 1988) (no prejudice where pretrial intervention would not delay trial).

While post-judgment motions to intervene are not *per se* untimely, they are not favored and will be granted only in unusual and extraordinary circumstances. *State ex rel. Napolitano v. Brown & Williamson Tobacco Corp.*, 196 Ariz. 382, 998 P.2d 1055 (2000); *Matter of One Cessna 206 Aircraft, FAA Registry No. N-72308, License No. U-206-1361*, 118 Ariz. 399, 577 P.2d 250 (1978); *John F. Long Homes, Inc. v. Holohan*, 97 Ariz. 31, 396

P.2d 394 (1964); *Weaver v. Synthes, Ltd. (U.S.A.)*, 162 Ariz. 442, 784 P.2d 268 (Ct. App. Div. 1 1989); *Gonzalez-Burgueno v. National Indem. Co.*, 134 Ariz. 383, 656 P.2d 1244 (Ct. App. Div. 2 1982); *Salvatierra v. National Indem. Co.*, 133 Ariz. 16, 648 P.2d 131 (Ct. App. Div. 2 1982); *Velasco v. Mallory*, 5 Ariz. App. 406, 427 P.2d 540 (1967).

For example, it was held not to be an abuse of discretion for the trial court to permit a nonparty public interest organization to intervene post-judgment, where such motion sought modification of a protective order entered before the case was settled and dismissed. *Zenith Electronics Corp. v. Ballinger*, 220 Ariz. 257, 204 P.3d 1106 (Ct. App. Div. 1 2009). In *Zenith*, the public interest organization argued the settlement operated to injure public health, safety and welfare because the settlement precluded the public disclosure of documents. *Zenith Electronics Corp. v. Ballinger*, 220 Ariz. 257, 204 P.3d 1106 (Ct. App. Div. 1 2009). Intervention on appeal, however, is not authorized or permissible. *Riley v. Cochise County*, 10 Ariz. App. 55, 455 P.2d 1005 (1969).

7. *Procedure After Intervention.* Under Rule 24(d), if the Court grants the motion to intervene, the intervenor's adversary (plaintiff or defendant) must be given a reasonable time, but not exceeding twenty (20) days, to respond to the intervenor's pleading.

8. *Appellate Review.* Denial of a motion to intervene is an appealable order. *Bechtel v. Rose In and For Maricopa County*, 150 Ariz. 68, 722 P.2d 236 (1986); *Allen v. Chon-Lopez*, 214 Ariz. 361, 153 P.3d 382 (Ct. App. Div. 2 2007). A subsequent ruling on the merits will not moot the issue as the proposed intervenor may appeal from the order denying intervention and from the judgment entered in the intervenor's absence. *Winner Enterprises, Ltd. v. Superior Court in and for County of Yavapai*, 159 Ariz. 106, 765 P.2d 116 (Ct. App. Div. 1 1988). An order denying a motion to intervene may also be reviewed on a petition for special action where an appeal would not be an equally plain, speedy or adequate remedy. *J.A.R. v. Superior Court In and For County of Maricopa*, 179 Ariz. 267, 877 P.2d 1323 (Ct. App. Div. 1 1994). The trial court's resolution of the issue of the timeliness of an application for intervention will be reviewed only for an abuse of discretion. *State ex rel. Napolitano v. Brown & Williamson Tobacco Corp.*, 196 Ariz. 382, 998 P.2d 1055 (2000); *Allen v. Chon-Lopez*, 214 Ariz. 361, 153 P.3d 382 (Ct. App. Div. 2 2007); *Purvis v. Hartford Acc. and Indem. Co.*, 179 Ariz. 254, 877 P.2d 827 (Ct. App. Div. 1 1994). A trial court's determination on whether the applicant has established a right to intervene will be reviewed *de novo*. *Dowling v. Stapley*, 221 Ariz. 251, 211 P.3d 1235 (Ct. App. Div. 1 2009); *Purvis v. Hartford Acc. and Indem. Co.*, 179 Ariz. 254, 877 P.2d 827 (Ct. App. Div. 1 1994).

Rule 25. Substitution of parties

(a) Death.

(1) If a party dies and the claim is not thereby extinguished, the court may order substitution of the proper parties. The motion for substitution may be made by any party or by the successors or representatives of the deceased party and, together with the notice of hearing, shall be served on the parties as provided in Rule 5 and upon persons not parties in the manner provided in Rules 4, 4.1 or 4.2, as applicable, of these rules for the service of a summons. Unless the motion for substitution is made not later than 90 days after the death is suggested upon the record by service of a statement of the fact of the death as provided herein for the service of the motion, the action shall be dismissed as to the deceased party.

(2) In the event of the death of one or more of the plaintiffs or of one or more of the defendants in an action in which the right sought to be enforced survives only to the surviving plaintiffs or only against the surviving defendants, the action does not abate. The death shall be suggested upon the record and the action shall proceed in favor of or against the surviving parties.

Amended March 26, 1963, effective June 1, 1963; Oct. 2, 1991, effective Dec. 1, 1991.

(b) Death of Defendant After Tort Action Commenced. An action to recover damages for injuries to the person, or death caused by the wrongful act, default or neglect of another, shall not abate by reason of the death of the defendant, and the decedent's personal representative may be substituted as defendant. If the action is against a receiver, assignee or trustee, and such receiver, assignee or trustee dies, resigns or is removed from office, the successor in office may be substituted as defendant. The action shall thereupon proceed to judgment as if the defendant had remained alive, or the original receiver, assignee or trustee had continued in office.

Amended Sept. 15, 1987, effective Nov. 15, 1987.

(c) Incompetency. If a party becomes incompetent, the court upon motion served as provided in subdivision (a) of this Rule may allow the action to be continued by or against the party's representative.

Amended Sept. 15, 1987, effective Nov. 15, 1987.

(d) Transfer of Interest. In case of any transfer of interest, the action may be continued by or against the original party, unless the court upon motion directs the person to whom the interest is transferred to be substituted in the action or joined with the original party. Service of the motion shall be made as provided in subdivision (a) of this Rule.

(e) Public Officers; Death or Separation From Office.

1. When a public officer is a party to an action in an official capacity and during its pendency dies, resigns, or otherwise ceases to hold office, the action does not abate and the officer's successor is automatically substituted as a party. Proceedings following the substitution shall be in the name of the substituted party, but any misnomer not affecting the substantial rights of the parties shall be disregarded. An order of substitution may be entered at any time, but the omission to enter such an order shall not affect the substitution.

2. A public officer who sues or is sued in an official capacity may be described as a party by the officer's official title rather than by name; but the court may require the officer's name to be added.

Amended July 14, 1961, effective Nov. 1, 1961; Sept. 15, 1987, effective Nov. 15, 1987.

STATE BAR COMMITTEE NOTES

1961 Amendment

Rule 25(e): This proposed amendment is designed to conform to changes in the Federal Rules. The official comment on the change in the Federal Rules is comprehensive, and is adopted.

This rule is needed as well to solve the problems of the state practice. Under our existing Rule, when a suit is brought by or against a public officer, that suit abates at the end of six months after the removal or retirement of that person from office unless he is a member of a continuing board, in which case this becomes immaterial. *Ethington v. Wright*, 66 Ariz. 382, 189 P.2d 209 (1948). In other words, if a suit were against a Recorder or a Sheriff, and there were a change in the occupancy, the suit would be totally lost if the mechanical step of substitution were not taken.

This problem has been one of continuing concern in Arizona. Prior to Rule 25(e), we had no method for substituting successors in office, and in a leading case, therefore, a suit was dismissed against an Arizona County Treasurer, a County Assessor, and a County Attorney, and it was held that a wholly new suit would have to be brought against their successors. *Irwin v. Wright*, 258 U.S. 219, 42 S. Ct. 293, 66 L. Ed. 573 (1922). This was followed in Ex parte *Ex parte La Prade*, 289 U.S. 444, 53 S. Ct. 682, 77 L. Ed. 1311 (1933). To meet the situation thus revealed by the two United States Supreme Court decisions, under the Revised Code of 1928, Section 3772, the Legislature provided that an action should not abate because an officer was a party, and instead provided for the possibility of substitution. (For the text, see the note to the 1939 Code at Section 21-530).

The Act just referred to was rendered obsolete by the Rules of Civil Procedure and our Court followed the present 25(e) in lieu of it. See: *Engle v. Scott*, 57 Ariz. 383, 392, 114 P.2d 236, 239 (1941). The current Code, has dropped the 1928 provision altogether.

1963 Amendment

[Rule 25(a)] Present Rule 25(a)(1), together with present Rule 6(b), results in an inflexible requirement that an action be dismissed as to a deceased party if substitution is not carried out within a fixed period measured from the time of the death. The hardships and inequities of this unyielding requirement plainly appear from the cases.

The amended rule establishes a time limit for the motion to substitute based not upon the time of the death, but rather upon the time information of the death is provided by means of a suggestion of death upon the record, i.e. service of a statement of the fact of the death. Cf. Ill.Ann.Stat., c. 110, section 54(2) (Smith-Hurd 1956). The motion may not be made later than 90 days after the service of the statement unless the period is extended pursuant to Rule 6(b), as amended.

A motion to substitute may be made by any party or by the representative of the deceased party without awaiting the suggestion of death. Indeed, the motion will usually be so made. If a party or the representative of the deceased party desires to limit the time within which another may make the motion, he may do so by suggesting the death upon the record.

A motion to substitute made within the prescribed time will ordinarily be granted, but under the permissive language of the first sentence of the amended rule ("the court may order") it may be denied by the court in the exercise of a sound discretion if made long after the death—as can occur if the suggestion of death is not made or is delayed—and circumstances have arisen rendering it unfair to allow substitution. Accordingly, a party interested in securing substitution under the amended rule should not assume that he can rest indefinitely awaiting the suggestion of death before he makes his motion to substitute.

Since the change eliminates the two-year provision and substitutes therefor the ninety-day period after the suggestion of death, it of course follows that the two-year cases are rendered obsolete. An example is *Shire v. Superior Court In and For Greenlee County*, 63 Ariz. 420, 162 P.2d 909 (1945). The amendment will not affect such a case as *Jasper v. Batt*, 76 Ariz. 328, 264 P.2d 409 (1953), which requires substitution in tort cases, since this decision deals with the right of substitution and not with the timing or technique of it, and the latter matters are the only ones within the rule revision.

AUTHORS' COMMENTS

Analysis

1. Scope and Purpose of Rule.
2. Comparison With Federal Rule.
3. Survival of Claims.
4. Death of a Party; Suggestion of Death on the Record.
5. Transfer of Interests.
6. Change of Public Official.

1. *Scope and Purpose of Rule.* Ariz. R. Civ. P. 25 deals generally with the subject of the substitution of parties, in those instances where the original named party dies, becomes incompetent, or consummates a transfer of interests affected by the litigation. It also covers the situation where a state official named individually but in an official capacity is succeeded in office. Rule

25 does not govern amendments to add parties or intervention.

2. *Comparison With Federal Rule.* ARCP 25 is substantially similar to FRCP 25. The Federal Rule does not contain the provision in ARCP 25(b), which provides that actions for personal injury do not abate upon the death of the defendant, but proceed against the personal representative as if the defendant had remained alive. ARCP 25(c), (d) and (e)(1) are generally the same as FRCP 25(b), (c) and (d), respectively. ARCP 25(e)(2) is substantively identical to FRCP 17(d).

In 2007, the language of FRCP 25 was amended as part of the general restyling of the Federal Rules of Civil Procedure to make the Federal Rules more easily understood and to make style and terminology consistent throughout the Federal Rules of Civil Procedure. Those stylistic modifications have not been incorporated into ARCP 25.

3. *Survival of Claims.* Ariz. R. Civ. P. 25 does not address whether a right or liability survives the death of a party. It only provides a vehicle, and specifies the procedure, for accomplishing a substitution where the right or liability does survive.

As a general rule, unless a statute specifically provides to the contrary, an action for personal injuries does not survive the death of the plaintiff, *Liberty Mut. Ins. Co. v. Thunderbird Bank*, 113 Ariz. 375, 555 P.2d 333 (1976); *Quintero v. Continental Rent-A-Car System, Inc.*, 105 Ariz. 135, 460 P.2d 189 (1969); *Harleysville Mut. Ins. Co. v. Lea*, 2 Ariz. App. 538, 410 P.2d 495 (1966); *Eades v. House*, 3 Ariz. App. 245, 413 P.2d 576 (1966); or the death of the tortfeasor. *Rodriquez v. Terry*, 79 Ariz. 348, 290 P.2d 248 (1955). The current statute governing the survival of claims and liabilities is A.R.S. § 14-3110, which provides that all claims and liabilities survive, except causes of action for breach of a promise to marry, seduction, libel, slander, separate maintenance, alimony, loss of consortium or invasion of the right of privacy.

The constitutionality of this statute's predecessor has been upheld. *Harrington v. Flanders*, 2 Ariz. App. 265, 407 P.2d 946 (1965). Under that statute, a decedent's personal representative may pursue a claim for personal injuries suffered by the decedent, but may not recover damages for pain and suffering or so-called "hedonic damages"—damages for loss of enjoyment of life. *Quintero v. Rogers*, 221 Ariz. 536, 212 P.3d 874 (Ct. App. Div. 1 2009). Actions for punitive damages, on the other hand, survive the death of the plaintiff as well as the death of the tortfeasor. *Quintero v. Rogers*, 221 Ariz. 536, 212 P.3d 874 (Ct. App. Div. 1 2009).

Because the elder abuse statute, A.R.S. § 46-455, expressly provides to victims of elder abuse and their representatives the right to recover damages for pain and suffering, even after the death of the abused victim, it controls over the provisions of A.R.S. § 14-3110, and such claims will survive the death of the victim. *In re Estate of Winn*, 214 Ariz. 149, 150 P.3d 236 (2007); *Matter of Guardianship/Conservatorship of Denton*, 190 Ariz. 152, 945 P.2d 1283 (1997). Claims for financial exploitation of a vulnerable adult brought under that statute survive as well. *In re Estate of Wyttenbach*, 219 Ariz. 120, 193 P.3d 814 (Ct. App. Div. 1 2008). In addition, an action for dissolution of a marriage abates, and the Superior Court loses subject matter jurisdiction over it, when one of the spouses involved dies before any order is entered, other than one for a preliminary injunction. *Van Emmerik v. Colosi*, 193 Ariz. 398, 972 P.2d 1034 (Ct. App. Div. 1 1998).

The survival statute neither creates a cause of action nor affects the running of the statute of limitations. *Matter of Chase's Estate*, 125 Ariz. 270, 609 P.2d 85 (Ct. App. Div. 1 1980). The statute also provides that, in an action for personal injuries, recovery for pain and suffering is barred by the death of the injured party. *Cf. also, Harrington v. Flanders*, 2 Ariz. App. 265, 407 P.2d 946 (1965). The remedy in that circumstance is through a claim for wrongful death. *Barragan v. Superior Court of Pima County*, 12 Ariz. App. 402, 470 P.2d 722 (Div. 2 1970).

4. *Death of a Party; Suggestion of Death on the Record.* The present version of Rule 25(a), adopted in 1963, establishes a time limit for effecting a substitution which runs, not from the actual date of death, but rather from the time notice of the death is provided through a suggestion of death upon the record. The former Rule required dismissal unless a motion for substitution was made within two years of the actual date of death. *Ray v. Rambaud*, 103 Ariz. 186, 438 P.2d 752 (1968). Under the present Rule, the action is to be dismissed unless a motion for substitution is made no later than ninety (90) days after the death is suggested on the record, but a formal suggestion of death must be filed and served to commence the running of that ninety-day period. *Varela v. Roman*, 156 Ariz. 476, 753 P.2d 166 (Ct. App. Div. 2 1987).

5. *Transfer of Interests.* Where there has been a transfer of interests affected by the action, the action continues by or against the transferor, unless the Court on motion directs either the substitution or joinder of the transferee. A "transfer of interest" under the Rule includes a corporate merger.

6. *Change of Public Official.* Rule 25(e) applies in those instances where a public officer has been named in the action individually, but in an official capacity. This is, of course, not necessary. Under Rule 25(e)(2), a public officer sued in an official capacity may be described by the title of the office held, rather than by name.

Strictly speaking, seeking the substitution of a successor in office by amendment or otherwise is an unnecessary formality. Under Rule 25(e)(1), a succession does not cause an action to abate and the successor "is automatically substituted as a party." The failure to seek or secure the entry of an order of substitution "shall not affect the [automatic] substitution."

V. DEPOSITIONS AND DISCOVERY

Rule 26. General provisions governing discovery

(a) Discovery Methods. Parties may obtain discovery by one or more of the following methods: depositions upon oral examination or written questions; written interrogatories; production of documents or things or permission to enter upon land or other property, for inspection and other purposes; physical and mental examinations; and requests for admission.

Added July 17, 1970, effective Nov. 1, 1970. Amended Aug. 7, 1984, effective Nov. 1, 1984.

(b) Discovery Scope and Limits. Unless otherwise limited by order of the court in accordance with these rules, the scope of discovery is as follows:

(1) *In General.*

(A) Parties may obtain discovery regarding any matter, not privileged, which is relevant to the subject matter involved in the pending action, whether it relates to the claim or defense of the party seeking discovery or to the claim or defense of any other party, including the existence, description, nature, custody, condition and location of any books, documents, or other tangible things and the identity and location of persons having knowledge of any discoverable matter. It is not ground for objection that the information sought will be inadmissible at the trial if the information sought appears reasonably calculated to lead to the discovery of admissible evidence.

(B) A party need not provide discovery of electronically stored information from sources that the party identifies as not reasonably accessible because of undue burden or expense. On motion to compel discovery or for a protective order, the party from whom discovery is sought must show that the information is not readily accessible because of undue burden or expense. If that showing is made, the court may nevertheless order disclosure or discovery from such sources if the requesting party shows good cause considering the limitations in the final paragraph of subsection (b)(1) of this Rule. The court may specify conditions for the disclosure or discovery.

(C) The frequency or extent of use of the discovery methods set forth in subdivision (a) may be limited by the court if it determines that: (i) the discovery sought is unreasonably cumulative or duplicative, or obtainable from some other source that is either more convenient, less burdensome, or less expensive; (ii) the party seeking discovery has had ample opportunity by discovery in the action to obtain the information sought; or (iii) the discovery is unduly burdensome or expensive, given the needs of the case, the amount in controversy, limitations on the parties' resources, and the importance of the issues at stake in the litigation. The court may act upon its own initiative after reasonable notice or pursuant to a motion under subdivision (c).

(2) *Insurance Agreements.* A party may obtain discovery of the existence and contents of any insurance agreement under which any person carrying on an insurance business may be liable to satisfy part or all of a judgment which may be entered in the action or to indemnify or reimburse for payments made to satisfy the judgment. Information concerning the insurance agreement is not by reason of disclosure admissible in evidence at trial. For purposes of this paragraph, an application for insurance shall not be treated as part of an insurance agreement.

(3) *Trial Preparation: Materials.* Subject to the provisions of subdivision (b)(4) of this rule, a party may obtain discovery of documents and tangible things otherwise discoverable under subdivision (b)(1) of this rule and prepared in anticipation of litigation or for trial by or for another party or by or for that other party's representative (including the other party's attorney, consultant, surety, indemnitor, insurer or agent) only upon a showing that the party seeking discovery has substantial need of the materials in the preparation of the party's case and that the party is unable without undue hardship to obtain the substantial equivalent of the materials by other means. In ordering discovery of such materials when the required showing has been made, the court shall protect against disclosure of the mental impressions, conclusions, opinions, or legal theories of an attorney or other representative of a party concerning the litigation.

A party may obtain without the required showing a statement concerning the action or its subject matter previously made by that party. Upon request, a person not a party may obtain without the required showing a statement concerning the action or its subject matter previously made by that person. If the request is refused, the person may move for a court order. The provisions of Rule 37(a)(4) apply to the award of expenses incurred in relation to the motion. For purposes of this paragraph, a statement previously made is (A) a written statement signed or otherwise adopted or approved by the person making it, or (B) a stenographic, mechanical, electrical, or other recording, or a transcription thereof, which is a substantially verbatim recital of an oral statement by the person making it and contemporaneously recorded.

(4) *Trial Preparation: Experts.*

(A) A party may depose any person who has been identified as an expert whose opinions may be presented at trial.

(B) A party may through interrogatories or by deposition discover facts known or opinions held by an expert who has been retained or specially employed by another party in anticipation of litigation or preparation for trial and who is not expected to be called as a witness at trial, only as provided in Rule 35(b) or upon a showing of exceptional circumstances under which it is impracticable for the party seeking discovery to obtain facts or opinions on the same subject by other means.

(C) Unless manifest injustice would result, (i) the court shall require that the party seeking discovery pay the expert a reasonable fee for time spent in responding to discovery under subdivisions (b)(4)(A) and (b)(4)(B) of this rule; and (ii) with respect to discovery obtained under subdivision (b)(4)(B) of this rule the court shall require, the party seeking discovery to pay the other party a fair portion of the fees and expenses reasonably incurred by the latter party in obtaining facts and opinions from the expert.

(D) In all cases including medical malpractice cases, each side shall presumptively be entitled to only one independent expert on an issue, except upon a showing of good cause. Where there are multiple parties on a side and the parties cannot agree as to which independent expert will be called on an issue, the court shall designate the independent expert to be called or, upon the showing of good cause, may allow more than one independent expert to be called.

In medical malpractice cases, each party shall presumptively be entitled to only one standard-of-care expert. A defendant may testify on the issue of that defendant's standard-of-care in addition to that defendant's independent expert witness and the court shall not be required to allow the plaintiff an additional expert witness on the issue of the standard-of-care.

Text of Rule 26(b)(5) applicable to those cases filed before April 15, 2014 that are not subject to the conditions stated in the November 27, 2013 Amended Order Regarding Applicability Provision, in R-13-0017.

See also, text of Rule 26(b)(5) applicable to cases filed on or after April 15, 2014 and to those cases filed before April 15, 2014 that are subject to the conditions stated in the November 27, 2013 Amended Order Regarding Applicability Provision, in R-13-0017.

(5) *Non-party at Fault.* Any party who alleges pursuant to A.R.S. § 12-2506(B) (as amended), that a person or entity not

currently or formerly named as a party was wholly or partially at fault in causing any personal injury, property damage or wrongful death for which damages are sought in the action shall provide the identity, location, and the facts supporting the claimed liability of such nonparty at the time of compliance with the requirements of Rule 38.1(b)(2) of these Rules, or within one hundred fifty (150) days after the filing of that party's answer, whichever is earlier. The trier of fact shall not be permitted to allocate or apportion any percentage of fault to any nonparty whose identity is not disclosed in accordance with the requirements of this subpart 5 except upon written agreement of the parties or upon motion establishing good cause, reasonable diligence, and lack of unfair prejudice to other parties.

Amended July 17, 1970, effective Nov. 1, 1970; Aug. 7, 1984, effective Nov. 1, 1984; Sept. 15, 1987, effective Nov. 15, 1987; May 3, 1989, effective July 1, 1989; Dec. 20, 1991, effective July 1, 1992; Oct. 9, 1996, effective Dec. 1, 1996; Oct. 10, 2000, effective Dec. 1, 2000; September 5, 2007, effective January 1, 2008; Sept. 2, 2010, effective Jan. 1, 2011.

Text of Rule 26(b)(5) applicable to cases filed on or after April 15, 2014 and to those cases filed before April 15, 2014 that are subject to the conditions stated in the November 27, 2013, Amended Order Regarding Applicability Provision, in R-13-0017.

See also, text of Rule 26(b)(5) applicable to those cases filed before April 15, 2014 that are not subject to the conditions stated in the November 27, 2013 Amended Order Regarding Applicability Provision, in R-13-0017.

(5) *Non-party at Fault.* Any party who alleges pursuant to A.R.S. § 12-2506(B), that a person or entity not currently or formerly named as a party was wholly or partially at fault in causing any personal injury, property damage or wrongful death for which damages are sought in the action shall provide the identity, location, and the facts supporting the claimed liability of such non-party within one hundred fifty (150) days after the filing of that party's answer. The trier of fact shall not be permitted to allocate or apportion any percentage of fault to any non-party whose identity is not disclosed in accordance with the requirements of this subsection except upon written agreement of the parties or upon motion establishing good cause, reasonable diligence, and lack of unfair prejudice to other parties.

Amended July 17, 1970, effective Nov. 1, 1970; Aug. 7, 1984, effective Nov. 1, 1984; Sept. 15, 1987, effective Nov. 15, 1987; May 3, 1989, effective July 1, 1989; Dec. 20, 1991, effective July 1, 1992; Oct. 9, 1996, effective Dec. 1, 1996; Oct. 10, 2000, effective Dec. 1, 2000; September 5, 2007, effective January 1, 2008; Sept. 2, 2010, effective Jan. 1, 2011; Aug. 28, 2013, effective April 15, 2014, subject to the conditions of Order No. R-13-0017.

(c) Protective Orders.

(1) Subject to paragraph (2) of this rule, upon motion by a party or by the person from whom discovery is sought, and for good cause shown, the court in which the action is pending or alternatively, on matters relating to a deposition, the court in the county where the deposition is to be taken may make any order which justice requires to protect a party or person from annoyance, embarrassment, oppression, or undue burden or expense, including one or more of the following: (1) that the discovery not be had; (2) that the discovery may be had only on specified terms and conditions, including a designation of the time or place; (3) that the discovery may be had only by a method of discovery other than that selected by the party seeking discovery; (4) that certain matters not be inquired into, or that the scope of the discovery be limited to certain matters; (5) that discovery be conducted with no one present except persons designated by the court; (6) that a deposition after being sealed be opened only by order of the court; (7) that a trade secret or other confidential research, development, or commercial information not be disclosed or be disclosed only in a designated way; (8) that the parties simultaneously file specified documents or information enclosed in sealed envelopes to be opened as directed by the court. If the motion for a protective order is denied in whole or in part, the court may, on such terms and conditions as are just, order that any party or person provide or permit discovery. The provisions of Rule 37(a)(4) apply to the award of expenses incurred in relation to the motion.

(2) Before entering an order in any way restricting a party or person from disclosing information or materials produced in discovery to a person who is not a party to the litigation in which the information or materials are being discovered or denying an intervener's request for access to such discovery materials, a court shall direct: (a) the party seeking confidentiality to show why a confidentiality order should be entered or continued; and (b) the party or intervener opposing confidentiality to show why a confidentiality order should be denied in whole or in part, modified or vacated. The burden of showing good cause for an order shall remain with the party seeking confidentiality. The court shall then make findings of fact concerning any relevant factors, including but not limited to: (i) any party's need to maintain the confidentiality of such information or materials; (ii) any nonparty's or intervener's need to obtain access to such information or materials; and (iii) any possible risk to the public health, safety or financial welfare to which such information or materials may relate or reveal. Any order restricting release of such information or materials to nonparties or interveners shall use the least restrictive means

to maintain any needed confidentiality. No such findings of fact are needed where the parties have stipulated to such an order or where a motion to intervene and to obtain access to materials subject to a confidentiality order are not opposed.

Amended July 17, 1970, effective Nov. 1, 1970; Oct. 28, 2002, effective Dec. 1, 2002; January 30, 2004, effective June 1, 2004.

(d) Sequence and Timing of Discovery. Unless the court upon motion, for the convenience of parties and witnesses and in the interests of justice, orders otherwise, methods of discovery may be used in any sequence and the fact that a party is conducting discovery, whether by deposition or otherwise, shall not operate to delay any other party's discovery.

Added July 17, 1970, effective Nov. 1, 1970.

(e) Supplementation of Responses. Except as provided in Rule 26.1 a party who has responded to a request for discovery with a response that was complete when made is under no duty to supplement the response to include information thereafter acquired, except as follows:

(1) A party is under a duty seasonably to supplement the response with respect to any question directly addressed to (A) the identity and location of persons having knowledge of discoverable matters, (B) the identity of each person expected to be called as an expert witness at trial, the subject matter on which the person is expected to testify and the substance of the person's testimony, (C) the identity of any other person expected to be called as a witness at trial and (D) the identity, location and the facts supporting the liability of any nonparty who is claimed to be wholly or partially at fault in causing any personal injury, property damage or wrongful death, pursuant to A.R.S. § 12-2506(B) (as amended). A party shall supplement responses with respect to any question directly addressed to (B), (C) or (D) prior to sixty (60) days before the date of trial. Any witness not identified in accordance with this Rule shall not be permitted to testify except for good cause shown or upon written agreement of the parties. The trier of fact shall not be permitted to allocate or apportion any percentage of fault to any nonparty whose identity is not disclosed in accordance with subpart (D) of this rule except for good cause shown or upon written agreement of the parties.

(2) A party is under a duty seasonably to amend a prior response if the party obtains information upon the basis of which (A) the party knows that the response was incorrect when made, or (B) the party knows that the response though correct when made is no longer true and the circumstances are such that a failure to amend the response is in substance a knowing

concealment.

(3) A duty to supplement responses may be imposed by order of the court, agreement of the parties, or at any time prior to trial through new requests for supplementation of prior responses.

Added July 17, 1970, effective Nov. 1, 1970. Amended July 27, 1978, effective Sept. 1, 1978; July 6, 1983, effective Sept. 7, 1983; Sept. 15, 1987, effective Nov. 15, 1987; May 1, 1989, effective July 1, 1989; Dec. 20, 1991, effective July 1, 1992; Oct. 9, 1996, effective Dec. 1, 1996; Oct. 10, 2000, effective Dec. 1, 2000.

(f) Discovery Requests, Responses, Objections and Sanctions. The court shall assess an appropriate sanction including any order under Rule 16(f) against any party or attorney who has engaged in unreasonable, groundless, abusive, or obstructionist conduct.

Added Aug. 7, 1984, effective Nov. 1, 1984. Amended Dec. 20, 1991, effective July 1, 1992.

(g) Discovery Motions. No discovery motion will be considered or scheduled unless a separate statement of moving counsel is attached thereto certifying that, after personal consultation and good faith efforts to do so, counsel have been unable to satisfactorily resolve the matter.

Added and effective June 27, 2001.

(h) [Deleted effective November 1, 1970].

HISTORICAL NOTES

[2014 Amendments]

[Rule 26(b)(5)] Arizona Supreme Court Order No. R-13-0017, issued Aug. 28, 2013, provided that the amendments of the order would be "effective on April 15, 2014 as to all cases filed on or after that date." The applicability provision of Order No. R-13-0017 was amended on Nov. 14, 2013, and subsequently amended on Nov. 27, 2013 to provide:

(1) The Amendments shall apply to all actions filed on or after April 15, 2014.

(2) Beginning on April 15, 2014, the Amendments also shall apply to any action filed prior to April 15, 2014 (a "pending action"), unless one of the following events has occurred before that date:

  (a) A party has filed a Motion to Set and Certificate of Readiness,

  (b) The parties have filed a Proposed Scheduling Order, or

  (c) The court has entered a Scheduling Order.

(3) If, in a pending action, one of the preceding events has not occurred before April 15, 2014, the parties shall file a Joint Report and a Proposed Scheduling Order in accordance with the Amendments by June 30, 2014, or within 270 days after the commencement of the action, whichever date is later. Otherwise, the court will place the action on the Dismissal Calendar in accordance with the Amendments.

(4) A trial court, in its discretion, may apply any of the Amendments to a case pending before April 15, 2014, even if the Amendments would not otherwise apply under paragraph (2) above. For example, if a party filed a Motion to Set and Certificate of Readiness before April 15, 2014, the

trial judge may set the matter for a trial setting conference under amended Rule 16(f), rather than place the case on the active calendar under pre-amendment Rule 38.1(c).

(5) Civil actions pending on the Inactive Calendar on April 15, 2014 shall be dismissed without prejudice on June 14, 2014, unless one of the actions set forth in subparts (1) - (4) of amended Rule 38.1(f) occurs before June 14, 2014.

STATE BAR COMMITTEE NOTES

1970 Amendments

Rule 26: The 1970 revision of rules is the first substantial alteration of discovery practice since the rules were first adopted in 1939. The 1970 revision includes some reorganization and redistribution of provisions within the discovery rules, which are, principally, Rules 26 through 37 of the Rules of Civil Procedure. The federal rules as revised are the subject of extensive annotations of greater length than is the normal Arizona practice. Major points of those notes plus matters of special application to Arizona are included in these notes. The Rule rearrangement is as follows:

Pre-1970 Rule No.	New Rule No.	Pre-1970 Rule No.	New Rule No.
26(a)	30(a), 31(a)	26(e)	32(b)
26(c)	30(c)	26(f)	32(c)
26(d)	32(a)	30(a)	30(b)
		30(c)	26(c)
		32	32(d)

Rule 26(a): This is a new subdivision enumerating discovery devices and is in accord with existing Arizona practice.

Rule 26(b): This subdivision is recast to cover the scope of discovery generally.

Rule 26(b)(2): This subdivision permits discovery of the existence and contents of insurance policies applicable to satisfy part or all of a judgment which may be obtained in the action. The rule alters to this extent the Arizona practice as declared in *Di Pietruntonio v. Superior Court In and For Maricopa County*, 84 Ariz. 291, 327 P.2d 746 (1958). However, the 1970 revision, which is based on the premise that in at least some instances the disclosure may aid settlement, accords with those elements of *Di Pietruntonio* which preclude examination into other financial assets of a defendant and which hold that the existence of casualty insurance is not a matter in which the jury has any concern whatsoever.

Rule 26(b)(3): This subdivision must be read in conjunction with Rule 34. The pre-1970 Rule 34 required a showing of "good cause" in court to require the production of documents. No such showing was required as a condition of either depositions or interrogatories. The good cause requirement unnecessarily consumed court time and was troublesome because of the obscurity of the term. The cases are fully analyzed in the annotations to the federal rule, but the practical consequence was that good cause was largely equated to simple relevance in connection with many documents, with a higher standard applied as to documents created for purposes of trial. The revised rules have therefore recognized this distinction. The requirement of good cause is totally eliminated from Rule 34 as applied to documents created for purposes of anything but trial. Such documents will be protected as against discovery abuses in the same way that all abuses may be prevented; a special good cause procedure is unnecessary.

However, the good cause standard is clarified, revised, and maintained as applied to documents created especially for trial.

Thus, revised Rule 26(b)(3) moves from the premise of the leading case of *Hickman v. Taylor*, 329 U.S. 495, 67 S. Ct. 385, 91 L. Ed. 451, 1947 A.M.C. 1 (1947), that strong protection is to be given to "work product." The Rule in providing that documents prepared in anticipation of litigation, whether by an attorney or other representative or directly interested person, shall be discoverable only upon a showing of substantial need, coupled with an inability to obtain the substantial equivalent of the materials without undue hardship, codifies the standard of *Southern Ry. Co. v. Lanham*, 403 F.2d 119, 12 Fed. R. Serv. 2d 860, 33 A.L.R.3d 427 (5th Cir. 1968). While the Rule is in specific accord with Lanham, it is in general accord with *Guilford Nat. Bank of Greensboro v. Southern Ry. Co.*, 297 F.2d 921, 5 Fed. R. Serv. 2d 575 (4th Cir. 1962), quoted at length and with approval in *Schlagenhauf v. Holder*, 379 U.S. 104, 117–118, 85 S. Ct. 234, 242–243, 13 L. Ed. 2d 152, 9 Fed. R. Serv. 2d 35A.1, Case 1 (1964).

The 1970 revised rule is generally in accord with existing Arizona decisions. The general approach to discovery is "liberal" as expressed in *Watts v. Superior Court In and For Maricopa County*, 87 Ariz. 1, 347 P.2d 565 (1959), and a considerable measure of discretion is maintained in the trial judge as that case declares. *Watts* recognized the interest of a party in getting a copy of his own statement, which he may have given to the other side. The Rule makes this an absolute right, so that if either party gives a statement to the other, he is entitled to a copy of it for the asking. The Rule broadens *Watts* somewhat by extending this right to any person to a copy of his own statement, if he desires; either a party or a non-party may compel delivery of his own statement to himself by court order.

The standards of the Rule are very much in accord with *Dean v. Superior Court In and For Maricopa County*, 84 Ariz. 104, 113, 324 P.2d 764, 770, 73 A.L.R.2d 1 (1958), followed, for illustration, in a case which would reach the same result under the revised rule, *Maricopa County v. Peterson*, 7 Ariz. App. 363, 439 P.2d 526 (1968). As in *Zimmerman v. Superior Court In and For Maricopa County*, 98 Ariz. 85, 402 P.2d 212, 18 A.L.R.3d 909 (1965), the Rule, while it gives strong protection to work product, does not extend the quality of absolute protection beyond the "mental impressions, conclusions, opinions, or legal theories" of the person who is entitled to this protection. The matter of production of impeachment materials, as in *Zimmerman v. Superior Court, supra*, or *State Farm Ins. Co. v. Roberts*, 97 Ariz. 169, 398 P.2d 671 (1965), is not touched in the Rule at all, so as to leave this matter to case-by-case development.

Rule 26(b)(4): This Rule, dealing with experts, is essentially similar to previous Arizona practice, but will require a slight modification. Under the Arizona practice, "the deposition of an expert may be taken under the same circumstances as any other witness;" *State ex rel. Willey v. Whitman*, 91 Ariz. 120, 124, 370 P.2d 273, 276 (1962). More limited views have been expressed in other parts of the country, see for example, *U.S. v. Certain Parcels of Land in City and County of San Francisco, State of Cal.*, 25 F.R.D. 192, 3 Fed. R. Serv. 2d 617 (N.D. Cal. 1959); *U.S. v. Certain Acres of Land in Decatur and Seminole Counties, Ga.*, 18 F.R.D. 98 (M.D. Ga. 1955).

The Rule resolves this conflict in favor of discovery of the experts. If the expert is to appear at trial, then a party may through interrogatory discover the name, subject matter, and substance of the scope of the expert's testimony. If he desires to go further and take a deposition, he may do so "upon motion." It is this requirement of "motion" which slightly modifies the existing Arizona practice, where no motion is required. This language in the Rule is deliberately intended to permit elasticity of interpretation in accordance with local wishes.

It is the express intention of the Arizona Bar, in recommending this Rule to the Arizona Supreme Court, that we do not deviate at all from our existing practice as expressed in *State v. Whitman, supra*. Because of our strong desire to maintain substantial uniformity between the State and Federal Rules, we keep the phrase "upon motion" in the Rule; but it is intended in this jurisdiction that the motion shall be perfunctory, and that it will be automatically granted, barring the most exceptional circumstances, if the parties are unable to stipulate to the appearance. The Bar reaffirms its belief in the sound practice that "the deposition of an expert may be taken under the same circumstances as any other witness." Under Arizona practice, the deposition of an expert will not be limited by the scope of the descriptive answer to the interrogatory, but may be examined upon any matter which would be permitted if he were cross-examined in open court at the conclusion of his main testimony.

On the other hand, an expert who may have been specifically retained for litigation, as, for example, to advise counsel generally, but who is not to be a witness, will be subject to discovery only "upon a showing of exceptional circumstances." The rule as amended is not intended to change or impair the scope of *State v. Whitman, supra*, in any way whatsoever.

A distinction is also made as to the pay of experts. Two time interludes are involved: First is the time the witness spends in the deposition; and second is the time he spends in preparing himself for the deposition. If the expert is to be a witness at trial, the adverse party taking his deposition need not pay for the time he has spent equipping himself to appear, in the belief that this time would be required in any case for his appearance for the party originally calling him. On the other hand, the time he spends in deposition on cross-examination is time which would not otherwise be required of him, and for this he should be compensated by the inquiring party, unless, at the discretion of the court, manifest injustice would result. In the event of discovery from a nonwitness expert, the court may also require payment for preparation time.

Rule 26(c): The provisions of pre-1970 Rule 30(c) are transferred to this subdivision (c), as part of the rearrangement of Rule 26. The subdivision recognizes the power of the county where a deposition is being taken as well as the county in which the action is pending to make protective orders; it thus alters the result in *Ward v. Stevens*, 86 Ariz. 222, 344 P.2d 491 (1959), which held that a Maricopa County judge could not quash a notice of deposition for that county when the case itself was pending in Pinal County. Insertions are made to avoid any implication that a protective order does not extend to "time" as well as to "place" or may not safeguard against "undue burden or expense."

Arizona's leading case under the previous form of this Rule is *State v. Mahoney*, 103 Ariz. 308, 441 P.2d 68 (1968), holding that a trial court has discretion to assess travel costs for the opponent's attorney, if the deposition is to be taken at a distant point. This case also holds that the asking party cannot be required to advance the other side's attorney's fees for the deposition. The new form of the Rule does not affect the principles of *Mahoney*.

Rule 26(d): In some parts of the country, discovery problems have arisen in connection with the order of discovery. In some instances, the priority practice of allowing first notices to control the order of depositions have been abused. This has not been the case in Arizona, where the priority system has worked well, and where order is usually settled by arrangement among the parties. This revision of the Rule is added to make clear that there is not any fixed priority in the sequence of discovery, and also to make clear and explicit the court's power to establish priorities by orders, when necessary for orderly administration of discovery.

Rule 26(e): If interrogatories are sent early in a case, and a protracted period passes before trial, there are occasions in which later knowledge or later events warrant a different answer from that originally given as correct. Yet the burden of reviewing answers to check them against change would be very heavy. Therefore, this subdivision provides that answers need not be supplemented, absent a new request which could be resisted by an application for a protective order if it is unreasonably burdensome, except in the circumstances set forth in the Rule. The answering party is, however, under a duty to supplement as to direct questions concerning the identity and location of persons having knowledge of discoverable matters, which includes non-expert witnesses, or as to experts who will be called at trial. Beyond this, there is a duty to supplement only when the answering party actually knows that a response was incorrect when made or that changing circumstances make a failure to amend a knowing concealment.

Rule 26(e)(2) does not impose a duty to check the accuracy of prior responses, and applies only to knowing concealment. Cf. *Kelch v. Courson*, 7 Ariz. App. 365, 439 P.2d 528, 533 (1968), opinion vacated on other grounds, 103 Ariz. 576, 447 P.2d 550 (1968) (overruled by, Heimke v. Munoz, 106 Ariz. 26, 470 P.2d 107 (1970)), holding that under Rule III(a)(5) of the Rules of Practice of the Superior Court, the trial court could take into account, in considering a motion for a new trial for failure to supplement interrogatories, whether the failure was "willful and deliberate or inadvertent."

1983 Amendment

Rule 26(e)(1): A party has a affirmative duty to disclose information which is the subject of this rule in a timely fashion. The primary duty is to supplement discovery responses concerning (B) and (C) seasonably after receiving the information. 8 C. Wright & A. Miller, Federal Practice and Procedure, § 2049 (1970). That duty may not be fulfilled by waiting until the last minute (e.g., 31 days before trial) to make the required disclosures. Similarly, in those courts opting for Rule V(b)(3)(i) or (ii), Uniform Rules of Practice, discovery responses concerning (B) and (C) should be seasonably supplemented, and information should not be withheld until the filing of the list of witnesses and exhibits required to be filed prior to the Motion to Set and Certificate of Readiness.

1984 Amendments

Rule 26(a) and (b): The 1984 amendments to Rule 26 are aimed at preventing both excess discovery and evasion of reasonable discovery devices. Deletion of "the frequency of use" from Rule 26(a) is intended to deal directly with the problems of duplicative and needless discovery. This change and others in Rule 26(b) should encourage judges to identify instances of unnecessary discovery and to limit the use of the various discovery devices accordingly.

New standards are added in Rule 26(b)(1) which courts will use in deciding whether to limit the frequency or extent of use of the various discovery methods. Subdivision (i) is intended to reduce redundancy in discovery and require counsel to be sensitive to the comparative costs of different methods of securing information. Subdivision (ii) also seeks to minimize repetitiveness and to oblige lawyers to think through their discovery activities in advance so that full utilization is made of each deposition, document request, or set of interrogatories. Subdivision (iii) addresses the problem of discovery that is disproportionate to the individual lawsuit as measured by various factors, e.g., its nature and complexity, the importance of the issues at stake, the financial position of the parties, etc. These standards must be applied in an even-handed manner to prevent use of discovery to wage a war of attrition or as a device to coerce a party, whether affluent or financially weak.

Acknowledging that discovery cannot always be self-regulating, the Rule contemplates earlier and greater judicial involvement in the discovery process. The court may act on motion or its own initiative.

Rule 26(f): This subsection was adopted in lieu of Federal Rule 26(g), which elaborates on the elements that must be certified in connection with discovery requests, responses and objections. The 1984 amendment to Rule 11 adequately accomplishes the purposes of Federal Rule 26(g).

The rejection of Federal Rule 26(g), and the concomitant loss of its language expressly requiring certification that the discovery request, response or objection is not unreasonable or unduly burdensome or expensive, is not intended to diminish the protection provided by Rule 26(c).

1989 Amendment

Rule 26(b)(5) is intended to be read in conjunction with the provisions of Rule 26(e)(1)(D), which requires the seasonable supplementation of responses to discovery requests addressed to the identity, location, and the facts supporting the asserted liability of any nonparty who is claimed to be wholly or partially at fault in causing any personal injury, property damage or wrongful death for which damages are claimed in the action, pursuant to A.R.S. § 12-2506(B) (as amended).

1991 Amendments

[Rule 26(b)(4)] The amendment to Rule 26(b)(4) must be read in conjunction with the amendment to Rule 43(g). The purpose of these two rules is to avoid unnecessary costs inherent in the retention of multiple independent expert witnesses. The words "independent expert" in this rule refer to a person who will offer opinion evidence who is retained for testimonial purposes and who is not a witness to the facts giving rise to the action. As used in this rule, the word "presumptively" is intended to mean that an additional expert on an issue can be used only upon a showing of good cause. Where an issue cuts across several professional disciplines, the court should be liberal in allowing expansion of the limitation upon experts established in the rule.

Rule 43(g) is intended to reinforce Rule 403 of the Arizona Rules of Evidence which gives the court discretion to exclude relevant evidence which represents . . . "needless presentation of cumulative evidence." By use of the word "shall" in Rule 43(g) it is the intent of the Committee to strongly urge trial judges to exclude testimony from independent experts on both sides which is cumulative except in those circumstances where the cause of justice requires.

There is no intent to preclude witnesses who in addition to their opinion testimony are factual witnesses. Under Rule 43(g), however, the court would exclude an independent expert witness whose opinion would simply duplicate that of the factual expert witness, except for good cause shown.

This amendment to Rule 26(b)(4) in combination with Rule 43(g) and Rule 16(c)(3) is intended to discourage the unnecessary retention of multiple independent expert witnesses and the discovery costs associated with listing multiple cumulative independent experts as witnesses. The Committee does not intend any change in the present rule regarding specially retained experts.

[Rule 26(f)] This rule is intended to give the court the authority to sanction any party or attorney who has engaged in unreasonable, groundless, abusive or obstructionist conduct. It is intended to allow the court all of the sanctions available under Rule 16(f). The rule is specifically intended to give the court express authority to deal with parties and attorneys whose unprofessional and unreasonable conduct has resulted in an abuse of the discovery process.

2000 Amendment

As part of the effort to consolidate formerly separate sets of procedural rules into either the Arizona Rules of Civil Procedure or the Rules of the Arizona Supreme Court, the Uniform Rules of Practice of the Superior Court were effectively transferred to one or the other of those existing sets of Rules. The provisions of former Rule V(a) of the Uniform Rules of Practice of the Superior Court, which required the filing, in certain counties, of a list of witnesses and exhibits as a predicate for submitting a Motion to Set and Certificate of Readiness, however, were not retained in that process. The Committee was of the view that this requirement had been rendered obsolete by the provisions of Rule 26.1, which requires the voluntary and seasonable disclosure of, inter alia, the identities of trial witnesses and exhibits. This necessitated the amendment of Rule 26(b)(5) to eliminate the former reference to Rule V(a) and to substitute in its place a reference to new Rule 38.1(b)(2) of the Arizona Rules of Civil Procedure.

Rule 26(b)(4) was amended to incorporate, as a new separate paragraph, the provisions of former Rule 1(D)(4) of the Uniform Rules of Practice for Medical Malpractice Cases. The Comment to that former Rule had observed that, if a medical malpractice case involved issues of nursing care, anesthesia, and general surgery, the plaintiff should be entitled to three standard-of-care experts and, similarly, if the hospital employed the nurse, anesthesiologist and surgeon and was the sole defendant, it would also be entitled to three standard-of-care experts. The addition of the phrase "except upon a showing of good cause" merely incorporates the standards of former Rule 43(g), which addressed the same subject and was abrogated as unnecessary. Finally, the provisions of Rule 26(e) were amended to reflect prior amendments to Rules 26.1 and 37 which require the disclosure of such information by no later than sixty (60) days prior to trial, without leave of court.

COURT COMMENT

1991 Amendments

[Rule 26(b)(4)] The above rule change was part of a comprehensive set of rule revisions proposed by the Special Bar Committee to Study Civil Litigation Abuse, Cost and Delay, which was specifically charged in March, 1990 with the task of proposing rules to reduce discovery abuse and to make the judicial system in Arizona more efficient, expeditious, and accessible to the people.

For more complete background information on the rule changes proposed by the Committee, see Court Comment to Rule 26.1.

2002 Amendment

The amendment to Rule 26(c) does not limit the discretion of trial judges to issue confidentiality orders in the appropriate case. Trial judges should look to federal case law to determine what factors, including the three listed in the rule, should be weighed in deciding whether to grant or modify a confidentiality order where parties contest the need for such an order. Trial judges also should look to federal case law to determine whether to permit nonparties to intervene and obtain access to information protected by such orders.

AUTHORS' COMMENTS

Analysis

1. Scope and Purpose of Rule.
2. Comparison With Federal Rule.
3. Available Discovery Devices.
4. Presumptive Discovery Limits.
5. Scope of Discovery in General.
6. Discovery of Impeachment Materials.
7. Discovery of Statements of a Party.
8. Non-party's Request for Non-party's Statement.
9. Discovery of Privileged Materials.

10. Discovery of Materials Prepared in Anticipation of Litigation.
11. Discovery of Trial Experts.
12. Discovery of Consulting Experts.
13. Discovery of Medical Records.
14. Discovery of Electronically Stored Information.
15. Court Control of Discovery Generally.
16. Protective Orders.
17. Stays of Discovery.
18. Control of the Place of Deposition.
19. Control of Methods for Conducting Discovery.
20. Protection of Trade Secrets and Other Confidential Information.
21. Sealing Discovery.
22. Control of Attendance at Depositions.
23. Control of Sequence and Scheduling of Discovery.
24. Supplementation of Discovery Responses.
25. Disclosure of Claims of Non-Party Liability; 2014 Rule Amendments.
26. Discovery Disputes.
27. Testifying treating physicians.
28. 2014 Rule Amendments: Effective Date and Applicability.

1. *Scope and Purpose of Rule.* The function of Rule 26, the initial discovery Rule, is to establish the general standards and procedures that will apply to the use, and disputes as to the misuse, of the particular discovery devices authorized by subsequent Rules.

2. *Comparison With Federal Rule.* There are now significant differences between ARCP 26 and FRCP 26, as a consequence of the 1992 Arizona discovery and court reform amendments, and the 1993, 2000, 2006, 2007 and 2010 amendments to the Federal Rules of Civil Procedure.

ARCP 26(a) is substantially identical to former FRCP 26(a). Amended FRCP 26(a), however, now requires the parties to make three separate categories of disclosures, at varying times, without awaiting a discovery request therefor: "initial disclosures," "expert testimony disclosures," and "pretrial disclosures." Arizona's mandatory disclosure Rule is ARCP 26.1, and the categories of information it requires be disclosed, do not entirely correspond to those in FRCP 26(a).

The defined scope of discovery, as set forth in the Arizona and Federal Rules, also differs between the two sets of rules. ARCP 26(b)(1) continues to define the scope of permissible discovery as encompassing "any matter, not privileged, which is relevant to the subject matter involved in the pending action. . . ." As a consequence of the 2000 amendment, however, FRCP 26(b)(1) limits the discovery which can be undertaken without leave of court to "any matter, not privileged, that is relevant to the claim or defense of any other party. . . ." The court may permit discovery into matters relevant to the "subject matter" involved in the action for good cause shown.

ARCP 26(b)(4)(D) now provides that each side in a case is presumptively entitled to only one independent expert on an "issue." The Federal Rule has no comparable provision.

ARCP 26(b)(5) requires that a party who wishes to claim a person or entity not a party to the action is wholly or partially responsible for the plaintiff's injuries or damages must disclose, generally within one hundred and fifty (150) days of the filing of that party's answer, the identity and location of the non-party claimed to be so responsible, and the facts supporting the claim. The Federal Rule has no comparable provision. Rather, FRCP 26(b)(5) establishes the procedural requirements for asserting privileges in response to discovery requests and with respect to required disclosures, which is essentially identical to ARCP 26.1(f).

While both ARCP 26(c) and FRCP 26(c) address protective orders, the Federal Rule requires that a motion for protective order be accompanied by a certification that the moving party has conferred or attempted to confer in good faith with the opposing party in an attempt to resolve the dispute. ARCP 26(c) has no such provision, but such a requirement is imposed by ARCP 36(g), and 37(a)(2)(C).

In addition, FRCP 26 has no provision corresponding to ARCP 26(c)(2), concerning confidentiality orders.

FRCP 26(d) provides that no discovery may be conducted before the parties conduct the discovery planning conference required by FRCP 26(f). ARCP 26 contains no such provision.

ARCP 26(e) generally requires the seasonable supplementation of prior discovery responses, and specifically requires that interrogatory responses as to the identity of both lay and expert witnesses must be supplemented, and all such witnesses be identified, at least sixty (60) days prior to trial. Any witness not identified as required by ARCP 26(e) may not testify at trial except upon agreement of the parties or a showing of good cause. This supplementation requirement also applies to discovery responses with respect to the identity and location of any non-party who is claimed to be wholly or partially responsible for the plaintiff's damages and with respect to the facts upon which such a claim is based. The corresponding Federal Rule, FRCP 26(e), now applies to all responses to all written discovery requests and to all disclosures mandated by FRCP 26(a), and requires supplementation of additional or corrective information not otherwise disclosed or revealed in discovery at "appropriate intervals."

ARCP 26(f) provides that the Court shall assess an appropriate sanction against any party who has engaged in unreasonable, groundless, abusive or obstructionist conduct. The corresponding federal provision, FRCP 26(g), provides, in detail, that all discovery requests and responses, and all disclosures, must be signed and that the signature of a discovery paper constitutes a certification that the paper signed is consistent with the Rules, is warranted by existing law, is not interposed for delay or any other improper purpose, and is not unreasonable or unduly burdensome. In the case of disclosures, the signature is a certification that the disclosure is complete and correct as of the time it is made. Sanctions may be awarded for a violation of the Federal Rule.

FRCP 26(f) requires the parties confer—a meeting is not required—not later than 21 days before a scheduling conference is to be held or a scheduling order is due, and that they develop and submit to the Court a written discovery and case management plan. ARCP 26 has no corresponding provision, but a discovery plan and schedule is one of the items that can be raised and discussed at the Comprehensive Pretrial Conference authorized by ARCP 16(c). *See* Section 3 of the *Authors' Comments* under ARCP 16.

ARCP 26 does not contain the provisions added in 2006 to FRCP 26(a)(1)(ii), (b)(2)(B), and (f) dealing with discovery of electronically stored information. *But see,* ARCP 16(c)(1), 26.1(a)(8), 26.1(a)(9), 33(c), 34(a), 37(g) and 45(c).

ARCP 26 also does not contain the stylistic and substantive amendments made in 2007 (various) or the substantive amendments made in 2010 (expert discovery).

3. *Available Discovery Devices.* As set forth in Ariz. R. Civ. P. 26(a), the available discovery devices are:

(1) "depositions upon examination or written questions;
(2) written interrogatories;
(3) production of documents or things or permission to enter upon land or other property, for inspection and other purposes;
(4) physical and mental examinations; and
(5) requests for admission."

While the parties nominally have the right to freely select which of these discovery devices are to be employed, and the use of one does not bar resort to others, *Hine v. Superior Court In and For Yuma County*, 18 Ariz. App. 568, 504 P.2d 509 (Div. 1 1972), that right was severely circumscribed by the 1992 amendments to various discovery rules, discussed in later Sections, which mandate disclosure, without request, of certain specified categories of information, and impose presumptive limits on the use of virtually all discovery devices. See also *Authors' Comments* to Rule 26.1.

In fact, there are instances where one of these discovery devices *must* be employed to secure information pertinent to pending litigation. In *Duquette v. Superior Court In and For County of Maricopa*, 161 Ariz. 269, 778 P.2d 634 (Ct. App. Div. 1 1989), the Court held that defense lawyers in a medical malpractice case could not conduct *ex parte* interviews of the plaintiff's treating physicians, without advance permission, but were limited to the use of the discovery procedures authorized by the Rules of Civil Procedure. *But see, Phoenix Children's Hosp., Inc. v. Grant*, 228 Ariz. 235, 265 P.3d 417 (Ct. App. Div. 1 2011). Counsel are also precluded from conducting *ex parte* interviews of former employees of corporate adversaries whose acts or omissions gave rise to the litigation or who have an ongoing relationship with their former employer in connection with the litigation. *Lang v. Superior Court, In and For County of Maricopa*, 170 Ariz. 602, 826 P.2d 1228 (Ct. App. Div. 1 1992).

4. *Presumptive Discovery Limits.* The circumstances under which the trial court will need to invoke its authority to control the use and scope of discovery were both narrowed and focused by the 1992 amendments to the discovery rules. Those amendments emanated from discovery and court reform recommendations from a Special Bar Committee to Study Civil Litigation Abuse, Cost and Delay and from the work of the Arizona Commission on the Courts. Rule 26.1 was adopted and mandates the disclosure, without request, of specified categories of information which would previously have been sought through the use of discovery. Correspondingly, the pertinent discovery rules were amended to impose the following presumptive limits on the use of discovery devices, which may only be exceeded by agreement of the parties or with leave from the Court:

(a) Depositions are limited to those of the parties, expert trial witnesses and custodians of documents;

(b) Depositions of any party or witness are not to exceed four (4) hours in length;

(c) A party may not serve on any other party more than forty (40) interrogatories;

(d) A party could not submit more than one request for production of documents and things, and that request could not include more than ten (10) distinct items or categories of items requested;

(e) A party may not submit more than twenty-five (25) requests for admissions.

The initially adopted presumptive limitation on requests for production and inspection has been slightly ameliorated by an amendment to Rule 34 which took effect on December 1, 1996. Under that amendment, a party may propound multiple requests for production, but these separate requests cannot cumulatively contain more than ten (10) specific requests for items to be produced and/or inspected.

Limits were also imposed upon the number of expert witnesses that may be called to testify. See the discussion in Section 11, *infra*. As noted, these are presumptive limits and may be exceeded by agreement of the parties or pursuant to order of the trial court.

5. *Scope of Discovery in General.* Rule 26(b) defines the overall scope of discovery, if permitted, and includes specific provisions concerning discovery of insurance agreements, (which are subject to disclosure in any event under Rule 26.1(a)(8)), materials prepared or generated in anticipation of litigation or preparation for trial, and discovery of experts. The amount of discovery that may be conducted in the ordinary civil case is initially controlled by the presumptive limits enacted by the 1992 amendments to the discovery rules, discussed above, which may only be exceeded by mutual agreement or with leave of the Court.

Generally, discovery may be had of "any matter" which is "not privileged" that is either "relevant to the subject matter" of the litigation or which "appears reasonably calculated to lead to the discovery of admissible evidence." The broad scope thus defined is a logical consequence of Arizona's adoption of a "notice pleading" regime. *U-Totem Store v. Walker*, 142 Ariz. 549, 691 P.2d 315 (Ct. App. Div. 2 1984). Correspondingly, parties to litigation have a duty to preserve evidence which they know, or reasonably should know, is relevant to the issues in the action, is reasonably calculated to lead to the discovery of admissible evidence, is reasonably likely to be requested during discovery and/or is the subject of a pending discovery request. *Souza v. Fred Carries Contracts, Inc.*, 191 Ariz. 247, 955 P.2d 3 (Ct. App. Div. 2 1997).

It is now, accordingly, axiomatic that the scope of discovery as defined by Rule 26(b) is to be construed broadly to facilitate the identification of issues, assist in the efficient resolution of disputes and to avoid trial becoming a guessing game. *Cornet Stores v. Superior Court In and For Yavapai County*, 108 Ariz. 84, 492 P.2d 1191 (1972); *Watts v. Superior Court In and For Maricopa County*, 87 Ariz. 1, 347 P.2d 565 (1959); *U-Totem Store v. Walker*,

142 Ariz. 549, 691 P.2d 315 (Ct. App. Div. 2 1984). In exercising its broad discretion in discovery matters, the trial court must always consider the danger of injecting collateral issues into a case. *Braillard v. Maricopa County*, 224 Ariz. 481, 232 P.3d 1263 (Ct. App. Div. 2 2010), review denied, (Jan. 4, 2011) and cert. denied, 131 S. Ct. 2911, 179 L. Ed. 2d 1247 (2011); *American Family Mut. Ins. Co. v. Grant*, 222 Ariz. 507, 217 P.3d 1212 (Ct. App. Div. 1 2009), citing *Mohn v. Hahnemann Medical College and Hosp. of Philadelphia*, 357 Pa. Super. 173, 515 A.2d 920 (1986).

The purpose of the discovery rules is to permit a party to become apprised of an opponent's case and be prepared to meet it. *Kott v. City of Phoenix*, 158 Ariz. 415, 763 P.2d 235 (1988). The fact that documents or information sought may not be admissible does not *ipso facto* make them nondiscoverable; similarly, the fact that information is discoverable does not thereby render it admissible. *Samaritan Health Services, Inc. v. Superior Court In and For Maricopa County*, 142 Ariz. 435, 690 P.2d 154 (Ct. App. Div. 1 1984). On the other hand, in a wrongful death medical malpractice action, the amounts paid by the defendant health care provider to settle prior malpractice cases establishes neither negligence nor gross negligence, and is not subject to discovery. *Miller v. Kelly*, 212 Ariz. 283, 130 P.3d 982 (Ct. App. Div. 2 2006).

In order to obtain discovery of an anonymous Internet speaker's identity, the requesting party must show: (1) the speaker has been given adequate notice and a reasonable opportunity to respond to the discovery request, (2) the requesting party's cause of action would survive a motion for summary judgment on elements not dependent on the speaker's identity, and (3) a balance of the parties' competing interests favors disclosure. *Mobilisa, Inc. v. Doe*, 217 Ariz. 103, 170 P.3d 712, 36 Media L. Rep. (BNA) 2007 (Ct. App. Div. 1 2007).

Discovery may even be conducted after judgment in aid of efforts at collection. *Ash v. Arnold*, 115 Ariz. 462, 565 P.2d 1323 (Ct. App. Div. 2 1977). In discovery matters, including rulings on assertion of a privilege, the trial court has broad discretion, which is reviewed only for abuse of discretion. *State Farm Mut. Auto. Ins. Co. v. Lee*, 199 Ariz. 52, 13 P.3d 1169 (2000); *Tritschler v. Allstate Ins. Co.*, 213 Ariz. 505, 144 P.3d 519 (Ct. App. Div. 2 2006), as corrected, (Dec. 19, 2006); *Green v. Nygaard*, 213 Ariz. 460, 143 P.3d 393 (Ct. App. Div. 2 2006).

The 2008 amendments added a new Rule 26(b)(1)(B), which provides that a party need not provide discovery of electronically stored information from sources that the party identifies as not reasonably accessible because of undue burden or expense. On a motion to compel such discovery, or on a motion for a protective order, the party from whom such discovery is sought has the burden of showing that the information is not reasonably accessible due to undue burden or expense. Even if such a showing is made, the court may nevertheless order discovery or disclosure if the requesting party shows good cause.

6. *Discovery of Impeachment Materials.* It was previously held that documents or other materials that are to be used *solely* for purposes of impeachment at trial were not discoverable. That exemption was limited, however, to matters that were not related to the substantive issues in the action and had potential probative value solely for impeachment purposes. *Helena Chemical Co. v. Coury Bros. Ranches, Inc.*, 126 Ariz. 448, 616 P.2d 908 (Ct. App. Div. 1 1980); *Zimmerman v. Superior Court In and For Maricopa County*, 98 Ariz. 85, 402 P.2d 212, 18 A.L.R.3d 909 (1965). Amendments to former Rules V(a) and VI(a) of the now abrogated Uniform Rules of Practice of the Superior Court deleted the special treatment accorded trial exhibits intended to be used solely for impeachment. One effect of these amendments is that such impeachment exhibits must now be listed in the pretrial statement required by Rule 16(d). It seems safe to assume that such impeachment exhibits would now be discoverable as well.

Generally, litigants are entitled to present evidence that tends to show bias or prejudice on the part of witnesses, including those who testify as experts. *American Family Mut. Ins. Co. v. Grant*, 222 Ariz. 507, 217 P.3d 1212 (Ct. App. Div. 1 2009). Courts have recognized, however, that overbroad discovery requests for this type of evidence can have a chilling effect on would-be experts. *American Family Mut. Ins. Co. v. Grant*, 222 Ariz. 507, 217 P.3d 1212 (Ct. App. Div. 1 2009). Accordingly, a party's need to conduct discovery for bias-related information must be balanced against competing interests, including the right of witnesses to be free from unduly intrusive or burdensome inquiries and the need to prevent broad-ranging discovery forays that serve to increase the cost, length and burden of litigation with little or no corresponding benefit. *American Family Mut. Ins. Co. v. Grant*, 222 Ariz. 507, 217 P.3d 1212 (Ct. App. Div. 1 2009).

7. *Discovery of Statements of a Party.* While Ariz. R. Civ. P. 26(b)(3) makes statements made by a party discoverable by that party, the rule does not specify any particular procedure to be followed to obtain such a statement. Ariz. R. Civ. P. 26.1(a)(5) does require, however, the parties to disclose, without request, the names and addresses of all persons who have given statements and the custodian of copies of the statements. Ariz. R. Civ. P. 26.1(a)(5) does not require, by its terms, that the statements be produced.

A formal request for production under Ariz. R. Civ. P. 34, obviously, would be appropriate. Informal requests for production of a party's statement are frequently made by informal, but documented, communications between counsel.

Regardless of the format of the request, production of the statement can be compelled before the party is required to submit to a deposition. *Tury v. Superior Court*, 19 Ariz. App. 169, 505 P.2d 1060 (Div. 1 1973).

A "statement" is, however, narrowly defined to encompass a written recitation signed or approved by the person making it, or a stenographic or other recording or a transcription thereof which constitutes a substantially verbatim recital of a person's oral statement. Difficult issues are presented where the "statement" sought is memorialized in an attorney's or investigator's notes or summary of an interview, which may also reflect the mental impressions or conclusions of the interviewer. In that instance, the "work product" privilege may be implicated and there may need to be redactions made, if possible, or other restrictions imposed to accommodate the privilege.

8. *Non-Party Request for Non-party's Statement.* Rule 26(b)(3) makes statements made by a person not a party to the action discoverable by that person. Since the person making the request is not a party, the discovery procedure of Rule 34, is not available, and the Rule does not specify any particular vehicle for making the request. A formal request filed with the Court and served on the parties can be utilized but an informal request is both typical and sufficient.

In the past, the usual, but not exclusive, catalyst for such a request was the scheduling of the deposition of the person who gave the statement. In that circumstance, a Motion for Protective Order can and should be made if an informal request for production of the witness' prior statement is not honored. Now, the name of any person who has given a statement concerning the subject matter of the action must be disclosed pursuant to Rule 26.1(a)(5). According to the Committee Notes that accompanied the 1996 amendments to the "disclosure" rules, that Rule does not require the automatic production of witness statements themselves, and that the issue of their actual production remains governed by Rule 26(b)(3).

9. *Discovery of Privileged Materials.* Rule 26(b) excludes from the scope of permissible discovery, by negative inference, matters subject to an evidentiary privilege. *Helge v. Druke*, 136 Ariz. 434, 666 P.2d 534 (Ct. App. Div. 2 1983). The privilege may be one recognized at common law, *cf.*, Rule 501, Arizona Rules of Evidence, or created by statute. Whether a privilege exists is a question of law subject to *de novo* review on appeal. *Lund v. Donahoe*, 227 Ariz. 572, 261 P.3d 456 (Ct. App. Div. 1 2011).

Privileges frequently invoked and enforced in discovery are: the attorney-client privilege; the accountant-client privilege, *cf.* A.R.S. § 32-749; and, the physician-patient privilege, *cf. Banta v. Superior Court of Maricopa County*, 112 Ariz. 544, 544 P.2d 653 (1976). Although the language of the Fifth Amendment refers only to criminal cases, the privilege against self-incrimination applies to civil proceedings as well and may be invoked in response to civil discovery requests that seek potentially incriminating information. *State v. Ott*, 167 Ariz. 420, 808 P.2d 305 (Ct. App. Div. 1 1990). A limited privilege also has been recognized for the deliberative processes of government agencies and officials. *Grimm v. Arizona Bd. of Pardons and Paroles*, 115 Ariz. 260, 564 P.2d 1227, 5 A.L.R.4th 757 (1977).

There are, of course, limitations on these privileges. The attorney-client privilege applies only to confidential communications between counsel and client in connection with securing and rendering legal advice. *State ex rel. Corbin v. Weaver*, 140 Ariz. 123, 680 P.2d 833 (Ct. App. Div. 2 1984). It will not necessarily insulate from discovery factual investigations made by the client or the client's insurer, the results of which are furnished to counsel. *Longs Drug Stores v. Howe*, 134 Ariz. 424, 657 P.2d 412 (1983); *Butler v. Doyle*, 112 Ariz. 522, 544 P.2d 204 (1975).

Similarly, the accountant-client privilege covers communications between the accountant and the client concerning the client's financial affairs, but not communications concerning the retention of the accountant to review financial records of third parties. *Brown v. Superior Court In and For Maricopa County*, 137 Ariz. 327, 670 P.2d 725 (1983). There is no privilege, or other discovery exemption, conferred upon the details of an otherwise discoverable settlement which includes a nondisclosure covenant. *Ingalls v. Superior Court in and for Pima County*, 117 Ariz. 448, 573 P.2d 522 (Ct. App. Div. 2 1977).

With regard to whether communications between corporate employees and counsel for the corporation will qualify for the corporation's attorney-client privilege, the Supreme Court previously held that the relevant inquiry concerned the nature and purpose of the communication rather than the identity or position of the corporate employee involved. *Samaritan Foundation v. Goodfarb*, 176 Ariz. 497, 862 P.2d 870, 26 A.L.R.5th 893 (1993), superseded by A.R.S. § 12-2234 (1994) with respect to civil cases. All communications initiated by the employee and made in confidence to counsel in which the communicating employee is directly seeking to secure or evaluate legal advice for the corporation, will be privileged. *Samaritan Foundation v. Goodfarb*, 176 Ariz. 497, 862 P.2d 870, 26 A.L.R.5th 893 (1993), superseded by A.R.S. § 12-2234 (1994) with respect to civil cases.

Under the *Samaritan* decision, where someone other than the employee initiated the communication, a factual communication by a corporate employee to corporate counsel would be within the corporation's privilege only if it concerned the employee's own conduct within the scope of his or her own employment and was made to assist the lawyer in assessing or responding to the legal consequences of that conduct for that corporate client. *Samaritan Foundation v. Goodfarb*, 176 Ariz. 497, 862 P.2d 870, 26 A.L.R. 5th 893 (1993), superseded by A.R.S. § 12-2234 (1994) with respect to civil cases. Communications from those who, but for their status as corporate officers, agents or employees, are mere witnesses, would not qualify for the absolute attorney-client privilege. *Samaritan Foundation v. Goodfarb*, 176 Ariz. 497, 862 P.2d 870, 26 A.L.R.5th 893 (1993), superseded by A.R.S. § 12-2234 (1994) with respect to civil cases.

In 1994, and apparently in response to the *Samaritan* decision, the Arizona Legislature amended A.R.S. § 12-2234, the statutory codification of the attorney-client privilege, to make all communications between corporate counsel and a corporate officer, employee or agent privileged if they were (1) for the purpose of providing legal advice to either the corporation or to the employee, or (2) for the purpose of obtaining information in order to provide such legal advice. *See also, Salvation Army v. Bryson*, 229 Ariz. 204, 273 P.3d 656 (Ct. App. Div. 2 2012) (finding the trial court abused its discretion in ordering the disclosure of summaries of interviews of corporate employees, even in redacted form, prepared by a private investigator at the direction of legal counsel because such communications are protected attorney-client communications protected by A.R.S. § 12-2234).

Each of the privileges in question can be waived by voluntary disclosure, or by putting the subject matter of the communication in direct issue in the action. *Alexander v. Superior Court In and For Maricopa County*, 141 Ariz. 157, 685 P.2d 1309 (1984); *Patania v. Silverstone*, 3 Ariz. App. 424, 415 P.2d 139 (1966) (rejected on other grounds by, Buffa v. Scott, 147 Ariz. 140, 708 P.2d 1331 (Ct. App. Div. 1 1985)).

The fact that privileged matters are included in a document does not necessarily protect the document from discovery in its entirety. Under certain circumstances, the questioned documents may be submitted for an in camera review by a judicial officer. See, *Lund v. Myers*, 232 Ariz. 309, 305 P.3d 374 (2013) (decided under Ariz. R. Civ. P. 26.1(f), trial court may review allegedly privileged document *only after* it determines such review is warranted). *Cf., Brown v. Superior Court In and For Maricopa County*, 137 Ariz. 327, 670 P.2d 725 (1983); *Pima County v. Harte*, 131 Ariz. 68, 638 P.2d 735 (Ct. App. Div. 2 1981); *Jolly v. Superior Court of Pinal County*, 112 Ariz. 186, 540 P.2d 658 (1975); *Tucson Medical Center Inc. v. Rowles*, 21 Ariz. App. 424, 520 P.2d 518

(Div. 2 1974); *City of Phoenix v. Peterson*, 11 Ariz. App. 136, 462 P.2d 829 (Div. 1 1969).

10. *Discovery of Materials Prepared in Anticipation of Litigation.* Rule 26(b)(3) is a partial codification of the work-product doctrine enunciated in *Hickman v. Taylor*, 329 U.S. 495, 67 S. Ct. 385, 91 L. Ed. 451, 1947 A.M.C. 1 (1947), and its progeny. *Cf., Dean v. Superior Court In and For Maricopa County*, 84 Ariz. 104, 324 P.2d 764, 73 A.L.R.2d 1 (1958); *Emergency Care Dynamics, Ltd. v. Superior Court In and For County of Maricopa*, 188 Ariz. 32, 932 P.2d 297, 1997-2 Trade Cas. (CCH) ¶ 71929 (Ct. App. Div. 1 1997). The protection provided by the work-product doctrine serves the primary purposes of preserving the integrity of the adversary system of litigation and permitting attorneys to adequately prepare for trial without fear that the results of their efforts will be available to their adversaries through discovery. *Brown v. Superior Court In and For Maricopa County*, 137 Ariz. 327, 670 P.2d 725 (1983); *Accomazzo v. Kemp, ex rel. County of Maricopa*, — P.3d —, 2014 WL 222783 (Ct. App. Div. 1 2014) ("To the extent that documents or other tangible items reflect [an attorney's] mental impressions, the work-product doctrine provides those items absolute protection from discovery."). Thus, an expert retained by counsel or by the client at counsel's direction to investigate and produce reports on technical aspects of specific litigation is considered part of the lawyer's investigative staff and the opinions and theories of the expert constitute protectable "work product." *State ex rel. Corbin v. Ybarra*, 161 Ariz. 188, 777 P.2d 686 (1989).

This does not mean, however, that all materials generated by counsel, or at counsel's direction, will be entitled to protection. *Zimmerman v. Superior Court In and For Maricopa County*, 98 Ariz. 85, 402 P.2d 212, 18 A.L.R.3d 909 (1965). For example, a lawyer's communications with an expert witness who has been retained to testify will not be immunized from discovery as work-product. *Emergency Care Dynamics, Ltd. v. Superior Court In and For County of Maricopa*, 188 Ariz. 32, 932 P.2d 297, 1997-2 Trade Cas. (CCH) ¶ 71929 (Ct. App. Div. 1 1997). On the other hand, such communications with an expert that is only a consultant, and not a testimonial expert, will be protected. *Emergency Care Dynamics, Ltd. v. Superior Court In and For County of Maricopa*, 188 Ariz. 32, 932 P.2d 297, 1997-2 Trade Cas. (CCH) ¶ 71929 (Ct. App. Div. 1 1997).

Under Rule 26(b)(3), limited protection is afforded to documents and tangible things "prepared in anticipation of litigation or for trial by or for another party or by or for that other party's representative. . . ." Whether this "work product" privilege applies is determined by the nature of the document and the factual setting of its preparation, including the nature of the event that prompted its preparation, whether it contains analyses or opinions or purely factual data, and whether it was requested or prepared at the specific instance of the party or an attorney or in the ordinary course of business. *Brown v. Superior Court In and For Maricopa County*, 137 Ariz. 327, 670 P.2d 725 (1983); *Accomazzo v. Kemp, ex rel. County of Maricopa*, __ P.3d __, 2014 WL 222783 (Ct. App. Div. 1 2014) ("To the extent that documents or other tangible items reflect [an attorney's] mental impressions, the work-product doctrine provides those items absolute protection from discovery."); *Salvation Army v. Bryson*, 229 Ariz. 204, 273 P.3d 656 (Ct. App. Div. 2 2012) (in contrast, a claim of attorney-client privilege "makes a discussion of substantial need and unavailability of the substantial equivalent irrelevant."), citing *Butler v. Doyle*, 112 Ariz. 522, 544 P.2d 204 (1975); *State ex rel. Corbin v. Weaver*, 140 Ariz. 123, 680 P.2d 833 (Ct. App. Div. 2 1984).

Discovery of trial preparation materials may be had only upon a dual showing by the party seeking discovery that there is a substantial need for the materials and that the party cannot obtain the substantial equivalent of the materials sought by other means without undue hardship. *Butler v. Doyle*, 112 Ariz. 522, 544 P.2d 204 (1975); *Salvation Army v. Bryson*, 229 Ariz. 204, 273 P.3d 656 (Ct. App. Div. 2 2012) (citing Rule 26(b)(3)). In the case of a party seeking production of witness interviews or statements, the fact that the witnesses have testified to conflicting versions of the same events may be sufficient. *Klaiber v. Orzel*, 148 Ariz. 320, 714 P.2d 813 (1986). *But cf., Lumber Country, Inc. v. Superior Court of State In and For Maricopa County*, 155 Ariz. 98, 745 P.2d 156 (Ct. App. Div. 1 1987).

Similarly, the fact that the statements were taken or given shortly after the events in question may give them a unique character which in and of itself justifies production. *Longs Drug Stores v. Howe*, 134 Ariz. 424, 657 P.2d 412 (1983); *Butler v. Doyle*, 112 Ariz. 522, 544 P.2d 204 (1975). *See also, Salvation Army v. Bryson*, 229 Ariz. 204, 273 P.3d 656 (Ct. App. Div. 2 2012) (observing that while the relationship of interviewed individuals to a corporate party is relevant to a claim such communications are protected by attorney-client privilege, such relationship is not relevant to a claim that summaries of such witness statements are protected by the work-product doctrine).

Even where the requisite showing is made to warrant the compelled production of trial preparation materials, special additional protection is given to "the mental impressions, conclusions, opinions or legal theories of an attorney or other representative of a party . . .", and the court is admonished by the Rule to guard against disclosure of such materials. *Longs Drug Stores v. Howe*, 134 Ariz. 424, 657 P.2d 412 (1983).

11. *Discovery of Trial Experts.* Before the 1996 amendment, Rule 26(b)(4) limited a party, without court order, to the use of interrogatories to discover the identity of an adversary's expert trial witnesses, the subject matter of the expert's anticipated testimony, and the substance of the facts and opinions to which the expert was expected to testify. The Rule was amended in 1996 to permit depositions of expert trial witnesses, which conformed to the prevalent practice under which depositions of such experts were routinely taken by agreement of the parties and/or through the use of subpoenas under Rules 30 and 45, without resorting to a motion seeking permission to do so. In fact, the presumptive limits on depositions imposed by the 1992 amendment to Rule 30(a), had already permitted the conduct of depositions of trial experts as of right.

It is settled that the opinions of a prospective expert witness are not protected by the "work product" privilege. *State ex rel. Willey v. Whitman*, 91 Ariz. 120, 370 P.2d 273 (1962). Moreover, the discoverability of the written reports generated by trial experts is governed by Rule 26(b)(4) rather than Rule 26(b)(3) and the party seeking them need not make a predicate showing of substantial need. *State ex rel. Miller v. Superior Court In and For Maricopa County*, 159 Ariz. 21, 764 P.2d 756 (Ct. App. Div. 1 1988), decision aff'd, 159 Ariz. 567, 769 P.2d 1013 (1989). The same rule applies to counsel's communications with an expert who has been retained to testify. *Emergency Care Dynamics, Ltd. v. Superior Court In and For County of Maricopa*, 188 Ariz. 32, 932 P.2d 297, 1997-2 Trade Cas. (CCH) ¶ 71929 (Ct. App. Div. 1 1997). On the other hand, an expert retained by counsel, or by the client at counsel's direction, to investigate and produce reports on technical aspects of specific litigation, and who is not expected to testify at trial, is considered part of counsel's "investigative staff," and the theories and opinions of such an expert constitute protectible "work product." *State ex rel. Corbin v. Ybarra*, 161 Ariz. 188, 777 P.2d 686 (1989); *Emergency Care Dynamics, Ltd. v. Superior Court In and For County of Maricopa*, 188 Ariz. 32, 932 P.2d 297, 1997-2 Trade Cas. (CCH) ¶ 71929 (Ct. App. Div. 1 1997).

A party waives the work product protection ordinarily afforded the work of a consulting expert when the party designates that expert to testify at trial. That work product protection can be reinstated by removing that designation before expert opinion evidence is offered from that witness through production of a report, responses to discovery or expert testimony. *Green v. Nygaard*, 213 Ariz. 460, 143 P.3d 393 (Ct. App. Div. 2 2006); *Arizona Minority Coalition for Fair Redistricting v. Arizona Independent Redistricting Com'n*, 211 Ariz. 337, 121 P.3d 843 (Ct. App. Div. 1 2005). It can also be restored by withdrawing an expert witness designation after that expert has testified for a limited purpose during a pretrial hearing and after the parties have resolved by stipulation the matter on which the expert previously testified. *Green v. Nygaard*, 213 Ariz. 460, 143 P.3d 393 (Ct. App. Div. 2 2006).

In some cases, a party may reinstate the privileges and discovery protections that apply to consulting experts by redesignating its expert from a testifying expert to a consulting expert before expert opinion evidence is offered through production of a report, discovery responses or testimony. *Para v. Anderson ex rel. County of Maricopa*, 231 Ariz. 91, 290 P.3d 1214 (Ct. App. Div. 1 2012), review granted, (Mar. 19, 2013), *citing*, Ariz. Minority Coalition for Fair Redistricting v. Ariz. Independent Redistricting Comm'n (Redistricting II), 211 Ariz. 337, 121 P.3d 843 (Ct. App. Div. 1 2005). A party may not reinstate the privileges and discovery protections that apply to consulting expert by redesignating an expert as a consultant once the expert's opinions have been disclosed. *Para v. Anderson ex rel. County of Maricopa*, 231 Ariz. 91, 290 P.3d 1214 (Ct. App. Div. 1 2012), review granted, (Mar. 19, 2013). Although a party may depose such redesignated expert, the trial court retains broad discretions under Ariz.R.Evid. 403 to control the use of such testimony at trial. *Para v. Anderson ex rel. County of Maricopa*, 231 Ariz. 91, 290 P.3d 1214 (Ct. App. Div. 1 2012), review granted, (Mar. 19, 2013).

Rule 26(b)(4)(C) provides that the Court shall require the party seeking further discovery of a trial expert to pay a reasonable fee for the time spent responding to the discovery, "unless manifest injustice would result." The Court also has the discretion to order the discovering party to pay the other party a fair portion of the fees and expenses incurred in obtaining the facts and opinions of the expert. A party cannot recover, as a taxable cost under A.R.S. § 12-332(A)(2), fees paid to that party's own expert in connection with a deposition of that expert conducted by that party for use at trial. *Schritter v. State Farm Mut. Auto. Ins. Co.*, 201 Ariz. 391, 36 P.3d 739 (2001). The provision in Rule 26 that a party seeking discovery from an expert must pay some or all of the expenses associated with that is not implicated, because a deposition of one's own expert is not conducted for discovery purposes. *Schritter v. State Farm Mut. Auto. Ins. Co.*, 201 Ariz. 391, 36 P.3d 739 (2001). Allowing a party to recover such costs would permit the recovery, under A.R.S. § 12-332(A)(2), of the functional equivalent of witness fees, which are not recoverable by reason of A.R.S. § 12-332(A)(1). *Schritter v. State Farm Mut. Auto. Ins. Co.*, 201 Ariz. 391, 36 P.3d 739 (2001).

The 1992 discovery and court reform amendments included the enactment of Rule 26(b)(4)(D) which provides that each *side* in a case is presumptively entitled to only one expert on an issue. A corresponding amendment was made to former Rule 43(g), Ariz.R.Civ.P. (Rule 43(g) was abrogated in 2000 because its provisions were entirely duplicative of those of Rule 26(b)(4)(D).) This Rule does not elaborate on what constitutes an "issue." An "independent expert" is defined in the Committee Comment as a "person who will offer opinion evidence who is retained for testimonial purposes and who is not a witness to the facts giving rise to the action." In cases where there are multiple parties on one side of the case, they may agree on a common expert but, if they cannot agree, the Court is to designate the common independent expert to be called. The Court may permit additional expert witnesses upon a showing of good cause. Moreover, the "one independent expert witness" limitation does not apply to or include an employee of a party whose opinions were formed during the course and scope of employment by that party. *Arizona Dept. of Revenue v. Superior Court In and For the County of Maricopa*, 189 Ariz. 49, 938 P.2d 98 (Ct. App. Div. 1 1997).

The Committee Comment to Rule 26(b)(4)(D) recognizes that there may be issues in a case that involve more than one professional discipline. In addition, there may be circumstances where it will be unfair and prejudicial to require multiple parties on one side of a case to use a common independent expert. Parties of course remain free to retain any number of consulting experts, who are not intended to testify, as they choose. The identities of such specially retained consulting experts need not be disclosed under Rule 26.1, Ariz.R.Civ.P.

A new paragraph was added to Rule 26(b)(4)(D), effective December 1, 2000, as a consequence of the Supreme Court's abrogation of the Uniform Rules of Practice for Medical Malpractice Cases as a separate set of procedural rules. The new paragraph, which incorporates the provisions of former Rule 1(D)(4) of the Medical Malpractice Rules, as they were commonly referred to. It provides that in medical malpractice cases, each party is presumptively entitled to only one expert witness on the applicable standard of care. The defendant, however, may also testify on the issue of that defendant's adherence to the standard of care, in addition to calling an independent expert witness on that issue, and the Court is not required, if that occurs, to allow the plaintiff an additional expert witness on the issue.

Generally, litigants are entitled to present evidence that tends to show bias or prejudice on the part of witnesses, including those who testify as experts. *American Family Mut. Ins. Co. v. Grant*, 222 Ariz. 507, 217 P.3d 1212 (Ct. App. Div. 1 2009). Courts have recognized, however, that overbroad discovery requests for this type of evidence can have a chilling effect on would-be experts. *American Family Mut. Ins. Co. v. Grant*, 222 Ariz. 507, 217 P.3d

1212 (Ct. App. Div. 1 2009). Accordingly, a party's need to conduct discovery for bias-related information must be balanced against competing interests, including the right of witnesses to be free from unduly intrusive or burdensome inquiries and the need to prevent broad-ranging discovery forays that serve to increase the cost, length and burden of litigation with little or no corresponding benefit. *American Family Mut. Ins. Co. v. Grant*, 222 Ariz. 507, 217 P.3d 1212 (Ct. App. Div. 1 2009).

12. *Discovery of Consulting Experts.* Rule 26(b)(4)(B) permits discovery of non-witness experts only upon a showing of "exceptional circumstances under which it is impracticable for the party seeking discovery to obtain facts or opinions on the same subject by other means." *Green v. Nygaard*, 213 Ariz. 460, 143 P.3d 393 (Ct. App. Div. 2 2006); *State ex rel. Miller v. Superior Court In and For Maricopa County*, 154 Ariz. 363, 742 P.2d 864 (Ct. App. Div. 1 1987). The standard is essentially the same as the showing required to secure discovery of trial preparation materials. *See* Rule 26(b)(3). Indeed, an expert retained by counsel, or by the client at counsel's direction, to investigate and produce reports on technical aspects of specific litigation, and who is not expected to testify at trial, is considered part of counsel's "investigative staff," and the theories and opinions of such an expert constitute protectible "work product." *State ex rel. Corbin v. Ybarra*, 161 Ariz. 188, 777 P.2d 686 (1989); *Emergency Care Dynamics, Ltd. v. Superior Court In and For County of Maricopa*, 188 Ariz. 32, 932 P.2d 297, 1997-2 Trade Cas. (CCH) ¶ 71929 (Ct. App. Div. 1 1997). Rule 26(b)(4)(B) also allows a party to obtain the facts and/or opinions of any expert who performed an examination under Rule 35(b).

A party waives the work product protection ordinarily afforded the work of a consulting expert when the party designates that expert to testify at trial. That work product protection can be reinstated by removing that designation before expert opinion evidence is offered from that witness through production of a report, responses to discovery or expert testimony. *Green v. Nygaard*, 213 Ariz. 460, 143 P.3d 393 (Ct. App. Div. 2 2006); *Arizona Minority Coalition for Fair Redistricting v. Arizona Independent Redistricting Com'n*, 211 Ariz. 337, 121 P.3d 843 (Ct. App. Div. 1 2005). It can also be restored by withdrawing an expert witness designation after that expert has testified for a limited purpose during a pretrial hearing and after the parties have resolved by stipulation the matter on which the expert previously testified. *Green v. Nygaard*, 213 Ariz. 460, 143 P.3d 393 (Ct. App. Div. 2 2006).

In some cases, a party may reinstate the privileges and discovery protections that apply to consulting experts by redesignating its expert from a testifying expert to a consulting expert before expert opinion evidence is offered through production of a report, discovery responses or testimony. *Para v. Anderson ex rel. County of Maricopa*, 231 Ariz. 91, 290 P.3d 1214 (Ct. App. Div. 1 2012), review granted, (Mar. 19, 2013), *citing*, Ariz. Minority Coalition for Fair Redistricting v. Ariz. Independent Redistricting Comm'n (Redistricting II), 211 Ariz. 337, 121 P.3d 843 (Ct. App. Div. 1 2005). A party may not reinstate the privileges and discovery protections that apply to consulting expert by redesignating an expert as a consultant once the expert's opinions have been disclosed. *Para v. Anderson ex rel. County of Maricopa*, 231 Ariz. 91, 290 P.3d 1214 (Ct. App. Div. 1 2012), review granted, (Mar. 19, 2013). Although a party may depose such redesignated expert, the trial court retains broad discretions under Ariz.R.Evid. 403 to control the use of such testimony at trial. *Para v. Anderson ex rel. County of Maricopa*, 231 Ariz. 91, 290 P.3d 1214 (Ct. App. Div. 1 2012), review granted, (Mar. 19, 2013).

Rule 26(b)(4)(C) provides that the Court *shall* require the party seeking further discovery of a trial expert a reasonable fee for the time spent responding to the discovery "unless manifest injustice would result." It is also virtually mandatory that the Court require that the party seeking discovery of consulting experts pay a fair portion of the fees and expenses reasonably incurred by the other party in obtaining facts and opinions from those experts.

13. *Discovery of Medical Records*. A patient's medical records are confidential and protected from discovery by statute. See A.R.S. §§ 12-2235, 12-2282(A), 12-2294.01. Notwithstanding that, medical records of a party, at least with respect to the medical condition which that party has put in issue, are freely discoverable. In fact, Rule 26.2(a)(1) requires the plaintiff, in a medical malpractice case, to serve upon the defendant(s), before the Comprehensive Pretrial Conference required by Rule 16(c), copies of all the medical records of plaintiff that are available and are relevant to the condition that is in issue in the case. See Section 3 of the *Authors' Comments* under Rule 26.2. This requirement would appear to be bottomed on the proposition that, by bringing the action and putting a certain medical condition in issue, the plaintiff has waived any privilege or confidentiality protection that pertains to medical records concerning that condition. On the other hand, A.R.S. § 12-2282 places certain specific requirements on subpoenas duces tecum issued to a health care provider and seeking the production of medical records. See discussion in Section 9 of the *Authors' Comments* under Rule 45.

In addition, non-party medical records, if relevant, may also be subject to discovery in spite of the statutory privilege, but only if the following precautions are taken: (1) all references to the name, address, marital status, occupation, or employment of the patient are removed; (2) after review, the records are filed with the Court and are not opened absent Court order; (3) no efforts are made to discover the identity of the patients or to contact them; and, (4) information from the records is not communicated to a non-party, except to experts and during trial. *Ziegler v. Superior Court In and For Pima County*, 134 Ariz. 390, 656 P.2d 1251 (Ct. App. Div. 2 1982); *C.B. v. Sabalos ex rel. County of Pima*, 198 Ariz. 115, 7 P.3d 124 (Ct. App. Div. 2 2000), review denied and opinion ordered not published, 199 Ariz. 164, 15 P.3d 276 (2000).

The discoverability of medical records may also be constrained, to an as yet undetermined degree, by the privacy provisions of the Health Insurance Portability and Accountability Act. *See* C. Tindall, HIPAA and Medical Records: A Primer for the Personal Injury Lawyer, 40-DEC Ariz. Att'y 32.

14. *Discovery of Electronically Stored Information.* "Electronic discovery" is the term that has come into vogue as a shorthand designation of the process of securing discovery and/or disclosure of documents and other information that has been generated by, and is stored on, computer systems and other digital devices. Effective January 1, 2008, the Arizona Supreme Court adopted a number of amendments to various provisions of the Arizona Rules of Civil Procedure to deal with this phenomenon.

Ariz. R. Civ. P. 16(b)(1)(B) authorizes the trial court at, or following a comprehensive pretrial conference, to enter orders establishing requirements for or limitations upon the discovery or disclosure of electronically stored information, including the form in which such information is to be produced, setting forth what measures the parties must take to preserve discoverable information that is electronically stored, and adopting any agreements between the parties concerning the assertion of claims of privilege as to such materials after it has been produced. The State Bar Committee Note accompanying that amendment stresses that, in entering preservation orders that might adversely impact the ongoing operation of a party's computer system, a court should consider the amount in controversy or type of relief requested, that preservation orders entered over objection should be narrowly tailored to the needs of the case, and that ex parte preservation orders should only be entered in exceptional circumstances.

Ariz. R. Civ. P. 26(b)(1)(B) provides that a party need not provide discovery of electronically stored information from sources the party identifies as not reasonably accessible because of undue burden and expense. On a motion to compel discovery or for a protective order, the party from which such discovery is sought has the burden of showing that the information is not reasonably accessible due to undue burden and expense. Even if such a showing is made, the court may nevertheless order discovery or disclosure if the requesting party shows good cause.

Ariz. R. Civ. P. 34(b) was amended to provide that a request for production of electronically stored information may specify the form or forms in which it is to be produced. The party to whom such a request is directed may object but must, in any event, specify the form it intends to use in producing such information. If the request for production does not specify a form for electronic information requested, then the information must be produced in a form in which it is ordinarily maintained or in a form that is reasonably usable.

Finally, Ariz. R. Civ. P. 37(g) specifies that, absent exceptional circumstances, a court may not impose sanctions for the failure to provide in discovery electronically stored information that has been lost as a result of the routine, good faith operation of an electronic information system.

15. *Court Control of Discovery Generally.* Rules 26(c) and (d) provide the trial court with the authority, in the appropriate case, to impose reasonable limitations on the use, scope and timing of discovery, and to otherwise control the discovery process to prevent "annoyance, embarrassment, oppression or undue burden or expense." *Cf., Southern Pac. Transp. Co. v. Veliz*, 117 Ariz. 199, 571 P.2d 696 (Ct. App. Div. 2 1977); *Hine v. Superior Court In and For Yuma County*, 18 Ariz. App. 568, 504 P.2d 509 (Div. 1 1972). In that regard, Rule 26 was substantially amended in 1984 in response to perceived discovery abuses. The final sentence of Rule 26(a), which discouraged the imposition of limitations on the frequency of use of discovery methods, was deleted, and the second paragraph was added to Rule 26(b) to give the trial court specific authority to limit the frequency or extent of use of discovery devices. *See,* State Bar Committee Note to 1984 Amendment to Rule 26(b). The circumstances under which the trial court will have the need or opportunity to invoke its authority to control the use and scope of discovery were drastically affected by the 1992 amendments to the discovery rules. See the discussion of those amendments in Section 4, *supra.*

In matters affecting discovery, however, the trial court is vested with a very broad discretion. *Twin City Fire Ins. Co. v. Burke*, 204 Ariz. 251, 63 P.3d 282 (2003); *State Farm Mut. Auto. Ins. Co. v. Lee*, 199 Ariz. 52, 13 P.3d 1169 (2000); *Brown v. Superior Court In and For Maricopa County*, 137 Ariz. 327, 670 P.2d 725 (1983); *Banta v. Superior Court of Maricopa County*, 112 Ariz. 544, 544 P.2d 653 (1976); *American Family Mut. Ins. Co. v. Grant*, 222 Ariz. 507, 217 P.3d 1212 (Ct. App. Div. 1 2009); *Reid v. Reid*, 222

Ariz. 204, 213 P.3d 353 (Ct. App. Div. 1 2009); *Felder v. Physiotherapy Associates*, 215 Ariz. 154, 158 P.3d 877 (Ct. App. Div. 1 2007); *Tritschler v. Allstate Ins. Co.*, 213 Ariz. 505, 144 P.3d 519 (Ct. App. Div. 2 2006), as corrected, (Dec. 19, 2006); *Green v. Nygaard*, 213 Ariz. 460, 143 P.3d 393 (Ct. App. Div. 2 2006); *Zuern By and Through Zuern v. Ford Motor Co.*, 188 Ariz. 486, 937 P.2d 676 (Ct. App. Div. 2 1996); *Rosner v. Denim & Diamonds, Inc.*, 188 Ariz. 431, 937 P.2d 353 (Ct. App. Div. 2 1996); *Soto v. Brinkerhoff*, 183 Ariz. 333, 903 P.2d 641 (Ct. App. Div. 2 1995); *Jackson v. American Credit Bureau, Inc.*, 23 Ariz. App. 199, 531 P.2d 932, 79 A.L.R.3d 841 (Div. 1 1975). The recent emphasis, however, has been upon reducing the burden of having the courts resolve every discovery dispute that arises and encouraging the parties to resolve them informally. In furtherance of that goal, both Rule 26(g) and Rule 37(a)(2)(C) provide that a discovery motion will be neither scheduled nor heard unless accompanied by a separate statement of counsel certifying that personal consultation between counsel and good faith efforts to resolve the dispute have been unsuccessful.

16. *Protective Orders.* Rule 26(c)(1) provides that a protective order may be entered to protect the person or party from whom the discovery is requested, from "annoyance, embarrassment, oppression, or undue burden or expense." A motion for a protective order directed at the taking of a deposition may be brought in the county where the deposition is scheduled.

There are any number of grounds upon which a protective order may be sought with respect to depositions, and the trial court has broad discretion in fashioning appropriate protective relief that may be less than, or different from, that requested by the moving party. *See, BNSF Ry. Co. v. Buttrick*, 228 Ariz. 449, 268 P.3d 400 (Ct. App. Div. 1 2011) ("To maintain the integrity of the discovery process and to ensure that no witness is harassed, the Arizona Rules of Civil Procedure grant trial courts broad discretion to issue protective orders."). The trial court must have jurisdiction, however, to enter such order. *BNSF Ry. Co. v. Buttrick*, 228 Ariz. 449, 268 P.3d 400 (Ct. App. Div. 1 2011) (finding the trial court exceeded its jurisdiction in granting a Rule 26(c) protective order).

The Arizona Supreme Court adopted an amendment to Rule 26(c), effective December 1, 2002, which may operate to restrict, to an as yet indeterminable extent, the ability to secure confidentiality or protective orders with respect to information and materials sought in discovery in civil litigation. The amendment makes existing Rule 26(c) subpart (1) of the Rule [apparently overlooking the fact that the Rule has existing numbered subparts], and adopts a new subpart 26(c)(2), which applies to orders which in any way restrict "a party or person from disclosing information or materials produced in discovery to a person who is not a party to the litigation" or deny "an intervener's request for access to such discovery materials." Before entering any such order, the court is to direct the party seeking confidentiality to show why a confidentiality order should be entered or continued, and the party or intervener opposing confidentiality to show why a confidentiality order should be denied in whole or in part, modified or vacated. The Rule was amended in 2004 to specify that the burden of showing good cause remains with the party seeking confidentiality.

Before entering a confidentiality order, a trial court must make findings of fact "concerning any relevant factors," including a party's need to maintain confidentiality, any nonparty's or intervener's need to obtain access to the materials, and "any possible risk to the public health, safety or financial welfare . . ." The Court Comment accompanying the amendment makes clear that these three listed factors are not exclusive, and counsels trial judges to consider federal case law to determine what other relevant factors to consider. In addition, "any order restricting release of such information or materials to nonparties or interveners shall use the least restrictive means to maintain any needed confidentiality."

The new subpart 26(c)(2) does contain a provision that the specified findings are not required where the parties have stipulated to a confidentiality order or where a motion to intervene and obtain access to materials subject to an existing confidentiality order is not opposed. Nominally, accordingly, it does not impact stipulated confidentiality orders, but it will apply to requests, from whatever source, to modify or vacate them. It also clearly places a burden on a party seeking confidentiality for discovery materials which the present rules do not impose.

17. *Stays of Discovery.* Discovery proceedings may be stayed pending other proceedings, such as criminal prosecutions related to the same matter, or pending the outcome of dispositive motions in the same case that might make such discovery unnecessary. *See,* Wright & Miller, *Federal Practice and Procedure: Civil* § 2040. There is no constitutional prohibition of parallel civil and criminal proceedings, and whether to grant a stay or continuance of the civil proceedings in that circumstance is a matter within the trial court's discretion. *State v. Ott*, 167 Ariz. 420, 808 P.2d 305 (Ct. App. Div. 1 1990). The court should consider whether the civil and criminal proceedings concern the same matter, whether the resolution of the criminal case would moot, clarify or simplify the matter, and whether there is a possibility that a party might exploit discovery in the civil proceedings for use in the criminal case. *State v. Ott*, 167 Ariz. 420, 808 P.2d 305 (Ct. App. Div. 1 1990). The civil proceedings should be

stayed if the conduct of parallel proceedings would substantially prejudice the defendant's rights. *State v. Ott*, 167 Ariz. 420, 808 P.2d 305 (Ct. App. Div. 1 1990).

18. *Control of the Place of Deposition.* Issues concerning the place where a deposition is to be conducted arise frequently in instances where the deposition of a party who does not reside in Arizona is noticed to be conducted in the State. A party does not have an absolute right to conduct the deposition of another party at the site of the forum; rather, the Court must weigh the party's preference for Arizona as the place for the deposition against the resulting burden on the party to be deposed. *Rogers v. Fenton*, 115 Ariz. 217, 564 P.2d 906 (Ct. App. Div. 2 1977). The fact that the party resisting the deposition is the plaintiff who instituted proceedings in Arizona is a factor to be considered.

The burden of out-of-state depositions can be alleviated, if appropriate, through cost allocation protective orders. It was held not to be an abuse of discretion for the trial court to order the defendant to pay in advance the travel expenses that would be incurred by plaintiff's counsel in attending the depositions of the defendant's witnesses by defendant's counsel. *State v. Mahoney*, 103 Ariz. 308, 441 P.2d 68 (1968); *City of Kingman v. Havatone*, 14 Ariz. App. 585, 485 P.2d 574 (Div. 1 1971). The Court can also order that the deposition be taken by written interrogatories, rather than upon oral examination, or by telephone.

19. *Control of Methods for Conducting Discovery.* Parties are usually free to decide which form of discovery they wish to utilize. However, Rule 26(c), recognizes that the person from whom the discovery is requested may ask the Court to mold the discovery to special needs or circumstances. For instance, expense of travel is a common ground given for the request that written interrogatories be used instead of depositions.

20. *Protection of Trade Secrets and Other Confidential Information.* Rule 26(c)(1)(7), provides that a protective order may be entered to protect the person or party from being forced to disclose trade secrets or confidential information. *Cornet Stores v. Superior Court In and For Yavapai County*, 108 Ariz. 84, 492 P.2d 1191 (1972). The Court may also establish limitations on the form of disclosure or use of such information to protect the interests of the person or party.

Rule 26(c)(1)(7) grants the Court authority to protect against the disclosure of "a trade secret or other confidential research, development, or commercial information. . . ." The details of a settlement of an earlier action, if otherwise discoverable, are not rendered privileged or confidential by reason of a nondisclosure covenant. *Ingalls v. Superior Court in and for Pima County*, 117 Ariz. 448, 573 P.2d 522 (Ct. App. Div. 2 1977).

21. *Sealing Discovery.* Rule 26(c)(1)(6) gives the Court implied authority to seal a deposition, the contents of which should not be disclosed to the public. It has been interpreted to authorize sealing responses to other forms of discovery requests as well. See Wright & Miller, *Federal Practice and Procedure: Civil* § 2042.

Rule 26(c)(1)(8), also provides for protective orders that "the parties simultaneously file specified documents or information enclosed in sealed envelopes to be opened as directed by the court." There are a variety of circumstances where such a procedure may be warranted. See Wright & Miller, *Federal Practice and Procedure: Civil* § 2044.

22. *Control of Attendance at Depositions.* A deposition is not a public proceeding, and the Court has the authority to exclude from attendance persons whose presence is not necessary or authorized. *Lewis R. Pyle Memorial Hosp. v. Superior Court of Arizona In and For Gila County*, 149 Ariz. 193, 717 P.2d 872 (1986). Because it is part of the judicial and litigation process, however, it is error to exercise that authority so as to exclude a party from any representation or participation at a deposition. *Montgomery Elevator Co. v. Superior Court of State, In and For Maricopa County*, 135 Ariz. 432, 661 P.2d 1133 (1983). Although, in a wrongful death action, only those categories of persons specified by statute are proper parties plaintiff, a statutory beneficiary of such an action is still a party to the case with respect to damages. Absent a clear conflict between beneficiaries, a statutory beneficiary and/or counsel may attend depositions in a wrongful death action, but may only participate in those portions of the deposition that relate to damages. *Williams v. Superior Court In and For County of Maricopa*, 169 Ariz. 468, 820 P.2d 332 (Ct. App. Div. 1 1991).

23. *Control of Sequence and Scheduling of Discovery.* Rule 26(d) articulates the general rule that discovery is not to be conducted in any arbitrary sequence or priority, but permits the Court to impose such a schedule for discovery where it is necessary "for the convenience of parties and witnesses" or "in the interests of justice." The Court also has authority to regulate the pace and timing of discovery by setting a schedule therefor at a scheduling or comprehensive conference held pursuant to Rule 16.

24. *Supplementation of Discovery Responses.* Rule 26(e) deals with a party's duty to supplement and update prior responses to written discovery requests. Under Rule 26(e)(1), there is an absolute duty, even in the absence of a request for supplementation, to supplement prior responses concerning (a) the identity and location of potential witnesses, (b) the identity of and anticipated testimony of expert witnesses, (c) the identity of other witnesses expected to be called at trial, and (d) the identity and

location of a person or entity not a party to the action who is claimed to be wholly or partially responsible for the claimant's injuries or damages, and the facts supporting such a claim. The identification of an individual as a lay witness does not permit a party to elicit opinion testimony from that witness as an expert at trial, even if that testimony is characterized as "lay opinion" testimony. *Kott v. City of Phoenix*, 158 Ariz. 415, 763 P.2d 235 (1988); *but cf. AMERCO v. Shoen*, 184 Ariz. 150, 907 P.2d 536 (Ct. App. Div. 1 1995), corrected, (Aug. 29, 1995).

Rule 26(e) was amended, effective December 1, 2000, to provide that prior discovery responses concerning the identity of lay witnesses, the identity and anticipated testimony of expert witnesses, and claims that a person or entity not a party to the action is wholly or partially fault for the plaintiff's injuries or damages must be supplemented by no later than sixty (60) days before trial. The purpose of the amendment was to bring Rule 26(e) into conformity with prior amendments to Rules 26.1 and 37 which require the disclosure of such information within that time frame.

While the Rule thus specifies time periods before trial by which supplementation must be made, the intent of the Rule is to have supplemental information furnished seasonably after it is acquired rather than at the last permissible minute. *See,* State Bar Committee Note to 1983 Amendment. Under Rule 26(e)(2), a duty to supplement prior responses on other subjects arises where the party acquires information that indicates a prior response was incorrect when made or would no longer be considered accurate. Such a duty would also arise where a party indicated in a prior response that the information requested was not available but would be furnished in the future. *Greco v. Manolakos*, 24 Ariz. App. 490, 539 P.2d 964 (Div. 2 1975). Under Rule 26(e)(3), a duty to supplement may be imposed through a formal request for supplementation, by the service of supplemental requests, or by the Court. The duty to supplement discovery responses under Rule 26(e) does not operate as a limitation on the obligation to supplement disclosures under Rule 26.1.

Whether sanctions should be imposed for failure to update interrogatory responses is a question committed to the trial court's discretion. *Mott's Inc. of Mississippi v. Coco's Family Restaurant*, 158 Ariz. 350, 762 P.2d 637 (Ct. App. Div. 2 1988). It was found not to be an abuse of that discretion to refuse to exclude a witness who had not been disclosed in answers to interrogatories when the witness was listed in the pretrial statement and there had been adequate opportunity to conduct the witness' deposition. *Mott's Inc. of Mississippi v. Coco's Family Restaurant*, 158 Ariz. 350, 762 P.2d 637 (Ct. App. Div. 2 1988).

25. *Disclosure of Claims of Non-Party Liability; 2014 Rule*

Amendments. A.R.S. § 12-2506(B) (as amended) specifies that the negligence or fault of a non-party may be considered by the trier of fact in assessing percentages of fault if the plaintiff has settled with such non-party or if "the defending party gives notice before trial, in accordance with requirements established by court rule, that a nonparty was wholly or partially or fault." *Cf. Zuern By and Through Zuern v. Ford Motor Co.*, 188 Ariz. 486, 937 P.2d 676 (Ct. App. Div. 2 1996).

To serve as the "court rule" contemplated by this legislation, the Arizona Supreme Court adopted, effective July 1, 1989, Ariz. R. Civ. P. 26(b)(5). As adopted, Rule 26(b)(5) set forth a general rule requiring the disclosure of such a claim within one hundred fifty (150) days after the filing of the answer of the party making the claim, or at the time of compliance with the requirements of Rule 38.1(b)(2), whichever is earlier.

Effective April 15, 2014, Rule 26(b)(5) was amended to provide that such notice must be filed within 150 days of the filing of the party's answer, and eliminated the reference to Rule 38.1(b)(2). The 2014 amendment to Rule 26(b)(5) was part of sweeping revisions made to Arizona's civil case managment and trial setting procedures, which, among other things, dispensed with the filing of motions to set and controverting certificates. Rule 26(b)(5), as amended effective April 15, 2014, applies to cases filed on or after April 15, 2014 and to those cases to conditions stated in the November 27, 2013 Amended Order Regarding Applicability Provision in R-13-0017. Pre-amendment Rule 26(b)(5) continues to apply to cases filed before April 15, 2014 that are not otherwise subject to conditions stated in the November 27, 2013, Amended Order Regarding Applicability Provision in R-13-0017.

The disclosure must ordinarily be specific, not generic, and must include not only the identity and location of the non-party claimed to be wholly or partially at fault, but also the facts relied upon to support that claim.

A nonparty at fault designation fails when it fails to state facts establishing the claim that the alleged nonparty is at fault. *Bowen Productions, Inc. v. French*, 231 Ariz. 424, 296 P.3d 87 (Ct. App. Div. 1 2013).

On the other hand, where the party making such a claim and disclosure has made duly diligent efforts to locate and specifically identify such nonparties and has been unsuccessful, it is not an abuse of discretion for the trial court to allow the jury to allocate fault to nonparties whose names and addresses have not been provided. *Rosner v. Denim & Diamonds, Inc.*, 188 Ariz. 431, 937 P.2d 353 (Ct. App. Div. 2 1996). Furthermore, a Rule 26(b)(5) notice of a non-party at fault, and timely Rule 26.1 disclosures must be read together, to determine the sufficiency of such notice. *Bowen*

Productions, Inc. v. French, 231 Ariz. 424, 296 P.3d 87 (Ct. App. Div. 1 2013). A facially vague notice of non-party at fault, however, cannot be revived by facially vague Rule 26.1 disclosures. *Scottsdale Ins. Co. v. Cendejas*, 220 Ariz. 281, 205 P.3d 1128 (Ct. App. Div. 1 2009).

Rule 26(b)(5) requires that any party who claims a person or entity not *currently or formerly named as a party* is wholly or partially at fault for causing damages claimed for personal injury, property damage or wrongful death must file a notice of a non-party at fault. *LyphoMed, Inc. v. Superior Court In and For County of Maricopa*, 172 Ariz. 423, 837 P.2d 1158 (Ct. App. Div. 1 1992) (Neither the Rule nor the statute it implements, however, require notice of a claim that another party is wholly or partially at fault). *See also*, *Bowen Productions, Inc. v. French*, 231 Ariz. 424, 296 P.3d 87 (Ct. App. Div. 1 2013) (observing that "[c]omparative fault principles do not apply in breach of contract cases.", citing *Fidelity and Deposit Co. of Maryland v. Bondwriter Southwest, Inc.*, 228 Ariz. 84, 263 P.3d 633 (Ct. App. Div. 1 2011), review denied, (Oct. 30, 2012). A defendant is not relieved of the need to file such a notice because another defendant has done so, even though the other defendant's notice identifies all of the non-parties that the defendant who failed to file a notice would name.

A defendant can name a nonparty at fault even if the plaintiff is prohibited from directly naming or recovering from such a nonparty. *Dietz v. General Elec. Co.*, 169 Ariz. 505, 821 P.2d 166 (1991); *A Tumbling-T Ranches v. Flood Control Dist. of Maricopa County*, 222 Ariz. 515, 217 P.3d 1220 (Ct. App. Div. 1 2009); *Larsen v. Nissan Motor Corp. in U.S.A.*, 194 Ariz. 142, 978 P.2d 119 (Ct. App. Div. 2 1998); *Ocotillo West Joint Venture v. Superior Court In and For County of Maricopa*, 173 Ariz. 486, 844 P.2d 653 (Ct. App. Div. 1 1992). Where the parties stipulate that a non-party was the proximate cause of the plaintiff's injuries, the jury must allocate some degree of fault to that non-party, and the jury's disregard of such a stipulation and assignment of 100% of the fault to the named defendants warrants a new trial on all issues. *Ogden v. J.M. Steel Erecting, Inc.*, 201 Ariz. 32, 31 P.3d 806 (Ct. App. Div. 1 2001).

In accordance with the 2011 amendments to Rule 26(b)(5), the fault of a person or entity not currently or formerly named as a party whose identity is not disclosed within the time periods set forth in Rule 26(b)(5) will be considered only upon the written agreement of the parties or upon motion establishing "good cause, reasonable diligence and lack of unfair prejudice to other parties." The 2011 amendment relaxes the harsh standard embodied by former Rule 26(b)(5). *See e.g.*, *Scottsdale Ins. Co. v. Cendejas*, 220 Ariz. 281, 205 P.3d 1128 (Ct. App. Div. 1 2009). Interpreting former Rule 26(b)(5), it had been held that in order to satisfy the then-applicable "newly discovered evidence exception", the "newly discovered evidence" establishing the nonparty's liability must be information that was unknown or unavailable through discovery to the party making the claim during the time frames specified in Rule 26(b)(5). *Soto v. Brinkerhoff*, 183 Ariz. 333, 903 P.2d 641 (Ct. App. Div. 2 1995). It is as yet unknown, but nonetheless seems likely, that this case may continue to have some viability when newly discovered evidence forms the basis of the "good cause" component of a motion brought pursuant to Rule 26(b)(5).

Joint liability and vicarious liability "are related but separate doctrines." *Wiggs v. City of Phoenix*, 198 Ariz. 367, 10 P.3d 625, 111 A.L.R.5th 815 (2000) (citing, *Srithong v. Total Investment Co.*, 23 Cal. App. 4th 721, 28 Cal. Rptr. 2d 672 (2d Dist. 1994); *State Farm Ins. Companies v. Premier Manufactured Systems, Inc.*, 213 Ariz. 419, 142 P.3d 1232, Prod. Liab. Rep. (CCH) P 17517 (Ct. App. Div. 1 2006), opinion aff'd, 217 Ariz. 222, 172 P.3d 410 (2007). The joint liability that was abolished by A.R.S. § 12-2506(D) is limited to "that class of joint tortfeasors whose independent negligence coalesced to form a single injury." *Wiggs v. City of Phoenix*, 198 Ariz. 367, 10 P.3d 625, 111 A.L.R.5th 815 (2000). The statute preserves joint liability both for true joint tortfeasors (those "acting in concert") and for those who are vicariously liable for the fault of others. *Wiggs v. City of Phoenix*, 198 Ariz. 367, 10 P.3d 625, 111 A.L.R.5th 815 (2000); *State Farm Ins. Companies v. Premier Manufactured Systems, Inc.*, 213 Ariz. 419, 142 P.3d 1232, Prod. Liab. Rep. (CCH) P 17517 (Ct. App. Div. 1 2006), opinion aff'd, 217 Ariz. 222, 172 P.3d 410 (2007). The comparative fault statute, thus, preserves vicarious liability for the negligence of an independent contractor, when the employer of that independent contractor had a non-delegable duty. *Wiggs v. City of Phoenix*, 198 Ariz. 367, 10 P.3d 625, 111 A.L.R.5th 815 (2000).

In *Wiggs*, the Supreme Court observed that it would make little legal or tactical sense to name as a non-party at fault the party (employee or independent contractor) whose conduct will be imputed to the employer, because the employer will be fully liable for that fault in any event.

26. *Discovery Disputes*. In October 2000, the Arizona Supreme Court approved a proposal to abrogate the Uniform Rules of Practice of the Superior Court, the Uniform Rules of Procedure for Medical Malpractice Cases, and the Uniform Rules of Procedure for Arbitration, and to transfer their provisions to either the Arizona Rules of Civil Procedure or the Rules of the Arizona Supreme Court. The provisions of former Rule IV(g) of the Uniform Rules of Practice of the Superior Court, which required a good faith attempt to resolve a discovery dispute as a condition of having a discovery motion scheduled or heard, were trans-

ferred, effective December 1, 2000, to Rule 37, as a new Rule 37(a)(2)(C). The language of that new Rule, however, was amended to suggest that its requirements only applied to motions brought under Rule 37, which overlooked the fact that "discovery motions," such as motions for a protective order, are brought under Rule 26 rather than Rule 37. To correct that apparent oversight, the Supreme Court promulgated, on June 27, 2001, Rule 26(g), to be effective upon promulgation, the provisions of which are identical to those of former Rule IV(g) of the Uniform Rules of Practice of the Superior Court. Under this Rule, any motion brought under Rule 26 seeking relief with respect to a discovery matter must be accompanied by, or have attached thereto, a separate statement signed by counsel for the moving party, certifying that counsel in the case have consulted personally and in good faith and have been unable to resolve the discovery issue satisfactorily.

27. *Testifying treating physicians.* A testifying treating physician is entitled to compensation only if the treating physician is serving as an expert witness as opposed to a fact witness. Whether a treating physician testifies as an expert or a fact witness depends on the context of the testimony. *Sanchez v. Gama*, 233 Ariz. 125, 310 P.3d 1 (Ct. App. Div. 1 2013), as amended, (Sept. 4, 2013). A fact witness is not entitled to be compensated as an expert; an expert witness is entitled to be compensated as an expert. *Sanchez v. Gama*, 233 Ariz. 125, 310 P.3d 1 (Ct. App. Div. 1 2013), as amended, (Sept. 4, 2013). Ariz. R. Civ. P. 26(b)(4) does not apply to treating physicians who testify as fact witnesses.

A treating physician is a fact witness if the physician is testifying as to the injury, the treatment and other facts within the treating physician's first-hand knowledge. Where expert testimony is developed for purposes of litigation and given at trial, then the treating physician is entitled to compensation. *Sanchez v. Gama*, 233 Ariz. 125, 310 P.3d 1 (Ct. App. Div. 1 2013), as amended, (Sept. 4, 2013). The trial court has discretion to make this determination, which likely will depend on the questions asked.

The court in *Sanchez* made clear that its decision was not intended to provide a platform by which litigants could obtain free expert testimony. In that regard, the court stated as follows:

> "Our holding in no way entitles parties to abuse physicians by compelling them to give uncompensated expert testimony. The Guidelines for Interprofessional Relationships in Legal Proceedings was an excellent attempt at compromise, and we encourage similar efforts of cooperation and good faith in the future. See Joint Committee on Interprofessional Relationships et al., Guidelines on Interprofessional Relationships in Legal Proceedings 1992/1993 (1993)."

28. *2014 Rule Amendments: Effective Date and Applicability.* On August 28, 2013, the Arizona Supreme Court adopted sweeping amendments to the case management and trial setting rules governing civil cases. The Promulgating Order specified such rules were adopted "effective on April 15, 2014 as to all cases filed on or after that date." *See,* August 28, 2013 Order entered in In the Matter of Petition to Amend Rules 16, 16.1, 26, 37, 38, 38.1, 72, 73, 74 and 77, Arizona Rules of Civil Procedure, R-13-0017. The applicability provision set forth in the Promulgating Order set up two procedural tracks for case management with the new rules governing cases file on or after April 15, 2014 and the "old" rules governing pre-April 15, 2014 cases.

To avoid any confusion potentially created by the two different tracks, the Court entered an order on November 14, 2013, amending the applicability provision. On November 27, 2013, the court entered a second order further refining the amended applicability provision. As a result, the Amendments are effective and applicable as follows:

"(1) The Amendments shall apply to all actions filed on or after April 15, 2014.

"(2) Beginning on April 15, 2014, the Amendments also shall apply to any action filed prior to April 15, 2014 (a "pending action"), unless one of the following events has occurred before that date:

(a) A party has filed a Motion to Set and Certificate of Readiness,

(b) The parties have filed a Proposed Scheduling Order, or

(c) The court has entered a Scheduling Order.

"(3) If, in a pending action, one of the preceding events has not occurred before April 15, 2014, the parties shall file a Joint Report and a Proposed Scheduling Order in accordance with the Amendments by June 30, 2014, or within 270 days after the commencement of the action, whichever date is later. Otherwise, the court will place the action on the Dismissal Calendar in accordance with the Amendments.

"(4) A trial court, in its discretion, may apply any of the Amendments to a case pending before April 15, 2014, even if the Amendments would not otherwise apply under paragraph (2) above. For example, if a party filed a Motion to Set and Certificate of Readiness before April 15, 2014, the trial judge may set the matter for a trial setting conference under amended Rule 16(f), rather than place the case on the active calendar under pre-amendment Rule 38.1(c).

"(5) Civil actions pending on the Inactive Calendar on April 15, 2014 shall be dismissed without prejudice on June 14, 2014, unless one of the actions set forth in subparts (1) - (4) of amended Rule 38.1(f) occurs before June 14, 2014."

Rule 26.1. Prompt disclosure of information

(a) Duty to Disclose, Scope. Within the times set forth in subdivision (b), each party shall disclose in writing to every other party:

(1) The factual basis of the claim or defense. In the event of multiple claims or defenses, the factual basis for each claim or defense.

(2) The legal theory upon which each claim or defense is based including, where necessary for a reasonable understanding of the claim or defense, citations of pertinent legal or case authorities.

(3) The names, addresses, and telephone numbers of any witnesses whom the disclosing party expects to call at trial with a fair description of the substance of each witness' expected testimony.

(4) The names and addresses of all persons whom the party believes may have knowledge or information relevant to the events, transactions, or occurrences that gave rise to the action, and the nature of the knowledge or information each such individual is believed to possess.

(5) The names and addresses of all persons who have given statements, whether written or recorded, signed or unsigned, and the custodian of the copies of those statements.

(6) The name and address of each person whom the disclosing party expects to call as an expert witness at trial, the subject matter on which the expert is expected to testify, the substance of the facts and opinions to which the expert is expected to testify, a summary of the grounds for each opinion, the qualifications of the witness and the name and address of the custodian of copies of any reports prepared by the expert.

(7) A computation and the measure of damage alleged by the disclosing party and the documents or testimony on which such computation and measure are based and the names, addresses, and telephone numbers of all damage witnesses.

(8) The existence, location, custodian, and general description of any tangible evidence, relevant documents, or electronically stored information that the disclosing party plans to use at trial and relevant insurance agreements.

(9) A list of the documents or electronically stored information or, in the case of voluminous documentary information or electronically stored information, a list of the categories of documents or electronically stored information, known by a

party to exist whether or not in the party's possession, custody or control and which that party believes may be relevant to the subject matter of the action, and those which appear reasonably calculated to lead to the discovery of admissible evidence, and the date(s) upon which those documents or electronically stored information will be made, or have been made, available for inspection, copying, testing or sampling. Unless good cause is stated for not doing so, a copy of the documents and electronically stored information listed shall be served with the disclosure. If production is not made, the name and address of the custodian of the documents and electronically stored information shall be indicated. A party who produces documents for inspection shall produce them as they are kept in the usual course of business.

(b) Time for Disclosure; a Continuing Duty.

(1) The parties shall make the initial disclosure required by subdivision (a) as fully as then possible within forty (40) days after the filing of a responsive pleading to the Complaint, Counterclaim, Crossclaim or Third Party Complaint unless the parties otherwise agree, or the Court shortens or extends the time for good cause. If feasible, counsel shall meet to exchange disclosures; otherwise, the disclosures shall be served as provided by Rule 5. In domestic relations cases involving children whose custody is at issue, the parties shall make disclosure regarding custody issues no later than 30 days after mediation of the custody dispute by the conciliation court or a third party results in written notice acknowledging that mediation has failed to settle the issues, or at some other time set by court order.

(2) The duty prescribed in subdivision (a) shall be a continuing duty, and each party shall make additional or amended disclosures whenever new or different information is discovered or revealed. Such additional or amended disclosures shall be made seasonably, but in no event more than thirty (30) days after the information is revealed to or discovered by the disclosing party. A party seeking to use information which that party first disclosed later than sixty (60) days before trial shall seek leave of court to extend the time for disclosure as provided in Rule 37(c)(2) or (c)(3).

(3) All disclosures shall include information and data in the possession, custody and control of the parties as well as that which can be ascertained, learned or acquired by reasonable inquiry and investigation.

(c) [Deleted effective December 1, 1996].

(d) Signed Disclosure. Each disclosure shall be made in writing under oath, signed by the party making the disclosure.

(e) [Deleted effective December 1, 1996].

(f) Claims of Privilege or Protection of Trial Preparation Materials.

(1) *Information Withheld.*

When information is withheld from disclosure or discovery on a claim that it is privileged or subject to protection as trial preparation materials, the claim shall be made expressly and shall be supported by a description of the nature of the documents, communications, or things not produced or disclosed that is sufficient to enable other parties to contest the claim.

(2) *Information Produced.*

If a party contends that information subject to a claim of privilege or of protection as trial-preparation materials has been inadvertently disclosed or produced in discovery, the party making the claim may notify any party that received the information of the claim and the basis for it. After being notified, a party must promptly return, sequester, or destroy the specified information and any copies it has made and may not use or disclose the information until the claim is resolved. A receiving party may promptly present the information to the court under seal for a determination of the claim. If the receiving party disclosed the information before being notified, it must take reasonable steps to retrieve it. The producing party must preserve the information until the claim is resolved.

(g) [Deleted effective December 1, 1996].

Rule 26.1 added Dec. 20, 1991, effective July 1, 1992; amended May 30, 1996, effective Dec. 1, 1996; Nov. 22, 1996, effective March 1, 1997; September 5, 2007, effective January 1, 2008.

STATE BAR COMMITTEE NOTES

1991 Promulgation

[Rule 26.1(a)] This addition to the rules is intended to require cooperation between counsel in the handling of civil litigation. The Committee has endeavored to set forth those items of information and evidence which should be promptly disclosed early in the course of litigation in order to avoid unnecessary and protracted discovery as well as to encourage early evaluation, assessment and possible disposition of the litigation between the parties.

It is the intent of the Committee that there be a reasonable and fair disclosure of the items set forth in Rule 26.1 and that the disclosure of that information be reasonably prompt. The intent of the Committee is to have newly discovered information exchanged with reasonable promptness and to preclude those attorneys and parties who intentionally withhold such information from offering it later in the course of litigation.

The Committee originally considered including in Rule 26.1(a)(5) a requirement for disclosure of all cases in which an expert had testified within the prior five (5) years. The Committee recognized in its deliberations that information as to such cases might be important in certain types of litigation and not in others. On balance, it was decided that it would be burdensome to require this information in all cases.

[Rule 26.1(b)] The Committee does not intend to affect in any way, any party's right to amend or move to amend or supplement pleadings as provided in Rule 15.

Rule 26.1(e) is intended specifically to deal with the party and/or attorney who makes intentionally inaccurate or misleading responses to discovery.

1996 Amendment

Rule 26.1(a)(3). With regard to the degree of specificity required for disclosing witness testimony, it is the intent of the rule that parties must disclose the substance of the witness' expected testimony. The disclosure must fairly apprise the parties of the information and opinion known by that person. It is not sufficient to simply describe the subject matter upon which the witness will testify.

Rule 26.1(a)(5) was not intended to require automatic production of statements. Production of statements remains subject to the provisions of Rule 26(b)(3).

Rule 26.1(a)(6). A specially retained expert as described in Rule 26(b)(4)(B) is not required to be disclosed under Rule 26.1.

2008 Amendment

As with its federal counterpart, the amendment is intended merely to place a "hold" on further use or dissemination of an inadvertently produced document that is subject to a privilege claim until a court resolves its status or the parties agree to an appropriate disposition. The amendment, however, "does not address whether the privilege or protection that is asserted after production was waived by the production." Fed. R. Civ. P. 26(b)(5)(B), Advisory Committee Notes on 2006 Amendment.

COURT COMMENT

1991 Promulgation

In March, 1990 the Supreme Court, in conjunction with the State Bar of Arizona, appointed the Special Bar Committee to Study Civil Litigation Abuse, Cost and Delay, which was specifically charged with the task of studying problems pertaining to abuse and delay in civil litigation and the cost of civil litigation.

Following extensive study, the Committee concluded that the American system of civil litigation was employing methods which were causing undue expense and delay and threatening to make the courts inaccessible to the average citizen. The Committee further concluded that certain adjustments in the system and the Arizona Rules of Civil Procedure were necessary to reduce expense, delay and abuse while preserving the traditional jury trial system as a means of resolution of civil disputes.

In September, 1990 the Committee proposed a comprehensive set of rule revisions, designed to make the judicial system in Arizona more efficient, more expeditious, less expensive, and more accessible to the people. It was the goal of the Committee to provide a framework which would allow sufficient discovery of facts and information to avoid "litigation by ambush." At the same time, the Committee wished to promote greater professionalism among counsel, with the ultimate goal of increasing voluntary cooperation and exchange of information. The intent of the amendments was to limit the adversarial nature of proceedings to those areas where there is a true and legitimate dispute between the parties, and to preclude hostile, unprofessional, and unnecessarily adversarial conduct on the part of counsel. It was also the intent of the rules that the trial courts deal in a strong and forthright fashion with discovery abuse and discovery abusers.

After a period of public comment and experimental implementation in four divisions of the Superior Court in Maricopa County, the rule changes proposed by the Committee were promulgated by the Court on December 18, 1991, effective July 1, 1992.

AUTHORS' COMMENTS

Analysis

1. *Scope and Purpose of Rule.* In December 1991, the Arizona Supreme Court adopted, to become effective July 1, 1992, a comprehensive package of discovery and court reform proposals which emanated from recommendations made by a Special Bar Committee to Study Civil Litigation Abuse, Cost and Delay, and from the work of the Arizona Commission on the Courts. Rule 26.1 was, and remains, the cornerstone of this effort.

The intent of Rule 26.1 is to reduce the abuse, cost and delay in modern civil litigation and to make the judicial system more efficient and accessible to the public. *Montgomery Ward & Co., Inc. v. Superior Court In and For County of Maricopa*, 176 Ariz. 619, 863 P.2d 911 (Ct. App. Div. 1 1993). The reforms required disclosure, without prior request, of information pertinent to the matter in controversy, placed presumptive limits on the amount of discovery that can be conducted, and provided lawyers with incentives, backed by the availability of meaningful sanctions, to cooperate rather than litigate. Amendments were also adopted to facilitate the prompt identification and disposition of cases subject to compulsory arbitration.

The admitted cornerstone of these reform measures, which were tested before adoption on an experimental basis in certain Divisions of the Maricopa County Superior Court, is Ariz. R. Civ. P. 26.1 which implements the mandatory disclosure requirements. The disclosure rules represent a policy that the facts and issues to be litigated must be fairly exposed, as should witnesses and exhibits, and the purpose is to give the parties a reasonable opportunity to prepare for trial or settlement, as well as to maximize the likelihood of a decision on the merits. *Gerow v. Covill*, 192 Ariz. 9, 960 P.2d 55 (Ct. App. Div. 1 1998), as amended, (Aug. 26, 1998). The Rule, however, does not apply in dependency proceedings in Juvenile Court. *S.S. v. Superior Court In and For County of Maricopa*, 178 Ariz. 423, 874 P.2d 980 (Ct. App. Div. 1 1994). Nor does the Rule apply to the uncontested probate of an estate. *In re Estate of Thurston*, 199 Ariz. 215, 16 P.3d 776 (Ct. App. Div. 1 2000). The disclosure requirements for such proceedings are those set forth in A.R.S. § 14-3706, and Rule 26.1 only comes into play when the probate proceedings become a disputed matter. *In re Estate of Thurston*, 199 Ariz. 215, 16 P.3d 776 (Ct. App. Div. 1 2000).

2. *Comparison With Federal Rule.* The Federal Rules of Civil Procedure do not have a provision that directly corresponds to ARCP 26.1, which sets forth the Arizona rule providing for mandatory disclosure obligations. The corresponding mandatory disclosure provision in the Federal Rules of Civil Procedure is FRCP 26(a), but the categories of information to be disclosed under FRCP 26(a) do not entirely correspond to those set forth in the Arizona Rule.

ARCP 26.1(f), which sets forth provisions for claims of privilege or protection of trial preparation materials with respect to mandatory disclosures or discovery, is essentially identical to FRCP 26(b)(5). Both rules provide procedures for withholding such information and for seeking protection if such information is inadvertently disclosed or produced.

3. *Disclosure Requirements.* As amended in 1996, Ariz. R. Civ. P. 26.1(a) specifies nine categories of information and/or documents that all parties must disclose, without request, in all civil cases. These are:

(1) the factual basis for each claim or defense asserted;

(2) the underlying legal theory on which each claim or defense is based including, where necessary, citations to pertinent legal authority;

(3) the names, addresses and phone numbers of any witnesses whom the party making the disclosure expects to call at trial, together with a "fair description of the substance of each such witness' expected testimony";

(4) the names and addresses of all persons whom the disclosing party believes may have "knowledge or information relevant to the events, transactions, or occurrences that gave rise to the action," together with a description of the nature of the information each such person is believed to have;

(5) the names and addresses of all persons who have given statements and the custodian of copies of such statements;

(6) the names and addresses of expert witnesses to be called at trial by the party making the disclosure, the subject matter on which the expert is to testify, the substance of the facts and

opinions to which the expert is expected to testify, a summary of the grounds for each opinion, the expert's qualifications, and the name and address of custodians of copies of any reports generated by the expert;

(7) a computation and the measure of damages alleged by the disclosing party, the documents and testimony on which those computations and measure are based, and the names, addresses and telephone numbers of all damage witnesses;

(8) the existence, location and a general description of any documents or tangible evidence the disclosing party plans to use at trial, and relevant insurance agreements; and,

(9) a list of documents or categories of documents known by the disclosing party to exist, whether or not in that party's possession, that may be relevant to the subject matter of the action or which appear reasonably calculated to lead to the discovery of admissible evidence, and the dates on which they have been or will be made available for inspection. This disclosure encompasses production of a copy of each document listed, absent a showing of good cause for not doing so, and, if production is not made, an identification of the custodian of such documents.

See *Englert v. Carondelet Health Network*, 199 Ariz. 21, 13 P.3d 763 (Ct. App. Div. 2 2000); *Link v. Pima County*, 193 Ariz. 336, 972 P.2d 669 (Ct. App. Div. 2 1998). The 2008 amendments clarify that the disclosure obligations imposed by paragraphs (8) and (9) apply to electronically stored information.

With respect to expert witness, under A.R.S. § 12-2603(a), a plaintiff who asserts a claim against a health care professional in a civil action must certify whether or not expert opinion testimony is necessary to prove the health care professional's standard of care or liability for the claim, and serve a preliminary expert opinion affidavit at the time of the initial disclosures under Rule 26.1, Ariz.R.Civ.P., if the claimant certifes such an opinion is needed. See *Jilly v. Rayes*, 221 Ariz. 40, 209 P.3d 176 (Ct. App. Div. 1 2009), upholding constitutionality of A.R.S. § 12-2603. Such affidavit must contain, at a minimum, four elements: (1) the expert's qualifications for providing an opinion on the standard of care, (2) the factual basis for the claim, (3) the facts that are claimed to have violated the standard of care, and (4) the manner in which those acts harmed the claimant. *Sanchez v. Old Pueblo Anesthesia, P.C.*, 218 Ariz. 317, 183 P.3d 1285 (Ct. App. Div. 2 2008). The rules do not require "scripting" of an expert's testimony, however. *Englert v. Carondelet Health Network*, 199 Ariz. 21, 13 P.3d 763 (Ct. App. Div. 2 2000). A party's disclosure obligations are not met, however, where disclosure of expert testimony is extremely general and the expert's deposition testimony fails to adequately supplement written disclosures. *Solimeno v. Yonan*, 224 Ariz. 74, 227 P.3d 481 (Ct. App. Div. 1 2010).

The phrasing selected for a description of certain of the categories of information to be disclosed leaves some ambiguities. In requiring the disclosure of the existence and custodian of statements, Rule 26.1(a)(5) includes statements "whether written or recorded, signed or unsigned," and it is not clear whether "statements" in this Rule is intended to be more encompassing than the definition of statements in the second paragraph of Rule 26(b)(3). A Committee Note which accompanied the 1996 amendments to Rule 26.1 clarified that the Rule is not intended to require the automatic production of witness statements, which remains subject to the standards of Rule 26(b)(3). A similar Committee Note to Rule 26.1(a)(6) explains that it does not require disclosure of a specially retained expert who is not expected to testify at trial. With respect to the disclosure requirements of Rule 26.1(a)(7), there is a question whether the disclosure requirements of Rule 26.1(a)(7) apply to a defendant who contests liability but intends to offer an alternative theory and calculation of damages.

The disclosure requirements with respect to relevant documents other than trial exhibits are particularly opaque, but should probably be given a practical construction. Every disclosing party should list the documents or, in the case of voluminous documents that fall within particular categories, provide a list of those categories of documents that are in that party's possession. A similar listing should be provided for documents or categories of documents of which the disclosing party is aware but which are not in that party's possession, together with the name and address of the custodian of such documents. In the case of documents in the disclosing party's possession which are not voluminous, copies should be produced with the disclosure unless good cause can be established for not doing so. In the case of voluminous documents or categories of documents, the disclosing party should advise when they have been, or will be, made available for inspection and copying.

It is readily apparent that not all of the categories of information or documents subject to disclosure under Rule 26.1(a) will be applicable in every case. For example, there may be no witness statements to disclose or applicable insurance coverage. In that situation, the wisest course is to state that there are none or that the disclosure requirement is inapplicable rather than ignoring the issue. With respect to trial witnesses, Rule 26.1 requires disclosure, in addition to the specified identifying information, only of the substance of witnesses' expected testimony, and not the specific details. *Jimenez v. Wal-Mart Stores, Inc.*, 206 Ariz.

424, 79 P.3d 673 (Ct. App. Div. 2 2003).

All that is required to trigger a duty to disclose under Rule 26.1(a)(4) or (9) is a determination that a person "may" have relevant knowledge or a document "may" have relevant content. *Norwest Bank (Minnesota), N.A. v. Symington*, 197 Ariz. 181, 3 P.3d 1101 (Ct. App. Div. 1 2000). "Relevance" for disclosure purposes is to be interpreted broadly. It is not limited to evidence that is admissible at trial, but also includes information that may be useful solely because it may reasonably lead to admissible evidence. *Norwest Bank (Minnesota), N.A. v. Symington*, 197 Ariz. 181, 3 P.3d 1101 (Ct. App. Div. 1 2000).

Because presumptive limits now apply to the traditional methods for discovery, the disclosure statement is the primary vehicle by which parties become informed of their opponent's case. *Bryan v. Riddel*, 178 Ariz. 472, 875 P.2d 131 (1994). Indeed, one of the goals of Rule 26.1 is to eliminate, or at least significantly reduce, the need to resort to various discovery devices in order to prepare a case for trial. *Zimmerman v. Shakman*, 204 Ariz. 231, 62 P.3d 976 (Ct. App. Div. 1 2003); *Norwest Bank (Minnesota), N.A. v. Symington*, 197 Ariz. 181, 3 P.3d 1101 (Ct. App. Div. 1 2000). The disclosures, accordingly, should fully and fairly expose the facts and issues to be litigated, as well as the witnesses and exhibits to be relied upon. *Norwest Bank (Minnesota), N.A. v. Symington*, 197 Ariz. 181, 3 P.3d 1101 (Ct. App. Div. 1 2000). Disclosure statements which merely refer to the complaint for the legal and factual basis for the plaintiff's claims, or merely incorporate prior interrogatory answers or refer to deposition transcripts as setting forth the subject matter of a witness' anticipated testimony, do not comply. *Norwest Bank (Minnesota), N.A. v. Symington*, 197 Ariz. 181, 3 P.3d 1101 (Ct. App. Div. 1 2000).

It has been held that litigants have a duty to preserve evidence which they know, or reasonably should know, is relevant in the action, is reasonably calculated to lead to the discovery of admissible evidence, is reasonably likely to be requested during discovery and/or is the subject of a pending discovery request. *Souza v. Fred Carries Contracts, Inc.*, 191 Ariz. 247, 955 P.2d 3 (Ct. App. Div. 2 1997). Undoubtedly, this same duty extends to evidence which falls within one of the categories of information subject to mandatory disclosure specified in Rule 26.1(a), which are in effect "standing" discovery requests.

4. *Signing of Disclosures; Filing*. Ariz. R. Civ. P. 26.1, as adopted, is slightly ambiguous on the issue of signature, and on the issue of whether disclosures are to be filed. Rule 26.1(d) states that each disclosure made is to be in writing, under oath, and signed by the *party* making the disclosure. Rule 26.1(e), however,

authorizes sanctions against a "party or attorney" who makes an inaccurate or misleading disclosure, and Rule 26.1(f) authorizes sanctions against a "party or attorney" who fails to comply with Rule 26.1. It may be that what was contemplated was the preparation and signature of the disclosure by counsel, with an accompanying verification signed by the party on whose behalf the disclosure is made, as is done in responding to interrogatories.

Rule 26.1 does not specifically address the issue whether the written disclosures made pursuant to the Rules are to be filed with the Court. Rule 26.1(b)(1) previously provided that, whenever a disclosure was made pursuant to the Rule, a "notice of disclosure" was to be filed. This provision was deleted in 1996, suggesting that such notices need no longer be prepared or filed. The disclosures themselves have not been expressly exempted from the filing requirement of Rule 5(g). The amendment to that Rule, which became effective June 1, 1993, directs that "discovery papers," which are defined to include "notices of service of any discovery or discovery response," are not to be filed. The amended Rule does not, however, mention Rule 26.1 disclosure statements or notices of service thereof. The prevailing practice is not to file disclosure statements as a matter of course.

5. *Extent of Duty of Disclosure*. It is readily apparent that, at the time disclosures are called for, a party must make disclosure of facts and information called for that is known to the party or the party's agents. A party cannot, however, evade the disclosure requirements by indifference or by ignoring the obvious.

Rule 26.1(b)(3) makes clear that disclosures must be not only of information that the disclosing party possesses, but also of facts and information which can be learned or acquired "by reasonable inquiry and investigation." *Link v. Pima County*, 193 Ariz. 336, 972 P.2d 669 (Ct. App. Div. 2 1998). The reasonableness of the inquiry actually conducted is an issue of fact for the trial court to resolve. *Scottsdale Princess Partnership v. Maricopa County*, 185 Ariz. 368, 916 P.2d 1084 (Ct. App. Div. 1 1995).

6. *Time of Disclosure*. Ariz. R. Civ. P. 26.1(b)(1) provides that the initial disclosure by the parties are to be made, as fully as then possible, within forty (40) days after the filing of a responsive pleading to the complaint, counterclaim, crossclaim or third-party complaint. Computation of this date will pose no problem in the case where the pleadings that initially frame the issues consist of a complaint and an answer. In that circumstance, the initial disclosure will be due within forty (40) days after the filing of the answer. If the answer, which is a responsive pleading, also contains a counterclaim and/or cross-claim and/or third-party complaint, all of which require responsive pleadings, the issue arises whether the initial disclosure is to be made within forty

(40) days of the filing of the answer or at some later point. If the initial disclosure is to be made within forty (40) days of filing of the answer, then the issue arises whether another disclosure must be made following the filing of responsive pleadings to any counterclaim, cross-claim or third-party complaint. Where such a situation arises, the parties would be well advised to attempt to agree upon a date for the initial disclosure.

7. *Duty to Supplement*. Under Ariz. R. Civ. P. 26.1(b)(2), the duty to make disclosures is a continuing one and additional or amended disclosures are to be made whenever new or different information is learned. *Link v. Pima County*, 193 Ariz. 336, 972 P.2d 669 (Ct. App. Div. 2 1998). The new or different information must be disclosed "seasonably" but in no event more than thirty (30) days after the information is discovered, and in no event later than sixty (60) days before trial, except by leave of court. Parties have come to expect that Rule 26.1 disclosure statements may be amended or supplemented many times during the course of a case.

Perhaps due to oversight, Rule 26.1(b)(2) was not amended to conform to the 2014 amendment of Rule 37(c)(2). For those civil cases subject to Rule 37(c)(2), as amended effective April 15, 2014, a party is required to obtain leave of court, upon motion, supported by affidavit, in order to utilize at trial information which is disclosed for the first time later than:

(i) the deadline set in the Scheduling Order or,

(ii) in the absence of such deadline, sixty (60) days before trial.

A prudent practitioner handling a case subject to the 2014 amended case management/trial setting rules would be wise to adhere to the requirements of Rule 37(c)(2) (amended 2014).

By Order dated November 22, 1996, the Arizona Supreme Court adopted, effective March 1, 1997, amendments to Rules 26.1(b) and 37, which specifically address the circumstances under which a party may be permitted to use at trial information which is disclosed for the first time within sixty (60) days before trial, or during trial. The amendments added a sentence to existing Rule 26.1(b)(2) specifying that a party seeking to use information which was first disclosed later than sixty (60) days before trial must obtain leave of court to extend the time for disclosure, as provided for in Rule 37(c)(2).

The 1996 Order also adopted an amendment to that Rule, Rule 37(c)(2), which provides that a party must obtain leave of court, upon motion, supported by affidavit, in order to utilize at trial information which is disclosed for the first time less than sixty (60) days before trial. The provision specifies that leave of court is not to be granted to use such late disclosed information unless the

Court finds that there was good cause for the late disclosure and for allowing the information to be used, and that the information was disclosed to the adverse party as soon as practicable after it was discovered.

In making these determinations, which are reviewed only for abuse of discretion, the trial court is to remember the goal of maximizing the likelihood of a decision on the merits, and it is not an abuse of discretion for the trial court to permit testimony from a witness identified as a trial witness in a supplemental disclosure statement only nine days before trial, where the witness had been disclosed in the joint pretrial statement and opposing counsel had adequate opportunity to conduct the witness' deposition. *In re Estate of Thurston*, 199 Ariz. 215, 16 P.3d 776 (Ct. App. Div. 1 2000).

At this same time, Rule 37(c)(3), was also adopted to specifically address the use of information which is disclosed for the first time during trial. Once again, the information cannot be used unless the party seeking to use it obtains leave of court upon motion, supported by affidavit, to extend the time for disclosure. The Court is not to grant such leave unless the Court finds that the information in question could not have been discovered and disclosed earlier even with due diligence, and that the information was disclosed immediately upon its discovery.

An additional disclosure obligation may be imposed by statute in actions against licensed professionals. In 2000, the Legislature amended A.R.S. § 12-2602 to address the concerns that lead to the original version being declared unconstitutional. Under the amended version, when a claim is asserted against a licensed professional in a civil action, the claimant must also certify, in a filed written statement, whether or not expert opinion is necessary to establish the licensed professional's standard of care. If the claimant certifies that such expert opinion is necessary, then the claimant must serve a preliminary expert opinion affidavit, together with the initial disclosures required by Rule 26.1. (Under the statute, multiple affidavits may be employed, if deemed necessary.) The court can also order that such a disclosure be made. If the required disclosure is not made, then the court, on motion of the professional or on its own motion, can dismiss the action without prejudice. As thus amended, the statute has been held not to conflict with any procedural rule, and to be otherwise constitutional. *Bertleson v. Sacks Tierney, P.A.*, 204 Ariz. 124, 60 P.3d 703 (Ct. App. Div. 1 2002).

8. *Privileged Materials.* Ariz. R. Civ. P. 26.1(f)(1) specifically addresses the situation where data or information subject to disclosure under Rule 26.1(a) is claimed to represent trial preparation materials or otherwise privileged matter. If information is

not disclosed because of a claim that it is privileged, the claim must be made expressly and supported by a non-privileged description of the materials withheld that is sufficient to enable other parties to contest whether the privilege was properly claimed.

Rule 26.1 does not remove or override any applicable privileges, such as the attorney-client privilege. That privilege protects against disclosure of communications between attorney and client, but does not protect against the disclosure of the underlying facts. *Samaritan Foundation v. Goodfarb*, 176 Ariz. 497, 862 P.2d 870, 26 A.L.R.5th 893 (1993). A client who has a duty to disclose facts in discovery is not relieved of that duty simply because those facts have been communicated to a lawyer. *Samaritan Foundation v. Goodfarb*, 176 Ariz. 497, 862 P.2d 870, 26 A.L.R. 5th 893 (1993).

The language of Rule 26.1(f)(1) states that it applies "[W]hen information is withheld from disclosure *or discovery* . . ." (Emphasis added). Although this provision was placed in the "disclosure rule," this language arguably makes its procedures and requirements applicable to privilege claims asserted in response to any discovery request as well.

9. *Inadvertent Production*. Ariz. R. Civ. P. 26.1(f)(2), added by the 2008 amendments, deals with the problem of inadvertent disclosure of privileged information. If a party claims that privileged information or trial preparation material has been inadvertently disclosed or produced during discovery, that party may notify any party who received the information of the claim and the basis for it.

A party who receives notice of such a claim must promptly "return, sequester or destroy" the specified information and any copies it has made, and may not use the information until the issue is resolved. The receiving party may promptly present the information to the court under seal for a determination, and the producing party must preserve the information until the claim is resolved. An essentially identical provision was added to the rule governing subpoenas as Ariz. R. Civ. P. 45(c)(5)(C)(ii). *See also, Lund v. Myers*, 232 Ariz. 309, 305 P.3d 374 (2013).

Lund concerned the inadvertent production of documents claimed to be subject to attorney-client privilege. Interpreting Ariz. R. Civ. P. 26.1(f)(2), the Arizona Supreme Court held the filing of inadvertently disclosed documents with trial court under seal did not constitute impermissible "use" of documents, as that word was used in the rule.

The *Lund* Court then addressed the issue of when, in deciding issues of privilege and waiver, a trial court may conduct an in camera inspection of the allegedly privileged documents inadvertently disclosed or produced. The Court held as follows:

1. As to each document at issue, the trial court first must determine whether in camera inspection is needed to resolve a claim of privilege. The trial court makes this determination based on its consideration of the privilege log, the opposing party's response to such privilege log and the parties' arguments on the issues of privilege and waiver.

2. If the trial court determines such in camera review is necessary, the trial court then must decide who will conduct such in camera review of the allegedly privileged documents: the trial judge or another judicial officer. If the trial judge conducts the in camera inspection and upholds the claim of privilege, the trial judge then will need to consider recusal or face a possible Rule 42(f) challenge based on claims of bias resulting from the review of such privileged documents.

Ariz. R. Civ. P. 45(c)(5)(C)(ii) is substantially identical to Ariz. R. Civ. P. 26.1(f)(2). Thus, the holding in *Lund* likely would apply in the case of privileged documents allegedly produced in response to a subpoena.

10. *Sanctions.* There were three provisions in the original Rule 26.1 that addressed the subject of sanctions for failure to comply with its terms. The first, former Rule 26.1(c), provided that the court was to exclude from evidence at trial any evidence offered by a party that was not disclosed in a timely fashion. See *Link v. Pima County*, 193 Ariz. 336, 972 P.2d 669 (Ct. App. Div. 2 1998). In addition, other parties could not examine witnesses called by the offending party to prove facts other than those disclosed by the offending party. This sanction of exclusion of evidence did not address the problem of a party's failure to disclose information harmful to that party's position which the offending party would prefer not to be admitted into evidence. The purpose of this mandatory sanction was to deter litigants and their counsel from withholding relevant information by precluding its later use at trial. *Bryan v. Riddel*, 178 Ariz. 472, 875 P.2d 131 (1994).

The second, former Rule 26.1(e), dealt with the situation where a party or attorney made a disclosure that the party or attorney knew or should have known was inaccurate and thereby caused an opposing party substantial and unnecessary investigation or discovery costs.

The third, former Rule 26.1(g) was the "general" sanction provision for any failure to comply with the provisions of Rule 26.1, and authorized the Court to enter any orders with respect to such conduct as were just, including any order provided for in Rule 16(f) [pre-04-15-2014 amendment rule]. That Rule, as thus incorporated, allowed the award of expenses, including attorneys' fees, incurred because of noncompliance with Rule 26.1. Any award of expenses a a sanction, however, was to bear some relationship to the expenses directly caused by the sanctionable conduct. *Taliaferro v. Taliaferro*, 188 Ariz. 333, 935 P.2d 911 (Ct. App. Div. 1 1996).

Effective December 1, 1996, all of the sanctions provisions contained in Rules 26.1(c), (e) and (g) were deleted from Rule 26.1, and replaced by new provisions added to Rule 37. Discussion of the standards that apply to awards of sanctions for failure to make required disclosures, or for making misleading disclosures, accordingly, is now contained in the *Authors' Comments* to Rule 37.

Although former Rule 26.1(c)'s prescribed sanction of the exclusion of undisclosed evidence was nominally mandatory, the Arizona Supreme Court noted that wooden application of that sanction could bring about results that were unduly harsh and inconsistent with the purposes of the disclosure rules. *Allstate Ins. Co. v. O'Toole*, 182 Ariz. 284, 896 P.2d 254 (1995); *Bryan v. Riddel*, 178 Ariz. 472, 875 P.2d 131 (1994). The Court has stressed that the intent of the new rules was not to produce the automatic forfeiture of substantive legal rights because of harmless human failings and that trial courts should take a "common sense" approach to the issue of whether to exclude undisclosed evidence. *Allstate Ins. Co. v. O'Toole*, 182 Ariz. 284, 896 P.2d 254 (1995); *Zimmerman v. Shakman*, 204 Ariz. 231, 62 P.3d 976 (Ct. App. Div. 1 2003).

The rules are to be interpreted and applied to maximize the likelihood of a decision on the merits and, in determining whether undisclosed evidence should be excluded, trial courts should examine not only the reason for the failure to disclose the evidence in a timely fashion, but also the degree of prejudice to the other side or the justice system, and whether the failure to disclose was purposeful or inadvertent. *Allstate Ins. Co. v. O'Toole*, 182 Ariz. 284, 896 P.2d 254 (1995); *Rivers v. Solley*, 217 Ariz. 528, 177 P.3d 270 (Ct. App. Div. 1 2008); *Perguson v. Tamis*, 188 Ariz. 425, 937 P.2d 347 (Ct. App. Div. 2 1996). In an appropriate case, however, exclusion of evidence remains an available remedy for a party's failure to comply with Rule 26.1's disclosure requirements. *Zuern By and Through Zuern v. Ford Motor Co.*, 188 Ariz. 486, 937 P.2d 676 (Ct. App. Div. 2 1996). A trial court's decision on a motion for sanctions for disclosure violations will not be disturbed on appeal absent an abuse of discretion. *Jimenez v. Wal-Mart Stores, Inc.*, 206 Ariz. 424, 79 P.3d 673 (Ct. App. Div. 2 2003); *Taeger v. Catholic Family and Community Services*, 196 Ariz. 285, 995 P.2d 721 (Ct. App. Div. 1 1999).

It has been held that before trial, a motion *in limine* is the proper way to raise the issue of the exclusion of evidence that has not been properly disclosed. *Zimmerman v. Shakman*, 204 Ariz. 231, 62 P.3d 976 (Ct. App. Div. 1 2003). The proper method for raising a claimed violation of the disclosure rules that is not discovered until *after* judgment is to file a motion for new trial or for relief from judgment. *In re Estate of Travers*, 192 Ariz. 333, 965 P.2d 67 (Ct. App. Div. 1 1998). A violation of Rule 26.1 by an intentional non-disclosure may entitle a party to relief under Rule 60(c)(3), but such a motion must be filed within six (6) months after the judgment becomes final. *In re Estate of Travers*, 192 Ariz. 333, 965 P.2d 67 (Ct. App. Div. 1 1998) (recognizing Rule 6(b) expressly bars the extension of time for filing a Rule 60(c) motion.). *See also, Andrew R. v. Arizona Dept. of Economic Sec.*, 223 Ariz. 453, 224 P.3d 950 (Ct. App. Div. 1 2010) (trial court lacked authority to grant Rule 60(c)(3) motion for relief from paternity judgment filed more than six months after entry of judgment). Relief may also be available under Rule 60(c)(3) where the failure to disclose was accidental, inadvertent and/or in good faith. *Norwest Bank (Minnesota), N.A. v. Symington*, 197 Ariz. 181, 3 P.3d 1101 (Ct. App. Div. 1 2000). Proof of misconduct alone, however, will not justify relief. The movant must also show that the failure to disclose substantially interfered with the moving party's ability to fully prepare for trial. *Norwest Bank (Minnesota), N.A. v. Symington*, 197 Ariz. 181, 3 P.3d 1101 (Ct. App. Div. 1 2000). To justify relief under that Rule, it is not necessary for there to be a showing that the outcome of the case would have been different but for the violation. *Breitbart-Napp v. Napp*, 216 Ariz. 74, 163 P.3d 1024 (Ct. App. Div. 1 2007).

As originally adopted, Rule 26.1 did not specifically authorize motions to compel disclosures but it was generally assumed that the trial court had the inherent authority to compel disclosures if requested to do so. That authority has now been made explicit by the adoption of a new provision in Rule 37(a)(2) specifically authorizing such motions.

Rule 26.2. Exchange of records and discovery limitations in medical malpractice cases

(a) Exchange of Records.

(1) Within five days of the date that plaintiff notifies the court pursuant to Rule 16(c) of these Rules that all served defendants have either answered or filed motions, plaintiff shall serve upon defendant copies of all of plaintiff's available medical records relevant to the condition which is the subject matter of the action.

(2) Within ten days of the date of service by plaintiff of such records, each defendant shall serve upon plaintiff copies of all of plaintiff's medical records relevant to the condition which is the subject matter of the action.

(3) In lieu of serving copies of the above-described records counsel may, before the date set for exchange of records, inquire of opposing counsel concerning the documents or electronically stored information which opposing counsel wishes produced and may then produce copies of only those records which are specifically requested.

(b) Discovery Limitations. Before the comprehensive pretrial conference contemplated by Rule 16(c) of these Rules, the parties may exchange the uniform interrogatories set forth in the Appendix and 10 additional non-uniform interrogatories. Any subparagraph of a non-uniform interrogatory will be treated as one non-uniform interrogatory. The parties may also submit a request for production of documents pursuant to Rule 34 of these Rules, requesting the following items:

1. A party's wage information where relevant.
2. Written or recorded statements by any party or witness including reports or statements of experts.
3. Any exhibits intended to be used at trial.
4. Incident reports.

In addition, the depositions of the parties and any known liability experts may be taken. No other discovery is permitted before the comprehensive pretrial conference except pursuant to stipulation of the parties, or, upon motion and a showing of good cause. Stipulations for additional discovery shall not be unreasonably withheld.

Rule 26.1 added Oct. 10, 2000, effective Dec. 1, 2000; amended Oct. 15, 2001, effective Dec. 1, 2001; September 5, 2007, effective January 1, 2008.

STATE BAR COMMITTEE NOTES

2000 Promulgation

New Rule 26.2 was promulgated in 2000 as part of the effort to consolidate formerly separate sets of procedural rules into either the Arizona Rules of Civil Procedure or the Rules of the Arizona Supreme Court, and essentially incorporates, without substantive change, the provisions of former Rules 1(B) and (C) of the Uniform Rules of Practice for Medical Malpractice Cases. Those Rules, originally promulgated in 1989, were the product of a special Committee appointed by the Arizona Supreme Court to study malpractice procedure. In the Preamble which accompanied those Rules, it was pointed out that the Committee had proposed certain presumptive limitations, but did not thereby intend to remove judicial discretion with respect to those limits. It was contemplated, however, that variation from the presumptive limits would occur only where there was an affirmative demonstration of good cause.

In a Comment to Rule 2 of the original Uniform Rules of Practice for Medical Malpractice Cases, which was effective January 1, 1990 and was amended effective July 1, 1992, the Committee stated the following, inter alia:

> " Paragraph B(1) of this rule [now Rule 26.2(a)(1)] requires the plaintiff to serve upon the defendant copies of all of plaintiff's available medical records relevant to the condition which is the subject matter of the action. The committee's intent is that counsel will make a reasonable effort to obtain relevant medical records and make them available under this rule.
>
> With regard to Rule C(1) [now Rule 26.2(b)(1)], it was never intended that the financial information of the defendant would be subject to a request for production unless there was a prima facie case for punitive damages.
>
> It is the intention of the Rule that witness statements will be produced and interrogatories may be propounded requesting a summary of the expected testimony of lay witnesses notwithstanding the ruling in *Sundt v. Farley*, 12 Ariz. App. 346, 470 P.2d 494 (Div. 2 1970).
>
> The term 'parties' when referring to depositions is intended to include the managing agent of any party, and any persons involved in the incident giving rise to the complaint.
>
> * * *
>
> The rule further contemplates full and complete answers to interrogatories in a timely manner. Absent a need for additional discovery, interrogatory answers should be sufficiently complete so that both sides can be informed of the claims and defenses of the other side."

AUTHORS' COMMENTS

Analysis

1. *History and Origin of Rule*. The Uniform Rules of Practice for Medical Malpractice Cases, which became effective January 1, 1990, were the product of a Special Committee appointed by the Arizona Supreme Court at the request of the Governor and the Thirty Ninth Legislature. The request, and the appointment of

the Committee, were in response to increasing concern over the rising costs of medical malpractice litigation and in anticipation of the legislative abolition of the system of having such claims presented first to a Medical Liability Review Panel. The charge to the Committee was to develop a set of procedures applicable only to cases involving claims of medical malpractice which would be more efficient and less expensive, without infringing on the substantive rights of the parties. The Rules applied to all cases involving allegations of malpractice by a health care provider.

As part of the 2000 effort to reduce the number of separate sets of rules applicable to civil cases, the Uniform Rules of Practice for Medical Malpractice Cases (along with the Uniform Rules of Practice of the Superior Court and the Uniform Rules of Procedure for Arbitration) were abrogated, and their provisions generally transferred to either the Arizona Rules of Civil Procedure or the Rules of the Arizona Supreme Court. Ariz. R. Civ. P. 26.2 essentially contains the provisions of Rules 1(B) and (C) of the former Uniform Rules of Practice for Medical Malpractice Cases.

2. *Comparison With Federal Rule.* The Federal Rules of Civil Procedure do not have a provision that corresponds to Rule 26.2.

3. *Discovery Permitted and Exchange of Records Required Prior to Comprehensive Pretrial Conference.* As is discussed in Section 4 of the *Authors' Comments* under Rule 16, the centerpiece of the procedural requirements applicable to medical malpractice cases is a Comprehensive Pretrial Conference which is to be convened and conducted shortly after such cases are at issue. The scheduling of, and the subjects to be discussed and resolved, at that Comprehensive Pretrial Conference, are now the subject of Rule 16(c). Ariz. R. Civ. P. 26.2 delineates the information that must be exchanged, and the discovery that may be conducted, so that the parties may be prepared for that Conference.

Within five (5) days of providing notice to the Court that answers or motions have been received from all defendants who have been served, the plaintiff is required, by Ariz. R. Civ. P. 26.2(a)(1), to serve upon the defendants copies of all the medical records of plaintiff that are available and that are relevant to the condition that is in issue in the case. Within ten (10) days of service of the plaintiff's medical records, each defendant is to serve on the plaintiff copies of medical records of the plaintiff which are relevant to the condition in issue. In lieu of serving copies of all such medical records, counsel may confer and agree to produce only those records which are specifically requested.

Ariz. R. Civ. P. 26.2(b) specifies the limited discovery that the parties may undertake prior to the conduct of the Comprehensive Pretrial Conference. The Appendix to the Rules contains three sets of uniform interrogatories for use in medical malpractice cases. (As part of the 2000 consolidation effort, these sets of uniform interrogatories were transferred to the Appendix of Forms following Rule 84.) To view these sets of uniform interrogatories, please see the current Edition of the publication *Arizona Rules of Court—State and Federal*. (The Court of Appeals has held that, as formulated, Interrogatory No. 17 of Set B of these uniform interrogatories seeks information protected from disclosure by the "peer review privilege," created by A.R.S. § 36-445.01. *Yuma Regional Medical Center v. Superior Court In and For County of Yuma*, 175 Ariz. 72, 852 P.2d 1256 (Ct. App. Div. 1 1993).

Prior to the Comprehensive Pretrial Conference, the parties may exchange those uniform interrogatories and ten (10) additional non-uniform interrogatories. Any subpart of a non-uniform interrogatory is considered a separate interrogatory. In addition, the parties may also submit a request for production under Rule 34, but it may only seek production of documents reflecting a party's wage information, if relevant; written or recorded statements of a party or witness, including statements and reports of experts; exhibits intended to be used at trial; and, incident reports. Finally, the parties may conduct, during this period, the depositions of the parties and the depositions of any identified experts on the issue of liability. The Committee Comment to the Rule explains that the term "parties" encompasses managing agents of parties and any persons involved in the incident giving rise to the litigation.

Ariz. R. Civ. P. 26.2(b) specifically provides that no other discovery is permitted prior to the Comprehensive Pretrial Conference except by stipulation of the parties. The 1992 amendment to the Rule added a provision that stipulations for additional discovery during this period are not to be unreasonably withheld. Presumably, however, absent such a stipulation, requests for admissions under Rule 36 may not be served prior to the Conference.

4. *Discovery Permitted After Comprehensive Pretrial Conference*. The 1992 amendments to the Uniform Rules of Practice for Medical Malpractice Cases added a specific provision to former Rule 1(D)(1), which is now Rule 16(c)(1), limiting the depositions that could be conducted following the Comprehensive Pretrial Conference to those specifically authorized by the Court at the Conference, except upon stipulation of the parties or with leave of Court based upon a showing of good cause. The Rules contain no specific provision similarly limiting the use of other forms of discovery following the Comprehensive Pretrial Conference. The sense of the Rules, however, would suggest that, absent an agreement of the parties or leave of Court, the only discovery that can be conducted between the Comprehensive Pretrial Conference and

the trial is that discussed at the Conference and included in the discovery schedule that is established at the Conference.

The Rules do contain a provision, added by the 1992 amendments, that stipulations to conduct additional discovery are not to be withheld unreasonably. That provision, however, was inserted into the provision which generally governed discovery *prior to* the Comprehensive Pretrial Conference (now Rule 26.2(b)), and it is not certain whether it was intended to apply to the conduct of discovery in subsequent stages of the case as well.

Rule 27. Depositions before action or pending appeal

(a) Before Action; Petition; Notice and Service; Order and Examination; Use of Deposition.

(1) A person who desires to perpetuate that person's own testimony or that of another person regarding any matter that may be cognizable in any court may file a verified petition in the superior court in the county of the residence of any expected adverse party. The petition shall be entitled in the name of the petitioner and shall show:

(i) That the petitioner expects to be a party to an action cognizable in a court but is presently unable to bring it or cause it to be brought.

(ii) The subject matter of the expected action and the petitioner's interest therein.

(iii) The facts which the petitioner desires to establish by the proposed testimony and the reasons for desiring to perpetuate it.

(iv) The names or a description of the persons the petitioner expects will be adverse parties and their addresses so far as known.

(v) The names and addresses of the persons to be examined and the substance of the testimony which the petitioner expects to elicit from each. The petition shall also ask for an order authorizing the petitioner to take the depositions of the persons to be examined named in the petition, for the purpose of perpetuating their testimony.

(2) The petitioner shall thereafter serve a notice upon each person named in the petition as an expected adverse party, together with a copy of the petition, stating that the petitioner will apply to the court, at a time and place named therein, for the order described in the petition. At least twenty days before the date of hearing the notice shall be served either within or without the state in the manner provided in Rule 4.1 or Rule 4.2 of these rules for service of summons, but if such service cannot with due diligence be made upon any expected adverse party named in the petition, the court may make such order as is just for service by publication or otherwise, and shall appoint, for persons not served in the manner provided in Rule 4.1 or Rule 4.2 an attorney who shall represent them, and, in case they are not otherwise represented, shall cross-examine the deponent. If any expected adverse party is a minor or incompetent, the provisions of Rule 17(g) shall apply.

(3) If the court is satisfied that the perpetuation of the testimony may prevent a failure or delay of justice, it shall make an order designating or describing the persons whose depositions may be taken and specifying the subject matter of the examination and whether the depositions shall be taken upon oral examination or written interrogatories. The depositions may then be taken in accordance with these Rules, and the court may make orders of the character provided for by Rules 34 and 35. For the purpose of applying these Rules to depositions for perpetuating testimony, each reference therein to the court in which the action is pending shall be deemed to refer to the court in which the petition for such deposition was filed.

(4) If a deposition to perpetuate testimony is taken under these Rules, it may be used in any action involving the same subject matter subsequently brought, in accordance with the provisions of Rule 32(a).

Amended Dec. 16, 1980, effective March 1, 1981; Sept. 15, 1987, effective Nov. 15, 1987; Oct. 2, 1991, effective Dec. 1, 1991; Oct. 9, 1996, effective Dec. 1, 1996.

(b) Pending Appeal. If an appeal has been taken from a judgment of a superior court or before taking an appeal if the time therefor has not expired, the court in which the judgment was rendered may allow the taking of the depositions of witnesses to perpetuate their testimony for use in the event of further proceedings in the court. In such case the party who desires to perpetuate the testimony may make a motion in the court for leave to take the depositions, upon the same notice and service thereof as if the action was pending in the court. The motion shall show the names and addresses of the persons to be examined, the substance of the testimony which the party expects to elicit from each and the reasons for perpetuating their testimony. If the court finds that the perpetuation of the testimony is proper to avoid a failure or delay of justice, it may make an order allowing the depositions to be taken and may make orders of the character provided for by Rules 34 and 35, and thereupon the depositions may be taken and used in the same manner and under the same conditions as are prescribed in these Rules for depositions taken in actions pending in the superior court.

Amended Sept. 15, 1987, effective Nov. 15, 1987.

AUTHORS' COMMENTS

Analysis

4. Petition to Perpetuate Testimony Pending Appeal.

1. *Scope and Purpose of Rule.* Ariz. R. Civ. P. 27 governs the taking of depositions in two distinct circumstances: (1) before an action is filed, and (2) after judgment and pending appeal. Under these relatively infrequent circumstances, the Rule provides a method to perpetuate testimony that might later become unavailable, but that is its sole purpose.

2. *Comparison With Federal Rule.* ARCP 27 is essentially identical to FRCP 27, there are certain differences, however.

In 2007, the language of FRCP 27 was amended as part of the general restyling of the Federal Rules of Civil Procedure to make the Federal Rules more easily understood and to make style and terminology consistent throughout the Federal Rules of Civil Procedure. Those stylistic modifications have not been incorporated into ARCP 27. In addition, and as a consequence of the 2009 amendments to FRCP 27, the time set in the former rule at 20 days was revised to 21 days. ARCP 27 has not been amended to alter this time period, which remains set at 20 days.

3. *Petition to Perpetuate Testimony Before Action is Filed.* A person may seek leave to conduct a deposition to perpetuate that person's, or another person's, testimony before an action is filed by filing a Petition in the Superior Court. The Petition, which is required to be verified, must:

(1) state that the petitioner expects to be a party to an action but is presently unable to bring it or to cause it to be brought;

(2) describe the subject matter of the expected action and the petitioner's interest in it;

(3) state the facts which the petitioner desires to establish in the testimony to be perpetuated and the reasons for seeking to perpetuate it;

(4) provide the names or a description of the expected adverse parties in the future action, and their addresses, to the extent they are known; and

(5) provide the names and addresses of the persons to be examined and the substance of the testimony to be elicited.

The Petition must be served in the manner contemplated by Ariz. R. Civ. P. 4.1 or 4.2, as applicable, at least twenty (20) days before the hearing on the Petition. If the Petition cannot be served on one or more expected adverse parties through the exercise of due diligence, the Court may order alternative service, including service by publication, and must appoint an attorney to represent the unserved expected adverse party(ies) and to cross-examine the deponent(s) whose testimony is to be perpetuated. If the Petition is granted, the deposition(s) taken may be used in any subsequent action in accordance with the provisions of Ariz. R. Civ. P. 32.

A petition to conduct depositions in contemplation of an action that is expected, but not yet instituted, is one addressed to the trial court's discretion. *High School Dist. No. 106, Pima County v. Civil Rights Division*, 121 Ariz. 444, 590 P.2d 1390, 19 Empl. Prac. Dec. (CCH) P 8986 (Ct. App. Div. 2 1979). Ariz. R. Civ. P. 27(a) is intended only to perpetuate testimony which, for reasons established to the satisfaction of the court, may not be available when the expected action is brought. It is not properly used as a discovery device to establish a cause of action and frame the complaint. *City of Phoenix v. Peterson*, 11 Ariz. App. 136, 462 P.2d 829 (Div. 1 1969).

4. *Petition to Perpetuate Testimony Pending Appeal*. Ariz. R. Civ. P. 27(b) authorizes the taking of depositions, where necessary to preserve testimony, in an action which is on appeal from a judgment that has been entered, upon motion and order of the trial court. The motion, the contents of which are specified in the Rule, is to be filed and served in the same fashion as if the action were still pending in the trial court. Any deposition taken pursuant to the authority conferred by this Rule may be used in accordance with the requirements of Ariz. R. Civ. P. 32.

Rule 28. Persons before whom depositions may be taken

(a) Within the United States; Commission or Letters Rogatory. Within the United States or within a territory or insular possession subject to the jurisdiction of the United States, depositions shall be taken before an officer authorized to administer oaths by the laws of the United States, the State of Arizona, or of the place where the examination is held, or before a person appointed by the court in which the action is pending. A person so appointed has power to administer oaths and take testimony. Depositions may be taken in this state or anywhere upon notice provided by these Rules without a commission, letters rogatory or other writ. The term officer as used in Rules 30, 31 and 32 includes a person appointed by the court or designated by the parties under Rule 29.

Upon proof that the notice to take a deposition outside this state has been given as provided by these Rules, the party seeking such deposition may, but is not required, after one full day's notice to the other parties, have issued by the clerk, in the form given in such notice, a commission or letters rogatory or other like writ either in lieu of the notice to take the deposition or supplementary thereto. Failure to file written objections to such form before or at the time of its issuance shall be a waiver of any objection thereto. Any objection shall be heard and determined forthwith by the court or judge thereof.

Amended July 6, 1983, effective Sept. 7, 1983.

(b) In Foreign Countries. In a foreign country, depositions may be taken (1) on notice before a person authorized to administer oaths in the place in which the examination is held, either by the law thereof or by the law of the United States, or (2) before a person commissioned by the court, and a person so commissioned shall have the power by virtue of the commission to administer any necessary oath and take testimony, or (3) pursuant to a letter rogatory. A commission or a letter rogatory shall be issued on application and notice and on terms that are just and appropriate. It is not requisite to the issuance of a commission or a letter rogatory that the taking of the deposition in any other manner is impracticable or inconvenient; and both a commission and a letter rogatory may be issued in proper cases. A notice or commission may designate the person before whom the deposition is to be taken either by name or descriptive title. A letter rogatory may be addressed "To the Appropriate Authority in (here name the country)." Evidence obtained in response to a letter rogatory need not be excluded merely for the reason that it is not a verbatim transcript or that the testimony was not taken under oath or for any similar departure from the requirements for depositions taken within the United States under these rules.

Amended March 26, 1963, effective June 1, 1963; Sept. 15, 1987, effective Nov. 15, 1987.

(c) Disqualification for Interest. No deposition shall be taken before a person who is a relative or employee or attorney or counsel of any of the parties, or is a relative or employee of such attorney or counsel, or is financially interested in the action.

STATE BAR COMMITTEE NOTES

1963 Amendment

[Rule 28(b)] The changes in this rule follow the Federal Committee's report and no longer confine the taking of depositions to United States foreign service officers. The changes are intended to enable the use of either depositions or letters rogatory as best accommodated by the legal system of the host country. The purpose is to minimize objections of host country courts to compelling witnesses to attend or testify in aid of litigation pending in Arizona courts. The last sentence of this rule is to be interpreted in the light of the amendment to Rule 26(e).

AUTHORS' COMMENTS

Analysis

1. Scope and Purpose of Rule.
2. Comparison With Federal Rule.
3. Commissions to Take Depositions.
4. Depositions in Foreign Countries.

1. *Scope and Purpose of Rule.* Ariz. R. Civ. P. 28 specifies the officials before whom depositions may be taken. Within the United States and its possessions depositions may be taken before an officer authorized to administer oaths by federal law or by the laws of the state or possession where the deposition is taken.

Depositions also may be taken before a person specially appointed by the Court in which the action is pending. Under Ariz. R. Civ. P. 28(c), a deposition may not be taken before a person who is a relative or employee of, or counsel for, one of the parties, who is a relative or employee of a party's counsel, or who has a financial interest in the action.

Persons wishing to take a deposition in another state should consult that state's rules to determine whether that state has adopted the Uniform Interstate Depositions and Discovery Act.

2. *Comparison With Federal Rule.* Despite structural differences, ARCP 28 is generally similar to FRCP 28, but there are differences. FRCP 28 does not have provisions corresponding to

the third sentence of the first paragraph and the second paragraph of ARCP 28(a). Also, as amended in 1993, FRCP 28(b) now allows depositions to be taken in foreign countries pursuant to any applicable treaty or convention, and refers to a "letter of request" rather than a "letter rotatory." The corresponding Arizona Rule, ARCP 28(b), last amended in 1987, does not include this language.

In 2007, the language of FRCP 28 was amended as part of the general restyling of the Federal Rules of Civil Procedure to make the Federal Rules more easily understood and to make style and terminology consistent throughout the Federal Rules of Civil Procedure. Those stylistic modifications have not been incorporated into ARCP 28.

3. *Commissions to Take Depositions.* The issuance of a commission is not required even for the taking of a deposition in another state. Regular notice of such a deposition is sufficient. If a commission is desired, it may be issued on one day's notice to the other parties, and any objections not made within that time are waived.

4. *Depositions in Foreign Countries.* The provisions of subpart (b) facilitate the taking of depositions in foreign countries, but do not assure that the deposition may be taken. Other than those countries which are signatories of the Hague Convention, many foreign countries do not permit depositions except through their local courts.

Although the Judge directs the issuance of a Letter Rogatory, the initial Letter Rogatory itself is actually signed and issued by the Clerk of the Court, with the Judge certifying the Clerk's signature. If the Letter Rogatory is directed to a jurisdiction whose official language is not English, the Letter Rogatory should be submitted to the Court both in English and in the language of the jurisdiction to which it is directed, and the Judge should be requested to order the Clerk to sign and issue both the original English Letter Rogatory and the translated copy of it.

Rule 29. Stipulations regarding discovery procedure

Unless the court orders otherwise, the parties may by stipulation (1) provide that depositions may be taken before any person, at any time or place, upon any notice, and in any manner and when so taken may be used like other depositions, and (2) modify the procedures provided by these rules for other methods of discovery, including extending the time provided in Rules 33, 34, and 36 for responses to discovery.

Amended July 17, 1970, effective Nov. 1, 1970.

STATE BAR COMMITTEE NOTES

1970 Amendment

Rule 29: In actual practice, stipulations are extensively made concerning discovery. This Rule recognizes that practice and encourages it. All stipulations are of course subject to the provisions of Rule 80(d) that any agreement to be binding if disputed should be either in writing or made orally in open court and entered in the minutes.

AUTHORS' COMMENTS

Analysis

1. *Scope and Purpose of Rule.* Ariz. R. Civ. P. 29 permits the parties to an action to enter into stipulations concerning the taking of depositions, and the procedures for other methods of discovery, that modify the otherwise applicable provisions of the Rules. While the Rule does not by its terms require that stipulations of this nature be approved by the Court, they should be filed with the Clerk as a record of the parties' agreement. The filing of such stipulations is either required or implied by Local Rule in certain Counties. *Cf.* Rule 5, Coconino County Superior Court Local Rules; Rule CV-4, Mohave County Superior Court Local Rules.

Rule 80(d) of the Arizona Rules of Civil Procedure, moreover, provides that no agreement between parties or counsel will be binding, if subsequently disputed, unless it is in writing or made orally in open court and entered in the minutes. *Cf. Canyon Contracting Co. v. Tohono O'Odham Housing Authority*, 172 Ariz. 389, 837 P.2d 750 (Ct. App. Div. 1 1992).

2. *Comparison With Federal Rule.* ARCP 29 addresses the same subject matter as FRCP 29, but there are differences in the

requirements imposed for discovery stipulations.

FRCP 29 requires that such stipulations be "written" and that stipulations extending the time to respond to interrogatories, requests for production and/or requests for admissions be approved by the Court, but only if the extension would interfere with a time set by the Court for completion of discovery, for hearing a motion or for trial. ARCP 29 does not specifically require that discovery stipulations be in writing, and does not require court approval for them. ARCP 80(d) however, provides that, if subsequently disputed, a stipulation is not binding unless it is in writing or made orally in open court and entered in the minutes. Cf. *Canyon Contracting Co. v. Tohono O'Odham Housing Authority*, 172 Ariz. 389, 837 P.2d 750 (Ct. App. Div. 1 1992).

In 2007, the language of FRCP 29 was amended as part of the general restyling of the Federal Rules of Civil Procedure to make the Federal Rules more easily understood and to make style and terminology consistent throughout the Federal Rules of Civil Procedure. Those stylistic modifications have not been incorporated into ARCP 29.

3. *Depositions Taken on Stipulation.* Ariz. R. Civ. P. 29 contemplates that depositions taken pursuant to stipulation are to be treated in the same fashion as noticed depositions in all other respects. Thus, unless addressed in the stipulation, the provisions of the Rules governing certification and delivery (Rules 30(f) and 31(b)), the use at trial of the deposition (Rule 32(a)), and objections to admissibility of the testimony (Rule 32(b)) remain applicable.

A stipulation concerning the taking of depositions implies a mutual obligation of reasonable cooperation to accomplish the goal of the stipulation. *Jones v. Queen Ins. Co.*, 76 Ariz. 212, 262 P.2d 250 (1953).

Rule 30. Depositions upon oral examination

(a) When Depositions May Be Taken. After commencement of the action, the testimony of parties or any expert witnesses expected to be called may be taken by deposition upon oral examination. Depositions of document custodians may be taken to secure production of documents and to establish evidentiary foundation. No other depositions shall be taken except upon: (1) agreement of all parties; (2) an order of the court following a motion demonstrating good cause, or (3) an order of the court following a Comprehensive Pretrial Conference pursuant to Rule 16(c).

If the plaintiff seeks to take a deposition prior to the expiration of 30 days after service of the summons and complaint upon any defendant or service which is completed under Rule 4.2 of these rules, leave of court, granted with or without notice, is required except that leave is not required: (1) if a defendant has served a notice of taking deposition or otherwise sought discovery or (2) if special notice is given as provided in subdivision (b)(2) of this rule. The attendance of witnesses may be compelled by subpoena as provided in Rule 45. The deposition of a person confined in prison may be taken only by leave of court on such terms as the court prescribes.

Amended July 17, 1970, effective Nov. 1, 1970; Oct. 2, 1991, effective Dec. 1, 1991; Dec. 20, 1991, effective July 1, 1992.

(b) Notice of Examination; General Requirements; Special Notice; Method of Recording; Production of Documents and Things; Deposition of Organization; Deposition by Telephone.

(1) Absent a stipulation of all parties to the action or an order of the court authorizing a briefer notice, a party desiring to take the deposition of any person upon oral examination shall give notice in writing to every other party to the action at least ten days prior to the date of the deposition. The notice shall state the date, time and place for taking the deposition, the name and address of each person to be examined, if known, and, if the name is not known, a general description sufficient to identify the person or the particular class or group to which the person belongs, and the name and address of the person before whom the deposition shall be taken. If a subpoena duces tecum is to be served on the person to be examined, the designation of the materials to be produced as set forth in the subpoena shall be attached to or included in the notice.

If the deposition is to be recorded by audio or audio-video, the notice shall state the technique for recording the deposition and the protocols to be used for such recording, the identity of the person recording the deposition, and the placement of camera(s), if any.

(2) Leave of court is not required for the taking of a deposition by plaintiff if the notice (A) states that the person to be examined is about to go out of the State of Arizona, and will be un-available for examination unless the person's deposition is taken before expiration of the 30-day period, and (B) sets forth facts to support the statement. The plaintiff's attorney shall sign the notice, and the attorney's signature constitutes a certification by the attorney that to the best of the attorney's knowledge, information, and belief the statement and supporting facts are true. The sanctions provided by Rule 11(a) are applicable to the certification.

If a party shows that when the party was served with notice under this subdivision (b)(2) the party was unable through the exercise of diligence to obtain counsel to represent the party at the taking of the deposition, the deposition may not be used against the party.

(3) The court may for cause shown enlarge or shorten the time for taking the deposition.

(4) Unless the parties stipulate or the court orders otherwise, the depositions shall be recorded by a certified court reporter and may also be recorded by audio or audio-video means.

When a deposition is recorded only by a certified court reporter, the party taking the deposition shall bear the cost of recording. If requested by one of the parties, the testimony shall be transcribed. If the testimony is transcribed, the party noticing the deposition or the party causing the deposition to be taken shall be responsible for the cost of the original transcript. A party may arrange to have a certified copy of the transcript made at the party's own expense. If audio or audio-video is additionally requested by one of the parties, the requesting party shall be responsible for the cost of such recording, and a party requesting an audio or audio-video copy of the deposition shall be responsible for the cost of the audio or audio-video copy.

When a deposition is recorded only by audio or audio-video means, the party noticing the deposition shall bear the cost of the recording. A party requesting an audio or audio-video copy of the deposition shall be responsible for the cost of the audio or audio-video copy. The stipulation or order shall designate the person before whom the deposition shall be taken, the manner of recording, preserving and filing the deposition, and may include other provisions to assure that the recorded testimony will be accurate and trustworthy. A party may arrange to have a certified transcript made at the party's own expense.

Any changes made by the witness, the witness' signature identifying the deposition as the witness' own or the statement of the officer that is required if the witness does not sign as provided in subdivision (e), and the certification of the officer required by subdivision (f) shall be set forth in a writing to accompany a deposition.

Unless otherwise agreed by the parties, a deposition shall be conducted before an officer appointed or designated under Rule 28 and shall begin with a statement or notation on the record by the officer that includes (A) the officer's name, certification number, if any, and business address; (B) the date, time and place of the deposition; (C) the name of the deponent; (D) the administration of the oath or affirmation to the deponent; and (E) an identification of all persons present. The officer shall repeat items (A) through (C) at the beginning of each unit of recorded tape or other recording medium. The appearance or demeanor of deponents or attorneys shall not be distorted through or sound-recording techniques. At the end of the deposition, the officer shall state or note on the record that the deposition is complete and shall set forth any stipulations made by counsel concerning the custody of the transcript or recording and the exhibits, or concerning other pertinent matters.

(5) The notice to a party deponent may be accompanied by a request made in compliance with Rule 34 for the production of documents and tangible things at the taking of the deposition. The procedure of Rule 34 shall apply to the request.

(6) A party may in the party's notice name as the deponent a public or private corporation or a partnership or association or governmental agency and designate with reasonable particularity the matters on which examination is requested. The organization so named shall designate one or more officers, directors, or managing agents, or other persons who consent to testify on its behalf, and may set forth, for each person designated, the matters on which that person will testify. The persons so designated shall testify as to matters known or reasonably available to the organization. This subdivision (b)(6) does not preclude taking a deposition by any other procedure authorized in these rules.

(7) The parties may stipulate or the court may order that a deposition be taken by telephone. For the purpose of this Rule and Rules 28(a), 37(a)(1), 45(c)(3)(A)(ii), and 45(e), a deposition is taken in the county where the deponent is to answer questions propounded to the deponent.

Amended July 17, 1970, effective Nov. 1, 1970; July 6, 1983, effective Sept. 7, 1983; Sept. 15, 1987, effective Nov. 15, 1987; March 12, 1990, effective June 1,

1990; Oct. 9, 1996, effective Dec. 1, 1996; Oct. 16, 2003, effective Dec. 1, 2003; Sept. 18, 2006, effective Jan. 1, 2007.

(c) Examination and Cross-Examination; Record of Examination; Oath; Objections. Examination and cross-examination of witnesses may proceed as permitted at the trial under the provisions of the Arizona Rules of Evidence. The examination shall commence at the time and place specified in the notice or within thirty minutes thereafter. And, unless otherwise stipulated or ordered, will be continued on successive days, except Saturdays, Sundays and legal holidays until completed. Any party not present within thirty minutes following the time specified in the notice of taking deposition waives any objection that the deposition was taken without that party's presence. The officer before whom the deposition is to be taken shall put the witness on oath and shall personally, or by someone acting under the officer's direction and in the officer's presence, record the testimony of the witness. If the deposition is taken telephonically and the witness is not physically in the presence of the officer before whom the deposition is to be taken, the officer may nonetheless place the witness under oath with the same force and effect as if the witness were physically present before the officer. The testimony shall be taken in accordance with subdivision (b)(4) of this rule.

All objections made at the time of the examination to the qualifications of the officer taking the deposition, or to the manner of taking it, or to the evidence presented, or to the conduct of any party, and any other objection to the proceedings, shall be noted by the officer upon the deposition. Evidence objected to shall be taken subject to the objections. The court shall assess an appropriate sanction, including a sanction provided for under Rule 16(f), against any party or attorney who has engaged in unreasonable, groundless, abusive or obstructionist conduct. In lieu of participating in the oral examination, parties may serve written questions in a sealed envelope on the party taking the deposition and the party taking the deposition shall transmit them to the officer, who shall propound them to the witness and record the answers verbatim.

Amended July 17, 1970, effective Nov. 1, 1970; July 23, 1976, effective Oct. 1, 1976; June 1, 1977, effective Sept. 1, 1977; April 18, 1979, effective July 1, 1979; Sept. 15, 1987, effective Nov. 15, 1987; Dec. 20, 1991, effective July 1, 1992; Sept. 18, 2006, effective Jan. 1, 2007.

Comment

The scope of discovery at depositions is governed by 16 A.R.S. Rules of Civil Procedure, Rule 26(b).

(d) Length of Deposition; Motion to Terminate or Limit Examination. Depositions shall be of reasonable length. The oral deposition of any party or witness, including expert witnesses, whenever taken, shall not exceed four (4) hours in length, except pursuant to stipulation of the parties, or, upon motion and a showing of good cause. The court shall impose sanctions pursuant to Rule 16(f) for unreasonable, groundless, abusive or obstructionist conduct.

At any time during the taking of the deposition, on motion of a party or of the deponent and upon a showing that the examination is being conducted in bad faith or in such manner as unreasonably to annoy, embarrass, or oppress the deponent or party, the court in which the action is pending or the court in the county where the deposition is being taken may order the officer conducting the examination to cease forthwith from taking the deposition, or may limit the scope and manner of the taking of the deposition as provided in Rule 26(c). If the order made terminates the examination, it shall be resumed thereafter only upon the order of the court in which the action is pending. Upon demand of the objecting party or deponent, the taking of the deposition shall be suspended for the time necessary to make a motion for an order. The provisions of Rule 37(a)(4) apply to the award of expenses incurred in relation to the motion.

Amended July 17, 1970, effective Nov. 1, 1970; Dec. 20, 1991, effective July 1, 1992.

(e) Submission to Witness; Changes; Signing. If requested by the deponent or a party before completion of the deposition, the deponent shall have 30 days after being notified by the officer that the transcript or recording is available in which to review the transcript or recording and, if there are changes in form or substance, to sign a statement reciting such changes and the reasons given by the deponent for making them. The officer shall indicate in the certificate prescribed by subdivision (f)(1) whether any review was requested and, if so, shall append any changes made by the deponent during the period allowed. If the witness does not submit such a statement or a written explanation why such statement cannot be submitted within the time period provided, the officer shall state on the record the fact of the refusal to submit a statement with the reason therefore, if any, and the deposition may then be used as fully as though signed unless on a motion to suppress under Rule 32(d)(4) the court holds that the reasons given for the refusal to submit a statement require rejection of the deposition in whole or in part.

Amended July 17, 1970, effective Nov. 1, 1970; Sept. 15, 1987, effective Nov. 15, 1987; Oct. 16, 2003, effective Dec. 1, 2003; Sept. 18, 2006, effective Jan. 1, 2007.

(f) Certification and Delivery by Officer; Exhibits; Copies.

(1) The officer must certify that the witness was duly sworn

by the officer and that the deposition is a true record of the testimony given by the witness. This certificate must be in writing and accompany the record of the deposition. Unless otherwise ordered by the court, the officer must securely seal the deposition in an envelope or package indorsed with the title of the action and marked "Deposition of [here insert name of witness]" and must promptly send it to the attorney who arranged for the transcript or recording, who must store it under conditions that will protect it against loss, destruction, tampering, or deterioration. Documents and things produced for inspection during the examination of the witness must, upon the request of a party, be marked for identification and annexed to the deposition and may be inspected and copied by any party, except that if the person producing the materials desires to retain them the person may (A) offer copies to be marked for identification and annexed to the deposition and to serve thereafter as originals if the person affords to all parties fair opportunity to verify the copies by comparison with the originals, or (B) offer the originals to be marked for identification, after giving to each party an opportunity to inspect and copy them, in which event the materials may then be used in the same manner as if annexed to the deposition. Any party may move for an order that the original be annexed to and returned with the deposition to the court, pending final disposition of the case.

(2) Unless otherwise ordered by the court or agreed by the parties, the officer shall retain stenographic notes and tapes of any deposition and a copy of the recording of any deposition taken by another method in such place and manner as to ensure their availability to the court or any party upon request. The officer shall retain stenographic notes, tapes, and copies of recordings taken by another method according to records retention and disposition schedules and purge lists adopted by the Supreme Court. Upon payment of reasonable charges therefor, the officer shall furnish a copy of the transcript or other recording of the deposition to any party or to the deponent.

(3) The party taking the deposition shall give prompt notice of its filing to all other parties.

Amended July 17, 1970, effective Nov. 1, 1970; Feb. 14, 1979, effective April 1, 1979; July 6, 1983, effective Sept. 7, 1983; Sept. 15, 1987, effective Nov. 15, 1987; Oct. 20, 1993, effective Dec. 1, 1993; Oct. 16, 2003, effective Dec. 1, 2003; September 27, 2005, effective December 1, 2005; Sept. 18, 2006, effective Jan. 1, 2007.

(g) Failure to Attend or to Serve Subpoena; Expenses.

(1) If the party giving the notice of the taking of a deposition fails to attend and proceed therewith and another party attends in person or by attorney pursuant to the notice, the court

may order the party giving the notice to pay to such other party the reasonable expenses incurred by that party and that party's attorney in attending, including reasonable attorney's fees.

(2) If the party giving the notice of the taking of a deposition of a witness fails to serve a subpoena upon the witness and the witness because of such failure does not attend, and if another party attends in person or by attorney because that party expects the deposition of that witness to be taken, the court may order the party giving the notice to pay to such other party the reasonable expenses incurred by that party and that party's attorney in attending, including reasonable attorney's fees.

Amended March 26, 1963, effective June 1, 1963; July 17, 1970, effective Nov. 1, 1970; Sept. 15, 1987, effective Nov. 15, 1987.

(h) [Deleted effective January 1, 2013].

(i) [Deleted effective November 1, 1970].

STATE BAR COMMITTEE NOTES

1963 Amendment

[Rule 30(f)] [The insertion of the words "or certified" preceding the word "mail"] * * * is unnecessary under Arizona law since our statutes already provide the use of certified mail, but it is made solely for the purpose of conformity.

1970 Amendments

Rule 30(a): This section covers the materials previously in Rule 26(a) with certain changes. The previous time for beginning the taking of depositions is extended to 30 days, running from service rather than the commencement of the action.

Rule 30(b): Subdivision: (1) adds that the notice of any materials to be subpoenaed shall be included with the notice of the deposition. Subdivision (2) permits depositions within the 30-day period without leave of court where there is a substantial and certified assurance by counsel that the person to be deposed is about to leave the jurisdiction. This provision comes from the admiralty practice, where it is necessary in connection with ships which may suddenly leave, but it may be equally applicable in a state with many tourists. Nonetheless, this practice is a rare exception, and the court is expected to enforce the disciplinary provisions against its abuse. Subdivision (4) is intended to permit experimentation with other forms of recording depositions other than stenographic testimony, but this is protected both by the requirement that it be ordered by the court, and that a party may use stenographic transcription in any case, if he desires. Subdivision (5) is intended to terminate the existing doubt as to whether a party may be compelled to produce documents at the deposition, and to permit their copying. The previous rules did not directly relate Rule 34 and the production of documents to depositions. The revised Rule does make clear that the deposition and document discovery procedures may be used together as to a party. Subdivision (6) deals with the problem which arises when a party desiring discovery does not know what individual in the responding organization should be called. He may, if he wishes, seek such information by interrogatory, and proceed without use of this subdivision, but if he desires to do so, the party may name the organization or government agency as the deponent, describe the matters on which examination is requested, and require the organization to produce the appropriately informed persons.

Rule 30(c) alters the existing practice under which depositions are almost automatically transcribed. In view of the many depositions taken from which nothing useful is discovered, the revised language provides that the transcription is to be performed if any party requests it. The fact of the request is relevant to the exercise of the court's discretion in determining who shall pay for transcription.

Rule 30(d) does not change existing practice, except to make clear that the sanctions of Rule 37(a)(4) will apply in connection with motions to terminate or eliminate examinations.

Rule 30(e): The provision relating to the refusal of a witness to sign his deposition is tightened through insertion of a 30-day time period.

Rule 30(f): This adds a provision codifying the best of existing practices concerning methods of handling exhibits at depositions. It also assures each party that he may inspect and copy documents and things produced by a nonparty witness in response to a subpoena duces tecum. The revision also protects the right of a witness to substitute copies for the purpose of marking, and to obtain return of exhibits where this may be important to him. This may be done by showing the original to the persons present at the deposition, giving them a fair opportunity to satisfy themselves as to the accuracy of the copy.

1983 Amendment

Rule 30(b)(4): The provision that the stipulation or order shall designate the person before whom the deposition is to be taken is added to encourage the naming of the recording technician as that person, eliminating the necessity of the presence of one whose only function is to administer the oath. See Rules 28(a) and 29.

1991 Amendments

Rule 30(a) is intended to address the problem of overuse of expensive and unnecessary depositions. Any party may take the deposition of any other party, including depositions taken under Rule 30(b)(6), the deposition of any disclosed expert, and the depositions of the custodian of documents without agreement or leave of court. Treating physicians are regarded as disclosed experts for purposes of this rule. Depositions of custodian taken as a matter of right shall be limited to questions necessary to secure the documents and to provide evidentiary foundation for their admissibility. The rule, along with Rule 26.1 and Rule 16, is intended to encourage voluntary disclosure of information between the parties and is further intended to require at a minimum consultation between counsel prior to the setting of depositions. Any party may take the deposition of any other party, including depositions taken under Rule 30(b)(6) and the deposition of any disclosed expert, without agreement or leave of court. Any other depositions must be taken either by agreement of the parties, upon motion and order of the court, or pursuant to an order of the court following a Comprehensive Pretrial Conference under Rule 16. Refusing to agree to the taking of a reasonable and necessary deposition should subject counsel to sanctions under Rule 26(f).

[Rule 30(d)] This rule, in conjunction with Rule 30(a), is intended to address the problem of overuse of depositions. Depositions are presumptively limited to four (4) hours. The Committee recognizes, however, that there are depositions which cannot be concluded within these presumptive limits. The presumptive limits can be exceeded upon stipulation of counsel. Counsel who refuse to agree to depositions which reasonably and necessarily require more than four (4) hours may subject themselves to sanctions pursuant to Rule 6(f). The court, upon motion and for good cause shown or as a part of the Comprehensive Pretrial Conference pursuant to Rule 16(c)(1), may prescribe the time limits. The Committee intends that there be professional cooperation between counsel in regulating the necessary length and scope of depositions.

COURT COMMENT

1991 Amendments

The above rule change was part of a comprehensive set of rule revisions proposed by the Special Bar Committee to Study Civil Litigation Abuse, Cost and Delay, which was specifically charged in March, 1990 with the task of proposing rules to reduce discovery abuse and to make the judicial system in Arizona more efficient, expeditious, and accessible to the people.

For more complete background information on the rule changes proposed by the Committee, see Court Comment to Rule 26.1.

AUTHORS' COMMENTS

Analysis

1. *Scope and Purpose of Rule.* Ariz. R. Civ. P. 30 sets forth procedures for, and requirements applicable to, the conduct of depositions upon oral examination. The scope of the discovery permitted during the course of such an oral examination is that defined by Ariz. R. Civ. P. 26(b). Whether and, if so, under what circumstances such a deposition may be used at a trial or other evidentiary hearing is controlled by Ariz. R. Civ. P. 32. Absent a stipulation of all parties or an order of the court permitting a shorter notice, at least ten (10) days' prior notice of a deposition must be provided.

2. *Comparison With Federal Rule.* While both ARCP 30 and FRCP 30 govern the conduct of depositions upon oral examina-

tion, they are now materially different as a consequence of the 1992 Arizona discovery and court reform amendments and the 1993 and 2007 amendments to the Federal Rules of Civil Procedure.

Initially, the Arizona version of the Rule contains a number of provisions not found in the Federal version. FRCP 30 does not contain:

(1) a provision such as in ARCP 30(b)(1), requiring ten days' notice of the taking of a deposition;

(2) provisions that a deposition shall commence within thirty (30) minutes of the time for which it is noticed, that any party not present by that time waives objection to the conduct of the deposition in the party's absence, and that depositions are to be conducted on successive business days until completed such as are contained in ARCP 30(c);

(3) a provision imposing a presumptive limit of four (4) hours on the length of any deposition such as is found in ARCP 30(d); or,

(4) a provision requiring court reporters to retain their original notes and stenographic tapes of depositions for a period of time specified by the Arizona Supreme Court, such as in ARCP 30(f)(2).

Both ARCP 30(a) and FRCP 30(a) impose presumptive limitations on the number of depositions that can be conducted in an action, but the limits imposed are quite different. ARCP 30(a) limits the depositions that can be conducted as of right, *i.e.*, without agreement of the parties or leave of Court, to those of parties to the action, disclosed expert witnesses and custodians of records. FRCP 30(a) requires a written stipulation or leave of court to conduct a deposition if the proposed deposition would result in more than ten (10) depositions being conducted by the plaintiffs, by the defendants, or by third-party defendants, to conduct a deposition of a person whose deposition has already been conducted in the action, or to conduct a deposition before the discovery planning conference required by amended FRCP 26(f), unless the deponent is about to leave the country.

Under ARCP 30(b)(4), depositions may be recorded by nonstenographic means absent a stipulation or court order. FRCP 32(a), as amended, permits the party noticing a deposition to specify in the notice the method by which the testimony is to be recorded, which may be by sound, video or stenographic means. Any other party may, with prior notice to the other parties and to the deponent, designate another method for recording the testimony, in addition to that specified in the deposition notice, at that party's expense.

FRCP 30(d)(1) requires that objections at depositions be stated concisely and in a non-argumentative and non-suggestive manner, and provides that witnesses at a deposition may not be instructed not to answer a question, except to preserve a privilege, to enforce a discovery limitation previously ordered by the Court, or to present a motion for protective order. The provisions in the Arizona Rules of Civil Procedure regulating the conduct of counsel and parties at depositions are contained in ARCP Rules 32(d)(3)(D) and (E).

ARCP 30(e) requires that the witness is to read and sign the transcript of the deposition, unless that requirement is waived by the parties. FRCP 30(e), as amended, only requires review and signature of the transcript by the witness where that is requested by the deponent or by a party before completion of the deposition.

In 2007, FRCP 30(b)(6) was amended to add "other entity" to the list of organizations that may be named as a deponent. ARCP 30(b)(6) has not been amended to add this language.

In addition, in 2007, the language of FRCP 30 was amended as part of the general restyling of the Federal Rules of Civil Procedure to make the Federal Rules more easily understood and to make style and terminology consistent throughout the Federal Rules of Civil Procedure. Those stylistic modifications have not been incorporated into ARCP 30.

3. *Presumptive Limit on Taking of Depositions.* The discovery and court reform amendments adopted by the Supreme Court, effective July 1, 1992, imposed presumptive limits on the use of all discovery devices, and particularly depositions. Under amended Ariz. R. Civ. P. 30(a), absent an agreement of the parties or leave of court, depositions as of right are authorized only of the parties to the action, disclosed expert witnesses, and custodians of documents, but only to secure production of documents and to establish evidentiary foundation. (Of course, following the 1996 amendments to Ariz. R. Civ. P. 45, it is no longer necessary to conduct the deposition of a custodian of records in order to secure the production of documents from a person or entity that is not a party to the action. See discussion in the *Authors' Comments* under Ariz. R. Civ. P. 45.) Moreover, under amended Rule 30(d), depositions that are taken are not to exceed four (4) hours in length, absent an agreement of the parties or leave of court. As noted, additional depositions, such as those of trial witnesses, or depositions exceeding the four hour limit, may be taken only by agreement or with the permission of the Court. The Committee Note to the amendments observes that parties should be subject to sanctions for unreasonably refusing to agree to reasonable and necessary depositions.

Depositions as of right are permitted of "parties" to the action, and it remains to be seen how broadly that will be construed in the case of corporate parties. An argument can be made that this provision must be construed in conjunction with Ariz. R. Civ. P. 30(b)(6), and that what is authorized are depositions of organizational representatives designated to testify on specified subject matters. On the other hand, the intent of the amendments, at least in part, was to encourage counsel to conduct discovery more informally, through interviews of witnesses, rather than through the expensive deposition process. Counsel are probably precluded from conducting *ex parte* interviews of former employees of corporate adversaries whose acts or omissions gave rise to the litigation or who have an ongoing relationship with their former employer in connection with the litigation. *Lang v. Superior Court, In and For County of Maricopa*, 170 Ariz. 602, 826 P.2d 1228 (Ct. App. Div. 1 1992). This preclusion would argue in favor of considering such former employees to be parties for purposes of the limitations imposed by Ariz. R. Civ. P. 30(a).

4. *Persons Authorized to Attend Depositions.* A deposition is not a public proceeding, and the Court has the authority to exclude from attendance persons whose presence is not necessary or authorized. *Lewis R. Pyle Memorial Hosp. v. Superior Court of Arizona In and For Gila County*, 149 Ariz. 193, 717 P.2d 872 (1986). The Court may not, however, exclude a party from any representation or participation at a deposition. *Montgomery Elevator Co. v. Superior Court of State, In and For Maricopa County*, 135 Ariz. 432, 661 P.2d 1133 (1983). While, in a wrongful death action, only those categories of persons specified by statute are proper parties plaintiff, the statutory beneficiaries of such an action are still parties to the case with respect to damages. Absent a clear conflict between beneficiaries, a statutory beneficiary and counsel may attend depositions in a wrongful death action, but may only participate in the portions of those depositions that relate to damage issues. *Williams v. Superior Court In and For County of Maricopa*, 169 Ariz. 468, 820 P.2d 332 (Ct. App. Div. 1 1991).

5. *Commencement of Taking of Depositions.* The general rule, set forth in Ariz. R. Civ. P. 30(a), is that the plaintiff may not conduct depositions, without a stipulation or leave of Court, until thirty (30) days after service of the summons and complaint upon any defendant. This limitation is removed if any defendant commences discovery during that period. There is also an exception, created by Ariz. R. Civ. P. 30(b)(2), where the witness to be examined is about to leave the State of Arizona. To invoke that exception, the notice of deposition must state the facts showing that the witness is to become unavailable.

Under Ariz. R. Civ. P. 30(c), depositions are to commence within thirty (30) minutes of the time for which they are noticed. That Rule also provides that depositions are to be conducted on successive business days until completed, but that particular requirement will be of limited application now that a presumptive four (4) hour limit on the length of depositions has been adopted.

While the plaintiff may commence depositions thirty (30) days after securing service upon *any* defendant, and not *all* defendants, the risk is that a deposition conducted that early in the action may not be used at trial against unserved defendants. *See* Ariz. R. Civ. P. 32(a).

6. *Depositions of Prisoners.* Ariz. R. Civ. P. 30(a) states that a deposition "of a person confined in prison may be taken only by leave of court on such terms as the court prescribes." Whether special cause must be shown for leave is not clear. The prudent course is to include in the motion a reason for taking the deposition. The Rule only authorizes the taking of the deposition in the institution in which the prisoner is confined. In exceptional circumstances, the taking of the testimony before the Court might be secured through a writ of *habeas corpus ad testificandum.*

7. *Notices of Depositions.* Notice of a deposition must be given in writing to every party to the action. An oral notice of deposition is insufficient and the opposing party is not thereby obligated to seek a protective order, but may have the deposition suppressed. *City of Kingman v. Havatone*, 14 Ariz. App. 585, 485 P.2d 574 (Div. 1 1971). The service of a notice of deposition of a party is sufficient to compel that party to appear for a deposition. In the case of a non-party witness, the notice serves only to advise the parties of the scheduling of the deposition; the appearance of the witness must be compelled by subpoena. Under the 1993 amendment to Ariz. R. Civ. P. 5(g), notices of deposition are no longer to be filed with the Court.

Before the 1990 amendment to Ariz. R. Civ. P. 30(b)(1), the rule was that reasonable notice of a deposition was required but that what constituted "reasonable" notice would depend upon the particular circumstances. Under this regime, it was held that as little as five days' notice was reasonable, *Copper State Bank v. Saggio*, 139 Ariz. 438, 679 P.2d 84 (Ct. App. Div. 2 1983); but that it was not an abuse of discretion for the trial court to refuse to permit a witness to be deposed on the evening before the witness' testimony at trial. *Ring v. Taylor*, 141 Ariz. 56, 685 P.2d 121 (Ct. App. Div. 1 1984). Ariz. R. Civ. P. 30(b)(1) was amended in 1990, however, to require ten days' prior notice of any deposition, absent a stipulation of all parties or an order of the Court permitting a shorter notice. Through application of the provisions of Ariz. R. Civ. P. 6(a), intermediate Saturdays, Sundays and legal holidays are not to be included, so that a party is generally entitled to ten business days' notice. *National Broker Associates, Inc. v. Marlyn Nutraceuticals, Inc.*, 211 Ariz. 210, 119 P.3d 477

(Ct. App. Div. 1 2005).

As a consequence of 2003 amendments to the Rule, it is now no longer necessary to secure an agreement of other counsel or a court order in order to record a deposition by other than stenographic means (*i.e.*, primarily, videotape). Under those amendments, however, all deposition notices must now specify "the time for recording the deposition and the protocols to be used for such recording, the identity of the person recording the deposition, and the placement of camera(s), if any . . ."

8. *Production of Documents at Deposition.* Under Ariz. R. Civ. P. 30(b)(5), the notice of a deposition of a party deponent may include a request that the party produce documents or other tangible items at the deposition. If that option is elected, however, the procedures of Rule 34 still apply, and the party deponent has (now) forty (40) days in which to respond to the request. This procedure cannot be altered or evaded through service of a subpoena *duces tecum* on a party deponent. *MacDonald v. Hyder*, 12 Ariz. App. 411, 471 P.2d 296 (Div. 1 1970).

The production of documents at a deposition of a non-party witness can only be secured through service of a subpoena *duces tecum* under Rule 45. The documents or other materials to be requested from the non-party witness must be described in the deposition notice, which is usually accomplished by attaching a copy of the subpoena *duces tecum* to be served.

9. *Rule 30(b)(6) Depositions.* Ariz. R. Civ. P. 30(b)(6) facilitates the conduct of depositions of "organizational" parties or witnesses, where the nature of the information sought to be discovered is known, but the party seeking to discover it does not know the name of a particular individual associated with the organization who is in a position to furnish it. In that circumstance, a party may issue and serve a notice of deposition in which the organization (public or private corporation, partnership, association or governmental agency) is named as the deponent and which specifies "with reasonable particularity the matters on which examination is requested." The organization named then has the obligation to designate one or more officers, directors or managing agents, or any other persons who agree to testify on the organization's behalf, and to produce them to testify as to matters specified in the notice that are known or reasonably available to the organization.

The production of an individual, in response to an Ariz. R. Civ. P. 30(b)(6) deposition notice, who is not an officer, director or managing agent of the party deponent, and who has no knowledge of the information or subjects of examination specified in the notice, is tantamount to a failure to appear for the deposition and warrants the imposition of sanctions. *Groat v. Equity Ameri-*

can Ins. Co., 180 Ariz. 342, 884 P.2d 228 (Ct. App. Div. 1 1994).

10. *Nonstenographic Recording of Depositions.* Amendments adopted to Rule 30 in 2003 abrogated the prior regime under which it was necessary to secure an agreement of counsel or a court order in order to record a deposition by other than stenographic means. In recent years, the most common form of nonstenographic recording of depositions has been by videotape. Accordingly, under the amendments, *all* notices of deposition must specify "the technique for recording the deposition and the protocols to be used for such recording, the identity of the person recording the deposition, [and] the placement of camera(s), if any . . ."

Unless there is an agreement of counsel or court order to the contrary, however, the deposition must also be stenographically recorded, and the party conducting the deposition is to bear the cost of recording. The officer recording the deposition, even one recorded purely stenographically, must read at the commencement of the deposition a statement that includes: (1) the officer's name and business address, (2) the date, time and place of the deposition, (3) the name of the deponent, (4) the administration of the oath or affirmation to the deponent, and (5) an identification of all persons present. Where the deposition is recorded by nonstenographic means, a statement containing the information in (1) through (3), *supra*, must be repeated "at the beginning of each unit of recorded tape or other recording medium." In addition, a sentence in the amended Rule requires that the appearance or demeanor of deponents may not be distorted through camera or sound-recording techniques.

The provisions of Rules 30(e) and 30(f), which concern the submission of the deposition to the witness and the delivery of completed depositions, were rewritten to accommodate the fact that there may be instances where there is no stenographic transcript to submit to the witness or deliver to counsel who arranged for the recording.

11. *Conduct of Depositions by Telephone.* Shortly before the adoption of Ariz. R. Civ. P. 30(b)(7), it was held that the trial court had the inherent authority to permit or require the conduct of depositions by telephone. *Wagner v. Casteel*, 136 Ariz. 29, 663 P.2d 1020 (Ct. App. Div. 2 1983). The subsequent amendment merely confirmed that authority, and clarified that the deposition was deemed taken in the county where the deponent is located during the examination. The taking of telephone depositions has been facilitated by the 1992 amendment to Ariz. R. Civ. P. 30(c), which authorizes the officer before whom a deposition is to be taken to place a witness at a telephone deposition under oath even though the witness is not physically in the presence of the

officer. Where depositions are conducted by telephone, however, the Court and the parties should consider the imposition of special restrictions, such as on the persons allowed to be present with the witness, for example, to insure the integrity of the proceedings.

12. *Use of Written Questions.* Where a party has a very limited interest in the testimony of a witness whose deposition upon oral examination has been noticed, Ariz. R. Civ. P. 30(c) provides an option to have written questions propounded to the witness by the court reporter and thereby avoid the expense of attending. The written questions are to be served on the party taking the deposition in a sealed envelope, and that party must transmit them to the court reporter or other officer before whom the deposition is to be conducted. This is quite distinct from the procedure followed where the entire deposition is taken upon written questions under Rule 31. *See* discussion in Section 4 of the *Authors' Comments* under Ariz. R. Civ. P. 31.

13. *Judicial Control of Depositions.* There are two separate Rules which provide a party and/or a non-party witness with vehicles for seeking judicial relief for a perceived discovery abuse in the scheduling and/or conduct of a deposition— Ariz. R. Civ. P. 26(c) and 30(d).

Where the problem associated with the conduct of a particular deposition, or of depositions in general, is known before the depositions commence, relief can and should be sought by seeking a protective order under Ariz. R. Civ. P. 26(c). Such an application for judicial relief may only be made in the court in which the action is pending.

Where the problem is not known, or does not arise, until the deposition actually commences, Ariz. R. Civ. P. 30(d) authorizes a party to demand that the deposition proceedings be suspended to permit application to the Court in the county where the action is pending, for an order terminating the deposition or limiting the scope of examination. The deposition proceedings must be suspended upon such demand, and the application for judicial relief may thereafter be made either in the Court in which the action is pending or in the Superior Court of the county where the deposition is being conducted, if different.

One or the other of these procedures, however, must be employed. A party or deponent who believes that a deposition is being conducted improperly or in bad faith, *e.g.*, in the presence of an unauthorized person or in contravention of a court order, must invoke either Ariz. R. Civ. P. 30(d) or Rule 26(c)—it is not proper to simply leave the deposition or to refuse to be deposed. *Lewis R. Pyle Memorial Hosp. v. Superior Court of Arizona In and For Gila County*, 149 Ariz. 193, 717 P.2d 872 (1986). If a protective order sought under Rule 30(d) terminates the examination, the deposition may be resumed only upon an order from the Court in which the action is pending.

14. *Judicial Control of Place of Deposition.* Issues concerning the place where a deposition is to be conducted arise frequently in instances where the deposition of a party who does not reside in Arizona is noticed to be conducted in the State. A party does not have an absolute right to conduct the deposition of another party at the site of the forum; rather, the Court must weigh the party's preference for Arizona as the place for the deposition against the resulting burden on the party to be deposed. *Rogers v. Fenton*, 115 Ariz. 217, 564 P.2d 906 (Ct. App. Div. 2 1977). The fact that the party resisting the deposition is the plaintiff who instituted proceedings in Arizona is a factor to be considered.

The burden of out-of-state depositions can be alleviated, if appropriate, through cost allocation protective orders. It was held not to be an abuse of discretion for the trial court to order the defendant to pay in advance the travel expenses that would be incurred by plaintiff's counsel in attending the depositions of the defendant's witnesses by defendant's counsel. *State v. Mahoney*, 103 Ariz. 308, 441 P.2d 68 (1968); *City of Kingman v. Havatone*, 14 Ariz. App. 585, 485 P.2d 574 (Div. 1 1971). The Court can also order that the deposition be taken by written interrogatories, rather than upon oral examination, or by telephone.

15. *Objections to Deposition Questions.* Testimony at a deposition is normally taken subject to objections stated on the record, and objections to the form of the questions or answers are waived unless stated at the time. *See,* Ariz. R. Civ. P. 32(d)(3)(B). As part of the discovery and court reform amendments, Ariz. R. Civ. P. 32(d)(3)(D) and (E) were adopted to regulate the conduct of attorneys in making objections at depositions. Objections to form are to be concise and are not to suggest answers to the witness. The defect in the form of the question or answer is not to be specified unless the party propounding the question so requests. Continuous and unwarranted conferences off the record between the deponent and counsel are prohibited and subject to sanctions.

16. *Review by Witness; Signing; Filing.* Details concerning the signing of depositions, or the waiver of those requirements, are typically handled orally by counsel and entered on the record at the deposition, rather than by filing a formal stipulation with the Court. A witness may make changes to the substance of the responses originally given at the deposition, but may thereafter be subject to impeachment on the basis of the original answers. *Valley Nat. Bank v. National Ass'n for Stock Car Auto Racing, Inc.*, 153 Ariz. 374, 736 P.2d 1186 (Ct. App. Div. 2 1987). Where a deposition has not been read and signed by the witness, and the

requirement has not been waived, the Court may consider the deposition in ruling on a motion for summary judgment. *Perez v. Tomberlin*, 86 Ariz. 66, 340 P.2d 982 (1959). The failure to move to have such an unsigned deposition suppressed, however, before it is considered on a motion for summary judgment operates as a waiver of the irregularity. *Brooker v. Hunter*, 22 Ariz. App. 510, 528 P.2d 1269 (Div. 1 1974), opinion approved of, 111 Ariz. 578, 535 P.2d 1051 (1975).

Under the amendment to Ariz. R. Civ. P. 5(g) which became effective June 1, 1993, depositions are no longer to be filed with the Court. The original transcript is instead delivered to the party who noticed the deposition to retain until the action proceeds to trial or is otherwise resolved. Corresponding technical amendments were subsequently made, deleting the second sentence of Ariz. R. Civ. P. 30(f)(1) and 30(f)(3) both of which imposed certain procedural requirements attendant upon, or preparatory to, the filing of depositions. The fact that discovery materials are not filed does not preclude use of them in connection with motions and other proceedings. *GM Development Corp. v. Community American Mortg. Corp.*, 165 Ariz. 1, 795 P.2d 827 (Ct. App. Div. 1 1990).

A 1999 amendment to former Rule XVIII of the now abrogated Uniform Rules of Practice of the Superior Court permitted the use of deposition transcripts that are reduced in size, consisting of not more than four pages of text printed on one 8½ by 11 inch page—so-called "condensed transcripts." This provision is now contained in Rule 91(h)(2) of the Rules of the Arizona Supreme Court.

17. *Failure of Party Noticing Deposition to Attend.* If the party giving notice of the taking of a deposition fails to attend and proceed at the noticed time and the attorney for the opposing party attends, the Court may order the party giving the notice to pay the expenses incurred by the opponent, including reasonable attorneys' fees. The issue of whether sanctions are appropriate and, if so, their nature and extent is one committed to the trial court's discretion. *Jones v. Queen Ins. Co.*, 76 Ariz. 212, 262 P.2d 250 (1953); *Nienstedt v. Wetzel*, 133 Ariz. 348, 651 P.2d 876, 33 A.L.R.4th 635 (Ct. App. Div. 1 1982); *Preston Motor Co., Inc. v. Palomares*, 133 Ariz. 245, 650 P.2d 1227, 34 U.C.C. Rep. Serv. 1184 (Ct. App. Div. 2 1982).

18. *Failure to Subpoena Witness for Deposition.* If a witness fails to attend because not subpoenaed by the party giving the notice, the court may order the party giving the notice to pay the reasonable expenses of a party who attends.

19. *Conduct of Local Depositions in Foreign Actions.* Before 2013, former Rule 30(h) set forth the procedure that governed the

conduct of depositions in Arizona relating to cases pending in 'foreign' jurisdictions. Effective January 1, 2013, this procedure is now governed by new Rule 45.1 ["Interstate Depositions and Discovery"], which is a modified version of the Uniform Interstate Depositions and Discovery Act, and replaces the cumbersome, and more limited, procedure formerly provided by Rule 30(h), Ariz. R. Civ. P. As a consequence, Rule 30(h) was deleted, Rule 45.1 was adopted and Rule 45(b) was amended to conform with the adoption of new Rule 45.1.

Rule 31. Depositions upon written questions

(a) Serving Questions; Notice. After commencement of the action, any party may take the testimony of any person, including a party, by deposition upon written questions. The attendance of witnesses may be compelled by the use of subpoena as provided in Rule 45. The deposition of a person confined in prison may be taken only by leave of court on such terms as the court prescribes.

A party desiring to take a deposition upon written questions shall serve them upon every other party with a notice stating (1) the name and address of the person who is to answer them, if known, and if the name is not known, a general description sufficient to identify the person or the particular class or group to which the person belongs, and (2) the name or descriptive title and address of the officer before whom the deposition is to be taken. A deposition upon written questions may be taken of a public or private corporation or a partnership or association or governmental agency in accordance with the provisions of Rule 30(b)(6).

Within 30 days after the notice and written questions are served, a party may serve cross questions upon all other parties. Within 10 days after being served with cross questions, a party may serve redirect questions upon all other parties. Within 10 days after being served with redirect questions, a party may serve recross questions upon all other parties. The court may for cause shown enlarge or shorten the time.

Amended July 17, 1970, effective Nov. 1, 1970; Sept. 15, 1987, effective Nov. 15, 1987.

(b) Officer to Take Responses and Prepare Record. A copy of the notice and copies of all questions served shall be delivered by the party taking the deposition to the officer designated in the notice, who shall proceed promptly, in the manner provided by Rule 30(c), (e), and (f), to take the testimony of the witness in response to the questions and to prepare, certify, and file or mail the deposition, attaching thereto the copy of the notice and the questions received by the officer.

Amended July 17, 1970, effective Nov. 1, 1970; Sept. 15, 1987, effective Nov. 15, 1987.

(c) [Deleted effective January 1, 2013].

(d) [Deleted effective November 1, 1970].

STATE BAR COMMITTEE NOTES

1970 Amendment

Rule 31: This little-used rule involving depositions upon written inquiries had previously termed those inquiries "interrogatories." This has created confusion with Rule 33, dealing with interrogatories not used in conjunction with a deposition. Therefore, the term "questions" has been substituted in the 1970 revision. The case of *Torosian v. Paulos*, 82 Ariz. 304, 314, 313 P.2d 382, 389 (1957), holding that in the circumstances of that case, it is not an abuse of discretion for the trial court to forbid the use of a written question deposition where the witness could have been called directly, and submitted to cross-examination, is unaffected by the change.

AUTHORS' COMMENTS

Analysis

1. Scope and Purpose of Rule.
2. Comparison With Federal Rule.
3. Comparison to Discovery by Interrogatories and to Depositions Upon Oral Examination.
4. Relationship of Rule 31 Depositions to Rule 30(c) Procedures.
5. Procedure for Conducting Deposition on Written Questions.
6. Disposition of Objections.
7. Applicability of Presumptive Limits on Depositions.

1. *Scope and Purpose of Rule.* Ariz. R. Civ. P. 30 governs the conduct of depositions upon *oral* examination of the deponent by counsel for the parties. Rule 31 authorizes an optional method for conducting depositions upon *written* questions determined in advance through the procedures set forth in the Rule. Although Rule 31(b) continues to refer to the "filing" of the deposition, the 1993 amendment to Ariz. R. Civ. P. 5(g) provides that depositions are no longer to be filed with the Court. Rule 31(c), which also referred to the "filing" of the deposition, was deleted effective January 1, 2013.

The fact that discovery materials are not filed does not preclude, however, use of such materials in connection with motions and other proceedings. *GM Development Corp. v. Community American Mortg. Corp.*, 165 Ariz. 1, 795 P.2d 827 (Ct. App. Div. 1 1990).

2. *Comparison With Federal Rule.* There are now significant differences between ARCP 31 and FRCP 31. The Arizona Rule does not contain any specific presumptive limitation on the number of depositions upon written questions that can be conducted in an action, and contemplates a period of fifty (50) days for the completion of the process of serving cross questions, redirect questions and recross questions. The Federal Rule, on

the other hand, limits the number of depositions on written questions that can be conducted in an action to the number of depositions permitted by FRCP 30(a). Those limits are discussed in Section 2 of the *Authors'* Comments under ARCP 30. In addition, the period contemplated by the amended Federal Rule for the service of cross questions, redirect questions and recross questions has been shortened to twenty-eight (28) days, as opposed to a period of fifty (50) days contemplated by ARCP 31.

In 2007, the language of FRCP 31 was amended as part of the general restyling of the Federal Rules of Civil Procedure to make the Federal Rules more easily understood and to make style and terminology consistent throughout the Federal Rules of Civil Procedure. Those stylistic modifications have not been incorporated into ARCP 31.

3. *Comparison to Discovery by Interrogatories and to Depositions Upon Oral Examination.* Although they share certain common characteristics, the discovery technique of depositions upon written questions, which is governed by Ariz. R. Civ. P. 31, should be distinguished from depositions upon oral examination under Ariz. R. Civ. P. 30 and from interrogatories propounded under Ariz. R. Civ. P. 33.

While both interrogatories under Ariz. R. Civ. P. 33 and depositions under Ariz. R. Civ. P. 31 entail propounding written questions to a person or entity possessed of relevant factual information, interrogatories may only be directed to a party, while Rule 31 permits the taking of testimony of both parties and witnesses. Moreover, answers to interrogatories under Rule 33 are prepared and served without the involvement of a deposition officer, and lack some degree of spontaneity.

Both Ariz. R. Civ. P. 31 and Ariz. R. Civ. P. 30 contemplate oral responses by the deponent recorded by a court reporter or other deposition officer. Where the deposition is upon written questions under Rule 31, however, the questions to be propounded are known in advance and there is ordinarily no opportunity for oral examination based upon the deponent's responses. The procedure for conducting a Rule 31 deposition is also more cumbersome, and the testimony may not be taken until the time periods for filing cross questions, and perhaps redirect and recross questions, have elapsed, unless the Court orders otherwise.

While depositions upon written questions eliminate the necessity, and concomitant expense, of appearances by counsel, they are generally not regarded as of equal effectiveness as a deposition upon oral examination, particularly in complex cases or where cross-examination is necessary. They are, however, an available and relatively inexpensive device where straightforward and/or uncontested matters must be established of record.

4. *Relationship of Rule 31 Depositions to Rule 30(c) Procedures.* The procedure established by Ariz. R. Civ. P. 31(a), where the initial notice specifies a deposition upon written questions, is quite distinct from the situation where the notice is for a deposition upon oral examination, and another party exercises the option granted by Ariz. R. Civ. P. 30(c) to waive participation and submit written questions. In the latter instance, the questions to be propounded are served upon the noticing party in a sealed envelope for delivery to the deposition officer, who propounds them to the deponent and records the responses.

Where the notice is for a deposition upon written questions under Rule 31, the questions to be propounded must be served with the notice. The notice must identify the deponent and the officer before whom the deposition is to be conducted, but need not designate the date, time or location of the deposition. It is contemplated that those specifics will be established after the cross, redirect and recross questions, if any, have been submitted.

5. *Procedure for Conducting Deposition on Written Questions.* A party desiring to take a deposition upon written questions must serve the questions to be propounded on other parties to the action, together with a notice specifying the person or entity to be deposed and the officer before whom the deposition is to be conducted. Any party who is served with a notice for a deposition upon written questions may serve cross questions within thirty (30) days, and redirect questions may be served by the noticing party within ten (10) days thereafter. Recross questions are authorized and must be served within ten (10) days after service of redirect questions. During this stage of the proceedings, a party may reframe the questions previously submitted if objection is made to them. Ariz. R. Civ. P. 31(a) authorizes the Court to enlarge or shorten the time for service of cross questions, redirect questions and recross questions "for cause shown."

Once these procedures have been completed, the party noticing the deposition is to deliver to the officer before whom it is to be conducted a copy of the notice of the deposition and copies of all questions served by the parties. That officer then convenes the deposition, propounds to the deponent the written questions that have been served, and records the testimony in the manner provided by Ariz. R. Civ. P. 30(c), (e) and (f).

6. *Disposition of Objections.* Ariz. R. Civ. P. 32(d)(3)(C) provides that: "Objections to the form of written questions submitted under Rule 31 are waived unless served in writing upon the party propounding them within the time allowed for serving the succeeding cross and within 5 days after service of the last questions authorized."

There is no specific provision in the Rules for a hearing on such objections and the Court would not normally rule upon them in advance of introduction of the deposition at the trial. Where the objection goes beyond the form of the question propounded, and would be rendered moot if not determined before the deposition, *i.e.*, an objection based upon a claim of privilege, the issue should be presented to the Court by a motion for a protective order.

7. *Applicability of Presumptive Limits on Depositions.* As discussed in the *Authors' Comments* to Ariz. R. Civ. P. 30, the discovery and court reform amendments adopted by the Arizona Supreme Court, effective July 1, 1992, imposed presumptive limits on the use of the authorized discovery devices, and particularly depositions. The amendments limited the depositions which could be conducted as of right to those of the parties, those of disclosed expert witnesses, and those of custodians of records (but only to secure production of documents and to establish evidentiary foundation), and provided that depositions that are conducted are not to exceed four (4) hours in length, absent an agreement of the parties or leave of Court. The amendments which imposed those limitations on the conduct of depositions were made, however, only to Ariz. R. Civ. P. 30, and no corresponding limiting amendment was made to Rule 31, leaving the question whether the limits apply to depositions conducted upon written questions.

The Committee Notes to the amendments do not specifically address the question, and there are cogent arguments that can be made on either side of the issue. On the one hand, the intent of the amendments was to limit the unfettered conduct of discovery depositions. Exempting depositions upon written questions from the limitations imposed may simply provide an unintended opportunity for evading them. For example, the conduct of a deposition of a party (permitted as of right under the amendments) could conceivably be used as a device for evading the limitation imposed by Ariz. R. Civ. P. 33.1 on the number of interrogatories that may be propounded. On the other hand, depositions upon written questions were never cited as a discovery device that had been subject to abuse, and the four (4) hour presumptive length limitation might prove difficult to administer and monitor in the case of such depositions. The issue may, in the final analysis, prove academic, as the limited utility of such depositions operates naturally to limit abuses of them.

Rule 32. Use of depositions in court proceedings

(a) Use of Depositions. At the trial or at any hearing, any part or all of a deposition, so far as admissible under the rules of evidence applied as though the witness were then present and testifying, may be used against any party who was present or represented at the taking of the deposition or who had reasonable notice thereof, and had an opportunity and similar motive to develop the testimony by direct, cross, or redirect examination. The party who seeks admission of the testimony by deposition may do so without proof of the deponent's unavailability to testify at trial. Nothing contained in this Rule shall be construed to limit, in any way, the right of any party to call the deposed witness to testify in person at trial.

If only part of a deposition is offered in evidence by a party, the court may require the offeror to introduce contemporaneously any other part which ought in fairness to be considered together with the part introduced.

Except as provided in Rule 56(e), the use of the deposition transcript may be supplemented with contemporaneously recorded audio and video files that may be synchronized to the deposition transcript, if any.

Substitution of parties pursuant to Rule 25 does not affect the right to use depositions previously taken; and, when an action has been brought in any court of the United States or of any state, and another action involving the same subject matter is afterward brought between the same parties or their representatives or successors in interest, all depositions lawfully taken and duly filed in the former action may be used in the latter as if originally taken therefor. A deposition previously taken may also be used as permitted by the Arizona Rules of Evidence.

Amended July 17, 1970, effective Nov. 1, 1970; July 6, 1983, effective Sept. 7, 1983; Sept. 15, 1987, effective Nov. 15, 1987; July 9, 1991, effective Oct. 1, 1991; July 30, 1991, effective Oct. 1, 1991; Oct. 3, 1994, effective Dec. 1, 1994; Oct. 9, 1996, effective Dec. 1, 1996; Sept. 18, 2006, effective Jan. 1, 2007

(b) Objections to Admissibility. Subject to the provisions of Rule 28(b) and subdivision (d)(3) of this rule, objection may be made at the trial or hearing to receiving in evidence any deposition or part thereof for any reason which would require the exclusion of the evidence if the witness were then present and testifying.

Amended March 26, 1963, effective June 1, 1963; July 17, 1970, effective Nov. 1, 1970; Oct. 9, 1996, effective Dec. 1, 1996.

(c) Form of Presentation. A party offering deposition testimony may offer it in the form permitted by Rules 30(b)(4) and 30(c). If deposition testimony is offered in any form for any purpose, the offering party shall provide the court with a transcript of the portions offered. In cases tried before a jury, if deposition testimony is to be offered for purposes other than impeachment and is available in non-stenographic form, it shall be presented to the jury in that form unless the court for good cause orders otherwise.

Added Oct. 9, 1996, effective Dec. 1, 1996.

(d) Effect of Errors and Irregularities in Depositions.

(1) *As to Notice.* All errors and irregularities in the notice for taking a deposition are waived unless written objection is promptly served upon the party giving the notice.

(2) *As to Disqualification of Officer.* Objection to taking a deposition because of disqualification of the officer before whom it is to be taken is waived unless made before the taking of the deposition begins or as soon thereafter as the disqualification becomes known or could be discovered with reasonable diligence.

(3) *As to Taking of Deposition.*

(A) Objections to the competency of a witness or to the competency, relevancy, or materiality of testimony are not waived by failure to make them before or during the taking of the deposition, unless the ground of the objection is one which might have been obviated or removed if presented at that time.

(B) Errors and irregularities occurring at the oral examination in the manner of taking the deposition, in the form of the questions or answers, in the oath or affirmation, or in the conduct of parties, and errors of any kind which might be obviated, removed, or cured if promptly presented, are waived unless seasonable objection thereto is made at the taking of the deposition.

(C) Objections to the form of written questions submitted under Rule 31 are waived unless served in writing upon the party propounding them within the time allowed for serving the succeeding cross or other questions and within 5 days after service of the last questions authorized.

(D) Objections to the form of the question or responsiveness of the answer shall be concise, and shall not suggest answers to the witness. No specification of the defect in the form of the question or the answer shall be stated unless requested by the party propounding the question. Argumentative interruptions shall not be permitted.

(E) Continuous and unwarranted off the record conferences between the deponent and counsel following the propounding of questions and prior to the answer or at any time during the deposition are prohibited. This conduct is subject to the proscriptions of Rule 32(d)(3)(D) and the sanctions prescribed in Rule 37.

(4) *As to Completion and Return of Deposition.* Errors and irregularities in the manner in which the testimony is transcribed or the deposition is prepared, signed, certified, sealed, indorsed, transmitted, filed, or otherwise dealt with by the officer under Rules 30 and 31 are waived unless a motion to suppress the deposition or some part thereof is made with reasonable promptness after such defect is, or with due diligence might have been, ascertained.

Amended July 17, 1970, effective Nov. 1, 1970; Dec. 20, 1991, effective July 1, 1992; Oct. 9, 1996, effective Dec. 1, 1996.

2004 COURT COMMENT

The verbatim reading of deposition transcripts at trial can be a tedious exercise for the jury that greatly reduces juror comprehension and attention. Deposition summaries are an effective means of giving a jury the information contained in deposition transcripts in an understandable and abbreviated form. Rule 1006, Rules of Evidence, already encourages the use of summaries of documents that "cannot be conveniently examined in court."

Parties are encouraged to agree upon and use a concise deposition summary instead of a verbatim reading of a deposition transcript. When considered necessary for jury comprehension or an efficient trial, the court may require the use of deposition summaries. *See* Rule 611, Arizona Rules of Evidence. Similarly, the court may require the editing of videotaped depositions to fairly and succinctly include only the important portions of the proceedings. Additionally, the introduction of important portions of deposition transcripts, which allows direct introduction of key questions and answers, is permitted.

STATE BAR COMMITTEE NOTES

1970 Amendments

Rule 32: The 1970 revision collects in one place the materials on use of depositions in court proceedings, which had previously been in Rule 26(d), (e), and (f), putting them together with what had previously been in Rule 32 on the effect of errors and irregularities in depositions. The change in Rule 32(a) making clear that the deposition shall be admissible so far as the testimony would be permitted if the witness were then present and testifying, accords with *Skok v. City of Glendale*, 3 Ariz. App. 254, 413 P.2d 585, 588 (1966), which holds that insofar as admissibility may be affected by changing events, it is the status of the matter at trial which is controlling. A deposition may be read even though the party is in court, *Southern Pac. Co. v. Cavallo*, 84 Ariz. 24, 323 P.2d 1 (1958), though it will not be reversible error if in all the circumstances the trial court directs live testimony. *Han v. Horwitz*, 2 Ariz. App. 245, 407 P.2d 786 (1965). The deposition is admissible to challenge inconsistent statements. *Bogard G.M.C. Co. v. Henley*, 92 Ariz. 107, 374 P.2d 660 (1962).

Use of depositions of witnesses, as distinguished from parties, remains somewhat more restricted, and the requirements of § 32(a)(3) must be met. If a deposition is offered under that provision, any necessary record must be made in the trial court to show the foundation, as, for example, absence; *Skok v. City of*

Glendale, 3 Ariz. App. 254, 413 P.2d 585, 589 (1966); *Slow Development Co. v. Coulter*, 88 Ariz. 122, 130, 353 P.2d 890, 895 (1960) (foundation held adequate though not detailed in opinion). A claim of self-incrimination at trial has been held an "exceptional circumstance" warranting use of a deposition, *Union Bank v. Safanie*, 5 Ariz. App. 342, 427 P.2d 146, 153 (1967).

In Sec. 32(a)(4) a somewhat greater measure of discretion in application is suggested by substituting, in lieu of "relevant" in the pre-1970 rule equivalent Sec. 26(d)(4), the test of fairness. See McCormick on Evidence, § 56, and Udall on Evidence, § 11, pp. 21–23.

Sec. 32(d)(3)(B) as to waiver of certain objections not made at the taking of the deposition has been held not to bar an objection to clearly inadmissible opinion evidence where the offeror offers the testimony not against the deponent party, but against a third party, and where the deponent is readily available to testify; *Finn v. J. H. Rose Truck Lines*, 1 Ariz. App. 27, 398 P.2d 935, 941 (1965). Nothing in the new rule affects any of the Arizona interpretations mentioned in this Note.

1991 Amendments

[Rule 32(d)(3)] The changes in Rule 32(d)(3) are again intended to reflect the requirement of professional conduct on the part of counsel engaged in the deposition process. The intent of this rule is that, absent a stipulation to the contrary, objections at depositions will be limited to those matters involving privilege against disclosure of information or to the form of the question or answer. If the question or answer is such that a rephrasing of either would make an objection to the form thereof inappropriate at trial, the party propounding the question may request specification of the defect in the form of the question. The party objecting must then specify the basis of the objection. Rule 32(d)(3)(D) was not intended to be all-inclusive of the conduct at depositions which could lead to sanctions under Rule 26(f). By way of example, continuous unwarranted conferences between counsel and the deponent following the propounding of questions and prior to the answer, could also be the kind of conduct prescribed by Rule 32(d)(3)(D) and Rule 26(f).

Note to 1991 Amendments amended May 30, 1996, effective Dec. 1, 1996.

COURT COMMENT

1991 Amendments

The above rule change was part of a comprehensive set of rule revisions proposed by the Special Bar Committee to Study Civil Litigation Abuse, Cost and Delay, which was specifically charged in March, 1990 with the task of proposing rules to reduce discovery abuse and to make the judicial system in Arizona more efficient, expeditious, and accessible to the people.

For more complete background information on the rule changes proposed by the Committee, see Court Comment to Rule 26.1.

AUTHORS' COMMENTS

Analysis

1. Scope and Purpose of Rule.
2. Comparison With Federal Rule.
3. Use of Depositions at Trial.
4. Offer of Additional Portions of Deposition.
5. Depositions Subject to Technical Defects.
6. Depositions Taken in Other Actions.

7. Conduct at Deposition; Objections to Questions.

1. *Scope and Purpose of Rule.* The principal focus of Ariz. R. Civ. P. 32 is on the circumstances under which a deposition may be used as evidence at the trial or other evidentiary proceeding in an action in which it is taken. A deposition is still primarily a discovery device, rather than a dress rehearsal for trial, and the fact that a party has the right to take a deposition does not mean that the deposition may be used as evidence. *Skok v. City of Glendale*, 3 Ariz. App. 254, 413 P.2d 585 (1966). If the conditions for evidentiary use of depositions established by Rule 32 and/or the Arizona Rules of Evidence are satisfied, however, depositions are freely admissible. *Edwards v. Van Voorhis*, 11 Ariz. App. 216, 463 P.2d 111 (Div. 1 1970).

2. *Comparison With Federal Rule.* There are now significant differences between the provisions of ARCP 32 and FRCP 32, as a consequence of the 1993 amendments to the Federal Rule and the 1994 amendments to the Arizona Rule.

FRCP 32(a)(3) permits the use of a deposition where the Court finds the witness is more than one hundred (100) miles from the place of trial. The Federal Rules of Civil Procedure do not have a rule that corresponds to ARCP 32(d)(3)(D) and (E), which provide that objections made at a deposition are not to suggest answers to the witness and which prohibit continuous and unwarranted conferences off the record between the deponent and counsel. The provision in the Federal Rules of Civil Procedure which roughly corresponds to the provisions of ARCP 32(d)(3)(D) and (E), regulating conduct of counsel and parties at depositions, is FRCP 30(d)(1).

The 1994 amendments to ARCP 32(a) eliminated the three subparts of the prior Rule which had set forth the specific conditions under which deposition testimony could be used at the trial of the matter. These subparts remain in the Federal Rule. ARCP 32(a) now simply provides that a deposition may be used against any party who was present at the taking of the deposition, or who had reasonable notice of it, and who had an opportunity and similar motive to develop the testimony by direct, cross or redirect examination. It is not necessary for the party offering the deposition testimony to show that the deponent is unavailable to testify. Any other party, however, may call the deponent to testify in person.

In 2007, the language of FRCP 32 was amended as part of the general restyling of the Federal Rules of Civil Procedure to make the Federal Rules more easily understood and to make style and terminology consistent throughout the Federal Rules of Civil

Procedure. Those stylistic modifications have not been incorporated into ARCP 32.

As a consequence of the 2009 amendments to FRCP 32, the times set in the former FRCP 32 for taking a deposition were revised. The time set in ARCP 32 for taking a deposition has not been similarly revised.

3. *Use of Depositions at Trial.* The 1994 amendments to Ariz. R. Civ. P. 32(a) eliminated the three subparts of the prior Rule which had set forth the specific conditions under which deposition testimony could be used at the trial of the matter. The Rule, as amended, now simply provides that a deposition may be used against any party who was present at the taking of the deposition, or who had reasonable notice of it, and who had an opportunity and similar motive to develop the testimony by direct, cross or redirect examination. It is no longer necessary for the party offering the deposition testimony to show that the deponent is unavailable to testify. Any other party, however, may call the deponent to testify in person.

The 1996 amendments adopted Ariz. R. Civ. P. 32(c) which in effect establishes a preference for presenting deposition testimony at jury trials in nonstenographic form, where the testimony is offered for purposes other than impeachment. Under the Rule, if a nonstenographic recording of the deposition is available, the testimony is to be offered in that form, unless the court directs otherwise. Regardless of the form in which, or the purpose for which, it is offered, when a party offers deposition testimony, the Court must be provided with a transcript of the portions offered.

A 1999 amendment to former Rule XVIII of the now abrogated Uniform Rules of Practice of the Superior Court permitted the use of deposition transcripts that are reduced in size, consisting of not more than four pages of text printed on one 8½ by 11 inch page—so-called "condensed transcripts." This provision is now contained in Rule 91(h)(2) of the Rules of the Arizona Supreme Court.

In 2004, the Supreme Court approved the addition of a Comment to the Rule, which encourages parties to agree upon and read to the jury concise summaries of depositions rather than employ the verbatim reading of transcripts. The Comment also notes that the trial court may require the use of such deposition summaries, and may also require the editing of videotaped depositions so that only the important portions are presented.

4. *Offer of Additional Portions of Deposition.* The 1994 amendments slightly reworded the provisions of former Ariz. R. Civ. P. 32(a)(4) and made it simply a separate paragraph of the Rule. It now provides that, if only a portion of a deposition is offered, the Court may require the offering party to introduce any other por-

tions that ought to be considered together with the portion initially offered. *See Ott v. Samaritan Health Service*, 127 Ariz. 485, 622 P.2d 44 (Ct. App. Div. 1 1980). As amended, the Rule specifies that any additional portions that the Court requires be introduced are to be introduced contemporaneously with the initial portion.

5. *Depositions Subject to Technical Defects.* The clear intent of Ariz. R. Civ. P. 32(d) is to insure that technical defects in deposition procedures are raised promptly, while there is an opportunity to cure them. Thus, where a party fails to move to suppress a deposition which has not been properly signed, before it is considered on a motion for summary judgment, that operates as a waiver of the irregularity. *Brooker v. Hunter*, 22 Ariz. App. 510, 528 P.2d 1269 (Div. 1 1974), opinion approved of, 111 Ariz. 578, 535 P.2d 1051 (1975). A stipulation that such a deposition may only be used at trial permits a court to consider it on a motion for summary judgment. *Brooker v. Hunter*, 22 Ariz. App. 510, 528 P.2d 1269 (Div. 1 1974), opinion approved of, 111 Ariz. 578, 535 P.2d 1051 (1975).

6. *Depositions Taken in Other Actions.* The deposition of a witness taken in another proceeding is, technically speaking, hearsay. Under the final paragraph of Ariz. R. Civ. P. 32(a), such a deposition may nevertheless be used if it was taken in a prior action involving the same subject matter between the same parties or their representatives or predecessors in interest.

The final sentence of Rule 32(a), additionally, specifies that a previously taken deposition may be used as permitted by the Arizona Rules of Evidence.

Contemporaneously with the adoption of the 1994 amendments to Rule 32(a), amendments were also adopted to Ariz. R. Evid. 803 and 804. The "former testimony" exception to the hearsay rule contained in former Ariz. R. Evid. 804(b)(1), which required that the declarant be "unavailable," was reworded and limited to criminal cases. Ariz. R. Evid. 803(25) was adopted, which establishes a "former testimony" exception to the hearsay rule in civil ("non-criminal") cases, and which does not require a showing that the declarant-deponent is "unavailable." All that is required is that the party against whom the former testimony is offered, or a predecessor in interest, had an opportunity and similar motive to develop the former testimony through direct, cross or redirect examination.

7. *Conduct at Deposition; Objections to Questions.* Testimony at a deposition is normally taken subject to objections stated on the record, and objections to the form of the questions or answers are waived unless stated at the time. Ariz. R. Civ. P. 32(d)(3)(B). As part of the discovery and court reform amendments adopted ef-

fective July 1, 1992, Ariz. R. Civ. P. 32(d)(3)(D) and (E) were added to regulate the conduct of attorneys in making objections at depositions. Objections to form are to be concise and are not to suggest answers to the witness. The defect in the form of the question or answer is not to be specified unless the party propounding the question so requests. Continuous and unwarranted conferences off the record between the deponent and counsel, particularly those conducted following a question and before an answer is given, are prohibited and subject to sanctions.

Rule 33. Interrogatories to parties

(a) Availability; Procedures for Use. Any party may serve upon any other party written interrogatories to be answered by the party served or, if the party served is a public or private corporation or a partnership or association of governmental agency, by any officer or agent, who shall furnish such information as is available to the party. Interrogatories may, without leave of court, be served upon the plaintiff after commencement of the action and upon any other party with or after service of the summons and complaint upon that party.

Each interrogatory shall be answered separately and fully in writing under oath, unless it is objected to, in which event the reasons for objection shall be stated in lieu of an answer. The answers are to be signed by the person making them, and the objections signed by the attorney making them. The party upon whom the interrogatories have been served shall serve a copy of the answers, and objections if any, within 40 days after the service of the interrogatories, except that a defendant may serve answers or objections within 60 days after service of the summons and complaint upon that defendant, or execution of a waiver of service, by that defendant. The court may allow a shorter or longer time. The party submitting the interrogatories may move for an order under Rule 37(a) with respect to any objection to or other failure to answer an interrogatory.

Amended July 17, 1970, effective Nov. 1, 1970; Dec. 20, 1991, effective July 1, 1992; Oct. 9, 1996, effective Dec. 1, 1996.

(b) Scope; Use at Trial. Interrogatories may relate to any matters which can be inquired into under Rule 26(b), and the answers may be used to the extent permitted by the rules of evidence.

An interrogatory otherwise proper is not necessarily objectionable merely because an answer to the interrogatory involves an opinion or contention that relates to fact or the application of law to fact, but the court may order that such an interrogatory need not be answered until after designated discovery has been completed or until a pretrial conference or other later time.

Amended July 17, 1970, effective Nov. 1, 1970.

(c) Option to Produce Business Records. Where the answer to an interrogatory may be derived or ascertained from the business records, including electronically stored information, of the party upon whom the interrogatory has been served or from an examination, audit or inspection of such business records, including a compilation, abstract or summary thereof, and the burden of deriving or ascertaining the answer is substantially the same for the party serving the interrogatory as for the party served, it is a sufficient answer to such interrogatory to specify the records from which the answer may be derived or ascertained and to afford to the party serving the interrogatory reasonable opportunity to examine, audit or inspect such records and to make copies, compilations, abstracts or summaries. A specification shall be in sufficient detail to permit the interrogating party to locate and to identify, as readily as can the party served, the records from which the answer may be derived or ascertained.

Amended July 17, 1970, effective Nov. 1, 1970; July 6, 1983, effective Sept. 7, 1983; September 5, 2007, effective January 1, 2008.

STATE BAR COMMITTEE NOTES

1970 Amendments

Rule 33: This Rule changes previous practice in numerous particulars.

Rule 33(a): This section permits service of interrogatories by the defendant immediately upon receipt of the complaint, and also permits service of interrogatories with the complaint. Abuse is avoided by extending the time to answer—all answer time is extended to thirty days, and a defendant need not respond at all until 45 days after completion of service of the summons and complaint upon him. In Arizona there has been no need felt for service of interrogatories with the complaint, so it is assumed that if need be, protective orders will be liberally given.

The practice prior to this amendment required a party objecting to an interrogatory to take his objection to court, thus forcing a considerable consumption of court time with resultant expense. The amendment reverses this procedure, providing that the objection should be stated with the answer. The inquiring party may then take the matter to court if he wishes. This is meant to encourage practical adjustments among the parties, but not to frustrate interrogatories by captious objections. Hence the Rule emphasizes by express reference that the party submitting the interrogatories may ask for full sanctions, with costs, under Rule 37(a) with respect to failures to answer or objections. The uniform interrogatories presently in use in Arizona should go far to avoid objections. The changes are similar in approach to those adopted in California in 1961. See Calif. Code Civ. Proc. § 2030(a).

Rule 33(b): This section provides that an interrogatory is not necessarily objectionable because it relates to opinion as well as fact. This does not change the Arizona rule, *State ex rel. Willey v. Whitman*, 91 Ariz. 120, 125, 370 P.2d 273, 277 (1962) though it does alter practice in some other parts of the country. To prevent abuse, the court may defer answers where the responding party cannot reasonably be expected to be prepared to respond on a mixed matter of fact and opinion, as with an expert; but this is not intended to delay discovery as it exists under present Arizona practice, nor to limit the provisions as to expert discovery in Rule 26.

Rule 33(c): This is a new subdivision, adapted from Calif. Code Civ. Proc. § 2030(c), relating especially to interrogatories which require a party to engage in burdensome or expensive research into his own business records in order to give an answer. This subdivision gives the party an option to make the records available and places the burden of research on the party who seeks the information. The interrogating party is protected against abusive use of this provision through the requirement that the burden of ascertaining the answer be substantially the same for both sides. A respondent may not impose on an interrogating party a mass of records as to which research is feasible only for one familiar with the records. At the same time, the respondent unable to invoke this subdivision still has the protection available to him under new Rule 26(c) against oppressive or unduly burdensome or expensive interrogatories. And even when the respondent successfully invokes the subdivision, the court is not deprived of its usual power, in appropriate cases, to require that the interrogating party reimburse the respondent for the expense of assembling his records and making them intelligible.

1983 Amendment

[Rule 33(c)] A party who is permitted by the terms of this subdivision to offer records for inspection in lieu of answering an interrogatory should offer them in a manner that permits the same direct and economical access that is available to the party. If the information sought exists in the form of compilations, abstracts or summaries then available to the responding party, those should be made available to the interrogating party. The final sentence is added to make it clear that a responding party has the duty to specify by category and location, the records from which answers to interrogatories can be derived or ascertained.

AUTHORS' COMMENTS

Analysis

1. *Scope and Purpose of Rule.* Ariz. R. Civ. P. 33 sets forth the procedure by which one party to an action may request any other party to answer specific written questions regarding such party's claims or defenses. The other party need not be, but generally is, an adverse party. Interrogatories under Rule 33 were intended to be a relatively inexpensive method for the parties to obtain information and, hopefully, narrow the issues for trial. They became, to varying degrees, however, subject to the abuse of propounding multiple sets of voluminous interrogatories. This phenomenon led to the imposition of presumptive limits on their use, as part of

the discovery and court reform amendments which became effective July 1, 1992.

2. *Comparison With Federal Rule.* There are now significant differences between ARCP 33 and FRCP 33, as a consequence of the 1992 Arizona court and discovery reform amendments and the 1993 amendments to the Federal Rules of Civil Procedure.

Under amended ARCP 33(a), answers and/or objections to interrogatories must be served within forty (40) days after service of the interrogatories, unless they are served with or shortly after service of the summons and complaint, in which event the defendant may serve answers and/or objections within sixty (60) days after service of the summons and complaint, or after that defendant executes a waiver of service. Under FRCP 33(a), as amended, the time period for responding and/or objecting to interrogatories is thirty (30) days. The provision which formerly authorized a longer period to respond to interrogatories served with or shortly after service of the summons and complaint was deleted, as interrogatories may now not be served until after conduct of the discovery planning conference required by FRCP 26(f).

FRCP 33(a), as amended, provides that, without leave of court or a written stipulation, a party may not serve upon any other party more than twenty-five (25) interrogatories, including all discrete subparagraphs. The provision in the Arizona Rules of Civil Procedure that imposes presumptive limits on the number of interrogatories that can be propounded, which are different, is ARCP 33.1, discussed *infra*.

FRCP 33(b) provides that, where an objection is made to an interrogatory, the objecting party is to answer the interrogatory to the extent that it is not objectionable, that all grounds for objection must be stated with specificity, and that any ground not stated is waived. There is no corresponding provision in the Arizona Rules of Civil Procedure. ARCP 33(b) roughly corresponds to FRCP 33(c). ARCP 33(c), which provides for the option of producing business records under specified circumstances, is similar to FRCP 33(d).

In 2007, the language of FRCP 33 was amended as part of the general restyling of the Federal Rules of Civil Procedure to make the Federal Rules more easily understood and to make style and terminology consistent throughout the Federal Rules of Civil Procedure. Those stylistic modifications have not been incorporated into ARCP 33.

3. *Scope of Discovery by Interrogatory.* The permissible scope of inquiry by means of interrogatories is that defined by Ariz. R. Civ. P. 26(b). It is proper to seek either facts or opinions, and the names and addresses of potential witnesses. *State ex rel. Willey v.*

Whitman, 91 Ariz. 120, 370 P.2d 273 (1962). An interrogatory which requires the responding party to predict the actual testimony of a witness, however, is objectionable. *Sundt v. Farley*, 12 Ariz. App. 346, 470 P.2d 494 (Div. 2 1970).

4. *Uniform v. Non-Uniform Interrogatories.* In Arizona, interrogatories may be either "uniform interrogatories" or "non-uniform interrogatories." As characterized by Ariz. R. Civ. P. 33.1(f), uniform interrogatories are those which have been "approved for use as a standard or guide in preparation by counsel of interrogatories. . . ." Uniform interrogatories, however, are not necessarily appropriate for and should not be automatically used in all cases.

The practitioner should use only those uniform interrogatories which fit the particular case. The Appendix of Forms following Ariz. R. Civ. P. 84 now contains the approved set of Uniform Personal Injury Interrogatories, Contract Litigation Interrogatories, and Domestic Relations Interrogatories, and three sets of Uniform Interrogatories for Use in Medical Malpractice Cases. Many of these Uniform Interrogatories were updated and amended effective January 1, 2009. A 2009 amendment to Rule 33.1 also makes clear that the categories or titles assigned to sets of uniform interrogatories is not intended to limit their use to the corresponding types of cases, and that they are presumptively valid if the information sought is discoverable.

Non-uniform interrogatories, on the other hand, are interrogatories which have been written especially for a particular case. A particular set of interrogatories propounded may include both uniform and non-uniform interrogatories.

5. *Presumptive Limits on Number of Interrogatories.* The court and discovery reform amendments adopted by the Supreme Court, effective July 1, 1992, severely limited the use of interrogatories as a discovery device. Ariz. R. Civ. P. 33.1(a) provides that, absent agreement or an order of court, a party may not serve upon any other party more than forty (40) interrogatories, which may be any combination of uniform and non-uniform interrogatories. See *Authors' Comments* to Ariz. R. Civ. P. 33.1. The time for answering interrogatories was also extended.

6. *Use of Interrogatory Responses at Trial.* Ariz. R. Civ. P. 33(b) provides that answers to interrogatories "may be used [at trial] to the extent permitted by the rules of evidence." When offered as substantive evidence by the answering party, they are hearsay. When offered by the answering party's opponent, however, they should be admissible as an admission under Ariz. R. Evid. 801(d)(2). *Barrett v. Melton*, 112 Ariz. 605, 545 P.2d 421 (1976); *Gordon v. Liguori*, 182 Ariz. 232, 895 P.2d 523 (Ct. App. Div. 1 1995). That may not be the case, however, where the responses

are more in the nature of alternative or contingent pleadings than admissions of fact. *Gordon v. Liguori*, 182 Ariz. 232, 895 P.2d 523 (Ct. App. Div. 1 1995).

7. *Service of Interrogatories.* The procedure for serving interrogatories varies according to whether the interrogatories being propounded are uniform interrogatories or non-uniform interrogatories. In the case of non-uniform interrogatories, under Ariz. R. Civ. P. 33.1(e), a party propounding such interrogatories is to serve the original and one copy upon the party to whom they are propounded, and is to serve a copy on all other parties to the action. An amendment to Ariz. R. Civ. P. 5(g), which became effective June 1, 1993, directs that "discovery papers," including interrogatories, answers to interrogatories and notices of service, are no longer to be filed with the Court. In a published Note to that amendment, and to a companion amendment to former Rule XVII, Uniform Rules of Practice of the Superior Court, the Supreme Court noted that there was no longer a need for parties to prepare Notices of Service of Non-Uniform Interrogatories and expressed the hope that parties would discontinue the practice of preparing and exchanging such notices.

In the case where uniform interrogatories are being propounded, Ariz. R. Civ. P. 33.1(f) prescribes that a party propounding uniform interrogatories is to serve a Notice of Service of Uniform Interrogatories upon each other party to the action. The Notice is to identify the party and attorney to whom the interrogatories are directed and specify the number of each uniform interrogatory that is being propounded. The Notice is not to be filed with the Court.

8. *Method for Answering and/or Objecting to Interrogatories.* Ariz. R. Civ. P. 33(a), sets forth the time within which to serve answers and objections to interrogatories.

Answers and objections should be served at the same time. Answers and/or objections must be served within forty (40) days of service of the interrogatories, unless the interrogatories are served with or shortly after the complaint, in which event the defendant may serve answers and/or objections within sixty (60) days after service of the summons and complaint, or the execution by that defendant of a waiver of service.

Objections are waived unless served within the time prescribed. Additional time to answer or object to interrogatories can be secured either by stipulation or motion.

Objections are usually stated in the space provided in the original set of interrogatories for a response, as is required by Ariz. R. Civ. P. 33.1(d). When an objection is made, the party submitting the interrogatories must take the procedural initiative to bring the objection before the Court by a motion to compel discovery.

The responding party need not answer the interrogatories to which an objection was made until ordered to do so by the Court, but has the burden of sustaining the objection. *Hine v. Superior Court In and For Yuma County*, 18 Ariz. App. 568, 504 P.2d 509 (Div. 1 1972). An unjustified objection may result in an order requiring the party whose conduct necessitated judicial intervention to pay expenses to the other party and possibly the award of other sanctions. See, Ariz. R. Civ. P. 37(b).

Answers to interrogatories must be signed by a party, or an officer of a party who has personal knowledge of the matters stated or is otherwise competent to testify thereto. *Johnson By and Through Johnson v. Svidergol*, 157 Ariz. 333, 757 P.2d 609 (Ct. App. Div. 2 1988).

In the case of a public or private corporation, partnership, association or governmental agency, Ariz. R. Civ. P. 33(a) provides that an officer or agent shall furnish the information available to such entity. The in-house counsel for such entity may be its agent and may answer for it.

If a third person is the source of the information set forth in such entity's answers, it may be desirable to identify such person and state that the information is derived from that source.

9. *Service of Interrogatory Responses.* The procedure for providing answers to interrogatories varies, depending upon whether uniform or non-uniform interrogatories have been propounded. In the case of uniform interrogatories, Ariz. R. Civ. P. 33.1(f)(3) requires the answering party to reproduce the text of each interrogatory propounded, insert the answers, serve the original interrogatories and answers on the propounding party, and a copy upon each other party. In the case of non-uniform interrogatories, the answering party inserts answers and/or objections in the space provided, and then serves a copy of the answers upon the propounding party and all other parties. In both cases, the answers are not filed with the court.

The fact that discovery requests and/or responses are not filed does not preclude use of them in connection with motions and other proceedings. *GM Development Corp. v. Community American Mortg. Corp.*, 165 Ariz. 1, 795 P.2d 827 (Ct. App. Div. 1 1990).

10. *Protective Relief From Interrogatories; Necessity.* Ariz. R. Civ. P. 26(c), provides, in part, that a party from whom discovery is sought may move for an order protecting such party from annoyance, embarrassment, oppression or undue burden or expense. Where interrogatories are deemed objectionable, however, the usual practice is simply to state objections within the time period prescribed rather than to seek protective relief from the Court in advance. A motion for protective order may be the preferable op-

tion, however, in the circumstance where a party, without prior agreement or leave of court, serves interrogatories that exceed in number those allowed by Ariz. R. Civ. P. 33.1(a).

11. *Option of Producing Business Records in Response to Interrogatories.* Under Ariz. R. Civ. P. 33(c), the responding party has an option to specify the business records from which answers to particular interrogatories may be derived, if the responding party is willing to give the interrogating party a reasonable opportunity to examine and copy such business records. A 2008 amendment to the Rule specifies that the term "business records" includes electronically stored information.

By its terms, Ariz. R. Civ. P. 33(c) provides the interrogating party with some protection against the improper use of this provision. Specifically, Rule 33(c) can be invoked only under circumstances where the burden of ascertaining the answer is substantially the same for the interrogating party as for the responding party. Thus, a responding party may not exercise this option and produce a volume of business records in lieu of answering the interrogatories where, as a practical matter, only someone familiar with such records is capable of deriving the requested information. If a responding party invokes Rule 33(c) in such a fashion, and the interrogating party disputes the exercise of such option, the interrogating party may file a motion to compel under Ariz. R. Civ. P. 37(a).

12. *Compelling Answers to Interrogatories.* Ariz. R. Civ. P. 37(a) provides that where particular interrogatories are not answered, or the answers are insufficient, or an objection is made, the interrogating party may move to compel. Ariz. R. Civ. P. 37(a)(3) specifies that evasive or cryptic answers are to be treated as a failure to answer. If the motion is granted, the Court should award the moving party its costs and expenses, including attorneys' fees, unless it finds such an award would be unjust. Where a party has failed to respond to an entire set of interrogatories, Ariz. R. Civ. P. 37(f) authorizes the Court to grant even greater sanctions, and specifically those authorized by Ariz. R. Civ. P. 37(b)(2)(A), (B), and (C).

The failure to respond to interrogatories, after being ordered to do so by the Court, is grounds for the imposition of sanctions under Ariz. R. Civ. P. 37(b)(2), including the entry of a default judgment. *Central Cycle Sales, Inc. v. Obert*, 23 Ariz. App. 378, 533 P.2d 686 (Div. 2 1975). A more extensive discussion of the sanctions available under Rule 37 and the procedures for securing them, is found in the *Authors' Comments* to that Rule.

Rule 33.1. Uniform and non-uniform interrogatories; limitations; procedure

(a) Presumptive Limitations. Except as provided in these Rules, a party shall not serve upon any other party more than forty (40) interrogatories, which may be any combination of uniform or non-uniform interrogatories. Any uniform interrogatory and its subparts shall be counted as one interrogatory. Any subpart to a non-uniform interrogatory shall be considered as a separate interrogatory. In the notice of service of uniform interrogatories, a propounding party may specifically limit the scope of the uniform interrogatory to request less information than called for in the uniform interrogatory, such as by requesting information only as to particular persons, events, or issues. Such limiting instructions do not transform the uniform interrogatory into a non-uniform interrogatory.

(b) Stipulations to Serve Additional Interrogatories. If a party believes that good cause exists for the service of more than forty (40) interrogatories upon any other party, that party shall consult with the party upon whom the additional interrogatories would be served and attempt to secure a written stipulation as to the number of additional interrogatories that may be served.

(c) Leave of Court to Serve Additional Interrogatories. If a stipulation permitting the service of additional interrogatories is not secured, a party desiring to serve additional interrogatories may do so only by leave of court. Upon written motion or application showing good cause therefor, the court in its discretion may grant to a party leave to serve a reasonable number of additional interrogatories upon any other party. The party seeking leave to serve additional interrogatories shall have the burden of establishing that the issues presented in the action warrant the service of additional interrogatories, or that such additional interrogatories are a more practical or less burdensome method of obtaining the information sought, or other good cause therefor. No such motion or application may be heard or considered by the court unless accompanied by the proposed additional interrogatories to be served, and by the certification of counsel required by Rule 37(a)(2)(C) of these Rules. The proposed additional interrogatories shall only be attached to the judge's copy of the motion and the copy served on opposing parties.

(d) Spacing. Whenever interrogatories are used, a space sufficient for the answer shall be left immediately below the question. The answering party shall insert the answer in the space below each interrogatory, or if it requires more space, on a separate sheet which restates the question before giving the answer.

(e) Nonuniform Interrogatories. The method of propounding and answering Nonuniform Interrogatories shall be as follows:

(1) A party propounding interrogatories, other than Uniform Interrogatories, shall serve upon the answering party and not the clerk of the court, the original and one copy of the interrogatories and shall serve a copy upon every other party.

(2) The answering party shall, within the time permitted by law, serve upon the propounding party and all other parties one copy of the interrogatories and typewritten answers.

(f) Uniform Interrogatories. The interrogatories set forth in the Appendix of Forms following these Rules are denominated as Uniform Interrogatories, and are approved for use as a standard or guide in preparation by counsel of interrogatories under Rule 33 of these Rules. The use of Uniform Interrogatories shall be governed by Rule 33 of these Rules, and this Rule. The use of Uniform Interrogatories is not mandatory. The interrogatories should serve as a guide only, and may or may not be approved as to either form or substance in a particular case. They are not to be used as a standard set of interrogatories for submission in all cases. Any uniform interrogatory may be used where it fits the legal or factual issues of the particular case, regardless of how the claims are designated. The method of propounding and answering Uniform Interrogatories shall be as follows:

(1) A party propounding Uniform Interrogatories shall serve a copy of a Notice of Service of Uniform Interrogatories upon each other party to the action.

(2) The Notice of Service of Uniform Interrogatories shall contain the names of the party and attorney to whom the request is made and the number only of each uniform interrogatory for which the propounding party requests an answer.

(3) The answering party shall:

(i) reproduce the text of each interrogatory requested and insert the answer below it;

(ii) serve the original upon the propounding party and a copy upon all other parties.

Added Dec. 20, 1991, effective July 1, 1992; amended Oct. 10, 2000, effective Dec. 1, 2000; Sept. 2008, effective Jan. 1, 2009.

STATE BAR COMMITTEE NOTES

1991 Promulgation

It is the Committee's belief that with the mandatory disclosure under Rule 26.1 and the addition of the revised uniform interrogatories for personal injury and wrongful death cases, adequate discovery can take place in the vast majority of civil cases through the use of available uniform interrogatories and the additional non-uniform interrogatories allowed by the rule. As is the case with depositions under Rule 30(a), if there is a reasonable need for additional interrogatories, they may be obtained by stipulation of counsel or by motion to the court on a showing of good cause. Refusing to agree to additional interrogatories which are reasonable and necessary should subject counsel to sanctions under Rule 16(f).

2000 Amendment

As part of the effort to consolidate formerly separate sets of procedural rules into either the Arizona Rules of Civil Procedure or the Rules of the Arizona Supreme Court, former Rule XVII of the Uniform Rules of Practice of the Superior Court was abrogated, and the provisions of former subparts (a), (c) and (d) of that Rule were added to Rule 33.1 as new subparts (d), (e), and (f). In a Court Comment that accompanied the 1993 amendment to former Rules XVII(c) and (d), proscribing the filing of certain documents, and a related amendment to Rule 5(g) of the Arizona Rules of Civil Procedure, it was noted that the amendments were intended to have a positive impact on the Superior Court clerks' offices, making their operations both more efficient and less costly. The Supreme Court observed that, as parties are no longer required to file Notices of Service of Interrogatories, and since all parties receive copies of Nonuniform Interrogatories, there is no longer a need for the preparation of Notices of Service of Nonuniform Interrogatories. The court expressed the hope that, in the interests of conservation and cost-savings, parties would discontinue the practice of preparing and serving those notices.

A technical amendment was made to Rule 33.1(c) to reflect the new location of former Rule IV(g) of the Uniform Rules of Practice of the Superior Court.

Committee Comment to 2009 Amendment

The uniform interrogatories stated in the Appendix of Forms under Rule 84 are for use in any litigation brought under the civil rules, and the category heading for each Form is suggestive in nature and not restrictive; no uniform interrogatory is limited by the nature of the cause of action. Further, in light of Rules 26.1 and 26.2 and their comments, use of the uniform interrogatories is presumptively deemed to not be harassing or overly broad, and their language is presumptively not vague or ambiguous. Disputes arising from the use of the interrogatories should be considered in light of the standard stated in Rule 26(b)(1).

COURT COMMENT

1991 Promulgation

The above rule change was part of a comprehensive set of rule revisions proposed by the Special Bar Committee to Study Civil Litigation Abuse, Cost and Delay, which was specifically charged in March, 1990 with the task of proposing rules to reduce discovery abuse and to make the judicial system in Arizona more efficient, expeditious, and accessible to the people.

For more complete background information on the rule changes proposed by the Committee, see Court Comment to Rule 26.1(a).

AUTHORS' COMMENTS

Analysis

1. Scope and Purpose of Rule.
2. Comparison With Federal Rule.
3. Limitations Imposed on Use of Interrogatories.

4. Procedure for Securing Permission to Exceed Limits.
5. Service of Interrogatories; Filing Not Permitted.
6. Method for Answering and/or Objecting to Interrogatories.
7. Service of Interrogatory Responses; Filing Not Permitted.

1. *Scope and Purpose of Rule.* The discovery and court reform amendments adopted by the Supreme Court, effective July 1, 1992, imposed presumptive limitations on the use of virtually all discovery devices, including interrogatories, which were generally considered to be one of the most overused and abused forms of civil discovery. The limits on the use of interrogatories, and the procedures for securing authority to exceed them, are contained in Ariz. R. Civ. P. 33.1.

2. *Comparison With Federal Rule.* The Federal Rules of Civil Procedure contain no provision which directly corresponds to ARCP 33.1, in its entirety. Amended FRCP 33(a) does impose, however, presumptive limitations on the number of interrogatories that can be propounded in an action.

3. *Limitations Imposed on Use of Interrogatories.* Ariz. R. Civ. P. 33.1(a) provides that a party is not to serve on any other party more than forty (40) interrogatories, which may be any combination of uniform or non-uniform interrogatories. A *uniform interrogatory* together with its subparts is counted as one interrogatory. Any subpart of a *non-uniform interrogatory*, however, is considered a separate interrogatory. A notice of service of a uniform interrogatory, however, may limit the scope of information sought and that does not operate to transform it into a non-uniform interrogatory.

4. *Procedure for Securing Permission to Exceed Limits.* If a party believes that there is good cause to serve more than forty (40) interrogatories upon another party, that party must first consult with the party on whom they are to be served and attempt to secure a written stipulation as to the number of additional interrogatories that may be served. Ariz. R. Civ. P. 33.1(b). If such a stipulation cannot be secured, the party must then seek leave of court to serve the additional interrogatories, and has the burden of establishing that the issues in the action warrant the use of additional interrogatories, or that the additional interrogatories are a more practical or less burdensome method of obtaining the information sought, or other good cause. Ariz. R. Civ. P. 33.1(c).

Any motion or application to the Court for leave to serve additional interrogatories must be accompanied by the certification of counsel required by Ariz. R. Civ. P. 26(g) and 37(a)(2)(C), and by the proposed additional interrogatories to be served. The proposed additional interrogatories are to be attached only to the judge's copy of the motion or application and to the copy served on other parties to the action.

5. *Service of Interrogatories; Filing Not Permitted.* The procedure for serving interrogatories varies according to whether the interrogatories being propounded are uniform interrogatories or non-uniform interrogatories. In the case of non-uniform interrogatories, under Ariz. R. Civ. P. 33.1(e), a party propounding such interrogatories is to serve the original and one copy upon the party to whom they are propounded, and is to serve a copy on all other parties to the action.

In the case where uniform interrogatories are being propounded, Ariz. R. Civ. P. 33.1(f) prescribes that a party propounding uniform interrogatories is to serve a Notice of Service of Uniform Interrogatories upon each other party to the action. The Notice is to identify the party and attorney to whom the interrogatories are directed and specify the number of each uniform interrogatory that is being propounded. A notice of service of a uniform interrogatory may limit the scope of information sought and that does not operate to transform it into a non-uniform interrogatory.

The notice of service of non-uniform interrogatories is not filed with the court. An amendment to Ariz. R. Civ. P. 5(g), which became effective June 1, 1993, directs that "discovery papers," including interrogatories, answers to interrogatories and notices of service, are no longer to be filed with the Court. In a published Note to that amendment, and to a companion amendment to former Rule XVII, Uniform Rules of Practice of the Superior Court, the Supreme Court noted that there was no longer a need for parties to prepare Notices of Service of Non-Uniform Interrogatories and expressed the hope that parties would discontinue the practice of preparing and exchanging such notices.

6. *Method for Answering and/or Objecting to Interrogatories.* Ariz. R. Civ. P. 33(a), sets forth the time within which to serve answers and objections to interrogatories. Answers and objections should be served at the same time. Answers and/or objections must be served within forty (40) days of service of the interrogatories, unless the interrogatories are served with or shortly after the complaint, in which event the defendant may serve answers and/or objections within sixty (60) days after service of the summons and complaint, or the execution by that defendant of a waiver of service. Objections are waived unless served within the time prescribed. Additional time to answer or object to interrogatories can be secured either by stipulation or motion.

The procedure for providing answers to interrogatories varies, depending upon whether uniform or non-uniform interrogatories have been propounded. In the case of uniform interrogatories, Ariz. R. Civ. P. 33.1(f)(3) requires the answering party to reproduce the text of each interrogatory propounded, insert the answers, serve the original interrogatories and answers on the propounding party, and a copy upon each other party. In the case of non-uniform interrogatories, the original is served upon the answering party, who must insert answers and/or objections in the space provided, and serve a copy of the answers upon the propounding party and all other parties. Objections are usually stated in the space provided in the original set of interrogatories for a response, as is required by Ariz. R. Civ. P. 33.1(d).

Objections are usually stated in the space provided in the original set of interrogatories for a response, as is required by Ariz. R. Civ. P. 33.1(d). When an objection is made, the party submitting the interrogatories must take the procedural initiative to bring the objection before the Court by a motion to compel discovery. The responding party need not answer the interrogatories to which an objection was made until ordered to do so by the Court, but has the burden of sustaining the objection. *Hine v. Superior Court In and For Yuma County*, 18 Ariz. App. 568, 504 P.2d 509 (Div. 1 1972). An unjustified objection may result in an order requiring the party whose conduct necessitated judicial intervention to pay expenses to the other party and possibly the award of other sanctions. *See*, Ariz. R. Civ. P. 37(b).

Answers to interrogatories must be signed by a party, or an officer of a party who has personal knowledge of the matters stated or is otherwise competent to testify thereto. *Johnson By and Through Johnson v. Svidergol*, 157 Ariz. 333, 757 P.2d 609 (Ct. App. Div. 2 1988). In the case of a public or private corporation, partnership, association or governmental agency, Rule 33(a) provides that an officer or agent shall furnish the information available to such entity. The in-house counsel for such entity may be its agent and may answer for it. If a third person is the source of the information set forth in such entity's answers, it may be desirable to identify such person and state that the information is derived from that source.

7. *Service of Interrogatory Responses; Filing Not Permitted.* The procedure for providing answers to interrogatories varies, depending upon whether uniform or non-uniform interrogatories have been propounded.

In the case of uniform interrogatories, Ariz. R. Civ. P. 33.1(f)(3) requires the answering party to reproduce the text of each interrogatory propounded, insert the answers, serve the original interrogatories and answers on the propounding party, and a copy upon each other party.

In the case of non-uniform interrogatories, the answering party inserts answers and/or objections in the space provided, and then serves a copy of the answers upon the propounding party and all other parties.

In both cases, the answers are served upon all parties, but not filed with the court. *See*, Ariz. R. Civ. P. 5(g).

The fact that discovery requests and/or responses are not filed does not preclude use of them in connection with motions and other proceedings. *GM Development Corp. v. Community American Mortg. Corp.*, 165 Ariz. 1, 795 P.2d 827 (Ct. App. Div. 1 1990).

Rule 34. Production of documents, electronically stored information, and things and entry upon land for inspection and other purposes

(a) Scope. Any party may serve on any other party requests (1) to produce and permit the party making the request, or someone acting on the requestor's behalf, to inspect, copy test or sample, any designated documents or electronically stored information, (including writings, drawings, graphs, charts, photographs, sound recordings, images, and other data or data compilations stored in any medium from which information can be obtained, translated through detection devices into reasonably usable form when translation is practicably necessary) or to inspect, copy, test, or sample any designated tangible things which constitute or contain matters within the scope of Rule 26(b) and which are in the possession, custody or control of the party upon whom the request is served; or (2) to permit entry upon designated land or other property in the possession or control of the party upon whom the request is served for the purpose of inspection and measuring, surveying, photographing, testing, or sampling the property or any designated object or operation thereon, within the scope of Rule 26(b).

Amended July 17, 1970, effective Nov. 1, 1970; Sept. 15, 1987, effective Nov. 15, 1987; Oct. 9, 1996, effective Dec. 1, 1996; September 5, 2007, effective January 1, 2008.

(b) Procedure and Limitations. The requests may, without leave of court, be served upon the plaintiff after commencement of the action and upon any other party with or after service of the summons and complaint upon that party. The requests shall set forth the items to be inspected either by individual item or by specific category, and describe each item and specific category with reasonable particularity. The request may specify the form or forms in which electronically stored information is to be produced. The request(s) shall not, without leave of court, cumulatively include more than ten (10) distinct items or specific categories of items. Each request shall specify a reasonable time, place, and manner of making the inspection and performing the related acts. If a party believes that good cause exists for more than ten (10) distinct items or categories of items, that party shall consult with the party upon whom a request would be served and attempt to secure a written stipulation to that effect. The party upon whom a request is served shall serve a written response within 40 days after the service of the request, except that a defendant may serve a response within 60 days after service of the summons and complaint upon that defendant, or execution of a waiver of service by that defendant. The court may allow a shorter or longer time. The response shall state, with respect to each item or category, that inspection and related activities will be permitted as requested or identify the reason for any objection, including any objection to the requested form or forms for producing electronically stored information. If objection is made to part of an item or category, the part shall be specified. If objection is made to the requested form or forms for producing electronically stored information—or if no form was specified in the request—the responding party must state the form or forms it intends to use. The party submitting a request may move for an order under Rule 37(a) with respect to any objection to or other failure to respond to the request or any part thereof, or any failure to permit inspection as requested. Unless the parties otherwise agree, or the court otherwise orders:

(1) a party who produces documents for inspection shall produce them as they are kept in the usual course of business or shall organize and label them to correspond with the categories in the request;

(2) if a request does not specify the form or forms for producing electronically stored information, a responding party must produce the information in a form or forms in which it is ordinarily maintained or in a form or forms that are reasonably usable; and

(3) a party need not produce the same electronically stored information in more than one form.

Amended July 17, 1970, effective Nov. 1, 1970; July 6, 1983, effective Sept. 7, 1983; Dec. 20, 1991, effective July 1, 1002; May 30, 1996, effective Dec. 1. 1996; September 5, 2007, effective January 1, 2008.

(c) Persons Not Parties. A person not a party to the action may be compelled to produce documents and things or to submit to an inspection as provided in Rule 45.

Amended July 17, 1970, effective Nov. 1, 1970; May 30, 1996, effective Dec. 1, 1996; Oct. 9, 1996, effective Dec. 1, 1996.

STATE BAR COMMITTEE NOTES

1970 Amendments

[Rule 34] The principal changes alter the pre-1970 Rule to eliminate "good cause" by transfer to Rule 26(b) of the portions relating to trial preparation; to have the Rule operate extra-judicially; to include sampling and testing as well as inspecting or photographing tangible things; and to make clear that the Rule does not preclude an independent action for discovery against persons not parties.

Rule 34 applies to electronic data compilations from which information can be obtained only with the use of detection devices. When the data can as a practical matter be made usable by the discovering party only through respondent's devices, respondent may be required to use his devices to translate the data into usable form, as by print-out.

[Rule 34(a)] This section eliminates the good cause requirement, which as to materials acquired in anticipation for trial is transferred to Rule 26(b); the matter is covered in the Note to that Rule. Arizona had previously concluded that "good cause" is too general a phrase to help much in concrete cases; see *State Farm Ins. Co. v. Roberts*, 97 Ariz. 169, 398 P.2d 671 (1965) and *Watts v. Superior Court In and For Maricopa County*, 87 Ariz. 1, 347 P.2d 565 (1959), holding that each good cause case depended heavily on its particular facts. The resolution of the problem adopted by this amendment makes the rule read about as Arizona had interpreted it in *Dean v. Superior Court In and For Maricopa County*, 84 Ariz. 104, 324 P.2d 764, 73 A.L.R.2d 1 (1958), that documents might be discovered where relevant or reasonably calculated to lead to admissible evidence.

The inclusion of testing and sampling of tangible things and objects or operations on land reflects a need frequently encountered by parties in preparation for trial. If the operation of a particular machine is the basis of a claim for negligent injury, it will often be necessary to test its operating parts or to sample and test the products it is producing. *Cf.* Mich.Gen.Ct.R. 310.1(1) (1963) (testing authorized).

[Rule 34(b)] This section includes the same timing provisions as Rule 33 on interrogatories. The same procedure for objections and for enforcing the request is also applied, so that it will be unnecessary to go to court for a production order in most cases. The requirements of reasonable particularity remain, as illustrated in *Phoenix General Hospital v. Superior Court of Maricopa County*, 1 Ariz. App. 298, 402 P.2d 233 (1965), writ rescinded, 98 Ariz. 262, 403 P.2d 815 (1965); *Industrial Commission v. Holohan*, 97 Ariz. 122, 397 P.2d 624 (1964); *Dean v. Superior Court In and For Maricopa County*, 84 Ariz. 104, 324 P.2d 764, 73 A.L.R.2d 1 (1958).

[Rule 34(c)] Rule 34 continues to apply only to parties. In the preparation of cases for trial it is occasionally necessary to enter land or inspect large tangible things in the possession of a person not a party. This section makes clear that the Rule does not prevent independent actions.

1983 Amendment

[Rule 34(b)] The last sentence is added to prevent the deliberate jumbling of documents.

1992 Supplemental Note

Rule 34 provides for the inspection and, if desired, copying of discoverable documents. The costs of copying should be borne by the party that requests that copies be made. If a party designates documents to be copied after a permitted inspection, or specifies in the request that copies of documents may be provided in response, that party should be responsible for any copying costs involved. If a party, in response to a request made under this rule, elects to furnish copies in lieu of permitting an inspection, that party should bear any copying or related costs incurred. Reference should be made to A.R.S. § 12-351 (costs of compliance with subpoena for production of documentary evidence; payment by requesting party; definitions) for guidelines as to what constitutes reasonable copying charges.

AUTHORS' COMMENTS

Analysis

2. Comparison With Federal Rule.
3. Limitations on Use of Requests for Production.
4. Presumptive Limits on Number of Requests for Production.
5. Procedure for Making Request; Contents.
6. Filing of Request/Response Not Permitted.
7. Procedure for Responding to Request.
8. Procedure for Production of Requested Documents.
9. Compelling Response to Request.
10. Time for Production.

1. *Scope and Purpose of Rule.* Rule 34 is a specific application of the general principles of discovery to documents and tangible objects. As with the other discovery rules, its purpose is to permit the issues to be simplified, the trial to be expedited and surprise to be minimized. The scope of what may be requested is defined by Ariz. R. Civ. P. 26.

2. *Comparison With Federal Rule.* There are now significant differences between ARCP 34 and FRCP 34, as a consequence of the 1992 Arizona discovery and court reform amendments and the 1993, 2006 and 2007 amendments to the Federal Rules of Civil Procedure.

ARCP 34(a) provides that a "party may serve on any other party *requests*" for production or inspection (emphasis supplied), while FRCP 34(a) refers to the service of "*a request.*" (emphasis supplied). This different terminology does not suggest any substantive difference.

ARCP 34(b), as amended, provides that a response to a request for production is to be made within forty (40) days after service of the request, unless the request is served with or shortly after the complaint, in which event the defendant may serve a response within sixty (60) days after service of the summons and complaint, or after the defendant executes a waiver of service. Under FRCP 34(b), as amended, the time period for responding and/or objecting to a request for production is thirty (30) days. The provision formerly authorizing a longer period to respond to a request served with or shortly after service of the summons and complaint was deleted, as such a request may now not be served until after conduct of the discovery planning conference required by FRCP 26(f). Amended FRCP 34(b) also contains a provision, not found in the Arizona Rule, that where an objection is made to a portion of the request, inspection is to be permitted for items requested that are not subject to the objection.

ARCP 34(b) contains a provision that, absent an agreement between the affected parties or leave of Court, a party may not submit Rule 34 requests which cumulatively request the production and/or inspection of more than ten (10) distinct items or categories of items requested. There is no similar provision in FRCP 34. ARCP 34 does not contain any provision comparable to that added to the federal rule by the 2006 amendments concerning the formats for the production of electronically stored information. ARCP 34(c), which is concerned with discovery from non-parties, is similar to FRCP 34(c).

In 2007, the language of FRCP 34 was amended as part of the general restyling of the Federal Rules of Civil Procedure to make the Federal Rules more easily understood and to make style and terminology consistent throughout the Federal Rules of Civil Procedure. Those stylistic modifications have not been incorporated into ARCP 34.

3. *Limitations on Use of Requests for Production.* Ariz. R. Civ. P. 34 is limited in that it may only be used to require a party to the action to produce documents and tangible things. A party desiring to inspect documents in the control of a non-party to a pending action must proceed under Ariz. R. Civ. P. 26 and 45. Moreover, Ariz. R. Civ. P. 34 establishes the exclusive procedure for securing production of documents from a party; its procedures may not be circumvented by service of a subpoena *duces tecum* upon a party. *MacDonald v. Hyder*, 12 Ariz. App. 411, 471 P.2d 296 (Div. 1 1970). The provisions of Ariz. R. Civ. P. 34(c) which formerly authorized an independent action to secure the production of documents or tangible objects were removed as part of the 1996 amendments to the Rule.

4. *Presumptive Limits on Number of Requests for Production.* The discovery and court reform amendments adopted by the Supreme Court, effective July 1, 1992, placed presumptive limits on the use of Rule 34 requests for production as well. The amendments originally provided that, absent an agreement between the affected parties or leave of court, a party could not submit more than one request for the production of documents and things and could not include within that request more than ten (10) distinct items or categories of items sought. This limitation was ameliorated slightly by an amendment to Ariz. R. Civ. P. 34 which became effective December 1, 1996. Under the Rule as amended, a party may propound multiple requests for production, but these separate requests cannot cumulatively include more than ten (10) specific requests for items to be produced and/or inspected.

This limitation, however, should not prove overly significant because the disclosure requirements of Ariz. R. Civ. P. 26.1 clearly contemplate that pertinent documents in a party's possession will be produced or made available for inspection and copying as part of the required disclosures. (In light of that, parties should be careful not to use one of their limited requests for production to seek production of documentary materials that are already subject to the mandatory disclosure requirements.) A party who nevertheless feels it is necessary to exceed these limits must first consult with the party upon whom the additional requests would be served and attempt to secure a written stipulation to that effect. If such a stipulation cannot be secured, then leave of court must be sought and obtained.

5. *Procedure for Making Request; Contents.* Under Ariz. R. Civ. P. 34(a), the party desiring the production of documents and tangible objects need only send a "Request for Production of Documents and Tangible Objects" to the party from whom such production is desired. The time limits for serving a written response to such Request are established by Rule 34(b). Consequently, there is no need to specify in the Request the time for serving a written response. Rule 34(b) does require, however, that the Request specify a reasonable time, place and manner of producing the requested documents, making the inspection and performing the related acts. If the time specified in the Request for such inspection or production is not reasonable, the written response should so state.

Ariz. R. Civ. P. 34(b) requires that the request "set forth the items to be inspected either by individual item or by specific category, and describe each item and specific category with reasonable particularity." The description of the documents or items to be produced should be as precise as possible so that the parties, and the Court, can determine what materials have been requested should a dispute arise. *Industrial Commission v. Holohan*, 97 Ariz. 122, 397 P.2d 624 (1964); *Dean v. Superior Court In and For Maricopa County*, 84 Ariz. 104, 324 P.2d 764, 73 A.L.R.2d 1 (1958); *Kirkpatrick v. Industrial Commission*, 10 Ariz. App. 564, 460 P.2d 670 (Div. 1 1969).

Ariz. R. Civ. P. 34(b) was amended, effective January 1, 2008, to provide that a request for production of electronically stored information may specify the form or forms in which it is to be produced. The party to whom such a request is directed may object but must, in any event, specify the form it intends to use in producing such information. If the request does not specify a form in which electronically stored information is to be produced, it must be produced in a form in which it is ordinarily maintained or in a form that is reasonably usable. Amended Rule 34(b)(3) provides that a party need not produce the same electronically stored information in more than one form.

6. *Filing of Request/Response Not Permitted.* Under Ariz. R. Civ. P. 5(g), discovery papers and any notices of service of such discovery or responses are served upon all parties, but not filed

with the court.

It has previously been held that the fact that discovery requests and responses are not filed does not preclude use of them in connection with motions and other proceedings. *GM Development Corp. v. Community American Mortg. Corp.*, 165 Ariz. 1, 795 P.2d 827 (Ct. App. Div. 1 1990).

7. *Procedure for Responding to Request.* Ariz. R. Civ. P. 34(b) provides that a party upon whom a Rule 34 request is served must serve a written response within forty (40) days after service of the request, except that a defendant may serve a response within sixty (60) days after service of the summons and complaint, or after execution by that defendant of a waiver of service. If no response is served, the requesting party can seek an order compelling production and sanctions under Ariz. R. Civ. P. 37(f), unless the party upon whom the request was served has first secured an appropriate protective order.

The written response may merely state that production or inspection will be permitted as requested, or it may state that the requested production or inspection will be permitted with some modification in time, place or manner of inspection. In this latter situation, an objection should be stated to the "time, place and manner" of inspection specified in the request. While it is typical for a Request for Production to set a date forty (40) days hence for the actual production of the documents requested, Ariz. R. Civ. P. 34(b) requires only that a response be filed, and not that actual production be either commenced or completed, within that time period. If the responding party cannot actually produce the records sought within forty (40) days, it is only necessary to serve a timely Rule 34(b) response stating that the documents requested will be made available, but objecting to the date specified in the Request for their actual production.

If a party objects to the production, inspection or copying of any item or category (or part thereof), the response should state such objection and the reasons for it. An objection should identify the particular document request to which it is directed. An objection is usually stated as part of the response to a Request for Production called for by Ariz. R. Civ. P. 34(b). An objection may be made on grounds which would otherwise provide the basis for a motion for protective order under Ariz. R. Civ. P. 26(c). If a party objects to the form or forms in which the request seeks the production of electronically stored information, the response must specify the form the party intends to use in producing such information. Whether a party should affirmatively seek protective relief under Rule 26(c), or merely state an objection in the response made under Rule 34(b), is a tactical question for counsel to resolve.

8. *Procedure for Production of Requested Documents*. Ariz. R. Civ. P. 34 authorizes only the inspection and copying of discoverable documents; it does not require that original documents be released to opposing counsel. *Nesmith v. Superior Court In and For County of Maricopa*, 164 Ariz. 70, 790 P.2d 768 (Ct. App. Div. 1 1990), redesignated as opinion and publication ordered, (Dec. 27, 1989). Documents produced pursuant to a request are to be produced as they are kept in the usual course of business, or are to be organized and labeled to correspond with the categories in the request. A Supplemental State Bar Committee Note to Rule 34, approved in 1992, makes clear that the responsibility for costs of copying documents rests with the party that decided to have copies made. If a party inspects documents made available pursuant to Rule 34 and requests that copies be made, that party should be responsible for the costs. If a party, in response to a request for inspection, elects to furnish copies of the documents requested, that party should be responsible for copying costs. A.R.S. § 12-351 sets forth guidelines for what constitutes reasonable copying charges.

9. *Compelling Response to Request.* Ariz. R. Civ. P. 34(b), provides, in part, that the party submitting a Request for Production of Documents may move for an order under Ariz. R. Civ. P. 37(a) with respect to any objection or other failure to respond to the Request or any part thereof, or any failure to permit inspection as requested. A party prevailing on such a motion may be awarded the expenses thereby incurred, including reasonable attorneys' fees.

10. *Time for Production.* While it is typical for a Request for Production to set a date forty (40) days hence for the actual production of the documents requested, Ariz. R. Civ. P. 34(b) requires only that a response be served, and not that actual production be commenced or completed within that time. If the responding party cannot actually produce the records sought within forty (40) days, it is only necessary to serve a timely Rule 34(b) response stating that the documents will be made available, but objecting to the date specified in the Request for their actual production.

Rule 35. Physical and mental examination of persons

(a) Order for Examination. When the mental or physical condition (including the blood group) of a party, or of a person in the custody or under the legal control of a party, is in controversy, the court in which the action is pending may order the party to submit to a physical or mental examination by a physician or psychologist or to produce for examination the person in the party's custody or legal control. The order may be made only on motion for good cause shown and upon notice to the person to be examined and to all parties and shall specify the time, place, manner, conditions, and scope of the examination and the person or persons by whom it is to be made. The person to be examined shall have the right to have a representative present during the examination, unless the presence of that representative may adversely affect the outcome of the examination. The person to be examined shall have the right to record by audiotape any physical examination. A mental examination may be recorded by audiotape, unless such recording may adversely affect the outcome of the examination. Upon good cause shown, a physical or mental examination may be video-recorded. A copy of any record made of a physical or mental examination shall be provided to any party upon request.

Amended July 17, 1970, effective Nov. 1, 1970; Sept. 15, 1987, effective Nov. 15, 1987; Oct. 1, 1992, effective Dec. 1, 1992.

(b) Report of Examiner.

(1) If requested by the party against whom an order is made under Rule 35(a) or the person examined, the party causing the examination to be made shall deliver to the requestor, within twenty days of the examination, a copy of a detailed written report of the examining licensed professional setting out the professional's findings, including the results of all tests made, diagnoses and conditions, together with like reports of all earlier examinations of the same condition and copies of all written or recorded notes filed out by the examiner and the person examined at the time of the examination, providing access to the original written or recorded notes for purposes of comparing same with the copies. After delivery the party causing the examination shall be entitled upon request to receive from the party against whom the order is made a like report of any examination, previously or thereafter made, of the same condition, unless, in the case of a report of examination of a person not a party, the party shows that such party is unable to obtain it. The court on motion may make an order against a

party requiring delivery of a report on such terms as are just, and if a physician or psychologist fails or refuses to make a report the court may exclude the physician's or psychologist's testimony if offered at the trial.

(2) By requesting and obtaining a report of the examination so ordered or by taking the deposition of the examiner, the party examined waives any privilege the party may have in that action or any other involving the same controversy, regarding the testimony of every other person who has examined or may thereafter examine the party in respect of the same mental or physical condition.

(3) This subdivision applies to examinations made by agreement of the parties, unless the agreement expressly provides otherwise. This subdivision does not preclude discovery of a report of an examining physician or psychologist or the taking of a deposition of the physician or psychologist in accordance with the provisions of any other rule.

Amended July 17, 1970, effective Nov. 1, 1970; Sept. 15, 1987, effective Nov. 15, 1987; Oct. 1, 1992, effective Dec. 1, 1992.

(c) Alternate Procedure; Notice of Examination; Objections.

(1) When the parties agree that a mental or physical examination is appropriate but do not agree as to the examining physician or psychologist, the party desiring the examination may seek it by giving reasonable notice in writing to every other party to the action not less than 30 days in advance. The notice shall specify the name of the person to be examined, the time, place and scope of the examination, and the person or persons by whom it is to be made. The person to be physically examined shall have the right to have a representative present during the examination, unless the presence of that representative may adversely affect the outcome of the examination. The person to be examined shall have the right to record by audiotape any physical examination. A mental examination may be recorded by audiotape, unless such recording may adversely affect the outcome of the examination. Upon good cause shown, a physical or mental examination may be videorecorded. A copy of any record made of a physical or mental examination shall be provided to any party upon request.

(2) Upon motion by a party or by the person to be examined, and for good cause shown, the court in which the action is pending may, in addition to other orders appropriate under subdivision (a) of this rule, make an order that the examination be made by a physician or psychologist other than the one specified in the notice. If a party after being served with a proper notice under this subdivision does not make a motion

under this rule, and fails to appear for the examination or to produce for the examination the person in the party's custody or legal control, the court in which the action is pending may on motion make such orders in regard to the failure as are just, such as those specified in Rule 37(f).

(3) The provisions of Rule 35(b) shall apply to an examination made under this subdivision.

Amended July 17, 1970, effective Nov. 1, 1970; Sept. 15, 1987, effective Nov. 15, 1987; Oct. 1, 1992, effective Dec. 1, 1992; Sept. 3, 2009, effective Jan. 1, 2010.

STATE BAR COMMITTEE NOTES

1970 Amendments

[Rule 35(a)] The pre-1970 Rule 35(a) provided only for an order requiring a party to submit to an examination. The 1970 revision settles that a parent or guardian suing to recover for injuries to a minor may be ordered to produce the minor for examination. Further, it expressly includes blood examination within the kinds of examinations that can be ordered under the rule.

The 1970 revision makes no change in the requirements of Rule 35 that, before a court order may issue, the relevant physical or mental condition must be shown to be "in controversy" and "good cause" must be shown for the examination. Thus, it has no effect on the recent decision of the Supreme Court in *Schlagenhauf v. Holder*, 379 U.S. 104, 85 S. Ct. 234, 13 L. Ed. 2d 152, 9 Fed. R. Serv. 2d 35A.1, Case 1 (1964). It also in no way affects *Martin v. Superior Court In and For Maricopa County*, 104 Ariz. 268, 451 P.2d 597, 33 A.L.R.3d 1005 (1969), on the discretion of the trial court as to choice of physician; or *Pedro v. Glenn*, 8 Ariz. App. 332, 446 P.2d 31 (1968) on persons entitled to be present.

Rule 35(b)(1): This subdivision as revised corrects an imbalance in Rule 35(b)(1) as it existed before 1970. Under that text, a party causing a Rule 35(a) examination to be made is required to furnish to the party examined, on request, a copy of the examining physician's report. If he delivers this copy, he is in turn entitled to receive from the party examined reports of all examinations of the same condition previously or later made. See e.g., *Simpson v. Heiderich*, 4 Ariz. App. 232, 419 P.2d 362 (1966). But the rule has not in terms entitled the examined party to receive from the party causing the Rule 35(a) examination any reports of earlier examinations of the same condition to which the latter may have access. The 1970 revision cures this defect. See La. Stat. Ann. Civ. Proc. art. 1495 (1960); Utah R. Civ. P. 35(c).

The rule specifies that the written report of the examining physician includes results of all tests made, such as results of x-rays and cardiograms. It also embodies changes required by the broadening of Rule 35(a) to take in persons who are not parties.

Rule 35(b)(2): The reference to "party examined" here includes the person produced under Rule 35(a).

Rule 35(b)(3): This confirms the existing practice that reports of examinations made by agreement are also subject to the rule.

Rule 35(c) is intended to encourage counsel to agree, whenever possible, on arrangements for a mental or physical examination. It provides for an examination on notice, rather than on motion under Rule 35(a), when the parties agree that an examination is appropriate but disagree only as to the identity of the examining physician. Rule 35(c) allows the party seeking the examination to designate the physician, subject to the right of the adverse party to object by motion. This rule provides precise procedures to carry out the general policy of

Martin v. Superior Court In and For Maricopa County, 104 Ariz. 268, 451 P.2d 597, 33 A.L.R.3d 1005 (1969). Rule 35(c) does not provide any greater right to an examination than otherwise exists under Rule 35(a), but does place upon the objecting party the burden of showing "good cause" as to the identity of the examiner. Rule 35(c) will hopefully reduce the necessity for going to court, but when resort to court is necessary, and the motion is granted, it is anticipated that the court will choose a mutually acceptable examiner.

AUTHORS' COMMENTS

Analysis

1. *Scope and Purpose of Rule.* Ariz. R. Civ. P. 35 authorizes, and establishes the procedures for securing, a physical or mental examination of a party or "a person in the custody or under the legal control" of a party, whenever the physical or mental condition of the person or party to be examined is in controversy.

A party desiring to have such an examination may proceed by motion and order under Ariz. R. Civ. P. 35(a) or, where the parties agree that an examination is appropriate, by notice under Ariz. R. Civ. P. 35(c). Ariz. R. Civ. P. 35(b) gives the examined party the right to secure the report of the ordered examination and any written or recorded notes generated during the course of the examination, and other parties the right to secure from the examined party reports of other examinations conducted of the same physical or mental condition.

By reason of Ariz. R. Civ. P. 5(g), requests for physical or mental examinations are served upon all parties, but not filed with the Court.

2. *Comparison With Federal Rule.* While both ARCP 35 and FRCP 35 deal with physical and mental examinations as a

discovery device, there are significant differences between them.

FRCP 35(a) authorizes examinations by "a suitably licensed or certified examiner." ARCP 35(a) only authorizes examinations by "a physician or psychologist." Under ARCP 35(b)(1), as amended effective December 1, 1992, where an examination is ordered, the party examined is entitled, upon request, to copies of all written or recorded notes completed by the examiner or the person examined at the time of the examination. The Federal Rules of Civil Procedure do not contain a similar provision.

Under the 1992 amendments to ARCP 35, whether the examination is ordered or conducted on notice pursuant to agreement, the person examined has the right to have a representative in attendance during the examination, unless that representative's attendance would have an adverse impact on the examination's outcome. The person examined may also record by audiotape any physical examination, and any mental examination, unless the recording would adversely affect the mental examination's outcome. For good cause shown, a physical or mental examination may be recorded by video. The Federal Rules of Civil Procedure do not contain a similar provision.

Finally, the Arizona Rule has a provision, ARCP 35(c), not found in the Federal Rule, specifying an alternate procedure for the conduct of physical and mental examinations where the parties agree that an examination is appropriate, but cannot agree on the examiner.

In 2007, the language of FRCP 35 was amended as part of the general restyling of the Federal Rules of Civil Procedure to make the Federal Rules more easily understood and to make style and terminology consistent throughout the Federal Rules of Civil Procedure. Those stylistic modifications have not been incorporated into ARCP 35.

3. *Requirements for Ordering Examination.* The 1992 amendment to Ariz. R. Civ. P. 35 authorizes examinations by "psychologists" in addition to "physicians." As articulated in a 1991 case decided before this amendment, three requirements are necessary for a court to order an examination pursuant to Rule 35: 1) the party's physical or mental condition must be in controversy; 2) the examiner must meet the professional qualifications required; and 3) good cause must be shown. *Avila v. Superior Court In and For County of Maricopa*, 169 Ariz. 49, 816 P.2d 946 (Ct. App. Div. 1 1991). (Rule 35 does not authorize use of a vocational rehabilitation specialist).

4. *Persons Subject to Examination.* The United States Supreme Court in *Schlagenhauf v. Holder*, 379 U.S. 104, 85 S. Ct. 234, 13 L. Ed. 2d 152, 9 Fed. R. Serv. 2d 35A.1, Case 1 (1964), made clear that the term "a party" employed in the Rule refers equally

to defendants and plaintiffs. Moreover, the party to be examined need not be aligned in opposition to the party moving for the examination. After the 1970 amendment to the Rule, it is clear that a minor may be examined in a suit by a parent or guardian for injuries to the minor. The trial court also has the inherent power, not grounded in or circumscribed by this Rule, to order a physical or mental examination to determine the capacity of a witness to testify at trial or deposition. *Lewin v. Jackson*, 108 Ariz. 27, 492 P.2d 406 (1972). Knowledge gained during a court directed physical or mental examination is not subject to a claim of privilege.

5. *Time for Seeking Examination.* Ariz. R. Civ. P. 35(a) does not establish any time parameters during which a motion for physical or mental examination is to be made, but it should be made in a timely fashion before trial. The motion may suggest the names of certain physicians as acceptable examiners, and may seek a variety of specific tests. The Court may, upon a sufficient showing, direct an examination that may be painful, but can deny the motion where the safety of a particular procedure requested is subject to question. The moving party must pay the expense of examination.

6. *Mental Examinations.* The 1992 amendments to Ariz. R. Civ. P. 35 authorize examinations conducted by a "psychologist," as well as by a physician. The Court's discretion to authorize the mental examination of a party is subject to the limitation that it must be exercised in a manner that is reasonable under the circumstances. *Pedro v. Glenn*, 8 Ariz. App. 332, 446 P.2d 31 (1968).

7. *Order Directing Examination.* Under Ariz. R. Civ. P. 35(a), the order directing the examination must "specify the time, place, manner, conditions, and scope of the examination and person or persons by whom it is to be made." As an alternative to specifying a precise date and time for conduct of the examination, the order can provide that the examination take place at a date and time agreed to by the parties, but no later than a specific date.

8. *Availability of Reports of Examination and Notes of Examiner.* The 1992 amendments to Ariz. R. Civ. P. 35 expanded the information available to the person examined. The party or person subjected to the examination has the right to receive "a detailed written report of the examining licensed professional" which includes the "findings, including the results of all tests made, diagnoses and conclusions, together with like reports of all earlier examinations of the same condition. . . ." This is to be delivered to the examined party making the request within twenty (20) days of the examination. In addition, the party or person making the request is to receive copies of "all written or

recorded notes filled out by the examiner and the person examined at the time of the examination," and is to be provided access to the originals of any such notes to permit comparisons with the copies provided.

9. *Reports of Other Examinations.* Once the examined party has received the report of the ordered examination, the party who requested the examination may secure from the examined party upon request "a like report of any examination, previously or thereafter made, of the same condition. . . ." This requirement is mandatory and bottomed on the notion that mutual knowledge of all relevant facts is essential to a fair trial. *Simpson v. Heiderich*, 4 Ariz. App. 232, 419 P.2d 362 (1966).

10. *Failure to Supply Examination Reports.* If a requested examination report is not supplied, Ariz. R. Civ. P. 35(b)(1) authorizes the Court to exclude the physician's testimony at trial. This provision may be invoked only when the doctor fails or refuses to make a report after being ordered to do so. *Simpson v. Heiderich*, 4 Ariz. App. 232, 419 P.2d 362 (1966). It does not apply where the examination of a plaintiff was not conducted pursuant to an order obtained by the defendant. *City of Scottsdale v. Kokaska*, 17 Ariz. App. 120, 495 P.2d 1327 (Div. 1 1972).

11. *Examination Upon Notice.* Ariz. R. Civ. P. 35(c) provides for an examination on notice, rather than by motion and order, when the parties agree that an examination is appropriate. If the person or party to be examined objects to the identity of the examining physician specified in the notice, the Court may order that it be conducted by a different physician, but only upon motion and for good cause shown.

12. *Selection of Examiner.* A party seeking an examination, whether by motion or notice, does not have an absolute right to select the examining physician or psychologist. When there is objection to the examination being conducted by a particular examiner, the court has the duty of determining whether appointment of that examiner will best serve the interests of justice. *Martin v. Superior Court In and For Maricopa County*, 104 Ariz. 268, 451 P.2d 597, 33 A.L.R.3d 1005 (1969). The Rule anticipates that the court will, in most instances, choose a mutually acceptable examiner. *See* State Bar Committee Note to 1970 Amendment. Prior to the 1992 amendments, it was held that, an examination by a vocational rehabilitation specialist was not authorized by the Rule. *Avila v. Superior Court In and For County of Maricopa*, 169 Ariz. 49, 816 P.2d 946 (Ct. App. Div. 1 1991).

13. *Attendance of Representative at Examination.* The 1992 amendments to Ariz. R. Civ. P. 35 added provisions to subparts (a) and (c), giving the person to be examined the right to have a representative present at the examination, unless the presence of

that representative may adversely affect the outcome of the examination. This right applies whether the examination is conducted pursuant to Court order or on notice pursuant to agreement of the parties.

14. *Recording of Examination.* The 1992 amendments also added provisions regarding the recording of the examination, which draw a distinction between physical and mental examinations. A person to be examined has the right to record any physical examination by audiotape. A mental examination may be similarly recorded, unless the recording may adversely affect the outcome of the examination. The amendments do not expressly limit the right to record mental examinations by audiotape to the person to be examined. A video recording of either a physical or mental examination is also authorized, but only for good cause shown. A copy of any recording of an examination is to be provided to any party upon request.

Rule 36. Requests for admission

(a) Request for Admission. A party may serve upon any other party a written request for the admission, for purposes of the pending action only, of the truth of any matters within the scope of Rule 26(b) set forth in the request that relate to statements or opinions of fact or of the application of law to fact, including the genuineness of any documents described in the request. Copies of documents shall be served with the request unless they have been or are otherwise furnished or made available for inspection and copying. The request may, without leave of court, be served upon the plaintiff after commencement of the action and upon any other party with or after service of the summons and complaint upon that party. Each matter of which an admission is requested shall be separately set forth. The matter is admitted unless, within 40 days after service of the request, or, in the case of a defendant, within 60 days after service of the summons and complaint upon that defendant, or execution of a waiver of service by that defendant, or within such shorter or longer time as the court may allow, the party to whom the request is directed serves upon the party requesting the admission a written answer or objection addressed to the matter, signed by the party or by the party's attorney. If objection is made, the reasons therefor shall be stated. The answer shall specifically deny the matter or set forth in detail the reasons why the answering party cannot truthfully admit or deny the matter. A denial shall fairly meet the substance of the requested admission, and when good faith requires that a party qualify an answer or deny only a part of the matter of which an admission is requested, the party shall specify so much of it as is true and qualify or deny the remainder. An answering party may not give lack of information or knowledge as a reason for failure to admit or deny unless the party states that the party has made reasonable inquiry and that the information known or readily obtainable by the party is insufficient to enable the party to admit or deny. A party who considers that a matter of which an admission has been requested presents a genuine issue for trial may not, on that ground alone, object to the request; the party may, subject to the provisions of Rule 37(e), deny the matter or set forth reasons why the party cannot admit or deny it. The party who has requested the admissions may move to determine the sufficiency of the answers or objections. Unless the court determines that an objection is justified, it shall order that an answer be served. If the court determines that an answer does not comply with the requirements of this rule, it may order either that the matter is admitted or that an amended answer be served. The court may, in lieu of these orders, determine that final disposition of the request be made at a pre-trial conference or at a designated time prior to trial. The provisions of Rule 37(a)(4) apply to the award of expenses incurred in relation to the motion.

Amended July 17, 1970, effective Nov. 1, 1970; Sept. 15, 1987, effective Nov. 15, 1987; Dec. 20, 1991, effective July 1, 1992; Oct. 9, 1996, effective Dec. 1, 1996.

(b) Procedure. Each request shall contain only one factual matter or request for genuineness of all documents or categories of documents. Each party without leave of court shall be entitled to submit no more than twenty-five (25) requests in any case except upon: (1) agreement of all parties; (2) an order of the court following a motion demonstrating good cause, or (3) an order of the court following a Comprehensive Pretrial Conference pursuant to Rule 16(c). Any interrogatories accompanying requests shall be deemed interrogatories under Rule 33.1.

Amended Dec. 20, 1991, effective July 1, 1992.

(c) Effect of Admission. Any matter admitted under this rule is conclusively established unless the court on motion permits withdrawal or amendment of the admission. Subject to the provisions of Rule 16 governing amendment of a pre-trial order, the court may permit withdrawal or amendment when the presentation of the merits of the action will be subserved thereby and the party who obtained the admission fails to satisfy the court that withdrawal or amendment will prejudice that party in maintaining the action or defense on the merits. Any admission made by a party under this rule is for the purpose of the pending action only and is not an admission for any other purpose nor may it be used against the party in any other proceeding.

Amended July 17, 1970, effective Nov. 1, 1970; Sept. 15, 1987, effective Nov. 15, 1987; Dec. 20, 1991, effective July 1, 1992.

STATE BAR COMMITTEE NOTES

1970 Amendments

[Rule 36] The purpose of the admission rule is to expedite trial and to relieve parties of unnecessary costs in proving facts, *Aetna Loan Co. v. Apache Trailer Sales*, 1 Ariz. App. 322, 402 P.2d 580 (1965), and it is the purpose of the 1970 revision to increase its use for these purposes. See generally Finman, The Request for Admissions in Federal Civil Procedure, 71 Yale L.J. 371 (1962).

[Rule 36(a)] The subdivision provides that a request may be made to admit any matters within the scope of Rule 26(b) that relate to statements or opinions of fact or of the application of law to fact. It thereby resolves conflicts in the court decisions as to whether a request to admit matters of "opinion" and matters involving "mixed law and fact" is proper under the rule, and accords with the general Arizona approach to discovery as to opinions; *State ex rel. Willey v. Whitman*, 91 Ariz. 120, 370 P.2d 273 (1962). See also Note on this matter in connection with Rule 33.

Courts have also divided on whether an answering party may properly object to requests for admission as to matters which that party regards as "in dispute." The proper response in such cases is an answer. The very purpose of the request is to ascertain whether the answering party is prepared to admit or regards the matter as presenting a genuine issue for trial. In his answer, the party may deny, or he may give as his reason for inability to admit or deny the existence of a genuine issue. The party runs no risk of sanctions if the matter is genuinely in issue, since Rule 37(c) provides a sanction of costs only when there are no good reasons for a failure to admit.

Another sharp split of authority exists on the question whether a party may base his answer on lack of information or knowledge without seeking out additional information. One line of cases has held that a party may answer on the basis of such knowledge as he has at the time he answers. A larger group of cases, supported by commentators, has taken the view that if the responding party lacks knowledge, he must inform himself in reasonable fashion. This is the Arizona view; see *Allison v. State*, 101 Ariz. 418, 421, 420 P.2d 289, 292 (1966), in which a refusal to look at a document "readily available" was held to amount to an admission.

The 1970 revision adopts the majority view, as in keeping with a basic principle of the discovery rules that a reasonable burden may be imposed on the parties when its discharge will facilitate preparation for trial and ease the trial process. The revised rule requires only that the answering party make reasonable inquiry and secure such knowledge and information as are readily obtainable by him.

The requirement that the answer to a request for admission be sworn is deleted, in favor of a provision that the answer be signed by the party or by his attorney. The provisions of Rule 36 make it clear that admissions function very much as pleadings do. Thus, when a party admits in part and denies in part, his admission is for purposes of the pending action only and may not be used against him in any other proceeding; *Phelps Dodge Corp. v. Superior Court In and For Cochise County*, 7 Ariz. App. 277, 438 P.2d 424 (1968) (abrogated by, State v. Ott, 167 Ariz. 420, 808 P.2d 305 (Ct. App. Div. 1 1990)). The broadening of the rule to encompass mixed questions of law and fact reinforces this feature. Rule 36 does not lack a sanction for false answers; Rule 37(c) furnishes an appropriate deterrent.

Changes are made in the sequence of procedures in Rule 36 so that they conform to the new procedures in Rules 33 and 34.

The requirement that the objecting party move automatically for a hearing on his objection is eliminated, and the burden is on the requesting party to move for an order. The change in the burden of going forward does not modify present law on burden of persuasion. The award of expenses incurred in relation to the motion is made subject to the comprehensive provisions of Rule 37(a)(4).

[Rule 36(b)] The rule does not now indicate the extent to which a party is bound by his admission.

The new provisions give an admission a conclusively binding effect, for purposes only of the pending action, unless the admission is withdrawn or amended. Unless the party securing an admission can depend on its binding effect, he cannot safely avoid the expense of preparing to prove the very matters on which he has secured the admission, and the purpose of the rule is defeated. Field & McKusick, Maine Civil Practice § 36.4 (1959); Finman, supra, 71 Yale L.J. 371, 418–426; Comment, 56 N.W. L. Rev. 679, 682–683 (1961).

Provision is made for withdrawal or amendment of an admission. This provision emphasizes the importance of having the action resolved on the merits, while at the same time assuring each party that justified reliance on an admission in preparation for trial will not operate to his prejudice; and the burden of justifying the withdrawal of the admission therefore is on the party who made it.

AUTHORS' COMMENTS

Analysis

1. *Scope and Purpose of Rule.* Ariz. R. Civ. P. 36 sets forth the procedure by which a party may request that another party admit: (1) the truthfulness of statements of fact; (2) the genuineness of documents; (3) the accuracy or legitimacy of opinions; and (4) the appropriate application of the law to the facts. This discovery device serves to narrow the issues and expedite the trial by eliminating the time and expense of proving facts and other matters which cannot be legitimately denied. *Aetna Loan Co. v. Apache Trailer Sales*, 1 Ariz. App. 322, 402 P.2d 580 (1965). Admissions may be used as a basis for a motion for summary or partial summary judgment, *Fleitz v. Van Westrienen*, 114 Ariz. 246, 560 P.2d 430 (Ct. App. Div. 1 1977), and are admissible at trial. *Downs v. Ziegler*, 13 Ariz. App. 387, 477 P.2d 261 (Div. 1 1970).

2. *Comparison With Federal Rule.* There are now significant differences between ARCP 36 and FRCP 36, as a consequence of the 1992 Arizona discovery and court reform amendments and the 1993 amendments to the Federal Rules of Civil Procedure.

Under amended ARCP 36(a), responses to requests for admissions must now be served within forty (40) days after service of the requests, unless they are served with or shortly after service of the summons and complaint, in which event the defendant may serve responses and/or objections within sixty (60) days after service of the summons and complaint, or after execution of a waiver of service. Under FRCP 36(a), as amended, the time period for responding and/or objecting to requests for admissions is thirty (30) days. The provision formerly authorizing a longer period to respond to requests served with or shortly after service of the summons and complaint was deleted, as such a request may now not be served until after conduct of the discovery planning conference required by FRCP 26(f).

ARCP 36(b) provides that, absent an agreement of *all* parties or leave of Court, a party may not serve more than twenty-five (25) requests for admissions and each such request may only address one factual matter. FRCP 36 does not contain a similar provision.

In 2007, the language of FRCP 36 was amended as part of the general restyling of the Federal Rules of Civil Procedure to make the Federal Rules more easily understood and to make style and terminology consistent throughout the Federal Rules of Civil Procedure. Those stylistic modifications have not been incorporated into ARCP 36.

3. *Presumptive Limits on Number of Requests.* The discovery and court reform amendments adopted by the Supreme Court, effective July 1, 1992, adopted Ariz. R. Civ. P. 36(b) which placed presumptive limits on the number of requests for admissions that can be served in a civil case. (Former Rule 36(b) was redesignated Rule 36(c) with no substantive change.) Without an agreement of the parties or leave of court, a party may not serve more than twenty-five (25) requests and each request may address only one factual matter.

The limitations thus imposed are easy to apply in cases involving a single plaintiff and a single defendant. In a multiple party case, however, it is not clear whether the twenty-five (25) request limit applies to the number of requests that can be served on any other individual party, or represents the number of requests that can be served on all parties. In that regard, amended Ariz. R. Civ. P. 36(b) requires that there be an agreement of *all* parties (or leave of Court) to exceed the twenty-five (25) request limit. By contrast, a party wishing to exceed the presumptive limits on the number of interrogatories that may be propounded or the limits on the number of requests for production that may be served need only secure the agreement of the party to whom the additional interrogatories or requests for production would be directed. *Cf.* Ariz. R. Civ. P. 33.1(b) and 34(b).

4. *Procedure for Making Requests; Standards.* Requests for admission may be served by any party upon any other party. The admissions sought must be relevant and not privileged. A request for admission may properly seek an admission on a matter of opinion as well as on matters involving mixed questions of law and fact, but may not seek admissions on questions of law unrelated to the facts of the case. *West v. Sundance Development Co.*, 169 Ariz. 579, 821 P.2d 240 (Ct. App. Div. 2 1991).

Each matter as to which an admission is requested must be set forth separately. Requests for admission should be simple and direct so that the answering party may admit or deny the request, or explain in a few words why the request cannot be answered. When an admission of the genuineness of a document is sought, a copy of the document in question must be attached as an exhibit to the Requests for Admission and served with them, unless the document has previously been furnished or made available for inspection and copying.

5. *Filing of Requests Not Permitted.* Under Ariz. R. Civ. P. 5(g), discovery papers and any notices of service of such discovery or responses are to be served upon all parties, but not filed with the court.

It has previously been held that the fact that discovery requests and responses are not filed does not preclude use of them in connection with motions and other proceedings. *GM Development Corp. v. Community American Mortg. Corp.*, 165 Ariz. 1, 795 P.2d 827 (Ct. App. Div. 1 1990).

6. *Responses to Requests for Admission.* The party served must respond to the request and admit or deny all matters which are not objectionable. Under amended Ariz. R. Civ. P. 36(a), responses to requests for admissions must now be served within forty (40) days after service of the requests, unless the requests are served with or shortly after service of the summons and complaint, in which event the defendant may serve responses and/or objections within sixty (60) days after service of the summons and complaint, or after execution of a waiver of service.

Under Rule 36, the response to a request for admission must:

(1) admit the matter;
(2) deny the matter;
(3) set forth the reason(s) why the matter cannot be truthfully admitted or denied; or
(4) state an objection.

In most cases, the response to a Request for Admission will be set forth on the original Request for Admission served upon the responding party.

In case of an improper request for admission, the procedure is to respond with an objection to that request. Objections may be included in the response together with the admissions, denials, and other responses, or may be set forth in a separate document served at the same time as the response.

Responses to Requests for Admission need not be verified or under oath, and may be signed by either the party responding or counsel. The signature of counsel or of an unrepresented party is, of course, subject to the requirements of Ariz. R. Civ. P. 11.

Rule 36(a) provides that a party may not object to a request merely because (a) the request goes to a disputed matter that presents a genuine issue of fact, or (b) the respondent lacks personal knowledge when the information is obtainable through reasonable inquiry. A party may object, however, on the grounds that the request seeks information beyond the scope of discovery defined by Ariz. R. Civ. P. 26(b), or that the request is so vague and ambiguous that it cannot be answered.

A request for an admission of law unrelated to the facts of the case is objectionable. *West v. Sundance Development Co.*, 169 Ariz. 579, 821 P.2d 240 (Ct. App. Div. 2 1991) (requests for admission which call for "bold legal conclusions unrelated to the facts", *i.e.*, admissions as to whether a party was negligent or that plaintiff is entitled to general damages, are not proper requests.).

When a request for admission seeks information that may tend to incriminate the party on whom the requests are served, that party may invoke the privilege against self-incrimination. The immunity inherent in the restricted use of admissions to the pending action is insufficient to protect the claimant against future criminal charges. *State v. Ott*, 167 Ariz. 420, 808 P.2d 305 (Ct. App. Div. 1 1990).

A party failing to respond in a timely manner to a Request for Admission will be deemed to have admitted the matter or matters covered in the Request. The admission is, however, only for the purposes of the pending action. *See*, Ariz. R. Civ. P. 36(c). When a party who requested an admission under Rule 36, which was denied, is forced to prove the matter at trial and does so, that party who made the request may apply to the Court, under Ariz. R. Civ. P. 37(e), for attorneys' fees incurred in making the proof. *West v. Sundance Development Co.*, 169 Ariz. 579, 821 P.2d 240 (Ct. App. Div. 2 1991).

7. *Duty of Inquiry.* Ariz. R. Civ. P. 36 expressly provides that an answering party "may not give lack of information or knowledge" as a response, unless such response also states that the party "has made reasonable inquiry and that the information known or readily obtainable . . . is insufficient" to enable the party to admit or deny the Request. The Rule thus does impose an obligation upon the responding party to conduct some reasonable investigation into the matters that are the subject of the request. See *Allison v. State*, 101 Ariz. 418, 420 P.2d 289 (1966). If the sufficiency of such a response is challenged, the party making it must be prepared to make a factual showing of the nature and extent of the reasonable inquiry conducted. *Fickett v. Superior Court of Pima County*, 27 Ariz. App. 793, 558 P.2d 988 (Div. 2 1976).

8. *Filing of Responses Not Permitted.* By reason of Ariz. R. Civ. P. 5(g), "discovery papers," including requests for admission, responses thereto, and notices of service of discovery requests and

responses, are to be served on all parties, but not filed with the Court.

9. *Remedies for Failure to Respond or for Deficient Responses.* Pursuant to Ariz. R. Civ. P. 36(a), a party who has requested the admissions may move to compel further responses to such requests or for an order that the matter is deemed admitted. A copy of the Request and the allegedly deficient response should accompany the motion.

10. *Withdrawal or Amendment of Responses.* Subject to certain limitations, Ariz. R. Civ. P. 36(c) confers upon the trial court the discretion to permit the withdrawal or amendment of a response to a request for admission. To grant relief from a response to a request for admission, the Court must determine that: (1) the presentation of the merits of the action will be promoted by the withdrawal or amendment of the response at issue; and (2) the party securing the admission has failed to demonstrate that it will be prejudiced by the withdrawal or amendment. *See also, DeLong v. Merrill*, 233 Ariz. 163, 310 P.3d 39 (Ct. App. Div. 2 2013) (trial court erred by failing to apply the Rule 36(c) factors in evaluating party's request to amend late 'responses' to requests for admission).

Rule 37. Failure to make disclosure or discovery; sanctions

(a) Motion for Order Compelling Disclosure or Discovery. A party, upon reasonable notice to other parties and all persons affected thereby, may apply for an order compelling disclosure or discovery as follows:

(1) *Appropriate Court.* An application for an order to a party may be made to the court in the county in which the action is pending, or, in matters relating to a deposition, to the court in the county where the deposition is being taken. An application for an order to a person who is not a party shall be made to the court in the county where the discovery is being, or is to be, taken.

(2) *Motion.*

(A) If a party fails to make a disclosure required by Rule 26.1, any other party may move to compel disclosure and for appropriate sanctions.

(B) If a deponent fails to answer a question propounded or submitted under Rule 30 or 31, or a corporation or other entity fails to make a designation under Rule 30(b)(6) or 31(a), or a party fails to answer an interrogatory submitted under Rule 33, or if a party, in response to a request for inspection submitted under Rule 34, fails to respond that inspection will be permitted as requested or fails to permit inspection as requested, the discovering party may move for an order compelling an answer, or a designation, or an order compelling inspection in accordance with the request. When taking a deposition on oral examination, the proponent of the question may complete or adjourn the examination before applying for an order.

(C) No motion brought under this Rule 37 will be considered or scheduled unless a separate statement of moving counsel is attached thereto certifying that, after personal consultation and good faith efforts to do so, counsel have been unable to satisfactorily resolve the matter.

(3) *Evasive or Incomplete Disclosure, Answer, or Response.* For purposes of this subdivision an evasive or incomplete disclosure, answer, or response is to be treated as a failure to disclose, answer, or respond.

(4) *Expenses and Sanctions.*

(A) If the motion is granted or if the disclosure or requested discovery is provided after the motion was filed, the court shall, after affording an opportunity to be heard, require the party or deponent whose conduct necessitated the motion or the party or attorney advising such conduct or both of them to pay the moving party the reasonable expenses incurred in making the motion, including attorney's fees, unless the court finds that the motion was filed without the movant's first making a good faith effort to obtain the disclosure or discovery without court action, or that the opposing party's nondisclosure, response, or objection was substantially justified or that other circumstances make an award of expenses unjust.

(B) If the motion is denied, the court may enter any protective order authorized under Rule 26(c) and shall, after affording an opportunity to be heard, require the moving party or the attorney filing the motion or both of them to pay to the party or deponent who opposed the motion the reasonable expenses incurred in opposing the motion, including attorney's fees, unless the court finds that the making of the motion was substantially justified or that other circumstances make an award of expenses unjust.

(C) If the motion is granted in part and denied in part, the court may enter any protective order authorized under Rule 26(c) and may, after affording an opportunity to be heard, apportion the reasonable expenses incurred in relation to the motion among the parties and persons in a just manner.

Amended July 17, 1970, effective Nov. 1, 1970; Sept. 15, 1987, effective Nov. 15, 1987; May 30, 1996, effective Dec. 1, 1996; Oct. 10, 2000, effective Dec. 1, 2000.

(b) Failure to Comply With Order.

(1) *Sanctions by Court in County Where Deposition Is Taken.* If a deponent fails to be sworn or to answer a question after being directed to do so by the court in the county in which the deposition is being taken, the failure may be considered a contempt of that court.

(2) *Sanctions by Court in Which Action Is Pending.* If a party or an officer, director, or managing agent of a party or a person designated under Rule 30(b)(6) or 31(a) to testify on behalf of a party fails to obey an order to provide or permit discovery, including an order made under subdivision (a) of this rule or Rule 35 the court in which the action is pending may make such orders in regard to the failure as are just, and among others the following:

(A) An order that the matters regarding which the order was made or any other designated facts shall be taken to be established for the purposes of the action in accordance with the claim of the party obtaining the order;

(B) An order refusing to allow the disobedient party to support or oppose designated claims or defenses, or prohibiting that party from introducing designated matters in evidence;

(C) An order striking out pleadings or parts thereof, or staying further proceedings until the order is obeyed, or dismissing the action or proceeding or any part thereof, or rendering a judgment by default against the disobedient party;

(D) In lieu of any of the foregoing orders or in addition thereto, an order treating as a contempt of court the failure to obey any orders except an order to submit to a physical or mental examination;

(E) Where a party has failed to comply with an order under Rule 35(a) requiring that party to produce another for examination, such orders as are listed in paragraphs (A), (B), and (C) of this subdivision, unless the party failing to comply shows that that party is unable to produce such person for examination.

In lieu of any of the foregoing orders or in addition thereto, the court shall require the party failing to obey the order or the attorney advising that party or both to pay the reasonable expenses, including attorney's fees, caused by the failure, unless the court finds that the failure was substantially justified or that other circumstances make an award of expenses unjust.

Amended July 17, 1970, effective Nov. 1, 1970; Sept. 15, 1987, effective Nov. 15, 1987.

(c) Failure to Disclose; False or Misleading Disclosure; Untimely Disclosure.

(1) A party who fails to timely disclose information required by Rule 26.1 shall not, unless such failure is harmless, be permitted to use as evidence at trial, at a hearing, or on a motion, the information or witness not disclosed, except by leave of court for good cause shown. A party or attorney who makes a disclosure pursuant to Rule 26.1 that the party or attorney knew or should have known was inaccurate or incomplete and thereby causes an opposing party to engage in investigation or discovery, shall be ordered by the court to reimburse the opposing party for the cost including attorney's fees of such investigation or discovery. In addition to or in lieu of these sanctions, the court on motion of a party or on the court's own motion, and after affording an opportunity to be heard, may impose other appropriate sanctions. In addition to requiring payment of reasonable expenses, including attorney's fees, caused by the failure, these sanctions may include any of the actions authorized under subparagraphs (A), (B) and (C) of subdivision (b)(2) of this Rule and may include informing the jury of the failure to make the disclosure.

Text of Rule 37(c)(2) applicable to those cases filed before April 15, 2014 that are not subject to the conditions stated in the November 27, 2013 Amended Order Regarding Applicability Provision, in R-13-0017.

See also, text of Rule 37(c)(2) applicable to cases filed on or after April 15, 2014 and to those cases filed before April 15, 2014 that are subject to the conditions stated in the November 27, 2013, Amended Order Regarding Applicability Provision, in R-13-0017.

(2) A party seeking to use information which that party first disclosed later than sixty (60) days before trial must obtain leave of court by motion, supported by affidavit, to extend the time for disclosure. Such information shall not be used unless the motion establishes and the court finds:

(i) that the information would be allowed under the standards of subsection (c)(1) notwithstanding the short time remaining before trial; and

(ii) that the information was disclosed as soon as practicable after its discovery.

Text of Rule 37(2)(c) applicable to cases filed on or after April 15, 2014 and to those cases filed before April 15, 2014 that are subject to the conditions stated in the November 27, 2013, Amended Order Regarding Applicability Provision, in R-13-0017.

See also, text of Rule 37(c)(2) applicable to those cases filed before April 15, 2014 that are not subject to the conditions stated in the November 27, 2013 Amended Order Regarding Applicability Provision, in R-13-0017.

(2) A party seeking to use information which that party first disclosed later than (A) the deadline set in a Scheduling Order, or (B) in the absence of such a deadline, sixty (60) days before trial must obtain leave of court by motion, supported by affidavit, to extend the time for disclosure. Such information shall not be used unless the motion establishes and the court finds:

(i) that the information would be allowed under the standards of subsection (c)(1); and

(ii) that the information was disclosed as soon as practicable after its discovery.

(3) A party seeking to use information which that party first disclosed during trial must obtain leave of court by motion, supported by affidavit, to extend the time for disclosure. Such information shall not be used unless the motion establishes and the court finds:

(i) that the information could not have been discovered and disclosed earlier even with due diligence; and

(ii) that the information was disclosed immediately upon

its discovery.

Amended July 17, 1970, effective Nov. 1, 1970; Sept. 15, 1987, effective Nov. 15, 1987; May 30, 1996, effective Dec. 1, 1996; Nov. 22, 1996, effective March 1, 1997; Aug. 28, 2013, effective April 15, 2014, subject to the conditions of Order No. R-13-0017.

(d) Failure to Disclose Unfavorable Information. A party's or attorney's knowing failure to timely disclose damaging or unfavorable information shall be grounds for imposition of serious sanctions in the court's discretion up to and including dismissal of the claim or defense.

Amended Nov. 22, 1996, effective March 1, 1997; Aug. 28, 2013, effective April 15, 2014.

(e) Expenses on Failure to Admit. If a party fails to admit the genuineness of any document or the truth of any matter as requested under Rule 36, and if the party requesting the admissions thereafter proves the genuineness of the document or the truth of the matter, the requesting party may apply to the court for an order requiring the other party to pay the reasonable expenses incurred in making that proof, including reasonable attorney's fees. The court shall make the order unless it finds that (1) the request was held objectionable pursuant to Rule 36(a), or (2) the admission sought was of no substantial importance, or (3) the party failing to admit had reasonable ground to believe that the party might prevail on the matter, or (4) there was other good reason for the failure to admit.

Amended Nov. 22, 1996, effective March 1, 1997.

(f) Failure of Party to Attend at Own Deposition or Serve Answer to Interrogatories or Respond to Request for Inspection. If a party or an officer, director, or managing agent of a party or a person designated under Rule 30(b)(6) or 31(a) to testify on behalf of a party fails (1) to appear before the officer who is to take the deposition, after being served with a proper notice, or (2) to serve answers or objections to interrogatories submitted under Rule 33, after proper service of the interrogatories, or (3) to serve a written response to a request for inspection submitted under Rule 34, after proper service of the request, the court in which the action is pending on motion may make such orders in regard to the failure as are just, and among others it may take any action authorized under paragraphs (A), (B), and (C) of subdivision (b)(2) of this rule. In lieu of any order or in addition thereto, the court shall require the party failing to act or the attorney advising that party or both to pay the reasonable expenses, including attorney's fees, caused by the failure, unless the court finds that the failure was substantially justified or that other circumstances make an award of expenses unjust.

The failure to act described in this subdivision may not be

excused on the ground that the discovery sought is objectionable unless the party failing to act has applied for a protective order as provided by Rule 26(c). Formerly Rule 37(d).

Amended July 17, 1970, effective Nov. 1, 1970; Sept. 15, 1987, effective Nov. 15, 1987. Redesignated 37(f) and amended Nov. 22, 1996, effective March 1, 1997.

(g) Electronically stored information. Absent exceptional circumstances, a court may not impose sanctions under these rules on a party for failing to provide electronically stored information lost as a result of the routine, good-faith operation of an electronic information system.

Added Sept. 5, 2007, effective Jan. 1, 2008.

HISTORICAL NOTES

[2014 Amendments]

[Rule 37(c)] Arizona Supreme Court Order No. R-13-0017, issued Aug. 28, 2013, provided that the amendments of the order would be "effective on April 15, 2014 as to all cases filed on or after that date." The applicability provision of Order No. R-13-0017 was amended on Nov. 14, 2013, and subsequently amended on Nov. 27, 2013 to provide:

(1) The Amendments shall apply to all actions filed on or after April 15, 2014.

(2) Beginning on April 15, 2014, the Amendments also shall apply to any action filed prior to April 15, 2014 (a "pending action"), unless one of the following events has occurred before that date:

  (a) A party has filed a Motion to Set and Certificate of Readiness,

  (b) The parties have filed a Proposed Scheduling Order, or

  (c) The court has entered a Scheduling Order.

(3) If, in a pending action, one of the preceding events has not occurred before April 15, 2014, the parties shall file a Joint Report and a Proposed Scheduling Order in accordance with the Amendments by June 30, 2014, or within 270 days after the commencement of the action, whichever date is later. Otherwise, the court will place the action on the Dismissal Calendar in accordance with the Amendments.

(4) A trial court, in its discretion, may apply any of the Amendments to a case pending before April 15, 2014, even if the Amendments would not otherwise apply under paragraph (2) above. For example, if a party filed a Motion to Set and Certificate of Readiness before April 15, 2014, the trial judge may set the matter for a trial setting conference under amended Rule 16(f), rather than place the case on the active calendar under pre-amendment Rule 38.1(c).

(5) Civil actions pending on the Inactive Calendar on April 15, 2014 shall be dismissed without prejudice on June 14, 2014, unless one of the actions set forth in subparts (1) - (4) of amended Rule 38.1(f) occurs before June 14, 2014.

STATE BAR COMMITTEE NOTES

1970 Amendment

[Rule 37] The general purpose of the 1970 revisions of this rule is to stiffen the sanctions for the occasional frustrations of discovery. A further change, largely of style, is the use of the term "failure" to comply in lieu of "refusal," to accord with *Societe Internationale Pour Participations Industrielles Et Commerciales, S. A. v. Rogers*, 357 U.S. 197, 78 S. Ct. 1087, 2 L. Ed. 2d 1255 (1958).

In case of non-performance of the duties itemized in Rule 37(a), the party seeking discovery may move for an order compelling performance. Under the pre-amendment practice, expenses are awarded only upon an affirmative finding that the losing party was without substantial justification. The amended rule slightly tilts the burden in that situation. With full realization that any discovery motion will necessarily put some cost on someone, the rule provides that the cost shall be borne by the loser unless the court affirmatively finds that his conduct was substantially justified. The change is intended to encourage judges to be more alert to discovery abuses, and should result in charging expenses where no genuine dispute exists. Expenses should ordinarily be awarded unless a court finds that the losing party acted justifiably.

The cost provision is carried over to the enforcement of court orders respecting discovery by Rule 37(b)(2). This is particularly appropriate where a court order is disobeyed; and so also under Rule 37(d) as to failures to attend a deposition or otherwise make responses.

While the rule should stiffen Arizona practice as to costs, it does not affect the results of any decided cases. Thus, where the question on the necessity to answer a question is close, *Hastings v. Thurston*, 100 Ariz. 302, 413 P.2d 767 (1966), or where the witness has an absolute right not to answer because of a claim of self-incrimination, *Buzard v. Griffin*, 89 Ariz. 42, 358 P.2d 155 (1960), there will be no sanctions. If a non-party witness refuses to cooperate in lawful discovery, he may be ordered to perform and may be charged expenses, and if he fails after order, he may be held in contempt; but unless such a witness is an agent of a party, the party cannot be penalized. *Milam v. Milam*, 101 Ariz. 323, 419 P.2d 502 (1966). The court retains a high degree of discretion as to sanctions, and may impose less drastic sanctions where a failure is from inability to comply, *Zakroff v. May*, 8 Ariz. App. 101, 443 P.2d 916 (1968). The assessment of expenses for unreasonable failure to admit accords with *Aetna Loan Co. v. Apache Trailer Sales*, 1 Ariz. App. 322, 402 P.2d 580 (1965).

1996 and 1997 Amendments

Subsection (c)(1) of the amended rule is intended to codify the holding of *Allstate Ins. Co. v. O'Toole*, 182 Ariz. 284, 896 P.2d 254 (1995), to the effect that information or witnesses disclosed in an untimely manner shall be excluded from evidence unless there is good cause for granting relief from the exclusion. Under the amended rule, a showing that the untimely disclosure is harmless would constitute grounds for granting relief from the sanction of exclusion. "Harmless" means the other party has a full and fair opportunity to investigate and rebut the new evidence. Factors to be considered in determining whether there is "good cause" for relief from exclusion include: the reason for the failure to disclose, the willfulness or inadvertence of the conduct, the prejudice to the proponent of the evidence from exclusion, the prejudice to the other party from late disclosure, attempts to resolve the dispute short of exclusion and the overall diligence of the parties. See Allstate. Late disclosure in a case "where the trial date has not yet been set" will be governed by Allstate.

Although the Allstate factors allow flexibility, those militating against the use of late disclosed evidence gain strength as the trial nears. Late disclosure will prejudice the opposing party if there is insufficient time to investigate fully and prepare rebuttal before the date for final supplementation of disclosures. Prejudice is also inherent when a trial must be continued after the parties have spent time and resources in preparation. The rule requires full, early and continuous disclosure. Gamesmanship at any stage of the proceedings should be addressed strongly. Even where there is good cause to refrain from excluding evidence, other sanctions may be appropriate.

Subsection (c)(2) addresses new information or areas of testimony disclosed for the first time after the date for final disclosure. Although disclosures should normally be completed 60 days before trial, there are some circumstances where it may be appropriate to extend the date for final disclosures. Because prejudice from the lateness of disclosure is so likely at this stage, however, the proponent of such evidence must make a substantially heightened showing of good cause or harmlessness under Allstate. A party seeking to use such information should disclose it as soon as practicable and then promptly file a motion and affidavit for leave to allow use of the information.

Circumstances warranting relief at this stage may exist, for example, where one party has disclosed substantial new evidence shortly before the final disclosure date. If allowed (and there would be substantial questions whether such a late disclosure of key information was seasonable), the other party may well be in a position where rebuttal evidence could not have been disclosed earlier even with due diligence. It may then be appropriate to extend disclosure for that party to allow rebuttal. Each case must be addressed under its own circumstances, giving due regard to the fact that the parties have had many months to complete disclosure and to the substantial risk of prejudice at this late stage of the proceedings. One party's lack of diligence must not be allowed to deprive the other party of a fair opportunity to investigate, rebut opposing evidence and prepare for trial.

Subsection (c)(3) addresses new information or areas of testimony first disclosed during trial. Prejudice at this point is inevitable. Such evidence should be excluded unless it would meet the standards to obtain a new trial for newly discovered evidence under Rule 59. If allowed, the court should be flexible in allowing a continuance or other means to prepare for rebuttal of the new matter.

The restrictions upon the use of evidence or information which has not been timely disclosed apply to the side that made the untimely disclosure. Adverse parties that wish to make use of such evidence or information should generally be free to do so in a manner that is otherwise consistent with the rules of procedure and evidence, upon such terms as will prevent any unfair surprise.

At any stage of the proceedings, disclosure means fairly apprising the other party of the substance of the expected evidence and testimony. Fair disclosure of the substance of evidence includes disclosing sufficient facts to allow an understanding of the substance and import of the evidence. Scripting or listing every detail is not required. Where substance is fairly disclosed, the details reasonably to be inferred from that substance are deemed disclosed. The test is whether the disclosure "fairly expose[s] the facts and issues to be litigated, as well as the witnesses and exhibits to be relied upon." *Bryan v. Riddel*, 178 Ariz. 472, 477, 875 P.2d 131, 136 (1994). For example, where a witness has died or become unavailable, a new witness should normally be allowed to provide the timely disclosed testimony. Similarly, a recently identified custodian should normally be allowed to lay foundation for previously disclosed documents. In these situations, the substance of the evidence was fairly disclosed. Objections on such matters of form, or to details fairly to be inferred from disclosure, are inappropriate and should be discouraged.

Imposition of the sanction of exclusion does not preclude the court from entering other sanctions pursuant to Rule 37(a)(4)(A), (B) or (C). In keeping with *Bryan v. Riddel*, 178 Ariz. 472, 875 P.2d 131 (1994), the committee wishes to reemphasize that the disclosure of the information need not be in a formal disclosure statement but can be in response to an interrogatory, request for production, request for admission, deposition, or an informal process so long as all parties are reasonably apprised of the identity of the witness, the information possessed by the witness, or other information sought to be admitted.

When the adequacy of the disclosure is contested, the burden shall be upon the proponent of the evidence to demonstrate that the substance of the offered evidence has been fairly disclosed to all parties.

2000 Amendment

As part of an effort to consolidate formerly separate sets of procedural rules into either the Arizona Rules of Civil Procedure or the Rules of the Arizona Supreme Court, the former Uniform Rules of Practice of the Superior Court were abrogated in their entirety. The provisions of former Rule IV(g) of those Rules, which required, as a condition of securing a hearing on any discovery motion, the filing of a separate statement of moving counsel attesting that, after personal consultation and good faith efforts to do so, counsel had been unable to resolve the matter satisfactorily, were added to Rule 37 as a new Rule 37(a)(2)(C). In the process, the coverage of the provision was expanded to apply, not just to "discovery motions," but to any motion brought under Rule 37.

AUTHORS' COMMENTS

Analysis

1. Scope and Purpose of Rule.
2. Comparison With Federal Rule.
3. Motions to Compel Discovery; Requirements.
4. Sanctions Available for Failure to Make Discovery.
5. Sanctions for Failure to Comply With Order Compelling Discovery.
6. Motions to Compel Disclosures.
7. Leave of Court to Make Late Disclosure.
8. Sanctions for Failure to Disclose or Misleading Disclosure; Exclusion of Evidence.
9. Sanctions Available under Rule 37(f).
10. Sanctions for Failure to Admit Requests for Admission.
11. Compelling Answers to Deposition Questions.
12. Selection of Appropriate Sanctions.
13. Exclusion of Evidence.
14. Striking of Answer.
15. Dismissal; Entry of Default.
16. 2014 Rule Amendments: Effective Date and Applicability.

1. *Scope and Purpose of Rule.* Ariz. R. Civ. P. 37 is the "enforcement arm" of the discovery rules—the vehicle for enforcing compliance with the parties' discovery obligations, and their obligation to make the disclosures mandated by Ariz. R. Civ. P. 26.1. Under Rule 37, the Court is empowered to order that a discovery request be complied with, and to apply one or more of a variety of sanctions to coerce that compliance. *State Farm Ins. Co. v. Roberts*, 97 Ariz. 169, 398 P.2d 671 (1965). The burden of persuasion is on the party who objected to the discovery in issue. *State ex rel. Babbitt v. Arnold*, 26 Ariz. App. 333, 548 P.2d 426 (Div. 2 1976).

2. *Comparison With Federal Rule.* As a consequence of the 1996 amendments, ARCP 37 is once again substantially identical

to FRCP 37, with some differences.

Ariz. R. Civ. P. 37 does not have a provision similar to FRCP 37(f), which authorizes the award of expenses as a sanction against any party who fails to participate in good faith in the framing of a discovery plan under FRCP 26(f).

In 2008, Arizona adopted ARCP 37(g), which in all material respects, is identical to FRCP 37(e). ARCP 37(g), and its federal counterpart FRCP 37(e), provide protection from discovery sanctions for the loss of discoverable electronic data from the routine, good faith operation of an information technology system.

The Federal commentary discussing the 2006 adoption of FRCP 37(e) and its intended scope with respect to electronically stored information, erroneously cites to FRCP 37(f) [which concerns the failure to participate in framing a discovery plan]. The Federal commentary should have cited to FRCP 37(e) [which concerns failure to provide electronically stored information].

FRCP 37(a)(2)(A), adopted as part of the 1993 amendments, and the contemporaneously amended FRCP 37(a)(2)(B), 37(c)(2) and 37(d), all contain a provision that any motion to compel or motion for sanctions must include a certification that the moving party has conferred or attempted to confer in good faith with the opposing party in an effort to resolve the controversy before bringing the motion. The comparable provision in the Arizona Rule is ARCP 37(a)(2)(C) (formerly Rule IV(g) of the now abrogated Uniform Rules of Practice of the Superior Court) which was added by amendment in 2000.

Amended ARCP 37(a)(4) now also contains a provision allowing the court to deny an award of expenses or sanctions on a motion to compel discovery or disclosure if it finds that the moving party did not make a good faith effort to obtain the materials sought before bringing the motion.

FRCP 37(c)(1) and ARCP 37(c)(1), are roughly comparable, but the Federal Rule does not contain provisions corresponding to ARCP 37(c)(2), 37(c)(3) and 37(d).

In 2007, the language of FRCP 37 was amended as part of the general restyling of the Federal Rules of Civil Procedure to make the Federal Rules more easily understood and to make style and terminology consistent throughout the Federal Rules of Civil Procedure. Those stylistic modifications have not been incorporated into ARCP 37.

In 2013, FRCP 37(b) was amended to conform to amendments made to FRCP 45, particularly the addition of FRCP 45(f) providing for transfer of a subpoena-related motion to the court where the action is pending. FRCP 37(b)(1) was amended to deal with contempt of orders entered after such a transfer. ARCP 37 does not contain a similar provision.

3. *Motions to Compel Discovery; Requirements.* Where there has been a failure to respond to an interrogatory, request for production or deposition question, or a failure to designate a deponent under Ariz. R. Civ. P. 30(b)(6), the party seeking the discovery can apply to the Court for an order compelling the discovery sought, and for the imposition of an appropriate sanction. An evasive or incomplete answer to a discovery request is considered a failure to respond. Ariz. R. Civ. P. 37(a)(2)(A) now also specifically authorizes motions to compel the disclosures required by Ariz. R. Civ. P. 26.1. The motion to compel discovery or disclosure is ordinarily to be made in the Court where the action is pending. In the case of a party's failure to respond to a deposition question, the motion may be made in the Superior Court for the county where the deposition is being conducted. Where a deponent who is not a party fails to respond to a deposition question, the motion *must* be brought in the county where the deposition is being taken.

Ariz. R. Civ. P. 37(a)(2)(C), which contains the provisions of former Rule IV(g) of the now abrogated Uniform Rules of Practice of the Superior Court, provides that discovery motions will not be "considered or scheduled unless a separate statement of moving counsel is attached thereto," which certifies that "after personal consultation and good faith efforts" to do so, counsel have been unable to satisfactorily resolve the discovery dispute which is the subject of the motion being submitted. Moreover, under Ariz. R. Civ. P. 37(a)(4)(A), added to the Rule in 1996, the failure of a party moving to compel discovery or a required disclosure to make a good faith effort to secure the discovery or disclosure sought without resorting to the Court, is grounds for denying an award of sanctions.

In addition, Rule 3.2(h) of the Maricopa County Superior Court Local Rules, and Rule 3.10, of the Pima County Superior Court Local Rules require that a motion for an order compelling discovery, brought pursuant to Rule 37(a)(2), must be accompanied by a separate statement in which the moving party sets forth, in separate, numbered paragraphs:

"(1) [T]he question propounded, the interrogatory submitted, the designation requested or the inspection requested;

(2) [T]he answer, designation or response received; and

(3) [T]he reason(s) why said answer, designation or response is deficient."

This requirement does not apply where there has been a complete and total failure to respond to a discovery request or set of discovery requests.

4. *Sanctions Available for Failure to Make Discovery.* The mildest of the available sanctions is an award of the costs and expenses, including reasonable attorneys' fees, incurred by the successful party on a motion to compel discovery or disclosure. This sanction is available where one of the following failures to make discovery is involved:

1) A deponent fails to answer a question propounded or submitted at a deposition, or gives an answer that is evasive or incomplete.

2) A corporation or other entity fails to designate a representative to testify on its behalf at a deposition.

3) A party fails to answer an interrogatory propounded under Rule 33.

4) A party, in response to a request for production or inspection under Rule 34, fails to state that inspection or production will be permitted, or fails to permit inspection or production as requested.

Under Ariz. R. Civ. P. 37(a)(4)(A), which was added to the Rule in 1996, an award of sanctions can be denied, if the Court finds that the party bringing the motion to compel disclosure or discovery failed to make a good faith effort to secure the discovery or disclosure informally without resorting to the Court for relief. Ariz. R. Civ. P. 37(g), added in 2008, provides that, absent exceptional circumstances, a court may not impose sanctions for the failure to provide in discovery electronically stored information that has been lost as the result of the routine, good faith operation of an electronic information system.

Ariz. R. Civ. P. 37(a) specifically authorizes the Court to award, to a party who successfully resists a motion to compel, the expenses thereby incurred, including reasonable attorneys' fees, unless it finds the bringing of the motion to be substantially justified. Where it is debatable whether a question was proper, however, the failure to answer may not subject the non-responding party to potential liability for an award of fees and costs. *Hastings v. Thurston*, 100 Ariz. 302, 413 P.2d 767 (1966).

5. *Sanctions for Failure to Comply With Order Compelling Discovery.* Ariz. R. Civ. P. 37(b) authorizes an additional array of sanctions which may be applied where a party has failed to comply with a previous order compelling discovery. In that circumstance, the Court is authorized to do one or more of the following:

1) Enter an order that the matters which were the subject of the prior order shall be deemed established against the recalcitrant party's position. *See,* Rule 37(b)(2)(A).

2) Enter an order precluding the recalcitrant party from asserting certain claims or defenses or introducing evidence with

respect to them. *See,* Rule 37(b)(2)(B).

3) Enter an order striking the pleadings or portions thereof of the recalcitrant party, or dismissing the action or portions thereof, or entering the default of the recalcitrant party. *See,* Rule 37(b)(2)(C).

4) Finding the recalcitrant party in contempt of court. *See,* Rule 37(b)(2)(D).

5) Enter orders listed in Rules 37(b)(2)(A), (B) and (C), in those cases where a party has failed to produce another for a Rule 35(a) examination. *See*, Rule 37(b)(2)(E).

The contempt sanction, under Rule 37(b)(2)(D), may not be employed for failure to obey an order to submit to a physical or mental examination. Similarly, a party who has failed to comply with an order to produce another for a physical or mental examination will not be subject to sanctions if an inability to comply is shown.

An award of sanctions under Ariz. R. Civ. P. 37(b) requires that there have been a violation of an order compelling discovery; an award of sanctions under Ariz. R. Civ. P. 37(f), discussed hereinafter, does not require disobedience of a prior order. *Verde Ditch Co. by Allert v. James*, 157 Ariz. 369, 758 P.2d 144 (Ct. App. Div. 1 1988).

6. *Motions to Compel Disclosures*. The 1996 amendment added Ariz. R. Civ. P. 37(a)(2)(A), which specifically authorizes motions to compel the disclosures required by Ariz. R. Civ. P. 26.1. Any party to the action can file such a motion to compel and/or for sanctions for a claimed failure to make the requisite disclosures. An evasive or incomplete disclosure is to be treated as a failure to disclose.

Sanctions for a failure to disclose are permitted if a motion to compel is granted or if the requested discovery or disclosure is provided after the motion is filed but before it is ruled upon, unless the court finds that the moving party did not make a good faith effort to obtain the discovery or disclosure before resorting to a motion, or that the non-disclosure or objection to discovery was substantially justified. Sanctions can include an award of expenses and attorney's fees. A trial court's decision on a motion for sanctions for disclosure violations will not be disturbed on appeal absent an abuse of discretion. *Taeger v. Catholic Family and Community Services*, 196 Ariz. 285, 995 P.2d 721 (Ct. App. Div. 1 1999).

7. *Leave of Court to Make Late Disclosure.* Under Ariz. R. Civ. P. 26.1, a party is required to disclose in a timely manner, *inter alia*, its claims and defenses, the factual bases for them, a fair description of each witness' expected testimony, and the substance of the facts and opinions of each expert's expected testimony.

Englert v. Carondelet Health Network, 199 Ariz. 21, 13 P.3d 763 (Ct. App. Div. 2 2000). If a party fails to do so, it is not permitted to use that information at trial absent specific extenuating circumstances. *Englert v. Carondelet Health Network*, 199 Ariz. 21, 13 P.3d 763 (Ct. App. Div. 2 2000).

By Order dated November 22, 1996, the Arizona Supreme Court adopted, effective March 1, 1997, amendments to Ariz. R. Civ. P. 26.1(b) and 37, which specifically address the circumstances under which a party may be permitted to use at trial information which is disclosed for the first time within sixty (60) days before trial, or during trial. The amendments added two new provisions dealing with the procedure for seeking leave of court to make disclosures (and, more importantly, to make use of the late disclosed information) after the nominal deadline of no later than sixty (60) days before the commencement of trial imposed by Ariz. R. Civ. P. 26.1(b)(2). The amendments also added a sentence to existing Rule 26.1(b)(2) specifying that a party seeking to use information which was first disclosed later than sixty (60) days before trial must obtain leave of court to extend the time for disclosure, as provided for in Ariz. R. Civ. P. 37(c)(2).

Ariz. R. Civ. P. 37(c)(2) governs late disclosure before trial as follows:

1. With respect to cases filed before April 15, 2014, and not otherwise subject to Ariz. R. Civ. P. 37(c)(2) (amended 2014), the provision requires a party obtain leave of court, upon motion, supported by affidavit, in order to utilize at trial information which is disclosed for the first time less than sixty (60) days before trial.
2. With respect to those cases subject to Ariz. R. Civ. P. 37(c)(2) (amended 2014), the provision requires a party obtain leave of court, upon motion, supported by affidavit, in order to utilize at trial information which is disclosed for the first time later than:
   - (i) the deadline set in the Scheduling Order or,
   - (ii) in the absence of such deadline, sixty (60) days before trial.

With respect to both categories of cases, Rule 37(c)(2) specifies that leave of court is not to be granted to use such late disclosed information unless the Court finds that the information would be allowed under Rule 37(c)(1) standards, and that the information was disclosed to the adverse party as soon as practicable after it was discovered.

Ariz. R. Civ. P. 37(c)(3) addresses the use of information which is disclosed for the first time at or during trial. Once again, the information cannot be used unless the party seeking to use it obtains leave of court upon motion, supported by affidavit, to extend the time for disclosure. The Court is not to grant such leave unless the Court finds that the information in question could not have been discovered and disclosed earlier even with due diligence, and that the information was disclosed immediately upon its discovery.

8. *Sanctions for Failure to Disclose or Misleading Disclosure; Exclusion of Evidence*. Ariz. R. Civ. P. 37(c) and (d) were added to Rule 37 by 1996 amendments which, *inter alia*, transferred from Ariz. R. Civ. P. 26.1 the provisions prescribing the sanctions available, and the procedure for seeking them, for failure to comply with the disclosure requirements imposed by that Rule. Under Ariz. R. Civ. P. 37(a)(2)(A), any party to the action may file a motion to compel and/or for sanctions for failure to make the requisite disclosures.

Ariz. R. Civ. P. 37(c)(1) now contains the sanction provisions for the failure to make timely disclosure of information as required by Ariz. R. Civ. P. 26.1. An evasive or incomplete disclosure is to be treated as a failure to disclose. Sanctions for a failure to disclose are permitted if a motion to compel is granted, or if the requested discovery or disclosure is provided after the motion is filed but before it is ruled upon, unless the Court finds that the moving party did not make a good faith effort to obtain the discovery or disclosure sought before resorting to a motion. Sanctions may include an award of expenses and attorneys' fees, unless the Court finds that the noncompliance with the disclosure requirements was substantially justified, or that other circumstances make an award of expenses and fees unjust. *Scottsdale Princess Partnership v. Maricopa County*, 185 Ariz. 368, 916 P.2d 1084 (Ct. App. Div. 1 1995). A trial court's decision on a motion for sanctions for disclosure violations will not be disturbed on appeal absent an abuse of discretion. *Taeger v. Catholic Family and Community Services*, 196 Ariz. 285, 995 P.2d 721 (Ct. App. Div. 1 1999).

Sanctions also may include any of those authorized by the other provisions of Ariz. R. Civ. P. 37, and can even include having the Court inform the jury of any failure to disclose. In addition, under the Rule, where a failure to disclose, or a misleading disclosure, results in a party being required to engage in investigation or to conduct discovery that should not have been necessary, the Court *must* direct the offending party to reimburse the other party for the expenses thereby incurred, including attorneys' fees. Such a monetary sanction, however, should bear some relationship to the expenses directly caused by the offending conduct. *Taliaferro v. Taliaferro*, 188 Ariz. 333, 935 P.2d 911 (Ct. App. Div. 1 1996).

Unless the failure to disclose is found by the trial judge to be harmless, a party failing to make a timely disclosure of evidence may not use that evidence at trial, at any hearing, or in connection with a motion, except with leave of court for good cause shown. *Marquez v. Ortega*, 231 Ariz. 437, 296 P.3d 100 (Ct. App. Div. 1 2013); *Englert v. Carondelet Health Network*, 199 Ariz. 21, 13 P.3d 763 (Ct. App. Div. 2 2000).

The accompanying Committee Note with respect to the 1996 amendments explains that these provisions are intended to codify the holding of the Arizona Supreme Court in *Allstate Ins. Co. v. O'Toole*, 182 Ariz. 284, 896 P.2d 254 (1995). In that decision, the Supreme Court observed that the wooden application of the sanction of exclusion of undisclosed evidence could bring about results that were unduly harsh and inconsistent with the purposes of the disclosure rules, and urged trial courts to take a "common sense" approach to the issue of whether undisclosed evidence should be excluded. The Committee Note goes on to explain that, in order to avoid the sanction of exclusion, the disclosure of information need not be in a formal disclosure statement, but can be in response to other discovery requests, or as part of an informal process, so long as all parties to the litigation are reasonably apprised of the information in question.

Although some form of notice and opportunity to be heard on the issue of the propriety of imposing sanctions should precede the imposition of sanctions, a hearing is not always required. *Marquez v. Ortega*, 231 Ariz. 437, 296 P.3d 100 (Ct. App. Div. 1 2013); *Lund v. Donahoe*, 227 Ariz. 572, 261 P.3d 456 (Ct. App. Div. 1 2011); *Precision Components, Inc. v. Harrison, Harper, Christian & Dichter, P.C.*, 179 Ariz. 552, 880 P.2d 1098 (Ct. App. Div. 2 1993); *Robinson v. Higuera*, 157 Ariz. 622, 760 P.2d 622 (Ct. App. Div. 1 1988) ("due process does not require a hearing in every case"). Whether a hearing is required depends on several factors: (1) the circumstances; (2) the severity of the sanctions under consideration; (3) the judge's knowledge of the facts and/or need for further inquiry. *Marquez v. Ortega*, 231 Ariz. 437, 296 P.3d 100 (Ct. App. Div. 1 2013); *Lund v. Donahoe*, 227 Ariz. 572, 261 P.3d 456 (Ct. App. Div. 1 2011)). Nevertheless, it has been held that when the issue concerns a party's bad faith or willful misconduct in violating a discovery order, fundamental fairness requires that the court hold an evidentiary hearing before entry of default judgment or dismissal. *Robinson v. Higuera*, 157 Ariz. 622, 760 P.2d 622 (Ct. App. Div. 1 1988).

The exclusion of evidence remains an available sanction, however, in an appropriate case. *Marquez v. Ortega*, 231 Ariz. 437, 296 P.3d 100 (Ct. App. Div. 1 2013); *Link v. Pima County*, 193 Ariz. 336, 972 P.2d 669 (Ct. App. Div. 2 1998); *Zuern By and Through Zuern v. Ford Motor Co.*, 188 Ariz. 486, 937 P.2d 676 (Ct. App. Div. 2 1996); *Perguson v. Tamis*, 188 Ariz. 425, 937

P.2d 347 (Ct. App. Div. 2 1996).

Finally, Rule 37(d) specifically states that a knowing failure to disclose damaging or unfavorable evidence can be grounds for the imposition of more serious sanctions, up to and including dismissal of a claim or defense.

Motions *in limine* have been employed in civil cases as a means to exclude evidence for violations of the disclosure rules. *Zimmerman v. Shakman*, 204 Ariz. 231, 62 P.3d 976 (Ct. App. Div. 1 2003). When a motion *in limine* is used to enforce the provisions of Rule 26.1, it is effectively a request for sanctions under Rule 37(c), and will be considered and reviewed using the standards developed under those Rules. *Zimmerman v. Shakman*, 204 Ariz. 231, 62 P.3d 976 (Ct. App. Div. 1 2003). The granting of a motion *in limine* for a violation of the disclosure rules, followed by a dismissal for lack of evidence, is the equivalent of a dismissal for nondisclosure and must be preceded by a hearing to determine whether the party or the party's attorney was at fault. *Zimmerman v. Shakman*, 204 Ariz. 231, 62 P.3d 976 (Ct. App. Div. 1 2003).

While a trial court's order of dismissal for discovery or disclosure violations will be upheld absent a clear abuse of discretion, the trial court's discretion to dismiss a case for such violations is more limited than when it employs lesser sanctions. *Zimmerman v. Shakman*, 204 Ariz. 231, 62 P.3d 976 (Ct. App. Div. 1 2003). Sanctions for abuses of discovery or disclosure must be appropriate and must be preceded by due process. *Zimmerman v. Shakman*, 204 Ariz. 231, 62 P.3d 976 (Ct. App. Div. 1 2003). There is little reason to completely bar the use of evidence when no trial or case dispositive motion is pending. *Zimmerman v. Shakman*, 204 Ariz. 231, 62 P.3d 976 (Ct. App. Div. 1 2003). On the other hand, if a trial is set or imminent, the possibility of prejudice increases. *Zimmerman v. Shakman*, 204 Ariz. 231, 62 P.3d 976 (Ct. App. Div. 1 2003).

9. *Sanctions Available Under Rule 37(f).* While Rule 37(b) by its terms applies to a failure to comply with a prior discovery order, the sanctions which it authorizes, with the exception of a citation for contempt, are also available in certain circumstances enumerated in Rule 37(f) (formerly Rule 37(d)), where no prior order has been entered, *Verde Ditch Co. by Allert v. James*, 157 Ariz. 369, 758 P.2d 144 (Ct. App. Div. 1 1988). Rule 37(f) authorizes the imposition of sanctions, even absent a prior order compelling discovery, in the following instances:

1) Where a party, or a representative of a corporate party, fails to appear for a properly noticed deposition;

2) Where a party fails to serve answers or objections to interrogatories under Rule 33; and

3) Where a party fails to serve a written response to a properly served Rule 34 request for production or inspection.

The production of an individual, in response to a Rule 30(b)(6) deposition notice, who is not an officer, director or managing agent of the party deponent, and who has no knowledge of the information or subjects of examination specified in the notice, is tantamount to a failure to appear for the deposition and warrants the imposition of sanctions. *Groat v. Equity American Ins. Co.*, 180 Ariz. 342, 884 P.2d 228 (Ct. App. Div. 1 1994).

10. *Sanctions for Failure to Admit Requests for Admission.* Rule 37(e) (formerly Rule 37(c)) deals specifically with the failure of a party to admit matters made the subject of a request for admissions under Rule 36. If the party seeking the admission subsequently proves the truth of the matter in question, the Court can award that party the expenses incurred in making that proof, including reasonable attorneys' fees, unless the Court finds that the request was objectionable, the matter was not of substantial importance, the party in question had good reason to believe they would prevail on the issue, or there were other good grounds for the failure to admit. *West v. Sundance Development Co.*, 169 Ariz. 579, 821 P.2d 240 (Ct. App. Div. 2 1991); *Aetna Loan Co. v. Apache Trailer Sales*, 1 Ariz. App. 322, 402 P.2d 580 (1965). Where the Court finds that the denial of a requested admission was not made in good faith, that is grounds for an award of expenses and fees. *Aetna Loan Co. v. Apache Trailer Sales*, 1 Ariz. App. 322, 402 P.2d 580 (1965).

11. *Compelling Answers to Deposition Questions.* Under Rule 37(a)(1), a motion to compel answers to deposition questions may be brought in the county where the deposition is being conducted, and must be brought there if the deponent is not a party. An evasive answer to a deposition question may be tantamount to a refusal to answer. Rule 37(a)(3); *Gulf Homes, Inc. v. Beron*, 141 Ariz. 624, 688 P.2d 632 (1984).

12. *Selection of Appropriate Sanctions.* The issue of what sanction, if any, to apply in any given circumstance is one committed to the trial court's discretion. *Twin City Fire Ins. Co. v. Burke*, 204 Ariz. 251, 63 P.3d 282 (2003); *Granger v. Wisner*, 134 Ariz. 377, 656 P.2d 1238 (1982); *AG Rancho Equipment Co. v. Massey-Ferguson, Inc.*, 123 Ariz. 122, 598 P.2d 100 (1979); *Jimenez v. Wal-Mart Stores, Inc.*, 206 Ariz. 424, 79 P.3d 673 (Ct. App. Div. 2 2003); *Birds Intern. Corp. v. Arizona Maintenance Co., Inc.*, 135 Ariz. 545, 662 P.2d 1052 (Ct. App. Div. 2 1983); *In re Marriage of Gove*, 117 Ariz. 324, 572 P.2d 458 (Ct. App. Div. 1 1977); *State ex rel. Babbitt v. Arnold*, 26 Ariz. App. 333, 548 P.2d 426 (Div. 2 1976); *Buchanan v. Jimenez*, 18 Ariz. App. 298, 501 P.2d 567 (Div. 2 1972). Any sanction that is awarded, however, must be

"appropriate" and should bear some relationship to the nature of the violation and the harm it caused. *Taliaferro v. Taliaferro*, 188 Ariz. 333, 935 P.2d 911 (Ct. App. Div. 1 1996). Rule 37(g), added in 2008, provides that, absent exceptional circumstances, a court may not impose sanctions for the failure to provide in discovery electronically stored information that has been lost as the result of the routine, good faith operation of an electronic information system.

Dismissal of the action, or the entry of a party's default, however, is a very drastic sanction that should only be invoked in extreme circumstances. *Austin v. City of Scottsdale*, 140 Ariz. 579, 684 P.2d 151, 46 A.L.R.4th 941 (1984); *Wayne Cook Enterprises, Inc. v. Fain Properties Ltd. Partnership*, 196 Ariz. 146, 993 P.2d 1110 (Ct. App. Div. 1 1999); *Lenze v. Synthes, Ltd.*, 160 Ariz. 302, 772 P.2d 1155 (Ct. App. Div. 1 1989); *Birds Intern. Corp. v. Arizona Maintenance Co., Inc.*, 135 Ariz. 545, 662 P.2d 1052 (Ct. App. Div. 2 1983); *Buchanan v. Jimenez*, 18 Ariz. App. 298, 501 P.2d 567 (Div. 2 1972); *Zakroff v. May*, 8 Ariz. App. 101, 443 P.2d 916 (1968). The propriety of this sanction is discussed more extensively in Section 15, *infra*.

The involvement of counsel is a factor to be considered. A party should not be unduly penalized for the conduct of counsel. *Birds Intern. Corp. v. Arizona Maintenance Co., Inc.*, 135 Ariz. 545, 662 P.2d 1052 (Ct. App. Div. 2 1983). In an appropriate case, the Court can award sanctions against counsel. *Golleher v. Horton*, 119 Ariz. 604, 583 P.2d 260 (Ct. App. Div. 1 1978). Parties representing themselves, however, are charged with knowledge of their obligations under the discovery rules and may be subjected to sanctions for failure to comply. *Copper State Bank v. Saggio*, 139 Ariz. 438, 679 P.2d 84 (Ct. App. Div. 2 1983). In the final analysis, the sanctions that are awarded must be appropriate to the nature, extent and impact of the violations found to have occurred, and must be preceded by due process. *Taliaferro v. Taliaferro*, 188 Ariz. 333, 935 P.2d 911 (Ct. App. Div. 1 1996); *Montgomery Ward & Co., Inc. v. Superior Court In and For County of Maricopa*, 176 Ariz. 619, 863 P.2d 911 (Ct. App. Div. 1 1993). The sanction that is appropriate and the process that is due depends upon the circumstances and the exercise of the trial court's sound discretion. The more severe the sanction contemplated, the more deliberate the process that is due and the more thorough the findings that should be made. *Montgomery Ward & Co., Inc. v. Superior Court In and For County of Maricopa*, 176 Ariz. 619, 863 P.2d 911 (Ct. App. Div. 1 1993).

13. *Exclusion of Evidence.* The exclusion of evidence is an appropriate sanction for a party's failure to produce documents in response to a Rule 34 request. *B & R Materials, Inc. v. U. S. Fidelity and Guaranty Co.*, 132 Ariz. 122, 644 P.2d 276 (Ct. App.

Div. 2 1982).

14. *Striking of Answer.* A party's right to due process limits the trial court's authority to strike a pleading. The trial court generally may not impose the ultimate sanction of striking a party's pleading without expressly finding that the *party* has obstructed discovery. *Montgomery Ward & Co., Inc. v. Superior Court In and For County of Maricopa*, 176 Ariz. 619, 863 P.2d 911 (Ct. App. Div. 1 1993). It has been held to be proper to strike a corporation's answer where, without good reason, a corporate officer failed to appear for a noticed deposition of the corporation. *American Title & Trust Co. v. Hughes*, 4 Ariz. App. 341, 420 P.2d 584 (1966).

15. *Dismissal; Entry of Default.* The drastic sanction of dismissal of the action, or the entry of party's default, should only be invoked in extreme circumstances. *Austin v. City of Scottsdale*, 140 Ariz. 579, 684 P.2d 151, 46 A.L.R.4th 941 (1984); *Souza v. Fred Carries Contracts, Inc.*, 191 Ariz. 247, 955 P.2d 3 (Ct. App. Div. 2 1997); *Birds Intern. Corp. v. Arizona Maintenance Co., Inc.*, 135 Ariz. 545, 662 P.2d 1052 (Ct. App. Div. 2 1983); *Buchanan v. Jimenez*, 18 Ariz. App. 298, 501 P.2d 567 (Div. 2 1972); *Zakroff v. May*, 8 Ariz. App. 101, 443 P.2d 916 (1968). Generally, before ordering such a sanction, the court should issue an Order to Show Cause and conduct a hearing into the circumstances of the party's conduct. *AG Rancho Equipment Co. v. Massey-Ferguson, Inc.*, 123 Ariz. 122, 598 P.2d 100 (1979); *Birds Intern. Corp. v. Arizona Maintenance Co., Inc.*, 135 Ariz. 545, 662 P.2d 1052 (Ct. App. Div. 2 1983). A party not guilty of bad faith or willful conduct should not suffer a dismissal for counsel's conduct. *Treadaway v. Meador*, 103 Ariz. 83, 436 P.2d 902 (1968); *Birds Intern. Corp. v. Arizona Maintenance Co., Inc.*, 135 Ariz. 545, 662 P.2d 1052 (Ct. App. Div. 2 1983).

Dismissal of an action for discovery misconduct is warranted only where the party personally shares complicity in the abusive behavior and, even then, other, less severe sanctions should be considered. *Groat v. Equity American Ins. Co.*, 180 Ariz. 342, 884 P.2d 228 (Ct. App. Div. 1 1994); *Nesmith v. Superior Court In and For County of Maricopa*, 164 Ariz. 70, 790 P.2d 768 (Ct. App. Div. 1 1990), redesignated as opinion and publication ordered, (Dec. 27, 1989). To sustain imposition of the sanction of dismissal for discovery or disclosure violations, the trial court must make an express finding that a party, as opposed to that party's counsel, has obstructed the discovery process. *Rivers v. Solley*, 217 Ariz. 528, 177 P.3d 270 (Ct. App. Div. 1 2008); *Wayne Cook Enterprises, Inc. v. Fain Properties Ltd. Partnership*, 196 Ariz. 146, 993 P.2d 1110 (Ct. App. Div. 1 1999). If there is a question as to whether the misconduct involved was that of the party or counsel, a hearing should be conducted to resolve it. *AG Rancho Equipment Co. v. Massey-Ferguson, Inc.*, 123 Ariz. 122, 598 P.2d 100 (1979);

Seidman v. Seidman, 222 Ariz. 408, 215 P.3d 382 (Ct. App. Div. 1 2009); *Zimmerman v. Shakman*, 204 Ariz. 231, 62 P.3d 976 (Ct. App. Div. 1 2003); *Weaver v. Synthes, Ltd. (U.S.A.)*, 162 Ariz. 442, 784 P.2d 268 (Ct. App. Div. 1 1989); *Lenze v. Synthes, Ltd.*, 160 Ariz. 302, 772 P.2d 1155 (Ct. App. Div. 1 1989); *Robinson v. Higuera*, 157 Ariz. 622, 760 P.2d 622 (Ct. App. Div. 1 1988).

Where the Court is satisfied, however, that there has been a conscious and purposeful frustration of the discovery rules by a party, dismissal or entry of a default is warranted. *Clark v. Clark*, 124 Ariz. 235, 603 P.2d 506 (1979); *Poleo v. Grandview Equities, Ltd.*, 143 Ariz. 130, 692 P.2d 309 (Ct. App. Div. 1 1984) ("the party whose pleadings have been stricken as a sanction under Rule 37 must be given notice of the application for judgment as required by Rule 55(b)(2) because that party has 'appeared' in the action."). An innocent failure to preserve evidence will generally not warrant the sanction of dismissal. *Souza v. Fred Carries Contracts, Inc.*, 191 Ariz. 247, 955 P.2d 3 (Ct. App. Div. 2 1997).

16. *2014 Rule Amendments: Effective Date and Applicability.* On August 28, 2013, the Arizona Supreme Court adopted sweeping amendments to the case management and trial setting rules governing civil cases. The Promulgating Order specified such rules were adopted "effective on April 15, 2014 as to all cases filed on or after that date." *See,* August 28, 2013 Order entered in In the Matter of Petition to Amend Rules 16, 16.1, 26, 37, 38, 38.1, 72, 73, 74 and 77, Arizona Rules of Civil Procedure, R-13-0017. The applicability provision set forth in the Promulgating Order set up two procedural tracks for case management with the new rules governing cases file on or after April 15, 2014 and the "old" rules governing pre-April 15, 2014 cases.

To avoid any confusion potentially created by the two different tracks, the Court entered an order on November 14, 2013, amending the applicability provision. On November 27, 2013, the court entered a second order further refining the amended applicability provision. As a result, the Amendments are effective and applicable as follows:

> "(1) The Amendments shall apply to all actions filed on or after April 15, 2014.
>
> "(2) Beginning on April 15, 2014, the Amendments also shall apply to any action filed prior to April 15, 2014 (a "pending action"), unless one of the following events has occurred before that date:
>
> (a) A party has filed a Motion to Set and Certificate of Readiness,
>
> (b) The parties have filed a Proposed Scheduling Order, or
>
> (c) The court has entered a Scheduling Order.
>
> "(3) If, in a pending action, one of the preceding events has not occurred before April 15, 2014, the parties shall file a Joint Report and a Proposed Scheduling Order in accordance with the Amendments by June 30, 2014, or within 270 days after the commencement of the action, whichever date is later. Otherwise, the court will place the action on the Dismissal Calendar in accordance with the Amendments.
>
> "(4) A trial court, in its discretion, may apply any of the Amendments to a case pending before April 15, 2014, even if the Amendments would not otherwise apply under

paragraph (2) above. For example, if a party filed a Motion to Set and Certificate of Readiness before April 15, 2014, the trial judge may set the matter for a trial setting conference under amended Rule 16(f), rather than place the case on the active calendar under pre-amendment Rule 38.1(c).

"(5) Civil actions pending on the Inactive Calendar on April 15, 2014 shall be dismissed without prejudice on June 14, 2014, unless one of the actions set forth in subparts (1) - (4) of amended Rule 38.1(f) occurs before June 14, 2014."

VI. TRIALS

Rule 38. Jury trial of right

(a) Right Preserved. The right of trial by jury shall be preserved inviolate to the parties.

Text of Rule 38(b) applicable to those cases filed before April 15, 2014 that are subject to the conditions stated in the November 27, 2013 Amended Order Regarding Applicability Provision, in R-13-0017.

See also, text of Rule 38(b) applicable to cases filed on or after April 15, 2014 and to those cases filed before April 15, 2014 that are subject to the conditions stated in the November 27, 2013, Amended Order Regarding Applicability Provision, in R-13-0017.

(b) Demand. Any person may demand a trial by jury of any issue triable of right by jury. The demand may be made by any party by serving upon the other party a demand therefor in writing at any time after the commencement of the action, but not later than the date of setting the case for trial or ten days after a motion to set the case for trial is served, whichever first occurs. The demand for trial by jury may be endorsed on or be combined with the motion to set, but shall not be endorsed on or be combined with any other motion or pleading filed with the court.

Amended July 14, 1961, effective Nov. 1, 1961.

Text of Rule 38(b) applicable to cases filed on or after April 15, 2014 and to those cases filed before April 15, 2014 that are subject to the conditions stated in the November 27, 2013, Amended Order Regarding Applicability Provision, in R-13-0017.

See also, text of Rule 38(b) applicable to those cases filed before April 15, 2014 that are not subject to the conditions stated in the November 27, 2013 Amended Order Regarding Applicability Provision, in R-13-0017.

(b) Demand. Any person may demand a trial by jury of any issue triable of right by jury. The demand may be made by any party by filing and serving a demand therefor in writing at any time after the commencement of the action, but not later than the date on which the court sets a trial date or ten days after the date a Joint Report and Proposed Scheduling Order under Rule 16(b) or Rule 16.3 are filed, whichever first occurs. The demand for trial by jury shall not be endorsed on or be combined with any other motion or pleading filed with the court.

Amended July 14, 1961, effective Nov. 1, 1961; Aug. 28, 2013, effective April 15, 2014, subject to the conditions of Order No. R-13-0017.

Text of Rule 38(c) applicable to those cases filed before April 15, 2014 that are not subject to the conditions stated in the November 27, 2013 Amended Order Regarding Applicability Provision, in R-13-0017.

See also, text of Rule 38(c) applicable to cases filed on or after April 15, 2014 and to those cases filed before April 15, 2014 that are subject to the conditions stated in the November 27, 2013, Amended Order Regarding Applicability Provision, in R-13-0017.

(c) Demand; Specification of Issues. In the demand a party may specify the issues which the party wishes so tried, otherwise the party shall be deemed to have demanded trial by jury for all the issues so triable. If the party has demanded trial by jury for only some of the issues, any other party within ten days after service of the demand or such lesser time as the court may order, may serve a demand for trial by jury of any other or all the issues of fact in the action.

Amended Sept. 15, 1987, effective Nov. 15, 1987.

Text of Rule 38(c) applicable to cases filed on or after April 15, 2014 and to those cases filed before April 15, 2014 that are subject to the conditions stated in the November 27, 2013, Amended Order Regarding Applicability Provision, in R-13-0017.

See also, text of Rule 38(c) applicable to those cases filed before April 15, 2014 that are not subject to the conditions stated in the November 27, 2013 Amended Order Regarding Applicability Provision, in R-13-0017.

(c) Demand; Specification of Issues. In the demand a party may specify the issues which the party wishes to have tried by a jury; otherwise the party shall be deemed to have demanded trial by jury for all the issues so triable. If the party has demanded trial by jury for only some of the issues, any other party may, within ten days after service of the demand or such lesser time as the court may order, serve a demand for trial by jury of any other or all issues of fact in the action triable by jury.

Amended Sept. 15, 1987, effective Nov. 15, 1987; Aug. 28, 2013, effective April 15, 2014, subject to the conditions of Order No. R-13-0017.

Text of Rule 38(d) applicable to those cases filed before April 15, 2014 that are not subject to the conditions stated in the November 27, 2013, Amended Order Regarding Applicability Provision, in R-13-0017.

See also, text of Rule 38(d) applicable to cases filed on or after

April 15, 2014 and to those cases filed before April 15, 2014 that are not subject to the conditions stated in the November 27, 2013, Order in R-13-0017.

(d) Waiver. The failure of a party to serve a demand as required by this Rule and to file it as required by Rule 5(g) constitutes a waiver by the party of trial by jury. A demand for trial by jury made as herein provided may not be withdrawn without the consent of the parties.

Amended Sept. 15, 1987, effective Nov. 15, 1987.

Text of Rule 38(d) applicable to cases filed on or after April 15, 2014 and to those cases filed before April 15, 2014 that are subject to the conditions stated in the November 27, 2013, Amended Order Regarding ApplicabilityProvision, in R-13-0017.

See also, text of Rule 38(d) applicable to those cases filed before April 15, 2014 that are not subject to the conditions stated in the November 27, 2013 Amended Order Regarding Applicability Provision, in R-13-0017.

(d) Waiver. A party waives a jury trial unless its demand is properly served and filed. A proper demand may be withdrawn only if the parties consent.

Amended Sept. 15, 1987, effective Nov. 15, 1987; Aug. 28, 2013, effective April 15, 2014, subject to the conditions of Order No. R-13-0017.

HISTORICAL NOTES

[2014 Amendments]

[Rule 38(b), (c), (d)] Arizona Supreme Court Order No. R-13-0017, issued Aug. 28, 2013, provided that the amendments of the order would be "effective on April 15, 2014 as to all cases filed on or after that date." The applicability provision of Order No. R-13-0017 was amended on Nov. 14, 2013, and subsequently amended on Nov. 27, 2013 to provide:

(1) The Amendments shall apply to all actions filed on or after April 15, 2014.

(2) Beginning on April 15, 2014, the Amendments also shall apply to any action filed prior to April 15, 2014 (a "pending action"), unless one of the following events has occurred before that date:

  (a) A party has filed a Motion to Set and Certificate of Readiness,

  (b) The parties have filed a Proposed Scheduling Order, or

  (c) The court has entered a Scheduling Order.

(3) If, in a pending action, one of the preceding events has not occurred before April 15, 2014, the parties shall file a Joint Report and a Proposed Scheduling Order in accordance with the Amendments by June 30, 2014, or within 270 days after the commencement of the action, whichever date is later. Otherwise, the court will place the action on the Dismissal Calendar in accordance with the Amendments.

(4) A trial court, in its discretion, may apply any of the Amendments to a case pending before April 15, 2014, even if the Amendments would not otherwise apply under paragraph (2) above. For example, if a party filed a Motion to Set and Certificate of Readiness before April 15, 2014, the

trial judge may set the matter for a trial setting conference under amended Rule 16(f), rather than place the case on the active calendar under pre-amendment Rule 38.1(c).

(5) Civil actions pending on the Inactive Calendar on April 15, 2014 shall be dismissed without prejudice on June 14, 2014, unless one of the actions set forth in subparts (1) - (4) of amended Rule 38.1(f) occurs before June 14, 2014.

STATE BAR COMMITTEE NOTES

1961 Amendment

[Rule 38(b)] Present Rule 38(b) is identical with the present Federal Rule 38(b), but does not conform with the present superior court practice in demanding trial by jury. For example Rule V of Supplemental Rules of the Superior Court of Maricopa County provides that after a case is at issue, either counsel may file a motion to set which will set forth whether a jury is requested.

Confusion sometimes arises when a demand for trial by jury, buried in the complaint or answer, is not brought to the attention of the court until the day set for trial and a jury is not then available. The amended rule eliminates this source of confusion by providing that the demand may not be endorsed on or be combined with any pleading or any motion except a motion to set.

AUTHORS' COMMENTS

Analysis

1. *Scope and Purpose of Rule.* The right to a trial by jury is a fundamental one, and the Arizona Constitution specifically provides that: "The right of trial by jury shall remain inviolate." Ariz. Const., Art. II, § 23. That constitutional provision, however, *preserves* the right to trial by jury *only* for those actions that were recognized at common law when the Arizona Constitution was adopted in 1910. *Life Investors Ins. Co. of America v. Horizon Resources Bethany, Ltd.*, 182 Ariz. 529, 898 P.2d 478 (Ct. App. Div. 1 1995); *In re Estate of Newman*, 219 Ariz. 260, 196 P.3d 863 (Ct. App. Div. 1 2008), as amended on other grounds, (July 17, 2008).

There is no right to a jury trial for purely statutory actions thereafter created, unless the statute itself confers one. *Life Investors Ins. Co. of America v. Horizon Resources Bethany, Ltd.*, 182 Ariz. 529, 898 P.2d 478 (Ct. App. Div. 1 1995); *In re Estate of Newman*, 219 Ariz. 260, 196 P.3d 863 (Ct. App. Div. 1 2008), as amended on other grounds, (July 17, 2008). Thus, for instance, there is no right to a jury trial in a paternity action. *Hoyle v. Superior Court In and For County of Maricopa*, 161 Ariz. 224, 778 P.2d 259 (Ct. App. Div. 1 1989) (no statutory or common law right to a trial by jury in a paternity case).

In addition, the legislature and the courts may prescribe procedures for invocation of the right to trial by jury and specify the circumstances where that right is waived. The primary provision of the Arizona Rules of Civil Procedure which accomplishes that is Ariz. R. Civ. P. 38.

Ariz. R. Civ. P. 38 is concerned with the procedures for making a demand for trial by jury. The procedures for securing an actual trial setting, whether a jury trial is demanded or not, are the subject of Ariz. R. Civ. P. 38.1.

2. *Comparison With Federal Rule.* ARCP 38(a), (c) and (d) are similar to FRCP 38(a), (c) and (d). The Arizona Rules of Civil Procedure do not contain a provision similar to FRCP 38(e), eschewing an intent to create a right to trial by jury for admiralty and maritime claims. The procedures for making a jury trial demand, however, differ markedly between the two Rules.

In 2007, the language of FRCP 38 was amended as part of the general restyling of the Federal Rules of Civil Procedure to make the Federal Rules more easily understood and to make style and terminology consistent throughout the Federal Rules of Civil Procedure. Those stylistic modifications have not been incorporated into ARCP 38.

3. *Procedure for Making Demand for Jury Trial.* The procedures for making a demand for a trial by jury are set forth in Ariz. R. Civ. P. 38(b) specifies that a demand for jury trial must be made as follows:

1. For cases not subject to the 2014 case management/trial setting rules, such demand must be made no later than the date of setting the case for trial or within ten (10) days after service of a motion to set a date for trial, whichever is later.
2. For those cases subject to the 2014 case management/trial setting rules, such demand must be made no later than the date upon which the court sets a trial date or 10 days after the date a Joint Report and Proposed Scheduling Order under Rule 16(b) (amended 2014) or Rule 16.3 (amended 2014) are filed, whichever first occurs.

A demand for jury trial must be in writing. An oral request is insufficient. *Cactus Corp. v. State ex rel. Murphy*, 14 Ariz. App. 38, 480 P.2d 375 (Div. 2 1971); *Smith v. Rabb*, 95 Ariz. 49, 386 P.2d 649 (1963). A jury demand also must be made separately and may not be endorsed on or combined with any other pleading. See Ariz. R. Civ. P. 38(b).

In an appropriate case, however, the trial court may order trial to a jury, even where no demand therefor has been made. Ariz. R. Civ. P. 39(j); *Valley Nat. Bank v. Witter*, 58 Ariz. 491, 121 P.2d 414 (1942). Where one party has demanded a jury trial of all issues, the adverse party may rely on that demand and need not make a separate one. *Stukey v. Stephens*, 37 Ariz. 514, 295 P. 973 (1931).

If the demand does not specify which issues are to be tried by a jury, then the demand is deemed to be a demand for jury trial as to all issues. If a party makes a demand for jury trial only with respect to certain specific issues, any other party has ten (10) days after service of the limited demand to make a demand for jury trial with respect to any additional issues. *See,* Ariz. R. Civ. P. 38(c).

4. *Effect of Demand.* Where a demand has been properly made, or the opportunity to make one is still available, the right to a jury may not be infringed. Thus, it is impermissible to consolidate the hearing on a request for preliminary injunction with the trial on the merits without notifying the parties and affording them the opportunity to demand a jury. *Paris-Phoenix Corp. v. Esper*, 112 Ariz. 320, 541 P.2d 917 (1975).

Similarly, a court may not unilaterally withdraw a case presenting factual issues from a jury, even in instances where the jury is advisory. *Slonsky v. Hunter*, 17 Ariz. App. 231, 496 P.2d 874 (Div. 1 1972); *Zimmer v. Salcido*, 9 Ariz. App. 416, 453 P.2d 245 (1969). Thus, it was error for a trial court to initially order the bifurcation of a breach of contract trial between the issues of liability and damages, and then vacate that order and appoint a special master to decide the issue of damages after the jury had found liability, because that operated to deprive the defendant of the right to a jury trial on an issue triable to a jury, *i.e.*, damages. *Chartone, Inc. v. Bernini*, 207 Ariz. 162, 83 P.3d 1103 (Ct. App. Div. 2 2004).

It is not a denial of the right to trial by jury, however, for the Court to preclude a plaintiff from appearing before a jury, where the sole issue being tried is liability and the plaintiff's comatose condition may be unduly prejudicial. *Morley v. Superior Court of Arizona In and For Maricopa County*, 131 Ariz. 85, 638 P.2d 1331, 27 A.L.R.4th 575 (1981).

Where one party has demanded a jury trial, the other parties to the action may rely on that demand and need not make a separate one. *Stukey v. Stephens*, 37 Ariz. 514, 295 P. 973 (1931). A subsequent unilateral withdrawal of that demand could deprive parties who relied on it of their right to trial by jury. Accordingly, Rule 38(d) specifies that a demand for jury trial, once made: "may not be withdrawn without the consent of the parties."

The Court may, under Rule 39(a)(2), strike or disregard a demand for jury trial where the matter, or particular issues, are not triable of right by a jury. Presumably, similar relief is available, and should be sought, where the demand is untimely.

5. *Waiver of Right to Trial by Jury*. The right to a jury trial may of course be waived, but only in the manner specified in Rule 38. *Wiseman v. Young*, 4 Ariz. App. 573, 422 P.2d 404 (1967). The failure to make a timely demand operates as a waiver. *Leigh v. Swartz*, 74 Ariz. 108, 245 P.2d 262 (1952); *Moran v. Jones*, 75 Ariz. 175, 178, 253 P.2d 891, 893 (1953) ("While the right to a trial by jury is a most substantial right, it may be waived by a failure to demand it."); *Mason v. Cansino*, 195 Ariz. 465, 990 P.2d 666 (Ct. App. Div. 2 1999); *Del Castillo v. Wells*, 22 Ariz. App. 41, 523 P.2d 92 (Div. 1 1974).

The plaintiff's failure to appear for the trial of a civil action for damages also operates as a waiver not only of the right to demand a jury trial, but also of the right to object to the withdrawal by the opposing party of a prior jury trial demand. *Health For Life Brands, Inc. v. Powley*, 203 Ariz. 536, 57 P.3d 726 (Ct. App. Div. 1 2002); *Bloch v. Bentfield*, 1 Ariz. App. 412, 403 P.2d 559 (1965).

Filing a Motion to Set and Certificate of Readiness in which it is stated that a jury trial is not demanded is an unequivocal waiver of the right to trial by jury. *Johnson v. Mofford*, 193 Ariz. 540, 975 P.2d 130 (Ct. App. Div. 1 1998).

6. *Relief From Waiver; Revival of Right to Trial by Jury*. The trial court has the discretion to relieve a party of a waiver of the right to trial by jury. *Hackin v. Pioneer Plumbing Supply Co.*, 10 Ariz. App. 150, 457 P.2d 312 (1969). The right to a jury trial, once waived, may also be revived, in whole or in part, by a subsequent amendment to the pleadings. *Hackin v. Pioneer Plumbing Supply Co.*, 10 Ariz. App. 150, 457 P.2d 312 (1969). Whether the right to a jury trial is revived generally, or only as to new issues raised by the amendments, turns on whether the basic nature of the case has been changed by the amendment. *Apache Playtime, Inc. v. Universal Playtime, Inc.*, 27 Ariz. App. 178, 552 P.2d 767 (Div. 1 1976); *Hackin v. Pioneer Plumbing Supply Co.*, 10 Ariz. App. 150, 457 P.2d 312 (1969).

7. *2014 Rule Amendments: Effective Date and Applicability*. On August 28, 2013, the Arizona Supreme Court adopted sweeping amendments to the case management and trial setting rules governing civil cases. The Promulgating Order specified such rules were adopted "effective on April 15, 2014 as to all cases filed on or after that date." *See,* August 28, 2013 Order entered in In the Matter of Petition to Amend Rules 16, 16.1, 26, 37, 38, 38.1, 72, 73, 74 and 77, Arizona Rules of Civil Procedure, R-13-0017. The applicability provision set forth in the Promulgating

Order set up two procedural tracks for case management with the new rules governing cases file on or after April 15, 2014 and the "old" rules governing pre-April 15, 2014 cases.

To avoid any confusion potentially created by the two different tracks, the Court entered an order on November 14, 2013, amending the applicability provision. On November 27, 2013, the court entered a second order further refining the amended applicability provision. As a result, the Amendments are effective and applicable as follows:

"(1) The Amendments shall apply to all actions filed on or after April 15, 2014.

"(2) Beginning on April 15, 2014, the Amendments also shall apply to any action filed prior to April 15, 2014 (a "pending action"), unless one of the following events has occurred before that date:

(a) A party has filed a Motion to Set and Certificate of Readiness,

(b) The parties have filed a Proposed Scheduling Order, or

(c) The court has entered a Scheduling Order.

"(3) If, in a pending action, one of the preceding events has not occurred before April 15, 2014, the parties shall file a Joint Report and a Proposed Scheduling Order in accordance with the Amendments by June 30, 2014, or within 270 days after the commencement of the action, whichever date is later. Otherwise, the court will place the action on the Dismissal Calendar in accordance with the Amendments.

"(4) A trial court, in its discretion, may apply any of the Amendments to a case pending before April 15, 2014, even if the Amendments would not otherwise apply under paragraph (2) above. For example, if a party filed a Motion to Set and Certificate of Readiness before April 15, 2014, the trial judge may set the matter for a trial setting conference under amended Rule 16(f), rather than place the case on the active calendar under pre-amendment Rule 38.1(c).

"(5) Civil actions pending on the Inactive Calendar on April 15, 2014 shall be dismissed without prejudice on June 14, 2014, unless one of the actions set forth in subparts (1) - (4) of amended Rule 38.1(f) occurs before June 14, 2014."

Rule 38.1. Setting of civil cases for trial; postponements (pre-2014 amendment)

Text of Rule 38.1 applicable to to those cases filed before April 15, 2014 that are not subject to the conditions stated in the November 27, 2013 Amended Order Regarding Applicability Provision, in R-13-0017.

See also, text of Rule 38.1 applicable to cases filed on or after April 15, 2014 and applicable to those cases filed before April 15, 2014 that are subject to the conditions stated in the November 27, 2013, Amended Order Regarding Applicability Provision, in R-13-0017.

(a) Motion to Set and Certificate of Readiness: Identification of Nonparty at Fault. In every civil case, counsel for plaintiff shall, or counsel for any other party may, file a Motion to Set and Certificate of Readiness. Service shall be in the manner prescribed by Rule 5 of these Rules. The form and contents of the Certificate of Readiness shall be as follows:

The undersigned attorney hereby certifies:

(1) That the issues in the above-captioned case have actually been joined;

(2) The largest award sought by any party, including punitive damages, but excluding interest, attorneys' fees, and costs, is $________. This case [is] [is not] subject to the mandatory arbitration provisions of Rules 72 through 76 [*sic*, Rules 72 through 77] of these Rules.

(3) That the status of discovery is as follows:

(i) In a court which requires such certification by local rule, the parties have completed, or will have had a reasonable opportunity to complete, the procedures under Rules 26 to 37 of these Rules within 60 days after the filing of the Certificate of Readiness; or

(ii) In a court which requires such certification by local rule, the parties have completed, or have had a reasonable opportunity to complete, the procedures under Rules 26 to 37 of these Rules at the time of filing of the Certificate of Readiness; or

(iii) In all other cases, the parties have completed, or will have had a reasonable opportunity to complete, the procedures under Rules 26 to 37 of these Rules prior to ten days before trial.

(4) That this case will be ready for trial on or after [DATE].

(5) That a trial by jury is [not] demanded (strike out the word "not" if a jury trial is demanded);

(6) That this cause may [not] be heard as a short cause within one hour [strike out the word "not" if the time required for trial will not exceed one hour];

(7) That the names, addresses and telephone numbers of the parties or their individual attorneys who are responsible for the conduct of the litigation are:—[insert the appropriate information]; and

(8) That this cause is entitled to a preference for trial by reason of the following statute or rule:—[insert statutory section or rule number if a preference is applicable].

____

Signature of Attorney

If the Motion to Set and Certificate of Readiness is filed by a defending party in a court which does not require the certification set forth in (a)(3)(i) or (ii) of this Rule, then the Certificate of Readiness shall also identify any nonparty who is alleged, pursuant to A.R.S. § 12-2506(B) (as amended), to be wholly or partially at fault in causing any personal injury, property damage or wrongful death for which damages are sought in the action.

Rule 38.1(a) added Oct. 10, 2000, effective Dec. 1, 2000.

(b) Controverting Certificate: Identification of Nonparty at Fault. Within ten days after a Motion to Set and Certificate of Readiness has been served:

(1) Counsel for any other party may file a Controverting Certificate which specifies the particular statements contained in the Certificate of Readiness to which objection is made, and the reasons therefor.

(2) In those courts which do not require the certification set forth in either subpart (a)(3)(i) or (ii) of this Rule, counsel for a defending party must, in a Controverting Certificate or separately, identify any nonparty who is alleged, pursuant to A.R.S. § 12-2506(B) (as amended), to be wholly or partially at fault in causing any personal injury, property damage or wrongful death for which damages are sought in the action.

The court shall thereupon enter an order, without oral argument, placing the case on the Active Calendar either immediately or, where good cause is shown, at a specified later date. No case shall be heard as a short cause if objection is made thereto in the Controverting Certificate.

Rule 38.1(b) added Oct. 10, 2000, effective Dec. 1, 2000.

(c) Active Calendar. Ten days after a Motion to Set and Certificate of Readiness has been served, if a Controverting Certificate has not been served, or otherwise by order of the court, the clerk of the court or court administrator shall place the case on the Active Calendar and shall stamp thereon a chronological list number which shall generally govern the priority of the case for trial, except as to those cases which are entitled to preference by statute or local rule, and except that short causes may be preferred for trial in accordance with local rules.
Rule 38.1(c) added Oct. 10, 2000, effective Dec. 1, 2000.

(d) Inactive Calendar. The clerk of the court or court administrator shall place on the Inactive Calendar every case in which a Motion to Set and Certificate of Readiness has not been served within nine months after the commencement thereof. All cases remaining on the Inactive Calendar for two months shall be dismissed without prejudice for lack of prosecution, and the court shall make an appropriate order as to any bond or other security filed therein, unless prior to the expiration of such two months period:

(1) a proper Motion to Set and Certificate of Readiness is served; or

(2) the court, on motion for good cause shown, orders the case to be continued on the Inactive Calendar for a specified period of time without dismissal; or

(3) a notice of decision has been filed with the clerk of court in a case assigned to arbitration.

Rule 38.1(d) added Oct. 10, 2000, effective Dec. 1, 2000.

(e) Notification. The clerk of the court or court administrator, whoever is designated by the presiding judge, shall promptly notify counsel in writing of the placing of cases on the Inactive Calendar, and no further notice shall be required prior to dismissal.
Rule 38.1(e) added Oct. 10, 2000, effective Dec. 1, 2000.

(f) Additional Discovery. In those cases in which the certification set forth in subpart (a)(3)(i) is required by local rule, all pretrial procedures under Rules 26 to 37 of these Rules shall be completed within 60 days after service of the Motion to Set and Certificate of Readiness. In those cases in which the certification set forth in subpart (a)(3)(ii) is required by local rule, all pretrial procedures under Rules 26 to 37 of these Rules shall be completed at the time of service of the Motion to Set and Certificate of Readiness. In all other cases, all pretrial procedures under Rules

26 to 37 of these Rules shall be completed prior to ten days before trial. Notwithstanding the foregoing, for good cause shown, the court may permit or the parties may stipulate that additional discovery procedures may be undertaken anytime prior to trial.
Rule 38.1(f) added Oct. 10, 2000, effective Dec. 1, 2000.

(g) Setting for Trial. Cases on the Active Calendar shall be set for trial as soon as possible. Preference shall be given to short causes and cases which by reason of statute, rule or court order are entitled to priority. Counsel shall be given at least thirty days notice of the trial date.
Rule 38.1(g) added Oct. 10, 2000, effective Dec. 1, 2000.

(h) Postponements. Unless otherwise provided by local rule, when an action has been set for trial on a specified date by order of the court, no postponement of the trial shall be granted except for sufficient cause, supported by affidavit, or by consent of the parties, or by operation of law.
Rule 38.1(h) added Oct. 10, 2000, effective Dec. 1, 2000.

(i) Application for Postponement: Grounds; Effect of Admission of Truth of Affidavit by Adverse Party. On an application for a postponement of the trial, if the ground for the application is the want of testimony, the party applying therefor shall make affidavit that such testimony is material showing the materiality thereof, and that the party has used due diligence to procure such testimony, stating such diligence and the cause of failure to procure such testimony, if known, and that such testimony cannot be obtained from any other source. If the ground for the application is the absence of a witness, the party applying shall state the name and residence of the witness, and what the party expects to prove by the witness. The application in either case shall also state that the postponement is not sought for delay only, but that justice may be done. If the adverse party admits that such testimony would be given and that it will be considered as actually given on the trial, or offered and overruled as improper, the trial shall not be postponed. Such testimony may be controverted as if the witness were personally present.
Rule 38.1(i) added Oct. 10, 2000, effective Dec. 1, 2000.

(j) Deposition of Witness or Party; Consent. The party obtaining a postponement shall, if required by the adverse party, consent that the testimony of any witness or adverse party in attendance be taken by deposition, without notice. The testimony so taken may be read on the trial by either party as if the witnesses were present.
Rule 38.1(j) added Oct. 10, 2000, effective Dec. 1, 2000.

(k) Scheduling Conflicts Between Courts.

(1) *Notice to the Court.* Upon learning of a scheduling conflict between a case in Superior Court and a case in United States District Court, or between cases in the Superior Courts of different counties, or between cases in different courts within a county, counsel has a duty to promptly notify the judges and other counsel involved in order that the conflict may be resolved.

(2) *Resolution of Conflicts.* Upon being advised of a scheduling conflict, the judges involved shall, if necessary, confer personally or by telephone in an effort to resolve the conflict. While neither federal nor state court cases have priority in scheduling, the following factors may be considered in resolving the conflict:

(A) the nature of the cases as civil or criminal, and the presence of any speedy trial problems;

(B) the length, urgency, or relative importance of the matters;

(C) a case which involves out-of-town witnesses, parties or counsel;

(D) the age of the cases;

(E) the matter which was set first;

(F) any priority granted by rule or statute;

(G) any other pertinent factor.

(3) *Inter-Division Conflicts.* Conflicts in scheduling between divisions of the same court may be governed by local rule or general order.

Rule 38.1(k) added Oct. 10, 2000, effective Dec. 1, 2000.

STATE BAR COMMITTEE NOTES

2000 Promulgation

As part of an effort to consolidate formerly separate sets of procedural rules into either the Arizona Rules of Civil Procedure or the Rules of the Arizona Supreme Court, the former Uniform Rules of Practice of the Superior Court were abrogated in their entirety. With one exception, the provisions of Rule V of those Rules were incorporated into a new Rule 38.1 of the Arizona Rules of Civil Procedure. The provisions of former Rule V(a) of the Uniform Rules of Practice of the Superior Court, which required the filing, in certain counties, of a list of witnesses and exhibits as a predicate for submitting a Motion to Set and Certificate of Readiness were not retained in the process. The Committee was of the view that this requirement had been rendered obsolete by the provisions of Rule 26.1, which requires the voluntary and seasonable disclosure of, inter alia, the identities of trial witnesses and exhibits. Changes were also made to the form of Motion to Set and Certificate of Readiness prescribed by what is now Rule 38.1(a) to reflect the abandonment of the witness and exhibit list requirement.

Some other changes were also made in this process. The provisions of former Rules V(b) through (i) of the Uniform Rules of Practice of the Superior Court became new Rules 38.1(a) through (h) of the Arizona Rules of Civil Procedure, and former Rule V(j) became new Rule 38.1(k). To ensure that all provisions relating to trial settings and securing trial continuances appeared in a single Rule, the provisions of former Rules 42(d) and (e) of the Arizona Rules of Civil Procedure were transferred to the new Rule 38.1, as subparts (i) and (j), respectively.

New Rule 38.1(g) continues to refer to alternative time frames by which discovery in a civil case "shall be completed," as did former Rule V(g) of the Uniform Rules of Practice of the Superior Court. A Supplemental State Bar Committee Note to former Rule V pointed out that "completed" signified that discovery requests had to be both propounded and answered, rather than simply propounded, by the date for the completion of discovery. This construction of the Rule should pertain to new Rule 38.1(g) as well.

This issue is of particular significance in the case of written discovery requests, where the party to whom they are directed is typically allowed, under the applicable Rules, a period of forty (40) days in which to respond. To interpret the date for the completion of discovery as merely establishing the deadline for service of such written discovery requests would make little sense, for example, in those courts which require only the certification set forth in what is now Rule 38.1(a)(3)(iii), that pretrial discovery procedures "shall be completed prior to ten days before trial." Under such an interpretation of the phrase "shall be completed," a written discovery request under Rule 33, 34 or 36 would be deemed timely if propounded more than ten (10) days prior to trial, even though the responses would not be due until after the trial had commenced. That is not what the Rule contemplates.

In order to satisfy the Rule, written discovery requests must be propounded sufficiently in advance of the discovery completion date to afford the party to whom they are directed the time for response prescribed by the Rules and to insure that the responses are due prior to the date for the completion of discovery. The propounding party may, of course, pursue any further proceedings under Rule 37 deemed necessary to secure a further response.

AUTHORS' COMMENTS

Analysis

1. *History and Origin of Rule*. Rule 38.1 was added to the Arizona Rules of Civil Procedure, effective December 1, 2000, as a consequence of the Arizona Supreme Court's approval of the

recommendations of what was known as the Civil Rules Consolidation Project. By an Order entered in October 2000, the Supreme Court abrogated the Uniform Rules of Practice of the Superior Court, the Uniform Rules of Procedure for Medical Malpractice Cases, and the Uniform Rules of Procedure for Arbitration, as separate sets of procedural rules, and transferred their provisions to either the Arizona Rules of Civil Procedure or the Rules of the Arizona Supreme Court.

The rationale used for determining the placement of rules was that rules affecting the processing of civil cases should be placed in the Arizona Rules of Civil Procedure, while rules that concerned only internal court administration should be placed in the Rules of the Arizona Supreme Court. Application of this rationale resulted, in some instances, in the transfer of certain provisions of the Arizona Rules of Civil Procedure to the Rules of the Arizona Supreme Court.

Rule 38.1 essentially incorporates, with one exception, the provisions of former Rule V of the now abrogated Uniform Rules of Practice of the Superior Court. Rule V was (and Rule 38.1 now is) the principal Rule governing the procedures for securing trial settings in civil cases and the consequences of failing to prepare cases for trial in a timely manner. It also contains provisions for resolving conflicting trial settings between different courts.

The provisions of former Rule V(a) of the Uniform Rules of Practice of the Superior Court, which required the filing, in certain counties, of a list of witness and exhibits as a predicate for submitting a Motion to Set and Certificate of Readiness were not retained in the process. The proponents of the consolidation proposal were of the view that this requirement had been rendered obsolete by the provisions of Ariz. R. Civ. P. 26.1, which requires the voluntary and seasonable disclosure of, *inter alia*, the identities of trial witnesses and exhibits. Changes were also made to the form of Motion to Set and Certificate of Readiness prescribed by what is now Ariz. R. Civ. P. 38.1(a) to reflect the abandonment of the witness and exhibit list requirement.

The provisions of former Rules V(b) through (i) of the Uniform Rules of Practice thus became Rules 38.1(a) through (h) of the Arizona Rules of Civil Procedure, and former Rule V(j) became new Rule 38.1(k). To ensure that all provisions relating to trial settings and securing trial continuances appeared in a single Rule, the provisions of former Rules 42(d) and (e) of the Arizona Rules of Civil Procedure were transferred to Ariz. R. Civ. P. 38.1 as subparts (i) and (j), respectively. Rule 42(c) was simply abrogated, because its provisions were identical to those of Rule V(i) of the Uniform Rules of Practice, which became Ariz. R. Civ. P. 38.1(h).

2. *Comparison With Federal Rule.* The Federal Rules of Civil Procedure do not have a provision that corresponds to ARCP 38.1.

3. *Securing Trial Settings; Motions to Set and Certificates of Readiness.* The prescribed method for securing a trial setting is by the filing of a Motion to Set and Certificate of Readiness, the contents of which are specifically set forth in Ariz. R. Civ. P. 38.1(a). The Motion to Set and Certificate of Readiness is also the predominant vehicle for requesting a trial by jury. One of the specified contents of the Motion to Set and Certificate of Readiness is a statement as to whether a trial by jury is demanded. If the party filing the Motion to Set does not demand a jury, and the adverse party desires a jury trial, that must be demanded in the Controverting Certificate contemplated by Ariz. R. Civ. P. 38.1(b) and discussed in Section 5, *infra.* Filing a Motion to Set in which it is stated that a jury trial is not demanded is an unequivocal waiver of the right to a jury trial. *Johnson v. Mofford*, 193 Ariz. 540, 975 P.2d 130 (Ct. App. Div. 1 1998).

In addition to stating whether a trial by jury is demanded, the Motion to Set and Certificate of Readiness must also specify, *inter alia,* that the issues in the case have actually been joined, the amount in controversy, the anticipated length of trial and whether the matter can be heard as a short cause, and whether the case is entitled to a preference for trial. The Motion and Certificate must also contain one of three alternative certifications by counsel as to the status of discovery, which are discussed in Section 3, *infra.*

The predecessor to this Rule, Rule V of the Uniform Rules of Practice of the Superior Court, was intended to standardize the inherent power of trial courts to dismiss cases for lack of prosecution. *BCAZ Corp. v. Helgoe*, 194 Ariz. 11, 976 P.2d 260 (Ct. App. Div. 1 1998), opinion supplemented on reh'g, (Mar. 25, 1999). It is designed to provide a convenient administrative practice to bring to the attention of the Court and the attorneys involved the fact that ample time has elapsed in which to prepare a case for trial.

Under Ariz. R. Civ. P. 38.1(d), all cases remaining on the Inactive Calendar for two months shall be dismissed without prejudice for lack of prosecution unless, prior to the expiration of that two months, a proper Motion to Set and Certificate of Readiness is filed or the Court, for good cause shown, continues the case on the Inactive Calendar. Whether such good cause is shown is a matter left to the sound discretion of the trial court.

Under Rule 38.1(b), upon the filing of a Controverting Certificate, the Court is to place the case on the Active Calendar immediately or, where good cause is shown, at a specified later date. Ariz. R. Civ. P. 38(d) does not, by its terms, permit the Court to refuse a party's request that the case be set for trial, assuming it has complied with the requirements of the Rule, even if the opposing party has filed a Controverting Certificate. *BCAZ Corp. v. Helgoe*, 194 Ariz. 11, 976 P.2d 260 (Ct. App. Div. 1 1998), opinion supplemented on reh'g, (Mar. 25, 1999). Under Ariz. R. Civ. P. 38.1(a), however, the failure to file a timely Motion to Set and Certificate of Readiness within the time frames specified will result in the dismissal of an action without prejudice, for failure to prosecute.

In theory, a Motion to Set and Certificate of Readiness may be filed at any time after the case is at issue, provided counsel consistent with Ariz. R. Civ. P. 11 is able to make the required certification as to the status of discovery. A Motion to Set and Certificate of Readiness *must* be filed within nine (9) months of the commencement of the action or the case will be placed on the Inactive Calendar and dismissed two months thereafter for want of prosecution. In cases where a counterclaim has been filed, it is not necessary that both the plaintiff and the counterclaimant comply with the requirements of the Rule; it is sufficient if either does. *Thompson v. Mecey*, 101 Ariz. 125, 416 P.2d 558 (1966).

4. *Alternative Certifications as to Status of Discovery*. Among the required contents of the Motion to Set and Certificate of Readiness is a certification by counsel as to the status of discovery. Three alternative certifications are specified, and the appropriate one to be employed depends upon the requirements of the Local Rules of the particular county in which the action is pending.

The first alternative, set forth in Ariz. R. Civ. P. 38.1(a)(3)(i), is that all discovery has been completed or the parties will have a reasonable opportunity to complete it within sixty (60) days. Only Maricopa, Santa Cruz and Yuma Counties have to date adopted a Local Rule requiring such a certification. *See* Rule 3.4, Maricopa County Superior Court Local Rules; Rule 10, Santa Cruz County Superior Court Local Rules; Rule 13, Yuma County Superior Court Local Rules.

The second alternative certification, specified in Ariz. R. Civ. P. 38.1(a)(3)(ii), is that all discovery procedures have been completed, or that there has been a reasonable opportunity to complete them, at the time the Motion to Set and Certificate of Readiness is filed. To date, no county has adopted a Local Rule which would require such a certification.

If the Local Rules are silent on the nature of the certification required, counsel must make the third alternative certification specified in Ariz. R. Civ. P. 38.1(a)(3)(iii), *viz.*, that the parties will have completed, or have had reasonable opportunity to complete, discovery prior to ten (10) days before trial. As noted, this is presently the certification required in all counties other than Maricopa, Santa Cruz and Yuma Counties.

In cases where the certification specified in Ariz. R. Civ. P. 38.1(a)(3)(i) is required, all discovery must be completed within sixty (60) days after the filing of the Motion to Set and Certificate of Readiness. In cases where the certification set forth in Ariz. R. Civ. P. 38.1(a)(3)(ii) is required, discovery must be completed at the time the Motion to Set and Certificate of Readiness is filed. In all other cases, discovery must be completed ten (10) days before trial. A State Bar Committee Note, which was adapted from one which accompanied former Rule V, explains that "completed" means that discovery requests must be both propounded and answered, rather than simply propounded, by the date established for the completion of discovery. Counsel must, accordingly, make sure that discovery requests are served sufficiently in advance of the date set for completion of discovery to insure that responses are due before that date. The party propounding the discovery may pursue remedies under Rule 37 to secure further responses even if the date for completion of discovery has passed.

Discovery may be conducted after the dates set by Ariz. R. Civ. P. 38.1(f) for the completion of discovery only upon stipulation of the parties or with leave of Court for good cause. Whether to permit such additional discovery is a matter committed to the trial court's discretion. *Ring v. Taylor*, 141 Ariz. 56, 685 P.2d 121 (Ct. App. Div. 1 1984); *Dykeman v. Ashton*, 8 Ariz. App. 327, 446 P.2d 26 (1968).

5. *Controverting Certificates.* If any party disagrees with the matters set forth in a Motion to Set and Certificate of Readiness that has been filed, that party may file, within ten (10) days after the filing of the Motion to Set and Certificate of Readiness, a Controverting Certificate which specifies the particular statements as to which there is disagreement and the reasons for the disagreement. As noted earlier, even though Ariz. R. Civ. P. 38(b) literally provides that a jury trial demand may not be endorsed on or combined with any motion or pleading other than the Motion to Set, the prevailing practice, where a party desires a jury trial and one has not been demanded in the opponent's Motion to Set and Certificate of Readiness, is to make the demand in the Controverting Certificate. After considering the Controverting Certificate, without oral argument, the Court may place the case on the Active Calendar immediately or at a specified later date, and may, if it chooses, conduct a hearing concerning the disagreement.

6. *Identification of Nonparty at Fault.* A.R.S. § 12-2506(B) (as amended) specifies that the negligence or fault of a nonparty may

be considered by the trier of fact in assessing percentages of fault if the plaintiff has settled with such a nonparty or if "the defending party gives notice before trial, in accordance with requirements established by court rule, that a nonparty was wholly or partially at fault." To serve as the primary "court rule" contemplated by this legislation, the Arizona Supreme Court adopted, effective July 1, 1989, Ariz. R. Civ. P. 26(b)(5), which adopts a general rule requiring the disclosure of such a claim within one hundred and fifty (150) days after the filing of the answer of the party making the claim.

At the same time, amendments were adopted to former Rule V of the Uniform Rules of Practice to impose a complementary disclosure requirement. In those counties which do not require the certification as to the status of discovery specified in what is now Ariz. R. Civ. P. 38.1(a)(3)(i) or 38.1(a)(3)(ii), *i.e.*, where the certification specified in Ariz. R. Civ. P. 38.1(a)(3)(iii) is required, a Motion to Set and Certificate of Readiness can theoretically be filed at any time. In those counties, the Motion to Set and Certificate of Readiness must identify any nonparty who is claimed to be wholly or partially at fault in causing the claimant's injuries or damages. This requirement applies even if there has been an earlier disclosure under Ariz. R. Civ. P. 26(b)(5) Accordingly, where the Motion to Set and Certificate of Readiness is filed in a case pending in such a county more than one hundred and fifty (150) days after the answer, there must be an essentially duplicative disclosure of any nonparty claimed to be wholly or partially at fault. A similar requirement pertains to Controverting Certificates by reason of Ariz. R. Civ. P. 38.1(b)(2).

7. *Active Calendar; Inactive Calendar; Dismissals for Failure to Prosecute; Relief From Dismissal; Savings Statute.* Cases are given trial settings by being placed on the Active Calendar. If a timely Motion to Set and Certificate of Readiness is filed, the case is to be placed on the Active Calendar within ten (10) days, if no Controverting Certificate is filed. If a Controverting Certificate is filed, the trial court is to determine whether and when the case is placed on the Active Calendar. Cases placed on the Active Calendar are assigned a chronological list number which governs their priority for trial, unless the case is entitled to a preferential trial setting by statute or Local Rule. Cases on the Active Calendar are to be set for trial as soon as is possible, and counsel are to be given at least thirty (30) days notice of the trial date assigned.

A Motion to Set and Certificate of Readiness must be filed within nine (9) months after the commencement of the action. If one is not filed within that time period, the case is to be placed on the Inactive Calendar. Cases which remain on the Inactive Calendar for two (2) months without a proper Motion to Set and

Certificate of Readiness being filed are to be dismissed without prejudice for lack of prosecution, unless the Court for good cause shown orders that the case be continued on the Inactive Calendar. A case assigned to mandatory arbitration is not to be dismissed if, during that two-month period, an arbitrator's notice of decision, required by Ariz. R. Civ. P. 76(a)(5), is filed with the clerk of court. The purpose of this Rule is to standardize to some degree the exercise of the Court's inherent power to dismiss cases for want of prosecution, and it is not intended to penalize parties for missing a deadline where the case is otherwise being actively pursued. *Walker v. Kendig*, 107 Ariz. 510, 489 P.2d 849 (1971); *Black v. Greer*, 17 Ariz. App. 383, 498 P.2d 225 (Div. 1 1972).

The provisions of the Rule calling for the dismissal of cases that remain on the Inactive Calendar for two months are not self-executing, and a written order of dismissal must be entered or the case remains on the Inactive Calendar and may be revived. *Campbell v. Deddens*, 93 Ariz. 247, 379 P.2d 963 (1963); *Blech v. Blech*, 6 Ariz. App. 131, 430 P.2d 710 (1967). While the Rule contemplates that an order dismissing the case will be routinely signed and entered, it is frequently the responsibility of counsel to bring to the Court's attention the fact that a matter has been on the Inactive Calendar for two months or more and/or to submit a formal written order of dismissal.

The Clerk or Court Administrator, if there is one, is to promptly notify counsel in writing when a case is placed on the Inactive Calendar. *American Asphalt & Grading Co. v. CMX, L.L.C.*, 227 Ariz. 117, 253 P.3d 1240 (2011). No further notice is required prior to dismissal. There is a rebuttable presumption that such a notice mailed by the Clerk or Court Administrator has been received by counsel. *Thompson v. Mecey*, 101 Ariz. 125, 416 P.2d 558 (1966); *Black v. Greer*, 17 Ariz. App. 383, 498 P.2d 225 (Div. 1 1972). Counsel who receives such a notice may file a Motion to Set and Certificate of Readiness, if the certifications required can be made, or move the Court for an Order continuing the case on the Inactive Calendar. Good cause must be shown for such relief, but the request is one directed to the discretion of the trial court. *Campbell v. Deddens*, 93 Ariz. 247, 379 P.2d 963 (1963).

The dismissal contemplated by Ariz. R. Civ. P. 38.1(d) is without prejudice. If the statute of limitations applicable to the claims asserted has not run, the action can simply be refiled if the plaintiff wishes to pursue it. If, however, the statute of limitations has expired, the order of dismissal, although nominally without prejudice, operates to bar further prosecution of the claim unless some relief from the dismissal is secured.

One potential avenue for relief is a motion to set aside the dismissal pursuant to Ariz. R. Civ. P. 60(c). *American Asphalt &*

Grading Co. v. CMX, L.L.C., 227 Ariz. 117, 253 P.3d 1240 (2011); *Thunderbird Farms v. Hernandez*, 11 Ariz. App. 383, 464 P.2d 829 (Div. 2 1970). The standards for granting relief under Ariz. R. Civ. P. 60(c), from an order dismissing a case for lack of prosecution are analogous to those applicable to securing relief from a default. *State ex rel. Corbin v. Marshall*, 161 Ariz. 429, 778 P.2d 1325 (Ct. App. Div. 1 1989); *Cline v. Ticor Title Ins. Co. of California*, 154 Ariz. 343, 742 P.2d 844 (Ct. App. Div. 1 1987).

Where relief from a dismissal for failure to prosecute is sought under Ariz. R. Civ. P. 60(c)(6), a plaintiff must show extraordinary circumstances of hardship or injustice justifying relief, and that: (1) plaintiff diligently and vigorously prosecuted the case, (2) the parties took reasonable steps to inform the Court of the status of the case, (3) substantial prejudice will result unless relief is granted, (4) plaintiff sought relief promptly, and (5) plaintiff has a meritorious claim. *Jepson v. New*, 164 Ariz. 265, 792 P.2d 728 (1990); *Copeland v. Arizona Veterans Memorial Coliseum and Exposition Center*, 176 Ariz. 86, 859 P.2d 196 (Ct. App. Div. 1 1993); *Copeland v. Arizona Veterans Memorial Coliseum and Expo Center*, 178 Ariz. 246, 872 P.2d 201 (1994); citing *Jepson v. New*, 164 Ariz. 265, 792 P.2d 728 (1990); *Hyman v. Arden-Mayfair, Inc.*, 150 Ariz. 444, 724 P.2d 63 (Ct. App. Div. 1 1986); *Resolution Trust Corp. v. Maricopa County*, 176 Ariz. 631, 863 P.2d 923 (Tax Ct. 1993).

Further, a party can obtain relief under Ariz. R. Civ. P. 60(c)(6) from a judgment entered due to his or her attorney's failure to act only if that attorney's failure to act is legally excusable. *Panzino v. City of Phoenix*, 196 Ariz. 442, 999 P.2d 198 (2000) (discussing, and disapproving, the "positive misconduct rule"). The rule in the discovery context that the sanction of dismissal should not be imposed for the attorney's misconduct has no application to dismissals for lack of prosecution. *Panzino v. City of Phoenix*, 196 Ariz. 442, 999 P.2d 198 (2000) (attorney conduct did not entitle client to relief from judgment under Rule 60(c)(6)).

The fact that the statute of limitations applicable to the claim has expired, so that the dismissal in fact operates with prejudice, does not in and of itself warrant relief. *Bickerstaff v. Denny's Restaurant, Inc.*, 141 Ariz. 629, 688 P.2d 637 (1984) (disapproved of on other grounds by, Panzino v. City of Phoenix, 196 Ariz. 442, 999 P.2d 198 (2000)); *Hyman v. Arden-Mayfair, Inc.*, 150 Ariz. 444, 724 P.2d 63 (Ct. App. Div. 1 1986). However, where the dismissal would be one without prejudice because the statute of limitations has run, the "trial court must take "an especially hard look at the actual circumstances of the case before it." *Jepson v. New*, 164 Ariz. 265, 792 P.2d 728 (1990), citing *Gorman v. City of Phoenix*, 152 Ariz. 179, 731 P.2d 74 (1987).

Relief should be granted in that instance, however, where the action has been vigorously pursued and dismissed due to inadvertence. *Gorman v. City of Phoenix*, 152 Ariz. 179, 731 P.2d 74 (1987). The plaintiff's failure to receive the prescribed notice that the case has been placed on the Inactive Calendar for impending dismissal is only one factor the trial court should consider in assessing the plaintiff's diligence. *Copeland v. Arizona Veterans Memorial Coliseum and Exposition Center*, 176 Ariz. 86, 859 P.2d 196 (Ct. App. Div. 1 1993).

An alternative, or companion, avenue for relief where a dismissal nominally without prejudice occurs after the expiration of the statute of limitations, is the Arizona "savings statute," A.R.S. § 12-504. *Jepson v. New*, 164 Ariz. 265, 792 P.2d 728 (1990) *Copeland v. Arizona Veterans Memorial Coliseum and Exposition Center*, 176 Ariz. 86, 859 P.2d 196 (Ct. App. Div. 1 1993). Under that statute, any action which was originally timely filed, and then dismissed, may be automatically reinstituted within six months of the dismissal, unless the dismissal was for one of the following reasons: (1) abatement, (2) voluntary dismissal, (3) dismissal for lack of prosecution, or (4) a judgment on the merits, regardless of whether the termination occurs before or after the limitations period has expired. *Janson on Behalf of Janson v. Christensen*, 167 Ariz. 470, 808 P.2d 1222 (1991).

Where the dismissal is for abatement, for lack of prosecution, or on motion for voluntary dismissal, A.R.S. § 12-504 permits the Court entering the original order of dismissal to permit the refiling of the action for a period of up to six (6) months following the dismissal. *Copeland v. Arizona Veterans Memorial Coliseum and Exposition Center*, 176 Ariz. 86, 859 P.2d 196 (Ct. App. Div. 1 1993). The permission to refile must, however, be contained in the original order of dismissal. Where there has been a dismissal for lack of prosecution under Rule 38.1(d), accordingly, the aggrieved party must secure an amendment of the order of dismissal to include language permitting it to be refiled pursuant to A.R.S. § 12-504.

By the statute's very terms, whether a party's right to refile a suit is absolute or discretionary depends upon the reason for termination of the action. *Schwartz v. Arizona Primary Care Physicians*, 192 Ariz. 290, 964 P.2d 491 (Ct. App. Div. 1 1998). If an action is terminated for insufficiency of process, rather than abatement, the statute entitles the plaintiff to reinstitute the action as a matter of right. *Schwartz v. Arizona Primary Care Physicians*, 192 Ariz. 290, 964 P.2d 491 (Ct. App. Div. 1 1998). The statute, by its terms, applies to an action that is timely filed and then terminated for one of the enumerated reasons, regardless of whether the termination occurs *before or after* the limitations period has expired. *Janson on Behalf of Janson v. Christensen*, 167 Ariz. 470, 808 P.2d 1222 (1991). The standards for securing relief are similar, but not identical, to Rule 60(c). It must be shown whether (1) plaintiff acted reasonably and in good faith, (2) plaintiff prosecuted the case diligently and vigorously, (3) a procedural impediment exists which affects plaintiff's ability to file a second action and (4) either party will be substantially prejudiced. *Jepson v. New*, 164 Ariz. 265, 792 P.2d 728 (1990); *Copeland v. Arizona Veterans Memorial Coliseum and Exposition Center*, 176 Ariz. 86, 859 P.2d 196 (Ct. App. Div. 1 1993); *Flynn v. Cornoyer-Hedrick Architects & Planners, Inc.*, 160 Ariz. 187, 772 P.2d 10 (Ct. App. Div. 1 1988), decision aff'd, 164 Ariz. 265, 792 P.2d 728 (1990). The plaintiff's failure to seek relief under A.R.S. § 12-504 until after expiration of the six-month period to refile authorized by the statute is evidence of a lack of the required diligence. *Copeland v. Arizona Veterans Memorial Coliseum and Exposition Center*, 176 Ariz. 86, 859 P.2d 196 (Ct. App. Div. 1 1993).

A dismissal order entered pursuant to the "savings statute," A.R.S. § 12-504, is both final and appealable, notwithstanding that such dismissal is without prejudice. *Short v. Dewald*, 226 Ariz. 88, 244 P.3d 92 (Ct. App. Div. 1 2010) (to interpret § 12-504 otherwise would render uncertain relief granted under the statute). An order denying relief under A.R.S. § 12-504 will be reversed on appeal only for an abuse of discretion. *Copeland v. Arizona Veterans Memorial Coliseum and Exposition Center*, 176 Ariz. 86, 859 P.2d 196 (Ct. App. Div. 1 1993).

8. *Securing Trial Settings in Arbitration Cases*. Ariz. R. Civ. P. 38.1(a) (former Rule V(b) of the now abrogated Uniform Rules of Practice of the Superior Court) requires that a Motion to Set and Certificate of Readiness is to be filed in "every civil case" to avoid dismissal for lack of prosecution. A case subject to compulsory arbitration is still a "civil case," and the time periods and procedures prescribed in Rule 38.1 remain fully applicable to them. *Martinez v. Binsfield*, 196 Ariz. 466, 999 P.2d 810 (2000). Indeed, at the time the provisions of former Rule 2(d) of the now abrogated Uniform Rules of Procedure for Arbitration were transferred to then new Ariz. R. Civ. P. 73(d), they were also amended to conform to the holding in *Martinez v. Binsfield*, 196 Ariz. 466, 999 P.2d 810 (2000), and to make clear that the time periods set forth in Rule 38.1 apply in cases subject to compulsory arbitration.

The procedure for securing a trial setting in a case which has been assigned to compulsory arbitration are part and parcel of the procedures for prosecuting an appeal from the award or other final disposition entered by the assigned arbitrator. See Rule 77 and accompanying *Authors' Comments*. The notice of appeal from the arbitrator's final decision is to be entitled "Appeal from Arbitration and Motion to Set for Trial," and is treated in all material respects as the Motion to Set and Certificate of Readiness required by Ariz. R. Civ. P. 38.1(a). See *Decola v. Freyer*, 198 Ariz. 28, 6 P.3d 333 (Ct. App. Div. 1 2000).

9. *Trial Continuances.* Under Ariz. R. Civ. P. 38.1(h), once a matter has been set for trial on a specified date, a continuance may only be granted for sufficient cause. The provision does not apply to adjournments of trials once commenced. *Bezat v. Home Owners' Loan Corporation*, 55 Ariz. 85, 98 P.2d 852 (1940). What constitutes good cause, and whether a continuance should be granted, are matters within the trial court's discretion, and will not be disturbed on appeal except for an abuse of that discretion. *Nordale v. Fisher*, 93 Ariz. 342, 380 P.2d 1003 (1963); *Yates v. Superior Court In and For Pima County*, 120 Ariz. 436, 586 P.2d 997 (Ct. App. Div. 2 1978); *Modla v. Parker*, 17 Ariz. App. 54, 495 P.2d 494 (Div. 1 1972); *Evans v. Scottsdale Plumbing Co.*, 10 Ariz. App. 184, 457 P.2d 724 (Div. 1 1969). A written motion, supported by affidavits as to the grounds for a continuance, is required. *Valley Nat. Bank of Arizona v. Meneghin*, 130 Ariz. 119, 634 P.2d 570 (1981).

Ariz. R. Civ. P. 38.1(h), (i) and (j) imply a heavy presumption against the granting of a trial continuance. Once a matter is set for trial, a continuance will not be granted unless sufficient cause is shown. *Valley Nat. Bank of Arizona v. Meneghin*, 130 Ariz. 119, 634 P.2d 570 (1981); *Aries v. Palmer Johnson, Inc.*, 153 Ariz. 250, 735 P.2d 1373, 4 U.C.C. Rep. Serv. 2d 85 (Ct. App. Div. 2 1987). Requesting a continuance by stipulation does not eliminate the need to show sufficient cause for it. Where a request for a continuance is based upon the absence of a witness, there must be a showing by affidavit of what the testimony of the absent witness would be, and when the witness will be available. *Miller v. Boeger*, 1 Ariz. App. 554, 405 P.2d 573 (1965).

There is no constitutional prohibition of parallel civil and criminal proceedings, and whether to grant a continuance or stay of the civil proceedings in that circumstance is a matter within the trial court's discretion. *State v. Ott*, 167 Ariz. 420, 808 P.2d 305 (Ct. App. Div. 1 1990). The court should consider whether the civil and criminal proceedings concern the same matter, whether resolution of the criminal case would moot, clarify or simplify the matter, and whether there is a possibility that a party might exploit discovery for use in the criminal case. *State v. Ott*, 167 Ariz. 420, 808 P.2d 305 (Ct. App. Div. 1 1990). The civil proceedings should be stayed if the conduct of parallel proceedings would substantially prejudice the defendant's rights. *State v. Ott*, 167 Ariz. 420, 808 P.2d 305 (Ct. App. Div. 1 1990).

10. *Scheduling Conflicts Between Courts; Notice of Calendar Conflict; Procedure for Resolving Calendar Conflicts.* Rule 38.1(k)

governs the procedures for resolving scheduling conflicts whether they arise between cases pending in the Superior Courts of different counties, between a case pending in the Superior Court and a case pending in the United States District Court for the District of Arizona, or between cases pending in different courts within the same county. While the criteria to be considered in resolving the conflict that are listed in Ariz. R. Civ. P. 38.1(k)(2) seem to be generally concerned with conflicts in the scheduling of trials or evidentiary hearings, calendar conflicts in the scheduling of other matters are covered by the Rule as well.

Once counsel becomes aware that the scheduling of a proceeding in one matter in which counsel has appeared conflicts with the scheduling of a matter in another case, counsel has the responsibility to promptly notify both the judges and all counsel involved in all matters affected by the conflict. Upon receiving such a notice, the judges in the matters involved are to confer and attempt to resolve the scheduling conflict. The Rule does not require that counsel be involved in, or be consulted with regard to, the attempted resolution. Ariz. R. Civ. P. 38.1(k)(2) lists the factors that are to be considered in resolving the conflict, and specifies that no particular priority is to be accorded to a matter because the case is pending in either state or federal court. The Superior Court in any county may, either by Local Rule or by general order, establish procedures for resolving calendar conflicts between different Divisions of that Superior Court.

Rule 38.1. Setting of civil cases for trial; postponements; scheduling conflicts; dismissal calendar (2014 amendment)

Text of Rule 38.1 applicable to cases filed on or after April 15, 2014 and to those cases filed before April 15, 2014 that are subject to the conditions stated in the November 27, 2013, Amended Order Regarding ApplicabilityProvision, in R-13-0017.

See also, text of Rule 38.1 applicable to those cases filed before April 15, 2014 that are not subject to the conditions stated in the November 27, 2013 Amended Order Regarding Applicability Provision, in R-13-0017.

(a) Setting for Trial. Civil actions shall be set for trial pursuant to Rule 16 or Rule 77. Preference shall be given to short causes and cases that by reason of statute, rule or court order are entitled to priority. The parties shall be given at least thirty days notice of the trial date.

Formerly Rule 38.1(g), added Oct. 10, 2000, effective Dec. 1, 2000. Renumbered Rule 38.1(a) and amended Aug. 28, 2013, effective April 15, 2014, subject to conditions of Order No. R-13-0017.

(b) Postponements. Unless otherwise provided by local rule, when an action has been set for trial on a specified date by order of the court, no postponement of the trial shall be granted except for sufficient cause, supported by affidavit, or by consent of the parties, or by operation of law.

Formerly Rule 38.1(h), added Oct. 10, 2000, effective Dec. 1, 2000. Renumbered Rule 38.1(b) and amended Aug. 28, 2013, effective April 15, 2014, subject to conditions of Order No. R-13-0017.

(c) Application for Postponement; Grounds; Effect of Admission of Truth of Affidavit by Adverse Party. On an application for a postponement of the trial, if the ground for the application is the want of testimony, the party applying therefor shall provide an affidavit showing the materiality of the testimony and that the party has used due diligence to procure such testimony, stating such diligence and the cause of failure to procure such testimony, if known, and that such testimony cannot be obtained from any other source. If the ground for the application is the absence of a witness, the party applying shall state the name and residence of the witness and what the party expects to prove by the witness. The application in either case shall also state that the postponement is not sought for delay only, but that justice may be done. If the adverse party admits that such testimony would be given and that it will be considered as actually given at the trial, or offered and overruled as improper, the trial shall not be postponed. Such testimony may be controverted as if the witness were personally present.

Formerly Rule 38.1(i), added Oct. 10, 2000, effective Dec. 1, 2000. Renumbered Rule 38.1(c) and amended Aug. 28, 2013, effective April 15, 2014, subject to conditions of Order No. R-13-0017.

(d) Deposition of Witness or Party; Consent. The party obtaining a postponement shall, if required by the adverse party, consent that the testimony of any witness or adverse party in attendance be taken by deposition. The testimony so taken may be read at the trial by either party as if the witnesses were present.

Formerly Rule 38.1(j), added Oct. 10, 2000, effective Dec. 1, 2000. Renumbered Rule 38.1(d) and amended Aug. 28, 2013, effective April 15, 2014, subject to conditions of Order No. R-13-0017.

(e) Scheduling conflicts between courts.

(1) *Notice to the court.* Upon learning of a scheduling conflict between a case in Superior Court and a case in United States District Court, or between cases in the Superior Courts of different counties, or between cases in different courts within a county, counsel shall promptly notify the judges and other counsel involved in order that the conflict may be resolved.

(2) *Resolution of conflicts.* Upon being advised of a scheduling conflict, the judges involved shall, if necessary, confer personally or by telephone in an effort to resolve the conflict. While neither federal nor state court cases have priority in scheduling, the following factors may be considered in resolving the conflict:

(A) the nature of the cases as civil or criminal, and the presence of any speedy trial problems;

(B) the length, urgency, or relative importance of the matters;

(C) a case which involves out-of-town witnesses, parties or counsel;

(D) the age of the cases;

(E) the matter which was set first;

(F) any priority granted by rule or statute; and

(G) any other pertinent factor.

(3) *Inter-division Conflicts.* Conflicts in scheduling between divisions of the same court may be governed by local rule or general order.

Formerly Rule 38.1(k), added Oct. 10, 2000, effective Dec. 1, 2000. Renumbered Rule 38.1(e) and amended Aug. 28, 2013, effective April 15, 2014, subject to conditions of Order No. R-13-0017.

(f) Dismissal Calendar. The clerk of the court or court administration shall place on the Dismissal Calendar every civil action in which a Joint Report and a Proposed Scheduling Order under Rule 16 or Rule 16.3 or an arbitrator's notice of decision under Rule 76 have not been filed with the court within 270 days after the commencement thereof, or in medical malpractice cases where the court has not set a Comprehensive Pretrial Conference within 270 days after the commencement thereof. A case remaining on the Dismissal Calendar for 60 days shall be dismissed without prejudice for lack of prosecution, and the court shall make an appropriate order as to any bond or other security filed therein, unless prior to the expiration of such 60-day period:

(1) a Joint Report and a Proposed Scheduling Order under Rule 16(b) or Rule 16.3 are filed with the court;

(2) in medical malpractice cases, the court sets a Comprehensive Pretrial Conference;

(3) the court, on motion for good cause shown, orders the case to be continued on the Dismissal Calendar for a specified period of time without dismissal; or

(4) a notice of decision has been filed with the clerk of the court in a case assigned to arbitration.

Added Aug. 28, 2013, effective April 15, 2014, subject to conditions of Order No. R-13-0017.

(g) Notification. The clerk of the court or court administrator, whoever is designated by the presiding judge, shall promptly notify counsel in writing when a case is placed on the Dismissal Calendar, and no further notice shall be required prior to dismissal.

Added Aug. 28, 2013, effective April 15, 2014, subject to conditions of Order No. R-13-0017.

HISTORICAL NOTES

[2014 Amendments]

[Rule 38.1] Arizona Supreme Court Order No. R-13-0017, issued Aug. 28, 2013, provided that the amendments of the order would be "effective on April 15, 2014 as to all cases filed on or after that date." The applicability provision of Order No. R-13-0017 was amended on Nov. 14, 2013, and subsequently amended on Nov. 27, 2013 to provide:

(1) The Amendments shall apply to all actions filed on or after April 15, 2014.

(2) Beginning on April 15, 2014, the Amendments also shall apply to any action filed prior to April 15, 2014 (a "pending action"), unless one of the following events has occurred before that date:

   (a) A party has filed a Motion to Set and Certificate of Readiness,

   (b) The parties have filed a Proposed Scheduling Order, or

   (c) The court has entered a Scheduling Order.

(3) If, in a pending action, one of the preceding events has not occurred before April 15, 2014, the parties shall file a Joint Report and a Proposed

Scheduling Order in accordance with the Amendments by June 30, 2014, or within 270 days after the commencement of the action, whichever date is later. Otherwise, the court will place the action on the Dismissal Calendar in accordance with the Amendments.

(4) A trial court, in its discretion, may apply any of the Amendments to a case pending before April 15, 2014, even if the Amendments would not otherwise apply under paragraph (2) above. For example, if a party filed a Motion to Set and Certificate of Readiness before April 15, 2014, the trial judge may set the matter for a trial setting conference under amended Rule 16(f), rather than place the case on the active calendar under pre-amendment Rule 38.1(c).

(5) Civil actions pending on the Inactive Calendar on April 15, 2014 shall be dismissed without prejudice on June 14, 2014, unless one of the actions set forth in subparts (1) - (4) of amended Rule 38.1(f) occurs before June 14, 2014.

AUTHORS' COMMENTS

Analysis

1. *Purpose and Scope of Rule*. Ariz. R. Civ. P. 38.1 (added 2014) was adopted as part of a larger project to align case management and trial setting procedures with current practice and, thereby, "acknowledge, by rule, what has become the reality in the vast majority of civil cases litigated in the State." *See,* Amended Petition filed In the Matter of Petition to Amend Rules 16, 16.1, 26, 37, 38, 38.1, 72, 73, 74 and 77, Arizona Rules of Civil Procedure, R-13-0017, page 2.

The general purpose of case management and trial setting procedures is discussed in the Authors' Comments to pre-2014 amendment Rules 16 and 38.1 applicable to cases filed before April 15, 2014, which are not otherwise subject to the R-13-0017 rule amendments.

2. *Comparison With Federal Rule*. There is no provision in the Federal Rules of Civil Procedure corresponding to ARCP 38.1 (added 2014).

3. *2014 Rule Amendments: Effective Date and Applicability*. On August 28, 2013, the Arizona Supreme Court adopted sweeping amendments to the case management and trial setting rules governing civil cases. The Promulgating Order specified such rules were adopted "effective on April 15, 2014 as to all cases filed on or after that date." *See,* August 28, 2013 Order entered in In the Matter of Petition to Amend Rules 16, 16.1, 26, 37, 38, 38.1, 72, 73, 74 and 77, Arizona Rules of Civil Procedure, R-13-0017. The applicability provision set forth in the Promulgating

Order set up two procedural tracks for case management with the new rules governing cases file on or after April 15, 2014 and the "old" rules governing pre-April 15, 2014 cases.

To avoid any confusion potentially created by the two different tracks, the Court entered an order on November 14, 2013, amending the applicability provision. On November 27, 2013, the court entered a second order further refining the amended applicability provision. As a result, the Amendments are effective and applicable as follows:

"(1) The Amendments shall apply to all actions filed on or after April 15, 2014.

"(2) Beginning on April 15, 2014, the Amendments also shall apply to any action filed prior to April 15, 2014 (a "pending action"), unless one of the following events has occurred before that date:

(a) A party has filed a Motion to Set and Certificate of Readiness,

(b) The parties have filed a Proposed Scheduling Order, or

(c) The court has entered a Scheduling Order.

"(3) If, in a pending action, one of the preceding events has not occurred before April 15, 2014, the parties shall file a Joint Report and a Proposed Scheduling Order in accordance with the Amendments by June 30, 2014, or within 270 days after the commencement of the action, whichever date is later. Otherwise, the court will place the action on the Dismissal Calendar in accordance with the Amendments.

"(4) A trial court, in its discretion, may apply any of the Amendments to a case pending before April 15, 2014, even if the Amendments would not otherwise apply under paragraph (2) above. For example, if a party filed a Motion to Set and Certificate of Readiness before April 15, 2014, the trial judge may set the matter for a trial setting conference under amended Rule 16(f), rather than place the case on the active calendar under pre-amendment Rule 38.1(c).

"(5) Civil actions pending on the Inactive Calendar on April 15, 2014 shall be dismissed without prejudice on June 14, 2014, unless one of the actions set forth in subparts (1) - (4) of amended Rule 38.1(f) occurs before June 14, 2014."

Rule 39. Trial by jury or by the court

(a) Trial by Jury. When trial by jury has been demanded as provided in Rule 38, the action shall be designated upon the docket as a jury action. The trial of all issues so demanded shall be by jury, unless:

1. The parties or their attorneys of record, by written stipulation filed with the court or by an oral stipulation made in open court and entered in the record, consent to trial by the court sitting without a jury, or

2. The court upon motion or of its own initiative finds that a right of trial by jury of some or all of those issues does not exist.

(b) Order of Trial by Jury; Questions by Jurors to Witnesses or the Court. The trial by a jury shall proceed in the following order, unless the court for good cause stated in the record, otherwise directs:

1. Immediately after the jury is sworn, the court shall instruct the jury concerning its duties, its conduct, the order of proceedings, the procedure for submitting written questions of witnesses or of the court as set forth in Rule 39(b)(10), and the elementary legal principles that will govern the proceeding.

2. The plaintiff or the plaintiff's counsel may read the complaint to the jury and make a statement of the case.

3. The defendant or the defendant's counsel may read the answer and may make a statement of the case to the jury, but may defer making such statement until after the close of the evidence on behalf of the plaintiff.

4. Other parties admitted to the action or their counsel may read their pleadings and may make a statement of their cases to the jury, but they may defer making such statement until after the close of the evidence on behalf of the plaintiff and defendant. The statement of such parties shall be in the order directed by the court.

5. The plaintiff shall then introduce evidence.

6. The defendant shall then introduce evidence.

7. The other parties, if any, shall then introduce evidence in the order directed by the court.

8. The plaintiff may then introduce rebutting evidence.

9. The defendant may then introduce rebutting evidence in support of the defendant's counterclaim(s), if any. Rebuttal evidence from other parties or with respect to cross-claims or third party complaints may be introduced with the permission

of the court in an order to be established at the court's discretion.

The statements to the jury shall be confined to a concise and brief statement of the facts which the parties propose to establish by evidence on the trial, and any party may decline to make such statement.

10. Jurors shall be permitted to submit to the court written questions directed to witnesses or to the court. Opportunity shall be given to counsel to object to such questions out of the presence of the jury. Notwithstanding the foregoing, for good cause the court may prohibit or limit the submission of questions to witnesses.

Amended July 14, 1961, effective Nov. 1, 1961; Sept. 15, 1987, effective Nov. 15, 1987; Oct. 24, 1995, effective Dec. 1, 1995.

(c) Omission of Testimony During Trial. The court may at any time before commencement of the argument, when it appears necessary to the due administration of justice, allow a party to supply an omission in the testimony upon such terms and limitations as the court prescribes.

Added as Rule 43(j). Renumbered as Rule 39(c) Sept. 15, 1987, effective Nov. 15, 1987.

(d) Verdict, Deliberations and Conduct of Jury; Sealed Verdict; Access to Juror Notes and Notebooks.

1. Before the jury begins deliberating, the court shall instruct the jury on the law, the appropriate procedures to be followed during deliberations, and the appropriate method for reporting the results of its deliberations. Such instructions shall be recorded or reduced to writing and made available to the jurors during deliberations.

2. When the jurors retire to deliberate, they shall be kept together in some convenient place in the charge of a proper officer. The court in its discretion may permit jurors to separate while not deliberating, or, on motion of any party, or the court may require them to be sequestered in the charge of a proper officer whenever they leave the courtroom or place of deliberation. The court shall admonish the jury not to converse among themselves or with anyone else on any subject connected with the trial while not deliberating, or to permit themselves to be exposed to any accounts of the proceeding, or to view the place or places where the events involved in the action occurred, until they have completed their deliberations.

3. The court shall not require a jury to deliberate after normal work hours unless the court, after consultation with the jury and the parties, determines that evening or weekend deliberations are necessary in the interest of justice and will

not impose an undue hardship upon the jurors.

4. The court may direct the jury to return a sealed verdict at such time as the court directs.

5. Jurors shall have access to their notes and notebooks during recesses, discussions and deliberations.

6. When dismissing a jury at the conclusion of the case, the court shall advise the jurors that they are discharged from service and, if appropriate, release them from their duty of confidentiality and explain their rights regarding inquiries from counsel, the media or any person.

Added as 39(c). Amended Oct. 28, 1980, effective Jan. 1, 1981. Renumbered as Rule 39(d) Sept. 15, 1987, effective Nov. 15, 1987. Amended Oct. 24, 1995, effective Dec. 1, 1995; September 16, 2008, effective January 1, 2009.

(e) Duty of Officer in Charge of Jury. The officer having the jurors under that officer's charge shall not allow any communication to be made to them, or make any, except to ask them if they have agreed upon their verdict, unless by order of the court, and shall not, before the verdict is rendered, communicate to any person the state of their deliberations or the verdict agreed upon.

Added as Rule 39(d). Renumbered as Rule 39(e) Sept. 15, 1987, effective Nov. 15, 1987.

(f) Admonition to Jurors; Juror Discussions. If the jurors are permitted to separate during the trial, they shall be admonished by the court that it is their duty not to converse with or permit themselves to be addressed by any person on any subject connected with the trial; except that the jurors shall be instructed that they will be permitted to discuss the evidence among themselves in the jury room during recesses from trial when all are present, as long as they reserve judgment about the outcome of the case until deliberations commence. Notwithstanding the foregoing, the jurors' discussion of the evidence among themselves during recesses may be limited or prohibited by the court for good cause.

Added as 39(c). Amended Oct. 28, 1980, effective Jan. 1, 1981. Renumbered as Rule 39(d) Sept. 15, 1987, effective Nov. 15, 1987. Amended Oct. 24, 1995, effective Dec. 1, 1995; September 16, 2008, effective January 1, 2009.

(g) Communication to Court by Jury. When the jurors desire to communicate with the court during retirement, they shall make their desire known to the officer having them in charge who shall inform the court and they may be brought into court, and through their foreman shall state to the court, either orally or in writing, what they desire to communicate.

Added as Rule 39(f). Renumbered as Rule 39(g) Sept. 15, 1987, effective Nov. 15, 1987.

(h) Assisting Jurors at Impasse. If the jury advises the court that it has reached an impasse in its deliberations, the court may, in the presence of counsel, inquire of the jurors to determine whether and how court and counsel can assist them in their deliberative process. After receiving the jurors' response, if any, the judge may direct that further proceedings occur as appropriate.

Added Oct. 24, 1995, effective 1995.

(i) Discharge of Jury; New Trial. The jurors may, after the action is submitted to them, be discharged by the court when they have been kept together for such time as to render it altogether improbable that they can agree, or when a calamity, sickness or accident may, in the opinion of the court, require it. When a jury has been discharged without having rendered a verdict the action may be tried again.

Added as Rule 39(g). Renumbered as Rule 39(h) Sept. 15, 1987, effective Nov. 15, 1987. Renumbered as Rule 39(i) Oct. 24, 1995, effective Dec. 1, 1995.

(j) Trial by the Court. Issues not demanded for trial by jury as provided in Rule 38 shall be tried by the court. Notwithstanding the failure of a party to demand a jury in an action in which such a demand might have been made of right, the court in its discretion upon motion may order a trial by jury of any or all issues.

Added as Rule 39(h). Renumbered as Rule 39(i) Sept. 15, 1987, effective Nov. 15, 1987. Renumbered as Rule 39(j) Oct. 24, 1995, effective Dec. 1, 1995.

(k) Procedure Applicable in Trial by the Court. The rules prescribed for trial of actions before a jury shall govern in trials by the court so far as applicable.

Added as Rule 39(i). Renumbered as Rule 39(j) Sept. 15, 1987, effective Nov. 15, 1987. Renumbered as Rule 39(k) Oct. 24, 1995, effective Dec. 1, 1995.

(*l*) [Abrogated Oct. 10, 2000, effective Dec. 1, 2000].

(m) Advisory Jury and Trial by Consent. In all actions not triable of right by a jury the court upon motion or of its own initiative may try any issue with an advisory jury or, the court, with the consent of both parties, may order a trial with a jury whose verdict has the same effect as if trial by jury had been a matter of right.

Added as Rule 39(k). Renumbered as Rule 39(l) Sept. 15, 1987, effective Nov. 15, 1987. Renumbered as Rule 39(m) Oct. 24, 1995, effective Dec. 1, 1995.

(n) Interrogatories When Equitable Relief Sought; Answers Advisory. In actions where equitable relief is sought, if a jury is demanded, and more than one material issue of fact is joined, the court may submit written interrogatories to the jury covering all or part of the issues of fact, and such interrogatories shall be answered by the jury. The interrogatories shall be approved by the court, and each interrogatory shall be confined to a single question of fact and shall be so framed that it can be answered yes or no, and shall be so answered. The answers shall be only advisory to the court.

Added as Rule 39(l). Renumbered as Rule 39(m) Sept. 15, 1987, effective Nov. 15, 1987. Renumbered as Rule 39(n) Oct. 24, 1995, effective Dec. 1, 1995.

(*o*) Arguments. The party having under the pleadings the burden of proof on the whole case shall be entitled to open and close the argument. Where there are several parties having several claims or defenses, and represented by different counsel, the court shall prescribe the order of argument among them.

Added as Rule 51(c). Renumbered as Rule 39(n) Sept. 15, 1987, effective Nov. 15, 1987. Renumbered as Rule 39(o) Oct. 24, 1995, effective Dec. 1, 1995.

(p) Note Taking by Jurors. The court shall instruct that the jurors may take notes regarding the evidence and keep the notes for the purpose of refreshing their memory for use during recesses, discussions and deliberations. The court shall provide materials suitable for this purpose. After the jury has rendered its verdict, the notes shall be collected by the bailiff or clerk who shall promptly destroy them.

Added Oct. 24, 1995, effective Dec. 1, 1995.

(q) Memoranda. No post trial memoranda shall be filed by counsel, other than memoranda in support of or in opposition to a motion pursuant to Rule 50(b), 52(b), 59 or 60 of these Rules, unless otherwise specifically directed by the trial judge.

Added Oct. 10, 2000, effective Dec. 1, 2000.

STATE BAR COMMITTEE NOTES

1961 Amendment

[Rule 39(b)] The word "may" has been substituted for "shall" at the appropriate place in each of the first three numbered provisions of proposed amended Rule 39(b) in order that the matter of reading pleadings to the jury may be left to the discretion of the party or his counsel instead of requiring the pleadings to be read to the jury as provided by the present rule.

2000 Amendment

As part of the 2000 effort to consolidate formerly separate sets of procedural rules into either the Arizona Rules of Civil Procedure or the Rules of the Arizona Supreme Court, the provisions of former Rule VIII(c) of the Uniform Rules of Practice of the Superior Court were added to Rule 39 as subpart (q), but revised to clarify that the Rule does not apply to memoranda filed in support of post-trial motions seeking relief from a verdict or judgment. The provisions of former Rules VIII(b) and (d) were simply abrogated, because they were essentially duplicative of the provisions of existing rules in the Arizona Rules of Civil Procedure.

The provisions of former Rule 39(l), which merely reiterated the requirement of Article VI, Section 21 of the Arizona Constitution that matters be decided within sixty (60) days of their submission to a judge or commissioner, were abrogated. The Rule was entirely duplicative of both Rule XIII of the Uniform Rules of Practice of the Superior Court and Rule 77(i) of the Arizona Rules of Civil Procedure. The Committee was of the view that, because the issue addressed was one affecting primarily the administration of the courts, any Rule on the subject should be contained in the Rules of the Arizona Supreme Court. Accordingly, a modified version of what was formerly Rule 77(i) of the Arizona Rules of Civil Procedure was added to the Rules of the Arizona Supreme Court as a new Rule 91(e).

COURT COMMENT

1995 Amendments

[Rule 39(b)(10)] The court should instruct the jury that any questions directed to witnesses or the court must be in writing, unsigned and given to the bailiff. The court should further instruct that, if a juror has a question for a witness or the court, the juror should hand it to the bailiff during a recess, or if the witness is about to leave the witness stand, the juror should signal to the bailiff. If the court determines that the juror's question calls for admissible evidence, the question should be asked by court or counsel in the court's discretion. Such question may be answered by stipulation or other appropriate means, including but not limited to additional testimony upon such terms and limitations as the court prescribes. If the court determines that the juror's question calls for inadmissible evidence, the question shall not be read or answered. If a juror's question is rejected, the jury should be told that trial rules do not permit some questions to be asked and that the jurors should not attach any significance to the failure of having their question asked.

[Rule 39(f)] In exercising its discretion to limit or prohibit jurors' permission to discuss the evidence among themselves during recesses, the trial court should consider the length of the trial, the nature and complexity of the issues, the makeup of the jury, and other factors that may be relevant on a case by case basis.

[Rule 39(h)] Many juries, after reporting to the judge that they have reached an impasse in their deliberations, are needlessly discharged very soon thereafter and a mistrial declared when it would be appropriate and might be helpful for the judge to offer some assistance in hopes of improving the chances of a verdict. The judge's offer would be designed and intended to address the issues that divide the jurors, if it is legally and practically possible to do so. The invitation to dialogue should not be coercive, suggestive or unduly intrusive.

The judge's response to the jurors' report of impasse could take the following form:

"This instruction is offered to help your deliberations, not to force you to reach a verdict.

"You may wish to identify areas of agreement and areas of disagreement. You may then wish to discuss the law and the evidence as they relate to areas of disagreement.

"If you still have disagreement, you may wish to identify for the court and counsel which issues or questions or law or fact you would like counsel or court to assist you with. If you elect this option, please list in writing the issues where further assistance might help bring about a verdict.

"I do not wish or intend to force a verdict. We are merely trying to be responsive to your apparent need for help. If it is reasonably probable that you could reach a verdict as a result of this procedure, it would be wise to give it a try."

If the jury identifies one or more issues that divide them, the court, with the help of the attorneys, can decide whether and how the issues can be addressed. Among the obvious options are the following; giving additional instructions; clarifying earlier instructions; directing the attorneys to make additional closing argument; reopening the evidence for limited purposes; or a combination of these measures. Of course, the court might decide that it is not legally or practically possible to respond to the jury's concerns.

[Rule 39(*o*)] The Court has discretion to give final instructions to the jury before closing arguments of counsel instead of after, in order to enhance jurors' ability to apply the applicable law to the facts. In that event, the court may wish to withhold giving the necessary procedural and housekeeping instructions until after closing arguments, in order to offset the impact of the last counsel's argument.

AUTHORS' COMMENTS

Analysis

1. *Scope and Purpose of Rule.* Rule 39, which deals, *inter alia,* with trials to the Court, the use of advisory juries, and the order of proof at and conduct of trials, is closely related to Rule 38. The legal issues likely to arise under Rule 39 are quite similar to those that arise under Rule 38, with the exceptions noted herein.

After a bench trial, the court must enter findings of fact and conclusions of law, when requested to do so before trial. *In re U.S. Currency in Amount of $26,980.00*, 199 Ariz. 291, 18 P.3d 85 (Ct. App. Div. 2 2000). The purpose of this requirement, which is discussed in detail in the *Authors' Comments* under Ariz. R. Civ. P. 52, is to enable appellate courts to examine the bases for the trial court's conclusions. *In re U.S. Currency in Amount of $26,980. 00*, 199 Ariz. 291, 18 P.3d 85 (Ct. App. Div. 2 2000).

2. *Comparison with Federal Rule.* ARCP 39(a), (j) and (m) are substantially the same as FRCP Rules 39(a), (b), and (c). The Federal Rules of Civil Procedure do not have provisions that cor-

respond to ARCP 39(b), (c), (d), (e), (f), (g), (h), (i), (k), (n), (o), (p), and (q).

In 2007, the language of FRCP 39 was amended as part of the general restyling of the Federal Rules of Civil Procedure to make the Federal Rules more easily understood and to make style and terminology consistent throughout the Federal Rules of Civil Procedure. Those stylistic modifications have not been incorporated into ARCP 39.

3. *Agreements to Waive Jury.* Under Ariz. R. Civ. P. 39(a)(1), a stipulation to waive a jury and conduct the trial to the Court must be in writing and filed with the Court, or made orally in open court and entered in the record. The memorialization of such an agreement in the Court's minute entries of pretrial conferences may not be sufficient. *Nackard v. Wolfswinkel*, 116 Ariz. 348, 569 P.2d 290 (Ct. App. Div. 1 1977).

4. *Effect of Improper or Untimely Jury Demand.* Ariz. R. Civ. P. 39(a)(2) contemplates striking a jury demand where the matter, or particular issues, are not triable of right to a jury. Presumably, such relief can also be granted, and probably should be sought, where an untimely demand for jury trial is made.

Under Ariz. R. Civ. P. 39(j), the Court may order a jury trial even in instances where the parties failed to make a timely demand therefor. A motion seeking such relief is addressed to the Court's sound discretion. *Valley Nat. Bank v. Witter*, 58 Ariz. 491, 121 P.2d 414 (1942).

5. *Use of Advisory Juries.* Ariz. R. Civ. P. 39(m) (formerly Rule 39(k)) authorizes the use of an advisory jury, in the Court's discretion, in "actions not triable of right by a jury," primarily equity cases. The verdict of such a jury, or its answers to submitted interrogatories, are advisory and not binding, and the judgment is deemed to be that of the Court based upon its own findings. *Graham v. Shooke*, 107 Ariz. 79, 482 P.2d 446 (1971); *Kostolansky v. Lesher*, 95 Ariz. 103, 387 P.2d 804 (1963); *Bohmfalk v. Vaughan*, 89 Ariz. 33, 357 P.2d 617 (1960); *Garden Lakes Community Ass'n, Inc. v. Madigan*, 204 Ariz. 238, 62 P.3d 983 (Ct. App. Div. 1 2003); *Wooldridge Const. Co. v. First Nat. Bank of Arizona*, 130 Ariz. 86, 634 P.2d 13 (Ct. App. Div. 1 1981); *Mullins v. Horne*, 120 Ariz. 587, 587 P.2d 773, 25 U.C.C. Rep. Serv. 358 (Ct. App. Div. 1 1978).

In addition, Rule 39(m) gives the trial court explicit authority to *sua sponte* conduct a bench trial in which an advisory jury addresses only certain of the issues presented. *Paul R. Peterson Const., Inc. v. Arizona State Carpenters Health and Welfare Trust Fund*, 179 Ariz. 474, 880 P.2d 694, 17 Employee Benefits Cas. (BNA) 2624 (Ct. App. Div. 1 1994).

Once an advisory jury has been empaneled, the case may not

be withdrawn from it so long as there are factual issues to be resolved. *Slonsky v. Hunter*, 17 Ariz. App. 231, 496 P.2d 874 (Div. 1 1972). Such a withdrawal from an advisory jury is permissible only where the Court would, with a common law jury, direct a verdict for a failure of proof. *Jones v. CPR Division, Upjohn Co.*, 120 Ariz. 147, 584 P.2d 611, Blue Sky L. Rep. (CCH) P 71445 (Ct. App. Div. 1 1978); *Han v. Horwitz*, 2 Ariz. App. 245, 407 P.2d 786 (1965).

An issue need not be submitted to an advisory jury where the parties have not requested a special interrogatory directed to it. *Milam v. Milam*, 101 Ariz. 323, 419 P.2d 502 (1966); *Hammontree v. Kenworthy*, 1 Ariz. App. 472, 404 P.2d 816 (1965). Interrogatories directed to issues of law can be excluded. *Tucson Federal Sav. & Loan Ass'n v. Sundell*, 106 Ariz. 137, 472 P.2d 6 (1970); *Edwards v. Van Voorhis*, 11 Ariz. App. 216, 463 P.2d 111 (Div. 1 1970).

6. *Trial to Jury by Consent.* Under Ariz. R. Civ. P. 39(m), the parties may agree to utilize a jury whose verdict will be binding, rather than advisory, in cases where there is no right to a jury. The use of such a jury may not, however, be ordered by the Court without the consent of the parties.

7. *Use of Juries in Actions Involving Equitable Claims.* Where both legal and equitable claims are pursued together, the jury may be permitted to consider all legal claims and all issues common to both claims. In such cases, the jury's finding becomes advisory as to the equitable relief sought. It is not proper, however, to use a general verdict form and to treat all claims as legal in nature and the jury's verdict as binding on all claims. *Timmons v. City of Tucson*, 171 Ariz. 350, 830 P.2d 871, 63 Fair Empl. Prac. Cas. (BNA) 11 (Ct. App. Div. 2 1991).

8. *Communications With Jurors.* Ariz. R. Civ. P. 39(g) prescribes that, when jurors wish to communicate with the Court during their deliberations, they should make their desire known to the officer in charge of the jury, generally the Court's bailiff, who is to so advise the court. The jurors may then be brought into open court to make their communication to the Court, either orally or in writing, through the jury foreman.

Indeed, Ariz. R. Civ. P. 51 was amended in 2009 to add a provision requiring that all communications between the Court and the jury be either in writing or on the record. Jurors are generally advised of these procedures before commencing their deliberations. It is error for the Court to respond to a substantive inquiry from the jury, or to refuse to respond, without advising counsel of the inquiry and securing their positions on how to respond. *Perkins v. Komarnyckyj*, 172 Ariz. 115, 834 P.2d 1260 (1992).

9. *Juror Notebooks.* Under Ariz. R. Civ. P. 39(p), adopted in 1995 as part of several "jury reform" amendments, jurors may take notes concerning the evidence presented and may use them to refresh their recollections during recesses, discussions and deliberations. The court must provide jurors with materials suitable for this purpose, and is to advise the jury in the preliminary instructions given after the jury is sworn that they are permitted to take such notes.

Ariz. R. Civ. P. 47(g) gives the trial court discretion to direct that exhibits and other documents be included in notebooks for use by the jurors during trial. Ariz. R. Civ. P. 39(d)(3) confirms that jurors are to have access to their notes and/or notebooks during recesses, discussions and deliberations. The Court Comment to a companion amendment to Ariz. R. Evid. 611(a) suggests that jurors be given copies of key trial exhibits either for temporary viewing or for retention in juror notebooks.

After the jury has rendered its verdict, the jury's notes and/or notebooks are to be collected and destroyed by the bailiff or clerk.

10. *Questions from Jurors.* As part of the 1995 "jury reform" amendments, Ariz. R. Civ. P. 39(b)(10) has been adopted, dealing with questions from jurors. It specifies that jurors are ordinarily to be permitted to submit to the Court written questions directed to witnesses or to the Court.

The Court can limit or prohibit the submission of questions from the jury to witnesses, but only for good cause shown. The Rule provides that counsel are to be given the opportunity to object to such questions outside the presence of the jury.

The Court's Comment to the 1995 amendments elaborates on the procedures to be followed to accommodate this right of the jurors to ask questions. Questions from the jury are to be submitted to the clerk or bailiff in writing and unsigned and before the testimony of the witness is completed.

If the Court determines that the question calls for admissible evidence, then the Court can propound the question to the witness, or permit counsel to do so. If the Court determines that the evidence the question calls for is inadmissible, it should explain that situation to the jury. A trial court's decision concerning whether or not to submit a juror's question to a witness will be reviewed on appeal only for an abuse of discretion. *Warner v. Southwest Desert Images, LLC*, 218 Ariz. 121, 180 P.3d 986 (Ct. App. Div. 2 2008).

11. *Predeliberation Discussions of Evidence.* As part of the 1995 "jury reform" amendments, Ariz. R. Civ. P. 39(f) was amended to provide that jurors are to be instructed that they may discuss the evidence among themselves in the jury room during recesses, so long as all jurors are present and they reserve judgment concern-

ing the outcome of the case until formal deliberations commence. For good cause shown, the court can prohibit or limit such predeliberation discussions of evidence.

12. *Jury Impasses*. The 1995 "jury reform" amendments added a Ariz. R. Civ. P. 39(h) which is intended to give the trial judge greater power and discretion to assist juries who have reached an impasse, rather than immediately directing a mistrial. Upon being advised that the jury is at an impasse, the trial court may, in the presence of counsel, inquire of the jury as to whether and how further proceedings might assist them in reaching a verdict. If the court determines that further proceedings might assist the jury in reaching a decision, it has the power to direct them.

The Court Comment to this particular amendment emphasizes that the inquiry of the jury that has reported an impasse should not be coercive, suggestive or unduly intrusive. As examples of further proceedings that might be ordered, if the court determines they would be helpful, the Court Comment mentions the giving of additional jury instructions and/or clarifying earlier instructions, reopening evidence for limited purposes, permitting additional closing argument, or some combination of these measures. These, or any other, steps should be taken only where the trial court determines that it is legally and/or practically possible to address the concerns that produced the impasse. If the jury is eventually discharged, and a mistrial ordered, such an order in effect grants a new trial and is an appealable order under A.R.S. § 12-2101(F)(1). *Hall Family Properties, Ltd. v. Gosnell Development Corp.*, 185 Ariz. 382, 916 P.2d 1098 (Ct. App. Div. 1 1995).

13. *Order of Proof.* Ariz. R. Civ. P. 39(b) generally specifies the following order of proof at civil trials:

(1) opening statement by plaintiff;
(2) opening statement by defendant, unless deferred;
(3) opening statements of other parties, if any, unless deferred;
(4) presentation of evidence by plaintiff;
(5) presentation of evidence by defendant;
(6) presentation of evidence by other parties, if any, in an order directed by the Court;
(7) presentation of rebuttal evidence by plaintiff; and
(8) presentation by defendant of rebuttal evidence on a counterclaim, if any.

The presentation of rebuttal evidence by other parties, if any, on any cross-claims or third-party claims is with the permission of, and in the order directed by, the trial court. Under Ariz. R. Evid. 611(a), the trial court may also control the method and order of the interrogation of witnesses, and may impose reasonable time limits on the trial or portions of it.

Ariz. R. Civ. P. 39(b) was amended in 1995, as part of the "jury reform" amendments, to specify that, immediately after the jury is sworn and before opening statements, the jury is to be instructed concerning its duties, the order that proceedings will follow, the procedure for submitting questions that the jurors wish to direct to witnesses or to the court, and the elementary legal principles that apply to the case. A virtually identical requirement was also added by amendment to Ariz. R. Civ. P. 51(a).

The trial judge has the discretion conferred by Ariz. R. Civ. P. 39, and also has discretion to alter the order of the presentation of evidence within the parameters specified by the Rule. *Podol v. Jacobs*, 65 Ariz. 50, 173 P.2d 758 (1946); *Aritex Land Co. v. Baker*, 14 Ariz. App. 266, 482 P.2d 875 (Div. 2 1971). Thus, the trial court can permit the presentation of evidence outside the order of proof contemplated by Ariz. R. Civ. P. 39(b), *Mackey v. Philzona Petroleum Co.*, 93 Ariz. 87, 378 P.2d 906 (1963). The trial court may also permit a party to re-open its case after resting, if the interests of justice require. *Heeter v. Moore Drug Co.*, 104 Ariz. 41, 448 P.2d 391 (1968); *Bowman v. Hall*, 83 Ariz. 56, 316 P.2d 484 (1957); *T.H. Properties v. Sunshine Auto Rental, Inc.*, 151 Ariz. 444, 728 P.2d 663 (Ct. App. Div. 2 1986).

The trial court also has considerable discretion to control the presentation of rebuttal evidence so as to confine it to its proper boundaries. Rebuttal evidence should be limited to evidence that addresses new matters brought out by the opposing party in the presentation of its case, and should not be a vehicle for simply repeating evidence that the party put on in its case-in-chief. *Catchings v. City of Glendale*, 154 Ariz. 420, 743 P.2d 400 (Ct. App. Div. 2 1987); *Deyoe v. Clark Equipment Co., Inc.*, 134 Ariz. 281, 655 P.2d 1333 (Ct. App. Div. 2 1982); *Lowery v. Turner*, 19 Ariz. App. 299, 506 P.2d 1084 (Div. 1 1973).

14. *Order of Argument.* Ariz. R. Civ. P. 39(*o*), which was formerly designated Rule 51(c), specifies that the party with the burden of proof on the whole case is entitled to open and close arguments to the jury. Where there are multiple parties and claims, the Court is to prescribe the order of argument.

The Court Comment to the 1995 "jury reform" amendments, which *inter alia* redesignated former Ariz. R. Civ. P. 39(n) as Ariz. R. Civ. P. 39(*o*), points out that the trial court has the discretion to give the jury its substantive jury instructions before rather than after closing arguments of counsel. The Court Comment suggests that, where that procedure is followed, the trial court may wish to withhold giving what it describes as the "procedural and housekeeping instructions" until after closing arguments, so that the jury hears from the court last before commencing its formal deliberations.

15. *Trial Time Limitations*. Ariz. R. Civ. P. 16(h), added by a 1995 amendment to the Rule, provides that the Court may impose "reasonable time limits on the trial proceedings or portions thereof." While trial courts have the discretion to place time limitations on trial proceedings to avoid undue delay, waste of time or needless presentation of cumulative evidence, any limits imposed must be reasonable under the circumstances and rigid limits are disfavored. *Gamboa v. Metzler*, 223 Ariz. 399, 224 P.3d 215 (Ct. App. Div. 1 2010); *Brown v. U.S. Fidelity and Guar. Co.*, 194 Ariz. 85, 977 P.2d 807 (Ct. App. Div. 1 1998), as amended, (Nov. 25, 1998) and as corrected, (Aug. 5, 1999). Any time limits imposed should be sufficiently flexible to allow for adjustment during trial. *Gamboa v. Metzler*, 223 Ariz. 399, 224 P.3d 215 (Ct. App. Div. 1 2010); *Brown v. U.S. Fidelity and Guar. Co.*, 194 Ariz. 85, 977 P.2d 807 (Ct. App. Div. 1 1998), as amended, (Nov. 25, 1998) and as corrected, (Aug. 5, 1999).

The time limitations imposed will be reviewed on appeal for abuse of discretion. *Gamboa v. Metzler*, 223 Ariz. 399, 224 P.3d 215 (Ct. App. Div. 1 2010); *Brown v. U.S. Fidelity and Guar. Co.*, 194 Ariz. 85, 977 P.2d 807 (Ct. App. Div. 1 1998), as amended, (Nov. 25, 1998) and as corrected, (Aug. 5, 1999). To merit reversal, a party must show they incurred some harm as a consequence of the court's time limitation. *Gamboa v. Metzler*, 223 Ariz. 399, 224 P.3d 215 (Ct. App. Div. 1 2010); *Brown v. U.S. Fidelity and Guar. Co.*, 194 Ariz. 85, 977 P.2d 807 (Ct. App. Div. 1 1998), as amended, (Nov. 25, 1998) and as corrected, (Aug. 5, 1999).

16. *Time Limits for Decision by Court*. Under Ariz. R. Civ. P. 39(j), where no demand for jury trial has been made, or the issues presented are not triable to a jury, the trial is to be to the Court. Trials to the Court are to be conducted in the same fashion as trials to a jury. Article VI, Section 21 of the Arizona Constitution requires that matters be decided within sixty (60) days of their submission to a Judge or Commissioner.

An action is not deemed submitted, however, until the time for filing any briefs required has expired. This Rule formerly contained a provision, Ariz. R. Civ. P. 39(*l*), making that requirement specifically applicable to trials to the Court. It was abrogated in 2000, because its provisions were entirely duplicative of both former Rule XIII of the now abrogated Uniform Rules of Practice of the Superior Court and Ariz. R. Civ. P. 77(i), which was also abrogated. A provision reflecting this constitutional requirement was added to the Rules of the Arizona Supreme Court as Rule 91(e).

17. *Post-Trial Memoranda*. Ariz. R. Civ. P. 39(q), which was

formerly Rule VIII(c) of the now abrogated Uniform Rules of Practice of the Superior Court, specifies that post-trial memoranda are not to be filed unless counsel are specifically directed to do so by the trial judge. Obviously, and by the express language of Rule 39(q), this provision does not apply to memoranda submitted in support of, or in opposition to, one of the post-trial motions authorized by Ariz. R. Civ. P. 50, 52, 59 or 60.

Rule 39.1. Trial of cases assigned to the Complex Civil Litigation Program

The court should employ trial procedures as are deemed necessary or appropriate to facilitate a just, speedy and efficient resolution of the case, including, but not limited to, time limits and allocation of trial time, sequencing of evidence and arguments, bifurcation of issues or claims, advance scheduling of witnesses and other evidence, pre-trial admission of exhibits or other evidence, electronic presentation of evidence, jury selection and juror participation issues and other means of managing or expediting the trial of a complex case.

Added Nov. 3, 2005, effective on an experimental basis nunc pro tunc from Nov. 22, 2002. Amended Sept. 1, 2011, effective on a permanent basis Jan. 1, 2012.

COMMENT

Justification for this rule: Rule 39.1 is intended to supplement the Arizona Rules of Civil Procedure in a manner that will provide judges and litigants with appropriate procedural mechanisms for the fair, efficient and expeditious management of discovery, disclosures, motions, service of documents and pleadings, communications between and among counsel and the court, trial, and other aspects of complex civil litigation. Other than as specifically set forth, cases assigned to the complex litigation program are not exempt from any normally applicable rule of procedure, except to the extent the trial judge may order otherwise. Rule 39.1 should be available to any trial judge who wishes to follow it, in whole or in part, in managing a civil dispute, even in cases that are not formally assigned to a complex litigation program.

AUTHORS' COMMENTS

Analysis

1. *Scope and Purpose of Rule.* By Administrative Order effective November 22, 2002, the Arizona Supreme Court adopted Rule 39.1, together with certain other rules, as part of an experimental program following the Court's approval of a report from the Complex Civil Litigation Court Evaluation Committee. *See*, Administrative Order No. 2002-107. By that same administrative order, the Court established a pilot program to experiment with a Complex Civil Litigation Court in the Maricopa County Superior Court and adopted, on an experimental basis, several rules of civil procedure to apply to cases in the Complex Civil Litigation Court. Administrative Order No. 2002-107 also adopted, on an experimental basis, a form for identifying cases eligible for the

program, which the Court set forth in an Appendix to the Order. *See* Ariz. R. Civ. P. 8(i)(8).

The Complex Civil Litigation Rules—designated as Ariz. R. Civ. P. 8(h)(3), 8(i), 16.3, and 39.1—were promulgated to facilitate the conduct of an experimental Complex Litigation Program in the Superior Court of Maricopa County, which was scheduled to run from January 1, 2003 and December 31, 2004. At the request of the Complex Civil Litigation Court Evaluation Committee, this experimental program was extended through December 31, 2010. On September 1, 2011, the Arizona Supreme Court made permanent the Complex Litigation pilot program. The Complex Civil Litigation Rules— Rule 8(h)(3), 8(i), 16.3, and 39.1—are effective January 1, 2012.

2. *Comparison With Federal Rule.* The Federal Rules of Civil Procedure do not have a provision that corresponds to ARCP 39.1.

Rule 40. Assignment of cases for trial

The superior courts shall provide by rule for the placing of actions upon the trial calendar:

1. Without request of the parties, or
2. Upon request of a party and notice to other parties, or
3. In such other manner as the court deems expedient.

AUTHORS' COMMENTS

Analysis

1. *Scope and Purpose of Rule.* Rule 40 provides the Superior Courts with the authority to adopt rules governing the procedure for having civil actions placed upon the trial calendar. The system adopted need not require a request of the parties. The system that has been adopted is that set forth in what is now Ariz. R. Civ. P. 38.1, See the *Authors' Comments* concerning that Rule.

2. *Comparison With Federal Rule.* ARCP 40 is substantially the same as FRCP 40, but the Arizona Rule does not have a provision giving preference to actions entitled to a trial preference by statute as does the Federal Rule.

In 2007, the language of FRCP 40 was amended as part of the general restyling of the Federal Rules of Civil Procedure to make the Federal Rules more easily understood and to make style and terminology consistent throughout the Federal Rules of Civil Procedure. Those stylistic modifications have not been incorporated into ARCP 40.

Rule 41. Dismissal of action

(a) Voluntary Dismissal; By Plaintiff or by Order of Court; Effect.

1. Subject to the provisions of Rule 23(c), or Rule 66(c), or of any statute, an action may be dismissed (A) by the plaintiff without order of court by filing a notice of dismissal at any time before service by the adverse party of an answer or of a motion for summary judgment, whichever first occurs, or (B) by order of the court pursuant to a stipulation of dismissal signed by all parties who have appeared in the action. Such an order may be signed by a judge or a duly authorized court commissioner, the clerk of court or a deputy clerk. Unless otherwise stated in the notice or order of dismissal, the dismissal is without prejudice, except that a notice of dismissal operates as an adjudication upon the merits when filed by a plaintiff who has once dismissed in any court of the United States or of any state an action based on or including the same claim.

2. Except as provided in paragraph 1 of this subdivision of this Rule, an action shall not be dismissed at the plaintiff's instance save upon order of the court and upon such terms and conditions as the court deems proper. If a counterclaim has been pleaded by a defendant prior to the service upon the defendant of the plaintiff's motion to dismiss, the action shall not be dismissed against the defendant's objection unless the counterclaim can remain pending for independent adjudication by the court. Unless otherwise specified in the order, a dismissal under this paragraph is without prejudice.

Amended Sept. 15, 1987, effective Nov. 15, 1987; Oct. 4, 1990, effective Dec. 1, 1990; June 17, 1999, effective Dec. 1, 1999.

(b) Involuntary Dismissal; Effect Thereof. For failure of the plaintiff to prosecute or to comply with these rules or any order of court, a defendant may move for dismissal of an action or of any claim against the defendant. Unless the court in its order for dismissal otherwise specifies, a dismissal under this subdivision and any dismissal not provided for in this rule, other than a dismissal for lack of jurisdiction, for improper venue, or for failure to join a party under Rule 19, operates as an adjudication upon the merits.

Amended March 26, 1963; July 1, 1966, effective Nov. 1, 1966; Sept. 15, 1987, effective Nov. 15, 1987; Oct. 9, 1996, effective Dec. 1, 1996.

(c) Dismissal of Counterclaim, Cross-Claim, or Third-Party Claim. The provisions of this Rule apply to the dismissal of any counterclaim, cross-claim, or third-party claim. A voluntary dismissal by the claimant alone pursuant to paragraph 1 of subdivision (a) of this Rule shall be made before a responsive pleading is served or, if there is none, before the introduction of evidence at the trial or hearing.

(d) Costs of Previously Dismissed Action. If a plaintiff who has once dismissed an action in any court commences an action based upon or including the same claim against the same defendant, the court may make such order for the payment of costs of the action previously dismissed as it may deem proper and may stay the proceedings in the action until plaintiff has complied with the order.

STATE BAR COMMITTEE NOTES

1963 Amendment

[Rule 41(b)] This amendment corrects the duplication in the existing rules. Under the rules without the amendment, a directed verdict at the end of plaintiff's presentation to the jury is covered by Rule 50(a) which deals especially with this subject. A defense motion for judgment at the end of plaintiff's presentation in a non-jury case is covered by Rule 41(b). But the language of 41(b) is broad enough to cover jury cases as well, so that the practical effect is that in a jury case the motion to dismiss, but for this amendment, could be made under both 41(b) and under Rule 50(a). The amendment eliminates this duplication, leaving directed verdicts in jury cases to Rule 50(a) and motions to dismiss at the end of plaintiff's case in nonjury cases to this rule.

1966 Amendment

[Rule 41(b)] The terminology of this rule is changed to accord with the language of Rule 19. It is intended that dismissal of an action for failure to join a party who is indispensable under Rule 19, shall not operate as an adjudication upon the merits.

1990 Amendment

[Rule 41(a)(1)] The 1990 amendment to Rule 41(a)(1) provides that a stipulated dismissal, which is necessary to voluntarily dismiss an action after an answer or motion for summary judgment has been served, becomes effective upon entry of an order of the court. This conforms the formal requirements and the effective date of Rule 41(a) stipulated dismissals to those of appealable orders under Rule 58(a). This amendment avoids the problem encountered in *Theriault v. Scottsdale Enterprises*, 157 Ariz. 77, 754 P.2d 1352 (Ct. App. Div. 2 1987).

AUTHORS' COMMENTS

Analysis

1. Scope and Purpose of Rule.
2. Comparison With Federal Rule.
3. Notice of Voluntary Dismissal Prior to Filing of Answer.
4. Voluntary Dismissal After Filing of Answer.
5. Effect of Voluntary Dismissal Generally.
6. Effect of Voluntary Dismissal on Counterclaims and Cross-Claims.

1. *Scope and Purpose of Rule.* Rule 41 governs generally the dismissal of actions, both voluntary and involuntary, which are dealt with in separate subparts of the Rule. While the Rule is perhaps most frequently invoked against complaints, Ariz. R. Civ. P. 41(c) makes clear that the provisions of Ariz. R. Civ. P. 41(a) and (b) apply to counterclaims, cross-claims or third-party claims as well.

2. *Comparison With Federal Rule.* ARCP 41 is substantially identical to FRCP 41, but there are some important differences. ARCP 41(a)(1) contains a provision, not found in the Federal Rule, that the Court, when presented with a stipulation for dismissal, is to enter a formal order of dismissal.

In addition, in 2007, the language of FRCP 41 was amended as part of the general restyling of the Federal Rules of Civil Procedure to make the Federal Rules more easily understood and to make style and terminology consistent throughout the Federal Rules of Civil Procedure. Those stylistic modifications have not been incorporated into ARCP 41.

3. *Notice of Voluntary Dismissal Prior to Filing of Answer.* Voluntary dismissals by the plaintiff are the subject of Ariz. R. Civ. P. 41(a), which draws a sharp distinction according to the state of the pleadings at the time the dismissal is sought. Before an answer or motion for summary judgment is served by the adverse party, the plaintiff can secure the voluntary dismissal of the action simply by filing a notice of dismissal. Ariz. R. Civ. P. 41(c) provides that the voluntary dismissal of a counterclaim, cross-claim or third-party claim by notice is to be made before a responsive pleading is served or, if there is none, before the introduction of evidence at trial.

A notice of voluntary dismissal is self-executing and there is no need for notice to the adverse party, a hearing, or an order of Court. *Goodman v. Gordon*, 103 Ariz. 538, 447 P.2d 230 (1968). Such a dismissal is without prejudice, but may only be sought once.

If an action has previously been filed in any court and voluntarily dismissed, a second voluntary dismissal of an action that has been reinstituted following the first will be an adjudication on the merits and with prejudice.

Where there has been a voluntary dismissal after the statute of limitations for the claim has expired, the plaintiff must apply for leave to refile under the "savings statute," A.R.S. § 12-504, discussed further hereinafter, which preserves the Court's power to place equitable conditions on the reinstitution of claims previously voluntarily dismissed. *Jepson v. New*, 160 Ariz. 193, 772 P.2d 16 (Ct. App. Div. 1 1989), vacated in part, 164 Ariz. 265, 792 P.2d 728 (1990); *Flynn v. Cornoyer-Hedrick Architects & Planners, Inc.*, 160 Ariz. 187, 772 P.2d 10 (Ct. App. Div. 1 1988), decision aff'd, 164 Ariz. 265, 792 P.2d 728 (1990); *Osuna v. Wal-Mart Stores, Inc.*, 214 Ariz. 286, 151 P.3d 1267 (Ct. App. Div. 2 2007). A dismissal order entered pursuant to the "savings statute," A.R.S. § 12-504, however, is both final and appealable, notwithstanding that such dismissal is without prejudice. *Short v. Dewald*, 226 Ariz. 88, 244 P.3d 92 (Ct. App. Div. 1 2010) (to interpret A.R.S. § 12-504 otherwise would render uncertain the relief granted under the statute).

4. *Voluntary Dismissal After Filing of Answer.* Once an answer or motion for summary judgment has been filed, the procedures of Ariz. R. Civ. P. 41(a)(2) control the securing of a voluntary dismissal. Such a dismissal is discretionary with the Court, requires a motion or other application, notice to the adverse party, a hearing and an order of the Court. *Goodman v. Gordon*, 103 Ariz. 538, 447 P.2d 230 (1968). The Court is empowered to set such terms and conditions upon the dismissal as it feels are proper.

In applying the Rule, a distinction must be drawn between voluntary dismissals *with* prejudice and those that are to be *without* prejudice. *Turf Paradise, Inc. v. Maricopa County*, 179 Ariz. 337, 878 P.2d 1375 (Ct. App. Div. 1 1994). The plaintiff has an absolute right to a voluntary dismissal with prejudice; the party against whom dismissal is sought has no grounds for objection when its rights are protected. *Turf Paradise, Inc. v. Maricopa County*, 179 Ariz. 337, 878 P.2d 1375 (Ct. App. Div. 1 1994).

In the case of voluntary dismissals without prejudice, the Court's discretion is guided and limited by the first proviso in the first sentence of Ariz. R. Civ. P. 41(a)(2), that the dismissal be on such terms and conditions as the Court deems proper. *Goodman v. Gordon*, 103 Ariz. 538, 447 P.2d 230 (1968); *Turf Paradise, Inc. v. Maricopa County*, 179 Ariz. 337, 878 P.2d 1375 (Ct. App. Div. 1 1994).

It is not an abuse of the Court's discretion under that provision to condition dismissal upon payment of the defendant's attorneys' fees. *Turf Paradise, Inc. v. Maricopa County*, 179 Ariz. 337, 878 P.2d 1375 (Ct. App. Div. 1 1994). Similarly, the payment of the costs incurred by the defendant is also a permissible condition for the Court to impose upon such a voluntary dismissal. *State ex rel. Corbin v. Portland Cement Ass'n*, 142 Ariz. 421, 690 P.2d 140, 1984-2 Trade Cas. (CCH) ¶ 66240 (Ct. App. Div. 1 1984). Correspondingly, the omission of such conditions upon a voluntary dismissal is not necessarily an abuse of discretion. *Goodman v. Gordon*, 103 Ariz. 538, 447 P.2d 230 (1968).

In exercising its discretion whether to permit a voluntary dismissal without prejudice after the issues are joined and, if so, upon what conditions, the trial court should weigh the competing equities and make the decision that is the fairest to all parties concerned, *State ex rel. Corbin v. Portland Cement Ass'n*, 142 Ariz. 421, 690 P.2d 140, 1984-2 Trade Cas. (CCH) ¶ 66240 (Ct. App. Div. 1 1984), it should particularly focus on whether the dismissal would violate any substantial rights of the defendant. *Schoolhouse Educational Aids, Inc. v. Haag*, 145 Ariz. 87, 699 P.2d 1318 (Ct. App. Div. 2 1985); *Penunuri v. Superior Court In and For Pima County*, 115 Ariz. 399, 565 P.2d 905 (Ct. App. Div. 2 1977).

Thus, a motion for voluntary dismissal was properly denied where it was sought so that the plaintiff could refile the same action after the effective date of a new statute which enacted a scheme of comparative negligence and eliminated contributory negligence as a full defense. *Cheney v. Arizona Superior Court for Maricopa County*, 144 Ariz. 446, 698 P.2d 691 (1985); *Crawford By and Through Crawford v. Superior Court In and For Pima County*, 144 Ariz. 498, 698 P.2d 743 (Ct. App. Div. 2 1984). The Court may also condition a voluntary dismissal upon the dismissal by the plaintiff of related claims in an action in federal court. *State ex rel. Corbin v. Portland Cement Ass'n*, 142 Ariz. 421, 690 P.2d 140, 1984-2 Trade Cas. (CCH) ¶ 66240 (Ct. App. Div. 1 1984).

5. *Effect of Voluntary Dismissal Generally*. Unless the order specifies to the contrary, a voluntary dismissal is without prejudice, and the same cause of action may be brought in a subsequent suit. *Airfreight Exp. Ltd v. Evergreen Air Center, Inc.*, 215 Ariz. 103, 158 P.3d 232 (Ct. App. Div. 2 2007); *Edgar v. Garrett*, 10 Ariz. App. 98, 456 P.2d 944 (1969). A dismissal with prejudice is, of course, an adjudication on the merits and *res judicata*. *Torres v. Kennecott Copper Corp.*, 15 Ariz. App. 272, 488 P.2d 477 (Div. 1 1971).

The plain language of Ariz. R. Civ. P. 41(a)(1) permits a plaintiff to voluntarily dismiss a case without a court order by filing a notice of dismissal before the adverse party serves an answer or motion for summary judgment. Such a voluntary dismissal does not, however, preclude the superior court from subsequently entering an award of attorneys' fees in favor of the adverse party. *Vicari v. Lake Havasu City*, 222 Ariz. 218, 213 P.3d 367 (Ct. App. Div. 1 2009). In this context, a claim that the superior court lacks such "jurisdiction" refers not to the power of the court to award attorneys' fees, but to the correctness of the court's decision to award fees on any basis.

6. *Effect of Voluntary Dismissal on Counterclaims and Cross-Claims.* The second sentence of Ariz. R. Civ. P. 41(a)(2) only comes into play where plaintiff seeks a voluntary dismissal after the defendant has pled a proper permissive or compulsory counterclaim. *Turf Paradise, Inc. v. Maricopa County*, 179 Ariz. 337, 878 P.2d 1375 (Ct. App. Div. 1 1994). That sentence of the Rule specifically provides that the voluntary dismissal by the plaintiff must leave pending for independent adjudication any counterclaim that has been filed, unless the defendant does not object to its dismissal. The dismissal of the complaint, whether voluntary or by stipulation, does not automatically require the dismissal of any pending cross-claims. *Hollar v. Wright*, 115 Ariz. 606, 566 P.2d 1352 (Ct. App. Div. 1 1977).

7. *Involuntary Dismissals Generally.* Ariz. R. Civ. P. 41(b) is the provision governing involuntary dismissals, and particularly those for failure to prosecute, failure to comply with an order of court or a provision of the Rules, and dismissals after the plaintiff has rested in a trial to the Court. Dismissals for failure to prosecute are clearly authorized in appropriate circumstances. *Union Interchange, Inc. v. Van Aalsburg*, 102 Ariz. 461, 432 P.2d 589 (1967); *Cooper v. Odom*, 6 Ariz. App. 466, 433 P.2d 646 (1967). Similarly, a dismissal may be entered for the willful violation of a court order, *Carman v. Hefter*, 136 Ariz. 597, 667 P.2d 1312 (1983), or even for failure to appear for a hearing after proper notice. *Troxler v. Holohan*, 9 Ariz. App. 304, 451 P.2d 662 (1969); *Long v. Arizona Portland Cement Co.*, 2 Ariz. App. 332, 408 P.2d 852 (1965).

For those cases filed before April 15, 2014 and not otherwise subject to the conditions stated in the November 27, 2013 Amended Order Regarding Applicability Provision in R-13-0017, pre-amendment Ariz. R. Civ. P. 38.1(d) applies and is designed to standardize the inherent power of trial courts to dismiss cases for lack of prosecution. *BCAZ Corp. v. Helgoe*, 194 Ariz. 11, 976 P.2d 260 (Ct. App. Div. 1 1998), opinion supplemented on reh'g, (Mar. 25, 1999). It is designed to provide a convenient administrative practice to bring to the attention of the Court and the attorneys involved the fact that ample time has elapsed in which to prepare a case for trial. Under Ariz. R. Civ. P. 38.1(d), all cases remaining on the Inactive Calendar for two months shall be dismissed without prejudice for lack of prosecution unless, prior to the expiration of that two months, a proper Motion to Set and Certificate of Readiness is filed or the Court, for good cause shown, continues the case on the Inactive Calendar. Whether such good cause is shown is a matter left to the sound discretion of the trial court.

For cases filed on or after April 15, 2014 and those cases subject to the conditions stated in the November 27, 2013 Amended Order Regarding Applicability Provision, Ariz. R. Civ. P. 38.1 (added 2014) applies. Specifically subpart (f) creates a Dismissal Calendar as the administrative tool for dispensing with cases for lack of prosecution.

Because it is not a final judgment, a dismissal without prejudice is not an appealable order. *McMurray v. Dream Catcher USA, Inc.*, 220 Ariz. 71, 202 P.3d 536 (Ct. App. Div. 2 2009). A dismissal without prejudice, however, may be final for purposes of an award of attorneys' fees. *McMurray v. Dream Catcher USA, Inc.*, 220 Ariz. 71, 202 P.3d 536 (Ct. App. Div. 2 2009).

8. *Motion for Dismissal at Close of Plaintiff's Case in Trials to the Court.* Prior to the 1996 amendment, Ariz. R. Civ. P. 41(b) contained provisions authorizing and governing motions for dismissal at the close of the plaintiff's case in trials to the court. Such motions were the rough equivalent of motions for a directed verdict in jury trials under Ariz. R. Civ. P. 50(a). *Rempt v. Borgeas*, 120 Ariz. 36, 583 P.2d 1356 (Ct. App. Div. 1 1978); State Bar Committee Note to 1963 Amendment. Those provisions of Rule 41(b) were deleted and in effect replaced by the amendments to Rule 50(a), which authorize motions for judgment as a matter of law when any party has been fully heard with respect to an issue, and by the adoption of new Ariz. R. Civ. P. 52(c) which authorizes a "judgment on partial findings" where the court grants a Rule 50 motion in nonjury trials.

Rule 52(c) carries forward the prior rule that, when it grants such a motion, the court need only make findings of fact and conclusions of law where they are requested before trial. *Cf. Amfac Elec. Supply Co. v. Ranier Const. Co.*, 123 Ariz. 413, 600 P.2d 26 (1979). Under the prior Rule, it was held that, in passing upon such a motion, the trial court can weigh the evidence and assess the credibility of witnesses. *Lehman v. Whitehead*, 1 Ariz. App. 355, 403 P.2d 8 (1965). Presumably, the Court also retains discretion to defer a ruling on a motion made at the close of the plaintiff's case until all the evidence has been received. *Phoenix Western Holding Corp. v. Gleeson*, 18 Ariz. App. 60, 500 P.2d 320 (Div. 1 1972).

9. *Effect of Involuntary Dismissal.* Unless the Court specifies otherwise, an involuntary dismissal is an adjudication on the

merits, and *res judicata*. *Cf. Matter of Forfeiture of $3,000.00 U.S. Currency*, 164 Ariz. 120, 791 P.2d 646 (Ct. App. Div. 2 1990). There are three exceptions specified in the Rule: dismissal for improper venue, for failure to join an indispensable party, and for lack of jurisdiction. *Cf. Chavez v. State of Ind. for Logansport State Hospital*, 122 Ariz. 560, 596 P.2d 698 (1979).

10. *Running of Statute of Limitations; Savings Statute.* Arizona has enacted a general "savings statute," A.R.S. § 12-504, to deal with the issue of the refiling of an action which was timely filed, but then dismissed after the date when the statute of limitations would bar it. *Jepson v. New*, 164 Ariz. 265, 792 P.2d 728 (1990); *Copeland v. Arizona Veterans Memorial Coliseum and Exposition Center*, 176 Ariz. 86, 859 P.2d 196 (Ct. App. Div. 1 1993). Any action which is timely filed and then dismissed may be refiled within six months of the dismissal, unless it was for one of the following reasons: 1) abatement, 2) voluntary dismissal, 3) lack of prosecution, or 4) a judgment on the merits, regardless of whether the termination occurs before or after the limitations period has expired. *Jepson v. New*, 164 Ariz. 265, 792 P.2d 728 (1990).

By the express language of the statute, whether a party's right to refile a suit is absolute or discretionary depends upon the reason for termination of the action. *Schwartz v. Arizona Primary Care Physicians*, 192 Ariz. 290, 964 P.2d 491 (Ct. App. Div. 1 1998). If an action is terminated for insufficiency of process, rather than abatement, the statute entitles the plaintiff to reinstitute the action as a matter of right. *Schwartz v. Arizona Primary Care Physicians*, 192 Ariz. 290, 964 P.2d 491 (Ct. App. Div. 1 1998).

The standards for securing relief under this statute are similar, but not identical, to Ariz. R. Civ. P. 60(c). It must be shown that (1) plaintiff acted reasonably and in good faith, (2) plaintiff prosecuted the case diligently and vigorously, (3) a procedural impediment exists which affects plaintiff's ability to file a second action and (4) either party will be substantially prejudiced. *Jepson v. New*, 164 Ariz. 265, 792 P.2d 728 (1990); *Copeland v. Arizona Veterans Memorial Coliseum and Exposition Center*, 176 Ariz. 86, 859 P.2d 196 (Ct. App. Div. 1 1993); *Flynn v. Cornoyer-Hedrick Architects & Planners, Inc.*, 160 Ariz. 187, 772 P.2d 10 (Ct. App. Div. 1 1988), decision aff'd, 164 Ariz. 265, 792 P.2d 728 (1990). The plaintiff's failure to seek relief under A.R. S. § 12-504 until after expiration of the six-month period to refile authorized by the statute is evidence of a lack of the required diligence. *Copeland v. Arizona Veterans Memorial Coliseum and Exposition Center*, 176 Ariz. 86, 859 P.2d 196 (Ct. App. Div. 1 1993).

In the case of an action terminated by abatement, voluntary dismissal or for failure to prosecute, the Court entering the dismissal may, in its discretion, grant a period of up to six (6) months for it to be refiled notwithstanding the statute of limitations. *Copeland v. Arizona Veterans Memorial Coliseum and Exposition Center*, 176 Ariz. 86, 859 P.2d 196 (Ct. App. Div. 1 1993). In those instances, the "savings" provision must be in the original order of dismissal, and the extended period granted to refile cannot be greater than six (6) months. *Cf. also Hosogai v. Kadota*, 145 Ariz. 227, 700 P.2d 1327 (1985).

There was initially a divergence of views between two Departments of Division One of the Arizona Court of Appeals concerning the standards to be applied by the trial court in determining whether to permit refiling under § 12-504. In *Flynn v. Cornoyer-Hedrick Architects & Planners, Inc.*, 160 Ariz. 187, 772 P.2d 10 (Ct. App. Div. 1 1988), decision aff'd, 164 Ariz. 265, 792 P.2d 728 (1990), which involved a dismissal for lack of prosecution after expiration of the statute of limitations, the Court held that the considerations bearing upon whether to permit refiling under A.R.S. § 12-504 were identical to those applied where relief from the dismissal was sought under Ariz. R. Civ. P. 60(c): whether the plaintiff could show good cause for the apparent lack of diligence. In *Jepson v. New*, 160 Ariz. 193, 772 P.2d 16 (Ct. App. Div. 1 1989), vacated in part, 164 Ariz. 265, 792 P.2d 728 (1990), which arose under similar circumstances, the Court disagreed that the Rule 60(c) standards were applicable, and held that the inquiry should focus on whether the defendant would suffer undue prejudice by permitting refiling under A.R.S. § 12-504.

In a consolidated appeal, the Supreme Court rejected the test for relief articulated in *Jepson*, and approved that enunciated in *Flynn, viz.*, that the plaintiff, to secure relief under the savings statute, must show that the plaintiff acted reasonably and in good faith and prosecuted the action vigorously and diligently. *Jepson v. New*, 160 Ariz. 193, 772 P.2d 16 (Ct. App. Div. 1 1989), vacated in part on other grounds, 164 Ariz. 265, 792 P.2d 728 (1990); *Flynn v. Cornoyer-Hedrick Architects & Planners, Inc.*, 160 Ariz. 187, 772 P.2d 10 (Ct. App. Div. 1 1988), decision aff'd, 164 Ariz. 265, 792 P.2d 728 (1990). The failure to seek relief until after expiration of the six-month period to refile authorized by the statute is evidence of the lack of the requisite diligence. *Copeland v. Arizona Veterans Memorial Coliseum and Exposition Center*, 176 Ariz. 86, 859 P.2d 196 (Ct. App. Div. 1 1993).

The "savings statute" does apply to actions originally instituted in other jurisdictions, even when that prior action has been dismissed for lack of personal jurisdiction. *Templer v. Zele*, 166 Ariz. 390, 803 P.2d 111 (Ct. App. Div. 2 1990); it does not apply where the prior action, wherever instituted, was terminated by an adjudication on the merits. *Matter of Forfeiture of $3,000.00 U.S. Currency*, 164 Ariz. 120, 791 P.2d 646 (Ct. App. Div. 2 1990).

The initial termination or dismissal of the action can have occurred before or after the limitations period has expired; it is not a prerequisite to relief under A.R.S. § 12-504 that the applicable statute of limitations has expired at the time of the initial termination. *Janson on Behalf of Janson v. Christensen*, 167 Ariz. 470, 808 P.2d 1222 (1991).

A dismissal order entered pursuant to the "savings statute," A.R.S. § 12-504, is both final and appealable, notwithstanding that such dismissal is without prejudice. *Short v. Dewald*, 226 Ariz. 88, 244 P.3d 92 (Ct. App. Div. 1 2010) (to interpret § 12-504 otherwise would render uncertain relief granted under the statute). *But see*, *McMurray v. Dream Catcher USA, Inc.*, 220 Ariz. 71, 202 P.3d 536 (Ct. App. Div. 2 2009) (a dismissal without prejudice is not final and, therefore, *generally* not appealable).

An order denying relief under A.R.S. § 12-504 will be reversed on appeal only for an abuse of discretion. *Copeland v. Arizona Veterans Memorial Coliseum and Exposition Center*, 176 Ariz. 86, 859 P.2d 196 (Ct. App. Div. 1 1993).

11. *Award of Costs of Prior Action.* Under the provisions of Ariz. R. Civ. P. 41(d), if a plaintiff who has once dismissed an action in any court commences an action based upon the same claim against the same defendant, the Court may make an order for the payment of taxable costs of the action previously dismissed, and may stay further proceedings until the plaintiff has complied.

12. *Dismissals on Stipulation.* A stipulation for dismissal should clearly state that it is intended to permit dismissal and must be signed by all parties who have appeared in the action. Ariz. R. Civ. P. 41(a)(1) provides that the dismissal is without prejudice unless it states otherwise. Nevertheless, if the dismissal is intended to be without prejudice, the usual and better practice is to state that in the stipulation. A stipulation for dismissal may be used for a counterclaim, cross-claim or third-party complaint. Rule 41(a)(1) was amended, effective December 1, 1990, to make it clear that, where a stipulation for dismissal is submitted, the Court is to enter a formal order of dismissal. An amendment to Rule 41(a)(1), which became effective December 1, 1999, authorizes the Clerk of the Court, or a Deputy Clerk, to sign such stipulated orders of dismissal as well.

13. *Dismissals of Less Than All Parties or Claims.* By its terms, Ariz. R. Civ. P. 41(a)(2), does not expressly address the dismissal of (a) individual parties, (b) a claim against one or more, but less than all, of multiple defendants, or (c) a portion of a claim for relief. Such a result can clearly be achieved by seeking an amendment to the Complaint, however, and should be permissible under Rule 41 as well.

14. *Dismissals for Failure to Prosecute.* Even though Ariz. R.

Civ. P. 41(b) is limited by its terms to dismissals on motion by defendant, the Court has inherent power to dismiss for lack of prosecution on its own motion. *See, Cooper v. Odom*, 6 Ariz. App. 466, 433 P.2d 646 (1967).

Rule 41(b) does not state a time period which constitutes unreasonable delay sufficient to authorize dismissal for want of prosecution. Ariz. R. Civ. P. 38.1 does address this issue.

For those cases filed before April 15, 2014 and not otherwise subject to the conditions stated in the November 27, 2013 Amended Order Regarding Applicability Provision in R-13-0017, pre-amendment Ariz. R. Civ. P. 38.1(d) applies and requires that the Clerk of the Court place on the Inactive Calendar "every case in which a Motion to Set and Certificate of Readiness has not been filed within nine months after the commencement thereof. . . ." In accordance with this mandate, the Clerk of the Court sends a notice to the parties advising that a particular matter has been placed on the Inactive Calendar and that such matter has been scheduled for dismissal without further notice on a particular date. Cases remaining on the Inactive Calendar for two months "shall be dismissed without prejudice for lack of prosecution" unless the Court extends the matter on the Inactive Calendar for a specified period of time without dismissal. See *Authors' Comments* to Rule 38.1, *supra*. Of course, there are other facts which may support a motion to dismiss for failure to prosecute, such as sustained periods of inactivity or lack of diligence in prosecuting the matter.

For cases filed on or after April 15, 2014 and those cases subject to the November 27, 2013 Amended Order Regarding Applicability Provision, Ariz. R. Civ. P. 38.1 (added 2014) applies. Specifically subpart (f) creates a Dismissal Calendar as the administrative tool for dispensing with cases for lack of prosecution.

The dismissal of a pleading for failure to comply with the Rules or an Order of Court is a matter within the Court's discretion. *See Carman v. Hefter*, 136 Ariz. 597, 667 P.2d 1312 (1983). Where dismissal is for failure to prosecute, the adverse party is considered the prevailing party and is entitled to recover costs and, if appropriate, attorneys' fees, even though the dismissal is without prejudice and the action may be reinstated. *Harris v. Reserve Life Ins. Co.*, 158 Ariz. 380, 762 P.2d 1334 (Ct. App. Div. 1 1988).

Rule 42. Consolidation; separate trials; change of judge

(a) Consolidation. When actions involving a common question of law or fact are pending before the court, it may order a joint hearing or trial of any or all the matters in issue in the actions, or it may order all the actions consolidated, and it may make such orders concerning proceedings therein as may tend to avoid unnecessary costs or delay.

(b) Separate Trials. The court, in furtherance of convenience or to avoid prejudice, or when separate trials will be conducive to expedition and economy, may order a separate trial of any claim, cross-claim, counterclaim, or third-party claim, or of any separate issue or of any number of claims, cross-claims, counterclaims, third-party claims, or issues, always preserving inviolate the right of trial by jury.

Amended July 1, 1966, effective Nov. 1, 1966.

(c) [Abrogated Oct. 10, 2000, effective Dec. 1, 2000].

(d) [Renumbered as Rule 38.1(i), effective Dec. 1, 2000].

(e) [Renumbered as Rule 38.1(j), effective Dec. 1, 2000].

(f) Change of Judge.

1. *Change as a Matter of Right.*

(A) Nature of Proceedings. In any action pending in superior court, except an action pending in the Arizona Tax Court, each side is entitled as a matter of right to a change of one judge and of one court commissioner. Each action, whether single or consolidated, shall be treated as having only two sides. Whenever two or more parties on a side have adverse or hostile interests, the presiding judge or that judge's designee may allow additional changes of judge as a matter of right but each side shall have the right to the same number of such changes. A party wishing to exercise that party's right to change of judge shall file a "Notice of Change of Judge." The notice may be signed by an attorney; it shall state the name of the judge to be changed; and it shall neither specify grounds nor be accompanied by an affidavit, such as required by subsection (f)(2) of this rule, but it shall contain a certification by the party filing the notice or by the attorney that (i) the notice is timely, (ii) the party has not waived the right under subsection (f)(1)(D) of the rule, and (iii) the party has not previously been granted a change of judge as a matter of right in the case. A judge may honor an informal request for change of judge. When a judge does so, the judge shall enter upon the record the date of the request and the name of the party requesting change of judge. Such action shall constitute an exercise of the requesting party's right to change of judge.

(B) Filing and Service. The notice shall be filed and copies served on the parties, the presiding judge, the noticed judge and the court administrator, if any, in accordance with Rule 5, Arizona Rules of Civil Procedure.

(C) Time. Failure to file a timely notice precludes change of judge as a matter of right. A notice is timely if filed sixty (60) or more days before the date set for trial. Whenever an assignment is made which identifies the judge for the first time or which changes the judge within sixty (60) days of the date set for trial, a notice shall be timely filed as to the newly assigned judge if filed within ten (10) days after such new assignment. A notice of change of judge is ineffective if filed within three (3) days of a scheduled proceeding unless the parties have received less than five (5) days' notice of that proceeding or the assignment of the judge. The filing of such an ineffective notice neither requires a change of judge nor precludes the party who filed it from subsequently filing a notice of change of judge that otherwise satisfies the requirements of this rule.

(D) Waiver. After a judge is assigned to preside at trial or is otherwise permanently assigned to the action, a party waives the right to change of that judge as a matter of right when:

(i) the party agrees to the assignment; or

(ii) after notice to the parties

(aa) the judge rules on any contested issue; or

(bb) the judge grants or denies a motion to dispose of one or more claims or defenses in the action; or

(cc) the judge holds a scheduled conference or contested hearing; or

(dd) trial commences.

Such waiver is to apply only to such assigned judge.

(E) Cases Remanded From Appellate Courts. When an action is remanded by an appellate court and the opinion or order requires a new trial on one or more issues, then all rights to change of judge are renewed and no event connected with the first trial shall constitute a waiver.

(F) Assignment of Action. At the time of the filing of a notice of change of judge, the parties shall inform the court in writing if they have agreed upon a judge who is available and is willing to have the action assigned to that judge. An agreement of all parties upon such judge may be honored and, if so, shall preclude further changes of judge as a matter of right unless the judge agreed upon becomes unavailable. If no judge has been agreed upon, then the presiding judge shall immediately reassign the action.

If a judge to whom an action has been assigned by agreement later becomes unavailable because of a change of calendar assignment, death, illness or other legal incapacity, the parties shall be restored to their several positions and rights under this rule as they existed immediately before the assignment of the action to such judge.

2. *Proceedings Based on Cause.*

(A) Grounds. Grounds for proceedings based upon cause are stated in A.R.S. § 12-409 and proceedings under that statute shall be governed by this rule.

(B) Filing and Service. An affidavit shall be filed and copies served on the parties, the presiding judge and the court administrator, if any, in accordance with Rule 5, Arizona Rules of Civil Procedure.

(C) Timeliness and Waiver. An affidavit shall be timely if filed and served within twenty days after discovery that grounds exist for change of judge. No event occurring before such discovery shall constitute waiver of rights to change of judge based on cause.

(D) Hearing and Assignment. If a party makes proper service of an affidavit that meets the requirements of A.R.S. § 12-409, the presiding judge or that judge's designee shall forthwith conduct or provide for a hearing to determine the issues connected with the affidavit. The hearing judge shall decide the issues by the preponderance of the evidence. Under § 12-409(B)(5) the sufficiency of any "cause to believe" shall be determined by an objective standard, not by reference to affiant's subjective belief. Following the hearing, the presiding judge or that judge's designee shall expeditiously reassign the action to the original judge or make a new assignment, depending on the findings of the hearing judge. If a new assignment is to be made, it shall be in accordance with the provisions of A.R.S. § 12-411.

3. *Duty of Judge After Filing of Notice or Affidavit.*

(A) When a notice or an affidavit for change of judge is timely filed, the judge named in the notice or affidavit shall proceed no further in the action except to make such temporary orders as may be absolutely necessary to prevent immediate and irreparable injury, loss or damage from occurring before the action can be transferred to another judge. However, if the named judge is the only judge in the county where the action is pending, that judge shall also perform the functions of the presiding judge.

(B) If the court determines that the party who filed the notice or affidavit is not entitled to a change of judge, then the judge named in the notice or affidavit shall proceed with the action.

Adopted Dec. 29, 1971, effective March 1, 1972. Amended March 1, 1983, effective June 1, 1983; Aug. 7, 1984, effective Nov. 1, 1984; Sept. 15, 1987, effective Nov. 15, 1987; June 27, 1989, effective Sept. 1, 1989; Oct. 4, 1990, effective Dec. 1, 1990; Oct. 28, 1996, effective Dec. 1, 1996.

STATE BAR COMMITTEE NOTES

1966 Amendment

[Rule 42(b)] While separation of issues for trial is not to be routinely ordered it is encouraged where experience has demonstrated its worth. However, in any such case, separation should not be allowed to deprive a party of the right to trial by jury where it would otherwise exist. See e.g., *United Air Lines, Inc. v. Wiener*, 286 F.2d 302 (9th Cir.1961).

1971 Amendments

[Rule 42(f)(1)(A)] This section codifies the right to change of judge without necessity for proof of grounds for disqualification. This right previously has been recognized in *Murray v. Thomas*, 80 Ariz. 378, 298 P.2d 795 (1956), *Marsin v. Udall*, 78 Ariz. 309, 279 P.2d 721 (1955), and *Conkling v. Crosby*, 29 Ariz. 60, 239 P. 506 (1925). A significant change is that affidavits of bias and prejudice are no longer required. Lawyers may sign the notice.

This rule adopts for changes of judge the two "sides" approach used for peremptory challenges to jurors in Rule 47(e). However, this section together with section (F) below is designed to be implemented and interpreted in such a way as to promote immediate agreement upon a trial judge whenever possible.

Voluntary disqualification upon oral request has been recognized as an exercise of the right to change of judge. *American Buyers Life Ins. Co. v. Superior Court In and For Maricopa County*, 84 Ariz. 377, 329 P.2d 1100 (1958).

[Rule 42(f)(1)(B)] This section is new.

[Rule 42(f)(1)(C)] Under this section, a notice is timely if it meets either of two conditions. It may be filed twenty days before the date set for trial. Because some calendar systems do not regularly identify the trial judge sufficiently far in advance of trial, and because there are frequently late changes in judicial responsibility, fairness to litigants requires that notices be timely as to newly assigned or identified judges after such new assignments. See *Marsin v. Udall*, 78 Ariz. 309, 279 P.2d 721 (1955), and *Newsom v. Superior Court In and For Maricopa County*, 102 Ariz. 95, 425 P.2d 422 (1967). When such an assignment occurs within twenty days before trial, the rule grants ten more days for this purpose. This section is designed to simplify the rules on timeliness without affecting the number of changes of judge permitted in any case. Waiver is treated separately in section (D) below and the provisions stated there operate independently of considerations of timeliness. A notice, although timely, may be inoperative because the right to change of judge has been waived.

[Rule 42(f)(1)(D)] Subsection (iv) is new [deleted]. Subsection (i) expressly includes affidavits as well as other types of evidence concerning the merits of the action. The remainder of the rule is consistent with existing case law. See, for example, *Marsin v. Udall*, 78 Ariz. 309, 279 P.2d 721 (1955).

[Rule 42(f)(1)(E)] *State v. Neil*, 102 Ariz. 110, 425 P.2d 842 (1967) requires change of judge following an appeal to be based upon cause. This section permits change of judge as a matter of right following an appeal if a new trial is required on one or more issues.

[Rule 42(f)(1)(F)] This section is new and is to be interpreted in conjunction with section 1(A) so as to promote immediate agreement upon a judge whenever possible.

[Rule 42(f)(2)(C)] This section is new.

[Rule 42(f)(2)(D)] This section is new. With part 1 of this rule covering change of judge as a matter of right, it is no longer appropriate for the affidavit itself to accomplish disqualification. When change of judge as a matter of right is no longer available to a litigant, actual disqualification must be asserted and proved. This may be done late in the proceedings if necessary. *Hendrickson v. Superior Court In and For Cochise County*, 85 Ariz. 10, 330 P.2d 507, 73 A.L.R.2d 1235 (1958) and *Conkling v. Crosby*, 29 Ariz. 60, 239 P. 506 (1925).

[Rule 42(f)(3) The exception for temporary orders is new. The remainder of this section is consistent with existing law; see *Truck Equipment Co. of Ariz. v. Vanlandingham*, 103 Ariz. 402, 442 P.2d 849 (1968), and Rule I, Uniform Rules of Practice of the Superior Court of Arizona, 17 A.R.S.

2000 Amendment

As part of the 2000 effort to consolidate formerly separate sets of procedural rules into either the Arizona Rules of Civil Procedure or the Rules of the Arizona Supreme Court, former Rule V of the Uniform Rules of Practice of the Superior Court, which dealt with the subject of securing a trial setting, was effectively transferred to the Arizona Rules of Civil Procedure. Rule 42(c) of the Arizona Rules of Civil Procedure was abrogated, because its provisions were duplicative of, indeed identical to, new Rule 38.1(h). In an effort to place provisions relating to trial continuances in a single Rule, and to give that Rule some internal logic, the provisions of Rules 42(d) and (e) of the Arizona Rules of Civil Procedure were transferred to new Rule 38.1 as subparts (i) and (j). The title of Rule 42 was also amended to eliminate the now anachronistic reference to "Postponements."

AUTHORS' COMMENTS

Analysis

1. *Scope and Purpose of Rule.* Rule 42 includes provisions dealing with the structuring of matters for trial, such as consolidation of cases, and the ordering of separate trials. The Rule's former provisions dealing with the procedures and standards for

securing trial continuances were transferred in 2000 to then new Ariz. R. Civ. P. 38.1. See the discussion of these subjects in Section 8 of the *Authors' Comments* under Rule 38.1. Ariz. R. Civ. P. 42 also includes a unique provision, Ariz. R. Civ. P. 42(f), which permits parties to litigation to secure a change of judge as a matter of right.

2. *Comparison With Federal Rule.* ARCP 42(a) and (b) are substantially identical to FRCP 42(a) and (b). The Federal Rules of Civil Procedure do not have a provision corresponding to ARCP 42(f).

In 2007, the language of FRCP 42 was amended as part of the general restyling of the Federal Rules of Civil Procedure to make the Federal Rules more easily understood and to make style and terminology consistent throughout the Federal Rules of Civil Procedure. Those stylistic modifications have not been incorporated into ARCP 42.

3. *Consolidation of Cases.* Ariz. R. Civ. P. 42(a) authorizes the consolidation of actions involving common questions of law or fact, but only contemplates the joining of actions which are independently viable. *Berge Ford, Inc. v. Maricopa County*, 172 Ariz. 483, 838 P.2d 822 (Tax Ct.1992). Whether actions should be consolidated under Rule 42(a) is a matter committed to the trial court's discretion and a consolidation order will be disturbed on appeal only for an abuse of that discretion. *Hancock v. McCarroll*, 188 Ariz. 492, 937 P.2d 682 (Ct. App. Div. 1 1996). Consolidation may be ordered for limited purposes. *Torosian v. Paulos*, 82 Ariz. 304, 313 P.2d 382 (1957). A consolidation does not merge the consolidated suits into a single cause, or change the rights or claims of the parties, and may be vacated or modified in light of subsequent developments. *Yavapai County v. Superior Court In and For Yavapai County*, 13 Ariz. App. 368, 476 P.2d 889 (Div. 1 1970).

Under A.R.S. § 12-406(B)(3), a trial court has discretion to order the transfer of a case from one county, where venue is proper, to another county for "good and sufficient cause." There is "good and sufficient cause" for directing such a transfer so that the case can be consolidated with another case arising out of the same underlying event, because such a consolidation will serve the interests of judicial economy, and will ensure that 100% of all damages are awarded, and no more, and properly allocated among all parties and nonparties at fault, as required by A.R.S. § 12-2506. *Behrens v. O'Melia*, 206 Ariz. 309, 78 P.3d 278 (Ct. App. Div. 1 2003).

4. *Separate Trials of Issues or Claims.* Rule 42(b) authorizes the trial court to direct separate trials of separate claims, or issues, where that will be conducive to expedition or economy.

Whether to order separate trials of particular issues or claims under Ariz. R. Civ. P. 42(b) is a discretionary determination that will not be disturbed absent an abuse of that discretion. *Williams for and on Behalf of Dixon v. Thude*, 180 Ariz. 531, 885 P.2d 1096 (Ct. App. Div. 1 1994), aff'd, 188 Ariz. 257, 934 P.2d 1349 (1997); *McElhanon v. Hing*, 151 Ariz. 386, 728 P.2d 256 (Ct. App. Div. 1 1985), judgment aff'd in part, vacated in part, 151 Ariz. 403, 728 P.2d 273 (1986); *Anderson Aviation Sales Co., Inc. v. Perez*, 19 Ariz. App. 422, 508 P.2d 87 (Div. 1 1973); *Purcell v. Zimbelman*, 18 Ariz. App. 75, 500 P.2d 335 (Div. 2 1972); *Ulan v. Richtars*, 8 Ariz. App. 351, 446 P.2d 255 (1968).

Separate trials are ordered for trial convenience and to avoid prejudice and confusion. The trial court has wide discretion to decide whether to exercise the power to separate the trial of any claim or issue. *McElhanon v. Hing*, 151 Ariz. 386, 728 P.2d 256 (Ct. App. Div. 1 1985), judgment aff'd in part, vacated in part on other grounds, 151 Ariz. 403, 728 P.2d 273 (1986); *Cota v. Harley Davidson, a Div. of AMF, Inc.*, 141 Ariz. 7, 684 P.2d 888 (Ct. App. Div. 2 1984). For example, if it is likely that trial of some issues will avoid an expensive and lengthy trial of additional issues, separate trials may be ordered. In particular instances a court may order separate trials of legal and equitable issues; separate trials of issues relating to jurisdiction or venue; separate trials of different issues on the merits; and separate trials of counter-claims, cross-claims, or third-party claims.

The Rule allows the trial court to bifurcate trial of the issues of liability and damages, where those issues are separate and distinct from one another. *Williams for and on Behalf of Dixon v. Thude*, 180 Ariz. 531, 885 P.2d 1096 (Ct. App. Div. 1 1994), aff'd, 188 Ariz. 257, 934 P.2d 1349 (1997). The Rule, however, directs that any separation of trials that is ordered must preserve "inviolate the right of trial by jury." In negligence actions, there is no constitutional requirement that the jury hear all the evidence, including evidence on damages, before deciding whether to apply the doctrine of contributory negligence. *Rosen v. Knaub*, 173 Ariz. 304, 842 P.2d 1317 (Ct. App. Div. 1 1992), opinion vacated on other grounds, 175 Ariz. 329, 857 P.2d 381, 24 A.L.R. 5th 909 (1993).

5. *Change of Judge on Notice.* Ariz. R. Civ. P. 42(f) permits each side to a controversy to secure a change of the judge to whom the matter is assigned as a matter of right, simply by filing a notice that the right is being exercised. Rule 42(f) was preceded by A.R.S. § 12-409, which required the filing of an affidavit of bias and prejudice, which had become something of a fiction. *Brush Wellman, Inc. v. Lee*, 196 Ariz. 344, 996 P.2d 1248 (Ct. App. Div. 2 2000). The adoption of Rule 42(f), accordingly, did not create a separate and distinct remedy from A.R.S. § 12-409; it merely

modified the procedure to be followed. *Brush Wellman, Inc. v. Lee*, 196 Ariz. 344, 996 P.2d 1248 (Ct. App. Div. 2 2000).

A minute entry assigning a matter to the "Probate Division" of the Superior Court is not an assignment to a particular judge within the meaning of Rule 42. *Jones v. Pima County*, 157 Ariz. 389, 758 P.2d 660 (Ct. App. Div. 2 1988). And, a change of the Tax Court Judge can only be secured through a challenge for cause under Ariz. R. Civ. P. 42(f)(2). *Mervyn's v. Superior Court In and For County of Maricopa*, 179 Ariz. 359, 879 P.2d 367 (Ct. App. Div. 1 1994). Similarly, a 2003 amendment to Rule 1(c) of the Rules of Procedure for Judicial Review of Administrative Decisions makes Rule 42(f) inapplicable to actions seeking review of administrative agency decisions.

The Notice of Change of Judge must name the judge to be changed, and must be served on the judge to whom it is directed, the presiding judge and the court administrator, if any. The 1996 amendments to Ariz. R. Civ. P. 42(f)(1)(A) changed the requirements concerning the prescribed contents of a formal notice of change of judge. A notice must now contain a "certification" by the party or that party's attorney: (1) that the notice is timely, (2) that the right to notice a change of judge has not previously been waived, and (3) that the party filing the notice has not previously been granted a change of judge as a matter of right in the case. Rule 42(f)(1)(A), however, also permits a judge to "honor an informal request for change of judge."

Notices of change of judge are viewed as entailing considerable administrative attention and inconvenience and, accordingly, there has been a reluctance to interpret the provisions of Ariz. R. Civ. P. 42(f) expansively. *Switzer v. Superior Court In and For County of Maricopa*, 176 Ariz. 285, 860 P.2d 1338 (Ct. App. Div. 1 1993). On the other hand, the interests of judicial economy has been held to be an improper ground for refusing to honor an otherwise proper notice of change of judge. *Lewis v. Kelliher*, 171 Ariz. 228, 829 P.2d 1274 (Ct. App. Div. 2 1992).

Issues concerning exercise of the right to a peremptory change of judge are frequently reviewed by special action. *Mann v. Superior Court In and For County of Maricopa*, 183 Ariz. 586, 905 P.2d 595 (Ct. App. Div. 1 1995). In fact, the Arizona Supreme Court has held that the trial court's failure to honor a proper notice of change of judge does not affect the subject matter jurisdiction of the Superior Court, and review of such a failure *must* be sought by petition for special action rather than by appeal following entry of final judgment. *Cypress on Sunland Homeowners Ass'n v. Orlandini*, 227 Ariz. 288, 257 P.3d 1168 (Ct. App. Div. 1 2011), review denied, (Oct. 25, 2011) (a denial of a peremptory notice of change of judge may only be reviewed by special action.);

Taliaferro v. Taliaferro, 186 Ariz. 221, 921 P.2d 21 (1996). *Cf. also Smith v. Mitchell*, 214 Ariz. 78, 148 P.3d 1151 (Ct. App. Div. 2 2006); *Anderson v. Contes*, 212 Ariz. 122, 128 P.3d 239 (Ct. App. Div. 1 2006); *Brush Wellman, Inc. v. Lee*, 196 Ariz. 344, 996 P.2d 1248 (Ct. App. Div. 2 2000); *Adrian S. v. Superior Court In and For County of Navajo*, 190 Ariz. 517, 950 P.2d 593 (Ct. App. Div. 1 1997). The appellate court reviews a denial of a change of judge as of right for an abuse of discretion, but reviews the trial court's interpretation of the rule regarding change of judge on remand *de novo*. *Smith v. Mitchell*, 214 Ariz. 78, 148 P.3d 1151 (Ct. App. Div. 2 2006).

Rule 42(f)(1)(E) provides that, when an action is remanded by an appellate court for a new trial on one or more issues, all rights to a change of judge are renewed and no event that occurred in the first trial is to constitute a waiver. This provision applies to remands for proceedings that represent de novo redeterminations of remanded issues. *Smith v. Mitchell*, 214 Ariz. 78, 148 P.3d 1151 (Ct. App. Div. 2 2006). It is not applicable, however, where the remand only contemplates a continuation of proceedings already conducted. *Anderson v. Contes*, 212 Ariz. 122, 128 P.3d 239 (Ct. App. Div. 1 2006).

6. *Timeliness of Notices of Change of Judge.* Unless earlier waived, the right must be exercised sixty (60) days or more before the date set for trial or within ten (10) days after receipt of a notice which changes the judge or identifies the judge for the first time within sixty (60) days of trial, and is waived if not timely filed. Ariz. R. Civ. P. 42(f)(1)(C); *Fendler v. Phoenix Newspapers Inc.*, 130 Ariz. 475, 636 P.2d 1257, 7 Media L. Rep. (BNA) 2569 (Ct. App. Div. 1 1981); *Harmon v. Harmon*, 126 Ariz. 242, 613 P.2d 1298 (Ct. App. Div. 2 1980). For purposes of applying this particular provision of the Rule, a judicial proceeding such as an order to show cause is not the same as a trial. *Mann v. Superior Court In and For County of Maricopa*, 183 Ariz. 586, 905 P.2d 595 (Ct. App. Div. 1 1995). By operation of Ariz. R. Civ. P. Rule 6(a), the date set for trial is excluded from the computation as "the day . . . from which the designated period of time begins to run. . . ." *Maciborski v. Chase Service Corp. of Arizona*, 161 Ariz. 557, 779 P.2d 1296 (Ct. App. Div. 1 1989).

The 1996 amendments to Ariz. R. Civ. P. 42(f)(1)(C) purport to have the timeliness of a notice of change of judge be controlled by when the parties receive notice of the assignment of any judge to a case, and not necessarily the trial judge, and may engender some confusion. The amended Rule is subject to the construction that, in order to be timely, a notice directed to the judge initially assigned to a case must be filed within ten (10) days after the parties receive notice of such assignment. That is not, however, what was intended, because the provision specifying that a notice is timely if filed sixty (60) or more days before the date set for trial was retained, and the amended Rule still speaks in terms of the timeliness of a notice directed to a "newly assigned" judge. Such a newly assigned judge remains susceptible to a notice of change of judge for ten (10) days after the assignment, and may not terminate that period of susceptibility by issuing an accelerated ruling, without prior notice to the parties, on a matter that the parties had been advised would not be reached until after the ten-day period had expired. *Williams v. Superior Court In and For County of Maricopa*, 190 Ariz. 80, 945 P.2d 391 (Ct. App. Div. 1 1997).

Even if it is otherwise timely, a notice of change of judge will be ineffective if it is filed within three (3) days of a scheduled proceeding (other than trial), unless the parties received less than five (5) days' notice of that proceeding or of the identity of the judge assigned to preside over it. In that circumstance, the judge to whom the notice is directed may preside at the proceeding in question, and the party filing it retains the right to subsequently file a notice of change of judge.

7. *Waiver of Right to Change of Judge on Notice.* The 1996 amendments made significant revisions to the "waiver" provisions of Ariz. R. Civ. P. 42(f)(1)(D). Under the amended Rule, a party now waives the right to notice a change of any judge who has been permanently assigned to the action, or who has been assigned to preside at trial, if the party has previously agreed that the action could be assigned to that judge, or if that judge, after notice to the parties (1) rules on any contested issue, (2) grants or denies a motion to dispose of one or more claims or defenses in the action, (3) holds a scheduled conference or contested hearing, or (4) commences trial.

Effective January 1, 2012, the Court amended Ariz. R. Civ. P. 77 to delete subparagraph (d), which set forth the change of judge provision then applicable to compulsory arbitration cases. As a consequence of this amendment, Rule 42(f)—and, not Rule 77(d)—applies to compulsory arbitration cases and, thus, governs whether a party in a compulsory arbitration case has the right to a change of judge or whether that right has been waived.

The waiver provisions of the Rule are intended to prohibit a party from peremptorily challenging a judge after discovering the judge's viewpoint on any significant aspect of the case. *Williams v. Superior Court In and For County of Maricopa*, 190 Ariz. 80, 945 P.2d 391 (Ct. App. Div. 1 1997). The point of the 1996 amendments to these provisions was to substitute the element of notice of a judge's decision for the element of participation before that judge in a contested proceeding, and thus obviate the strategem of a party not participating in a proceeding and then exercising the right to notice a judge after learning of the judge's decision. *Williams v. Superior Court In and For County of Maricopa*, 190 Ariz. 80, 945 P.2d 391 (Ct. App. Div. 1 1997).

Under the prior version of the Rule, it was held that a "contested matter" implied an issue in dispute between the parties which was heard or resolved at the proceeding in question. *Lewis v. Kelliher*, 171 Ariz. 228, 829 P.2d 1274 (Ct. App. Div. 2 1992); *Sarchett v. Superior Court In and For County of Maricopa*, 168 Ariz. 321, 812 P.2d 1139 (Ct. App. Div. 1 1991). It was also held that the waiver provisions added by the 1990 amendments to Rule 42(f) could be applied to a notice of change of judge filed after their effective date, even though the activity claimed to constitute a waiver had occurred before they became effective. *Sarchett v. Superior Court In and For County of Maricopa*, 168 Ariz. 321, 812 P.2d 1139 (Ct. App. Div. 1 1991). Thus, a party whose case is consolidated with an action in which a party on the same "side" has already exercised the right to a peremptory change of judge does not have the right to file a Rule 42 notice of change of judge. *Huerta v. Nelson*, 222 Ariz. 44, 213 P.3d 193 (Ct. App. Div. 1 2009).

8. *Revival of Right to Notice of Change of Judge*. Ariz. R. Civ. P. 42(f)(1)(E) provides that the right to notice a change of judge, even if waived or exercised, is revived where an action is remanded by an appellate court "and the opinion or order requires a new trial on one or more issues." This provision applies to remands for proceedings that represent *de novo* redeterminations of remanded issues. *Smith v. Mitchell*, 214 Ariz. 78, 148 P.3d 1151 (Ct. App. Div. 2 2006); *Anderson v. Contes*, 212 Ariz. 122, 128 P.3d 239 (Ct. App. Div. 1 2006). This provision is not applicable, however, where the remand only contemplates a continuation of proceedings already conducted. *Anderson v. Contes*, 212 Ariz. 122, 128 P.3d 239 (Ct. App. Div. 1 2006). The provision also does not apply to the declaration of mistrials. *King v. Superior Court In and For Maricopa County*, 108 Ariz. 492, 502 P.2d 529, 60 A.L.R.3d 172 (1972). It is applicable, however, where the remand is occasioned by the reversal of a prior summary judgment which was a final adjudication on the merits and disposed of all claims at issue. *Valenzuela v. Brown*, 186 Ariz. 105, 919 P.2d 1376 (Ct. App. Div. 2 1996).

Notwithstanding the plain language of the Rule, the Court of Appeals has held that Ariz. R. Civ. P. 42(f)(1)(E) does not revive the right to a peremptory notice of change of judge on remand from an appellate court where a party exercised the right to a peremptory change of judge in proceedings before the appeal. *Brush Wellman, Inc. v. Lee*, 196 Ariz. 344, 996 P.2d 1248 (Ct. App. Div. 2 2000). *See also, State ex rel. Thomas v. Gordon*, 213 Ariz. 499, 144 P.3d 513 (Ct. App. Div. 1 2006); *Smith v. Mitchell*, 214 Ariz.

78, 148 P.3d 1151 (Ct. App. Div. 2 2006). The Court reasoned that a contrary result would make the Rule conflict with the provisions of A.R.S. § 12-411, which allows but a single change of judge. *Brush Wellman, Inc. v. Lee*, 196 Ariz. 344, 996 P.2d 1248 (Ct. App. Div. 2 2000). To avoid the apparent conflict between the rule and the statute, the *Wellman* Court reasoned, that Rule 42(f)(1)(E) provides that a party's right to a change of judge is renewed after a case has been remanded to the trial court for "a new trial on one or more issues." But, if the right to a change of judge was previously exercised, it is not renewed upon remand. *Brush Wellman, Inc. v. Lee*, 196 Ariz. 344, 996 P.2d 1248 (Ct. App. Div. 2 2000).

9. *Number of Notices Allowed in Multiple Party Cases; Newcomers.* For purposes of Rule 42, each action is treated as having two sides, but the Presiding Judge may allow additional changes to be exercised where parties nominally on the same side have adverse or hostile interests. *Switzer v. Superior Court In and For County of Maricopa*, 176 Ariz. 285, 860 P.2d 1338 (Ct. App. Div. 1 1993); *Huerta v. Nelson*, 222 Ariz. 44, 213 P.3d 193 (Ct. App. Div. 1 2009). Thus, Subsection (A) of Ariz. R. Civ. P. 42(f)(1) grants the right to file a notice of change of judge to each *side* in a case, while Subsection (D) provides that a *party* waives the right to file a notice of change of judge under certain specified circumstances. *Cf. Switzer v. Superior Court In and For County of Maricopa*, 176 Ariz. 285, 860 P.2d 1338 (Ct. App. Div. 1 1993). The use of the word "party" in Ariz. R. Civ. P. 42(f)(1)(D) is not necessarily inconsistent with the use of the word "side" in Rule 42(f)(1)(A). *Switzer v. Superior Court In and For County of Maricopa*, 176 Ariz. 285, 860 P.2d 1338 (Ct. App. Div. 1 1993).

Read together, these provisions of the Rule simply mean that each side has a peremptory notice and that any party can either exercise or waive the right to such a notice, even though the other parties do not concur and may not even have been parties at the time the exercise or waiver occurred. *Switzer v. Superior Court In and For County of Maricopa*, 176 Ariz. 285, 860 P.2d 1338 (Ct. App. Div. 1 1993); *Huerta v. Nelson*, 222 Ariz. 44, 213 P.3d 193 (Ct. App. Div. 1 2009). The Rule thus treats all parties with similar interests as one side entitled to only one notice of change of judge, and represents a compromise between the interests of litigants who would like a free hand in selecting their forum and the interests of the courts in efficient administration of cases. *Switzer v. Superior Court In and For County of Maricopa*, 176 Ariz. 285, 860 P.2d 1338 (Ct. App. Div. 1 1993).

A party who is brought into an action after some other party on its side of the case has exercised or waived the right to notice a change of judge may be deprived of a right that might otherwise have been available. *Switzer v. Superior Court In and For County of Maricopa*, 176 Ariz. 285, 860 P.2d 1338 (Ct. App. Div. 1 1993). The apparent harshness of this aspect of the Rule's operation is ameliorated by the fact that, if the newcomer's interests are inconsistent with those of other parties on the same side, or if the judge is biased against the newcomer, the newcomer may still secure relief under the provisions of Rule 42(f)(1)(A) or Rule 42(f)(2). *Switzer v. Superior Court In and For County of Maricopa*, 176 Ariz. 285, 860 P.2d 1338 (Ct. App. Div. 1 1993); *Huerta v. Nelson*, 222 Ariz. 44, 213 P.3d 193 (Ct. App. Div. 1 2009).

10. *Stipulation to Reassignment.* The 1996 amendments to Rule 42(f) changed the requirement that agreements upon the judge to whom a case could be reassigned were to be honored. Under the version of Ariz. R. Civ. P. 42(f)(1)(F) in effect before its amendment in December 1, 1996, when one party exercised the right to a change of judge, the parties could agree upon the judge to whom the action should be reassigned, providing that judge was willing to accept it, and such an agreement was to be honored, even if it called for the assignment of the action to a judge from another county. *City of Tucson v. Birdsall*, 109 Ariz. 581, 514 P.2d 714 (1973). Indeed, the practice of encouraging judges to decline to accept such reassignments was criticized as circumventing the Rule's mandatory provisions. *Dunn By and Through Dunn v. Superior Court In and For County of Maricopa*, 160 Ariz. 311, 772 P.2d 1164 (Ct. App. Div. 1 1989).

The amended Rule 42(f)(1)(F) now merely provides that such an agreement on the reassignment of the action "may" be honored. If the agreement is honored, that operates to preclude subsequent notices of change of judge unless the matter is subsequently reassigned to a different judge.

11. *Opposition to Notice of Change of Judge.* There is no express provision in Ariz. R. Civ. P. 42(f)(1) for resisting a notice of change of judge or specifying when such an opposition must be made. It has been held that Rule 42(f)(1) implicitly authorizes the filing of an opposition to an adversary's notice of change of judge and that such an opposition must be filed within the time period prescribed by Rule 7.1, for responding to civil motions, which is currently ten (10) days. *Guberman v. Chatwin*, 19 Ariz. App. 590, 509 P.2d 721 (Div. 1 1973). Typically, however, the reassignment of the case to a new judge occurs before that ten-day period expires, so any opposition to a notice of change of judge should be made expeditiously, to avoid a jurisdictional hiatus and uncertainty as to the identity of the judge with authority to rule upon pending matters in the case.

Objections to the notice of change of judge are to be resolved by the judge to whom the notice was directed. *Anderson v. Contes*, 212 Ariz. 122, 128 P.3d 239 (Ct. App. Div. 1 2006); *Dunn By and*

Through Dunn v. Superior Court In and For County of Maricopa, 160 Ariz. 311, 772 P.2d 1164 (Ct. App. Div. 1 1989); *Guberman v. Chatwin*, 19 Ariz. App. 590, 509 P.2d 721 (Div. 1 1973) (reasoning the noticed judge is best qualified to decide timeliness and waiver issues under Rule 42(f)). The Presiding Judge does not have authority to overrule a fellow judge's rulings on issues concerning the timeliness of a notice. *Dunn By and Through Dunn v. Superior Court In and For County of Maricopa*, 160 Ariz. 311, 772 P.2d 1164 (Ct. App. Div. 1 1989).

Ariz. R. Civ. P. 42(f)(3)(B), added by the 1996 amendments, specifies that, where an improper or ineffective notice of change is filed, the judge to whom that notice was directed is to proceed with the action.

12. *Change of Judge for Cause.* The grounds for change of judge for cause are set forth in A.R.S. § 12-409. Upon the filing of an Affidavit, the judge to whom the case is assigned shall not hear any further proceedings until the application for change of judge is decided. Ariz. R. Civ. P. 42(f)(3).

Ariz. R. Civ. P. 42(f)(2)(D), as amended in 1996, contemplates that the Presiding Judge, or another judge designated by the Presiding Judge, will either conduct a hearing to decide the issues raised by the affidavit, or appoint another judge to do so. Such a hearing may not be necessary, however, if the Presiding Judge determines that the affidavits submitted in support of the request are insufficient on their face to make a *prima facie* showing of grounds for actual disqualification. *Mervyn's v. Superior Court In and For County of Maricopa*, 179 Ariz. 359, 879 P.2d 367 (Ct. App. Div. 1 1994). The Presiding Judge, or the Presiding Judge's designee, makes the ultimate decision on disqualification, based upon the findings made by the judge who conducted the hearing, if one is required.

A provision added by the 1996 amendments specifies that the decision whether to disqualify a judge for cause must be based on an "objective standard" rather than upon the subjective beliefs of the party who made the challenge. A judge's legitimate exercise of judicial discretion cannot constitute the bias and prejudice required to secure a change of judge for cause. *Mervyn's v. Superior Court In and For County of Maricopa*, 179 Ariz. 359, 879 P.2d 367 (Ct. App. Div. 1 1994). Ariz. R. Civ. P. 42(f)(3)(B), added by the 1996 amendments, confirms that, where a challenge to a judge based upon cause is unsuccessful, the judge who was the subject of the challenge is to proceed with the action.

Rule 43. Witnesses; evidence

(a) Definition of Witness. A witness is a person whose declaration under oath or affirmation is received as evidence for any purpose, whether such declaration is made on oral examination or by deposition or affidavit.

(b) Affirmation in Lieu of Oath. Whenever under these Rules an oath is required to be taken, a solemn affirmation may be accepted in lieu thereof.

(c) Interpreters. The court may appoint an interpreter of its own selection and may fix the interpreter's reasonable compensation. The compensation shall be paid out of funds provided by law or by one or more of the parties as the court may direct, and may be taxed ultimately as costs, in the discretion of the court.

Former Rule 43(c) deleted June 1, 1977, effective Sept. 1, 1977. New Rule 43(c) adopted and amended Sept. 15, effective Nov. 15, 1987.

(d) Limitation on Examination of Witness; Exception. Only one attorney on each side shall conduct the examination of a witness until such examination is completed, except when the court grants permission for other attorneys to conduct the examination.

(e) [Deleted effective September 1, 1977].

(f) Form and Admissibility of Evidence. In all trials the testimony of witnesses shall be taken orally in open court, unless otherwise provided by these rules or the Arizona Rules of Evidence.

Amended June 1, 1977, effective Sept., 1977; Oct. 10, 2000, effective Dec. 1, 2000.

(g) [Abrogated Oct. 10, 2000, effective Dec. 1, 2000].

(h) [Deleted effective Sept. 1, 1977].

(i) Evidence on Motions. When a motion is based on facts not appearing of record the court may hear the matter on affidavits presented by the respective parties, but the court may direct that the matter be heard wholly or partly on oral testimony or depositions.

(j) [Renumbered as Rule 39(c)].

(k) Preservation of Verbatim Recording of Court Proceedings.

(1) The official verbatim recording of any court proceeding is an official record of the court. The original of such verbatim recording shall be kept by the person who recorded it, a court-

designated custodian, or the Clerk of the Superior Court in such place or places as shall be designated by the court. Unless the court specifies a different period for the retention of such verbatim recording, it shall be retained according to the records retention and disposition schedules and purge lists adopted by the Supreme Court.

(2) If a court reporter's verbatim recording has been delivered to the Clerk of the Superior Court or court-designated custodian and is to be transcribed, the court reporter who made the recording shall be given the first opportunity to make the transcription, unless that court reporter has been dismissed or has otherwise terminated the position as court reporter for the Superior Court or is unavailable for any other reason.

Added Feb. 14, 1979, effective April 1, 1979. Amended Sept. 15, 1987, effective Nov. 1987; Sept. 27, 2005, effective Dec. 1, 2005.

STATE BAR COMMITTEE NOTES

1977 Amendment

[Rule 43(c)] Deleted incident to adoption of the Arizona Rules of Evidence.

[Rule 43(f)] The last three sentences of Rule 43(f) have been deleted incident to the adoption of the Arizona Rules of Evidence. A corresponding deletion was made in the applicable Federal rules.

1987 Amendment

Rule 43(c) is essentially the same as Rule 43(f) of the Federal Rules of Civil Procedure.

1991 Amendment

[Rule 43(g)] The 1991 amendment to Rule 43(g) must be read in conjunction with the 1991 amendment to Rules 16(c)(3) and 26(b)(4). As noted in the comment to Rule 26(b)(4), where an issue cuts across several professional disciplines, the court should be liberal in allowing expansion of the limitation upon experts set forth in this rule.

2000 Amendment

As part of the process of consolidating formerly separate sets of procedural rules into either the Arizona Rules of Civil Procedure or the Rules of the Arizona Supreme Court, an effort was also made to eliminate duplicative and unnecessary provisions. The second sentence of Rule 43(f) was, accordingly, eliminated, because it essentially expressed the same thought as both Rule 77(j) of the Arizona Rules of Civil Procedure and Rule XIX of the Uniform Rules of Practice of the Superior Court. The provisions of those two Rules were consolidated and incorporated into a new Rule 91(f) of the Rules of the Arizona Supreme Court. Rule 43(g) was also eliminated, because its limitations on the use of expert testimony were essentially duplicative of the more specific limitations contained in amended Rule 26(b)(4)(D).

COURT COMMENT

1991 Amendment

[Rule 43(g)] The above rule change was part of a comprehensive set of rule revisions proposed by the Special Bar Committee to Study Civil Litigation Abuse, Cost and Delay, which was specifically charged in March, 1990 with the task of proposing rules to reduce discovery abuse and to make the judicial system in Arizona more efficient, expeditious, and accessible to the people.

For more complete background information on the rule changes proposed by the Committee, see Court Comment to Rule 26.1.

AUTHORS' COMMENTS

Analysis

1. Scope and Purpose of Rule.
2. Comparison With Federal Rule.
3. Witnesses; Examination of Witnesses.
4. Evidence on Motions.
5. Interpreters.

1. *Scope and Purpose of Rule.* Rule 43 is a collection of miscellaneous provisions bearing on the receipt of evidence and the conduct of evidentiary proceedings. Many of its former provisions were deleted as unnecessary and duplicative contemporaneously with the adoption of the Arizona Rules of Evidence.

2. *Comparison With Federal Rule.* ARCP 43(b), (c) and (i) are substantially identical to FRCP 43(b), (d) and (e), respectively. ARCP 43(f) is similar to FRCP 43(a), but the Arizona Rule does not contain the provision added to the Federal Rule allowing the trial court to permit testimony to be presented by contemporaneous transmission from a different location. The Federal Rules of Civil Procedure do not contain provisions corresponding to ARCP 43(a), (d), and (k).

In addition, in 2007, the language of FRCP 43 was amended as part of the general restyling of the Federal Rules of Civil Procedure to make the Federal Rules more easily understood and to make style and terminology consistent throughout the Federal Rules of Civil Procedure. Those stylistic modifications have not been incorporated into ARCP 43.

3. *Witnesses; Examination of Witnesses.* The term "witness" is defined in Rule 43(a) to include any person whose declaration under oath is received as evidence for any purpose, whether by oral examination, by deposition or by affidavit. Rule 43(b) provides that a "solemn affirmation" may be substituted whenever an oath is required under the Rules of Civil Procedure. Thus, the administration of an oath which ended, "So help you God", has been held to not violate either the United States or state constitutions insofar as an affirmation is permitted in lieu of such oath. *State v. Albe*, 10 Ariz. App. 545, 460 P.2d 651 (Div. 1 1969). *Cf. also*, Ariz.R.Evid. 603.

Rule 611(a), Ariz. R. Evid. gives the trial court authority and discretion to control the interrogation of witnesses. That discretion is guided, however, by Rule 43(d), which provides that, in multiple party cases, only one attorney on each side may conduct the examination, or cross-examination, of a witness unless the Court directs otherwise. This provision is frequently invoked as the basis for counsel insisting that the examination of a witness at a deposition be conducted exclusively by one attorney for each party.

4. *Evidence on Motions.* While Rule 43(f) evidences a preference for receiving the testimony of witnesses at trial orally in open court, Rule 43(i) provides for more flexibility where facts are to be established for purposes of a motion. In that case, the Court may hear the matter on affidavits submitted by the parties, and also has the option of directing that the matter be heard wholly or partially on oral testimony or depositions.

5. *Interpreters.* Under Rule 43(c), the Court has the authority, where necessary or desirable, to appoint an interpreter of its own selection. The Court can direct that the interpreter's compensation be paid by one or more of the parties and/or be taxed as costs in the action. The situations where interpreters may or must be appointed are discussed in the *Authors' Comments* to Rule 604, Ariz. R. Evid.

Rule 44. Proof of records; determination of foreign law

(a) Records of Public Officials. The records required to be made and kept by a public officer of the state, county, municipality, or any body politic, and copies thereof certified under the hand and seal of the public officer having custody of such records, shall be received in evidence as prima facie evidence of the facts therein stated.

(b) Deleted Sept. 1, 1977 incident to adoption of Arizona Rules of Evidence.

(c) Proof of Records of Notaries Public. Declarations and protests made and acknowledgments taken by notaries public, and certified copies of their records and official papers, shall be received in evidence as prima facie evidence of the facts therein stated.

(d) - (i). Deleted Sept. 1, 1977 incident to adoption of Arizona Rules of Evidence.

(j) Deleted effective Nov. 1, 1967.

(k) Proof of Appointment of Executor, Administrator, or Guardian; Letters or Certificate. Whenever it is necessary to make proof of the appointment and qualification of an executor, administrator or guardian, the letters issued in the manner provided by law, or a certificate of the proper clerk under official seal that the letters issued, shall be sufficient evidence of the appointment and qualification of the executor, administrator or guardian.

Amended Sept. 15, 1987, effective Nov. 15, 1987.

(*l*) Deleted effective Sept. 1, 1977.

(m) Comparison of Handwriting. In any action comparison of a disputed writing with any writing proved to the satisfaction of the judge to be genuine shall be permitted to be made by witnesses, and such writings and the evidence of witnesses respecting them may be submitted to the court and jury as evidence of the genuineness or otherwise of the writing in dispute.

(n)–(s) Deleted Sept. 1, 1977 incident to adoption of Arizona Rules of Evidence.

AUTHORS' COMMENTS

Analysis

1. Scope and Purpose of Rule.

2. Comparison With Federal Rule.
3. Records of Public Officials; Notaries Public.
4. Proof of Appointment.
5. Handwriting Comparisons.

1. *Scope and Purpose of Rule.* Rule 44 formerly contained a number of provisions specifying the standard of proof for various types of documentary materials. Most of its provisions were deleted as unnecessary and duplicative contemporaneously with the adoption of the Arizona Rules of Evidence. The remnants concern proof of official records, proof of records acknowledged before notaries public, proof of the appointment of a legal representative, and handwriting comparisons.

2. *Comparison With Federal Rule.* ARCP 44 differs significantly from FRCP 44. While both ARCP 44(a) and FRCP 44(a) deal with the proof of official records, their provisions are markedly different. The Arizona Rules of Civil Procedure do not contain provisions that correspond to FRCP 44(b) and (c). Similarly, the Federal Rules of Civil Procedure do not contain provisions corresponding to ARCP 44(c), (k) and (m).

In addition, in 2007, the language of FRCP 44 was amended as part of the general restyling of the Federal Rules of Civil Procedure to make the Federal Rules more easily understood and to make style and terminology consistent throughout the Federal Rules of Civil Procedure. Those stylistic modifications have not been incorporated into ARCP 44.

3. *Records of Public Officials; Notaries Public.* Records that are required to be made and maintained by governmental bodies or public officers, and certified copies of those records, may be received in evidence as *prima facie* evidence of the facts stated therein. The same standard applies to declarations and protests made and acknowledged before notaries public. These provisions of Rules 44(a) and (c) are essentially duplicative of Rules 902(4) and 902(8), Ariz. R. Evid. See discussion in Sections 4 and 5 of the *Authors' Comments* to Rule 902, Ariz. R. Evid.

4. *Proof of Appointment.* Where it is necessary to prove the appointment of an executor, administrator or guardian, it is sufficient to offer the letter of appointment, or a certificate of the appropriate court clerk that the letters were issued.

5. *Handwriting Comparisons.* Rule 44(m) deals specifically with the situation where the authenticity of a handwritten document is in dispute. The judge is first to find that a writing has been shown to be genuine, and thereafter witnesses are permitted to compare the written document thus found to be genuine with the writing that is in dispute. This subject is also covered by Rules

901(b)(2) and (3), Ariz. R. Evid., and discussed in Section 5 of the *Authors' Comments* to Rule 901, Ariz. R. Evid.

Rule 44.1. Determination of foreign law

A party who intends to raise an issue concerning the law of a foreign country shall give notice by pleadings or other reasonable written notice. The court, in determining foreign law, may consider any relevant material or source, including testimony, whether or not submitted by a party or admissible under the Arizona Rules of Evidence. The court's determination shall be treated as a ruling on a question of law.

Added June 1, 1977, effective Sept. 1, 1977; amended Sept. 15, 1987, effective Nov. 15, 1987.

COMMENT

[Rule 44.1] Historically, laws of foreign nations and even laws of some United States jurisdictions were treated as matters which had to be proved as facts are proved. With modern availability of sources of law, this is no longer appropriate. Arizona has, for some time, treated matters of the law of foreign nations as questions of law rather than questions of fact. Since the law of foreign nations can be much more difficult to ascertain than the law of United States jurisdictions, a separate rule stating that law of other United States jurisdictions should also be treated as a question of law, rather than fact, is considered unnecessary.

AUTHORS' COMMENTS

Analysis

1. Scope and Purpose of Rule.
2. Comparison With Federal Rule.
3. Procedure for Determining Foreign Law.

1. *Scope and Purpose of Rule.* Rule 44.1 is a special provision establishing the procedure for resolving issues concerning the law of a foreign country.

2. *Comparison With Federal Rule.* ARCP 44.1 is substantially identical to FRCP 44.1.

In 2007, the language of FRCP 44.1 was amended as part of the general restyling of the Federal Rules of Civil Procedure to make the Federal Rules more easily understood and to make style and terminology consistent throughout the Federal Rules of Civil Procedure. Those stylistic modifications have not been incorporated into ARCP 44.1.

3. *Procedure for Determining Foreign Law.* A party who intends to raise issues concerning the law of a foreign country must provide written notice of that, either in the pleadings or in some other fashion. The Court is then to determine the foreign law and, in doing so, may consider any relevant source, including

testimony, which need not be admissible under the Arizona Rules of Evidence. *Dayka & Hackett, LLC v. Del Monte Fresh Produce N.A., Inc.*, 228 Ariz. 533, 269 P.3d 709, 76 U.C.C. Rep. Serv. 2d 637 (Ct. App. Div. 2 2012), review denied, (May 30, 2012). The matters properly considered can include affidavits from experts concerning the foreign law to be determined. *Gemstar Ltd. v. Ernst & Young*, 185 Ariz. 493, 917 P.2d 222 (1996). A determination of foreign law is to be treated as a ruling on a question of law, which departs from and abandons the historical practice where foreign law was proven as a matter of fact.

Rule 45. Subpoena

(a) Form; Issuance.

(1) *General Requirements.* Every subpoena shall:

(A) state the name of the Arizona court from which it is issued;

(B) state the title of the action, the name of the court in which it is pending, and its civil action number;

(C) command each person to whom it is directed to do the following at a specified time and place:

(i) attend and give testimony at a hearing, trial, or deposition; or

(ii) produce and permit inspection, copying, testing, or sampling designated documents, electronically stored information or tangible things in that person's possession, custody or control; or

(iii) permit the inspection of premises; and

(D) be substantially in the form set forth in Rule 84, Form 9.

(2) *Issuance by Clerk.* The clerk shall issue a signed but otherwise blank subpoena to a party requesting it, and that party shall complete the subpoena before service. The State Bar of Arizona may also issue signed subpoenas on behalf of the clerk through an online subpoena issuance service approved by the Supreme Court of Arizona.

(b) For Attendance of Witnesses at Hearing, Trial or Deposition; Objections.

(1) *Issuing Court.* A subpoena commanding a person to attend and give testimony at a hearing or trial shall issue from the superior court for the county in which the hearing or trial is to be held. A subpoena commanding a person to attend and give testimony at a deposition shall issue from the superior court for the county in which the case is pending.

(2) *Combining or Separating a Command to Produce or to Permit Inspection.* A command to produce documents, electronically stored information, or tangible things, or to permit the inspection of premises, may be joined with a command to attend and give testimony at a hearing, trial, or deposition, or may be set out in a separate subpoena.

(3) *Place of Appearance.*

(A) Trial Subpoena. Subject to Rule 45(e)(2)(B)(iii), a subpoena commanding a person to attend and give testimony at a trial may require the subpoenaed person to travel from anywhere within the state.

(B) Hearing or Deposition Subpoena. A subpoena commanding a person who is neither a party nor a party's officer to attend and give testimony at a hearing or deposition may not require the subpoenaed person to travel to a place other than:

(i) the county in which the person resides or transacts business in person;

(ii) the county in which the person is served with a subpoena, or within forty miles from the place of service; or

(iii) such other convenient place fixed by a court order.

(4) *Command to Attend a Deposition—Notice of Recording Method.* A subpoena commanding a person to attend and give testimony at a deposition shall state the method for recording the testimony.

(5) *Objections; Appearance Required.* Objections to a subpoena commanding a person to attend and give testimony at a hearing, trial, or deposition shall be made by timely motion in accordance with Rule 45(e)(2). Unless excused from doing so by the party or attorney serving a subpoena, by a court order, or by any other provision of this Rule, a person who is properly served with a subpoena is required to attend and give testimony at the date, time and place specified in the subpoena.

(c) For Production of Documentary Evidence or for Inspection of Premises; Duties in Responding to Subpoena; Objections; Production to Other Parties.

(1) *Issuing Court.* If separate from a subpoena commanding a person to attend and give testimony at a hearing, trial or deposition, a subpoena commanding a person to produce designated documents, electronically stored information or tangible things, or to permit the inspection of premises, shall issue from the superior court for the county in which the production or inspection is to be made.

(2) *Specifying the Form for Electronically Stored Information.* A subpoena may specify the form or forms in which electronically stored information is to be produced.

(3) *Appearance Not Required.* A person commanded to produce documents, electronically stored information or tangible things, or to permit the inspection of premises, need not appear in person at the place of production or inspection unless the subpoena commands the person to attend and give testimony at a hearing, trial or deposition.

(4) *Production of Documents.* A person responding to a subpoena to produce documents shall produce them as they are

kept in the usual course of business or shall organize and label them to correspond with the categories in the demand.

(5) *Objections.*

(A) Form and Time for Objection.

(i) A person commanded to produce documents, electronically stored information or tangible items, or to permit the inspection of premises, may serve upon the party or attorney serving the subpoena an objection to producing, inspecting, copying, testing or sampling any or all of the designated materials; to inspecting the premises; or to producing electronically stored information in the form or forms requested. The objection shall set forth the basis for the objection, and shall include the name, address, and telephone number of the person, or the person's attorney, serving the objection.

(ii) The objection shall be served upon the party or attorney serving the subpoena before the time specified for compliance or within 14 days after the subpoena is served, whichever is earlier.

(iii) An objection also may be made to that portion of a subpoena that commands the person to produce and permit inspection, copying, testing, or sampling if it is joined with a command to attend and give testimony at a hearing, trial or deposition, but making such an objection does not suspend or modify a person's obligation to attend and give testimony at the date, time and place specified in the subpoena.

(B) Procedure After an Objection Is Made.

(i) If an objection is made, the party or attorney serving the subpoena shall not be entitled to compliance with those portions of the subpoena that are subject to the objection, except pursuant to an order of the issuing court.

(ii) The party serving the subpoena may move for an order under Rule 37(a) to compel compliance with the subpoena. The motion shall comply with Rule 37(a)(2)(C), and shall be served on the subpoenaed person and all other parties in accordance with Rule 5(c).

(iii) Any order to compel entered by the court shall protect any person who is neither a party nor a party's officer from undue burden or expense resulting from the production, inspection, copying, testing, or sampling commanded.

(C) Claiming Privilege or Protection.

(i) When information subject to a subpoena is withheld on a claim that it is privileged or subject to protection as trial-preparation materials, the claim shall be made expressly and shall be supported by a description of the nature of the documents, communications, or things not produced that is sufficient to enable the demanding party to contest the claim.

(ii) If a person contends that information that is subject to a claim of privilege or of protection as trial-preparation material has been inadvertently produced in response to a subpoena, the person making the claim may notify any party that received the information of the claim and the basis for it. After being notified, a party must promptly return, sequester, or destroy the specified information and any copies it has and may not use or disclose the information until the claim is resolved. A receiving party may promptly present the information to the court under seal for a determination of the claim. If the receiving party disclosed the information before being notified, it must take reasonable steps to retrieve it. The person who produced the information must preserve the information until the claim is resolved.

(6) *Production to Other Parties.* Unless otherwise stipulated by the parties or ordered by the court, documents, electronically stored information and tangible things that are obtained in response to a subpoena shall be made available to all other parties in accordance with Rule 26.1(a) and (b).

(d) Service.

(1) *General Requirements; Tendering Fees.* A subpoena may be served by any person who is not a party and is not less than eighteen years of age. Serving a subpoena requires delivering a copy to the named person and, if the subpoena requires that person's attendance, tendering to that person the fees for one day's attendance and the mileage allowed by law.

(2) *Exceptions to Tendering Fees.* When the subpoena commands the appearance of a party at a trial or hearing, or is issued on behalf of the state or any of its officers or agencies, fees and mileage need not be tendered.

(3) *Service on Other Parties.* A copy of every subpoena shall be served on every other party in accordance with Rule 5(c).

(4) *Service within the State.* A subpoena may be served anywhere within the state.

(5) *Proof of Service.* Proving service, when necessary, requires filing with the clerk of the court of the county in which the case is pending a statement showing the date and manner of service and of the names of the persons served. The statement must be certified by the person who served the subpoena.

(e) Protection of Persons Subject to Subpoenas; Motion

to Quash or Modify.

(1) *Avoiding Undue Burden or Expense; Sanctions.* A party or an attorney responsible for the service of a subpoena shall take reasonable steps to avoid imposing undue burden or expense on a person subject to that subpoena. The issuing court shall enforce this duty and impose upon the party or attorney who breaches this duty an appropriate sanction, which may include, but is not limited to, lost earnings and a reasonable attorneys' fee.

(2) *Quashing or Modifying a Subpoena.*

(A) When Required. On the timely filing of a motion to quash or modify a subpoena, the superior court of the county in which the case is pending or from which a subpoena was issued shall quash or modify the subpoena if:

(i) it fails to allow a reasonable time for compliance;

(ii) it commands a person who is neither a party nor a party's officer to travel to a location other than the places specified in Rule 45(b)(3)(B);

(iii) it requires disclosure of privileged or other protected matter, if no exception or waiver applies; or

(iv) it subjects a person to undue burden.

(B) When Permitted. On the timely filing of a motion to quash or modify a subpoena, and to protect a person subject to or affected by a subpoena, the superior court of the county in which the case is pending or from which a subpoena was issued may quash or modify the subpoena if:

(i) it requires disclosing a trade secret or other confidential research, development, or commercial information;

(ii) it requires disclosing an unretained expert's opinion or information that does not describe specific occurrences in dispute and results from the expert's study that was not requested by a party;

(iii) it requires a person who is neither a party nor a party's officer to incur substantial travel expense; or

(iv) justice so requires.

(C) Specifying Conditions as an Alternative. In the circumstances described in Rule 45(e)(2)(B), the court may, instead of quashing or modifying a subpoena, order appearance or production under specified conditions, including any conditions and limitations set forth in Rule 26(c), as the court deems appropriate:

(i) if the party or attorney serving the subpoena shows a substantial need for the testimony or material that cannot be otherwise met without undue hardship; and

(ii) if the person's travel expenses or the expenses resulting from the production are at issue, the party or attorney serving the subpoena assures that the subpoenaed person will be reasonably compensated.

(D) Time for Motion. A motion to quash or modify a subpoena must be filed before the time specified for compliance or within 14 days after the subpoena is served, whichever is earlier.

(E) Service of Motion. Any motion to quash or modify a subpoena shall be served on the party or the attorney serving the subpoena in accordance with Rule 5(c). The party or attorney who served the subpoena shall serve a copy of any such motion on all other parties in accordance with Rule 5(c).

(f) Contempt. The issuing court may hold in contempt a person, who having been served, fails without adequate excuse to obey a subpoena. A failure to obey must be excused if the subpoena purports to require a person who is neither a party nor a party's officer to attend or produce at a location other than the places specified in Rule 45(b)(3)(B).

(g) Failure to Produce Evidence. If a person fails to produce a document, electronically stored information, or a tangible thing requested in a subpoena, secondary evidence of the item's content may be offered in evidence at trial.

Amended July 17, 1970, effective Nov. 1, 1970; July 6, 1983, effective Sept. 7, 1983; Sept. 15, 1987, effective Nov. 15, 1987; Oct. 9, 1996, effective Dec. 1, 1996; June 9, 2005, effective December 1, 2005; September 5, 2007, effective January 1, 2008; Sept. 2, 2010, effective Jan. 1, 2011.

STATE BAR COMMITTEE NOTES

1970 Amendment

Rule 45(e)(1): This provision deals with the subpoena of materials to be brought to a deposition. The provisions in revised Rule 30(f) for copying documents at a deposition apply to documents produced in response to a subpoena under revised Rule 45(e)(1). The Arizona Supreme Court has held that the pre-1970 Rules 34 and 45 should be interpreted together, and on the same standard; *State Farm Ins. Co. v. Roberts*, 97 Ariz. 169, 398 P.2d 671 (1965). This remains true, though the standard itself is now somewhat changed, the standard for most documents coming from revised Rule 34, and for those prepared in anticipation of trial from revised Rule 26. Rule 45(e)(2) is wholly unaffected by this revision.

1996 Amendments

To the extent that a person who is not a party or an officer of a party is commanded by subpoena only to produce documents, the reimbursement to which that person is entitled for the costs incurred in complying with the subpoena is governed by A.R.S. § 12-351. The provisions of Rule 45(c)(1) and Rule 45(c)(2)(B) do not alter the statutory provisions of A.R.S. § 12-351, but rather apply to subpoenas commanding testimony (in the case of Rule 45(c)(1)) and to nonmonetary measures to protect against "significant expense" resulting from a subpoena commanding production of documents (in the case of Rule 45(c)(2)(B)).

AUTHORS' COMMENTS

Analysis

1. *Scope and Purpose of Rule.* The procedures for securing, serving, resisting and enforcing subpoenas, whether for trial or discovery depositions, are the subject of Rule 45. The subpoena is the vehicle for compelling the attendance of witnesses, and the production of documents from non-parties.

A case decided before the 2011 amendments to Rule 45 held that a subpoena is issued by the Clerk of the Court, but has the force of law. *Ingalls v. Superior Court in and for Pima County*, 117 Ariz. 448, 573 P.2d 522 (Ct. App. Div. 2 1977). Logically, this holding extends to subpoenas issued, pursuant to Ariz. R. Civ. P. 45(a)(2) (2011), by the State Bar of Arizona on behalf of the clerk of court.

2. *Comparison With Federal Rule.* In 2011, ARCP 45 was amended, reorganized, restyled and renumbered. As a consequence, of these amendments, which became effective January 1, 2011, ARCP 45 and FRCP 45 remain similar in general content, but the two rules are now quite dissimilar in many respects.

As part of the 2011 structural reorganization of the Arizona Rule, ARCP 45 now separately states the rights and obligations of the parties with respect to: (1) subpoenas for attendance at hearing, trial, or deposition ("attendance" subpoenas) [ARCP 45(b)] and (2) subpoenas for the production of documents or inspection of premises [ARCP 45(c)]. This organizational approach serves to make the rule more easily understood. The Federal Rule is structured differently.

ARCP 45(a)(1)(D), as amended in 2011, provides that a subpoena must be substantially in the form set forth in ARCP 84, Form 9. In contrast, FRCP 45(a)(1)(A)(iv) provides merely that a subpoena must set forth the text of FRCP 45(c) and (d), and does not provide a uniform form for use.

FRCP 45(a)(3) permits attorneys, under specified circumstances, to issue and sign subpoenas. The Arizona Rules do not contain a similar provision. However, ARCP 45(a)(2) provides that the Arizona State Bar, through an online subpoena issuance service, may issue signed subpoenas on behalf of the clerk. The Federal Rules do not have a similar provision.

Under ARCP 45(b)(1), a subpoena for attendance at a deposition is to be issued from the Superior Court for the county in which the case is pending. The Federal Rule, FRCP 45(a)(2)(B), requires such subpoena be issued from the District Court for the District in which the deposition is to be taken.

ARCP 45(b)(3)(B)(ii) provides that a subpoena issued for the purpose of testimony at a hearing or deposition may not require a person who is neither a party nor a party's officer to travel more than forty (40) miles from the place of service. The mileage limitation in the corresponding Federal Rule is one hundred (100) miles from the place of service. *See*, FRCP 45(c)(3)(A)(ii).

The 2011 amendments to ARCP 45 added a new provision, ARCP 45(b)(4), requiring that a deposition subpoena state the method for recording the testimony. This new provision in the Arizona rule is essentially identical to FRCP 45(a)(1)(B).

As a result of the 2011 amendments, the procedures set forth in the Arizona Rule for objecting to an attendance subpoena or a subpoena *duces tecum* are now quite different from the corresponding procedures set forth in the Federal Rule. The procedure for objecting to an attendance subpoena is governed by ARCP 45(b)(5), which now makes clear that any such objection must be made by motion and must be timely filed in accordance with ARCP 45(e)(2). ARCP 45(b)(5) also specifically requires a properly served witness to attend and give testimony unless excused from doing so by agreement of the party serving the subpoena, by court order or by some other provision of the rule. FRCP 45 does not contain provisions that correspond to Arizona's procedures.

The procedure for objecting to a subpoena *duces tecum* is governed by ARCP 45(c), which retains the ability of the objecting party to serve a letter objection. ARCP 45(c)(5)(A) sets forth, in detail, the form and time for objecting to a command to produce documents or permit inspection and, ARCP 45(c)(5)(B) sets forth the procedures for what is to happen *after* an objection is made. In this latter regard, and among other things, ARCP 45(c)(5)(B)(ii) expressly requires compliance with Rule 37(a)(2)(C) [the "personal consultation" requirement] before a motion to compel is filed. The Federal Rule does not contain provisions that directly correspond to Arizona's procedures.

The procedures set forth in ARCP 45(e), relating to motions to quash or modify a subpoena, generally correspond to FRCP 45(c)(3). The Federal Rule does not have a provision, however, establishing time limits for filing a motion to quash or modify a subpoena [ARCP 45(e)(2)(D)].

ARCP 45(f), which sets forth the scope of the court's authority to hold a person in contempt, is essentially identical to FRCP 45(e).

Finally, the Federal Rule does not have a provision that corresponds to ARCP 45(g), formerly ARCP 45(f), which provides that, where a witness fails to produce documents in response to a subpoena *duces tecum* for trial, secondary evidence of the documents may be received. *Cf. also*, Rule 1004, Ariz. R. Evid.

In 2013, FRCP 45 was amended to clarify sweeping amendments made to FRCP in 1991. As noted in the first paragraph of the Comment to the 2013 Amendments, the amendments "recognize the court where the action is pending as the issuing court, permit nationwide service of subpoena, and collect in a new subdivision (c) the previously scattered provisions regarding place of compliance." Some, but not all of the amendments are unique to federal practice.

3. *Subpoenas—Form; Issuance*. As a consequence of the 2011 amendments, effective January 1, 2011, every subpoena must be substantially in the form set forth in Ariz. R. Civ. P. 84, Form 9. *See*, Ariz. R. Civ. P. 45(a)(1)(D). The Arizona State Bar's website has this form available in a convenient, fill-in the blank format. The Arizona State Bar's website is: http://www.azbar.org.

Ariz. R. Civ. P. 45(a)(2), as amended in 2011, sets forth the methods for securing the issuance of a subpoena. That rule provides that the Clerk shall issue a signed, but otherwise blank, subpoena to a requesting party and the party then completes the subpoena before service. Alternatively, the rule provides that a requesting party may secure a subpoena from the Arizona State Bar, through its online subpoena issuance service. Again, this convenient, fill-in the blank form, can be found on the State Bar's website: http://www.azbar.org.

Finally, if the party securing the issuance of the subpoena desires to enforce the subpoena, if necessary, through the issuance of a Civil Arrest Warrant, authorized by Ariz.R.Civ.P. 64.1, the subpoena must contain a warning that failure to appear in response thereto may result in the issuance and service of such a warrant. See the *Authors' Comments* to Ariz.R.Civ.P. 64.1.

4. *Subpoenas for Attendance of Witnesses at Hearing, Deposition or Trial; Objections; Attendance Required*. Effective January 1, 2011, Ariz. R. Civ. P. 45(b) now sets forth the procedures governing subpoenas issued for attendance at a hearing, trial or deposition ("attendance" subpoenas). Rule 45(b) retained many of the provisions contained in the former rule relating to attendance subpoenas. There are differences, however, between new Rule

45(b) and its predecessor provisions, in addition to those differences resulting from the 2011 reorganization, restyling and renumbering of former Rule 45.

Rule 45(b) is similar to its predecessor in that Ariz. R. Civ. P. 45(b)(3)(A), as renumbered in 2011, still provides that a subpoena to appear for a trial can compel attendance anywhere within the state; and, Ariz. R. Civ. P. 45(b)(3)(B)(i) and (ii), as renumbered in 2011, still provide that a subpoena issued for the purpose of testimony at a hearing or deposition may not require a person who is neither a party nor a party's officer to travel to a place other than the county in which the person resides or transacts business in person or more than forty (40) miles from the place of service.

The 2011 amendments, however, resulted in two important modifications to the procedures governing attendance subpoenas. First, a new provision was added [Rule 45(b)(4)] that requires a deposition subpoena state the method for recording the testimony. Second, the 2011 amendments modified the procedures for objecting to an attendance subpoena and clarified a recipient's continuing obligation after an objection is made. Thus, Rule 45(b)(5), the rule now governing objections to attendance subpoenas, expressly provides that an objection to an attendance subpoena must be made by motion and must be timely filed in accordance with Rule 45(e)(2). In turn, Rule 45(e)(2)(D) provides that the motion objecting to the subpoena must be filed *before* the time specified for compliance or within 14 days after the subpoena is served, which ever is earlier.

In addition, Rule 45(b)(5) expressly requires the witness to attend and give testimony *unless* excused from doing so by agreement of the party serving the subpoena, by court order or by some other provision of the rule. *But see*, discussion in Section 9 of the *Authors' Comments* under this Rule 45 ["*Subpoenas for Media Witnesses*"].

Consistent with its predecessor, Rule 45(e)(2)(B)(iii), as renumbered in 2011, permits the Court to quash a trial or deposition subpoena if it would require a person who is neither a party nor a party's officer to incur "substantial travel expense." Alternatively, if the party who procured issuance of the subpoena shows a substantial need for the testimony that cannot otherwise be met without undue hardship, the trial court is still permitted to condition the person's attendance on the receipt of an assurance that the person subpoenaed will be "reasonably compensated." *See*, Ariz. R. Civ. P. 45(e)(2)(C).

Ariz. R. Civ. P. 45(f), which is essentially identical to former Rule 45(e), authorizes the Court to hold a person in contempt for failing to obey a subpoena without adequate excuse. *See also*,

Jolly v. Superior Court of Pinal County, 112 Ariz. 186, 540 P.2d 658 (1975) (A witness may be subject to sanctions for failure to appear if an order quashing or modifying the subpoena has not been secured.).

Subpoenas for the attendance of trial witnesses should be secured and served promptly, and may be quashed or modified where they do not give the prospective trial witnesses adequate advance notice. *Cf. Parkinson v. Farmers Ins. Co.*, 122 Ariz. 343, 594 P.2d 1039 (Ct. App. Div. 2 1979).

5. *Service of Subpoenas.* The requirements for service of a subpoena differ from those for service of process under Rule 4. Rule 4(d) provides that process may be served only by (1) a sheriff or deputy sheriff, (2) a certified (formerly, "registered") private process server, or (3) a person at least twenty-one years of age specially appointed for that purpose. Under Ariz. R. Civ. P. 45(d), however, a subpoena may be served by "any person who is not a party and is not less than eighteen years of age." While Rules 4, 4.1 and 4.2 enumerate a number of methods for service of process, a subpoena must be delivered to the person named therein, and be accompanied by a tender of the fees for one day's attendance and applicable mileage. A.R.S. § 12-303. Rule 45(d), as renumbered in 2011, provides that a copy of every subpoena shall be served on every other party in accordance with Ariz. R. Civ. P. 5(c).

6. *Subpoenas for Production of Documentary Evidence or for Inspection of Premises; Generally; Objections.* As a consequence of the 2011 amendments to the Arizona Rules of Civil Procedure, new Ariz. R. Civ. P. 45(c) now sets forth the procedures governing subpoenas for the production of documentary evidence or inspection of premises. Rule 45(c) retained many of the provisions contained in the former rule. But, there are differences between new Rule 45(c) and its predecessor provisions, in addition to those differences resulting from the 2011 reorganization, restyling and renumbering of former Rule 45.

Rule 45(c) is similar to its predecessor provisions in many respects. Thus, Ariz. R. Civ. P. 45(c)(1), as renumbered in 2011, still allows a subpoena for the production or inspection of documentary materials, or for the inspection of premises, to be issued separately from a subpoena to appear for a hearing, trial or deposition. *Compare*, former Rule 45(a)(2). Ariz. R. Civ. P. 45(c)(2), as renumbered in 2011, still provides that a subpoena *duces tecum* may specify the form of producing electronically stored information. *Compare*, former Rule 45(a)(1)(C). Ariz. R. Civ. P. 45(c)(3), as renumbered in 2011, still provides that a recipient need not appear in person unless otherwise commanded to give testimony at a trial, hearing or deposition. *Compare*, former Rule 45(c)(2)(A). Ariz. R. Civ. P. 45(c)(4) provides, as did its predecessor, that the recipient must produce the requested information either as usually kept or categorized as specified in the subpoena. *Compare*, former Rule 45(d)(1). Ariz. R. Civ. P. 45(c)(5)(A), as renumbered in 2011, still allows the recipient to serve a letter objection; a motion is not required. *Compare*, former Rule 45(c)(2)(B).

The procedures for objecting to a subpoena for production of documents or inspection of premises are now governed by Ariz. R. Civ. P. 45(c)(5), and now differ in one important respect from the corresponding procedures set forth in former Rule 45(c)(2). Specifically, the 2011 amendments resulted in the adoption of Ariz. R. Civ. P. 45(c)(5)(B)(ii), which imposes upon the party or attorney serving the subpoena the "personal consultation" requirement set forth in Ariz. R. Civ. P. 37(a)(2)(C), before a motion to compel is filed.

The 2011 amendments do not appear to change or supplant the provisions of A.R.S. § 12-351. That statute provides that a non-party witness may charge a party procuring the issuance of a subpoena *duces tecum* "all reasonable costs" incurred in locating and producing documents pursuant to a subpoena, not to exceed ten cents per page copying charges and ten dollars per hour for clerical costs. Under the statute, the subpoenaed person may demand payment simultaneously with actual delivery of the documents. While it is not clear that this statute was intended to apply to trial subpoenas *duces tecum*, its literal language encompasses them.

A subpoena *duces tecum* must describe the documents or other materials it seeks with reasonable particularity. *Helge v. Druke*, 136 Ariz. 434, 666 P.2d 534 (Ct. App. Div. 2 1983). A subpoena *duces tecum* may not be served on a party under Ariz. R. Civ. P. 45 to avoid the procedures of Ariz. R. Civ. P. 34. *MacDonald v. Hyder*, 12 Ariz. App. 411, 471 P.2d 296 (Div. 1 1970).

7. *Claims of Privilege; Inadvertent Production*. Ariz. R. Civ. P. 45(c)(5)(C)(i), as renumbered in 2011, deals expressly with the situation where materials are withheld from production in response to a subpoena because they are considered to be privileged or entitled to protection as trial preparation materials. The Rule requires that such a claim be made expressly, and be supported by a description of the nature of the documents, communications or other materials not produced that is sufficient to enable the party seeking their production to contest the claim.

Rule 45(c)(5)(C)(ii), as renumbered in 2011, was added as now former Rule 45(d)(2)(B), in 2008. Rule 45(c)(5)(C)(ii) (2011), like its predecessor, is substantially identical to Ariz. R. Civ. P. 26.1(f)(2) and deals with the situation where a party believes it has inadvertently produced or disclosed, in response to a subpoena, information that is privileged or entitled to protection as trial preparation material. Where that occurs, the responding party may notify any party who received the information of the claim and the basis for it. A party who receives a notice of such a claim must promptly return, sequester or destroy the specified information and any copies it has, and may not use or disclose the information until the issue is resolved. The receiving party may promptly present the information to the court under seal for a determination, and the producing party must preserve the information until the claim is resolved.

Rule 26.1(f)(2)(2008) sets forth an essentially identical provision and governs inadvertent production made during the Rule 26.1 disclosure process. *See also, Lund v. Myers*, 232 Ariz. 309, 305 P.3d 374 (2013). *Lund* concerned the inadvertent production of documents claimed to be subject to attorney-client privilege. Interpreting Ariz. R. Civ. P. 26.1(f)(2), the Arizona Supreme Court held the filing of inadvertently disclosed documents with trial court under seal did not constitute impermissible "use" of documents, as that word is used in the rule.

The *Lund* Court then addressed the issue of when, in deciding issues of privilege and waiver, a trial court may conduct an in camera inspection of the allegedly privileged documents inadvertently disclosed or produced. The Court held as follows:

1. As to each document at issue, the trial court first must determine whether in camera inspection is needed to resolve a claim of privilege. The trial court makes this determination based on its consideration of the privilege log, the opposing party's response to such privilege log and the parties' arguments on the issues of privilege and waiver.

2. If the trial court determines such in camera review is necessary, the trial court then must decide who will conduct such in camera review of the allegedly privileged documents: the trial judge or another judicial officer. If the trial judge conducts the in camera inspection and upholds the claim of privilege, the trial judge then will need to consider recusal or face a possible Rule 42(f) challenge based on claims of bias resulting from the review of such privileged documents.

Ariz. R. Civ. P. 45(c)(5)(C)(ii) is substantially identical to Ariz. R. Civ. P. 26.1(f)(2). Thus, the holding in *Lund* likely would apply in the case of privileged documents allegedly produced in response to a subpoena.

8. *Subpoenas for Media Witnesses.* A.R.S. § 12-2214 requires a special affidavit in connection with the issuance of a subpoena directed to a "person engaged in gathering, reporting, writing, editing, publishing or broadcasting news to the public," which

seeks matters related to those activities. The affidavit, which must be attached to the subpoena, must set forth:

1. A list of each item of documentary and evidentiary information sought from the person subpoenaed.
2. The affiant's statement that the affiant or his representative has attempted to obtain each item of information from all other available sources, specifying which items the affiant has been unable to obtain.
3. The identity of the other sources from which the affiant or his representative has attempted to obtain the information.
4. The affiant's statement that the information sought is relevant and material to the affiant's cause of action or defense.
5. The affiant's statement that the information sought is not protected by any lawful privilege.
6. The affiant's statement that the subpoena is not intended to interfere with the gathering, writing, editing, publishing, broadcasting and disseminating of news to the public as protected by the first amendment, Constitution of the United States, or by article II, section 6, Constitution of Arizona.

If the affidavit is controverted or a motion to quash the subpoena or for a protective order is filed by the person subpoenaed, the subpoena need not be honored until the issues are resolved by the Court. *See,* A.R.S. § 12-2214. The statute does not apply to subpoenas issued by a grand jury or to subpoenas issued by a magistrate conducting a criminal investigation. If the requisite affidavit is made, the burden then shifts to the media witness subject to the subpoena to controvert it. *Bartlett v. Superior Court In and For Pima County*, 150 Ariz. 178, 722 P.2d 346 (Ct. App. Div. 2 1986).

Rule 45.1. Interstate depositions and discovery

(a) Definitions. In this Rule:

(1) Foreign jurisdiction means a state other than this state.

(2) Foreign subpoena means a subpoena issued under authority of a court of record of a foreign jurisdiction.

(3) Person means an individual, corporation, business trust, estate, trust, partnership, limited liability company, association, joint venture, public corporation, government, or governmental subdivision, agency or instrumentality, or any other legal or commercial entity.

(4) State means a state of the United States, the District of Columbia, Puerto Rico, the United States Virgin Islands, a federally recognized Indian tribe, or any territory or insular possession subject to the jurisdiction of the United States.

(5) Subpoena means a document, however denominated, issued under authority of a court of record requiring a person to:

(A) attend and give testimony at a deposition;

(B) produce and permit inspection and copying of designated books, documents, records, electronically stored information; or tangible things in the possession, custody, or control of the person; or

(C) permit inspection of premises under the control of the person.

(b) Issuance of Subpoena.

(1) To request issuance of a subpoena under this rule, a party must present a foreign subpoena to a clerk of court in the county in which discovery is sought to be conducted in this state. The foreign subpoena must include the following phrase below the case number: "For the Issuance of an Arizona Subpoena Under Ariz. R. Civ. P. 45.1." A request for the issuance of a subpoena under this rule does not constitute an appearance in the courts of this state.

(2) When a party presents a foreign subpoena to a clerk of court in this state, the clerk shall promptly issue a signed but otherwise blank subpoena to the party requesting it, and that party shall complete the subpoena before service.

(3) A subpoena under subsection (b)(2) must:

(A) state the name of the Arizona court issuing it;

(B) bear the caption and case number of the out-of-state case to which it relates, identifying (before the case number) the foreign jurisdiction and court where the case is pending;

(C) accurately incorporate the discovery requested in the

foreign subpoena;

(D) contain or be accompanied by the names, addresses, and telephone numbers of all counsel of record in the proceeding to which the subpoena relates and of any party not represented by counsel;

(E) comply with the form specified in Rule 45(a)(1) and otherwise required in Rule 45; and

(F) not request discovery exceeding the discovery authorized in Rule 45.

(c) Service of Subpoena. A subpoena issued by a clerk of court under subsection (b) of this rule must be served in compliance with Rule 45(d).

(d) Deposition, Production, and Inspection. Rule 45 applies to subpoenas issued under subsection (b) of this rule. Depositions and other discovery taken pursuant to this rule shall be conducted consistent with, and subject to the limitations in, the Arizona Rules of Civil Procedure, including but not limited to Rules 26, 28, 30, 31, and 32.

(e) Motion or Application to a Court. A motion or application to the court for a protective order or to enforce, quash, or modify a subpoena issued by a clerk of court under subsection (b) must comply with the rules or statutes of this state and be filed with the court in the county in which discovery is to be conducted. Any such motion or application must be filed as a separate civil action bearing the caption that appears on the subpoena. The following phrase must appear below the case number of the newly filed action: "Motion or Application Related to a Subpoena Issued Under Ariz. R. Civ. P. 45.1." Any later motion or application relating to the same subpoena must be filed in the same action.

Added August 30, 2012, effective January 1, 2013.

Comment to 2013 Amendment

This rule derives from the Uniform Interstate Depositions and Discovery Act, 13 Pt.2 Uniform Laws Annotated 59 (West 2011 Supp.). In applying and construing this rule, consideration should be given to the need to promote uniformity of the law with respect to its subject matter among states that adopt or enact it.

AUTHORS' COMMENTS

Analysis

1. *Scope and Purpose of Rule.* Effective January 1, 2013, the Arizona Supreme Court adopted Ariz. R. Civ. P. 45.1 ["Interstate Depositions and Discovery"] to govern the procedures for obtaining a subpoena to take depositions and certain other discovery in Arizona related to civil proceedings pending in an out-of-state proceeding. As adopted, Rule 45.1 is a modified version of the Uniform Interstate Depositions and Discovery Act, and replaces the cumbersome, and more limited, procedure formerly provided by Ariz. R. Civ. P. 30(h).

As the title to Rule 45.1 explicitly states Rule 45.1 also provides a procedural mechanism for specified discovery (production and premises inspection) to be taken in Arizona with respect to a matter pending in a foreign jurisdiction. This is a broader scope than former Rule 30(h), the predecessor to Rule 45.1, in that the former rule concerned only depositions conducted in Arizona related to a case pending in a foreign jurisdiction,

In adopting Ariz. R. Civ. P. 45.1, the Court also deleted Rule 30(h), and made a minor modification to Rule 45(b) to accommodate the requirement, set forth in Rule 45.1, that the superior court, in the county in which the discovery will be conducted, issue the Rule 45.1 subpoena, which subpoena is to be in the form specified by Ariz. R. Civ. P. 45.

The 2013 Comment to the rule states that "[i]n applying and construing this rule, consideration should be given to the need to promote uniformity of the law with respect to its subject matter among states that adopt or enact it."

2. *Comparison with Federal Rule.* The Federal Rules of Civil Procedure do not have a provision that corresponds to Ariz. R. Civ. P. 45.1.

3. *Conduct of Local Depositions and Discovery in Actions Pending in Foreign Jurisdictions.* To secure a subpoena for the deposition or discovery in Arizona relating to an out-of state civil proceeding, the party in the out-of-state case simply presents the foreign subpoena to a clerk of court in the county in which discovery is sought to be conducted in this state. The foreign subpoena is not filed with the clerk. Rule 45.1(b)(1) requires that, below the case number of the foreign case, the foreign subpoena must include the following phrase: "*For the Issuance of an Arizona Subpoena under Ariz.R.Civ.P. 45.1.*" A request for the issuance of a Rule 45.1 subpoena does not constitute an appearance in the courts of the State. *See,* Rule 45.1(b)(1).

Once received, and consistent with Ariz. R. Civ. P. 45.1(b)(2) the clerk will issue a "signed but otherwise blank subpoena to the party requesting it, and that party shall complete the subpoena before service."

Ariz. R. Civ. P. 45.1(b)(3) sets forth the requirements of a subpoena issued by the clerk of this state, which subpoena must:

(1) state the name of the Arizona court issuing the subpoena;
(2) bear the caption and other specified information identifying the foreign jurisdiction and court where the case is pending;
(3) incorporate accurately the discovery requested in the foreign subpoena presented to the clerk of the issuing court;
(4) contain or be accompanied by the specified contact information for all counsel of record to which the subpoena relates and of any party not represented by counsel;
(5) be in the form required by Ariz. R. Civ. P. 45(a)(1) and as otherwise provided in Rule 45; and,
(6) not request discovery broader than that authorized in Rule 45.

A subpoena issued by a clerk of court under Rule 45.1(b)(2) is served pursuant to Rule 45(d). *See,* Ariz. R. Civ. P. 45.1(c).

Depositions, production of documents and premises inspections are to be conducted consistent with, and subject to the limitations, in the Arizona Rules of Civil Procedure. *See,* Ariz. R. Civ. P. 45.1(d).

By its terms, Rule 45.1 is limited to *intrastate* depositions and discovery. 28 U.S.C.A. § 1782, enacted in 1948, provides the procedure for the deposition of any witness residing within the United States for use in any civil action pending in any court in a foreign country. This statute provides, among other things, that the deposition may be taken before a person authorized to administer oaths designated by the district court of any district where the witness resides or may be found. 28 U.S.C.A. § 1782 also expressly shields privileged material.

4. *Motion or Application for Protective Order, or to Enforce, Quash or Modify a Subpoena.* Ariz. R. Civ. P. 45.1(e) sets forth the procedures to be followed in the event it becomes necessary to obtain a protective order, or to enforce, quash or modify a subpoena issued under Rule 45.1(b)(2). Specifically, the party seeking relief may file a motion or application with the court in the county in which the discovery is to be conducted. The motion or application is filed as a separate civil action bearing the caption shown on the subpoena, and the following phrase must appear below the case number of the newly filed action: "*Motion or Application Related to a Subpoena Issued Under Ariz.R.Civ.P. 45.1.*"

Any later motion or application relating to the same subpoena is filed in the same action. *See,* Ariz. R. Civ. P. 45.1(e). Rule 45.1 does not specify the procedure to be followed after the commencement of a separate civil action under Rule 45.1(e), but it is reasonably likely that the Arizona Rules of Civil Procedure will govern to such action, to the extent applicable.

To appear in court on any such matter, an out-of state attorney would have to comply with Arizona's *pro hac vice* procedures.

Rule 46. Exceptions unnecessary

Formal exceptions to rulings or orders of the court are unnecessary. It is sufficient that a party, at the time the ruling or order of the court is made or sought, makes known to the court the action which the party desires the court to take or the party's objection to the action of the court and the grounds therefor. If a party has no opportunity to object to a ruling or order at the time it is made, the absence of an objection does not thereafter prejudice the party.

Amended Sept. 15, 1987, effective Nov. 15, 1987.

AUTHORS' COMMENTS

Analysis

1. Scope and Purpose of Rule.
2. Comparison With Federal Rule.

1. *Scope and Purpose of Rule.* Rule 46 merely abolishes the unnecessarily formalistic procedure of requiring counsel to take an "exception" to rulings and orders of the Court in order to preserve an objection for appeal. The Rule does not, however, eliminate the requirement that an objection to an action taken by the Court, and the grounds therefor, be made known to the Court. *Moran v. Jones*, 75 Ariz. 175, 253 P.2d 891 (1953).

2. *Comparison With Federal Rule.* ARCP 46 is substantially identical to FRCP 46. In 2007, the language of FRCP 46 was amended as part of the general restyling of the Federal Rules of Civil Procedure to make the Federal Rules more easily understood and to make style and terminology consistent throughout the Federal Rules of Civil Procedure. Those stylistic modifications have not been incorporated into ARCP 46.

Rule 47. Jurors

(a) Trial Jury Procedure; List; Striking; Oath.

1. When an action is called for trial by jury, the clerk shall prepare and deposit in a box ballots containing the names of the jurors summoned who have appeared and have not been excused. The clerk shall then draw from the box as many names of jurors as the court directs. If the ballots are exhausted before the jury is completed, the court shall order to be forthwith drawn in the manner provided for other drawings of jurors, but without notice and without the attendance of officers other than the clerk, as many qualified persons as necessary to complete the jury.

2. Alternatively, in any court where data processing equipment is used and random selection of trial jurors can be accomplished by such equipment, the court may direct the jury commissioner to cause a list of jurors to be printed, at random, by the use of such equipment and delivered to the court. The clerk shall then read the names of jurors in the order printed. If the number of names appearing on the printed form is exhausted before the jury selection is completed the court shall order additional jurors drawn in the same manner.

3. After the jury is completed, the clerk shall make a list thereof and deliver it to the parties for peremptory challenges. The parties shall exercise their challenges by alternate strikes, beginning with the plaintiff, until the peremptory challenges are exhausted. Failure of a party to exercise a challenge in turn shall operate as a waiver of remaining challenges but shall not deprive the other party of that other party's full number of challenges. The list shall then be delivered to the clerk who shall call the first eight names remaining on the list who shall constitute the trial jury, and to whom an oath or affirmation shall then be administered in substance as follows: "You do solemnly swear (or affirm) that you will give careful attention to the proceedings, follow the court's instructions, including the admonition, and render a verdict in accordance with the law and evidence presented to you, so help you God." If a juror affirms, the clause "so help you God" shall be omitted.

Amended Aug. 28, 2013, effective January 1, 2014.

4. The court shall furnish counsel with the name, zip code, employment status, occupation, employer, residency status, education level, prior jury duty experience, and felony conviction status of prospective jurors in writing before the voir dire

examination is conducted on the day when jury selection is commenced within a specific time schedule as established by the court. The court shall keep all jurors' home and business telephone numbers and addresses confidential unless good cause is shown to the court which would require such disclosure.

Amended July 14, 1961, effective Nov. 1, 1961; April 3, 1978, effective May 1, 1978; Sept. 15, 1987, effective Nov. 15, 1987; Oct. 24, 1995, effective Dec. 1, 1995.

(b) Voir Dire Oath; Examination of Jurors; Brief Opening Statements.

1. Prior to examination of jurors with respect to their qualifications, an oath or examination shall be administered in substance as follows: "You do solemnly swear (or affirm) that you will well and truly answer all questions touching your qualifications to serve as a trial juror in the cause now on trial, so help you God." If a juror affirms, the clause "so help you God" shall be omitted.

2. Upon request and with the court's consent, the parties may present brief opening statements to the entire jury panel, prior to voir dire. The court may require counsel to present such opening statements.

3. The court shall control voir dire and conduct a thorough oral examination of prospective jurors. Upon the request of any party, the court shall permit that party a reasonable time to conduct a further oral examination of the prospective jurors. In courts of record, voir dire shall be conducted on the record unless waived by the parties on the record. The court may impose reasonable limitations with respect to questions allowed during a party's examination of the prospective jurors. The court shall ensure the privacy of prospective jurors is reasonably protected. The court may terminate or limit voir dire on grounds of abuse. Nothing in this Rule shall preclude the use of written questionnaires to be completed by the prospective jurors, in addition to oral examination. The court may permit written questions to be submitted following review and approval by the court.

Amended July 14, 1961, effective Nov. 1, 1961; July 9, 1991, effective Sept. 1, 1991; Oct. 24, 1995, effective Dec. 1, 1995; Sept. 16, 2008, effective January 1, 2009.

(c) Grounds of Challenge for Cause. Challenges to jurors for cause in civil actions may be taken on one or more of the following grounds:

1. Want of any qualifications prescribed by statute to render a person competent as a juror.

2. Standing in the relation of guardian and ward, master and servant, employer and clerk, or principal and agent to either

party, or being a member of a family of either party, or a partner in business with either party, or when a surety on a bond or obligation for either party.

3. Having served as a juror or been a witness on a previous trial between the same parties in the same action.

4. Having formed or expressed an unqualified opinion or belief as to the merits of the action or showing such a state of mind as will preclude the juror from rendering a just verdict, but in the trial of any action the fact that a person called as a juror has formed an opinion or impression based upon rumor or newspaper statements about the truth of which that person has expressed no opinion shall not disqualify that person to serve as a juror in such action, if the person, upon oath, states that the person believes the person can fairly and impartially render a verdict therein in accordance with the law and evidence, and the court is satisfied of the truth of such statement.

5. The existence of a state of mind evincing enmity or bias for or against either party.

6. The presence of any grounds for disqualification specified in A.R.S. § 21-211.

Amended Sept. 15, 1987, effective Nov. 15, 1987.

(d) Extent of Examination; Trial of Challenge. The examination of the jurors touching their qualifications to serve shall not be restricted to the grounds of challenge for cause, but may extend to any legitimate inquiry which might disclose a basis for exercise of a peremptory challenge. Challenges for cause shall be tried by the court. Upon the trial of the challenge to an individual juror for cause the juror challenged and any other material witness produced by the parties shall be examined on oath by the court and may be so examined by either party.

(e) Manner of Challenging; Number of Peremptory Challenges. Each side shall be entitled to four peremptory challenges. For the purposes of this rule, each case, whether a single action or two or more actions consolidated or consolidated for trial, shall be treated as having only two sides. Whenever it appears that two or more parties on a side have an adverse or hostile interest, the court may allow additional peremptory challenges, but each side shall have an equal number of peremptory challenges. If the parties on a side are unable to agree upon the allocation of peremptory challenges among themselves, the allocation shall be determined by the court. Any individual party, without consent of any other party, may challenge for cause.

Amended July 1, 1968, effective Jan. 1, 1969.

(f) Alternate Jurors. The court may direct that not more than six jurors in addition to the regular jury be called and impanelled to sit as alternate jurors. Alternate jurors shall be drawn in the same manner, shall have the same qualifications, shall be subject to the same examination and challenges, shall take the same oath, and shall have the same functions, powers, facilities, and privileges as the regular jurors. If alternate jurors are impanelled, their identity shall not be determined until the end of trial. At the time of impanelment, the trial judge should inform the jurors that at the end of the case, the alternates will be determined by lot in a drawing held in open court. The trial judge shall also explain the need for alternate jurors and the procedure regarding alternates to be followed at the end of trial. The alternate, or alternates, upon being physically excused by the court at the end of trial, shall be instructed to continue to observe the admonitions to jurors until they are informed that a verdict has been returned or the jury discharged. In the event a deliberating juror is excused due to inability or disqualification to perform required duties, the court may substitute an alternate juror, choosing from among the alternates in the order previously designated, unless disqualified, to join in the deliberations. If an alternate joins the deliberations, the jury shall be instructed to begin deliberations anew. Each side is entitled to 1 peremptory challenge in addition to those otherwise allowed by law if 1 or 2 alternate jurors are to be impanelled, 2 peremptory challenges if 3 or 4 alternate jurors are to be impanelled, and 3 peremptory challenges if 5 or 6 alternate jurors are to be impanelled.

Amended July 1, 1966, effective Nov. 1, 1966; Oct. 24, 1995, effective Dec. 1, 1995.

(g) Juror Notebooks. In its discretion, the court may authorize documents and exhibits to be included in notebooks for use by the jurors during trial to aid them in performing their duties.

Added Oct. 24, 1995, effective Dec. 1, 1995.

STATE BAR COMMITTEE NOTES

1961 Amendments

Rule 47(a)(2) now compels the plaintiff to exercise all of his peremptory challenges prior to the defendant. Proposed amended Rule 47(a)(2) [now (3)] provides that the parties shall exercise their peremptory challenges alternately. Under the present rule, while the plaintiff receives the same number of peremptory challenges as the defendant, the order of exercising them resulted in an obvious inequity. The purpose of the proposed rule is to eliminate this inequity by giving both parties peremptory challenges which are not only equal in number but also in practical weight and value.

The amended rule is patterned substantially but not exactly after the rule presently in effect in the State of Oregon (O.R.S. 17.160). A review of the rules and customs of some forty jurisdictions in the United States indicates that 31 states have the "alternative challenge" system. In only one other jurisdiction, is plaintiff required to exercise all of his peremptory challenges prior to defendant.

Present Rule 47(a)(2) provides for the substance of the oath to be administered to the jury. The present form of oath requires that the plaintiff and defendant be named. This not only unduly complicates administration of the oath by the clerk of the court, especially where the parties are several and may involve crossclaimants, counterclaimants, etc., but also may be subject to error in that certain parties have often been eliminated or added. The change in juror's oath proposed herein conforms very closely to that administered in criminal cases under Criminal Rule 230-A [see, now Rules Cr.Proc., Rule 18.6].

Rule 47(b) now contains only that portion appearing as proposed 47(b)(2). The new portion consisting of 47(b)(1) provides for voir dire oath to be administered to the jury prior to examination of jurors as to qualifications. Although such oath has been administered as a matter of practice by many of our courts in civil proceedings, a requirement for it is not now provided in the Rules. This requirement substantially conforms with that presently prescribed for criminal proceedings by Criminal Rule 217 [see, now, Rules Cr.Proc., Rule 18.5].

1966 Amendment

[Rule 47(f)] The amendment is made for the purpose of conformity with the Federal Rule. The revision of this subdivision brings it into line with a revision of Rule 24(c) of the Federal Rules of Criminal Procedure proposed by the Advisory Committee on Criminal Rules. Rule 24(c) now allows four alternate jurors, as contrasted with the two allowed in civil cases, and it is proposed to increase the number to a maximum of six in all cases. The Note of the Advisory Committee on Criminal Rules points to experience demonstrating that four alternates may not be enough in some lengthy criminal trials; and the same may be said of civil trials. The Note adds:

> "The words 'or are found to be' are added to the second sentence to make clear that an alternate juror may be called in the situation where it is first discovered during the trial that a juror was unable or disqualified to perform his duties at the time he was sworn."

1968 Amendment

[Rule 47(e)] The original rule required several parties on a side to join in each peremptory challenge. This frequently caused problems when parties on the same side of a case had interests adverse or hostile to each other. Provisions for additional peremptory challenges where there are multiple parties on a side are not unusual. See, for example, 28 U.S.C.A. § 1870; Ill. Anno. Stats., Ch. 110, § 66 [now, Smith-Hurd Illinois Annotated Statutes ch. 110, par. 2-1106]; and Rule 543(a)(4), Maryland Rules of Procedure.

The provision that each case shall be treated as having only two sides is intended to forestall any contention that there may be more than two sides because of cross-claims or third party claims. Before additional peremptory challenges may be allowed the court must determine whether any parties on a side have adverse or hostile interests. The number of additional peremptory challenges allowed is discretionary with the court.

1987 Amendment

Rule 47(c)(6) is intended to eliminate any possible ambiguity, or perceived conflict, between the provisions of the Rule and A.R.S. § 21-211.

1991 Amendment

The 1991 amendment substituted a new version of Rule 47(b)(2) for the former version, which operated to make voir dire examination of prospective jurors by counsel discretionary with the court. The new version makes clear that counsel have a *right* to conduct voir dire examination of prospective jurors, subject to the court's authority to set reasonable limitations thereon and to prevent abuses.

COURT COMMENT

1995 Amendments

[Rule 47(a)(1)] Prior to the 1995 amendment, Rule 47(a)(1) was read to require trial judges to use the traditional "strike and replace" method of jury selection, where only a portion of the jury panel is examined, the remaining jurors being called upon to participate in jury selection only upon excusal for cause of a juror in the initial group. Challenges for cause are heard and decided with the jurors being examined in the box. A juror excused for cause leaves the courtroom in the presence and view of the other panel members, after which the excused juror's position is filled by a panel member who responds to all previous and future questions of the potential jurors.

The purpose of this amendment is to allow the trial judge to use the "struck" method of selection if the judge chooses. This procedure is thought by some to offer more advantages than the "strike and replace" method. See T. Munsterman, R. Strand and J. Hart, The Best Method of Selecting Jurors, The Judges' Journal 9 (Summer 1990); A.B.A. Standards Relating to Juror Use and Management, Standard 7, at 68–74 (1983); and "The Jury Project," Report to the Chief Judge of the State of New York 58–60 (1984).

The "struck" method calls for all of the jury panel members to participate in voir dire examination by the judge and counsel. Although the judge may excuse jurors for cause in the presence of the panel, challenges for cause are usually reserved until the examination of the panel has been completed and a recess taken. Following disposition of the for cause challenges, the juror list is given to counsel for the exercise of their peremptory strikes. When all the peremptory strikes have been taken, and all legal issues arising therefrom have been resolved, the clerk calls the first eight names remaining on the list, plus the number of alternate jurors thought necessary by the judge, who shall be the trial jury.

[Rule 47(b)(2)] Under the 1995 amendment to Rule 47(b)(2), the judge can control the length and content of the parties' voir dire. The court should instruct counsel that voir dire is permitted to enable counsel to propound questions seeking relevant information from and about the jurors but not to ask questions intended to impart information or arguments to the jurors. The court should be particularly sensitive to the prejudice which can arise from voir dire by an unrepresented party.

[Rule 47(g)] In trials of unusual duration or involving complex issues, juror notebooks are a significant aid to juror comprehension and recall of evidence. At a minimum notebooks should contain: (1) a copy of the preliminary jury instructions, (2) jurors' notes, (3) witnesses' names, photographs and/or biographies, (4) copies of key documents and an index of all exhibits, (5) a glossary of technical terms, and (6) a copy of the court's final instructions. The preliminary jury instructions should be removed, discarded and replaced by the final jury instructions before the latter are read to the jury by the court.

AUTHORS' COMMENTS

Analysis

6. Challenges of Jurors for Cause.
7. Peremptory Challenges of Prospective Jurors.
8. Alternate Jurors.

1. *Scope and Purpose of Rule.* Rule 47 contains a number of specific provisions governing the manner in which trial jurors are selected in civil cases. Rule 47(a) specifies the procedure for selection of jury panels, for affording an opportunity for challenges to jurors, and for swearing the jurors eventually selected. Rule 47(c) sets forth the grounds upon which a juror may be challenged for cause, but Rule 47(d) specifies that the examination of the panel is not restricted to those grounds, and that any challenges for cause are to be tried to the Court.

Under Rule 47(e), each side is also entitled to four peremptory challenges. A party is entitled to a fair and impartial jury, but the failure to make a timely objection to the manner in which the jury is being empaneled operates as a waiver of any irregularity. *Moran v. Jones*, 75 Ariz. 175, 253 P.2d 891 (1953).

2. *Comparison With Federal Rule.* Although both ARCP 47 and FRCP 47 deal with the subject of trial jurors, these two rules bear almost no resemblance to each other, particularly after the 1991 amendment to the Federal Rule which eliminated the use of alternate jurors and the 1995 "jury reform" amendments to the Arizona Rule.

The only common provision deals with the right of the parties to conduct voir dire, and those provisions differ substantively. ARCP 47(b)(3) requires the Court to allow the parties a reasonable time to examine prospective trial jurors; under FRCP 47(a) it remains discretionary with the trial court whether to permit parties or their counsel to conduct any such examination.

3. *Alternative Methods for Selecting Jurors.* Before the 1995 "jury reform" amendments, Rule 47(a)(1) was generally interpreted as requiring trial judges to use the "strike and replace" method for selecting the trial jury from the pool of jurors summoned for that purpose. Under that method, only a portion of the pool of jurors is subjected to *voir dire* examination, and the remaining jurors only participate if one of those originally selected for examination is excused, for cause or other considerations.

The 1995 amendment to Rule 47(a)(1) gives trial judges discretion and authority to employ the alternative "struck" method for jury selection. Under the "struck" method, the entire jury pool participates in the *voir dire* examination. Challenges for cause are then heard and decided. The list of remaining jurors is then provided to counsel for the exercise of their peremptory strikes.

The clerk then calls the first eight names that remain on the jury list, plus the number of alternates the judge has decided to employ, and that constitutes the trial jury.

4. *Pre-Voir Dire Opening Statements.* As part of the 1995 "jury reform" amendments, Rule 47(b)(2) was amended to insert a provision that permits the parties, with the Court's permission, to present brief opening statements to the entire pool of potential jurors before the commencement of the *voir dire* examination to select the eventual jury. The amendment also authorizes the Court, on its own motion, to require the parties to make such pre-*voir dire* opening statements.

5. *Voir Dire Examination of Prospective Jurors.* The purpose of permitting examination of the jury panel on their qualifications to serve as trial jurors is to permit the parties to intelligently exercise their right to challenge jurors, either for cause or peremptorily. *Wilson v. Wiggins*, 54 Ariz. 240, 94 P.2d 870 (1939). Under Rule 47(d), examination is not limited to the grounds of challenge for cause, and parties have the right on *voir dire* to ascertain whether any jurors have an interest in the case which would influence their verdict. *Dunipace v. Martin*, 73 Ariz. 415, 242 P.2d 543 (1952).

Rule 47(b) was amended in 1991 to discourage what was becoming a frequent practice of having the *voir dire* examination of prospective jurors conducted exclusively by the Court. Under that amendment, the Court was to conduct a preliminary oral examination of prospective jurors, and was then to permit the parties, on request, to conduct a further oral examination of the prospective jurors, subject to any limitations the Court had imposed on the questions that could be asked.

Rule 47(b) was again amended as part of the 1995 "jury reform" amendments. Under the Rule as amended, the Court is to initially conduct a "thorough" oral examination of the prospective jurors. The parties are then to be permitted to conduct a further oral examination, but the Court retains the right to impose reasonable limitations on the questions that can be asked. In addition, the Court may terminate or limit *voir dire* examination by the parties for abuse. The Court Comment to that amendment indicates that the Court should advise the parties and counsel that the purpose of *voir dire* examination is to elicit pertinent information from the jurors, and not to impart information or arguments to the prospective jury panel.

The 1995 amendment to Rule 47(b)(2) retained the provision added by the 1991 amendment which indirectly authorized the use of written questionnaires to be completed by prospective jurors. In addition, Rule 47(a)(4) was added, which provides that the Court is to furnish counsel, on the date set for jury selection but before the commencement of *voir dire*, with the name, zip code, employment status, occupation, employer, residency status, education level, prior jury experience, and felony conviction status of the prospective jurors who will constitute the jury pool. The jurors' home and business telephone numbers and addresses are to be kept confidential, absent a showing of good cause to the Court for their disclosure.

The Rule was again amended in 2009 to make it even clearer that the court is to control the conduct of voir dire, and is to ensure that the privacy of prospective jurors is reasonably protected. The amendment also added a requirement that voir dire in courts of record be conducted on the record unless the parties formally waive that requirement.

6. *Challenges of Jurors for Cause.* There is no limit on the number of challenges for cause that a party may make, but the grounds of challenge are those specified in Rule 47(c) and A.R.S. § 21-211. They include: relationship to the parties, prior service as a juror in the same matter, and bias or prejudice. The fact that a juror has formed an opinion or impression about the case from rumors or media stories is not *ipso facto* grounds for disqualification if the juror states under oath that he or she can fairly and impartially render a verdict and the Court is satisfied that that is the case.

Jurors who are insured by an insurance company that is a party in a case, however, have a direct financial interest in the outcome if they know or have reason to believe that their premiums may increase depending on the outcome, and it is an abuse of discretion for the trial court to fail to excuse such jurors for cause. *Lopez v. Farmers Ins. Co. of Arizona*, 177 Ariz. 371, 868 P.2d 954 (Ct. App. Div. 1 1993).

A juror's affidavit or testimony is admissible to show improper acts by third parties or the failure by *that juror* to disclose bias and prejudice upon *voir dire* examination. *Richtmyre v. State*, 175 Ariz. 489, 858 P.2d 322 (Ct. App. Div. 1 1993); *Brooks v. Zahn*, 170 Ariz. 545, 826 P.2d 1171 (Ct. App. Div. 1 1991). Testimony or an affidavit from one juror is not admissible to show another juror's failure to disclose bias and prejudice. *Richtmyre v. State*, 175 Ariz. 489, 858 P.2d 322 (Ct. App. Div. 1 1993); *Brooks v. Zahn*, 170 Ariz. 545, 826 P.2d 1171 (Ct. App. Div. 1 1991).

A juror is competent to offer testimony to impeach a verdict in a civil case only on the question whether any outside influence was improperly brought to the jury's attention. *Brooks v. Zahn*, 170 Ariz. 545, 826 P.2d 1171 (Ct. App. Div. 1 1991). Specialized knowledge possessed by a juror, however, and discussed during deliberations cannot be categorized as extrinsic and extraneous information. *Brooks v. Zahn*, 170 Ariz. 545, 826 P.2d 1171 (Ct. App. Div. 1 1991).

The purpose of giving parties both challenges for cause and peremptory challenges is to secure a fair and impartial jury. *Wilson v. Wiggins*, 54 Ariz. 240, 94 P.2d 870 (1939). Challenges for cause are, however, to be tried to the court, and the denial or allowance of a challenge is a matter committed to the trial court's discretion. *J. & B. Motors v. Margolis*, 75 Ariz. 392, 257 P.2d 588, 38 A.L.R.2d 946 (1953); *Lopez v. Farmers Ins. Co. of Arizona*, 177 Ariz. 371, 868 P.2d 954 (Ct. App. Div. 1 1993); *Lindley v. Northwest Hosp. & Medical Center, Inc.*, 164 Ariz. 133, 791 P.2d 659 (Ct. App. Div. 2 1990). It is grounds for reversal to force a party to use peremptory challenges to strike jurors who should have been removed for cause. *Lindley v. Northwest Hosp. & Medical Center, Inc.*, 164 Ariz. 133, 791 P.2d 659 (Ct. App. Div. 2 1990).

7. *Peremptory Challenges of Prospective Jurors.* The right to exercise peremptory challenges is one of the most important rights granted to litigants in the effort to insure a fair and impartial jury. *Lindley v. Northwest Hosp. & Medical Center, Inc.*, 164 Ariz. 133, 791 P.2d 659 (Ct. App. Div. 2 1990); *Board of Trustees Eloy Elementary School Dist. v. McEwen*, 6 Ariz. App. 148, 430 P.2d 727 (1967); *but cf. Moran v. Jones*, 75 Ariz. 175, 253 P.2d 891 (1953).

Under Rule 47(e), each side is entitled to four peremptory challenges, but each case is presumptively viewed as having only two sides. (The number of peremptory challenges allowed increases if alternate jurors are seated, according to the formula set forth in Rule 47(f).)

If the trial court finds that parties nominally on the same "side" have adverse or hostile interests, it may allow additional peremptory challenges, but the same number must be granted to both "sides." Rule 47(a)(3) prescribes that peremptory challenges are to be exercised by the parties alternately in turns, and the failure of a party to exercise a challenge in turn operates as a waiver of any challenges remaining. Rule 47(a)(3).

8. *Alternate Jurors.* The court may sit up to six (6) additional jurors as alternates, who are to be selected in the same manner as regular jurors. The number of peremptory challenges permitted each side increases according to the number of alternate jurors seated, as specified in Rule 47(f).

The procedures for selecting and using alternate jurors were altered significantly by the 1995 "jury reform" amendments to Rule 47(f). Before the amendments, the identities of those selected as alternate jurors were known from the conclusion of the jury selection process, and alternate jurors replaced regular jurors in the order in which the alternates were called. Under Rule 47(f), as amended, the identity of the alternate jurors is not determined until the end of the trial, when they are to be selected by lot in a drawing held in open court.

Alternates thus selected who are physically excused at that point are to be instructed to continue to observe the Court's admonitions to the jurors until they are advised that a verdict has been returned or the jury has been discharged. If a juror selected for deliberations is excused before a verdict is reached, the Court may then substitute an alternate juror, in an order previously determined. If an alternate is thus substituted, the jury is to be instructed to begin deliberations anew.

Rule 48. Juries of less than eight; majority verdict

The parties may stipulate that the jury shall consist of any number less than eight but not less than three, or that a verdict or a finding of a stated majority of the jurors shall be taken as the verdict or finding of the jury.

Amended Sept. 15, 1987, effective Nov. 15, 1987.

AUTHORS' COMMENTS

Analysis

1. *Scope and Purpose of Rule.* In Arizona, the size, and degree of unanimity required, of civil juries is governed by statute, A.R.S. § 21-102(C). Rule 48 was amended in 1987 to conform its title and text to the current statutory provision that civil juries consist of eight (8) persons. The parties may stipulate to a smaller jury panel, but not one of less than three (3). The parties may also stipulate as to the number of jurors necessary for the rendering of a verdict, whether the jury panel consists of eight (8) members or a lesser number that has been agreed to. Absent a stipulation to the number of jurors required to reach a verdict, the concurrence of six (6) jurors is required. A.R.S. § 21-102(C).

Jurors who vote against finding liability during the course of deliberations should nevertheless participate in the determination of the amount of damages to be awarded, and it is fundamental error to instruct the jury otherwise. *Perkins v. Komarnyckyj*, 172 Ariz. 115, 834 P.2d 1260 (1992). The constitutional right of trial by jury carries with it the right to have every issue tried by the jury that has been empaneled, not by two-thirds or three-fourths, or any other fraction of that jury. Depriving the parties of their right to have all the jurors participate in deciding all of the issues is inherently prejudicial and fundamental error, requiring reversal without any further showing of prejudice. *Perkins v. Komarnyckyj*, 172 Ariz. 115, 834 P.2d 1260 (1992).

2. *Comparison With Federal Rule.* In addition to structural difference, ARCP 48 differs materially from FRCP 48. As a consequence of the 1991 amendments to the Federal Rule which reflected the elimination of alternate jurors. The Arizona Rule assumes a standard jury size of eight (8) persons, and permits the parties to stipulate to a jury of less than eight (8) but not less

than three (3) persons. As amended, FRCP 48 permits the Court to seat a jury of between six (6) and twelve (12) persons, and provides that all jurors are to deliberate, unless excused, that verdicts must be unanimous, and that a verdict may not be taken from a jury of less than six (6) members.

In 2009, FRCP 48 was amended to include a new provision that allows a court on its own to poll the jury and requires polling at a parties' request. As explained in the 2009 Comment to this amendment, FRCP 48(c) was drawn, with minor revisions, from Rule 31(d), Federal Rules of Criminal Procedure. ARCP 48 does not contain a similar provision. *Cf.* Rule 23.4, Arizona Rules of Criminal Procedure.

Rule 49. Special and general verdicts and interrogatories

(a) Return of Verdict by Six or More Jurors; Presentation in Court. When eight jurors have been impaneled to try the action, and if there has been no stipulation as provided in Rule 48 entered in the minutes of the trial as provided by A.R.S. § 21-102, the concurrence of six or more jurors shall be sufficient to render a verdict therein. When the eight jurors unanimously agree upon a verdict, the verdict shall be signed by the foreman and returned into court. When the jurors do not unanimously agree upon a verdict, but six or more agree, the jurors who agree shall each sign the verdict agreed upon, then notify the court of that fact, and thereupon the jury shall be returned into court and deliver to the court the verdict so signed. The court shall receive and cause the verdict to be read and recorded, and judgment shall be entered thereon.

Amended Sept. 15, 1987, effective Nov. 15, 1987.

(b) Proceedings on Return of Verdict. When the jurors have agreed upon a verdict, they shall be conducted into court by the officer having them in charge. The clerk shall read the verdict and shall inquire of the jury, or jurors agreeing, if it is their verdict. If any such juror disagrees as to the verdict, the jury shall again retire to consider the case further, but if no juror disagrees, the court shall receive the verdict and order it to be entered in the minutes, and the jury shall be discharged. Where a verdict is rendered by six or more jurors the verdict shall be received unless a juror signing the verdict disagrees therewith.

Amended Sept. 15, 1987, effective Nov. 15, 1987.

(c) Defective or Nonresponsive Verdict. If the verdict is informal or defective, the court may direct it to be reformed at the bar, and where there has been a manifest miscalculation of interest, the court may direct a computation thereof at the bar, and the verdict may, if the jury assents thereto, be reformed in accordance with such computation. If the verdict is not responsive to the issue submitted to the jury, the court shall call the jurors' attention thereto, and send them back for further deliberation.

(d) Fixing Amount of Recovery. When a verdict is found for the plaintiff in an action for recovery of money, and for the defendant upon a counterclaim or cross-claim for recovery of money, the jury shall find the amount of recovery on each claim, and the court shall render judgment in favor of the party entitled thereto for the difference in the amounts of such verdicts.

(e) Special Form of Verdict Not Required. No special form of verdict is required. Where there has been a substantial compliance with the law in rendering a verdict, the judgment shall be rendered and entered thereon notwithstanding a defect in the form of the verdict.

(f) Polling Jury; Procedure. When the verdict is announced either party may require the jury to be polled, which shall be done by the clerk asking each juror separately if the verdict returned is that juror's verdict. If any juror answers in the negative, the jury shall again be sent out for further deliberation, but if each juror concurs in the verdict it shall be received and noted in the minutes, except as provided by subdivision (c) of this Rule, and the jury shall be discharged.

Amended Sept. 15, 1987, effective Nov. 15, 1987; Jan 26, 2004, effective June 1, 2004.

(g) Special Verdicts and Interrogatories. The court may require a jury to return only a special verdict in the form of a special written finding upon each issue of fact. In that event the court may submit to the jury written questions susceptible of categorical or other brief answer or may submit written forms of the several special findings which might properly be made under the pleadings and evidence, or it may use such other method of submitting the issues and requiring the written findings thereon as it deems most appropriate. The court shall give to the jury such explanation and instruction concerning the matter thus submitted as may be necessary to enable the jury to make its findings upon each issue. If in so doing the court omits any issue of fact raised by the pleadings or by the evidence, each party waives the right to a trial by jury of the issue so omitted unless before the jury retires the party demands its submission to the jury. As to an issue omitted without such demand the court may make a finding, or, if it fails to do so, it shall be deemed to have made a finding in accord with the judgment on the special verdict.

Amended Sept. 15, 1987, effective Nov. 15, 1987.

(h) General Verdict Accompanied by Answer to Interrogatories. The court may submit to the jury, together with appropriate forms for a general verdict, written interrogatories upon one or more issues of fact the decision of which is necessary to a verdict. The court shall give such explanation or instruction as may be necessary to enable the jury both to make answers to the interrogatories and to render a general verdict, and the court shall direct the jury both to make written answers and to render a general verdict. When the general verdict and the answers are harmonious, the court shall direct the entry of the appropriate judgment upon the verdict and answers. When the answers are consistent with each other but one or more is inconsistent with the general verdict, the court may direct the entry of judgment in accordance with the answers, notwithstanding the general verdict or may return the jury for further consideration of its answers and verdict or may order a new trial. When the answers are inconsistent with each other and one or more is likewise inconsistent with the general verdict, the court shall not direct the entry of judgment but may return the jury for further consideration of its answers and verdict or may order a new trial.

Amended Sept. 15, 1987, effective Nov. 15, 1987.

AUTHORS' COMMENTS

Analysis

1. *Scope and Purpose of Rule.* Rule 49 deals generally with forms of verdict and contemplates three basic alternatives. Under Rule 49(e), there is no special form of verdict that is required in any given instance. A party desiring a particular form of verdict must submit the issue and verdict forms to the trial court or the issue is waived for any appeal. *Kelman v. Bohi*, 27 Ariz. App. 24, 550 P.2d 671 (Div. 1 1976).

There is little Arizona case law on the interplay between jury instructions and forms of verdict. The purpose of jury instructions is to inform the jury of the applicable law in understandable terms. The form of verdict is then used by the jury to record its decision made pursuant to the instructions it has received from the Court. Any instructions to the jury contained in the verdict form are to be considered together with the instructions as a whole. *Mullin v. Brown*, 210 Ariz. 545, 115 P.3d 139 (Ct. App. Div. 2 2005).

2. *Comparison With Federal Rule.* ARCP 49(g) is essentially the same as FRCP 49(a); and, ARCP 49(h) is substantially identical to FRCP 49(b). The Federal Rules of Civil Procedure, however, do not contain provisions that correspond to ARCP 49(a) to (f).

In 2007, the language of FRCP 49 was amended as part of the

general restyling of the Federal Rules of Civil Procedure to make the Federal Rules more easily understood and to make style and terminology consistent throughout the Federal Rules of Civil Procedure. Those stylistic modifications have not been incorporated into ARCP 49.

3. *General Verdicts.* The most common form of verdict employed is the general verdict. A general verdict implies a finding by the jury on every essential fact in favor of the prevailing party. *King & Johnson Rental Equipment Co. v. Superior Court, In and For Pima County*, 123 Ariz. 256, 599 P.2d 212 (1979). Where the jury renders a verdict that determines liability but awards damages that are clearly an arithmetic error, the trial court may correct that on a motion seeking that relief. *Banner Realty, Inc. v. Turek*, 113 Ariz. 62, 546 P.2d 798 (1976). An inconsistent verdict, however, cannot stand. *Gonzales v. City of Tucson*, 124 Ariz. 450, 604 P.2d 1161 (Ct. App. Div. 2 1979).

Similarly, a verdict, like a judgment, may not be based upon a contingency. Where a trial court determines that the true intent of the jury was to make a contingent award, it must order a new trial. *Wright v. Mayberry*, 158 Ariz. 387, 762 P.2d 1341 (Ct. App. Div. 1 1988). The failure to request reformation, or resubmission to the jury, of such a defective verdict, does not necessarily result in a waiver of the objection. *Wright v. Mayberry*, 158 Ariz. 387, 762 P.2d 1341 (Ct. App. Div. 1 1988). See the discussion in Section 8, *infra*.

In the absence of a request for an instruction that the jury bring in a separate verdict on each count, or motion for a directed verdict on each count, where several counts, issues, or theories are tried and submitted to the jury, a general verdict will stand if the evidence on one count, issue, or theory is sufficient to sustain the verdict. *Dunlap v. Jimmy GMC of Tucson, Inc.*, 136 Ariz. 338, 666 P.2d 83 (Ct. App. Div. 2 1983); *Murcott v. Best Western Intern., Inc.*, 198 Ariz. 349, 9 P.3d 1088, 16 I.E.R. Cas. (BNA) 1277 (Ct. App. Div. 1 2000), as amended on other grounds, (Oct. 16, 2000) (appellate court "will uphold a general verdict if evidence on any one count, issue or theory sustains the verdict."); *Reese v. Cradit*, 12 Ariz. App. 233, 469 P.2d 467 (Div. 2 1970).

If counsel for a defendant wants to preserve for appeal an issue whether any count, issue or theory was erroneously submitted for the jury's consideration, it may be necessary for counsel to request a special verdict and/or object to the use of a general verdict form, even if the issue has previously been raised on a motion for judgment as a matter of law. *Mullin v. Brown*, 210 Ariz. 545, 115 P.3d 139 (Ct. App. Div. 2 2005); *Dunlap v. Jimmy GMC of Tucson, Inc.*, 136 Ariz. 338, 666 P.2d 83 (Ct. App. Div. 2 1983).

4. *General Verdicts in Cases Involving Equitable Claims.* Where both legal and equitable claims are pursued together, the jury may be permitted to consider all legal claims and all issues common to both claims. In such cases, the jury's finding becomes advisory as to the equitable relief sought. It is not proper, however, to use a general verdict form and to treat all claims as legal in nature and the jury's verdict as binding on all claims. *Timmons v. City of Tucson*, 171 Ariz. 350, 830 P.2d 871, 63 Fair Empl. Prac. Cas. (BNA) 11 (Ct. App. Div. 2 1991).

5. *Special Verdicts.* Under Rule 49(g), the trial court can require a special verdict consisting of written findings, generally in the form of answers to questions, on each issue of fact presented. In an action at law, a special verdict is binding on the Court if there is evidence to support it. *Deyoe v. Clark Equipment Co., Inc.*, 134 Ariz. 281, 655 P.2d 1333 (Ct. App. Div. 2 1982); *Commercial Credit Equipment Corp. v. Kelland*, 101 Ariz. 477, 421 P.2d 325 (1966). Any fact issues not submitted to the jury are deemed to have been resolved by the trial court in a fashion that supports the judgment entered. *Kammert Bros. Enterprises, Inc. v. Tanque Verde Plaza Co.*, 4 Ariz. App. 349, 420 P.2d 592 (1966), vacated on other grounds, 102 Ariz. 301, 428 P.2d 678 (1967).

The issues are generally submitted to the jury in the form of questions that can be answered "yes" or "no" or with some other brief response. The questions can be purely factual in nature, or a mixture of fact and law. The jury should be instructed as to how to complete the questions and as to the definitions of any special legal terms employed in the questions.

If the Court omits from the issues or questions submitted to the jury any issue of fact raised by the pleadings or the evidence, a party must demand that the issue be submitted to the jury before it retires for its deliberations and the failure to do so operates as a waiver of the right to trial by jury on the issue omitted. *See,* Ariz. R. Civ. P. 49(g). A trial court's decision to submit special interrogatories to the jury will be reviewed on appeal only for an abuse of discretion. *Lohmeier v. Hammer*, 214 Ariz. 57, 148 P.3d 101 (Ct. App. Div. 1 2006).

Any fact issues not submitted to the jury are deemed to have been resolved by the trial court in a fashion that supports the judgment entered. *Kammert Bros. Enterprises, Inc. v. Tanque Verde Plaza Co.*, 4 Ariz. App. 349, 420 P.2d 592 (1966), vacated on other grounds, 102 Ariz. 301, 428 P.2d 678 (1967).

6. *General Verdicts With Interrogatories.* The final alternative is that authorized by Rule 49(h), a general verdict, together with written interrogatories for the jurors to answer. Whether to submit written interrogatories is discretionary with the trial court, and its determination to do so will be reversed on appeal

only for an abuse of that discretion. *Lohmeier v. Hammer*, 214 Ariz. 57, 148 P.3d 101 (Ct. App. Div. 1 2006). Such a verdict form may create difficulty where the responses to the interrogatories are not consistent with the general verdict returned.

Where the jury's answers to interrogatories are consistent with each other, but inconsistent with the general verdict, the Court may (1) enter judgment in accordance with the interrogatory answers, (2) order further deliberations by the jury, or (3) order a new trial. Where the answers are internally inconsistent, however, the Court may not enter a judgment but is limited to directing further deliberations or ordering a new trial. A signed order granting a mistrial under Rule 49(h) in effect grants a new trial and is an appealable order under A.R.S. § 12-2101(F)(1). *Hall Family Properties, Ltd. v. Gosnell Development Corp.*, 185 Ariz. 382, 916 P.2d 1098 (Ct. App. Div. 1 1995). Whether to grant a mistrial or new trial under this section of the Rule is a decision committed to the trial court's discretion and will be disturbed on appeal only for an abuse of that discretion. *Hall Family Properties, Ltd. v. Gosnell Development Corp.*, 185 Ariz. 382, 916 P.2d 1098 (Ct. App. Div. 1 1995).

7. *Use of Juror Testimony to Impeach Verdict.* Testimony or affidavits from jurors will not be admitted to impeach a verdict unless they involve matters that are not inherent in the verdict. *Brooks v. Zahn*, 170 Ariz. 545, 826 P.2d 1171 (Ct. App. Div. 1 1991); *Maxwell v. Aetna Life Ins. Co.*, 143 Ariz. 205, 693 P.2d 348 (Ct. App. Div. 1 1984); *Ott v. Samaritan Health Service*, 127 Ariz. 485, 622 P.2d 44 (Ct. App. Div. 1 1980); *Valley Nat. Bank of Arizona v. Haney*, 27 Ariz. App. 692, 558 P.2d 720 (Div. 1 1976). A juror's testimony is admissible to show an error in the judgment as not confirming to the jury's findings, improper acts by third parties, or failure by *that juror* to disclose bias and prejudice. *Richtmyre v. State*, 175 Ariz. 489, 858 P.2d 322 (Ct. App. Div. 1 1993); *Brooks v. Zahn*, 170 Ariz. 545, 826 P.2d 1171 (Ct. App. Div. 1 1991).

A juror is competent to offer testimony to impeach a verdict in a civil case only on the question whether any outside influence was improperly brought to the jury's attention. *Brooks v. Zahn*, 170 Ariz. 545, 826 P.2d 1171 (Ct. App. Div. 1 1991). Specialized knowledge possessed by a juror, however, and discussed during deliberations cannot be categorized as extrinsic and extraneous information. *Brooks v. Zahn*, 170 Ariz. 545, 826 P.2d 1171 (Ct. App. Div. 1 1991).

8. *Inconsistent Verdicts; Nonresponsive Verdicts.* Rule 49(c) provides that, if a verdict is not responsive to the issue submitted, the Court is to call that to the jury's attention and send the jurors back for further deliberations. When a verdict is nonre-

sponsive, resubmission to the jury is appropriate to give the jury an opportunity to decide the case properly and prevent unnecessary litigation. *Piper v. Bear Medical Systems, Inc.*, 180 Ariz. 170, 883 P.2d 407, Prod. Liab. Rep. (CCH) P 13766 (Ct. App. Div. 1 1993).

Where a jury fails to specify the disposition of a counterclaim in its verdict, the verdict is nonresponsive within the meaning of Rule 49(c). A party who fails to ask the trial court to call the jurors' attention to the oversight and to send them back for further deliberations, however, cannot raise that issue as error on appeal. *Farmers Ins. Co. v. Tallsalt*, 191 Ariz. 177, 953 P.2d 921 (Ct. App. Div. 1 1997), vacated in part on other grounds, 192 Ariz. 129, 962 P.2d 203 (1998);

Similarly, where inconsistent verdicts are returned, the error may be capable of correction by resubmission to the jury if it is raised as soon as the verdicts are returned, and the failure to do so may constitute a waiver of the defect. *Gonzalez v. Gonzalez*, 181 Ariz. 32, 887 P.2d 562 (Ct. App. Div. 2 1994). Requiring that an objection to a defective verdict be made at trial provides the trial court with an opportunity to correct the error with minimal effort and expense, particularly when the defect or inconsistency is one that can be readily corrected by further deliberations on the part of the jury. *Trustmark Ins. Co. v. Bank One, Arizona, NA*, 202 Ariz. 535, 48 P.3d 485, 48 U.C.C. Rep. Serv. 2d 276 (Ct. App. Div. 1 2002), as corrected, (June 19, 2002).

Rule 50. Judgment as a matter of law in actions tried by jury; alternative motion for new trial; conditional rulings

(a) Judgment as a Matter of Law.

(1) If during a trial by jury a party has been fully heard on an issue and there is no legally sufficient evidentiary basis for a reasonable jury to find for that party on that issue, the court may determine the issue against the party and may grant a motion for judgment as a matter of law against that party with respect to a claim or defense that cannot under the controlling law be maintained or defeated without a favorable finding on that issue.

(2) Motions for judgment as a matter of law may be made at any time before submission of the case to the jury. Such a motion shall specify the judgment sought and the law and the facts on which the moving party is entitled to the judgment.

(b) Renewal of Motion for Judgment After Trial; Alternative Motion for New Trial.

If the court does not grant a motion for judgment as a matter of law made under Rule 50(a), the court is considered to have submitted the action to the jury subject to the court's later deciding the legal questions raised by the motion. Such a motion may be renewed by service and filing not later than 15 days after the entry of judgment. A motion for a new trial under Rule 59 may be joined with a renewal of the motion for judgment as a matter of law, or a new trial may be requested in the alternative. If a verdict was returned, the court may, in disposing of the renewed motion, allow the judgment to stand or may reopen the judgment and either order a new trial or direct the entry of judgment as a matter of law. If no verdict was returned, the court may, in disposing of the renewed motion, direct the entry of judgment as a matter of law or may order a new trial.

(c) Same: Conditional Rulings on Grant of Motion for Judgment as a Matter of Law.

(1) If the renewed motion for judgment as a matter of law is granted, the court shall also rule on the motion for new trial, if any, by determining whether it should be granted if the judgment is thereafter vacated or reversed, and shall specify the grounds for granting or denying the motion for the new trial. If the motion for new trial is thus conditionally granted, the order thereon does not affect the finality of the judgment. In case the motion for new trial has been conditionally granted and the judgment is reversed on appeal, the new trial shall proceed un-

less the appellate court has otherwise ordered. In case the motion for new trial has been conditionally denied, the appellee on appeal may assert error in that denial; and if the judgment is reversed on appeal, subsequent proceedings shall be in accordance with the order of the appellate court.

(2) The party against whom judgment as a matter of law has been rendered may serve a motion for a new trial pursuant to Rule 59 not later than 15 days after entry of the judgment.

(d) Same: Denial of Motion for Judgment as a Matter of Law. If the motion for judgment as a matter of law is denied, the party who prevailed on that motion may, as appellee, assert grounds entitling the party to a new trial in the event the appellate court concludes that the trial court erred in denying the motion for judgment. If the appellate court reverses the judgment, nothing in this rule precludes it from determining that the appellee is entitled to a new trial, or from directing the trial court to determine whether a new trial shall be granted.

Rule 50 added July 14, 1961, effective on and after midnight Oct. 31, 1961. Amended March 26, 1963, effective June 1, 1963; July 23, 1976, effective Oct. 1, 1976; Sept. 15, 1987, effective Nov. 15, 1987; Oct. 9, 1996, effective Dec. 1, 1996; Sept. 3, 2009, effective Jan. 1, 2010.

STATE BAR COMMITTEE NOTES

1961 Amendment

[Rule 50(e)] Rule 50(c) [renumbered 50(e) on March 26, 1963, effective June 1, 1963] is new and is proposed by the Committee to recognize the existing practice under which some judges enter an order for a directed verdict without requiring the foreman's signature. The practice will remain discretionary with the judge.

1963 Amendments

[Rule 50(b, c, d, e)] A motion for judgment notwithstanding the verdict will not lie unless it was preceded by a motion for a directed verdict made at the close of all the evidence.

The amendment of the second sentence of this subdivision sets the time limit for making the motion for judgment n.o.v. at 10 [now 15] days after the reception of the verdict. Thus the time provision is made consistent with that contained in Rule 59(b) (time for motion for new trial) and Rule 52(b) (time for motion to amend findings by the court).

Deals with the situation where a party joins a motion for a new trial with his motion for judgment n.o.v., or prays for a new trial in the alternative, and the motion for judgment n.o.v. is granted. The procedure to be followed in making rulings on the motion for the new trial, and the consequences of the rulings thereon, were set out in *Montgomery Ward & Co. v. Duncan*, 311 U.S. 243, 61 S. Ct. 189, 85 L. Ed. 147 (1940), and have been further elaborated in later cases. This same rule and practice has been adopted in Arizona in *Zugsmith v. Mullins*, 81 Ariz. 185, 188–189, 303 P.2d 261, 263–264 (1956), which expressly adopts the Montgomery Ward rule.

By this rule change we put into the rule what was required in the Montgomery Ward case, supra, and in our own Zugsmith decision.

An extensive note illuminating the rule is attached to the Federal rule, and we incorporate it as our own.

2010 Amendment

This amendment eliminates the need to make a motion for judgment as a matter of law at the close of all the evidence as a prerequisite to renewing a motion made earlier during trial, as the former rule had been interpreted by cases such as *Ash v. Flieger*, 118 Ariz. 547, 578 P.2d 628 (Ct. App. Div. 2 1978).

AUTHORS' COMMENTS

Analysis

1. *Scope and Purpose of Rule.* Before its amendment in 1996, Rule 50 treated together two motions which, although made at separate times, operated in tandem to raise the issue of the sufficiency of a party's evidence to sustain a verdict in that party's favor: motions for a directed verdict and motions for judgment notwithstanding the verdict. The 1996 amendments to Rule 50 abandoned the terminology "motion for directed verdict" and "motion for judgment notwithstanding the verdict" in favor of a unitary "motion for judgment as a matter of law." The 1996 amendments to Rule 50 were adopted to make it conform more closely to Fed.R.Civ.P. 50, which rule been amended in 1991.

Under the amended Rule, a motion for judgment as a matter of law may be made, at any time before a case is submitted to the jury, when a party has been fully heard with respect to an issue. If the motion is well taken, the Court may determine the issue against a party, and may enter judgment as a matter of law with respect to any claim or defense that cannot be maintained (or defeated) without a favorable finding on that issue. A motion for judgment as a matter of law made at the close of all the evidence which is denied may be renewed by the filing and service of such a renewal no later than fifteen (15) days after the entry of judgment. This renewal of a motion for judgment as a matter of law is the equivalent of the former motion for judgment notwithstanding the verdict.

2. *Comparison With Federal Rule.* Despite structural differ-

ences, the provisions of ARCP 50 are now essentially identical to those of FRCP 50. The only substantive difference between them is the prescribed time periods in which a motion for judgment as a matter of law must be renewed and in which a party against whom a renewed motion for judgment as a matter of law has been granted must move for a new trial.

Under the Arizona Rule, the prescribed time period for taking such steps is no later than 15 days after entry of judgment; the prescribed time period in the corresponding Federal Rule is no later than 28 days after entry of judgment. Before FRCP 50 was amended in 2009, the rule provided a 10-day time period for filing a Rule 50 post-judgment motion.

The commentary to the 2009 Amendment to the FRCP 50 states the 10-day time period was expanded to 28 days because experience had shown that, in many cases, it was not possible to prepare a satisfactory post-judgment motion in the 10 days provided. ARCP 50 has not been amended to similarly expand the time period for filing a Rule 50 post-judgment motion, which remains at 15 days.

In 2007, the language of FRCP 50 was amended as part of the general restyling of the Federal Rules of Civil Procedure to make the Federal Rules more easily understood and to make style and terminology consistent throughout the Federal Rules of Civil Procedure. Those stylistic modifications have not been incorporated into ARCP 50.

3. *Motion for Judgment as a Matter of Law; Timing*. The motion for directed verdict which former Rule 50 authorized could be made after the conclusion of an opponent's presentation of evidence, at the conclusion of the presentation of all evidence, or both. The new "motion for judgment as a matter of law" referred to in the amended Rule, which in effect replaces the former motions for directed verdict, can be made at any time, before the case is submitted to the jury, when a party "has been fully heard on an issue." The point when that occurs is, to some degree, discretionary with the trial judge, and will not necessarily coincide with the point at which one party or another rests its case.

Another significant difference between the two motions is the fact that, whereas a "motion for directed verdict" sought a disposition in the moving party's favor on the entire case or portions thereof, a "motion for judgment as a matter of law" may be directed to specific issues, claims and defenses.

Rule 50(b) was amended in 2010 to make clear that, when a Rule 50(a) motion for judgment as a matter of law is made at a point before the close of the evidence, and is denied, the court is deemed to have submitted the action to the jury subject to later addressing the legal issues raised, and such a motion need not be made again at the close of evidence in order to preserve the right to renew the motion after the verdict is rendered.

As a general rule, the denial of a motion for summary judgment is not reviewable on appeal from a final judgment entered after a trial on the merits. *John C. Lincoln Hosp. and Health Corp. v. Maricopa County*, 208 Ariz. 532, 96 P.3d 530 (Ct. App. Div. 1 2004), as amended, (Sept. 1, 2004). Accordingly, in cases which proceed to trial, a party who wants to preserve for appeal an issue on which summary judgment was denied, with the possible exception of a purely legal issue, must do so by reasserting it in a motion for judgment as a matter of law under Rule 50, or in some other post-trial motion. *John C. Lincoln Hosp. and Health Corp. v. Maricopa County*, 208 Ariz. 532, 96 P.3d 530 (Ct. App. Div. 1 2004), as amended on other grounds, (Sept. 1, 2004).

4. *Standards for Judgment as a Matter of Law.* As described in earlier Sections, the 1996 amendments to Rule 50 substituted what is termed a "motion for judgment as a matter of law" for the former "motion for a directed verdict."

The Rule itself states that a motion for judgment as a matter of law is to be granted with respect to an issue if the Court finds that "there is no legally sufficient evidentiary basis for a reasonable jury to find for that party on that issue." *See Desert Mountain Properties Ltd. Partnership v. Liberty Mut. Fire Ins. Co.*, 225 Ariz. 194, 236 P.3d 421 (Ct. App. Div. 1 2010), review granted in part, (Mar. 15, 2011) and opinion aff'd, 226 Ariz. 419, 250 P.3d 196 (2011); *Felder v. Physiotherapy Associates*, 215 Ariz. 154, 158 P.3d 877 (Ct. App. Div. 1 2007), citing *Orme School v. Reeves*, 166 Ariz. 301, 309, 802 P.2d 1000, 1008, 64 Ed. Law Rep. 1221 (1990).

That standard seems at least similar, if not identical, to that employed by Arizona's appellate courts in articulating when a motion for directed verdict should be granted. Moreover, the language of the amended Rule is identical to that adopted by the 1991 amendments to FCRP Rule 50, and the Advisory Committee Notes to those amendments made clear that no change in existing legal standards was intended.

Although the terminology of the Rule is not always consistently applied, it has been recognized that the standards for granting a motion or renewed motion for judgment as a matter of law are the same as those for granting the former motion for directed verdict. *Warner v. Southwest Desert Images, LLC*, 218 Ariz. 121, 180 P.3d 986 (Ct. App. Div. 2 2008); *Murcott v. Best Western Intern., Inc.*, 198 Ariz. 349, 9 P.3d 1088, 16 I.E.R. Cas. (BNA) 1277 (Ct. App. Div. 1 2000), as amended, (Oct. 16, 2000).

Thus, as with motions for directed verdict, when considering a motion for judgment as a matter of law, a trial court may not weigh the credibility of witnesses or resolve conflicts of evidence and reasonable inferences drawn therefrom. *See Estate of Reinen v. Northern Arizona Orthopedics, Ltd.*, 198 Ariz. 283, 9 P.3d 314 (2000); *Thompson v. Better-Bilt Aluminum Products Co., Inc.*, 171 Ariz. 550, 832 P.2d 203, 7 I.E.R. Cas. (BNA) 1017, 126 Lab. Cas. (CCH) P 57536 (1992); *McBride v. Kieckhefer Associates, Inc.*, 228 Ariz. 262, 265 P.3d 1061 (Ct. App. Div. 1 2011), review denied, (Apr. 24, 2012).

In contrast, in ruling on a motion for new trial, a trial court may evaluate the credibility of witness and weigh the evidence to determine if the verdict is against the weight of the evidence and contrary to justice. *Reeves v. Markle*, 119 Ariz. 159, 579 P.2d 1382 (1978); *Thompson v. Better-Bilt Aluminum Products Co., Inc.*, 171 Ariz. 550, 832 P.2d 203, 7 I.E.R. Cas. (BNA) 1017, 126 Lab. Cas. (CCH) P 57536 (1992); *McBride v. Kieckhefer Associates, Inc.*, 228 Ariz. 262, 265 P.3d 1061 (Ct. App. Div. 1 2011), review denied, (Apr. 24, 2012).

A motion for judgment as a matter of law admits the truth of all competent evidence introduced by the party opposing the motion, and all reasonable inferences to be drawn therefrom. *Robertson v. Sixpence Inns of America, Inc.*, 163 Ariz. 539, 789 P.2d 1040 (1990); *Chambers v. Western Arizona CATV*, 130 Ariz. 605, 638 P.2d 219 (1981); *Byrns v. Riddell, Inc.*, 113 Ariz. 264, 550 P.2d 1065 (1976); *Hlavaty v. Song*, 107 Ariz. 606, 491 P.2d 460 (1971); *E. L. Jones Const. Co. v. Noland*, 105 Ariz. 446, 466 P.2d 740 (1970); *Morris v. Ortiz*, 103 Ariz. 119, 437 P.2d 652, 35 A.L.R.3d 747 (1968); *Daugherty v. Montgomery Ward*, 102 Ariz. 267, 428 P.2d 419 (1967).

The evidence is to be viewed in the light most favorable to that party. *Brand v. J. H. Rose Trucking Co.*, 102 Ariz. 201, 427 P.2d 519 (1967); *Davis v. Weber*, 93 Ariz. 312, 380 P.2d 608 (1963); *Security Title Agency, Inc. v. Pope*, 219 Ariz. 480, 200 P.3d 977, 27 I.E.R. Cas. (BNA) 1811 (Ct. App. Div. 1 2008); *Warne Investments, Ltd. v. Higgins*, 219 Ariz. 186, 195 P.3d 645 (Ct. App. Div. 1 2008); *Warner v. Southwest Desert Images, LLC*, 218 Ariz. 121, 180 P.3d 986 (Ct. App. Div. 2 2008); *State v. City of Kingman*, 217 Ariz. 485, 176 P.3d 53 (Ct. App. Div. 1 2008); *Brown v. U.S. Fidelity and Guar. Co.*, 194 Ariz. 85, 977 P.2d 807 (Ct. App. Div. 1 1998), as amended, (Nov. 25, 1998) and as corrected, (Aug. 5, 1999); *State ex rel. Miller v. Wells Fargo Bank of Arizona, N.A.*, 194 Ariz. 126, 978 P.2d 103 (Ct. App. Div. 1 1998); *Shoen v. Shoen*, 191 Ariz. 64, 952 P.2d 302 (Ct. App. Div. 1 1997); *McCleaf v. State*, 190 Ariz. 167, 945 P.2d 1298 (Ct. App. Div. 1 1997), as amended, (Feb. 13, 1997).

The motion should only be granted if the facts produced in support of the claim have so little probative value, given the quantum of evidence required, that reasonable people could not agree with the conclusion advanced by the proponent of the claim or defense. *Shoen v. Shoen*, 191 Ariz. 64, 952 P.2d 302 (Ct. App. Div. 1 1997); *Gemstar Ltd. v. Ernst & Young*, 185 Ariz. 493, 917 P.2d 222 (1996); *McBride v. Kieckhefer Associates, Inc.*, 228 Ariz. 262, 265 P.3d 1061 (Ct. App. Div. 1 2011), review denied, (Apr. 24, 2012); *A Tumbling-T Ranches v. Flood Control Dist. of Maricopa County*, 222 Ariz. 515, 217 P.3d 1220 (Ct. App. Div. 1 2009); *Security Title Agency, Inc. v. Pope*, 219 Ariz. 480, 200 P.3d 977, 27 I.E.R. Cas. (BNA) 1811 (Ct. App. Div. 1 2008); *State v. City of Kingman*, 217 Ariz. 485, 176 P.3d 53 (Ct. App. Div. 1 2008); *Felder v. Physiotherapy Associates*, 215 Ariz. 154, 158 P.3d 877 (Ct. App. Div. 1 2007); *Acuna v. Kroack*, 212 Ariz. 104, 128 P.3d 221 (Ct. App. Div. 2 2006). This is essentially the same test as that for granting summary judgment. *Roberson v. Wal-Mart Stores, Inc.*, 202 Ariz. 286, 44 P.3d 164, 18 I.E.R. Cas. (BNA) 1196 (Ct. App. Div. 1 2002).

A trial court's award of a directed verdict was reviewed on appeal *de novo,* employing the same standard. *Gemstar Ltd. v. Ernst & Young*, 185 Ariz. 493, 917 P.2d 222 (1996); *Shuck v. Texaco Refining & Marketing, Inc.*, 178 Ariz. 295, 872 P.2d 1247 (Ct. App. Div. 1 1994).

That *de novo* standard for appellate review has now been applied to trial court rulings on motions for judgment as a matter of law as well. *McBride v. Kieckhefer Associates, Inc.*, 228 Ariz. 262, 265 P.3d 1061 (Ct. App. Div. 1 2011), review denied, (Apr. 24, 2012); *A Tumbling-T Ranches v. Flood Control Dist. of Maricopa County*, 222 Ariz. 515, 217 P.3d 1220 (Ct. App. Div. 1 2009); *Warner v. Southwest Desert Images, LLC*, 218 Ariz. 121, 180 P.3d 986 (Ct. App. Div. 2 2008); *State v. City of Kingman*, 217 Ariz. 485, 176 P.3d 53 (Ct. App. Div. 1 2008); *Dawson v. Withycombe*, 216 Ariz. 84, 163 P.3d 1034 (Ct. App. Div. 1 2007); *Felder v. Physiotherapy Associates*, 215 Ariz. 154, 158 P.3d 877 (Ct. App. Div. 1 2007); *Crackel v. Allstate Ins. Co.*, 208 Ariz. 252, 92 P.3d 882 (Ct. App. Div. 2 2004); *Barrett v. Harris*, 207 Ariz. 374, 86 P.3d 954 (Ct. App. Div. 1 2004); *Golonka v. General Motors Corp.*, 204 Ariz. 575, 65 P.3d 956, Prod. Liab. Rep. (CCH) P 16561 (Ct. App. Div. 1 2003); *Roberson v. Wal-Mart Stores, Inc.*, 202 Ariz. 286, 44 P.3d 164, 18 I.E.R. Cas. (BNA) 1196 (Ct. App. Div. 1 2002); *Trustmark Ins. Co. v. Bank One, Arizona, NA*, 202 Ariz. 535, 48 P.3d 485, 48 U.C.C. Rep. Serv. 2d 276 (Ct. App. Div. 1 2002), as corrected, (June 19, 2002); *Saucedo ex rel. Sinaloa v. Salvation Army*, 200 Ariz. 179, 24 P.3d 1274 (Ct. App. Div. 1 2001); *Monaco v. HealthPartners of Southern Arizona*, 196 Ariz. 299, 995 P.2d 735 (Ct. App. Div. 2 1999).

Judgments as a matter of law are not to be used, however, as substitutes for jury trials simply because the trial judge believed the moving party would win or should win the jury's verdict.

Potter v. H. Kern Wisner, M.D., P.C., 170 Ariz. 331, 823 P.2d 1339 (Ct. App. Div. 1 1991). If reasonable minds could differ on whether a verdict contrary to the motion can be sustained, the motion should be denied. *Dietz v. Waller*, 141 Ariz. 107, 685 P.2d 744 (1984); *Arizona Public Service Co. v. Brittain*, 107 Ariz. 278, 486 P.2d 176 (1971); *Sturm v. Heim*, 95 Ariz. 300, 389 P.2d 702 (1964); *Fedie v. Travelodge Intern., Inc.*, 162 Ariz. 263, 782 P.2d 739 (Ct. App. Div. 2 1989); *Kuhnke v. Textron, Inc.*, 140 Ariz. 587, 684 P.2d 159 (Ct. App. Div. 1 1984); *Gibson v. Boyle*, 139 Ariz. 512, 679 P.2d 535 (Ct. App. Div. 1 1983).

On appeal, the granting or denial of a motion for judgment as a matter of law is reviewed *de novo*. *McBride v. Kieckhefer Associates, Inc.*, 228 Ariz. 262, 265 P.3d 1061 (Ct. App. Div. 1 2011), review denied, (Apr. 24, 2012); *A Tumbling-T Ranches v. Flood Control Dist. of Maricopa County*, 222 Ariz. 515, 217 P.3d 1220 (Ct. App. Div. 1 2009); *United Dairymen of Arizona v. Schugg*, 212 Ariz. 133, 128 P.3d 756, 2006-1 Trade Cas. (CCH) ¶ 75120 (Ct. App. Div. 1 2006); *Mullin v. Brown*, 210 Ariz. 545, 115 P.3d 139 (Ct. App. Div. 2 2005); *Anderson v. Nissei ASB Mach. Co., Ltd.*, 197 Ariz. 168, 3 P.3d 1088, Prod. Liab. Rep. (CCH) P 15732 (Ct. App. Div. 1 1999); *Johnson v. Pankratz*, 196 Ariz. 621, 2 P.3d 1266 (Ct. App. Div. 1 2000); *Taeger v. Catholic Family and Community Services*, 196 Ariz. 285, 995 P.2d 721 (Ct. App. Div. 1 1999).

Where such a motion has been granted, the evidence, and all reasonable inferences that can be drawn from it, are viewed in the light most favorable to the non-moving party. *McBride v. Kieckhefer Associates, Inc.*, 228 Ariz. 262, 265 P.3d 1061 (Ct. App. Div. 1 2011), review denied, (Apr. 24, 2012); *Security Title Agency, Inc. v. Pope*, 219 Ariz. 480, 200 P.3d 977, 27 I.E.R. Cas. (BNA) 1811 (Ct. App. Div. 1 2008); *Murcott v. Best Western Intern., Inc.*, 198 Ariz. 349, 9 P.3d 1088, 16 I.E.R. Cas. (BNA) 1277 (Ct. App. Div. 1 2000), as amended, (Oct. 16, 2000); *Taeger v. Catholic Family and Community Services*, 196 Ariz. 285, 995 P.2d 721 (Ct. App. Div. 1 1999).

5. *Renewal of Motion for Judgment as a Matter of Law; Timing*. Rule 50(b) was amended in 2010 to make clear that, when a motion for judgment as a matter of law is made at a point before the close of the evidence, and is denied, the court is deemed to have submitted the action to the jury subject to later addressing the legal issues raised, and such a motion need not be made again at the close of evidence in order to preserve the right to renew it after the verdict is rendered.

Rule 50(b) requires, however, such motion must be formally renewed after verdict in order to bring those questions back before the Court for disposition. *Marquette Venture Partners II,*

L.P. v. Leonesio, 227 Ariz. 179, 254 P.3d 418 (Ct. App. Div. 1 2011).

The filing and service of a renewal of a formerly denied motion for judgment as a matter of law, if necessary, may be done at any time after the jury's verdict is returned, but must be done no later than fifteen (15) days after the entry of judgment.

The trial court was granted limited authority to enlarge that period by the 1994 amendment to Rule 6(b). The circumstances under which such an extension to submit a renewed motion for judgment as a matter of law under Rule 50(b) can be secured are discussed in Section 5 of the *Authors' Comments* under Rule 6.

6. *Relationship of Motion for Judgment as a Matter of Law and Renewal of Motion*. Under the terminology employed in former Rule 50, a motion for judgment notwithstanding the verdict was considered to be merely a renewal of a motion for directed verdict, and designed as a vehicle for allowing the Court to reconsider the issue of the sufficiency of the opponent's evidence after an opportunity for mature deliberation. *Bond v. Cartwright Little League, Inc.*, 112 Ariz. 9, 536 P.2d 697 (1975). The amended Rule now makes that explicit. What is the equivalent, under the amended Rule, of the former motion for judgment notwithstanding the verdict is the "renewal" of a motion for judgment as a matter of law unsuccessfully made at the close of all the evidence.

Under former Rule 50, a motion for judgment notwithstanding the verdict could not be made unless the moving party had previously moved for a directed verdict at the close of the evidence. *Rodriguez v. Williams*, 107 Ariz. 458, 489 P.2d 268 (1971); *Standard Chartered PLC v. Price Waterhouse*, 190 Ariz. 6, 945 P.2d 317 (Ct. App. Div. 1 1996), as corrected on denial of reconsideration, (Jan. 13, 1997); *Ash v. Flieger*, 118 Ariz. 547, 578 P.2d 628 (Ct. App. Div. 2 1978); *Dodge City Motors, Inc. v. Rogers*, 16 Ariz. App. 24, 490 P.2d 853 (Div. 1 1971); *Loya v. Fong*, 1 Ariz. App. 482, 404 P.2d 826 (1965).

Indeed, the scope and grounds of a motion for judgment notwithstanding the verdict were ordinarily limited to the matters raised by the motion for directed verdict. *Standard Chartered PLC v. Price Waterhouse*, 190 Ariz. 6, 945 P.2d 317 (Ct. App. Div. 1 1996), as corrected on denial of reconsideration, (Jan. 13, 1997).

Rule 50(b) was amended in 2010 to make clear that, when a motion for judgment as a matter of law is made at a point before the close of the evidence, and is denied, the court is deemed to have submitted the action to the jury subject to later addressing the legal issues raised, and such a motion need not be made again at the close of evidence in order to preserve the right to renew it after the verdict is rendered. The motion, however, must be formally renewed in order to bring those questions back before the Court for disposition.

7. *Standards for Renewed Motion for Judgment as a Matter of Law*. As described in earlier Sections, the 1996 amendments substituted the "renewal" of a prior unsuccessful "motion for judgment as a matter of law" for what was formerly called a motion for judgment notwithstanding the verdict. It has now been recognized that renewals of motions for judgment as a matter of law are to be determined according to the same standard as applies to the original motion. *Murcott v. Best Western Intern., Inc.*, 198 Ariz. 349, 9 P.3d 1088, 16 I.E.R. Cas. (BNA) 1277 (Ct. App. Div. 1 2000), as amended on other grounds, (Oct. 16, 2000).

That is consistent with case law developed under the former Rule, under which it was held that the standards to be applied in deciding motions for judgment notwithstanding the verdict were identical to those applicable to motions for directed verdict. *Piper v. Bear Medical Systems, Inc.*, 180 Ariz. 170, 883 P.2d 407, Prod. Liab. Rep. (CCH) P 13766 (Ct. App. Div. 1 1993); *Esplendido Apartments v. Metropolitan Condominium Ass'n of Arizona II*, 158 Ariz. 487, 763 P.2d 983 (Ct. App. Div. 2 1988), opinion vacated on other grounds, 161 Ariz. 325, 778 P.2d 1221 (1989).

The evidence is to be viewed in the light most favorable to upholding the verdict. *Graber v. City of Peoria*, 156 Ariz. 553, 753 P.2d 1209 (Ct. App. Div. 2 1988). If reasonable minds could differ on the evidence in support of the verdict, the motion should be denied. *Shafer v. Monte Mansfield Motors*, 91 Ariz. 331, 372 P.2d 333 (1962); *Huggins v. Deinhard*, 127 Ariz. 358, 621 P.2d 45 (Ct. App. Div. 1 1980); *Hurvitz v. Coburn*, 117 Ariz. 300, 572 P.2d 128 (Ct. App. Div. 2 1977); *In re Accomazzo's Estate*, 16 Ariz. App. 211, 492 P.2d 460 (Div. 1 1972); *In re Frick's Estate*, 13 Ariz. App. 247, 475 P.2d 732 (Div. 1 1970). In reviewing the denial such a motion, the evidence and all reasonable inferences therefrom were to be viewed in the light most favorable to the nonmoving party.

In *Shoen v. Shoen*, 191 Ariz. 64, 952 P.2d 302 (Ct. App. Div. 1 1997), the Court of Appeals clarified prior confusion concerning the proper scope of appellate review of the denial of a motion for judgment notwithstanding the verdict that had been created by an earlier decision in *Nelson v. Phoenix Resort Corp.*, 181 Ariz. 188, 888 P.2d 1375 (Ct. App. Div. 1 1994). In *Shoen v. Shoen*, the Court noted that the standards for granting motions for judgment notwithstanding the verdict were the same as the standards for granting motions for a directed verdict.

Accordingly, the Court concluded, there should be a similar symmetry between the standards for appellate review of dispositions of these two types of motions. Because rulings on motions for a directed verdict were reviewed *de novo*, that same *de novo* standard should apply to review of dispositions of motions for judgment notwithstanding the verdict. *Shoen v. Shoen*, 191 Ariz. 64, 952 P.2d 302 (Ct. App. Div. 1 1997). *Cf. also State ex rel. Miller v. Wells Fargo Bank of Arizona, N.A.*, 194 Ariz. 126, 978 P.2d 103 (Ct. App. Div. 1 1998).

8. *Renewed Motion for Judgment as a Matter of Law and Motion for New Trial Combined.* Under amended Rule 50(b), the post-trial renewal of a motion for judgment as a matter of law may be combined with a motion for new trial under Rule 59. In the event the court grants a renewed motion for judgment as a matter of law, Ariz. R. Civ. P 50(c) requires the court to enter a conditional ruling on the motion for new trial as well.

Under the prior version of the Rule, it was held that it was not inconsistent for a trial court to grant a motion for judgment notwithstanding the verdict and conditionally deny a new trial. *Adroit Supply Co. v. Electric Mut. Liability Ins. Co.*, 112 Ariz. 385, 542 P.2d 810 (1975); *Times Mirror Co. v. Sisk*, 122 Ariz. 174, 593 P.2d 924 (Ct. App. Div. 2 1978). The conditional ruling is, in any event, not a bar to any arguments the parties may wish to make on appeal, and the appellate court is free to make its own determination on the issue.

Rule 50(c)(2) expressly authorizes a motion for new trial by a party against whom a motion for judgment as a matter of law has been granted. Such a motion must be brought no later than fifteen (15) days after the entry of judgment.

Rule 51. Instructions to jury; objections; arguments

(a) Instructions to Jury; Objection. Immediately after the jury is sworn, the court shall instruct the jury concerning its duties, its conduct, the order of proceedings, the procedure for submitting written questions of witnesses or of the court as set forth in Rule 39(b)(10), the procedure for note-taking, the nature of evidence and its evaluation, any issues to be addressed, and the elementary legal principles that will govern the proceeding. The instructions shall be provided in a manner that makes them as readily understandable as possible by individuals unfamiliar with the legal system. Prior to the commencement of a jury trial or at such other time during the trial as the court reasonably directs, any party may file written requests that the court instruct the jury on the law as set forth in the requests. Counsel shall be deemed to have waived request for other instructions except those which could not reasonably have been anticipated prior to trial. The court shall inform counsel of its proposed action upon the requests prior to their arguments to the jury. The court, at its election, may instruct the jury before or after argument, or both. No party may assign as error the giving or the failure to give an instruction unless that party objects thereto before the jury retires to consider its verdict, stating distinctly the matter objected to and the grounds of the objection. Opportunity shall be given to make the objection out of hearing of the jury. All communications between the court and members of the jury panel shall be in writing or on the record.

Amended Sept. 15, 1987, effective Nov. 15, 1987; Oct. 24, 1995, effective Dec. 1, 1995; September 2008, effective January 1, 2009.

(b) Instructions to Jury; Notations; Filing Transcript.

1. The court shall either give or refuse the instruction as requested, or shall modify the instruction, indicating on the record the modifications made and give it as modified. The court's instructions may be used by the parties in the argument to the jury.

2. The written instructions shall be filed among the papers in the action and constitute a part of the record. At the request and cost of either party, the entire instructions given by the court shall be transcribed by the reporter and filed with the clerk.

3. The court's preliminary and final instructions on the law shall be in written form and a copy of the instructions shall be furnished to each juror before being read by the court. Upon retiring for deliberations the jurors shall take with them all

jurors' copies of final written instructions given by the court. In limited jurisdiction courts, the court may record jury instructions on audiotape and provide these audio instructions to the jury for their use during deliberations.

Amended Sept. 15, 1987, effective Nov. 15, 1987; Oct. 24, 1995, effective Dec. 1, 1995; Sept. 18, 2006, effective Jan. 1, 2007.

(c) [Renumbered as Rule 39(n), effective Nov. 15, 1987].

(d) [Deleted May 1, 1989, effective July 1, 1989].

AUTHORS' COMMENTS

Analysis

1. *Scope and Purpose of Rule.* One of the most important aspects of the trial process is the rendering, at the close of evidence, of the Court's instructions to the jury, which advises the jurors of the principles of law they are to apply to the facts as they find them from the evidence. *Eldredge v. Miller*, 78 Ariz. 140, 277 P.2d 239 (1954). Rule 51 establishes the procedures for submitting proposed instructions, settling on the instructions to be given, and recording any objections thereto. It is also proper for the trial court to instruct the jury *sua sponte* on acceptable methods for the jury to communicate with the Court. *Harrington v. Beauchamp Enterprises*, 158 Ariz. 118, 761 P.2d 1022 (1988).

2. *Comparison With Federal Rule.* As a consequence of the 1995 "jury reform" amendments to ARCP 51, and the 2003 amendments to FRCP 51, there are both substantive and structural difference between the two rules. Both ARCP 51 and FRCP 51 deal with the subject of jury instructions, but the Federal Rule now contains specific provisions dealing with the subject of objecting to instructions, and preserving claimed error in the instructions for appeal, for which there are no counterparts in the Arizona Rule.

The requirement in ARCP 51 that the jury be given preliminary instructions concerning its duties immediately after being sworn is not found in FRCP 51. In addition, the Arizona Rule requires that proposed jury instructions be submitted before the commencement of trial, whereas the amended Federal Rule only requires the submission of jury instructions to the jury "at the close of evidence or at an earlier reasonable time that the court directs."

3. *Timing and Form of Proposed Jury Instructions.* Rule 51(a), as amended as part of the 1995 "jury reform" amendments, now specifies that any party may file, before the commencement of trial or at such other time as the Court directs, written requests for particular instructions to be given to the jury. The Rule also provide that any request for an instruction or an interrogatory not submitted in accordance with those requirements is deemed to have been waived, unless the instruction or interrogatory desired is one that could not have been reasonably anticipated before trial. This requirement also applies to specialized forms of verdict which any party seeks to have used. *Kelman v. Bohi*, 27 Ariz. App. 24, 550 P.2d 671 (Div. 1 1976).

The usual, and better, practice has been for each requested instruction to be separately numbered and set forth on a separate page, with citations to the source of the instruction, or other authority for giving it, and lines for the Court and parties to note whether the requested instruction was given, given as modified, or refused. This practice may be eliminated over time, however, in light of the 1987 amendment to Rule 51(b), which merely requires the trial court to note modifications "on the record."

The Superior Courts in several Counties have adopted Local Rules which address the timing and/or form of proposed jury instructions. The Cochise, Coconino and Mohave County Superior Courts require that proposed jury instructions be submitted to the trial judge, unless otherwise ordered, by the morning of the first day of trial. Rule 24, Cochise County Superior Court Local Rules; Rule 7(B), Coconino County Superior Court Local Rules; Rule CV-5(B), Mohave County Superior Court Local Rules. Apache County requires that proposed jury instructions be submitted to the judge on the Friday preceding the first day of trial. Rule 23(b), Apache County Superior Court Local Rules. The Maricopa, Pinal and Santa Cruz County Superior Courts have Local Rules which specify the form of proposed jury instructions, but not the time for submitting them. Rule 2.9(b), Maricopa County Superior Court Local Rules; Rule 2.14(b), Pinal County Superior Court Local Rules; Rule 6.3, Santa Cruz County Superior Court Local Rules.

4. *Standards for Settling Jury Instructions.* Instructions should be framed in clear, comprehensible everyday English. *Petefish By*

and Through Clancy v. Dawe, 137 Ariz. 570, 672 P.2d 914 (1983). A provision added to the Rule in 2009 requires that the instructions "be provided in a manner that makes them as readily understandable as possible by individuals unfamiliar with the legal system. Instructions given to the jury will be reviewed as a whole and the test on appeal is whether the entire charge, viewed as a whole, gives the jury the proper rules of law to apply. *Dawson v. Withycombe*, 216 Ariz. 84, 163 P.3d 1034 (Ct. App. Div. 1 2007); *State Farm Fire & Cas. In. Co. v. Grabowski*, 214 Ariz. 188, 150 P.3d 275 (Ct. App. Div. 1 2007), as amended, (Jan. 29, 2007); *Mullin v. Brown*, 210 Ariz. 545, 115 P.3d 139 (Ct. App. Div. 2 2005); *Crackel v. Allstate Ins. Co.*, 208 Ariz. 252, 92 P.3d 882 (Ct. App. Div. 2 2004); *Lifeflite Medical Air Transport, Inc. v. Native American Air Services, Inc.*, 198 Ariz. 149, 7 P.3d 158, R.I.C.O. Bus. Disp. Guide (CCH) P 9919 (Ct. App. Div. 1 2000); *State ex rel. Miller v. Wells Fargo Bank of Arizona, N.A.*, 194 Ariz. 126, 978 P.2d 103 (Ct. App. Div. 1 1998); *Sheppard v. Crow-Barker Paul No. 1 Ltd. Partnership*, 192 Ariz. 539, 968 P.2d 612 (Ct. App. Div. 1 1998); *Pima County v. Gonzalez*, 193 Ariz. 18, 969 P.2d 183 (Ct. App. Div. 2 1998); *Barnes v. Outlaw*, 188 Ariz. 401, 937 P.2d 323 (Ct. App. Div. 2 1996), as amended on denial of reconsideration, (Nov. 8, 1996) and opinion vacated in part on other grounds, 192 Ariz. 283, 964 P.2d 484 (1998); *Thompson v. Better-Bilt Aluminum Products Co., Inc.*, 187 Ariz. 121, 927 P.2d 781, 11 I.E.R. Cas. (BNA) 971 (Ct. App. Div. 1 1996), as corrected, (Apr. 8, 1996); *Haynes v. Syntek Finance Corp.*, 184 Ariz. 332, 909 P.2d 399 (Ct. App. Div. 1 1995). Counsel should be, and almost invariably are, advised of the final instructions to be given so that they can argue the facts accordingly in closing argument. *Eldredge v. Miller*, 78 Ariz. 140, 277 P.2d 239 (1954). In that regard, the 1987 amendment to Rule 51(a) gives the Court the option to give its instructions either before or after argument, or both.

The jury must be instructed on all phases of the law which have some bearing on the evidence. *Gemstar Ltd. v. Ernst & Young*, 185 Ariz. 493, 917 P.2d 222 (1996); *DeMontiney v. Desert Manor Convalescent Center Inc.*, 144 Ariz. 6, 695 P.2d 255 (1985); *A Tumbling-T Ranches v. Flood Control Dist. of Maricopa County*, 222 Ariz. 515, 217 P.3d 1220 (Ct. App. Div. 1 2009); *Miel v. State Farm Mut. Auto. Ins. Co.*, 185 Ariz. 104, 912 P.2d 1333 (Ct. App. Div. 1 1995); *AMERCO v. Shoen*, 184 Ariz. 150, 907 P.2d 536 (Ct. App. Div. 1 1995), corrected, (Aug. 29, 1995); *Newell v. Town of Oro Valley*, 163 Ariz. 527, 789 P.2d 394 (Ct. App. Div. 2 1990); *Baroldy v. Ortho Pharmaceutical Corp.*, 157 Ariz. 574, 760 P.2d 574, Prod. Liab. Rep. (CCH) P 11732 (Ct. App. Div. 1 1988); *Hallmark v. Allied Products Corp.*, 132 Ariz. 434, 646 P.2d 319 (Ct. App. Div. 1 1982); *Barker v. James*, 15 Ariz. App. 83, 486

P.2d 195 (Div. 1 1971); *Towers v. Johnson*, 11 Ariz. App. 455, 465 P.2d 592 (Div. 1 1970).

A trial court must give a requested instruction if (1) the evidence presented supports the instruction, (2) the instruction is proper under the law, and (3) the instruction pertains to an issue that is not dealt with in any other instruction. *Brethauer v. General Motors Corp.*, 221 Ariz. 192, 211 P.3d 1176 (Ct. App. Div. 1 2009); *Brown v. U.S. Fidelity and Guar. Co.*, 194 Ariz. 85, 977 P.2d 807 (Ct. App. Div. 1 1998), as amended, (Nov. 25, 1998) and as corrected, (Aug. 5, 1999); *State ex rel. Miller v. Wells Fargo Bank of Arizona, N.A.*, 194 Ariz. 126, 978 P.2d 103 (Ct. App. Div. 1 1998); *Dunn v. Maras*, 182 Ariz. 412, 897 P.2d 714 (Ct. App. Div. 1 1995). If there is any evidence tending to establish the theory posed in the instruction, it should be given, even if contradictory facts are presented. *Cotterhill v. Bafile*, 177 Ariz. 76, 865 P.2d 120 (Ct. App. Div. 1 1993); *Czarnecki v. Volkswagen of America*, 172 Ariz. 408, 837 P.2d 1143, Prod. Liab. Rep. (CCH) P 13137 (Ct. App. Div. 1 1991); *Timmons v. City of Tucson*, 171 Ariz. 350, 830 P.2d 871, 63 Fair Empl. Prac. Cas. (BNA) 11 (Ct. App. Div. 2 1991). In a negligence action, the trial court is not required to advise the jury of the nature of the legal duty imposed, but must give instructions as to any specific standard of care that applies under the circumstances. *Ballesteros v. State*, 161 Ariz. 625, 780 P.2d 458 (Ct. App. Div. 2 1989).

The trial court can properly refuse to give an instruction which may represent a perfectly accurate statement of law but which does not apply to the facts of the case. *O'Rielly Motor Co. v. Rich*, 3 Ariz. App. 21, 411 P.2d 194 (1966). In fact, it is reversible error to give an instruction on a legal theory as to which no substantial evidence was received. *Pima County v. Gonzalez*, 193 Ariz. 18, 969 P.2d 183 (Ct. App. Div. 2 1998); *Kemp v. Pinal County*, 13 Ariz. App. 121, 474 P.2d 840 (Div. 2 1970); *Rowley v. Rowley*, 7 Ariz. App. 418, 440 P.2d 54 (1968). In that circumstance, such an instruction merely invites the jury to speculate about nonexistent circumstances. *Higgins v. Assmann Electronics, Inc.*, 217 Ariz. 289, 173 P.3d 453 (Ct. App. Div. 1 2007); *City of Phoenix v. Clauss*, 177 Ariz. 566, 869 P.2d 1219 (Ct. App. Div. 1 1994). This rule applies even though the issue was presented in the pleadings. *Ong v. Pepsi Cola Metropolitan Bottling Co., Inc.*, 18 Ariz. App. 457, 503 P.2d 415 (Div. 1 1972). Quite obviously, the trial court must refuse to give an instruction that does not correctly state the law. *Bike Fashion Corp. v. Kramer*, 202 Ariz. 420, 46 P.3d 431 (Ct. App. Div. 1 2002).

The evidence presented, however, should be viewed in the strongest manner that supports the theory of the party requesting the instruction and, if any evidence establishes that theory, the instruction should be given. *Gemstar Ltd. v. Ernst & Young*,

185 Ariz. 493, 917 P.2d 222 (1996); *Cotterhill v. Bafile*, 177 Ariz. 76, 865 P.2d 120 (Ct. App. Div. 1 1993); *Czarnecki v. Volkswagen of America*, 172 Ariz. 408, 837 P.2d 1143, Prod. Liab. Rep. (CCH) P 13137 (Ct. App. Div. 1 1991); *Timmons v. City of Tucson*, 171 Ariz. 350, 830 P.2d 871, 63 Fair Empl. Prac. Cas. (BNA) 11 (Ct. App. Div. 2 1991); *Newell v. Town of Oro Valley*, 163 Ariz. 527, 789 P.2d 394 (Ct. App. Div. 2 1990); *Baroldy v. Ortho Pharmaceutical Corp.*, 157 Ariz. 574, 760 P.2d 574, Prod. Liab. Rep. (CCH) P 11732 (Ct. App. Div. 1 1988).

Failure to instruct the jury on a claim that has been asserted and on which evidence has been presented is tantamount to granting a directed verdict. The giving of an instruction, however, which misleads the jury as to the applicable law to apply, to the prejudice of a party, is reversible error. *American Pepper Supply Co. v. Federal Ins. Co.*, 208 Ariz. 307, 93 P.3d 507 (2004); *Fridena v. Evans*, 127 Ariz. 516, 622 P.2d 463, 12 A.L.R.4th 46 (1980) ("A trial court is not required to instruct a jury on every refinement of law; and, it must refuse to give an instruction that does not correctly state the law"); *Taylor v. DiRico*, 124 Ariz. 513, 606 P.2d 3 (1980); *Maricopa County v. Barkley*, 168 Ariz. 234, 812 P.2d 1052 (Ct. App. Div. 1 1990).

Rule 51(b)(3), adopted as part of the 1995 "jury reform" amendments, requires that the Court's preliminary and final instructions to the jury be in written form, and that a copy of the instructions be furnished to each juror before they are read. When they retire for deliberations, the jurors are to take with them their copies of the final written instructions given by the Court. In limited jurisdiction courts, the jury instructions may be recorded on audio tape and the instructions may be provided to the jury in that form for their use during deliberations.

5. *Forms of Verdict.* There is very little Arizona case law on the interplay between jury instructions and forms of verdict. The purpose of jury instructions is to inform the jury, in understandable terms, of the principles of law to be applied, according to the claims asserted. The form of verdict is then used by the jury to record the decision it makes pursuant to the instructions given by the Court. Any instructions to the jury in the verdict form are to be considered together with the instructions as a whole. *Mullin v. Brown*, 210 Ariz. 545, 115 P.3d 139 (Ct. App. Div. 2 2005).

6. *Objections to Proposed Instructions; Waiver.* Rule 51(a) specifies that a party waives any objection to the giving or omission of an instruction unless an objection is made before the jury retires, stating the precise grounds for and nature of the objection. The purpose of this requirement is to insure that the trial court has the benefit of counsel's views before instructions are settled and given, and to prevent error that could be cured at that point.

Edward Greenband Enterprises of Arizona v. Pepper, 112 Ariz. 115, 538 P.2d 389 (1975); *Milam v. Milam*, 101 Ariz. 323, 419 P.2d 502 (1966); *Williams for and on Behalf of Dixon v. Thude*, 180 Ariz. 531, 885 P.2d 1096 (Ct. App. Div. 1 1994), aff'd, 188 Ariz. 257, 934 P.2d 1349 (1997); *Copeland v. City of Yuma*, 160 Ariz. 307, 772 P.2d 1160 (Ct. App. Div. 1 1989); *Nielson v. Flashberg*, 101 Ariz. 335, 419 P.2d 514 (1966); *L.B. Nelson Corp. of Tucson v. Western American Financial Corp.*, 150 Ariz. 211, 722 P.2d 379 (Ct. App. Div. 2 1986); *Packard v. Reidhead*, 22 Ariz. App. 420, 528 P.2d 171 (Div. 1 1974); *Purcell v. Zimbelman*, 18 Ariz. App. 75, 500 P.2d 335 (Div. 2 1972).

A general objection to the effect that the instruction does not correctly state the law is not sufficient. *Grant v. Arizona Public Service Co.*, 133 Ariz. 434, 652 P.2d 507 (1982); *Rhue v. Dawson*, 173 Ariz. 220, 841 P.2d 215 (Ct. App. Div. 1 1992). A party must distinctly identify the aspect of the instruction which is deemed objectionable and the precise nature and grounds for the objection. *Williams for and on Behalf of Dixon v. Thude*, 180 Ariz. 531, 885 P.2d 1096 (Ct. App. Div. 1 1994), aff'd, 188 Ariz. 257, 934 P.2d 1349 (1997); *Rhue v. Dawson*, 173 Ariz. 220, 841 P.2d 215 (Ct. App. Div. 1 1992); *Czarnecki v. Volkswagen of America*, 172 Ariz. 408, 837 P.2d 1143, Prod. Liab. Rep. (CCH) P 13137 (Ct. App. Div. 1 1991); *Rodriguez v. Schlittenhart*, 161 Ariz. 609, 780 P.2d 442 (Ct. App. Div. 2 1989); *White v. Mitchell*, 157 Ariz. 523, 759 P.2d 1327 (Ct. App. Div. 1 1988); *Rhodes v. El Rancho Markets*, 9 Ariz. App. 576, 454 P.2d 1016 (1969).

For example, the claim that the evidence is insufficient to warrant submitting the issue of punitive damages to the jury does not preserve for appeal a challenge to the wording of the punitive damages instruction. *White v. Mitchell*, 157 Ariz. 523, 759 P.2d 1327 (Ct. App. Div. 1 1988). To the contrary, a party dissatisfied with the formulation of an instruction the trial court proposes to give must submit other instructions for the trial court to consider. *White v. Mitchell*, 157 Ariz. 523, 759 P.2d 1327 (Ct. App. Div. 1 1988). On the other hand, a party which requests and submits an instruction on consequential damages is deemed to have admitted that there is evidence to support the claim and cannot later contend that there was insufficient evidence to warrant the instruction or to support a recovery. *Walter v. Simmons*, 169 Ariz. 229, 818 P.2d 214 (Ct. App. Div. 1 1991).

Generally, the failure to object in proper fashion to a proposed instruction, or the omission of a proposed instruction, before the jury retires bars any challenge to the instructions on appeal. *Czarnecki v. Volkswagen of America*, 172 Ariz. 408, 837 P.2d 1143, Prod. Liab. Rep. (CCH) P 13137 (Ct. App. Div. 1 1991); *Copeland v. City of Yuma*, 160 Ariz. 307, 772 P.2d 1160 (Ct. App. Div. 1 1989); *White v. Mitchell*, 157 Ariz. 523, 759 P.2d 1327 (Ct.

App. Div. 1 1988); *United Bank of Ariz. v. Wine*, 18 Ariz. App. 23, 499 P.2d 754 (Div. 1 1972). One exception to this rule is where the instruction given, or the omission of an instruction, constitutes fundamental and prejudicial error. *Williams for and on Behalf of Dixon v. Thude*, 180 Ariz. 531, 885 P.2d 1096 (Ct. App. Div. 1 1994), aff'd, 188 Ariz. 257, 934 P.2d 1349 (1997); *Ruiz v. Faulkner*, 12 Ariz. App. 352, 470 P.2d 500 (Div. 1 1970); *Moore v. Gray*, 3 Ariz. App. 309, 414 P.2d 158 (1966).

Fundamental error is that which goes to the very foundation of a case, or takes an essential right from a party, or deprives a party of a fair trial. Fundamental error is not waived even in the absence of an objection, and must be considered by the Court *sua sponte* even when not raised on appeal. *Salt River Project Agr. Imp. and Power Dist. v. Westinghouse Elec. Corp.*, 176 Ariz. 383, 861 P.2d 668, Prod. Liab. Rep. (CCH) P 13562 (Ct. App. Div. 2 1993).

The doctrine of "fundamental error," however, is one applied very sparingly, and only in circumstances of severe prejudice. *Bradshaw v. State Farm Mut. Auto. Ins. Co.*, 157 Ariz. 411, 758 P.2d 1313 (1988); *Moser v. Mardian Const. Co.*, 20 Ariz. App. 27, 509 P.2d 1064 (Div. 1 1973). It is fundamental error to instruct the jury that jurors who vote against finding liability during the course of deliberations should not participate in the determination of the amount of damages to be awarded. *Perkins v. Komarnyckyj*, 172 Ariz. 115, 834 P.2d 1260 (1992).

The constitutional right of trial by jury carries with it the right to have every issue tried by the jury that has been empaneled, not by two-thirds or three-fourths, or any other fraction of that jury. Depriving the parties of their right to have all the jurors participate in deciding all of the issues is inherently prejudicial and fundamental error, requiring reversal without any further showing of prejudice. *Perkins v. Komarnyckyj*, 172 Ariz. 115, 834 P.2d 1260 (1992).

An appellate court will ordinarily not overturn a verdict on the basis of jury instructions unless there is substantial doubt whether the jury was properly guided. *Wendland v. AdobeAir, Inc.*, 223 Ariz. 199, 221 P.3d 390 (Ct. App. Div. 1 2009); *Hudgins v. Southwest Airlines, Co.*, 221 Ariz. 472, 212 P.3d 810 (Ct. App. Div. 1 2009); *Bike Fashion Corp. v. Kramer*, 202 Ariz. 420, 46 P.3d 431 (Ct. App. Div. 1 2002); *Link v. Pima County*, 193 Ariz. 336, 972 P.2d 669 (Ct. App. Div. 2 1998); *Republic Ins. Co. v. Feidler*, 193 Ariz. 8, 969 P.2d 173 (Ct. App. Div. 1 1998), review denied and opinion ordered not published, 199 Ariz. 472, 19 P.3d 613 (1999); *Barnes v. Outlaw*, 188 Ariz. 401, 937 P.2d 323 (Ct. App. Div. 2 1996), as amended on denial of reconsideration, (Nov. 8, 1996) and opinion vacated in part, 192 Ariz. 283, 964 P.2d 484

(1998); *Thompson v. Better-Bilt Aluminum Products Co., Inc.*, 187 Ariz. 121, 927 P.2d 781, 11 I.E.R. Cas. (BNA) 971 (Ct. App. Div. 1 1996), as corrected, (Apr. 8, 1996); *City of Phoenix v. Clauss*, 177 Ariz. 566, 869 P.2d 1219 (Ct. App. Div. 1 1994). Quite obviously, a party is precluded from complaining of instructions given at that party's request. *Roscoe v. Schoolitz*, 105 Ariz. 310, 464 P.2d 333 (1970); *Walter v. Simmons*, 169 Ariz. 229, 818 P.2d 214 (Ct. App. Div. 1 1991); *Verdugo v. Po Shing Gee*, 4 Ariz. App. 113, 417 P.2d 747 (1966).

By reason of a provision unique to Arizona's Constitution, Article 18, Section 5, the presence or absence of assumption of the risk (and of contributory negligence) and its effect, if any, on a plaintiff's recovery, are matters exclusively for the jurors to decide. *Estate of Reinen v. Northern Arizona Orthopedics, Ltd.*, 198 Ariz. 283, 9 P.3d 314 (2000). Jury instructions which violate this principle have uniformly been held to constitute fundamental, prejudicial error, and to warrant reversal. *Estate of Reinen v. Northern Arizona Orthopedics, Ltd.*, 198 Ariz. 283, 9 P.3d 314 (2000).

7. *Procedure for Making Objections to Proposed Jury Instructions.* While it is clearly better, for record purposes, for objections to proposed instructions to be submitted formally in advance of argument, it is frequently not possible to do so and the usual practice is for proposed instructions to be argued and settled orally to the Court, with a reporter present to transcribe the proceedings. The Supreme Court has recognized this practice, but stressed the importance of making a full and complete record, before a court reporter, of the parties' positions on proposed instructions and the trial court's rulings. *Gosewisch v. American Honda Motor Co., Inc.*, 153 Ariz. 400, 737 P.2d 376, Prod. Liab. Rep. (CCH) P 11531, 83 A.L.R.4th 53 (1987); *but cf. Hiett v. Howard*, 17 Ariz. App. 1, 494 P.2d 1347 (Div. 1 1972).

8. *Copies of Instructions for Jurors.* As part of the 1995 "jury reform" amendments, Rule 51(b)(3) was adopted, which requires that the Court's preliminary and final instructions to the jury be in written form, and that a copy of the instructions be furnished to each juror before they are read. When they retire for deliberations, the jurors are to take with them their copies of the final written instructions. In limited jurisdiction courts, the jury instructions may be recorded on audio tape and the instructions may be provided to the jury in that form for their use during deliberations.

9. *Communications and Questions From Jurors.* It is not at all uncommon for jurors, during the course of their deliberations, to communicate questions to the trial court concerning the jury instructions or other matters of concern to them. It is proper for

the trial court to instruct the jury on acceptable methods for them to communicate with the Court. *Harrington v. Beauchamp Enterprises*, 158 Ariz. 118, 761 P.2d 1022 (1988). It is clear error for the trial court, however, to respond to a substantive inquiry from the jury without consulting counsel for the parties. *Perkins v. Komarnyckyj*, 172 Ariz. 115, 834 P.2d 1260 (1992). In many cases, the failure to respond to such an inquiry may in effect be a communication.

Even if the trial judge has no intention of responding to the jury's question, and does not respond, the judge must still inform the parties of the communication and allow them to voice their positions and/or concerns for the record. *Perkins v. Komarnyckyj*, 172 Ariz. 115, 834 P.2d 1260 (1992). A 2009 amendment to Rule 51(a) added a provision requiring that communications between the court and members of the jury be in writing or on the record.

10. *Objections to Arguments of Counsel.* In 1989, the Arizona Supreme Court abrogated the provisions of former Rule 51(d), which, read literally, prohibited the interruption of the arguments of counsel "except for the purpose of raising a question of law." While the Rule discouraged contemporaneous objections to counsel's argument, and implied that such objections were preserved, except for an otherwise undefined category of objections that raised "questions of law," the Rule in fact had never been interpreted and operated as a blanket prohibition upon objections during argument. *Copeland v. City of Yuma*, 160 Ariz. 307, 772 P.2d 1160 (Ct. App. Div. 1 1989). It is generally assumed that prior case law on the necessity for and timeliness of objections to argument, which effectively ignored Rule 51(d), will survive its abrogation.

There is authority to the effect that an objection to perceived misconduct of counsel during argument must be made at the time the misconduct occurs, or it is waived. *Kelch v. Courson*, 103 Ariz. 576, 447 P.2d 550 (1968) (overruled by, Heimke v. Munoz, 106 Ariz. 26, 470 P.2d 107 (1970)). Generally, however, such objections have been treated as timely and adequately preserved if raised, through a motion for mistrial or otherwise, before the case is submitted to the jury. *Grant v. Arizona Public Service Co.*, 133 Ariz. 434, 652 P.2d 507 (1982).

Rule 52. Findings by the court; judgment on partial findings

(a) Effect. In all actions tried upon the facts without a jury or with an advisory jury, the court, if requested before trial, shall find the facts specially and state separately its conclusions of law thereon, and judgment shall be entered pursuant to Rule 58; and in granting or refusing interlocutory injunctions the court shall similarly set forth the findings of fact and conclusions of law which constitute the grounds of its action. Requests for findings are not necessary for purposes of review. Findings of fact, whether based on oral or documentary evidence, shall not be set aside unless clearly erroneous, and due regard shall be given to the opportunity of the trial court to judge the credibility of witnesses. The findings of a master, to the extent that the court adopts them, shall be considered as the findings of the court. It will be sufficient if the findings of fact and conclusions of law are stated orally and recorded in open court following the close of the evidence or appear in an opinion or minute entry or memorandum of decision filed by the court. Findings of fact and conclusions of law are unnecessary on decisions of motions under Rule 12 or 56 or any other motion except as provided in subdivision (c) of this rule.

Amended Aug. 7, 1984, effective Nov. 1, 1984; Oct. 9, 1996, effective Dec. 1, 1996.

(b) Amendment. Upon motion of a party made not later than 15 days after entry of judgment the court may amend its findings or make additional findings and may amend the judgment accordingly. The motion may be made with a motion for a new trial pursuant to Rule 59. When findings of fact are made in actions tried by the court without a jury, the question of the sufficiency of the evidence to support the findings may thereafter be raised whether or not the party raising the question has made in the superior court an objection to such findings or has made a motion to amend them or a motion for judgment.

Amended July 23, 1976, effective Oct. 1, 1976; Oct. 9, 1996, effective Dec. 1, 1996.

(c) Judgment on Partial Findings. If during a trial without a jury a party has been fully heard on an issue and the court after determining the facts finds against the party on that issue, the court may enter judgment as a matter of law against that party with respect to a claim or defense that cannot under the controlling law be maintained or defeated without a favorable finding on that issue, or the court may decline to render any judgment until the close of all the evidence. Such a judgment shall be supported by findings of fact and conclusions of law if requested as required by subdivision (a) of this rule.

Added Oct. 9, 1996, effective Dec. 1, 1996.

(d) Submission on Agreed Statement of Facts. The parties to an action may submit the matter in controversy to the court upon an agreed statement of facts, signed by them and filed with the clerk and the court shall render judgment thereon as in other cases. The agreed statement, certified by the court to be correct, and the judgment shall constitute the record of the action.

Added as Rule 52(c). Renumbered as rule 52(d) and amended Oct. 9, 1996, effective Dec. 1, 1996.

STATE BAR COMMITTEE NOTES

1984 Amendment

[Rule 52(a)] The amendment expressly authorizes superior court judges to state findings of fact and conclusions of law orally or in a minute entry. This change comports with judicial construction of the current rule, and thus does not alter Arizona practice. See *Lane v. Hognason*, 12 Ariz. App. 330, 470 P.2d 478 (Div. 2 1970), opinion supplemented on reh'g, 13 Ariz. App. 120, 474 P.2d 839 (Div. 2 1970), in which the minute entry procedure was approved. This rule does not preclude the settling of findings of fact and conclusions of law with advice of counsel.

AUTHORS' COMMENTS

Analysis

1. *Scope and Purpose of Rule.* Rule 52 generally governs the procedures for securing, or for dispensing with, specific findings of fact in actions tried to the Court or with an advisory jury.

2. *Comparison With Federal Rule.* Despite structural differences, ARCP 52 and FRCP 52 are substantially similar, but there are some significant differences. ARCP 52(a) provides that findings of fact and conclusions of law are required in trials to the

Court only "if requested before trial." That requirement also is found in ARCP 52(c), governing judgment on partial findings. Neither FRCP 52(a) nor FRCP 52(c) contains such a provision.

While phrased differently, ARCP 52(b) and FRCP 52(b) are substantively identical, except for the time period specified for making a motion to alter or amend findings. Under the Arizona Rule, such a motion must be made no later than 15 days after entry of judgment; the time period specified in the Federal Rule is no later than 28 days after entry of judgment. Before FRCP 52(a) was amended in 2009, the rule provided a 10-day time period for filing a Rule 52 post-judgment motion. The commentary to the 2009 Amendment to FRCP 52 states the 10-day time period was expanded to 28 days because experience had shown that, in many cases, it was not possible to prepare a satisfactory post-judgment motion in the 10 days provided. ARCP 52 has not been amended to similarly expand the time period for filing a Rule 52 post-judgment motion, which remains at 15 days.

ARCP 52(c) is essentially the same as FRCP 52(c), but there are differences. In 2009, FRCP 52(c) was amended to replace the phrase "*judgment as a matter of law*" with the word "*judgment*" to avoid any confusion with a FRCP 50 judgment as a matter of law in a jury case. The Federal Commentators stated "the standards that govern judgment as a matter of law in a jury case have no bearing on a decision under Rule 52(c)." ARCP 52(c) has not been amended to conform with its federal counterpart.

There is no provision in the Federal Rules of Civil Procedure corresponding to ARCP 52(d) [Submission on Agreed Statement of Facts].

In 2007, the language of FRCP 52 was amended as part of the general restyling of the Federal Rules of Civil Procedure to make the Federal Rules more easily understood and to make style and terminology consistent throughout the Federal Rules of Civil Procedure. Those stylistic modifications have not been incorporated into ARCP 52.

3. *When Findings Required.* Rule 52 requires the trial court to make findings of fact where they are requested by one of the parties before trial. *Fritts v. Ericson*, 87 Ariz. 227, 349 P.2d 1107 (1960); *Miller v. McAlister*, 151 Ariz. 435, 728 P.2d 654 (Ct. App. Div. 1 1986). Where such a request is made, the trial court is only required to make findings on the ultimate facts, not each subsidiary evidentiary fact on which the ultimate facts are based. *In re U.S. Currency in Amount of $26,980.00*, 199 Ariz. 291, 18 P.3d 85 (Ct. App. Div. 2 2000). Findings of fact must be made, whether requested or not, where the Court grants or refuses a preliminary injunction. *Bayless Inv. & Trading Co. v. Bekins Moving & Storage Co.*, 26 Ariz. App. 265, 547 P.2d 1065 (Div. 1

1976).

Before the 1996 amendment to the Rule, it was held that the Rule has no application to dispositions on summary judgment, which are not "tried upon the facts without a jury." *Orkin Exterminating Co., Inc. v. Robles*, 128 Ariz. 132, 624 P.2d 329 (Ct. App. Div. 2 1980). The 1996 amendments added, *inter alia*, the final sentence of Rule 52(a) which specifies that findings of fact and conclusions of law are unnecessary on the decision of any motion except the motion for judgment as a matter of law in nonjury trials implicitly authorized by Rule 52(c).

While not specified in Rule 52, it has been previously held that a trial court is also required to make appropriate findings of fact and conclusions of law in awarding attorneys' fees under either A.R.S. § 12-341.01(C) or § 12-349 (amended 2013), or under Ariz.R.Civ.P. 11, *State v. Richey*, 160 Ariz. 564, 774 P.2d 1354 (1989). Rule 54(g), adopted in 1996, which dealt specifically with claims for attorneys' fees, provided that, in determining such claims, the court "shall find the facts and state its conclusions of law as provided in Rule 52(a)." *See also*, A.R.S. § 12-350. This language was removed from the Rule by the 1999 amendment, placing in an uncertain status the continuing vitality of earlier cases which held that findings and conclusions were required in this situation. Since 1999, the courts that have addressed the issue have confirmed that findings and conclusions are required. *Bennett v. Baxter Group, Inc.*, 223 Ariz. 414, 224 P.3d 230 (Ct. App. Div. 2 2010); *Johnson v. Mohave County*, 206 Ariz. 330, 78 P.3d 1051 (Ct. App. Div. 1 2003).

The 1996 amendment added to Rule 52(a) the phrase, taken from FCRP Rule 52(a), that: "Requests for findings are not necessary for purposes of review." The significance of this phrase in the Federal Rule, which does not require a request for findings and conclusions, is relatively easy to discern. Under the Arizona Rule, however, except in the case where the Court grants or denies an interlocutory injunction, findings of fact and conclusions of law are, by Rule, not necessary unless they are requested before trial and decisions in cases where such a request is not made are obviously subject to review. Whether this new phrase was intended to have any significance other than a statement of the obvious remains to be seen.

4. *Purpose of Findings.* Several purposes are served by the requirement that the trial court state separately its findings of fact and conclusions of law.

First, a defeated party may more easily determine whether the case presents issues appropriate for appellate review. *Miller v. Board of Sup'rs of Pinal County*, 175 Ariz. 296, 855 P.2d 1357, 84 Ed. Law Rep. 549 (1993).

Second, findings and conclusions clarify what has been decided and provide guidance in applying the doctrines of *res judicata* and collateral estoppel. *Miller v. Board of Sup'rs of Pinal County*, 175 Ariz. 296, 855 P.2d 1357, 84 Ed. Law Rep. 549 (1993).

Third, the requirement prompts judges to consider issues more carefully because they are required to state not only the end results of their inquiry, but also the process by which they reached it. *Miller v. Board of Sup'rs of Pinal County*, 175 Ariz. 296, 855 P.2d 1357, 84 Ed. Law Rep. 549 (1993).

Finally, and most importantly, findings and conclusions permit an appellate court to examine more closely the basis on which the trial court reached its eventual judgment. *Miller v. Board of Sup'rs of Pinal County*, 175 Ariz. 296, 855 P.2d 1357, 84 Ed. Law Rep. 549 (1993); *City of Phoenix v. Consolidated Water Co.*, 101 Ariz. 43, 415 P.2d 866 (1966); *Ellingson v. Fuller*, 20 Ariz. App. 456, 513 P.2d 1339 (Div. 1 1973); *In re U.S. Currency in Amount of $26,980.00*, 199 Ariz. 291, 18 P.3d 85 (Ct. App. Div. 2 2000). To satisfy this purpose of the requirement, the trial court's findings must encompass all of the "ultimate" facts necessary to resolve the disputed issues in the case and be sufficiently specific and comprehensive to allow an appellate court to test the validity of the judgment. *Miller v. Board of Sup'rs of Pinal County*, 175 Ariz. 296, 855 P.2d 1357, 84 Ed. Law Rep. 549 (1993); *Elliott v. Elliott*, 165 Ariz. 128, 796 P.2d 930 (Ct. App. Div. 1 1990). Correspondingly, findings of fact must be based on more than a one-sided presentation of the evidence and, where factual issues are disputed, all parties must be given a reasonable opportunity to present evidence. *McCarthy Western Constructors, Inc. v. Phoenix Resort Corp.*, 169 Ariz. 520, 821 P.2d 181 (Ct. App. Div. 1 1991), redesignated as opinion and publication ordered, (Apr. 2, 1991).

When the trial court has failed to comply with Rule 52(a), the proper remedy is to be tailored to each case. *Miller v. Board of Sup'rs of Pinal County*, 175 Ariz. 296, 855 P.2d 1357, 84 Ed. Law Rep. 549 (1993). Where possible, when a trial court in a non-jury case fails to make, or makes insufficient, findings of fact and conclusions of law, a reviewing court should remand the case to the trial court for further findings. *Miller v. Board of Sup'rs of Pinal County*, 175 Ariz. 296, 855 P.2d 1357, 84 Ed. Law Rep. 549 (1993); *City of Tucson v. Whiteco Metrocom, Inc.*, 194 Ariz. 390, 983 P.2d 759 (Ct. App. Div. 2 1999), redesignated as opinion and publication ordered, (Apr. 14, 1999). While that is what is ordinarily done, an appellate court may also proceed to decide the appeal without those findings where the record is clear and/or the facts are not seriously in dispute and it is, accordingly, in a position to do so. In that circumstance, the failure of the trial court to make requested findings and conclusions will not be in and of itself grounds for reversal. *Miller v. Board of Sup'rs of*

Pinal County, 175 Ariz. 296, 855 P.2d 1357, 84 Ed. Law Rep. 549 (1993); *City of Phoenix v. Consolidated Water Co.*, 101 Ariz. 43, 415 P.2d 866 (1966); *Willow Creek Leasing, Inc. v. Bartzen*, 154 Ariz. 339, 742 P.2d 840 (Ct. App. Div. 1 1987).

The trial court's failure to make the required findings may, absent those circumstances, however, be reversible error and grounds for directing the entry of judgment in favor of the aggrieved party. *Miller v. Board of Sup'rs of Pinal County*, 175 Ariz. 296, 855 P.2d 1357, 84 Ed. Law Rep. 549 (1993). If the trial court's basis for a conclusion is unclear, however, an appellate court may not affirm simply because it may find some possible basis for the conclusion in the record. *Kelsey v. Kelsey*, 186 Ariz. 49, 918 P.2d 1067 (Ct. App. Div. 1 1996).

Where no findings are requested or made, the appellate court will presume that the trial court found every fact necessary to support its judgment, and will affirm if there is any proper basis for doing so. *Garden Lakes Community Ass'n, Inc. v. Madigan*, 204 Ariz. 238, 62 P.3d 983 (Ct. App. Div. 1 2003); *Horton v. Mitchell*, 200 Ariz. 523, 29 P.3d 870 (Ct. App. Div. 1 2001); *Crye v. Edwards*, 178 Ariz. 327, 873 P.2d 665 (Ct. App. Div. 1 1993); *Able Distributing Co., Inc. v. James Lampe, General Contractor*, 160 Ariz. 399, 773 P.2d 504 (Ct. App. Div. 1 1989).

5. *Standards for Appellate Review of Findings.* Findings of fact, "whether based on oral or documentary evidence," are not to be set aside unless they are clearly erroneous, and will generally be sustained if there is any reasonable evidence to support them. *In re Estate of Pouser*, 193 Ariz. 574, 975 P.2d 704 (1999); *Valley Medical Specialists v. Farber*, 194 Ariz. 363, 982 P.2d 1277, 15 I.E.R. Cas. (BNA) 419 (1999); *Sholes v. Fernando*, 228 Ariz. 455, 268 P.3d 1112 (Ct. App. Div. 2 2011); *In re Estate of Jung*, 210 Ariz. 202, 109 P.3d 97 (Ct. App. Div. 1 2005); *In re Estate of Zaritsky*, 198 Ariz. 599, 12 P.3d 1203 (Ct. App. Div. 1 2000); *Najar v. State*, 198 Ariz. 345, 9 P.3d 1084 (Ct. App. Div. 2 2000); *SAL Leasing, Inc. v. State ex rel. Napolitano*, 198 Ariz. 434, 10 P.3d 1221 (Ct. App. Div. 1 2000); *Ahwatukee Custom Estates Management Ass'n, Inc. v. Turner*, 196 Ariz. 631, 2 P.3d 1276 (Ct. App. Div. 1 2000).

A finding is "clearly erroneous" when the reviewing court is left with the definite and firm conviction that a mistake has been made. *Najar v. State*, 198 Ariz. 345, 9 P.3d 1084 (Ct. App. Div. 2 2000); *Civil Rights Div. of Arizona Dept. of Law v. Amphitheater Unified School Dist. No. 10*, 140 Ariz. 83, 680 P.2d 517, 17 Ed. Law Rep. 657, 33 Fair Empl. Prac. Cas. (BNA) 1135 (Ct. App. Div. 2 1983); *Arizona Tank Lines, Inc. v. Arizona Corp. Commission*, 18 Ariz. App. 390, 502 P.2d 539 (Div. 1 1972); *Park Central Development Co. v. Roberts Dry Goods, Inc.*, 11 Ariz. App. 58, 461

P.2d 702 (Div. 1 1969).

In addition, an appellate court assumes that the trial court found every fact necessary to sustain the judgment, and there is implied in every judgment, in addition to the express findings made, any additional finding necessary to sustain the judgment, if reasonably supported by the evidence, and not in conflict with the express findings. *John C. Lincoln Hosp. and Health Corp. v. Maricopa County*, 208 Ariz. 532, 96 P.3d 530 (Ct. App. Div. 1 2004), as amended, (Sept. 1, 2004). This requires a litigant to object to inadequate findings at the trial court level, so that the trial court will have an opportunity to correct them, and failure to do so constitutes a waiver. *John C. Lincoln Hosp. and Health Corp. v. Maricopa County*, 208 Ariz. 532, 96 P.3d 530 (Ct. App. Div. 1 2004), as amended on other grounds, (Sept. 1, 2004).

The deferential "clearly erroneous" standard does not apply to conclusions of law, findings that combine both statements of fact and law, and findings which are induced by an erroneous view of the law. *Enterprise Leasing Co. of Phoenix v. Ehmke*, 197 Ariz. 144, 3 P.3d 1064, 15 I.E.R. Cas. (BNA) 1496, 55 U.S.P.Q.2d 1303, 139 Lab. Cas. (CCH) P 58794 (Ct. App. Div. 1 1999); *Mohave Elec. Co-op., Inc. v. Byers*, 189 Ariz. 292, 942 P.2d 451 (Ct. App. Div. 1 1997); *State Farm Fire and Cas. Co. v. Brown*, 183 Ariz. 518, 905 P.2d 527 (Ct. App. Div. 1 1995); *Lee Development Co. v. Papp*, 166 Ariz. 471, 803 P.2d 464 (Ct. App. Div. 2 1990). An appellate court is not bound by a trial court's legal conclusion and, where the trial court's decision is purely one of law, the appellate court is free to substitute its own judgment. *State Farm Fire and Cas. Co. v. Brown*, 183 Ariz. 518, 905 P.2d 527 (Ct. App. Div. 1 1995); *Passey v. Great Western Associates II*, 174 Ariz. 420, 850 P.2d 133 (Ct. App. Div. 1 1993); *Valley Nat. Bank of Arizona v. Insurance Co. of North America*, 172 Ariz. 212, 836 P.2d 425 (Ct. App. Div. 1 1992). The "clearly erroneous" standard will apply, however, to a finding of fact which is mistakenly designated as a conclusion of law. *Schade v. Diethrich*, 158 Ariz. 1, 760 P.2d 1050 (1988).

Specific findings are not required, except in rulings on requests for preliminary injunctions, where they have not been requested in a timely manner. *Lenslite Co. v. Zocher*, 95 Ariz. 208, 388 P.2d 421 (1964). In that event, it will be assumed by a reviewing court that the trial court found every fact necessary to sustain the judgment and the judgment will be upheld if there is any reasonable evidence to support it. *Garden Lakes Community Ass'n, Inc. v. Madigan*, 204 Ariz. 238, 62 P.3d 983 (Ct. App. Div. 1 2003); *A.R. Teeters & Associates, Inc. v. Eastman Kodak Co.*, 172 Ariz. 324, 836 P.2d 1034 (Ct. App. Div. 1 1992); *Able Distributing Co., Inc. v. James Lampe, General Contractor*, 160 Ariz. 399, 773 P.2d 504 (Ct. App. Div. 1 1989); *Ellingson v. Sloan*, 22 Ariz. App. 383,

527 P.2d 1100 (Div. 1 1974); *Wilson v. Tucson General Hospital*, 18 Ariz. App. 31, 499 P.2d 762 (Div. 2 1972); *Fleming v. Becker*, 14 Ariz. App. 347, 483 P.2d 579 (Div. 1 1971); *Kay v. Biggs*, 13 Ariz. App. 172, 475 P.2d 1 (Div. 1 1970). The trial court will be affirmed where it has reached the correct conclusion, even though it gave a wrong or insufficient reason. *Chandler Medical Bldg. Partners v. Chandler Dental Group*, 175 Ariz. 273, 855 P.2d 787 (Ct. App. Div. 1 1993); *Passey v. Great Western Associates II*, 174 Ariz. 420, 850 P.2d 133 (Ct. App. Div. 1 1993).

6. *Form of Findings.* The potential burden of preparing separate detailed findings of fact in every case where they are requested was partially alleviated by the 1984 amendment to Rule 52(a) which permits the findings of the Court to be "stated orally and recorded in open court" or included in "an opinion or minute entry or memorandum of decision. . . ." In fact, the amendment endorsed what had already been the practice. *See* State Bar Committee Note to 1984 Amendment.

7. *Amendment of Findings.* Rule 52(b) authorizes a motion to amend findings or for additional findings, which must be brought within fifteen (15) days of the entry of judgment. The trial court was granted limited authority to enlarge that period by the 1994 amendment to Ariz.R.Civ.P. 6(b). The circumstances under which such an extension to file a motion under Rule 52(b) can be secured are discussed in Section 5 of the *Authors' Comments* under Rule 6.

A timely motion under Rule 52(b) extends the time period for filing a notice of appeal until thirty days from its disposition. Rule 9(b)(2), Ariz. R. Civ. App. Pr. A motion to amend findings is not proper, however, where there has been no initial request that findings be made. *United Leasing, Inc. v. Commonwealth Land Title Agency of Tucson, Inc.*, 134 Ariz. 385, 656 P.2d 1246 (Ct. App. Div. 2 1982).

An objection that the judgment was against the weight of the evidence may also be raised in a motion for new trial brought under Ariz.R.Civ.P. 59, even though such an objection was not raised to any proposed findings submitted to the Court. *Gerow v. Covill*, 192 Ariz. 9, 960 P.2d 55 (Ct. App. Div. 1 1998), as amended, (Aug. 26, 1998). Raising such an objection in that fashion will preserve the issue for appeal. *Gerow v. Covill*, 192 Ariz. 9, 960 P.2d 55 (Ct. App. Div. 1 1998), as amended on other grounds, (Aug. 26, 1998).

8. *Motions for Judgment as a Matter of Law; Judgments on Partial Findings.* Rule 52(c), which authorizes "judgments on partial findings," was added by the 1996 amendments to the Rule, to bring it into greater conformity with Fed.R.Civ.P. 52. The intent of the provision is to authorize "motions for judgment as a

matter of law," created by the 1996 amendment to Ariz.R.Civ.P. 50(a), in nonjury trials, even though it does not explicitly do so. In effect, the Rule replaces the provision in Rule 41(b), which was deleted as part of the 1996 amendments, which authorized motions for dismissal at the conclusion of the plaintiff's case in trials to the Court. The new "motion for judgment as a matter of law" can be made at any time when a party "has been fully heard on an issue." The point when that occurs is, to some degree, discretionary with the trial judge, and will not necessarily coincide with the point at which one party rests its case. A "directed verdict" in a trial to the court based on the insufficiency of the evidence may be treated as a judgment on partial findings under this Rule. *Johnson v. Pankratz*, 196 Ariz. 621, 2 P.3d 1266 (Ct. App. Div. 1 2000).

If the Court finds against a party with respect to an issue as to which that party has been fully heard, it may enter a judgment against that party with respect to any claim or defense that cannot, as a matter of law, be maintained or defeated without a favorable finding on that issue. Such a judgment on partial findings may be entered against either plaintiffs or defendants. Alternatively, the Court can decline to render any judgment until the close of all the evidence.

In determining such a motion for judgment as a matter of law in nonjury trials, the Court must make findings of fact and state conclusions of law "if requested" as required by Rule 52(a), *i.e.*, before trial. This may require parties, if they desire findings of fact and conclusions of law in the event a motion for judgment as a matter of law is made and decided during a trial to the Court, to make protective requests for them before trial commences.

9. *Submission of Matter on Agreed Statement of Facts.* Rule 52(c) authorizes the parties to submit a matter to the court for decision on an agreed statement of facts. Where that procedure is invoked, the trial court may not go beyond the stipulated facts submitted and may not take additional evidence. *Bishop v. Department of Public Safety*, 122 Ariz. 512, 596 P.2d 38 (Ct. App. Div. 2 1979); *Clayton v. Communications Capital Corp.*, 7 Ariz. App. 449, 440 P.2d 330 (1968).

Rule 53. Masters

(a) Appointment.

(1) Unless a statute provides otherwise, a court may appoint a master only to:

(A) perform duties consented to by the parties;

(B) hold trial proceedings and make or recommend findings of fact and conclusions of law on issues to be decided by the court without a jury if appointment is warranted by

(i) some exceptional condition or

(ii) the need to perform an accounting or resolve a difficult computation of damages; or

(C) address pretrial and post-trial matters that cannot be addressed effectively and timely by an available superior court judge in the county in which the court sits.

(2) A master shall not have a relationship to the parties, counsel, action or court that would require disqualification of a judge under Rule 81 of the Rules of the Supreme Court of Arizona unless the parties consent with the court's approval to appointment of a particular person after disclosure of any potential grounds for disqualification.

(3) In appointing a master, the court shall consider the fairness of imposing the likely expenses on the parties and must protect against unreasonable expense or delay.

Amended Sept. 15, 1987, effective Nov. 15, 1987; Sept. 27, 2005, effective Jan. 1, 2006.

(b) Order appointing master.

(1) *Notice.* The court shall give the parties notice and an opportunity to be heard before appointing a master. A party may suggest candidates for appointment.

(2) *Contents.* The order appointing a master shall direct the master to proceed with all reasonable diligence and must state:

(A) the master's duties, including any investigation or enforcement duties, and any limits on the master's authority under Rule 53(c);

(B) the circumstances, if any, in which the master may communicate ex parte with the court or a party;

(C) the nature of the materials to be preserved and filed as the record of the master's activities;

(D) the time limits, method of filing the record, other procedures, and standards for reviewing the master's orders, findings and recommendations; and

(E) the basis, terms, and procedure for fixing the master's compensation under Rule 53(i).

(3) *Acceptance of Appointment.* Before accepting an appointment as a master, the prospective appointee shall file an affidavit or declaration disclosing whether there is any ground for disqualification under Rule 81 of the Rule of the Supreme Court of Arizona. If a potential ground for disqualification is disclosed, the prospective appointee shall not proceed with the appointment unless the parties have consented (with the court's approval) to waive the ground for disqualification.

Amended Aug, 30, 2012, effective Jan. 1, 2013.

(4) *Amendment.* The order appointing a master may be amended at any time after notice to the parties and an opportunity to be heard.

Amended September 27, 2005, effective January 1, 2006.

(c) Master's authority. Unless the appointing order expressly directs otherwise, a master has authority to regulate all proceedings and take all appropriate measures to perform fairly and efficiently the assigned duties. The master may by order impose upon a party any noncontempt sanction provided by Rules 37 or 45, and may recommend a contempt sanction against a party and sanctions (including contempt) against a nonparty.

Amended Sept. 15, 1987, effective Nov. 15, 1987; Sept. 27, 2005, effective Jan. 1, 2006.

(d) Meetings and evidentiary hearings.

(1) *Meetings.* When a master is appointed, the clerk shall forthwith furnish the master with a copy of the appointing order. Upon receipt thereof, unless the appointing order otherwise provides, the master shall forthwith set a time and place for the first meeting of the parties or their attorneys, to be held within twenty days after the date of the appointing order, and shall notify the parties or their attorneys. It is the duty of the master to proceed with all reasonable diligence. Either party, on notice to the parties and master, may apply to the court for an order requiring the master to speed the proceedings and, if applicable, make the report. If a party fails to appear at the time and place appointed, the master may proceed ex parte or, in the master's discretion, adjourn the proceedings to a future day, giving notice to the absent party of the adjournment.

(2) *Evidentiary hearings.* Unless the appointing order expressly directs otherwise, a master conducting an evidentiary hearing may exercise the power of the appointing court to compel, take and record evidence.

Amended Sept. 15, 1987, effective Nov. 15, 1987; Sept. 27, 2005, effective Jan. 1, 2006.

(e) Master's orders. A master who makes an order shall file the order and promptly serve a copy on each party. The clerk shall enter the order on the docket.

Amended Sept. 15, 1987, effective Nov. 15, 1987; Sept. 27, 2005, effective Jan. 1, 2006.

(f) Draft reports. Before filing a report, a master may submit a draft of the report to the parties for the purpose of receiving comments.

Amended Sept. 15, 1987, effective Nov. 15, 1987; Sept. 27, 2005, effective Jan. 1, 2006.

(g) Master's reports. A master shall report to the court as required by the order of appointment. The master shall file the report and promptly serve a copy of the report on each party, unless the court directs otherwise.

Amended Sept. 15, 1987, effective Nov. 15, 1987; Sept. 27, 2005, effective Jan. 1, 2006.

(h) Action on master's order, report or recommendations.

(1) *Time to object or move.* A party may file objections to—or a motion to adopt or modify—the master's final order, report, or recommendations no later than 10 days from the time the master's final order, report, or recommendations are served, unless the court sets a different time.

(2) *Fact findings.* The court shall decide all objections to findings of fact made or recommended by a master under the clearly erroneous standard, unless the parties stipulate with the court's consent that:

(A) the master's findings will be reviewed de novo, or

(B) the findings of a master will be final.

(3) *Legal conclusions.* The court shall decide de novo all objections to conclusions of law made or recommended by a master.

(4) *Procedural matters.* Unless the order of appointment establishes a different standard of review, the court may set aside a master's ruling on a procedural matter only for an abuse of discretion.

(5) *Action.* In acting on a master's final order, report, or recommendations, the court shall consider and rule upon any objections and motions filed by the parties, and may adopt or affirm, modify, wholly or partly reject or reverse, or resubmit to the master with instructions.

Amended Sept. 27, 2005, effective Jan. 1, 2006.

(i) Compensation.

(1) *Fixing compensation.* The court shall fix the master's compensation before or after judgment on the basis and terms stated in the order of appointment, but the court may set a new basis and terms after providing notice to the parties and an opportunity to be heard.

(2) *Payment.* The compensation fixed under Rule 53(i)(1) must be paid either:

(A) by a party or parties; or

(B) from a fund or subject matter of the action within the court's control.

(3) *Allocation.* If a master's compensation is to be paid by a party or the parties, the court shall allocate payment of the master's compensation among the parties and may consider the nature and amount of the controversy, the means of the parties, the extent to which any party is more responsible than other parties for the reference to or use of a master, and any other factor the court deems relevant. An interim allocation may be amended by the court after providing notice to the parties and an opportunity to be heard.

Amended Sept. 27, 2005, effective Jan. 1, 2006.

(j) Repealed Sept. 27, 2005, effective Jan. 1, 2006.

(k) Repealed Sept. 27, 2005, effective Jan. 1, 2006.

STATE BAR COMMITTEE NOTE

2005 Amendment

Rule 53 was extensively revised to incorporate most, but not all, of the December 2003 amendments to Rule 53 of the Federal Rules of Civil Procedure. Where the provisions of this rule are similar to those found in Federal Rule 53, a court may look to federal precedent and the advisory committee notes to Federal Rule 53 for guidance in interpreting this Rule.

The subdivision (d) provisions for evidentiary hearings are reduced from the extensive provisions previously set forth in Rule 53. This simplification of the rule is not intended to diminish the authority that may be delegated to a master. Reliance is placed on the broad and general terms of the master's authority set forth in amended Rule 53(c).

The amendments to the rule require in several places that a court must give the parties "an opportunity to be heard" before taking a specified action. This requirement can be satisfied by giving the parties an opportunity to make written submissions to the court and does not require the court to hold a hearing before taking action.

AUTHORS' COMMENTS

Analysis

3. Orders Appointing Masters.
4. Proceedings Upon Appointment; Report of Master.
5. Setting Master's Compensation.

1. *Scope and Purpose of Rule*. Superior court judges have clear authority, which is constitutional in origin, to appoint masters, subject to restrictions to be established by Supreme Court rule. Ariz. Const. Art. 6, 24. The Rule which implements this authority, Rule 53, was extensively amended in 2005 to bring it into greater conformity with the corresponding provision of the Federal Rules of Civil Procedure. While the amendment significantly restructured the Rule, it retained the sense that appointment of masters is to be the exception rather than the rule.

Unless a statute provides otherwise, masters may only be appointed to perform duties to which the parties to the case have consented, to address pretrial and post-trial matters that cannot be addressed effectively and timely by an available Superior Court judge in the county where the action is pending, or to hold trial proceedings and make or recommend findings of fact and conclusions of law on issues to be decided by the court. The latter type of appointment may only be made in cases to be tried to the court without a jury, and only where appointment is warranted by some exceptional condition or the need to perform an accounting or to resolve a difficult damages computation. This is consistent with the prior Rule, under which it was found to be error for a trial court to initially order the bifurcation of a breach of contract trial between the issues of liability and damages, and then vacate that order and appoint a special master to decide the issues of damages after the jury had found liability. Such an order was not authorized by the Rule, and also operated to deprive the defendant of the right to a jury trial on an issue triable to a jury. *Chartone, Inc. v. Bernini*, 207 Ariz. 162, 83 P.3d 1103 (Ct. App. Div. 2 2004).

The master cannot have a relationship to the parties, court or counsel that would require the disqualification of a judge, unless the parties consent to the appointment of such a person after disclosure of the grounds for disqualification. In appointing a master, the court is directed to consider the fairness of imposing the likely expense on the parties, and must protect against unreasonable expense or delay. Before appointing a master, the court must give the parties notice and an opportunity to be heard on the subject.

2. *Comparison With Federal Rule*. In 2006, ARCP 53 was amended to adopt most, but not all of the 2003 amendments to FRCP 53. And, for a time, ARCP 53 and FRCP 53 were similar,

but even then there were both stylistic and substantive differences.

As a consequence of an amendment to Ariz. R. Civ. P. 53(b), effective January 1, 2013, Ariz. R. Civ. P. 53(b) and Fed. R. Civ. P. 53(b) are dissimilar.

3. *Orders Appointing Masters.* The vehicle for the appointment of a master is an order entered by the court. Such an order may now be entered before the prospective master files a conflicts disclosure affidavit, as required by former Rule 53 (b)(3). Ariz. R. Civ. P. 53(b)(3), as amended effective January 1, 2013, now allows the court to enter an order appointing a master without first requiring a conflicts disclosure affidavit from the prospective master. Before accepting such appointment, however, Ariz. R. Civ. P. 53(b) (2013) requires the prospective master to file an affidavit disclosing whether there are any grounds for disqualification under Rule 81 of the Rules of the Arizona Supreme Court.

The order of appointment is to specify

(1) the special master's duties, including any investigation or enforcement duties, any limits on the special master's authority;
(2) the circumstances, if any, in which the special master may communicate ex parte with the court or a party;
(3) the nature of the materials to be preserved and filed as the record of the master's activities, the time limits;
(4) method of filing the record and standards for reviewing the master's orders, findings and recommendations; and
(5) the basis, terms and procedure for fixing the special master's compensation.

An order appointing a master is not an appealable order. *Bolon v. Pennington*, 3 Ariz. App. 433, 415 P.2d 148 (1966).

4. *Proceedings Upon Appointment; Report of Master.* Unless the order of appointment provides otherwise, a master has authority to regulate all proceedings and take all appropriate measures to perform the duties assigned. The master is to schedule and conduct the first meeting with the parties and their counsel within twenty (20) days after the date of the appointing order. A master conducting an evidentiary hearing may exercise the power of the appointing court to compel, take and record evidence. The master may by order impose upon a party any sanction, except contempt, authorized by Ariz.R.Civ.P. 37 or 45, and may recommend a sanction of contempt against a party and sanctions (including contempt) against a nonparty.

A master must report to the court as required by the order of appointment. This report, and any other report the master chooses to submit, must be filed and served on the parties promptly. A master may circulate a draft of any report to the parties for comment before finalizing it. A party may file objections to, or a motion to adopt or modify, the master's final order, report or recommendations no later than ten (10) days from the time it is served, unless a different time is set by the court. All objections to findings of fact made or recommended by the master are to be decided by application of the "clearly erroneous" standard, unless the parties agree that they shall be final or reviewed *de novo*. *Cf. Brown v. Brown*, 15 Ariz. App. 333, 488 P.2d 689 (Div. 1 1971); *Hurst v. Hurst*, 1 Ariz. App. 603, 405 P.2d 913 (1965). Conclusions of law made or recommended by the master are reviewed *de novo*.

The court may adopt or affirm, modify, wholly or partly reject or reverse the master's order, or resubmit the matter to the master with instructions. Unless the order of appointment provides otherwise, a master's ruling on a "procedural matter" may be set aside only for an abuse of discretion. It is not error for the trial court to reject a master's report even though no objections have been filed. *Miner v. Rogers*, 115 Ariz. 463, 565 P.2d 1324 (Ct. App. Div. 2 1977). Under the prior version of the Rule, it was held that a master's report could only be approved after a "hearing," and the failure to conduct one deprived the report of its status and precluded it from constituting the findings of the court. *Wood v. Holiday Mobile Home Resorts, Inc.*, 128 Ariz. 274, 625 P.2d 337 (Ct. App. Div. 1 1980).

5. *Setting the Master's Compensation*. The court is to fix the master's compensation on the basis and terms set forth in the order of appointment, which may be amended following notice to the parties and providing them an opportunity to be heard. The master's compensation must be paid either by a party or parties or from a fund or subject matter of the action within the court's control. If the master's compensation is to be paid by a party or the parties, the court can allocate payment among the parties and, in doing so, may consider the nature and amount of the controversy, the means of the parties, the extent to which any party is more responsible than the others for the reference to a master, and any other factor the court deems relevant. The matter of assessing responsibility for the master's fees and expenses is committed to the trial court's discretion. *Hanner v. Hanner*, 95 Ariz. 191, 388 P.2d 239 (1964); *Brown v. Brown*, 15 Ariz. App. 333, 488 P.2d 689 (Div. 1 1971).

VII. JUDGMENT

Rule 54. Judgments; costs; attorney's fees

(a) Definition; Form. "Judgment" as used in these Rules includes a decree and an order from which an appeal lies. A judgment shall not contain a recital of pleadings, the report of a master, or the record of prior proceedings.

(b) Judgment Upon Multiple Claims or Involving Multiple Parties. When more than one claim for relief is presented in an action, whether as a claim, counterclaim, cross-claim, or third-party claim, or when multiple parties are involved, the court may direct the entry of final judgment as to one or more but fewer than all of the claims or parties only upon an express determination that there is no just reason for delay and upon an express direction for the entry of judgment. In the absence of such determination and direction, any order or other form of decision, however designated, which adjudicates fewer than all the claims or the rights and liabilities of fewer than all the parties shall not terminate the action as to any of the claims or parties, and the order or other form of decision is subject to revision at any time before the entry of judgment adjudicating all the claims and the rights and liabilities of all the parties. For purposes of this subsection, a claim for attorneys' fees may be considered a separate claim from the related judgment regarding the merits of a cause.

Amended July 14, 1961, effective Nov. 1, 1961; June 17, 1999, effective Dec. 1, 1999.

(c) Judgment Upon All Claims and Parties. A judgment shall not be final unless the court states that no further matters remain pending and that judgment is entered pursuant to Rule 54(c).

Former Rule 54(c) deleted Sept. 15, 1987, effective Oct. 1, 1987. New Rule 54(c) added Aug. 28, 2013, effective Jan. 1, 2014.

(d) Demand for Judgment. A judgment by default shall not be different in kind from or exceed in amount that prayed for in the demand for judgment. Except as to a party against whom a judgment is entered by default, every final judgment shall grant the relief to which the party in whose favor it is rendered is entitled, even if the party has not demanded such relief in the party's pleadings.

Amended Sept. 15, 1987, effective Oct. 1, 1987.

(e) Entry of Judgment After Death of Party. Judgment may be entered after the death of a party upon a verdict or decision upon an issue of fact rendered in the party's lifetime.

Amended Sept. 15, 1987, effective Oct. 1, 1987.

(f) Costs.

(1) A party who claims costs shall file a statement of costs and serve a copy thereof on the opposing party. The statement shall be filed and served within ten days after judgment, unless for good cause shown the time is extended by the court. At any time within five days after receipt of the copy of the statement of costs, the opposing party may file objections to the statement serving a copy thereof on the party claiming such costs. The court shall pass upon the objections and by its order correct the statement of costs to the extent that it requires correction.

(2) In medical malpractice cases only, witness fees, set forth in A.R.S. § 12-332(a)(1) as taxable costs in the Superior Court, shall include reasonable fees paid expert witnesses for testifying at trial.

Amended and effective July 1, 1970. Amended Sept. 15, 1987, effective Oct. 1, 1987; Oct. 10, 2000, effective Dec. 1, 2000.

(g) Attorneys' Fees.

(1) *Claims for Attorneys' Fees.* A claim for attorneys' fees shall be made in the pleadings.

(2) *Time of Determination.* When attorneys' fees are claimed, the determination as to the claimed attorneys' fees shall be made after a decision on the merits of the cause. The motion for attorneys' fees shall be filed within 20 days from the clerk's mailing of a decision on the merits of the cause, unless extended by the trial court.

(3) *Method of Establishing Claim.* A motion for attorneys' fees may be supported by affidavit and exhibits or, at the discretion of the court, by testimony. If the motion is contested, opposing parties may respond to the motion, and a hearing may be granted in the discretion of the court. In addition, the court may refer issues relating to the value of services to a special master under Rule 53.

(4) *Scope.* The provisions of subparagraphs (1) through (3) do not apply to claims for fees and expenses as sanctions pursuant to statute or rule, or to causes in which the substantive law governing the action provides for the recovery of such fees as an element of damages to be proved at trial.

Added Oct. 9, 1996, effective Dec. 1, 1996. Amended June 17, 1999, effective Dec. 1, 1999.

STATE BAR COMMITTEE NOTES

1961 Amendment

[Rule 54(b)] The Arizona State Bar Committee adopts as its own the relevant materials from the comment of the Federal Committee whose note in the relevant portion is as follows:

"This rule permitting appeal, upon the trial court's determination of 'no just reason for delay,' from a judgment upon one or more but less than all the claims in an action, has generally been given a sympathetic construction by the courts and its validity is settled. *Reeves v. Beardall, [62 S.Ct. 1085] 316 U.S. 283 [86 L.Ed. 1478] (1942)*; *Sears, Roebuck & Co. v. Mackey, [76 S.Ct. 895] 351 U.S. 427 [100 L.Ed. 1297] (1956)*; *Cold Metal Process Co. v. United Engineering & Foundry Co., [76 S.Ct. 904] 351 U.S. 445 [100 L.Ed. 1311] (1956)*.

"A serious difficulty has, however, arisen because the rule speaks of claims but nowhere mentions parties. A line of cases has developed in the circuits consistently holding the rule to be inapplicable to the dismissal, even with the requisite trial court determination, of one or more but less than all defendants jointly charged in an action, i.e., charged with various forms of concerted or related wrongdoing or related liability. See: *Mull v. Ackerman*, 279 F.2d 25 (2d Cir.1960); *Richards v. Smith*, 276 F.2d 652, 3 Fed. R. Serv. 2d 848 (5th Cir. 1960); *Hardy v. Bankers Life & Cas. Co.*, 222 F.2d 827 (7th Cir.1955); *Steiner v. 20th Century-Fox Film Corp.*, 220 F.2d 105 (9th Cir.1955). For purposes of Rule 54(b) it was arguable that there were as many 'claims' as there were parties defendant and that the rule in its present text applied where less than all of the parties were dismissed, cf. *United Artists Corp. v. Masterpiece Productions*, 221 F.2d 213, 215, 105 U.S.P.Q. 52 (2d Cir. 1955); *Bowling Machines, Inc. v. First Nat. Bank of Boston*, 283 F.2d 39 (1st Cir. 1960); but the Courts of Appeals are now committed to an opposite view.

"The danger of hardship through delay of appeal until the whole action is concluded may be at least as serious in the multiple-parties situations as in multiple-claims cases, see *Pabellon v. Grace Line*, 191 F.2d 169, 179, 1951 A.M.C. 1751 (2d Cir. 1951), and courts and commentators have urged that Rule 54(b) be changed to take in the former. See: *Reagan v. Traders & General Ins. Co.*, 255 F.2d 845 (5th Cir.1958); *Meadows v. Greyhound Corporation*, 235 F.2d 233 (5th Cir. 1956); *Steiner v. 20th Century-Fox Film Corp., supra*; 6 Moore's Federal Practice Par. 54.34(2) (2d ed.1953); 3 Barron & Holtzoff, Federal Practice & Procedure Sec. 1193.2 (Wright ed. 1958); Developments in the Law—Multiparty Litigation, 71 Harv.L.Rev. 874, 981 (1958); Note, 62 Yale L.J. 263, 271 (1953); Ill.Ann.Stat. ch. 110, Sec. 50(2) (Smith-Hurd 1956). The amendment accomplishes this purpose by referring explicitly to parties."

1970 Amendment

[Rule 54(f)] (1) Rule 54(f). The amended rule is designed expressly to settle the present conflict between this rule and A.R.S. § 12-346 pertaining to statements of costs.

(2) Prior to this amendment, Rule 54(f) provided that costs could be taxed by the clerk on one day's notice. There is no similar provision in A.R.S. § 12-346.

(3) A.R.S. § 12-346 provides that the statement of costs shall be filed and served within ten days after judgment, unless for good cause shown the time is extended by the court. Prior to this amendment, Rule 54(f) placed no time limit upon filing the statement of costs.

(4) The five-day period provided in the original Rule 54(f) and A.R.S. § 12-346 for objecting to the statement of costs began to run from differing events. The amendment to Rule 54(f) eliminates this procedural inconsistency.

(5) The original Rule 54(f) provided that costs against the state, its officers, and agencies could be imposed only to the extent permitted by law. This portion

of the rule has been deleted by the amendment since the subject is completely covered in A.R.S. § 12-345.

(6) In *Hurst v. Hurst*, 1 Ariz. App. 227, 401 P.2d 232 (1965), opinion supplemented on reh'g, 1 Ariz. App. 603, 405 P.2d 913 (1965), the Court of Appeals held that under the provisions of the original Rule 54(f), which provided that costs should be allowed to the prevailing party "unless the court otherwise directs," the taxing of costs in favor of the prevailing party was discretionary with the trial court. No similar language is found in A.R.S. § 12-346 giving the court the same discretion in the matter of taxing costs. Therefore, in order to eliminate the conflict and avoid the possibility of altering a substantive right by a rule of procedure, the discretionary language has been omitted by the amendment to Rule 54(f).

(7) The substantive law on taxing costs is covered in A.R.S. § 12-341 through A.R.S. § 12-347. Reference should be had to these sections to determine when and to what extent a party has the right to costs in a given case.

1999 Amendments

[Rule 54(b)] Typically, the court will render its decision on attorneys' fees after the decision on the merits of the cause, but before the entry of judgment. *See*, Rule 58, Ariz. R. Civ. P. This procedure will allow an attorneys' fee award (if any) to be included in the judgment so that all issues may be addressed on appeal. In some cases, however, there may be good reasons to enter an immediate judgment on the merits of a cause, while leaving attorneys' fees issues to be addressed later. Rule 54(b) was amended in 1999 to permit that approach. Under the amended rule, the trial judge may certify the "merits" judgment for immediate entry and appeal before such judge renders a decision on the attorneys' fees issues. The trial court will retain jurisdiction to address the attorneys' fee issue after the appeal of a Rule 54(b) certified judgment on the merits. This amendment changes the result in *Trebilcox v. Brown & Bain, P.A.*, 133 Ariz. 588, 653 P.2d 45 (Ct. App. Div. 1 1982) (disavowed by, Western Technologies, Inc. v. Sverdrup & Parcel, Inc., 154 Ariz. 1, 739 P.2d 1318 (Ct. App. Div. 1 1986)) and (disapproved of by, Barmat v. John and Jane Doe Partners A-D, 155 Ariz. 519, 747 P.2d 1218 (1987)), which interpreted the prior version of Rule 54(b).

[Rule 54(g)] The 1999 amendments to Rule 54(g) clarify that claims for attorneys' fees under A.R.S. § 12-341.01 or other similar grounds must be timely asserted in the pleadings. The Committee notes that the amendment to Rule 54(g) differs from Rule 3.7(e), Local Rules of Practice for Maricopa County Superior Court.

Rule 54(g) was also amended expressly to provide that the rule does not apply to attorneys' fees and costs sought as sanctions pursuant to statute or rule. The amendment was adopted to avoid confusion of the type discussed in *Monti v. Monti*, 186 Ariz. 432, 924 P.2d 122 (Ct. App. Div. 1 1996).

2000 Amendment

Rule 54(f)(2) was adopted as part of the effort to consolidate formerly separate sets of procedural rules into either the Arizona Rules of Civil Procedure or the Rules of the Arizona Supreme Court, and contains the provisions of former Rule 4 of the Uniform Rules of Practice for Medical Malpractice Cases. Existing Rule 54(f) was simply redesignated as Rule 54(f)(1).

In a Comment to the original Uniform Rules of Practice for Medical Malpractice Cases, which was effective January 1, 1990 and was amended effective July 1, 1992, the Committee stated the following concerning Rule 4 [now Rule 54(f)(2)]: "This rule allows for the inclusion of reasonable fees paid expert witnesses. Any party may challenge the reasonableness of the fees charged by the expert witness for testifying at trial."

AUTHORS' COMMENTS

Analysis

1. *Scope and Purpose of Rule.* Rule 54 governs the form and significance of formal judgments. As defined by Rule 54(a), a judgment is "a decree and an order from which an appeal lies." It is the act of the Court which fixes the rights and liabilities of the parties and determines the controversy at hand. *State v. Birmingham*, 96 Ariz. 109, 392 P.2d 775 (1964); *Wolf Corp. v. Louis*, 11 Ariz. App. 352, 464 P.2d 672 (Div. 2 1970). The procedures for securing the entry of formal judgments are the subject of Ariz. R. Civ. P. 58.

2. *Comparison With Federal Rule.* ARCP 54(a), (b), and (d) are essentially the same as FRCP 54(a), (b), and (c). FRCP 54(b) does not contain the last sentence set forth in ARCP 54(b), which provides that a claim for attorney's fees may be considered a separate claim from the related judgment on the merits. FRCP 54 does not contain a provision similar to ARCP 54(c) (added 2014).

ARCP 54(f) provides that a party claiming costs must file a statement of costs within 10 days after judgment is rendered. The adverse party has five days in which to object to the statement of costs. FRCP 54(d)(1) is the corresponding provision in the Federal Rule, but it does not specify a time period in which a party is to file a statement of costs. FRCP 54(d)(1) does provide that costs are ordinarily to be allowed to the prevailing party and that they may be taxed by the Clerk on 14 days' notice. Pursuant to FRCP 54(d)(1), a motion to review the Clerk's taxation of costs must be made within five days thereafter. FRCP 54 does not contain a provision that corresponds to ARCP 54(e).

As a consequence of the 1996 and 1999 amendments, ARCP Rule 54(g) governs requests for awards of attorney's fees and roughly corresponds to FRCP 54(d)(2). FRCP 54(d)(2)(B) requires that a motion seeking an attorneys' fee award be filed no later than 14 days after entry of judgment. The corresponding Arizona provision, ARCP Rule 54(g), requires that a motion seeking an award of attorneys' fees be filed "within 20 days from the clerk's mailing of a decision on the merits of the cause," unless the court sets a different date.

3. *Form of Judgment.* The form of judgment, and the procedures for securing its entry, are governed by Ariz. R. Civ. P. 58. No particular form is required, and the designation "Judgment" need not be employed. To be effective, however, a judgment must (1) be in writing, (2) be signed, and (3) be filed with the Clerk of the Court. *Lamb v. Superior Court In and For Maricopa County*, 127 Ariz. 400, 621 P.2d 906 (1980); *Spriggel v. Maricopa County*, 15 Ariz. App. 162, 487 P.2d 8 (Div. 1 1971). It is customary for a judgment to contain a brief and succinct recital of the proceedings that led to its entry. Under Rule 54(a), however, a judgment may not "contain a recital of pleadings, the report of a master, or the record of prior proceedings."

As a consequence of the 1996 and 1999 amendments, ARCP Rule 54(g) governs requests for awards of attorney's fees and roughly corresponds to FRCP Rule 54(d)(2). FRCP Rule 54(d)(2)(B) requires that a motion seeking an attorneys' fee award be filed no later than 14 days after entry of judgment. The corresponding Arizona provision, ARCP Rule 54(g)(2), requires that a motion seeking an award of attorneys' fees be filed "within 20 days from the clerk's mailing of a decision on the merits of the cause," unless the court sets a different date.

The terms of a judgment should be clear and concise. Where there is an ambiguity, however, the judgment will be construed in light of the proceedings that led to its entry and in light of what the judgment was intended to accomplish. *Benson v. State ex rel. Eyman*, 108 Ariz. 513, 502 P.2d 1332 (1972); and, if possible, in a fashion that sustains the judgment. *Title Ins. Co. of Minnesota v. Acumen Trading Co., Inc.*, 121 Ariz. 525, 591 P.2d 1302 (1979). Conditional judgments are generally void. *Gerow v. Covill*, 192 Ariz. 9, 960 P.2d 55 (Ct. App. Div. 1 1998), as amended, (Aug. 26, 1998). Exceptions to this general rule are: (1) alternative or conditional judgments from which the rights and obligations of the parties thereto can be readily determined, and

(2) equitable judgments. *Gerow v. Covill*, 192 Ariz. 9, 960 P.2d 55 (Ct. App. Div. 1 1998), as amended on other grounds, (Aug. 26, 1998).

The parol evidence rule does not apply to judgments, and a court may not consider evidence extrinsic to the record to resolve the meaning of a judgment. *In re Marriage of Zale*, 193 Ariz. 246, 972 P.2d 230 (1999). A judgment is an act of the Court which fixes clearly the rights and liabilities of the parties in the matter before it, and not the product of a negotiated contract to which the Court is merely a party. Applying the parol evidence rule to judgments would make the Court little more than another party to a contract, would impinge upon the finality of judgments, and would allow impermissible collateral attacks on judgments. *In re Marriage of Zale*, 193 Ariz. 246, 972 P.2d 230 (1999).

A.R.S. § 12-2101 permits appeals to be taken from certain "orders" which are not typically embodied in formal judgments. The term "judgment," however, has been defined to include "any appealable order, whether denominated an order, a judgment, a decree, or otherwise." Rule 2(d), Ariz. R. Civ. App. P. Those orders listed in A.R.S. § 12-2101, accordingly, such as an order denying a motion to compel arbitration, are "an order from which an appeal lies" and, thus, judgments within the meaning of this Rule. *Holm Development and Management, Inc. v. Superior Court In and For County of Maricopa*, 161 Ariz. 376, 778 P.2d 1272 (Ct. App. Div. 1 1989). *Cf. also, Dusold v. Porta-John Corp.*, 167 Ariz. 358, 807 P.2d 526 (Ct. App. Div. 1 1990). Even if an order contains an appealable determination, it must be in appealable form to constitute a judgment. *Hamilton Mines Corp. v. Price*, 14 Ariz. App. 186, 481 P.2d 872 (Div. 1 1971); *Wiltbank v. Lyman Water Co.*, 13 Ariz. App. 485, 477 P.2d 771 (Div. 1 1970).

4. *Significance of Entry of Judgment.* The date of the entry of judgment is of critical significance because it typically commences the running of the time period for post-trial motions or prosecuting appeals and the date of entry will determine whether motions for post-verdict relief and/or the filing of a notice of appeal are timely. *City of Tucson v. Wondergem*, 4 Ariz. App. 291, 419 P.2d 552 (1966). On the other hand, it has been held that a stipulation for the dismissal of a counterclaim, which was the sole remaining claim in the action, was effective to terminate the action upon its filing and that the time for appeal ran from that date and *not* from the date of entry of the subsequent judgment formally disposing of the action. *Theriault v. Scottsdale Enterprises*, 157 Ariz. 77, 754 P.2d 1352 (Ct. App. Div. 2 1987). (The 1990 amendment to Ariz. R. Civ. P. 41(a)(1), which requires the Court to enter a formal order of dismissal when such a stipulation is presented, probably obviates the occurrence of circumstances that led to the result reached in *Theriault*.)

The date of entry of a judgment is the date the judgment is file-stamped by the Clerk of the Court. *Haroutunian v. Valueoptions, Inc.*, 218 Ariz. 541, 189 P.3d 1114 (Ct. App. Div. 2 2008); *Schoenfelder v. Arizona Bank*, 161 Ariz. 601, 780 P.2d 434, 8 U.C.C. Rep. Serv. 2d 771 (Ct. App. Div. 1 1989), opinion vacated in part on other grounds, 165 Ariz. 79, 796 P.2d 881, 12 U.C.C. Rep. Serv. 2d 469 (1990). *See also, Valley Nat. Bank of Arizona v. Meneghin*, 130 Ariz. 119, 634 P.2d 570 (1981) ("the court renders judgment, . . . and the clerk of the court enters the judgment").

Arizona does not follow the "one final judgment" rule. The second sentence of Rule 54(b) does not require the entry of a single judgment adjudicating all claims by all parties. *Hill v. City of Phoenix*, 193 Ariz. 570, 975 P.2d 700 (1999). In the absence of a certification under Rule 54(b), all judgments become effective upon the entry of a subsequent judgment that terminates the last unadjudicated claim. *Cristall v. Cristall*, 225 Ariz. 591, 242 P.3d 1060 (Ct. App. Div. 1 2010), review denied, (May 24, 2011); *Hill v. City of Phoenix*, 193 Ariz. 570, 975 P.2d 700 (1999). Counsel have been urged, however, to avoid, where reasonably possible, the submission of separate judgments on different dates. *Hill v. City of Phoenix*, 193 Ariz. 570, 975 P.2d 700 (1999).

While Ariz. R. Civ. P. 58(e) requires the Clerk to mail a notice of entry of judgment to the parties, specifying the date of entry, the time for filing post-judgment motions and for taking an appeal commences to run on the date of entry even though that notice is not received. *Park v. Strick*, 137 Ariz. 100, 669 P.2d 78 (1983); *Old Pueblo Transit Co. v. Corp. Com'n of Ariz.*, 73 Ariz. 32, 236 P.2d 1018 (1951); *Lone Mountain Ranch, Inc. v. Dillingham Inv., Inc.*, 131 Ariz. 583, 643 P.2d 28 (Ct. App. Div. 2 1982).

5. *Minute Entry as Judgment.* An unsigned order or minute entry is not a judgment, may not be appealed, and is subject to being vacated or modified. *Phillips v. Adler*, 134 Ariz. 480, 657 P.2d 893 (Ct. App. Div. 2 1982). A minute entry that is signed and filed, however, does constitute a judgment, and the time for filing post-judgment motions and/or prosecuting an appeal runs from the time of filing. *Focal Point, Inc. v. Court of Appeals of State of Ariz., Div. One*, 149 Ariz. 128, 717 P.2d 432 (1986).

6. *Effect of Judgment.* A final judgment on the merits rendered without fraud or collusion by a court of competent jurisdiction settles, and is *res judicata* as to, every claim or demand decided, as well as every claim or demand that could have been decided, in the action. *In re General Adjudication of All Rights to Use Water In Gila River System and Source*, 212 Ariz. 64, 127 P.3d 882 (2006); *Peterson v. Newton*, 232 Ariz. 593, 307 P.3d 1020 (Ct. App. Div. 1 2013); *PFS v. Industrial Com'n of Arizona*, 191 Ariz. 274, 955 P.2d 30 (Ct. App. Div. 1 1997); *Hall v. Lalli*, 191 Ariz.

104, 952 P.2d 748 (Ct. App. Div. 2 1997), aff'd, 194 Ariz. 54, 977 P.2d 776 (1999); *Norriega v. Machado*, 179 Ariz. 348, 878 P.2d 1386 (Ct. App. Div. 1 1994); *Matusik v. Arizona Public Service Co.*, 141 Ariz. 1, 684 P.2d 882 (Ct. App. Div. 1 1984); *Noble v. Industrial Com'n of Arizona*, 140 Ariz. 571, 683 P.2d 1173 (Ct. App. Div. 1 1984); *Fed Mart v. Industrial Com'n of Arizona*, 135 Ariz. 533, 662 P.2d 1040 (Ct. App. Div. 1 1982); *Application of Stone*, 14 Ariz. App. 109, 481 P.2d 280 (Div. 1 1971).

A judgment which is void on its face may be attacked at any time; otherwise, the judgment is voidable and only subject to direct attack by appeal. *School Dist. No. 1 of Navajo County v. Snowflake Union High School Dist. of Navajo County*, 100 Ariz. 389, 414 P.2d 985 (1966); *Cooper v. Commonwealth Title of Ariz.*, 15 Ariz. App. 560, 489 P.2d 1262 (Div. 1 1971).

A judgment is presumed to be correct if there is any reasonable evidence in the record to sustain it. *Hutcherson v. City of Phoenix*, 192 Ariz. 51, 961 P.2d 449 (1998); *Rhue v. Dawson*, 173 Ariz. 220, 841 P.2d 215 (Ct. App. Div. 1 1992); *Employers' Liability Assur. Corp. v. Glens Falls Ins. Co.*, 12 Ariz. App. 362, 470 P.2d 682 (Div. 2 1970); *Davies v. Courtney*, 11 Ariz. App. 248, 463 P.2d 554 (Div. 2 1970). A stipulated or consent judgment is conclusive as to the parties stipulating to its entry. *Industrial Park Corp. v. U. S. I. F. Palo Verde Corp.*, 19 Ariz. App. 342, 507 P.2d 681 (Div. 1 1973).

7. *Judgments Nunc Pro Tunc.* The authority of the Court to enter judgments *nunc pro tunc,* and the circumstances where it is appropriate to do so, are discussed in Section 6 of the *Authors' Comments* under Rule 58.

8. *Interest on Judgments; Prejudgment Interest.* Most civil judgments accrue interest at the rate of ten per cent (10%) *per annum*, unless a different rate has been contracted for in writing. A.R.S. § 44-1201. Judgments in condemnation actions instituted by the Department of Transportation bear interest at the rates prescribed in A.R.S. § 28-7101. Interest on judgments entered in condemnation proceedings instituted by a county, city or town bear interest at the "prime rate charged by banks on short-term business loans." A.R.S. §§ 9-409, 11-269.03. Judgments in medical malpractice cases accrue interest at a rate equal to three percentage points above the federal postjudgment rate in effect on the date the judgment is entered. A.R.S. § 12-352. Judgments accrue interest, from the date of entry until satisfied.

Prejudgment interest is also allowed as a matter of right on liquidated claims, both in contract and tort actions. *Alta Vista Plaza, Ltd. v. Insulation Specialists Co., Inc.*, 186 Ariz. 81, 919 P.2d 176 (Ct. App. Div. 2 1995), as corrected on reconsideration, (Nov. 30, 1995); *Paul R. Peterson Const., Inc. v. Arizona State*

Carpenters Health and Welfare Trust Fund, 179 Ariz. 474, 880 P.2d 694, 17 Employee Benefits Cas. (BNA) 2624 (Ct. App. Div. 1 1994). This rule applies even if the award of such interest may increase the award against the surety on a conservator's bond above the penal sum of the bond. *In re Guardianship of Pacheco*, 219 Ariz. 421, 199 P.3d 676 (Ct. App. Div. 2 2008). Such interest is in the nature of compensation for use by the defendant of money to which the plaintiff is entitled. *Dawson v. Withycombe*, 216 Ariz. 84, 163 P.3d 1034 (Ct. App. Div. 1 2007). Prejudgment interest, however, does not run on an administrative civil penalty, unless the relevant statute so provides, because it is not a loan, indebtedness, judgment or other obligation within the meaning of A.R.S. § 44-1201. *State ex rel. Arizona Structural Pest Control Com'n v. Taylor*, 223 Ariz. 486, 224 P.3d 983 (Ct. App. Div. 1 2010).

A claim is "liquidated" if the sum is certain, or the evidence furnishes data which, if believed, makes it possible to compute the amount due with exactness, without reliance upon opinion or discretion. *Scottsdale Ins. Co. v. Cendejas*, 220 Ariz. 281, 205 P.3d 1128 (Ct. App. Div. 1 2009); *John C. Lincoln Hosp. and Health Corp. v. Maricopa County*, 208 Ariz. 532, 96 P.3d 530 (Ct. App. Div. 1 2004), as amended, (Sept. 1, 2004); *Alta Vista Plaza, Ltd. v. Insulation Specialists Co., Inc.*, 186 Ariz. 81, 919 P.2d 176 (Ct. App. Div. 2 1995), as corrected on reconsideration, (Nov. 30, 1995); *Hyatt Regency Phoenix Hotel Co. v. Winston & Strawn*, 184 Ariz. 120, 907 P.2d 506 (Ct. App. Div. 1 1995); *Canal Ins. Co. v. Pizer*, 183 Ariz. 162, 901 P.2d 1192 (Ct. App. Div. 1 1995); *Patterson v. Bianco*, 167 Ariz. 249, 805 P.2d 1070 (Ct. App. Div. 2 1991); *Lee Development Co. v. Papp*, 166 Ariz. 471, 803 P.2d 464 (Ct. App. Div. 2 1990). In other words, the amount owed is known or knowable, without reliance on opinion or discretion.

The fact that the amount awarded differs from the amount claimed does not necessarily preclude an award of prejudgment interest. *Paul R. Peterson Const., Inc. v. Arizona State Carpenters Health and Welfare Trust Fund*, 179 Ariz. 474, 880 P.2d 694, 17 Employee Benefits Cas. (BNA) 2624 (Ct. App. Div. 1 1994). In Arizona, prejudgment interest generally accrues from the date of demand, not from the date of loss. *Alta Vista Plaza, Ltd. v. Insulation Specialists Co., Inc.*, 186 Ariz. 81, 919 P.2d 176 (Ct. App. Div. 2 1995), as corrected on reconsideration, (Nov. 30, 1995). Demand can be made by demanding payment or by the filing of a complaint. *Alta Vista Plaza, Ltd. v. Insulation Specialists Co., Inc.*, 186 Ariz. 81, 919 P.2d 176 (Ct. App. Div. 2 1995), as corrected on reconsideration, (Nov. 30, 1995) (disallowing prejudgment interest from date of demand letter because demand letter failed to provide sufficient information on amount owed); *Paul R. Peterson Const., Inc. v. Arizona State Carpenters Health and Welfare Trust Fund*, 179 Ariz. 474, 880 P.2d 694, 17 Employee Benefits Cas. (BNA) 2624 (Ct. App. Div. 1 1994).

On appeal, the entitlement to an award of prejudgment interest is reviewed *de novo*. *John C. Lincoln Hosp. and Health Corp. v. Maricopa County*, 208 Ariz. 532, 96 P.3d 530 (Ct. App. Div. 1 2004), as amended on other grounds, (Sept. 1, 2004). The amount of a judgment to be paid pursuant to a "Damron-Morris" agreement is not liquidated, however, unless and until the court determines whether the amount of the proposed settlement is reasonable. *Pueblo Santa Fe Townhomes Owners' Ass'n v. Transcontinental Ins. Co.*, 218 Ariz. 13, 178 P.3d 485 (Ct. App. Div. 1 2008).

9. *Rule 54(b): Judgments on Less Than All Claims and/or for Less Than All Parties.* Under Rule 54(b), a judgment that resolves some but less than all of a party's claims, or all of a party's claims but against less than all parties, is not final or appealable unless the trial court (a) makes an express determination to that effect, and (b) directs the entry of judgment. *Stevens v. Mehagian's Home Furnishings, Inc.*, 90 Ariz. 42, 365 P.2d 208 (1961); *Maria v. Najera*, 222 Ariz. 306, 214 P.3d 394 (Ct. App. Div. 1 2009); *North Star Development Corp. v. Wolfswinkel*, 146 Ariz. 406, 706 P.2d 732 (Ct. App. Div. 2 1985); *Tarnoff v. Jones*, 15 Ariz. App. 88, 486 P.2d 200 (Div. 1 1971); *Ulan v. Kay*, 5 Ariz. App. 395, 427 P.2d 376 (1967); *Cordoba v. Wiswall*, 5 Ariz. App. 265, 425 P.2d 576 (1967). This is the case even if the judgment against one of several defendants is taken by default. *Sullivan & Brugnatelli Advertising Co., Inc. v. Century Capital Corp.*, 153 Ariz. 78, 734 P.2d 1034 (Ct. App. Div. 1 1986). For purposes of applying the Rule's requirements, entities or persons named in the pleadings who have not been served are not considered "parties." *McHazlett v. Otis Engineering Corp.*, 133 Ariz. 530, 652 P.2d 1377 (1982).

Rule 54(b) was promulgated to relieve parties of the delay caused by the ongoing litigation of other claims and represents a compromise between the rule against deciding piecemeal appeals and the desirability of having a final judgment in some situations involving multiple claims or parties. *Southern California Edison Co. v. Peabody Western Coal Co.*, 194 Ariz. 47, 977 P.2d 769 (1999), as amended, (May 19, 1999) (Rule 54(b) "is designed as a compromise between the policy against interlocutory appeals and the desirability, in a few cases, of an immediate appeal to prevent an injustice."). It allows a trial court to certify finality to a judgment which disposes of one or more, but not all, of the multiple claims, if the Court determines there is no just reason for delay and directs the entry of judgment. *Davis v. Cessna Aircraft Corp.*, 168 Ariz. 301, 812 P.2d 1119 (Ct. App. Div. 1 1991).

A judgment entered with the language specified in the Rule is in effect a final judgment, albeit with respect to only a portion of the case, and enforceable through execution, garnishment and other judgment collection procedures. A Rule 54(b) determination is unnecessary, however, if a statute renders the order in question appealable as of right. *People of Faith, Inc. v. Arizona Dept. of Revenue*, 164 Ariz. 102, 791 P.2d 369 (Ct. App. Div. 1 1990).

The purpose of the Rule is to prevent wholesale piecemeal appeals by imposing the trial court's supervision over what can be immediately appealed. *McHazlett v. Otis Engineering Corp.*, 133 Ariz. 530, 652 P.2d 1377 (1982); *Terrazas v. Superior Court, Maricopa County, Division Five*, 112 Ariz. 434, 543 P.2d 120 (1975). Whether or not to make the requisite determination is an issue committed to the trial court's sound discretion. *Continental Cas. v. Superior Court, In and For Maricopa County*, 130 Ariz. 189, 635 P.2d 174 (1981); *GM Development Corp. v. Community American Mortg. Corp.*, 165 Ariz. 1, 795 P.2d 827 (Ct. App. Div. 1 1990). Generally, the determination should be made, however, only where there is some hardship that will be suffered from the delay in securing an appealable judgment. *Pulaski v. Perkins*, 127 Ariz. 216, 619 P.2d 488 (Ct. App. Div. 1 1980). The determination is not proper where only one alternative theory of recovery, and not an entire claim, has been resolved. *McAlister v. Citibank (Arizona), a Subsidiary of Citicorp*, 171 Ariz. 207, 829 P.2d 1253 (Ct. App. Div. 1 1992); *Marshall v. Williams*, 128 Ariz. 511, 627 P.2d 242 (Ct. App. Div. 1 1981).

The trial court need not formulate its determination using the precise language of the Rule—it is sufficient if there is a clear expression of an intent to make the judgment immediately appealable. *Arizona Bank v. Superior Court In and For Maricopa County*, 17 Ariz. App. 115, 495 P.2d 1322 (Div. 1 1972). The determination is unnecessary where the interlocutory order is made appealable by statute. *People of Faith, Inc. v. Arizona Dept. of Revenue*, 164 Ariz. 102, 791 P.2d 369 (Ct. App. Div. 1 1990); *Bulova Watch Co. v. Super City Dept. Stores of Ariz., Inc.*, 4 Ariz. App. 553, 422 P.2d 184 (1967).

On the other hand, the fact that the trial court inserts in its order or judgment the language specified in Rule 54(b) will not by itself insure that the judgment will be immediately appealable. *Davis v. Cessna Aircraft Corp.*, 168 Ariz. 301, 812 P.2d 1119 (Ct. App. Div. 1 1991); *Egan-Ryan Mechanical Co. v. Cardon Meadows Development Corp.*, 169 Ariz. 161, 818 P.2d 146 (Ct. App. Div. 1 1990); *Sisemore v. Farmers Ins. Co. of Arizona*, 161 Ariz. 564, 779 P.2d 1303 (Ct. App. Div. 1 1989).

The insertion of the language specified in Rule 54(b) will render a judgment or order immediately appealable only if it disposes of an entire claim. *Sisemore v. Farmers Ins. Co. of Arizona*, 161

Ariz. 564, 779 P.2d 1303 (Ct. App. Div. 1 1989) (judgment rejecting plaintiffs' request for punitive damages was not appealable because a request for punitive damages "is not a separate claim for relief under Rule 54(b)"). *Compare*, *James v. State*, 215 Ariz. 182, 158 P.3d 905 (Ct. App. Div. 2 2007) (judgment eliminating any and all claims against one of multiple defendants was appealable because such judgment ultimately disposed of that defendant's claim and, thus, was a final judgment).

The certification also must be substantively warranted. *Musa v. Adrian*, 130 Ariz. 311, 636 P.2d 89 (1981); *Southwest Gas Corp. v. Irwin ex rel. County of Cochise*, 229 Ariz. 198, 273 P.3d 650 (Ct. App. Div. 2 2012). In that regard, a claim is separable when the nature of the claim already determined is "such that no appellate court would have to decide the same issues more than once even if there [a]re subsequent appeals." *Southwest Gas Corp. v. Irwin ex rel. County of Cochise*, 229 Ariz. 198, 273 P.3d 650 (Ct. App. Div. 2 2012), citing *Continental Cas. v. Superior Court, In and For Maricopa County*, 130 Ariz. 189, 635 P.2d 174 (1981).

Multiple claims for relief exist when the facts give rise to more than one legal right or cause of action—the determination rests on whether the claims could be separately enforced. *Southwest Gas Corp. v. Irwin ex rel. County of Cochise*, 229 Ariz. 198, 273 P.3d 650 (Ct. App. Div. 2 2012), citing *Continental Cas. v. Superior Court, In and For Maricopa County*, 130 Ariz. 189, 635 P.2d 174 (1981) (a claim is separable when the nature of the claim already determined is "such that no appellate court would have to decide the same issues more than once even if there [a]re subsequent appeals"); *Salerno v. Atlantic Mut. Ins. Co.*, 198 Ariz. 54, 6 P.3d 758 (Ct. App. Div. 1 2000); *Davis v. Cessna Aircraft Corp.*, 168 Ariz. 301, 812 P.2d 1119 (Ct. App. Div. 1 1991); *Sisemore v. Farmers Ins. Co. of Arizona*, 161 Ariz. 564, 779 P.2d 1303 (Ct. App. Div. 1 1989).

An order which merely eliminates a potential remedy or one alternative theory of recovery, but does not dispose of a claim entirely should not be certified as final under Rule 54(b). *McAlister v. Citibank (Arizona), a Subsidiary of Citicorp*, 171 Ariz. 207, 829 P.2d 1253 (Ct. App. Div. 1 1992); *Marshall v. Williams*, 128 Ariz. 511, 627 P.2d 242 (Ct. App. Div. 1 1981). Where a claim that is disposed of, however, is clearly separate and distinct from the claims that remain pending, and there is little likelihood that an appellate court would be faced with the same issues in a subsequent appeal, it is appropriate to make that disposition immediately appealable. *GM Development Corp. v. Community American Mortg. Corp.*, 165 Ariz. 1, 795 P.2d 827 (Ct. App. Div. 1 1990).

A.R.S. § 12-2101(A)(6) [as renumbered in 2011] creates a statutory exception to the final judgment rule, and allows a party to appeal from an interlocutory judgment which finally resolves the parties' rights as to liability, leaving unresolved the issues of damages. Appeals under this statute are not limited to cases in which an accounting or similar equitable proceeding has been ordered to determine the amount of the recovery. *Bilke v. State*, 206 Ariz. 462, 80 P.3d 269 (2003) (citing to A.R.S. § 12-2101(G) (2003), " 'an interlocutory judgment which determines the rights of the parties and directs . . . [a] proceeding to determine the amount of the recovery' can be appealed if the trial court, in the exercise of its sound discretion, expressly directs that the only issue remaining is the amount of recovery.").

Although Rule 54(b) does not expressly refer to the statute, the rule and the statute should be read together, and it is appropriate for a trial court to include the language specified in Rule 54(b) which resolves the issue of liability with respect to one of multiple claims in a case, even though the issue of damages remains to be resolved. *Salerno v. Atlantic Mut. Ins. Co.*, 198 Ariz. 54, 6 P.3d 758 (Ct. App. Div. 1 2000).

To make the interlocutory judgment appealable under this statute, the trial judge must use express language that the judgment has finally determined the rights of the parties and is subject to an interlocutory appeal. *Bilke v. State*, 206 Ariz. 462, 80 P.3d 269 (2003). A Rule 54(b) certification is not necessary but it would, if made, satisfy the finality requirement, as would other express language indicating finality on the question of the rights of the parties. *Bilke v. State*, 206 Ariz. 462, 80 P.3d 269 (2003).

Similarly, a prayer or claim for punitive damages is not a separate claim from the underlying cause of action, and a dismissal of a punitive damage claim cannot be made immediately appealable simply by the inclusion of the language specified in Rule 54(b). *Sisemore v. Farmers Ins. Co. of Arizona*, 161 Ariz. 564, 779 P.2d 1303 (Ct. App. Div. 1 1989). Under the 1999 amendment to Rule 54(b), a claim for attorneys' fees can now be in effect considered a claim separate from the claim on the merits, which was not formerly the case. *See* discussion in Section 12, *infra*, and *Maciborski v. Chase Service Corp. of Arizona*, 161 Ariz. 557, 779 P.2d 1296 (Ct. App. Div. 1 1989). The purpose of those amendments was to permit a trial court, in the rare case in which a judgment on the merits of a cause would be appropriate before the resolution of attorneys' fees, to certify the entry of a "merits" judgment under this Rule and retain jurisdiction to resolve fees issues. *National Broker Associates, Inc. v. Marlyn Nutraceuticals, Inc.*, 211 Ariz. 210, 119 P.3d 477 (Ct. App. Div. 1 2005).

The final sentence of Rule 54(b), and the accompanying State Bar Committee Note, provide a trial court with discretion to treat a claim for attorneys' fees as a separate claim, for purposes of Rule 54(b), only in the context of a related judgment regarding the merits of a cause. *Kim v. Mansoori*, 214 Ariz. 457, 153 P.3d 1086 (Ct. App. Div. 2 2007). There is no support for entering an appealable judgment on an attorneys' fee claim in the absence of a resolution on the merits. *Kim v. Mansoori*, 214 Ariz. 457, 153 P.3d 1086 (Ct. App. Div. 2 2007).

Parties cannot employ Rule 54(b) as a creative device for securing advisory appellate court opinions. Where the trial court has denied a motion for summary judgment, which is not an appealable order, the parties cannot thereafter stipulate to the entry of a summary judgment in favor of the previously unsuccessful moving party, and to the inclusion in that judgment of the language required by Rule 54(b), as a means for securing an appellate court's views on the issue presented. *Sorensen v. Farmers Ins. Co. of Arizona*, 191 Ariz. 464, 957 P.2d 1007 (Ct. App. Div. 1 1997).

10. *Rule 54(c): Judgment Upon All Claims and Parties.* In order to simplify procedures for perfecting an appeal and to avoid unfairness, confusion and judicial inefficiencies caused by the "premature" filing of a notice of appeal, Ariz. R. Civ. P. 54(c) was added effective January 1, 2014, to facilitate the effectiveness of a simultaneous amendment to Ariz. R. Civ. App. P. 9. The amendments are consistent with the federal approach, which provides a procedure for curing technical jurisdictional defects caused by the premature filing of a notice of appeal.

Rule 54(c) was adopted to require a judgment, to be final, must include a statement from the trial court that "no further matters remain pending and that the judgment is entered pursuant to Rule 54(c)". The expectation is that such certification will provide certainty as to whether a judgment was a "final" judgment and assist in the implementation of the amendment to ARCAP 9.

As written, however, Ariz. R. Civ. P. 54(c) is ambiguous. Rule 54(c) merely requires the "court state" such matters. Rule 54(c) does not expressly require a final judgment include such language. Thus, a judicial statement made on the record to this effect arguably might suffice. Having said that, it appears the intent of the adoption of Rule 54(c) is that such statement by the court must be included in the judgment itself, if the judgment is to be considered a "final judgment". As a cautionary measure, therefore practitioners are urged to include the language from Rule 54(c) in those case where the judgment to be entered is intended to be a final judgment, including final judgments on default, pretrial motions, trial motions, jury verdicts or decisions by the court, post-trial motions.

As indicated, the more important 2014 amendment is to

ARCAP 9, which is similar to Federal Rule of Civil Appellate Procedure 4(a)(4), and which added a new provision ARCAP 9(b)(2)(B). Thus, under ARCAP 9 as amended, there are now procedures in place to avoid the results that occurred in *Barassi v. Matison*, 130 Ariz. 418, 636 P.2d 1200 (1981); *Craig v. Craig*, 227 Ariz. 105, 253 P.3d 624 (2011); *Fields v. Oates*, 230 Ariz. 411, 286 P.3d 160 (Ct. App. Div. 1 2012) (in the absence of Rule 54(b) language in the judgment/signed order, a notice of appeal filed while a claim for attorneys' fees is pending is a nullity and appellate court lacks jurisdiction to hear the matter); *Santee v. Mesa Airlines, Inc.*, 229 Ariz. 88, 270 P.3d 915 (Ct. App. Div. 2 2012), review denied, (May 30, 2012) (notice of appeal filed before ruling on Rule 68(g) motion was premature and failed to vest the appellate court with jurisdiction); *Engel v. Landman*, 221 Ariz. 504, 212 P.3d 842 (Ct. App. Div. 1 2009); *Baumann v. Tuton*, 180 Ariz. 370, 884 P.2d 256 (Ct. App. Div. 1 1994) (Premature filing of notice of appeal while motion for new trial was pending in trial court did not confer jurisdiction upon appellate court).

11. *Taxation of Costs.* Rule 54(f) is concerned only with the procedures for securing the taxation of costs. In civil proceedings, the term "costs" is a term of art which refers to expenses incurred in litigation that a prevailing party is allowed to recover from the losing party, which are limited to those expenses listed in A.R.S. §§ 12-331 to 333. *Heatec, Inc. v. R.W. Beckett Corp.*, 219 Ariz. 293, 197 P.3d 754, Prod. Liab. Rep. (CCH) P 18040 (Ct. App. Div. 1 2008). The nature of the costs that are properly taxable is governed by statute. A.R.S. § 12-341 makes it mandatory that the successful party in a civil action recover from the adversary all costs (as distinguished from attorneys' fees) incurred therein. *Graville v. Dodge*, 195 Ariz. 119, 985 P.2d 604 (Ct. App. Div. 1 1999); *Roddy v. County of Maricopa*, 184 Ariz. 625, 911 P.2d 631 (Ct. App. Div. 1 1996).

The trial court has discretion to determine who is the "prevailing party," and the recovery of costs is equally available to those who successfully defend an action as to those who seek affirmative relief. *Hooper v. Truly Nolen of America, Inc.*, 171 Ariz. 692, 832 P.2d 709 (Ct. App. Div. 1 1992). A party who recovers judgment for only a part of a demand or claim or who is held to be more than 50% at fault, is nevertheless the prevailing party and entitled to recover costs. *Ayala v. Olaiz*, 161 Ariz. 129, 776 P.2d 807 (Ct. App. Div. 1 1989). Similarly, a plaintiff who receives a favorable verdict and judgment is the prevailing party and entitled to recover all taxable costs, even if the amount of that verdict is less than pretrial settlements received by that plaintiff which would reduce the damage award to zero. *McEvoy v. Aerotek, Inc.*, 201 Ariz. 300, 34 P.3d 979 (Ct. App. Div. 1 2001). Jury fees may not be assessed against the prevailing party, and any local

Superior Court Rule purporting to permit such an assessment is invalid. *Roddy v. County of Maricopa*, 184 Ariz. 625, 911 P.2d 631 (Ct. App. Div. 1 1996). Conversely, a party cannot recover its litigation costs unless a statutory basis exists for recovery. *Ahwatukee Custom Estates Management Ass'n, Inc. v. Bach*, 193 Ariz. 401, 973 P.2d 106 (1999).

In civil proceedings, the term "costs" is a term of art which refers to expenses incurred in litigation that a prevailing party is allowed to recover from the losing party, and which are limited to those expenses listed in A.R.S. §§ 12-331 to 333. *Heatec, Inc. v. R.W. Beckett Corp.*, 219 Ariz. 293, 197 P.3d 754, Prod. Liab. Rep. (CCH) P 18040 (Ct. App. Div. 1 2008). A.R.S. § 12-332 sets forth several categories of costs that are taxable in the Superior Court. Under A.R.S. § 12-332(A)(2), these include the costs of taking depositions. The cost of depositions may include the travel expenses of an attorney to attend another party's deposition taken outside Arizona. *Ponderosa Plaza v. Siplast*, 181 Ariz. 128, 888 P.2d 1315 (Ct. App. Div. 1 1993).

Expenses not enumerated in § 12-332 are generally not recoverable as costs and the enumerated expenses do not include the travel expenses of out-of-state witnesses to attend trial. *Ponderosa Plaza v. Siplast*, 181 Ariz. 128, 888 P.2d 1315 (Ct. App. Div. 1 1993). *See also, Motzer v. Escalante*, 228 Ariz. 295, 265 P.3d 1094 (Ct. App. Div. 2 2011) (cost of preparing juror notebooks not recoverable if not ordered by the court or agreed to by the parties). The reimbursement of such expenses, accordingly, is not a recoverable cost. *Ponderosa Plaza v. Siplast*, 181 Ariz. 128, 888 P.2d 1315 (Ct. App. Div. 1 1993). The term "costs" is generally viewed as not encompassing attorneys' fees, even where they are recoverable by statute or rule. *Boltz & Odegaard v. Hohn*, 148 Ariz. 361, 714 P.2d 854 (Ct. App. Div. 1 1985).

A.R.S. § 12-332(A)(1) and (2) include as recoverable costs the "fees of officers and witnesses" and the "cost of taking depositions." A party cannot recover, as a taxable cost under A.R.S. § 12-332(A)(2), however, fees paid to that party's own expert in connection with a deposition of that expert conducted by that party for use at trial. *Schritter v. State Farm Mut. Auto. Ins. Co.*, 201 Ariz. 391, 36 P.3d 739 (2001). The provision in Rule 26 that a party seeking discovery from an expert must pay some or all of the expenses associated with that is not implicated, because a deposition of one's own expert is not conducted for discovery purposes. *Schritter v. State Farm Mut. Auto. Ins. Co.*, 201 Ariz. 391, 36 P.3d 739 (2001). Allowing a party to recover such costs would permit the recovery, under A.R.S. § 12-332(A)(2), of the functional equivalent of witness fees, which are not recoverable by reason of A.R.S. § 12-332(A)(1). *Schritter v. State Farm Mut. Auto. Ins. Co.*, 201 Ariz. 391, 36 P.3d 739 (2001).

The cost recovery statute does not permit the recovery of expenses incurred for photocopying, long distance telephone calls, messenger and delivery charges, and telecopier and facsimile charges. *Ahwatukee Custom Estates Management Ass'n, Inc. v. Bach*, 193 Ariz. 401, 973 P.2d 106 (1999). Again, those non-taxable costs cannot be recovered as part of an award of attorneys' fees, because to permit that would undermine the legislative intent expressed in A.R.S. § 12-332.

The accepted definition of "attorneys' fees" has been fees charged by an attorney for rendering services that reflect and depend upon the attorney's training and legal skill. Attorney's fees awards may properly include charges for legal assistant and law clerk services, and charges for computerized legal research, but such awards may not include non-taxable costs that are really part of overhead. *Ahwatukee Custom Estates Management Ass'n, Inc. v. Bach*, 193 Ariz. 401, 973 P.2d 106 (1999); *Matter of Liquidation of Azstar Cas. Co. Inc.*, 189 Ariz. 27, 938 P.2d 76 (Ct. App. Div. 1 1996). Finally, A.R.S. § 12-332(A)(6) does permit the assessment as a taxable cost of the fees of a court-appointed expert witness. *Graville v. Dodge*, 195 Ariz. 119, 985 P.2d 604 (Ct. App. Div. 1 1999).

Rule 54(f)(2), adopted in 2000, which was formerly Rule 4 of the Uniform Rules of Practice for Medical Malpractice Cases, creates a special category of recoverable costs, but only in medical malpractice cases. Under the Rule, reasonable fees paid to expert witnesses for testifying at trial in medical malpractice cases are considered taxable costs. This provision permits the recovery only of expert fees for the time spent actually testifying at trial, and not for time spent by the expert preparing to testify. *Levy v. Alfaro*, 215 Ariz. 443, 160 P.3d 1201 (Ct. App. Div. 1 2007); *Foster ex rel. Foster v. Weir*, 212 Ariz. 193, 129 P.3d 482 (Ct. App. Div. 2 2006).

A party claiming costs must file a statement of costs within ten (10) days after the entry of judgment, and the opposing party must file objections, if any, within five (5) days after receipt of that statement. The court then rules on any such objections. If no objections are filed, then costs are taxed automatically and the court need not be involved.

12. *Procedure for Seeking Awards of Attorneys' Fees.* Ariz. R. Civ. P. 54(g)(1), requires that a claim for attorneys' fees, to be preserved, be stated in the pleadings. *Cf., Balestrieri v. Balestrieri*, 232 Ariz. 25, 300 P.3d 560 (Ct. App. Div. 1 2013). Where a defendant files a motion to dismiss in lieu of an answer, such defendant must assert a claim for attorney's fees at the time the motion is filed or forfeit any claim to such fees. 232 Ariz. 25, 300 P.3d 560 (Ct. App. Div. 1 2013). A defendant does not submit

itself to the jurisdiction of the court by filing a request for fees with the motion to dismiss. *Balestrieri v. Balestrieri*, 232 Ariz. 25, 300 P.3d 560 (Ct. App. Div. 1 2013).

A motion seeking an award of attorneys' fees must be filed within twenty (20) days after the mailing by the Clerk of the Court of a decision on the merits, unless the trial court prescribes a longer period. Rule 54(g)(2). The trial court has the discretion, under Rule 54(g)(2), to extend the time for requesting attorney's fees, even if such request is made after the time specified for making the application. *Aztar Corp. v. U.S. Fire Ins. Co.*, 223 Ariz. 463, 224 P.3d 960 (Ct. App. Div. 1 2010). The motion may be supported by affidavit and exhibits or, at the trial court's discretion, by testimony. Rule 54(g)(3).

A fee application must contain sufficient detail to enable the trial court to assess the reasonableness of the amount sought, and counsel should specify the type of legal service provided, the attorney providing the service, and the time spent in providing the service. *State ex rel. Goddard v. Gravano*, 210 Ariz. 101, 108 P.3d 251 (Ct. App. Div. 1 2005) (trial court's determination of 'reasonableness' upheld even though supporting affidavit only included general descriptions of the work performed; evidentiary hearing was not requested); *Orfaly v. Tucson Symphony Society*, 209 Ariz. 260, 99 P.3d 1030 (Ct. App. Div. 2 2004). It has been held that an award of attorneys' fees may include charges for computerized legal research. *Ahwatukee Custom Estates Management Ass'n, Inc. v. Bach*, 193 Ariz. 401, 973 P.2d 106 (1999); *Matter of Liquidation of Azstar Cas. Co. Inc.*, 189 Ariz. 27, 938 P.2d 76 (Ct. App. Div. 1 1996). Opposing parties may respond to the motion and contest the award, and the Court may, in its discretion, conduct a hearing on the issue.

The trial court also retains the discretion to refer issues relating to the value of the legal services rendered to a special master appointed under Ariz. R. Civ. P. 53. *Orfaly v. Tucson Symphony Society*, 209 Ariz. 260, 99 P.3d 1030 (Ct. App. Div. 2 2004).

The provision specifying that these procedures are inapplicable where an award of attorneys' fees is sought as a sanction under an applicable statute or rule, and to causes in which fees may be recovered as an element of damages to be proven at trial is set forth in Rule 54(g)(4).

The requirement in Rule 54(g)(2) that claims for attorneys' fees be made after a decision on the merits does not necessarily mean that the substantive merits of the underlying claim must be finally adjudicated before any fees may be awarded. *Britt v. Steffen*, 220 Ariz. 265, 205 P.3d 357 (Ct. App. Div. 1 2008). A dismissal of an action for failure to prosecute does not deprive the Superior Court of jurisdiction to consider a timely application for award of attorneys' fees and to award such fees if warranted. *Britt v. Steffen*, 220 Ariz. 265, 205 P.3d 357 (Ct. App. Div. 1 2008); cf. also *McMurray v. Dream Catcher USA, Inc.*, 220 Ariz. 71, 202 P.3d 536 (Ct. App. Div. 2 2009). While the plain language of Rule 41(a)(1) permits a plaintiff to voluntarily dismiss a case by filing a notice of dismissal before the adverse party serves an answer or motion for summary judgment, such a voluntary dismissal does not preclude the Superior Court from subsequently entering an award of attorneys' fees in favor of the adverse party. *Vicari v. Lake Havasu City*, 222 Ariz. 218, 213 P.3d 367 (Ct. App. Div. 1 2009).

Before the adoption of Rule 54(g), it was held that, in awarding attorneys' fees under either A.R.S. §§ 12-341.01(C) or 12-349 (amended 2013), or under Ariz. R. Civ. P. 11, the trial court was required to make findings of fact and conclusions of law, but that requirement could be waived by a failure to object. *Trantor v. Fredrikson*, 179 Ariz. 299, 878 P.2d 657 (1994); *State v. Richey*, 160 Ariz. 564, 774 P.2d 1354 (1989); *Bennett v. Baxter Group, Inc.*, 223 Ariz. 414, 224 P.3d 230 (Ct. App. Div. 2 2010); *Johnson v. Mohave County*, 206 Ariz. 330, 78 P.3d 1051 (Ct. App. Div. 1 2003). That requirement was in effect carried forward in the version of Rule 54(g) adopted in 1996, and appears to have survived the 1999 amendments to that Rule. *Bennett v. Baxter Group, Inc.*, 223 Ariz. 414, 224 P.3d 230 (Ct. App. Div. 2 2010); *Johnson v. Mohave County*, 206 Ariz. 330, 78 P.3d 1051 (Ct. App. Div. 1 2003). *See also*, A.R.S. § 12-350.

A trial court's decision to deny a request for an award of attorneys' fees is reviewed on appeal only for an abuse of discretion, and will be upheld if there is any reasonable basis to do so. *Radkowsky v. Provident Life & Acc. Ins. Co.*, 196 Ariz. 110, 993 P.2d 1074 (Ct. App. Div. 1 1999), as amended, (June 29, 1999). Essentially, the same standard applies to a trial court's decision to award fees, and its determination of the amount to award. *Orfaly v. Tucson Symphony Society*, 209 Ariz. 260, 99 P.3d 1030 (Ct. App. Div. 2 2004).

13. *Bases for Awarding Attorneys' Fees in Civil Actions.* As stated by the Court in *London v. Green Acres Trust*, 159 Ariz. 136, 145, 765 P.2d 538, 547 (Ct. App. Div. 1 1988): "The general rule regarding attorneys' fees, sometimes referred to as the 'American Rule,' is that, absent a statute or contract, the prevailing litigant is ordinarily not entitled to collect attorney's fees from the losers." See also *Kromko v. Superior Court In and For County of Maricopa*, 168 Ariz. 51, 811 P.2d 12 (1991); *Marcus v. Fox*, 150 Ariz. 333, 723 P.2d 682 (1986); *Kaufmann v. Cruikshank*, 222 Ariz. 488, 217 P.3d 438 (Ct. App. Div. 2 2009); *McMurray v. Dream Catcher USA, Inc.*, 220 Ariz. 71, 202 P.3d 536 (Ct. App. Div. 2 2009); *Schwab Sales, Inc. v. GN Const. Co., Inc.*, 196 Ariz. 33, 992 P.2d 1128 (Ct. App. Div. 2 1998); *Lewin v. Miller*

Wagner & Co., Ltd., 151 Ariz. 29, 725 P.2d 736 (Ct. App. Div. 1 1986). Both the Arizona Supreme Court and the Arizona Court of Appeals, however, have had occasion to observe that the prior prevalence of the so-called "American Rule" in Arizona has been significantly eroded, both by the enactment of fee-shifting statutes and the recognition and/or application of various common law doctrines that constitute exceptions to it. *Wagenseller v. Scottsdale Memorial Hosp.*, 147 Ariz. 370, 710 P.2d 1025, 1 I.E.R. Cas. (BNA) 526, 119 L.R.R.M. (BNA) 3166, 103 Lab. Cas. (CCH) P 55511 (1985); *New Pueblo Constructors, Inc. v. State*, 144 Ariz. 95, 696 P.2d 185 (1985); *Arnold v. Arizona Dept. of Health Services*, 160 Ariz. 593, 775 P.2d 521 (1989).

Arizona has recognized, to one degree or another, five (5) separate common law or equitable doctrines that, where the conditions for invoking them are satisfied, permit the Court to award the prevailing party its attorneys' fees even though no statute, rule or contract calls for that: (1) the "common fund" doctrine; (2) the "substantial benefit" doctrine; (3) the "private attorney general" doctrine; (4) the "tort of another" doctrine; and, (5) the "bad faith" exception.

("Common Fund" Doctrine)

The Arizona Supreme Court first recognized and applied the "common fund" doctrine in *Zeckendorf v. Steinfeld*, 15 Ariz. 335, 138 P. 1044 (1914), judgment aff'd, appeal dismissed, 239 U.S. 26, 36 S. Ct. 14, 60 L. Ed. 125 (1915). This was a shareholders' derivative action in which the Court determined that "right and justice" required that the benefitted company reimburse the plaintiff for the legal costs incurred in securing a recovery for the company which benefitted the company and all its shareholders. *Zeckendorf v. Steinfeld*, 15 Ariz. 335, 138 P. 1044 (1914), judgment aff'd, appeal dismissed, 239 U.S. 26, 36 S. Ct. 14, 60 L. Ed. 125 (1915).

In *State v. Boykin*, 112 Ariz. 109, 538 P.2d 383 (1975), the Arizona Supreme Court, in declining to apply the "common fund" doctrine, indicated that it agreed with the rationale for the doctrine articulated in the decision of the United States Supreme Court in *Mills v. Electric Auto-Lite Co.*, 396 U.S. 375, 90 S. Ct. 616, 24 L. Ed. 2d 593, Fed. Sec. L. Rep. (CCH) P 92556 (1970), which held that an award of attorney's fees to a plaintiff might be appropriate where the plaintiff had successfully prosecuted litigation that (1) conferred a substantial benefit, (2) upon members of an ascertainable class, and (3) the Court's jurisdiction made possible an award which would spread the costs proportionately among the beneficiaries. In *Kadish v. Arizona State Land Dept.*, 155 Ariz. 484, 747 P.2d 1183, 44 Ed. Law Rep. 701 (1987), judgment aff'd, 490 U.S. 605, 109 S. Ct. 2037, 104 L. Ed. 2d 696,

53 Ed. Law Rep. 384 (1989), the Court discussed that the plaintiffs were seeking an award of their attorneys' fees under the "substantial benefit" doctrine, but did so in a fashion that confused it with the "common fund" doctrine. In any event, a majority of the Justices could not concur in any resolution of the question, so attorneys' fees were not awarded until the litigation was remanded.

In *Kerr v. Killian*, 197 Ariz. 213, 3 P.3d 1133 (Ct. App. Div. 1 2000), the Court of Appeals held that a court may award attorneys' fees, under the "common fund" doctrine, to counsel for the prevailing side whose efforts in litigation create or preserve a common fund from which others who have undertaken no risk or cost will nevertheless benefit. The Court pointed out that the purpose of the doctrine is to compensate counsel for producing such benefits and to preclude the unjust enrichment of those who receive the benefits of the fund created and/or preserved. Thus, the "common fund doctrine" is a general rule of equity that a person or persons who employ attorneys for the preservation of a common fund may be entitled to have their attorneys' fees paid out of that fund. *Hobson v. Mid-Century Ins. Co.*, 199 Ariz. 525, 19 P.3d 1241 (Ct. App. Div. 2 2001). The court's equitable powers may not be invoked, however, to reduce the amount of a workmen's compensation carrier's statutory lien on the proceeds of a recovery from a third party by a portion of the fees incurred in securing that recovery. *Hobson v. Mid-Century Ins. Co.*, 199 Ariz. 525, 19 P.3d 1241 (Ct. App. Div. 2 2001).

The "common fund" doctrine is an equitable exception to the general rule that, absent a statute or contract, each side in a litigated case must bear its own attorneys' fees. *Charles I. Friedman, P.C. v. Microsoft Corp.*, 213 Ariz. 344, 141 P.3d 824, 2006-2 Trade Cas. (CCH) ¶ 75406 (Ct. App. Div. 1 2006); *Valder Law Offices v. Keenan Law Firm*, 212 Ariz. 244, 129 P.3d 966 (Ct. App. Div. 1 2006); *Burke v. Arizona State Retirement System*, 206 Ariz. 269, 77 P.3d 444 (Ct. App. Div. 2 2003). The doctrine allows a court to award attorneys' fees to counsel for the prevailing side whose efforts create or preserve a common fund from which others who have undertaken no risk or cost will nevertheless benefit. *Charles I. Friedman, P.C. v. Microsoft Corp.*, 213 Ariz. 344, 141 P.3d 824, 2006-2 Trade Cas. (CCH) ¶ 75406 (Ct. App. Div. 1 2006); *Valder Law Offices v. Keenan Law Firm*, 212 Ariz. 244, 129 P.3d 966 (Ct. App. Div. 1 2006); *Burke v. Arizona State Retirement System*, 206 Ariz. 269, 77 P.3d 444 (Ct. App. Div. 2 2003). It serves the twofold purpose of compensating counsel for producing benefits for a class and preventing the unjust enrichment of the class members who receive them. *Valder Law Offices v. Keenan Law Firm*, 212 Ariz. 244, 129 P.3d 966 (Ct. App. Div. 1 2006); *Burke v. Arizona State Retirement System*, 206 Ariz. 269, 77 P.3d

444 (Ct. App. Div. 2 2003). The award is from the common fund created, and is not against the opposing party. *Valder Law Offices v. Keenan Law Firm*, 212 Ariz. 244, 129 P.3d 966 (Ct. App. Div. 1 2006); *Burke v. Arizona State Retirement System*, 206 Ariz. 269, 77 P.3d 444 (Ct. App. Div. 2 2003). The doctrine, accordingly, is a mechanism for fee-spreading, not fee-shifting; it requires reimbursement of fees by the prevailing party, not the losing party. *Valder Law Offices v. Keenan Law Firm*, 212 Ariz. 244, 129 P.3d 966 (Ct. App. Div. 1 2006); *Burke v. Arizona State Retirement System*, 206 Ariz. 269, 77 P.3d 444 (Ct. App. Div. 2 2003).

The doctrine's operation is not limited to class actions; it can theoretically be applied in wrongful death actions where the conditions for its proper application are satisfied. *Valder Law Offices v. Keenan Law Firm*, 212 Ariz. 244, 129 P.3d 966 (Ct. App. Div. 1 2006). The policies against enhancement of a fee award, through the use of multipliers, applied in the context of determining fees under the statutory fee-shifting schemes, are not applicable to fees awarded under the common fund doctrine. *Charles I. Friedman, P.C. v. Microsoft Corp.*, 213 Ariz. 344, 141 P.3d 824, 2006-2 Trade Cas. (CCH) ¶ 75406 (Ct. App. Div. 1 2006). In the common fund context, courts have authority and discretion to enhance a lodestar by use of a multiplier based on risk, result and quality of services performed. *Charles I. Friedman, P.C. v. Microsoft Corp.*, 213 Ariz. 344, 141 P.3d 824, 2006-2 Trade Cas. (CCH) ¶ 75406 (Ct. App. Div. 1 2006).

("Substantial Benefit" Doctrine)

In *Hartman v. Oatman Gold Min. & Mill. Co.*, 22 Ariz. 476, 198 P. 717 (1921), the Court again permitted reimbursement of the plaintiff's fees, even though the litigation had neither brought a fund into the Court nor added to the assets of the corporation. The Court found a substantial benefit to the stockholders in the enhanced value of the remaining shares, and reasoned that the award served to spread the costs proportionately among those shares. Subsequent development suggests that the result in Hartman was justifiable, not by application of the "common fund" doctrine, but rather the "substantial benefit" doctrine.

In *Kadish v. Arizona State Land Dept.*, 155 Ariz. 484, 747 P.2d 1183, 44 Ed. Law Rep. 701 (1987), judgment aff'd, 490 U.S. 605, 109 S. Ct. 2037, 104 L. Ed. 2d 696, 53 Ed. Law Rep. 384 (1989) (1989), the Court discussed that the plaintiffs were seeking an award of their attorneys' fees under the "substantial benefit" doctrine, but did so in a fashion that confused it with the "common fund" doctrine. In any event, a majority of the Justices could not concur in any resolution of the question, so attorneys' fees were not awarded until the litigation was remanded.

("Private Attorney General" Doctrine)

The "private attorney general" doctrine was first adopted and applied in *Arnold v. Arizona Dept. of Health Services*, 160 Ariz. 593, 775 P.2d 521 (1989), in which private parties had successfully prosecuted a class action on behalf of approximately 4,500 chronically mentally ill indigents who claimed that state and county governmental agencies had breached a statutory duty to provide them, and others similarly situated, with adequate mental health care. The trial court had awarded plaintiffs their attorneys' fees against the State based on A.R.S. § 12-348, and then held that the county defendants should be responsible for one-third of the fees awarded on the basis of the "private attorney general" doctrine. The Arizona Supreme Court affirmed, noting that some of its prior decisions had discussed the doctrine and recognized its existence, but had never actually applied it. Recognizing that the decision whether or not to apply the doctrine involved weighing the interests in encouraging public interest litigation against the interest in preserving the "American Rule" concerning attorneys' fee awards, the Court noted that there had already been significant erosion of the "American Rule," and that its vitality was outweighed in that case by the societal interest in public service litigation.

In *Arizona Center For Law In Public Interest v. Hassell*, 172 Ariz. 356, 837 P.2d 158, 23 Envtl. L. Rep. 20348 (Ct. App. Div. 1 1991), the Court of Appeals approved an award of fees, on the basis of the "private attorney general" doctrine, to a public interest law firm that had successfully challenged the constitutionality of certain legislation that permitted the disposal of public trust lands in the beds of certain watercourses in the state. Subsequently, in *Kadish v. Arizona State Land Dept.*, 177 Ariz. 322, 868 P.2d 335 (Ct. App. Div. 1 1993), the Court held that the plaintiffs and the Arizona Center for Law in the Public Interest should receive, under the "private attorney general" doctrine, an award of their attorneys' fees incurred in their long and ultimately successful challenge to the constitutionality of Arizona's fixed mining royalty statutory provisions. The Court held that the litigation satisfied all the criteria that were required for application of the doctrine, which the Court described as follows: (1) the resolution of the litigation benefitted a large number of people in the state, including taxpayers and public school students, (2) the vindication of the right asserted was of societal importance, and (3) vindication of the right asserted required a legal challenge to a statute adopted by the state legislature and thus could only have been privately enforced. Interestingly, the Court rejected the argument that an award of fees against the State based on the "private attorney general" doctrine was pre-empted by A.R.S. § 12-348 and that the State

Land Department should not be liable for the fee award because its status in the litigation was that of a "nominal party."

("Tort of Another" Doctrine)

The "tort of another" doctrine was first recognized by the Supreme Court in *U.S. Fidelity & Guar. Co. v. Frohmiller*, 71 Ariz. 377, 227 P.2d 1007 (1951), where the Court explained: "It is generally held that where the wrongful act of the defendant has involved the plaintiff in litigation with others or placed him in such relation with others as makes it necessary to incur expenses to protect his interest, such costs and expenses, including attorneys' fees, should be treated as the legal consequences of the original wrongful act and may be recovered as damages." *U.S. Fidelity & Guar. Co. v. Frohmiller*, 71 Ariz. 377, 380, 227 P.2d 1007, 1009 (1951). The doctrine was subsequently applied in *Collins v. First Financial Services, Inc.*, 168 Ariz. 484, 815 P.2d 411 (Ct. App. Div. 1 1991), where the Court indicated that, in order to recover attorneys' fees under this exception, the plaintiff must show that: (1) the plaintiff became involved in a legal dispute because of the defendant's tortious conduct; (2) the dispute was with a third party; (3) the plaintiff incurred attorneys' fees in connection with that dispute; (4) the expenditure of attorneys' fees was a foreseeable or necessary result of the defendant's tortious conduct; and, (5) the claimed fees were reasonable. *Collins v. First Financial Services, Inc.*, 168 Ariz. 484, 486, 815 P.2d 411, 413-14 (Ct. App. Div. 1 1991).

Finally, in *London v. Green Acres Trust*, 159 Ariz. 136, 765 P.2d 538 (Ct. App. Div. 1 1988), a successful class action brought against sellers of funeral services and related items for violations of endowment care statutes, securities statutes and the Arizona Consumer Fraud Act, the Court noted that there were several bases upon which the plaintiffs might be awarded their attorneys' fees incurred in the litigation. Initially, the Court pointed out: "There is indeed an equitable exception to the American Rule which permits recovery of fees and expenses in this case: the bad faith exception." *London v. Green Acres Trust*, 159 Ariz. 136, 146, 765 P.2d 538, 548 (Ct. App. Div. 1 1988). The Court noted that there were very few Arizona cases which discussed that exception, but attributed that to the fact that it had been partially codified in A.R.S. § 12-341.01(C), which permits the award of attorneys' fees where the action or defense is groundless or not made in good faith. The Court noted, however, that there was at least one Arizona case— *Taylor v. Southern Pac. Transp. Co.*, 130 Ariz. 516, 637 P.2d 726 (1981)—which had recognized and applied it.

(Award of Statutory Fees in Contract Actions)

As both the Arizona Supreme Court and the Arizona Court of

Appeals have had occasion to observe, the Arizona Legislature has also enacted a number of statutes that permit or require an award of attorneys' fees to the prevailing party in specified categories of cases. Thus, in *New Pueblo Constructors, Inc. v. State*, 144 Ariz. 95, 111, 696 P.2d 185, 201 (1985), the Supreme Court observed that: "The Arizona Legislature has enacted more than sixty statutes authorizing recovery of attorneys' fees . . . ." Subsequently, in *Arnold v. Arizona Dept. of Health Services*, 160 Ariz. 593, 609, 775 P.2d 521, 537 (1989), the Court of Appeals noted that: "In Arizona, we have at least 73 statutes providing for fee-shifting . . ." This Section will discuss only those statutory provisions which are most frequently invoked as the basis for an award of fees.

Perhaps the most frequently invoked fee-shifting statute is A.R.S. § 12-341.01(A), which provides that: "In any contested action arising out of a contract, express or implied, the court may award the successful party reasonable attorney's fees." The plain language of the statute thus grants a trial court authority to award attorneys' fees in a claim arising out of an implied contract. *Tritschler v. Allstate Ins. Co.*, 213 Ariz. 505, 144 P.3d 519 (Ct. App. Div. 2 2006), as corrected, (Dec. 19, 2006). Subpart (B) of the statute specifies that: "The award of reasonable attorney's fees awarded pursuant to subsection A should be made to mitigate the burden of the expense of litigation to establish a just claim or a just defense. It need not equal or relate to the attorney's fees actually paid or contracted, but such award may not exceed the amount paid or agreed to be paid."

In light of this statutory language, the Arizona courts have consistently held that a fee award under the statute may not exceed, and conversely need not equal, the amount of fees which the litigant actually incurred. *Associated Indem. Corp. v. Warner*, 143 Ariz. 567, 694 P.2d 1181 (1985); *Sparks v. Republic Nat. Life Ins. Co.*, 132 Ariz. 529, 647 P.2d 1127 (1982); *Jerman v. O'Leary*, 145 Ariz. 397, 701 P.2d 1205 (Ct. App. Div. 2 1985). Subpart (D) specifies that any award of fees under this statutory provision is to be made by the Court and not by a jury. Assuming that the standards of the statute are met, there is nothing that precludes an award of fees under it against the State. *New Pueblo Constructors, Inc. v. State*, 144 Ariz. 95, 696 P.2d 185 (1985).

One issue which has been a relatively frequent focus of litigation under this statute is the circumstances under which a claim will be deemed to be one "arising out of a contract, express or implied." In *ASH, Inc. v. Mesa Unified School Dist. No. 4*, 138 Ariz. 190, 673 P.2d 934, 15 Ed. Law Rep. 560 (Ct. App. Div. 1 1983), the Court suggested that an action could be deemed to be one "arising out" of a contract if the action was one in which a contract was "a factor causing the dispute." This view of the statute was criticized subsequently as representing an overly broad interpretation of the phrase, and as being inconsistent with the decision in *Sparks v. Republic Nat. Life Ins. Co.*, 132 Ariz. 529, 647 P.2d 1127 (1982). *Marcus v. Fox*, 150 Ariz. 333, 723 P.2d 682 (1986).

The Court in *Marcus* also rejected the argument, which found some support in earlier decisions, that an award of fees under A.R.S. § 12-341.01(A) would only be proper in cases in which a contract is actually breached. The Court concluded that the appropriate test was whether the cause of action in question could not have existed but for the existence of a contract. See also *Keystone Floor & More, LLC v. Arizona Registrar of Contractors*, 223 Ariz. 27, 219 P.3d 237 (Ct. App. Div. 1 2009), as amended, (July 15, 2009); *Burke v. Arizona State Retirement System*, 206 Ariz. 269, 77 P.3d 444 (Ct. App. Div. 2 2003); *Schwab Sales, Inc. v. GN Const. Co., Inc.*, 196 Ariz. 33, 992 P.2d 1128 (Ct. App. Div. 2 1998).

The contract must be the basis for the action, and not just a factual predicate for it. *Chaurasia v. General Motors Corp.*, 212 Ariz. 18, 126 P.3d 165 (Ct. App. Div. 1 2006). The statute does not apply, however, in cases where a recovery is based on the doctrine of promissory estoppel, which provides an equitable remedy but is not a theory of contractual liability. *Double AA Builders, Ltd. v. Grand State Const. L.L.C.*, 210 Ariz. 503, 114 P.3d 835 (Ct. App. Div. 1 2005).

The fee statute does not apply to purely statutory causes of action, even if a contract is a factual predicate to the action, but not the essential basis of it. *Hanley v. Pearson*, 204 Ariz. 147, 61 P.3d 29 (Ct. App. Div. 1 2003). A successful party on a contract claim may recover not only attorneys' fees expended on that claim, but also fees expended litigating an "interwoven" tort claim. *Arizona Tile, L.L.C. v. Berger*, 223 Ariz. 491, 224 P.3d 988 (Ct. App. Div. 1 2010), as amended on other grounds, (Feb. 8, 2010); *Modular Mining Systems, Inc. v. Jigsaw Technologies, Inc.*, 221 Ariz. 515, 212 P.3d 853 (Ct. App. Div. 2 2009); *Ramsey Air Meds, L.L.C. v. Cutter Aviation, Inc.*, 198 Ariz. 10, 6 P.3d 315 (Ct. App. Div. 1 2000). The tort claim will be considered "interwoven," however, only if the tort could not exist but for the breach or avoidance of a contract. *Arizona Tile, L.L.C. v. Berger*, 223 Ariz. 491, 224 P.3d 988 (Ct. App. Div. 1 2010), as amended on other grounds, (Feb. 8, 2010); *Modular Mining Systems, Inc. v. Jigsaw Technologies, Inc.*, 221 Ariz. 515, 212 P.3d 853 (Ct. App. Div. 2 2009); *Robert E. Mann Const. Co. v. Liebert Corp.*, 204 Ariz. 129, 60 P.3d 708 (Ct. App. Div. 1 2003). When an action arising out of a contract has been dismissed without prejudice for failure to prosecute, the defendant is still considered a successful party for purposes of the statute, even though such a dismissal does not operate as an adjudication on the merits. *Britt v. Steffen*, 220 Ariz. 265, 205 P.3d 357 (Ct. App. Div. 1 2008).

On the other hand, the Arizona courts have rejected the notion, particularly in cases involving professionals, that claims of negligent performance of a contract are ones arising out of contract. In *Lewin v. Miller Wagner & Co., Ltd.*, 151 Ariz. 29, 725 P.2d 736 (Ct. App. Div. 1 1986), an accounting malpractice action, the trial court had awarded the successful plaintiffs their attorneys' fees on the grounds that the action arose out of the contract between the plaintiffs and the defendant for the performance of accounting services. The Court of Appeals agreed that there clearly had been a contract between the parties for the performance of accounting services, and that the law does impose upon the accountant who is a party to such a contract a duty to perform the services in accordance with a standard of reasonable care or suffer liability for failure to do so. It went on to hold, however, that was not a sufficient basis to award fees under the statute. The very same result was reached, based upon essentially the same reasoning, where a legal malpractice action was claimed to be one "arising out" of the contract to perform legal services. *Barmat v. John and Jane Doe Partners A-D*, 155 Ariz. 519, 747 P.2d 1218 (1987); *cf. also Desilva v. Baker*, 208 Ariz. 597, 96 P.3d 1084 (Ct. App. Div. 1 2004). The fact that an attorney may have carried out a task which the attorney agreed to perform in a negligent manner does not change the gravamen of the action from tort to contract. *Keonjian v. Olcott*, 216 Ariz. 563, 169 P.3d 927 (Ct. App. Div. 2 2007).

An award of fees under the statute is discretionary rather than mandatory. *Hall v. Read Development, Inc.*, 229 Ariz. 277, 274 P.3d 1211 (Ct. App. Div. 1 2012), as amended, (Apr. 26, 2012) and review denied, (Aug. 28, 2012). Such an award will be reviewed on appeal only for an abuse of discretion. *Robert E. Mann Const. Co. v. Liebert Corp.*, 204 Ariz. 129, 60 P.3d 708 (Ct. App. Div. 1 2003). The leading case concerning the factors the trial court should take into account in exercising its discretion whether or not to award fees remains *Associated Indem. Corp. v. Warner*, 143 Ariz. 567, 694 P.2d 1181 (1985), where the Court indicated that the following factors should be taken into account:

1. Whether litigation could have been avoided or settled and whether the successful party's efforts were completely superfluous in achieving the result;
2. Whether assessing fees against the unsuccessful party would cause an extreme hardship;
3. Whether the successful party prevailed with respect to all of the relief sought;
4. Whether the legal question presented was novel and whether

such claim or defense had previously been adjudicated in Arizona; and

5. Whether a fee award would discourage other parties with tenable claims or defenses from litigating or defending legitimate contract issues.

Associated Indem. Corp. v. Warner, 143 Ariz. 567, 570, 694 P.2d 1181, 1184 (1985). See also *Wagenseller v. Scottsdale Memorial Hosp.*, 147 Ariz. 370, 710 P.2d 1025, 1 I.E.R. Cas. (BNA) 526, 119 L.R.R.M. (BNA) 3166, 103 Lab. Cas. (CCH) P 55511 (1985).

The attorneys' fees awarded must be reasonable. Under A.R.S. § 12-341.01(B), as earlier noted, the fees awarded may not exceed the amount actually paid by the claimant. The fact that the fees requested exceed the amount in dispute, however, does not mean that they are unreasonable. *Wagner v. Casteel*, 136 Ariz. 29, 663 P.2d 1020 (Ct. App. Div. 2 1983). The most definitive articulation of the standards for determining the reasonableness of requested attorneys' fee awards, and the support that the claimant must provide for any such request, remains the decision in *Schweiger v. China Doll Restaurant, Inc.*, 138 Ariz. 183, 673 P.2d 927 (Ct. App. Div. 1 1983).

The Court held that the starting point for determining reasonableness was the actual billing rate charged by the lawyer or lawyers involved in the matter. The Court then indicated that applications for the award of attorneys' fees should be supported by an affidavit of counsel indicating the type of services provided, the date the service was provided, the identity of the attorney providing the service (if more than one attorney was involved), and the time spent in providing the service. The Court also pointed out that any fee application must be in sufficient detail to permit the Court to evaluate the reasonableness of the time spent on individual tasks and on the entire matter, and cautioned practitioners to prepare summaries from contemporaneous time records indicating the work performed. See also *Orfaly v. Tucson Symphony Society*, 209 Ariz. 260, 99 P.3d 1030 (Ct. App. Div. 2 2004); *Burke v. Arizona State Retirement System*, 206 Ariz. 269, 77 P.3d 444 (Ct. App. Div. 2 2003); Note, *Statutory Attorney's Fees in Arizona: An Analysis of A.R.S. Section 12-341.01*, 24 Ariz. L. Rev. 659 (1982). In cases where fees are not paid on an hourly basis, such as contingency fee cases, the most useful starting point for determining the amount of a reasonable fee is the number of hours reasonably expended on the matter multiplied by a reasonable hourly rate. *Bogard v. Cannon & Wendt Elec. Co., Inc.*, 221 Ariz. 325, 212 P.3d 17 (Ct. App. Div. 1 2009). It is not necessarily an abuse of discretion for the trial court to rely upon counsel's reconstructed timekeeping records in performing this calculation. *Bogard v. Cannon & Wendt Elec. Co., Inc.*, 221

Ariz. 325, 212 P.3d 17 (Ct. App. Div. 1 2009).

A.R.S. § 12-341.01(C) is a separate subsection of that same statute which authorizes awards of attorney's fees in actions found to be groundless or to have been brought in bad faith. Specifically, it provides: "Reasonable attorney's fees shall be awarded by the court in any contested action upon clear and convincing evidence that the claim or defense constitutes harassment, is groundless and not made in good faith. In making such award, the court may consider such evidence as it deems appropriate and shall receive this evidence during trial on the merits of the cause, or separately, regarding the amount of such fees as it deems in the best interest of the litigating parties."

The Court of Appeals has stated unequivocally that an award of fees under this statute is "punitive in nature." *Wean Water, Inc. v. Sta-Rite Industries, Inc.*, 141 Ariz. 315, 318, 686 P.2d 1285, 1288 (Ct. App. Div. 1 1984). Accordingly, a fee award under this statute need not be designed to compensate the party wronged by the conduct the statute proscribes, or measured with that goal in mind. The statute applies to "any contested action," regardless of the nature of the claims or defenses asserted. *White v. Kaufmann*, 133 Ariz. 388, 652 P.2d 127 (1982); *Nationwide Resources Corp. v. Ngai*, 129 Ariz. 226, 630 P.2d 49 (Ct. App. Div. 2 1981). The state may be subject to an award of fees under this statute, and may recover fees under it as well. *New Pueblo Constructors, Inc. v. State*, 144 Ariz. 95, 696 P.2d 185 (1985). The statute may be applied on appeal, as well as in actions brought in Superior Court. *Boone v. Grier*, 142 Ariz. 178, 688 P.2d 1070 (Ct. App. Div. 1 1984).

The terminology employed in the statute ("shall be awarded") means that, once a court has found that the statutory criteria have been met, an award of reasonable attorneys' fees is mandatory. *Associated Indem. Corp. v. Warner*, 143 Ariz. 567, 568, 694 P.2d 1181, 1182, (1985); *White v. Kaufmann*, 133 Ariz. 388, 652 P.2d 127 (1982). The statute applies only when it is shown, by clear and convincing evidence, that a claim or defense: (1) constitutes harassment, (2) is groundless, and (3) is not made in good faith. All three elements must be established to support a fee award. *State v. Richey*, 160 Ariz. 564, 774 P.2d 1354 (1989); *Rowland v. Great States Ins. Co.*, 199 Ariz. 577, 20 P.3d 1158 (Ct. App. Div. 2 2001), as corrected, (May 24, 2001); *McKesson Chemical Co., a div. of Foremost-McKesson, Inc. v. Van Waters & Rogers*, 153 Ariz. 557, 739 P.2d 211 (Ct. App. Div. 1 1987). In *Gilbert v. Board of Medical Examiners of State of Ariz.*, 155 Ariz. 169, 745 P.2d 617 (Ct. App. Div. 1 1987), superseded by statute as stated in, *Goodman v. Samaritan Health System*, 195 Ariz. 502, 990 P.2d 1061 (Ct. App. Div. 1 1999), the Court held that the appropriate standard for measuring "good faith" was a subjective one, *i.e.*, whether the particular attorney or party in the action knew that the action was not being brought in good faith, not whether a "reasonable" attorney would have known that the claim was frivolous or improper, but acknowledged that such subjective bad faith would ordinarily have to be proven by reference to objective factors.

A separate statute which authorizes the award of attorneys' fees, in addition to other penalties, for the bringing of meritless claims is A.R.S. § 12-349 (amended 2013). Subparagraph (A) of that statute provides that, in any civil action commenced in a court of record, the court shall assess reasonable attorney's fees and, at the court's discretion, double damages of not to exceed five thousand dollars ($5,000) against any attorney or party, including the state or any political subdivision, who is found to have done any of the following:

1. Brings or defends a claim without substantial justification;
2. Brings or defends a claim solely or primarily for delay or harassment;
3. Unreasonably expands or delays the proceeding;
4. Engages in abuse of discovery.

"Without substantial justification" is defined in the statute to mean that the claim or defense is groundless and is not made in good faith. A.R.S. § 12-349 (amended 2013). Effective January 1, 2013, the definition of "without substantial justification" set forth in subparagraph (F) was amended to delete the phrase "constitutes harassment." Each element must be proven by a preponderance of the evidence, and the absence of one element renders the statute inapplicable. *Johnson v. Mohave County*, 206 Ariz. 330, 78 P.3d 1051 (Ct. App. Div. 1 2003). Subpart (C) of the statute also provides that attorney's fees may not be assessed if, after filing an action, a voluntary dismissal is filed for any claim or defense within a reasonable time after the attorney or party filing the dismissal knew or reasonably should have known that the claim or defense was without substantial justification.

In *Solimeno v. Yonan*, 224 Ariz. 74, 227 P.3d 481 (Ct. App. Div. 1 2010), the Court of Appeals affirmed an award of attorney's fees and costs under A.R.S. § 12-349(A)(3) as a sanction following a mistrial based on defendants' failure to disclose. The court further found Ariz. R. Civ. P. 37(c) provided an additional basis for the award of attorney's fees and costs as a sanction, under the circumstances presented in that case. *Solimeno v. Yonan*, 224 Ariz. 74, 227 P.3d 481 (Ct. App. Div. 1 2010).

A.R.S. § 12-350 provides that, in awarding attorney's fees under A.R.S. § 12-349 (amended 2013) the Court must set forth the specific reasons for the award, and may take into account the following factors in determining whether such an award is warranted:

1. The extent of any effort made to determine the validity of a claim before the claim was asserted;
2. The extent of any effort made after the commencement of an action to reduce the number of claims or defenses being asserted or to dismiss claims or defenses found not to be valid;
3. The availability of facts to assist a party in determining the validity of a claim or defense;
4. The relative financial positions of the parties involved;
5. Whether the action was prosecuted, in whole or in part, in bad faith;
6. Whether issues of fact determinative of the validity of a party's claim or defense were reasonably in conflict;
7. The extent to which the party prevailed with respect to the amount and number of claims in controversy; and
8. The amount and conditions of any offer of judgment or settlement as related to the amount and conditions of the ultimate relief granted by the court.

The failure of a party, however, to object to the absence of specific findings constitutes a waiver of this requirement, and that party is precluded from raising on appeal the trial court's failure to comply with the specificity requirement. *Johnson v. Mohave County*, 206 Ariz. 330, 78 P.3d 1051 (Ct. App. Div. 1 2003). It has been held that the same issues and concerns are involved, where a party requests sanctions under A.R.S. § 12-349 (amended 2013), as where the request is based upon Rule 11. *See e.g.*, *Harris v. Reserve Life Ins. Co.*, 158 Ariz. 380, 762 P.2d 1334 (Ct. App. Div. 1 1988).

A.R.S. § 12-348 authorizes awards of attorneys' fees and expenses in favor of a private party who has prevailed in certain types of actions commenced by or against certain governmental entities. The purpose of the statute has been found to be to encourage individuals aggrieved by governmental action to assert their rights. *Estate of Walton*, 164 Ariz. 498, 794 P.2d 131 (1990); *New Pueblo Constructors, Inc. v. State*, 144 Ariz. 95, 696 P.2d 185 (1985). The statute is mandatory, however, and an award of attorneys' fees is required when a party, including a county officer, other than the state or a city or town or county prevails on the merits in one of the categories of actions covered by the statute. *Hounshell v. White*, 219 Ariz. 381, 199 P.3d 636 (Ct. App. Div. 1 2008). The statute does not authorize an award of fees if the governmental entity prevails; nor does it authorize awards of fees to a party who intervenes on the side of the agency against a party seeking judicial review. *Grand Canyon Trust v. Arizona*

Corp. Com'n, 210 Ariz. 30, 107 P.3d 356 (Ct. App. Div. 1 2005).

"Fees and other expenses" is defined by the statute, and specifically A.R.S. § 12-348 (I)(1), to include the reasonable expenses of expert witnesses, the reasonable cost of any study found by the court to be necessary for the preparation of the prevailing private party's case, and reasonable and necessary attorney's fees. A.R.S. § 12-348(E)(1) specifies that an award of expert expenses may not be at a rate which exceeds the highest rate of compensation for experts paid by the state, or a city, town or county. In addition, A.R.S. § 12-348(H)(3) specifies that an award is not to include the fees and expenses incurred in making an application for an award under the statute. The fact that, because of some of the exceptions discussed below, a party does not qualify for an award of fees and expenses under A.R.S. § 12-348, does not preclude an award based upon other statutes, or based upon one of the equitable theories previously discussed in this section. *Kadish v. Arizona State Land Dept.*, 177 Ariz. 322, 868 P.2d 335 (Ct. App. Div. 1 1993).

The statute draws an initial distinction between cases where such fee awards are nominally mandatory, and those where they are expressly discretionary. Thus, A.R.S. § 12-348(A) provides that a court "shall award fees and other expenses to any party other than this state or a city, town or county" which prevails on the merits in the following types of actions:

1. A civil action brought against the party by the state or a city, town or county;
2. A court proceeding brought to secure judicial review of any state agency decision;
3. A proceeding brought under A.R.S. § 41-1034;
4. A special action proceeding brought by the private party to challenge an action by the state against the party; and
5. An appeal by the state from a decision by the personnel board under title 41, chapter 4, article 6 of the Arizona Revised Statutes.

A party who successfully challenges rules and regulations issued by the Arizona Corporation Commission is entitled to recover its attorneys' fees under this statute. *Phelps Dodge Corp. v. Arizona Elec. Power Co-op., Inc.*, 207 Ariz. 95, 83 P.3d 573 (Ct. App. Div. 1 2004), as amended on denial of reconsideration, (Mar. 15, 2004). Under A.R.S. § 12-348(E)(2), an award of attorneys' fees made under subsection (A) of the statute may not exceed the amount which the prevailing party has paid or agreed to pay, or a maximum amount of seventy-five dollars per hour, unless the court specifically finds that an increase in the cost of living, or some special factor, such as a limited availability of qualified attorneys to handle the type of case involved, justifies a higher fee. The trial court's decision not to award fees at a rate higher than the statutory rate of $75 per hour is reviewed on appeal only for an abuse of discretion. *Phelps Dodge Corp. v. Arizona Elec. Power Co-op., Inc.*, 207 Ariz. 95, 83 P.3d 573 (Ct. App. Div. 1 2004), as amended on denial of reconsideration, (Mar. 15, 2004). Moreover, any award under subsection (A) made against a city, town or county (but not the state) is subject to a maximum limit of $10,000. See *Bromley Group, Ltd. v. Arizona Dept. of Revenue*, 170 Ariz. 532, 826 P.2d 1158 (Ct. App. Div. 1 1991).

A.R.S. § 12-348(B) makes an award of fees and other expenses discretionary "to any party, other than this state or a city, town or county" who prevails on the merits "in an action brought by the party against the state or a city, town or county challenging the assessment or collection of taxes." A judgment entered pursuant to an acceptance of an offer of judgment under Ariz. R. Civ. P. 68 does represent an "adjudication on the merits" within the meaning of A.R.S. § 12–348(B)(1), and will support an award of attorneys' fees against a public entity in a case covered by the statute. *4501 Northpoint LP v. Maricopa County*, 212 Ariz. 98, 128 P.3d 215 (2006). A discretionary award under subsection (B) may not, under A.R.S. § 12-348(E)(3), exceed the amount the prevailing party has paid or agreed to pay, or a maximum amount of one hundred dollars an hour. Moreover, under A.R.S. § 12-348(E)(5), awards under this section against the state, or a city, town or county may not exceed $30,000. This statutory limitation is not retroactive, and only applies to attorneys' fees and not other recoverable expenses. *Aida Renta Trust v. Maricopa County*, 221 Ariz. 603, 212 P.3d 941 (Ct. App. Div. 1 2009), as amended, (July 22, 2009).

Notwithstanding the facially mandatory nature of awards under subsection (A) of the statute, A.R.S. § 12-348(C) provides that a court may, in its discretion, deny an award of fees and expenses, if it finds that:

1. The prevailing party unduly and unreasonably protracted the final resolution of the matter; or
2. The reason that the party prevailed is attributable to an intervening change in the law; or
3. The prevailing party refused an offer of settlement that was at least as favorable to the party as the relief ultimately granted.

Obviously, a finding of any of the foregoing would also justify a denial of a discretionary fee award under subsection (B).

Finally, A.R.S. § 12-348(H) provides that the statute will not apply to the following types and categories of proceedings:

1. An action arising from proceedings in which the role of the state, city, town or county was to determine the eligibility or entitlement of an individual to a monetary benefit or its equivalent, to adjudicate a dispute or issue between private parties, or to fix a rate;
2. Proceedings brought by the state, or by a city, town or county, pursuant to title 13 or title 28 of the Arizona Revised Statutes;
3. Proceedings involving eminent domain, foreclosure, collection of judgment debts;
4. Proceedings in which the state, city, town or county is a nominal party;
5. Proceedings brought by a city, town or county to collect taxes, or pursuant to traffic ordinances; and
6. Proceedings brought by a city, town or county on ordinances which contain a criminal penalty or fine for violations of them.

A.R.S. § 12-348 was intended to be a "very broad" exception to the American Rule, which normally bars attorneys' fee awards to prevailing parties in civil litigation. *Estate of Walton*, 164 Ariz. 498, 794 P.2d 131 (1990); *New Pueblo Constructors, Inc. v. State*, 144 Ariz. 95, 696 P.2d 185 (1985). It is, however, a very complicated statute which has been frequently amended and/or restructured since its initial adoption, making the task of applying earlier precedents to the current statutory provisions a difficult one.

A.R.S. § 12-348.1, a new statute enacted in 2012, provides that notwithstanding A.R.S. § 12-348, in addition to any statutory costs that may be awarded, the court shall award reasonable attorney's fees to the successful party in any civil action brought by an agency, department, board or commission of the State of Arizona, a city, town or county, governmental officer or an association of governmental entities against such other governmental entity(ies).

A.R.S. § 12-2030(A) provides that a court must award fees and other expenses to a party that prevails in a civil action against the state or any political subdivision to compel a state or other public officer to perform an act imposed by law as a duty. This provision, however, is limited to actions that are in the nature of *mandamus*, and does not apply to actions to secure recovery on a demand which a county has refused to pay, as that is not a ministerial act. *John C. Lincoln Hosp. and Health Corp. v. Maricopa County*, 208 Ariz. 532, 96 P.3d 530 (Ct. App. Div. 1 2004), as amended, (Sept. 1, 2004). To recover fees under this statute, plaintiffs must show that they (1) prevailed on the merits, (2) in a civil action, (3) filed against the State or a political subdivision of the State (4) to compel a State officer or any officer of a political subdivision to perform a duty imposed by law. *Bilke v. State*, 221 Ariz. 60, 209 P.3d 1056 (Ct. App. Div. 1 2009). The action does not necessarily have to be styled as one for mandamus. *Bilke v. State*, 221 Ariz. 60, 209 P.3d 1056 (Ct. App. Div. 1 2009).

There are a variety of provisions in the Arizona Rules of Civil Procedure which authorize the imposition of sanctions, which may include awards of attorneys' fees, for the filing and/or pursuit of non-meritorious claims or positions, for failure to comply with discovery and/or disclosure obligations, and for failure to participate in certain pretrial proceedings in good faith. *See* Rules 11, 16 and 37, Arizona Rules of Civil Procedure. These provisions are discussed in the *Authors' Comments* following those Rules.

Attorneys' fees may be recovered for prosecution of an appeal, if an award of fees is authorized by statute, decisional law or contract. They must, however, be requested in the manner prescribed in Rule 21(c), Ariz. R. Civ. App. Pr., which requires that a request for an award of fees be made in the briefs filed on appeal, or in a written motion served before oral argument or submission of the appeal without argument. If a party fails to request an award of fees in that manner, that party cannot on remand request that the trial court award fees incurred on the appeal, and is also precluded from seeking fees incurred in the trial court after remand. *Robert E. Mann Const. Co. v. Liebert Corp.*, 204 Ariz. 129, 60 P.3d 708 (Ct. App. Div. 1 2003).

In cases where federal jurisdiction is based on diversity of citizenship, a federal court should apply a state statute permitting the recovery of attorneys' fees. *See Alyeska Pipeline Service Co. v. Wilderness Society*, 421 U.S. 240, 95 S. Ct. 1612, 44 L. Ed. 2d 141, 7 Env't. Rep. Cas. (BNA) 1849, 10 Fair Empl. Prac. Cas. (BNA) 826, 11 Empl. Prac. Dec. (CCH) P 10842, 5 Envtl. L. Rep. 20286 (1975); *Apollo Group, Inc. v. Avnet, Inc.*, 58 F.3d 477, Prod. Liab. Rep. (CCH) P 14249, 26 U.C.C. Rep. Serv. 2d 1099 (9th Cir. 1995); *Marvin Johnson, P.C. v. Shoen*, 888 F. Supp. 1009 (D. Ariz. 1995). In cases involving both federal claims and pendent state claims, A.R.S. § 12-341.01(A) has been found to be applicable as to the state-law claims. *Nelson v. Pima Community College*, 83 F.3d 1075, 109 Ed. Law Rep. 598 (9th Cir. 1996); *Moses v. Phelps Dodge Corp.*, 826 F. Supp. 1234, 73 Fair Empl. Prac. Cas. (BNA) 739 (D. Ariz. 1993).

14. *Judgments for Future Damages.* A.R.S. § 12-582(A) permits any party in a medical malpractice action to elect to receive or pay future damages for economic losses in periodic installments. "Future damages" is defined in A.R.S. § 12-581(4) as loss arising

from bodily injury which accrues after trial of the medical malpractice claim. If future damages are awarded in the action, the trial court must enter a judgment according to the procedures, and in the form, specified in A.R.S. § 12-586.

15. *Foreign Judgments*. The Full Faith and Credit Clause of the United States Constitution (Art. IV, § 1) obliges the states to respect and enforce judgments rendered in the courts of their sister states. *Springfield Credit Union v. Johnson*, 123 Ariz. 319, 599 P.2d 772 (1979); *Cho v. American Bonding Co.*, 190 Ariz. 593, 951 P.2d 468 (Ct. App. Div. 1 1997); *Giehrl v. Royal Aloha Vacation Club, Inc.*, 188 Ariz. 456, 937 P.2d 378 (Ct. App. Div. 1 1997); *Oyakawa v. Gillett*, 175 Ariz. 226, 854 P.2d 1212 (Ct. App. Div. 1 1993); *Tarnoff v. Jones*, 17 Ariz. App. 240, 497 P.2d 60 (Div. 1 1972). The Clause was intended to in effect nationalize the principle of *res judicata*. *Giehrl v. Royal Aloha Vacation Club, Inc.*, 188 Ariz. 456, 937 P.2d 378 (Ct. App. Div. 1 1997). This requires that a judgment rendered in one state's courts be accorded in the other states the same validity and effect as it had in the state in which it was rendered. *Springfield Credit Union v. Johnson*, 123 Ariz. 319, 599 P.2d 772 (1979); *Giehrl v. Royal Aloha Vacation Club, Inc.*, 188 Ariz. 456, 937 P.2d 378 (Ct. App. Div. 1 1997); *Oyakawa v. Gillett*, 175 Ariz. 226, 854 P.2d 1212 (Ct. App. Div. 1 1993). This is true even when the cause of action underlying the judgment is barred by the public policy of the state in which enforcement of the judgment is sought. *Oyakawa v. Gillett*, 175 Ariz. 226, 854 P.2d 1212 (Ct. App. Div. 1 1993). The foreign state's judgment need not be enforced, however, if the rendering court lacked personal or subject matter jurisdiction, if the judgment was obtained through fraud or is otherwise invalid or unenforceable, or if the defendant's due process rights were violated. *Giehrl v. Royal Aloha Vacation Club, Inc.*, 188 Ariz. 456, 937 P.2d 378 (Ct. App. Div. 1 1997); *Pioneer Federal Sav. Bank v. Driver*, 166 Ariz. 585, 804 P.2d 118 (Ct. App. Div. 1 1990).

While a foreign nation's judgment will not be enforced if it results from prejudice, fraud, unfairness or irregularities in the proceedings, this does not require that an Arizona court conduct a detailed review of the proceedings that resulted in the foreign judgment and decline to recognize it upon the merest suggestion of prejudice or fraud. *Alberta Securities Com'n v. Ryckman*, 200 Ariz. 540, 30 P.3d 121 (Ct. App. Div. 1 2001). There is a strong presumption of the validity of a foreign judgment, and a party challenging it must point to specific grounds, and evidence supporting them, for overcoming that presumption. *Alberta Securities Com'n v. Ryckman*, 200 Ariz. 540, 30 P.3d 121 (Ct. App. Div. 1 2001). When a judgment debtor has already had an opportunity to seek relief from a foreign nation's judgment in that nation's courts but has not pursued it, a court in the United States is not required to provide a second opportunity to do so. *Alberta Securities Com'n v. Ryckman*, 200 Ariz. 540, 30 P.3d 121 (Ct. App. Div. 1 2001).

A defendant served with a suit in one state may either appear and litigate that state's jurisdiction in that suit, or let that suit go to judgment by default and collaterally attack the resulting default judgment for lack of jurisdiction. If one state court determines, in default proceedings, that it has personal jurisdiction over the defendant, and a second state court determines, in a proceeding in which both parties appear and litigate the matter, that the first court lacked personal jurisdiction over the defendant, Arizona will give Full Faith and Credit to the judgment of the second court that made its determination with both parties present to litigate the issue. *Giehrl v. Royal Aloha Vacation Club, Inc.*, 188 Ariz. 456, 937 P.2d 378 (Ct. App. Div. 1 1997).

The procedures for seeking enforcement in Arizona of a judgment secured in another state are discussed in Section 11 of the *Authors' Comments* to Rule 69.

16. *Judgments of Tribal Courts*. The Arizona courts have long followed the rule that judgments rendered by the courts of Indian tribes are not entitled to Full Faith and Credit, but will be honored and enforced only under principles of comity. *Tracy v. Superior Court of Maricopa County*, 168 Ariz. 23, 810 P.2d 1030 (1991); *Begay v. Miller*, 70 Ariz. 380, 222 P.2d 624 (1950); *Brown v. Babbitt Ford, Inc.*, 117 Ariz. 192, 571 P.2d 689, 23 U.C.C. Rep. Serv. 266 (Ct. App. Div. 1 1977). The Supreme Court "codified" that doctrine, and established separate procedures for seeking enforcement of tribal *civil* judgments, by its adoption of the Rules of Procedure for the recognition of Tribal Court Judgments, which become effective on December 1, 2000. The Rules were not intended to be the exclusive means for seeking the enforcement of tribal court judgments, and they do not apply where a tribal court judgment is invoked to support the defense of collateral estoppel. *Beltran v. Harrah's Arizona Corp.*, 220 Ariz. 29, 202 P.3d 494 (Ct. App. Div. 2 2008).

Rule 2(a) of those Rules defines "tribal court" to include "any court or other tribunal of any federally recognized Indian nation, tribe, pueblo, band or Alaska native village. . . ." Rule 2(b) defines "tribal judgment" as "any final written judgment decree or order of a tribal court duly authenticated in accordance with the laws and procedures of the tribe or tribal court." Under Rule 3, a person seeking to enforce such a judgment is to file it with the Clerk of the Superior Court in any county, together with an affidavit setting forth the name and last known address of the party seeking enforcement and the "responding party" (presumably the party against whom the judgment is to be enforced). The party seeking enforcement is also to serve upon the responding party a notice of filing, and a copy of the tribal judgment. Service is to be accomplished in accordance with the requirements of Rule 4.1. Alternatively, the party seeking enforcement may mail the notice of filing and a copy of the tribal judgment to the responding party at that party's last known address, by certified mail, return receipt requested. If the responding party is the State of Arizona, or any of its officers, employees, departments or agencies, then service can be accomplished by mailing to the office of the Attorney General. Proof of service or mailing must be filed with the Clerk. The notice of filing must contain the name and address of the enforcing party and of the enforcing party's attorney, if any, and the full text of Ariz. R. Civ. P. 4, 5(a) and 5(b).

Rule 4 requires that any objection to enforcement of the tribal judgment be filed within twenty (20) days after service, or receipt of the mailing, of the notice of filing, or within twenty-five (25) days of the date of mailing, whichever is later. If no timely objection is filed, then, under Rule 5(a), the Clerk is to issue a certification to that effect and the tribal judgment shall have the same force and effect as a judgment, order or decree issued by a court of the State of Arizona. If an objection is filed, the Superior Court may set a time for a reply and/or set the matter for hearing.

Under Rule 5(c), the Superior Court *must* decline to enforce the tribal judgment if it finds that (1) the tribal court entering the judgment lacked personal or subject matter discretion, or (2) the defendant was not afforded due process in the proceedings resulting in the entry of the judgment. Under Rule 5(d), the Superior Court *may*, in its discretion, decline to enforce the tribal judgment if it finds that: (1) the tribal judgment was obtained through extrinsic fraud; (2) the tribal judgment conflicts with another final judgment that is entitled to recognition; (3) the tribal judgment is inconsistent with the parties' contractual choice of forum; *or* (4) recognition of the judgment, or the cause of action upon which it is based, would be contrary to the fundamental public policy of the United States or the State of Arizona.

Under Rule 6, if the party objecting to enforcement demonstrates that an appeal from the judgment is pending or will be taken, or that a stay of execution upon the judgment has been granted, then the Superior Court is to stay enforcement of it until it has become final, or the stay upon execution expires or is vacated. Rule 7 grants the Superior Court authority to contact the tribal court judge who issued the judgment, after notice to the parties, to attempt to resolve any issues regarding it that may arise.

17. *Premature Notice of Appeal of Final Judgment.* In order to

simplify procedures for perfecting an appeal and to avoid unfairness, confusion and judicial inefficiencies caused by the "premature" filing of a notice of appeal, Ariz. R. Civ. P. 54(c) was added effective January 1, 2014, to facilitate the effectiveness of a simultaneous amendment to Ariz. R. Civ. App. P. 9, also amended effective January 1, 2014. The amendment to ARCAP 9 is the meat-and-potatoes of this effort. The 2014 amendments are consistent with the federal approach, which provides a relatively easy procedure for curing technical jurisdictional defects caused by the premature filing of a notice of appeal.

Rule 54(c) was adopted, therefore, to require that a judgment, in order to be final, must include a statement from the trial court that "no further matters remain pending and that the judgment is entered pursuant to Rule 54(c). The apparent expectation is that this statement will provide certainty as to whether a judgment is a "final" judgment and, as such, will assist in the implementation of the amendment to ARCAP 9.

As written, however, Ariz. R. Civ. P. 54(c) (added 2014) is ambiguous. Rule 54(c) merely requires the "court state" such matters. Rule 54(c) does not expressly require a final judgment include such language. Thus, a judicial statement made on the record to this effect arguably might suffice. Having said that, it appears the intent of the adoption of Rule 54(c) is that such statement by the court must be included in the judgment itself, if the judgment is to be considered a "final judgment". As a cautionary measure, therefore practitioners are urged to include the language from Rule 54(c) in those case where the judgment to be entered is intended to be a final judgment, including final judgments on default, pretrial motions, trial motions, jury verdicts or decisions by the court, post-trial motions.

As indicated earlier, the more important 2014 amendment in this procedural arena is to ARCAP 9. Amended ARCAP 9 added a new provision ARCAP 9(b)(2)(B), which is similar to Federal Rule of Civil Appellate Procedure 4(a)(4). Thus, under ARCAP 9 as amended, there are now procedures in place to avoid the results that occurred in *Barassi v. Matison*, 130 Ariz. 418, 636 P.2d 1200 (1981) ("appellate courts lack jurisdiction when 'a litigant attempts to appeal where a motion is still pending in the trial court or where there is no final judgment' "); *Craig v. Craig*, 227 Ariz. 105, 253 P.3d 624 (2011); *Fields v. Oates*, 230 Ariz. 411, 286 P.3d 160 (Ct. App. Div. 1 2012) (in the absence of Rule 54(b) language in the judgment or signed order, a notice of appeal filed while a claim for attorneys' fees is pending is a nullity and appellate court lacks jurisdiction to hear the matter); *Santee v. Mesa Airlines, Inc.*, 229 Ariz. 88, 270 P.3d 915 (Ct. App. Div. 2 2012), review denied, (May 30, 2012) (notice of appeal filed before ruling on Rule 68(g) motion was premature and failed to vest the appellate court with jurisdiction); *Engel v. Landman*, 221 Ariz. 504, 212 P.3d 842 (Ct. App. Div. 1 2009) ("[O]utside the slim exception announced in *Barassi*, premature notices of appeal are ineffective because they disrupt the court process and prevent two courts from assuming jurisdiction and acting at the same time."); *Baumann v. Tuton*, 180 Ariz. 370, 884 P.2d 256 (Ct. App. Div. 1 1994) (Premature filing of notice of appeal while motion for new trial was pending in trial court did not confer jurisdiction upon appellate court).

Rule 55. Default

(a) Application and Entry. When a party against whom a judgment for affirmative relief is sought has failed to plead or otherwise defend as provided by these Rules, the clerk shall enter that party's default in accordance with the procedures set forth below. All requests for entry of default shall be by written application to the clerk of the court in which the matter is pending.

(1) *Notice.*

(i) To the Party. When the whereabouts of the party claimed to be in default are known by the party requesting the entry of default, a copy of the application for entry of default shall be mailed to the party claimed to be in default.

(ii) Represented Party. When a party claimed to be in default is known by the party requesting the entry of default to be represented by an attorney, whether or not that attorney has formally appeared, a copy of the application shall also be sent to the attorney for the party claimed to be in default. Nothing herein shall be construed to create any obligation to undertake any affirmative effort to determine the existence or identity of counsel representing the party claimed to be in default.

(iii) Whereabouts of Unrepresented Party Unknown. If the whereabouts of a party claimed to be in default are unknown to the party requesting the entry of default and the identity of counsel for that party is also not known to the requesting party, the application for entry of default shall so state.

(iv) Other Parties. Nothing in this Rule relieves a party requesting entry of default from the requirements of Rule 5(a) as to service on other parties.

(2) *Entry of Default.* The acceptance by the clerk of the filing of the application for entry of default constitutes the entry of default.

(3) *Effective Date of Default.* A default entered by the clerk shall be effective ten (10) days after the filing of the application for entry of default.

(4) *Effect of Responsive Pleading.* A default shall not become effective if the party claimed to be in default pleads or otherwise defends as provided by these Rules prior to the expiration of ten (10) days from the filing of the application for entry of default.

(5) *Applicability.* The provisions of this rule requiring notice prior to the entry of default shall apply only to a default sought

and entered pursuant to this rule.

Amended July 2, 1985, effective Oct. 1, 1985; Sept. 15, 1987, effective Nov. 15, 1987. Rule 55(a)(1)(iv) added Sept. 1, 2011, effective Jan. 1. 2012. Rule 55(a)(2) added Aug. 30, 2012, effective January 1, 2013.

(b) Judgment by Default. Judgment by default may be entered as follows:

1. *By Motion.* When the plaintiff's claim against a defendant is for a sum certain or for a sum which can by computation be made certain, the Court upon motion of the plaintiff and upon affidavit of the amount due shall enter judgment for that amount and costs against the defendant, if the defendant has been defaulted for failure to appear and is not an infant or incompetent person. If the claim states a specific sum of attorneys' fees which will be sought in the event judgment is rendered by default, and if such award is allowed by law and is supported by the affidavit, the judgment may include an award of reasonable attorneys' fees not to exceed the amount of the demand therefor. If the claim requests an award of attorneys' fees, but fails to specify the amount of such fees that will be sought in the event judgment is rendered by default, the judgment may include an award of attorneys' fees, if such an award is allowed by law and the reasonable amount therefor is established by affidavit, where the defendant has not entered an appearance in the action.

2. *By Hearing.* In all other cases the party entitled to a judgment shall apply to the court therefor, but no judgment by default shall be entered against an infant or incompetent person unless represented in the action by a general guardian, or other such representative who has appeared therein. If the party against whom judgment by default is sought has appeared in the action, that party or, if appearing by representative, that party's representative, shall be served with written notice of the application for judgment at least three days prior to the hearing on such application. If, in order to enable the court to enter judgment or to carry it into effect, it is necessary to take an account or to determine the amount of damages or to establish the truth of any averment by evidence or to make an investigation of any other matter, the court may conduct such hearings or order such references as it deems necessary and proper and shall accord a right of trial by jury to the parties when required by law.

Amended Oct. 21, 1975, effective Jan. 1, 1976; Aug. 7, 1984, effective Nov. 1, 1984; Sept. 15, 1987, effective Nov. 15, 1987; Oct. 4, 1990 effective Dec. 1 1990; Feb. 25, 1991, effective May 1, 1991; July 16, 1992, effective Dec. 1, 1992; Sept. 16, 2008, effective Jan. 1, 2009.

(c) Setting Aside Default. For good cause shown the court may set aside an entry of default and, if a judgment by default has been entered, may likewise set it aside in accordance with Rule 60(c).

(d) Plaintiffs, Counterclaimants, Cross-Claimants. The provisions of this Rule apply whether the party entitled to the judgment by default is a plaintiff, a third-party plaintiff, or a party who has pleaded a cross-claim or counterclaim. In all cases a judgment by default is subject to the limitations of Rule 54(d).

(e) Judgment Against the State. No judgment by default shall be entered against the state or an officer or agency thereof unless the claimant establishes a claim or right to relief by evidence satisfactory to the court.

Amended Sept. 15, 1987, effective Nov. 15, 1987.

(f) Judgment When Service by Publication; Statement of Evidence. Where service of process has been made by publication and no answer has been filed within the time prescribed by law, judgment shall be rendered as in other cases, but a record of the proceedings, in a form approved by the court, shall be maintained by the clerk of the court unless designated otherwise by the court.

Amended Sept. 18, 2006, effective Jan. 1, 2007.

STATE BAR COMMITTEE NOTES

1984 Amendment

[Rule 55(b)] The amendment to Rule 55(b)(1) is intended to avoid the result suggested by dicta in *Monte Produce, Inc. v. Delgado*, 126 Ariz. 320, 614 P.2d 862 (Ct. App. Div. 2 1980), that a default judgment including attorneys' fees may not be obtained by motion without a hearing unless the amount of attorneys' fees is liquidated. The amendment is intended to permit the court to consider and rule upon the issue of attorneys' fees by motion, even though it may be an unliquidated claim, where the complaint gives notice of an amount sought in the event of default. The amendment does not attempt to change the substantive law in regard to liquidated or unliquidated damages.

A party desiring to preserve his right to prove the amount of reasonable attorneys' fees to which he is entitled at the time of default, without the limitation set by a prayer for a specific amount, may plead entitlement to an unspecified reasonable amount of attorneys' fees with knowledge that he must proceed by hearing pursuant to 55(b)(2) upon default.

AUTHORS' COMMENTS

Analysis

1. Scope and Purpose of Rule.
2. Comparison With Federal Rule.
3. Application for Entry of Default; Service.
4. Procedure for Entry of Default.
5. Effect of Entry of Default.

1. *Scope and Purpose of Rule.* Terminating an action at the trial court level where the party against whom the action has been instituted has failed or refused to defend is a two-stage process: (1) securing the entry of that party's default, and (2) securing the entry of a default judgment against that party. The procedures for accomplishing both are governed by Rule 55.

The appellate courts have drawn a distinction between a default judgment entered by the Court and an entry of default by the Clerk. An order *setting aside a default judgment* is appealable as a special order after judgment, under A.R.S. § 12-2101(C). *Master Financial, Inc. v. Woodburn*, 208 Ariz. 70, 90 P.3d 1236 (Ct. App. Div. 1 2004), as amended, (June 7, 2004). An order *vacating the entry of default* is not appealable, and can only be reviewed on a petition for special action. *Master Financial, Inc. v. Woodburn*, 208 Ariz. 70, 90 P.3d 1236 (Ct. App. Div. 1 2004), as amended, (June 7, 2004).

2. *Comparison With Federal Rule.* There are significant differences between the procedural requirements imposed by ARCP 55 and those imposed by FRCP 55.

With respect to the procedural requirements to secure the entry of default (as opposed to default judgment), the Arizona Rule, ARCP 55(a), requires that, when the whereabouts of a party claimed to be in default is known or that party is known to be represented by counsel in the matter, a copy of an application for entry of default must be sent to the attorney and/or the party claimed to be in default. Any default entered pursuant to the application does not become effective for a period of ten (10) days after the filing of the application. Filing a responsive pleading or otherwise defending within that 10-day period prevents the default from becoming effective. The Federal Rule, FRCP 55, provides simply that the Clerk is to enter the default of a party shown by affidavit to have failed to plead or otherwise defend.

With respect to the procedural requirements to secure the entry of default judgment, FRCP 55(b)(1) allows the Clerk to enter default judgments where the amount claimed is a sum certain. ARCP 55(b)(1), on the other hand, contemplates that the Court will enter such default judgments.

ARCP 55(b)(2), (c), and (e) are similar to FRCP 55(b)(2), (c), and (e). FRCP 54 does not have provisions that correspond to ARCP 55(d) and (f).

3. *Application for Entry of Default; Service.* The manner in which the first step—the entry of default—is accomplished was significantly revised by the 1985 amendment to Rule 55(a). Under prior practice, the entry of a default was essentially a ministerial task performed by the Clerk of the Court when presented with a proper Application for Entry of Default, and an Affidavit establishing that the party whose default was to be entered had failed to appear. There was no requirement of notice to the party in default.

As amended in 1985, Rule 55(a) requires that a copy of the Application for Entry of Default be mailed to the party claimed to be in default, if that party's whereabouts are known. Rule 55(a) does not require, however, that the application specify the effective date of the default or advise the party in default that the effective date may be delayed or avoided by appearing and defending within ten (10) days of the application. *State ex rel. Corbin v. Marshall*, 161 Ariz. 429, 778 P.2d 1325 (Ct. App. Div. 1 1989). Many practitioners do include this information in the application.

Rule 55(a) also provides that a copy must be mailed to the attorney for the party, if the party seeking the default knows that the party to be defaulted is represented by counsel. Rule 55(a) specifically states that it does not impose any affirmative obligation to ascertain the existence or identity of counsel representing the party to be defaulted. If neither the party's whereabouts nor the identity of counsel is known, the Application for Entry of Default must so state. *See,* Rule 55(a)(1)(iii). Effective January 1, 2012, Rule 55(a)(1) was amended to clarify that applications for entry of default must be served on all parties consistent with Ariz. R. Civ. P. 5(a), not just the party against whom default is sought. *See*, Rule 55(a)(1)(iv).

By clear and necessary implication, the failure to serve a copy of the Application for Entry of Default, where required under amended Rule 55(a), will be a sufficient basis for setting the default aside. *See also, Champlin v. Bank of America, N.A.*, 231 Ariz. 265, 293 P.3d 541 (Ct. App. Div. 2 2013); *Ruiz v. Lopez*, 225 Ariz. 217, 236 P.3d 444 (Ct. App. Div. 1 2010), review denied, (Jan. 4, 2011).

4. *Procedures for Entry of Default.* The basic procedure outlined in Ariz. R. Civ. P. 55(a) for securing the entry of default is as

follows:

1. Application for Entry of Default. The party seeking the entry of default files an application for the entry of default. Ariz. R. Civ. P. 55(a).

2. Notice to Defaulting Party; Other Parties.

2.1. Whereabouts of defaulting party known. The party seeking the entry of default must mail a copy of the application for entry of default to the defaulting party. Ariz. R. Civ. P. 55(a)(1)(i). The defaulting party must be given notice of the application for entry of default before or simultaneously with the filing of the application. Ariz. R. Civ. P. 55(a)(5). *See also, Champlin v. Bank of America, N.A.*, 231 Ariz. 265, 293 P.3d 541 (Ct. App. Div. 2 2013) ("Rule 55 plainly requires 'notice prior to entry of default,'" citing Ariz. R. Civ. P. 55(a)(4) [sic, Ariz. R. Civ. P. 55(a)(5)].

2.2. Represented party. If the party seeking the entry of default knows the defaulting party is represented by an attorney, the party seeking the entry of default also must send a copy of the application to such attorney. Ariz. R. Civ. P. 55(a)(1)(ii).

2.3. Whereabouts of defaulting party and identity of counsel for defaulting party unknown. In this circumstance, the application for entry of judgment shall so state. Ariz. R. Civ. P. 55(a)(1)(iii).

2.4. Other parties. Consistent with Ariz. R. Civ. P. 5(a), the party seeking the entry of default also must send a copy of the application to all other parties. Ariz. R. Civ. P. 55(a)(1)(iv).

3. Entry of Default. The acceptance by the clerk of application for entry of default constitutes the entry of default. Ariz. R. Civ. P. 55(a)(2). The default entered by the clerk becomes effective 10-days after the filing of the application or entry of default. Ariz. R. Civ. P. 55(a)(3).

4. Default Judgment after Grace Period. If the party claimed to be in default fails to appear during the 10-day grace period, the default as entered by the Clerk becomes effective 10-days after the application for entry of default is filed. Ariz. R. Civ. P. 55(a)(3), (4). *See also, Champlin v. Bank of America, N.A.*, 231 Ariz. 265, 293 P.3d 541 (Ct. App. Div. 2 2013); *Estate of Lewis v. Lewis*, 229 Ariz. 316, 275 P.3d 615 (Ct. App. Div. 2 2012); *Corbet v. Superior Court In and For County of Maricopa*, 165 Ariz. 245, 798 P.2d 383 (Ct. App. Div. 1 1990).

This 10-day grace period is computed in accordance with Rule 6(a) so that weekends and holidays are excluded. *Corbet v. Superior Court In and For County of Maricopa*, 165 Ariz. 245, 798 P.2d 383 (Ct. App. Div. 1 1990). Because that 10-day period runs from the *filing* of the application for entry of default, however, Rule 6(e) does not apply, even if the application is served by mail. *Baker Intern. Associates, Inc. v. Shanwick Intern. Corp.*, 174 Ariz. 580, 851 P.2d 1379 (Ct. App. Div. 1 1993). Thus, the entry-of-default clock starts running immediately upon filing of the application under Rule 55(a)(2) and no extra days are added even if the application is served by mail.

If, within that 10-day grace period, the party in default "pleads or otherwise defends," the default does not become effective and is, essentially, null and void. In that circumstance, the trial court has no discretion to refuse to vacate any default that has been entered. *Corbet v. Superior Court In and For County of Maricopa*, 165 Ariz. 245, 798 P.2d 383 (Ct. App. Div. 1 1990).

This 10-day grace period gives the defaulting party a second chance simply by filing a responsive pleading or by otherwise defending against the action. *Waltner v. JPMorgan Chase Bank, N.A.*, 231 Ariz. 484, 297 P.3d 176 (Ct. App. Div. 1 2013) (moving for summary judgment constitutes "otherwise defend[ing]" against an action). It effectively extends the time to answer under Rule 12(a). *General Elec. Capital Corp. v. Osterkamp*, 172 Ariz. 185, 836 P.2d 398 (Ct. App. Div. 2 1992).

The party must, however, both appear *and* defend within the grace period allowed. A notice of appearance, for instance, is not a pleading and does not qualify as otherwise defending against the action. As such, it will not prevent the entry of default from becoming effective or the rendering of a default judgment. *Arizona Dept. of Revenue v. Superior Court In and For Arizona Tax Court*, 165 Ariz. 47, 796 P.2d 479 (Ct. App. Div. 1 1990); *Suncor Development Co. v. Maricopa County*, 163 Ariz. 403, 788 P.2d 136 (Tax Ct.1990). On the other hand, a timely filed motion for summary judgment will toll the time for filing an answer and satisfy Rule 55(a). *Waltner v. JPMorgan Chase Bank, N.A.*, 231 Ariz. 484, 297 P.3d 176 (Ct. App. Div. 1 2013).

Rule 4.2(b) specifies that, where direct service is made on a defendant outside the State of Arizona, an affidavit of service must be filed "before any default may be had on such service." The affidavit is to show the circumstances that warranted use of that method of service and must attach a separate affidavit from the process server who accomplished service on the defendant. This provision, however, was not intended to confer any substantive rights on a defendant who is properly served in that fashion, and the fact that the specified affidavits are not filed until after a default is taken is not in and of itself grounds for setting that default aside. *Creach v. Angulo*, 186 Ariz. 548, 925 P.2d 689 (Ct. App. Div. 1 1996), decision approved, 189 Ariz. 212, 941 P.2d 224 (1997).

5. *Effect of Entry of Default.* A default, when properly entered, is a judicial admission of all well-pleaded facts in the complaint or other pleading seeking affirmative relief, except those as to the amount the plaintiff or other party is entitled to recover, unless the claim is a liquidated one. *Reed v. Frey*, 10 Ariz. App. 292, 458 P.2d 386 (1969). Those judicial admissions are not, however, binding on a co-defendant, even if the co-defendant's liability is derivative. *American Nat. Rent-A-Car, Inc. v. McNally*, 8 Ariz. App. 208, 445 P.2d 91 (1968), judgment vacated on other grounds, 104 Ariz. 301, 451 P.2d 882 (1969).

The entry of default, and any resulting judgment, are ineffective and void, however, if the party moving for default fails to provide notice in accordance with Rule 55(a). *See also, Champlin v. Bank of America, N.A.*, 231 Ariz. 265, 293 P.3d 541 (Ct. App. Div. 2 2013); *Ruiz v. Lopez*, 225 Ariz. 217, 236 P.3d 444 (Ct. App. Div. 1 2010), review denied, (Jan. 4, 2011) (Rule 55(a) permits entry of default only upon proper notice to defaulting party).

After a party's default has been properly entered, the next step in the procedure is to secure the entry of default judgment. Rule 55(b) establishes two separate and distinct procedures for securing the entry of default judgment. Rule 55(b)(1) governs the procedure for securing judgment against a defaulted party in a liquidated damages case; and, Rule 55(b)(2) establishes the procedure for securing judgment against a defaulted party in an unliquidated damages case. The associated procedures are discussed in Sections 6 and 7 of this chapter.

6. *Entry of Default Judgment By Motion.* Rule 55(b)(1) governs the procedure for securing the entry of default judgment in cases where default has been entered against a non-minor/incompetent defendant for failure to appear and the claimed damages are for a sum certain or for a sum which can be made certain by calculation, *i.e.*, liquidated damages. By its express terms, Rule 55(b)(1) permits the court to enter a default judgment against such defendant in the amount of such liquidated damages upon motion supported by affidavit as to the amount due.

In 2012, a divergence of views emerged between two panels of Division One of the Arizona Court of Appeals on the issue of whether a damages hearing is required in liquidated damages cases where defaulted party enters an appearance after the entry of default but before the entry of default judgment. A brief summary to the two cases follows:

(1) In *BYS Inc. v. Smoudi*, 228 Ariz. 573, 269 P.3d 1197 (Ct. App. Div. 1 2012), as amended, (Mar. 13, 2012), a Division One panel held that, under Rule 55(b)(2), a defaulted party who has appeared in an action after the entry of default and before the entry of default judgment is entitled to notice and

an opportunity to be heard at a hearing on damages regardless of the nature of the claimed damages, *i.e.*, liquidated or unliquidated.

(2) In *Searchtoppers.com, L.L.C. v. TrustCash LLC*, 231 Ariz. 236, 293 P.3d 512 (Ct. App. Div. 1 2012), a different Division One panel discussed and then declined to follow the *BYS* court's interpretation of Rule 55(b) in what the court described as a "factually analogous case." In *Searchtoppers* the Division One panel essentially held that Rule 55(b)(1) applies to liquidated damages cases and Rule 55(b)(2) applies to unliquidated damages cases. Thus, the court concluded, a defaulted party who has appeared in an action after the entry of default and before the entry of default judgment in a liquidated damages case is not entitled to a hearing on the amount of the liquidated damages.

Neither decision has been appealed. On December 13, 2013, the Arizona State Bar filed a Rule 28 petition to amend Rule 55(b)(1) to address this ambiguity in Rule 55(b)(1).

7. *Entry of Default Judgment by Hearing.* Where the claim is unliquidated, the party securing the default must proceed under Rule 55(b)(2), which requires application to the Court and a hearing. If the party in default has by now entered an appearance in the action, through the filing of a late answer or otherwise, written notice of the application and hearing must be provided at least 3-days in advance of the hearing date. *Tarr v. Superior Court In and For Pima County*, 142 Ariz. 349, 690 P.2d 68 (1984); *McClintock v. Serv-Us Bakers*, 103 Ariz. 72, 436 P.2d 891 (1968); *BYS Inc. v. Smoudi*, 228 Ariz. 573, 269 P.3d 1197 (Ct. App. Div. 1 2012), as amended, (Mar. 13, 2012); *Poleo v. Grandview Equities, Ltd.*, 143 Ariz. 130, 692 P.2d 309 (Ct. App. Div. 1 1984) ("the party whose pleadings have been stricken as a sanction under Rule 37 must be given notice of the application for judgment as required by Rule 55(b)(2) because that party has 'appeared' in the action.").

Failure to adhere to these requirements may render the eventual judgment a nullity, or provide grounds for setting it aside. *BYS Inc. v. Smoudi*, 228 Ariz. 573, 269 P.3d 1197 (Ct. App. Div. 1 2012), as amended, (Mar. 13, 2012); *Gustafson v. McDade*, 26 Ariz. App. 322, 548 P.2d 415 (Div. 1 1976); *City of Phoenix v. Collar, Williams & White Engineering, Inc.*, 12 Ariz. App. 510, 472 P.2d 479 (Div. 1 1970); *Austin v. State ex rel. Herman*, 10 Ariz. App. 474, 459 P.2d 753 (Div. 2 1969). In large counties, the Notice should specify the Division of the Court where, and the Judge or Commissioner before whom, the hearing will take place. *Lawrence v. Burke*, 6 Ariz. App. 228, 431 P.2d 302 (1967).

The defaulted party is allowed to participate in the hearing by cross-examination and otherwise. *Tarr v. Superior Court In and For Pima County*, 142 Ariz. 349, 690 P.2d 68 (1984); *Arizona Dept. of Revenue v. Superior Court In and For Arizona Tax Court*, 165 Ariz. 47, 796 P.2d 479 (Ct. App. Div. 1 1990) (Rule 55(e): "No judgment against the state or an officer or agency thereof unless the claimant establishes a claim or right to relief by evidence satisfactory to the court."); *Dungan v. Superior Court In and For Pinal County*, 20 Ariz. App. 289, 512 P.2d 52 (Div. 2 1973). The Court must exercise some discretion in determining what relief is to be granted, and should not merely endorse the claimant's requests. *Daou v. Harris*, 139 Ariz. 353, 678 P.2d 934 (1984); *Hilgeman v. American Mortg. Securities, Inc.*, 196 Ariz. 215, 994 P.2d 1030 (Ct. App. Div. 2 2000); *Dungan v. Superior Court In and For Pinal County*, 20 Ariz. App. 289, 290, 512 P.2d 52, 53 (Div. 2 1973) (the hearing on damages must be more than "a one-sided presentation by the party seeking the default judgment"); *Mayhew v. McDougall*, 16 Ariz. App. 125, 491 P.2d 848 (Div. 2 1971) (determining damages in a default setting when the amount is unliquidated requires judicial discretion). In any event, the limitations of Rule 54(d) apply.

Under Rule 54(d), a default judgment may not be different in kind from or exceed in amount that prayed for in the demand for judgment. That Rule serves the goal of due process by preventing a plaintiff from securing a result in a default proceeding without giving a defendant notice of the risk presented. *Kline v. Kline*, 221 Ariz. 564, 212 P.3d 902 (Ct. App. Div. 1 2009).

There are no special pleading requirements for punitive damages, however, and a general prayer for punitive damages is sufficient to put the defendant on notice that such damages may be awarded. *Kline v. Kline*, 221 Ariz. 564, 212 P.3d 902 (Ct. App. Div. 1 2009); *Tarnoff v. Jones*, 17 Ariz. App. 240, 497 P.2d 60 (Div. 1 1972). The fact that punitive damages are included in a default judgment does not eliminate the need for effective appellate review to insure that the award comports with constitutional standards. *Hilgeman v. American Mortg. Securities, Inc.*, 196 Ariz. 215, 994 P.2d 1030 (Ct. App. Div. 2 2000). When the record developed at the default judgment hearing is inadequate for a meaningful evaluation of the constitutionality of a punitive damages award, that award will be set aside. *Hilgeman v. American Mortg. Securities, Inc.*, 196 Ariz. 215, 994 P.2d 1030 (Ct. App. Div. 2 2000).

8. *Entry of Default Judgment Against the State.* Rule 55(e) clearly suggests that a hearing will be necessary where a default judgment is sought against the state, or a state officer or agency, whether the claim is liquidated or unliquidated. That provision specifies that a default judgment may not be entered against the state, a state officer or state agency unless the claimant estab-

lishes a claim or right to relief "by evidence satisfactory to the court."

9. *Securing An Award of Attorneys' Fees in Default Judgments.* The process by which a party can secure an award of attorneys' fees in a default judgment in cases where such fees are recoverable has evolved over the years. In *Monte Produce, Inc. v. Delgado*, 126 Ariz. 320, 614 P.2d 862 (Ct. App. Div. 2 1980), the Court intimated that attorneys' fees were always an unliquidated claim on which a hearing was required. In response to that decision, a sentence was added to Rule 55(b)(1) providing that, if the pleading of the party securing the default set forth a specific sum that would be sought for attorneys' fees in the event of a default and the amount of such fees was supported by affidavit, a default judgment including an award of attorneys' fees in that amount could be entered on motion without the necessity of a hearing. It was believed that this type of procedure would also assure compliance with the requirement of Rule 54(d) that a default judgment "not be different in kind from or exceed in amount that prayed for in the demand for judgment."

Experience showed, however, that such claims were rarely contested and that a good deal of judicial time was being devoted to the conduct of perfunctory hearings on the amount of attorneys' fees to be awarded on liquidated claims. Accordingly, Rule 55(b)(1) was amended, effective December 1, 1992, to add the final sentence. This provision permits a default judgment entered on motion to include an award of attorneys' fees, even though the amount of such fees to be sought is not specified in the pleadings of the party securing the default, provided they are recoverable by law and the amount sought and the reasonableness thereof is established by affidavit. For some reason, the amendment left intact the provision that had been added in 1984. The procedure contemplated by that provision, however, pursuant to which a party specified in its pleadings the amount of attorneys' fees that would be sought in the event of a default, would seem to be of limited practical utility in light of the amendment.

10. *Effect of Default Judgments.* A default judgment is *res judicata* and of the same force and effect as if the action had been tried on the merits. *Technical Air Products, Inc. v. Sheridan-Gray, Inc.*, 103 Ariz. 450, 445 P.2d 426 (1968); *Tarnoff v. Jones*, 17 Ariz. App. 240, 497 P.2d 60 (Div. 1 1972). It is void, however, if service of process was not properly made upon, or if the court lacks personal jurisdiction over, the party against whom it is entered. *Tonner v. Paradise Valley Magistrate's Court*, 171 Ariz. 449, 831 P.2d 448 (Ct. App. Div. 1 1992); *Sprang v. Petersen Lumber, Inc.*, 165 Ariz. 257, 798 P.2d 395 (Ct. App. Div. 1 1990); *French v. Angelic*, 137 Ariz. 244, 669 P.2d 1021 (Ct. App. Div. 1 1983); *Austin v. State ex rel. Herman*, 10 Ariz. App. 474, 459 P.2d

753 (Div. 2 1969). Thus, a default judgment entered against a defendant over whom the trial court lacked personal jurisdiction, because service by publication was not authorized, is void and all acts performed pursuant to such a judgment, including execution thereon, are without legal effect. *Sprang v. Petersen Lumber, Inc.*, 165 Ariz. 257, 798 P.2d 395 (Ct. App. Div. 1 1990). Further, the violation of the notice requirements set forth in Rule 55(a) render any resulting default judgment void and without legal effect. *Ruiz v. Lopez*, 225 Ariz. 217, 236 P.3d 444 (Ct. App. Div. 1 2010), review denied, (Jan. 4, 2011).

11. *Setting Aside Entry of Default and/or Default Judgment.* A party seeking relief from a default judgment must move to set aside the entry of default or the default judgment, or both. A default judgment may not be appealed unless there has been a motion in the trial court to set it aside. *Byrer v. A. B. Robbs Trust Co.*, 105 Ariz. 457, 466 P.2d 751 (1970); *Sears Roebuck and Co. v. Walker*, 127 Ariz. 432, 621 P.2d 938 (Ct. App. Div. 1 1980); *Mercantile Nat. Life Ins. Co. v. Villalba*, 18 Ariz. App. 179, 501 P.2d 20 (Div. 2 1972). The foregoing rule does not apply where the default judgment was entered as a discovery sanction rather than as a consequence of a failure to appear and defend. *Sears Roebuck and Co. v. Walker*, 127 Ariz. 432, 621 P.2d 938 (Ct. App. Div. 1 1980). The motion may be brought by an insurer on behalf of its insured. *Evans v. Arthur*, 139 Ariz. 362, 678 P.2d 943 (1984); *Camacho v. Gardner*, 104 Ariz. 555, 456 P.2d 925 (1969); *Echols v. State Farm Mut. Auto. Ins. Co.*, 152 Ariz. 384, 732 P.2d 1122 (Ct. App. Div. 2 1986); *Beal v. State Farm Mut. Auto. Ins. Co.*, 151 Ariz. 514, 729 P.2d 318 (Ct. App. Div. 1 1986); *Koven v. Saberdyne Systems, Inc.*, 128 Ariz. 318, 625 P.2d 907 (Ct. App. Div. 1 1980).

While a motion to set aside an entry of default is based on Rule 55(c), and a motion to set aside a default judgment is brought pursuant to Ariz.R.Civ.P. 60(c), the standards for relief are the same under both Rules. *Richas v. Superior Court of Arizona In and For Maricopa County*, 133 Ariz. 512, 652 P.2d 1035 (1982). The moving party has the burden of demonstrating that there are grounds for relief. *State ex rel. Corbin v. Marshall*, 161 Ariz. 429, 778 P.2d 1325 (Ct. App. Div. 1 1989).

The failure to serve a copy of the application for entry of default where, and as, required by Rule 55(a) will render the entry of default, and any resulting judgment, void *Ruiz v. Lopez*, 225 Ariz. 217, 236 P.3d 444 (Ct. App. Div. 1 2010), review denied, (Jan. 4, 2011).

12. *Showing Required to Set Aside Default Generally.* There are three essential requirements. A party seeking relief from an entry of default or a default judgment must (1) move promptly to

have the default or default judgment set aside and show both (2) that the failure to defend was the result of excusable neglect *and* (3) that there exists a meritorious defense to the claims. *Richas v. Superior Court of Arizona In and For Maricopa County*, 133 Ariz. 512, 652 P.2d 1035 (1982); *Western Coach Corp. v. Mark V Mobile Homes Sales, Inc.*, 23 Ariz. App. 546, 534 P.2d 760 (Div. 1 1975); *Phillips v. Findlay*, 19 Ariz. App. 348, 507 P.2d 687 (Div. 2 1973); *Arizona State Tax Commission v. Catalina Sav. & Loan Ass'n*, 16 Ariz. App. 398, 493 P.2d 944 (Div. 2 1972); *Smith v. Monroe*, 15 Ariz. App. 366, 488 P.2d 1003 (Div. 2 1971); *but cf. Peralta v. Heights Medical Center, Inc.*, 485 U.S. 80, 108 S. Ct. 896, 99 L. Ed. 2d 75 (1988).

When a party demonstrates that either the entry of default or the entry of default judgment is void, however, the trial court must set aside the default judgment. The failure to serve a copy of the application for entry of default where, and as, required by Rule 55(a) will render the entry of default, and any resulting judgment, void. *Ruiz v. Lopez*, 225 Ariz. 217, 236 P.3d 444 (Ct. App. Div. 1 2010), review denied, (Jan. 4, 2011) (Rule 55(a) permits entry of default only upon proper notice to defaulting party.).

The appellate courts have drawn a distinction between a default judgment entered by the court and an entry of default by the clerk. An order setting aside a default judgment is appealable as a special order after judgment, under A.R.S. § 12-2101(C). *Master Financial, Inc. v. Woodburn*, 208 Ariz. 70, 90 P.3d 1236 (Ct. App. Div. 1 2004), as amended, (June 7, 2004). An order vacating the entry of default is not appealable, and can only be reviewed on a petition for special action. *Master Financial, Inc. v. Woodburn*, 208 Ariz. 70, 90 P.3d 1236 (Ct. App. Div. 1 2004), as amended on other grounds, (June 7, 2004).

13. *Excusable Neglect*. The showing of excusable neglect requires a presentation of the circumstances that led to the default and will vary from case to case. The test is whether the acts of the party defaulted were those of a reasonably prudent person under the circumstances. *Daou v. Harris*, 139 Ariz. 353, 678 P.2d 934 (1984); *Gray v. Dillon*, 97 Ariz. 16, 396 P.2d 251 (1964); *State ex rel. Husky v. Oaks*, 3 Ariz. App. 174, 412 P.2d 743 (1966). Mere carelessness is not excusable neglect. *Kohlbeck v. Handley*, 3 Ariz. App. 469, 415 P.2d 483, 21 A.L.R.3d 1248 (1966).

Because the 1985 amendment to the Rule, which added the 10-day grace period, gives a defaulting party an automatic second chance to avoid the entry of default from becoming effective, the burden of establishing a basis for setting aside the default will be greater than before the Rule was amended. *General Elec. Capital*

Corp. v. Osterkamp, 172 Ariz. 185, 836 P.2d 398 (Ct. App. Div. 2 1992). The amendment virtually eliminates any claim of lack of notice as a basis for setting aside a default, and the party who fails to defend, even within the 10-day grace period, will have difficulty showing that such failure was the result of excusable neglect. *General Elec. Capital Corp. v. Osterkamp*, 172 Ariz. 185, 836 P.2d 398 (Ct. App. Div. 2 1992); *Ruiz v. Lopez*, 225 Ariz. 217, 236 P.3d 444 (Ct. App. Div. 1 2010), review denied, (Jan. 4, 2011). Once the grace period has expired, the defaulting party's burden and the trial court's analysis should be no different than when relief is sought from a final judgment under Rule 60(c). *General Elec. Capital Corp. v. Osterkamp*, 172 Ariz. 185, 836 P.2d 398 (Ct. App. Div. 2 1992); *Ruiz v. Lopez*, 225 Ariz. 217, 236 P.3d 444 (Ct. App. Div. 1 2010), review denied, (Jan. 4, 2011). An attorney's reliance on the erroneous belief that Rule 6(e) extended the time for filing an answer under Rule 55(a)(3) does not constitute excusable neglect. *Baker Intern. Associates, Inc. v. Shanwick Intern. Corp.*, 174 Ariz. 580, 851 P.2d 1379 (Ct. App. Div. 1 1993).

14. *Meritorious Defense.* The requirement of a showing of the existence of a meritorious defense is an independent one. The nature of the defense must be shown through facts established by affidavits or testimony from witnesses or others with personal knowledge thereof. *United Imports and Exports, Inc. v. Superior Court of State In and For Maricopa County*, 134 Ariz. 43, 653 P.2d 691 (1982); *Richas v. Superior Court of Arizona In and For Maricopa County*, 133 Ariz. 512, 652 P.2d 1035 (1982); *Echols v. State Farm Mut. Auto. Ins. Co.*, 152 Ariz. 384, 732 P.2d 1122 (Ct. App. Div. 2 1986); *Cota v. Southern Arizona Bank & Trust Co.*, 17 Ariz. App. 326, 497 P.2d 833 (Div. 2 1972); *Parag v. Walters*, 11 Ariz. App. 276, 464 P.2d 347 (Div. 2 1970). The affidavit of the party's counsel, if not based on personal knowledge, will not be sufficient. *Brandt v. Daman Trailer Sales, Inc.*, 116 Ariz. 421, 569 P.2d 851 (Ct. App. Div. 2 1977); *Parag v. Walters*, 11 Ariz. App. 276, 464 P.2d 347 (Div. 2 1970). It has been held to be a denial of due process of law, however, to require a showing of the existence of a meritorious defense where the default has been entered without proper notice. *Peralta v. Heights Medical Center, Inc.*, 485 U.S. 80, 108 S. Ct. 896, 99 L. Ed. 2d 75 (1988).

15. *Standards for Setting Aside Defaults.* A motion to set aside the entry of default or default judgment is addressed to the trial court's discretion, and the eventual determination will not be disturbed on appeal absent an abuse of that discretion. *Daou v. Harris*, 139 Ariz. 353, 678 P.2d 934 (1984); *DeHoney v. Hernandez*, 122 Ariz. 367, 595 P.2d 159 (1979); *Daystar Investments, L.L.C. v. Maricopa County Treasurer*, 207 Ariz. 569, 88 P.3d 1181 (Ct. App. Div. 1 2004); *Douglas v. Lease Investors, Inc.*, 19 Ariz. App. 87, 504 P.2d 1310 (Div. 2 1973); *Payne v. Payne*, 12 Ariz. App.

434, 471 P.2d 319 (Div. 2 1970); *Prell v. Amado*, 2 Ariz. App. 35, 406 P.2d 237 (1965). That discretion is to be guided by equitable principles and the policy of the law that disputes should be resolved on their merits rather than by default. *Ramada Inns, Inc. v. Lane & Bird Advertising, Inc.*, 102 Ariz. 127, 426 P.2d 395 (1967); *U-Totem Store v. Walker*, 142 Ariz. 549, 691 P.2d 315 (Ct. App. Div. 2 1984); *Cota v. Southern Arizona Bank & Trust Co.*, 17 Ariz. App. 326, 497 P.2d 833 (Div. 2 1972); *Smith v. Monroe*, 15 Ariz. App. 366, 488 P.2d 1003 (Div. 2 1971); *Wellton-Mohawk Irr. and Drainage Dist. v. McDonald*, 1 Ariz. App. 508, 405 P.2d 299 (1965). An order setting aside a default judgment is an appealable order; an order vacating the entry of default is not. *Sanders v. Cobble*, 154 Ariz. 474, 744 P.2d 1 (1987).

Rule 4.2(b) specifies that, where direct service is made on a defendant outside the State of Arizona, an affidavit of service must be filed "before any default may be had on such service." The affidavit is to show the circumstances that warranted use of that method of service and must attach a separate affidavit from the process server who accomplished service on the defendant. This provision, however, was not intended to confer any substantive rights on a defendant who is properly served in that fashion, and the fact that the specified affidavits are not filed until after a default is taken is not in and of itself grounds for setting that default aside. *Creach v. Angulo*, 186 Ariz. 548, 925 P.2d 689 (Ct. App. Div. 1 1996), decision approved, 189 Ariz. 212, 941 P.2d 224 (1997).

16. *Setting Aside Default Where Service Made by Publication.* A default or default judgment will be set aside where service by publication was utilized in circumstances not authorized by Rule 4.1 or 4.2. *Preston v. Denkins*, 94 Ariz. 214, 382 P.2d 686 (1963); *Sprang v. Petersen Lumber, Inc.*, 165 Ariz. 257, 798 P.2d 395 (Ct. App. Div. 1 1990). Under Ariz.R.Civ.P. 59(j), the defendant against whom a default judgment has been entered based upon service by publication has one year to seek a new trial. *Master Financial, Inc. v. Woodburn*, 208 Ariz. 70, 90 P.3d 1236 (Ct. App. Div. 1 2004), as amended, (June 7, 2004).

Rule 56. Summary judgment

(a) Motion for Summary Judgment or Partial Summary Judgment. A party may move for summary judgment, identifying each claim or defense—or the part of each claim or defense—on which summary judgment is sought. The court shall grant summary judgment if the moving party shows that there is no genuine dispute as to any material fact and the moving party is entitled to judgment as a matter of law. The court should state on the record the reasons for granting or denying the request.

(b) Time to File a Motion.

(1) A claimant may move for summary judgment with or without supporting affidavits:

(A) after the expiration of 20 days from the service of process upon the adverse party, but no sooner than the date on which the answer is due, or

(B) after service of a Rule 12(b)(6) motion to dismiss or a motion for summary judgment by the adverse party.

(2) Any other party may move for summary judgment, with or without supporting affidavits, at any time after the action is commenced.

(3) A motion by any party shall be filed no later than the dispositive motion deadline set by the court or local rule, or in the absence of such a deadline, 90 days before the date set for trial.

(c) Motion and Proceedings

(1) Upon timely request by any party, the court shall set a time for hearing on the motion, provided, however, that the court need not conduct a hearing if it determines that the motion should be denied or if the motion is uncontested. If no request for a hearing is made, the court may, in its discretion, set a time for such hearing.

(2) A party opposing the motion must file its response and any supporting materials within 30 days after service of the motion. The moving party shall have 15 days after service of the response in which to serve a reply memorandum and any supporting materials. These time periods may be shortened or enlarged by a filed stipulation of the parties or by court order; provided, however, that court approval is required for any stipulated extensions to a briefing schedule that would purport to make a reply or other memorandum due less than five days before a hearing date previously set by the court, or would require postponement of a scheduled hearing date or other modifications to an existing case scheduling order.

(3) Any party filing a motion for summary judgment shall set forth, in a statement separate from the memorandum of law, the specific facts relied upon in support of the motion. The facts shall be stated in concise, numbered paragraphs. As to each fact, the statement shall refer to the specific portion of the record where the fact may be found. Any party opposing a motion for summary judgment shall file a statement in the form prescribed by this Rule, specifying those paragraphs in the moving party's statement of facts which are disputed, and also setting forth those facts which establish a genuine issue of material fact or otherwise preclude summary judgment in favor of the moving party. In the alternative, the movant and the party opposing the motion shall file a joint statement in the form prescribed by this Rule, setting forth those material facts as to which there is no genuine dispute. The joint statement may provide that any stipulation of fact is not intended to be binding for any purpose other than the motion for summary judgment.

(4) Objections to the admissibility of evidence on motions for summary judgment shall be governed by Rule 7.1(f)(2), except that an objection may be included in a party's response to another party's separate statement of material facts in lieu of (or in addition to) including it in the party's responsive memorandum. Any objection presented in the party's response to the separate statement of material facts must be stated concisely.

(d) Declining to Grant All the Requested Relief. If the court does not grant all the relief requested by the motion, or if on independent consideration pursuant to section (h) of this Rule judgment is not rendered on the whole case, the court may enter an order stating any material fact—including an item of damages or other relief—that is not genuinely in dispute and treating the fact as established in the case.

(e) Form of Affidavits and Depositions; Further Testimony; Defense Required.

(1) An affidavit used to support or oppose a motion shall be made on personal knowledge, set out facts that would be admissible in evidence, and show that the affiant is competent to testify on the matters stated. If a paper or part of a paper is referred to in an affidavit, a properly authenticated copy shall be attached to or served with the affidavit.

(2) Affidavits may be supplemented or opposed by depositions, answers to interrogatories, additional affidavits or other materials that would be admissible in evidence.

(3) If all or part of a deposition is submitted in support of or in opposition to a motion for summary judgment, the offering

party must submit a written transcript of the testimony. An electronic recording of the testimony may be submitted only if the offering party contends that the written transcript is erroneous.

(4) When a motion for summary judgment is made and supported as provided in this Rule, an opposing party may not rely merely on allegations or denials of its own pleading; rather, its response must, by affidavits or as otherwise provided in this Rule, set forth specific facts showing a genuine issue for trial. If the opposing party does not so respond, summary judgment, if appropriate, shall be entered against that party.

(f) When Facts are Unavailable to the Nonmovant; Request for Rule 56(f) Relief and Expedited Hearing

(1) If a party opposing summary judgment files a request for relief and expedited hearing under this Rule, along with a supporting affidavit showing that, for specified reasons, it cannot present evidence essential to justify its opposition, the court may, after holding a hearing:

(A) defer considering the motion for summary judgment and allow time to obtain affidavits or to take discovery before a response to the motion is required;

(B) deny the requested relief and require a response to the motion for summary judgment by a date certain; or

(C) issue any other appropriate order.

(2) Unless otherwise ordered by the court, the filing of a request for relief and affidavit under this section does not by itself extend the date by which the party opposing summary judgment must file a memorandum and separate statement of facts as prescribed in section (c) of this Rule.

(3) No request for relief will be considered and no hearing will be scheduled unless the request for relief is accompanied by a separate statement of counsel seeking the relief certifying that, after personal consultation and good-faith efforts to do so, the parties have been unable to satisfactorily resolve the matter.

(4) The party moving for summary judgment is not required to file a response to the request for relief or affidavit unless otherwise ordered by the court. If such a party elects to file a response, it must be filed no later than two days before the hearing scheduled to consider the requested relief.

(5) Except as provided in subsection (3), the court shall hold an expedited hearing concerning the requested relief, in person or by telephone, within seven days after the filing of a request for hearing by the party seeking the relief. If the court's calendar does not allow a hearing within seven days, a later date may be set.

(g) Affidavits Made in Bad Faith. If satisfied that an affidavit under this Rule is submitted in bad faith or solely for delay, the court may order the submitting party to pay the other party the reasonable expenses, including attorney's fees, it incurred as a result, or may impose other appropriate sanctions. The court shall allow notice and a reasonable time to respond before imposing any sanctions pursuant to this section.

(h) Judgment Independent of the Motion or Based on Materials Not Cited in the Motion. After giving notice and a reasonable time to respond, the court may:

(1) grant summary judgment for a nonmovant;

(2) grant the motion on grounds not raised by a party; or

(3) consider summary judgment after identifying for the parties material facts that may not be genuinely in dispute.

Amended March 26, 1963, effective June 1, 1963; March 21, 1980, effective June 1, 1980; Sept. 15, 1987, effective Nov. 15, 1987; Oct. 9, 1996, effective Dec. 1, 1996; Oct. 10, 2000, effective Dec. 1, 2000; Oct. 16, 2003, effective Dec. 1, 2003; January 20, 2006, effective June 1, 2006; Aug. 30, 2012, eff. Jan. 1, 2013. Rule 56(c)(4) added August 28, 2013, effective January 1, 2014.

STATE BAR COMMITTEE NOTES

1963 Amendments

[Rule 56(c)] By the amendment "answers to interrogatories" are included among the materials which may be considered on motion for summary judgment. The phrase was inadvertently omitted from the rule, see 3 Barron & Holtzoff, Federal Practice & Procedure 159–60 (Wright ed.1958), and the courts have generally reached by interpretation the result which will hereafter be required by the text of the amended rule. See Propriety of considering answers to interrogatories in determining motion for summary judgment, 74 A.L.R.2d 984.

The amendment is declaratory of existing Arizona practice. Under our decisions "the entire record" is to be examined in connection with a motion for summary judgment. *Malta v. Phoenix Title & Trust Co.*, 76 Ariz. 116, 118, 259 P.2d 554, 556 (1953); *Stevens v. Anderson*, 75 Ariz. 331, 256 P.2d 712 (1953).

[Rule 56(e)] The words "answers to interrogatories" are added in the third sentence of this subdivision to conform to the amendment of subdivision (c), and the wording of the last two sentences has been changed to conform to the wording of subdivision (e) of the federal rule.

2000 Amendment

As part of the effort to consolidate formerly separate sets of procedural rules into either the Arizona Rules of Civil Procedure or the Rules of the Arizona Supreme Court, the provisions of former Rule IV(f) of the Uniform Rules of Practice of the Superior Court, which required the submission of separate statements of facts and supporting record references, both in support of and in opposition to, motions for summary judgment, were incorporated into a new subpart (c)(2) of Rule 56 of the Arizona Rules of Civil Procedure, which deals generally with the subject of summary judgment motions. Existing Rule 56(c) was redesignated as Rule 56(c)(1), with no change.

2005 Amendment (sic)

(Amendment effective, June 1, 2006)

The amendments to Rules 56(a) and (b), requiring a motion for summary judgment to be filed 90 days prior to the trial date, change the practice of permitting the superior court to adopt local rules setting deadlines for the filing of summary judgment motions. Such amendment does not, however, preclude the superior court from enlarging the period for filing a summary judgment motion pursuant to Rule 6(b) of these rules.

The amendment to Rule 56(c)(1), to extend the deadlines for filing summary judgment responses and replies, is made to conform to the practice in the local federal courts, as well as to ensure that parties have sufficient time to brief summary judgment motions.

Comment to 2013 Amendments to Rule 56

Rule 56 is revised in several respects. The language of some sections is updated and simplified to conform to the 2010 restyling of Rule 56 of the Federal Rules of Civil Procedure, with no intended substantive change to Arizona's rule or summary judgment procedure. These revisions are selective and reflect a determination that fundamental differences between Arizona's rule and the counterpart federal rule weigh against wholesale adoption of the federal rule amendments. In addition, a number of other changes have been made to improve or clarify Arizona's summary judgment practice.

Section (a). The standard for granting summary judgment has been moved from section (c) to section (a). In addition, the language of new section (a) has been modified to conform to the language of Federal Rule of Civil Procedure 56(a). These changes are stylistic and are not intended to alter the substantive requirements for obtaining summary judgment as developed in Arizona case law, including *Orme School v. Reeves*, 166 Ariz. 301, 802 P.2d 1000, 64 Ed. Law Rep. 1221 (1990) and its progeny. Likewise, the new language, which recognizes the availability of partial summary judgment, is not intended to change existing Arizona law.

Section (b). Section (b) incorporates aspects of former sections (a) and (b), governing when a claimant and defending party, respectively, may move for summary judgment. Former section (a) restricted a claimant's ability to move for summary judgment until after the answer was due or the adverse party moved for summary judgment, while section (b) allowed a defending party to move for summary judgment at any time. The amendment additionally authorizes a claimant to move for summary judgment after an opposing party moves to dismiss under Rule 12(b)(6). Subsection (3) is modified to clarify that any dispositive motion cut-off established by the court will control over the 90—day period provided in the rule.

Section (c). Section (c)(1) is modified to clarify certain hearing and briefing requirements. The standard for granting summary judgment has been moved to section (a).

Section (d). Section (d) is modified to conform to the stylistic revisions to Federal Rule of Civil Procedure 56(g), which simplified the language of this section and made it more concise. No substantive change is intended. Section (d) cross-references new section (h), which allows the court to grant summary judgment on independent consideration in appropriate circumstances.

Section (e). The first sentence of section (e) is modified to conform to the stylistic revisions to similar language contained in Federal Rule of Civil Procedure 56(c)(4). Other stylistic revisions were made to the remainder of the section to make it easier to understand. No substantive change is intended.

Section (f). Section (f) is modified in several significant respects. Subsection (1) has been modified to set forth a uniform procedure requiring the filing of a request for Rule 56(f) relief and expedited hearing, along with a supporting Rule 56(f) affidavit. Subsection (1) also requires a hearing before relief can be granted. Subsection (2) clarifies that absent a court order extending the time for response, filing a request for Rule 56(f) relief does not extend the date for opposing a motion for summary judgment. Subsection (3), modeled after Arizona Rule of Civil Procedure 26(g), requires a party seeking relief to attempt to resolve the issue by good-faith personal consultation with the opposing party and to submit a separate certification regarding such consultation with its Rule 56(f) affidavit. Subsection (4) provides that the party moving for summary judgment is generally not required to file a response to the request for Rule 56(f) relief; but, if it chooses to do so, it must file the response within two days of the scheduled hearing. Finally, subsection (5) adopts an expedited hearing procedure, requiring courts to hold a telephonic or in-person hearing within seven days after any hearing request filed by the party seeking the relief. These procedures are intended to facilitate resolution of section (f) disputes and minimize the need for court intervention. Section (f) affidavits must continue to satisfy the specificity requirements set forth in existing Arizona case law. *E.g.*, *Simon v. Safeway, Inc.*, 217 Ariz. 330, 173 P.3d 1031 (Ct. App. Div. 2 2007).

Section (g). Section (g) is modified to conform to the stylistic revisions to counterpart Federal Rule of Civil Procedure 56(h), which simplified the language of this section and made it more concise. Additionally, section (g)'s reference to the sanction of "contempt" has been eliminated. The rule allows "other appropriate sanctions," leaving it to the court to determine whether a sanction of contempt is warranted by the applicable substantive law. The language of section (g) also has been modified to make clear that notice and an opportunity to respond are required before the court may impose any sanctions.

Section (h). New section (h) is based on counterpart Federal Rule of Civil Procedure 56(f). The section recognizes the court's inherent authority to dispose of matters on summary judgment on the court's own initiative, where appropriate. The section (h) procedure strikes a balance between the court's inherent power and the rights of litigants, by requiring notice and a hearing before the court may grant summary judgment for a nonmovant, grant a motion on grounds not raised by a party, or otherwise consider summary judgment on the court's own initiative.

AUTHORS' COMMENTS

Analysis

1. *Scope and Purpose of Rule.* Ariz. R. Civ. P. 56 establishes

the procedures and general standard for securing an award of summary judgment. Effective January 1, 2013, Rule 56 was revised and restructured in several important respects. Certain revisions were made to conform to the 2010 restyling of Fed. R. Civ. P. 56. Other revisions, such as the amendment to Ariz. R. Civ. P. 56(f), were made to "improve or clarify Arizona's summary judgment procedure." *See*, Comment to 2013 Amendments to Rule 56.

2. *Comparison With Federal Rule.* As a consequence of the extensive amendments to Ariz. R. Civ. P. 56, effective January 1, 2013, Arizona's summary judgment rule is similar to its federal counterpart, but there are important differences.

Ariz. R. Civ. P. 56(a), (d), (e)(1) and (h) are substantially identical to Fed. R. Civ. P. 56(a), (g), (c)(4) and (f), respectively. The summary judgment standard, previously expressed in Rule 56(c), was moved to Ariz. R. Civ. P. 56(a) and modified to conform to the language of Fed. R. Civ. P. 56(a).

Subpart (b) of the two rules differ primarily in the time frames they establish for the filing of summary judgment motions. Ariz. R. Civ. P. 56(b)(1) (amended 2013) provides that a *claimant* may file a motion for summary judgment (A) after the expiration of 20 days from service of the claim on the adverse party, but not sooner than the date on which the answer is due, or (B) the adverse party files a motion for summary judgment or a Rule 12(b)(6) motion to dismiss. Ariz. R. Civ. P. 56(b)(2) (amended 2013) provides that *any other party* may move for summary judgment at anytime. All such motions must be filed no later than 90 days before trial, unless a different time is specified by local rule or court order. *See,* Ariz. R. Civ. P. 56(b)(3). In contrast, Fed. R. Civ. P. 56(b) allows any party to file a motion for summary judgment "at any time until 30 days after the close of all discovery."

Arizona's summary judgment rule does not have a provision comparable to Fed. R. Civ. P. 56(c), which federal rule sets forth procedures for supporting factual positions and objecting that a "fact" is not supported by admissible evidence. Similarly, the federal summary judgment rule does not have a provision comparable to Ariz. R. Civ. P. 56(c).

Before it was amended effective January 1, 2013, Ariz. R. Civ. P. 56(f) was substantially identical to Fed. R. Civ. P. 56(d). Effective January 1, 2013, however, Ariz. R. Civ. P. 56(f) was amended to clarify ambiguities and provide a uniform procedure for addressing requests for Rule 56(f) relief when facts are unavailable to the nonmovant. As amended, Ariz.R.Civ.P. 56(f) sets forth an expedited procedure for the hearing and resolution of such requests. Rule 56(f) now expressly requires the party seeking relief to confer with the other side in an effort to resolve the dispute. If such efforts fail, the requesting party must submit a separate certificate to that effect along with the Rule 56(f) request. As a result of this amendment, the two provisions differ substantially.

In 2007, the language of FRCP 56 was amended as part of the general restyling of the Federal Rules of Civil Procedure to make the Federal Rules more easily understood and to make style and terminology consistent throughout the Federal Rules of Civil Procedure. Those stylistic modifications have not been incorporated into ARCP 56.

3. *Nature of Summary Judgment; Standards for Award.* Summary judgment is a disposition which effectively removes the controversy from the province of the trier of fact, and resolves it as a matter of law. Ariz. R. Civ. P. 56(a) sets forth the standard for granting summary judgment and provides that the court shall grant summary judgment when the record satisfies the court that "there is no genuine dispute as to any material fact and the moving party is entitled to judgment as a matter of law." Ariz. R. Civ. P. 56(a). *Parkway Bank and Trust Co. v. Zivkovic*, 232 Ariz. 286, 304 P.3d 1109 (Ct. App. Div. 1 2013) (noting that, as a result of the 2013 amendments, former Rule 56(c) was renumbered as Rule 56(a), and that the word "dispute" was substituted for the word "issue.").

Rule 56 was extensively amended in 2013, but such amendments did not alter the "substantive requirements for obtaining summary judgment as developed in Arizona case law, ..." *See* Comment to 2013 Amendments to Rule 56. *City of Phoenix v. Garretson*, 232 Ariz. 115, 302 P.3d 640 (Ct. App. Div. 1 2013), review granted, (Nov. 26, 2013).

Case law discussing the summary judgment standard under former Rule 56(c) include: *See also, Wells Fargo Bank v. Arizona Laborers, Teamsters and Cement Masons Local No. 395 Pension Trust Fund*, 201 Ariz. 474, 38 P.3d 12, 27 Employee Benefits Cas. (BNA) 1811 (2002), as corrected, (Apr. 9, 2002); *Samsel v. Allstate Ins. Co.*, 204 Ariz. 1, 59 P.3d 281 (2002); *Arizona Dept. of Admin. v. Cox*, 222 Ariz. 270, 213 P.3d 707 (Ct. App. Div. 2 2009); *Modular Mining Systems, Inc. v. Jigsaw Technologies, Inc.*, 221 Ariz. 515, 212 P.3d 853 (Ct. App. Div. 2 2009); *Sage v. Blagg Appraisal Co., Ltd.*, 221 Ariz. 33, 209 P.3d 169 (Ct. App. Div. 1 2009); *Tilley v. Delci*, 220 Ariz. 233, 204 P.3d 1082 (Ct. App. Div. 1 2009); *Havasupai Tribe of Havasupai Reservation v. Arizona Bd. of Regents*, 220 Ariz. 214, 204 P.3d 1063, 243 Ed. Law Rep. 889 (Ct. App. Div. 1 2008); *Chalpin v. Snyder*, 220 Ariz. 413, 207 P.3d 666 (Ct. App. Div. 1 2008); *Highland Village Partners, L.L.C. v. Bradbury & Stamm Const. Co., Inc.*, 219 Ariz. 147, 195 P.3d 184 (Ct. App. Div. 1 2008); *Arab Monetary Fund v. Hashim*, 219 Ariz. 108, 193

P.3d 802 (Ct. App. Div. 1 2008); *Haab v. County of Maricopa*, 219 Ariz. 9, 191 P.3d 1025 (Ct. App. Div. 1 2008); *In re Estate of Parker*, 217 Ariz. 563, 177 P.3d 305 (Ct. App. Div. 1 2008); *Best v. Edwards*, 217 Ariz. 497, 176 P.3d 695 (Ct. App. Div. 1 2008); *Maxfield v. Martin*, 217 Ariz. 312, 173 P.3d 476 (Ct. App. Div. 1 2007); *Keonjian v. Olcott*, 216 Ariz. 563, 169 P.3d 927 (Ct. App. Div. 2 2007); *Tierra Ranchos Homeowners Ass'n v. Kitchukov*, 216 Ariz. 195, 165 P.3d 173 (Ct. App. Div. 1 2007); *Banner Health v. Medical Sav. Ins. Co.*, 216 Ariz. 146, 163 P.3d 1096 (Ct. App. Div. 1 2007); *PLM Tax Certificate Program 1991-92, L.P. v. Schweikert*, 216 Ariz. 47, 162 P.3d 1267 (Ct. App. Div. 1 2007).

The cases cited above, and prior precedents, however, must be read and evaluated in light of the reevaluation and clarification by the Arizona Supreme Court of the purposes of, and standards for awarding, summary judgments.

In *Orme School v. Reeves*, 166 Ariz. 301, 802 P.2d 1000, 64 Ed. Law Rep. 1221 (1990), the Court noted that motions for summary judgment under Rule 56 and motions for directed verdict under Rule 50 both serve the same purpose of removing meritless claims from the civil justice system, and share the same underlying theory that, under the established facts presented, the moving party is entitled to judgment as a matter of law. Accordingly, the trial courts were directed, in considering motions for summary judgment, to apply the same standards as for a directed verdict, even though that might entail evaluating the evidence to some degree. *See Matos v. City of Phoenix*, 176 Ariz. 125, 859 P.2d 748, 2 A.D. Cas. (BNA) 1458 (Ct. App. Div. 2 1993); *Plattner v. State Farm Mut. Auto. Ins. Co.*, 168 Ariz. 311, 812 P.2d 1129 (Ct. App. Div. 1 1991).

While trial courts were cautioned not to use summary judgment proceedings as a substitute for jury trials, the motion should be granted if the facts produced in support of the claim or defense have so little probative value, given the quantum of evidence required, that reasonable people could not agree with the conclusion advanced by the proponent of the claim or defense. *See Andrews v. Blake*, 205 Ariz. 236, 69 P.3d 7 (2003); *Sanchez v. City of Tucson*, 191 Ariz. 128, 953 P.2d 168 (1998); *Estate of Hernandez by Hernandez-Wheeler v. Flavio*, 187 Ariz. 506, 930 P.2d 1309, 115 Ed. Law Rep. 1067 (1997); *Riley, Hoggatt & Suagee, P.C. v. English*, 177 Ariz. 10, 864 P.2d 1042 (1993); *In re Estate of Olson*, 223 Ariz. 441, 224 P.3d 938 (Ct. App. Div. 1 2010); *Dube v. Desai*, 218 Ariz. 362, 186 P.3d 587, 233 Ed. Law Rep. 954 (Ct. App. Div. 2 2008); *Nolan v. Starlight Pines Homeowners Ass'n*, 216 Ariz. 482, 167 P.3d 1277 (Ct. App. Div. 1 2007); *Grafitti-Valenzuela ex rel. Grafitti v. City of Phoenix*, 216 Ariz. 454, 167 P.3d 711 (Ct. App. Div. 1 2007); *Airfreight Exp. Ltd v. Evergreen Air Center, Inc.*, 215 Ariz. 103, 158 P.3d 232 (Ct.

App. Div. 2 2007). A motion for summary judgment may be brought "upon all or any part" of a claim or defense. Even where the motion is for a complete summary judgment, the Court has discretion to grant it only in part. *Madden v. Barnes*, 8 Ariz. App. 404, 446 P.2d 510 (1968).

In determining whether there are any factual 'disputes' (which is the word now used in Rule 56), to resolve, the Court is to view the matters of record in the light most favorable to the party opposing the summary judgment motion. *Espinoza v. Schulenburg*, 212 Ariz. 215, 129 P.3d 937 (2006); *Hohokam Irr. and Drainage Dist. v. Arizona Public Service Co.*, 204 Ariz. 394, 64 P.3d 836 (2003); *Andrews v. Blake*, 205 Ariz. 236, 69 P.3d 7 (2003); *Samsel v. Allstate Ins. Co.*, 204 Ariz. 1, 59 P.3d 281 (2002); *Gunnell v. Arizona Public Service Co.*, 202 Ariz. 388, 46 P.3d 399 (2002); *Walk v. Ring*, 202 Ariz. 310, 44 P.3d 990 (2002); *Wells Fargo Bank v. Arizona Laborers, Teamsters and Cement Masons Local No. 395 Pension Trust Fund*, 201 Ariz. 474, 38 P.3d 12, 27 Employee Benefits Cas. (BNA) 1811 (2002), as corrected, (Apr. 9, 2002); *Stoecker v. Brush Wellman, Inc.*, 194 Ariz. 448, 984 P.2d 534 (1999); *Aida Renta Trust v. Maricopa County*, 221 Ariz. 603, 212 P.3d 941 (Ct. App. Div. 1 2009), as amended, (July 22, 2009); *Modular Mining Systems, Inc. v. Jigsaw Technologies, Inc.*, 221 Ariz. 515, 212 P.3d 853 (Ct. App. Div. 2 2009); *Sage v. Blagg Appraisal Co., Ltd.*, 221 Ariz. 33, 209 P.3d 169 (Ct. App. Div. 1 2009); *Messina v. Midway Chevrolet Co.*, 221 Ariz. 11, 209 P.3d 147 (Ct. App. Div. 1 2008); *Tilley v. Delci*, 220 Ariz. 233, 204 P.3d 1082 (Ct. App. Div. 1 2009); *Ratliff v. Hardison*, 219 Ariz. 441, 199 P.3d 696 (Ct. App. Div. 2 2008); *Chalpin v. Snyder*, 220 Ariz. 413, 207 P.3d 666 (Ct. App. Div. 1 2008); *Chapman v. The Westerner*, 220 Ariz. 52, 202 P.3d 517 (Ct. App. Div. 2 2008); *Dube v. Desai*, 218 Ariz. 362, 186 P.3d 587, 233 Ed. Law Rep. 954 (Ct. App. Div. 2 2008); *In re Estate of Parker*, 217 Ariz. 563, 177 P.3d 305 (Ct. App. Div. 1 2008); *Maxfield v. Martin*, 217 Ariz. 312, 173 P.3d 476 (Ct. App. Div. 1 2007); *Simon v. Safeway, Inc.*, 217 Ariz. 330, 173 P.3d 1031 (Ct. App. Div. 2 2007); *Law v. Verde Valley Medical Center*, 217 Ariz. 92, 170 P.3d 701 (Ct. App. Div. 1 2007); *Kaman Aerospace v. Arizona Bd. of Regents*, 217 Ariz. 148, 171 P.3d 599, 227 Ed. Law Rep. 296 (Ct. App. Div. 2 2007); *Keonjian v. Olcott*, 216 Ariz. 563, 169 P.3d 927 (Ct. App. Div. 2 2007); *Nolan v. Starlight Pines Homeowners Ass'n*, 216 Ariz. 482, 167 P.3d 1277 (Ct. App. Div. 1 2007); *Tierra Ranchos Homeowners Ass'n v. Kitchukov*, 216 Ariz. 195, 165 P.3d 173 (Ct. App. Div. 1 2007); *Banner Health v. Medical Sav. Ins. Co.*, 216 Ariz. 146, 163 P.3d 1096 (Ct. App. Div. 1 2007); *Robson Ranch Quail Creek, LLC v. Pima County*, 215 Ariz. 545, 161 P.3d 588 (Ct. App. Div. 2 2007); *Aranda v. Cardenas*, 215 Ariz. 210, 159 P.3d 76 (Ct. App. Div. 2 2007); *Allstate Indem. Co. v. Ridgely*, 214 Ariz. 440, 153

P.3d 1069 (Ct. App. Div. 2 2007); *Acosta v. Phoenix Indem. Ins. Co.*, 214 Ariz. 380, 153 P.3d 401 (Ct. App. Div. 2 2007); *City of Bisbee v. Arizona Water Co.*, 214 Ariz. 368, 153 P.3d 389 (Ct. App. Div. 2 2007); *Center Bay Gardens, L.L.C. v. City of Tempe City Council*, 214 Ariz. 353, 153 P.3d 374 (Ct. App. Div. 1 2007), as amended, (Feb. 6, 2007); *Gorney v. Meaney*, 214 Ariz. 226, 150 P.3d 799 (Ct. App. Div. 2 2007); *Stein v. Sonus USA, Inc.*, 214 Ariz. 200, 150 P.3d 773 (Ct. App. Div. 2 2007).

If there is any genuine issue, or dispute, as to a material fact to be resolved, or any doubt as to whether such a material factual issue is present, the motion should be denied. *Gatecliff v. Great Republic Life Ins. Co.*, 170 Ariz. 34, 821 P.2d 725 (1991); *Wisener v. State*, 123 Ariz. 148, 598 P.2d 511 (1979); *Livingston v. Citizen's Utility, Inc.*, 107 Ariz. 62, 481 P.2d 855 (1971); *Nanini v. Nanini*, 166 Ariz. 287, 802 P.2d 438 (Ct. App. Div. 2 1990); *MH Inv. Co. v. Transamerica Title Ins. Co.*, 162 Ariz. 569, 785 P.2d 89 (Ct. App. Div. 2 1989); *Federoff By and Through Roberts v. Aetna Cas. and Sur. Co.*, 163 Ariz. 371, 788 P.2d 104 (Ct. App. Div. 2 1989); *Gesina v. General Elec. Co.*, 162 Ariz. 35, 780 P.2d 1376, 117 Lab. Cas. (CCH) P 56490 (Ct. App. Div. 2 1989).

Even where the facts are undisputed, a genuine dispute as to conflicting inferences to be drawn from them precludes an award of summary judgment. *Executive Towers v. Leonard*, 7 Ariz. App. 331, 439 P.2d 303 (1968). On the other hand, a motion for summary judgment should not be denied simply on the speculation that some slight doubt, some scintilla of evidence, or some dispute over irrelevant or immaterial facts might blossom into a real controversy in the midst of trial. *Orme School v. Reeves*, 166 Ariz. 301, 802 P.2d 1000, 64 Ed. Law Rep. 1221 (1990); *Shaw v. Petersen*, 169 Ariz. 559, 821 P.2d 220 (Ct. App. Div. 1 1991); *State ex rel. Arizona Dept. of Revenue v. Care Const. Corp.*, 166 Ariz. 294, 802 P.2d 445 (Ct. App. Div. 1 1990).

The fact that both sides to the controversy file opposing cross-motions for summary judgment does not constrain the trial court to grant either motion if it determines that a genuine issue of material fact exists. *Grain Dealers Mut. Ins. Co. v. James*, 118 Ariz. 116, 575 P.2d 315 (1978); *Phoenix Control Systems, Inc. v. Insurance Co. of North America*, 161 Ariz. 420, 778 P.2d 1316 (Ct. App. Div. 1 1989), decision rev'd on other grounds, 165 Ariz. 31, 796 P.2d 463 (1990). Correspondingly, a party who files an unsuccessful motion for summary judgment is not estopped from arguing that a genuine issue of material fact exists and bars an adversary's cross-motion. *Phoenix Control Systems, Inc. v. Insurance Co. of North America*, 165 Ariz. 31, 796 P.2d 463 (1990); *Cambridge Co., Ltd. v. Arizona Lawn Sprinklers, Inc.*, 166 Ariz. 269, 801 P.2d 504 (Ct. App. Div. 2 1990). A summary judgment is a disposition on the merits and will support application of the doctrines of *res judicata* or collateral estoppel. *Grand v. Cigna Property and Cas. Companies*, 172 Ariz. 419, 837 P.2d 1154 (Ct. App. Div. 2 1992).

4. *Time for Motion; Briefing Schedule; Requirement of Separate Statements of Facts.* Under Ariz. R. Civ. P. 56(b)(1), as amended effective January 1, 2013, a claimant may file a motion for summary judgment:

(1) after the expiration of 20 days from service of the claim on the adverse party, but not sooner than the date on which the answer is due; or

(2) the adverse party files a motion for summary judgment or a Rule 12(b)(6) motion to dismiss.

Any other party may move for summary judgment at anytime, including before filing an answer. Ariz. R. Civ. P. 56(b)(2) (2013). All motions for summary judgment must be led no later than the deadline set by the court or by local rule, or in the absence of such deadline, no later than 90 days before trial. See, Ariz. R. Civ. P. 56(b)(3) (2013).

A party opposing a motion for summary judgment has 30 days after service of the motion to file and serve a response and any supporting material. The moving party has 15 days thereafter to serve its reply and any supporting material. This briefing schedule is more generous than the schedule prescribed for responding to civil motions by Rule 7.1(a). Ariz. R. Civ. P. 56(c)(2) (2013) [former Rule 56(c)(1)].

Ariz. R. Civ. P. 56 (c)(2) also permits the parties to stipulate to an extension of the briefing schedule but requires the parties file any such stipulation. Court approval of any such stipulated briefing schedule is required if such stipulation "would purport to make a reply or other memorandum due less than 5 days before a hearing date previously set by the court or would require postponement of a scheduled hearing date or other modifications to an existing case scheduling order."

Under Ariz. R. Civ. P. 56(c)(3) [former Rule 56(c)(2)], a motion for summary judgment must be accompanied by a separate statement of the specific facts upon which the moving party relies in support of the motion. The facts are to be stated in concise and numbered paragraphs, with accompanying references to the specific portion of the record which establishes them. A motion for summary judgment which is not accompanied by this separate statement of facts is appropriately treated as a motion for judgment on the pleadings under Ariz. R. Civ. P. 12(c). *Wieman v. Roysden*, 166 Ariz. 281, 802 P.2d 432 (Ct. App. Div. 1 1990). The party opposing the motion also must file a separate statement, in the same format, specifying those paragraphs of the moving party's factual statement that are disputed, and setting forth any additional facts relied upon as precluding the award of summary judgment. If the parties desire, they may submit a separate joint factual statement. *See*, Ariz. R. Civ. P. 56(c)(3) (former Rule 56(c)(2)).

5. *Burden on Party Seeking Summary Judgment.* The burden of persuasion on the party seeking summary judgment is heavy. *Wells Fargo Bank, N.A. v. Allen*, 231 Ariz. 209, 292 P.3d 195 (Ct. App. Div. 1 2012) (the party moving for summary judgment bears the burden of persuasion); *Comerica Bank v. Mahmoodi*, 224 Ariz. 289, 229 P.3d 1031 (Ct. App. Div. 1 2010); *National Bank of Arizona v. Thruston*, 218 Ariz. 112, 180 P.3d 977 (Ct. App. Div. 1 2008), as amended on other grounds, (Jan. 23, 2008). While this showing is usually made, at least in part, by affidavits accompanying the motion, the submission of affidavits is not a prerequisite. *Cagle v. Home Ins. Co.*, 14 Ariz. App. 360, 483 P.2d 592 (Div. 1 1971). It is sufficient if the party moving for summary judgment points out, by specific reference to the relevant discovery, that no evidence exists to support an essential element of a claim or defense. *Mohave Elec. Co-op., Inc. v. Byers*, 189 Ariz. 292, 942 P.2d 451 (Ct. App. Div. 1 1997); *Hydroculture, Inc. v. Coopers & Lybrand*, 174 Ariz. 277, 848 P.2d 856 (Ct. App. Div. 1 1992); *Pima County v. State*, 174 Ariz. 402, 850 P.2d 115 (Ct. App. Div. 1 1992). A party moving for summary judgment is not required to present the trial court with evidence negating affirmative defenses; the proponent of an affirmative defense has the burden of proof with respect to it. *National Bank of Arizona v. Thruston*, 218 Ariz. 112, 180 P.3d 977 (Ct. App. Div. 1 2008), as amended, (Jan. 23, 2008).

To carry its initial burden, a plaintiff who seeks summary judgment must submit "undisputed admissible evidence that would compel any reasonable juror to find in its favor on every element of its claim." *Wells Fargo Bank, N.A. v. Allen*, 231 Ariz. 209, 292 P.3d 195 (Ct. App. Div. 1 2012), citing, *Comerica Bank v. Mahmoodi*, 224 Ariz. 289, 229 P.3d 1031 (Ct. App. Div. 1 2010); *National Bank of Arizona v. Thruston*, 218 Ariz. 112, 180 P.3d 977 (Ct. App. Div. 1 2008), as amended, (Jan. 23, 2008). Although it may be well-accepted logic that if a plaintiff cannot establish a *prima facie* case, the defendant is entitled to judgment as a matter of law, the inverse of that logic is not true for motions brought by a plaintiff. *Comerica Bank v. Mahmoodi*, 224 Ariz. 289, 229 P.3d 1031 (Ct. App. Div. 1 2010) ("It is not the law that where the plaintiff *does* establish a case that would warrant submission to a jury, it is necessarily entitled to judgment as a matter of law in the absence of rebuttal evidence by the defense.").

Where affidavits are employed, they must be based on the affiant's personal knowledge, and set forth facts that would be admissible in evidence. *Portonova v. Wilkinson*, 128 Ariz. 501,

627 P.2d 232 (1981); *Hegel v. O'Malley Ins. Co., Inc.*, 122 Ariz. 52, 593 P.2d 275 (1979); *Wells Fargo Bank, N.A. v. Allen*, 231 Ariz. 209, 292 P.3d 195 (Ct. App. Div. 1 2012); *Airfreight Exp. Ltd v. Evergreen Air Center, Inc.*, 215 Ariz. 103, 158 P.3d 232 (Ct. App. Div. 2 2007); *Madsen v. Western American Mortg. Co.*, 143 Ariz. 614, 694 P.2d 1228 (Ct. App. Div. 1 1985); *Briskman v. Del Monte Mortg. Co.*, 10 Ariz. App. 263, 458 P.2d 130 (Div. 1 1969); *Hay v. Duskin*, 9 Ariz. App. 599, 455 P.2d 281 (1969); *Madsen v. Fisk*, 5 Ariz. App. 65, 423 P.2d 141 (1967); *7-G Ranching Co. v. Stites*, 4 Ariz. App. 228, 419 P.2d 358 (1966).

The affidavit of an attorney is insufficient except where the facts set out are based upon the attorney's personal knowledge. *Tilley v. Delci*, 220 Ariz. 233, 204 P.3d 1082 (Ct. App. Div. 1 2009). *See also*, *Wells Fargo Bank, N.A. v. Allen*, 231 Ariz. 209, 292 P.3d 195 (Ct. App. Div. 1 2012) (supporting paralegal affidavit, insufficient).

It is not sufficient to simply state the affiant's conclusions. *Harmon v. Szrama*, 102 Ariz. 343, 429 P.2d 662 (1967); *Wells Fargo Bank, N.A. v. Allen*, 231 Ariz. 209, 292 P.3d 195 (Ct. App. Div. 1 2012); *Chess v. Pima County*, 126 Ariz. 233, 613 P.2d 1289 (Ct. App. Div. 2 1980); *Feuchter v. Bazurto*, 22 Ariz. App. 427, 528 P.2d 178 (Div. 2 1974); *Herring v. Railway Exp. Agency, Inc.*, 13 Ariz. App. 28, 474 P.2d 35 (Div. 1 1970); *Equitable Life & Cas. Ins. Co. v. Rutledge*, 9 Ariz. App. 551, 454 P.2d 869 (1969). Conclusions expressed from documents as to which the affiant cannot establish the requisite foundation to remove their hearsay character, are insufficient to support summary judgment. *Wells Fargo Bank, N.A. v. Allen*, 231 Ariz. 209, 292 P.3d 195 (Ct. App. Div. 1 2012); *Villas at Hidden Lakes Condominiums Ass'n v. Geupel Const. Co., Inc.*, 174 Ariz. 72, 847 P.2d 117 (Ct. App. Div. 1 1992).

Similarly, if a party fails to demonstrate adequate foundation for an affidavit from an expert that is submitted either in support of, or in opposition to, a motion for summary judgment, that affidavit cannot be considered. *Ulibarri v. Gerstenberger*, 178 Ariz. 151, 871 P.2d 698 (Ct. App. Div. 1 1993) (rejected by, Logerquist v. Danforth, 188 Ariz. 16, 932 P.2d 281 (Ct. App. Div. 2 1996)).

It is not an infrequent practice for parties to submit depositions, or portions of depositions, in support of their separate statement of undisputed material facts. Ariz. R. Civ. P. 56(e) was amended in 2003, however, to specify that only a written deposition or portion thereof, and not an electronic recording, can be submitted in support of or in opposition to a motion for summary judgment, unless a party claims the written transcript is inaccurate. The 2013 amendment of Rule 56(e) did not substantively change this provision.

Ariz. R. Civ. P. 56(c)(4), adopted effective January 1, 2014, provides that the procedure for objecting to the admissibility of evidence submitted in connection with a motion for summary judgment is governed by Ariz. R. Civ. 7.1(f)(2) (2014), except that any such objection may be included in a party's response to a separate statement of facts in lieu of including any such objection in the responsive memoranda.

6. *Burden on Party Opposing Summary Judgment.* Where a moving party makes a *prima facie* showing of the absence of any genuine dispute of fact, the adverse party may not simply rest on the pleadings, but must show by competent evidence specific facts that create a genuine issue for trial. *MacConnell v. Mitten*, 131 Ariz. 22, 638 P.2d 689 (1981); *W. J. Kroeger Co. v. Travelers Indem. Co.*, 112 Ariz. 285, 541 P.2d 385 (1975); *Markel v. Transamerica Title Ins. Co.*, 103 Ariz. 353, 442 P.2d 97 (1968) (overruled on other grounds by, Burch & Cracchiolo, P.A. v. Pugliani, 144 Ariz. 281, 697 P.2d 674 (1985)); *Eastwood Elec. Co. v. R. L. Branaman Contractor, Inc.*, 102 Ariz. 406, 432 P.2d 139 (1967); *Ancell v. Union Station Associates, Inc.*, 166 Ariz. 457, 803 P.2d 450 (Ct. App. Div. 2 1990); *GM Development Corp. v. Community American Mortg. Corp.*, 165 Ariz. 1, 795 P.2d 827 (Ct. App. Div. 1 1990); *Burrington v. Gila County*, 159 Ariz. 320, 767 P.2d 43 (Ct. App. Div. 2 1988); *Diamond v. Kenner*, 140 Ariz. 524, 683 P.2d 323 (Ct. App. Div. 2 1984); *Joseph v. Markovitz*, 27 Ariz. App. 122, 551 P.2d 571 (Div. 1 1976); *Ong Hing v. Arizona Harness Raceway, Inc.*, 10 Ariz. App. 380, 459 P.2d 107 (Div. 1 1969).

In resisting summary judgment, the adverse party need not reveal its entire case; it need only present sufficient evidence to demonstrate that there is a genuine factual dispute as to a material fact. *Tobel v. State, Arizona Dept. of Public Safety*, 189 Ariz. 168, 939 P.2d 801 (Ct. App. Div. 1 1997); *Mohave Elec. Co-op., Inc. v. Byers*, 189 Ariz. 292, 942 P.2d 451 (Ct. App. Div. 1 1997).

While Ariz. R. Civ. P. 56(e)(4) (2013) requires a response by the party opposing a motion for summary judgment, there is nothing in the Rule which requires the submission or inclusion of affidavits. *See also, Maxwell v. Fidelity Financial Services, Inc.*, 184 Ariz. 82, 907 P.2d 51, 28 U.C.C. Rep. Serv. 2d 806 (1995). Rather, Rule 56(e)(4) mandates that the adverse party support its position either by affidavits *or* as otherwise provided in the Rule. If the respondent demonstrates by way of deposition testimony, answers to interrogatories or other discovery materials, that there exists a genuine issue of material fact, then no affidavits are required and entry of summary judgment is inappropriate. *Maxwell v. Fidelity Financial Services, Inc.*, 184 Ariz. 82, 907 P.2d 51, 28 U.C.C. Rep. Serv. 2d 806 (1995).

It is not an infrequent practice for parties to submit depositions, or portions of depositions, in support of their oppositions to summary judgment motions. Ariz. R. Civ. P. 56(e) was amended in 2003, however, to specify that only a written deposition or portion thereof, and not an electronic recording, can be submitted in support of or in opposition to a motion for summary judgment, unless a party claims the written transcript is inaccurate. The 2013 amendment of Rule 56(e) did not substantively change this provision.

An award of summary judgment will not be affirmed on appeal, however, even in the absence of controverting evidence, if the motion and the evidence cited in support of the motion are insufficient to show that no genuine issue of material fact exists or that the moving party is entitled to judgment as a matter of law. Thus, a plaintiff responding to a motion for summary judgment need not present a *prima facie* case unless the motion and supporting papers adequately challenges the plaintiff's ability to do so. *Hydroculture, Inc. v. Coopers & Lybrand*, 174 Ariz. 277, 848 P.2d 856 (Ct. App. Div. 1 1992). In responding to a motion for summary judgment in a medical malpractice case, on the other hand, a plaintiff must show that expert testimony is available to establish that the defendant provider's treatment fell below the applicable standard of care. *McGuire By and Through McGuire v. DeFrancesco*, 168 Ariz. 88, 811 P.2d 340 (Ct. App. Div. 1 1990).

The failure to file a response to a motion for summary judgment will not lead inevitably to the entry of summary judgment in favor of the moving party if the moving party has not made a *prima facie* showing of the absence of a factual dispute. *United Bank of Arizona v. Allyn*, 167 Ariz. 191, 805 P.2d 1012 (Ct. App. Div. 1 1990); *Strategic Development and Const., Inc. v. 7th & Roosevelt Partners, LLC*, 224 Ariz. 60, 226 P.3d 1046 (Ct. App. Div. 1 2010). While Ariz. R. Civ. P. 56(e)(4) (2013) says that a party opposing a motion for summary judgment may not rest on the allegations and denials in its pleadings, this simply means that a nonmoving party who fails to respond does so at its peril. *Schwab v. Ames Const.*, 207 Ariz. 56, 83 P.3d 56 (Ct. App. Div. 1 2004). If a moving party's summary judgment motion fails to show an entitlement to judgment, the nonmoving party need not respond to controvert the motion, and the trial court is still required to determine the moving party's entitlement to the relief requested. *Strategic Development and Const., Inc. v. 7th & Roosevelt Partners, LLC*, 224 Ariz. 60, 226 P.3d 1046 (Ct. App. Div. 1 2010); *Schwab v. Ames Const.*, 207 Ariz. 56, 83 P.3d 56 (Ct. App. Div. 1 2004).

A defendant has standing to resist a co-defendant's motion for summary judgment, for its success may bar subsequent assertions that the moving defendant was the party responsible for the plaintiff's damages. *Wisener v. State*, 123 Ariz. 148, 598 P.2d

511 (1979); *Matusik v. Arizona Public Service Co.*, 141 Ariz. 1, 684 P.2d 882 (Ct. App. Div. 1 1984); *Rigney v. Superior Court In and For Pima County*, 17 Ariz. App. 546, 499 P.2d 160 (Div. 2 1972).

7. *Objections to Admission of Evidence.* Effective January 1, 2014, the Arizona Supreme Court adopted two rules pertaining to the procedures for stating objections to evidence on motions. Ariz. R. Civ. P. 7.1(f)(2) sets forth the general rule for all such objections, and Ariz. R. Civ. P. 56(c)(4) sets forth a nuance applicable only to objections to evidence submitted in connection with summary judgment motions.

Thus, Rule 7.1(f)(2) (added 2014) states the requirements and procedures for objecting to evidence on written motion as follows:

1. objections to the admissibility of evidence offered in support of, or opposition to, a motion must be made in the objecting party's response or reply and *not* in a separate filing;
2. any response to such objection must be in a party's reply memorandum and *not* in a separate filing;
3. where evidence is offered for the first time in the reply, the objecting party, within 5 days after service of the reply, may file a separate objection limited in scope to the newly offered evidence and limited in length to 3 pages; and
4. no other briefing is permitted unless authorized by the court.

With respect to evidentiary objections on motions for summary judgment, Rule 56(c)(4) (added 2014) confirms that Rule 7.1 (f)(2) (added 2014) applies to evidentiary objections on motions for summary judgment. Rule 56(c)(4) also allows, however, a party to include objections in that party's response to the opposing party's separate statement of facts, if such objections are stated "concisely."

8. *Role of Court.* If there is no genuine issue of material fact, the Court may award summary judgment either for or against the moving party, even if there has been no cross-motion filed. *Trimmer v. Ludtke*, 105 Ariz. 260, 462 P.2d 809 (1969); *Markel v. Transamerica Title Ins. Co.*, 103 Ariz. 353, 442 P.2d 97 (1968) (overruled on other grounds by, Burch & Cracchiolo, P.A. v. Pugliani, 144 Ariz. 281, 697 P.2d 674 (1985)); *Giovanelli v. First Federal Sav. and Loan Ass'n of Phoenix*, 120 Ariz. 577, 587 P.2d 763 (Ct. App. Div. 1 1978); *Johnson v. Collins*, 11 Ariz. App. 327, 464 P.2d 647 (Div. 2 1970). Summary judgment can also be awarded on part of a claim. *See,* Ariz. R. Civ. P. 56(a); *Madden v. Barnes*, 8 Ariz. App. 404, 446 P.2d 510 (1968).

The award of summary judgment is not a sanction, and the trial court is not required to conduct a hearing to determine whether a party or its attorney is at fault for a deficient response to a summary judgment motion. *Tilley v. Delci*, 220 Ariz. 233, 204 P.3d 1082 (Ct. App. Div. 1 2009).

The fact that both sides to the controversy file opposing cross-motions for summary judgment, however, does not constrain the trial court to grant either motion if it determines that a genuine issue of material fact exists. *Phoenix Control Systems, Inc. v. Insurance Co. of North America*, 161 Ariz. 420, 778 P.2d 1316 (Ct. App. Div. 1 1989), decision rev'd on other grounds, 165 Ariz. 31, 796 P.2d 463 (1990). Correspondingly, a party who files an unsuccessful motion for summary judgment is not estopped from arguing that a genuine issue of material fact exists and bars an adversary's cross-motion. *Phoenix Control Systems, Inc. v. Insurance Co. of North America*, 161 Ariz. 420, 778 P.2d 1316 (Ct. App. Div. 1 1989), decision rev'd on other grounds, 165 Ariz. 31, 796 P.2d 463 (1990).

While summary judgment is not usually awarded in negligence cases, it is appropriate when there are no material factual disputes and the summary judgment standard is met. *Sallomi v. Phoenix Newspapers, Inc.*, 160 Ariz. 144, 771 P.2d 469, 16 Media L. Rep. (BNA) 1529 (Ct. App. Div. 2 1989); *Dolezal v. Carbrey*, 161 Ariz. 365, 778 P.2d 1261 (Ct. App. Div. 1 1989); *United Services Auto. Ass'n v. Parry*, 158 Ariz. 83, 761 P.2d 157 (Ct. App. Div. 2 1988); *Morrell v. St. Luke's Medical Center*, 27 Ariz. App. 486, 556 P.2d 334 (Div. 1 1976); *Choisser v. State ex rel. Herman*, 12 Ariz. App. 259, 469 P.2d 493 (Div. 1 1970); *Hackin v. Rupp*, 9 Ariz. App. 354, 452 P.2d 519 (1969). While that determination should be based on the entire record in the case, it is counsel's burden to bring issues of fact to the Court's attention. *Gatecliff v. Great Republic Life Ins. Co.*, 170 Ariz. 34, 821 P.2d 725 (1991); *Chanay v. Chittenden*, 115 Ariz. 32, 563 P.2d 287 (1977); *White v. Lewis*, 167 Ariz. 76, 804 P.2d 805 (Ct. App. Div. 1 1990).

Similarly, Arizona's constitutional provision making the defense of assumption of the risk a question of fact in all cases (Article 18, Section 5) essentially precludes the award of summary judgment with respect to contractual waivers of liability. *Phelps v. Firebird Raceway, Inc.*, 210 Ariz. 403, 111 P.3d 1003 (2005).

The burden on the Court is further eased by Ariz. R. Civ. P. 56(c)(3) (2013) (formerly, Rule 56(c)(2)), which requires both the moving party and that party's opponent to submit separate statements of facts which are claimed to be disputed or undisputed, as the case may be, with appropriate references to the record. A motion for summary judgment that is not accompanied by this requisite separate statement of facts is to be treated as a motion for judgment on the pleadings pursuant to Ariz. R. Civ. P. 12(c).

Wieman v. Roysden, 166 Ariz. 281, 802 P.2d 432 (Ct. App. Div. 1 1990).

9. *Partial Findings of Facts Not in Controversy.* Where the Court finds that the existence of material factual issues precludes an award of summary judgment, Rule 56(d) nevertheless requires that the Court, if practicable, make an order setting forth the facts not in controversy which are to be deemed established for further proceedings. While this requirement is not strictly mandatory, neither is it an empty formality and it should be complied with unless it is impracticable to do so. *Kelman v. Bohi*, 27 Ariz. App. 24, 550 P.2d 671 (Div. 1 1976).

10. *Partial Summary Judgment.* As amended effective January 1, 2013, Ariz. R. Civ. P. 56(a) provides that a party may move for summary judgment on "each claim or defense—or part of each claim or defense." Even where the motion is for a complete summary judgment, the Court has discretion to grant it only in part. *Madden v. Barnes*, 8 Ariz. App. 404, 446 P.2d 510 (1968).

The last sentence of former Rule 56(c)(1) (the predecessor of Ariz. R. Civ. P. 56(a)) expressly authorized the court to enter a partial summary judgment, interlocutory in nature, "on the issue of liability alone although there is a genuine issue as to the amount of damages." This provision did not survive the 2013 amendments.

11. *Form of* Affidavits. It is relatively common practice for the parties to attempt to meet their respective burdens of showing the presence or absence of a material factual dispute, at least in part, by the submission of affidavits. The submission of affidavits is not required, however, if the existence of a genuine issue of material fact can be shown through other discovery materials. *Maxwell v. Fidelity Financial Services, Inc.*, 184 Ariz. 82, 907 P.2d 51, 28 U.C.C. Rep. Serv. 2d 806 (1995).

Ariz. R. Civ. P. 56(e)(1) requires that any affidavits submitted "set out such facts that would be admissible in evidence, and show that the affiant is competent to testify on the matters stated." Where affidavits are employed, accordingly, they must be based on the affiant's personal knowledge, and set forth facts that would be admissible in evidence. *See,* Ariz. R. Civ. P. 56(e)(1) (2013). *See also, Portonova v. Wilkinson*, 128 Ariz. 501, 627 P.2d 232 (1981); *Hegel v. O'Malley Ins. Co., Inc.*, 122 Ariz. 52, 593 P.2d 275 (1979); *Airfreight Exp. Ltd v. Evergreen Air Center, Inc.*, 215 Ariz. 103, 158 P.3d 232 (Ct. App. Div. 2 2007); *Villas at Hidden Lakes Condominiums Ass'n v. Geupel Const. Co., Inc.*, 174 Ariz. 72, 847 P.2d 117 (Ct. App. Div. 1 1992); *Madsen v. Western American Mortg. Co.*, 143 Ariz. 614, 694 P.2d 1228 (Ct. App. Div. 1 1985); *Hay v. Duskin*, 9 Ariz. App. 599, 455 P.2d 281 (1969); *Madsen v. Fisk*, 5 Ariz. App. 65, 423 P.2d 141 (1967); *7-G Ranch-*

ing Co. v. Stites, 4 Ariz. App. 228, 419 P.2d 358 (1966).

Affidavits, including those from experts, that only set forth ultimate facts or conclusions of law can neither support nor defeat a motion for summary judgment. *Florez v. Sargeant*, 185 Ariz. 521, 917 P.2d 250 (1996); *Harmon v. Szrama*, 102 Ariz. 343, 429 P.2d 662 (1967); *Chess v. Pima County*, 126 Ariz. 233, 613 P.2d 1289 (Ct. App. Div. 2 1980); *Feuchter v. Bazurto*, 22 Ariz. App. 427, 528 P.2d 178 (Div. 2 1974); *Herring v. Railway Exp. Agency, Inc.*, 13 Ariz. App. 28, 474 P.2d 35 (Div. 1 1970); *Equitable Life & Cas. Ins. Co. v. Rutledge*, 9 Ariz. App. 551, 454 P.2d 869 (1969). Similarly, if a party fails to demonstrate adequate foundation for an affidavit from an expert that is submitted in response to a motion for summary judgment, that affidavit may not be considered. *Ulibarri v. Gerstenberger*, 178 Ariz. 151, 871 P.2d 698 (Ct. App. Div. 1 1993) (rejected by, Logerquist v. Danforth, 188 Ariz. 16, 932 P.2d 281 (Ct. App. Div. 2 1996)).

Ariz. R. Civ. P. 56(c)(4), adopted effective January 1, 2014, provides that the procedure for objecting to the admissibility of evidence submitted in connection with a motion for summary judgment is governed by Ariz. R. Civ. 7.1(f)(2) (2014), except that any such objection may be included in a party's response to a separate statement of facts in lieu of including any such objection in the responsive memoranda.

The parties cannot thwart the purposes of Rule 56 by creating issues of fact through affidavits that contradict their own deposition testimony and any affidavit which does contradict prior deposition testimony should be disregarded for purposes of summary judgment. *Allstate Indem. Co. v. Ridgely*, 214 Ariz. 440, 153 P.3d 1069 (Ct. App. Div. 2 2007); *MacLean v. State Dept. of Educ.*, 195 Ariz. 235, 986 P.2d 903, 9 A.D. Cas. (BNA) 1284 (Ct. App. Div. 2 1999), as corrected, (Aug. 27, 1999); *Wright v. Hills*, 161 Ariz. 583, 780 P.2d 416 (Ct. App. Div. 2 1989), abrogated on other grounds by *James, Cooke & Hobson, Inc. v. Lake Havasu Plumbing & Fire Protection*, 177 Ariz. 316, 868 P.2d 329 (Ct. App. Div. 1 1993), and *MacLean v. State Dept. of Educ.*, 195 Ariz. 235, 986 P.2d 903, 9 A.D. Cas. (BNA) 1284 (Ct. App. Div. 2 1999), as corrected, (Aug. 27, 1999). Such an inconsistent affidavit may only preclude an award of summary judgment if the affiant was confused at the prior deposition and the affidavit satisfactorily explains those aspects of the deposition testimony affected by the confusion, or if the affiant lacked access to material facts at the time of the deposition and the affidavit sets forth the newly discovered evidence that explains the inconsistency. *Allstate Indem. Co. v. Ridgely*, 214 Ariz. 440, 153 P.3d 1069 (Ct. App. Div. 2 2007); *MacLean v. State Dept. of Educ.*, 195 Ariz. 235, 986 P.2d 903, 9 A.D. Cas. (BNA) 1284 (Ct. App. Div. 2 1999), as corrected, (Aug. 27, 1999); *Wright v. Hills*, 161 Ariz. 583, 780 P.2d 416 (Ct.

App. Div. 2 1989), abrogated on other grounds by *James, Cooke & Hobson, Inc. v. Lake Havasu Plumbing & Fire Protection*, 177 Ariz. 316, 868 P.2d 329 (Ct. App. Div. 1 1993), and *MacLean v. State Dept. of Educ.*, 195 Ariz. 235, 986 P.2d 903, 9 A.D. Cas. (BNA) 1284 (Ct. App. Div. 2 1999), as corrected, (Aug. 27, 1999). This "sham affidavit" rule should not be applied, however, to preclude consideration of deposition testimony that contradicts a party's prefiling *ex parte* sworn statement. *Allstate Indem. Co. v. Ridgely*, 214 Ariz. 440, 153 P.3d 1069 (Ct. App. Div. 2 2007).

12. *Unavailability of Affidavits.* Where a party opposing a motion for summary judgment is unable to secure affidavits or other evidence necessary to justify a good faith opposition, the Court may order a continuance to permit opportunity to do so, under Rule 56(f). *Magellan South Mountain Ltd. Partnership v. Maricopa County*, 192 Ariz. 499, 968 P.2d 103 (Ct. App. Div. 1 1998); *Heuisler v. Phoenix Newspapers, Inc.*, 168 Ariz. 278, 812 P.2d 1096, 18 Media L. Rep. (BNA) 2305 (Ct. App. Div. 1 1991); *Boatman v. Samaritan Health Services, Inc.*, 168 Ariz. 207, 812 P.2d 1025 (Ct. App. Div. 2 1990); *Wells Fargo Credit Corp. v. Smith*, 166 Ariz. 489, 803 P.2d 900 (Ct. App. Div. 1 1990). The purpose of Ariz. R. Civ. P. 56(f) is to insure that a diligent party is given a reasonable opportunity to prepare that party's case. *Simon v. Safeway, Inc.*, 217 Ariz. 330, 173 P.3d 1031 (Ct. App. Div. 2 2007); *Hunter Contracting Co., Inc. v. Superior Court In and For County of Maricopa*, 190 Ariz. 318, 947 P.2d 892 (Ct. App. Div. 1 1997).

The Rule 56(f) procedure was substantially amended effective January 1, 2013. Among other things, the procedure under Rule 56(f) now makes clear that the submission of a Rule 56(f) request, in and of itself, does not relieve the party opposing the summary judgment motion from responding to the summary judgment motion. A Rule 56(f) request for relief will not be considered, and a hearing will not be scheduled, unless the request is accompanied by a separate statement of counsel seeking relief certifying that the parties have been unable to resolve the matter, after personal consultation and good faith efforts. The certification requirement is similar to that imposed by Ariz. R. Civ. P. 26(g).

In addition, under this new procedure, the party moving for summary judgment is generally not required to file a response to the Rule 56(f) request but a hearing is required before relief can be granted. In this latter respect, Rule 56(f), as amended, provides that the court hold an expedited telephonic or in-person hearing within seven days after the filing of a request; if the court's calendar does not allow such hearing within 7 days, the court may set a later date for the hearing.

To succeed under Ariz. R. Civ. P. 56(f), the party requesting

Rule 56(f) relief, must file a request for relief and expedited hearing. The request for relief must be supported by an affidavit that sets forth the specific reasons the requesting party requires the relief. Under established case law, the affidavit should address the following:

(1) the particular evidence that is beyond that party's control;
(2) the location of the evidence;
(3) what the party believes the evidence will reveal;
(4) the methods to be used to obtain it; and,
(5) an estimate of the time the conduct of the additional discovery will require.

Simon v. Safeway, Inc., 217 Ariz. 330, 173 P.3d 1031 (Ct. App. Div. 2 2007); *Grand v. Nacchio*, 214 Ariz. 9, 147 P.3d 763, Blue Sky L. Rep. (CCH) P 74608 (Ct. App. Div. 2 2006); *Alberta Securities Com'n v. Ryckman*, 200 Ariz. 540, 30 P.3d 121 (Ct. App. Div. 1 2001); *Magellan South Mountain Ltd. Partnership v. Maricopa County*, 192 Ariz. 499, 968 P.2d 103 (Ct. App. Div. 1 1998); *Lewis v. Oliver*, 178 Ariz. 330, 873 P.2d 668 (Ct. App. Div. 1 1993); *Bobo v. John W. Lattimore, Contractor*, 12 Ariz. App. 137, 468 P.2d 404 (Div. 1 1970).

The failure to file a motion to continue and an appropriate affidavit setting forth specific reasons why delay is warranted entitles the trial court to proceed to a ruling. *Heuisler v. Phoenix Newspapers, Inc.*, 168 Ariz. 278, 812 P.2d 1096, 18 Media L. Rep. (BNA) 2305 (Ct. App. Div. 1 1991); *Boatman v. Samaritan Health Services, Inc.*, 168 Ariz. 207, 812 P.2d 1025 (Ct. App. Div. 2 1990); *Wells Fargo Credit Corp. v. Smith*, 166 Ariz. 489, 803 P.2d 900 (Ct. App. Div. 1 1990).

A party who fails to seek relief under Rule 56(f) may not simply file affidavits after the hearing on the motion for summary judgment, unless their contents constitute newly discovered evidence which could not previously have been obtained by due diligence. *Phil W. Morris Co. v. Schwartz*, 138 Ariz. 90, 673 P.2d 28 (Ct. App. Div. 1 1983).

A request for such a continuance is addressed to the trial court's discretion, and its ruling on a Rule 56(f) application will not be disturbed on appeal absent an abuse of that discretion. *Simon v. Safeway, Inc.*, 217 Ariz. 330, 173 P.3d 1031 (Ct. App. Div. 2 2007); *Alberta Securities Com'n v. Ryckman*, 200 Ariz. 540, 30 P.3d 121 (Ct. App. Div. 1 2001); *Lewis v. Oliver*, 178 Ariz. 330, 873 P.2d 668 (Ct. App. Div. 1 1993). Moreover, if, in order to respond to a motion, a responding party requires more discovery and that party fails to file an appropriate Rule 56(f) motion, such failure constitutes a waiver of this issue on appeal. *Edwards v. Board of Supervisors of Yavapai County*, 224 Ariz. 221, 229 P.3d

233 (Ct. App. Div. 1 2010). A trial court's ruling on a Rule 56(f) application will not be disturbed on appeal absent an abuse of discretion. *Birth Hope Adoption Agency, Inc. v. Doe*, 190 Ariz. 285, 947 P.2d 859 (Ct. App. Div. 1 1997); *Lewis v. Oliver*, 178 Ariz. 330, 873 P.2d 668 (Ct. App. Div. 1 1993).

13. *Affidavits Submitted in Bad Faith.* Rule 56(g) provides that if the Court finds that affidavits are presented in bad faith or solely for the purpose of delay, it shall order the offending party to pay to that party's adversary the reasonable expenses caused by the filing of the affidavits, including attorneys' fees. The offending party or attorney may also be adjudged in contempt.

14. *Appellate Review of Summary Judgment Dispositions.* Appellate review of an award of summary judgment is *de novo*, both as to whether there are any genuine issues of material fact, and as to whether the moving party was entitled to judgment as a matter of law. *Espinoza v. Schulenburg*, 212 Ariz. 215, 129 P.3d 937 (2006); *Hohokam Irr. and Drainage Dist. v. Arizona Public Service Co.*, 204 Ariz. 394, 64 P.3d 836 (2003); *Andrews v. Blake*, 205 Ariz. 236, 69 P.3d 7 (2003); *Wells Fargo Bank v. Arizona Laborers, Teamsters and Cement Masons Local No. 395 Pension Trust Fund*, 201 Ariz. 474, 38 P.3d 12, 27 Employee Benefits Cas. (BNA) 1811 (2002), as corrected, (Apr. 9, 2002); *Estate of Hernandez by Hernandez-Wheeler v. Flavio*, 187 Ariz. 506, 930 P.2d 1309, 115 Ed. Law Rep. 1067 (1997); *Broemmer v. Abortion Services of Phoenix, Ltd.*, 173 Ariz. 148, 840 P.2d 1013, 24 A.L.R. 5th 793 (1992); *Arizona Dept. of Admin. v. Cox*, 222 Ariz. 270, 213 P.3d 707 (Ct. App. Div. 2 2009); *Aida Renta Trust v. Maricopa County*, 221 Ariz. 603, 212 P.3d 941 (Ct. App. Div. 1 2009), as amended, (July 22, 2009); *Sage v. Blagg Appraisal Co., Ltd.*, 221 Ariz. 33, 209 P.3d 169 (Ct. App. Div. 1 2009); *Messina v. Midway Chevrolet Co.*, 221 Ariz. 11, 209 P.3d 147 (Ct. App. Div. 1 2008); *Tilley v. Delci*, 220 Ariz. 233, 204 P.3d 1082 (Ct. App. Div. 1 2009); *Havasupai Tribe of Havasupai Reservation v. Arizona Bd. of Regents*, 220 Ariz. 214, 204 P.3d 1063, 243 Ed. Law Rep. 889 (Ct. App. Div. 1 2008); *Chalpin v. Snyder*, 220 Ariz. 413, 207 P.3d 666 (Ct. App. Div. 1 2008); *Highland Village Partners, L.L.C. v. Bradbury & Stamm Const. Co., Inc.*, 219 Ariz. 147, 195 P.3d 184 (Ct. App. Div. 1 2008); *Arab Monetary Fund v. Hashim*, 219 Ariz. 108, 193 P.3d 802 (Ct. App. Div. 1 2008); *Haab v. County of Maricopa*, 219 Ariz. 9, 191 P.3d 1025 (Ct. App. Div. 1 2008); *Dube v. Desai*, 218 Ariz. 362, 186 P.3d 587, 233 Ed. Law Rep. 954 (Ct. App. Div. 2 2008); *In re Estate of Parker*, 217 Ariz. 563, 177 P.3d 305 (Ct. App. Div. 1 2008); *Best v. Edwards*, 217 Ariz. 497, 176 P.3d 695 (Ct. App. Div. 1 2008); *Maxfield v. Martin*, 217 Ariz. 312, 173 P.3d 476 (Ct. App. Div. 1 2007); *Law v. Verde Valley Medical Center*, 217 Ariz. 92, 170 P.3d 701 (Ct. App. Div. 1 2007); *Kaman Aerospace v. Arizona Bd. of Regents*, 217 Ariz. 148, 171

P.3d 599, 227 Ed. Law Rep. 296 (Ct. App. Div. 2 2007); *Keonjian v. Olcott*, 216 Ariz. 563, 169 P.3d 927 (Ct. App. Div. 2 2007); *Nolan v. Starlight Pines Homeowners Ass'n*, 216 Ariz. 482, 167 P.3d 1277 (Ct. App. Div. 1 2007); *Tierra Ranchos Homeowners Ass'n v. Kitchukov*, 216 Ariz. 195, 165 P.3d 173 (Ct. App. Div. 1 2007); *Banner Health v. Medical Sav. Ins. Co.*, 216 Ariz. 146, 163 P.3d 1096 (Ct. App. Div. 1 2007); *PLM Tax Certificate Program 1991–92, L.P. v. Schweikert*, 216 Ariz. 47, 162 P.3d 1267 (Ct. App. Div. 1 2007); *Airfreight Exp. Ltd v. Evergreen Air Center, Inc.*, 215 Ariz. 103, 158 P.3d 232 (Ct. App. Div. 2 2007); *Lopez v. Cole*, 214 Ariz. 536, 155 P.3d 1060 (Ct. App. Div. 1 2007); *Acosta v. Phoenix Indem. Ins. Co.*, 214 Ariz. 380, 153 P.3d 401 (Ct. App. Div. 2 2007); *Center Bay Gardens, L.L.C. v. City of Tempe City Council*, 214 Ariz. 353, 153 P.3d 374 (Ct. App. Div. 1 2007), as amended, (Feb. 6, 2007).

However, the Court will not consider new factual theories raised for the first time on an appeal from the award of summary judgment. *Napier v. Bertram*, 191 Ariz. 238, 954 P.2d 1389 (1998). The trial court will be affirmed if it reached the correct result, even if it did so for the incorrect reason. *In re Estate of Lamparella*, 210 Ariz. 246, 109 P.3d 959 (Ct. App. Div. 1 2005), as amended, (June 20, 2005); *Guo v. Maricopa County Medical Center*, 196 Ariz. 11, 992 P.2d 11, 5 Wage & Hour Cas. 2d (BNA) 1864, 139 Lab. Cas. (CCH) P 58812 (Ct. App. Div. 1 1999); *Citibank (Arizona) v. Van Velzer*, 194 Ariz. 358, 982 P.2d 833, 36 U.C.C. Rep. Serv. 2d 145 (Ct. App. Div. 2 1998); *Link v. Pima County*, 193 Ariz. 336, 972 P.2d 669 (Ct. App. Div. 2 1998); *Hill v. Safford Unified School Dist.*, 191 Ariz. 110, 952 P.2d 754, 124 Ed. Law Rep. 721 (Ct. App. Div. 2 1997); *Gonzalez v. Satrustegui*, 178 Ariz. 92, 870 P.2d 1188 (Ct. App. Div. 1 1993); *Chandler Medical Bldg. Partners v. Chandler Dental Group*, 175 Ariz. 273, 855 P.2d 787 (Ct. App. Div. 1 1993). If the entry of summary judgment by the trial court is determined to be error, the appellate court may either vacate the award or, if appropriate, it may direct the entry of summary judgment in favor of the opposing party. *Havasu Springs Resort Co. v. La Paz County*, 199 Ariz. 349, 18 P.3d 143 (Ct. App. Div. 1 2001); *PNL Asset Management Co., LLC v. Brendgen & Taylor Partnership*, 193 Ariz. 126, 970 P.2d 958 (Ct. App. Div. 1 1998), as amended, (Jan. 5, 1999) and as amended, (Mar. 2, 1999); *Anderson v. Country Life Ins. Co.*, 180 Ariz. 625, 886 P.2d 1381 (Ct. App. Div. 1 1994).

The award of summary judgment does, of course, ordinarily result in the entry of a judgment that is subject to appeal. The denial of a motion for summary judgment is generally neither appealable nor subject to review in an appeal from a final judgment in the same action, except in very limited circumstances. *Fernandez v. Garza*, 93 Ariz. 318, 380 P.2d 778 (1963); *Martin v. Schroeder*,

209 Ariz. 531, 105 P.3d 577 (Ct. App. Div. 2 2005); *Woodty v. Weston's Lamplighter Motels*, 171 Ariz. 265, 830 P.2d 477 (Ct. App. Div. 1 1992); *Fleitz v. Van Westrienen*, 114 Ariz. 246, 560 P.2d 430 (Ct. App. Div. 1 1977); *but cf. Roosevelt Sav. Bank of City of New York v. State Farm Fire & Cas. Co.*, 27 Ariz. App. 522, 556 P.2d 823 (Div. 1 1976). Accordingly, in cases which have gone to trial, a party who wants to preserve a summary judgment issue for appeal, with the possible exception of a purely legal issue, must do so by reasserting it in a Rule 50 motion for judgment as a matter of law, or some other appropriate post-trial motion. *Bogard v. Cannon & Wendt Elec. Co., Inc.*, 221 Ariz. 325, 212 P.3d 17 (Ct. App. Div. 1 2009); *John C. Lincoln Hosp. and Health Corp. v. Maricopa County*, 208 Ariz. 532, 96 P.3d 530 (Ct. App. Div. 1 2004), as amended, (Sept. 1, 2004).

The sole avenue for appellate relief from an interlocutory order denying a motion for summary judgment is by petition for special action. *Lavit v. Superior Court In and For County of Maricopa*, 173 Ariz. 96, 839 P.2d 1141 (Ct. App. Div. 1 1992). Appellate courts have been cautioned to decline to exercise jurisdiction over special action petitions requesting review of such a denial of a motion for summary judgment in all but the most exceptional cases. *Piner v. Superior Court In and For County of Maricopa*, 192 Ariz. 182, 962 P.2d 909 (1998); *City of Phoenix v. Yarnell*, 184 Ariz. 310, 909 P.2d 377 (1995); *Sanchez v. Coxon*, 175 Ariz. 93, 854 P.2d 126 (1993); *Cardon v. Cotton Lane Holdings, Inc.*, 173 Ariz. 203, 841 P.2d 198 (1992); *Flood Control Dist. of Maricopa County v. Gaines*, 202 Ariz. 248, 43 P.3d 196 (Ct. App. Div. 1 2002); *Salt River Valley Water Users' Ass'n v. Superior Court, In and For County of Maricopa*, 178 Ariz. 70, 870 P.2d 1166 (Ct. App. Div. 1 1993); *Lavit v. Superior Court In and For County of Maricopa*, 173 Ariz. 96, 839 P.2d 1141 (Ct. App. Div. 1 1992).

Acceptance of such a petition may be appropriate where the issue presented is purely a question of law, where the trial court's decision on the issue appears to be incorrect, where the resolution of the issue will terminate the litigation, and where the petitioner cannot obtain justice by any other means, including appeal. *Cardon v. Cotton Lane Holdings, Inc.*, 173 Ariz. 203, 841 P.2d 198 (1992); *Callan v. Bernini*, 213 Ariz. 257, 141 P.3d 737 (Ct. App. Div. 2 2006). Thus, a defendant who has unsuccessfully asserted a qualified tort immunity defense through a motion for summary judgment has no adequate remedy at law by direct appeal after trial, and special action relief is appropriate to enforce such a claim. *Samaritan Health System v. Superior Court of State of Ariz.*, 194 Ariz. 284, 981 P.2d 584 (Ct. App. Div. 1 1998); *Darragh v. Superior Court In and For County of Maricopa*, 183 Ariz. 79, 900 P.2d 1215 (Ct. App. Div. 1 1995); *Salt River Valley Water*

Users' Ass'n v. Superior Court, In and For County of Maricopa, 178 Ariz. 70, 870 P.2d 1166 (Ct. App. Div. 1 1993).

The denial of a motion for summary judgment, however, is reviewed only for an abuse of discretion. *Sonoran Desert Investigations, Inc. v. Miller*, 213 Ariz. 274, 141 P.3d 754 (Ct. App. Div. 2 2006); *Blanchard v. Show Low Planning and Zoning Com'n*, 196 Ariz. 114, 993 P.2d 1078 (Ct. App. Div. 1 1999); *Samaritan Health System v. Superior Court of State of Ariz.*, 194 Ariz. 284, 981 P.2d 584 (Ct. App. Div. 1 1998).

A party cannot obtain appellate review of an adverse partial summary judgment ruling by dismissing the remaining claims without prejudice with the intention of refiling them following an appeal. *Grand v. Nacchio*, 214 Ariz. 9, 147 P.3d 763, Blue Sky L. Rep. (CCH) P 74608 (Ct. App. Div. 2 2006).

Parties cannot employ Ariz. R. Civ. P. 54(b) as a creative device for securing advisory appellate court opinions. Where the trial court has denied a motion for summary judgment, which is not an appealable order, the parties cannot thereafter stipulate to the entry of a summary judgment in favor of the previously unsuccessful moving party, and to the inclusion in that judgment of the language required by Rule 54(b), as a means for securing an appellate court's views on the issue presented. *Sorensen v. Farmers Ins. Co. of Arizona*, 191 Ariz. 464, 957 P.2d 1007 (Ct. App. Div. 1 1997).

Rule 57. Declaratory judgments

The procedure for obtaining a declaratory judgment shall be in accordance with these Rules, and the right to trial by jury may be demanded under the circumstances and in the manner provided in Rule 38 and subdivisions (a), (h), and (k) of Rule 39. The existence of another adequate remedy does not preclude a judgment for declaratory relief in cases where it is appropriate. The court may order a speedy hearing of an action for a declaratory judgment and may advance it on the calendar.

AUTHORS' COMMENTS

Analysis

1. *Scope and Purpose of Rule.* Rule 57 authorizes, by implication, the entry of declaratory judgments and confirms that the Rules of Civil Procedure are fully applicable to declaratory judgment actions. Arizona has adopted the Uniform Declaratory Judgments Act, codified at A.R.S. §§ 12-1831 *et seq.,* which governs the substantive aspects of actions seeking declaratory relief. The Act is to be construed liberally, and a justiciable controversy will be found to exist if there is an assertion of a right, status or legal relation in which the plaintiff has a definite interest and a denial of it by the opposing party. *State ex rel. Montgomery v. Mathis*, 231 Ariz. 103, 290 P.3d 1226 (Ct. App. Div. 1 2012); *Keggi v. Northbrook Property and Cas. Ins. Co.*, 199 Ariz. 43, 13 P.3d 785 (Ct. App. Div. 1 2000).

Actions brought for a declaratory judgment proceed as other civil suits and, if otherwise available, a jury trial may be requested. The fact that the party seeking declaratory relief may have another adequate remedy available is not a bar to the action, and it is not uncommon for a claim for declaratory relief to be combined with other causes of action.

A declaratory judgment is given the same force and effect as any other civil judgment, and is *res judicata* as to the issues raised by the parties and resolved by the Court. *Lisitzky v. Brady*, 38 Ariz. 337, 300 P. 177 (1931). *See also Adams v. Bear*, 87 Ariz. 288, 350 P.2d 751 (1960). Ordinarily, in a declaratory judgment action concerning the proper interpretation of a contract, the prevailing party can seek an award of attorney's fees. *Republic Ins. Co. v. Feidler*, 193 Ariz. 8, 969 P.2d 173 (Ct. App. Div. 1 1998), review denied and opinion ordered not published, 199 Ariz. 472, 19 P.3d 613 (1999).

As a consequence of the supplementary relief statute, A.R.S. § 12-1838, the court in a declaratory judgment action may also grant monetary relief. *Associated Aviation Underwriters v. Wood*, 209 Ariz. 137, 98 P.3d 572 (Ct. App. Div. 2 2004).

2. *Comparison With Federal Rule.* ARCP 57 is essentially the same as FRCP 57.

In 2007, the language of FRCP 57 was amended as part of the general restyling of the Federal Rules of Civil Procedure to make the Federal Rules more easily understood and to make style and terminology consistent throughout the Federal Rules of Civil Procedure. Those stylistic modifications have not been incorporated into ARCP 57.

3. *Nature of Action for Declaratory Relief.* A declaratory judgment action is designed to permit the adjudication of rights or status without the necessity of a prior breach or injury. *Elkins v. Vana*, 25 Ariz. App. 122, 541 P.2d 585 (Div. 2 1975). The declaratory judgment in a sense renders the Court's opinion on a controversy, without providing coercive relief by directing that action be taken. *Black v. Siler*, 96 Ariz. 102, 392 P.2d 572 (1964); *Lecky v. Staley*, 6 Ariz. App. 556, 435 P.2d 63 (1967). A declaratory judgment is, however, *res judicata*. *Lisitzky v. Brady*, 38 Ariz. 337, 300 P. 177 (1931). *See also Adams v. Bear*, 87 Ariz. 288, 350 P.2d 751 (1960).

Arizona does not have a statute of limitations that expressly applies to declaratory judgment actions. And, thus, the question of "whether and when statutes of limitations are applicable to declaratory relief actions is a less than clear area of the law." *Canyon del Rio Investors, L.L.C. v. City of Flagstaff*, 227 Ariz. 336, 258 P.3d 154 (Ct. App. Div. 1 2011) (quoting, *Western Cas. & Sur. Co. v. Evans*, 130 Ariz. 333, 636 P.2d 111 (Ct. App. Div. 1 1981).

Arizona's courts, however, "have determined the appropriate limitations period by 'examining the substance of that action to identify the relationship out of which the claim arises and the relief sought." *Canyon del Rio Investors, L.L.C. v. City of Flagstaff*, 227 Ariz. 336, 258 P.3d 154 (Ct. App. Div. 1 2011), quoting, *Vales v. Kings Hill Condominium Ass'n*, 211 Ariz. 561, 125 P.3d 381 (Ct. App. Div. 1 2005); *La Canada Hills Ltd. Partnership v. Kite*, 217 Ariz. 126, 171 P.3d 195 (Ct. App. Div. 2 2007), quoting, *Vales v. Kings Hill Condominium Ass'n*, 211 Ariz. 561, 125 P.3d 381 (Ct. App. Div. 1 2005). Declaratory judgment actions filed within the time limitation most analogous to the action have generally been treated as timely. *Canyon del Rio Investors, L.L.C. v. City of Flagstaff*, 227 Ariz. 336, 258 P.3d 154 (Ct. App. Div. 1 2011) (holding, after consideration of justiciability, exhaustion, and limitations that a claim for declaratory judgment concerning a zoning ordinance cannot be time-barred if it is brought before a related damage action accrues or within the applicable statute of limitations after the statute of limitations accrues). *La Canada Hills Ltd. Partnership v. Kite*, 217 Ariz. 126, 171 P.3d 195 (Ct. App. Div. 2 2007).

4. *Requirement of an Actual Controversy.* The dispute which the Court is asked to resolve must be a justiciable controversy. When a breach or actual injury does occur, however, a coercive cause of action may be brought and maintained even though declaratory relief has been requested. *Canyon del Rio Investors, L.L.C. v. City of Flagstaff*, 227 Ariz. 336, 258 P.3d 154 (Ct. App. Div. 1 2011) (quoting, *Western Cas. & Sur. Co. v. Evans*, 130 Ariz. 333, 636 P.2d 111 (Ct. App. Div. 1 1981).

This requirement, however, is not constitutionally driven insofar as Arizona's constitution does not contain a "case or controversy" requirement. *State v. B Bar Enterprises, Inc.*, 133 Ariz. 99, 649 P.2d 978 (1982); *State ex rel. Montgomery v. Mathis*, 231 Ariz. 103, 290 P.3d 1226 (Ct. App. Div. 1 2012).

The dispute giving rise to a declaratory judgment action must be an actual, existing dispute based on an existing state of facts rather than a factual scenario which may or may not arise in the future, *Moore v. Bolin*, 70 Ariz. 354, 220 P.2d 850 (1950); *American Federation of State, County and Mun. Employees, AFL-CIO, Council 97 v. Lewis*, 165 Ariz. 149, 797 P.2d 6 (Ct. App. Div. 1 1990); *Lake Havasu Resort, Inc. v. Commercial Loan Ins. Corp.*, 139 Ariz. 369, 678 P.2d 950 (Ct. App. Div. 1 1983); *Richey v. City of Phoenix*, 18 Ariz. App. 208, 501 P.2d 49 (Div. 1 1972); between parties whose positions and interests are truly adversarial, *Riley v. Cochise County*, 10 Ariz. App. 55, 455 P.2d 1005 (1969).

A mere difference of opinion on an issue will not give the Court jurisdiction to grant declaratory relief. *Arizona State Bd. of Directors for Junior Colleges v. Phoenix Union High School Dist. of Maricopa County*, 102 Ariz. 69, 424 P.2d 819 (1967); *Moore v. Bolin*, 70 Ariz. 354, 220 P.2d 850 (1950); *Manning v. Reilly*, 2 Ariz. App. 310, 408 P.2d 414 (1965). No action may be brought under the Declaratory Judgments Act for a declaratory judgment which is merely advisory or which will merely address an abstract or hypothetical question. *Moore v. Bolin*, 70 Ariz. 354, 220 P.2d 850 (1950); *Manning v. Reilly*, 2 Ariz. App. 310, 408 P.2d 414 (1965).

A.R.S. § 12-1836 provides that the Court may refuse to entertain a declaratory judgment action where such a judgment would not terminate the uncertainty or controversy giving rise to the proceeding. See *Morton v. Pacific Const. Co.*, 36 Ariz. 97, 283 P. 281 (1929). The question whether a declaratory judgment would or would not terminate the controversy giving rise to the action is a matter best resolved early in the litigation.

Where a declaratory judgment action challenges the constitutionality of a state statute or rule, A.R.S. § 12-1841(A) requires that the Arizona Attorney General be served with the pleading, motion or other document which raises that issue. There must also be attached to that pleading, motion or other document, as a cover page when it is served, a Notice of Claim of Unconstitutionality, the contents of which are prescribed in A.R.S. § 12-1841(B).

Rule 57.1. Declaration of factual innocence

a. Scope of Rule. This rule governs the determination of factual innocence of a person who claims pursuant to A.R.S. § 12-771 that the person's personal identifying information was taken, and as a result the person's name was used by another person who was arrested, cited, or charged with a criminal offense, or entered as of record in a judgment of guilt in a criminal case.

b. Filing. A petition brought under this rule shall be filed in the superior court in the county in which the other person was arrested for, or cited or charged with, a criminal offense. The petition shall be assigned a civil case number. If applicable, the petition shall state the specific court location where the underlying charge was filed, or the judgment of guilt was entered, and the case number of that prior filing. The petition shall identify, as applicable, the names and mailing addresses of all persons and entities entitled under A.R.S. § 12-771(H) to notice of a finding of factual innocence. The petition shall be captioned: In re: (name of petitioner).

c. Service. The petitioner shall serve the petition in the manner prescribed by A.R.S. § 12-771 and by these rules.

d. Redacted Filings and Filings Under Seal. A person may request, and the court may order, that a filing containing potentially sensitive identifying information such as the person's birth date, social security number, or financial account numbers, be filed or retained in redacted form or under seal.

e. Transmission of Records. If the petition is related to a charge filed in a justice of the peace court or a municipal court, the clerk of the superior court shall request the justice of the peace or presiding officer of the municipal court to transmit a copy of the file to the clerk's office.

f. Discovery and Disclosure. Discovery may be conducted and disclosure under Rule 26.1 may be required only upon stipulation of the parties, or by order of the court.

g. Evidence. The petitioner must establish factual innocence by clear and convincing evidence.

h. Hearing and Determination.

1. The court may hold a hearing to determine the petitioner's factual innocence.

2. The court may enter an order pursuant to this rule upon submission of proof by affidavit.

3. At any hearing, the victim of the offense identified in a judgment of guilt, or committed by the person arrested for, or

cited or charged with, a criminal offense, has a right to be present and to be heard at the hearing.

i. Order. On a finding of factual innocence related to an arrest, citation, or charge, the court shall notify the following persons, if applicable: the petitioner; the prosecuting agency which filed the charge; the law enforcement agency which made the arrest or issued the citation; the defense attorney.

Adopted on emergency basis effective Jan. 1, 2009. Adopted on a permanent basis and amended Sept. 3, 2009, effective Jan. 1, 2010.

AUTHORS' COMMENTS

Analysis

1. *Scope and Purpose of Rule.* Rule 57.1, and the companion Rule 57.2, was adopted by the Arizona Supreme Court on an emergency basis, effective January 1, 2009, to facilitate victims of identity theft taking advantage of certain legislation passed during 2008, and codified at A.R.S. §§ 12-771 and 772. The legislation, and this Rule, applies to persons whose personal information has been taken and whose name has been used by a person who has been arrested for or charged with a criminal offense, or adjudged guilty of a crime.

The Petition to establish the wronged person's factual innocence of the charges involved is to be filed in the Superior Court for the county where the criminal proceedings took place. The person's factual innocence must be proven by clear and convincing evidence.

The language of the Rule suggests that the petitioner need not be the victim of the underlying identity theft, although it seems likely that the victim will be the person who most frequently invokes these procedures. The Rule also suggests that the discovery rules do not apply, and that discovery is to be authorized either by stipulation of the parties or by Court order.

2. *Comparison With Federal Rule.* The Federal Rules of Civil Procedure do not have a provision that corresponds to ARCP 57.1.

Rule 57.2. Declaration of factual improper party status

a. Scope of Rule. This rule governs petitions alleging factual improper party status pursuant to A.R.S. § 12-772, if as a result of a person's personal identifying information being taken, the person's name was entered as of record in a civil action or judgment.

b. Filing. A petition brought under this rule shall be filed in the superior court for the county in which the petitioner's name was entered as of record in a civil action or judgment because of alleged improper use of the petitioner's personal identifying information. The petition shall be assigned a civil case number. The petition shall state the specific court location where the underlying action was filed, and the case number of the prior filing. The petition shall be captioned: In re: (name of petitioner).

c. Service. The petitioner shall serve the petition in the manner prescribed by these rules on all parties in the civil action in which the petitioner's identity was allegedly used.

d. Redacted Filings and Filings Under Seal. A person may request, and the court may order, that a filing containing potentially sensitive identifying information such as the person's birth date, social security number, or financial account numbers, be filed or retained in redacted form or under seal.

e. Transmission of Records. If the petition is related to a case filed in a justice of the peace court, the clerk of the superior court shall request the justice of the peace to transmit a copy of the file to the clerk's office.

f. Discovery and Disclosure. Discovery proceedings may be conducted and disclosure under Rule 26.1 may be required only upon stipulation of the interested parties, or by order of the court.

g. Evidence. The petitioner must establish improper party status by clear and convincing evidence.

h. Hearing and Determination.

1. The court may hold a hearing on the petition.

2. The court may enter an order pursuant to this rule upon submission of proof by affidavit.

i. Order. The court shall provide notice of the court's findings to the petitioner and to all parties in the civil action in which the petitioner's identity was allegedly used.

Adopted on emergency basis effective Jan. 1, 2009. Adopted on a permanent basis and amended Sept. 3, 2009, effective Jan. 1, 2010.

AUTHORS' COMMENTS

Analysis

1. *Scope and Purpose of Rule.* Ariz. R. Civ. P. 57.2, and the companion Rule 57.1, was adopted by the Supreme Court on an emergency basis, effective January 1, 2009, to facilitate victims of identity theft taking advantage of certain legislation passed during 2008, and codified at A.R.S. §§ 12-771 and 772. While Rule 57.1 deals with the situation where personal information has been taken and the name of the identity theft victim has been used by a person who has been arrested for or charged with a criminal offense, or adjudged guilty of a crime, Rule 57.2 is concerned with the situation where the theft has resulted in the victim's being improperly named in a civil action or judgment. The Petition to establish the wronged person's improper status as a party is to be filed in the Superior Court for the county where the underlying civil proceedings took place. The fact that the person has been improperly named in a civil action or judgment must be proven by clear and convincing evidence.

As distinguished from Rule 57.1, the language of this Rule suggests that the petitioner is to be the victim of the identity theft who has been improperly named in the civil proceedings. Rule 57.2 also suggests that the discovery rules do not apply, but rather discovery is to be authorized either by stipulation of the parties or order of the Court in which the Petition is filed.

2. *Comparison With Federal Rule.* The Federal Rules of Civil Procedure do not have a provision that corresponds to ARCP 57.2.

Rule 58. Entry of judgment

(a) Service of Form of Judgment; Entry. Proposed forms of judgment shall be served upon all parties and counsel. Except as provided in Rule 54(b), a party seeking attorneys' fees shall provide in the form of judgment for an award of attorneys' fees in an amount to be entered by the court. Except as provided in subsection (f) of this rule, all judgments shall be in writing and signed by a judge or a court commissioner duly authorized to do so. The filing with the clerk of the judgment constitutes entry of such judgment, and the judgment is not effective before such entry, except that in such circumstances and on such notice as justice may require, the court may direct the entry of a judgment nunc pro tunc, and the reasons for such direction shall be entered of record. The entry of the judgment shall not be delayed for taxing costs.

Amended July 14, 1961, effective Nov. 1, 1961; amended effective Nov. 1, 1967; June 1, 1970. Amended Sept. 23, 1994, effective Dec. 1, 1994; Oct. 3, 1996, effective Dec. 1, 1996; June 17, 1999, effective Dec. 1, 1999; Oct. 2000, effective Dec. 1, 2000. Amended and effective May 9, 2001. Amended Aug. 28, 2013, effective Jan. 1, 2014.

(b) Remittitur; Procedure; Effect on Right of Appeal.

1. A party in whose favor a verdict or judgment has been rendered may, in open court, or in writing filed with the clerk, remit any part of the verdict or judgment. The remittitur shall be entered on the judgment docket and in the minutes, and execution shall thereafter issue for the balance only of the judgment after deducting the amount remitted.

2. The remittitur shall not affect the right of the opposite party to appeal from the judgment, and for that purpose the amount of the original judgment shall be considered the amount in controversy.

Amended Sept. 20, 2006, effective Jan. 1, 2007.

(c) Enforcement of Judgment; Special Writ. The court shall cause the judgment to be carried into execution. When the judgment is for personal property, and it is shown by the pleadings and found that the property has a special value to the plaintiff, or prevailing party, the court may award the plaintiff, or prevailing party, a special writ for the seizure and delivery of the property and may, in addition to the other relief granted, enforce its judgment in the manner provided by law.

(d) Objections to Form.

1. In case of a judgment other than for money or costs, or

that all relief be denied, the judgment shall not be settled, approved and signed until the expiration of five days after the proposed form thereof has been served upon opposing counsel unless the opposite party or that party's counsel endorses on the judgment an approval as to form. The five-day provision may be waived by the court only upon an express written finding by minute order or otherwise of necessity to shorten time or to enter judgment without notice.

2. If objection to the form of the judgment is made within the time provided in paragraph 1 of this subdivision, the party submitting the proposed form of judgment may respond to the objection within five (5) days after service thereof, and the matter shall thereafter be presented to the court for determination, without oral argument, unless the court otherwise directs.

3. The requirements of this Rule shall not apply to parties in default.

Amended and effective Nov. 1, 1967. Amended June 27, 1991, effective July 1, 1991.

(e) Minute Entries; Notice of Entry of Judgments. The clerk shall distribute, either by U.S. mail, electronic mail, or attorney drop box copies of all minute entries to all parties. Immediately upon the entry of a judgment as defined in Rule 54(a), the clerk shall distribute, either by U.S. mail, electronic mail, or attorney drop box a notice of the entry of judgment stating the date of entry, in the manner provided for in Rule 5, to every party who is not in default for failure to appear, and shall make a record of the distribution. Any party may in addition serve a notice of such entry, in the manner provided in Rule 5 for the service of papers. In the case of a judgment in the form of a minute entry, the date of entry shall be the date on which the clerk affixes a file stamp on the minute entry. Lack of notice of the entry by the clerk does not affect the time to appeal or relieve or authorize the court to relieve a party for failure to appeal within the time allowed, except as provided in Rule 9(a), Arizona Rules of Civil Appellate Procedure.

Notice of the entry of judgment shall be accomplished by any of the following:

1. a specifically designated notice form;
2. a minute entry;
3. a conformed copy of the file stamped judgment.

Added Oct. 10, 2000, effective Dec. 1, 2000. Amended Oct. 4, 2004, effective Dec. 1, 2004.

(f) Entry of Judgment in Habeas Corpus Proceedings. A judgment in habeas corpus proceedings need not be signed, and shall be final when entered in the minutes of the court.

Added as 58(e) Oct. 3, 1996, effective Dec. 1, 1996. Renumbered as 58(f) Oct. 10, 2000, effective Dec. 1, 2000.

(g) Entry of Judgment. Except as provided in Rule 54(b), a judgment shall not be entered until claims for attorneys' fees have been resolved and are addressed in the judgment. Entry of judgment shall not be delayed nor the time for appeal extended in order to tax costs.

Added as 58(f) Oct. 3, 1996, effective Dec. 1, 1996. Amended June 17, 1999, effective Dec. 1, 1999. Renumbered as 58(f) Oct. 10, 2000, effective Dec. 1, 2000.

COURT COMMENT

1994 Amendment

[Rule 58(a)] The 1994 amendment, requiring forms of judgment to be served upon all parties and counsel, is designed to address a problem experienced by practitioners, whereby they were not receiving notice of entry of judgment in some cases and their clients' rights to appeal were jeopardized. See also, Rule 9(a), ARCAP, and Rules 6(b) and 77(g), Rules of Civil Procedure, as amended effective December 1, 1994.

STATE BAR COMMITTEE NOTES

1961 Amendment

[Rule 58(a)] Proposed amended Rule 58(a) will require that all judgments, which are defined by Rule 54(a) to include decrees and appealable orders, be in writing and signed by a judge or, where he is so authorized, by a court commissioner. It also provides that the filing of the signed judgment with the clerk constitutes the entry of the judgment.

Under the present rule judgments for money or costs only, or denying all relief, are not required to be in writing, but are required to be entered by the clerk in the civil docket upon receipt of the direction of the court. The notation in the docket constitutes entry of such judgments. *Harbel Oil Co. v. Steele*, 81 Ariz. 104, 301 P.2d 757 (1956). Other judgments have to be in writing, approved and signed by the judge, and are entered when thereafter filed with the clerk. *Black v. Industrial Commission of Ariz.*, 83 Ariz. 121, 317 P.2d 553, 70 A.L.R.2d 1119 (1957) (overruled on other grounds by, Hash's Estate v. Henderson, 109 Ariz. 174, 507 P.2d 99 (1973)).

The primary purpose of the amended rule is to formalize by a writing all judgments, decrees and appealable orders, and to fix the crucial act of entry of every judgment, decree or appealable order by reference to the date of its filing, rather than, as now in some cases, to the date it is noted clerically in the docket book. Under the present rule it is this less certain, and often unascertainable, date of notation that starts the time to appeal from a judgment or order that is not required to be in writing and signed by a judge. *Harbel Oil Co. v. Steele*, 81 Ariz. 104, 301 P.2d 757 (1956); and execution of such a judgment before that date is not proper, *Jackson v. Sears, Roebuck & Co.*, 83 Ariz. 20, 315 P.2d 871, 65 A.L.R.2d 1158 (1957).

The amended rule will have other beneficial effects. Thus, a formal judgment will facilitate its recording to become a lien on real property (see A.R.S. section 33-961) as well as a suit on the judgment in this or another state. Further, the amended rule will eliminate some of the uncertainty that now exists in respect of orders of dismissal, which are not appealable, see e.g., *Meloy v. Saint Paul Mercury Indem. Co.*, 72 Ariz. 406, 236 P.2d 732 (1951); *Reed v. Coyner Crop Dusters*, 83 Ariz. 153, 317 P.2d 944 (1957); *Miller v. Arizona Bank*, 45 Ariz. 297, 43 P.2d 518 (1935), unless the order, recorded under the present rule only as a minute entry, is also a direction for judgment. Compare: *State Bd. of Barber Examiners v. Edwards*, 76 Ariz. 27, 258 P.2d 418 (1953), and *Southwestern Freight Lines v. Shafer*, 57 Ariz. 111, 111 P.2d 625 (1941) with *Gillespie Land & Irr. Co. v. Buckeye Irr. Co.*, 69 Ariz. 367, 213 P.2d 902 (1950). Formalization of the order in a written instrument renders it a simple task to make the order of dismissal specifically also a judgment of dismissal, which is appealable. Thus, although the amended rule will not affect the appealability of orders (see A.R.S. section 12-2101), it will insure that until an appealable order or judgment is signed by a judge and filed with the clerk, the time to appeal will not begin to run, and an appeal filed before these acts are completed will be premature.

Nor will there be a problem under the amended rule, as there is under the present rule, whether a judge's oral opinion, noted as a minute entry and entered in the civil docket, is itself the order of judgment. See: *Ollason v. Glasscock*, 26 Ariz. 193, 224 P. 284 (1924); see also, e.g., *Schwartz v. Schwerin*, 85 Ariz. 242, 336 P.2d 144 (1959). No act or declaration of the judge or notation by the clerk will under the amended rule constitute a judgment or appealable order, unless a form of judgment or order is signed by the judge and filed with the clerk. Further, under the amended rule there will be no requirement of a "direction" of the court, apart from the signing of the order or judgment.

The amended rule will not require interlocutory, nonappealable orders, whether made before, during or after trial, to be in writing and signed by the judge. These orders will be reviewable only when properly assigned as error on appeal from the final judgment (see A.R.S. section 12-2102). Where an order is appealable (such as one granting or refusing a new trial or granting a motion in arrest of judgment, see A.R.S. section 12-2101), subsection F, paragraph 1, it will have to be signed by separate instrument, or where appropriate will have to be incorporated in the final judgment entered on the verdict or decision after trial.

Under the amended rule, as under the present rule, orders denying post-trial motions on the grounds specified in sub-paragraphs (i), (ii) or (iii) of paragraph 2 of Rule 73(b) will not be appealable but timely motions made on these grounds will extend the time for appeal until the entry of the order (see Rule 73(b)). Under both the present and the amended rule, such orders, as true with all non-appealable orders, need not be in writing, and will be entered when noted in the docket book. *Harbel Oil Co. v. Steele, supra.* Consideration has been given for making provision that these few non-appealable orders also be in writing, but this has been deemed unnecessary, for the reason that the entry of the final judgment on the merits, which judgment must be in writing, will permit appeal and execution. The only effect of the entry of such orders will be to stop the running of the extended time for appeal.

Under both the present and the amended rule, entry of judgment need not await the taxation of costs, but the judgment may, of course, include all costs taxed before the judgment is signed. The taxing of costs by the clerk is not appealable. *Dawson v. Lail*, 1 Ariz. 490, 3 P. 399 (1884) and consequently, need not be signed by a judge under amended Rule 58(a). It is clear that the costs taxed by the clerk and noted in the civil docket can be made the basis of an execution, and it seems unnecessary, for the sole purpose of providing a more certain date for the execution of costs, to change the present practice, and require that all costs, even those taxed without objection, be included in the final judgment, with the resultant delay in the entry of the judgment, or be noted in a separate form of order or judgment signed by the judge and filed with the clerk.

An order entered on a motion (under Rule 54(f)) to review the costs taxed by the clerk is appealable and must, under the amended Rule 58(a), be signed by a judge and filed with the clerk. Thus, where the judgment will not include the costs, it will be this signed order, entered when filed with the clerk, from which an appeal must be taken to obtain appellate review of the propriety of the costs.

Although it has been held that entry of judgment is not effective until the judgment fee has been paid, compare: *Southwestern Freight Lines v. Shafer*, 57 Ariz. 111, 111 P.2d 625 (1941) with *Sligh v. Watson*, 67 Ariz. 95, 191 P.2d 724 (1948), the recent enactment of Senate Bill 71, 25th Legislature, 1st Regular Session (Laws 1961, chapter 103), which eliminates, from and after June 30, 1961, any fee for entry of judgment, makes unnecessary any reference in the amended Rule 58(a) to payment of a judgment fee.

It may be noted that present Rule 58(d) requires notice of settlement only of judgments other than for money or costs only, or denying all relief. The proposed amendment to Rule 58(a) will not affect 58(d), and thus the court will be able to sign judgments for money or costs, or denying all relief, without notice.

1967 Amendment

[Rule 58(d)] The amendment to this rule relieves trial judges of a handicap upon their capacity to make orders effective immediately or in less than five days where necessary. As the language read prior to the amendment, the court had no power to modify the five-day provision; *Haechler v. Andrews*, 2 Ariz. App. 395, 409 P.2d 315 (1965). This opinion pointed out that under the rule as it existed, a judge could not shorten time even if an injunction were to be issued. The amendment gives the court needed discretion to cover emergency situations in fewer than five days. The five-day rule is generally regarded as highly desirable, and the amendment is not intended to be used except where some sound reason exists for exercising this special power. To insure that the exercise of the power to dispense with the five-day requirement is not casually exercised, an express finding of necessity to shorten time or enter judgment without notice is required. The procedure of Rule 65(d) requiring best efforts to give notice or reasons for not doing so should be followed in this connection also. The amendment does not affect in any way the decision in *Patch v. Buros*, 2 Ariz. App. 585, 410 P.2d 703 (1966) on the effect of this rule.

1970 Amendment

[Rule 58(a)] *Black v. Industrial Commission of Ariz.*, 83 Ariz. 121, 317 P.2d 553, 70 A.L.R.2d 1119 (1957) (overruled by, Hash's Estate v. Henderson, 109 Ariz. 174, 507 P.2d 99 (1973)) has been viewed by some as prohibiting the entry of an order or judgment nunc pro tunc in Arizona. The purpose of the amendment is to reject the basis for that view and to adopt the rationale of the dissenting opinion of Justice Struckmeyer in that case. The amendment does not specify the conditions, circumstances and effects involving the entry of a judgment or order nunc pro tunc. These are best determined by reference to the considerable body of law on the subject. See e.g. *Mitchell v. Overman*, 103 U.S. 62, 26 L. Ed. 369, 1880 WL 18766 (1880); 6A Moore's Federal Practice (2nd ed.), para. 58.08; 1 Freeman, Judgments, (5th ed. 1925), chapter III, sections 121 to 139. The right of a party to appeal will not be cut off and rights acquired by third persons without notice will not be affected adversely by an entry nunc pro tunc. See Freeman, supra, sections 138 and 139. The record of the reasons required by the amendment shall include not only the circumstances for entry of the judgment but also the reasons for the kind of notice given and if no notice is required the reasons for dispensing with notice.

1996 Amendment

[Rule 58(e)] This rule change is in accordance with *Sims v. Ryan*, 181 Ariz. 330, 890 P.2d 625 (Ct. App. Div. 1 1995), which held that, because of the special nature of habeas proceedings, a signed judgment is not a jurisdictional prerequisite to a habeas appeal. An order of judgment is "entered in the minutes of the court" within the meaning of Rule 58(e) at the time of the last official date on the minute entry. See, *Matter of Maricopa County Juvenile Action No. JS-8441*,

174 Ariz. 341, 849 P.2d 1371 (1992).

1999 Amendments

[Rule 58(a)] Except in the Rule 54(b) situation, amended Rule 58(a) now requires parties submitting forms of judgment to include a provision for attorneys' fees and a blank space in the form of judgment where the court may fill in the amount awarded. If the trial judge determines that fees will not be awarded, the trial judge shall so signify by inserting an amount of "0" or similar designation in the space provided in the form of judgment. Although, by statute, costs may be taxed after judgment, it may be efficient for parties to also include a blank space in the initial form of judgment for taxation of costs.

[Rule 58(g)] In 1996, the Committee recommended the adoption of new Rule 58(f) not only to conform with the newly adopted federal practice, but also to assist in reducing the time required for appeal. Since December 1996, experience with the new procedure, and changes in the Arizona Rules of Civil Appellate Procedure demonstrated that the new rule was not achieving its intended goals. Accordingly, in 1999, Rule 58(f) was amended to provide that a judgment should not normally be entered until all attorneys' fees issues have been resolved and can be addressed in the judgment. This procedure will allow all issues to be addressed efficiently in a single appeal, and will avoid the problem identified in *Mark Lighting Fixture Co., Inc. v. General Elec. Supply Co., a Div. of General Elec. Co.*, 155 Ariz. 27, 745 P.2d 85 (1987) (holding that the trial court lacked jurisdiction to award attorneys' fees after judgment absent a timely motion to alter or amend judgment). In the rare case in which a judgment on the merits of a cause would be appropriate prior to the resolution of attorneys' fees, the trial court may certify the entry of a "merits" judgment under Rule 54(b).

2000 Amendment

As part of the effort to consolidate formerly separate sets of procedural rules into either the Arizona Rules of Civil Procedure or the Rules of the Arizona Supreme Court, Rule 77 of the Arizona Rules of Civil Procedure was effectively abrogated through the transfer of virtually all of its subparts to a new Rule 91 of the Rules of the Arizona Supreme Court. Because Rule 77(g) did not deal primarily with matters of court administration, however, the Committee concluded that it should remain in the Arizona Rules of Civil Procedure, and should be incorporated into Rule 58, which deals with the entry of judgments, as a new subpart (e). Existing subparts (e) and (f) of the Rule were redesignated as Rules 58(f) and (g), respectively.

AUTHORS' COMMENTS

Analysis

11. Interest; Prejudgment Interest.
12. Remittitur Procedure.
13. Special Writs.

1. *Scope and Purpose of Rule.* Rule 58 deals generally with the procedures for securing the entry of judgment in an action. The "rendition" of judgment and the "entry" of judgment are not, however, synonymous terms, and entry of judgment must be accomplished as required by Rule 58. *Devenir Associates v. City of Phoenix*, 169 Ariz. 500, 821 P.2d 161 (1991); *Valley Nat. Bank of Arizona v. Meneghin*, 130 Ariz. 119, 634 P.2d 570 (1981); *Fridena v. Maricopa County*, 18 Ariz. App. 527, 504 P.2d 58 (Div. 1 1972).

Once a judgment has been entered, it may be corrected, if irregular or erroneous, only by some proper proceeding for that purpose. *Egan-Ryan Mechanical Co. v. Cardon Meadows Development Corp.*, 169 Ariz. 161, 818 P.2d 146 (Ct. App. Div. 1 1990). A judgment against an insured defendant will be binding upon, and have preclusive effect against, an insurer who has refused to defend after a proper tender of the defense, but only if the insured defended the action with due diligence and reasonable prudence. *Falcon v. Beverly Hills Mortg. Corp.*, 168 Ariz. 527, 815 P.2d 896 (1991). The exercise of due diligence is a question of fact, and a finding of fraud or collusion is not a necessary predicate for finding a lack of due diligence. *Falcon v. Beverly Hills Mortg. Corp.*, 168 Ariz. 527, 815 P.2d 896 (1991).

A statutory exception to the principle that only final judgments are appealable is found in A.R.S. § 12-2101(A)(6) [as renumbered in 2011], which provides that interlocutory judgments can be appealed when the trial judge has signed an order that contains language indicating that the judgment is a final determination of the rights of the parties, and the only remaining issue is the amount of recovery. *Salerno v. Atlantic Mut. Ins. Co.*, 198 Ariz. 54, 6 P.3d 758 (Ct. App. Div. 1 2000) [citing, A.R.S. § 12-2101(G) (2000)]. To make the interlocutory judgment appealable under this statute, the trial judge must use express language that the judgment has finally determined the rights of the parties and is subject to an interlocutory appeal. *Bilke v. State*, 206 Ariz. 462, 80 P.3d 269 (2003). A Rule 54(b) certification is not necessary but would, if made, satisfy the statutory requirement. *Bilke v. State*, 206 Ariz. 462, 80 P.3d 269 (2003). Appeals under the statute are not limited to cases in which an accounting or similar equitable proceeding has been ordered to determine the amount of recovery. *Bilke v. State*, 206 Ariz. 462, 80 P.3d 269 (2003).

At the appellate level, there is an initial presumption that a judgment is correct and there will be implied for every judgment, in addition to the express findings made by the Court, any additional findings necessary to sustain the judgment, if reasonably supported by the evidence and not in conflict with the express findings. *Navajo Nation v. MacDonald*, 180 Ariz. 539, 885 P.2d 1104, R.I.C.O. Bus. Disp. Guide (CCH) P 8679 (Ct. App. Div. 1 1994); *A.R. Teeters & Associates, Inc. v. Eastman Kodak Co.*, 172 Ariz. 324, 836 P.2d 1034 (Ct. App. Div. 1 1992); *General Elec. Capital Corp. v. Osterkamp*, 172 Ariz. 191, 836 P.2d 404 (Ct. App. Div. 2 1992). This rule requires a litigant to object to inadequate findings at the trial court level so that the court will have an opportunity to correct them, and failure to do so constitutes a waiver. *John C. Lincoln Hosp. and Health Corp. v. Maricopa County*, 208 Ariz. 532, 96 P.3d 530 (Ct. App. Div. 1 2004), as amended, (Sept. 1, 2004).

On appeal from a judgment entered on a jury verdict, the evidence, and all reasonable inferences arising therefrom, are viewed in a light most favorable to the prevailing party. *Hutcherson v. City of Phoenix*, 192 Ariz. 51, 961 P.2d 449 (1998); *Mealey v. Arndt*, 206 Ariz. 218, 76 P.3d 892 (Ct. App. Div. 1 2003); *Warrington v. Tempe Elementary School Dist. No. 3*, 197 Ariz. 68, 3 P.3d 988, 146 Ed. Law Rep. 508 (Ct. App. Div. 1 1999); *Pima County v. Gonzalez*, 193 Ariz. 18, 969 P.2d 183 (Ct. App. Div. 2 1998); *Gemstar Ltd. v. Ernst & Young*, 183 Ariz. 148, 901 P.2d 1178 (Ct. App. Div. 1 1995), opinion vacated on other grounds, 185 Ariz. 493, 917 P.2d 222 (1996); *Navajo Nation v. MacDonald*, 180 Ariz. 539, 885 P.2d 1104, R.I.C.O. Bus. Disp. Guide (CCH) P 8679 (Ct. App. Div. 1 1994); *Bank One, Arizona v. Rouse*, 181 Ariz. 36, 887 P.2d 566 (Ct. App. Div. 1 1994); *Callender v. Transpacific Hotel Corp.*, 179 Ariz. 557, 880 P.2d 1103 (Ct. App. Div. 2 1993); *Lopez v. Farmers Ins. Co. of Arizona*, 177 Ariz. 371, 868 P.2d 954 (Ct. App. Div. 1 1993).

A valid and final judgment on the merits rendered without fraud or collusion by a court of competent jurisdiction is conclusive as to every issue decided and every issue raised by the record that could have been decided. *Norriega v. Machado*, 179 Ariz. 348, 878 P.2d 1386 (Ct. App. Div. 1 1994); *Heinig v. Hudman*, 177 Ariz. 66, 865 P.2d 110 (Ct. App. Div. 1 1993). Such a judgment will also support the defense of *res judicata*, or claim preclusion, but only between those who were parties to the judgment or their privies. *PFS v. Industrial Com'n of Arizona*, 191 Ariz. 274, 955 P.2d 30 (Ct. App. Div. 1 1997).

The parol evidence rule does not apply to judgments, and a court may not consider evidence extrinsic to the record to resolve the meaning of a judgment. *In re Marriage of Zale*, 193 Ariz. 246, 972 P.2d 230 (1999). A judgment is an act of the Court which fixes clearly the rights and liabilities of the parties in the matter before it, and not the product of a negotiated contract to which the Court is merely a party. Applying the parol evidence rule to judgments would make the Court little more than another party to a contract, would impinge upon the finality of judgments, and would allow impermissible collateral attacks on judgments. *In re Marriage of Zale*, 193 Ariz. 246, 972 P.2d 230 (1999).

As a general rule, conditional judgments are void. *Gerow v. Covill*, 192 Ariz. 9, 960 P.2d 55 (Ct. App. Div. 1 1998), as amended, (Aug. 26, 1998). That will not be the case, however, where the alternative or conditional judgment is of such a nature that it is possible to determine from the terms of the judgment the rights and obligations of the parties to the action in which the judgment was entered. *Gerow v. Covill*, 192 Ariz. 9, 960 P.2d 55 (Ct. App. Div. 1 1998), as amended on other grounds, (Aug. 26, 1998). Equitable judgments constitute another exception to the general rule. *Gerow v. Covill*, 192 Ariz. 9, 960 P.2d 55 (Ct. App. Div. 1 1998), as amended on other grounds, (Aug. 26, 1998).

A recorded satisfaction of judgment ordinarily signals the end of the cause of action on which the judgment was based, and is *prima facie* evidence that the judgment creditor has received payment of the amount of the judgment or its equivalent. *Brewer v. Gerson*, 190 Ariz. 164, 945 P.2d 1295 (1997). That will not be the case, however, where, before the filing of the satisfaction of judgment, the underlying judgment is set aside by court order. *Brewer v. Gerson*, 190 Ariz. 164, 945 P.2d 1295 (1997). In that circumstance, the satisfaction of judgment does not extinguish the underlying cause of action. *Brewer v. Gerson*, 190 Ariz. 164, 945 P.2d 1295 (1997).

The granting of a motion for new trial has the effect of vacating a judgment previously entered. *Nielson v. Patterson*, 204 Ariz. 530, 65 P.3d 911 (2003). Accordingly, when the party, whose verdict and judgment have in effect been set aside, appeals from the award of a new trial, it is not necessary for the party who secured a new trial to file a protective cross-appeal to preserve the right to challenge the verdict and judgment in the event the new trial order is reversed on appeal. *Nielson v. Patterson*, 204 Ariz. 530, 65 P.3d 911 (2003). If the new trial order is reversed on appeal, the judgment would be reinstated and the party against whom the judgment was reinstated can appeal at that point. *Nielson v. Patterson*, 204 Ariz. 530, 65 P.3d 911 (2003).

2. *Comparison With Federal Rule.* ARCP 58 and FRCP 58 deal with the same subject matter of entry of judgments, but there are significant differences between the two rules. ARCP 58(a), which roughly corresponds with FRCP 58(a), provides that all judgments must be signed by a Judge or Commissioner, and are only filed and entered on the docket by the Clerk. ARCP 58(a) contains a provision for judgments *nunc pro tunc*, and also specifies that

the entry of judgment is not to be delayed for the taxing of costs. A 1994 amendment to ARCP 58 added a provision, subpart (d), requiring that all proposed forms of judgment submitted to the Court for entry be served upon all parties and counsel. ARCP 58(d) further specifies the procedures and time frames for making and resolving objections to proposed forms of judgment.

The prescribed procedures for securing the formal entry of judgment under the Federal Rules of Civil Procedure differ markedly from those prescribed by the Arizona Rules of Civil Procedure. FRCP 58, as amended in 2002, still provides that, in cases where a jury returns a general verdict or the Court enters an award of a sum certain or denies all relief, a judgment is to be prepared and entered by the Clerk without further direction from the Court. In other cases, including where the jury returns a special verdict, the court must approve the form of judgment.

The provision that attorneys should not submit, unless directed to do so, proposed forms of judgment has been eliminated from the Federal Rule. *See*, FRCP 58(d). A judgment or amended judgment must be set forth on a separate document, but this requirement does not apply to an order disposing of a motion for judgment as a matter of law, to amend or make additional findings, for an award of attorneys' fees, for a new trial, to alter or amend a judgment, or for relief from a judgment under FRCP 60. A party may request that such a judgment be set forth in a separate document. If a timely motion for award of attorney's fees is made after entry of judgment, but before a notice of appeal is filed, the court may direct that the motion be treated as one brought under Rule 59 which extends the time for taking an appeal.

FRCP 58 does not have any provisions that directly correspond to ARCP Rules 58(b), (c), (d), (e), (f) or (g).

In 2007, the language of FRCP 58 was amended as part of the general restyling of the Federal Rules of Civil Procedure to make the Federal Rules more easily understood and to make style and terminology consistent throughout the Federal Rules of Civil Procedure. Those stylistic modifications have not been incorporated into ARCP 58.

3. *Significance of Date of Entry of Judgment; Notice*. The date of the entry of judgment is of critical significance because it typically commences the running of the time period for post-trial motions or prosecuting appeals and the date of entry will determine whether motions for post-verdict relief and/or the filing of a notice of appeal are timely. *Haroutunian v. Valueoptions, Inc.*, 218 Ariz. 541, 189 P.3d 1114 (Ct. App. Div. 2 2008); *City of Tucson v. Wondergem*, 4 Ariz. App. 291, 419 P.2d 552 (1966).

On the other hand, it has been held that a stipulation for the dismissal of a counterclaim, which was the sole remaining claim in the action, was effective to terminate the action upon its filing and that the time for appeal ran from that date and *not* from the date of entry of the subsequent judgment formally disposing of the action. *Theriault v. Scottsdale Enterprises*, 157 Ariz. 77, 754 P.2d 1352 (Ct. App. Div. 2 1987). (The 1990 amendment to Rule 41(a)(1), which requires the Court to enter a formal order of dismissal when such a stipulation is presented, probably obviates the occurrence of the circumstances which led to the result reached in *Theriault*.)

The date of entry of a judgment is the date the judgment is file-stamped by the Clerk of the Court. *Haroutunian v. Valueoptions, Inc.*, 218 Ariz. 541, 189 P.3d 1114 (Ct. App. Div. 2 2008); *Schoenfelder v. Arizona Bank*, 161 Ariz. 601, 780 P.2d 434, 8 U.C.C. Rep. Serv. 2d 771 (Ct. App. Div. 1 1989), opinion vacated in part on other grounds, 165 Ariz. 79, 796 P.2d 881, 12 U.C.C. Rep. Serv. 2d 469 (1990). *See also, Valley Nat. Bank of Arizona v. Meneghin*, 130 Ariz. 119, 634 P.2d 570 (1981) ("the court renders judgment, . . . and the clerk of the court enters the judgment"). A 1994 amendment to Ariz.R.Civ.P 58(e) specifies that, where the judgment is in the form of a signed minute entry, the date of entry is the date that the Clerk affixes a file stamp on the minute entry.

While Rule 58(e) requires the Clerk to mail a notice of entry of judgment to the parties, specifying the date of entry, the time for filing post-judgment motions and for taking an appeal commences to run on the date of entry even though that notice is not received. *Park v. Strick*, 137 Ariz. 100, 669 P.2d 78 (1983); *Old Pueblo Transit Co. v. Corp. Com'n of Ariz.*, 73 Ariz. 32, 236 P.2d 1018 (1951); *Lone Mountain Ranch, Inc. v. Dillingham Inv., Inc.*, 131 Ariz. 583, 643 P.2d 28 (Ct. App. Div. 2 1982). As a consequence of the 1994 amendments to Ariz.R.Civ.P. 6(b) and to Ariz.R.Civ.P. 9(a), these time periods may now be extended where a party entitled to receive notice of entry of judgment does not receive it within twenty-one (21) days of its entry and no party would be prejudiced by such an extension. The circumstances under which such an extension can be granted are discussed in Section 5 of the *Authors' Comments* under Ariz.R.Civ.P. 6.

A sentence was contemporaneously added to former Ariz.R.Civ.P. 77(g) (which is now Rule 58(e)), which authorizes any party to serve a notice of entry of judgment and thereby either preclude such an extension or minimize the period during which one can be sought and secured. If a litigant cannot satisfy the time constraints in those amended Rules, it may still apply under Rule 60(c)(6) to have the judgment vacated and re-entered in order to start the time for taking an appeal running anew. *Decola v. Freyer*, 198 Ariz. 28, 6 P.3d 333 (Ct. App. Div. 1 2000).

Rule 58(a) was also amended in 1994 to require that proposed forms of judgment be served upon all parties and counsel, even if the parties to be served would have no right to object to the form of judgment under Rule 58(d)(1). The purpose of adding this requirement was to help prevent parties from losing their rights to appeal from the judgment eventually entered. *State v. Empire American Bail Bonds, Inc.*, 191 Ariz. 218, 953 P.2d 1271 (Ct. App. Div. 1 1998). The requirement applies to bond forfeiture proceedings which, although they occur in the context of a criminal case, remain civil in nature. *State v. Eazy Bail Bonds*, 224 Ariz. 227, 229 P.3d 239 (Ct. App. Div. 1 2010) (Bond forfeiture proceedings are civil in nature and, thus, the rules of civil procedure apply); *State v. Empire American Bail Bonds, Inc.*, 191 Ariz. 218, 953 P.2d 1271 (Ct. App. Div. 1 1998).

Rule 58(e) was amended in 2004 to give the Clerks of the Superior Court greater flexibility in, and more options for, distributing notices of the entry of judgment. The amendment specifies that distribution of the notice of entry of judgment may be by United States mail, by electronic mail, or by leaving a copy in the proper attorney drop box. That amendment also provides that notice of the entry of judgment can be accomplished by the Clerk distributing (1) a specially designated notice form, (2) a minute entry, or (3) a conformed copy of the file stamped judgment.

Arizona does not follow the "one final judgment" rule. The last sentence of Rule 54(b) does not require the entry of a single judgment adjudicating all claims by all parties. *Hill v. City of Phoenix*, 193 Ariz. 570, 975 P.2d 700 (1999). In the absence of a certification under Rule 54(b), all judgments become effective upon the entry of a subsequent judgment that terminates all remaining claims. *Cristall v. Cristall*, 225 Ariz. 591, 242 P.3d 1060 (Ct. App. Div. 1 2010), review denied, (May 24, 2011); *Hill v. City of Phoenix*, 193 Ariz. 570, 975 P.2d 700 (1999). Counsel have been urged, however, to avoid, where reasonably possible, the use of separate judgments entered upon separate dates. *Hill v. City of Phoenix*, 193 Ariz. 570, 975 P.2d 700 (1999).

4. *Form of Judgment.* No particular form of judgment is required, and the designation "Judgment" need not be employed. To be effective, however, a judgment generally must (1) be in writing, (2) be signed, and (3) be filed with the Clerk of the Court. *Lamb v. Superior Court In and For Maricopa County*, 127 Ariz. 400, 621 P.2d 906 (1980); *Jackson v. Sears, Roebuck & Co.*, 83 Ariz. 20, 315 P.2d 871, 65 A.L.R.2d 1158 (1957); *ABC Supply, Inc. v. Edwards*, 191 Ariz. 48, 952 P.2d 286 (Ct. App. Div. 1 1996), on reconsideration in part, (Oct. 30, 1997); *Spriggel v. Maricopa County*, 15 Ariz. App. 162, 487 P.2d 8 (Div. 1 1971). To be a final judgment, compliance with Ariz. R. Civ. P. 54(c) (2014) is

required. In that regard, Rule 54(c) provides that a judgment is not final "unless the court states that no further matters remain pending and that the judgment is entered pursuant to Rule 54(c)." A prudent practitioner will include such representation in any proposed form of judgment submitted to the court.

A judgment does not bind the assets of a marital community unless both spouses have been joined as parties to the action. *Heinig v. Hudman*, 177 Ariz. 66, 865 P.2d 110 (Ct. App. Div. 1 1993); *Flexmaster Aluminum Awning Co., Inc. v. Hirschberg*, 173 Ariz. 83, 839 P.2d 1128 (Ct. App. Div. 1 1992); *Spudnuts, Inc. v. Lane*, 139 Ariz. 35, 676 P.2d 669 (Ct. App. Div. 2 1984). A 1994 amendment to what was then Rule 77(g), and is now Ariz.R.Civ.P. 58(e) specifies that, where the judgment is in the form of a signed minute entry, the date of entry is the date that the Clerk affixes a file stamp on the minute entry.

A judgment issued electronically and containing an electronic signature of the issuing judge satisfies the requirement of Rule 58(a) that final judgments be in writing and signed by the judge. *Haywood Securities, Inc. v. Ehrlich*, 214 Ariz. 114, 149 P.3d 738 (2007). In construing the Rule, the focus is on the intent of the judge, and the phrase "signed by a judge" encompasses more than manual signatures. *Haywood Securities, Inc. v. Ehrlich*, 214 Ariz. 114, 149 P.3d 738 (2007). The defining characteristic of the requirement that a judgment be "signed" is that the document have affixed to it in some form the name of the issuing judge in a fashion that evidences an intent to authenticate it. *Haywood Securities, Inc. v. Ehrlich*, 214 Ariz. 114, 149 P.3d 738 (2007).

5. *Minute Entry as Judgment.* Before 1986, there was a difference of opinion between the two Divisions of the Court of Appeals as to whether a signed minute entry could constitute a judgment within the meaning of Rules 54(a) and 58(a). In *Stoneberg v. Northwood*, 121 Ariz. 230, 589 P.2d 473 (Ct. App. Div. 2 1978), Division II held that a signed minute entry was an appealable order. Subsequently, in *Johnson v. Nelson*, 128 Ariz. 587, 627 P.2d 1085 (Ct. App. Div. 1 1981) (rejected by, Focal Point, Inc. v. Court of Appeals of State of Ariz., Div. One, 149 Ariz. 128, 717 P.2d 432 (1986)), Division I held, to the contrary, that a judgment had to be a separate and discrete instrument from a signed minute entry. The Supreme Court, in *Focal Point, Inc. v. Court of Appeals of State of Ariz., Div. One*, 149 Ariz. 128, 717 P.2d 432 (1986), resolved the controversy by adopting Division II's view that a minute entry order that is signed by the Court and filed with the Clerk does constitute a formal judgment, and the time for filing post-judgment motions and/or prosecuting an appeal runs from the time of filing. The rule announced in *Focal Point* applies retroactively. *Mark Lighting Fixture Co., Inc. v. General Elec. Supply Co., a Div. of General Elec. Co.*, 155 Ariz. 27, 745

P.2d 85 (1987). As amended, Rule 58(e) now specifies that a judgment that is in the form of a signed minute entry is deemed entered on the date the Clerk affixes a file stamp on the minute entry.

Except in habeas corpus proceedings, an unsigned order or minute entry is not a judgment and is subject to being vacated or modified. *Phillips v. Adler*, 134 Ariz. 480, 657 P.2d 893 (Ct. App. Div. 2 1982); *Forquer v. Pinal County*, 22 Ariz. App. 266, 526 P.2d 1064 (Div. 1 1974). Accordingly, an unsigned minute entry is not an appealable order, and an appeal taken from it does not vest jurisdiction in the appellate court. *Hall Family Properties, Ltd. v. Gosnell Development Corp.*, 185 Ariz. 382, 916 P.2d 1098 (Ct. App. Div. 1 1995); *Rancho Pescado, Inc. v. Northwestern Mut. Life Ins. Co.*, 140 Ariz. 174, 680 P.2d 1235 (Ct. App. Div. 1 1984); *Spriggel v. Maricopa County*, 15 Ariz. App. 162, 487 P.2d 8 (Div. 1 1971); *Thomas v. Western Sav. & Loan Ass'n*, 6 Ariz. App. 511, 433 P.2d 1003 (1967); *Zoellner v. Zoellner*, 4 Ariz. App. 561, 422 P.2d 392 (1967); *In re Anonymous*, 4 Ariz. App. 170, 418 P.2d 416 (1966). An appeal taken from such a minute entry need not be dismissed as premature, however, where a formal judgment is subsequently entered and no party is prejudiced by the irregularity. *Barassi v. Matison*, 130 Ariz. 418, 636 P.2d 1200 (1981).

Rule 58(f) provides that a judgment in a *habeas corpus* proceeding need not be signed and is deemed final (and appealable) when it is entered in the minutes of the court.

6. *Notice of Entry of Judgments*. The usual fashion in which Judges of the Superior Court memorialize their rulings on motions and other proceedings is by minute entry. The subject of providing notice to the parties of rulings by the Court and of the entry of judgment was previously addressed in Rule 77(g). As part of the effort in 2000 to consolidate previously separate sets of procedural rules into either the Arizona Rules of Civil Procedure or the Rules of the Arizona Supreme Court, former Rule 77(g) was renumbered as Ariz.R.Civ.P. 58(e). Under Rule 58(e), the Clerk is directed to distribute copies of all minute entries to all parties to the action. Rule 58(e) also requires the Clerk to immediately distribute to the parties a notice of the entry of judgment.

A 2004 amendment to the Rule specifies that such distribution may be by U.S. mail, by electronic mail, or by leaving a copy in the proper attorney drop box. That amendment also provided that notice of the entry of judgment can be accomplished by the Clerk distributing (1) a specially designated notice form, (2) a minute entry, or (3) a conformed copy of the file stamped judgment.

A 1994 amendment to former Rule 77(g), which has been retained in new Rule 58(e), added a sentence which authorizes any party to serve notice of the entry of judgment as well. The date of entry of a judgment is the date the judgment is file-stamped by the Clerk of the Court. *Haroutunian v. Valueoptions, Inc.*, 218 Ariz. 541, 189 P.3d 1114 (Ct. App. Div. 2 2008); *Schoenfelder v. Arizona Bank*, 161 Ariz. 601, 780 P.2d 434, 8 U.C.C. Rep. Serv. 2d 771 (Ct. App. Div. 1 1989), opinion vacated in part on other grounds, 165 Ariz. 79, 796 P.2d 881, 12 U.C.C. Rep. Serv. 2d 469 (1990).

Rule 58(e) now specifies that a judgment that is in the form of a signed minute entry is deemed entered on the date the Clerk affxes a file stamp on the minute entry. The date of the entry of judgment is of critical significance because it typically commences the running of the time period for post-trial motions and/or for prosecuting appeals, and the date of entry will determine whether motions for post-verdict relief and/or the filing of a notice of appeal are timely. *City of Tucson v. Wondergem*, 4 Ariz. App. 291, 419 P.2d 552 (1966); *Haroutunian v. Valueoptions, Inc.*, 218 Ariz. 541, 189 P.3d 1114 (Ct. App. Div. 2 2008). By its very terms, Ariz.R.Civ.P. 6(e) does not apply and the applicable time period is not extended because the notice is transmitted by mail. Moreover, these time periods commence on the date of entry of judgment even though the notice of entry is not actually received. *Park v. Strick*, 137 Ariz. 100, 669 P.2d 78 (1983); *Old Pueblo Transit Co. v. Corp. Com'n of Ariz.*, 73 Ariz. 32, 236 P.2d 1018 (1951); *PNL Credit L.P. v. Southwest Pacific Investments, Inc.*, 179 Ariz. 259, 877 P.2d 832 (Ct. App. Div. 1 1994); *Lone Mountain Ranch, Inc. v. Dillingham Inv., Inc.*, 131 Ariz. 583, 643 P.2d 28 (Ct. App. Div. 2 1982).

As a consequence of the 1994 amendments to Rule 6(b) and to Rule 9(a), Ariz. R. Civ. App. P., the time periods for filing post-trial motions and/or notices of appeal may now be extended where a party entitled to receive notice of entry of judgment does not receive it within twenty-one (21) days of its entry and no party would be prejudiced by such an extension. The circumstances under which such an extension can be granted are discussed in Section 5 of the *Authors' Comments* under Rule 6. If a litigant cannot satisfy the time constraints in those amended Rules, such litigant may still apply under Rule 60(c)(6) to have the judgment vacated and re-entered in order to start the time for taking an appeal running anew. *Decola v. Freyer*, 198 Ariz. 28, 6 P.3d 333 (Ct. App. Div. 1 2000).

7. *Judgments Nunc Pro Tunc.* Rule 58(a) authorizes the Court to direct entry of a judgment *nunc pro tunc,* "in such circumstances and on such notice as justice may require. . . ." A judgment *nunc pro tunc* may be entered to correct a clerical error,

and to record the fact that a judgment was previously rendered but not entered of record due to an oversight. *Valley Nat. Bank of Arizona v. Meneghin*, 130 Ariz. 119, 634 P.2d 570 (1981); *Hash's Estate v. Henderson*, 109 Ariz. 174, 507 P.2d 99 (1973), decision modified on denial of reh'g, 109 Ariz. 258, 508 P.2d 334 (1973). Such a procedure has been frequently employed where a decree of dissolution or for legal separation has been made, but not formally entered, and one or both of the former spouses has remarried or is deceased. *Drahos v. Rens*, 149 Ariz. 248, 717 P.2d 927 (Ct. App. Div. 2 1985); *DeForest v. DeForest*, 143 Ariz. 627, 694 P.2d 1241 (Ct. App. Div. 1 1985); *Allen v. Allen*, 129 Ariz. 112, 628 P.2d 995 (Ct. App. Div. 1 1981). A *nunc pro tunc* order cannot be used to retroactively decrease an award of child support where the change is not justified by a prior clerical error or oversight. *Hatch v. Hatch*, 113 Ariz. 130, 547 P.2d 1044 (1976).

8. *Procedure for Securing Entry of Judgment.* In Arizona, formal judgments are generally prepared by the parties rather than the Court, and the procedures for securing settlement and approval are set forth in Rule 58(d). Under Rule 58(a), as amended in 1994, all proposed forms of judgment must be served upon all parties and counsel, even if the parties to be served would have no right to object to the form of judgment under Rule 58(d)(1). *State v. Empire American Bail Bonds, Inc.*, 191 Ariz. 218, 953 P.2d 1271 (Ct. App. Div. 1 1998).

The purpose of adding this requirement was to help prevent parties from losing their rights to appeal from the judgment eventually entered. *State v. Empire American Bail Bonds, Inc.*, 191 Ariz. 218, 953 P.2d 1271 (Ct. App. Div. 1 1998). This requirement also applies to bond forfeiture proceedings which, although such proceedings occur in the context of a criminal case, they remain civil in nature. *State v. Eazy Bail Bonds*, 224 Ariz. 227, 229 P.3d 239 (Ct. App. Div. 1 2010) (Bond forfeiture proceedings are civil in nature and, thus, the rules of civil procedure apply); *State v. Empire American Bail Bonds, Inc.*, 191 Ariz. 218, 953 P.2d 1271 (Ct. App. Div. 1 1998).

A judgment for money, for costs, or denying all relief, may be signed and entered by the Court upon presentation. All other judgments may not be signed until five (5) days after service of the proposed judgment upon opposing counsel, unless the approval of opposing counsel is endorsed upon the judgment or the waiting period is waived by the Court. The five-day provision does not apply to a proposed judgment which merely embodies revisions dictated by the Court's rulings on objections to a prior proposed judgment. *Rexing v. Rexing*, 11 Ariz. App. 285, 464 P.2d 356 (Div. 1 1970). Rule 58(f), adopted effective December 1, 1996, provides that the entry of judgment is not to be delayed, nor the time for appeal extended, in order to tax costs or to award fees.

The party against whom the judgment is to be entered may file objections to the proposed form of judgment during that five-day waiting period. If such an objection is filed, the party who submitted the proposed form of judgment then has five (5) days in which to respond, and the issue as to the proper form of judgment is then to be determined by the Court without oral argument, unless the Court directs it. If, on the basis of the objections, the Court makes revisions to the proposed form of judgment, that does not inaugurate yet another five-day waiting period. *Rexing v. Rexing*, 11 Ariz. App. 285, 464 P.2d 356 (Div. 1 1970).

The failure to honor the five-day waiting period for objections to be made is not in and of itself reversible error, unless prejudice to a party's interests is shown to result therefrom. *City of Phoenix v. Geyler*, 144 Ariz. 323, 697 P.2d 1073 (1985); *Dawe v. City of Scottsdale*, 119 Ariz. 486, 581 P.2d 1136 (1978); *Gutierrez v. Gutierrez*, 20 Ariz. App. 388, 513 P.2d 677 (Div. 2 1973); *Green Reservoir Flood Control Dist. v. Willmoth*, 15 Ariz. App. 406, 489 P.2d 69 (Div. 2 1971); *Rexing v. Rexing*, 11 Ariz. App. 285, 464 P.2d 356 (Div. 1 1970). *Foster v. Ames*, 5 Ariz. App. 1, 422 P.2d 731 (1967); *Patch v. Buros*, 2 Ariz. App. 585, 410 P.2d 703 (1966); *cf. also, Staffco, Inc. v. Maricopa Trading Co.*, 122 Ariz. 353, 595 P.2d 31 (1979). Rule 58(d) does not require that a proposed judgment be signed after five days even if no objection thereto is received. *Thomas v. Western Sav. & Loan Ass'n*, 6 Ariz. App. 511, 433 P.2d 1003 (1967).

An amendment to Rule 5 which became effective June 1, 1999 added Rule 5(j), which imposes some very specific and detailed requirements for the form of proposed orders and judgments. They are to be prepared as a separate document, and cannot be included as part of any motion, stipulation or other document that is filed. To the left of the center of the page, starting at line one, the submitting attorney must place, single spaced, that attorney's name, address, phone number, State Bar of Arizona attorney identification number, State Bar of Arizona law firm identification number (if applicable), and an identification of the party being represented by the submitting attorney.

The title of the Court is to be centered on line 6, again single-spaced. The title of the action or proceeding is to be below the title of the Court and to the left of the center of the page. Opposite the title, in the space to the right of the center of the page, the submitting party is to place the case number of the action or proceeding. Immediately below the case number, there is to be a brief description of the nature of the document. Finally, the Rule requires that there must be at least two lines of text on the signature page.

Proposed forms of orders and judgments are to be served upon all parties and counsel simultaneously with their submission to the Court for consideration. They are not to be filed or docketed until after the Judge has decided to sign, modify or reject them. At that point, an unsigned order or form of judgment may be filed, if necessary to preserve the record on an issue for appeal. Both Rule 58(a) and Rule 5(j) require that proposed forms of judgment be served upon all parties to the action. Rule 5(j) extends that requirement to proposed forms of orders as well. *See* the discussion in Section 14 of the *Authors' Comments* under Rule 5(j).

9. *Judgments Against Marital Communities*. A debt incurred during the marriage for the benefit of the marital community is presumed to be a community obligation, unless clear and convincing evidence exists to the contrary, and a judgment for such debt may be enforced against community property. *Arab Monetary Fund v. Hashim*, 219 Ariz. 108, 193 P.3d 802 (Ct. App. Div. 1 2008). A creditor must join both spouses before the creditor may obtain and enforce a judgment against the marital community property, even where the judgment is for a separate premarital debt of one of the spouses. *Heinig v. Hudman*, 177 Ariz. 66, 865 P.2d 110 (Ct. App. Div. 1 1993); *Flexmaster Aluminum Awning Co., Inc. v. Hirschberg*, 173 Ariz. 83, 839 P.2d 1128 (Ct. App. Div. 1 1992).

A premarital debt of one spouse can be recovered from community property, but only to the extent of the debtor spouse's contribution to the community. *Arab Monetary Fund v. Hashim*, 219 Ariz. 108, 193 P.3d 802 (Ct. App. Div. 1 2008). The other spouse's interest in the community property includes a due process right to litigate the premarital debt and the value of the debtor spouse's contribution to the marital community. *Heinig v. Hudman*, 177 Ariz. 66, 865 P.2d 110 (Ct. App. Div. 1 1993); *Flexmaster Aluminum Awning Co., Inc. v. Hirschberg*, 173 Ariz. 83, 839 P.2d 1128 (Ct. App. Div. 1 1992). Although a creditor cannot summarily convert a separate judgment into one against the community, an independent action may be brought to establish the liability of the spouse who was not, or could not have been, joined in the initial action. *Heinig v. Hudman*, 177 Ariz. 66, 865 P.2d 110 (Ct. App. Div. 1 1993).

A creditor, who secures a judgment against one of the marital partners *prior to* the marriage, however, for a separate premarital debt, may enforce that judgment against the community without bringing an independent action naming the nondebtor spouse. *CBM of Arizona, Inc. v. Sevier*, 184 Ariz. 503, 910 P.2d 654 (Ct. App. Div. 2 1996). Where such a judgment has been obtained prior to the marriage, both spouses are limited to those defenses which may be raised against the judgment, such as satisfaction or nonrenewal. Additionally, with respect to the community property which may be reached to satisfy the judgment, both spouses have the right to litigate the extent of the debtor spouse's contribution to the community. *CBM of Arizona, Inc. v. Sevier*, 184 Ariz. 503, 910 P.2d 654 (Ct. App. Div. 2 1996).

10. *Attorneys' Fees in Judgments.* All proposed forms of judgment submitted in cases in which attorneys' fees are sought by the prevailing party are to provide a space "for an award of attorneys' fees in an amount to be entered by the court." Rule 58(a). Amended Rule 58(g) provides that a judgment is normally not to be entered until claims for attorneys' fees have been resolved and are addressed in the judgment.

The sole exception is where the Court determines that the judgment on the merits should be certified for immediate appeal, under the provisions of Rule 54(b), before attorneys' fees issues are resolved. *National Broker Associates, Inc. v. Marlyn Nutraceuticals, Inc.*, 211 Ariz. 210, 119 P.3d 477 (Ct. App. Div. 1 2005). To facilitate use of that exception, Rule 54(b) has been amended by the inclusion of a new sentence, which states: "For purposes of this subsection, a claim for attorneys' fees may be considered a separate claim from the related judgment regarding the merits of a cause." The Comment accompanying this particular amendment specifically notes that it changes the result reached in *Trebilcox v. Brown & Bain, P.A.*, 133 Ariz. 588, 653 P.2d 45 (Ct. App. Div. 1 1982) (disavowed by, Western Technologies, Inc. v. Sverdrup & Parcel, Inc., 154 Ariz. 1, 739 P.2d 1318 (Ct. App. Div. 1 1986)) and (disapproved of by, Barmat v. John and Jane Doe Partners A-D, 155 Ariz. 519, 747 P.2d 1218 (1987)), construing the prior version of Rule 54(b).

The procedures for establishing entitlement to an award of attorneys' fees remain relatively unchanged. A motion seeking an award of attorneys' fees must still be made, but it must now be filed within twenty (20) days after the mailing by the Clerk of the Court of a decision on the merits, unless the trial court prescribes a longer period. Rule 54(g)(2). The motion may be supported by affidavit or exhibits or, at the trial court's discretion, by testimony. Rule 54(g)(3).

Opposing parties may respond to the motion and contest the award, and the Court may, in its discretion, conduct a hearing on the issue. The trial court also retains the discretion to refer issues relating to the value of the legal services rendered to a special master appointed under Rule 53. The provision specifying that these procedures are inapplicable where an award of attorneys' fees is sought as a sanction under an applicable statute or rule, and to causes in which fees may be recovered as an element of damages to be proven at trial, has been retained as new Rule 54(g)(4).

Neither the 1996 nor 1999 amendments purported to change the rule that an award of attorneys' fees may include charges for computerized legal research. *Matter of Liquidation of Azstar Cas. Co. Inc.*, 189 Ariz. 27, 938 P.2d 76 (Ct. App. Div. 1 1996).

It remains unclear whether, following adoption of the 1999 amendments, a motion to alter or amend a judgment that is entered but for some reason does not address a requested attorneys' fee award, will still be proper. Before the adoption of these various amendments, the appropriate vehicle for a post-judgment objection to the amount of attorneys' fees awarded was, and probably remains, either a motion for new trial or a motion to alter or amend the judgment. *PNL Credit L.P. v. Southwest Pacific Investments, Inc.*, 179 Ariz. 259, 877 P.2d 832 (Ct. App. Div. 1 1994). Such a motion, if timely filed, will operate to extend the time for filing a notice of appeal. *PNL Credit L.P. v. Southwest Pacific Investments, Inc.*, 179 Ariz. 259, 877 P.2d 832 (Ct. App. Div. 1 1994).

Before the adoption of Rule 54(g), it was held that, in awarding attorneys' fees under either A.R.S. § 12-341.01(C) or § 12-349 (amended 2013) or under Rule 11, the trial court was required to make findings of fact and conclusions of law, but that requirement could be waived by a failure to object. *Trantor v. Fredrikson*, 179 Ariz. 299, 878 P.2d 657 (1994); *State v. Richey*, 160 Ariz. 564, 774 P.2d 1354 (1989); *Bennett v. Baxter Group, Inc.*, 223 Ariz. 414, 224 P.3d 230 (Ct. App. Div. 2 2010); *Johnson v. Mohave County*, 206 Ariz. 330, 78 P.3d 1051 (Ct. App. Div. 1 2003). That requirement was in effect carried forward in the version of Rule 54(g) adopted in 1996, and appears to have survived the 1999 amendments to that Rule. *Bennett v. Baxter Group, Inc.*, 223 Ariz. 414, 224 P.3d 230 (Ct. App. Div. 2 2010); *Johnson v. Mohave County*, 206 Ariz. 330, 78 P.3d 1051 (Ct. App. Div. 1 2003). *See also*, A.R.S. § 12-350.

A trial court's decision to deny a request for an award of attorneys' fees will be reviewed on appeal only for an abuse of discretion, and will be sustained if there is any reasonable basis for upholding it. *Radkowsky v. Provident Life & Acc. Ins. Co.*, 196 Ariz. 110, 993 P.2d 1074 (Ct. App. Div. 1 1999), as amended, (June 29, 1999).

11. *Interest; Prejudgment Interest.* Judgments bear interest at a rate specified by statute from the date of entry until satisfied. A.R.S. § 44-1201. In Arizona, however, prejudgment interest is a matter of right on a liquidated claim, regardless of whether it sounds in contract or in tort. *Alta Vista Plaza, Ltd. v. Insulation Specialists Co., Inc.*, 186 Ariz. 81, 919 P.2d 176 (Ct. App. Div. 2 1995), as corrected on reconsideration, (Nov. 30, 1995); *Canal Ins. Co. v. Pizer*, 183 Ariz. 162, 901 P.2d 1192 (Ct. App. Div. 1

1995). That holds true even where the award of prejudgment interest will increase the award against the surety on a conservator's bond above the penal sum of that bond. *In re Guardianship of Pacheco*, 219 Ariz. 421, 199 P.3d 676 (Ct. App. Div. 2 2008). Prejudgment interest, however, does not run on an administrative civil penalty, unless the relevant statute so provides, because it is not a loan, indebtedness, judgment or other obligation within the meaning of A.R.S. § 44-1201. *State ex rel. Arizona Structural Pest Control Com'n v. Taylor*, 223 Ariz. 486, 224 P.3d 983 (Ct. App. Div. 1 2010).

A claim is liquidated if the evidence furnishes data which, if believed, makes it possible to compute the amount due with exactness, without reliance upon opinion or discretion. *Scottsdale Ins. Co. v. Cendejas*, 220 Ariz. 281, 205 P.3d 1128 (Ct. App. Div. 1 2009); *Alta Vista Plaza, Ltd. v. Insulation Specialists Co., Inc.*, 186 Ariz. 81, 919 P.2d 176 (Ct. App. Div. 2 1995), as corrected on reconsideration, (Nov. 30, 1995); *Hyatt Regency Phoenix Hotel Co. v. Winston & Strawn*, 184 Ariz. 120, 907 P.2d 506 (Ct. App. Div. 1 1995); *Canal Ins. Co. v. Pizer*, 183 Ariz. 162, 901 P.2d 1192 (Ct. App. Div. 1 1995); *Patterson v. Bianco*, 167 Ariz. 249, 805 P.2d 1070 (Ct. App. Div. 2 1991); *Lee Development Co. v. Papp*, 166 Ariz. 471, 803 P.2d 464 (Ct. App. Div. 2 1990). The prevailing party in such a case is entitled to prejudgment interest even if interest is not specifically requested in the complaint. A good faith dispute as to liability does not preclude an award of prejudgment interest on a liquidated claim. *Hyatt Regency Phoenix Hotel Co. v. Winston & Strawn*, 184 Ariz. 120, 907 P.2d 506 (Ct. App. Div. 1 1995); *Employers Mut. Cas. Co. v. McKeon*, 170 Ariz. 75, 821 P.2d 766 (Ct. App. Div. 1 1991).

Similarly, the fact that the amount awarded differs from the amount claimed does not necessarily preclude an award of prejudgment interest. *Paul R. Peterson Const., Inc. v. Arizona State Carpenters Health and Welfare Trust Fund*, 179 Ariz. 474, 880 P.2d 694, 17 Employee Benefits Cas. (BNA) 2624 (Ct. App. Div. 1 1994). All that is required is for the plaintiff to provide a basis for a precise calculation that would make the amount of damages readily ascertainable by reference to an agreement between the parties or through simple computation. *Paul R. Peterson Const., Inc. v. Arizona State Carpenters Health and Welfare Trust Fund*, 179 Ariz. 474, 880 P.2d 694, 17 Employee Benefits Cas. (BNA) 2624 (Ct. App. Div. 1 1994).

In Arizona, prejudgment interest generally accrues from the date of demand, not from the date of the loss. *Scottsdale Ins. Co. v. Cendejas*, 220 Ariz. 281, 205 P.3d 1128 (Ct. App. Div. 1 2009) (Prejudgment interest on a liquidated claim accrues from the date of demand of a sum certain, but the amount of the claim must be capable of exact calculation on the date of accrual); *Alta*

Vista Plaza, Ltd. v. Insulation Specialists Co., Inc., 186 Ariz. 81, 919 P.2d 176 (Ct. App. Div. 2 1995), as corrected on reconsideration, (Nov. 30, 1995). A demand can be made by demanding payment or by the filing of a complaint. *Alta Vista Plaza, Ltd. v. Insulation Specialists Co., Inc.*, 186 Ariz. 81, 919 P.2d 176 (Ct. App. Div. 2 1995), as corrected on reconsideration, (Nov. 30, 1995) (disallowing prejudgment interest from date of demand letter because demand letter failed to provide sufficient information on amount owed); *Paul R. Peterson Const., Inc. v. Arizona State Carpenters Health and Welfare Trust Fund*, 179 Ariz. 474, 880 P.2d 694, 17 Employee Benefits Cas. (BNA) 2624 (Ct. App. Div. 1 1994).

12. *Remittitur Procedure.* The trial court has the initial responsibility for reducing an excessive verdict, and its determination in that regard will generally not be disturbed except for an abuse of discretion. *Torres for and on Behalf of Torres v. North American Van Lines, Inc.*, 135 Ariz. 35, 658 P.2d 835 (Ct. App. Div. 2 1982); *Arizona Container Corp. v. Consolidated Freightways*, 22 Ariz. App. 11, 522 P.2d 772 (Div. 2 1974). Even if a remittitur is ordered, the defendant on appeal may still challenge the entire verdict as being the result of passion and prejudice. *Sequoia Mfg. Co., Inc. v. Halec Const. Co., Inc.*, 117 Ariz. 11, 570 P.2d 782 (Ct. App. Div. 1 1977). Remittitur procedure is discussed more extensively in Section 9 of the *Authors' Comments* under Rule 59.

13. *Special Writs.* Rule 58(c) speaks of the enforcement of judgments for personal property by a special writ for seizure and delivery of the property, a remedy analogous to replevin. In Arizona, replevin is a "provisional remedy," which may be exercised before actual judgment. The plaintiff seeking the remedy of replevin must comply both with the general statutory requirements for "provisional remedies," A.R.S. §§ 12-1301 *et seq.*, and the specific statutory provisions applicable to replevin actions, A.R.S. §§ 12-1301, *et seq.*

A writ of replevin cannot be executed unless and until the plaintiff posts a bond for not less than double the value of the property to be seized. A.R.S. § 12-1302. The defendant may retain the property, and avoid seizure thereof, by posting a bond of similar amount. A.R.S. § 12-1304. A more extensive discussion of replevin procedures can be found in Sections 11–13 of the *Authors' Comments* under Rule 64.

Rule 59. New trial; amendment of judgment

(a) Procedure; Grounds. A verdict, decision or judgment may be vacated and a new trial granted on motion of the aggrieved party for any of the following causes materially affecting that party's rights:

1. Irregularity in the proceedings of the court, referee, jury or prevailing party, or any order or abuse of discretion, whereby the moving party was deprived of a fair trial.

2. Misconduct of the jury or prevailing party.

3. Accident or surprise which could not have been prevented by ordinary prudence.

4. Material evidence, newly discovered, which with reasonable diligence could not have been discovered and produced at the trial.

5. Excessive or insufficient damages.

6. Error in the admission or rejection of evidence, error in the charge to the jury, or in refusing instructions requested, or other errors of law occurring at the trial or during the progress of the action.

7. That the verdict is the result of passion or prejudice.

8. That the verdict, decision, findings of fact, or judgment is not justified by the evidence or is contrary to law.

Amended Sept. 15, 1987, effective Nov. 15, 1987.

(b) Scope. A new trial may be granted to all or any of the parties and on all or part of the issues in an action in which there has been a trial by jury, for any of the reasons for which new trials are authorized by law or rule of court. On a motion for a new trial in an action tried without a jury, the court may open the judgment if one has been entered, take additional testimony, amend findings of fact and conclusions of law or make new findings and conclusions, and direct the entry of a new judgment.

(c) Contents of Motion; Amendment; Rulings Reviewable.

1. The motion for new trial shall be in writing, shall specify generally the grounds upon which the motion is based, and may be amended at any time before it is ruled upon by the court.

2. Upon the general ground that the court erred in admitting or rejecting evidence, the court shall review all rulings during the trial upon objections to evidence.

3. Upon the general ground that the court erred in charging the jury and in refusing instructions requested, the court shall

review the charge and the rulings refusing an instruction requested.

4. Upon the general ground that the verdict, decision, findings of fact, or judgment is not justified by the evidence, the court shall review the sufficiency of the evidence.

(d) Time for Motion. A motion for new trial shall be filed not later than 15 days after entry of the judgment.

Amended July 14, 1961, effective Nov. 1, 1961; July 23, 1976, effective Oct. 1, 1976.

(e) [Deleted effective November 1, 1967].

(f) Time for Serving Affidavits. When a motion for new trial is based upon affidavits they shall be served with the motion. The opposing party has ten days after such service within which to serve opposing affidavits, which period may be extended for an additional period not exceeding twenty days either by the court for good cause shown or by the parties by written stipulation. The court may permit reply affidavits.

(g) On Initiative of Court. Not later than 15 days after entry of judgment the court of its own initiative may order a new trial for any reason for which it might have granted a new trial on motion of a party. After giving the parties notice and an opportunity to be heard on the matter, the court may grant a motion for a new trial, timely served, for a reason not stated in the motion. In either case, the court shall specify in the order the grounds therefor.

(h) Questions to Be Considered in New Trial. A new trial, if granted, shall be only a new trial of the question or questions with respect to which the verdict or decision is found erroneous, if separable. If a new trial is ordered because the damages are excessive or inadequate and granted solely for that reason, the verdict shall be set aside only in respect of the damages, and shall stand in all other respects.

(i) Motion on Ground of Excessive or Inadequate Damages.

1. When a motion for new trial is made upon the ground that the damages awarded are either excessive or insufficient, the court may grant the new trial conditionally upon the filing within a fixed period of time of a statement by the party adversely affected by reduction or increase of damages accepting that amount of damages which the court shall designate. If such a statement is filed within the prescribed time, the motion for new trial shall be regarded as denied as of the date of such filing. If no statement is filed, the motion for new trial shall be regarded as granted as of the date of the expiration of the time period within which a statement could have been filed. No fur-

ther written order shall be required to make an order granting or denying the new trial final. If the conditional order of the court requires a reduction of or increase in damages, then the new trial will be granted in respect of the damages only and the verdict shall stand in all other respects.

2. If a statement of acceptance is filed by the party adversely affected by reduction or increase of damages, and the other party thereafter perfects an appeal, the party filing such statement may nevertheless cross-appeal and the perfecting of a cross-appeal shall be deemed to revoke the consent to the decrease or increase in damages.

(j) After Service By Publication.

1. When judgment has been rendered on service by publication, and the defendant has not appeared, a new trial may be granted upon application of the defendant for good cause shown by affidavit, made within one year after rendition of the judgment.

2. Execution of the judgment shall not be stayed unless the defendant gives bond, approved by the clerk, in double the amount of the judgment or value of the property adjudged, payable to the plaintiff in the judgment, conditioned that the party will prosecute the application for new trial to effect, and will satisfy such judgment as may be rendered by the court should its decision be against the defendant.

(k) Number of New Trials. Not more than two new trials shall be granted to either party in the same action, except when the jury has been guilty of some misconduct or has erred in matters of law.

(*l*) Motion to Alter or Amend a Judgment. A motion to alter or amend the judgment shall be filed not later than 15 days after entry of judgment.

(m) Specification of Grounds of New Trial in Order. No order granting a new trial shall be made and entered unless the order specifies with particularity the ground or grounds on which the new trial is granted.

STATE BAR COMMITTEE NOTES

1961 Amendment

[Rule 59(d)] The time within which to move for relief on the ground of newly discovered evidence will be covered by adding a proposed amendment to Rule 60(c). The State Bar Committee recommends this amendment to Rule 59(d) only if Rule 60(c) is amended. [Rule 60(c) was amended in 1961.]

1966 Amendment

[Rule 59(g)] This rule is taken from Federal Rule 59(d).

By narrow interpretation of Rule 59, it has been held that the trial court is without power to grant a motion for a new trial, timely served, by an order made more than 10 days after entry of judgment, based upon a ground not stated in the motion but perceived and relied on by the trial court sua sponte.

The result is undesirable. Just as the court has power under the present text of Rule 59 to grant a new trial of its own initiative within the 10 [now 15] days, so it should have power, when an effective new trial motion has been made and is pending, to decide it on grounds though meritorious by the court although not advanced in the motion. The second sentence added by amendment to Rule 59(g) confirms the court's power in the latter situation, with provision that the parties be afforded a hearing before the power is exercised.

The importance of setting forth the grounds of a new trial in any such order under Rule 59 is established in *Yoo Thun Lim v. Crespin*, 100 Ariz. 80, 411 P.2d 809 (1966), holding inadequate a grant of such a motion which merely refers to the grounds set forth in the motion without specifying them.

1967 Amendment

[Rule 59(i)] 1. Existing Rule 59(i) governs remittitur practice on motion for new trial. The existing rule provides the remittitur orders shall be so drafted that if the condition is not accepted, "a new trial *will be* granted" or "*will be* denied." The practical effect of this language is to require that the orders be in the future tense. That is to say, a preliminary order is issued calling for the remittitur (or the additur), and then some later order must be entered actually disposing of the new trial motion. The rule has been so construed. *Harris v. Howard P. Foley Co.*, 2 Ariz. App. 389, 409 P.2d 309 (1965).

The existing rule clearly does seem to contemplate future tense orders. This form of the order is regarded as highly undesirable, both because it requires that there be a second written instrument executed by the court and because it invites uncertainty as to when the order becomes effective. The Committee adopts the view of the California Court in *Chapman v. Municipal Court, City of Los Angeles, Los Angeles County*, 91 Cal. App. 2d 689, 205 P.2d 712, 715 (2d Dist. 1949).

When an order is granted in the present tense, it is granted and nothing further is required; upon failure to remit the order becomes absolute; *Ex parte Smith*, 228 Ala. 232, 153 So. 152, 153 (1934) and numerous citations; 66 C.J.S. 529; 46 C.J.S. 433, n. 83. But when the order is granted with a future tense, the question does arise as to whether some additional order is needed. *Jennings v. Superior Court in and for Los Angeles County*, 134 Cal. App. 300, 25 P.2d 246 (2d Dist. 1933).

Under the revised rule, a proper remittitur or additur order will provide that a motion for new trial is granted unless the designated condition is met within the time provided. No second order will be required. The order will become final either upon the filing of the remittitur or additur statement, or upon the expiration of the time within which to do so, with no further action required.

2. The previous rule provided that in case of a new trial because of rejection of a remittitur, the new trial would be only on the issue of damages; but it had no equivalent provision for additur. The amendment treats the two the same in this regard.

3. In *State ex rel. Herman v. Tucson Title Ins. Co.*, 101 Ariz. 415, 420 P.2d 286 (1966), the Supreme Court held that under the existing Rule 59(i) a consent to a remittitur was binding, notwithstanding a subsequent appeal by the moving party. Thus, it was held that the consent to the remittitur estopped the party in whose favor the judgment had been entered from taking a cross-appeal from the order. In many cases one of the primary reasons for consenting to a remittitur is the hope of thereby ending the litigation and avoiding an appeal by the moving party. If, despite the opposing party's consent to the remittitur, the moving party nevertheless perfects an appeal, the party consenting to the remittitur should have the right to cross-appeal from the order.

AUTHORS' COMMENTS

Analysis

1. *Scope and Purpose of Rule.* Rule 59, which delineates the authority of the trial court to direct a new trial of a matter, is an all-purpose vehicle which allows the Court to review and correct any errors in its proceedings which have had a material effect on the outcome and to insure that substantial justice has been done before an appeal becomes necessary. *King v. Superior Court*, 138 Ariz. 147, 673 P.2d 787 (1983); *Maganas v. Northroup*, 112 Ariz. 46, 537 P.2d 595 (1975).

2. *Comparison With Federal Rule.* There are significant differences between ARCP 59 and FRCP 59. The Federal Rule does not contain provisions that correspond to ARCP 59(a), (c), (h), (i), (j), (k), and (m).

ARCP 59(b) is generally similar, but not identical, to FRCP 59(a). And, ARCP 59(d), (f), (g), and (l) are substantially identical to FRCP 59(b), (c), (d), and (e), respectively.

The time period prescribed in the Arizona Rule, however, for the filing of a motion for new trial [ARCP 59(d)], for the filing of a motion to alter or amend a judgment [ARCP 59(l), and for the Court to grant a new trial on its own initiative [ARCP 59(g)] is no later than 15 days after entry of judgment. As a consequence of the 2009 amendments, the corresponding time period prescribed in the Federal Rule is no later than 28 days following entry of judgment.

Before FRCP 59 was amended in 2009, the rule provided a 10-day time period for filing Rule 59 post-judgment motions. The commentary to the 2009 Amendment to the FRCP 59 states the 10-day time period was expanded to 28 days because experience had shown that, in many cases, it was not possible to prepare a satisfactory post-judgment motion in the 10 days then provided. ARCP 59 has not been amended to similarly expand the time period for filing a Rule 59 post-judgment motion, which remains at 15 days.

The time period prescribed by ARCP 59(f) for serving affidavits also differs from its Federal counterpart. ARCP 59(f) provides that if a motion for new trial is based on affidavits, the opposing party must serve opposing affidavits within 10 days after service, or 20 days if extended by the court or written stipulation of the parties. FRCP 59(f) provides such opposing affidavits must be filed within 14 days after service.

In 2007, the language of FRCP 59 was amended as part of the general restyling of the Federal Rules of Civil Procedure to make the Federal Rules more easily understood and to make style and terminology consistent throughout the Federal Rules of Civil Procedure. Those stylistic modifications have not been incorporated into ARCP 59.

3. *Motions for New Trial Generally.* A request for new trial usually emanates from the party or parties dissatisfied with the result, and is frequently brought in combination with the renewal of a motion for judgment as a matter of law (formerly a motion for judgment notwithstanding the verdict) under Rule 50(b). Unlike the motion for judgment notwithstanding the verdict, however, a motion for new trial does not require that any prior foundational motion, such as a motion for mistrial or motion for judgment as a matter of law (formerly a motion for directed verdict), have been made. *Smith v. Moroney*, 79 Ariz. 35, 282 P.2d 470 (1955); *Miller v. Palmer*, 143 Ariz. 84, 691 P.2d 1112 (Ct. App. Div. 1 1984); *Pierce v. Lopez*, 16 Ariz. App. 54, 490 P.2d 1182 (Div. 2 1971) (disapproved of on other grounds by, Ontiveros v. Borak, 136 Ariz. 500, 667 P.2d 200 (1983)).

In fact, a "motion for new trial" is almost a misnomer, as Rule 59 requires neither a motion nor that there have been a trial. A motion for new trial is the proper means by which to challenge an order granting summary judgment. *Farmers Ins. Co. of Arizona v. Vagnozzi*, 132 Ariz. 219, 644 P.2d 1305 (1982); *Engineers v. Sharpe*, 117 Ariz. 413, 573 P.2d 487 (1977); *Maganas v. Northroup*, 112 Ariz. 46, 537 P.2d 595 (1975); *Tripati v. Forwith*, 223 Ariz. 81, 219 P.3d 291 (Ct. App. Div. 1 2009); *Maria v. Najera*, 222 Ariz. 306, 214 P.3d 394 (Ct. App. Div. 1 2009); *Ulibarri v.*

Gerstenberger, 178 Ariz. 151, 871 P.2d 698 (Ct. App. Div. 1 1993) (rejected by, Logerquist v. Danforth, 188 Ariz. 16, 932 P.2d 281 (Ct. App. Div. 2 1996)); *Matter of Estate of Craig*, 174 Ariz. 228, 848 P.2d 313 (Ct. App. Div. 1 1992); *Union Rock & Materials Corp. v. Scottsdale Conference Center*, 139 Ariz. 268, 678 P.2d 453 (Ct. App. Div. 1 1983); or, against a dismissal for failure to comply with a discovery order. *J-R Const. Co. v. Paddock Pool Const. Co.*, 128 Ariz. 343, 625 P.2d 932 (Ct. App. Div. 1 1981).

Under Rule 59(g), the trial court has explicit authority to order a new trial on its own initiative. *Johnson v. Elliott*, 112 Ariz. 57, 537 P.2d 927 (1975). Under Rule 59(h), a new trial should be limited to the question or questions which were affected by the grounds found to warrant a new trial, if they are separable.

The proper method for raising an alleged violation of the disclosure requirements of Ariz.R.Civ.P. 26.1 that is not discovered until *after* the entry of judgment is to file a Rule 59 post-trial motion for new trial or a Rule 60 motion for relief from the judgment. *In re Estate of Travers*, 192 Ariz. 333, 965 P.2d 67 (Ct. App. Div. 1 1998). A motion for new trial must be made no later than fifteen (15) days after the judgment is entered.

A violation of Rule 26.1 by intentional non-disclosure may also entitle a party to relief under Rule 60(c)(3), and such a motion must be filed within six (6) months after the judgment becomes final. *In re Estate of Travers*, 192 Ariz. 333, 965 P.2d 67 (Ct. App. Div. 1 1998) (recognizing Rule 6(b) expressly bars the extension of time for filing a Rule 60(c) motion). *See also*, *Andrew R. v. Arizona Dept. of Economic Sec.*, 223 Ariz. 453, 224 P.3d 950 (Ct. App. Div. 1 2010) (trial court lacked authority to grant Rule 60(c)(3) motion for relief from paternity judgment filed more than six months after entry of judgment).

The denial of a motion for new trial is an appealable order. An order granting a new trial is also appealable pursuant to A.R.S. § 12-2101(F). *Davis v. Davis*, 195 Ariz. 158, 985 P.2d 643 (Ct. App. Div. 1 1999). A.R.S. § 12-2101(F), however, does not authorize an appeal from an order denying a motion for new trial which was directed to a partial summary judgment which only disposed of three of plaintiff's claims and left a counterclaim undecided. *Maria v. Najera*, 222 Ariz. 306, 214 P.3d 394 (Ct. App. Div. 1 2009). An order granting a mistrial prior to judgment being entered, however, is not the grant of a new trial and is not appealable. *Davis v. Davis*, 195 Ariz. 158, 985 P.2d 643 (Ct. App. Div. 1 1999). An appeal from the denial of a motion for new trial may only be taken from a signed order denying the motion, and the time for appeal does not commence to run until that occurs. *Tripati v. Forwith*, 223 Ariz. 81, 219 P.3d 291 (Ct. App. Div. 1 2009).

The granting of a motion for new trial has the effect of vacating a judgment previously entered. *Nielson v. Patterson*, 204 Ariz. 530, 65 P.3d 911 (2003). Accordingly, when the party whose verdict and judgment have in effect been set aside appeals from the award of a new trial, it is not necessary for the party who secured a new trial to file a protective cross-appeal to preserve the right to challenge the verdict and judgment in the event the new trial order is reversed on appeal. *Nielson v. Patterson*, 204 Ariz. 530, 65 P.3d 911 (2003). If the new trial order is reversed on appeal, the judgment would be reinstated and the party against whom the judgment was reinstated can appeal at that point. *Nielson v. Patterson*, 204 Ariz. 530, 65 P.3d 911 (2003).

4. *Grounds for New Trial Generally.* Rule 59(a) specifies eight separate grounds for requesting or ordering a new trial: (1) irregularity in the proceedings, (2) misconduct of jury or the prevailing party, (3) accident or surprise at trial, (4) newly discovered evidence, (5) excessive or insufficient damages, (6) errors in evidentiary rulings or instructing the jury, (7) a verdict resulting from passion or prejudice, and (8) that the verdict or decision is not justified by the evidence. It is not uncommon for a new trial motion to cite several of these as grounds for relief.

5. *Misconduct of Jury or Prevailing Party.* Where there has been misconduct of the prevailing party or that party's counsel, a new trial is warranted if the right to a fair trial has been materially affected. *Colfer v. Ballantyne*, 89 Ariz. 408, 363 P.2d 588 (1961); *Miller v. Palmer*, 143 Ariz. 84, 691 P.2d 1112 (Ct. App. Div. 1 1984). A new trial should not be granted as a disciplinary measure, but only where the trial court is satisfied that the misconduct probably affected the verdict. *Brethauer v. General Motors Corp.*, 221 Ariz. 192, 211 P.3d 1176 (Ct. App. Div. 1 2009); *Bledsoe v. Salt River Valley Water Users' Ass'n*, 179 Ariz. 469, 880 P.2d 689 (Ct. App. Div. 2 1994); *Walter v. Simmons*, 169 Ariz. 229, 818 P.2d 214 (Ct. App. Div. 1 1991); *Dykeman By and Through Dykeman v. Engelbrecht*, 166 Ariz. 398, 803 P.2d 119 (Ct. App. Div. 1 1990); *Maxwell v. Aetna Life Ins. Co.*, 143 Ariz. 205, 693 P.2d 348 (Ct. App. Div. 1 1984); *Ring v. Taylor*, 141 Ariz. 56, 685 P.2d 121 (Ct. App. Div. 1 1984).

The fact that the misconduct may have had a tendency to influence the result is not sufficient. *Grant v. Arizona Public Service Co.*, 133 Ariz. 434, 652 P.2d 507 (1982). If the misconduct is serious, however, the trial judge should resolve any doubt as to whether prejudice resulted in favor of the aggrieved party. *Leavy v. Parsell*, 188 Ariz. 69, 932 P.2d 1340 (1997).

An appellate court will defer to the trial court's ruling on alleged misconduct of counsel unless it is clear that the trial court abused its discretion.

The trial court should take into account whether the misconduct was flagrant or intentional, whether it was calculated to create sympathy or bias, and whether it was successful in doing so. *Sanchez v. Stremel*, 95 Ariz. 392, 391 P.2d 557, 10 A.L.R.3d 1324 (1964); *Bledsoe v. Salt River Valley Water Users' Ass'n*, 179 Ariz. 469, 880 P.2d 689 (Ct. App. Div. 2 1994); *Tanner v. Pacioni*, 3 Ariz. App. 297, 413 P.2d 863 (1966). Where the misconduct occurs during the argument of counsel, the objection may be waived if not made at the time the misconduct occurs. *Kelch v. Courson*, 103 Ariz. 576, 447 P.2d 550 (1968) (overruled on other grounds by, Heimke v. Munoz, 106 Ariz. 26, 470 P.2d 107 (1970)). *Cf. also, Grant v. Arizona Public Service Co.*, 133 Ariz. 434, 652 P.2d 507 (1982). Prompt objection to improper closing argument permits the trial court to impose restraints upon counsel once it appears that argument is proceeding past legitimate boundaries. *Monaco v. HealthPartners of Southern Arizona*, 196 Ariz. 299, 995 P.2d 735 (Ct. App. Div. 2 1999). Generally, however, it is sufficient if the objection is raised before the case is submitted to the jury. *Copeland v. City of Yuma*, 160 Ariz. 307, 772 P.2d 1160 (Ct. App. Div. 1 1989); *Liberatore v. Thompson*, 157 Ariz. 612, 760 P.2d 612 (Ct. App. Div. 1 1988).

It is improper to permit counsel to use a videotaped computer simulation of an accident in rebuttal closing argument, where the proper foundation for the simulation was not established at trial and there has been no opportunity for cross-examination of it. *Bledsoe v. Salt River Valley Water Users' Ass'n*, 179 Ariz. 469, 880 P.2d 689 (Ct. App. Div. 2 1994). Such a simulation is not simply another type of pedagogical device, such as a chart or diagram, which counsel may utilize in argument. *Bledsoe v. Salt River Valley Water Users' Ass'n*, 179 Ariz. 469, 880 P.2d 689 (Ct. App. Div. 2 1994).

An allegation of jury misconduct, such as the introduction and consideration of extraneous information, must be supported by sworn affidavits to warrant ordering a new trial. *Kirby v. Rosell*, 133 Ariz. 42, 648 P.2d 1048 (Ct. App. Div. 1 1982); *Foster v. Camelback Management Co.*, 132 Ariz. 462, 646 P.2d 893 (Ct. App. Div. 2 1982); *but cf., Wasko v. Frankel*, 116 Ariz. 288, 569 P.2d 230 (1977) (abrogated by, State v. Hickman, 205 Ariz. 192, 68 P.3d 418 (2003)).

Whether a juror's misconduct warrants a new trial is a decision committed to the discretion of the trial court. *Elliott v. Videan*, 164 Ariz. 113, 791 P.2d 639 (Ct. App. Div. 2 1989). There are two separate standards to govern that decision. In cases of juror misconduct not involving the consideration of extraneous information, the moving party must make an affirmative showing that prejudice probably resulted from the misconduct. *Dunn v. Maras*, 182 Ariz. 412, 897 P.2d 714 (Ct. App. Div. 1 1995). Where the juror misconduct involves the submission and consideration of extraneous information, however, the prohibition upon juror testimony makes it impossible to prove the extent of any prejudice, and the moving party consequently need only show a reasonable possibility that prejudice resulted. *Dunn v. Maras*, 182 Ariz. 412, 897 P.2d 714 (Ct. App. Div. 1 1995). Prejudice resulting from an improper communication to the jury can almost be "conclusively presumed" when the nature of the violation of the prohibition on *ex parte* communications with the jury deprives the Court of the ability to determine the extent of the actual prejudice. *Perez By and Through Perez v. Community Hosp. of Chandler, Inc.*, 187 Ariz. 355, 929 P.2d 1303 (1997) ("prejudice can be conclusively presumed when nature of error deprives court of ability to determine extent of prejudice.").

In general, testimony from a juror about any matter discussed in the sanctity of the jury room during deliberations is inadmissible to impeach a verdict. A juror's testimony is admissible to show an error in the judgment as not conforming to the jury's findings, improper acts by third parties or failure by the juror submitting the affidavit to disclose bias and prejudice upon *voir dire* inquiry, but not to show another juror's failure to disclose bias and prejudice. *Richtmyre v. State*, 175 Ariz. 489, 858 P.2d 322 (Ct. App. Div. 1 1993); *Brooks v. Zahn*, 170 Ariz. 545, 826 P.2d 1171 (Ct. App. Div. 1 1991).

To obtain a new trial based on a juror's failure to answer honestly a question on *voir dire,* a party must show that misconduct occurred and that it resulted in probable prejudice. *Richtmyre v. State*, 175 Ariz. 489, 858 P.2d 322 (Ct. App. Div. 1 1993); *Brooks v. Zahn*, 170 Ariz. 545, 826 P.2d 1171 (Ct. App. Div. 1 1991). The denial of a motion for a new trial based on claimed juror misconduct will not be set aside absent a clear abuse of discretion. *Richtmyre v. State*, 175 Ariz. 489, 858 P.2d 322 (Ct. App. Div. 1 1993); *Brooks v. Zahn*, 170 Ariz. 545, 826 P.2d 1171 (Ct. App. Div. 1 1991).

6. *Accident, Surprise, Newly Discovered Evidence.* To sustain a motion for new trial, the accident or surprise must derive from an incident or event that could not have been discovered or anticipated and rectified before trial. *Pacht v. Morris*, 107 Ariz. 392, 489 P.2d 29 (1971); *Board of Trustees Eloy Elementary School Dist. v. McEwen*, 6 Ariz. App. 148, 430 P.2d 727 (1967). Relief should be granted only where the verdict was probably influenced by the incident. *Simpson v. Heiderich*, 4 Ariz. App. 232, 419 P.2d 362 (1966).

In a similar vein, the claimed newly discovered evidence must have been in existence at the time of trial, not discoverable through the exercise of due diligence, and of such a character that it would probably change the result. *Black v. Black*, 114 Ariz. 282, 560 P.2d 800 (1977); *Matos v. City of Phoenix*, 176 Ariz. 125, 859 P.2d 748, 2 A.D. Cas. (BNA) 1458 (Ct. App. Div. 2 1993); *Boatman v. Samaritan Health Services, Inc.*, 168 Ariz. 207, 812 P.2d 1025 (Ct. App. Div. 2 1990); *Peabody Coal Co. v. State*, 158 Ariz. 190, 761 P.2d 1094 (Ct. App. Div. 1 1988); *Wendling v. Southwest Sav. and Loan Ass'n*, 143 Ariz. 599, 694 P.2d 1213 (Ct. App. Div. 1 1984); *Rustin v. Cook*, 143 Ariz. 486, 694 P.2d 316 (Ct. App. Div. 2 1984); *Lake Havasu Resort, Inc. v. Commercial Loan Ins. Corp.*, 139 Ariz. 369, 678 P.2d 950 (Ct. App. Div. 1 1983); *Roberts v. Morgensen Motors*, 135 Ariz. 162, 659 P.2d 1307, 35 U.C.C. Rep. Serv. 836 (Ct. App. Div. 1 1982); *Ghyselinck v. Buchanan*, 13 Ariz. App. 125, 474 P.2d 844 (Div. 1 1970). A new trial should not be granted if the newly discovered evidence is merely cumulative of evidence that was available and offered, or is material only to a collateral issue. *Schmerfeld v. Hendry*, 74 Ariz. 159, 245 P.2d 420 (1952) (overruled on other grounds by, Rosen v. Knaub, 175 Ariz. 329, 857 P.2d 381, 24 A.L.R.5th 909 (1993)); *Ohio Farmers Ins. Co. v. Norman*, 122 Ariz. 330, 594 P.2d 1026 (Ct. App. Div. 2 1979); *State v. Long*, 12 Ariz. App. 170, 468 P.2d 621 (Div. 1 1970); *Horne v. Timbanard*, 6 Ariz. App. 518, 434 P.2d 520 (1967).

An application for new trial will also be denied where it appears that the degree of activity or diligence which led to the discovery of the evidence after trial would have produced it had such diligence been exercised before trial. *Tamsen v. Weber*, 166 Ariz. 364, 802 P.2d 1063 (Ct. App. Div. 1 1990). A party fails to employ due diligence if the party fails to make any reasonable effort to obtain critical evidence, or attempts to discover it from only one source when several are available. *Tamsen v. Weber*, 166 Ariz. 364, 802 P.2d 1063 (Ct. App. Div. 1 1990). Whether or not the moving party exercised due diligence is a question of fact for the trial court to resolve. *Estate of Page v. Litzenburg*, 177 Ariz. 84, 865 P.2d 128 (Ct. App. Div. 1 1993).

7. *Errors in Evidentiary Rulings or Instructions to Jury.* A request for new trial on the grounds of erroneous evidentiary rulings or errors in giving or refusing jury instructions permits the trial court to review the propriety of the proceedings that led to the verdict. Indeed, under Rule 59(c), where these are cited as the grounds for awarding a new trial, the Court is to "review all rulings during the trial upon objections to evidence" and "review the charge [to the jury] and the rulings refusing an instruction requested." Rulings on the admission or exclusion of evidence will not be disturbed absent an abuse of the trial court's discretion that resulted in prejudice to the moving party. *Gemstar Ltd. v. Ernst & Young*, 185 Ariz. 493, 917 P.2d 222 (1996); *Hudgins v. Southwest Airlines, Co.*, 221 Ariz. 472, 212 P.3d 810 (Ct. App.

Div. 1 2009); *Belliard v. Becker*, 216 Ariz. 356, 166 P.3d 911 (Ct. App. Div. 1 2007); *Girouard v. Skyline Steel, Inc.*, 215 Ariz. 126, 158 P.3d 255 (Ct. App. Div. 1 2007); *Lohmeier v. Hammer*, 214 Ariz. 57, 148 P.3d 101 (Ct. App. Div. 1 2006); *Acuna v. Kroack*, 212 Ariz. 104, 128 P.3d 221 (Ct. App. Div. 2 2006); *John C. Lincoln Hosp. and Health Corp. v. Maricopa County*, 208 Ariz. 532, 96 P.3d 530 (Ct. App. Div. 1 2004), as amended, (Sept. 1, 2004); *Larsen v. Decker*, 196 Ariz. 239, 995 P.2d 281 (Ct. App. Div. 1 2000), amended, (Feb. 22, 2000); *Brown v. U.S. Fidelity and Guar. Co.*, 194 Ariz. 85, 977 P.2d 807 (Ct. App. Div. 1 1998), as amended, (Nov. 25, 1998) and as corrected, (Aug. 5, 1999); *State ex rel. Miller v. Wells Fargo Bank of Arizona, N.A.*, 194 Ariz. 126, 978 P.2d 103 (Ct. App. Div. 1 1998); *Sheppard v. Crow-Barker Paul No. 1 Ltd. Partnership*, 192 Ariz. 539, 968 P.2d 612 (Ct. App. Div. 1 1998).

Moreover, an objection to the admission of evidence must be made on the record to support a finding of error and may not be made for the first time on appeal, unless the admission or exclusion of evidence amounted to "fundamental error," a doctrine that is applied sparingly in civil cases. *Brown v. U.S. Fidelity and Guar. Co.*, 194 Ariz. 85, 977 P.2d 807 (Ct. App. Div. 1 1998), as amended, (Nov. 25, 1998) and as corrected, (Aug. 5, 1999); *Rhue v. Dawson*, 173 Ariz. 220, 841 P.2d 215 (Ct. App. Div. 1 1992). The fact that a party may have waived an objection to certain evidence by failing to object to its admission at an initial trial of a matter does not preclude that party from objecting to its admission at a retrial of the case. *Jimenez v. Wal-Mart Stores, Inc.*, 206 Ariz. 424, 79 P.3d 673 (Ct. App. Div. 2 2003).

The standard for review of challenged jury instructions is whether the instructions, considered as a whole, misled the jury as to the proper rules of law to apply. *Sheppard v. Crow-Barker Paul No. 1 Ltd. Partnership*, 192 Ariz. 539, 968 P.2d 612 (Ct. App. Div. 1 1998); *Terry v. Gaslight Square Associates*, 182 Ariz. 365, 897 P.2d 667 (Ct. App. Div. 2 1994); *Callender v. Transpacific Hotel Corp.*, 179 Ariz. 557, 880 P.2d 1103 (Ct. App. Div. 2 1993); *Rodriguez v. Schlittenhart*, 161 Ariz. 609, 780 P.2d 442 (Ct. App. Div. 2 1989). Similarly, Rule 59(c)(3) does not require the trial court to review the propriety of all instructions given, if the objecting party has failed to preserve the objection in the manner required by Rule 51(a). *White v. Mitchell*, 157 Ariz. 523, 759 P.2d 1327 (Ct. App. Div. 1 1988).

To sustain a new trial, any perceived error must result in prejudice amounting to material error. *Reeves v. Markle*, 119 Ariz. 159, 579 P.2d 1382 (1978); *Johnson v. Elliott*, 112 Ariz. 57, 537 P.2d 927 (1975); *Callender v. Transpacific Hotel Corp.*, 179 Ariz. 557, 880 P.2d 1103 (Ct. App. Div. 2 1993); *Marcal Ltd. Partnership v. Title Ins. Co. of Minnesota*, 150 Ariz. 191, 722 P.2d 359

(Ct. App. Div. 2 1986); *Long v. Corvo*, 131 Ariz. 216, 639 P.2d 1041 (Ct. App. Div. 2 1981). Whether the claimed error was prejudicial will not be presumed, but must appear affirmatively from the record. *Republic Ins. Co. v. Feidler*, 193 Ariz. 8, 969 P.2d 173 (Ct. App. Div. 1 1998), review denied and opinion ordered not published, 199 Ariz. 472, 19 P.3d 613 (1999).

The failure of a party to object to a jury instruction is a waiver of the issue, however, unless giving the instruction constitutes fundamental error. *Bradshaw v. State Farm Mut. Auto. Ins. Co.*, 157 Ariz. 411, 758 P.2d 1313 (1988); *Copeland v. City of Yuma*, 160 Ariz. 307, 772 P.2d 1160 (Ct. App. Div. 1 1989). Fundamental error is that which goes to the very foundation of a case, or takes an essential right from a party, or deprives a party of a fair trial or a constitutional right. *Salt River Project Agr. Imp. and Power Dist. v. Westinghouse Elec. Corp.*, 176 Ariz. 383, 861 P.2d 668, Prod. Liab. Rep. (CCH) P 13562 (Ct. App. Div. 2 1993).

Fundamental error is not waived even in the absence of an objection, and must be considered by the Court *sua sponte* even when not raised on appeal. *Salt River Project Agr. Imp. and Power Dist. v. Westinghouse Elec. Corp.*, 176 Ariz. 383, 861 P.2d 668, Prod. Liab. Rep. (CCH) P 13562 (Ct. App. Div. 2 1993). The doctrine of fundamental error is applied sparingly in civil cases. *Bradshaw v. State Farm Mut. Auto. Ins. Co.*, 157 Ariz. 411, 758 P.2d 1313 (1988).

It is fundamental error to instruct the jury that jurors who vote against finding liability during the course of deliberations should not participate in the determination of the amount of damages to be awarded. *Perkins v. Komarnyckyj*, 172 Ariz. 115, 834 P.2d 1260 (1992). The constitutional right of trial by jury carries with it the right to have every issue tried by the jury that has been empaneled, not by two-thirds or three-fourths, or any other fraction of that jury. Depriving the parties of their right to have all the jurors participate in deciding all of the issues is inherently prejudicial and fundamental error, requiring reversal without any further showing of prejudice. *Perkins v. Komarnyckyj*, 172 Ariz. 115, 834 P.2d 1260 (1992).

It is also error for the trial court to respond to an inquiry from the jury regarding substantive legal issues or matters of substantial procedural importance without first notifying counsel and giving them the opportunity to state their positions and/or make whatever record is appropriate. *Perkins v. Komarnyckyj*, 172 Ariz. 115, 834 P.2d 1260 (1992). Indeed, in many cases, the failure to respond to an inquiry from the jury may in effect itself be a communication. Even if the trial court has no intention of responding to the jury, the judge must inform the parties of the inquiry and allow them to voice their positions or concerns for the record. *Perkins v. Komarnyckyj*, 172 Ariz. 115, 834 P.2d 1260 (1992).

It is not an abuse of discretion, however, to award a new trial where the trial court failed to give an instruction warranted by the evidence and the legal theories of the party requesting it. *Cotterhill v. Bafile*, 177 Ariz. 76, 865 P.2d 120 (Ct. App. Div. 1 1993); *Ross v. Bartz*, 158 Ariz. 305, 762 P.2d 592 (Ct. App. Div. 2 1988). While, generally, a party may not sit by and allow error to be committed and then move for a new trial on that ground, a trial court does have discretion to reach the merits of a motion for new trial or remittitur in favor of the moving party even though that party clearly waived or invited the error claimed. *Walter v. Simmons*, 169 Ariz. 229, 818 P.2d 214 (Ct. App. Div. 1 1991).

8. *Verdict Resulting From Passion or Prejudice.* While it is frequently relied upon as a basis for claiming that a verdict was the result of passion or prejudice, the size of the jury award alone is inconclusive as to whether it was produced by passion or prejudice. *Hutcherson v. City of Phoenix*, 192 Ariz. 51, 961 P.2d 449 (1998). Thus, the inquiry undertaken by the trial court where such a claim is made is related to that required where a party requests a new trial on the grounds of excessive or insufficient damages. While the trial court has some discretion in this area, *cf. Alires v. Southern Pac. Co.*, 100 Ariz. 6, 409 P.2d 714 (1966), generally a verdict should not be set aside without attempting an additur or remittitur unless the trial court concludes that the verdict was the result of passion or prejudice. *Maxwell v. Aetna Life Ins. Co.*, 143 Ariz. 205, 693 P.2d 348 (Ct. App. Div. 1 1984); *Young Candy & Tobacco Co. v. Montoya*, 91 Ariz. 363, 372 P.2d 703 (1962); *Flieger v. Reeb*, 120 Ariz. 31, 583 P.2d 1351 (Ct. App. Div. 2 1978); *Jackson v. Mearig*, 17 Ariz. App. 94, 495 P.2d 864 (Div. 1 1972).

A verdict should not be set aside unless the size of the verdict, considered together with other factors affecting the integrity of the proceedings, is so unreasonable and outrageous as to shock the conscience of the Court. *Higgins v. Assmann Electronics, Inc.*, 217 Ariz. 289, 173 P.3d 453 (Ct. App. Div. 1 2007); *Acuna v. Kroack*, 212 Ariz. 104, 128 P.3d 221 (Ct. App. Div. 2 2006); *Larsen v. Decker*, 196 Ariz. 239, 995 P.2d 281 (Ct. App. Div. 1 2000), amended, (Feb. 22, 2000); *Sheppard v. Crow-Barker Paul No. 1 Ltd. Partnership*, 192 Ariz. 539, 968 P.2d 612 (Ct. App. Div. 1 1998); *Olson v. Walker*, 162 Ariz. 174, 781 P.2d 1015, 12 A.L.R. 5th 1020 (Ct. App. Div. 1 1989); *Gonzales v. Arizona Public Service Co.*, 161 Ariz. 84, 775 P.2d 1148 (Ct. App. Div. 2 1989); *Mammo v. State*, 138 Ariz. 528, 675 P.2d 1347 (Ct. App. Div. 1 1983); *Linsenmeyer v. Hancock*, 23 Ariz. App. 444, 533 P.2d 1181 (Div. 1 1975); *Pumphrey v. Dynek*, 10 Ariz. App. 241, 457 P.2d

954 (Div. 2 1969). The size of the verdict alone is not dispositive. *Hutcherson v. City of Phoenix*, 192 Ariz. 51, 961 P.2d 449 (1998); *Olson v. Walker*, 162 Ariz. 174, 781 P.2d 1015, 12 A.L.R.5th 1020 (Ct. App. Div. 1 1989); *Waqui v. Tanner Bros. Contracting Co., Inc.*, 121 Ariz. 323, 589 P.2d 1355 (Ct. App. Div. 2 1979). Neither is the length of the jury's deliberations. *Stallcup v. Rathbun*, 76 Ariz. 63, 258 P.2d 821 (1953); *Suciu v. AMFAC Distributing Corp.*, 138 Ariz. 514, 675 P.2d 1333 (Ct. App. Div. 2 1983).

9. *Excessive or Insufficient Damages; Additur or Remittitur; Conditional New Trial Orders.* Under Rule 59(a)(5), a claim of "excessive or insufficient damages" is an independent basis for seeking a new trial. The trial court has the initial responsibility for adjusting an excessive or inadequate verdict, and its decisions in that regard will be disturbed on appeal only for an abuse of discretion. *Bradshaw v. State Farm Mut. Auto. Ins. Co.*, 157 Ariz. 411, 758 P.2d 1313 (1988); *Bond v. Cartwright Little League, Inc.*, 112 Ariz. 9, 536 P.2d 697 (1975); *Creamer v. Troiano*, 108 Ariz. 573, 503 P.2d 794 (1972); *Sheppard v. Crow-Barker Paul No. 1 Ltd. Partnership*, 192 Ariz. 539, 968 P.2d 612 (Ct. App. Div. 1 1998); *Gonzales v. Arizona Public Service Co.*, 161 Ariz. 84, 775 P.2d 1148 (Ct. App. Div. 2 1989); *Duncan v. State*, 157 Ariz. 56, 754 P.2d 1160 (Ct. App. Div. 2 1988); *Torres for and on Behalf of Torres v. North American Van Lines, Inc.*, 135 Ariz. 35, 658 P.2d 835 (Ct. App. Div. 2 1982); *Arizona Container Corp. v. Consolidated Freightways*, 22 Ariz. App. 11, 522 P.2d 772 (Div. 2 1974); *Braun v. Moreno*, 11 Ariz. App. 509, 466 P.2d 60 (Div. 2 1970). This is particularly the case where a verdict quantifies intangible damages or where punitive damages are concerned. *Bradshaw v. State Farm Mut. Auto. Ins. Co.*, 157 Ariz. 411, 758 P.2d 1313 (1988).

The verdict should be adjusted where there has been an obvious exclusion of an item of recoverable damages. *Tryon v. Naegle*, 20 Ariz. App. 138, 510 P.2d 768 (Div. 1 1973). On the other hand, where the trial court determines that the intent of the jury was to compensate for a contingent future damage or injury, the verdict may not be adjusted and the only alternative is to grant a new trial. *Wright v. Mayberry*, 158 Ariz. 387, 762 P.2d 1341 (Ct. App. Div. 1 1988). Where the trial court has refused to interfere with the jury's determination of damages, however, an appellate court will interpose its own judgment only if it is convinced that the verdict is either so excessive or so inadequate as to suggest passion or prejudice. *Hyatt Regency Phoenix Hotel Co. v. Winston & Strawn*, 184 Ariz. 120, 907 P.2d 506 (Ct. App. Div. 1 1995).

The trial court may review an award of punitive damages and exercise its power of remittitur to reduce a verdict it finds excessive. The amount of punitive damages awarded should be based in part on the defendant's wealth in order to achieve the appropriate level of punitive effect. In a civil racketeering action, both punitive damages and treble damages are recoverable because the treble damages awarded under the statute are remedial and supplemental to other damages recovered. *Rhue v. Dawson*, 173 Ariz. 220, 841 P.2d 215 (Ct. App. Div. 1 1992). The trial court, however, may review the amount of punitive damages awarded in light of the trebled compensatory damages to ensure that the former are not excessive. *Rhue v. Dawson*, 173 Ariz. 220, 841 P.2d 215 (Ct. App. Div. 1 1992).

The procedure for awarding a new trial on the grounds of excessive or insufficient damages is governed by Rule 59(i). Rule 59(i) was amended in 1967 to eliminate the need to couch conditional new trial orders in the future tense, which contemplated, or at least implied, a second order which actually disposed of the new trial motion. Under the present Rule, the trial court can issue a single order which requires acceptance of the remittitur or additur within a prescribed time and specifies the disposition of the motion for new trial if the acceptance is not timely filed. See *State Bar Committee Note* to 1967 Amendment to Rule 59(i).

The Court may, and should, grant the new trial conditionally unless the party affected files, within a time fixed by the Court, a statement accepting the reduction or increase in the jury's award which the Court has determined is appropriate. *Barnes v. City of Tucson*, 157 Ariz. 566, 760 P.2d 566 (Ct. App. Div. 2 1988). Obviously, this procedure should not be invoked where the trial court has found the verdict to be the result of passion or prejudice. *Hancock v. Linsenmeyer*, 15 Ariz. App. 296, 488 P.2d 501 (Div. 1 1971); *Howard P. Foley Co. v. Harris*, 10 Ariz. App. 78, 456 P.2d 398 (1969).

If the statement of acceptance of an increase or reduction in the jury's verdict is filed within the prescribed period of time, the party who moved for a new trial may nevertheless appeal from the resulting denial of the motion. *Sequoia Mfg. Co., Inc. v. Halec Const. Co., Inc.*, 117 Ariz. 11, 570 P.2d 782 (Ct. App. Div. 1 1977). The party who filed the acceptance may then cross-appeal, which operates to revoke the acceptance where the cross-appeal is directed to that issue. *Flory v. Silvercrest Industries, Inc.*, 129 Ariz. 574, 633 P.2d 383, 31 U.C.C. Rep. Serv. 1256 (1981); *Duncan v. State*, 157 Ariz. 56, 754 P.2d 1160 (Ct. App. Div. 2 1988); *Mammo v. State*, 138 Ariz. 528, 675 P.2d 1347 (Ct. App. Div. 1 1983); *Waqui v. Tanner Bros. Contracting Co., Inc.*, 121 Ariz. 323, 589 P.2d 1355 (Ct. App. Div. 2 1979). That will not be the case, however, where the party accepting the remittitur prosecutes an appeal but does not put the propriety of the remittitur in issue. *Duke v. Cochise County*, 189 Ariz. 35, 938 P.2d 84 (Ct. App. Div. 2 1996).

Under the express provisions of Rule 59(i)(1), a new trial

granted on the grounds of excessive or inadequate damages is with respect to the issue of damages only. The verdict stands in all other respects. A trial court can grant a new trial solely on the issue of damages, except where the issues of liability and damages are so inextricably intertwined that a fair trial cannot be given on the issue of damages alone. *Martinez v. Schneider Enterprises, Inc.*, 178 Ariz. 346, 873 P.2d 684 (Ct. App. Div. 1 1994).

An order limiting a new trial to only part of the issues is within the sound discretion of the trial court and will not be overturned on appeal absent an abuse of that discretion. *Martinez v. Schneider Enterprises, Inc.*, 178 Ariz. 346, 873 P.2d 684 (Ct. App. Div. 1 1994).

10. *Verdict Not Justified by the Evidence.* A motion for new trial on the grounds that the verdict or decision is not justified by the evidence is addressed to the trial court's discretion and may be made even if there was no prior motion for directed verdict. *Singleton v. Valianos*, 84 Ariz. 51, 323 P.2d 697 (1958); *Dawson v. Withycombe*, 216 Ariz. 84, 163 P.3d 1034 (Ct. App. Div. 1 2007); *Larsen v. Decker*, 196 Ariz. 239, 995 P.2d 281 (Ct. App. Div. 1 2000), amended, (Feb. 22, 2000); *Styles v. Ceranski*, 185 Ariz. 448, 916 P.2d 1164 (Ct. App. Div. 1 1996); *Smith v. Johnson*, 183 Ariz. 38, 899 P.2d 199 (Ct. App. Div. 1 1995), corrected, (July 21, 1995); *Walter v. Simmons*, 169 Ariz. 229, 818 P.2d 214 (Ct. App. Div. 1 1991). The denial of such a motion will be disturbed on appeal only if it reflects a manifest abuse of discretion. *Ogden v. J.M. Steel Erecting, Inc.*, 201 Ariz. 32, 31 P.3d 806 (Ct. App. Div. 1 2001).

Case law on the subject reflects at times conflicting articulations concerning the role of the trial court in assessing the evidence when considering a new trial motion brought on this particular ground. One line of cases states that the trial court in that situation sits, in a very real sense, as the (in Arizona) "ninth juror," and is free to weigh the evidence and determine independently whether it supports the verdict. *Hutcherson v. City of Phoenix*, 192 Ariz. 51, 961 P.2d 449 (1998); *State v. Ross*, 97 Ariz. 51, 396 P.2d 619 (1964) (overruled in part by, Yoo Thun Lim v. Crespin, 100 Ariz. 80, 411 P.2d 809 (1966)); *Crowe v. Miller*, 27 Ariz. App. 453, 555 P.2d 1141 (Div. 1 1976).

Other decisions suggest that, when the sufficiency of the evidence upon which a verdict rests is questioned, the trial court is not to reweigh and resolve conflicts in the evidence and substitute its own conclusions for those reached by the jury, but is only to examine the record to determine whether substantial evidence was presented to support that verdict. *Republic Ins. Co. v. Feidler*, 193 Ariz. 8, 969 P.2d 173 (Ct. App. Div. 1 1998), review denied and opinion ordered not published, 199 Ariz. 472, 19 P.3d 613 (1999); *Callender v. Transpacific Hotel Corp.*, 179 Ariz. 557, 880 P.2d 1103 (Ct. App. Div. 2 1993).

It is not an abuse of discretion to order a new trial where the evidence is in conflict, or even where the evidence for and against the verdict is "equiponderant." *Joy v. Raley*, 24 Ariz. App. 584, 540 P.2d 710 (Div. 1 1975); *Cano v. Neill*, 12 Ariz. App. 562, 473 P.2d 487 (Div. 1 1970); *Hammontree v. Kenworthy*, 1 Ariz. App. 472, 404 P.2d 816 (1965). The burden rests upon the party pursuing a claim, however, to present sufficient evidence to permit a properly instructed jury to return a meaningful verdict, and a new trial is not required when a party has had a full and complete opportunity to present its case but does not do so. *A.R. Teeters & Associates, Inc. v. Eastman Kodak Co.*, 172 Ariz. 324, 836 P.2d 1034 (Ct. App. Div. 1 1992).

A claim that a jury's allocation of fault, rather than its monetary verdict, is against the weight of the evidence is properly brought as a motion for new trial under Rule 59(a)(8). *Hutcherson v. City of Phoenix*, 188 Ariz. 183, 933 P.2d 1251 (Ct. App. Div. 1 1996), vacated on other grounds, 192 Ariz. 51, 961 P.2d 449 (1998). Confusion of the jury is also a proper basis for concluding that a verdict is "not justified by the evidence or is contrary to law" within the meaning of the Rule. *Standard Chartered PLC v. Price Waterhouse*, 190 Ariz. 6, 945 P.2d 317 (Ct. App. Div. 1 1996), as corrected on denial of reconsideration, (Jan. 13, 1997).

Sufficiency of the evidence objections can be made the subject of a motion for new trial following a trial to the court, even when they have not been raised as objections to proposed findings of fact and conclusions of law. *Gerow v. Covill*, 192 Ariz. 9, 960 P.2d 55 (Ct. App. Div. 1 1998), as amended, (Aug. 26, 1998). Raising the issue in that fashion will operate to preserve it for appeal. *Gerow v. Covill*, 192 Ariz. 9, 960 P.2d 55 (Ct. App. Div. 1 1998), as amended on other grounds, (Aug. 26, 1998).

11. *Effect of Filing Motion for New Trial on Time for Appeal.* The filing of a timely motion for new trial extends the time for filing a notice of appeal until thirty (30) days after its disposition. Rule 9, Ariz. R. Civ. App. Proc. (This is not the case, however, with respect to post-judgment motions in Justice Court, where the time for taking an appeal to the Superior Court is governed by the Superior Court Rules of Appellate Procedure—Civil. *JNS Holding Corp. v. Superior Court In and For County of Maricopa*, 183 Ariz. 98, 900 P.2d 1234 (Ct. App. Div. 1 1995).)

To effectively extend the time for appeal, however, the motion, however captioned, must refer to Rule 59 and cite one of the grounds for relief specified in Rule 59(a). *Farmers Ins. Co. of Arizona v. Vagnozzi*, 132 Ariz. 219, 644 P.2d 1305 (1982); *Hegel v. O'Malley Ins. Co., Inc., Agents and Brokers*, 117 Ariz. 411, 573 P.2d 485 (1977), opinion after reinstatement of appeal, 122 Ariz. 52, 593 P.2d 275 (1979); *State ex rel. Corbin v. Tolleson*, 152 Ariz. 376, 732 P.2d 1114 (Ct. App. Div. 1 1986); *Molever v. Roush*, 152 Ariz. 367, 732 P.2d 1105 (Ct. App. Div. 1 1986); *Ray Korte Chevrolet v. Simmons*, 117 Ariz. 202, 571 P.2d 699 (Ct. App. Div. 1 1977); *but cf. Matter of Balcomb's Estate*, 114 Ariz. 519, 562 P.2d 399 (Ct. App. Div. 1 1977).

A notice of appeal that is filed while a motion for new trial is still pending is premature, is ineffective to confer jurisdiction on the appellate court, and does not constitute abandonment of the new trial motion. *Baumann v. Tuton*, 180 Ariz. 370, 884 P.2d 256 (Ct. App. Div. 1 1994).

The granting of a motion for new trial has the effect of vacating a judgment previously entered. *Nielson v. Patterson*, 204 Ariz. 530, 65 P.3d 911 (2003). Accordingly, when the party whose verdict and judgment have in effect been set aside appeals from the award of a new trial, it is not necessary for the party who secured a new trial to file a protective cross-appeal to preserve the right to challenge the verdict and judgment in the event the new trial order is reversed on appeal. *Nielson v. Patterson*, 204 Ariz. 530, 65 P.3d 911 (2003).

If the new trial order is reversed on appeal, the judgment would be reinstated and the party against whom the judgment was reinstated can appeal at that point. *Nielson v. Patterson*, 204 Ariz. 530, 65 P.3d 911 (2003).

The appropriate vehicle for a post-judgment objection to the amount of attorneys' fees awarded and included in a judgment is either a motion for new trial or a motion to alter or amend the judgment. *PNL Credit L.P. v. Southwest Pacific Investments, Inc.*, 179 Ariz. 259, 877 P.2d 832 (Ct. App. Div. 1 1994). Such a motion, if timely filed, will operate to extend the time for filing a notice of appeal. *PNL Credit L.P. v. Southwest Pacific Investments, Inc.*, 179 Ariz. 259, 877 P.2d 832 (Ct. App. Div. 1 1994).

12. *Time for Filing Motion for New Trial.* Under Rule 59(d), the motion for new trial must be filed "not later than 15 days after entry of the judgment." *Welch v. McClure*, 123 Ariz. 161, 598 P.2d 980 (1979). It was formerly held that this time period was to be strictly applied, and Rule 6 formerly provided that this time period could not be enlarged by the trial court. *Edwards v. Young*, 107 Ariz. 283, 486 P.2d 181 (1971); *Egan-Ryan Mechanical Co. v. Cardon Meadows Development Corp.*, 169 Ariz. 161, 818 P.2d 146 (Ct. App. Div. 1 1990); *Foster v. Camelback Management Co.*, 132 Ariz. 462, 646 P.2d 893 (Ct. App. Div. 2 1982); *Harold Laz Advertising Co. v. Dumes*, 2 Ariz. App. 236, 407 P.2d 777 (1965). The trial court was granted limited authority to enlarge that pe-

riod by the 1994 amendment to Rule 6(b). The circumstances under which such an extension can be secured are discussed in Section 5 of the *Authors' Comments* under Rule 6.

A motion is timely if filed after the jury's verdict is rendered but before entry of judgment. *Farmers Ins. Co. of Arizona v. Vagnozzi*, 132 Ariz. 219, 644 P.2d 1305 (1982); *Dunahay v. Struzik*, 96 Ariz. 246, 393 P.2d 930 (1964). A timely motion for new trial may, under Rule 59(c)(1), "be amended at any time before it is ruled upon by the court."

13. *Discretion of Court.* The trial court is vested with a very broad discretion in resolving motions for new trial. Thus, in ruling on a motion for new trial, a trial court may evaluate the credibility of witness and may weigh the evidence to determine if the verdict is against the weight of the evidence and contrary to justice. *Reeves v. Markle*, 119 Ariz. 159, 579 P.2d 1382 (1978); *Thompson v. Better-Bilt Aluminum Products Co., Inc.*, 171 Ariz. 550, 832 P.2d 203, 7 I.E.R. Cas. (BNA) 1017, 126 Lab. Cas. (CCH) P 57536 (1992); *McBride v. Kieckhefer Associates, Inc.*, 228 Ariz. 262, 265 P.3d 1061 (Ct. App. Div. 1 2011), review denied, (Apr. 24, 2012).

The role of the trial court when considering a motion for new trial is in direct contrast to the trial court's role when considering a motion for judgment as a matter of law. Specifically, when considering a motion for judgment as a matter of law, the trial court may not may not weigh the credibility of witnesses or resolve conflicts of evidence and reasonable inferences drawn therefrom. *See Estate of Reinen v. Northern Arizona Orthopedics, Ltd.*, 198 Ariz. 283, 9 P.3d 314 (2000); *Thompson v. Better-Bilt Aluminum Products Co., Inc.*, 171 Ariz. 550, 832 P.2d 203, 7 I.E.R. Cas. (BNA) 1017, 126 Lab. Cas. (CCH) P 57536 (1992); *McBride v. Kieckhefer Associates, Inc.*, 228 Ariz. 262, 265 P.3d 1061 (Ct. App. Div. 1 2011), review denied, (Apr. 24, 2012).

A trial court's decisions will not be disturbed absent an abuse of that discretion. *Hutcherson v. City of Phoenix*, 192 Ariz. 51, 961 P.2d 449 (1998); *Reeves v. Markle*, 119 Ariz. 159, 579 P.2d 1382 (1978); *McBride v. Kieckhefer Associates, Inc.*, 228 Ariz. 262, 265 P.3d 1061 (Ct. App. Div. 1 2011), review denied, (Apr. 24, 2012); *White v. Greater Arizona Bicycling Ass'n*, 216 Ariz. 133, 163 P.3d 1083 (Ct. App. Div. 2 2007) (overruled by, Walsh v. Advanced Cardiac Specialists Chartered, 229 Ariz. 193, 273 P.3d 645 (2012)); *Dawson v. Withycombe*, 216 Ariz. 84, 163 P.3d 1034 (Ct. App. Div. 1 2007); *Mullin v. Brown*, 210 Ariz. 545, 115 P.3d 139 (Ct. App. Div. 2 2005); *Jimenez v. Wal-Mart Stores, Inc.*, 206 Ariz. 424, 79 P.3d 673 (Ct. App. Div. 2 2003); *Henry ex rel. Estate of Wilson v. HealthPartners of Southern Arizona*, 203 Ariz. 393, 55 P.3d 87 (Ct. App. Div. 2 2002); *Najar v. State*, 198 Ariz. 345, 9

P.3d 1084 (Ct. App. Div. 2 2000); *Monaco v. HealthPartners of Southern Arizona*, 196 Ariz. 299, 995 P.2d 735 (Ct. App. Div. 2 1999); *Harris v. Harris*, 195 Ariz. 559, 991 P.2d 262 (Ct. App. Div. 1 1999); *State ex rel. Miller v. Wells Fargo Bank of Arizona, N.A.*, 194 Ariz. 126, 978 P.2d 103 (Ct. App. Div. 1 1998).

On appeal, an appellate court will view the evidence in the light most favorable to sustaining the verdict. *Hutcherson v. City of Phoenix*, 192 Ariz. 51, 961 P.2d 449 (1998); *Mealey v. Arndt*, 206 Ariz. 218, 76 P.3d 892 (Ct. App. Div. 1 2003); *Pima County v. Gonzalez*, 193 Ariz. 18, 969 P.2d 183 (Ct. App. Div. 2 1998); *Styles v. Ceranski*, 185 Ariz. 448, 916 P.2d 1164 (Ct. App. Div. 1 1996); *Bank One, Arizona v. Rouse*, 181 Ariz. 36, 887 P.2d 566 (Ct. App. Div. 1 1994); *Lopez v. Farmers Ins. Co. of Arizona*, 177 Ariz. 371, 868 P.2d 954 (Ct. App. Div. 1 1993). Generally, however, subject to the provisions of Rule 59(m), greater deference is given to a ruling granting a new trial. *Grant v. Arizona Public Service Co.*, 133 Ariz. 434, 652 P.2d 507 (1982); *Caldwell v. Tremper*, 90 Ariz. 241, 367 P.2d 266 (1962); *Englert v. Carondelet Health Network*, 199 Ariz. 21, 13 P.3d 763 (Ct. App. Div. 2 2000); *State Farm Fire and Cas. Co. v. Brown*, 183 Ariz. 518, 905 P.2d 527 (Ct. App. Div. 1 1995); *Walter v. Simmons*, 169 Ariz. 229, 818 P.2d 214 (Ct. App. Div. 1 1991); *Liberatore v. Thompson*, 157 Ariz. 612, 760 P.2d 612 (Ct. App. Div. 1 1988); *Koepnick v. Sears Roebuck & Co.*, 158 Ariz. 322, 762 P.2d 609 (Ct. App. Div. 1 1988); *Melcher v. Melcher*, 137 Ariz. 210, 669 P.2d 987 (Ct. App. Div. 2 1983).

An order granting a new trial cannot be reversed on a ground that was not presented to and considered by the trial court. *Anderson v. Preferred Stock Food Markets, Inc.*, 175 Ariz. 208, 854 P.2d 1194 (Ct. App. Div. 1 1993). The fact that the trial court could leave a verdict undisturbed does not mean it was error to disturb it. *Bradshaw v. State Farm Mut. Auto. Ins. Co.*, 157 Ariz. 411, 758 P.2d 1313 (1988).

The Court may, under Rule 59(g), order a new trial upon its own initiative, but only for one of the grounds for which a new trial could have been granted upon motion. *Johnson v. Elliott*, 112 Ariz. 57, 537 P.2d 927 (1975). A motion for new trial may also be granted only with respect to certain issues. *Reed v. Hyde*, 15 Ariz. App. 203, 487 P.2d 424 (Div. 1 1971); *Tucson Rapid Transit Co. v. Tocci*, 3 Ariz. App. 330, 414 P.2d 179 (1966). Partial new trials, however, are not recommended and should only be granted when the issues are not inextricably intertwined and can be separated without prejudice to the parties. *Englert v. Carondelet Health Network*, 199 Ariz. 21, 13 P.3d 763 (Ct. App. Div. 2 2000). Where the action is one that was tried to the Court without a jury, the Court can grant a new trial or open the original judgment and enter a new one. *Krug v. Porter*, 83 Ariz. 108, 317 P.2d 543 (1957); *Freese v. Bassett Furniture Industries*, 78 Ariz. 70,

275 P.2d 758 (1954). Rule 59(k) limits the number of new trials that may be granted in the same action to two, unless the jury has been guilty of misconduct.

The denial of a motion for new trial is an appealable order. An order granting a new trial is also appealable pursuant to A.R.S. § 12-2101(F). *Davis v. Davis*, 195 Ariz. 158, 985 P.2d 643 (Ct. App. Div. 1 1999). That statutory provision, however, applies only to orders entered after an actual trial, and does not confer appellate jurisdiction over an order denying a new trial from a non-final partial summary judgment on liability. An order granting a mistrial before judgment being entered, however, is not the grant of a new trial and is not appealable. *Davis v. Davis*, 195 Ariz. 158, 985 P.2d 643 (Ct. App. Div. 1 1999).

14. *Specification of Grounds for Awarding New Trial.* Rule 59(m) requires that any order granting a new trial specify "with particularity the ground or grounds on which the new trial is granted." *Powell v. Klein*, 11 Ariz. App. 360, 464 P.2d 806 (Div. 2 1970) (overruled on other grounds by, Reeves v. Markle, 119 Ariz. 170, 580 P.2d 2 (Ct. App. Div. 2 1977)); *Heaton v. Waters*, 8 Ariz. App. 256, 445 P.2d 458 (1968). The particularity requirement means the reasons must be stated "in detail." *Reeves v. Markle*, 119 Ariz. 159, 579 P.2d 1382 (1978); *Smith v. Tang*, 100 Ariz. 196, 412 P.2d 697 (1966); *Nordensson v. Nordensson*, 146 Ariz. 544, 707 P.2d 948 (Ct. App. Div. 2 1985); *Brooks v. De La Cruz*, 12 Ariz. App. 591, 473 P.2d 793 (Div. 1 1970). Where the order fails to specify the grounds for granting a new trial, the verdict of the jury will be presumed correct on appeal, and the burden shifts to the party who secured the new trial order to sustain that order. *Brooks v. De La Cruz*, 12 Ariz. App. 591, 473 P.2d 793 (Div. 1 1970); *Montalvo v. Hartford Fire Ins. Co.*, 5 Ariz. App. 419, 427 P.2d 553 (1967).

The purpose of requiring the trial court to state the grounds for granting a new trial with specificity is to narrow the issues on appeal. *Martinez v. Schneider Enterprises, Inc.*, 178 Ariz. 346, 873 P.2d 684 (Ct. App. Div. 1 1994); *Liberatore v. Thompson*, 157 Ariz. 612, 760 P.2d 612 (Ct. App. Div. 1 1988); *Koepnick v. Sears Roebuck & Co.*, 158 Ariz. 322, 762 P.2d 609 (Ct. App. Div. 1 1988). Where the grounds are stated with the requisite specificity, the appellate court may not reverse unless a clear abuse of discretion is shown; when the trial court sets forth grounds that fail the specificity requirement, the burden shifts to the appellee to show that the trial court did not err; where the trial court sets forth both specific and nonspecific grounds for the decision, the reviewing court will assume that the trial court relied only on the specific grounds and ignore the nonspecific; when no grounds are stated, the new trial order is a nullity. *Esplendido Apartments v. Metropolitan Condominium Ass'n of Arizona II*, 161 Ariz. 325,

778 P.2d 1221 (1989); *Montalvo v. Hartford Fire Ins. Co.*, 5 Ariz. App. 419, 427 P.2d 553 (1967).

15. *Use of Affidavits.* Where affidavits are employed in support of a new trial motion, they must be served with the motion and the adverse party has ten (10) days to serve affidavits in opposition. Under Rule 59(f), this period may be extended an additional twenty (20) days by stipulation or by the Court, upon motion for good cause.

16. *Default Judgments Where Service by Publication.* Rule 59(j) deals specifically with the situation where a default judgment has been secured against a defendant who was served by publication. Within one year after the judgment is rendered, the defendant may secure a new trial upon application "for good cause shown by affidavit. . . ." *See Master Financial, Inc. v. Woodburn*, 208 Ariz. 70, 90 P.3d 1236 (Ct. App. Div. 1 2004), as amended, (June 7, 2004). Execution of the judgment will not be stayed, however, unless the defendant posts a bond for "double the amount of the judgment or value of the property adjudged. . . ." The provisions of Rule 59(j) are essentially duplicative of A.R.S. § 12-1560.

17. *Motion to Alter or Amend Judgment; Appeal.* A motion to alter or amend a judgment under Rule 59(*l*) must be made no later than fifteen (15) days after entry of the judgment. This time limitation is to be strictly applied. *Harold Laz Advertising Co. v. Dumes*, 2 Ariz. App. 236, 407 P.2d 777 (1965). The trial court was granted limited authority to enlarge that period by the 1994 amendment to Ariz.R.Civ.P. 6(b). The circumstances under which such an extension can be secured are discussed in Section 5 of the *Authors' Comments* under Rule 6. Amendment of a judgment may also be secured under Rule 52(b), where there have been findings of fact entered by the Court. In addition, the correction of clerical or mathematical errors in the final judgment may be sought under Rules 60(a) and (b).

There are now specific Rules establishing procedures for seeking an award of attorneys' fees where such awards are allowed to the prevailing party. These Rules and procedures are discussed in Section 12 of the *Authors' Comments* under Rule 54 and in Section 9 of the *Authors' Comments* under Rule 58. The appropriate vehicle for a post-judgment objection to the amount of attorneys' fees awarded and included in the judgment is either a motion for new trial or a motion to alter or amend the judgment. *PNL Credit L.P. v. Southwest Pacific Investments, Inc.*, 179 Ariz. 259, 877 P.2d 832 (Ct. App. Div. 1 1994). Such a motion, if timely filed, will operate to extend the time for filing a notice of appeal. *PNL Credit L.P. v. Southwest Pacific Investments, Inc.*, 179 Ariz. 259, 877 P.2d 832 (Ct. App. Div. 1 1994).

Rule 60. Relief from judgment or order

(a) Clerical mistakes. Clerical mistakes in judgments, orders, or other parts of the record and errors therein arising from oversight or omission may be corrected by the court at any time of its own initiative or on motion of any party and after such notice, if any, as the court orders. During pendency of an appeal, such mistakes may be so corrected before the appeal is docketed in the appellate court, and thereafter while the appeal is pending may be so corrected with leave of the appellate court.

(b) Correction of error in record of judgment

1. When a mistake in a judgment is corrected as provided by subdivision (a) of this Rule, thereafter the execution shall conform to the judgment as corrected.

2. Where there is a mistake, miscalculation or misrecital of a sum of money, or of a name, and there is among the records of the action a verdict or instrument of writing whereby such judgment may be safely corrected, the court shall on application and after notice, correct the judgment accordingly.

(c) Mistake; inadvertence; surprise; excusable neglect; newly discovered evidence; fraud, etc. On motion and upon such terms as are just the court may relieve a party or a party's legal representative from a final judgment, order or proceeding for the following reasons: (1) mistake, inadvertence, surprise or excusable neglect; (2) newly discovered evidence which by due diligence could not have been discovered in time to move for a new trial under Rule 59(d); (3) fraud (whether heretofore denominated intrinsic or extrinsic), misrepresentation or other misconduct of an adverse party; (4) the judgment is void; (5) the judgment has been satisfied, released or discharged, or a prior judgment on which it is based has been reversed or otherwise vacated, or it is no longer equitable that the judgment should have prospective application; or (6) any other reason justifying relief from the operation of the judgment. The motion shall be filed within a reasonable time, and for reasons (1), (2) and (3) not more than six months after the judgment or order was entered or proceeding was taken. A motion under this subdivision does not affect the finality of a judgment or suspend its operation. This rule does not limit the power of a court to entertain an independent action to relieve a party from a judgment, order or proceeding, or to grant relief to a defendant served by publication as provided by Rule 59(j) or to set aside a judgment for fraud upon the court. The procedure for obtaining any relief from a judgment shall be by motion as prescribed in these rules or by an independent action.

Rule 60 amended July 14, 1961, effective Nov. 1, 1961; July 23, 1976, effective Oct. 1, 1976; Sept. 15, 1987, effective Nov. 15, 1987.

(d) Reversed judgment of foreign state. When a judgment has been rendered upon the judgment of another state or foreign country, and the foreign judgment is thereafter reversed or set aside by a court of such state or foreign country, the court in which judgment was rendered in this state shall set aside, vacate and annul its judgment.

STATE BAR COMMITTEE NOTES

1961 Amendment

[Rule 60(c)] The present Rule 60(c) is in the form of its federal counterpart (Rule 60(b)) as originally adopted in 1937. It provides only one basis for relief by motion of a party: that the judgment, order or proceeding had been taken against him through his "mistake, inadvertence, surprise or excusable neglect."

The Federal Rule was amended extensively in 1946. The principal changes were:

1. Application of the Rule was specifically limited to final judgments, orders or proceedings.

2. Relief could be obtained by a party whether the mistake, etc. was his or that of others and could be obtained from a judgment taken by him, as well as one taken against him.

3. Five new bases for relief were added: (a) newly discovered evidence; (b) fraud, misrepresentation or other misconduct of an adverse party; (c) the judgment is void; (d) the judgment has been set aside, released or discharged, or a prior judgment upon which it is based has been reversed or otherwise vacated, or it is no longer equitable that the judgment should have effective application; and (e) any other reason justifying relief from the operation of the judgment.

4. A motion for relief on the grounds of mistake, etc., newly discovered evidence or fraud, was to be made within one year after the judgment, order or proceeding was entered or taken. A motion on any other grounds was to be made within a reasonable time.

5. Various common law writs for relief from judgments and orders were abolished and relief from a judgment was limited to motion or an independent action.

The Arizona Rule, as proposed to be revised, would differ from the Federal Rule in that the time for moving for relief for mistake, etc., newly discovered evidence or fraud, would be six months, and no provision abolishing various common law writs was considered necessary because such writs have long since been superseded by the practice of applying to the court by motion for the relief sought.

The present Rule authorizes the court to set aside within one year a judgment obtained against a defendant not actually personally notified. When judgment has been rendered on service by publication and the defendant has not appeared, he may, for good cause shown by affidavit made within one year after rendition of judgment, obtain a new trial. See Rule 59(j). The proposed amendment limits the court's authority to set aside a judgment obtained against a defendant not personally notified to cases arising under Rule 59(j).

AUTHORS' COMMENTS

Analysis

1. *Scope and Purpose of Rule.* As its title implies, Rule 60 is the vehicle for securing corrections to, or relief from, a judgment or order that has been formally entered by the trial court. Rule 60 is intended to permit relief from judgments or orders that are legally proper, but incorrect or unjust due to circumstances that can be corrected at the trial court level rather than by direct legal review. *Tippit v. Lahr*, 132 Ariz. 406, 646 P.2d 291 (Ct. App. Div. 2 1982).

A Rule 60 motion may not be used as a substitute for appeal, however, in order to litigate issues already resolved by the trial court, *Arizona Property and Cas. Ins. Guar. Fund v. Lopez*, 177 Ariz. 1, 864 P.2d 558 (Ct. App. Div. 2 1993); *Tovrea v. Nolan*, 178 Ariz. 485, 875 P.2d 144 (Ct. App. Div. 2 1993); *Budreau v. Budreau*, 134 Ariz. 539, 658 P.2d 192 (Ct. App. Div. 2 1982); *Andrews v. Andrews*, 126 Ariz. 55, 612 P.2d 511 (Ct. App. Div. 1 1980); or as a substitute for other procedures authorized under Rules 50 and 59 for securing post-trial relief, *Craig v. Superior Court In and For Pima County*, 141 Ariz. 387, 687 P.2d 395 (Ct. App. Div. 2 1984).

Both the denial of a motion for relief under Rule 60(c), and an order under Rule 60(c) setting aside a dismissal of an action, are appealable as a "special order made after final judgment" within the meaning of A.R.S. § 12-2101(C). *Johnson v. Elson*, 192 Ariz. 486, 967 P.2d 1022 (Ct. App. Div. 1 1998); *M & M Auto Storage Pool, Inc. v. Chemical Waste Management, Inc.*, 164 Ariz. 139, 791 P.2d 665 (Ct. App. Div. 1 1990). Where a notice of appeal is filed before a pending motion brought under Rule 60 is decided by the trial court, and another notice of appeal is not filed after the trial court's decision on the motion is issued, the appellate court does not have jurisdiction to review that decision. *Navajo Nation v. MacDonald*, 180 Ariz. 539, 885 P.2d 1104, R.I.C.O. Bus. Disp. Guide (CCH) P 8679 (Ct. App. Div. 1 1994).

Where the grounds for relief under Rule 60(c) arise while the judgment is on appeal, a motion should be made in the appellate court to revest jurisdiction in the trial court to entertain an appropriate motion. *Budreau v. Budreau*, 134 Ariz. 539, 658 P.2d 192 (Ct. App. Div. 2 1982). A trial court's decision to grant or deny a motion brought under Rule 60(c) is reviewed only for an abuse of discretion. *Johnson v. Elson*, 192 Ariz. 486, 967 P.2d 1022 (Ct. App. Div. 1 1998).

Rule 60(c) expressly provides that it "does not limit the power of a court to entertain an independent action to relieve a party from a judgment, order or proceeding. . . ." *Master Financial, Inc. v. Woodburn*, 208 Ariz. 70, 90 P.3d 1236 (Ct. App. Div. 1 2004), as amended, (June 7, 2004); *Fischer v. Sommer*, 160 Ariz. 530, 774 P.2d 834 (Ct. App. Div. 1 1989). Rule 60(d) authorizes relief from foreign judgments under specified circumstances.

2. *Comparison With Federal Rule.* ARCP 60(a) and FRCP 60(a), are essentially the same. ARCP 60(c) is substantially similar to FRCP 60(b) and (c). ARCP 60(c), however, requires that motions to set aside a judgment for mistake, inadvertence, surprise, excusable neglect, newly discovered evidence, or fraud must be made within six (6) months after the judgment was entered. FRCP 60(c)(1) allows motions for relief upon those grounds to be made up to one year following the entry of judgment. The Federal Rule does not have any provisions that correspond to ARCP 60(b) and (d); and, the Arizona Rule does not have any provisions that correspond to FRCP 60(d) or (e).

In 2007, the language of FRCP 60 was amended as part of the general restyling of the Federal Rules of Civil Procedure to make the Federal Rules more easily understood and to make style and terminology consistent throughout the Federal Rules of Civil Procedure. Those stylistic modifications have not been incorporated into ARCP 60.

3. *Rule 60(a)—Correcting Clerical Mistakes in Judgments.* Rule 60(a) permits the trial court, on motion or upon its own initiative, to correct clerical mistakes that are the result of an oversight or omission. Rule 60(a) only authorizes the correction of "clerical" errors—to show what the Court actually decided but did not correctly represent in the written judgment. It may not be used to correct "judicial" errors—to supply something that the Court could have decided, but did not. *Minjares v. State*, 223 Ariz. 54,

219 P.3d 264 (Ct. App. Div. 1 2009); *Egan-Ryan Mechanical Co. v. Cardon Meadows Development Corp.*, 169 Ariz. 161, 818 P.2d 146 (Ct. App. Div. 1 1990). A purely clerical error may also be corrected on appeal, even if not raised at the lower court level, but a "judgmental" error is waived if not objected to in the trial court. *Ace Automotive Products, Inc. v. Van Duyne*, 156 Ariz. 140, 750 P.2d 898 (Ct. App. Div. 1 1987).

For example, it is appropriate to afford relief under Rule 60(a) where a default judgment has incorporated an obvious error in the principal amount of the note sued upon. *Perry v. Safety Federal Sav. and Loan Ass'n of Kansas City*, 25 Ariz. App. 443, 544 P.2d 267 (Div. 1 1976). Similarly, Rule 60(a) permits, on a proper showing, the correction of the record to reflect the timely filing of a judgment renewal affidavit which was originally misfiled or misplaced by the Clerk. *Crye v. Edwards*, 178 Ariz. 327, 873 P.2d 665 (Ct. App. Div. 1 1993).

Rule 60(a) cannot, however, be used to change the identities of defendants subject to a stock transfer order, *Harold Laz Advertising Co. v. Dumes*, 2 Ariz. App. 236, 407 P.2d 777 (1965); to change the amount of damages actually awarded, *Fernandez v. Garza*, 88 Ariz. 214, 354 P.2d 260 (1960); or, to change an award which the jury intended but which is legally improper. *Wright v. Mayberry*, 158 Ariz. 387, 762 P.2d 1341 (Ct. App. Div. 1 1988). Similarly, a Rule 60(a) order cannot retroactively change a child support award where there is no evidence that the change was to correct a clerical error. *Hatch v. Hatch*, 113 Ariz. 130, 547 P.2d 1044 (1976).

4. *Rule 60(b)—Correcting Miscalculations or Misrecitals.* Rule 60(b) permits the court to correct obvious miscalculations or misrecitals, and provides that, where a judgment is corrected under Rule 60(a) or (b), any execution thereon must conform to the judgment as corrected.

Relief from a judgment that has been entered but is based upon errors in calculation may also be secured under Rule 60(c)(1). *Martin v. Martin*, 182 Ariz. 11, 893 P.2d 11 (Ct. App. Div. 1 1994). A motion under that Rule, however, must be filed within six (6) months after the judgment is entered. *Martin v. Martin*, 182 Ariz. 11, 893 P.2d 11 (Ct. App. Div. 1 1994).

5. *Rule 60(c)—Relief From Judgments in General.* The principal provision of Rule 60 is Rule 60(c) which permits relief from a judgment for the following specified reasons: 1) mistake, inadvertence or excusable neglect, 2) newly discovered evidence, 3) fraud, misrepresentation or other misconduct, 4) that the judgment is void, 5) satisfaction or release of the judgment or 6) any other grounds warranting relief.

A motion brought pursuant to Rule 60(c) must be brought

within a reasonable time, and the trial court has discretion to determine whether the delay in bringing the motion was reasonable. *United Imports and Exports, Inc. v. Superior Court of State In and For Maricopa County*, 134 Ariz. 43, 653 P.2d 691 (1982); *Brooks v. Consolidated Freightways Corp. of Delaware*, 173 Ariz. 66, 839 P.2d 1111 (Ct. App. Div. 1 1992). The Court must, however, vacate a judgment that is void, even if the party delayed unreasonably in requesting that relief. *Martin v. Martin*, 182 Ariz. 11, 893 P.2d 11 (Ct. App. Div. 1 1994); *Brooks v. De La Cruz*, 12 Ariz. App. 591, 473 P.2d 793 (Div. 1 1970); *Darnell v. Denton*, 137 Ariz. 204, 669 P.2d 981 (Ct. App. Div. 2 1983).

Where the judgment from which relief is sought is one that was entered pursuant to a mandate from an appellate court, relief may now be sought directly in the trial court and it is no longer necessary to first obtain permission from the appellate court and/or to seek recall of the mandate. *U S West Communications, Inc. v. Arizona Dept. of Revenue*, 199 Ariz. 101, 14 P.3d 292 (2000). A Rule 60(c) motion may be entertained although directed at a judgment that has already been affirmed on appeal. *Minjares v. State*, 223 Ariz. 54, 219 P.3d 264 (Ct. App. Div. 1 2009).

The purpose of Rule 60(c) is to provide relief where mistakes and errors occur despite a party's diligent efforts to comply with the rules. By its very terms, the Rule only provides the potential for relief where a party's conduct is excusable. *Panzino v. City of Phoenix*, 196 Ariz. 442, 999 P.2d 198 (2000); *In re Marriage of Worcester*, 192 Ariz. 24, 960 P.2d 624 (1998). It is axiomatic that one who knowingly and intentionally perpetrated a fraud on another party and the court can never be entitled to relief under the Rule. *In re Marriage of Worcester*, 192 Ariz. 24, 960 P.2d 624 (1998).

The precise scope of relief available under Rule 60(c) defies neat encapsulation, but it was primarily intended to allow relief from judgments that, although perhaps legally faultless, are unjust because of extraordinary circumstances that cannot be remedied by legal review. *Minjares v. State*, 223 Ariz. 54, 219 P.3d 264 (Ct. App. Div. 1 2009) (relief granted where judgment, correct when entered, became incorrect due to incorrect interest calculation).

Rule 60(c) may be utilized to reopen the trial court's approval of a property settlement agreement, even though that agreement has not been incorporated or merged into a judgment of dissolution. *Breitbart-Napp v. Napp*, 216 Ariz. 74, 163 P.3d 1024 (Ct. App. Div. 1 2007). The Superior Court does not have jurisdiction under Rule 60(c)(5), however, to modify a spousal maintenance award entered pursuant to an agreement which the parties have agreed would not be subject to modification, as permitted by A.R.S. §§ 25-319(C) and 25-317(G). *In re Marriage of Waldren*, 217 Ariz. 173, 171 P.3d 1214 (2007).

A trial court may vacate and re-enter a judgment under Rule 60(c) to effectively extend the time for taking an appeal. To obtain such relief, in addition to a showing of compelling circumstances to secure relief from a judgment, a party must also demonstrate (1) that it did not receive notice that judgment had been entered, (2) that it promptly filed a motion after actually receiving such notice, (3) that it exercised due diligence, or had reason for the lack thereof, and (4) that no party would be prejudiced. *Haroutunian v. Valueoptions, Inc.*, 218 Ariz. 541, 189 P.3d 1114 (Ct. App. Div. 2 2008).

Where the grounds for relief are reasons 1, 2, or 3, the motion must be brought within six (6) months after entry of the judgment under attack. *Andrew R. v. Arizona Dept. of Economic Sec.*, 223 Ariz. 453, 224 P.3d 950 (Ct. App. Div. 1 2010) (finding time barred, Rule 60(c)(3) motion challenging paternity filed more than six months after execution of an acknowledgment of paternity); *ABC Supply, Inc. v. Edwards*, 191 Ariz. 48, 952 P.2d 286 (Ct. App. Div. 1 1996), on reconsideration in part, (Oct. 30, 1997). These time limits may not be avoided merely by asserting that relief is sought under clause 6—"any other reason justifying relief," when the grounds upon which relief is actually sought are among those enumerated in clauses 1–5. *Edsall v. Superior Court In and For Pima County*, 143 Ariz. 240, 693 P.2d 895 (1984); *Dunn v. Law Offices of Ramon R. Alvarez, P. C.*, 119 Ariz. 437, 581 P.2d 282 (Ct. App. Div. 2 1978); *Vander Wagen v. Hughes*, 19 Ariz. App. 155, 505 P.2d 1046 (Div. 1 1973).

The trial court may consider, however, a factor relevant to relief under clauses 1–5 in determining whether there are extraordinary circumstances warranting relief under clause 6. *M & M Auto Storage Pool, Inc. v. Chemical Waste Management, Inc.*, 164 Ariz. 139, 791 P.2d 665 (Ct. App. Div. 1 1990). The fact that the trial court has retained jurisdiction to modify the terms of a decree of dissolution, as authorized by A.R.S. § 25-327, does not obviate the need to find one of the conditions specified in Rule 60(c) for relief from a judgment. *Schmidt v. Schmidt*, 158 Ariz. 496, 763 P.2d 992 (Ct. App. Div. 1 1988).

Both the denial of a motion for relief under Rule 60(c), and an order setting aside a dismissal of an action, are appealable as a "special order made after final judgment." *Johnson v. Elson*, 192 Ariz. 486, 967 P.2d 1022 (Ct. App. Div. 1 1998); *M & M Auto Storage Pool, Inc. v. Chemical Waste Management, Inc.*, 164 Ariz. 139, 791 P.2d 665 (Ct. App. Div. 1 1990). If a notice of appeal is filed while a Rule 60 motion is pending before the trial court and not yet decided, a subsequent notice of appeal must be filed after the trial court's decision is issued in order to confer on the appellate court jurisdiction to review that decision. *Navajo Nation v. MacDonald*, 180 Ariz. 539, 885 P.2d 1104, R.I.C.O. Bus. Disp. Guide (CCH) P 8679 (Ct. App. Div. 1 1994).

Rule 60(c) does not provide a remedy for a party seeking to set aside a satisfaction of judgment; in that instance, the party is seeking to enforce, rather than avoid, the judgment. *W.F. Conelly Const. Co. v. L. Harvey Concrete, Inc.*, 162 Ariz. 574, 785 P.2d 94 (Ct. App. Div. 2 1989). Similarly, Rule 60(c) has no application to petitions for enforcement of a judgment. *Daley v. Earven*, 166 Ariz. 461, 803 P.2d 454 (Ct. App. Div. 2 1990). A trial court's decision to grant or deny a motion brought pursuant to Rule 60(c) will be reviewed only for an abuse of discretion. *Johnson v. Elson*, 192 Ariz. 486, 967 P.2d 1022 (Ct. App. Div. 1 1998).

6. *Rule 60(c)(1)—Mistake, Inadvertence, Surprise or Excusable Neglect; Generally*. Generally, a party seeking relief from a default judgment under Rule 60(c)(1) (or, for that matter, the entry of default) must establish that (1) the failure to answer within the time required by law was due to excusable neglect, (2) relief was promptly sought, and (3) a meritorious defense to the action existed. *Master Financial, Inc. v. Woodburn*, 208 Ariz. 70, 90 P.3d 1236 (Ct. App. Div. 1 2004), as amended, (June 7, 2004). A defendant's neglect or inadvertence is compared to that of a reasonably prudent person under the circumstances. *Master Financial, Inc. v. Woodburn*, 208 Ariz. 70, 90 P.3d 1236 (Ct. App. Div. 1 2004), as amended, (June 7, 2004), as amended on other grounds, (June 7, 2004). Rule 60(c)(1) does not provide, however, for relief from judgments entered based on the statute of limitations when a complaint is untimely filed due to alleged "excusable neglect" of office staff. *Porter v. Spader*, 225 Ariz. 424, 239 P.3d 743 (Ct. App. Div. 1 2010).

An attorney's misunderstanding or ignorance of the requirements of the Arizona Rules of Civil Procedure is not the type of excuse contemplated in Rule 60(c) as a sufficient ground for vacating entry of default or default judgment. *Baker Intern. Associates, Inc. v. Shanwick Intern. Corp.*, 174 Ariz. 580, 851 P.2d 1379 (Ct. App. Div. 1 1993); *General Elec. Capital Corp. v. Osterkamp*, 172 Ariz. 185, 836 P.2d 398 (Ct. App. Div. 2 1992); *General Elec. Capital Corp. v. Osterkamp*, 172 Ariz. 191, 836 P.2d 404 (Ct. App. Div. 2 1992). An insurer may secure relief from a default of its insured if it did not have notice of the claim, and even though the insured's neglect was not excusable. *Beal v. State Farm Mut. Auto. Ins. Co.*, 151 Ariz. 514, 729 P.2d 318 (Ct. App. Div. 1 1986).

A defaulted defendant generally must show that it acted promptly in seeking relief from the entry of default. *Hilgeman v. American Mortg. Securities, Inc.*, 196 Ariz. 215, 994 P.2d 1030

(Ct. App. Div. 2 2000). A motion under Rule 60(c)(1) to set aside a default judgment for excusable neglect is timely if filed within six (6) months after entry of the judgment, even if that is more than six (6) months following the entry of default. *Harper v. Canyon Land Development, LLC*, 219 Ariz. 535, 200 P.3d 1032 (Ct. App. Div. 1 2008).

The decision whether to set aside an entry of default judgment is left to the sound discretion of the trial court and review is limited to a finding of a clear abuse of that discretion. *General Elec. Capital Corp. v. Osterkamp*, 172 Ariz. 185, 836 P.2d 398 (Ct. App. Div. 2 1992).

7. *Rule 60(c)(1), (6)—Failure to Prosecute.* A Rule 60(c) motion may be utilized for relief from an order of dismissal for failure to file a timely Motion to Set and Certificate of Readiness, as required by Ariz.R.Civ.P. 38.1(a). *American Asphalt & Grading Co. v. CMX, L.L.C.*, 227 Ariz. 117, 253 P.3d 1240 (2011); *Copeland v. Arizona Veterans Memorial Coliseum and Exposition Center*, 176 Ariz. 86, 859 P.2d 196 (Ct. App. Div. 1 1993); *Thunderbird Farms v. Hernandez*, 11 Ariz. App. 383, 464 P.2d 829 (Div. 2 1970). Where a case has been placed on the Inactive Calendar, and then dismissed as required by Rule 38.1(d), relief and reinstatement can be secured under Rule 60(c), under standards analogous to those applicable to securing relief from a default. *State ex rel. Corbin v. Marshall*, 161 Ariz. 429, 778 P.2d 1325 (Ct. App. Div. 1 1989); *Cline v. Ticor Title Ins. Co. of California*, 154 Ariz. 343, 742 P.2d 844 (Ct. App. Div. 1 1987). A Rule 60(c) motion may also be employed to secure relief from a dismissal for failure to serve within prescribed time limits, but the showing necessary to secure relief is roughly similar. *Maher v. Urman*, 211 Ariz. 543, 124 P.3d 770 (Ct. App. Div. 2 2005).

Where relief from a dismissal for failure to prosecute is sought under Rule 60(c)(6), a plaintiff must show extraordinary circumstances of hardship or injustice justifying relief, and that: (1) plaintiff diligently and vigorously prosecuted the case, (2) the parties took reasonable steps to inform the Court of the status of the case, (3) substantial prejudice will result unless relief is granted, (4) plaintiff sought relief promptly, and (5) plaintiff has a meritorious claim. *Jepson v. New*, 164 Ariz. 265, 792 P.2d 728 (1990); *Copeland v. Arizona Veterans Memorial Coliseum and Exposition Center*, 176 Ariz. 86, 859 P.2d 196 (Ct. App. Div. 1 1993); *Hyman v. Arden-Mayfair, Inc.*, 150 Ariz. 444, 724 P.2d 63 (Ct. App. Div. 1 1986); *Resolution Trust Corp. v. Maricopa County*, 176 Ariz. 631, 863 P.2d 923 (Tax Ct. 1993).

Further, a party can obtain relief under Rule 60(c)(6) from a judgment entered due to his or her attorney's failure to act only if that attorney's failure to act is legally excusable. *Panzino v. City of Phoenix*, 196 Ariz. 442, 999 P.2d 198 (2000) (discussing, and disapproving, the "positive misconduct rule"). The fact that the statute of limitations applicable to the claim has expired, so that the dismissal in fact operates with prejudice, does not in and of itself warrant relief. *Bickerstaff v. Denny's Restaurant, Inc.*, 141 Ariz. 629, 688 P.2d 637 (1984) (disapproved of on other grounds by, Panzino v. City of Phoenix, 196 Ariz. 442, 999 P.2d 198 (2000)); *Hyman v. Arden-Mayfair, Inc.*, 150 Ariz. 444, 724 P.2d 63 (Ct. App. Div. 1 1986). Relief should be granted in that instance, however, where the action has been vigorously pursued and dismissed due to inadvertence. *Gorman v. City of Phoenix*, 152 Ariz. 179, 731 P.2d 74 (1987).

Rule 60(c) does not require extraordinary vigilance, but carelessness does not equate with excusable neglect. *Ulibarri v. Gerstenberger*, 178 Ariz. 151, 871 P.2d 698 (Ct. App. Div. 1 1993) (rejected by, Logerquist v. Danforth, 188 Ariz. 16, 932 P.2d 281 (Ct. App. Div. 2 1996)). Neglect is excusable when it is such as might be the act of a reasonably prudent person in the same circumstances. *Ulibarri v. Gerstenberger*, 178 Ariz. 151, 871 P.2d 698 (Ct. App. Div. 1 1993) (rejected on other grounds by, Logerquist v. Danforth, 188 Ariz. 16, 932 P.2d 281 (Ct. App. Div. 2 1996)).

The plaintiff's failure to receive the prescribed notice that the case has been placed on the Inactive Calendar for impending dismissal is only one factor the trial court should consider in assessing the plaintiff's diligence. *Copeland v. Arizona Veterans Memorial Coliseum and Exposition Center*, 176 Ariz. 86, 859 P.2d 196 (Ct. App. Div. 1 1993). An insurer without notice may secure relief even if the insured's neglect is not excusable. *Beal v. State Farm Mut. Auto. Ins. Co.*, 151 Ariz. 514, 729 P.2d 318 (Ct. App. Div. 1 1986).

The rule followed in the discovery context that the sanction of dismissal should not be imposed for the attorney's misconduct has no application to dismissals for lack of prosecution. *Panzino v. City of Phoenix*, 196 Ariz. 442, 999 P.2d 198 (2000).

A party may obtain relief under Rule 60(c)(6) from a judgment entered due to his or her attorney's failure to act only if that attorney's failure to act is legally excusable. *Panzino v. City of Phoenix*, 196 Ariz. 442, 999 P.2d 198 (2000) (discussing, and disapproving, the "positive misconduct rule").

8. *Rule 60(c)(2)—Newly Discovered Evidence.* Where the motion for relief is based upon the grounds of newly discovered evidence, the evidence relied upon must have been in existence at the time of trial, *Rogers v. Ogg*, 101 Ariz. 161, 416 P.2d 594 (1966) (overruled by, U S West Communications, Inc. v. Arizona Dept. of Revenue, 199 Ariz. 101, 14 P.3d 292 (2000); and must not have

been discoverable through the exercise of due diligence. *Catalina Foothills Ass'n, Inc. v. White*, 132 Ariz. 427, 646 P.2d 312 (Ct. App. Div. 2 1982); *Rhodes v. Hirsch*, 5 Ariz. App. 583, 429 P.2d 470 (1967). Such asserted "newly discovered evidence," accordingly, may not consist of events occurring after the entry of judgment. *OPI Corp. v. Pima County*, 176 Ariz. 625, 863 P.2d 917 (Tax Ct. 1993). Similarly, factual matters cited as the basis for a Rule 60(c) motion will not be considered "newly discovered evidence" where the moving party did not exercise due diligence in conducting or attempting any discovery in a timely fashion. *Tovrea v. Nolan*, 178 Ariz. 485, 875 P.2d 144 (Ct. App. Div. 2 1993).

A motion seeking relief under Rule 60(c)(2) based upon newly discovered evidence must be brought within six (6) months of the order from which relief is sought—there is no discovery rule which makes the motion timely if brought within six (6) months of discovery of the new evidence. *McKernan v. Dupont*, 192 Ariz. 550, 968 P.2d 623 (Ct. App. Div. 1 1998) (disapproved of on other grounds by, Panzino v. City of Phoenix, 196 Ariz. 442, 999 P.2d 198 (2000)).

9. *Rule 60(c)(3)—Fraud or Other Misconduct.* To obtain relief under Rule 60(c)(3), the moving party must (1) have a meritorious defense, (2) that the party was prevented from fully presenting before judgment, (3) because of the adverse party's fraud, misrepresentation or misconduct. *Estate of Page v. Litzenburg*, 177 Ariz. 84, 865 P.2d 128 (Ct. App. Div. 1 1993). "Other misconduct" within the meaning of the Rule need not amount to fraud or intentional misrepresentation, but may include even accidental omissions. *Estate of Page v. Litzenburg*, 177 Ariz. 84, 865 P.2d 128 (Ct. App. Div. 1 1993). The failure to disclose or produce evidence requested in discovery can constitute misconduct justifying relief. *Estate of Page v. Litzenburg*, 177 Ariz. 84, 865 P.2d 128 (Ct. App. Div. 1 1993). Fraud as a basis for relief must be shown by clear and convincing evidence, and will not be presumed from receipt of erroneous testimony. *Lake v. Bonham*, 148 Ariz. 599, 716 P.2d 56 (Ct. App. Div. 2 1986).

The proper method for raising an alleged violation of the disclosure requirements of Ariz.R.Civ.P. 26.1 which is not discovered until *after* the entry of judgment is to file either a motion for new trial, which must be made within fifteen (15) days after the entry of judgment, or a motion under Rule 60(c) for relief from the judgment. *In re Estate of Travers*, 192 Ariz. 333, 965 P.2d 67 (Ct. App. Div. 1 1998). A violation of Rule 26.1 through intentional non-disclosure also may entitle a party to relief under Rule 60(c)(3), and such a motion must be filed within six (6) months after the judgment becomes final. *In re Estate of Travers*, 192 Ariz. 333, 965 P.2d 67 (Ct. App. Div. 1 1998) (recognizing Rule 6(b) expressly bars the extension of time for filing a Rule 60(c) motion.). *See also*, *Andrew R. v. Arizona Dept. of Economic Sec.*, 223 Ariz. 453, 224 P.3d 950 (Ct. App. Div. 1 2010) (trial court lacked authority to grant Rule 60(c)(3) motion for relief from paternity judgment filed more than six months after entry of judgment).

Relief also may be available under Rule 60(c)(3) where the failure to disclose was accidental, inadvertent and/or in good faith. *Norwest Bank (Minnesota), N.A. v. Symington*, 197 Ariz. 181, 3 P.3d 1101 (Ct. App. Div. 1 2000). Proof of misconduct alone, however, will not justify relief. The movant must also show that the failure to disclose substantially interfered with the moving party's ability to fully prepare for trial. *Norwest Bank (Minnesota), N.A. v. Symington*, 197 Ariz. 181, 3 P.3d 1101 (Ct. App. Div. 1 2000).

10. *Rule 60(c)(4), (5)—Void or Satisfied Judgment.* A party seeking relief from a judgment claimed to be void must (and should) proceed under Rule 60(c)(4) rather than under Rule 60(c)(6). *Brooks v. Consolidated Freightways Corp. of Delaware*, 173 Ariz. 66, 839 P.2d 1111 (Ct. App. Div. 1 1992). A judgment or order is "void" if the Court entering it lacked jurisdiction over the subject matter, over the party against whom it was entered, or to render the particular judgment or order entered. *Master Financial, Inc. v. Woodburn*, 208 Ariz. 70, 90 P.3d 1236 (Ct. App. Div. 1 2004), as amended, (June 7, 2004); *Martin v. Martin*, 182 Ariz. 11, 893 P.2d 11 (Ct. App. Div. 1 1994).

If a judgment or order is void, the trial court has no discretion and must vacate it. *Ezell v. Quon*, 224 Ariz. 532, 233 P.3d 645 (Ct. App. Div. 1 2010); *Springfield Credit Union v. Johnson*, 123 Ariz. 319, 599 P.2d 772 (1979); *Preston v. Denkins*, 94 Ariz. 214, 382 P.2d 686 (1963); *Martin v. Martin*, 182 Ariz. 11, 893 P.2d 11 (Ct. App. Div. 1 1994). There is no time limit within which a motion for relief under Rule 60(c)(4) must be brought, and the Court must grant relief from a judgment or order that is void even if the party seeking relief delayed unreasonably in doing so. *Martin v. Martin*, 182 Ariz. 11, 893 P.2d 11 (Ct. App. Div. 1 1994); *Brooks v. Consolidated Freightways Corp. of Delaware*, 173 Ariz. 66, 839 P.2d 1111 (Ct. App. Div. 1 1992).

A party seeking relief from a void default judgment need not show that their failure to file a timely answer was excusable, that they acted promptly in seeking relief, or that they had a meritorious defense. *Master Financial, Inc. v. Woodburn*, 208 Ariz. 70, 90 P.3d 1236 (Ct. App. Div. 1 2004), as amended on other grounds, (June 7, 2004). By contrast, a party must request relief under Rule 60(c)(6) within a reasonable time and the trial court has discretion to determine whether or not a delay in seeking relief is reasonable. *Delbridge v. Salt River Project Agr. Imp.*

and Power Dist., 182 Ariz. 46, 893 P.2d 46 (Ct. App. Div. 1 1994); *Martin v. Martin*, 182 Ariz. 11, 893 P.2d 11 (Ct. App. Div. 1 1994); *Brooks v. De La Cruz*, 12 Ariz. App. 591, 473 P.2d 793 (Div. 1 1970).

A claim that a judgment has been satisfied must be supported by a formal, filed satisfaction of judgment. *Koepke v. Carter Hawley Hale Stores, Inc.*, 140 Ariz. 420, 682 P.2d 425 (Ct. App. Div. 1 1984). A Rule 60(c) motion, however, is not the appropriate vehicle for seeking to set aside a satisfaction of judgment. *W.F. Conelly Const. Co. v. L. Harvey Concrete, Inc.*, 162 Ariz. 574, 785 P.2d 94 (Ct. App. Div. 2 1989).

11. *Rule 60(c)(6)—Other Grounds Justifying Relief.* Relief granted on the basis of Clause 6 is usually reserved for cases where none of the particular reasons for relief described in clauses 1 through 5 of the Rule are applicable and the motion raises extraordinary circumstances of hardship or injustice. *Davis v. Davis*, 143 Ariz. 54, 691 P.2d 1082 (1984); *Webb v. Erickson*, 134 Ariz. 182, 655 P.2d 6 (1982); *Hilgeman v. American Mortg. Securities, Inc.*, 196 Ariz. 215, 994 P.2d 1030 (Ct. App. Div. 2 2000); *In re Estate of Travers*, 192 Ariz. 333, 965 P.2d 67 (Ct. App. Div. 1 1998); *Hyman v. Arden-Mayfair, Inc.*, 150 Ariz. 444, 724 P.2d 63 (Ct. App. Div. 1 1986). *But see, Amanti Elec., Inc. v. Engineered Structures, Inc.*, 229 Ariz. 430, 276 P.3d 499 (Ct. App. Div. 2 2012) (stating that even when relief may have been available under Rule 60(c)(1)-(5), but for the fact that the time limits of the rule had elapsed, this circumstance does not necessarily preclude relief under Rule 60(c)(6) if such motion also raises exceptional additional circumstances that convince the court relief should be granted in the interest of justice); *Roll v. Janca*, 22 Ariz. App. 335, 527 P.2d 294 (Div. 1 1974) ('despite availability of relief under Rule 60(c)(4), relief also available pursuant to Rule 60(c)(6) "under circumstances going beyond" foregoing clauses of rule').

In determining whether Rule 60(c)(6) relief is appropriate, the trial court must consider the "totality of facts and circumstances" presented. *Amanti Elec., Inc. v. Engineered Structures, Inc.*, 229 Ariz. 430, 276 P.3d 499 (Ct. App. Div. 2 2012), quoting *Roll v. Janca*, 22 Ariz. App. 335, 527 P.2d 294 (Div. 1 1974). In the 1982 case of *Webb v. Erickson,* the Arizona Supreme Court affirmed the trial court's order vacating a judgment against a garnishee three and a half years after its entry upon the basis of excusable neglect where there were "extraordinary circumstances" and lack of notice of entry of judgment. *Webb v. Erickson*, 134 Ariz. 182, 655 P.2d 6 (1982). The Court in *Webb* stated that none of those factors alone would be sufficient to invoke equitable relief, but in combination they created a unique situation so that the trial court did not abuse its discretion in granting relief under the sixth ground.

To obtain Rule 60(c)(6) relief from a dismissal for lack of prosecution, a plaintiff must show extraordinary circumstances of hardship or injustice justifying relief as well as proof that: (1) plaintiff diligently and vigorously prosecuted the case; (2) the parties took reasonable steps to inform the court of the case status; (3) substantial prejudice will result unless relief is granted; (4) plaintiff sought relief promptly and (5) plaintiff has a meritorious claim. *Jepson v. New*, 164 Ariz. 265, 792 P.2d 728 (1990); *Copeland v. Arizona Veterans Memorial Coliseum and Exposition Center*, 176 Ariz. 86, 859 P.2d 196 (Ct. App. Div. 1 1993); *Hyman v. Arden-Mayfair, Inc.*, 150 Ariz. 444, 724 P.2d 63 (Ct. App. Div. 1 1986). Establishing a "meritorious defense" as a foundation for relief under Rule 60(c)(6) does not require a showing that the moving party is likely to prevail on the merits; the moving party need only demonstrate by "affidavit, deposition, or testimony some facts which, if proved at trial, would constitute a viable defense." *United Imports and Exports, Inc. v. Superior Court of State In and For Maricopa County*, 134 Ariz. 43, 653 P.2d 691 (1982).

In, and of itself, the failure to receive the notice of entry of judgment required by former Rule 77(g) (now, Ariz.R.Civ.P. 58(e)), is not sufficient. *Park v. Strick*, 137 Ariz. 100, 669 P.2d 78 (1983); *Lone Mountain Ranch, Inc. v. Dillingham Inv., Inc.*, 131 Ariz. 583, 643 P.2d 28 (Ct. App. Div. 2 1982).

Where a party has not been afforded the requisite five days' notice of a proposed form of judgment under Ariz.R.Civ.P. 58(d) and can demonstrate prejudice, relief should be granted. *Dawe v. City of Scottsdale*, 119 Ariz. 486, 581 P.2d 1136 (1978); *Gutierrez v. Gutierrez*, 20 Ariz. App. 388, 513 P.2d 677 (Div. 2 1973); *Green Reservoir Flood Control Dist. v. Willmoth*, 15 Ariz. App. 406, 489 P.2d 69 (Div. 2 1971).

A motion for relief under Rule 60(c)(6) must be filed within a "reasonable time" after the judgment is entered. *Harper v. Canyon Land Development, LLC*, 219 Ariz. 535, 200 P.3d 1032 (Ct. App. Div. 1 2008); *Hilgeman v. American Mortg. Securities, Inc.*, 196 Ariz. 215, 994 P.2d 1030 (Ct. App. Div. 2 2000).

A trial court's disposition of a motion brought pursuant to Rule 60(c)(6) will not be disturbed on appeal absent an abuse of discretion. *Delbridge v. Salt River Project Agr. Imp. and Power Dist.*, 182 Ariz. 46, 893 P.2d 46 (Ct. App. Div. 1 1994); *Martin v. Martin*, 182 Ariz. 11, 893 P.2d 11 (Ct. App. Div. 1 1994).

12. *Effect of Savings Statute.* An alternative, or companion, avenue for relief where a dismissal for failure to prosecute, which is nominally without prejudice, occurs after the expiration of the statute of limitations, is the Arizona "savings statute," A.R.S.

§ 12-504, which authorizes the court entering the dismissal to allow a period of up to six (6) months for the claim to be reinstated. By the terms of the statute itself, whether a party's right to refile a suit is absolute or discretionary depends upon the reason for the initial termination of the action. If the initial termination was for insufficiency of process, rather than abatement for failure to serve or prosecute, the statute entitles the plaintiff to refile the action as a matter of right. *Schwartz v. Arizona Primary Care Physicians*, 192 Ariz. 290, 964 P.2d 491 (Ct. App. Div. 1 1998).

There was a divergence of views between two Departments of Division One of the Arizona Court of Appeals concerning the standards to be applied in deciding whether to grant relief under A.R.S. § 12-504 in that circumstance. In *Flynn v. Cornoyer-Hedrick Architects & Planners, Inc.*, 160 Ariz. 187, 772 P.2d 10 (Ct. App. Div. 1 1988), decision aff'd, 164 Ariz. 265, 792 P.2d 728 (1990), the Court held that the inquiry was essentially the same as where relief was sought under Rule 60(c), and the plaintiff must show excusable neglect and due diligence. The Court in *Jepson v. New*, 160 Ariz. 193, 772 P.2d 16 (Ct. App. Div. 1 1989), vacated in part, 164 Ariz. 265, 792 P.2d 728 (1990), however, disagreed that the inquiry was identical to that under Rule 60(c), and held that the test for granting relief under A.R.S. § 12-504 was whether the defendant would be unduly prejudiced by permitting refiling of the action. In a consolidated appeal, the Supreme Court rejected the test for relief articulated in *Jepson I*, and approved that enunciated in *Flynn*, *viz.*, that, to secure relief under the statute, the plaintiff must show that the plaintiff acted reasonably and in good faith and prosecuted the action vigorously and diligently. *Jepson v. New*, 164 Ariz. 265, 792 P.2d 728 (1990). The plaintiff's failure to seek relief under A.R.S. § 12-504 until after expiration of the six-month period to refile authorized by the statute is evidence of a lack of the required diligence. *Copeland v. Arizona Veterans Memorial Coliseum and Exposition Center*, 176 Ariz. 86, 859 P.2d 196 (Ct. App. Div. 1 1993).

The "savings statute" applies to actions originally instituted in other jurisdictions, even where they have been dismissed for lack of personal jurisdiction, *Templer v. Zele*, 166 Ariz. 390, 803 P.2d 111 (Ct. App. Div. 2 1990); it may not be employed where the prior action has been terminated in an adjudication on the merits. *Matter of Forfeiture of $3,000.00 U.S. Currency*, 164 Ariz. 120, 791 P.2d 646 (Ct. App. Div. 2 1990). Where there has been a dismissal or abatement for failure to secure timely service, relief may be available under the statute, but the plaintiff must show an inability to effect service despite diligent efforts to do so. *Maher v. Urman*, 211 Ariz. 543, 124 P.3d 770 (Ct. App. Div. 2 2005). The statute, by its terms, applies to an action that is timely filed and then terminated for one of the enumerated reasons, regardless of whether the termination occurs before or after the limitations period has expired. *Janson on Behalf of Janson v. Christensen*, 167 Ariz. 470, 808 P.2d 1222 (1991). An order denying relief under A.R.S. § 12-504 will be reversed on appeal only for an abuse of discretion. *Maher v. Urman*, 211 Ariz. 543, 124 P.3d 770 (Ct. App. Div. 2 2005); *Copeland v. Arizona Veterans Memorial Coliseum and Exposition Center*, 176 Ariz. 86, 859 P.2d 196 (Ct. App. Div. 1 1993). The statute does not apply when the trial court has made a final adjudication on the merits. *Tilley v. Delci*, 220 Ariz. 233, 204 P.3d 1082 (Ct. App. Div. 1 2009).

13. *Relief From Foreign Judgment.* The Full Faith and Credit Clause, U.S. Const., Art. IV, § 1, requires that Arizona courts accord a foreign judgment the same validity and effect as they would have in the state rendering it. *Springfield Credit Union v. Johnson*, 123 Ariz. 319, 599 P.2d 772 (1979); *Cho v. American Bonding Co.*, 190 Ariz. 593, 951 P.2d 468 (Ct. App. Div. 1 1997); *Oyakawa v. Gillett*, 175 Ariz. 226, 854 P.2d 1212 (Ct. App. Div. 1 1993); *Tarnoff v. Jones*, 17 Ariz. App. 240, 497 P.2d 60 (Div. 1 1972). The Clause was intended to nationalize the doctrine of *res judicata*. *Giehrl v. Royal Aloha Vacation Club, Inc.*, 188 Ariz. 456, 937 P.2d 378 (Ct. App. Div. 1 1997). An Arizona court must set aside an Arizona judgment that is based upon a foreign judgment that has been set aside or reversed.

Arizona courts are not required, however, to give full faith and credit to judgments of courts of foreign nations. Such a judgment will be honored if the Arizona court is convinced that the foreign nation's court had jurisdiction and there was an opportunity for a full and fair trial without prejudice. *Rotary Club of Tucson v. Chaprales Ramos de Pena*, 160 Ariz. 362, 773 P.2d 467 (Ct. App. Div. 2 1989). Foreign judgments, however, may be attacked if the rendering court lacked jurisdiction over the person or the subject matter, if the judgment was obtained through lack of due process or was the result of extrinsic fraud, or if the judgment was invalid or unenforceable. *Cho v. American Bonding Co.*, 190 Ariz. 593, 951 P.2d 468 (Ct. App. Div. 1 1997); *Pioneer Federal Sav. Bank v. Driver*, 166 Ariz. 585, 804 P.2d 118 (Ct. App. Div. 1 1990). If an Arizona court finds that the notice given to the defendant in the foreign tribunal failed to satisfy constitutional due process standards, it may properly refuse to give the foreign court's judgment full faith and credit. *Pioneer Federal Sav. Bank v. Driver*, 166 Ariz. 585, 804 P.2d 118 (Ct. App. Div. 1 1990). These issues are discussed further in the *Authors' Comments* under Rule 69.

Rule 61. Harmless error

No error in either the admission or the exclusion of evidence and no error or defect in any ruling or order or in anything done or omitted by the court or by any of the parties is ground for granting a new trial or for setting aside a verdict or for vacating, modifying or otherwise disturbing a judgment or order, unless refusal to take such action appears to the court inconsistent with substantial justice. The court at every stage of the proceeding must disregard any error or defect in the proceeding which does not affect the substantial rights of the parties.

AUTHORS' COMMENTS

Analysis

1. *Scope and Purpose of Rule.* Rule 61 merely articulates the general principle, which imbues the application of several other Rules, that it is not the occurrence of error, but rather its prejudicial effect, that warrants relief from the prior resolution of the parties' claims. Thus, a verdict is not to be set aside, a new trial is not to be granted, and a judgment is not to be vacated or disturbed unless the Court determines that to refuse to do so would be inconsistent with substantial justice.

2. *Comparison With Federal Rule.* ARCP 61 is essentially identical to FRCP 61.

In 2007, the language of FRCP 61 was amended as part of the general restyling of the Federal Rules of Civil Procedure to make the Federal Rules more easily understood and to make style and terminology consistent throughout the Federal Rules of Civil Procedure. Those stylistic modifications have not been incorporated into ARCP 61.

Rule 62. Stay of proceedings to enforce a judgment

(a) Stay in Injunctions and Receiverships. Unless otherwise ordered by the court, an interlocutory or final judgment in an action for an injunction or in a receivership action shall not be stayed during the period after its entry and until an appeal is taken or during the pendency of an appeal. The provisions of subdivision (c) of this Rule govern the suspending, modifying, restoring, or granting of an injunction during the pendency of an appeal.

(b) Stay on Motion for New Trial or for Judgment. In its discretion and on such conditions for the security of the adverse party as are proper, the court may stay the execution of or any proceedings to enforce a judgment pending the disposition of a motion for a new trial or to alter or amend a judgment made pursuant to Rule 59, or of a motion for relief from a judgment or order made pursuant to subdivisions (a) and (c) of Rule 60, or of a motion for judgment in accordance with a motion for judgment as a matter of law made pursuant to Rule 50, or of a motion for amendment to the findings or for additional findings made pursuant to Rule 52(b), or when justice so requires in other cases until such time as the court may fix.

Amended July 14, 1961, effective Nov. 1, 1961; Feb. 26, 1992, effective May 1, 1992; Jan. 26, 1993, effective June 1, 1993; Oct. 9, 1996, effective Dec. 1, 1996; Oct. 14, 1997, effective Oct. 15, 1997.

(c) Injunction Pending Appeal. When an appeal is taken from an interlocutory or final judgment granting, dissolving, or denying an injunction, the court in its discretion may suspend, modify, restore, or grant an injunction during the pendency of the appeal upon such terms as to bond or otherwise as it considers proper for the security of the rights of the adverse party.

(d) and (e) [Deleted effective January 1, 1978].

(f) Stay of Judgment Directing Execution of Instrument; Sale of Perishable Property and Disposition of Proceeds.

1. If the judgment or order appealed from directs the execution of a conveyance or other instrument, the execution of the judgment or order shall not be stayed by the appeal until the instrument is executed and deposited with the clerk of the superior court to abide the judgment of the supreme court.

2. A judgment or order directing the sale of perishable property shall not be stayed, but the proceeds of the sale shall be deposited with the clerk of the superior court to abide the appeal.

(g) Stay in Favor of the State or Agency or Political Subdivision Thereof. Money judgments against the state or agency or political subdivision thereof, are automatically stayed when an appeal is filed. Judgments against the state or agency or political subdivision thereof other than money judgments are not automatically stayed when an appeal is filed, but as to them, no bond can be required if a stay is ordered.

Amended Feb. 26, 1992, effective May 1, 1992.

(h) [Deleted effective January 1, 1978].

(i) Stay of Judgment Under Rule 54(b). When a court has ordered a final judgment under the conditions stated in Rule 54(b), the court may stay enforcement of that judgment until the entering of a subsequent judgment or judgments and may prescribe such conditions as are necessary to secure the benefit thereof to the party in whose favor the judgment is entered.

Amended July 14, 1961, effective Nov. 1, 1961.

(j) Stay of Judgments In Rem. No execution or other process shall issue on judgments in rem disposing of an interest in property in connection with which a proper claim was timely filed and the claimant is not in default until 15 days after the time for filing a notice of appeal begins. Within such 15-day period, no such judgment shall be self-executing.

Added Jan. 26, 1993, effective June 1, 1993.

STATE BAR COMMITTEE NOTES

1961 Amendment

[Rule 62(i)] The changes in Rule 62(i) conform to the amendment of Rule 54(b). Since it is amended to cover cases of both multiple claims and multiple parties, the restriction of Rule 62(i) to multiple claims situations must also be adjusted.

COURT COMMENT

1993 Amendment

[Rule 62(j)] The jurisdictional rule announced in In the *Matter of One Hundred Thirteen Thousand Eight Hundred Eighty-Eight Dollars ($113,888.00) U.S. Currency*, 168 Ariz. 229, 812 P.2d 1047 (Ct. App. Div. 1 1990) (overruled by, Matter of One Single Family Residence and Real Property Located at 15453 North Second Avenue, 185 Ariz. 35, 912 P.2d 39 (Ct. App. Div. 1 1996)) is drawn into question by *Republic Nat. Bank of Miami v. U.S.*, 506 U.S. 80, 113 S. Ct. 554, 121 L. Ed. 2d 474, 1993 A.M.C. 2010 (1992). However, as noted in Republic National Bank of Miami, irrespective of the court's jurisdiction over an appeal, loss of control of the res could effectively deprive a party of a remedy. Rule 62(j) is designed to preserve the appeal as an efficacious remedy.

AUTHORS' COMMENTS

Analysis

1. Scope and Purpose of Rule.

1. *Scope and Purpose of Rule.* Rule 62 must be considered in conjunction with Rule 7 of the Arizona Rules of Civil Appellate Procedure to which several former provisions of Rule 62 were transferred in 1978. Together, these two Rules define the procedures for securing a stay of a judgment, or an injunction, pending an appeal.

2. *Comparison With Federal Rule.* There are significant substantive and structural differences between ARCP 62 and FRCP 62.

ARCP 62(a) does not contain the provision found in FRCP 62(a) that automatically stays execution upon judgments, not otherwise excepted by the rule, for 14 days after their entry. And FRCP 62(a) no longer contains the final sentence found in ARCP 62(a). In 2007, FRCP 62 was amended to delete that final sentence, which referred to Rule 62(c), as unnecessary because FRCP 62(c) "governs of its own force." ARCP 62(a) has not been amended to conform to its federal counterpart.

Despite structural differences, ARCP 62(b) and FRCP 62(b) are substantially similar in content. ARCP 62(c) is similar, but not identical, to FRCP 62(c). For instance, ARCP 62(c) does not contain the provision found in FRCP 62(c) dealing with stays when appeals are taken from district courts composed of three judges.

Before 1978, former ARCP 62(d), (e), and (h) were substantially similar to current FRCP 62(d) and (g); but, in 1978, those rules were abrogated upon the adoption of the Arizona Rules of Civil Appellate Procedure. FRCP 62 does not have a provision that directly corresponds to ARCP 62(f) [Stay of Judgment Directing Execution of Instrument; Sale of Perishable Property and Disposition of Proceeds]. ARCP 62 does not have a provision that directly corresponds to FRCP 62(f) [Stay in Favor of Debtor Under State Law].

ARCP 62(g) and FRCP 62(e) deal with the same subject matter, stays of judgments against the government, but their provisions are substantively different. ARCP 62(i) is substantially identical to FRCP 62(h). FRCP 62 does not have a provision that corresponds to ARCP 62(j).

In 2007, the language of FRCP 62 was amended as part of the general restyling of the Federal Rules of Civil Procedure to make the Federal Rules more easily understood and to make style and terminology consistent throughout the Federal Rules of Civil Procedure. Those stylistic modifications have not been incorporated into ARCP 62.

3. *Stay of Execution on Judgments Generally.* Arizona has not adopted the first sentence of Rule 62(a) of the Federal Rules of Civil Procedure, which provides an automatic stay of execution upon a judgment "until the expiration of 10 days after its entry." In Arizona, accordingly, a judgment creditor may commence enforcement and/or collection procedures immediately upon the entry of a judgment, even though the judgment debtor has fifteen (15) days thereafter in which to renew a previously unsuccessful motion for judgment as a matter of law and/or file a motion for new trial, and at least thirty days thereafter to file a notice of appeal. *Salt River Sand and Rock Co. v. Dunevant*, 222 Ariz. 102, 213 P.3d 251 (Ct. App. Div. 1 2009); *Bruce Church, Inc. v. Superior Court In and For County of Yuma*, 160 Ariz. 514, 774 P.2d 818 (Ct. App. Div. 1 1989). Execution upon a judgment may be stayed by the trial court pending disposition of post-trial or post-judgment motions, and is automatically stayed by the filing of a *supersedeas* bond as contemplated by Rule 7, Ariz. R. Civ. App. Pr.

That Rule contemplates that issues concerning the form and sufficiency of the bond to be posted pending appeal are ordinarily to be resolved by the trial court. Normally, a *supersedeas* bond should be posted in an amount which secures the total judgment together with an amount which reasonably covers costs, interest and any damages which might be attributed to the delay in collection pending appeal. *Salt River Sand and Rock Co. v. Dunevant*, 222 Ariz. 102, 213 P.3d 251 (Ct. App. Div. 1 2009); *Bruce Church, Inc. v. Superior Court In and For County of Yuma*, 160 Ariz. 514, 774 P.2d 818 (Ct. App. Div. 1 1989). Particularized objections to the bond posted are to be filed no later than ten (10) days after the bond is served, and the trial court must conduct a hearing on the objections within ten (10) days after they are served. Rule 7(a)(3), Ariz. R. Civ. App. Pr. The trial court has the authority and discretion to fashion substitute security but, if it chooses to explore such alternatives, it must provide notice, an opportunity to respond, and a hearing. *Bruce Church, Inc. v. Superior Court In and For County of Yuma*, 160 Ariz. 514, 774 P.2d 818 (Ct. App. Div. 1 1989) (the trial court may certainly pursue alternatives to the usual cash bond, if it finds the existence of extraordinary facts and circumstances call for departure). The judgment debtor has the burden of providing reasons for departure from the bond requirement and the obligation of presenting an alternative method of security that is reasonably calculated to preserve the *status quo* pending appeal. *Salt River Sand and Rock Co. v. Dunevant*, 222 Ariz. 102, 213 P.3d 251 (Ct. App. Div. 1 2009); *Bruce Church, Inc. v. Superior Court In and For County of Yuma*, 160 Ariz. 514, 774 P.2d 818 (Ct. App. Div. 1 1989).

4. *Stay of Enforcement of Judgments Pending Post-Trial Proceedings and/or Appeal.* Rule 62(b) provides the trial court with limited authority to stay proceedings to enforce a judgment pending the disposition of those post-trial motions specified therein, "on such conditions for the security of the adverse party as are proper. . . ." Depending upon the length of time the Court anticipates will be necessary to secure such a disposition, it may be impractical to require the posting of a bond.

After the disposition of such motions, or if no such motions are filed, a stay of execution or enforcement may only be secured as specified in Rule 7, Ariz. R. Civ. App. Pr. Generally, this requires the posting of a *supersedeas* bond, as contemplated by Rule 7(a), although Rule 7(c) recognizes the power of the appellate court to "stay proceedings during the pendency of an appeal . . .", apparently without requiring a bond. The *supersedeas* bond should normally be in an amount which secures the entire judgment plus interest, and any costs or other damages that might result from the stay of execution pending appeal.

The trial court has both authority and discretion to fashion substitute or alternative security but, if it chooses to explore such alternatives, it must provide notice to the judgment creditor and a hearing. The judgment debtor has the burden of proving reasons for departure from the bond requirement and the obligation to present alternative methods for providing security that are reasonably calculated to preserve the *status quo* pending appeal. *Salt River Sand and Rock Co. v. Dunevant*, 222 Ariz. 102, 213 P.3d 251 (Ct. App. Div. 1 2009); *Bruce Church, Inc. v. Superior Court In and For County of Yuma*, 160 Ariz. 514, 774 P.2d 818 (Ct. App. Div. 1 1989).

In determining whether to order alternate security, a court must balance the judgment creditor's right to collect the monetary judgment against the judgment debtor's right to pursue appellate relief. *Salt River Sand and Rock Co. v. Dunevant*, 222 Ariz. 102, 213 P.3d 251 (Ct. App. Div. 1 2009).

5. *Stays Where Injunctive Relief Involved.* Rule 62(c) authorizes the trial court to "suspend, modify, restore, or grant an injunction" pending an appeal from an order or judgment "granting,

dissolving, or denying an injunction." Rule 7(c), Ariz. R. Civ. App. Pr. recognizes a similar power of the appellate court to "suspend, modify, restore or grant an injunction during the pendency of an appeal, or to make any order appropriate to preserve the status quo . . .", but requires that any application for such relief "be made in the first instance in the superior court."

6. *Stays in Favor of Governmental Entities.* The provisions of Rule 62(g) were amended in their entirety, effective May 1, 1992. Under the amended Rule, monetary judgments against the state, a state agency or a political subdivision of the state, are automatically stayed when an appeal is filed.

The Rule is silent on whether execution can proceed before a notice of appeal is filed, but such action would appear to be contrary to the sense of the Rule. Similarly, the Rule does not specify whether or not a bond is required for such a stay. Judgments against governmental entities for other than monetary relief are not automatically stayed when an appeal is taken. A stay can be applied for, however, and, if it is granted, the Rule specifies that no bond is required.

In direct-condemnation actions governed by A.R.S. §§ 12-1111 to 12-1130, A.R.S. § 12-1127(B) provides for the payment of a condemnation award upon application by the condemnee, even if the condemning authority is prosecuting an appeal on the grounds that the award was excessive. A.R.S. § 12-1127(B) conflicts with the provisions of Rule 62(g), but the statute confers a substantive right to receive payment pending appeal, and thus controls over the Rule. *City of Phoenix v. Johnson*, 220 Ariz. 189, 204 P.3d 447 (Ct. App. Div. 1 2009).

In an inverse condemnation action, however, there is no statutory counterpart to A.R.S. § 12-1127(B). Thus, in an inverse condemnation action, if judgment is entered for the value of the land taken (which the county-defendant pays) and litigation expenses (which the county-defendant does not pay but appeals), Rule 62(g) operates to automatically stay enforcement of the unpaid amount of the judgment; and, an order to pay the remaining amounts due under the judgment despite the pending appeal is error. *Pima County v. McCarville ex rel. County of Pinal*, 224 Ariz. 366, 231 P.3d 370 (Ct. App. Div. 2 2010).

7. *Stay of Enforcement of Judgments Involving Less Than All Parties or Less Than All Claims.* If the Court in a case involving multiple claims and/or multiple parties enters a judgment as to one or more but fewer than all claims or parties and makes the determination and direction as to immediate entry contemplated by Rule 54(b), that judgment becomes final and appealable, and may be enforced as such.

Rule 62(i) permits the trial court, in its discretion, to stay enforcement proceedings until all claims against all parties are resolved. In granting such a stay, the trial court "may prescribe such conditions as are necessary to secure the benefit thereof to the party in whose favor the judgment is entered."

8. *Stays of Judgments in Rem.* Under Rule 62(j), effective June 1, 1993, there can be no execution on a judgment *in rem* disposing of an interest in property for a period of fifteen (15) days from the date of its entry if a timely claim to the property was filed and the claimant is not in default.

9. *Jurisdiction After Appeal Taken.* The general rule is that an appeal divests the trial court of jurisdiction except for matters in furtherance of the appeal or to enter orders to perpetuate the testimony of witnesses pursuant to Rule 27(b), and the trial court has no power to enter a new judgment related to the subject matter of a judgment pending an appeal. *Lightning A Ranch Venture v. Tankersley*, 161 Ariz. 497, 779 P.2d 812 (Ct. App. Div. 2 1989); *Holm Development and Management, Inc. v. Superior Court In and For County of Maricopa*, 161 Ariz. 376, 778 P.2d 1272 (Ct. App. Div. 1 1989). A flexible approach is to be taken in applying this rule; the trial court retains jurisdiction to act so long as the act cannot negate the decision in a pending appeal or frustrate the appeal process. *State v. O'Connor*, 171 Ariz. 19, 827 P.2d 480 (Ct. App. Div. 1 1992).

In the case of an appeal taken from the issuance of a preliminary injunction, the trial court retains jurisdiction with respect to the balance of the case, but is divested of jurisdiction with respect to the injunction. *State ex rel. Corbin v. Tolleson*, 152 Ariz. 376, 732 P.2d 1114 (Ct. App. Div. 1 1986). After an appeal has been taken, the trial court may only modify the injunction to preserve the *status quo*. *State ex rel. Corbin v. Tolleson*, 152 Ariz. 376, 732 P.2d 1114 (Ct. App. Div. 1 1986). A motion to dissolve or modify an injunction, brought pursuant to Rule 62(c), does *not* extend the time for taking an appeal. *Nu-Tred Tire Co., Inc. v. Dunlop Tire & Rubber Corp.*, 118 Ariz. 417, 577 P.2d 268 (Ct. App. Div. 1 1978). The trial court generally does not lose jurisdiction when an appeal is taken from the denial of a request for an injunction. *Holm Development and Management, Inc. v. Superior Court In and For County of Maricopa*, 161 Ariz. 376, 778 P.2d 1272 (Ct. App. Div. 1 1989).

Rule 63. Disability of a judge

If a trial or hearing has been commenced and the judge is unable to proceed, any other judge may proceed with it upon certifying familiarity with the record and determining that the proceedings in the case may be completed without prejudice to the parties. In a hearing or trial without a jury, the successor judge shall at the request of a party recall any witness whose testimony is material and disputed and who is available to testify again without undue burden. The successor judge may also recall any other witness.

Amended Sept. 15, 1987, effective Nov. 15, 1987; Oct. 9, 1996, effective Dec. 1, 1996.

STATE BAR COMMITTEE NOTE

1996 Amendment

The 1996 Amendment to Rule 63 substantially displaces the former Rule. The amendment adopts the present Federal Rule 63 in its entirety. The Committee recommends review of the Advisory Committee Notes following the 1991 Amendment to the existing Federal Rule.

AUTHORS' COMMENTS

Analysis

1. Scope and Purpose of Rule.
2. Comparison With Federal Rule.

1. *Scope and Purpose of Rule.* Rule 63 deals with the situation where a judge to whom a case has been assigned dies or becomes incapacitated before matters in the case are fully resolved. Before December 1, 1996, the Rule permitted the substitution of a new judge regularly sitting in or assigned to the same Court, but only where the originally assigned judge died or became incapacitated after a case had been tried and only to complete whatever post-trial duties remained to be performed. The Rule was intended to avoid the waste and expense that would be entailed by automatically requiring the parties to start the trial anew before another judge, if a replacement judge was in a position to complete the matter. *Daru v. Martin*, 89 Ariz. 373, 363 P.2d 61 (1961).

The coverage of the Rule was significantly expanded by an amendment which became effective December 1, 1996. Under the amended Rule, a new judge may be substituted for one who has died or become incapacitated at any time after a trial or hearing commences, if the substitute judge determines that the substitution will not prejudice the parties. Where such a substitution occurs during the course of a hearing or a trial without a jury, the successor judge must, at the request of any party, recall any witness whose testimony is material and disputed and who is available to testify again without undue burden. The successor judge has discretion to recall any other witness as well. Under the amended Rule, there is no requirement that the successor judge be one regularly assigned to or sitting in the Court in which the action is pending.

Before the adoption of the 1996 amended version of Rule 63, the Arizona Supreme Court took the view that, when a trial judge's handling of a case ceases before the judge is able to make any findings of fact from the evidence, it was an abuse of discretion to refuse to grant a new trial. *Daru v. Martin*, 89 Ariz. 373, 363 P.2d 61 (1961). *See also*, *Davis v. Davis*, 195 Ariz. 158, 985 P.2d 643 (Ct. App. Div. 1 1999). Unlike former Rule 63, the current version of Rule 63 (as amended) does not limit the reasons for withdrawal of the prior judge before a successor may step in. The rule (as amended), therefore, would apply in the instance of a recusal of the predecessor judge. *Davis v. Davis*, 195 Ariz. 158, 985 P.2d 643 (Ct. App. Div. 1 1999).

2. *Comparison With Federal Rule*. As a consequence of the 1996 amendment to the Arizona Rule, ARCP 63 is now once again substantially identical to FRCP 63. In fact, the State Bar Committee Note to the 1996 amendment so notes.

In 2007, however, the language of FRCP 63 was amended as part of the general restyling of the Federal Rules of Civil Procedure to make the Federal Rules more easily understood and to make style and terminology consistent throughout the Federal Rules of Civil Procedure. Those stylistic modifications have not been incorporated into ARCP 63.

VIII. PROVISIONAL AND FINAL REMEDIES AND SPECIAL PROCEEDINGS

Rule 64. Seizure of person or property

At the commencement of and during the course of an action, all remedies providing for seizure of person or property for the purpose of securing satisfaction of the judgment ultimately to be entered in the action are available under the circumstances and in the manner provided by law. The remedies thus available include arrest, attachment, garnishment, replevin, sequestration, and other corresponding or equivalent remedies, however designated and regardless of whether the remedy is ancillary to an action or must be obtained by an independent action.

AUTHORS' COMMENTS

Analysis

21. Proceedings Upon Answer; Objection to Writ of Garnishment of Non-Earnings.
22. Discharge of Garnishee.
23. Garnishments of Earnings Generally; Scope of Remedy; Application for Writ.
24. Issuance of Writ of Garnishment of Earnings.
25. Service Requirements for Writ of Garnishment of Earnings.
26. Notice to Debtor of Writ of Garnishment of Earnings; Effect of Service of Writ.
27. Answer to Writ of Garnishment of Earnings.
28. Proceedings Upon Answer.
29. Objection to Writ or Answer.
30. Resolution of Objections to Writ of Garnishment of Earnings.
31. Order for Continuing Lien on Earnings; Effect.

1. *Scope and Purpose of Rule.* Rule 64 merely provides that the Rules of Civil Procedure do not limit or affect the availability of whatever prejudgment remedies "are available under the circumstances and in the manner provided by law" for "securing satisfaction of the judgment ultimately to be entered in the action.. . ." The procedures for securing remedies to enforce or collect a judgment already entered are the subject of Ariz.R.Civ.P. 69 and 70.

2. *Comparison With Federal Rule.* Despite structural differences, ARCP 64 and ARCP 64 are substantially identical. In 2007, however, the language of FRCP 64 was amended as part of the general restyling of the Federal Rules of Civil Procedure to make the Federal Rules more easily understood and to make style and terminology consistent throughout the Federal Rules of Civil Procedure. Those stylistic modifications have not been incorporated into ARCP 64.

3. *General Prerequisites for Provisional Remedies.* The principal prejudgment remedies are attachment, replevin, and non-earnings garnishments, which are generally classified as "provisional remedies." A.R.S. § 12-2401(3). (A garnishment of earnings may only be employed as a post-judgment collection device, A.R.S. §§ 12-1598 *et seq.*). An application for any of these remedies must be in accordance with the statutory requirements for provisional remedies, A.R.S. §§ 12-2401 *et seq.* In addition, the application must also satisfy the specific statutory requirements for attachment, replevin and non-earnings garnishments set forth in A.R.S. §§ 12-1521 *et seq.*, 12-1301 *et seq.*, and 12-1570 *et seq.*, respectively.

4. *Notice Requirements.* A "provisional remedy" may be secured either with or without prior notice to the person whose property

is to be seized. A.R.S. §§ 12-2401, et seq. The remedy may be secured without notice only when the party seeking the remedy establishes by affidavit that one of the following situations pertains:

1. The party against whom the remedy is sought is about to leave the state permanently and has refused to secure the debt, or has secreted property to defraud creditors, or has disposed of or is about to dispose of property to defraud creditors; or
2. The moving party is the owner of or otherwise entitled to possession of certain property, and the requirements for replevin have been satisfied; or
3. A provisional remedy is necessary to obtain jurisdiction.

The applicant must serve the party against whom the remedy is sought with notice of the seizure at the time it takes place or within three (3) days thereafter.

In addition, at the time the application is filed, the Justice of the Peace or Superior Court Clerk is to address a statutorily prescribed notice to the party against whom the remedy is sought. A.R.S. §§ 12-2402(E), 12-2405. That party may move to quash the order allowing the remedy immediately and it is to be heard within five (5) days. A.R.S. § 12-2402(C).

An application for a provisional remedy with notice need only state that the statutory requirements for the particular remedy sought have been met. The application and a notice of issuance are to be served upon the party against whom the remedy is sought. In addition, that party is to receive, from the Clerk or Justice of the Peace, a statutorily prescribed notice. A.R.S. §§ 12-2403, 12-2405. A hearing on the application is to be conducted within five (5) days after filing a request for hearing, absent an agreement of the parties to a later date. A.R.S. § 12-2410. The hearing cannot be waived. A.R.S. § 12-2412.

5. *Attachment Generally*. As noted earlier, attachment has been classified as a "provisional remedy" subject to the general requirements of A.R.S. §§ 12-2401 *et seq.,* as well as the particularized requirements of A.R.S. §§ 12-1521 *et seq.* The fact that a dispute is subject to contractual arbitration does not preclude recourse to the provisional remedy of attachment. The legal merits of the underlying claim are left to the arbitrator to resolve. *Bancamerica Commercial Corp. v. Brown*, 167 Ariz. 308, 806 P.2d 897 (Ct. App. Div. 2 1990). As noted below, a trial court may only issue a writ of attachment in a contract action if the debt is not fully secured by real or personal property. A.R.S. § 12-1521; *Tenet Healthsystem TGH, Inc. v. Silver*, 203 Ariz. 217, 52 P.3d 786 (Ct. App. Div. 2 2002). For purposes of determining whether there is sufficient security for a debt, a guaranty is viewed as an agreement separate from the principal debt, and is not to be taken into

account in determining whether the debt is fully secured. *Howard v. Associated Grocers*, 123 Ariz. 593, 601 P.2d 593 (1979); *Tenet Healthsystem TGH, Inc. v. Silver*, 203 Ariz. 217, 52 P.3d 786 (Ct. App. Div. 2 2002); *Phoenix Arbor Plaza, Ltd. v. Dauderman*, 163 Ariz. 27, 785 P.2d 1215 (Ct. App. Div. 1 1989).

6. *Purpose of Prejudgment Attachment; Prerequisites.* Attachment is a remedy designed to insure that property of the defendant remains available as security for satisfaction of any judgment that may be entered in favor of the plaintiff. It is only authorized in the following situations:

1. In an action on a contract for debt which is not fully secured by real or personal property.
2. Where the defendant is about to dispose of property or remove it beyond the court's jurisdiction.
3. In an action against a nonresident defendant or a foreign corporation.
4. In an action upon a judgment.

A.R.S. § 12-1521.

Where the plaintiff establishes by affidavit that one or more of these requirements is satisfied, the Clerk of the Superior Court or Justice of the Peace issues a writ of attachment. A.R.S. § 12-1522. For purposes of determining whether there is sufficient security for a debt, a guaranty is viewed as an agreement separate from the principal debt, and is not to be taken into account in determining whether the debt is fully secured. *Tenet Healthsystem TGH, Inc. v. Silver*, 203 Ariz. 217, 52 P.3d 786 (Ct. App. Div. 2 2002).

7. *Prejudgment Attachment Where Debt Not Yet Due.* A writ of attachment may issue even though the debt or demand of the plaintiff is not yet due. In that case, however, the supporting affidavit must establish:

1. That the defendant is indebted to the plaintiff upon a contract, express or implied, for the direct payment of money [stating the amount of the debt] and that the debt is not due.
2. That the contract creating the debt was made in the state, or that the debt is payable here.
3. That payment of the debt is not secured by a mortgage, pledge or lien.
4. That there are no legal setoffs or counterclaims against the debt.
5. That the defendant:

(a) is about to leave the state permanently and has refused to secure the debt, or

(b) secreted defendant's property for the purpose of

defrauding defendant's creditors, or

(c) that defendant is about to remove defendant's property from the state without leaving sufficient property remaining for payment of defendant's debts, or

(d) has disposed of defendant's property wholly or in part with intent to defraud defendant's creditors, or

(e) is about to dispose of defendant's property with intent to defraud defendant's creditors.

A.R.S. § 12-1523(B).

The affidavit must also state that the attachment is not sought to injure or harass the defendant and that the debt will probably be lost unless an attachment issues. A.R.S. § 12-1523(C). While a writ of attachment may issue where the claimed debt is not yet due, a final judgment may not be entered against the defendant until the debt or demand is due. A.R.S. § 12-1523(A).

8. *Attachment Bond.* Before the writ can be issued, the plaintiff must post a bond in favor of the defendant for the amount claimed in the action. A.R.S. § 12-1524. If the requisite bond and affidavit have not been filed, the writ may be quashed upon motion. A.R.S. § 12-1525(A).

9. *Issuance and Execution of Writ of Attachment.* The writ, when issued, directs the Sheriff or Constable to whom it is addressed to attach so much of the property of the defendant as can be located which will be sufficient to satisfy the plaintiff's demands and the probable costs of the action. A.R.S. § 12-1526.

The plaintiff may secure the issuance of successive and/or several writs in different counties. A.R.S. § 12-1528(A). The Sheriff or Constable executes the writ by levying upon property in the same manner as with a writ of execution. A.R.S. §§ 12-1529(A), 12-1530(A). The officer may seize and retain personal property until final judgment is entered. A.R.S. § 12-1530(C).

10. *Securing Release of Property Seized Under Writ of Attachment.* A defendant can replevy property which has been levied upon, and not claimed or sold, by posting a bond for either double the amount of the debt to plaintiff or for the value of the property, as estimated by the Sheriff or Constable. A.R.S. § 12-1536.

11. *Replevin Generally; Prerequisites.* Replevin, which is governed by the provisions of A.R.S. §§ 12-1301 *et seq.,* is available as a remedy where the complaint in the action seeks possession of specific personal property. A.R.S. § 12-1301. In order to secure prejudgment possession of the property in question, the plaintiff must comply with the requirements of A.R.S. §§ 12-2401 *et seq.*, and file an affidavit, in accordance with A.R.S. § 12-1301, establishing that the plaintiff owns or is entitled to possession of

the property claimed, that the defendant is wrongfully detaining it, and the value of the property.

12. *Issuance of Writ of Replevin.* When those requirements are met, the court issues a writ of replevin, directing the appropriate Sheriff or Constable to seize the property and deliver it to the plaintiff. A.R.S. § 12-1302.

13. *Bond Requirements for Writ of Replevin.* No actual seizure may take place, however, until the plaintiff posts a bond on replevin for at least twice the stated value of the property to be seized. A.R.S. § 12-1303. The defendant can avoid delivery of the seized property by furnishing to the Sheriff or Constable, within two (2) days after the seizure, a redelivery bond in favor of the plaintiff in an amount at least twice the claimed value of the property. A.R.S. § 12-1304.

14. *Garnishment Generally.* The garnishment remedy in Arizona is governed by statutes, A.R.S. §§ 12-1570 et seq., which statutes draw sharp distinctions between garnishments of earnings and garnishments directed to other categories of money or property.

The garnishment statutes were extensively revised, effective March 12, 1986, to draw even sharper distinctions between garnishments of earnings and garnishments directed to other categories of money or property. *Frazer, Ryan, Goldberg, Keyt and Lawless v. Smith*, 184 Ariz. 181, 907 P.2d 1384 (Ct. App. Div. 1 1995). Notwithstanding the statutory overlay, a garnishment proceeding is civil in nature and subject to the provisions of the Arizona Rules of Civil Procedure, including the discovery sanction provisions of Rule 37. *Groat v. Equity American Ins. Co.*, 180 Ariz. 342, 884 P.2d 228 (Ct. App. Div. 1 1994).

Garnishment is a remedy which seeks to seize, or otherwise control, money or property in the possession of a third party, which is owed to, or held by that third party on behalf or for the account of, a defendant or judgment debtor. The effect of a writ of garnishment is to impound any asset of the defendant which is found to be in the garnishee's hands pending resolution of the garnishor's claims. *Able Distributing Co., Inc. v. James Lampe, General Contractor*, 160 Ariz. 399, 773 P.2d 504 (Ct. App. Div. 1 1989).

The liability of the garnishee is to be determined according to the facts as they were found to exist at the time the writ was served, and a claim acquired by a garnishee against the judgment debtor generally cannot be used as a setoff, unless the garnishee's claim arises out of the same contract that gives rise to the garnishee's liability to the judgment debtor. *Able Distributing Co., Inc. v. James Lampe, General Contractor*, 160 Ariz. 399, 773 P.2d 504 (Ct. App. Div. 1 1989). A garnishor has the burden of proving the existence of a debt owed by the garnishee to the debtor. *Falcon v. Beverly Hills Mortg. Corp.*, 168 Ariz. 527, 815 P.2d 896 (1991). Because garnishment proceedings are purely statutory, there is no right to a trial by jury. *Parking Concepts, Inc. v. Sheldon*, 193 Ariz. 432, 973 P.2d 1189 (Ct. App. Div. 1 1998), not designated for publication, (Mar. 23, 1999).

Before a debt or obligation can be subject to garnishment, it must be, at the time the writ is secured, existing, ascertainable and not contingent upon other events. *Premier Financial Services v. Citibank (Arizona)*, 185 Ariz. 80, 912 P.2d 1309 (Ct. App. Div. 1 1995); *Davidson-Chudacoff/Kol-Pak of Arizona, Inc. v. Pioneer Hotel Co.*, 129 Ariz. 254, 630 P.2d 550 (Ct. App. Div. 1 1981). A debt that is contingent upon other events is not subject to a writ of garnishment, but a debt is only considered to be contingent if it is one which may never become due and payable. *Able Distributing Co., Inc. v. James Lampe, General Contractor*, 160 Ariz. 399, 773 P.2d 504 (Ct. App. Div. 1 1989). Similarly, an unliquidated debt is generally not subject to garnishment, but the fact that parties dispute a claim does not *ipso facto* render it unliquidated. *Able Distributing Co., Inc. v. James Lampe, General Contractor*, 160 Ariz. 399, 773 P.2d 504 (Ct. App. Div. 1 1989).

A judgment creditor of a limited partnership can use a garnishment proceeding to prove and collect funds that were wrongfully distributed to a limited partner. *Retzke v. Larson*, 166 Ariz. 446, 803 P.2d 439 (Ct. App. Div. 1 1990). No separate action is required to prove a wrongful distribution of partnership assets. *Retzke v. Larson*, 166 Ariz. 446, 803 P.2d 439 (Ct. App. Div. 1 1990). Legal action to prove a fraudulent conveyance need not be separate from the garnishment proceeding but the burden of proof is on the creditor to show a debt properly subject to garnishment. *Retzke v. Larson*, 166 Ariz. 446, 803 P.2d 439 (Ct. App. Div. 1 1990).

When a judgment creditor, after initiating a garnishment against the unrestricted bank account of the judgment debtor, discovers that the judgment debtor does not own the bulk of the funds in the account, but merely holds them to accomplish a transaction on behalf of another, the judgment debtor does not subject itself to liability to that other person or entity for conversion by pursuing the garnishment remedy. *Universal Marketing and Entertainment, Inc. v. Bank One of Arizona, N.A.*, 203 Ariz. 266, 53 P.3d 191 (Ct. App. Div. 1 2002). A writ of garnishment to collect on a registered foreign judgment cannot be enforced against a community property bank account, where the judgment is based on a guaranty signed by only one spouse and both spouses were not joined in the foreign action. *Rackmaster Systems, Inc. v. Maderia*, 219 Ariz. 60, 193 P.3d 314 (Ct. App. Div. 1 2008).

The qualified immunity of the state from garnishment is not a defense personal to the state; it is a specific limitation on the statutory garnishment procedure and an exception to the state's sovereign immunity. *State v. Peruskov*, 166 Ariz. 28, 800 P.2d 15 (Ct. App. Div. 1 1990). In a proceeding to garnish an inmate bank account administered by the Department of Corrections, the inmate-debtor has standing to raise the state's qualified immunity from garnishment and the state may not, merely by answering the writ, effectively waive its qualified immunity. *State v. Peruskov*, 166 Ariz. 28, 800 P.2d 15 (Ct. App. Div. 1 1990).

An Arizona court does not have jurisdiction to issue a writ of garnishment to attach a bank account in an out-of-state branch of an interstate bank which does business in Arizona. *Desert Wide Cabling & Installation, Inc. v. Wells Fargo & Co., N.A.*, 191 Ariz. 516, 958 P.2d 457 (Ct. App. Div. 1 1998), as corrected, (June 23, 1998). The validity of an attachment or garnishment served on an interstate bank is determined by the law of the state in which the process issues. A.R.S. § 12-1577(A), which specifies the sole method of serving a writ of garnishment on a bank, specifies that the writ may be served "at any office or branch thereof located in the county where such service is made." That language indicates that the Legislature was referring only to counties in Arizona, and not to counties in other states as well. *Desert Wide Cabling & Installation, Inc. v. Wells Fargo & Co., N.A.*, 191 Ariz. 516, 958 P.2d 457 (Ct. App. Div. 1 1998), as corrected, (June 23, 1998).

15. *Non-Earnings Garnishment; Scope of Remedy.* The procedures for non-earnings garnishments are set forth in A.R.S. §§ 12-1570 to 12-1597. Disposable earnings lose that character, and the protections against garnishment contained in A.R.S. § 12-1598.10, once they are disbursed into an individual's bank account. *Frazer, Ryan, Goldberg, Keyt and Lawless v. Smith*, 184 Ariz. 181, 907 P.2d 1384 (Ct. App. Div. 1 1995). A non-earnings garnishment may be used as a device for collection of a judgment or as a prejudgment provisional remedy. While the statutory provisions speak of garnishing money or property in the hands of the garnishee that is due to a "judgment debtor," that term is defined by A.R.S. § 12-1570(5) to include a defendant against whom a prejudgment provisional remedy order has been entered pursuant to A.R.S. §§ 12-2401 *et seq.*

16. *Contents of Application for Writ of Garnishment of Non-Earnings.* An application for a non-earnings writ of garnishment must be in writing, and contain at least the following:

(1) a statement that the applicant is a judgment creditor;

(2) a statement that the applicant has reason to believe that the garnishee owes the judgment debtor monies which are

not earnings, or holds monies on behalf of the judgment debtor, or has possession of personal property which belongs to the judgment debtor, or is a corporation in which the judgment debtor owns shares;

(3) a statement of the total amount currently due on the underlying judgment and the rate at which interest accrues, or the amount claimed in the complaint; and

(4) the garnishee's address.

A.R.S. § 12-1572. In addition, if the garnishment is sought as a provisional remedy before judgment, the applicant must post a bond in favor of the defendant for the amount of the debt claimed. A.R.S. § 12-1573.

17. *Issuance of Writ of Garnishment of Non-Earnings.* If the application complies with the requirements of A.R.S. §§ 12-1572 and 12-1573, the Clerk of the Superior Court or Justice of the Peace issues a writ of garnishment and a summons addressed to the garnishee. A.R.S. §§ 12-1571, 12-1574. The writ of garnishment must specify:

(1) the amount currently due on the underlying judgment and the rate at which interest is accruing thereon;

(2) the name and address of the garnishee or authorized agent;

(3) the name and address of the judgment creditor and the creditor's counsel, if any; and,

(4) the last known mailing address of the judgment debtor.

A.R.S. § 12-1574(B).

18. *Service Requirements for Writ of Garnishment of Non-Earnings.* The creditor/applicant must serve upon the garnishee, in the same manner as required for a summons, two (2) copies of the summons and writ of garnishment as issued, four (4) copies of the form for answer, two (2) copies of the standard form of notice to judgment debtor and request for hearing, and one copy of the standard instructions for the garnishee. A.R.S. § 12-1574(C).

Under A.R.S. § 12-1596(A), the Superior Court or Justice of the Peace must maintain, and provide to parties at no cost, copies of a notice to judgment debtor and request for hearing form, an answer form, and a form of instructions to the garnishee.

Once served with the papers specified in A.R.S. § 12-1574(C), the garnishee must deliver to the judgment debtor, through one of the means of delivery specified in A.R.S. § 12-1570(1), a copy of the summons, writ of garnishment and notice to judgment debtor and request for hearing form, within three (3) business days. A.R.S. § 12-1574(D).

The notice to judgment debtor and request for hearing form must contain, at the top of the first page, a Spanish translation of a warning and instruction notice, the text of which is set out in the statutes. A.R.S. § 12-1596(D).

19. *Effect of Service of Writ of Garnishment of Non-Earnings; Release of Writ.* The effect of a writ of garnishment is to impound any asset of the judgment debtor which is found to be in the garnishee's hands pending resolution of the garnishor's claims. *Able Distributing Co., Inc. v. James Lampe, General Contractor*, 160 Ariz. 399, 773 P.2d 504 (Ct. App. Div. 1 1989). Once service of the papers specified in A.R.S. § 12-1574(C) has been made on the garnishee, the garnishee may not pay or release to the judgment debtor any non-exempt money or personal property, and any such payment or transfer is voidable. A.R.S. § 12-1578(A). In the case of a prejudgment garnishment, the judgment debtor can secure the release through replevin of the money or property garnished, by posting a bond in favor of the judgment creditor for double the amount of the debt or the value of the property garnished as determined by the Court or Justice of the Peace. A.R.S. § 12-1578(C).

20. *Answer to Writ of Garnishment of Non-Earnings.* The garnishee must answer the writ within ten (10) days of service. A.R.S. § 12-1578.01. The answer must be signed by the garnishee under oath, and contain the following:

(1) Whether, at the time the writ was served, the garnishee had possession of any money or property due or belonging to the judgment debtor.

(2) If so, the amount of money and/or a description of the items of personal property so held.

(3) The amount of money and/or a list of items of personal property withheld by the garnishee in response to the writ.

(4) The amount of money and/or a list of the items of personal property not withheld and the reasons for not doing so.

(5) Whether the garnishee is a corporation in which the judgment debtor owns shares or has any other proprietary interest and, if so, the number and type of shares and/or the nature of the interest.

(6) The identity of any other persons or entities indebted to, or in possession of personal property of, the judgment debtor.

(7) The garnishee's name, address and telephone number.

(8) The date and method of delivery to the judgment debtor of a copy of the writ and notice to judgment debtor form, and

(9) The date and manner of delivery to the judgment creditor and to the judgment debtor of a copy of the answer.

A.R.S. § 12-1579. If the garnishee fails to answer the writ within the time period prescribed, the judgment creditor may petition the Court for an order directing the garnishee to appear or file and serve an answer. If the garnishee fails to respond to such an order, the Court may enter a default judgment against the garnishee for the full amount of any judgment entered against the judgment debtor, regardless of the amount for which the garnishee would have been liable had the writ been answered. A.R.S. § 12-1583. *Cf. Postal Instant Press, Inc. v. Corral Restaurants, Inc.*, 186 Ariz. 535, 925 P.2d 260 (1996), opinion supplemented on reconsideration, 187 Ariz. 487, 930 P.2d 1001 (1997).

21. *Proceedings Upon Answer; Objection to Writ of Garnishment of Non-Earnings.* If any party has an objection to the writ of garnishment or to the contents of the garnishee's answer, or claims that the property garnished should be exempt, that party must file a written objection and request for hearing within ten (10) days after receipt of the garnishee's answer. A hearing on the objection must be held within five (5) business days of the request, but may be continued for good cause. A.R.S. § 12-1580. It is appropriate for the Court, in a hearing requested on an objection to a writ of garnishment, to resolve all issues relevant to a final determination of a garnishee's rights, including whether a garnished debt is contingent or unliquidated. *Able Distributing Co., Inc. v. James Lampe, General Contractor*, 160 Ariz. 399, 773 P.2d 504 (Ct. App. Div. 1 1989). There is no right to a trial by jury. *Parking Concepts, Inc. v. Sheldon*, 193 Ariz. 432, 973 P.2d 1189 (Ct. App. Div. 1 1998), not designated for publication, (Mar. 23, 1999).

If the garnishee's answer reflects that the garnishee did not possess or control money or personal property due to or held for the judgment debtor at the time the writ was served, and a timely objection is not made, the Court is to enter an order discharging the garnishee. A.R.S. § 12-1581(A). If the answer reflects that the garnishee was indebted to the judgment debtor at the time the writ was served, the Court, on application of the judgment creditor, is to enter a judgment on the writ for the amount held or owed by the garnishee but not for more than the current outstanding balance of the judgment or debt, unless an objection to the answer is made. A.R.S. § 12-1584.

If the garnishee's answer reflects that the garnishee was holding personal property of the judgment debtor at the time the writ was served, and no objection to the answer is made, the Court is to enter an order that the garnishee hold that property pending service of a writ of special execution pursuant to A.R.S. § 12-1554. Such a writ then must be served within ninety (90) days, or the garnishee is discharged. A.R.S. § 12-1585.

The liability of the garnishee is to be determined according to the facts as they were found to exist at the time the writ was served, and a claim acquired by a garnishee against the judgment debtor after the writ was served generally cannot be employed as a setoff. *Able Distributing Co., Inc. v. James Lampe, General Contractor*, 160 Ariz. 399, 773 P.2d 504 (Ct. App. Div. 1 1989). Any issues relevant to a final determination of the garnishee's rights and obligations should be resolved in the hearing on any objections to the writ contemplated by A.R.S. § 12-1584(A). *Able Distributing Co., Inc. v. James Lampe, General Contractor*, 160 Ariz. 399, 773 P.2d 504 (Ct. App. Div. 1 1989).

22. *Discharge of Garnishee.* The failure of the judgment creditor to secure an order or judgment against the garnishee within ninety (90) days after the garnishee's answer is filed results in the discharge and release of the garnishee on the writ, unless an objection to the answer is filed. This provision does not apply where the property or money is being held by the garnishee for the judgment debtor's trustee in bankruptcy, or pursuant to A.R.S. §§ 12-2401 *et seq.* A.R.S. § 12-1587. Under A.R.S. § 12-1582, a garnishment action in which the garnishee has answered may not be dismissed without notice to the garnishee, and an opportunity to be heard on the question of costs and attorneys' fees recoverable by the garnishee. The statute does not specify whether such costs and fees must be prayed for in the answer.

The compliance of the garnishee with an order of judgment entered by the Court on a writ of garnishment is a sufficient defense to any claim by the judgment debtor against the garnishee for the money or property that was the subject of the garnishment. A.R.S. § 12-1592.

23. *Garnishments of Earnings Generally; Scope of Remedy; Application for Writ.* As noted earlier, the 1986 amendments to the garnishment statute made more specific the procedures for obtaining, and the limitations upon, a garnishment of earnings. Such garnishments are governed by the provisions of A.R.S. §§ 12-1598 to 12-1598.16. The limitations on garnishments of earnings set forth in these statutory provisions do not apply, however, to disposable earnings that have been deposited into a debtor's bank account. *Frazer, Ryan, Goldberg, Keyt and Lawless v. Smith*, 184 Ariz. 181, 907 P.2d 1384 (Ct. App. Div. 1 1995).

An earnings garnishment may only be employed as a device for enforcing the collection of a judgment—it is not available as a prejudgment remedy. A writ of garnishment for earnings may be issued by the Clerk of the Superior Court or a Justice of the Peace. A.R.S. § 12-1598.02. To secure the issuance of a writ of garnishment for earnings, the judgment creditor must make an application in writing which states the following:

(1) That the applicant has secured a money judgment in an

action in which the applicant was a party.

(2) That a demand has been made on the judgment debtor for payment of the judgment, but the judgment debtor has not paid it or has not made payments of the non-exempt portions of the debtor's earnings toward the judgment.

(3) The amount of the outstanding balance due on the judgment.

(4) That the garnishee is believed to be the judgment debtor's employer or indebted to the judgment debtor for amounts which represent disposable earnings; and

(5) The name and address of the garnishee.

A.R.S. § 12-1598.03. The caption of any pleadings in connection with the writ of garnishment must identify the judgment creditor and the judgment debtor as such. A.R.S. § 12-1598.04(E).

24. *Issuance of Writ of Garnishment of Earnings.* Upon receipt of an application, the Clerk or Justice of the Peace issues a writ of garnishment which is in the form of a summons to the garnishee and is served, together with the other papers specified in the statute, in the same manner. The writ of garnishment must specify: (1) the amount currently due on the judgment and the rate at which interest is accruing thereon, (2) the name and address of the garnishee or authorized agent, (3) the name and address of the judgment creditor and the creditor's counsel, if any, and (4) the last known mailing address of the judgment debtor. A.R.S. § 12-1598.04(B).

25. *Service Requirements for Writ of Garnishment of Earnings.* The judgment creditor must serve upon the garnishee, in the same manner as required for a summons, two (2) copies of the summons and writ of garnishment as issued, a copy of the underlying judgment, four (4) copies of the form for answer, two (2) copies of the standard form of the initial notice to judgment debtor and request for hearing, two (2) copies of the standard instructions for the garnishee, and four (4) copies of the non-exempt earnings statement. A.R.S. § 12-1598.04(C).

Under A.R.S. § 12-1598.16(A), the Clerk of the Superior Court or Justice of the Peace must maintain, and provide to the parties at no cost, copies of the initial notice and notice to judgment debtor and request for hearing form, the answer form, the form of instructions to the garnishee and the form of non-exempt earnings statements.

26. *Notice to Debtor of Writ of Garnishment of Earnings; Effect of Service of Writ.* In addition to serving on the garnishee the papers specified in A.R.S. § 12-1598.04(C), the judgment creditor must also deliver to the judgment debtor within three (3) days, through one of the means specified in A.R.S. § 12-1598(2), a copy

of the writ, and the initial notice to judgment debtor and request for hearing form. A.R.S. § 12-1598.04(D).

Once served, the writ constitutes an initial lien on non-exempt earnings of the judgment debtor which remains effective for a period of forty-five (45) days, unless continued in effect or quashed by the Court. A.R.S. § 12-1598.05(A).

27. *Answer to Writ of Garnishment of Earnings.* The garnishee must answer the writ within ten (10) days of service. A.R.S. § 12-1598.06. The answer must be signed by the garnishee under oath, and state the following information:

(1) Whether the judgment debtor was an employee of the garnishee at the time the writ was served.

(2) Whether the garnishee expects to owe earnings to the judgment debtor within sixty (60) days after service.

(3) A statement of the efforts made to determine the identity of the judgment debtor, if the answer states that the garnishee has been unable to do so.

(4) The dates of the next two paydays after service of the writ.

(5) The nature and duration of the pay period for the judgment debtor.

(6) The amount which the writ indicated to be the outstanding amount due on the judgment.

(7) Whether the judgment debtor is subject to an existing wage assignment, garnishment or levy and, if so, the name, address and telephone number of the creditor.

(8) The garnishee's name, address and telephone number.

(9) The date and means by which a copy of the answer was delivered to the judgment creditor and judgment debtor.

A.R.S. § 12-1598.08(B).

The answer must be delivered to the judgment creditor and judgment debtor. In addition, the garnishee is to deliver to the judgment debtor, at the same time, a copy of the notice to judgment debtor and request for hearing form. A.R.S. § 12-1598.08(C).

When a garnishee fails to answer a writ of garnishment, a claimant may petition the Court for an "order" requiring the garnishee to answer or otherwise appear. A.R.S. § 12-1598.13(H). If, after proper service of that order, the garnishee fails to file and serve an answer to the writ or otherwise appear, the Court may enter judgment against the garnishee for the full amount of the underlying judgment against the debtor, regardless of the amount for which the garnishee would have been liable had the writ been answered. *Postal Instant Press, Inc. v. Corral Restaurants, Inc.*, 186 Ariz. 535, 925 P.2d 260 (1996), opinion supplemented on reconsideration, 187 Ariz. 487, 930 P.2d 1001

(1997).

28. *Proceedings Upon Answer.* If the answer indicates that the judgment debtor was not an employee of the garnishee at the time the writ was served, or that the garnishee would not owe earnings to the judgment debtor within sixty (60) days after service, or has been unable to determine the identity of the judgment debtor, and no objection to the answer is made, the Court is to enter judgment discharging the garnishee. A.R.S. § 12-1598.09.

If, on the other hand, the answer indicates that the judgment debtor was employed by the garnishee, or that the garnishee owed earnings to the judgment debtor at the time of service, or would owe such earnings during the next sixty (60) days, and no objection is made, the Court, on application of the judgment creditor, is to order any non-exempt earnings held by the garnishee transferred to the judgment creditor, and that the garnishment constitutes a continuing lien against the judgment debtor's non-exempt earnings. A.R.S. § 12-1598.10(A).

29. *Objection to Writ or Answer.* Any party who objects to the writ of garnishment or the garnishee's answer may file a written objection and request for hearing, in the general form prescribed in A.R.S. § 12-1598.16 and supplied by the Clerk or Justice of the Peace, no later than ten (10) days after receipt of the garnishee's answer or non-exempt earnings statement. A.R.S. § 12-1598.07(A).

The grounds for objection must be stated in writing, but other grounds may be relied upon at the hearing. A.R.S. § 12-1598.07(C). A hearing on the objection must be commenced within ten (10) days after it is received by the Court but may be continued for good cause. A.R.S. § 12-1598.07(B).

30. *Resolution of Objections to Writ of Garnishment of Earnings.* At the hearing, the Court must determine whether the writ is valid against the judgment debtor, the amount outstanding on the underlying judgment, whether the judgment debtor was an employee of the garnishee at the time the writ was served, and/or whether the garnishee owes the judgment debtor wages, or would owe such wages during the sixty (60) days following service. A.R.S. § 12-1598.10(B).

If the requisite predicate findings are made, the Court is to order non-exempt earnings held by the garnishee transferred to the judgment debtor and that the writ constitutes a continuing lien. A.R.S. § 12-1598.10(C).

31. *Order for Continuing Lien on Earnings; Effect.* When the Court orders that a writ is to constitute a continuing lien, that lien remains in effect until one of the following occurs:

(1) the underlying judgment is satisfied, vacated or expires;

(2) the proceedings are stayed by a court of competent jurisdiction;

(3) the judgment debtor leaves the employ of the garnishee for a period of more than sixty (60) days;

(4) the judgment debtor fails to earn non-exempt earnings for at least sixty (60) days; or

(5) the garnishment is released or quashed. A.R.S. § 12-1598.10(D).

If no objection is made to the garnishee's answer, and no order for continuing lien is entered within forty-five (45) days after the garnishee's answer is filed, any earnings held by the garnishee are to be released to the judgment debtor and the garnishee is discharged from any liability on the writ. A.R.S. § 12-1598.10(E).

As long as the continuing lien is in effect:

(1) The garnishee must pay any nonexempt earnings earned by the judgment debtor to the judgment creditor and the balance to the judgment debtor. Contemporaneously, the garnishee is to deliver to both the judgment creditor and the judgment debtor a copy of a completed form of nonexempt earnings statement such as is prescribed in A.R.S. § 12-1598.16. *See,* A.R.S. § 12-1598.10(E).

(2) The judgment creditor must issue a report in writing to the garnishee and the judgment debtor within twenty-one days after the end of each calendar quarter. The judgment creditor must provide to the garnishee and the judgment debtor within 21 days after the end of each quarter a written report specifying the following:

(a) The beginning and ending date of the reporting period for that report. The beginning date of the first reporting period is the date the writ was served.

(b) The date and amount of each payment received during the reporting period.

(c) The total amount credited to the judgment balance for that reporting period.

(d) The interest accrued during that reporting period.

(e) The total outstanding balance due on the judgment as of the ending date of the reporting period. A.R.S. § 12-1598.12(A), 12-1598(C).

(3) Within twenty-one (21) days after receipt of a payment that reduces the balance outstanding to $500.00 or less, and within the first 10 days of each calendar month thereafter until the judgment is satisfied, the judgment creditor must provide a written report to the garnishee and the judgment debtor specifying the following:

(a) The beginning and ending date of the reporting period

for that report. The beginning date of the first reporting period is the date the writ was served.

(b) The date and amount of each payment received during the reporting period.

(c) The total amount credited to the judgment balance for that reporting period.

(d) The interest accrued during that reporting period.

(e) The total outstanding balance due on the judgment as of the ending date of the reporting period. A.R.S. § 12-1598.12(B), 12-1598(C).

As soon as the judgment is satisfied or expires, the judgment creditor must file and serve a satisfaction or release of the judgment. *See,* A.R.S. § 12-1598.12(E).

Rule 64.1. Civil arrest warrant

(a) Definition. A "civil arrest warrant" is an order issued in a non-criminal matter, directed to any peace officer in the state, to arrest the individual named therein and bring such person before the court.

Added March 27, 1985, effective June 1, 1985.

(b) When Issued. The court may, on motion of a party or on its own motion, issue a civil arrest warrant if it finds that the person for whom the warrant is sought:

(1) Having been ordered by the court to appear personally at a specific time and location, and having received actual notice of such order, including a warning that failure to appear may result in the issuance of a civil arrest warrant, has failed to appear as ordered; or

(2) Having been served personally with a subpoena to appear in person, at a specific time and location, which contains a warning that failure to appear may result in the issuance of a civil arrest warrant, has failed to appear.

Added March 27, 1985, effective June 1, 1985; Feb. 18, 1992, effective May 1, 1992.

(c) Content of Warrant. The civil arrest warrant shall be ordered by the judge and issued by the clerk. It shall contain the name of the person to be arrested and a description by which such person can be identified with reasonable certainty. It shall command that the person named be brought before the judge or, if the judge is absent or unable to act, the nearest or most accessible judge in the same county. The warrant shall set forth a bond in a reasonable amount to guarantee the appearance of the arrested person, or an order that the arrested person be held without bond until the arrested person is seen by a judge.

Added March 27, 1985, effective June 1, 1985; amended Sept. 15, 1987, effective Nov. 15, 1987.

(d) Time and Manner of Execution. A civil arrest warrant is executed by the arrest of the person named therein. Unless the court otherwise directs upon a showing of good cause, a civil arrest warrant shall not be executed between the hours of ten p.m. and six-thirty a.m. The arrested person shall be brought immediately before the issuing judge if it is reasonably possible to do so. In any event, the arrested person shall be brought before the issuing judge, or a judge in the county of arrest, within 24 hours of the execution of the warrant. If the person is arrested in a county other than the county of issue, the arresting officer shall notify the sheriff in the county of issue who shall, as soon as possible, take custody of the arrested person and transport the arrested person to the issuing judge.

Added March 27, 1985, effective June 1, 1985. Amended Sept. 15, 1987, effective Nov. 15, 1987.

(e) Duty of Court After Execution of Warrant. The judge shall advise the arrested person of the nature of the proceedings, release the arrested person on the least onerous terms and conditions which reasonably guarantee the required appearance, and set the date of the next court appearance.

Added March 27, 1985, effective June 1, 1985. Amended Sept. 15, 1987, effective Nov. 15, 1987.

(f) Forfeiture of Bond. The procedure for the forfeiture of bonds in criminal cases shall apply.

Added March 27, 1985, effective June 1, 1985.

AUTHORS' COMMENTS

Analysis

1. *Scope and Purpose of Rule.* Rule 64.1 was adopted in 1985 to codify the authority for the long-standing practice, previously and still based on the Court's inherent authority, of issuing "body attachments" which direct the arrest of persons who have disobeyed an official command from the Court to appear. It was amended in 1992 to clarify the scope of its application.

2. *Comparison With Federal Rule.* The Federal Rules of Civil Procedure do not have a provision that corresponds to ARCP Rule 64.1.

3. *Issuance of Civil Arrest Warrant; Requirements.* Rule 64.1(b) permits a court to issue a civil arrest warrant "in a non-criminal matter." *State v. Jones*, 188 Ariz. 534, 937 P.2d 1182 (Ct. App. Div. 1 1996) (abrogated by, State v. Ferrero, 229 Ariz. 239, 274 P.3d 509 (2012)). Specifically, a civil arrest warrant may be issued where (1) a person has failed to appear after receiving actual notice of an order of the Court directing that person to appear personally at a specific time and location, or (2) a person has failed to appear after having been served personally with a subpoena to appear at a specific time and location. *See*, *State v. Jones*, 188 Ariz. 534, 937 P.2d 1182 (Ct. App. Div. 1 1996)

(abrogated by, State v. Ferrero, 229 Ariz. 239, 274 P.3d 509 (2012)). To support issuance of a civil arrest warrant, the order or subpoena must contain a warning that failure to appear in response thereto may result in the issuance of a civil arrest warrant.

4. *Execution of Civil Arrest Warrant.* A civil arrest warrant is not to be executed between the hours of 10:00 p.m. and 6:30 a.m., unless the issuing Court finds good cause to direct otherwise. The person arrested is to be brought promptly to the issuing judge, or another judge in the county, if the issuing judge is unavailable, for establishing the terms of release.

The Rule does not prescribe the period of time that a civil arrest warrant remains in effect. The form of Civil Arrest Warrant currently in use at the Maricopa County Superior Court provides for automatic expiration after one (1) year.

Rule 65. Injunctions

(a) Preliminary Injunction; Notice.

(1) *Notice.* No preliminary injunction shall be issued without notice to the adverse party.

(2) *Consolidation of Hearing With Trial on Merits.* Before or after the commencement of the hearing of an application for a preliminary injunction, the court may order the trial of the action on the merits to be advanced and consolidated with the hearing of the application. Even when this consolidation is not ordered, any evidence received upon an application for a preliminary injunction which would be admissible upon the trial on the merits becomes part of the record on the trial and need not be repeated upon the trial. This subdivision (a)(2) shall be so construed and applied as to save to the parties any rights they may have to trial by jury.

Amended July 1, 1966, effective Nov. 1, 1966.

(b) [Deleted Sept. 15, 1987, effective November, 15, 1987].

(c) Motion to Dissolve or Modify. Motions to dissolve or modify a preliminary injunction may be heard after an answer is filed, upon notice to the opposite party. If, upon hearing the motion, it appears that there is not sufficient grounds for the injunction, it shall be dissolved, or if it appears that the injunction is too broad, it shall be modified. A denial of the material allegations of the complaint shall not be sufficient ground for dissolution of a preliminary injunction unless the answer denying the allegations is verified.

Amended Sept. 15, 1987, effective Nov. 15, 1987.

(d) Temporary Restraining Order; Notice; Hearing; Duration. A temporary restraining order may be granted without written or oral notice to the adverse party or that party's attorney only if (1) it clearly appears from specific facts shown by affidavit or by the verified complaint that immediate and irreparable injury, loss or damage will result to the applicant before the adverse party or that party's attorney can be heard in opposition, and (2) the applicant's attorney certifies to the court in writing the efforts, if any, which have been made to give the notice or the reasons supporting the claim that notice should not be required. Every temporary restraining order granted without notice shall be indorsed with the date and hour of issuance; shall be filed forthwith in the clerk's office and entered of record; shall define the injury and state why it is irreparable and why the order was granted without notice; and shall expire by its terms within such time after entry, not to exceed 10 days, as the court fixes, unless within the time so fixed the order, for good cause shown, is extended for a like period or unless the party against whom the order is directed consents that it may be extended for a longer period. The reasons for the extension shall be entered of record. In case a temporary restraining order is granted without notice, the motion for a preliminary injunction shall be set down for hearing at the earliest possible time and takes precedence of all matters except older matters of the same character, and when the motion comes on for hearing the party who obtained the temporary restraining order shall proceed with the application for a preliminary injunction and, if the party does not do so, the court shall dissolve the temporary restraining order. On 2 days' notice to the party who obtained the temporary restraining order without notice or on such shorter notice to that party as the court may prescribe, the adverse party may appear and move its dissolution or modification and in that event the court shall proceed to hear and determine such motion as expeditiously as the ends of justice require.

Amended July 1, 1966, effective Nov. 1, 1966; amended Sept. 15, 1987, effective Nov. 15, 1987.

(e) Security. No restraining order or preliminary injunction shall issue except upon the giving of security by the applicant, in such sum as the court deems proper, for the payment of such costs and damages as may be incurred or suffered by any party who is found to have been wrongfully enjoined or restrained. No such security shall be required of the State or of an officer or agency thereof.

The provisions of Rule 65.1 apply to a surety upon a bond or undertaking under this rule.

Amended July 1, 1966, effective Nov. 1, 1966.

(f) [Deleted effective November 1, 1967].

(g) Security on Injunction Restraining Collection of Money; Injunction Made Permanent.

1. Upon dissolution of a preliminary injunction or temporary restraining order restraining the collection of money, if the action is continued over for trial, the court shall require the defendant to give security to be approved by the court, and payable to the plaintiff in the amount previously enjoined and such additional amount as the court requires, and conditioned upon refunding to the plaintiff the amount of money, interest and costs which may be collected by the plaintiff in the action in the event a permanent injunction is ordered on final hearing.

2. If a permanent injunction is ordered on final hearing, the

court shall, on motion of the plaintiff, enter judgment against the principal and surety giving the security for the amount shown to have been collected and to which the plaintiff appears entitled.

Amended Sept. 15, 1987, effective Nov. 15, 1987.

(h) Form and Scope of Injunction or Restraining Order. Every order granting an injunction and every restraining order shall set forth the reasons for its issuance and shall be specific in terms. It shall describe in reasonable detail, and not by reference to the complaint or other document, the act or acts sought to be restrained, and it is binding only upon the parties to the action, their officers, agents, servants, employees, and attorneys, and upon those persons in active concert or participation with them who receive actual notice of the order by personal service or otherwise.

(i) Writs of Injunction; Where Returnable; Several Parties. Writs of injunction granted to stay proceedings in an action, or to stay execution of a judgment, shall be returnable to and tried in the court where the action is pending or the judgment was rendered.

(j) Disobedience of Injunction as Contempt; Order to Show Cause; Warrant; Attachment; Punishment.

1. Disobedience of an injunction may be punished by the court as a contempt.

2. When a party in whose favor an injunction has been issued files an affidavit that the party against whom the injunction was issued is guilty of disobeying the injunction and describes the acts constituting such disobedience, the court may order the person so charged to show cause at the time and place the court directs why such disobedient party should not be adjudged in contempt of the court which issued the injunction.

3. The order, with a copy of the affidavit, shall be served upon the person charged with the contempt within sufficient time to enable that person to prepare and make return to the order.

4. If such person fails or refuses to make return to the order to show cause a warrant of arrest may issue directing the sheriff or any constable of the county where the alleged contemnor resides or may be found, to arrest and bring the alleged contemnor before the court at a time and place directed by the court, and such person may be required to give bail for attendance at the trial and submission to the final judgment of the court.

5. If the alleged contemnor is a corporation, an attachment

for sequestration of the property of the corporation may be issued upon refusal or failure to appear.

6. Upon the appearance of the alleged contemnor, or at the trial of the issue, the court shall hear the evidence, and if the person enjoined has disobeyed the injunction that person may be committed to jail until that person is purged of the contempt as may be directed by the court or until that person is discharged by law.

Amended Sept. 15, 1987, effective Nov. 15, 1987.

STATE BAR COMMITTEE NOTES

1966 Amendments

[Rule 65(a)] This new subdivision [(a)(2) added in 1966] provides express authority for consolidating the hearing of an application for a preliminary injunction with the trial on the merits. The authority can be exercised with particular profit when it appears that a substantial part of the evidence offered on the application will be relevant to the merits and will be presented in such form as to qualify for admission on the trial proper. Repetition of evidence is thereby avoided. The fact that the proceedings have been consolidated should cause no delay in the disposition of the application for the preliminary injunction, for the evidence will be directed in the first instance to that relief, and the preliminary injunction, if justified by the proof, may be issued in the course of the consolidated proceedings. Furthermore, to consolidate the proceedings will tend to expedite the final disposition of the action. It is believed that consolidation can be usefully availed of in many cases.

The subdivision further provides that even when consolidation is not ordered, evidence received in connection with an application for a preliminary injunction which would be admissible on the trial on the merits forms part of the trial record. This evidence need not be repeated on the trial. On the other hand, repetition is not altogether prohibited. That would be impractical and unwise. For example, a witness testifying comprehensively on the trial who has previously testified upon the application for a preliminary injunction might sometimes be hamstrung in telling his story if he could not go over some part of his prior testimony to connect it with his present testimony. So also, some repetition of testimony may be called for where the trial is conducted by a judge who did not hear the application for the preliminary injunction. In general, however, repetition can be avoided with an increase of efficiency in the conduct of the case and without any distortion of the presentation of evidence by the parties.

[Rule 65(d)] In view of the possibly drastic consequences of a temporary restraining order, the opposition should be heard, if feasible, before the order is granted. Many judges have properly insisted that, when time does not permit formal notice of the application to the averse party, some expedient, such as telephonic notice to the attorney for the adverse party, be resorted to if this can reasonably be done. On occasion, however, temporary restraining orders have been issued without any notice when it was feasible for some fair, although informal, notice to be given.

Heretofore the first sentence of subdivision (b), in referring to a notice "served" on the "adverse party" on which a "hearing" could be held, perhaps invited the interpretation that the order might be granted without notice if the circumstances did not permit of a formal hearing on the basis of a formal notice. The subdivision is amended to make it plain that informal notice, which may be communicated to the attorney rather than the adverse party, is to be preferred to no notice at all.

Before notice can be dispensed with, the applicant's counsel must give his certificate as to any efforts made to give notice and the reasons why notice should not be required. This certificate is in addition to the requirement of an affidavit or verified complaint setting forth the facts as to the irreparable injury which would result before the opposition could be heard.

The amended subdivision continues to recognize that a temporary restraining order may be issued without any notice. In domestic relations cases, there may be a reasonable fear of bodily harm, and this is expressly regarded as one kind of irreparable injury which, if supported by affidavit and certificate, justifies a temporary restraining order without notice.

[Rule 65(e)] This section refers to Rule 65.1 which covers enforcement of surety claims in any surety situation under the rules, including injunctions.

1967 Amendment

[Rule 65(f)] In the Arizona Rules of Civil Procedure, there are two duplicating rules dealing with security on injunctions. Rule 65(e) is taken verbatim from the Federal Rule and, read in concert with Rule 65.1, provides that there shall be security on all restraining orders and preliminary injunctions, with provision for proceeding against sureties. These provisions were amended to make them absolutely uniform with the Federal Rule in 1966. In addition, Rule 65(f) provides for security in case of restraint against the execution of a money judgment or the collection of a debt. This provision is drawn from old Arizona statutes.

Rule 65(f) does not exist in the federal procedure, and as a possibly confusing duplication should be eliminated.

The Committee further believes that this deletion will have the effect of eliminating a difference of interpretation between the State and the Federal Rules as reflected in *Bayham v. Funk*, 3 Ariz. App. 220, 413 P.2d 279 (1966), which at least to some extent draws on Rule 65(f) for its conclusion. The Federal cases hold that the rule requiring security does not mean that the order is unenforceable if a judge does not require a security; see the cases collected in the dissenting opinion in *Bayham v. Funk, supra*.

This Committee believes that there should be security in the case of every injunction, but further believes that if in some instance security is omitted, the proper remedy is either a motion for security or an appeal, but not disobedience of the order. The Committee has not recommended any alteration in the language of Rule 65 to deal expressly with this point because it believes that greater value lies in keeping the rules uniform, but it does believe that, since the court in *Bayham v. Funk* relied to some extent in reaching a result different from the Federal interpretation on Rule 65(f), the repeal of the special Arizona provision may result in a different result in the *Bayham v. Funk* situation.

1987 Amendment

[Rule 65(c)] The 1987 amendment to Rule 65(c), and the contemporaneous abrogation of Rule 65(b), were intended to eliminate duplication and possible confusion. No substantive change was intended.

AUTHORS' COMMENTS

Analysis

1. *Scope and Purpose of Rule.* Rule 65 is concerned generally with the procedures for securing injunctive relief, and particularly with situations where a party desires injunctive relief *pendente lite.* The power to grant an injunction is both statutory, A.R.S. §§ 12-1801 *et seq.* and inherent. *Town of Chino Valley v. State Land Dept.*, 119 Ariz. 243, 580 P.2d 704, 11 Env't. Rep. Cas. (BNA) 1668 (1978); *see also, State ex rel. Corbin v. Portland Cement Ass'n*, 142 Ariz. 421, 690 P.2d 140, 1984-2 Trade Cas. (CCH) ¶ 66240 (Ct. App. Div. 1 1984).

An injunction may be negative, restraining actual or threatened conduct by a party, or mandatory, wherein the Court compels positive action by the party enjoined. *State ex rel. Corbin v. Portland Cement Ass'n*, 142 Ariz. 421, 690 P.2d 140, 1984-2 Trade Cas. (CCH) ¶ 66240 (Ct. App. Div. 1 1984). Generally, under both Rule 65 and the injunction statute, A.R.S. § 12-1801, there must be some action or threatened action to enjoin as a necessary predicate to the action. *Dowling v. Stapley*, 218 Ariz. 80, 179 P.3d 960, 230 Ed. Law Rep. 794 (Ct. App. Div. 1 2008).

Where a negative injunction is sought, the plaintiff bears the burden of showing that the defendant is likely to engage in the conduct to be enjoined. *Modular Mining Systems, Inc. v. Jigsaw Technologies, Inc.*, 221 Ariz. 515, 212 P.3d 853 (Ct. App. Div. 2 2009); *State ex rel. Babbitt v. Goodyear Tire & Rubber Co.*, 128 Ariz. 483, 626 P.2d 1115 (Ct. App. Div. 1 1981).

An injunction may not issue, however, to stay a judicial proceeding (unless necessary to prevent a multiplicity of such proceedings), to prevent enforcement of a statute by public officials, to prevent breach of a contract that cannot be specifically enforced, to prevent the lawful exercise of a public or private office, or to prevent a legislative act by a municipal corporation. A.R.S. § 12-1802. A.R.S. §§ 12-1802(4) and (6) do not, however, prevent a Superior Court from granting injunctive relief against public officials who act illegally, exceed their statutory authority, or exercise their discretion arbitrarily or unreasonably. *Wallace v. Shields*, 175 Ariz. 166, 854 P.2d 1152 (Ct. App. Div. 1 1992).

2. *Comparison With Federal Rule.* ARCP 65(a), (d), (e), and (h) are substantially identical to FRCP 65(a), (b), (c), and (d), with two important exceptions. First, in order to secure the issuance of a temporary restraining order without notice, FRCP 65(b)(1)(B) requires that the applicant's attorney certify to the court *both* the efforts that have been made to give notice *and* the reasons why notice should not be required. ARCP 65(d)(2), the corresponding Arizona Rule, merely requires the applicant's attorney certify *either* the efforts undertaken to give notice *or* the reasons why notice should not be required. This difference in the Arizona Rule suggests that a temporary restraining order without notice may be sought without undertaking any efforts to give notice.

Second, ARCP 65(d) provides, among other things, that every temporary restraining order shall expire by its terms, not to exceed 10 days. Until the 2009 amendments to the Federal Rules of Civil Procedure, FRCP 65(b)(2) similarly provided that a temporary restraining order entered without notice would expire by its terms, not to exceed 10-days. As a consequence of the 2009 amendments to FRCP 65, however, the time period was extended to 14 days. ARCP 65 has not been amended to similarly extend this time period, which remains set at 10 days.

FRCP 65 does not have any provisions that directly correspond to ARCP Rules. 65(c), (g), (i), and (j). ARCP 65 does not have any provision that correspond to FRCP 65(e) and (f).

In 2007, the language of FRCP 65 was amended as part of the general restyling of the Federal Rules of Civil Procedure to make the Federal Rules more easily understood and to make style and terminology consistent throughout the Federal Rules of Civil Procedure. Those stylistic modifications have not been incorporated into ARCP 65.

3. *Verification of Pleadings.* A complaint seeking injunctive relief need not be verified. *Barnet v. Board of Medical Examiners*, 121 Ariz. 338, 590 P.2d 454 (1979). Where an injunction is sought before final judgment, however, the complaint in the action must be supported by affidavit, or verified by at least one of the plaintiffs. *Barnet v. Board of Medical Examiners*, 121 Ariz. 338, 590 P.2d 454 (1979); *Foster v. Thunderbird Irr. Water Delivery Dist. of Pinal County No. 3*, 125 Ariz. 324, 609 P.2d 594 (Ct. App. Div. 2 1980); A.R.S. § 12-1803.

Where a complaint seeking injunctive relief is verified, the answer must also be verified, unless the requirement is waived. Rule 11(c), Ariz.R.Civ.P. *Barnet v. Board of Medical Examiners*, 121 Ariz. 338, 590 P.2d 454 (1979).

4. *Forms and Types of Interlocutory Injunctions.* As is the case under its counterpart in the Federal Rules of Civil Procedure,

Rule 65 contemplates two separate types of interlocutory injunction: a preliminary injunction and a temporary restraining order.

Every preliminary injunction or temporary restraining order must, under Rule 65(h), state the reasons for its issuance and specify the conduct enjoined. *Miller v. Board of Sup'rs of Pinal County*, 175 Ariz. 296, 855 P.2d 1357, 84 Ed. Law Rep. 549 (1993). The failure to comply with these requirements does not render the injunctive order void, but may detract from its effectiveness. *North Star Development Corp. v. Wolfswinkel*, 146 Ariz. 406, 706 P.2d 732 (Ct. App. Div. 2 1985); *State v. Nettz*, 114 Ariz. 296, 560 P.2d 814 (Ct. App. Div. 2 1977); *Laks v. Laks*, 25 Ariz. App. 58, 540 P.2d 1277 (Div. 2 1975).

Rule 65(h) specifies that a properly issued injunction or restraining order binds not only the party to whom it is directed but also that party's "officers, agents, servants, employees and attorneys, and . . . those persons in active concert or participation with them who receive actual notice of the order by personal service or otherwise." This presupposes, however, that the party enjoined is subject to the jurisdiction of the Court. *Bussart v. Superior Court In and For Yavapai County*, 11 Ariz. App. 348, 464 P.2d 668 (Div. 1 1970).

An injunction, even one issued under the harassment statute, A.R.S. § 12-809, cannot properly restrain or restrict pure political speech. *LaFaro v. Cahill*, 203 Ariz. 482, 56 P.3d 56 (Ct. App. Div. 1 2002).

An injunction which restrains a party from breaching a contract is frequently characterized as an order of specific performance. *The Power P.E.O., Inc. v. Employees Ins. of Wausau*, 201 Ariz. 559, 38 P.3d 1224 (Ct. App. Div. 1 2002). There are five requirements for granting specific performance of a contract: (1) there must be a binding contract; (2) the terms of that contract must be certain and fair; (3) the party seeking specific performance must not have acted inequitably; (4) specific performance must not inflict hardship on the party enjoined or on the public that outweighs the anticipated benefit to the party seeking specific performance; and, (5) there must be no adequate remedy at law. *The Power P.E.O., Inc. v. Employees Ins. of Wausau*, 201 Ariz. 559, 38 P.3d 1224 (Ct. App. Div. 1 2002).

Under A.R.S. § 12-2101(F)(2), an order granting an injunction is an appealable order. *LaFaro v. Cahill*, 203 Ariz. 482, 56 P.3d 56 (Ct. App. Div. 1 2002). The fact that an injunction may be subject to modification does not affect its appealability. *LaFaro v. Cahill*, 203 Ariz. 482, 56 P.3d 56 (Ct. App. Div. 1 2002).

5. *Purpose of Preliminary Injunctions.* The purpose of a preliminary injunction is to preserve the *status quo* and/or to prevent ir-

reparable loss or injury until a full trial on the merits of the controversy can be held. Because of its potential duration, a preliminary injunction may not issue without notice to the adverse party and an opportunity to be heard in opposition. *Nu-Tred Tire Co., Inc. v. Dunlop Tire & Rubber Corp.*, 118 Ariz. 417, 577 P.2d 268 (Ct. App. Div. 1 1978). The requirement of Rules 65(a)(1) and 65(a)(2) that there be a hearing on an application for a preliminary injunction requires that the party opposing the preliminary injunction be given an opportunity to be heard and present testimony when there are disputed issues of fact. *McCarthy Western Constructors, Inc. v. Phoenix Resort Corp.*, 169 Ariz. 520, 821 P.2d 181 (Ct. App. Div. 1 1991), redesignated as opinion and publication ordered, (Apr. 2, 1991). The usual procedure is to secure issuance of an Order to Show Cause which schedules the preliminary injunction hearing.

The issue of injunctive relief is moot when the events make it absolutely clear that the allegedly wrongful behavior could not reasonably be expected to recur. *Modular Mining Systems, Inc. v. Jigsaw Technologies, Inc.*, 221 Ariz. 515, 212 P.3d 853 (Ct. App. Div. 2 2009); *SAL Leasing, Inc. v. State ex rel. Napolitano*, 198 Ariz. 434, 10 P.3d 1221 (Ct. App. Div. 1 2000). Factors that may point to a danger of future transgressions include past violations, involuntary cessation of the violations, and their continuance in disregard of the litigation. *Modular Mining Systems, Inc. v. Jigsaw Technologies, Inc.*, 221 Ariz. 515, 212 P.3d 853 (Ct. App. Div. 2 2009); *SAL Leasing, Inc. v. State ex rel. Napolitano*, 198 Ariz. 434, 10 P.3d 1221 (Ct. App. Div. 1 2000).

6. *Standards for Preliminary Injunctive Relief.* The traditional equitable criteria for granting preliminary injunctive relief are:

(1) a strong likelihood of success on the merits;

(2) the possibility of irreparable harm to the plaintiff, not remedied by damages, if relief is not granted;

(3) a balance of hardships favoring the plaintiff; and

(4) in certain cases, advancement of the public interest.

TP Racing, L.L.L.P. v. Simms, 232 Ariz. 489, 307 P.3d 56 (Ct. App. Div. 1 2013); *Arizona Association of Providers for Persons with Disabilities v. State*, 223 Ariz. 6, 219 P.3d 216 (Ct. App. Div. 1 2009); *LaFaro v. Cahill*, 203 Ariz. 482, 56 P.3d 56 (Ct. App. Div. 1 2002); *Kromko v. City of Tucson*, 202 Ariz. 499, 47 P.3d 1137 (Ct. App. Div. 2 2002), redesignated as opinion, (June 11, 2002); *The Power P.E.O., Inc. v. Employees Ins. of Wausau*, 201 Ariz. 559, 38 P.3d 1224 (Ct. App. Div. 1 2002); *Powell-Cerkoney v. TCR-Montana Ranch Joint Venture, II*, 176 Ariz. 275, 860 P.2d 1328 (Ct. App. Div. 1 1993); *Shoen v. Shoen*, 167 Ariz. 58, 804 P.2d 787, Fed. Sec. L. Rep. (CCH) P 95683 (Ct. App. Div. 1 1990).

Whether or not an injunction should issue is a matter committed to the trial court's discretion, and its determination in that regard will be disturbed generally only for an abuse of that discretion. *Valley Medical Specialists v. Farber*, 194 Ariz. 363, 982 P.2d 1277, 15 I.E.R. Cas. (BNA) 419 (1999); *Clay v. Arizona Interscholastic Ass'n, Inc.*, 161 Ariz. 474, 779 P.2d 349, 56 Ed. Law Rep. 308 (1989); *Gillespie Land & Irr. Co. v. Gonzalez*, 93 Ariz. 152, 379 P.2d 135 (1963); *Dowling v. Stapley*, 218 Ariz. 80, 179 P.3d 960, 230 Ed. Law Rep. 794 (Ct. App. Div. 1 2008); *Garden Lakes Community Ass'n, Inc. v. Madigan*, 204 Ariz. 238, 62 P.3d 983 (Ct. App. Div. 1 2003); *Horton v. Mitchell*, 200 Ariz. 523, 29 P.3d 870 (Ct. App. Div. 1 2001); *Town of Tortolita v. Napolitano*, 199 Ariz. 556, 20 P.3d 599 (Ct. App. Div. 1 2001). *Ahwatukee Custom Estates Management Ass'n, Inc. v. Turner*, 196 Ariz. 631, 2 P.3d 1276 (Ct. App. Div. 1 2000); *Berry v. Foster*, 180 Ariz. 233, 883 P.2d 470, 95 Ed. Law Rep. 699 (Ct. App. Div. 2 1994); *Shoen v. Shoen*, 167 Ariz. 58, 804 P.2d 787, Fed. Sec. L. Rep. (CCH) P 95683 (Ct. App. Div. 1 1990); *Cochise County v. Broken Arrow Baptist Church*, 161 Ariz. 406, 778 P.2d 1302 (Ct. App. Div. 2 1989); *Financial Associates, Inc. v. Hub Properties, Inc.*, 143 Ariz. 543, 694 P.2d 831 (Ct. App. Div. 2 1984); *American Credit Bureau, Inc. v. Carter*, 11 Ariz. App. 145, 462 P.2d 838 (Div. 1 1969); *Cochise County ex rel. Riley v. Board of Sup'rs of Cochise County*, 7 Ariz. App. 571, 442 P.2d 129 (1968).

Review on appeal will be *de novo*, however, where the underlying issues in the case involve only matters of statutory interpretation and application. *Garden Lakes Community Ass'n, Inc. v. Madigan*, 204 Ariz. 238, 62 P.3d 983 (Ct. App. Div. 1 2003); *Kromko v. City of Tucson*, 202 Ariz. 499, 47 P.3d 1137 (Ct. App. Div. 2 2002), redesignated as opinion, (June 11, 2002). The specific issue whether a party has an adequate remedy at law will also be subject to *de novo* review. *The Power P.E.O., Inc. v. Employees Ins. of Wausau*, 201 Ariz. 559, 38 P.3d 1224 (Ct. App. Div. 1 2002).

An abuse of discretion occurs if the trial court: (1) applies the incorrect substantive law or preliminary injunction standard; (2) bases its decision on a clearly erroneous finding of fact that is material to the decision to grant or deny the injunction; or, (3) applies an acceptable preliminary injunction standard in a manner that results in an abuse of discretion. *McCarthy Western Constructors, Inc. v. Phoenix Resort Corp.*, 169 Ariz. 520, 821 P.2d 181 (Ct. App. Div. 1 1991), redesignated as opinion and publication ordered, (Apr. 2, 1991). Under the provisions of A.R.S. § 12-2101 (F)(2), orders "[G]ranting or dissolving an injunction, or refusing to grant or dissolve an injunction . . ." are orders from which an appeal may be taken. The fact that an injunction may be subject to modification does not affect its appealability. *LaFaro v. Cahill*, 203 Ariz. 482, 56 P.3d 56 (Ct. App. Div. 1 2002).

Prior case law that a preliminary injunction was rendered ineffective by the failure of the trial court to require the posting of a bond or other security was based on former Rule 65(f), which was abrogated in 1967. *Matter of Wilcox Revocable Trust*, 192 Ariz. 337, 965 P.2d 71 (Ct. App. Div. 1 1998). The Comment to that change makes clear that, although a bond or some other form of security should be required as a condition for issuance of a preliminary injunction, it is no longer the case that a preliminary injunction has no force or effect if a security bond is for some reason not required or posted.

7. *Findings of Fact and Conclusions of Law.* Rule 52(a), Ariz.R.Civ.P. specifies that, in granting or denying preliminary injunctions, the Court must set forth the findings of fact and conclusions of law which constitute the grounds for its action. *Miller v. Board of Sup'rs of Pinal County*, 175 Ariz. 296, 855 P.2d 1357, 84 Ed. Law Rep. 549 (1993). A trial judge's conclusions underlying an order denying an application for a preliminary injunction, however, do not operate as the "law of the case" so as to prevent another trial judge who later considers a motion for summary judgment in the same case from conducting an independent legal analysis of the issues. *Powell-Cerkoney v. TCR-Montana Ranch Joint Venture, II*, 176 Ariz. 275, 860 P.2d 1328 (Ct. App. Div. 1 1993).

A party requesting a preliminary injunction assumes a lesser burden of proof of probable success on the merits than does a party moving for summary judgment, who must establish entitlement to final judgment on the merits. *Powell-Cerkoney v. TCR-Montana Ranch Joint Venture, II*, 176 Ariz. 275, 860 P.2d 1328 (Ct. App. Div. 1 1993).

The legal standard against which the trial judge measures the evidentiary showing thus varies substantially, and the issues the judges presiding over these two proceedings are asked to consider cannot be viewed as identical. *Powell-Cerkoney v. TCR-Montana Ranch Joint Venture, II*, 176 Ariz. 275, 860 P.2d 1328 (Ct. App. Div. 1 1993).

Moreover, affording "law of the case" effect to legal conclusions reached in preliminary injunction proceedings would effectively avoid the restrictions inherent in Rule 65(a)(2), which preclude a trial judge from reaching a final decision on the merits in a preliminary injunction hearing unless that hearing has been properly consolidated with the trial on the merits. *Powell-Cerkoney v. TCR-Montana Ranch Joint Venture, II*, 176 Ariz. 275, 860 P.2d 1328 (Ct. App. Div. 1 1993).

On appeal, a trial judge's findings made in granting or denying a preliminary injunction will be binding unless they are clearly contrary to the evidence. *SAL Leasing, Inc. v. State ex rel.*

Napolitano, 198 Ariz. 434, 10 P.3d 1221 (Ct. App. Div. 1 2000).

8. *Consolidation of Hearing on Preliminary Injunction With Trial on the Merits.* In the interests of expediting the final resolution of the dispute, and particularly in instances where most of the evidence that bears upon the controversy will be presented at the preliminary injunction hearing, the Court may order that the hearing be consolidated with the full trial on the merits. *Riess v. City of Tucson*, 19 Ariz. App. 579, 509 P.2d 651 (Div. 2 1973). The Court may not order such a consolidation, however, without notifying the parties and affording them an opportunity to demand a trial by jury. *Paris-Phoenix Corp. v. Esper*, 112 Ariz. 320, 541 P.2d 917 (1975). Even where such a consolidation is not ordered, evidence received during the preliminary injunction hearing which would be admissible at the trial on the merits becomes part of the record and need not be offered and received again at trial.

9. *Modification or Dissolution of Preliminary Injunction.* Between the date of its issuance and the trial on the merits, a preliminary injunction may be dissolved or modified upon application of the enjoined party, after an answer is filed. If the basis for securing a modification or dissolution is the fact that the material allegations of the complaint have been denied, the answer must be verified. A trial court's order dissolving a preliminary injunction is generally reviewed for an abuse of discretion, except that issues of law involved in that determination will be reviewed *de novo*. *Griffis v. Pinal County*, 213 Ariz. 300, 141 P.3d 780 (Ct. App. Div. 2 2006), opinion vacated on other grounds, 215 Ariz. 1, 156 P.3d 418, 35 Media L. Rep. (BNA) 1726 (2007).

Rule 65(c), which authorizes an application to dissolve or modify preliminary injunctions, does not provide a vehicle for attacking the original basis for the injunction on grounds that were available when the request for injunctive relief was first heard. *Town of Tortolita v. Napolitano*, 199 Ariz. 556, 20 P.3d 599 (Ct. App. Div. 1 2001). Rather, it serves the much more limited purpose of providing a means to show that changed circumstances, including matters which could not reasonably have been raised at the preliminary injunction hearing, or changes in the law, require that the injunction be modified or dissolved. *TP Racing, L.L.L.P. v. Simms*, 232 Ariz. 489, 307 P.3d 56 (Ct. App. Div. 1 2013); *Town of Tortolita v. Napolitano*, 199 Ariz. 556, 20 P.3d 599 (Ct. App. Div. 1 2001).

10. *Purpose of Temporary Restraining Order.* A temporary restraining order is the vehicle for preserving the *status quo* between the time of commencement of the action and the hearing on an application for preliminary injunction. While Rule 65(d) deals mostly with the requirements for securing a temporary

restraining order without notice, that procedure should be the exception rather than the rule, and the adverse party should be given the opportunity to be heard on the application, if it is feasible to do so. See *State Bar Committee Note* to 1966 Amendment.

11. *Issuance of Temporary Restraining Order Without Notice.* A temporary restraining order may be secured without notice to the adverse party only if (1) specific facts are established, by affidavit or a verified pleading, that the party seeking the order will suffer immediate and irreparable injury before the adverse party can be given an opportunity to be heard, and (2) the applicant's attorney files a written certification as to either the efforts that have been made to provide notice or the reasons notice should not be required. The issuance of a temporary restraining order without notice should be the exception rather than the rule, and the requirements of Rule 65(d) for securing such an order are to be scrupulously observed. *Bussart v. Superior Court In and For Yavapai County*, 11 Ariz. App. 348, 464 P.2d 668 (Div. 1 1970). A temporary restraining order may not be issued solely on the basis of an affidavit without any complaint having been filed. *Bryant v. Bloch Companies*, 166 Ariz. 46, 800 P.2d 33 (Ct. App. Div. 1 1990).

12. *Duration of Temporary Restraining Order.* A temporary restraining order issued without notice may not be in effect for longer than ten (10) days, unless the Court grants an extension for good cause shown or the adverse party consents to an extension. Ariz. R. Civ. P. 65(d). The application for a preliminary injunction in such a case is to be set for hearing at the earliest possible time and granted precedence over all other matters, except older matters of the same character.

A temporary restraining order issued without notice may be dissolved on two (2) days' notice to the party who secured it, and such a dissolution or modification can be based upon the pleadings alone. *Nu-Tred Tire Co., Inc. v. Dunlop Tire & Rubber Corp.*, 118 Ariz. 417, 577 P.2d 268 (Ct. App. Div. 1 1978).

13. *Security; Bonds for Injunctions.* Under Rule 65(e), a condition for securing any restraining order or preliminary injunction is the posting by the applicant of security, usually an injunction bond, in an amount fixed by the Court "for the payment of such costs and damages as may be incurred or suffered by any party who is found to have been wrongfully enjoined or restrained." The amount of the bond fixed by the Court limits the surety's liability, but not the amount of wrongful injunction damages that may be recovered. *Smith v. Coronado Foothills Estates Homeowners Ass'n Inc.*, 117 Ariz. 171, 571 P.2d 668 (1977). The recovery can include the attorneys' fees incurred in securing dissolution of the injunction. *U.S. Fidelity & Guar. Co. v. Frohmiller*, 71 Ariz.

377, 227 P.2d 1007 (1951); *Mason Dry Goods Co. v. Ackel*, 30 Ariz. 7, 243 P. 606 (1926). The surety's liability on the bond may be enforced by motion in the same action in which the injunction was secured, by proceeding under Rule 65.1, Ariz.R.Civ.P.

Prior case law that a preliminary injunction was rendered ineffective by the failure of the trial court to require the posting of a bond or other security was based on former Rule 65(f), which was abrogated in 1967. *Matter of Wilcox Revocable Trust*, 192 Ariz. 337, 965 P.2d 71 (Ct. App. Div. 1 1998). The Comment to that change makes clear that, although a bond or some other form of security should be required as a condition for issuance of a preliminary injunction, it is no longer the case that a preliminary injunction has no force or effect if a security bond is for some reason not required or posted.

14. *Disobedience of injunction as contempt.* Disobedience of an injunction may be punished as a contempt of court. Ariz. R. Civ. P. 65(j)(1). *See also, Green v. Lisa Frank, Inc.*, 221 Ariz. 138, 211 P.3d 16 (Ct. App. Div. 2 2009) (acknowledging limitations prescribed by language of Rule 65(j) and discussing inherent authority of the court to dismiss an action for failure to comply with injunctive orders). The party in whose favor the injunction was issued and who believes the injunction has been violated, must file an affidavit stating that the party against whom the injunction was issued is guilty of disobeying it, and describing the acts claimed to constitute disobedience of the injunction. Ariz. R. Civ. P. 65(j)(2).

Upon receipt of such affidavit, the Court may order the person charged with such disobedience to appear and show cause why that person should not be adjudged in contempt, and that order to show cause is to be served upon the person charged with contempt in sufficient time to enable that person to prepare and make a return. Ariz. R. Civ. P. 65(j)(2).

If the person against whom the injunction was issued fails to appear or make return on the order to show cause, the Court may direct that person's arrest. If the claimed contemnor is a corporation and fails to appear, an attachment for sequestration of the corporation's property may issue. Ariz. R. Civ. P. 65(j)(4) and (5).

If, upon appearance, the person against whom the injunction was issued is found to have disobeyed it, the Court may commit that person to jail until the contempt is purged in a fashion the Court directs, or until that person is discharged by law. Ariz. R. Civ. P. 65(j)(6).

Rule 65.1. Security; proceedings against sureties

Whenever these rules, including the Injunction Rule and any other relating to security, require or permit the giving of security by a party, and security is given in the form of a bond or stipulation or other undertaking with one or more sureties, each surety submits to the jurisdiction of the court and irrevocably appoints the clerk of the court as the surety's agent upon whom any papers affecting the surety's liability on the bond or undertaking may be served. The surety's liability may be enforced on motion without the necessity of an independent action. The motion and such notice of the motion as the court prescribes may be served on the clerk of the court, who shall forthwith mail copies to the sureties if their addresses are known.

Added July 1, 1966, effective Nov. 1, 1966; amended Sept. 15, 1987, effective Nov. 15, 1987.

STATE BAR COMMITTEE NOTES

1966 Addition

[Rule 65.1] This section integrates the procedure on both injunction bonds and appeal bonds and eliminates confusion as to the proper method of obtaining service and permitting enforcement of such bonds.

AUTHORS' COMMENTS

Analysis

1. *Scope and Purpose of Rule.* When an injunction or restraining order is dissolved, set aside or vacated, the party enjoined may recover damages for having been wrongfully enjoined from the party who procured the injunction. Hence the requirement of Ariz.R.Civ.P. Rule 65(e), that security be posted as a condition of securing a restraining order or preliminary injunction. Rule 65.1 merely allows the liability of the surety to be enforced by motion in the action in which the injunction was secured to avoid the need for filing an independent action.

Prior case law that a preliminary injunction was rendered ineffective by the failure of the trial court to require the posting of a bond or other security was based on former Rule 65(f), which was abrogated in 1967. *Matter of Wilcox Revocable Trust*, 192 Ariz. 337, 965 P.2d 71 (Ct. App. Div. 1 1998). The Comment to that change makes clear that, although a bond or some other form of security should be required as a condition for issuance of a preliminary injunction, it is no longer the case that a preliminary injunction has no force or effect if a security bond is for some reason not required or posted.

2. *Comparison With Federal Rule.* ARCP 65.1 is substantially identical to FRCP 65.1. In 2007, however, the language of FRCP 65.1 was amended as part of the general restyling of the Federal Rules of Civil Procedure to make the Federal Rules more easily understood and to make style and terminology consistent throughout the Federal Rules of Civil Procedure. Those stylistic modifications have not been incorporated into ARCP 65.1.

3. *Amounts Recoverable; Attorneys' Fees; Liability of Principal.* While the surety's liability may be limited to the penal sum of the bond posted, the amount of damages recoverable against the principal is not limited by the amount of the bond. *Smith v. Coronado Foothills Estates Homeowners Ass'n Inc.*, 117 Ariz. 171, 571 P.2d 668 (1977). Any recovery over and above the bond amount, however, is the responsibility of the principal, not the surety.

The recovery may also include the attorneys' fees incurred in securing dissolution of the injunction. *Mason Dry Goods Co. v. Ackel*, 30 Ariz. 7, 243 P. 606 (1926). This is a well-recognized exception to the general rule that attorneys' fees are only recoverable where authorized by contract or statute. *U.S. Fidelity & Guar. Co. v. Frohmiller*, 71 Ariz. 377, 227 P.2d 1007 (1951). The fees recoverable are only those incurred in procuring the dissolution of the injunction, however, and not the fees incurred in the general defense of the case, which must be segregated. *Hammond v. A.J. Bayless Markets*, 58 Ariz. 58, 117 P.2d 490 (1941); *Jacobson v. Laurel Canyon Mining Co.*, 27 Ariz. 546, 234 P. 823 (1925); *State v. Williams*, 12 Ariz. App. 498, 472 P.2d 109 (Div. 1 1970).

Rule 65.2. Action pursuant to A.R.S. § 23-212

(a) Commencement of Action. An action brought by the county attorney pursuant to A.R.S. § 23-212 shall be commenced by filing a verified complaint with the clerk of the superior court. The attorney signing the complaint shall verify that the attorney believes the assertions in the complaint to be true on the basis of a reasonably diligent inquiry.

(b) Contents of Complaint. A complaint filed under this Rule shall include the following:

(1) The name and address(es) of the employer;

(2) Specification of one or more business licenses subject to suspension or revocation under A.R.S. § 23-212 that are held by the employer, and the identity and address of the licensing agency(ies), including the identity(ies) and mailing address(es) of the agency official(s) authorized to accept service under this Rule;

(3) A statement of specific facts alleged to show that one or more employees are unauthorized aliens;

(4) A statement of specific facts alleged to show that the employer intentionally or knowingly employed one or more unauthorized aliens; and

(5) In the case of an action for a second violation of A.R.S. § 23-212, the case number of the first action and the date of the order or judgment finding a first violation of A.R.S. § 23-212. The complaint shall also include as an attachment a copy of the court's order or judgment finding a first violation of A.R.S. § 23-212.

(c) Nature of Proceedings. An action brought pursuant to A.R.S. § 23-212 shall be denominated as a civil action and assigned a specific sub-category code for purposes of case tracking. An action brought pursuant to A.R.S. § 23-212 shall be heard and decided by the court sitting without a jury, except as otherwise permitted by Rule 39(m).

(d) Venue. An action brought pursuant to A.R.S. § 23-212 shall be brought against the employer by the county attorney in the county where the unauthorized alien employee is or was employed by the employer. If the employee is or was employed by the employer in more than one county, the action shall be proper in any county in which the employee is or was employed by the employer.

(e) Expedited Proceedings. The court shall expedite an action brought pursuant to A.R.S. § 23-212.

(f) Scheduling Conference. Simultaneously with the filing of the complaint required by subsection (a) of this Rule, the county attorney shall file an application and submit a form of order requesting the court to set a date for a scheduling conference to determine the schedule for expedited proceedings. A copy of the signed order shall be served on the employer and may be served with the complaint. At the scheduling conference, the court may address the matters set forth in Rule 16(b) and may set such additional hearings as it deems necessary. On or before the date of the scheduling conference, the employer shall file and serve a written disclosure of the identity of all business licenses that it holds in this State.

(g) Evidentiary Hearing; Summary Judgment. The court may not order a license suspension or license revocation pursuant to A.R.S. § 23-212 without first affording the parties the opportunity for an evidentiary hearing, unless all parties waive the hearing. Rule 56 shall not apply to these proceedings except upon the agreement of all parties.

(h) Standard of Proof. All factual issues required to be determined by the court shall be determined by a preponderance of the evidence.

(i) Applicability of Rules of Evidence. Except as provided in A.R.S. § 23-212(H), the Arizona Rules of Evidence shall apply to proceedings under this Rule.

(j) Enforcement of Court Orders.

(1) After the entry of an order under A.R.S. § 23-212(F)(1) or A.R.S. § 23-212(F)(2) for a first violation, if an employer fails to file a timely sworn affidavit required by A.R.S. § 23-212(F)(1)(c) or A.R.S. § 23-212(F)(2)(d), the county attorney shall file an application for an order to show cause why the employer's licenses with the appropriate licensing agencies should not be suspended beyond any period prescribed in any prior court order. The application shall be accompanied by an affidavit or other proof demonstrating that the employer has failed to file the required sworn affidavit and shall set forth the identity and address of any appropriate licensing agency, including the identity and mailing address of the agency official authorized to accept service under this Rule.

(2) Within five (5) days after service of an application for an order to show cause, the employer may file an opposition to the relief sought in the application and to any further license suspension on the ground that the employer has filed an affidavit meeting the requirements of A.R.S. § 23-212(F)(1)(c) or A.R.S. § 23-212(F)(2)(d). If such an opposition is timely filed, the court shall hold a hearing and shall not order any further license suspension until it renders its decision on whether to

grant the relief sought in the application. If no opposition is timely filed or if the court grants the relief sought in the application, the court shall order the appropriate licensing agencies to suspend indefinitely all applicable licenses held by the employer.

(3) After the entry of an order suspending a license for a first violation for failure to file a required sworn affidavit, the employer may, by motion or stipulation, seek relief from the order on the ground that the employer has filed a sworn affidavit required by A.R.S § 23-212(F)(1)(c) or A.R.S. § 23-212(F)(2)(d). If such a showing is made and subject to the completion of any term of license suspension ordered under A.R.S. § 23-212(F)(1)(d) or A.R.S. § 23-212(F)(2)(c), the court shall enter an order terminating any further license suspension.

(4) The clerk of the superior court shall distribute by any method authorized by Rule 58(e) a certified copy of any order suspending or revoking a license, or terminating a license suspension, entered under this Rule or A.R.S. § 23-212 to the parties, the Arizona Attorney General, and any licensing agency ordered to suspend an employer's license.

(k) Action for Second Violation. An action alleging a second violation under A.R.S. § 23-212(F)(3) shall be filed and served as a new action.

(l) Requirement of Electronic or Facsimile Service. After a party has appeared in a proceeding brought under this Rule, any papers served on that party by mail under Rule 5(c) shall also be served at the same time by electronic mail or by facsimile, or as agreed to by the parties or ordered by the court. If the party on whom service is to be made does not have access to electronic mail or facsimile, then service shall be made as otherwise provided by Rule 5(c).

(m) Fees. The court shall assess such fees in these proceedings as may be prescribed by A.R.S. §§ 12-284, 12-284.01, and 12-284.02.

Added December 14, 2007, effective January 1, 2008.

COURT COMMENT

This Rule applies only to actions filed pursuant to A.R.S. § 23-212. The rule is intended to supplement, not supplant, statutory procedures.

AUTHORS' COMMENTS

Analysis

1. *Scope and Purpose of Rule*. Rule 65.2, as its title suggests,

deals only with proceedings brought to enforce the provisions of the so-called "employer sanctions" statute, A.R.S. § 23-212, enacted by the Legislature in 2007. That statute provides for the forfeiture of licenses by employers found to employ undocumented immigrants. Although there was pending litigation to enjoin enforcement of that statute, the Supreme Court, out of an abundance of caution, adopted Rule 65.2 on an emergency basis in December 2007. There are no reported cases interpreting or applying this rule.

2. *Comparison With Federal Rule*. The Federal Rules of Civil Procedure do not have a provision that corresponds to ARCP 65.2.

Rule 66. Receivers

(a) Application; Verification; Service; Notice; Restraining Order. An application for the appointment of a receiver may be included in a verified complaint or may be made by separate and independent verified application after a complaint has been filed. No application shall be considered unless served upon the adverse party except where (A) at least ten days after filing the application, the applicant files a sworn affidavit showing that all reasonable efforts having been made, personal service on the adverse party cannot be made within the state or by direct service out of state; or (B) there is substantial cause for appointing a receiver before service can otherwise be made. If application for appointment of a receiver without notice is made, the court shall require and the applicant shall file in the court a bond in such amount as the court shall fix, with such surety as the court shall approve, conditioned to indemnify the defendant for such costs, and all damages as may be occasioned by the seizure, taking and detention of the defendant's property; or, if the defendant is available for service, the court may order a hearing on the application in less than ten days. No application for a receivership under this rule shall be entertained where Rule 65 is applicable.

Amended and effective Nov. 1, 1967.

(b) Appointment; Oath; Bond; Certificate.

1. The court shall not appoint as receiver a party, an officer or employee of a party, an attorney for a party, or a person interested in the action; provided, however, that after such notice as the court shall find is adequate, and if no party shall have objected, the court may appoint an employee of a party or an officer of a corporate party, or a person otherwise interested in the action, in a case in which the court finds that the property has been abandoned or that duties of the receiver will consist chiefly of physical preservation of the property (including crops growing thereon), collection of rents or the maturing, harvesting and disposition of crops then growing thereon.

2. Before entering upon the prescribed duties, the receiver shall file a bond to be approved by the court in the amount fixed by the order of appointment, conditioned that the receiver will faithfully discharge the duties of the receiver in the action and obey the orders of the court. The receiver shall make an oath to the same effect, which shall be endorsed on the bond. The clerk shall thereupon deliver to the receiver a certificate of appointment. The certificate shall contain a description of the property involved in the action.

Amended and effective Nov. 1, 1967. Amended Sept. 15, 1987, effective Nov. 15, 1987.

(c) Powers; Termination; Governing Law.

1. The receiver may, subject to control of the court, commence and defend actions. The receiver shall take and keep possession of the property, receive rents, collect debts and perform such other duties respecting the property as authorized by the court.

2. The court may at any time suspend a receiver and may, upon notice, remove a receiver and appoint another.

3. A receivership may be terminated upon motion served with at least ten days notice upon all parties who have appeared in the proceedings. The court in the notice of hearing may require that a final account and report be filed and served, and may require the filing of written objections thereto. In the termination proceedings, the court shall take such evidence as is appropriate and shall make such order as is just concerning its termination, including all necessary orders on the fees and costs of the receivership.

4. In all matters relating to the appointment of receivers, to their powers, duties and liabilities, and to the power of the court, the principles of equity shall govern when applicable.

(d) Procedure. An action wherein a receiver has been appointed shall not be dismissed except by order of the court. The practice in the administration of estates by receivers or by similar officers appointed by the court shall be in accordance with the practice heretofore followed. In all other respects the action in which the appointment of a receiver is sought or which is brought by or against a receiver is governed by these rules.

STATE BAR COMMITTEE NOTES

1967 Amendments

[Rule 66(a, b, c, d)] This Rule merges and revises the former Rule 66 on receivers and ARS § 12-1242, also dealing with receivers. It completely replaces the statutory provision, which hereafter will be of no force and effect. ARS § 12-1241, of course, still remains in effect.

The principal changes are that ARS § 12-1242, as revised, becomes § 66(a) of the rule on receivers. The former Rule 66(a), with the addition of language permitting the appointment of the enumerated persons in certain cases, becomes Rule 66(b). The former Rule 66(b), which dealt with removal of receivers but did not cover other aspects of termination, is revised to cover termination as well and becomes Rule 66(c). The former Rule 66(c) is retained without alteration as Rule 66(d).

The actual changes of consequence thus are restricted to new sections 66(a) and 66(c).

These are:

1. The statute required that the application be separate from the complaint. This serves no useful purpose if the application is made simultaneously, and the normal equity practice should be followed of including the ap-

plication in the verified complaint and of obtaining a show cause order for consideration of the receivership. This will avoid a duplicating and unnecessary document.

2. The statute required service on an adverse party before the matter can be heard. Service should be required whenever the adverse party can be reached. However, if the adverse party is out of state or is otherwise unavailable or unknown, the practical result of this requirement is that property may deteriorate entirely during the pendency of the publication period. The change eliminates that hazard and still preserves personal service wherever it is practicably possible. Normally deterioration or dissipation of assets can be controlled by injunctive relief prior to the hearing on the receivership, and the rule makes this the preferred practice. However, in case of an emergency in which for some reason injunctive relief is not suitable, the rule expressly permits the court to shorten time for the hearing on the receivership and further provides, in language taken from the Federal Bankruptcy Act, 11 U.S.C. § 109(§ 69(a) of the Bankruptcy Act) [repealed; see, now 11 U.S.C.A. § 303(e)] for an appropriate bond.

3. The statutory affidavit conflicted with the normal method of handling interlocutory equity proceedings in this state on the basis of testimony alone. The rule contemplates procedure as on a preliminary injunction, usually on the basis of testimony but with affidavits permitted.

4. The statute permitted what was in effect a temporary restraining order, without normal safeguards. This power is preserved by the rule, but subject to the Rule 65 provisions on notice, bond, et cetera.

5. There has been no written practice on termination of receiverships. The rule codifies the best existing actual practice.

AUTHORS' COMMENTS

Analysis

1. *Scope and Purpose of Rule.* The substantive and jurisdictional requirements for securing the appointment of a receiver are set forth both in Rule 66 and in A.R.S. § 12-1241. The procedures for securing such an appointment are addressed in Rule 66 which, in effect, supersedes and replaces A.R.S. § 12-1242. *First Phoenix Realty Investments v. Superior Court In and For County of Maricopa*, 173 Ariz. 265, 841 P.2d 1390 (Ct. App. Div. 1 1992).

2. *Comparison With Federal Rule.* ARCP 66(d) is substantially the same as FRCP 66. The Federal Rule does not have provisions, however, that correspond to ARCP 66(a), (b), and (c). In ad-

dition, in 2007, the language of FRCP 66 was amended as part of the general restyling of the Federal Rules of Civil Procedure to make the Federal Rules more easily understood and to make style and terminology consistent throughout the Federal Rules of Civil Procedure. Those stylistic modifications have not been incorporated into ARCP 66.

3. *Nature and Purpose of Remedy.* The appointment of a receiver is an equitable remedy. *First Phoenix Realty Investments v. Superior Court In and For County of Maricopa*, 173 Ariz. 265, 841 P.2d 1390 (Ct. App. Div. 1 1992). A receiver is often used to protect a creditor with an interest in the property at issue from irreparable loss by preventing the dissipation or waste of the assets. The appointment of a receiver is designed to protect property subject to pending litigation, and such an appointment is not proper where there is no pending action or where the property is adequate security and is being properly operated and maintained. *Dart v. Western Sav. & Loan Ass'n*, 103 Ariz. 170, 438 P.2d 407 (1968); *First Phoenix Realty Investments v. Superior Court In and For County of Maricopa*, 173 Ariz. 265, 841 P.2d 1390 (Ct. App. Div. 1 1992). A receiver may be appointed to manage the judicial dissolution and winding up of the affairs of an Arizona general partnership. *Gravel Resources of Arizona v. Hills*, 217 Ariz. 33, 170 P.3d 282 (Ct. App. Div. 1 2007).

4. *Prerequisites for Securing Appointment of Receiver.* A.R.S. § 12-1241 previously authorized the Superior Court to appoint a receiver in a pending action when "no other adequate remedy is given by law for the protection and preservation of property or the rights of the parties therein, pending litigation in respect thereto." Applying that version of the statute, it was held that the Superior Court may appoint a receiver where there is:

(1) a pending action over which the Court has jurisdiction; and

(2) no other adequate remedy at law.

See Ferguson v. Superior Court of Maricopa County, 76 Ariz. 31, 258 P.2d 421 (1953); *Wingfoot Cal. Homes Co. v. Valley Nat. Bank of Phoenix*, 74 Ariz. 287, 248 P.2d 738 (1952); *United Sanders Stores v. Messick*, 39 Ariz. 323, 6 P.2d 430 (1931).

The statute has since been amended to delete that language "when no adequate remedy is given by law for the protection and preservation of property or the rights of the parties therein, pending litigation in respect thereto," and substituted in its place the phrase "even if the action includes no other claim for relief." This statutory elimination of the "no other adequate remedy at law" requirement would appear to broaden the universe of cases in which a receiver may be appointed, and it is no longer necessary for a petitioner to show irreparable harm or the lack of an adequate legal remedy to secure the appointment of a receiver. *Gravel Resources of Arizona v. Hills*, 217 Ariz. 33, 170 P.3d 282 (Ct. App. Div. 1 2007). The foreclosure statute was also amended to in effect overrule legislatively the decision in *First Phoenix Realty Investments v. Superior Court In and For County of Maricopa*, 173 Ariz. 265, 841 P.2d 1390 (Ct. App. Div. 1 1992), which held that receivers could not be appointed in nonjudicial foreclosure proceedings. Statutory authority for the appointment of receivers in such situations is now furnished by A.R.S. § 33-807(C).

5. *Procedure for Securing Appointment of Receiver; Contents of Application; Verification; Service.* A.R.S. § 12-1242 provided that an application for the appointment of a receiver had to be in writing and supported by affidavit. Rule 66(a), which replaced A.R.S. § 12-1242, provides that an application for the appointment of a receiver *may* be included in a verified complaint, but the Court of Appeals has held that the Rule contemplates that the "complaint" is a different document from the receivership "application." *First Phoenix Realty Investments v. Superior Court In and For County of Maricopa*, 173 Ariz. 265, 841 P.2d 1390 (Ct. App. Div. 1 1992). The verified complaint should allege that "no other adequate remedy is given by law for the protection and preservation of the property at issue or the rights of the parties therein" and that "the provisions of Ariz.R.Civ.P. 65, are inapplicable." If the request for an appointment of a receiver is made in a verified complaint, the verified complaint should be filed and served together with the appropriate documents necessary to secure a hearing on the request for a receivership.

Generally, a receiver is appointed, if at all, following (1) notice of the requested appointment to all parties having an interest in the property at issue, and (2) a hearing on the application at which the appointment of the receiver may be contested. A.R.S. § 12-1242 stated that the application for appointment was to be "served upon the adverse party, together with reasonable notice of the time of hearing." Under Rule 66(a), however, the *ex parte* appointment of a receiver is possible where sufficient emergency conditions exist. Such an appointment does not violate due process. *Sato v. First Nat. Bank of Ariz.*, 12 Ariz. App. 263, 469 P.2d 829 (Div. 1 1970).

Specifically, the Court may consider an application for the appointment of a receiver which has not been served on the adverse party, if (1) at least ten (10) days after filing the application, the applicant files an affidavit showing that, despite all reasonable efforts having been made, personal service on the adverse party cannot be made within the state or by direct service out of state; or (2) there is substantial cause for appointing a receiver before service can otherwise be made.

If difficulties in securing service form the basis of the request for appointment of a receiver without notice, then the applicant must wait ten (10) days after filing the original application before making such request. This application must be verified and must be supported by an affidavit setting forth the nature of the efforts made to secure service. On the other hand, if the justification is the existence of "substantial cause" for the appointment of a receiver without notice, then the applicant may make such request immediately. The application must, however, be verified. Ariz. R. Civ. P. 66(a).

6. *Role and Powers of Receiver.* A receiver is a ministerial officer of the Court and may only act in accordance with and subject to the orders of the Court. *Stowell v. Arizona Sav. & Loan Ass'n*, 93 Ariz. 310, 380 P.2d 606 (1963). Rule 66(b) requires the receiver to post a bond and be sworn before undertaking any official action. Thereafter, the receiver is issued a Certificate of Appointment, which describes the property at issue. In practice, a certified copy of the order of appointment often serves as the "Certificate of Appointment." A receiver stands in the shoes of the entity it represents, and may bring, defend or settle claims on that entity's behalf. *Gravel Resources of Arizona v. Hills*, 217 Ariz. 33, 170 P.3d 282 (Ct. App. Div. 1 2007).

The appointment of a receiver is discretionary with the Court. If appointed, the receiver is generally a disinterested person. If no party objects after adequate notice, however, then the Court may appoint an officer or employee of a party or a person otherwise interested in the action as the receiver in a case where the Court finds either that (1) the property at issue has been abandoned or (2) the "duties of the receiver will consist chiefly of physical preservation of the property (including crops growing thereon), collection of rents or the maturing, harvesting and disposition of crops then growing thereon." Rule 66(b)(1).

7. *Removal of Receiver.* Rule 66(c)(2) provides that the "court may at any time suspend a receiver and may, upon notice, remove a receiver and appoint another."

8. *Dismissal of Action in Which Receiver Appointed.* An action in which a receiver has been appointed under Rule 66 may not be dismissed except by Court order. *See* Rules 41(a)(1) and 66(d).

Rule 67. Deposit in court; security for costs

(a) By Leave of Court. In an action in which any part of the relief sought is a judgment for a sum of money or the disposition of a sum of money or the disposition of any other thing capable of delivery, a party, upon notice to every other party, and by leave of court, may deposit with the court all or any part of such sum or thing.

Amended Nov. 15, 1978, effective Feb. 1, 1979.

(b) By Order of Court. When it is admitted by the pleading or examination of a party that the party has in the party's possession, or under the party's control money or other things capable of delivery which are the subject of litigation, and held by the party as trustee for another party, or which belong or are due to another party, the court may order the money or things to be deposited in court or delivered to such party upon such conditions as may be just and subject to the further order of the court.

Amended Nov. 15, 1978, effective Feb. 1, 1979; Sept. 15, 1987, effective Nov. 15, 1987.

(c) Custody; Duties of Clerk. When any money, debt, instrument of writing or other article is paid or deposited in court to abide the result of legal proceedings, the clerk shall seal the article in a package, and deposit it in a safe or bank, subject to the control of the court, and enter in the records of the action a statement showing each item of money or property received, and the disposition thereof. If the deposit is money the court may order the clerk to deposit it with the county treasurer, who shall receive and hold it subject to the order of the court.

(d) Security for Costs; When Required; Bond and Conditions. At any time before trial of an issue of law or fact, on motion of the defendant, supported by affidavit showing that the plaintiff is not the owner of property within the state out of which the costs could be made by execution sale, the court shall order the plaintiff to give security for the costs of the action. The court shall fix the amount of the security, the time within which it shall be given and it shall be given upon condition that the plaintiff will pay all costs that may be adjudged against the plaintiff, and authorize judgment against the sureties, if a written undertaking. If the plaintiff fails so to do within the time fixed by the court, the court shall order the action dismissed without notice.

Amended Nov. 15, 1978, effective Feb. 1, 1979; Sept. 15, 1987, effective Nov. 15, 1987.

(e) Inability to Give Security; Proof; Objection and Examination. If the plaintiff, within five days after the order, makes strict proof of inability to give the security, the order to give security shall be vacated. The proof may be made by affidavit, but if objection thereto is made by the defendant, the plaintiff shall submit to the court at a time designated by the court, when the plaintiff shall be examined orally as to the inability to give such security.

Amended Nov. 15, 1978, effective Feb. 1, 1979; Sept. 15, 1987, effective Nov. 15, 1987.

(f) Exemptions; Exceptions.

1. The following shall not be required to give security for costs:

(i) The state.

(ii) A county.

(iii) A board or commission of the state or county, or an officer of such board or commission acting in an official capacity.

(iv) An executor, administrator or guardian appointed under the laws of this state.

2. When the costs are secured by an attachment bond or other bond no further security shall be required.

3. An intervener, and a defendant seeking judgment against the plaintiff on a counterclaim, though the plaintiff has discontinued the plaintiff's action, shall be required to give security as is required of a plaintiff.

Amended Nov. 15, 1978, effective Feb. 1, 1979; Sept. 15, 1987, effective Nov. 15, 1987.

AUTHORS' COMMENTS

Analysis

1. *Scope and Purpose of Rule.* Two separate subjects are covered by Rule 67: (1) the deposit into Court of money or property that is the subject of the dispute, and (2) the circumstances under

which a plaintiff may be required to post a bond as security for the defendant's anticipated costs.

2. *Comparison With Federal Rule.* ARCP 67(a) corresponds to FRCP 67, but their provisions are slightly different. The Federal Rule has provisions, not contained in ARCP 67(a), requiring service of an order permitting a deposit on the Clerk of the Court and requiring that funds deposited with the Court be placed in an interest-bearing account or invested in interest-bearing securities. The Federal Rule does not have provisions that correspond to ARCP 67(b), (c), (d), (e), and (f). (In the District of Arizona, a procedure for requiring a nonresident plaintiff to post security for costs has been enacted by Local Rule. *See*, L. R. Civ. 54.1(c), Local Rules of Practice of the United States District Court for the District of Arizona.)

In addition, in 2007, the language of FRCP 67 was amended as part of the general restyling of the Federal Rules of Civil Procedure to make the Federal Rules more easily understood and to make style and terminology consistent throughout the Federal Rules of Civil Procedure. Those stylistic modifications have not been incorporated into ARCP 67.

3. *Voluntary Deposits in Court.* Under Rule 67(a), where all or part of the relief sought in an action is "a judgment for a sum of money or the disposition of a sum of money or the disposition of any other thing capable of delivery," any party may, with leave of the Court and notice to the other parties, deposit the money or property in dispute, or any part of it, with the Court.

4. *Deposits by Order of Court.* The Court may order a deposit, under Rule 67(b), of money or property that is the subject of litigation, where a party admits possession or control of it. The Court may also order the money or property delivered to the party claiming it "upon such conditions as may be just."

5. *Procedure Upon Deposit.* Where property capable of delivery is deposited with the Court, Rule 67(c) requires the Clerk to seal it and deposit it in a safe or bank, and maintain a record of the deposit and disposition. In the case of money that is deposited, the Court may order the Clerk to deposit it with the County Treasurer.

6. *Motion for Security for Costs.* Ariz. R. Civ. P. 67(d) and (e) govern the procedures for requiring the posting of security for costs. Recently, the Court of Appeals upheld the constitutionality of Rule 66(d). *Thiele v. City of Phoenix*, 232 Ariz. 40, 301 P.3d 206 (Ct. App. Div. 1 2013) (Rule 67(d) did not unconstitutionally infringe on resident's fundament rights or create an invidious classification).

To secure such a cost bond, the defendant must make a motion, supported by affidavit, showing that the plaintiff does not own property in the state that can be subjected to execution to satisfy an award of costs. It is the general and accepted practice for the supporting affidavit to estimate the costs the moving defendant anticipates will be incurred. Such a motion is not a responsive pleading and will not alone forestall the entry of the defendant's default. *Whitlock v. Boyer*, 77 Ariz. 334, 271 P.2d 484 (1954). The motion may be made at any time before trial, and is not precluded by the fact that discovery has commenced. *Wright v. Sears, Roebuck & Co.*, 116 Ariz. 391, 569 P.2d 821 (1977).

If the motion is properly supported, the Court must order the plaintiff "to give security for the costs of the action." The Court is to establish the amount of the security required, and the time within which it must be filed.

In determining the amount of Rule 67(d) security to be required, the trial court must consider the estimated taxable costs of the litigation, and may consider only those expenses that qualify as costs under statute. *Thiele v. City of Phoenix*, 232 Ariz. 40, 301 P.3d 206 (Ct. App. Div. 1 2013). A.R.S. § 12-332 (2003) sets forth those items that constitute taxable costs and permits the recovery of expenses for officers and witnesses, depositions, referees, certified records or papers, and other expenses resulting from court orders (including mandatory filing fees) or from agreements between the parties. A.R.S. § 12-332(A).

As a result of a recent case, trial courts, and litigants, now have guidance as to the factors that go into fixing the amount of security. Thus, a trial court should consider the following factors in determining the amount of the security to be imposed:

(1) complexity and size of the case,
(2) number of parties involved,
(3) likely number of depositions needed,
(4) projected cost of transcripts, and
(5) any other factors pertinent to the estimated taxable costs of the defendant.

See Thiele v. City of Phoenix, 232 Ariz. 40, 301 P.3d 206 (Ct. App. Div. 1 2013) (citing, *Hytken v. Wake*, 68 P.3d 508, 512 (Colo. App. 2002) and, McAuliffe and Wahl, 2 *Arizona Practice: Civil Trial Practice,* § 13.14 (2d ed. 2001).

Rule 67(d) "costs" do not include attorneys' fees, even in an action where such fees are recoverable as costs, such as one under A.R.S. § 12-341.01. *Sweis v. Chatwin*, 120 Ariz. 249, 253–54, 585 P.2d 269 (Ct. App. Div. 1 1978) (holding a trial court erroneously considered attorneys' fees in setting a cost bond).

The plaintiff must be given a reasonable time to comply with the order. *Wright v. Sears, Roebuck & Co.*, 116 Ariz. 391, 569 P.2d 821 (1977).

7. *Failure to Post Security for Costs.* If the plaintiff fails to file the security within the period prescribed, and does not invoke the procedures of Rule 67(e), the action is to be dismissed without notice. *Union Interchange, Inc. v. Benton*, 100 Ariz. 33, 410 P.2d 477 (1966); *Flynn v. Johnson*, 3 Ariz. App. 369, 414 P.2d 757 (1966).

8. *Claim of Inability to Post Security for Costs.* Rule 67(e) permits the plaintiff to avoid, or at least forestall, the requirement to post such security by making "strict proof," by affidavit or otherwise, of an "inability to give the security." Such proof must be submitted within five (5) days after the order requiring security and, if it is, the order is vacated. If the defendant objects to the plaintiff's proof, however, the Court must order the plaintiff to appear at a designated time to be examined orally concerning the claimed inability to give security. *McCarthy v. Arnold*, 150 Ariz. 208, 722 P.2d 376 (Ct. App. Div. 2 1986). This is a mandatory requirement of the Rule, and not discretionary with the trial court. *McCarthy v. Arnold*, 150 Ariz. 208, 722 P.2d 376 (Ct. App. Div. 2 1986).

Rule 68. Offer of judgment

(a) Time for Making; Procedure. At any time more than 30 days before the trial begins, any party may serve upon any other party an offer to allow judgment to be entered in the action. However, in cases subject to arbitration, no offer of judgment may be made during the period beginning 25 days before the arbitration hearing and ending upon the date of the filing of any notice of appeal of an award pursuant to Rule 77(a).

Amended Sept. 1, 2011, effective Jan. 1, 2012.

(b) Contents of Offer. If any portion of an offer made under this Rule is for the entry of a monetary judgment, the monetary award to be made shall be set forth in the offer as a specifically stated sum. which shall be inclusive of all damages, taxable court costs, interest, and attorney's fees, if any, sought in the case. The offeror may choose to exclude an amount for attorney's fees, but must specifically so state in the offer. If the offeror excludes an amount for attorney's fees in the offer, and the offeree accepts the offer, then either party may apply to the court for an award of attorney's fees, if otherwise allowed by statute, contract or otherwise. The offer need not be apportioned by claim.

(c) Acceptance of Offer; Entry of Judgment. If, while an offer remains effective within the meaning of this rule, the offeree serves written notice that the offer is accepted, then either party may file the offer together with proof of acceptance, and a judgment complying with the requirements of Rule 58(a) shall be entered.

(d) Rejection of Offer; Waiver of Objections. An offer that is not accepted while it remains effective within the meaning of this Rule shall be deemed rejected. Evidence of the rejected offer shall not be admissible except in a proceeding to determine sanctions under this Rule. If the offeree has any objection(s) to the validity of the offer, the offeree must serve upon the offeror, within ten days after service of the offer, written notice of any such objection(s). Unless the offeree notifies the offeror of any objection as provided under this subsection, the offeree waives the right to do so in any proceeding to determine sanctions under this rule.

(e) Multiple Offerors. Multiple parties may make a joint unapportioned offer of judgment to a single offeree.

(f) Multiple Offerees. Unapportioned offers may not be made to multiple offerees. However, one or more parties may make to two or more other parties an apportioned offer of judgment that is conditioned upon acceptance by all the offerees. Each offeree may serve a separate written notice of acceptance of the offer. If fewer than all offerees accept, then the offeror may nevertheless enforce any number of the acceptances if (i) the offer discloses that the offeror may exercise this option, and (ii) the offeror serves written notice of final acceptance no later than 10 days after the expiration of the effective period of the offer. The sanctions provided in this Rule apply to each offeree who did not accept the unapportioned offer.

(g) Sanctions. If the offeree rejects an offer and does not later obtain a more favorable judgment other than pursuant to this Rule, the offeree must pay, as a sanction, reasonable expert witness fees and double the taxable costs, as defined in A.R.S. § 12-332, incurred by the offeror after making the offer and prejudgment interest on unliquidated claims to accrue from the date of the offer. If the judgment includes an award of taxable costs or attorney's fees, only those taxable costs and attorney's fees determined by the court as having been reasonably incurred as of the date the offer was made shall be considered in determining if the judgment is more favorable than the offer. The determination whether a sanction should be imposed after an arbitration hearing shall be made by reference to the judgment ultimately entered, whether on the award itself pursuant to Rule 76(c) or after an appeal of the award pursuant to Rule 77.

Amended Sept. 1, 2011, effective Jan. 1, 2012.

(h) Effective Period of Offers; Subsequent Offers; Offers on Damages. An offer of judgment made pursuant to this Rule shall remain effective for 30 days after it is served, except that (i) an offer made within 60 days after service of the summons and complaint shall remain effective for 60 days after service, (ii) an offer made within 45 days of trial shall remain effective for 15 days after service, and (iii) in a case subject to arbitration, an offer that has not previously expired shall expire at 5:00 p.m. on the fifth day before the arbitration hearing. If the effective period is enlarged by the court, the offeror may withdraw the offer at any time after expiration of the initial effective period and prior to acceptance of the offer. The fact that an offer has been rejected does not preclude a subsequent offer. When the liability of one party to another has been determined by verdict or order or judgment, but the amount or extent of the liability remains to be determined by further proceedings, any party may make an offer of judgment, which shall have the same effect as an offer made before trial if it is served within a reasonable time not fewer than 10 days before the commencement of hearings to determine the amount or extent of liability.

Amended Sept. 1, 2011, effective Jan. 1, 2012.

Rule 68 amended July 1, 1966, effective Nov. 1, 1966; Sept. 15, 1987, effective Nov. 15, 1987; Feb. 14, 1990, effective May 1, 1990; June 8, 1990, effective Sept. 1, 1990; March 23, 1992, effective June 1, 1992; Sept. 30, 1993, effective Dec. 1, 1993; September 5, 2007, effective January 1, 2008.

STATE BAR COMMITTEE NOTES

1966 Amendment

This rule differs from the Federal Rule which authorizes the clerk to enter judgment when an offer of judgment is accepted. This rule requires that when an offer of judgment is accepted, "a judgment complying with the requirements of Rule 58(a) shall be entered." It was felt that adoption of the language of the Federal Rule might imply an authority of the clerk to enter a judgment without complying with Rule 58(a).

1990 Amendment

The term "costs" used in Rule 68 does not include attorney's fees, even if they are recoverable in the action. See *Boltz & Odegaard v. Hohn*, 148 Ariz. 361, 714 P.2d 854 (Ct. App. Div. 1 1985). To eliminate confusion in cases where such fees are recoverable, and to facilitate their disposition through the offer of judgment procedure, the 1990 amendment to Rule 68 added the requirement that, in cases where attorney's fees are sought, the offer of judgment specify what disposition is to be made of such claims if the offer is accepted.

1992 Amendments

In connection with the 1990 amendments to Rule 68, which made the offer of judgment procedure bilateral and provided for the award of double costs for failure to accept an offer of judgment that was the same as, or less than, the relief eventually obtained, the Arizona Supreme Court called for consideration of further amendments to make the offer of judgment procedure an even more effective vehicle for the settlement of claims. The 1992 amendments to the Rule were proposed in response to that request.

The intent of the 1992 amendments was to increase the sanctions associated with failures to accept offers of judgment to include reasonable expert witness fees incurred after the offer was made, and post-offer prejudgment interest on unliquidated claims. An effort was also made to simplify the task involved in determining whether an award is to be made under the Rule. The procedure for making an offer, the time periods when an offer remains effective, and the procedure for securing the entry of a judgment once an offer is accepted remain unchanged.

An offer of judgment in the ordinary case in which a monetary award is sought should now simply be for a specific stated sum. If the judgment finally obtained is equal to, or more favorable to the offeror than, the offer that was made, the offeror is entitled to an award of (a) double the amount of statutory taxable costs incurred after the offer was made, (b) reasonable expert witness fees incurred after the offer was made, and (c), in the case of unliquidated claims, an award of prejudgment interest computed from the date of the offer. The intent was to award prejudgment interest, where appropriate under Rule 68, only on unliquidated claims, or on the unliquidated portions of claims that are partially liquidated, and the rule specifically provides that prejudgment interest is not to be awarded, as a sanction under Rule 68, on those portions of the judgment that already include a prejudgment interest award.

The term "costs" in Rule 68 does not include attorney's fees, even if they are recoverable in the action. *See Boltz & Odegaard v. Hohn*, 148 Ariz. 361, 714 P.2d 854 (Ct. App. Div. 1 1985). In cases which involve a claim for attorney's fees, the procedure of having the offer of judgment specify an alternative for disposition of such a claim has been abandoned in favor of setting forth separate requirements and procedures to be followed in such cases. In an action involving a claim for attorney's fees, the offer of judgment must set forth and state separately the amount of attorney's fees to be awarded and the monetary award to be made to the offeror if the offer is accepted. Such an offer may be accepted in whole or in part. If the offer is accepted in its entirety, the procedure for filing the offer and proof of acceptance with the court, and securing the entry of an appropriate judgment, is the same as in other cases. The party to whom such an offer is made, however, has the option to accept only that portion of the offer which states the amount of the monetary award to be made on the underlying claims. If such a partial acceptance is elected and made, the Rule specifies the procedure to be followed to have the court determine whether attorney's fees are to be awarded and, if so, the amount. The Rule does not authorize a partial acceptance of that portion of such an offer that states the attorney's fees to be awarded upon acceptance, and any such partial acceptance should be considered a nullity. To insure comparability, in cases where attorney's fees are sought, in determining whether an award under Rule 68 is warranted, the court should exclude attorney's fees from the comparison, and compare the result obtained on the underlying claims with that portion of the offer stating the amount that will be accepted with respect to those claims.

2007 Amendments

The former subsection (c) regarding attorney's fees has been deleted. Under the amended rule, unless specifically stated otherwise, all offers include an amount for attorney's fees if an award of fees has been sought in the action. In determining whether sanctions are appropriate, the court may require a hearing to determine the amount of attorney's fees reasonably incurred as of the date the offer was made. *Cf.* Rule 54(g)(3). In subsections (e) and (f), provisions for joint and apportioned offers have been added. The "taxable costs" awarded as sanctions under subsection (g) would not preclude an award of costs otherwise available under A.R.S. § 12-341 to the "successful party." *Drozda v. McComas*, 181 Ariz. 82, 85, 887 P.2d 612, 615 (Ct. App. Div. 1 1994).

AUTHORS' COMMENTS

Analysis

1. Scope and Purpose of Rule.
2. Comparison With Federal Rule.
3. History of Rule.
4. Offer of Judgment Procedure; Non-Arbitration Cases.
5. Offer of Judgment Procedure; Arbitration Cases.
6. Effect of Complete Acceptance of Offer.
7. Effect of Failure to Accept Offer.
8. Offer of Judgment Procedure in Cases Involving Claims for Attorney's Fees; History.
9. Offers in Multiple Party Cases; Joint Offers; Apportioned Offers.
10. Offers of Judgment on Damages.
11. Filing of Offers of Judgment.
12. Relationship to Amended Attorney's Fees Statute.

1. *Scope and Purpose of Rule.* The policy behind Rule 68, which authorizes the making of offers of judgment, is to encourage

settlements and thereby avoid the burden and expense of protracted litigation. *Digirolamo v. Superior Court In and For County of Mohave*, 173 Ariz. 7, 839 P.2d 427 (Ct. App. Div. 1 1991). The Rule was amended extensively in 1990, and again in 1992, to make the offer of judgment a more effective device for facilitating the settlement of litigation. The Rule was once again extensively amended in 2008. In 2012, the Court amended Rule 68 to clarify the procedure by which offers of judgment may be made in arbitration cases, and to adopt corresponding amendments to Rule 74.

2. *Comparison With Federal Rule.* ARCP 68 and FRCP 68 are radically different. The Federal Rule only authorizes offers of judgment by a party defending against a claim, does not separately address cases involving claims for attorney's fees, and provides that, if the judgment finally obtained by the offeree is not more favorable than the offer, the offeree must pay only the actual costs incurred by the offeror after the making of the offer.

Under the Arizona Rule, an offer of judgment may be made by "any party." In cases involving claims for attorney's fees, unless specifically stated otherwise, all offers include an amount for attorney's fees. The offer may exclude an amount for attorney's fees, but that must be specifically stated in the offer. If attorney's fees are excluded and the offer is accepted, either party may apply to the court for an award of attorney's fees. Under Arizona's rule, the sanctions for failing to accept an offer which is less favorable to the offeror than the judgment eventually obtained are more severe, and include double the costs incurred by the offeror after the offer was made, reasonable expert witness fees incurred after the offer was made, and prejudgment interest on unliquidated claims accruing from the date of the offer. The time periods in which an offer can be made and during which it is effective also differ between the two Rules.

In addition, in 2007, the language of FRCP 68 was amended as part of the general restyling of the Federal Rules of Civil Procedure to make the Federal Rules more easily understood and to make style and terminology consistent throughout the Federal Rules of Civil Procedure. Those stylistic modifications have not been incorporated into ARCP 68.

3. *History of Rule.* Before 1990, Rule 68, like its counterpart in the Federal Rules of Civil Procedure, only authorized offers of judgment to be made by "a party defending against a claim." The limitation was in part dictated by the fact that the only sanction which the Rule provided for the failure to accept an offer of judgment was an award of costs. As a party pursuing a claim would, upon prevailing, recover costs in any event, there would be no incentive for such a party to make use of the offer of judgment

device.

The Rule was amended, effective May 1, 1990, to allow an offer of judgment to be made by "any party" to an action. (An essentially technical further amendment to the Rule was made effective September 1, 1990.) The incentive for a party pursuing a claim to use the offer of judgment procedure was provided by increasing the penalties attendant upon failing to accept such an offer. Under the Rule as amended in 1990, if the offer of judgment was not accepted, and the eventual judgment obtained was equal to, or more favorable to the party making the offer than, the terms of the offer, the party to whom the offer was made was to pay *double* the offeror's costs incurred after the making of the offer. The 1990 amendments also changed the period when an offer of judgment was deemed to be effective, altered the time frames when an offer could be made, and instituted special provisions concerning the mandated contents of an offer when made in a case where attorney's fees were claimed.

The Rule was again extensively amended, effective June 1, 1992. Significant changes were made to the procedures for making offers of judgment in cases involving claims for attorney's fees. These changes are discussed in Section 7 of these Comments. The penalties potentially associated with the failure to accept an offer were also dramatically increased. Under the 1992 amendments, if an offer of judgment is not accepted, and the eventual judgment that is obtained is equal to, or more favorable to the party making the offer than, the terms of the offer, the party to whom the offer was made must pay double the costs incurred by the offeror after the offer was made, reasonable expert witness fees incurred by the offeror after the offer was made, and prejudgment interest on unliquidated claims which is to accrue from the date of the offer.

The 1990 and 1992 amendments each increased the potential penalties attendant upon failing to accept an offer of judgment. It has now been held that the 1992 amendments to the Rule cannot be applied retroactively to offers of judgment made before their effective date (June 1, 1992), because that would require the offeree to bear the burden of an unknown and unanticipated risk. *Drozda v. McComas*, 181 Ariz. 82, 887 P.2d 612 (Ct. App. Div. 1 1994). Should the issue ever arise, presumably the same rule of non-retroactivity would pertain and neither the 1990 nor the 1992 amendments would apply to offers of judgment made before May 1, 1990, the effective date of the 1990 amendments.

Rule 68 was again amended, effective January 1, 2008. The 2008 amendments abandoned the regime established in 1992 with respect to claims for attorneys' fees and, thus, then existing subpart (c) was abrogated. As amended, Rule 68(b) provides that, unless otherwise stated, an offer of judgment is inclusive of all damages, taxable costs, interest and attorney's fees, if any, sought in the action. The offeror still has the option of having the offer not include attorney's fees, but must state explicitly in the offer that it does not include them. If the offer does exclude attorney's fees in that fashion, and it is accepted, then either party may apply to the court for an attorney's fee award, if authorized by statute, contract or otherwise.

As a further consequence of the 2008 amendments, Rule 68(e) now states unequivocally that multiple parties may make a joint unapportioned offer to a single offeree. The initial sentence of Rule 68(f) bars unapportioned offers made to multiple offerees. It goes on to provide, however, that one or more parties may make to two or more parties an apportioned offer that is made conditional upon acceptance by all the offerees.

In 2012, the Court amended Rule 68 to clarify the procedure by which offers of judgment may be made in arbitration cases, and to adopt corresponding amendments to Rule 74. Although not expressly stated in the amendments to Rule 68, the corresponding amendment to Rule 74(g) reveals that the 2012 amendment to Rule 68 is intended to apply to compulsory arbitration cases under A.R.S. § 12-133 and these rules, as well as cases referred to arbitration by Agreement of Arbitration.

4. *Offer of Judgment Procedure; Non-Arbitration Cases.* Under the amended Rule, an offer of judgment is an offer communicated to an adverse party to "allow judgment to be entered in the action." An implicit rather than explicit requirement of the Rule is that an offer of judgment be in writing. *Davis v. Discount Tire Co.*, 182 Ariz. 571, 898 P.2d 520 (Ct. App. Div. 1 1995). The Arizona version of Rule 68 requires certain specificity. First, the offer must contain a specific monetary sum to settle the asserted causes of action. Second, the offer must be specific enough so that it can be determined, at the time of judgment, whether the offer or the judgment favored the offeree. Lastly, the offer must be sufficiently specific to support entry of a judgment based upon an acceptance. *Greenwald v. Ford Motor Co.*, 196 Ariz. 123, 993 P.2d 1087 (Ct. App. Div. 1 1999). If the offer is for the entry of a monetary judgment, then it is deemed to include all damages, taxable court costs, interest, and attorney's fees, if any, sought in the case, unless the offer specifically excludes any attorney's fees that have been sought.

The fact that an offer of judgment is conditioned upon the offeree's agreement not to disclose the fact or amount of the offer does not render it unenforceable. *Powers v. Taser Intern., Inc.*, 217 Ariz. 398, 174 P.3d 777 (Ct. App. Div. 1 2007), as corrected, (Jan. 4, 2008). Rule 68(b) provides that, when an offer of judgment is accepted, either party may file the offer and acceptance and secure the entry of a judgment, but the language of the Rule is permissive and does not require either party to file the offer. *Powers v. Taser Intern., Inc.*, 217 Ariz. 398, 174 P.3d 777 (Ct. App. Div. 1 2007), as corrected, (Jan. 4, 2008). A stipulation for dismissal that embodied none of the offer of judgment's terms could also be employed. *Powers v. Taser Intern., Inc.*, 217 Ariz. 398, 174 P.3d 777 (Ct. App. Div. 1 2007), as corrected, (Jan. 4, 2008).

Rule 68 requires that an offer of judgment be served, though it is not filed, and contemplates service in accordance with the omnibus service provisions of Ariz.R.Civ.P. 5(c). *McEvoy v. Aerotek, Inc.*, 201 Ariz. 300, 34 P.3d 979 (Ct. App. Div. 1 2001). Although service by mail pursuant to that Rule is deemed effective upon mailing, the trial court retains discretion to relieve a party of the consequences of failing to respond to an offer of judgment that was served by mail, if that party provides proof that it was not in fact received. *McEvoy v. Aerotek, Inc.*, 201 Ariz. 300, 34 P.3d 979 (Ct. App. Div. 1 2001).

An offer of judgment made pursuant to amended Rule 68 remains effective for thirty (30) days after it is served, except in the case where the offer is made within sixty (60) days after service of the summons and complaint, in which case the offer remains effective for sixty (60) days after service. An offer that is made within forty-five (45) days of trial is only effective for fifteen (15) days. Under the prior Rule, an offer of judgment was considered irrevocable during the then prescribed effective period. *Mubi v. Broomfield*, 108 Ariz. 39, 492 P.2d 700 (1972); *Twin City Const. of Fargo, North Dakota v. Cantor*, 22 Ariz. App. 133, 524 P.2d 967 (Div. 1 1974); *but cf. Preuss v. Stevens*, 150 Ariz. 6, 721 P.2d 664 (Ct. App. Div. 2 1986). The amendments to the Rule do not purport to change that.

Where a motion for summary judgment encompasses the same issues as those contained in a pending offer of judgment, however, the intervening entry of summary judgment precludes a party's ability to accept the offer. *Wersch v. Radnor/Landgrant-a Phoenix Partnership*, 192 Ariz. 99, 961 P.2d 1047 (Ct. App. Div. 1 1997). It does not matter whether the summary judgment order has as yet been signed and rendered appealable. *Wersch v. Radnor/Landgrant-a Phoenix Partnership*, 192 Ariz. 99, 961 P.2d 1047 (Ct. App. Div. 1 1997). The language in the Rule that an offer is to "remain effective" for thirty (30) days only forbids the offeror from withdrawing or revoking the offer during that period, and does not address the effect of an intervening judgment. *Wersch v. Radnor/Landgrant-a Phoenix Partnership*, 192 Ariz. 99, 961 P.2d 1047 (Ct. App. Div. 1 1997).

An offer of judgment on damages made following a determination of liability must be made no later than ten (10) days before the commencement of any hearing to determine the amount of damages. Rule 68, however, does not allow a party to make a post-judgment offer of judgment, while a case is on appeal and in anticipation of a remand. *Conant v. Whitney*, 190 Ariz. 290, 947 P.2d 864 (Ct. App. Div. 1 1997).

The change allowing bilateral offers of judgment may place the recipient party at a disadvantage when an adverse party serves an offer of judgment at an early stage of the proceedings, because the parties may not be in equal positions to evaluate the merits of the case. In such circumstances, the trial court has the authority to enlarge the time period during which an offer of judgment remains effective and may be accepted. *Digirolamo v. Superior Court In and For County of Mohave*, 173 Ariz. 7, 839 P.2d 427 (Ct. App. Div. 1 1991). Rule 68(e), now Rule 68(h), was amended in 1993, however, to provide that, where the Court does enlarge the time period during which an offer of judgment is effective and may be accepted, the party who made the offer may withdraw it after the initial, unextended effective period and before it is accepted.

5. *Offer of Judgment Procedure; Arbitration Cases.* In 2012, the Court amended Rule 68 to clarify the procedure by which offers of judgment may be made in arbitration cases, and to adopt corresponding amendments to Rule 74. Although not expressly stated in the amendments to Rule 68, the corresponding amendment to Rule 74(g) reveals that the 2012 amendment to Rule 68 is intended to apply to compulsory arbitration cases under A.R.S. § 12-133 and these rules as well as cases referred to arbitration by Agreement of Arbitration.

As a consequence of the 2012 amendments, Rule 68(a) includes a specific provision which prohibits making a Rule 68 offer of judgment in arbitration cases during the period of time "beginning 25 days before the arbitration hearing and ending upon the date of the filing of any notice of appeal of an award pursuant to Rule 77(a)." The rule, as amended, does not expressly prohibit making a Rule 68 offer of judgment at any other time. Rule 68(h), as amended, includes a provision addressing the effective period of an offer made in an arbitration case. As such, in a case subject to arbitration, a Rule 68 "offer that has not previously expired shall expire at 5:00 p.m. on the fifth day before the arbitration hearing."

6. *Effect of Complete Acceptance of Offer.* If the offer is accepted by the party to whom it is made while it is still effective, then either party may file the offer and acceptance, and a judgment embodying the terms of the offer is entered. The acceptance of an offer must be by written notice, must be unambiguous and

unconditional, and must be effectively communicated to the offering party during the period the offer remains in effect. *Mubi v. Broomfield*, 108 Ariz. 39, 492 P.2d 700 (1972); *Smith v. Hurley*, 121 Ariz. 164, 589 P.2d 38 (Ct. App. Div. 1 1978). The judgment that is entered does represent an "adjudication on the merits" within the meaning of A.R.S. § 12–348(B)(1), and will support an award of attorney's fees against a city, county or state in a case covered by that statute. *4501 Northpoint LP v. Maricopa County*, 212 Ariz. 98, 128 P.3d 215 (2006).

7. *Effect of Failure to Accept Offer.* An offer that is not accepted within the specified time period is deemed rejected. *Mubi v. Broomfield*, 108 Ariz. 39, 492 P.2d 700 (1972); *Twin City Const. of Fargo, North Dakota v. Cantor*, 22 Ariz. App. 133, 524 P.2d 967 (Div. 1 1974). An offer that is not accepted may not be admitted into evidence except in a proceeding to determine sanctions, and may not be considered in determining whether or not an additur should be granted. *State v. Burton*, 20 Ariz. App. 491, 514 P.2d 244 (Div. 2 1973).

Rule 68 necessarily implies that an offeree must have the legal ability to accept an offer of judgment before sanctions may be imposed. *Warner v. Southwest Desert Images, LLC*, 218 Ariz. 121, 180 P.3d 986 (Ct. App. Div. 2 2008). The penalties of Rule 68 are a sanction, and due process demands that, before a party may properly be sanctioned, it must have had the ability to avoid that. *Warner v. Southwest Desert Images, LLC*, 218 Ariz. 121, 180 P.3d 986 (Ct. App. Div. 2 2008). An offeree whose recovery is subject to a workmens' compensation carrier's lien cannot settle that claim by accepting an offer of judgment without the carrier's approval. Such a plaintiff seeking to avoid the imposition of Rule 68 sanctions must demonstrate that it timely sought approval for an offer of judgment it intended to accept; it is not sufficient that the plaintiff merely notified the lien holder of the defendant's offer of judgment. *Warner v. Southwest Desert Images, LLC*, 218 Ariz. 121, 180 P.3d 986 (Ct. App. Div. 2 2008).

The consequences of the increased penalties are ameliorated to some degree where the offeree is the party who ultimately prevails in the action. If the offeree is the successful party, but recovers less than the amount set forth in a previously and properly made offer of judgment, the offeree will be liable to the offeror for post-offer expert witness fees and double the offeror's post-offer costs. In that circumstance, however, the offeree is still the prevailing party and entitled to recover costs incurred both before and after the offer was made. *Davis v. Discount Tire Co.*, 182 Ariz. 571, 898 P.2d 520 (Ct. App. Div. 1 1995); *Drozda v. McComas*, 181 Ariz. 82, 887 P.2d 612 (Ct. App. Div. 1 1994).

When a party is awarded sanctions under Rule 68(g), those

sanctions should be applied to offset any verdict in favor of the party who failed to accept the offer of judgment. *Langerman Law Offices, P.A. v. Glen Eagles at Princess Resort, LLC*, 220 Ariz. 252, 204 P.3d 1101 (Ct. App. Div. 1 2009). If the amount of those sanctions exceeds the jury's verdict plus the amount of taxable costs, the plaintiff's attorney has no common law charging lien because there is no net judgment to which it can attach. *Langerman Law Offices, P.A. v. Glen Eagles at Princess Resort, LLC*, 220 Ariz. 252, 204 P.3d 1101 (Ct. App. Div. 1 2009).

An award of sanctions under Rule 68 in condemnation actions is not necessarily precluded by the provisions of A.R.S. § 12-1128. *Salt River Project Agricultural Improvement and Power Dist. v. Miller Park, L.L.C.*, 218 Ariz. 246, 183 P.3d 497 (2008). The plain language of what is now Rule 68(g) allows the trial court to award reasonable expert witness fees as a sanction for failure to accept an offer of judgment. The trial court has broad discretion in determining the amount of such fees to award, and the exercise of that discretion will be disturbed on appeal only for an abuse of that discretion. *Lohmeier v. Hammer*, 214 Ariz. 57, 148 P.3d 101 (Ct. App. Div. 1 2006). The Rule does not limit such an award to those fees incurred for the time spent testifying. *Levy v. Alfaro*, 215 Ariz. 443, 160 P.3d 1201 (Ct. App. Div. 1 2007). The limitations of Rule 54(f)(2) only apply in medical malpractice cases, and do not operate as a limit on the sanctions that can be awarded under Rule 68. *Levy v. Alfaro*, 215 Ariz. 443, 160 P.3d 1201 (Ct. App. Div. 1 2007). In fact, an award of expert witness fees as a sanction under Rule 68 is not limited to those experts who testify. *Scottsdale Ins. Co. v. Cendejas*, 220 Ariz. 281, 205 P.3d 1128 (Ct. App. Div. 1 2009).

Under Rule 68(g), as amended effective January 1, 2008, if the eventual judgment includes an award of taxable costs or attorney's fees, only those taxable costs and attorney's fees determined by the court as having been reasonably incurred as of the date the offer was made shall be considered in determining whether that judgment was more favorable than the offer. *Berry v. 352 E. Virginia, L.L.C.*, 228 Ariz. 9, 261 P.3d 784 (Ct. App. Div. 1 2011).

In determining whether attorneys' fees are awardable under A.R.S § 12-341.01(A), the "judgment finally obtained" includes attorney's fees, taxable costs and prejudgment interest, if any. *Hall v. Read Development, Inc.*, 229 Ariz. 277, 274 P.3d 1211 (Ct. App. Div. 1 2012), as amended, (Apr. 26, 2012) and review denied, (Aug. 28, 2012). This methodology makes a distinction is made between the "judgment" and the "verdict." *Hall v. Read Development, Inc.*, 229 Ariz. 277, 274 P.3d 1211 (Ct. App. Div. 1 2012), as amended, (Apr. 26, 2012) and review denied, (Aug. 28, 2012). It also "fulfills the purposes of the statute and provides an accurate comparison of the settlement offer with the final judgment, ensuring the final judgment includes only those attorneys' fees and costs that were incurred at the time of the settlement offer and included in the final settlement figure." *Hall v. Read Development, Inc.*, 229 Ariz. 277, 274 P.3d 1211 (Ct. App. Div. 1 2012), as amended, (Apr. 26, 2012) and review denied, (Aug. 28, 2012). *Cf. Hales v. Humana of Arizona, Inc.*, 186 Ariz. 375, 923 P.2d 841 (Ct. App. Div. 2 1996) (explaining that former Rule 68(d) "requires an 'apples to apples' comparison between the judgment and the offer").

With respect to determining prejudgment interest on remand, the judgment entered on the appellate court's mandate—and not the 'initial judgment' vacated by a grant of new trial—is the judgment that governs to award of prejudgment interest. *Metzler v. BCI Coca-Cola Bottling Co. of Los Angeles, Inc.*, 230 Ariz. 26, 279 P.3d 1188 (Ct. App. Div. 2 2012) (In determining whether Rule 68 sanctions should be imposed after a trial de novo following an arbitration hearing, the trial court must: (1) compare the arbitration award with the judgment on the trial de novo, (2) determine and deduct from such judgment any Rule 77(f) sanctions, and (3) consider whether Rule 68 sanctions are applicable, *i.e.*, compare final judgment on trial *de novo* to Rule 68 offer of judgment.). *Metzler v. BCI Coca-Cola Bottling Co. of Los Angeles, Inc.*, 233 Ariz. 133, 310 P.3d 9 (Ct. App. Div. 2 2013) (prejudgment interest imposed as a sanction under Ariz. R. Civ. P. 68(g) is interest on an "obligation" calculated at 10% per annum pursuant to A.R.S. § 44-1201(A), and is not interest "on a judgment" calculated at 1% plus prime pursuant to A.R.S. § 44-1201(B)).

As a consequence of the amendments to Rule 68(g), effective January 1, 2012, in arbitration cases the determination whether a sanction should be imposed is made with reference to the judgment ultimately entered, regardless of whether the ultimate judgment was entered on the award itself or entered on the award after an appeal pursuant to Rule 77. In those circumstances where Rule 68(g) sanctions may be involved, Rule 68(g) expressly provides that the court determine whether to impose a sanction under Rule 68(g) only after first complying with Rule 77(f). *See also, Bradshaw v. Jasso-Barajas*, 231 Ariz. 197, 291 P.3d 991 (Ct. App. Div. 1 2013) (In determining whether Rule 68 sanctions should be imposed after a *trial de novo* following an arbitration hearing, the trial court must: (1) compare the arbitration award with the judgment on the trial *de novo*, (2) determine and deduct from such judgment any Rule 77(f) sanctions, and (3) consider whether Rule 68 sanctions are applicable, *i.e.*, compare final judgment on trial *de novo* to Rule 68 offer of judgment.).

8. *Offer of Judgment Procedure in Cases Involving Claims for Attorney's Fees; History.* Under the prior Rule, it was held that

the term "costs" did not include attorney's fees, even where they were recoverable by statute. *Boltz & Odegaard v. Hohn*, 148 Ariz. 361, 714 P.2d 854 (Ct. App. Div. 1 1985). To eliminate further confusion in cases where attorney's fees are sought and recoverable, the Rule was amended in 1990 to require that, in those cases, an offer of judgment specify what disposition was to be made of such claims in the event the offer was accepted. Under the Rule as amended in 1990, if the action was one in which attorney's fees were sought and recoverable, any offer of judgment had to specify one of three alternative ways in which the attorney's fees claim would be disposed of, either (a) the amount of attorney's fees to be awarded if the offer was accepted, or (b) that the offer as stated included any attorney's fees sought in the action, or (c) that if the offer was accepted, the issue of entitlement to and the amount of attorney's fees to be awarded would be determined in subsequent judicial proceedings.

The foregoing requirements applied to offers made during the period of time in which the 1990 amendments were in effect. The 1992 amendments to Rule 68 once again changed the procedures for making offers of judgment in cases involving claims for attorney's fees. Under the Rule as amended in 1992, in such cases the offer of judgment was required to state *both* the amount of any monetary award to be made on the causes of action asserted *and* the amount of the attorney's fees to be awarded if the offer was accepted. If the offer is accepted *in toto,* then either party could file the offer together with proof of acceptance and secure the entry of judgment. The offeree, however, had the option of partially accepting only that portion of the offer setting the monetary award to be made on the underlying claims.

This regime was abandoned by the 2008 amendments to the Rule, and subpart (c) was abrogated. As amended, Rule 68(a) provides that, unless otherwise stated, an offer of judgment is inclusive of all damages, taxable costs, interest and attorney's fees, if any, sought in the action. The offeror still has the option of having the offer not include attorney's fees, but must state explicitly in the offer that it does not include them. If the offer does exclude attorney's fees in that fashion, and it is accepted, then either party may apply to the court for an attorney's fee award, if authorized by statute, contract or otherwise.

9. *Offers in Multiple Party Cases; Joint Offers; Apportioned Offers*. Before the 2008 amendments to the Rule, it was held that an unapportioned offer of judgment made on behalf of, or to, multiple claimants did not comply with the spirit of the Rule, and would not support an award of sanctions. *Gamez v. Brush Wellman, Inc.*, 201 Ariz. 266, 34 P.3d 375 (Ct. App. Div. 2 2001), redesignated as opinion, (Nov. 14, 2001); *Duke v. Cochise County*, 189 Ariz. 35, 938 P.2d 84 (Ct. App. Div. 2 1996). An offeree pre-

sented with such an unapportioned offer cannot make a meaningful choice between accepting the offer on any single claim or continuing the litigation to judgment on all claims.

Imposing sanctions for failing to accept what is in effect an unspecified and unapportioned offer deprives the offeree of the opportunity to assess the chance of doing better at trial against one or more of the parties covered by the joint offer. On the other hand, requiring joint offers to be allocated between multiple parties or claims places no greater burden on the party or parties making the offer. *Duke v. Cochise County*, 189 Ariz. 35, 938 P.2d 84 (Ct. App. Div. 2 1996). Accordingly, it was held that offer of judgment in a wrongful death action brought on behalf of more than one beneficiary must be apportioned among the beneficiaries, or it lacks the specificity Rule 68 requires. *Greenwald v. Ford Motor Co.*, 196 Ariz. 123, 993 P.2d 1087 (Ct. App. Div. 1 1999).

This principle, however, did not apply to an unapportioned offer made in a case in which a parent is suing on behalf of a minor child, even though the suit seeks recovery both for the costs of medical care paid by the parent, and for the injuries to the minor child. *Sheppard v. Crow-Barker Paul No. 1 Ltd. Partnership*, 192 Ariz. 539, 968 P.2d 612 (Ct. App. Div. 1 1998). An award of sanctions may be appropriate where the joint unapportioned offer provided the offerees with the ability to make a meaningful choice between accepting or rejecting the offer and going forward with the litigation. *Girouard v. Skyline Steel, Inc.*, 215 Ariz. 126, 158 P.3d 255 (Ct. App. Div. 1 2007). When a purported class representative accepts an unapportioned offer of judgment, that party relinquishes both the personal claim against the defendant(s) and a claim to proceed on behalf of a class, and lacks standing to appeal from the judgment entered on the offer and acceptance. *Douglas v. Governing Bd. of Window Rock Consol. School Dist. No. 8*, 221 Ariz. 104, 210 P.3d 1275, 246 Ed. Law Rep. 435 (Ct. App. Div. 1 2009).

The 2008 amendments to Rule 68 codified these precedents only in part. Rule 68(e) now states unequivocally that multiple parties may make a joint unapportioned offer to a single offeree. Although the initial sentence of Rule 68(f) bars unapportioned offers made to multiple offerees, the sentence goes on to provide, however, that one or more parties may make to two or more parties an apportioned offer that is made conditional upon acceptance by all the offerees. Each of those offerees may serve a separate written notice of acceptance. If fewer than all offerees accept, the offeror may still enforce any number of acceptances if the offer states that the offeror may exercise that option, and the offeror serves written notice of final acceptance not later than ten (10) days after expiration of the effective date of the offer. Sanctions may be awarded against any offeree who did not accept such an offer.

10. *Offers of Judgment on Damages.* Where only the issue of liability has been determined by a verdict or decision, an offer of judgment may be made as to the amount of damages to be recovered. Such an offer must be made not fewer than ten (10) days before the commencement of any hearing to determine the amount or extent of damages liability. Rule 68, however, does not allow a party to make a post-judgment offer of judgment, while a case is on appeal and in anticipation of a remand. *Conant v. Whitney*, 190 Ariz. 290, 947 P.2d 864 (Ct. App. Div. 1 1997).

11. *Filing of Offers of Judgment.* An offer of judgment is served, but not filed unless and until it is accepted, and is specifically exempted from the general filing requirements of Ariz.R.Civ.P. 5(g). Rule 68 contemplates service in accordance with the omnibus service provisions of Ariz.R.Civ.P. 5(c). *McEvoy v. Aerotek, Inc.*, 201 Ariz. 300, 34 P.3d 979 (Ct. App. Div. 1 2001). Although service by mail pursuant to that Rule is deemed effective upon mailing, the trial court retains discretion to relieve a party of the consequences of failing to respond to an offer of judgment that was served by mail, if that party provides proof that it was not in fact received. *McEvoy v. Aerotek, Inc.*, 201 Ariz. 300, 34 P.3d 979 (Ct. App. Div. 1 2001). If the offer is accepted, both the offer and the acceptance are to be filed to secure entry of a judgment.

12. *Relationship to Amended Attorney's Fees Statute.* In 1999, the Arizona Legislature amended the principal attorney's fees statute, A.R.S. § 12-341.01(A), by adding the following language as a new second sentence:

> If a written settlement offer is rejected and the judgment finally obtained is equal to or more favorable to the offeror than an offer made in writing to settle any contested action arising out of a contract, the offeror is deemed to be the successful party from the date of the offer and the court may award the successful party reasonable attorney's fees.

This statute, as amended, still applies only to actions arising out of a contract, but the recovery available goes well beyond what is available under Ariz. R. Civ. P. 68. In contrast, the recovery available under Rule 68 is limited to "reasonable" expert witness fees and double the costs, as defined by A.R.S. 12-332, incurred after the making of an Offer of Judgment which the offeree does not improve upon at the end of the case. Rule 68 does not call for an award of attorneys' fees.

Under the statute, as amended, a plaintiff who ultimately prevails in such an action will be deemed the successful party and entitled to ask for a discretionary award of attorneys' fees in any event, whether the verdict or judgment is more or less than a written settlement offer made during the course of the action. On the other hand, in the situation where the plaintiff in such an action makes a written settlement offer that is rejected by the defendant, and the verdict or judgment turns out to be less than the amount of the offer, the defendant will not be entitled to ask for an award of fees—only the offeror can make such a request.

The statute comes into play whenever there is an "offer made in writing to settle" the action. It is not limited to, but it would seem to include, formal Rule 68 Offers of Judgment. While the amendment to the statute is not artfully worded, it seems to provide that, if a defendant in a contract action makes a written settlement offer during the course of the case which is rejected, and the plaintiff's ultimate recovery is less than the amount of the offer, then the defendant is entitled to seek a discretionary award of attorneys' fees incurred from and after the date the offer was made.

The statute does not seem to require the offer to settle be in the form of a formal Rule 68 Offer of Judgment. If the settlement offer is not in the form of an offer of judgment, however, then an offeror may only be entitled to seek an award of attorneys' fees, which is discretionary with the Court, and not the sanctions provided for in Rule 68, which are mandatory. On the other hand, a settlement offer made for the purposes of putting a defendant in a position to secure an attorneys' fees award under this statute need not specify how much of the offer is for damages and how much for attorneys' fees, as Rule 68 requires for Offers of Judgment in such cases.

Under the express wording of A.R.S. § 12-341.01(A), if the offer is more favorable than the "judgment finally obtained," then the offeror is deemed to be the successful party and may be awarded reasonably attorney's fees. For purposes of making this determination, a recent court of appeals decision has interpreted this statute to require a comparison of the amount of the settlement offer with the amount of the 'judgment finally obtained"—not the 'verdict finally obtained'. *Hall v. Read Development, Inc.*, 229 Ariz. 277, 274 P.3d 1211 (Ct. App. Div. 1 2012), as amended, (Apr. 26, 2012) and review denied, (Aug. 28, 2012). Thus, if attorney's fees are awarded in the judgment, such sums must be included in the comparison. *Hall v. Read Development, Inc.*, 229 Ariz. 277, 274 P.3d 1211 (Ct. App. Div. 1 2012), as amended, (Apr. 26, 2012) and review denied, (Aug. 28, 2012). Similarly, if taxable costs and prejudgment interest are included in the 'judgment finally obtained' such sums also must be included in the comparison. *Berry v. 352 E. Virginia, L.L.C.*, 228 Ariz. 9, 261 P.3d 784 (Ct. App. Div. 1 2011).

Rule 69. Execution

Process to enforce a judgment for the payment of money shall be a writ of execution, unless the court directs otherwise. The procedure on execution, in proceedings supplementary to and in aid of a judgment, and in proceedings on and in aid of execution shall be as provided by law. In aid of the judgment or execution, the judgment creditor or a successor in interest when that interest appears of record, may obtain discovery from any person, including the judgment debtor, in the manner provided in these Rules or otherwise by law.

Amended July 17, 1970, effective Nov. 1, 1970; Sept. 15, 1987, effective Nov. 15, 1987.

STATE BAR COMMITTEE NOTES

1970 Amendment

The amendment makes clear that discovery is available to a judgment creditor.

AUTHORS' COMMENTS

Analysis

1. Scope and Purpose of Rule.
2. Comparison With Federal Rule.
3. Period for Execution on Judgments.
4. Recording of Judgments.
5. Renewal of Judgments.
6. Writ of General Execution.
7. Writ of Special Execution.
8. Levy and Return on Writ of Execution.
9. Notice and Conduct of Execution Sales.
10. Satisfaction of Judgment.
11. Enforcement of Foreign Judgments.
12. Judgments of Tribal Courts.

1. *Scope and Purpose of Rule.* Rule 69 merely provides that the procedures for enforcing judgments "shall be as provided by law." In Arizona, the procedures for securing both prejudgment and post-judgment remedies are prescribed by statute. The "provisional remedies" of replevin and garnishment of non-earnings may also be employed post-judgment, where appropriate, and execution is the post-judgment functional equivalent of attachment. The prejudgment use of these remedies is discussed in the *Authors' Comments* under Ariz.R.Civ.P. 64. Garnishments of earnings may only be employed to collect on a judgment.

2. *Comparison With Federal Rule.* Despite structural differences, ARCP 69 and FRCP 69 are substantially identical. The sole substantive difference is that the Arizona Rule does not contain the provision in the Federal Rule incorporating the applicable procedures of the state in which the district court sits.

In 2007, the language of FRCP 69 was amended as part of the general restyling of the Federal Rules of Civil Procedure to make the Federal Rules more easily understood and to make style and terminology consistent throughout the Federal Rules of Civil Procedure. Those stylistic modifications have not been incorporated into ARCP 69.

3. *Period for Execution on Judgments.* The procedures for securing writs of execution are set forth in A.R.S. §§ 12-1551 *et seq.* A judgment is initially effective for five years from the date of its entry, and execution must be accomplished within that period. A.R.S. § 12-1551(B). The five-year period is in the nature of a statute of limitations, however, and does not begin to run until the judgment can be enforced or sued upon, *i.e.,* following a stay pending an appeal. *Groves v. Sorce*, 161 Ariz. 619, 780 P.2d 452 (Ct. App. Div. 2 1989); *North Star Development Corp. v. Wolfswinkel*, 146 Ariz. 406, 706 P.2d 732 (Ct. App. Div. 2 1985).

In applying this provision and its predecessors to judgments payable in installments, such as judgments for child support or for alimony, etc., the rule has consistently been that the five-year limitations period begins to run from the period fixed for each installment as it becomes due. *Johnson v. Johnson*, 195 Ariz. 389, 988 P.2d 621 (Ct. App. Div. 1 1999).

4. *Recording of Judgments.* A judgment creditor who desires that a judgment become a lien on real property of the judgment debtor can accomplish that by recording a certified copy of the judgment in the office of the county recorder in each county in which the judgment debtor has, or might have, real property. A.R.S. § 33-961(A). The certified copy of the judgment tendered for recording must contain the following information: (1) the title of the court in which it was entered and the civil action number; (2) the date the judgment was entered and the docket record which reflects that; (3) the names of both the judgment creditor and the judgment debtor; (4) the amount of the judgment; and, (5) the judgment creditor's attorney of record. A.R.S. § 33-961(A).

Under A.R.S. §§ 33-963 and 33-964(A), a judgment that is recorded in the manner prescribed by A.R.S. § 33-961 becomes a lien on the real property of the judgment debtor for a period of five (5) years from the date the judgment was entered. The automatic stay imposed when a judgment debtor files for bankruptcy protection extends the effectiveness of a judgment beyond the five-year statutory period for a period of time equal to that during which the stay was in effect. It does not, however, extend the deadline for filing an affidavit of renewal of the judgment. *In re Smith*, 209 Ariz. 343, 101 P.3d 637 (2004).

As discussed in Section 5, *infra*, a judgment may be renewed either by filing suit on it or by filing an affidavit of renewal with the Clerk of the appropriate Court. A.R.S. §§ 12-1611, 1612(A). Such a renewal, however, does not automatically extend the judgment lien created by the recording of the original judgment. *Hall v. World Sav. and Loan Ass'n*, 189 Ariz. 495, 943 P.2d 855 (Ct. App. Div. 1 1997), disapproved of on other grounds, *Fidelity Nat. Financial Inc. v. Friedman*, 225 Ariz. 307, 238 P.3d 118 (2010). In order to extend that judgment lien, the judgment creditor must record in the proper county recorder's office an affidavit of renewal of the judgment. *Hall v. World Sav. and Loan Ass'n*, 189 Ariz. 495, 943 P.2d 855 (Ct. App. Div. 1 1997), disapproved of on other grounds, *Fidelity Nat. Financial Inc. v. Friedman*, 225 Ariz. 307, 238 P.3d 118 (2010); A.R.S. § 12-1613(C).

The perfection of a judgment lien does not disable the judgment debtor from transferring real property subject to the lien, but such a transfer to a third party does not immunize the liened property from execution. Under A.R.S. § 12-1553(2), where a judgment lien has been perfected against the judgment debtor, the judgment creditor may satisfy the judgment by executing against any real property that belonged to the judgment debtor when the judgment was recorded, even if the judgment debtor later transfers the liened property to a third party. *Byers v. Wik*, 169 Ariz. 215, 818 P.2d 200 (Ct. App. Div. 1 1991).

Any judgment or decree that requires the payment of money which is thus recorded, and any recorded renewal of such a judgment or decree, must be attached to a separate "Judgment Information Statement" which contains the following information, if known: (1) the correct name and last known address of each judgment debtor; (2) the name and address of the judgment creditor; (3) the amount of the judgment; (4) the social security number, date of birth and driver license number of any judgment debtor who is a natural person; and, (5) whether enforcement of the judgment has been stayed and, if so, the date the stay expires. A.R.S. § 33-967. If any of the specified information is not known, the judgment creditor should specify that in the Judgment Information Statement, and the judgment debtor's social security number is only to be included if the judgment debtor provided it voluntarily.

Another statute, A.R.S. § 33-968, deals with the situation where a recorded monetary judgment appears to create a lien on real property of an individual who is not the judgment debtor, but whose name is similar to, or the same as, the judgment debtor's.

In that circumstance, the "erroneously identified" property owner may deliver to the judgment creditor reasonable proof that the property owner is not in fact the judgment debtor and a written demand for a recordable document that releases the lien of the judgment with respect to the property. The judgment creditor is required to provide such a recordable release of the lien within fifteen (15) days of receipt of such a demand, and may be liable for any damages that result from a failure to do so. Where the misidentification is the consequence of the misidentified individual having been the victim of identify theft, that individual may have to invoke the procedures furnished by A.R.S. § 12-772 and Ariz.R.Civ.P. 57.2.

5. *Renewal of Judgments.* In Arizona, monetary judgments expire if they are not renewed every five (5) years. *Fidelity Nat. Financial Inc. v. Friedman*, 225 Ariz. 307, 238 P.3d 118 (2010); *Cristall v. Cristall*, 225 Ariz. 591, 242 P.3d 1060 (Ct. App. Div. 1 2010), review denied, (May 24, 2011); *Crye v. Edwards*, 178 Ariz. 327, 873 P.2d 665 (Ct. App. Div. 1 1993). A judgment may be renewed by instituting an action on it within the five-year period. A.R.S. § 12-1611. *Fidelity Nat. Financial Inc. v. Friedman*, 225 Ariz. 307, 238 P.3d 118 (2010). Collection activities, such as writs of garnishment and other efforts to discover assets, do not constitute an action on a judgment and, thus, do not serve to renew a judgment, *Fidelity Nat. Financial Inc. v. Friedman*, 225 Ariz. 307, 238 P.3d 118 (2010). Further, a related lawsuit filed in a State other than Arizona does not serve to renew an Arizona judgment. *Fidelity Nat. Financial Inc. v. Friedman*, 225 Ariz. 307, 238 P.3d 118 (2010). A judgment may also be renewed for an additional five years by filing an Affidavit for Renewal. A.R.S. § 12-1612; *Fidelity Nat. Financial Inc. v. Friedman*, 225 Ariz. 307, 238 P.3d 118 (2010). The Affidavit must be filed within a ninety-day period *prior* to the expiration of the judgment or any renewal period. *Mobile Discount Corp. v. Hargus*, 156 Ariz. 559, 753 P.2d 1215 (Ct. App. Div. 2 1988). The Affidavit, which may be made by the judgment creditor or a personal representative or assignee of the judgment creditor, must set forth the following:

(1) The names of the parties to the action in which the judgment was rendered.

(2) The name of the Court in which the judgment was docketed and the number and page of the docket in which it was entered.

(3) If the judgment has been recorded, the name of the county in which it has been so recorded and the number and page of the book in which it was recorded.

(4) The name of the owner of the judgment and, if the owner is not the judgment creditor, the source and succession of the

owner's title.

(5) Whether or not any execution upon the judgment is outstanding and unreturned.

(6) The date and amount of all payments upon the judgment, and a statement that such payments have been credited.

(7) Whether or not there are any set-offs or counterclaims in favor of the judgment debtor and, if so, the amount thereof.

(8) The exact amount currently due upon the judgment after allowances for set-offs and counterclaims.

A.R.S. § 12-1612. A judgment for child support need not be renewed, except as required by A.R.S. § 12-2453(E). A.R.S. § 12-1551(D). *Murren v. Murren*, 191 Ariz. 335, 955 P.2d 973 (Ct. App. Div. 1 1998). The renewal statute by affidavit, A.R.S. § 12-1612(B), does not begin to run until any and all objections to domestication are resolved and final judgment is entered. *Cristall v. Cristall*, 225 Ariz. 591, 242 P.3d 1060 (Ct. App. Div. 1 2010), review denied, (May 24, 2011).

The statutes governing the renewal of judgments clearly require that the affidavit of renewal is to be filed with the Clerk of the Superior Court in the same county in which the judgment was docketed, so that it can be maintained with other records concerning that judgment. *J.C. Penney v. Lane*, 197 Ariz. 113, 3 P.3d 1033 (Ct. App. Div. 1 1999). One of the purposes of this requirement is to give notice to the judgment debtor and other interested parties of the status of the judgment. *J.C. Penney v. Lane*, 197 Ariz. 113, 3 P.3d 1033 (Ct. App. Div. 1 1999).

Filing an affidavit of renewal in a county other than the county in which the judgment was rendered will not give interested parties notice of the judgment's status. *J.C. Penney v. Lane*, 197 Ariz. 113, 3 P.3d 1033 (Ct. App. Div. 1 1999). Accordingly, an affidavit of renewal of a judgment which contains an improper caption and is filed in a county other than the county in which the judgment was rendered is ineffective. *J.C. Penney v. Lane*, 197 Ariz. 113, 3 P.3d 1033 (Ct. App. Div. 1 1999).

A judgment creditor's ability to enforce a judgment during the initial or a subsequent statutory five-year period, whether because of a bankruptcy stay or other reasons, does not extend the deadline imposed by A.R.S. 12–1551 and 12–1612 to file a renewal affidavit. The filing of a renewal affidavit is simply a ministerial action intended in part to alert interested parties to the existence of the judgment; it serves a notice function and does not seek to enforce the judgment. *In re Smith*, 209 Ariz. 343, 101 P.3d 637 (2004); Cf, *State ex rel. Indus. Com'n of Arizona v. Galloway*, 224 Ariz. 325, 230 P.3d 708 (Ct. App. Div. 1 2010) (discussing premature filing of renewal affidavit).

6. *Writ of General Execution.* A writ of execution to enforce a

judgment may be either general or special. A general writ of execution directs the Sheriff or other officer to satisfy the judgment from the property of the judgment debtor without specifying the property to be executed upon. A.R.S. § 12-1552(A)(1). The writ must state the amount of the judgment and costs and the amount due, and requires the Sheriff or Constable to satisfy it from the personal property of the judgment debtor and, if sufficient personal property cannot be located, from real property of the judgment debtor. A.R.S. § 12-1553. A writ of general execution may be issued to the Sheriff of any county, and several and successive writs may be issued to different counties until the judgment is satisfied. A.R.S. § 12-1557(A).

Community property generally cannot be reached to satisfy a judgment entered against only one spouse. *Heinig v. Hudman*, 177 Ariz. 66, 865 P.2d 110 (Ct. App. Div. 1 1993). A creditor must join both spouses as defendants before the creditor may obtain and execute upon a judgment against the marital community, even where the judgment is for a separate premarital debt of one of the parties. *Flexmaster Aluminum Awning Co., Inc. v. Hirschberg*, 173 Ariz. 83, 839 P.2d 1128 (Ct. App. Div. 1 1992); *Spudnuts, Inc. v. Lane*, 139 Ariz. 35, 676 P.2d 669 (Ct. App. Div. 2 1984).

A judgment against one spouse cannot be converted into one against the community without regard to the absent spouse's right to procedural due process, which requires that that spouse have an opportunity to litigate the underlying liability and/or the value of the judgment debtor spouse's contribution to the community. *Heinig v. Hudman*, 177 Ariz. 66, 865 P.2d 110 (Ct. App. Div. 1 1993); *Flexmaster Aluminum Awning Co., Inc. v. Hirschberg*, 173 Ariz. 83, 839 P.2d 1128 (Ct. App. Div. 1 1992). Although a creditor cannot summarily convert a separate judgment into one against the community, an independent action may be brought to establish the liability of the spouse who was not, or could not have been, joined in the initial action. *Heinig v. Hudman*, 177 Ariz. 66, 865 P.2d 110 (Ct. App. Div. 1 1993).

A creditor, who secures a judgment against one of the marital partners *prior to* the marriage, however, for a separate premarital debt, may enforce that judgment against the community without bringing an independent action naming the nondebtor spouse. *CBM of Arizona, Inc. v. Sevier*, 184 Ariz. 503, 910 P.2d 654 (Ct. App. Div. 2 1996). Where such a judgment has been obtained prior to the marriage, both spouses are limited to those defenses which may be raised against the judgment, such as satisfaction or nonrenewal. Additionally, with respect to the community property which may be reached to satisfy the judgment, both spouses have the right to litigate the extent of the debtor spouse's contribution to the community estate. *CBM of Arizona, Inc. v. Sevier*, 184 Ariz. 503, 910 P.2d 654 (Ct. App. Div. 2 1996).

7. *Writ of Special Execution.* A writ of special execution directs the Sheriff or other officer to sell certain specific property, or to deliver it to the party who has been adjudged to be entitled to it. A.R.S. § 12-1552(A)(2). The writ must set forth the substance of the provisions of the judgment which require the sale or delivery of specific property, and requires the Sheriff to sell or deliver the property as the judgment directs. A.R.S. § 12-1554. A writ of special execution may be issued only to the Sheriff of the county where the property is located.

8. *Levy and Return on Writ of Execution.* A.R.S. § 12-1555(A) requires that an execution be made returnable to the Clerk of the Court issuing it not less than ten (10) nor more than ninety (90) days after its receipt. The return should describe the actions taken pursuant to the writ. The Sheriff levies upon property of the judgment debtor, according to its character, in the manner specified in A.R.S. § 12-1559. Sales of property under execution must be conducted according to the procedures specified in A.R.S. §§ 12-1621 *et seq.*

Where the Sheriff's return on the sale indicates that a surplus was realized, the trial court must determine whether there was in fact a surplus and, if so, what disposition should be made of it. *Regional Inv. Co. v. SMK Investments, Inc.*, 129 Ariz. 5, 628 P.2d 42 (Ct. App. Div. 2 1980); *Imperial-Yuma Production Credit Ass'n v. Nussbaumer*, 22 Ariz. App. 485, 528 P.2d 871 (Div. 1 1974). Property sold at execution may be redeemed by the judgment debtor or a successor in interest, or by a junior lienholder, within six (6) months after the date of the sale, unless the Court, as part of the judgment, determined that the property was abandoned and not used for agricultural purposes. A.R.S. §§ 12-1281, 12-1282.

An Arizona court does not have jurisdiction to issue a writ of garnishment to attach a bank account in an out-of-state branch of an interstate bank which does business in Arizona. *Desert Wide Cabling & Installation, Inc. v. Wells Fargo & Co., N.A.*, 191 Ariz. 516, 958 P.2d 457 (Ct. App. Div. 1 1998), as corrected, (June 23, 1998). The validity of an attachment or garnishment served on an interstate bank is determined by the law of the state in which the process issues. A.R.S. § 12-1577(A), which specifies the sole method of serving a writ of garnishment on a bank, specifies that the writ may be served "at any office or branch thereof located in the county where such service is made." That language indicates that the Legislature was referring only to counties in Arizona, and not to counties in other states as well. *Desert Wide Cabling & Installation, Inc. v. Wells Fargo & Co., N.A.*, 191 Ariz. 516, 958 P.2d 457 (Ct. App. Div. 1 1998), as corrected, (June 23, 1998).

9. *Notice and Conduct of Execution Sales.* The statutory

requirements for notices of execution sales distinguish between three types of property: perishable personal property, non-perishable personal property, and real property. A.R.S. § 12-1621.

For perishable personal property, the notice must be posted in three public places, two of which must be in the precinct and the third of which must be at or near the courthouse door. The notices must be posted "for such period of time before the sale as is reasonable, considering the character and condition of the property." A.R.S. § 12-1621(A)(1). For non-perishable personal property, the posting requirement is the same, except the notice must be posted for "ten days successively before the sale." A.R.S. § 12-1621(A)(2). A sale of personal property, whether perishable or not, may be conducted on the premises where it is taken, the courthouse door, or any other place where, because of the nature of the property, it is convenient to show it to prospective purchasers. A.R.S. § 12-1621(C).

In the case of real property, the notice must also be posted in three public places in the county, one of which must be at or near the courthouse door, for "not less than fifteen days successively" prior to the sale. In addition, the notice must be published in a newspaper "for three weeks before the day of sale." A.R.S. § 12-1621(A)(3). Sales of real property must be conducted at or near the courthouse door of the county where the property is located. A.R.S. § 12-1621(C).

The notice must identify the judgment, including its amount, the parties and the Court in which it was rendered, and must particularly describe the property to be sold. In the case of real property, this must include its legal description and, if possible, the street address or its identifiable location. A.R.S. § 12-1621(B).

The perfection of a judgment lien does not disable the judgment debtor from transferring real property subject to the lien, but such a transfer to a third-party does not immunize the liened property from execution. Under A.R.S. § 12-1553(2), where a judgment lien has been perfected against the judgment debtor, the judgment creditor may satisfy the judgment by executing on any real property that belonged to the judgment debtor when the judgment was recorded, even if the judgment debtor transferred the liened property to a third party after the judgment was recorded. *Byers v. Wik*, 169 Ariz. 215, 818 P.2d 200 (Ct. App. Div. 1 1991).

While notice of an execution sale by posting and publication is constitutionally sufficient notice to the judgment debtor and the judgment debtor has no due process right to actual notice of an execution sale, a third-party who was not a party to the underlying adjudication and whose name and address were available on the public record of documents affecting title to the property has a right to reasonable prior notice of the execution sale either by mail or by some other means equally likely to provide actual notice. *Byers v. Wik*, 169 Ariz. 215, 818 P.2d 200 (Ct. App. Div. 1 1991).

The procedures for the actual conduct of the sale are set forth in A.R.S. § 12-1622. The sale must be conducted between the hours of 10:00 a.m. and 4:00 p.m., and all sales must be made at public auction to the highest bidder. A.R.S. § 12-1622(A). Once sufficient property has been sold to satisfy the judgment and costs, no more property is to be sold. A.R.S. § 12-1622(B). Where the sale is of real property that can be sold in separate parcels, it can be sold separately at the direction of the judgment debtor, who may also specify the order in which the parcels are to be sold. A.R.S. § 12-1622(G).

Where the Sheriff's return on the sale indicates that a surplus was realized, but that is disputed or there are competing claimants to the surplus, the trial court must determine whether there in fact was a surplus and, if so, the appropriate disposition of it. *Regional Inv. Co. v. SMK Investments, Inc.*, 129 Ariz. 5, 628 P.2d 42 (Ct. App. Div. 2 1980); *Imperial-Yuma Production Credit Ass'n v. Nussbaumer*, 22 Ariz. App. 485, 528 P.2d 871 (Div. 1 1974).

10. *Satisfaction of Judgment.* A satisfaction of judgment is a discharge of an obligation by payment of the amount due. The term is also used to refer to the document that is filed indicating the judgment has been paid. *W.F. Conelly Const. Co. v. L. Harvey Concrete, Inc.*, 162 Ariz. 574, 785 P.2d 94 (Ct. App. Div. 2 1989).

A recorded satisfaction of judgment ordinarily signals the end of the cause of action on which the judgment was based, and is *prima facie* evidence that the judgment creditor has received payment of the amount of the judgment or its equivalent. *Brewer v. Gerson*, 190 Ariz. 164, 945 P.2d 1295 (1997). That will not be the case, however, where, prior to the filing of the satisfaction of judgment, the underlying judgment is set aside by court order. *Brewer v. Gerson*, 190 Ariz. 164, 945 P.2d 1295 (1997). In that circumstance, the satisfaction of judgment does not extinguish the underlying cause of action. *Brewer v. Gerson*, 190 Ariz. 164, 945 P.2d 1295 (1997).

The doctrine of "satisfaction of judgment" provides that, if one joint tortfeasor satisfies a judgment obtained by the plaintiff, all other tortfeasors are discharged from liability and the plaintiff has no further cause of action. *Bridgestone/Firestone North America Tire, L.L.C. v. Naranjo*, 206 Ariz. 447, 79 P.3d 1206, Prod. Liab. Rep. (CCH) P 16845 (Ct. App. Div. 2 2003). This doctrine also survives the abolition of joint and several liability, and the adoption of a comparative fault regime, in situations where the plaintiff has obtained a judgment for the total damages suffered from an indivisible injury against only one party at fault, and that judgment is satisfied. *Bridgestone/Firestone North America Tire, L.L.C. v. Naranjo*, 206 Ariz. 447, 79 P.3d 1206, Prod. Liab. Rep. (CCH) P 16845 (Ct. App. Div. 2 2003). The satisfaction of that judgment extinguishes any claim against other parties at fault. *Bridgestone/Firestone North America Tire, L.L.C. v. Naranjo*, 206 Ariz. 447, 79 P.3d 1206, Prod. Liab. Rep. (CCH) P 16845 (Ct. App. Div. 2 2003).

11. *Enforcement of Foreign Judgments.* The Full Faith and Credit Clause of the United States Constitution obliges the states to respect and enforce judgments rendered in the courts of their sister states, and effectively nationalizes the principle of *res judicata*. *Springfield Credit Union v. Johnson*, 123 Ariz. 319, 599 P.2d 772 (1979); *Giehrl v. Royal Aloha Vacation Club, Inc.*, 188 Ariz. 456, 937 P.2d 378 (Ct. App. Div. 1 1997); *Oyakawa v. Gillett*, 175 Ariz. 226, 854 P.2d 1212 (Ct. App. Div. 1 1993); *Tarnoff v. Jones*, 17 Ariz. App. 240, 497 P.2d 60 (Div. 1 1972). This requires that a judgment validly rendered in one state's courts be accorded in the other states the same validity and effect as it had in the state in which it was rendered. *Springfield Credit Union v. Johnson*, 123 Ariz. 319, 599 P.2d 772 (1979); *Giehrl v. Royal Aloha Vacation Club, Inc.*, 188 Ariz. 456, 937 P.2d 378 (Ct. App. Div. 1 1997); *Oyakawa v. Gillett*, 175 Ariz. 226, 854 P.2d 1212 (Ct. App. Div. 1 1993).

Similarly, where an arbitration award is reviewed in a state court, as part of a confirmation proceeding, the courts of other states are required to give the same effect to the resulting state court judgment as it would have in the rendering state's own courts. *Cho v. American Bonding Co.*, 190 Ariz. 593, 951 P.2d 468 (Ct. App. Div. 1 1997). This is true even when the cause of action underlying the judgment is barred by the public policy of the state in which enforcement of the judgment is sought. *Cho v. American Bonding Co.*, 190 Ariz. 593, 951 P.2d 468 (Ct. App. Div. 1 1997).

The foreign state's judgment need not be enforced, however, if the rendering court lacked personal or subject matter jurisdiction, if the judgment was obtained through fraud or is invalid or unenforceable, or if the defendant's due process rights were violated. *Cho v. American Bonding Co.*, 190 Ariz. 593, 951 P.2d 468 (Ct. App. Div. 1 1997); *Pioneer Federal Sav. Bank v. Driver*, 166 Ariz. 585, 804 P.2d 118 (Ct. App. Div. 1 1990).

A defendant served with a lawsuit in another state may litigate that state's jurisdiction in that suit, or may let the suit go to judgment by default and collaterally attack jurisdiction when the plaintiff attempts to enforce the default judgment. *Giehrl v. Royal Aloha Vacation Club, Inc.*, 188 Ariz. 456, 937 P.2d 378 (Ct. App.

Div. 1 1997). If one state court determines, in default proceedings, that it has jurisdiction over the defendant, and a second state court determines, in a proceeding in which both parties are present and litigating the matter, that the first court lacked jurisdiction over the defendant's person, Arizona will give full faith and credit to the judgment of the second court that made its determination with both parties present to litigate jurisdiction.

A judgment obtained in the courts of another state may be enforced in Arizona either by bringing an independent action on the judgment or by utilizing the procedures of the Uniform Enforcement of Foreign Judgments Act, A.R.S. §§ 12-1701 to 12-1708. *C & J Travel, Inc. v. Shumway*, 161 Ariz. 33, 775 P.2d 1097 (Ct. App. Div. 2 1989). The effect of filing a foreign judgment under the Act is to transform it into a valid Arizona judgment subject to the same procedures for enforcement as a judgment rendered by an Arizona court. *C & J Travel, Inc. v. Shumway*, 161 Ariz. 33, 775 P.2d 1097 (Ct. App. Div. 2 1989). Arizona's version of the Act requires that notice of filing of a foreign judgment must be sent to the judgment debtor's last known post office address. Actual notice is not required. While a person's post office address and residence address are not always the same, given that constitutional considerations do not require notice to the debtor of post-judgment proceedings, the judgment creditor, in the absence of information to the contrary, may presume that mail addressed to a residence will be delivered. *Douglas N. Higgins, Inc. v. Songer*, 171 Ariz. 8, 827 P.2d 469 (Ct. App. Div. 1 1991).

The purpose of the Uniform Enforcement of Foreign Judgments Act is to provide the states with a speedy and economical method of enforcing foreign judgments. Although filing a judgment under the Uniform Act "domesticates" it for purposes of enforcement, it remains a foreign judgment subject to A.R.S. § 12-544(3), which prescribes a four-year statute of limitations for actions to enforce foreign judgments. *Citibank (South Dakota), N.A. v. Phifer*, 181 Ariz. 5, 887 P.2d 5 (Ct. App. Div. 2 1994). Arizona may constitutionally apply its own statute of limitations, even if that operates to bar enforcement of foreign judgments filed under the Act. *Citibank (South Dakota), N.A. v. Phifer*, 181 Ariz. 5, 887 P.2d 5 (Ct. App. Div. 2 1994).

Difficult questions arise where efforts are made to enforce against a marital community in Arizona the provisions of a judgment rendered against only one spouse in a non-community property state. A spouse not named in the foreign action cannot be added as a party to an action on the judgment in Arizona, and a judgment against only one spouse thereby converted into one against the community, without regard to the procedural due process rights of the absent spouse. *C & J Travel, Inc. v. Shumway*,

161 Ariz. 33, 775 P.2d 1097 (Ct. App. Div. 2 1989). A judgment rendered in another state against only one spouse can be enforced against community property, however, without offending due process, where a statute of the rendering jurisdiction authorizes judgment against the community through a suit that names only one spouse, and thereby gives notice to all married persons that an action on a community obligation may proceed against only one spouse and that the resulting judgment will bind the community of both spouses. *Oyakawa v. Gillett*, 175 Ariz. 226, 854 P.2d 1212 (Ct. App. Div. 1 1993).

A.R.S. § 25-215(C) provides that "the community property is liable for a spouse's debts incurred outside of this state during the marriage which would have been community debts if incurred in this state." With the enactment of that provision, the Arizona Legislature gave practical effect to the Full Faith and Credit Clause and specifically decided that Arizona's community property laws may not be used to make Arizona a haven for debtors from non-community property states. *National Union Fire Ins. Co. of Pittsburgh, Pa. v. Greene*, 195 Ariz. 105, 985 P.2d 590 (Ct. App. Div. 1 1999).

While A.R.S. § 25-215(D) provides that community property cannot be liable for a judgment unless both spouses are joined in the underlying action, that is not a proper ground to deny enforcement of a judgment rendered in a jurisdiction in which both spouses could not have been joined in the underlying action. Under the Full Faith and Credit Clause, a foreign judgment may not be attacked on the basis that it does not comply with the law of the state in which the judgment creditor seeks to enforce it, and an Arizona court may not impress Arizona procedural law upon a foreign judgment and refuse to recognize that judgment merely because Arizona law was not followed in obtaining it. The spouse not joined in the foreign action, however, must be given a meaningful opportunity to be heard before that spouse can be deprived of that spouse's equal interest in the community property. *National Union Fire Ins. Co. of Pittsburgh, Pa. v. Greene*, 195 Ariz. 105, 985 P.2d 590 (Ct. App. Div. 1 1999).

A creditor, who secures a judgment against one of the marital partners *prior to* the marriage, however, for a separate premarital debt, may enforce that judgment against the community without bringing an independent action naming the nondebtor spouse. *CBM of Arizona, Inc. v. Sevier*, 184 Ariz. 503, 910 P.2d 654 (Ct. App. Div. 2 1996). Where such a judgment has been obtained before the marriage, both spouses are limited to those defenses which may be raised against the judgment, such as satisfaction or nonrenewal.

Additionally, with respect to the community property that may be reached to satisfy the judgment, both spouses have the right to litigate the extent of the debtor spouse's contribution to the community. *CBM of Arizona, Inc. v. Sevier*, 184 Ariz. 503, 910 P.2d 654 (Ct. App. Div. 2 1996).

The fact that a spouse was not joined as a party in the proceedings in a foreign nation that resulted in a judgment does not preclude recognition of it in Arizona and enforcement of it against community property. *CBM of Arizona, Inc. v. Sevier*, 184 Ariz. 503, 910 P.2d 654 (Ct. App. Div. 2 1996). A judgment rendered against one spouse in a non-community property jurisdiction may be enforced against Arizona community property as long as (1) the obligation on which the foreign judgment was based would have been a community obligation if it had been incurred in Arizona, and (2) the non-defendant spouse is joined in the Arizona domestication action and has an opportunity to contend that the foreign judgment was based on an obligation of the other spouse that would have been separate if incurred in Arizona. *CBM of Arizona, Inc. v. Sevier*, 184 Ariz. 503, 910 P.2d 654 (Ct. App. Div. 2 1996). A writ of garnishment to collect on a registered foreign judgment cannot be enforced against a community property bank account, however, where the judgment is based on a guaranty signed by only one spouse and both spouses were not joined in the foreign action. *Rackmaster Systems, Inc. v. Maderia*, 219 Ariz. 60, 193 P.3d 314 (Ct. App. Div. 1 2008).

Arizona courts are not required to give full faith and credit to judgments of courts of foreign nations. Such a foreign judgment will be recognized only if the Arizona court is convinced that the foreign court had jurisdiction and that there was an opportunity for a full and fair trial without prejudice in the foreign court or system of law. *Rotary Club of Tucson v. Chaprales Ramos de Pena*, 160 Ariz. 362, 773 P.2d 467 (Ct. App. Div. 2 1989).

While a foreign nation's judgment will not be enforced if it results from prejudice, fraud, unfairness or irregularities in the proceedings, this does not require that an Arizona court review the proceedings that resulted in the foreign judgment and decline to recognize is upon the merest suggestion of prejudice or fraud. *Alberta Securities Com'n v. Ryckman*, 200 Ariz. 540, 30 P.3d 121 (Ct. App. Div. 1 2001). There is a strong presumption of the validity of a foreign judgment and a party challenging it must point so specific grounds, and evidence supporting them, for overcoming that presumption. *Alberta Securities Com'n v. Ryckman*, 200 Ariz. 540, 30 P.3d 121 (Ct. App. Div. 1 2001).

12. *Judgments of Tribal Courts*. The Arizona courts have long followed the rule that judgments rendered by the courts of Indian tribes are not entitled to Full Faith and Credit, but will be honored and enforced only under principles of comity. *Tracy v.*

Superior Court of Maricopa County, 168 Ariz. 23, 810 P.2d 1030 (1991); *Begay v. Miller*, 70 Ariz. 380, 222 P.2d 624 (1950); *Beltran v. Harrah's Arizona Corp.*, 220 Ariz. 29, 202 P.3d 494 (Ct. App. Div. 2 2008); *Brown v. Babbitt Ford, Inc.*, 117 Ariz. 192, 571 P.2d 689, 23 U.C.C. Rep. Serv. 266 (Ct. App. Div. 1 1977). The Supreme Court "codified" that doctrine, and established separate procedures for seeking enforcement of tribal *civil* judgments, by its adoption of the Rules of Procedure for the Recognition of Tribal Court Judgments, which become effective on December 1, 2000. The Rules were not intended to be the exclusive means for seeking the enforcement of tribal court judgments, and they do not apply where a tribal court judgment is invoked to support the defense of collateral estoppel. *Beltran v. Harrah's Arizona Corp.*, 220 Ariz. 29, 202 P.3d 494 (Ct. App. Div. 2 2008).

Rule 2(a) of those Rules defines "tribal court" to include "any court or other tribunal of any federally recognized Indian nation, tribe, pueblo, band or Alaska native village.. . ." Rule 2(b) defines "tribal judgment" as "any final written judgment decree or order of a tribal court duly authenticated in accordance with the laws and procedures of the tribe or tribal court."

Under Rule 3, a person seeking to enforce such a judgment is to file it with the Clerk of the Superior Court in any county, together with an affidavit setting forth the name and last known address of the party seeking enforcement and the "responding party" (presumably the party against whom the judgment is to be enforced). The party seeking enforcement is also to serve upon the responding party a notice of filing, and a copy of the tribal judgment. Service is to be accomplished in accordance with the requirements of Rule 4.1.

Alternatively, the party seeking enforcement may mail the notice of filing and a copy of the tribal judgment to the responding party at that party's last known address, by certified mail, return receipt requested. If the responding party is the State of Arizona, or any of its officers, employees, departments or agencies, then service can be accomplished by mailing to the office of the Attorney General. Proof of service or mailing must be filed with the Clerk. The notice of filing must contain the name and address of the enforcing party and of the enforcing party's attorney, if any, and the full text of Ariz.R.Civ.P. 4, 5(a) and 5(b).

Rule 4 requires that any objection to enforcement of the tribal judgment be filed within twenty (20) days after service, or receipt of the mailing, of the notice of filing, or within twenty-five (25) days of the date of mailing, whichever is later. If no timely objection is filed, then, under Rule 5(a), the Clerk is to issue a certification to that effect and the tribal judgment shall have the same force and effect as a judgment, order or decree issued by a court of the State of Arizona. If an objection is filed, the Superior Court may set a time for a reply and/or set the matter for hearing.

Under Rule 5(c), the Superior Court *must* decline to enforce the tribal judgment if it finds that (1) the tribal court entering the judgment lacked personal or subject matter discretion, or (2) the defendant was not afforded due process in the proceedings resulting in the entry of the judgment.

Under Rule 5(d), the Superior Court *may*, in its discretion, decline to enforce the tribal judgment if it finds that: (1) the tribal judgment was obtained through extrinsic fraud; (2) the tribal judgment conflicts with another final judgment that is entitled to recognition; (3) the tribal judgment is inconsistent with the parties' contractual choice of forum; *or* (4) recognition of the judgment, or the cause of action upon which it is based, would be contrary to the fundamental public policy of the United States or the State of Arizona.

Under Rule 6, if the party objecting to enforcement demonstrates that an appeal from the judgment is pending or will be taken, or that a stay of execution upon the judgment has been granted, then the Superior Court is to stay enforcement of it until it has become final, or the stay upon execution expires or is vacated. Rule 7 grants the Superior Court authority to contact the tribal court judge who issued the judgment, after notice to the parties, to attempt to resolve any issues regarding it that may arise.

Rule 70. Judgment for specific acts; vesting title

1. If a judgment directs a party to execute a conveyance of land or to deliver deeds or other documents or to perform any other specific act and the party fails to comply within the time specified, the court may direct the act to be done at the cost of the disobedient party by some other person appointed by the court and the act when so done has like effect as if done by the party. On application of the party entitled to performance, the clerk shall issue a writ of attachment or sequestration against the property of the disobedient party to compel obedience to the judgment. The court may also in proper cases adjudge the party in contempt.

2. If real or personal property is within the state, the court in lieu of directing a conveyance thereof may enter a judgment divesting the title of any party and vesting it in others and such judgment has the effect of a conveyance executed in due form of law. When any order or judgment is for the delivery of possession, the party in whose favor it is entered is entitled to a writ of execution or assistance upon application to the clerk.

AUTHORS' COMMENTS

Analysis

1. *Scope and Purpose of Rule.* Rule 70 enumerates enforcement options available to the Court in the specific situation where the relief awarded is to transfer land to, or perform some specific act for the benefit of, the prevailing party. If the judgment or decree initially entered directs the losing party to execute a conveyance of and/or deliver deeds for property, or to perform an act, and the losing party fails to comply, the Court may appoint a third party to comply with the judgment, at the expense of the disobedient party.

As an alternative, where the case concerns Arizona property, the Court may initially enter a decree or judgment which itself divests the losing party of title and vests it in others.

2. *Comparison With Federal Rule.* Despite structural differences, ARCP 70 and FRCP 70 are substantially identical.

In 2007, however, the language of FRCP 70 was amended as part of the general restyling of the Federal Rules of Civil Procedure to make the Federal Rules more easily understood and to make style and terminology consistent throughout the Federal Rules of Civil Procedure. Those stylistic modifications have not been incorporated into ARCP 70. Finally, for reasons that are not clear, the titles to the 2 rules differ.

Rule 70.1. Application to transfer structured settlement payment rights

Every application for approval of the transfer of structured settlement rights filed pursuant to A.R.S. Sec. 12-2901 et seq. shall include:

(a) Payee's Declaration in Support of Application, signed under oath by the payee, that sets forth the following information:

(1) The payee's name, address and age.

(2) The payee's marital status, and, if married or separated, the name of the payee's spouse.

(3) The names, ages, and Place(s) of residence of the payee's minor children and other dependents, if any.

(4) The payee's monthly income and sources of income, and, if presently married, the monthly income and sources of income of the payee's spouse.

(5) Whether the payee is subject to any child support or spousal maintenance orders, and, if so, for each such order:

(A) The amount of the obligation, to whom it is payable, and whether there are arrearages, and, if so, the amount; and

(B) The jurisdiction and name of the court that entered the order, the case number of the action in which the order was entered, the parties to such action, and the date the order was entered.

(6) Whether the payee is subject to any orders in any civil, probate, or criminal case which requires the payee to pay money to any person, and, if so, for each such order:

(A) The amount of the obligation, to whom it is payable, and whether there are arrearages and, if so, the amount; and

(B) The jurisdiction and name of the court that entered the order, the case number of the action in which the order was entered, the parties to such action, and the date when the order was entered.

(7) Whether there has been any previous application to any court or responsible administrative authority for approval of a transfer of payment rights under the structured settlement that is the subject of the application, and, if so, for each such application:

(A) The jurisdiction and name of the court or responsible administrative authority that considered the application, the case number of the action in which the application was submitted, the parties to such action, and the date when the application was filed; and

(B) Whether the application was approved or disapproved, the date of the order approving or disapproving the transfer, and, if approved:

(i) The name of the transferee and the payment amount(s) and due dates of the payments involved in the transfer; and

(ii) The amount of money the payee received from the transferee for the transfer, if any, and the manner in which the money was used.

(8) Whether the payee has ever transferred payment rights under the structured settlement without court approval or the approval of a responsible administrative authority, and, if so, for each such transfer:

(A) The name of the transferee and the payment amount(s) and due dates of the payments involved in the transfer; and

(B) The amount of money the payee received from the transferee for the transfer, if any, and the manner in which the money was used.

(9) The payee's reasons for the proposed transfer of payment rights and the payee's plans for using the proceeds from the transfer.

(10) Whether the payee intends to use the proceeds from the proposed transfer to pay debts, and, if so, the amount of each such debt, the name and address of the creditor to whom it is owed, and, if applicable, the rate at which interest is accruing on such debt.

(b) A Transferee's Declaration in Support of Application, signed under oath by the transferee, that states that:

(1) After making reasonable inquiry, the transferee is not aware of any prior transfers of structured settlement rights by the payee other than those disclosed in Payee's Declaration in Support of Application;

(2) the transferee has complied with its obligations under A.R.S. § 12-2901, et seq.; and

(3) To the best of the transferee's knowledge after making reasonable inquiry, the proposed transfer would not contravene any applicable law, statute, or the order of any court or other governmental authority.

Rule 70.1 added September 2008, effective January 1, 2009.

AUTHORS' COMMENTS

Analysis

1. *Scope and Purpose of Rule.* It is not uncommon for personal injury actions, particularly where the nature of the injuries sustained may require long-term medical care, to be settled on a basis which calls for the plaintiff to receive periodic payments over a length of time. Such "structured settlements" are typically funded through the purchase by the settling defendant(s) of an annuity from an insurance company which makes the payments called for. It is also not an infrequent occurrence for the plaintiff entitled to receive such payments to subsequently, either due to changed circumstances, to want to effect a transfer to receive such periodic payments, either in whole or in part, to a third party.

The Legislature adopted specific requirements governing the approval of such transfers in 2002 as A.R.S. §§ 12-2901 to 2904. Under A.R.S. § 12-2902(A), such a transfer is not effective, and a settlement obligor or annuity issuer has no obligation to make payments to the transferee "unless the transfer has been authorized in advance in a final order of a court of competent jurisdiction or responsible administrative authority." A.R.S. § 12-2903(A) grants the Superior Court jurisdiction over any application for approval of such a transfer. While the statute specifies the findings that a court or administrative agency is required to make as a condition of granting such approval, see A.R.S. § 12-2902(B), it is silent as to the nature of the information that the court is to be provided in support of an application for approval.

Rule 70.1 thus serves several purposes—to insure that the court asked to approve such a transfer is provided with the information necessary to make an informed determination as to whether such a transfer is in the best interests of the payee under the settlement, to rectify an apparent legislative oversight in that regard, and to bring a much needed uniformity to the form and contents of an application to transfer the rights to receive payments under a prior structured settlement.

2. *Comparison With Federal Rule.* The Federal Rules of Civil Procedure do not have a provision that corresponds to ARCP 70.1.

Rule 71. Process in behalf of and against persons not parties

When an order is made in favor of a person who is not a party to the action, that person may enforce obedience to the order by the same process as if a party, and, when obedience to an order may be lawfully enforced against a person who is not a party, that person is liable to the same process for enforcing obedience to the order as if a party.

Amended Sept. 15, 1987, effective Nov. 15, 1987.

AUTHORS' COMMENTS

Analysis

1. *Scope and Purpose of Rule.* Rule 71 makes enforcement procedures available both against and in favor of persons who are not parties to an action, under the circumstances delineated in the Rule. A non-party may invoke court process to enforce the terms of a judicial order which is made in favor of that non-party. Non-parties may be subjected to court process for the enforcement of orders or judgments which "may be lawfully enforced against" them.

2. *Comparison With Federal Rule.* ARCP 71 and FRCP 71 are substantially identical.

In 2007, however, the language of FRCP 71 was amended as part of the general restyling of the Federal Rules of Civil Procedure to make the Federal Rules more easily understood and to make style and terminology consistent throughout the Federal Rules of Civil Procedure. Those stylistic modifications have not been incorporated into ARCP 71. Finally, the titles to the 2 rules are different.

IX. COMPULSORY ARBITRATION

Rule 72. Compulsory arbitration; arbitration by reference; alternative dispute resolution; determination of suitability for arbitration

(a) Decision to Provide for Compulsory Arbitration. Rules 72 through 77 of these rules shall apply when the Superior Court in a county, by a majority vote of the judges thereof, decides to provide for arbitration of claims and establishes jurisdictional limits by rule of court pursuant to A.R.S. § 12-133. Such decision to provide for arbitration shall be incorporated into a Superior Court order which shall be filed with the Clerk of the Supreme Court, and a copy thereof shall be filed with the Clerk of the Superior Court of the applicable county. All other provisions of the Arizona Rules of Civil Procedure that are not inconsistent with Rules 72 through 77 shall be applicable to all cases in arbitration.

(b) Compulsory Arbitration. Civil cases which meet both of the following conditions, except appeals from municipal or justice courts, shall be submitted to arbitration in accordance with the provisions of A.R.S. § 12-133:

(1) No party seeks affirmative relief other than a money judgment; and

(2) No party seeks an award in excess of the jurisdictional limit for arbitration set by applicable local rule of the Superior Court.

For purposes of this provision, "award" and "affirmative relief" include punitive damages, but do not include interest, attorneys' fees or costs.

(c) Arbitration by Agreement of Reference. Any claim may at any time, whether or not suit has been filed, be referred to arbitration by Agreement of Reference signed by all parties or their counsel. If suit has not been filed, the Agreement of Reference shall define the issues involved for determination in the arbitration proceedings and may contain stipulations with respect to agreed facts, issues or defenses. In such cases, the Agreement of Reference shall take the place of the pleadings in the case and shall be filed and assigned a civil case number. Filing an Agreement of Reference shall not relieve any party from paying the required filing fee. Filing of an Agreement of Reference shall have the same effect on the running of the statute of limitations as the filing of a civil complaint.

Text of Rule 72(d) applicable to those cases filed before April 15,

2014 that are not subject to the conditions stated in the November 27, 2013 Amended Order Regarding Applicability Provision, in R-13-0017.

See also, text of Rule 72(d) applicable to cases filed on or after April 15, 2014 and applicable to those cases filed before April 15, 2014 that are subject to the conditions stated in the November 27, 2013, Amended Order Regarding Applicability Provision, in R-13-0017.

(d) Alternative Dispute Resolution.

(1) Compulsory arbitration under A.R.S. § 12-133 and these rules is not binding. Any party may appeal and all appeals are de novo on the law and facts. Therefore, before a hearing in accordance with Rule 75 of these rules is held, counsel for the parties, or the parties if not represented by counsel, shall confer regarding the feasibility of resolving their dispute through another form of alternative dispute resolution, including but not limited to private mediation or binding arbitration with a mediator or arbitrator agreed to by the parties.

(2) The court shall waive the arbitration requirement if the parties file a written stipulation to participate in good faith in an alternative dispute resolution proceeding, and the court approves the method selected by the parties. The stipulation shall identify the specific alternative dispute resolution method selected. The court may waive the arbitration requirement for other good cause upon stipulation of all parties. If the alternative dispute resolution method selected under this Rule fails, the case shall be set for trial in accordance with Rule 38.1 of these Rules and shall not be subject to the rules governing compulsory arbitration.

Text of Rule 72(d) applicable to cases filed on or after April 15, 2014 and to those cases filed before April 15, 2014 that are subject to the conditions stated in the November 27, 2013, Amended Order Regarding Applicability Provision, in R-13-0017.

See also, text of Rule 72(d) applicable to those cases filed before April 15, 2014 that are not subject to the conditions stated in the November 27, 2013 Amended Order Regarding Applicability Provision, in R-13-0017.

(d) Alternative Dispute Resolution.

(1) Compulsory arbitration under A.R.S. § 12-133 and these rules is not binding. Any party may appeal and all appeals are de novo on the law and facts. Therefore, before a hearing in accordance with Rule 75 of these rules is held, counsel for the parties, or the parties if not represented by counsel, shall confer regarding the feasibility of resolving their dispute through an-

other form of alternative dispute resolution, including but not limited to private mediation or binding arbitration with a mediator or arbitrator agreed to by the parties.

(2) The court shall waive the arbitration requirement if the parties file a written stipulation to participate in good faith in an alternative dispute resolution proceeding, and the court approves the method selected by the parties. The stipulation shall identify the specific alternative dispute resolution method selected. The court may waive the arbitration requirement for other good cause upon stipulation of all parties. If the alternative dispute resolution method selected under this Rule fails, the case shall be set for trial in accordance with Rule 16 of these Rules and shall not be subject to the rules governing compulsory arbitration.

(e) Procedure for Determining Suitability for Arbitration.

(1) At the time of filing the complaint, the plaintiff shall also file a separate certificate on compulsory arbitration with the Clerk of the Superior Court in the following form:

> "The undersigned certifies that he or she knows the dollar limits and any other limitations set forth by the local rules of practice for the applicable superior court, and further certifies that this case (is) (is not) subject to compulsory arbitration, as provided by Rules 72 through 77 of the Arizona Rules of Civil Procedure."

(i) The certificate on compulsory arbitration must be served upon the defendant at the time of service of the complaint. It, and any controverting certificate of a party represented by an attorney, shall be signed by at least one attorney of record in the attorney's individual name. A party who is not represented by an attorney shall sign the party's certificate on compulsory arbitration or controverting certificate.

(ii) The signature of an attorney or party constitutes a certification by the signer that the signer has considered the applicability of both the local rules of practice for the appropriate superior court and Rules 72 through 77 of the Arizona Rules of Civil Procedure; that the signer has read the certificate on compulsory arbitration or controverting certificate; that to the best of the signer's knowledge, information and belief, formed after reasonable inquiry, it is warranted; and that the allegation as to arbitrability is not set forth for any improper purpose. The provisions of Rule 11(a) of these Rules apply to every certificate on compulsory arbitration and controverting certificate filed under this rule.

(iii) The certificate on compulsory arbitration shall not be admissible at any hearing on the merits.

(2) If the defendant disagrees with the plaintiff's assertion as to arbitrability, the defendant shall file a controverting certificate that specifies the particular reason for the defendant's disagreement with plaintiff's certificate. The defendant's certificate shall be filed with the answer and a copy or copies shall be served upon the plaintiff.

(3) If conflicting certificates are filed, the matter shall be referred to the judge to whom the case has been assigned for determination of the issues raised thereby. If the judge determines that the case is subject to compulsory arbitration, it shall proceed to arbitration as provided in these rules.

(4) A party or attorney is under a duty to seasonably amend a prior certificate on compulsory arbitration if the party or attorney obtains information upon the basis of which (a) the party or attorney knows the certificate was incorrect when filed or (b) the party or attorney knows that the certificate, though correct when filed, is no longer true.

(5) The court may, on its own motion, or upon the motion of either party at any time after the close of pleadings, determine that the case is subject to compulsory arbitration, and in that event, the court may order that the case proceed to arbitration as provided in these rules.

(6) At such time as the arbitrator renders a decision, should the arbitrator find that the appropriate award exceeds the limit for compulsory arbitration set by local rule or statute, the arbitrator shall enter an award for the full amount.

(7) If the court finds that an attorney or party has made an allegation as to arbitrability which was not made in good faith or failed to amend seasonably as required, the court, upon motion or upon its own initiative, shall make such orders with regard to such conduct as are just, including, among others, any action authorized under Rule 11(a) of these Rules.

Rule 72 added Oct. 10, 2000, effective Dec. 1, 2000. Amended September 5, 2007, effective January 1, 2008; Aug. 28, 2013, effective April 15, 2014, subject to conditions of Order No. R-13-0017.

HISTORICAL NOTES

[2014 Amendments]

[Rule 72] Arizona Supreme Court Order No. R-13-0017, issued Aug. 28, 2013, provided that the amendments of the order would be "effective on April 15, 2014 as to all cases filed on or after that date." The applicability provision of Order No. R-13-0017 was amended on Nov. 14, 2013, and subsequently amended on Nov. 27, 2013 to provide:

(1) The Amendments shall apply to all actions filed on or after April 15, 2014.

(2) Beginning on April 15, 2014, the Amendments also shall apply to any action filed prior to April 15, 2014 (a "pending action"), unless one of the following events has occurred before that date:

(a) A party has filed a Motion to Set and Certificate of Readiness,

(b) The parties have filed a Proposed Scheduling Order, or

(c) The court has entered a Scheduling Order.

(3) If, in a pending action, one of the preceding events has not occurred before April 15, 2014, the parties shall file a Joint Report and a Proposed Scheduling Order in accordance with the Amendments by June 30, 2014, or within 270 days after the commencement of the action, whichever date is later. Otherwise, the court will place the action on the Dismissal Calendar in accordance with the Amendments.

(4) A trial court, in its discretion, may apply any of the Amendments to a case pending before April 15, 2014, even if the Amendments would not otherwise apply under paragraph (2) above. For example, if a party filed a Motion to Set and Certificate of Readiness before April 15, 2014, the trial judge may set the matter for a trial setting conference under amended Rule 16(f), rather than place the case on the active calendar under pre-amendment Rule 38.1(c).

(5) Civil actions pending on the Inactive Calendar on April 15, 2014 shall be dismissed without prejudice on June 14, 2014, unless one of the actions set forth in subparts (1) - (4) of amended Rule 38.1(f) occurs before June 14, 2014.

STATE BAR COMMITTEE NOTES

2000 Promulgation and Amendments

As part of the effort to consolidate formerly separate sets of procedural rules into either the Arizona Rules of Civil Procedure or the Rules of the Arizona Supreme Court, the Uniform Rules of Procedure for Arbitration, as recently amended, were effectively transferred to the Arizona Rules of Civil Procedure and placed in a section of those rules which had formerly been concerned with appeals in civil cases. The rules in Section IX had been abrogated effective January 1, 1978, at the time of the adoption of the Arizona Rules of Civil Appellate Procedure. In the 2000 Amendments, Section IX of the rules was renamed "Section IX: Compulsory Arbitration." New Rule 72, with certain stylistic and technical revisions, contains the provisions formerly contained in Rule 1, and certain of the provisions formerly contained in Rule 3, of the Uniform Rules of Procedure for Arbitration.

[Rule 72(d)] New Rule 72(d) was added, by a 2000 amendment to what was then Rule 1 of the Uniform Rules of Procedure for Arbitration, to require that, in cases otherwise subject to compulsory arbitration, the parties discuss the use of alternative dispute resolution ("ADR") methods. Possible ADR methods include, but are not limited to, private mediation, binding arbitration and/or summary jury trial. Consistent with A.R.S. § 12-133(b), new Rule 72(d)(2) provides that, if all parties stipulate in writing and if the court approves the ADR method selected by the parties, then the court shall waive the arbitration requirement. Good cause for waiving the arbitration requirement is not limited, however, to participating in an alternative dispute resolution process. If, following participation in the court approved ADR method, the case is not settled, the case shall be set for trial in accordance with Rule 38.1 of these Rules and shall not be subject to the rules governing compulsory arbitration.

2007 Amendments

The 2007 amendments are the result of work of the Committee on Compulsory Arbitration in the Superior Court appointed by Chief Justice Ruth V. McGregor in November 2005. The amendments seek to clarify, reorganize, and improve the rules to avoid unnecessary delay and expense in arbitrated matters.

AUTHORS' COMMENTS

Analysis

1. *Background of Arbitration Statutes and Rules.* Before January 1, 2011, consensual arbitration of disputes as an alternative to court proceedings was authorized by statute in Arizona in A.R.S. §§ 12-1501 through 12-1518. Effective January 1, 2011, Arizona adopted the Revised Uniform Arbitration Act (the "RUAA"). *See*, A.R.S. §§ 12-3001 to 12-3029. A.R.S. § 12-3003 governs the applicability of the statute to existing and future contractual agreements to arbitrate.

Specifically, A.R.S. § 12-3003(A)(1) states that the statute applies to agreements to arbitrate made on or after January 1, 2011 and A.R.S. § 12-3003(A)(2) states that it applies to agreements to arbitrate entered into *before* January 1, 2011, only if all parties agree to the agreement or the proceeding agree "in a record." A.R.S. § 12-3003(A)(3) states that the statute governs an agreement to arbitrate *whenever* made. It remains to be seen how a court will reconcile the apparent inconsistency, assuming it becomes an issue.

By its express terms, the RUAA does not apply to agreements to arbitrate made before January 1, 2011. *See*, A.R.S. § 12-3003. The RUAA also does not apply to: (1) employer-employee agreements, (2) insurance contracts, (3) agreements between a national bank/savings association and customer and (4) arbitrations conducted or administered by specified self-regulatory organizations. *See*, A.R.S. § 12-3003(B). Rather, the RUAA provides that A.R.S. §§ 12-1501 et seq. will govern those arbitration agreements described above in (2), (3) and (4). *See*, A.R.S. § 12-3003(C).

To date, there is only one reported appellate court decision addressing disputes related to the RUAA. *Sun Valley Ranch 308 Ltd. Partnership ex rel. Englewood Properties, Inc. v. Robson*, 231 Ariz. 287, 294 P.3d 125 (Ct. App. Div. 1 2012). In *Sun Valley*, the appellate court held that the broad arbitration clause in the limited partnership agreement required the arbitration of disputes arising under an associated construction contract which arose out or related to the partnership agreement, which did not have such provision.

Arbitration has been, and clearly is, recognized as playing an important role in dispute resolution. *Broemmer v. Abortion Services of Phoenix, Ltd.*, 173 Ariz. 148, 840 P.2d 1013, 24 A.L.R. 5th 793 (1992). There has also been a steadily increasing legislative awareness of, and emphasis upon, *requiring* the use of arbitration as a means for resolving relatively minor disputes, and thereby maximizing the use of the judicial resources within the Superior Court system. The underlying assumption for this development is the thought that something short of a full-blown adversary adjudicatory proceeding is a more efficient and cost-effective means for resolving relatively minor civil disputes. *Martinez v. Binsfield*, 196 Ariz. 466, 999 P.2d 810 (2000). As the caseload of the Superior Court continues to escalate, this trend toward encouraging and/or mandating arbitration will undoubtedly continue.

In 1971, the Legislature enacted A.R.S. § 12-133, which permitted the Superior Court in any county to adopt a Local Rule requiring parties to submit a dispute to binding arbitration where the amount in controversy was $3,000 or less. The original version of the Uniform Rules of Procedure for Arbitration was adopted shortly thereafter. By successive amendments to the statute, the "jurisdictional threshold" of the amount in controversy that will potentially make a matter subject to mandatory court-annexed arbitration has been increased to $5,000, then to $15,000, to $50,000, and finally to $65,000. The operative language of the statute has also been changed to place greater emphasis upon requiring arbitration, As amended, A.R.S. § 12-133(A) *requires* the Superior Court in each county, by Local Rule, to: "1. Establish jurisdictional limits of not to exceed fifty thousand dollars for submission of disputes to arbitration.," and "2. Require arbitration in all cases which are filed in superior court in which the court finds or the parties agree that the amount in controversy does not exceed the jurisdictional limit."

In anticipation that the legislative increase of the "jurisdictional amount" for imposing mandatory arbitration would result in a corresponding increase in the number of matters submitted to arbitration for resolution, the Uniform Rules of Procedure for Arbitration were substantially amended in 1987. The amended Rules were designed to expedite cases subject to compulsory arbitration and to provide more procedural structure, while preserving the desired informality of the arbitration process. The Rules were again amended, effective August 1, 1991, to facilitate the early identification of those cases subject to compulsory arbitration.

As the culmination of what was informally referred to as the Civil Rules Consolidation Project, the Uniform Rules of Procedure for Arbitration were abrogated by the Supreme Court in their entirety, effective December 1, 2000, and their provisions effectively transferred to Rules 72 through 76 of the Arizona Rules of Civil Procedure (now, Ariz. R. Civ. P. 72 through 77). The Rules were then extensively amended and expanded in 2008 as a result of the work of the Committee on Compulsory Arbitration in the Superior Court appointed by the Chief Justice in November 2005.

At the time of this consolidation, there was also pending before the Court a proposal to amend the existing Uniform Rules of Procedure for Arbitration which the Court also approved. The amendments thereby made were simply incorporated into the amended provision in its new location. Thus, Rule 72(d)(2) provides that, if all parties stipulate in writing to use another alternative dispute resolution method, and the Court approves the method selected, then the Court shall waive the arbitration requirement.

Rule 73(b)(1) lowered the experience requirements for eligibility to serve as an arbitrator from five (5) years of practice to four (4) years. The Rules made it clear that the time periods for processing civil cases, set forth in Ariz.R.Civ.P. 38.1, are fully applicable to cases subject to mandatory arbitration, and in effect conformed the Rules to the decision (issued while the proposed amendments were pending) in *Martinez v. Binsfield*, 196 Ariz. 466, 999 P.2d 810 (2000).

2. *Comparison With Federal Rule*. The Federal Rules of Civil Procedure do not have a provision that corresponds to ARCP 72.

3. *Cases Subject to Mandatory Arbitration*. Both A.R.S. § 12-133 and Rule 72(b) specify that a case will be subject to mandatory arbitration and the procedures of Rules 72 through 77, if two separate conditions are satisfied: (1) no party to the action seeks affirmative relief other than a monetary judgment, and (2) no party seeks an award which exceeds the "jurisdictional limit" for arbitration established by Local Rule of the Superior Court for the county in which the action is filed.

Ariz. R. Civ. P. 72(b) expressly excludes appeals from municipal or justice courts from mandatory arbitration.

As a result of the quasi-mandatory nature of A.R.S. § 12-133(A), as amended, all of Arizona's fifteen County Superior Courts have, as of the present time, adopted either a Local Rule or, in one case, an Administrative Order, requiring arbitration in specified classes of cases, but the dollar amount in controversy which determines whether arbitration is required varies from county to county. The current limits or thresholds applicable in the

Superior Court for each county are as follows:[1]

Apache	$10,000
Cochise	$50,000
Coconino	$65,000
Gila	$25,000
Graham	$30,000
Greenlee	$1,000
La Paz	$25,000
Maricopa	$50,000
Mohave	$50,000
Navajo	Unknown
Pima	$50,000
Pinal	$40,000
Santa Cruz	$1,000
Yavapai	$65,000
Yuma	$50,000

4. *Procedure for Identifying Cases Subject to Compulsory Arbitration*. Under the former Rules, the only vehicle, and generally the first opportunity, for the Court to be called upon to decide whether a case was subject to compulsory arbitration was the Motion to Set and Certificate of Readiness required by former Rule V(b) of the Uniform Rules of Practice of the Superior Court, (which is now pre-2014 amendment Ariz. R. Civ. P. 38.1(a)) which was, in many cases, not filed until discovery in the action had been substantially completed. This was inconsistent with the goal of having arbitration function as a less expensive and more expeditious vehicle for resolving relatively minor controversies.

[Rule 72]

[1]See Rule 8, Apache County Superior Court Local Rules; Rule 11, Cochise County Superior Court Local Rules; Rule 16, Coconino County Superior Court Local Rules; Rule 13(A), Gila County Superior Court Local Rules; Rule 2.1, Graham County Superior Court Local Rules; Rule 7, Greenlee County Superior Court Local Rules; Rule 10, La Paz County Superior Court Local Rules; Rule 3.10, Maricopa County Superior Court Local Rules; Rule CV-6, Mohave County Superior Court Local Rules; Rule 4.2, Pima County Superior Court Local Rules; Rule 2.20, Pinal County Superior Court Local Rules; Rule 5, Santa Cruz County Superior Court Local Rules; Rule 10.3, Yavapai County Superior Court Local Rules; Rule 10, Yuma County Superior Court Local Rules.

The Coconino County Local Rule states that "the amount in controversy [may] not exceed the limit set in A.R.S. § 12-133, ..." Currently, the limit set by A.R.S. § 12-133 is $65,000.00.

The Superior Court, Navajo County has adopted its arbitration limit by Administrative Order rather than by a published Local Rule. As a result, practitioners are advised to check with the Superior Court, Navajo County re any amendments to the Administrative Order pertaining to arbitration limitations.

The 1991 amendments to the former Uniform Rules of Procedure for Arbitration, accordingly, added provisions to facilitate the earlier identification of cases subject to compulsory arbitration.

Under what is now Ariz. R. Civ. P. 72(e), a separate Certificate on Compulsory Arbitration must be filed at the time of the filing of the Complaint, stating whether or not the case is subject to compulsory arbitration. This requirement is repeated and reconfirmed in Ariz. R. Civ. P. 5(i). If the defendant disagrees with the assertions as to arbitrability in the Certificate on Compulsory Arbitration, a Controverting Certificate must be filed with the answer.

If the Certificate on Compulsory Arbitration asserts that the case is subject to compulsory arbitration, and no Controverting Certificate is filed, then the case is to be assigned to arbitration. (In fact, in that instance, the Maricopa County Superior Court requires the defendant to file and serve, and to provide to the Court Administrator, a certification of the defendant's agreement with the plaintiff's certificate. Rule 3.10(c), Maricopa County Superior Court Local Rules.) If the defendant files a Controverting Certificate, the issue of arbitrability is to be resolved by the Judge to whom the case is assigned. If the Certificate asserts that the matter is *not* subject to compulsory arbitration, and is not controverted, the regular procedures for processing civil cases apply. The Court may, on its own motion, however, determine that a case is subject to compulsory arbitration. Once a case is determined to be subject to compulsory arbitration, it is to be processed in accordance with Rules 72 through 77.

The parties or their attorneys are under a duty to amend a Certificate on Compulsory Arbitration or Controverting Certificate if they subsequently obtain information indicating that the Certificate or Controverting Certificate was incorrect when filed, or was correct when filed but is no longer accurate. Under Rule 72(e)(7), the Court may impose sanctions for an allegation as to arbitrability which was not made in good faith, or for the failure to seasonably amend a Certificate or Controverting Certificate.

5. *Arbitration by Agreement of Reference*. Rule 72(c) permits the parties to agree to submit a case to mandatory arbitration by filing an Agreement of Reference. Such a submission to arbitration may be made with respect to "any claim" and "at any time." Thus, an Agreement of Reference may be used for cases that have not yet been filed. In that circumstance, the Agreement of Reference is to define the issues to be resolved in arbitration, may contain stipulations as to facts, issues or defenses, and takes the place of pleadings in the case. Rule 72(c) provides that the filing of an Agreement of Reference in such a case ends the running

of the statute of limitations.

An Agreement of Reference is merely a particularized form of arbitration agreement. Presumably, where the parties submit a dispute to court-annexed arbitration under this Rule 72(c), the standards and procedures of Rules 72 through 77, rather than those set forth in either A.R.S. §§ 12-1501 *et seq.* or A.R.S. §§ 12-3001 *et seq.*, will apply.

6. *Authority of Arbitrator to Exceed Jurisdictional Limits.* Typically an action is made subject to compulsory arbitration because there has been a concession by the parties, or a determination by the Court, that the amount in controversy does not exceed the jurisdictional threshold for arbitration set by the applicable Local Rules. That concession or determination, however, is not binding on the arbitrator appointed to hear the matter. Under Rule 72(e)(6), if the arbitrator finds that the appropriate award to be made exceeds the limits established for mandatory arbitration, the arbitrator is to enter an award for the full amount found to be justified by the evidence.

7. *2014 Rule Amendments: Effective Date of Rule; Applicability.* On August 28, 2013, the Arizona Supreme Court adopted sweeping amendments to the case management and trial setting rules governing civil cases. The Promulgating Order specified such rules were adopted "effective on April 15, 2014 as to all cases filed on or after that date." *See,* August 28, 2013 Order entered in In the Matter of Petition to Amend Rules 16, 16.1, 26, 37, 38, 38.1, 72, 73, 74 and 77, Arizona Rules of Civil Procedure, R-13-0017. The applicability provision set forth in the Promulgating Order set up two procedural tracks for case management with the new rules governing cases file on or after April 15, 2014 and the "old" rules governing pre-April 15, 2014 cases.

To avoid any confusion potentially created by the two different tracks, the Court entered an order on November 14, 2013, amending the applicability provision. On November 27, 2013, the court entered a second order further refining the amended applicability provision. As a result, the Amendments are effective and applicable as follows:

"(1) The Amendments shall apply to all actions filed on or after April 15, 2014.

"(2) Beginning on April 15, 2014, the Amendments also shall apply to any action filed prior to April 15, 2014 (a "pending action"), unless one of the following events has occurred before that date:

(a) A party has filed a Motion to Set and Certificate of Readiness,

(b) The parties have filed a Proposed Scheduling Order, or

(c) The court has entered a Scheduling Order.

"(3) If, in a pending action, one of the preceding events has not occurred before April 15, 2014, the parties shall file a Joint Report and a Proposed Scheduling Order in accordance with the Amendments by June 30, 2014, or within 270 days after the commencement of the action, whichever date is later. Otherwise, the court will place the action on the Dismissal Calendar in accordance with the Amendments.

"(4) A trial court, in its discretion, may apply any of the Amendments to a case pending before April 15, 2014, even if the Amendments would not otherwise apply under paragraph (2) above. For example, if a party filed a Motion to Set and Certificate of Readiness before April 15, 2014, the trial judge may set the matter for a trial setting conference under amended Rule 16(f), rather than place the case on the active calendar under pre-amendment Rule 38.1(c).

"(5) Civil actions pending on the Inactive Calendar on April 15, 2014 shall be dismissed without prejudice on June 14, 2014, unless one of the actions set forth in subparts (1) - (4) of amended Rule 38.1(f) occurs June 14, 2014."

Rule 73. Appointment of arbitrators

Text of Rule 73(a) applicable to those cases filed before April 15, 2014 that are not subject to the conditions stated in the November 27, 2013 Amended Order Regarding Applicability Provision, in R-13-0017.

See also, text of Rule 73(a) applicable to cases filed on or after April 15, 2014 and applicable to those cases filed before April 15, 2014 that are subject to the conditions stated in the November 27, 2013, Amended Order Regarding Applicability Provision, in R-13-0017.

(a) Lawyer or Non-lawyer Arbitrators. The parties, by written stipulation and by written consent of the proposed arbitrator filed with the Clerk of the Superior Court with conformed copies to the Superior Court Administrator, may agree that the case be assigned to a single lawyer or non-lawyer arbitrator named in the stipulation. All other cases subject to arbitration shall be heard by an arbitrator selected as provided below.

Text of Rule 73(a) applicable to cases filed on or after April 15, 2014 and to those cases filed before April 15, 2014 that are subject to the conditions stated in the November 27, 2013, Amended Order Regarding Applicability Provision, in R-13-0017.

See also, text of Rule 73(a) applicable to those cases filed before April 15, 2014 that are not subject to the conditions stated in the November 27, 2013 Amended Order Regarding Applicability Provision, in R-13-0017.

(a) Lawyer or Non-lawyer Arbitrators. The parties, by written stipulation and by written consent of the proposed arbitrator filed with the clerk of the court with conformed copies to the court administrator, may agree that the case be assigned to a single lawyer or non-lawyer arbitrator named in the stipulation. All other cases subject to arbitration shall be heard by an arbitrator selected as provided below.

Text of Rule 73(b) applicable to those cases filed before April 15, 2014 that are not subject to the conditions stated in the November 27, 2013 Amended Order Regarding Applicability Provision, in R-13-0017.

See also, text of Rule 73(b) applicable to cases filed on or after April 15, 2014 and applicable to those cases filed before April 15, 2014 that are subject to the conditions stated in the November 27,

2013, Amended Order Regarding Applicability Provision, in R-13-0017.

(b) List of Arbitrators. Except as the parties may stipulate under the provisions of subdivision (a) of this Rule, the arbitrator shall be appointed by the Court Administrator or Superior Court Clerk from a list of persons, as provided by local rule, which shall include the following:

(1) all residents of the county in which the court is located who, for at least four years, have been active members of the State Bar of Arizona.

(2) other active and inactive members of the State Bar of Arizona residing anywhere in Arizona, and members of any other federal court or state bar, who have agreed to serve as arbitrators in the county where the action is pending.

Text of Rule 73(b) applicable to cases filed on or after April 15, 2014 and to those cases filed before April 15, 2014 that are subject to the conditions stated in the November 27, 2013, Amended Order Regarding Applicability Provision, in R-13-0017.

See also, text of Rule 73(b) applicable to those cases filed before April 15, 2014 that are not subject to the conditions stated in the November 27, 2013 Amended Order Regarding Applicability Provision, in R-13-0017.

(b) List of Arbitrators. Except as the parties may stipulate under the provisions of section (a) of this Rule, the arbitrator shall be appointed by the clerk of court or court administrator from a list of persons, as provided by local rule, which shall include the following:

(1) all residents of the county in which the court is located who, for at least four years, have been active members of the State Bar of Arizona.

(2) other active and inactive members of the State Bar of Arizona residing anywhere in Arizona, and members of any other federal court or state bar, who have agreed to serve as arbitrators in the county where the court is located.

Text of Rule 73(c) applicable to those cases filed before April 15, 2014 that are not subject to the conditions stated in the conditions stated in the November 27, 2013, Amended Order Regarding Applicability Provision, in R-13-0017.

See also, text of Rule 73(c) applicable to cases filed on or after April 15, 2014 and applicable to those cases filed before April 15, 2014 that are subject to the November 27, 2013 Amended Order Regarding Applicability Provision, in R-13-0017.

(c) Appointment of Arbitrator From List; Timing of As-

signment; Notice of Appointment; Right to Peremptory Strike.

(1) *Appointment of Arbitrator from List.* The Superior Court Administrator or Superior Court Clerk, under the supervision of the Presiding Judge or that judge's designee, shall prepare a list of arbitrators who may be designated as to the area of concentration, specialty or expertise. By means of a method of selecting names at random from the list of arbitrators, the Superior Court Administrator or Superior Court Clerk shall select and assign to each case one name from the list of arbitrators.

(2) *Timing of Assignment.* Assignment to arbitration shall take place as soon as is feasible after the answer and controverting certificate are filed and in any event no later than 120 days thereafter.

(3) *Notice of Appointment of Arbitrator.* The Superior Court Administrator or Superior Court Clerk shall promptly notify the parties of the name of the arbitrator by mailing written notice to the parties and the arbitrator. The notice from the Superior Court Administrator or Superior Court Clerk shall advise the parties that the time periods specified for placing a case on the inactive calendar in Rule 38.1(d) of these rules shall apply.

(4) *Right to Peremptory Strike.* Within ten days after the mailing of such notice, or within ten days after the appearance of a party, if the arbitrator was appointed before that party appeared, either side may peremptorily strike the assigned arbitrator and request that a new arbitrator be appointed. Each side shall have the right to only one peremptory strike in any one case. A motion for recusal or motion to strike for cause shall toll the time to exercise a peremptory strike.

Text of Rule 73(c) applicable to cases filed on or after April 15, 2014 and to those cases filed before April 15, 2014 that are subject to the conditions stated in the November 27, 2013, Amended Order Regarding Applicability Provision, in R-13-0017.

See also, text of Rule 73(c) applicable to those cases filed before April 15, 2014 that are not subject to the conditions stated in the November 27, 2013 Amended Order Regarding Applicability Provision, in R-13-0017.

(c) Appointment of Arbitrator From List; Timing of Appointment; Notice of Appointment; Right to Peremptory Strike.

(1) *Appointment of Arbitrator from List.* The clerk of court or court administrator, under the supervision of the presiding judge or that judge's designee, shall prepare a list of arbitra-

tors who may be designated by their area of concentration, specialty or expertise. The clerk of court or court administrator shall randomly select and then assign to each case one arbitrator from the list.

(2) *Timing of Appointment.* Appointment of an arbitrator to a case shall occur no later than 120 days after an answer is filed.

(3) *Notice of Appointment of Arbitrator.* The clerk of court or court administrator shall promptly mail written notice of the arbitrator selected to the parties and the arbitrator. The written notice shall advise the parties that the time periods specified in Rule 38.1(f) of these Rules for placing a case on the Dismissal Calendar shall apply.

(4) *Right to Peremptory Strike.* Within ten days after the mailing of the notice of appointment of arbitrator, or within ten days after the appearance of a party, if the arbitrator was appointed before that party appeared, either side may peremptorily strike the assigned arbitrator and request that a new arbitrator be appointed. Each side shall have the right to only one peremptory strike in any one case. A motion for recusal or motion to strike for cause shall toll the time to exercise a peremptory strike.

Text of Rule 73(d) applicable to those cases filed before April 15, 2014 that are not subject to the conditions stated in the November 27, 2013 Amended Order Regarding Applicability Provision, in R-13-0017.

See also, text of Rule 73(d) applicable to cases filed on or after April 15, 2014 and applicable to those cases filed before April 15, 2014 that are subject to the conditions stated in the November 27, 2013, Amended Order Regarding Applicability Provision, in R-13-0017.

(d) Disqualifications and Excuses.

(1) Upon written motion and a finding of good cause therefor, the Presiding Judge or that judge's designee may excuse a lawyer from the list.

(2) An arbitrator, after selection, may be disqualified from serving in a particular assigned case upon motion of either party to the judge assigned to the case, for an ethical conflict of interest or other good cause shown as defined in A.R.S. §§ 12-409 or 21-211, submitted in accord with the procedure set out in Rule 42(f)(2) of these Rules.

(3) An arbitrator may be excused by the presiding judge or that judge's designee from serving in a particular assigned case upon a showing by the arbitrator that such individual has completed contested hearings and ruled as an arbitrator pursuant to these Rules in two or more cases assigned during the

current calendar year or shall be excused on a detailed showing that such individual has an ethical conflict of interest or other good cause shown as defined in A.R.S. §§ 12-409 or 21-211, submitted in accord with the procedure set out in Rule 42(f)(2) of these Rules.

(4) After an arbitrator has been disqualified or excused under these rules, a new arbitrator shall be appointed in accordance with the procedure set forth in subdivision (c) of this Rule.

Rule 73 added Oct. 10, 2000, effective Dec. 1, 2000. Amended September 5, 2007, effective January 1, 2008.

Text of Rule 73(d) applicable to cases filed on or after April 15, 2014 and to those cases filed before April 15, 2014 that are subject to the conditions stated in the November 27, 2013, Amended Order Regarding Applicability Provision, in R-13-0017.

See also, text of Rule 73(d) applicable to those cases filed before April 15, 2014 that are not subject to the conditions stated in the November 27, 2013 Amended Order Regarding Applicability Provision, in R-13-0017.

(d) Disqualifications and Excuses.

(1) Upon written motion and a finding of good cause therefor, the presiding judge or that judge's designee may excuse a lawyer from the list of arbitrators.

(2) An arbitrator, after appointment, may be disqualified from serving in a particular assigned case upon motion of either party to the judge assigned to the case, for an ethical conflict of interest or other good cause shown as defined in A.R.S. §§ 12-409 or 21-211, submitted in accord with the procedure set out in Rule 42(f)(2) of these Rules.

(3) An arbitrator may be excused by the presiding judge or that judge's designee from serving in a particular assigned case upon a showing by the arbitrator that such individual has completed contested hearings and ruled as an arbitrator pursuant to these Rules in two or more cases assigned during the current calendar year and shall be excused on a detailed showing that such individual has an ethical conflict of interest or other good cause shown as defined in A.R.S. §§ 12-409 or 21-211, submitted in accord with the procedure set out in Rule 42(f)(2) of these Rules.

(4) After an arbitrator has been disqualified or excused from a particular case under this section (d), a new arbitrator shall be appointed in accordance with the procedure set forth in section (c) of this Rule.

Rule 73 added Oct. 10, 2000, effective Dec. 1, 2000. Amended September 5, 2007, effective January 1, 2008; Aug. 28, 2013, effective April 15, 2014, subject to conditions of Order No. R-13-0017.

HISTORICAL NOTES

[2014 Amendments]

[Rule 73] Arizona Supreme Court Order No. R-13-0017, issued Aug. 28, 2013, provided that the amendments of the order would be "effective on April 15, 2014 as to all cases filed on or after that date." The applicability provision of Order No. R-13-0017 was amended on Nov. 14, 2013, and subsequently amended on Nov. 27, 2013 to provide:

(1) The Amendments shall apply to all actions filed on or after April 15, 2014.

(2) Beginning on April 15, 2014, the Amendments also shall apply to any action filed prior to April 15, 2014 (a "pending action"), unless one of the following events has occurred before that date:
  (a) A party has filed a Motion to Set and Certificate of Readiness,
  (b) The parties have filed a Proposed Scheduling Order, or
  (c) The court has entered a Scheduling Order.

(3) If, in a pending action, one of the preceding events has not occurred before April 15, 2014, the parties shall file a Joint Report and a Proposed Scheduling Order in accordance with the Amendments by June 30, 2014, or within 270 days after the commencement of the action, whichever date is later. Otherwise, the court will place the action on the Dismissal Calendar in accordance with the Amendments.

(4) A trial court, in its discretion, may apply any of the Amendments to a case pending before April 15, 2014, even if the Amendments would not otherwise apply under paragraph (2) above. For example, if a party filed a Motion to Set and Certificate of Readiness before April 15, 2014, the trial judge may set the matter for a trial setting conference under amended Rule 16(f), rather than place the case on the active calendar under pre-amendment Rule 38.1(c).

(5) Civil actions pending on the Inactive Calendar on April 15, 2014 shall be dismissed without prejudice on June 14, 2014, unless one of the actions set forth in subparts (1) - (4) of amended Rule 38.1(f) occurs before June 14, 2014, subject to conditions of Order No. R-13-0017.

STATE BAR COMMITTEE NOTES

2000 Promulgation and Amendment

As part of the effort to consolidate formerly separate sets of procedural rules into either the Arizona Rules of Civil Procedure or the Rules of the Arizona Supreme Court, the Uniform Rules of Procedure for Arbitration, as recently amended, were effectively transferred to the Arizona Rules of Civil Procedure and placed in a Section of those Rules which had formerly been concerned with appeals in civil cases. The Rules in that Section IX had been abrogated effective January 1, 1978, at the time of the adoption of the Arizona Rules of Civil Appellate Procedure. In the 2000 amendments, Section IX of the Rules was renamed "Section IX. Compulsory Arbitration."

New Rule 73, with certain revisions, contains the provisions formerly contained in Rule 2 of the Uniform Rules of Procedure for Arbitration dealing with the process for selection of the arbitrator to be appointed in a case subject to compulsory arbitration. A State Bar Committee Note to that former Rule 2 had pointed out that it is the obligation of all qualified lawyers to serve as arbitrators and that only exceptional circumstances should justify removal of an attorney from the list from which arbitrators are selected.

2007 Amendments

[Rule 73(d)] [renumbered as 73(c)(3) in the 2007 amendments] The provisions of former Rule 2(d) of the Uniform Rules of Procedure for Arbitration (now new Rule 73(d)) [renumbered in 2007 as 73(c)(3)] were amended in 2000 to conform to the holding of *Martinez v. Binsfield*, 196 Ariz. 466, 999 P.2d 810 (2000), and to make clear that the time periods set forth in Rule 38.1 of these Rules [former Uniform Rule V] apply in every civil case including those subject to compulsory arbitration.

[Rule 73(e)] [renumbered as 73(d) in the 2007 amendments] The provisions of former Rule 2(e)(3) of the Uniform Rules of Procedure for Arbitration (now new Rule 73(e)(3)) [renumbered in 2007 as 73(d)(3)] were edited in 2000 to render them gender neutral.

AUTHORS' COMMENTS

Analysis

1. *Scope and Purpose of Rule.* Rule 73(a) defines the procedures for selecting the individual who will serve as the arbitrator for the dispute. It was promulgated in 2000, and essentially contains the provisions formerly located in Rule 2 of the Uniform Rules of Procedure for Arbitration. The former Uniform Rules of Procedure for Arbitration were amended in 1991 to provide that matters assigned to compulsory arbitration are now to be heard by a single arbitrator rather than a panel of three arbitrators. The 1991 amendments also streamlined the procedures for selecting that arbitrator. Under the procedure in the Rules before these amendments, it was not uncommon for it to take longer to resolve a matter through compulsory arbitration than through a trial.

2. *Comparison With Federal Rule.* The Federal Rules of Civil Procedure do not have a provision that corresponds to ARCP 73.

3. *Selection of Arbitrators; From List.* Rule 73 defines the procedures for selecting the individual who will serve as the arbitrator for the dispute. Former Rule 2 of the Uniform Rules of Procedure for Arbitration was amended in 1991 to provide that matters assigned to compulsory arbitration were to be heard by a single arbitrator rather than by a panel of three arbitrators. The 1991 amendments also streamlined the procedures for selecting that arbitrator. Former Rule 2 was transferred to the Arizona Rules of Civil Procedure as a new Rule 73, effective December 1, 2000. Contemporaneously, the Rule was amended to increase the

pool of attorneys from which arbitrators can be selected, and to further facilitate the process of securing the expeditious appointment of an arbitrator in cases subject to compulsory arbitration.

Generally, and as otherwise provided by local rule, arbitrators are selected from a list of potential arbitrators maintained by the Clerk or, if there is one, by the Court Administrator of the Superior Court in each county. At a minimum, that list is to be comprised of the following two components: (1) all residents of the county in which the Superior Court sits who have been active members of the State Bar of Arizona for at least four years; and (2) other active and inactive members of the State Bar of Arizona residing anywhere in Arizona, together with members of the Bar of any other state, and members of the Bar of any federal court who have indicated to the Court their agreement to serve as court-appointed arbitrators. A lawyer may be excused from the list only by "written motion" to the Presiding Judge of the Superior Court, or that judge's designee, involved and upon a finding by the Presiding Judge of good cause for excusing the individual from service as a potential arbitrator. *See*, Ariz.R.Civ.P. 73(d)(1).

A.R.S. § 12-133(C) provides that each Superior Court is to maintain a "list of qualified arbitrators within its jurisdiction who have agreed to serve as arbitrators." This does not signify, however, that the Superior Court can only appoint arbitrators from that list of volunteers. *Scheehle v. Justices of the Supreme Court of the State of Arizona*, 211 Ariz. 282, 120 P.3d 1092 (2005). Resolving a question certified to it by the United States Court of Appeals for the Ninth Circuit, the Arizona Supreme Court had held that this statute does not authorize requiring attorneys to serve as arbitrators in court-annexed mandatory arbitration programs. *Scheehle v. Justices of Supreme Court of State of Arizona*, 203 Ariz. 520, 57 P.3d 379 (2002). In a subsequent decision, the Court held that, as part of its constitutional function of regulating an integrated judiciary, the Court has the inherent power to regulate the practice of law, and that includes the power and authority to require lawyers to serve as arbitrators in court-annexed arbitration programs. *Scheehle v. Justices of the Supreme Court of the State of Arizona*, 211 Ariz. 282, 120 P.3d 1092 (2005).

4. *Procedure for Appointing Arbitrator From List.* Once a matter has been assigned to compulsory arbitration, the Clerk or Court Administrator selects a potential arbitrator at random from the list of persons available, and notifies the parties of the identity of the individual thus selected. Within ten (10) days after the mailing of that notice, or within ten (10) days after a party appears if an arbitrator has been appointed prior to that appearance, either side may peremptorily strike the arbitrator

assigned. If that occurs, the appointment procedure commences anew, and in the same manner, but each side may only exercise one peremptory strike of a potential arbitrator.

It is, of course, perfectly possible that both sides to the controversy may exercise their peremptory strike directed to the initial potential arbitrator selected. If that occurs, because each side may exercise the right of peremptory strike only once, the individual next selected by the Clerk or Court Administrator from the arbitration list will be the arbitrator appointed to serve. If for some reason that individual is unacceptable to both sides, the parties retain the option to stipulate to a different arbitrator. Former Rule 2 of the Uniform Rules of Procedure for Arbitration provided that such a stipulation could only be entered into up to thirty (30) days after an appointment of an arbitrator, but that limitation was eliminated when the Rule was transferred to the Arizona Rules of Civil Procedure.

5. *Notice of Appointment of Arbitrator*. Once the procedures of Rule 73(c) have been completed, and an arbitrator has been selected, the Clerk or Court Administrator is to notify the parties in writing of the assignment of the case to that arbitrator. Under the Rules, the date on which the arbitrator is appointed dictates the time frames within which the arbitration hearing must be conducted, and the date by which an award must be made.

The notice is also to advise the parties that the time periods specified for placing a case on the Inactive Calendar in Ariz.R.Civ.P. 38.1(d) apply notwithstanding that the case is subject to mandatory arbitration. See *Martinez v. Binsfield*, 196 Ariz. 466, 999 P.2d 810 (2000). The former requirement that the Clerk or Court Administrator also furnish the parties with a form by which they could stipulate to waive the right to appeal from the arbitration award, if they desire, was eliminated in 2000. Under Ariz.R.Civ.P. 77(e), the parties do retain the right to stipulate in writing, at any time before the entry of an award, that the award or other final disposition will be binding.

6. *Disqualifications and Excuses; Procedure for Filling Vacancies; Peremptory Strikes.* Rule 73(d)(3) provides that an individual may be excused from serving in a particular case, by the Presiding Judge or that Judge's designee, upon a showing that the individual has completed contested hearings and ruled as an arbitrator in two or more cases assigned during the current calendar year, or upon a detailed showing that the individual has an ethical conflict of interest, or other good cause as defined in A.R.S. § 12-409 or 21-211. An individual also may seek to be excused from the list of potential arbitrators itself by written application to the Presiding Judge and a showing of good cause.

An arbitrator, once appointed, may only be disqualified for an ethical conflict of interest or other good cause as defined in A.R.S. § 12-409 or A.R.S. § 21-211. An application for such disqualification must be made to the Judge to whom the case is assigned, and must comply with the procedural requirements for challenging a judge for cause set forth in Ariz.R.Civ.P. 42(f)(2).

The former Uniform Rules of Procedure for Arbitration did not specify the relationship, if any, between the right to a peremptory challenge of a potential arbitrator and the right to disqualify an appointed arbitrator for cause, and had no provision for raising the potential disqualification issue before the selection of the eventual arbitrator. This placed a party who believed there were grounds for disqualifying a selected arbitrator in an anomalous situation. If the Clerk or Court Administrator selected from the list of arbitrators an individual whom one party believed was subject to a disqualification motion, that party could wait to see if the other side exercised a peremptory challenge to that individual, or could exercise its own peremptory challenge. If that party did so, however, it did not get another. If it did not, and the other side also did not, that party ran the risk that the Court would not agree with the claimed grounds for disqualification in question.

That situation was dealt with by an amendment to former Rule 2 of the Uniform Rules of Procedure for Arbitration effected contemporaneously with its transfer to the Arizona Rules of Civil Procedure. Ariz.R.Civ.P. 73(c)(4) now provides that the filing of a motion for recusal tolls the time in which a party must exercise its right to a peremptory strike. That suggests that, if the Clerk or Court Administrator initially selects as the arbitrator an individual that a party believes is subject to disqualification, the motion to disqualify can, and should, be brought at that time. If the motion is unsuccessful, the moving party retains the right to a peremptory strike of the individual selected.

If an arbitrator, once selected, is disqualified or excused from service, the vacancy is to be filled by repeating the procedures for the initial selection of an arbitrator set forth in Rule 73(c). The formulation of Rule 72(c)(4) implies that, in that situation, the parties retain their right to one peremptory challenge of an arbitrator candidate.

7. *Selection of Arbitrator; By Stipulation.* Rule 73(a) permits the parties by written stipulation, and with the written consent of the proposed arbitrator, to agree the case may be assigned to the lawyer or non-lawyer named in the stipulation, who will conduct the arbitration governed by Rules 72 through 77. The stipulated agreement must name the proposed arbitrator, must contain the written consent of the proposed arbitrator and must be filed with the Clerk of the Superior Court with conformed cop-

ies delivered to the Superior Court Administrator.

The limitation in former Rule 2(a) of the Uniform Rules of Procedure for Arbitration that such a stipulation could only be filed up to thirty (30) days after an arbitrator was appointed was eliminated in 2000. Permitting the parties to stipulate to an arbitrator even after one has been appointed provides an avenue for relief in the situation where pursuit of the normal appointment procedures results in the selection of an arbitrator who is, for some reason, unacceptable to both sides to the controversy.

8. *2014 Rule Amendments: Effective Date and Applicability*. On August 28, 2013, the Arizona Supreme Court adopted sweeping amendments to the case management and trial setting rules governing civil cases. The Promulgating Order specified such rules were adopted "effective on April 15, 2014 as to all cases filed on or after that date." *See,* August 28, 2013 Order entered in In the Matter of Petition to Amend Rules 16, 16.1, 26, 37, 38, 38.1, 72, 73, 74 and 77, Arizona Rules of Civil Procedure, R-13-0017. The applicability provision set forth in the Promulgating Order set up two procedural tracks for case management with the new rules governing cases file on or after April 15, 2014 and the "old" rules governing pre-April 15, 2014 cases.

To avoid any confusion potentially created by the two different tracks, the Court entered an order on November 14, 2013, amending the applicability provision. On November 27, 2013, the court entered a second order further refining the amended applicability provision. As a result, the Amendments are effective and applicable as follows:

> "(1) The Amendments shall apply to all actions filed on or after April 15, 2014.
>
> "(2) Beginning on April 15, 2014, the Amendments also shall apply to any action filed prior to April 15, 2014 (a "pending action"), unless one of the following events has occurred before that date:
>
> (a) A party has filed a Motion to Set and Certificate of Readiness,
>
> (b) The parties have filed a Proposed Scheduling Order, or
>
> (c) The court has entered a Scheduling Order.
>
> "(3) If, in a pending action, one of the preceding events has not occurred before April 15, 2014, the parties shall file a Joint Report and a Proposed Scheduling Order in accordance with the Amendments by June 30, 2014, or within 270 days after the commencement of the action, whichever date is later. Otherwise, the court will place the action on the Dismissal Calendar in accordance with the Amendments.
>
> "(4) A trial court, in its discretion, may apply any of the Amendments to a case pending before April 15, 2014, even if the Amendments would not otherwise apply under paragraph (2) above. For example, if a party filed a Motion to Set and Certificate of Readiness before April 15, 2014, the trial judge may set the matter for a trial setting conference under amended Rule 16(f), rather than

place the case on the active calendar under pre-amendment Rule 38.1(c).

"(5) Civil actions pending on the Inactive Calendar on April 15, 2014 shall be dismissed without prejudice on June 14, 2014, unless one of the actions set forth in subparts (1) - (4) of amended Rule 38.1(f) occurs before June 14, 2014."

Rule 74. Powers of arbitrator; scheduling of arbitration hearing; permitted rulings by arbitrator; time for filing summary judgment motion; receipt of court file; settlement of cases; offer of judgment

(a) Powers of Arbitrator. The arbitrator shall have the power to administer oaths or affirmations to witnesses, to determine the admissibility of evidence, and to decide the law and the facts of the case submitted.

(b) Scheduling of Arbitration Hearing. The arbitrator shall fix a time for hearing, which hearing shall commence not fewer than 60 days, nor more than 120 days after the appointment of the arbitrator. The arbitrator shall, unless waived by the parties, give at least 30 days' notice in writing to the parties of the time and place of the hearing. Subject to Rule 38.1 of these rules, the arbitrator may shorten or extend these time periods for good cause. No hearings shall be held on Saturdays, Sundays, legal holidays, or evenings, except upon agreement by counsel for all parties and the arbitrator.

(c) Rulings by Arbitrator.

Text of Rule 74(c)(1) applicable to those cases filed before April 15, 2014 that are not subject to the conditions stated in the November 27, 2013 Amended Order Regarding Applicability Provision, in R-13-0017.

See also, text of Rule 74(c)(1) applicable to cases filed on or after April 15, 2014 and applicable to those cases filed before April 15, 2014 that are subject to the conditions stated in the November 27, 2013, Amended Order Regarding Applicability Provision, in R-13-0017.

(1) *Authorized Rulings.* After a case has been assigned to an arbitrator, the arbitrator shall make all legal rulings, including rulings on motions, except:

(A) motions to continue on the inactive calendar or otherwise extend time allowed under Rule 38.1 of these rules;

(B) motions to consolidate cases under Rule 42 of these rules;

(C) motions to dismiss;

(D) motions to withdraw as attorney of record under Rule 5.1 of these rules;

(E) motions for summary judgment that, if granted, would dispose of the entire case as to any party; or

(F) motions for sanctions under Rule 68 of these rules.

Text of Rule 74(c)(1) applicable to cases filed on or after April 15, 2014 and to those cases filed before April 15, 2014 that are subject to the conditions stated in the November 27, 2013, Amended Order Regarding Applicability Provision, in R-13-0017.

See also, text of Rule 74(c)(1) applicable to those cases filed before April 15, 2014 that are not subject to the conditions stated in the November 27, 2013 Amended Order Regarding Applicability Provision, in R-13-0017.

(c) Rulings by Arbitrator.

(1) *Authorized Rulings*. After a case has been assigned to an arbitrator, the arbitrator shall make all legal rulings, including rulings on motions, except:

(A) motions to continue on the Dismissal Calendar or otherwise extend time allowed under Rule 38.1 of these Rules;

(B) motions to consolidate cases under Rule 42 of these Rules;

(C) motions to dismiss;

(D) motions to withdraw as attorney of record under Rule 5.1 of these rules; or

(E) motions for summary judgment that, if granted, would dispose of the entire case as to any party.

(2) *Procedure*. The parties shall serve upon the arbitrator copies of documents requiring the arbitrator's consideration. Telephonic motions and testimony are acceptable and appropriate.

(3) *Discovery Motions*. In ruling on motions pertaining to discovery, the arbitrator shall consider that the purpose of compulsory arbitration is to provide for the efficient and inexpensive handling of small claims and shall limit discovery whenever appropriate to insure compliance with the purposes of compulsory arbitration.

(4) *Interlocutory Appeal of Discovery Ruling*. If an arbitrator makes a discovery ruling requiring the disclosure of matters that a party claims are privileged or otherwise protected from disclosure under applicable law, the party may appeal the ruling by filing a motion with the assigned trial judge within ten days after the arbitrator transmits the ruling to the parties. No party shall be required to respond to the motion unless ordered to do so by the court. No such motion, however, shall be granted without the court first providing an opportunity for response. The arbitrator's ruling shall be subject to de novo review by the court. If the court finds that the motion was frivolous or was

filed for the purpose of delay or harassment, the court shall impose sanctions on the party filing the motion, including an award of reasonable attorneys' fees incurred in responding to the motion. The time for conducting an arbitration hearing set forth in Rule 74(b) shall be tolled during the pendency of any such motion.

(d) Time for Filing Summary Judgment Motion. If a motion for summary judgment is filed, the original shall be filed no fewer than 20 days prior to the date for hearing. A copy of the motion shall be served upon the arbitrator and trial judge. If the court finds the motion is frivolous or was filed for the purpose of delay or harassment, the court shall impose sanctions on the party filing the motion, including an award of reasonable attorneys' fees incurred in responding to the motion. The time for conducting an arbitration shall be tolled during the pendency of any such motion.

(e) Receipt of Court File. If the arbitrator believes that the file contains materials needed to conduct the arbitration hearing, the arbitrator shall, within four days prior to the date of the hearing, sign for and receive from the Superior Court Clerk the original superior court file. If the clerk maintains an electronic court record, the arbitrator shall have access to the original if available, or to a certified copy of the file either by print-outs of said documents or on alternative media. The clerk may deliver the documents electronically to any arbitrator who files a consent, either traditionally or electronically. Alternatively, the arbitrator may order the parties to provide the arbitrator with those pleadings and other documents the arbitrator deems necessary to complete the arbitration hearing.

(f) Settlement of Cases Assigned to Arbitration. If the parties to a case assigned to arbitration settle, they shall file with the court an appropriate stipulation and order of dismissal and shall mail a copy to the arbitrator. Upon entry of the order the arbitration is terminated.

(g) Offer of Judgment. Any party to an action either subject to compulsory arbitration under A.R.S. § 12-133 and these rules or referred to arbitration by Agreement of Reference may serve upon any other party an offer of judgment pursuant to Rule 68.

Added Oct. 10, 2000, effective Dec. 1, 2000. Amended Sept. 18, 2006, effective Jan. 1, 2007; Sept. 5, 2007, effective Jan. 1, 2008; Sept. 1, 2011, effective Jan. 1, 2012; Aug. 28, 2013, effective April 15, 2014, subject to conditions of Order No. R-13-0017.

HISTORICAL NOTES

[2014 Amendments]

[Rule 74] Arizona Supreme Court Order No. R-13-0017, issued Aug. 28, 2013, provided that the amendments of the order would be "effective on April 15, 2014 as to all cases filed on or after that date." The applicability provision of

Order No. R-13-0017 was amended on Nov. 14, 2013, and subsequently amended on Nov. 27, 2013 to provide:

(1) The Amendments shall apply to all actions filed on or after April 15, 2014.

(2) Beginning on April 15, 2014, the Amendments also shall apply to any action filed prior to April 15, 2014 (a "pending action"), unless one of the following events has occurred before that date:
   (a) A party has filed a Motion to Set and Certificate of Readiness,
   (b) The parties have filed a Proposed Scheduling Order, or
   (c) The court has entered a Scheduling Order.

(3) If, in a pending action, one of the preceding events has not occurred before April 15, 2014, the parties shall file a Joint Report and a Proposed Scheduling Order in accordance with the Amendments by June 30, 2014, or within 270 days after the commencement of the action, whichever date is later. Otherwise, the court will place the action on the Dismissal Calendar in accordance with the Amendments.

(4) A trial court, in its discretion, may apply any of the Amendments to a case pending before April 15, 2014, even if the Amendments would not otherwise apply under paragraph (2) above. For example, if a party filed a Motion to Set and Certificate of Readiness before April 15, 2014, the trial judge may set the matter for a trial setting conference under amended Rule 16(f), rather than place the case on the active calendar under pre-amendment Rule 38.1(c).

(5) Civil actions pending on the Inactive Calendar on April 15, 2014 shall be dismissed without prejudice on June 14, 2014, unless one of the actions set forth in subparts (1) - (4) of amended Rule 38.1(f) occurs before June 14, 2014.

STATE BAR COMMITTEE NOTES

2000 Promulgation and Amendment

As part of the effort to consolidate formerly separate sets of procedural rules into either the Arizona Rules of Civil Procedure or the Rules of the Arizona Supreme Court, the Uniform Rules of Procedure for Arbitration, as recently amended, were effectively transferred to the Arizona Rules of Civil Procedure and placed in a Section of those Rules which had formerly been concerned with appeals in civil cases. The Rules in that Section IX had been abrogated effective January 1, 1978, at the time of the adoption of the Arizona Rules of Civil Appellate Procedure. In the 2000 amendments, Section IX of the Rules was renamed "Section IX. Compulsory Arbitration."

New Rule 74(a) [renumbered in 2007 as 74(c)], with some revisions, contains most of the provisions formerly contained in Rule 3 of the Uniform Rules of Procedure for Arbitration. The provision in former Rule 3 concerning the continuing applicability of the Arizona Rules of Civil Procedure was incorporated into new Rule 72(a). The provision of former Rule 3 concerning the legal status of rulings made by the arbitrator in cases where an appeal is taken from the arbitration award was incorporated into new Rule 76(c) [renumbered in 2007 as Rule 77(c)]. Similarly, the provision of former Rule 3 concerning the legal status of discovery conducted while the case was assigned to arbitration was incorporated into new Rule 76(c) [renumbered in 2007 as Rule 77(c)].

Rules 74(b) through 74(k) contain the provisions of former Rules 4(a) through (j), respectively, of the Uniform Rules of Procedure for Arbitration. [Rule 74(d) was renumbered in 2007 as Rule 74(a), and Rule 74(i) was renumbered as Rule 74(e). Rules 74(c), (e) through (h), (j), and (k) were moved and renumbered as Rules 75 (a) and (c) through (g).]

[Rule 74(a)] [renumbered in 2007 as Rule 74(c)] Former Rule 3 of the

Uniform Rules of Procedure for Arbitration (now new Rule 74(a)) [renumbered in 2007 as Rule 74(c)] was amended in 2000 to make clear that, after a case has been assigned to an arbitrator, the arbitrator hears and rules on all motions except those described in the Rule. Under Rule 74(a) [renumbered in 2007 as Rule 74(c)], an arbitrator has the authority to enter an award or other final disposition which becomes binding if not timely appealed. Rule 74(a) [renumbered in 2007 as Rule 74(c) provides further, however, that an arbitrator is not authorized to enter a judgment including a default judgment, a stipulated judgment, or a judgment of dismissal.

[Rule 74(b)] [Former Rule 4(a) of the Uniform Rules of Procedure for Arbitration (now new Rule 74(b)) was amended in 2000 to provide that an arbitrator's authority to shorten or lengthen the time periods is subject to Rule 38.1 of these Rules.

Rule 74(h)] [renumbered in 2007 as Rule 75(f)] Former Rule 4(g) of the Uniform Rules of Procedure for Arbitration (now new Rule 74(h)) [renumbered in 2007 as Rule 75(f)] was amended in 2000 to require that the arbitrator refer all proceedings concerning any defaulted defendant(s) to the trial court. The amendment alters former Rule 4(g), which had permitted an arbitrator to assess, as part of the award, damages against any defaulted defendant(s).

[Rule 74(i)] [renumbered in 2007 as Rule 74(e)] Former Rule 4(h) of the Uniform Rules of Procedure for Arbitration (now new Rule 74(i)) [renumbered in 2007 as Rule 74(e)] was amended in 2000 to provide the arbitrator with the option of reviewing the original court file or directing the parties to provide the arbitrator with those pleadings and other documents the arbitrator deems necessary to the arbitration hearing. As a result of this amendment, the arbitrator is no longer required to obtain the original file from the court.

2007 Amendments

[Rule 74(c)] Rule 74(c)(1) (formerly Rule 74(a)) expands the types of motions on which the arbitrator may not rule to include motions to dismiss, motions to withdraw as attorney of record, and dispositive motions for summary judgment. New Rule 74(c)(4) creates an appeal to the trial judge from a ruling by the arbitrator on discovery motions when a party believes the information sought to be discovered is privileged or otherwise protected by law.

[Rule 74(e)] Rule 74(e) (formerly Rule 74(i)) was amended to allow the clerk of the court to deliver the record to the arbitrator in an electronic format, with consent of the arbitrator, or to allow the arbitrator access to an original electronic court record either by print-outs of the documents or on alternative media.

AUTHORS' COMMENTS

Analysis

10. 2014 Rule Amendments: Effective Date and Applicability.

1. *Scope and Purpose of Rule*. Ariz.R.Civ.P. 74, as extensively amended in 2008, contains the provisions delineating the role and powers of the arbitrator, and governing the scheduling of the arbitration hearing. It contains the provisions of former Rules 74(a) and 74(i). The remaining provisions of former Rule 74 were made part of current Ariz.R.Civ.P. 75.

In 2012, the Court amended Ariz.R.Civ.P. 68 to clarify the procedure by which offers of judgment may be made in arbitration cases, and to adopt corresponding amendments to Rule 74. Although not expressly stated in the amendments to Rule 68, the corresponding amendment to Rule 74(g) reveals that the 2012 amendment to Rule 68 is intended to apply to compulsory arbitration cases under A.R.S. § 12-133 and these rules as well as cases referred to arbitration by Agreement of Arbitration.

2. *Comparison With Federal Rule*. The Federal Rules of Civil Procedure do not have a provision that corresponds to ARCP 74.

3. *Role of Arbitrator*. The pre-hearing processing of a case assigned to mandatory arbitration is primarily governed by what are now Rules 72 through 77 of the Arizona Rules of Civil Procedure. Rule 72(a) provides that all other provisions of the Arizona Rules of Civil Procedure, where not inconsistent, are applicable to cases subject to mandatory arbitration.

The assigned arbitrator functions as a surrogate trial judge, albeit with circumscribed powers, is to be served with copies of all pleadings, motions and other papers that require the arbitrator's consideration, and makes most legal rulings. Rulings on issues of law made by the arbitrator are not binding on the court or the parties on appeal.

4. *Powers of Arbitrator; Limitations*. In setting and conducting the arbitration hearing, the assigned arbitrator continues to function as a surrogate trial judge. The arbitrator schedules and presides over the arbitration hearing, has the power to administer oaths and affirmations, rules on the admissibility of evidence, and renders a decision based on the evidence submitted and the applicable law.

The arbitrator rules on all motions, except those motions specifically reserved for decision by the assigned trial judge. The 2008 and 2012 amendments expanded the types of motions on which the arbitrator does not have authority to rule. As set forth in amended Rule 74(c)(1), these motions are as follows:

(1) motions to continue the case on the inactive calendar or otherwise extend time allowed under Ariz.R.Civ.P.

38.1;

(2) motions to consolidate cases under Ariz.R.Civ.P. 42;
(3) motions to dismiss;
(4) motions by counsel to withdraw as attorney of record brought under Ariz.R.Civ.P. 5.1;
(5) motions for summary judgment that, if granted, would dispose of the entire case as to any party; and
(6) motions for sanctions under Rule 68.

With respect to Rule 68 sanction motions, on August 28, 2013, Rule 74(c)(1)(F) was deleted effective April 15, 2014, as to all cases filed on or after April 15, 2014 and to those cases subject to the November 27, 2013 Amended Order Regarding Applicability Provision in R-13-0017. Thus, with respect to those cases to which the 2014 case management/trial setting amendments apply, an arbitrator will no longer be authorized to rule on motions for Rule 68 sanctions if the case was filed on or after April 15, 2014. With respect to those cases to which the 2014 case management/ trial setting amendments do not apply, the arbitration rules continue to permit arbitrators to decide Rule 68 motions for sanctions.

Certain of these limitations on the arbitrator's authority are consistent with the Supreme Court's decision in *Martinez v. Binsfield*, 196 Ariz. 466, 999 P.2d 810 (2000). In that decision, the Court held that the time limitations specified in former Rule V of the Uniform Rules of Practice of the Superior Court (now Ariz.R.Civ.P. 38.1) were fully applicable to civil cases subject to mandatory arbitration. The Court also held that, while former Rule 3 of the Uniform Rules of Procedure for Arbitration provided that, once the case was assigned to arbitration, the arbitrator was to make all legal rulings, including rulings on motions, that authority extended to legal rulings in aid of arbitration, and did not include the authority to continue cases on the Inactive Calendar, or to otherwise extend the deadlines set forth in former Rule V of the Uniform Rules of Practice.

5. *Scheduling of Arbitration Hearings*. The arbitrator sets the schedule for the conduct of the arbitration hearing. Under amended Rule 74(b), the hearing must commence not less than 60 days and not more than 120 days after the arbitrator is appointed. the parties are to be given at least 30 days written notice of the time and place for the hearing, unless the parties waive that requirement. Hearings are not to be conducted on Saturdays, Sundays, or legal holidays, or during the evenings, unless the parties and the arbitrator agree to such scheduling.

The arbitrator presides at the hearing, administers oaths and rules on the admissibility of evidence. Subpoenas for the attendance of witnesses are issued by the Clerk of the Court.

6. *Discovery Rulings; Interlocutory Appeals.* The arbitrator makes all rulings on matters pertaining to the conduct of discovery while the case is assigned to arbitration. Rule 74(c)(3) cautions arbitrators, in considering discovery issues, to take into account that the purpose of arbitration is to provide a less expensive and more efficient method for resolving disputes and to limit discovery, where appropriate, to serve that end. If an appeal is taken from the arbitration award, any discovery taken while the matter was assigned to arbitration may be used in proceedings on appeal in the Superior Court.

The 2008 amendments added a new Rule 74(c)(4) which authorizes interlocutory appeals from an arbitrator's decision on a discovery matter that requires the disclosure of matters that a party claims are privileged or otherwise protected from disclosure. The aggrieved party may appeal such a ruling by filing a motion with the assigned trial judge within ten (10) days after the arbitrator transmits the challenged ruling to the parties. No party is required to respond to the motion unless the trial judge orders that a response be made, but no such motion shall be granted without providing an opportunity for a response. If the trial court finds that the motion was frivolous or was filed for the purpose of delay or harassment, it must impose sanctions upon the party filing it, including an award of attorneys' fees incurred in responding to it. The time for conducting the arbitration hearing is tolled while any such motion is pending.

7. *Summary Judgment Motions.* As discussed in Section 4, *supra*, under Rule 74(c)(1)(E), the arbitrator does not have authority to rule on motions for summary judgment which, if granted, would dispose of the entire case as to any party. Such motions are to be heard and decided by the assigned trial judge, and must be filed no later than 20 days prior to the date set for the arbitration hearing. *See*, Rule 74(d). A copy of any such motion must be served upon the trial judge and the arbitrator. The time for conducting the arbitration hearing is to be tolled while the motion is pending. If the trial judge finds that the motion is frivolous, or was filed for the purpose of delay or harassment, it must impose sanctions upon the party filing it, including an award of attorneys' fees incurred in responding to it.

8. Offer of Judgment. In 2012, the Court amended Ariz.R.Civ.P. 68 to clarify the procedure by which offers of judgment may be made in arbitration cases, and to adopt corresponding amendments to Rule 74. Although not expressly stated in the amendments to Rule 68, the corresponding amendment to Rule 74(g) reveals that the 2012 amendment to Rule 68 is intended to apply to compulsory arbitration cases under A.R.S. § 12-133 and these rules as well as cases referred to arbitration by Agreement of Arbitration.

As a consequence of the 2012 amendments, Rule 68(a) includes a specific provision which prohibits making a Rule 68 offer of judgment in arbitration cases during the period of time "beginning 25 days before the arbitration hearing and ending upon the date of the filing of any notice of appeal of an award pursuant to Rule 77(a)." The rule, as amended, does not expressly prohibit making a Rule 68 offer of judgment at any other time. Rule 68(h), as amended, includes a provision addressing the effective period of an offer made in an arbitration case. As such, in a case subject to arbitration, a Rule 68 "offer that has not previously expired shall expire at 5:00 p.m. on the fifth day before the arbitration hearing."

Under Rule 68(g), as amended in 2012, in arbitration cases, the determination whether a sanction should be imposed is made with reference to the judgment ultimately entered, regardless of whether the ultimate judgment was entered on the award itself or entered on the award after an appeal pursuant to Rule 77.

9. *Settlement of Cases Assigned to Arbitration.* In most cases, the settlement of a civil cases contemplates the filing of a stipulation for the entry of an order dismissing the case with prejudice, and the subsequent entry of such an order. Under Rule 74(f), added by the 2008 amendments, if the parties to a case assigned to arbitration settle, they are to file an appropriate stipulation an order with the court, and mail a copy to the arbitrator. The arbitration terminates upon entry of an order of dismissal pursuant to the settlement.

10. *2014 Rule Amendments: Effective Date and Applicability.* On August 28, 2013, the Arizona Supreme Court adopted sweeping amendments to the case management and trial setting rules governing civil cases. The Promulgating Order specified such rules were adopted "effective on April 15, 2014 as to all cases filed on or after that date." *See,* August 28, 2013 Order entered in In the Matter of Petition to Amend Rules 16, 16.1, 26, 37, 38, 38.1, 72, 73, 74 and 77, Arizona Rules of Civil Procedure, R-13-0017. The applicability provision set forth in the Promulgating Order set up two procedural tracks for case management with the new rules governing cases file on or after April 15, 2014 and the "old" rules governing pre-April 15, 2014 cases.

To avoid any confusion potentially created by the two different tracks, the Court entered an order on November 14, 2013, amending the applicability provision. On November 27, 2013, the court entered a second order further refining the amended applicability provision. As a result, the Amendments are effective and applicable as follows:

"(1) The Amendments shall apply to all actions filed on or after April 15, 2014.

"(2) Beginning on April 15, 2014, the Amendments also shall apply to any action filed prior to April 15, 2014 (a "pending action"), unless one of the following events has occurred before that date:

(a) A party has filed a Motion to Set and Certificate of Readiness,

(b) The parties have filed a Proposed Scheduling Order, or

(c) The court has entered a Scheduling Order.

"(3) If, in a pending action, one of the preceding events has not occurred before April 15, 2014, the parties shall file a Joint Report and a Proposed Scheduling Order in accordance with the Amendments by June 30, 2014, or within 270 days after the commencement of the action, whichever date is later. Otherwise, the court will place the action on the Dismissal Calendar in accordance with the Amendments.

"(4) A trial court, in its discretion, may apply any of the Amendments to a case pending before April 15, 2014, even if the Amendments would not otherwise apply under paragraph (2) above. For example, if a party filed a Motion to Set and Certificate of Readiness before April 15, 2014, the trial judge may set the matter for a trial setting conference under amended Rule 16(f), rather than place the case on the active calendar under pre-amendment Rule 38.1(c).

"(5) Civil actions pending on the Inactive Calendar on April 15, 2014 shall be dismissed without prejudice on June 14, 2014, unless one of the actions set forth in subparts (1) - (4) of amended Rule 38.1(f) occurs before June 14, 2014."

Rule 75. Hearing procedures

(a) Issuance of Subpoenas. The Clerk of the Superior Court shall issue subpoenas in matters assigned to an arbitrator, and the subpoenas shall be served and enforceable as provided by law.

(b) Initial Disclosure. Within 30 days of service of an answer, the plaintiff and answering defendant shall make the initial disclosure required by Rule 26.1.

(c) Pre-hearing Statement. Not less than ten days before the date set for hearing, counsel who will present the case at the arbitration hearing shall, after conferring, prepare and submit to the arbitrator a joint written pre-hearing statement which shall contain a brief statement of the nature of the claim or defense, a list of witnesses and exhibits, a brief description of the subject matter of the testimony of each witness who will be called to testify, and an estimate as to the length of time that will be required for the arbitration hearing. In preparing the pre-hearing statement required by this Rule, counsel shall consider that the purpose of compulsory arbitration is to provide for the efficient and inexpensive handling of claims. Agreement on facts and issues is encouraged. No witness or exhibit shall be used at the hearing other than those listed and exchanged, except for good cause shown or upon written agreement of the parties.

Motions potentially dispositive of the case shall be set for a hearing, and lawyers shall notify their respective clients of the time and place of hearing, encouraging them to attend.

(d) Evidence. The Arizona Rules of Evidence shall apply to arbitration hearings.

(e) Documentary Evidence. The Arbitrator shall admit into evidence without further proof the following documents, if relevant, and if listed in the pre-hearing statement, unless it is shown that any such document is not what it appears to be and the objection is set forth in the pre-hearing statement.

(1) Hospital bills on the official letterhead or billhead of the hospital, when dated and itemized.

(2) Bills of doctors and dentists, when dated and containing a statement showing the date of each visit and the charge therefor.

(3) Bills of registered nurses, licensed practical nurses, or physical therapists, when dated and containing an itemized statement of the days and hours of service and the charges therefor.

(4) Bills for medicine, eyeglasses, prosthetic devices, medical belts or similar items, when dated and itemized.

(5) Property repair bills or estimates, when dated and itemized, setting forth the charges for labor and material. In the case of an estimate, the party intending to offer the estimate shall serve upon the adverse party a copy of the estimate, a statement indicating whether or not the property was repaired, and, if so, whether the estimated repairs were made in full or in part and the cost thereof.

(6) Testimony of any witness given in a deposition taken pursuant to these Rules, whether or not such witness is available to appear in person.

(7) A sworn written statement by an expert, other than a doctor's medical report, whether or not such expert is available to appear in person, provided that such statement is signed by the expert and contains a summary of the expert's qualifications. If any such statement contains the expert's opinions, it shall also state the grounds for each such opinion, including a summary of the facts upon which each opinion is based.

(8) In actions involving personal injury, doctors' medical reports may be offered and received in evidence without further proof, and may be given the weight to which the arbitrator deems them entitled, provided that a copy of said report has been filed and served upon the adverse party at least twenty days prior to the date of the hearing. The adverse party may not object to the admissibility of the report unless the adverse party files and serves written objection thereto within ten days from the receipt of said copy stating the objections, and the grounds therefor, that will be made if the report is offered at the time of the hearing.

(9) Records of regularly conducted business activity as contemplated by Rule 803(6) of the Arizona Rules of Evidence.

(10) A sworn statement of any witness, other than an expert witness, who is listed in the pre-hearing statement, whether or not such witness is available to appear in person.

(f) Assessment of Damages Against Defaulted Parties. In cases involving more than one defendant, where a default has been entered against one or more, but less than all, of the defendants prior to the arbitration hearing, the arbitrator shall refer all further proceedings involving the defaulted defendant(s) to the trial court. The arbitrator shall continue to serve and shall proceed with the arbitration for the remaining parties.

(g) Record of Proceedings. The arbitrator shall not be required to make a record of the proceedings. If any party desires the presence of a reporter, such party shall pay for and provide the reporter. The charges of the reporter shall not be considered costs in the case.

(h) Failure to Appear or Participate in Good Faith at Hearing. Failure to appear at a hearing or to participate in good faith at a hearing which has been set in accordance with subparagraph (b) of this Rule shall constitute a waiver of the right to appeal absent a showing of good cause. If the judge finds that further proceedings before the arbitrator are appropriate, the case shall be remanded to the assigned arbitrator.

Added September 5, 2007, effective January 1, 2008.

STATE BAR COMMITTEE NOTES

2007 Amendments

[Rule 75] New Rule 75 represents a reorganization of the rules and includes provisions contained in former Rule 74, paragraphs (c), (e) through (h), (j), and (k).

AUTHORS' COMMENTS

Analysis

1. Scope and Purpose of Rule.
2. Comparison With Federal Rule.
3. Pre-Hearing Statements.
4. Parties in Default.
5. Admissibility of Evidence.
6. Record of Proceedings.
7. Failure to Appear at Hearing; Failure to Participate in Good Faith.

1. *Scope and Purpose of Rule.* This nominally new Rule, promulgated as part of the 2008 amendments, contains the provisions governing the conduct of the actual arbitration hearing. In actuality, however, it represents primarily simply a reorganization of the provisions of what was formerly Rule 74. Former Rules 74(c), (e), (f), (g), (h), (j) and (k) became, without substantive change, then new Rules 75(a), (c), (d), (e), (f), (g), and (h), respectively. Rule 75(b) provides that, in cases assigned to arbitration, the plaintiff and any answering defendant will make the initial disclosures called for by Ariz.R.Civ.P. 26.1, within thirty (30) days after service of that answer.

2. *Comparison With Federal Rule.* The Federal Rules of Civil Procedure do not have a provision that corresponds to ARCP 75.

3. *Pre-Hearing Statements.* Rule 75(c) requires that counsel who will present the case at the arbitration hearing must confer, and prepare and submit to the arbitrator, a written joint pre-hearing statement. That pre-hearing statement, which now must

be submitted not less than ten (10) days before the date set for the arbitration hearing, must contain the following:

(1) a brief statement of the nature of all claims or defenses;

(2) a list of witnesses and exhibits;

(3) a brief description of the subject matter of the testimony of each witness who will be called to testify; and,

(4) an estimate as to the length of time that will be required for the arbitration hearing.

A witness or exhibit not identified in the pre-hearing statement may not be used at the hearing except for good cause or upon written agreement of the parties.

Under Rule 75(e), a relaxed standard of admissibility will apply to certain specified categories of exhibits, if they are listed in the pre-hearing statement and no foundational objection is stated in the pre-hearing statement.

4. *Admissibility of Evidence.* Rule 75(d) makes the Arizona Rules of Evidence applicable to arbitration hearings. The Rules, however, specifically relax the standards for admissibility of certain specified categories of documents.

Under Rule 75(e), the following categories of exhibits are to be admitted into evidence, if they are relevant and are listed in the pre-hearing statement:

1. Dated and itemized hospital bills on the hospital's official letterhead.
2. Dated and itemized bills from doctors and dentists.
3. Dated and itemized bills of registered nurses, licensed practical nurses or physical therapists.
4. Dated and itemized bills for medicine, eyeglasses, prosthetic devices, and similar items.
5. Dated and itemized property repair bills and estimates.
6. The sworn testimony of a witness in a deposition conducted pursuant to the Arizona Rules of Civil Procedure, even if the witness is available to testify in person.
7. A sworn statement signed by an expert, other than a doctor's medical report, which states the grounds for the expert's opinions, if any, and includes a summary of the facts upon which the opinion is based, even if the expert is available to testify in person.
8. Records of regularly conducted business activity as described in Rule 803(6) of the Arizona Rules of Evidence.
9. A sworn statement of any lay witness, whether or not the witness is available to appear in person.

A separate provision, Rule 75(e)(8), governs doctors' medical reports and provides that they may be received in evidence, provided that a copy has been served upon the adverse party at least twenty (20) days before the hearing and no objection thereto is made.

The relaxed standard for admissibility will not apply, however, if it is shown that the document offered is not what it appears to be *and* an appropriate objection to the document was listed in the pre-hearing statement.

5. *Parties in Default*. Former Rule 4(g) of the now abrogated Uniform Rules of Procedure for Arbitration provided that in multi-defendant cases, if a default had been entered against one or more defendants the arbitrator could, as part of the arbitration award, assess damages against the defaulted defendant(s). That authority was eliminated when the arbitration rules were effectively transferred to the Arizona Rules of Civil Procedure.

Ariz. R. Civ. P. 75(f) now governs this situation and provides that the arbitrator is to refer all further proceedings involving the defaulted defendant(s) to the Superior Court. The arbitrator is to continue to serve and proceed with the arbitration for the remaining parties.

6. *Record of Proceedings*. The arbitrator is not required to make a record of the proceedings at the arbitration hearing. If a party desires to have a court reporter record the proceedings, that party must arrange for the court reporter and pay any applicable charges. Court reporter's charges, moreover, are not taxable as costs in the case.

7. *Failure to Appear at Hearing; Failure to Participate in Good Faith*. Former Rule 7(a) of the Uniform Rules of Procedure for Arbitration (now Ariz.R.Civ.P. 77(a)) was amended in 1990 to effectively overrule the anomalous result in *Chevron U.S.A., Inc. v. Thompson*, 145 Ariz. 85, 699 P.2d 1316 (Ct. App. Div. 2 1985), which held that a party need not participate in the arbitration hearing in order to prosecute an appeal. The 1991 amendments to the former Uniform Rules of Procedure for Arbitration added a new Rule 4(j), now Ariz.R.Civ.P. 75(h), which confirmed and extended that change.

Under Rule 75(h), the failure to appear at the arbitration hearing or the failure to participate in the hearing in good faith constitutes a waiver of the right to appeal absent a showing of good cause. If the judge finds such good cause, and concludes that further proceedings before the arbitrator are required, the case is to be remanded to the assigned arbitrator.

Rules 75(h) and 77(a) do not impermissibly abridge the statutory right to appeal from arbitration awards or the constitutional right to trial by jury. *Graf v. Whitaker*, 192 Ariz. 403, 966 P.2d 1007 (Ct. App. Div. 1 1998). While the Rules do not quantify the degree of participation required, when read together, they require more than minimal participation in arbitration proceedings; both require a party to participate in good faith in order to satisfy the spirit of the arbitration requirement. *Romer-Pollis v. Ada*, 223 Ariz. 300, 222 P.3d 916 (Ct. App. Div. 1 2009); *Graf v. Whitaker*, 192 Ariz. 403, 966 P.2d 1007 (Ct. App. Div. 1 1998). Whether a party has participated in good faith "is a factual determination to be made on a case-by-case basis." *Romer-Pollis v. Ada*, 223 Ariz. 300, 222 P.3d 916 (Ct. App. Div. 1 2009), citing *Lane v. City of Tempe*, 202 Ariz. 306, 44 P.3d 986 (2002).

Nonetheless, Rules 77(a) and 75(h) do not unconditionally require a personal appearance at the arbitration hearing by a party who wishes to preserve the right to appeal; appearances can be made through counsel. *Lane v. City of Tempe*, 202 Ariz. 306, 44 P.3d 986 (2002) (It is not the case that the physical appearance of a party at the arbitration hearing is never required.); *Sabori v. Kuhn*, 199 Ariz. 330, 18 P.3d 124 (Ct. App. Div. 1 2001).

In most cases, what constitutes good faith participation is a matter of fairness and common sense. *Lane v. City of Tempe*, 202 Ariz. 306, 44 P.3d 986 (2002). A trial court's determination that a party has waived the right to appeal by failing to participate at the arbitration hearing is reviewed on appeal for an abuse of discretion. *Lane v. City of Tempe*, 202 Ariz. 306, 44 P.3d 986 (2002).

Where a party has been subjected to, and participated in, prehearing discovery, and the opposing party had notice and an opportunity to subpoena that party to appear, a party's failure to personally appear for the arbitration hearing will not operate to waive the right to appeal. *Lane v. City of Tempe*, 202 Ariz. 306, 44 P.3d 986 (2002) Similarly, where a party cannot appear personally at the time set by the arbitrator for the conduct of the hearing, and offers to appear and be cross-examined telephonically, it is an abuse of discretion for the arbitrator to deny that opportunity, and for the trial court to find a waiver of the right to appeal on that basis. *Sabori v. Kuhn*, 199 Ariz. 330, 18 P.3d 124 (Ct. App. Div. 1 2001).

Rule 76. Notice of disposition; failure of arbitrator to file award; judgment; dismissal; compensation of arbitrators

(a) Notice of Decision and Filing of Award or Other Final Disposition. Within ten days after completion of the hearing, the arbitrator shall:

(1) render a decision;

(2) return the original superior court file by messenger or certified mail to the Superior Court Clerk;

(3) notify the parties that their exhibits are available for retrieval;

(4) notify the parties of the decision in writing (a letter to the parties or their counsel shall suffice); and

(5) file the notice of decision with the court.

Within ten days of the notice of decision, either party may submit to the arbitrator a proposed form of award or other final disposition, including any form of award for attorneys' fees and costs whether arising out of an offer of judgment, sanctions or otherwise, an affidavit in support of attorneys' fees if such fees are recoverable, and a verified statement of costs. Within five days of receipt of the foregoing, the opposing party may file objections. Within ten days of receipt of the objections, the arbitrator shall pass upon the objections and file one signed original award or other final disposition with the Clerk of the Superior Court, and on the same day shall mail or deliver copies thereof to all parties or their counsel.

(b) Failure of Arbitrator to File Award. Unless a formal award or stipulation for entry of another form of relief is filed with the court within 50 days from the date of filing the notice of decision, the notice of decision shall constitute the award of the arbitrator.

(c) Judgment. Upon expiration of the time for appeal, if no appeal has been filed, any party may file to have judgment entered upon the award.

(d) Dismissal upon Failure to Apply for Entry of Judgment. If no application for entry of judgment has been filed within 120 days from the date of the filing of the notice of decision, and no appeal is pending, the case shall be dismissed.

(e) Referral of Case to Judge. If the arbitrator does not file an award or other final disposition with the Clerk of the Superior Court within 145 days after the first appointment of an arbitrator, the Superior Court Clerk or the Court Administrator shall refer the case to the judge to whom the case has been assigned for appropriate action.

(f) Amount of Compensation for Arbitrators. An arbitrator assigned to serve in a case subject to the provisions of Rules 72 through 77 of these Rules shall receive as compensation for services in each case a fee not to exceed the amount allowed by A.R.S. § 12-133(G) per day for each day, or part thereof, necessarily expended in the hearing of the case. For purposes of this Rule 76(f), "hearing" means any fact-finding proceeding, or oral argument that results in the filing of an award or other final disposition, or at which the parties agree to settle and stipulate to dismiss the case. The fee to be paid in each county shall be decided by a majority vote of the judges thereof and the amount that is decided upon shall be incorporated into a superior court order filed with the Clerk of the Supreme Court, and a copy thereof shall be filed with the Clerk of the Superior Court of the applicable county. When more than one case arising out of the same transaction is heard at the same hearing or hearings, it shall be considered as one case insofar as compensation of the arbitrator is concerned.

(g) Payment of Compensation. The arbitrator shall not be entitled to receive the compensation prescribed in subparagraph (f) of this Rule until after an award or other final disposition is filed with the Clerk of the Superior Court; or, if the parties agree to settle and stipulate to dismiss the case at a proceeding before the arbitrator, until after the case has been dismissed.

Added as Rule 75 Oct. 10, 2000, effective Dec. 1, 2000. Renumbered as 76 and amended September 5, 2007, effective January 1, 2008.

STATE BAR COMMITTEE NOTES

2000 Promulgation and Amendment

As part of the effort to consolidate formerly separate sets of procedural rules into either the Arizona Rules of Civil Procedure or the Rules of the Arizona Supreme Court, the Uniform Rules of Procedure for Arbitration, as recently amended, were effectively transferred to the Arizona Rules of Civil Procedure and placed in a Section of those Rules which had formerly been concerned with appeals in civil cases. The rules in that Section had been abrogated effective January 1, 1978, at the time of the adoption of the Arizona Rules of Civil Appellate Procedure. In the 2000 amendments, Section IX of the Rules was renamed "Section IX. Compulsory Arbitration."

New Rules 75(a) through (c) [Rule 75(a) was renumbered in 2007 as Rule 76(a); Rules 75(b) and (c) were abrogated] contain the provisions formerly contained in Rule 5(a) through (c) of the Uniform Rules of Procedure for Arbitration. Former Rule 5(d) was simply eliminated as duplicative and unnecessary.

New Rules 75(d) and (e) [renumbered in 2007 as Rules 76(f) and (g)], contain, as amended, the provision formerly contained in Rules 6(a) and (b) of the Uniform Rules of Procedure for Arbitration.

[Rule 75(a)] [renumbered in 2007 as Rule 76(a)] Former Rule 5(a), now new Rule 75(a) [renumbered in 2007 as Rule 76(a)], was amended and restructured in 2000 to more clearly state the arbitrator's duties and responsibilities following the arbitration hearing.

[Rule 75(d)] [renumbered in 2007 as Rule 76(f)], Former Rule 6(a), now new Rule 75(d) [renumbered in 2007 as Rule 76(f)], was amended in 2000 to make clear that assigned arbitrators are entitled to the compensation provided for in A.R.S. § 12-133(G) when their work results in an award or other final disposition, or a settlement, without a traditional "hearing" or fact-finding proceeding.

AUTHORS' COMMENTS

Analysis

1. *Scope and Purpose of Rule.* Rule 76 was originally promulgated in 2000 as Rule 75 and was essentially a composite of the provisions of Rules 5 and 6 of the former Uniform Rules of Procedure for Arbitration. Then Rule 75 was renumbered as Rule 76 and amended in some important particulars in 2008. Rule 76 now prescribes the procedure for the issuance and finalization of the arbitrator's award or other final disposition of the matter, and also addresses the issue of the arbitrator's compensation and when it is payable.

2. *Comparison With Federal Rule.* The Federal Rules of Civil Procedure do not have a provision that corresponds to ARCP 76.

3. *Procedure for Settling and Filing Arbitration Award.* Rule 76(a) provides that within ten (10) days after the completion of the hearing, the arbitrator must accomplish the following steps:

(1) render a decision;

(2) return the original court file to the Clerk of the Superior Court by messenger or by certified mail;

(3) notify the parties that the exhibits received in evidence at the arbitration hearing are available to be retrieved;

(4) notify the parties in writing of the arbitrator's decision; and

(5) file a notice of decision with the court.

Rule 76(a)(4) specifies that the written notice to the parties of the decision may be in the form of a letter to the parties or their counsel.

Rule 76(a) provides that within ten (10) days of the notice of the arbitrator's decision, the prevailing party is to submit a proposed form of award or other final disposition, including any form of award for attorneys' fees and costs regardless of the basis for claiming them, an affidavit in support of any claim for attorneys' fees, and a verified statement of costs. *Aqua Management, Inc. v. Abdeen*, 224 Ariz. 91, 227 P.3d 498 (Ct. App. Div. 1 2010) (under Rule 76(a), the term "arbitration award" includes any award of attorney's fees and costs); *Decola v. Freyer*, 198 Ariz. 28, 6 P.3d 333 (Ct. App. Div. 1 2000), (interpreting former Rule 5(a) of the Uniform Rules of Procedure for Arbitration). While the Rule does not specify that date from which this ten-day period begins to run, the language of the Rule suggests that it runs from the date upon which the notice of decision is *issued*, rather than from the date of its receipt.

The opposing party may file any objections to the proposed award, the request for attorneys' fees, the supporting affidavit and/or the verified statement of costs within five (5) days of the *receipt* of them. Within ten (10) days of the *receipt* of such objections, the arbitrator is to pass upon them, and file with the Clerk of the Superior Court a signed original award or other final disposition. A copy of the final award or other final disposition is to be mailed to the parties by the arbitrator on the same day it is filed. *Decola v. Freyer*, 198 Ariz. 28, 6 P.3d 333 (Ct. App. Div. 1 2000), (interpreting former Rule 5(a) of the Uniform Rules of Procedure for Arbitration). Under the time frames set forth in the Rule, this entire process can take 25-35 days following the completion of the arbitration hearing itself.

As amended in 2008, Rules 76(b) through (e) spell out how an arbitration case is to be finalized if the arbitrator and/or the parties do not strictly adhere to the procedures contemplated in Rule 76(a). Under Rule 76(b), unless a formal award or stipulation for some other form of relief is filed with the court within 50 days from the date the arbitrator's notice of decision is filed, then that notice of decision is to constitute the award of the arbitrator.

Rule 76(c) specifies that, upon the expiration of the time for appeal, if no such appeal has been taken, then any party may file to have judgment entered upon the arbitration award.

Rule 76(d) provides that, if no application for entry of judgment has been filed within 120 days of the filing of the notice of decision, then the case is to be dismissed. (This suggests that a party must take affirmative steps to have a judgment entered on the award and the failure to do so within 120 days of the notice of decision makes the case subject to dismissal. A provision of the statute which authorizes the mandatory arbitration program, specifically A.R.S. § 12-133(E), provides that the court is to "enter the award in its record of judgments" and that: "The award has the effect of a judgment upon the parties unless reversed on appeal.")

4. *Time Limit for Arbitrator's Award.* Rule 76(e) contemplates that the arbitrator's award or other final disposition will be made and filed within 145 days after the arbitrator is appointed. At that point, if an award or other final disposition has not been made and filed, the Clerk or Court Administrator is to refer the case to the Judge to whom it is assigned for appropriate action. As a practical matter, this time limitation could prove very difficult to meet unless where the hearing is not scheduled as early as is possible and/or where multiple hearing days are required to complete the proceedings.

Under Ariz.R.Civ.P. 74(b), the arbitration hearing is to be conducted no later than one hundred and twenty (120) days after the arbitrator is appointed. Under Ariz.R.Civ.P. 76(e), the case is to be referred back to the judge to whom it is assigned if the arbitrator fails to file an award or other final disposition within 145 days after an arbitrator is first appointed. Given that the process prescribed by Rule 76(a) for finalizing an award after the arbitrator issues a decision can take 25-35 days, an arbitrator who schedules the hearing for a date during the latter stages of the period permitted under Rule 74(b) will either be unable, as a practical matter, to meet the overall 145 day limitation contemplated by Rule 76(e), or may have to reach a decision and/or resolve objections to a proposed form of award and/or applications for attorneys' fees and statements of costs in less than the time permitted by Rule 76(a). This will almost certainly be the case if multiple days are required to complete the arbitration hearing. Presumably, the Judge to whom the case is assigned can and will take such circumstances into account in deciding what, if any action, is appropriate when an award or other final disposition is not filed by the arbitrator within 145 days after the arbitrator's appointment.

5. *Effect of Award.* Under Rule 76(c), if an appeal is not taken from the arbitration award in the manner and within the time frames specified in Ariz.R.Civ.P. 77, then either party may file to have judgment entered upon the arbitration award. Rule 76(d) then provides that, if no application for entry of judgment has been filed within 120 days of the filing of the notice of decision, then the case is to be dismissed. (This suggests that a party must take affirmative steps to have a judgment entered on the award and the failure to do so within 120 days of the notice of decision makes the case subject to dismissal. A provision of the statute which authorizes the mandatory arbitration program, specifically A.R.S. § 12-133(E), provides that the court is to "enter the award in its record of judgments" and that: "The award has the effect of a judgment upon the parties unless reversed on appeal.")

In addition, the filing of the final arbitration award operates to divest the arbitrator of jurisdiction over the matter and revest it in the Superior *Varga v. Hebern*, 116 Ariz. 539, 570 P.2d 226 (Ct. App. Div. 1 1977), disagreed with on other grounds, *Riendeau v. Wal-Mart Stores, Inc.*, 223 Ariz. 540, 225 P.3d 597 (Ct. App. Div. 1 2010). An arbitrator has no jurisdiction to consider a motion for new trial, and the filing of such a motion will not operate to extend the time for taking an appeal. *Diggs Realty and Ins. v. Pertile*, 114 Ariz. 85, 559 P.2d 205 (Ct. App. Div. 2 1977).

6. *Compensation of Arbitrators*. The arbitrator is compensated at a fixed daily fee for each day, or part of a day, necessarily expended in the hearing of the case. Rule 76(f) specifies that, for purposes of computing the compensation to be paid to the arbitrator, "hearing" includes "any fact-finding proceeding, or oral argument that results in the filing of an award or other final disposition, or at which the parties agree to settle and stipulate to dismiss the case."

The daily fee is to be set by a majority vote of the Judges of the Superior Court in each county, but may not exceed the statutory maximum of $140.00 per day established in A.R.S. § 12-133(G). The arbitrator is not entitled to receive the compensation due until after an award or other final disposition is filed with the Clerk of the Superior Court, or, in the case where the arbitrator has presided over a proceeding at which the parties agree to settle and dismiss the case, until after the case has been dismissed. A.R.S. § 12-133(G) provides that the arbitrator's compensation is not to be taxed as costs in the case. Both a separate section of that statute, A.R.S. § 12-133(I), however, as well as Ariz.R.Civ.P. 77(f), contemplate that the compensation paid the arbitrator may be taxed against the appellant, under specified circumstances, as costs on appeal.

A 2009 amendment to Rule 45 of the Rules of the Supreme Court added a new subpart (a)(4) which provides that an active member of the State Bar of Arizona who serves as an arbitrator under Rule 73 "is eligible for two hours of continuing legal education activity credit," but any such credit is "in lieu of financial compensation" otherwise to be paid such arbitrators. The amended Rule provides that such a credit is to be claimed as self-study, but does not address how this is to be accounted for, if at all, in determining what costs are to be taxed in the arbitration which provided the right to claim it.

Rule 77. Right of appeal

Text of Rule 77(a) applicable to those cases filed before April 15, 2014 that are not subject to the conditions stated in the November 27, 2013 Amended Order Regarding Applicability Provision, in R-13-0017.

See also, text of Rule 77(b) applicable to cases filed on or after April 15, 2014 and applicable to those cases filed before April 15, 2014 that are subject to the conditions stated in the November 27, 2013, Amended Order Regarding Applicability Provision, in R-13-0017.

(a) Notice of Appeal. Any party who appears and participates in the arbitration proceedings may appeal from the award or other final disposition by filing a notice of appeal with the Clerk of the Superior Court within 20 days after the filing of the award or 20 days after the date upon which the notice of decision becomes an award under Rule 76(b), whichever occurs first. The notice of appeal shall be entitled "Appeal from Arbitration and Motion to Set for Trial" and shall request that the case be set for trial in the Superior Court and state whether a jury trial is requested and the estimated length of trial. The Appeal from Arbitration and Motion to Set for Trial shall serve in place of a Motion to Set and Certificate of Readiness under Rule 38.1(a) of these Rules.

Text of Rule 77(a) applicable to cases filed on or after April 15, 2014 and to those cases filed before April 15, 2014 that are subject to the conditions stated in the November 27, 2013, Amended Order Regarding Applicability Provision, in R-13-0017.

See also, text of Rule 77(a) applicable to those cases filed before April 15, 2014 that are not subject to the conditions stated in the November 27, 2013 Amended Order Regarding Applicability Provision, in R-13-0017.

(a) Notice of Appeal. Any party who appears and participates in the arbitration proceedings may appeal from the award or other final disposition by filing a notice of appeal with the clerk of the superior court within 20 days after the award is filed or 20 days after the date upon which the notice of decision becomes an award under Rule 76(b), whichever occurs first. The notice of appeal shall be entitled "Appeal from Arbitration and Motion to Set for Trial" and shall request that the case be set for trial in the Superior Court and state whether a jury trial is requested and the estimated length of trial.

Text of Rule 77(b) applicable to those cases filed before April 15, 2014 that are not subject to the conditions stated in the November 27, 2013 Amended Order Regarding Applicability Provision, in R-13-0017.

See also, text of Rule 77(b) applicable to cases filed on or after April 15, 2014 and applicable to those cases filed before April 15, 2014 that are subject to the conditions stated in the November 27, 2013, Amended Order Regarding Applicability Provision, in R-13-0017.

(b) Deposit on Appeal. At the time of filing the notice of appeal, and as a condition of filing, the appellant shall deposit with the Clerk of the Superior Court a sum equal to one hearing day's compensation of the arbitrator, but not exceeding ten percent of the amount in controversy. If the court finds that the appellant is unable to make such deposit by reason of lack of funds, the court shall allow the filing of the appeal without deposit.

Text of Rule 77(b) applicable to cases filed on or after April 15, 2014 and to those cases filed before April 15, 2014 that are subject to the conditions stated in the November 27, 2013, Amended Order Regarding Applicability Provision, in R-13-0017.

See also, text of Rule 77(b) applicable to those cases filed before April 15, 2014 that are not subject to the conditions stated in the November 27, 2013 Amended Order Regarding Applicability Provision, in R-13-0017.

(b) Deposit on Appeal. At the time of ling the notice of appeal, and as a condition of filing, the appellant shall deposit with the Clerk of the Superior Court a sum equal to one hearing day's compensation of the arbitrator, but not exceeding ten percent of the amount in controversy. If the court finds that the appellant is unable to make such deposit by reason of lack of funds, the court shall allow the filing of the appeal without deposit.

(c) Appeals *De Novo*. All appeals shall be *de novo* on law and facts. Any legal rulings and factual findings made by the arbitrator shall not be binding on the court or the parties, and any discovery had while the case was assigned to arbitration may be used in the superior court proceeding.

(d) [Deleted].

(e) Waiver of Right to Appeal. At any time prior to the entry of an award or other final disposition by the arbitrator, the parties may stipulate in writing that the award or other final disposition so entered shall be binding upon the parties. No appeal or collateral attack upon the award or other final disposition may be thereafter taken except as allowed by A.R.S. § 12-1501, et seq.

(f) Costs and Fees on Appeal. The deposit provided for in subparagraph (b) of this Rule shall be refunded to the appellant if the judgment on the trial *de novo* is at least twenty-three percent (23%) more favorable than the monetary relief, or more favorable than the other type of relief, granted by the arbitration award or other final disposition. If the judgment on the trial *de novo* is not more favorable by at least twenty-three percent (23%) than the monetary relief, or more favorable than the other relief, granted by the arbitration award or other final disposition, the court shall order the deposit to be used to pay, or that the appellant pay if the deposit is insufficient, the following costs and fees unless the court finds on motion that the imposition of the costs and fees would create such a substantial economic hardship as not to be in the interests of justice:

(1) to the county, the compensation actually paid to the arbitrator;

(2) to the appellee, those costs taxable in civil actions together with reasonable attorneys' fees as determined by the trial judge for services necessitated by the appeal; and

(3) reasonable expert witness fees incurred by the appellee in connection with the appeal.

Upon final disposition of the case and lacking an order from the court for the disposition of the deposit provided for in paragraph (b) of this rule, the clerk of court shall refund the deposit to the party making the deposit.

Upon final disposition of the case and lacking an order from the court for the disposition of the deposit provided for in paragraph (b) of this rule, the clerk of court shall refund the deposit to the party making the deposit.

(g) Discovery and Listing of Witnesses and Exhibits. In all cases in which an appeal is taken from the arbitration award, the parties shall proceed as follows:

(1) The appellant shall simultaneously with the filing of the Appeal from Arbitration and Motion to Set for Trial referenced above also file a list of witnesses and exhibits intended to be used at trial that complies with the requirements of Rule 26.1 of these Rules. If the appellant fails or elects not to file such a list of witnesses and exhibits together with the Appeal from Arbitration and Motion to Set for Trial, then the witnesses and exhibits intended to be used at trial by appellant shall be deemed to be those set forth in any such list previously filed in the action or in the pre-hearing statement submitted pursuant to Rule 75(c) of these Rules.

(2) Within 20 days after service of the Appeal from Arbitration and Motion to Set for Trial, appellee shall serve a list of witnesses and exhibits intended to be used at trial that complies with the requirements of Rule 26.1 of these rules. If

the appellee fails or elects not to file such a list of witnesses and exhibits, then the witnesses and exhibits intended to be used at trial by appellee shall be deemed to be those set forth in any such list previously filed in the action or in the prehearing statement submitted pursuant to Rule 76(e) of these Rules.

(3) The parties shall have 80 days from the filing of the Appeal from Arbitration and Motion to Set for Trial to complete discovery, pursuant to Rules 26 through 37 of these Rules.

(4) For good cause shown the court may extend the time for discovery set forth in subsection (3) above and/or allow a supplemental list of witnesses and exhibits to be filed.

Added Oct. 10, 2000, effective Dec. 1, 2000. Amended and renumbered as Rule 77 September 5, 2007, effective January 1, 2008. Amended Sept. 1, 2011, effective Jan. 1, 2012; Aug. 2013, effective April 15, 2014, subject to conditions of Order No. R-13-0017.

HISTORICAL NOTES

[2014 Amendments]

[Rule 77] Arizona Supreme Court Order No. R-13-0017, issued Aug. 28, 2013, provided that the amendments of the order would be "effective on April 15, 2014 as to all cases filed on or after that date." The applicability provision of Order No. R-13-0017 was amended on Nov. 14, 2013, and subsequently amended on Nov. 27, 2013 to provide:

(1) The Amendments shall apply to all actions filed on or after April 15, 2014.

(2) Beginning on April 15, 2014, the Amendments also shall apply to any action filed prior to April 15, 2014 (a "pending action"), unless one of the following events has occurred before that date:

   (a) A party has filed a Motion to Set and Certificate of Readiness,

   (b) The parties have filed a Proposed Scheduling Order, or

   (c) The court has entered a Scheduling Order.

(3) If, in a pending action, one of the preceding events has not occurred before April 15, 2014, the parties shall file a Joint Report and a Proposed Scheduling Order in accordance with the Amendments by June 30, 2014, or within 270 days after the commencement of the action, whichever date is later. Otherwise, the court will place the action on the Dismissal Calendar in accordance with the Amendments.

(4) A trial court, in its discretion, may apply any of the Amendments to a case pending before April 15, 2014, even if the Amendments would not otherwise apply under paragraph (2) above. For example, if a party filed a Motion to Set and Certificate of Readiness before April 15, 2014, the trial judge may set the matter for a trial setting conference under amended Rule 16(f), rather than place the case on the active calendar under pre-amendment Rule 38.1(c).

(5) Civil actions pending on the Inactive Calendar on April 15, 2014 shall be dismissed without prejudice on June 14, 2014, unless one of the actions set forth in subparts (1) - (4) of amended Rule 38.1(f) occurs before June 14, 2014.

STATE BAR COMMITTEE NOTES

2000 Promulgation and Amendment

As part of the effort to consolidate formerly separate sets of procedural rules into either the Arizona Rules of Civil Procedure or the Rules of the Arizona

Supreme Court, the Uniform Rules of Procedure for Arbitration, as recently amended, were effectively transferred to the Arizona Rules of Civil Procedure and placed in a Section of those Rules which had formerly been concerned with appeals in civil cases. The rules in that Section had been abrogated effective January 1, 1978, at the time of the adoption of the Arizona Rules of Civil Appellate Procedure. In the 2000 amendments, Section IX of the Rules was renamed "Section IX. Compulsory Arbitration."

New Rules 76(a) through (g) [renumbered in 2007 as Rules 77(a) through (g)] contain the provisions formerly contained in Rules 7(a) through (g) of the Uniform Rules of Procedure for Arbitration, with modifications to reflect their new placement. The sentence from former Rule 3 of the Uniform Rules of Procedure for Arbitration which dealt with the precedential effect of rulings by the arbitrator, and the use of discovery taken while a case was assigned to arbitration, was placed in new Rule 76(c) [renumbered in 2007 as Rule 77(c)].

AUTHORS' COMMENTS

Analysis

1. *Scope and Purpose of Rule.* The predecessor to Ariz. R. Civ. P. 77 (then- Rule 76) was promulgated in 2000, and contained the provisions of Rule 7 of the former Uniform Rules of Procedure for Arbitration. It was renumbered as Rule 77 as part of the 2008 amendments to the rules governing cases assigned to arbitration.

Rule 77 specifies the procedures for taking an appeal from an arbitration award, or other final disposition by the arbitrator, and prescribes the course and nature of the proceedings that are to take place in the Superior Court in cases appealed from arbitration awards.

2. *Comparison With Federal Rule.* The Federal Rules of Civil Procedure do not have a provision that corresponds to ARCP 77.

3. *Procedure for Taking Appeal from Arbitration Award.* A party desiring to appeal from an arbitration award must file, within twenty (20) days after the award is filed or the notice of decision becomes the award by operation of Rule 76(b), a notice of appeal, which is to be entitled "Appeal from Arbitration and Motion to Set for Trial," and which is treated in all material respects as the Motion to Set and Certificate of Readiness required by

Ariz. R. Civ. P. 38.1(a) for cases filed before April 15, 2014 that are not otherwise subject to conditions stated in the November 27, 2013, Order in R-13-0017. See *Decola v. Freyer*, 198 Ariz. 28, 6 P.3d 333 (Ct. App. Div. 1 2000).

Because the twenty (20) day period runs from the "filing" of the award or other final disposition, rather than from its service, the provisions of Ariz.R.Civ.P. 6(e) do not apply, and no extra time is provided if the award is served by mail. *Anderson v. Fidelity Southern Ins. Corp.*, 119 Ariz. 563, 582 P.2d 653 (Ct. App. Div. 1 1978). The parties may also file lists of witnesses and exhibits intended to be used at trial. See discussion in Section 4, *infra*.

Arizona courts disfavor hypertechnical arguments that needlessly deprive litigants of the right to an appeal. Accordingly, a notice of appeal that is filed more than twenty (20) days after the arbitrator mails a copy of the arbitration award to the parties, but before the award is actually *filed*, is premature rather than tardy, but nevertheless effective. *Guinn v. Schweitzer*, 190 Ariz. 116, 945 P.2d 837 (Ct. App. Div. 1 1997) (premature appeal not jurisdictionally defective). It is the *filing* of the arbitration award or other final disposition, not the *mailing* of it, that commences the running of the period in which to take an appeal from it. *Guinn v. Schweitzer*, 190 Ariz. 116, 945 P.2d 837 (Ct. App. Div. 1 1997).

Similarly, because Rule 6(b) grants the superior court authority to enlarge time, the superior court has jurisdiction to consider an appeal from compulsory arbitration, even if the the notice of appeal was premature and the submission of a cost bond was untimely. *Riendeau v. Wal-Mart Stores, Inc.*, 223 Ariz. 540, 225 P.3d 597 (Ct. App. Div. 1 2010). In so holding, the *Riendeau* court expressly disagreed with its sister court's holding in *Varga v. Hebern*, 116 Ariz. 539, 570 P.2d 226 (Ct. App. Div. 1 1977). The *Varga* court held that the failure to timely pay a cost bond is a jurisdictional defect that prevents the appellate court from hearing an appeal from compulsory arbitration.

The arbitration rules are silent about whether and under what circumstances relief can be granted to a litigant who has received no notice that the appeal time is running because of the filing of the award. *Decola v. Freyer*, 198 Ariz. 28, 6 P.3d 333 (Ct. App. Div. 1 2000). If the party appealing the award failed to receive notice of the filing of the arbitration award, however, the superior court has discretion to grant an extension of time to appeal an arbitration award in circumstances where the party appealing the award has acted diligently and no prejudice to the other party is shown. *Decola v. Freyer*, 198 Ariz. 28, 6 P.3d 333 (Ct. App. Div. 1 2000).

4. *Deposit on Appeal*. Under Rule 77(b), the Appeal from

Arbitration and Motion to Set for Trial must be accompanied by the deposit with the Clerk of the Superior Court of a sum equal to one hearing day's compensation for the arbitrator, but not exceeding ten percent (10%) of the amount in controversy. The Court may allow the filing of an appeal without this deposit, if it finds that the appellant lacks the funds to make it.

5. *Waiver of Right to Appeal: Failure to Participate.* A 1990 amendment to what was then Rule 7(a) of the former Uniform Rules of Procedure for Arbitration (now Rule 77(a)) limited the right to appeal to a party who appears and participates in the arbitration proceedings, and effectively precludes the anomalous result reached in *Chevron U.S.A., Inc. v. Thompson*, 145 Ariz. 85, 699 P.2d 1316 (Ct. App. Div. 2 1985). Moreover, under what is now Ariz.R.Civ.P. 75(h), the failure of a party to appear at an arbitration hearing or to participate in the hearing in good faith operates as a waiver of the right to appeal, absent a showing of good cause. *Romer-Pollis v. Ada*, 223 Ariz. 300, 222 P.3d 916 (Ct. App. Div. 1 2009). It has been determined that the predecessors to these Rules did not impermissibly abridge the statutory right to appeal from arbitration awards or the constitutional right to trial by jury. *Graf v. Whitaker*, 192 Ariz. 403, 966 P.2d 1007 (Ct. App. Div. 1 1998).

While the rules do not quantify the degree of participation in the hearing that is required, when read together, the Rules require more than minimal participation in arbitration proceedings; both require a party to participate in good faith in order to satisfy the spirit of the arbitration requirement. *Romer-Pollis v. Ada*, 223 Ariz. 300, 222 P.3d 916 (Ct. App. Div. 1 2009).

Rules 77(a) and 75(h) do not unconditionally require a personal appearance at the arbitration hearing by a party who wishes to preserve the right to appeal; appearances can be made through counsel. *Lane v. City of Tempe*, 202 Ariz. 306, 44 P.3d 986 (2002); *Sabori v. Kuhn*, 199 Ariz. 330, 18 P.3d 124 (Ct. App. Div. 1 2001). In most cases, what constitutes good faith participation is a matter of fairness and common sense. *Lane v. City of Tempe*, 202 Ariz. 306, 44 P.3d 986 (2002). It is not the case that the physical appearance of a party at the arbitration hearing is never required. *Lane v. City of Tempe*, 202 Ariz. 306, 44 P.3d 986 (2002).

Where a party has been subjected to, and participated in, prehearing discovery, and the opposing party had notice and an opportunity to subpoena that party to appear, a party's failure to personally appear for the arbitration hearing will not operate to waive the right to appeal. *Lane v. City of Tempe*, 202 Ariz. 306, 44 P.3d 986 (2002). Similarly, where a party cannot appear personally at the time set by the arbitrator for the conduct of the hearing, and offers to appear and be cross-examined telephonically, it is an abuse of discretion for the arbitrator to deny that opportunity, and for the trial court to find a waiver of the right to appeal on that basis. *Sabori v. Kuhn*, 199 Ariz. 330, 18 P.3d 124 (Ct. App. Div. 1 2001).

An appeal may be taken to the Superior Court from a court-appointed arbitrator's denial of a motion to compel binding arbitration. *Western Agr. Ins. Co. v. Chrysler Corp.*, 198 Ariz. 64, 6 P.3d 768 (Ct. App. Div. 1 2000). The time for taking such an appeal is governed, not by the provisions of Rule 77(a), but by A.R.S. § 12-2101.01, which provides that a notice of appeal must be filed no later than thirty (30) days after the entry of the judgment or order from which the appeal is being taken. *Western Agr. Ins. Co. v. Chrysler Corp.*, 198 Ariz. 64, 6 P.3d 768 (Ct. App. Div. 1 2000).

A trial court's determination that a party has waived the right to appeal by failing to participate at the arbitration hearing is reviewed on appeal for an abuse of discretion. *Lane v. City of Tempe*, 202 Ariz. 306, 44 P.3d 986 (2002).

6. *Waiver of Right to Appeal: Written Stipulation*. Rule 77(e) provides that the parties may stipulate in writing, "at any time" before an award or other final disposition is entered, that the eventual award or other final disposition will be binding. In that event, the award or other final disposition is subject to appeal or collateral attack only on the grounds set forth in A.R.S. §§ 12-1501 *et seq*.

The provision of former Rule 2(d) of the Uniform Rules of Procedure for Arbitration that required the Clerk, at the time the parties were advised of the identity of the appointed arbitrator, to also furnish the parties with forms that would permit them to stipulate to waive the right to appeal, was eliminated when the arbitration rules were transferred to the Arizona Rules of Civil Procedure.

7. *Procedure on Appeal*. All appeals to the Superior Court from mandatory arbitration proceedings are *de novo* both as to the facts and the law. *See*, Ariz. R. Civ. P. 77(c). Appeals from arbitration are handled as ordinary civil cases, but on an accelerated schedule. It is now established that the time periods for processing a civil case set forth in what is now Ariz. R. Civ. P. 38.1, are fully applicable to mandatory arbitration cases. *Martinez v. Binsfield*, 196 Ariz. 466, 999 P.2d 810 (2000). See also Ariz.R.Civ.P. 73(c).

Rule 77(g)(1) provides that, simultaneously with the filing of the Appeal from Arbitration and Motion to Set for Trial, the appellant is also to file a list of witnesses and exhibits intended to be used at trial, which list must comply with the requirements of Rule 26.1. *Cosper v. Rea ex rel. County of Maricopa*, 228 Ariz.

555, 269 P.3d 1179 (2012) (witness list may be supplemented only for good cause under Rule 77(g)(4)). The appellee is to file such a list of witnesses and exhibits within twenty (20) days after service of the Appeal from Arbitration and Motion to Set for Trial. Either party may elect, however, not to file such a list.

If a party elects not to file a list of witnesses and exhibits, or simply fails to do so, then the witnesses and exhibits which that party intends to use at trial in the Superior Court are deemed to be those contained in any similar list filed during the course of the arbitration proceedings, or those set forth in the pre-hearing statement required by Ariz.R.Civ.P. 75(c). *See*, Rule 77(g)(1). *Cosper v. Rea ex rel. County of Maricopa*, 228 Ariz. 555, 269 P.3d 1179 (2012) (witness list may be supplemented only for good cause under Rule 77(g)(4)).

Rule 77(g)(3) provides that the parties have a period of 80 days following the filing of the Appeal from Arbitration and Motion to Set for Trial to complete any discovery they wish, and are permitted to conduct. The submission and supplementation of witness and exhibit lists is governed, however, by Rule 77(g)(1) and not Rule 77(g)(3). *Cosper v. Rea ex rel. County of Maricopa*, 228 Ariz. 555, 269 P.3d 1179 (2012).

If an appeal is taken from an arbitration award, any discovery taken while the matter was assigned to arbitration may be used in proceedings on appeal in the Superior Court. Rulings on issues of law made by the arbitrator are not binding on the Superior Court or the parties on appeal.

Any party who appears and participates in good faith in the arbitration proceedings, and who timely appeals from the arbitration award or other final disposition, is entitled to a trial *de novo* on the facts and law of all claims, including the claims of a non-appealing plaintiff against a non-appealing co-defendant. *Valler v. Lee*, 190 Ariz. 391, 949 P.2d 51 (Ct. App. Div. 2 1997). In the context of compulsory arbitration, an "appeal" is not a request for review, but rather a demand for trial *de novo*. While arbitration is mandatory in cases subject to the particular Local Rule on the subject, absent a stipulation by the parties, the resulting award or other final disposition is not binding if a timely appeal is filed. *Valler v. Lee*, 190 Ariz. 391, 949 P.2d 51 (Ct. App. Div. 2 1997). The right to trial *de novo* is essential to the constitutionality of the compulsory arbitration regime. *Valler v. Lee*, 190 Ariz. 391, 949 P.2d 51 (Ct. App. Div. 2 1997).

On the other hand, when the facts or theories of liability differ as unrelated claims between the parties, the law does not require that an appeal from an arbitration award be *de novo* as to all parties. *Orlando v. Superior Court ex rel. County of Maricopa*, 194 Ariz. 96, 977 P.2d 818 (Ct. App. Div. 1 1998). In that circumstance, where joinder is not required, as it would be if issues of comparative fault were involved, an appeal of an arbitration award or other final disposition will only be effective as to the party or parties named in that appeal. *Orlando v. Superior Court ex rel. County of Maricopa*, 194 Ariz. 96, 977 P.2d 818 (Ct. App. Div. 1 1998).

Because an appeal results in a trial *de novo*, an arbitrator's conclusion that the claim of the prevailing party did not depend upon the existence of an express or implied contract does not prevent the Superior Court from considering that issue anew and awarding fees. *Schwab Sales, Inc. v. GN Const. Co., Inc.*, 196 Ariz. 33, 992 P.2d 1128 (Ct. App. Div. 2 1998). The fact that the prevailing party does not cross-appeal from an arbitrator's denial of an award of attorneys' fees does not preclude the Superior Court from granting them. *Schwab Sales, Inc. v. GN Const. Co., Inc.*, 196 Ariz. 33, 992 P.2d 1128 (Ct. App. Div. 2 1998). Such a limitation would be contrary to the mandate that appeals from arbitration awards be *de novo*. *Schwab Sales, Inc. v. GN Const. Co., Inc.*, 196 Ariz. 33, 992 P.2d 1128 (Ct. App. Div. 2 1998).

The superior court has the inherent authority to allow a party to dismiss its own appeal from an arbitration award, in circumstances where no pleading other than the notice of appeal has been filed, no further proceedings have taken place, and no prejudice will result to the opposing party. *Carlisle v. Petrosky*, 212 Ariz. 323, 131 P.3d 495 (Ct. App. Div. 1 2006).

Neither the Legislature nor the Supreme Court has limited post-arbitration trials to the evidence presented at the arbitration hearing, and a party appealing from an arbitration award may encounter additional legal and factual claims at the trial *de novo*. *Poulson v. Ofack*, 220 Ariz. 294, 205 P.3d 1141 (Ct. App. Div. 1 2009); *Valler v. Lee*, 190 Ariz. 391, 949 P.2d 51 (Ct. App. Div. 2 1997). The options for addressing such concerns, however, do not include waiving or limiting the sanctions provisions of the statute or Rule 77(f). *Poulson v. Ofack*, 220 Ariz. 294, 205 P.3d 1141 (Ct. App. Div. 1 2009) (holding, the plain language of A.R.S. § 12-133(I) and Rule 77(f) mandates a trial court order payment of fees and costs if party appealing an arbitration award does not better its position at trial in excess of the required percentage, unless such order would cause a substantial economic hardship).

8. *Costs on Appeal*. 1991 amendments to former Rule 7(f), which have been retained in Rule 77(f), sought to provide disincentives to prosecuting appeals from arbitration awards in two separate ways: (1) by increasing the costs and fees that could be taxed against the appellant on appeal, and (2) by making the appellant responsible for those increased fees and costs, in most cases, unless the appeal resulted in an improvement in the appellant's

position.

Rule 77(f) provides that, if the result achieved on appeal is not at least 23% more favorable to the appellant than the monetary relief secured in the arbitration (*i.e.*, 23% less than an award in arbitration against the appellant, or 23% more than an arbitration award in favor of the appellant, then the appellant is to pay the arbitrator's compensation, the appellee's taxable costs, the reasonable attorneys' fees incurred by the appellee for services necessitated by the appeal, and reasonable expert witness fees incurred by the appellee in connection with the appeal).

Subpart (I) of the statute which authorizes the mandatory arbitration program, A.R.S. § 12-133, was amended in 2007 to provide that the appellant was to be responsible for these fees and costs, unless the result achieved on appeal was not at least 23% more favorable than the arbitration award. As part of the 2008 amendments, Rule 77(f) was amended to conform to the statute. The deposit posted by the appellant is to be used to pay these fees and costs but, if it is insufficient (which it generally will be), then the appellant is to pay them, unless the Superior Court finds that the imposition of these fees and costs would impose a substantial economic hardship on the appellant.

Rule 77(f) (and A.R.S. § 12-133(I)) also provides that these increased fees and costs are to be awarded against the appellant if the nonmonetary relief secured on appeal is not more favorable than the nonmonetary relief secured in arbitration. *Poulson v. Ofack*, 220 Ariz. 294, 205 P.3d 1141 (Ct. App. Div. 1 2009) (holding, the plain language of A.R.S. § 12-133(I) and Rule 77(f) mandates a trial court order payment of fees and costs if party appealing an arbitration award does not better its position at trial in excess of the required percentage, unless such order would cause a substantial economic hardship).

A finding of "substantial economic hardship" is based on the financial circumstances of the party facing the imposition of fees and costs and not the alleged impact on the verdict of the admission of untimely disclosed evidence. *Poulson v. Ofack*, 220 Ariz. 294, 205 P.3d 1141 (Ct. App. Div. 1 2009). Given that one of the requirements for referring a case to compulsory arbitration, under Rule 72(b)(1), is that no party seeks affirmative relief other than a monetary judgment, this aspect of this provision will rarely, if ever, come into play.

In determining whether or not the result on the trial *de novo* is sufficiently more favorable to the appellant to avoid the award of the appellee's reasonable attorneys' fees and expert witness fees incurred on appeal, the trial court is required, by the literal provisions of Rule 77(f), to draw a comparison between the "arbitration award" and the "judgment on trial *de novo*." In drawing that comparison, the trial court must calculate the percentage reduction between the arbitration award (including the attorney's fees and costs portions, *i.e.*, taxable costs and expert witness fees) and the judgment (including the prejudgment interest portion). *Aqua Management, Inc. v. Abdeen*, 224 Ariz. 91, 227 P.3d 498 (Ct. App. Div. 1 2010); *Vega v. Sullivan*, 199 Ariz. 504, 19 P.3d 645 (Ct. App. Div. 2 2001).

In those circumstances where Rule 68(g) sanctions may be involved, Rule 68(g) expressly provides that the court determine whether to impose a sanction under Rule 68(g) only after first complying with Rule 77(f). *See also*, *Bradshaw v. Jasso-Barajas*, 231 Ariz. 197, 291 P.3d 991 (Ct. App. Div. 1 2013) (In determining whether Rule 68 sanctions should be imposed after a trial de novo following an arbitration hearing, the trial court must: (1) compare the arbitration award with the judgment on the trial de novo, (2) determine and deduct from such judgment any Rule 77(f) sanctions, and (3) consider whether Rule 68 sanctions are applicable, *i.e.,* compare final judgment on trial *de novo* to Rule 68 offer of judgment.).

Generally, post-judgment interest does not represent a portion of the monetary relief granted by an arbitration award [Rule 77(f)] and should not be included in the Rule 77(f) analysis. A prejudgment interest provision is an integral part of the monetary relief granted in either an arbitration award or judgment. A post-judgment interest provision, on the other hand, is (a) collateral to to the monetary relief granted in an underlying judgment or arbitration award, and (b) an enforcement mechanism designed to encourage timely satisfaction of the judgment. *Aqua Management, Inc. v. Abdeen*, 224 Ariz. 91, 227 P.3d 498 (Ct. App. Div. 1 2010); *Vega v. Sullivan*, 199 Ariz. 504, 19 P.3d 645 (Ct. App. Div. 2 2001).

In circumstances where the arbitrator has awarded one or both parties $0 at the conclusion of the arbitration proceedings, in order for the appellant of such award to avoid paying attorneys' fees, the appellant must obtain a judgment greater than $0. *Farmers Ins. Co. v. Tallsalt*, 192 Ariz. 129, 962 P.2d 203 (1998); *Freeman v. Sorchych*, 226 Ariz. 242, 245 P.3d 927 (Ct. App. Div. 1 2011), review denied, (Aug. 31, 2011).

In that regard, Rule 77(f) (formerly Rule 7(f) of the Uniform Rules of Procedure for Arbitration) provides that the appellant must pay the appellee's attorneys' and reasonable expert witness fees unless the appellant obtains a judgment that is more favorable by at least 23% than the monetary relief granted by the arbitration award. While the use of the phrase "monetary relief" may suggest a number that is greater than zero, zero is a number as well, and where the arbitrator awarded the appellant nothing, any award in excess of that will exceed the arbitration award by 23%. *Farmers Ins. Co. v. Tallsalt*, 192 Ariz. 129, 962 P.2d 203 (1998) (suggesting a wholesale review of Rule 7(f), now Rule 77(f), may be in order to address the issue of appeals from arbitration awards entered in the amount of zero dollars).

9. *2014 Rule Amendments: Effective and Applicability*. On August 28, 2013, the Arizona Supreme Court adopted sweeping amendments to the case management and trial setting rules governing civil cases. The Promulgating Order specified such rules were adopted "effective on April 15, 2014 as to all cases filed on or after that date." *See,* August 28, 2013 Order entered in In the Matter of Petition to Amend Rules 16, 16.1, 26, 37, 38, 38.1, 72, 73, 74 and 77, Arizona Rules of Civil Procedure, R-13-0017. The applicability provision set forth in the Promulgating Order set up two procedural tracks for case management with the new rules governing cases file on or after April 15, 2014 and the "old" rules governing pre-April 15, 2014 cases.

To avoid any confusion potentially created by the two different tracks, the Court entered an order on November 14, 2013, amending the applicability provision. On November 27, 2013, the court entered a second order further refining the amended applicability provision. As a result, the Amendments are effective and applicable as follows:

"(1) The Amendments shall apply to all actions filed on or after April 15, 2014.

"(2) Beginning on April 15, 2014, the Amendments also shall apply to any action filed prior to April 15, 2014 (a "pending action"), unless one of the following events has occurred before that date:

(a) A party has filed a Motion to Set and Certificate of Readiness,

(b) The parties have filed a Proposed Scheduling Order, or

(c) The court has entered a Scheduling Order.

"(3) If, in a pending action, one of the preceding events has not occurred before April 15, 2014, the parties shall file a Joint Report and a Proposed Scheduling Order in accordance with the Amendments by June 30, 2014, or within 270 days after the commencement of the action, whichever date is later. Otherwise, the court will place the action on the Dismissal Calendar in accordance with the Amendments.

"(4) A trial court, in its discretion, may apply any of the Amendments to a case pending before April 15, 2014, even if the Amendments would not otherwise apply under paragraph (2) above. For example, if a party filed a Motion to Set and Certificate of Readiness before April 15, 2014, the trial judge may set the matter for a trial setting conference under amended Rule 16(f), rather than place the case on the active calendar under pre-amendment Rule 38.1(c).

"(5) Civil actions pending on the Inactive Calendar on April 15, 2014 shall be dismissed without prejudice on June 14, 2014, unless one of the actions set forth in subparts (1) - (4) of amended Rule 38.1(f) occurs before June 14, 2014."

X. GENERAL PROVISIONS

Rule 78. [Abrogated]

AUTHORS' NOTE

By Order entered on October 10, 2000, the Arizona Supreme Court abrogated in their entirety the Uniform Rules of Practice of the Superior Court, the Uniform Rules of Procedure for Arbitration, and the Uniform Rules of Practice for Medical Malpractice Cases, effective December 1, 2000. The provisions of these formerly separate sets of rules were generally transferred to either the Arizona Rules of Civil Procedure or the Rules of the Arizona Supreme Court. The guiding principles for this consolidation effort were that (1) rules whose subject matter was adequately covered by other existing rules should simply be eliminated, (2) provisions in the sets of rules to be consolidated that had a bearing on the manner on the manner in which civil litigants and/or their counsel are to conduct civil litigation should be placed in the Arizona Rules of Civil Procedure, and (3) rule provisions that dealt primarily with the internal workings of the Superior Courts should be placed in the Rules of the Arizona Supreme Court. Consistent application of these principles resulted in the transfer of certain provisions of the Arizona Rules of Civil Procedure as well, including Rule 78.

The "*2000 Rules Consolidation Correlation Table*" is reprinted herein and follows the Arizona Rules of Civil Procedure in the Volume.

The discussion concerning civil motion practice generally, can now be found in the *Authors' Comments* under Ariz.R.Civ.P. 7.1. The discussion concerning "Notice of Orders; Notice of Entry of Judgment" is now Section 6 of the *Authors' Comments* under Ariz.R.Civ.P. 58.

Rule 79. [Abrogated]

AUTHORS' NOTE

By Order entered on October 10, 2000, the Arizona Supreme Court abrogated in their entirety the Uniform Rules of Practice of the Superior Court, the Uniform Rules of Procedure for Arbitration, and the Uniform Rules of Practice for Medical Malpractice Cases, effective December 1, 2000. The provisions of these formerly separate sets of rules were generally transferred to either the Arizona Rules of Civil Procedure or the Rules of the Arizona Supreme Court.

The guiding principles for this consolidation effort were that (1) rules whose subject matter was adequately covered by other existing rules should simply be eliminated, (2) provisions in the sets of rules to be consolidated that had a bearing on the manner on the manner in which civil litigants and/or their counsel are to conduct civil litigation should be placed in the Arizona Rules of Civil Procedure, and (3) rule provisions that dealt primarily with the internal workings of the Superior Courts should be placed in the Rules of the Arizona Supreme Court.

Consistent application of these principles resulted in the transfer of certain provisions of the Arizona Rules of Civil Procedure as well, including Rule 79.

The "*2000 Rules Consolidation Correlation Table*" is reprinted herein and follows the Arizona Rules of Civil Procedure in the Volume.

Rule 80. General provisions

(a) Conduct in Trial. Trials shall be conducted in an orderly, courteous and dignified manner. Arguments and remarks shall be addressed to the court, except that by permission of the court counsel may make proper inquiries or ask questions of opposing counsel.

(b) Exclusion of Minors From Trial. When an action or proceeding of a scandalous or obscene nature is to be tried, the court or referee may exclude from the courtroom minors whose presence is not necessary as parties or witnesses.

(c) [Abrogated June 27, 1991 on an emergency basis; abrogation adopted in final form on July 7, 1992].

(d) Agreement or Consent of Counsel or Parties. No agreement or consent between parties or attorneys in any matter is binding if disputed, unless it is in writing, or made orally in open court, and entered in the minutes.

(e) [Abrogated May 1, 1989, effective July 1, 1989].

(f) [Deleted Sept. 16, 2008 effective Jan. 1, 2009].

(g) Officer of Court or Attorney as Surety. No officer or attorney of the court shall be accepted as surety upon an undertaking or bond in a judicial action or proceeding.

(h) Lost Records; Method of Supplying; Substitution of Copies; Hearing if Correctness Denied.

1. When the records and papers of an action or proceeding, or part thereof, are lost or destroyed either before or after the trial or hearing, they may be supplied by either party on motion addressed to the court on three days notice to an adverse party. The motion shall be signed and verified, and shall state the loss or destruction of the records or papers, and shall be accompanied by certified copies of the originals, if obtainable, and if not, then copies duplicating the originals as nearly as possible.

2. If the adverse party admits the correctness of the copies and the court is satisfied that they are copies in substance of the original, the court shall order the copies substituted for the originals. If their correctness is denied, or if the court finds them not correct, it shall hear evidence and correct copies shall be made under the direction of the judge. The substituted copies shall be filed with the clerk and shall constitute a part of the record in the action or proceeding, and shall have the force and effect of the originals.

(i) Unsworn Declarations Under Penalty of Perjury.

Wherever, under any of these rules, or under any rule, regulation, order, or requirement made pursuant to these rules, any matter is required or permitted to be supported, evidenced, established, or proved by the sworn written declaration, verification, certificate, statement, oath, or affidavit of the person making the same (other than a deposition, or an oath of office, or an oath required to be taken before a specified official other than a notary public), such matter may, with like force and effect, be supported, evidenced, established, or proved by the unsworn written declaration, certificate, verification, or statement, subscribed by such person as true under penalty of perjury, and dated, in substantially the following form:

"I declare (or certify, verify or state) under penalty of perjury that the foregoing is true and correct. Executed on (date).

(Signature)."

Amended May 1, 1989, effective July 1, 1989; June 27, 1991 on an emergency basis; amendment adopted in final form July 7, 1992; amended May 30, 1996, effective Dec. 1, 1996.

AUTHORS' COMMENTS

Analysis

1. Scope and Purpose of Rule.
2. Comparison With Federal Rule.
3. Conduct of Counsel.
4. Stipulations and Agreements.
5. Replacing Lost Records.
6. Unsworn Declarations.

1. *Scope and Purpose of Rule.* Rule 80 is a collection of miscellaneous provisions, most of which deal with particular aspects of the conduct of counsel.

2. *Comparison With Federal Rule.* ARCP 80 and FRCP 80 are entirely different. The Arizona Rule does not contain the sole remaining subpart of the Federal Rule, and the Federal Rule contains none of the provisions of the Arizona Rule.

3. *Conduct of Counsel.* Rule 80(g) precludes an attorney from serving as a surety on a bond or undertaking furnished in connection with a judicial proceeding.

The overriding mandate of Rule 80(a) is that trials are to be conducted in an "orderly, courteous, and dignified manner." The misconduct of counsel during the course of trial may, under certain circumstances, furnish grounds for the award of a new trial. See the discussion of this issue in Section 5 of the *Authors'*

Comments under Ariz.R.Civ.P. 59.

4. *Stipulations and Agreements.* Rule 80(d) provides that an agreement between counsel or parties, if subsequently disputed, will not be binding unless it is in writing, or made orally in open court and entered in the minutes. The purpose of the Rule is to prevent disputes as to the existence and/or terms of such agreements and to relieve the trial court of the burden of attempting to resolve them. *Hackin v. Rupp*, 9 Ariz. App. 354, 452 P.2d 519 (1969). Accordingly, the terms of the Rule are to be strictly enforced. *Canyon Contracting Co. v. Tohono O'Odham Housing Authority*, 172 Ariz. 389, 837 P.2d 750 (Ct. App. Div. 1 1992). Where the parties have entered into a stipulation in accordance with the terms of the Rule, they will be bound by it unless relieved of its effect by the Court. *Peart v. Superior Court In and For Mohave County*, 6 Ariz. App. 6, 429 P.2d 498 (1967).

The Rule fully applies to settlement agreements. *Canyon Contracting Co. v. Tohono O'Odham Housing Authority*, 172 Ariz. 389, 837 P.2d 750 (Ct. App. Div. 1 1992). *See also, Cosper v. Rea ex rel. County of Maricopa*, 228 Ariz. 555, 269 P.3d 1179 (2012) (accepting as binding between the parties a settlement agreement counsel for both parties entered into the court record). Where the existence and/or terms of an alleged settlement agreement are disputed, it will not be enforced unless it is in writing or recorded in the Court minutes. *Canyon Contracting Co. v. Tohono O'Odham Housing Authority*, 172 Ariz. 389, 837 P.2d 750 (Ct. App. Div. 1 1992).

Rule 80(d) does not apply where the existence and terms of the settlement are not in dispute, and the only issue concerns the attorney's authority to bind the client to the settlement. *Perry v. Ronan*, 225 Ariz. 49, 234 P.3d 617 (Ct. App. Div. 1 2010); *Hays v. Fischer*, 161 Ariz. 159, 777 P.2d 222 (Ct. App. Div. 1 1989). In that regard, an attorney's authority to bind his or her client by stipulation or other agreement is governed by the principles of agency. *Panzino v. City of Phoenix*, 196 Ariz. 442, 999 P.2d 198 (2000) (general rules of agency apply to attorney-client relationship); *Balmer v. Gagnon*, 19 Ariz. App. 55, 504 P.2d 1278 (Div. 2 1973). An attorney has apparent and/or implied actual authority, manifested by the client's act of retaining the attorney, to do that which attorneys are normally authorized to do in the course of litigation, and to bind the client thereto. *Garn v. Garn*, 155 Ariz. 156, 745 P.2d 604 (Ct. App. Div. 1 1987).

The attorney is generally not authorized, however, merely by being retained to handle litigation, to impair a client's substantial rights or the cause of action itself without the client's express consent. *United Liquor Co. v. Stephenson*, 84 Ariz. 1, 322 P.2d 886 (1958). Thus, an attorney has no implied or apparent authority to settle or compromise a claim and may not stipulate to a compromise settlement of a pending lawsuit without the client's express, actual authorization. *Garn v. Garn*, 155 Ariz. 156, 745 P.2d 604 (Ct. App. Div. 1 1987). But, when a client expressly authorizes his or her attorney to settle a lawsuit and the attorney acts in conformity with this authority, the attorney's action in settling the case is binding on the client. *United Liquor Co. v. Stephenson*, 84 Ariz. 1, 322 P.2d 886 (1958) (party bound by settlement because she had authorized attorneys to settle and settlement not "grossly unfair"); *Garn v. Garn*, 155 Ariz. 156, 745 P.2d 604 (Ct. App. Div. 1 1987).

5. *Replacing Lost Records.* Rule 80(h) sets forth a rarely invoked procedure for the replacement of records in an action or proceeding where such records have been lost or destroyed. Any party may present the issue to the Court by motion, which must be verified and accompanied by certified copies of the records in question, if possible, or by copies which duplicate the originals as nearly as possible. If the correctness of the submitted copies is disputed, the Court is to resolve the issue and may conduct an evidentiary hearing for that purpose.

6. *Unsworn Declarations.* Ariz. R. Civ. P. 80(i) permits unsworn declarations to be used in place of formal, sworn declarations, verifications, certificates or affidavits where such are required under the Rules to support, establish, evidence or prove any matter. The unsworn declaration must be subscribed by the person making it as true under penalty of perjury, in substantially the form specified in the Rule. *See, Airfreight Exp. Ltd v. Evergreen Air Center, Inc.*, 215 Ariz. 103, 158 P.3d 232 (Ct. App. Div. 2 2007) (undated declarations do not meet the requirements of Rule 80(i)). Claimed deficiencies to a Rule 80(i) declaration may be waived by failure to move to strike or object. *Airfreight Exp. Ltd v. Evergreen Air Center, Inc.*, 215 Ariz. 103, 158 P.3d 232 (Ct. App. Div. 2 2007). *See also,* Ariz. R. Civ. P. 7.1(f) (added 2014).

Rule 81. When rules applicable

These Rules govern all actions or proceedings brought after they take effect and also all further actions or proceedings then pending, except to the extent that in the opinion of the court their application in a particular action or proceeding pending when the rules take effect would not be feasible or would work injustice, in which event the former procedure applies.

Rule 81.1. Juvenile emancipation

Juvenile emancipation proceedings shall conform to the provisions of these rules, except as provided for in Part V, Rules of Proc. Juv. Court.

Added Sept. 5, 2007, effective Jan. 1, 2008.

Rule 82. Jurisdiction and venue unaffected

These Rules shall not be construed to extend or limit the jurisdiction of superior courts or venue of actions therein.

AUTHORS' COMMENTS

Analysis

1. *Scope and Purpose of Rule.* The subject matter jurisdiction of a trial court is to be determined from sources other than procedural rules. *See* 12 Wright & Miller, Federal Practice and Procedure, § 3141 at 210–11 (1973). In Arizona, this principle is codified in Ariz.R.Civ.P. 82. *Encinas v. Pompa*, 189 Ariz. 157, 939 P.2d 435, R.I.C.O. Bus. Disp. Guide (CCH) P 9287 (Ct. App. Div. 1 1997) (A.R.S. § 13-2314.04(H) impermissibly impacts superior court jurisdiction by limiting such jurisdiction under the guise of a procedural rule, a direct conflict with Rule 82). Moreover, the Arizona Rules of Civil Procedure do not create substantive rights. See Ariz. Const., Art. VI, § 5(5); Ariz. R. Civ. P. 82; see also A.R.S. § 12-109(A) (1992). *Arizona Dept. of Revenue v. Dougherty*, 200 Ariz. 515, 29 P.3d 862 (2001).

2. *Comparison With Federal Rule.* The Federal Rules of Civil Procedure do not have a provision that corresponds to Ariz.R.Civ.P. 82.

Rule 83. Local rules by superior courts

With the approval of a majority of the judges of the county, the presiding judge shall supplement these rules by local rules, not inconsistent with the provisions of these Rules, which shall be promulgated and published upon approval of the Chief Justice of the Supreme Court.

Amended Oct. 10, 2000, effective Dec. 1, 2000.

STATE BAR COMMITTEE NOTES

2000 Amendment

As part of the effort to consolidate formerly separate sets of procedural rules into either the Arizona Rules of Civil Procedure or the Rules of the Arizona Supreme Court, the Uniform Rules of Practice of the Superior Court were effectively eliminated. Both Rule I(a)(5) and Rule XIV of those Rules, and Rule 83 of the Arizona Rules of Civil Procedure, provided authority for the Presiding Judge in each County to promulgate Local Rules for the Superior Court in that County. Former Rule XIV of the Uniform Rules of Practice of the Superior Court, however, more accurately described current practice with respect to the adoption of such Local Rules in that it specified that such Local Rules (1) are to be promulgated by the Presiding Judge, (2) need the approval of the majority of the judges sitting in that County, and (3) must also be approved by the Chief Justice of the Arizona Supreme Court. The effect of the 2000 amendment, accordingly, was to repeal the language of Rule 83 of the Arizona Rules of Civil Procedure, and to substitute in its place a slightly modified version of the language of former Rule XIV, so that the Rule would be consistent with current practice.

AUTHORS' COMMENTS

Analysis

1. *Scope and Purpose of Rule.* Rule 83 authorizes the Superior Court in each county to adopt Local Rules governing practice in that court, so long as they are not inconsistent with the Arizona Rules of Civil Procedure. The Rule was amended in 2000 to substitute, with minor modifications, the language of former Rule XIV of the Uniform Rules of the Superior Court because the latter more accurately described current practice with respect to the adoption of such Local Rules.

Local Rules are promulgated by the Presiding Judge but must first be approved by a majority of the judges of the Superior Court for the county, and by the Chief Justice of the Supreme Court. *State, ex rel. Romley v. Ballinger*, 209 Ariz. 1, 97 P.3d 101 (2004). Proposed amendments to existing Local Rules and proposed new

Local Rules of the Superior Court for a particular county are not considered to be subject to the provisions of Rule 28, Rules of the Supreme Court and are not circulated for comment as required by that Rule.

The Superior Courts in each of the fifteen counties have adopted Local Rules which should be consulted for matters that are pending in that particular county.

2. *Comparison With Federal Rule.* Both ARCP 83 and FRCP 83 authorize individual courts within the court system to adopt Local Rules to govern particular aspects of practice and procedure in those courts. The procedures contemplated for adopting such Local Rules, however, are quite different. For example, FRCP 83(a)(1) provides that there must be "appropriate public notice and an opportunity to comment" in connection with the adoption or amendment of Local Rules of a United States District Court. There is no such requirement applicable to the adoption or amendment of Local Rules in the Superior Court for an individual county. The Arizona Rule also does not have provisions corresponding to FRCP 83(a)(2) and 83(b), added to the Federal Rule by the 1995 amendments.

Rule 84. Forms

The forms contained in the Appendix of Forms are sufficient under the rules and are intended to indicate the simplicity and brevity of statement which the rules contemplate.

Added Oct. 9, 1996, effective Dec. 1, 1996.

STATE BAR COMMITTEE NOTE

1996 Amendment

The 1996 adoption of Rule 84 was part of a comprehensive set of rule revisions proposed by the State Bar of Arizona. Such comprehensive revisions were intended to bring the Arizona Rules of Civil Procedure in line with the 1991 and 1993 amendments to the Federal Rules of Civil Procedure. Specifically, Rule 84 was adopted to conform to the 1995 amendment of Rule 4.1(c) and Rule 4.2(c) concerning the promulgation of Form 1 ("Notice of Lawsuit and Request for Waiver of Service of Summons") and Form 2 ("Waiver of Service and Summons").

Consistent with 1946 Advisory Committee Note, which accompanies Rule 84 of the Federal Rules of Civil Procedure, the forms contained in the Appendix of Forms are sufficient to withstand attack under the rules under which they are drawn, and, to that event, the practitioner using them may rely upon them. A practitioner is not required, however, to use such forms.

State Bar Committee Note adopted Oct. 31, 1996 on an emergency basis, effective Dec. 1, 1996.

AUTHORS' COMMENTS

Analysis

1. *Scope and Purpose of Rule*. Rule 84 was adopted in 1996 as part of omnibus amendments to the Arizona Rules of Civil Procedure intended to eliminate many of the differences between the Arizona Rules of Civil Procedure and the Federal Rules of Civil Procedure. These differences resulted from the 1991 and 1993 amendments to the Federal Rules of Civil Procedure. As adopted, Rule 84 refers to an Appendix of Forms that are deemed sufficient under the Rules.

"Form 1. Notice of Lawsuit and Request for Waiver of Summons" and "Form 2. Waiver of Service of Summons" are the approved Forms for complying with the requirements of Ariz.R.Civ.P. 4.1(c) and 4.2(c). (As promulgated, Form 2 was separated into two separate Forms, but they comprise only a single "Waiver of Service of Summons.")

Form 3, formerly the Joint Dispute Resolution Statement to

the Court, required by former Rule 16(g), was abrogated August 30, 2012, effective January 1, 2013.

The sets of Uniform Interrogatories which were formerly contained as Appendices to the Uniform Rules of Practice of the Superior Court and to the Uniform Rules of Practice for Medical Malpractice Cases were transferred here as Forms 4, 5, and 6 as part of the 2000 Civil Rules Consolidation Project. Forms 4, 5 and 6 were amended effective January 1, 2009.

Form 8 (Notice of Limited Scope Representation, was adopted effective) January 1, 2009.

Form 9 (Subpoena in a Civil Case) was adopted effective January 1, 2011.

Form 10 (Certification of a Complex Case) was adopted on a permanent basis effective January 1, 2012.

Forms 11, 12 and 13 were adopted in connection with the adoption of new and amended rules governing pretrial case management and trial setting. These forms set forth the forms approved by the Arizona Supreme Court for the parties' Joint Report and Proposed Scheduling Order.

Forms 11(a) and (b) are for use in expedited cases. Forms 12(a) and (b) are for use in standard cases. Forms 13(a) and 13(b) are for use in complex cases. Parties are required to file their Joint Report and Proposed Scheduling Order on the appropriate Rule 84 form depending on the classification of their case, *i.e.*, expedited, standard or complex. The forms are effective April 15, 2014 and apply to cases filed on or after that date, and to those cases subject to the 2014 case management/trial setting rule amendments. *See*, November 27, 2013 Amended Order Regarding Applicability Provision, in R-13-0017.

2. *Comparison with Federal Rule*. The text of ARCP 84 is essentially the same as FRCP 84.

Rule 85. Title

These Rules may be known and cited as the Rules of Civil Procedure.

Rule 86. Effective date

These Rules shall take effect and be in force on and after midnight December 31, 1955.

2000 RULES CONSOLIDATION CORRELATION TABLE

The 2000 rules consolidation effort seeks to incorporate the provisions of the Uniform Rules of Practice of the Superior Court, the Uniform Rules of Procedure for Arbitration, and the Uniform Rules of Practice for Medical Malpractice Cases, which now exist as separate sets of procedural rules, into either the Arizona Rules of Civil Procedure or the Rules of the Arizona Supreme Court. The guiding principles for this consolidation initiative were that (1) rules whose subject matter was adequately covered by other existing rules should simply be eliminated, (2) provisions in the sets of rules to be consolidated that had a bearing on the manner in which civil litigants and/or their counsel are to conduct civil litigation should be placed in the Arizona Rules of Civil Procedure, and (3) rule provisions that dealt primarily with the internal workings of the Superior Courts, and had at most an indirect impact on how litigants and/or their counsel interact with the judicial system, should be placed in the Rules of the Arizona Supreme Court. Consistent application of these principles resulted in a need to transfer and/or renumber certain existing provisions of the Arizona Rules of Civil Procedure and, in one instance, to renumber an existing provision in the Rules of the Arizona Supreme Court.

The Correlation Table which follows indicates what disposition is to be made of the provisions of the Uniform Rules of Practice of the Superior Court, the Uniform Rules of Procedure for Arbitration and the Uniform Rules of Practice for Medical Malpractice Cases, which are to be eliminated as separate sets of rules, and of the provisions of the Arizona Rules of Civil Procedure and of the Rules of the Arizona Supreme Court which are incidentally affected in the process. In describing the "New Location" of the rules impacted by the consolidation process, the Arizona Rules of Civil Procedure has been abbreviated as "ARCP," and the Rules of the Arizona Supreme Court as "RASC."

Arizona Rules of Civil Procedure

Former Rule	New Location (2000)
Rule 6(c)	Abrogated[1]
Rule 7(b)(1)	Rule 7.1(a), ARCP
Rule 7(b)(2)	Rule 7.1(a), ARCP
Rule 7(b)(3)	Rule 7.1(a), ARCP
Rule 7(c)	Rule 7(b), ARCP
Rule 16(a)(5)	Rule 16.1(g), ARCP
Rule 16(c)	Rule 16(b), ARCP
Rule 16.1	Rule 16.2, ARCP
Rule 39(*l*)	Abrogated[2]
Rule 42(c)	Abrogated[3]
Rule 42(d)	Rule 38.1(i), ARCP
Rule 42(e)	Rule 38.1(j), ARCP
Rule 43(g)	Abrogated[4]
Rule 54(f)	Rule 54(f)(1), ARCP
Rule 56(c)	Rule 56(c)(1), ARCP
Rule 58(e)	Rule 58(f), ARCP

[1]Former Rule 6(c) was abrogated because its provisions, with one exception, were plainly inconsistent with the provisions of Rule IV of the Uniform Rules of Practice of the Superior Court, and with actual civil motion practice. A modified version of the provision of former Rule 6(c) dealing with the time for filing of affidavits in support of, or in opposition to, civil motions, was incorporated into Rule 7.1(a).

[2]The provisions of former Rule 39(*l*) were entirely duplicative of both Rule XIII of the Uniform Rules of Practice of the Superior Court and Rule 77(i) of the Arizona Rules of Civil Procedure. A modified version of the latter Rule was added to the Rules of the Arizona Supreme Court as a Rule 91(e), and the other two Rules were simply eliminated.

[3]The provisions of former Rule 42(c) were duplicative of, indeed identical to, the provisions of former Rule V(i) of the Uniform Rules of Practice of the Superior Court, which became Rule 38.1(h) of the Arizona Rules of Civil Procedure.

[4]Rule 43(g) was eliminated because its limitations on the use of expert testimony were essentially duplicative of the more specific limitations contained in Rule 26(b)(4)(D).

Former Rule	New Location (2000)
Rule 58(f)	Rule 58(g), ARCP
Rule 77(a)	Rule 91(a), RASC
Rule 77(b)	Rule 91(b), RASC
Rule 77(c)	Rule 91(c), RASC
Rule 77(d)	Rule 91(d), RASC
Rule 77(e)	Rule 95(d), RASC
Rule 77(f)	Rule 94(b), RASC
Rule 77(g)	Rule 58(e), ARCP
Rule 77(h)	Rule 95(e), RASC
Rule 77(i)	Rule 91(e), RASC
Rule 77(j)	Rule 91(f), RASC
Rule 78	Rule 7.1(c), ARCP
Rule 79(a)	Rule 94(c), RASC
Rule 79(b)	Rule 94(d), RASC
Rule 79(c)	Rule 94(e), RASC
Rule 79(d)	Rule 94(f), RASC
Rule 79(e)	Rule 91(g), RASC
Rule 79(f)	Rule 94(g), RASC
Rule 79(g)	Rule 94(h), RASC
Rule 83	Abrogated[5]

Uniform Rules of Practice of the Superior Court

Former Rule	New Location (2000)
Uniform Rule I(a)	Rule 92(a), RASC[6]
Uniform Rule I(b)	Rule 92(b), RASC

[5]The provisions of former Rule 83 were effectively replaced by the provisions formerly contained in Rule XIV of the Uniform Rules of Practice of the Superior Court.

[6]Rule I(a)(5) of the Uniform Rules of Practice of the Superior Court was not retained, because its provisions were arguably inconsistent with current practice with respect to the adoption and promulgation of Local Rules, and were deemed unnecessary in light of the adoption of Rule 83 of the Arizona Rules of Civil Procedure.

Former Rule	New Location (2000)
Uniform Rule II(a)	Rule 93(a)(1), RASC
Uniform Rule II(b)	Rule 93(a)(2), RASC
Uniform Rule II(c)	Rule 93(a)(3), RASC
Uniform Rule II(d)	Rule 93(a)(4), RASC
Uniform Rule II(e)	Rule 93(a)(5), RASC
Uniform Rule II(f)	Rule 93(a)(6), RASC
Uniform Rule II(g)	Rule 93(a)(7), RASC
Uniform Rule II(h)	Rule 93(a)(8), RASC
Uniform Rule II(i)	Rule 93(a)(9), RASC
Uniform Rule III(a)	Rule 94(a)(1), RASC
Uniform Rule III(b)	Rule 94(a)(2), RASC
Uniform Rule III(c)	Rule 94(a)(3), RASC
Uniform Rule IV(a)	Rule 7.1(a), ARCP
Uniform Rule IV(b)	Rule 7.1(b), ARCP
Uniform Rule IV(c)	Rule 93(b), RASC
Uniform Rule IV(d)	Rule 7.1(d), ARCP
Uniform Rule IV(e)	Abrogated[7]
Uniform Rule IV(f)	Rule 56(c)(2), ARCP
Uniform Rule IV(g)	Rules 26(g), 37(a)(2)(C), ARCP
Uniform Rule IV(h)	Rule 7.1 (e), ARCP
Uniform Rule V(a)	Abrogated[8]
Uniform Rule V(b)	Rule 38.1(a), ARCP
Uniform Rule V(c)	Rule 38.1(b), ARCP

---

[7]The retention of former Rule IV(e) of the Uniform Rules of Practice of the Superior Court, which authorized the scheduling of a special pretrial conference for the hearing of repeated or multiple motions, was deemed unnecessary, and potentially confusing, in light of the expanded permissible scope of pretrial conferences scheduled pursuant to Rule 16 of the Arizona Rules of Civil Procedure.

[8]The provisions of former Rule V(a) of the Uniform Rules of Practice of the Superior Court required the filing, in certain counties, of a list of witnesses and exhibits as a predicate for submitting a Motion to Set and Certificate of Readiness. The Committee was of the view that this requirement had been rendered obsolete by the provisions of Rule 26.1 of the Arizona Rules of Civil Procedure, which requires the voluntary and seasonable disclosure of, inter alia, the identities of trial witnesses and exhibits, and by Rule 16(d), which requires the filing of a joint pretrial statement.

Former Rule	**New Location (2000)**
Uniform Rule V(d)	Rule 38.1(c), ARCP
Uniform Rule V(e)	Rule 38.1(d), ARCP
Uniform Rule V(f)	Rule 38.1(e), ARCP
Uniform Rule V(g)	Rule 38.1(f), ARCP
Uniform Rule V(h)	Rule 38.1(g), ARCP
Uniform Rule V(i)	Rule 38.1(h), ARCP
Uniform Rule V(j)	Rule 38.1(k), ARCP
Uniform Rule VI(a)	Rule 16(d), ARCP
Uniform Rule VI(b)	Rule 16(d), ARCP
Uniform Rule VI(c)	Abrogated[9]
Uniform Rule VI(d)	Rule 16(f), ARCP
Uniform Rule VI(e)	Rules 16.1(a) to (c), (f), (h), ARCP
Uniform Rule VII	Rule 92(c), RASC
Uniform Rule VIII(a)	Rule 16(d), ARCP
Uniform Rule VIII(b)	Abrogated[10]
Uniform Rule VIII(c)	Rule 39(q), ARCP
Uniform Rule VIII(d)	Abrogated[11]
Uniform Rule IX	Rule 91(i), RASC
Uniform Rule X(a)	Rule 95(a), RASC
Uniform Rule X(b)	Rule 95(b), RASC
Uniform Rule X(c)	Rule 95(c), RASC

[9]The provisions of former Rule VI(c) of the Uniform Rules of Practice of the Superior Court were essentially duplicative of the provisions of Rules 16(a) to (c) of the Arizona Rules of Civil Procedure.

[10]Former Rule VIII(b) of the Uniform Rules of Practice of the Superior Court was entirely duplicative of the provisions of Rule 51(a) of the Arizona Rules of Civil Procedure.

[11]Former Rule VIII(d) of the Uniform Rules of Practice of the Superior Court was entirely duplicative of the provisions of Rule 47(b) of the Arizona Rules of Civil Procedure.

Former Rule	New Location (2000)
Uniform Rule XI	Abrogated[12]
Uniform Rule XII(a)	Rule 5.1(b), ARCP
Uniform Rule XII(b)	Rule 5.1(c), ARCP
Uniform Rule XII(c)	Rule 5.1(a), ARCP
Uniform Rule XII(d)	Rule 8(h), ARCP
Uniform Rule XIII	Abrogated[13]
Uniform Rule XIV	Rule 83, ARCP
Uniform Rule XV	Abrogated[14]
Uniform Rule XVI	Abrogated[15]
Uniform Rule XVII(a)	Rule 33.1(d), ARCP
Uniform Rule XVII(b)	Abrogated[16]
Uniform Rule XVII(c)	Rule 33.1(e), ARCP
Uniform Rule XVII(d)	Rule 33.1(f), ARCP
Uniform Rule XVII, Appendix	Appendix of Forms, Rule 84 ARCP

[12]The provisions of former Rule XI of the Uniform Rules of Practice of the Superior Court were essentially duplicative of provisions contained in Rule 79(a) of the Arizona Rules of Civil Procedure, which became Rule 94(c) of the Rules of the Arizona Supreme Court.

[13]The provisions of former Rule XIII of the Uniform Rules of Practice of the Superior Court were duplicative of both Rule 39(*l*) of the Arizona Rules of Civil Procedure, which was abrogated, and Rule 77(i) of those Rules, which became Rule 91(e) of the Rules of the Arizona Supreme Court.

[14]The provisions of former Rule XV of the Uniform Rules of Practice of the Superior Court merely set forth the effective date of those Rules. As the Rules were to be eliminated as a separate set of rules, there was no need to retain this provision.

[15]The provisions of former Rule XVI of the Uniform Rules of Practice of the Superior Court had been deleted effective September 7, 1983. There was, accordingly, no need to relocate this provision as part of the consolidation process.

[16]The provisions of former Rule XVII(b) of the Uniform Rules of Practice of the Superior Court specified that the service of interrogatories and responses was to be made in accordance with Rule 5 of the Arizona Rules of Civil Procedure. As this and certain other Uniform Rules were incorporated into the Arizona Rules of Civil Procedure, the continued reference to Rule 5 was unnecessary.

Former Rule	**New Location (2000)**
Uniform Rule XVIII(a)	Rule 91(h)(1), RASC
Uniform Rule XVIII(b)	Rule 91(h)(2), RASC
Uniform Rule XIX	Rule 91(f), RASC

Uniform Rules of Procedure for Arbitration

Former Rule	**New Location (2000)**
Arb Rule 1(a)	Rule 72(a), ARCP
Arb Rule 1(b)	Rule 72(b), ARCP
Arb Rule 1(c)	Rule 72(c), ARCP
Arb Rule 1(d)	Rule 72(d), ARCP
Arb Rule 1(e)	Rule 72(e), ARCP
Arb Rule 2(a)	Rule 73(a), ARCP
Arb Rule 2(b)	Rule 73(b), ARCP
Arb Rule 2(c)	Rule 73(c), ARCP
Arb Rule 2(d)	Rule 73(d), ARCP
Arb Rule 2(e)	Rule 73(e), ARCP
Arb Rule 3	Rules 72(a), 74(a), 76(c), ARCP
Arb Rule 4(a)	Rule 74(b), ARCP
Arb Rule 4(b)	Rule 74(c), ARCP
Arb Rule 4(c)	Rule 74(d), ARCP
Arb Rule 4(d)	Rule 74(e), ARCP
Arb Rule 4(e)	Rule 74(f), ARCP
Arb Rule 4(f)	Rule 74(g), ARCP
Arb Rule 4(g)	Rule 74(h), ARCP
Arb Rule 4(h)	Rule 74(i), ARCP
Arb Rule 4(i)	Rule 74(j), ARCP
Arb Rule 4(j)	Rule 74(k), ARCP
Arb Rule 5(a)	Rule 75(a), ARCP
Arb Rule 5(b)	Rule 75(b), ARCP
Arb Rule 5(c)	Rule 75(c), ARCP

Former Rule	New Location (2000)
Arb Rule 5(d)	Abrogated[17]
Arb Rule 6(a)	Rule 75(d), ARCP
Arb Rule 6(b)	Rule 75(e), ARCP
Arb Rule 7(a)	Rule 76(a), ARCP
Arb Rule 7(b)	Rule 76(b), ARCP
Arb Rule 7(c)	Rule 76(c), ARCP
Arb Rule 7(d)	Rule 76(d), ARCP
Arb Rule 7(e)	Rule 76(e), ARCP
Arb Rule 7(f)	Rule 76(f), ARCP
Arb Rule 7(g)	Rule 76(g), ARCP

Uniform Rules of Practice for Medical Malpractice Cases

Former Rule	New Location (2000)
Med Mal Rule 1(A)	Rule 16(c), ARCP
Med Mal Rule 1(B)	Rule 26.2(A), ARCP
Med Mal Rule 1(C)	Rule 26.2(B), ARCP
Med Mal Rule 1(D)	Rules 16(c), 26(b)(4), ARCP[18]
Med Mal Rule 1(E)	Abrogated[19]

[17]The provisions of former Rule 5(d) of the Uniform Rules of Procedure for Arbitration called for a Statement of Costs to be filed within ten (10) days after the filing of the arbitration award. An identical requirement was imposed by Rule 5(a) of those Rules, which has been transferred to Rule 75(a) of the Arizona Rules of Civil Procedure. Former Rule 5(d) was actually abrogated as part of amendments to the Uniform Rules of Procedure for Arbitration which were implemented together with, and as part of, the "consolidation amendments."

[18]The only provision of former Rule 1(D) of the Uniform Rules of Practice for Medical Malpractice Cases placed in Rule 26(b)(4) of the Arizona Rules of Civil Procedure was former Rule 1(D)(4). Former Medical Malpractice Rule 1(D)(9) and Rule 1(D)(10) were eliminated as outmoded and/or unnecessary. The balance of the provisions of former Rule 1(D) were placed in Rule 16(c) of the Arizona Rules of Civil Procedure.

[19]The provisions of former Rule 1(E) of the Uniform Rules of Practice for Medical Malpractice Cases were essentially duplicative of the provisions of Rule 16(f) of the Arizona Rules of Civil Procedure, as amended.

Former Rule	New Location (2000)
Med Mal Rule 2	Rules 16.1(a), (c), (d), (e), (g), ARCP
Med Mal Rule 3	Abrogated[20]
Med Mal Rule 4	Rule 54(f)(2), ARCP
Uniform Interrogatories for Use in Medical Malpractice Cases	Appendix of Forms, Rule 84, ARCP

Rules of the Arizona Supreme Court

Former Rule	New Location (2000)
Rule 91, RASC	Rule 96, RASC

[20]Former Rule 3 of the Uniform Rules of Practice for Medical Malpractice Cases was eliminated as having served its intended purpose, and now serving only to impose an unnecessary burden on the court and litigants.

ARIZONA RULES OF EVIDENCE

Research Note

See Arizona Revised Statutes Annotated, *Volume 17A, for historical notes, comments, and judicial constructions.*

See McAuliffe and Wahl, Arizona Practice—Law of Evidence, 4th Ed. (Revised), *for discussion of the Arizona Rules of Evidence.*

Use Westlaw® *to find recent cases citing provisions of the Arizona Rules of Evidence. In addition, use* Westlaw *to find a specific term or to update a rule; see the AZ-RULES and AZ-ORDERS SCOPE screens for further information.*

ARTICLE I. GENERAL PROVISIONS

ARTICLE II. JUDICIAL NOTICE

ARTICLE III. PRESUMPTIONS IN CIVIL ACTIONS AND PROCEEDINGS

ARTICLE IV. RELEVANCY AND ITS LIMITS

ARTICLE V. PRIVILEGES

ARTICLE VI. WITNESSES

ARTICLE VII. OPINIONS AND EXPERT TESTIMONY

ARTICLE VIII. HEARSAY

ARTICLE IX. AUTHENTICATION AND IDENTIFICATION

ARTICLE X. CONTENTS OF WRITINGS, RECORDINGS, AND PHOTOGRAPHS

ARTICLE XI. MISCELLANEOUS RULES

ARTICLE I. GENERAL PROVISIONS

Prefatory Comment to 2012 Amendments

The 2012 amendments to the Arizona Rules of Evidence make three different kinds of changes: (1) the Arizona rules have generally been restyled so that they correspond to the Federal Rules of Evidence as restyled. These "restyling" changes are not meant to change the admissibility of evidence; (2) in several instances, the Arizona rules have also been amended to "conform" to the federal rules, and these changes may alter the way in which evidence is admitted (see, e.g., Rule 702); and (3) in some instances, the Arizona rules either retain language that is distinct from the federal rules (see, e.g., Rule 404), or deliberately depart from the language of the federal rules (see, e.g., Rule 412).

The Court has generally adopted the federal rules as restyled, with the following exceptions: Rule 103(d) (Fundamental Error); Rule 302; Rule 404 (Character and Other Acts Evidence); Rule 408(a)(2) (Criminal Use Exception); Rule 611(b) (Scope of Cross-Examination); Rule 706(c) (Compensation for Expert Testimony); Rule 801(d)(1)(A) (Prior Inconsistent Statements as Non-Hearsay); Rule 803(25) (Former testimony in non-criminal action or proceeding); and Rule 804(b)(1) (Former testimony in a criminal case). The restyling is intended to make the rules more easily understood and to make style and terminology consistent throughout the rules and with the restyled Federal Rules. Restyling changes are intended to be stylistic only, and not intended to change any ruling on the admissibility of evidence.

The Court has adopted conforming changes to Rule 103 (Rulings on Evidence); Rule 201 (Judicial Notice); Rule 301 (Presumptions); Rule 407 (Subsequent Remedial Measures); Rule 410 (Plea Discussions); Rules 412–415; Rule 606 (Juror's Competency as a Witness); Rule 608 (Character Evidence); Rule 609 (Impeachment by Criminal Conviction); Rule 611 (Mode of Presenting Evidence); Rule 615 (Excluding Witnesses); Rule 701 (Opinion Testimony by Lay Witnesses); Rule 702 (Testimony by Expert Witnesses); Rule 704(b) (Opinion on an Ultimate Issue—Exception); Rule 706 (Court Appointed Experts); Rule 801(d)(2) (Definitions That Apply to This Article; Exclusions from Hearsay); Rule 803(6)(A), (6)(D) and (24) (Hearsay Exceptions Regardless of Unavailability); Rule 804 (b)(1), (b)(3) and (b)(7) (Hearsay Exceptions When Declarant Unavailable); and Rule 807 (Residual Exception).

Conforming changes that are not merely restyling, as well as deliberate departures from the language of the federal rules, are noted at the outset of the comment to the corresponding Arizona rule.

Where the language of an Arizona rule parallels that of a federal rule, federal court decisions interpreting the federal rule are persuasive but not binding with respect to interpreting the Arizona rule.

Added Sept. 8, 2011, effective Jan. 1, 2012. Amended Aug. 30, 2012, effective Jan. 1, 2013.

Rule 101. Scope; Definitions

(a) Scope. These rules apply to proceedings in courts in the State of Arizona. The specific courts and proceedings to which the rules apply, along with exceptions, are set out in Rule 1101.

(b) Definitions. In these rules:

(1) "civil case" means a civil action or proceeding;

(2) "criminal case" includes a criminal proceeding;

(3) "public office" includes a public agency;

(4) "record" includes a memorandum, report, or data compilation;

(5) a "rule prescribed by the Supreme Court" means a rule adopted by the Arizona Supreme Court; and

(6) a reference to any kind of written material or any other medium includes electronically stored information.

Amended Sept. 8, 2011, effective Jan. 1, 2012.

Comment to 2012 Amendment

The language of Rule 101 has been amended, and definitions have been added, to conform to the federal restyling of the Evidence Rules to make them more easily understood and to make style and terminology consistent throughout the rules. These changes are intended to be stylistic only. There is no intent to change any result in any ruling on evidence admissibility.

Comment to Original 1977 Rule

These rules apply in all courts, record and nonrecord, in Arizona.

AUTHORS' COMMENTS

Analysis

1. *Scope and Origin of Arizona Rules of Evidence.* The Arizona Rules of Evidence were adopted effective September 1, 1977, fol-

lowing the adoption of the Federal Rules of Evidence, on which they were closely modeled. Ariz.R.Evid. 101, which cross-references Rule 1101, specifies that the Rules govern proceedings in courts in the State of Arizona.

Rule 1101 makes clear that the Rules are applicable in proceedings before magistrates, court commissioners and in the Justice Courts. *Arizona State Hospital/Arizona Community Protection and Treatment Center v. Klein*, 231 Ariz. 467, 296 P.3d 1003 (Ct. App. Div. 1 2013) (The Arizona Rules of Evidence "apply to proceedings in courts in the State of Arizona" subject to certain exceptions.).

The Rules apply in all civil proceedings, and in all criminal proceedings except as otherwise provided in the Arizona Rules of Criminal Procedure. The Rules, other than the rules with respect to privileges, do not apply in grand jury proceedings. *See,* Ariz. R. Evid. 1101(d); *Franzi v. Superior Court of Arizona In and For Pima County*, 139 Ariz. 556, 679 P.2d 1043 (1984) ("[H]earsay evidence in a grand jury proceeding is not objectionable."). In addition, Rule 104(a) specifies that the Rules do not apply where the Court is called upon to make preliminary determinations as to the admissibility of evidence.

Rule 75(d) specifically makes the Arizona Rules of Evidence applicable to arbitration hearings. Rule 75(e) of those rules, however, also provide for relaxed requirements for the admissibility of certain specified categories of documents. Finally, in family law cases, the rules of evidence apply in those circumstances, and to the extent, provided in Rule 2(B) of the Arizona Family Law Rules.

2. *Similarity to Federal Rules of Evidence.* Effective January 1, 2012, and with few exceptions, the Arizona Supreme Court amended and/or restyled the Arizona Rules of Evidence in their entirety. The Court did not amend Arizona Rule 404, and did not adopt Federal Rules of Evidence 412 to 415. Rule 502 was amended to add a hyphen between the words "work" and "product" in the text of the rule. The Arizona Supreme Court did not make that same stylistic amendment, however, to the title of Rule 502. That approach is consistent with the federal approach, which also did not hyphenate "work product" in the title to Federal Rule of Evidence 502.

As explained in the Prefatory Comments to 2012 Amendments, the 2012 amendments to the Arizona Rules of Evidence consist of three different types of changes: (1) restyling amendments to correspond to the Federal Rules of Evidence, but not intended to change the admissibility of evidence; (2) conforming amendments to correspond with the Federal Rules of Evidence, which may alter the admissibility of evidence (*see, e.g.,* Rule 702); and (3) amendments that retain language distinct from the Federal Rules of Evidence or deliberately depart from the Federal Rules of Evidence. As a result of these amendments, the Arizona Rules of Evidence as a whole bear a greater resemblance to the Federal Rules of Evidence than the Arizona Rules of Civil Procedure bear to the Federal Rules of Civil Procedure.

The Federal Rules of Evidence, however, were legislatively enacted; while, the Arizona Rules of Evidence were adopted and promulgated solely by the Arizona Supreme Court. While the United States Supreme Court, in construing a provision of the Federal Rules of Evidence, must consider Congressional purpose and intent, the Arizona Supreme Court, in construing the Arizona Rules of Evidence, looks only to the text of the Rule and its own intent in adopting or amending it. *State v. Bible*, 175 Ariz. 549, 858 P.2d 1152 (1993). Thus, in interpreting any of the Arizona Rules of Evidence, the Arizona Supreme Court considers decisions interpreting a corresponding Federal Rule of Evidence as persuasive, but not controlling. *Shotwell v. Donahoe*, 207 Ariz. 287, 85 P.3d 1045, 93 Fair Empl. Prac. Cas. (BNA) 658 (2004); *State ex rel. Miller v. Tucson Associates Ltd. Partnership*, 165 Ariz. 519, 799 P.2d 860 (Ct. App. Div. 2 1990). Stated another way, Arizona Supreme Court is not bound by the United States Supreme Court's non-constitutional interpretations of a corresponding provision of the Federal Rules of Evidence. *State v. Terrazas*, 189 Ariz. 580, 944 P.2d 1194 (1997); *State v. Bible*, 175 Ariz. 549, 858 P.2d 1152 (1993). *See*, *Logerquist v. McVey*, 196 Ariz. 470, 1 P.3d 113 (2000) (interpreting Arizona's Rule 702 differently than its Federal counterpart).

3. *Comparison With Federal Rule.* Effective January 1, 2012, the Arizona Supreme Court added definitions and amended Rule 101 to conform to the federal restyling of the Evidence Rules, an effort undertaken to make the evidence rules more easily understood and to make style and terminology consistent throughout. The 2012 Comment states the stylistic amendments are not intended to "change any result in any ruling on evidence admissibility."

Following the 2012 restyling amendments, the language of Rule 101 remains identical to its federal counterpart, Fed. R. Evid. 101, except for changes necessary to adapt the Rule to the Arizona court system.

Although Rule 101 parallels its federal counterpart, "federal court decisions interpreting the federal rule are persuasive but not binding with respect to interpreting the Arizona rule." *See,* Prefatory Comment to 2012 Amendments. *See also, State v. Terrazas*, 189 Ariz. 580, 944 P.2d 1194 (1997) (The Arizona Supreme Court is "not bound by the United States Supreme Court's non-

constitutional construction of the Federal Rules of Evidence when [the Arizona Supreme Court construes] the Arizona Rules of Evidence."), citing, *State v. Bible*, 175 Ariz. 549, 858 P.2d 1152 (1993); *State v. Salazar-Mercado*, 232 Ariz. 256, 304 P.3d 543 (Ct. App. Div. 2 2013). Practitioners are urged to keep this legal tenet in mind as they research federal case law interpreting a federal evidentiary rule that corresponds to an Arizona evidentiary rule.

4. *Relationship of Rules to Statutory Provisions.* Rules of Evidence have been held to be a species of "procedural rule," and the Arizona Rules of Evidence were adopted pursuant to the Arizona Supreme Court's exclusive constitutional authority to regulate procedural matters in any court in the state. Ariz. Const. Art. VI, § 5(5); *Seisinger v. Siebel*, 220 Ariz. 85, 203 P.3d 483 (2009) (the "rules of evidence have generally been regarded as procedural in nature"), quoting *State ex rel. Collins v. Seidel*, 142 Ariz. 587, 590, 691 P.2d 678, 681 (1984); *Lear v. Fields*, 226 Ariz. 226, 245 P.3d 911 (Ct. App. Div. 2 2011), review denied, (Sept. 20, 2011); *State v. Robinson*, 153 Ariz. 191, 735 P.2d 801 (1987) (rejected by, Cassidy v. State, 74 Md. App. 1, 536 A.2d 666 (1988)); *Readenour v. Marion Power Shovel, a Div. of Dresser Industries, Inc.*, 149 Ariz. 442, 719 P.2d 1058, Prod. Liab. Rep. (CCH) P 11012 (1986); *In re Jonah T.*, 196 Ariz. 204, 994 P.2d 1019 (Ct. App. Div. 1 1999); *Matter of One (1) Rolex Brand Man's Watch*, 176 Ariz. 294, 860 P.2d 1347 (Ct. App. Div. 1 1993).

The determination of whether a statute unduly infringes upon the rulemaking power of the court requires an analysis of both the challenged statute and the rule then at issue. *Seisinger v. Siebel*, 220 Ariz. 85, 203 P.3d 483 (2009). The first step in the analysis is to determine whether the rule and the statute can be harmonized; if it is possible to harmonize the statute with the rule, then there is no conflict and the analysis ends. *See*, *Seisinger v. Siebel*, 220 Ariz. 85, 203 P.3d 483 (2009). If the statute and the rule cannot be harmonized, then the analysis turns to whether the statute at issue is substantive or procedural in nature. *Seisinger v. Siebel*, 220 Ariz. 85, 203 P.3d 483 (2009). Substantive law, which is the province of the Legislative branch, "creates, defines and regulates rights." *Seisinger v. Siebel*, 220 Ariz. 85, 203 P.3d 483 (2009).

With respect to the rules of evidence, and particularly in the area of the hearsay rules, the Court views the process of defining what is reliable and admissible evidence, and establishing processes to test that reliability, as inherently and exclusively judicial functions, and has tended to guard its rule-making prerogatives somewhat more zealously. *State v. Robinson*, 153 Ariz. 191, 735 P.2d 801 (1987) (rejected on other grounds by, Cassidy v. State, 74 Md. App. 1, 536 A.2d 666 (1988)); *Matter of One (1) Rolex Brand Man's Watch*, 176 Ariz. 294, 860 P.2d 1347

(Ct. App. Div. 1 1993); *Wieseler v. Prins*, 167 Ariz. 223, 805 P.2d 1044 (Ct. App. Div. 1 1990). Evidentiary rules adopted by statute will be honored only if they represent "reasonable and workable" arrangements that supplement rather than contradict the Rules of Evidence, and the appellate courts have upheld such statutes on this basis as not violating the separation of powers doctrine. *Seisinger v. Siebel*, 220 Ariz. 85, 203 P.3d 483 (2009) (statute establishing requirements for introducing expert testimony on standard of care in medical malpractice cases); *Readenour v. Marion Power Shovel, a Div. of Dresser Industries, Inc.*, 149 Ariz. 442, 719 P.2d 1058, Prod. Liab. Rep. (CCH) P 11012 (1986) (post-sale product modifications inadmissible); *State ex rel. Collins v. Seidel*, 142 Ariz. 587, 691 P.2d 678 (1984) (alternative foundational requirements for admissibility of breathalyzer tests); *Borja v. Phoenix General Hosp., Inc.*, 151 Ariz. 302, 727 P.2d 355 (Ct. App. Div. 2 1986) (admissibility of medical liability review panel findings).

The legislature, however, may not define what is relevant and admissible in a manner that conflicts with the Rules of Evidence, and the appellate courts have on occasions declared unconstitutional statutes which it perceived as having crossed that line. *State v. Robinson*, 153 Ariz. 191, 735 P.2d 801 (1987) (rejected on other grounds by, Cassidy v. State, 74 Md. App. 1, 536 A.2d 666 (1988)) (hearsay exception for minors' statements describing sexual abuse); *Barsema v. Susong*, 156 Ariz. 309, 751 P.2d 969 (1988) (statute precluding receipt of evidence that witness in medical malpractice case is insured by same carrier as defendant); *Lear v. Fields*, 226 Ariz. 226, 245 P.3d 911 (Ct. App. Div. 2 2011), review denied, (Sept. 20, 2011) (holding unconstitutional, A.R.S. § 12-2203, a statute purporting to govern as a general rule of evidence the admissibility of expert testimony in any civil or criminal action).

Rule 102. Purpose

These rules should be construed so as to administer every proceeding fairly, eliminate unjustifiable expense and delay, and promote the development of evidence law, to the end of ascertaining the truth and securing a just determination.

Amended Sept. 8, 2011, effective Jan. 1, 2012.

Comment to 2012 Amendment

The language of Rule 102 has been amended to conform to the federal restyling of the Evidence Rules to make them more easily understood and to make style and terminology consistent throughout the rules. These changes are intended to be stylistic only. There is no intent to change any result in any ruling on evidence admissibility.

AUTHORS' COMMENTS

Analysis

1. *Scope and Purpose of Rule.* Ariz.R.Evid. 102 prescribes that the Arizona Rules of Evidence are to be construed to afford litigants fairness in judicial proceedings, to eliminate unjustifiable expense and delay, and to promote the growth and development of the law of evidence as a vehicle for ascertaining truth and insuring justice. *Shotwell v. Donahoe*, 207 Ariz. 287, 85 P.3d 1045, 93 Fair Empl. Prac. Cas. (BNA) 658 (2004) (hearsay exceptions that favor admission must be "counterbalanced by [analysis of the proffered evidence under] Rules 102 and 403", citing Comment to Rule 801); *State v. Carr*, 154 Ariz. 468, 743 P.2d 1386 (1987) (discussing the balancing tests inherent in Rules 102 and 403 with respect to the admission and exclusion of alleged prior inconsistent statement); *State v. Cruz*, 128 Ariz. 538, 627 P.2d 689 (1981) ("Like all other rules [of evidence] which favor the admission of evidence, the exceptions to the hearsay rule are counterbalanced by Rules 102 and 403." (quoting the Comment to Original 1977 Rule)). This is consistent with the admonition in Rule 1 of the Arizona Rules of Civil Procedure which provides that the rules of civil procedure are to be construed to "secure the just, speedy and inexpensive determination of every action."

2. *Comparison With Federal Rule.* Effective January 1, 2012, the Arizona Supreme Court amended Rule 102 to conform to the federal restyling of the Federal Rules of Evidence, an effort undertaken to make the evidence rules more easily understood and

to make style and terminology consistent throughout. The 2012 Comment states the stylistic amendments are not intended to "change any result in any ruling on evidence admissibility."

Following the 2012 restyling amendments, which included the addition of definitions, the language of Rule 102 remains identical to its federal counterpart, Fed. R. Evid. 102.

Although Rule 102 parallels its federal counterpart, "federal court decisions interpreting the federal rule are persuasive but not binding with respect to interpreting the Arizona rule." *See,* Prefatory Comment to 2012 Amendments. *See also, State v. Terrazas*, 189 Ariz. 580, 944 P.2d 1194 (1997) (The Arizona Supreme Court is "not bound by the United States Supreme Court's non-constitutional construction of the Federal Rules of Evidence when [the Arizona Supreme Court construes] the Arizona Rules of Evidence."), citing, *State v. Bible*, 175 Ariz. 549, 858 P.2d 1152 (1993); *State v. Salazar-Mercado*, 232 Ariz. 256, 304 P.3d 543 (Ct. App. Div. 2 2013). Practitioners are urged to keep this legal tenet in mind as they research federal case law interpreting a federal evidentiary rule that corresponds to an Arizona evidentiary rule.

Rule 103. Rulings on Evidence

(a) Preserving a Claim of Error. A party may claim error in a ruling to admit or exclude evidence only if the error affects a substantial right of the party and:

(1) if the ruling admits evidence, a party, on the record:

(A) timely objects or moves to strike; and

(B) states the specific ground, unless it was apparent from the context; or

(2) if the ruling excludes evidence, a party informs the court of its substance by an offer of proof, unless the substance was apparent from the context.

(b) Not Needing to Renew an Objection or Offer of Proof. Once the court rules definitively on the record—either before or at trial—a party need not renew an objection or offer of proof to preserve a claim of error for appeal.

(c) Court's Statement About the Ruling; Directing an Offer of Proof. The court may make any statement about the character or form of the evidence, the objection made, and the ruling. The court may direct that an offer of proof be made in question-and-answer form.

(d) Preventing the Jury from Hearing Inadmissible Evidence. To the extent practicable, the court must conduct a jury trial so that inadmissible evidence is not suggested to the jury by any means.

(e) Taking Notice of Fundamental Error. A court may take notice of an error affecting a fundamental right, even if the claim of error was not properly preserved.

Amended Sept. 8, 2011, effective Jan. 1, 2012.

Comment to 2012 Amendment

Subsection (b) has been added to conform to Federal Rule of Evidence 103(b).

Additionally, the language of Rule 103 has been amended to conform to the federal restyling of the Evidence Rules to make them more easily understood and to make style and terminology consistent throughout the rules. These changes are intended to be stylistic only. There is no intent in the restyling to change any result in any ruling on evidence admissibility.

The substance of subsection (e) (formerly subsection (d)), which refers to "fundamental error," has not been changed to conform to the federal rule, which refers to "plain error," because Arizona and federal courts have long used different terminology in this regard.

AUTHORS' COMMENTS

Analysis

2. Comparison With Federal Rule.
3. Objections to Admission of Evidence; Necessity; Specificity; Timing.
4. Objections to Exclusion of Evidence; Offers of Proof; Necessity; Procedure.
5. Reversals for Erroneous Admission or Exclusion of Evidence; Fundamental Error.

1. *Scope and Purpose of Rule.* Rule 103 is concerned with the mechanics of making and recording objections to the admission and exclusion of evidence. An objection to the admission of evidence, and an offer of proof when evidence is excluded, are necessary to preserve the issue of error in those decisions for appeal. *Montano v. Scottsdale Baptist Hospital, Inc.*, 119 Ariz. 448, 581 P.2d 682 (1978); *Brown v. U.S. Fidelity and Guar. Co.*, 194 Ariz. 85, 977 P.2d 807 (Ct. App. Div. 1 1998), as amended, (Nov. 25, 1998) and as corrected, (Aug. 5, 1999); *Rhue v. Dawson*, 173 Ariz. 220, 841 P.2d 215 (Ct. App. Div. 1 1992); *Gaston v. Hunter*, 121 Ariz. 33, 588 P.2d 326 (Ct. App. Div. 1 1978); *Hall v. Keller*, 9 Ariz. App. 584, 455 P.2d 266 (1969). The fact that a party may have waived an objection to certain evidence by failing to object to its admission at an initial trial of a matter does not preclude that party from objecting to its admission at a retrial of the matter. *Jimenez v. Wal-Mart Stores, Inc.*, 206 Ariz. 424, 79 P.3d 673 (Ct. App. Div. 2 2003). Under Ariz.R.Civ.P. 46, if an appropriate objection has been made, a formal exception to the ruling made is not necessary.

Whether proffered evidence is to be admitted or excluded is a matter committed to the trial court's sound discretion. *Gemstar Ltd. v. Ernst & Young*, 185 Ariz. 493, 917 P.2d 222 (1996); *Pipher v. Loo*, 221 Ariz. 399, 212 P.3d 91 (Ct. App. Div. 1 2009); *Belliard v. Becker*, 216 Ariz. 356, 166 P.3d 911 (Ct. App. Div. 1 2007); *Girouard v. Skyline Steel, Inc.*, 215 Ariz. 126, 158 P.3d 255 (Ct. App. Div. 1 2007); *Lohmeier v. Hammer*, 214 Ariz. 57, 148 P.3d 101 (Ct. App. Div. 1 2006); *Acuna v. Kroack*, 212 Ariz. 104, 128 P.3d 221 (Ct. App. Div. 2 2006); *John C. Lincoln Hosp. and Health Corp. v. Maricopa County*, 208 Ariz. 532, 96 P.3d 530 (Ct. App. Div. 1 2004), as amended, (Sept. 1, 2004); *Golonka v. General Motors Corp.*, 204 Ariz. 575, 65 P.3d 956, Prod. Liab. Rep. (CCH) P 16561 (Ct. App. Div. 1 2003); *Zimmerman v. Shakman*, 204 Ariz. 231, 62 P.3d 976 (Ct. App. Div. 1 2003); *Elia v. Pifer*, 194 Ariz. 74, 977 P.2d 796 (Ct. App. Div. 1 1998); *Brown v. U.S. Fidelity and Guar. Co.*, 194 Ariz. 85, 977 P.2d 807 (Ct. App. Div. 1 1998), as amended, (Nov. 25, 1998) and as corrected, (Aug. 5, 1999); *State ex rel. Miller v. Wells Fargo Bank of Arizona, N.A.*, 194 Ariz. 126, 978 P.2d 103 (Ct. App. Div. 1 1998); *Sheppard v.*

Crow-Barker Paul No. 1 Ltd. Partnership, 192 Ariz. 539, 968 P.2d 612 (Ct. App. Div. 1 1998). Those decisions are, of course, not made in a vacuum but are assisted by the arguments and objections of counsel.

2. *Comparison With Federal Rule.* As a consequence of the 2012 amendments, the language of Rule 103 is identical to its federal counterpart, Fed. R. Evid. 103.

Until the 2012 amendments, Arizona's rule differed from the Federal rule in that Arizona had not adopted the 2000 federal amendment to Fed. R. Evid.103, which added a provision to former Fed. R. Evid.103(a) obviating the need for the renewal of objections or offers of proof where the trial court has made a "definitive ruling" admitting or excluding evidence. As part of the 2012 amendments, Arizona adopted this provision as new subsection (b) [Not Needing To Renew an Objection Or Offer Of Proof] to conform with Fed. R. Evid. 103(b), as restyled. Arizona's adoption of this new provision imposes the obligation on a party to seek clarification as to whether an *in limine* or other evidentiary ruling is "definitive" where there is any doubt on that issue.

In addition, effective January 1, 2012, the Arizona Supreme Court amended Rule 103 to conform to the federal restyling of the Evidence Rules to make the rules more easily understood and to make style and terminology consistent throughout. The 2012 Comment states the stylistic amendments are not intended to "change any result in any ruling on evidence admissibility."

Although Rule 103 parallels its federal counterpart, "federal court decisions interpreting the federal rule are persuasive but not binding with respect to interpreting the Arizona rule." *See,* Prefatory Comment to 2012 Amendments. *See also, State v. Terrazas*, 189 Ariz. 580, 944 P.2d 1194 (1997) (The Arizona Supreme Court is "not bound by the United States Supreme Court's nonconstitutional construction of the Federal Rules of Evidence when [the Arizona Supreme Court construes] the Arizona Rules of Evidence."), citing, *State v. Bible*, 175 Ariz. 549, 858 P.2d 1152 (1993); *State v. Salazar-Mercado*, 232 Ariz. 256, 304 P.3d 543 (Ct. App. Div. 2 2013). Practitioners are urged to keep this legal tenet in mind as they research federal case law interpreting a federal evidentiary rule that corresponds to an Arizona evidentiary rule.

3. *Objections to Admission of Evidence; Necessity; Specificity; Timing.* In order to give the trial court opportunity to avoid error, and to preserve the issue for appeal, a party against whom assertedly objectionable evidence is offered must make a timely objection to its admission. *Brown v. U.S. Fidelity and Guar. Co.*, 194 Ariz. 85, 977 P.2d 807 (Ct. App. Div. 1 1998), as amended, (Nov. 25, 1998) and as corrected, (Aug. 5, 1999). As a consequence of the 2012 addition of Rule 103(b), it is no longer necessary to

renew an objection or offer of proof to preserve a claim of error for appeal.

The objection must specify the grounds and bases for objection; it is not sufficient to simply assert that the evidence is irrelevant, incompetent and/or immaterial. *Bradshaw v. State Farm Mut. Auto. Ins. Co.*, 157 Ariz. 411, 758 P.2d 1313 (1988); *Hawkins v. Allstate Ins. Co.*, 152 Ariz. 490, 733 P.2d 1073 (1987); *Grant v. Arizona Public Service Co.*, 133 Ariz. 434, 652 P.2d 507 (1982); *Johnson v. Elliott*, 112 Ariz. 57, 537 P.2d 927 (1975); *Tucson Federal Sav. & Loan Ass'n v. Aetna Inv. Corp.*, 74 Ariz. 163, 245 P.2d 423 (1952). An objection to evidence which states the wrong ground for objection does not preserve for appeal what would constitute a proper ground for objection to the evidence. *State ex rel. Miller v. Tucson Associates Ltd. Partnership*, 165 Ariz. 519, 799 P.2d 860 (Ct. App. Div. 2 1990); *Shell Oil Co. v. Gutierrez*, 119 Ariz. 426, 581 P.2d 271 (Ct. App. Div. 2 1978).

The objection must be made in a timely manner, and almost always before the evidence is received. A party cannot wait until the trial is over to see what the result will be and, at that point, move for a new trial on the grounds of evidentiary errors. *Estate of Reinen v. Northern Arizona Orthopedics, Ltd.*, 198 Ariz. 283, 9 P.3d 314 (2000); *Rustin v. Cook*, 143 Ariz. 486, 694 P.2d 316 (Ct. App. Div. 2 1984).

If a party does not have an opportunity to object before the receipt of the evidence, then that party must make a timely motion to strike the evidence, or for a mistrial, in order to preserve the issue. *Rutledge v. Arizona Bd. of Regents*, 147 Ariz. 534, 711 P.2d 1207, 29 Ed. Law Rep. 1161 (Ct. App. Div. 1 1985). The failure to make an appropriate objection or a motion to strike operates as a waiver of any claim of error in the admission of the evidence. *Bradshaw v. State Farm Mut. Auto. Ins. Co.*, 157 Ariz. 411, 758 P.2d 1313 (1988) (general objection insufficient); *Starkins v. Bateman*, 150 Ariz. 537, 724 P.2d 1206 (Ct. App. Div. 1 1986) (hearsay evidence admitted without objection becomes competent evidence admissible for all purposes); *Schneider v. Cessna Aircraft Co.*, 150 Ariz. 153, 722 P.2d 321, Prod. Liab. Rep. (CCH) P 10743 (Ct. App. Div. 1 1985); *Maxwell v. Aetna Life Ins. Co.*, 143 Ariz. 205, 693 P.2d 348 (Ct. App. Div. 1 1984); *Goldthorpe v. Farmers Ins. Exchange*, 19 Ariz. App. 366, 507 P.2d 978 (Div. 2 1973).

Any bench conference held to conduct argument and/or to make a ruling with respect to an objection must be held on the record, but outside the presence or hearing of the jury. *Archer v. Board of Sup'rs of Pima County*, 166 Ariz. 106, 800 P.2d 972 (1990); *Gosewisch v. American Honda Motor Co., Inc.*, 153 Ariz. 400, 737 P.2d 376, Prod. Liab. Rep. (CCH) P 11531, 83 A.L.R.4th 53 (1987); *Rodriguez v. Schlittenhart*, 161 Ariz. 609, 780 P.2d 442 (Ct. App.

Div. 2 1989); *Copeland v. City of Yuma*, 160 Ariz. 307, 772 P.2d 1160 (Ct. App. Div. 1 1989).

There are circumstances where both practical and strategic considerations make it unworkable to comply with the literal requirements of those doctrines. Where a subject which a party considers irrelevant and/or prejudicial will be gone into repeatedly by that party's opponent, and the Court rules the evidence admissible, requiring the aggrieved party to make an objection and/or conduct a bench conference or sidebar argument on the record every time the subject is addressed would serve only to unduly lengthen the trial, and might force that party to appear unduly disruptive in the jury's eyes. Ariz.R.Civ.P. 7.2 specifically authorizes the filing of motions *in limine*, which were a time-honored practice where a party anticipates an evidentiary problem in advance. *State ex rel. Berger v. Superior Court In and For Maricopa County*, 108 Ariz. 396, 499 P.2d 152 (1972); *Zimmerman v. Shakman*, 204 Ariz. 231, 62 P.3d 976 (Ct. App. Div. 1 2003); *Shuck v. Texaco Refining & Marketing, Inc.*, 178 Ariz. 295, 872 P.2d 1247 (Ct. App. Div. 1 1994).

A specific motion in limine directed to categories or types of evidence which is denied removes the necessity for making repeated objections to the evidence in question. *Gibson v. Gunsch*, 148 Ariz. 416, 714 P.2d 1311 (Ct. App. Div. 1 1985). Similarly, an adverse ruling on a challenged class of evidence eliminates the need for objection to that class of evidence when offered through other witnesses. *Padilla v. Southern Pac. Transp. Co.*, 131 Ariz. 533, 642 P.2d 878 (Ct. App. Div. 2 1982). In such a situation, it is prudent for counsel to record a continuing objection on the record and secure the trial court's concurrence in that procedure. *Starkins v. Bateman*, 150 Ariz. 537, 724 P.2d 1206 (Ct. App. Div. 1 1986).

Such motions *in limine* have also been employed in civil cases as a means to exclude evidence from trial for violations of the disclosure rules. *Zimmerman v. Shakman*, 204 Ariz. 231, 62 P.3d 976 (Ct. App. Div. 1 2003). When a motion *in limine* is used to enforce the provisions of Ariz.R.Civ.P. 26.1, governing disclosure of evidence, it is effectively a request for sanctions under Ariz.R.Civ.P. 37(c). *Zimmerman v. Shakman*, 204 Ariz. 231, 62 P.3d 976 (Ct. App. Div. 1 2003). As such, it must be considered and reviewed using the standards that have been developed in cases construing those two Rules. *Zimmerman v. Shakman*, 204 Ariz. 231, 62 P.3d 976 (Ct. App. Div. 1 2003).

4. *Objections to Exclusion of Evidence; Offers of Proof; Necessity; Procedure.* When the trial court's ruling excludes evidence, the party offering the evidence must make an offer of proof in order to preserve any claim that the exclusion of the evidence was reversible error. *A Tumbling-T Ranches v. Flood Control Dist. of*

Maricopa County, 222 Ariz. 515, 217 P.3d 1220 (Ct. App. Div. 1 2009); *Stewart v. Woodruff*, 19 Ariz. App. 190, 505 P.2d 1081 (Div. 2 1973); *Sulpher Springs Valley Elec. Co-op., Inc. v. Verdugo*, 14 Ariz. App. 141, 481 P.2d 511 (Div. 2 1971). The 2012 adoption of Rule 103(b) provides that a claim of error with respect to a definitive ruling is preserved for review when the party has otherwise satisfied the objection or offer of proof requirements of Rule 103(a). If, on the other hand, the court has reserved its ruling or indicated the ruling was provisional, the prudent practitioner should bring the issue to the court's attention to ensure the issue is preserved for review.

An offer of proof is simply a detailed description of what the proposed evidence is; and such offer is necessary to make an adequate record. *A Tumbling-T Ranches v. Flood Control Dist. of Maricopa County*, 222 Ariz. 515, 217 P.3d 1220 (Ct. App. Div. 1 2009). Such a formal offer of proof may not, however, be necessary where the purpose and substance of the proposed evidence can be ascertained from the context in which it was offered and/or discussions held on the record at the time. *Watson v. Southern Pac. Co.*, 62 Ariz. 29, 152 P.2d 665 (1944); *Molloy v. Molloy*, 158 Ariz. 64, 761 P.2d 138 (Ct. App. Div. 1 1988); *Block v. Meyer*, 144 Ariz. 230, 696 P.2d 1379 (Ct. App. Div. 1 1985); *Hinson v. Phoenix Pie Co.*, 3 Ariz. App. 523, 416 P.2d 202 (1966).

The purpose of the offer of proof is to give the trial court an opportunity to reconsider its initial ruling and to insure an adequate record for appellate review of the issue. *Musgrave v. Karis*, 63 Ariz. 417, 163 P.2d 278 (1945); *Williams v. Long*, 1 Ariz. App. 330, 402 P.2d 1006 (1965). Accordingly, an offer of proof cannot be made after the trial has been concluded. *Deyoe v. Clark Equipment Co., Inc.*, 134 Ariz. 281, 655 P.2d 1333 (Ct. App. Div. 2 1982).

The failure to make any offer of proof operates as a waiver of any claim of error in the exclusion of the evidence in question. *Chapman v. Levi-Strauss*, 145 Ariz. 411, 701 P.2d 1219 (Ct. App. Div. 2 1985); *Shell Oil Co. v. Gutierrez*, 119 Ariz. 426, 581 P.2d 271 (Ct. App. Div. 2 1978). A request to make an offer of proof is not a motion that is deemed denied—there must be a ruling on the request to preserve the issue. *McElwain v. Schuckert*, 13 Ariz. App. 468, 477 P.2d 754 (Div. 1 1970). It is error for the trial court to refuse to grant a party an opportunity to make an offer of proof, unless the evidence being offered is clearly inadmissible for any purpose. *Lappin v. Lappin*, 18 Ariz. App. 444, 503 P.2d 402 (Div. 2 1972).

Both the offer of proof and any request to make it should be made outside the presence or hearing of the jury, and on the record. The offer of proof can be made either through a statement of counsel as to what the rejected evidence would be, or through the actual presentation of the evidence in question through a witness. The clearly better practice is for the trial court to hear the actual offer of proof rather than having it placed on the record in the judge's absence. *State v. Belcher*, 109 Ariz. 551, 514 P.2d 472 (1973). The offer, however made, must show what specific facts would be established and how they are relevant to the issues. *Caldwell v. Tilford*, 90 Ariz. 202, 367 P.2d 239 (1961); *Gaston v. Hunter*, 121 Ariz. 33, 588 P.2d 326 (Ct. App. Div. 1 1978). Where the testimony of a witness is involved, the offer of proof must also show that there is a proper foundation for the testimony. *Jones v. Pak-Mor Mfg. Co.*, 145 Ariz. 121, 700 P.2d 819, 51 A.L.R.4th 1167 (1985).

Where the issue is the foundation for the admission of scientific evidence, whether that showing should be made outside the jury's presence is discretionary with the trial court. *State v. Bible*, 175 Ariz. 549, 858 P.2d 1152 (1993). While there is admittedly a potential for reversible error, should the jury hear evidence later determined to be inadmissible, the trial court is nevertheless not required to hold a foundational hearing outside the jury's presence. *State v. Bible*, 175 Ariz. 549, 858 P.2d 1152 (1993).

5. *Reversals for Erroneous Admission or Exclusion of Evidence; Fundamental Error.* Not every error in the admission or exclusion of evidence will result in the reversal of the eventual judgment. Rule 103(a) specifies that error may not be predicated on rulings admitting or excluding evidence unless a "substantial right of the party is affected."

Over the years, case law has developed two related lines of cases addressing the standard for determining when decisions concerning the admission or exclusion of evidence will be affirmed, the application of which may depend on the circumstances presented. Under one line of cases, the trial court's evidentiary rulings will be affirmed on appeal absent a clear abuse of discretion and resulting prejudice to a party. *Gemstar Ltd. v. Ernst & Young*, 185 Ariz. 493, 917 P.2d 222 (1996); *Pipher v. Loo*, 221 Ariz. 399, 212 P.3d 91 (Ct. App. Div. 1 2009); *Elia v. Pifer*, 194 Ariz. 74, 977 P.2d 796 (Ct. App. Div. 1 1998); *State ex rel. Miller v. Wells Fargo Bank of Arizona, N.A.*, 194 Ariz. 126, 978 P.2d 103 (Ct. App. Div. 1 1998); *Sheppard v. Crow-Barker Paul No. 1 Ltd. Partnership*, 192 Ariz. 539, 968 P.2d 612 (Ct. App. Div. 1 1998). Under a second line of cases, the trial court's discretion will be affirmed on appeal absent a clear abuse of discretion or legal error, and resulting prejudice. *Bogard v. Cannon & Wendt Elec. Co., Inc.*, 221 Ariz. 325, 212 P.3d 17 (Ct. App. Div. 1 2009); *Lohmeier v. Hammer*, 214 Ariz. 57, 148 P.3d 101 (Ct. App. Div. 1 2006); *John C. Lincoln Hosp. and Health Corp. v. Maricopa County*, 208 Ariz. 532, 96 P.3d 530 (Ct. App. Div. 1 2004), as amended on other grounds, (Sept. 1, 2004); *Yauch v. Southern Pacific Transp. Co.*, 198 Ariz. 394, 10 P.3d 1181 (Ct. App. Div. 2 2000).

Reversal for evidentiary errors to which a timely and appropriate objection was made will be required, however, where the evidence received or excluded affects a substantial right or the appellate court is convinced that the admission or exclusion of the evidence affected the result. *Carter-Glogau Laboratories, Inc. v. Construction, Production & Maintenance Laborers' Local 383*, 153 Ariz. 351, 736 P.2d 1163, 126 L.R.R.M. (BNA) 2752 (Ct. App. Div. 1 1986); *Good v. City of Glendale*, 150 Ariz. 218, 722 P.2d 386 (Ct. App. Div. 2 1986); *Wean Water, Inc. v. Sta-Rite Industries, Inc.*, 141 Ariz. 315, 686 P.2d 1285 (Ct. App. Div. 1 1984).

A party will be relieved of the failure to object to evidentiary rulings and relief nevertheless granted only where "fundamental rights" are affected. The doctrine of "fundamental error," recognized in Rule 103(d), however, is applied very sparingly in civil cases. *Bradshaw v. State Farm Mut. Auto. Ins. Co.*, 157 Ariz. 411, 758 P.2d 1313 (1988); *Salt River Project Agr. Imp. and Power Dist. v. Westinghouse Elec. Corp.*, 176 Ariz. 383, 861 P.2d 668, Prod. Liab. Rep. (CCH) P 13562 (Ct. App. Div. 2 1993); *Copeland v. City of Yuma*, 160 Ariz. 307, 772 P.2d 1160 (Ct. App. Div. 1 1989).

Rule 104. Preliminary Questions

(a) In General. The court must decide any preliminary question about whether a witness is qualified, a privilege exists, or evidence is admissible. In so deciding, the court is not bound by evidence rules, except those on privilege.

(b) Relevance That Depends on a Fact. When the relevance of evidence depends on whether a fact exists, proof must be introduced sufficient to support a finding that the fact does exist. The court may admit the proposed evidence on the condition that the proof be introduced later.

(c) Conducting a Hearing So That the Jury Cannot Hear It. The court must conduct any hearing on a preliminary question so that the jury cannot hear it if:

(1) the hearing involves the admissibility of a confession;

(2) a defendant in a criminal case is a witness and so requests; or

(3) justice so requires.

(d) Cross-Examining a Defendant in a Criminal Case. By testifying on a preliminary question, a defendant in a criminal case does not become subject to cross-examination on other issues in the case.

(e) Evidence Relevant to Weight and Credibility. This rule does not limit a party's right to introduce before the jury evidence that is relevant to the weight or credibility of other evidence.

Amended Oct. 19, 1988, effective Nov. 1, 1988; Sept. 8, 2011, effective Jan. 1, 2012.

Comment to 2012 Amendment

The language of Rule 104 has been amended to conform to the federal restyling of the Evidence Rules to make them more easily understood and to make style and terminology consistent throughout the rules. These changes are intended to be stylistic only. There is no intent to change any result in any ruling on evidence admissibility.

AUTHORS' COMMENTS

Analysis

1. *Scope and Purpose of Rule.* Rule 104 establishes that, where a factual predicate is required for the admission of evidence, determinations as to the presence or absence of those factual predicates are to be made by the Court. In making determinations on such "preliminary questions," the Court is not bound by the Rules of Evidence, except those with respect to privileges. Thus, the Court may consider hearsay in deciding whether the circumstances are present for applying one of the exceptions to the hearsay rule. *Cf., State v. Edwards*, 136 Ariz. 177, 665 P.2d 59 (1983); *State v. Spratt*, 126 Ariz. 184, 613 P.2d 848 (Ct. App. Div. 2 1980).

2. *Comparison With Federal Rule.* Effective January 1, 2012, the Arizona Supreme Court amended Rule 104 to conform to the federal restyling of the Evidence Rules to make the rules more easily understood and to make style and terminology consistent throughout. The 2012 Comment states the stylistic amendments are not intended to "change any result in any ruling on evidence admissibility."

Following the 2012 restyling amendments, the language of Rule 104 remains identical to its federal counterpart, Ariz. R. Evid. 104.

Although Rule 104 parallels its federal counterpart, "federal court decisions interpreting the federal rule are persuasive but not binding with respect to interpreting the Arizona rule." *See,* Prefatory Comment to 2012 Amendments. *See also, State v. Terrazas*, 189 Ariz. 580, 944 P.2d 1194 (1997) (The Arizona Supreme Court is "not bound by the United States Supreme Court's nonconstitutional construction of the Federal Rules of Evidence when [the Arizona Supreme Court construes] the Arizona Rules of Evidence."), citing, *State v. Bible*, 175 Ariz. 549, 858 P.2d 1152 (1993); *State v. Salazar-Mercado*, 232 Ariz. 256, 304 P.3d 543 (Ct. App. Div. 2 2013). Practitioners are urged to keep this legal tenet in mind as they research federal case law interpreting a federal evidentiary rule that corresponds to an Arizona evidentiary rule.

3. *Role of Court in Determining Admissibility; Procedure.* Decisions on the admissibility of evidence are committed to the sound discretion of the trial court. *Gemstar Ltd. v. Ernst & Young*, 185 Ariz. 493, 917 P.2d 222 (1996); *Belliard v. Becker*, 216 Ariz. 356, 166 P.3d 911 (Ct. App. Div. 1 2007); *Girouard v. Skyline Steel, Inc.*, 215 Ariz. 126, 158 P.3d 255 (Ct. App. Div. 1 2007); *Lohmeier v. Hammer*, 214 Ariz. 57, 148 P.3d 101 (Ct. App. Div. 1 2006); *Acuna v. Kroack*, 212 Ariz. 104, 128 P.3d 221 (Ct. App. Div. 2 2006); *Elia v. Pifer*, 194 Ariz. 74, 977 P.2d 796 (Ct. App. Div. 1 1998); *Brown v. U.S. Fidelity and Guar. Co.*, 194 Ariz. 85, 977 P.2d 807 (Ct. App. Div. 1 1998), as amended, (Nov. 25, 1998) and

as corrected, (Aug. 5, 1999); *State ex rel. Miller v. Wells Fargo Bank of Arizona, N.A.*, 194 Ariz. 126, 978 P.2d 103 (Ct. App. Div. 1 1998); *Sheppard v. Crow-Barker Paul No. 1 Ltd. Partnership*, 192 Ariz. 539, 968 P.2d 612 (Ct. App. Div. 1 1998); *Cervantes v. Rijlaarsdam*, 190 Ariz. 396, 949 P.2d 56 (Ct. App. Div. 2 1997); *Conant v. Whitney*, 190 Ariz. 290, 947 P.2d 864 (Ct. App. Div. 1 1997).

Where the admissibility of evidence turns on the presence or absence of predicate facts, the determination as to whether those predicates have been established is always for the Court. *W. R. Skousen Contractor, Inc. v. Gray*, 26 Ariz. App. 100, 546 P.2d 369 (Div. 1 1976). Perhaps the most common example, cited in the Rule itself, is the decision concerning the qualifications of an expert to offer particular opinion testimony. *Bliss v. Treece*, 134 Ariz. 516, 658 P.2d 169 (1983); *Clearwater v. State Farm Mut. Auto. Ins. Co.*, 161 Ariz. 590, 780 P.2d 423 (Ct. App. Div. 2 1989), opinion vacated in part on other grounds, 164 Ariz. 256, 792 P.2d 719 (1990). In essence, the Court decides whether the facts permitting certain evidence to be admitted have been shown; the jury decides whether to credit the evidence.

The proponent of the evidence has the burden of establishing the predicates for its admissibility. *DeElena v. Southern Pac. Co.*, 121 Ariz. 563, 592 P.2d 759 (1979). The opponent of the evidence has the burden of raising the issue of whether the requisite predicate facts have been established. In the case of documentary evidence that is offered, that should be done by an appropriate objection. Where objectionable testimony is offered, the issue may be raised by an objection, or by a request to *voir dire* the witness, an examination out of order for the limited purpose of showing that the predicates for admissibility are absent. If permitted, *voir dire* is not cross-examination, and must be requested and conducted before the questioned evidence is admitted. If the interests of justice require, *voir dire* examinations into a witness' qualifications or other conditions of admissibility should be conducted out of the presence of the jury.

Where the issue is the foundation for the admission of scientific evidence, whether that showing should be made outside the jury's presence is discretionary with the trial court. *State v. Bible*, 175 Ariz. 549, 858 P.2d 1152 (1993). While there is admittedly a potential for reversible error, should the jury hear evidence later determined to be inadmissible, the trial court is nevertheless not required to hold a foundational hearing outside the jury's presence. *State v. Bible*, 175 Ariz. 549, 858 P.2d 1152 (1993).

4. *Conditional Admission; Motion to Strike.* Where the predicates for admission of evidence have not been established at the time the evidence is offered, the Court may nevertheless allow it

to be received on condition that evidence establishing the predicate facts will be forthcoming at a later point in the proceedings. Generally, the trial court will require an avowal of counsel to that effect. If the predicate facts are not subsequently established, the party against whom the evidence was offered and received must move to strike it, or the objection may be waived.

5. *Parol Evidence Rule; Standardized Agreements.* There has been considerable controversy and debate over the scope and proper application of the "parol evidence rule." *Taylor v. State Farm Mut. Auto. Ins. Co.*, 175 Ariz. 148, 854 P.2d 1134 (1993). Where the provisions of a contract or other written agreement are in issue, the role of the Court and, if necessary, the trier of fact is to ascertain and effectuate the intention of the parties at the time the agreement was entered into. *Taylor v. State Farm Mut. Auto. Ins. Co.*, 175 Ariz. 148, 854 P.2d 1134 (1993); *Aboud v. DeConcini*, 173 Ariz. 315, 842 P.2d 1328 (Ct. App. Div. 2 1992). The parol evidence rule merely defines what extrinsic evidence, other than the contract or written agreement itself, is admissible on the issue of the proper interpretation of it. *Taylor v. State Farm Mut. Auto. Ins. Co.*, 175 Ariz. 148, 854 P.2d 1134 (1993). The parol evidence rule does not apply to judgments, and a court may not consider evidence extrinsic to the record to resolve the meaning of a judgment. *In re Marriage of Zale*, 193 Ariz. 246, 972 P.2d 230 (1999).

The traditional view has been that a written agreement adopted by the parties is to be treated as an integrated contract and the intent of the parties is to be derived from the terms expressed within the four corners of the instrument itself. *Statewide Ins. Corp. v. Dewar*, 143 Ariz. 553, 694 P.2d 1167 (1984); *Darner Motor Sales, Inc. v. Universal Underwriters Ins. Co.*, 140 Ariz. 383, 682 P.2d 388 (1984); *Estate of Tovrea v. Nolan*, 173 Ariz. 568, 845 P.2d 494 (Ct. App. Div. 1 1992). Extrinsic evidence of prior and contemporaneous negotiations, subsequent conduct and/or other surrounding circumstances was not admissible unless the court determined that the contract language in issue was ambiguous or subject to more than one reasonable construction. *Leo Eisenberg & Co., Inc. v. Payson*, 162 Ariz. 529, 785 P.2d 49 (1989); *Leikvold v. Valley View Community Hosp.*, 141 Ariz. 544, 688 P.2d 170, 1 I.E.R. Cas. (BNA) 1749, 116 L.R.R.M. (BNA) 2193, 100 Lab. Cas. (CCH) P 55456 (1984); *Estate of Tovrea v. Nolan*, 173 Ariz. 568, 845 P.2d 494 (Ct. App. Div. 1 1992); *Aboud v. DeConcini*, 173 Ariz. 315, 842 P.2d 1328 (Ct. App. Div. 2 1992); *Koenen v. Royal Buick Co.*, 162 Ariz. 376, 783 P.2d 822, 11 U.C.C. Rep. Serv. 2d 1096 (Ct. App. Div. 2 1989); *Continental Bank v. Guaranty Warehouse Corp.*, 153 Ariz. 522, 738 P.2d 1129 (Ct. App. Div. 2 1987); *Jeski v. American Exp. Co.*, 147 Ariz. 19, 708 P.2d 110 (Ct. App. Div. 1 1985). Arizona law concerning the parol evidence rule departs significantly from this traditional model.

Arizona has always permitted parol evidence to be received on the issue whether the written agreement is truly an integrated statement of the parties' bargain. *Burkons v. Ticor Title Ins. Co. of California*, 168 Ariz. 345, 813 P.2d 710 (1991); *Darner Motor Sales, Inc. v. Universal Underwriters Ins. Co.*, 140 Ariz. 383, 682 P.2d 388 (1984); *Anderson v. Preferred Stock Food Markets, Inc.*, 175 Ariz. 208, 854 P.2d 1194 (Ct. App. Div. 1 1993); *American Nat. Fire Ins. Co. v. Esquire Labs of Arizona, Inc.*, 143 Ariz. 512, 694 P.2d 800 (Ct. App. Div. 2 1984).

Arizona, however, also follows the so-called "Corbin approach" to contract interpretation, and permits the consideration of extrinsic evidence, not only on the issue of contract integration, but on the issue of contract interpretation as well and without the necessity of a threshold finding of contract ambiguity. *Taylor v. State Farm Mut. Auto. Ins. Co.*, 175 Ariz. 148, 854 P.2d 1134 (1993); *Darner Motor Sales, Inc. v. Universal Underwriters Ins. Co.*, 140 Ariz. 383, 682 P.2d 388 (1984); *Smith v. Melson, Inc.*, 135 Ariz. 119, 659 P.2d 1264 (1983); *Nahom v. Blue Cross and Blue Shield of Arizona, Inc.*, 180 Ariz. 548, 885 P.2d 1113 (Ct. App. Div. 1 1994); *American Nat. Fire Ins. Co. v. Esquire Labs of Arizona, Inc.*, 143 Ariz. 512, 694 P.2d 800 (Ct. App. Div. 2 1984). In Arizona, thus, in interpreting the provisions of either a negotiated or standardized agreement, the Court's consideration is not limited to the text of the agreement itself. *Taylor v. State Farm Mut. Auto. Ins. Co.*, 175 Ariz. 148, 854 P.2d 1134 (1993); *Darner Motor Sales, Inc. v. Universal Underwriters Ins. Co.*, 140 Ariz. 383, 682 P.2d 388 (1984); *Smith v. Melson, Inc.*, 135 Ariz. 119, 659 P.2d 1264 (1983); *Nahom v. Blue Cross and Blue Shield of Arizona, Inc.*, 180 Ariz. 548, 885 P.2d 1113 (Ct. App. Div. 1 1994); *American Nat. Fire Ins. Co. v. Esquire Labs of Arizona, Inc.*, 143 Ariz. 512, 694 P.2d 800 (Ct. App. Div. 2 1984).

Procedurally, the trial court receives the proffered parol evidence, not only on the issue of whether the parties intended the written agreement to be an integrated statement of their bargain, but also on the issue whether the contract language is reasonably susceptible to the interpretation advocated by the proponent of the evidence. *Taylor v. State Farm Mut. Auto. Ins. Co.*, 175 Ariz. 148, 854 P.2d 1134 (1993); *American Nat. Fire Ins. Co. v. Esquire Labs of Arizona, Inc.*, 143 Ariz. 512, 694 P.2d 800 (Ct. App. Div. 2 1984). Parol evidence is admissible, and may be considered by the trier of fact, in determining the meaning intended by the parties, if the contract language is susceptible to more than one reasonable interpretation. *Taylor v. State Farm Mut. Auto. Ins. Co.*, 175 Ariz. 148, 854 P.2d 1134 (1993). The parol evidence rule still bars the receipt of evidence that supports an interpretation to which the Court determines the contract language is not reasonably susceptible. *Taylor v. State Farm Mut. Auto. Ins. Co.*, 175 Ariz. 148, 854 P.2d 1134 (1993).

The Court may not always be in a position to determine the issue of admissibility when such parol evidence is initially offered. In that circumstance, the trial judge has discretion to admit the evidence conditionally subject to a later determination of relevance, or to consider it outside the presence of the jury. *Taylor v. State Farm Mut. Auto. Ins. Co.*, 175 Ariz. 148, 854 P.2d 1134 (1993). Whether the contract language is reasonably susceptible to the interpretation advocated by the proponent of the parol evidence, however, remains a question of law for the Court. *Pasco Industries, Inc. v. Talco Recycling, Inc.*, 195 Ariz. 50, 985 P.2d 535, 1998-2 Trade Cas. (CCH) ¶ 72377 (Ct. App. Div. 1 1998); *Nahom v. Blue Cross and Blue Shield of Arizona, Inc.*, 180 Ariz. 548, 885 P.2d 1113 (Ct. App. Div. 1 1994).

In determining whether an ambiguity exists in an insurance policy, the language is examined from the viewpoint of one not trained in law or in the business of insurance. *Samsel v. Allstate Ins. Co.*, 204 Ariz. 1, 59 P.3d 281 (2002); *Liristis v. American Family Mut. Ins. Co.*, 204 Ariz. 140, 61 P.3d 22 (Ct. App. Div. 1 2002), redesignated as opinion, (Dec. 26, 2002) and as amended, (Dec. 26, 2002) and (rejected by, DeVore v. American Family Mut. Ins. Co., 383 Ill. App. 3d 266, 322 Ill. Dec. 490, 891 N.E.2d 505 (2d Dist. 2008)); *National Bank of Arizona v. St. Paul Fire and Marine Ins. Co.*, 193 Ariz. 581, 975 P.2d 711 (Ct. App. Div. 1 1999). When the policy language is clear, the court may not invent ambiguity and then resolve it to find coverage where none exists under the policy. Provisions of insurance policies are to be construed according to their plain and ordinary meaning. *Samsel v. Allstate Ins. Co.*, 204 Ariz. 1, 59 P.3d 281 (2002).

In the case of standardized agreements containing boilerplate language, such as many personal insurance policies, the Arizona courts will construe a clause that is reasonably subject to different interpretations by examining the language of the clause, public policy considerations and the purpose of the underlying transaction. *State Farm Mut. Auto. Ins. Co. v. Wilson*, 162 Ariz. 251, 782 P.2d 727 (1989); *Arizona Property and Cas. Ins. Guar. Fund v. Helme*, 153 Ariz. 129, 735 P.2d 451, 64 A.L.R.4th 651 (1987) (rejected by, Buysse v. Baumann-Furrie & Co., 448 N.W.2d 865 (Minn. 1989)); *Transamerica Ins. Group v. Meere*, 143 Ariz. 351, 694 P.2d 181 (1984).

In addition, Arizona adheres to the "doctrine of reasonable expectations" articulated in the *Restatement (Second) of Contracts*, § 211. *Gordinier v. Aetna Cas. & Sur. Co.*, 154 Ariz. 266, 742 P.2d 277 (1987); *Darner Motor Sales, Inc. v. Universal Underwriters*

Ins. Co., 140 Ariz. 383, 682 P.2d 388 (1984). Under this doctrine, courts will give effect to a boilerplate provision in a standardized agreement unless the drafter of the provision had reason to believe that the other party would not have assented to the term had that party been aware of its presence and significance. *Phoenix Control Systems, Inc. v. Insurance Co. of North America*, 165 Ariz. 31, 796 P.2d 463 (1990); *Gilbreath Through Hassl v. St. Paul Fire and Marine Ins. Co.*, 141 Ariz. 92, 685 P.2d 729 (1984); *Gordinier v. Aetna Cas. & Sur. Co.*, 154 Ariz. 266, 742 P.2d 277 (1987); *Darner Motor Sales, Inc. v. Universal Underwriters Ins. Co.*, 140 Ariz. 383, 682 P.2d 388 (1984).

Boilerplate insurance policy terms, particularly those excluding coverage, will not be enforced if they cannot be understood by the reasonably intelligent consumer or if the insurer's actions create a reasonable impression of coverage in the minds of a reasonable insured. *Anderson v. Country Life Ins. Co.*, 180 Ariz. 625, 886 P.2d 1381 (Ct. App. Div. 1 1994).

Parol evidence is obviously admissible to demonstrate the drafter's reason to believe that the other party would not have assented and/or that other party's "reasonable expectations." *Gordinier v. Aetna Cas. & Sur. Co.*, 154 Ariz. 266, 742 P.2d 277 (1987); *Darner Motor Sales, Inc. v. Universal Underwriters Ins. Co.*, 140 Ariz. 383, 682 P.2d 388 (1984); *Services Holding Co., Inc. v. Transamerica Occidental Life Ins. Co.*, 180 Ariz. 198, 883 P.2d 435 (Ct. App. Div. 1 1994). Reason to believe the signing party would not have agreed to the term may be (1) shown by the parties' negotiations, (2) inferred from the circumstances of the transaction, (3) inferred from the fact that the term is bizarre or oppressive, (4) inferred from the fact that the term eviscerates the non-standard terms to which the parties explicitly agreed, or (5) inferred if the term frustrates the dominant purpose of the transaction. *State Farm Fire & Cas. In. Co. v. Grabowski*, 214 Ariz. 188, 150 P.3d 275 (Ct. App. Div. 1 2007), as amended, (Jan. 29, 2007); *Harrington v. Pulte Home Corp.*, 211 Ariz. 241, 119 P.3d 1044 (Ct. App. Div. 1 2005). Application of the "doctrine of reasonable expectations" is not limited to the situation where the boilerplate clause in question is ambiguous or where there has been a misrepresentation as to its significance by the drafting party. *Averett v. Farmers Ins. Co. of Arizona*, 177 Ariz. 531, 869 P.2d 505 (1994); *Gordinier v. Aetna Cas. & Sur. Co.*, 154 Ariz. 266, 742 P.2d 277 (1987); *Services Holding Co., Inc. v. Transamerica Occidental Life Ins. Co.*, 180 Ariz. 198, 883 P.2d 435 (Ct. App. Div. 1 1994).

The reasonable expectations of coverage on the part of an insured may estop an insurer from denying coverage under the terms of an insurance policy. An insurance policy may not be interpreted so as to defeat the reasonable expectations of the insured. *Samsel v. Allstate Ins. Co.*, 204 Ariz. 1, 59 P.3d 281 (2002). The expectations to be realized, however, must have been induced by the making of a promise and be something more than the fervent hopes usually engendered by suffering a loss. *American Family Mut. Ins. Co. v. White*, 204 Ariz. 500, 65 P.3d 449 (Ct. App. Div. 1 2003).

Application of the "reasonable expectations" doctrine in this context has been limited to the following situations: (1) where the contract terms, although not ambiguous to the Court, cannot be understood by the reasonably intelligent consumer who might check on his or her rights, the Court will interpret them in light of objective, reasonable expectations of the average insured; (2) where the insured did not receive full and adequate notice of the policy term in question, and the provision is either unusual or unexpected, or one that emasculates coverage; (3) where some activity which can reasonably be attributed to the insurer would create an objective impression of coverage in the mind of a reasonable insured; and, (4) where some activity reasonably attributable to the insurer has induced a particular insured to reasonably believe that he or she has coverage, although such coverage is expressly and unambiguously denied by the insurer. The doctrine of "reasonable expectations" operates to relieve a party from clauses in an agreement which that party did not negotiate, probably did not read, and probably would not have understood in any event. *Philadelphia Indem. Ins. Co. v. Barerra*, 200 Ariz. 9, 21 P.3d 395 (2001).

This doctrine of "reasonable expectations" and the doctrine of "unconscionability" are two separate and distinct grounds for invalidating a contract or limiting its enforcement. Even if a contract provision is consistent with the reasonable expectations of the parties, it may nevertheless be found unenforceable if it is unconscionable or oppressive. *Maxwell v. Fidelity Financial Services, Inc.*, 184 Ariz. 82, 907 P.2d 51, 28 U.C.C. Rep. Serv. 2d 806 (1995). The issue of unconscionability is one for the court to resolve. *Maxwell v. Fidelity Financial Services, Inc.*, 184 Ariz. 82, 907 P.2d 51, 28 U.C.C. Rep. Serv. 2d 806 (1995); *Nelson v. Rice*, 198 Ariz. 563, 12 P.3d 238 (Ct. App. Div. 2 2000). Substantive unconscionability, which concerns the actual terms of the contract and examines the relative fairness of the obligations assumed, is sufficient to invalidate a contract; there need not be an additional showing of procedural unconscionability. *Maxwell v. Fidelity Financial Services, Inc.*, 184 Ariz. 82, 907 P.2d 51, 28 U.C.C. Rep. Serv. 2d 806 (1995); *Harrington v. Pulte Home Corp.*, 211 Ariz. 241, 119 P.3d 1044 (Ct. App. Div. 1 2005).

Rule 105. Limiting Evidence That Is Not Admissible Against Other Parties or for Other Purposes

If the court admits evidence that is admissible against a party or for a purpose—but not against another party or for another purpose—the court, on timely request, must restrict the evidence to its proper scope and instruct the jury accordingly.

Amended Sept. 8, 2011, effective Jan. 1, 2012.

Comment to 2012 Amendment

The language of Rule 105 has been amended to conform to the federal restyling of the Evidence Rules to make them more easily understood and to make style and terminology consistent throughout the rules. These changes are intended to be stylistic only. There is no intent to change any result in any ruling on evidence admissibility.

AUTHORS' COMMENTS

Analysis

1. *Scope and Purpose of Rule.* Rule 105 presupposes, properly, that evidence admissible for one purpose but not for others is properly received, but directs the Court, upon request, to instruct the jury as to the limited purpose for which the evidence was received and to consider it solely for that purpose. The Rule is for the protection of, and is most frequently invoked, by the party against whom such evidence is offered.

2. *Comparison With Federal Rule.* Effective January 1, 2012, the Arizona Supreme Court amended Rule 105 to conform to the federal restyling of the Evidence Rules to make the rules more easily understood and to make style and terminology consistent throughout. The 2012 Comment states the stylistic amendments are not intended to "change any result in any ruling on evidence admissibility."

Following the 2012 restyling amendments, the language of Rule 105 remains identical to its federal counterpart, Fed. R. Evid. 105.

Although Rule 105 parallels its federal counterpart, "federal court decisions interpreting the federal rule are persuasive but

not binding with respect to interpreting the Arizona rule." *See,* Prefatory Comment to 2012 Amendments. *See also, State v. Terrazas*, 189 Ariz. 580, 944 P.2d 1194 (1997) (The Arizona Supreme Court is "not bound by the United States Supreme Court's non-constitutional construction of the Federal Rules of Evidence when [the Arizona Supreme Court construes] the Arizona Rules of Evidence."), citing, *State v. Bible*, 175 Ariz. 549, 858 P.2d 1152 (1993); *State v. Salazar-Mercado*, 232 Ariz. 256, 304 P.3d 543 (Ct. App. Div. 2 2013). Practitioners are urged to keep this legal tenet in mind as they research federal case law interpreting a federal evidentiary rule that corresponds to an Arizona evidentiary rule.

3. *Admissibility of Evidence for Limited Purpose.* Evidence which is admissible for one purpose, but inadmissible for others, is nevertheless to be received. *Readenour v. Marion Power Shovel, a Div. of Dresser Industries, Inc.*, 149 Ariz. 442, 719 P.2d 1058, Prod. Liab. Rep. (CCH) P 11012 (1986); *Rossell v. Volkswagen of America*, 147 Ariz. 160, 709 P.2d 517, Prod. Liab. Rep. (CCH) P 10752 (1985); *Alires v. Southern Pac. Co.*, 93 Ariz. 97, 378 P.2d 913 (1963) (disapproved of by, Miller v. State of Okl., 240 F. Supp. 263 (E.D. Okla. 1965)); *Rhue v. Dawson*, 173 Ariz. 220, 841 P.2d 215 (Ct. App. Div. 1 1992); *Gaston v. Hunter*, 121 Ariz. 33, 588 P.2d 326 (Ct. App. Div. 1 1978).

4. *Limiting Instruction; Purpose; Need to Request.* Where evidence is admitted for a limited purpose, the jury is generally not aware of that and there is a danger that it will be considered for purposes for which it was not admissible, unless the jury is advised that the evidence was only admitted for a limited purpose or purposes, and instructed that they should consider it only for the purpose(s) for which it was admitted. Rule 105 provides that the Court must give the jury such a limiting instruction, when requested to do so by a party who desires to limit the evidence's impact. *Readenour v. Marion Power Shovel, a Div. of Dresser Industries, Inc.*, 149 Ariz. 442, 719 P.2d 1058, Prod. Liab. Rep. (CCH) P 11012 (1986).

The theory behind the Rule is that such a limiting instruction negates any prejudicial effect the evidence might have. There is also a presumption that, when evidence is admitted for a limited purpose, the jury follows a limiting instruction given by the Court. *Bledsoe v. Salt River Valley Water Users' Ass'n*, 179 Ariz. 469, 880 P.2d 689 (Ct. App. Div. 2 1994). *Baroldy v. Ortho Pharmaceutical Corp.*, 157 Ariz. 574, 760 P.2d 574, Prod. Liab. Rep. (CCH) P 11732 (Ct. App. Div. 1 1988). Such a limiting instruction, however, must be requested.

When evidence exceeds the purpose for which it is admissible, a party is required to object and the objection must be specific as to those portions of the evidence that are claimed to be inadmissible. *Rhue v. Dawson*, 173 Ariz. 220, 841 P.2d 215 (Ct. App. Div. 1 1992). Moreover, the failure to object to the content of the limiting instruction given, or to suggest an alternate instruction, operates as a waiver of objections to the instruction given. *Baroldy v. Ortho Pharmaceutical Corp.*, 157 Ariz. 574, 760 P.2d 574, Prod. Liab. Rep. (CCH) P 11732 (Ct. App. Div. 1 1988).

5. *Receipt of Limited Purpose Evidence in Court Trials.* In trials to the Court, where evidence is improperly received, there is a presumption that the Court considered only the competent and properly admitted evidence in rendering its judgment. *DeForest v. DeForest*, 143 Ariz. 627, 694 P.2d 1241 (Ct. App. Div. 1 1985). Where evidence is received in a trial to the Court which is admissible only for a limited purpose, there is a similar presumption that the Court considered it only for the purpose for which it was properly admissible. *Christmas v. Turkin*, 148 Ariz. 602, 716 P.2d 59 (Ct. App. Div. 2 1986); *Wineinger v. Wineinger*, 137 Ariz. 194, 669 P.2d 971 (Ct. App. Div. 2 1983). The presumption is, however, rebuttable by a showing that erroneously admitted evidence affected the trial court's decision. *Murphy v. Yeast*, 59 Ariz. 281, 126 P.2d 313 (1942).

Rule 106. Remainder of or Related Writings or Recorded Statements

If a party introduces all or part of a writing or recorded statement, an adverse party may require the introduction, at that time, of any other part—or any other writing or recorded statement—that in fairness ought to be considered at the same time.

Amended Oct. 19, 1988, effective Nov. 1, 1988; Sept. 8, 2011, effective Jan. 1, 2012.

Comment to 2012 Amendment

The language of Rule 106 has been amended to conform to the federal restyling of the Evidence Rules to make them more easily understood and to make style and terminology consistent throughout the rules. These changes are intended to be stylistic only. There is no intent to change any result in any ruling on evidence admissibility.

AUTHORS' COMMENTS

Analysis

1. Scope and Purpose of Rule.
2. Comparison With Federal Rule.

1. *Scope and Purpose of Rule.* Rule 106 provides that when a writing or recorded statement, or any part thereof, is introduced into evidence, any party may require the introduction of other parts of the writing or statement, or other writings or recorded statements, which ought to be considered together with the writing, statement or part thereof that has been introduced. It is designed to protect against misleading the trier of fact by having certain forms of evidence received and considered out of context. Similar protection is provided with respect to the use of portions of depositions in court proceedings by the second paragraph of Ariz. R. Civ. P. 32(a).

In order to invoke the Rule, the party against whom the evidence is offered should make an appropriate objection. The receipt of additional writings or statements, or of additional portions of the writing or statement introduced, is not automatic. The additional portions to be offered must themselves be admissible, and the Court must determine that the additional matters should in fairness be considered contemporaneously with the matter originally offered.

2. *Comparison With Federal Rule.* Effective January 1, 2012, the Arizona Supreme Court amended Rule 106 to conform to the federal restyling of the Evidence Rules to make the rules more

easily understood and to make style and terminology consistent throughout. The 2012 Comment states the stylistic amendments are not intended to "change any result in any ruling on evidence admissibility."

Following the 2012 restyling amendments, the language of Rule 106 remains identical to its federal counterpart, Fed. R. Evid. 106.

Although Rule 106 parallels its federal counterpart, "federal court decisions interpreting the federal rule are persuasive but not binding with respect to interpreting the Arizona rule." *See,* Prefatory Comment to 2012 Amendments. *See also, State v. Terrazas*, 189 Ariz. 580, 944 P.2d 1194 (1997) (The Arizona Supreme Court is "not bound by the United States Supreme Court's non-constitutional construction of the Federal Rules of Evidence when [the Arizona Supreme Court construes] the Arizona Rules of Evidence."), citing, *State v. Bible*, 175 Ariz. 549, 858 P.2d 1152 (1993); *State v. Salazar-Mercado*, 232 Ariz. 256, 304 P.3d 543 (Ct. App. Div. 2 2013). Practitioners are urged to keep this legal tenet in mind as they research federal case law interpreting a federal evidentiary rule that corresponds to an Arizona evidentiary rule.

ARTICLE II. JUDICIAL NOTICE

Rule 201. Judicial Notice of Adjudicative Facts

(a) Scope. This rule governs judicial notice of an adjudicative fact only, not a legislative fact.

(b) Kinds of Facts That May Be Judicially Noticed. The court may judicially notice a fact that is not subject to reasonable dispute because it:

(1) is generally known within the trial court's territorial jurisdiction; or

(2) can be accurately and readily determined from sources whose accuracy cannot reasonably be questioned.

(c) Taking Notice. The court:

(1) may take judicial notice on its own; or

(2) must take judicial notice if a party requests it and the court is supplied with the necessary information.

(d) Timing. The court may take judicial notice at any stage of the proceeding.

(e) Opportunity to Be Heard. On timely request, a party is entitled to be heard on the propriety of taking judicial notice and the nature of the fact to be noticed. If the court takes judicial notice before notifying a party, the party, on request, is still entitled to be heard.

(f) Instructing the Jury. In a civil case, the court must instruct the jury to accept the noticed fact as conclusive. In a criminal case, the court must instruct the jury that it may or may not accept the noticed fact as conclusive.

Amended Sept. 8, 2011, effective Jan. 1, 2012.

Comment to 2012 Amendment

The last sentence of subsection (f) (formerly subsection (g)) has been added to conform to Federal Rule of Evidence 201(f), as restyled.

Additionally, the language of Rule 201 has been amended to conform to the federal restyling of the Evidence Rules to make them more easily understood and to make style and terminology consistent throughout the rules. These changes are intended to be stylistic only. There is no intent in the restyling to change any result in any ruling on evidence admissibility.

AUTHORS' COMMENTS

Analysis

3. Adjudicative v. Legislative Facts.
4. Requirements for Taking Judicial Notice.
5. Procedure for Taking of Judicial Notice; Effect of Taking Judicial Notice; Instructions to Jury.
6. Judicial Notice of Court Records and Files; Judicial Notice by Appellate Courts.
7. Other Matters Judicially Noticed.

1. *Scope and Purpose of Rule.* The device of taking judicial notice of facts, partially codified in Rule 201, is an evidentiary shortcut which relieves the parties of the burden and expense of putting on proof of relevant matters which are either obvious or not subject to reasonable dispute. Absent agreement of the parties, portions of the record not admitted in evidence at trial have no evidentiary value unless they are the proper subject of judicial notice. *Gersten v. Gersten*, 223 Ariz. 99, 219 P.3d 309 (Ct. App. Div. 1 2009).

2. *Comparison With Federal Rule.* Effective January 1, 2012, the Arizona Supreme Court amended Rule 201 to conform to the federal restyling of the Evidence Rules to make the rules more easily understood and to make style and terminology consistent throughout. The 2012 Comment states the stylistic amendments are not intended to "change any result in any ruling on evidence admissibility."

Until the 2012 amendments, Arizona's rule differed from the Federal rule in that Arizona had not adopted either the introductory phrase, or the final sentence of, Fed. R. Evid. 201(f) [formerly, Rule 201(g)]. As part of the 2012 amendments, Arizona amended Rule 201(f) [formerly, Rule 201(g)] to conform to Fed. R. Evid. 201(f), as restyled.

Following the 2012 amendments, the language of Rule 201 remains substantially identical to its federal counterpart, Fed. R. Evid. 201.

Although Rule 201 parallels its federal counterpart, "federal court decisions interpreting the federal rule are persuasive but not binding with respect to interpreting the Arizona rule." *See,* Prefatory Comment to 2012 Amendments. *See also, State v. Terrazas*, 189 Ariz. 580, 944 P.2d 1194 (1997) (The Arizona Supreme Court is "not bound by the United States Supreme Court's non-constitutional construction of the Federal Rules of Evidence when [the Arizona Supreme Court construes] the Arizona Rules of Evidence."), citing, *State v. Bible*, 175 Ariz. 549, 858 P.2d 1152 (1993); *State v. Salazar-Mercado*, 232 Ariz. 256, 304 P.3d 543 (Ct. App. Div. 2 2013). Practitioners are urged to keep this legal tenet in mind as they research federal case law interpreting a federal evidentiary rule that corresponds to an Arizona evidentiary rule.

3. *Adjudicative v. Legislative Facts.* Rule 201 applies to judicial notice of so-called "adjudicative facts"—facts which are relevant to determining the rights and liabilities of the parties in a particular case. The Advisory Committee Note to Rule 201 of the Federal Rules of Evidence distinguishes "adjudicative facts," which it describes as "the facts of the particular case" from so-called "legislative facts," which it describes as "those which have relevance to legal reasoning and the lawmaking process, whether in the formulation of a legal principle or ruling by a judge or court or in the enactment of a legislative body." The categories are not necessarily discrete. Facts of which a Court may take judicial notice in establishing a legal principle or reaching a ruling may, in a separate context and proceeding, be relevant, and appropriately noticed as evidence, to determine the rights of the parties in a particular case.

4. *Requirements for Taking Judicial Notice.* In order to be judicially noticed, the fact in question must be one which is not subject to reasonable dispute. *Beyerle Sand & Gravel, Inc. v. Martinez*, 118 Ariz. 60, 574 P.2d 853 (Ct. App. Div. 2 1977). *See also, In re Roy L.*, 197 Ariz. 441, 4 P.3d 984, 990 (Ct. App. Div. 1 2000), corrected, (Feb. 3, 2000) (appellate court may take judicial notice of matters trial court could have, even if trial court did not). As formulated in the Rule, the facts must be generally known in the area of the Court's jurisdiction or readily and accurately ascertainable by reference to authorities whose accuracy cannot be reasonably disputed.

A high degree of the probability of the truth of the fact is not enough; the fact to be noticed must not be subject to reasonable dispute. *Phelps Dodge Corp. v. Ford*, 68 Ariz. 190, 203 P.2d 633 (1949). Further, it is neither necessary nor sufficient that the trial judge personally knows the fact in question to be true—the predicate for taking judicial notice can and should be established by reference to reliable and readily accessible sources. *Utah Const. Co. v. Berg*, 68 Ariz. 285, 205 P.2d 367 (1949).

5. *Procedure for Taking of Judicial Notice; Effect of Taking Judicial Notice; Instructions to Jury.* Judicial notice may be taken at any stage of the proceedings. A request to the Court to take judicial notice is not necessary, as the Court has discretion to take judicial notice, whether it is requested to do so or not. If a request to take judicial notice is made, however, and the Court is supplied with the necessary information to determine that the standards for taking judicial notice have been met, then the taking of judicial notice is mandatory. The opponent of the party requesting that judicial notice be taken is entitled to be heard on the issue of whether the fact in question is not subject to reason-

able dispute.

A fact judicially noticed is conclusively established, and evidence cannot thereafter be received to dispute it. *Phelps Dodge Corp. v. Ford*, 68 Ariz. 190, 203 P.2d 633 (1949); *Bade v. Drachman*, 4 Ariz. App. 55, 417 P.2d 689 (1966). The jury is to be instructed to accept any fact judicially noticed as conclusively established.

6. *Judicial Notice of Court Records and Files; Judicial Notice by Appellate Courts*. It is perfectly appropriate for appellate courts to take judicial notice. *Miceli v. Industrial Com'n of Arizona*, 135 Ariz. 71, 659 P.2d 30 (1983); *Hovatter v. Shell Oil Co.*, 111 Ariz. 325, 529 P.2d 224 (1974); *Southwestern Freight Lines v. Floyd*, 58 Ariz. 249, 119 P.2d 120 (1941). Rule 201 allows an appellate court to take judicial notice of any matter of which the trial court could take notice, even if the trial court was never asked to do so. *Reeck v. Mendoza*, 232 Ariz. 299, 304 P.3d 1122 (Ct. App. Div. 1 2013); *In re Sabino R.*, 198 Ariz. 424, 10 P.3d 1211 (Ct. App. Div. 1 2000); *Matheny v. Gila County*, 147 Ariz. 359, 710 P.2d 469 (Ct. App. Div. 2 1985); *State v. McGuire*, 124 Ariz. 64, 601 P.2d 1348 (Ct. App. Div 2 1978).

Both an appellate court and the Superior Court can take judicial notice of records of actions in the Superior Court. *City of Phoenix v. Superior Court In and For Maricopa County*, 110 Ariz. 155, 515 P.2d 1175 (1973); *In re Sabino R.*, 198 Ariz. 424, 10 P.3d 1211 (Ct. App. Div. 1 2000); *Schuldes v. National Sur. Corp.*, 27 Ariz. App. 611, 557 P.2d 543 (Div. 1 1976); *Pierpont v. Hydro Mfg. Co., Inc.*, 22 Ariz. App. 252, 526 P.2d 776 (Div. 1 1974); *Visco v. Universal Refuse Removal Co.*, 11 Ariz. App. 73, 462 P.2d 90 (Div. 1 1969). An appellate court may take notice of matters that are of record in a separate appeal. *Boy v. Fremont Indem. Co.*, 154 Ariz. 334, 742 P.2d 835 (Ct. App. Div. 1 1987).

Notice can be taken that testimony was given, or allegations made, in a separate case, but not that the testimony is true or that the allegations are accurate. *Matter of Ronwin*, 139 Ariz. 576, 680 P.2d 107 (1983). Judicial notice may not, however, be taken of the unpublished decision of a federal court. *Kriz v. Buckeye Petroleum Co., Inc.*, 145 Ariz. 374, 701 P.2d 1182 (1985).

Judicial notice may be taken of the laws of the State of Arizona, *Earhart v. Frohmiller*, 65 Ariz. 221, 178 P.2d 436 (1947); of the laws of another State, *Prudential Ins. Co. of America v. O'Grady*, 97 Ariz. 9, 396 P.2d 246 (1964); of the published Code of the City of Phoenix, *Roseland v. City of Phoenix*, 14 Ariz. App. 117, 481 P.2d 288 (Div. 1 1971); and, of the records of State agencies, *Adams v. Bolin*, 74 Ariz. 269, 247 P.2d 617, 33 A.L.R.2d 1102 (1952); *Hernandez v. Frohmiller*, 68 Ariz. 242, 204 P.2d 854 (1949). The law of a foreign nation, however, is to be determined as prescribed in Ariz.R.Civ.P. 44.1. The Court of Appeals, however, cannot take judicial notice of what is represented to be census data presented in an affidavit which leaves unanswered questions as to the foundation for the data used and fails to explain how it was compiled and what it represents. *City of Tucson v. Woods*, 191 Ariz. 523, 959 P.2d 394 (Ct. App. Div. 1 1997).

7. *Other Matters Judicially Noticed.* The case law evidences that a wide variety of subjects have been the subject of judicial notice by the Arizona courts. Examples of matters and facts that have been judicially noticed include:

(1) CT Corporation serves as the statutory agent for many companies, *Hughes Air Corp. v. Maricopa County Superior Court*, 114 Ariz. 412, 561 P.2d 736 (1977) (disapproved of by, Ritchie v. Grand Canyon Scenic Rides, 165 Ariz. 460, 799 P.2d 801 (1990));

(2) general inflationary trends, *Bade v. Drachman*, 4 Ariz. App. 55, 417 P.2d 689 (1966);

(3) there has been a general increase in the cost of living, *Beck v. Jaeger*, 124 Ariz. 316, 604 P.2d 18 (Ct. App. Div. 2 1979);

(4) general weather patterns in Arizona, *Maricopa Utilities Co. v. Cline*, 60 Ariz. 209, 134 P.2d 156 (1943);

(5) geographical boundaries and locations, *Treadway v. Industrial Commission*, 69 Ariz. 301, 213 P.2d 373 (1950); *Silva v. Menderson*, 41 Ariz. 258, 17 P.2d 809 (1933);

(6) average life expectancies from standard mortality tables, *Rodgers v. Bryan*, 82 Ariz. 143, 309 P.2d 773 (1957);

(7) the time of sunset on a particular day, *Southwestern Freight Lines v. Floyd*, 58 Ariz. 249, 119 P.2d 120 (1941);

(8) that pools can become dirty without negligence on the part of the owner, *Williams by Williams v. Stewart*, 145 Ariz. 602, 703 P.2d 546 (Ct. App. Div. 2 1985);

(9) that public funds are limited, *Vegodsky v. City of Tucson*, 1 Ariz. App. 102, 399 P.2d 723 (1965); official census data, *State ex rel. Corbin v. Sabel*, 138 Ariz. 253, 674 P.2d 316 (Ct. App. Div. 2 1983);

(10) the birth date and age of a purported juvenile, *In re Sabino R.*, 198 Ariz. 424, 10 P.3d 1211 (Ct. App. Div. 1 2000);

(11) that Phoenix has experienced significant growth, *City of Phoenix v. Lopez*, 77 Ariz. 146, 268 P.2d 323 (1954);

(12) the numbering system for public highways, *Campbell v. Superior Court In and For Pinal County*, 18 Ariz. App. 216, 501 P.2d 57 (Div. 2 1972);

(13) the continued participation of the University of Arizona in intercollegiate basketball competition, *University of Arizona v. Pima County*, 150 Ariz. 184, 722 P.2d 352, 34 Ed. Law Rep. 280 (Ct. App. Div. 2 1986).

ARTICLE III. PRESUMPTIONS IN CIVIL ACTIONS AND PROCEEDINGS

Rule 301. Presumptions in Civil Cases Generally

In a civil case, unless a statute or these rules provide otherwise, the party against whom a presumption is directed has the burden of producing evidence to rebut the presumption. But this rule does not shift the burden of persuasion, which remains on the party who had it originally.

Amended Sept. 8, 2011, effective Jan. 1, 2012.

Comment to 2012 Amendment

The language of this rule has been added to conform to Federal Rule of Evidence 301, as restyled.

AUTHORS' COMMENTS

Analysis

1. *Scope and Purpose of Rule.* Rule 301 governs presumptions in civil cases generally.

2. *Comparison With Federal Rule.* Effective January 1, 2012, the Arizona Supreme Court adopted Rule 301, the language of which parallels its federal counterpart, Fed. R. Evid. 301, as restyled.

Although Rule 301 parallels its federal counterpart, "federal court decisions interpreting the federal rule are persuasive but not binding with respect to interpreting the Arizona rule." *See,* Prefatory Comment to 2012 Amendments. *See also, State v. Terrazas*, 189 Ariz. 580, 944 P.2d 1194 (1997) (The Arizona Supreme Court is "not bound by the United States Supreme Court's non-constitutional construction of the Federal Rules of Evidence when [the Arizona Supreme Court construes] the Arizona Rules of Evidence."), citing, *State v. Bible*, 175 Ariz. 549, 858 P.2d 1152 (1993); *State v. Salazar-Mercado*, 232 Ariz. 256, 304 P.3d 543 (Ct. App. Div. 2 2013). Practitioners are urged to keep this legal tenet in mind as they research federal case law interpreting a federal evidentiary rule that corresponds to an Arizona evidentiary rule.

3. *Presumptions Pre-Adoption of Rule 301.* In Arizona, before

the 2012 adoption of Rule 301, presumptions were established, and governed by case law and, in many instances, by statute. Securing a clear understanding of the case law that has developed concerning presumptions is rendered difficult by the fact that the term "presumption" has been used to describe a wide variety of things, not all of which are true presumptions. In addition, over time, there developed a variety of categories to which so-called "presumptions" are assigned, such as "permissive," "mandatory," "conclusive" or "irrebuttable," and "statutory."

A presumption is merely a procedural device for shifting either the burden of going forward with evidence or the burden of proof, or both. A presumption confers on the party who properly invokes it, or in whose favor it operates, a procedural advantage which that party's adversary must overcome. What that adversary must do in order to avoid the effect of the presumption depends on the nature of the presumption involved. If the presumption is one characterized as "conclusive" or "irrebuttable," then there is nothing the adversary can do to overcome it, as any evidence contradicting the presumption will be deemed immaterial. An "irrebuttable" presumption is really not a presumption at all, but rather a rule of law.

If the presumption is one that shifts the burden of going forward with evidence, then the adversary of the party who is the beneficiary of the presumption must adduce competent evidence contradicting the matter to be presumed. If the presumption is one which shifts both the burden of going forward with evidence and the burden of proof, then the adversary must produce sufficient competent evidence to support a verdict contrary to the presumption. An example of the latter type of presumption is the presumption that parties act with due care. *Englehart v. Jeep Corp.*, 122 Ariz. 256, 594 P.2d 510 (1979); *Sheehan v. Pima County*, 135 Ariz. 235, 660 P.2d 486 (Ct. App. Div. 2 1982).

Many, but not all, presumptions are factually based. Where such a presumption is involved, once a basic or "triggering" fact is established, the trier of fact is to assume that a presumed fact has been established as well. *Starkweather v. Conner*, 44 Ariz. 369, 38 P.2d 311 (1934). An example of such a presumption is that property acquired during the marriage and/or held in the joint names of the spouses is community property. *Mitchell v. Mitchell*, 152 Ariz. 317, 732 P.2d 208, 77 A.L.R.4th 633 (1987); *Eng v. Stein*, 123 Ariz. 343, 599 P.2d 796 (1979); *Elia v. Pifer*, 194 Ariz. 74, 977 P.2d 796 (Ct. App. Div. 1 1998); *Heinig v. Hudman*, 177 Ariz. 66, 865 P.2d 110 (Ct. App. Div. 1 1993); *Bianco v. Patterson*, 159 Ariz. 472, 768 P.2d 204 (Ct. App. Div. 2 1989); *Delozier v. Evans*, 158 Ariz. 490, 763 P.2d 986 (Ct. App. Div. 1 1988); *Valladee v. Valladee*, 149 Ariz. 304, 718 P.2d 206 (Ct. App. Div. 1 1986). A party need only present proof that particular property was acquired during marriage, or that title to the property was held in the joint names of the spouses, and the community nature of the property will be presumed.

Where the presumption is factually based, the trier of fact is to assume that the presumed fact has been established until the adversary produces evidence to contradict either the presumed fact or the basic, "triggering" fact. If the basic fact is disputed, the presumption operates only if the trier of fact finds the basic or "triggering" fact to be true. If the basic fact is conceded or established by evidence that is not contradicted, the presumption can be rendered inoperative by producing evidence to contradict the presumed fact. The quality of evidence required to avoid the presumption, *e.g.,* any evidence, substantial evidence, or clear and convincing evidence, will depend on the nature and strength of the presumption involved. Even if the presumption becomes inoperative, the evidence introduced to establish the basic "triggering" fact remains for the trier of fact to consider for whatever probative value it may have, and the presumed fact can still be found if that is a permissible inference to draw from the evidence.

Examples of certain presumptions that have been recognized in the Arizona case law include:

1. Statutes are constitutional. *Rochlin v. State*, 112 Ariz. 171, 540 P.2d 643 (1975); *New Times, Inc. v. Arizona Bd. of Regents*, 110 Ariz. 367, 519 P.2d 169 (1974).

2. People are presumed to know the law and its requirements. *Frazier v. Industrial Com'n of Arizona*, 145 Ariz. 488, 702 P.2d 717 (Ct. App. Div. 1 1985); *Cooper v. Arizona Western College Dist. Governing Bd.*, 125 Ariz. 463, 610 P.2d 465 (Ct. App. Div. 1 1980).

3. Acts taken by public officials in their official capacity are correct. *Sandblom v. Corbin*, 125 Ariz. 178, 608 P.2d 317 (Ct. App. Div. 1 1980).

4. A testator has testamentary capacity. *Matter of Estate of Thorpe*, 152 Ariz. 341, 732 P.2d 571 (Ct. App. Div. 1 1986).

5. A testator who includes a time-of-death marital deduction provision in a will intends the current unlimited marital deduction to apply. *In re Estate of Pouser*, 193 Ariz. 574, 975 P.2d 704 (1999).

6. A grantor of real property cannot adversely possess the property conveyed as against its grantee. *Ziggy's Opportunities, Inc. v. I-10 Indus. Park Developers*, 152 Ariz. 104, 730 P.2d 281 (Ct. App. Div. 1 1986).

7. Debts incurred during marriage are community debts. *Arab Monetary Fund v. Hashim*, 219 Ariz. 108, 193 P.3d 802 (Ct. App. Div. 1 2008); *Schlaefer v. Financial Management Service, Inc.*, 196 Ariz. 336, 996 P.2d 745 (Ct. App. Div. 1 2000);

Gutierrez v. Gutierrez, 193 Ariz. 343, 972 P.2d 676 (Ct. App. Div. 1 1998).

8. A corporate agent will communicate to the corporation information received by the agent that is necessary for the protection of the corporation's interests. *Fridena v. Evans*, 127 Ariz. 516, 622 P.2d 463, 12 A.L.R.4th 46 (1980); *Baroldy v. Ortho Pharmaceutical Corp.*, 157 Ariz. 574, 760 P.2d 574, Prod. Liab. Rep. (CCH) P 11732 (Ct. App. Div. 1 1988).

9. A prior industrial injury finally determined by the Industrial Commission to have resulted in a scheduled permanent disability is conclusively presumed to have caused a permanent loss of earning capacity. *PFS v. Industrial Com'n of Arizona*, 191 Ariz. 274, 955 P.2d 30 (Ct. App. Div. 1 1997).

10. A prior nonindustrial injury that would, if it were an industrial injury, have been scheduled under Arizona law is only rebuttably—not conclusively— presumed to have caused a permanent loss of earning capacity. *PFS v. Industrial Com'n of Arizona*, 191 Ariz. 274, 955 P.2d 30 (Ct. App. Div. 1 1997).

11. A worker's actual post-injury earnings are presumed to establish the worker's residual earning capacity, but that presumption is rebuttable. *Reavis v. Industrial Com'n of Arizona*, 196 Ariz. 280, 995 P.2d 716 (Ct. App. Div. 1 1999).

12. In civil cases, children under ten (10) years of age are only presumed to be incompetent to serve as witnesses. That presumption, however can be rebutted by a showing that permits the trial judge to fnd the witness competent. A.R.S. § 12-2202(2); *State v. Schossow*, 145 Ariz. 504, 703 P.2d 448 (1985).

Rule 302. Applying State Law to Presumptions in Civil Cases

Not adopted.

Comment to 2012 Amendment

Federal Rule of Evidence 302 has not been adopted because it is inapplicable to state court proceedings.

Comment to Original 1977 Rule

Federal Rule of Evidence 302 was not adopted because of the non-adoption of Rule 301. No other purpose was intended.

ARTICLE IV. RELEVANCY AND ITS LIMITS

Rule 401. Test for "Relevant Evidence"

Evidence is relevant if:

(a) it has any tendency to make a fact more or less probable than it would be without the evidence; and

(b) the fact is of consequence in determining the action.

Amended Sept. 8, 2011, effective Jan. 1, 2012.

Comment to 2012 Amendment

The language of Rule 401 has been amended to conform to the federal restyling of the Evidence Rules to make them more easily understood and to make style and terminology consistent throughout the rules. These changes are intended to be stylistic only. There is no intent to change any result in any ruling on evidence admissibility.

AUTHORS' COMMENTS

Analysis

1. *Scope and Purpose of Rule.* Rule 402 establishes "relevance" as the touchstone for the admissibility of evidence. Rule 401 defines "relevance" to include evidence that satisfies two criteria: (1) the evidence has a tendency to prove or disprove a fact, *i.e.,* probative value; and, (2) the fact to be proven, viewed in the context of other facts proven or to be proven and the applicable law, is of consequence in the action, *i.e.,* materiality. The adoption of Rule 401 in 1977, however, did not a change in the law, but rather the articulation of a single, concise standard for determining relevance that was consistent with established principles. *Brown v. General Foods Corp.*, 117 Ariz. 530, 573 P.2d 930 (Ct. App. Div. 1 1978).

2. *Comparison With Federal Rule.* Effective January 1, 2012, the Arizona Supreme Court amended Rule 401 to conform to the federal restyling of the Evidence Rules to make the rules more

easily understood and to make style and terminology consistent throughout. The 2012 Comment states the stylistic amendments are not intended to "change any result in any ruling on evidence admissibility."

Following the 2012 restyling amendments, the language of Rule 401 remains identical to its federal counterpart, Fed. R. Evid. 401.

Although Rule 401 parallels its federal counterpart, "federal court decisions interpreting the federal rule are persuasive but not binding with respect to interpreting the Arizona rule." *See,* Prefatory Comment to 2012 Amendments. *See also, State v. Terrazas*, 189 Ariz. 580, 944 P.2d 1194 (1997) (The Arizona Supreme Court is "not bound by the United States Supreme Court's non-constitutional construction of the Federal Rules of Evidence when [the Arizona Supreme Court construes] the Arizona Rules of Evidence."), citing, *State v. Bible*, 175 Ariz. 549, 858 P.2d 1152 (1993); *State v. Salazar-Mercado*, 232 Ariz. 256, 304 P.3d 543 (Ct. App. Div. 2 2013). Practitioners are urged to keep this legal tenet in mind as they research federal case law interpreting a federal evidentiary rule that corresponds to an Arizona evidentiary rule.

3. *General Standards of Relevance/Admissibility.* To satisfy the express standard established by Rule 401, evidence need only have any tendency to make the existence of any fact that is of consequence to the determination of the action more probable or less probable than it would be without the evidence. *See also*, *McMurtry v. Weatherford Hotel, Inc.*, 231 Ariz. 244, 293 P.3d 520 (Ct. App. Div. 1 2013) (vacating trial court's admission of alcohol abuse and attendance at alcohol awareness class after DUI citation and remanding with direction to balance the probative value of such evidence against its prejudicial effect under Ariz. R. Evid. 403); *State v. Cooperman*, 230 Ariz. 245, 282 P.3d 446 (Ct. App. Div. 2 2012), review granted in part, (Mar. 19, 2013) and aff'd, 232 Ariz. 347, 306 P.3d 4 (2013). *See also*, *United Ins. Co. v. Lutz*, 227 Ariz. 411, 258 P.3d 229 (Ct. App. Div. 1 2011) (citing Rule 401, relevant evidence is evidence having "any tendency to make the existence of any fact that is of consequence to the determination of the action more probable or less probable than it would be without the evidence"); *Brethauer v. General Motors Corp.*, 221 Ariz. 192, 211 P.3d 1176 (Ct. App. Div. 1 2009).

The Arizona Supreme Court has opined that this is not a particularly high standard. *State v. Oliver*, 158 Ariz. 22, 28, 760 P.2d 1071, 1077 (1988). *See also*, *State v. Cooperman*, 230 Ariz. 245, 282 P.3d 446 (Ct. App. Div. 2 2012), review granted in part, (Mar. 19, 2013) and aff'd, 232 Ariz. 347, 306 P.3d 4 (2013), citing *State v. Oliver*, 158 Ariz. 22, 28, 760 P.2d 1071, 1077 (1988).

It is not necessary that the evidence in and of itself be sufficient to support a finding of that fact; it is enough if the evidence renders the fact more probable or less probable than it would be without the evidence being received. *Hawkins v. Allstate Ins. Co.*, 152 Ariz. 490, 733 P.2d 1073 (1987); *Reader v. General Motors Corp.*, 107 Ariz. 149, 483 P.2d 1388, 54 A.L.R.3d 1068 (1971); *Acuna v. Kroack*, 212 Ariz. 104, 128 P.3d 221 (Ct. App. Div. 2 2006); *Brown v. U.S. Fidelity and Guar. Co.*, 194 Ariz. 85, 977 P.2d 807 (Ct. App. Div. 1 1998), as amended, (Nov. 25, 1998) and as corrected, (Aug. 5, 1999).

The fact to be inferred from the evidence must be material, *i.e.*, "of consequence in the action." The materiality of a fact will be defined by the law applicable to the claims and defenses properly raised by the pleadings. Evidence is admissible if it is relevant to facts supporting any theory of recovery. *Rossell v. Volkswagen of America*, 147 Ariz. 160, 709 P.2d 517, Prod. Liab. Rep. (CCH) P 10752 (1985). Evidence need only have "any tendency" to make an inference of a material fact more or less probable, a minimal test which places substantial discretion in the trial judge.

Under Rule 403, the trial judge can refuse to admit otherwise relevant evidence where its probative value is outweighed by the danger of unfair prejudice, confusion of the issues, or undue delay. The trial judge can even refuse to admit evidence which the parties have agreed is admissible. *Matter of Swartz*, 141 Ariz. 266, 686 P.2d 1236 (1984).

4. *Negative Evidence.* Most evidence is positive evidence, *i.e.*, testimony of witnesses concerning events they observed or in which they participated. Negative evidence, *e.g.*, testimony that a witness did *not* observe the occurrence of a particular event, has probative value only when supported by sufficient foundation that the witness' position was such that the witness would have observed the event had it taken place. *Mast v. Standard Oil Co. of California*, 140 Ariz. 1, 680 P.2d 137 (1984); *Alires v. Southern Pac. Co.*, 100 Ariz. 6, 409 P.2d 714 (1966); *Jeune v. Del E. Webb Const. Co.*, 76 Ariz. 418, 265 P.2d 1076 (1954).

Thus, while evidence of the absence of accidents involving a particular product may be admissible in a product liability action, the proponent of such evidence must establish that, if there had been such accidents involving the product in question, the witness called to establish prior product safety would have known of them. *Jimenez v. Sears, Roebuck and Co.*, 180 Ariz. 432, 885 P.2d 120, Prod. Liab. Rep. (CCH) P 13925 (Ct. App. Div. 2 1994), vacated in part, 183 Ariz. 399, 904 P.2d 861, Prod. Liab. Rep. (CCH) P 14382 (1995). The scale tips strongly, however, against the admission of this type of evidence because the absence of actual accidents does not necessarily negate the possibility of near-accidents resulting from a dangerous condition, and a very careful and thorough foundation must be established before it can be admitted. *Isbell ex rel. Isbell v. State*, 198 Ariz. 291, 9 P.3d 322 (2000).

5. *Impeachment Evidence.* Substantive evidence is evidence which has probative value on the facts that are material under the legal principles applicable to the claims and defenses of the parties. Impeachment evidence attacks the credibility of the other party's proof. Given the rule that a witness' credibility is not to be attacked on purely collateral matters, the two categories of evidence are not always discrete, and a good deal of evidence which attacks the credibility of the opponent's evidence will also have independent substantive probative value. *Zimmerman v. Superior Court In and For Maricopa County*, 98 Ariz. 85, 402 P.2d 212, 18 A.L.R.3d 909 (1965); *Helena Chemical Co. v. Coury Bros. Ranches, Inc.*, 126 Ariz. 448, 616 P.2d 908 (Ct. App. Div. 1 1980).

Within the limits defined by Rules 608 and 609, evidence that tests, sustains or questions the credibility of witnesses is admissible for impeachment or rebuttal purposes. A party can prove events that would show bias, prejudice, interest or corruption of a witness. *Barsema v. Susong*, 156 Ariz. 309, 751 P.2d 969 (1988); *Jones v. Munn*, 140 Ariz. 216, 681 P.2d 368 (1984); *Foulk v. Kotz*, 138 Ariz. 159, 673 P.2d 799 (Ct. App. Div. 2 1983). A party may introduce specific instances of a witness' conduct if they are inconsistent with the witness' testimony, but not on a purely collateral matter. *Public Service Co. of Oklahoma v. Bleak*, 134 Ariz. 311, 656 P.2d 600 (1982); *Nienstedt v. Wetzel*, 133 Ariz. 348, 651 P.2d 876, 33 A.L.R.4th 635 (Ct. App. Div. 1 1982).

6. *Demonstrative Evidence.* Demonstrative evidence permits the trier of fact to itself observe a matter that is in issue rather than simply hear it described by the testimony of witnesses. Demonstrative evidence can be either "real," *i.e.,* an actual scene or object in issue, or "illustrative," *i.e.,* evidence used to illustrate the testimony of witnesses.

Photographs or movies of a scene or object can be both real and illustrative. The foundation required for the use of such evidence is that a witness familiar with the scene or object at the time in issue establish through testimony that the photograph or movie is an accurate depiction of the scene or object at the time. *Stroud v. Dorr-Oliver, Inc.*, 112 Ariz. 403, 542 P.2d 1102 (1975); *Higgins v. Arizona Sav. and Loan Ass'n*, 90 Ariz. 55, 365 P.2d 476 (1961); *Slow Development Co. v. Coulter*, 88 Ariz. 122, 353 P.2d 890 (1960); *Gonzales v. Arizona Public Service Co.*, 161 Ariz. 84, 775 P.2d 1148 (Ct. App. Div. 2 1989); *Trevizo v. Astec Industries, Inc.*, 156 Ariz. 320, 751 P.2d 980 (Ct. App. Div. 2 1987). The individual who took the photographs need not be the person who verifies it at trial, and the verifying witness is not required to have been present when the photographs were taken, provided that the witness can attest that the photographs accurately depict the scene or object depicted. *Lohmeier v. Hammer*, 214 Ariz. 57, 148 P.3d 101 (Ct. App. Div. 1 2006).

Witnesses can also use sketches, diagrams, models and other visual aids to illustrate or explain their testimony, but such materials are not necessarily admissible as exhibits in the case. *Rossell v. Volkswagen of America*, 147 Ariz. 160, 709 P.2d 517, Prod. Liab. Rep. (CCH) P 10752 (1985); *Wait v. City of Scottsdale*, 127 Ariz. 107, 618 P.2d 601 (1980); *Slow Development Co. v. Coulter*, 88 Ariz. 122, 353 P.2d 890 (1960).

Computer simulations are a form of demonstrative evidence, and their use is generally permissible, provided foundational requirements are satisfied. *Bledsoe v. Salt River Valley Water Users' Ass'n*, 179 Ariz. 469, 880 P.2d 689 (Ct. App. Div. 2 1994). The proponent of such evidence must show, at a minimum, that the simulation fairly represents what it depicts, whether through the computer expert who prepared it or some other witness qualified to so testify, and the opposing party must be afforded the opportunity for cross-examination. *Bledsoe v. Salt River Valley Water Users' Ass'n*, 179 Ariz. 469, 880 P.2d 689 (Ct. App. Div. 2 1994).

7. *Evidence of Defendant's Financial Condition.* In normal circumstances, a defendant's financial condition would not be probative of a material issue, and its relevance might be outweighed by the risk of unfair prejudice and confusion of the issues. Where punitive damages are sought, however, evidence of a defendant's wealth or poverty is admissible on the issue of the amount of such damages, if any, to award. *Hawkins v. Allstate Ins. Co.*, 152 Ariz. 490, 733 P.2d 1073 (1987); *Grant v. Arizona Public Service Co.*, 133 Ariz. 434, 652 P.2d 507 (1982); *Rodriguez v. Schlittenhart*, 161 Ariz. 609, 780 P.2d 442 (Ct. App. Div. 2 1989); *Liberatore v. Thompson*, 157 Ariz. 612, 760 P.2d 612 (Ct. App. Div. 1 1988); *White v. Mitchell*, 157 Ariz. 523, 759 P.2d 1327 (Ct. App. Div. 1 1988). Given the risk of prejudice, however, the better and more frequent practice is for the trial court to require a *prima facie* showing of evidence sufficient to support a punitive damages award before allowing such financial evidence to be introduced.

Rule 402. General Admissibility of Relevant Evidence

Relevant evidence is admissible unless any of the following provides otherwise:

- the United States or Arizona Constitution;
- an applicable statute;
- these rules; or
- other rules prescribed by the Supreme Court.

Irrelevant evidence is not admissible.

Amended Sept. 8, 2011, effective Jan. 1, 2012.

Comment to 2012 Amendment

The language of Rule 402 has been amended to conform to the federal restyling of the Evidence Rules to make them more easily understood and to make style and terminology consistent throughout the rules. These changes are intended to be stylistic only. There is no intent to change any result in any ruling on evidence admissibility.

AUTHORS' COMMENTS

Analysis

1. *Scope and Purpose of Rule.* Rule 402 simply declares that relevant evidence is admissible, except as otherwise provided in the United States Constitution, the Arizona Constitution, or applicable statutes or rules. Rule 401 defines the standard for determining relevance. Subject to the protections of Rules 105 and 403, evidence should be received if it is admissible for any purpose. *Readenour v. Marion Power Shovel, a Div. of Dresser Industries, Inc.*, 149 Ariz. 442, 719 P.2d 1058, Prod. Liab. Rep. (CCH) P 11012 (1986).

The corollary, also expressed in the Rule, is that evidence that is irrelevant is not admissible. *Newell v. Town of Oro Valley*, 163 Ariz. 527, 789 P.2d 394 (Ct. App. Div. 2 1990); *Good v. City of Glendale*, 150 Ariz. 218, 722 P.2d 386 (Ct. App. Div. 2 1986). Where one party, however, has injected irrelevant or improper evidence, that may open the door to permitting that party's adversary the right to respond. *Pool v. Superior Court In and For Pima County*, 139 Ariz. 98, 677 P.2d 261 (1984); *Elia v. Pifer*, 194 Ariz. 74, 977 P.2d 796 (Ct. App. Div. 1 1998). The trial judge has discretion to reject evidence even if the parties have stipulated to its receipt. *Matter of Swartz*, 141 Ariz. 266, 686 P.2d 1236 (1984).

Evidence of other similar accidents at or near the place suffered by persons other than the plaintiff, at different times, but not too remote in time, may be admissible. *Slow Development Co. v. Coulter*, 88 Ariz. 122, 353 P.2d 890 (1960); *Wiggs v. City of Phoenix*, 197 Ariz. 358, 4 P.3d 413 (Ct. App. Div. 1 1999), opinion vacated on other grounds, 198 Ariz. 367, 10 P.3d 625, 111 A.L.R. 5th 815 (2000). Before such evidence can be admitted, a proper foundation must be established, tending to prove the existence of a defective or dangerous condition, knowledge or notice of the dangerous condition, or negligence in permitting it to continue. *Wiggs v. City of Phoenix*, 197 Ariz. 358, 4 P.3d 413 (Ct. App. Div. 1 1999), opinion vacated on other grounds, 198 Ariz. 367, 10 P.3d 625, 111 A.L.R.5th 815 (2000).

2. *Comparison With Federal Rule.* Effective January 1, 2012, the Arizona Supreme Court amended Rule 402 to conform to the federal restyling of the Evidence Rules to make the rules more easily understood and to make style and terminology consistent throughout. The 2012 Comment states the stylistic amendments are not intended to "change any result in any ruling on evidence admissibility."

Following the 2012 restyling amendments, the language of Rule 402 remains identical to its federal counterpart, Fed. R. Evid. 402, except for editorial changes to adapt the rule to the Arizona court system.

Although Rule 402 parallels its federal counterpart, "federal court decisions interpreting the federal rule are persuasive but not binding with respect to interpreting the Arizona rule." *See,* Prefatory Comment to 2012 Amendments. *See also, State v. Terrazas*, 189 Ariz. 580, 944 P.2d 1194 (1997) (The Arizona Supreme Court is "not bound by the United States Supreme Court's non-constitutional construction of the Federal Rules of Evidence when [the Arizona Supreme Court construes] the Arizona Rules of Evidence."), citing, *State v. Bible*, 175 Ariz. 549, 858 P.2d 1152 (1993); *State v. Salazar-Mercado*, 232 Ariz. 256, 304 P.3d 543 (Ct. App. Div. 2 2013). Practitioners are urged to keep this legal tenet in mind as they research federal case law interpreting a federal evidentiary rule that corresponds to an Arizona evidentiary rule.

3. *Effect of Statutory Provisions.* As it is phrased, Rule 402 purports to defer to statutory provisions declaring evidence inadmissible. Such deference has been exercised where a statute recognizes or creates an evidentiary privilege, but a court rule concerning the admissibility of evidence will control over a statute that directly conflicts with it. *Barsema v. Susong*, 156 Ariz. 309, 751 P.2d 969 (1988); *Readenour v. Marion Power Shovel, a*

Div. of Dresser Industries, Inc., 149 Ariz. 442, 719 P.2d 1058, Prod. Liab. Rep. (CCH) P 11012 (1986); *Borja v. Phoenix General Hosp., Inc.*, 151 Ariz. 302, 727 P.2d 355 (Ct. App. Div. 2 1986).

4. *Conditional Relevance.* The proponent of evidence has the burden of establishing the predicates for its admissibility. *DeElena v. Southern Pac. Co.*, 121 Ariz. 563, 592 P.2d 759 (1979). Where the relevance and admissibility of evidence turns on the presence or absence of predicate facts, the determination as to whether those predicates have been established is always for the Court. *W. R. Skousen Contractor, Inc. v. Gray*, 26 Ariz. App. 100, 546 P.2d 369 (Div. 1 1976). Where the predicates for admission of evidence have not been established at the time the evidence is offered, the Court may nevertheless allow it to be received on condition that evidence establishing the predicate facts will be forthcoming at a later point in the proceedings. Rule 104(b), Ariz. R. Evid. Generally, the trial court will require an avowal of counsel to that effect. If the predicate facts are not subsequently established, the party against whom the evidence was offered and received must move to strike it, or the objection may be waived.

Rule 403. Excluding Relevant Evidence for Prejudice, Confusion, Waste of Time, or Other Reasons

The court may exclude relevant evidence if its probative value is substantially outweighed by a danger of one or more of the following: unfair prejudice, confusing the issues, misleading the jury, undue delay, wasting time, or needlessly presenting cumulative evidence.

Amended Sept. 8, 2011, effective Jan. 1, 2012.

Comment to 2012 Amendment

The language of Rule 403 has been amended to conform to the federal restyling of the Evidence Rules to make them more easily understood and to make style and terminology consistent throughout the rules. These changes are intended to be stylistic only. There is no intent to change any result in any ruling on evidence admissibility.

AUTHORS' COMMENTS

Analysis

1. *Scope and Purpose of Rule.* Rule 403 grants the trial court both discretion and authority to protect the integrity of the fact-finding process through the exclusion of otherwise relevant evidence if its probative value is substantially outweighed by one of the negative factors specified in the Rule. The Rule contemplates that the trial court will arrive at its decision through a process of balancing the relative probative value of the evidence in question against the risk of unfair prejudice, jury confusion or undue delay.

2. *Comparison With Federal Rule.* Effective January 1, 2012, the Arizona Supreme Court amended Rule 403 to conform to the federal restyling of the Evidence Rules to make the rules more easily understood and to make style and terminology consistent throughout. The 2012 Comment states the stylistic amendments are not intended to "change any result in any ruling on evidence admissibility."

Following the 2012 restyling amendments, the language of Rule 403 remains identical to its federal counterpart, Fed. R. Evid. 403.

Although Rule 403 parallels its federal counterpart, "federal court decisions interpreting the federal rule are persuasive but

not binding with respect to interpreting the Arizona rule." *See,* Prefatory Comment to 2012 Amendments. *See also, State v. Terrazas*, 189 Ariz. 580, 944 P.2d 1194 (1997) (The Arizona Supreme Court is "not bound by the United States Supreme Court's non-constitutional construction of the Federal Rules of Evidence when [the Arizona Supreme Court construes] the Arizona Rules of Evidence."), citing, *State v. Bible*, 175 Ariz. 549, 858 P.2d 1152 (1993); *State v. Salazar-Mercado*, 232 Ariz. 256, 304 P.3d 543 (Ct. App. Div. 2 2013). Practitioners are urged to keep this legal tenet in mind as they research federal case law interpreting a federal evidentiary rule that corresponds to an Arizona evidentiary rule.

3. *Standards for Exclusion.* Rule 403 allows the trial court to exclude relevant evidence if its probative value is outweighed by any of six considerations:

(1) danger of unfair prejudice;
(2) danger of confusion of the issues;
(3) danger of misleading the jury;
(4) considerations of undue delay;
(5) considerations of waste of time; or,
(6) needless presentation of cumulative evidence. Rules 404 and 407 through 411 are really particularized applications of the first three of these considerations to frequently encountered situations.

Although trial court should make a record of its Rule 403 determinations, the failure to do so is not necessarily reversible error. *See Salt River Project Agricultural Improvement and Power Dist. v. Miller Park, L.L.C.*, 218 Ariz. 246, 183 P.3d 4 (2008).

The "unfair prejudice" to which the Rule refers is an undue tendency of the evidence to suggest or invite a decision on an improper, basis, such as emotion, sympathy or horror. *Shotwell v. Donahoe*, 207 Ariz. 287, 85 P.3d 1045, 93 Fair Empl. Prac. Cas. (BNA) 658 (2004); *State v. Schurz*, 176 Ariz. 46, 859 P.2d 156 (1993); *Hudgins v. Southwest Airlines, Co.*, 221 Ariz. 472, 212 P.3d 810 (Ct. App. Div. 1 2009); *Higgins v. Assmann Electronics, Inc.*, 217 Ariz. 289, 173 P.3d 453 (Ct. App. Div. 1 2007).

Not all harmful evidence is unfairly prejudicial; evidence which is relevant and material will generally be adverse to the opponent of the party offering it and, in that sense, "prejudicial." That form of "prejudice" is not the basis for exclusion under Rule 403. *State v. Salamanca*, 233 Ariz. 292, 311 P.3d 1105 (Ct. App. Div. 1 2013) (trial court did not abuse its discretion in finding that any prejudice caused by admission of unredacted text messages was outweighed by the probative value of such text messages). *Henry ex rel. Estate of Wilson v. HealthPartners of Southern Arizona*, 203 Ariz. 393, 55 P.3d 87 (Ct. App. Div. 2 2002), quoting *Yauch v.*

Southern Pacific Transp. Co., 198 Ariz. 394, 10 P.3d 1181 (Ct. App. Div. 2 2000).

"Confusion of the issues" refers to the introduction of extraneous or collateral issues and does not encompass conflicting evidence on material issues. *State ex rel. McDougall v. Municipal Court of City of Phoenix*, 153 Ariz. 111, 735 P.2d 141 (Ct. App. Div. 1 1986); *Schneider v. Cessna Aircraft Co.*, 150 Ariz. 153, 722 P.2d 321, Prod. Liab. Rep. (CCH) P 10743 (Ct. App. Div. 1 1985); *Chapman v. Levi-Strauss*, 145 Ariz. 411, 701 P.2d 1219 (Ct. App. Div. 2 1985).

The trial court can exclude evidence of instances of conduct that would be admissible impeachment under Rule 608(b), even past examples of untruthfulness on the part of a witness, if receipt of the evidence would unduly delay the trial. *Delozier v. Evans*, 158 Ariz. 490, 763 P.2d 986 (Ct. App. Div. 1 1988); *Block v. Meyer*, 144 Ariz. 230, 696 P.2d 1379 (Ct. App. Div. 1 1985). The Court also may exclude evidence that is purely cumulative, although the admission of repetitive evidence does not require a reversal. *State ex rel. La Sota v. Arizona Licensed Beverage Ass'n, Inc.*, 128 Ariz. 515, 627 P.2d 666, 1981-1 Trade Cas. (CCH) ¶ 63933 (1981); *Elia v. Pifer*, 194 Ariz. 74, 977 P.2d 796 (Ct. App. Div. 1 1998).

Even relevant testimony admissible pursuant to Rule 702, however, may be excluded, pursuant to Rule 403, if its probative value is substantially outweighed by the danger of unfair prejudice, confusion of the issues, or misleading the jury. *State v. Sosnowicz*, 229 Ariz. 90, 270 P.3d 917 (Ct. App. Div. 1 2012); *State v. Chappell*, 225 Ariz. 229, 236 P.3d 1176, 1182–83 (2010), cert. denied, 131 S. Ct. 1485, 179 L. Ed. 2d 320 (2011). Moreover, there is nothing in Rule 403 which precludes the exclusion of evidence merely because an expert has relied on the data. *Brethauer v. General Motors Corp.*, 221 Ariz. 192, 211 P.3d 1176 (Ct. App. Div. 1 2009).

While the possibility of undue delay is an appropriate factor for the trial court to consider in applying Rule 403, before excluding seemingly extraneous evidence, the trial court should take into account the right to cross-examine. *Gasiorowski v. Hose*, 182 Ariz. 376, 897 P.2d 678 (Ct. App. Div. 1 1994).

Other Rule 403 cases excluding evidence when the danger of prejudice, confusion or delay substantially outweighed the probative value of the evidence include the following:

(1) *State v. Delahanty*, 226 Ariz. 502, 250 P.3d 1131 (2011), cert. denied, 132 S. Ct. 143, 181 L. Ed. 2d 61 (2011) (unconfirmed statement that the witness suffered from schizophrenia excluded under Rule 403);

(2) *State v. Abdi*, 226 Ariz. 361, 248 P.3d 209 (Ct. App. Div. 2

2011) (citing Rule 403, relevant evidence may be excluded if its probative value is substantially outweighed by the danger of unfair prejudice or needless presentation of cumulative evidence);

(3) *Boy v. I.T.T. Grinnell Corp.*, 150 Ariz. 526, 724 P.2d 612, Prod. Liab. Rep. (CCH) P 10636, 61 A.L.R.4th 137 (Ct. App. Div. 1 1986);

(4) *Jones v. Pak-Mor Mfg. Co.*, 145 Ariz. 121, 700 P.2d 819, 51 A.L.R.4th 1167 (1985);

(5) *Bledsoe v. Salt River Valley Water Users' Ass'n*, 179 Ariz. 469, 880 P.2d 689 (Ct. App. Div. 2 1994);

(6) *West Pinal Family Health Center, Inc. v. McBryde*, 162 Ariz. 546, 785 P.2d 66 (Ct. App. Div. 2 1989);

(7) *Dunlap v. Jimmy GMC of Tucson, Inc.*, 136 Ariz. 338, 666 P.2d 83 (Ct. App. Div. 2 1983);

(8) *Hallmark v. Allied Products Corp.*, 132 Ariz. 434, 646 P.2d 319 (Ct. App. Div. 1 1982).

The decision whether to admit or exclude the questioned evidence is one committed to the trial court's discretion, and that decision will be disturbed on appeal only for an abuse of that discretion. *State v. Cooperman*, 230 Ariz. 245, 282 P.3d 446 (Ct. App. Div. 2 2012), review granted in part, (Mar. 19, 2013) and aff'd, 232 Ariz. 347, 306 P.3d 4 (2013) (the trial court "has broad discretion to determine the admissibility of evidence and is best suited to conduct any balancing of probative value and prejudicial effect."); *Gemstar Ltd. v. Ernst & Young*, 185 Ariz. 493, 917 P.2d 222 (1996); *Bradshaw v. State Farm Mut. Auto. Ins. Co.*, 157 Ariz. 411, 758 P.2d 1313 (1988); *Readenour v. Marion Power Shovel, a Div. of Dresser Industries, Inc.*, 149 Ariz. 442, 719 P.2d 1058, Prod. Liab. Rep. (CCH) P 11012 (1986); *Brethauer v. General Motors Corp.*, 221 Ariz. 192, 211 P.3d 1176 (Ct. App. Div. 1 2009); *Elia v. Pifer*, 194 Ariz. 74, 977 P.2d 796 (Ct. App. Div. 1 1998); *Brown v. U.S. Fidelity and Guar. Co.*, 194 Ariz. 85, 977 P.2d 807 (Ct. App. Div. 1 1998), as amended, (Nov. 25, 1998) and as corrected, (Aug. 5, 1999); *State ex rel. Miller v. Wells Fargo Bank of Arizona, N.A.*, 194 Ariz. 126, 978 P.2d 103 (Ct. App. Div. 1 1998); *Sheppard v. Crow-Barker Paul No. 1 Ltd. Partnership*, 192 Ariz. 539, 968 P.2d 612 (Ct. App. Div. 1 1998); *Cervantes v. Rijlaarsdam*, 190 Ariz. 396, 949 P.2d 56 (Ct. App. Div. 2 1997); *Conant v. Whitney*, 190 Ariz. 290, 947 P.2d 864 (Ct. App. Div. 1 1997); *Monthofer Investments Ltd. Partnership v. Allen*, 189 Ariz. 422, 943 P.2d 782 (Ct. App. Div. 1 1997); *AMERCO v. Shoen*, 184 Ariz. 150, 907 P.2d 536 (Ct. App. Div. 1 1995), corrected, (Aug. 29, 1995).

Rule 404. Character evidence not admissible to prove conduct; exceptions; other crimes

(a) Character Evidence Generally. Evidence of a person's character or a trait of character is not admissible for the purpose of proving action in conformity therewith on a particular occasion, except:

(1) *Character of Accused or Civil Defendant.* Evidence of a pertinent trait of character offered by an accused, or by the prosecution to rebut the same, or evidence of the aberrant sexual propensity of the accused or a civil defendant pursuant to Rule 404(c);

(2) *Character of Victim.* Evidence of a pertinent trait of character of the victim of the crime offered by an accused, or by the prosecution to rebut the same, or evidence of a character trait of peacefulness of the victim offered by the prosecution in a homicide case to rebut evidence that the victim was the first aggressor;

(3) *Character of Witness.* Evidence of the character of a witness, as provided in Rules 607, 608, and 609.

(b) Other Crimes, Wrongs, or Acts. Except as provided in Rule 404(c), evidence of other crimes, wrongs, or acts is not admissible to prove the character of a person in order to show action in conformity therewith. It may, however, be admissible for other purposes, such as proof of motive, opportunity, intent, preparation, plan, knowledge, identity, or absence of mistake or accident.

(c) Character Evidence in Sexual Misconduct Cases. In a criminal case in which a defendant is charged with having committed a sexual offense, or a civil case in which a claim is predicated on a party's alleged commission of a sexual offense, evidence of other crimes, wrongs, or acts may be admitted by the court if relevant to show that the defendant had a character trait giving rise to an aberrant sexual propensity to commit the offense charged. In such a case, evidence to rebut the proof of other crimes, wrongs, or acts, or an inference therefrom, may also be admitted.

(1) In all such cases, the court shall admit evidence of the other act only if it first finds each of the following:

(A) The evidence is sufficient to permit the trier of fact to find that the defendant committed the other act.

(B) The commission of the other act provides a reasonable basis to infer that the defendant had a character trait giving rise to an aberrant sexual propensity to commit the crime charged.

(C) The evidentiary value of proof of the other act is not substantially outweighed by danger of unfair prejudice, confusion of issues, or other factors mentioned in Rule 403. In making that determination under Rule 403, the court shall also take into consideration the following factors, among others:

(i) remoteness of the other act;

(ii) similarity or dissimilarity of the other act;

(iii) the strength of the evidence that defendant committed the other act;

(iv) frequency of the other acts;

(v) surrounding circumstances;

(vi) relevant intervening events;

(vii) other similarities or differences;

(viii) other relevant factors.

(D) The court shall make specific findings with respect to each of (A), (B), and (C) of Rule 404(c)(1).

(2) In all cases in which evidence of another act is admitted pursuant to this subsection, the court shall instruct the jury as to the proper use of such evidence.

(3) In all criminal cases in which the state intends to offer evidence of other acts pursuant to this subdivision of Rule 404, the state shall make disclosure to the defendant as to such acts as required by Rule 15.1, Rules of Criminal Procedure, no later than 45 days prior to the final trial setting or at such later time as the court may allow for good cause. The defendant shall make disclosure as to rebuttal evidence pertaining to such acts as required by Rule 15.2, no later than 20 days after receipt of the state's disclosure or at such other time as the court may allow for good cause. In all civil cases in which a party intends to offer evidence of other acts pursuant to this subdivision of Rule 404, the parties shall make disclosure as required by Rule 26.1, Rules of Civil Procedure, no later than 60 days prior to trial, or at such later time as the court may allow for good cause shown.

(4) As used in this subsection of Rule 404, the term "sexual offense" is as defined in A.R.S. § 13-1420(C) and, in addition, includes any offense of first-degree murder pursuant to A.R.S. Sec. 13-1105(A)(2) of which the predicate felony is sexual conduct with a minor under Sec. 13-1405, sexual assault under Sec. 13-1406, or molestation of a child under Sec. 13-1410.

Amended Oct. 19, 1988, effective Nov. 1, 1988; amended Aug. 19, 1997, effective Dec. 1, 1997.

Comment to 2012 Amendment

The language of Rule 404 has not been changed in any manner.

Comment to 1997 Amendment

Subsection (c) is intended to codify and supply an analytical framework for the application of the rule created by case law in *State v. Treadaway*, 116 Ariz. 163, 568 P.2d 1061 (1977), and *State v. McFarlin*, 110 Ariz. 225, 517 P.2d 87 (1973). The rule announced in *Treadway* and *McFarlin* and here codified is an exception to the common-law rule forbidding the use of evidence of other acts for the purpose of showing character or propensity.

Subsection (1)(B) of Rule 404(c) is intended to modify the *Treadway* rule by permitting the court to admit evidence of remote or dissimilar other acts providing there is a "reasonable" basis, by way of expert testimony or otherwise, to support relevancy, *i.e.*, that the commission of the other act permits an inference that defendant had an aberrant sexual propensity that makes it more probable that he or she committed the sexual offense charged. The *Treadway* requirement that there be expert testimony in all cases of remote or dissimilar acts is hereby eliminated.

The present codification of the rule permits admission of evidence of the other act either on the basis of similarity or closeness in time, supporting expert testimony, or other reasonable basis that will support such an inference. To be admissible in a criminal case, the relevant prior bad act must be shown to have been committed by the defendant by clear and convincing evidence. *State v. Terrazas*, 189 Ariz. 580, 944 P.2d 1194 (1997).

Notwithstanding the language in *Treadway*, the rule does not contemplate any bright line test of remoteness or similarity, which are solely factors to be considered under subsection (1)(C) of Rule 404(c). A medical or other expert who is testifying pursuant to Rule 404(c) is not required to state a diagnostic conclusion concerning any aberrant sexual propensity of the defendant so long as his or her testimony assists the trier of fact and there is other evidence which satisfies the requirements of subsection (1)(B).

Subsection (1)(C) of the rule requires the court to make a Rule 403 analysis in all cases. The rule also requires the court in all cases to instruct the jury on the proper use of any other act evidence that is admitted. At a minimum, the court should instruct the jury that the admission of the other acts does not lessen the prosecution's burden to prove the defendant's guilt beyond a reasonable doubt, and that the jury may not convict the defendant simply because it finds that he committed the other act or had a character trait that predisposed him to commit the crime charged.

Comment to Original 1977 Rule

State ex rel. Pope v. Superior Court, In and For Mohave County, 113 Ariz. 22, 545 P.2d 946, 94 A.L.R.3d 246 (1976) is consistent with and interpretative of Rule 404(a)(2).

Application

Applicable to cases pending on and after that date [Dec. 1, 1997], except civil cases as to which the final trial date is set to occur between December 1, 1997 and February 1, 1998 and criminal cases as to which the final trial date is set to occur between December 1, 1997 and January 15, 1998.

AUTHORS' COMMENTS

Analysis

4. Proof of Other Crimes or Wrongful Acts.
5. Proof of Other Accidents or Conditions.
6. Evidence of Aberrant Sexual Propensity.

1. *Scope and Purpose of Rule.* Rule 404 covers two separate subjects: (1) the admissibility of evidence of a person's character as substantive evidence; and, (2) the admissibility of evidence of other crimes or instances of misconduct for purposes other than proof of character. "Character" is a description of a person's general disposition, as distinguished from "habit," which describes that person's regular response to a recurring specific situation. *Boswell v. Phoenix Newspapers, Inc.*, 152 Ariz. 1, 730 P.2d 178 (Ct. App. Div. 1 1985), approved as supplemented, 152 Ariz. 9, 730 P.2d 186, 13 Media L. Rep. (BNA) 1785 (1986); *Gasiorowski v. Hose*, 182 Ariz. 376, 897 P.2d 678 (Ct. App. Div. 1 1994).

2. *Comparison With Federal Rule.* The language of Rule 404 was not restyled or amended in 2012 to conform with its federal counterpart. As a result, Ariz.R.Evid. 404 and Fed.R.Evid. 404 remain quite dissimilar. The Federal Rule does not contain the matters added by the 1997 amendments to the Arizona Rule, which added provisions that would permit the admission, under the circumstances specified in Rule 404(c), Ariz. R. Evid., of evidence of other crimes, wrongs or acts that show a defendant's "aberrant sexual propensity" to commit a sexual offense. Thus, the Federal Rule does not contain a provision comparable to Rule 404(c), Ariz. R. Evid., or the conforming phrases added to Rules 404(a)(1) and 404(b), Ariz. R. Evid. by those amendments.

The provisions added to the Arizona Rule by the 1997 amendments are roughly similar, in certain limited respects, to the provisions added to the Federal Rules of Evidence in 1994. Rule 415, Fed. R. Evid. permits the introduction, in civil cases in which a claim for relief is predicated on a party's alleged commission of conduct constituting the offense of sexual assault or child molestation, of evidence of the party's commission of another offense or offenses of sexual assault or child molestation. These provisions of Arizona Rule 404, discussed in Section 6, *infra*, would permit a somewhat broader range of sexual misconduct evidence to be admitted than would the Federal Rule, but also requires much more detailed findings by the trial court before such evidence is admitted. The provisions of the Arizona Rule are not at all similar to Rule 412, Fed. R. Evid., which only permits the introduction, in very limited circumstances, of evidence of past sexual misconduct by a *victim* of a crime in criminal cases.

Arizona has not adopted the final phrase of Rule 404(b), Fed. R. Evid., added by a 1991 amendment, which requires the prosecution in a criminal case to give the accused, upon request, reasonable notice, generally before trial, of the evidence of other crimes of the accused it intends to introduce at trial. There is a prior disclosure requirement, however, for evidence of other crimes, wrongs or acts tending to show an "aberrant sexual propensity" that is to be offered pursuant to the authority conferred by Rule 404(c), Ariz. R. Evid.

Arizona also has not adopted the 2000 amendment to Rule 404(a)(1), Fed. R. Evid., which permits the prosecution in criminal cases to offer evidence of a pertinent character trait of the accused where evidence of that character trait of the alleged victim has been offered by the accused and admitted. Finally, Arizona has not adopted the 2006 amendments to Rule 404(a)(1) and (2), which expressly limit the applications of those exceptions to criminal cases.

3. *Proof of Character as Substantive Evidence.* Rule 404(a) governs use of character evidence substantively. The use of character for purposes of impeachment of a witness is governed by Rules 608 and 609. The Rule is specifically concerned with the use of character circumstantially, *i.e.,* to prove that a person acted in conformity with that person's character on a particular occasion. Such evidence is rarely, if ever, admissible for that purpose. *State v. Cota*, 229 Ariz. 136, 272 P.3d 1027 (2012), cert. denied, 133 S. Ct. 107, 184 L. Ed. 2d 49 (2012) (Rule 404(b) did not prohibit the admission of evidence of defendant's flight, because the evidence was not used "to prove the character of a person in order to show action in conformity therewith."); *Lee v. Hodge*, 180 Ariz. 97, 882 P.2d 408 (1994); *Hudgins v. Southwest Airlines, Co.*, 221 Ariz. 472, 212 P.3d 810 (Ct. App. Div. 1 2009). The concern with evidence of that nature is not with its reliability, but rather that its slight probative value on the issue of whether a specific incident occurred, or occurred in a certain way, is outweighed by the risk that jurors will decide matters on the basis of the person's character rather than on the basis of other evidence of greater probative value. *Elia v. Pifer*, 194 Ariz. 74, 977 P.2d 796 (Ct. App. Div. 1 1998).

Rule 404(a) thus states a broad rule of inadmissibility for such evidence for that purpose, subject to four exceptions, two of which apply only in criminal cases. The third exception, which is applicable in civil cases, is for the use of such evidence for impeachment of a witness, which is governed by Rules 608 and 609. The fourth exception, added by the 1997 amendments, for evidence of other crimes, wrongs or acts that tend to show a defendant's "aberrant sexual propensity," applies in both civil and criminal cases. That provision is discussed further in Section 6, *infra*.

As a general rule, accordingly, the circumstantial use of

character evidence for other than impeachment purposes is permissible only in criminal cases. *Delozier v. Evans*, 158 Ariz. 490, 763 P.2d 986 (Ct. App. Div. 1 1988) (evidence of party's combative nature when intoxicated properly excluded); *Gibson v. Gunsch*, 148 Ariz. 416, 714 P.2d 1311 (Ct. App. Div. 1 1985) (evidence of plaintiff's peaceful character properly excluded in assault case); *Blankinship v. Duarte*, 137 Ariz. 217, 669 P.2d 994 (Ct. App. Div. 2 1983) (evidence of defendant's peaceful character not admissible in civil assault case).

There may be categories of cases where character or a character trait can be an essential element of a claim or defense, such as in actions for libel or slander. In those circumstances, proof of character may be received, but it must be shown in accordance with the standards of Rule 405.

4. *Proof of Other Crimes or Wrongful Acts.* Rule 404(b), which does apply in civil cases, provides that evidence of crimes or misconduct other than that at issue in the litigation cannot be used to prove character as circumstantial evidence, but may be admissible for other purposes. *State v. Payne*, 233 Ariz. 484, 314 P.3d 1239 (2013). ("When other act evidence is admissible but prejudicial, the trial court must 'limit the evidence to its probative essence (motive) by excluding irrelevant or inflammatory detail.' "); *State v. Ferrero*, 229 Ariz. 239, 274 P.3d 509 (2012) ("Rule 404(b) prohibits evidence of other crimes, wrongs, or acts to prove the defendant's character to act in a certain way, but may allow such evidence for other purposes, such as showing 'motive, opportunity, intent, preparation, plan, knowledge, identity, or absence of mistake or accident'."); *State v. Hausner*, 230 Ariz. 60, 280 P.3d 604 (2012); *Cal X-Tra v. W.V.S.V. Holdings, L.L.C.*, 229 Ariz. 377, 276 P.3d 11 (Ct. App. Div. 1 2012), review denied, (Dec. 4, 2012); *Hudgins v. Southwest Airlines, Co.*, 221 Ariz. 472, 212 P.3d 810 (Ct. App. Div. 1 2009) (evidence of wrongful acts admitted as proof of the absence of mistake); *Brown v. U.S. Fidelity and Guar. Co.*, 194 Ariz. 85, 977 P.2d 807 (Ct. App. Div. 1 1998), as amended, (Nov. 25, 1998) and as corrected, (Aug. 5, 1999). Such evidence that tends to show a defendant's "aberrant sexual propensity" may also be admitted subject to the conditions specified in Rule 404(c). See discussion in Section 6, *infra*.

Evidence of other crimes or wrongful acts that are not relevant to any issue being litigated has the effect of demonstrating that the party against whom it is offered has a bad character, which the Rule expressly prohibits. *Lee v. Hodge*, 180 Ariz. 97, 882 P.2d 408 (1994); *Elia v. Pifer*, 194 Ariz. 74, 977 P.2d 796 (Ct. App. Div. 1 1998); *Henson v. Triumph Trucking, Inc.*, 180 Ariz. 305, 884 P.2d 191 (Ct. App. Div. 2 1994). Accordingly, the trial court should give a limiting instruction when such evidence is received for other purposes.

Evidence of other wrongful acts, such as prior fraudulent misrepresentations, has been admitted to show motive, intent, a conscious plan, as well as to establish the predicate for an award of punitive damages. *Hawkins v. Allstate Ins. Co.*, 152 Ariz. 490, 733 P.2d 1073 (1987) (insurer's past claims adjustment practices); *Crackel v. Allstate Ins. Co.*, 208 Ariz. 252, 92 P.3d 882 (Ct. App. Div. 2 2004); *Lang v. Superior Court, In and For County of Maricopa*, 170 Ariz. 602, 826 P.2d 1228 (Ct. App. Div. 1 1992) (seller's past deceptive sales practices); *Warfel v. Cheney*, 157 Ariz. 424, 758 P.2d 1326, 85 A.L.R.4th 349 (Ct. App. Div. 1 1988); *Cassell v. General Motors Corp.*, 154 Ariz. 75, 740 P.2d 496 (Ct. App. Div. 2 1987); *Mister Donut of America, Inc. v. Harris*, 150 Ariz. 347, 723 P.2d 696 (Ct. App. Div. 1 1985), opinion vacated on other grounds, 150 Ariz. 321, 723 P.2d 670 (1986) (similar fraudulent misrepresentations); *Dunlap v. Jimmy GMC of Tucson, Inc.*, 136 Ariz. 338, 666 P.2d 83 (Ct. App. Div. 2 1983) (past deceptive sales practices); *but cf. Rutledge v. Arizona Bd. of Regents*, 147 Ariz. 534, 711 P.2d 1207, 29 Ed. Law Rep. 1161 (Ct. App. Div. 1 1985) (evidence of abusive acts toward others properly excluded in assault action).

There is nothing in Rule 404(b) which explicitly requires that the prior bad acts be substantially similar to the subsequently alleged acts. *Lee v. Hodge*, 180 Ariz. 97, 882 P.2d 408 (1994). Evidence of other crimes, wrongs or acts thus may be admissible if: (1) the evidence is related to a material fact, (2) the evidence tends to make the existence of a material fact more or less probable without the evidence, (3) the material fact that is rendered more or less probable is something other than a party's propensity to act in accordance with a certain character, and (4) the probative value of the evidence substantially outweighs the danger of unfair prejudice. *Lee v. Hodge*, 180 Ariz. 97, 882 P.2d 408 (1994). In addition, there must be enough of a relationship between the prior bad acts and the current allegations that the evidence of the prior acts helps prove a material fact other than a person's character and a propensity to act in accordance with that character. *Lee v. Hodge*, 180 Ariz. 97, 882 P.2d 408 (1994).

Where the evidence of prior bad acts is not offered for one of the alternative purposes sanctioned in Rule 404(b), *e.g.*, to show motive, intent, opportunity, etc., but rather to show a habit or routine practice, its admissibility should be analyzed under Rule 406 rather than under Rule 404. *Gasiorowski v. Hose*, 182 Ariz. 376, 897 P.2d 678 (Ct. App. Div. 1 1994). When the trial court determines that proffered evidence falls within one of the Rule 404(b) exceptions, however, it must also decide whether the probative value of the evidence is substantially outweighed by the danger of unfair prejudice or other considerations implicated by Rule 403. *Hudgins v. Southwest Airlines, Co.*, 221 Ariz. 472, 212 P.3d 810 (Ct. App. Div. 1 2009).

5. *Proof of Other Accidents or Conditions.* Proof of accidents or conditions other than those at issue in a particular case is admissible where the prior accidents occurred under similar conditions and for similar reasons as the accident in issue and the evidence is offered to show the dangerousness of a condition and/or notice to the defendant of the condition. *Porter By and Through Porter v. Superior Court In and For Pima County (Price Co.)*, 144 Ariz. 346, 697 P.2d 1096 (1985) (notice of other similar accidents); *Grant v. Arizona Public Service Co.*, 133 Ariz. 434, 652 P.2d 507 (1982) (evidence of prior accidents admissible on issue of foreseeability); *Burgbacher v. Mellor*, 112 Ariz. 481, 543 P.2d 1110 (1975) (knowledge of dangerous condition); *Trevizo v. Astec Industries, Inc.*, 156 Ariz. 320, 751 P.2d 980 (Ct. App. Div. 2 1987) (knowledge and/or foreseeability of risk); *Johnson v. Tucson Estates, Inc.*, 140 Ariz. 531, 683 P.2d 330 (Ct. App. Div. 2 1984) (notice and dangerous nature of condition); *but cf. Chapman v. Levi-Strauss*, 145 Ariz. 411, 701 P.2d 1219 (Ct. App. Div. 2 1985) (general statistics on burn injuries from clothing properly excluded).

It is prejudicial error, however, to permit such evidence to be admitted without a foundational showing that the prior accidents occurred under conditions that were substantially similar to the accident in issue. *Wiggs v. City of Phoenix*, 197 Ariz. 358, 4 P.3d 413 (Ct. App. Div. 1 1999), opinion vacated on other grounds, 198 Ariz. 367, 10 P.3d 625, 111 A.L.R.5th 815 (2000); *Cotterhill v. Bafile*, 177 Ariz. 76, 865 P.2d 120 (Ct. App. Div. 1 1993); *Rodriguez v. Schlittenhart*, 161 Ariz. 609, 780 P.2d 442 (Ct. App. Div. 2 1989).

The Arizona Supreme Court has overruled the prior doctrine that proof of the absence of prior accidents is *per se* inadmissible. *Jones v. Pak-Mor Mfg. Co.*, 145 Ariz. 121, 700 P.2d 819, 51 A.L.R. 4th 1167 (1985). Accordingly, where a case involves claims of defective design, evidence of the product's prior safety history, whether it consists of the existence or absence of prior accidents, is admissible. *Boy v. I.T.T. Grinnell Corp.*, 150 Ariz. 526, 724 P.2d 612, Prod. Liab. Rep. (CCH) P 10636, 61 A.L.R.4th 137 (Ct. App. Div. 1 1986); *Schneider v. Cessna Aircraft Co.*, 150 Ariz. 153, 722 P.2d 321, Prod. Liab. Rep. (CCH) P 10743 (Ct. App. Div. 1 1985). The scale tips strongly, however, against the admission of this type of evidence because the absence of actual accidents does not necessarily negate the possibility of near-accidents resulting from a dangerous condition, and a very careful and thorough foundation must be established before it can be admitted. *Isbell ex rel. Isbell v. State*, 198 Ariz. 291, 9 P.3d 322 (2000). That issue is discussed in Section 4 of the *Authors' Com-*

ments under Rule 401, Ariz. R. Evid.

6. *Evidence of Aberrant Sexual Propensity*. Rule 404(a)(1) was amended in 1997 to permit the admission, in certain civil cases, of evidence of the defendant's "aberrant sexual propensity" under the conditions specified in Rule 404(c), added by the same amendment. *State v. Rhodes*, 219 Ariz. 476, 200 P.3d 973 (Ct. App. Div. 1 2008) (in sexual misconduct cases, Rule 404(c) supplements Rule 404(a)(1), and does not supercede it). *See also, State v. Lehr*, 227 Ariz. 140, 254 P.3d 379 (2011), cert. denied, 132 S. Ct. 403, 181 L. Ed. 2d 263 (2011) (discussing the admission of evidence showing the defendant had a character trait giving rise to an aberrant sexual propensity in cases involving sexual offense charges); *State v. Dixon*, 226 Ariz. 545, 250 P.3d 1174 (2011), cert. denied, 132 S. Ct. 456, 181 L. Ed. 2d 297 (2011) (discussing standard for admission of Rule 404(c) evidence and, in first degree murder case, upholding admission of other rape evidence). *See also, State v. Aguilar*, 209 Ariz. 40, 97 P.3d 865 (2004) (discussing Rule 404(c) requirements). Rule 404(c) permits the introduction of evidence of "other crimes, wrongs, or acts" in civil cases in which a claim is predicated on a party's alleged commission of a "sexual offense," as that term is defined in A.R.S. § 13-1420(C), if it is relevant to show that the defendant had a character trait "giving rise to an aberrant sexual propensity to commit the offense charged."

Before such evidence can be admitted, the trial court must first make specific written findings that: (1) the evidence is sufficient to permit the trier of fact to find that the defendant committed the "other act"; (2) the commission of the other act provides a reasonable basis to infer that the defendant had a character trait giving rise to an "aberrant sexual propensity" to commit the offense charged; and, (3) the evidentiary value of the proof of the "other act" is not substantially outweighed by the danger of unfair prejudice or by the other factors listed in Rule 403. In all cases in which such evidence is admitted, the trial court is to instruct the jury as to the proper use of it, and evidence to rebut the proof of the other crimes, wrongs or acts may also be admitted.

Rule 404(c)(3) specifies that, in civil cases where a party intends to offer evidence of this nature, disclosure of the evidence must be made as required by Ariz.R.Civ.P. 26.1, no later than sixty (60) days before trial, or at such later time as the court may permit for good cause shown. A technical amendment was also made to Rule 404(b), simply adding a reference to the Rule 404(c). The Order adopting the 1997 amendments specified that they were to become effective December 1, 1997, and were to apply to all civil cases pending on that date, except cases in which the final trial date had been set for between December 1, 1997 and February 1, 1998.

Rule 405. Methods of Proving Character

(a) By Reputation or Opinion. When evidence of a person's character or character trait is admissible, it may be proved by testimony about the person's reputation or by testimony in the form of an opinion. On cross-examination of the character witness, the court may allow an inquiry into relevant specific instances of the person's conduct.

(b) By Specific Instances of Conduct. When a person's character or character trait is an essential element of a charge, claim, or defense, or pursuant to Rule 404(c), the character or trait may also be proved by relevant specific instances of the person's conduct.

Amended Oct. 19, 1988, effective November 1, 1988; Aug. 19, 1997, effective Dec. 1, 1997; Sept. 8, 2011, effective Jan. 1, 2012.

Comment to 2012 Amendment

The language of Rule 405 has been amended to conform to the federal restyling of the Evidence Rules to make them more easily understood and to make style and terminology consistent throughout the rules. These changes are intended to be stylistic only. There is no intent to change any result in any ruling on evidence admissibility.

Application

Applicable to cases pending on and after that date [Dec. 1, 1997], except civil cases as to which the final trial date is set to occur between December 1, 1997 and February 1, 1998 and criminal cases as to which the final trial date is set to occur between December 1, 1997 and January 15, 1998.

AUTHORS' COMMENTS

Analysis

1. Scope and Purpose of Rule.
2. Comparison With Federal Rule.
3. Proof of Character Generally.
4. Proof of Other Specific Instances of Conduct.

1. *Scope and Purpose of Rule.* Rule 405 defines acceptable methods for proving a person's character in those instances where evidence of character is admissible. It carries forward the distinction between the use of character as circumstantial evidence and situations where character is directly in issue for purposes of when specific instances of conduct other than that involved in the litigation will be admissible. Rule 405 concerns only the proof of character *per se*; it does not govern proof of specific instances of other conduct that may be admissible for other purposes under the standards of Rule 404(b).

2. *Comparison With Federal Rule.* Effective January 1, 2012, the Arizona Supreme Court amended Rule 405 to conform to the federal restyling of the Evidence Rules to make the rules more easily understood and to make style and terminology consistent throughout. The 2012 Comment states the stylistic amendments are not intended to "change any result in any ruling on evidence admissibility."

Following the 2012 restyling amendments, the language of Rule 405 remains substantially identical to its federal counterpart, Fed. R. Evid. 405, with the exception that the Federal Rule does not contain the phrase added to the Arizona Rule in 1997 referring to Rule 404(c).

Although Rule 405 parallels its federal counterpart, "federal court decisions interpreting the federal rule are persuasive but not binding with respect to interpreting the Arizona rule." *See,* Prefatory Comment to 2012 Amendments. *See also, State v. Terrazas,* 189 Ariz. 580, 944 P.2d 1194 (1997) (The Arizona Supreme Court is "not bound by the United States Supreme Court's non-constitutional construction of the Federal Rules of Evidence when [the Arizona Supreme Court construes] the Arizona Rules of Evidence."), citing, State v. Bible, 175 Ariz. 549, 858 P.2d 1152 (1993); *State v. Salazar-Mercado*, 232 Ariz. 256, 304 P.3d 543 (Ct. App. Div. 2 2013). Practitioners are urged to keep this legal tenet in mind as they research federal case law interpreting a federal evidentiary rule that corresponds to an Arizona evidentiary rule.

3. *Proof of Character Generally.* The traditional method for proving a person's character was through proof of that person's reputation in a relevant community. Reputation witnesses could be called who were familiar with the expressed views of others concerning the character of the person in question, or concerning a particular, relevant character trait, and, provided the requisite foundation were established, would report the composite community hearsay. *Cf., e.g., Selby v. Savard*, 134 Ariz. 222, 655 P.2d 342 (1982). Such evidence was often disguised opinion, and Rule 405 now straightforwardly permits character to be established by opinion evidence. *Cf. State v. Miller*, 128 Ariz. 112, 624 P.2d 309 (Ct. App. Div. 1 1980).

4. *Proof of Other Specific Instances of Conduct.* Specific instances of a person's conduct other than that involved in the litigation may be brought out on direct examination only where the person's character or a character trait of the person is an essential element of a claim or defense in the case. *Scott v. Allstate Ins. Co.*, 27 Ariz. App. 236, 553 P.2d 1221 (Div. 1 1976). Where a witness is called to testify about a person's reputation or to express an opinion about a person's character, however, inquiry may be made into specific instances of other conduct by that

person on cross-examination.

Rule 406. Habit; Routine Practice

Evidence of a person's habit or an organization's routine practice may be admitted to prove that on a particular occasion the person or organization acted in accordance with the habit or routine practice. The court may admit this evidence regardless of whether it is corroborated or whether there was an eyewitness.

Amended Sept. 8, 2011, effective Jan. 1, 2012.

Comment to 2012 Amendment

The language of Rule 406 has been amended to conform to the federal restyling of the Evidence Rules to make them more easily understood and to make style and terminology consistent throughout the rules. These changes are intended to be stylistic only. There is no intent to change any result in any ruling on evidence admissibility.

AUTHORS' COMMENTS

Analysis

1. *Scope and Purpose of Rule.* Rule 406 provides that the habit of a person or its "corporate equivalent," the routine practice of an organization, is admissible to demonstrate that the person or organization acted in conformity with the habit or routine on a particular occasion. The sense of the Rule is that such a habit or routine practice is a more reliable indicator of a person's or organization's conduct in a particular situation because of its repetitive nature and the focus on a specific and frequently recurring set of circumstances.

2. *Comparison With Federal Rule.* Effective January 1, 2012, the Arizona Supreme Court amended Rule 406 to conform to the federal restyling of the Evidence Rules to make the rules more easily understood and to make style and terminology consistent throughout. The 2012 Comment states the stylistic amendments are not intended to "change any result in any ruling on evidence admissibility."

Following the 2012 restyling amendments, the language of Rule 406 remains identical to its federal counterpart, Fed. R. Evid. 406.

Although Rule 406 parallels its federal counterpart, "federal court decisions interpreting the federal rule are persuasive but

not binding with respect to interpreting the Arizona rule." *See,* Prefatory Comment to 2012 Amendments. *See also, State v. Terrazas*, 189 Ariz. 580, 944 P.2d 1194 (1997) (The Arizona Supreme Court is "not bound by the United States Supreme Court's non-constitutional construction of the Federal Rules of Evidence when [the Arizona Supreme Court construes] the Arizona Rules of Evidence."), citing, *State v. Bible*, 175 Ariz. 549, 858 P.2d 1152 (1993); *State v. Salazar-Mercado*, 232 Ariz. 256, 304 P.3d 543 (Ct. App. Div. 2 2013). Practitioners are urged to keep this legal tenet in mind as they research federal case law interpreting a federal evidentiary rule that corresponds to an Arizona evidentiary rule.

3. *Habit v. Character.* Rule 406 does not provide any definition of "habit" or "routine practice" so as to distinguish these concepts from character. Character is a person's general disposition; habit is that person's regular response to a repeated specific situation. *Boswell v. Phoenix Newspapers, Inc.*, 152 Ariz. 1, 730 P.2d 178 (Ct. App. Div. 1 1985), approved as supplemented, 152 Ariz. 9, 730 P.2d 186, 13 Media L. Rep. (BNA) 1785 (1986); *Gasiorowski v. Hose*, 182 Ariz. 376, 897 P.2d 678 (Ct. App. Div. 1 1994).

4. *Specific Applications of Rule.* In general, Rule 406 is a useful tool where a witness does not have a specific recollection of how that witness, or the organization with which that witness is associated, acted on a particular occasion or in connection with a particular transaction. To qualify as "habit," Rule 406 contemplates the behavior be "semi-automatic and regular" in nature. *State v. Slover*, 220 Ariz. 239, 204 P.3d 1088 (Ct. App. Div. 2 2009).

If the occasion or transaction is a recurring one, the witness can testify to that witness' habit, or the organization's routine course of conduct, in such a situation. Thus, evidence of the routine practice of an organization of collecting letters and mailing them once they are signed is admissible to show that a particular letter, shown to have been signed, was in fact mailed. *Consolidated Motors v. Skousen*, 56 Ariz. 481, 109 P.2d 41, 132 A.L.R. 1040 (1941). In addition, proof of a manufacturer's routine quality control procedures has been found admissible to show the improbability of a product defect occurring during the manufacturing process. *Brown v. General Foods Corp.*, 117 Ariz. 530, 573 P.2d 930 (Ct. App. Div. 1 1978).

Rule 407. Subsequent Remedial Measures

When measures are taken that would have made an earlier injury or harm less likely to occur, evidence of the subsequent measures is not admissible to prove:

- negligence;
- culpable conduct;
- a defect in a product or its design; or
- a need for a warning or instruction.

But the court may admit this evidence for another purpose, such as impeachment or—if disputed—proving ownership, control, or the feasibility of precautionary measures.

Amended Sept. 8, 2011, effective Jan. 1, 2012.

Comment to 2012 Amendment

This rule has been amended to conform to Federal Rule of Evidence 407 in order to provide greater clarity regarding the applicable scope of the rule.

Additionally, the language of Rule 407 has been amended to conform to the federal restyling of the Evidence Rules to make them more easily understood and to make style and terminology consistent throughout the rules. These changes are intended to be stylistic only. There is no intent in the restyling to change any result in any ruling on evidence admissibility.

Rule 407 previously provided that evidence was not excluded if offered for a purpose not explicitly prohibited by the rule. To improve the language of the rule, it now provides that the court may admit evidence if offered for a permissible purpose. There is no intent to change the process for admitting evidence covered by the rule. It remains the case that if offered for an impermissible purpose, it must be excluded, and if offered for a purpose not barred by the rule, its admissibility remains governed by the general principles of Rules 402, 403, 801, etc.

AUTHORS' COMMENTS

Analysis

1. *Scope and Purpose of Rule.* Rule 407 codifies the familiar rule that post-accident remedial measures are not admissible to demonstrate negligence or that a product was unreasonably dangerous. The "remedial measures" encompassed by the Rule include not only design changes, but also other remedial measures such as the posting of warning notices, the conduct of

safety studies and similar measures.

In a case of first impression, the Arizona Supreme Court held that Rule 407 requires the exclusion of evidence of subsequent remedial measures to prove a party's negligence or culpable conduct, even when such measures are taken without specific knowledge of, or for reasons unrelated to, the event in question. *Johnson v. State, Dept. of Transp.*, 224 Ariz. 554, 233 P.3d 1133 (2010).

Arguably, such remedial measures can be an admission of negligence or culpability. The rationale of the Rule, however, is that there can be a variety of reasons why such subsequent measures are taken, not all of which are consistent with a recognition of potential liability. The Rule is intended in part to encourage the implementation of safety measures by removing the disincentive posed by the possibility that such measures can subsequently be admitted at a trial as evidence of an admission of liability. Such evidence can be admitted, however, if it is pertinent to other issues that are in dispute or for purposes of impeachment.

A statute applicable to product liability actions, A.R.S. § 12-687, provides that evidence of a "product safety analysis or review" or of "reasonable remedial measures" taken as a consequence of such a product safety analysis or review is not admissible to show negligence or that the product was defective or unreasonably dangerous. Under the statute, however, such evidence may be admitted if offered for other purposes, such as to show the feasibility of precautionary measures, or for impeachment purposes.

2. *Comparison With Federal Rule.* Effective January 1, 2012, the Arizona Supreme Court amended Rule 407 to conform to the federal restyling of the Evidence Rules to make the rules more easily understood and to make style and terminology consistent throughout. The 2012 Comment states the stylistic amendments are not intended to "change any result in any ruling on evidence admissibility."

As a consequence of the 2012 amendments, the language of Rule 407 is identical to its federal counterpart, Fed. R. Evid. 407.

Previously, Ariz. R. Evid. Rule 407 provided that evidence was not excluded if offered for a purpose not expressly prohibited by the rule. To clarify this language, and consistent with the language of its federal counterpart, the rule now provides the court may admit evidence if offered for a permissible purpose. As noted in the Comment to the 2012 amendments, it remains the case that evidence offered for an impermissible purpose must be excluded. The admissibility of evidence offered for a purpose not barred by the rule "remains governed by the general principles of

Rules 402, 403, 801, etc." *See*, Comment to 2012 Amendment.

Although Rule 407 parallels its federal counterpart, "federal court decisions interpreting the federal rule are persuasive but not binding with respect to interpreting the Arizona rule." *See,* Prefatory Comment to 2012 Amendments. *See also, State v. Terrazas*, 189 Ariz. 580, 944 P.2d 1194 (1997) (The Arizona Supreme Court is "not bound by the United States Supreme Court's non-constitutional construction of the Federal Rules of Evidence when [the Arizona Supreme Court construes] the Arizona Rules of Evidence."), citing, *State v. Bible*, 175 Ariz. 549, 858 P.2d 1152 (1993); *State v. Salazar-Mercado*, 232 Ariz. 256, 304 P.3d 543 (Ct. App. Div. 2 2013). Practitioners are urged to keep this legal tenet in mind as they research federal case law interpreting a federal evidentiary rule that corresponds to an Arizona evidentiary rule.

3. *Post-Sale Design Changes in Products Liability Cases.* Although the rule has been relaxed in some other jurisdictions, in Arizona, in products liability cases, post-sale design changes are not admissible if offered to demonstrate that the product in question was unreasonably dangerous before the changes. *Readenour v. Marion Power Shovel, a Div. of Dresser Industries, Inc.*, 149 Ariz. 442, 719 P.2d 1058, Prod. Liab. Rep. (CCH) P 11012 (1986); *Volz v. Coleman Co., Inc.*, 155 Ariz. 563, 748 P.2d 1187, Prod. Liab. Rep. (CCH) P 10977 (Ct. App. Div. 1 1986), judgment aff'd in part, rev'd in part, 155 Ariz. 567, 748 P.2d 1191, Prod. Liab. Rep. (CCH) P 11608 (1987); *Hallmark v. Allied Products Corp.*, 132 Ariz. 434, 646 P.2d 319 (Ct. App. Div. 1 1982); *Hohlenkamp v. Rheem Mfg. Co.*, 134 Ariz. 208, 655 P.2d 32 (Ct. App. Div. 2 1982).

In point of fact, Rule 407 only applies to product changes or modifications made after the event that is in issue. The extension of its qualified prohibition on the admission of such evidence to include changes or modifications made after the product was first *sold* was accomplished by statute, A.R.S. § 12-686(2). The constitutionality of that statute was upheld in *Readenour v. Marion Power Shovel, a Div. of Dresser Industries, Inc.*, 149 Ariz. 442, 719 P.2d 1058, Prod. Liab. Rep. (CCH) P 11012 (1986).

As is the case for other subsequent remedial measures, however, this rule with respect to post-sale design changes is not one of *per se* inadmissibility. Such changes may be admissible to show notice of a defect in the product and/or the feasibility of posting warnings concerning the product. *Readenour v. Marion Power Shovel, a Div. of Dresser Industries, Inc.*, 149 Ariz. 442, 719 P.2d 1058, Prod. Liab. Rep. (CCH) P 11012 (1986); *Baroldy v. Ortho Pharmaceutical Corp.*, 157 Ariz. 574, 760 P.2d 574, Prod. Liab. Rep. (CCH) P 11732 (Ct. App. Div. 1 1988).

4. *Admissibility of Subsequent Remedial Measures for Other*

Purposes. By its express terms, Rule 407 allows evidence of subsequent remedial measures to be admitted in negligence and products liability cases "when offered for another purpose." *Grant v. Arizona Public Service Co.*, 133 Ariz. 434, 652 P.2d 507 (1982). Such evidence may be admissible to show the defendant's control of the premises or product, where control is in dispute. *Sullins v. Third and Catalina Const. Partnership*, 124 Ariz. 114, 602 P.2d 495 (Ct. App. Div. 1 1979). Such evidence also may be admissible for impeachment purposes. *Johnson v. State, Dept. of Transp.*, 224 Ariz. 554, 233 P.3d 1133 (2010) (discussing circumstances under which subsequent remedial measures may and may not be used as proper impeachment evidence and observing that even if admissible for another purpose, a trial court may exclude such evidence under Rule 403); *Slow Development Co. v. Coulter*, 88 Ariz. 122, 353 P.2d 890 (1960).

Whether to permit such evidence to be introduced for such "other purpose" is a decision committed to the trial court's discretion, and some care must be exercised to insure that the asserted "other purpose" is not a mere subterfuge. *Hallmark v. Allied Products Corp.*, 132 Ariz. 434, 646 P.2d 319 (Ct. App. Div. 1 1982). At the very least, the matter for which the evidence assertedly has probative value should be one that is in dispute. Where evidence of subsequent remedial measures is admitted, the trial court must, upon request, give the jury a limiting instruction. *Readenour v. Marion Power Shovel, a Div. of Dresser Industries, Inc.*, 149 Ariz. 442, 719 P.2d 1058, Prod. Liab. Rep. (CCH) P 11012 (1986); *Baroldy v. Ortho Pharmaceutical Corp.*, 157 Ariz. 574, 760 P.2d 574, Prod. Liab. Rep. (CCH) P 11732 (Ct. App. Div. 1 1988). Rule 407 does not permit a party who performed subsequent remedial measures to introduce evidence of them in order to deter or prevent an award of punitive damages. *Monaco v. HealthPartners of Southern Arizona*, 196 Ariz. 299, 995 P.2d 735 (Ct. App. Div. 2 1999).

Rule 408. Compromise Offers and Negotiations

(a) Prohibited Uses. Evidence of the following is not admissible—on behalf of any party—either to prove or disprove the validity or amount of a disputed claim or to impeach by a prior inconsistent statement or a contradiction:

(1) furnishing, promising, or offering—or accepting, promising to accept, or offering to accept—a valuable consideration in compromising or attempting to compromise the claim; and

(2) conduct or a statement made during compromise negotiations about the claim.

(b) Exceptions. The court may admit this evidence for another purpose, such as proving a witness's bias or prejudice, negating a contention of undue delay, or proving an effort to obstruct a criminal investigation or prosecution.

Amended Sept. 3, 2009, effective Jan. 1, 2010; Sept. 8, 2011, effective Jan. 1, 2012.

Comment to 2012 Amendment

The 2012 amendment does not include any substantive changes and does not include the "criminal use exception" in Federal Rule of Evidence 408(a)(2).

Otherwise, the language of Rule 408 has been amended to conform to the federal restyling of the Evidence Rules to make them more easily understood and to make style and terminology consistent throughout the rules. These changes are intended to be stylistic only. There is no intent to change any result in any ruling on evidence admissibility.

Rule 408 previously provided that evidence was not excluded if offered for a purpose not explicitly prohibited by the rule. To improve the language of the rule, it now provides that the court may admit evidence if offered for a permissible purpose. There is no intent to change the process for admitting evidence covered by the rule. It remains the case that if offered for an impermissible purpose, it must be excluded, and if offered for a purpose not barred by the rule, its admissibility remains governed by the general principles of Rules 402, 403, 801, etc.

The reference to "liability" has been deleted on the ground that the deletion makes the rule flow better and easier to read, and because "liability" is covered by the broader term "validity." Courts have not made substantive decisions on the basis of any distinction between validity and liability. No change in current practice or in the coverage of the rule is intended.

AUTHORS' COMMENTS

Analysis

5. "Gallagher" Agreements.

1. *Scope and Purpose of Rule.* Rule 408 renders compromise and settlement negotiations inadmissible to show either the defendant's liability or the invalidity of the plaintiff's claim or of the amount claimed. Absent such a Rule, offers to settle could be construed as admissions of liability by the defendant, or admissions by a plaintiff that the claim was not worth the amount claimed. The Rule states what has long been the law, *viz.,* that such negotiations are not admissible for that purpose. *Schneider v. McAleer*, 39 Ariz. 190, 4 P.2d 903 (1931). That, of course, does not necessarily mean that they are not discoverable. *Cf., Ingalls v. Superior Court in and for Pima County*, 117 Ariz. 448, 573 P.2d 522 (Ct. App. Div. 2 1977). In a wrongful death medical malpractice action, however, information concerning amounts paid by the defendant doctor to settle prior malpractice cases would establish neither negligence nor gross negligence and, consequently, is not discoverable. *Miller v. Kelly*, 212 Ariz. 283, 130 P.3d 982 (Ct. App. Div. 2 2006) Additionally, the Rule permits the admission into evidence of the fact of settlement, where that evidence is offered for some purpose other than to establish liability for, or invalidity of, a claim. *Henry ex rel. Estate of Wilson v. HealthPartners of Southern Arizona*, 203 Ariz. 393, 55 P.3d 87 (Ct. App. Div. 2 2002).

The Rule is based on the belief that offers to settle, or to accept settlements, may be motivated by considerations other than a recognition of liability or of the invalidity of a claim. The Rule is also consistent with the policy of the law to encourage the consensual settlement of disputes, and serves to facilitate the conduct of settlement negotiations.

2. *Comparison With Federal Rule.* Effective January 1, 2012, the Arizona Supreme Court amended Rule 408 to conform to the federal restyling of the Evidence Rules to make the rules more easily understood and to make style and terminology consistent throughout. The 2012 Comment states the stylistic amendments are not intended to "change any result in any ruling on evidence admissibility."

Rule 408 was amended further, in conformance with its federal counterpart, to delete reference to the word "liability." Relying on the rationale for the federal amendment, the word "liability" was deleted because the rule flows better without the word and because "liability" is covered by the broader term "validity." The 2012 Comment to this rule amendment notes that courts have not made any substantive decisions on the basis of any distinction between the two words.

As a result of the 2012 amendments, Rule 408 is substantially identical to Fed. R. Evid. 408, although there are minor differences. The 2012 amendment to Rule 408 does not include the "criminal use exception" in Fed. R. Evid. 408(a)(2).

Previously, Arizona Rule of Evidence 408 provided that evidence was not excluded if offered for a purpose not expressly prohibited by the rule. To clarify this language, and consistent with the language of its federal counterpart, the rule now provides the court may admit evidence if offered for a permissible purpose. As noted in the Comment to the 2012 amendments, it remains the case that evidence offered for an impermissible purpose must be excluded. The admissibility of evidence offered for a purpose not barred by the rule "remains governed by the general principles of Rules 402, 403, 801, etc." *See*, Comment to 2012 Amendment.

Although Rule 408 parallels its federal counterpart, "federal court decisions interpreting the federal rule are persuasive but not binding with respect to interpreting the Arizona rule." *See,* Prefatory Comment to 2012 Amendments. *See also, State v. Terrazas*, 189 Ariz. 580, 944 P.2d 1194 (1997) (The Arizona Supreme Court is "not bound by the United States Supreme Court's non-constitutional construction of the Federal Rules of Evidence when [the Arizona Supreme Court construes] the Arizona Rules of Evidence."), citing, *State v. Bible*, 175 Ariz. 549, 858 P.2d 1152 (1993); *State v. Salazar-Mercado*, 232 Ariz. 256, 304 P.3d 543 (Ct. App. Div. 2 2013). Practitioners are urged to keep this legal tenet in mind as they research federal case law interpreting a federal evidentiary rule that corresponds to an Arizona evidentiary rule.

3. *Matters Covered by Rule.* The Rule encompasses: (1) offers of settlement, whether emanating from the party asserting a claim or the party defending; and, (2) conduct or statements made during the course of settlement negotiations. *State ex rel. Miller v. Superior Court*, 189 Ariz. 228, 941 P.2d 240 (Ct. App. Div. 1 1997). Rule 408 represented a departure from the prior rule that unequivocal admissions of fact made during the course of settlement negotiations were admissible. *Gallagher v. Viking Supply Corp.*, 3 Ariz. App. 55, 411 P.2d 814, 15 A.L.R.3d 1 (1966).

Under Rule 408, as amended in 2010, all statements made in that context are inadmissible when offered for the purposes cited, including impeachment purposes. For discussion of cases decided before the 2010 amendment to Rule 408, see, *State ex rel. Miller v. Superior Court*, 189 Ariz. 228, 941 P.2d 240 (Ct. App. Div. 1 1997); *Berthot v. Courtyard Properties, Inc.*, 138 Ariz. 566, 675 P.2d 1385 (Ct. App. Div. 1 1983). The Supreme Court had held Rule 408 did not preclude the use of a notice of claim submitted to a governmental entity to impeach a claimant who testified inconsistently therewith at trial. *Hernandez v. State*, 203 Ariz. 196, 52 P.3d 765 (2002). The 2010 amendments to the Rule effectively overrule the result reached in the *Hernandez* decision. *But see*, *Johnson v. State, Dept. of Transp.*, 224 Ariz. 554, 233 P.3d 1133 (2010).

The Rule is unclear on the subject of its applicability to settlements and/or settlement negotiations with persons not parties to the litigation in which the evidence is offered. It has been held that offers to settle similar claims with persons other than the parties to the litigation are irrelevant and immaterial. *Cf. Southern Pac. Transp. Co. v. Veliz*, 117 Ariz. 199, 571 P.2d 696 (Ct. App. Div. 2 1977). On the other hand, a settlement agreement between the plaintiff and a defendant/third-party plaintiff may be admissible, unless its probative value is substantially outweighed by the danger of unfair prejudice. *Monthofer Investments Ltd. Partnership v. Allen*, 189 Ariz. 422, 943 P.2d 782 (Ct. App. Div. 1 1997).

Settlement negotiations may now be held under the auspices, or at least with the participation, of the Court in settlement conferences. Consistently with this Rule, Ariz.R.Civ.P. 16.1(c) specifies that no part of any settlement conference memorandum shall be admissible at trial, and Rule 16.1(e) requires the court presiding over a settlement conference to order that all discussions at the conference shall be confidential among the parties, their counsel and the court.

4. *Limitations on Exclusion of Settlement Discussions.* The protections of Rule 408 can be waived by the parties. *Youngren v. Rezzonico*, 25 Ariz. App. 304, 543 P.2d 142 (Div. 1 1975). The Rule applies only to statements made in the context of actual settlement negotiations and not statements made in other contexts. *J. & B. Motors v. Margolis*, 75 Ariz. 392, 257 P.2d 588, 38 A.L.R.2d 946 (1953). Thus, it is not an uncommon practice to include in correspondence transmitting settlement positions and/or at meetings or conferences held to discuss settlement a statement formally invoking the protections of Rule 408. The Rule does not, however, protect from disclosure or admission at trial factual information revealed during the course of settlement negotiations which is otherwise discoverable.

The Rule does not preclude evidence of settlement negotiations when offered for purposes other than to show liability or the invalidity of a claim. *Henry ex rel. Estate of Wilson v. HealthPartners of Southern Arizona*, 203 Ariz. 393, 55 P.3d 87 (Ct. App. Div. 2 2002). As examples of such other purposes, the Rule lists: (1) to prove bias or prejudice on the part of a witness, (2) to rebut a claim of undue delay, and (3) to prove an effort to obstruct a criminal investigation or prosecution. This list is illustrative, not exhaustive. *Cf. Bradshaw v. State Farm Mut. Auto. Ins. Co.*, 157 Ariz. 411, 758 P.2d 1313 (1988) (settlement discussions in other case admissible on issue of probable cause in later malicious prosecution action); *Truck Ins. Exchange v. Hale*, 95 Ariz. 76, 386 P.2d 846 (1963) (admissible to show waiver of requirement for proof of loss); *Leigh v. Swartz*, 74 Ariz. 108, 245 P.2d 262 (1952) (admissible to show fraud); *Burris v. City of Phoenix*, 179 Ariz. 35, 875 P.2d 1340, 2 A.D. Cas. (BNA) 1251, 63 Empl. Prac. Dec. (CCH) P 42761 (Ct. App. Div. 1 1993) (admissible on issue of mitigation of damages in wrongful termination case); *DeForest v. DeForest*, 143 Ariz. 627, 694 P.2d 1241 (Ct. App. Div. 1 1985) (admissible to show knowledge of spousal maintenance requirement); *Campbell v. Mahany*, 127 Ariz. 332, 620 P.2d 711 (Ct. App. Div. 2 1980).

5. *"Gallagher" Agreements.* Rule 408 generally bars the receipt of evidence of compromise and settlement negotiations when offered by and/or against the parties who participated in them or on whose behalf they were conducted. Different considerations apply, however, when what is in issue is an actual settlement reached between the plaintiff and one or more of, but less than all, multiple defendants.

Not all settlements are reached on the basis that, in exchange for payment of an agreed upon sum by the defendant, the plaintiff will release and dismiss the pending claim as to that defendant. Deriving their name from the decision in *City of Tucson v. Gallagher*, 108 Ariz. 140, 493 P.2d 1197, 65 A.L.R.3d 597 (1972), the term "Gallagher agreement" came to be used to describe a variety of alternative arrangements which generally required the settling co-defendant to remain as a party to the case and/or to participate in the trial, and which dealt with how the settling co-defendant's monetary liability to the plaintiff, if any, would be handled after the jury's verdict was rendered. *Mustang Equipment, Inc. v. Welch*, 115 Ariz. 206, 564 P.2d 895 (1977); *Ring v. Taylor*, 141 Ariz. 56, 685 P.2d 121 (Ct. App. Div. 1 1984).

If the agreement is supported by consideration and confers an immediate benefit upon the plaintiff, then it must be disclosed to all remaining parties to the case "at the earliest possible opportunity," or it will be held unenforceable. *Mustang Equipment, Inc. v. Welch*, 115 Ariz. 206, 564 P.2d 895 (1977); *Ring v. Taylor*, 141 Ariz. 56, 685 P.2d 121 (Ct. App. Div. 1 1984). This is the case even where the terms of the agreement do not encourage fraud or collusion and provide no incentive to the settling defendant to enhance the plaintiff's verdict. *Mustang Equipment, Inc. v. Welch*, 115 Ariz. 206, 564 P.2d 895 (1977). Whether the terms of such an agreement should be disclosed to the jury is discretionary with the trial court, but the Court of Appeals has suggested that such disclosure may be not only permissible, but mandatory, where the agreeing co-defendant can improve that defendant's financial position by insuring a verdict of a certain amount, or over a certain amount, against a non-agreeing defendant. *Sequoia Mfg. Co., Inc. v. Halec Const. Co., Inc.*, 117 Ariz. 11, 570 P.2d 782 (Ct. App. Div. 1 1977); *but cf., Taylor v. DiRico*, 124 Ariz. 513, 606 P.2d 3 (1980).

An agreement between defendants not to present at trial evidence of each other's negligence, however, has been held not to upset the parties' normal adversarial relationship, and evidence of such an agreement may properly be precluded. *Gordon v. Liguori*, 182 Ariz. 232, 895 P.2d 523 (Ct. App. Div. 1 1995). On the other hand, a settlement agreement between the plaintiff and a defendant/third-party plaintiff is admissible unless its probative value is substantially outweighed by the danger of unfair prejudice. *Monthofer Investments Ltd. Partnership v. Allen*, 189 Ariz. 422, 943 P.2d 782 (Ct. App. Div. 1 1997).

Rule 409. Offers to Pay Medical and Similar Expenses

Evidence of furnishing, promising to pay, or offering to pay medical, hospital, or similar expenses resulting from an injury is not admissible to prove liability for the injury.

Amended Sept. 8, 2011, effective Jan. 1, 2012.

Comment to 2012 Amendment

The language of Rule 409 has been amended to conform to the federal restyling of the Evidence Rules to make them more easily understood and to make style and terminology consistent throughout the rules. These changes are intended to be stylistic only. There is no intent to change any result in any ruling on evidence admissibility.

AUTHORS' COMMENTS

Analysis

1. Scope and Purpose of Rule.
2. Comparison With Federal Rule.

1. *Scope and Purpose of Rule.* Rule 409, which is, in a sense, merely a particularized application of Rule 408, bars the receipt of evidence of the payment of, and of offers or promises to pay, medical expenses occasioned by an injury, when offered to prove liability. The Rule recognizes that such payments may very well be made for reasons unrelated to a perceived potential liability for them, and that the benefits of removing a disincentive to assist injured persons outweigh whatever probative value such evidence might have on issues of liability.

Essentially the same result would pertain through the operation of A.R.S. §§ 12-2301 and 12-2302, which bar evidence of advance payments made by or on behalf of a defendant for the benefit of persons asserting claims for damages, and provide for a credit against any judgment eventually awarded equal to the amount or value of any such advance payments.

2. *Comparison With Federal Rule.* Effective January 1, 2012, the Arizona Supreme Court amended Rule 409 to conform to the federal restyling of the Evidence Rules to make the rules more easily understood and to make style and terminology consistent throughout. The 2012 Comment states the stylistic amendments are not intended to "change any result in any ruling on evidence admissibility."

Following the 2012 restyling amendments, the language of Rule 409 remains identical to its federal counterpart, Fed. R.

Evid. 409.

Although Rule 409 parallels its federal counterpart, "federal court decisions interpreting the federal rule are persuasive but not binding with respect to interpreting the Arizona rule." *See,* Prefatory Comment to 2012 Amendments. *See also, State v. Terrazas*, 189 Ariz. 580, 944 P.2d 1194 (1997) (The Arizona Supreme Court is "not bound by the United States Supreme Court's non-constitutional construction of the Federal Rules of Evidence when [the Arizona Supreme Court construes] the Arizona Rules of Evidence."), citing, *State v. Bible*, 175 Ariz. 549, 858 P.2d 1152 (1993); *State v. Salazar-Mercado*, 232 Ariz. 256, 304 P.3d 543 (Ct. App. Div. 2 2013). Practitioners are urged to keep this legal tenet in mind as they research federal case law interpreting a federal evidentiary rule that corresponds to an Arizona evidentiary rule.

Rule 410. Pleas, Plea Discussions and Related Statements

(a) Prohibited Uses. Except as otherwise provided by statute, in a civil or criminal case, or administrative proceeding, evidence of the following is not admissible against the defendant who made the plea or participated in the plea discussions:

(1) a guilty plea that was later withdrawn;

(2) a nolo contendere or no contest plea;

(3) a statement made during a proceeding on either of those pleas under Arizona Rule of Criminal Procedure 17.4 or a comparable federal procedure; or

(4) a statement made during plea discussions with an attorney for the prosecuting authority if the discussions did not result in a guilty plea or they resulted in a later-withdrawn guilty plea.

(b) Exceptions. The court may admit a statement described in Rule 410(a)(3) or (4):

(1) in any proceeding in which another statement made during the same plea or plea discussions has been introduced, if in fairness the statements ought to be considered together; or

(2) in a criminal proceeding for perjury or false statement, if the defendant made the statement under oath, on the record, and with counsel present.

Amended Sept. 8, 2011, effective Jan. 1, 2012.

Comment to 2012 Amendment

This rule has been amended to conform to Federal Rule of Evidence 410, including the addition of subdivision (b)(2) and the Arizona-specific provision in subdivision (a)(3).

Additionally, the language of Rule 410 has been amended to conform to the federal restyling of the Evidence Rules to make them more easily understood and to make style and terminology consistent throughout the rules. These changes are intended to be stylistic only. There is no intent in the restyling to change any result in any ruling on evidence admissibility.

Arizona Rule of Criminal Procedure 17.4(f) has also been amended to conform to its federal counterpart, Fed. R. Crim. P. 11(f).

AUTHORS' COMMENTS

Analysis

1. *Scope and Purpose of Rule; Limitations.* Rule 410 is the coun-

terpart to Rule 408 for "settlement negotiations," *i.e.,* plea bargaining, in the context of criminal cases. The Rule recognizes the need to encourage, or at least the need to not discourage, disposition of criminal cases through the plea bargaining process.

Rule 410 declares inadmissible the following categories of evidence: (1) evidence of a guilty plea that is subsequently withdrawn; (2) pleas of *nolo contendere* or no contest; (3) offers to plead guilty, *nolo contendere* or no contest to the crime charged or any other crime; and, (4) statements made in connection with such offers and negotiations. The Rule is roughly consistent with Rule 17.4(f), Ariz.Crim.P. and is absolute—there are no provisions authorizing the receipt of such evidence when offered for "other purposes."

Under the Rule, guilty pleas that are not withdrawn are admissible as admissions, but pleas of *nolo contendere* are not. A conviction entered on a plea of *nolo contendere,* however, is admissible as impeachment evidence under Rule 609. *Wilson v. Riley Whittle, Inc.*, 145 Ariz. 317, 701 P.2d 575 (Ct. App. Div. 2 1984). Such a conviction will also not be excluded where it is made admissible by a regulatory statute. *Bear v. Nicholls*, 142 Ariz. 560, 691 P.2d 326 (Ct. App. Div. 1 1984).

The Rule includes within its coverage statements made during the course of plea negotiations, and Arizona has not adopted the provision in Rule 410 of the Federal Rules of Evidence limiting the exclusionary protection to statements made to an attorney for the prosecuting authority. *See* discussion in Section 2, *infra.* To be entitled to protection under the Arizona Rule, however, the statement in question must be one made in the context of actual negotiations of a plea bargain. *State v. Stuck*, 154 Ariz. 16, 739 P.2d 1333 (Ct. App. Div. 1 1987); *State v. Sweet*, 143 Ariz. 289, 693 P.2d 944 (Ct. App. Div. 2 1984), aff'd in part, modified in part and remanded, 143 Ariz. 266, 693 P.2d 921 (1985).

2. *Comparison With Federal Rule.* Effective January 1, 2012, the Arizona Supreme Court amended Rule 410 to conform to the federal restyling of the Evidence Rules to make the rules more easily understood and to make style and terminology consistent throughout. The 2012 Comment states the stylistic amendments are not intended to "change any result in any ruling on evidence admissibility."

As a consequence of the 2012 amendments, the language of Ariz. R. Evid. 410 is substantially similar to its federal counterpart, Fed. R. Evid. 410. The 2012 amendments included the addition of subparagraph (b)(2) and the Arizona-specific provision in subparagraph (a)(3). Additionally, Ariz. R. Crim. P. 17.4(f) was amended to conform to its counterpart, Fed. R. Crim. P. 11(f).

Although Rule 410 parallels its federal counterpart, "federal

court decisions interpreting the federal rule are persuasive but not binding with respect to interpreting the Arizona rule." *See,* Prefatory Comment to 2012 Amendments. *See also, State v. Terrazas*, 189 Ariz. 580, 944 P.2d 1194 (1997) (The Arizona Supreme Court is "not bound by the United States Supreme Court's non-constitutional construction of the Federal Rules of Evidence when [the Arizona Supreme Court construes] the Arizona Rules of Evidence."), citing, *State v. Bible*, 175 Ariz. 549, 858 P.2d 1152 (1993); *State v. Salazar-Mercado*, 232 Ariz. 256, 304 P.3d 543 (Ct. App. Div. 2 2013). Practitioners are urged to keep this legal tenet in mind as they research federal case law interpreting a federal evidentiary rule that corresponds to an Arizona evidentiary rule.

Rule 411. Liability Insurance

Evidence that a person was or was not insured against liability is not admissible to prove whether the person acted negligently or otherwise wrongfully. But the court may admit this evidence for another purpose, such as proving a witness's bias or prejudice or proving agency, ownership, or control.

Amended Oct. 19, 1988, effective Nov. 1, 1988; Sept. 8, 2011, effective Jan. 1, 2012.

Comment to 2012 Amendment

The language of Rule 411 has been amended to conform to the federal restyling of the Evidence Rules to make them more easily understood and to make style and terminology consistent throughout the rules. These changes are intended to be stylistic only. There is no intent to change any result in any ruling on evidence admissibility.

Rule 411 previously provided that evidence was not excluded if offered for a purpose not explicitly prohibited by the rule. To improve the language of the rule, it now provides that the court may admit evidence if offered for a permissible purpose. There is no intent to change the process for admitting evidence covered by the rule. It remains the case that if offered for an impermissible purpose, it must be excluded, and if offered for a purpose not barred by the rule, its admissibility remains governed by the general principles of Rules 402, 403, 801, etc.

AUTHORS' COMMENTS

Analysis

1. Scope and Purpose of Rule.
2. Comparison With Federal Rule.
3. Mention of Insurance as Grounds for Mistrial and/or New Trial.
4. Exceptions to Rule of Inadmissibility.

1. *Scope and Purpose of Rule.* Rule 411 recognizes the familiar doctrine that the presence or absence of liability insurance coverage for the defendant which is applicable to the claim being litigated is inadmissible on the issue of the defendant's fault. Insurance coverage is irrelevant to a determination of a party's legal liability. The reasoning behind the Rule is that admitting evidence of liability insurance creates an unacceptable risk that the jury, either in finding liability or in determining the amount of the award to make, will be influenced by the fact that an insurance policy is available to pay any award made. *Muehlebach v. Mercer Mortuary & Chapel, Inc.*, 93 Ariz. 60, 378 P.2d 741 (1963). The Rule, however, eschews adopting a regime of blanket exclusion of such evidence, and permits it to be admitted if it is

shown to be pertinent to other issues, such as agency, ownership or control, or to show bias and prejudice of a witness.

2. *Comparison With Federal Rule.* Effective January 1, 2012, the Arizona Supreme Court amended Rule 411 to conform to the federal restyling of the Evidence Rules to make the rules more easily understood and to make style and terminology consistent throughout. The 2012 Comment states the stylistic amendments are not intended to "change any result in any ruling on evidence admissibility."

Following the 2012 amendments, the language of Rule 411 remains identical to its federal counterpart, Fed. R. Evid. 411.

Previously, Rule 411 provided that evidence was not excluded if offered for a purpose not expressly prohibited by the rule. To clarify this language, and consistent with the language of its federal counterpart, the rule now provides the court may admit evidence if offered for a permissible purpose. As noted in the Comment to the 2012 amendments, it remains the case that evidence offered for an impermissible purpose must be excluded. The admissibility of evidence offered for a purpose not barred by the rule "remains governed by the general principles of Rules 402, 403, 801, etc." *See*, Comment to 2012 Amendment.

Although Rule 411 parallels its federal counterpart, "federal court decisions interpreting the federal rule are persuasive but not binding with respect to interpreting the Arizona rule." *See,* Prefatory Comment to 2012 Amendments. *See also, State v. Terrazas*, 189 Ariz. 580, 944 P.2d 1194 (1997) (The Arizona Supreme Court is "not bound by the United States Supreme Court's nonconstitutional construction of the Federal Rules of Evidence when [the Arizona Supreme Court construes] the Arizona Rules of Evidence."), citing, *State v. Bible*, 175 Ariz. 549, 858 P.2d 1152 (1993); *State v. Salazar-Mercado*, 232 Ariz. 256, 304 P.3d 543 (Ct. App. Div. 2 2013). Practitioners are urged to keep this legal tenet in mind as they research federal case law interpreting a federal evidentiary rule that corresponds to an Arizona evidentiary rule.

3. *Mention of Insurance as Grounds for Mistrial and/or New Trial.* The rule concerning the mention at trial of the subject of the defendant's insurance, if any, has evolved. In earlier times, the rule was that any mention, implication or suggestion of the existence of liability insurance covering the defendant was virtually an automatic ground for declaring a mistrial or awarding a new trial. *Cf., Carman v. Hefter*, 136 Ariz. 597, 667 P.2d 1312 (1983); *Michael v. Cole*, 122 Ariz. 450, 595 P.2d 995 (1979). The inflexibility of that rule eroded over time, and now the mere mention of insurance will not require declaration of a mistrial or a new trial, unless prejudice resulting from it is shown. *Michael v. Cole*, 122 Ariz. 450, 595 P.2d 995 (1979); *Sheppard v. Crow-Barker*

Paul No. 1 Ltd. Partnership, 192 Ariz. 539, 968 P.2d 612 (Ct. App. Div. 1 1998); *Anderson Aviation Sales Co., Inc. v. Perez*, 19 Ariz. App. 422, 508 P.2d 87 (Div. 1 1973). Whether such prejudice has resulted is a decision within the discretion of the trial judge.

This evolution does not signal an opening of the doors to free discussion of insurance before the jury. To the contrary, counsel have been admonished to take "affirmative precautions" to avoid eliciting testimony which mentions insurance. *E. L. Jones Const. Co. v. Noland*, 105 Ariz. 446, 466 P.2d 740 (1970). In assessing whether prejudice has resulted from the mention of insurance, the trial judge will take into account whether there are indications that it was invited by counsel. *Muehlebach v. Mercer Mortuary & Chapel, Inc.*, 93 Ariz. 60, 378 P.2d 741 (1963); *Dunipace v. Martin*, 73 Ariz. 415, 242 P.2d 543 (1952).

Rule 411 specifically applies to "insurance against liability" and does not mention health insurance. *Cervantes v. Rijlaarsdam*, 190 Ariz. 396, 949 P.2d 56 (Ct. App. Div. 2 1997). Even in that context, prejudice is not presumed from the improper admission of insurance-related evidence, and the mere mention of health insurance will not be automatic grounds for a mistrial. *Cervantes v. Rijlaarsdam*, 190 Ariz. 396, 949 P.2d 56 (Ct. App. Div. 2 1997).

4. *Exceptions to Rule of Inadmissibility.* Rule 411 bars the introduction of evidence of liability insurance when offered "upon the issue whether the person acted negligently or otherwise wrongfully." The Rule permits such evidence to be received where offered on other issues, and cites as examples issues such as agency, ownership and control. Evidence of liability insurance will also be admissible as impeachment, to suggest bias and prejudice on the part of a witness employed by the liability insurance carrier. *Barsema v. Susong*, 156 Ariz. 309, 751 P.2d 969 (1988); *Jones v. Munn*, 140 Ariz. 216, 681 P.2d 368 (1984); *Foulk v. Kotz*, 138 Ariz. 159, 673 P.2d 799 (Ct. App. Div. 2 1983). In fact, the Arizona Supreme Court declared a statute which barred the receipt of evidence of medical malpractice liability insurance coverage for any purpose, A.R.S. § 12-569, unconstitutional due to its conflict with Rule 411. *Barsema v. Susong*, 156 Ariz. 309, 751 P.2d 969 (1988).

Rule 412. Sex-Offense Cases: The Victim's Sexual Behavior or Predisposition

Not adopted.

Comment to 2012 Amendment

Federal Rule of Evidence 412 has not been adopted. *See*, A.R.S. § 13-1421 (Evidence relating to victim's chastity; pretrial hearing).

Rule 413. Similar Crimes in Sexual-Assault Cases

Not adopted.

Comment to 2012 Amendment

Federal Rule of Evidence 413 has not been adopted. *See,* Ariz. R. Evid. 404(c).

Rule 414. Similar Crimes in Child-Molestation Cases

Not adopted.

Comment to 2012 Amendment

Federal Rule of Evidence 414 has not been adopted. *See,* Ariz. R. Evid. 404(c).

Rule 415. Similar Acts in Civil Cases Involving Sexual Assault or Child Molestation

Not adopted.

Comment to 2012 Amendment

Federal Rule of Evidence 415 has not been adopted. *See,* Ariz. R. Evid. 404(c).

ARTICLE V. PRIVILEGES

Rule 501. Privilege in General

The common law—as interpreted by Arizona courts in the light of reason and experience—governs a claim of privilege unless any of the following provides otherwise:

- the United States or Arizona Constitution;
- an applicable statute; or
- rules prescribed by the Supreme Court.

Amended Sept. 8, 2011, effective Jan. 1, 2012.

Comment to 2012 Amendment

The language of Rule 501 has been amended to conform to the federal restyling of the Evidence Rules to make them more easily understood and to make style and terminology consistent throughout the rules. These changes are intended to be stylistic only. There is no intent to change any result in any ruling on evidence admissibility.

AUTHORS' COMMENTS

Analysis

1. Scope and Purpose of Rule.
2. Comparison With Federal Rule.
3. Privileges Generally.
4. Common Interest Doctrine
5. Physician-Patient Privilege.
6. Psychologist-Patient Privilege.
7. Medical Peer Review Committees.
8. Discovery of Medical Records.
9. Marital Privileges.
10. Privilege for Communications With Clergy.
11. Accountant-Client Privilege.
12. Journalists' Sources.
13. Confidential Informants.
14. Privilege Against Self-Incrimination.
15. Legislative Speech or Debate.
16. Confidentiality of Certain Governmental Records.

1. *Scope and Purpose of Rule.* Rule 501 merely provides that, except as otherwise dictated by constitutional or statutory provisions, privileges are governed by the common law as it has been developed, or may be developed in the future, in decisional law. It

essentially leaves the existing state of the law with respect to evidentiary privileges untouched, and allows for its unfettered future development.

2. *Comparison With Federal Rule.* Effective January 1, 2012, the Arizona Supreme Court amended Rule 501 to conform to the federal restyling of the Evidence Rules to make the rules more easily understood and to make style and terminology consistent throughout. The 2012 Comment states the stylistic amendments are not intended to "change any result in any ruling on evidence admissibility."

Following the 2012 restyling amendments, the language of Rule 501 remains similar to its federal counterpart, Fed. R. Evid. 501, except for changes necessary to adapt the rule to the Arizona court system. For instance, there was no need for the Arizona Rule to incorporate the last provision in the Federal Rule that requires the application of state law, in civil cases, with respect to privileges where claims and defenses governed by state law are litigated in federal courts.

Although the thrust of Rule 501 is the same as its federal counterpart, "federal court decisions interpreting the federal rule are persuasive but not binding with respect to interpreting the Arizona rule." *See,* Prefatory Comment to 2012 Amendments. *See also, State v. Terrazas*, 189 Ariz. 580, 944 P.2d 1194 (1997) (The Arizona Supreme Court is "not bound by the United States Supreme Court's non-constitutional construction of the Federal Rules of Evidence when [the Arizona Supreme Court construes] the Arizona Rules of Evidence."), citing, *State v. Bible*, 175 Ariz. 549, 858 P.2d 1152 (1993); *State v. Salazar-Mercado*, 232 Ariz. 256, 304 P.3d 543 (Ct. App. Div. 2 2013). Practitioners are urged to keep this legal tenet in mind as they research federal case law interpreting a federal evidentiary rule that corresponds to an Arizona evidentiary rule.

3. *Privileges Generally.* A privilege is a right which a person, generally referred to as the holder of the privilege, has to prevent the revelation of otherwise material and relevant evidence, not because the evidence in question is unreliable or of questionable probative value, but rather to protect and encourage certain relationships and activities at the potential cost of shielding pertinent information from the trier of fact. Most privileges that have been recognized concern communications occurring during the course of one of the protected relationships, and it is generally held that the privilege shields the content of the communication, but not the fact that it took place or the surrounding circumstances. *Granger v. Wisner*, 134 Ariz. 377, 656 P.2d 1238 (1982). In fact, that type of information is frequently determinative of whether a privilege applies and/or has been properly

invoked.

Privileges can be created by statute and, in Arizona, there are a number of statutory provisions either creating or recognizing evidentiary privileges. *Jolly v. Superior Court of Pinal County*, 112 Ariz. 186, 540 P.2d 658 (1975); *Humana Hosp. Desert Valley v. Superior Court of Arizona In and For Maricopa County*, 154 Ariz. 396, 742 P.2d 1382 (Ct. App. Div. 1 1987). The language of Rule 501 also strongly suggests that privileges can be limited by statute as well. By statute, only the attorney-client privilege and the privilege for communications with members of the clergy apply in any litigation or administrative proceeding in which "a child's neglect, dependency, abuse or abandonment is an issue." A.R.S. §§ 8-546.04(C); 13-3620(F), (G).

Privileges can also be recognized or created by the courts. The Arizona Supreme Court has set forth four criteria for the recognition of an evidentiary privilege for communications: (1) the communication must originate in circumstances indicating that the parties were confident it would remain confidential; (2) such confidentiality is essential to the full maintenance of the relationship in connection with which the communication occurred; (3) the relationship is one which the community believes should be fostered; and, (4) the injury to the relationship that would occur from disclosure would be greater than the countervailing benefit to the litigation process. *City of Tucson v. Superior Court In and For County of Pima*, 167 Ariz. 513, 809 P.2d 428 (1991).

A privilege must be claimed by the holder of the privilege or it is waived. *Tripp v. Chubb*, 69 Ariz. 31, 208 P.2d 312 (1949). Such a waiver can be express, or implied from the failure to object to testimony on matters subject to the privilege. *Throop v. F. E. Young & Co.*, 94 Ariz. 146, 382 P.2d 560 (1963). Generally, once a privilege is waived, it cannot be reasserted.

If the holder of the privilege is deceased, the holder's heirs or personal representative may assert it. *Schornick v. Schornick*, 25 Ariz. 563, 220 P. 397, 31 A.L.R. 159 (1923). If the holder of the privilege is incompetent, it may be claimed by a duly appointed guardian. *Lewin v. Jackson*, 108 Ariz. 27, 492 P.2d 406 (1972); *Lietz v. Primock*, 84 Ariz. 273, 327 P.2d 288, 67 A.L.R.2d 1262 (1958). While the party making the protected communication is the privilege holder, others may raise the issue of privilege, or at least call it to the Court's attention, where the holder of the privilege is not a party or not present to protect it. *Lipschultz v. Superior Court, In and For Maricopa County*, 128 Ariz. 16, 623 P.2d 805 (1981); *Tucson Medical Center, Inc. v. Misevch*, 113 Ariz. 34, 545 P.2d 958 (1976); *Hospital Corp. of America v. Superior Court of Pima County*, 157 Ariz. 210, 755 P.2d 1198 (Ct. App. Div. 2 1988).

Once an assertion of privilege is made, whether there is a privilege and whether it applies in the particular situation presented are issues of law for the Court. *State ex rel. Babbitt v. Arnold*, 26 Ariz. App. 333, 548 P.2d 426 (Div. 2 1976); *Gordon v. Industrial Commission*, 23 Ariz. App. 457, 533 P.2d 1194 (Div. 1 1975); *Blazek v. Superior Court In and For County of Maricopa*, 177 Ariz. 535, 869 P.2d 509 (Ct. App. Div. 1 1994). Privileges are to be strictly construed and the burden of sustaining the existence and applicability of a privilege is on the person claiming it. *Throop v. F. E. Young & Co.*, 94 Ariz. 146, 382 P.2d 560 (1963); *G & S Investments v. Belman*, 145 Ariz. 258, 700 P.2d 1358 (Ct. App. Div. 2 1984). Evidentiary privileges are narrowly construed because they operate to deprive the fact finder of information that is relevant to the issues before it and impede the search for the truth. *Arizona Independent Redistricting Com'n v. Fields*, 206 Ariz. 130, 75 P.3d 1088 (Ct. App. Div. 1 2003).

If the claim of privilege is sustained, it is improper to comment on its invocation in the presence of the jury. *State v. Holsinger*, 124 Ariz. 18, 601 P.2d 1054 (1979). Where a claim of privilege is overruled, a petition for special action is the appropriate vehicle for seeking appellate relief for a party ordered to divulge what that party believes is privileged material. *Twin City Fire Ins. Co. v. Burke*, 204 Ariz. 251, 63 P.3d 282 (2003); *Green v. Nygaard*, 213 Ariz. 460, 143 P.3d 393 (Ct. App. Div. 2 2006); *State ex rel. Thomas v. Schneider*, 212 Ariz. 292, 130 P.3d 991 (Ct. App. Div. 1 2006); *Arizona Independent Redistricting Com'n v. Fields*, 206 Ariz. 130, 75 P.3d 1088 (Ct. App. Div. 1 2003); *Sun Health Corp. v. Myers*, 205 Ariz. 315, 70 P.3d 444 (Ct. App. Div. 1 2003), redesignated as opinion, (June 12, 2003) and as amended, (June 12, 2003); *Ulibarri v. Superior Court in and for County of Coconino*, 184 Ariz. 382, 909 P.2d 449 (Ct. App. Div. 1 1995), corrected, (Aug. 22, 1995); *Blazek v. Superior Court In and For County of Maricopa*, 177 Ariz. 535, 869 P.2d 509 (Ct. App. Div. 1 1994).

There are other evidentiary rules, which are not called privileges but are at least analogous to them, in that their application results in the exclusion of otherwise material and probative evidence in order to foster an activity or relationship. Examples of such privilege analogs include Rule 407's limitations on the admission of evidence of product modifications or other remedial measures, the exclusion of evidence of offers to settle and settlement negotiations, mandated by Rule 408, and the exclusion of evidence of plea bargaining negotiations under Rule 410. *See Readenour v. Marion Power Shovel, a Div. of Dresser Industries, Inc.*, 149 Ariz. 442, 446, 719 P.2d 1058, 1062, Prod. Liab. Rep. (CCH) P 11012 (1986). The Arizona "Dead Man's Statute," A.R.S. § 12-2251, which serves quite different interests, excludes evidence of a witness' communications or transactions with a decedent. *Cf. Bostwick v. Jasin*, 170 Ariz. 15, 821 P.2d 282 (Ct. App. Div. 2 1991). *See* discussion of this statute in Section 5 of the *Authors' Comments* to Rule 601, Ariz. R. Evid. These rules and statutes do not create "true" privileges, however, for they do not necessarily protect the excluded evidence from discovery. *Cf. Ingalls v. Superior Court in and for Pima County*, 117 Ariz. 448, 573 P.2d 522 (Ct. App. Div. 2 1977).

4. *"Common Interest" Doctrine*. The "common interest" doctrine, as it has been recognized and defined in § 76(1) of the *Restatement (Third) of the Law Governing Lawyers*, does not create a privilege, but rather extends the scope of the attorney-client and work-product privileges. *Arizona Independent Redistricting Com'n v. Fields*, 206 Ariz. 130, 75 P.3d 1088 (Ct. App. Div. 1 2003). It is an exception to the rule that communications between a person and a lawyer representing another person are not privileged. *Arizona Independent Redistricting Com'n v. Fields*, 206 Ariz. 130, 75 P.3d 1088 (Ct. App. Div. 1 2003). The purpose of the "common interest" doctrine is to permit persons with common interests to share privileged attorney-client communications and work-product in order to coordinate their respective positions without destroying the privilege. *Arizona Independent Redistricting Com'n v. Fields*, 206 Ariz. 130, 75 P.3d 1088 (Ct. App. Div. 1 2003).

Exchanged communications subject to the "common interest" doctrine must themselves be privileged as well as related to the parties' common interest, which may be legal, factual or strategic. *Arizona Independent Redistricting Com'n v. Fields*, 206 Ariz. 130, 75 P.3d 1088 (Ct. App. Div. 1 2003). Communications solely among clients are not protected by the doctrine. *Arizona Independent Redistricting Com'n v. Fields*, 206 Ariz. 130, 75 P.3d 1088 (Ct. App. Div. 1 2003). Moreover, the doctrine protects only those communications made to facilitate the rendition of legal services to each of the clients involved. *Arizona Independent Redistricting Com'n v. Fields*, 206 Ariz. 130, 75 P.3d 1088 (Ct. App. Div. 1 2003).

5. *Physician-Patient Privilege*. The privilege for confidential communications between doctor and patient has long been recognized in Arizona both by case law and statute. *Barnes v. Outlaw*, 188 Ariz. 401, 937 P.2d 323 (Ct. App. Div. 2 1996), as amended on denial of reconsideration, (Nov. 8, 1996) and opinion vacated in part on other grounds, 192 Ariz. 283, 964 P.2d 484 (1998); A.R.S. §§ 12-2235; 13-4062(4). The purpose of the privilege is to insure full and frank disclosure by the patient to the physician so that the patient can receive the best possible medical care. *Carondelet Health Network v. Miller*, 221 Ariz. 614, 212 P.3d 952 (Ct. App. Div. 2 2009); *State ex rel. Udall v. Superior Court In and For County of Apache*, 183 Ariz. 462, 904 P.2d 1286

(Ct. App. Div. 1 1995). *Lewin v. Jackson*, 108 Ariz. 27, 492 P.2d 406 (1972).

The privilege is not limited, however, to physician-patient communications; it applies as well to information acquired or generated by the physician as a result of examination of the patient and testing. *Ornelas v. Fry*, 151 Ariz. 324, 727 P.2d 819 (Ct. App. Div. 1 1986). One case suggests that the privilege protects from disclosure the names of a medical malpractice defendant's other patients, but not their medical records. *Ziegler v. Superior Court of State, In and For Pima County*, 131 Ariz. 250, 640 P.2d 181 (1982); *but cf. Hospital Corp. of America v. Superior Court of Pima County*, 157 Ariz. 210, 755 P.2d 1198 (Ct. App. Div. 2 1988). Because the privilege is a creature of statute, however, it is to be strictly construed. *State ex rel. Udall v. Superior Court In and For County of Apache*, 183 Ariz. 462, 904 P.2d 1286 (Ct. App. Div. 1 1995); *Benton v. Superior Court in and for County of Navajo*, 182 Ariz. 466, 897 P.2d 1352 (Ct. App. Div. 1 1994). By statute, the privilege does not apply in any proceeding involving issues of child abuse. *State ex rel. Udall v. Superior Court In and For County of Apache*, 183 Ariz. 462, 904 P.2d 1286 (Ct. App. Div. 1 1995).

The examination by and consultation with the physician must be private and confidential—the presence of third parties who are strangers to the relationship destroys it. *Banta v. Superior Court of Maricopa County*, 112 Ariz. 544, 544 P.2d 653 (1976). The privilege does not apply to an examination ordered by the Court to determine a person's physical condition. *Lewin v. Jackson*, 108 Ariz. 27, 492 P.2d 406 (1972). The fact that the substance of the communication, or other information secured by the physician, however, is recorded in the physician's office records or in hospital records that are available to others involved to varying degrees in the treatment of the patient does not make the privilege inapplicable. *Tucson Medical Center, Inc. v. Misevch*, 113 Ariz. 34, 545 P.2d 958 (1976).

In fact, in most circumstances, a hospital must assert the privilege in order to protect the patient. *Tucson Medical Center, Inc. v. Misevch*, 113 Ariz. 34, 545 P.2d 958 (1976); *Tucson Medical Center Inc. v. Rowles*, 21 Ariz. App. 424, 520 P.2d 518 (Div. 2 1974). Patient records in the custody of hospitals retain their confidential nature even if furnished to regulatory authorities. A.R.S. §§ 36-404; 36-1451.01(C), (D), (E). Accordingly, there are special requirements applicable to subpoenas duces tecum issued to health care providers seeking production of medical records which are designed to provide the patient with an opportunity to object and/or raise the privilege. A.R.S. § 12-2294.01. These special statutory provisions are discussed in Section 9 of the *Authors' Comments* to Rule 45. A hospital does not, however, have a duty to assert the patient's privilege when served with a search warrant for medical records. *Samaritan Health Services v. City of Glendale*, 148 Ariz. 394, 714 P.2d 887 (Ct. App. Div. 1 1986); *cf. also Linch v. Thomas-Davis Medical Centers, P.C.*, 186 Ariz. 545, 925 P.2d 686 (Ct. App. Div. 2 1996). The privilege also does not prevent the compelled disclosure of the identity of a hospital patient who shared a room with the decedent in a wrongful death action and was a witness to events taking place in that room. *Carondelet Health Network v. Miller*, 221 Ariz. 614, 212 P.3d 952 (Ct. App. Div. 2 2009).

The privilege can be waived by the patient, either expressly or by implication. There is an implied waiver where the patient voluntarily testifies to communications that would be subject to the privilege's protection. A.R.S. § 12-2336; *but cf. Styers v. Superior Court In and For County of Mohave*, 161 Ariz. 477, 779 P.2d 352 (Ct. App. Div. 1 1989). Similarly, a waiver may be implied by failing to object to testimony from the physician concerning privileged matters. *Throop v. F. E. Young & Co.*, 94 Ariz. 146, 382 P.2d 560 (1963); *Patania v. Silverstone*, 3 Ariz. App. 424, 415 P.2d 139 (1966) (rejected on other grounds by, Buffa v. Scott, 147 Ariz. 140, 708 P.2d 1331 (Ct. App. Div. 1 1985)). A waiver of the privilege is a condition to receiving reports of certain medical examinations under Ariz.R.Civ.P. 35(b).

There is some authority that the privilege is waived by putting the holder's medical condition in issue in litigation, *Bain v. Superior Court In and For Maricopa County*, 148 Ariz. 331, 714 P.2d 824 (1986), and that the failure to object to deposition testimony by the physician concerning the condition in issue is also a waiver. *Patania v. Silverstone*, 3 Ariz. App. 424, 415 P.2d 139 (1966) (rejected on other grounds by, Buffa v. Scott, 147 Ariz. 140, 708 P.2d 1331 (Ct. App. Div. 1 1985)). The later cases, however, suggest that putting a medical condition in issue in litigation is a waiver only of the right to object on the grounds of privilege to discovery requests concerning that medical condition, and that deposition testimony concerning that condition is not voluntary and, therefore, not a waiver. *Duquette v. Superior Court In and For County of Maricopa*, 161 Ariz. 269, 778 P.2d 634 (Ct. App. Div. 1 1989); *Buffa v. Scott*, 147 Ariz. 140, 708 P.2d 1331 (Ct. App. Div. 1 1985). In any event, the waiver is only with respect to the mental or physical condition that has been put in issue.

6 *Psychologist-Patient Privilege.* Arizona has a statutory privilege for confidential communications between licensed psychologists and their patients in connection with consultation and treatment. A.R.S. § 32-2085. The privilege also covers patients' records. The courts have held that the psychologist-patient privilege serves purposes identical to those underlying the physician-

patient privilege. *Linch v. Thomas-Davis Medical Centers, P.C.*, 186 Ariz. 545, 925 P.2d 686 (Ct. App. Div. 2 1996). Interestingly enough, however, the statute puts such communications between psychologists and their patients "on the same basis as those provided by law between an attorney and client." *Linch v. Thomas-Davis Medical Centers, P.C.*, 186 Ariz. 545, 925 P.2d 686 (Ct. App. Div. 2 1996). The privilege enhances the effective diagnosis and treatment of illness by ensuring that people requiring a psychologist's attention will not be deterred out of fear that their condition may create public embarrassment or humiliation. *Blazek v. Superior Court In and For County of Maricopa*, 177 Ariz. 535, 869 P.2d 509 (Ct. App. Div. 1 1994). A patient consents to the disclosure of privileged information by (1) expressly waiving the privilege in writing or in open court; or (2) pursuing a course of conduct that is inconsistent with observance of the privilege, such as by placing the underlying psychological condition at issue as a claim or defense. *Blazek v. Superior Court In and For County of Maricopa*, 177 Ariz. 535, 869 P.2d 509 (Ct. App. Div. 1 1994). The scope of such an implied waiver of the privilege is limited to those communications which concern the specific condition which the patient has placed in issue. *Blazek v. Superior Court In and For County of Maricopa*, 177 Ariz. 535, 869 P.2d 509 (Ct. App. Div. 1 1994). The psychologist-patient privilege will not prevent a seizure of medical records pursuant to a duly issued search warrant. *Linch v. Thomas-Davis Medical Centers, P.C.*, 186 Ariz. 545, 925 P.2d 686 (Ct. App. Div. 2 1996).

In addition to the physician-patient and psychologist-patient privileges, Arizona has also recognized, by statute, the confidential nature of the relationship between other behavioral health providers and their clients, A.R.S. § 32-3283, including counselors and "marriage therapists." A.R.S. §§ 32-3301, 32-3311; *Barnes v. Outlaw*, 188 Ariz. 401, 937 P.2d 323 (Ct. App. Div. 2 1996), as amended on denial of reconsideration, (Nov. 8, 1996) and opinion vacated in part, 192 Ariz. 283, 964 P.2d 484 (1998).

7. *Medical Peer Review Committees.* By statute, proceedings before medical peer review committees at hospitals, as well as the records and materials prepared in connection therewith, are confidential and exempt from discovery. A.R.S. § 36-445.01. The statute also exempts members of such medical peer review committees from subpoenas to testify concerning the activities of those committees. A.R.S. § 36-445.01. A very similar privilege pertains to the activities of "quality assurance" committees. A.R.S. §§ 36-441(B); 36-2403.

The privilege applies both to the review and investigation conducted by such committees of the background and credentials of applicants for hospital staff privileges, as well as their review of the quality of care rendered by those who have already been granted staff privileges. *John C. Lincoln Hosp. and Health Center v. Superior Court In and For County of Maricopa*, 159 Ariz. 456, 768 P.2d 188 (Ct. App. Div. 1 1989); *Humana Hosp. Desert Valley v. Superior Court of Arizona In and For Maricopa County*, 154 Ariz. 396, 742 P.2d 1382 (Ct. App. Div. 1 1987). The privilege does not, however, immunize from disclosure all information such committees may consider. *Tucson Medical Center, Inc. v. Misevch*, 113 Ariz. 34, 545 P.2d 958 (1976). The privilege does protect from disclosure the names of participants in a peer review proceeding and a listing of any written or documentary items submitted to the committee, but does not protect information that originated outside the peer review process and is discoverable from other sources. *Yuma Regional Medical Center v. Superior Court In and For County of Yuma*, 175 Ariz. 72, 852 P.2d 1256 (Ct. App. Div. 1 1993).

Similarly privileged are a hospital's communications to the Board of Medical Examiners (BOMEX) relating to the suspension of the staff privileges of a doctor. *Sun Health Corp. v. Myers*, 205 Ariz. 315, 70 P.3d 444 (Ct. App. Div. 1 2003), redesignated as opinion, (June 12, 2003) and as amended, (June 12, 2003). A.R.S. § 32-1451.01(C) establishes the general rule that documents submitted to BOMEX as a result of an investigation are absolutely privileged. A.R.S. § 32-1451.01(E) creates an exception for material which was not privileged in its original form.

8. *Discovery of Medical Records*. A patient's medical records are confidential and protected from discovery by statute. A.R.S. § 12-2292 covers records maintained in any form that relate to the physical or mental health of a patient and are maintained for purposes of treatment or diagnosis. *Schoeneweis v. Hamner*, 223 Ariz. 169, 221 P.3d 48, 38 Media L. Rep. (BNA) 1001 (Ct. App. Div. 1 2009) (holding medical record statutes inapplicable to public records requests for autopsy reports because "a determination of the cause of death is not made for the purposes of diagnosis or treatment."); *Catrone v. Miles*, 215 Ariz. 446, 160 P.3d 1204, 220 Ed. Law Rep. 925 (Ct. App. Div. 1 2007) (holding the statutory medical privilege for medical records does not protect special education records because the "formulation of an educational plan for students with disabilities in a school setting is not the same as the diagnosis and treatment of a person with disabilities in a medical setting.").

Notwithstanding that, medical records of a party, at least with respect to the medical condition which that party has put in issue, are freely discoverable. In fact, Rule 26.2(a)(1) requires the plaintiff, in a medical malpractice case, to serve upon the defendant(s), before the Comprehensive Pretrial Conference required by Ariz.R.Civ.P. 16(c), copies of all the medical records of plaintiff that are available and are relevant to the condition that is in issue in the case. See Section 3 of the *Authors' Comments* under Ariz.R.Civ.P. 26.2. This requirement would appear to be bottomed on the proposition that, by bringing the action and putting a certain medical condition in issue, the plaintiff has waived any privilege or confidentiality protection that pertains to medical records concerning that condition. On the other hand, A.R.S. § 12-2282 places certain specific requirements on subpoenas *duces tecum* issued to a health care provider and seeking the production of medical records. See discussion in Section 9 of the *Authors' Comments* under Ariz.R.Civ.P. 45.

In addition, non-party medical records, if relevant, may also be subject to discovery in spite of the statutory privilege, but only if the following precautions are taken: (1) all references to the name, address, marital status, occupation, or employment of the patient are removed; (2) after review, the records are filed with the Court and are not opened absent Court order; (3) no efforts are made to discover the identity of the patients or to contact them; and, (4) information from the records is not communicated to a non-party, except to experts and during trial. *Ziegler v. Superior Court In and For Pima County*, 134 Ariz. 390, 656 P.2d 1251 (Ct. App. Div. 2 1982); *C.B. v. Sabalos ex rel. County of Pima*, 198 Ariz. 115, 7 P.3d 124 (Ct. App. Div. 2 2000), review denied and opinion ordered not published, 199 Ariz. 164, 15 P.3d 276 (2000).

9. *Marital Privileges.* There are two separate privileges that center around the marital relationship: the so-called anti-marital fact privilege [A.R.S. § 12-2231] and the marital communications privilege [A.R.S. § 12-2232]. *In re MH 2007-000937*, 218 Ariz. 517, 189 P.3d 1090 (Ct. App. Div. 1 2008); *Blazek v. Superior Court In and For County of Maricopa*, 177 Ariz. 535, 869 P.2d 509 (Ct. App. Div. 1 1994). The anti-marital fact privilege and the marital communications privilege are found in A.R.S. § 13-4062(1). As a result of a 2009 amendment to A.R.S. § 13-4062(1), the marital communications privilege is unavailable if (1) the testifying spouse makes voluntary statements to law enforcement about events or about statements the other spouse made about those events or (2) either spouse request to testify. A.R.S. § 13-4062(1)(a)(b). *See also, State v. Carver*, 227 Ariz. 438, 258 P.3d 256 (Ct. App. Div. 1 2011).

The accepted policy underlying the privilege is to promote family harmony and encourage spouses to share confidences and secrets. *In re MH 2007-000937*, 218 Ariz. 517, 189 P.3d 1090 (Ct. App. Div. 1 2008); *Ulibarri v. Superior Court in and for County of Coconino*, 184 Ariz. 382, 909 P.2d 449 (Ct. App. Div. 1 1995), corrected, (Aug. 22, 1995). This stated policy, however, has been subject to criticism. *State v. Williams*, 133 Ariz. 220, 650 P.2d 1202 (1982); *State v. Whitaker*, 112 Ariz. 537, 544 P.2d 219 (1975)

("The [marital] privilege has sometimes been defended on the ground that it protects family harmony. But family harmony is nearly always past saving when the spouse is willing to aid the prosecution." quoting McCormick, Evidence 2nd Ed. 1972, § 66 at 145–146); *In re MH 2007-000937*, 218 Ariz. 517, 189 P.3d 1090 (Ct. App. Div. 1 2008) (discussing both *State v. Williams* and *State v. Whitaker*).

In civil actions, and absent an exception, the anti-marital fact privilege gives a party spouse the right to prevent to other spouse from being examined in a court proceeding held during the marriage. *In re MH 2007-000937*, 218 Ariz. 517, 189 P.3d 1090 (Ct. App. Div. 1 2008); *Blazek v. Superior Court In and For County of Maricopa*, 177 Ariz. 535, 538, 869 P.2d 509, 512 (Ct. App. Div. 1 1994). By contrast, the marital communications privilege prevents a spouse during the marriage or afterward from being examined as to any communication made by one to the other during the marriage, without the consent of the other. *In re MH 2007-000937*, 218 Ariz. 517, 189 P.3d 1090 (Ct. App. Div. 1 2008); *Blazek v. Superior Court In and For County of Maricopa*, 177 Ariz. 535, 538, 869 P.2d 509, 512 (Ct. App. Div. 1 1994).

The anti-marital fact privilege ceases, accordingly, upon divorce or dissolution of the marriage. *Posner v. New York Life Ins. Co.*, 56 Ariz. 202, 106 P.2d 488 (1940); *Blazek v. Superior Court In and For County of Maricopa*, 177 Ariz. 535, 869 P.2d 509 (Ct. App. Div. 1 1994). In addition, the privilege does not apply to *de facto* marriages. *State v. Watkins*, 126 Ariz. 293, 614 P.2d 835 (1980).

The anti-marital fact privilege also does apply in mental health proceedings for court-ordered treatment initiated by a petition filed pursuant to A.R.S. § 36-522. *In re MH 2007-000937*, 218 Ariz. 517, 189 P.3d 1090 (Ct. App. Div. 1 2008). The statutes creating the privilege contain no substantive testimonial limitation. The words "for or against" do not mean "favorable or unfavorable." They mean simply "on behalf of" a spouse or "on behalf of a party opposing" a spouse. The privilege forbids any testimony, not just damaging testimony, as to events which occurred during marriage unless the non-testifying spouse consents. *State ex rel. Woods v. Cohen*, 173 Ariz. 497, 844 P.2d 1147 (1992).

The anti-marital fact privilege is subject to a number of statutory exceptions. In civil cases, the most important exception where the privilege is completely unavailable is when one spouse has brought an action against the other. A.R.S. § 12-2232(a). The 2009 amendment to A.R.S. § 12-2232 deleted an exception previously provided for damages suits for alienation of affections or adultery.

The marital communications privilege, recognized in A.R.S.

§ 12-2232, protects what one spouse says to the other in confidence during the course of the marriage, but will not protect communications made when third parties are present. *Arizona Title Guarantee & Trust Co. v. Wagner*, 75 Ariz. 82, 251 P.2d 897 (1952). The marital communications privilege protects only what was said and does not preclude testimony concerning the conduct of one spouse that the other spouse observed. *Posner v. New York Life Ins. Co.*, 56 Ariz. 202, 106 P.2d 488 (1940); *Blazek v. Superior Court In and For County of Maricopa*, 177 Ariz. 535, 538, 869 P.2d 509, 512 (Ct. App. Div. 1 1994).

Arizona does not recognize an exception to the marital communications privilege for statements made during periods of separation, or when the marriage has been "irretrievably broken," but the marriage has not yet been formally dissolved. *Blazek v. Superior Court In and For County of Maricopa*, 177 Ariz. 535, 869 P.2d 509 (Ct. App. Div. 1 1994). Unlike the antimarital fact privilege, the marital communications privilege survives the termination of the marital relationship. *Posner v. New York Life Ins. Co.*, 56 Ariz. 202, 106 P.2d 488 (1940); *Ulibarri v. Superior Court in and for County of Coconino*, 184 Ariz. 382, 909 P.2d 449 (Ct. App. Div. 1 1995), corrected, (Aug. 22, 1995), corrected, (Aug. 22, 1995); *Blazek v. Superior Court In and For County of Maricopa*, 177 Ariz. 535, 869 P.2d 509 (Ct. App. Div. 1 1994).

A separate statute, A.R.S. § 13-3620, makes the privileges inapplicable in any civil or criminal litigation or proceeding in which the neglect, dependency, abuse or abandonment of a child is in issue.

10. *Privilege for Communications With Clergy*. There is a statutory privilege for a confession or similar communication made to a member of the clergy "in the course of a discipline enjoined by the church." A.R.S. §§ 12-2233; 13-4062(3). This is one of the privileges which does apply in cases involving issues of child neglect and/or child abuse. A.R.S. §§ 8-546.04; 13-3620(A), (H). The privilege belongs to the person making the confession and cannot be asserted by the clergy if the holder of the privilege has waived it. *Church of Jesus Christ of Latter-Day Saints v. Superior Court In and For Maricopa County*, 159 Ariz. 24, 764 P.2d 759 (Ct. App. Div. 1 1988).

A determination of whether the clergy-penitent privilege applies involves a three-step inquiry: (1) Is the person who received the confession a "clergyman or priest"?; (2) Was the confession made while the clergyman or priest was acting in a professional capacity?; and (3) Was the confession made in the course of a discipline enjoined by the church to which the clergyman or priest belongs? *State v. Archibeque*, 223 Ariz. 231, 221 P.3d 1045 (Ct. App. Div. 1 2009). If the answer to all three inquiries is in the affirmative, then the clergy-penitent privilege applies unless it is waived. *State v. Archibeque*, 223 Ariz. 231, 221 P.3d 1045 (Ct. App. Div. 1 2009). The presence of the clergyman's wife during the confession does not operate as a waiver if the penitent believed the communication would remain private and that belief is reasonable. *State v. Archibeque*, 223 Ariz. 231, 221 P.3d 1045 (Ct. App. Div. 1 2009).

The privilege exists because of a belief that people should be encouraged to discuss their "flawed behavior" with individuals who, within the spiritual traditions and doctrines of their faith, are qualified and capable of encouraging the communicants to abandon and perhaps make amends for wrongful and destructive behavior. *Waters v. O'Connor*, 209 Ariz. 380, 103 P.3d 292 (Ct. App. Div. 1 2004). While the term "clergyman" is not limited to members of religious organizations having an ordained clergy, the privilege should not be expanded to include communications with individuals who are not qualified to provide the type of advice the privilege is intended to foster. *Waters v. O'Connor*, 209 Ariz. 380, 103 P.3d 292 (Ct. App. Div. 1 2004). Whether a person is a clergyman of a particular religious organization should be determined by that organization's ecclesiastical rules, customs and laws. *Waters v. O'Connor*, 209 Ariz. 380, 103 P.3d 292 (Ct. App. Div. 1 2004).

11. *Accountant-Client Privilege.* This statutory privilege protects from disclosure confidential information acquired by public accountants during the course of their employment in that capacity. A.R.S. § 32-749. The privilege has been held not to apply in criminal cases. *State v. O'Brien*, 123 Ariz. 578, 601 P.2d 341 (Ct. App. Div. 2 1979). The privilege covers communications between the public accountant and the client concerning the client's financial affairs, but not communications concerning retention of the accountant to review the financial records of third parties. *Brown v. Superior Court In and For Maricopa County*, 137 Ariz. 327, 670 P.2d 725 (1983).

12. *Journalists' Sources.* A.R.S. § 12-2237 protects from compelled disclosure sources of information obtained by media reporters for publication or broadcasting. The privilege applies in any legal proceeding or trial whatsoever, including hearings before legislative committees. In addition, there are special requirements applicable to securing the issuance of subpoenas directed to a "person engaged in gathering, reporting, writing, editing, publishing or broadcasting news to the public." A.R.S. § 12-2214. These special requirements are discussed in Section 10 of the *Authors' Comments* under Ariz.R.Civ.P. 45.

The privilege belongs to the reporter and is rooted in the public interest in allowing journalists to collect news from sources who would not otherwise disclose information if they were publicly identified. *Flores v. Cooper Tire and Rubber Co.*, 218 Ariz. 52, 178 P.3d 1176, 36 Media L. Rep. (BNA) 1710 (Ct. App. Div. 1 2008). A reporter does not waive this privilege by disclosing that the information for a story came from a "whistle-blower," without disclosing that person's identity. *Flores v. Cooper Tire and Rubber Co.*, 218 Ariz. 52, 178 P.3d 1176, 36 Media L. Rep. (BNA) 1710 (Ct. App. Div. 1 2008).

13. *Confidential Informants.* The identity of a confidential informant who furnishes information to law enforcement agencies, and who is not called to testify, is privileged unless the failure to disclose the informant's identity would infringe the constitutional rights of the accused. Rule 15.4(b)(2), Ariz. R. Crim. P.

14. *Privilege Against Self-Incrimination.* The privilege against self-incrimination is constitutional in origin. U.S. Const. Amend. V; Ariz. Const. Art. 2, Sec. 10. In Arizona, it is also recognized by statute. A.R.S. § 13-117. The privilege has two separate aspects: (1) that a person may not be compelled to testify as to potentially incriminating matters, *Rivera v. City of Douglas*, 132 Ariz. 117, 644 P.2d 271 (Ct. App. Div. 2 1982); and, (2) the right of a criminal defendant not to testify at all in the defense of the criminal charges. A party who invokes the privilege against self-incrimination cannot be subjected to any penalty for remaining silent. *Wohlstrom v. Buchanan*, 180 Ariz. 389, 884 P.2d 687 (1994).

The testimony sought from the witness need not be directly incriminating; a witness can invoke the privilege and refuse to answer questions if the answers might provide a link in a chain of evidence needed to sustain criminal charges. The failure to assert the privilege, however, operates as a waiver. *State v. Tudgay*, 128 Ariz. 1, 623 P.2d 360 (1981). Such a waiver occurs by the voluntary giving of any testimony about the potentially incriminating subject matter. *Gilbert v. McGhee*, 111 Ariz. 121, 524 P.2d 157 (1974). Absent such a waiver, the invocation of the privilege should be overruled only where it is indisputably clear that the answer sought cannot possibly have a tendency to incriminate the witness. The privilege against self-incrimination can be invoked in response to discovery requests in civil cases. *State v. Ott*, 167 Ariz. 420, 808 P.2d 305 (Ct. App. Div. 1 1990).

15. *Legislative Speech or Debate.* Although it found the privilege inapplicable in the situation presented, in *Steiger v. Superior Court for Maricopa County*, 112 Ariz. 1, 536 P.2d 689 (1975), the Arizona Supreme Court held that the Speech or Debate Clause, U.S. Const. Art. 1, § 6, protects members of the United States Congress and their legislative aides from inquiry into their

legislative acts and their motivation for performing them. *But cf. Yuma Greyhound Park, Inc. v. Hardy*, 106 Ariz. 178, 472 P.2d 47 (1970). The privilege does not encompass every activity in which a member of the Congress engages, but only acts generally and traditionally performed in connection with the legislative process.

The "legislative privilege" stems from the doctrine of legislative immunity, which in turn springs from the common law and is embodied in the Speech or Debate Clause and the principles underlying the government's separation of powers. *Arizona Independent Redistricting Com'n v. Fields*, 206 Ariz. 130, 75 P.3d 1088 (Ct. App. Div. 1 2003). The privilege does not cloak all things that are in any way related to the legislative process. *Arizona Independent Redistricting Com'n v. Fields*, 206 Ariz. 130, 75 P.3d 1088 (Ct. App. Div. 1 2003). Rather, the privilege extends to matters beyond pure speech and debate in the legislature only when such matters are an integral part of the deliberative process relating to proposed legislation or other matters placed within the jurisdiction of the legislature. *Arizona Independent Redistricting Com'n v. Fields*, 206 Ariz. 130, 75 P.3d 1088 (Ct. App. Div. 1 2003). In appropriate circumstances, the legislative privilege protects against disclosure of documents. *Arizona Independent Redistricting Com'n v. Fields*, 206 Ariz. 130, 75 P.3d 1088 (Ct. App. Div. 1 2003). To the extent the legislative privilege protects against inquiry about a legislative act or communications about that act, the privilege also shields from disclosure documentation reflecting those acts or communications. *Arizona Independent Redistricting Com'n v. Fields*, 206 Ariz. 130, 75 P.3d 1088 (Ct. App. Div. 1 2003).

A legislator may invoke the privilege to shield from inquiry the acts of independent contractors retained by that legislator that would be privileged legislative conduct if personally performed by the legislator. *Arizona Independent Redistricting Com'n v. Fields*, 206 Ariz. 130, 75 P.3d 1088 (Ct. App. Div. 1 2003). If that consultant, however, is designated as a testifying, rather than a consulting, expert, then the privilege is waived as to communications with that expert or any materials reviewed by that expert that relate to the subject of the expert's testimony. *Arizona Independent Redistricting Com'n v. Fields*, 206 Ariz. 130, 75 P.3d 1088 (Ct. App. Div. 1 2003).

16. *Confidentiality of Certain Governmental Records.* As a general rule, government records are available for public inspection. A.R.S. § 39-121. While there is a presumption that records received by the courts are public records, that must be balanced against the state's legitimate interests in preserving the confidentiality of ongoing criminal investigations. *Phoenix Newspapers, Inc. v. Superior Court In and For County of Maricopa*, 180 Ariz. 159, 882 P.2d 1285, 22 Media L. Rep. (BNA) 1531 (Ct.

App. Div. 1 1993). Certain statutes, moreover, confer varying degrees of confidentiality on certain categories of documents collected and/or generated by governmental agencies. These include, for example, investigative materials of the Board of Medical Examiners, A.R.S. §§ 32-1451.01(C), (D), (E); child welfare agency records, A.R.S. § 8-519(C); grand jury proceedings, A.R.S. § 13-2812(A); Rules 12.8(c), 12.25(A), Ariz. R. Crim. P.; certain records of the Department of Health Services, A.R.S. § 36-404; Juvenile Court dispositions, A.R.S. § 8-207(C); investigations of the Division of Occupational Safety and Health, A.R.S. § 23-408(E); tax returns and reports, A.R.S. §§ 42-108, 42-223(B), 43-381; and, vital statistics records and information, A.R.S. § 36-340(A). The degree and duration of the protection granted to the records in question will depend on the phrasing of the statute involved. *Grossman v. Westmoreland II Investors*, 123 Ariz. 223, 599 P.2d 179 (1979); *Industrial Commission v. Superior Court In and For Maricopa County*, 122 Ariz. 374, 595 P.2d 166 (1979).

Rule 502. Attorney-Client Privilege and Work Product; Limitations on Waiver

The following provisions apply, in the circumstances set out, to disclosure of a communication or information covered by the attorney-client privilege or work-product protection:

(a) Disclosure made in an Arizona proceeding; scope of a waiver.

When the disclosure is made in an Arizona proceeding and waives the attorney-client privilege or work-product protection, the waiver extends to an undisclosed communication or information in an Arizona proceeding only if:

(1) the waiver is intentional;

(2) the disclosed and undisclosed communications or information concern the same subject matter; and

(3) they ought in fairness to be considered together.

(b) Inadvertent disclosure.

When made in an Arizona proceeding, the disclosure does not operate as a waiver in an Arizona proceeding if:

(1) the disclosure is inadvertent;

(2) the holder of the privilege or protection took reasonable steps to prevent disclosure; and

(3) the holder promptly took reasonable steps to rectify the error, including (if applicable) following Arizona Rule of Civil Procedure 26.1(f)(2).

(c) Disclosure made in a proceeding in federal court or another state.

When the disclosure is made in a proceeding in federal court or another state and is not the subject of a court order concerning waiver, the disclosure does not operate as a waiver in an Arizona proceeding if the disclosure:

(1) would not be a waiver under this rule if it had been made in an Arizona proceeding; or

(2) is not a waiver under the law governing the federal or state proceeding where the disclosure occurred.

(d) Controlling effect of a court order.

An Arizona court may order that the privilege is not waived by disclosure connected with the litigation pending before the court - in which event the disclosure is also not a waiver in any other proceeding.

(e) Controlling effect of a party agreement.

An agreement on the effect of disclosure in an Arizona proceeding is binding only on the parties to the agreement, unless it is incorporated into a court order.

(f) Definitions.

In this rule:

(1) "attorney-client privilege" means the protection that applicable law provides for confidential attorney-client communications: and

(2) "work-product protection" means the protection that applicable law provides for tangible material (or its intangible equivalent) prepared in anticipation of litigation or for trial.

Added Sept. 3, 2009, effective Jan. 1, 2010. Amended Sept. 8, 2011, effective Jan. 1, 2012.

AUTHORS' COMMENTS

Analysis

1. Scope and Purpose of Rule.
2. Comparison With Federal Rule.
3. Attorney-Client Privilege.
4. Work-Product Protection.

1. *Scope and Purpose of Rule.* One of the perhaps unanticipated consequences of our society's wholesale move into the "digital age" is that an increasing volume of discovery is directed to the production of "electronically stored information," which some estimate may now comprise almost 80% of the universe of documents subject to discovery. Cogent evidence indicates that counsel faced with a discovery request for such materials have felt compelled to conduct extensive, expensive and time-consuming reviews of such information out of a concern that the production of materials subject to the attorney-client privilege or entitled to work-product protection will be held to constitute the waiver of such privileges generally and will not be limited to the particular communications disclosed or their subject matter. This Rule addresses this problem for disclosures or production made in an "Arizona proceeding," and some federal proceedings. It is modeled on Rule 502 added to the Federal Rules of Evidence by legislation in 2009, and effectively abolishes the "general waiver" rule.

The Rule addresses both "intentional" and "inadvertent" disclosures of privileged materials. Under subpart (a) of the Rule, the "intentional" disclosures of a privileged communication will constitute a waiver of the privilege for undisclosed communications *only if* the disclosed and undisclosed communications or information concern the same subject matter and they ought in fairness to be considered together by the trier of fact.

Subpart (b) of the Rule provides that the inadvertent disclosure of privileged information or communications does not operate as a waiver of protection for undisclosed communications at all, *provided* the holder of the privilege took reasonable steps to prevent disclosure *and* the holder also took reasonable steps to rectify the error, including (if applicable) providing the notice and taking the other steps required by Rule 26.1(f)(2) of the Arizona Rules of Civil Procedure. *See also, Lund v. Myers*, 232 Ariz. 309, 305 P.3d 374 (2013).

Subpart (c) provides that, where the disclosure occurs in a proceeding in federal court or the court of another state, and there is no court order governing the waiver issue, it does not operate as a waiver in an Arizona proceeding if it would not have been a waiver in an Arizona proceeding by application of Rule 502 *or* if it is not a waiver under the law applicable to the federal or state proceeding where it occurred.

Subpart (d) provides that an Arizona court may order that a privilege is not waived by disclosure in litigation pending before it and that order controls the issue in any other proceeding. Subpart (e) authorizes parties to a proceeding to enter into agreements concerning the effect of disclosure of privileged materials, *but* such an agreement will only be binding on the parties to it *unless* it is incorporated into a court order.

2. *Comparison With Federal Rule.* As noted, Rule 502, Ariz.R.Evid is modeled on a provision added to the Federal Rules of Evidence legislatively as Rule 502, and the two Rules are substantially identical. The Arizona Rule is understandably limited to the impact of privilege waivers that take place in Arizona proceedings; the Federal Rule is not subject to such a limitation.

Although not noted by way of a Comment, effective January 1, 2012, the Arizona Supreme Court amended Ariz. R. Evid. 502 to conform to Fed. R. Evid. 502. The amendment consisted of inserting a hyphen between the words "work" and "product" in the text of the rule. The Arizona Supreme Court did not make that same stylistic amendment, however, to the title of Rule 502. That approach is consistent with the federal approach, which also did not hyphenate "work product" in the title to Rule 502.

3. *Attorney-Client Privilege.* The ancient common law privilege applicable to communications between counsel and client has been recognized in Arizona both by decisional law and by statute. A.R.S. §§ 12-2234; 13-4062(2). The purpose of the privilege is to protect advice given and/or information exchanged during the course of the attorney-client relationship and to encourage candor by the client with counsel. *Ulibarri v. Superior Court in and for County of Coconino*, 184 Ariz. 382, 909 P.2d 449 (Ct. App. Div. 1

1995), corrected, (Aug. 22, 1995). The privilege, accordingly, has been viewed as central to the effective delivery of legal services. *Samaritan Foundation v. Goodfarb*, 176 Ariz. 497, 862 P.2d 870, 26 A.L.R.5th 893 (1993).

Factual information communicated by the client to the lawyer is not necessarily immunized from discovery from the client. The privilege simply precludes compelling the lawyer to reveal it. *Zork Hardware Co. v. Gottlieb*, 170 Ariz. 5, 821 P.2d 272 (Ct. App. Div. 2 1991); *Certainteed Corp. v. United Pacific Ins. Co.*, 158 Ariz. 273, 762 P.2d 560 (Ct. App. Div. 2 1988). Thus, the transmittal of pre-existing documents to counsel does not make them subject to the attorney-client privilege. *State ex rel. Corbin v. Weaver*, 140 Ariz. 123, 680 P.2d 833 (Ct. App. Div. 2 1984). Similarly, the privilege does not protect information learned by the lawyer from third parties. *Granger v. Wisner*, 134 Ariz. 377, 656 P.2d 1238 (1982). Ariz.R.Civ.P. 26.1, accordingly, does not remove or override the attorney-client privilege, or any other privilege. *Samaritan Foundation v. Goodfarb*, 176 Ariz. 497, 862 P.2d 870, 26 A.L.R.5th 893 (1993). A client who has a duty to disclose facts in discovery is not relieved of that duty simply because those facts have been communicated to a lawyer. *Samaritan Foundation v. Goodfarb*, 176 Ariz. 497, 862 P.2d 870, 26 A.L.R. 5th 893 (1993).

The applicability of the privilege is not destroyed by the fact that the communication from the client is revealed by the lawyer to clerical employees, or by their presence when the communication takes place. The statute itself extends the privilege's protection to a lawyer's "secretary, stenographer or clerk." Recognizing the modern realities of the practice of law and the necessary role of nonlawyer assistants in it, the Court of Appeals has held that the privilege extends to a client's confidential communications to a lawyer's paralegal or secretary. *Smart Industries Corp., Mfg. v. Superior Court In and For County of Yuma*, 179 Ariz. 141, 876 P.2d 1176 (Ct. App. Div. 1 1994); *Samaritan Foundation v. Superior Court In and For County of Maricopa*, 173 Ariz. 426, 844 P.2d 593 (Ct. App. Div. 1 1992), aff'd in part, vacated in part, 176 Ariz. 497, 862 P.2d 870, 26 A.L.R.5th 893 (1993). On the other hand, information which is provided by an insured to an insurance adjuster is not privileged, even if it is to be transmitted to a lawyer retained to defend the insured. *Longs Drug Stores v. Howe*, 134 Ariz. 424, 657 P.2d 412 (1983); *Butler v. Doyle*, 112 Ariz. 522, 544 P.2d 204 (1975); *State v. Superior Court, In and For Pima County*, 120 Ariz. 501, 586 P.2d 1313 (Ct. App. Div. 2 1978).

The privilege extends to communications made in confidence for the purposes of obtaining legal advice, even if an attorney-client relationship is not eventually formed. *Alexander v. Superior*

Court In and For Maricopa County, 141 Ariz. 157, 685 P.2d 1309 (1984); *State ex rel. Corbin v. Weaver*, 140 Ariz. 123, 680 P.2d 833 (Ct. App. Div. 2 1984).

Consultations with a lawyer to secure personal or business advice, however, are not within the scope of the privilege. *G & S Investments v. Belman*, 145 Ariz. 258, 700 P.2d 1358 (Ct. App. Div. 2 1984); *State ex rel. Corbin v. Weaver*, 140 Ariz. 123, 680 P.2d 833 (Ct. App. Div. 2 1984). The privilege also will not apply to communications which are made in furtherance of a crime or fraud. *Buell v. Superior Court of Maricopa County*, 96 Ariz. 62, 391 P.2d 919 (1964); *Pearce v. Stone*, 149 Ariz. 567, 720 P.2d 542 (Ct. App. Div. 1 1986). The "crime-fraud" exception to the privilege will only be applied, however, where there is a *prima facie* showing that the attorney was retained by the client for the express purpose of promoting intended or continuing criminal or fraudulent activity. *State v. Fodor*, 179 Ariz. 442, 880 P.2d 662 (Ct. App. Div. 1 1994). A party relying on this exception need not establish actual fraud by clear and convincing evidence; the party need only present *prima facie* evidence to show that the charge has some foundation in fact. *Kline v. Kline*, 221 Ariz. 564, 212 P.3d 902 (Ct. App. Div. 1 2009).

Two situations which have presented difficult issues of determining the identity of the client and which communications are privileged are where the lawyer undertakes (1) joint representation of multiple clients and/or (2) the representation of corporate clients. In the case of joint representation of multiple clients with respect to a matter, communications with the lawyer will not be privileged as between the joint clients, but will be as against third parties. *Alexander v. Superior Court In and For Maricopa County*, 141 Ariz. 157, 685 P.2d 1309 (1984); *Hellyer v. Hellyer*, 129 Ariz. 453, 632 P.2d 263 (Ct. App. Div. 2 1981); *Hahman v. Hahman*, 129 Ariz. 101, 628 P.2d 984 (Ct. App. Div. 2 1981); *Nichols v. Elkins*, 2 Ariz. App. 272, 408 P.2d 34 (1965).

The scope of the attorney-client privilege where the client is a corporate entity was addressed comprehensively by the Arizona Supreme Court in its decision in *Samaritan Foundation v. Goodfarb*, 176 Ariz. 497, 862 P.2d 870, 26 A.L.R.5th 893 (1993). The Court held that, in order to determine whether communications between corporate employees and counsel for the corporation will qualify for the corporation's attorney-client privilege, the relevant inquiry concerns the nature and purpose of the communication rather than the identity or position of the corporate employee involved. *Samaritan Foundation v. Goodfarb*, 176 Ariz. 497, 862 P.2d 870, 26 A.L.R.5th 893 (1993).

All communications initiated by the employee and made in confidence to counsel in which the communicating employee is directly seeking to secure or evaluate legal advice for the corporation, will be privileged. *Samaritan Foundation v. Goodfarb*, 176 Ariz. 497, 862 P.2d 870, 26 A.L.R.5th 893 (1993). Where someone other than the employee initiates the communication, a factual communication by a corporate employee to corporate counsel will be within the corporation's privilege only if it concerns the employee's own conduct within the scope of his or her own employment and is made to assist the lawyer in assessing or responding to the legal consequences of that conduct for that corporate client. *Samaritan Foundation v. Goodfarb*, 176 Ariz. 497, 862 P.2d 870, 26 A.L.R.5th 893 (1993). The Court was quite specific that counsel's self-initiated interviews of corporate officers, agents or employees who were mere witnesses to events of legal significance to the corporation, would not qualify for the corporation's attorney-client privilege. *Samaritan Foundation v. Goodfarb*, 176 Ariz. 497, 862 P.2d 870, 26 A.L.R.5th 893 (1993).

A subsequent legislative amendment to A.R.S. § 12-2234, the statutory codification of the attorney-client privilege in civil cases, however, makes all communications between corporate counsel and a corporate officer, employee or agent privileged if they were (1) for the purpose of providing legal advice to either the corporation or to the employee, or (2) for the purpose of obtaining information in order to provide such legal advice. This legislative redefinition of the scope of the privilege differs from that adopted by the Court in *Samaritan Foundation* in its treatment as privileged of the one category of communications which the Court specifically found not to qualify for privileged status—counsel's interviews of corporate employees or agents who are mere witnesses to events. *Samaritan Foundation v. Goodfarb*, 176 Ariz. 497, 862 P.2d 870, 26 A.L.R.5th 893 (1993). The statute which defines the scope of the privilege in criminal cases, A.R.S. § 13-4062(2), was not similarly amended. Accordingly, the scope of the attorney-client privilege for corporations in criminal cases is defined by A.R.S. § 13-4062(2) and the *Samaritan Foundation* decision. *Roman Catholic Diocese of Phoenix v. Superior Court ex rel. County of Maricopa*, 204 Ariz. 225, 62 P.3d 970 (Ct. App. Div. 1 2003).

In assessing whether a city attorney's communications with city officers or employees will be protected by the city's attorney-client privilege, Arizona follows a functional approach. *State ex rel. Thomas v. Schneider*, 212 Ariz. 292, 130 P.3d 991 (Ct. App. Div. 1 2006). If the communication concerns the employee's own conduct within the scope of employment and is made to assist the lawyer in assessing or responding to the legal consequences of that conduct, then the communication falls within the city's privilege. *State ex rel. Thomas v. Schneider*, 212 Ariz. 292, 130 P.3d 991 (Ct. App. Div. 1 2006).

The attorney-client privilege is waived if the client voluntarily testifies to communications subject to the privilege. *Alexander v. Superior Court In and For Maricopa County*, 141 Ariz. 157, 685 P.2d 1309 (1984); *Tripp v. Chubb*, 69 Ariz. 31, 208 P.2d 312 (1949); A.R.S. § 12-2234. Waiver may also result where the client injects into the dispute the advice of counsel as a basis for acting. *Elia v. Pifer*, 194 Ariz. 74, 977 P.2d 796 (Ct. App. Div. 1 1998); *Ulibarri v. Superior Court in and for County of Coconino*, 184 Ariz. 382, 909 P.2d 449 (Ct. App. Div. 1 1995), corrected, (Aug. 22, 1995). The privilege can also be waived by the client's failure to object to testimony by the attorney as to privileged matters. *United California Bank v. Prudential Ins. Co. of America*, 140 Ariz. 238, 681 P.2d 390 (Ct. App. Div. 1 1983). There is an implied waiver of the privilege where the client legally attacks the quality of the lawyer's representation. *State v. Zuck*, 134 Ariz. 509, 658 P.2d 162 (1982); *Waitkus v. Mauet*, 157 Ariz. 339, 757 P.2d 615 (Ct. App. Div. 2 1988). The privilege may also be waived by showing privileged materials to a witness to refresh the witness' recollection, and thereby making them subject to production under Rule 612. *Samaritan Health Services, Inc. v. Superior Court In and For Maricopa County*, 142 Ariz. 435, 690 P.2d 154 (Ct. App. Div. 1 1984).

There are several competing tests for when there has been an implied waiver of the attorney-client privilege. Under the restrictive approach, the privilege is not deemed waived unless the holder of the privilege has expressly waived it or has impliedly waived it by directly injecting the advice of counsel as an issue in litigation. The intermediate test, which is the one followed in Arizona, considers the following factors: (1) assertion of the privilege was a result of some affirmative act, such as filing suit or raising an affirmative defense by the asserting party; (2) that affirmative act put the protected information at issue by making it relevant; and, (3) application of the privilege would deprive a party of information vital to a claim or defense.

Essentially, a party will not be allowed to assert the privilege when doing so places the claimant in such a position, with reference to the evidence, that it would be unfair and inconsistent to permit the privilege to be asserted. *Twin City Fire Ins. Co. v. Burke*, 204 Ariz. 251, 63 P.3d 282 (2003); *State Farm Mut. Auto. Ins. Co. v. Lee*, 199 Ariz. 52, 13 P.3d 1169 (2000). Where a party claims that its actions were both objectively and subjectively reasonable and taken in good faith based on its evaluation of the law, and part of that evaluation included receiving advice from counsel, that party may not assert privilege as a bar to prevent discovery of the information, including communications with counsel, in the party's possession when they made the determination that their actions were permitted by law. *Twin City Fire Ins.*

Co. v. Burke, 204 Ariz. 251, 63 P.3d 282 (2003); *State Farm Mut. Auto. Ins. Co. v. Lee*, 199 Ariz. 52, 13 P.3d 1169 (2000).

There is now a specific rule, Ariz.R.Civ.P. 26.1(f)(2) (2008), that specifies the procedures to be followed where a party contends that information subject to a claim of privilege or protection has been inadvertently disclosed or produced in discovery. Similarly, Ariz. R. Civ. P. 45(c)(5)(C)(ii) (2011), which is substantially identical to Rule 26.1(f)(2), concerns the inadvertent production of documents in response to a subpoena. *See also, Lund v. Myers*, 232 Ariz. 309, 305 P.3d 374 (2013).

Lund concerned the inadvertent production of documents claimed to be subject to attorney-client privilege. Interpreting Ariz. R. Civ. P. 26.1(f)(2), the Arizona Supreme Court held the filing under seal of inadvertently disclosed documents with the trial court did not constitute an impermissible "use" of documents, as that word is used in the rule.

The *Lund* Court then addressed the issue of when, in deciding issues of privilege and waiver, a trial court may conduct an in camera inspection of the allegedly privileged documents inadvertently disclosed or produced. The Court held as follows:

1. As to each document at issue, the trial court first must determine whether in camera inspection is needed to resolve a claim of privilege. The trial court makes this determination based on its consideration of the privilege log, the opposing party's response to such privilege log and the parties' arguments on the issues of privilege and waiver.

2. If the trial court determines such in camera review is necessary, the trial court then must decide who will conduct such in camera review of the allegedly privileged documents: the trial judge or another judicial officer. If the trial judge conducts the in camera inspection and upholds the claim of privilege, the trial judge then will need to consider recusal or face a possible Rule 42(f) challenge based on claims of bias resulting from the review of such privileged documents.

Lund v. Myers, 232 Ariz. 309, 305 P.3d 374 (2013). Ariz. R. Civ. P. 45(c)(5)(C)(ii) is substantially identical to Ariz. R. Civ. P. 26.1(f)(2).

4. *Work-Product Doctrine.* Rule 26(b)(3) represents a partial codification of the work-product doctrine enunciated in *Hickman v. Taylor*, 329 U.S. 495, 67 S. Ct. 385, 91 L. Ed. 451, 1947 A.M.C. 1 (1947), and its progeny. *Cf. Dean v. Superior Court In and For Maricopa County*, 84 Ariz. 104, 324 P.2d 764, 73 A.L.R.2d 1 (1958); *Emergency Care Dynamics, Ltd. v. Superior Court In and For County of Maricopa*, 188 Ariz. 32, 932 P.2d 297, 1997-2 Trade Cas. (CCH) ¶ 71929 (Ct. App. Div. 1 1997). The work-product doctrine is intended to preserve the integrity of the adversary

system of litigation and to permit attorneys to adequately prepare for trial without fear that the results of their efforts will be available to their adversaries through discovery. *Brown v. Superior Court In and For Maricopa County*, 137 Ariz. 327, 670 P.2d 725 (1983).

Under Rule 26(b)(3), limited protection is afforded to documents and tangible things "prepared in anticipation of litigation or for trial by or for another party or by or for that other party's representative.. . ." An expert retained by counsel or by the client at counsel's direction to investigate and produce reports on technical aspects of specific litigation is considered part of the lawyer's investigative staff and the opinions and theories of such an expert constitute protectible work-product. *State ex rel. Corbin v. Ybarra*, 161 Ariz. 188, 777 P.2d 686 (1989). This does not mean, however, that all materials generated by counsel, or at counsel's direction, will be entitled to protection. *Zimmerman v. Superior Court In and For Maricopa County*, 98 Ariz. 85, 402 P.2d 212, 18 A.L.R.3d 909 (1965). For example, the "work-product" doctrine does not immunize from discovery a lawyer's written or oral communications with an expert who has been hired to provide expert testimony, even if that expert has also been retained to consult with counsel as well. *Emergency Care Dynamics, Ltd. v. Superior Court In and For County of Maricopa*, 188 Ariz. 32, 932 P.2d 297, 1997-2 Trade Cas. (CCH) ¶ 71929 (Ct. App. Div. 1 1997). Such communications may be protected, however, if the expert is only a consulting, and not a testimonial, expert. *Emergency Care Dynamics, Ltd. v. Superior Court In and For County of Maricopa*, 188 Ariz. 32, 932 P.2d 297, 1997-2 Trade Cas. (CCH) ¶ 71929 (Ct. App. Div. 1 1997).

A party waives the work-product protection ordinarily afforded the work of a consulting expert when the party designates that expert to testify at trial. *Green v. Nygaard*, 213 Ariz. 460, 143 P.3d 393 (Ct. App. Div. 2 2006). That work-product protection can be reinstated by removing that designation before expert opinion evidence is offered from that witness through production of a report, responses to discovery or expert testimony. *Green v. Nygaard*, 213 Ariz. 460, 143 P.3d 393 (Ct. App. Div. 2 2006); *Arizona Minority Coalition for Fair Redistricting v. Arizona Independent Redistricting Com'n*, 211 Ariz. 337, 121 P.3d 843 (Ct. App. Div. 1 2005). It can also be restored by withdrawing an expert witness designation after that expert has testified for a limited purpose during a pretrial hearing and after the parties have resolved by stipulation the matter on which the expert previously testified. *Green v. Nygaard*, 213 Ariz. 460, 143 P.3d 393 (Ct. App. Div. 2 2006).

Whether the work-product doctrine applies is determined by the nature of the document and the factual setting of its preparation, whether it contains analyses or opinions or purely factual data, and whether it was requested or prepared at the specific instance of the party or an attorney or in the ordinary course of business. *State ex rel. Corbin v. Weaver*, 140 Ariz. 123, 680 P.2d 833 (Ct. App. Div. 2 1984); *Brown v. Superior Court In and For Maricopa County*, 137 Ariz. 327, 670 P.2d 725 (1983); *Accomazzo v. Kemp, ex rel. County of Maricopa*, ___ P.3d ___, 2014 WL 222783 (Ct. App. Div. 1 2014) ("To the extent that documents or other tangible items reflect [an attorney's] mental impressions, the work-product doctrine provides those items absolute protection from discovery."); *Salvation Army v. Bryson*, 229 Ariz. 204, 273 P.3d 656 (Ct. App. Div. 2 2012) (a claim of attorney-client privilege "makes a discussion of substantial need and unavailability of the substantial equivalent irrelevant."), citing *Butler v. Doyle*, 112 Ariz. 522, 544 P.2d 204; *State ex rel. Corbin v. Weaver*, 140 Ariz. 123, 680 P.2d 833 (Ct. App. Div. 2 1984).

The privilege accorded such materials is a qualified privilege, but disclosure of trial preparation materials may be had only upon a dual showing by the party seeking disclosure: (1) that there is a substantial need for the materials sought, and (2) that the party cannot obtain the substantial equivalent of the materials by other means without undue hardship. In the case of a party seeking production of witness interviews or statements, the fact that the witnesses have testified to conflicting versions of the same events may be sufficient. *Klaiber v. Orzel*, 148 Ariz. 320, 714 P.2d 813 (1986); *but cf. Lumber Country, Inc. v. Superior Court of State In and For Maricopa County*, 155 Ariz. 98, 745 P.2d 156 (Ct. App. Div. 1 1987). Similarly, the fact that the statements in question were taken shortly after the events in question may give them a unique character which in and of itself justifies production. *Longs Drug Stores v. Howe*, 134 Ariz. 424, 657 P.2d 412 (1983); *Butler v. Doyle*, 112 Ariz. 522, 544 P.2d 204 (1975). Even where the requisite showing is made to warrant the compelled production of trial preparation materials, special additional protection is given to "the mental impressions, conclusions, opinions or legal theories of an attorney or other representative of a party . . .". Ariz.R.Civ.P. 26(b)(3) specifically admonishes the Court to guard against disclosure of such materials. *Longs Drug Stores v. Howe*, 134 Ariz. 424, 657 P.2d 412 (1983); *Accomazzo v. Kemp, ex rel. County of Maricopa*, ___ P.3d ___, 2014 WL 222783 (Ct. App. Div. 1 2014) ("To the extent that documents or other tangible items reflect [an attorney's] mental impressions, the work-product doctrine provides those items absolute protection from discovery.").

There is now a specific rule, Ariz.R.Civ.P. 26.1(f)(2) 2008, that specifies the procedures to be followed where a party contends that information subject to a claim of privilege or protection has been inadvertently disclosed or produced in discovery. Ariz. R. Civ. P. 45(c)(5)(C)(ii) (2011), which is substantially identical to Rule 26.1(f)(2), concerns the inadvertent production of documents in response to a subpoena. *See also, Lund v. Myers*, 232 Ariz. 309, 305 P.3d 374 (2013).

Lund concerned the inadvertent production of documents claimed to be subject to attorney-client privilege. Interpreting Ariz. R. Civ. P. 26.1(f)(2), the Arizona Supreme Court held the filing under seal of inadvertently disclosed documents with the trial court did not constitute impermissible "use" of documents, as that word is used in the rule.

The *Lund* Court then addressed the issue of when, in deciding issues of privilege and waiver, a trial court may conduct an in camera inspection of the allegedly privileged documents inadvertently disclosed or produced. The Court held as follows:

1. As to each document at issue, the trial court first must determine whether in camera inspection is needed to resolve a claim of privilege. The trial court makes this determination based on its consideration of the privilege log, the opposing party's response to such privilege log and the parties' arguments on the issues of privilege and waiver.
2. If the trial court determines such in camera review is necessary, the trial court then must decide who will conduct such in camera review of the allegedly privileged documents: the trial judge or another judicial officer. If the trial judge conducts the in camera inspection and upholds the claim of privilege, the trial judge then will need to consider recusal or face a possible Rule 42(f) challenge based on claims of bias resulting from the review of such privileged documents.

Ariz. R. Civ. P. 45(c)(5)(C)(ii) is substantially identical to Ariz. R. Civ. P. 26.1(f)(2). Thus, the holding in *Lund* likely would apply in the case of privileged documents allegedly produced in response to a subpoena.

ARTICLE VI. WITNESSES

Rule 601. Competency to Testify in General

Every person is competent to be a witness unless these rules or an applicable statute provides otherwise.

Amended Sept. 8, 2011, effective Jan. 1, 2012.

Comment to 2012 Amendment

The language of Rule 601 has been amended to conform to the federal restyling of the Evidence Rules to make them more easily understood and to make style and terminology consistent throughout the rules. These changes are intended to be stylistic only. There is no intent to change any result in any ruling on evidence admissibility.

AUTHORS' COMMENTS

Analysis

1. Scope and Purpose of Rule.
2. Comparison With Federal Rule.
3. Statutory Abolition of Common Law Disqualifications of Witnesses.
4. Persons of Unsound Mind and Minor Children.
5. The Dead Man's Statute.

1. *Scope and Purpose of Rule.* Rule 601 preserves existing rules concerning the competency of witnesses, by providing that all persons are competent to serve as witnesses except as provided by statute or by the Rules of Evidence. A "witness" is defined by Ariz.R.Civ.P. 43(a) to include any person whose declaration under oath is received as evidence for any purpose, whether by oral examination, by deposition or by affidavit.

2. *Comparison With Federal Rule.* Effective January 1, 2012, the Arizona Supreme Court amended Ariz.R.Evid. 601 to conform to the federal restyling of the Evidence Rules to make the rules more easily understood and to make style and terminology consistent throughout. The 2012 Comment states the stylistic amendments are not intended to "change any result in any ruling on evidence admissibility."

Following the 2012 amendments, Rule 601 and Fed. R. Evid. 601 remain slightly different. The Arizona Rule authorizes exceptions to the general rule of universal competency to be created "by statute." The Federal Rule has no such provision. In addition, Arizona understandably did not adopt the second sentence of the Federal Rule, which requires the application of state law concerning the competence of witnesses in civil actions involving claims or defenses governed by state law.

3. *Statutory Abolition of Common Law Disqualifications of Witnesses.* A.R.S. § 12-2201(A) provides that every person, including a party, may testify in any civil or criminal proceeding, except as otherwise provided by law. Rules 605 and 606, however, operate to disqualify the trial judge and trial jurors as witnesses in the action in which they are sitting in that capacity. Similarly, by case law, a member of the Arizona Legislature is not competent to testify regarding the intent of the Legislature in passing a law. *Golder v. Department of Revenue, State Bd. of Tax Appeals*, 123 Ariz. 260, 599 P.2d 216 (1979); *City of Tucson v. Woods*, 191 Ariz. 523, 959 P.2d 394 (Ct. App. Div. 1 1997).

A.R.S. § 12-2201(B) abolishes the common law disqualifications for parties, persons with an interest in the proceedings or the outcome, and persons accused or convicted of a crime. It also precludes finding a witness incompetent to testify on the basis of that person's religious beliefs or lack thereof. Consistently therewith, under both Rule 603 and Ariz.R.Civ.P. 43(b), a solemn affirmation to tell the truth may be accepted from a witness in lieu of an oath. A.R.S. § 13-4061 simply provides that every person is competent to be a witness in a criminal trial.

Except in the case of minors, discussed in Section 4 *infra,* a person is presumed to be competent to testify as a witness in a civil proceeding, and competency is to be determined at the time testimony is given. *Zimmer v. Peters*, 176 Ariz. 426, 861 P.2d 1188 (Ct. App. Div. 1 1993). There is a notable distinction between competency and credibility. Competency, which is a question of law for the Court, involves only a very limited inquiry into a witness' capacity or ability to observe, recollect and communicate with reference to the events that are the subject of the witness' testimony. *Zimmer v. Peters*, 176 Ariz. 426, 861 P.2d 1188 (Ct. App. Div. 1 1993). Credibility, on the other hand, is a question to be determined by the trier of fact, and examines the reliability of the witness' testimony. In general, when a proposed witness' competency is called into question, discretion should be exercised in favor of allowing the witness to testify, and a determination as to a witness' competency will not be overturned absent an abuse of discretion. *Zimmer v. Peters*, 176 Ariz. 426, 861 P.2d 1188 (Ct. App. Div. 1 1993). A trial court should not, however, preclude a witness from testifying without first having conducted a meaningful inquiry into the witness' competency and it is an abuse of discretion to do so. *Zimmer v. Peters*, 176 Ariz. 426, 861 P.2d 1188 (Ct. App. Div. 1 1993).

Prior common law disqualifications of witnesses are now only matters that may be used to impeach a witness' credibility, and affect only the weight to be accorded the witness' testimony, not its competence or admissibility. *Schornick v. Schornick*, 25 Ariz. 563, 220 P. 397, 31 A.L.R. 159 (1923); *Maricopa County v. Barkley*, 168 Ariz. 234, 812 P.2d 1052 (Ct. App. Div. 1 1990).

4. *Persons of Unsound Mind and Minor Children.* A.R.S. § 12-2202 provides that persons of unsound mind, and children under ten (10) years of age who appear incapable of receiving just impressions of the facts or of relating them truthfully, may not be witnesses in civil cases. The corresponding provisions in the statute applicable to criminal cases, A.R.S. § 13-4061, were removed in 1985.

Even in civil cases, the prohibition is neither absolute nor automatic. The trial court must determine the competence of such witnesses to testify after an inquiry conducted outside the presence and hearing of the jury. *Montgomery Elevator Co. v. Superior Court of State, In and For Maricopa County*, 135 Ariz. 432, 661 P.2d 1133 (1983); *State v. Brown*, 102 Ariz. 87, 425 P.2d 112 (1967); *Davis v. Weber*, 93 Ariz. 312, 380 P.2d 608 (1963). The trial judge's determinations as to the competency of witnesses will be disturbed on appeal only for an abuse of discretion. *Zimmer v. Peters*, 176 Ariz. 426, 861 P.2d 1188 (Ct. App. Div. 1 1993); *Tanner Companies v. Arizona State Land Dept.*, 142 Ariz. 183, 688 P.2d 1075 (Ct. App. Div. 2 1984).

In civil cases, children under ten (10) years of age are only presumed to be incompetent to serve as witnesses. That presumption, however can be rebutted by a showing that permits the trial judge to find the witness competent. *State v. Schossow*, 145 Ariz. 504, 703 P.2d 448 (1985). Even if no objection is raised, the trial court has a mandatory duty to question the minor witness' competence and to examine such witnesses to determine if they have the requisite mental capacity to understand, recall and relate their knowledge and observations truthfully and accurately. *Toney v. Bouthillier*, 129 Ariz. 402, 631 P.2d 557 (Ct. App. Div. 1 1981). A witness cannot be rejected as incompetent to testify purely on the basis of age. *Litzkuhn v. Clark*, 85 Ariz. 355, 339 P.2d 389 (1959).

The rule, and the required procedure, is now different in criminal cases due to the 1985 revision to A.R.S. § 13-4061, which provides for universal competence of witnesses. The revision repealed, for criminal cases, the presumption that a child under ten (10) years of age was incompetent as a witness, and removed the duty of the trial court to question and determine such a minor witness' competence. Whether to do so is now discretionary with the trial court. *Escobar v. Superior Court of State of Ariz. In and For Maricopa County*, 155 Ariz. 298, 746 P.2d 39 (Ct. App. Div. 1 1987); *State v. Superior Court In and For Pima County*, 149 Ariz.

397, 719 P.2d 283, 60 A.L.R.4th 353 (Ct. App. Div. 2 1986).

5. *The Dead Man's Statute.* A.R.S. § 12-2251 provides that, in an action by or against a personal representative or guardian, neither party may testify to any transaction or communication with the decedent or ward. Despite its facial breadth, the statute is of limited application, and subject to numerous exceptions.

The statute does not apply where the witness is called by the opposing party, or required to testify by the Court. *Bostwick v. Jasin*, 170 Ariz. 15, 821 P.2d 282 (Ct. App. Div. 2 1991). The trial court also has discretion to admit such testimony where, in the trial court's judgment, there is sufficient corroborating evidence or when the interests of justice require. *Fridena v. Evans*, 127 Ariz. 516, 622 P.2d 463, 12 A.L.R.4th 46 (1980); *Condos v. Felder*, 92 Ariz. 366, 377 P.2d 305 (1962); *Estate of Page v. Litzenburg*, 177 Ariz. 84, 865 P.2d 128 (Ct. App. Div. 1 1993); *Mahan v. First Nat. Bank of Arizona*, 139 Ariz. 138, 677 P.2d 301 (Ct. App. Div. 1 1984); *Matter of Mustonen's Estate*, 130 Ariz. 283, 635 P.2d 876 (Ct. App. Div. 2 1981); *Cachenos v. Baumann*, 25 Ariz. App. 502, 544 P.2d 1103 (Div. 1 1976). It may even be an abuse of that discretion to exclude such testimony when an injustice thereby results. *Estate of Calligaro v. Owen*, 159 Ariz. 498, 768 P.2d 660 (Ct. App. Div. 1 1988); *G & S Investments v. Belman*, 145 Ariz. 258, 700 P.2d 1358 (Ct. App. Div. 2 1984).

The statute only applies in actions involving third parties in which the personal representative or guardian is suing or being sued in that capacity. *Carrillo v. Taylor*, 81 Ariz. 14, 299 P.2d 188 (1956); *Robson v. Daily*, 61 Ariz. 225, 147 P.2d 491 (1944). Thus, it does not apply to will contests and other matters that are heard in the probate action itself. *In re Welch's Estate*, 60 Ariz. 215, 134 P.2d 701 (1943). Finally, the statute does not preclude testimony to an independent fact that does not involve a transaction or communication with the ward or decedent. *Kerwin v. Bank of Douglas*, 93 Ariz. 269, 379 P.2d 978, 13 A.L.R.3d 398 (1963); *Estate of Calligaro v. Owen*, 159 Ariz. 498, 768 P.2d 660 (Ct. App. Div. 1 1988).

Rule 602. Need for Personal Knowledge

A witness may testify to a matter only if evidence is introduced sufficient to support a finding that the witness has personal knowledge of the matter. Evidence to prove personal knowledge may consist of the witness's own testimony. This rule does not apply to a witness's expert testimony under Rule 703.

Amended Oct. 19, 1988, effective Nov. 1, 1988; Sept. 8, 2011, effective Jan. 1, 2012.

Comment to 2012 Amendment

The language of Rule 602 has been amended to conform to the federal restyling of the Evidence Rules to make them more easily understood and to make style and terminology consistent throughout the rules. These changes are intended to be stylistic only. There is no intent to change any result in any ruling on evidence admissibility.

AUTHORS' COMMENTS

Analysis

1. Scope and Purpose of Rule.
2. Comparison With Federal Rule.
3. Foundational Requirements for Witnesses.
4. Negative Evidence; Foundation Required.
5. Hypnotically Induced Recollection.

1. *Scope and Purpose of Rule.* Rule 602 states the well established rule that a witness who testifies to factual matters that can be perceived by the senses must have actually observed the matters testified to. Except in the case of expert witnesses, whose testimony is governed by Rules 702 and 703, the testimony of a witness must be based on that witness' personal observation of and/or participation in events, and not on the reports of others. *Selby v. Savard*, 134 Ariz. 222, 655 P.2d 342 (1982).

2. *Comparison With Federal Rule.* Effective January 1, 2012, the Arizona Supreme Court amended Rule 602 to conform to the federal restyling of the Evidence Rules to make the rules more easily understood and to make style and terminology consistent throughout. The 2012 Comment states the stylistic amendments are not intended to "change any result in any ruling on evidence admissibility."

Following the 2012 restyling amendments, the language of Rule 602 remains identical to its federal counterpart, Fed. R. Evid. 602.

Although Rule 602 parallels its federal counterpart, "federal

court decisions interpreting the federal rule are persuasive but not binding with respect to interpreting the Arizona rule." *See,* Prefatory Comment to 2012 Amendments. *See also, State v. Terrazas*, 189 Ariz. 580, 944 P.2d 1194 (1997) (The Arizona Supreme Court is "not bound by the United States Supreme Court's non-constitutional construction of the Federal Rules of Evidence when [the Arizona Supreme Court construes] the Arizona Rules of Evidence."), citing, *State v. Bible*, 175 Ariz. 549, 858 P.2d 1152 (1993); *State v. Salazar-Mercado*, 232 Ariz. 256, 304 P.3d 543 (Ct. App. Div. 2 2013). Practitioners are urged to keep this legal tenet in mind as they research federal case law interpreting a federal evidentiary rule that corresponds to an Arizona evidentiary rule.

3. *Foundational Requirements for Witnesses.* As a general rule, a witness' lack of first hand knowledge of events or conditions renders that witness' testimony about them incompetent. *Selby v. Savard*, 134 Ariz. 222, 655 P.2d 342 (1982); *Evans v. Bernhard*, 23 Ariz. App. 413, 533 P.2d 721 (Div. 1 1975). Before a witness is permitted to testify about facts or events, there must be evidence that the witness observed them or had the opportunity to observe them. Such a showing, commonly referred to as "foundation," may be made, but need not be, by the witness' own testimony.

4. *Negative Evidence; Foundation Required.* Most evidence is positive evidence, *i.e.,* testimony of witnesses concerning events which they observed or in which they participated. Negative evidence, *e.g.,* testimony that a witness did *not* observe the occurrence of a particular event or transaction, has probative value only when supported by sufficient foundation that the position of the witness was such that the witness would have observed the event or transaction had it taken place. *Mast v. Standard Oil Co. of California*, 140 Ariz. 1, 680 P.2d 137 (1984); *Alires v. Southern Pac. Co.*, 100 Ariz. 6, 409 P.2d 714 (1966); *Jeune v. Del E. Webb Const. Co.*, 76 Ariz. 418, 265 P.2d 1076 (1954); *Byars v. Arizona Public Service Co.*, 24 Ariz. App. 420, 539 P.2d 534 (Div. 1 1975).

5. *Hypnotically Induced Recollection.* The hypnotically induced recollections of a witness are not admissible in either civil or criminal cases. *State ex rel. Collins v. Superior Court, In and For Maricopa County*, 132 Ariz. 180, 644 P.2d 1266 (1982); *Lemieux v. Superior Court of Arizona In and For Maricopa County*, 132 Ariz. 214, 644 P.2d 1300, 31 A.L.R.4th 1231 (1982). A witness who has been hypnotized to refresh recollection may testify as to matters that the witness was able to recall and relate before undergoing such hypnosis, provided the matters were recorded before hypnosis in a written, taped or videotaped statement. *State ex rel. Neely v. Sherrill*, 165 Ariz. 508, 799 P.2d 849 (1990); *State ex rel. Collins v. Superior Court, In and For Maricopa County*, 132 Ariz. 180, 644 P.2d 1266 (1982); *Lemieux v. Superior Court of Arizona In and For Maricopa County*, 132 Ariz. 214, 644 P.2d

1300, 31 A.L.R.4th 1231 (1982). The party offering the hypnotically refreshed testimony must have made an appropriate record, by written statement, tape recording or (preferably) videotape, of the substance of the witness' prehypnotic knowledge and recollection so that that recall can be shown. *Ulibarri v. Gerstenberger*, 178 Ariz. 151, 871 P.2d 698 (Ct. App. Div. 1 1993) (rejected on other grounds by, Logerquist v. Danforth, 188 Ariz. 16, 932 P.2d 281 (Ct. App. Div. 2 1996)).

Rule 603. Oath or Affirmation to Testify Truthfully

Before testifying, a witness must give an oath or affirmation to testify truthfully. It must be in a form designed to impress that duty on the witness's conscience.

Amended Oct. 19, 1988, effective Nov. 1, 1988; Sept. 8, 2011, effective Jan. 1, 2012.

Comment to 2012 Amendment

The language of Rule 603 has been amended to conform to the federal restyling of the Evidence Rules to make them more easily understood and to make style and terminology consistent throughout the rules. These changes are intended to be stylistic only. There is no intent to change any result in any ruling on evidence admissibility.

AUTHORS' COMMENTS

Analysis

1. *Scope and Purpose of Rule.* Rule 603 requires that a witness, before testifying, take an oath or solemn affirmation to testify truthfully. In Arizona, this requirement is constitutional in origin. Ariz. Const. Art. 2, Sec. 7. Consistent with the modern view that a witness' religious beliefs, or lack thereof, are not dispositive of a witness' competence to testify, a solemn affirmation may be accepted in lieu of an oath. Ariz.R.Civ.P. 43(b); A.R.S. § 1-215(22). The oath or affirmation, however, is taken or made under penalty of perjury. A.R.S. § 12-2221(A). Any irregularity in the swearing of a witness, or in failing to do so, is waived if the witness then proceeds to testify without objection. *State v. Navarro*, 132 Ariz. 340, 645 P.2d 1254 (Ct. App. Div. 2 1982).

2. *Comparison With Federal Rule.* Effective January 1, 2012, the Arizona Supreme Court amended Rule 603 to conform to the federal restyling of the Evidence Rules to make the rules more easily understood and to make style and terminology consistent throughout. The 2012 Comment states the stylistic amendments are not intended to "change any result in any ruling on evidence admissibility."

Following the 2012 restyling amendments, the language of Rule 603 remains identical to its federal counterpart, Fed. R. Evid. 603.

Although Rule 603 parallels its federal counterpart, "federal court decisions interpreting the federal rule are persuasive but

not binding with respect to interpreting the Arizona rule." *See,* Prefatory Comment to 2012 Amendments. *See also, State v. Terrazas*, 189 Ariz. 580, 944 P.2d 1194 (1997) (The Arizona Supreme Court is "not bound by the United States Supreme Court's non-constitutional construction of the Federal Rules of Evidence when [the Arizona Supreme Court construes] the Arizona Rules of Evidence."), citing, *State v. Bible*, 175 Ariz. 549, 858 P.2d 1152 (1993); *State v. Salazar-Mercado*, 232 Ariz. 256, 304 P.3d 543 (Ct. App. Div. 2 2013). Practitioners are urged to keep this legal tenet in mind as they research federal case law interpreting a federal evidentiary rule that corresponds to an Arizona evidentiary rule.

Rule 604. Interpreters

An interpreter must be qualified and must give an oath or affirmation to make a true translation.

Amended Oct. 19, 1988, effective Nov. 1, 1988; Sept. 8, 2011, effective Jan. 1, 2012.

Comment to 2012 Amendment

The language of Rule 604 has been amended to conform to the federal restyling of the Evidence Rules to make them more easily understood and to make style and terminology consistent throughout the rules. These changes are intended to be stylistic only. There is no intent to change any result in any ruling on evidence admissibility.

AUTHORS' COMMENTS

Analysis

1. *Scope and Purpose of Rule.* Rule 604 simply provides that an interpreter, when one is required, must be shown to be qualified and must take an oath or affirmation, as would a witness, before serving.

2. *Comparison With Federal Rule.* Effective January 1, 2012, the Arizona Supreme Court amended Rule 604 to conform to the federal restyling of the Evidence Rules to make the rules more easily understood and to make style and terminology consistent throughout. The 2012 Comment states the stylistic amendments are not intended to "change any result in any ruling on evidence admissibility."

Following the 2012 restyling amendments, the language of Rule 604 remains identical to its federal counterpart, Fed. R. Evid. 604.

Although Rule 604 parallels its federal counterpart, "federal court decisions interpreting the federal rule are persuasive but not binding with respect to interpreting the Arizona rule." *See,* Prefatory Comment to 2012 Amendments. *See also, State v. Terrazas*, 189 Ariz. 580, 944 P.2d 1194 (1997) (The Arizona Supreme Court is "not bound by the United States Supreme Court's non-constitutional construction of the Federal Rules of Evidence when [the Arizona Supreme Court construes] the Arizona Rules of Evidence."), citing, *State v. Bible*, 175 Ariz. 549, 858 P.2d 1152

(1993); *State v. Salazar-Mercado*, 232 Ariz. 256, 304 P.3d 543 (Ct. App. Div. 2 2013). Practitioners are urged to keep this legal tenet in mind as they research federal case law interpreting a federal evidentiary rule that corresponds to an Arizona evidentiary rule.

3. *Authority to Appoint Interpreter; When Required; Qualifications.* Rule 604 provides that an interpreter must be shown to be qualified to serve, as would any other expert witness. *State v. Burris*, 131 Ariz. 563, 643 P.2d 8 (Ct. App. Div. 2 1982). The assessment of an individual's qualifications to serve as an interpreter is a matter committed to the trial court's discretion. *In re MH 2007-001895*, 221 Ariz. 346, 212 P.3d 38 (Ct. App. Div. 1 2009). The burden is on the party complaining of an interpreter's performance to show that it was deficient. *Gallegos v. Garcia*, 14 Ariz. App. 85, 480 P.2d 1002 (Div. 1 1971).

In addition, Ariz.R.Civ.P. 43(c) gives the Court the authority to appoint an interpreter where necessary or desirable, and provides that the Court can direct that the interpreter's compensation be paid by one or more of the parties and/or be taxed as costs in the action. Cf. also, A.R.S. § 12-241. An interpreter must be appointed where a deaf person is a participant in legal proceedings as a party, witness or attorney. A.R.S. § 12-242. An interpreter may be appointed for a deaf juror. *State v. Marcham*, 160 Ariz. 52, 770 P.2d 356 (Ct. App. Div. 1 1988).

Rule 605. Judge's Competency as a Witness

The judge presiding at trial may not testify as a witness at the trial. A party need not object to preserve the issue.

Amended Sept. 8, 2011, effective Jan. 1, 2012.

Comment to 2012 Amendment

The language of Rule 605 has been amended to conform to the federal restyling of the Evidence Rules to make them more easily understood and to make style and terminology consistent throughout the rules. These changes are intended to be stylistic only. There is no intent to change any result in any ruling on evidence admissibility.

AUTHORS' COMMENTS

Analysis

1. Scope and Purpose of Rule.
2. Comparison With Federal Rule.
3. Testimony in Other Proceedings.

1. *Scope and Purpose of Rule.* Rule 605 provides that the trial judge may not testify as a witness in a trial over which that judge is presiding. The Rule preserves both the fact and the appearance of judicial impartiality. It also avoids what would be at best the awkward situation of forcing the parties to object to the trial judge's testimony and/or having the trial judge rule on those objections. A violation of this Rule is fundamental error, and no objection is required to secure reversal.

2. *Comparison With Federal Rule.* Effective January 1, 2012, the Arizona Supreme Court amended Rule 605 to conform to the federal restyling of the Evidence Rules to make the rules more easily understood and to make style and terminology consistent throughout. The 2012 Comment states the stylistic amendments are not intended to "change any result in any ruling on evidence admissibility."

As a consequence of the 2012 amendments, Ariz. R. Evid. 605 and Fed. R. Evid. 605 are now slightly different. The Arizona Rule uses the phrase "[t]he judge presiding at trial may not . . .," while the Federal Rule uses the phrase "[t]he presiding judge may not . . .." The difference is one of style and not substance.

Although Rule 605 parallels its federal counterpart, "federal court decisions interpreting the federal rule are persuasive but not binding with respect to interpreting the Arizona rule." *See,* Prefatory Comment to 2012 Amendments. *See also, State v. Terrazas*, 189 Ariz. 580, 944 P.2d 1194 (1997) (The Arizona Supreme

Court is "not bound by the United States Supreme Court's non-constitutional construction of the Federal Rules of Evidence when [the Arizona Supreme Court construes] the Arizona Rules of Evidence."), citing, *State v. Bible*, 175 Ariz. 549, 858 P.2d 1152 (1993); *State v. Salazar-Mercado*, 232 Ariz. 256, 304 P.3d 543 (Ct. App. Div. 2 2013). Practitioners are urged to keep this legal tenet in mind as they research federal case law interpreting a federal evidentiary rule that corresponds to an Arizona evidentiary rule.

3. *Testimony in Other Proceedings.* By its terms, Rule 605 applies only to testimony from a judge in a trial (and presumably any other proceeding) over which she or he is presiding. A judge may, however, testify about earlier proceedings in a case, in a subsequent hearing or proceedings over which a different judge is presiding. *DeForest v. DeForest*, 143 Ariz. 627, 694 P.2d 1241 (Ct. App. Div. 1 1985). In *DeForest*, the Court approved the use of judicial testimony to establish the terms and rendition of a prior judgment in a dissolution case.

In *Phillips v. Clancy*, 152 Ariz. 415, 733 P.2d 300 (Ct. App. Div. 1 1986), the Court noted that other jurisdictions had permitted judicial testimony (1) as to factual matters brought out in a former proceeding, and (2) in situations where the impressions of the judge are sought on issues such as the reputation or credibility of a witness at an earlier trial. The Court specifically precluded the use of judicial testimony, however, in a legal malpractice action arising out of litigation over which the judge/prospective witness presided, to establish what the judge would have done had the claimed malpractice not occurred. *Phillips v. Clancy*, 152 Ariz. 415, 733 P.2d 300 (Ct. App. Div. 1 1986). *See also Reed v. Mitchell & Timbanard, P.C.*, 183 Ariz. 313, 903 P.2d 621 (Ct. App. Div. 1 1995).

Rule 606. Juror's Competency as a Witness

(a) At the Trial. A juror may not testify as a witness before the other jurors at the trial. If a juror is called to testify, the court must give a party an opportunity to object outside the jury's presence.

(b) During an Inquiry into the Validity of a Verdict in a Civil Case.

(1) **Prohibited Testimony or Other Evidence**. During an inquiry into the validity of a verdict in a civil case, a juror may not testify about any statement made or incident that occurred during the jury's deliberations; the effect of anything on that juror's or another juror's vote; or any juror's mental processes concerning the verdict or indictment. The court may not receive a juror's affidavit or evidence of a juror's statement on these matters.

(2) **Exceptions**. A juror may testify about whether:

(A) extraneous prejudicial information was improperly brought to the jury's attention;

(B) an outside influence was improperly brought to bear on any juror; or

(C) a mistake was made in entering the verdict on the verdict form.

Rule 606(b) amended Oct. 19, 1988, effective Nov. 1, 1988; Sept. 8, 2011, effective Jan. 1, 2012.

Comment to 2012 Amendment

This rule has been amended to conform to Federal Rule of Evidence 606, including the addition of subdivision (b)(2)(C). However, subsection (b) has not been applied to criminal cases, as is done in Federal Rule of Evidence 606(b), because the matter is covered by Arizona Rule of Criminal Procedure 24.1(d).

Additionally, the language of Rule 606 has been amended to conform to the federal restyling of the Evidence Rules to make them more easily understood and to make style and terminology consistent throughout the rules. These changes are intended to be stylistic only. There is no intent in the restyling to change any result in any ruling on evidence admissibility.

AUTHORS' COMMENTS

Analysis

1. Scope and Purpose of Rule.
2. Comparison With Federal Rule.
3. Trial Juror as Witness.
4. Use of Juror Testimony to Impeach Verdict.

1. *Scope and Purpose of Rule.* Rule 606 addresses two different but related subjects: (1) the competence of a trial juror as a witness in the case in which that juror is sitting, and (2) the competence of testimony from a trial juror with respect to the validity of a verdict rendered in a civil action.

2. *Comparison With Federal Rule.* Effective January 1, 2012, the Arizona Supreme Court amended and restyled Rule 606 to conform to its federal counterpart, Fed. R. Evid. 606. As a result, Ariz. R. Evid. 606(a) remains identical to Fed. R. Evid. 606(a).

Ariz. R. Evid. 606(b) continues to be limited to civil cases, while Fed. R. Evid. 606(b) applies to both civil and criminal cases. As noted in the Comment to 2012 Amendment, the Arizona Supreme Court did not apply subsection (b) to criminal cases, as Fed. R. Evid. 606(b) does, because that matter is covered by Ariz. R. Crim. P. 24.1(d).

In addition, the Arizona Rule now contains a new provision, similar to Fed. R. Evid. 606(b)(2)(C). Thus, Ariz. R. Evid. 606(b)(2) permits juror testimony on the question whether the verdict rendered was the result of a clerical mistake. Former Ariz. R. Evid. 606(b) did not permit such testimony.

Although Rule 606 parallels its federal counterpart, "federal court decisions interpreting the federal rule are persuasive but not binding with respect to interpreting the Arizona rule." *See,* Prefatory Comment to 2012 Amendments. *See also, State v. Terrazas*, 189 Ariz. 580, 944 P.2d 1194 (1997) (The Arizona Supreme Court is "not bound by the United States Supreme Court's non-constitutional construction of the Federal Rules of Evidence when [the Arizona Supreme Court construes] the Arizona Rules of Evidence."), citing, *State v. Bible*, 175 Ariz. 549, 858 P.2d 1152 (1993); *State v. Salazar-Mercado*, 232 Ariz. 256, 304 P.3d 543 (Ct. App. Div. 2 2013). Practitioners are urged to keep this legal tenet in mind as they research federal case law interpreting a federal evidentiary rule that corresponds to an Arizona evidentiary rule.

3. *Trial Juror as Witness.* Rule 606(a) bars trial jurors from testifying as witnesses in the case in which they are sitting as jurors. If a juror is called to testify, the opposing party must be given the opportunity to object outside the presence of the jury.

4. *Use of Juror Testimony to Impeach Verdict.* Misconduct by trial jurors is one of the grounds upon which a verdict may be set aside and a new trial granted. Ariz.R.Civ.P. 59(a)(2). To warrant the granting of a new trial, however, an allegation of jury misconduct must be supported by sworn affidavits or testimony. *Kirby v. Rosell*, 133 Ariz. 42, 648 P.2d 1048 (Ct. App. Div. 1 1982); *Foster v. Camelback Management Co.*, 132 Ariz. 462, 646 P.2d 893 (Ct. App. Div. 2 1982). Whether jury misconduct, if established, warrants the granting of a new trial is a decision commit-

ted to the discretion of the trial court. *Elliott v. Videan*, 164 Ariz. 113, 791 P.2d 639 (Ct. App. Div. 2 1989).

The earlier rule was that testimony from jurors, or juror affidavits, could not be used at all to impeach or explain a verdict. *Wasko v. Frankel*, 116 Ariz. 288, 569 P.2d 230 (1977) (abrogated by, State v. Hickman, 205 Ariz. 192, 68 P.3d 418 (2003)); *Valley Nat. Bank of Arizona v. Haney*, 27 Ariz. App. 692, 558 P.2d 720 (Div. 1 1976); *Johnson v. Harris*, 23 Ariz. App. 103, 530 P.2d 1136 (Div. 2 1975); *Board of Trustees Eloy Elementary School Dist. v. McEwen*, 6 Ariz. App. 148, 430 P.2d 727 (1967). The prohibition extended to all matters discussed by the jury in arriving at its verdict. *Valley Nat. Bank of Arizona v. Haney*, 27 Ariz. App. 692, 558 P.2d 720 (Div. 1 1976).

That earlier absolute rule was relaxed by the adoption of Rule 606(b) and of Ariz. R. Crim. P. 24.1(d). Now, in civil cases, a juror may testify as to whether extraneous information was brought to the jurors' attention during deliberations; whether any outside influence was brought to bear on the jurors; and whether a mistake was made in entering the verdict on the verdict form.

Testimony from a juror about any matter discussed in the jury room during jury deliberations remains inadmissible unless one of the limited exceptions in Rule 606(b) applies. *Dunn v. Maras*, 182 Ariz. 412, 897 P.2d 714 (Ct. App. Div. 1 1995); *Richtmyre v. State*, 175 Ariz. 489, 858 P.2d 322 (Ct. App. Div. 1 1993); *Maxwell v. Aetna Life Ins. Co.*, 143 Ariz. 205, 693 P.2d 348 (Ct. App. Div. 1 1984); *Kirby v. Rosell*, 133 Ariz. 42, 648 P.2d 1048 (Ct. App. Div. 1 1982). A trial court may not consider a juror affidavit that would not be admissible under Rule 606(b), and the submission of such an affidavit for the trial court's consideration indicates a serious dearth of either competence or ethics. *Martinez v. Schneider Enterprises, Inc.*, 178 Ariz. 346, 873 P.2d 684 (Ct. App. Div. 1 1994). Thus, the trial court may not consider affidavits or testimony from jurors that jurors did not consider improperly admitted evidence, *Taylor v. Southern Pac. Transp. Co.*, 130 Ariz. 516, 637 P.2d 726 (1981); that a verdict was a quotient verdict, *Moorer v. Clayton Mfg. Corp.*, 128 Ariz. 565, 627 P.2d 716 (Ct. App. Div. 2 1981); or, that the trial court's failure to answer jurors' questions had an effect on the verdict, *Ott v. Samaritan Health Service*, 127 Ariz. 485, 622 P.2d 44 (Ct. App. Div. 1 1980).

A juror's testimony is admissible, however, to show an error in the judgment as not conforming to the jury's findings, improper acts by third parties, or that extraneous information, *i.e.,* matters not received in evidence, was considered by the jury. *Dunn v. Maras*, 182 Ariz. 412, 897 P.2d 714 (Ct. App. Div. 1 1995); *Kirby v. Rosell*, 133 Ariz. 42, 648 P.2d 1048 (Ct. App. Div. 1 1982); *Foster v. Camelback Management Co.*, 132 Ariz. 462, 646 P.2d

893 (Ct. App. Div. 2 1982). Where extraneous information has been submitted to and considered by the jury, a party seeking a new trial on that basis need only show a reasonable possibility that prejudice resulted. *Dunn v. Maras*, 182 Ariz. 412, 897 P.2d 714 (Ct. App. Div. 1 1995); *Hallmark v. Allied Products Corp.*, 132 Ariz. 434, 646 P.2d 319 (Ct. App. Div. 1 1982). Specialized knowledge possessed by a juror and discussed during deliberations does not qualify as extrinsic and extraneous material. *Brooks v. Zahn*, 170 Ariz. 545, 826 P.2d 1171 (Ct. App. Div. 1 1991).

Testimony or an affidavit from a juror is admissible to show the failure *by that juror, i.e.,* the juror furnishing the testimony or affidavit, to disclose bias and prejudice during *voir dire* examination of the jury panel, but it is not admissible to show the failure of other jurors to do so. *Richtmyre v. State*, 175 Ariz. 489, 858 P.2d 322 (Ct. App. Div. 1 1993); *Brooks v. Zahn*, 170 Ariz. 545, 826 P.2d 1171 (Ct. App. Div. 1 1991).

Rule 607. Who May Impeach a Witness

Any party, including the party that called the witness, may attack the witness's credibility.

Amended Oct. 19, 1988, effective Nov. 1, 1988; Sept. 8, 2011, effective Jan. 1, 2012.

Comment to 2012 Amendment

The language of Rule 607 has been amended to conform to the federal restyling of the Evidence Rules to make them more easily understood and to make style and terminology consistent throughout the rules. These changes are intended to be stylistic only. There is no intent to change any result in any ruling on evidence admissibility.

AUTHORS' COMMENTS

Analysis

1. Scope and Purpose of Rule.
2. Comparison With Federal Rule.
3. Grounds for and Methods of Impeachment Generally.
4. Impeachment for Bias or Prejudice.
5. Impeachment of Ability to Perceive.
6. Impeachment by Prior Inconsistent Statement or Conduct.

1. *Scope and Purpose of Rule.* Rule 607 abolished the common law prohibition on a party impeaching a witness which that party had called to testify, except in the case of surprise. *Cf., e.g., State v. Lane*, 69 Ariz. 236, 211 P.2d 821 (1949). Under Rule 607, the credibility of a witness may be attacked by any party to the action.

2. *Comparison With Federal Rule.* Effective January 1, 2012, the Arizona Supreme Court amended Rule 607 to conform to the federal restyling of the Evidence Rules to make the rules more easily understood and to make style and terminology consistent throughout. The 2012 Comment states the stylistic amendments are not intended to "change any result in any ruling on evidence admissibility."

Following the 2012 restyling amendments, the language of Rule 607 remains identical to its federal counterpart, Fed. R. Evid. 607.

Although Rule 607 parallels its federal counterpart, "federal court decisions interpreting the federal rule are persuasive but not binding with respect to interpreting the Arizona rule." *See,* Prefatory Comment to 2012 Amendments. *See also, State v. Terrazas*, 189 Ariz. 580, 944 P.2d 1194 (1997) (The Arizona Supreme Court is "not bound by the United States Supreme Court's non-

constitutional construction of the Federal Rules of Evidence when [the Arizona Supreme Court construes] the Arizona Rules of Evidence."), citing, *State v. Bible*, 175 Ariz. 549, 858 P.2d 1152 (1993); *State v. Salazar-Mercado*, 232 Ariz. 256, 304 P.3d 543 (Ct. App. Div. 2 2013). Practitioners are urged to keep this legal tenet in mind as they research federal case law interpreting a federal evidentiary rule that corresponds to an Arizona evidentiary rule.

3. *Grounds for and Methods of Impeachment Generally.* Pure impeachment evidence is that which is solely an attack on the credibility of a witness. *Watts v. Golden Age Nursing Home*, 127 Ariz. 255, 619 P.2d 1032 (1980). In light of the general prohibition on impeachment of a witness on a purely collateral matter, *Montano v. Scottsdale Baptist Hospital, Inc.*, 119 Ariz. 448, 581 P.2d 682 (1978), most impeachment evidence, particularly that which contradicts what a witness has said, will have some substantive value as well, and is not evidence introduced or used "solely" for impeachment purposes. *Zimmerman v. Superior Court In and For Maricopa County*, 98 Ariz. 85, 402 P.2d 212, 18 A.L.R.3d 909 (1965); *Helena Chemical Co. v. Coury Bros. Ranches, Inc.*, 126 Ariz. 448, 616 P.2d 908 (Ct. App. Div. 1 1980); *Ries v. McComb*, 25 Ariz. App. 554, 545 P.2d 65 (Div. 1 1976). In fact, one test for whether impeachment material delves improperly into collateral matters is whether the fact sought to be proven for impeachment purposes could be admitted for another, independent purpose. *Public Service Co. of Oklahoma v. Bleak*, 134 Ariz. 311, 656 P.2d 600 (1982).

There are several categories of impeachment evidence, including: (a) evidence which shows bias and/or prejudice on the part of the witness; (b) evidence which shows a witness' mental or sensory deficiencies and/or questions the witness' ability to observe, perceive, recall or recount events; (c) evidence which independently contradicts the accuracy of the facts to which the witness has testified; (d) evidence which attacks the character of the witness by showing the witness' poor reputation for veracity or specific instances of the witness' misconduct; and, (e) evidence of a prior statement by the witness which is inconsistent with the witness' current testimony. The manner in which many of these grounds for impeachment may be established is governed by Rules 404, 405, 608, 609, 613, and 801(d) of the Rules of Evidence.

Impeachment evidence must, however, be relevant and not divert the fact finding process into the determination of matters which are wholly collateral to the issues presented. *Public Service Co. of Oklahoma v. Bleak*, 134 Ariz. 311, 656 P.2d 600 (1982); *Montano v. Scottsdale Baptist Hospital, Inc.*, 119 Ariz. 448, 581 P.2d 682 (1978).

4. *Impeachment for Bias or Prejudice.* A witness' motives for

testifying, and matters that would show bias or prejudice in favor of or against a party, are proper subjects of impeachment, even though the subject matter may appear collateral to the issues in the case. *Barsema v. Susong*, 156 Ariz. 309, 751 P.2d 969 (1988); *Ring v. Taylor*, 141 Ariz. 56, 685 P.2d 121 (Ct. App. Div. 1 1984); *Foulk v. Kotz*, 138 Ariz. 159, 673 P.2d 799 (Ct. App. Div. 2 1983); *Gonzales v. City of Tucson*, 124 Ariz. 450, 604 P.2d 1161 (Ct. App. Div. 2 1979). This would obviously include whether the witness personally had a financial interest in the outcome of the litigation. *Cottonwood Estates, Inc. v. Paradise Builders, Inc.*, 128 Ariz. 99, 624 P.2d 296 (1981).

While litigants are generally entitled to present evidence that tends to show bias or prejudice on the part of witnesses, including those who testify as experts, a party's need to conduct discovery for bias-related information must be balanced against competing interests, including the right of witnesses to be free from unduly intrusive or burdensome inquiries and the need to prevent broad-ranging discovery forays that serve to increase the cost, length and burden of litigation with little or no corresponding benefit. *American Family Mut. Ins. Co. v. Grant*, 222 Ariz. 507, 217 P.3d 1212 (Ct. App. Div. 1 2009). Courts have recognized that such overbroad discovery requests have a chilling effect on would-be experts. *American Family Mut. Ins. Co. v. Grant*, 222 Ariz. 507, 217 P.3d 1212 (Ct. App. Div. 1 2009).

5. *Impeachment of Ability to Perceive.* For impeachment purposes, it is permissible to show facts that would show that the witness' ability to perceive and/or recall the events to which the witness has testified was impaired, such as by being under the influence of drugs or alcohol or by reason of some physical impairment. *Yoo Thun Lim v. Crespin*, 100 Ariz. 80, 411 P.2d 809 (1966); *Martinez v. Jordan*, 27 Ariz. App. 254, 553 P.2d 1239 (Div. 1 1976).

6. *Impeachment by Prior Inconsistent Statement or Conduct.* Under Rule 801(d)(1), the prior inconsistent statement of a witness is admissible both for substantive and for impeachment purposes. *State v. Skinner*, 110 Ariz. 135, 515 P.2d 880 (1973). It is also permissible to show prior conduct of a witness that is inconsistent with the witness' present testimony. *Public Service Co. of Oklahoma v. Bleak*, 134 Ariz. 311, 656 P.2d 600 (1982); *Chavez v. Pima County*, 107 Ariz. 358, 488 P.2d 978 (1971); *Rodriguez v. Schlittenhart*, 161 Ariz. 609, 780 P.2d 442 (Ct. App. Div. 2 1989); *Martinez v. Jordan*, 27 Ariz. App. 254, 553 P.2d 1239 (Div. 1 1976).

Rehabilitation of a witness by the proof of a prior consistent statement is permitted only where there is an assertion that the witness' trial testimony is a recent fabrication and/or the witness denies making the prior inconsistent statement. *Ray Korte Chevrolet v. Simmons*, 117 Ariz. 202, 571 P.2d 699 (Ct. App. Div. 1 1977); *but cf. Trevizo v. Astec Industries, Inc.*, 156 Ariz. 320, 751 P.2d 980 (Ct. App. Div. 2 1987).

Rule 608. A Witness's Character for Truthfulness or Untruthfulness

(a) Reputation or Opinion Evidence. A witness's credibility may be attacked or supported by testimony about the witness's reputation for having a character for truthfulness or untruthfulness, or by testimony in the form of an opinion about that character. But evidence of truthful character is admissible only after the witness's character for truthfulness has been attacked.

(b) Specific Instances of Conduct. Except for a criminal conviction under Rule 609, extrinsic evidence is not admissible to prove specific instances of a witness's conduct in order to attack or support the witness's character for truthfulness. But the court may, on cross-examination, allow them to be inquired into if they are probative of the character for truthfulness or untruthfulness of:

(1) the witness; or

(2) another witness whose character the witness being cross-examined has testified about.

By testifying on another matter, a witness does not waive any privilege against self-incrimination for testimony that relates only to the witness's character for truthfulness.

Amended Oct. 19, 1988, effective Nov. 1, 1988; Sept. 8, 2011, effective Jan. 1, 2012.

Comment to 2012 Amendment

This rule has been amended to conform to Federal Rule of Evidence 608, including changing two references to "credibility" to "character for truthfulness" in subsection (b). Additionally, the language of Rule 608 has been amended to conform to the federal restyling of the Evidence Rules to make them more easily understood and to make style and terminology consistent throughout the rules. These changes are intended to be stylistic only. There is no intent in the restyling to change any result in any ruling on evidence admissibility.

Comment to Original 1977 Rule

State ex rel. Pope v. Superior Court, In and For Mohave County, 113 Ariz. 22, 545 P.2d 946, 94 A.L.R.3d 246 (1976) is consistent with and interpretative of Rule 608(b).

AUTHORS' COMMENTS

Analysis

5. Methods of Rehabilitation.

1. *Scope and Purpose of Rule.* Rule 608 governs the methods for impeaching a witness through evidence of the witness' poor reputation for veracity, or through evidence of specific instances of the witness' misconduct (other than criminal convictions) in the past. The Rule, on balance, represents a relaxation of the prior doctrine that a witness' past acts of untruthfulness were not admissible to attack the witness' credibility. *State v. Hatton*, 116 Ariz. 142, 568 P.2d 1040 (1977). Rule 608 does not limit impeachment by other means or on other grounds, and has no application where the past acts of misconduct sought to be introduced are convictions of a crime. That situation is controlled by Rule 609.

2. *Comparison With Federal Rule.* Effective January 1, 2012, the Arizona Supreme Court amended and restyled Rule 608 to conform to its federal counterpart, Fed. R. Evid. 608. As a result of the 2012 amendments and restyling, Ariz. R. Evid. 608 and Fed. R. Evid. 608 are substantially identical. The 2012 Comment states the stylistic amendments are not intended to "change any result in any ruling on evidence admissibility."

The 2012 amendment substitutes, in two places, the phrase "character for truthfulness" for the term "credibility" in subsection (b) of former Ariz. R. Evid. 608, conforming Arizona's rule to Fed. R. Evid. 608(b). The Comment to 2012 Amendment states that the changes to Rule 608 are intended to be stylistic only and not intended to change any result in any ruling on evidence admissibility.

As a consequence of the 2012 restyling amendments, the language of Rule 608 is identical to its federal counterpart, Fed. R. Evid. 608.

Although Rule 608 parallels its federal counterpart, "federal court decisions interpreting the federal rule are persuasive but not binding with respect to interpreting the Arizona rule." *See,* Prefatory Comment to 2012 Amendments. *See also, State v. Terrazas*, 189 Ariz. 580, 944 P.2d 1194 (1997) (The Arizona Supreme Court is "not bound by the United States Supreme Court's non-constitutional construction of the Federal Rules of Evidence when [the Arizona Supreme Court construes] the Arizona Rules of Evidence."), citing, *State v. Bible*, 175 Ariz. 549, 858 P.2d 1152 (1993); *State v. Salazar-Mercado*, 232 Ariz. 256, 304 P.3d 543 (Ct. App. Div. 2 2013). Practitioners are urged to keep this legal tenet in mind as they research federal case law interpreting a federal evidentiary rule that corresponds to an Arizona evidentiary rule.

3. *Proof of Witness' Character for Veracity.* It has long been the

rule that one witness could testify as to the poor reputation of another witness for truthfulness. Rule 608(a) expanded past doctrine and practice by permitting opinion evidence, as well as reputation evidence, on the character of a witness for veracity. See discussion in Section 3 of the *Authors' Comments* to Rule 405, Ariz. R. Evid. If opinion evidence on this subject is offered, it must have sufficient foundation and be directed to the witness' character for veracity, not the truthful nature of the witness' specific testimony. The character of the witness may not be proven by evidence of specific instances of conduct.

Rule 608(a) permits opinion or reputation evidence that supports the credibility of a witness, but only after the character of the witness has been attacked.

4. *Proof of Specific Instances of Witness' Conduct.* The circumstances under which specific instances of a witness' misconduct, other than criminal convictions, may be delved into are governed by Rule 608(b). The Rule permits only cross-examination of a witness concerning past conduct of that witness, or past conduct of another witness whose character for veracity was the subject of the witness' testimony, if (1) the past conduct is probative of truthfulness or untruthfulness, and (2) the trial court in its discretion permits it. *Henson v. Triumph Trucking, Inc.*, 180 Ariz. 305, 884 P.2d 191 (Ct. App. Div. 2 1994).

As noted, Rule 608(b) permits only cross-examination on the subject; if denied, the past misconduct cannot be proven by extrinsic evidence. If the inquiry is permitted by the trial court, the past acts in question must show actual falsification or at least a willingness to do so. *Cf. Amburgey v. Holan Division of Ohio Brass Co.*, 124 Ariz. 531, 606 P.2d 21 (1980). The sexual misconduct of a witness is not probative of veracity and is not a proper subject of inquiry under this Rule. *State v. Oliver*, 158 Ariz. 22, 760 P.2d 1071 (1988); *State ex rel. Pope v. Superior Court, In and For Mohave County*, 113 Ariz. 22, 545 P.2d 946, 94 A.L.R.3d 246 (1976). Similarly, evidence of the misuse of prescription medicine two to eight years before an accident is not probative of truthfulness and, consequently, not admissible under this Rule. *Henson v. Triumph Trucking, Inc.*, 180 Ariz. 305, 884 P.2d 191 (Ct. App. Div. 2 1994).

The examiner must have some basis in fact for the inquiry before making it. *Foulk v. Kotz*, 138 Ariz. 159, 673 P.2d 799 (Ct. App. Div. 2 1983). The trial court can preclude the inquiry if, in its judgment, the value of the evidence of past acts of the witness' untruthfulness is outweighed by considerations of delay of the trial. *Block v. Meyer*, 144 Ariz. 230, 696 P.2d 1379 (Ct. App. Div. 1 1985).

5. *Methods of Rehabilitation.* Where the credibility of a witness

has been attacked by evidence of this or a similar nature, the witness can be rehabilitated either by showing that the impeaching evidence is untrue, or by showing that the witness is nonetheless worthy of belief. Nominally, rehabilitation of a witness is only proper after the witness' credibility has been attacked, but it is permissible, and not at all unusual, to have the witness on direct examination admit and explain the impeaching facts. Introduction of opinion or reputation evidence of a witness' good character for veracity is proper rehabilitation. *Blankinship v. Duarte*, 137 Ariz. 217, 669 P.2d 994 (Ct. App. Div. 2 1983).

Rule 609. Impeachment by Evidence of Criminal Conviction

(a) In General. The following rules apply to attacking a witness's character for truthfulness by evidence of a criminal conviction:

(1) for a crime that, in the convicting jurisdiction, was punishable by death or by imprisonment for more than one year, the evidence:

(A) must be admitted, subject to Rule 403, in a civil case or in a criminal case in which the witness is not a defendant; and

(B) must be admitted in a criminal case in which the witness is a defendant, if the probative value of the evidence outweighs its prejudicial effect to that defendant; and

(2) for any crime regardless of the punishment, the evidence must be admitted if the court can readily determine that establishing the elements of the crime required proving—or the witness's admitting—a dishonest act or false statement.

(b) Limit on Using the Evidence After 10 Years. This subsection (b) applies if more than 10 years have passed since the witness's conviction or release from confinement for it, whichever is later. Evidence of the conviction is admissible only if:

(1) its probative value, supported by specific facts and circumstances, substantially outweighs its prejudicial effect; and

(2) the proponent gives an adverse party reasonable written notice of the intent to use it so that the party has a fair opportunity to contest its use.

(c) Effect of a Pardon, Annulment, or Certificate of Rehabilitation. Evidence of a conviction is not admissible if:

(1) the conviction has been the subject of a pardon, annulment, certificate of rehabilitation, or other equivalent procedure based on a finding that the person has been rehabilitated, and the person has not been convicted of a later crime punishable by death or by imprisonment for more than one year; or

(2) the conviction has been the subject of a pardon, annulment, or other equivalent procedure based on a finding of innocence.

(d) Juvenile Adjudications. Evidence of a juvenile adjudication is admissible under this rule only if:

(1) it is offered in a criminal case;

(2) the adjudication was of a witness other than the defendant;

(3) an adult's conviction for that offense would be admissible to attack the adult's credibility; and

(4) admitting the evidence is necessary to fairly determine guilt or innocence.

(e) *Pendency of an Appeal.* A conviction that satisfies this rule is admissible even if an appeal is pending. Evidence of the pendency is also admissible.

Amended Oct. 19, 1988, effective Nov. 1, 1988; Sept. 8, 2011, effective Jan. 1, 2012.

Comment to 2012 Amendment

This rule has been amended to conform to Federal Rule of Evidence 609, including changing "credibility" to "character for truthfulness" in subsection (a) and adding language to the last clause of subdivision (a)(2) to clarify that this evidence must be admitted "if the court can readily determine that establishing the elements of the crime required proving—or the witness's admitting—a dishonest act or false statement."

Additionally, the language of Rule 609 has been amended to conform to the federal restyling of the Evidence Rules to make them more easily understood and to make style and terminology consistent throughout the rules. These changes are intended to be stylistic only. There is no intent in the restyling to change any result in any ruling on evidence admissibility.

Added Sept. 8, 2011, effective Jan. 1, 2012. Amended Aug. 30, 2012, effective Jan. 1, 2013

Comment to Original 1977 Rule

Subsection (d) is contrary to the provisions of A.R.S. § 8-207, but in criminal cases due process may require that the fact of a juvenile adjudication be admitted to show the existence of possible bias and prejudice. *Davis v. Alaska*, 415 U.S. 308, 94 S. Ct. 1105, 39 L. Ed. 2d 347 (1974). The fact of a juvenile delinquency adjudication may not be used to impeach the general credibility of a witness. The admission of such evidence may be necessary to meet due process standards.

AUTHORS' COMMENTS

Analysis

1. *Scope and Purpose of Rule.* Rule 609 governs impeachment of a witness through evidence that the witness has been convicted of a crime. The Rule applies to all witnesses, including criminal defendants who choose to testify in their defense. It represents

one of the limited instances where specific acts of misconduct by a witness are admissible to impeach credibility, and the only instance where a specific act of misconduct may be proven for that purpose by independent evidence. *Amburgey v. Holan Division of Ohio Brass Co.*, 124 Ariz. 531, 606 P.2d 21 (1980). The Rule applies to civil cases, but the issue arises most frequently in criminal proceedings.

2. *Comparison With Federal Rule.* Effective January 1, 2012, the Arizona Supreme Court restyled Rule 609 to conform to its federal counterpart, Fed. R. Evid. 609. The 2012 Comment states the stylistic amendments are not intended to "change any result in any ruling on evidence admissibility."

In addition, in 2012, Ariz. R. Evid. 609 was amended in three important ways.

First, Rule 609 was amended to substitutes the phrase "character for truthfulness" for the term "credibility" in subsection (a) of Ariz. R. Evid. 609, which amendment is consistent with the language used in Fed. R. Evid. 609(a).

Second, Rule 609(a) conforms with its federal counterpart in that it now sets a standard for the use of criminal convictions to impeach what the Rule now terms as "character for truthfulness" [fka, "credibility"], depending upon whether the witness whose credibility to be impeached is merely a witness or is the accused in a criminal case, and depending upon the crime for which the conviction was entered.

Third, Rule 609 was amended to add language to the last clause of subdivision (a)(2), which expressly provides that "for any crime regardless of the punishment, the evidence must be admitted if the court can readily determine that establishing the elements of the crime required proving—or the witness's admitting—a dishonest act or false statement."

Effective January 1, 2013, the Arizona Supreme Court amended the Comment to 2012 Amendment to clarify that evidence of convictions involving a dishonest act or false statement *must* be admitted "if the court can readily determine that establishing the elements of the crime required proving—or the witness's admitting—a dishonest act of false statement." *See,* Ariz. R. Evid. 609(a)(2).

Under Rule 609, as amended in 2012, where the "character for truthfulness" of the accused is to be impeached by showing a conviction for a crime punishable by death or imprisonment in excess of one year, the trial court must first determine that the probative value of the conviction outweighs its prejudicial impact. The use of such a conviction to impeach the credibility of an ordinary witness is subject only to the general balancing test of Ariz. R. Evid. 403. There are no restrictions on the use of convictions of crimes involving dishonesty for impeachment purposes or false statement. *Cf. Green v. Bock Laundry Mach. Co.*, 490 U.S. 504, 109 S. Ct. 1981, 104 L. Ed. 2d 557, 27 Fed. R. Evid. Serv. 577 (1989) (construing Federal Rule before 1990 amendment).

Although Rule 609 parallels its federal counterpart, "federal court decisions interpreting the federal rule are persuasive but not binding with respect to interpreting the Arizona rule." *See,* Prefatory Comment to 2012 Amendments. *See also, State v. Terrazas*, 189 Ariz. 580, 944 P.2d 1194 (1997) (The Arizona Supreme Court is "not bound by the United States Supreme Court's non-constitutional construction of the Federal Rules of Evidence when [the Arizona Supreme Court construes] the Arizona Rules of Evidence."), citing, *State v. Bible*, 175 Ariz. 549, 858 P.2d 1152 (1993); *State v. Salazar-Mercado*, 232 Ariz. 256, 304 P.3d 543 (Ct. App. Div. 2 2013). Practitioners are urged to keep this legal tenet in mind as they research federal case law interpreting a federal evidentiary rule that corresponds to an Arizona evidentiary rule.

3. *Use of Criminal Conviction for Impeachment of Witness Generally.* The law concerning the effect of a prior criminal conviction on the testimony of a witness has evolved. At common law, convicted felons were incompetent to serve as witnesses. Gradually, the conviction of a witness for a felony came to be viewed as a fact bearing on the witness' credibility, rather than a disqualification of the witness entirely. *State v. Hull*, 60 Ariz. 124, 132 P.2d 436 (1942).

Rule 609(a) expands the range of crimes that can be used to impeach a witness beyond felonies to some misdemeanors. Under Rule 609(a), a witness may be impeached, provided the trial court permits it, on the basis of (1) a conviction of a crime punishable by death or by imprisonment for a period in excess of one year under the law under which the conviction was entered, and (2) on the basis of conviction of a crime involving a lesser potential punishment if the crime involved "dishonesty or false statement." To fall into the latter category, the crime must involve an element of deceit, untruthfulness or falsification. *Blankinship v. Duarte*, 137 Ariz. 217, 669 P.2d 994 (Ct. App. Div. 2 1983). A conviction for tax evasion has been held to meet this standard. *Blankinship v. Duarte*, 137 Ariz. 217, 669 P.2d 994 (Ct. App. Div. 2 1983).

If the impeachment is allowed by the trial court, the fact of the conviction can be elicited from the witness during cross-examination, or proven by extrinsic evidence. Notwithstanding the provisions of Rule 410, convictions entered on pleas of *nolo contendere* are admissible for impeachment purposes. *Wilson v. Riley Whittle, Inc.*, 145 Ariz. 317, 701 P.2d 575 (Ct. App. Div. 2 1984). Under Rule 609(e), the fact that a conviction is on appeal does not render it inadmissible, but if evidence of such a conviction is allowed, then evidence of the appeal becomes admissible as well.

4. *Use of Older Convictions.* Rule 609(b) places somewhat greater restrictions on the use of criminal convictions of a witness where more than ten (10) years have elapsed since the date of the conviction or the witness' release from confinement, whichever is later. In that circumstance, the conviction may not be used unless the Court determines that the conviction's probative value *substantially* outweighs its prejudicial effect. This is consistent with the notion that a criminal conviction's probative value regarding a witness' credibility declines as it becomes more remote in time. *Blankinship v. Duarte*, 137 Ariz. 217, 669 P.2d 994 (Ct. App. Div. 2 1983); *cf. also, Sibley v. Jeffreys*, 76 Ariz. 340, 264 P.2d 831 (1953). The presence of "exceptional circumstances" is required to warrant the use of a conviction that is over ten (10) years old. *Blankinship v. Duarte*, 137 Ariz. 217, 669 P.2d 994 (Ct. App. Div. 2 1983). Under the Rule, there also must be prior notice given of an intent to use such an older conviction for impeachment, which is not required by Rule 609(a).

5. *Use of Juvenile Adjudications.* Rule 609(d) provides that evidence of juvenile adjudications is generally not admissible, and specifies no exceptions applicable in civil cases. In criminal cases, evidence of a juvenile adjudication with respect to a witness other than the accused may be used if it would be admissible to impeach an adult and the Court determines that it is necessary to a fair determination of the issues. This potential for the admission of juvenile adjudications under the stated circumstances creates a potential conflict between the Rule and the provisions of A.R.S. § 8-207(B).

6. *Effect of Pardons, Annulments, Rehabilitation.* A conviction may not be used for impeachment if it has been set aside, annulled or pardoned on the basis of a finding of innocence or that the witness has been rehabilitated. *Blankinship v. Duarte*, 137 Ariz. 217, 669 P.2d 994 (Ct. App. Div. 2 1983).

7. *Discretion of Court.* Unlike the corresponding Federal Rule, Rule 609 places the discretion of the trial court as a screen or filter on any use of a prior criminal conviction to impeach a witness' credibility. *Cf., e.g., Green v. Bock Laundry Mach. Co.*, 490 U.S. 504, 109 S. Ct. 1981, 104 L. Ed. 2d 557, 27 Fed. R. Evid. Serv. 577 (1989) (construing Federal Rule 609 before 1990 amendment). Even if the other conditions of Rule 609 are satisfied, a criminal conviction of a witness may not be used for impeachment unless the Court determines that its probative value outweighs its prejudicial effect. *Wilson v. Riley Whittle, Inc.*, 145 Ariz. 317, 701 P.2d 575 (Ct. App. Div. 2 1984); *Quinonez*

for and on Behalf of Quinonez v. Andersen, 144 Ariz. 193, 696 P.2d 1342 (Ct. App. Div. 1 1984). In the case of an older conviction, the Court must determine that its use *substantially* outweighs its prejudicial impact.

Any felony conviction has probative value on credibility. *Wilson v. Riley Whittle, Inc.*, 145 Ariz. 317, 701 P.2d 575 (Ct. App. Div. 2 1984). The burden is on the party seeking to use evidence of a witness' prior conviction, however, to demonstrate that its probative value overrides its prejudicial impact. *State v. Wilson*, 128 Ariz. 422, 626 P.2d 152 (Ct. App. Div. 2 1981). The trial court has a wide discretion in this area to either permit or refuse the evidence, and it need not make specific findings to support its decision. *Mulhern v. City of Scottsdale*, 165 Ariz. 395, 799 P.2d 15 (Ct. App. Div. 2 1990); *Wilson v. Riley Whittle, Inc.*, 145 Ariz. 317, 701 P.2d 575 (Ct. App. Div. 2 1984); *State v. Dixon*, 126 Ariz. 613, 617 P.2d 779 (Ct. App. Div. 2 1980). The Rule does not specify the criteria that are to guide the exercise of that discretion, but it is permissible to take into account the recency of the conviction, *Segovia v. Industrial Commission*, 119 Ariz. 231, 580 P.2d 369 (Ct. App. Div. 1 1978); and, the degree to which the witness' credibility is an important issue in the case, *Blankinship v. Duarte*, 137 Ariz. 217, 669 P.2d 994 (Ct. App. Div. 2 1983).

Rule 610. Religious Beliefs or Opinions

Evidence of a witness's religious beliefs or opinions is not admissible to attack or support the witness's credibility.

Amended Oct. 19, 1988, effective Nov. 1, 1988; Sept. 8, 2011, effective Jan. 1, 2012.

Comment to 2012 Amendment

The language of Rule 610 has been amended to conform to the federal restyling of the Evidence Rules to make them more easily understood and to make style and terminology consistent throughout the rules. These changes are intended to be stylistic only. There is no intent to change any result in any ruling on evidence admissibility.

AUTHORS' COMMENTS

Analysis

1. *Scope and Purpose of Rule.* Rule 610 prohibits the introduction of evidence of a witness' religious beliefs or opinions for the purpose of either bolstering or attacking the witness' credibility. *State v. West*, 168 Ariz. 292, 812 P.2d 1110 (Ct. App. Div. 1 1991). It is improper to question a witness about the witness' religious beliefs for that purpose, and such references to a witness' religious beliefs constitute fundamental error. *State v. Thomas*, 130 Ariz. 432, 636 P.2d 1214, 27 A.L.R.4th 1158 (1981); *State v. Crum*, 150 Ariz. 244, 722 P.2d 971 (Ct. App. Div. 2 1986). The inquiry may be permissible, however, if the evidence of the witness' religious beliefs is probative of some material fact and is not introduced to bolster or attack credibility. *State v. Stone*, 151 Ariz. 455, 728 P.2d 674 (Ct. App. Div. 1 1986); *State v. West*, 168 Ariz. 292, 812 P.2d 1110 (Ct. App. Div. 1 1991).

2. *Comparison With Federal Rule.* Effective January 1, 2012, the Arizona Supreme Court amended Rule 610 to conform to the federal restyling of the Evidence Rules to make the rules more easily understood and to make style and terminology consistent throughout. The 2012 Comment states the stylistic amendments are not intended to "change any result in any ruling on evidence admissibility."

Following the 2012 restyling amendments, the language of Rule 610 remains identical to its federal counterpart, Fed. R. Evid. 610.

Although Rule 610 parallels its federal counterpart, "federal

court decisions interpreting the federal rule are persuasive but not binding with respect to interpreting the Arizona rule." *See,* Prefatory Comment to 2012 Amendments. *See also, State v. Terrazas*, 189 Ariz. 580, 944 P.2d 1194 (1997) (The Arizona Supreme Court is "not bound by the United States Supreme Court's non-constitutional construction of the Federal Rules of Evidence when [the Arizona Supreme Court construes] the Arizona Rules of Evidence."), citing, *State v. Bible*, 175 Ariz. 549, 858 P.2d 1152 (1993); *State v. Salazar-Mercado*, 232 Ariz. 256, 304 P.3d 543 (Ct. App. Div. 2 2013). Practitioners are urged to keep this legal tenet in mind as they research federal case law interpreting a federal evidentiary rule that corresponds to an Arizona evidentiary rule.

Rule 611. Mode and Order of Examining Witnesses and Presenting Evidence

(a) Control by the Court; Purposes. The court should exercise reasonable control over the mode and order of examining witnesses and presenting evidence so as to:

(1) make those procedures effective for determining the truth;

(2) avoid wasting time; and

(3) protect witnesses from harassment or undue embarrassment.

(b) Scope of cross-examination. A witness may be cross-examined on any relevant matter.

(c) Leading Questions. Leading questions should not be used on direct examination except as necessary to develop the witness's testimony. Ordinarily, the court should allow leading questions:

(1) on cross-examination; and

(2) when a party calls a hostile witness, an adverse party, or a witness identified with an adverse party.

Amended Oct. 19, 1988, effective Nov. 1, 1988; Oct. 24, 1995, effective Dec. 1, 1995; Sept. 8, 2011, effective Jan. 1, 2012.

Comment to 2012 Amendment

This rule has been amended to conform to Federal Rule of Evidence 611, except for subsection (b), which has not been changed.

Additionally, the language of subsections (a) and (c) has been amended to conform to the federal restyling of the Evidence Rules to make them more easily understood and to make style and terminology consistent throughout the rules. These changes are intended to be stylistic only. There is no intent in the restyling to change any result in any ruling on evidence admissibility.

The 2012 amendment of Rule 611(a) is not intended to diminish a trial court's ability to impose reasonable time limits on trial proceedings, which is otherwise provided for by rules of procedure. Similarly, the 2012 amendment of Rule 611(c) is not intended to change existing practice under which a witness called on direct examination and interrogated by leading questions may be interrogated by leading questions on behalf of the adverse party as well.

Comment to Rule 611(a), 1995 Amendment

Following are suggested procedures for effective document control:

(1) The trial judge should become involved as soon as possible, and no later than the pretrial conference, in controlling the number of documents to be used at trial.

(2) For purposes of trial, only one number should be applied to a document whenever referred to.

(3) Copies of key trial exhibits should be provided to the jurors for temporary viewing or for keeping in juror notebooks.

(4) Exhibits with text should and, on order of the court, shall be highlighted to direct jurors' attention to important language. Where important to an understanding of the document, that language should be explained dur-

ing the course of trial.

(5) At the close of evidence in a trial involving numerous exhibits, the trial judge shall ensure that a simple and clear retrieval system, e.g., an index, is provided to the jurors to assist them in finding exhibits during deliberations.

Comment to Original 1977 Rule

The last sentence of (c) changes the Arizona Supreme Court's holding in *J. & B. Motors v. Margolis*, 75 Ariz. 392, 257 P.2d 588, 38 A.L.R.2d 946 (1953).

AUTHORS' COMMENTS

Analysis

1. Scope and Purpose of Rule.
2. Comparison With Federal Rule.
3. Judicial Control of Order of Proof.
4. Judicial Control of Examination of Witnesses Generally.
5. Use of Leading Questions in Examination of Witnesses.
6. Scope of Cross-Examination.

1. *Scope and Purpose of Rule.* Rule 611 confers on the trial court broad authority and responsibility to control courtroom proceedings to insure that they remain focused on the issues properly presented and are conducted in a fair and efficient manner. Trial judges are functionaries of justice, not referees at prize fights, and the trial judge has an affirmative obligation to control the courtroom to ensure a fair trial. *State v. Bible*, 175 Ariz. 549, 858 P.2d 1152 (1993). The Rule also addresses the proper scope of cross-examination, and the use of leading questions in the examination of witnesses.

2. *Comparison With Federal Rule.* As a consequence of the 2012 conforming and restyling amendments, Rule 611(a) and Rule 611(c) are identical to their federal counterparts, Fed. R. Evid. 611(a) and (c). The 2012 Comment states the restyling amendments to subsections (a) are not intended to diminish a court's ability to impose reasonable time limits; and similar amendments to subsection (c) are not intended to change existing practice.

Ariz. R. Evid. 611(b), was not amended in 2012 and, thus, continues to permit cross-examination of a witness on any relevant matter. Fed. R. Evid. 611(b), however, limits the scope of cross-examination of a witness to the subject matter of the witness's direct testimony.

Although subsections (a) and (c) of Rule 611 parallel their federal counterparts, "federal court decisions interpreting the federal rule are persuasive but not binding with respect to interpreting the Arizona rule." *See,* Prefatory Comment to 2012

Amendments. *See also, State v. Terrazas*, 189 Ariz. 580, 944 P.2d 1194 (1997) (The Arizona Supreme Court is "not bound by the United States Supreme Court's non-constitutional construction of the Federal Rules of Evidence when [the Arizona Supreme Court construes] the Arizona Rules of Evidence."), citing, *State v. Bible*, 175 Ariz. 549, 858 P.2d 1152 (1993); *State v. Salazar-Mercado*, 232 Ariz. 256, 304 P.3d 543 (Ct. App. Div. 2 2013). Practitioners are urged to keep this legal tenet in mind as they research federal case law interpreting a federal evidentiary rule that corresponds to an Arizona evidentiary rule.

3. *Judicial Control of Order of Proof.* Rule 39(b) generally specifies the following order of proof at civil trials: (1) opening statement by plaintiff; (2) opening statement by defendant, unless deferred; (3) opening statements of other parties, if any, unless deferred; (4) presentation of evidence by plaintiff; (5) presentation of evidence by defendant; (6) presentation of evidence by other parties, if any, in an order directed by the Court; (7) presentation of rebuttal evidence by plaintiff; and, (8) presentation by defendant of rebuttal evidence on a counterclaim, if any. As a consequence of the 1995 amendments to Ariz.R.Civ.P. 39, the jury is to be instructed concerning its duties, the order that proceedings will follow, the procedure for submitting questions from the jurors, and the elementary legal principles that apply to the case, immediately after the jury is sworn and before opening statements. The presentation of rebuttal evidence by other parties, if any, on any cross-claims or third-party claims is with the permission of, and in the order directed by, the trial court.

As part of the 1995 "jury reform" amendments, a sentence was added to Rule 611(a) which grants the trial judge power and discretion to impose reasonable time limits on the trial proceedings or any portion thereof. A Court Comment that accompanied that particular amendment also delineated certain procedures which trial judges should consider implementing for controlling documents in complex or document-intensive cases.

Those same amendments added an identical provision as Ariz.R.Civ.P. 16(h). While trial courts have the discretion, under these Rules, to place time limitations on trial proceedings to avoid undue delay, waste of time or needless presentation of cumulative evidence, any limits imposed must be reasonable under the circumstances and rigid limits are disfavored. *Gamboa v. Metzler*, 223 Ariz. 399, 224 P.3d 215 (Ct. App. Div. 1 2010) (trial court within its discretion to stop cross-examination in light of parties' agreed upon witness schedule); *Brown v. U.S. Fidelity and Guar. Co.*, 194 Ariz. 85, 977 P.2d 807 (Ct. App. Div. 1 1998), as amended, (Nov. 25, 1998) and as corrected, (Aug. 5, 1999). Any time limits imposed should be sufficiently flexible to allow for adjustment during trial. *Gamboa v. Metzler*, 223 Ariz. 399, 224

P.3d 215 (Ct. App. Div. 1 2010); *Brown v. U.S. Fidelity and Guar. Co.*, 194 Ariz. 85, 977 P.2d 807 (Ct. App. Div. 1 1998), as amended, (Nov. 25, 1998) and as corrected, (Aug. 5, 1999).

The time limitations imposed will be reviewed on appeal for abuse of discretion. *Gamboa v. Metzler*, 223 Ariz. 399, 224 P.3d 215 (Ct. App. Div. 1 2010); *Brown v. U.S. Fidelity and Guar. Co.*, 194 Ariz. 85, 977 P.2d 807 (Ct. App. Div. 1 1998), as amended, (Nov. 25, 1998) and as corrected, (Aug. 5, 1999). To merit reversal, a party must show they incurred some harm as a consequence of the court's time limitation. *Gamboa v. Metzler*, 223 Ariz. 399, 224 P.3d 215 (Ct. App. Div. 1 2010); *Brown v. U.S. Fidelity and Guar. Co.*, 194 Ariz. 85, 977 P.2d 807 (Ct. App. Div. 1 1998), as amended, (Nov. 25, 1998) and as corrected, (Aug. 5, 1999).

The trial judge also has discretion to alter the order of the presentation of evidence within the parameters specified by the Rule. *Podol v. Jacobs*, 65 Ariz. 50, 173 P.2d 758 (1946); *Aritex Land Co. v. Baker*, 14 Ariz. App. 266, 482 P.2d 875 (Div. 2 1971). Thus, the trial court can permit the presentation of evidence outside the order of proof contemplated by Ariz.R.Civ.P. 39(b). *Mackey v. Philzona Petroleum Co.*, 93 Ariz. 87, 378 P.2d 906 (1963). The trial court may also permit a party to re-open its case after resting, if the interests of justice require. *Heeter v. Moore Drug Co.*, 104 Ariz. 41, 448 P.2d 391 (1968); *Bowman v. Hall*, 83 Ariz. 56, 316 P.2d 484 (1957); *T.H. Properties v. Sunshine Auto Rental, Inc.*, 151 Ariz. 444, 728 P.2d 663 (Ct. App. Div. 2 1986).

The trial court has considerable discretion to control the presentation of rebuttal evidence so as to confine it to its proper boundaries. Rebuttal evidence should be limited to evidence that addresses new matters brought out by the opposing party in the presentation of its case, and should not be a vehicle for simply repeating evidence that the party put on its case-in-chief. *Catchings v. City of Glendale*, 154 Ariz. 420, 743 P.2d 400 (Ct. App. Div. 2 1987); *Deyoe v. Clark Equipment Co., Inc.*, 134 Ariz. 281, 655 P.2d 1333 (Ct. App. Div. 2 1982); *Lowery v. Turner*, 19 Ariz. App. 299, 506 P.2d 1084 (Div. 1 1973).

4. *Judicial Control of Examination of Witnesses Generally.* The mandatory wording of Rule 611(a) suggests that the Court is more than a passive observer of trial proceedings and has an affirmative duty to insure that the trial is conducted efficiently and fairly. *State v. Bible*, 175 Ariz. 549, 858 P.2d 1152 (1993); *Pool v. Superior Court In and For Pima County*, 139 Ariz. 98, 677 P.2d 261 (1984); *State v. Mendez*, 2 Ariz. App. 77, 406 P.2d 427 (1965). Under Ariz.R.Civ.P. 43(d), only one attorney from each side can conduct the examination of a witness, unless the Court in its discretion permits other attorneys to participate.

The trial judge also has the authority to both protect and

control witnesses. The Court can preclude the use of argumentative questions, which have been held to be an improper mode of examination. *State v. Bible*, 175 Ariz. 549, 858 P.2d 1152 (1993); *Pool v. Superior Court In and For Pima County*, 139 Ariz. 98, 677 P.2d 261 (1984); *Gosewisch v. American Honda Motor Co., Inc.*, 153 Ariz. 389, 737 P.2d 365, Prod. Liab. Rep. (CCH) P 10819 (Ct. App. Div. 2 1985), opinion vacated in part on other grounds, 153 Ariz. 400, 737 P.2d 376, Prod. Liab. Rep. (CCH) P 11531, 83 A.L.R.4th 53 (1987). The Court may also strike a witness' nonresponsive answers and, if a witness evidences a propensity to make improper remarks, may direct that the witness' videotaped testimony be shown to the jury. *Rutledge v. Arizona Bd. of Regents*, 147 Ariz. 534, 711 P.2d 1207, 29 Ed. Law Rep. 1161 (Ct. App. Div. 1 1985).

5. *Use of Leading Questions in Examination of Witnesses.* Rule 611(c) states the general rule that leading questions are ordinarily not to be used in the direct examination of a witness. Such questions, however, may be permitted when doing so will serve "the ends of justice," *State v. King*, 66 Ariz. 42, 182 P.2d 915 (1947). Moreover, it is error to permit a leading question when the answer suggested "had already been received as the result of proper questioning." *State v. Garcia*, 141 Ariz. 97, 685 P.2d 734 (1984). The use of leading questions is, of course, proper during cross-examination.

A leading question is one that suggests the answer to the witness, although not all questions that can be answered with a simple affirmative or negative response are leading. *State v. Simoneau*, 98 Ariz. 2, 401 P.2d 404 (1965); *Wackerman v. Wackerman*, 16 Ariz. App. 382, 493 P.2d 928 (Div. 1 1972). Leading questions may be used in direct examination where that is necessary to develop the witness' testimony. *Preston v. Denkins*, 94 Ariz. 214, 382 P.2d 686 (1963); *Ball v. State*, 43 Ariz. 556, 33 P.2d 601 (1934). Leading questions are often permitted to establish preliminary or foundational matters. *Wackerman v. Wackerman*, 16 Ariz. App. 382, 493 P.2d 928 (Div. 1 1972).

An exception to the general prohibition of leading questions on direct examination which is recognized by the Rule itself is where a party calls as a witness an adverse party, a representative or managing agent of an adverse party, or a witness whose interests are identified with an adverse party. Where such a witness is called, the interrogation, which is nominally a direct examination, may be conducted through the use of leading questions. *Slow Development Co. v. Coulter*, 88 Ariz. 122, 353 P.2d 890 (1960); *City of Tucson v. Koerber*, 82 Ariz. 347, 313 P.2d 411 (1957); *Bogard GMC Co. v. Henley*, 2 Ariz. App. 223, 407 P.2d 412 (1965).

The trial court has discretion to determine whether the witness called is an adverse party or the managing agent of an adverse party. *Embry v. General Motors Corp.*, 115 Ariz. 433, 565 P.2d 1294 (Ct. App. Div. 2 1977) (overruled by, Gosewisch v. American Honda Motor Co., Inc., 153 Ariz. 400, 737 P.2d 376, Prod. Liab. Rep. (CCH) P 11531, 83 A.L.R.4th 53 (1987)). The burden is on the party seeking to conduct the direct examination through leading questions to establish that the witness is hostile or adverse. *General Petroleum Corp. v. Barker*, 77 Ariz. 235, 269 P.2d 729 (1954).

If the direct examination is allowed to proceed through the use of leading questions, the adverse party may then conduct its examination of the witness through leading questions as well. This provision of Rule 611(c) effectively overrules the result in *J. & B. Motors v. Margolis*, 75 Ariz. 392, 257 P.2d 588, 38 A.L.R.2d 946 (1953).

6. *Scope of Cross-Examination.* The right to cross-examination recognized in Rule 611(b) is fundamental and may even be an element of the due process of law. *Forman v. Creighton School Dist. No. 14*, 87 Ariz. 329, 351 P.2d 165 (1960); *Town of El Mirage v. Industrial Commission of Arizona*, 127 Ariz. 377, 621 P.2d 286 (Ct. App. Div. 1 1980); *cf. also,* Ariz. Const. Art. 2, Sec. 24. There is no rule, however, that requires that cross-examination of a witness be conducted. *City of Tucson v. Gallagher*, 108 Ariz. 140, 493 P.2d 1197, 65 A.L.R.3d 597 (1972).

Unlike its counterpart in the Federal Rules of Evidence, Rule 611(b) does not limit the scope of cross-examination to matters covered in the witness' direct testimony, but permits it to be conducted "on any relevant matter." Counsel are, accordingly, to be accorded a wide latitude in the conduct of cross-examination. *Watts v. Golden Age Nursing Home*, 127 Ariz. 255, 619 P.2d 1032 (1980).

While the right to conduct cross-examination cannot be denied altogether, cross-examination can, in the trial court's discretion, be subjected to reasonable limitations that take into account its importance in the fact finding process. *Middleton v. Green*, 35 Ariz. 205, 276 P. 322 (1929); *Block v. Meyer*, 144 Ariz. 230, 696 P.2d 1379 (Ct. App. Div. 1 1985); *Johnson v. University Hosp.*, 148 Ariz. 37, 712 P.2d 950 (Ct. App. Div. 1 1985) (disapproved of on other grounds by, Dunn v. Carruth, 162 Ariz. 478, 784 P.2d 684 (1989)); *Pyeatte v. Pyeatte*, 21 Ariz. App. 448, 520 P.2d 542, 84 A.L.R.3d 486 (Div. 2 1974). The trial court's decisions concerning the scope of cross-examination will not be disturbed on appeal absent a showing from the record of an abuse of discretion. *Cervantes v. Rijlaarsdam*, 190 Ariz. 396, 949 P.2d 56 (Ct. App. Div. 2 1997).

It is improper to ask questions during cross-examination that insinuate the existence of facts that will not be the subject of proof. *Taylor v. Cate*, 117 Ariz. 367, 573 P.2d 58 (1977); *Ruth v. Rhodes*, 66 Ariz. 129, 185 P.2d 304 (1947); *Foulk v. Kotz*, 138 Ariz. 159, 673 P.2d 799 (Ct. App. Div. 2 1983). Cross-examination also may not be used as a subterfuge for putting before the jury evidence which the Court has previously excluded. *Sharman v. Skaggs Companies, Inc.*, 124 Ariz. 165, 602 P.2d 833 (Ct. App. Div. 2 1979).

Recross-examination is permitted only where the redirect examination of the witness introduces new matters not covered in the direct and cross-examination of the witness. *General Petroleum Corp. v. Barker*, 77 Ariz. 235, 269 P.2d 729 (1954).

Rule 612. Writing Used to Refresh a Witness's Memory

(a) Scope. This rule gives an adverse party certain options when a witness uses a writing to refresh memory:

(1) while testifying; or

(2) before testifying, if the court decides that justice requires the party to have those options.

(b) Adverse Party's Options; Deleting Unrelated Matter. An adverse party is entitled to have the writing produced at the hearing, to inspect it, to cross-examine the witness about it, and to introduce in evidence any portion that relates to the witness's testimony. If the producing party claims that the writing includes unrelated matter, the court must examine the writing in camera, delete any unrelated portion, and order that the rest be delivered to the adverse party. Any portion deleted over objection must be preserved for the record.

(c) Failure to Produce or Deliver the Writing. If a writing is not produced or is not delivered as ordered, the court may issue any appropriate order. But if the prosecution does not comply in a criminal case, the court must strike the witness's testimony or—if justice so requires—declare a mistrial.

Amended Oct. 19, 1988, effective Nov. 1, 1988; Sept. 8, 2011, effective Jan. 1, 2012.

Comment to 2012 Amendment

The language of Rule 612 has been amended to conform to the federal restyling of the Evidence Rules to make them more easily understood and to make style and terminology consistent throughout the rules. These changes are intended to be stylistic only. There is no intent to change any result in any ruling on evidence admissibility.

Comment to Original 1977 Rule

Subparagraphs (1) and (2) of Federal Rule 612 have been reversed in order to clarify the intent of the rule which is to invoke the court's discretion concerning matters used before testifying and to have production as a matter of right of materials used while testifying. The word "action" in the second sentence of the rule replaces "testimony" in the Federal Rule to accord with the broader scope of cross-examination used in Arizona.

AUTHORS' COMMENTS

Analysis

1. *Scope and Purpose of Rule.* Rule 612 governs the procedures

to be followed where a written document or documents are used to refresh the recollection of a witness either before or during the witness' testimony. The writing used must be one that prompts a present recollection to which the witness can then testify. The document does not, by that reason alone, become admissible. In fact, it is improper to use inadmissible hearsay, such as a newspaper article, to attempt to refresh a witness' recollection while the witness is testifying. *Cf. Tuzon v. MacDougall*, 137 Ariz. 482, 671 P.2d 923 (Ct. App. Div. 1 1983).

Where a document is used to refresh a witness' recollection, opposing counsel has the right to have the document produced, to inspect it, to cross-examine the witness with respect to it, and to have introduced into evidence those portions which relate to the testimony of the witness. The Court can excise from the document, before it is thus introduced, those portions which do not relate to the subject matter of the action, but any portions thus excised must be made part of the record on appeal.

If the document or documents used to refresh a witness' recollection are or contain matters subject to the attorney-client or work-product protection, the privilege/protection is effectively waived, and the document or documents must be produced to opposing counsel, as the Rule requires. *Samaritan Health Services, Inc. v. Superior Court In and For Maricopa County*, 142 Ariz. 435, 690 P.2d 154 (Ct. App. Div. 1 1984).

2. *Comparison With Federal Rule.* Effective January 1, 2012, the Arizona Supreme Court amended Rule 612 to conform to the federal restyling of the Evidence Rules to make the rules more easily understood and to make style and terminology consistent throughout. The 2012 Comment states the stylistic amendments are not intended to "change any result in any ruling on evidence admissibility."

As a consequence of the 2012 restyling amendments, the language of Rule 612 is substantially identical to its federal counterpart, Fed. R. Evid. 612, except the Arizona Rule does not contain the exception for the provisions of the Jencks Act, 18 U.S.C.A. § 3500, contained in the Federal Rule.

Although Rule 612 parallels its federal counterpart, "federal court decisions interpreting the federal rule are persuasive but not binding with respect to interpreting the Arizona rule." *See,* Prefatory Comment to 2012 Amendments. *See also, State v. Terrazas*, 189 Ariz. 580, 944 P.2d 1194 (1997) (The Arizona Supreme Court is "not bound by the United States Supreme Court's nonconstitutional construction of the Federal Rules of Evidence when [the Arizona Supreme Court construes] the Arizona Rules of Evidence."), citing, *State v. Bible*, 175 Ariz. 549, 858 P.2d 1152 (1993); *State v. Salazar-Mercado*, 232 Ariz. 256, 304 P.3d 543 (Ct.

App. Div. 2 2013). Practitioners are urged to keep this legal tenet in mind as they research federal case law interpreting a federal evidentiary rule that corresponds to an Arizona evidentiary rule.

Rule 613. Witness's Prior Statements

(a) Showing or Disclosing the Statement During Examination. When examining a witness about the witness's prior statement, a party need not show it or disclose its contents to the witness. But the party must, on request, show it or disclose its contents to an adverse party's attorney.

(b) Extrinsic Evidence of a Prior Inconsistent Statement. Extrinsic evidence of a witness's prior inconsistent statement is admissible only if the witness is given an opportunity to explain or deny the statement and an adverse party is given an opportunity to examine the witness about it, or if justice so requires. This subdivision (b) does not apply to an opposing party's statement under Rule 801(d)(2).

Amended Oct. 19, 1988, effective Nov. 1, 1988; Sept. 8, 2011, effective Jan. 1, 2012.

Comment to 2012 Amendment

The language of Rule 613 has been amended to conform to the federal restyling of the Evidence Rules to make them more easily understood and to make style and terminology consistent throughout the rules. These changes are intended to be stylistic only. There is no intent to change any result in any ruling on evidence admissibility.

AUTHORS' COMMENTS

Analysis

1. *Scope and Purpose of Rule.* Rule 613 is concerned primarily with the mechanical aspects of impeaching a witness through the use of a prior statement made by the witness which is claimed to be inconsistent with the witness' testimony. Such a statement can be, under Rule 801(d)(1), admitted for both substantive and impeachment purposes. *Reed v. Hinderland*, 135 Ariz. 213, 660 P.2d 464, 37 A.L.R.4th 555 (1983). A statement need not be flatly contradictory of a witness' testimony to be considered inconsistent. *Trickel v. Rainbo Baking Co. of Phoenix*, 100 Ariz. 222, 412 P.2d 852 (1966); *State ex rel. Morrison v. Jay Six Cattle Co.*, 88 Ariz. 97, 353 P.2d 185 (1960). The inconsistency, if any, however may not be with respect to a matter that is purely col-

lateral to the issues addressed by the witness' testimony.

2. *Comparison With Federal Rule.* Effective January 1, 2012, the Arizona Supreme Court amended Rule 613 to conform to the federal restyling of the Evidence Rules to make the rules more easily understood and to make style and terminology consistent throughout. The 2012 Comment states the stylistic amendments are not intended to "change any result in any ruling on evidence admissibility."

Following the 2012 restyling amendments, the language of Rule 613 remains identical to its federal counterpart, Fed. R. Evid. 613.

Although Rule 613 parallels its federal counterpart, "federal court decisions interpreting the federal rule are persuasive but not binding with respect to interpreting the Arizona rule." *See,* Prefatory Comment to 2012 Amendments. *See also, State v. Terrazas*, 189 Ariz. 580, 944 P.2d 1194 (1997) (The Arizona Supreme Court is "not bound by the United States Supreme Court's non-constitutional construction of the Federal Rules of Evidence when [the Arizona Supreme Court construes] the Arizona Rules of Evidence."), citing, *State v. Bible*, 175 Ariz. 549, 858 P.2d 1152 (1993); *State v. Salazar-Mercado*, 232 Ariz. 256, 304 P.3d 543 (Ct. App. Div. 2 2013). Practitioners are urged to keep this legal tenet in mind as they research federal case law interpreting a federal evidentiary rule that corresponds to an Arizona evidentiary rule.

3. *Disclosure of Prior Statement.* The prior, assertedly inconsistent statements of the witness need not be shown to the witness. *Cf. Lynn v. Helitec Corp.*, 144 Ariz. 564, 698 P.2d 1283 (Ct. App. Div. 1 1984). They must, however, be shown to opposing counsel upon request. *But see, Wells v. Fell*, 231 Ariz. 525, 297 P.3d 931 (Ct. App. Div. 2 (2013) ((1) discussing the disclosure of impeachment evidence in civil and criminal cases; and (2) rejecting prior case law suggesting disclosure at trial obviates any substantial need for pretrial disclosure).

4. *Use of Extrinsic Evidence to Prove Prior Inconsistent Statement.* Before extrinsic evidence of a prior inconsistent statement may be admitted, the witness must be given the opportunity to explain the prior statement or to deny making it, and opposing counsel must be given the opportunity to interrogate the witness with respect to it, unless the interests of justice require a different procedure. This requirement does not apply to a prior statement which is an admission of a party. *Lynn v. Helitec Corp.*, 144 Ariz. 564, 698 P.2d 1283 (Ct. App. Div. 1 1984).

By implication, if the witness denies making the statement, extrinsic evidence of it can be received. If the witness admits making the statement, proof of it by extrinsic evidence is, strictly speaking, unnecessary. Even if the making of the prior statement is admitted, however, the trial court can nevertheless allow extrinsic evidence of it to be admitted, if the jury must determine which of the witness' statements is the truth. *State v. Woods*, 141 Ariz. 446, 687 P.2d 1201 (1984). A prior inconsistent statement is not conclusive, but is simply to be given whatever weight the trier of fact determines is appropriate. *Ohio Farmers Ins. Co. v. Norman*, 122 Ariz. 330, 594 P.2d 1026 (Ct. App. Div. 2 1979).

Rule 614. Court's Calling or Examining a Witness

(a) Calling. The court may call a witness on its own or at a party's request. Each party is entitled to cross-examine the witness.

(b) Examining. The court may examine a witness regardless of who calls the witness.

(c) Objections. A party may object to the court's calling or examining a witness either at that time or at the next opportunity when the jury is not present.

Amended Sept. 8, 2011, effective Jan. 1, 2012.

Comment to 2012 Amendment

The language of Rule 614 has been amended to conform to the federal restyling of the Evidence Rules to make them more easily understood and to make style and terminology consistent throughout the rules. These changes are intended to be stylistic only. There is no intent to change any result in any ruling on evidence admissibility.

AUTHORS' COMMENTS

Analysis

1. *Scope and Purpose of Rule.* Rule 614 grants the trial court authority and discretion to call its own witnesses, as well as to interrogate witnesses called by any party or by the Court. Any objections to the Court's calling or interrogation of witnesses are to be made at the time, or at the next available opportunity when the jury is not present. When witnesses are called by the Court, all parties are entitled to cross-examine.

In its calling or interrogation of witnesses, the Court must be careful not to show or imply any partiality to any party's position on the issues in the case. *Ruth v. Rhodes*, 66 Ariz. 129, 185 P.2d 304 (1947); *Tom Reed Gold Mines Co. v. Brady*, 55 Ariz. 133, 99 P.2d 97, 127 A.L.R. 905 (1940). It was previously held that the Court had the authority to permit jurors to submit written questions which the Court could then put to the witness, if appropriate. *State v. LeMaster*, 137 Ariz. 159, 669 P.2d 592 (Ct. App. Div. 1 1983). That authority has now been codified and confirmed in Ariz.R.Civ.P. 39(b)(10). See the discussion in Section of the *Authors' Comments* to Ariz.R.Civ.P. 39.

2. *Comparison With Federal Rule.* Effective January 1, 2012, the Arizona Supreme Court amended Rule 614 to conform to the

federal restyling of the Evidence Rules to make the rules more easily understood and to make style and terminology consistent throughout. The 2012 Comment states the stylistic amendments are not intended to "change any result in any ruling on evidence admissibility."

Following the 2012 restyling amendments, the language of Rule 614 remains identical to its federal counterpart, Fed. R. Evid. 614.

Although Rule 614 parallels its federal counterpart, "federal court decisions interpreting the federal rule are persuasive but not binding with respect to interpreting the Arizona rule." *See,* Prefatory Comment to 2012 Amendments. *See also, State v. Terrazas*, 189 Ariz. 580, 944 P.2d 1194 (1997) (The Arizona Supreme Court is "not bound by the United States Supreme Court's non-constitutional construction of the Federal Rules of Evidence when [it construes] the Arizona Rules of Evidence."), citing, *State v. Bible*, 175 Ariz. 549, 858 P.2d 1152 (1993); *State v. Salazar-Mercado*, 232 Ariz. 256, 304 P.3d 543 (Ct. App. Div. 2 2013). Practitioners are urged to keep this legal tenant in mind as they research federal case law interpreting a federal evidentiary rule that corresponds to an Arizona evidentiary rule. *See also, Authors' Comments*, Ariz. R. Evid. 101, Section 2, *supra*.

Rule 615. Excluding Witnesses

At a party's request, the court must order witnesses excluded so that they cannot hear other witnesses' testimony. Or the court may do so on its own. But this rule does not authorize excluding:

(a) a party who is a natural person;

(b) an officer or employee of a party that is not a natural person, after being designated as the party's representative by its attorney;

(c) a person whose presence a party shows to be essential to presenting the party's claim or defense;

(d) a person authorized by statute to be present; or

(e) a victim of crime, as defined by applicable law, who wishes to be present during proceedings against the defendant.

Amended Oct. 19, 1988, effective Nov. 1, 1988; Nov. 12, 1991, effective Dec. 31, 1991; Sept. 8, 2011, eective Jan. 1, 2012.

Comment to 2012 Amendment

This rule has been amended to conform to Federal Rule of Evidence 615, including the addition of subsection (d).

Subsection (e) (formerly subsection (d)), which is a uniquely Arizona provision, has been retained but amended to reflect that "a victim of crime" means a crime victim "as defined by applicable law," which includes any applicable rule, statute, or constitutional provision. The rule previously provided that "a victim of crime" would be "as defined by Rule 39(a), Rules of Criminal Procedure."

Additionally, the language of Rule 615 has been amended to conform to the federal restyling of the Evidence Rules to make them more easily understood and to make style and terminology consistent throughout the rules. These changes are intended to be stylistic only. There is no intent in the restyling to change any result in any ruling on evidence admissibility.

Comment to 1991 Amendment

The 1991 amendment to Rule 615 was necessary in order to conform the rule to the victim's right to be present at criminal proceedings, recognized in Ariz. Const. Art. II, § 2.1(A)(3).

AUTHORS' COMMENTS

Analysis

1. *Scope and Purpose of Rule.* Rule 615 governs the long-recognized practice of excluding witnesses from the courtroom during trial proceedings in order to prevent collusion and to discourage fabrication or tailoring of testimony. The exclusion of witnesses is not automatic—it must be requested by one of the

parties, although the Court has discretion to order it on its own motion.

Once such a request is made, exclusion of witnesses is mandatory, but a party must show prejudice resulting from the trial court's refusal to honor such a request in order to secure reversal on that basis. *Kosidlo v. Kosidlo*, 125 Ariz. 32, 607 P.2d 15 (Ct. App. Div. 2 1979), decision disapproved in part on other grounds, 125 Ariz. 18, 607 P.2d 1 (1979). If an exclusion order is entered, and a witness violates it by appearing in the courtroom during trial before testifying, the Court can refuse to permit the witness to testify. *Allison v. Ovens*, 4 Ariz. App. 496, 421 P.2d 929 (1966), vacated in part on other grounds, 102 Ariz. 520, 433 P.2d 968 (1967) (overruled in part by, Young v. Bach, 107 Ariz. 180, 484 P.2d 176 (1971)).

The Rule does not authorize the exclusion of a party, the exclusion of an officer or employee designated as the representative of a party that is not a natural person, or the exclusion of a person whose presence is shown to be essential to the presentation of a party's case. Thus, even though an exclusion order has been requested and made, the Court can permit one side's expert witness to hear or review the testimony of the opposing side's expert in order to be in a position to suggest areas for cross-examination. *McGuire v. Caterpillar Tractor Co.*, 151 Ariz. 420, 728 P.2d 290, Prod. Liab. Rep. (CCH) P 11010 (Ct. App. Div. 2 1986).

Recently, issues have surfaced concerning the possible use of portable electronic devices by a non-excluded persons attending a trial who then communicates electronically with an excluded witness who is waiting to testify in that case. Despite the modern day twist, this situation is similar, but not identical, to a non-excluded person in the courtroom walking outside the courtroom and communicating with the excluded witness about the trial. Ariz.R.Evid. 615 does not specifically address, and there are no reported Arizona cases discussing, this issue. An admonition on this specific topic, therefore, maybe the best way to deal with this issue.

Under a 1991 amendment to the Rule, the Court may not exclude the victim of a crime who wishes to be present during proceedings against the defendant accused of committing it.

2. *Comparison With Federal Rule.* Effective January 1, 2012, the Arizona Supreme Court amended Rule 615 to conform to its federal counterpart, Fed. R. Evid. 615. This amendment resulted in the inclusion of new subsection (d), which prevents the exclusion of persons authorized by statute.

As a consequence of the 2012 amendment, subsections (a), (b), (c) and (d) of Ariz. R. Evid. 615 are now identical to subsections (a), (b), (c) and (d) of Fed. R. Evid. 615.

The 2012 amendments retained former Rule 615(d) [now denominated as Rule 615(e)], but amended that provision to provide that "a victim of crime" means a crime victim "as defined by applicable law." The 2012 Comment explains that "applicable law" includes any applicable rule, statute or constitutional provision. The 2012 Comment to Rule 615 further notes that the rule had previously provided that a "victim of crime" would be "as defined by Rule 39(a), Rules of Criminal Procedure."

Although subsections (a) to (d) of Rule 615 parallel their federal counterparts, "federal court decisions interpreting the federal rule are persuasive but not binding with respect to interpreting the Arizona rule." *See,* Prefatory Comment to 2012 Amendments. *See also, State v. Terrazas*, 189 Ariz. 580, 944 P.2d 1194 (1997) (The Arizona Supreme Court is "not bound by the United States Supreme Court's non-constitutional construction of the Federal Rules of Evidence when [the Arizona Supreme Court construes] the Arizona Rules of Evidence."), citing, *State v. Bible*, 175 Ariz. 549, 858 P.2d 1152 (1993); *State v. Salazar-Mercado*, 232 Ariz. 256, 304 P.3d 543 (Ct. App. Div. 2 2013). Practitioners are urged to keep this legal tenet in mind as they research federal case law interpreting a federal evidentiary rule that corresponds to an Arizona evidentiary rule.

ARTICLE VII. OPINIONS AND EXPERT TESTIMONY

Introductory Note to Original 1977 Rules: Problems of Opinion Testimony

The rules in this article are designed to avoid unnecessary restrictions concerning the admissibility of opinion evidence; however, as this note makes clear, an adverse attorney may, by timely objection, invoke the court's power to require that before admission of an opinion there be a showing of the traditional evidentiary prerequisites. Generally, it is not intended that evidence which would have been inadmissible under pre-existing law should now become admissible.

A major objective of these rules is to eliminate or sharply reduce the use of hypothetical questions. With these rules, hypothetical questions should seldom be needed and the court will be expected to exercise its discretion to curtail the use of hypothetical questions as inappropriate and premature jury summations. Ordinarily, a qualified expert witness can be asked whether he has an opinion on a particular subject and then what that opinion is. If an objection is made and the court determines that the witness should disclose the underlying facts or data before giving the opinion, the witness should identify the facts or data necessary to the opinion.

In jury trials, if there is an objection and if facts or data upon which opinions are to be based have not been admitted in evidence at the time the opinion is offered, the court may admit the opinion subject to later admission of the underlying facts or data; however, the court will be expected to exercise its discretion so as to prevent the admission of such opinions if there is any serious question concerning the admissibility, under Rule 703 or otherwise, of the underlying facts or data.

Added Sept. 8, 2011, effective Jan. 1, 2012. Amended Aug. 30, 2012, effective Jan. 1, 2013.

Rule 701. Opinion Testimony by Lay Witnesses

If a witness is not testifying as an expert, testimony in the form of an opinion is limited to one that is:

(a) rationally based on the witness's perception;

(b) helpful to clearly understanding the witness's testimony or to determining a fact in issue; and

(c) not based on scientific, technical, or other specialized knowledge within the scope of Rule 702.

Amended Oct. 19, 1988, effective Nov. 1, 1988; Sept. 8, 2011, effective Jan. 1, 2012.

Comment to 2012 Amendment

The 2012 amendment of Rule 701 adopts Federal Rule of Evidence 701, as restyled.

AUTHORS' COMMENTS

Analysis

1. *Scope and Purpose of Rule.* Rule 701 deals with the subject of opinion testimony by lay witnesses. There is a strong preference that the testimony of lay witnesses be confined to factual matters they have observed or perceived or events in which they have participated. This preference is premised on the theory that the members of the jury are as qualified as the lay witness to draw inferences and conclusions from the facts which the witness has observed. The line between facts observed/perceived and opinions drawn from such observations/perceptions is at times a difficult line to draw and enforce, however, particularly because lay witnesses are prone to express their observations and perceptions in terms of the conclusions they have drawn from them.

Rule 701 recognizes that it is almost inevitable that testimony from lay witnesses will involve, to some degree, their opinions, and seeks to limit such testimony to those opinions that are rationally based on the witness' perceptions and helpful to an understanding of the witness' testimony or to the determination of a fact that is in issue. It is the trial court's function to keep lay witnesses' testimony, where possible, focused on what the witness has observed and perceived.

2. *Comparison With Federal Rule.* Effective January 1, 2012, the Arizona Supreme Court amended Rule 701 to adopt Federal Rule of Evidence 701, as restyled.

Before the 2012 amendment, Arizona's Rule 701 did not contain a provision comparable to Fed. R. Evid. 701(c), which provides that lay opinion testimony, to be admissible as such, may not be based upon "scientific, technical or other specialized knowledge within the scope of Rule 702." In addition, and while not mentioned in the 2012 Comment, the 2012 amendment of Rule 701 resulted in the deletion of the word *inferences,* presumably for the same reason the word *inference* was deleted from Ariz. R. Evid. 703 to 705.

As a result of the 2012 amendment, the language of Arizona's Rule 701 is now identical to the language of its federal counterpart and includes the proviso that lay opinion testimony may not be based upon knowledge that falls within the scope of 702.

The Federal Rules of Evidence also do not have an introductory note, such as the "Introductory Note to Original 1977 Rules: Problems of Opinion Testimony" that precedes and pertains to Ariz. R. Evid. 701 to 706 dealing with opinion testimony.

Although Rule 701 parallels its federal counterpart, "federal court decisions interpreting the federal rule are persuasive but not binding with respect to interpreting the Arizona rule." *See,* Prefatory Comment to 2012 Amendments. *See also, State v. Terrazas*, 189 Ariz. 580, 944 P.2d 1194 (1997) (The Arizona Supreme Court is "not bound by the United States Supreme Court's nonconstitutional construction of the Federal Rules of Evidence when [the Arizona Supreme Court construes] the Arizona Rules of Evidence."), citing, *State v. Bible*, 175 Ariz. 549, 858 P.2d 1152 (1993); *State v. Salazar-Mercado*, 232 Ariz. 256, 304 P.3d 543 (Ct. App. Div. 2 2013). Practitioners are urged to keep this legal tenet in mind as they research federal case law interpreting a federal evidentiary rule that corresponds to an Arizona evidentiary rule.

3. *Conditions for Admissibility of Lay Opinion.* Rule 701 establishes three separate circumstances, each of which must be presented, where a lay witness is permitted to express an opinion drawn from the witness' observations: (1) where the opinion is rationally based on the witness' perception; (2) where it is helpful to a clear understanding of the witness' testimony or to a determination of a fact in issue; and (3) the opinion is one that is not based on scientific, technical, or other specialized knowledge within the scope of Rule 702.

The first circumstance is really a foundational requirement, *i.e.,* there must be a showing that the opinion is actually based on the witness' factual perceptions. *Lewis v. N.J. Riebe Enterprises, Inc.*, 170 Ariz. 384, 825 P.2d 5 (1992); *Rimondi v. Briggs*, 124 Ariz. 561, 606 P.2d 412 (1980); *Eldredge v. Miller*, 78 Ariz. 140, 277 P.2d 239 (1954); *Alires v. Southern Pac. Co.*, 93 Ariz. 97, 378 P.2d 913 (1963) (disapproved of by, Miller v. State of Okl., 240 F. Supp. 263 (E.D. Okla. 1965)); *Southwestern Freight Lines v. Floyd*, 58 Ariz. 249, 119 P.2d 120 (1941); *Pincock v. Dupnik*, 146 Ariz. 91, 703 P.2d 1240 (Ct. App. Div. 2 1985); *Groener v. Briehl*, 135 Ariz. 395, 661 P.2d 659 (Ct. App. Div. 1 1983); *Globe American Cas. Co. v. Lyons*, 131 Ariz. 337, 641 P.2d 251, 33 A.L.R.4th 972 (Ct. App. Div. 1 1981) (rejected by, State Farm Fire & Cas. Co. v. Wicka, 474 N.W.2d 324 (Minn. 1991)). Additionally, there must be a showing, or it must be apparent from the testimony, that the extent of the witness' perceptions and/or experience were sufficient to permit the rational drawing of the inference and/or formation of the opinion the witness intends to express. *Pulliam v. Pulliam*, 139 Ariz. 343, 678 P.2d 528 (Ct. App. Div. 2 1984); *Groener v. Briehl*, 135 Ariz. 395, 661 P.2d 659 (Ct. App. Div. 1 1983).

Second, the opinion must be one that will assist the trier of fact in understanding the witness' testimony; it should not simply consist of the witness telling the jurors how to decide the case. *Groener v. Briehl*, 135 Ariz. 395, 661 P.2d 659 (Ct. App. Div. 1 1983); *Ingrum v. Tucson Yellow Cab Co.*, 131 Ariz. 523, 642 P.2d 868 (Ct. App. Div. 2 1981).

Whether a lay witness is qualified to offer a particular opinion and whether a sufficient foundation has been established as to the basis for the opinion are preliminary determinations to be made by the trial court under Rule 104(a). *Groener v. Briehl*, 135 Ariz. 395, 661 P.2d 659 (Ct. App. Div. 1 1983). A lay witness is not qualified to draw legal conclusions. *Young v. Environmental Air Products, Inc.*, 136 Ariz. 206, 665 P.2d 88 (Ct. App. Div. 2 1982), aff'd as modified, 136 Ariz. 158, 665 P.2d 40 (1983). The trial court can exclude, under Rule 403, a lay opinion for which there is sufficient foundation if its prejudicial effect outweighs its probative value. *Kassman v. Busfield Enterprises, Inc.*, 131 Ariz. 163, 639 P.2d 353 (Ct. App. Div. 2 1981).

The third circumstance was adopted by the Arizona Supreme Court in 2012 and conforms with Fed. R. Evid. 701(c). To date, there are no reported cases interpreting Rule 701(c) (as amended). Insofar as federal case law is *persuasive, but not controlling*, this section will be updated as Arizona case law interpreting Rule 701 gives guidance.

4. *Examples of Permitted Lay Opinion Testimony—Pre 2012 Amendment.* Perhaps the most recognized example of a situation where lay opinion testimony is permitted is the rule that an owner of property may express an opinion as to its value. *Atkinson v. Marquart*, 112 Ariz. 304, 541 P.2d 556 (1975); *Madisons Chevrolet, Inc. v. Donald*, 109 Ariz. 100, 505 P.2d 1039 (1973); *Acheson v. Shafter*, 107 Ariz. 576, 490 P.2d 832 (1971); *Board of Regents of the University and State Colleges of Ariz. v. Cannon*, 86 Ariz. 176, 342 P.2d 207 (1959); *Town of Paradise Valley v. Laughlin*, 174 Ariz. 484, 851 P.2d 109 (Ct. App. Div. 1 1992); *Maricopa County v. Barkley*, 168 Ariz. 234, 812 P.2d 1052 (Ct. App. Div. 1 1990); *United California Bank v. Prudential Ins. Co. of America*, 140 Ariz. 238, 681 P.2d 390 (Ct. App. Div. 1 1983); *King v. O'Rielly Motor Co.*, 16 Ariz. App. 518, 494 P.2d 718 (Div. 2 1972). The basis on which the owner arrived at that opinion of

value bears only on the weight to be given the opinion, not its admissibility. *Santa Fe Pac. R. Co. v. Cord*, 14 Ariz. App. 254, 482 P.2d 503 (Div. 1 1971).

Other matters which have been recognized to be potentially proper subjects for lay opinion testimony, provided that a sufficient foundation for it is established, include: the speed of a vehicle, *Eldredge v. Miller*, 78 Ariz. 140, 277 P.2d 239 (1954); *Ring v. Taylor*, 141 Ariz. 56, 685 P.2d 121 (Ct. App. Div. 1 1984); *but cf. Townsend v. Whatton*, 21 Ariz. App. 556, 521 P.2d 1014 (Div. 2 1974); intoxication or sobriety of an individual, *Esquivel v. Nancarrow*, 104 Ariz. 209, 450 P.2d 399 (1969); *Morales v. Bencic*, 12 Ariz. App. 40, 467 P.2d 752 (Div. 1 1970); and, the mental condition, sanity or insanity of another person, *Wigley v. Whitten*, 78 Ariz. 88, 276 P.2d 517 (1954), opinion adhered to on reh'g, 78 Ariz. 224, 278 P.2d 412 (1955); *In re Wagner's Estate*, 75 Ariz. 135, 252 P.2d 789 (1953); *Sapp v. Lifrand*, 44 Ariz. 321, 36 P.2d 794 (1934); *Starkins v. Bateman*, 150 Ariz. 537, 724 P.2d 1206 (Ct. App. Div. 1 1986).

Rule 702. Testimony by Expert Witnesses

A witness who is qualified as an expert by knowledge, skill, experience, training, or education may testify in the form of an opinion or otherwise if:

(a) the expert's scientific, technical, or other specialized knowledge will help the trier of fact to understand the evidence or to determine a fact in issue;

(b) the testimony is based on sufficient facts or data;

(c) the testimony is the product of reliable principles and methods; and

(d) the expert has reliably applied the principles and methods to the facts of the case.

Amended Sept. 8, 2011, effective Jan. 1, 2012.

Comment to 2012 Amendment

The 2012 amendment of Rule 702 adopts Federal Rule of Evidence 702, as restyled. The amendment recognizes that trial courts should serve as gatekeepers in assuring that proposed expert testimony is reliable and thus helpful to the jury's determination of facts at issue. The amendment is not intended to supplant traditional jury determinations of credibility and the weight to be afforded otherwise admissible testimony, nor is the amendment intended to permit a challenge to the testimony of every expert, preclude the testimony of experience-based experts, or prohibit testimony based on competing methodologies within a field of expertise. The trial court's gatekeeping function is not intended to replace the adversary system. Cross-examination, presentation of contrary evidence, and careful instruction on the burden of proof are the traditional and appropriate means of attacking shaky but admissible evidence.

A trial court's ruling finding an expert's testimony reliable does not necessarily mean that contradictory expert testimony is not reliable. The amendment is broad enough to permit testimony that is the product of competing principles or methods in the same field of expertise. Where there is contradictory, but reliable, expert testimony, it is the province of the jury to determine the weight and credibility of the testimony.

This comment has been derived, in part, from the Committee Notes on Rules—2000 Amendment to Federal Rule of Evidence 702.

AUTHORS' COMMENTS

Analysis

8. Weight Accorded Expert Testimony.
9. Examples of Permitted Expert Testimony—Construing Rule 702 before the 2012 Amendment.
10. Limitations on Use of Expert Witnesses.

1. *Scope and Purpose of Rule.* Arizona Rule of Evidence 702 expressly permits opinion testimony from experts who are not necessarily percipient witnesses, but who have, by reason of their experience, training or education, technical, scientific or other specialized knowledge that will help the trier of fact in understanding the issues to be resolved. Even relevant testimony, however, admissible pursuant to Rule 702 may be excluded, pursuant to Rule 403, if its probative value is substantially outweighed by the danger of unfair prejudice, confusion of the issues, or misleading the jury. *State v. Sosnowicz*, 229 Ariz. 90, 270 P.3d 917 (Ct. App. Div. 1 2012); *State v. Chappell*, 225 Ariz. 229, 236 P.3d 1176, 1182–83 (2010), cert. denied, 131 S. Ct. 1485, 179 L. Ed. 2d 320 (2011).

In 2012, the Arizona Rules of Evidence were modified to bring them in line with the Federal Rules of Evidence. The 2012 amendment of Ariz. R. Evid. 702 adopted Fed. R. Evid. 702. *See* Comment to 2012 Amendment. This amendment shifts the standard for the admissibility of expert witness testimony from the "general acceptance" test expressed in *Frye* to the "reliability" test expressed in *Daubert*. *See, Frye v. U.S.*, 293 F. 1013, 34 A.L.R. 145 (App. D.C. 1923) (rejected by, State v. Walstad, 119 Wis. 2d 483, 351 N.W.2d 469 (1984)) and (rejected by, State v. Brown, 297 Or. 404, 687 P.2d 751 (1984)) and (rejected by, Nelson v. State, 628 A.2d 69 (Del. 1993)) and (rejected by, State v. Alberico, 1993-NMSC-047, 116 N.M. 156, 861 P.2d 192 (1993)) and (rejected by, State v. Moore, 268 Mont. 20, 885 P.2d 457 (1994)) and (rejected by, State v. Faught, 127 Idaho 873, 908 P.2d 566 (1995)) and (rejected by, People v. Shreck, 22 P.3d 68, 90 A.L.R. 5th 765 (Colo. 2001)) and *Daubert v. Merrell Dow Pharmaceuticals, Inc.*, 509 U.S. 579, 113 S. Ct. 2786, 125 L. Ed. 2d 469, 27 U.S.P. Q.2d 1200, Prod. Liab. Rep. (CCH) P 13494, 37 Fed. R. Evid. Serv. 1, 23 Envtl. L. Rep. 20979 (1993), respectively.

Whether, and to what extent, however, Arizona's court will rely on federal case law in interpreting Arizona Rule of Evidence 702 is unknown. The Prefatory Comments to the 2012 Amendments states: "Where the language of an Arizona rule parallels that of a federal rule, federal court decisions interpreting the federal rule are persuasive but not binding with respect to interpreting the Arizona rule." *See also, State v. Terrazas*, 189 Ariz. 580, 944 P.2d 1194 (1997) (The Arizona Supreme Court is "not bound by the United States Supreme Court's non-constitutional construction of the Federal Rules of Evidence when [it construes] the Arizona Rules of Evidence."), citing, *State v. Bible*, 175 Ariz. 549, 858 P.2d 1152 (1993); *State v. Bernstein*, __ P.3d __, 2014 WL 118106 (Ct. App. Div. 1 2014), citing *Arizona State Hospital/Arizona Community Protection and Treatment Center v. Klein*, 231 Ariz. 467, 296 P.3d 1003 (Ct. App. Div. 1 2013) ("'federal court decisions interpreting [Federal Rule of Evidence 702] are persuasive but not binding' in interpreting Arizona Rule of Evidence 702". Similarly, advisory committee notes to Federal Rule of Evidence 702 provide guidance in interpreting Arizona Rule of Evidence 702. *See State v. Salazar-Mercado*, 232 Ariz. 256, 304 P.3d 543 (Ct. App. Div. 2 2013). Practitioners are urged to keep this legal tenent in mind as they research federal case law interpreting a federal evidentiary rule that corresponds to an Arizona evidentiary rule.

2. *Comparison With Federal Rule.* Effective January 1, 2012, the Arizona Supreme Court amended Rule 702 to 'adopt' its federal counterpart, Fed. R. Evid. 702, as restyled. As a result of the 2012 amendment, the language of Ariz. R. Evid. 702 is once again identical to its federal counterpart, Fed. R. Evid. 702.

Under Rule 702 (as amended), the admissibility of expert witness testimony is no longer governed by the "general acceptance" standard announced in Frye v. U.S., 293 F. 1013, 34 A.L.R. 145 (App. D.C. 1923) (rejected by, State v. Walstad, 119 Wis. 2d 483, 351 N.W.2d 469 (1984)) and (rejected by, State v. Brown, 297 Or. 404, 687 P.2d 751 (1984)) and (rejected by, Nelson v. State, 628 A.2d 69 (Del. 1993)) and (rejected by, State v. Alberico, 1993-NMSC-047, 116 N.M. 156, 861 P.2d 192 (1993)) and (rejected by, State v. Moore, 268 Mont. 20, 885 P.2d 457 (1994)) and (rejected by, State v. Faught, 127 Idaho 873, 908 P.2d 566 (1995)) and (rejected by, People v. Shreck, 22 P.3d 68, 90 A.L.R. 5th 765 (Colo. 2001)). Rather, the admissibility of such testimony is now governed by the "reliability" standard announced in *Daubert v. Merrell Dow Pharmaceuticals, Inc.*, 509 U.S. 579, 113 S. Ct. 2786, 125 L. Ed. 2d 469, 27 U.S.P.Q.2d 1200, Prod. Liab. Rep. (CCH) P 13494, 37 Fed. R. Evid. Serv. 1, 23 Envtl. L. Rep. 20979 (1993), and codified in Fed. R. Evid. 701 and 702.

3. *History of 2012 Amendment of Rule 702.* The admissibility of expert opinion testimony is governed by Ariz. R. Evid. 702, which was amended quite strikingly in 2011, effective January 1, 2012, to adopt Federal Rule of Evidence, as restyled. See, Comment to 2012 Amendment. Under amended Ariz. R. Evid. 702, expert opinion testimony is admissible if:

1. the witness is qualified as an expert and the testimony will help the trier of fact to understand the evidence or determine a fact issue;

2. the testimony is based on sufficient facts or data;
3. the testimony is the product of reliable principles and methods; and
4. the expert has reliably applied the principles and methods to the facts of the case.

In its 2012 amendment of Rule 702, the Arizona Supreme Court abandoned the "general acceptance" test rooted in *Frye v. U.S.*, 293 F. 1013, 34 A.L.R. 145 (App. D.C. 1923) (rejected by, State v. Walstad, 119 Wis. 2d 483, 351 N.W.2d 469 (1984)) and (rejected by, State v. Brown, 297 Or. 404, 687 P.2d 751 (1984)) and (rejected by, Nelson v. State, 628 A.2d 69 (Del. 1993)) and (rejected by, State v. Alberico, 1993-NMSC-047, 116 N.M. 156, 861 P.2d 192 (1993)) and (rejected by, State v. Moore, 268 Mont. 20, 885 P.2d 457 (1994)) and (rejected by, State v. Faught, 127 Idaho 873, 908 P.2d 566 (1995)) and (rejected by, People v. Shreck, 22 P.3d 68, 90 A.L.R.5th 765 (Colo. 2001)) and used in Arizona dating back to 1962 to determine the admissibility of scientific expert opinion testimony. *Logerquist v. McVey*, 196 Ariz. 470, 1 P.3d 113 (2000), superceded by rule, (("Arizona adopted *Frye* in 1962."), citing *State v. Valdez*, 91 Ariz. 274, 371 P.2d 894 (1962)).

In its place, the Court adopted the 'reliability' test expressed in Federal Rule of Evidence 702, which federal rule essentially codifies the holdings of the U.S. Supreme Court in *Daubert/Joiner/Kumho Tire. See,* Comment to the 2012 Amendment of Ariz. R. Evid. 702; *Daubert v. Merrell Dow Pharmaceuticals, Inc.*, 509 U.S. 579, 113 S. Ct. 2786, 125 L. Ed. 2d 469, 27 U.S.P.Q.2d 1200, Prod. Liab. Rep. (CCH) P 13494, 37 Fed. R. Evid. Serv. 1, 23 Envtl. L. Rep. 20979 (1993); *General Elec. Co. v. Joiner*, 522 U.S. 136, 118 S. Ct. 512, 139 L. Ed. 2d 508, 18 O.S.H. Cas. (BNA) 1097, Prod. Liab. Rep. (CCH) P 15120, 48 Fed. R. Evid. Serv. 1, 28 Envtl. L. Rep. 20227, 177 A.L.R. Fed. 667 (1997); *Kumho Tire Co., Ltd. v. Carmichael*, 526 U.S. 137, 119 S. Ct. 1167, 143 L. Ed. 2d 238, 50 U.S.P.Q.2d 1177, Prod. Liab. Rep. (CCH) P 15470, 50 Fed. R. Evid. Serv. 1373, 29 Envtl. L. Rep. 20638 (1999). *See also, Lear v. Fields*, 226 Ariz. 226, 245 P.3d 911 (Ct. App. Div. 2 2011), review denied, (Sept. 20, 2011) for a comparative discussion of the then-Arizona *Frye* "general acceptance" test with the federal *Daubert/Kumho Tire* "reliability" test for the admissibility of expert witness testimony.

Arizona did not come early, or easily, to its conversion to the federal standard. For many decades before 1993, both the Arizona courts and the federal courts utilized the *Frye* test for determining the admissibility of scientific expert opinion testimony. The *Frye* test called for a judicial determination as to whether the expert offering the testimony relied upon scientific theories or processes that were "generally accepted in the relevant scientific community." *Frye v. U.S.*, 293 F. 1013, 34 A.L.R. 145 (App. D.C. 1923) (rejected by, State v. Walstad, 119 Wis. 2d 483, 351 N.W.2d 469 (1984)) and (rejected by, State v. Brown, 297 Or. 404, 687 P.2d 751 (1984)) and (rejected by, Nelson v. State, 628 A.2d 69 (Del. 1993)) and (rejected by, State v. Alberico, 1993-NMSC-047, 116 N.M. 156, 861 P.2d 192 (1993)) and (rejected by, State v. Moore, 268 Mont. 20, 885 P.2d 457 (1994)) and (rejected by, State v. Faught, 127 Idaho 873, 908 P.2d 566 (1995)) and (rejected by, People v. Shreck, 22 P.3d 68, 90 A.L.R.5th 765 (Colo. 2001)). In June 1993, however, the U.S. Supreme Court altered this landscape with its decision in *Daubert v. Merrell Dow Pharmaceuticals, Inc.*, 509 U.S. 579, 113 S. Ct. 2786, 125 L. Ed. 2d 469, 27 U.S.P. Q.2d 1200, Prod. Liab. Rep. (CCH) P 13494, 37 Fed. R. Evid. Serv. 1, 23 Envtl. L. Rep. 20979 (1993).

In *Daubert*, the U.S. Supreme Court held the *Frye* "general acceptance" test had been superceded by the Federal Rules of Evidence, adopted in 1975. *Daubert v. Merrell Dow Pharmaceuticals, Inc.*, 509 U.S. 579, 113 S. Ct. 2786, 125 L. Ed. 2d 469, 27 U.S.P. Q.2d 1200, Prod. Liab. Rep. (CCH) P 13494, 37 Fed. R. Evid. Serv. 1, 23 Envtl. L. Rep. 20979 (1993) (finding that nothing in the text of Federal Rule of Evidence 702, or its drafting history, established "general acceptance" as an "absolute prerequisite to admissibility" of expert witness testimony.). The Court interpreted the then federal Rule 702 to impose a "gatekeeper" duty upon federal trial judges to ensure the relevance and reliability of scientific testimony. *Daubert v. Merrell Dow Pharmaceuticals, Inc.*, 509 U.S. 579, 113 S. Ct. 2786, 125 L. Ed. 2d 469, 27 U.S.P. Q.2d 1200, Prod. Liab. Rep. (CCH) P 13494, 37 Fed. R. Evid. Serv. 1, 23 Envtl. L. Rep. 20979 (1993) ("under the Rules, the trial judge must ensure that any and all scientific testimony or evidence admitted is not only relevant, but reliable").

The U.S. Supreme Court, thus, rejected the *Frye* test, in favor of a "flexible" test that required federal trial court judges serve as gatekeepers in making the preliminary assessment of whether the underlying reasoning or methodology employed by the expert is "scientifically valid." *Daubert v. Merrell Dow Pharmaceuticals, Inc.*, 509 U.S. 579, 113 S. Ct. 2786, 125 L. Ed. 2d 469, 27 U.S.P. Q.2d 1200, Prod. Liab. Rep. (CCH) P 13494, 37 Fed. R. Evid. Serv. 1, 23 Envtl. L. Rep. 20979 (1993) ("The inquiry envisioned by Rule 702 is, we emphasize, a flexible one. Its overarching subject is the scientific validity—and thus the evidentiary relevance and reliability—of the principles that underlie a proposed submission."). The U.S. Supreme Court later extended the scope of *Daubert* in *General Elec. Co. v. Joiner*, 522 U.S. 136, 118 S. Ct. 512 (1997) (federal trial judge's reliability determination applied to both conclusions and methodology), and *Kumho*

Tire Co., Ltd. v. Carmichael, 526 U.S. 137, 119 S. Ct. 1167 (1999) (*Daubert* applies to all forms of expert evidence). Fed. R. Evid. 702 was amended in 2001 essentially to "codify" the approach taken by these U.S. Supreme Court decisions. *Manpower, Inc. v. Insurance Co. of Pennsylvania*, 732 F.3d 796 (7th Cir. 2013) ("*Daubert* . . . is essentially codified in the current version of Rule 702", citing *Lees v. Carthage College*, 714 F.3d 516, 521 (7th Cir. 2013); *U.S. v. Nacchio*, 555 F.3d 1234 (10th Cir. 2009); *Massachusetts Mut. Life Ins. Co. v. Residential Funding Co., LLC*, — F.Supp.2d —, 2013 WL 6490125 (D.Mass. 2013) (Federal Rule of Evidence 702 codified *Daubert* and its progeny).

In August 1993, six weeks after the U.S. Supreme Court's decision in *Daubert*, the Arizona Supreme Court considered the *Daubert* opinion, as it might apply to Arizona's then-identical, and now former, Rule 702. *State v. Bible*, 175 Ariz. 549, 858 P.2d 1152 (1993). In *State v. Bible*, the Arizona Supreme Court declined to follow *Daubert* and reaffirmed that the *Frye* test would continue to apply in Arizona.

In 2000, the Arizona Supreme Court returned to the issue of the differing standards for the admissibility of expert witness testimony. *Logerquist v. McVey*, 196 Ariz. 470, 1 P.3d 113 (2000), superceded by rule. This time, in *Logerquist*, the Arizona Supreme Court emphatically rejected the *Daubert/Joiner/Kumho Tire* test, upheld the *Frye* test and limited the types of expert evidence to which the *Frye* test was to be applied to those involving scientific theories or processes.

By way of background, *Logerquist* involved the interlocutory review of a trial court order excluding expert testimony concerning plaintiff's "repressed memory" after applying the 'general acceptance' test expressed in *Frye*. In *Logerquist*, the Arizona Supreme Court held that the trial court had erred in applying the *Frye* test at all, holding that *Frye* applied only to the use of "novel scientific theories or processes to produce results," and not to testimony or conclusions based on experience and observation about human behavior for the purpose of explaining that behavior. *Logerquist v. McVey*, 196 Ariz. 470, 1 P.3d 113 (2000), superceded by rule.

After deciding the issue presented on appeal, the *Logerquist* court went on to address, however, the comparative merits of both the *Frye* and *Daubert/Joiner/Kumho Tire* tests. The Court rejected the federal test announced in *Daubert/Joiner/Kumho Tire* and firmly held that the *Frye* test would remain the test in Arizona for the admissibility of scientific evidence. Briefly summarized, the *Logerquist* court's articulated reasons to reaffirm *Frye* were as follows:

(1) the experience with the *Frye* test in Arizona had not been

unsatisfactory;

(2) trial judges are not, as a group, necessarily more qualified than jurors to distinguish good science from bad science;

(3) trial judges do not have the time to conduct the hearings which *Kumho Tire* contemplates in every case in which expert testimony is to be offered;

(4) giving trial judges the power to determine reliability and credibility of a qualified expert witness would be inconsistent with the Arizona constitutional mandate that juries determine questions of fact; and,

(5) allowing judges to pass on the weight or credibility of an expert's testimony would cross the line between the judicial task of ruling on the foundation and relevance of evidence, and the jury's function of assessing the credibility of evidence admitted.

The *Logerquist* decision was not a unanimous decision. It also was not the end of the debate.

Following the 2000 decision in *Logerquist*, the debate over the competing evidentiary tests persisted. Then, in 2010, the Arizona Legislature enacted, and the Governor signed into law, A.R.S. § 12-2203, which purported to adopt for civil and criminal cases the federal evidentiary test set forth in Fed. R. Evid. 702, as amended in 2000, and expressed in *Daubert/Joiner/Kumho Tire*. The constitutionality of A.R.S. § 12-2203 was quickly challenged. *Lear v. Fields*, 226 Ariz. 226, 245 P.3d 911 (Ct. App. Div. 2 2011), review denied, (Sept. 20, 2011). On appeal, the statute was declared unconstitutional under the separation of powers doctrine because the statute impinged upon the Arizona Supreme Court's constitutionally conferred rule-making authority.

The debate ended in 2011, when the Arizona Supreme Court amended Ariz. R. Evid. 702 to adopt Fed. R. Evid. 702, effective January 1, 2012. As a consequence of this amendment, and as earlier noted, the 'general acceptance' test expressed in *Frye* is no longer the standard for the admissibility of expert witness testimony in Arizona. Rather, going forward, the 'reliability' test set forth in Fed. R. Evid. 702 and expressed in *Daubert/Joiner/Kumho Tire* (and their progeny) will govern the admissibility of expert witness testimony in Arizona's court. Ariz. R. Evid. 702 (2012).

4. *Qualifications Required for Experts.* Both before and after the 2012 amendment to Ariz. R. Evid. 702, a foundation must be established for the testimony of the particular expert witness in order for that witness in order for that witness to qualify to testify as an expert. Such foundation involves proof of an expert witness' qualifications. On this point, Ariz. R. Evid. 702 (2012) continues

to require that an expert witness qualify as such by reason of "knowledge, skill, experience, training or education." *See,* Ariz. R. Evid. 702(a) (2012); *State v. Cooperman*, 230 Ariz. 245, 282 P.3d 446 (Ct. App. Div. 2 2012), review granted in part, (Mar. 19, 2013) and aff'd, 232 Ariz. 347, 306 P.3d 4 (2013). *See also, Ulibarri v. Gerstenberger*, 178 Ariz. 151, 871 P.2d 698 (Ct. App. Div. 1 1993) (rejected on other grounds by, Logerquist v. Danforth, 188 Ariz. 16, 932 P.2d 281 (Ct. App. Div. 2 1996)).

Under Rule 702, an expert witness is one who possesses skill and knowledge "superior to that of [people] in general." *State v. Keener*, 110 Ariz. 462, 520 P.2d 510 (1974) ("An expert witness is one who possesses skill and knowledge superior to that of [people] in general."); *Good v. City of Glendale*, 150 Ariz. 218, 722 P.2d 386 (Ct. App. Div. 2 1986). To qualify as an expert, the witness need not have the highest possible qualifications or highest degree of skill or knowledge; rather, it is sufficient the witness have a skill and knowledge superior to that of persons in general. *McMurtry v. Weatherford Hotel, Inc.*, 231 Ariz. 244, 293 P.3d 520 (Ct. App. Div. 1 2013); *Pincock v. Dupnik*, 146 Ariz. 91, 703 P.2d 1240 (Ct. App. Div. 2 1985); *Godwin v. Farmers Ins. Co. of America*, 129 Ariz. 416, 631 P.2d 571 (Ct. App. Div. 1 1981) (Educational attainments are not a prerequisite, and a person can be qualified as an expert by reason of experience alone.). The courts have reasoned that the lack of a professional degree or experience goes to the weight of the testimony before the trier of fact, rather than its admissibility. *McMurtry v. Weatherford Hotel, Inc.*, 231 Ariz. 244, 293 P.3d 520 (Ct. App. Div. 1 2013) (The degree of an expert's qualification goes to the weight given the testimony, not its admissibility.); *State v. Macumber*, 112 Ariz. 569, 544 P.2d 1084 (1976); *State v. Mosley*, 119 Ariz. 393, 581 P.2d 238 (1978); *State v. Garrison*, 120 Ariz. 255, 585 P.2d 563 (1978); *City of Phoenix v. Brown*, 88 Ariz. 60, 352 P.2d 754 (1960); *Perguson v. Tamis*, 188 Ariz. 425, 937 P.2d 347 (Ct. App. Div. 2 1996); *Smith v. John C. Lincoln Hospital*, 118 Ariz. 549, 578 P.2d 630 (Ct. App. Div. 1 1978).

Thus, an expert need not be a professional or the most qualified person to offer opinions in the particular area of expertise. *McMurtry v. Weatherford Hotel, Inc.*, 231 Ariz. 244, 293 P.3d 520 (Ct. App. Div. 1 2013) (holding, the 2012 amendments did not change the outcome on the facts presented). *See also*, *State v. Garrison*, 120 Ariz. 255, 585 P.2d 563 (1978), citing *City of Phoenix v. Brown*, 88 Ariz. 60, 352 P.2d 754 (1960) ("While this witness did not have the best possible qualifications nor the highest degree of skill or knowledge, [the witness] did possess skill and knowledge superior to that of [people] in general."); *State v. Macumber*, 112 Ariz. 569, 544 P.2d 1084 (1976) (expert may be a lay person who has specialized knowledge acquired through actual experience or careful study, which will assist the jury); *Lay v. City of Mesa*, 168 Ariz. 552, 815 P.2d 921 (Ct. App. Div. 1 1991) (expert may be qualified to testify on basis of actual experience or careful study); *Maricopa County v. Barkley*, 168 Ariz. 234, 812 P.2d 1052 (Ct. App. Div. 1 1990) (A witness may qualify to give an expert opinion by reason of "real world" experience as well as by academic study.); *Good v. City of Glendale*, 150 Ariz. 218, 722 P.2d 386 (Ct. App. Div. 2 1986) ("It is not necessary that the witness have the highest possible qualifications or highest degree of skill or knowledge; rather, it is merely sufficient that the witness have a skill and knowledge superior to that of persons in general.").

Ariz. R. Evid. 702(a) (2012) requires that any such expert testimony "help" the trier of fact to understand the evidence or determine a fact issue. The 2012 amendment did not materially change this requirement in that former Rule 702 used virtually identical language to define this requirement, but used the word 'assist' instead of the word 'help.' *Compare*, Rule 702(a), Ariz. R. Evid. (2012) with former Ariz. R. Evid. 702. *See also*, *State v. Sosnowicz*, 229 Ariz. 90, 270 P.3d 917 (Ct. App. Div. 1 2012). Thus, under former Rule 702, and under Ariz. R. Evid. 702(a) (2012), expert opinion testimony is inadmissible if special knowledge is not required to help the trier of fact understand the evidence or determine a particular issue. *Alires v. Southern Pac. Co.*, 93 Ariz. 97, 378 P.2d 913 (1963) (disapproved of by, Miller v. State of Okl., 240 F. Supp. 263 (E.D. Okla. 1965)) ("The principle to be applied is that where the facts can be intelligently described to the jurors and understood by them and they can form a reasonable opinion for themselves, the opinion of experts will be rejected."); *Messina v. Midway Chevrolet Co.*, 221 Ariz. 11, 209 P.3d 147 (Ct. App. Div. 1 2008) (The threshold test for expert testimony is whether it will assist the trier of fact); *Adams v. Amore*, 182 Ariz. 253, 895 P.2d 1016 (Ct. App. Div. 1 1994); *Rabe v. Cut and Curl of Plaza 75, Inc.*, 148 Ariz. 552, 715 P.2d 1240 (Ct. App. Div. 2 1986) (expert testimony properly excluded); *Pincock v. Dupnik*, 146 Ariz. 91, 703 P.2d 1240 (Ct. App. Div. 2 1985) (expert testimony excluded); *Shell Oil Co. v. Gutierrez*, 119 Ariz. 426, 581 P.2d 271 (Ct. App. Div. 2 1978).

A separate foundational requirement is that the expert's opinions be based on facts or data reasonably relied upon by experts in the same field. *Standard Chartered PLC v. Price Waterhouse*, 190 Ariz. 6, 945 P.2d 317 (Ct. App. Div. 1 1996), as corrected on denial of reconsideration, (Jan. 13, 1997), (defense accounting firm expert relied on filed and signed tax return, which suggested information's trustworthiness); *Adams v. Amore*, 182 Ariz. 253, 895 P.2d 1016 (Ct. App. Div. 1 1994); *Davis v. Cessna Aircraft Corp.*, 182 Ariz. 26, 893 P.2d 26, Prod. Liab. Rep.

(CCH) P 14038 (Ct. App. Div. 1 1994). Foundational objections to the bases for an expert's testimony serve a useful purpose when there is a legitimate foundational question to explore. *Sheppard v. Crow-Barker Paul No. 1 Ltd. Partnership*, 192 Ariz. 539, 968 P.2d 612 (Ct. App. Div. 1 1998). To make such objections, however, merely to force one's adversary to "do it the hard way" wastes court time and client dollars. *Sheppard v. Crow-Barker Paul No. 1 Ltd. Partnership*, 192 Ariz. 539, 968 P.2d 612 (Ct. App. Div. 1 1998).

While there is no *per se* rule of admissibility on the expert's personal practices, there may be situations where how a testifying expert approaches a medical problem may be relevant and of assistance to the jury in determining what the standard of care requires or to evaluate the expert's credibility. *Smethers v. Campion*, 210 Ariz. 167, 108 P.3d 946 (Ct. App. Div. 1 2005).

In addition, A.R.S. § 12-2604 establishes minimum qualifications for standard of care experts in medical malpractice cases. *Baker v. University Physicians Healthcare*, 231 Ariz. 379, 296 P.3d 42 (2013) (rejecting various constitutional challenges to A.R.S. § 12-2604). The statute was enacted to "ensure that physicians testifying as experts have sufficient expertise to truly assist the fact-finder on issues of standard of care and proximate causation." *Baker v. University Physicians Healthcare*, 231 Ariz. 379, 296 P.3d 42 (2013) (interpreting A.R.S. § 12-2604 to require that testifying experts in medical malpractice cases specialize "in the same specialty or claimed specialty" as treating physician only when the care or treatment at issue is within that specialty and interpreting the meaning of "specialist" and "specialty" to include subspecialties); *Cornerstone Hosp. of Southeast Arizona, L.L.C. v. Marner ex rel. County of Pima*, 231 Ariz. 67, 290 P.3d 460 (Ct. App. Div. 2 2012)) (citations omitted) (addressing qualifications of registered nurse to testify about the standard of care applicable to any registered nurse, licensed practical nurse or certified nurse assistant). *See also*, *Lo v. Lee*, 231 Ariz. 484, 297 P.3d 176 (2013) (A.R.S. § 12-2604(A) only requires expert to have a specialty that matches the specialized standard of care relevant to the medical treatment that gave rise to the action).

The party seeking to introduce expert opinion testimony has the burden of establishing both the need for it and the qualifications of the particular witness to provide it. *Ulibarri v. Gerstenberger*, 178 Ariz. 151, 871 P.2d 698 (Ct. App. Div. 1 1993) (rejected on other grounds by, Logerquist v. Danforth, 188 Ariz. 16, 932 P.2d 281 (Ct. App. Div. 2 1996)); *Gaston v. Hunter*, 121 Ariz. 33, 588 P.2d 326 (Ct. App. Div. 1 1978).

5. *Scientific Evidence: Post-2012 Amendments.* Effective January 1, 2012, the Arizona Supreme Court amended Rule 702 to

conform to Federal Rule of Evidence 702, i.e., the codification of the U.S. Supreme Court's decisions in *Daubert v. Merrell Dow Pharmaceuticals, Inc.*, 509 U.S. 579, 113 S. Ct. 2786 (1993) (holding *Frye's* "general acceptance" test had been superseded by the adoption of the Federal Rules of Evidence) and *Kumho Tire Co., Ltd. v. Carmichael*, 526 U.S. 137, 119 S. Ct. 1167 (1999) (holding the "gatekeeping" function assigned to federal trial courts by *Daubert* applied not only to "scientific knowledge," but also to testimony based upon "technical, or other specialized knowledge," i.e. to all expert evidence).

As of the date of this submission, the Arizona Supreme Court has not addressed Rule 702 (2012) in the context of a civil case, and there are but a few appellate decisions addressing Rule 702 (2012) in such setting. Accordingly, to provide more insight into the decisional evolution of Rule 702, a summary of both civil and certain criminal cases discussing Rule 702 (2012) is set forth below as follows:

(1) *State v. Miller*, — P.3d —, 2013 WL 6842566 (2013). The Arizona Supreme Court held the "2012 amendment to Rule 702 is not a new constitutional rule." Accordingly, the Court declined to retroactively apply Rule 702 (as amended 2012).

(2) *State v. Bernstein*, — P.3d —, 2014 WL 118106 (Ct. App. Div. 1 2014). State established under Rule 702 (2012) that the challenged blood alcohol content test results were admissible. In reaching this conclusion, the appellate court, among other things, examined Fed.R.Evid. 702 and found that the federal rule did not codify the non-exclusive factors for determining whether scientific evidence is admissible as set forth in the United States Supreme Court's decision in Daubert, and is "broad enough to require consideration of any or all of the . . . factors where appropriate."

(3) *State v. Buccheri-Bianca*, 233 Ariz. 324, 312 P.3d 123 (Ct. App. Div. 2 2013). Rule 702 (2012) does not prohibit generalized expert testimony, and thus "does not effect a 'sea change' in Arizona's well-established framework for evaluating the admissibility of generalized expert testimony." In support of its decision, the appellate court relied on *State v. Salazar-Mercado*, 232 Ariz. 256, 304 P.3d 543 (Ct. App. Div. 2 2013).

(4) *State v. Perez*, 233 Ariz. 38, 308 P.3d 1189 (Ct. App. Div. 2 2013). The appellate court upheld the exclusion of polygraph test results under Rule 702 (2012).

(5) *Arizona State Hospital/Arizona Community Protection and Treatment Center v. Klein*, 231 Ariz. 467, 296 P.3d 1003 (Ct. App. Div. 1 2013). Rule 702 (2012) applies to expert

testimony in discharge hearings brought pursuant to A.R.S. § 36-3714.

(6) *McMurtry v. Weatherford Hotel, Inc.*, 231 Ariz. 244, 293 P.3d 520 (Ct. App. Div. 1 2013). The court of appeals upheld admissibility of testimony from hospital industry expert under Rule 702 (2012), which is consistent with prior decisions under former Rule 702.

6. *Discretion of Trial Court.* Following the 2012 amendment of Rule 702, the trial court continues to have considerable discretion to determine whether there is a need for expert testimony on a particular subject and whether the particular expert witness possesses the requisite qualifications to provide it. *Escamilla v. Cuello*, 230 Ariz. 202, 282 P.3d 403 (2012).

A trial court's decision to admit or exclude expert testimony is reviewed for abuse of discretion. *State v. Bernstein*, — P.3d —, 2014 WL 118106 (Ct. App. Div. 1 2014) (appellate court reviews "a fact-based 'decision to permit or exclude expert testimony for an abuse of discretion' "); *Escamilla v. Cuello*, 230 Ariz. 202, 282 P.3d 403 (2012). If the trial court bases its decision on a question of law, such ruling is reviewed *de novo*. *McMurtry v. Weatherford Hotel, Inc.*, 231 Ariz. 244, 293 P.3d 520 (Ct. App. Div. 1 2013).

7. *Consulting Experts.* A single expert may be named as either a consulting expert or a testifying expert, but not both. *Emergency Care Dynamics, Ltd. v. Superior Court In and For County of Maricopa*, 188 Ariz. 32, 932 P.2d 297, 1997-2 Trade Cas. (CCH) ¶ 71929 (Ct. App. Div. 1 1997). Thus, in a case where the defendant planned to call as an expert a witness who had previously consulted with counsel for the plaintiff concerning serving as an expert, the trial court had discretion to condition allowing the witness to testify on there being no references made to the prior consultation. *Granger v. Wisner*, 134 Ariz. 377, 656 P.2d 1238 (1982).

In some cases, a party may reinstate the privileges and discovery protections that apply to consulting experts by redesignating its expert from a testifying expert to a consulting expert before expert opinion evidence is offered through production of a report, discovery responses or testimony. *Para v. Anderson ex rel. County of Maricopa*, 231 Ariz. 91, 290 P.3d 1214 (Ct. App. Div. 1 2012), review granted, (Mar. 19, 2013), *citing, Arizona Minority Coalition for Fair Redistricting v. Arizona Independent Redistricting Com'n*, 211 Ariz. 337, 121 P.3d 843 (Ct. App. Div. 1 2005). A party may not reinstate the privileges and discovery protections that apply to consulting expert by redesignating an expert as a consultant once the expert's opinions have been disclosed. *Para v. Anderson ex rel. County of Maricopa*, 231 Ariz. 91, 290 P.3d 1214 (Ct. App. Div. 1 2012), review granted, (Mar. 19, 2013). Although a party may depose such redesignated expert, the trial court retains broad discretions under Ariz. R. Evid. 403 to control the use of such testimony at trial. *Para v. Anderson ex rel. County of Maricopa*, 231 Ariz. 91, 290 P.3d 1214 (Ct. App. Div. 1 2012), review granted, (Mar. 19, 2013).

In *Seisinger v. Siebel*, 220 Ariz. 85, 203 P.3d 483 (2009), the Supreme Court held that the provisions of A.R.S. § 12-2604(A), which purported to establish the standards for admitting medical expert testimony in medical malpractice cases, were substantive in nature and not an unconstitutional infringement on the Court's rule-making powers because the challenged statute defined the evidence required to establish a breach of the standard of care in that type of case. *But see*, *Lear v. Fields*, 226 Ariz. 226, 245 P.3d 911 (Ct. App. Div. 2 2011), review denied, (Sept. 20, 2011) (holding unconstitutional, A.R.S. § 12-2203, a statute purporting to govern as a general rule of evidence the admissibility of expert testimony in any civil or criminal action).

8. *Weight Accorded Expert Testimony.* Uncontradicted expert testimony may be controlling evidence where a material issue is one on which expert guidance is required. *McNeely v. Industrial Commission*, 108 Ariz. 453, 501 P.2d 555 (1972); *Asbestos Engineering & Supply Co. v. Industrial Commission of Arizona*, 131 Ariz. 558, 642 P.2d 903 (Ct. App. Div. 1 1982). Generally, however, the trier of fact is free to disregard or discount expert evidence where it is equivocal, contradicted or where its factual predicate is disputed. *City Consumer Services, Inc. v. Metcalf*, 161 Ariz. 1, 775 P.2d 1065 (1989); *Stainless Specialty Mfg. Co. v. Industrial Com'n of Arizona*, 144 Ariz. 12, 695 P.2d 261 (1985); *Matter of Estate of Thorpe*, 152 Ariz. 341, 732 P.2d 571 (Ct. App. Div. 1 1986); *Tucson Unified School Dist. v. Industrial Com'n of Arizona*, 138 Ariz. 1, 672 P.2d 953 (Ct. App. Div. 1 1983); *Butler v. Wong*, 117 Ariz. 395, 573 P.2d 86 (Ct. App. Div. 2 1977); *Fleitz v. Van Westrienen*, 114 Ariz. 246, 560 P.2d 430 (Ct. App. Div. 1 1977). While expert testimony stating there was a *possible* causal connection between the defendant's negligence and the plaintiff's injuries is not, in and of itself, sufficient to support a finding of liability, it may be sufficient if supported by other evidence of causation. *Kennecott Copper Corp. v. McDowell*, 100 Ariz. 276, 413 P.2d 749 (1966); *Ideal Food Products Co. v. Rupe*, 76 Ariz. 175, 261 P.2d 992 (1953); *Butler v. Wong*, 117 Ariz. 395, 573 P.2d 86 (Ct. App. Div. 2 1977); *Coca-Cola Bottling Co. of Tucson v. Fitzgerald*, 3 Ariz. App. 303, 413 P.2d 869 (1966).

9. *Examples of Permitted Expert Testimony—Construing Rule 702 before the 2012 Amendment.* The Arizona cases decided under the *Frye* test before the 2012 amendment of Rule 702 present a bewildering variety of diverse subjects, too numerous to list here,

on which expert opinion testimony has been held to be admissible/inadmissible. Examples are as follows:

(1) the reconstruction of automobile accidents, *Englehart v. Jeep Corp.*, 122 Ariz. 256, 594 P.2d 510 (1979); *American Honda Motor Co., Inc. v. Smith*, 110 Ariz. 593, 521 P.2d 1139 (1974);

(2) the standard of due care applicable to health care providers, *Taylor v. DiRico*, 124 Ariz. 513, 606 P.2d 3 (1980);

(3) product safety, *Brown v. Sears, Roebuck & Co.*, 136 Ariz. 556, 667 P.2d 750 (Ct. App. Div. 1 1983); *Hohlenkamp v. Rheem Mfg. Co.*, 123 Ariz. 535, 601 P.2d 298 (Ct. App. Div. 2 1979);

(4) the value of property, *Golder v. Department of Revenue, State Bd. of Tax Appeals*, 123 Ariz. 260, 599 P.2d 216 (1979); *State ex rel. Morrison v. Jay Six Cattle Co.*, 88 Ariz. 97, 353 P.2d 185 (1960); *Maricopa County v. Barkley*, 168 Ariz. 234, 812 P.2d 1052 (Ct. App. Div. 1 1990);

(5) causation or lack thereof, *Rayner v. Stauffer Chemical Co.*, 120 Ariz. 328, 585 P.2d 1240 (Ct. App. Div. 1 1978); *Butler v. Wong*, 117 Ariz. 395, 573 P.2d 86 (Ct. App. Div. 2 1977);

(6) the present economic value of a future stream of income, *Southern Pac. Transp. Co. v. Lueck*, 111 Ariz. 560, 535 P.2d 599 (1975);

(7) the effect of water on concrete, *Glowacki v. A.J. Bayless Markets, Inc.*, 76 Ariz. 295, 263 P.2d 799 (1953);

(8) commercially reasonable banking practices, *Cook v. Great Western Bank & Trust*, 141 Ariz. 80, 685 P.2d 145, 39 U.C.C. Rep. Serv. 214 (Ct. App. Div. 1 1984);

(9) testamentary capacity, *Matter of Estate of Thorpe*, 152 Ariz. 341, 732 P.2d 571 (Ct. App. Div. 1 1986);

(10) whether a particular intersection was dangerous, *Dunham v. Pima County*, 161 Ariz. 304, 778 P.2d 1200 (1989);

(11) whether the actions of an insurance company constituted bad faith, *Clearwater v. State Farm Mut. Auto. Ins. Co.*, 161 Ariz. 590, 780 P.2d 423 (Ct. App. Div. 2 1989), opinion vacated in part, 164 Ariz. 256, 792 P.2d 719 (1990);

(12) videotaped computer simulation, *Bledsoe v. Salt River Valley Water Users' Ass'n*, 179 Ariz. 469, 880 P.2d 689 (Ct. App. Div. 2 1994);

(13) deficiencies of eyewitness testimony, *State v. Chapple*, 135 Ariz. 281, 660 P.2d 1208 (1983).

10. *Limitations on Use of Expert Witnesses.* The years preceding the 2012 amendment of Ariz. R. Evid. 702 have witnessed an

ever increasing use and reliance upon expert testimony in civil cases, and a proliferation in the number of areas in which expert testimony is claimed to be permissible and appropriate. This has caused considerable concern, in Arizona and elsewhere, over the contribution this phenomenon has made to the escalating costs of civil litigation. In Arizona, the response has been reform efforts to place presumptive limits on the use of expert witnesses in civil cases.

These reform efforts commenced in 1990 with the adoption of the former Uniform Rules of Practice for Medical Malpractice Cases. Rule 1(D)(4) of those Rules provided that the trial court was to limit the number of expert witnesses that the parties could call at trial, that each *party* was presumptively entitled to only one expert witness on the issue of the standard of care, and that each *side* was presumptively entitled to only one expert witness on any other issue. This Rule was made part of Ariz. R. Civ. P. 26(b)(4)(D), discussed *infra*, as part of the 2000 civil rules consolidation effort.

These limitations on experts in medical malpractice cases served in part as the model for limitations imposed on the use of expert witnesses in civil cases generally by the court and discovery reform amendments to the Arizona Rules of Civil Procedure which became effective on July 1, 1992. Ariz. R. Civ. P. 43(g) provided that, absent a showing of good cause, the Court was not to allow opinion evidence on the same issue from more than one independent expert witness per side. (This "one independent expert witness" limitation does not apply to or include an employee of a party whose opinions were formed during the course and scope of employment by that party. *Arizona Dept. of Revenue v. Superior Court In and For the County of Maricopa*, 189 Ariz. 49, 938 P.2d 98 (Ct. App. Div. 1 1997). Ariz. R. Civ. P. 26(b)(4)(D) confirmed that each *side* is presumptively entitled to only one expert witness on an issue and that, in multiple party cases where the parties cannot agree on a single expert witness to call, the Court is to designate the independent expert or, upon a showing of good cause, may allow more than one expert to be called on an issue. In 2000, as part of the 2000 civil rules consolidation, Ariz. R. Civ. P. 43(g) was abrogated, because its provisions were essentially duplicative of those of Ariz. R. Civ. P. 26(b)(4)(D).

Rule 703. Bases of an Expert's Opinion Testimony

An expert may base an opinion on facts or data in the case that the expert has been made aware of or personally observed. If experts in the particular field would reasonably rely on those kinds of facts or data in forming an opinion on the subject, they need not be admissible for the opinion to be admitted. But if the facts or data would otherwise be inadmissible, the proponent of the opinion may disclose them to the jury only if their probative value in helping the jury evaluate the opinion substantially outweighs their prejudicial effect.

Amended Oct. 19, 1988, effective Nov. 1, 1988; Sept. 3, 2009, effective Jan. 1, 2010; Sept. 8, 2011, effective Jan. 1, 2012.

Comment to 2012 Amendment

The language of Rule 703 has been amended to conform to the federal restyling of the Evidence Rules to make them more easily understood and to make style and terminology consistent throughout the rules. These changes are intended to be stylistic only. There is no intent to change any result in any ruling on evidence admissibility.

All references to an "inference" have been deleted on the grounds that the deletion made the rule flow better and easier to read, and because any "inference" is covered by the broader term "opinion." Courts have not made substantive decisions on the basis of any distinction between an opinion and an inference. No change in current practice is intended.

Comment to Original 1977 Rule

This rule, along with others in this article, is designed to expedite the reception of expert testimony. Caution is urged in its use. Particular attention is called to the Advisory Committee's Note to the Federal Rules of Evidence which accompanies Federal Rule 703. In addition, it should be emphasized that the standard "if of a type reasonably relied upon by experts in the particular field" is applicable to both sentences of the rule. The question of whether the facts or data are of a type reasonably relied upon by experts is in all instances a question of law to be resolved by the court prior to the admission of the evidence. If the facts or data meet this standard and form the basis of admissible opinion evidence they become admissible under this rule for the limited purpose of disclosing the basis for the opinion unless they should be excluded pursuant to an applicable constitutional provision, statute, rule or decision.

Evidence which is inadmissible except as it may qualify as being "reasonably relied upon by experts in the particular field" has traditionally included such things as certain medical reports and comparable sales in condemnation actions.

AUTHORS' COMMENTS

Analysis

4. Manner of Presentation of Expert Testimony.
5. Permissible Bases for Expert Opinion Under Rule 703.
6. Unadmitted and/or Inadmissible Matters as Basis for Expert Opinion.

1. *Scope and Purpose of Rule.* Rule 703 governs the extent to which an expert may state an opinion that is based on information other than what the expert has personally observed. Despite the statement in the *Introductory Note: Problems of Opinion Testimony* which precedes Rule 701 that it "was not intended that evidence which would have been inadmissible under preexisting law should now become admissible," Rule 703 has, at least in part, produced exactly that result. The 2010 amendment of Ariz. R. Evid. 703, which appears to have survived the 2012 restyling amendments, attempts to address this problem by adding a new requirement for the admissibility of such information and testimony.

2. *Comparison With Federal Rule.* Effective January 1, 2012, the Arizona Supreme Court amended Rule 703 to conform to the federal restyling of the Evidence Rules to make the rules more easily understood and to make style and terminology consistent throughout. The 2012 Comment states the stylistic amendments are not intended to "change any result in any ruling on evidence admissibility."

In addition to the restyling amendments, Rule 703 was amended to delete all references to an "inference." Consistent with the 2011 comment to the Federal Rule, the 2012 Comment to the Arizona Rule explains that the deletion made the rule flow better and easier to read, and because any "inference" is covered by the broader term "opinion." *See* Comment to 2012 Amendment. The 2012 Comment further notes the amendment [deleting the word *inference*] was not intended to change current practice.

Following the 2012 restyling amendments, the language of Rule 703 is again identical to its federal counterpart, Fed. R. Evid. 703.

Although Rule 703 parallels its federal counterpart, "federal court decisions interpreting the federal rule are persuasive but not binding with respect to interpreting the Arizona rule." *See,* Prefatory Comment to 2012 Amendments. *See also, State v. Terrazas*, 189 Ariz. 580, 944 P.2d 1194 (1997) (The Arizona Supreme Court is "not bound by the United States Supreme Court's nonconstitutional construction of the Federal Rules of Evidence when [the Arizona Supreme Court construes] the Arizona Rules of Evidence."), citing, *State v. Bible*, 175 Ariz. 549, 858 P.2d 1152 (1993); *State v. Salazar-Mercado*, 232 Ariz. 256, 304 P.3d 543 (Ct.

App. Div. 2 2013). Practitioners are urged to keep this legal tenet in mind as they research federal case law interpreting a federal evidentiary rule that corresponds to an Arizona evidentiary rule.

3. *Prior Practice re Presentation of Expert Testimony; Use of Hypothetical Questions.* Both before and after the adoption of Ariz. R. Evid. 703, it has been permissible for an expert witness to base opinions on that witness' personal knowledge and first-hand observations, *e.g.,* the treating physician. Before the adoption of Rule 703, an expert could also express opinions based on facts that had been observed by others, but those facts and observations had to have been received in evidence. *American Honda Motor Co., Inc. v. Smith*, 110 Ariz. 593, 521 P.2d 1139 (1974); *Schmidt v. Gibbons*, 101 Ariz. 222, 418 P.2d 378 (1966); *Gray v. Woods*, 84 Ariz. 87, 324 P.2d 220 (1958). One recognized exception was that a medical expert was permitted to base an opinion, at least in part, on the medical history provided by the patient. *Wise v. Monteros*, 93 Ariz. 124, 379 P.2d 116 (1963).

The then prevailing practice was to present the opinion testimony of expert witnesses through the device of hypothetical questions in which the expert was asked to assume certain facts to be true, to indicate whether, on that assumption, the expert had an opinion, and, if so, what that opinion was. *Rayner v. Stauffer Chemical Co.*, 120 Ariz. 328, 585 P.2d 1240 (Ct. App. Div. 1 1978); *Erickson v. Waller*, 116 Ariz. 476, 569 P.2d 1374 (Ct. App. Div. 1 1977). The hypothetical could be based on matters in evidence of which the expert had no personal knowledge, and did not need to include all the evidence in the case. *Larriva v. Widmer*, 101 Ariz. 1, 415 P.2d 424 (1966); *Decker v. Ramenofsky*, 91 Ariz. 97, 370 P.2d 258 (1962); *Rayner v. Stauffer Chemical Co.*, 120 Ariz. 328, 585 P.2d 1240 (Ct. App. Div. 1 1978); *Erickson v. Waller*, 116 Ariz. 476, 569 P.2d 1374 (Ct. App. Div. 1 1977). The hypothetical had to be based, however, on facts that had been, or would be, received in evidence. *American Honda Motor Co., Inc. v. Smith*, 110 Ariz. 593, 521 P.2d 1139 (1974).

The hypothetical question was really a device for permitting the expert to express an opinion without in effect having to vouch for the credibility of witnesses who had established the facts on which the expert's opinion was based. *Cf. Reeves v. Markle*, 119 Ariz. 159, 579 P.2d 1382 (1978); *City of Yuma v. Evans*, 85 Ariz. 229, 336 P.2d 135 (1959).

The hypothetical question asked of an expert witness is the exception to the rule of simplicity in direct examination. Hypothetical questions are necessarily complex and must be carefully prepared in advance of trial. The question may be based in whole or in part upon proof in the case of which the expert has no firsthand knowledge, such as facts or data made known to the expert at trial. *See,* Rule 703, Ariz.R.Evid. (2012). This requires the witness to assume that certain evidence is true. Often the question calls for the witness to utilize a combination of factors in answering the question, such as training and experience, first-hand examination, tests, observations, and certain other evidence in the case which is assumed to be true. *Rayner v. Stauffer Chemical Co.*, 120 Ariz. 328, 585 P.2d 1240 (Ct. App. Div. 1 1978); *Erickson v. Waller*, 116 Ariz. 476, 569 P.2d 1374 (Ct. App. Div. 1 1977).

4. *Manner of Presentation of Expert Testimony.* According to the *Introductory Note: Problems of Opinion Testimony,* a stated "major objective" of the rules on opinion testimony is "to eliminate or sharply reduce the use of hypothetical questions." Such hypothetical questions had become, at best, cumbersome vehicles for the presentation of opinion evidence and, at worst, "inappropriate and premature jury summations." While a stated objective of the rules on opinion testimony was to, in this fashion, eliminate or sharply reduce the use of hypothetical questions, the rules did not forbid their use altogether. *See, Smith v. John C. Lincoln Hospital*, 118 Ariz. 549, 578 P.2d 630 (Ct. App. Div. 1 1978).

Two separate evidence rules operate in tandem to accomplish the objective of reducing the perceived need for hypothetical questions. First, Ariz. R. Evid. 703 permits an expert to base an opinion on facts or data made known to the expert, which facts/data may be inadmissible if the facts or data are of a type "experts in the particular field would reasonably rely upon in forming an opinion on the subject, ..."—but, only if the probative value of such facts and data "substantially outweighs their prejudicial effect." Second, Ariz. R. Evid. 705 permits an expert to testify to an opinion without first testifying to the facts or data on which it was based, unless the Court orders otherwise. The expert may be required to disclose those facts/data on cross-examination. Thus, an expert could theoretically simply state on direct examination the opinions which the expert had formed without explaining the bases therefor. The premise is that any weaknesses in the foundation for the expert's opinion could be brought out on cross-examination.

5. *Permissible Bases for Expert Opinion Under Rule 703.* Under Ariz. R. Evid. 703 (2012), an expert may base an opinion upon: (1) facts or data admitted into evidence, (2) facts or data the expert has been made aware of or personally observed, and/or (3) facts or data of a type reasonably relied upon by experts in the particular field, which need not be admissible in evidence. *State v. Joseph*, 230 Ariz. 296, 283 P.3d 27 (2012), cert. denied, 133 S. Ct. 936, 184 L. Ed. 2d 733 (2013) ("expert testimony that discusses reports and opinions of another is admissible under

[Arizona Rule of Evidence 703] if the expert reasonably relied on these matters in reaching his own conclusion." *citing*, *State v. Smith*, 215 Ariz. 221, 159 P.3d 531 (2007) and *Williams v. Illinois*, 132 S. Ct. 2221, 2228, 183 L. Ed. 2d 89 (2012) ("Out-of-court statements that are related by the expert solely for the purpose of explaining the assumptions on which that opinion rests are not offered for their truth and thus fall outside the scope of the Confrontation Clause."). *See also*, cases decided interpreting former Ariz. R. Evid. 702 as follows: *Pipher v. Loo*, 221 Ariz. 399, 212 P.3d 91 (Ct. App. Div. 1 2009); *Cervantes v. Rijlaarsdam*, 190 Ariz. 396, 949 P.2d 56 (Ct. App. Div. 2 1997); *Standard Chartered PLC v. Price Waterhouse*, 190 Ariz. 6, 945 P.2d 317 (Ct. App. Div. 1 1996), as corrected on denial of reconsideration, (Jan. 13, 1997) (defense accounting firm expert relied on filed and signed tax return, which suggested information's trustworthiness); *Adams v. Amore*, 182 Ariz. 253, 895 P.2d 1016 (Ct. App. Div. 1 1994); *Davis v. Cessna Aircraft Corp.*, 182 Ariz. 26, 893 P.2d 26, Prod. Liab. Rep. (CCH) P 14038 (Ct. App. Div. 1 1994); *Lynn v. Helitec Corp.*, 144 Ariz. 564, 698 P.2d 1283 (Ct. App. Div. 1 1984).

Mere reliance by an expert on data in reaching an opinion, however, does not automatically make that data admissible at trial. *Brethauer v. General Motors Corp.*, 221 Ariz. 192, 211 P.3d 1176 (Ct. App. Div. 1 2009).

The Comment to Original 1977 Rule explains that the standard "if of a type reasonably relied upon by experts in the particular field" applies to both sentences of the Rule, so that both facts perceived by the expert and facts placed in evidence by others and made known to the expert must satisfy that standard as well. Whether that standard is satisfied is an issue of law for the Court.

No serious problem is presented if the facts upon which the expert bases an opinion are ones of which the expert has firsthand knowledge, *e.g.*, *Rayner v. Stauffer Chemical Co.*, 120 Ariz. 328, 585 P.2d 1240 (Ct. App. Div. 1 1978); or, if the facts have been admitted into evidence through competent proof. Issues do arise, however, where the expert bases an opinion on facts or data that have not been admitted into evidence and/or are inadmissible. If such facts or data are relied upon, and meet the standard of being of a type reasonably relied upon by experts in the field involved, then they become admissible, not as substantive evidence, but for the limited purpose of showing the basis for the expert's opinion. *Lynn v. Helitec Corp.*, 144 Ariz. 564, 698 P.2d 1283 (Ct. App. Div. 1 1984); *Hernandez v. Faker*, 137 Ariz. 449, 671 P.2d 427 (Ct. App. Div. 2 1983). It has been recognized that this aspect of the Rules on opinion testimony poses the danger of providing a vehicle for the evasion of other provisions of the Rules of Evidence which preclude the admission of hearsay and other types of evidence that are considered unreliable. *Lynn v. Helitec Corp.*, 144 Ariz. 564, 698 P.2d 1283 (Ct. App. Div. 1 1984). See discussion in Section 6, *infra*.

Foundational objections to the bases for an expert's testimony serve a useful purpose when there is a legitimate foundational question to explore. *Sheppard v. Crow-Barker Paul No. 1 Ltd. Partnership*, 192 Ariz. 539, 968 P.2d 612 (Ct. App. Div. 1 1998). To make such objections, however, merely to force one's adversary to "do it the hard way" wastes court time and client dollars. *Sheppard v. Crow-Barker Paul No. 1 Ltd. Partnership*, 192 Ariz. 539, 968 P.2d 612 (Ct. App. Div. 1 1998).

6. *Unadmitted and/or Inadmissible Matters as Basis for Expert Opinion.* Rule 703 was amended in 2011, effective January 1, 2012. The 2012 Comment to Rule 703 state that the restyling amendments were not intended to "change any result in any ruling on evidence admissibility" and the deletion of the word *inference* was not intended to "change current practice . . . ." Thus, amended Rule 703 will continue to permit an expert's opinion to be based on facts that are not in evidence and, in certain circumstances, on facts that are not admissible.

The issue of whether and, if so, when an expert may base an opinion on facts or data that have not been admitted into evidence and/or are inadmissible is complicated by certain observations made in the *Introductory Note: Problems of Opinion Testimony* with which Article VII of the Arizona Rules of Evidence begins. The final paragraph of that *Introductory Note* seems to contemplate objections if the facts or data upon which an expert's opinion are to be based have not been admitted in evidence at the time the opinion is offered, provides that the Court may allow admission of the opinion subject to later admission of the underlying facts, and cautions that the Court should prevent the admission of the opinion if there is any serious question as to the admissibility of the underlying facts or data. At first blush, these statements are subject to the interpretation that an expert may only base an opinion on matters that are properly admissible in evidence.

The statements in the *Introductory Note* should be read as referring to the limited admissibility for such materials authorized by Rules 703 and 705. Under Rules 703–705, facts or data on which the expert opinion is based may be unadmitted or inadmissible, but can be revealed to the trier of fact, not as substantive evidence, but for the limited purpose of showing the basis for the expert's opinion. *Lynn v. Helitec Corp.*, 144 Ariz. 564, 698 P.2d 1283 (Ct. App. Div. 1 1984); *Hernandez v. Faker*, 137 Ariz. 449, 671 P.2d 427 (Ct. App. Div. 2 1983).

Before Rule 703 was amended in 2010, there was a recognized

danger that this aspect of the Rules would permit presentation to the trier of fact of matters that other evidentiary rules would exclude as unreliable. *Lynn v. Helitec Corp.*, 144 Ariz. 564, 698 P.2d 1283 (Ct. App. Div. 1 1984). That was particularly true in light of the latitude to be given to experts to explain the bases of their opinions. *Cf. Mohave Elec. Co-op., Inc. v. Byers*, 189 Ariz. 292, 942 P.2d 451 (Ct. App. Div. 1 1997). The sole protection provided was cogent and strict application of the requirement of Rule 703 that such non-admitted and inadmissible matters be of a type reasonably relied upon by experts in the particular field. *Cervantes v. Rijlaarsdam*, 190 Ariz. 396, 949 P.2d 56 (Ct. App. Div. 2 1997); *Standard Chartered PLC v. Price Waterhouse*, 190 Ariz. 6, 945 P.2d 317 (Ct. App. Div. 1 1996), as corrected on denial of reconsideration, (Jan. 13, 1997).

Arizona's appellate courts had held that, if such foundation for the expert's opinion was lacking, the opinions should not be admitted. *Adams v. Amore*, 182 Ariz. 253, 895 P.2d 1016 (Ct. App. Div. 1 1994); *Davis v. Cessna Aircraft Corp.*, 182 Ariz. 26, 893 P.2d 26, Prod. Liab. Rep. (CCH) P 14038 (Ct. App. Div. 1 1994). The Supreme Court cautioned that trial courts should employ their discretion to prevent the admission of opinions where there is a serious question as to the admissibility of the underlying facts and/or data. *Florez v. Sargeant*, 185 Ariz. 521, 917 P.2d 250 (1996).

Under this standard, experts have been permitted to rely upon medical laboratory reports prepared by others, *State v. Villafuerte*, 142 Ariz. 323, 690 P.2d 42 (1984); medical records, *Hernandez v. Faker*, 137 Ariz. 449, 671 P.2d 427 (Ct. App. Div. 2 1983); official schedules of billboard reproduction costs, *City of Scottsdale v. Eller Outdoor Advertising Co. of Ariz., Inc.*, 119 Ariz. 86, 579 P.2d 590 (Ct. App. Div. 1 1978); official wage rate publications, *Ehman v. Rathbun*, 116 Ariz. 460, 569 P.2d 1358 (Ct. App. Div. 2 1977); factual findings in authorized government investigations, *State ex rel. Miller v. Tucson Associates Ltd. Partnership*, 165 Ariz. 519, 799 P.2d 860 (Ct. App. Div. 2 1990); and, generally accepted scientific principles recorded in authoritative literature, *Reeves v. Markle*, 119 Ariz. 159, 579 P.2d 1382 (1978); *State v. Superior Court, In and For Pima County*, 152 Ariz. 327, 732 P.2d 218 (Ct. App. Div. 2 1986); *Gaston v. Hunter*, 121 Ariz. 33, 588 P.2d 326 (Ct. App. Div. 1 1978).

Under the same standard, experts have not been permitted to rely on the unsubstantiated hearsay reports of others, *State ex rel. Ordway v. McRae*, 122 Ariz. 325, 594 P.2d 1021 (Ct. App. Div. 2 1979); *Ehman v. Rathbun*, 116 Ariz. 460, 569 P.2d 1358 (Ct. App. Div. 2 1977); *but cf. Matter of Olivas' Estate*, 132 Ariz. 61, 643 P.2d 1031 (Ct. App. Div. 2 1982); or, surveys that were shown to be unreliable and untrustworthy, *Gosewisch v. Ameri-*

can Honda Motor Co., Inc., 153 Ariz. 389, 737 P.2d 365, Prod. Liab. Rep. (CCH) P 10819 (Ct. App. Div. 2 1985), opinion vacated in part, 153 Ariz. 400, 737 P.2d 376, Prod. Liab. Rep. (CCH) P 11531, 83 A.L.R.4th 53 (1987).

It also had been held that, in forming an opinion, an expert should not rely on evidence which Rule 404(b), Ariz. R. Evid. renders inadmissible, and should not be permitted to disclose that evidence to jurors as part of the basis for the expert's opinion. *Henson v. Triumph Trucking, Inc.*, 180 Ariz. 305, 884 P.2d 191 (Ct. App. Div. 2 1994). While it is permissible for an expert to rely on general opinions of other experts who do not testify, where an expert merely serves as a vehicle for the introduction of another non-testifying expert's opinion on an issue in the case, such testimony has been held to be hearsay. *State v. Lundstrom*, 161 Ariz. 141, 776 P.2d 1067, 89 A.L.R.4th 437 (1989).

One of the more persistent and vexing problems that has been encountered in the application of the provisions of the evidence rules governing the admission of expert testimony has been that an expert is permitted to base her or his opinion on information and evidence that would not be admissible independently, but only to explain the basis for the expert's opinion. There have been instances of abuse of this regime where experts have been used as conduits for putting before juries information which is not admissible and should not be admitted, and an instruction to the jury that the information can only be considered in evaluating the merits of the expert's opinion has not always been effective.

The 2010 amendment to Rule 703, which appears to have survived the 2012 restyling amendment to Rule 703, attempts to address this problem by adding a new requirement for the admissibility of such information and testimony. Before facts or data that would otherwise be inadmissible are disclosed to a jury by the proponent of an opinion, the trial court must first make a determination "that their probative value in helping the jury evaluate the opinion substantially outweighs their prejudicial effect." This is then an additional hurdle that must be cleared for this evidence to be admitted, and is in addition to the requirement that the facts or data be of the type reasonably relied upon by experts in the particular field in forming opinions upon the subject. As a result of the 2012 amendments, the quoted language of Rule 703, adopted in 2010, was restyled and amended, but the underlying meaning was not changed.

Determining whether an expert's opinion will be of assistance is a matter within the sound discretion of the trial court, and its decision will not be disturbed on appeal absent a clear abuse of that discretion. *Messina v. Midway Chevrolet Co.*, 221 Ariz. 11,

209 P.3d 147 (Ct. App. Div. 1 2008). Further, a trial court's decision to admit or exclude expert testimony is reviewed for abuse of discretion. *State v. Bernstein*, ___ P.3d ___, 2014 WL 118106 (Ct. App. Div. 1 2014) (appellate court reviews "a fact-based 'decision to permit or exclude expert testimony for an abuse of discretion' "); *McMurtry v. Weatherford Hotel, Inc.*, 231 Ariz. 244, 293 P.3d 520 (Ct. App. Div. 1 2013); *Escamilla v. Cuello*, 230 Ariz. 202, 282 P.3d 403 (2012).

Rule 704. Opinion on an Ultimate Issue

(a) In General—Not Automatically Objectionable. An opinion is not objectionable just because it embraces an ultimate issue.

(b) Exception. In a criminal case, an expert witness must not state an opinion about whether the defendant did or did not have a mental state or condition that constitutes an element of the crime charged or of a defense. Those matters are for the trier of fact alone.

Amended Sept. 8, 2011, effective Jan. 1, 2012.

Comment to 2012 Amendment

Subsection (b) has been added to conform to Federal Rule of Evidence 704, which was amended in 1984 to add comparable language. The new language in the Arizona rule is considered to be consistent with current Arizona law.

Additionally, the language of Rule 704 has been amended to conform to the federal restyling of the Evidence Rules to make them more easily understood and to make style and terminology consistent throughout the rules. These changes are intended to be stylistic only. There is no intent in the restyling to change any result in any ruling on evidence admissibility.

The Court deleted the reference to an "inference" on the grounds that the deletion made the rule flow better and easier to read, and because any "inference" is covered by the broader term "opinion." Courts have not made substantive decisions on the basis of any distinction between an opinion and an inference. No change in current practice is intended.

Comment to Original 1977 Rule

Some opinions on ultimate issues will be rejected as failing to meet the requirement that they assist the trier of fact to understand the evidence or to determine a fact in issue. Witnesses are not permitted as experts on how juries should decide cases.

AUTHORS' COMMENTS

Analysis

1. *Scope and Purpose of Rule.* The adoption of Ariz. R. Evid. 704 abolishes the prior common law doctrine that a witness could not express an opinion on the ultimate issue to be resolved in the action. *Cf., e.g., Duncan v. Mack*, 59 Ariz. 36, 122 P.2d 215 (1942). Under Rule 704, neither lay nor expert opinion is to be automatically excluded simply "because it embraces an ultimate issue to be decided by the trier of fact." *See,* Ariz. R. Evid. 704(a). The 1977 Comment to Rule 704 cautions, however, that "[w]itnesses

are not permitted as experts on how juries should decide cases." *State v. Sosnowicz*, 229 Ariz. 90, 270 P.3d 917 (Ct. App. Div. 1 2012)(quoting the Comment to Original 1977 Rule [704] with approval).

2. *Comparison With Federal Rule.* Effective January 1, 2012, the Arizona Supreme Court amended Rule 704 to conform to the federal restyling of the Evidence Rules to make the rules more easily understood and to make style and terminology consistent throughout. The 2012 Comment states the stylistic amendments are not intended to "change any result in any ruling on evidence admissibility."

In addition to the restyling amendments, Rule 704 was amended to delete all references to an "inference." Consistent with the 2011 comment to the Federal Rule, the 2012 Comment to the Arizona Rule explains that the deletion made the rule flow better and easier to read, and because any "inference" is covered by the broader term "opinion." *See* Comment to 2012 Amendment. The 2012 Comment further notes the amendment [deleting the word *inference*] was not intended to change current practice.

To conform with Fed. R. Evid. 704, the Court also added subparagraph (b), which deals with expert testimony in criminal cases on the mental state or condition of the accused, to Rule 704. The 2012 Comment states this amendment is consistent with current Arizona law.

Following the 2012 restyling amendments, the language of Rule 704 remains identical to its federal counterpart, Fed. R. Evid. 704.

Although Rule 704 parallels its federal counterpart, "federal court decisions interpreting the federal rule are persuasive but not binding with respect to interpreting the Arizona rule." *See,* Prefatory Comment to 2012 Amendments. *See also, State v. Terrazas*, 189 Ariz. 580, 944 P.2d 1194 (1997) (The Arizona Supreme Court is "not bound by the United States Supreme Court's non-constitutional construction of the Federal Rules of Evidence when [the Arizona Supreme Court construes] the Arizona Rules of Evidence."), citing, *State v. Bible*, 175 Ariz. 549, 858 P.2d 1152 (1993); *State v. Salazar-Mercado*, 232 Ariz. 256, 304 P.3d 543 (Ct. App. Div. 2 2013). Practitioners are urged to keep this legal tenet in mind as they research federal case law interpreting a federal evidentiary rule that corresponds to an Arizona evidentiary rule.

3. *Opinion Evidence on Ultimate Issues in the Action.* Ariz. R. Evid. 704 (2012) allows both lay and expert opinion on the ultimate issue to be decided in a case, if that question is not one which can be resolved through application of the knowledge and experience of the average juror, and the trial court determines that opinion testimony on the issue will be of assistance to the

jury in resolving it. *Dunham v. Pima County*, 161 Ariz. 304, 778 P.2d 1200 (1989); *Bliss v. Treece*, 134 Ariz. 516, 658 P.2d 169 (1983); *State v. Sosnowicz*, 229 Ariz. 90, 270 P.3d 917 (Ct. App. Div. 1 2012); *Baroldy v. Ortho Pharmaceutical Corp.*, 157 Ariz. 574, 760 P.2d 574, Prod. Liab. Rep. (CCH) P 11732 (Ct. App. Div. 1 1988); *cf. also Newell v. Town of Oro Valley*, 163 Ariz. 527, 789 P.2d 394 (Ct. App. Div. 2 1990); *Continental Bank v. Wa-Ho Truck Brokerage*, 122 Ariz. 414, 595 P.2d 206, 26 U.C.C. Rep. Serv. 101 (Ct. App. Div. 1 1979). Of course, the trier of fact is not bound to agree with the expert's opinion on the issue. *Cook v. Great Western Bank & Trust*, 141 Ariz. 80, 685 P.2d 145, 39 U.C.C. Rep. Serv. 214 (Ct. App. Div. 1 1984).

The prior common law prohibition was based on the concern that the rendering of such opinions by witnesses invaded the province of the jury. *Duncan v. Mack*, 59 Ariz. 36, 122 P.2d 215 (1942). The 1977 adoption of Rule 704 was not predicated upon the evaporation of that concern; nor did it signal a new era of *carte blanche* admissibility for opinions of that nature. In fact, the 1977 Comment to Rule 704 itself points out that some opinions on ultimate issues will and should be excluded for failing to be of assistance to the jury, and cautions that: "Witnesses are not permitted as experts on how juries should decide cases." *State v. Chappell*, 225 Ariz. 229, 236 P.3d 1176 (2010), cert. denied, 131 S. Ct. 1485, 179 L. Ed. 2d 320 (2011), quoting the 1977 Comment with approval; *State v. Sosnowicz*, 229 Ariz. 90, 270 P.3d 917 (Ct. App. Div. 1 2012) (Although an expert's opinion may embrace an ultimate issue, under Rule 704 an expert is not permitted to tell a jury how to decide a case).

Decided under former Rule 704, it had been held that testimony by an expert witness that encompasses an ultimate issue is generally admissible when it alludes to an inference that the trier of fact should make, or uses a term that has both a lay factual meaning and a legal meaning, and it is clear that the witness is using only the factual term. *Webb v. Omni Block, Inc.*, 216 Ariz. 349, 166 P.3d 140 (Ct. App. Div. 1 2007). The current version of Rule 704 deleted the references to an "inference" on the grounds that "the deletion made the rule flow better and easier to read, and because any 'inference' is covered by the broader term "opinion." *See* Comment to 2012 Amendment to Rule 704.

Ariz. R. Evid. 704 does not permit the admission of expert opinion testimony couched in legal conclusions that simply opine how the jury should decide a case. *Webb v. Omni Block, Inc.*, 216 Ariz. 349, 166 P.3d 140 (Ct. App. Div. 1 2007). So for example, expert testimony that apportions percentages of fault to the parties and non-parties improperly invades the province of the jury and constitutes inadmissible legal conclusions. *Webb v. Omni Block, Inc.*, 216 Ariz. 349, 166 P.3d 140 (Ct. App. Div. 1 2007).

Finally, the standards for admissibility contained in Rule 702 must still be met for opinions on ultimate issues in the case. Moreover, because of the danger that the opinion will involve an expert in effect telling the jury how the case, in that expert's opinion, should be decided, the trial court is to pay particular care to insure that the ultimate issue to be determined is one which requires specialized knowledge and one on which the jury will require the assistance of expert opinion. *Pool v. Superior Court In and For Pima County*, 139 Ariz. 98, 677 P.2d 261 (1984). If, in the Court's judgment, that standard is not met, the opinion should not be allowed, *Pincock v. Dupnik*, 146 Ariz. 91, 703 P.2d 1240 (Ct. App. Div. 2 1985); *Groener v. Briehl*, 135 Ariz. 395, 661 P.2d 659 (Ct. App. Div. 1 1983); *Young v. Environmental Air Products, Inc.*, 136 Ariz. 206, 665 P.2d 88 (Ct. App. Div. 2 1982), aff'd as modified, 136 Ariz. 158, 665 P.2d 40 (1983); *Ingrum v. Tucson Yellow Cab Co.*, 131 Ariz. 523, 642 P.2d 868 (Ct. App. Div. 2 1981); *Carlson v. Tucson Racquet and Swim Club, Inc.*, 127 Ariz. 247, 619 P.2d 756 (Ct. App. Div. 2 1980); *Shaner v. Tucson Airport Authority, Inc.*, 117 Ariz. 444, 573 P.2d 518 (Ct. App. Div. 2 1977); *Jamas v. Krpan*, 116 Ariz. 216, 568 P.2d 1114 (Ct. App. Div. 1 1977).

Rule 705. Disclosing the Facts or Data Underlying an Expert's Opinion

Unless the court orders otherwise, an expert may state an opinion—and give the reasons for it—without first testifying to the underlying facts or data. But the expert may be required to disclose those facts or data on cross-examination.

Amended Oct. 19, 1988, effective Nov. 1, 1988; Sept. 3, 2009, effective Jan. 1, 2010; Sept. 8, 2011, effective Jan. 1, 2012.

Comment to 2012 Amendment

The language of Rule 705 has been amended to conform to the federal restyling of the Evidence Rules to make them more easily understood and to make style and terminology consistent throughout the rules. These changes are intended to be stylistic only. There is no intent to change any result in any ruling on evidence admissibility.

The reference to an "inference" has been deleted on the grounds that the deletion made the rule flow better and easier to read, and because any "inference" is covered by the broader term "opinion." Courts have not made substantive decisions on the basis of any distinction between an opinion and an inference. No change in current practice is intended.

AUTHORS' COMMENTS

Analysis

1. Scope and Purpose of Rule.
2. Comparison With Federal Rule.
3. Disclosure of Bases for Expert Opinion.

1. *Scope and Purpose of Rule.* Ariz. R. Evid. 705 provides that an expert may testify to an opinion without prior disclosure of the underlying facts or data on which the opinion is based, unless the Court requires prior disclosure. The expert may be required to disclose the underlying facts or data on cross-examination.

Ariz. R. Evid. 705 operates in tandem with Ariz. R. Evid. 703 to facilitate the presentation of expert opinion testimony, and to eliminate or sharply reduce the need to present such testimony through the vehicle of hypothetical questions. Many of the issues that arise under both these Rules are discussed in the *Authors' Comments* to Rule 703, Ariz. R. Evid.

2. *Comparison With Federal Rule.* Effective January 1, 2012, the Arizona Supreme Court amended Rule 705 to conform to the federal restyling of the Evidence Rules to make the rules more easily understood and to make style and terminology consistent throughout. The 2012 Comment states the stylistic amendments are not intended to "change any result in any ruling on evidence

admissibility."

In addition to the restyling amendments, Rule 705 was amended to delete all references to an "inference." Consistent with the 2011 comment to the Federal Rule, the 2012 Comment to the Arizona Rule explains that the deletion made the rule flow better and easier to read, and because any "inference" is covered by the broader term "opinion." *See* Comment to 2012 Amendment. The 2012 Comment further notes the amendment [deleting the word *inference*] was not intended to change current practice.

Following 2012 restyling amendments, the language of Ariz. R. Evid. 705 remains identical to its federal counterpart, Fed. R. Evid. 705.

Although Rule 705 parallels its federal counterpart, "federal court decisions interpreting the federal rule are persuasive but not binding with respect to interpreting the Arizona rule." *See,* Prefatory Comment to 2012 Amendments. *See also, State v. Terrazas*, 189 Ariz. 580, 944 P.2d 1194 (1997) (The Arizona Supreme Court is "not bound by the United States Supreme Court's non-constitutional construction of the Federal Rules of Evidence when [the Arizona Supreme Court construes] the Arizona Rules of Evidence."), citing, *State v. Bible*, 175 Ariz. 549, 858 P.2d 1152 (1993); *State v. Salazar-Mercado*, 232 Ariz. 256, 304 P.3d 543 (Ct. App. Div. 2 2013). Practitioners are urged to keep this legal tenet in mind as they research federal case law interpreting a federal evidentiary rule that corresponds to an Arizona evidentiary rule.

3. *Disclosure of Bases for Expert Opinion.* At least in theory, Rule 705 permits an expert to take the stand and testify to the opinions that the expert has formulated that are relevant to the issues in the cases, without first testifying to the underlying facts or data on which that opinion is based, unless the Court requires a prior disclosure. *Continental Bank v. Wa-Ho Truck Brokerage*, 122 Ariz. 414, 595 P.2d 206, 26 U.C.C. Rep. Serv. 101 (Ct. App. Div. 1 1979). *But see,* Ariz. R. Civ. P. 26.1(a)(6).

As a practical matter, however, that is rarely what occurs. While the Rule does not require a prior disclosure or explanation of the underlying bases for the expert's opinion, it does not forbid it either and these matters can be covered during the direct examination of the expert. *Lynn v. Helitec Corp.*, 144 Ariz. 564, 698 P.2d 1283 (Ct. App. Div. 1 1984); *Hernandez v. Faker*, 137 Ariz. 449, 671 P.2d 427 (Ct. App. Div. 2 1983). Generally, expert witnesses will provide at least some explanation of the bases for their opinions so that the jury is in a position to determine what weight to accord them. In fact, experts are to be given some degree of latitude to explain the bases for their opinions. *Mohave Elec. Co-op., Inc. v. Byers*, 189 Ariz. 292, 942 P.2d 451 (Ct. App. Div. 1 1997). An expert may not rely on, however, or disclose to the jury as part of the basis for the expert's opinion, information which would be inadmissible under Rule 404(b), Ariz. R. Evid. *Henson v. Triumph Trucking, Inc.*, 180 Ariz. 305, 884 P.2d 191 (Ct. App. Div. 2 1994).

Under the Rule, the expert is required to disclose the underlying facts or data on cross-examination. *Florez v. Sargeant*, 185 Ariz. 521, 917 P.2d 250 (1996); *Cervantes v. Rijlaarsdam*, 190 Ariz. 396, 949 P.2d 56 (Ct. App. Div. 2 1997). The word "disclose" used in the Rule is a bit of a misnomer, as counsel conducting the cross-examination, at least in civil cases, can and should already know the bases of the expert's opinions through the pursuit of discovery. The identities of experts to be called at trial, the subject matter of the experts' testimony, the substance of the facts and opinions to which the experts are expected to testify, and a summary of the grounds for each opinion are among the matters which the parties are required to disclose under Ariz.R.Civ.P. 26.1(a)(6). In addition, even under amended Ariz.R.Civ.P. 30(a), the parties still retain the right to conduct the deposition of "any expert witness expected to be called" at trial.

It is clearly proper to cross-examine an expert at trial as to the facts and data underlying the expert's opinion. The Court can exclude the expert's testimony, or portions of it, if the expert refuses to disclose the underlying data. *Gaston v. Hunter*, 121 Ariz. 33, 588 P.2d 326 (Ct. App. Div. 1 1978). When an expert bases an opinion on hearsay evidence, the hearsay objection does not apply to the cross-examination of that expert witness. *Cervantes v. Rijlaarsdam*, 190 Ariz. 396, 949 P.2d 56 (Ct. App. Div. 2 1997). It is not proper to cross-examine an expert on the basis of facts or data which the expert did not consider in forming the opinion as a device for putting inadmissible matter before the jury. *Sharman v. Skaggs Companies, Inc.*, 124 Ariz. 165, 602 P.2d 833 (Ct. App. Div. 2 1979); *State ex rel. Ordway v. McRae*, 122 Ariz. 325, 594 P.2d 1021 (Ct. App. Div. 2 1979). An expert witness may be cross-examined on any other relevant matter properly within the scope of cross-examination. *Purcell v. Zimbelman*, 18 Ariz. App. 75, 500 P.2d 335 (Div. 2 1972); *Zier v. Shamrock Dairy of Phoenix, Inc.*, 4 Ariz. App. 382, 420 P.2d 954 (1966).

Rule 706. Court Appointed Expert Witnesses

(a) Appointment Process. On a party's motion or on its own, the court may order the parties to show cause why expert witnesses should not be appointed and may ask the parties to submit nominations. The court may appoint any expert that the parties agree on and any of its own choosing. But the court may only appoint someone who consents to act.

(b) Expert's Role. The court must inform the expert of the expert's duties. The court may do so in writing and have a copy filed with the clerk or may do so orally at a conference in which the parties have an opportunity to participate. The expert:

(1) must advise the parties of any findings the expert makes;

(2) may be deposed by any party;

(3) may be called to testify by the court or any party; and

(4) may be cross-examined by any party, including the party that called the expert.

(c) Compensation. The expert is entitled to a reasonable compensation, as set by the court. Except as otherwise provided by law, appointment of an expert by the court is subject to the availability of funds or the agreement of the parties concerning compensation.

(d) Disclosing the Appointment to the Jury. The court may authorize disclosure to the jury that the court appointed the expert.

(e) Parties' Choice of Their Own Experts. This rule does not limit a party in calling its own experts.

Amended Oct. 19, 1988, effective Nov. 1, 1988; Sept. 8, 2011, effective Jan. 1, 2012.

Comment to 2012 Amendment

The language of subsection (c) of Rule 706 has been amended to provide, consistent with Federal Rule of Evidence 706, that an expert is entitled to a reasonable compensation, as set by the court.

Additionally, the language of subsections (a), (b), (d), and (e) of the rule has been amended to conform to the federal restyling of the Evidence Rules to make them more easily understood and to make style and terminology consistent throughout the rules. These changes are intended to be stylistic only. There is no intent in the restyling to change any result in any ruling on evidence admissibility.

Comment to Original 1977 Rule

Federal Rule of Evidence 706(b) is appropriate in Federal Courts where the funds to compensate experts are made available by statute. Such funds are not generally available in Arizona except in capital offenses, A.R.S. § 13-673; sanity hearings, A.R.S. § 13-1674; medical liability review panels, A.R.S. § 12-567(B)(4) and (M); and mental health proceedings, A.R.S. § 36-545.04. Therefore, Arizona

Rule of Evidence 706(a) was prefaced by the availability of these funds or the compensation of the experts to be agreed upon, and Federal Rule of Evidence 706(b) was not adopted, and paragraphs numbered (c) and (d) were renumbered paragraphs (b) and (c) respectively.

AUTHORS' COMMENTS

Analysis

1. *Scope and Purpose of Rule.* Rule 706 allows the Court to appoint experts, subject to the availability of funds or an agreement of the parties concerning compensation, either on its own motion or on motion of one of the parties. If the Court determines that a court-appointed expert is required, then the Court can request that the parties nominate candidates, and the Court can appoint an expert on whom the parties agree or one of its own selection.

The deposition of an expert appointed by the Court may be taken by any party, and the expert may be called to testify at trial by any party or by the Court. Regardless of who calls the expert as a witness at trial, each party may conduct cross-examination. It is in the trial court's discretion whether to advise the jury that the expert in question was one appointed by the Court. Nothing in the Rule limits the parties from calling experts of their own selection.

There are certain other instances where the Court can become involved in the selection of experts. An interpreter is, in a sense, an expert witness. Ariz.R.Civ.P. 43(c) gives the Court the authority to appoint an interpreter where necessary or desirable, and provides that the Court can direct that the interpreter's compensation be paid by one or more of the parties and/or taxed as costs in the action. *Cf. also,* Ariz. R. Evid. 604; A.R.S. § 12-241. An interpreter must be appointed where a deaf person is a participant in legal proceedings as a party, witness or attorney. A.R.S. § 12-242. An interpreter may be appointed for a deaf juror. *State v. Marcham*, 160 Ariz. 52, 770 P.2d 356 (Ct. App. Div. 1 1988).

Under Ariz.R.Civ.P. 26(b)(4)(D), where multiple parties on one side of a case cannot agree on the single independent expert witness which that side can call on an issue, the Court can designate the expert or, for good cause shown, allow more than one independent expert witness to be called. Finally, Ariz.R.Civ.P. 35(c)(2) contemplates that, under some circumstances, the Court can determine the physician or psychologist who will conduct the independent medical examination authorized by Rule 35.

2. *Comparison With Federal Rule.* Effective January 1, 2012,

the Arizona Supreme Court amended Ariz. R. Evid. 706(a), (b), (d) and (e) to conform to the federal restyling of the Evidence Rules to make the rules more easily understood and to make style and terminology consistent throughout. The 2012 Comment states the stylistic amendments are not intended to "change any result in any ruling on evidence admissibility."

Due to differences concerning the availability of funding for experts appointed by the Court, Arizona did not amend Rule 706(c) to conform to its federal counterpart, Fed. R. Evid. 706(c), except a provide that an expert is entitled to reasonable compensation, as set by the court. Further, Fed. R. Evid. 706(c) does not contain the last sentence of Ariz. R. Evid. 706(c), which provides that the appointment of experts by the Court is subject to the availability of funds or an agreement of the parties regarding the expert's compensation.

Following the 2012 restyling amendments, the language of Ariz. R. Evid. 706(a), (b), (d) and (e) correspond, and are identical, to Fed. R. Evid. 706(a), (b), (d) and (e). As noted above, Rule 706(c) is substantially different from its federal counterpart.

Although the language of Ariz. R. Evid. 706(a), (b), (d) and (e) correspond, and are identical, to Fed. R. Evid. 706(a), (b), (d) and (e), "federal court decisions interpreting the federal rule are persuasive but not binding with respect to interpreting the Arizona rule." *See,* Prefatory Comment to 2012 Amendments. *See also, State v. Terrazas*, 189 Ariz. 580, 944 P.2d 1194 (1997) (The Arizona Supreme Court is "not bound by the United States Supreme Court's non-constitutional construction of the Federal Rules of Evidence when [the Arizona Supreme Court construes] the Arizona Rules of Evidence."), citing, *State v. Bible*, 175 Ariz. 549, 858 P.2d 1152 (1993); *State v. Salazar-Mercado*, 232 Ariz. 256, 304 P.3d 543 (Ct. App. Div. 2 2013). Practitioners are urged to keep this legal tenet in mind as they research federal case law interpreting a federal evidentiary rule that corresponds to an Arizona evidentiary rule.

ARTICLE VIII. HEARSAY

Rule 801. Definitions that Apply to This Article; Exclusions from Hearsay

(a) Statement. "Statement" means a person's oral assertion, written assertion, or nonverbal conduct, if the person intended it as an assertion.

(b) Declarant. "Declarant" means the person who made the statement.

(c) Hearsay. "Hearsay" means a statement that:

(1) the declarant does not make while testifying at the current trial or hearing; and

(2) a party offers in evidence to prove the truth of the matter asserted in the statement.

(d) Statements That Are Not Hearsay. A statement that meets the following conditions is not hearsay:

(1) **A Declarant-Witness's Prior Statement**. The declarant testifies and is subject to cross-examination about a prior statement, and the statement:

(A) is inconsistent with the declarant's testimony;

(B) is consistent with the declarant's testimony and is offered to rebut an express or implied charge that the declarant recently fabricated it or acted from a recent improper influence or motive in so testifying; or

(C) identifies a person as someone the declarant perceived earlier.

(2) **An Opposing Party's Statement**. The statement is offered against an opposing party and:

(A) was made by the party in an individual or representative capacity;

(B) is one the party manifested that it adopted or believed to be true;

(C) was made by a person whom the party authorized to make a statement on the subject;

(D) was made by the party's agent or employee on a matter within the scope of that relationship and while it existed; or

(E) was made by the party's coconspirator during and in furtherance of the conspiracy.

The statement must be considered but does not by itself establish the declarant's authority under (C); the existence or scope of the relationship under (D); or the existence of the conspiracy or participation in it under (E).

Amended Oct. 19, 1988, effective Nov. 1, 1988; Sept. 8, 2011, effective Jan. 1, 2012.

Comment to 2012 Amendment

The last sentence of Rule 801(d)(2) has been added to conform to Federal Rule of Evidence 801(d)(2). The amendment does not, however, include the requirement in Federal Rule of Evidence 801(d)(1)(A) that a prior inconsistent statement be "given under oath" to be considered as non-hearsay.

Otherwise, the language of Rule 801 has been amended to conform to the federal restyling of the Evidence Rules to make them more easily understood and to make style and terminology consistent throughout the rules. These changes are intended to be stylistic only. There is no intent in the restyling to change any result in any ruling on evidence admissibility.

Statements falling under the hearsay exclusion provided by Rule 801(d)(2) are no longer referred to as "admissions" in the title to the subdivision. The term "admissions" is confusing because not all statements covered by the exclusion are admissions in the colloquial sense—a statement can be within the exclusion even if it "admitted" nothing and was not against the party's interest when made. The term "admissions" also raises confusion in comparison with the Rule 804(b)(3) exception for declarations against interest. No change in application of the exclusion is intended.

Comment to Original 1977 Rule

Evidence which is admissible under the hearsay rules may be inadmissible under some other rule or principle. A notable example is the confrontation clause of the Constitution as applied to criminal cases. The definition of "hearsay" is a utilitarian one. The exceptions to the hearsay rule are based upon considerations of reliability, need, and experience. Like all other rules which favor the admission of evidence, the exceptions to the hearsay rule are counterbalanced by Rules 102 and 403.

Rule 801(d). This subsection of the rule has been modified and is consistent with the United States Supreme Court's version of the Rule and *State v. Skinner*, 110 Ariz. 135, 515 P.2d 880 (1973).

AUTHORS' COMMENTS

Analysis

1. *Scope and Purpose of Rule.* Rule 801 is primarily definitional. The first three subparts of the Rule define the terms that are

central to the operation and application of the hearsay rule: "statement," "declarant," and "hearsay" itself. Rule 801(d) then excludes from the definition of hearsay certain prior statements made by witnesses, statements made, adopted or authorized by an adverse party, and certain statements made during the course of and in furtherance of a conspiracy.

Rule 801(d)'s exclusion of these categories of statements from the definition of hearsay has the same practical effect as if they had been classified as exceptions to the hearsay rule under Rules 803 or 804. Thus, to the extent that Rule 804(b)(3) provides an exception from the hearsay rule for statements against interest made by an adverse party, it is partially duplicative of Rule 801(d)(2)(A).

2. *Comparison With Federal Rule.* Effective January 1, 2012, the Arizona Supreme Court amended Rule 801 to conform to the federal restyling of the Evidence Rules to make the rules more easily understood and to make style and terminology consistent throughout. The 2012 Comment states the stylistic amendments are not intended to "change any result in any ruling on evidence admissibility."

In addition to the restyling amendments, in 2012, Rule 801(d)(2) was amended to conform with Fed. R. Evid. 801(d)(2) to remove the reference to "admission" in the title to the subdivision in that such term was deemed confusing because, as explained in the comment to the 2012 amendment, not all statements covered by the section are "admissions in the colloquial sense."

The Arizona Supreme Court also added, in 2012, a sentence to the end of Rule 801(d)(2) to conform to Fed. R. Evid. 801(d)(2). Thus, where an opposing party's statement is offered pursuant to subdivisions (C), (D) or (E) of that rule, the declarant's statement may be considered, but will not be in and of itself sufficient to establish the declarant's authority, agency or employment relationship, or the existence of a conspiracy.

As a consequence of the 2012 amendments, the only difference between Ariz. R. Evid. 801 and Fed. R. Evid. 801 is in the provisions of Rule 801(d)(1)(A). Arizona did not adopt as part of its version of this particular Rule the phrase in the Federal Rule which requires that the prior inconsistent statement of a witness, in order to be excluded from the definition of hearsay, must have been made under oath, subject to the penalty of perjury, in a deposition or at a trial, hearing or other evidentiary proceeding. This was due to the fact that, in *State v. Skinner*, 110 Ariz. 135, 515 P.2d 880 (1973), the Arizona Supreme Court had approved and adopted the standard set forth in the then proposed Rule 801(d)(1)(A) of the Federal Rules, before Congress added the limiting language. *But cf., State v. Cruz*, 128 Ariz. 538, 627 P.2d

689 (1981). *See,* Rule 801, Comment to Original 1977 Rule.

The 2012 Comment to Rule 801 states that "no change in the application is intended."

Although Rule 801 parallels its federal counterpart, "federal court decisions interpreting the federal rule are persuasive but not binding with respect to interpreting the Arizona rule." *See,* Prefatory Comment to 2012 Amendments. *See also, State v. Terrazas*, 189 Ariz. 580, 944 P.2d 1194 (1997) (The Arizona Supreme Court is "not bound by the United States Supreme Court's non-constitutional construction of the Federal Rules of Evidence when [the Arizona Supreme Court construes] the Arizona Rules of Evidence."), citing, *State v. Bible*, 175 Ariz. 549, 858 P.2d 1152 (1993); *State v. Salazar-Mercado*, 232 Ariz. 256, 304 P.3d 543 (Ct. App. Div. 2 2013). Practitioners are urged to keep this legal tenet in mind as they research federal case law interpreting a federal evidentiary rule that corresponds to an Arizona evidentiary rule.

3. *Definition of Hearsay; Assertive Conduct as Hearsay.* As amended effective January 1, 2012, "hearsay" is defined in Rule 801(c) as a statement made by a person other than the person testifying at the current trial or hearing, which a party offers in evidence to prove the truth of the mater asserted in the statement. *State v. Palmer*, 229 Ariz. 64, 270 P.3d 891 (Ct. App. Div. 2 2012), review denied, (Aug. 28, 2012) (2012 stylistic change to Rule 801(a) "clarifies that all assertions [oral/written assertions and nonverbal conduct] must be intended as such to constitute a "statement."). *Cf., Crackel v. Allstate Ins. Co.*, 208 Ariz. 252, 92 P.3d 882 (Ct. App. Div. 2 2004) (construing the Arizona Rules of Evidence before 2012 amendment); *Schneider v. Cessna Aircraft Co.*, 150 Ariz. 153, 722 P.2d 321, Prod. Liab. Rep. (CCH) P 10743 (Ct. App. Div. 1 1985) (construing the Arizona Rules of Evidence before 2012 amendment). Virtually every document generated in connection with the events in issue that is offered into evidence will satisfy this definition, and can only be admitted if it is not offered to prove the truth of the matters contained therein, if it is excluded from the definition of hearsay by Rule 801(d), or if it qualifies for one of the exceptions in Rule 803 or 804. *Cf., Villas at Hidden Lakes Condominiums Ass'n v. Geupel Const. Co., Inc.*, 174 Ariz. 72, 847 P.2d 117 (Ct. App. Div. 1 1992).

True hearsay is considered an unreliable source of information for the trier of fact because it is not subject to cross-examination, which may point out deficiencies in the declarant's perceptions, recall or articulation of events, or other matters that undercut the probative value of the evidence. In addition, the trier of fact will have no opportunity to view and assess the demeanor of the hearsay declarant. *State v. Allen*, 157 Ariz. 165, 755 P.2d 1153 (1988); *Larsen v. Decker*, 196 Ariz. 239, 995 P.2d 281 (Ct. App.

Div. 1 2000), amended, (Feb. 22, 2000).

The definition of a hearsay statement in Rule 801(a) includes nonverbal conduct if it is intended by the actor as an assertion. *State v. Palmer*, 229 Ariz. 64, 270 P.3d 891 (Ct. App. Div. 2 2012), review denied, (Aug. 28, 2012) (2012 stylistic change to Rule 801(a) "clarifies that all assertions [oral/written assertions and nonverbal conduct] must be intended as such to constitute a "statement."). Assertive conduct is conduct which is arguably based on or prompted by the actor's belief or perception of a matter, which is offered as circumstantial evidence of the matter perceived or believed. *State v. Chavez*, 225 Ariz. 442, 239 P.3d 761 (Ct. App. Div. 1 2010) (upholding the admission of text messages from unidentified senders indicating the defendant had drugs for sale, on the ground the text messages were not offered to prove the truth of the matter they asserted, *i.e.,* that the prospective buyers wanted to purchase drugs from the defendant). An example is the failure to call a witness who could corroborate a party's version of events supporting an inference that the witness' testimony was either non-corroborative or positively harmful. *State ex rel. McDougall v. Corcoran*, 153 Ariz. 157, 735 P.2d 767 (1987); *Williams v. Williams*, 86 Ariz. 201, 344 P.2d 161 (1959).

Almost all conduct can arguably qualify as assertive conduct, so the Rule eschews too broad a definition of such conduct as inadmissible hearsay. To constitute hearsay, the conduct in question must have been *intended* by the actor to be an assertion, and the party claiming evidence of such conduct should be excluded has the burden to show that to be the case. *State v. Palmer*, 229 Ariz. 64, 270 P.3d 891 (Ct. App. Div. 2 2012), review denied, (Aug. 28, 2012) (2012 stylistic change to Rule 801(a) "clarifies that all assertions [oral/written assertions and nonverbal conduct] must be intended as such to constitute a "statement.").

4. *Admissibility When Offered for Other Purposes.* By definition, the rule excluding hearsay does not apply when an otherwise hearsay statement is offered for some purpose other than to prove the truth of the spoken or written words. Stated another way, the hearsay rule may not apply where the claimed significance of the oral or written statement is simply the fact that it was made rather than the truth or accuracy of its contents.

One circumstance where that will be the case is when the words in the statement have independent legal significance, such as in the formation of a contract. *Ruhsam v. Ruhsam*, 110 Ariz. 326, 518 P.2d 576 (1974), opinion supplemented on denial of reh'g, 110 Ariz. 426, 520 P.2d 298 (1974); *In re Guardianship of Sorrells*, 58 Ariz. 25, 117 P.2d 96 (1941); *U. S. Fidelity & Guaranty Co. v. Davis*, 3 Ariz. App. 259, 413 P.2d 590 (1966). Another example of this category of statement is an acknowledgment of a debt barred by the statute of limitations. *Bulmer v. Belcher*, 22 Ariz. App. 394, 527 P.2d 1237 (Div. 2 1974). In an action for fraud, the allegedly fraudulent statements will be offered even though they are claimed to be false. *Miller v. Boeger*, 1 Ariz. App. 554, 405 P.2d 573 (1965). The same is the case when the defendant's allegedly slanderous statements are offered in a defamation action.

Another common category is when the statements are offered to prove their effect on persons who heard them or read them, *i.e.,* where the state of mind of the audience is in issue. *Public Service Co. of Oklahoma v. Bleak*, 134 Ariz. 311, 656 P.2d 600 (1982); *Cashway Concrete & Materials v. Sanner Contracting Co.*, 158 Ariz. 81, 761 P.2d 155 (Ct. App. Div. 2 1988); *Rutledge v. Arizona Bd. of Regents*, 147 Ariz. 534, 711 P.2d 1207, 29 Ed. Law Rep. 1161 (Ct. App. Div. 1 1985). For example, a consultant's otherwise hearsay account of what consultant was told by City staff was admissible to show the consultant's state of mind with respect to the plan consultant created and City adopted on consultant's advise. *Home Builders Ass'n of Cent. Arizona v. City of Goodyear*, 223 Ariz. 193, 221 P.3d 384 (Ct. App. Div. 1 2009). And, hearsay statements to a former plaintiff or prosecuting authority will be admissible to establish probable cause and/or reasonable belief in a subsequent action for malicious prosecution. *Walker v. State*, 161 Ariz. 621, 780 P.2d 454 (Ct. App. Div. 2 1989); *Tate v. Connel*, 3 Ariz. App. 534, 416 P.2d 213 (1966). Similarly, the contents of a judicial order which are not offered for the truth of the matters asserted, but rather for their effect on the party subject to it, are not subject to the hearsay exclusion rule. *Crackel v. Allstate Ins. Co.*, 208 Ariz. 252, 92 P.3d 882 (Ct. App. Div. 2 2004). There is also some authority that, where a person's state of mind is in issue, statements made by that person may be admissible as circumstantial evidence on that issue. *Barnette v. McNulty*, 21 Ariz. App. 127, 516 P.2d 583 (Div. 2 1973); *Valley Nat. Bank v. Hay*, 13 Ariz. App. 39, 474 P.2d 46 (Div. 1 1970).

A closely related category is out-of-court statements which are offered to prove the hearer's or reader's knowledge of the subject matter of the statement. *Rutledge v. Arizona Bd. of Regents*, 147 Ariz. 534, 711 P.2d 1207, 29 Ed. Law Rep. 1161 (Ct. App. Div. 1 1985). These types of statements pose a particular difficulty, because in cases where an otherwise hearsay statement is offered to prove the hearer's knowledge of a fact, the truth or accuracy of the fact is frequently also in issue. For example, in a products liability case, whether a product was defective and whether the manufacturer was aware of the defect may both be in issue. The obvious danger is that a statement made to the manufacturer concerning a defect in the product could be considered by the trier of fact not only on the issue of whether the manufacturer had notice, but also on the issue of whether the product was defective. *Readenour v. Marion Power Shovel, a Div. of Dresser Industries, Inc.*, 149 Ariz. 442, 719 P.2d 1058, Prod. Liab. Rep. (CCH) P 11012 (1986); *Volz v. Coleman Co., Inc.*, 155 Ariz. 563, 748 P.2d 1187, Prod. Liab. Rep. (CCH) P 10977 (Ct. App. Div. 1 1986), judgment aff'd in part, rev'd in part, 155 Ariz. 567, 748 P.2d 1191, Prod. Liab. Rep. (CCH) P 11608 (1987). A limiting instruction can be requested, and should be given, but may not be completely effective.

5. *Prior Inconsistent Statements of Witnesses.* Rule 801(d)(1)(A) excludes from the definition of hearsay prior statements made by a witness who is present and subject to cross-examination, which are inconsistent with the witness' present testimony. *See also*, *State v. Hausner*, 230 Ariz. 60, 280 P.3d 604 (2012) ("A claimed inability to recall, when disbelieved by the trial judge, may be viewed as inconsistent with previous statements." *citing*, *State v. King*, 180 Ariz. 268, 275, 883 P.2d 1024, 1031 (1994). Such statements are admissible both substantively and for impeachment purposes.

Under Rule 613(b), the statement need not be shown to the witness, but it must be given to opposing counsel upon request. The witness must be given an opportunity to explain or deny the statement before extrinsic evidence of it can be received. *Lynn v. Helitec Corp.*, 144 Ariz. 564, 698 P.2d 1283 (Ct. App. Div. 1 1984). That is not required, however, where the witness is a party and the prior inconsistent statement is a party admission. *Lynn v. Helitec Corp.*, 144 Ariz. 564, 698 P.2d 1283 (Ct. App. Div. 1 1984). The inconsistent statement may be, and frequently is, from the witness' deposition. *Volz v. Coleman Co., Inc.*, 155 Ariz. 563, 748 P.2d 1187, Prod. Liab. Rep. (CCH) P 10977 (Ct. App. Div. 1 1986), judgment aff'd in part, rev'd in part, 155 Ariz. 567, 748 P.2d 1191, Prod. Liab. Rep. (CCH) P 11608 (1987). Under Arizona's version of this particular Rule, however, it is not necessary that the witness' prior inconsistent statement have been made under oath.

6. *Prior Consistent Statements of Witnesses.* Under Rule 801(d)(1)(B), prior out-of-court statements of a witness that are consistent with the witness' testimony are excluded from the definition of hearsay when they are offered to rebut an express or implied charge that the witness' testimony is a recent fabrication or the result of improper influence or motive. Prior consistent statements offered to rehabilitate a witness in that circumstance are also useable as substantive evidence. The statement must, however, have been made before the witness' motive to fabricate testimony arose. *Starkins v. Bateman*, 150 Ariz. 537, 724 P.2d 1206 (Ct. App. Div. 1 1986); *Ray Korte Chevrolet v. Simmons*, 117

Ariz. 202, 571 P.2d 699 (Ct. App. Div. 1 1977); *but cf., Trevizo v. Astec Industries, Inc.*, 156 Ariz. 320, 751 P.2d 980 (Ct. App. Div. 2 1987).

7. *Statements by Party Opponent.* Rule 801(d)(2)(A) excludes from the definition of hearsay statements made by one party that are offered into evidence by the opposing party. *Cal X-Tra v. W.V.S.V. Holdings, L.L.C.*, 229 Ariz. 377, 276 P.3d 11 (Ct. App. Div. 1 2012), review denied, (Dec. 4, 2012); *State v. Far West Water & Sewer Inc.*, 224 Ariz. 173, 228 P.3d 909, 2010 O.S.H. Dec. (CCH) P 33057 (Ct. App. Div. 1 2010), as amended on other grounds, (May 4, 2010) (corporate president's statements made in his representative capacity and within the scope of his authority to an investigator were the statements of the corporate defendant and, thus, were not hearsay; Rule 801(d)(2)(D)).

Such statements are admissible even though the party-declarant is available and in court. *Rimondi v. Briggs*, 124 Ariz. 561, 606 P.2d 412 (1980); *Bogard G.M.C. Co. v. Henley*, 92 Ariz. 107, 374 P.2d 660 (1962); *Hellyer v. Hellyer*, 129 Ariz. 453, 632 P.2d 263 (Ct. App. Div. 2 1981); *Needel v. Needel*, 15 Ariz. App. 471, 489 P.2d 729 (Div. 2 1971) (disapproved of on other grounds by, Becchelli v. Becchelli, 109 Ariz. 229, 508 P.2d 59 (1973)). Such statements are admissible both substantively and for purposes of impeachment. *Nystrom v. Massachusetts Cas. Ins. Co.*, 148 Ariz. 208, 713 P.2d 1266 (Ct. App. Div. 1 1986).

A statement by a party opponent is admissible regardless of its reliability. *Walls v. Arizona Dept. of Public Safety*, 170 Ariz. 591, 826 P.2d 1217 (Ct. App. Div. 1 1991). Thus, it is not necessary to show that the party had personal knowledge of the subjects addressed in the statement. Although this subpart of the Rule is captioned *"Admission by Party Opponent,"* the statement need not be one against the party's interest at the time. The statement also need not be contemporaneous with the events or matters that the statement concerns. *Prophet v. S. H. Kress Co.*, 106 Ariz. 504, 479 P.2d 167 (1970); *Nystrom v. Massachusetts Cas. Ins. Co.*, 148 Ariz. 208, 713 P.2d 1266 (Ct. App. Div. 1 1986); *Mastick v. State*, 118 Ariz. 366, 576 P.2d 1366 (Ct. App. Div. 2 1978). The statement can also be an expression of opinion by the party, if that is relevant to the issues in the action. *Alires v. Southern Pac. Co.*, 93 Ariz. 97, 378 P.2d 913 (1963) (disapproved of by, Miller v. State of Okl., 240 F. Supp. 263 (E.D. Okla. 1965)); *Thomas v. Bowman*, 24 Ariz. App. 322, 538 P.2d 409 (Div. 1 1975).

The statement can, but need not, be formal, such as a signed statement, answers to interrogatories, or testimony at a deposition or trial. *Barrett v. Melton*, 112 Ariz. 605, 545 P.2d 421 (1976); *Kelch v. Courson*, 103 Ariz. 576, 447 P.2d 550 (1968) (overruled by, Heimke v. Munoz, 106 Ariz. 26, 470 P.2d 107 (1970)); *Borbon v. City of Tucson*, 27 Ariz. App. 550, 556 P.2d 1153 (Div. 2 1976); *Dykeman v. Ashton*, 8 Ariz. App. 327, 446 P.2d 26 (1968). The fact that a document is found in a party's files is not sufficient to qualify it as a statement, unless the document was one made or authorized by the party. *Markiewicz v. Salt River Valley Water Users' Ass'n*, 118 Ariz. 329, 576 P.2d 517 (Ct. App. Div. 1 1978). *See* also, *Cal X-Tra v. W.V.S.V. Holdings, L.L.C.*, 229 Ariz. 377, 276 P.3d 11 (Ct. App. Div. 1 2012), review denied, (Dec. 4, 2012).

Responses of a party to interrogatories are ordinarily admissible against that party as statements of an opposing party, *See*, Rule 801(d)(2) (as amended 2012); *Gordon v. Liguori*, 182 Ariz. 232, 895 P.2d 523 (Ct. App. Div. 1 1995). *See also*, *Ryan v. San Francisco Peaks Trucking Co., Inc.*, 228 Ariz. 42, 262 P.3d 863 (Ct. App. Div. 1 2011), review denied, (Feb. 15, 2012) (Disclosure statement admissible as admission under Rule 801(d)(2)(D) but are not conclusive). That may not be the case, however, where the responses are more in the nature of an alternative contingent pleading than an admission. *Gordon v. Liguori*, 182 Ariz. 232, 895 P.2d 523 (Ct. App. Div. 1 1995).

A statement by a party will not be conclusive or dispositive of an issue. The party can deny making the statement, can explain or clarify it, or reject its accuracy, even if the statement was one made under oath. *Heth v. Del Webb's Highway Inn*, 102 Ariz. 330, 429 P.2d 442 (1967); *Fox v. Weissbach*, 76 Ariz. 91, 259 P.2d 258 (1953); *Rogers v. Greer*, 70 Ariz. 264, 219 P.2d 760 (1950); *Porter v. Porter*, 67 Ariz. 273, 195 P.2d 132 (1948); *Husky Fence Co., Inc. v. Industrial Com'n of Arizona*, 138 Ariz. 21, 672 P.2d 973 (Ct. App. Div. 1 1983); *Ohio Farmers Ins. Co. v. Norman*, 122 Ariz. 330, 594 P.2d 1026 (Ct. App. Div. 2 1979); *Leone v. Precision Plumbing and Heating of Southern Arizona, Inc.*, 121 Ariz. 514, 591 P.2d 1002 (Ct. App. Div. 2 1979); *Ness v. Greater Arizona Realty, Inc.*, 117 Ariz. 357, 572 P.2d 1195 (Ct. App. Div. 2 1977); *Gallagher v. Viking Supply Corp.*, 3 Ariz. App. 55, 411 P.2d 814, 15 A.L.R.3d 1 (1966).

8. *Adopted/Authorized Statements by an Opposing Party; Statements by Agent or Employee.* Rule 801(d)(2) excludes from the definition of hearsay not only statements actually made by a party, but also statements adopted by a party, statements by persons authorized to speak on behalf of a party, and statements made by an agent or employee of a party "concerning a matter within the scope of the agency or employment." Thus, a party's silence or failure to act in response to a statement or an event that calls for such a response may be an admission. *Ruth v. Rhodes*, 66 Ariz. 129, 185 P.2d 304 (1947).

Statements made by an attorney retained to represent a party have been admitted as statements authorized by that party. *Reed v. Hinderland*, 135 Ariz. 213, 660 P.2d 464, 37 A.L.R.4th 555 (1983); *Copeland v. City of Yuma*, 160 Ariz. 307, 772 P.2d 1160 (Ct. App. Div. 1 1989). Thus, an attorney's letter to an administrative agency on behalf of a client may be admissible against the client under Rule 801(d)(2)(D), as an admission, if the letter was written during the course of the attorney-client relationship and involved a matter within the scope of the attorney's agency. *Bogue v. Better-Bilt Aluminum Co.*, 179 Ariz. 22, 875 P.2d 1327, 3 A.D. Cas. (BNA) 137 (Ct. App. Div. 1 1994). A disclosure statement also may be admissible under Rule 801(d)(2)(D). *Ryan v. San Francisco Peaks Trucking Co., Inc.*, 228 Ariz. 42, 262 P.3d 863 (Ct. App. Div. 1 2011), review denied, (Feb. 15, 2012). Similarly, statements in pleadings filed on behalf of a party will be admissible if it is shown that the party adopted or approved them. *Fridena v. Evans*, 127 Ariz. 516, 622 P.2d 463, 12 A.L.R.4th 46 (1980); *Starkovich v. Noye*, 111 Ariz. 347, 529 P.2d 698 (1974); *Ulibarri v. Gerstenberger*, 178 Ariz. 151, 871 P.2d 698 (Ct. App. Div. 1 1993) (rejected on other grounds by, Logerquist v. Danforth, 188 Ariz. 16, 932 P.2d 281 (Ct. App. Div. 2 1996)); *Black v. Perkins*, 163 Ariz. 292, 787 P.2d 1088 (Ct. App. Div. 2 1989); *Fridenmaker v. Valley Nat. Bank of Arizona*, 23 Ariz. App. 565, 534 P.2d 1064 (Div. 1 1975).

Rule 801(d)(2)(C) excludes from the definition of hearsay, and thereby allows the statements made by a party's agent or employee, but only if the party authorized the agent or employee to speak on the subject. *Shuck v. Texaco Refining & Marketing, Inc.*, 178 Ariz. 295, 872 P.2d 1247 (Ct. App. Div. 1 1994). The Rule's requirement that the declarant have "speaking authority" has operated to exclude highly probative statements made by knowledgeable agents because it could not be shown that the principal had authorized the agent to make the particular statement in question. *Shuck v. Texaco Refining & Marketing, Inc.*, 178 Ariz. 295, 872 P.2d 1247 (Ct. App. Div. 1 1994). Dissatisfaction with this aspect of the Rule led to the adoption of subpart (d)(2)(D) of the Rule. *Shuck v. Texaco Refining & Marketing, Inc.*, 178 Ariz. 295, 872 P.2d 1247 (Ct. App. Div. 1 1994).

Rule 801(d)(2)(D), which excludes from the definition of hearsay statements made by an agent or employee concerning a matter within the scope of the agency or employment, is substantially broader than Rule 801(d)(2)(C). *Shuck v. Texaco Refining & Marketing, Inc.*, 178 Ariz. 295, 872 P.2d 1247 (Ct. App. Div. 1 1994). *See also Brooks v. Neer*, 46 Ariz. 144, 47 P.2d 452 (1935). Whereas the focus of Rule 801(d)(2)(C) is the employee's authority to make the statement, the focus of Rule 801(d)(2)(D) is the content of the statement and whether it relates to some aspect of the employer's business that is within the scope of the employee's activities. *Shuck v. Texaco Refining & Marketing, Inc.*, 178 Ariz.

295, 872 P.2d 1247 (Ct. App. Div. 1 1994).

The proponent of evidence under Rule 801(d)(2)(D) must only make a foundational showing that the statement: (1) was made by the opposing party's agent or servant, (2) was made during the existence of the agency relationship, and (3) concerned a matter within the scope of the agency or employment. *Daly v. Williams*, 78 Ariz. 382, 280 P.2d 701 (1955); *Walter v. Southern Arizona School for Boys, Inc.*, 77 Ariz. 141, 267 P.2d 1076 (1954); *Podol v. Jacobs*, 65 Ariz. 50, 173 P.2d 758 (1946); *Henry ex rel. Estate of Wilson v. HealthPartners of Southern Arizona*, 203 Ariz. 393, 55 P.3d 87 (Ct. App. Div. 2 2002); *Formento v. Encanto Business Park*, 154 Ariz. 495, 744 P.2d 22 (Ct. App. Div. 2 1987), opinion supplemented, (Aug. 4, 1987); *Hudlow v. American Estate Life Ins. Co.*, 22 Ariz. App. 246, 526 P.2d 770 (Div. 1 1974); *Sears Roebuck & Co. v. Jackson*, 21 Ariz. App. 176, 517 P.2d 529 (Div. 1 1973).

The declarant need not have personal knowledge of the matter asserted in the statement for it to be admissible under the party opponent rule. *Henry ex rel. Estate of Wilson v. HealthPartners of Southern Arizona*, 203 Ariz. 393, 55 P.3d 87 (Ct. App. Div. 2 2002). Such evidence may emanate from the pleadings of a party, whether signed by the party or the party's counsel. *Henry ex rel. Estate of Wilson v. HealthPartners of Southern Arizona*, 203 Ariz. 393, 55 P.3d 87 (Ct. App. Div. 2 2002).

Such an agency can be proven by circumstantial evidence, and even by hearsay. *Bank of America, National Trust and Sav. Ass'n v. Barnett*, 87 Ariz. 96, 348 P.2d 296 (1960); *Maynard v. Hall*, 61 Ariz. 32, 143 P.2d 884, 150 A.L.R. 618 (1943); *Little v. Brown*, 40 Ariz. 206, 11 P.2d 610 (1932); *Shuck v. Texaco Refining & Marketing, Inc.*, 178 Ariz. 295, 872 P.2d 1247 (Ct. App. Div. 1 1994); *Phoenix Western Holding Corp. v. Gleeson*, 18 Ariz. App. 60, 500 P.2d 320 (Div. 1 1972). The statement in question, however, must have been made while the agency or employment relationship still existed—statements by former employees will not qualify. *Gibraltar Escrow Co. v. Thomas J. Grosso Inv., Inc.*, 4 Ariz. App. 490, 421 P.2d 923 (1966).

9. *Statements by Co-Conspirator in Furtherance of Conspiracy.* What could be viewed as a particular type of authorized admission or statement by a party's agent is covered in Rule 801(d)(2)(E), which excludes from the definition of hearsay statements made by a party's co-conspirator during the course and in furtherance of a conspiracy. *State v. Baumann*, 125 Ariz. 404, 610 P.2d 38 (1980). While this type of statement is more frequently encountered in criminal cases, the Rule is fully applicable in civil cases. *Sheet Metal Workers Intern. Ass'n v. Nichols*, 89 Ariz. 187, 360 P.2d 204, 47 L.R.R.M. (BNA) 2856, 42 Lab. Cas.

(CCH) P 50176 (1961); *Consolidated Tungsten Mines, Inc. v. Frazier*, 87 Ariz. 128, 348 P.2d 734 (1960). To secure the admission of such a statement, it must be shown that there was a conspiracy, and that the declarant and the party were both participants in it. *State ex rel. La Sota v. Arizona Licensed Beverage Ass'n, Inc.*, 128 Ariz. 515, 627 P.2d 666, 1981-1 Trade Cas. (CCH) ¶ 63933 (1981).

Rule 802. The Rule Against Hearsay

Hearsay is not admissible unless any of the following provides otherwise:

- an applicable constitutional provision or statute;
- these rules; or
- other rules prescribed by the Supreme Court.

Amended Sept. 8, 2011, effective Jan. 1, 2012.

Comment to 2012 Amendment

The language of Rule 802 has been amended to conform to the federal restyling of the Evidence Rules to make them more easily understood and to make style and terminology consistent throughout the rules. These changes are intended to be stylistic only. There is no intent to change any result in any ruling on evidence admissibility.

AUTHORS' COMMENTS

Analysis

1. *Scope and Purpose of Rule.* Rule 802 merely states the general rule that hearsay is not admissible, except as permitted by constitutional provisions, statutes or by other rules.

2. *Comparison With Federal Rule.* Effective January 1, 2012, the Arizona Supreme Court amended Rule 802 to conform to the federal restyling of the Evidence Rules to make the rules more easily understood and to make style and terminology consistent throughout. The 2012 Comment states the stylistic amendments are not intended to "change any result in any ruling on evidence admissibility."

Following the 2012 restyling amendments, the language of Rule 802 remains identical to its federal counterpart, Fed. R. Evid. 802, except for editorial differences necessary to adapt the Rule to the Arizona court system, and the Arizona exception that permits the receipt of hearsay when allowed by "applicable constitutional provision."

Although Rule 802 parallels its federal counterpart, "federal court decisions interpreting the federal rule are persuasive but not binding with respect to interpreting the Arizona rule." *See,* Prefatory Comment to 2012 Amendments. *See also, State v. Terra-*

zas, 189 Ariz. 580, 944 P.2d 1194 (1997) (The Arizona Supreme Court is "not bound by the United States Supreme Court's non-constitutional construction of the Federal Rules of Evidence when [the Arizona Supreme Court construes] the Arizona Rules of Evidence."), citing, *State v. Bible*, 175 Ariz. 549, 858 P.2d 1152 (1993); *State v. Salazar-Mercado*, 232 Ariz. 256, 304 P.3d 543 (Ct. App. Div. 2 2013). Practitioners are urged to keep this legal tenet in mind as they research federal case law interpreting a federal evidentiary rule that corresponds to an Arizona evidentiary rule.

3. *Instances Where Hearsay Admissible.* As discussed in Section 4 of the *Authors' Comments* to Rule 801, hearsay is admissible when offered for some purpose other than to prove the truth of the matter asserted in the hearsay statement. Under Rule 104(a), hearsay may also be considered by the Court in making preliminary determinations concerning the admissibility of evidence.

By statute, hearsay is admissible in administrative hearings. A.R.S. § 41-1062(A)(1). It has been held, however, that that statute only authorizes the receipt of hearsay which has circumstantial guarantees of reliability. *Wieseler v. Prins*, 167 Ariz. 223, 805 P.2d 1044 (Ct. App. Div. 1 1990); *Plowman v. Arizona State Liquor Bd.*, 152 Ariz. 331, 732 P.2d 222 (Ct. App. Div. 2 1986). It has even been intimated that statutory exceptions to the hearsay rule will be found unconstitutional unless the hearsay evidence they permit has guarantees of trustworthiness similar or equivalent to those of the exceptions recognized by Rules 803 and 804. *Matter of One (1) Rolex Brand Man's Watch*, 176 Ariz. 294, 860 P.2d 1347 (Ct. App. Div. 1 1993).

Ariz.R.Civ.P. 75(e) (formerly Rule 4(d) of the now abrogated Uniform Rules of Procedure for Arbitration) authorizes the receipt into evidence at the arbitration hearing of several categories of documents which would be inadmissible as hearsay at trial, provided they are listed in the pre-hearing statement and no objection as to their authenticity is made. These include depositions of witnesses who are available to testify, sworn statements of witnesses and sworn written statements of experts. Ariz.R.Civ.P. 75(e)(6), (7), (10). See further discussion in the *Authors' Comments* under Ariz.R.Civ.P. 75.

Affidavits fall within the definition of hearsay in Rule 801(c). The Arizona Rules of Civil Procedure, however, authorize the use of affidavits to establish service of process by someone other than the sheriff or a deputy sheriff, Ariz.R.Civ.P. 4(g); to establish the grounds for issuance of a temporary restraining order without notice, Ariz.R.Civ.P. 65(d); to support or oppose a motion for summary judgment, Ariz.R.Civ.P. 56(e); and, in the Court's discretion, to establish facts pertinent to the resolution of other civil motions, Ariz.R.Civ.P. 43(i).

4. *Effect of Improper Admission of Hearsay.* Hearsay which is admitted without objection is competent proof, but may not be sufficient, in and of itself, to sustain a party's burden of proof. *State v. Allen*, 157 Ariz. 165, 755 P.2d 1153 (1988); *State v. McGann*, 132 Ariz. 296, 645 P.2d 811 (1982); *Starkins v. Bateman*, 150 Ariz. 537, 724 P.2d 1206 (Ct. App. Div. 1 1986).

The improper admission of hearsay evidence will generally not result in a reversal where no prejudice results, as where the facts established by the hearsay were not truly controverted, *Public Service Co. of Oklahoma v. Bleak*, 134 Ariz. 311, 656 P.2d 600 (1982); where the hearsay concerned a collateral issue, *Rutledge v. Arizona Bd. of Regents*, 147 Ariz. 534, 711 P.2d 1207, 29 Ed. Law Rep. 1161 (Ct. App. Div. 1 1985); where the hearsay evidence was cumulative of other, competent proof, *Mott's Inc. of Mississippi v. Coco's Family Restaurant*, 158 Ariz. 350, 762 P.2d 637 (Ct. App. Div. 2 1988); *Borja v. Phoenix General Hosp., Inc.*, 151 Ariz. 302, 727 P.2d 355 (Ct. App. Div. 2 1986); or, where the admission of the evidence was otherwise harmless error, *Starkins v. Bateman*, 150 Ariz. 537, 724 P.2d 1206 (Ct. App. Div. 1 1986).

Rule 803. Exceptions to the Rule Against Hearsay— Regardless of Whether the Declarant Is Available as a Witness

The following are not excluded by the rule against hearsay, regardless of whether the declarant is available as a witness:

(1) Present Sense Impression. A statement describing or explaining an event or condition, made while or immediately after the declarant perceived it.

(2) Excited Utterance. A statement relating to a startling event or condition, made while the declarant was under the stress of excitement that it caused.

(3) Then-Existing Mental, Emotional, or Physical Condition. A statement of the declarant's then-existing state of mind (such as motive, intent, or plan) or emotional, sensory, or physical condition (such as mental feeling, pain, or bodily health), but not including a statement of memory or belief to prove the fact remembered or believed unless it relates to the validity or terms of the declarant's will.

(4) Statement Made for Medical Diagnosis or Treatment. A statement that:

(A) is made for—and is reasonably pertinent to—medical diagnosis or treatment; and

(B) describes medical history; past or present symptoms or sensations; their inception; or their general cause.

(5) Recorded Recollection. A record that:

(A) is on a matter the witness once knew about but now cannot recall well enough to testify fully and accurately;

(B) was made or adopted by the witness when the matter was fresh in the witness's memory; and

(C) accurately reflects the witness's knowledge.

If admitted, the record may be read into evidence but may be received as an exhibit only if offered by an adverse party.

(6) Records of a Regularly Conducted Activity. A record of an act, event, condition, opinion, or diagnosis if:

(A) the record was made at or near the time by—or from information transmitted by—someone with knowledge;

(B) the record was kept in the course of a regularly conducted activity of a business, organization, occupation, or calling, whether or not for profit;

(C) making the record was a regular practice of that activity;

(D) all these conditions are shown by the testimony of the custodian or another qualified witness, or by a certification that complies with Rule 902(11) or (12) or with a statute permitting certification; and

(E) neither the source of information nor the method or circumstances of preparation indicate a lack of trustworthiness.

(7) Absence of a Record of a Regularly Conducted Activity. Evidence that a matter is not included in a record described in paragraph (6) if:

(A) the evidence is admitted to prove that the matter did not occur or exist;

(B) a record was regularly kept for a matter of that kind; and

(C) neither the possible source of the information nor other circumstances indicate a lack of trustworthiness.

(8) Public Records. A record or statement of a public office if:

(A) it sets out:

(i) the office's activities;

(ii) a matter observed while under a legal duty to report, but not including, in a criminal case, a matter observed by law-enforcement personnel; or

(iii) in a civil case or against the government in a criminal case, factual findings from a legally authorized investigation; and

(B) neither the source of information nor other circumstances indicate a lack of trustworthiness.

(9) Public Records of Vital Statistics. A record of a birth, death, or marriage, if reported to a public office in accordance with a legal duty.

(10) Absence of a Public Record. Testimony—or a certification under Rule 902—that a diligent search failed to disclose a public record or statement:

(A) the testimony or certification is admitted to prove that

(i) the record or statement does not exist; or

(ii) a matter did not occur or exist, if a public office regularly kept a record or statement for a matter of that kind; and

(B) in a criminal case, a prosecutor who intends to offer a certification provides written notice of that intent at least 20 days before trial, and the defendant does not object in writing within 10 days of receiving the notice—unless the court sets a different time for the notice or the objection.

Rule 803(10) amended Aug. 28, 2013, effective Jan. 1, 2014.

(11) Records of Religious Organizations Concerning Personal or Family History. A statement of birth, legitimacy, ancestry, marriage, divorce, death, relationship by blood or marriage, or similar facts of personal or family history, contained in a regularly kept record of a religious organization.

(12) Certificates of Marriage, Baptism, and Similar Ceremonies. A statement of fact contained in a certificate:

(A) made by a person who is authorized by a religious organization or by law to perform the act certified;

(B) attesting that the person performed a marriage or similar ceremony or administered a sacrament; and

(C) purporting to have been issued at the time of the act or within a reasonable time after it.

(13) Family Records. A statement of fact about personal or family history contained in a family record, such as a Bible, genealogy, chart, engraving on a ring, inscription on a portrait, or engraving on an urn or burial marker.

(14) Records of Documents That Affect an Interest in Property. The record of a document that purports to establish or affect an interest in property if:

(A) the record is admitted to prove the content of the original recorded document, along with its signing and its delivery by each person who purports to have signed it;

(B) the record is kept in a public office; and

(C) a statute authorizes recording documents of that kind in that office.

(15) Statements in Documents That Affect an Interest in Property. A statement contained in a document that purports to establish or affect an interest in property if the matter stated was relevant to the document's purpose—unless later dealings with the property are inconsistent with the truth of the statement or the purport of the document.

(16) Statements in Ancient Documents. A statement in a document that is at least 20 years old and whose authenticity is established.

(17) Market Reports and Similar Commercial Publications. Market quotations, lists, directories, or other compilations that are generally relied on by the public or by persons in particular occupations.

(18) Statements in Learned Treatises, Periodicals, or Pamphlets. A statement contained in a treatise, periodical, or pamphlet if:

(A) the statement is called to the attention of an expert witness on cross-examination or relied on by the expert on direct examination; and

(B) the publication is established as a reliable authority by the expert's admission or testimony, by another expert's testimony, or by judicial notice.

If admitted, the statement may be read into evidence but not received as an exhibit.

(19) Reputation Concerning Personal or Family History. A reputation among a person's family by blood, adoption, or marriage—or among a person's associates or in the community—concerning the person's birth, adoption, legitimacy, ancestry, marriage, divorce, death, relationship by blood, adoption, or marriage, or similar facts of personal or family history.

(20) Reputation Concerning Boundaries or General History. A reputation in a community—arising before the controversy—concerning boundaries of land in the community or customs that affect the land, or concerning general historical events important to that community, state, or nation.

(21) Reputation Concerning Character. A reputation among a person's associates or in the community concerning the person's character.

(22) Judgment of a Previous Conviction. Evidence of a final judgment of conviction if:

(A) the judgment was entered after a trial or guilty plea, but not a nolo contendere plea;

(B) the conviction was for a crime punishable by death or by imprisonment for more than a year;

(C) the evidence is admitted to prove any fact essential to the judgment; and

(D) when offered by the prosecutor in a criminal case for a purpose other than impeachment, the judgment was against the defendant.

The pendency of an appeal may be shown but does not affect admissibility.

(23) Judgments Involving Personal, Family, or General History or a Boundary. A judgment that is admitted to prove a matter of personal, family, or general history, or boundaries, if the matter:

(A) was essential to the judgment; and

(B) could be proved by evidence of reputation.

(24) [Other exceptions.] [Transferred to Rule 807.]

(25) Former testimony (non-criminal action or proceeding). Except in a criminal action or proceeding, testimony given as a witness at another hearing of the same or different proceeding, or in a deposition taken in compliance with law in the course of the same or another proceeding, if the party against whom the testimony is now offered, or a predecessor in interest, had an opportunity and similar motive to develop the testimony by direct, cross, or redirect examination.

Amended Oct. 19, 1988, effective Nov. 1, 1988; Oct. 3, 1994, effective Dec. 1, 1994; Oct. 16, 2003, effective Dec. 1, 2003; Sept. 8, 2011, effective Jan. 1, 2012.

Comment to 2014 Amendment

Rule 803(10) has been amended to incorporate, with minor variations, a "notice-and-demand" procedure that was approved in *Melendez-Diaz v. Massachusetts*, 557 U.S. 305, 129 S. Ct. 2527, 174 L. Ed. 2d 314 (2009). This amendment is not intended to alter any otherwise applicable disclosure requirements.

Added Aug. 28, 2013, effective Jan. 1, 2014.

Comment to 2012 Amendment

To conform to Federal Rule of Evidence 803(6)(A), as restyled, the language "first hand knowledge" in Rule 803(6)(b) has been changed to "knowledge" in amended Rule 803(6)(A). The new language is not intended to change the requirement that the record be made by—or from information transmitted by–someone with personal or first hand knowledge.

To conform to Federal Rule of Evidence 803(24) and 807, Rule 803(24) has been deleted and transferred to Rule 807.

Rule 803(25) has not been amended to conform to the federal rules.

Otherwise, the language of Rule 803 has been amended to conform to the federal restyling of the Evidence Rules to make them more easily understood and to make style and terminology consistent throughout the rules. These changes are intended to be stylistic only. There is no intent in the restyling to change any result in any ruling on evidence admissibility.

Added Sept. 8, 2011, effective Jan. 1, 2012. Amended Aug. 30, 2012, effective Jan. 1, 2013.

Comment to 1994 Amendment

For provisions governing former testimony in criminal actions or proceedings, see Rule 804(b)(1) and Rule 19.3(c), Rules of Criminal Procedure.

AUTHORS' COMMENTS

Analysis

10. Learned Treatises.
11. Reputation as to Character.
12. Former Testimony.

1. *Scope and Purpose of Rule.* Following the 2012 amendments, Rule 803 lists twenty-four specific exceptions to the rule excluding hearsay. Former Rule 803(24) set forth the "residual exception" that permitted the trial court to allow receipt of hearsay that did not satisfy one of the specific exceptions if the statement had the equivalent circumstantial guarantees of trustworthiness. In 2012, the provisions of Rule 803(24) were combined with Rule 804(b)(7) and transferred to new Rule 807, to conform to its federal counterpart.

The hearsay rules represent a peculiarly judicial function—defining what evidence is reliable and establishing judicial processes to test that reliability. *Matter of One (1) Rolex Brand Man's Watch*, 176 Ariz. 294, 860 P.2d 1347 (Ct. App. Div. 1 1993). Virtually all documents are hearsay and will be admissible only if offered for a non-hearsay purpose or if one of the exceptions to the hearsay rule listed in Rules 803 and 804 is shown to be applicable, or Rule 807 applies. *Cf. Villas at Hidden Lakes Condominiums Ass'n v. Geupel Const. Co., Inc.*, 174 Ariz. 72, 847 P.2d 117 (Ct. App. Div. 1 1992) (decided before the 2012 adoption of Rule 807).

Hearsay is admissible only if it falls within one of the specific exceptions recognized in Rules 803 and 804. *Matter of One (1) Rolex Brand Man's Watch*, 176 Ariz. 294, 860 P.2d 1347 (Ct. App. Div. 1 1993). The theoretical basis for most of the exceptions is the belief that the specified circumstances under which the statement was made provide a guarantee of the statement's trustworthiness, and negate to an acceptable level the dangers of poor perception and/or memory and insincerity. Statutory exceptions to the hearsay rule will not be constitutional unless they require similar or equivalent guarantees of trustworthiness. *Matter of One (1) Rolex Brand Man's Watch*, 176 Ariz. 294, 860 P.2d 1347 (Ct. App. Div. 1 1993). Any exceptions, however, only bar the application of the hearsay rule. Other rules may preclude the admissibility of the evidence, such as the rules that the statement must be based on first-hand knowledge and must be relevant. *State v. Dixon*, 107 Ariz. 415, 489 P.2d 225 (1971); *State v. Hughes*, 120 Ariz. 120, 584 P.2d 584 (Ct. App. Div. 2 1978). Even if a document qualifies for an exception, moreover, it must still be authenticated under the standards of Rule 901 or 902.

Many of the exceptions to the hearsay rule seldom come into play and/or are relatively straightforward in their application.

The specific Comments which follow will address only those exceptions that are most frequently invoked in civil cases.

2. *Comparison With Federal Rule.* Effective January 1, 2012, the Arizona Supreme Court amended Rule 803 to conform to the federal restyling of the Evidence Rules to make the rules more easily understood and to make style and terminology consistent throughout. The 2012 Comment states the stylistic amendments are not intended to "change any result in any ruling on evidence admissibility."

Consistent with the Court's 2012 restyling efforts, the term "first hand knowledge" in Ariz. R. Evid. 803(6)(A) [Records Of A Regularly Conducted Activity] was changed to "knowledge." The Comment explains that the new language is not intended to change the requirement that the "record be made by—or from information transmitted by—someone with personal or first hand knowledge."

In 2012, the Arizona Supreme Court also transferred the provision formerly set forth in Rule 803(24) [Other Exceptions] to newly adopted Rule 807 [Residual Exception] to conform to similar amendments made to Fed. R. Evid. 803(24) and 807.

Rule 803(25) was not amended to conform to the federal rules.

As a consequence of the 2012 amendments, the principal difference between Rule 803 and Fed. R. Evid. 803 is that the Federal Rule does not contain a provision corresponding to Rule 803(25), added to the Arizona Rule by a 1994 amendment. Ariz. R. Evid. 803(25) creates an exception to the hearsay rule, applicable only in civil ("non-criminal") cases, for former testimony, even though the witness-declarant is available to testify in person.

To the extent Rule 803 parallels its federal counterpart, "federal court decisions interpreting the federal rule are persuasive but not binding with respect to interpreting the Arizona rule." *See,* Prefatory Comment to 2012 Amendments. *See also, State v. Terrazas*, 189 Ariz. 580, 944 P.2d 1194 (1997) (The Arizona Supreme Court is "not bound by the United States Supreme Court's non-constitutional construction of the Federal Rules of Evidence when [the Arizona Supreme Court construes] the Arizona Rules of Evidence."), citing, *State v. Bible*, 175 Ariz. 549, 858 P.2d 1152 (1993); *State v. Salazar-Mercado*, 232 Ariz. 256, 304 P.3d 543 (Ct. App. Div. 2 2013). Practitioners are urged to keep this legal tenet in mind as they research federal case law interpreting a federal evidentiary rule that corresponds to an Arizona evidentiary rule.

3. *Present Sense Impressions.* The exception to the hearsay rule for statements that describe or explain an event or condition being perceived or experienced by the declarant assumes that the relative contemporaneity of the event and the statement will give

the statement an element of spontaneity that reduces the risk of fabrication. *State v. Rendon*, 148 Ariz. 524, 715 P.2d 777 (Ct. App. Div. 2 1986). The event that prompted the statement need not be a startling one. The statement can be one made "immediately" after perceiving the event or experiencing the condition, but it has not been definitively established how soon after the event the statement must be made to qualify for the exception. *Trevizo v. Astec Industries, Inc.*, 156 Ariz. 320, 751 P.2d 980 (Ct. App. Div. 2 1987).

For example, a text message sent by the victim stating that victim and defendant "are fighting" constituted a present-sense impression under Rule 803(1), Ariz. R. Evid. *State v. Damper*, 223 Ariz. 572, 225 P.3d 1148 (Ct. App. Div. 1 2010).

4. *Excited Utterances.* To qualify as an excited utterance under Rule 803(2), hearsay statements must meet three requirements: (1) there must be a startling event; (2) the words must be spoken soon after the event so that the declarant does not have time to fabricate the declarations; and, (3) the words spoken must relate to the startling event. *State v. Hausner*, 230 Ariz. 60, 280 P.3d 604 (2012) (statements of shooting victims/witnesses constituted excited utterances, shooting incidents were startling events, victims/witnesses made their statements soon after such incidents, and statements related to the events); *State v. Ruelas*, 174 Ariz. 37, 846 P.2d 850 (Ct. App. Div. 1 1992); *Peagler v. Phoenix Newspapers, Inc.*, 131 Ariz. 308, 640 P.2d 1110, 8 Media L. Rep. (BNA) 1209 (Ct. App. Div. 1 1981). The theory of the exception is that the startling event will produce a condition in the declarant which negates the possibility of reflection and fabrication. *Lewin v. Miller Wagner & Co., Ltd.*, 151 Ariz. 29, 725 P.2d 736 (Ct. App. Div. 1 1986).

The declarant need not be a participant in the startling event, and can be simply a witness to it, but it must be shown that the declarant was in fact startled or excited by it. *Warfield v. Shell Oil Co.*, 106 Ariz. 181, 472 P.2d 50 (1970); *Ehman v. Rathbun*, 116 Ariz. 460, 569 P.2d 1358 (Ct. App. Div. 2 1977); *Sears Roebuck & Co. v. Jackson*, 21 Ariz. App. 176, 517 P.2d 529 (Div. 1 1973). There is no fixed limit as to the amount of time that can elapse between the event and the statement, and a statement is not necessarily inadmissible as an excited utterance because it was made in response to a question. *State v. Ruelas*, 174 Ariz. 37, 846 P.2d 850 (Ct. App. Div. 1 1992). Whether the standards for application of the exception are satisfied is a matter committed to the trial court's discretion. *Musgrave v. Karis*, 63 Ariz. 417, 163 P.2d 278 (1945); *Byars v. Arizona Public Service Co.*, 24 Ariz. App. 420, 539 P.2d 534 (Div. 1 1975).

5. *Statements of Mental, Emotional or Physical Condition.* This

exception is particularly helpful, if not necessary, where the declarant's state of mind is an issue, but that must be in issue or the statements are not relevant. *Trevizo v. Astec Industries, Inc.*, 156 Ariz. 320, 751 P.2d 980 (Ct. App. Div. 2 1987). The exception is also related to, but distinct from, statements used as circumstantial evidence of a person's state of mind. This exception embraces only a statement as to the *present* (not past) statement of mind or physical condition of the declarant.

Where the statements are offered to prove the impact upon, or the state of mind of, the persons who heard them or read them, they are not hearsay. *Rutledge v. Arizona Bd. of Regents*, 147 Ariz. 534, 711 P.2d 1207, 29 Ed. Law Rep. 1161 (Ct. App. Div. 1 1985). On the other hand, if they are offered not just to show the declarant's belief, but also to prove the facts that justified that belief, the exception does not apply and they should be excluded. *Hudlow v. American Estate Life Ins. Co.*, 22 Ariz. App. 246, 526 P.2d 770 (Div. 1 1974). Statements of intent may be allowed as proof of performance of the intended act. *Ray Korte Chevrolet v. Simmons*, 117 Ariz. 202, 571 P.2d 699 (Ct. App. Div. 1 1977).

6. *Statements for Purposes of Medical Diagnosis or Treatment.* Unlike the exception in Rule 803(3) for statements as to state of mind, mental or physical condition, this exception applies to statements as to past symptoms and medical history as well as statements as to the declarant's present condition. It also includes statements made to expert witnesses for purposes of diagnosis. Before adoption of the Rule, these types of statements were only admissible to the extent an expert had relied upon them as the basis for forming a relevant opinion. *Wise v. Monteros*, 93 Ariz. 124, 379 P.2d 116 (1963).

7. *Recorded Recollection.* The application of this hearsay exception must be distinguished from the situation contemplated by Rule 612 where a document is used to refresh a witness' recollection and successfully does so. In that circumstance, the evidence that is received is the witness' testimony based upon the refreshed recollection, and not the document that was used to refresh it.

This exception deals with the situation where a document records what a witness once knew but simply cannot independently recall. There need not be a total lack of memory, just an inability on the part of the witness to testify fully and accurately. *DeForest v. DeForest*, 143 Ariz. 627, 694 P.2d 1241 (Ct. App. Div. 1 1985). The document in question need not be one that was created by or at the direction of the witness, if the witness read it at the time and approved it as accurate. The contents of the document need not have been adopted contemporaneously with the events described, but the adoption by the witness must have been at a time when the events were fresh in the witness' mind. The document can only be read into evidence; it is not admitted unless it is offered by the adverse party.

Under this exception, a law-enforcement officer testifying during a criminal trial may read his or her report as evidence as a "recorded recollection," provided all the other preconditions of Rule 803(5) are satisfied. *Goy v. Jones*, 205 Ariz. 421, 72 P.3d 351 (Ct. App. Div. 1 2003). For the report to be admitted into evidence as an exhibit, however, the standards of Rule 803(8) must be satisfied. *Goy v. Jones*, 205 Ariz. 421, 72 P.3d 351 (Ct. App. Div. 1 2003).

8. *Records of Regularly Conducted Activity.* Rule 803(6) codifies an exception to the hearsay rule that has long been recognized. Even before the promulgation of the Rules of Evidence, Arizona had adopted (but has since repealed) its version of the Uniform Business Records as Evidence Act in what was formerly A.R.S. § 12-2262. Former A.R.S. § 12-2262(B) provided that the record of any act, condition or event was competent evidence if made in the regular course of business, at or near the time of the act, condition or event, and if the Court determined that the sources of information, and the method and time of preparation were such as to justify admission of the record. Rule 803(6) is somewhat more specific concerning the foundational requirements that must be shown to qualify for the exception, and expands the concept of "business" to include any "business, institution, association, profession, occupation and calling of every kind, whether or not conducted for profit."

To qualify for this exception to the hearsay rule, the record in question must be made and kept as part of a regular practice of a business activity, as thus broadly defined. *Consolidated Tungsten Mines, Inc. v. Frazier*, 87 Ariz. 128, 348 P.2d 734 (1960). If the record is not one that is routinely prepared, or is otherwise untrustworthy, it may be excluded as hearsay. *Starkovich v. Noye*, 111 Ariz. 347, 529 P.2d 698 (1974). The fact that a document is kept with the records of a business does not *ipso facto* qualify it as a business record entitled to the exemption. *Villas at Hidden Lakes Condominiums Ass'n v. Geupel Const. Co., Inc.*, 174 Ariz. 72, 847 P.2d 117 (Ct. App. Div. 1 1992); *Transamerica Ins. Co. v. Trout*, 145 Ariz. 355, 701 P.2d 851 (Ct. App. Div. 1 1985); *Markiewicz v. Salt River Valley Water Users' Ass'n*, 118 Ariz. 329, 576 P.2d 517 (Ct. App. Div. 1 1978).

Rule 803(6)(A) requires that the record must have been created "at or near the time" of the event reported, but there is no definitive test as to how close in time the event and the creation of the record must occur. *Wells Fargo Bank, N.A. v. Allen*, 231 Ariz. 209, 292 P.3d 195 (Ct. App. Div. 1 2012). It is within the trial court's discretion to determine whether a record was or was not made at or near the time of the events it records. *Standard Chartered PLC v. Price Waterhouse*, 190 Ariz. 6, 945 P.2d 317 (Ct. App. Div. 1 1996), as corrected on denial of reconsideration, (Jan. 13, 1997). A lapse of seven (7) days did not defeat application of the exception in *Lenslite Co. v. Zocher*, 95 Ariz. 208, 388 P.2d 421 (1964); but a delay of fifty-nine days was held to be outside the parameters of the Rule in *Kemp v. Pinal County*, 8 Ariz. App. 41, 442 P.2d 864 (1968). The contents of the business record must also shown to be probative concerning an issue in the case. *Larsen v. Decker*, 196 Ariz. 239, 995 P.2d 281 (Ct. App. Div. 1 2000), amended, (Feb. 22, 2000).

In its former version of the Rule, Arizona required that the record or memorandum must have been made by, or from information transmitted by, a person with *first hand* knowledge acquired in the course of a regularly conducted business activity. The 2012 amendments to Rule 803(6) substituted the phrase person with *first hand* knowledge with the phrase someone *with knowledge*. The 2012 Comment states that the amendment was stylistic only and there was "no intent in the restyling to change any result in any ruling on evidence admissibility."

Thus, statements made by one external to the business that are included in a business record are inadmissible unless offered simply to prove that the statement was made, or unless some other exception to the hearsay rule applies. Similarly, a statement that is contained in a business record, but is based on firsthand knowledge not acquired in the course of a regularly conducted business activity, cannot be received to prove the truth of the statement. *Baker v. Leight*, 91 Ariz. 112, 370 P.2d 268 (1962); *Horizon Corp. v. Home Ins. Co.*, 20 Ariz. App. 162, 511 P.2d 175, 68 A.L.R.3d 1064 (Div. 2 1973); *cf. also, Starkovich v. Noye*, 111 Ariz. 347, 529 P.2d 698 (1974). The fact that a statement in a business record is self-serving does not make the hearsay exception inapplicable. *Drumwright v. Lynn Engineering & Mfg., Inc.*, 14 Ariz. App. 282, 482 P.2d 891 (Div. 1 1971).

Before a business record can be admitted as an exception to the hearsay rule, the trial court must be satisfied that the Rule's conditions concerning the circumstances of the record's preparation and the source of the information contained therein have been met. Neither the person who witnessed the matters recorded nor the person who created the record are necessary foundational witnesses. The requisite foundation must, however, be established by someone who has personal knowledge or is otherwise familiar with how the record was prepared or with the practice of the business concerning the preparation of records of that type. *Sitton v. Deutsche Bank Nat. Trust Co.*, 233 Ariz. 215, 311 P.3d 237 (Ct. App. Div. 1 2013) (finding custodian of records declaration contained sufficient foundation to support the admission of business records); *Wells Fargo Bank, N.A. v. Allen*, 231 Ariz. 209, 292 P.3d 195 (Ct. App. Div. 1 2012) (discussing purpose and content of the custodian of records affidavit); *Lenslite Co. v. Zocher*, 95 Ariz. 208, 388 P.2d 421 (1964); *Colvin v. Westinghouse Elec. Corp.*, 79 Ariz. 275, 288 P.2d 490 (1955); *Taeger v. Catholic Family and Community Services*, 196 Ariz. 285, 995 P.2d 721 (Ct. App. Div. 1 1999); *GM Development Corp. v. Community American Mortg. Corp.*, 165 Ariz. 1, 795 P.2d 827 (Ct. App. Div. 1 1990); *Matter of Estate of Walton*, 163 Ariz. 51, 785 P.2d 1239 (Ct. App. Div. 2 1989), opinion vacated in part on other issue, 164 Ariz. 498, 794 P.2d 131 (1990); *Continental Tel. Co. of the West v. Blazzard*, 149 Ariz. 1, 716 P.2d 62 (Ct. App. Div. 2 1986); *Merrick v. U. S. Rubber Co.*, 7 Ariz. App. 433, 440 P.2d 314 (1968).

Some examples of the types of business records that have been held to qualify for this hearsay exception include:

(1) invoices and shipping records, *Holt v. Western Farm Services, Inc.*, 110 Ariz. 276, 517 P.2d 1272 (1974); *Colvin v. Westinghouse Elec. Corp.*, 79 Ariz. 275, 288 P.2d 490 (1955);

(2) appraisal reports, *Higgins v. Arizona Sav. and Loan Ass'n*, 90 Ariz. 55, 365 P.2d 476 (1961);

(3) hauling records, *Builders Supply Corp. v. Shipley*, 86 Ariz. 153, 341 P.2d 940 (1959);

(4) time records, *Lenslite Co. v. Zocher*, 95 Ariz. 208, 388 P.2d 421 (1964);

(5) school attendance records, *Snyder v. Beers*, 1 Ariz. App. 497, 405 P.2d 288 (1965);

(6) a credit card report prepared for litigation from databases compiled during the ordinary course of business, *State v. Parker*, 231 Ariz. 391, 296 P.3d 54 (2013);

(7) testing reports, *Rayner v. Stauffer Chemical Co.*, 120 Ariz. 328, 585 P.2d 1240 (Ct. App. Div. 1 1978);

(8) equipment installation records, *Packard v. Reidhead*, 22 Ariz. App. 420, 528 P.2d 171 (Div. 1 1974).

To qualify for this exception to the hearsay rule, statements recorded in minutes of a meeting of a corporate Board of Directors must be shown to be "business records," and must be authenticated. *Taeger v. Catholic Family and Community Services*, 196 Ariz. 285, 995 P.2d 721 (Ct. App. Div. 1 1999).

9. *Public Records and Reports.* Rule 803(8) provides an exception to the hearsay rule for the types of records and reports generated and maintained by public officers and agencies, unless the sources of information and/or other circumstances indicate a lack

of trustworthiness. *Larsen v. Decker*, 196 Ariz. 239, 995 P.2d 281 (Ct. App. Div. 1 2000), amended, (Feb. 22, 2000). Such records and reports must still, however, be properly authenticated under Rules 901 and 902 or Ariz.R.Civ.P. 44(a). *Rodriguez v. Williams*, 107 Ariz. 458, 489 P.2d 268 (1971). If the trustworthiness and authentication prerequisites are satisfied, then both facts and conclusions contained in the record or report are admissible. *Larsen v. Decker*, 196 Ariz. 239, 995 P.2d 281 (Ct. App. Div. 1 2000), amended on other grounds, (Feb. 22, 2000). The exception is justified by an assumption that public officials perform their duties properly and probably do not independently recall details reflected in public records they have created. *Hudgins v. Southwest Airlines, Co.*, 221 Ariz. 472, 212 P.3d 810 (Ct. App. Div. 1 2009). The fact that a police report was not prepared until seven weeks after the interview recorded does not necessarily make it or its sources untrustworthy. *Hudgins v. Southwest Airlines, Co.*, 221 Ariz. 472, 212 P.3d 810 (Ct. App. Div. 1 2009).

With respect to certain types of public records and reports, the Rule draws distinctions as to their admissibility between civil and criminal cases. For example, police and law enforcement reports, such as accident reports, qualify for the hearsay exception set forth in Rule 803(8)(B) in civil cases, but not in criminal cases. *Parsons v. Smithey*, 109 Ariz. 49, 504 P.2d 1272, 54 A.L.R.3d 964 (1973); *Killingsworth v. Nottingham*, 18 Ariz. App. 356, 501 P.2d 1197 (Div. 2 1972). Similarly, Rule 803(8)(C) exempts from the hearsay rule reports setting forth factual findings resulting from an investigation made pursuant to authority granted by law, but only in civil cases and when offered *against* the government in criminal cases. *See Borja v. Phoenix General Hosp., Inc.*, 151 Ariz. 302, 727 P.2d 355 (Ct. App. Div. 2 1986). *Dicta* in certain earlier cases suggested that this exception encompassed only the government agency's factual findings, and did not include a government agency's conclusions. *Davis v. Cessna Aircraft Corp.*, 182 Ariz. 26, 893 P.2d 26, Prod. Liab. Rep. (CCH) P 14038 (Ct. App. Div. 1 1994); *Steed v. Cuevas*, 24 Ariz. App. 547, 540 P.2d 166 (Div. 1 1975). These suggestions were disapproved in *Larsen v. Decker*, 196 Ariz. 239, 995 P.2d 281 (Ct. App. Div. 1 2000), amended, (Feb. 22, 2000).

While a determination by the Equal Employment Opportunity Commission of reasonable cause to believe discrimination has occurred may be trustworthy, Rule 803(8)(C) creates an exemption only from the requirements of the hearsay rule and does not render any document satisfying the requirements of that rule automatically admissible without regard to the resolution of other evidentiary objections that may be made. *Shotwell v. Donahoe*, 207 Ariz. 287, 85 P.3d 1045, 93 Fair Empl. Prac. Cas. (BNA) 658 (2004). Such determinations are not *per se* admissible in Title VII employment discrimination cases brought in Arizona state courts. *Shotwell v. Donahoe*, 207 Ariz. 287, 85 P.3d 1045, 93 Fair Empl. Prac. Cas. (BNA) 658 (2004).

10. *Learned Treatises.* Rule 803(18) permits the introduction of portions of learned treatises or other authoritative publications which are called to an expert's attention during cross-examination or are relied upon by the expert during direct examination. The particular statements relied upon can be read to the jury, but neither the treatise or publication itself nor the selected statements are admissible as exhibits. *Cf. Rossell v. Volkswagen of America*, 147 Ariz. 160, 709 P.2d 517, Prod. Liab. Rep. (CCH) P 10752 (1985); *Schneider v. Cessna Aircraft Co.*, 150 Ariz. 153, 722 P.2d 321, Prod. Liab. Rep. (CCH) P 10743 (Ct. App. Div. 1 1985). Where voluminous materials of this nature are involved, the trial court can order the disclosure before trial of what will be offered so that issues of admissibility can be resolved before the actual offer. *Chapman v. Levi-Strauss*, 145 Ariz. 411, 701 P.2d 1219 (Ct. App. Div. 2 1985).

11. *Reputation as to Character.* This exception to the hearsay rule accommodates the proof of character through reputation evidence which is authorized by Rule 404(a). The codification of an exception to the hearsay rule for this category of evidence is an acknowledgment that what the reputation witness purports to know and report to the trier of fact is really the collective hearsay of the community concerning a person's character.

12. *Former Testimony.* Contemporaneously with the adoption of the 1994 amendments to Ariz.R.Civ.P. 32(a), amendments were also adopted to Rules 803 and 804, Ariz. R. Evid. The "former testimony" exception to the hearsay rule contained in former Rule 804(b)(1), which required that the declarant be "unavailable," was reworded and limited to criminal cases. Rule 803(25) was adopted, which established a "former testimony" exception to the hearsay rule applicable only in civil ("non-criminal") cases, and which does not require a showing that the declarant is "unavailable." All that is required is that the party against whom the former testimony is offered, or a predecessor in interest, had an opportunity and similar motive to develop the former testimony through direct, cross or redirect examination. See also the discussion in Section 6 of the *Authors' Comments* under Ariz.R.Civ.P. 32.

Rule 804. Exceptions to the Rule Against Hearsay—When the Declarant is Unavailable as a Witness

(a) Criteria for Being Unavailable. A declarant is considered to be unavailable as a witness if the declarant:

(1) is exempted from testifying about the subject matter of the declarant's statement because the court rules that a privilege applies;

(2) refuses to testify about the subject matter despite a court order to do so;

(3) testifies to not remembering the subject matter;

(4) cannot be present or testify at the trial or hearing because of death or a then-existing infirmity, physical illness, or mental illness; or

(5) is absent from the trial or hearing and the statement's proponent has not been able, by process or other reasonable means, to procure:

(A) the declarant's attendance, in the case of a hearsay exception under Rule 804(b)(1) or (5); or

(B) the declarant's attendance or testimony, in the case of a hearsay exception under Rule 804(b)(2), (3), or (4).

But this subsection (a) does not apply if the statement's proponent procured or wrongfully caused the declarant's unavailability as a witness in order to prevent the declarant from attending or testifying.

(b) The Exceptions. The following are not excluded by the rule against hearsay if the declarant is unavailable as a witness:

(1) **Former Testimony in a Criminal Case**. Testimony that:

(A) was made under oath by a party or witness during a previous judicial proceeding or a deposition under Arizona Rule of Criminal Procedure 15.3 shall be admissible in evidence if:

(i) The party against whom the former testimony is offered was a party to the action or proceeding during which a statement was given and had the right and opportunity to cross-examine the declarant with an interest and motive similar to that which the party now has (no person who was unrepresented by counsel at the proceeding during which a statement was made shall be deemed to have had the right and opportunity to cross-examine the declarant, unless such representation was waived) and

(ii) The declarant is unavailable as a witness, or is present and subject to cross-examination.

(B) The admissibility of former testimony under this subsection is subject to the same limitations and objections as though the declarant were testifying at the hearing, except that the former testimony offered under this subsection is not subject to:

(i) Objections to the form of the question which were not made at the time the prior testimony was given.

(ii) Objections based on competency or privilege which did not exist at the time the former testimony was given.

(2) **Statement Under the Belief of Imminent Death**. In a prosecution for homicide or in a civil case, a statement that the declarant, while believing the declarant's death to be imminent, made about its cause or circumstances.

(3) **Statement Against Interest**. A statement that:

(A) a reasonable person in the declarant's position would have made only if the person believed it to be true because, when made, it was so contrary to the declarant's proprietary or pecuniary interest or had so great a tendency to invalidate the declarant's claim against someone else or to expose the declarant to civil or criminal liability; and

(B) is supported by corroborating circumstances that clearly indicate its trustworthiness, if it is offered in a criminal case as one that tends to expose the declarant to criminal liability.

(4) **Statement of Personal or Family History**. A statement about:

(A) the declarant's own birth, adoption, legitimacy, ancestry, marriage, divorce, relationship by blood, adoption, or marriage, or similar facts of personal or family history, even though the declarant had no way of acquiring personal knowledge about that fact; or

(B) another person concerning any of these facts, as well as death, if the declarant was related to the person by blood, adoption, or marriage or was so intimately associated with the person's family that the declarant's information is likely to be accurate.

(5) **[Formerly (7) Other exceptions.]** [Transferred to Rule 807.]

(6) **Statement Offered Against a Party That Wrongfully Caused the Declarant's Unavailability**. A statement offered against a party that wrongfully caused—or acquiesced in wrongfully causing—the declarant's unavailability as a witness, and did so intending that result.

Amended Oct. 19, 1988, effective Nov. 1, 1988; Oct. 3, 1994, effective Dec. 1,

1994; Sept. 3, 2009, effective Jan. 1, 2010; Sept. 8, 2011, effective Jan. 1, 2012.

Comment to 2012 Amendment

Rule 804(b)(3) has been amended to conform to Federal Rule of Evidence 804(b)(3), as amended effective December 1, 2010.

Rule 804(b)(1) has been amended to incorporate the language of Arizona Rule of Criminal Procedure 19.3(c), but has not been amended to conform to the federal rules.

To conform to Federal Rule of Evidence 804(b)(5) and 807, Rule 804(b)(7) has been deleted and transferred to Rule 807.

Otherwise, the language of Rule 804 has been amended to conform to the federal restyling of the Evidence Rules to make them more easily understood and to make style and terminology consistent throughout the rules. These changes are intended to be stylistic only. There is no intent in the restyling to change any result in any ruling on evidence admissibility.

Amended Aug. 30, 2012, effective Jan. 1, 2013.

Comment to 1994 Amendment

For provisions governing former testimony in non-criminal actions or proceedings, *see* Rule 803(25).

AUTHORS' COMMENTS

Analysis

1. *Scope and Purpose of Rule.* Rule 804 defines five specific exceptions to the hearsay rule which can be invoked only when the declarant is *not* available as a witness under the tests set forth in subpart (a) of the Rule. Before it was amended effective January 1, 2012, Rule 804 also provided for a sixth exception -- the "residual" exception. This exception, former Rule 804(b)(7), permitted the Court to admit other hearsay statements if such statements had the "equivalent circumstantial guarantees of trustworthiness." To conform to its federal counterpart, Rule 804(b)(7) was deleted and transferred to Rule 807, as restyled.

2. *Comparison With Federal Rule.* Effective January 1, 2012, the Arizona Supreme Court amended Rule 804 to conform to the federal restyling of the Evidence Rules to make the rules more easily understood and to make style and terminology consistent throughout. The 2012 Comment states the stylistic amendments are not intended to "change any result in any ruling on evidence admissibility."

In 2012, Rule 804 was amended in three other ways. First, Rule 804(b)(1) was amended to incorporate the language of Ariz. R. Crim. P. 19.3(c), which addresses, in criminal proceedings, the "former testimony" hearsay exception, where the declarant is required to be unavailable. Second, Rule 804(b)(3) [Statement Against Interest] was amended to conform to the 2010 amendment to Fed. R. Evid. 804(b)(3). Third, the Court transferred the provision formerly set forth in Ariz. R. Evid. 804(b)(7) [Other Exceptions] to newly adopted Ariz. R. Evid. 807 [Residual Exception] to conform to similar amendments made to Fed. R. Evid. 804(b)(5) and 807.

As a consequence of the 2012 amendments, Ariz. R. Evid. 804 and Fed. R. Evid. 804 are substantially identical, except for the provisions of Rule 804(b)(1) [Former Testimony in a Criminal Case].

To the extent Rule 804 parallels its federal counterpart, "federal court decisions interpreting the federal rule are persuasive but not binding with respect to interpreting the Arizona rule." *See,* Prefatory Comment to 2012 Amendments. *See also, State v. Terrazas*, 189 Ariz. 580, 944 P.2d 1194 (1997) (The Arizona Supreme Court is "not bound by the United States Supreme Court's non-constitutional construction of the Federal Rules of Evidence when [the Arizona Supreme Court construes] the Arizona Rules of Evidence."), citing, *State v. Bible*, 175 Ariz. 549, 858 P.2d 1152 (1993); *State v. Salazar-Mercado*, 232 Ariz. 256, 304 P.3d 543 (Ct. App. Div. 2 2013). Practitioners are urged to keep this legal tenet in mind as they research federal case law interpreting a federal evidentiary rule that corresponds to an Arizona evidentiary rule.

3. *Unavailability of Declarant.* The hearsay exceptions listed in Rule 804 apply only when the hearsay declarant is unavailable as a witness. As defined in the Rule, "unavailable" does not necessarily mean that the witness is absent from or unable to be summoned to the proceedings. A witness suffering periodic episodes of amnesia as a consequence of a traumatic injury is properly determined to be "unavailable" for purposes of the Rule. *Ruvalcaba By and Through Stubblefield v. Ruvalcaba*, 174 Ariz. 436, 850 P.2d 674 (Ct. App. Div. 1 1993). Rule 804(a) sets forth the following non-exclusive list of situations where the hearsay declarant will be considered "unavailable" as a witness:

(1) where the declarant has successfully invoked a privilege concerning the subject matter of the hearsay statement to be offered, *cf., e.g., State v. LaGrand*, 153 Ariz. 21, 734 P.2d 563 (1987); *Union Bank v. Safanie*, 5 Ariz. App. 342, 427 P.2d 146 (1967);

(2) where a witness persists in a refusal to testify concerning

the subject matter of the hearsay statement despite being ordered by the Court to do so;

(3) where the declarant testifies to a lack of memory as to the subject matter of the hearsay statement;

(4) where the declarant cannot attend the proceedings due to death or due to physical or mental infirmity, *cf., e.g., In re Guardianship of Sorrells*, 58 Ariz. 25, 117 P.2d 96 (1941); *W.R.Skousen Contractors, Inc. v. Chatter*, 24 Ariz. App. 153, 536 P.2d 722 (Div. 1 1975); and

(5) where the declarant is not present and the proponent of the hearsay statement has been unable to procure the declarant's attendance through service of process or other reasonable means, *cf., e.g., Slow Development Co. v. Coulter*, 88 Ariz. 122, 353 P.2d 890 (1960); *Delozier v. Evans*, 158 Ariz. 490, 763 P.2d 986 (Ct. App. Div. 1 1988); *Erickson v. Waller*, 116 Ariz. 476, 569 P.2d 1374 (Ct. App. Div. 1 1977); *Edwards v. Van Voorhis*, 11 Ariz. App. 216, 463 P.2d 111 (Div. 1 1970); *Deike v. Great Atlantic & Pac. Tea Co.*, 3 Ariz. App. 430, 415 P.2d 145 (1966).

If the condition which renders the declarant unavailable is one that has been procured or created by the proponent of the statement, in order to prevent the witness from appearing and testifying, then Rule 804 will not apply, and the hearsay rule will operate to preclude receipt of the evidence.

4. *Former Testimony.* Contemporaneously with the adoption of the 1994 amendments to Ariz.R.Civ.P. 32(a), amendments were also adopted to Rules 803 and 804, Ariz. R. Evid. The "former testimony" exception to the hearsay rule contained in Rule 804(b)(1), which applies where the declarant is unavailable, now applies only in criminal cases. As amended in 2012, Rule 804(b)(1) sets forth the language of Ariz. R. Crim. P. 19.3(c) governing the admissibility of such former testimony in criminal proceedings.

Rule 803(25) was adopted, establishing a "former testimony" hearsay exception, which is applicable only in civil ("non-criminal") cases and which does not require a showing that the declarant is unavailable. This "former testimony" exception is discussed in Section 12 of the *Authors' Comments* under Rule 803, Ariz. R. Evid.

5. *Dying Declarations.* Rule 804(b)(2) allows an exception to the hearsay rule for statements made by a declarant "while believing that the declarant's death was imminent.. . ." The theory underlying this exception is that where there is a belief of impending death, a declarant lacks a motive to misstate the truth. *State v. Hughes*, 120 Ariz. 120, 584 P.2d 584 (Ct. App. Div. 2 1978).

For this exception to apply, it must be shown, generally by

circumstantial evidence, that the declarant believed death to be imminent, and the statement must concern the cause or circumstances of that impending death. *State v. Adamson*, 136 Ariz. 250, 665 P.2d 972 (1983); *Collins v. State*, 37 Ariz. 353, 294 P. 625 (1930); *State v. Ruelas*, 174 Ariz. 37, 846 P.2d 850 (Ct. App. Div. 1 1992). It must also be shown that the declarant was sufficiently in possession of the declarant's mental faculties to realize what was being said. *Macias v. State*, 39 Ariz. 303, 6 P.2d 423 (1931).

Before the adoption of the Rules of Evidence, the hearsay exception for such dying declarations was recognized only in criminal prosecutions for homicide. Rule 804(b)(2) specifically makes the exception available in any "civil action or proceeding." *But cf., State v. Ruelas*, 174 Ariz. 37, 846 P.2d 850 (Ct. App. Div. 1 1992).

6. *Statements Against Declarant's Interest.* Rule 804(b)(3), which was amended in 2012 to conform with Fed. R. Evid. 803(b)(3), provides an exception from the hearsay rule for statements that are against the declarant's pecuniary or proprietary interests at the time they are made. *In re Guardianship of Sorrells*, 58 Ariz. 25, 117 P.2d 96 (1941). The Rule expanded prior doctrine on the subject by including within its scope statements that tended to subject the declarant to civil or criminal liability. *Cf., e.g., Deike v. Great Atlantic & Pac. Tea Co.*, 3 Ariz. App. 430, 415 P.2d 145 (1966). The exception is, of course, unnecessary where the statement against interest is that of a party-opponent, as Rule 801(d)(2) excludes such statements from the definition of hearsay.

For the exception to apply, the declarant must be unavailable. *Konow v. Southern Pac. Co.*, 105 Ariz. 386, 465 P.2d 366 (1970); *State v. Machado*, 226 Ariz. 281, 246 P.3d 632 (2011) (statements made during anonymous telephone call admitted as statement against penal interest under Rule 804(b)(3) where statements were obtained pursuant to a warrant and prosecutor conceded that such statements were against the penal interest of the declarant and the declarant was unavailable). *See also, State v. Parker*, 231 Ariz. 391, 296 P.3d 54 (2013). Once received, the statements are neither conclusive nor dispositive; they can be contradicted or rebutted by the party against whom they are offered. *Ohio Farmers Ins. Co. v. Norman*, 122 Ariz. 330, 594 P.2d 1026 (Ct. App. Div. 2 1979); *Gallagher v. Viking Supply Corp.*, 3 Ariz. App. 55, 411 P.2d 814, 15 A.L.R.3d 1 (1966).

Where such a statement is offered in a criminal case to exculpate the accused, there is a special requirement that the trial court must determine whether the independent corroborating and contradicting evidence would lead a reasonable person to conclude that the statement could be true. *State v. LaGrand*, 153

Ariz. 21, 734 P.2d 563 (1987).

7. *Forfeiture-by-Wrongdoing Exception.* The forfeiture-by-wrongdoing exception to the hearsay rule permits admission of statements offered against a party that has engaged in wrongdoing where such wrongdoing "resulted in the unavailability of the declarant as a witness." *See,* Ariz. R. Evid. 804(b)(6). This exception is not limited to the trial for which the defendant silenced the witness, but permits such hearsay in all other relevant circumstances. *State v. Miller,* —— *Ariz.* ——, 316 P.3d 1219 (2013) (Rule 804(b)(6) is not limited to the trial for which the defendant silenced the witness; *State v. Benson*, 232 Ariz. 452, 307 P.3d 19 (2013).

Ariz. R. Evid. 804(b)(6) itself sets forth 4 factors to consider in evaluating this exception to the hearsay rule:

1. Witness unavailability;
2. Wrongdoing on the part of the party against whom the statement is offered;
3. Caused or acquiesced in witness tampering; and
4. Intention on the party of the party against whom the statement is offered to procure the witness' unavailability.

State v. Franklin, 232 Ariz. 556, 307 P.3d 983 (Ct. App. Div. 1 2013).

Rule 805. Hearsay Within Hearsay

Hearsay within hearsay is not excluded by the rule against hearsay if each part of the combined statements conforms with an exception to the rule.

Amended Sept. 8, 2011, effective Jan. 1, 2012.

Comment to 2012 Amendment

The language of Rule 805 has been amended to conform to the federal restyling of the Evidence Rules to make them more easily understood and to make style and terminology consistent throughout the rules. These changes are intended to be stylistic only. There is no intent to change any result in any ruling on evidence admissibility.

AUTHORS' COMMENTS

Analysis

1. *Scope and Purpose of Rule.* Rule 805 addresses the admissibility of multiple levels of hearsay, *e.g.*, where a witness present and in court proposes to testify to a statement made to that witness by another person, and the statement in question in turn reported to the witness a hearsay statement made by yet a third person, which is offered to prove the truth of its contents. In that circumstance, both statements must qualify for one of the exceptions to the hearsay rule set forth in Rules 803 and 804. *Cf., e.g., State v. McGann*, 132 Ariz. 296, 645 P.2d 811 (1982); *English-Clark v. City of Tucson*, 142 Ariz. 522, 690 P.2d 1235 (Ct. App. Div. 2 1984).

2. *Comparison With Federal Rule.* Effective January 1, 2012, the Arizona Supreme Court amended Rule 805 to conform to the federal restyling of the Evidence Rules to make the rules more easily understood and to make style and terminology consistent throughout. The 2012 Comment states the stylistic amendments are not intended to "change any result in any ruling on evidence admissibility."

Following the 2012 restyling amendments, the language of Rule 805 remains identical to its federal counterpart, Fed. R. Evid. 805.

Although Rule 805 parallels its federal counterpart, "federal court decisions interpreting the federal rule are persuasive but not binding with respect to interpreting the Arizona rule." *See*, Prefatory Comment to 2012 Amendments. *See also, State v. Terra-*

zas, 189 Ariz. 580, 944 P.2d 1194 (1997) (The Arizona Supreme Court is "not bound by the United States Supreme Court's non-constitutional construction of the Federal Rules of Evidence when [the Arizona Supreme Court construes] the Arizona Rules of Evidence."), citing, *State v. Bible*, 175 Ariz. 549, 858 P.2d 1152 (1993); *State v. Salazar-Mercado*, 232 Ariz. 256, 304 P.3d 543 (Ct. App. Div. 2 2013). Practitioners are urged to keep this legal tenet in mind as they research federal case law interpreting a federal evidentiary rule that corresponds to an Arizona evidentiary rule.

Rule 806. Attacking and Supporting the Declarant's Credibility

When a hearsay statement—or a statement described in Rule 801(d)(2)(C), (D), or (E)—has been admitted in evidence, the declarant's credibility may be attacked, and then supported, by any evidence that would be admissible for those purposes if the declarant had testified as a witness. The court may admit evidence of the declarant's inconsistent statement or conduct, regardless of when it occurred or whether the declarant had an opportunity to explain or deny it. If the party against whom the statement was admitted calls the declarant as a witness, the party may examine the declarant on the statement as if on cross-examination.

Amended Oct. 19, 1988, effective Nov. 1, 1988; Sept. 8, 2011, effective Jan. 1, 2012.

Comment to 2012 Amendment

The language of Rule 806 has been amended to conform to the federal restyling of the Evidence Rules to make them more easily understood and to make style and terminology consistent throughout the rules. These changes are intended to be stylistic only. There is no intent to change any result in any ruling on evidence admissibility.

AUTHORS' COMMENTS

Analysis

1. Scope and Purpose of Rule.
2. Comparison With Federal Rule.

1. *Scope and Purpose of Rule.* The principle underlying the complex language of Rule 806 is a simple one—when a hearsay statement is admitted pursuant to one of the exceptions set forth in Rules 803 and 804, the declarant who actually made the statement is treated as a witness in the proceedings, and the credibility of that declarant can be attacked or supported as with any other witness. One practical exception recognized by the Rule itself is that the declarant-witness need not be given the opportunity to explain or deny a prior inconsistent statement before extrinsic evidence of it can be received, as would be required by Rule 613(b) in the case of a witness who appears and testifies. The Rule essentially codified pre-existing law. *Cf., State v. Owen*, 101 Ariz. 156, 416 P.2d 589 (1966).

2. *Comparison With Federal Rule.* Effective January 1, 2012, the Arizona Supreme Court amended Rule 806 to conform to the

federal restyling of the Evidence Rules to make the rules more easily understood and to make style and terminology consistent throughout. The 2012 Comment states the stylistic amendments are not intended to "change any result in any ruling on evidence admissibility."

Following the 2012 restyling amendments, the language of Rule 806 remains identical to its federal counterpart, Fed. R. Evid. 806.

Although Rule 806 parallels its federal counterpart, "federal court decisions interpreting the federal rule are persuasive but not binding with respect to interpreting the Arizona rule." *See,* Prefatory Comment to 2012 Amendments. *See also, State v. Terrazas*, 189 Ariz. 580, 944 P.2d 1194 (1997) (The Arizona Supreme Court is "not bound by the United States Supreme Court's non-constitutional construction of the Federal Rules of Evidence when [the Arizona Supreme Court construes] the Arizona Rules of Evidence."), citing, *State v. Bible*, 175 Ariz. 549, 858 P.2d 1152 (1993); *State v. Salazar-Mercado*, 232 Ariz. 256, 304 P.3d 543 (Ct. App. Div. 2 2013). Practitioners are urged to keep this legal tenet in mind as they research federal case law interpreting a federal evidentiary rule that corresponds to an Arizona evidentiary rule.

Rule 807. Residual Exception

When a hearsay statement—or a statement described in Rule 801(d)(2)(C), (D), or (E)—has been admitted in evidence, the declarant's credibility may be attacked, and then supported, by any evidence that would be admissible for those purposes if the declarant had testified as a witness. The court may admit evidence of the declarant's inconsistent statement or conduct, regardless of when it occurred or whether the declarant had an opportunity to explain or deny it. If the party against whom the statement was admitted calls the declarant as a witness, the party may examine the declarant on the statement as if on cross-examination.

Added Sept. 8, 2011, effective Jan. 1, 2012.

Comment to 2012 Amendment

Rule 807 has been adopted to conform to Federal Rule of Evidence 807, as restyled.

AUTHORS' COMMENTS

Analysis

1. *Scope and Purpose of Rule*. As a result of the 2012 amendments to Arizona's Rules of Evidence, the contents of former Rules 803(24) and 804(b)(7) were combined and transferred to new Rule 807, which now provides the "residual" exception to the hearsay rule. As such, Rule 807 allows the trial court to permit hearsay evidence to be received in other circumstances in which it has "equivalent circumstantial guarantees of trustworthiness," provided that advance notice of the proposed offer is provided to the adverse party.

2. *Comparison With Federal Rule*. The language of Rule 807 is identical to its federal counterpart, Fed. R. Evid. 807, as restyled. Nonetheless, as noted in the Prefatory Comments to the 2012 Amendments: "[W]here the language of an Arizona rule parallels that of a federal rule, federal court decisions interpreting the federal rule are persuasive but not binding with respect to interpreting the Arizona rule." *See also, State v. Terrazas*, 189 Ariz. 580, 944 P.2d 1194 (1997) (The Arizona Supreme Court is "not bound by the United States Supreme Court's non-

constitutional construction of the Federal Rules of Evidence when [the Arizona Supreme Court construes] the Arizona Rules of Evidence."), citing, *State v. Bible*, 175 Ariz. 549, 858 P.2d 1152 (1993); *State v. Salazar-Mercado*, 232 Ariz. 256, 304 P.3d 543 (Ct. App. Div. 2 2013). Practitioners are urged to keep this legal tenet in mind as they research federal case law interpreting a federal evidentiary rule that corresponds to an Arizona evidentiary rule.

3. *Residual Exception*. Whether a hearsay statement has equivalent circumstantial guarantees of trustworthiness must be determined by the trial court from the circumstances surrounding the making of the statement itself, and not from other extrinsic evidence that may corroborate the statement. *Ruvalcaba By and Through Stubblefield v. Ruvalcaba*, 174 Ariz. 436, 850 P.2d 674 (Ct. App. Div. 1 1993). *See also, State v. Roque*, 213 Ariz. 193, 141 P.3d 368 (2006); *State v. Ramirez*, 142 Ariz. 171, 688 P.2d 1063 (Ct. App. Div. 2 1984) (addressing reliability under evidence rule 804(b)(5), a residual exception for hearsay with "equivalent circumstantial guarantees of trustworthiness").

A party intending to offer a hearsay statement in reliance on this residual exception must provide the adverse party with reasonable advance notice of that before the trial or hearing, so that the adverse party has a fair opportunity to prepare to meet it. The failure to provide the advance notice which the Rule requires is sufficient grounds to exclude the evidence. *Starkins v. Bateman*, 150 Ariz. 537, 724 P.2d 1206 (Ct. App. Div. 1 1986). Surveys are not admissible under this exception unless they were conducted independently of the case and counsel, and in strict accordance with accepted survey and statistical techniques. *Gosewisch v. American Honda Motor Co., Inc.*, 153 Ariz. 389, 737 P.2d 365, Prod. Liab. Rep. (CCH) P 10819 (Ct. App. Div. 2 1985), opinion vacated in part on other grounds, 153 Ariz. 400, 737 P.2d 376, Prod. Liab. Rep. (CCH) P 11531, 83 A.L.R.4th 53 (1987).

ARTICLE IX. AUTHENTICATION AND IDENTIFICATION

Rule 901. Authenticating and Identifying Evidence

(a) In General. To satisfy the requirement of authenticating or identifying an item of evidence, the proponent must produce evidence sufficient to support a finding that the item is what the proponent claims it is.

(b) Examples. The following are examples only—not a complete list—of evidence that satisfies the requirement:

(1) **Testimony of a Witness with Knowledge**. Testimony that an item is what it is claimed to be.

(2) **Nonexpert Opinion About Handwriting**. A nonexpert's opinion that handwriting is genuine, based on a familiarity with it that was not acquired for the current litigation.

(3) **Comparison by an Expert Witness or the Trier of Fact**. A comparison with an authenticated specimen by an expert witness or the trier of fact.

(4) **Distinctive Characteristics and the Like**. The appearance, contents, substance, internal patterns, or other distinctive characteristics of the item, taken together with all the circumstances.

(5) **Opinion About a Voice**. An opinion identifying a person's voice—whether heard firsthand or through mechanical or electronic transmission or recording—based on hearing the voice at any time under circumstances that connect it with the alleged speaker.

(6) **Evidence About a Telephone Conversation**. For a telephone conversation, evidence that a call was made to the number assigned at the time to:

(A) a particular person, if circumstances, including self-identification, show that the person answering was the one called; or

(B) a particular business, if the call was made to a business and the call related to business reasonably transacted over the telephone.

(7) **Evidence About Public Records**. Evidence that:

(A) a document was recorded or filed in a public office as authorized by law; or

(B) a purported public record or statement is from the office where items of this kind are kept.

(8) **Evidence About Ancient Documents or Data Compilations**. For a document or data compilation, evidence that it:

(A) is in a condition that creates no suspicion about its authenticity;

(B) was in a place where, if authentic, it would likely be; and

(C) is at least 20 years old when offered.

(9) **Evidence About a Process or System**. Evidence describing a process or system and showing that it produces an accurate result.

(10) **Methods Provided by a Statute or Rule**. Any method of authentication or identification allowed by a statute or a rule prescribed by the Supreme Court.

Amended Sept. 8, 2011, effective Jan. 1, 2012.

Comment to 2012 Amendment

The language of Rule 901 has been amended to conform to the federal restyling of the Evidence Rules to make them more easily understood and to make style and terminology consistent throughout the rules. These changes are intended to be stylistic only. There is no intent to change any result in any ruling on evidence admissibility.

Comment to Original 1977 Rule

This rule is declaratory of general evidence law and deals only with identification or authentication and not with grounds for admissibility.

AUTHORS' COMMENTS

Analysis

1. *Purpose and Scope of Rule.* Rule 901 articulates the requirement of, and the standards for, the authentication of evidence, and provides, in subpart (b), ten specific illustrations of acceptable methods for the authentication of certain types of evidence.

2. *Comparison With Federal Rule.* Effective January 1, 2012, the Arizona Supreme Court amended Rule 901 to conform to the federal restyling of the Evidence Rules to make the rules more easily understood and to make style and terminology consistent throughout. The 2012 Comment states the stylistic amendments

are not intended to "change any result in any ruling on evidence admissibility."

Following the 2012 restyling amendments, the language of Rule 901 remains identical to its federal counterpart, Fed. R. Evid. 901, except for minor differences in the title of the rule and editorial changes necessary to adapt the Rule to the Arizona court system.

Although Rule 901 parallels its federal counterpart, "federal court decisions interpreting the federal rule are persuasive but not binding with respect to interpreting the Arizona rule." *See,* Prefatory Comment to 2012 Amendments. *See also, State v. Terrazas*, 189 Ariz. 580, 944 P.2d 1194 (1997) (The Arizona Supreme Court is "not bound by the United States Supreme Court's non-constitutional construction of the Federal Rules of Evidence when [the Arizona Supreme Court construes] the Arizona Rules of Evidence."), citing, *State v. Bible*, 175 Ariz. 549, 858 P.2d 1152 (1993); *State v. Salazar-Mercado*, 232 Ariz. 256, 304 P.3d 543 (Ct. App. Div. 2 2013). Practitioners are urged to keep this legal tenet in mind as they research federal case law interpreting a federal evidentiary rule that corresponds to an Arizona evidentiary rule.

3. *Requirement of Authentication Generally; Role of Court.* Tangible evidence can only be relevant and admissible if it is in fact what it purports to be. Such evidence, accordingly, must be authenticated before it can be admitted. *Taeger v. Catholic Family and Community Services*, 196 Ariz. 285, 995 P.2d 721 (Ct. App. Div. 1 1999). The requirement of authentication may also be an issue with certain forms of "intangible" evidence, such as telephone conversations, where the witness testifying to the contents of the conversation did not physically observe the other participant(s).

While the requirement of authentication is frequently discussed as an aspect of relevance, it is really a separate condition precedent to the admissibility of evidence. *State v. Lavers*, 168 Ariz. 376, 814 P.2d 333 (1991). The fact that evidence is properly authenticated does not guarantee its relevance and admissibility.

As phrased by Rule 901(a), the requirement of authentication is satisfied by "evidence sufficient to support a finding that the item is what the proponent claims it is." *See also, State v. Forde*, 315 P.3d 1200 (2014) (sufficient evidence produced to authenticate text message); *State v. Damper*, 223 Ariz. 572, 225 P.3d 1148 (Ct. App. Div. 1 2010) (text message sent by deceased victim authenticated by testimony of recipient sufficient to permit jury to conclude the witness received the text message sent by victim). In determining whether proffered evidence has been property authenticated, trial courts consider the facts and circumstances in each case together with the purpose for which the evidence is offered. *State v. Haight-Gyuro*, 218 Ariz. 356, 186 P.3d 33 (Ct. App. Div. 2 2008). The trial court does not determine authenticity, but only whether there is sufficient evidence for the trier of fact to determine whether the item is authentic. *State v. Lavers*, 168 Ariz. 376, 814 P.2d 333 (1991). By phrasing the requirement in terms of "evidence sufficient to support a finding" of authenticity, Rule 901(a) suggests that evidence of authenticity must be admissible, and that hearsay evidence cannot be considered for this purpose.

An objection of "no foundation" is not sufficient to preserve issues of authenticity for appeal. The objection must specify the particular deficiencies in the proof of authenticity that are claimed. *Packard v. Reidhead*, 22 Ariz. App. 420, 528 P.2d 171 (Div. 1 1974).

4. *Tangible Objects; Documents.* Under Rule 901(b)(1), tangible objects or documents may be authenticated by witnesses who can identify the object or document to be what it is claimed to be. *Cal X-Tra v. W.V.S.V. Holdings, L.L.C.*, 229 Ariz. 377, 276 P.3d 11 (Ct. App. Div. 1 2012), review denied, (Dec. 4, 2012), review denied, (Dec. 4, 2012) (documents on computer disk properly authenticated). Under Rule 901(b)(4), this can be done by testimony as to the appearance, contents or other distinctive characteristics of the object or document. *Cf. Barrow v. Arizona Bd. of Regents*, 158 Ariz. 71, 761 P.2d 145, 49 Ed. Law Rep. 761 (Ct. App. Div. 2 1988); *but cf. Posner v. New York Life Ins. Co.*, 56 Ariz. 202, 106 P.2d 488 (1940).

Where the document or tangible object has been removed or seized from its original location or custodian, it may be necessary to establish a chain of custody from the time of the original movement or seizure. *State ex rel. Corbin v. Goodrich*, 151 Ariz. 118, 726 P.2d 215, Blue Sky L. Rep. (CCH) P 72397 (Ct. App. Div. 2 1986).

To be admissible, a photograph must be a reasonably faithful representation of the object depicted and aid the jury in understanding the testimony or in evaluating the issues. *Lohmeier v. Hammer*, 214 Ariz. 57, 148 P.3d 101 (Ct. App. Div. 1 2006). The individual who took the photograph need not be the person who verifies it at trial, and the verifying witness is not required to have been present when the photograph was taken, provided that the witness can attest that the photograph accurately depicts the scene or object depicted. *Lohmeier v. Hammer*, 214 Ariz. 57, 148 P.3d 101 (Ct. App. Div. 1 2006). *See also, State v. King*, 226 Ariz. 253, 245 P.3d 938 (Ct. App. Div. 2 2011) (videotaped demonstrations properly authenticated).

5. *Authentication of Handwriting.* Handwritten documents, or handwritten entries on documents, may be authenticated by a

witness who is familiar with the handwriting and can identify the person whose handwriting it is. Rule 901(b)(2) permits non-expert opinions on the authenticity of handwriting, provided that the witness' familiarity with the handwriting in question was not acquired for purposes of the litigation. *Johnson v. Maehling*, 123 Ariz. 15, 597 P.2d 1 (1979).

Under both Rule 901(b)(3) and Ariz.R.Civ.P. 44(m), a handwritten document or entry may also be authenticated by comparing the matter offered with a specimen that has been proven to be genuine to the trial court's satisfaction. Rule 901(b)(3) permits such a comparison to be made by an expert witness.

6. *Voice Identification.* This particular authenticity issue is presented where a witness to a conversation did not physically observe the other party to the conversation, as will be the case with most telephone conversations. Rule 901(b)(6) provides one method for establishing authenticity in that circumstance, but it only applies where a call is placed *to* a party whose identity must be authenticated.

Rule 901(b)(5) permits voice identification by a witness familiar with the alleged speaker's voice. *Cavanagh v. Ohio Farmers Ins. Co.*, 20 Ariz. App. 38, 509 P.2d 1075 (Div. 2 1973). *See also, State v. Miller*, 226 Ariz. 202, 245 P.3d 887 (Ct. App. Div. 2 2010) (person monitoring wiretap calls allowed to testify defendant's voice was same voice on jail calls and law enforcement interviews). There is no provision in the Rules which provides that such a voice identification may not be predicated upon a familiarity with the voice that was acquired for purposes of the litigation.

7. *Ancient Documents.* Rule 901(b)(8) creates a method for the authentication of those ancient documents that qualify for the exception to the hearsay rule recognized in Rule 803(16). The Rules of Evidence reduced the required age of such "ancient documents" from thirty (30) to twenty (20) years. *Markiewicz v. Salt River Valley Water Users' Ass'n*, 118 Ariz. 329, 576 P.2d 517 (Ct. App. Div. 1 1978).

Rule 902. Evidence That Is Self-Authenticating

The following items of evidence are self-authenticating; they require no extrinsic evidence of authenticity in order to be admitted:

(1) **Domestic Public Documents That Are Sealed and Signed**. A document that bears:

(A) a seal purporting to be that of the United States; any state, district, commonwealth, territory, or insular possession of the United States; the former Panama Canal Zone; the Trust Territory of the Pacific Islands; a political subdivision of any of these entities; or a department, agency, or officer of any entity named above; and

(B) a signature purporting to be an execution or attestation.

(2) **Domestic Public Documents That Are Not Sealed but Are Signed and Certified**. A document that bears no seal if:

(A) it bears the signature of an officer or employee of an entity named in Rule 902(1)(A); and

(B) another public officer who has a seal and official duties within that same entity certifies under seal—or its equivalent—that the signer has the official capacity and that the signature is genuine.

(3) **Foreign Public Documents**. A document that purports to be signed or attested by a person who is authorized by a foreign country's law to do so. The document must be accompanied by a final certification that certifies the genuineness of the signature and official position of the signer or attester—or of any foreign official whose certificate of genuineness relates to the signature or attestation or is in a chain of certificates of genuineness relating to the signature or attestation. The certification may be made by a secretary of a United States embassy or legation; by a consul general, vice consul, or consular agent of the United States; or by a diplomatic or consular official of the foreign country assigned or accredited to the United States. If all parties have been given a reasonable opportunity to investigate the document's authenticity and accuracy, the court may, for good cause, either:

(A) order that it be treated as presumptively authentic without final certification; or

(B) allow it to be evidenced by an attested summary with or without final certification.

(4) **Certified Copies of Public Records**. A copy of an of-

ficial record—or a copy of a document that was recorded or filed in a public office as authorized by law—if the copy is certified as correct by:

(A) the custodian or another person authorized to make the certification; or

(B) a certificate that complies with Rule 902(1), (2), or (3), a statute, or a rule prescribed by the Supreme Court.

(5) **Official Publications**. A book, pamphlet, or other publication purporting to be issued by a public authority.

(6) **Newspapers and Periodicals**. Printed material purporting to be a newspaper or periodical.

(7) **Trade Inscriptions and the Like**. An inscription, sign, tag, or label purporting to have been affixed in the course of business and indicating origin, ownership, or control.

(8) **Acknowledged Documents**. A document accompanied by a certificate of acknowledgment that is lawfully executed by a notary public or another officer who is authorized to take acknowledgments.

(9) **Commercial Paper and Related Documents**. Commercial paper, a signature on it, and related documents, to the extent allowed by general commercial law.

(10) **Presumptions Under a Statute**. A signature, document, or anything else that a statute declares to be presumptively or prima facie genuine or authentic.

(11) **Certified Domestic Records of a Regularly Conducted Activity**. The original or a copy of a domestic record that meets the requirements of Rule 803(6)(A)–(C), as shown by a certification of the custodian or another qualified person that complies with a statute or a rule prescribed by the Supreme Court. Before the trial or hearing, the proponent must give an adverse party reasonable written notice of the intent to offer the record—and must make the record and certification available for inspection—so that the party has a fair opportunity to challenge them.

(12) **Certified Foreign Records of a Regularly Conducted Activity**. In a civil case, the original or a copy of a foreign record that meets the requirements of Rule 902(11), modified as follows: the certification, rather than complying with a statute or Supreme Court rule, must be signed in a manner that, if falsely made, would subject the maker to a criminal penalty in the country where the certification is signed. The proponent must also meet the notice requirements of Rule 902(11).

Amended Oct. 19, 1988, effective Nov. 1, 1988; Oct. 16, 2003, effective Dec. 1, 2003; Jan. 26, 2004, effective June 1, 2004; Sept. 8, 2011, effective Jan. 1, 2012.

Comment to 2012 Amendment

The language of Rule 902 has been amended to conform to the federal restyling of the Evidence Rules to make them more easily understood and to make style and terminology consistent throughout the rules. These changes are intended to be stylistic only. There is no intent to change any result in any ruling on evidence admissibility.

Comment to Original 1977 Rule

The language "general commercial law" in (9) is carried forward from the Federal Rule. In Arizona, the reference is to the Uniform Commercial Code as adopted in this State.

AUTHORS' COMMENTS

Analysis

1. *Scope and Purpose of Rule.* Rule 902 provides twelve instances where documents will be self-authenticating, in the sense that extrinsic evidence of their authenticity will not be required as a condition precedent to their admission. These include various categories of domestic and foreign public documents, certified copies of public records, official publications, newspapers and periodicals, trade inscriptions, signs and labels, acknowledged documents, certain commercial documents, and documents presumed to be authentic by statute.

2. *Comparison With Federal Rule.* Effective January 1, 2012, the Arizona Supreme Court amended Rule 902 to conform to the federal restyling of the Evidence Rules to make the rules more easily understood and to make style and terminology consistent throughout. The 2012 Comment states the stylistic amendments are not intended to "change any result in any ruling on evidence admissibility."

Following the 2012 restyling amendments, the language of Rule 902 remains identical to its federal counterpart, Fed. R. Evid. 902, except for editorial differences necessary to adapt the Rule to the Arizona court system [Rule 902(10)].

Although Rule 902 parallels its federal counterpart, "federal court decisions interpreting the federal rule are persuasive but not binding with respect to interpreting the Arizona rule." *See,* Prefatory Comment to 2012 Amendments. *See also, State v. Terrazas*, 189 Ariz. 580, 944 P.2d 1194 (1997) (The Arizona Supreme

Court is "not bound by the United States Supreme Court's non-constitutional construction of the Federal Rules of Evidence when [the Arizona Supreme Court construes] the Arizona Rules of Evidence."), citing, *State v. Bible*, 175 Ariz. 549, 858 P.2d 1152 (1993); *State v. Salazar-Mercado*, 232 Ariz. 256, 304 P.3d 543 (Ct. App. Div. 2 2013). Practitioners are urged to keep this legal tenet in mind as they research federal case law interpreting a federal evidentiary rule that corresponds to an Arizona evidentiary rule.

3. *Public Documents.* Public documents have been deemed entitled to relaxed standards for authentication due to the perceived unlikelihood that public officials would falsify public records for court proceedings, and because of the disruption in the conduct of public business that might result from requiring public officials or employees to appear personally and testify to the authenticity of such records. The records and reports of public agencies also qualify for an exception to the hearsay rule under Rule 803(8).

The authenticity of public documents may be established by a certification under seal in the manner specified in Rules 902(1), (2) or (3), as applicable. *Cf. also* Ariz.R.Civ.P. 44(a). Rule 902(5) also specifies, as self-authenticating, official publications purporting to be issued by public authority. *Schneider v. Cessna Aircraft Co.*, 150 Ariz. 153, 722 P.2d 321, Prod. Liab. Rep. (CCH) P 10743 (Ct. App. Div. 1 1985).

4. *Certified Copies of Public Records.* A seal or attestation is sufficient to authenticate the originals of public documents. A variety of provisions, including Rule 902(4), permit the receipt into evidence, without further proof of authenticity, of the duly certified copies of records of public agencies. *Cf.* Ariz.R.Civ.P. 44(a); A.R.S. § 12-2263.

5. *Acknowledged Documents.* Rule 902(8) provides for self-authentication of documents that are accompanied "by a certificate of acknowledgment executed in the manner provided by law by a notary public" or other authorized official. A.R.S. § 12-2261 provides that every written instrument, except promissory notes, bills of exchange and last wills and testaments, may be acknowledged and, when thus acknowledged, are to be received in evidence without further proof of execution. A.R.S. § 33-511 specifies the categories of officials who are authorized to acknowledge instruments. Arizona has also adopted the Uniform Recognition of Acknowledgments Act, A.R.S. §§ 33-501 to 33-508 which, *inter alia,* provides forms and procedures for the acknowledgment of instruments.

6. *Certified Records of Regularly Conducted Activity.* In 2003, the Arizona Supreme Court amended Rule 902 to add domestic business records to the closed list of those documents deemed to

be self-authenticating. The authentication requirement is satisfied when the custodian of the proffered document, or other qualified person, provides a written declaration that the records were properly prepared in the regular course of business. Although not stated in the Rule, good practice dictates that any such declaration is prepared to meet the requirements of Ariz.R.Civ.P. 80(i). A party intending to introduce evidence through Rule 902(11) must give written notice of that intent, and must make the record and authenticating declaration available sufficiently in advance of the offer of the evidence to provide the adverse party with a fair opportunity to challenge them.

In 2004, six months after adding subpart (11) with respect to domestic business records, the Court again amended Rule 902 to add foreign business records to the self-authenticating documents list. As with domestic business records, authentication is provided when the custodian of the proffered document, or other qualified person, provides a written declaration that the records were properly prepared in the regular course of business. A party intending to introduce evidence under Rule 902(12) must give written notice of that intent and must make the record and authenticating declaration available sufficiently in advance of the offer of the evidence to provide the adverse party with a fair opportunity to challenge it.

Rule 903. Subscribing Witness's Testimony

A subscribing witness's testimony is necessary to authenticate a writing only if required by the law of the jurisdiction that governs its validity.

Amended Sept. 8, 2011, effective Jan. 1, 2012.

Comment to 2012 Amendment

The language of Rule 903 has been amended to conform to the federal restyling of the Evidence Rules to make them more easily understood and to make style and terminology consistent throughout the rules. These changes are intended to be stylistic only. There is no intent to change any result in any ruling on evidence admissibility.

AUTHORS' COMMENTS

Analysis

1. *Scope and Purpose of Rule.* Rule 903 merely eliminates the necessity for securing the testimony of a subscribing witness to authenticate a document, unless such testimony is required by the laws of the jurisdiction whose law governs the issue of the document's validity.

2. *Comparison With Federal Rule.* Effective January 1, 2012, the Arizona Supreme Court amended Rule 903 to conform to the federal restyling of the Evidence Rules to make the rules more easily understood and to make style and terminology consistent throughout. The 2012 Comment states the stylistic amendments are not intended to "change any result in any ruling on evidence admissibility."

Following the 2012 restyling amendments, the language of Rule 903 remains identical to its federal counterpart, Fed. R. Evid. 903.

Although Rule 903 parallels its federal counterpart, "federal court decisions interpreting the federal rule are persuasive but not binding with respect to interpreting the Arizona rule." *See,* Prefatory Comment to 2012 Amendments. *See also, State v. Terrazas*, 189 Ariz. 580, 944 P.2d 1194 (1997) (The Arizona Supreme Court is "not bound by the United States Supreme Court's non-constitutional construction of the Federal Rules of Evidence when [the Arizona Supreme Court construes] the Arizona Rules of Evidence."), citing, State v. Bible, 175 Ariz. 549, 858 P.2d 1152 (1993); *State v. Salazar-Mercado*, 232 Ariz. 256, 304 P.3d 543 (Ct.

App. Div. 2 2013). Practitioners are urged to keep this legal tenet in mind as they research federal case law interpreting a federal evidentiary rule that corresponds to an Arizona evidentiary rule.

ARTICLE X. CONTENTS OF WRITINGS, RECORDINGS, AND PHOTOGRAPHS

Rule 1001. Definitions That Apply to This Article

In this article:

(a) A "**writing**" consists of letters, words, numbers, or their equivalent set down in any form.

(b) A "**recording**" consists of letters, words, numbers, or their equivalent recorded in any manner.

(c) A "**photograph**" means a photographic image or its equivalent stored in any form.

(d) An "**original**" of a writing or recording means the writing or recording itself or any counterpart intended to have the same effect by the person who executed or issued it. For electronically stored information, "original" means any printout—or other output readable by sight—if it accurately reflects the information. An "original" of a photograph includes the negative or a print from it.

(e) A "**duplicate**" means a counterpart produced by a mechanical, photographic, chemical, electronic, or other equivalent process or technique that accurately reproduces the original.

Amended Sept. 8, 2011, effective Jan. 1, 2012.

Comment to 2012 Amendment

The language of Rule 1001 has been amended to conform to the federal restyling of the Evidence Rules to make them more easily understood and to make style and terminology consistent throughout the rules. These changes are intended to be stylistic only. There is no intent to change any result in any ruling on evidence admissibility.

AUTHORS' COMMENTS

Analysis

1. Scope and Purpose of Rule.
2. Comparison With Federal Rule.

1. *Scope and Purpose of Rule.* Rule 1001 merely provides the definitions of the terms that will have significance in the application and construction of the remaining Rules in Chapter X, which *inter alia,* codify a modified version of the so-called "best evidence rule": "writings," "recordings," "photographs," "original," and

"duplicate." The definitions are largely self-explanatory.

2. *Comparison With Federal Rule.* Effective January 1, 2012, the Arizona Supreme Court amended Rule 1001 to conform to the federal restyling of the Evidence Rules to make the rules more easily understood and to make style and terminology consistent throughout. The 2012 Comment states the stylistic amendments are not intended to "change any result in any ruling on evidence admissibility."

Following the 2012 restyling amendments, the language of Rule 1001 remains identical to its federal counterpart, Fed. R. Evid. 1001.

Although Rule 1001 parallels its federal counterpart, "federal court decisions interpreting the federal rule are persuasive but not binding with respect to interpreting the Arizona rule." *See,* Prefatory Comment to 2012 Amendments. *See also, State v. Terrazas*, 189 Ariz. 580, 944 P.2d 1194 (1997) (The Arizona Supreme Court is "not bound by the United States Supreme Court's non-constitutional construction of the Federal Rules of Evidence when [the Arizona Supreme Court construes] the Arizona Rules of Evidence."), citing, *State v. Bible*, 175 Ariz. 549, 858 P.2d 1152 (1993); *State v. Salazar-Mercado*, 232 Ariz. 256, 304 P.3d 543 (Ct. App. Div. 2 2013). Practitioners are urged to keep this legal tenet in mind as they research federal case law interpreting a federal evidentiary rule that corresponds to an Arizona evidentiary rule.

Rule 1002. Requirement of the Original

An original writing, recording, or photograph is required in order to prove its content unless these rules or an applicable statute provides otherwise.

Amended Sept. 8, 2011, effective Jan. 1, 2012.

Comment to 2012 Amendment

The language of Rule 1002 has been amended to conform to the federal restyling of the Evidence Rules to make them more easily understood and to make style and terminology consistent throughout the rules. These changes are intended to be stylistic only. There is no intent to change any result in any ruling on evidence admissibility.

AUTHORS' COMMENTS

Analysis

1. Scope and Purpose of Rule.
2. Comparison With Federal Rule.
3. Best Evidence Rule; Limitations.

1. *Scope and Purpose of Rule.* Rule 1002 is the codification of the so-called "best evidence rule," which requires that the original of a document is to be used for proof of its terms or contents, unless one of the exceptions applies. Under Rule 1001(3), a copy or counterpart executed as an original is considered to be an original. *Cf., M. Karam & Sons Mercantile Co. v. Serrano*, 51 Ariz. 397, 77 P.2d 447 (1938). The Rule applies not just to documents, but to all recordings and writings as described in Rule 1001(1).

2. *Comparison With Federal Rule.* Effective January 1, 2012, the Arizona Supreme Court amended Rule 1002 to conform to the federal restyling of the Evidence Rules to make the rules more easily understood and to make style and terminology consistent throughout. The 2012 Comment states the stylistic amendments are not intended to "change any result in any ruling on evidence admissibility."

Following the 2012 restyling amendments, the language of Rule 1002 remains identical to its federal counterpart, Fed. R. Evid. 1002, except for changes necessary to adapt it to the Arizona court system.

Although Rule 1002 parallels its federal counterpart, "federal court decisions interpreting the federal rule are persuasive but not binding with respect to interpreting the Arizona rule." *See,* Prefatory Comment to 2012 Amendments. *See also, State v. Terra-*

zas, 189 Ariz. 580, 944 P.2d 1194 (1997) (The Arizona Supreme Court is "not bound by the United States Supreme Court's non-constitutional construction of the Federal Rules of Evidence when [the Arizona Supreme Court construes] the Arizona Rules of Evidence."), citing, *State v. Bible*, 175 Ariz. 549, 858 P.2d 1152 (1993); *State v. Salazar-Mercado*, 232 Ariz. 256, 304 P.3d 543 (Ct. App. Div. 2 2013). Practitioners are urged to keep this legal tenet in mind as they research federal case law interpreting a federal evidentiary rule that corresponds to an Arizona evidentiary rule.

3. *Best Evidence Rule; Limitations.* The "best evidence rule" is actually one of fairly limited application, and is not a principle which governs all forms of evidence. The rule only requires that, unless an exception applies, proof of the terms of a document must be made by production and introduction of the original of the document. *Higgins v. Arizona Sav. and Loan Ass'n*, 90 Ariz. 55, 365 P.2d 476 (1961). The rule only applies, however, when the terms or contents of a writing are to be proven, rather than that it was signed or sent. *Higgins v. Arizona Sav. and Loan Ass'n*, 90 Ariz. 55, 365 P.2d 476 (1961); *Mitchell v. Emblade*, 80 Ariz. 398, 298 P.2d 1034 (1956), adhered to in part on reh'g, 81 Ariz. 121, 301 P.2d 1032 (1956) (overruled in part by, State v. Grilz, 136 Ariz. 450, 666 P.2d 1059 (1983)); *International Life Ins. Co. v. Sorteberg*, 70 Ariz. 92, 216 P.2d 702 (1950), opinion modified on reh'g, 70 Ariz. 171, 217 P.2d 1038 (1950); *Duncan v. Mack*, 59 Ariz. 36, 122 P.2d 215 (1942); *MH Inv. Co. v. Transamerica Title Ins. Co.*, 162 Ariz. 569, 785 P.2d 89 (Ct. App. Div. 2 1989); *Berthot v. Courtyard Properties, Inc.*, 138 Ariz. 566, 675 P.2d 1385 (Ct. App. Div. 1 1983).

For example, where a party wished to prove simply the fact of a prior conviction rather than the contents of the document that officially recorded it, the best evidence rule was held not to apply. *W.F. Dunn, Sr. & Son v. Industrial Com'n of Arizona*, 160 Ariz. 343, 773 P.2d 241 (Ct. App. Div. 1 1989). The rule also does not preclude a witness from summarizing information taken from voluminous reports and records, provided the information is admissible and the records and reports are available to the adverse party for inspection. *Rayner v. Stauffer Chemical Co.*, 120 Ariz. 328, 585 P.2d 1240 (Ct. App. Div. 1 1978).

Rule 1003. Admissibility of Duplicates

A duplicate is admissible to the same extent as the original unless a genuine question is raised about the original's authenticity or the circumstances make it unfair to admit the duplicate.

Amended Sept. 8, 2011, effective Jan. 1, 2012.

Comment to 2012 Amendment

The language of Rule 1003 has been amended to conform to the federal restyling of the Evidence Rules to make them more easily understood and to make style and terminology consistent throughout the rules. These changes are intended to be stylistic only. There is no intent to change any result in any ruling on evidence admissibility.

AUTHORS' COMMENTS

Analysis

1. Scope and Purpose of Rule.
2. Comparison With Federal Rule.

1. *Scope and Purpose of Rule.* Rule 1003 mollifies to a great extent the potential impact of the best evidence rule, by providing that a duplicate of a document will be admissible to the same extent as the original, with two exceptions. The two exceptions are: (1) where there is a genuine question raised as to the authenticity of the original, and (2) where, under the circumstances, it would be unfair to permit the duplicate to be admitted in lieu of the original. The latter exception may apply where there is a demonstrable need for the trier of fact to examine the original, due to corrections, alterations or color-coded markings or notations. The Rule is consistent with prior law which permitted the use of copies in lieu of originals. *Cf. Hackin v. Gaynes*, 103 Ariz. 13, 436 P.2d 127 (1968); *M. Karam & Sons Mercantile Co. v. Serrano*, 51 Ariz. 397, 77 P.2d 447 (1938).

2. *Comparison With Federal Rule.* Effective January 1, 2012, the Arizona Supreme Court amended Rule 1003 to conform to the federal restyling of the Evidence Rules to make the rules more easily understood and to make style and terminology consistent throughout. The 2012 Comment states the stylistic amendments are not intended to "change any result in any ruling on evidence admissibility."

Following the 2012 restyling amendments, the language of Rule 1003 remains identical to its federal counterpart, Fed. R. Evid. 1003.

Although Rule 1003 parallels its federal counterpart, "federal

court decisions interpreting the federal rule are persuasive but not binding with respect to interpreting the Arizona rule." *See,* Prefatory Comment to 2012 Amendments. *See also, State v. Terrazas*, 189 Ariz. 580, 944 P.2d 1194 (1997) (The Arizona Supreme Court is "not bound by the United States Supreme Court's non-constitutional construction of the Federal Rules of Evidence when [the Arizona Supreme Court construes] the Arizona Rules of Evidence."), citing, *State v. Bible*, 175 Ariz. 549, 858 P.2d 1152 (1993); *State v. Salazar-Mercado*, 232 Ariz. 256, 304 P.3d 543 (Ct. App. Div. 2 2013). Practitioners are urged to keep this legal tenet in mind as they research federal case law interpreting a federal evidentiary rule that corresponds to an Arizona evidentiary rule.

Rule 1004. Admissibility of Other Evidence of Contents

An original is not required and other evidence of the content of a writing, recording, or photograph is admissible if:

(a) all the originals are lost or destroyed, and not by the proponent acting in bad faith;

(b) an original cannot be obtained by any available judicial process;

(c) the party against whom the original would be offered had control of the original; was at that time put on notice, by pleadings or otherwise, that the original would be a subject of proof at the trial or hearing; and fails to produce it at the trial or hearing; or

(d) the writing, recording, or photograph is not closely related to a controlling issue.

Amended Oct. 19, 1988, effective Nov. 1, 1988; Sept. 8, 2011, effective Jan. 1, 2012.

Comment to 2012 Amendment

The language of Rule 1004 has been amended to conform to the federal restyling of the Evidence Rules to make them more easily understood and to make style and terminology consistent throughout the rules. These changes are intended to be stylistic only. There is no intent to change any result in any ruling on evidence admissibility.

AUTHORS' COMMENTS

Analysis

1. Scope and Purpose of Rule.
2. Comparison With Federal Rule.
3. Where Secondary Evidence of Contents Admissible.

1. *Scope and Purpose of Rule.* Ariz. R. Evid. 1004 defines four (4) separate circumstances where the best evidence rule is waived, and proof of the contents of a document may be made by secondary evidence. Because an original includes duplicates, by operation of Ariz. R. Evid. 1003, the four circumstances represent situations where neither an original nor a duplicate of a writing is required. In fact, the phrasing of the Rule, for the most part, appears to assume that no duplicates of the writing are available.

2. *Comparison With Federal Rule.* Effective January 1, 2012, the Arizona Supreme Court amended Ariz. R. Evid. 1004 to conform to the federal restyling of the Evidence Rules to make the rules more easily understood and to make style and terminol-

ogy consistent throughout. The 2012 Comment states the stylistic amendments are not intended to "change any result in any ruling on evidence admissibility."

Following the 2012 restyling amendments, the language of Rule 1004 remains identical to its federal counterpart, Fed. R. Evid. 1004.

Although Ariz. R. Evid. 1004 parallels its federal counterpart, "federal court decisions interpreting the federal rule are persuasive but not binding with respect to interpreting the Arizona rule." *See,* Prefatory Comment to 2012 Amendments. *See also, State v. Terrazas*, 189 Ariz. 580, 944 P.2d 1194 (1997) (The Arizona Supreme Court is "not bound by the United States Supreme Court's non-constitutional construction of the Federal Rules of Evidence when [the Arizona Supreme Court construes] the Arizona Rules of Evidence."), citing, *State v. Bible*, 175 Ariz. 549, 858 P.2d 1152 (1993); *State v. Salazar-Mercado*, 232 Ariz. 256, 304 P.3d 543 (Ct. App. Div. 2 2013). Practitioners are urged to keep this legal tenet in mind as they research federal case law interpreting a federal evidentiary rule that corresponds to an Arizona evidentiary rule.

3. *Where Secondary Evidence of Contents Admissible.* The four circumstances defined by the Rule where the best evidence rule, even as modified by Ariz. R. Evid. 1003, will not apply are:

(1) where all originals of the document have been lost or destroyed, unless the proponent of the document was the instigator of the destruction in bad faith, *cf., In re Schade's Estate*, 87 Ariz. 341, 351 P.2d 173 (1960); *Gonzalez v. Satrustegui*, 178 Ariz. 92, 870 P.2d 1188 (Ct. App. Div. 1 1993);

(2) where the primary evidence is out of the jurisdiction of the court and it is "impossible to obtain it"; *cf., Johnson v. State*, 33 Ariz. 354, 264 P. 1083 (1928);

(3) where the original of the document was in the custody or subject to the control of the party against whom it was to be offered, that party was placed on notice that the contents of the document would be a subject of proof at the trial or hearing, and that party nevertheless did not produce the original, *cf., Johnson v. State*, 33 Ariz. 354, 264 P. 1083 (1928); *Jones v. Stanley*, 27 Ariz. 381, 233 P. 598 (1925) (receipt of "parol" evidence); or,

(4) where the document, recording or photograph is not closely related to a controlling issue in the case.

Consistent with Ariz. R. Evid. 1004(2), Ariz. R. Civ. P. 45(f), provides that where there has been a failure to comply with a subpoena *duces tecum*, secondary evidence of the documents or records subpoenaed may be received.

Where there is a dispute as to whether a document ever existed, the party seeking to invoke Ariz. R. Evid. 1004 must make a showing that the document did in fact once exist. If a party produces competent evidence that a document existed, and one of the conditions specified in Rule 1004 is applicable, then oral testimony as to the contents of the document will be admissible. *Jones v. Stanley*, 27 Ariz. 381, 233 P. 598 (1925); *Gonzalez v. Satrustegui*, 178 Ariz. 92, 870 P.2d 1188 (Ct. App. Div. 1 1993); *Combs v. Lufkin*, 123 Ariz. 210, 598 P.2d 1029 (Ct. App. Div. 2 1979).

Rule 1005. Copies of Public Records to Prove Content

The proponent may use a copy to prove the content of an official record—or of a document that was recorded or filed in a public office as authorized by law—if these conditions are met: the record or document is otherwise admissible; and the copy is certified as correct in accordance with Rule 902(4) or is testified to be correct by a witness who has compared it with the original. If no such copy can be obtained by reasonable diligence, then the proponent may use other evidence to prove the content.

Amended Sept. 8, 2011, effective Jan. 1, 2012.

Comment to 2012 Amendment

The language of Rule 1005 has been amended to conform to the federal restyling of the Evidence Rules to make them more easily understood and to make style and terminology consistent throughout the rules. These changes are intended to be stylistic only. There is no intent to change any result in any ruling on evidence admissibility.

AUTHORS' COMMENTS

Analysis

1. Scope and Purpose of Rule.
2. Comparison With Federal Rule.

1. *Scope and Purpose of Rule.* Ariz. R. Evid. 1005 permits proof of the contents of official records to be made by certified or compared copies or, if such copies cannot be secured through the exercise of reasonable diligence, by other secondary evidence. The Rule accommodates the fact that, in most instances, removal and introduction of the originals of the official records of public agencies would be neither wise nor feasible. It also effectuates the policies underlying Rule 902(4) by specifically exempting self-authenticating certified copies of public records from the best evidence rule. The Rule codifies a preference for the use of certified or compared copies over other forms of secondary evidence. A similar rule applies, by statute, to the records of health care providers, A.R.S. § 12-2284.

2. *Comparison With Federal Rule.* Effective January 1, 2012, the Arizona Supreme Court amended Ariz. R. Evid. 1005 to conform to the federal restyling of the Evidence Rules to make the rules more easily understood and to make style and terminology consistent throughout. The 2012 Comment states the stylistic amendments are not intended to "change any result in any ruling

on evidence admissibility."

Following the 2012 restyling amendments, the language of Rule 1005 remains identical to its federal counterpart, Fed. R. Evid. 1005.

Although Ariz. R. Evid. 1005 parallels its federal counterpart, "federal court decisions interpreting the federal rule are persuasive but not binding with respect to interpreting the Arizona rule." *See,* Prefatory Comment to 2012 Amendments. *See also, State v. Terrazas*, 189 Ariz. 580, 944 P.2d 1194 (1997) (The Arizona Supreme Court is "not bound by the United States Supreme Court's non-constitutional construction of the Federal Rules of Evidence when [the Arizona Supreme Court construes] the Arizona Rules of Evidence."), citing, *State v. Bible*, 175 Ariz. 549, 858 P.2d 1152 (1993); *State v. Salazar-Mercado*, 232 Ariz. 256, 304 P.3d 543 (Ct. App. Div. 2 2013). Practitioners are urged to keep this legal tenet in mind as they research federal case law interpreting a federal evidentiary rule that corresponds to an Arizona evidentiary rule.

Rule 1006. Summaries to Prove Content

The proponent may use a summary, chart, or calculation to prove the content of voluminous writings, recordings, or photographs that cannot be conveniently examined in court. The proponent must make the originals or duplicates available for examination or copying, or both, by other parties at a reasonable time or place. And the court may order the proponent to produce them in court.

Amended Sept. 8, 2011, effective Jan. 1, 2012.

Comment to 2012 Amendment

The language of Rule 1006 has been amended to conform to the federal restyling of the Evidence Rules to make them more easily understood and to make style and terminology consistent throughout the rules. These changes are intended to be stylistic only. There is no intent to change any result in any ruling on evidence admissibility.

Comment to Original 1977 Rule

This rule is not intended to change foundation requirements for summaries. The person creating a summary will ordinarily be required to lay the foundation and be available for cross-examination.

AUTHORS' COMMENTS

Analysis

1. *Scope and Purpose of Rule.* Ariz. R. Evid. 1006 permits the contents of voluminous writings, recordings or photographs to be admitted through summaries, charts or calculations. *See, State v. Parker*, 231 Ariz. 391, 296 P.3d 54 (2013) (credit card report prepared for litigation from databases compiled during the ordinary course of business held admissible; report also admissible under Rule 1006 insofar as report simply repeated information admissible as a business record). *Cf., e.g., Collison v. International Ins. Co.*, 58 Ariz. 156, 118 P.2d 445 (1941); *Rayner v. Stauffer Chemical Co.*, 120 Ariz. 328, 585 P.2d 1240 (Ct. App. Div. 1 1978). As a practical matter, truly voluminous materials of this nature will not be particularly useful to the trier of fact unless they are summarized.

A Committee Comment to the Rule cautions that the Rule was not intended to change foundational requirements for summaries, which ordinarily must be established by the person who created the summary and who is then available for cross-examination.

Whether a sufficient foundation has been established for the introduction of a summary is a matter committed to the trial court's discretion. *John C. Lincoln Hosp. and Health Corp. v. Maricopa County*, 208 Ariz. 532, 96 P.3d 530 (Ct. App. Div. 1 2004), as amended, (Sept. 1, 2004). The Rule itself requires that the records, or copies, from which the summary was prepared must be made available to the adverse party for inspection and copying, which provides the adverse party with the data required to challenge the accuracy of the offered summary. *Crackel v. Allstate Ins. Co.*, 208 Ariz. 252, 92 P.3d 882 (Ct. App. Div. 2 2004).

2. *Comparison With Federal Rule.* Effective January 1, 2012, the Arizona Supreme Court amended Ariz. R. Evid. 1006 to conform to the federal restyling of the Evidence Rules to make the rules more easily understood and to make style and terminology consistent throughout. The 2012 Comment states the stylistic amendments are not intended to "change any result in any ruling on evidence admissibility."

Following the 2012 restyling amendments, the language of Rule 1006 remains identical to its federal counterpart, Fed. R. Evid. 1006.

Although Ariz. R. Evid. 1006 parallels its federal counterpart, "federal court decisions interpreting the federal rule are persuasive but not binding with respect to interpreting the Arizona rule." *See,* Prefatory Comment to 2012 Amendments. *See also, State v. Terrazas*, 189 Ariz. 580, 944 P.2d 1194 (1997) (The Arizona Supreme Court is "not bound by the United States Supreme Court's non-constitutional construction of the Federal Rules of Evidence when [the Arizona Supreme Court construes] the Arizona Rules of Evidence."), citing, *State v. Bible*, 175 Ariz. 549, 858 P.2d 1152 (1993); *State v. Salazar-Mercado*, 232 Ariz. 256, 304 P.3d 543 (Ct. App. Div. 2 2013). Practitioners are urged to keep this legal tenet in mind as they research federal case law interpreting a federal evidentiary rule that corresponds to an Arizona evidentiary rule.

Rule 1007. Testimony or Statement of a Party to Prove Content

The proponent may prove the content of a writing, recording, or photograph by the testimony, deposition, or written statement of the party against whom the evidence is offered. The proponent need not account for the original.

Amended Oct. 19, 1988, effective Nov. 1, 1988; Sept. 8, 2011, effective Jan. 1, 2012.

Comment to 2012 Amendment

The language of Rule 1007 has been amended to conform to the federal restyling of the Evidence Rules to make them more easily understood and to make style and terminology consistent throughout the rules. These changes are intended to be stylistic only. There is no intent to change any result in any ruling on evidence admissibility.

AUTHORS' COMMENTS

Analysis

1. *Scope and Purpose of Rule.* Ariz. R. Evid. 1007 provides that an admission of an opposing party under oath, in testimony at a trial or deposition, or in writing is admissible to prove the contents of writings, recordings or photographs. Such an admission may be used to prove the contents of such documents even where the originals are available. The oral admission of an adverse party not under oath does not meet the requirements of this Rule, but may be admissible under Rules 801(b)(2) and 1004.

2. *Comparison With Federal Rule.* Effective January 1, 2012, the Arizona Supreme Court amended Ariz. R. Evid. 1007 to conform to the federal restyling of the Evidence Rules to make the rules more easily understood and to make style and terminology consistent throughout. The 2012 Comment states the stylistic amendments are not intended to "change any result in any ruling on evidence admissibility."

Following the 2012 restyling amendments, the language of Rule 1007 remains identical to its federal counterpart, Fed. R. Evid. 1007.

Although Ariz. R. Evid. 1007 parallels its federal counterpart, "federal court decisions interpreting the federal rule are persuasive but not binding with respect to interpreting the Arizona rule." *See,* Prefatory Comment to 2012 Amendments. *See also, State v. Terrazas*, 189 Ariz. 580, 944 P.2d 1194 (1997) (The Arizona Supreme Court is "not bound by the United States Supreme Court's non-constitutional construction of the Federal Rules of Evidence when [the Arizona Supreme Court construes] the Arizona Rules of Evidence."), citing, *State v. Bible*, 175 Ariz. 549, 858 P.2d 1152 (1993); *State v. Salazar-Mercado*, 232 Ariz. 256, 304 P.3d 543 (Ct. App. Div. 2 2013). Practitioners are urged to keep this legal tenet in mind as they research federal case law interpreting a federal evidentiary rule that corresponds to an Arizona evidentiary rule.

Rule 1008. Functions of the Court and Jury

Ordinarily, the court determines whether the proponent has fulfilled the factual conditions for admitting other evidence of the content of a writing, recording, or photograph under Rule 1004 or 1005. But in a jury trial, the jury determines—in accordance with Rule 104(b)—any issue about whether:

(a) an asserted writing, recording, or photograph ever existed;

(b) another one produced at the trial or hearing is the original; or

(c) other evidence of content accurately reflects the content.

Amended Sept. 8, 2011, effective Jan. 1, 2012.

Comment to 2012 Amendment

The language of Rule 1008 has been amended to conform to the federal restyling of the Evidence Rules to make them more easily understood and to make style and terminology consistent throughout the rules. These changes are intended to be stylistic only. There is no intent to change any result in any ruling on evidence admissibility.

AUTHORS' COMMENTS

Analysis

1. *Scope and Purpose of Rule.* Ariz. R. Evid. 1008 is merely a particularized explanation of how Rule 104 will operate in circumstances where application of the best evidence rule is in issue. The Rule allocates to the Court the responsibility for determining whether the conditions for the admission of secondary evidence of the contents of writings have been met, and whether the secondary evidence offered is admissible. The trier of fact determines issues as to whether a writing ever existed, whether any other writing produced is in fact the original, and whether the contents of the writing have been accurately proven by secondary evidence. Essentially, the Court decides whether secondary evidence of the contents of documents is admissible, and the trier of fact determines what weight to give it.

2. *Comparison With Federal Rule.* Effective January 1, 2012, the Arizona Supreme Court amended Rule 1008 to conform to the federal restyling of the Evidence Rules to make the rules more easily understood and to make style and terminology consistent throughout. The 2012 Comment states the stylistic amendments are not intended to "change any result in any ruling on evidence

admissibility."

Following the 2012 restyling amendments, the language of Rule 1008 remains identical to its federal counterpart, Fed. R. Evid. 1008.

Although Ariz. R. Evid. 1008 parallels its federal counterpart, "federal court decisions interpreting the federal rule are persuasive but not binding with respect to interpreting the Arizona rule." *See,* Prefatory Comment to 2012 Amendments. *See also, State v. Terrazas*, 189 Ariz. 580, 944 P.2d 1194 (1997) (The Arizona Supreme Court is "not bound by the United States Supreme Court's non-constitutional construction of the Federal Rules of Evidence when [the Arizona Supreme Court construes] the Arizona Rules of Evidence."), citing, *State v. Bible*, 175 Ariz. 549, 858 P.2d 1152 (1993); *State v. Salazar-Mercado*, 232 Ariz. 256, 304 P.3d 543 (Ct. App. Div. 2 2013). Practitioners are urged to keep this legal tenet in mind as they research federal case law interpreting a federal evidentiary rule that corresponds to an Arizona evidentiary rule.

ARTICLE XI. MISCELLANEOUS RULES

Rule 1101. Applicability of the Rules

(a) Courts and magistrates. These rules apply to all courts of the State and to magistrates, and court commissioners and justices of the peace, masters and referees in actions, cases, and proceedings and to the extent hereinafter set forth. The terms "judge" and "court" in these rules include magistrates, court commissioners and justices of the peace.

(b) Proceedings generally. These rules apply generally to civil actions and proceedings, to contempt proceedings except those in which the court may act summarily, and to criminal cases and proceedings except as otherwise provided in the Arizona Rules of Criminal Procedure.

(c) Rule of privilege. The rule with respect to privileges applies at all stages of all actions, cases, and proceedings.

(d) Exceptions. These rules—except those on privilege—do not apply to grand jury proceedings.

Amended Sept. 8, 2011, effective Jan. 1, 2012.

Comment to 2012 Amendment

The title and language of Rule 1101(d) have been amended to conform to the federal restyling of the Evidence Rules to make them more easily understood and to make style and terminology consistent throughout the rules. These changes are intended to be stylistic only. There is no intent to change any result in any ruling on evidence admissibility.

No changes have been made to Rule 1101(a), (b), and (c).

Comment to Original 1977 Rule

Federal Rule 1101 has been supplanted by one that conforms to Arizona state practice. *See also* Ariz. R. Crim. P. 19.3.

AUTHORS' COMMENTS

Analysis

1. *Scope and Purpose of Rule.* Ariz. R. Evid. 1101 is the substantive provision establishing the scope of the applicability of the Arizona Rules of Evidence. Rule 101 essentially incorporates its provisions.

2. *Comparison With Federal Rule.* Effective January 1, 2012, the title and the language of Ariz. R. Evid. 1101(d) was amended to conform to the federal restyling of the Evidence Rules. The 2012 Comment states the stylistic amendments are not intended to "change any result in any ruling on evidence admissibility." No changes were made in 2012 to Rule 1101(a), (b), and (c).

Following the 2012 restyling amendments, Rules 1101(c) and (d) are substantially identical to Fed. R. Evid. 1101(c) and (d)(2), but other differences remain between Rule 1101 and its federal counterpart, Fed. R. Evid. 1101. Rule 1101(b) incorporates significant editorial revisions to adapt the Rule to the Arizona court system. Also, Rule 1101(b) does not contain a provision making the Rule applicable to admiralty and maritime cases, and provides that the Rules do not apply where "otherwise provided in the Arizona Rules of Criminal Procedure." Finally, the Arizona Rule does not have provisions corresponding to Rule 1101(d)(1), (d)(2) and (e) of the Federal Rules of Evidence.

3. *Applicability of Rules of Evidence.* Ariz. R. Evid. 101 and Ariz. R. Evid. 1101 make the Arizona Rules of Evidence applicable to all civil and criminal proceedings, except as may be otherwise provided. For instance:

(1) Rule 101 specifies that the Arizona Rules of Evidence govern proceedings in courts in the State of Arizona; and

(2) Rule 1101 makes clear that the Rules apply in proceedings before magistrates, court commissioners and in Justice Courts.

In addition, the Arizona Rules of Evidence either do not apply or their application is limited in the following circumstances:

1. The rules of evidence, other than the rules with respect to privileges, do not apply in grand jury proceedings. See, Ariz. R. Evid. 1101(d). *See also, Franzi v. Superior Court of Arizona In and For Pima County*, 139 Ariz. 556, 679 P.2d 1043 (1984) (to fulfill its function "the grand jury has the right to every person's evidence, absent a constitutional, common law, or statutory privilege.").

2. The rules of evidence, except those relating to privileges, do not apply where the Court is called upon to make preliminary determinations as to the admissibility of evidence. *See,* Ariz. R. Evid. 104(a).

3. The rules of evidence apply to arbitration hearings, but in a limited fashion. The rules of civil procedure governing arbitration hearingso provide for relaxed requirements for the admissibility of certain specified categories of documents. *See* Ariz. R. Civ. P. 75(e).

4. The rules of evidence apply in family law cases in the circumstances, and to the extent, provided in Rule 2(B) of the

Arizona Family Law Rules.

5. The Arizona Rules of Evidence do not apply in administrative hearings concerning workers' compensation claims. *State, Div. of Finance v. Industrial Com'n of Arizona*, 159 Ariz. 553, 769 P.2d 461 (Ct. App. Div. 1 1989), citing A.R.S. § 23-941(F).

Rule 1102. Amendments

These rules may be amended as provided in Rule 28, Rules of the Supreme Court.

Amended Sept. 8, 2011, effective Jan. 1, 2012.

Comment to 2012 Amendment

Rule 1102 has been added to be consistent with Federal Rule of Evidence 1102, as restyled.

Rule 1103. Title

These rules may be cited as the Arizona Rules of Evidence.

Amended Sept. 8, 2011, effective Jan. 1, 2012.

Comment to 2012 Amendment

The language of Rule 1103 has been amended to conform to the federal restyling of the Evidence Rules to make them more easily understood and to make style and terminology consistent throughout the rules. These changes are intended to be stylistic only. There is no intent to change any result in any ruling on evidence admissibility.

Table of Laws and Rules

UNITED STATES CONSTITUTION

	Sec.
Art. 1, § 6	501
Amend. 1	45(g)
Amend. 14	4.2(m)
Art. IV, § 1	54(g)(4), 60(d)
Amend. V	501

BANKRUPTCY ACT

Sec.	Sec.
69(a)	66(d)

UNITED STATES CODE ANNOTATED

11 U.S.C.A.	Sec.
109	66(d)
303(e)	66(d)

18 U.S.C.A.	Sec.
3500	612(c)

28 U.S.C.A.	Sec.
1608	4.2(*l*)
1782	45.1(e)
1870	47(g)

42 U.S.C.A.	Sec.
1983	3

FEDERAL RULES OF CIVIL PROCEDURE

Rule	Sec.
1	1
2	2
3	3
4	4.1(m), 4(i)
4(a)(4)	54(g)(4)
4(c)(2)(C)	4.1(m)
4(d)	4.1(m), 4.2(m)
4(e)	4.2(m)
4(f)	4.2(m)
4(g)	4.2(m)
4(h)(2)	4.2(m)
4(j)	4.2(m)
4(k)	4.2(m)
4.1	4.1(m), 4(i)
5	5(j)(2)(B)
5(a)	5(j)(2)(B)
5(d)	38(d)
5(d)(1)	5(j)(2)(B)
5(e)	5(j)(2)(B)
6(d)	6(f), 7.1(g)
7	7(b)
7(a)	7(b)
7(b)	7(b)
7.1	7.1(g)
8	8(i)(8)
8(b)(6)	8(i)(8)
8(c)	8(i)(8)
9(a) to (g)	9(i)(9)
9(h)	9(i)(9)
10(a)	10(f)
10(b)	10(f)
10(c)	10(f)

FEDERAL RULES OF CIVIL PROCEDURE—Continued

FEDERAL RULES OF CIVIL PROCEDURE—Continued

FEDERAL RULES OF CIVIL PROCEDURE—Continued

FEDERAL RULES OF CRIMINAL PROCEDURE

FEDERAL RULES OF EVIDENCE

FEDERAL RULES OF EVIDENCE—Continued

FEDERAL RULES OF EVIDENCE—Continued

Rule	Sec.
1101	1101(d)
1101(c)	1101(d)
1101(d)(2)	1101(d)
1101(e)	1101(d)
1102	1102

SENATE BILLS

No.	Sec.
71	58(g)

ARIZONA CONSTITUTION

	Sec.
Art. II, § 2.1(A)(3)	615(e)
Art. II, § 2.1(D)	1
Art. II, § 6	45(g)
Art. II, § 7	603
Art. II, § 10	501
Art. II, § 23	38(d)
Art. II, § 24	611(c)(2)
Art. VI, § 1	1
Art. VI, § 3	1
Art. VI, § 5	1
Art. VI, § 5(5)	101(b)(6)
Art. VI, § 14(1)	1
Art. VI, § 14(3)	1
Art. VI, § 14(11)	1
Art. VI, § 16	1
Art. VI, § 19	1
Art. VI, § 20	1
Art. VI, § 21	1, 39(q)
Art. VI, § 30(A)	1
Art. VI, § 32(B)	1
Art. VI, § 32(c)	1
Art. VI	53(k)
Art. XVIII, § 5	8(i)(8), 13(i), 14(b), 16.2(c), 51(d)
Art. XXIV	53(k)

ARIZONA REVISED STATUTES

Sec.	Sec.
1-205	4.2(m)
1-215(22)	603
Ch. 4, art. 6	54(g)(4)
Ch. 5, art. 12	8(i)(8)
8-207	609(e)
8-207(B)	609(e)
8-207(C)	501
8-519(C)	501
8-546.04	501
8-546.04(C)	501
9-409	54(g)(4)
10-110	9(i)(9)
10-111	9(i)(9)
10-202	4.1(m)
10-501	4.1(m)
10-504	4.1(m)
10-742	23.1
10-1502(A)	9(i)(9)
10-1502(B)	9(i)(9)
10-1503	4.1(m)
10-1510	4.1(m)
11-269.03	54(g)(4)
11-413.01	6(f)
11-622	3
11-630(A)	3
Title 12	1

ARIZONA REVISED STATUTES—Continued

ARIZONA REVISED STATUTES—Continued

ARIZONA REVISED STATUTES—Continued

ARIZONA REVISED STATUTES—Continued

ARIZONA REVISED STATUTES—Continued

ARIZONA REVISED STATUTES—Continued

ARIZONA SUPREME COURT RULES

ARIZONA RULES OF CIVIL APPELLATE PROCEDURE

ARIZONA RULES OF CIVIL PROCEDURE

ARIZONA RULES OF CIVIL PROCEDURE—Continued

ARIZONA RULES OF CIVIL PROCEDURE—Continued

ARIZONA RULES OF CIVIL PROCEDURE—Continued

ARIZONA RULES OF CIVIL PROCEDURE—Continued

Rule	Sec.
26(b)	26(h), 30(c), 30(h)(i), 33(b), 33(c), 34(a), 34(c), 36(a), 36(c)
26(b)(1)	26(h), 33.1(f)(3)(ii)
26(b)(2)	26(h)
26(b)(3)	26.1(g), 26(h)
26(b)(4)	16(b)(3), 16(h), 26(h), 43(k)(2), 86
26(b)(4)(B)	26.1(g), 26(h)
26(b)(4)(C)	26(h)
26(b)(4)(D)	16(c)(4), 26(h), 43(k)(2), 86, 702(d)
26(b)(5)	26(h), 38.1(k)(3)
26(c)	26(h), 30(d), 30(h)(i), 33(c), 34(c), 37(a)(4)(B), 37(a)(4)(C), 37(f)
26(c)(1)	26(h)
26(c)(1)(6)	26(h)
26(c)(1)(7)	26(h)
26(c)(2)	26(h)
26(d)	26(h), 32(d)(4)
26(e)	16(h), 26(h), 28(c), 32(d)(4)
26(e)(1)	26(h)
26(e)(1)(D)	26(h)
26(e)(2)	26(h)
26(e)(3)	26(h)
26(f)	26(h), 32(d)(4)
26(g)	26(h), 33.1(f)(3)(ii), 56(h)(3), 86
26.1	4(i), 7.2(f), 16(b)(13), 16(h), 26.1(g), 26(e), 26(h), 30(h)(i), 32(d)(4), 33.1(f)(3)(ii), 34(c), 37(a)(2)(A), 37(c)(1), 37(g), 38.1(k)(3), 43(k)(2), 57.1(f), 57.2(f), 60(d), 77(g)(1), 86, 404(c)(3)
26.1(a)	26.1(g), 33.1(f)(3)(ii)
26.1(a)(3)	26.1(g)
26.1(a)(4)	26.1(g)
26.1(a)(5)	26.1(g), 26(h)
26.1(a)(6)	26.1(g), 705
26.1(a)(7)	26.1(g)
26.1(a)(8)	26(h)
26.1(a)(9)	26.1(g), 26(h)
26.1(b)	26.1(g), 37(g)
26.1(b)(1)	26.1(g)
26.1(b)(2)	26.1(g), 37(g)
26.1(b)(3)	26.1(g)
26.1(c)	26.1(g)
26.1(d)	26.1(g)
26.1(e)	26.1(g)
26.1(f)	26.1(g), 26(h)
26.1(f)(1)	26.1(g), 26(h)
26.1(f)(2)	26.1(g), 26(h), 45(g), 501, 502(b)(3), 502(f)(2)
26.1(g)	26.1(g)
26.2	26.2(b)(4), 33.1(f)(3)(ii)
26.2(a)	16(h), 86
26.2(a)(1)	26.2(b)(4), 26(h)
26.2(a)(2)	16(c)(1)
26.2(b)	16(h), 26.2(b)(4), 86
26.2(b)(1)	26.2(b)(4)
27	27(b)
27(a)	27(b)
27(b)	27(b), 62(j)
28	28(c), 30(b)(4)
28(a)	28(c), 30(b)(7), 30(h)(i)
28(b)	28(c), 32(b)
28(c)	28(c)
29	28(a), 29, 30(h)(i)
30	26(h), 28(a), 30(h)(i), 31(d), 32(d)(4), 37(a)(2)(B)
30(a)	26(h), 30(h)(i), 33.1(f)(3)(ii)
30(b)	26(h), 30(h)(i)
30(b)(1)	30(h)(i)
30(b)(2)	30(h)(i)
30(b)(4)	30(h)(i), 32(c)
30(b)(5)	30(h)(i)
30(b)(6)	30(h)(i), 31(a), 37(a)(2)(B), 37(b)(2), 37(f), 37(g)
30(b)(7)	30(h)(i)
30(c)	26(h), 30(h)(i), 31(b), 31(d), 32(c)
30(d)	30(h)(i)
30(e)	30(h)(i), 31(b), 31(d)
30(f)	30(h)(i), 31(b), 31(d), 45(g)
30(f)(1)	30(h)(i)
30(f)(2)	30(h)(i)
30(f)(3)	30(h)(i)
30(h)	30(h)(i), 45.1(e)

ARIZONA RULES OF CIVIL PROCEDURE—Continued

ARIZONA RULES OF CIVIL PROCEDURE—Continued

ARIZONA RULES OF CIVIL PROCEDURE—Continued

ARIZONA RULES OF CIVIL PROCEDURE—Continued

ARIZONA RULES OF CIVIL PROCEDURE—Continued

ARIZONA RULES OF CIVIL PROCEDURE—Continued

ARIZONA RULES OF CRIMINAL PROCEDURE

ARIZONA RULES OF CRIMINAL PROCEDURE—Continued

ARIZONA RULES OF EVIDENCE

ARIZONA RULES OF EVIDENCE—Continued

ARIZONA RULES OF EVIDENCE—Continued

Rule	Sec.
1101(d)	101(b)(6), 1101(d)

ARIZONA RULES OF PROCEDURE FOR SPECIAL ACTIONS

Rule	Sec.
2(b)	24(d)

ARIZONA RULES OF JUVENILE PROCEDURE

Rule	Sec.
Part V	81.1

ARIZONA UNIFORM RULES OF PRACTICE OF THE SUPERIOR COURT

Rule	Sec.
7.1	42(f)(3)(B)
38.1(d)	38.1(k)(3)
I	42(f)(3)(B)
I(a)(5)	86
III(a)(5)	26(h)
IV	6(f), 86
IV(b)	7.1(g)
IV(d)	7.1(g)
IV(h)	7.1(g)
V	38.1(k)(3)
V(a)	26(h)
V(b)(3)(i)	26(h)
V(b)(3)(ii)	26(h)
V(i)	38.1(k)(3)
XIII	39(q), 86
XIV	86
XIX	43(k)(2)
XVII	5(j)(2)(B)
XVII(c)(1)	5(j)(2)(B)

ARIZONA UNIFORM RULES OF PROCEDURE FOR ARBITRATION

Rule	Sec.
3	74(g)

APACHE COUNTY SUPERIOR COURT RULES

Rule	Sec.
2	7.1(g)
8	72(e)(7)
10(c)	7.1(g)
20(a)	16(h)
23(b)	51(d)

CALIFORNIA CODE OF CIVIL PROCEDURE

Sec.	Sec.	Sec.	Sec.
2030(a)	33(c)	2030(c)	33(c)

COCHISE COUNTY SUPERIOR COURT RULES

Rule	Sec.	Rule	Sec.
2(a)	7.1(g)	11	72(e)(7)
2(c)	7.1(g)	22	16(h)
2(d)	7.1(g)	24	51(d)

COCONINO COUNTY SUPERIOR COURT RULES

Rule	Sec.	Rule	Sec.
4(D)	7.1(g)	16	72(e)(7)
5	29		

GILA COUNTY SUPERIOR COURT RULES

Rule	Sec.	Rule	Sec.
2	7.1(g)	16(B)	7.1(g)
13(A)	72(e)(7)		

GRAHAM COUNTY SUPERIOR COURT RULES

Rule	Sec.	Rule	Sec.
1.13(B)	7.1(g)	2.1	72(e)(7)

LA PAZ COUNTY SUPERIOR COURT RULES

Rule	Sec.	Rule	Sec.
2(a)	7.1(g)	4	16(h)
2(b)	7.1(g)	7(B)	51(d)
3.2(d)	7.1(g)	10	72(e)(7)

MARICOPA COUNTY SUPERIOR COURT RULES

Rule	Sec.	Rule	Sec.
2.9(b)	51(d)	3.4	38.1(k)(3)
2.10(c)	1	3.7(e)	54(g)(4)
3.2(d)	7.1(g)	3.10	72(e)(7)
3.2(f)	7.1(g)	3.10(c)	72(e)(7)
3.2(h)	37(g)	5	38(d)

MOHAVE COUNTY SUPERIOR COURT RULES

Rule	Sec.	Rule	Sec.
7(B)	16(h)	CV-4	29
CV-1(A)	7.1(g)	CV-5(B)	51(d)
CV-1(B)	7.1(g)	CV-6	72(e)(7)

PIMA COUNTY SUPERIOR COURT RULES

Rule	Sec.	Rule	Sec.
2.1	7.1(g)	4.2	72(e)(7)
3.8(a)	7.1(g)		

PINAL COUNTY SUPERIOR COURT RULES

Rule	Sec.	Rule	Sec.
1.3(a)	7.1(g)	2.14(b)	51(d)
1.3(b)	7.1(g)	2.20	72(e)(7)
2.5(b)	7.1(g)		

SANTA CRUZ COUNTY SUPERIOR COURT RULES

Rule	Sec.	Rule	Sec.
1.2(a)	7.1(g)	8.2(a)	7.1(g)
5	72(e)(7)	8.3	7.1(g)
6.3	51(d)	10	38.1(k)(3)
8.1	7.1(g)		

YAVAPAI COUNTY SUPERIOR COURT RULES

Rule	Sec.	Rule	Sec.
2(B)	7.1(g)	6(A)	16(h)
2(C)	7.1(g)	10.3	72(e)(7)
2(E)	7.1(g)		

YUMA COUNTY SUPERIOR COURT RULES

Rule	Sec.	Rule	Sec.
2(a)	7.1(g)	13	38.1(k)(3)
10	72(e)(7)		

RESTATEMENT SECOND, JUDGMENTS

Sec.	Sec.
61	8(i)(8)

ILLINOIS REVISED STATUTES

Ill. Ann. Stat.	Sec.
Ch. 110, § 50(2)	54(g)(4)
Ch. 110, § 54(2)	25(e)(2)
Ch. 110, § 66	47(g)
Ch. 110, par. 2-1106	47(g)

LOUISIANA CODE OF CIVIL PROCEDURE ANNOTATED

Art.	Sec.
1495	35(c)(3)

OHIO RULES OF CIVIL PROCEDURE

Rule	Sec.
4.2(14)	4.1(m)

OREGON REVISED STATUTES

Sec.	Sec.
17.160	47(g)

UTAH RULES OF CIVIL PROCEDURE

Rule	Sec.
35(c)	35(c)(3)

Table of Cases

A

Ahwatukee Custom Estates Management Ass'n, Inc. v. Turner, 196 Ariz. 631, 2 P.3d 1276 (Ct. App. Div. 1 2000)—52(d), 65(j)(6)
Aida Renta Trust v. Maricopa County, 221 Ariz. 603, 212 P.3d 941 (Ct. App. Div. 1 2009)—54(g)(4), 56(h)(3)
Airfreight Exp. Ltd v. Evergreen Air Center, Inc., 215 Ariz. 103, 158 P.3d 232 (Ct. App. Div. 2 2007)—8(i)(8), 12(i), 41(d), 56(h)(3), 80(i)
A.J. Bayless Markets, Inc. v. Superior Court of Pima County, 145 Ariz. 285, 700 P.2d 1385 (Ct. App. Div. 2 1985)—23(f)
Albers v. Edelson Technology Partners L.P., 201 Ariz. 47, 31 P.3d 821, 111 A.L.R.5th 715 (Ct. App. Div. 1 2001)—12(i), 23.1
Alberta Securities Com'n v. Ryckman, 200 Ariz. 540, 30 P.3d 121 (Ct. App. Div. 1 2001)—54(g)(4), 56(h)(3), 69
Aldabbagh v. Arizona Dept. of Liquor Licenses and Control, 162 Ariz. 415, 783 P.2d 1207 (Ct. App. Div. 2 1989)—12(i)
Alexander v. Superior Court In and For Maricopa County, 141 Ariz. 157, 685 P.2d 1309 (1984)—26(h), 501
Alires v. Southern Pac. Co., 93 Ariz. 97, 378 P.2d 913 (1963)—105, 701(c), 702(d), 801(d)(2)(E)
Alires v. Southern Pac. Co., 100 Ariz. 6, 409 P.2d 714 (1966)—59(m), 401(b), 602
Allen v. Allen, 129 Ariz. 112, 628 P.2d 995 (Ct. App. Div. 1 1981)—58(g)
Allen v. Chon-Lopez, 214 Ariz. 361, 153 P.3d 382 (Ct. App. Div. 2 2007)—24(d)
Allen v. Superior Court of Maricopa County, 86 Ariz. 205, 344 P.2d 163 (1959)—3
Allison v. Ovens, 4 Ariz. App. 496, 421 P.2d 929 (1966)—615(e)
Allison v. State, 101 Ariz. 418, 420 P.2d 289 (1966)—12(i), 36(c)
Allison Steel Mfg. Co. v. Superior Court of Maricopa County, Division Three, 20 Ariz. App. 185, 511 P.2d 198 (Div. 1 1973)—14(b)
Allstate Indem. Co. v. Ridgely, 214 Ariz. 440, 153 P.3d 1069 (Ct. App. Div. 2 2007)—56(h)(3)
Allstate Ins. Co. v. O'Toole, 182 Ariz. 284, 896 P.2d 254 (1995)—26.1(g), 37(g)
Alta Vista Plaza, Ltd. v. Insulation Specialists Co., Inc., 186 Ariz. 81, 919 P.2d 176 (Ct. App. Div. 2 1995)—54(g)(4), 58(g)
Althaus v. Cornelio, 203 Ariz. 597, 58 P.3d 973 (Ct. App. Div. 2 2002)—8(i)(8)
Alyeska Pipeline Service Co. v. Wilderness Society, 421 U.S. 240, 95 S. Ct. 1612, 44 L. Ed. 2d 141, 7 Env't. Rep. Cas. (BNA) 1849, 10 Fair Empl. Prac. Cas. (BNA) 826, 11 Empl. Prac. Dec. (CCH) ¶ 10842, 5 Envtl. L. Rep. 20286 (1975)—54(g)(4)
Amanti Elec., Inc. v. Engineered Structures, Inc., 229 Ariz. 430, 276 P.3d 499 (Ct. App. Div. 2 2012)—60(d)
Amburgey v. Holan Division of Ohio Brass Co., 124 Ariz. 531, 606 P.2d 21 (1980)—608(b)(2), 609(e)
Amchem Products, Inc. v. Windsor, 521 U.S. 591, 117 S. Ct. 2231, 138 L. Ed. 2d 689, 37 Fed. R. Serv. 3d 1017, 28 Envtl. L. Rep. 20173 (1997)—23(f)
AMCOR Inv. Corp. v. Cox Ariz. Publications, Inc., 158 Ariz. 566, 764 P.2d 327, 16 Media L. Rep. (BNA) 1059 (Ct. App. Div. 2 1988)—8(i)(8)
AMERCO v. Shoen, 184 Ariz. 150, 907 P.2d 536 (Ct. App. Div. 1 1995)—26(h), 51(d), 403
American and Foreign Ins. Co. v. Allstate Ins. Co., 139 Ariz. 223, 677 P.2d 1331 (Ct. App. Div. 1 1983)—14(b)

Andrew R. v. Arizona Dept. of Economic Sec., 223 Ariz. 453, 224 P.3d 950 (Ct. App. Div. 1 2010)—6(f), 26.1(g), 59(m), 60(d)

Andrews v. Andrews, 126 Ariz. 55, 612 P.2d 511 (Ct. App. Div. 1 1980)—60(d)

Andrews v. Blake, 205 Ariz. 236, 69 P.3d 7 (2003)—56(h)(3)

Andrew S. Arena, Inc. v. Superior Court In and For County of Maricopa, 163 Ariz. 423, 788 P.2d 1174 (1990)—23(f)

Andrews ex rel. Woodard v. Eddie's Place, Inc., 199 Ariz. 240, 16 P.3d 801 (Ct. App. Div. 2 2000)—8(i)(8)

Angus Medical Co. v. Digital Equipment Corp., 173 Ariz. 159, 840 P.2d 1024, 17 U.C.C. Rep. Serv. 2d 724 (Ct. App. Div. 1 1992)—8(i)(8)

Anonymous, In re, 4 Ariz. App. 170, 418 P.2d 416 (1966)—58(g)

Anserv Ins. Services, Inc. v. Albrecht In and For County of Maricopa, 192 Ariz. 48, 960 P.2d 1159 (1998)—1, 8(i)(8)

Apache County v. Superior Court In and For County of Maricopa, 163 Ariz. 54, 785 P.2d 1242 (Ct. App. Div. 1 1989)—18(b), 20(b)

Apache Playtime, Inc. v. Universal Playtime, Inc., 27 Ariz. App. 178, 552 P.2d 767 (Div. 1 1976)—38(d)

Apollo Group, Inc. v. Avnet, Inc., 58 F.3d 477, Prod. Liab. Rep. (CCH) ¶ 14249, 26 U.C.C. Rep. Serv. 2d 1099 (9th Cir. 1995)—54(g)(4)

Appleton's Estate, In re, 15 Ariz. App. 490, 489 P.2d 864 (Div. 1 1971)—1

Aqua Management, Inc. v. Abdeen, 224 Ariz. 91, 227 P.3d 498 (Ct. App. Div. 1 2010)—76(g), 77(g)(4)

Arab Monetary Fund v. Hashim, 219 Ariz. 108, 193 P.3d 802 (Ct. App. Div. 1 2008)—56(h)(3), 58(g), 301

Aranda v. Cardenas, 215 Ariz. 210, 159 P.3d 76 (Ct. App. Div. 2 2007)—9(i)(9), 56(h)(3)

Archer v. Board of Sup'rs of Pima County, 166 Ariz. 106, 800 P.2d 972 (1990)—103(e)

Aries v. Palmer Johnson, Inc., 153 Ariz. 250, 735 P.2d 1373, 4 U.C.C. Rep. Serv. 2d 85 (Ct. App. Div. 2 1987)—12(i), 13(i), 38.1(k)(3)

Aritex Land Co. v. Baker, 14 Ariz. App. 266, 482 P.2d 875 (Div. 2 1971)—39(q), 611(c)(2)

Arizona Association of Providers for Persons with Disabilities v. State, 223 Ariz. 6, 219 P.3d 216 (Ct. App. Div. 1 2009)—12(i), 65(j)(6)

Arizona Bank v. Superior Court In and For Maricopa County, 17 Ariz. App. 115, 495 P.2d 1322 (Div. 1 1972)—54(g)(4)

Arizona Bd. of Regents for and on Behalf of University of Arizona v. State ex rel. State of Ariz. Public Safety Retirement Fund Manager Adm'r, 160 Ariz. 150, 771 P.2d 880, 53 Ed. Law Rep. 260 (Ct. App. Div. 1 1989)—19(d)

Arizona Center For Law In Public Interest v. Hassell, 172 Ariz. 356, 837 P.2d 158, 23 Envtl. L. Rep. 20348 (Ct. App. Div. 1 1991)—54(g)(4)

Arizona Container Corp. v. Consolidated Freightways, 22 Ariz. App. 11, 522 P.2d 772 (Div. 2 1974)—58(g), 59(m)

Arizona Dept. of Admin. v. Cox, 222 Ariz. 270, 213 P.3d 707 (Ct. App. Div. 2 2009)—56(h)(3)

Arizona Dept. of Economic Sec. v. Superior Court In and For County of Maricopa, 178 Ariz. 236, 871 P.2d 1172 (Ct. App. Div. 1 1994)—17(j)

Arnold v. Arizona Dept. of Health Services, 160 Ariz. 593, 775 P.2d 521 (1989)—54(g)(4)

Arnold v. Van Ornum, 4 Ariz. App. 89, 417 P.2d 723 (1966)—7.1(g)

Arpaio v. Maricopa County Bd. of Supervisors, 225 Ariz. 358, 238 P.3d 626 (Ct. App. Div. 1 2010)—3

A.R. Teeters & Associates, Inc. v. Eastman Kodak Co., 172 Ariz. 324, 836 P.2d 1034 (Ct. App. Div. 1 1992)—52(d), 58(g), 59(m)

Asbestos Engineering & Supply Co. v. Industrial Commission of Arizona, 131 Ariz. 558, 642 P.2d 903 (Ct. App. Div. 1 1982)—702(d)

Ash v. Arnold, 115 Ariz. 462, 565 P.2d 1323 (Ct. App. Div. 2 1977)—26(h)

Ash v. Flieger, 118 Ariz. 547, 578 P.2d 628 (Ct. App. Div. 2 1978)—50(d)

ASH, Inc. v. Mesa Unified School Dist. No. 4, 138 Ariz. 190, 673 P.2d 934, 15 Ed. Law Rep. 560 (Ct. App. Div. 1 1983)—54(g)(4)

Associated Aviation Underwriters v. Wood, 209 Ariz. 137, 98 P.3d 572 (Ct. App. Div. 2 2004)—7(b), 8(i)(8), 57

Associated Indem. Corp. v. Warner, 143 Ariz. 567, 694 P.2d 1181 (1985)—54(g)(4)

Associated Students of University of Arizona v. Arizona Bd. of Regents, 120 Ariz. 100, 584 P.2d 564 (Ct. App. Div. 2 1978)—17(j), 23.2

Astorga v. Wing, 211 Ariz. 139, 118 P.3d 1103 (Ct. App. Div. 1 2005)—12(i)

Atkinson v. Marquart, 112 Ariz. 304, 541 P.2d 556 (1975)—701(c)

A Tumbling-T Ranches v. Flood Control Dist. of Maricopa County, 220 Ariz. 202, 204 P.3d 1051 (Ct. App. Div. 1 2008)—8(i)(8), 14(b)

A Tumbling-T Ranches v. Flood Control Dist. of Maricopa County, 222 Ariz. 515, 217 P.3d 1220 (Ct. App. Div. 1 2009)—8(i)(8), 13(i), 14(b), 16.2(c), 26(h), 50(d), 51(d), 103(e)

A. Uberti and C. v. Leonardo, 181 Ariz. 565, 892 P.2d 1354, Prod. Liab. Rep. (CCH) ¶ 14198 (1995)—4.2(m)

Austin v. City of Scottsdale, 140 Ariz. 579, 684 P.2d 151, 46 A.L.R.4th 941 (1984)—37(g)

Austin v. CrystalTech Web Hosting, 211 Ariz. 569, 125 P.3d 389 (Ct. App. Div. 1 2005)—4.2(m)

Austin v. State ex rel. Herman, 10 Ariz. App. 474, 459 P.2d 753 (Div. 2 1969)—4(i), 55(f)

Averett v. Farmers Ins. Co. of Arizona, 177 Ariz. 531, 869 P.2d 505 (1994)—104(e)

Avila v. Superior Court In and For County of Maricopa, 169 Ariz. 49, 816 P.2d 946 (Ct. App. Div. 1 1991)—35(c)(3)

Ayala v. Olaiz, 161 Ariz. 129, 776 P.2d 807 (Ct. App. Div. 1 1989)—54(g)(4)

Azstar Cas. Co. Inc., Matter of Liquidation of, 189 Ariz. 27, 938 P.2d 76 (Ct. App. Div. 1 1996)—54(g)(4), 58(g)

Aztar Corp. v. U.S. Fire Ins. Co., 223 Ariz. 463, 224 P.3d 960 (Ct. App. Div. 1 2010)—54(g)(4)

B

Babbitt, State ex rel. v. Arnold, 26 Ariz. App. 333, 548 P.2d 426 (Div. 2 1976)—37(g), 501

Babbitt, State ex rel. v. Goodyear Tire & Rubber Co., 128 Ariz. 483, 626 P.2d 1115 (Ct. App. Div. 1 1981)—65(j)(6)

Barnes v. Outlaw, 188 Ariz. 401, 937 P.2d 323 (Ct. App. Div. 2 1996)—51(d), 501
Barnes v. Vozack, 113 Ariz. 269, 550 P.2d 1070 (1976)—15(d)
Barnet v. Board of Medical Examiners, 121 Ariz. 338, 590 P.2d 454 (1979)—8(i)(8), 11(c), 65(j)(6)
Barnette v. McNulty, 21 Ariz. App. 127, 516 P.2d 583 (Div. 2 1973)—801(d)(2)(E)
Baroldy v. Ortho Pharmaceutical Corp., 157 Ariz. 574, 760 P.2d 574, Prod. Liab. Rep. (CCH) ¶ 11732 (Ct. App. Div. 1 1988)—51(d), 105, 301, 407, 704(b)
Barragan v. Superior Court of Pima County, 12 Ariz. App. 402, 470 P.2d 722 (Div. 2 1970)—25(e)(2)
Barrett v. Harris, 207 Ariz. 374, 86 P.3d 954 (Ct. App. Div. 1 2004)—50(d)
Barrett v. Melton, 112 Ariz. 605, 545 P.2d 421 (1976)—33(c), 801(d)(2)(E)
Barrow v. Arizona Bd. of Regents, 158 Ariz. 71, 761 P.2d 145, 49 Ed. Law Rep. 761 (Ct. App. Div. 2 1988)—11(c), 901(b)(10)
Barry v. Alberty, 173 Ariz. 387, 843 P.2d 1279 (Ct. App. Div. 1 1992)—6(f)
Barsema v. Susong, 156 Ariz. 309, 751 P.2d 969 (1988)—101(b)(6), 401(b), 402, 411, 607
Bartlett v. Superior Court In and For Pima County, 150 Ariz. 178, 722 P.2d 346 (Ct. App. Div. 2 1986)—45(g)
Bates v. Bates, 1 Ariz. App. 165, 400 P.2d 593 (1965)—8(i)(8)
Batton v. Tennessee Farmers Mut. Ins. Co., 153 Ariz. 268, 736 P.2d 2 (1987)—4.2(m)
Batty v. Glendale Union High School Dist. No. 205, 221 Ariz. 592, 212 P.3d 930, 247 Ed. Law Rep. 456 (Ct. App. Div. 1 2009)—4.1(m)
Baumann v. Tuton, 180 Ariz. 370, 884 P.2d 256 (Ct. App. Div. 1 1994)—54(g)(4), 59(m)
Baxter v. Harrison, 83 Ariz. 354, 321 P.2d 1019 (1958)—9(i)(9), 12(i)
Bayham v. Funk, 3 Ariz. App. 220, 413 P.2d 279 (1966)—1, 65(j)(6)
Bayless Inv. & Trading Co. v. Bekins Moving & Storage Co., 26 Ariz. App. 265, 547 P.2d 1065 (Div. 1 1976)—52(d)
BCAZ Corp. v. Helgoe, 194 Ariz. 11, 976 P.2d 260 (Ct. App. Div. 1 1998)—7.1(g), 11(c), 38.1(k)(3), 41(d)
Beal v. State Farm Mut. Auto. Ins. Co., 151 Ariz. 514, 729 P.2d 318 (Ct. App. Div. 1 1986)—55(f), 60(d)
Bear v. Nicholls, 142 Ariz. 560, 691 P.2d 326 (Ct. App. Div. 1 1984)—410(b)(2)
Bechtel v. Rose In and For Maricopa County, 150 Ariz. 68, 722 P.2d 236 (1986)—24(d)
Beck v. Jaeger, 124 Ariz. 316, 604 P.2d 18 (Ct. App. Div. 2 1979)—201(f)
Beckwith v. Clevenger Realty Co., 89 Ariz. 238, 360 P.2d 596 (1961)—15(d)
Begay v. Miller, 70 Ariz. 380, 222 P.2d 624 (1950)—54(g)(4), 69
Behrens v. O'Melia, 206 Ariz. 309, 78 P.3d 278 (Ct. App. Div. 1 2003)—12(i), 13(i), 14(b), 16.2(c), 42(f)(3)(B)
Belen Loan Investors, LLC v. Bradley, 231 Ariz. 448, 296 P.3d 984 (Ct. App. Div. 2 2012)—3, 8(i)(8), 12(i)
Bell Atlantic Corp. v. Twombly, 550 U.S. 544, 127 S. Ct. 1955, 167 L. Ed. 2d 929, 2007-1 Trade Cas. (CCH) ¶ 75709, 68 Fed. R. Serv. 3d 661 (2007)—8(i)(8), 12(i)
Belliard v. Becker, 216 Ariz. 356, 166 P.3d 911 (Ct. App. Div. 1 2007)—59(m), 103(e), 104(e)

Beltran v. Harrah's Arizona Corp., 220 Ariz. 29, 202 P.3d 494 (Ct. App. Div. 2 2008)—8(i)(8), 19(d), 54(g)(4), 69

Beltran v. Roll, 39 Ariz. 417, 7 P.2d 248 (1932)—10(f)

Bender v. Bender, 123 Ariz. 90, 597 P.2d 993 (Ct. App. Div. 1 1979)—9(i)(9)

Bennett v. Appaloosa Horse Club, 201 Ariz. 372, 35 P.3d 426 (Ct. App. Div. 1 2001)—4.2(m)

Bennett v. Baxter Group, Inc., 223 Ariz. 414, 224 P.3d 230 (Ct. App. Div. 2 2010)—52(d), 54(g)(4), 58(g)

Bennett v. Brownlow, 211 Ariz. 193, 119 P.3d 460 (2005)—12(i)

Benson v. State ex rel. Eyman, 108 Ariz. 513, 502 P.2d 1332 (1972)—54(g)(4)

Benton v. Superior Court in and for County of Navajo, 182 Ariz. 466, 897 P.2d 1352 (Ct. App. Div. 1 1994)—501

Berg v. Hohenstein, 13 Ariz. App. 583, 479 P.2d 730 (Div. 1 1971)—9(i)(9)

Berge Ford, Inc. v. Maricopa County, 172 Ariz. 483, 838 P.2d 822 (Tax Ct.1992)—42(f)(3)(B)

Berger, State ex rel. v. Superior Court In and For Maricopa County, 108 Ariz. 396, 499 P.2d 152 (1972)—7.2(f), 103(e)

Berry v. 352 E. Virginia, L.L.C., 228 Ariz. 9, 261 P.3d 784 (Ct. App. Div. 1 2011)—68(h)

Berry v. Foster, 180 Ariz. 233, 883 P.2d 470, 95 Ed. Law Rep. 699 (Ct. App. Div. 2 1994)—65(j)(6)

Berthot v. Courtyard Properties, Inc., 138 Ariz. 566, 675 P.2d 1385 (Ct. App. Div. 1 1983)—408(b), 1002

Bertleson v. Sacks Tierney, P.A., 204 Ariz. 124, 60 P.3d 703 (Ct. App. Div. 1 2002)—1, 8(i)(8), 26.1(g)

Best v. Edwards, 217 Ariz. 497, 176 P.3d 695 (Ct. App. Div. 1 2008)—56(h)(3)

Better Homes Const., Inc. v. Goldwater, 203 Ariz. 295, 53 P.3d 1139 (Ct. App. Div. 1 2002)—8(i)(8)

Beverage v. Pullman & Comley, LLC, 232 Ariz. 414, 306 P.3d 71 (Ct. App. Div. 1 2013)—4.2(m)

Beyerle Sand & Gravel, Inc. v. Martinez, 118 Ariz. 60, 574 P.2d 853 (Ct. App. Div. 2 1977)—201(f)

Bezat v. Home Owners' Loan Corporation, 55 Ariz. 85, 98 P.2d 852 (1940)—38.1(k)(3)

Biaett v. Phoenix Title & Trust Co., 70 Ariz. 164, 217 P.2d 923, 22 A.L.R.2d 615 (1950)—5(j)(2)(B), 5.1(d), 13(i)

Bianco v. Patterson, 159 Ariz. 472, 768 P.2d 204 (Ct. App. Div. 2 1989)—301

Bickerstaff v. Denny's Restaurant, Inc., 141 Ariz. 629, 688 P.2d 637 (1984)—38.1(k)(3), 60(d)

Bike Fashion Corp. v. Kramer, 202 Ariz. 420, 46 P.3d 431 (Ct. App. Div. 1 2002)—51(d)

Bilke v. State, 206 Ariz. 462, 80 P.3d 269 (2003)—54(g)(4), 58(g)

Bilke v. State, 221 Ariz. 60, 209 P.3d 1056 (Ct. App. Div. 1 2009)—54(g)(4)

Bill Alexander Ford, Lincoln Mercury, Inc. v. Casa Ford, Inc., 187 Ariz. 616, 931 P.2d 1126, Prod. Liab. Rep. (CCH) ¶ 14727 (Ct. App. Div. 1 1996)—8(i)(8), 13(i), 14(b)

Bils v. Bils, 200 Ariz. 45, 22 P.3d 38 (2001)—4.2(m)

Bils v. Nixon, Hargrave, Devans & Doyle, 179 Ariz. 523, 880 P.2d 743 (Ct. App. Div. 2 1994)—4.2(m), 12(i)

Bird v. Rothman, 128 Ariz. 599, 627 P.2d 1097 (Ct. App. Div. 2 1981)—11(c)

Birds Intern. Corp. v. Arizona Maintenance Co., Inc., 135 Ariz. 545, 662 P.2d 1052 (Ct. App. Div. 2 1983)—37(g)

Birth Hope Adoption Agency, Inc. v. Doe, 190 Ariz. 285, 947 P.2d 859 (Ct. App. Div. 1 1997)—12(i), 56(h)(3)

Bisaillon v. Casares, 165 Ariz. 359, 798 P.2d 1368 (Ct. App. Div. 2 1990)—15(d)

Bisbee, City of v. Arizona Water Co., 214 Ariz. 368, 153 P.3d 389 (Ct. App. Div. 2 2007)—56(h)(3)

Bishop v. Department of Public Safety, 122 Ariz. 512, 596 P.2d 38 (Ct. App. Div. 2 1979)—52(d)

Bishop v. Marks, 117 Ariz. 50, 570 P.2d 821 (Ct. App. Div. 2 1977)—8(i)(8)

Bishop v. Pecanic, 193 Ariz. 524, 975 P.2d 114 (Ct. App. Div. 1, 1998)—8(i)(8), 13(i), 14(b), 16.2(c)

Black v. Black, 114 Ariz. 282, 560 P.2d 800 (1977)—59(m)

Black v. Greer, 17 Ariz. App. 383, 498 P.2d 225 (Div. 1 1972)—38.1(k)(3)

Black v. Industrial Commission of Ariz., 83 Ariz. 121, 317 P.2d 553, 70 A.L.R.2d 1119 (1957)—58(g)

Black v. Perkins, 163 Ariz. 292, 787 P.2d 1088 (Ct. App. Div. 2 1989)—801(d)(2)(E)

Black v. Siler, 96 Ariz. 102, 392 P.2d 572 (1964)—57

Blair v. Burgener, 226 Ariz. 213, 245 P.3d 898 (Ct. App. Div. 2 2010)—4.1(m)

Blakely Oil, Inc. v. Crowder, 80 Ariz. 72, 292 P.2d 842 (1956)—14(b)

Blanchard v. Show Low Planning and Zoning Com'n, 196 Ariz. 114, 993 P.2d 1078 (Ct. App. Div. 1 1999)—12(i), 56(h)(3)

Blankenbaker v. Jonovich, 203 Ariz. 226, 52 P.3d 795 (Ct. App. Div. 1 2002)—12(i)

Blankinship v. Duarte, 137 Ariz. 217, 669 P.2d 994 (Ct. App. Div. 2 1983)—404(c)(4), 608(b)(2), 609(e)

Blazek v. Superior Court In and For County of Maricopa, 177 Ariz. 535, 869 P.2d 509 (Ct. App. Div. 1 1994)—501

Blech v. Blech, 6 Ariz. App. 131, 430 P.2d 710 (1967)—38.1(k)(3)

Bledsoe v. Salt River Valley Water Users' Ass'n, 179 Ariz. 469, 880 P.2d 689 (Ct. App. Div. 2 1994)—59(m), 105, 401(b), 403, 702(d)

Bliss v. Treece, 134 Ariz. 516, 658 P.2d 169 (1983)—104(e), 702(d), 704(b)

Bloch v. Bentfield, 1 Ariz. App. 412, 403 P.2d 559 (1965)—38(d)

Block v. Meyer, 144 Ariz. 230, 696 P.2d 1379 (Ct. App. Div. 1 1985)—103(e), 403, 608(b)(2), 611(c)(2)

Blumenthal v. Teets, 155 Ariz. 123, 745 P.2d 181 (Ct. App. Div. 1 1987)—15(d), 23.1

BNSF Ry. Co. v. Buttrick, 228 Ariz. 449, 268 P.3d 400 (Ct. App. Div. 1 2011)—26(h)

Boatman v. Samaritan Health Services, Inc., 168 Ariz. 207, 812 P.2d 1025 (Ct. App. Div. 2 1990)—12(i), 56(h)(3), 59(m)

Bobo v. John W. Lattimore, Contractor, 12 Ariz. App. 137, 468 P.2d 404 (Div. 1 1970)—56(h)(3)

Bogard v. Cannon & Wendt Elec. Co., Inc., 221 Ariz. 325, 212 P.3d 17 (Ct. App. Div. 1 2009)—7.1(g), 54(g)(4), 56(h)(3), 103(e)

Bogard GMC Co. v. Henley, 2 Ariz. App. 223, 407 P.2d 412 (1965)—611(c)(2)
Bogard G.M.C. Co. v. Henley, 92 Ariz. 107, 374 P.2d 660 (1962)—32(d)(4), 801(d)(2)(E)
Bogue v. Better-Bilt Aluminum Co., 179 Ariz. 22, 875 P.2d 1327, 3 A.D. Cas. (BNA) 137 (Ct. App. Div. 1 1994)—801(d)(2)(E)
Bohmfalk v. Vaughan, 89 Ariz. 33, 357 P.2d 617 (1960)—7(b), 39(q)
Bohn v. Waddell, 164 Ariz. 74, 790 P.2d 772 (Tax Ct. 1990)—23(f)
Bohn, Estate of v. Waddell, 174 Ariz. 239, 848 P.2d 324, 16 Employee Benefits Cas. (BNA) 2877 (Ct. App. Div. 1 1992)—23(f)
Bolin v. Superior Court In and For Maricopa County, 85 Ariz. 131, 333 P.2d 295 (1958)—19(d)
Bolon v. Pennington, 3 Ariz. App. 433, 415 P.2d 148 (1966)—53(k)
Boltz & Odegaard v. Hohn, 148 Ariz. 361, 714 P.2d 854 (Ct. App. Div. 1 1985)—54(g)(4), 68(h)
Bond v. Cartwright Little League, Inc., 112 Ariz. 9, 536 P.2d 697 (1975)—50(d), 59(m)
Bonner v. Minico, Inc., 159 Ariz. 246, 766 P.2d 598 (1988)—12(i)
Boone v. Grier, 142 Ariz. 178, 688 P.2d 1070 (Ct. App. Div. 1 1984)—54(g)(4)
Boone v. Superior Court In and For Maricopa County, 145 Ariz. 235, 700 P.2d 1335 (1985)—11(c), 12(i)
Borbon v. City of Tucson, 27 Ariz. App. 550, 556 P.2d 1153 (Div. 2 1976)—801(d)(2)(E)
Borja v. Phoenix General Hosp., Inc., 151 Ariz. 302, 727 P.2d 355 (Ct. App. Div. 2 1986)—101(b)(6), 402, 802, 803
Bostwick v. Jasin, 170 Ariz. 15, 821 P.2d 282 (Ct. App. Div. 2 1991)—501, 601
Boswell v. Phoenix Newspapers, Inc., 152 Ariz. 1, 730 P.2d 178 (Ct. App. Div. 1 1985)—404(c)(4), 406
Bothell v. Two Point Acres, Inc., 192 Ariz. 313, 965 P.2d 47 (Ct. App. Div. 2 1998)—8(i)(8)
Bowen v. Graham, 140 Ariz. 593, 684 P.2d 165 (Ct. App. Div. 1 1984)—4.1(m)
Bowen Productions, Inc. v. French, 231 Ariz. 424, 296 P.3d 87 (Ct. App. Div. 1 2013)—8(i)(8), 26(h)
Bowling Machines, Inc. v. First Nat. Bank of Boston, 283 F.2d 39 (1st Cir. 1960)—54(g)(4)
Bowman v. Hall, 83 Ariz. 56, 316 P.2d 484 (1957)—39(q), 611(c)(2)
Boy v. Fremont Indem. Co., 154 Ariz. 334, 742 P.2d 835 (Ct. App. Div. 1 1987)—201(f)
Boy v. I.T.T. Grinnell Corp., 150 Ariz. 526, 724 P.2d 612, Prod. Liab. Rep. (CCH) ¶ 10636, 61 A.L.R.4th 137 (Ct. App. Div. 1 1986)—403, 404(c)(4)
Boydston v. Strole Development Co., 193 Ariz. 47, 969 P.2d 653 (1998)—5(j)(2)(B)
Bradshaw v. Jasso-Barajas, 231 Ariz. 197, 291 P.3d 991 (Ct. App. Div. 1 2013)—68(h), 77(g)(4)
Bradshaw v. State Farm Mut. Auto. Ins. Co., 157 Ariz. 411, 758 P.2d 1313 (1988)—13(i), 51(d), 59(m), 103(e), 403, 408(b)
Braillard v. Maricopa County, 224 Ariz. 481, 232 P.3d 1263 (Ct. App. Div. 2 2010)—26(h)
Brand v. Dolgin, 17 Ariz. App. 154, 496 P.2d 144 (Div. 1 1972)—12(i)
Brand v. J. H. Rose Trucking Co., 102 Ariz. 201, 427 P.2d 519 (1967)—50(d)

Brandt v. Daman Trailer Sales, Inc., 116 Ariz. 421, 569 P.2d 851 (Ct. App. Div. 2 1977)—55(f)

Braun v. Moreno, 11 Ariz. App. 509, 466 P.2d 60 (Div. 2 1970)—59(m)

Brazee v. Morris, 68 Ariz. 224, 204 P.2d 475 (1949)—8(i)(8)

Breitbart-Napp v. Napp, 216 Ariz. 74, 163 P.3d 1024 (Ct. App. Div. 1 2007)—26.1(g), 60(d)

Brennan v. Western Sav. and Loan Ass'n, 22 Ariz. App. 293, 526 P.2d 1248 (Div. 1 1974)—4.1(m), 10(f)

Brethauer v. General Motors Corp., 221 Ariz. 192, 211 P.3d 1176 (Ct. App. Div. 1 2009)—51(d), 59(m), 401(b), 403, 703

Brewer v. Gerson, 190 Ariz. 164, 945 P.2d 1295 (1997)—58(g), 69

Bridgestone/Firestone North America Tire, L.L.C. v. Naranjo, 206 Ariz. 447, 79 P.3d 1206, Prod. Liab. Rep. (CCH) ¶ 16845 (Ct. App. Div. 2 2003)—8(i)(8), 13(i), 14(b), 16.2(c), 69

Briskman v. Del Monte Mortg. Co., 10 Ariz. App. 263, 458 P.2d 130 (Div. 1 1969)—56(h)(3)

Bristol v. Moser, 55 Ariz. 185, 99 P.2d 706 (1940)—17(j)

Britt v. Steffen, 220 Ariz. 265, 205 P.3d 357 (Ct. App. Div. 1 2008)—11(c), 54(g)(4)

Broemmer v. Abortion Services of Phoenix, Ltd., 173 Ariz. 148, 840 P.2d 1013, 24 A.L.R.5th 793 (1992)—56(h)(3), 72(e)(7)

Bromley Group, Ltd. v. Arizona Dept. of Revenue, 170 Ariz. 532, 826 P.2d 1158 (Ct. App. Div. 1 1991)—54(g)(4)

Brooker v. Hunter, 22 Ariz. App. 510, 528 P.2d 1269 (Div. 1 1974)—30(h)(i), 32(d)(4)

Brooks v. Consolidated Freightways Corp. of Delaware, 173 Ariz. 66, 839 P.2d 1111 (Ct. App. Div. 1 1992)—60(d)

Brooks v. De La Cruz, 12 Ariz. App. 591, 473 P.2d 793 (Div. 1 1970)—59(m), 60(d)

Brooks v. Neer, 46 Ariz. 144, 47 P.2d 452 (1935)—801(d)(2)(E)

Brooks v. Zahn, 170 Ariz. 545, 826 P.2d 1171 (Ct. App. Div. 1 1991)—47(g), 49(h), 59(m), 606(b)(2)(C)

Brosie v. Stockton, 105 Ariz. 574, 468 P.2d 933 (1970)—12(i)

Brown v. Babbitt Ford, Inc., 117 Ariz. 192, 571 P.2d 689, 23 U.C.C. Rep. Serv. 266 (Ct. App. Div. 1 1977)—54(g)(4), 69

Brown v. Brown, 15 Ariz. App. 333, 488 P.2d 689 (Div. 1 1971)—53(k)

Brown v. General Foods Corp., 117 Ariz. 530, 573 P.2d 930 (Ct. App. Div. 1 1978)—401(b), 406

Brown v. Industrial Com'n of Arizona, 199 Ariz. 521, 19 P.3d 1237 (Ct. App. Div. 2 2001)—8(i)(8)

Brown v. Sears, Roebuck & Co., 136 Ariz. 556, 667 P.2d 750 (Ct. App. Div. 1 1983)—702(d)

Brown v. Superior Court In and For Maricopa County, 137 Ariz. 327, 670 P.2d 725 (1983)—26(h), 501

Brown v. U.S. Fidelity and Guar. Co., 194 Ariz. 85, 977 P.2d 807 (Ct. App. Div. 1 1998)—16(h), 39(q), 50(d), 51(d), 59(m), 103(e), 104(e), 401(b), 403, 404(c)(4), 611(c)(2)

Bruce Church, Inc. v. Superior Court In and For County of Yuma, 160 Ariz. 514, 774 P.2d 818 (Ct. App. Div. 1 1989)—62(j)

C

Cacho v. Superior Court In and For County of Maricopa, 170 Ariz. 30, 821 P.2d 721 (1991)—12(i)

Cactus Corp. v. State ex rel. Murphy, 14 Ariz. App. 38, 480 P.2d 375 (Div. 2 1971)—38(d)

Cagle v. Carr, 101 Ariz. 225, 418 P.2d 381 (1966)—15(d)

Cagle v. Home Ins. Co., 14 Ariz. App. 360, 483 P.2d 592 (Div. 1 1971)—56(h)(3)

Calderon v. Calderon, 9 Ariz. App. 538, 454 P.2d 586 (1969)—16(h)

Caldwell v. Tilford, 90 Ariz. 202, 367 P.2d 239 (1961)—103(e)

Caldwell v. Tremper, 90 Ariz. 241, 367 P.2d 266 (1962)—59(m)

Callan v. Bernini, 213 Ariz. 257, 141 P.3d 737 (Ct. App. Div. 2 2006)—56(h)(3)

Callanan v. Sun Lakes Homeowners' Ass'n No. 1, Inc., 134 Ariz. 332, 656 P.2d 621 (Ct. App. Div. 1 1982)—23.1

Callender v. Transpacific Hotel Corp., 179 Ariz. 557, 880 P.2d 1103 (Ct. App. Div. 2 1993)—58(g), 59(m)

Calligaro, Estate of v. Owen, 159 Ariz. 498, 768 P.2d 660 (Ct. App. Div. 1 1988)—601

Cal X-Tra v. W.V.S.V. Holdings, L.L.C., 229 Ariz. 377, 276 P.3d 11 (Ct. App. Div. 1 2012)—404(c)(4), 801(d)(2)(E), 901(b)(10)

Camacho v. Gardner, 104 Ariz. 555, 456 P.2d 925 (1969)—55(f)

Cambridge Co., Ltd. v. Arizona Lawn Sprinklers, Inc., 166 Ariz. 269, 801 P.2d 504 (Ct. App. Div. 2 1990)—56(h)(3)

Campbell v. Deddens, 21 Ariz. App. 295, 518 P.2d 1012 (Div. 2 1974)—15(d)

Campbell v. Deddens, 93 Ariz. 247, 379 P.2d 963 (1963)—38.1(k)(3)

Campbell v. Mahany, 127 Ariz. 332, 620 P.2d 711 (Ct. App. Div. 2 1980)—408(b)

Campbell v. Superior Court In and For Pinal County, 18 Ariz. App. 216, 501 P.2d 57 (Div. 2 1972)—201(f)

Campbell v. SZL Properties, Ltd., 204 Ariz. 221, 62 P.3d 966 (Ct. App. Div. 1 2003)—8(i)(8)

Canal Ins. Co. v. Pizer, 183 Ariz. 162, 901 P.2d 1192 (Ct. App. Div. 1 1995)—22(b), 54(g)(4), 58(g)

C & J Travel, Inc. v. Shumway, 161 Ariz. 33, 775 P.2d 1097 (Ct. App. Div. 2 1989)—17(j), 69

Cannon v. Hirsch Law Office, P.C., 222 Ariz. 171, 213 P.3d 320 (Ct. App. Div. 1 2009)—8(i)(8)

Cano v. Neill, 12 Ariz. App. 562, 473 P.2d 487 (Div. 1 1970)—59(m)

Canyon Contracting Co. v. Tohono O'Odham Housing Authority, 172 Ariz. 389, 837 P.2d 750 (Ct. App. Div. 1 1992)—29, 80(i)

Canyon del Rio Investors, L.L.C. v. City of Flagstaff, 227 Ariz. 336, 258 P.3d 154 (Ct. App. Div. 1 2011)—12(i), 57

Capin v. S & H Packing Co., Inc., 130 Ariz. 441, 636 P.2d 1223 (Ct. App. Div. 2 1981)—9(i)(9)

Cardon v. Cotton Lane Holdings, Inc., 173 Ariz. 203, 841 P.2d 198 (1992)—56(h)(3)

Cardona v. Kreamer, 225 Ariz. 143, 235 P.3d 1026 (2010)—4.2(m)

Cargill, Inc. v. Sabine Trading & Shipping Co., Inc., 756 F.2d 224, 1985 A.M.C. 1634, 40 Fed. R. Serv. 2d 1476 (2d Cir. 1985)—12(i)

Carlisle v. Petrosky, 212 Ariz. 323, 131 P.3d 495 (Ct. App. Div. 1 2006)—77(g)(4)

Carlson v. Brown, 118 Ariz. 387, 576 P.2d 1387 (Ct. App. Div. 1 1978)—12(i)

Carlson v. Tucson Racquet and Swim Club, Inc., 127 Ariz. 247, 619 P.2d 756 (Ct. App. Div. 2 1980)—704(b)
Carlton v. Emhardt, 138 Ariz. 353, 674 P.2d 907 (Ct. App. Div. 2 1983)—16(h)
Carman v. Hefter, 136 Ariz. 597, 667 P.2d 1312 (1983)—41(d), 411
Carondelet Health Network v. Miller, 221 Ariz. 614, 212 P.3d 952 (Ct. App. Div. 2 2009)—501
Carpinteiro v. Tucson School Dist. No. 1 of Pima County, 18 Ariz. App. 283, 501 P.2d 459 (Div. 2 1972)—23(f)
Carrillo v. State, 169 Ariz. 126, 817 P.2d 493 (Ct. App. Div. 1 1991)—15(d)
Carrillo v. Taylor, 81 Ariz. 14, 299 P.2d 188 (1956)—601
Carter-Glogau Laboratories, Inc. v. Construction, Production & Maintenance Laborers' Local 383, 153 Ariz. 351, 736 P.2d 1163, 126 L.R.R.M. (BNA) 2752 (Ct. App. Div. 1 1986)—103(e)
Cashway Concrete & Materials v. Sanner Contracting Co., 158 Ariz. 81, 761 P.2d 155 (Ct. App. Div. 2 1988)—801(d)(2)(E)
Cassell v. General Motors Corp., 154 Ariz. 75, 740 P.2d 496 (Ct. App. Div. 2 1987)—404(c)(4)
Cassidy's Estate, In re, 77 Ariz. 288, 270 P.2d 1079 (1954)—9(i)(9), 12(i)
Catalina Foothills Ass'n, Inc. v. White, 132 Ariz. 427, 646 P.2d 312 (Ct. App. Div. 2 1982)—60(d)
Catchings v. City of Glendale, 154 Ariz. 420, 743 P.2d 400 (Ct. App. Div. 2 1987)—39(q), 611(c)(2)
Catrone v. Miles, 215 Ariz. 446, 160 P.3d 1204, 220 Ed. Law Rep. 925 (Ct. App. Div. 1 2007)—501
Cavanagh v. Ohio Farmers Ins. Co., 20 Ariz. App. 38, 509 P.2d 1075 (Div. 2 1973)—901(b)(10)
C.B. v. Sabalos ex rel. County of Pima, 198 Ariz. 115, 7 P.3d 124 (Ct. App. Div. 2 2000)—26(h), 501
CBM of Arizona, Inc. v. Sevier, 184 Ariz. 503, 910 P.2d 654 (Ct. App. Div. 2 1996)—17(j), 19(d), 58(g), 69
CDT, Inc. v. Addison, Roberts & Ludwig, C.P.A., P.C., 198 Ariz. 173, 7 P.3d 979 (Ct. App. Div. 2 2000)—8(i)(8)
Cella Barr Associates, Inc. v. Cohen, 177 Ariz. 480, 868 P.2d 1063 (Ct. App. Div. 1 1994)—8(i)(8), 13(i), 14(b), 16.2(c)
Center Bay Gardens, L.L.C. v. City of Tempe City Council, 214 Ariz. 353, 153 P.3d 374 (Ct. App. Div. 1 2007)—12(i), 56(h)(3)
Central Arizona Light & Power Co. v. Akers, 45 Ariz. 526, 46 P.2d 126 (1935)—9(i)(9)
Central Cycle Sales, Inc. v. Obert, 23 Ariz. App. 378, 533 P.2d 686 (Div. 2 1975)—33(c)
Certainteed Corp. v. United Pacific Ins. Co., 158 Ariz. 273, 762 P.2d 560 (Ct. App. Div. 2 1988)—8(i)(8), 501
Cervantes v. Rijlaarsdam, 190 Ariz. 396, 949 P.2d 56 (Ct. App. Div. 2 1997)—104(e), 403, 411, 611(c)(2), 703, 705
Chaffin v. Commissioner of Arizona Dept. of Real Estate, 164 Ariz. 474, 793 P.2d 1141 (Ct. App. Div. 1 1990)—24(d)
Chalpin v. Snyder, 220 Ariz. 413, 207 P.3d 666 (Ct. App. Div. 1 2008)—10(f), 11(c), 56(h)(3)

Chambers v. Western Arizona CATV, 130 Ariz. 605, 638 P.2d 219 (1981)—50(d)

Champlin v. Bank of America, N.A., 231 Ariz. 265, 293 P.3d 541 (Ct. App. Div. 2 2013)—55(f)

Chanay v. Chittenden, 115 Ariz. 32, 563 P.2d 287 (1977)—56(h)(3)

Chandler Medical Bldg. Partners v. Chandler Dental Group, 175 Ariz. 273, 855 P.2d 787 (Ct. App. Div. 1 1993)—52(d), 56(h)(3)

Chaney Bldg. Co. v. City of Tucson, 148 Ariz. 571, 716 P.2d 28 (1986)—8(i)(8)

Chapman v. Levi-Strauss, 145 Ariz. 411, 701 P.2d 1219 (Ct. App. Div. 2 1985)—103(e), 403, 404(c)(4), 803

Chapman v. Municipal Court, City of Los Angeles, Los Angeles County, 91 Cal. App. 2d 689, 205 P.2d 712 (2d Dist. 1949)—59(m)

Chapman v. The Westerner, 220 Ariz. 52, 202 P.3d 517 (Ct. App. Div. 2 2008)—56(h)(3)

Chappell v. Wenholz, 226 Ariz. 309, 247 P.3d 192 (Ct. App. Div. 1 2011)—8(i)(8), 13(i), 14(b), 16.2(c)

Charles I. Friedman, P.C. v. Microsoft Corp., 213 Ariz. 344, 141 P.3d 824, 2006-2 Trade Cas. (CCH) ¶ 75406 (Ct. App. Div. 1 2006)—54(g)(4)

Chartone, Inc. v. Bernini, 207 Ariz. 162, 83 P.3d 1103 (Ct. App. Div. 2 2004)—38(d), 53(k)

Chase's Estate, Matter of, 125 Ariz. 270, 609 P.2d 85 (Ct. App. Div. 1 1980)—25(e)(2)

Chaurasia v. General Motors Corp., 212 Ariz. 18, 126 P.3d 165 (Ct. App. Div. 1 2006)—54(g)(4)

Chavez v. Pima County, 107 Ariz. 358, 488 P.2d 978 (1971)—607

Chavez v. State of Ind. for Logansport State Hospital, 122 Ariz. 560, 596 P.2d 698 (1979)—41(d)

Cheney v. Arizona Superior Court for Maricopa County, 144 Ariz. 446, 698 P.2d 691 (1985)—41(d)

Chess v. Pima County, 126 Ariz. 233, 613 P.2d 1289 (Ct. App. Div. 2 1980)—56(h)(3)

Chevron U.S.A., Inc. v. Thompson, 145 Ariz. 85, 699 P.2d 1316 (Ct. App. Div. 2 1985)—75(h), 77(g)(4)

Chino Valley, Town of v. State Land Dept., 119 Ariz. 243, 580 P.2d 704, 11 Env't. Rep. Cas. (BNA) 1668 (1978)—65(j)(6)

Chirco Const. Co., Inc. v. Stewart Title and Trust of Tucson, 129 Ariz. 187, 629 P.2d 1023 (Ct. App. Div. 2 1981)—14(b)

Cho v. American Bonding Co., 190 Ariz. 593, 951 P.2d 468 (Ct. App. Div. 1 1997)—9(i)(9), 54(g)(4), 60(d), 69

Choisser v. State ex rel. Herman, 12 Ariz. App. 259, 469 P.2d 493 (Div. 1 1970)—7.1(g), 56(h)(3)

Christmas v. Turkin, 148 Ariz. 602, 716 P.2d 59 (Ct. App. Div. 2 1986)—105

Chrysler Corp. v. McCarthy, 14 Ariz. App. 536, 484 P.2d 1065 (Div. 1 1971)—14(b)

Church v. Rawson Drug & Sundry Co., 173 Ariz. 342, 842 P.2d 1355 (Ct. App. Div. 1 1992)—8(i)(8), 13(i), 14(b), 16.2(c)

Church of Jesus Christ of Latter-Day Saints v. Superior Court In and For Maricopa County, 159 Ariz. 24, 764 P.2d 759 (Ct. App. Div. 1 1988)—501

Citibank (Arizona) v. Van Velzer, 194 Ariz. 358, 982 P.2d 833, 36 U.C.C. Rep. Serv. 2d 145 (Ct. App. Div. 2 1998)—56(h)(3)

Citibank (South Dakota), N.A. v. Phifer, 181 Ariz. 5, 887 P.2d 5 (Ct. App. Div. 2 1994)—8(i)(8), 69

Citizens' Committee for Recall of Jack Williams v. Marston, 109 Ariz. 188, 507 P.2d 113 (1973)—12(i)

City Consumer Services, Inc. v. Metcalf, 161 Ariz. 1, 775 P.2d 1065 (1989)—702(d)

Civil Rights Div. of Arizona Dept. of Law v. Amphitheater Unified School Dist. No. 10, 140 Ariz. 83, 680 P.2d 517, 17 Ed. Law Rep. 657, 33 Fair Empl. Prac. Cas. (BNA) 1135 (Ct. App. Div. 2 1983)—52(d)

Clark v. Clark, 124 Ariz. 235, 603 P.2d 506 (1979)—37(g)

Clark v. Wesendorf, 35 Ariz. 172, 275 P. 925 (1929)—9(i)(9)

Clark Equipment Co. v. Arizona Property and Cas. Ins. Guar. Fund, 189 Ariz. 433, 943 P.2d 793 (Ct. App. Div. 1 1997)—3

Clay v. Arizona Interscholastic Ass'n, Inc., 161 Ariz. 474, 779 P.2d 349, 56 Ed. Law Rep. 308 (1989)—65(j)(6)

Clayton v. Communications Capital Corp., 7 Ariz. App. 449, 440 P.2d 330 (1968)—52(d)

Clearwater v. State Farm Mut. Auto. Ins. Co., 161 Ariz. 590, 780 P.2d 423 (Ct. App. Div. 2 1989)—104(e), 702(d)

Cline v. Ticor Title Ins. Co. of California, 154 Ariz. 343, 742 P.2d 844 (Ct. App. Div. 1 1987)—38.1(k)(3), 60(d)

Clogher v. Winston and Strawn, 181 Ariz. 372, 891 P.2d 240 (Ct. App. Div. 2 1995)—17(j)

Clouse ex rel. Clouse v. State, 199 Ariz. 196, 16 P.3d 757 (2001)—3, 8(i)(8)

Coast to Coast Marketing Co., Inc. v. G & S Metal Products Co., Inc., 130 Ariz. 506, 637 P.2d 308 (Ct. App. Div. 2 1981)—12(i)

Coca-Cola Bottling Co. of Tucson v. Fitzgerald, 3 Ariz. App. 303, 413 P.2d 869 (1966)—702(d)

Cochise County v. Borowiec, 162 Ariz. 192, 781 P.2d 1379 (Ct. App. Div. 2 1989)—12(i)

Cochise County v. Broken Arrow Baptist Church, 161 Ariz. 406, 778 P.2d 1302 (Ct. App. Div. 2 1989)—65(j)(6)

Cochise County ex rel. Riley v. Board of Sup'rs of Cochise County, 7 Ariz. App. 571, 442 P.2d 129 (1968)—65(j)(6)

Cochise Hotels, Inc. v. Douglas Hotel Operating Co., 83 Ariz. 40, 316 P.2d 290 (1957)—13(i)

Coconino County v. Antco, Inc., 214 Ariz. 82, 148 P.3d 1155 (Ct. App. Div. 1 2006)—12(i)

Cohen v. Barnard, Vogler & Co., 199 Ariz. 16, 13 P.3d 758 (Ct. App. Div. 1 2000)—4.2(m)

Colboch v. Aviation Credit Corp., 64 Ariz. 88, 166 P.2d 584 (1946)—8(i)(8), 11(c), 12(i)

Cold Metal Process Co. v. United Engineering & Foundry Co., 76 S.Ct. 904, 351 U.S. 445, 100 L.Ed. 1311 (1956)—54(g)(4)

Coleman v. City of Mesa, 230 Ariz. 352, 284 P.3d 863 (2012)—3, 8(i)(8), 12(i)

Colfer v. Ballantyne, 89 Ariz. 408, 363 P.2d 588 (1961)—59(m)

Collins v. First Financial Services, Inc., 168 Ariz. 484, 815 P.2d 411 (Ct. App. Div. 1 1991)—54(g)(4)

Collins v. State, 37 Ariz. 353, 294 P. 625 (1930)—804(b)(6)

Collins, State ex rel. v. Seidel, 142 Ariz. 587, 691 P.2d 678 (1984)—101(b)(6)

Collins, State ex rel. v. Superior Court, In and For Maricopa County, 132 Ariz. 180, 644 P.2d 1266 (1982)—602

Collison v. International Ins. Co., 58 Ariz. 156, 118 P.2d 445 (1941)—1006

Colorado Cas. Ins. Co. v. Safety Control Co., Inc., 230 Ariz. 560, 288 P.3d 764 (Ct. App. Div. 1 2012)—17(j)

Columbia Group, Inc. v. Jackson, 151 Ariz. 86, 725 P.2d 1120 (Ct. App. Div. 2 1985)—5(j)(2)(B)

Colvin v. Westinghouse Elec. Corp., 79 Ariz. 275, 288 P.2d 490 (1955)—803

Combs v. Lufkin, 123 Ariz. 210, 598 P.2d 1029 (Ct. App. Div. 2 1979)—1004(d)

Comerica Bank v. Mahmoodi, 224 Ariz. 289, 229 P.3d 1031 (Ct. App. Div. 1 2010)—56(h)(3)

Commercial Credit Equipment Corp. v. Kelland, 101 Ariz. 477, 421 P.2d 325 (1966)—49(h)

Commercial Union Ins. Co. v. Lewis and Roca, 183 Ariz. 250, 902 P.2d 1354 (Ct. App. Div. 1 1995)—8(i)(8)

Conant v. Whitney, 190 Ariz. 290, 947 P.2d 864 (Ct. App. Div. 1 1997)—68(h), 104(e), 403

Condos v. Felder, 92 Ariz. 366, 377 P.2d 305 (1962)—601

Conkling v. Crosby, 29 Ariz. 60, 239 P. 506 (1925)—42(f)(3)(B)

Consolidated Motors v. Skousen, 56 Ariz. 481, 109 P.2d 41, 132 A.L.R. 1040 (1941)—406

Consolidated Tungsten Mines, Inc. v. Frazier, 87 Ariz. 128, 348 P.2d 734 (1960)—801(d)(2)(E), 803

Consolidated Zicam Product Liability Cases, In re, 212 Ariz. 85, 127 P.3d 903 (Ct. App. Div. 1 2006)—4.2(m), 12(i)

Continental Bank v. Guaranty Warehouse Corp., 153 Ariz. 522, 738 P.2d 1129 (Ct. App. Div. 2 1987)—104(e)

Continental Bank v. Wa-Ho Truck Brokerage, 122 Ariz. 414, 595 P.2d 206, 26 U.C.C. Rep. Serv. 101 (Ct. App. Div. 1 1979)—704(b), 705

Continental Cas. v. Superior Court, In and For Maricopa County, 130 Ariz. 189, 635 P.2d 174 (1981)—54(g)(4)

Continental Tel. Co. of the West v. Blazzard, 149 Ariz. 1, 716 P.2d 62 (Ct. App. Div. 2 1986)—803

Continental Townhouses East Unit One Ass'n v. Brockbank, 152 Ariz. 537, 733 P.2d 1120, 73 A.L.R.4th 921 (Ct. App. Div. 1 1986)—23(f)

Cook v. Great Western Bank & Trust, 141 Ariz. 80, 685 P.2d 145, 39 U.C.C. Rep. Serv. 214 (Ct. App. Div. 1 1984)—702(d), 704(b)

Cook v. Superior Court of Maricopa County, 135 Ariz. 1, 658 P.2d 801 (1983)—10(f), 15(d)

Cooney v. Phoenix Newspapers, Inc., 160 Ariz. 139, 770 P.2d 1185 (Ct. App. Div. 2 1989)—8(i)(8)

Coonley & Coonley v. Turck, 173 Ariz. 527, 844 P.2d 1177 (Ct. App. Div. 1 1993)—12(i)

D

Daou v. Harris, 139 Ariz. 353, 678 P.2d 934 (1984)—1, 55(f)
Darnell v. Denton, 137 Ariz. 204, 669 P.2d 981 (Ct. App. Div. 2 1983)—60(d)
Darner Motor Sales, Inc. v. Universal Underwriters Ins. Co., 140 Ariz. 383, 682 P.2d 388 (1984)—8(i)(8), 104(e)
Darragh v. Superior Court In and For County of Maricopa, 183 Ariz. 79, 900 P.2d 1215 (Ct. App. Div. 1 1995)—56(h)(3)
Dart v. Western Sav. & Loan Ass'n, 103 Ariz. 170, 438 P.2d 407 (1968)—66(d)
Daru v. Martin, 89 Ariz. 373, 363 P.2d 61 (1961)—63
Daubert v. Merrell Dow Pharmaceuticals, Inc., 509 U.S. 579, 113 S. Ct. 2786, 125 L. Ed. 2d 469, 27 U.S.P.Q.2d 1200, Prod. Liab. Rep. (CCH) ¶ 13494, 37 Fed. R. Evid. Serv. 1, 23 Envtl. L. Rep. 20979 (1993)—702(d)
Daugherty v. Montgomery Ward, 102 Ariz. 267, 428 P.2d 419 (1967)—50(d)
Davidson v. All State Materials Co., 101 Ariz. 375, 419 P.2d 732 (1966)—12(i)
Davidson-Chudacoff/Kol-Pak of Arizona, Inc. v. Pioneer Hotel Co., 129 Ariz. 254, 630 P.2d 550 (Ct. App. Div. 1 1981)—64
Davies v. Courtney, 11 Ariz. App. 248, 463 P.2d 554 (Div. 2 1970)—54(g)(4)
Davis v. Alaska, 415 U.S. 308, 94 S. Ct. 1105, 39 L. Ed. 2d 347 (1974)—609(e)
Davis v. Cessna Aircraft Corp., 168 Ariz. 301, 812 P.2d 1119 (Ct. App. Div. 1 1991)—54(g)(4)
Davis v. Cessna Aircraft Corp., 182 Ariz. 26, 893 P.2d 26, Prod. Liab. Rep. (CCH) ¶ 14038 (Ct. App. Div. 1 1994)—702(d), 703, 803
Davis v. Davis, 143 Ariz. 54, 691 P.2d 1082 (1984)—60(d)
Davis v. Davis, 195 Ariz. 158, 985 P.2d 643 (Ct. App. Div. 1 1999)—8(i)(8), 59(m), 63
Davis v. Davis, 230 Ariz. 333, 284 P.3d 23 (Ct. App. Div. 1 2012)—4(i)
Davis v. Discount Tire Co., 182 Ariz. 571, 898 P.2d 520 (Ct. App. Div. 1 1995)—68(h)
Davis v. Weber, 93 Ariz. 312, 380 P.2d 608 (1963)—50(d), 601
Dawe v. City of Scottsdale, 119 Ariz. 486, 581 P.2d 1136 (1978)—58(g), 60(d)
Dawson v. Lail, 1 Ariz. 490, 3 P. 399 (1884)—58(g)
Dawson v. Withycombe, 216 Ariz. 84, 163 P.3d 1034 (Ct. App. Div. 1 2007)—50(d), 51(d), 54(g)(4), 59(m)
Day v. Wiswall, 11 Ariz. App. 306, 464 P.2d 626 (Div. 2 1970)—2
Dayka & Hackett, LLC v. Del Monte Fresh Produce N.A., Inc., 228 Ariz. 533, 269 P.3d 709, 76 U.C.C. Rep. Serv. 2d 637 (Ct. App. Div. 2 2012)—44.1
Daystar Investments, L.L.C. v. Maricopa County Treasurer, 207 Ariz. 569, 88 P.3d 1181 (Ct. App. Div. 1 2004)—55(f)
Dean v. Superior Court In and For Maricopa County, 84 Ariz. 104, 324 P.2d 764, 73 A.L.R.2d 1 (1958)—26(h), 34(c), 501
Decca Design Build, Inc. v. American Auto. Ins. Co., 206 Ariz. 301, 77 P.3d 1251 (Ct. App. Div. 1 2003)—8(i)(8)
Decker v. Ramenofsky, 91 Ariz. 97, 370 P.2d 258 (1962)—703
Decola v. Freyer, 198 Ariz. 28, 6 P.3d 333 (Ct. App. Div. 1 2000)—38.1(k)(3), 58(g), 76(g), 77(g)(4)
DeElena v. Southern Pac. Co., 121 Ariz. 563, 592 P.2d 759 (1979)—104(e), 402
Deer Valley Unified School Dist. No. 97 v. Houser, 214 Ariz. 293, 152 P.3d 490, 25 I.E.R. Cas. (BNA) 1491 (2007)—3

DeForest v. DeForest, 143 Ariz. 627, 694 P.2d 1241 (Ct. App. Div. 1 1985)—58(g), 105, 408(b), 605, 803

DeHoney v. Hernandez, 122 Ariz. 367, 595 P.2d 159 (1979)—55(f)

Deike v. Great Atlantic & Pac. Tea Co., 3 Ariz. App. 430, 415 P.2d 145 (1966)—804(b)(6)

Delbridge v. Salt River Project Agr. Imp. and Power Dist., 182 Ariz. 46, 893 P.2d 46 (Ct. App. Div. 1 1994)—60(d)

Del Castillo v. Wells, 22 Ariz. App. 41, 523 P.2d 92 (Div. 1 1974)—1, 38(d)

DeLoach v. Alfred, 192 Ariz. 28, 960 P.2d 628 (1998)—8(i)(8)

Delozier v. Evans, 158 Ariz. 490, 763 P.2d 986 (Ct. App. Div. 1 1988)—301, 403, 404(c)(4), 804(b)(6)

DeMontiney v. Desert Manor Convalescent Center Inc., 144 Ariz. 6, 695 P.2d 255 (1985)—51(d)

Denbo v. Badger, 18 Ariz. App. 426, 503 P.2d 384 (Div. 2 1972)—9(i)(9)

Denton, Matter of Guardianship/Conservatorship of, 190 Ariz. 152, 945 P.2d 1283 (1997)—25(e)(2)

DeSela, Estate of v. Prescott Unified School Dist. No. 1, 226 Ariz. 387, 249 P.3d 767, 265 Ed. Law Rep. 1241 (2011)—3, 12(i)

Desert Mountain Properties Ltd. Partnership v. Liberty Mut. Fire Ins. Co., 225 Ariz. 194, 236 P.3d 421 (Ct. App. Div. 1 2010)—50(d)

Desert Wide Cabling & Installation, Inc. v. Wells Fargo & Co., N.A., 191 Ariz. 516, 958 P.2d 457 (Ct. App. Div. 1 1998)—64, 69

Desilva v. Baker, 208 Ariz. 597, 96 P.3d 1084 (Ct. App. Div. 1 2004)—54(g)(4)

Devenir Associates v. City of Phoenix, 169 Ariz. 500, 821 P.2d 161 (1991)—58(g)

Dewey v. Arnold, 159 Ariz. 65, 764 P.2d 1124 (Ct. App. Div. 2 1988)—15(d)

Deyoe v. Clark Equipment Co., Inc., 134 Ariz. 281, 655 P.2d 1333 (Ct. App. Div. 2 1982)—39(q), 49(h), 103(e), 611(c)(2)

Diamond v. Kenner, 140 Ariz. 524, 683 P.2d 323 (Ct. App. Div. 2 1984)—56(h)(3)

Dietz v. General Elec. Co., 169 Ariz. 505, 821 P.2d 166 (1991)—8(i)(8), 13(i), 14(b), 16.2(c), 26(h)

Dietz v. Waller, 141 Ariz. 107, 685 P.2d 744 (1984)—50(d)

Diggs Realty and Ins. v. Pertile, 114 Ariz. 85, 559 P.2d 205 (Ct. App. Div. 2 1977)—76(g)

Digirolamo v. Superior Court In and For County of Mohave, 173 Ariz. 7, 839 P.2d 427 (Ct. App. Div. 1 1991)—6(f), 68(h)

Di Pietruntonio v. Superior Court In and For Maricopa County, 84 Ariz. 291, 327 P.2d 746 (1958)—26(h)

Dixon v. Feffer, 84 Ariz. 308, 327 P.2d 994 (1958)—8(i)(8), 18(b)

Dixon v. Picopa Const. Co., 160 Ariz. 251, 772 P.2d 1104 (1989)—4(i), 4.1(m), 4.2(m)

Dodge City Motors, Inc. v. Rogers, 16 Ariz. App. 24, 490 P.2d 853 (Div. 1 1971)—50(d)

Doe v. Roe, 191 Ariz. 313, 955 P.2d 951 (1998)—8(i)(8)

Doe ex rel. Doe v. State, 200 Ariz. 174, 24 P.3d 1269, 155 Ed. Law Rep. 1424 (2001)—12(i)

Dolezal v. Carbrey, 161 Ariz. 365, 778 P.2d 1261 (Ct. App. Div. 1 1989)—56(h)(3)

Dombey v. Phoenix Newspapers, Inc., 147 Ariz. 61, 708 P.2d 742, 12 Media L. Rep. (BNA) 1201 (Ct. App. Div. 1 1985)—17(j)

Double AA Builders, Ltd. v. Grand State Const. L.L.C., 210 Ariz. 503, 114 P.3d 835 (Ct. App. Div. 1 2005)—54(g)(4)

Douglas v. Governing Bd. of Window Rock Consol. School Dist. No. 8, 206 Ariz. 344, 78 P.3d 1065, 182 Ed. Law Rep. 624 (Ct. App. Div. 1 2003)—12(i)

Douglas v. Governing Bd. of Window Rock Consol. School Dist. No. 8, 221 Ariz. 104, 210 P.3d 1275, 246 Ed. Law Rep. 435 (Ct. App. Div. 1 2009)—23(f), 68(h)

Douglas v. Lease Investors, Inc., 19 Ariz. App. 87, 504 P.2d 1310 (Div. 2 1973)—55(f)

Douglas N. Higgins, Inc. v. Songer, 171 Ariz. 8, 827 P.2d 469 (Ct. App. Div. 1 1991)—15(d), 69

Dowling v. Stapley, 218 Ariz. 80, 179 P.3d 960, 230 Ed. Law Rep. 794 (Ct. App. Div. 1 2008)—65(j)(6)

Dowling v. Stapley, 221 Ariz. 251, 211 P.3d 1235 (Ct. App. Div. 1 2009)—24(d)

Downs v. Ziegler, 13 Ariz. App. 387, 477 P.2d 261 (Div. 1 1970)—36(c)

Drahos v. Rens, 149 Ariz. 248, 717 P.2d 927 (Ct. App. Div. 2 1985)—58(g)

Dressler v. Morrison, 212 Ariz. 279, 130 P.3d 978 (2006)—12(i)

Drozda v. McComas, 181 Ariz. 82, 887 P.2d 612 (Ct. App. Div. 1 1994)—68(h)

Drumwright v. Lynn Engineering & Mfg., Inc., 14 Ariz. App. 282, 482 P.2d 891 (Div. 1 1971)—803

Dube v. Desai, 218 Ariz. 362, 186 P.3d 587, 233 Ed. Law Rep. 954 (Ct. App. Div. 2 2008)—3, 56(h)(3)

Dube v. Likins, 216 Ariz. 406, 167 P.3d 93, 224 Ed. Law Rep. 408 (Ct. App. Div. 2 2007)—12(i)

Duke v. Cochise County, 189 Ariz. 35, 938 P.2d 84 (Ct. App. Div. 2 1996)—59(m), 68(h)

Dunahay v. Struzik, 96 Ariz. 246, 393 P.2d 930 (1964)—59(m)

Dunbar v. Dunbar, 102 Ariz. 352, 429 P.2d 949 (1967)—8(i)(8)

Duncan v. Mack, 59 Ariz. 36, 122 P.2d 215 (1942)—704(b), 1002

Duncan v. State, 157 Ariz. 56, 754 P.2d 1160 (Ct. App. Div. 2 1988)—59(m)

Dungan v. Superior Court In and For Pinal County, 20 Ariz. App. 289, 512 P.2d 52 (Div. 2 1973)—55(f)

Dunham v. Pima County, 161 Ariz. 304, 778 P.2d 1200 (1989)—702(d), 704(b)

Dunipace v. Martin, 73 Ariz. 415, 242 P.2d 543 (1952)—47(g), 411

Dunlap v. City of Phoenix, 169 Ariz. 63, 817 P.2d 8 (Ct. App. Div. 1 1990)—7.1(g)

Dunlap v. Fort Mohave Farms, Inc., 89 Ariz. 387, 363 P.2d 194 (1961)—8(i)(8)

Dunlap v. Jimmy GMC of Tucson, Inc., 136 Ariz. 338, 666 P.2d 83 (Ct. App. Div. 2 1983)—49(h), 403, 404(c)(4)

Dunn v. Carruth, 162 Ariz. 478, 784 P.2d 684 (1989)—12(i)

Dunn v. Law Offices of Ramon R. Alvarez, P. C., 119 Ariz. 437, 581 P.2d 282 (Ct. App. Div. 2 1978)—60(d)

Dunn v. Maras, 182 Ariz. 412, 897 P.2d 714 (Ct. App. Div. 1 1995)—51(d), 59(m), 606(b)(2)(C)

Dunn By and Through Dunn v. Superior Court In and For County of Maricopa, 160 Ariz. 311, 772 P.2d 1164 (Ct. App. Div. 1 1989)—42(f)(3)(B)

Duquette v. Superior Court In and For County of Maricopa, 161 Ariz. 269, 778 P.2d 634 (Ct. App. Div. 1 1989)—26(h), 501

E

El Mirage, Town of v. Industrial Commission of Arizona, 127 Ariz. 377, 621 P.2d 286 (Ct. App. Div. 1 1980)—611(c)(2)

ELM Retirement Center, LP v. Callaway, 226 Ariz. 287, 246 P.3d 938 (Ct. App. Div. 1 2010)—12(i)

Emblen v. Southern Adjustment Bureau, Inc., 1 Ariz. App. 359, 403 P.2d 294 (1965)—9(i)(9)

Embry v. General Motors Corp., 115 Ariz. 433, 565 P.2d 1294 (Ct. App. Div. 2 1977)—611(c)(2)

Emergency Care Dynamics, Ltd. v. Superior Court In and For County of Maricopa, 188 Ariz. 32, 932 P.2d 297, 1997-2 Trade Cas. (CCH) ¶ 71929 (Ct. App. Div. 1 1997)—26(h), 501, 702(d)

Emmett McLoughlin Realty, Inc. v. Pima County, 203 Ariz. 557, 58 P.3d 39 (Ct. App. Div. 2 2002)—12(i)

Employers' Liability Assur. Corp. v. Glens Falls Ins. Co., 12 Ariz. App. 362, 470 P.2d 682 (Div. 2 1970)—54(g)(4)

Employers Mut. Cas. Co. v. McKeon, 170 Ariz. 75, 821 P.2d 766 (Ct. App. Div. 1 1991)—58(g)

Employers Mut. Liability Ins. Co. of Wis. v. Advance Transformer Co., 15 Ariz. App. 1, 485 P.2d 591 (Div. 2 1971)—13(i), 14(b)

Encinas v. Pompa, 189 Ariz. 157, 939 P.2d 435, R.I.C.O. Bus. Disp. Guide (CCH) ¶ 9287 (Ct. App. Div. 1 1997)—1, 82

Eng v. Stein, 123 Ariz. 343, 599 P.2d 796 (1979)—301

Engel v. Landman, 221 Ariz. 504, 212 P.3d 842 (Ct. App. Div. 1 2009)—54(g)(4)

Engineers v. Sharpe, 117 Ariz. 413, 573 P.2d 487 (1977)—59(m)

Engle v. Scott, 57 Ariz. 383, 114 P.2d 236 (1941)—25(e)(2)

Engle Bros., Inc. v. Superior Court In and For Pima County, 23 Ariz. App. 406, 533 P.2d 714 (Div. 2 1975)—12(i)

Englehart v. Jeep Corp., 122 Ariz. 256, 594 P.2d 510 (1979)—301, 702(d)

Englert v. Carondelet Health Network, 199 Ariz. 21, 13 P.3d 763 (Ct. App. Div. 2 2000)—26.1(g), 37(g), 59(m)

English-Clark v. City of Tucson, 142 Ariz. 522, 690 P.2d 1235 (Ct. App. Div. 2 1984)—805

Enterprise Leasing Co. of Phoenix v. Ehmke, 197 Ariz. 144, 3 P.3d 1064, 15 I.E.R. Cas. (BNA) 1496, 55 U.S.P.Q.2d 1303, 139 Lab. Cas. (CCH) ¶ 58794 (Ct. App. Div. 1 1999)—52(d)

Enyart v. Transamerica Ins. Co., 195 Ariz. 71, 985 P.2d 556 (Ct. App. Div. 1,1998)—8(i)(8)

Equal Employment Opportunity Commission v. Wah Chang Albany Corp., 499 F.2d 187, 8 Fair Empl. Prac. Cas. (BNA) 203, 8 Empl. Prac. Dec. (CCH) ¶ 9477, 18 Fed. R. Serv. 2d 1099 (9th Cir. 1974)—8(i)(8), 9(i)(9)

Equitable Life & Cas. Ins. Co. v. Rutledge, 9 Ariz. App. 551, 454 P.2d 869 (1969)—56(h)(3)

Erickson v. Waller, 116 Ariz. 476, 569 P.2d 1374 (Ct. App. Div. 1 1977)—703, 804(b)(6)

Escamilla v. Cuello, 230 Ariz. 202, 282 P.3d 403 (2012)—702(d), 703

Escobar v. Superior Court of State of Ariz. In and For Maricopa County, 155 Ariz. 298, 746 P.2d 39 (Ct. App. Div. 1 1987)—601

ESI Ergonomic Solutions, LLC v. United Artists Theatre Circuit, Inc., 203 Ariz. 94, 50 P.3d 844 (Ct. App. Div. 1 2002)—23(f)

Espinoza v. Schulenburg, 212 Ariz. 215, 129 P.3d 937 (2006)—56(h)(3)

Esplendido Apartments v. Metropolitan Condominium Ass'n of Arizona II, 158 Ariz. 487, 763 P.2d 983 (Ct. App. Div. 2 1988)—50(d)

Esplendido Apartments v. Metropolitan Condominium Ass'n of Arizona II, 161 Ariz. 325, 778 P.2d 1221 (1989)—59(m)

Esquivel v. Nancarrow, 104 Ariz. 209, 450 P.2d 399 (1969)—701(c)

Estes Co. v. Aztec Const., Inc., 139 Ariz. 166, 677 P.2d 939 (Ct. App. Div. 1 1983)—14(b)

Ethington v. Wright, 66 Ariz. 382, 189 P.2d 209 (1948)—25(e)(2)

Evans v. Arthur, 139 Ariz. 362, 678 P.2d 943 (1984)—55(f)

Evans v. Bernhard, 23 Ariz. App. 413, 533 P.2d 721 (Div. 1 1975)—602

Evans v. Mason, 82 Ariz. 40, 308 P.2d 245, 65 A.L.R.2d 936 (1957)—2

Evans v. Scottsdale Plumbing Co., 10 Ariz. App. 184, 457 P.2d 724 (Div. 1 1969)—5.1(d), 38.1(k)(3)

Evans Withycombe, Inc. v. Western Innovations, Inc., 215 Ariz. 237, 159 P.3d 547 (Ct. App. Div. 1 2006)—8(i)(8), 14(b)

Evergreen West, Inc. v. Boyd, 167 Ariz. 614, 810 P.2d 612 (Ct. App. Div. 2 1991)—3

Ewing v. Goettl's Metal Products Co., 116 Ariz. 484, 569 P.2d 1382 (Ct. App. Div. 1 1977)—14(b)

Executive Towers v. Leonard, 7 Ariz. App. 331, 439 P.2d 303 (1968)—56(h)(3)

Ezell v. Quon, 224 Ariz. 532, 233 P.3d 645 (Ct. App. Div. 1 2010)—60(d)

F

4501 Northpoint LP v. Maricopa County, 212 Ariz. 98, 128 P.3d 215 (2006)—54(g)(4), 68(h)

Fairway Constructors, Inc. v. Ahern, 193 Ariz. 122, 970 P.2d 954, 48 U.S.P.Q.2d 1951 (Ct. App. Div. 1 1998)—12(i)

Faith, Inc., People of v. Arizona Dept. of Revenue, 164 Ariz. 102, 791 P.2d 369 (Ct. App. Div. 1 1990)—54(g)(4)

Falcon v. Beverly Hills Mortg. Corp., 166 Ariz. 311, 802 P.2d 1010 (Ct. App. Div. 2 1990)—14(b)

Falcon v. Beverly Hills Mortg. Corp., 168 Ariz. 527, 815 P.2d 896 (1991)—58(g), 64

Falcon ex rel. Sandoval v. Maricopa County, 213 Ariz. 525, 144 P.3d 1254 (2006)—3, 4.1(m)

Farmers Ins. Co. v. Tallsalt, 191 Ariz. 177, 953 P.2d 921 (Ct. App. Div. 1 1997)—49(h)

Farmers Ins. Co. v. Tallsalt, 192 Ariz. 129, 962 P.2d 203 (1998)—77(g)(4)

Farmers Ins. Co. of Arizona v. Vagnozzi, 132 Ariz. 219, 644 P.2d 1305 (1982)—59(m)

Farris v. Advantage Capital Corp., 217 Ariz. 1, 170 P.3d 250 (2007)—3

Federal Housing Adm'r v. Christianson, 26 F. Supp. 419, 1 Fed. R. Serv. 304, 1 Fed. R. Serv. 305 (D. Conn. 1939)—18(b)

Federoff By and Through Roberts v. Aetna Cas. and Sur. Co., 163 Ariz. 371, 788 P.2d 104 (Ct. App. Div. 2 1989)—56(h)(3)
Fedie v. Travelodge Intern., Inc., 162 Ariz. 263, 782 P.2d 739 (Ct. App. Div. 2 1989)—50(d)
Fed Mart v. Industrial Com'n of Arizona, 135 Ariz. 533, 662 P.2d 1040 (Ct. App. Div. 1 1982)—54(g)(4)
Felder v. Physiotherapy Associates, 215 Ariz. 154, 158 P.3d 877 (Ct. App. Div. 1 2007)—26(h), 50(d)
Fendler v. Phoenix Newspapers Inc., 130 Ariz. 475, 636 P.2d 1257, 7 Media L. Rep. (BNA) 2569 (Ct. App. Div. 1 1981)—42(f)(3)(B)
Ferguson v. Superior Court of Maricopa County, 76 Ariz. 31, 258 P.2d 421 (1953)—66(d)
Fernandez v. Garza, 88 Ariz. 214, 354 P.2d 260 (1960)—60(d)
Fernandez v. Garza, 93 Ariz. 318, 380 P.2d 778 (1963)—56(h)(3)
Fernandez v. Takata Seat Belts, Inc., 210 Ariz. 138, 108 P.3d 917 (2005)—12(i), 23(f)
Ferris v. Hawkins, 135 Ariz. 329, 660 P.2d 1256 (Ct. App. Div. 1 1983)—8(i)(8)
Feuchter v. Bazurto, 22 Ariz. App. 427, 528 P.2d 178 (Div. 2 1974)—56(h)(3)
Fickett v. Superior Court of Pima County, 27 Ariz. App. 793, 558 P.2d 988 (Div. 2 1976)—36(c)
Fidelity and Deposit Co. of Maryland v. Bondwriter Southwest, Inc., 228 Ariz. 84, 263 P.3d 633 (Ct. App. Div. 1 2011)—8(i)(8), 26(h)
Fidelity Nat. Financial Inc. v. Friedman, 225 Ariz. 307, 238 P.3d 118 (2010)—69
Fidelity Sec. Life Ins. Co. v. State, Dept. of Ins., 191 Ariz. 222, 954 P.2d 580 (1998)—12(i)
Fields v. Oates, 230 Ariz. 411, 286 P.3d 160 (Ct. App. Div. 1 2012)—54(g)(4)
Financial Associates, Inc. v. Hub Properties, Inc., 143 Ariz. 543, 694 P.2d 831 (Ct. App. Div. 2 1984)—65(j)(6)
Finn v. J. H. Rose Truck Lines, 1 Ariz. App. 27, 398 P.2d 935 (1965)—32(d)(4)
First Bank of Ariz. v. Otis Elevator Co., 2 Ariz. App. 596, 411 P.2d 34 (1966)—14(b)
First Nat. Bank of Arizona v. Superior Court of Maricopa County, 112 Ariz. 292, 541 P.2d 392 (1975)—2
First Phoenix Realty Investments v. Superior Court In and For County of Maricopa, 173 Ariz. 265, 841 P.2d 1390 (Ct. App. Div. 1 1992)—66(d)
Fischer v. Sommer, 160 Ariz. 530, 774 P.2d 834 (Ct. App. Div. 1 1989)—60(d)
Flagstaff, City of v. Babbitt, 8 Ariz. App. 123, 443 P.2d 938 (1968)—12(i), 19(d)
Fleitz v. Van Westrienen, 114 Ariz. 246, 560 P.2d 430 (Ct. App. Div. 1 1977)—36(c), 56(h)(3), 702(d)
Fleming v. Becker, 14 Ariz. App. 347, 483 P.2d 579 (Div. 1 1971)—52(d)
Flexmaster Aluminum Awning Co., Inc. v. Hirschberg, 173 Ariz. 83, 839 P.2d 1128 (Ct. App. Div. 1 1992)—17(j), 19(d), 58(g), 69
Flieger v. Reeb, 120 Ariz. 31, 583 P.2d 1351 (Ct. App. Div. 2 1978)—59(m)
Flood Control Dist. of Maricopa County v. Gaines, 202 Ariz. 248, 43 P.3d 196 (Ct. App. Div. 1 2002)—3, 8(i)(8), 56(h)(3)
Flores v. Cooper Tire and Rubber Co., 218 Ariz. 52, 178 P.3d 1176, 36 Media L. Rep. (BNA) 1710 (Ct. App. Div. 1 2008)—501
Florez v. Sargeant, 185 Ariz. 521, 917 P.2d 250 (1996)—56(h)(3), 703, 705

Flory v. Silvercrest Industries, Inc., 129 Ariz. 574, 633 P.2d 383, 31 U.C.C. Rep. Serv. 1256 (1981)—59(m)
Floyd v. Donahue, 186 Ariz. 409, 923 P.2d 875 (Ct. App. Div. 1 1996)—8(i)(8)
Flynn v. Cornoyer-Hedrick Architects & Planners, Inc., 160 Ariz. 187, 772 P.2d 10 (Ct. App. Div. 1 1988)—38.1(k)(3), 41(d), 60(d)
Flynn v. Johnson, 3 Ariz. App. 369, 414 P.2d 757 (1966)—67(f)(3)
Flynn v. Rogers, 172 Ariz. 62, 834 P.2d 148 (1992)—8(i)(8)
Focal Point, Inc. v. Court of Appeals of State of Ariz., Div. One, 149 Ariz. 128, 717 P.2d 432 (1986)—54(g)(4), 58(g)
Folk v. City of Phoenix, 27 Ariz. App. 146, 551 P.2d 595 (Div. 1 1976)—3, 8(i)(8), 12(i)
Foman v. Davis, 371 U.S. 178, 83 S. Ct. 227 (1962)—15(d)
Food for Health Co., Inc. v. 3839 Joint Venture, 129 Ariz. 103, 628 P.2d 986 (Ct. App. Div. 1 1981)—12(i)
Foremost-McKesson Corp. v. Allied Chemical Co., 140 Ariz. 108, 680 P.2d 818 (Ct. App. Div. 2 1983)—8(i)(8)
Forman v. Creighton School Dist. No. 14, 87 Ariz. 329, 351 P.2d 165 (1960)—611(c)(2)
Formento v. Encanto Business Park, 154 Ariz. 495, 744 P.2d 22 (Ct. App. Div. 2 1987)—801(d)(2)(E)
Forquer v. Pinal County, 22 Ariz. App. 266, 526 P.2d 1064 (Div. 1 1974)—58(g)
Foster v. Ames, 5 Ariz. App. 1, 422 P.2d 731 (1967)—58(g)
Foster v. Camelback Management Co., 132 Ariz. 462, 646 P.2d 893 (Ct. App. Div. 2 1982)—59(m), 606(b)(2)(C)
Foster v. Thunderbird Irr. Water Delivery Dist. of Pinal County No. 3, 125 Ariz. 324, 609 P.2d 594 (Ct. App. Div. 2 1980)—65(j)(6)
Foster ex rel. Foster v. Weir, 212 Ariz. 193, 129 P.3d 482 (Ct. App. Div. 2 2006)—54(g)(4)
Fotinos v. Baker, 164 Ariz. 447, 793 P.2d 1114 (Ct. App. Div. 2 1990)—8(i)(8)
Foulk v. Kotz, 138 Ariz. 159, 673 P.2d 799 (Ct. App. Div. 2 1983)—401(b), 411, 607, 608(b)(2), 611(c)(2)
Fox v. Weissbach, 76 Ariz. 91, 259 P.2d 258 (1953)—801(d)(2)(E)
Francisco v. State, 113 Ariz. 427, 556 P.2d 1 (1976)—4(i), 4.2(m)
Frank v. Solomon, 94 Ariz. 55, 381 P.2d 591 (1963)—8(i)(8), 15(d)
Franzi v. Superior Court of Arizona In and For Pima County, 139 Ariz. 556, 679 P.2d 1043 (1984)—101(b)(6), 1101(d)
Frazer, Ryan, Goldberg, Keyt and Lawless v. Smith, 184 Ariz. 181, 907 P.2d 1384 (Ct. App. Div. 1 1995)—64
Frazier v. Industrial Com'n of Arizona, 145 Ariz. 488, 702 P.2d 717 (Ct. App. Div. 1 1985)—301
Freeman v. Sorchych, 226 Ariz. 242, 245 P.3d 927 (Ct. App. Div. 1 2011)—77(g)(4)
Freese v. Bassett Furniture Industries, 78 Ariz. 70, 275 P.2d 758 (1954)—59(m)
French v. Angelic, 137 Ariz. 244, 669 P.2d 1021 (Ct. App. Div. 1 1983)—55(f)
Frick's Estate, In re, 13 Ariz. App. 247, 475 P.2d 732 (Div. 1 1970)—50(d)
Fridena v. Evans, 127 Ariz. 516, 622 P.2d 463, 12 A.L.R.4th 46 (1980)—51(d), 301, 601, 801(d)(2)(E)
Fridena v. Maricopa County, 18 Ariz. App. 527, 504 P.2d 58 (Div. 1 1972)—58(g)

G

GM Development Corp. v. Community American Mortg. Corp., 165 Ariz. 1, 795 P.2d 827 (Ct. App. Div. 1 1990)—30(h)(i), 31(d), 33(c), 33.1(f)(3)(ii), 34(c), 36(c), 54(g)(4), 56(h)(3), 803

Godbey v. Roosevelt School Dist. No. 66 of Maricopa County, 131 Ariz. 13, 638 P.2d 235, 1 Ed. Law Rep. 1326, 25 Wage & Hour Cas. (BNA) 1011 (Ct. App. Div. 1 1981)—23(f)

Goddard, State ex rel. v. Gravano, 210 Ariz. 101, 108 P.3d 251 (Ct. App. Div. 1 2005)—54(g)(4)

Godwin v. Farmers Ins. Co. of America, 129 Ariz. 416, 631 P.2d 571 (Ct. App. Div. 1 1981)—702(d)

Goff v. Superior Courts In and For Pima and Maricopa Counties, 2 Ariz. App. 344, 409 P.2d 60 (1965)—12(i)

Golder v. Department of Revenue, State Bd. of Tax Appeals, 123 Ariz. 260, 599 P.2d 216 (1979)—601, 702(d)

Goldthorpe v. Farmers Ins. Exchange, 19 Ariz. App. 366, 507 P.2d 978 (Div. 2 1973)—103(e)

Golleher v. Horton, 119 Ariz. 604, 583 P.2d 260 (Ct. App. Div. 1 1978)—16(h), 37(g)

Golonka v. General Motors Corp., 204 Ariz. 575, 65 P.3d 956, Prod. Liab. Rep. (CCH) ¶ 16561 (Ct. App. Div. 1 2003)—50(d), 103(e)

Gomez v. Leverton, 19 Ariz. App. 604, 509 P.2d 735, 85 A.L.R.3d 158 (Div. 2 1973)—12(i)

Gomez v. Maricopa County, 175 Ariz. 469, 857 P.2d 1323 (Ct. App. Div. 1 1993)—17(j)

Gonzales v. Arizona Public Service Co., 161 Ariz. 84, 775 P.2d 1148 (Ct. App. Div. 2 1989)—9(i)(9), 17(j), 59(m), 401(b)

Gonzales v. City of Tucson, 124 Ariz. 450, 604 P.2d 1161 (Ct. App. Div. 2 1979)—49(h), 607

Gonzales v. Whitney, 90 Ariz. 324, 367 P.2d 668 (1961)—1

Gonzalez v. Gonzalez, 181 Ariz. 32, 887 P.2d 562 (Ct. App. Div. 2 1994)—49(h)

Gonzalez v. Satrustegui, 178 Ariz. 92, 870 P.2d 1188 (Ct. App. Div. 1 1993)—56(h)(3), 1004(d)

Gonzalez v. Tidelands Motor Hotel Co., Inc., 123 Ariz. 217, 598 P.2d 1036 (Ct. App. Div. 2 1979)—10(f)

Gonzalez-Burgueno v. National Indem. Co., 134 Ariz. 383, 656 P.2d 1244 (Ct. App. Div. 2 1982)—24(d)

Good v. City of Glendale, 150 Ariz. 218, 722 P.2d 386 (Ct. App. Div. 2 1986)—103(e), 402, 702(d)

Goodman v. Cushman, 92 Ariz. 276, 376 P.2d 394 (1962)—23.1

Goodman v. Gordon, 103 Ariz. 538, 447 P.2d 230 (1968)—41(d)

Goodman v. Samaritan Health System, 195 Ariz. 502, 990 P.2d 1061 (Ct. App. Div. 1 1999)—11(c), 54(g)(4)

Gordinier v. Aetna Cas. & Sur. Co., 154 Ariz. 266, 742 P.2d 277 (1987)—104(e)

Gordon v. Industrial Commission, 23 Ariz. App. 457, 533 P.2d 1194 (Div. 1 1975)—501

Gordon v. Liguori, 182 Ariz. 232, 895 P.2d 523 (Ct. App. Div. 1 1995)—33(c), 408(b), 801(d)(2)(E)

Gorman v. City of Phoenix, 152 Ariz. 179, 731 P.2d 74 (1987)—38.1(k)(3), 60(d)

Gorman v. Pima County, 230 Ariz. 506, 287 P.3d 800 (Ct. App. Div. 2 2012)—8(i)(8)

Gorney v. Meaney, 214 Ariz. 226, 150 P.3d 799 (Ct. App. Div. 2 2007)—56(h)(3)

Gosewisch v. American Honda Motor Co., Inc., 153 Ariz. 389, 737 P.2d 365, Prod. Liab. Rep. (CCH) ¶ 10819 (Ct. App. Div. 2 1985)—611(c)(2), 703, 807

Gosewisch v. American Honda Motor Co., Inc., 153 Ariz. 400, 737 P.2d 376, Prod. Liab. Rep. (CCH) ¶ 11531, 83 A.L.R.4th 53 (1987)—51(d), 103(e)

Gould v. Tibshraeny, 21 Ariz. App. 146, 517 P.2d 104 (Div. 1 1973)—10(f)

Gove, In re Marriage of, 117 Ariz. 324, 572 P.2d 458 (Ct. App. Div. 1 1977)—37(g)

Goy v. Jones, 205 Ariz. 421, 72 P.3d 351 (Ct. App. Div. 1 2003)—803

Graber v. City of Peoria, 156 Ariz. 553, 753 P.2d 1209 (Ct. App. Div. 2 1988)—50(d)

Graf v. Whitaker, 192 Ariz. 403, 966 P.2d 1007 (Ct. App. Div. 1 1998)—1, 75(h), 77(g)(4)

Grafitti-Valenzuela ex rel. Grafitti v. City of Phoenix, 216 Ariz. 454, 167 P.3d 711 (Ct. App. Div. 1 2007)—56(h)(3)

Graham v. Goodyear Aerospace Corp., Arizona Division, 120 Ariz. 275, 585 P.2d 884 (Ct. App. Div. 1 1978)—15(d)

Graham v. Shooke, 107 Ariz. 79, 482 P.2d 446 (1971)—2, 39(q)

Grain Dealers Mut. Ins. Co. v. James, 118 Ariz. 116, 575 P.2d 315 (1978)—56(h)(3)

Grand v. Cigna Property and Cas. Companies, 172 Ariz. 419, 837 P.2d 1154 (Ct. App. Div. 2 1992)—56(h)(3)

Grand v. Nacchio, 214 Ariz. 9, 147 P.3d 763, Blue Sky L. Rep. (CCH) ¶ 74608 (Ct. App. Div. 2 2006)—56(h)(3)

Grand v. Nacchio, 225 Ariz. 171, 236 P.3d 398, Blue Sky L. Rep. (CCH) ¶ 74862 (2010)—15(d)

Grand Canyon Trust v. Arizona Corp. Com'n, 210 Ariz. 30, 107 P.3d 356 (Ct. App. Div. 1 2005)—54(g)(4)

Granger v. Wisner, 134 Ariz. 377, 656 P.2d 1238 (1982)—37(g), 501, 702(d)

Grant v. Arizona Public Service Co., 133 Ariz. 434, 652 P.2d 507 (1982)—16(h), 51(d), 59(m), 103(e), 401(b), 404(c)(4), 407

Gravel Resources of Arizona v. Hills, 217 Ariz. 33, 170 P.3d 282 (Ct. App. Div. 1 2007)—66(d)

Graville v. Dodge, 195 Ariz. 119, 985 P.2d 604 (Ct. App. Div. 1 1999)—54(g)(4)

Gray v. Dillon, 97 Ariz. 16, 396 P.2d 251 (1964)—55(f)

Gray v. Woods, 84 Ariz. 87, 324 P.2d 220 (1958)—703

Greco v. Manolakos, 24 Ariz. App. 490, 539 P.2d 964 (Div. 2 1975)—26(h)

Green v. Bock Laundry Mach. Co., 490 U.S. 504, 109 S. Ct. 1981, 104 L. Ed. 2d 557, 27 Fed. R. Evid. Serv. 577 (1989)—609(e)

Green v. Lisa Frank, Inc., 221 Ariz. 138, 211 P.3d 16 (Ct. App. Div. 2 2009)—9(i)(9), 65(j)(6)

Green v. Nygaard, 213 Ariz. 460, 143 P.3d 393 (Ct. App. Div. 2 2006)—26(h), 501

Green Reservoir Flood Control Dist. v. Willmoth, 15 Ariz. App. 406, 489 P.2d 69 (Div. 2 1971)—15(d), 58(g), 60(d)

Greenwald v. Ford Motor Co., 196 Ariz. 123, 993 P.2d 1087 (Ct. App. Div. 1 1999)—68(h)

Griffis v. Pinal County, 213 Ariz. 300, 141 P.3d 780 (Ct. App. Div. 2 2006)—65(j)(6)

Grimm v. Arizona Bd. of Pardons and Paroles, 115 Ariz. 260, 564 P.2d 1227, 5 A.L.R.4th 757 (1977)—26(h)

Groat v. Equity American Ins. Co., 180 Ariz. 342, 884 P.2d 228 (Ct. App. Div. 1 1994)—30(h)(i), 37(g), 64

Grobe v. McBryde, 105 Ariz. 577, 468 P.2d 936 (1970)—10(f), 15(d)

Groener v. Briehl, 135 Ariz. 395, 661 P.2d 659 (Ct. App. Div. 1 1983)—701(c), 704(b)

Grossman v. Westmoreland II Investors, 123 Ariz. 223, 599 P.2d 179 (1979)—501

Groves v. Sorce, 161 Ariz. 619, 780 P.2d 452 (Ct. App. Div. 2 1989)—69

Grubb & Ellis Management Services, Inc. v. 407417 B.C., L.L.C., 213 Ariz. 83, 138 P.3d 1210 (Ct. App. Div. 1 2006)—14(b)

G.T. Helicopters, Inc. v. Helicopters, Ltd., 135 Ariz. 380, 661 P.2d 230 (Ct. App. Div. 1 1983)—4.2(m)

Guberman v. Chatwin, 19 Ariz. App. 590, 509 P.2d 721 (Div. 1 1973)—42(f)(3)(B)

Guerrero v. Copper Queen Hospital, 112 Ariz. 104, 537 P.2d 1329 (1975)—8(i)(8)

Guertin v. Dixon, 177 Ariz. 40, 864 P.2d 1072 (Ct. App. Div. 2 1993)—8(i)(8)

Guilford Nat. Bank of Greensboro v. Southern Ry. Co., 297 F.2d 921, 5 Fed. R. Serv. 2d 575 (4th Cir. 1962)—26(h)

Guinn v. Schweitzer, 190 Ariz. 116, 945 P.2d 837 (Ct. App. Div. 1 1997)—77(g)(4)

Gulf Homes, Inc. v. Beron, 141 Ariz. 624, 688 P.2d 632 (1984)—37(g)

Gull v. Constam, 105 F. Supp. 107 (D. Colo. 1952)—9(i)(9)

Guminski v. Arizona State Veterinary Medical Examining Bd., 201 Ariz. 180, 33 P.3d 514 (Ct. App. Div. 1 2001)—12(i)

Gunnell v. Arizona Public Service Co., 202 Ariz. 388, 46 P.3d 399 (2002)—8(i)(8), 13(i), 14(b), 16.2(c), 56(h)(3)

Guo v. Maricopa County Medical Center, 196 Ariz. 11, 992 P.2d 11, 5 Wage & Hour Cas. 2d (BNA) 1864, 139 Lab. Cas. (CCH) ¶ 58812 (Ct. App. Div. 1 1999)—56(h)(3)

Gustafson v. McDade, 26 Ariz. App. 322, 548 P.2d 415 (Div. 1 1976)—55(f)

Gust, Rosenfeld & Henderson v. Prudential Ins. Co. of America, 182 Ariz. 586, 898 P.2d 964 (1995)—8(i)(8)

Gutierrez v. Gutierrez, 20 Ariz. App. 388, 513 P.2d 677 (Div. 2 1973)—58(g), 60(d)

Gutierrez v. Gutierrez, 193 Ariz. 343, 972 P.2d 676 (Ct. App. Div. 1 1998)—301

H

Haab v. County of Maricopa, 219 Ariz. 9, 191 P.3d 1025 (Ct. App. Div. 1 2008)—3, 56(h)(3)

Hackin v. First Nat. Bank of Ariz., Phoenix, 5 Ariz. App. 379, 427 P.2d 360 (1967)—5.1(d)

Hackin v. Gaynes, 103 Ariz. 13, 436 P.2d 127 (1968)—1003

Hackin v. Pioneer Plumbing Supply Co., 10 Ariz. App. 150, 457 P.2d 312 (1969)—38(d)

Hackin v. Rupp, 9 Ariz. App. 354, 452 P.2d 519 (1969)—56(h)(3), 80(i)

Haechler v. Andrews, 2 Ariz. App. 395, 409 P.2d 315 (1965)—58(g)

Hahman v. Hahman, 129 Ariz. 101, 628 P.2d 984 (Ct. App. Div. 2 1981)—501

Hales v. Humana of Arizona, Inc., 186 Ariz. 375, 923 P.2d 841 (Ct. App. Div. 2 1996)—68(h)

Hall v. Keller, 9 Ariz. App. 584, 455 P.2d 266 (1969)—103(e)
Hall v. Lalli, 191 Ariz. 104, 952 P.2d 748 (Ct. App. Div. 2 1997)—8(i)(8), 54(g)(4)
Hall v. Read Development, Inc., 229 Ariz. 277, 274 P.3d 1211 (Ct. App. Div. 1 2012)—54(g)(4), 68(h)
Hall v. Romero, 141 Ariz. 120, 685 P.2d 757 (Ct. App. Div. 1 1984)—9(i)(9)
Hall v. World Sav. and Loan Ass'n, 189 Ariz. 495, 943 P.2d 855 (Ct. App. Div. 1 1997)—69
Hall Family Properties, Ltd. v. Gosnell Development Corp., 185 Ariz. 382, 916 P.2d 1098 (Ct. App. Div. 1 1995)—39(q), 49(h), 58(g)
Hallmark v. Allied Products Corp., 132 Ariz. 434, 646 P.2d 319 (Ct. App. Div. 1 1982)—51(d), 403, 407, 606(b)(2)(C)
Hamilton Mines Corp. v. Price, 14 Ariz. App. 186, 481 P.2d 872 (Div. 1 1971)—54(g)(4)
Hamman-McFarland Lumber Co. v. Arizona Equipment Rental Co., 16 Ariz. App. 188, 492 P.2d 437 (Div. 1 1972)—17(j)
Hammond v. A.J. Bayless Markets, 58 Ariz. 58, 117 P.2d 490 (1941)—65.1
Hammontree v. Kenworthy, 1 Ariz. App. 472, 404 P.2d 816 (1965)—39(q), 59(m)
Han v. Horwitz, 2 Ariz. App. 245, 407 P.2d 786 (1965)—32(d)(4), 39(q)
Hancock v. Linsenmeyer, 15 Ariz. App. 296, 488 P.2d 501 (Div. 1 1971)—59(m)
Hancock v. McCarroll, 188 Ariz. 492, 937 P.2d 682 (Ct. App. Div. 1 1996)—42(f)(3)(B)
Hanley v. Pearson, 204 Ariz. 147, 61 P.3d 29 (Ct. App. Div. 1 2003)—54(g)(4)
Hanner v. Hanner, 95 Ariz. 191, 388 P.2d 239 (1964)—53(k)
Hansson v. Arizona State Bd. of Dental Examiners, 195 Ariz. 66, 985 P.2d 551 (Ct. App. Div. 1 1998)—8(i)(8)
Harbel Oil Co. v. Steele, 81 Ariz. 104, 301 P.2d 757 (1956)—58(g)
Hardy v. Bankers Life & Cas. Co., 222 F.2d 827 (7th Cir.1955)—54(g)(4)
Harleysville Mut. Ins. Co. v. Lea, 2 Ariz. App. 538, 410 P.2d 495 (1966)—25(e)(2)
Harmon v. Harmon, 126 Ariz. 242, 613 P.2d 1298 (Ct. App. Div. 2 1980)—42(f)(3)(B)
Harmon v. Szrama, 102 Ariz. 343, 429 P.2d 662 (1967)—56(h)(3)
Harold Laz Advertising Co. v. Dumes, 2 Ariz. App. 236, 407 P.2d 777 (1965)—59(m), 60(d)
Haroutunian v. Valueoptions, Inc., 218 Ariz. 541, 189 P.3d 1114 (Ct. App. Div. 2 2008)—1, 6(f), 54(g)(4), 58(g), 60(d)
Harper v. Canyon Land Development, LLC, 219 Ariz. 535, 200 P.3d 1032 (Ct. App. Div. 1 2008)—60(d)
Harrington v. Beauchamp Enterprises, 158 Ariz. 118, 761 P.2d 1022 (1988)—51(d)
Harrington v. Flanders, 2 Ariz. App. 265, 407 P.2d 946 (1965)—25(e)(2)
Harrington v. Pulte Home Corp., 211 Ariz. 241, 119 P.3d 1044 (Ct. App. Div. 1 2005)—23(f), 104(e)
Harris v. Cochise Health Systems, 215 Ariz. 344, 160 P.3d 223 (Ct. App. Div. 2 2007)—3, 12(i)
Harris v. Harris, 195 Ariz. 559, 991 P.2d 262 (Ct. App. Div. 1 1999)—12(i), 59(m)
Harris v. Howard P. Foley Co., 2 Ariz. App. 389, 409 P.2d 309 (1965)—59(m)
Harris v. Reserve Life Ins. Co., 158 Ariz. 380, 762 P.2d 1334 (Ct. App. Div. 1 1988)—11(c), 41(d), 54(g)(4)

Harsh Bldg. Co. v. Bialac, 22 Ariz. App. 591, 529 P.2d 1185 (Div. 1 1975)—16(h)
Hartman v. Oatman Gold Min. & Mill. Co., 22 Ariz. 476, 198 P. 717 (1921)—54(g)(4)
Hash's Estate v. Henderson, 109 Ariz. 174, 507 P.2d 99 (1973)—58(g)
Hastings v. Thurston, 100 Ariz. 302, 413 P.2d 767 (1966)—37(g)
Hatch v. Hatch, 113 Ariz. 130, 547 P.2d 1044 (1976)—58(g), 60(d)
Hatch Companies Contracting, Inc. v. Arizona Bank, 170 Ariz. 553, 826 P.2d 1179 (Ct. App. Div. 1 1991)—3
Hauskins v. McGillicuddy, 175 Ariz. 42, 852 P.2d 1226 (Ct. App. Div. 1 1992)—3
Havasupai Tribe of Havasupai Reservation v. Arizona Bd. of Regents, 220 Ariz. 214, 204 P.3d 1063, 243 Ed. Law Rep. 889 (Ct. App. Div. 1 2008)—3, 8(i)(8), 56(h)(3)
Havasu Springs Resort Co. v. La Paz County, 199 Ariz. 349, 18 P.3d 143 (Ct. App. Div. 1 2001)—56(h)(3)
Hawkins v. Allstate Ins. Co., 152 Ariz. 490, 733 P.2d 1073 (1987)—103(e), 401(b), 404(c)(4)
Hawkins v. State, Dept. of Economic Sec., 183 Ariz. 100, 900 P.2d 1236, 68 Fair Empl. Prac. Cas. (BNA) 1178 (Ct. App. Div. 2 1995)—8(i)(8)
Hay v. Duskin, 9 Ariz. App. 599, 455 P.2d 281 (1969)—56(h)(3)
Haynes v. Anderson & Strudwick, Inc., 508 F. Supp. 1303, Fed. Sec. L. Rep. (CCH) ¶ 97905 (E.D. Va. 1981)—9(i)(9)
Haynes v. Syntek Finance Corp., 184 Ariz. 332, 909 P.2d 399 (Ct. App. Div. 1 1995)—15(d), 51(d)
Hays v. Fischer, 161 Ariz. 159, 777 P.2d 222 (Ct. App. Div. 1 1989)—80(i)
Haywood Securities, Inc. v. Ehrlich, 214 Ariz. 114, 149 P.3d 738 (2007)—1, 58(g)
Hazine v. Montgomery Elevator Co., 176 Ariz. 340, 861 P.2d 625, Prod. Liab. Rep. (CCH) ¶ 13676, 30 A.L.R.5th 729 (1993)—8(i)(8)
H.B.H. v. State Farm Fire and Cas. Co., 170 Ariz. 324, 823 P.2d 1332 (Ct. App. Div. 1 1991)—24(d)
HCZ Const., Inc. v. First Franklin Financial Corp., 199 Ariz. 361, 18 P.3d 155 (Ct. App. Div. 1 2001)—3
Health For Life Brands, Inc. v. Powley, 203 Ariz. 536, 57 P.3d 726 (Ct. App. Div. 1 2002)—12(i), 38(d)
Heatec, Inc. v. R.W. Beckett Corp., 219 Ariz. 293, 197 P.3d 754, Prod. Liab. Rep. (CCH) ¶ 18040 (Ct. App. Div. 1 2008)—54(g)(4)
Heaton v. Waters, 8 Ariz. App. 256, 445 P.2d 458 (1968)—59(m)
Heat Pump Equipment Co. v. Glen Alden Corp., 93 Ariz. 361, 380 P.2d 1016 (1963)—1
Heeter v. Moore Drug Co., 104 Ariz. 41, 448 P.2d 391 (1968)—39(q), 611(c)(2)
Hegel v. O'Malley Ins. Co., Inc., 122 Ariz. 52, 593 P.2d 275 (1979)—8(i)(8), 56(h)(3)
Hegel v. O'Malley Ins. Co., Inc., Agents and Brokers, 117 Ariz. 411, 573 P.2d 485 (1977)—59(m)
Heinig v. Hudman, 177 Ariz. 66, 865 P.2d 110 (Ct. App. Div. 1 1993)—8(i)(8), 19(d), 58(g), 69, 301
Helena Chemical Co. v. Coury Bros. Ranches, Inc., 126 Ariz. 448, 616 P.2d 908 (Ct. App. Div. 1 1980)—16(h), 26(h), 401(b), 607
Helge v. Druke, 136 Ariz. 434, 666 P.2d 534 (Ct. App. Div. 2 1983)—26(h), 45(g)

Helicopteros Nacionales de Colombia, S.A. v. Hall, 466 U.S. 408, 104 S. Ct. 1868, 80 L. Ed. 2d 404 (1984)—4.2(m)
Hellyer v. Hellyer, 129 Ariz. 453, 632 P.2d 263 (Ct. App. Div. 2 1981)—501, 801(d)(2)(E)
Henderson Realty v. Mesa Paving Co., Inc., 27 Ariz. App. 299, 554 P.2d 895 (Div. 1 1976)—14(b)
Hendrickson v. Superior Court In and For Cochise County, 85 Ariz. 10, 330 P.2d 507, 73 A.L.R.2d 1235 (1958)—42(f)(3)(B)
Henry ex rel. Estate of Wilson v. HealthPartners of Southern Arizona, 203 Ariz. 393, 55 P.3d 87 (Ct. App. Div. 2 2002)—59(m), 403, 408(b), 801(d)(2)(E)
Henson v. Triumph Trucking, Inc., 180 Ariz. 305, 884 P.2d 191 (Ct. App. Div. 2 1994)—404(c)(4), 608(b)(2), 703, 705
Herman, State ex rel. v. Tucson Title Ins. Co., 101 Ariz. 415, 420 P.2d 286 (1966)—59(m)
Hernandez v. Faker, 137 Ariz. 449, 671 P.2d 427 (Ct. App. Div. 2 1983)—703, 705
Hernandez v. Frohmiller, 68 Ariz. 242, 204 P.2d 854 (1949)—201(f)
Hernandez v. Maricopa County Superior Court, 108 Ariz. 422, 501 P.2d 6 (1972)—15(d)
Hernandez v. State, 203 Ariz. 196, 52 P.3d 765 (2002)—408(b)
Hernandez by Hernandez-Wheeler, Estate of v. Flavio, 187 Ariz. 506, 930 P.2d 1309, 115 Ed. Law Rep. 1067 (1997)—56(h)(3)
Herring v. Railway Exp. Agency, Inc., 13 Ariz. App. 28, 474 P.2d 35 (Div. 1 1970)—56(h)(3)
Herstam v. Deloitte & Touche, LLP, 186 Ariz. 110, 919 P.2d 1381 (Ct. App. Div. 1 1996)—13(i), 14(b), 16.2(c)
Heth v. Del Webb's Highway Inn, 102 Ariz. 330, 429 P.2d 442 (1967)—801(d)(2)(E)
Heuisler v. Phoenix Newspapers, Inc., 168 Ariz. 278, 812 P.2d 1096, 18 Media L. Rep. (BNA) 2305 (Ct. App. Div. 1 1991)—11(c), 56(h)(3)
Hibbs v. Calcot, Ltd., 166 Ariz. 210, 801 P.2d 445 (Ct. App. Div. 1 1990)—7.1(g)
Hibbs ex rel. Arizona Dept. of Revenue v. Chandler Ginning Co., 164 Ariz. 11, 790 P.2d 297 (Ct. App. Div. 1 1990)—12(i)
Hickman v. Taylor, 329 U.S. 495, 67 S. Ct. 385, 91 L. Ed. 451, 1947 A.M.C. 1 (1947)—26(h), 501
Hiett v. Howard, 17 Ariz. App. 1, 494 P.2d 1347 (Div. 1 1972)—51(d)
Higgins v. Arizona Sav. and Loan Ass'n, 90 Ariz. 55, 365 P.2d 476 (1961)—401(b), 803, 1002
Higgins v. Assmann Electronics, Inc., 217 Ariz. 289, 173 P.3d 453 (Ct. App. Div. 1 2007)—51(d), 59(m), 403
Highland Village Partners, L.L.C. v. Bradbury & Stamm Const. Co., Inc., 219 Ariz. 147, 195 P.3d 184 (Ct. App. Div. 1 2008)—56(h)(3)
High School Dist. No. 106, Pima County v. Civil Rights Division, 121 Ariz. 444, 590 P.2d 1390, 19 Empl. Prac. Dec. (CCH) ¶ 8986 (Ct. App. Div. 2 1979)—27(b)
Hilgeman v. American Mortg. Securities, Inc., 196 Ariz. 215, 994 P.2d 1030 (Ct. App. Div. 2 2000)—4(i), 4.2(m), 55(f), 60(d)
Hill v. Chubb Life American Ins. Co., 178 Ariz. 37, 870 P.2d 1133 (Ct. App. Div. 1 1993)—11(c)

Hill v. City of Phoenix, 193 Ariz. 570, 975 P.2d 700 (1999)—54(g)(4), 58(g)

Hill v. Favour, 52 Ariz. 561, 84 P.2d 575 (1938)—22(b)

Hill v. Safford Unified School Dist., 191 Ariz. 110, 952 P.2d 754, 124 Ed. Law Rep. 721 (Ct. App. Div. 2 1997)—56(h)(3)

Hill Bros. Chemical Co. v. Grandinetti, 123 Ariz. 84, 597 P.2d 987 (Ct. App. Div. 1 1979)—4(i), 22(b)

Himes v. Safeway Ins. Co., 205 Ariz. 31, 66 P.3d 74 (Ct. App. Div. 1 2003)—24(d)

Hine v. Superior Court In and For Yuma County, 18 Ariz. App. 568, 504 P.2d 509 (Div. 1 1972)—26(h), 33(c), 33.1(f)(3)(ii)

Hinson v. Phoenix Pie Co., 3 Ariz. App. 523, 416 P.2d 202 (1966)—103(e)

Hinton v. Hotchkiss, 65 Ariz. 110, 174 P.2d 749 (1946)—1

Hitching Post Lodge, Inc. v. Kerwin, 101 Ariz. 402, 420 P.2d 273 (1966)—15(d)

Hlavaty v. Song, 107 Ariz. 606, 491 P.2d 460 (1971)—50(d)

Hmielewski v. Maricopa County, 192 Ariz. 1, 960 P.2d 47 (Ct. App. Div. 1 1997)—11(c)

Hobson v. Mid-Century Ins. Co., 199 Ariz. 525, 19 P.3d 1241 (Ct. App. Div. 2 2001)—54(g)(4)

Hoffman v. Halden, 268 F.2d 280, 2 Fed. R. Serv. 2d 241 (9th Cir. 1959)—10(f)

Hogan v. Washington Mut. Bank, N.A., 230 Ariz. 584, 277 P.3d 781 (2012)—3, 8(i)(8)

Hohlenkamp v. Rheem Mfg. Co., 123 Ariz. 535, 601 P.2d 298 (Ct. App. Div. 2 1979)—702(d)

Hohlenkamp v. Rheem Mfg. Co., 134 Ariz. 208, 655 P.2d 32 (Ct. App. Div. 2 1982)—407

Hohokam Irr. and Drainage Dist. v. Arizona Public Service Co., 204 Ariz. 394, 64 P.3d 836 (2003)—56(h)(3)

Hollar v. Wright, 115 Ariz. 606, 566 P.2d 1352 (Ct. App. Div. 1 1977)—13(i), 41(d)

Holm Development and Management, Inc. v. Superior Court In and For County of Maricopa, 161 Ariz. 376, 778 P.2d 1272 (Ct. App. Div. 1 1989)—54(g)(4), 62(j)

Holmes v. Hoemako Hospital, 117 Ariz. 403, 573 P.2d 477, 7 A.L.R.4th 1231 (1977)—13(i), 14(b)

Holt v. Western Farm Services, Inc., 110 Ariz. 276, 517 P.2d 1272 (1974)—803

Home Builders Ass'n of Cent. Arizona v. City of Goodyear, 223 Ariz. 193, 221 P.3d 384 (Ct. App. Div. 1 2009)—801(d)(2)(E)

Home Builders Ass'n of Cent. Arizona v. Kard, 219 Ariz. 374, 199 P.3d 629 (Ct. App. Div. 1 2008)—3

Home Federal Sav. and Loan Ass'n v. Pleasants, 23 Ariz. App. 467, 534 P.2d 275 (Div. 2 1975)—23(f)

Home Indem. Co. v. Bush, 20 Ariz. App. 355, 513 P.2d 145 (Div. 1 1973)—9(i)(9)

Home Ins. Co. v. Balfour-Guthrie Ins. Co., 13 Ariz. App. 327, 476 P.2d 533 (Div. 1 1970)—15(d)

Hooper v. Truly Nolen of America, Inc., 171 Ariz. 692, 832 P.2d 709 (Ct. App. Div. 1 1992)—54(g)(4)

Horizon Corp. v. Home Ins. Co., 20 Ariz. App. 162, 511 P.2d 175, 68 A.L.R.3d 1064 (Div. 2 1973)—803

Horne v. Timbanard, 6 Ariz. App. 518, 434 P.2d 520 (1967)—8(i)(8), 59(m)

Horton v. Mitchell, 200 Ariz. 523, 29 P.3d 870 (Ct. App. Div. 1 2001)—52(d), 65(j)(6)

Hoskinson Through Fleming v. State of Cal., 168 Ariz. 250, 812 P.2d 1068 (Ct. App. Div. 2 1990)—4.2(m)

Hosogai v. Kadota, 145 Ariz. 227, 700 P.2d 1327 (1985)—41(d)

Hospital Corp. of America v. Superior Court of Pima County, 157 Ariz. 210, 755 P.2d 1198 (Ct. App. Div. 2 1988)—501

Hounshell v. White, 219 Ariz. 381, 199 P.3d 636 (Ct. App. Div. 1 2008)—54(g)(4)

Hovatter v. Shell Oil Co., 111 Ariz. 325, 529 P.2d 224 (1974)—201(f)

Howard v. Associated Grocers, 123 Ariz. 593, 601 P.2d 593 (1979)—64

Howard P. Foley Co. v. Harris, 10 Ariz. App. 78, 456 P.2d 398 (1969)—59(m)

Howell v. Hodap, 221 Ariz. 543, 212 P.3d 881 (Ct. App. Div. 1 2009)—8(i)(8)

Howland v. State, 169 Ariz. 293, 818 P.2d 1169 (Ct. App. Div. 1 1991)—3, 12(i)

Hoyle v. Superior Court In and For County of Maricopa, 161 Ariz. 224, 778 P.2d 259 (Ct. App. Div. 1 1989)—38(d)

HSL Linda Gardens Properties, Ltd. v. Freeman, 176 Ariz. 206, 859 P.2d 1339 (Ct. App. Div. 2 1993)—8(i)(8)

Hudgins v. Southwest Airlines, Co., 221 Ariz. 472, 212 P.3d 810 (Ct. App. Div. 1 2009)—51(d), 59(m), 403, 404(c)(4), 803

Hudlow v. American Estate Life Ins. Co., 22 Ariz. App. 246, 526 P.2d 770 (Div. 1 1974)—801(d)(2)(E), 803

Huerta v. Nelson, 222 Ariz. 44, 213 P.3d 193 (Ct. App. Div. 1 2009)—1, 42(f)(3)(B)

Huff v. Flynn, 48 Ariz. 175, 60 P.2d 931 (1936)—7(b)

Huggins v. Deinhard, 127 Ariz. 358, 621 P.2d 45 (Ct. App. Div. 1 1980)—50(d)

Hughes Air Corp. v. Maricopa County Superior Court, 114 Ariz. 412, 561 P.2d 736 (1977)—15(d), 201(f)

Hughes Aircraft Co v. Industrial Commission, 125 Ariz. 1, 606 P.2d 819 (Ct. App. Div. 1 1979)—8(i)(8)

Hullett v. Cousin, 204 Ariz. 292, 63 P.3d 1029 (2003)—8(i)(8)

Humana Hosp. Desert Valley v. Superior Court of Arizona In and For Maricopa County, 154 Ariz. 396, 742 P.2d 1382 (Ct. App. Div. 1 1987)—501

Hunter Contracting Co., Inc. v. Superior Court In and For County of Maricopa, 190 Ariz. 318, 947 P.2d 892 (Ct. App. Div. 1 1997)—8(i)(8), 56(h)(3)

Hunt Inv. Co. v. Eliot, 154 Ariz. 357, 742 P.2d 858 (Ct. App. Div. 1 1987)—17(j)

Hurst v. Hurst, 1 Ariz. App. 227, 401 P.2d 232 (1965)—54(g)(4)

Hurst v. Hurst, 1 Ariz. App. 603, 405 P.2d 913 (1965)—53(k)

Hurvitz v. Coburn, 117 Ariz. 300, 572 P.2d 128 (Ct. App. Div. 2 1977)—50(d)

Huskie v. Ames Bros. Motor and Supply Co., Inc., 139 Ariz. 396, 678 P.2d 977, 38 U.C.C. Rep. Serv. 618 (Ct. App. Div. 1 1984)—15(d)

Husky v. Lee, 2 Ariz. App. 129, 406 P.2d 847 (1965)—12(i)

Husky Fence Co., Inc. v. Industrial Com'n of Arizona, 138 Ariz. 21, 672 P.2d 973 (Ct. App. Div. 1 1983)—801(d)(2)(E)

Husky, State ex rel. v. Oaks, 3 Ariz. App. 174, 412 P.2d 743 (1966)—55(f)

Hutchens v. Linden, 159 Ariz. 388, 767 P.2d 1178 (Ct. App. Div. 2 1988)—22(b)

Hutcherson v. City of Phoenix, 188 Ariz. 183, 933 P.2d 1251 (Ct. App. Div. 1 1996)—59(m)

Hutcherson v. City of Phoenix, 192 Ariz. 51, 961 P.2d 449 (1998)—8(i)(8), 13(i), 14(b), 16.2(c), 54(g)(4), 58(g), 59(m)

Hyatt Regency Phoenix Hotel Co. v. Winston & Strawn, 184 Ariz. 120, 907 P.2d 506 (Ct. App. Div. 1 1995)—17(j), 54(g)(4), 58(g), 59(m)

Hydroculture, Inc. v. Coopers & Lybrand, 174 Ariz. 277, 848 P.2d 856 (Ct. App. Div. 1 1992)—56(h)(3)

Hyman v. Arden-Mayfair, Inc., 150 Ariz. 444, 724 P.2d 63 (Ct. App. Div. 1 1986)—38.1(k)(3), 60(d)

Hytken v. Wake, 68 P.3d 508 (Colo. App. 2002)—67(f)(3)

I

Ideal Food Products Co. v. Rupe, 76 Ariz. 175, 261 P.2d 992 (1953)—702(d)

Imperial-Yuma Production Credit Ass'n v. Nussbaumer, 22 Ariz. App. 485, 528 P.2d 871 (Div. 1 1974)—69

INA Ins. Co. of North America v. Valley Forge Ins. Co., 150 Ariz. 248, 722 P.2d 975 (Ct. App. Div. 1 1986)—14(b)

Indus. Com'n of Arizona, State ex rel. v. Galloway, 224 Ariz. 325, 230 P.3d 708 (Ct. App. Div. 1 2010)—69

Industrial Commission v. Holohan, 97 Ariz. 122, 397 P.2d 624 (1964)—34(c)

Industrial Commission v. Superior Court In and For Maricopa County, 122 Ariz. 374, 595 P.2d 166 (1979)—501

Industrial Commission v. Superior Court In and For Pima County, 5 Ariz. App. 100, 423 P.2d 375 (1967)—12(i)

Industrial Park Corp. v. U. S. I. F. Palo Verde Corp., 19 Ariz. App. 342, 507 P.2d 681 (Div. 1 1973)—54(g)(4)

Ingalls v. Superior Court in and for Pima County, 117 Ariz. 448, 573 P.2d 522 (Ct. App. Div. 2 1977)—26(h), 45(g), 408(b), 501

Ingrum v. Tucson Yellow Cab Co., 131 Ariz. 523, 642 P.2d 868 (Ct. App. Div. 2 1981)—701(c), 704(b)

International Life Ins. Co. v. Sorteberg, 70 Ariz. 92, 216 P.2d 702 (1950)—1002

Inter-Tel, Inc. v. Bank of America, Arizona, 195 Ariz. 111, 985 P.2d 596 (Ct. App. Div. 1 1999)—8(i)(8)

Irby Const. Co. v. Arizona Dept. of Revenue, 184 Ariz. 105, 907 P.2d 74 (Ct. App. Div. 1 1995)—8(i)(8)

Irwin v. Wright, 258 U.S. 219, 42 S. Ct. 293, 66 L. Ed. 573 (1922)—25(e)(2)

Isbell ex rel. Isbell v. State, 198 Ariz. 291, 9 P.3d 322 (2000)—401(b), 404(c)(4)

Ivancovich v. Meier, 122 Ariz. 346, 595 P.2d 24 (1979)—19(d)

J

Jackson v. American Credit Bureau, Inc., 23 Ariz. App. 199, 531 P.2d 932, 79 A.L.R.3d 841 (Div. 1 1975)—26(h)

Jackson v. Chandler, 204 Ariz. 135, 61 P.3d 17 (2003)—8(i)(8)

Jackson v. Mearig, 17 Ariz. App. 94, 495 P.2d 864 (Div. 1 1972)—59(m)

Jackson v. Sears, Roebuck & Co., 83 Ariz. 20, 315 P.2d 871, 65 A.L.R.2d 1158 (1957)—58(g)

Jacobson v. Laurel Canyon Mining Co., 27 Ariz. 546, 234 P. 823 (1925)—65.1

Jamas v. Krpan, 116 Ariz. 216, 568 P.2d 1114 (Ct. App. Div. 1 1977)—704(b)

James v. State, 215 Ariz. 182, 158 P.3d 905 (Ct. App. Div. 2 2007)—54(g)(4)
James, Cooke & Hobson, Inc. v. Lake Havasu Plumbing & Fire Protection, 177 Ariz. 316, 868 P.2d 329 (Ct. App. Div. 1 1993)—8(i)(8), 11(c), 56(h)(3)
J. & B. Motors v. Margolis, 75 Ariz. 392, 257 P.2d 588, 38 A.L.R.2d 946 (1953)—47(g), 408(b), 611(c)(2)
Janson on Behalf of Janson v. Christensen, 167 Ariz. 470, 808 P.2d 1222 (1991)—38.1(k)(3), 41(d), 60(d)
J.A.R. v. Superior Court In and For County of Maricopa, 179 Ariz. 267, 877 P.2d 1323 (Ct. App. Div. 1 1994)—24(d)
Jasper v. Batt, 76 Ariz. 328, 264 P.2d 409 (1953)—25(e)(2)
J.C. Penney v. Lane, 197 Ariz. 113, 3 P.3d 1033 (Ct. App. Div. 1 1999)—69
Jenkins v. First Baptist Church of Scottsdale, 166 Ariz. 243, 801 P.2d 478 (Ct. App. Div. 1 1990)—1
Jennings v. Superior Court in and for Los Angeles County, 134 Cal. App. 300, 25 P.2d 246 (2d Dist. 1933)—59(m)
Jepson v. New, 160 Ariz. 193, 772 P.2d 16 (Ct. App. Div. 1 1989)—41(d), 60(d)
Jepson v. New, 164 Ariz. 265, 792 P.2d 728 (1990)—38.1(k)(3), 41(d), 60(d)
Jerger v. Rubin, 106 Ariz. 114, 471 P.2d 726 (1970)—8(i)(8)
Jerman v. O'Leary, 145 Ariz. 397, 701 P.2d 1205 (Ct. App. Div. 2 1985)—54(g)(4)
Jeski v. American Exp. Co., 147 Ariz. 19, 708 P.2d 110 (Ct. App. Div. 1 1985)—104(e)
Jeune v. Del E. Webb Const. Co., 76 Ariz. 418, 265 P.2d 1076 (1954)—401(b), 602
Jilly v. Rayes, 221 Ariz. 40, 209 P.3d 176 (Ct. App. Div. 1 2009)—8(i)(8), 26.1(g)
Jimenez v. Sears, Roebuck and Co., 180 Ariz. 432, 885 P.2d 120, Prod. Liab. Rep. (CCH) ¶ 13925 (Ct. App. Div. 2 1994)—401(b)
Jimenez v. Sears, Roebuck and Co., 183 Ariz. 399, 904 P.2d 861, Prod. Liab. Rep. (CCH) ¶ 14382 (1995)—8(i)(8), 13(i), 14(b), 16.2(c)
Jimenez v. Wal-Mart Stores, Inc., 206 Ariz. 424, 79 P.3d 673 (Ct. App. Div. 2 2003)—26.1(g), 37(g), 59(m), 103(e)
JNS Holding Corp. v. Superior Court In and For County of Maricopa, 183 Ariz. 98, 900 P.2d 1234 (Ct. App. Div. 1 1995)—59(m)
Jobe v. King, 129 Ariz. 195, 629 P.2d 1031 (Ct. App. Div. 2 1981)—14(b)
Joel Erik Thompson, Ltd. v. Holder, 192 Ariz. 348, 965 P.2d 82 (Ct. App. Div. 1 1998)—8(i)(8)
John C. Lincoln Hosp. and Health Center v. Superior Court In and For County of Maricopa, 159 Ariz. 456, 768 P.2d 188 (Ct. App. Div. 1 1989)—501
John C. Lincoln Hosp. and Health Corp. v. Maricopa County, 208 Ariz. 532, 96 P.3d 530 (Ct. App. Div. 1 2004)—50(d), 52(d), 54(g)(4), 56(h)(3), 58(g), 59(m), 103(e), 1006
John F. Long Homes, Inc. v. Holohan, 97 Ariz. 31, 396 P.2d 394 (1964)—24(d)
Johnson v. Collins, 11 Ariz. App. 327, 464 P.2d 647 (Div. 2 1970)—56(h)(3)
Johnson v. Elliott, 112 Ariz. 57, 537 P.2d 927 (1975)—59(m), 103(e)
Johnson v. Elson, 192 Ariz. 486, 967 P.2d 1022 (Ct. App. Div. 1 1998)—60(d)
Johnson v. Harris, 23 Ariz. App. 103, 530 P.2d 1136 (Div. 2 1975)—606(b)(2)(C)
Johnson v. Johnson, 195 Ariz. 389, 988 P.2d 621 (Ct. App. Div. 1 1999)—8(i)(8), 69
Johnson v. Maehling, 123 Ariz. 15, 597 P.2d 1 (1979)—901(b)(10)

K

Kassman v. Busfield Enterprises, Inc., 131 Ariz. 163, 639 P.2d 353 (Ct. App. Div. 2 1981)—701(c)

Kaufmann v. Cruikshank, 222 Ariz. 488, 217 P.3d 438 (Ct. App. Div. 2 2009)—54(g)(4)

Kay v. Biggs, 13 Ariz. App. 172, 475 P.2d 1 (Div. 1 1970)—52(d)

Keck v. Kelley, 16 Ariz. App. 163, 492 P.2d 412 (Div. 1 1972)—8(i)(8)

Keeton v. Hustler Magazine, Inc., 465 U.S. 770, 104 S. Ct. 1473, 79 L. Ed. 2d 790, 10 Media L. Rep. (BNA) 1405 (1984)—4.2(m)

Keggi v. Northbrook Property and Cas. Ins. Co., 199 Ariz. 43, 13 P.3d 785 (Ct. App. Div. 1 2000)—57

Kelch v. Courson, 7 Ariz. App. 365, 439 P.2d 528 (1968)—26(h)

Kelch v. Courson, 103 Ariz. 576, 447 P.2d 550 (1968)—51(d), 59(m), 801(d)(2)(E)

Kellner v. Lewis, 130 Ariz. 465, 636 P.2d 1247 (Ct. App. Div. 2 1981)—10(f)

Kelman v. Bohi, 27 Ariz. App. 24, 550 P.2d 671 (Div. 1 1976)—49(h), 51(d), 56(h)(3)

Kelsey v. Kelsey, 186 Ariz. 49, 918 P.2d 1067 (Ct. App. Div. 1 1996)—52(d)

Kemp v. Pinal County, 8 Ariz. App. 41, 442 P.2d 864 (1968)—803

Kemp v. Pinal County, 13 Ariz. App. 121, 474 P.2d 840 (Div. 2 1970)—51(d)

Kennecott Copper Corp. v. McDowell, 100 Ariz. 276, 413 P.2d 749 (1966)—702(d)

Keonjian v. Olcott, 216 Ariz. 563, 169 P.3d 927 (Ct. App. Div. 2 2007)—8(i)(8), 54(g)(4), 56(h)(3)

Kerr v. Killian, 197 Ariz. 213, 3 P.3d 1133 (Ct. App. Div. 1 2000)—54(g)(4)

Kerwin v. Bank of Douglas, 93 Ariz. 269, 379 P.2d 978, 13 A.L.R.3d 398 (1963)—601

Keystone Floor & More, LLC v. Arizona Registrar of Contractors, 223 Ariz. 27, 219 P.3d 237 (Ct. App. Div. 1 2009)—54(g)(4)

Kiley v. Jennings, Strouss & Salmon, 187 Ariz. 136, 927 P.2d 796 (Ct. App. Div. 1 1996)—8(i)(8)

Killingsworth v. Nottingham, 18 Ariz. App. 356, 501 P.2d 1197 (Div. 2 1972)—803

Kim v. Mansoori, 214 Ariz. 457, 153 P.3d 1086 (Ct. App. Div. 2 2007)—54(g)(4)

King v. O'Rielly Motor Co., 16 Ariz. App. 518, 494 P.2d 718 (Div. 2 1972)—701(c)

King v. Superior Court, 138 Ariz. 147, 673 P.2d 787 (1983)—8(i)(8), 59(m)

King v. Superior Court In and For Maricopa County, 108 Ariz. 492, 502 P.2d 529, 60 A.L.R.3d 172 (1972)—42(f)(3)(B)

King v. Titsworth, 221 Ariz. 597, 212 P.3d 935 (Ct. App. Div. 1 2009)—7(b)

King v. Uhlmann, 103 Ariz. 136, 437 P.2d 928 (1968)—12(i), 19(d)

King & Johnson Rental Equipment Co. v. Superior Court, In and For Pima County, 123 Ariz. 256, 599 P.2d 212 (1979)—14(b), 49(h)

Kingman, City of v. Havatone, 14 Ariz. App. 585, 485 P.2d 574 (Div. 1 1971)—26(h), 30(h)(i)

Kirby v. Rosell, 133 Ariz. 42, 648 P.2d 1048 (Ct. App. Div. 1 1982)—59(m), 606(b)(2)(C)

Kirkland v. Bianco, 595 F. Supp. 797, 39 Fair Empl. Prac. Cas. (BNA) 1306 (S.D. N.Y. 1984)—9(i)(9)

Kirkpatrick v. Industrial Commission, 10 Ariz. App. 564, 460 P.2d 670 (Div. 1 1969)—34(c)

Klaiber v. Orzel, 148 Ariz. 320, 714 P.2d 813 (1986)—26(h), 501

Kline v. Kline, 221 Ariz. 564, 212 P.3d 902 (Ct. App. Div. 1 2009)—4.1(m), 5(j)(2)(B), 55(f), 501

Knox v. Knox, 137 Ariz. 494, 671 P.2d 935 (Ct. App. Div. 2 1983)—4(i)

Koenen v. Royal Buick Co., 162 Ariz. 376, 783 P.2d 822, 11 U.C.C. Rep. Serv. 2d 1096 (Ct. App. Div. 2 1989)—104(e)

Koepke v. Carter Hawley Hale Stores, Inc., 140 Ariz. 420, 682 P.2d 425 (Ct. App. Div. 1 1984)—60(d)

Koepnick v. Sears Roebuck & Co., 158 Ariz. 322, 762 P.2d 609 (Ct. App. Div. 1 1988)—59(m)

Kohlbeck v. Handley, 3 Ariz. App. 469, 415 P.2d 483, 21 A.L.R.3d 1248 (1966)—55(f)

Konow v. Southern Pac. Co., 105 Ariz. 386, 465 P.2d 366 (1970)—804(b)(6)

Kosidlo v. Kosidlo, 125 Ariz. 32, 607 P.2d 15 (Ct. App. Div. 2 1979)—615(e)

Kosman v. State, 199 Ariz. 184, 16 P.3d 211 (Ct. App. Div. 1 2000)—3, 8(i)(8)

Kostolansky v. Lesher, 95 Ariz. 103, 387 P.2d 804 (1963)—2, 39(q)

Kott v. City of Phoenix, 158 Ariz. 415, 763 P.2d 235 (1988)—26(h)

Koven v. Saberdyne Systems, Inc., 128 Ariz. 318, 625 P.2d 907 (Ct. App. Div. 1 1980)—55(f)

Kremser v. Quarles & Brady, L.L.P., 201 Ariz. 413, 36 P.3d 761 (Ct. App. Div. 1 2001)—12(i)

Kriz v. Buckeye Petroleum Co., Inc., 145 Ariz. 374, 701 P.2d 1182 (1985)—14(b), 201(f)

Kromko v. City of Tucson, 202 Ariz. 499, 47 P.3d 1137 (Ct. App. Div. 2 2002)—65(j)(6)

Kromko v. Superior Court In and For County of Maricopa, 168 Ariz. 51, 811 P.2d 12 (1991)—54(g)(4)

Krug v. Porter, 83 Ariz. 108, 317 P.2d 543 (1957)—59(m)

Kuhn v. St. Joseph's Hosp. and Medical Center, 194 Ariz. 465, 984 P.2d 551 (Ct. App. Div. 1 1998)—16(h)

Kuhnke v. Textron, Inc., 140 Ariz. 587, 684 P.2d 159 (Ct. App. Div. 1 1984)—50(d)

Kumho Tire Co., Ltd. v. Carmichael, 526 U.S. 137, 119 S. Ct. 1167, 143 L. Ed. 2d 238, 50 U.S.P.Q.2d 1177, Prod. Liab. Rep. (CCH) ¶ 15470, 50 Fed. R. Evid. Serv. 1373, 29 Envtl. L. Rep. 20638 (1999)—702(d)

Kyles v. Contractors/Engineers Supply, Inc., 190 Ariz. 403, 949 P.2d 63 (Ct. App. Div. 2 1997)—8(i)(8)

L

LaBombard v. Samaritan Health System, 195 Ariz. 543, 991 P.2d 246 (Ct. App. Div. 1 1998)—8(i)(8)

La Canada Hills Ltd. Partnership v. Kite, 217 Ariz. 126, 171 P.3d 195 (Ct. App. Div. 2 2007)—8(i)(8), 57

LaFaro v. Cahill, 203 Ariz. 482, 56 P.3d 56 (Ct. App. Div. 1 2002)—65(j)(6)

Lake v. Bonham, 148 Ariz. 599, 716 P.2d 56 (Ct. App. Div. 2 1986)—60(d)

Lake Havasu Community Hosp., Inc. v. Arizona Title Ins. and Trust Co., 141 Ariz. 363, 687 P.2d 371 (Ct. App. Div. 1 1984)—16(h)

Lake Havasu Resort, Inc. v. Commercial Loan Ins. Corp., 139 Ariz. 369, 678 P.2d 950 (Ct. App. Div. 1 1983)—57, 59(m)

Lakritz v. Superior Court In and For County of Coconino, 179 Ariz. 598, 880 P.2d 1144 (Ct. App. Div. 1 1994)—12(i)

Laks v. Laks, 25 Ariz. App. 58, 540 P.2d 1277 (Div. 2 1975)—65(j)(6)

Lamb v. Superior Court In and For Maricopa County, 127 Ariz. 400, 621 P.2d 906 (1980)—54(g)(4), 58(g)

Lamparella, In re Estate of, 210 Ariz. 246, 109 P.3d 959 (Ct. App. Div. 1 2005)—56(h)(3)

Landry v. Superior Court In and For Pima County, 125 Ariz. 337, 609 P.2d 607 (Ct. App. Div. 2 1980)—3

Lane v. City of Tempe, 202 Ariz. 306, 44 P.3d 986 (2002)—75(h), 77(g)(4)

Lane v. Elco Industries, Inc., 134 Ariz. 361, 656 P.2d 650 (Ct. App. Div. 1 1982)—10(f)

Lane v. Hognason, 12 Ariz. App. 330, 470 P.2d 478 (Div. 2 1970)—52(d)

Lang v. Superior Court, In and For County of Maricopa, 170 Ariz. 602, 826 P.2d 1228 (Ct. App. Div. 1 1992)—26(h), 30(h)(i), 404(c)(4)

Langerman Law Offices, P.A. v. Glen Eagles at Princess Resort, LLC, 220 Ariz. 252, 204 P.3d 1101 (Ct. App. Div. 1 2009)—68(h)

Lansford v. Harris, 174 Ariz. 413, 850 P.2d 126 (Ct. App. Div. 1, 1992)—8(i)(8), 13(i)

Lappin v. Lappin, 18 Ariz. App. 444, 503 P.2d 402 (Div. 2 1972)—103(e)

La Prade, Ex parte, 289 U.S. 444, 53 S. Ct. 682, 77 L. Ed. 1311 (1933)—25(e)(2)

La Prade, State ex rel. v. Smith, 43 Ariz. 343, 31 P.2d 102 (1934)—8(i)(8)

Larriva v. Widmer, 101 Ariz. 1, 415 P.2d 424 (1966)—703

Larsen v. Decker, 196 Ariz. 239, 995 P.2d 281 (Ct. App. Div. 1 2000)—59(m), 801(d)(2)(E), 803

Larsen v. Nissan Motor Corp. in U.S.A., 194 Ariz. 142, 978 P.2d 119 (Ct. App. Div. 2 1998)—8(i)(8), 13(i), 14(b), 16.2(c), 26(h)

Lasley v. Helms, 179 Ariz. 589, 880 P.2d 1135 (Ct. App. Div. 1 1994)—8(i)(8)

La Sota, State ex rel. v. Arizona Licensed Beverage Ass'n, Inc., 128 Ariz. 515, 627 P.2d 666, 1981-1 Trade Cas. (CCH) ¶ 63933 (1981)—403, 801(d)(2)(E)

Lavit v. Superior Court In and For County of Maricopa, 173 Ariz. 96, 839 P.2d 1141 (Ct. App. Div. 1 1992)—56(h)(3)

Law v. Verde Valley Medical Center, 217 Ariz. 92, 170 P.3d 701 (Ct. App. Div. 1 2007)—8(i)(8), 13(i), 14(b), 16.2(c), 56(h)(3)

Lawrence v. Burke, 6 Ariz. App. 228, 431 P.2d 302 (1967)—24(d), 55(f)

Lay v. City of Mesa, 168 Ariz. 552, 815 P.2d 921 (Ct. App. Div. 1 1991)—702(d)

L.B. Nelson Corp. of Tucson v. Western American Financial Corp., 150 Ariz. 211, 722 P.2d 379 (Ct. App. Div. 2 1986)—51(d)

Leal v. Allstate Ins. Co., 199 Ariz. 250, 17 P.3d 95 (Ct. App. Div. 1 2000)—12(i)

Lear v. Fields, 226 Ariz. 226, 245 P.3d 911 (Ct. App. Div. 2 2011)—101(b)(6), 702(d)

Leavy v. Parsell, 188 Ariz. 69, 932 P.2d 1340 (1997)—59(m)

Lebaron Properties, LLC v. Jeffrey S. Kaufman, Ltd., 223 Ariz. 227, 221 P.3d 1041 (Ct. App. Div. 1 2009)—3

Lebrecht v. O'Hagan, 96 Ariz. 288, 394 P.2d 216 (1964)—24(d)

Lecky v. Staley, 6 Ariz. App. 556, 435 P.2d 63 (1967)—57

Lee v. Hodge, 180 Ariz. 97, 882 P.2d 408 (1994)—404(c)(4)

M

Maldonado v. Southern Pac. Transp. Co., 129 Ariz. 165, 629 P.2d 1001 (Ct. App. Div. 2 1981)—3, 8(i)(8)

Mallamo v. Hartman, 70 Ariz. 294, 219 P.2d 1039 (1950)—7(b), 7.1(g)

Mallamo v. Hartman, 70 Ariz. 420, 222 P.2d 797 (1950)—12(i)

Malta v. Phoenix Title & Trust Co., 76 Ariz. 116, 259 P.2d 554 (1953)—56(h)(3)

Mammo v. State, 138 Ariz. 528, 675 P.2d 1347 (Ct. App. Div. 1 1983)—59(m)

M & M Auto Storage Pool, Inc. v. Chemical Waste Management, Inc., 164 Ariz. 139, 791 P.2d 665 (Ct. App. Div. 1 1990)—60(d)

Mann v. Superior Court In and For County of Maricopa, 183 Ariz. 586, 905 P.2d 595 (Ct. App. Div. 1 1995)—42(f)(3)(B)

Manning v. Reilly, 2 Ariz. App. 310, 408 P.2d 414 (1965)—57

Manor v. Stevens, 61 Ariz. 511, 152 P.2d 133 (1944)—2

Manterola v. Farmers Ins. Exchange, 200 Ariz. 572, 30 P.3d 639 (Ct. App. Div. 2 2001)—12(i)

Manufacturers' Lease Plans, Inc. v. Alverson Draughon College, 115 Ariz. 358, 565 P.2d 864 (1977)—4.2(m)

Mara M. v. Arizona Dept. of Economic Sec., 201 Ariz. 503, 38 P.3d 41 (Ct. App. Div. 1 2002)—5(j)(2)(B)

Marcal Ltd. Partnership v. Title Ins. Co. of Minnesota, 150 Ariz. 191, 722 P.2d 359 (Ct. App. Div. 2 1986)—59(m)

Marcus v. Fox, 150 Ariz. 333, 723 P.2d 682 (1986)—54(g)(4)

Maria v. Najera, 222 Ariz. 306, 214 P.3d 394 (Ct. App. Div. 1 2009)—54(g)(4), 59(m)

Maricopa County, Matter of, Juvenile Action No. JS-834, 26 Ariz. App. 485, 549 P.2d 580 (Div. 1 1976)—1

Maricopa County v. Arizona Tax Court, 162 Ariz. 64, 781 P.2d 41 (Ct. App. Div. 1 1989)—4.1(m), 5(j)(2)(B)

Maricopa County v. Barkley, 168 Ariz. 234, 812 P.2d 1052 (Ct. App. Div. 1 1990)—12(i), 51(d), 601, 701(c), 702(d)

Maricopa County v. Cities and Towns of Avondale, et al., Wickenburg, 12 Ariz. App. 109, 467 P.2d 949 (Div. 1 1970)—8(i)(8)

Maricopa County v. Peterson, 7 Ariz. App. 363, 439 P.2d 526 (1968)—26(h)

Maricopa County Juvenile Action No. JS-8441, Matter of, 174 Ariz. 341, 849 P.2d 1371 (1992)—58(g)

Maricopa Utilities Co. v. Cline, 60 Ariz. 209, 134 P.2d 156 (1943)—201(f)

Markel v. Transamerica Title Ins. Co., 103 Ariz. 353, 442 P.2d 97 (1968)—56(h)(3)

Markiewicz v. Salt River Valley Water Users' Ass'n, 118 Ariz. 329, 576 P.2d 517 (Ct. App. Div. 1 1978)—23(f), 801(d)(2)(E), 803, 901(b)(10)

Mark Lighting Fixture Co., Inc. v. General Elec. Supply Co., a Div. of General Elec. Co., 155 Ariz. 27, 745 P.2d 85 (1987)—58(g)

Marquette Venture Partners II, L.P. v. Leonesio, 227 Ariz. 179, 254 P.3d 418 (Ct. App. Div. 1 2011)—50(d)

Marquez v. Ortega, 231 Ariz. 437, 296 P.3d 100 (Ct. App. Div. 1 2013)—37(g)

Marshall v. Superior Court, Maricopa County, 131 Ariz. 379, 641 P.2d 867 (1982)—15(d)

Marshall v. Williams, 128 Ariz. 511, 627 P.2d 242 (Ct. App. Div. 1 1981)—54(g)(4)

Marsin v. Udall, 78 Ariz. 309, 279 P.2d 721 (1955)—42(f)(3)(B)

McCarthy Western Constructors, Inc. v. Phoenix Resort Corp., 169 Ariz. 520, 821 P.2d 181 (Ct. App. Div. 1 1991)—52(d), 65(j)(6)

McCauley's Estate, In re, 101 Ariz. 8, 415 P.2d 431 (1966)—15(d)

McClanahan v. Cochise College, 25 Ariz. App. 13, 540 P.2d 744 (Div. 2 1975)—8(i)(8)

McCleaf v. State, 190 Ariz. 167, 945 P.2d 1298 (Ct. App. Div. 1 1997)—50(d)

McClintock v. Serv-Us Bakers, 103 Ariz. 72, 436 P.2d 891 (1968)—55(f)

McCloud v. State, Ariz. Dept. of Public Safety, 217 Ariz. 82, 170 P.3d 691 (Ct. App. Div. 2 2007)—3, 8(i)(8)

McDermott, Inc. v. AmClyde, 511 U.S. 202, 114 S. Ct. 1461, 128 L. Ed. 2d 148, Prod. Liab. Rep. (CCH) ¶ 13826, 1994 A.M.C. 1521 (1994)—16.2(c)

McDougall, State ex rel. v. Corcoran, 153 Ariz. 157, 735 P.2d 767 (1987)—801(d)(2)(E)

McDougall, State ex rel. v. Municipal Court of City of Phoenix, 153 Ariz. 111, 735 P.2d 141 (Ct. App. Div. 1 1986)—403

McDougall, State ex rel. v. Superior Court In and For County of Maricopa, 173 Ariz. 385, 843 P.2d 1277 (Ct. App. Div. 1 1992)—8(i)(8), 11(c)

McElhanon v. Hing, 151 Ariz. 386, 728 P.2d 256 (Ct. App. Div. 1 1985)—11(c), 42(f)(3)(B)

McElwain v. Schuckert, 13 Ariz. App. 468, 477 P.2d 754 (Div. 1 1970)—103(e)

McEvoy v. Aerotek, Inc., 201 Ariz. 300, 34 P.3d 979 (Ct. App. Div. 1 2001)—5(j)(2)(B), 54(g)(4), 68(h)

McGough v. Insurance Co. of North America, 143 Ariz. 26, 691 P.2d 738 (Ct. App. Div. 1 1984)—24(d)

McGuire v. Caterpillar Tractor Co., 151 Ariz. 420, 728 P.2d 290, Prod. Liab. Rep. (CCH) ¶ 11010 (Ct. App. Div. 2 1986)—615(e)

McGuire By and Through McGuire v. DeFrancesco, 168 Ariz. 88, 811 P.2d 340 (Ct. App. Div. 1 1990)—56(h)(3), 702(d)

McHazlett v. Otis Engineering Corp., 133 Ariz. 530, 652 P.2d 1377 (1982)—54(g)(4)

McKernan v. Dupont, 192 Ariz. 550, 968 P.2d 623 (Ct. App. Div. 1 1998)—60(d)

McKesson Chemical Co., a div. of Foremost-McKesson, Inc. v. Van Waters & Rogers, 153 Ariz. 557, 739 P.2d 211 (Ct. App. Div. 1 1987)—54(g)(4)

McKillip v. Smitty's Super Valu, Inc., 190 Ariz. 61, 945 P.2d 372 (Ct. App. Div. 1 1997)—8(i)(8), 13(i), 14(b), 16.2(c)

McMurray v. Dream Catcher USA, Inc., 220 Ariz. 71, 202 P.3d 536 (Ct. App. Div. 2 2009)—12(i), 41(d), 54(g)(4)

McMurtry v. Weatherford Hotel, Inc., 231 Ariz. 244, 293 P.3d 520 (Ct. App. Div. 1 2013)—401(b), 702(d), 703

McNeely v. Industrial Commission, 108 Ariz. 453, 501 P.2d 555 (1972)—702(d)

McNutt v. Department of Revenue of State of Ariz., 196 Ariz. 255, 995 P.2d 691 (Ct. App. Div. 1 1998)—1, 12(i)

Meadows v. Greyhound Corporation, 235 F.2d 233 (5th Cir. 1956)—54(g)(4)

Mealey v. Arndt, 206 Ariz. 218, 76 P.3d 892 (Ct. App. Div. 1 2003)—58(g), 59(m)

Mehlhorn v. Pima County, 194 Ariz. 140, 978 P.2d 117 (Ct. App. Div. 2 1998)—1

Meineke v. Twin City Fire Ins. Co., 181 Ariz. 576, 892 P.2d 1365 (Ct. App. Div. 1 1994)—8(i)(8)

Miller, State ex rel. v. Tucson Associates Ltd. Partnership, 165 Ariz. 519, 799 P.2d 860 (Ct. App. Div. 2 1990)—101(b)(6), 103(e), 703

Miller, State ex rel. v. Wells Fargo Bank of Arizona, N.A., 194 Ariz. 126, 978 P.2d 103 (Ct. App. Div. 1 1998)—50(d), 51(d), 59(m), 103(e), 104(e), 403

Mills v. Electric Auto-Lite Co., 396 U.S. 375, 90 S. Ct. 616, 24 L. Ed. 2d 593, Fed. Sec. L. Rep. (CCH) ¶ 92556 (1970)—54(g)(4)

Miner v. Rogers, 115 Ariz. 463, 565 P.2d 1324 (Ct. App. Div. 2 1977)—53(k)

Mining Investment Group, LLC v. Roberts, 217 Ariz. 635, 177 P.3d 1207 (Ct. App. Div. 1 2008)—3

Minjares v. State, 223 Ariz. 54, 219 P.3d 264 (Ct. App. Div. 1 2009)—8(i)(8), 60(d)

Mister Donut of America, Inc. v. Harris, 150 Ariz. 347, 723 P.2d 696 (Ct. App. Div. 1 1985)—404(c)(4)

Mitchell v. City of Nogales, 83 Ariz. 328, 320 P.2d 955 (1958)—24(d)

Mitchell v. Emblade, 80 Ariz. 398, 298 P.2d 1034 (1956)—1002

Mitchell v. Gamble, 207 Ariz. 364, 86 P.3d 944, 186 Ed. Law Rep. 564 (Ct. App. Div. 2 2004)—12(i)

Mitchell v. Mitchell, 152 Ariz. 317, 732 P.2d 208, 77 A.L.R.4th 633 (1987)—301

Mitchell v. Overman, 103 U.S. 62, 26 L. Ed. 369, 1880 WL 18766 (1880)—58(g)

M. Karam & Sons Mercantile Co. v. Serrano, 51 Ariz. 397, 77 P.2d 447 (1938)—1002, 1003

Mobile Community Council for Progress, Inc. v. Brock, 211 Ariz. 196, 119 P.3d 463 (Ct. App. Div. 1 2005)—12(i)

Mobile Discount Corp. v. Hargus, 156 Ariz. 559, 753 P.2d 1215 (Ct. App. Div. 2 1988)—69

Mobile Discount Corp. v. Schumacher, 139 Ariz. 15, 676 P.2d 649 (Ct. App. Div. 2 1983)—8(i)(8)

Mobilisa, Inc. v. Doe, 217 Ariz. 103, 170 P.3d 712, 36 Media L. Rep. (BNA) 2007 (Ct. App. Div. 1 2007)—26(h)

Modern Views of State Courts as to Whether Consent Judgment is Entitled to Res Judicata or Collateral Estoppel Effect, 91 A.L.R.3d 1170—8(i)(8)

Modla v. Parker, 17 Ariz. App. 54, 495 P.2d 494 (Div. 1 1972)—38.1(k)(3)

Modular Mining Systems, Inc. v. Jigsaw Technologies, Inc., 221 Ariz. 515, 212 P.3d 853 (Ct. App. Div. 2 2009)—54(g)(4), 56(h)(3), 65(j)(6)

Mohave Concrete and Materials, Inc. v. Scaramuzzo, 154 Ariz. 28, 739 P.2d 1345 (Ct. App. Div. 1 1987)—13(i), 15(d)

Mohave County v. James R. Brathovde Family Trust, 187 Ariz. 318, 928 P.2d 1247 (Ct. App. Div. 1 1996)—12(i)

Mohave Disposal, Inc. v. City of Kingman, 186 Ariz. 343, 922 P.2d 308 (1996)—12(i)

Mohave Elec. Co-op., Inc. v. Byers, 189 Ariz. 292, 942 P.2d 451 (Ct. App. Div. 1 1997)—8(i)(8), 52(d), 56(h)(3), 702(d), 703, 705

Mohn v. Hahnemann Medical College and Hosp. of Philadelphia, 357 Pa. Super. 173, 515 A.2d 920 (1986)—26(h)

Molever v. Roush, 152 Ariz. 367, 732 P.2d 1105 (Ct. App. Div. 1 1986)—59(m)

Molloy v. Molloy, 158 Ariz. 64, 761 P.2d 138 (Ct. App. Div. 1 1988)—103(e)

Monaco v. HealthPartners of Southern Arizona, 196 Ariz. 299, 995 P.2d 735 (Ct. App. Div. 2 1999)—50(d), 59(m), 407

Montalvo v. Hartford Fire Ins. Co., 5 Ariz. App. 419, 427 P.2d 553 (1967)—59(m)

Morton v. Pacific Const. Co., 36 Ariz. 97, 283 P. 281 (1929)—57
Moser v. Mardian Const. Co., 20 Ariz. App. 27, 509 P.2d 1064 (Div. 1 1973)—51(d)
Moses v. Phelps Dodge Corp., 826 F. Supp. 1234, 73 Fair Empl. Prac. Cas. (BNA) 739 (D. Ariz. 1993)—54(g)(4)
Mott's Inc. of Mississippi v. Coco's Family Restaurant, 158 Ariz. 350, 762 P.2d 637 (Ct. App. Div. 2 1988)—26(h), 802
Motzer v. Escalante, 228 Ariz. 295, 265 P.3d 1094 (Ct. App. Div. 2 2011)—54(g)(4)
Moulton v. Napolitano, 205 Ariz. 506, 73 P.3d 637 (Ct. App. Div. 1 2003)—12(i)
Mountain States Tel. & Tel. Co. v. Arizona Corp. Com'n, 160 Ariz. 350, 773 P.2d 455 (1989)—24(d)
MT Builders, L.L.C. v. Fisher Roofing, Inc., 219 Ariz. 297, 197 P.3d 758 (Ct. App. Div. 1 2008)—14(b)
Mubi v. Broomfield, 108 Ariz. 39, 492 P.2d 700 (1972)—68(h)
Muchesko v. Muchesko, 191 Ariz. 265, 955 P.2d 21 (Ct. App. Div. 1 1997)—3
Muehlebach v. Mercer Mortuary & Chapel, Inc., 93 Ariz. 60, 378 P.2d 741 (1963)—411
Mulhern v. City of Scottsdale, 165 Ariz. 395, 799 P.2d 15 (Ct. App. Div. 2 1990)—609(e)
Mull v. Ackerman, 279 F.2d 25 (2d Cir.1960)—54(g)(4)
Mullane v. Central Hanover Bank & Trust Co., 339 U.S. 306, 70 S. Ct. 652, 94 L. Ed. 865 (1950)—4.1(m)
Mulleneaux v. State, 190 Ariz. 535, 950 P.2d 1156 (Ct. App. Div. 1 1997)—3
Mullin v. Brown, 210 Ariz. 545, 115 P.3d 139 (Ct. App. Div. 2 2005)—49(h), 50(d), 51(d), 59(m)
Mullins v. Horne, 120 Ariz. 587, 587 P.2d 773, 25 U.C.C. Rep. Serv. 358 (Ct. App. Div. 1 1978)—39(q)
Murcott v. Best Western Intern., Inc., 198 Ariz. 349, 9 P.3d 1088, 16 I.E.R. Cas. (BNA) 1277 (Ct. App. Div. 1 2000)—16(h), 49(h), 50(d)
Murphey v. Valenzuela, 95 Ariz. 30, 386 P.2d 78 (1963)—3
Murphy v. Board of Medical Examiners of State of Ariz., 190 Ariz. 441, 949 P.2d 530 (Ct. App. Div. 1 1997)—8(i)(8)
Murphy v. Yeast, 59 Ariz. 281, 126 P.2d 313 (1942)—105
Murray v. Thomas, 80 Ariz. 378, 298 P.2d 795 (1956)—42(f)(3)(B)
Murren v. Murren, 191 Ariz. 335, 955 P.2d 973 (Ct. App. Div. 1 1998)—69
Musa v. Adrian, 130 Ariz. 311, 636 P.2d 89 (1981)—54(g)(4)
Musgrave v. Karis, 63 Ariz. 417, 163 P.2d 278 (1945)—103(e), 803
Musgrove v. Leonard, 97 Ariz. 44, 396 P.2d 614 (1964)—8(i)(8), 18(b)
Mustang Equipment, Inc. v. Welch, 115 Ariz. 206, 564 P.2d 895 (1977)—408(b)
Mustonen's Estate, Matter of, 130 Ariz. 283, 635 P.2d 876 (Ct. App. Div. 2 1981)—601
Myers v. Wood, 174 Ariz. 434, 850 P.2d 672 (Ct. App. Div. 2 1992)—8(i)(8)

N

Nackard v. Wolfswinkel, 116 Ariz. 348, 569 P.2d 290 (Ct. App. Div. 1 1977)—39(q)

Nahom v. Blue Cross and Blue Shield of Arizona, Inc., 180 Ariz. 548, 885 P.2d 1113 (Ct. App. Div. 1 1994)—104(e)

Najar v. State, 198 Ariz. 345, 9 P.3d 1084 (Ct. App. Div. 2 2000)—52(d), 59(m)

Nangle v. Farmers Ins. Co. of Arizona, 205 Ariz. 517, 73 P.3d 1252 (Ct. App. Div. 1 2003)—8(i)(8)

Nanini v. Nanini, 166 Ariz. 287, 802 P.2d 438 (Ct. App. Div. 2 1990)—56(h)(3)

Napier v. Bertram, 191 Ariz. 238, 954 P.2d 1389 (1998)—12(i), 56(h)(3)

Napolitano, State ex rel. v. Brown & Williamson Tobacco Corp., 196 Ariz. 382, 998 P.2d 1055 (2000)—24(d)

Nataros v. Superior Court of Maricopa County, 113 Ariz. 498, 557 P.2d 1055 (1976)—13(i)

National Bank of Arizona v. St. Paul Fire and Marine Ins. Co., 193 Ariz. 581, 975 P.2d 711 (Ct. App. Div. 1 1999)—104(e)

National Bank of Arizona v. Thruston, 218 Ariz. 112, 180 P.3d 977 (Ct. App. Div. 1 2008)—56(h)(3)

National Broker Associates, Inc. v. Marlyn Nutraceuticals, Inc., 211 Ariz. 210, 119 P.3d 477 (Ct. App. Div. 1 2005)—30(h)(i), 54(g)(4), 58(g)

National Homes Corp. v. Totem Mobile Home Sales, Inc., 140 Ariz. 434, 682 P.2d 439 (Ct. App. Div. 1 1984)—12(i)

National Union Fire Ins. Co. of Pittsburgh, Pa. v. Greene, 195 Ariz. 105, 985 P.2d 590 (Ct. App. Div. 1 1999)—69

Nationwide Resources Corp. v. Ngai, 129 Ariz. 226, 630 P.2d 49 (Ct. App. Div. 2 1981)—54(g)(4)

Natseway v. City of Tempe, 184 Ariz. 374, 909 P.2d 441 (Ct. App. Div. 1 1995)—8(i)(8), 13(i), 14(b), 16.2(c)

Navajo Nation v. MacDonald, 180 Ariz. 539, 885 P.2d 1104, R.I.C.O. Bus. Disp. Guide (CCH) ¶ 8679 (Ct. App. Div. 1 1994)—58(g), 60(d)

Needel v. Needel, 15 Ariz. App. 471, 489 P.2d 729 (Div. 2 1971)—801(d)(2)(E)

Neely, State ex rel. v. Brown, 177 Ariz. 6, 864 P.2d 1038 (1993)—1

Neely, State ex rel. v. Sherrill, 165 Ariz. 508, 799 P.2d 849 (1990)—602

Neiderhiser v. Henry's Drive-In, Inc., 96 Ariz. 305, 394 P.2d 420 (1964)—12(i)

Neil v. Kavena, 176 Ariz. 93, 859 P.2d 203 (Ct. App. Div. 1 1993)—8(i)(8), 13(i), 14(b), 16.2(c)

Nelson v. Phoenix Resort Corp., 181 Ariz. 188, 888 P.2d 1375 (Ct. App. Div. 1 1994)—50(d)

Nelson v. Pima Community College, 83 F.3d 1075, 109 Ed. Law Rep. 598 (9th Cir. 1996)—54(g)(4)

Nelson v. Rice, 198 Ariz. 563, 12 P.3d 238 (Ct. App. Div. 2 2000)—104(e)

Nesmith v. Superior Court In and For County of Maricopa, 164 Ariz. 70, 790 P.2d 768 (Ct. App. Div. 1 1990)—34(c), 37(g)

Ness v. Greater Arizona Realty, Inc., 117 Ariz. 357, 572 P.2d 1195 (Ct. App. Div. 2 1977)—13(i), 801(d)(2)(E)

Ness v. Western Sec. Life Ins. Co., 174 Ariz. 497, 851 P.2d 122, R.I.C.O. Bus. Disp. Guide (CCH) ¶ 8086 (Ct. App. Div. 1 1992)—9(i)(9)

Newell v. Town of Oro Valley, 163 Ariz. 527, 789 P.2d 394 (Ct. App. Div. 2 1990)—51(d), 402, 704(b)

Newman, In re Estate of, 219 Ariz. 260, 196 P.3d 863 (Ct. App. Div. 1 2008)—1, 38(d)

New Pueblo Constructors, Inc. v. State, 144 Ariz. 95, 696 P.2d 185 (1985)—54(g)(4)

Newsom v. Superior Court In and For Maricopa County, 102 Ariz. 95, 425 P.2d 422 (1967)—42(f)(3)(B)

New Times, Inc. v. Arizona Bd. of Regents, 110 Ariz. 367, 519 P.2d 169 (1974)—301

Nichols v. Elkins, 2 Ariz. App. 272, 408 P.2d 34 (1965)—501

Nielson v. Flashberg, 101 Ariz. 335, 419 P.2d 514 (1966)—51(d)

Nielson v. Patterson, 204 Ariz. 530, 65 P.3d 911 (2003)—58(g), 59(m)

Nienstedt v. Wetzel, 133 Ariz. 348, 651 P.2d 876, 33 A.L.R.4th 635 (Ct. App. Div. 1 1982)—8(i)(8), 30(h)(i), 401(b)

Nikolous v. Superior Court In and For Maricopa County, 157 Ariz. 256, 756 P.2d 925 (1988)—13(i), 14(b)

Noble v. Industrial Com'n of Arizona, 140 Ariz. 571, 683 P.2d 1173 (Ct. App. Div. 1 1984)—54(g)(4)

Nolan v. Starlight Pines Homeowners Ass'n, 216 Ariz. 482, 167 P.3d 1277 (Ct. App. Div. 1 2007)—56(h)(3)

Nolde v. Frankie, 192 Ariz. 276, 964 P.2d 477, 129 Ed. Law Rep. 837 (1998)—8(i)(8)

Nordale v. Fisher, 93 Ariz. 342, 380 P.2d 1003 (1963)—38.1(k)(3)

Nordensson v. Nordensson, 146 Ariz. 544, 707 P.2d 948 (Ct. App. Div. 2 1985)—59(m)

Norman v. Del Elia, 111 Ariz. 480, 533 P.2d 537 (1975)—16(h)

Norriega v. Machado, 179 Ariz. 348, 878 P.2d 1386 (Ct. App. Div. 1 1994)—8(i)(8), 54(g)(4), 58(g)

Northern Propane Gas Co. v. Kipps, 127 Ariz. 522, 622 P.2d 469 (1980)—4.2(m)

North Star Development Corp. v. Wolfswinkel, 146 Ariz. 406, 706 P.2d 732 (Ct. App. Div. 2 1985)—15(d), 54(g)(4), 65(j)(6), 69

Norwest Bank (Minnesota), N.A. v. Symington, 197 Ariz. 181, 3 P.3d 1101 (Ct. App. Div. 1 2000)—26.1(g), 60(d)

Nu-Tred Tire Co., Inc. v. Dunlop Tire & Rubber Corp., 118 Ariz. 417, 577 P.2d 268 (Ct. App. Div. 1 1978)—62(j), 65(j)(6)

Nystrom v. Massachusetts Cas. Ins. Co., 148 Ariz. 208, 713 P.2d 1266 (Ct. App. Div. 1 1986)—801(d)(2)(E)

O

O'Brien v. Scottsdale Discount Corp., 14 Ariz. App. 224, 482 P.2d 473 (Div. 2 1971)—13(i)

Occhino v. Occhino, 164 Ariz. 482, 793 P.2d 1149 (Ct. App. Div. 2 1990)—8(i)(8)

Occidental Chemical Co. v. Connor, 124 Ariz. 341, 604 P.2d 605 (1979)—13(i)

O'Connor, Cavanagh, Anderson, Westover, Killingsworth & Beshears, P.A. v. Bonus Utah, Inc., 156 Ariz. 171, 750 P.2d 1374 (Ct. App. Div. 2 1988)—4.2(m)

Ocotillo West Joint Venture v. Superior Court In and For County of Maricopa, 173 Ariz. 486, 844 P.2d 653 (Ct. App. Div. 1 1992)—26(h)

Ogden v. J.M. Steel Erecting, Inc., 201 Ariz. 32, 31 P.3d 806 (Ct. App. Div. 1 2001)—13(i), 14(b), 16.2(c), 26(h), 59(m)

Oglesby v. Chandler, 37 Ariz. 1, 288 P. 1034 (1930)—19(d)

Owens v. City of Phoenix, 180 Ariz. 402, 884 P.2d 1100 (Ct. App. Div. 1 1994)—8(i)(8)

Oyakawa v. Gillett, 175 Ariz. 226, 854 P.2d 1212 (Ct. App. Div. 1 1993)—9(i)(9), 54(g)(4), 60(d), 69

P

Pabellon v. Grace Line, 191 F.2d 169, 1951 A.M.C. 1751 (2d Cir. 1951)—54(g)(4)

Pacheco, In re Guardianship of, 219 Ariz. 421, 199 P.3d 676 (Ct. App. Div. 2 2008)—54(g)(4), 58(g)

Pacht v. Morris, 107 Ariz. 392, 489 P.2d 29 (1971)—59(m)

Pacific Guano Co. v. Pinal County Land Co., 1 Ariz. App. 34, 399 P.2d 122 (1965)—13(i)

Packard v. Reidhead, 22 Ariz. App. 420, 528 P.2d 171 (Div. 1 1974)—51(d), 803, 901(b)(10)

Padilla v. Southern Pac. Transp. Co., 131 Ariz. 533, 642 P.2d 878 (Ct. App. Div. 2 1982)—103(e)

Page, Estate of v. Litzenburg, 177 Ariz. 84, 865 P.2d 128 (Ct. App. Div. 1 1993)—1, 8(i)(8), 59(m), 60(d), 601

PAM Transport v. Freightliner Corp., 182 Ariz. 132, 893 P.2d 1295 (1995)—8(i)(8), 13(i), 14(b), 16.2(c)

Panzino v. City of Phoenix, 196 Ariz. 442, 999 P.2d 198 (2000)—38.1(k)(3), 60(d), 80(i)

Para v. Anderson ex rel. County of Maricopa, 231 Ariz. 91, 290 P.3d 1214 (Ct. App. Div. 1 2012)—26(h), 702(d)

Paradise Valley, Town of v. Laughlin, 174 Ariz. 484, 851 P.2d 109 (Ct. App. Div. 1 1992)—701(c)

Parag v. Walters, 11 Ariz. App. 276, 464 P.2d 347 (Div. 2 1970)—55(f)

Pargman v. Vickers, 208 Ariz. 573, 96 P.3d 571 (Ct. App. Div. 1 2004)—15(d)

Paris-Phoenix Corp. v. Esper, 112 Ariz. 320, 541 P.2d 917 (1975)—38(d), 65(j)(6)

Park v. Strick, 137 Ariz. 100, 669 P.2d 78 (1983)—6(f), 54(g)(4), 58(g), 60(d)

Park Central Development Co. v. Roberts Dry Goods, Inc., 11 Ariz. App. 58, 461 P.2d 702 (Div. 1 1969)—52(d)

Parker, In re Estate of, 217 Ariz. 563, 177 P.3d 305 (Ct. App. Div. 1 2008)—56(h)(3)

Parker v. Vanell, 170 Ariz. 350, 824 P.2d 746 (1992)—16.2(c)

Parking Concepts, Inc. v. Sheldon, 193 Ariz. 432, 973 P.2d 1189 (Ct. App. Div. 1 1998)—64

Parkinson v. Farmers Ins. Co., 122 Ariz. 343, 594 P.2d 1039 (Ct. App. Div. 2 1979)—45(g)

Parks v. Macro-Dynamics, Inc., 121 Ariz. 517, 591 P.2d 1005 (Ct. App. Div. 2 1979)—12(i)

Parkway Bank and Trust Co. v. Zivkovic, 232 Ariz. 286, 304 P.3d 1109 (Ct. App. Div. 1 2013)—56(h)(3)

Parra v. Continental Tire North America, Inc., 222 Ariz. 212, 213 P.3d 361 (Ct. App. Div. 1 2009)—12(i)

Parrish v. United Bank of Arizona, 164 Ariz. 18, 790 P.2d 304 (Ct. App. Div. 2 1990)—8(i)(8)

Parsons v. Maricopa County, 176 Ariz. 307, 860 P.2d 1360 (Tax Ct.1993)—18(b)

Parsons v. Smithey, 109 Ariz. 49, 504 P.2d 1272, 54 A.L.R.3d 964 (1973)—803

Pasco Industries, Inc. v. Talco Recycling, Inc., 195 Ariz. 50, 985 P.2d 535, 1998-2 Trade Cas. (CCH) ¶ 72377 (Ct. App. Div. 1 1998)—16.2(c), 104(e)

Passey v. Great Western Associates II, 174 Ariz. 420, 850 P.2d 133 (Ct. App. Div. 1 1993)—52(d)

Patania v. Silverstone, 3 Ariz. App. 424, 415 P.2d 139 (1966)—26(h), 501

Patch v. Buros, 2 Ariz. App. 585, 410 P.2d 703 (1966)—58(g)

Patterson v. Bianco, 167 Ariz. 249, 805 P.2d 1070 (Ct. App. Div. 2 1991)—54(g)(4), 58(g)

Patterson v. City of Phoenix, 103 Ariz. 64, 436 P.2d 613 (1968)—10(f)

Paul R. Peterson Const., Inc. v. Arizona State Carpenters Health and Welfare Trust Fund, 179 Ariz. 474, 880 P.2d 694, 17 Employee Benefits Cas. (BNA) 2624 (Ct. App. Div. 1 1994)—8(i)(8), 39(q), 54(g)(4), 58(g)

Payne v. Payne, 12 Ariz. App. 434, 471 P.2d 319 (Div. 2 1970)—55(f)

Payne v. Pennzoil Corp., 138 Ariz. 52, 672 P.2d 1322 (Ct. App. Div. 2 1983)—12(i)

Peabody Coal Co. v. State, 158 Ariz. 190, 761 P.2d 1094 (Ct. App. Div. 1 1988)—59(m)

Peagler v. Phoenix Newspapers, Inc., 131 Ariz. 308, 640 P.2d 1110, 8 Media L. Rep. (BNA) 1209 (Ct. App. Div. 1 1981)—803

Pearce v. Stone, 149 Ariz. 567, 720 P.2d 542 (Ct. App. Div. 1 1986)—501

Peart v. Superior Court In and For Mohave County, 6 Ariz. App. 6, 429 P.2d 498 (1967)—80(i)

Pedro v. Glenn, 8 Ariz. App. 332, 446 P.2d 31 (1968)—35(c)(3)

Pegler v. Sullivan, 6 Ariz. App. 338, 432 P.2d 593 (1967)—12(i)

Penunuri v. Superior Court In and For Pima County, 115 Ariz. 399, 565 P.2d 905 (Ct. App. Div. 2 1977)—41(d)

Peralta v. Heights Medical Center, Inc., 485 U.S. 80, 108 S. Ct. 896, 99 L. Ed. 2d 75 (1988)—55(f)

Perez v. Tomberlin, 86 Ariz. 66, 340 P.2d 982 (1959)—30(h)(i)

Perez By and Through Perez v. Community Hosp. of Chandler, Inc., 187 Ariz. 355, 929 P.2d 1303 (1997)—59(m)

Perguson v. Tamis, 188 Ariz. 425, 937 P.2d 347 (Ct. App. Div. 2 1996)—16(h), 26.1(g), 37(g), 702(d)

Perkins v. Komarnyckyj, 172 Ariz. 115, 834 P.2d 1260 (1992)—39(q), 48, 51(d), 59(m)

Perry v. County of Maricopa, 167 Ariz. 458, 808 P.2d 343 (Ct. App. Div. 2 1991)—6(f)

Perry v. Ronan, 225 Ariz. 49, 234 P.3d 617 (Ct. App. Div. 1 2010)—80(i)

Perry v. Safety Federal Sav. and Loan Ass'n of Kansas City, 25 Ariz. App. 443, 544 P.2d 267 (Div. 1 1976)—60(d)

Petefish By and Through Clancy v. Dawe, 137 Ariz. 570, 672 P.2d 914 (1983)—51(d)

Peters v. M & O Const., Inc., 119 Ariz. 34, 579 P.2d 72 (Ct. App. Div. 1 1978)—3

Peterson v. Newton, 232 Ariz. 593, 307 P.3d 1020 (Ct. App. Div. 1 2013)—8(i)(8), 54(g)(4)

Pettit v. Pettit, 218 Ariz. 529, 189 P.3d 1102 (Ct. App. Div. 1 2008)—8(i)(8)

PFS v. Industrial Com'n of Arizona, 191 Ariz. 274, 955 P.2d 30 (Ct. App. Div. 1 1997)—8(i)(8), 54(g)(4), 58(g), 301

Phelps v. Firebird Raceway, Inc., 210 Ariz. 403, 111 P.3d 1003 (2005)—8(i)(8), 56(h)(3)
Phelps Dodge Corp. v. Arizona Elec. Power Co-op., Inc., 207 Ariz. 95, 83 P.3d 573 (Ct. App. Div. 1 2004)—54(g)(4)
Phelps Dodge Corp. v. Ford, 68 Ariz. 190, 203 P.2d 633 (1949)—201(f)
Phelps Dodge Corp. v. Superior Court In and For Cochise County, 7 Ariz. App. 277, 438 P.2d 424 (1968)—36(c)
Philadelphia Indem. Ins. Co. v. Barerra, 200 Ariz. 9, 21 P.3d 395 (2001)—104(e)
Phillips v. Adler, 134 Ariz. 480, 657 P.2d 893 (Ct. App. Div. 2 1982)—54(g)(4), 58(g)
Phillips v. Clancy, 152 Ariz. 415, 733 P.2d 300 (Ct. App. Div. 1 1986)—605
Phillips v. Findlay, 19 Ariz. App. 348, 507 P.2d 687 (Div. 2 1973)—55(f)
Phil W. Morris Co. v. Schwartz, 138 Ariz. 90, 673 P.2d 28 (Ct. App. Div. 1 1983)—56(h)(3)
Phoenix Airport Travelodge v. Dolgin, 12 Ariz. App. 358, 470 P.2d 506 (Div. 2 1970)—4(i), 12(i)
Phoenix Arbor Plaza, Ltd. v. Dauderman, 163 Ariz. 27, 785 P.2d 1215 (Ct. App. Div. 1 1989)—64
Phoenix, City of v. Brown, 88 Ariz. 60, 352 P.2d 754 (1960)—702(d)
Phoenix, City of v. Clauss, 177 Ariz. 566, 869 P.2d 1219 (Ct. App. Div. 1 1994)—51(d)
Phoenix, City of v. Collar, Williams & White Engineering, Inc., 12 Ariz. App. 510, 472 P.2d 479 (Div. 1 1970)—55(f)
Phoenix, City of v. Consolidated Water Co., 101 Ariz. 43, 415 P.2d 866 (1966)—52(d)
Phoenix, City of v. Fields, 219 Ariz. 568, 201 P.3d 529 (2009)—3, 8(i)(8), 23(f)
Phoenix, City of v. Garretson, 232 Ariz. 115, 302 P.3d 640 (Ct. App. Div. 1 2013)—56(h)(3)
Phoenix, City of v. Geyler, 144 Ariz. 323, 697 P.2d 1073 (1985)—58(g)
Phoenix, City of v. Johnson, 220 Ariz. 189, 204 P.3d 447 (Ct. App. Div. 1 2009)—62(j)
Phoenix, City of v. Kenly, 21 Ariz. App. 394, 519 P.2d 1159 (Div. 1 1974)—14(b)
Phoenix, City of v. Linsenmeyer, 86 Ariz. 328, 346 P.2d 140 (1959)—8(i)(8)
Phoenix, City of v. Lopez, 77 Ariz. 146, 268 P.2d 323 (1954)—201(f)
Phoenix, City of v. Peterson, 11 Ariz. App. 136, 462 P.2d 829 (Div. 1 1969)—26(h), 27(b)
Phoenix, City of v. Sanner, 54 Ariz. 363, 95 P.2d 987 (1939)—9(i)(9)
Phoenix, City of v. Superior Court In and For Maricopa County, 110 Ariz. 155, 515 P.2d 1175 (1973)—201(f)
Phoenix, City of v. Yarnell, 184 Ariz. 310, 909 P.2d 377 (1995)—56(h)(3)
Phoenix Control Systems, Inc. v. Insurance Co. of North America, 161 Ariz. 420, 778 P.2d 1316 (Ct. App. Div. 1 1989)—56(h)(3)
Phoenix Control Systems, Inc. v. Insurance Co. of North America, 165 Ariz. 31, 796 P.2d 463 (1990)—56(h)(3), 104(e)
Phoenix General Hospital v. Superior Court of Maricopa County, 1 Ariz. App. 298, 402 P.2d 233 (1965)—34(c)
Phoenix Metals Corp. v. Roth, 79 Ariz. 106, 284 P.2d 645 (1955)—5(j)(2)(B)

Phoenix Newspapers, Inc. v. Department of Corrections, State of Ariz., 188 Ariz. 237, 934 P.2d 801 (Ct. App. Div. 1 1997)—8(i)(8)

Phoenix Newspapers, Inc. v. Superior Court In and For County of Maricopa, 180 Ariz. 159, 882 P.2d 1285, 22 Media L. Rep. (BNA) 1531 (Ct. App. Div. 1 1993)—1, 501

Phoenix Western Holding Corp. v. Gleeson, 18 Ariz. App. 60, 500 P.2d 320 (Div. 1 1972)—41(d), 801(d)(2)(E)

Pierce v. Lopez, 16 Ariz. App. 54, 490 P.2d 1182 (Div. 2 1971)—59(m)

Pierpont v. Hydro Mfg. Co., Inc., 22 Ariz. App. 252, 526 P.2d 776 (Div. 1 1974)—201(f)

Pima County v. Gonzalez, 193 Ariz. 18, 969 P.2d 183 (Ct. App. Div. 2 1998)—51(d), 58(g), 59(m)

Pima County v. Harte, 131 Ariz. 68, 638 P.2d 735 (Ct. App. Div. 2 1981)—26(h)

Pima County v. McCarville ex rel. County of Pinal, 224 Ariz. 366, 231 P.3d 370 (Ct. App. Div. 2 2010)—62(j)

Pima County v. State, 174 Ariz. 402, 850 P.2d 115 (Ct. App. Div. 1 1992)—8(i)(8), 56(h)(3)

Pinal County v. Adams, 13 Ariz. App. 571, 479 P.2d 718 (Div. 1 1971)—13(i), 14(b)

Pincock v. Dupnik, 146 Ariz. 91, 703 P.2d 1240 (Ct. App. Div. 2 1985)—701(c), 702(d), 704(b)

Piner v. Superior Court In and For County of Maricopa, 192 Ariz. 182, 962 P.2d 909 (1998)—8(i)(8), 13(i), 14(b), 16.2(c), 56(h)(3)

Pingitore v. Town of Cave Creek, 194 Ariz. 261, 981 P.2d 129 (Ct. App. Div. 1 1998)—8(i)(8)

Pintek v. Superior Court In and For Cochise County, 78 Ariz. 179, 277 P.2d 265 (1954)—24(d)

Pioneer Federal Sav. Bank v. Driver, 166 Ariz. 585, 804 P.2d 118 (Ct. App. Div. 1 1990)—4.1(m), 9(i)(9), 54(g)(4), 60(d), 69

Pioneer Nat. Trust Co. of Arizona v. Pioneer Nat. Trust Co. of Arizona, 115 Ariz. 511, 566 P.2d 312 (Ct. App. Div. 2 1977)—21

Piper v. Bear Medical Systems, Inc., 180 Ariz. 170, 883 P.2d 407, Prod. Liab. Rep. (CCH) ¶ 13766 (Ct. App. Div. 1 1993)—49(h), 50(d)

Pipher v. Loo, 221 Ariz. 399, 212 P.3d 91 (Ct. App. Div. 1 2009)—103(e), 702(d), 703

Planning Group of Scottsdale, L.L.C. v. Lake Mathews Mineral Properties, Ltd., 226 Ariz. 262, 246 P.3d 343 (2011)—4.2(m)

Plattner v. State Farm Mut. Auto. Ins. Co., 168 Ariz. 311, 812 P.2d 1129 (Ct. App. Div. 1 1991)—56(h)(3)

PLM Tax Certificate Program 1991-92, L.P. v. Schweikert, 216 Ariz. 47, 162 P.3d 1267 (Ct. App. Div. 1 2007)—56(h)(3)

Plowman v. Arizona State Liquor Bd., 152 Ariz. 331, 732 P.2d 222 (Ct. App. Div. 2 1986)—802

Plummer v. Chemical Bank, 668 F.2d 654, 27 Fair Empl. Prac. Cas. (BNA) 1169, 27 Empl. Prac. Dec. (CCH) ¶ 32321 (2d Cir. 1982)—23(f)

PNL Asset Management Co., LLC v. Brendgen & Taylor Partnership, 193 Ariz. 126, 970 P.2d 958 (Ct. App. Div. 1 1998)—56(h)(3)

PNL Credit L.P. v. Southwest Pacific Investments, Inc., 179 Ariz. 259, 877 P.2d 832 (Ct. App. Div. 1 1994)—58(g), 59(m)

Pochiro v. Prudential Ins. Co. of America, 827 F.2d 1246, 9 Fed. R. Serv. 3d 266 (9th Cir. 1987)—13(i)

Podol v. Jacobs, 65 Ariz. 50, 173 P.2d 758 (1946)—39(q), 611(c)(2), 801(d)(2)(E)

Polacke v. Superior Court In and For County of Maricopa, 170 Ariz. 217, 823 P.2d 84 (Ct. App. Div. 1 1991)—4.2(m)

Poleo v. Grandview Equities, Ltd., 143 Ariz. 130, 692 P.2d 309 (Ct. App. Div. 1 1984)—37(g), 55(f)

Pompa v. Superior Court In and For the County of Maricopa, 187 Ariz. 531, 931 P.2d 431 (Ct. App. Div. 1 1997)—1

Ponderosa Plaza v. Siplast, 181 Ariz. 128, 888 P.2d 1315 (Ct. App. Div. 1 1993)—54(g)(4)

Pool v. Superior Court In and For Pima County, 139 Ariz. 98, 677 P.2d 261 (1984)—402, 611(c)(2), 704(b)

Pope, State ex rel. v. Superior Court, In and For Mohave County, 113 Ariz. 22, 545 P.2d 946, 94 A.L.R.3d 246 (1976)—404(c)(4), 608(b)(2)

Porter v. Porter, 67 Ariz. 273, 195 P.2d 132 (1948)—801(d)(2)(E)

Porter v. Spader, 225 Ariz. 424, 239 P.3d 743 (Ct. App. Div. 1 2010)—60(d)

Porter v. Triad of Arizona (L.P.), 203 Ariz. 230, 52 P.3d 799 (Ct. App. Div. 1 2002)—8(i)(8), 17(j)

Porter By and Through Porter v. Superior Court In and For Pima County (Price Co.), 144 Ariz. 346, 697 P.2d 1096 (1985)—404(c)(4)

Portonova v. Wilkinson, 128 Ariz. 501, 627 P.2d 232 (1981)—56(h)(3)

Posner v. New York Life Ins. Co., 56 Ariz. 202, 106 P.2d 488 (1940)—501, 901(b)(10)

Postal Instant Press, Inc. v. Corral Restaurants, Inc., 186 Ariz. 535, 925 P.2d 260 (1996)—4(i), 4.1(m), 64

Potter v. H. Kern Wisner, M.D., P.C., 170 Ariz. 331, 823 P.2d 1339 (Ct. App. Div. 1 1991)—50(d)

Poulson v. Ofack, 220 Ariz. 294, 205 P.3d 1141 (Ct. App. Div. 1 2009)—77(g)(4)

Pouser, In re Estate of, 193 Ariz. 574, 975 P.2d 704 (1999)—52(d), 301

Powell v. Klein, 11 Ariz. App. 360, 464 P.2d 806 (Div. 2 1970)—59(m)

Powell-Cerkoney v. TCR-Montana Ranch Joint Venture, II, 176 Ariz. 275, 860 P.2d 1328 (Ct. App. Div. 1 1993)—7.1(g), 65(j)(6)

Power P.E.O., Inc., The v. Employees Ins. of Wausau, 201 Ariz. 559, 38 P.3d 1224 (Ct. App. Div. 1 2002)—65(j)(6)

Powers v. Taser Intern., Inc., 217 Ariz. 398, 174 P.3d 777 (Ct. App. Div. 1 2007)—68(h)

Precision Components, Inc. v. Harrison, Harper, Christian & Dichter, P.C., 179 Ariz. 552, 880 P.2d 1098 (Ct. App. Div. 2 1993)—11(c), 37(g)

Prell v. Amado, 2 Ariz. App. 35, 406 P.2d 237 (1965)—55(f)

Premier Financial Services v. Citibank (Arizona), 185 Ariz. 80, 912 P.2d 1309 (Ct. App. Div. 1 1995)—64

Preston v. Denkins, 94 Ariz. 214, 382 P.2d 686 (1963)—55(f), 60(d), 611(c)(2)

Preston v. Kindred Hospitals West, L.L.C., 225 Ariz. 223, 236 P.3d 450 (Ct. App. Div. 1 2010)—17(j)

Preston v. Kindred Hospitals West, L.L.C., 226 Ariz. 391, 249 P.3d 771 (2011)—15(d), 17(j)

Preston Motor Co., Inc. v. Palomares, 133 Ariz. 245, 650 P.2d 1227, 34 U.C.C. Rep. Serv. 1184 (Ct. App. Div. 2 1982)—30(h)(i)

Preuss v. Stevens, 150 Ariz. 6, 721 P.2d 664 (Ct. App. Div. 2 1986)—68(h)

Price v. Reynolds Metals Co., 69 F. Supp. 82 (E.D. N.Y. 1946)—12(i)

Pritchard v. State, 163 Ariz. 427, 788 P.2d 1178 (1990)—3, 8(i)(8), 12(i)

Property at 6757 S. Burcham Ave., In re, 204 Ariz. 401, 64 P.3d 843 (Ct. App. Div. 2 2003)—1

Prophet v. S. H. Kress Co., 106 Ariz. 504, 479 P.2d 167 (1970)—801(d)(2)(E)

Prudential Ins. Co. of America v. O'Grady, 97 Ariz. 9, 396 P.2d 246 (1964)—201(f)

Pruitt v. Pavelin, 141 Ariz. 195, 685 P.2d 1347 (Ct. App. Div. 1 1984)—9(i)(9)

Prutch v. Town of Quartzsite, 231 Ariz. 431, 296 P.3d 94 (Ct. App. Div. 1 2013)—7(b), 8(i)(8), 12(i)

Public Service Co. of Oklahoma v. Bleak, 134 Ariz. 311, 656 P.2d 600 (1982)—401(b), 607, 801(d)(2)(E), 802

Pueblo Santa Fe Townhomes Owners' Ass'n v. Transcontinental Ins. Co., 218 Ariz. 13, 178 P.3d 485 (Ct. App. Div. 1 2008)—3, 8(i)(8), 54(g)(4)

Pulaski v. Perkins, 127 Ariz. 216, 619 P.2d 488 (Ct. App. Div. 1 1980)—54(g)(4)

Pulliam v. Pulliam, 139 Ariz. 343, 678 P.2d 528 (Ct. App. Div. 2 1984)—701(c)

Pumphrey v. Dynek, 10 Ariz. App. 241, 457 P.2d 954 (Div. 2 1969)—59(m)

Puntel v. Kirtides, 89 Ariz. 361, 362 P.2d 737 (1961)—15(d)

Purcell v. Zimbelman, 18 Ariz. App. 75, 500 P.2d 335 (Div. 2 1972)—42(f)(3)(B), 51(d), 705

Purcell, State ex rel. v. Superior Court In and For Maricopa County, 107 Ariz. 224, 485 P.2d 549 (1971)—1

Purvis v. Hartford Acc. and Indem. Co., 179 Ariz. 254, 877 P.2d 827 (Ct. App. Div. 1 1994)—24(d)

Pyeatte v. Pyeatte, 21 Ariz. App. 448, 520 P.2d 542, 84 A.L.R.3d 486 (Div. 2 1974)—611(c)(2)

Q

Quinonez for and on Behalf of Quinonez v. Andersen, 144 Ariz. 193, 696 P.2d 1342 (Ct. App. Div. 1 1984)—609(e)

Quintero v. Continental Rent-A-Car System, Inc., 105 Ariz. 135, 460 P.2d 189 (1969)—25(e)(2)

Quintero v. Rogers, 221 Ariz. 536, 212 P.3d 874 (Ct. App. Div. 1 2009)—25(e)(2)

Qwest Corp. v. Kelly, 204 Ariz. 25, 59 P.3d 789 (Ct. App. Div. 2 2002)—12(i)

R

Rabe v. Cut and Curl of Plaza 75, Inc., 148 Ariz. 552, 715 P.2d 1240 (Ct. App. Div. 2 1986)—702(d)

Rackmaster Systems, Inc. v. Maderia, 219 Ariz. 60, 193 P.3d 314 (Ct. App. Div. 1 2008)—1, 64, 69

Radkowsky v. Provident Life & Acc. Ins. Co., 196 Ariz. 110, 993 P.2d 1074 (Ct. App. Div. 1 1999)—54(g)(4), 58(g)

Ramada Inns, Inc. v. Lane & Bird Advertising, Inc., 102 Ariz. 127, 426 P.2d 395 (1967)—5(j)(2)(B), 55(f)

Ramsey Air Meds, L.L.C. v. Cutter Aviation, Inc., 198 Ariz. 10, 6 P.3d 315 (Ct. App. Div. 1 2000)—54(g)(4)

Rancho Pescado, Inc. v. Northwestern Mut. Life Ins. Co., 140 Ariz. 174, 680 P.2d 1235 (Ct. App. Div. 1 1984)—58(g)

Rashedi v. General Bd. of Church of Nazarene, 203 Ariz. 320, 54 P.3d 349 (Ct. App. Div. 1 2002)—12(i)

Ratliff v. Hardison, 219 Ariz. 441, 199 P.3d 696 (Ct. App. Div. 2 2008)—56(h)(3)

Ray v. Mangum, 163 Ariz. 329, 788 P.2d 62 (1989)—8(i)(8)

Ray v. Rambaud, 103 Ariz. 186, 438 P.2d 752 (1968)—25(e)(2)

Ray Korte Chevrolet v. Simmons, 117 Ariz. 202, 571 P.2d 699 (Ct. App. Div. 1 1977)—59(m), 607, 801(d)(2)(E), 803

Rayner v. Stauffer Chemical Co., 120 Ariz. 328, 585 P.2d 1240 (Ct. App. Div. 1 1978)—702(d), 703, 803, 1002, 1006

Readenour v. Marion Power Shovel, a Div. of Dresser Industries, Inc., 149 Ariz. 442, 719 P.2d 1058, Prod. Liab. Rep. (CCH) ¶ 11012 (1986)—101(b)(6), 105, 402, 403, 407, 501, 801(d)(2)(E)

Reader v. General Motors Corp., 107 Ariz. 149, 483 P.2d 1388, 54 A.L.R.3d 1068 (1971)—401(b)

Reader v. Magma-Superior Copper Co., 110 Ariz. 115, 515 P.2d 860 (1973)—23(f)

Reagan v. Traders & General Ins. Co., 255 F.2d 845 (5th Cir.1958)—54(g)(4)

Reavis v. Industrial Com'n of Arizona, 196 Ariz. 280, 995 P.2d 716 (Ct. App. Div. 1 1999)—301

Reed v. Coyner Crop Dusters, 83 Ariz. 153, 317 P.2d 944 (1957)—58(g)

Reed v. Frey, 10 Ariz. App. 292, 458 P.2d 386 (1969)—55(f)

Reed v. Hinderland, 135 Ariz. 213, 660 P.2d 464, 37 A.L.R.4th 555 (1983)—613(b), 801(d)(2)(E)

Reed v. Hyde, 15 Ariz. App. 203, 487 P.2d 424 (Div. 1 1971)—59(m)

Reed v. Mitchell & Timbanard, P.C., 183 Ariz. 313, 903 P.2d 621 (Ct. App. Div. 1 1995)—8(i)(8), 605

Reese v. Cradit, 12 Ariz. App. 233, 469 P.2d 467 (Div. 2 1970)—18(b), 49(h)

Reeves v. Arizona Aggregate Ass'n Health and Welfare Fund, 102 Ariz. 595, 435 P.2d 829, 67 L.R.R.M. (BNA) 2624, 57 Lab. Cas. (CCH) ¶ 12387 (1967)—9(i)(9)

Reeves v. Beardall, 62 S.Ct. 1085, 316 U.S. 283, 86 L.Ed. 1478 (1942)—54(g)(4)

Reeves v. Markle, 119 Ariz. 159, 579 P.2d 1382 (1978)—50(d), 59(m), 703

Regional Inv. Co. v. SMK Investments, Inc., 129 Ariz. 5, 628 P.2d 42 (Ct. App. Div. 2 1980)—69

Reid v. Reid, 222 Ariz. 204, 213 P.3d 353 (Ct. App. Div. 1 2009)—26(h)

Reinen, Estate of v. Northern Arizona Orthopedics, Ltd., 198 Ariz. 283, 9 P.3d 314 (2000)—8(i)(8), 50(d), 51(d), 59(m), 103(e)

R.E. Monks Const. Co. v. Aetna Cas. & Sur. Co., 189 Ariz. 575, 944 P.2d 517 (Ct. App. Div. 1 1997)—8(i)(8)

Rempt v. Borgeas, 120 Ariz. 36, 583 P.2d 1356 (Ct. App. Div. 1 1978)—41(d)

Republic Ins. Co. v. Feidler, 193 Ariz. 8, 969 P.2d 173 (Ct. App. Div. 1 1998)—51(d), 57, 59(m)

Roberto F. v. Arizona Dept. of Economic Sec., 232 Ariz. 45, 301 P.3d 211 (Ct. App. Div. 1 2013)—24(d)
Roberts v. Kino Community Hosp., 159 Ariz. 333, 767 P.2d 56 (Ct. App. Div. 2 1988)—11(c)
Roberts v. Morgensen Motors, 135 Ariz. 162, 659 P.2d 1307, 35 U.C.C. Rep. Serv. 836 (Ct. App. Div. 1 1982)—59(m)
Roberts v. Robert, 215 Ariz. 176, 158 P.3d 899 (Ct. App. Div. 1 2007)—4.1(m)
Robert Schalkenbach Foundation v. Lincoln Foundation, Inc., 208 Ariz. 176, 91 P.3d 1019 (Ct. App. Div. 1 2004)—8(i)(8), 12(i)
Robertson v. Sixpence Inns of America, Inc., 163 Ariz. 539, 789 P.2d 1040 (1990)—50(d)
Robinson v. Higuera, 157 Ariz. 622, 760 P.2d 622 (Ct. App. Div. 1 1988)—16(h), 37(g)
Robson v. Daily, 61 Ariz. 225, 147 P.2d 491 (1944)—601
Robson Ranch Quail Creek, LLC v. Pima County, 215 Ariz. 545, 161 P.3d 588 (Ct. App. Div. 2 2007)—56(h)(3)
Rochlin v. State, 112 Ariz. 171, 540 P.2d 643 (1975)—301
Roddy v. County of Maricopa, 184 Ariz. 625, 911 P.2d 631 (Ct. App. Div. 1 1996)—54(g)(4)
Roden v. Roden, 190 Ariz. 407, 949 P.2d 67 (Ct. App. Div. 1 1997)—1
Rodgers v. Bryan, 82 Ariz. 143, 309 P.2d 773 (1957)—201(f)
Rodriguez v. Rodriguez, 8 Ariz. App. 5, 442 P.2d 169 (1968)—12(i)
Rodriguez v. Schlittenhart, 161 Ariz. 609, 780 P.2d 442 (Ct. App. Div. 2 1989)—51(d), 59(m), 103(e), 401(b), 404(c)(4), 607
Rodriguez v. Williams, 107 Ariz. 458, 489 P.2d 268 (1971)—50(d), 803
Rodriquez v. Terry, 79 Ariz. 348, 290 P.2d 248 (1955)—25(e)(2)
Roer v. Buckeye Irr. Co., 167 Ariz. 545, 809 P.2d 970 (Ct. App. Div. 2 1990)—8(i)(8)
Rogers v. Fenton, 115 Ariz. 217, 564 P.2d 906 (Ct. App. Div. 2 1977)—26(h), 30(h)(i)
Rogers v. Greer, 70 Ariz. 264, 219 P.2d 760 (1950)—801(d)(2)(E)
Rogers v. Ogg, 101 Ariz. 161, 416 P.2d 594 (1966)—60(d)
Roland v. Bernstein, 171 Ariz. 96, 828 P.2d 1237 (Ct. App. Div. 2 1991)—8(i)(8), 13(i), 14(b), 16.2(c)
Roll v. Janca, 22 Ariz. App. 335, 527 P.2d 294 (Div. 1 1974)—60(d)
Rollin v. William v. Frankel & Co., Inc., 196 Ariz. 350, 996 P.2d 1254 (Ct. App. Div. 2 2000)—4.2(m)
Roman Catholic Diocese of Phoenix v. Superior Court ex rel. County of Maricopa, 204 Ariz. 225, 62 P.3d 970 (Ct. App. Div. 1 2003)—501
Romer-Pollis v. Ada, 223 Ariz. 300, 222 P.3d 916 (Ct. App. Div. 1 2009)—75(h), 77(g)(4)
Romley, State ex rel. v. Ballinger, 209 Ariz. 1, 97 P.3d 101 (2004)—1, 83
Romley, State ex rel. v. Johnson, 196 Ariz. 52, 993 P.2d 453 (Ct. App. Div. 1 1998)—1
Romley, State ex rel. v. Superior Court In and For County of Maricopa, 168 Ariz. 167, 812 P.2d 985 (1991)—1
Romo v. Reyes, 26 Ariz. App. 374, 548 P.2d 1186 (Div. 2 1976)—8(i)(8), 15(d)
Ronwin, Matter of, 139 Ariz. 576, 680 P.2d 107 (1983)—201(f)

Roosevelt Sav. Bank of City of New York v. State Farm Fire & Cas. Co., 27 Ariz. App. 522, 556 P.2d 823 (Div. 1 1976)—56(h)(3)

Roscoe v. Schoolitz, 105 Ariz. 310, 464 P.2d 333 (1970)—51(d)

Roseland v. City of Phoenix, 14 Ariz. App. 117, 481 P.2d 288 (Div. 1 1971)—201(f)

Rosen v. Knaub, 173 Ariz. 304, 842 P.2d 1317 (Ct. App. Div. 1 1992)—42(f)(3)(B)

Rosenberg v. Rosenberg, 123 Ariz. 589, 601 P.2d 589 (1979)—8(i)(8)

Rosner v. Denim & Diamonds, Inc., 188 Ariz. 431, 937 P.2d 353 (Ct. App. Div. 2 1996)—1, 8(i)(8), 13(i), 14(b), 16.2(c), 26(h)

Ross v. Bartz, 158 Ariz. 305, 762 P.2d 592 (Ct. App. Div. 2 1988)—59(m)

Ross v. Ross, 96 Ariz. 249, 393 P.2d 933 (1964)—12(i)

Rossell v. Volkswagen of America, 147 Ariz. 160, 709 P.2d 517, Prod. Liab. Rep. (CCH) ¶ 10752 (1985)—105, 401(b), 803

Rotary Club of Tucson v. Chaprales Ramos de Pena, 160 Ariz. 362, 773 P.2d 467 (Ct. App. Div. 2 1989)—9(i)(9), 60(d), 69

Rouzaud v. Marek, 166 Ariz. 375, 802 P.2d 1074 (Ct. App. Div. 1 1990)—4(i)

Rowland v. Great States Ins. Co., 199 Ariz. 577, 20 P.3d 1158 (Ct. App. Div. 2 2001)—54(g)(4)

Rowland v. Kellogg Brown and Root, Inc., 210 Ariz. 530, 115 P.3d 124 (Ct. App. Div. 2 2005)—8(i)(8)

Rowley v. Rowley, 7 Ariz. App. 418, 440 P.2d 54 (1968)—51(d)

Rowley Plastering Co., Inc. v. Marvin Gardens Development Corp., 180 Ariz. 212, 883 P.2d 449 (Ct. App. Div. 1 1994)—16.2(c)

Roy L., In re, 197 Ariz. 441, 4 P.3d 984 (Ct. App. Div. 1 2000)—201(f)

Rudy v. Meshorer, 146 Ariz. 467, 706 P.2d 1234 (Ct. App. Div. 2 1985)—702(d)

Rugee v. Hadley Products, 73 Ariz. 362, 241 P.2d 798, 33 A.L.R.2d 468 (1952)—23.1

Ruhsam v. Ruhsam, 110 Ariz. 326, 518 P.2d 576 (1974)—801(d)(2)(E)

Ruiz v. Faulkner, 12 Ariz. App. 352, 470 P.2d 500 (Div. 1 1970)—51(d)

Ruiz v. Lopez, 225 Ariz. 217, 236 P.3d 444 (Ct. App. Div. 1 2010)—55(f)

Rustin v. Cook, 143 Ariz. 486, 694 P.2d 316 (Ct. App. Div. 2 1984)—59(m), 103(e)

Ruth v. Rhodes, 66 Ariz. 129, 185 P.2d 304 (1947)—611(c)(2), 614(c), 801(d)(2)(E)

Rutherford v. Rutherford, 193 Ariz. 173, 971 P.2d 220 (Ct. App. Div. 1 1998)—4(i), 12(i)

Rutledge v. Arizona Bd. of Regents, 147 Ariz. 534, 711 P.2d 1207, 29 Ed. Law Rep. 1161 (Ct. App. Div. 1 1985)—103(e), 404(c)(4), 611(c)(2), 801(d)(2)(E), 802, 803

Ruvalcaba By and Through Stubblefield v. Ruvalcaba, 174 Ariz. 436, 850 P.2d 674 (Ct. App. Div. 1 1993)—17(j), 804(b)(6), 807

Ryan v. San Francisco Peaks Trucking Co., Inc., 228 Ariz. 42, 262 P.3d 863 (Ct. App. Div. 1 2011)—801(d)(2)(E)

S

7-G Ranching Co. v. Stites, 4 Ariz. App. 228, 419 P.2d 358 (1966)—56(h)(3)

Sabino R., In re, 198 Ariz. 424, 10 P.3d 1211 (Ct. App. Div. 1 2000)—201(f)

Sabori v. Kuhn, 199 Ariz. 330, 18 P.3d 124 (Ct. App. Div. 1 2001)—75(h), 77(g)(4)

Safeway Ins. Co. v. Collins, 192 Ariz. 262, 963 P.2d 1085 (Ct. App. Div. 1 1998)—17(j)

Safeway Stores, Inc. v. Maricopa County Superior Court, 19 Ariz. App. 210, 505 P.2d 1383 (Div. 1 1973)—3, 11(c)

Safeway Stores, Inc. v. Ramirez, 1 Ariz. App. 117, 400 P.2d 125 (1965)—4.1(m)

Sage v. Blagg Appraisal Co., Ltd., 221 Ariz. 33, 209 P.3d 169 (Ct. App. Div. 1 2009)—56(h)(3)

Salerno v. Atlantic Mut. Ins. Co., 198 Ariz. 54, 6 P.3d 758 (Ct. App. Div. 1 2000)—54(g)(4), 58(g)

Salerno v. Espinoza, 210 Ariz. 586, 115 P.3d 626 (Ct. App. Div. 1 2005)—3

Salica v. Tucson Heart Hosp.-Carondelet, L.L.C., 224 Ariz. 414, 231 P.3d 946 (Ct. App. Div. 2 2010)—8(i)(8), 13(i), 14(b), 16.2(c)

SAL Leasing, Inc. v. State ex rel. Napolitano, 198 Ariz. 434, 10 P.3d 1221 (Ct. App. Div. 1 2000)—52(d), 65(j)(6)

Sallomi v. Phoenix Newspapers, Inc., 160 Ariz. 144, 771 P.2d 469, 16 Media L. Rep. (BNA) 1529 (Ct. App. Div. 2 1989)—11(c), 56(h)(3)

Salt River Project Agricultural Improvement and Power Dist. v. Miller Park, L.L.C., 218 Ariz. 246, 183 P.3d 497 (2008)—68(h)

Salt River Project Agr. Imp. and Power Dist. v. City of Scottsdale, 24 Ariz. App. 254, 537 P.2d 982 (Div. 1 1975)—14(b)

Salt River Project Agr. Imp. and Power Dist. v. Westinghouse Elec. Corp., 176 Ariz. 383, 861 P.2d 668, Prod. Liab. Rep. (CCH) ¶ 13562 (Ct. App. Div. 2 1993)—51(d), 59(m), 103(e)

Salt River Project/Bechtel Corp. v. Industrial Com'n of Arizona, 179 Ariz. 280, 877 P.2d 1336 (Ct. App. Div. 1 1994)—8(i)(8)

Salt River Sand and Rock Co. v. Dunevant, 222 Ariz. 102, 213 P.3d 251 (Ct. App. Div. 1 2009)—62(j)

Salt River Valley Water Users' Ass'n v. Superior Court, In and For County of Maricopa, 178 Ariz. 70, 870 P.2d 1166 (Ct. App. Div. 1 1993)—56(h)(3)

Salvatierra v. National Indem. Co., 133 Ariz. 16, 648 P.2d 131 (Ct. App. Div. 2 1982)—24(d)

Salvation Army v. Bryson, 229 Ariz. 204, 273 P.3d 656 (Ct. App. Div. 2 2012)—26(h)

Samaritan Foundation v. Goodfarb, 176 Ariz. 497, 862 P.2d 870, 26 A.L.R.5th 893 (1993)—26(h), 26.1(g), 501

Samaritan Foundation v. Superior Court In and For County of Maricopa, 173 Ariz. 426, 844 P.2d 593 (Ct. App. Div. 1 1992)—501

Samaritan Health Services v. City of Glendale, 148 Ariz. 394, 714 P.2d 887 (Ct. App. Div. 1 1986)—501

Samaritan Health Services, Inc. v. Superior Court In and For Maricopa County, 142 Ariz. 435, 690 P.2d 154 (Ct. App. Div. 1 1984)—26(h), 501, 612(c)

Samaritan Health System v. Superior Court of State of Ariz., 194 Ariz. 284, 981 P.2d 584 (Ct. App. Div. 1 1998)—56(h)(3)

Samsel v. Allstate Ins. Co., 204 Ariz. 1, 59 P.3d 281 (2002)—56(h)(3), 104(e)

Sanchez v. City of Tucson, 191 Ariz. 128, 953 P.2d 168 (1998)—8(i)(8), 13(i), 14(b), 16.2(c), 56(h)(3)

Sanchez v. Coxon, 175 Ariz. 93, 854 P.2d 126 (1993)—56(h)(3)

Sanchez v. Gama, 233 Ariz. 125, 310 P.3d 1 (Ct. App. Div. 1 2013)—26(h)

School Dist. No. 1 of Navajo County v. Snowflake Union High School Dist. of Navajo County, 100 Ariz. 389, 414 P.2d 985 (1966)—54(g)(4)

Schoolhouse Educational Aids, Inc. v. Haag, 145 Ariz. 87, 699 P.2d 1318 (Ct. App. Div. 2 1985)—41(d)

Schornick v. Schornick, 25 Ariz. 563, 220 P. 397, 31 A.L.R. 159 (1923)—501, 601

Schritter v. State Farm Mut. Auto. Ins. Co., 201 Ariz. 391, 36 P.3d 739 (2001)—26(h), 54(g)(4)

Schuldes v. National Sur. Corp., 27 Ariz. App. 611, 557 P.2d 543 (Div. 1 1976)—201(f)

Schwab v. Ames Const., 207 Ariz. 56, 83 P.3d 56 (Ct. App. Div. 1 2004)—7.1(g), 56(h)(3)

Schwab Sales, Inc. v. GN Const. Co., Inc., 196 Ariz. 33, 992 P.2d 1128 (Ct. App. Div. 2 1998)—54(g)(4), 77(g)(4)

Schwartz v. Arizona Primary Care Physicians, 192 Ariz. 290, 964 P.2d 491 (Ct. App. Div. 1 1998)—4(i), 12(i), 38.1(k)(3), 41(d), 60(d)

Schwartz v. Schwerin, 85 Ariz. 242, 336 P.2d 144 (1959)—8(i)(8), 58(g)

Schweber Electronics v. National Semiconductor Corp., 174 Ariz. 406, 850 P.2d 119 (Ct. App. Div. 1 1992)—14(b)

Schweiger v. China Doll Restaurant, Inc., 138 Ariz. 183, 673 P.2d 927 (Ct. App. Div. 1 1983)—54(g)(4)

Scott v. Allstate Ins. Co., 27 Ariz. App. 236, 553 P.2d 1221 (Div. 1 1976)—405(b)

Scottsdale, City of v. Eller Outdoor Advertising Co. of Ariz., Inc., 119 Ariz. 86, 579 P.2d 590 (Ct. App. Div. 1 1978)—703

Scottsdale, City of v. Kokaska, 17 Ariz. App. 120, 495 P.2d 1327 (Div. 1 1972)—35(c)(3)

Scottsdale Ins. Co. v. Cendejas, 220 Ariz. 281, 205 P.3d 1128 (Ct. App. Div. 1 2009)—8(i)(8), 26(h), 54(g)(4), 58(g), 68(h)

Scottsdale Memorial Health Systems, Inc. v. Clark, 157 Ariz. 461, 759 P.2d 607 (1988)—10(f)

Scottsdale Princess Partnership v. Maricopa County, 185 Ariz. 368, 916 P.2d 1084 (Ct. App. Div. 1 1995)—26.1(g), 37(g)

Searchtoppers.com, L.L.C. v. TrustCash LLC, 231 Ariz. 236, 293 P.3d 512 (Ct. App. Div. 1 2012)—55(f)

Sears Roebuck & Co. v. Jackson, 21 Ariz. App. 176, 517 P.2d 529 (Div. 1 1973)—801(d)(2)(E), 803

Sears, Roebuck & Co. v. Mackey, 76 S.Ct. 895, 351 U.S. 427, 100 L.Ed. 1297 (1956)—54(g)(4)

Sears Roebuck and Co. v. Walker, 127 Ariz. 432, 621 P.2d 938 (Ct. App. Div. 1 1980)—16(h), 55(f)

Security Sav. and Loan Ass'n v. Fenton, 167 Ariz. 268, 806 P.2d 362 (Ct. App. Div. 2 1990)—3

Security Title Agency, Inc. v. Pope, 219 Ariz. 480, 200 P.3d 977, 27 I.E.R. Cas. (BNA) 1811 (Ct. App. Div. 1 2008)—8(i)(8), 13(i), 14(b), 16.2(c), 50(d)

Segovia v. Industrial Commission, 119 Ariz. 231, 580 P.2d 369 (Ct. App. Div. 1 1978)—609(e)

Seidman v. Seidman, 222 Ariz. 408, 215 P.3d 382 (Ct. App. Div. 1 2009)—37(g)

Seisinger v. Siebel, 220 Ariz. 85, 203 P.3d 483 (2009)—1, 101(b)(6), 702(d)

Selby v. Savard, 134 Ariz. 222, 655 P.2d 342 (1982)—405(b), 602

Silva v. Menderson, 41 Ariz. 258, 17 P.2d 809 (1933)—201(f)
Simer v. Rios, 661 F.2d 655, 32 Fed. R. Serv. 2d 781, 68 A.L.R. Fed. 235 (7th Cir. 1981)—23(f)
Simon v. Safeway, Inc., 217 Ariz. 330, 173 P.3d 1031 (Ct. App. Div. 2 2007)—56(h)(3)
Simpson v. Heiderich, 4 Ariz. App. 232, 419 P.2d 362 (1966)—35(c)(3), 59(m)
Sims v. Ryan, 181 Ariz. 330, 890 P.2d 625 (Ct. App. Div. 1 1995)—58(g)
Singleton v. Valianos, 84 Ariz. 51, 323 P.2d 697 (1958)—59(m)
Sirek v. Fairfield Snowbowl, Inc., 166 Ariz. 183, 800 P.2d 1291 (Ct. App. Div. 1 1990)—8(i)(8), 12(i), 15(d)
Sisemore v. Farmers Ins. Co. of Arizona, 161 Ariz. 564, 779 P.2d 1303 (Ct. App. Div. 1 1989)—54(g)(4)
Sitton v. Deutsche Bank Nat. Trust Co., 233 Ariz. 215, 311 P.3d 237 (Ct. App. Div. 1 2013)—7.1(g), 201(f), 803
Skates v. Stockton, 140 Ariz. 505, 683 P.2d 304 (Ct. App. Div. 2 1984)—12(i)
Skok v. City of Glendale, 3 Ariz. App. 254, 413 P.2d 585 (1966)—32(d)(4)
Sligh v. Watson, 67 Ariz. 95, 191 P.2d 724 (1948)—58(g)
Sligh v. Watson, 69 Ariz. 373, 214 P.2d 123 (1950)—8(i)(8)
Slonsky v. Hunter, 17 Ariz. App. 231, 496 P.2d 874 (Div. 1 1972)—2, 38(d), 39(q)
Slovenic Nat. Ben. Soc. v. Dabcevich, 30 Ariz. 294, 246 P. 765 (1926)—9(i)(9)
Slow Development Co. v. Coulter, 88 Ariz. 122, 353 P.2d 890 (1960)—32(d)(4), 401(b), 402, 407, 611(c)(2), 804(b)(6)
Smart Industries Corp., Mfg. v. Superior Court In and For County of Yuma, 179 Ariz. 141, 876 P.2d 1176 (Ct. App. Div. 1 1994)—501
Smethers v. Campion, 210 Ariz. 167, 108 P.3d 946 (Ct. App. Div. 1 2005)—702(d)
Smith, Ex parte, 228 Ala. 232, 153 So. 152 (1934)—59(m)
Smith, In re, 209 Ariz. 343, 101 P.3d 637 (2004)—69
Smith v. CIGNA HealthPlan of Arizona, 203 Ariz. 173, 52 P.3d 205, 19 I.E.R. Cas. (BNA) 41, 170 L.R.R.M. (BNA) 2884, 147 Lab. Cas. (CCH) ¶ 59642, 120 A.L.R.5th 757 (Ct. App. Div. 2 2002)—8(i)(8)
Smith v. Continental Bank, 130 Ariz. 320, 636 P.2d 98 (1981)—15(d)
Smith v. Coronado Foothills Estates Homeowners Ass'n Inc., 117 Ariz. 171, 571 P.2d 668 (1977)—65(j)(6), 65.1
Smith v. Hurley, 121 Ariz. 164, 589 P.2d 38 (Ct. App. Div. 1 1978)—68(h)
Smith v. John C. Lincoln Hospital, 118 Ariz. 549, 578 P.2d 630 (Ct. App. Div. 1 1978)—702(d), 703
Smith v. Johnson, 183 Ariz. 38, 899 P.2d 199 (Ct. App. Div. 1 1995)—59(m)
Smith v. Lucia, 173 Ariz. 290, 842 P.2d 1303 (Ct. App. Div. 1 1992)—11(c)
Smith v. Melson, Inc., 135 Ariz. 119, 659 P.2d 1264 (1983)—104(e)
Smith v. Mitchell, 214 Ariz. 78, 148 P.3d 1151 (Ct. App. Div. 2 2006)—42(f)(3)(B)
Smith v. Monroe, 15 Ariz. App. 366, 488 P.2d 1003 (Div. 2 1971)—55(f)
Smith v. Moroney, 79 Ariz. 35, 282 P.2d 470 (1955)—59(m)
Smith v. Payne, 156 Ariz. 506, 753 P.2d 1162 (1988)—12(i)
Smith v. Rabb, 95 Ariz. 49, 386 P.2d 649 (1963)—14(b), 19(d), 38(d)
Smith v. Superior Equipment Co., 102 Ariz. 320, 428 P.2d 998 (1967)—8(i)(8)
Smith v. Tang, 100 Ariz. 196, 412 P.2d 697 (1966)—59(m)
Smoole v. Maricopa County, 177 Ariz. 185, 866 P.2d 167 (Tax Ct.1993)—7.1(g)

Snyder v. Beers, 1 Ariz. App. 497, 405 P.2d 288 (1965)—803
Societe Internationale Pour Participations Industrielles Et Commerciales, S. A. v. Rogers, 357 U.S. 197, 78 S. Ct. 1087, 2 L. Ed. 2d 1255 (1958)—37(g)
Solimeno v. Yonan, 224 Ariz. 74, 227 P.3d 481 (Ct. App. Div. 1 2010)—26.1(g), 54(g)(4)
Solomon v. Findley, 165 Ariz. 45, 796 P.2d 477 (Ct. App. Div. 2 1990)—12(i)
Sonoran Desert Investigations, Inc. v. Miller, 213 Ariz. 274, 141 P.3d 754 (Ct. App. Div. 2 2006)—8(i)(8), 56(h)(3)
Sorensen v. Farmers Ins. Co. of Arizona, 191 Ariz. 464, 957 P.2d 1007 (Ct. App. Div. 1 1997)—54(g)(4), 56(h)(3)
Sorrells, In re Guardianship of, 58 Ariz. 25, 117 P.2d 96 (1941)—801(d)(2)(E), 804(b)(6)
Soto v. Brinkerhoff, 183 Ariz. 333, 903 P.2d 641 (Ct. App. Div. 2 1995)—26(h)
Southern Arizona School For Boys, Inc. v. Chery, 119 Ariz. 277, 580 P.2d 738 (Ct. App. Div. 2 1978)—9(i)(9)
Southern California Edison Co. v. Peabody Western Coal Co., 194 Ariz. 47, 977 P.2d 769 (1999)—54(g)(4)
Southern Pac. Co. v. Cavallo, 84 Ariz. 24, 323 P.2d 1 (1958)—32(d)(4)
Southern Pac. Transp. Co. v. Lueck, 111 Ariz. 560, 535 P.2d 599 (1975)—702(d)
Southern Pac. Transp. Co. v. Veliz, 117 Ariz. 199, 571 P.2d 696 (Ct. App. Div. 2 1977)—26(h), 408(b)
Southern Ry. Co. v. Lanham, 403 F.2d 119, 12 Fed. R. Serv. 2d 860, 33 A.L.R.3d 427 (5th Cir. 1968)—26(h)
Southwestern Freight Lines v. Floyd, 58 Ariz. 249, 119 P.2d 120 (1941)—201(f), 701(c)
Southwestern Freight Lines v. Shafer, 57 Ariz. 111, 111 P.2d 625 (1941)—58(g)
Southwest Gas Corp. v. Irwin ex rel. County of Cochise, 229 Ariz. 198, 273 P.3d 650 (Ct. App. Div. 2 2012)—54(g)(4)
Southwest Soil Remediation, Inc. v. City of Tucson, 201 Ariz. 438, 36 P.3d 1208 (Ct. App. Div. 2 2001)—12(i), 15(d)
Souza v. Fred Carries Contracts, Inc., 191 Ariz. 247, 955 P.2d 3 (Ct. App. Div. 2 1997)—26(h), 26.1(g), 37(g)
Spain v. General Motors Corp., Chevrolet Motor Div., 171 Ariz. 226, 829 P.2d 1272 (Ct. App. Div. 2 1992)—8(i)(8)
Sparks v. Republic Nat. Life Ins. Co., 132 Ariz. 529, 647 P.2d 1127 (1982)—54(g)(4)
Speer v. Donfeld, 193 Ariz. 28, 969 P.2d 193 (Ct. App. Div. 2 1998)—5.1(d)
Spiegel v. Board of Sup'rs of Maricopa County, 175 Ariz. 479, 857 P.2d 1333 (Tax Ct. 1993)—3, 4(i)
Sprang v. Petersen Lumber, Inc., 165 Ariz. 257, 798 P.2d 395 (Ct. App. Div. 1 1990)—4(i), 4.1(m), 55(f)
Spriggel v. Maricopa County, 15 Ariz. App. 162, 487 P.2d 8 (Div. 1 1971)—54(g)(4), 58(g)
Springfield Credit Union v. Johnson, 123 Ariz. 319, 599 P.2d 772 (1979)—54(g)(4), 60(d), 69
Spudnuts, Inc. v. Lane, 131 Ariz. 424, 641 P.2d 912 (Ct. App. Div. 2 1982)—9(i)(9)
Spudnuts, Inc. v. Lane, 139 Ariz. 35, 676 P.2d 669 (Ct. App. Div. 2 1984)—4.1(m), 17(j), 19(d), 21, 58(g), 69

Srithong v. Total Investment Co., 23 Cal. App. 4th 721, 28 Cal. Rptr. 2d 672 (2d Dist. 1994)—8(i)(8), 13(i), 14(b), 16.2(c), 26(h)
S.S. v. Superior Court In and For County of Maricopa, 178 Ariz. 423, 874 P.2d 980 (Ct. App. Div. 1 1994)—26.1(g)
Staffco, Inc. v. Maricopa Trading Co., 122 Ariz. 353, 595 P.2d 31 (1979)—18(b), 20(b), 58(g)
Stainless Specialty Mfg. Co. v. Industrial Com'n of Arizona, 144 Ariz. 12, 695 P.2d 261 (1985)—702(d)
Stallcup v. Rathbun, 76 Ariz. 63, 258 P.2d 821 (1953)—59(m)
Standage v. Jaburg & Wilk, P.C., 177 Ariz. 221, 866 P.2d 889 (Ct. App. Div. 1 1993)—11(c)
Standage Ventures, Inc. v. State, 114 Ariz. 480, 562 P.2d 360 (1977)—8(i)(8)
Standard Chartered PLC v. Price Waterhouse, 190 Ariz. 6, 945 P.2d 317 (Ct. App. Div. 1 1996)—8(i)(8), 13(i), 14(b), 16.2(c), 50(d), 59(m), 702(d), 703, 803
Starkins v. Bateman, 150 Ariz. 537, 724 P.2d 1206 (Ct. App. Div. 1 1986)—103(e), 701(c), 801(d)(2)(E), 802, 807
Starkovich v. Noye, 111 Ariz. 347, 529 P.2d 698 (1974)—801(d)(2)(E), 803
Starkweather v. Conner, 44 Ariz. 369, 38 P.2d 311 (1934)—301
State v. Abdi, 226 Ariz. 361, 248 P.3d 209 (Ct. App. Div. 2 2011)—403
State v. Adamson, 136 Ariz. 250, 665 P.2d 972 (1983)—804(b)(6)
State v. Aguilar, 209 Ariz. 40, 97 P.3d 865 (2004)—404(c)(4)
State v. Albe, 10 Ariz. App. 545, 460 P.2d 651 (Div. 1 1969)—43(k)(2)
State v. Allen, 157 Ariz. 165, 755 P.2d 1153 (1988)—801(d)(2)(E), 802
State v. Archibeque, 223 Ariz. 231, 221 P.3d 1045 (Ct. App. Div. 1 2009)—501
State v. Baumann, 125 Ariz. 404, 610 P.2d 38 (1980)—801(d)(2)(E)
State v. B Bar Enterprises, Inc., 133 Ariz. 99, 649 P.2d 978 (1982)—57
State v. Bejarano, 158 Ariz. 253, 762 P.2d 540 (1988)—1
State v. Belcher, 109 Ariz. 551, 514 P.2d 472 (1973)—103(e)
State v. Bible, 175 Ariz. 549, 858 P.2d 1152 (1993)—101(b)(6), 102, 103(e), 104(e), 105, 106, 201(f), 301, 401(b), 402, 403, 406, 407, 408(b), 409, 410(b)(2), 411, 501, 602 to 605, 606(b)(2)(C), 607, 608(b)(2), 609(e), 610, 611(c)(2), 612(c), 613(b), 614(c), 615(e), 701(c), 702(d), 703, 704(b), 705, 706(e), 801(d)(2)(E), 802, 803, 804(b)(6), 805 to 807, 901(b)(10), 902, 1001(e), 1002, 1003, 1004(d), 1005 to 1007, 1008(c)
State v. Bigger, 227 Ariz. 196, 254 P.3d 1142 (Ct. App. Div. 2 2011)—702(d), 703
State v. Birmingham, 96 Ariz. 109, 392 P.2d 775 (1964)—1, 54(g)(4)
State v. Blazak, 105 Ariz. 216, 462 P.2d 84 (1969)—1
State v. Boykin, 112 Ariz. 109, 538 P.2d 383 (1975)—54(g)(4)
State v. Brown, 102 Ariz. 87, 425 P.2d 112 (1967)—601
State v. Burris, 131 Ariz. 563, 643 P.2d 8 (Ct. App. Div. 2 1982)—604
State v. Burton, 20 Ariz. App. 491, 514 P.2d 244 (Div. 2 1973)—68(h)
State v. Burton, 144 Ariz. 248, 697 P.2d 331 (1985)—7.2(f)
State v. Carr, 154 Ariz. 468, 743 P.2d 1386 (1987)—102
State v. Carver, 227 Ariz. 438, 258 P.3d 256 (Ct. App. Div. 1 2011)—501
State v. Chappell, 225 Ariz. 229, 236 P.3d 1176 (2010)—403, 702(d), 704(b)
State v. Chapple, 135 Ariz. 281, 660 P.2d 1208 (1983)—702(d)
State v. Chavez, 225 Ariz. 442, 239 P.3d 761 (Ct. App. Div. 1 2010)—801(d)(2)(E)

State v. Long, 12 Ariz. App. 170, 468 P.2d 621 (Div. 1 1970)—59(m)
State v. Lundstrom, 161 Ariz. 141, 776 P.2d 1067, 89 A.L.R.4th 437 (1989)—703
State v. Machado, 226 Ariz. 281, 246 P.3d 632 (2011)—804(b)(6)
State v. Macumber, 112 Ariz. 569, 544 P.2d 1084 (1976)—702(d)
State v. Mahoney, 103 Ariz. 308, 441 P.2d 68 (1968)—26(h), 30(h)(i)
State v. Marcham, 160 Ariz. 52, 770 P.2d 356 (Ct. App. Div. 1 1988)—604, 706(e)
State v. McFarlin, 110 Ariz. 225, 517 P.2d 87 (1973)—404(c)(4)
State v. McGann, 132 Ariz. 296, 645 P.2d 811 (1982)—802, 805
State v. Mendez, 2 Ariz. App. 77, 406 P.2d 427 (1965)—611(c)(2)
State v. Miller, 128 Ariz. 112, 624 P.2d 309 (Ct. App. Div. 1 1980)—405(b)
State v. Miller, 226 Ariz. 202, 245 P.3d 887 (Ct. App. Div. 2 2010)—901(b)(10)
State v. Mosley, 119 Ariz. 393, 581 P.2d 238 (1978)—702(d)
State v. Navarro, 132 Ariz. 340, 645 P.2d 1254 (Ct. App. Div. 2 1982)—603
State v. Neil, 102 Ariz. 110, 425 P.2d 842 (1967)—42(f)(3)(B)
State v. Nettz, 114 Ariz. 296, 560 P.2d 814 (Ct. App. Div. 2 1977)—65(j)(6)
State v. O'Brien, 123 Ariz. 578, 601 P.2d 341 (Ct. App. Div. 2 1979)—501
State v. O'Connor, 171 Ariz. 19, 827 P.2d 480 (Ct. App. Div. 1 1992)—62(j)
State v. Oliver, 158 Ariz. 22, 760 P.2d 1071 (1988)—401(b), 608(b)(2)
State v. Ott, 167 Ariz. 420, 808 P.2d 305 (Ct. App. Div. 1 1990)—26(h), 36(c), 38.1(k)(3), 501
State v. Owen, 101 Ariz. 156, 416 P.2d 589 (1966)—806
State v. Palmer, 229 Ariz. 64, 270 P.3d 891 (Ct. App. Div. 2 2012)—801(d)(2)(E)
State v. Patterson, 222 Ariz. 574, 218 P.3d 1031 (Ct. App. Div. 1 2009)—1
State v. Payne, 232 Ariz. 360, 306 P.3d 17 (2013)—404(c)(4)
State v. Peruskov, 166 Ariz. 28, 800 P.2d 15 (Ct. App. Div. 1 1990)—64
State v. Pierce, 59 Ariz. 411, 129 P.2d 916 (1942)—1
State v. Ramirez, 142 Ariz. 171, 688 P.2d 1063 (Ct. App. Div. 2 1984)—807
State v. Rendon, 148 Ariz. 524, 715 P.2d 777 (Ct. App. Div. 2 1986)—803
State v. Rhodes, 219 Ariz. 476, 200 P.3d 973 (Ct. App. Div. 1 2008)—404(c)(4)
State v. Richey, 160 Ariz. 564, 774 P.2d 1354 (1989)—52(d), 54(g)(4), 58(g)
State v. Robinson, 153 Ariz. 191, 735 P.2d 801 (1987)—101(b)(6)
State v. Roque, 213 Ariz. 193, 141 P.3d 368 (2006)—807
State v. Ross, 97 Ariz. 51, 396 P.2d 619 (1964)—59(m)
State v. Ruelas, 174 Ariz. 37, 846 P.2d 850 (Ct. App. Div. 1 1992)—803, 804(b)(6)
State v. Schossow, 145 Ariz. 504, 703 P.2d 448 (1985)—301, 601
State v. Schurz, 176 Ariz. 46, 859 P.2d 156 (1993)—403
State v. Shipman, 208 Ariz. 474, 94 P.3d 1169 (Ct. App. Div. 2 2004)—11(c)
State v. Simoneau, 98 Ariz. 2, 401 P.2d 404 (1965)—611(c)(2)
State v. Skinner, 110 Ariz. 135, 515 P.2d 880 (1973)—607, 801(d)(2)(E)
State v. Slover, 220 Ariz. 239, 204 P.3d 1088 (Ct. App. Div. 2 2009)—406
State v. Smith, 215 Ariz. 221, 159 P.3d 531 (2007)—703
State v. Sosnowicz, 229 Ariz. 90, 270 P.3d 917 (Ct. App. Div. 1 2012)—403, 702(d), 704(b)
State v. Spratt, 126 Ariz. 184, 613 P.2d 848 (Ct. App. Div. 2 1980)—104(e)
State v. Stone, 151 Ariz. 455, 728 P.2d 674 (Ct. App. Div. 1 1986)—610
State v. Stuck, 154 Ariz. 16, 739 P.2d 1333 (Ct. App. Div. 1 1987)—410(b)(2)

State Farm Ins. Companies v. Premier Manufactured Systems, Inc., 217 Ariz. 222, 172 P.3d 410 (2007)—13(i), 14(b), 16.2(c)
State Farm Mut. Auto. Ins. Co. v. Lee, 199 Ariz. 52, 13 P.3d 1169 (2000)—26(h), 501
State Farm Mut. Auto. Ins. Co. v. Paynter, 118 Ariz. 470, 577 P.2d 1089 (Ct. App. Div. 1 1978)—24(d)
State Farm Mut. Auto. Ins. Co. v. Wilson, 162 Ariz. 251, 782 P.2d 727 (1989)—104(e)
Statewide Ins. Corp. v. Dewar, 143 Ariz. 553, 694 P.2d 1167 (1984)—104(e)
Steed v. Cuevas, 24 Ariz. App. 547, 540 P.2d 166 (Div. 1 1975)—803
Steiger v. Superior Court for Maricopa County, 112 Ariz. 1, 536 P.2d 689 (1975)—501
Stein v. Sonus USA, Inc., 214 Ariz. 200, 150 P.3d 773 (Ct. App. Div. 2 2007)—56(h)(3)
Steiner v. 20th Century-Fox Film Corp., 220 F.2d 105 (9th Cir.1955)—54(g)(4)
Stevens v. Anderson, 75 Ariz. 331, 256 P.2d 712 (1953)—56(h)(3)
Stevens v. Mehagian's Home Furnishings, Inc., 90 Ariz. 42, 365 P.2d 208 (1961)—54(g)(4)
Stewart v. Woodruff, 19 Ariz. App. 190, 505 P.2d 1081 (Div. 2 1973)—103(e)
Stoecker v. Brush Wellman, Inc., 194 Ariz. 448, 984 P.2d 534 (1999)—56(h)(3)
Stone, Application of, 14 Ariz. App. 109, 481 P.2d 280 (Div. 1 1971)—54(g)(4)
Stone v. Arizona Highway Commission, 93 Ariz. 384, 381 P.2d 107 (1963)—12(i)
Stoneberg v. Northwood, 121 Ariz. 230, 589 P.2d 473 (Ct. App. Div. 2 1978)—58(g)
Stowell v. Arizona Sav. & Loan Ass'n, 93 Ariz. 310, 380 P.2d 606 (1963)—66(d)
Stoyer v. Doctors Hospital, Inc., 15 Ariz. App. 255, 488 P.2d 191, 55 A.L.R.3d 295 (Div. 1 1971)—16(h)
Strategic Development and Const., Inc. v. 7th & Roosevelt Partners, LLC, 224 Ariz. 60, 226 P.3d 1046 (Ct. App. Div. 1 2010)—6(f), 12(i), 56(h)(3)
Strawberry Water Co. v. Paulsen, 220 Ariz. 401, 207 P.3d 654 (Ct. App. Div. 1 2008)—12(i)
Stroud v. Dorr-Oliver, Inc., 112 Ariz. 403, 542 P.2d 1102 (1975)—401(b)
Stukey v. Stephens, 37 Ariz. 514, 295 P. 973 (1931)—2, 38(d)
Stulce v. Salt River Project Agr. Imp. and Power Dist., 197 Ariz. 87, 3 P.3d 1007 (Ct. App. Div. 1 1999)—3, 8(i)(8)
Sturm v. Heim, 95 Ariz. 300, 389 P.2d 702 (1964)—50(d)
Styers v. Superior Court In and For County of Mohave, 161 Ariz. 477, 779 P.2d 352 (Ct. App. Div. 1 1989)—501
Styles v. Ceranski, 185 Ariz. 448, 916 P.2d 1164 (Ct. App. Div. 1 1996)—59(m)
Suciu v. AMFAC Distributing Corp., 138 Ariz. 514, 675 P.2d 1333 (Ct. App. Div. 2 1983)—59(m)
Sullins v. Third and Catalina Const. Partnership, 124 Ariz. 114, 602 P.2d 495 (Ct. App. Div. 1 1979)—407
Sullivan & Brugnatelli Advertising Co., Inc. v. Century Capital Corp., 153 Ariz. 78, 734 P.2d 1034 (Ct. App. Div. 1 1986)—54(g)(4)
Sulpher Springs Valley Elec. Co-op., Inc. v. Verdugo, 14 Ariz. App. 141, 481 P.2d 511 (Div. 2 1971)—103(e), 702(d)

Summit Properties, Inc. v. Wilson, 26 Ariz. App. 550, 550 P.2d 104 (Div. 1 1976)—8(i)(8)

Suncor Development Co. v. Maricopa County, 163 Ariz. 403, 788 P.2d 136 (Tax Ct.1990)—55(f)

Sundt v. Farley, 12 Ariz. App. 346, 470 P.2d 494 (Div. 2 1970)—26.2(b)(4), 33(c)

Sun Health Corp. v. Myers, 205 Ariz. 315, 70 P.3d 444 (Ct. App. Div. 1 2003)—501

Sun Valley Ranch 308 Ltd. Partnership ex rel. Englewood Properties, Inc. v. Robson, 231 Ariz. 287, 294 P.3d 125 (Ct. App. Div. 1 2012)—72(e)(7)

Sun World Corp. v. Pennysaver, Inc., 130 Ariz. 585, 637 P.2d 1088 (Ct. App. Div. 1 1981)—10(f), 12(i)

Suttle v. Seely, 94 Ariz. 161, 382 P.2d 570 (1963)—8(i)(8)

Swartz, Matter of, 141 Ariz. 266, 686 P.2d 1236 (1984)—401(b), 402

SWC Baseline & Crismon Investors, L.L.C. v. Augusta Ranch Ltd. Partnership, 228 Ariz. 271, 265 P.3d 1070 (Ct. App. Div. 1 2011)—15(d)

Sweis v. Chatwin, 120 Ariz. 249, 585 P.2d 269 (Ct. App. Div. 1 1978)—67(f)(3)

Swichtenberg v. Brimer, 171 Ariz. 77, 828 P.2d 1218 (Ct. App. Div. 1 1991)—12(i)

Switzer v. Superior Court In and For County of Maricopa, 176 Ariz. 285, 860 P.2d 1338 (Ct. App. Div. 1 1993)—42(f)(3)(B)

T

$3,000.00 U.S. Currency, Matter of Forfeiture of, 164 Ariz. 120, 791 P.2d 646 (Ct. App. Div. 2 1990)—41(d), 60(d)

Taeger v. Catholic Family and Community Services, 196 Ariz. 285, 995 P.2d 721 (Ct. App. Div. 1 1999)—26.1(g), 37(g), 50(d), 803, 901(b)(10)

Taliaferro v. Taliaferro, 186 Ariz. 221, 921 P.2d 21 (1996)—42(f)(3)(B)

Taliaferro v. Taliaferro, 188 Ariz. 333, 935 P.2d 911 (Ct. App. Div. 1 1996)—11(c), 16(h), 26.1(g), 37(g)

Tamsen v. Weber, 166 Ariz. 364, 802 P.2d 1063 (Ct. App. Div. 1 1990)—59(m)

Tanner v. Pacioni, 3 Ariz. App. 297, 413 P.2d 863 (1966)—59(m)

Tanner Companies v. Arizona State Land Dept., 142 Ariz. 183, 688 P.2d 1075 (Ct. App. Div. 2 1984)—601, 702(d)

Tarnoff v. Jones, 15 Ariz. App. 88, 486 P.2d 200 (Div. 1 1971)—54(g)(4)

Tarnoff v. Jones, 17 Ariz. App. 240, 497 P.2d 60 (Div. 1 1972)—54(g)(4), 55(f), 60(d), 69

Tarr v. Superior Court In and For Pima County, 142 Ariz. 349, 690 P.2d 68 (1984)—55(f)

Tate v. Connel, 3 Ariz. App. 534, 416 P.2d 213 (1966)—801(d)(2)(E)

Taylor v. Cate, 117 Ariz. 367, 573 P.2d 58 (1977)—611(c)(2)

Taylor v. DiRico, 124 Ariz. 513, 606 P.2d 3 (1980)—51(d), 408(b), 702(d)

Taylor v. Fireman's Fund Ins. Co. of Canada, 161 Ariz. 432, 778 P.2d 1328 (Ct. App. Div. 2 1989)—4.2(m), 12(i)

Taylor v. Jarrett, 191 Ariz. 550, 959 P.2d 807 (Ct. App. Div. 1 1998)—4(i), 12(i)

Taylor v. Southern Pac. Transp. Co., 130 Ariz. 516, 637 P.2d 726 (1981)—54(g)(4), 606(b)(2)(C)

Taylor v. State Farm Mut. Auto. Ins. Co., 175 Ariz. 148, 854 P.2d 1134 (1993)—104(e)

Taylor v. State Farm Mut. Auto. Ins. Co., 185 Ariz. 174, 913 P.2d 1092 (1996)—8(i)(8)

Technical Air Products, Inc. v. Sheridan-Gray, Inc., 103 Ariz. 450, 445 P.2d 426 (1968)—13(i), 55(f)

Tempe Corporate Office Bldg. v. Arizona Funding Services, Inc., 167 Ariz. 394, 807 P.2d 1130 (Ct. App. Div. 1 1991)—8(i)(8)

Templer v. Zele, 166 Ariz. 390, 803 P.2d 111 (Ct. App. Div. 2 1990)—41(d), 60(d)

Tenet Healthsystem TGH, Inc. v. Silver, 203 Ariz. 217, 52 P.3d 786 (Ct. App. Div. 2 2002)—64

Terrazas v. Superior Court, Maricopa County, Division Five, 112 Ariz. 434, 543 P.2d 120 (1975)—54(g)(4)

Terry v. Gaslight Square Associates, 182 Ariz. 365, 897 P.2d 667 (Ct. App. Div. 2 1994)—59(m)

Theriault v. Scottsdale Enterprises, 157 Ariz. 77, 754 P.2d 1352 (Ct. App. Div. 2 1987)—41(d), 54(g)(4), 58(g)

Thiele v. City of Phoenix, 232 Ariz. 40, 301 P.3d 206 (Ct. App. Div. 1 2013)—67(f)(3)

Thielking v. Kirschner, 176 Ariz. 154, 859 P.2d 777 (Ct. App. Div. 1 1993)—6(f)

Third & Catalina Associates v. City of Phoenix, 182 Ariz. 203, 895 P.2d 115, 63 A.L.R.5th 879 (Ct. App. Div. 1 1994)—8(i)(8)

Thomas v. Bowman, 24 Ariz. App. 322, 538 P.2d 409 (Div. 1 1975)—801(d)(2)(E)

Thomas v. First Interstate Bank of Arizona, N.A., 187 Ariz. 488, 930 P.2d 1002, 54 A.L.R.5th 827 (Ct. App. Div. 2 1996)—8(i)(8), 13(i), 14(b), 16.2(c)

Thomas v. Western Sav. & Loan Ass'n, 6 Ariz. App. 511, 433 P.2d 1003 (1967)—58(g)

Thomas, State ex rel. v. Gordon, 213 Ariz. 499, 144 P.3d 513 (Ct. App. Div. 1 2006)—42(f)(3)(B)

Thomas, State ex rel. v. Schneider, 212 Ariz. 292, 130 P.3d 991 (Ct. App. Div. 1 2006)—501

Thompson v. Better-Bilt Aluminum Products Co., Inc., 171 Ariz. 550, 832 P.2d 203, 7 I.E.R. Cas. (BNA) 1017, 126 Lab. Cas. (CCH) ¶ 57536 (1992)—50(d), 59(m)

Thompson v. Better-Bilt Aluminum Products Co., Inc., 187 Ariz. 121, 927 P.2d 781, 11 I.E.R. Cas. (BNA) 971 (Ct. App. Div. 1 1996)—51(d)

Thompson v. Mecey, 101 Ariz. 125, 416 P.2d 558 (1966)—38.1(k)(3)

Thornton v. Marsico, 5 Ariz. App. 299, 425 P.2d 869 (1967)—14(b)

Thorpe, Matter of Estate of, 152 Ariz. 341, 732 P.2d 571 (Ct. App. Div. 1 1986)—301, 702(d)

T.H. Properties v. Sunshine Auto Rental, Inc., 151 Ariz. 444, 728 P.2d 663 (Ct. App. Div. 2 1986)—39(q), 611(c)(2)

Throop v. F. E. Young & Co., 94 Ariz. 146, 382 P.2d 560 (1963)—501

Thunderbird Farms v. Hernandez, 11 Ariz. App. 383, 464 P.2d 829 (Div. 2 1970)—38.1(k)(3), 60(d)

Thurston, In re Estate of, 199 Ariz. 215, 16 P.3d 776 (Ct. App. Div. 1 2000)—26.1(g)

Tierra Ranchos Homeowners Ass'n v. Kitchukov, 216 Ariz. 195, 165 P.3d 173 (Ct. App. Div. 1 2007)—56(h)(3)

Trantor v. Fredrikson, 179 Ariz. 299, 878 P.2d 657 (1994)—54(g)(4), 58(g)
Travers, In re Estate of, 192 Ariz. 333, 965 P.2d 67 (Ct. App. Div. 1 1998)—26.1(g), 59(m), 60(d)
Treadaway v. Meador, 103 Ariz. 83, 436 P.2d 902 (1968)—37(g)
Treadway v. Industrial Commission, 69 Ariz. 301, 213 P.2d 373 (1950)—201(f)
Trebilcox v. Brown & Bain, P.A., 133 Ariz. 588, 653 P.2d 45 (Ct. App. Div. 1 1982)—54(g)(4), 58(g)
Trevizo v. Astec Industries, Inc., 156 Ariz. 320, 751 P.2d 980 (Ct. App. Div. 2 1987)—401(b), 404(c)(4), 607, 801(d)(2)(E), 803
Tri-City Property Management Services, Inc. v. Research Products Corp., 149 Ariz. 596, 721 P.2d 144, 42 U.C.C. Rep. Serv. 1606 (Ct. App. Div. 2 1986)—17(j), 19(d)
Trickel v. Rainbo Baking Co. of Phoenix, 100 Ariz. 222, 412 P.2d 852 (1966)—613(b)
Trimmer v. Ludtke, 105 Ariz. 260, 462 P.2d 809 (1969)—56(h)(3)
Tripati v. Forwith, 223 Ariz. 81, 219 P.3d 291 (Ct. App. Div. 1 2009)—59(m)
Tripp v. Chubb, 69 Ariz. 31, 208 P.2d 312 (1949)—501
Tritschler v. Allstate Ins. Co., 213 Ariz. 505, 144 P.3d 519 (Ct. App. Div. 2 2006)—8(i)(8), 26(h), 54(g)(4)
Troxler v. Holohan, 9 Ariz. App. 304, 451 P.2d 662 (1969)—5.1(d), 41(d)
Truck Equipment Co. of Ariz. v. Vanlandingham, 103 Ariz. 402, 442 P.2d 849 (1968)—14(b), 42(f)(3)(B)
Truck Ins. Exchange v. Hale, 95 Ariz. 76, 386 P.2d 846 (1963)—408(b)
Trujillo v. Brasfield, 119 Ariz. 8, 579 P.2d 46 (Ct. App. Div. 2 1978)—15(d)
Trustees Eloy Elementary School Dist., Board of v. McEwen, 6 Ariz. App. 148, 430 P.2d 727 (1967)—47(g), 59(m), 606(b)(2)(C)
Trustmark Ins. Co. v. Bank One, Arizona, NA, 202 Ariz. 535, 48 P.3d 485, 48 U.C.C. Rep. Serv. 2d 276 (Ct. App. Div. 1 2002)—49(h), 50(d)
Tryon v. Naegle, 20 Ariz. App. 138, 510 P.2d 768 (Div. 1 1973)—59(m)
Tucson, City of v. Birdsall, 109 Ariz. 581, 514 P.2d 714 (1973)—42(f)(3)(B)
Tucson, City of v. Clear Channel Outdoor, Inc., 209 Ariz. 544, 105 P.3d 1163 (2005)—3, 8(i)(8)
Tucson, City of v. Gallagher, 108 Ariz. 140, 493 P.2d 1197, 65 A.L.R.3d 597 (1972)—408(b), 611(c)(2)
Tucson, City of v. Koerber, 82 Ariz. 347, 313 P.2d 411 (1957)—611(c)(2)
Tucson, City of v. Superior Court In and For County of Pima, 161 Ariz. 441, 778 P.2d 1337 (Ct. App. Div. 2 1989)—8(i)(8), 14(b), 16.2(c)
Tucson, City of v. Superior Court In and For County of Pima, 165 Ariz. 236, 798 P.2d 374 (1990)—13(i), 14(b), 16.2(c)
Tucson, City of v. Superior Court In and For County of Pima, 167 Ariz. 513, 809 P.2d 428 (1991)—501
Tucson, City of v. Whiteco Metrocom, Inc., 194 Ariz. 390, 983 P.2d 759 (Ct. App. Div. 2 1999)—8(i)(8), 52(d)
Tucson, City of v. Wondergem, 4 Ariz. App. 291, 419 P.2d 552 (1966)—54(g)(4), 58(g)
Tucson, City of v. Woods, 191 Ariz. 523, 959 P.2d 394 (Ct. App. Div. 1 1997)—201(f), 601

U

United Bank of Arizona v. Allyn, 167 Ariz. 191, 805 P.2d 1012 (Ct. App. Div. 1 1990)—56(h)(3)

United California Bank v. Prudential Ins. Co. of America, 140 Ariz. 238, 681 P.2d 390 (Ct. App. Div. 1 1983)—501, 701(c)

United Dairymen of Arizona v. Schugg, 212 Ariz. 133, 128 P.3d 756, 2006-1 Trade Cas. (CCH) ¶ 75120 (Ct. App. Div. 1 2006)—50(d)

United Imports and Exports, Inc. v. Superior Court of State In and For Maricopa County, 134 Ariz. 43, 653 P.2d 691 (1982)—55(f), 60(d)

United Ins. Co. v. Lutz, 227 Ariz. 411, 258 P.3d 229 (Ct. App. Div. 1 2011)—401(b)

United Leasing, Inc. v. Commonwealth Land Title Agency of Tucson, Inc., 134 Ariz. 385, 656 P.2d 1246 (Ct. App. Div. 2 1982)—52(d)

United Liquor Co. v. Stephenson, 84 Ariz. 1, 322 P.2d 886 (1958)—80(i)

United Metro Materials, Inc. v. Pena Blanca Properties, L.L.C., 197 Ariz. 479, 4 P.3d 1022 (Ct. App. Div. 1 2000)—6(f)

United Pacific/Reliance Ins. Co. v. Kelley, 127 Ariz. 87, 618 P.2d 257 (Ct. App. Div. 1 1980)—17(j), 24(d)

United Sanders Stores v. Messick, 39 Ariz. 323, 6 P.2d 430 (1931)—66(d)

United Services Auto. Ass'n v. Parry, 158 Ariz. 83, 761 P.2d 157 (Ct. App. Div. 2 1988)—56(h)(3)

Universal Marketing and Entertainment, Inc. v. Bank One of Arizona, N.A., 203 Ariz. 266, 53 P.3d 191 (Ct. App. Div. 1 2002)—12(i), 64

University and State Colleges of Ariz., Board of Regents of the v. Cannon, 86 Ariz. 176, 342 P.2d 207 (1959)—701(c)

U.S. v. Certain Acres of Land in Decatur and Seminole Counties, Ga., 18 F.R.D. 98 (M.D. Ga. 1955)—26(h)

U.S. v. Certain Parcels of Land in City and County of San Francisco, State of Cal., 25 F.R.D. 192, 3 Fed. R. Serv. 2d 617 (N.D. Cal. 1959)—26(h)

U.S. Currency in Amount of $26,980.00, In re, 199 Ariz. 291, 18 P.3d 85 (Ct. App. Div. 2 2000)—39(q), 52(d)

U. S. Fidelity & Guaranty Co. v. Davis, 3 Ariz. App. 259, 413 P.2d 590 (1966)—801(d)(2)(E)

U.S. Fidelity & Guar. Co. v. Frohmiller, 71 Ariz. 377, 227 P.2d 1007 (1951)—54(g)(4), 65(j)(6), 65.1

U S West Communications, Inc. v. Arizona Dept. of Revenue, 199 Ariz. 101, 14 P.3d 292 (2000)—1, 60(d)

Utah Const. Co. v. Berg, 68 Ariz. 285, 205 P.2d 367 (1949)—201(f)

U-Totem Store v. Walker, 142 Ariz. 549, 691 P.2d 315 (Ct. App. Div. 2 1984)—26(h), 55(f)

Uyleman v. D.S. Rentco, 194 Ariz. 300, 981 P.2d 1081 (Ct. App. Div. 1 1999)—8(i)(8), 15(d)

V

Valder Law Offices v. Keenan Law Firm, 212 Ariz. 244, 129 P.3d 966 (Ct. App. Div. 1 2006)—54(g)(4)

Valencia Energy Co. v. Arizona Dept. of Revenue, 191 Ariz. 565, 959 P.2d 1256 (1998)—8(i)(8)

Vinson v. Marton & Associates, 159 Ariz. 1, 764 P.2d 736 (Ct. App. Div. 1 1988)—8(i)(8), 15(d), 18(b)

Visco v. Universal Refuse Removal Co., 11 Ariz. App. 73, 462 P.2d 90 (Div. 1 1969)—201(f)

Volkswagenwerk Aktiengesellschaft v. Schlunk, 486 U.S. 694, 108 S. Ct. 2104, 100 L. Ed. 2d 722, 11 Fed. R. Serv. 3d 417 (1988)—4.2(m)

Volz v. Coleman Co., Inc., 155 Ariz. 563, 748 P.2d 1187, Prod. Liab. Rep. (CCH) ¶ 10977 (Ct. App. Div. 1 1986)—407, 702(d), 801(d)(2)(E)

W

Wackerman v. Wackerman, 16 Ariz. App. 382, 493 P.2d 928 (Div. 1 1972)—611(c)(2)

Waddell v. Titan Ins. Co., Inc., 207 Ariz. 529, 88 P.3d 1141 (Ct. App. Div. 1 2004)—24(d)

Wagenseller v. Scottsdale Memorial Hosp., 147 Ariz. 370, 710 P.2d 1025, 1 I.E.R. Cas. (BNA) 526, 119 L.R.R.M. (BNA) 3166, 103 Lab. Cas. (CCH) ¶ 55511 (1985)—54(g)(4)

Wagner v. Casteel, 136 Ariz. 29, 663 P.2d 1020 (Ct. App. Div. 2 1983)—9(i)(9), 30(h)(i), 54(g)(4)

Wagner's Estate, In re, 75 Ariz. 135, 252 P.2d 789 (1953)—701(c)

Wait v. City of Scottsdale, 127 Ariz. 107, 618 P.2d 601 (1980)—401(b)

Waitkus v. Mauet, 157 Ariz. 339, 757 P.2d 615 (Ct. App. Div. 2 1988)—501

Waldren, In re Marriage of, 217 Ariz. 173, 171 P.3d 1214 (2007)—1, 60(d)

Walk v. Ring, 202 Ariz. 310, 44 P.3d 990 (2002)—8(i)(8), 56(h)(3)

Walker v. Dallas, 146 Ariz. 440, 706 P.2d 1207 (1985)—4.1(m), 4.2(m)

Walker v. Kendig, 107 Ariz. 510, 489 P.2d 849 (1971)—38.1(k)(3)

Walker v. State, 161 Ariz. 621, 780 P.2d 454 (Ct. App. Div. 2 1989)—801(d)(2)(E)

Wallace v. Shields, 175 Ariz. 166, 854 P.2d 1152 (Ct. App. Div. 1 1992)—65(j)(6)

Walls v. Arizona Dept. of Public Safety, 170 Ariz. 591, 826 P.2d 1217 (Ct. App. Div. 1 1991)—15(d), 801(d)(2)(E)

Walter v. Simmons, 169 Ariz. 229, 818 P.2d 214 (Ct. App. Div. 1 1991)—51(d), 59(m)

Walter v. Southern Arizona School for Boys, Inc., 77 Ariz. 141, 267 P.2d 1076 (1954)—801(d)(2)(E)

Walters v. First Federal Sav. and Loan Ass'n of Phoenix, 131 Ariz. 321, 641 P.2d 235 (1982)—16(h)

Waltner v. JPMorgan Chase Bank, N.A., 231 Ariz. 484, 297 P.3d 176 (Ct. App. Div. 1 2013)—12(i), 55(f)

Walton, Estate of, 164 Ariz. 498, 794 P.2d 131 (1990)—54(g)(4)

Walton, Matter of Estate of, 163 Ariz. 51, 785 P.2d 1239 (Ct. App. Div. 2 1989)—803

Waqui v. Tanner Bros. Contracting Co., Inc., 121 Ariz. 323, 589 P.2d 1355 (Ct. App. Div. 2 1979)—59(m)

Ward v. Stevens, 86 Ariz. 222, 344 P.2d 491 (1959)—26(h)

Wareing v. Falk, 182 Ariz. 495, 897 P.2d 1381 (Ct. App. Div. 1 1995)—8(i)(8), 13(i), 14(b), 16.2(c)

Wenrich v. Household Finance Corp., 5 Ariz. App. 335, 426 P.2d 671 (1967)—9(i)(9), 12(i)
Wersch v. Radnor/Landgrant-a Phoenix Partnership, 192 Ariz. 99, 961 P.2d 1047 (Ct. App. Div. 1 1997)—68(h)
West v. Sundance Development Co., 169 Ariz. 579, 821 P.2d 240 (Ct. App. Div. 2 1991)—36(c), 37(g)
Western Agr. Ins. Co. v. Chrysler Corp., 198 Ariz. 64, 6 P.3d 768 (Ct. App. Div. 1 2000)—77(g)(4)
Western Cable v. Industrial Com'n of Arizona, 144 Ariz. 514, 698 P.2d 759 (Ct. App. Div. 1 1985)—8(i)(8)
Western Cas. & Sur. Co. v. Evans, 130 Ariz. 333, 636 P.2d 111 (Ct. App. Div. 1 1981)—57
Western Coach Corp. v. Mark V Mobile Homes Sales, Inc., 23 Ariz. App. 546, 534 P.2d 760 (Div. 1 1975)—55(f)
Western Sav. and Loan Ass'n v. Diamond Lazy K Guest Ranch, Inc., 18 Ariz. App. 256, 501 P.2d 432 (Div. 1 1972)—1
West Pinal Family Health Center, Inc. v. McBryde, 162 Ariz. 546, 785 P.2d 66 (Ct. App. Div. 2 1989)—3, 403
W.F. Conelly Const. Co. v. L. Harvey Concrete, Inc., 162 Ariz. 574, 785 P.2d 94 (Ct. App. Div. 2 1989)—60(d), 69
W.F. Dunn, Sr. & Son v. Industrial Com'n of Arizona, 160 Ariz. 343, 773 P.2d 241 (Ct. App. Div. 1 1989)—1002
White v. Greater Arizona Bicycling Ass'n, 216 Ariz. 133, 163 P.3d 1083 (Ct. App. Div. 2 2007)—59(m)
White v. Kaufmann, 133 Ariz. 388, 652 P.2d 127 (1982)—54(g)(4)
White v. Lewis, 167 Ariz. 76, 804 P.2d 805 (Ct. App. Div. 1 1990)—56(h)(3)
White v. Mitchell, 157 Ariz. 523, 759 P.2d 1327 (Ct. App. Div. 1 1988)—51(d), 59(m), 401(b)
Whitlock v. Boyer, 77 Ariz. 334, 271 P.2d 484 (1954)—67(f)(3)
Widoff v. Wiens, 202 Ariz. 383, 45 P.3d 1232 (Ct. App. Div. 1 2002)—12(i), 17(j)
Wieman v. Roysden, 166 Ariz. 281, 802 P.2d 432 (Ct. App. Div. 1 1990)—8(i)(8), 11(c), 12(i), 56(h)(3)
Wieseler v. Prins, 167 Ariz. 223, 805 P.2d 1044 (Ct. App. Div. 1 1990)—101(b)(6), 802
Wiggs v. City of Phoenix, 197 Ariz. 358, 4 P.3d 413 (Ct. App. Div. 1 1999)—402, 404(c)(4)
Wiggs v. City of Phoenix, 198 Ariz. 367, 10 P.3d 625, 111 A.L.R.5th 815 (2000)—8(i)(8), 13(i), 14(b), 16.2(c), 26(h)
Wigley v. Whitten, 78 Ariz. 88, 276 P.2d 517 (1954)—701(c)
Wilcox Revocable Trust, Matter of, 192 Ariz. 337, 965 P.2d 71 (Ct. App. Div. 1 1998)—1, 65(j)(6), 65.1
Willey, State ex rel. v. Whitman, 91 Ariz. 120, 370 P.2d 273 (1962)—26(h), 33(c), 36(c)
Williams v. Illinois, 132 S. Ct. 2221, 183 L. Ed. 2d 89 (2012)—703
Williams v. Lakeview Co., 199 Ariz. 1, 13 P.3d 280 (2000)—4.2(m)
Williams v. Long, 1 Ariz. App. 330, 402 P.2d 1006 (1965)—103(e)
Williams v. Superior Court In and For County of Maricopa, 169 Ariz. 468, 820 P.2d 332 (Ct. App. Div. 1 1991)—26(h), 30(h)(i)

Williams v. Superior Court In and For County of Maricopa, 190 Ariz. 80, 945 P.2d 391 (Ct. App. Div. 1 1997)—42(f)(3)(B)

Williams v. Thude, 188 Ariz. 257, 934 P.2d 1349 (1997)—8(i)(8), 13(i), 14(b), 16.2(c)

Williams v. Williams, 86 Ariz. 201, 344 P.2d 161 (1959)—801(d)(2)(E)

Williams by Williams v. Stewart, 145 Ariz. 602, 703 P.2d 546 (Ct. App. Div. 2 1985)—201(f)

Williams for and on Behalf of Dixon v. Thude, 180 Ariz. 531, 885 P.2d 1096 (Ct. App. Div. 1 1994)—42(f)(3)(B), 51(d)

Williamson v. Columbia Gas & Elec. Corp., 186 F.2d 464 (3d Cir. 1950)—10(f)

William Z. v. Arizona Dept. of Economic Sec., 192 Ariz. 385, 965 P.2d 1224 (Ct. App. Div. 1 1998)—24(d)

Willow Creek Leasing, Inc. v. Bartzen, 154 Ariz. 339, 742 P.2d 840 (Ct. App. Div. 1 1987)—52(d)

Wilmot v. Wilmot, 203 Ariz. 565, 58 P.3d 507 (2002)—12(i)

Wilshire Ins. Co. v. S.A., 224 Ariz. 97, 227 P.3d 504 (Ct. App. Div. 1 2010)—14(b)

Wilson v. Bramblett, 91 Ariz. 284, 371 P.2d 1014 (1962)—18(b)

Wilson v. Riley Whittle, Inc., 145 Ariz. 317, 701 P.2d 575 (Ct. App. Div. 2 1984)—410(b)(2), 609(e)

Wilson v. Tucson General Hospital, 18 Ariz. App. 31, 499 P.2d 762 (Div. 2 1972)—52(d)

Wilson v. Wiggins, 54 Ariz. 240, 94 P.2d 870 (1939)—47(g)

Wiltbank v. Lyman Water Co., 13 Ariz. App. 485, 477 P.2d 771 (Div. 1 1970)—54(g)(4)

Wineinger v. Wineinger, 137 Ariz. 194, 669 P.2d 971 (Ct. App. Div. 2 1983)—105

Wingfoot Cal. Homes Co. v. Valley Nat. Bank of Phoenix, 74 Ariz. 287, 248 P.2d 738 (1952)—66(d)

Wingfoot California Homes Co. v. Valley Nat. Bank of Phoenix, 80 Ariz. 133, 294 P.2d 370 (1956)—8(i)(8)

Winn, In re Estate of, 214 Ariz. 149, 150 P.3d 236 (2007)—17(j), 25(e)(2)

Winner Enterprises, Ltd. v. Superior Court in and for County of Yavapai, 159 Ariz. 106, 765 P.2d 116 (Ct. App. Div. 1 1988)—24(d)

Wise v. Monteros, 93 Ariz. 124, 379 P.2d 116 (1963)—703, 803

Wiseman v. Young, 4 Ariz. App. 573, 422 P.2d 404 (1967)—38(d)

Wisener v. State, 123 Ariz. 148, 598 P.2d 511 (1979)—56(h)(3)

W. J. Kroeger Co. v. Travelers Indem. Co., 112 Ariz. 285, 541 P.2d 385 (1975)—13(i), 56(h)(3)

Wohlstrom v. Buchanan, 180 Ariz. 389, 884 P.2d 687 (1994)—501

Wolf Corp. v. Louis, 11 Ariz. App. 352, 464 P.2d 672 (Div. 2 1970)—54(g)(4)

Wolfinger v. Cheche, 206 Ariz. 504, 80 P.3d 783 (Ct. App. Div. 1 2003)—11(c)

Wonders v. Pima County, 207 Ariz. 576, 89 P.3d 810 (Ct. App. Div. 2 2004)—12(i)

Wood v. Holiday Mobile Home Resorts, Inc., 128 Ariz. 274, 625 P.2d 337 (Ct. App. Div. 1 1980)—53(k)

Woods, State ex rel. v. Cohen, 173 Ariz. 497, 844 P.2d 1147 (1992)—501

Woodty v. Weston's Lamplighter Motels, 171 Ariz. 265, 830 P.2d 477 (Ct. App. Div. 1 1992)—56(h)(3)

Wooldridge Const. Co. v. First Nat. Bank of Arizona, 130 Ariz. 86, 634 P.2d 13 (Ct. App. Div. 1 1981)—39(q)
Worcester, In re Marriage of, 192 Ariz. 24, 960 P.2d 624 (1998)—60(d)
Wright v. Demeter, 8 Ariz. App. 65, 442 P.2d 888 (1968)—16(h)
Wright v. Hills, 161 Ariz. 583, 780 P.2d 416 (Ct. App. Div. 2 1989)—11(c), 56(h)(3)
Wright v. Mayberry, 158 Ariz. 387, 762 P.2d 1341 (Ct. App. Div. 1 1988)—49(h), 59(m), 60(d)
Wright v. Sears, Roebuck & Co., 116 Ariz. 391, 569 P.2d 821 (1977)—67(f)(3)
W. R. Skousen Contractor, Inc. v. Gray, 26 Ariz. App. 100, 546 P.2d 369 (Div. 1 1976)—104(e), 402
W.R.Skousen Contractors, Inc. v. Chatter, 24 Ariz. App. 153, 536 P.2d 722 (Div. 1 1975)—804(b)(6)
Wustrack v. Clark, 18 Ariz. App. 407, 502 P.2d 1084 (Div. 1 1972)—1
Wyatt v. Wehmueller, 163 Ariz. 12, 785 P.2d 581 (Ct. App. Div. 1 1989)—3
Wyttenbach, In re Estate of, 219 Ariz. 120, 193 P.3d 814 (Ct. App. Div. 1 2008)—25(e)(2)

Y

Yarbrough v. Montoya-Paez, 214 Ariz. 1, 147 P.3d 755 (Ct. App. Div. 2 2006)—12(i)
Yates v. Superior Court In and For Pima County, 120 Ariz. 436, 586 P.2d 997 (Ct. App. Div. 2 1978)—38.1(k)(3)
Yauch v. Southern Pacific Transp. Co., 198 Ariz. 394, 10 P.3d 1181 (Ct. App. Div. 2 2000)—103(e), 403
Yavapai County v. Superior Court In and For Yavapai County, 13 Ariz. App. 368, 476 P.2d 889 (Div. 1 1970)—42(f)(3)(B)
Yes on Prop 200 v. Napolitano, 215 Ariz. 458, 160 P.3d 1216 (Ct. App. Div. 1 2007)—12(i)
Yollin v. City of Glendale, 219 Ariz. 24, 191 P.3d 1040 (Ct. App. Div. 1 2008)—3
Yoo Thun Lim v. Crespin, 100 Ariz. 80, 411 P.2d 809 (1966)—59(m), 607
Young v. Bishop, 88 Ariz. 140, 353 P.2d 1017 (1960)—8(i)(8), 10(f)
Young v. Environmental Air Products, Inc., 136 Ariz. 206, 665 P.2d 88 (Ct. App. Div. 2 1982)—13(i), 14(b), 701(c), 704(b)
Young v. Rose, 230 Ariz. 433, 286 P.3d 518 (Ct. App. Div. 1 2012)—10(f)
Young Candy & Tobacco Co. v. Montoya, 91 Ariz. 363, 372 P.2d 703 (1962)—59(m)
Youngren v. Rezzonico, 25 Ariz. App. 304, 543 P.2d 142 (Div. 1 1975)—408(b)
Yslava v. Hughes Aircraft Co., 188 Ariz. 380, 936 P.2d 1274, 45 Env't. Rep. Cas. (BNA) 1315 (1997)—8(i)(8), 13(i), 14(b), 16.2(c)
Yuma, City of v. Evans, 85 Ariz. 229, 336 P.2d 135 (1959)—703
Yuma Greyhound Park, Inc. v. Hardy, 106 Ariz. 178, 472 P.2d 47 (1970)—501
Yuma Regional Medical Center v. Superior Court In and For County of Yuma, 175 Ariz. 72, 852 P.2d 1256 (Ct. App. Div. 1 1993)—16(h), 26.2(b)(4), 501

Z

Zakroff v. May, 8 Ariz. App. 101, 443 P.2d 916 (1968)—16(h), 37(g)
Zale, In re Marriage of, 193 Ariz. 246, 972 P.2d 230 (1999)—54(g)(4), 58(g), 104(e)

Index

DEPOSITIONS—Cont'd